# LABELS USED IN THE DICTIONARY

APPROVING and DISAPPROVING

Words and phrases are labeled APPROVING or DISAPPROVING if people use them in order to show that they approve or disapprove of someone or something. For example, both **childlike** and **childish** are used for describing behavior that is typical of a child, but **childlike** shows approval, and **childish** shows disapproval.

FORMAL

Formal words and phrases such as **await** and **moreover** are used only in speech and writing that is formal or official, for example in essays or announcements.

HUMOROUS

Humorous words and phrases such as **clear as mud** are intended to be funny.

INFORMAL

Informal words and phrases such as **grungy** and **long shot** are used in informal conversations and unofficial writing such as letters to friends. Do not use these words and phrases in essays.

LAW

Words and phrases labeled LAW have a special legal meaning.

LITERARY

Literary words and phrases such as **foe** and **inferno** are used mostly in poetry and other types of literature. They are not usually suitable for essays.

NONSTANDARD

Nonstandard words and phrases do not follow the rules of grammar, but are still used a lot. For example, many people use **real** instead of **really**. Do not use nonstandard language in essays.

...o make
...e often
...her
...nd phrases
that only p..........................) be offensive.

OLD-FASHIONED

Old-fashioned words and phrases are ones that people still know, but that are not used very often in modern speech or writing.

SLANG

Slang words and phrases are ones that are not acceptable in many situations, because they are only used by particular groups of people (such as young people), or because they are extremly informal or not very polite. Be very careful when using these words and phrases, and do not use them in essays.

SPOKEN

Spoken words and phrases such as **I mean** and **by the way** are hardly ever used in writing. They are always informal, unless they have the label SPOKEN FORMAL. Do not use these words and phrases in essays.

TABOO

Taboo words and phrases are extremely rude, offensive to everyone, and should be avoided.

TECHNICAL

Technical words and phrases such as **larynx** and **certificate of deposit** relate to particular subjects, such as science, medicine, language study etc.

TRADEMARK

A trademark is a special name for a product that a company owns. It must always be spelled in a particular way, and cannot be used by anyone else in the names of similar products.

NEW EDITION

# LONGMAN

# DICTIONARY *of*

# AMERICAN

# ENGLISH

*Your Complete Guide to American English*

 LONGMAN

**Longman Dictionary of American English**

First published 1983
Second edition 1997

ISBN
0-8013-1823-8 (Paper)
0-8013-1409-7 (Hardcover)

Headwords that the editors have reason to believe
constitute trademarks have been described as such.
However, neither the presence or absence of such
description should be regarded as affecting the legal
status of any trademark.

Library of Congress Cataloging-in-Publication Data
Longman Dictionary of American English—New ed., 2nd ed.
ISBN 0-8013-1409-7 (hardcover)
ISBN 0-8013-1823-8 (softcover)
1. English language—United States—Dictionaries
2. English language—Textbooks for foreign speakers
PE2835.L6     1997     423′.1—dc21     96-51562  CIP

Typeset by  Morton Word Processing Ltd.
              RVC Associates Ltd.

Printed in the USA

Addison Wesley Longman
10 Bank Street, White Plains, N.Y. 10606-1951, USA
Edinburgh Gate, Harlow, Essex CM20 2JE, UK

8910-DOH-01009998

# Table of Contents

Short forms used in the Dictionary . . . . . . . . . . . . . . . . . . .inside front cover
Grammar codes used in the Dictionary . . . . . . . . . . . . . .inside front cover
Labels used in the Dictionary . . . . . . . . . . . . . . . . . . . . . . . . . . . . . . . . . . . .i
Acknowledgments . . . . . . . . . . . . . . . . . . . . . . . . . . . . . . . . . . . . . . . . . . .vi
Preface . . . . . . . . . . . . . . . . . . . . . . . . . . . . . . . . . . . . . . . . . . . . . . . . . . . . .ix
Key to the Dictionary . . . . . . . . . . . . . . . . . . . . . . . . . . . . . . . . . . . . . . . . .x
Dictionary Skills Workbook . . . . . . . . . . . . . . . . . . . . . . . . . . . . . . . . . .xiii
Answer Key . . . . . . . . . . . . . . . . . . . . . . . . . . . . . . . . . . . . . . . . . . . . . . .xxiv

**The Dictionary A-Z** . . . . . . . . . . . . . . . . . . . . . . . . . . . . . . . . . . . . . . . . .1

Study Notes
    Adjective word order . . . . . . . . . . . . . . . . . . . . . . . . . . . . . . .456
    Capitalization . . . . . . . . . . . . . . . . . . . . . . . . . . . . . . . . . . . . .456
    Comparatives . . . . . . . . . . . . . . . . . . . . . . . . . . . . . . . . . . . .457
    Modal verbs . . . . . . . . . . . . . . . . . . . . . . . . . . . . . . . . . . . . .458
    Numbers . . . . . . . . . . . . . . . . . . . . . . . . . . . . . . . . . . . . . . . .460
    Phrasal verbs . . . . . . . . . . . . . . . . . . . . . . . . . . . . . . . . . . . .462
    Intensifiers . . . . . . . . . . . . . . . . . . . . . . . . . . . . . . . . . . . . . .463
    Prepositions . . . . . . . . . . . . . . . . . . . . . . . . . . . . . . . . . . . . .464
    Quantity . . . . . . . . . . . . . . . . . . . . . . . . . . . . . . . . . . . . . . . .466
    Verbs . . . . . . . . . . . . . . . . . . . . . . . . . . . . . . . . . . . . . . . . . .468
Illustrations
    Cars . . . . . . . . . . . . . . . . . . . . . . . . . . . . . . . . . . . . . . . . . . .469
    Fruit and vegetables . . . . . . . . . . . . . . . . . . . . . . . . . . . . . .470
    Houses . . . . . . . . . . . . . . . . . . . . . . . . . . . . . . . . . . . . . . . . .471
    Sports . . . . . . . . . . . . . . . . . . . . . . . . . . . . . . . . . . . . . . . . . .472
    Verbs of movement . . . . . . . . . . . . . . . . . . . . . . . . . . . . . . .473

Word building . . . . . . . . . . . . . . . . . . . . . . . . . . . . . . . . . . . . . . . . . . . .929
Irregular verbs . . . . . . . . . . . . . . . . . . . . . . . . . . . . . . . . . . . . . . . . . . .931
Pronunciation . . . . . . . . . . . . . . . . . . . . . . . . . . . . . . . . . . . . . . . . . . .934
Pronunciation table . . . . . . . . . . . . . . . . . . . . . . . . . . . . .inside back cover

# Acknowledgments

**Editorial Directors**
Della Summers
Adam Gadsby

**Editorial Manager**
Wendalyn Nichols

**Senior Editor**
Karen Stern

**Lexicographers**
Rebecca Campbell
Robert Clevenger
Dewayne Crawford
Dileri Borunda Johnston
Carol Pomeroy Zhong

**Publishing Management**
Joanne Dresner
Allen Ascher

**Design**
Jenny Fleet
Carolyn Viola John

**Project Manager**
Alan Savill

**Administrative Assistant**
Sandra Rootsey

**Senior Lexicographer**
Karen Cleveland Marwick

**Associate Lexicographer**
Sue Engineer

**Pronunciation Editor**
Rebecca Dauer, PhD

**Corpus development**
Steve Crowdy
Denise Denney

**Production**
Clive McKeough
Patrice Fraccio

**Illustrator**
Len Shalansky

**Production Editor**
Claire Parkyns

**Keyboarder**
Pauline Savill

# Acknowledgments

The Publishers would like to thank:

▪ Professor Jack du Bois of the University of California at Santa Barbara, for the development of the Longman Corpus of Spoken American English. This unique corpus, developed especially for the *Longman Dictionary of American English*, consists of 5 million words of everyday conversation by US speakers of English. The corpus was designed to provide a representative sample of the US population, by age, sex, region, educational attainment and ethnic origin. Volunteers were selected to wear a digital cassette recorder and record their conversations over a two-week period. The tapes were then transcribed and built into a computer system so that the lexicographic team could analyze exactly how native speakers use the language.

▪ the thousands of teachers and students from around the world who have contributed scripts for the Longman Learner's Corpus. This corpus consists of 8 million words of writing in English by learners, and helps lexicographers to analyze what students know and where they have difficulty.

▪ the Linguistic Data Consortium for texts included in the 80-million-word Longman Corpus of Written American English

▪ the many teachers and students who have taken part in the development of the new edition of the dictionary. This has included focus groups, questionnaires, student vocabulary notebooks (in which students kept a record of which words they looked up), classroom piloting of material, and written feedback on text by teachers.

Nancy Ackles, University of Washington Extension, Seattle
Thomas W. Adams, University of Pennsylvania
Monica Alcarez-Snow, California State University, Fullerton
Isabella Anikst, American Language Center, University of California, Los Angeles Extension
Cathrine Berg, Drexel University, Philadelphia
Gretchen Bitterlin, San Diego Community College
Donna Brinton, University of California, Los Angeles
Arlene Bublick, William Rainey Harper College, Palatine, Illinois
Christine Bunn, City College of San Francisco
Dorothy Burak, University of California, San Diego
Rand Burger, California State Polytechnicall, Pomona University
Laura Cameron, A.C.E. Language Institute, Seattle Pacific University
Sarah Canady, Bellevue Community College, Seattle
Jane Cater, A.C.E. Language Institute, Seattle Pacific University
Rick Chapman, California State University, Fullerton
Martha Compton, University of California, Irvine
Jan Copeland, Long Beach City College, Long Beach, California
Patrick Cox, Houston Community College
Nick Crump, Merritt College, Oakland
Catherine Crystal, Laney College, Oakland
Kevin G. Curry, Wichita State University, Kansas
Susan Davis, EF International
Carlos C. Delgado, North Valley Occupational Center, Mission Hills, California
Carolyn Dupaquier, California State University, Fullerton
Nancy Dyer, A.C.E. Language Institute, Seattle Pacific University
Julie Easton, Adult Education Center, Santa Monica
Gerry Eldred, Long Beach City College, Long Beach, California
Rita Esquivel, Adult Education Center, Santa Monica
Mary Fitzpatrick, College of Marin, Novato
Annette Fruehan, Orange Coast College, California
Caroline Gibbs, College of Marin, Novato
Janet Goodwin, University of California, Los Angeles
Lisa Hale, St Giles College, London
James Harris, Rancho Santiago College, Santa Ana
Tamara Hefter, Truman College, Chicago
Patti Heiser, University of Washington Extension
Julie Herrmann, A.C.E. Language Institute, Seattle Pacific University
Wayne Heuple, A.C.E. Language Institute, Seattle Pacific University
Kathi Holper, William Rainey Harper College, Palatine, Illinois
Barbara Howard, Daley College ALSP, Chicago
Kathryn Howard
Leann Howard, San Diego Community College

# Acknowledgments

Stephanie Howard, American Language Center, University of California, Los Angeles Extension

Gail Hutchins, East San Jose College

Susan Jamieson, Bellevue Community College

Jeff Janulis, Daley College, Chicago

Linda Jensen, University of California, Los Angeles

Winston Joffrion, Bellevue Community College, Bellevue

Deborah Jonas, California State University, Long Beach

Kathryn Curry Keesler, Orange Coast College

Barbara Logan, A.C.E. Language Institute, Seattle Pacific University

Walter Lowe, Bellevue Community College, Bellevue

Lynne Lucas, Daley College ALSP, Chicago

Robyn Mann, William Rainey Harper College, Palatine, Illinois

Anne McGinley, San Diego State University

Elaine McVey, San Diego State University

Amy Meepoe, University of California, Los Angeles

Andy Muller, A.C.E. Language Institute, Seattle Pacific University

Jill Neely, Merritt College, Oakland

Maura Newberry, University of California, Los Angeles

Yvonne Nishio, Evans Community Adult School, Los Angeles

Roxanne Nuhaily, University of California, San Diego

Carla Nyssen, California State University, Long Beach

David Olsher, University of California, Los Angeles

Jorge Perez, Southwestern College, San Diego

Ellen Pentkowski, Truman College, Chicago

Eileen Prince Lou, Northeastern University, Boston

Nancy Quinn, Truman College, Chicago

Ralph Radell, Bunker Hill Community College, Boston

Eva Ramirez, Laney College, Oakland

Alison Rice, Hunter College

Lenore Richmond, California State University, Fullerton

Jane Rinaldi, California State Polytechnic University, Pomona

Bruce Rindler, CELOP, Boston University

Shirley Roberts, Long Beach City College, Long Beach

William Robertson, Northeastern University, Boston

Bonnie Rose, University of Denver

Teresa Ross, California State University, Long Beach

Paul Safstrom, South Seattle Community College

Karen Santiago, American Language Academy, Philadelphia

Irene Schoenberg, Hunter College, New York

Esther Sunde, South Seattle Community College, Seattle

Barbara Swartz, Northeastern University, Boston

Priscilla Taylor, California State University, Los Angeles

Elizabeth Terplan, College of Marin, Novato, California

Bill Trimble, Modesto Junior College

Wendy Walsh, College of Marin, Novato, California

Colleen Weldele, Palomar College, San Marcos, California

Sabella Wells, A.C.E. Language Institute, Seattle Pacific University

Madeleine Youmans, Long Beach City College, Long Beach

Christine Zilkow, California State University, Fullerton

Janet Zinner, Northeastern University, Boston

Jean Zukowski-Faust, Northern Arizona University

Yuri Komuro, for assistance in compiling the results of teacher questionnaires and student word diaries

Norma A. Register, PhD, for advice on coverage of socially sensitive language

# Preface

This new edition of the *Longman Dictionary of American English,* the foremost ESL dictionary, has been specially researched and written to meet the real needs of students of English as a second or foreign language.

## Real Language

The new edition of the *Dictionary* is based on the authentic language data in the Longman Corpus Network. Longman's unique computerized language database contains over 328 million words from all types of written texts, and from real conversations recorded across the US.

The Corpus tells us how frequently words and phrases are used, so there's no guesswork in deciding what words and phrases students need to know most. The Corpus shows which grammar patterns are the most important to illustrate. It shows important new words and idioms that people use every day, and words that are frequently used together (called *collocations*). We take our example sentences from the Corpus, and this makes the language come alive as never before.

## Real Clarity

The definitions in the *Dictionary* are written using only the 2000 most common English words—the Longman Defining Vocabulary. Longman pioneered the use of a limited vocabulary as the best way to guarantee that definitions are clear and easy to understand.

The comprehensive grammatical information in the *Dictionary* is easy to understand and use. Important patterns are highlighted in the example sentences, so that you can see at a glance how to use a word in a sentence.

The meaning you want is easy to find in the *Dictionary.* Words that have a large number of meanings have short, clear *Signposts* to guide you to the right meaning quickly.

## Real Help

The new edition of the Dictionary is the result of extensive research into student needs and abilities, and has been tested in schools and colleges all over the US.

The writers have also used their knowledge from years of ESL teaching to analyze the Longman Learner's Corpus, which is a computerized collection of over 8 million words of writing in English by learners of the language. By studying the errors students make in essays and exams, the writers were able to give clear, helpful usage information throughout the *Dictionary*—in the definitions, example sentences, study notes, and usage notes—to help students avoid common errors.

Use the exercises in the Dictionary Skills Workbook on pages xiii-xxvi to learn how to get the most from your *Dictionary.* The grammar codes and labels are inside the front cover, and the IPA (International Phonetic Alphabet) pronunciation charts are inside the back cover, so they are always easy to find and use.

Whether you are writing a report, sending an e-mail, or chatting with friends, the *Longman Dictionary of American English* will help you choose the right words, understand them clearly, and use them correctly.

# Key to the Dictionary

This Key is a quick guide to the way information is shown in this dictionary. For longer explanations and practice exercises, look up each subject in the Dictionary Skills Workbook on pages xiii-xxvi.

## SPELLING AND FINDING WORDS—workbook pages xiii-xiv

### Different spellings

**gan·gling** /'gæŋglɪŋ/, **gan·gly** /'gæŋgli/ *adj* unusually tall and thin and unable to move gracefully: *a gangly teenager*

Different spellings are shown here —see page xiii

### Irregular plurals

**medium²** *n* **1** *plural* **media** a way of communicating or expressing something: *The Internet is a powerful advertising medium.* **2** *plural* **media** the material, paints etc. that an artist uses: *This sculptor's favorite medium is wood.* **3** *plural* **mediums** someone who claims to speak to dead people and receive messages from them

Is the plural **media** or **mediums?** The correct spelling is shown here —see page xiv

### Irregular verbs and verb spellings

**sing** /sɪŋ/ *v* **sang, sung, singing** **1** [I,T] to make musical sounds, songs etc. with your voice: *Do you like singing folk songs?* | *Jana sings in the church choir.*

Does the spelling change? We show it here if it does —see page xiv

### Irregular comparatives and superlatives

**bad¹** /bæd/ *adj* **worse, worst** **1** not good and unpleasant: *I'm afraid I have some bad news for you.* | *a really bad smell*

Does the form of the word change? We show it here if it does —see page xiv

## SOUND AND STRESS—workbook pages xv-xvi

### Sound

**air·plane** /'ɛrpleɪn/ *n* a vehicle that flies by using wings and one or more engines; plane

The pronunciation of each word is shown like this —see page xv

### Stress

**e·lec·tion** /ɪ'lɛkʃən/ *n* an occasion when you vote in order to choose someone for an official position: *The election results are still coming in.*

Do you say **elec**tion or e**lec**tion? —see page xv

## FINDING AND UNDERSTANDING MEANINGS—workbook pages xvi-xviii

### Clear and simple explanations

**kay·ak** /'kaɪæk/ *n* a CANOE (=type of boat) usually for one person, that is enclosed and has a hole for that person to sit in

Word meanings are simply explained and easy to understand. Words that you may not know are written in large letters like this. You can find these words in the dictionary —see page xvi

### More than one meaning

**favorite²** *n* **1** someone or something that you like more than any other one of its kind: *I like all her books, but this one is my favorite.* **2** someone who receives more attention and approval than is fair: *Teachers shouldn't have*

Many words have more than one meaning. The first meaning is the most common one, but don't forget to check the others too —see page xvii

## Idiomatic expressions

**calm**[3] *n* **1** [singular, U] a time that is quiet and peaceful **2 the calm before the storm** a peaceful situation just before a big problem or

Phrases that have special meanings are shown like this —see page xvii

## Signposts

**school**[1] /skul/ *n*
**1** ▶BUILDING◀ [C,U] a place where children are taught: *Which school did you go to?* I *I can*

These words help you find the meaning you want quickly —see page xviii

## UNDERSTANDING THE GRAMMAR—workbook pages xviii-xx

### Parts of speech

**o·ver·night**[2] /'ouvɚ,naɪt/ *adj* continuing all night: *an overnight flight to Japan*

These letters tell you if the word is a noun, a verb, an adjective etc. —see page xviii

### Word families

*street lights* **3** unkind, cruel, or strict: *harsh criticism* I *harsh unfair laws* **–harshly** *adv* **–harshness** *n* [U]

Words that are part of the same word family and that have different parts of speech are often shown like this —see page xviii

### Nouns

**pit·y**[1] /'pɪti/ *n* **1** [U] sympathy for someone who is suffering or unhappy: *I don't need your pity!* **2** [singular] a sad or unfortunate situ-

These codes tell you how you can use the noun. [U] and [singular] mean you cannot use this meaning in the plural —see page xix

### Verbs

**cheat**[1] /tʃit/ *v* **1** [I] to behave in a dishonest way in order to win or gain something: *He always cheats when we play cards.* **2** [T] to

These codes tell you if the verb is followed by an object. [I] means you cannot use it with an object, and [T] means you must use it with an object —see page xix

### Phrasal verbs

**check on** sb/sth *phr v* [T] to make sure that someone or something is doing what he, she, or

These letters tell you that the object of the phrasal verb can be a person (sb) or a thing (sth) —see page xx

**dawn on** sb *phr v* [T] to realize something: *It suddenly dawned on me that he was right.*

These letters tell you that the object can only follow the preposition when you say **dawn on** —see page xx

**rinse** sth ↔ **out** *phr v* [T] to wash something with clean water but not soap: *Please rinse out your bottles before recycling them.*

These letters tell you that you can say **rinse something out** or **rinse out something** —see page xx

## USING THE WORDS CORRECTLY—workbook pages xx-xxi

### Examples of use

**certain**[2] *adj* **1** completely sure and without any doubts: *I'm not certain (that) he's telling me the truth.* I *No one was certain what to expect.* I *Are you certain about that?* **2** *knowI*

Many helpful example sentences show you how to use the word. Grammar patterns are shown in ***dark letters*** —see page xx

# Key to the Dictionary

### Frequent phrases

**2 ▶MAIN IDEA◀** the main meaning or idea in something that is said or done: *Get to the point!* (=say your idea directly) | *The point is that I don't trust him anymore.* | *What's your point?* | *That's beside the point.* (=it does not relate to the subject)

Clear explanations like this help you understand common phrases that are used with the word —see page xx

### Usage notes

USAGE NOTE **gain**, **earn**, and **win**

Use **gain** to talk about gradually getting more of something, such as an ability or quality: *You'll gain a lot of experience working here.* Use **earn** to talk about getting money by working: *She earns about*

Usage notes help you avoid common mistakes with using words
Some explain the meaning and use of similar words
Some explain the difficult grammar of a particular word
Others explain words that are used in a special way in American English
—see page xxi

### Usage hints

*you speak any foreign languages?" "Yes, I speak French."* ✗ DON'T SAY "I speak French language." ✗ **2** [U] the system of written and

Usage hints help you avoid common mistakes with particular words —see page xxi

---

## CHOOSING THE RIGHT WORD—workbook pages xxii-xxiii

### Labels such as FORMAL, INFORMAL, and SPOKEN

**guy** /gaɪ/ *n* **1** INFORMAL a man: *I'm going out with a few guys from work tonight.* | *Some guy wanted to talk to you.* **2 you guys/those guys** SPOKEN said when talking to or about two or more

Would it be correct to use this word in an essay? —see page xxii

### Synonyms

**elementary school** /..'.. ,./ *n* a school in the US for the first six or eight years of a child's education; GRADE SCHOOL

This shows another word you can use in the same way, that has a similar meaning

**fac·sim·i·le** /fæk'sɪməli/ *n* **1** an exact copy of a picture, piece of writing etc. **2** ⇨ FAX

This shows a word that is much more common, and means the same thing —see page xxii

### Opposites

**large** /lɑrdʒ/ *adj* **1** big, or bigger than usual in size, number, or amount: *I'd like a large pepperoni pizza, please.* | *What's the largest city in Canada?* −opposite SMALL −see usage note

This shows a word with the opposite meaning —see page xxiii

### "See also" cross-references

**mint¹** /mɪnt/ *n* **1** a candy with a sweet hot taste: *an after dinner mint* **2** [U] a plant with sweet hot-tasting leaves used in cooking and making medicine −see also PEPPERMINT, SPEARMINT **3 a mint** INFORMAL a large amount

This shows words that are related to the word **mint**

### "Compare" cross-references

**in·ter·pret·er** /ɪn'tɚprətɚ/ *n* someone who changes the spoken words of one language into another −compare TRANSLATOR

This shows a word that might be confused with the word **interpreter** —see page xxiii

# Dictionary Skills Workbook

This dictionary is full of information that makes spoken and written English easier to understand and use correctly. Use the exercises in this workbook to learn how to find and use the information you want.

## SPELLING AND FINDING WORDS

### The alphabet

The words in this dictionary are listed in alphabetical order. Here is the English alphabet:

Lowercase letters          a b c d e f g h i j k l m n o p q r s t u v w x y z

Uppercase or capital letters    A B C D E F G H I J K L M N O P Q R S T U V W X Y Z

### Compounds

Sometimes two words have a special meaning when they are used together. They can be written as two words, like **ice cream**, or with a HYPHEN, like **role-play**. In this dictionary, words like these are listed alphabetically as though they were just one word, like this:

> **forward⁴** *n* in basketball, one of two players
> **for·ward·ing ad·dress** /ˌ... '.., ˌ... .'./ *n* an
> **forward-look·ing** /'.. ˌ../, **forward-thinking**
> **fos·sil** /'fɑsəl/ *n* part of an animal or plant that

### Phrasal verbs

Two- and three-word verbs that are related to the main verb are listed separately, under the main verb, like this:

> **chime²** *v* [I,T] to make a ringing (RING) sound, especially in order to show what time it is: *The clock chimed six.*
> **chime in** *phr v* [I] to agree with what someone has just said, often by repeating it or adding to it

### Abbreviations

Abbreviations are also listed alphabetically:

> **ba·zaar** /bəˈzɑr/ *n* **1** an occasion when a lot
> **BB gun** /'bibi ˌgʌn/ *n* a gun that uses air
> **BBQ** /'bɑrbɪˌkyu/ a written abbreviation for

---

**EXERCISE 1**     Put these words in the order that you can find them in the dictionary.

pay       _____pawn_____

pay-TV    _____

pay off    _____

payroll    _____

pea        _____

PE         _____

pay dirt    _____

pay up     _____

pawn      _____

### Different spellings

If you look up the word **ambiance** in the dictionary, you will see that there are two different spellings for this word. Both of them are correct, but **ambiance** is the more common one, so it is written first:

> **am·bi·ance**, ambience /'æmbiəns, 'ɑmbiɑns/ *n* [U] the way a place makes you feel: *the*

## Dictionary Skills Workbook

### Irregular plurals

Most nouns form their plural by adding **-s** or **-es**. However, some nouns have special plural forms. When the plural of a noun is not formed by adding **-s** or **-es**, this dictionary shows the irregular plural form·

**child** /tʃaɪld/ *n, plural* **children** /'tʃɪldrən/
**1** a young person who is not yet fully grown:

### Irregular verbs and verb spellings

Most verbs form the past tense and PAST PARTICIPLE by adding **-ed** and the PRESENT PARTICIPLE by adding **-ing**, such as **helped**, **have helped**, **be helping**. However, some verbs have special forms. When a verb is irregular, this dictionary shows the irregular verb form:

**grow** /groʊ/ *v* **grew, grown, growing** [I]
**1** ▶DEVELOP◀ to develop and become bigger or longer over time, or to make something do

Sometimes only the spelling is irregular in the past tense and past participle. This shows that the spelling of **spot** changes when you add **-ed** or **-ing**:

**spot²** *v* **-tted, -tting** [T]  **1** to notice or recognize something that is difficult to see, or that

### Irregular comparatives and superlatives

Most adjectives and adverbs form the COMPARATIVE by adding **-er** and the SUPERLATIVE by adding **-est**, for example **mild, milder, mildest**. However, some of these have special forms. When the comparative or superlative of an adjective or adverb is irregular, this dictionary shows the irregular form:

**good¹** /gʊd/ *adj* **better, best**
**1** ▶HIGH IN QUALITY◀ of a high standard: *His score on the test was very good.* | *Thanks, Maria, you did a good job.* ✗ DON'T SAY "You

### Common spelling changes

Many spelling changes are the result of regular rules, and are therefore not shown in this dictionary as irregular forms. For example:

"Drop the **-y** and add **-ies**":      **party,** *plural* **parties**
"Drop the **-y** and add **-ied**":      **study,** *past tense* **studied**
"Drop the **-e** and add **-ing**":      **amaze,** *present participle* **amazing**
"Drop the **-e** and add **-er** or **-est**":      **sane,** *comparative* **saner,** *superlative* **sanest**

---

**EXERCISE 2**    Write the correct form of each word in the correct column. (Irregular spelling patterns are shown in the dictionary, and regular ones are not.)

| verb | past tense | past participle | present participle |
|------|-----------|-----------------|--------------------|
| take | took | | |
| make | | | making |
| eat | | | |
| lag | | lagged | |
| carry | | | |

| adjective | comparative | superlative |
|-----------|-------------|-------------|
| mad | madder | |
| tiny | | |
| bad | | |
| crazy | | craziest |
| funny | | |

| noun | plural |
|------|--------|
| domino | |
| knife | |
| candy | candies |
| axis | |
| aircraft | |

# Dictionary Skills Workbook

## SOUND AND STRESS

### Vowels and consonants

The pronunciation of a word is shown between sloping lines, like this: /..../

**phone**[1] /foʊn/ *n* **1** a piece of equipment that you use in order to talk with someone in another

On the inside back cover of this dictionary is a list of the special alphabet in PHONETIC letters that we have used for showing pronunciation. Next to each SYMBOL (=special letter) is a common word that shows what the sound is like. Because many different letters can have the same sound in English, the list also shows different ways of spelling the same sounds:

| vowels | | consonants | |
|---|---|---|---|
| Symbol | Key Word | Symbol | Key Word |
| aʊ | about, how | m | men, some |
| eɪ | date, paid | f | fan, photograph |

**EXERCISE 3A     VOWELS: Use this exercise to learn some of the most common symbols.**

Put the words below under the correct vowel symbol, by looking in the dictionary to see which sound each word uses.

said    need    awful    glue    new    bet    field    thought    boot    even    seed    soft
clean    dead    mood    true    do    ever    next    taught    went    malt

| /i/ | /ɛ/ | /ɔ/ | /u/ |
|---|---|---|---|
| need | said | awful | glue |

**EXERCISE 3B     CONSONANTS: Use this exercise to learn how some common sounds can be spelled.**

Put the words below under the correct consonant symbol, by looking in the dictionary to see which sound each word starts with.

kite    night    city    cool    noon    knead    pneumatic    key    science    psyche
cyberspace    cream    color    seal

| /s/ | /k/ | /n/ |
|---|---|---|
| city | kite | night |

## STRESS

Many words contain more than one SYLLABLE (=part that has a vowel sound). The words **agree, announce,** and **around** all have two syllables. If you look at the pronunciation guides for these words, you will see that they have a sign /ˈ/ in front of their second syllables. This means that when we say these words, we put more STRESS (=force) on the syllable with the sign in front of it:

**agree** /əˈgri/    **announce** /əˈnaʊns/    **around** /əˈraʊnd/

# Dictionary Skills Workbook

Look at the pronunciation guides for the words **airfare**, **bookstore**, and **forty**. When we say these words, the stress is on the first syllable of these words, so the sign is at the beginning:

**airfare** /'ɛrfɛr/   **bookstore** /'bʊkstɔr/   **forty** /'fɔrt̬i/

For more information on stress, see page 934.

**EXERCISE 4**   Look up the pronunciation guides for the words listed below. All of them have more than one syllable, so look for the sign /'/. Underline the part of the word that has the stress put on it:

ga<u>ze</u>bo    horizon    mercury    successfully

## Words with the same spelling, but different sounds or stress

When two words are spelled the same but have different sounds or stress patterns, this dictionary shows them like this:

**de·fense**¹ /dɪˈfɛns/ *n* **1** [U] the act of pro-

**de·fense**² /ˈdifɛns/ *n* [U] the players in a

**EXERCISE 5**   Use your dictionary to check the stress and pronunciation of *record, increase, permit,* and *upset* in the sentences below. Underline the syllable where the stress should be put on these words in each sentence.

*We keep a careful **<u>rec</u>ord** of our household expenses.*

*We carefully **record** all our household expenses.*

*The Governor does not want a tax **increase**.*

*The Governor does not want taxes to **increase**.*

*You need a special **permit** to park here.*

*They only **permit** employees to park here.*

*Sorry, I didn't mean to **upset** you.*

*Sorry, I didn't mean to cause a big **upset**.*

## Syllables and hyphenation

It helps to learn the pronunciation of a long word if you start by saying it one syllable at a time. This dictionary uses DOTs (=small round marks) between the syllables of words to show where the syllables are:

**in·her·i·tance** /ɪnˈhɛrɪtəns/ *n*

Say each syllable slowly:

> in  her  i  tance
>
> ɪn  'hɛr  ɪ  təns

Now say the word quickly. Remember to put the stress on /hɛr/: **in<u>her</u>itance**

The dots also show you where you can break a word at the end of a line of writing:

*Milton's aunt left him a large **inher-itance** when she died.*

*Milton's aunt left him a large **inheri-tance** when she died.*

✗ Do not break a word after only one letter, and do not leave just one letter on the new line, after the hyphen.✗

## FINDING AND UNDERSTANDING MEANINGS

### The defining vocabulary

This dictionary makes it easy for you to understand the meanings of words - their DEFINITIONS - because the definitions have been written using a defining vocabulary of only 2000 common words.

For example, look at the entry for **ice cream**. Because there are no difficult words used in the definition, you do not have to look up other words to understand what it means.

**ice cream** /'. ./ *n* [U] a frozen sweet food made of milk or cream and sugar, usually with

If it is impossible to avoid using a more difficult word in a definition, that word is shown in CAPITAL LETTERS like this. You can find this word in the dictionary, and many words like this have short explanations after them.

**tom·a·hawk** /ˈtɑmə,hɔk/ *n* a HATCHET (=type of weapon) used by some Native Americans in

**EXERCISE 6**    Use your dictionary to answer these questions by looking up the words shown in dark letters and reading their definitions.

1. What type of things would use a **beacon** to guide them? *Answer: boats, planes, etc.*

2. If you **stride**, how do you walk?

3. How would you play a **cymbal**?

4. If two things are **diametrically** opposed, are they similar or different?

5. When might you say "good **riddance**"?

6. How many quarts make up a **gallon**?

7. Does a **plaintive** sound seem happy or sad?

8. What might make you **wince**?

## More than one meaning

Many words have more than one meaning. When this is true, you should read through all the meanings until you find the one that correctly explains the use of the word you are looking for. To help you find the meaning you want quickly, this dictionary puts the most frequent meaning first, the second most frequent meaning second, and so on.

For example, at the noun **rap**, the first meaning listed is the musical meaning, because people use that meaning the most. The second meaning listed is the noise, because that is the next most frequent meaning.

> **rap**[1] /ræp/ *n* **1** [C,U] a type of popular music in which the words are not sung, but spoken in time to music with a steady beat **2** a quick light hit or knock: *a* ***rap at*** *the door*

**EXERCISE 7A**    Look up these words in the dictionary. How many meanings does each one have?

setting __3__    beaker _____    pouch _____

dizzy _____    language _____    gloom _____

**EXERCISE 7B**    In the sentences below, the words in dark letters all have more than one meaning. Look them up in the dictionary and decide which meaning correctly explains the use of the word in these sentences. Then, write the number of that meaning next to the sentence.

1. Polish the tiles with an **abrasive** cleaner.    __2__

2. She won a scholarship to a **ballet** school in Vienna.    _____

3. The camping equipment is out in the **garage**.    _____

4. The pills come in childproof **packaging**.    _____

5. Cut the dough into **diamonds** and place on a cookie sheet.    _____

## Idiomatic expressions

Some meanings in this dictionary start with a phrase in **dark letters**. This shows that the phrase is a very common expression, which has its own meaning.

For example, look at the entry for the verb **jog**. The expression **jog sb's memory** is listed as a separate meaning, because you cannot guess the meaning of this phrase, even if you know all the words in it.

> **jog**[1] /dʒɑg/ *v* **-gged, -gging 1** [I] to run slowly and in a steady way, especially for exercise: *Julie jogs every morning.* —see picture on page 473 **2 jog sb's memory** to make someone remember something: *This picture*

These phrases are all shown at the first important word in the phrase, so for example **join the club!** is at the main word **join**, and **you name it** is at the main word **name**. In some phrases, you have a choice of words to use, for example **keep/lose your head**. This phrase is shown at the word **head**. (Words such as prepositions and verbs like *make, get,* and *go* are usually not the most important word in the phrase.)

# Dictionary Skills Workbook

**EXERCISE 8** Look up the phrases below in the dictionary. Next to each phrase, write the main word where the phrase is shown.

| phrase | main word | phrase | main word |
|---|---|---|---|
| go against the grain | *grain* | hit the sack | |
| take sb for granted | | for sale | |
| kick/break the habit | | ulterior motive/reason | |
| early bird | | under the weather | |

## Signposts

Some words have so many meanings that it can be difficult to find the one you are looking for. In this dictionary, words with many meanings that are clearly different from each other have special, short words called *signposts* at the beginning of each meaning. These help you find the meaning you want more quickly.

For example, the noun **school** has several very different meanings. Some meanings are special phrases, and the other meanings have signposts.

**school**¹ /skul/ *n*
1 ▶BUILDING◀ [C,U] a place where children
2 ▶TIME AT SCHOOL◀ [U] the time spent at
3 ▶TEACHERS/STUDENTS◀ the students and
4 in school attending a school: *Are your boys*

## UNDERSTANDING THE GRAMMAR

This dictionary makes it easier to understand the grammar of words.

### Parts of speech

The first thing this dictionary tells you is whether a word is a noun, a verb, an adjective etc. Some of the parts of speech are written as complete words. The most common parts of speech are written as short forms; look at the list on the inside front cover for these.

**EXERCISE 9** Look up the words in the first column in the dictionary. Write the part of speech next to each one, in the second column. If the part of speech has a short form, write it in the third column.

| word | part of speech | short form | word | part of speech | short form |
|---|---|---|---|---|---|
| also | *adverb* | *adv* | excellent | | |
| although | | | you | | |
| may | | | several | | |
| aluminum | | | hundred | | |
| consider | | | run into | | |
| a/an | | | do¹ | | |
| the | | | at | | |
| every | | | wow | | |

## Word families

Many words in English have several different forms, which are often made by adding a group of letters to the end of a word. For example, you can add **-ly** to the adjective **sweet** to make the adverb **sweetly**, or you can add **-ness** to make the noun **sweetness**.

Sometimes, a word like **sweetly** does not change very much in meaning from the main word **sweet**. It only means "in a sweet way." Related words like this are shown at the end of the entry for the main word:

**sweet** /swit/ *adj* **1** having a taste like sugar:

to eat sweet foods **5** making you feel pleased and satisfied: *Revenge is sweet!* **—sweetly** *adv* **—sweetness** *n* [U]

Related words are only shown if they are frequent, and they are put in frequency order so you can tell which one is more common.

Some related words are so common that they are shown as main words. Words like this may have several meanings, or special usage that you need to know about.

**mil·i·tant**[1] /ˈmɪlətənt/ *adj* willing to use force or violence: *Militant groups were still protesting against the new law.* **–militancy** *n* [U]

**un·for·tu·nate** /ʌnˈfɔrtʃənɪt/ *adj* **1** hap-

**un·for·tu·nate·ly** /ʌnˈfɔrtʃənɪtli/ *adv* used

There is a list of word endings at the back of this dictionary on page 930. This list tells you what the endings mean, and gives you examples of words that are made with them.

**EXERCISE 10**   Look up the words in the first column in the dictionary. At the end of the entry for the main word, you will find words that are related to it. Write the different forms of the word in the columns on the right. Not every word will have related words in every column.

| word | adj | adv | n | n | v |
|------|-----|-----|---|---|---|
| barbarian | barbarous | | | | |
| respectable | | | | | |
| eccentric | | | | | |
| takeout | | | | | |
| perplex | | | | | |
| babysit | | | | | |
| careless | | | | | |
| magnet | | | | | |
| permanent | | | | | |

## Nouns

If the word you look up is a noun, this dictionary shows you whether it has a plural form or not.

Nouns that have a plural form are COUNTABLE nouns, and do not have a grammar sign.

Nouns that do not have a plural form are UNCOUNTABLE nouns, and are shown with the sign [U].

Some nouns can be both countable and uncountable, and are shown with the sign [C,U].

Other nouns are only [singular] or [plural].

See the Study Notes on page 466 for more information about nouns.

**car** /kɑr/ *n* **1** a vehicle with four wheels and an engine, used for traveling from one place to

**air**[1] /ɛr/ *n* **1** [U] the mixture of gases that we breathe and that surrounds the Earth: *Let's go*

**fash·ion**[1] /ˈfæʃən/ *n* **1** [C,U] the popular style of clothes, hair, behavior etc. at a particular

**past**[3] *n* [singular] **1** the time that existed before now: *People travel more now than they did*

**re·sour·ces** /ˈriˌsɔrsɪz/ *n* [plural] all the money, property, skills etc. that you have avail-

## Verbs

If the word you look up is a verb, this dictionary tells you what kind of a verb it is.

Verbs that are not followed by an object are INTRANSITIVE verbs, and are shown with the sign [I].

Verbs that must be followed by an object are TRANSITIVE verbs, and are shown with the sign [T].

Some verbs can be both intransitive and transitive, and are shown with the sign [I,T].

LINKING verbs are shown with the sign [linking verb].

See the Study Notes on page 468 for more information about verbs.

**daw·dle** /ˈdɔdl/ *v* [I] INFORMAL to waste time by doing things too slowly: *Stop dawdling; we'll be*

**needle**[2] *v* [T] INFORMAL to deliberately annoy someone by making a lot of unkind remarks or

**fin·ish**[1] /ˈfɪnɪʃ/ *v* **1** [I,T] to come to the end of doing or making something, so it is complete:

**seem** /sim/ *v* [linking verb] **1** to appear to be a particular thing or to have a particular quality

# Dictionary Skills Workbook

## Phrasal verbs

This dictionary helps you to put the object in the correct position when you are using a phrasal verb. The short forms **sb** and **sth** tell you whether the object can be only a person (**sb**), only a thing (**sth**), or either a person or a thing (**sb/sth**).

Sometimes the object can only follow the phrasal verb:

> **take after** sb *phr v* [T] to look or behave like another member of your family: *Jenny takes*

Sometimes the object can only come between the parts of the phrasal verb:

> **cheer** sb **on** *phr v* [T] to encourage someone by cheering for him/her: *Hansen's family was*

Sometimes a phrasal verb has more than one object:

> **read** sth **into** sth *phr v* [T] to think that a situation, action etc. means more than it really does:

Sometimes the object can either come between the parts of the phrasal verb, or follow it. The sign (↔) tells you that the object is not fixed:

> **pick** sth ↔ **over** *phr v* [T] to carefully examine a group of things in order to choose only the

See the Study Note on page 462 for more information about phrasal verbs.

---

**EXERCISE 11**    Read each sentence below and look up the word in dark letters in the dictionary. If the word is used correctly in the sentence, put a check (✓) next to the sentence. If it is used incorrectly, write a new, correct sentence on a sheet of paper.

1. It's only $3.50 - that's a **chickenfeed.**          _____
2. Tell him that Melanie sends her **regard.**          _____
3. He's just trying to **protect** his little sister.          _____
4. We decided it was best not to **interfere** their affairs.          _____
5. We can eat as soon as **I heat up** the tortillas.          _____
6. Stand on the corner so you can **flag** the bus **down.**          _____
7. I need a new car - mine is **falling apart.**          _____
8. It was her personality that **endeared to** the students.          _____

---

## USING THE WORDS CORRECTLY

This dictionary makes it easier to use words correctly in speech and writing.

### Examples of use

Example sentences show you how a word is typically used. Grammar patterns and frequent phrases are shown in **dark letters** so you can see clearly what the patterns are.

> **half·way** /ˌhæf'weɪ◂/ *adj, adv* **1** at the middle point between two places or two points: *Their boat was **halfway across** the lake when it*

Example sentences can show typical prepositions that a word is used with:

> **sip**² *n* a very small amount of a drink: *He took a **sip of** coffee.*

They can also show verbs, nouns, adjectives etc. that are usually used with the main word:

> jured: *The tests show some **brain/liver damage**. | Was there any **damage to** your car ? | The earthquake **caused serious/severe damage** to the*

### Frequent phrases

Some common phrases that are used with main words are not very easy to understand. This dictionary gives clear explanations next to these phrases so that it is easier to understand the usage.

> **date**¹ /deɪt/ *n* **1** a particular day of the month or of the year, shown by a number: *"What's today's date?" "It's August 11th." | Have you **set a date** (=chosen a day) for the wedding?* **2** an

**EXERCISE 12**  Look up the words in dark letters in the dictionary and answer the questions.

1. Does someone <u>do</u> a **crime** or <u>commit</u> a crime?    *Answer:  someone commits a crime.*

2. Draw a line under the most common prepositions that are used with the verb **work:**

    on      by      with      for      to      along      at

3. Does something <u>have</u> an **effect** or <u>give</u> an effect?

4. Does an object have **sentimental** <u>worth</u> or sentimental <u>value</u>?

5. Do we say "**prevent** someone to do something" or "prevent someone from doing something"?

## Usage notes and culture notes

The usage notes in this dictionary help you avoid the most common mistakes that are made in using words, by giving longer explanations when this is important.

Some sets of words are very easy to confuse with each other.

> **USAGE NOTE affect and effect**
> Use the verb **affect** to talk about making

Some words have very difficult grammar that needs more explanation.

> **USAGE NOTE all**
> **All** is used with a singular verb with un-countable nouns: *All the money is gone.* It

Some words are used in a special way in American English.

> **CULTURE NOTE soda, soda pop, pop, and soft drink**
> All of these words mean the same thing,

Culture notes tell you useful things to know about North American culture, such as how people expect you to behave:

> **CULTURE NOTE getting attention in a restaurant**
> In the US and Canada, when you are in a

## Usage hints

In this dictionary, many words also have short hints about common mistakes.

The following usage hint means that it is wrong to say *Butter wasn't in the shopping list.*

> remember them: *Make a list of the equipment you'll need.* | *Butter wasn't on the shopping list.*
> ✗ DON'T SAY "in the list." ✗

**EXERCISE 13**  Read each sentence below and look up the usage note for the word in dark letters in the dictionary. If the word is used correctly in the sentence, put a check (✓) next to the sentence. If it is used incorrectly, write a new, correct sentence below the incorrect sentence.

1. I'm **gonna** the movies tomorrow night.    _____

   _____

2. Please **remember** me to mail this letter.    _____

   _____

3. Renata always tries **hard** to do her best.    _____

   _____

4. My new **pair** of jeans are dirty.    _____

   _____

# Dictionary Skills Workbook

## CHOOSING THE RIGHT WORD

### SPOKEN, INFORMAL AND FORMAL

It is not always easy to know which words are acceptable to use in essays, formal letters etc. This dictionary helps you choose the right word for the right situation.

The label SPOKEN tells you that this word or phrase is not written very often at all, and cannot be used in an essay.

> **4** [T] SPOKEN to like something or someone: *You really dig her, don't you?*

The label INFORMAL tells you that this word or phrase may be written, but that it is still not good to use it in an essay.

> **clicked. 3** [I] INFORMAL to like someone and share his/her ideas, opinions etc.: *We clicked the first time we met.*

The label FORMAL tells you that this word is used in official documents or in formal writing. You can usually use these words in essays, but be careful not to use too many of them.

> **re·vere** /rɪˈvɪr/ v [T] FORMAL to greatly respect and admire someone: *He was revered as a*

Most words and phrases have no label, and are the best ones to use in an essays, because they are neither too informal nor too formal.

> *happy?* **8 think well/highly of** to admire or approve of someone or his/her work: *People had always thought highly of her grandmother.*

**EXERCISE 14**  Look up the words and phrases below in the dictionary. Put a check (✓) next to each one that would be acceptable to use in an essay. If you are not sure about whether a formal word is acceptable or not, ask your teacher.

| | |
|---|---|
| mess up | noteworthy |
| ruin | noticeable |
| spoil | negate |
| wreck | stop |
| merit | desist |
| deserve | knock it off |
| be worth it | quit |

## Synonyms

Words that are very similar in meaning are called SYNONYMS. Many words have synonyms, but the words are usually used in very different ways. To help you avoid choosing the wrong word, this dictionary shows synonyms only when they are used in similar ways.

For example, the only difference between **wing it** and **improvise** is that **wing it** is an INFORMAL phrase. The entry for **wing it** is labeled INFORMAL, so the synonym IMPROVISE is shown. The word **improvise** can be used in exactly the same way: *"Just improvise, you'll be fine!"*

> **wing²** v **1 wing it** INFORMAL to do or say something without any planning or preparation; IMPROVISE: *"I can't give a speech!" "Just wing it, you'll be fine!"* **2** [I] LITERARY to fly

Sometimes there is a synonym that is much less common than a main word, although the two words mean exactly the same thing. This dictionary shows the synonym, but tells you which main word to look up in order to find the definition.

For example, the word **pool** is much more common than the phrase **swimming pool**. So, the entry for **swimming pool** tells you that you can find the definition at **pool.**

> **swimming pool** /ˈ.. ˌ./ n ⇨ POOL¹

You can find much more information in the Usage Notes about special groups of synonyms.

## Opposites

This dictionary shows whether an opposite is formed with common prefixes such as **un-** and **non-,** or with more unusual prefixes such as **ir-** and **il-.**

An opposite is usually shown at the end of an entry.

> **leg·i·ble** /'lɛdʒəbəl/ *adj* written or printed clearly enough for you to read: *His writing was barely legible.* —**legibly** *adv* —opposite ILLEGIBLE

An opposite is shown at a particular meaning if the opposites for different meanings are different, or if the opposite is not used very often with the other meanings.

> **hard¹** /hɑrd/ *adj*
> **1 ▶FIRM TO TOUCH◄** firm and stiff, and difficult to cut, press down, or break: *I can't sleep on a hard mattress.* | *hard candy* | *The plums are still too hard to eat.* —opposite SOFT
> **2 ▶DIFFICULT◄** difficult to do or understand: *It was the hardest class he'd ever had.* | *It's **hard** to say* (=difficult to know) *when Glenn will be back.* | *It is **hard for** me to understand why this happened.* —opposite EASY¹

## "See also" cross-references

Sometimes the word or meaning you are looking for may not be shown at the main word you looked up. This dictionary tells you where to look for these words and meanings.

Many nouns have a plural form that has its own meaning. These nouns are shown as main words. If you look up the singular form first, the dictionary will tell you where to find the plural form.

> **flu·id¹** /'fluɪd/ *n* [C,U] a liquid: *It is a clear fluid that smells of alcohol.* —see also FLUIDS

Sometimes a phrase is at another entry. If you look up one word in the phrase, the dictionary tells you where to find that phrase.

> **grind·stone** /'graɪndstoʊn/ *n* a large round stone that is turned like a wheel and is used for making tools sharp —see also **keep your nose to the grindstone** (NOSE¹)

The dictionary also tells you where to look for a word with a similar spelling, or an entry that includes the word you are looking up.

> **kar·at** /'kærət/ *n* a unit for measuring how pure a piece of gold is —see also CARAT

> **lag²** *n* a delay between two events —see also JET LAG

## "Compare" cross-references

Sometimes the word or meaning you are looking up is related in a special way to another word or meaning. This dictionary makes it easy for you to compare these words and meanings, and to choose the right one.

Some words are used in similar ways, but mean slightly different things.

> **Jun·ior** /'dʒunyɚ/, *written abbreviation* **Jr.** *adj* used after the name of a man who has the same name as his father: *William Jones Jr.* —compare SENIOR

Some words are not exact opposites, but their meanings are different from another word in a special way.

> **in·tran·si·tive verb** /.,... './ *n* TECHNICAL in grammar, an intransitive verb has a subject but no object. In the sentence, "They arrived early," "arrive" is an intransitive verb —compare TRANSITIVE VERB —see study note on page 468

Some words are easily confused with each other.

> **im·ply** /ɪm'plaɪ/ *v* [T] to suggest that something is true without saying or showing it directly: *He implied that the money hadn't been lost, but was stolen.* —compare INFER

# Dictionary Skills Workbook: Answers

## ANSWERS TO THE WORKBOOK EXERCISES

### EXERCISE 1

| | |
|---|---|
| pay | pawn |
| pay-TV | pay |
| pay off | pay off |
| payroll | pay up |
| pea | pay dirt |
| PE | payroll |
| pay dirt | pay-TV |
| pay up | PE |
| pawn | pea |

### EXERCISE 2

| verb | past tense | past participle | present participle |
|---|---|---|---|
| take | took | taken | taking |
| make | made | made | making |
| eat | ate | eaten | eating |
| lag | lagged | lagged | lagging |
| carry | carried | carried | carrying |

| adjective | comparative | superlative |
|---|---|---|
| mad | madder | maddest |
| tiny | tinier | tiniest |
| bad | worse | worst |
| crazy | crazier | craziest |
| funny | funnier | funniest |

| noun | plural |
|---|---|
| domino | dominos |
| knife | knives |
| candy | candies |
| axis | axes |
| aircraft | aircraft |

### EXERCISE 3A

| /i/ | /ɛ/ | /ɔ/ | /u/ |
|---|---|---|---|
| need | said | awful | glue |
| field | bet | thought | new |
| even | dead | soft | boot |
| seed | ever | taught | mood |
| clean | next | malt | true |
| | went | | do |

### EXERCISE 3B

| /s/ | /k/ | /n/ |
|---|---|---|
| city | kite | night |
| science | cool | noon |
| psyche | key | knead |
| cyberspace | cream | pneumatic |
| seal | color | |

### EXERCISE 4  ga<u>ze</u>bo    ho<u>ri</u>zon    <u>mer</u>cury    suc<u>cess</u>fully

### EXERCISE 5  <u>record</u>    re<u>cord</u>;    <u>increase</u>    in<u>crease</u>;    <u>permit</u>    per<u>mit</u>;    up<u>set</u>    <u>upset</u>

### EXERCISE 6
1. boats, planes, etc.
2. with quick long steps
3. by hitting it with a stick or hitting two of them together
4. different
5. when you are glad someone or something has gone away
6. four
7. sad
8. pain or embarrassment

## EXERCISE 7A

setting ___3___    beaker ___1___    poach ___2___
dizzy ___2___    language ___5___    gloom ___2___

## EXERCISE 7B

| | |
|---|---|
| 1.  Polish the tiles with an **abrasive** cleaner. | 2 |
| 2.  She won a scholarship to a **ballet** school in Vienna. | 2 |
| 3.  The camping equipment is out in the **garage**. | 1 |
| 4.  The pills come in childproof **packaging**. | 1 |
| 5.  Cut the dough into **diamonds** and place on a cookie sheet. | 2 |

## EXERCISE 8

| phrase | main word | phrase | main word |
|---|---|---|---|
| go against the grain | grain | hit the sack | hit |
| take sb for granted | grant | for sale | sale |
| kick/break the habit | habit | ulterior motive/reason | ulterior |
| early bird | early | under the weather | weather |

## EXERCISE 9

| word | part of speech | short form | word | part of speech | short form |
|---|---|---|---|---|---|
| also | adverb | adv | excellent | adjective | adj |
| although | conjunction | | you | pronoun | pron |
| may | modal verb | | several | quantifier | |
| aluminum | noun | n | hundred | number | |
| consider | verb | v | run into | phrasal verb | phr v |
| a/an | indefinite article, determiner | | do¹ | auxiliary verb | |
| the | definite article, determiner | | at | preposition | prep |
| every | determiner | | wow | interjection | |

## EXERCISE 10

| word | adj | adv | n | n | v |
|---|---|---|---|---|---|
| barbarian | barbarous | | | | |
| respectable | | respectably | respectability | | |
| eccentric | | | eccentricity | | |
| takeout | take-out | | | | |
| perplex | perplexed | | perplexity | | |
| babysit | | | babysitter | babysitting | |
| careless | | carelessly | carelessness | | |
| magnet | | | | | magnetize |
| permanent | | | permanence | | |

# Dictionary Skills Workbook: Answers

**EXERCISE 11**

The wrong sentences are **1**, **2**, **4**, and **8**.  They should look like this:

1. It's only  $3.50 - that's chickenfeed.

2. Tell him that Melanie sends her regards.

4. We decided it was best not to interfere in their affairs.

8. It was her personality that endeared her to the students.

**EXERCISE 12**

1. someone commits a crime

2. for, at, *and* with

3. something has an effect

4. sentimental value

5. prevent someone from doing something

**EXERCISE 13**

The wrong sentences are **1**, **2**, and **4**.  They should look like this:

1. I'm going to the movies tomorrow night.

2. Please remind me to mail this letter.

4. My new pair of jeans is dirty.

**EXERCISE 14**

The acceptable words are:

ruin, spoil, merit, deserve, be worth it, noticeable, negate, stop

The formal words that may be acceptable are:

noteworthy, desist

**A, a** /eɪ/ the first letter of the English alphabet

**A** /eɪ/ n **1** the best grade that can be given to a student's work: *I got an "A" on my math test!* | *Rick was an A student* (=always received the best grades) *in high school.* **2** the sixth note in the musical SCALE of C, or the musical KEY based on this note

**a** /ə; *strong* eɪ/ also **an** (BEFORE A VOWEL SOUND) *indefinite article, determiner* **1** used before a noun to show that you are talking about a general type of thing, not a specific thing: *Do you have a car?* | *I'll find you a pencil.* —compare THE¹ **2 a)** one: *a thousand dollars* | *a dozen eggs* **b)** used before some words that show how much of something there is: *a few weeks from now* | *a little water* | *a lot of people* **3** used before a noun that is one of many similar things, people, events, times etc: *I'd like to be a teacher.* | *This is a very good wine.* **4** every or each: *A square has 4 sides.* **5** once a week/$100 a day etc. one time each week, $100 a day etc.; per **6** used before two nouns that are frequently mentioned together: *a cup and saucer* | *a knife and fork* **7 a)** used before the -ing form of some verbs when they are used as nouns: *a loud screeching of brakes* **b)** used before some singular nouns that are actions: *Take a look at that!*

> **USAGE NOTE a or an**
>
> Before you decide whether to use **a** or **an** before a word, you have to know how the word is pronounced. If the word starts with a vowel sound, use **an**: *an apple* | *an hour* | *an MBA*. If the word starts with a consonant sound, use **a**: *a house* | *a CD* | *a unit*

**AA** n Associate of Arts; a college degree given after two years of study, usually at a COMMUNITY COLLEGE

**a·back** /ə'bæk/ *adv* **be taken aback** to be very surprised, often in an unpleasant way: *I was taken aback by Linda's anger.*

**ab·a·cus** /'æbəkəs/ n a frame with balls that slide along BARs to help you count, add etc.

**a·ban·don** /ə'bændən/ v [T] **1** to leave someone or something you are responsible for; DESERT: *She just abandoned her family!* **2** to stop doing or using something because of problems: *The policy had to be abandoned.* —**abandonment** n [U]

**a·ban·doned** /ə'bændənd/ *adj* not being used or taken care of any longer: *an abandoned building/child*

**a·bashed** /ə'bæʃt/ *adj* feeling or looking shy or ashamed: *an abashed grin* —opposite UN-ABASHED

**a·bate** /ə'beɪt/ v [I] FORMAL to become less loud, strong, painful etc.: *Public anger does not appear to be abating.* —compare UNABATED

**ab·bey** /'æbi/ n a building in which NUNs or MONKs lived, especially in past times

**ab·bre·vi·ate** /ə'briviˌeɪt/ v [T] FORMAL to make a word, story etc. shorter

**ab·bre·vi·a·tion** /əˌbriviˈeɪʃən/ n the short form of a word used in writing. For example, Mr. is the abbreviation of Mister

**ABC** n [U] American Broadcasting Company; one of the national companies that broadcasts television and radio programs in the US

**ABC's** /ˌeɪbiˈsiz/ n [plural] the letters of the English alphabet: *a three-year old learning her ABC's*

**ab·di·cate** /'æbdɪˌkeɪt/ v [I,T] to give up a high position, or refuse responsibility for something —**abdication** /ˌæbdɪˈkeɪʃən/ n [C,U]

**ab·do·men** /'æbdəmən/ n TECHNICAL the part of your body between your chest and your legs —**abdominal** /æbˈdɑmənəl, əb-/ *adj*

**ab·duct** /əbˈdʌkt, æb-/ v [T] to take someone away illegally and by force; KIDNAP —**abduction** /-ˈdʌkʃən/ n [U]

**ab·er·ra·tion** /ˌæbəˈreɪʃən/ n [C,U] a situation or action that is different from what you expect or what is normal: *a minor aberration in the plan*

**a·bet** /ə'bɛt/ v **-tted, -tting** [T] ⇨ **aid and abet** (AID²)

**ab·hor** /əbˈhɔr, æb-/ v **-rred, -rring** [T] FORMAL to hate something: *Smith abhorred slavery for moral reasons.*

**ab·hor·rent** /əbˈhɔrənt, -ˈhɑr-, æb-/ *adj* FORMAL an idea that is abhorrent is one you hate —**abhorrence** n [U]

**a·bide** /ə'baɪd/ v [T] **sb can't abide sth** used in order to say that someone does not like someone or something at all: *I can't abide his stupid jokes.*

**abide by** sth *phr v* [T] to obey a law, agreement etc.: *If you're going to live here, you will abide by my rules!*

**a·bid·ing** /ə'baɪdɪŋ/ *adj* LITERARY continuing for a long time

**a·bil·i·ty** /ə'bɪləti/ n [C,U] the mental skill or physical power to do something: *A manager must have the ability to communicate well.* | *a young girl with great musical ability*

> **USAGE NOTE ability, skill, talent, knack**
>
> Use these words to talk about how well someone does something. An **ability** is what you can do with your mind or your body: *artistic ability* | *athletic ability*. You

A

can lose your **ability** to do something: *Ryan lost the ability to walk after his skiing accident.* A **skill** is something that you do very well because you have learned and practiced it: *I'm taking this class to improve my writing skills.* **Talent** is a natural ability to do something well: *Joan has a real talent for music.* **Knack** is a more informal word than **talent**: *Kate has a knack for decorating.*

**ab·ject** /'æbdʒɛkt, æb'dʒɛkt/ *adj* **1** abject conditions are severe or extreme: *abject poverty* **2** abject behavior shows that you do not respect yourself: *an abject apology* –**abjectly** *adv*

**a·blaze** /ə'bleɪz/ *adj* **1** **be ablaze** to be burning: *The old house was quickly ablaze.* **2** **be ablaze with** to be very bright with color or light: *a garden ablaze with summer flowers*

**a·ble** /'eɪbəl/ *adj* **1** **able to do sth** having the power, skill, or time to do something: *Will you be able to come tonight? | I was just able to reach the handle.* –opposite UNABLE **2** intelligent or skilled: *an able student* –see study note on page 458

**ab·nor·mal** /æb'nɔrməl/ *adj* different from what usually happens or what ought to be: *abnormal levels of chemicals in the water* –**abnormally** *adv* –**abnormality** /ˌæbnɔr-'mæləti, -nɚ-/ *n* [C,U]

**a·board** /ə'bɔrd/ *adv prep* on or onto a ship, plane, or train: *A reporter aboard the President's plane asked the question.*

**a·bode** /ə'boʊd/ *n* FORMAL the place where you live

**a·bol·ish** /ə'bɑlɪʃ/ *v* [T] to officially end a law, system etc: *Welfare programs cannot be abolished that quickly.* –**abolition** /ˌæbə'lɪʃən/ *n* [U]: *the abolition of slavery* –**abolitionist** *n*

**a·bom·i·na·ble** /ə'bɑmənəbəl/ *adj* extremely unpleasant, or of very bad quality

**ab·o·rig·i·nal** /ˌæbə'rɪdʒənəl/ *adj* relating to the people or animals that have lived in a place from the earliest times

**ab·o·rig·i·ne** /ˌæbə'rɪdʒəni/ *n* a member of the people who have lived in Australia from the earliest times

**a·bort** /ə'bɔrt/ *v* [T] **1** to end an activity because it would be too difficult or dangerous to continue: *The Reagan administration had to abort plans to sell public lands.* **2** to deliberately end a PREGNANCY when the baby is still too young to live –compare MISCARRY

**a·bor·tion** /ə'bɔrʃən/ *n* [C,U] the act of ABORTing a baby: *She was told about the dangers of having an abortion.*

**a·bor·tive** /ə'bɔrtɪv/ *adj* an abortive action or plan is not successful

**a·bound** /ə'baʊnd/ *v* [I] LITERARY to exist in large numbers: *Images of African life abound in her books.*

**a·bout¹** /ə'baʊt/ *prep* **1** on or dealing with a particular subject: *I'll call you and tell you all about it later. | a book about how the universe began* **2** in the nature or character of a person or thing: *There's something weird about that guy.* **3** **what about/how about** SPOKEN **a)** used in order to make a suggestion: *How about coming to my house after we're done here? | What about bringing a potato salad?* **b)** used in order to ask for news, or for a suggestion: *What about Jack? We can't just leave him here.* **4** SPOKEN used in order to introduce a subject: *About those tickets, I do want to buy one.*

**about²** *adv* **1** a little more or less than a particular number or amount; APPROXIMATELY: *I live about 10 miles from here.* **2** almost: *Dinner's about ready. Come and sit down.*

**about³** *adj* **1** **be about to do sth** to be just ready to start doing something: *We were about to leave, when Jerry arrived.* **2** **not be about to do sth** to be very unwilling to do something: *I'm not about to give him any more money!*

**above**

The picture is above / over the mantlepiece.

The dog jumped over the wall.

**a·bove¹** /ə'bʌv/ *prep* **1** in or to a higher position than something else: *Raise your arm above your head.* **2** at or to a higher number, amount, or level than something else: *Temperatures rose above freezing today. | 50 feet above ground* **3** louder or higher in PITCH than other sounds: *He couldn't hear her voice above the noise.* **4** **above all** FORMAL most importantly: *Above all, I would like to thank my parents.* **5** **above suspicion/criticism etc.** so honest or good that no one can doubt you

**above²** *adv* **1** more or higher than a particular number, amount, or level: *Males aged 18 and above could be drafted.* **2** in an earlier part of something you are reading: *The graph above shows the growth in pollution levels.* **3** in a higher place than something else: *The sound came from the room above.*

**a·bove·board** /ə'bʌvˌbɔrd/ *adj* honest and legal: *The agreement seems to be aboveboard.*

**a·bra·sive** /ə'breɪsɪv, -zɪv/ *adj* **1** rude and annoying: *an abrasive personality* **2** having a rough surface that can be used for rubbing things off other surfaces —**abrasively** *adv*

**a·breast** /ə'brɛst/ *adv* **1** **keep abreast of** to know the most recent facts about a subject: *I assume you will keep us abreast of his progress.* **2** next to someone or something, usually in a line, and facing the same direction: *Patrol cars were lined up four abreast.*

**a·bridge** /ə'brɪdʒ/ *v* [T] to make a book, play etc. shorter, keeping the general meaning the same: *the abridged version of the dictionary* —compare UNABRIDGED

**a·broad** /ə'brɔd/ *adv* in or to a foreign country: *He suggested that his son **go abroad** for a year.*

**a·brupt** /ə'brʌpt/ *adj* **1** sudden and unexpected: *an abrupt change in the attitudes of voters* **2** not polite or friendly, especially because you do not want to waste time: *She was abrupt on the phone the first time we talked.* —**abruptly** *adv*

**ab·scess** /'æbsɛs/ *n* a place on your body that is swollen and contains a poisonous liquid

**ab·scond** /əb'skɑnd, æb-/ *v* [I] FORMAL to leave a place secretly because you have done something wrong

**ab·sence** /'æbsəns/ *n* **1** [C,U] the state of being away from a place, or the time you are away: *The vice president will handle things **in my absence**.* | *frequent **absences from** work* **2** [U] the lack of something: *the absence of evidence of murder*

**ab·sent** /'æbsənt/ *adj* **1** not here: *Most of the class was absent with flu today.* **2** **absent look/smile/expression** a look etc. that shows you are not thinking about what is happening

**ab·sen·tee** /ˌæbsən'ti/ *n* FORMAL someone who is supposed to be in a place but is absent

**absentee bal·lot** /ˌ... '../ *n* a process by which people can send their votes by mail because they will be away during an election

**ab·sen·tee·ism** /ˌæbsən'tiɪzəm/ *n* [U] regular absence from work or school without a good reason

**ab·sent·ly** /'æbsənt͡li/ *adv* in a way that shows you are not interested in or not thinking about what is happening: *Jason patted his son absently.*

**absent-mind·ed** /ˌ... '..◂/ *adj* often forgetting or not noticing things because you are thinking of something else —**absent-mindedly** *adv*

**ab·so·lute** /'æbsə,lut, ˌæbsə'lut/ *adj* **1** complete or total: *The show was an absolute disaster the first night.* | *absolute authority* **2** definite and not likely to change: *I can't give you any absolute promises.*

**ab·so·lute·ly** /ˌæbsə'lutli, 'æbsə,lutli/ *adv* **1** completely or totally: *Are you absolutely sure?* | *The two women had absolutely nothing*

(=nothing at all) *in common.* —compare RELATIVELY **2** **Absolutely!** SPOKEN said when you agree completely, or used in order to emphasize the answer "yes": *"I wondered if I could talk to you?" "Absolutely, come in!"* **3** **Absolutely not!** SPOKEN said when you disagree completely, or used in order to add emphasis when you say "no"

**ab·solve** /əb'zɑlv, 'sɑlv/ *v* [T] FORMAL to formally forgive someone or say that s/he is not guilty

**ab·sorb** /əb'sɔrb, -'zɔrb/ *v* [T] **1** if something absorbs a liquid, it takes in the liquid through its surface: *The towel absorbed most of the water.* **2** to interest someone very much: *I was completely absorbed in the book.* **3** to understand something: *She's a good student who absorbs ideas quickly.* —**absorption** /-'ɔrpʃən/ *n* [U]

absorb

absorbent cloth

**ab·sorb·ent** /əb'sɔrbənt, -'zɔr-/ *adj* something that is absorbent can take in liquid through its surface: *absorbent diapers*

**ab·sorb·ing** /əb'sɔrbɪŋ, -'zɔr-/ *adj* so interesting that you do not notice or think about other things: *an absorbing article*

**ab·stain** /əb'steɪn/ *v* [I] **1** to not vote: *Three members of the committee abstained.* **2** to not allow yourself to do something —**abstention** /əb'stɛnʃən/ *n* [C,U]

**ab·sti·nence** /'æbstənəns/ *n* [U] the practice of not doing something you enjoy, or the length of time you do this —**abstinent** *adj*

**ab·stract¹** /əb'strækt, æb-, 'æbstrækt/ *adj* **1** existing as a general idea, or based on general ideas rather than a specific example or real event: *Beauty is an abstract idea.* | *an abstract argument about justice* **2** abstract art is made of shapes and patterns that do not look like real things or people —**abstraction** /əb'strækʃən/ *n* [C,U]

**abstract²** *n* a short written statement of the most important ideas in a long piece of writing

**ab·surd** /əb'səd, -'zəd/ *adj* seeming completely unreasonable or silly: *an absurd situation* | *an absurd hat* —**absurdly** *adv* —**absurdity** *n* [C,U]

**a·bun·dance** /ə'bʌndəns/ *n* [singular, U] FORMAL a large quantity of something: *an abundance of wavy red hair* | *Wild flowers grow in abundance on the hillsides.*

**a·bun·dant** /ə'bʌndənt/ *adj* more than enough in quantity: *an abundant supply of fresh fruit*

**a·bun·dant·ly** /ə'bʌndəntli/ *adv* completely, or in large amounts: *Kaplan made it abundantly clear that we weren't welcome.*

**A**

**a·buse**[1] /ə'byus/ *n* **1** [C,U] the use of something in a way it should not be used: *The newspapers are calling the President's action an* **abuse** *of power.* | *There has been a decrease in the amount of* **drug abuse** *in schools.* **2** [U] cruel or violent treatment of someone, usually by someone in a position of authority: *statistics on* **child abuse** *in middle class homes* | **sexual abuse** (=using sex in a way that is unacceptable or violent) **3** [U] unkind or cruel things someone says to another person

**a·buse**[2] /ə'byuz/ *v* [T] **1** to do cruel or violent things to someone: *He used to get drunk and abuse his wife.* **2** to use something too much or in the wrong way: *The laws are meant to prevent people from abusing the tax system.* | *He had been abusing drugs since the age of 12.* **3** to say cruel or unkind things to someone

**a·bu·sive** /ə'byusɪv/ *adj* using cruel words or physical violence: *an abusive husband*

**a·bys·mal** /ə'bɪzməl/ *adj* very bad: *The food at school was abysmal.*

**a·byss** /ə'bɪs/ *n* **1** a deep space that seems to have no bottom, usually in the ocean or mountains **2** LITERARY a very dangerous, frightening, sad etc. situation: *an abyss of loneliness*

**AC** *n* [U] alternating current; the type of electric current used in buildings for electrical equipment –compare DC

**ac·a·dem·ic**[1] /,ækə'dɛmɪk/ *adj* relating to teaching or studying subjects such as science, English, mathematics etc., especially in a college or university: *The academic year starts September 3rd.*

**academic**[2] *n* a teacher in a college or university

**a·cad·e·my** /ə'kædəmi/ *n* **1** a school, especially one that trains students in a special art or skill **2** an organization of people who want to encourage the progress of art, science, literature etc.

**ac·cel·er·ate** /ək'sɛlə,reɪt/ *v* **1** [I] if a vehicle or its driver accelerates, it moves faster: *Mel accelerated as she drove onto the highway.* | *a plane accelerating rapidly towards take-off* **2** [I,T] to happen at a faster rate than usual, or to make something do this: *We tried to accelerate the process by heating the chemicals.* –**acceleration** /ək,sɛlə'reɪʃən/ *n* [U]

**ac·cel·er·a·tor** /ək'sɛlə,reɪtɚ/ *n* the PEDAL in a car that you push to increase its speed –see picture on page 469

**ac·cent**[1] /'æksɛnt/ *n* **1** a way of speaking that someone has because of where s/he was born or lives: *a strong southern accent* **2** the part of a word that you emphasize when you say it: *The accent in the word "important" is on the second syllable.* **3** a mark written above some letters (such as à or ê) that shows what type of sound to make when you say it

**ac·cent**[2] /'æksɛnt, æk'sɛnt/ *v* [T] to emphasize a word or part of a word: *In the word "baby" you accent the first syllable.*

**ac·cent·ed** /'æksɛntɪd/ *adj* a language that is accented is spoken with an ACCENT from another country: *heavily accented English*

**ac·cen·tu·ate** /ək'sɛntʃu,eɪt, æk-/ *v* [T] to make something easier to notice: *Her scarf accentuated the blue of her eyes.*

**ac·cept** /ək'sɛpt/ *v* **1** [I,T] to take something that someone offers you: *Mr. Ryan wouldn't accept any money from us.* | *The company offered him the job, but he decided not to accept.* **2** [I,T] to agree to do something or to allow a plan to happen: *You shouldn't have accepted when he offered you a ride home.* | *Will the City Council accept the changes in the rules?* **3** [I,T] to agree, admit, or believe that something, often something unpleasant, is true: *I accept that we've made mistakes, but it's nothing we can't fix.* | *Barbara wouldn't accept her husband's death for months afterwards.* **4** [T] to let someone join an organization, university etc.: *I've been accepted at Harvard.* **5** [T] to let someone new become part of a group or society and to treat him/her in the same way as other members: *It was a long time before the other kids at school accepted him.* **6** [T] to let customers use a particular type of money to pay for something: *We don't accept credit cards.* **7** **accept responsibility** FORMAL to agree that you are responsible for something: *I won't accept responsibility for something I didn't do!*

**ac·cept·a·ble** /ək'sɛptəbəl/ *adj* **1** good enough for a particular purpose: *The paper was acceptable, but it wasn't her best work.* **2** acceptable behavior is considered to be morally or socially good enough: *Smoking isn't acceptable any more in many places in America.* –**acceptability** /ək,sɛptə'bɪləti/ *n* [U] –opposite UNACCEPTABLE

**ac·cept·ance** /ək'sɛptəns/ *n* [U] **1** the act of agreeing that an idea, statement, explanation etc. is right or true: *the White House's acceptance of a new bill from the Senate* **2** the act of agreeing to do, use, or take something: *I was surprised at her acceptance of my offer to help her.* **3** the process of allowing someone to become part of a group or society: *the immigrants' gradual acceptance into the community* **4** **gain/find acceptance** to become popular or liked: *Home computers first gained wide acceptance in the 1980s.* **5** the state of accepting an unpleasant situation, without getting angry or upset about it

**ac·cess**[1] /'æksɛs/ *n* [U] **1** the ability, chance, or right to use something: *Students need to* **have access to** *a computer system.* **2** the way in which you can enter a building or get to a place –see also **gain access** (GAIN)

**access**[2] *v* [T] to find and use information, especially on a computer: *I couldn't access the file.*

**ac·ces·si·ble** /ək'sɛsəbəl/ *adj* **1** able to be easily opened, used, traveled to etc.: *The national park is not accessible by road.* | *A college education wasn't accessible to women until the 1920s.* **2** easy to understand and enjoy: *I thought his first book was more accessible than the second.* –**accessibility** /ək,sɛsə'bɪləṭi/ *n* [U] –opposite INACCESSIBLE

**ac·ces·so·ry** /ək'sɛsəri/ *n* **1** [C usually plural] something such as a belt, jewelry etc. that you wear or carry because it is attractive: *a dress with matching accessories* **2** something that you add to a machine, tool, car etc. to make it more useful **3** LAW someone who helps a criminal

**ac·ci·dent** /'æksədənt, -,dɛnt/ *n* **1** a situation in which someone is hurt or something is damaged without anyone intending it to happen: *She didn't do it on purpose, it was an accident.* | *I was in an accident* (=involved in a car accident) *on the way home from work.* **2** **by accident** in a way that is not intended or planned: *I discovered by accident that he'd lied to me.*

**ac·ci·den·tal** /,æksə'dɛnṭəl/ *adj* not intended to happen: *Most accidental deaths occur at work.* –**accidentally** *adv*

**accident-prone** /'... ,./ *adj* likely to have accidents: *an accident-prone child*

**ac·claim**[1] /ə'kleɪm/ *v* [T] **be acclaimed (as)** to be praised very much, especially for particular qualities: *Landry was being acclaimed as the best coach around.*

**acclaim**[2] *n* [U] strong praise for a person, idea, book etc.

**ac·claimed** /ə'kleɪmd/ *adj* praised by a lot of people: *Rodzinki's latest film has been highly/ widely acclaimed.*

**ac·cli·mate** /'æklə,meɪt/, **ac·cli·ma·tize** /ə-'klaɪmə,taɪz/ *v* [I,T] to become used to the weather, way of living etc. in a new place, or to make someone do this: *It takes the astronauts a day to get acclimated to conditions in space.* –**acclimatization** /ə,klaɪməti'zeɪʃən/ *n* [U]

**ac·co·lade** /'ækə,leɪd/ *n* [C usually plural] FORMAL strong praise and approval

**ac·com·mo·date** /ə'kamə,deɪt/ *v* [T] **1** to have enough space for a particular number of people or things: *The auditorium can accommodate 300 people.* **2** to give someone a place to stay, live, or work: *A new dorm was built to accommodate graduate students.* **3** to do what someone wants or needs in order to help him/her or satisfy him/her: *If you need more time, we'll try to accommodate you.*

**ac·com·mo·dat·ing** /ə'kamə,deɪṭɪŋ/ *adj* helpful and willing to do what someone else wants

**ac·com·mo·da·tion** /ə,kamə'deɪʃən/ *n* [U] **1** also **accommodations** a place to live, stay, or work in: *Accommodation will be provided for all new students.* **2** a way of solving a problem between two people or groups so that both are satisfied

**ac·com·pa·ni·ment** /ə'kʌmpənimənt/ *n* **1** music played along with someone while s/he sings or plays an instrument: *a tune with a simple guitar accompaniment* **2** something that is served or used with something else: *This wine makes a nice accompaniment to fish.*

**ac·com·pa·nist** /ə'kʌmpənɪst/ *n* someone who plays a musical instrument while another person sings or plays the main tune

**ac·com·pa·ny** /ə'kʌmpəni/ *v* [T] **1** FORMAL to go somewhere with someone, especially in order to help or take care of him/her: *Children under 12 must be accompanied by an adult.* **2** to happen or exist at the same time: *Tonight, heavy rains accompanied by high winds will make driving difficult.* **3** to play music along with someone who is playing or singing the main tune

**ac·com·plice** /ə'kamplɪs/ *n* someone who helps someone do something wrong or illegal

**ac·com·plish** /ə'kamplɪʃ/ *v* [T] to succeed in doing something, especially after trying hard to do it; achieve: *We've accomplished our goal of raising $45,000.*

**ac·com·plished** /ə'kamplɪʃt/ *adj* very skillful: *an accomplished musician*

**ac·com·plish·ment** /ə'kamplɪʃmənt/ *n* **1** something you achieve or are able to do well, especially after a lot of effort: *Playing the piano is one of her many accomplishments.* **2** [U] the act of accomplishing something: *I'm looking for a job that gives me more of a sense of accomplishment.* (=a feeling that you have achieved something)

**ac·cord**[1] /ə'kɔrd/ *n* FORMAL **1** **of sb's own accord** without being asked; willingly: *I didn't say anything. He left of his own accord.* **2** [C,U] the state of agreeing about something, or a particular agreement: *The committee's report is completely in accord with our suggestions.*

**accord**[2] *v* FORMAL [T] to treat someone or something in a particular way, or to give someone a prize, reward etc.: *He was accorded the honor in 1972.*

**ac·cord·ance** /ə'kɔrdns/ *n* [U] the state of agreeing about something: *The amount of money varies in accordance with what each family needs.*

**ac·cord·ing·ly** /ə'kɔrdɪŋli/ *adv* **1** in a way that is suitable for a particular situation: *If you break the rules, you will be punished accordingly.* **2** as a result of something; therefore: *He knows how the Democrats like to work. Accordingly, he can help the Republicans defeat them.*

**according to** /.'... ./ *prep* **1** as shown by something or said by someone: *According to our records, you still have six of our* *books.* | *According to Angel, she's a great teacher.* **2** in a way that is suitable to a particular situation: *You will be paid according to the amount of work you do.*

**ac·cor·di·on** /ə'kɔrdiən/ *n* a musical instrument that you pull in and out while pushing buttons to produce different notes

**ac·cost** /ə'kɔst, ə'kɑst/ *v* [T] to go up to someone you do not know and speak to him/her in a threatening way: *I was accosted by a man asking for money.*

**ac·count**[1] /ə'kaʊnt/ *n* **1** a sum of money you keep in a bank, that you can add to or take from: *I don't have much money in my account.* | *He couldn't remember his account number.* | **checking account** (=one that you can take money out of at any time) | **savings account** (=one in which you save money so that the amount increases) **2** a written or spoken description of an event or situation: *Can you give us an account of what happened?* | *By/from all accounts* (=according to what everyone says), *Frank was once a great player.* **3** [C,U] an agreement that allows you to buy goods and pay for them later: *buying a dishwasher on account* | *Please settle your account* (=pay all you owe) *as soon as possible.* **4** take sth into account/take account of sth to consider particular facts when you make a judgment or decision about something: *The tax is unfair because it does not take account of people's ability to pay.* **5** an agreement to sell goods or services to someone over a period of time: *Our sales manager won five new accounts this year.* **6** not on my/his etc. account SPOKEN said when you do not want someone to do something for you unless s/he really wants to: *Don't stay up late on my account.* **7** on no account FORMAL used in order to say that someone must not do something for any reason: *On no account should anyone go near the building.* —see also ACCOUNTS

**account**[2] *v* [T]
**account for** sth *phr v* [T] to give a reason for something that has happened: *How do you account for the $20 that's missing?*

**ac·count·a·bil·i·ty** /ə,kaʊntə'bɪləti/ *n* [U] a system that allows you to know who is responsible for a particular action: *There is no accountability in our department.*

**ac·count·a·ble** /ə'kaʊntɹəbəl/ *adj* responsible for the effects of your actions and willing to explain them: *If anything happens to Max, I'll hold you accountable!* (=consider you responsible) —opposite UNACCOUNTABLE

**ac·count·ant** /ə'kaʊntənt, ə'kaʊnt⌐nt/ *n* someone whose job is to take care of financial accounts

**ac·count·ing** /ə'kaʊntɪŋ/ *n* [U] the profession of being an ACCOUNTANT, or the activity of dealing with financial accounts

**ac·counts** /ə'kaʊnts/ *n* [plural] a record of the money that a company has received and the money it has spent: *last year's accounts*

**ac·cred·i·ta·tion** /ə,krɛdə'teɪʃən/ *n* [U] official approval for a person or organization

**ac·cred·it·ed** /ə'krɛdɪtɪd/ *adj* having official approval as being of a high standard: *an accredited journalist/school*

**ac·crue** /ə'kru/ *v* [I,T] to increase over a period of time: *tax benefits that accrue to investors*

**ac·cu·mu·late** /ə'kyumyə,leɪt/ *v* [I,T] to gradually increase in quantity or size, or to make something do this: *Dirt and dust had accumulated in the corners of the room.* | *Myers accumulated a huge debt from gambling.* —**accumulation** /ə,kyumyə'leɪʃən/ *n* [C,U]

**ac·cu·ra·cy** /'ækyərəsi/ *n* [U] the quality of being accurate: *The bombs can be aimed with amazing accuracy.* —opposite INACCURACY

**ac·cu·rate** /'ækyərɪt/ *adj* exactly correct: *an accurate report of what happened* —**accurately** *adv* —opposite INACCURATE

**ac·cu·sa·tion** /,ækyə'zeɪʃən/ *n* a statement saying that someone has done something wrong or illegal: *Serious accusations have been made against the Attorney General.*

**ac·cuse** /ə'kyuz/ *v* [T] to make a statement saying that someone has done something wrong or illegal: *Norton was accused of murder.* | *Are you accusing me of cheating?* —**accuser** *n*

**ac·cused** /ə'kyuzd/ *n* LAW **the accused** the person or people who are being tried (TRY) for a crime in a court of law

**ac·cus·tom** /ə'kʌstəm/ *v* [T] to make yourself or another person become used to something: *They'll have to accustom themselves to working harder.*

**ac·cus·tomed** /ə'kʌstəmd/ *adj* FORMAL **be accustomed to (doing) sth** to be used to something: *Ed's eyes quickly became/got/grew accustomed to the dark room.* —opposite UNACCUSTOMED

**ace**[1] /eɪs/ *n* **1** a playing card with one mark on it, that has the highest or lowest value in a game: *the ace of spades* **2** a first hit in tennis or VOLLEYBALL that is hit so well that your opponent cannot hit it back **3** ace in the hole a secret advantage: *Money was Brown's ace in the hole; he could afford an expensive campaign.*

**ace**[2] *adj* INFORMAL **ace pilot/player etc.** someone who has a lot of skill as a pilot, player etc.

**ace**[3] *v* [T] INFORMAL to get the best grade possible on a test, piece of written work etc.: *Danny aced the spelling test.*

**a·cer·bic** /ə'sɚbɪk/ *adj* criticizing in a smart but unkind way: *Simon was known for his acerbic theater reviews.*

**ache**[1] /eɪk/ *n* **1** headache/backache/toothache a continuous pain in your head, back

A

etc. **2** a continuous dull pain: *an ache in the knee* —**achy** *adj*: *My arm feels all achy.*

**ache**[2] *v* [I] **1** to feel a continuous dull pain: *I ache all over.* **2 ache to do sth** to want to do something very much: *Jenny was aching to go home.*

**a·chieve** /əˈtʃiv/ *v* [T] to succeed in doing or getting something as a result of your actions: *You'll never achieve anything if you don't work harder.* | *We've achieved excellent sales this year.* —**achiever** *n*: *a high achiever* —**achievable** *adj*

**a·chieve·ment** /əˈtʃivmənt/ *n* **1** something important that you succeed in doing through skill and hard work: *Winning the championship is quite an achievement.* **2** [U] success in doing or getting what you worked for: *the achievement of a goal*

**ac·id**[1] /ˈæsɪd/ *n* **1** [C,U] a chemical substance that can produce salts or burn holes in the things it touches: *hydrochloric/citric acid* **2 acid test** a situation that proves whether something is true or is as good as it is supposed to be **3** [U] SLANG the drug LSD

**acid**[2] *adj* **1** having a very sour or bitter taste **2 acid remark/comment** something you say that uses humor in an unkind way —**acidity** /əˈsɪdəti/ *n* [U]

**acid rain** /ˌ.. ˈ./ *n* [U] rain that damages the environment because it contains acid, especially from factory smoke

**ac·knowl·edge** /əkˈnɑlɪdʒ/ *v* [T] **1** to accept or admit that something is true or that a situation exists: *Angie acknowledged that she had made a mistake.* **2** to officially accept that a government, court, leader etc. has legal authority: *They are refusing to acknowledge the court's decision.* **3** to state that you have received something: *The author wishes to acknowledge the help of the Art Museum.* **4** to show someone that you have seen him/her or heard what s/he has said: *Tina didn't even acknowledge me.*

**ac·knowl·edg·ment** /əkˈnɑlɪdʒmənt/ *n* something given, done, or said to thank someone or to show that something has been received: *I haven't received an acknowledgment of my letter yet.*

**ac·ne** /ˈækni/ *n* [U] a skin disease that causes small red spots to appear, especially on someone's face

**a·corn** /ˈeɪkɔrn/ *n* the nut of the OAK tree

**a·cous·tic** /əˈkustɪk/ *adj* **1** relating to sound and the way people hear things **2** an acoustic musical instrument does not have its sound made louder electronically

**a·cous·tics** /əˈkustɪks/ *n* [plural] **1** the scientific study of sound **2** the qualities of a room, such as its shape and size, that affect the way sound is heard in it

**ac·quaint** /əˈkweɪnt/ *v* [T] to know about something, because you have read about it, used it etc.: *We have already acquainted ourselves with the facts.*

**ac·quaint·ance** /əˈkweɪnt̚ns/ *n* someone you know, but not very well: *an acquaintance of mine*

**ac·quaint·ed** /əˈkweɪnt̚ɪd/ *adj* **1 get acquainted** to meet someone and start to know more about him/her: *How did you two get acquainted?* **2 be acquainted (with sb)** to know someone, but not well: *Yes, I'm acquainted with Roger.*

**ac·qui·esce** /ˌækwiˈɛs/ *v* [I] FORMAL to agree with someone without arguing or complaining, often when you do not want to —**acquiescence** *n* [U]

**ac·quire** /əˈkwaɪɚ/ *v* [T] **1** to get something, either by buying it or through hard work: *Think about the skills you have acquired, and how you can use them.* **2 an acquired taste** something that you only begin to like after you have tried it a few times: *Whiskey is often an acquired taste.*

**ac·qui·si·tion** /ˌækwəˈzɪʃən/ *n* FORMAL **1** [U] the act of getting something: *the acquisition of new companies* **2** something that you have gotten: *a recent acquisition*

**ac·quit** /əˈkwɪt/ *v* [T] to decide in a court of law that someone is not guilty of a crime: *Simmons was acquitted of murder.* —opposite CONVICT[1]

**ac·quit·tal** /əˈkwɪt̬l/ *n* [C,U] an official announcement in a court of law that someone is not guilty —opposite CONVICTION

**a·cre** /ˈeɪkɚ/ *n* a unit for measuring an area of land, equal to 4,840 square yards or about 4,047 square meters

**a·cre·age** /ˈeɪkərɪdʒ/ *n* [U] the area of a piece of land measured in ACRES

**ac·rid** /ˈækrɪd/ *adj* having a very strong and unpleasant smell or taste that hurts your nose or throat: *a cloud of acrid smoke*

**ac·ri·mo·ni·ous** /ˌækrəˈmoʊniəs/ *adj* if an argument, meeting etc. is acrimonious, the people involved are extremely angry and not kind to each other: *an acrimonious divorce*

**ac·ri·mo·ny** /ˈækrəˌmoʊni/ *n* [U] FORMAL very angry feelings between people, often strongly expressed

**ac·ro·bat** /ˈækrəˌbæt/ *n* someone who does difficult physical actions such as walking on his/her hands or balancing on a high rope —**acrobatic** /ˌækrəˈbætɪk/ *adj*

**ac·ro·bat·ics** /ˌækrəˈbætɪks/ *n* [plural] the skill or tricks of an ACROBAT

**ac·ro·nym** /ˈækrənɪm/ *n* a word that is made from the first letters of a group of words. For example, NATO is an acronym for the North Atlantic Treaty Organization

**a·cross**[1] /əˈkrɔs/ *prep* **1** going, looking, moving etc. from one side of something to the other side: *Vince stared across the canyon.* | *flying across the Atlantic* –see picture at OVER[1] **2** on or toward the opposite side of something: *Andy lives across the street from us.* | *The school is all the way across town.* **3** reaching or spreading from one side of an area to the other: *There was only one bridge across the bay.* **4** in every part of an organization or government· *Changes will have to be made across the board.* (=affecting everyone)

**across**[2] *adv* **1** from one side of something to the other: *The road's too busy to walk across.* **2 10 feet/5 miles etc. across** measuring 10 feet, 5 miles etc. from one side to the other: *At its widest point, the river is 2 miles across.* **3 across from** opposite something or someone: *One kid sitting across from me was really noisy.*

**a·cryl·ic** /ə'krılık/ *adj* acrylic paints, cloth etc. are made from a chemical substance

**act**[1] /ækt/ *v* **1** [I] to behave in a particular way: *She always acts shy when she's on the phone.* | *Pam's just acting like a baby.* **2** [I] to do something: *They think doctors can't act as managers.* | *We're acting on the advice of our lawyer.* (=doing what s/he says) **3** [I,T] to perform as a character in a play or movie: *I did a little acting in high school.* **4** [I] to produce a particular effect: *Salt acts as a preservative.*

**act** sth ↔ **out** *phr v* [T] to show how an event happened by performing it like a play: *The third graders acted out the story of the first Thanksgiving.*

**act up** *phr v* [I] INFORMAL to behave badly or not work correctly: *The car's acting up again.*

**act**[2] *n* **1** a particular type of action: *an act of cruelty* **2** also **Act** a law that has been officially passed by the government: *the Civil Rights Act* **3** also **Act** one of the main parts into which a play, OPERA etc. is divided: *Hamlet kills the king in Act 5.* **4** the performance of one of the singers, groups of musicians etc. in a show: *a comedy act* **5** [singular] insincere behavior that is meant to have a particular effect: *He doesn't care, Laura - it's just an act.* **6 get your act together** INFORMAL to do things in a more organized or effective way: *If Julie doesn't get her act together, she'll never graduate.* **7 get in on the act** INFORMAL to try to get advantages from an activity that someone else has started, especially when s/he does not want you to

---

**USAGE NOTE act and action**

Use **action** as a countable noun when it means the same as **act**: *a kind act* | *a kind action.* Use **act** in some fixed phrases when it means a particular type of action: *an act of friendship* | *an act of war* | *He was caught in the act of stealing.* **Act** is always countable, but **action** can be un-

countable: *What we need now is quick action.*

**act·ing**[1] /'æktıŋ/ *adj* **acting manager/ director etc.** someone who replaces the manager etc. for a short time

**acting**[2] *n* [U] the job or skill of representing a character, especially in a play or movie

**ac·tion** /'ækʃən/ *n* **1** something that you do: *His quick actions probably saved my life.* **2** [U] the process of doing things for a particular purpose: *We must take action* (=start doing something) *before it's too late.* | *It's time to put the plan into action.* (=do things to make it happen) –opposite INACTION **3** [singular, U] the way in which something moves, works, or has an effect on something else: *The rock is worn down by the action of the falling water.* **4 out of action** INFORMAL not working because of damage or injury: *My car's out of action.* | *Jim will be out of action for two weeks.* **5 the action** INFORMAL exciting and important things that are happening: *New York's where the action is.* **6 in action** doing a particular job or activity: *a chance to see ski jumpers in action* **7** [C,U] fighting during a war: *Ann's husband was killed in action.* –see usage note at ACT[2]

**ac·ti·vate** /'æktə,veɪt/ *v* [T] FORMAL to make something start working: *This switch activates the radar.* –**activation** /,æktə'veɪʃən/ *n* [U]

**ac·tive**[1] /'æktɪv/ *adj* **1** always doing things, or always ready and able to do something: *Grandpa's active for his age.* | *an active volcano* **2** TECHNICAL able or ready to operate: *The alarm is now active.*

**active**[2] *n* **the active (voice)** TECHNICAL in grammar, in the active voice, the subject of the sentence does the action of the verb. In the sentence, "They grow oranges in California," the verb is in the active voice –compare PASSIVE[2]

**ac·tiv·ist** /'æktəvɪst/ *n* someone who works to achieve social or political change –**activism** *n* [U]

**ac·tiv·i·ty** /æk'tɪvəti/ *n* **1** [U] movement and action: *the noise and activity of the city* | *a day full of activity* **2** [C,U] things that you do for pleasure, or because you want to achieve something: *after-school activities* | *an increase in terrorist activity*

**ac·tor** /'æktɚ/ *n* someone who performs in a play, movie etc.

**ac·tress** /'æktrɪs/ *n* a woman who performs in a play, movie etc.

**ac·tu·al** /'æktʃuəl, 'ækʃuəl/ *adj* real, especially when compared with what is believed, expected, or intended: *Were those his actual words?* | *Well, the actual cost is a lot higher than they say.*

**ac·tu·al·i·ty** /,ækʃu'æləti/ *n* **in actuality** real-

**ly:** *I always thought that making wine was complicated, when in actuality it's simple.*

**ac·tu·al·ly** /ˈæktʃuəli, -tʃəli, ˈækʃuəli, -ʃəli/ *adv* **1** used in order to emphasize an opinion or give new information: *I do actually think that things have improved.* | *Actually, a lot of Vancouver's restaurants are non-smoking.* **2** used when you are telling or asking someone what the truth about something is: *Is George actually 65?* | *Actually, I forgot to get the milk.* **3** although it may seem strange: *Pete was actually polite for once!*

**a·cu·men** /əˈkyumən, ˈækyəmən/ *n* [U] the ability to think quickly and make good judgments: *business acumen*

**ac·u·punc·ture** /ˈækyəˌpʌŋktʃɚ/ *n* [U] a method used in Chinese medicine in which needles are put into someone's body in order to treat pain or illness

**a·cute** /əˈkyut/ *adj* **1** very serious or severe: *acute pain* **2** showing an ability to clearly understand things: *an acute observation* **3** showing an ability to notice small differences in sound, taste etc.: *acute hearing* **4** TECHNICAL a disease or illness that is acute quickly becomes dangerous: *acute tuberculosis* —compare CHRONIC **5** TECHNICAL an acute angle is less than 90 degrees —**acutely** *adv*: *acutely embarrassed*

**A.D.** Anno Domini; used in order to show that a date is a particular number of years after the birth of Christ: *in the first century A.D.* —compare B.C

**ad** /æd/ *n* INFORMAL ⇨ ADVERTISEMENT

**ad·age** /ˈædɪdʒ/ *n* a well-known phrase that says something wise; PROVERB

**ad·a·mant** /ˈædəmənt/ *adj* FORMAL determined not to change your opinion, decision etc.: *Ann was adamant (that) she would not go with us.* —**adamantly** *adv*

**Ad·am's ap·ple** /ˈædəmz ˌæpəl/ *n* the part of your body at the front of your neck that sticks out slightly and moves when you talk or swallow

**a·dapt** /əˈdæpt/ *n* **1** [I] to change your behavior or ideas to fit a new situation: *The kids are having trouble adapting to their new school.* **2** [T] to change something so that it is suitable for a new need or purpose: *Mom's chili recipe is adapted from my Grandma's.* —**adaptation** /ˌædəpˈteɪʃən, ˌædæp-/ *n* [C,U]: *a film adaptation of "Huckleberry Finn"*

**a·dapt·a·ble** /əˈdæptəbəl/ *adj* able to change in order to be suitable or successful in new or different situations —**adaptability** /əˌdæptəˈbɪləti/ *n* [U]

**a·dapt·er** /əˈdæptɚ/ *n* something that is used for connecting two pieces of equipment, especially if they are different sizes or power levels

**add** /æd/ *v* [T] **1** to put something together with something else or with a group of other things: *Do you want to add your name to the mailing list?* | *Add one egg to the flour mixture.* **2** to put numbers or amounts together and then calculate the total: *If you add 5 and 3 you get 8.* **3** to say more about something when you are speaking: *The Judge added that this case was one of the worst she had ever tried.* **4** **add insult to injury** to make a situation even more upsetting for someone who has been badly or unfairly treated

**add to** sth *phr v* [T] to increase something: *The change of plans only added to our confusion.*

**add up** *phr v* **1** [I,T] **add** sth ↔ **up**] to put numbers or amounts together and then calculate the total: *We're now adding up the latest figures.* **2** **not add up** to not seem true or reasonable: *Her story just doesn't add up.*

**ad·dict** /ˈædɪkt/ *n* someone who is unable to stop a harmful habit, such as taking drugs: *a heroin/cocaine addict*

**ad·dict·ed** /əˈdɪktɪd/ *adj* unable to stop taking drugs or doing something harmful: *Marvin was addicted to sleeping pills.*

**ad·dic·tion** /əˈdɪkʃən/ *n* [C,U] the need to have something regularly because you are ADDICTED to it: *drug addiction* | *his addiction to alcohol*

**ad·dic·tive** /əˈdɪktɪv/ *adj* making you ADDICTED to something: *a highly addictive drug*

**ad·di·tion** /əˈdɪʃən/ *n* **1** **in addition** used in order to add another fact to what has already been mentioned. *In addition to his job, Harvey also coaches Little League.* | *In addition, you need a driver's license.* **2** [U] the adding together of several numbers or amounts **3** something added: *She was an important addition to our group.*

**ad·di·tion·al** /əˈdɪʃənəl/ *adj* more than what was agreed or expected: *We were charged an additional $50 in late fees.*

**ad·di·tive** /ˈædətɪv/ *n* a substance, especially a chemical, added to a food or drink in order to improve it, add color, preserve it etc.

**ad·dress¹** /əˈdrɛs, ˈædrɛs/ *n* the details of where someone lives or works, including the number of a building, name of the street and town etc.: *I forgot to give Damien my new address.*

**address²** *v* [T] **1** **address a problem/question/issue etc.** to try to find a way to solve a problem, answer a difficult question etc.: *Special meetings address the concerns of new members.* **2** FORMAL to speak directly to a person or a group: *A guest speaker then addressed the audience.* **3** to write a name and address on an envelope, package etc.: *There's a letter here addressed to you.* **4** to use a particular name or title when speaking or writing to someone: *The President should be addressed as "Mr. President."*

**address**³ /ə'drɛs/ *n* a formal speech: *the Gettysburg Address*

**a·dept** /ə'dɛpt/ *adj* good at doing something that needs care or skill: *Melissa was quickly becoming an adept skier.| He is adept at cooking Polish dishes.* **–adeptly** *adv*

**ad·e·quate** /'ædəkwɪt/ *adj* **1** enough for a particular purpose: *We have not been given adequate information.| Her income is hardly adequate to pay the bills.* **2** fairly good, but not excellent: *an adequate performance* **–adequately** *adv* **–opposite** INADEQUATE

**ad·here** /əd'hɪr/ *v* [I] to stick firmly to something
 **adhere to** sth *phr v* [I] to continue to behave according to a particular rule, agreement, or belief: *Not all the states adhered to the treaty.*

**ad·her·ence** /əd'hɪrəns/ *n* [U] the act of behaving according to particular rules, ideas, or beliefs: *a strict adherence to religious beliefs*

**ad·her·ent** /əd'hɪrənt/ *n* someone who agrees with and supports a particular idea, opinion, or political party

**ad·he·sion** /əd'hiʒən/ *n* [U] the ability of one thing to stick to another thing

**ad·he·sive** /əd'hisɪv, -zɪv/ *n* a substance that can stick things together, such as glue **–adhesive** *adj*: *adhesive tape*

**ad hoc** /ˌæd 'hɑk/ *adj* done or arranged only when a situation makes something necessary, and without any previous planning: *an ad hoc committee* **–ad hoc** *adv*

**ad·ja·cent** /ə'dʒeɪsənt/ *adj* very close to something, or next to it: *A fire broke out in the building adjacent to the police station.*

**ad·jec·tive** /'ædʒɪktɪv, 'ædʒətɪv/ *n* TECHNICAL in grammar, a word that describes a noun or pronoun. In the sentence "I bought a new car," "new" is an adjective **–see study note on page 456**

**ad·join·ing** /ə'dʒɔɪnɪŋ/ *adj* next to something, and connected to it: *a bedroom with an adjoining bathroom* **–adjoin** *v* [T]

**ad·journ** /ə'dʒɚn/ *v* [I,T] to stop a meeting for a short time: *This court is adjourned until 2:30 p.m. tomorrow.| The assembly adjourned for an hour.* **–adjournment** *n* [C,U]

**ad·ju·di·cate** /ə'dʒudɪˌkeɪt/ *v* [I,T] FORMAL to judge something such as a competition, or to make an official decision **–adjudicator** *n*

**ad·junct** /'ædʒʌŋkt/ *n* **1** someone such as a doctor or teacher who works at a hospital, university etc. for a few hours a week, in addition to having another job **2 an adjunct to sth** something that is added or joined to something else, but is not part of it. **–adjunct** *adj*: *an adjunct professor*

**ad·just** /ə'dʒʌst/ *v* **1** [T] to make small changes to the position of something in order to improve it: *Where's the thing for adjusting the car seat?* **2** [I] to make small changes to the way you do things in order to feel more

comfortable in a new situation or condition: *We're finally getting adjusted to all the heat.* **–adjustable** *adj*

**ad·just·ment** /ə'dʒʌstmənt/ *n* [C,U] **1** a small change made to a machine or system: *We've made some adjustments to our original calculations.* **2** a change in the way you behave or think, made when your situation changes: *It hasn't been an easy adjustment to his new job.*

**ad·lib** /ˌæd'lɪb/ *v* [I,T] to say something in a speech or a performance without preparing or planning it **–ad lib** *adj adv*

**ad·min·is·ter** /əd'mɪnəstɚ/ *v* [T] **1** to manage and organize the affairs of a company, government etc. **2** FORMAL to give someone a medicine or drug

**ad·min·is·tra·tion** /əd,mɪnə'streɪʃən/ *n* [U] **1** the management or organization of the affairs of a company, government etc. **2 the Administration** the part of the national, state, or city government that is controlled by the president, GOVERNOR, or MAYOR: *the Kennedy Administration* **–administrative** /əd'mɪnə,streɪtɪv, -strə-/ *adj*

**ad·min·is·tra·tor** /əd'mɪnə,streɪtɚ/ *n* someone who manages or organizes the affairs of a company, government etc.

**ad·mi·ra·ble** /'ædmərəbəl/ *adj* having a good quality that you respect and admire: *an admirable achievement | She never bragged, which was admirable of her.*

**ad·mi·ral, Ad·mi·ral** /'ædmərəl/ *n* an officer who has the second highest rank in the Navy

**ad·mi·ra·tion** /ˌædmə'reɪʃən/ *n* [U] a feeling of approval and respect for something or someone: *Dylan had a deep admiration for Auden's later work.*

**ad·mire** /əd'maɪɚ/ *v* [T] **1** to approve of and respect someone or something: *Mark Twain is often admired for his humor.* **2** to look at someone or something because you think it is beautiful or impressive: *We stopped halfway up the hill to admire the view.* **–admirer** *n*: *I'm a great admirer of Melville.*

**ad·mis·si·ble** /əd'mɪsəbəl/ *adj* FORMAL acceptable or allowed, especially in a court of law: *admissible evidence* **–opposite** INADMISSIBLE

**ad·mis·sion** /əd'mɪʃən/ *n* **1** a statement saying that something bad or slightly unpleasant is true: *If he resigns, it will be an admission of guilt.* **2** [U] permission that is given to someone to study at a college, be treated in a hospital, join a club etc.: *Tom has applied for admission to the graduate program at Northwestern.* **3** the price charged when you go to a movie, sports event, concert etc.: *Admission $6.50* **–compare** ADMITTANCE

**USAGE NOTE admission and admittance**
 **Admission** is the price that you pay when

you go into a place such as a museum, concert etc.: *The price of admission is $10.* **Admittance** is the permission that you need in order to enter a place or join an organization. It is usually used on signs in the phrase "No Admittance" to tell people that they cannot enter a place.

**ad·mis·sions** /əd'mɪʃənz/ *n* [plural] the process of letting people study at a college, be treated at a hospital, join a club etc., or the number of people who do this: *Admissions dropped by 13% last year.*

**ad·mit** /əd'mɪt/ *v* -tted, -tting [T] **1** to agree or say that something is true, although you do not want to: *You have to admit that Sheila has a good point.* | *He was wrong, but he won't admit it.* | *They said how hard it was to admit to being an alcoholic.* **2** to say that you did something wrong or are guilty of a crime; CONFESS: *He'll never admit to the murder.* **3** to let someone enter a place, study at a college, be treated in a hospital, join a club etc.: *Only ticket holders will be admitted into the stadium.*

**ad·mit·tance** /əd'mɪt⁻ns/ *n* [U] permission to enter a place: *Most journalists were unable to gain admittance backstage.* −compare ADMISSION −see usage note at ADMISSION

**ad·mit·ted·ly** /əd'mɪtɪdli/ *adv* used when admitting that something is true: *Our net profit this year is admittedly much smaller than we had expected.*

**ad·mon·ish** /əd'manɪʃ/ *v* [T] LITERARY to warn someone, or to tell him/her that s/he has done something wrong −admonition /ˌædmə'nɪʃən/ **admonishment** /əd'manɪʃmənt/ *n* [C,U]

**a·do·be** /ə'doubi/ *n* [U] a material made of clay and STRAW, used for building houses

**a·do·les·cence** /ˌædl'ɛsəns/ *n* the period of time, from about 13 to 17 years of age, when a young person is developing into an adult

**ad·o·les·cent** /ˌædl'ɛsənt/ *n* a young person who is developing into an adult −adolescent *adj*

**a·dopt** /ə'dapt/ *v* [T] **1** to legally have someone else's child become a part of your family: *Melissa was adopted when she was only two.* **2** to begin to have or use an idea, plan, or way of doing something: *They've been forced to adopt stricter rules.* **3** to formally approve and accept something: *A "no smoking" policy has recently been adopted at work.* −adoption /ə'dapʃən/ *n* [C,U]: *She's put her baby up for adoption.* −adopted *adj*: *their adopted daughter*

**a·dop·tive** /ə'daptɪv/ *adj* having adopted a child: *an adoptive parent*

**a·dor·a·ble** /ə'dɔrəbəl/ *adj* a word meaning very attractive and pleasant, used especially to describe young children and pets: *What an adorable little puppy!*

**ad·o·ra·tion** /ˌædə'reɪʃən/ *n* [U] great love and admiration

**a·dore** /ə'dɔr/ *v* [T] **1** to love and admire someone very much: *Tim absolutely adores his older brother.* **2** to like something very much: *I adore the place. It has such a great atmosphere.*

**a·dorn** /ə'dɔrn/ *v* [T] FORMAL to decorate something: *carvings that adorn the church walls*

**a·dorn·ment** /ə'dɔrnmənt/ *n* **1** something that is used as jewelry or to decorate a thing or place **2** [U] the act of adorning something

**a·dren·a·line** /ə'drɛnl-ɪn/ *n* [U] a chemical produced by your body that makes your heart beat faster and gives you extra strength when you are afraid, excited, or angry

**a·drift** /ə'drɪft/ *adv* **1** not tied to anything, and moved around by the ocean or wind **2** not having any aims, or not following an earlier plan: *The schedule has gone adrift.* −adrift *adj*

**a·droit** /ə'drɔɪt/ *adj* able to use your hands skillfully, or to think and use words quickly: *an adroit negotiator* −adroitly *adv*

**ad·u·la·tion** /ˌædʒə'leɪʃən/ *n* [U] praise and admiration that is more than what someone deserves

**a·dult**¹ /ə'dʌlt, 'ædʌlt/ *n* a person or animal that has finished growing

**adult**² *adj* **1** completely grown: *an adult male frog* **2** typical of an adult, or suitable for an adult: *Children should take half the adult dose.* | *an adult view of the world*

**a·dul·ter·ate** /ə'dʌltəˌreɪt/ *v* [T] to make something less pure by adding a substance of a lower quality to it −adulteration /əˌdʌltə'reɪʃən/ *n* [U] −compare UN-ADULTERATED

**a·dul·ter·y** /ə'dʌltəri/ *n* [U] a sexual relationship between someone who is married and someone who is not that person's husband or wife −adulterous *adj*

**ad·vance**¹ /əd'væns/ *n* **1 in advance** before something happens or is expected to happen: *The quiche can be made in advance.* **2** [C,U] a change, discovery, or invention that makes something develop or improve: *advances in medicine* **3** movement forward to a new position: *the army's advance into enemy territory* **4** [C usually singular] money paid to someone before the usual time: *I asked for an advance on my salary.*

**advance**² *v* **1** [I] to move forward to a new position: *Troops advanced on* (=moved forward while attacking) *the rebel forces.* | *Stanford advanced to the playoffs.* **2** [I,T] to improve, help, or develop: *research to advance our understanding of genetics* **3** [T] to suggest a plan or idea so that people can consider it: *arguments advanced by the Libertarians* −advancement *n* [U]

**advance**³ *adj* happening before something else: *advance warning of a hurricane*

**ad·vanced** /əd'vænst/ *adj* **1** using the most modern ideas, equipment, and methods: *the most advanced computer on the market* **2** studying or relating to a school subject at a difficult level: *an advanced student | advanced physics*

**ad·van·ces** /əd'vænsɪz/ *n* [plural] efforts to start a sexual relationship with someone

**ad·van·tage** /əd'væntɪdʒ/ *n* **1** something that helps you to be better or more successful than others: *Her education gave her an advantage over the other applicants.* **2** take advantage of sth to use a situation or thing to help you do or get something you want: *You should definitely take advantage of a chance to study abroad.* **3** [C,U] a good or useful quality that something has: *the advantages of living in a big city* **4** take advantage of sb to treat someone unfairly or to control a particular situation in order to get what you want: *I don't mind helping, but I resent being taken advantage of.* **5 to your advantage** useful or helpful to you: *It's to your advantage to arrive early.* −**advantageous** /ˌædvæn'teɪdʒəs, -vən-/ *adj* −opposite DISADVANTAGE

**ad·vent** /'ædvɛnt/ *n* the start of an important event or period, or the first time an invention is used: *the advent of television*

**ad·ven·ture** /əd'vɛntʃə/ *n* [C,U] an exciting experience in which dangerous or unusual things happen, or the act of having these experiences

**ad·ven·tur·er** /əd'vɛntʃərə/ *n* someone who enjoys traveling and doing exciting things

**ad·ven·ture·some** /əd'vɛntʃəsəm/ *adj* enjoying exciting and slightly dangerous activities

**ad·ven·tur·ous** /əd'vɛntʃərəs/ *adj* exciting and slightly dangerous: *an adventurous expedition up the Amazon*

**ad·verb** /'ædvəb/ *n* TECHNICAL in grammar, a word or a group of words that describes or adds to the meaning of a verb, an adjective, another adverb, or a sentence. For example, "slowly" in "He walked slowly" and "very" in "It was a very nice day" are adverbs −**adverbial** /əd'vəbiəl/ *adj*

**ad·ver·sar·y** /'ædvəˌsɛri/ *n* FORMAL a country or person you are fighting or competing with

**ad·verse** /əd'vəs, æd-, 'ædvəs/ *adj* FORMAL not favorable: *adverse publicity*

**ad·ver·si·ty** /əd'vəsəti, æd-/ *n* [C,U] difficulties or problems that seem to be caused by bad luck

**ad·ver·tise** /'ædvəˌtaɪz/ *v* **1** [I,T] to use an advertisement to tell people about a product, event, or service in order to persuade them to buy or use it : *a new shampoo being advertised on TV* **2** [I] to make an announcement in a newspaper asking for someone to work for you, or for something that you need: *They're advertising for an accountant.* −**advertiser** *n*

**ad·ver·tise·ment** /ˌædvə'taɪzmənt/ *n* a set of words or pictures in a newspaper, magazine etc. that gives information about a product, event, or service in order to persuade people to buy or use it −compare COMMERCIAL²

**ad·ver·tis·ing** /'ædvəˌtaɪzɪŋ/ *n* [U] the activity or business of advertising things on television, in newspapers etc.

**ad·vice** /əd'vaɪs/ *n* [U] an opinion you give someone about what s/he should do: *Did you follow/take your father's advice? | If you want my advice, I think you should move.| Let me give you some advice.| He offered them one piece of advice: Don't panic.*

**ad·vise** /əd'vaɪz/ *v* **1** [I,T] to tell someone what you think s/he should do: *Doctors advised her to have the operation.| Franklin advises us on financial matters.* **2** [T] to inform someone of something: *You will be advised when the shipment arrives.*

**ad·vis·er** /əd'vaɪzə/ **advisor** *n* someone whose job is to give advice about a particular subject: *our adviser on foreign affairs| an academic advisor*

**ad·vi·so·ry** /əd'vaɪzəri/ *adj* having the purpose of giving advice: *an advisory committee*

**ad·vo·cate**¹ /'ædvəˌkeɪt/ *v* [T] to strongly support a particular way of doing things: *Buchanan advocates tougher trade policies.* −**advocacy** /'ædvəkəsi/ *n* [U]

**ad·vo·cate**² /'ædvəkət, -ˌkeɪt/ *n* **1** someone who strongly supports a particular way of doing things: *an advocate of prison reform* **2** LAW a lawyer who speaks in a court of law

**aer·i·al** /'ɛriəl/ *adj* from the air or happening in the air: *aerial photographs | aerial stunts*

**ae·ro·bic** /ə'roʊbɪk, ɛ-/ *adj* relating to exercises that strengthen your heart and lungs

**ae·ro·bics** /ə'roʊbɪks, ɛ-/ *n* [U] a very active type of physical exercise done to music, usually in a class

**aer·o·dy·nam·ics** /ˌɛroʊdaɪ'næmɪks/ *n* [U] the scientific study of how objects move through the air −**aerodynamic** *adj*

**aer·o·sol** /'ɛrəˌsɔl, -ˌsɑl/ *n* [U] a small metal container from which a liquid can be forced out using high pressure: *an aerosol hairspray*

**aer·o·space** /'ɛroʊˌspeɪs/ *adj* involving the designing and building of aircraft and space vehicles: *the aerospace industry*

**aes·thet·ic** /ɛs'θɛtɪk, ɪs-/ *adj* ⇨ ESTHETIC

**aes·thet·ics** /ɛs'θɛtɪks, ɪs-/ *n* [U] ⇨ ESTHETICS

**a·far** /ə'fɑr/ *adv* LITERARY **from afar** from a long distance away

**AFC** American Football Conference; a group of teams that is part of the NFL

**af·fa·ble** /'æfəbəl/ *adj* friendly and easy to talk to: *an affable guy* −**affably** *adv*

**af·fair** /əˈfɛr/ *n* **1** an event or a set of related events, especially unpleasant ones: *The Watergate affair brought down the Nixon administration.* **2** a secret sexual relationship between two people, when at least one of them is married to someone else: *I heard that Ed is **having an affair**.*

**af·fairs** /əˈfɛrz/ *n* [plural] events or activities relating to a particular subject that a person, business, government etc. deals with: *affairs of state* (=government business) | *I've never been good at dealing with financial affairs.*

**af·fect** /əˈfɛkt/ *v* [T] **1** to do something that produces a change in someone or something: *The disease affected his breathing.* **2** to make someone feel strong emotions: *I was deeply affected by the news of Paul's death.* —compare EFFECT²

> **USAGE NOTE affect and effect**
>
> Use the verb **affect** to talk about making changes, and the noun **effect** to talk about the results of changes: *Do you think the changes in the law will **affect** us?* | *I don't know what **effect** they will have.* **Effect** can be used as a verb, but only in very formal English.

**af·fec·ta·tion** /ˌæfɛkˈteɪʃən/ *n* [C,U] an action or type of behavior that is not sincere —compare UNAFFECTED

**af·fect·ed** /əˈfɛktɪd/ *adj* not sincere: *an affected laugh*

**af·fec·tion** /əˈfɛkʃən/ *n* [C,U] a feeling of gentle love and caring: *Bart felt great affection for/towards the old woman.* | *He doesn't **show affection** easily.*

**af·fec·tion·ate** /əˈfɛkʃənɪt/ *adj* showing gentle love toward people: *an affectionate child* —affectionately *adv*

**af·fi·da·vit** /ˌæfəˈdeɪvɪt/ *n* LAW a written statement about something that you swear is true and that can be used in a court of law

**af·fil·i·ate¹** /əˈfɪliˌeɪt/ *v* **be affiliated with/to** to be a member of or closely related to a larger organization: *a TV station affiliated to CBS* —affiliation /əˌfɪliˈeɪʃən/ *n* [C,U]: *What are Jean's political affiliations?*

**affiliate²** *n* a small company or organization that is controlled by a larger one

**af·fin·i·ty** /əˈfɪnəti/ *n* [C,U] **1** a strong feeling that you like and understand someone or something, especially because you have similar qualities, interests, or ideas: *The two men have an affinity for hiking and mountain biking.* **2** a close similarity or relationship between two things

**af·firm** /əˈfɔm/ *v* [T] FORMAL to state publicly that something is true: *The President affirmed his intention to reduce taxes.* —affirmation /ˌæfɔˈmeɪʃən/ *n* [C,U]

**af·firm·a·tive** /əˈfɔmətɪv/ *adj* FORMAL a word, sign etc. that is affirmative means "yes" —affirmatively *adv*

**affirmative ac·tion** /.ˌ... ˈ../ *n* [U] the practice of choosing people for jobs, education etc. who have been treated unfairly because of their race, sex etc.

**af·fix** /əˈfɪks/ *v* [T] FORMAL to fasten or stick something to something else

**af·flict** /əˈflɪkt/ *v* [T usually passive] FORMAL to make someone have serious problems: *a child afflicted by/with blindness*

**af·flic·tion** /əˈflɪkʃən/ *n* [C,U] FORMAL something that causes pain or makes you unhappy

**af·flu·ent** /ˈæfluənt/ *adj* having plenty of money, or other possessions: *an affluent suburb of Baltimore* —affluence *n* [U]

**af·ford** /əˈfɔrd/ *v* [T] **can afford a)** to have enough money to buy something: *I can't **afford** to buy a new car.* | *Do you think we can afford a computer now?* **b)** to be able to do something or let something happen without risk or damage to yourself: *I can't afford any more time away from work.* | *We can't **afford to** offend regular customers.*

**af·ford·a·ble** /əˈfɔrdəbəl/ *adj* not expensive: *We had trouble finding an affordable hotel.*

**af·front** /əˈfrʌnt/ *n* [C usually singular] a remark or action that offends or insults someone: *Borrowing money was an **affront to** his pride.*

**a·float** /əˈfloʊt/ *adj* **1** having enough money to stay out of debt: *Smaller companies can barely **stay afloat** in this market.* **2** floating on water

**AFN** Armed Forces Network; a company that broadcasts American radio programs all over the world

**a·fraid** /əˈfreɪd/ *adj* **1** very frightened about something, because you think something bad may happen: *Small children are often **afraid of** the dark.* | *Mary's **afraid to** walk home alone.* | *A lot of people there are **afraid for** their lives.* (=afraid they will be killed) —opposite UNAFRAID **2** very worried about what might happen: *A lot of workers are **afraid of** losing their jobs.* | *I didn't say anything because I was **afraid (that)** the other kids would laugh at me.* **3 I'm afraid** SPOKEN used in order to politely tell someone something that may annoy, upset, or disappoint him/her: *I'm afraid (that) this is a "no smoking" area.* | *"Are we late?" "**I'm afraid so**" (=yes) "Are there any tickets left?" "**I'm afraid not**." (=no)*

**a·fresh** /əˈfrɛʃ/ *adv* FORMAL done again from the beginning, especially in a new way: *We decided to move to Texas and **start afresh**.*

**Africa** /ˈæfrɪkə/ *n* one of the seven CONTINENTs, that includes land south of Europe and west of the Indian Ocean

**Af·ri·can¹** /ˈæfrɪkən/ *adj* relating to or coming from Africa

**African**² *n* someone from Africa

**Af·ro-A·mer·i·can** /ˌæfrou-əˈmɛrɪkən/ *n* an American whose family originally came from Africa −**Afro-American** *adj*

**af·ter**¹ /ˈæftɚ/ *prep* **1** when a particular time or event has happened: *We're going out after the soccer game.* | *A month/year after the fire, the house was rebuilt.* **2** following someone or something in a series of things: *Whose name is after mine on the list?* **3 after 10 minutes/3 hours etc.** when a particular amount of time has passed: *After a while, the woman returned.* **4** used when telling time to say how many minutes past the hour it is: *It's ten after five.* **5 day after day/year after year etc.** continuing for a very long time: *Day after day we waited, hoping she'd call.* **6 one after the other** following just behind or a short amount of time later than the one before: *We led the horses one after the other out of the barn.* **7** because of: *After his insults, I don't see why I should be nice to him!* **8** in spite of: *After all the trouble I had, Reese didn't even say thank you.* **9 be after sb** to be looking for someone or something: *The FBI is after him for fraud.* **10 be after sth** to be trying to get something that belongs to someone else: *You're just after my money!* **11 after all a)** in spite of what you think, or what you thought was true: *Rita didn't have my pictures after all. Jake did.* | *Don't worry too much. After all, it's not your problem.* **b)** in spite of what you expected: *It didn't rain after all.* −compare BEFORE¹, SINCE²

---

**USAGE NOTE** **after an hour** and **in an hour**

Use these phrases to talk about the time when you plan to do something. However, compare the sentences: *We'll leave after an hour* and *We'll leave in an hour.* In the first sentence the speaker is planning how long to stay in a place before going there. In the second sentence, the speaker is already at a place and is deciding how much longer to stay there.

---

**after**² *conjunction* when a particular time has passed, or an event has happened: *Regan changed his name after he left Poland.* | *He discovered the jewel was fake 10 days/3 weeks after he bought it.*

**after**³ *adv* later than someone or something else: *Gina came on Monday, and I got here the day after.*

**af·ter·ef·fect** /ˈæftɚəˌfɛkt/ *n* [C usually plural] an unpleasant effect that remains after the condition or event that caused it: *the aftereffects of the drought last summer*

**af·ter·life** /ˈæftɚˌlaɪf/ *n* [singular] the life that some people believe you have after death

**af·ter·math** /ˈæftɚˌmæθ/ *n* [singular] the period of time after something bad has hap-

pened: *the danger of fire in the aftermath of the earthquake*

**af·ter·noon** /ˌæftɚˈnun/ *n* [C,U] the period of time between 12 o'clock and the evening: *a class on Friday afternoon* | *We should get there about 3 in the afternoon.* | *Can you go swimming this afternoon?* (=today in the afternoon) −**afternoon** *adj*: *an afternoon snack* ✗ DON'T SAY *"next/last afternoon"* ✗

**af·ter·shave** /ˈæftɚˌʃeɪv/ *n* [C,U] a liquid with a pleasant smell that a man puts on his face after he SHAVEs

**af·ter·taste** /ˈæftɚˌteɪst/ *n* [C usually singular] a taste that stays in your mouth after you eat or drink something: *a drink with a sour aftertaste*

**af·ter·thought** /ˈæftɚˌθɔt/ *n* something thought of, mentioned, or added later, especially something that was not part of an original plan: *The bar was only added as an afterthought.*

**af·ter·ward** /ˈæftɚwɚd/ **afterwards** *adv* after something else has happened; later: *We met at school but didn't get married until two years afterward.*

**a·gain** /əˈgɛn/ *adv* **1** one more time: *Could you say that again? I couldn't hear you.* **2** at another time: *Thanks for coming! Please come again.* **3** in the same way, situation, or place as before: *Is it already time to do taxes again?* | *Susan's home again, after studying in Europe.* **4 again and again** repeating many times: *I've tried again and again to contact her.* −see also **but then (again)** (BUT¹)

**a·gainst** /əˈgɛnst/ *prep* **1** touching, pushing on, hitting etc. another surface: *The cat's fur felt soft against her face.* | *waves slapping against the boat* | *Sheldon leaned lazily against the wall.* **2** opposed to or disagreeing with an idea, belief etc.: *Everyone was against closing the factory.* | **against the law** (=illegal) **3** in a way that has a bad or unfair effect: *discrimination against racial minorities* **4** fighting or competing with someone or something: *He was injured in the game against the Cowboys.* | *the battle against inflation* **5** in the opposite direction from something: *At least my drive to work is against the traffic.* **6 have sth against sb/sth** to dislike or disapprove of someone or something: *I have nothing against people making money, but they ought to pay taxes on it.*

**age**¹ /eɪdʒ/ *n* **1** [C,U] the period of time that someone has lived or that something has existed, usually expressed as a number of years: *Patrick is my age.* (=the same age as me) | *Jamie won his first tournament at the age of 15.* | *Most kids start kindergarten at age 5.* | *girls who become mothers at an early age* (=very young) | *Stop messing around and act your age!* (=behave in a way that is suitable for how old you are) | *Judy's very smart for her age.* (=compared to others of the same age) **2** [C,U] one of the particular periods of someone's life: *Who will look after* *you in old age?* | *voting/drinking/retirement age* (=when you can legally vote, drink alcohol, etc.) | *I'm sorry, but you're* **under age.** (=too young to be legally allowed to do something) **3** [C usually singular] a particular period of history: *the computer age* **4 be/come of age** to be or become old enough that you are considered to be a responsible adult **5** [U] the state of being old: *a letter that was brown with age* **6 age group/bracket** the people between two particular ages, considered as a group: *a book for children in the 8-12 age group* −see also AGES

**age**² *v* **1** [I,T] to become older and weaker, or to make someone seem this way: *After his wife's death, he aged quickly.* **2** to improve or develop in quality and taste over a period of time: *a wine that has aged well* −**aging** *adj*: *an aging movie star*

**aged**¹ /eɪdʒd/ *adj* **aged 5/15/50 etc.** 5, 15 etc. years old: *a game for children aged 12 and over*

**a·ged**² /'eɪdʒɪd/ *adj* **1** very old: *an aged man* **2 the aged** old people

**age·less** /'eɪdʒlɪs/ *adj* never seeming old or old-fashioned: *an ageless song*

**a·gen·cy** /'eɪdʒənsi/ *n* **1** a business that provides a particular service: *an employment agency* **2** an organization or department, especially within a government, that does a specific job: *the UN agency responsible for helping refugees*

**a·gen·da** /ə'dʒɛndə/ *n* **1** a list of the subjects to be discussed at a meeting: *Let's move on to item five* **on the agenda.** **2 on the agenda** being considered and discussed as something to do: *Health care reforms are* **on top of the agenda/high on the agenda.** (=very important)

**a·gent** /'eɪdʒənt/ *n* **1** a person or company that helps another person or company deal with business problems, finding work etc.: *I got a call from my agent about a job.* | *We're acting as* **agents for** *Mr. Rogers.* **2** someone who works for a government or police department in order to get secret information about another country or an organization **3** something that makes something else happen: *an agent for change* | *bleaching agent*

**ag·es** /'eɪdʒɪz/ *n* [plural] a long time: *It's been ages since I played volleyball.*

**ag·gra·vate** /'ægrə,veɪt/ *v* [T] **1** to make a bad situation worse: *The doctors say her condition is aggravated by stress.* **2** to annoy someone: *Jerry really aggravates me sometimes.* −**aggravating** *adj* −**aggravation** /,ægrə'veɪʃən/ *n* [C,U]

**vated,** but a person is **annoyed** or **irritated.**

**ag·gres·sion** /ə'grɛʃən/ *n* [U] angry or threatening behavior, especially in which you attack someone: *bombings and other* **acts of aggression**

**ag·gres·sive** /ə'grɛsɪv/ *adj* **1** forceful and showing that you are determined to succeed: *Borland's aggressive sales tactics* **2** always ready to argue with people or attack them: *Ricky's aggressive behavior on the playground is causing problems.* −**aggressively** *adv* −**aggressiveness** *n* [U]

**ag·gres·sor** /ə'grɛsɚ/ *n* [U] a person or country that begins a fight or war with another person or country

**ag·grieved** /ə'grivd/ *adj* feeling angry or unhappy because you think you have been unfairly treated

**a·ghast** /ə'gæst/ *adj* suddenly feeling or looking shocked

**ag·ile** /'ædʒəl, 'ædʒaɪl/ *adj* **1** able to move quickly and easily **2** able to think quickly and intelligently: *She's 92, but still mentally agile.* −**agility** /ə'dʒɪləti/ *n* [U]

**ag·i·tate** /'ædʒə,teɪt/ *v* **1** [I] to argue strongly in public for social or political changes: *workers* **agitating for** *higher pay* **2** [T] to make someone feel anxious, nervous, or upset −**agitation** /,ædʒə'teɪʃən/ *n* [U]

**ag·i·tat·ed** /'ædʒə,teɪtɪd/ *adj* very anxious, nervous, or upset

**ag·i·ta·tor** /'ædʒə,teɪtɚ/ *n* DISAPPROVING someone who does things to make people pay attention to and change social or political problems

**ag·nos·tic** /æg'nɑstɪk, əg-/ *n* someone who believes that people cannot know whether God exists or not −**agnostic** *adj* −**agnosticism** /æg'nɑstə,sɪzəm, əg-/ *n* [U]

**a·go** /ə'goʊ/ *adj* used in order to show how far back in the past something happened: *Jeff left for work* **10 minutes/2 hours ago.** | *We went to Maine once, but it was* **a long time ago.** | *I had the tickets* **a minute ago!** | *Scott's dad called* **a little while ago.**

**a·gon·ize** /'ægə,naɪz/ *v* [I] to think about a decision very carefully and with a lot of effort:

*Will has been* **agonizing about/over** *whether to get married.*

**a·gon·iz·ing** /'ægə,naɪzɪŋ/ *adj* extremely painful or difficult: *It was an agonizing decision to disconnect their son's life support system.* **–agonizingly** *adv*

**ag·o·ny** /'ægəni/ *n* [C,U] very severe pain or suffering: *The poor guy was* **in agony**.

**a·gree** /ə'gri/ *v* **1** [I,T] to have the same opinion about something: *Oh, I* **agree with** *you on that.* | *Most experts* **agree that** *global warming is a serious problem.* | *Mike and I certainly don't* **agree on/about** *everything.* ✗ DON'T SAY "I am agree" ✗ **–opposite** DISAGREE **2** [I,T] to make a decision with someone or say yes to someone after a discussion with him/her: *She* **agreed to** *stay home with Charles.* | *We* **agreed on** *a price for the car.* | *You know Dad won't* **agree to** *getting you a motorbike.* **3** [I] if two pieces of information agree, they say the same thing: *Your story doesn't* **agree with** *what the police have said.*

**agree with** *phr v* [T] **1** to believe that something is right: *I don't* **agree with** *spanking children.* **2 not agree with sb** to make you feel sick: *Some dairy products* **don't agree with** *me.*

**a·gree·a·ble** /ə'griəbəl/ *adj* **1** nice, acceptable, or enjoyable: *agreeable weather* **–opposite** DISAGREEABLE **2 be agreeable to sth** to be willing to do or accept something: *Are you sure Johnson is agreeable to the idea?* **–agreeably** *adv*

**a·greed** /ə'grid/ *adj* having been discussed and accepted: *an agreed price*

**a·gree·ment** /ə'grimənt/ *n* **1** an arrangement or promise to do something, made by two or more people, countries, organizations etc.: *Lawyers on both sides finally* **reached an agreement.** **2** [U] a situation in which two or more people have the same opinion as each other: *Not all scholars are* **in agreement** *on this point.* **–opposite** DISAGREEMENT

**ag·ri·cul·ture** /'ægrɪ,kʌltʃɚ/ *n* [U] the science or practice of farming, especially of growing crops **–agricultural** /,ægrə'kʌl-tʃərəl/ *adj*

**ah** /ɑ/ INTERJECTION said in order to express surprise, pity, dislike, pleasure etc.: *Ah, what a cute kid!*

**a·ha** /ɑ'hɑ/ INTERJECTION said in order to express surprise, satisfaction, or understanding: *Aha! So that's where you've been hiding!*

**a·head** /ə'hɛd/ *adv* **1** in front of someone or something: *Do you see that red convertible* **ahead of** *us?* | *Just* **up ahead** *and to the right is my old school.* **2** before an event or a particular time: *You can make the pie crust* **ahead of time.** | *At this point we're* **ahead of** *schedule.* **3** into the future: *Eddy never* **looks/plans ahead.** **4 go ahead a)** SPOKEN used in order to tell someone s/he can do something: *Go*

*ahead and help yourself to some punch.* **b)** used in order to say you are going to start doing something: *I'll go ahead and start the coffee.* **5** more advanced, developed, successful etc. than someone or something else: *Jane is* **ahead of** *the rest of her class.* **6 get/keep ahead** to succeed or to continue to succeed: *Stick with me if you want to get ahead in the world, kid.*

**aid¹** /eɪd/ *n* **1** [U] money, food, or services that are given by an organization to help people: *sending aid to the earthquake victims* **2** [U] help or support given to someone: *financial aid* **3** [C,U] a thing that helps you do something: *notebooks and study aids* | *bacteria viewed* **with the aid of** *a microscope* **4 in aid of** intended to help: *a fundraiser in aid of the Red Cross* **5 come/go to sb's aid** FORMAL to help someone

**aid²** *v* [T] **1** FORMAL to help or give support to someone **2 aid and abet** LAW to help someone do something illegal

**aide** /eɪd/ *aid n* someone whose job is to help someone in a more important position: *a nurse's aide*

**AIDS** /eɪdz/ *n* [U] Acquired Immune Deficiency Syndrome; a very serious disease that stops your body from defending itself against infection

**ail·ing** /'eɪlɪŋ/ *adj* weak or sick, and not getting stronger or better: *the country's ailing economy*

**ail·ment** /'eɪlmənt/ *n* an illness that is not very serious

**aim¹** /eɪm/ *v* **1** [I] to plan or intend to achieve something: *a program* **aimed at** *creating more jobs* | *We're* **aiming to** *qualify for the summer Olympics.* **2** [I] to do or say something to a particular person or group, in order to influence them, annoy them etc.: *a TV commercial* **aimed at** *teenagers* **3** [I,T] to point a weapon at a person or thing you want to hit: *A gun was* **aimed at** *his head.*

**aim²** *n* **1** something you are trying to do or get: *I flew to California* **with the aim of** *finding a job.* **2 take aim** to point a weapon at someone or something **3** someone's ability to hit something by throwing or shooting something at it: *Mabel's aim has improved.*

**aim·less** /'eɪmlɪs/ *adj* without a clear purpose or reason **–aimlessly** *adv*

**ain't** /eɪnt/ *v* SPOKEN NONSTANDARD a short form of "am not," "is not," "are not," "has not," or "have not": *Ain't that the truth!*

**air¹** /ɛr/ *n* **1** [U] the mixture of gases that we breathe and that surrounds the Earth: *Let's go outside and get some* **fresh air.** **2** [U] the space above the ground or around things: *tossing a ball into the air* **3 by air** traveling by or using a plane: *Are you shipping that box by air or by land?* **4** [singular] a general appearance

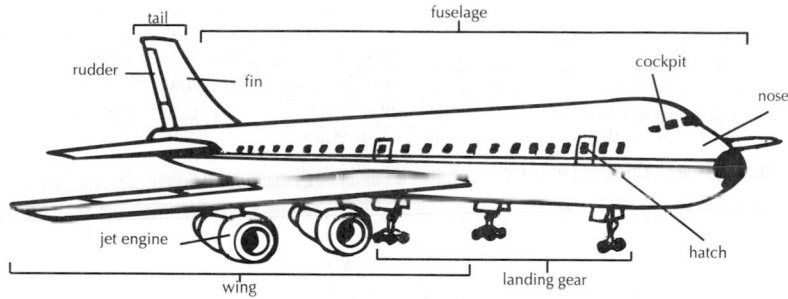

or feeling: *an **air** of mystery **about** her*  **5 it's up in the air** SPOKEN used to say that something has not been decided yet  **6 be on/off the air** to be broadcasting or to stop broadcasting  **7** SPOKEN ⇨ AIR CONDITIONING  −see also **thin air** (THIN)

**air**[2] *v*  **1** [T] to broadcast a program on television or radio: *Star Trek was first aired in 1966.*  **2** [T] to make your opinions, ideas, complaints etc. known to other people: *You will all get a chance to **air your views**.*  **3** [I,T] also **air** sth ↔ **out** to make a room, clothes, BLANKETs etc. smell fresh by letting air, especially from outdoors, go through them  −**airing** *n* [U]

**air·bag** /'ɛrbæg/ *n* a bag in a car that fills with air to protect people in an accident

**air·borne** /'ɛrbɔrn/ *adj* flying or floating in the air: *They'll serve drinks once we're airborne.*

**air con·di·tion·er** /'. .,.../ *n* a machine that makes the air in a room, car etc. stay cool

**air con·di·tion·ing** /'. .,.../ *n* [U] a system of machines that makes the air in a room, building etc. stay cool  −**air conditioned** *adj*

**air·craft** /'ɛrkræft/ *n, plural* **aircraft** a plane or any vehicle that can fly

**aircraft car·ri·er** /'.. .,.../ *n* a type of ship that has a large flat surface that planes fly from

**air·fare** /'ɛrfɛr/ *n* [U] the price of a plane trip

**air·field** /'ɛrfild/ *n* a place where military planes or small planes fly from

**Air Force** /'. ,./ *n* **the Air Force** the military organization of the US that uses planes when fighting a war

**air·head** /'ɛr,hɛd/ *n* SLANG someone who is stupid

**air·i·ly** /'ɛrəli/ *adv* in a way that shows that you are not serious or do not care very much: *"Oh, just do whatever you want," she said airily.*

**air·less** /'ɛrlɪs/ *adj* without fresh air: *a hot airless room*

**air·line** /'ɛrlaɪn/ *n* a business that regularly flies passengers to different places by plane

**air·lin·er** /'ɛr,laɪnɚ/ *n* a large plane for passengers

**air·mail** /'ɛrmeɪl/ *n* [U] letters, packages etc.

that are sent to another country by plane, or the system of doing this  −**airmail** *adj, adv*

**air·plane** /'ɛrpleɪn/ *n* a vehicle that flies by using wings and one or more engines; plane

**air·port** /'ɛrpɔrt/ *n* a place where planes fly from

**air raid** /'. ,./ *n* an attack by military planes

**airs** /ɛrz/ *n* [plural] the things someone does and says in order to seem more important than s/he really is: *Monica has been **putting on airs** ever since she moved to Beverly Hills.*

**air·space** /'ɛrspeɪs/ *n* [U] the sky above a particular country, considered to be controlled by that country

**air strike** /'. ./ *n* an attack on a place in which military aircraft drop bombs on it

**air·strip** /'ɛrstrɪp/ *n* a long narrow piece of land that has been cleared so that planes can fly from it

**air·tight** /'ɛr,taɪt, ,ɛr'taɪt/ *adj* **1** not allowing air to get in or out: *airtight containers*  **2** having no mistakes or weaknesses: *an airtight argument/excuse*

**air time** /'. ./ *n* [U] the period of time or the amount of time during a day that a radio or television station broadcasts its programs: *Thirty seconds of air time will cost $1500.*

**air·waves** /'ɛrweɪvz/ *n* [plural] INFORMAL all the programs that are broadcast on radio and television

**air·y** /'ɛri/ *adj* an airy room, building etc. has a lot of space and fresh air

**aisle** /aɪl/ *n* a long passage between rows of seats in a theater, church, bus, plane etc.

**a·jar** /ə'dʒɑr/ *adj* a door or window that is ajar is not completely closed

**ajar**

**AK** the written abbreviation of Alaska

**a.k.a.** *adv* the abbreviation of "also known as"; used when giving someone's real name together with the name s/he is known by: *John Phillips, a.k.a. The Mississippi Mauler*

**a·kin** /ə'kɪn/ *adj* FORMAL **akin to** similar to

something: *His music is much more akin to jazz than rock.*

**AL** the written abbreviation of Alabama

**à la carte** /ˌɑləˈkɑrt, ˌælə-, ˌɑlɑ-/ *adj* food in a restaurant that is à la carte has its own separate price for each dish —**à la carte** *adv*

**a·lac·ri·ty** /əˈlækrəti/ *n* [U] FORMAL eager willingness to do something: *Thomas agreed with alacrity.*

**à la mode** /ˌɑləˈmoʊd, ˌælə-, ˌɑlɑ-/ *adj* served with ice cream

**a·larm**[1] /əˈlɑrm/ *n* [U] **1** something such as a bell, loud noise, or light that warns people of danger: *a fire/burglar alarm* | *a car alarm* (=one attached to your car) **2** INFORMAL ⇨ ALARM CLOCK **3** a feeling of fear or anxiety because something dangerous might happen: *Calm down! There's no cause for alarm.* **4** raise/ sound the alarm to warn everyone about something bad or dangerous that is happening: *They first sounded the alarm about the problem of nuclear waste in 1955.*

**alarm**[2] *v* [T] to make someone feel very worried or anxious: *Local residents have been alarmed by the recent police activity.* —**alarmed** *adj*

**alarm clock** /.ˈ. ˌ./ *n* a clock that will make a noise at a particular time to wake you up

**a·larm·ing** /əˈlɑrmɪŋ/ *adj* very frightening or worrying: *an alarming increase in violent crime*

**a·larm·ist** /əˈlɑrmɪst/ *adj* making people unnecessarily worried about dangers that do not exist —**alarmist** *n*

**a·las** /əˈlæs/ *interjection* LITERARY said in order to express sadness

**al·be·it** /ɔlˈbiɪt, æl-/ *conjunction* FORMAL although

**al·bi·no** /ælˈbaɪnoʊ/ *n* a person or animal with a GENETIC condition that makes the skin and hair extremely pale or white

**al·bum** /ˈælbəm/ *n* **1** a group of songs or pieces of music recorded by a particular performer or group on a record, CD, or tape: *Do you have Neil Young's new album?* **2** a book in which you put photographs, stamps etc. that you want to keep

**al·co·hol** /ˈælkəˌhɔl, -ˌhɑl/ *n* **1** [U] drinks such as beer, wine, WHISKEY etc. that contain a substance that can make you drunk: *We do not serve alcohol to people under age 21.* **2** [C,U] a chemical substance that can be used for cleaning medical or industrial equipment

**al·co·hol·ic**[1] /ˌælkəˈhɔlɪk, -ˈhɑ-/ *n* someone who cannot stop the habit of drinking too much alcohol: *His father was an alcoholic.*

**alcoholic**[2] *adj* containing alcohol or relating to alcohol: *an alcoholic beverage* —opposite NON-ALCOHOLIC

**al·co·hol·is·m** /ˈælkəhɔˌlɪzəm, -hɑ-/ *n* [U] the medical condition of being an alcoholic

**al·cove** /ˈælkoʊv/ *n* a small place in a wall of a room that is built further back than the rest of the wall

**al·der·man** /ˈɔldəmən/, **al·der·wo·man** /ˈɔldəˌwʊmən/ *n* a low level city or town government official who is elected

**ale** /eɪl/ *n* [U] a type of beer with a slightly bitter taste

**a·lert**[1] /əˈlət/ *adj* **1** always watching and ready to notice anything strange, unusual, dangerous etc.: *Cyclists must always be alert to the dangers on a busy road.* **2** able to think quickly and clearly: *I didn't feel alert enough to do any more work.*

**alert**[2] *v* [T] **1** to officially warn someone of a problem or of possible danger: *An unnamed woman alerted the police about the bomb.* **2** to make someone notice something important, dangerous etc.: *A large sign alerts drivers to bad road conditions.*

**alert**[3] *n* **1** be on the alert to be ready to notice and deal with a problem: *Police are on the alert for trouble.* **2** a warning to be ready for possible danger: *The FBI put out an alert for a man seen near the crime.*

**al·fal·fa sprout** /ælˈfælfə spraʊt/ *n* a very small plant, eaten raw as a vegetable in SALADs

**al·gae** /ˈældʒi/ *n* [U] a very simple plant without stems or leaves that lives in or near water

**al·ge·bra** /ˈældʒəbrə/ *n* [U] a type of mathematics that uses letters and signs to represent numbers and values —**algebraic** /ˌældʒəˈbreɪ-ɪk/ *adj*

**al·go·rithm** /ˈælgəˌrɪðəm/ *n* a set of mathematical instructions that are done in a particular order

**a·li·as**[1] /ˈeɪliəs, ˈeɪlyəs/ *prep* used when giving a criminal's real name together with the name s/he uses: *the spy Margaret Zelle, alias Mata Hari*

**alias**[2] *n* a false name, usually used by a criminal

**al·i·bi** /ˈæləˌbaɪ/ *n* proof that someone was not where a crime happened and is therefore not guilty of the crime

**a·li·en**[1] /ˈeɪliən, ˈeɪlyən/ *adj* **1** very different or strange: *Her way of life is totally alien to me.* **2** relating to creatures from other worlds

**alien**[2] *n* **1** someone who lives or works in a country but is not a citizen: *State authorities are not dealing well with the problem of illegal aliens.* **2** a creature that comes from another world

**a·li·en·ate** /ˈeɪliəˌneɪt, ˈeɪlyə-/ *v* [T] to make someone stop feeling friendly or stop feeling like s/he belongs in a group: *We don't want to alienate kids who already have problems at school.* —**alienation** /ˌeɪliəˈneɪʃən, -ˌeɪlyə-/ *n* [U]

**a·light**[1] /əˈlaɪt/ *adj* **1** burning: *Several cars were set alight by rioters.* **2** someone whose face or eyes are alight is happy or excited

**alight**² *v* [I] FORMAL   **1 alight on/upon sth** if a bird, insect etc. alights on something, it stops flying in order to stand on a surface   **2 alight from** to step out of a vehicle at the end of a trip

**a·lign** /əˈlaɪn/ *v* [I,T]   **1** to work together with another person or group because you have the same aims: *Five Democrats have aligned themselves with the Republicans on this vote.*   **2** to arrange something so that it is in the same line as something else: *It looks like your wheels need aligning.* **–alignment** *n* [C,U]: *a close alignment between Syria and Egypt*

**a·like**¹ /əˈlaɪk/ *adj* almost exactly the same; similar: *All the new cars look alike to me.*

**alike**² *adv*   **1** in a similar way, or in the same way: *When we were younger, we dressed alike.*   **2** equally: *The new rule was criticized by teachers and students alike.*

**al·i·mo·ny** /ˈæləˌmoʊni/ *n* [singular] money that someone has to pay regularly to his/her former wife or husband after a DIVORCE

**a·live** /əˈlaɪv/ *adj*   **1** living and not dead: *They didn't expect to find anyone alive after the explosion.* | *I'm amazed my plants have stayed alive in this weather.*   **2** continuing to exist: *Let's keep the traditions of the Inuit alive.*   **3** full of activity or interest: *The streets come alive after ten o'clock.* | *The stadium was alive with excitement.*   **4** be alive and well healthy or successful: *Grandpa is alive and well at the age of 85.*

**al·ka·li** /ˈælkəˌlaɪ/ *n* [C,U] a substance that forms a chemical salt when combined with an acid **–alkaline** *adj*

**all**¹ /ɔl/ *determiner*   **1** the whole of an amount or time: *All the money is gone.* | *We've spent it all.* | *I've been waiting all day/week.* | *Bill talks about work all the time.* (=very often or too much)   **2** every one of a group of things or people: *Answer all twenty questions.* | *Nearly/almost all my teachers are married.* | *Have you told them all?* –see usage note at EACH¹   **3 all kinds of/all sorts of** very many different types of things, people, or places: *We saw all kinds of animals on our field trip.*   **4 for all...** in spite of a particular fact or situation: *For all his faults, he's a good father.*   **5 go all out** to do all you can to succeed: *To win the race, you have to go all out from the very start.* –see study note on page 466

---

**USAGE NOTE all**

**All** is used with a singular verb with uncountable nouns: *All the money is gone.* It is used with a plural verb with countable nouns: *All the people have gone.*

---

**all**² *adv*   **1** completely, entirely: *I walked all alone in the woods.* | *The judges were dressed all in black.*   **2 all over a)** everywhere on a surface or in a place: *The grave was decorated*  all over with flowers. | *We looked all over the place for it.* **b)** finished: *I used to travel a lot, but that's all over now.*   **3 be all over sb** to be kissing or touching someone a lot in a sexual way: *He was all over Pam last night in the bar.*   **4** used in order to say that both sides have the same number of points in a game: *The score was 10-all at half time.*   **5 all but** almost completely. *The wine left a stain that was all but impossible to get rid of.*   **6 all along** the whole time: *I knew all along that I couldn't trust him.*   **7 all of a sudden** in a very quick and surprising way: *All of a sudden I realized that the car in front of me was stopped.* –see also **after all** (AFTER¹) –see usage notes at ALREADY, ALTOGETHER

**all**³ *pron*   **1** everyone; everything: *Mandy thinks she knows it all.* | *All of the books were overdue.* –see usage note at EACH¹   **2 not at all** not in any way: *The snow didn't affect us at all.* | *He's not at all happy.*   **3 at all** used in questions to mean "in any way": *Did the new drugs help her at all?*   **4 all in all** considering everything: *It wasn't funny, but all in all it was a good movie.*

**Al·lah** /ˈælə, ˈɑlə/ *n* the name used in Islam for God

**all-A·mer·i·can** /ˌ. .ˈ...◂/ *adj* typical of America or Americans: *an all-American girl*

**all-a·round** /ˌ. .ˈ.◂/ *adj* good at doing many different things, especially in sports: *the best all-around player*

**al·lay** /əˈleɪ/ *v* [T] to make the effect of an unpleasant feeling or situation less strong: *The report allayed fears/worries etc. about the economy.*

**all-clear** /ˌ. ˈ./ *n* permission to begin doing something: *We have to wait for the all-clear from the safety committee before we can start.*

**al·le·ga·tion** /ˌæləˈgeɪʃən/ *n* a statement that someone has done something illegal, which is not supported by proof: *allegations of child abuse*

**al·lege** /əˈlɛdʒ/ *v* [T] to say that something is true without showing proof: *Baldwin is alleged to have killed two people.*

**al·leged** /əˈlɛdʒd/ *adj* supposed to be true, but not proven: *the group's alleged connections with organized crime*

**al·leg·ed·ly** /əˈlɛdʒɪdli/ *adv* used when repeating what other people say is true, when it has not been proven to be true: *He was arrested for allegedly raping a woman.*

**al·le·giance** /əˈlidʒəns/ *n* loyalty to or support for a leader, country, belief etc.

**al·le·go·ry** /ˈæləˌgɔri/ *n* [C,U] a story, poem, painting etc. in which the events and characters represent good and bad qualities **–allegorical** /ˌæləˈgɔrɪkəl/ *adj*

**al·ler·gic** /əˈlɔrdʒɪk/ *adj*   **1** having an ALLERGY: *Are you allergic to anything?*

A

**2** caused by an ALLERGY: *an allergic reaction to the bee sting*

**al·ler·gy** /ˈælədʒi/ *n* a condition that makes you ill when you eat, touch, or breathe a particular thing: *an allergy to cats*

**al·le·vi·ate** /əˈliviˌeɪt/ *v* [T] to make something less bad or severe: *Aspirin should alleviate the pain.* | *The road was built to alleviate traffic problems.*

**al·ley** /ˈæli/ *n* a narrow street between buildings

**al·li·ance** /əˈlaɪəns/ *n* a close agreement or connection between people, countries etc.: *the NATO alliance*

**al·lied** /əˈlaɪd, ˈælaɪd/ *adj* joined or closely related, especially by a political or military agreement: *allied forces* | *The two leaders were closely allied during the Gulf War.*

**al·li·ga·tor** /ˈæləˌgeɪtɚ/ *n* a large REPTILE (=type of animal) with a long body, a long mouth, and sharp teeth, that lives in hot wet areas of the US and China

**all-in·clu·sive** /ˌ. .ˈ...◂/ *adj* including everything: *The price is all-inclusive - it covers your hotel, flight, and food.*

**al·lo·cate** /ˈæləˌkeɪt/ *v* [T] to decide to allow a particular amount of money, time etc. to be used for a particular purpose: *The hospital has allocated $500,000 for cancer research.*

**al·lo·ca·tion** /ˌæləˈkeɪʃən/ *n* [C,U] the amount of something that is ALLOCATED, or the decision to allocate: *the allocation of state funds to the university*

**al·lot** /əˈlɑt/ *v* **-tted, -tting** [T] to ALLOCATE something: *Each person was allotted nine tickets.* | *He allotted 20 minutes a day to his exercises.* **–allotment** *n* [C,U]: *a decrease in the allotment of funds*

**al·low** /əˈlaʊ/ *v* [T] **1** to give someone permission to do something or have something: *Smoking is not allowed.* | *You're allowed one candy bar after lunch.* **2** to let someone go somewhere: *You're not allowed in here.* **3** to make it possible for something to happen: *I can't allow the situation to get any worse.* **4** to let someone have an amount of time or money for a particular purpose: *Allow ten days for delivery.* | *Allow yourself enough time to shop.*

**allow for** sb/sth *phr v* [T] to consider the possible effects of something and make plans to deal with it: *Even allowing for delays, we should finish early.*

**al·low·a·ble** /əˈlaʊəbəl/ *adj* acceptable according to particular rules: *allowable vacation time*

**al·low·ance** /əˈlaʊəns/ *n* **1** [C,U] money you are given regularly or for a special reason: *How much allowance do your parents give you?* | *a travel allowance* **2 make allowances for** to consider the facts about someone or something when making judgments or deci-

sions: *He's so tired I'll make allowances for him.*

**al·loy** /ˈælɔɪ/ *n* a metal made by mixing two or more different metals

**all right** /ˌ. ˈ./ *adj, adv* SPOKEN **1** acceptable, but not excellent: *"How's the food?" "It's all right, but I've had better."* **2** not hurt, not upset, or not having problems: *Sue, are you all right?* | *Did everything go all right* (=happen without any problems) *with your test?* **3** used in order to say you agree with a plan, suggestion etc.: *"Let's go now." "All right."* **4 that's all right a)** used in order to reply when someone thanks you: *"Thanks for your help!" "That's all right."* **b)** used in order to tell someone you are not angry when s/he says s/he is sorry: *"Sorry I'm late!" "That's all right."* **5** used in order to say or ask whether something is convenient for you: *Would that bar on Front Street be all right to meet in?* **6 is it all right if...** used in order to ask for someone's permission to do something: *Is it all right if I close the window?* **7** used in order to ask if someone has understood something: *You should do this exercise by yourself, all right?* **8** used in order to say you are happy about something: *"I got the job!" "All right!"* **9 be doing all right** to be successful in your job or life

---

**USAGE NOTE all right and alright**

**All right** is the usual way we spell this phrase: *Don't worry. I'm all right.* | *All right, let's go!* Many teachers think that **alright** is incorrect in formal writing.

---

**al·lude** /əˈlud/ *v*

**allude to** sb/sth *phr v* [T] FORMAL to talk about something in an indirect way

**al·lure**[1] /əˈlʊr/ *n* [singular, U] a pleasant or exciting quality that attracts people: *the allure of travel*

**allure**[2] *v* [T] to attract someone by seeming to offer something pleasant or exciting **–alluring** *adj: an alluring smile*

**al·lu·sion** /əˈluʒən/ *n* [C,U] FORMAL the act of speaking or writing in an indirect way about something: *His poetry is full of allusions to other literature.* **–allusive** /əˈlusɪv/ *adj*

**al·ly**[1] /əˈlaɪ, ˈælaɪ/ *n* a person or country that helps another, especially in war: *the US and its European allies*

**ally**[2] *v* [I,T] **ally yourself to/with** to join with other people or countries to help each other

**al·ma ma·ter** /ˌælmə ˈmɑtɚ, ˌɑl-/ *n* [singular, U] FORMAL **1** the school, college, or university where you used to study: *He returned to his alma mater to teach.* **2** the official song of a school, college, or university

**al·ma·nac** /ˈɔlməˌnæk/ *n* **1** a book giving a list of the days of a year, times the sun rises and sets, changes in the moon etc. **2** a book giving information about a particular subject or activity: *a farmers' almanac*

**al·might·y** /ɔl'maɪti/ *adj* **1** having the power to do anything: *Almighty God* **2** very important or powerful: *the almighty dollar*

**al·mond** /'amənd, 'æm-/ *n* a flat white nut with a slightly sweet taste, or the tree on which these nuts grow

**al·most** /'ɔlmoust, ɔl'moust/ *adv* nearly but not quite: *Are we almost there?* |*Almost all children like to read.*

**alms** /amz/ *n* [plural] OLD-FASHIONED money, food etc. given to poor people

**a·loft** /ə'lɔft/ *adv* LITERARY high up in the air

**a·lo·ha** /ə'louha/ *interjection* used in order to say hello or goodbye in Hawaii

**a·lone** /ə'loun/ *adj* **1** away from other people: *She lives alone.* **2** only: *He alone can do the job.* (=he is the only one who can do it) **3 leave sb alone** to stop annoying someone: *Go away and leave me alone.* **4 leave sth alone** to not touch something: *Leave that alone! It's mine.*

**a·long¹** /ə'lɔŋ/ *prep* **1** by the side of something and from one part of it to another part of it: *We took a walk along the river.*| *She looked anxiously along the line of faces.* **2** in a line next to or on something: *They've put up a fence along the road.*|*photographs arranged along the wall* **3** at a particular place on something, usually something long: *The house is somewhere along this road.*

**along²** *adv* **1** going forward in time or direction: *I was driving along, listening to the radio.* **2 go/come/be along** to go to, come to, or be in the place where something is happening: *We're going out - you're welcome to come along!* **3 along with** in addition to and at the same time: *There has been a sudden rise in the number of rapes, along with other forms of violence.* –see also **all along** (ALL²) **get along** (GET)

**a·long·side** /ə,lɔŋ'saɪd/ *adv prep* close to and in line with the edge of something: *a boat tied up alongside the dock*

**a·loof¹** /ə'luf/ *adv* apart from other people, not doing things with them: *She keeps aloof from us.*

**aloof²** *adj* staying apart from other people, especially because you think you are better than they are: *Your friend Jack seems pretty aloof.*

**a·loud** /ə'laud/ *adv* **1** in a voice that you can hear: *Will you please read the poem aloud?* **2** in a loud voice: *James cried aloud with pain.*

**al·pha·bet** /'ælfə,bɛt/ *n* a set of letters in a particular order, used in writing a language: *the Greek alphabet*

**al·pha·bet·i·cal** /,ælfə'bɛtɪkəl/ *adj* arranged according to the letters of the alphabet: *The dictionary is in alphabetical order.* –**alphabetically** *adv*

**al·pine** /'ælpaɪn/ *adj* being in or related to the Alps or other high mountains: *alpine flowers*

**al·read·y** /ɔl'rɛdi/ *adv* **1** before a particular time: *By the time he arrived, the room was already crowded.* **2** before: *We've been there already.* **3** sooner than expected: *I've forgotten the number already.*|*Is he leaving already?* **4** SPOKEN said in order to emphasize that you are annoyed: *"Cindy, come on! All right already! Stop rushing me!"* –see usage note at JUST¹

### USAGE NOTE all ready and already

Use **all ready** as an adjective phrase to say that someone is ready to do something, or that something is completely prepared: *We're all ready to go now.* | *Dinner is all ready.* Use **already** as an adverb to talk about something that has happened: *John has already seen the movie.*

**al·right** /ɔl'raɪt/ *adv* ⇨ ALL RIGHT –see usage note at ALL RIGHT

**al·so** /'ɔlsou/ *adv* **1** in addition; too: *We specialize in shoes, but we also sell accessories.* **2** used in order to say that one thing or fact is the same as another one: *My father also died of a heart attack.*

**al·tar** /'ɔltɚ/ *n* a table or raised structure used in a religious ceremony

**al·ter** /'ɔltɚ/ *v* [I,T] to change in some way: *The design has been altered slightly.*

**al·ter·a·tion** /,ɔltə'reɪʃən/ *n* [C,U] a change in something, or the act of changing it: *Alterations to clothes can be expensive.*

**al·ter·ca·tion** /,ɔltɚ'keɪʃən/ *n* FORMAL a noisy argument

**al·ter·nate¹** /'ɔltɚ,neɪt/ *v* **1** [I] to follow regularly, first one thing and then the other thing happening: *Jenny kept alternating between leaving and staying.* **2** [T] to do or use first one thing and then the other: *Alternate the layers of pasta and meat sauce.* –**alternation** /,ɔltɚ'neɪʃən/ *n* [C,U]

**alternate²** *adj* **1** happening in a regular way, first one thing and then the other thing: *alternate rain and sunshine* **2** able to be used instead of something or someone else: *an alternate method of payment*

**al·ter·na·tive¹** /ɔl'tɚnətɪv/ *adj* **1** an alternative plan, idea etc. can be used instead of another one: *an alternative way home* **2** an alternative system or solution is considered to be simpler or more natural than the old one: *alternative sources of energy* **3** different from what is usual or accepted: *alternative medicine* –**alternatively** *adv*

**alternative²** *n* something you can choose to do or use instead of something else: *He has the alternative of living at home or renting an apartment.*|*There's no alternative to your* plan. | *I have no alternative but to report you to the police.*

---

### USAGE NOTE alternative

Use **alternative** to talk about a choice between two things: *If we don't drive, what's the alternative?* We sometimes say "What are the alternatives?" when there are several choices, but many teachers think that this is incorrect.

---

**al·though** /ɔl'ðoʊ/ *conjunction* **1** in spite of the fact that; though: *Although the car's old, it still runs well.* **2** but; HOWEVER: *Patty might have left, although I'm not sure.* —see also THOUGH¹

**al·ti·tude** /'æltə,tud/ *n* the height of something above sea level: *flying at high/low altitude*

**al·to** /'æltoʊ/ *n* [C,U] a female singer with a low voice, or the line of a piece of music that this person sings

**al·to·geth·er** /,ɔltə'gɛðɚ, 'ɔltə,gɛðɚ/ *adv* **1** a word meaning "completely", used in order to emphasize what you are saying: *Bradley seems to have disappeared altogether.* **2** considering everything or the whole amount: *There were five people altogether.* | *It did rain a lot, but altogether it was a good trip.*

---

### USAGE NOTE altogether and all together

Use **altogether** as an adverb to talk about the total amount or number of something: *There were 50 guests altogether at the wedding.* Use **all together** as an adjective phrase to say that things or people are together in a group: *Try to keep the pieces of the puzzle all together.*

---

**al·tru·ism** /'æltru,ɪzəm/ *n* [U] the practice of thinking of the needs of other people before thinking of your own —**altruist** *n* —**altruistic** /,æltru'ɪstɪk/ *adj*

**a·lu·mi·num** /ə'lumənəm/ *n* [U] a silver-white metal that is an ELEMENT, and that is light and easily bent

**al·ways** /'ɔlweɪz, -wɪz, -wɪz/ *adv* **1** at all times, or each time: *Always lock the car doors at night in the city.* **2** for a very long time, or as long as you can remember: *He said he'd always love her.* | *I've always wanted to go to China.* **3** happening continuously, especially in an annoying way: *The stupid car is always breaking down!* **4 you could always...** SPOKEN said in order to make a polite suggestion: *You could always try calling her.*

---

### USAGE NOTE always

Use **always** between the auxiliary or modal verb and the main verb: *I can always tell when he's lying.* ✗ DON'T SAY "I always can tell." ✗ Use **always** after the verb "to be" when it is the main verb in a sentence:

---

*The twins are always together.* ✗ DON'T SAY "They always are together." ✗

**AM** /,eɪ 'ɛm‹ / amplitude modulation; a system of broadcasting radio programs in which the strength of the radio waves varies —compare EM

**a.m.** /,eɪ 'ɛm/ LATIN the abbreviation of "ante meridiem"; used after numbers to show times from MIDNIGHT until just before NOON: *I start work at 9:00 a.m.* —see also P.M.

**am** /m, əm; *strong* æm/ the first person singular and present tense of the verb BE

**a·mal·gam·ate** /ə'mælgə,meɪt/ *v* [I,T] to join to form a bigger organization —**amalgamation** /ə,mælgə'meɪʃən/ *n* [C,U]

**a·mass** /ə'mæs/ *v* [T] to gather together or collect money or information in large amounts: *amassing evidence for the case*

**am·a·teur¹** /'æmətʃɚ/ *adj* doing something for enjoyment, but not for money: *an amateur boxer/musician*

**amateur²** *n* **1** someone who does something because they enjoy it, but not for money —compare PROFESSIONAL² **2** someone who does not have experience or skill in a particular activity: *Don't have your tattoo done by an amateur.* —**amateurish** *adj*

**a·maze** /ə'meɪz/ *v* [T] to make someone feel great surprise: *The variety of food at the cafe never ceases to amaze me.* (=always surprises me)

**a·mazed** /ə'meɪzd/ *adj* **be amazed** to be very surprised: *We were amazed at how quickly the kids learned.* | *I'm amazed (that) you remember him.* | *We were amazed to hear/see that he was alive.*

**a·maze·ment** /ə'meɪzmənt/ *n* [U] the state or feeling of being AMAZED: *We watched the dancers in/with amazement.*

**a·maz·ing** /ə'meɪzɪŋ/ *adj* making someone feel very surprised: *The computers are absolutely amazing!*

**a·maz·ing·ly** /ə'meɪzɪŋli/ *adv* in an AMAZING way: *an amazingly skilled athlete* | *Amazingly enough, he lived to tell his story.*

**am·bas·sa·dor** /æm'bæsədɚ, əm-/ *n* an important official who represents his/her country in another country: *the Mexican ambassador to Canada* —**ambassadorial** /æm,bæsə'dɔriəl/ *adj*

**am·bi·ance, ambience** /'æmbiəns, 'ambiəns/ *n* [U] the way a place makes you feel: *the restaurant's friendly ambiance*

**am·bi·dex·trous** /,æmbɪ'dɛkstrəs/ *adj* able to use both hands with equal skill

**am·bi·gu·i·ty** /,æmbə'gyuɪti/ *n* [C,U] the state of being AMBIGUOUS: *There were some ambiguities in the letter.* | *the ambiguity of her words*

**am·big·u·ous** /æm'bɪgyuəs/ *adj* an ambiguous remark, word etc. is not clear because it could have more than one meaning –opposite UNAMBIGUOUS

**am·bi·tion** /æmˈbɪʃən/ *n* **1** [U] the quality of being determined to succeed: *Saul has no ambition at all.* **2** a strong desire to do or achieve something: *Her ambition is to climb Mount Everest.*

**am·bi·tious** /æmˈbɪʃəs/ *adj* **1** needing a lot of skill and effort to achieve something: *The goals we set were too ambitious.* **2** having a strong desire to be successful or powerful: *He is young and very ambitious.* –**ambitiously** *adv*

**am·biv·a·lent** /æmˈbɪvələnt/ *adj* not sure whether you like something or not: *I think Carla's ambivalent about getting married.* –**ambivalence** *n* [U]

**am·ble** /ˈæmbəl/ *v* [I] to walk slowly in a relaxed way: *He ambled down the street, smoking a cigarette.*

**am·bu·lance** /ˈæmbyələns/ *n* a special vehicle for taking sick or injured people to the hospital

**am·bush**[1] /ˈæmbʊʃ/ *n* an attack against someone, in which the attackers have been hiding: *Two soldiers were killed in an ambush near the border.*

**ambush**[2] *v* [T] to attack someone from a place where you have been hiding

**a·me·lio·rate** /əˈmilyəˌreɪt/ *v* [I,T] FORMAL to make something better –**amelioration** /əˌmilyəˈreɪʃən/ *n* [U]

**a·men** /ˌeɪˈmɛn, ˌɑ-/ *interjection* said at the end of a prayer to express agreement or the hope that it will be true

**a·me·na·ble** /əˈminəbəl, əˈmɛ-/ *adj* willing to listen to or do something: *I'm sure they'll be amenable to your suggestions.*

**a·mend** /əˈmɛnd/ *v* [T] to make small changes or improvements, especially in the words of a law: *The statute has been amended several times.*

**a·mend·ment** /əˈmɛndmənt/ *n* [C,U] a change, especially in the words of a law: *an amendment to the new banking bill*

**a·mends** /əˈmɛndz/ *n* **make amends** to do something that shows you are sorry for something: *I tried to make amends by inviting him to lunch.*

**a·men·i·ty** /əˈmɛnəti, əˈmi-/ *n* [C usually plural] something in a place that makes living there enjoyable and pleasant: *The hotel's amenities include a pool and two bars.*

**A·mer·i·can**[1] /əˈmɛrɪkən/ *n* someone from the US

**American**[2] *adj* relating to or coming from the US: *American cars*

**A·mer·i·ca·na** /əˌmɛrəˈkɑnə/ *n* [U] objects, styles, stories etc. that are typical of America

**American dream** /.ˌ... ˈ./ *n* [singular] **the American Dream** belief that everyone in the

US has the opportunity to be successful if s/he works hard

**American In·di·an** /.ˌ... ˈ.../ *n* ⇨ NATIVE AMERICAN

**A·mer·i·can·ism** /əˈmɛrɪkəˌnɪzəm/ *n* an English word or phrase that is used in the US

**A·mer·i·can·i·za·tion** /əˌmɛrɪkənɪˈzeɪʃən/ *n* [U] change in a foreign society that is influenced by American values: *They don't like the Americanization of European culture.*

**A·mer·i·cas** /əˈmɛrɪkəz/ *n* [plural] **the Americas** North, Central, and South America considered together as a whole

**a·mi·a·ble** /ˈeɪmiəbəl/ *adj* friendly and pleasant: *an amiable child* –**amiably** *adv*

**am·i·ca·ble** /ˈæmɪkəbəl/ *adj* done without arguments: *an amicable divorce*

**a·mid** /əˈmɪd/, **a·midst** /əˈmɪdst/ *prep* FORMAL among or in the middle of: *surviving amid the horrors of World War I*

**a·miss** /əˈmɪs/ *adj* **be amiss** FORMAL to be a problem or to be wrong: *She sensed something was amiss.*

**am·mo** /ˈæmoʊ/ *n* [U] INFORMAL ammunition

**am·mo·nia** /əˈmoʊnyə/ *n* [U] a gas or liquid with a strong unpleasant smell, used in cleaning

**am·mu·ni·tion** /ˌæmyəˈnɪʃən/ *n* [U] **1** things such as bullets, bombs etc. that are fired from guns **2** information that can be used in order to criticize someone: *The press has lots of ammunition to use against Ramirez.*

**am·ne·sia** /æmˈniʒə/ *n* [U] the medical condition of not being able to remember anything

**am·ne·si·ac** /æmˈniziˌæk, -ʒi-/ *n* someone with AMNESIA

**am·nes·ty** /ˈæmnəsti/ *n* [C,U] an official order forgiving criminals or freeing prisoners, especially people who have opposed the government

**a·moe·ba** /əˈmibə/ *n* a very small creature that has only one cell

**a·mok** /əˈmʌk, əˈmɑk/ *adv* **run amok** to behave or happen in an uncontrolled way

**a·mong** /əˈmʌŋ/, **a·mongst** /əˈmʌŋst/ *prep* **1** in a particular group of people or things: *rising unemployment among men under 25* | *Relax, you're among friends here.* | *They were talking amongst themselves.* (=a group of people were talking) **2** in the middle of, through, or between: *We looked for the watch among the bushes.* | *He stood among the huge piles of papers, frowning.* **3** used when mentioning one or two people or things from a larger group: *Swimming and diving are among the most popular Olympic events.* | *We discussed, among other things, ways to raise money.*

**a·mor·al** /eɪˈmɔrəl, -ˈmɑr-/ *adj* not moral: *amoral actions/behavior*

**am·o·rous** /ˈæmərəs/ *adj* full of sexual desire or feelings of love

**a·mor·phous** /əˈmɔrfəs/ *adj* FORMAL without a fixed form or shape, or without clear organization

**a·mount¹** /əˈmaʊnt/ *n* how much of something there is, or how much is needed: *I was surprised at the large **amount** of trash on the streets.* | *Please pay the full amount.*

---
**USAGE NOTE** amount and number
---

Use **amount** with uncountable nouns: *a large amount of money.* Use **number** with countable nouns: *a number of cities*

**amount²** *v*

**amount to** sth *phr v* [T] **1** amount to sth to mean something without saying it directly: *What he said **amounted to** an apology.* **2** to add up to a total of a particular amount: *Jenny's debts **amount to** over $1000.*

**amp** /æmp/, **ampere** *n* a unit for measuring an electric current

**am·phet·a·mine** /æmˈfɛtəˌmin, -mɪn/ *n* [C,U] a drug that gives people more energy and makes them feel excited

**am·phib·i·an** /æmˈfɪbiən/ *n* an animal such as a FROG that can live on land and in water

**am·phib·i·ous** /æmˈfɪbiəs/ *adj* **1** an amphibious vehicle can travel on land and water **2** an amphibious animal can live on land and in water

**am·phi·the·a·ter** /ˈæmfəˌθiətɚ/ *n* a large structure with rows of seats that curve partly around a central space, used for performances

**am·ple** /ˈæmpəl/ *adj* **1** more than enough: *There's ample room in here for everyone.* **2** ample belly/bosom etc. an expression meaning that a part of someone's body is large, used in order to be polite –**amply** *adv*

**am·pli·fi·er** /ˈæmpləˌfaɪɚ/ *n* a piece of electronic equipment that makes an electrical sound signal stronger, so that it is loud enough to hear

**am·pli·fy** /ˈæmpləˌfaɪ/ *v* [T] **1** to make something louder or stronger: *We may need to amplify your voice on the tape.* **2** FORMAL to explain something in more detail –**amplification** /ˌæmpləfəˈkeɪʃən/ *n* [singular, U]

**am·pu·tate** /ˈæmpyəˌteɪt/ *v* [I,T] to cut off a part of someone's body for medical reasons –**amputation** /ˌæmpyəˈteɪʃən/ *n* [C,U]

**am·pu·tee** /ˌæmpyəˈti/ *n* someone who has a part of his/her body cut off for medical reasons

**a·muck** /əˈmʌk/ *adv* ⇨ AMOK

**a·muse** /əˈmyuz/ *v* [T] **1** to make someone laugh or smile: *Harry's jokes always amused me.* **2** to make the time pass in an enjoyable way for someone: *I've been trying to find ways to **keep** the kids **amused**.*

**a·muse·ment** /əˈmyuzmənt/ *n* **1** [U] the feeling you get when something makes you laugh or smile: *"You're not asking me for help, are you?" she said **with amusement**.* **2** [C,U] something such as a movie or a sports game that makes the time pass in an enjoyable way: *What do you do **for amusement** in this town?*

**amusement park** /.ˈ.. ./ *n* a large park where people can play games of skill, go on large rides, and see performances

amusement park

**a·mus·ing** /əˈmyuzɪŋ/ *adj* funny and entertaining: *I didn't **find** your comment **amusing**.* (=did not think it was funny)

**an** /ən; *strong* æn/ *determiner* a word meaning "a," used when the following word begins with a vowel sound: *an orange* | *an X-ray of her chest* | *an hour before the movie* –see usage note at A

**a·nach·ro·nism** /əˈnækrəˌnɪzəm/ *n* someone or something that is or seems to be in the wrong historical time: *Tourists in their modern clothes seem an anachronism in the tiny old town.* –**anachronistic** /əˌnækrəˈnɪstɪk/ *adj*

**an·a·gram** /ˈænəˌgræm/ *n* a word or phrase made by changing the order of the letters in another word or phrase: *"Silent" is an anagram of "listen."*

**a·nal** /ˈeɪnl/ *n* **1** SLANG showing too much concern with small details in a way that annoys other people: *Don't be so anal.* **2** relating to the ANUS

**an·al·ge·sic** /ˌænlˈdʒizɪk/ *n* TECHNICAL a drug that reduces pain

**a·nal·o·gous** /əˈnæləgəs/ *adj* FORMAL similar to another situation or thing: *The system works in a way that is **analogous to** a large clock.*

**a·nal·o·gy** /əˈnælədʒi/ *n* [C,U] a comparison between two situations, processes etc. that seem similar: *We can **draw an analogy** between the brain and a computer.*

**a·nal·y·sis** /əˈnæləsɪs/ *n* [C,U] **1** the careful examination of something in order to understand it better or explain what it consists of: *an analysis of the test results* **2** ⇨ PSYCHOANALYSIS

**an·a·lyst** /ˈænl-ɪst/ *n* **1** someone whose job is to ANALYZE things: *a financial analyst* **2** ⇨ PSYCHOANALYST

**an·a·lyt·ic·al** /ˌænlˈɪtɪkəl/, **analytic** *adj* using methods that help you examine things carefully: *an analytical mind* | *an analytic method*

**an·a·lyze** /ˈænlˌaɪz/ *v* [T] **1** to examine or think about something carefully in order to understand it: *We're trying to analyze what went wrong.* | *The patient's blood is then tested and analyzed.* **2** to examine someone's mental or emotional problems using PSYCHOANALYSIS

**an·ar·chy** /ˈænɚki/ *n* [U] **1** a situation in which no one obeys rules or laws: *Officials are worried that the fighting in the city could lead to anarchy.* **2** a situation in which there is no government in a country −**anarchic** /æ'nɑrkɪk/ *adj*

**a·nath·e·ma** /ə'næθəmə/ *n* [singular, U] FORMAL something that is completely the opposite of what you believe in: *liberal values that were anathema to conservative voters*

**a·nat·o·my** /ə'næṭəmi/ *n* **1** [U] the scientific study of the structure of the body **2** [C usually singular] the structure of a living thing, organization, or social group, and how it works: *the anatomy of modern society* −**anatomical** /ˌænə'tɑmɪkəl/ *adj*

**an·ces·tor** /'æn,sɛstəʳ/ *n* a member of your family who lived in past times: *My ancestors were Italian.* −**ancestral** /æn'sɛstrəl/ *adj* −compare DESCENDANT

**an·ces·try** /'æn,sɛstri/ *n* [U] the members of your family who lived in past times: *people of Scottish ancestry*

**an·chor**[1] /'æŋkəʳ/ *n* **1** someone who reads the news on television or radio and is in charge of the program: *the local evening news anchor* **2** a heavy metal object that is lowered into the water to prevent a ship or boat from moving

**anchor**[2] *v* [I, T] **1** to lower the anchor on a ship or boat to keep it from moving: *Three tankers were anchored in the harbor.* **2** to fasten something firmly to something so that it cannot move: *The main rope anchors the tent to the ground.*

**an·chor·man** /'æŋkəʳmən/, **an·chor·wom·an** /'æŋkəʳˌwʊmən/ *n* ⇨ ANCHOR[1]

**an·cho·vy** /'æn,tʃouvi, -tʃə-, æn'tʃouvi/ *n* [C,U] a very small ocean fish that tastes very salty

**an·cient** /'eɪnʃənt/ *adj* **1** happening or existing very far back in history: *ancient Rome* **2** HUMOROUS very old: *I parked my ancient little car next to a big new Jaguar.* −compare ANTIQUE −see also OLD

**and** /ən, n, ənd; *strong* ænd/ *conjunction* **1** used in order to join two words or parts of sentences: *a peanut butter and jelly sandwich* | *They have two kids, a boy and a girl.* | *Martha is going to cook, and Tom is going to help her.* **2** used in order to say that one thing happens after another: *Grant knocked and went in.* **3** SPOKEN used instead of "to" after "come," "go," "try," and some other verbs: *Try and finish your homework before dinner, okay?* | *A guy comes every Sunday and cuts my grass for me.* **4** used when adding numbers: *Six and four make ten.* | *a hundred and thirty dollars* **5** used in order to say that one thing is caused by something else: *I missed supper and I'm starving!*

**and·ro·gyn·ous** /æn'drɑdʒənəs/ *adj* **1** someone who is androgynous looks both female and male **2** an androgynous plant or animal has both male and female parts

**an·droid** /'ændrɔɪd/ *n* a ROBOT that looks completely human

**an·ec·dot·al** /ˌænɪk'dout̯l/ *adj* consisting of stories based on someone's personal experience: *The report is based on anecdotal evidence. It can't be called scientific!*

**an·ec·dote** /'ænɪkˌdout/ *n* a short interesting story about a particular person or event

**a·ne·mi·a** /ə'nimiə/ *n* [U] the unhealthy condition of not having enough red cells in your blood −**anemic** *adj*

**an·es·the·sia** /ˌænəs'θiʒə/ *n* [U] the use of ANESTHETICs in medicine

**an·es·thet·ic** /ˌænəs'θɛt̯ɪk/ *n* [C,U] a drug that stops feelings of pain, used during a medical operation: *local anesthetic* (=affecting part of your body) | *general anesthetic* (=affecting all of your body)

**a·nes·thet·ist** /ə'nɛsθəˌtɪst/ *n* someone whose job is to give ANESTHETIC to people in hospitals

**a·nes·the·tize** /ə'nɛsθəˌtaɪz/ *v* [T] to make someone unable to feel pain or strong emotions

**a·new** /ə'nu/ *adv* LITERARY in a new or different way; again: *She started life anew in New York.*

**an·gel** /'eɪndʒəl/ *n* **1** a spirit who lives with God in heaven, usually represented as a person with wings and dressed in white **2** SPOKEN someone who is very kind or helpful: *Oh, thanks! You're an angel!* −**angelic** /æn'dʒɛlɪk/ *adj*

**an·ger**[1] /'æŋgəʳ/ *n* [U] a strong feeling of wanting to hurt or criticize someone because s/he has done something bad to you or been unkind to you: *Paul had punched the wall in anger.* | *I try not to react to her with anger.*

**anger**[2] *v* [T] to make someone feel angry: *The court's decision angered environmentalists.*

**an·gle**[1] /'æŋgəl/ *n* **1** the space between two lines or surfaces that meet or cross each other, measured in degrees: *an angle of 90 degrees* | *a 45-degree angle* −see also RIGHT ANGLE **2** **at an angle** not upright or straight: *The plant was growing at an angle.* **3** a way of considering a problem or situation: *We need to look at this from a new angle.*

**angle**[2] *v* [T] to turn or move something so that it is at an angle: *You could angle the table away from the wall.*

**angle for** sth *phr v* [T] to try to get something without asking for it directly: *I think she's angling for an invitation to the party.*

**An·gli·can** /'æŋglɪkən/ *adj* relating to the main British or Canadian Protestant Church −**Anglican** *n*

**an·gling** /'æŋglɪŋ/ *n* [U] fishing with a hook and a line −**angle** *v* [I] −**angler** *n*

**an·go·ra** /æŋ'gɔrə/ *n* [U] wool or thread made from the fur of some goats or rabbits

**an·gry** /'æŋgri/ *adj* feeling or showing anger: *I'm so angry with/at her!* | *My parents were* really **angry about** my bad grades. —**angrily** adv

**angst** /'ɑŋst, 'æŋst/ n [U] strong feelings of anxiety and sadness because you are worried about your life

**an·guish** /'æŋgwɪʃ/ n [U] very great pain or worry: the anguish of the hostages' families —**anguished** adj: anguished cries for help

**an·gu·lar** /'æŋgyələ/ adj **1** having sharp corners: an angular shape **2** very thin, and without much flesh on your bones: a tall angular young man

**an·i·mal**[1] /'ænəməl/ n **1** any living creature like a cow or dog, that is not a bird, insect, fish, or person: farm animals | wild animals **2** any living creature that can move around: Humans are highly intelligent animals. **3** INFORMAL someone who behaves in a cruel, violent, or rude way: Stay away from that crowd - they're a bunch of animals. —see also **party animal** (PARTY)

**animal**[2] adj **1** relating to or made from animals: animal fats **2 animal urges/instincts etc.** human feelings, desires etc. that relate to sex, food, and other basic needs

**an·i·mate**[1] /'ænə,meɪt/ v [T] to make something seem to have more life or energy: Laughter animated his face.

**an·i·mate**[2] /'ænəmɪt/ adj FORMAL living —opposite INANIMATE

**an·i·mat·ed** /'ænə,meɪt̬ɪd/ adj **1** full of interest and energy: an animated debate **2 animated cartoon/film etc.** a movie in which pictures, clay models etc. seem to move and talk —**animatedly** adv

**an·i·ma·tion** /,ænə'meɪʃən/ n [U] **1** energy and excitement: talking with animation **2** the process of making ANIMATED movies

**an·i·mos·i·ty** /,ænə'mɑsət̬i/ n [C,U] FORMAL strong dislike or hatred

**an·kle** /'æŋkəl/ n the joint between your foot and your leg —see picture at BODY

**an·nals** /'ænlz/ n [plural] **in the annals of history/science etc.** in the whole history of a particular subject

**an·nex**[1] /ə'nɛks, 'ænɛks/ v [T] to take control of a country or area next to your own, especially by using force —**annexation** /,ænɪk'seɪʃən, ,ænɛk-/ n [C,U]

**annex**[2] n a separate building that has been added to a larger one

**an·ni·hi·late** /ə'naɪə,leɪt/ v [T] to destroy something or defeat someone completely: Both forts were nearly annihilated. —**annihilation** /ə,naɪə'leɪʃən/ n [U]

**an·ni·ver·sa·ry** /,ænə'vɝsəri/ n a date on which something important or special happened in an earlier year: our wedding anniversary —compare BIRTHDAY

**an·nounce** /ə'naʊns/ v [T] **1** to officially and publicly tell people about something: The

police **announced that** an arrest would be made within 24 hours. **2** to say something in a loud or angry way: Randy suddenly **announced (that)** he was leaving.

**an·nounce·ment** /ə'naʊnsmənt/ n **1** an official public statement: We all waited for the captain to **make an announcement**. | I didn't hear the **announcement that** the store was closing. **2** [U] the act of telling people something publicly: the announcement of the winners

**an·nounc·er** /ə'naʊnsə/ n someone who gives people news or tells them what is happening at an event, during a broadcast etc.

**an·noy** /ə'nɔɪ/ v [T] to make someone feel slightly angry about something; IRRITATE: You're beginning to annoy me!

**an·noy·ance** /ə'nɔɪəns/ n **1** [U] the feeling of being slightly angry; IRRITATION: Mia's annoyance never showed. **2** something that makes you slightly angry: The kids next door are a constant annoyance.

**an·noyed** /ə'nɔɪd/ adj slightly angry: I'm **getting annoyed with** her. | Ben was **annoyed at** his mother. | Joel is really **annoyed about** the mess we left. | My sister's **annoyed (that)** we didn't call.

**an·noy·ing** /ə'nɔɪ-ɪŋ/ adj making you feel slightly angry; IRRITATING: an annoying habit | **It's annoying that** we didn't know about this before. —**annoyingly** adv

**an·nu·al**[1] /'ænyuəl/ adj **1** happening once a year: the annual conference **2** calculated over a period of one year: my annual income —**annually** adv

**annual**[2] n **1** a plant that lives for one year or season **2** a book that is produced once a year with the same title but with different stories, pictures etc. that relate to that year

**an·nu·i·ty** /ə'nuət̬i/ n an amount of money that is paid each year to someone from an INVESTMENT

**an·nul** /ə'nʌl/ v -lled, -lling [T] TECHNICAL to officially state that a marriage or legal agreement no longer exists —**annulment** n [C,U]

**a·noint** /ə'nɔɪnt/ v [T] to put oil or water on someone's head or body during a religious ceremony —**anointment** n [C,U]

**a·nom·a·ly** /ə'nɑməli/ n [C,U] FORMAL something that is very noticeable because it is so different from what is usual: Women firefighters are still an anomaly in a largely male profession.

**a·non** /ə'nɑn/ the written abbreviation of ANONYMOUS

**a·non·ym·i·ty** /,ænə'nɪmət̬i/ n [U] **1** the state of not having your name known: The author prefers anonymity. **2** the state of not having any unusual or interesting features: the drab anonymity of the city

**a·non·y·mous** /ə'nɑnəməs/ adj **1** not known by name: an anonymous writer **2** done, made, or given by someone whose name is not known: *an anonymous letter* **3** without interesting features or qualities: *an anonymous black car* **–anonymously** *adv*

**a·no·rex·i·a** /ˌænəˈrɛksiə/ *n* [U] a mental illness that makes people stop eating

**a·no·rex·ic** /ˌænəˈrɛksɪk/ *adj* having ANOREXIA, or relating to anorexia **–anorexic** *n*

**an·oth·er** /əˈnʌðə/ *determiner, pron* **1** one more person or thing of the same kind: *Do you want another beer?* | *I'll cancel that check and send you another.* **2** a different person or thing: *Is there another room we could use?* | *You'll just have to find another job.* **3** something in addition to a particular amount, distance, period of time etc.: *We'll wait another ten minutes.* –see also **one after the other/one after another** (ONE²) ONE ANOTHER –see usage note at OTHER¹

**an·swer¹** /ˈænsə/ *v* **1** [I,T] to reply to something that someone has asked or written: *I can't really answer your question.* | *Why don't you answer me?* | *He answered that he did not know.* **2** to reply to a question in a test, competition etc.: *Please answer questions 1-20.* **3 answer the telephone/door** to pick up the telephone when it rings or go to the door when someone knocks or rings a bell **4** to react to something that someone else has done: *The army answered by firing into the crowd.*

**answer back** *phr v* [I,T] to reply to someone in a rude way: *Don't answer back, young man!*

**answer for** sth *phr v* [T] **1** to explain why you did something or why something happened, and be punished if necessary: *One day you'll have to answer for this.* | *That sister of yours has a lot to answer for.* **2 answer for sb/sth** to say you are sure that someone will do something or that s/he has particular qualities: *I can answer for his honesty.*

**answer to** sb *phr v* to be judged by someone, especially someone you work for: *Wharton doesn't answer to anyone.*

---

**USAGE NOTE** answer, reply, respond

When you are asked a question you can **answer** or **reply**: *"Are you coming?" "Yes,"* *he replied.* | *She reluctantly answered his question.* ✗ DON'T SAY "answered to his question." ✗ **Respond** means the same thing, but it is more formal: *We would like to thank everyone who responded to our survey.*

---

**answer²** *n* **1** [C,U] a reply to what someone asks or writes: *Give me an answer as soon as possible.* | *I told you before, the answer is no!* | *In answer to your question, I think Paul's right.* **2** a reply to a question in a test, competition etc.: *What was the answer to question 7?* **3** something that you get as a result of thinking or calculating with numbers:\*The answer is 255.*

**4** something that solves a problem: *A new car would be the answer to all our problems.* **5** a reaction to something: *Jim's answer to their threat was to run.*

**an·swer·a·ble** /ˈænsərəbəl/ *adj* **be answerable (to sb) for** sth to have to explain your actions to someone: *You're all answerable for anything that goes wrong.*

**an·swer·ing ma·chine** /ˈ... .ˌ../ *n* a machine that records your telephone calls when you cannot answer them

**ant** /ænt/ *n* a common small black or red insect that lives in groups

**an·tac·id** /ˌæntˈæsɪd/ *n* a drug that gets rid of the burning feeling in your stomach when you have eaten too much, drunk too much alcohol etc.

**an·tag·o·nism** /ænˈtægəˌnɪzəm/ *n* [U] strong opposition to or hatred of someone else: *Polucci's antagonism towards the press is obvious.* | *There has always been antagonism between the two groups.*

**an·tag·o·nist** /ænˈtægənɪst/ *n* your opponent in an argument, fight etc.

**an·tag·o·nis·tic** /ænˌtægəˈnɪstɪk/ *adj* showing opposition to or hatred of someone or something: *His reactions to the teacher's questions were always antagonistic.* **–antagonistically** *adv*

**an·tag·o·nize** /ænˈtægəˌnaɪz/ *v* [T] to make someone feel angry with you: *Don't try to antagonize me.*

**Ant·arc·tic** /æntˈɑrktɪk, ænˈɑrtɪk/ *n* **the Antarctic** the very cold, most southern part of the world **–antarctic** *adj*

**Ant·arc·ti·ca** /æntˈɑrktɪkə, -ˈɑrtɪkə/ *n* one of the seven CONTINENTs, that is the most southern area of land on earth

**an·te** /ˈænti/ *n* **up/raise the ante** to increase your demands or try to get more things from a situation: *They've upped the ante by making a $120 million bid to buy the company.*

**ant·eat·er** /ˈænˌtitə/ *n* an animal that has a very long nose and eats small insects

**an·te·lope** /ˈænt̬əlˌoʊp/ *n* an animal that has long horns, can run very fast, and is very graceful

**an·ten·na** /ænˈtɛnə/ *n* **1** a piece of equipment on a television, car, roof etc. for receiving or sending radio or television signals –see picture on page 471 **2** *plural* **antennae** one of two long thin things like hairs on an insect's head, that it uses to feel things

**an·them** /ˈænθəm/ *n* **1** a formal or religious song **2** a song that a particular group of people consider to be very important to them: *an anthem for our generation*

**ant·hill** /ˈæntˌhɪl/ *n* a small pile of dirt on the ground over the place where ANTs live

**an·thol·o·gy** /ænˈθɑlədʒi/ *n* a set of stories,

poems etc. by different people collected together in one book

**an·thro·pol·o·gy** /ˌænθrə'pɑlədʒi/ *n* [U] the scientific study of people, their societies, beliefs etc. **–anthropologist** *n* **–anthropological** /ˌænθrəpə'lɑdʒɪkəl/ *adj*

**an·ti·air·craft** /ˌænti'ɛrkræft/ *adj* able to be used against enemy aircraft: *antiaircraft missiles*

**an·ti·bi·ot·ic** /ˌæntibaɪ'uṭɪk, ˌæntaɪ-/ *n* [C usually plural] a drug that is used in order to kill BACTERIA and cure infections **–antibiotic** *adj*

**an·ti·bod·y** /'ænti,bɑdi/ *n* a substance produced by your body to fight disease

**an·tic·i·pate** /æn'tɪsə,peɪt/ *v* [T] **1** to expect something to happen: *They anticipate trouble when the factory opens up again.| It's anticipated that grain prices will fall.* **2** to expect that something will happen and do something to prepare for it or prevent it: *We're trying to anticipate what questions we'll be asked.| Anticipating that the enemy would cross the river, they destroyed the bridge.*

**an·tic·i·pa·tion** /æn,tɪsə'peɪʃən/ *n* [U] the act of expecting something to happen: *Roy bought a new car in anticipation of his promotion.*

**an·ti·cli·max** /ˌænti'klaɪmæks/ *n* [C,U] something that seems disappointing because it happens after something that was much better: *After all the advertising, the concert itself was kind of an anticlimax.* **–anticlimactic** /ˌæntiklaɪ'mæktɪk/ *adj*

**an·tics** /'æntɪks/ *n* [plural] behavior that seems strange, funny, silly, or annoying: *Larry's antics last night really annoyed me.*

**an·ti·de·pres·sant** /ˌæntidɪ'prɛsənt, ˌæntaɪ-/ *n* [C,U] a drug used for treating DEPRESSION (=a mental illness that makes people very unhappy) **–antidepressant** *adj*

**an·ti·dote** /'ænti,doʊt/ *n* **1** a substance that stops the effects of a poison: *There's no antidote to these chemical weapons.* **2** something that makes an unpleasant situation better: *Laughter is one of the best antidotes to stress.*

**an·ti·freeze** /'ænti,friz/ *n* [U] a substance that is put in the water in car engines to stop it from freezing

**an·ti·his·ta·mine** /ˌænti'hɪstəmin, -min/ *n* [C,U] a drug that is used for treating an ALLERGY or COLD (=common illness) **–antihistamine** *adj*

**an·tip·a·thy** /æn'tɪpəθi/ *n* [U] FORMAL a feeling of strong dislike or opposition

**an·ti·per·spi·rant** /ˌænti'pɚspərənt/ *n* [U] a substance that prevents you from sweating (SWEAT)

**an·ti·quat·ed** /'ænti,kweɪṭɪd/ *adj* old-fashioned and not suitable for modern needs or conditions: *antiquated laws*

**an·tique** /æn'tik/ *n* a piece of furniture, jewelry etc. that is old and usually valuable: *price-*

*less antiques* **–antique** *adj*: *an antique table* **–compare** ANCIENT

**an·tiq·ui·ty** /æn'tɪkwəti/ *n* **1** [U] ancient times: *a tradition that stretches back into antiquity* **2** [U] the state of being very old: *a building of great antiquity* **3** [C usually plural] a building or object made in ancient times: *a collection of Roman antiquities*

**an·ti-Sem·i·tism** /ˌænti'sɛmə,tɪzəm, ˌæntaɪ-/ *n* [U] hatred of Jewish people **–anti-Semitic** /ˌæntisə'mɪṭɪk, ˌæntaɪ-/ *adj*

**an·ti·sep·tic** /ˌæntə'sɛptɪk/ *n* a chemical substance that prevents a wound from becoming infected **–antiseptic** *adj*: *antiseptic lotion*

**an·ti·so·cial** /ˌænti'soʊʃəl, ˌæntaɪ-/ *adj* **1** unwilling to meet people and talk to them: *Jane's friendly, but her husband's a little antisocial.* **2** not caring if you cause problems for other people: *Some people think smoking in public is antisocial.*

**an·tith·e·sis** /æn'tɪθəsɪs/ *n* FORMAL the exact opposite of something: *Her style of writing is the antithesis of Dickens'.*

**an·ti·trust** /ˌænti'trʌst, ˌæntaɪ-/ *adj* preventing one company from unfairly controlling prices: *antitrust laws*

**ant·ler** /'æntˈlɚ/ *n* one of the two horns that look like tree branches on the head of animals such as DEER

**an·to·nym** /'æntə,nɪm/ *n* TECHNICAL a word that means the opposite of another word. For example, "war" is the antonym of "peace" **–opposite** SYNONYM

**a·nus** /'eɪnəs/ *n* the hole in your body through which solid waste leaves your BOWELS

**an·vil** /'ænvɪl/ *n* a heavy iron block on which pieces of metal are shaped using a hammer

**anx·i·e·ty** /æŋ'zaɪəti/ *n* **1** [C,U] a strong feeling of worry about something: *fears and anxieties| The public's anxiety about job security is increasing.* **2** [U] a feeling of wanting to do something very much, but being worried that you will not succeed: *In her anxiety to make us comfortable, she managed to make us nervous.*

**anx·ious** /'æŋkʃəs, 'æŋʃəs/ *adj* **1** very worried about something, or showing that you are worried: *June's anxious about the results of her blood test.| an anxious look* **2** feeling strongly that you want something to happen, especially in order to improve a bad situation: *Ralph is anxious to prove that he can do the job.| His parents were anxious that he be given another chance.* **–see** usage note at NERVOUS

**an·y¹** /'ɛni/ *quantifier pron* **1** a word meaning "some," used in negative statements and questions: *Is there any coffee left? | Do you want any? | I don't think that will make any difference.| Are any of Norm's relatives coming for Christmas?* **2** used in order to say that it does not matter which person or thing you choose from a group: *Any of the restaurants in China-town would be fine.* | *There are bad things about any job.* −see also **in any case** (CASE[1]) **at any rate** (RATE[1]) −see usage notes at EITHER[2], SOME[1] −see study note on page 466

**any**[2] *adv* used in negative statements to mean "at all": *I don't see how things could be any worse.* | *Sandra couldn't walk any farther without a rest.*

**an·y·bod·y** /ˈɛniˌbɑdi, -ˌbʌdi, -bədi/ *pron* INFORMAL ⇨ ANYONE −see usage notes at ANYONE, SOME[1]

**an·y·how** /ˈɛniˌhaʊ/ *adv* INFORMAL ⇨ ANYWAY

**an·y·more** /ˌɛniˈmɔr/ *adv* **not anymore** used in order to say that something happened or was true before, but is not now: *Frank doesn't live here anymore.*

**an·y·one** /ˈɛniˌwʌn, -wən/ *pron* **1** a word meaning "any person" or "any people," used when it does not matter exactly who: *Anyone can learn to swim in just a few lessons.* | *Why would anyone want to do that?* **2** used in questions and negative statements to mean "a person": *Is anyone home?* | *She'd just moved and didn't know anyone.* −see usage note at PRONOUN

> ### USAGE NOTE anyone and anybody
>
> Use **anyone**, **someone**, **no one**, **anywhere**, **somewhere** and **nowhere** in all types of writing and in speech. We often use **anybody**, **somebody**, **nobody**, **anyplace**, **someplace** and **no place** in speech. They can also be used in informal writing, but not in formal writing.

**an·y·place** /ˈɛniˌpleɪs/ *adv* INFORMAL ⇨ ANYWHERE −see usage note at ANYONE

**an·y·thing** /ˈɛniˌθɪŋ/ *pron* **1** used in questions and negative statements to mean "something": *Do you need anything from the store?* | *Her dad didn't know anything about it.* **2** any thing, event, situation etc., when it does not matter exactly which: *That cat will eat anything.* | *I could have told him almost anything, and he would have believed me.* **3 or anything** SPOKEN said when there are several things or ideas that are possible: *Do you want a Coke or anything?* | *It wasn't like we were going steady or anything.* **4 anything like** used in questions and negative statements to mean "similar to": *Carrie doesn't look anything like her sister.* **5 anything goes** used in order to say that anything is possible: *Don't worry about what to wear - anything goes at Ben's parties.*

**an·y·way** /ˈɛniˌweɪ/ *adv* in spite of something: *The bride's mother was sick, but they had the wedding anyway.*

SPOKEN PHRASES
**1** used in order to continue a story or change the subject of a conversation: *I think* she's Lori's age, but anyway, she just had a baby.* | *Anyway, where do you want to go for lunch?* **2** used when you are saying something to support what you have just said: *We decided to sell it because nobody uses it anyway.* **3** used in order to find out the real reason for something: *What were you doing at his house anyway?*

**an·y·where** /ˈɛniˌwɛr/ *adv* **1** in or to any place, when it does not matter exactly where: *Fly anywhere in the US for only $170 with this special offer.* **2** used in questions and negative statements to mean "somewhere" or "nowhere": *I can't find my keys anywhere.* | *Are you going anywhere exciting on vacation this year?* **3 not anywhere near** not at all similar to something else: *The new car doesn't have anywhere near the power our last one had.* **4 not get anywhere** SPOKEN to not be successful at something: *I'm trying to set up a meeting, but I don't seem to be getting anywhere.* −see usage note at ANYONE

**a·part** /əˈpɑrt/ *adv* **1** separated by distance or time: *The two towns are 15 miles apart.* | *Our birthdays are only two days apart.* | *We try to keep the cats apart as much as possible because they fight.* **2** separated into many pieces: *He had to take the camera apart to fix it.* −see also **fall apart** (FALL[1]) **3 apart from a)** except for: *Apart from a couple of spelling mistakes, your paper looks fine.* **b)** in addition to: *What do you do for fun? Apart from volleyball, I mean.*

**a·part·heid** /əˈpɑrtaɪt, -teɪt, -taɪd/ *n* [U] a system in which the different races in a country are separated from each other

**a·part·ment** /əˈpɑrtˈmənt/ *n* a place to live that consists of a set of rooms in a large building

**apartment build·ing** /.ˈ.. ˌ../ *n* **apartment house** /.ˈ.. ˌ./ a building that is divided into separate apartments −see picture on page 471

**apartment com·plex** /.ˈ.. ˌ../ *n* a group of apartment buildings built at the same time in the same area

**ap·a·thet·ic** /ˌæpəˈθɛtɪk/ *adj* not interested in something: *Too many of our students are apathetic about learning.*

**ap·a·thy** /ˈæpəθi/ *n* [U] the feeling of not being interested in something or not caring about life: *public apathy about the coming election*

**ape** /eɪp/ *n* **1** a large monkey without a tail or with a very short tail, such as a GORILLA **2 go ape/apeshit** SLANG to become very angry or excited

**a·per·i·tif** /əˌpɛrəˈtif, ɑ-/ *n* a small alcoholic drink that you have before a meal

**ap·er·ture** /ˈæpətʃər/ *n* a small opening, especially one that lets light into a camera

**A**

**a·pex** /ˈeɪpɛks/ *n* **1** the top or highest part of something: *the apex of the pyramid* **2** the most successful part of something: *the apex of her career*

**aph·o·rism** /ˈæfəˌrɪzəm/ *n* a short expression that says something true

**aph·ro·dis·i·ac** /ˌæfrəˈdiziˌæk, -ˈdɪ-/ *n* a food or drug that makes someone feel sexual excitement —**aphrodisiac** *adj*

**a·piece** /əˈpis/ *adv* each: *Oranges are 20¢ apiece.* (=for each one) | *We gave $10 apiece for the gift.* (=each of us gave $10)

**a·plomb** /əˈplɑm, əˈplʌm/ *n* [U] FORMAL **with aplomb** in a confident or skillful way, especially in a difficult situation: *She answered all their questions with great aplomb.*

**a·po·ca·lypse** /əˈpɑkəlɪps/ *n* [U] **1** a dangerous situation that results in great destruction, death, or harm **2 the Apocalypse** the religious idea of the destruction and end of the world —**apocalyptic** /əˌpɑkəˈlɪptɪk/ *adj*

**a·po·lit·i·cal** /ˌeɪpəˈlɪtɪkəl/ *adj* not having any interest in or connection with politics

**a·pol·o·get·ic** /əˌpɑləˈdʒɛtɪk/ *adj* showing or saying that you are sorry about something: *He was really apologetic about forgetting my birthday.* —**apologetically** *adv*

**a·pol·o·gize** /əˈpɑləˌdʒaɪz/ *v* [I] to say that you are sorry about something that you have done, said etc.: *Shawn apologized for being mean.* | *Apologize to your sister now!*

---

**USAGE NOTE apologizing**

Say **I'm sorry** or **excuse me** when you make a small mistake: *I'm sorry - I didn't mean to step on your foot.* | *"You're blocking the entrance." "Oh, excuse me."* Use **I'm sorry** to apologize when you have done something wrong or upset someone: *I'm sorry about all the mess.* If you are late, say **I'm sorry** and give a reason: *I'm sorry I'm late. The traffic was bad.* In formal speech and writing, use **I apologize**: *I apologize for the inconvenience.*

---

**a·pol·o·gy** /əˈpɑlədʒi/ *n* **-ies** something that you say or write to show that you are sorry: *I owe you an apology for snapping at you.* | *I hope you will accept my apology for missing our appointment.*

**ap·o·plec·tic** /ˌæpəˈplɛktɪk/ *adj* **1** so angry you cannot control yourself **2** seeming to have had a STROKE

**ap·o·plex·y** /ˈæpəˌplɛksi/ *n* [U] ⇨ STROKE¹

**a·pos·tle** /əˈpɑsəl/ *n* **1** one of the 12 men chosen by Christ to teach his message **2** someone who believes strongly in a new idea and tries to persuade other people to believe it —**apostolic** /ˌæpəˈstɑlɪk/ *adj*

**a·pos·tro·phe** /əˈpɑstrəfi/ *n* **a)** the mark (') used in writing to show that one or more letters

or figures are missing, such as don't (=do not) or '96 (=1896/1996 etc.) **b)** the same mark used before or after the letter "s" to show that something belongs or relates to someone: *Mandy's coat* | *the workers' strike* **c)** the same sign used before "s" to show the plural of letters and numbers: *4 A's and 2 B's on my report card*

**ap·pall** /əˈpɔl/ *v* [T] to shock someone greatly: *We were appalled at/by the treatment of the refugees.*

**ap·pall·ing** /əˈpɔlɪŋ/ *adj* **1** shocking or terrible: *animals kept in appalling conditions* **2** INFORMAL very bad: *an appalling movie* —**appallingly** *adv*

**ap·pa·rat·us** /ˌæpəˈrætəs, -ˈreɪtəs/ *n, plural* **apparatus** *or* **apparatuses** [C,U] a set of instruments, tools, machines etc. used for a particular purpose: *an apparatus for breathing under water*

**ap·par·el** /əˈpærəl/ *n* [U] a word meaning clothing, used in stores: *men's/children's apparel*

**ap·par·ent** /əˈpærənt, əˈpɛr-/ *adj* **1** easily seen or understood: *Her embarrassment was apparent to everyone in the room.* | *Suddenly for no apparent reason* (=without a clear reason) *he began to shout at her.* **2** seeming to be true or real, although it may not really be: *We were fooled by his apparent lack of fear.*

**ap·par·ent·ly** /əˈpærəntˈli, əˈpɛr-/ *adv* **1** according to what you have heard is true, although you are not completely sure about it: *She apparently caught him in bed with another woman.* | *Apparently, Susan's living in Madrid now.* **2** according to the way something appears or someone looks, although it may not really be true: *We waited in apparently endless lines at the airport.*

**ap·pa·ri·tion** /ˌæpəˈrɪʃən/ *n* ⇨ GHOST

**ap·peal¹** /əˈpil/ *v* [I] **1** to make an urgent public request for money, information etc.: *Police are appealing to the public for information.* | *The water company appealed to everyone to save water.* **2 appeal to sb** to seem attractive or interesting to someone: *The program should appeal to older viewers.* | *The clothes don't appeal to me.* **3** to make a request to a higher court to change the decision of a lower court: *The defense is certain to appeal against the conviction.*

**appeal²** *n* **1** an urgent public request for money, information etc.: *UNICEF is launching* (=starting) *an appeal for the flood victims.* **2** [U] the quality that makes you like or want something: *sex appeal* **3** [C,U] a request to a higher court to change the decision of a lower court: *an appeal to the Supreme Court*

**ap·peal·ing** /əˈpilɪŋ/ *adj* attractive or interesting: *I found his smile very appealing.* | *The package should make it more* *appealing to kids.* –**appealingly** *adv* –opposite UNAPPEALING

**ap·pear** /ə'pɪr/ *v* [I] **1** to begin to be seen: *Suddenly, clouds began to appear in the sky.* | *A face appeared at the window.* **2** to seem: *The man appeared to be dead.* | *The noise appeared to come from the closet.* **3** to take part in a movie, television program, play etc.: *He'll be appearing in a new Broadway musical this fall* **4** to happen, exist, or become available for the first time: *Irving's novel is soon to appear in paperback.* **5** to be present officially, especially in a court of law: *Foster had to appear before the Senate subcommittee to testify.*

**ap·pear·ance** /ə'pɪrəns/ *n* **1** the way someone or something looks or seems to other people: *Here are six ways to improve your personal appearance.* | *The Christmas lights gave the house a festive appearance.* **2** an arrival by someone or something: *the sudden appearance of several reporters at the hospital* **3** the point at which something begins to exist or starts being used: *Viewing has increased since the appearance of cable TV.* **4** a public performance in a film, play, concert etc.: *his first appearance on stage* **5** the act of arriving at or attending an event because you think you should: *I put in an appearance at the wedding but did not stay long.*

**ap·pease** /ə'piz/ *v* [T] to do something or give someone something to make him/her less angry: *We changed the title to appease the critics.* –**appeasement** *n*

**ap·pel·late** /ə'pɛlɪt/ *adj* LAW able to change a decision that was made earlier in a court of law: *the appellate court* | *an appellate judge*

**ap·pend** /ə'pɛnd/ *v* [T] FORMAL to add something to a piece of writing: *Please see the conditions appended to this contract.*

**ap·pend·age** /ə'pɛndɪdʒ/ *n* something that is added or attached to something larger or more important

**ap·pen·di·ci·tis** /ə,pɛndə'saɪtɪs/ *n* [U] an illness in which your APPENDIX swells and becomes painful

**ap·pen·dix** /ə'pɛndɪks/ *n* **1** a small organ in your body that has little or no use **2** *plural* **appendixes** *or* **appendices** a part at the end of a book that has additional information

**ap·pe·tite** /'æpə,taɪt/ *n* [C,U] a strong desire or liking for something, especially food: *Don't eat now, you'll ruin/spoil your appetite.* | *Marcy seems to have lost her appetite for travel.*

**ap·pe·tiz·er** /'æpə,taɪzɚ/ *n* a small dish of food served at the beginning of a meal

**ap·pe·tiz·ing** /'æpə,taɪzɪŋ/ *adj* food that is appetizing looks or smells very good

**ap·plaud** /ə'plɔd/ *v* [T] **1** to hit your open hands together to show that you have enjoyed a play, concert, speaker etc.; CLAP **2** FORMAL to

express strong approval of an idea, plan etc.: *We applaud the company's efforts to improve safety.*

**ap·plause** /ə'plɔz/ *n* [U] the sound of people hitting their hands together in order to show that they enjoy or approve of something: *There was whistling and applause as the band got ready to play.* | *Let's give Rodney a big round of applause!*

**ap·ple** /'æpəl/ *n* a hard round red or green fruit that is white inside, or the tree this fruit grows on –see picture on page 470

**ap·ple·sauce** /'æpəl,sɔs/ *n* [U] a food made from crushed cooked apples

**ap·pli·ance** /ə'plaɪəns/ *n* a piece of electrical equipment such as a REFRIGERATOR or a DISHWASHER, used in people's homes –see usage note at MACHINE[1]

**ap·pli·ca·ble** /'æplɪkəbəl, ə'plɪkəbəl/ *adj* **1** affecting a particular person, group, or situation: *These tax laws are not applicable to foreigners.* **2** suitable for a particular situation: *That argument is not applicable here.*

**ap·pli·cant** /'æplɪkənt/ *n* someone who has formally asked for a job, place at a college etc., especially by writing a letter

**ap·pli·ca·tion** /,æplɪ'keɪʃən/ *n* **1** a formal, usually written, request for a job, place at a college etc.: *It took me three hours to fill in my Stanford application form.* **2** a piece of SOFTWARE **3** [C,U] the use of a machine, idea etc. for a practical purpose: *There are limits to the application of his theory.* **4** [C,U] the act of putting something like paint, medicine etc. on to a surface

**ap·pli·ca·tor** /'æplɪ,keɪtɚ/ *n* a special brush or tool used for putting paint, glue, medicine etc. on something: *It comes with its own special applicator.*

**ap·plied** /ə'plaɪd/ *adj* a subject such as applied mathematics or applied science is studied for a practical purpose

**ap·ply** /ə'plaɪ/ *v* **1** [I] to make a formal, especially written, request for a job, place at a college etc.: *Good luck applying for that job!* **2** [I,T] to affect or be suitable for a particular person, group, or situation: *The 20% discount only applies to club members.* **3** [T] to use a method, idea etc. in a particular situation, activity, or process: *I should be able to apply what I'm learning now in my job.* **4** [T] to put something such as paint, medicine etc. on a surface: *Be careful not to apply too much glue.* **5** [T] **apply yourself (to sth)** to work very hard and very carefully, especially for a long time: *I wish John would apply himself a little more!*

**ap·point** /ə'pɔɪnt/ *v* [T] **1** to choose someone for a job, position, etc.: *They've appointed a new principal at Ralston Elementary.* **2** FORMAL to arrange or decide a time or place for something to happen: *Judge Bailey appointed a new*

A

time for the trial. —**appointed** adj: We met at the appointed time.

**ap·point·ee** /ə‚pɔɪn'ti/ n someone who is chosen to do a particular job: a Presidential appointee

**ap·point·ment** /ə'pɔɪntˀmənt/ n **1** a meeting that has been arranged for a particular time and place: I'd like to **make an appointment with** Dr. Hanson. (=arrange to see the doctor) | I'm sorry I **missed** our appointment. (=did not go to meet someone) | Roy is bad at **keeping appointments**. (=remembering to meet people as arranged) | She had to call a client to **cancel an appointment**. (=say she could not come) **2** [C,U] the act of choosing someone for a job, position etc.: the **appointment of** a new Supreme Court Justice **3 by appointment** after arranging to meet at a particular time: Dr. Sutton will only see you by appointment.

**appointment book** /.'.. ‚./ n a book you keep at work with a CALENDAR in it, in which you write meetings, events, and other things you plan to do

**ap·por·tion** /ə'pɔrʃən/ v [T] FORMAL to decide how something should be divided between various people: The district has to find a better way to **apportion** funds **among** schools.

**ap·prais·al** /ə'preɪzəl/ n [C,U] an official judgment about how valuable, effective, or successful someone or something is: You should get an **appraisal** of Grandma's watch. (=find out how much it is worth)

**ap·praise** /ə'preɪz/ v [T] to make an APPRAISAL of someone or something: The furniture was **appraised** at $14,000. | We're waiting for the report before appraising the situation.

**ap·pre·cia·ble** /ə'priʃəbəl/ adj large enough to be noticed, felt, or considered important: There's been no appreciable change in the patient's condition.

**ap·pre·ci·ate** /ə'priʃi‚eɪt/ v **1** [T] to be grateful for something: Mom really appreciated the flowers you sent. **2** [T] to understand and enjoy the good qualities or value of something: All the bad weather here makes me appreciate home. **3 I would appreciate it if** used in order to politely ask for something: I'd really appreciate it if you could drive Kathy to school today. **4** [T] to understand a difficult situation or problem: You don't seem to **appreciate how** hard this is for us. **5** [I] to gradually increase in value: Your investment should appreciate by 10% over the next five years. —opposite DEPRECIATE

**ap·pre·ci·a·tion** /ə‚priʃi'eɪʃən, ə‚pri-/ n [singular, U] **1** something you say or do to thank someone or show you are grateful: I'd like to **show/express** my appreciation for everything you've done. **2** an understanding of a difficult situation or problem: I've **gained** a new appreciation of the problems Ellen has faced. **3** the enjoyment you feel when you recognize the

good qualities of something: As he grew older, his **appreciation for** his home town grew. **4** a rise in the value of something: the **appreciation** of the dollar **against** the yen

**ap·pre·cia·tive** /ə'priʃətɪv/ adj feeling or showing how much you enjoy, admire, or feel grateful for something or someone —**appreciatively** adv

**ap·pre·hend** /‚æprɪ'hɛnd/ v [T] FORMAL to find a criminal and take him/her to prison; ARREST

**ap·pre·hen·sion** /‚æprɪ'hɛnʃən/ n [U] **1** anxiety or fear, especially about the future: News of the plane crash increased Tim's apprehension about flying. **2** [C,U] FORMAL the act of catching a criminal

**ap·pre·hen·sive** /‚æprɪ'hɛnsɪv/ adj worried or anxious, especially about the future: She felt apprehensive at the thought of Mark's reaction. —**apprehensively** adv

**ap·pren·tice** /ə'prɛntɪs/ n someone who works for an employer for an agreed amount of time, usually for low pay, in order to learn a particular skill

**ap·pren·tice·ship** /ə'prɛntɪˌʃɪp/ n [C,U] the job of being an APPRENTICE, or the time spent as one

**ap·prise** /ə'praɪz/ v [T] FORMAL to formally or officially tell someone about something: Mrs. Bellamy has **been apprised** of the situation.

**ap·proach**[1] /ə'proʊtʃ/ v **1** [I,T] to move closer to someone or something: We watched as their car approached. | A man approached me, asking if I'd seen a little girl. **2** [T] to ask someone for something when you are not sure if s/he will do what you want: She's been approached by two schools about teaching jobs. **3** [I,T] to almost be a particular time, age, amount, temperature etc.: It's now approaching seven o'clock. **4** [T] to begin to deal with something: What's the best way to approach the problem?

**approach**[2] n **1** a way of doing something or dealing with a problem: a creative **approach to** teaching science **2** [U] the act of coming closer in time or distance: The air got colder with **the approach of** winter. **3** a road or path leading to a place: The easiest **approach to** the beach is from down here.

**ap·proach·a·ble** /ə'proʊtʃəbəl/ adj **1** friendly and easy to talk to: Dr. Grieg seems very approachable. **2** able to be reached: The castle was only approachable via a bridge.

**ap·pro·ba·tion** /‚æprə'beɪʃən/ n [U] FORMAL praise or approval —opposite DISAPPROBATION

**ap·pro·pri·ate**[1] /ə'proʊpriɪt/ adj suitable for a particular time, situation, or purpose: My mother didn't think my shoes were **appropriate for** church. —**appropriately** adv —**appropriateness** n [U] —opposite INAPPROPRIATE

Use these words to talk about things or people that are right or acceptable for a particular situation. Use **appropriate** to talk about a person's clothes or behavior: *an appropriate dress for the party.* Use **suitable** to say that something has the right qualities for a particular person or purpose: *a suitable school for the children.* Use **suited** to say that a person has the right qualities to do something: *He'd be well suited to the job.*

**ap·pro·pri·ate²** /əˈproupriˌeɪt/ v [T] FORMAL **1** to keep something such as money separate to be used for a particular purpose: *Congress appropriated funds for new laboratories in Hawaii.* **2** a word meaning to steal something, used in order to avoid saying this directly

**ap·prov·al** /əˈpruvəl/ n [U] **1** the belief that someone or something is good or doing something right: *It took three years to win/earn my father-in-law's approval.* **2** official permission: *We have to get approval from the council.*

**ap·prove** /əˈpruv/ v **1** [I] to believe that someone or something is good or acceptable: *I don't approve of drunk drivers.* **2** [T] to officially agree to something: *Congress approved an amendment to the Social Security Act.*

**ap·prox** adv the written abbreviation of APPROXIMATELY

**ap·prox·i·mate¹** /əˈprɑksəmɪt/ adj an approximate number, amount, or time is not exact. *What is the approximate cost of the materials?*

**approximate²** /əˈprɑksəˌmeɪt/ v FORMAL **approximate sth** to become similar to but not exactly the same as something else: *We try to give the animals food that approximates what they would eat in the wild.* **−approximation** /əˌprɑksəˈmeɪʃən/ n [C,U]

**ap·prox·i·mate·ly** /əˈprɑksəmɪtˌli/ adv a little bit more or less than an exact number, amount etc.; about: *Approximately 35% of the students come from Japan.*

**ap·ri·cot** /ˈeɪprɪˌkɑt, ˈæ-/ n a small soft yellow-orange fruit with a single large seed −see picture on page 470

**A·pril** /ˈeɪprəl/ written abbreviation **Apr.** n the fourth month of the year −see usage note at JANUARY

**April Fool's Day** /ˌ.. ˈ. ˌ./ n April 1 in the US and Canada, a day for playing funny tricks on people

**a·pron** /ˈeɪprən/ n a piece of clothing you wear to protect your clothes when you cook

**apt** /æpt/ adj **1 apt to** likely to do something: *If your camp is clean, you're less apt to attract bears.* **2** exactly right for a particular situation or purpose: *an apt remark* **3** able to learn or understand things quickly: *an apt pupil* −**aptly** adv

**apt.** n the written abbreviation of APARTMENT

**ap·ti·tude** /ˈæptəˌtud/ n [C,U] a natural ability or skill, especially in learning: *Ginny seems to have a real aptitude for painting.*

**aptitude test** /ˈ.. ˌ./ n a test used for finding out what someone's best skills are: *the Scholastic Aptitude Test*

**a·quar·i·um** /əˈkwɛriəm/ n **1** a clear glass or plastic container for fish or other water animals to live in **2** a building with many large aquariums where people go to look at fish or other water animals

**A·quar·i·us** /əˈkwɛriəs/ n **1** [singular] the eleventh sign of the ZODIAC, represented by a person pouring water **2** someone born between January 20 and February 18

**a·quat·ic** /əˈkwætɪk, əˈkwɑtɪk/ adj living or happening in water: *aquatic plants | aquatic sports*

**aq·ue·duct** /ˈækwəˌdʌkt/ n a structure like a bridge for carrying water across a valley

**AR** the written abbreviation of Arkansas

**Ar·a·bic numeral** /ˌærəbɪk ˈnumərəl/ n the sign 1, 2, 3, 4, 5, 6, 7, 8, 9, or 0, or a combination of these signs, used as a number −see also ROMAN NUMERAL

**ar·a·ble** /ˈærəbəl/ adj arable land is suitable for growing crops

**ar·bi·ter** /ˈɑrbətɚ/ n **1** a person or organization that settles an argument between two groups or people **2** an arbiter of style, fashion, taste etc. influences society's opinions about what is fashionable

**ar·bi·trar·y** /ˈɑrbəˌtrɛri/ adj based on personal opinions rather than having good reasons: *Their reasons for firing Mr. Casey seemed arbitrary.* −**arbitrarily** /ˌɑrbəˈtrɛrəli/ adv −**arbitrariness** /ˌɑrbəˈtrɛrinɪs/ n [U]

**ar·bi·trate** /ˈɑrbəˌtreɪt/ v [I,T] to be a judge in an argument because both sides have asked for this −**arbitrator** n

**ar·bi·tra·tion** /ˌɑrbəˈtreɪʃən/ n the process in which someone tries to help two opposing sides settle an argument

**arc** /ɑrk/ n part of a circle or any curved line

**ar·cade** /ɑrˈkeɪd/ n **1** a special room or small building where people go to play VIDEO GAMEs **2** a passage or side of a building that has small stores next to it and is covered with an ARCHed roof

**arch¹** /ɑrtʃ/ n, plural **arches 1** a curved structure at the top of a door, window, bridge etc., or something that has this curved shape **2** the curved middle part of the bottom of your foot −**arched** adj: *an arched doorway*

**arch²** v [I,T] to make something form an ARCH, or be in the shape of an arch: *The cat arched her back and hissed.*

A

**ar·chae·ol·o·gy,** archeology /ˌɑrkiˈɑlədʒi/ n [U] the study of ancient societies by examining what remains of their buildings, graves, tools etc. —**archaeological** /ˌɑrkiəˈlɑdʒɪkəl/ adj —**archaeologist** /ˌɑrkiˈɑlədʒɪst/ n

**ar·cha·ic** /ɑrˈkeɪ-ɪk/ adj belonging to the past, or old-fashioned and no longer used

**arch·bish·op** /ˌɑrtʃˈbɪʃəp‹/ n a priest with a very high rank

**ar·chi·pel·a·go** /ˌɑrkəˈpɛləˌgoʊ/ n a group of small islands

**ar·chi·tect** /ˈɑrkəˌtɛkt/ n someone whose job is to design buildings

**ar·chi·tec·ture** /ˈɑrkəˌtɛktʃə/ n [U] 1 the style and design of a building or buildings: medieval architecture | the architecture of Venice 2 the art and practice of planning and designing buildings —**architectural** /ˌɑrkəˈtɛktʃərəl/ adj

**ar·chives** /ˈɑrkaɪvz/ n [plural] a large number of records, reports, letters etc. relating to the history of a country, organization, family etc., or the place where these records are stored

**arch·way** /ˈɑrtʃweɪ/ n a passage or entrance under an ARCH or arches

**Arc·tic** /ˈɑrktɪk, -tɪk/ n the Arctic the most northern part of the earth, including parts of Alaska and Greenland, and the sea called the Arctic Ocean —**arctic** adj

**ar·dent** /ˈɑrdnt/ adj having very strong feelings of admiration or determination about someone or something: He's an ardent supporter of his son's baseball team. —**ardently** adv

**ar·dor** /ˈɑrdə/ n [U] very strong feelings of admiration, excitement, or love: He pursued her with surprising ardor.

**ar·du·ous** /ˈɑrdʒuəs/ adj needing a lot of hard and continuous effort: an arduous task | an arduous climb

**are** /ə; strong ɑr/ the present tense plural of BE

**ar·e·a** /ˈɛriə/ n 1 a particular part of a place, city, country etc.: Mom grew up in the Portland area. 2 a part of a house, office, park etc. that is used for a particular purpose: Their apartment has a large dining area. 3 a particular subject or type of activity: She talked about literary theory - her area of study. 4 the size of a flat surface, calculated by multiplying its length by its width

**area code** /ˈ... ˌ./ n the three numbers before a telephone number when you telephone someone outside your local area in the US

**a·re·na** /əˈrinə/ n 1 a building with a large flat central area surrounded by raised seats, used for sports or entertainment 2 **the political/public/national arena** all the people and activities relating to politics or public life: Our mayor has been in the political arena for over 12 years.

**aren't** /ˈɑrənt/ 1 the short form of "are not": Things aren't the same since you left. 2 the short form of "am not," used in asking questions: I'm in big trouble, aren't I?

**ar·gu·a·ble** /ˈɑrgyuəbəl/ adj 1 not at all certain, and therefore easy to doubt: Some of the paintings in the gallery are of arguable value. 2 **it is arguable that...** used in order to give good reasons why something might be true: It's arguable that the new law will make things worse.

**ar·gu·a·bly** /ˈɑrgyuəbli/ adv able to be argued or proven true: Wagner is arguably the best athlete in the school.

**ar·gue** /ˈɑrgyu/ v 1 [I] to disagree with someone, usually by talking or shouting in an angry way, or getting upset: Mom and Dad always seem to be **arguing over/about** the bills. 2 [I,T] to clearly explain or prove why you think something is true or should be done: It can be **argued that** most teachers are underpaid. | I couldn't **argue the point** because I didn't know anything about it.

**ar·gu·ment** /ˈɑrgyəmənt/ n 1 a disagreement, especially one in which people talk loudly: Jodie and I had a really big argument last night. 2 a set of explanations you use to try to prove that something is right or wrong, true or false etc.: the **arguments for/against** becoming a vegetarian

**ar·gu·men·ta·tive** /ˌɑrgyəˈmɛntətɪv/ adj liking to argue

**a·ri·a** /ˈɑriə/ n a song that is sung by only one person in an OPERA

**ar·id** /ˈærɪd/ adj 1 getting very little rain, and therefore very dry: arid land | an arid climate 2 unable to produce anything new, exciting, or useful: arid discussions

**Ar·ies** /ˈɛriz/ n 1 [singular] the first sign of the ZODIAC, represented by a RAM 2 someone born between March 21 and April 19

**a·rise** /əˈraɪz/ v [I] 1 to happen or appear: the problems that arise from losing a job 2 LITERARY to get up

**ar·is·toc·ra·cy** /ˌærəˈstɑkrəsi/ n the people in the highest social class, who traditionally have a lot of land, money, and power

**ar·is·to·crat** /əˈrɪstəˌkræt/ n someone who belongs to the highest social class —**aristocratic** /əˌrɪstəˈkrætɪk/ adj

**a·rith·me·tic¹** /əˈrɪθməˌtɪk/ n [U] the science of numbers involving adding, dividing, multiplying etc. —compare MATHEMATICS

**ar·ith·met·ic²** /ˌærɪθˈmɛtɪk/ adj involving or relating to ARITHMETIC —**arithmetically** adv

**arm¹** /ɑrm/ n 1 one of the two long parts of your body between your shoulders and your hands: a broken arm | I had a pile of books **in my arms**. | John and Marsha walked away **arm in arm**. (=with their arms bent around each other's) | She **took** him **by the arm** (=led him by holding his arm) and pushed him out the door. —see picture at BODY 2 a part of something that is shaped like or moves like an arm: *the arm of a chair* **3** ⇨ SLEEVE **4 be up in arms** INFORMAL to be very angry and ready to argue or fight: *The whole town is up in arms about the decision to build a new highway.* **5** a particular part of a group: *the political arm of the terrorist organization*

**arm²** *v* [T] to give someone the weapons or information s/he needs: *arming the local people with rifles | Jess armed himself with all the facts he needed to prove his case.*

**ar·ma·dil·lo** /ˌɑrməˈdɪloʊ/ *n* a small animal with a pointed nose and a hard shell that lives in hot dry parts of North and South America

**ar·ma·ments** /ˈɑrməmənts/ *n* [plural] weapons and military equipment: *nuclear armaments*

**arm·band** /ˈɑrmbænd/ *n* a band of material that you wear around your arm, for example to show that someone you love has died

**arm·chair** /ˈɑrmtʃɛr/ *n* a chair with sides that you can rest your arms on

**armed** /ɑrmd/ *adj* **1** carrying one or more weapons: *an armed guard | The suspect is armed with a shotgun.* | *armed robbery* (=stealing using guns) | *The fort was heavily armed.* (=had a lot of weapons) **2** having or knowing something useful: *I went to the meeting armed with all the facts I could find.*

**armed forc·es** /ˌ. ˈ../ *n* [plural] **the armed forces** a country's military organizations

**arm·ful** /ˈɑrmfʊl/ *n* the amount of something that you can hold in one or both arms: *an armful of books*

**arm·hole** /ˈɑrmˌhoʊl/ *n* a hole in a shirt, coat etc. that you put your arm through

**ar·mi·stice** /ˈɑrməstɪs/ *n* an agreement to stop fighting, usually for a specific period of time

**ar·mor** /ˈɑrmɚ/ *n* [U] **1** metal or leather clothing worn in past times by men and horses in battle: *a suit of armor* **2** a strong layer of metal that protects vehicles, ships, and aircraft

**ar·mored** /ˈɑrmɚd/ *adj* protected against bullets or other weapons by a strong layer of metal: *an armored car*

**ar·mor·y** /ˈɑrməri/ *n* a place where weapons are stored

**arm·pit** /ˈɑrmˌpɪt/ *n* **1** the hollow place under your arm where it joins your body – see picture at BODY **2** SLANG a very unpleasant or ugly place: *This town is the armpit of the state.*

**arms** /ɑrmz/ *n* [plural] weapons used for fighting wars

**arms con·trol** /ˈ. .ˌ./ *n* [U] the attempt by powerful countries to limit the number of war weapons that exist

**arms race** /ˈ. ˌ./ *n* a struggle between two or more unfriendly countries to produce more and better weapons than the others

**ar·my** /ˈɑrmi/ *n* **1** the part of a country's military force that is trained to fight on land: *Our* son is *in the army.* | *The two armies advanced across Europe.* **2** a large group of people or animals involved in the same activity: *an army of ants*

**a·ro·ma** /əˈroʊmə/ *n* a strong pleasant smell: *the aroma of fresh coffee* –**aromatic** /ˌærəˈmætɪk/ *adj*: *aromatic oils* –see usage note at SMELL²

**a·ro·ma·ther·a·py** /əˌroʊməˈθɛrəpi/ *n* [U] the use of pleasant-smelling oils to help you feel more healthy –**aromatherapist** *n*

**a·rose** /əˈroʊz/ *v* the past tense of ARISE

**a·round** /əˈraʊnd/ *adv, prep* **1** on all sides of something, so that it is surrounded: *We put a fence around the yard.* | *Mario put his arms around her.* **2** to or in many parts of a place, room etc.: *Stan showed me around the office.* | *an international company with offices all around* (=in all parts of) *the world* **3** in or near a particular place: *Is there a bank around here?* **4 around 10/6/200 etc.** used when you do not know an exact number, to give a number that is close to it; APPROXIMATELY: *Dodger Stadium seats around 50,000 people.* **5** in a circular movement: *Water pushes the wheel around.* **6** along the outside of a place, instead of through it: *We had to go around to the back of the house.* **7** so as to be turned in the opposite direction: *I'll turn the car around and pick you up at the door.* **8 be around a)** to be present in the same place as you: *It was 11:30 at night, and nobody was around.* **b)** to exist or be available to use: *That joke's been around for years.* | *I think the B52's were the best band around at the time.* **9 10 feet/3 inches etc. around** measuring a particular distance on the outside of a round object: *Redwood trees can measure 30 or 40 feet around.* **10 around and around** continuing to move in circles: *We drove around and around the block, looking for the house.* –see also **around the clock** (CLOCK¹)

**a·rou·sal** /əˈraʊzəl/ *n* [U] excitement, especially sexual excitement

**a·rouse** /əˈraʊz/ *v* [T] **1** to make someone have a particular feeling: *Her behavior aroused the suspicions of the police.* **2** to make someone feel sexually excited **3** FORMAL to wake someone up

**ar·raign** /əˈreɪn/ *v* [T] LAW to make someone come to a court of law to hear what the court says his/her crime is –**arraignment** *n* [C,U]

**ar·range** /əˈreɪndʒ/ *v* **1** [I,T] to make plans for something to happen: *Jeff will arrange our flights.* | *We've arranged to go to the cabin this weekend.* | *I've arranged for Mark to join us.* | *We still have to arrange where to meet.* **2** [T] to put a group of things or people in a particular order or position: *The file is arranged alphabetically.* **3** [T] to write or change a piece of music so that it is suitable for a particular instrument

A

**ar·range·ment** /ə'reɪndʒmənt/ n **1** [C usually plural] the things that you must organize for something to happen: *travel arrangements* | *making arrangements for the wedding* **2** [C,U] something that has been agreed on: *We have a special arrangement with the bank.* | *I'm sure we can come to some arrangement.* **3** [C,U] a group of things in a particular order or position, or the activity of arranging things in this way: *a flower arrangement* **4** [C,U] a piece of music that has been written or changed for a particular instrument

**ar·ray¹** /ə'reɪ/ n **1** an attractive collection or group: *a dazzling array of acting talent* **2** [C,U] LITERARY clothes worn for a special occasion

**array²** v [T] FORMAL **1** to arrange something in an attractive way **2** to dress someone in a particular type of clothes

**ar·rears** /ə'rɪrz/ n [plural] **1** be in arrears to owe someone more money than you should because your payment is late: *We're six weeks in arrears with the rent.* **2** money that is owed and should have been paid: *mortgage arrears*

**ar·rest¹** /ə'rɛst/ v [T] **1** to catch someone and take him/her away because s/he is believed to be guilty of a crime: *The police arrested Eric for shoplifting.* **2** FORMAL to stop something happening or make it happen more slowly: *The drug is used to arrest the spread of the disease.*

**arrest²** n [C,U] the act of taking someone away and guarding him/her because s/he is believed to be guilty of a crime: *The police expect to make an arrest soon.* | *Don't move, you're under arrest!*

**ar·riv·al** /ə'raɪvəl/ n **1** [U] the act of arriving somewhere: *The arrival of our flight was delayed.* | *Shortly after our arrival in Toronto, Lisa got sick.* **2** the arrival of the time when a new idea, method, product etc. is first used or discovered: *The arrival of the personal computer changed the way we work.* **3** a person or thing that has arrived: *Congratulations on your new arrival!* (=new baby)

**ar·rive** /ə'raɪv/ v [I] **1** to get to a place: *Your letter arrived last week.* | *What time does the plane arrive in New York?* | *We arrived at Mom's two hours late.* **2** to happen: *At last the big day arrived!* **3** arrive at a conclusion/decision to decide what to do about something after a lot of effort **4** to begin to exist, or start being used: *Our toy sales have doubled since computer games arrived.* | *It was just past midnight when the baby arrived.* (=was born) **5** INFORMAL to succeed: *Moving into my new office, I knew I'd finally arrived.*

**ar·ro·gance** /'ærəgəns/ n [U] the quality of being ARROGANT: *I can't stand her arrogance.*

**ar·ro·gant** /'ærəgənt/ adj believing that you are more important than anyone else, or showing this quality: *an arrogant selfish man* | *arrogant smile* —**arrogantly** adv

**ar·row** /'æroʊ/ n **1** a weapon like a thin straight stick with a point at one end and feathers at the other that you shoot with a BOW **2** a sign (→), used in order to show the direction or position of something

**ar·se·nal** /'ɑrsnl/ n a large number of weapons, or the building where they are stored

**ar·se·nic** /'ɑrsənɪk, 'ɑrsnɪk/ n [U] a very poisonous chemical that is often used for killing rats

**ar·son** /'ɑrsən/ n [U] the crime of deliberately making something burn, especially a building —**arsonist** n

**art** /ɑrt/ n **1** [U] the use of drawing, painting etc. to represent things or express ideas: *Steve's studying art at college.* **2** [U] things that are produced by art, such as drawings, paintings etc.: *modern art* | *an art exhibition* | *Several famous works of art were stolen from the museum.* **3** [C,U] the skill involved in making or doing something: *the art of writing*

**ar·ter·y** /'ɑrtəri/ n **1** one of the tubes that carries blood from your heart to the rest of your body —compare VEIN **2** a main road, railroad line, or river, considered as a way to carry people, goods etc. —**arterial** /ɑr'tɪriəl/ adj

**ar·thri·tis** /ɑr'θraɪtɪs/ n [U] a disease that causes pain and swelling in the joints of your body —**arthritic** /ɑr'θrɪtɪk/ adj: *arthritic fingers*

**ar·ti·choke** /'ɑrtɪˌtʃoʊk/ n a green round vegetable with thick pointed leaves and a firm base —see picture on page 470

**ar·ti·cle** /'ɑrtɪkəl/ n **1** a piece of writing in a newspaper, magazine etc.: *Did you read that article on the space shuttle?* **2** a thing, especially one of a group of things: *an article of clothing* **3** TECHNICAL in grammar, a word used before a noun to show whether the noun is a particular example of something (definite article) or a general example (indefinite article). In the sentence "I saw the woman", the word "the" is a definite article. In the sentence "I saw a woman," the word "a" is an indefinite article

**ar·tic·u·late¹** /ɑr'tɪkyəlɪt/ adj expressing or able to express thoughts and feelings clearly: *a bright and articulate child* —**articulately** adv

**ar·tic·u·late²** /ɑr'tɪkjyəˌleɪt/ v [I,T] to express something very clearly: *It's hard to articulate what I'm feeling.* | *You have to articulate* (=speak clearly) *if you want to be heard.* —**articulation** /ɑrˌtɪkyə'leɪʃən/ n [U]

**ar·ti·fact** /'ɑrtɪˌfækt/ n a small object that was made and used a long time ago, especially one that is studied by scientists: *Egyptian artifacts*

**ar·ti·fi·cial** /ˌɑrtə'fɪʃəl/ adj **1** not natural, but made by people: *artificial sweeteners* | *an artificial leg* **2** not natural or sincere: *an artificial smile* —**artificially** adv: *artificially colored*

**artificial in·tel·li·gence** /,.... .'.../ n [U] the study of how to make computers do things that people can do, such as make decisions or see things

**artificial res·pi·ra·tion** /,.... .'.., .,.. ..'../ n [U] a method of helping someone who is nearly dead breathe again by blowing air into his/her mouth

**ar·til·ler·y** /ɑr'tɪləri/ n [U] large guns, either on wheels or fixed in one place

**ar·ti·san** /'ɑrtəzən, -sən/ n someone who does work with his/her hands that needs skill; CRAFTSMAN

**art·ist** /'ɑrtɪst/ n someone who produces or performs any type of art, including painting, drawing, music, dance etc.

**ar·tis·tic** /ɑr'tɪstɪk/ adj 1 showing skill or imagination in an art: I never knew you were so artistic. 2 relating to art or with the practice of being an artist: artistic freedom –**artistically** adv

**art·ist·ry** /'ɑrtəstri/ n [U] skill in a particular ARTISTIC activity: an example of the painter's artistry

**arts** /ɑrts/ n [plural] 1 **the arts** painting, music, literature etc. all considered together: government funding for the arts 2 subjects of study that are not considered scientific, such as history, languages etc.: an arts degree

**art·sy** /'ɑrtsi/ adj INFORMAL interested in art, or seeming to know a lot about art: He's not a businessman - he's sort of artsy.

**art·work** /'ɑrtwɝk/ n 1 [U] the pictures or decorations that are included in a book, a magazine etc.: The artwork is the best thing in this book. 2 [C,U] paintings and other pieces of art: damaged paintings and other artwork | His private collection includes artworks by Dufy and Miro.

**as**[1] /əz; strong æz/ adv, prep 1 used when comparing things, or saying that they are like each other in some way: These houses aren't as old as the ones downtown. | He was as surprised as anyone when they offered him the job. | You can use cherries instead of plums - they work just as well. 2 used when describing what someone's job, duty, or position is: In the past, women were mainly employed as secretaries or teachers. | The kids dressed up as animals for Halloween. 3 used when describing the way something is being used or considered: John used an old blanket as a tent. | Settlers saw the wilderness as dangerous rather than beautiful. –see also as **long as** (LONG[2]) **as a matter of fact** (MATTER[1]) **such as** (SUCH) **as well as** (WELL[1])

USAGE NOTE as, like and so

Use **as** and **like** to make comparisons: He's as good as a professional golfer. | He plays golf like a professional. ✗ DON'T SAY

"He's so good as a professional." ✗ The sentence He plays golf as a professional means that he is a professional golfer.

**as**[2] conjunction 1 used when comparing things, or saying that they are like each other in some way: I can't run nearly as fast as I used to. | I'll be there as soon as I can. 2 In the way or manner mentioned: Leave things as they are until the police come. | As I said earlier, this research has just started. 3 while something is happening: Be patient with your puppy as he adjusts to his new home. | The phone rang just as I was leaving. 4 **as if/though** in a way that suggests that something is true: They all looked as if they were scared. 5 **as to** concerning or regarding a particular thing: The President asked for opinions as to the likelihood of war. | She offered no explanation as to why she'd left so suddenly. 6 **as of today/December 12th/ next spring etc.** starting at a particular time and continuing from that time: The pay raise will come into effect as of January. 7 **as for sb/sth** concerning a person or subject that is connected with what you were talking about before: As for racism, much progress has been made, but there is still much to do. 8 **as it is** according to the situation that exists: We were saving money to go to Hawaii, but as it is we can only afford a camping trip. 9 because: James decided not to go out as he was still really tired. –see also **as well** (WELL[1]) **so as (not) to do sth** (SO[1])

**a.s.a.p** n the abbreviation of "as soon as possible": Please reply a.s.a.p.

**as·bes·tos** /æs'bɛstəs, æz-, əs-, ɑz-/ n [U] a substance that does not burn easily, which was used in some clothing and building material

**as·cend** /ə'sɛnd/ v [I,T] FORMAL to move up or move to the top of something: The plane ascended rapidly. –opposite DESCEND

**as·cen·dan·cy** /ə'sɛndənsi/, **ascendency** n [U] a position of power, influence, or control: the ascendancy of Japanese industry

**as·cent** /ə'sɛnt, 'æsɛnt/ n 1 the act of moving or climbing up: a successful ascent of the mountain 2 [U] the process of becoming more important or successful: Jerry's quick ascent into management surprised no one. 3 a path or road that goes gradually up: a steep ascent –opposite DESCENT

**as·cer·tain** /,æsɚ'teɪn/ v [T] FORMAL to discover or find out something: School officials are trying to ascertain the facts.

**as·cet·ic** /ə'sɛtɪk/ adj living a simple strict life, usually for religious reasons –**ascetic** n –**asceticism** /ə'sɛtə,sɪzəm/ n [U]

**as·cribe** /ə'skraɪb/ v [T] FORMAL

**ascribe sth to sb/sth** phr v [T] FORMAL to believe that something happens or exists because of someone or something else: Carter ascribed his problems **to** a lack of money. –**ascribable** adj

**a·sex·u·al** /eɪˈsɛkʃuəl/ *adj* without sex, sex organs, or sexual activity

**ash** /æʃ/ *n, plural* **ashes** [C,U] **1** the soft gray powder that remains after something has been burned: *cigarette ash* **2** a type of forest tree, or the hard wood of this tree —see also ASHES

**a·shamed** /əˈʃeɪmd/ *adj* **1** feeling embarrassed or guilty about something: *Mike felt ashamed of his old clothes.* | *You should be ashamed of yourself, acting like that!* | *Fred was ashamed to admit his mistake.* **2 be ashamed of sb** feeling upset because someone embarrasses you: *Helen felt ashamed of her parents.* —see usage note at GUILTY

**ash·en** /ˈæʃən/ *adj* very pale because of shock or fear: *her ashen face*

**ash·es** /ˈæʃɪz/ *n* [plural] the ASH that remains after the body of a dead person has been burned: *We scattered my father's ashes over the lake.*

**a·shore** /əˈʃɔr/ *adv* onto or toward the shore of a lake, river, sea, or ocean: *Brian pulled the boat ashore.*

**ash·tray** /ˈæʃtreɪ/ *n* a small dish for cigarette ASHes

**A·sia** /ˈeɪʒə/ *n* one of the seven CONTINENTS, that includes land between the Ural mountains and the Pacific Ocean

**A·sian** /ˈeɪʒən/ *adj* relating to or coming from Asia

**A·sian-A·mer·i·can** /ˌ.. .ˈ.../ *n* an American whose family originally came from Asia — **Asian-American** *adj*

**a·side¹** /əˈsaɪd/ *adv* **1** to the side: *Jim stepped aside to let me pass.* **2 put/set sth aside** to not use something, especially money, so that it can be used for a particular purpose later: *I try to set aside $30 a week for my vacation.* | *A room was set aside for the tests.* **3 aside from** ⇨ **apart from** (APART)

**aside²** *n* a remark you make in a quiet voice so that only a few people can hear

**ask** /æsk/ *v* [I,T] **1** to make a request for someone to tell you something: *"What's your name?" she asked.* | *Can I ask a question?* | *He asked how this could have happened.* | *Visitors often ask about the place.* | *You should ask around* (=ask a lot of people) *before deciding.* **2** to make a request for help, advice, information etc.: *If you need anything, just ask.* | *Ask Paula to mail the letters.* | *Some people don't like to ask for help.* | *Ask your Dad if we can borrow his car.* | *All I ask is that you be faithful to me.* **3** to invite someone to go somewhere: *Jerry would like to ask her out.* | *Why don't you ask them over for dinner?* **4** to want a particular amount of money for something you are selling: *He's asking $2000 for that old car!* **5 If you ask me** used in order to emphasize your own opinion: *If you ask me, he's crazy.* **6 Don't ask me!** SPOKEN said when you do not know the answer to a question and are annoyed

that someone has asked: *"When will Vicky get home?" "Don't ask me!"* **7 be asking for trouble** to be behaving in a way that will probably cause trouble: *Allowing campus police to have guns is just asking for trouble.* —see usage note at RECOMMEND

**a·skance** /əˈskæns/ *adv* **look askance (at)** to look at or consider something in a way that shows you do not believe it or approve of it

**a·skew** /əˈskyu/ *adv* not exactly straight or level: *His coat was wrinkled and his hat was askew.*

**a·sleep** /əˈslip/ *adj* **1** sleeping: *Be quiet. The baby is asleep.* | *Look at Jerry. He's fast/sound asleep.* (=sleeping very deeply) **2 fall asleep** to begin to sleep: *I always fall asleep watching TV.* **3** if your arm or leg is asleep, it has been in one position too long so that you cannot feel anything

**as·par·a·gus** /əˈspærəgəs/ *n* [U] a slightly bitter green vegetable shaped like a small stick with a point on one end —see picture on page 470

**as·pect** /ˈæspɛkt/ *n* one of the parts or features of a situation, idea, problem etc: *The committee discussed several aspects of the traffic problem.*

**as·pen** /ˈæspən/ *n* a tall thin straight tree that grows in the western US, with leaves that make a pleasant noise in the wind

**as·per·sion** /əˈspɚʒən, -ʃən/ *n* FORMAL **cast aspersions on** to suggest that someone is not very good at something

**as·phalt** /ˈæsfɔlt/ *n* [U] a black sticky substance that gets hard when it dries, used for making the surface of roads

**as·phyx·i·ate** /əˈsfɪksiˌeɪt, æ-/ *v* [I,T] FORMAL to be unable to breathe or to make someone unable to breathe, often resulting in death; SUFFOCATE — **asphyxiation** /əˌsfɪksiˈeɪʃən/ *n* [U]

**as·pi·ra·tion** /ˌæspəˈreɪʃən/ *n* a strong desire to have or achieve something: *Annette has aspirations to become a writer.*

**as·pire** /əˈspaɪɚ/ *v* [I] to have a strong desire to do something important: *Milligan aspires to be Governor of the state.*

**as·pi·rin** /'æsprɪn/ *n, plural* **aspirins** or **aspi-rin** [C,U] a drug that reduces pain and fever

**as·pir·ing** /ə'spaɪrɪŋ/ *adj* an aspiring actor, politician etc. is trying to become an actor, politician etc.

**ass** /æs/ *n* **1** ⇨ DONKEY

---
SPOKEN PHRASES
**2** an impolite word for the part of your body that you sit on: *Jamie fell right on his ass.* **3 your ass/his ass etc.** used in many impolite phrases as a way of talking to or about someone: *Get your ass in gear!* (=hurry up) **4** SLANG used in order to emphasize an adjective: *That's one big ass car!*

---

**as·sail·ant** /ə'seɪlənt/ *n* FORMAL someone who attacks someone else

**as·sas·sin** /ə'sæsən/ *n* someone who murders a ruler or politician, usually for political reasons

**as·sas·si·nate** /ə'sæsə,neɪt/ *v* [T] to murder a ruler or politician, usually for political reasons –**assassination** /ə,sæsə'neɪʃən/ *n* [C,U]

**as·sault¹** /ə'sɔlt/ *n* [C,U] a violent attack on someone: *He served three years in prison for assault.* | *an increase in sexual assaults*

**assault²** *v* [T] to attack someone violently: *Demonstrators assaulted some of the policemen.*

**as·sem·bly** /ə'sɛmbli/ *n* [C,U] **1** a meeting of a group of people for a particular purpose: *The school assembly begins at 9 o'clock.* **2** the name of the group of people who are elected to make laws in some states: *the New York State Assembly*

**as·sem·bly·man** /ə'sɛmblimən/, **as·sem·bly·wo·man** /ə'sɛmbli,wʊmən/ *n* a member of a state assembly

**as·sent** /ə'sɛnt/ *v* [I] FORMAL to agree to a suggestion, idea etc –**assent** *n* [U] –opposite DISSENT²

**as·sert** /ə'sət/ *v* **1** [T] to state an opinion or belief firmly: *Professsor Ross asserts that American schools are not strict enough.* **2** [T] to behave in a way that shows your right to do or have something: *The president tried to assert his power over the military.* **3 assert yourself** to behave in a determined way so that no one makes you do things you do not want to do: *Don't be afraid to assert yourself in the interview.*

**as·ser·tion** /ə'səʃən/ *n* [C,U] something that you say or write that you strongly believe: *He repeated his assertion that he was innocent.*

**as·ser·tive** /ə'sətɪv/ *adj* behaving confidently so that people pay attention to what you say: *Kramer's more assertive than I am.* –**assertively** *adv* –**assertiveness** *n* [U]

**as·sess** /ə'sɛs/ *v* [T] **1** to make a judgment about a person or situation after thinking carefully about it: *Psychologists will assess the child's behavior.* | *We're trying to assess what*

went wrong. **2** to judge the quality, amount, or value of something: *They assessed the house at $90,000.* –**assessment** *n* [C,U]

**as·set** /'æsɛt/ *n* **1** something that a company owns, that can be sold to pay debts **2** someone or something that is useful in helping you succeed or deal with problems: *A sense of humor is a real asset.* | *You're an asset to the company, George.* –compare LIABILITY

**ass·hole** /'æs,hoʊl/ *n* SPOKEN OFFENSIVE **1** someone who annoys you: *Get out of my way, asshole!* **2** ⇨ANUS

**as·sign** /ə'saɪn/ *v* [T] **1** to give someone a job to do: *Guards were assigned to the President.* **2** to give something to someone so s/he can use it for a particular purpose: *They assigned me a small room.*

**as·sign·ment** /ə'saɪnmənt/ *n* **1** a job or piece of work that you are given to do: *The newspaper is sending her on a special assignment to China.* | *a homework assignment* **2** the act of giving people particular jobs to do: *the assignment of chores*

**as·sim·i·late** /ə'sɪmə,leɪt/ *v* **1** [I,T] to accept someone completely as a member of a group, or to become an accepted member of a group: *As the immigrants were assimilated into the US, they stopped speaking their languages.* **2** [T] to completely understand new facts and information, and be able to use them: *The person we need for the job must be able to assimilate new ideas quickly.* –**assimilation** /ə,sɪmə'leɪʃən/ *n* [U]

**as·sist** /ə'sɪst/ *v* [I,T] to help someone do something that needs special skills: *Two nurses assisted Dr. Bernard in performing the operation.* –see usage note at HELP¹

**as·sist·ance** /ə'sɪstəns/ *n* [U] help or support: *The company provides assistance for new computer users.* | *Can I be of any assistance?* (=a formal phrase meaning "Can I help you?")

**as·sist·ant** /ə'sɪstənt/ *n* someone who helps someone else who has a higher rank: *a sales assistant* | *the assistant manager*

**as·so·ci·ate¹** /ə'soʊʃi,eɪt, -si,eɪt/ *v* **1** [I,T] to make a connection in your mind between one thing or person and another: *I always associate summer with travel.* **2 be associated with** to be connected with a particular subject, activity, group etc: *health problems associated with tobacco* **3 associated with sb** to spend time with or work with someone: *She had been associated with the Paris fashion designers for years.*

**as·so·ci·ate²** /ə'soʊʃiɪt, -siɪt/ *n* someone whom you work or do business with: *a business associate*

**Associate of Arts** /.,... . './, **Associate degree** *n* a college degree given after two years of study, usually at a COMMUNITY COLLEGE

A

**as·so·ci·a·tion** /əˌsousiˈeɪʃən, -ʃiˈeɪ-/ *n*
**1** an organization that consists of people who
have the same aims or interests: *an association
for librarians* **2 in association with** together
with someone or something else: *Community
groups are working in association with the
schools.* **3** a connection in your mind between
two things: *Los Angeles has happy associations
for me.*

**as·sort·ed** /əˈsɔrtɪd/ *adj* of various different
types: *a box of assorted cookies*

**as·sort·ment** /əˈsɔrⁿmənt/ *n* a mixture of
various things or of different types of the same
thing: *an assortment of chocolates*

**as·sume** /əˈsum/ *v* [T] **1** to think that something is true although you have no proof: *Your
light wasn't on so I assumed (that) you were
out.* | *Assuming (that) Dad agrees, when do you
want to shop for cars?* **2** to start to do a job,
sometimes when you do not have the right to:
*Stalin assumed power/control in 1941.*
**3 assume an air/expression of** to pretend to
have a particular quality: *Andy assumed an air
of innocence when the teacher walked by.* **4** to
start having a particular quality or appearance:
*Her family life assumed more importance after
the accident.*

**as·sumed** /əˈsumd/ *adj* **an assumed name/
identity** a false name

**as·sump·tion** /əˈsʌmpʃən/ *n* something that
you think is true although you have no proof:
*How could you make an assumption about her
without meeting her!*

**as·sur·ance** /əˈʃʊrəns/ *n* **1** a promise that
you give to someone to make him/her feel less
worried: *We need an assurance that you can
pay off your loan.* **2** [U] confidence in your
own abilities: *Cindy answered their questions
with quiet assurance.*

**as·sure** /əˈʃʊr/ *v* [T] **1** to make someone feel
less worried by promising that something is
definitely true: *The doctors assured me that her
life was not in danger.* | *The concert won't be
canceled, I can assure you.* **2** to make something certain to happen or be achieved: *The new
contract means that the future of the company is
assured.*

**as·sured** /əˈʃʊrd/ *adj* certain to be achieved:
*an assured victory* **–assuredly** /əˈʃʊrɪdli/ *adv*

**as·ter·isk** /ˈæstərɪsk/ *n* a mark like a star (*)
used in order to show something interesting or
important

**as·ter·oid** /ˈæstəˌrɔɪd/ *n* one of the many
small PLANETs between Jupiter and Mars

**asth·ma** /ˈæzmə/ *n* [U] an illness that causes
difficulties in breathing **–asthmatic**
/æzˈmætɪk/ *adj*

**as·ton·ish** /əˈstanɪʃ/ *v* [T] to surprise someone very much: *Grandma was astonished by
how much Hal could eat.* | *I was astonished to
learn that she was only 22.*

**as·ton·ished** /əˈstanɪʃt/ *adj* very surprised
about something: *Parker seemed astonished
that someone wanted to buy the house.*

**as·ton·ish·ing** /əˈstanɪʃɪŋ/ *adj* so surprising
that it is difficult to believe: *astonishing news*
**–astonishingly** *adv*

**as·ton·ish·ment** /əˈstanɪʃmənt/ *n* [U] great
surprise: *To our astonishment, Sue won the
race.*

**as·tound** /əˈstaʊnd/ *adj* to make someone feel
very surprised or shocked: *My brother's decision astounded us all.*

**as·tound·ing** /əˈstaʊndɪŋ/ *adj* so surprising
or shocking that it is difficult to believe: *his
astounding success* **–astoundingly** *adv*

**a·stray** /əˈstreɪ/ *adv* **1 go astray** to become
lost: *One of the documents we sent them has
gone astray.* **2 lead sb astray** OFTEN HUMOROUS
to persuade someone to believe something that
is not true or to do something wrong: *I think
Mom's worried I'll be led astray if I live alone!*

**a·stride** /əˈstraɪd/ *adv*
having one leg on each
side of something: *sitting
astride a horse*

astride

**as·trin·gent** /əˈstrɪn-
dʒənt/ *adj* **1** criticizing
someone very severe-
ly: *astringent remarks*
**2** TECHNICAL able to make
your skin less oily or stop a
wound from bleeding: *an astringent cream*

**as·trol·o·gy** /əˈstralədʒi/ *n* [U] the study of
the movements of the stars and their influence on people or events **–astrological**
/ˌæstrəˈladʒɪkəl/ *adj* **–astrologist** /əˈstral-
ədʒɪst/ *n*

**as·tro·naut** /ˈæstrəˌnɔt, -ˌnat/ *n* someone
who travels and works in a SPACECRAFT

**as·tro·nom·i·cal** /ˌæstrəˈnamɪkəl/ *adj*
**1** extremely large in amount: *astronomical
prices* **2** relating to the study of the stars

**as·tron·o·my** /əˈstranəmi/ *n* [U] the scientific
study of the stars **–astronomer** *n*

**As·tro·Turf** /ˈæstrouˌtɚf/ *n* [U] TRADEMARK a
type of artificial grass that people play sports on

**as·tute** /əˈstut/ *adj* very good at using your
knowledge in order to become successful: *an
astute journalist* **–astutely** *adv*

**a·sy·lum** /əˈsaɪləm/ *n* **1** [U] protection that a
government gives to someone who escapes from
a country for political reasons **2** OLD-FASHIONED
a hospital for people with mental illnesses

**at** /ət; *strong* æt/ *prep* **1** used in order to
show the position of someone or something, or
where something is happening: *Meet me at my
house.* | *There was a long line at the bank.* | *A lot
of people were at the funeral.* **2** when it is a
particular time: *The movie starts at 8:00.* | *Alison
gets lonely at Christmas.* **3** toward someone or
something: *Jake shot at the deer but*

*missed.* | *Stop shouting at me!* **4** because of someone or something: *None of the kids laughed at his joke.* | *Jenny, I'm surprised at you!* **5** used in order to show what you are considering when making a judgment about someone's ability: *How's Brian doing at his new job?* | *Debbie is good/bad at math.* **6** used in order to show what someone is doing or the state someone or something is in: *I'm sorry, Mr. Rivers is at lunch* (=eating lunch). | *Many children are still at risk of disease.* **7** used in order to show a price, rate, speed, level, age etc.: *Gas is selling at about $1.25 a gallon.* | *I started school at age five.* —see also **at all** (ALL³) **at first** (FIRST¹) **at least** (LEAST¹)

**ate** /eɪt/ the past tense of EAT

**a·the·ist** /'eɪθiɪst/ *n* someone who does not believe in the existence of God —**atheism** *n* [U]

**ath·lete** /'æθlit/ *n* someone who is good at sports

**ath·let·ic** /æθ'lɛtɪk/ *adj* **1** able to play a particular sport or a lot of sports very well **2** having a healthy body with very strong muscles

**ath·let·ics** /æθ'lɛtɪks/ *n* [U] physical activities such as sports and exercises: *high school athletics*

**At·lan·tic O·cean** /ət‚læntɪk 'oʊʃən/ *n* **the Atlantic** the large ocean between North and South America in the west, and Europe and Africa in the east

**at·las** /'ætləs/ *n* a book of maps: *a world atlas*

**ATM** *n* Automated Teller Machine; a machine outside of a bank that you use to get money out of your account

**at·mos·phere** /'æt mɔs‚fɪr/ *n* [C,U] **1** the feeling that an event, situation, or place gives you: *The atmosphere at home's been really depressing since you left.* **2 the atmosphere** the mixture of gases that surrounds the Earth **3** the air inside a room: *a smoky atmosphere* —**atmospheric** /‚æt məs'fɪrɪk ◂/ *adj*

**at·om** /'ætəm/ *n* one of the smallest parts that any substance can be divided into, that combines with other atoms to make a MOLECULE —**atomic** /ə'tamɪk/ *adj*

**a·tom·ic bomb** /.‚.. './ *n* a very powerful bomb that causes an explosion by splitting ATOMS

**a·tomic en·er·gy** /.‚.. '.../ *n* [U] the power that comes from splitting atoms, often used in making electricity

**a·tone** /ə'toʊn/ *v* [I] FORMAL to do something to show that you are sorry for doing something wrong —**atonement** *n* [U]

**a·tro·cious** /ə'troʊʃəs/ *adj* extremely bad: *atrocious weather/behavior* —**atrociously** *adv*

**a·troc·i·ty** /ə'trɑsəti/ *n* [C,U] an extremely cruel or violent action: *the atrocities of war*

**at·tach** /ə'tætʃ/ *v* **1** [T] to make something stick to or be connected with something else: *Please attach a photograph to your application form.* **2 get attached to** to like someone or something, especially more than you should: *As a doctor I cannot get too attached to my patients.* **3 attach importance/blame etc.** to believe that someone or something is important, valuable, guilty etc.: *They seem to attach more importance to money than to happiness.*

attach

**at·ta·ché** /‚ætæ'ʃeɪ, ‚ætə-/ *n* someone who works in an EMBASSY, and deals with a particular area of knowledge: *a military attaché*

**at·tach·ment** /ə'tætʃmənt/ *n* **1** [U] a strong feeling of loyalty, love, or friendship for someone or something: *a mother's deep attachment to her baby* —opposite DETACHMENT **2** a piece of equipment that you attach to a machine to make it do different things: *attachments for the food processor*

**at·tack¹** /ə'tæk/ *n* **1** [C,U] a violent action that is intended to damage someone or something: *There have been several attacks on foreigners recently.* | *The city is under attack.* (=being attacked) **2** [C,U] strong criticism: *an attack on the government's welfare policy* **3** a sudden short period of time when you suffer from an illness, or feel frightened or worried: *an attack of asthma* | *panic attacks* —**attacker** *n* —see also HEART ATTACK

**attack²** *v* **1** [I,T] to try to hurt someone physically, especially by using a weapon: *Dan was attacked as he got into his car.* **2** [T] to severely criticize someone or something: *Newspapers attacked the President for failing to cut taxes.* **3** [T] if an illness attacks a part of your body, it damages it: *The AIDS virus attacks the body's immune system.*

**at·tain** /ə'teɪn/ *v* [T] to succeed in getting something you want, especially after trying for a long time: *More women are attaining high positions in business.* —**attainable** *adj* —**attainment** *n* [C,U]

**at·tempt¹** /ə'tɛmpt/ *v* [T] to try to do something: *I never would have attempted to climb that mountain!*

**attempt²** *n* **1** an act of trying to do something: *Can't you make an attempt to be nice to your sister?* **2 an attempt on sb's life** an action intended to kill someone, especially someone important

**at·tend** /ə'tɛnd/ *v* [T] **1** to go to an event, such as a meeting, wedding etc.: *Most of the people who attended the concert were teenagers.* **2** to regularly go to an institution, such as a school or church: *All students must attend*

A

*classes regularly.* **3** to take care of someone: *a doctor attending one of her patients*

**attend to** sb/sth *phr v* [T] to deal with someone or something: *Do our public schools* **attend to** *our children's needs?*

**at·tend·ance** /ə'tɛndəns/ *n* **1** [C,U] the act of regularly going to an institution, such as a school or church: *A child's* **attendance at** *school is required by law.* **2** [singular] the number of people who attend an event, such as a meeting, concert etc.: *Be quiet while I* **take attendance.** (=count how many students are in class today)

**at·tend·ant** /ə'tɛndənt/ *n* someone whose job is to take care of someone or something: *a parking lot attendant*

**at·ten·tion** /ə'tɛnʃən/ *n* [U] **1** the state of watching, listening to, noticing, or thinking about something: *Sorry, what did you say? I wasn't* **paying attention.** | *Charlie tried to* **catch/get/attract** *our* **attention.** (=make us notice him) **2** the special care or interest you give to someone or something: *Johnny always has to be* **the center of attention.** (=the person everyone notices) | *The back yard really needs some attention - it's full of weeds.* **3 (could I have your) attention, please** SPOKEN used in order to ask people to be quiet and to listen to what you are going to say **4 stand at/to attention** used in order to tell a soldier to stand up straight and stay still

**at·ten·tive** /ə'tɛntɪv/ *adj* carefully listening to or watching someone because you are interested in what s/he is doing: *an attentive audience* **−attentively** *adv* **−attentiveness** *n* [U]

**at·test** /ə'tɛst/ *v* [I,T] **1** to prove something or show that something is true: *The crowd of people waiting outside his door* **attests to** *this young star's popularity.* **2** to say officially that something is true, especially in a court of law

**at·tic** /'ætɪk/ *n* a space or room at the top of a house, usually used for storing things

**attic**

**at·tire** /ə'taɪɚ/ *n* [U] FORMAL clothes

**at·ti·tude** /'ætə,tud/ *n* **1** [C,U] the opinions and feelings that you usually have about a particular thing, idea, or person: *Pete has a really negative* **attitude toward/about** *work.* **2** [C,U] the way that you behave towards someone or in a situation: *Their whole attitude changed once they found out Ron was rich.* | *Cathy has a real* **attitude problem.** (=she is not helpful or pleasant to be with) **3** INFORMAL the confidence to do unusual and exciting things without caring what other people think: *a young singer* **with attitude**

**at·tor·ney** /ə'tɚni/ *n* ⇨ LAWYER

**attorney gen·er·al** /ə.,.. '.../ *n* the chief lawyer in a state, or of the government in the US

**at·tract** /ə'trækt/ *v* **1** [T] to make someone interested in something, or to make him/her want to be involved in something: *Disneyland attracts millions of tourists each year.* | *The story* **attracted** *a lot of* **attention** *from the media.* **2 be attracted to sb** to like someone and want to have a romantic or sexual relationship with him/her: *I was immediately attracted to him.* **3** [T] to make something move toward another thing: *Your perfume is attracting the bees.*

**at·trac·tion** /ə'trækʃən/ *n* **1** [U] the feeling of liking someone or something very much: *I can't understand Beth's* **attraction** *to Stan.* **2** something interesting or fun to see or do: *hundreds of attractions at the county fair* **3** [U] the ability to make things move toward each other: *magnetic attraction*

**at·trac·tive** /ə'træktɪv/ *adj* **1** pretty or beautiful, especially in a sexual way: *an attractive young woman/man* **2** pleasant to look at: *an attractive location for a wedding* **3** good enough to make people interested: *an attractive salary/offer* **−opposite** UNATTRACTIVE

**at·trib·u·ta·ble** /ə'trɪbyətəbəl/ *adj* **attributable to sth** likely to be caused by something

**at·trib·ute¹** /ə'trɪbyut/ *v*
**attribute** sth **to** sb/sth *phr v* [T] to say that someone or something is responsible for something: *Many diseases can be attributed to stress.* | *a painting attributed to Rembrandt* **−attribution** /,ætrə'byuʃən/ *n* [U]

**at·trib·ute²** /'ætrə,byut/ *n* a good or useful quality that someone or something has

**at·trib·u·tive** /ə'trɪbyətɪv/ *adj* TECHNICAL in grammar, an attributive adjective or noun comes before the noun or phrase it describes. In the sentence "I heard a funny story," the word "funny" is attributive

**at·tuned** /ə'tund/ *adj* so familiar with someone or something that you know how to deal with him, her, or it: *It took me a while to become* **attuned to** *the strong southern accent.*

**au·burn** /'ɔbɚn/ *n* [U] a red-brown color **−auburn** *adj*: *auburn hair*

**auc·tion** /'ɔkʃən/ *n* a public meeting where art, furniture, land etc. is sold to the person who offers the most money **−auction** *v* [T]

**auc·tion·eer** /,ɔkʃə'nɪr/ *n* someone who is in charge of an auction

**au·da·cious** /ɔ'deɪʃəs/ *adj* brave and shocking: *audacious behavior* **−audaciously** *adv*

**au·dac·i·ty** /ɔ'dæsəti/ *n* [U] the courage to take risks and do things that are shocking or rude: *I can't believe he* **had the audacity to** *call your father at 3 a.m.*

**au·di·ble** /'ɔdəbəl/ *adj* able to be heard: *Her voice was barely audible.* **−audibly** *adj* **−opposite** INAUDIBLE

**au·di·ence** /'ɔdiəns/ *n* **1** the people watching or listening to a concert, speech, movie etc.: *There were over 500 people in the audience.* **2** the number or the type of people in an audience: *Cartoons usually attract a younger audience.* **3** a formal meeting with someone who is very important: *an audience with the Pope*

**au·di·o** /'ɔdiou/ *adj* relating to recording and broadcasting sound — compare VIDEO¹

**au·di·o·vis·u·al** /,ɔdiou'vɪʒuəl/ *adj* involving the use of recorded pictures and sound: *audiovisual materials for use in the language lab*

**au·dit** /'ɔdɪt/ *v* [T] **1** to check that a company's financial records are correct **2** to study a subject at college without getting a grade for it — **audit** *n* — **auditor** *n*

**au·di·tion**¹ /ɔ'dɪʃən/ *n* a short performance by an actor, singer etc. that is judged in order to decide if s/he should act in a play, sing in a concert etc.

**audition**² *v* [I,T] to perform in an AUDITION or judge someone in an audition

**au·di·to·ri·um** /,ɔdɪ'tɔriəm/ *n* a large room, especially in a school or in a movie theater, where people sit to watch a performance

**aug·ment** /ɔg'mɛnt/ *v* [T] FORMAL to increase the amount of something

**Au·gust** /'ɔgəst/ written abbreviation **Aug.** *n* the eighth month of the year — see usage note at JANUARY

**aunt** /ænt, ɑnt/ *n* the sister of your mother or father, or the wife of your UNCLE — see picture at FAMILY

**au·ra** /'ɔrə/ *n* a quality or feeling that seems to come from a person or place: *There's an aura of mystery around the castle.*

**au·ral** /'ɔrəl/ *adj* related to the ear or the sense of hearing: *aural skills*

**aus·pic·es** /'ɔspəsɪz, -,siz/ *n* [plural] FORMAL help and support, especially from an organization: *The research was done **under the auspices of** Harvard Medical School.*

**aus·pi·cious** /ɔ'spɪʃəs/ *adj* showing that something is likely to be successful: *an auspicious beginning to her career* — opposite INAUSPICIOUS

**aus·tere** /ɔ'stɪr/ *adj* **1** very strict and very serious: *a cold austere woman* **2** plain and simple and without any decoration: *an austere style of painting* **3** without a lot of comfort or enjoyment: *They lived an austere life.*

**aus·ter·i·ty** /ɔ'stɛrəti/ *n* [U] **1** bad economic conditions in which people do not have enough money to live **2** the quality of being AUSTERE: *She spoke with austerity.* | *the austerity of the church's architecture*

**Aus·tra·lia** /ɑs'treɪliə/ *n* one of the seven CONTINENTS, that is also its own country

**Aus·tra·li·an** /ɑs'treɪliən/ *adj* relating to or coming from Australia

**au·then·tic** /ɔ'θɛnɪɪk/ *adj* **1** done or made in a traditional way: *authentic Indian food* **2** proven to be made by a particular person; GENUINE: *an authentic Renoir painting* — **authentically** *adv*

**au·then·ti·cate** /ɔ'θɛnɪɪ,keɪt/ *v* [T] to prove that something is real and not a copy

**au·then·ti·ci·ty** /,ɔθɛn'tɪsəti/ *n* [U] the quality of being real or true and not a copy. *Tests confirmed the book's authenticity.*

**au·thor** /'ɔθɚ/ *n* someone who writes a book, story, article, play etc.

**au·thor·i·tar·i·an** /ə,θɔrə'tɛriən, ə,θɑr-/ *adj* forcing people to obey rules and laws that are often wrong or unfair: *an authoritarian government* — **authoritarian** *n*: *Papa was a strict authoritarian.*

**au·thor·i·ta·tive** /ə'θɔrə,teɪtɪv, ə'θɑr-/ *adj* respected and trusted as being true, or making people respect and obey you: *an authoritative account of the country's history* | *an authoritative voice* — **authoritatively** *adv*

**au·thor·i·ty** /ə'θɔrəti, ə'θɑr-/ *n* **1** [U] the power or right to control and command people: *You have no **authority over** me!* | *Who's **in authority** here?* **2 the authorities** the people or organizations that are in charge of a particular place — see usage note at OFFICER

**au·thor·i·za·tion** /,ɔθərə'zeɪʃən/ *n* [C,U] official permission to do something: *You'll need authorization from the Director to do that.*

**au·thor·ize** /'ɔθə,raɪz/ *v* **1 be authorized to** to have the power to give official permission for something: *I'm not authorized to sign this.* **2** [T] to give official permission for something: *Can you authorize my expenses?*

**au·to** /'ɔtou/ *adj* relating to cars: *auto parts*

**au·to·bi·og·ra·phy** /,ɔtəbaɪ'ɑgrəfi/ *n* a book about your life, written by yourself — **autobiographical** /,ɔtə,baɪə'græfɪkəl/ *adj*

**au·toc·ra·cy** /ɔ'tɑkrəsi/ *n* [C,U] a system of government in which one person or group has unlimited power, or a country governed in this way

**au·to·crat·ic** /,ɔtə'krætɪk/ *adj* **1** giving orders to people without considering their opinions: *an autocratic style of management* **2** having unlimited control over a country, or showing this quality: *an autocratic government* — **autocrat** /'ɔtə,kræt/ *n*

**au·to·graph**¹ /'ɔtəgræf/ *n* a famous person's name, written in his/her own writing: *I have Keanu Reeves' autograph!*

**autograph**² *v* [T] if a famous person autographs something, s/he writes his/her name on it: *Please, will you autograph my baseball?*

**au·to·mate** /'ɔtə,meɪt/ *v* [T] to change to a system in which work is done by machines instead of people: *They automated the factory ten years ago.* — **automation** /,ɔtə'meɪʃən/ *n* [U]

**au·to·mat·ic**[1] /ˌɔtəˈmætɪk / *adj* **1** an automatic machine is designed to operate by itself after you start it: *an automatic timer* **2** certain to happen: *We get an automatic pay increase every year.* **3** done without thinking: *At first, driving is hard, but then it just becomes automatic.* –**automatically** *adv*

**automatic**[2] *n* **1** a car with a system of GEARs that operate themselves **2** a gun that can shoot bullets continuously

**au·to·mo·bile** /ˌɔtəməˈbil, ˈɔtəməˌbil/ *n* a car

**au·to·mo·tive** /ˌɔtəˈmoʊtɪv/ *adj* relating to cars: *the automotive industry*

**au·ton·o·mous** /ɔˈtɑnəməs/ *adj* having the power or freedom to do what you want, especially to govern your own country: *an autonomous nation* –**autonomously** *adv*

**au·ton·o·my** /ɔˈtɑnəmi/ *n* [U] the freedom or power to do what you want

**au·top·sy** /ˈɔˌtɑpsi/ *n* an examination of a dead body to discover the cause of death

**au·to·work·er** /ˈɔtoʊˌwɚkɚ/ *n* someone whose job is to make cars

**au·tumn** /ˈɔtəm/ *n* ⇒ FALL[2] –**autumnal** /ɔˈtʌmnəl/ *adj*

**aux·il·ia·ry** /ɔgˈzɪləri, -ˈzɪlyəri/ *adj* ready to be used in an urgent situation: *The factory has an auxiliary power supply.* –**auxiliary** *n*

**auxiliary verb** /.ˈ... ˌ./ *n* TECHNICAL in grammar, verbs such as "be," "do," "have," and the MODAL VERBs that are used with another verb to show the tense, person, mood etc.

**AV** the abbreviation of AUDIOVISUAL: *the company's AV department*

**a·vail**[1] /əˈveɪl/ *n* **to no avail** without success: *We searched everywhere to no avail.*

**avail**[2] *v* **avail yourself of sth** FORMAL to accept an offer or use an opportunity to do something: *Avail yourself of every chance to improve your English.*

**a·vail·a·ble** /əˈveɪləbəl/ *adj* **1** able to be used or obtained: *The database in the library is available to anyone.| When will the video be available?* **2** free to see or talk to someone: *I'm available after lunch.* **3** free to start a romantic relationship with someone new: *I'd ask her for a date if I thought she was available.* –**availability** /əˌveɪləˈbɪləti/ *n* [U] –opposite UNAVAILABLE

**av·a·lanche** /ˈævəˌlæntʃ, -ˌlantʃ/ *n* **1** a large amount of snow, ice, and rocks that fall down the side of a mountain **2** **an avalanche of** a very large number of things that happen or arrive at the same time: *An avalanche of letters came in from 101 FM listeners.*

**a·vant-garde** /ˌævɑntˈgɑrd , ˌa-/ *adj* extremely modern and often strange or shocking: *avant-garde music/art*

**av·a·rice** /ˈævərɪs/ *n* [U] FORMAL an extreme desire for wealth; GREED –**avaricious** /ˌævəˈrɪʃəs/ *adj*

**Ave.** the written abbreviation of AVENUE

**a·venge** /əˈvɛndʒ/ *v* [T] LITERARY to do something to hurt or punish someone because s/he has harmed or offended you –**avenger** *n*

**av·e·nue** /ˈævəˌnu/ *n* **1** also **Avenue** a street in a town or city: *Fifth Avenue* **2** a possible way of achieving something: *We explored every avenue, but couldn't find a solution.*

**av·erage**[1] /ˈævrɪdʒ/ *adj* **1** calculated by adding several quantities together and then dividing by the number of quantities: *What's the average rainfall for May?* **2** having qualities that are typical: *"How tall is he?" "Oh, average."* **3** not special or unusual in any way: *It wasn't a great book - just average.*

**average**[2] *n* **1** the amount calculated by adding several quantities together and then dividing by the number of quantities: *The average of 3, 8, and 10 is 7.* **2** **on average** based on a calculation that shows what usually happens: *On average, women live longer than men.* **3** [C,U] the usual level or amount: *Annette is an above average student.* (=better than the average)

**average**[3] *v* [T] **1** to do or have something usually: *I average about 10 cigarettes a day.* **2** to calculate the average of quantities
　**average out** *phr v* [I] to result in a particular average amount: *Our weekly profits average out at about $750.*

**a·verse** /əˈvɚs/ *adj* **not be averse to** used in order to say that you do not mind doing something: *I don't drink much, but I'm not averse to the occasional glass of wine.*

**a·ver·sion** /əˈvɚʒən/ *n* [singular, U] a strong dislike of something or someone: *Mary has an aversion to cats.*

**a·vert** /əˈvɚt/ *v* [T] **1** to prevent something from happening: *The whole thing could've been averted if you'd listened to us.* **2** **avert your eyes/gaze** to look away from something you do not want to see

**a·vi·a·tion** /ˌeɪviˈeɪʃən/ *n* [U] the science or practice of flying or making aircraft

**a·vi·a·tor** /ˈeɪviˌeɪtɚ/ *n* OLD-FASHIONED the pilot of an aircraft

**av·id** /ˈævɪd/ *adj* **avid reader/collector/fan etc.** someone who does something a lot because s/he enjoys it: *an avid collector of coins*

**av·o·ca·do** /ˌævəˈkɑdoʊ, ˌɑ-/ *n* [C,U] a firm green fruit, eaten as a vegetable

**a·void** /əˈvɔɪd/ *v* [T] **1** to make an effort not to do something or to stop something from happening: *Exercise will help you avoid heart disease.| Avoid drinking alcohol while taking this medicine.* ✗ DON'T SAY "avoid to do something" ✗ **2** to deliberately stay away from someone or something: *I was told to avoid stress.* –**avoidable** *adj* –**avoidance** *n* [U]

**a·vow** /əˈvaʊ/ v [T] FORMAL to say or admit something publicly –**avowal** n [C,U]

**a·vowed** /əˈvaʊd/ adj said or admitted publicly: an avowed atheist –**avowedly** /əˈvaʊɪdli/ adv

**a·wait** /əˈweɪt/ v [T] FORMAL  **1** to wait for something: Briggs is awaiting trial for murder.  **2** to be about to happen to someone: A terrible surprise awaited them.

**a·wake**[1] /əˈweɪk/ adj  **1** not sleeping: I was **wide awake** (=completely awake) before dawn.  **2** **be awake to sth** FORMAL to understand a situation and its possible effects

**awake**[2] v awoke, awoken [I,T] LITERARY  **1** to stop sleeping: The noise awoke me.  **2** to suddenly begin to feel an emotion, or to make someone do this

**a·wak·en** /əˈweɪkən/ v ⇨ AWAKE[2]
**awaken sb/sth to** phr v [T] FORMAL to begin to understand a situation and its possible effects, or to make someone do this: Churches are **awakening to** the needs of their older members.

**a·wak·en·ing** /əˈweɪkənɪŋ/ n a situation when you suddenly realize that you understand or feel something: Anyone who thinks that this job is easy will have a **rude awakening**. (=a time when s/he suddenly realizes that it is not easy)

**a·ward**[1] /əˈwɔrd/ v [T] to officially give someone an award: He was awarded the Nobel Prize.|A large sum of money was **awarded to** the survivors.

**award**[2] n a prize or money given to someone for a special reason: the **award for** best actor|an **award of** $10,000 to each victim

**a·ware** /əˈwɛr/ adj realizing that something is true, exists, or is happening: Are you **aware of** the dangers of smoking?|Were you **aware (that)** your son has been taking drugs?|Sheila is very **politically/environmentally aware**. (=she knows a lot about what is happening in politics etc.)|"Are there any more problems?" "Not that I'm aware of." –opposite UNAWARE

**a·ware·ness** /əˈwɛrnɪs/ n [U] knowledge or understanding of a particular subject or situation: The TV ads are meant to **raise** the public's **awareness** of environmental issues.

**a·wash** /əˈwɑʃ, əˈwɔʃ/ adj  **1** **awash with/in** too full of something: TV is awash with talk shows.  **2** covered with water or another liquid

**a·way**[1] /əˈweɪ/ adv  **1** to or at a different place from someone or something: Go away!|Diane drove away quickly.|Move away from the fire!  **2** **3 miles/40 feet etc. away** at a particular distance from a place: a town about 50 miles **away from** Chicago  **3** into a safe or enclosed place: Put all your toys away now, please.  **4** **2 days/3 weeks etc. away** at a particular time in the future: Christmas is only a month away.  **5** not at home or in your usual place of work: I'm sorry, Ms. Parker is away

this week.  **6** completely gone or used up: All the water had boiled away.|The music died away.  **7** all the time, or continuously: He's been working away on the patio all day.

**away**[2] adj playing on your opponent's sports field rather than your own: The **away team** is ahead by four runs. –opposite HOME[3]

**awe** /ɔ/ n [U]  **1** a feeling of great respect and admiration, and sometimes a slight fear: The beauty of the chapel **filled** them **with awe**.  **2** **be/stand in awe of sb** to respect someone and be slightly afraid of him/her –**awed** adj: an awed silence

**awe-in·spir·ing** /ˈ. .ˌ../ adj making you feel awe: an awe-inspiring achievement

**awe·some** /ˈɔsəm/ adj  **1** so impressive, serious, or difficult that it makes you feel awe: an awesome responsibility  **2** SLANG extremely good: That concert was awesome!

**awe·struck** /ˈɔstrʌk/ adj feeling great awe: We gazed awestruck at the pyramids.

**aw·ful**[1] /ˈɔfəl/ adj  **1** very bad or unpleasant: an awful movie|This soup tastes awful!  **2** SPOKEN used in order to emphasize how much of something there is, or how good, bad etc. something is: I have **an awful lot** (=a very large amount) of work to do.  **3** **look/feel awful** to look or feel sick

**awful**[2] adv SPOKEN NONSTANDARD very: She's awful cute.

**aw·fully** /ˈɔfli/ adv SPOKEN very: Helen looks awfully tired.

**a·while** /əˈwaɪl/ adv for a period of time, when you cannot say exactly how long: Gil stood at the window awhile, watching for Sarah.

**awk·ward** /ˈɔkwəd/ adj  **1** making you feel so embarrassed that you are not sure what to do or say: There was an awkward pause in the conversation.  **2** causing a problem or making things difficult: This is kind of an awkward time for me, could I call you back?|You're just **being awkward**! (=causing problems intentionally)  **3** difficult to use or handle: an awkward-sized box  **4** moving or behaving in a way that does not seem relaxed or comfortable: an awkward teenager –**awkwardly** adv –**awkwardness** n [U]

**awn·ing** /ˈɔnɪŋ/ n a sheet of material outside a store, tent etc. used for protection from the sun or the rain

**a·woke** /əˈwoʊk/ v the past tense of AWAKE

**a·wok·en** /əˈwoʊkən/ v the PAST PARTICIPLE of AWAKE

**AWOL** /ˈeɪˌwɔl/ adj Absent With Out Leave; absent from your military group without permission: Private Ames has **gone AWOL**.

**a·wry** /əˈraɪ/ adj LITERARY **go awry** to not happen in the way that was planned

**axe**[1], **ax** /æks/ n  **1** a tool with a heavy metal blade on a long handle, used for cutting wood  **2** **give sb/sth the axe** INFORMAL to dismiss

someone from his/her job, or get rid of something: *The TV station gave Brown the axe.*
**3 have an axe to grind** to do or say something again and again because you want people to accept your ideas or beliefs: *I have no political axe to grind.*

**axe², ax** *v* [T] INFORMAL to suddenly dismiss someone from his/her job, or get rid of something: *Did you hear they're axing 500 jobs?*

**ax·i·om** /ˈæksiəm/ *n* a rule or principle that is considered by most people to be true

**ax·i·o·mat·ic** /ˌæksiəˈmætɪk/ *adj* a principle that is axiomatic does not need to be proved because people can see that it is true —**axiomatically** *adv*

**ax·is** /ˈæksɪs/ *n, plural* **axes 1** the imaginary line around which something turns, for example the Earth **2** a line at the side or bottom of a GRAPH that you measure the positions of points on

axis

**ax·le** /ˈæksəl/ *n* the BAR that connects two wheels on a vehicle

**aye** /aɪ/ *adv* SPOKEN FORMAL used in order to say yes, especially when voting

**AZ** the written abbreviation of Arizona

# B

**B, b** /bi/ the second letter of the English alphabet

**B** /bi/ *n* **1** the second highest grade you can get on a test or piece of school work **2** [C,U] the seventh note in the musical SCALE of C, or the musical KEY based on this note

**b** the written abbreviation of born: *A. Lincoln, b. 1809*

**B.A.** *n* Bachelor of Arts; a university degree in a subject such as history or literature —compare B.S.

**baa** /bɑ, bæ/ *v* [I] to make the sound a sheep makes

**bab·ble** /ˈbæbəl/ *v* [I,T] to talk a lot in a way that does not make sense: *a baby just beginning to babble* —**babble** *n* [C,U]

**babe** /beɪb/ *n* **1** SPOKEN an attractive young man or woman: *Brad's a total babe.* **2** SPOKEN a way of speaking to someone you like and know well: *Hey, babe, how are you?* **3** SPOKEN a way of speaking to a woman, often considered offensive **4** LITERARY a baby

**ba·boon** /bæˈbun/ *n* a large African or South Asian monkey with a small tail

**ba·by** /ˈbeɪbi/ *n* **1** a very young child who has not yet learned to talk: *Joyce **had a baby*** (=gave birth to a baby) *in September.* | *Pam is **expecting a baby**.* (=will have a baby) | *a crying baby* **2** a very young animal or plant: *baby birds* **3** SPOKEN **a)** a way of speaking to someone you love: *Bye, baby. I'll be back by six.* **b)** a way of speaking to a woman, often considered offensive **4** SPOKEN a word meaning someone who behaves in a stupid or silly way, used especially by children **5 baby boom** a time when a lot of babies are born in a particular country

**baby boom·er** /ˈ.. ˌ../ *n* INFORMAL someone born between 1946 and 1965, when a lot of babies were born

**baby car·riage** /ˈ.. ˌ../, **baby bug·gy** /ˈbeɪbi ˌbʌgi/ *n* a small bed with wheels, used for pushing a baby around outdoors

**ba·by·ish** /ˈbeɪbiɪʃ/ *adj* DISAPPROVING like a baby or suitable for a baby: *babyish games*

**ba·by·sit** /ˈbeɪbiˌsɪt/ *v* **babysat, babysat, babysitting** [I,T] to take care of someone's children while the parents are not at home —**babysitter** *n* —**babysitting** *n* [U]

**ba·by·talk** /ˈbeɪbiˌtɔk/ *n* [U] words or sounds that you make when talking to a baby

**bach·e·lor** /ˈbætʃələ, ˈbætʃlə/ *n* a man who is not married

**bachelor par·ty** /ˈ... ˌ../ *n* a party given for a man the night before his wedding

**bach·e·lor's de·gree** /ˈ... ˌ./ *n* ⇨ B.A.

**back¹** /bæk/ *n*
**1** ▸BODY◂ **a)** the part of a person's or animal's body that goes from the neck to the BUTTOCKs or the tail: *My back was really aching.* | *The cat arched its back and hissed.* **b)** the bone that goes from your neck to your BUTTOCKs: *He broke his back in a motorcycle accident.*
**2** ▸PART OF STH◂ [singular, U] the part of something that is furthest from the way that it moves or faces: *a grocery list on the back of an envelope* | *The index is at the back of the book.* | *The pool's **in back of** the house.* | *Kids should always wear seat belts, even **in back**.* (=in the seats behind the driver in a car) | *Tom's working on the car **out back**.* (=behind a house or other building) —opposite FRONT¹
**3** ▸SEAT◂ the part of a seat that you lean against when you are sitting
**4 behind sb's back** without the person who is concerned knowing about what is being said or done: *I can't believe she said that about me behind my back!*
**5 at/in the back of your mind** a thought or feeling at the back of your mind is affecting you, although you are not thinking about it directly: *There was always a slight fear in the back of his mind.*
**6 get off my back!** SPOKEN said when you want someone to stop telling you to do something: *I'll*

*do it in a minute. Just get off my back!*

**7 be on sb's back** SPOKEN to keep telling someone to do something, in a way that annoys him/her: *The boss has been on my back about being late.*

**8 have your back to the wall** INFORMAL to be in a very difficult situation: *A lot of small businesses have their backs to the wall in this slow economy.* –see also **turn your back (on)** (TURN¹)

**back²** *adv* **1** where someone or something was before: *Put the milk back in the refrigerator.* | *Roger said he'd be back in an hour.* **2** in or into the condition that someone or something was in before: *I woke up at 5 a.m. and couldn't get back to sleep.* **3** in the direction that is behind you: *George glanced back to see if he was still being followed.* **4** as a reply or reaction to what someone has done: *Can you call me back later?* | *Sarah smiled, and the boy grinned back.* **5** away from the front of something or away from a person or thing: *Her hair was pulled back in a ponytail.* | *Stand back from the fire!* **6** in or toward an earlier time: *This all happened about three years back.* **7 back and forth** in one direction and then in the opposite direction: *He walked back and forth across the floor.*

**back³** *v* **1** [I,T] to move in the direction that is behind you, or to make someone or something move in this way: *Teresa backed the car down the narrow driveway.* | *We slowly backed away from the snake.* **2** [T] to support someone or something, especially by using your money or power: *The bill is backed by several environmental groups.* **3** [T] to risk money on the team, person, horse etc. that you think will win something: *Which team did you back in the Superbowl?*

**back down** *phr v* [I] to accept defeat or admit that you are wrong in an argument or fight: *Rosen backed down when he saw how big the other guy was.*

**back off** *phr v* [I] **1** to move in the direction that is behind you, away from something: *Back off a little, you're too close.* **2** to stop trying to make someone do or think something: *Back off! I don't need your advice.*

**back onto** sth *phr v* [T] to have something very near to the back: *These houses back onto a busy road.*

**back out** *phr v* [I] to decide not to do something you promised to do: *They backed out of the deal at the last minute.*

**back up** *phr v* **1** [T **back** sb/sth ↔ **up**] to support what someone is doing or saying, or show that it is true: *He had evidence on video to back up his claim.* **2** [I,T **back** sth ↔ **up**] to make a car go backward **3** [I] to move in the direction that is behind you: *Back up a little so they can get by.* **4** [I,T **back** sth ↔ **up**] to make a copy

of information on a computer **5 be backed up** traffic that is backed up is moving very slowly

**back⁴** *adj* **1** in the back or behind something: *the back door* **2 back street/road** a street or road that is away from the main streets of a town or area **3 back rent/taxes/pay** money that someone owes for rent, tax etc. from an earlier date: *We owe $350 in back taxes!*

**back·ache** /ˈbækeɪk/ *n* [C,U] a dull pain or general pain in your back

**back·bit·ing** /ˈbækˌbaɪtɪŋ/ *n* [U] criticism of someone who is not present: *The coach made sure there was never any backbiting in the locker room.*

**back·bone** /ˈbækboʊn/ *n* **1** ⇨ SPINE **2 the backbone of** the most important part of an activity, group, or set of ideas, on which other parts depend: *The cocoa industry is the backbone of Ghana's economy.* **3** [U] courage and determination: *Fight for what you believe - show some backbone!*

**back·break·ing** /ˈbækˌbreɪkɪŋ/ *adj* backbreaking work is very difficult and tiring

**back·date** /ˌbækˈdeɪt/ *v* [T] to write an earlier date on a document or check than the date when it was really written: *a pay increase backdated to January*

**back·drop** /ˈbækdrɑp/ *n* **1** the conditions in which something happens, and which help to explain it: *The company's growth must be seen against the backdrop of the city's economic expansion.* **2** a painted cloth behind a stage, or the area behind something you are looking at

**back·er** /ˈbækɚ/ *n* someone who supports a plan, organization, country etc., especially by providing money: *financial backers of the new gun club* (=people who give money to the club)

**back·fire** /ˈbækfaɪɚ/ *v* [I] **1** if a plan or action backfires, it has an effect that is the opposite of what you intended **2** if a car backfires, it makes a sudden loud noise because the engine is not working correctly

**back·gam·mon** /ˈbækˌgæmən/ *n* [U] a game for two players, using flat round pieces and DICE on a special board

**back·ground** /ˈbækgraʊnd/ *n* **1** the type of education, experiences, and family that someone has: *The kids here have very different religious backgrounds* **2** the sounds, things, movements etc. that are in or happening in a place or picture but that are not the main thing you see or hear: *I could hear cars honking in the background.* **3** [singular, U] ⇨ BACKDROP

**back·hand·ed** /ˈbækˌhændɪd/ *adj* **backhanded compliment** a statement that seems to express praise or admiration, but is actually insulting

**back·ing** /ˈbækɪŋ/ *n* **1** [U] support or help, especially with money: *The agency has provided financial backing for the project.* **2** material that is used to make the back of an object

**back·lash** /ˈbæklæʃ/ *n* [singular] a strong reaction against a particular event, decision, or social development: *a political backlash against immigrants*

**back·log** /ˈbæklɔg, -lag/ *n* work that still needs to be done and should have been done earlier: *a huge backlog of orders from customers*

**back·pack**[1] /ˈbækpæk/ *n* a bag you carry on your back when you are walking or camping

**backpack**[2] *v* [I] to go walking and camping carrying a BACKPACK – **backpacker** *n* – **backpacking** *n* [U]

**back seat** /ˌ. ˈ.◂/ *n* **1** the seat behind where the driver sits in a car **2 back seat driver** someone who gives unwanted advice to the driver of a car **3 take a back seat** to accept or be put in a less important position: *His career has taken a back seat while he helps raise his two children.*

**back·side** /ˈbæksaɪd/ *n* INFORMAL the part of your body on which you sit

**back·space** /ˈbækspeɪs/ *v* [I] to move backward toward the beginning of the line that you are typing (TYPE) on a computer or TYPEWRITER

**back·stage** /ˌbækˈsteɪdʒ/ *adv* in or toward the area behind the stage in a theater

**back-to-back** /ˌ. . ˈ.◂/ *adj, adv* **1** happening one after the other: *We played two concerts back-to-back.* | *back-to-back baseball games* **2** with someone's or something's back against another person's or thing's back: *The chairs were placed back-to-back.*

**back·track** /ˈbæktræk/ *v* [I] **1** to go back the way you have just come: *We had to backtrack about a mile.* **2** to do or say something again in a different way: *The witness backtracked, adding some new facts to his story.*

**back·up** /ˈbækʌp/ *n* **1** a copy of something that you can use if the original thing is lost or does not work: *Make a backup of any work you do on the computer.* **2** [C,U] someone or something that provides help or support when it is needed: *Several police cars provided backup for the officers.*

**back·ward**[1] /ˈbækwɚd/ **backwards** *adv* **1** in the direction that is behind you: *She took a step backwards, startled.* –opposite FORWARD[1] **2** toward the beginning or the past: *Can you say the alphabet backward?* –opposite FORWARD[1] **3** with the back part in front: *Your t-shirt is on backwards.*

**backward**[2] *adj* **1** made toward the direction that is behind you: *She left without a backward glance.* **2** developing slowly and less successfully than others: *a backward child*

**back·wa·ter** /ˈbækˌwɔtɚ, -ˌwɑ-/ *n* a town or place far away from cities, where not much happens

**back·woods** /ˌbækˈwʊdz◂/ *n* [plural] an area in the forest that is far from any towns – **backwoods** *adj*: *a backwoods town*

**back·yard, back yard** /ˌbækˈyɑrd◂/ *n* the area of land behind a house

**ba·con** /ˈbeɪkən/ *n* [U] long thin pieces of SALTed or SMOKED meat from the back or sides of a pig

**bac·te·ri·a** /bækˈtɪriə/ *n* [plural] very small living things, some of which can cause disease

**bad**[1] /bæd/ *adj* **worse, worst 1** not good and unpleasant: *I'm afraid I have some bad news for you.* | *a really bad smell* **2** low in quality or below an acceptable standard: *She was the worst teacher I ever had.* | *Brian is really bad at sports.* **3** damaging or harmful: *Smoking is bad for your health.* | *Pollution in the lake is having a bad effect on fish stocks.* **4** serious or severe: *a bad cold* | *The traffic near the airport was even worse today than it was yesterday.* **5 too bad** SPOKEN said when you are sorry that something unpleasant has happened to someone: *It's too bad she had to give up teaching when she got sick.* **6** not fit to eat: *The milk has gone bad.* **7 feel bad** to feel ashamed or sorry about something: *I felt really bad about missing your birthday.* **8** permanently injured or not working correctly: *The fever left him with a bad heart.* **9 not bad** SPOKEN used when you think something is acceptable: *"How are you?" "Oh, not bad."* **10** *comparative* **badder,** *superlative* **baddest** SLANG extremely good: *That's a bad song!* **11 bad language/words** swearing or rude words **12 bad off** NONSTANDARD ⇨ **badly off** (BADLY)

**bad**[2] *adv* SPOKEN NONSTANDARD ⇨ BADLY

**badge** /bædʒ/ *n* a small piece of metal that you wear or carry to show people that you work for a particular organization: *a police officer's badge*

**badg·er** /ˈbædʒɚ/ *n* an animal with black and white fur that lives in holes in the ground

**bad·lands** /ˈbædlændz/ *n* [plural] an area of rocks and hills where no crops can be grown

**bad·ly** /ˈbædli/ *adv* **worse, worst 1** in an unsatisfactory or unsuccessful way: *a badly written book* | *I sing very badly.* ✗ DON'T SAY "I sing very bad." ✗ –opposite WELL[1] **2** very much or seriously: *The refugees badly need food and clean water.* **3 badly off** not having things or money that you need: *The tax changes left many middle-class Americans worse off.*

**bad·min·ton** /ˈbædˌmɪntⁿn/ *n* [U] a game in which players hit a small object with feathers across a net and try not to let it touch the ground

**bad·mouth** /ˈbædmaʊθ/ *v* [T] INFORMAL to talk about someone in a way that criticizes him/her: *Ken's in trouble for badmouthing one of his employees.*

**baf·fle** /ˈbæfəl/ *v* [T] if something baffles you, you cannot understand it at all – **baffling** *adj*

**baf·fled** /ˈbæfəld/ *adj* unable to understand something at all: *Scientists are completely baffled by the results.*

**bag**[1] /bæg/ *n* **1** a container made of paper, plastic, cloth etc. that opens at the top: *a shopping bag | packing a bag for the weekend* **2** the amount a bag can hold: *two bags of rice per family* **3 in the bag** certain to be won or to be a success: *We thought we had the game in the bag, but they beat us.* **4 bags** dark circles or loose skin under your eyes

**bag**[2] *v* **-gged, -gging** [T] **1** to put things in a bag: *He got a job bagging groceries at the supermarket.* **2** SPOKEN to decide not to do something: *I'm tired of waiting. Bag this - I'm leaving.*

**ba·gel** /'beɪgəl/ *n* a type of bread that is shaped like a ring –see picture at BREAD

**bag·ful** /'bægfʊl/ *n* the amount a bag can hold

**bag·gage** /'bægɪdʒ/ *n* [U] **1** all the bags, boxes etc. that someone carries when s/he is traveling **2** beliefs, opinions, and experiences from the past that influence the way a person or society behaves or thinks: *cultural baggage*

**Bag·gies** /'bægiz/ *n* [plural] TRADEMARK small plastic bags used for keeping food in – **baggie** *n*

**bag·gy** /'bægi/ *adj* hanging in loose folds: *a baggy t-shirt*

**bag la·dy** /'. ‚../ *n* INFORMAL an impolite word for a woman who lives on the street and carries all her possessions with her

**bag·pipes** /'bægpaɪps/ *n* [plural] a Scottish musical instrument which is played by forcing air out of a bag through pipes

**bail**[1] /beɪl/ *n* [U] money left with a court of law so that someone can be let out of prison while waiting for his/her TRIAL: *The prisoner was let out on bail.* | *Marshall's father stood/posted bail for him.* (=paid the bail)

**bail**[2] *v* [I, T] to remove water from the bottom of a boat

**bail out** *phr v* **1** [T **bail** sb/sth **out**] to do something to help someone out of trouble, especially financial problems: *bailing out a company* **2** [T **bail** sb ↔ **out**] to give money to a court of law so that someone can leave prison until his/her TRIAL **3** [I] INFORMAL to escape from a situation that you no longer want to be involved in: *After ten years in the business, McArthur is bailing out.* **4** [T **bail** sth ↔ **out**] to remove water from the bottom of a boat **5** [I] to escape from a plane using a PARACHUTE

**bail·out** /'beɪlaʊt/ *n* a situation in which someone provides money to help someone else who has financial problems: *the government bailout of the savings and loan organizations*

**bait**[1] /beɪt/ *n* [singular, U] **1** food used for attracting fish, animals, or birds so that you can catch them **2** something you use in order to try to make someone do something or buy something: *He made the CD player sound so good, I took the bait and bought it.*

**bait**[2] *v* [T] **1** to put food on a hook to catch fish, or in a trap to catch animals **2** to laugh at or TEASE someone in an unkind way

**bake** /beɪk/ *v* [I,T] to cook food in an OVEN, using dry heat: *I'm baking a cake for Laurie.*

**bak·er** /'beɪkɚ/ *n* someone whose job is to BAKE bread, cakes, cookies etc.

**bak·er·y** /'beɪkəri/ *n* a place where bread, cakes, cookies etc. are made and sold

**bake sale** /'. ‚./ *n* an occasion when the members of a school group, church organization etc. make sweet foods and sell them in order to make money for the organization

**bal·ance**[1] /'bæləns/ *n* **1** [singular, U] a state in which your weight is evenly spread so that you are steady and not likely to fall: *Billy was walking on top of the fence and lost his balance.* (=was unable to stay steady) | *Tricia could not keep her balance* (=could not stay steady), *and fell on the ice.* | *I was still off balance* (=unable to stay steady) *when he hit me again.* **2** [singular] a state in which opposite qualities or influences have or are given equal importance: *The car's designers wanted to strike a balance between safety and style.* (=make sure that two things have equal importance) **3** the amount of something that remains after some has been used or spent: *a bank balance* (=the money you have left in the bank) **4 be/hang in the balance** to be in a situation where the result of something could be good or bad: *With the war still going, thousands of peoples' lives hang in the balance.*

**balance**[2] *v* **1** [I,T] to get into a steady position, without falling to one side or the other, or to put something in this position: *The man balanced a spinning plate on a tall stick.* **2** [I,T] to have equal amounts of money being paid and spent, or to make two amounts of money equal: *Congress is attempting to balance the budget.* **3** [T] to give equal importance to two or more things: *A working mother has to balance her home life with a career.* **4** [T] to consider one thing in relation to something else: *The need for a new road must be balanced against the damage to the environment.*

**bal·anced** /'bælənst/ *adj* **1** giving equal attention to all sides or opinions; fair: *balanced reporting of the election campaign* **2** including the right amount of different kinds of things or people: *a balanced diet*

**balance sheet** /'.. ‚./ *n* a written statement of the money and property a business has, and how much money it has paid for goods and services

**bal·co·ny** /'bælkəni/ *n* **1** a structure built onto the outside of a high window, so that you can stand or sit outside –see picture on page 471 **2** the seats upstairs in a theater

**bald** /bɔld/ *adj* **1** having little or no hair on your head **2** not having enough of the substance that normally covers something: *bald tires*

**bald ea·gle** /'. ˌ../ *n* a large North American wild bird that represents the US on money, official signs etc.

**bald·ing** /'bɔldɪŋ/ *adj* becoming BALD

**bale** /beɪl/ *n* a large amount of something such as paper or HAY that is tied tightly together

**bale·ful** /'beɪlfəl/ *adj* expressing a desire to harm someone: *a baleful look*

**balk** /bɔk/ *v* [I] to refuse to do something unpleasant or difficult: *Several managers balked at enforcing the decision.* —**balky** *adj*

**ball** /bɔl/ *n* **1** a round object that is thrown, hit, kicked etc. in a game, or any object shaped like this: *yellow tennis balls* | *a ball of yarn* **2 on the ball** INFORMAL able to think or act quickly: *If we had been on the ball, this might not have happened.* **3 have a ball** INFORMAL to have a very good time: *We had a ball last night!* **4 set/start the ball rolling** to begin an activity or event: *You set the ball rolling, and we'll help you out when you need us.* **5** a ball that is thrown toward the hitter outside the correct area in baseball **6** a large formal occasion where people dance **7 the ball of the foot/hand/thumb** the rounded part at the base of your largest toe or at the base or top of your thumb —see also BALLS **play ball** (PLAY¹)

**bal·lad** /'bæləd/ *n* **1** a simple song, especially about love **2** a short story in the form of a poem

**bal·le·ri·na** /ˌbælə'rinə/ *n* a female BALLET dancer

**bal·let** /bæ'leɪ, 'bæleɪ/ *n* **1** a performance in which a story is told using dance and music, without any speaking: *the ballet "Swan Lake"* **2** [U] this type of dancing as an art form **3** a group of ballet dancers who work together: *the Bolshoi ballet*

**ball game** /'. ./ *n* **1** a game of baseball, basketball, or football **2 a whole new ball game/a different ball game** a situation that is very different from the one you were in before: *I've used word processors, but this is a whole new ball game.*

**bal·lis·tic** /bə'lɪstɪk/ *adj* **go ballistic** SPOKEN to suddenly become very angry

**bal·lis·tics** /bə'lɪstɪks/ *n* [U] the study of how objects move through the air when they are thrown or shot from a gun

**bal·loon¹** /bə'lun/ *n* **1** a small brightly colored rubber bag that can be filled with air **2** ⇨ HOT AIR BALLOON

**balloon²** *v* [I] to become larger in size or amount

**bal·lot** /'bælət/ *n* **1** a piece of paper that you use to vote **2** [C,U] a system of voting in secret, or an occasion when you vote in this way:

*We're holding a ballot to decide the chairmanship.*

**ballot box** /'.. ˌ./ *n* **1 the ballot box** the process of voting, or the time when voting happens: *The voters will give their opinion of the Governor at the ballot box.* **2** a box that BALLOT papers are put in during the vote

**ball park** /'. ˌ./ *n* **1** a field for playing baseball, with seats for people to watch the game **2 a ball park figure/estimate** a number or amount that is almost but not exactly correct: *Can you give us a ball park figure?* **3 in the (right) ball park** INFORMAL close to the amount, price etc. that is correct: *"Does $3000 sound too high?" "No, that's in the right ball park."*

**ball·point pen** /ˌbɔlpɔɪnt 'pɛn/ *n* a pen with a small ball at the end that rolls ink onto the paper

**ball·room** /'bɔlrum/ *n* a large room where formal dances take place

**balls** /bɔlz/ *n* [plural] **1** SPOKEN an impolite word for TESTICLES **2** SLANG courage and determination: *It took balls to be that tough with Mr. Dozier.*

**balm** /bɑm/ *n* [U] an oily liquid that you rub onto your skin to reduce pain

**balm·y** /'bɑmi/ *adj* balmy weather or air is warm and pleasant

**ba·lo·ney** /bə'louni/ *n* [U] **1** INFORMAL something that is silly or not true: *His explanation sounded like a bunch of baloney to me.* **2** NONSTANDARD ⇨ BOLOGNA

**bam·boo** /ˌbæm'bu‹ / *n* [C,U] a tall plant with hard hollow stems, often used for making furniture

**bam·boo·zle** /bæm'buzəl/ *v* [T] INFORMAL to trick or confuse someone

**ban¹** /bæn/ *n* an official order that does not allow something to be used or done: *a global ban on nuclear testing*

**ban²** *v* **-nned, -nning** [T] to say that something must not be done, used etc.: *The city council banned smoking in public areas in 1995.*

**ba·nal** /bə'næl, bə'nɑl, 'beɪnl/ *adj* ordinary and not interesting: *a banal love song* —**banality** /bə'næləti/ [C,U]

**ba·nan·a** /bə'nænə/ *n* **1** a long curved yellow fruit —see picture on page 470 **2 go bananas** to get very excited, upset, or angry: *The kids went bananas and tore open the boxes.*

**band¹** /bænd/ *n* **1** a group of musicians, especially a group that plays popular music —compare ORCHESTRA **2** a group of people who work together to achieve the same aims: *a small band of terrorists* **3** a piece of material that forms a circle: *Her hair was pulled back with a rubber band.* **4** a line of a different color; STRIPE: *a fish with a black band along its back* **5** one of the parts or groups that something is divided into: *My new job puts us in a higher tax band.*

**band²** v
**band together** *phr v* [I] to join with other people in order to work toward achieving an aim: *150 families have **banded together** to try to keep drug dealers out of the neighborhood.*

**ban·dage¹** /ˈbændɪdʒ/ *n* a piece of cloth that you wrap around an injured part of someone's body

**bandage²** v [T] to put a BANDAGE on a part of someone's body that is injured

**Band-Aid** /ˈbænd eɪd/ *n* TRADEMARK a small piece of material that sticks to your skin to cover small wounds

**ban·dan·na** /bænˈdænə/ *n* a square piece of colored cloth that you can wear over your head or around your neck

**ban·dit** /ˈbændɪt/ *n* OLD-FASHIONED someone who robs people

**band·stand** /ˈbændstænd/ *n* a small building in a park that has a roof but no walls, used for musical performances

**band·wag·on** /ˈbænd,wægən/ *n* **jump/climb on the bandwagon** to start doing something because a lot of other people are doing it: *Like many companies, PELCO has jumped on the environmental bandwagon.* (=started to give attention to the environment)

**ban·dy** /ˈbændi/ v
**bandy** sth **about/around** *phr v* [T] to mention people or facts, especially to seem important or interesting: *Her name was **bandied about** in connection with the recent scandal.*

**bane** /beɪn/ *n* **bane of sb's existence** HUMOROUS someone or something that causes you problems: *Physics was the bane of my existence in high school.*

**bang¹** /bæŋ/ v **1** [I,T] to make a loud noise, especially by hitting something against something hard: *Larren was **banging on** the wall with his fist.|The screen door banged shut behind him.* **2** [T] to hit a part of your body against something hard and hurt it: *I banged my knee on the corner of the bed.*

bang

**bang²** *n* **1** a sudden loud noise, usually made by something hard hitting something else or by something exploding: *The door slammed shut **with a bang**.* **2 get a bang out of sth** SPOKEN to enjoy something very much: *I really got a bang out of seeing those guys last night!* **3 with a bang** in a way that is very exciting or noticeable: *He began his presidential campaign **with a bang**.* —see also BANGS

**bang³** *adv* INFORMAL directly or exactly: *They've built a parking lot bang in the middle of town.*

**bang⁴** *interjection* said in order to make the sound of a gun or bomb: *"Bang! Bang! You're dead!" Tommy shouted.*

**banged-up** /ˌ. ˈ.◂/ *adj* INFORMAL damaged or injured: *a banged-up old car*

**bangs** /bæŋz/ *n* [plural] hair that is cut straight across your FOREHEAD —see picture at HAIRSTYLE

**ban·ish** /ˈbænɪʃ/ v [T] to punish someone by making him/her leave a place and stay out of it for a long time: *The king banished Roderigo from the court.*

**ban·is·ter** /ˈbænəstəʳ/ *n* a row of upright pieces of wood or metal with a BAR along the top that you hold onto when using a set of stairs

**ban·jo** /ˈbændʒoʊ/ *n* a musical instrument with four or more strings, a circular body, and a long neck

**bank¹** /bæŋk/ *n* **1** a business that keeps and lends money, or the office or building belonging to this business: *I went to the bank at noon to deposit my check.* **2** land along the side of a river or lake: *trees lining the river bank* —see usage note at SHORE **3 blood/sperm/organ etc. bank** a place where human blood etc. is stored until someone needs it **4** a large number of machines etc. arranged close together in a row: *a bank of television screens along the wall* **5** a large pile of snow, sand etc. **6 cloud/fog etc. bank** a lot of clouds, thick mist etc. that you can see the edge of

**bank²** v **1** [I] to make a plane, car etc. slope to one side when it is turning: *The lead plane banked and turned toward Honolulu.* **2** [I,T] to put or keep money in a bank: *Do you **bank at** First National?* **3** [I] to have steep sides like a hill: *The race track banks steeply in the third turn.* **4** [T] also **bank up** to put a lot of wood, coal etc. on a fire to keep it burning for a long time
**bank on** sb/sth *phr v* [T] to depend on something happening or someone doing something: *We were **banking on** Jesse being here to help.*

**bank·er** /ˈbæŋkəʳ/ *n* someone who works in a bank in an important position

**bank·ing** /ˈbæŋkɪŋ/ *n* [U] the business of a bank

**bank·rupt¹** /ˈbæŋkrʌpt/ *adj* unable to pay your debts: *Many small businesses **went bankrupt** during the recession.*

**bankrupt²** v [T] to make someone become bankrupt

**bank·rupt·cy** /ˈbæŋk,rʌptsi/ *n* [C,U] a situation in which you officially say that you are unable to pay your debts: *The company lost so much money it was forced to **declare bankruptcy**.*

**bank tell·er** /ˈ. ,../ *n* ⇨ TELLER

**ban·ner¹** /ˈbænəʳ/ *n* **1** a long piece of cloth on which something is written, often carried between two poles: *voters waving election banners* **2** LITERARY a flag **3** a belief or principle: *Civil rights groups have achieved a* *lot* **under the banner of** *fair and equal treatment.*

**banner**[2] *adj* excellent: *a banner year for American soccer*

**ban·quet** /'bæŋkwɪt/ *n* a formal meal for many people

**ban·ter** /'bæntɚ/ *n* [U] conversation that has a lot of jokes in it –**banter** *v* [I]

**bap·tism** /'bæptɪzəm/ *n* [C,U] a Christian ceremony in which someone is touched or covered with water to welcome him/her into the Christian faith –**baptismal** /bæp'tɪzməl/ *adj*

**Bap·tist** /'bæptɪst/ *adj* relating to the Protestant church whose members believe that BAPTISM is only for people old enough to understand its meaning

**bap·tize** /'bæptaɪz, bæp'taɪz/ *v* [T] to perform a BAPTISM

**bar**[1] /bɑr/ *n* **1** a place that serves alcoholic drinks, where you go to meet other people: *We went to that bar called the Owl last night.* **2** the long table inside a bar where alcoholic drinks are sold and served: *O'Keefe stood at the bar, drinking and watching the girls.* **3** a small block of solid material that is longer than it is wide: *a bar of soap | a candy bar* **4 behind bars** in prison **5 the bar** the profession of being a lawyer, or lawyers considered as a group –see also SALAD BAR, SNACK BAR

**bar**[2] *v* **-rred, -rring** [T] **1** to put a piece of wood or metal across a door or window to prevent people from going in or out **2** to officially prevent something from happening or someone from doing something: *Photographers are barred from taking pictures inside the courtroom.*

**bar·bar·i·an** /bɑr'bɛriən/ *n* someone who is considered to be bad because s/he is violent, does not respect people's ideas or property etc.: *You're behaving like a barbarian!* –**barbarous** /'bɑrbərəs/ *adj*

**bar·bar·ic** /bɑr'bærɪk, -'bɛrɪk/ *adj* violent and cruel: *a barbaric act of terrorism*

**bar·be·cue**[1] /'bɑrbɪ,kyu/ *n* **1** a party at which food is cooked and eaten outdoors: *We're having a barbecue on Saturday.* **2** a metal frame for cooking food on outdoors

**barbecue**[2] *v* [T] to cook food outdoors on a BARBECUE

**barbed wire** /,bɑrbd 'waɪɚ/ *n* [U] wire with short sharp points on it, usually used for making fences

**bar·bell** /'bɑrbɛl/ *n* a long piece of metal with heavy round pieces at each end, that you lift to become stronger

**bar·ber** /'bɑrbɚ/ *n* a man whose job is to cut men's hair

**bar·bi·tu·rate** /bɑr'bɪtʃərɪt/ *n* [C,U] a drug that makes people calm or makes them sleep

**bar code** /'. ,./ *n* a group of thin and thick lines on a product that a computer in a store reads to find the price and other information

**bare**[1] /bɛr/ *adj* **1** not covered by clothes: *bare legs/feet/shoulders* –compare NAKED **2** empty, or not covered by anything: *bare and treeless hills* **3** having or including only the least amount of something that you need: *The refugees took only the bare necessities/ essentials.* (=the most necessary things they owned) | *a report giving just the bare facts*

**bare**[2] *v* [T] to let something that is not usually seen be seen by uncovering it: *The dog bared its teeth and growled.*

**bare·back** /'bɛrbæk/ *adj, adv* on a horse without a SADDLE: *riding bareback*

**bare-bones** /'. ,./ *adj* INFORMAL having only the most basic things, information, qualities etc. that are needed: *a bare-bones style of drawing | a bare-bones existence*

**bare·foot** /'bɛrfʊt/ *adj, adv* not wearing any shoes or socks: *We walked barefoot in the sand | barefoot children*

**bare·ly** /'bɛrli/ *adv* **1** hardly existing, happening, true etc.; just: *She was barely 18 when she had her first child. | I could barely stay awake.* **2** used in order to emphasize that something happens immediately after a previous action: *He'd barely sat down when she started asking questions.* –compare RARELY

**barf** /bɑrf/ *v* [I] SPOKEN ⇨ VOMIT[1] –**barf** *n* [U]

**bar·gain**[1] /'bɑrgən/ *n* **1** something bought for less than its usual price: *At $8500, this car is a real bargain.* **2** an agreement to do something in return for something else: *Let's make/ strike a bargain - you'll shop and I'll cook. | The company drove a hard bargain in the negotiations.* (=they made sure the agreement was favorable to them) –**bargainer** *n*

**bargain**[2] *v* [I] **1** to discuss the conditions of a sale, agreement etc.: *The players were bargaining with the owners for higher pay.* **2 more than sb bargained for** INFORMAL more difficult than you expected: *I got more than I bargained for in this job.*

**bargain on** sth *phr v* [T] to expect that something will happen and make it part of your plans: *I hadn't really bargained on things being so expensive there.*

**bar·gain·ing chip** /'... ,./ *n* something that one person or group in a business deal or political agreement has, that can be used in order to gain an advantage in the deal: *The country's oil supply will be used as a bargaining chip in the talks.*

**barge**[1] /bɑrdʒ/ *n* a boat with a flat bottom, used for carrying goods

**barge**[2] *v* [I] INFORMAL to walk somewhere quickly, often pushing against people or things: *Dana barged past the guards at the door.*

**barge in/into** *phr v* [I] to interrupt someone or go into a place when you were not invited:

*Matt's mom barged in on them while they were in bed.*

**bar·i·tone** /'bærəˌtoʊn/ *n* a man who sings in a low voice –compare BASS¹ (2)

**bark¹** /bɑrk/ *v* **1** [I] to make the sound that a dog makes **2** [T] also **bark out** to say something quickly in a loud voice: *"What's your name?" barked the officer.* **3 be barking up the wrong tree** INFORMAL to have a wrong idea or be making a mistake about something: *I realize now that I was barking up the wrong tree.*

**bark²** *n* **1** the sound a dog makes **2** [U] the outer cover on the TRUNK and branches of a tree **3 sb's bark is worse than his/her bite** SPOKEN used in order to say that someone talks more angrily than s/he behaves

**bar·ley** /'bɑrli/ *n* [C,U] a plant that produces a grain used in making food and alcohol

**barn** /bɑrn/ *n* a large building on a farm for storing crops or keeping animals in

**bar·na·cle** /'bɑrnəkəl/ *n* a small sea animal with a hard shell that sticks firmly to rocks, boats etc.

**barn·yard** /'bɑrnyɑrd/ *n* the area on a farm around a BARN

**ba·rom·e·ter** /bə'rɑmətɚ/ *n* an instrument for measuring changes in the air pressure and weather, or for calculating height above sea level –**barometric** /ˌbærə'mɛtrɪk/ *adj*

**ba·roque** /bə'roʊk/ *adj* relating to the very decorated style of art, music, buildings etc. that was common in Europe in the 17th century

**bar·racks** /'bærɪks/ *n* [plural] a group of buildings in which soldiers live

**bar·rage** /bə'rɑʒ/ *n* **1** a lot of actions, sounds, questions etc. that happen very quickly after each other: *a barrage of insults/abuse* **2** the continuous shooting of guns

**bar·rel¹** /'bærəl/ *n* **1** a large container with curved sides and a flat top and bottom: *a barrel for collecting rain water* **2** a unit used for measuring liquids, especially oil, equal to about 42 gallons or 159 liters **3** the part of a gun that the bullets are shot through **4 not be a barrel of laughs** SPOKEN HUMOROUS to not be enjoyable: *The meeting wasn't exactly a barrel of laughs.* **5 have sb over a barrel** INFORMAL to put someone in a situation where s/he is forced to do something: *I didn't really want to work overtime, but my boss had me over a barrel.*

**barrel²** *v* [I] to move very fast in a vehicle: *We were barreling down the road at 90 miles an hour.*

**bar·ren** /'bærən/ *adj* land that is barren cannot grow plants

**bar·rette** /bə'rɛt/ *n* a small plastic or metal object for holding your hair in a particular position

**bar·ri·cade¹** /'bærəˌkeɪd/ *n* something that is put across a road, door etc. for a short time to prevent people from going past

**barricade²** *v* [T] to build a BARRICADE: *Winters barricaded the door with the bookcase.*

**bar·ri·er** /'bæriɚ/ *n* **1** something such as a rule, situation, or problem that prevents or limits what people can do: *an attempt to reduce trade barriers* **2** a type of fence that prevents people from passing through a place: *The police put up barriers to hold back the crowds.* **3** a physical object that separates two areas, groups of people etc.: *The Alps form a natural barrier across Europe.*

**bar·ring** /'bɑrɪŋ/ *prep* unless there are: *Barring any last minute problems, we should finish Friday.*

**bar·ri·o** /'bæriˌoʊ/ *n* an area in a city where many poor, Spanish-speaking people live

**bar·room** /'bɑrˌrum/ *adj* INFORMAL happening in a BAR: *a barroom conversation*

**bar·tend·er** /'bɑrˌtɛndɚ/ *n* someone whose job is to make and serve drinks in a BAR

**bar·ter** /'bɑrtɚ/ *v* [I,T] to exchange goods, work, or services for other goods or services instead of money

**base¹** /beɪs/ *v* [T] to use a city, town etc. as your main place of business or activities: *a law firm based in Denver*

**base sth on/upon sth** *phr v* [T] to do something or develop something using a particular piece of information as the reason or starting point: *Discrimination based on race or sex is forbidden by law.* | *The movie was based on Amelia Earhart's life.*

**base²** *n*

**1** ►LOWEST PART◄ the lowest part or surface of something, especially the part on which it stands or where it is attached to something else: *a black vase with a round base* | *Waves crashed against the base of the cliff.* | *the base of the skull*

**2** ►MAIN PART◄ all the people, companies, money etc. that form the main part of something: *Roosevelt had a broad base of political support.* | *an attempt to improve the economic base* (=things that produce jobs and money) *of inner-city areas* | *The country's manufacturing base* (=companies that make things) *shrank by 15% during the recession.*

**3** ►COMPANY◄ the main place where the work of a company or organization is done: *Microsoft's base is in Redmond.*

**4** ►MILITARY◄ a permanent place where people in the army, navy etc. live and work

**5** ►IDEAS◄ something from which new things or ideas develop or are made: *Both French and Spanish come from a Latin base.*

**6 off base** INFORMAL completely wrong: *The estimate he gave for painting the house seems way off base.*

**7 touch/cover all the bases** to do or think about something thoroughly, so that all possible problems are dealt with: *OK, I think we've covered all the bases - we should be ready for*

*whatever happens.*

**8** ►SUBSTANCE/MIXTURE◄ the main part of something, to which other things can be added: *paints with a water base*

**9** ►BASEBALL◄ one of the four places that a player must touch in order to get a point

**base·ball** /'beɪsbɔl/ *n* **1** [U] an outdoor game in which two teams of nine players try to get points by hitting a ball and running around four bases −see picture on page 472 **2** the ball used in this game

**base·ment** /'beɪsmənt/ *n* a room or rooms in a building that are under the level of the ground −see picture on page 471

**bas·es** /'beɪsiz/ the plural of BASIS

**bash**[1] /bæʃ/ *v* [I,T] **1** to hit someone or something hard, causing pain or damage: *He bashed his toe on the coffee table.* **2** to criticize someone or something a lot: *The local newspaper has recently been bashing the city's court system.*

**bash**[2] *n* INFORMAL a large party: *They're having a big bash over at the club tonight.*

**bash·ful** /'bæʃfəl/ *adj* easily embarrassed; shy

**bash·ing** /'bæʃɪŋ/ *n* [U] **gay-bashing/ liberal-bashing etc.** the act of criticizing or physically attacking a particular person or group of people: *The police say they think the attack was an incident of gay-bashing.*

**ba·sic** /'beɪsɪk/ *adj* **1** forming the main or most necessary part of something: *the basic principles of mathematics* | *There are two basic problems here.* **2** simple or not fully developed: *basic health care for children* −see also BASICS

**ba·si·cally** /'beɪsɪkli/ *adv* **1** SPOKEN used when giving the most important reason or fact about something, or a simple explanation of something: *Well, basically the teacher said he'll need extra help with math.* **2** in the main or most important ways: *Norwegian and Danish are basically the same.*

**ba·sics** /'beɪsɪks/ *n* [plural] **1 the basics** the most important part of something, from which other things, ideas etc. can develop: *a class in the basics of first aid* **2 get/go back to basics** to return to teaching or doing the most important or the simplest part of something: *If you really want to learn this, we'll have to go back to basics.*

**ba·sin** /'beɪsən/ *n* **1** a large area of land that is lower in the center than at the edges: *the Amazon basin* **2** a large bowl, especially one for water

**ba·sis** /'beɪsɪs/ *n, plural* **bases** /'beɪsiz/ **1 on the basis of** because of a particular fact or reason: *Employers may not discriminate on the basis of race or sex.* **2 on a weekly/ informal/freelance etc. basis** happening at a particular time or in a particular way: *Meetings are held on a monthly basis.* **3** the information

or ideas from which something develops: *The fear of Communism* **formed the basis of** *American foreign policy at that time.*

**bask** /bæsk/ *v* [I] **1** to enjoy sitting or lying somewhere warm: *a snake basking in the sun* **2** to enjoy the attention or approval of someone: *She basked in her mother's praise.*

**bas·ket** /'bæskɪt/ *n* **1** a container made of thin pieces of dried plants, wire etc. woven together, used for carrying or holding things: *a basket full of fruit* **2** a net with a hole at the bottom, through which you throw the ball in basketball −see picture at NET

**bas·ket·ball** /'bæskɪt,bɔl/ *n* **1** [U] a game in which two teams of five players try to get points by throwing a ball through a net −see picture on page 472 **2** the ball used in this game

**basket case** /'.. ,./ *n* INFORMAL someone who is so nervous and worried that s/he cannot deal with a situation: *Mom was a complete basket case at our wedding.*

**bass**[1] /beɪs/ *n* **1** a type of electric GUITAR with four strings that plays low notes **2** a man who sings the lowest range of musical notes **3** [U] the lower half of the whole range of musical notes **4** ⇨ DOUBLE BASS −**bass** *adj*: *a bass guitar/drum*

**bass**[2] /bæs/ *n* [C,U] a fish that lives both in the sea and in rivers, lakes etc., or the meat from this fish

**bas·si·net** /,bæsɪ'nɛt/ *n* a small bed that looks like a basket, used for a very young baby

**bas·soon** /bə'sun, bæ-/ *n* a long wooden musical instrument with a low sound, played by blowing into a thin curved metal pipe and pressing buttons

**bas·tard** /'bæstɚd/ *n* **1** SPOKEN a rude word for a man you do not like or are angry with: *You stupid bastard!* **2** OLD-FASHIONED someone whose parents were not married when s/he was born

**bat**[1] /bæt/ *n* **1** a long wooden stick used for hitting the ball in baseball **2** a small animal like a mouse with wings, that flies at night **3 right off the bat** SPOKEN done immediately: *She said yes right off the bat!* **4 like a bat out of hell** SPOKEN very fast: *He came running out of the house like a bat out of hell.* **5 be at bat** to be the person who is trying to hit the ball in baseball

**bat**[2] *v* **-tted, -tting 1** [I] to hit a ball with a bat: *Brent is up to bat next.* (=he will try to hit the ball next) **2 bat your eyes/eyelashes** to open and close your eyes quickly, especially to try to look sexually attractive: *She's always batting her eyelashes at Tom.* **3** [I,T] to hit something lightly with your hand: *kittens batting at balls of paper* **4 without batting an eye** INFORMAL without showing any emotion or guilty feelings: *He used to tell the worst lies* *without batting an eye.* **5 go to bat for sb** INFORMAL to help someone and give him/her support: *Andy really went to bat for me with my manager.* **6 bat a thousand** INFORMAL to be very successful

**batch** /bætʃ/ *n* **1** a group of things or people that you deal with at the same time: *the latest batch of reports* **2** a number of things made at the same time: *a batch of cookies*

**bat·ed** /ˈbeɪt̬ɪd/ *adj* **with bated breath** in a very excited and anxious way: *I waited for her answer with bated breath.*

**bath** /bæθ/ *n, plural* **baths** /bæðz, bæθs/ **1** an act of washing your body in a bathtub: *You need to take a bath before you go to bed. | Dan, will you give the kids a bath tonight?* (=wash them) **2** water that you sit or lie in to wash yourself: *I love to sit and soak in a hot bath. | Lisa ran a bath* (=put water in a bathtub) *for herself.*

**bathe** /beɪð/ *v* **1** [I] to wash your whole body: *Water was scarce, and we only bathed once a week.* **2** [T] to wash someone else, usually in a bathtub **3** [T] to wash an injury with a liquid medicine **4 be bathed in** to be lit in a particular type of light: *The beach sparkled, bathed in the clear light of morning.*

**bathing suit** /ˈbeɪðɪŋ ˌsut/ *n* a piece of clothing you wear for swimming

**bath·robe** /ˈbæθroʊb/ *n* a long loose piece of clothing made of thick cloth, worn especially before or after you take a SHOWER or bath

**bath·room** /ˈbæθrum/ *n* **1** the room in a house where there is a toilet and usually a bathtub or a SHOWER and SINK **2 go to the bathroom** to use the toilet: *Mommy, I have to go to the bathroom!* –compare RESTROOM –see usage note at TOILET

**bath·tub** /ˈbæθtʌb/ *n* a large container you fill with water to sit in and wash yourself in

**ba·tik** /bəˈtik, bæ-/ *n* [C,U] a method of using WAX to put colored patterns on cloth, or cloth that has been colored in this way

**ba·ton** /bəˈtɑn/ *n* **1** a short stick, used by the leader of a group of musicians to direct the music **2** a metal stick that you spin and throw into the air

**bat·tal·ion** /bəˈtælyən/ *n* a large group of soldiers that is formed from several smaller groups

**bat·ter**[1] /ˈbæt̬ɚ/ *n* **1** [C,U] a mixture of flour, eggs, milk etc. used for making cakes, some kinds of bread etc. **2** the person who is trying to hit the ball in baseball –see picture on page 472

**bat·ter**[2] *v* [I,T] to hit someone or something hard, usually in a way that injures or damages him, her, or it: *Waves were battering against the rocks.* –**battering** *n* [C,U]

**bat·tered** /ˈbæt̬ɚd/ *adj* **1** old and slightly damaged: *a battered old paperback book*

**2 battered woman/child** etc. a woman etc. who has been violently hurt by someone that s/he lives with

**bat·ter·y** /ˈbæt̬əri/ *n* **1** an object that provides electricity for something such as a radio or car **2** [U] the crime of beating someone **3** a set of many things of the same type: *a battery of medical tests* **4** several large guns used together

**bat·tle**[1] /ˈbæt̬l/ *n* **1** [C,U] a fight between two armies, especially during a longer war: *the battle of Bunker Hill | Thousands of soldiers were killed in battle.* (–during a war or battle) **2** a situation in which two people or groups compete or argue with each other: *a long and costly legal battle* **3** an attempt to solve a difficult problem: *the battle against racial discrimination*

**battle**[2] *v* [I,T] to try very hard to achieve something when this is very difficult: *My mother battled bravely against breast cancer for years.*

**bat·tle·ground** /ˈbæt̬lˌɡraʊnd/, **bat·tle·field** /ˈbæt̬lˌfild/ *n* **1** a subject that people argue about: *Prayer in schools has become a political battleground.* **2** a place where a battle has been fought

**bat·tle·ship** /ˈbæt̬lˌʃɪp/ *n* a very large ship used in wars

**baud rate** /ˈbɔd ˌreɪt/ *n* TECHNICAL a measurement of how fast information is sent to or from a computer

**bawd·y** /ˈbɔdi/ *adj* bawdy songs, jokes etc. are about sex

**bawl** /bɔl/ *v* [I] INFORMAL to cry in a noisy way: *By the end of the movie I was bawling.*

**bawl** sb ↔ **out** *phr v* [T] INFORMAL to speak angrily to someone because s/he has done something wrong: *Mom bawled me out for not cleaning my room.*

**bay** /beɪ/ *n* **1** a part of the ocean that is enclosed by a curve in the land **2 keep/hold sth at bay** to prevent something dangerous or unpleasant from happening or coming too close: *The dogs kept the intruder at bay.* **3** an area used for a special purpose that is partly separated from the area surrounding it: *the plane's cargo bay*

**bay·o·net** /ˈbeɪənɪt, -ˌnɛt, ˌbeɪəˈnɛt/ *n* a long knife attached to the end of a RIFLE (=type of gun)

**bay·ou** /ˈbaɪu, ˈbaɪoʊ/ *n* a large area of slow moving water in the Gulf states of the US with plants growing out of it –compare SWAMP[1]

**ba·zaar** /bəˈzɑr/ *n* **1** an occasion when a lot of people sell various things to collect money for a good purpose: *the annual church bazaar* **2** a place, usually outdoors, where a lot of different things are sold, especially in the Middle East

**BB gun** /ˈbibi ˌɡʌn/ *n* a gun that uses air pressure to shoot small metal balls

**BBQ** /ˈbɑrbɪˌkyu/ a written abbreviation for BARBECUE

**B.C.** *adv* Before Christ; used in order to show that a date is a particular number of years before the birth of Christ: *The Great Pyramid dates from around 2600 B.C.* –compare A.D.

**be**¹ /bi/ *auxiliary verb*
PRESENT TENSE

| singular | plural |
|---|---|
| I **am**, I'**m** | we **are**, we'**re** |
| you **are**, you'**re** | you **are**, you'**re** |
| he/she/it **is**, | |
| he'**s**/she'**s**/it'**s** | they **are**, they'**re** |

PAST TENSE

| singular | plural |
|---|---|
| I **was** | we **were** |
| you **were** | you **were** |
| he/she/it **was** | they **were** |

| PAST PARTICIPLE | **been** |
|---|---|
| PRESENT PARTICIPLE | **being** |
| NEGATIVE *short forms* | **aren't, isn't, wasn't, weren't** |

**1** used with a PRESENT PARTICIPLE to form the continuous tenses of verbs: *Jane was reading by the fire.* | *Don't talk to me while I'm* (=I am) *working.* **2** used with a PAST PARTICIPLE to form the PASSIVE: *Smoking is not permitted on this flight.* **3** used in order to show what might happen in the future, in CONDITIONAL sentences: *If I were rich, I'd buy myself a Rolls Royce.* **4** used in order to show what you expect will happen in the future: *I'll be* (=I will be) *leaving tomorrow.* **5 is to/are to/were to etc.** FORMAL used in order to say what must happen or what has been arranged: *The children are to go to bed by 8:00.* –see also BEEN

**be**² *v* **1** [I, linking verb] used in order to give the name, date, or position of something or someone, or to describe it in some way: *January is the first month of the year.* | *The concert was last night.* | *Julie wants to be a doctor.* | *Where is Tom?* | *It's* (=it is) *going to be hot today.* | *I'm* (=I am) *hungry.* **2 there is/are/were etc.** used in order to show that something or someone exists: *Last night there were only eight people at choir practice.* | *There's* (=there is) *a hole in the knee of your jeans.* –see also **let sb/sth be** (LET) –compare BECOME

**beach** /bitʃ/ *n* an area of sand or small stones at the edge of an ocean or a lake

**beach ball** /ˈ. ˌ./ *n* a large plastic ball that you fill with air and play with at the beach

**bea·con** /ˈbikən/ *n* a flashing light, used as a signal to warn or guide boats, planes etc.

**bead** /bid/ *n* **1** a small ball of plastic, wood, glass etc., usually used for making jewelry **2** a small drop of liquid: *beads of sweat*

**bead·y** /ˈbidi/ *adj* beady eyes are small and shiny

**bea·gle** /ˈbigəl/ *n* a dog that has smooth fur, large ears, and short legs, sometimes used in hunting

**beak** /bik/ *n* the hard pointed mouth of a bird –see picture at BILL¹

**beak·er** /ˈbikɚ/ *n* a glass cup with straight sides used in a LABORATORY (=place where people do scientific tests)

**beam**¹ /bim/ *n* **1** a line of light shining from something such as the sun, a lamp etc.: *The beam of the flashlight flickered and went out.* | *a laser beam* **2** a long heavy piece of wood or metal used in building houses, bridges etc. **3** a line of energy or light that you cannot see

**beam**² *v* **1** [I] to smile or look at someone in a very happy way: *Uncle Willie beamed at us proudly.* **2** [I,T] to send out energy, light, radio, or television signals etc.: *the first broadcast beamed across the Atlantic*

**bean** /bin/ *n* **1 a)** the seed of one of many types of PEA plants, that is cooked as a food **b)** a POD (=seed case) from one of these plants that is eaten as a vegetable when it is young **2** a plant that produces these beans **3** a seed used in making some types of food or drinks: *coffee beans* **4 not know/care beans (about sth)** to not know anything or care about someone or something: *He doesn't care beans about his family.*

**bear**¹ /bɛr/ *v* **bore, borne, bearing** [T]
**1** ▶BE RESPONSIBLE◀ FORMAL to be responsible for or accept something: *In this case, you must bear some of the blame yourself.*
**2** ▶DEAL WITH STH◀ to bravely accept or deal with a painful or unpleasant situation: *The pain was almost more than she could bear.*
**3 bear a resemblance/relation etc. to sth** to be similar to something, or to be related to someone or something in some way: *The final script bore no resemblance to the one he'd originally written.*
**4 bear (sth) in mind** to consider a fact when you are deciding or judging something: *Bear in mind that this method does not always work.*
**5 bear fruit a)** if a plan or decision bears fruit, it is successful **b)** if a tree bears fruit, it grows it
**6** ▶MARK/NAME◀ FORMAL to have or show a particular mark, name, piece of information etc.: *He bore the scars for the rest of his life.*
**7 can't bear** to dislike something a lot, and get upset or annoyed about it: *She was the kind of person who couldn't bear to throw anything away.*
**8** ▶WEIGHT◀ to support the weight of something: *The ice wasn't thick enough to bear his weight.*
**9 bear with me** SPOKEN used in order to politely ask someone to be patient while you do something: *Bear with me for a minute while I check the files.*
**10 bear right/left** to turn right or left: *Bear*

*left where the road divides.*

**11** ▶BABY◀ FORMAL to give birth to a baby

**12** ▶CARRY◀ FORMAL to carry something: *The seeds are borne long distances by the wind.*
–see also **bring sth to bear (on)** (BRING)

**bear down on** sb/sth *phr v* [T] to move quickly toward someone or something, especially in a threatening way: *We ran as the truck bore down on us.*

**bear** sb/sth **out** *phr v* [T] to show that something is true: *Research bears out the claim that boys receive more attention in the classroom.*

---

**USAGE NOTE  bear, stand, tolerate, put up with**

Use these words to talk about accepting or dealing with a bad situation. **Bear** is more formal, and means that someone is being brave: *The pain was almost too much to bear.* **Stand** is usually used in the phrase "can't stand": *I can't stand this noise!* **Tolerate** and **put up with** mean the same thing, but **tolerate** is more formal: *Why do you put up with being treated so badly?* | *I'm surprised she tolerates his behavior.* ✗ DON'T SAY "support" instead of any of these words. ✗

---

**bear²** *n* **1** a large strong heavy animal with thick fur that eats fruit, insects, and some flesh **2** INFORMAL something very difficult to do or deal with: *That last test was a real bear!*

**bear·a·ble** /'bɛrəbəl/ *adj* a situation that is bearable is difficult or unpleasant but can be accepted or dealt with: *His letters made her loneliness bearable.* –opposite UNBEARABLE

**beard** /bɪrd/ *n* the hair that grows over a man's chin –**bearded** *adj* –see picture at HAIRSTYLE

**bear·er** /'bɛrɚ/ *n* **1** FORMAL someone who owns a legal document such as a PASSPORT **2** LITERARY someone who brings you something such as a message, letter etc: *the bearer of bad news* **3** someone who carries something: *a flag bearer* –see also PALLBEARER

**bear hug** /'. ,./ *n* the action of putting your arms around someone and holding him/her very tightly, especially to show loving feelings

**bear·ing** /'bɛrɪŋ/ *n* **1** have a bearing on sth to have some influence on or to be related to something: *The new information has no bearing on the case.* **2** get/lose your bearings to find out exactly where you are, or to not know exactly where you are: *Apparently the boat lost its bearings in the fog.* **3** [singular, U] the way someone moves or stands: *an elderly man with a military bearing*

**bear·ish** /'bɛrɪʃ/ *adj* relating to a decrease in prices in the STOCK MARKET: *The market has been bearish this week.* –compare BULLISH

**bear mar·ket** /,. '../ *n* a situation in which the

value of SHARES in business decreases –compare BULL MARKET

**beast** /bist/ *n* LITERARY an animal, especially a wild or dangerous one

**beat¹** /bit/ *v* beat, beat, beaten

**1** ▶DEFEAT◀ [T] to defeat someone in a game, competition etc., or to do better than someone or something. *Stein beat me at chess in 44 moves.* | *Hank Aaron finally beat the record for home runs set by Babe Ruth.*

**2** ▶HIT SB◀ [T] to hit someone many times with your hand, a stick etc.: *He used to come home drunk and beat us.*

**3** ▶HIT STH◀ [I,T] to hit something regularly or continuously: *waves beating on/against the shore*

**4** ▶FOOD◀ [I,T] to mix foods together quickly using a fork or a special kitchen tool: *Beat the eggs and add them to the sugar mixture.*

**5** ▶SOUND◀ [I,T] to make a regular sound or movement, or to make something do this: *My heart seemed to be beating much too fast.* | *beating time on the drum* (=making regular sounds for other musicians to follow)

**6** beat around the bush to avoid talking about the main point of a subject, often because it is unpleasant or embarrassing: *Stop beating around the bush, and say it!*

**7** beat the rush INFORMAL to do something early in order to avoid problems because later everyone will be doing it: *Shop early and beat the Christmas rush!*

---

SPOKEN PHRASES

**8** [T] to be better or more enjoyable than something else: *It's not the greatest job, but it beats waitressing for the rest of my life.* | *You can't beat* (=nothing is better than) *San Diego for good weather.*

**9** (it) beats me used in order to say that you cannot understand or do not know something: *"What kind of books does she write?" "Beats me. She makes good money, though."*

**10** beat it! an impolite way to tell someone to leave

---

–see also **off the beaten track/path** (BEATEN) –see usage note at HIT¹

**beat down** *phr v* [I] **1** if the sun beats down, it shines brightly and makes things hot **2** if the rain beats down, it rains very hard

**beat** sb/sth ↔ **off** *phr v* [T] to hit someone who is attacking you until s/he goes away

**beat** sb ↔ **out** *phr v* [T] INFORMAL to defeat someone in a competition: *By winning the game, Notre Dame beat out Georgia Tech for the number one position in the country.*

**beat** sb **to** sth *phr v* [T] to get or do something before someone else is able to: *I called to ask about buying the car, but someone had beaten me to it.*

**beat** sb ↔ **up** *phr v* [T] **1** to hit someone until they are badly hurt: *My boyfriend went crazy and beat me up.* **2 beat yourself up** to blame yourself too much for something bad that has happened: *Don't beat yourself up over this!*

**beat up on** sb *phr v* [T] to hit someone younger or weaker than you until s/he is badly hurt

**beat**[2] *n* **1** one of a series of regular movements, sounds, or hitting actions: *a strong heart beat | the beat of the drum* **2 a)** [singular] the main pattern of strong musical notes that are repeated in a piece of music: *The song has a beat you can dance to.* **b)** one of the notes in this pattern **3** [singular] a subject or an area of a city that someone is responsible for as his/her job: *journalists covering the political beat | a police officer on the beat* (=working in his/her area)

**beat**[3] *adj* INFORMAL very tired: *You look beat!*

**beat·en** /ˈbitʰn/ *adj* **off the beaten track/ path** far away from places that people usually visit: *a little hotel off the beaten track*

**beat·er** /ˈbitɚ/ *n* **1** a kitchen tool that is used for mixing foods together **2 wife/child beater** someone who hits his wife or his/her child

**beat·ing** /ˈbitɪŋ/ *n* **take a beating** to be defeated or criticized very badly: *The soccer team took a beating in the semifinals.*

**beat-up** /ˌ. ˈ.◂ / *adj* INFORMAL old and slightly damaged: *a beat-up old car*

**beaut** /byut/ *n* [singular] SPOKEN something that is very good: *That last catch was a beaut.*

**beau·ti·cian** /byuˈtɪʃən/ *n* OLD-FASHIONED ➪ HAIRDRESSER

**beau·ti·ful** /ˈbyuṭəfəl/ *adj* **1** a woman, girl, or child who is beautiful is very attractive to look at: *the most beautiful woman in the world | What a beautiful baby!* **2** very attractive to look at or good to listen to: *a beautiful gray wool dress | beautiful music | The views from the mountaintop were beautiful.*

**USAGE NOTE** beautiful, pretty, handsome, good-looking, cute

Use these words to say that someone is attractive. **Beautiful** is a very strong word meaning "extremely attractive": *a beautiful movie star.* **Pretty, handsome, good-looking,** and **cute** are all less strong ways of describing attractive people, and are used more often than **beautiful**. Use **pretty** only for describing younger women and girls. Use **handsome** for describing men, although we sometimes use it for describing attractive older women. Use **good-looking** for both men and women. Use **cute** for babies, children, and young men and women.

**beau·ty** /ˈbyuṭi/ *n* **1** [U] a quality that things, places, or people have that makes them very attractive to look at: *a woman of great beauty | the beauty of America's national parks* **2** [U] a quality that something such as a poem, piece of music etc. has that gives you a feeling of pleasure: *the beauty of Keats' poetry* **3** INFORMAL something that is very good: *His new car's a beauty.* **4 the beauty of** a good quality that makes something especially suitable or useful: *The beauty of this type of exercise is that you can do it anywhere.* **5** OLD-FASHIONED a woman who is very beautiful

**beauty sa·lon** /ˈ.. ˌ./, **beauty parlor** /ˈ.. ˌ../ *n* ➪ SALON

**bea·ver** /ˈbivɚ/ *n* an animal with thick fur, a flat tail, and sharp teeth that it uses to cut down trees for building DAMs

**be·bop** /ˈbibɑp/ *n* a style of JAZZ music

**be·came** /bɪˈkeɪm/ *v* the past tense of BECOME

**be·cause** /bɪˈkɔz, -ˈkʌz/ *conjunction* **1** for the reason that: *You can't go, because you're too young.* **2 because of** as a result of a particular thing or of someone's actions: *We weren't able to have the picnic because of the rain.* −see also **just because** (JUST)

**beck·on** /ˈbɛkən/ *v* [I,T] to move your hand or arm to show that you want someone to move toward you: *He beckoned her to join him. | He beckoned to her.*

**be·come** /bɪˈkʌm/ *v* **became, become, becoming 1** [linking verb] to begin to be something, or to develop in a particular way: *The weather had become warmer. | In 1960 Kennedy became the first Catholic president. | It is becoming harder to find good housing for low-income families. | She started to become anxious about her son ✗ DON'T SAY "She started to be anxious about her son." ✗* **2 what/whatever became of...?** used in order to ask what happened to a person or thing: *Whatever became of Grandma's dishes?* **3** [T] FORMAL to be suitable for someone: *I don't think that dress becomes you, dear.*

**USAGE NOTE** become, get, and go

Use these words to talk about situations or states that develop. **Become** is more formal: *He's becoming very successful. | Prague has become popular with tourists.* **Get** is more informal: *It's getting dark outside. | I'm getting hungry.* Use **go** in some fixed expressions: *Have you gone crazy?*

**be·com·ing** /bɪˈkʌmɪŋ/ *adj* OLD-FASHIONED becoming clothes or styles look attractive on you

**bed**[1] /bɛd/ *n* **1** [C,U] a piece of furniture for sleeping on: *an old brass bed | I was lying in bed reading. | She looked like she had just gotten out of bed. | What time do you usually put the kids to bed? | Jamie usually goes to bed around seven o'clock. | Sara, have you made your bed yet?* (=pulled the sheets etc. into place) *| Come* *on, it's **time for bed.*** (=time to go to sleep) **2 go to bed with sb** INFORMAL to have sex with someone **3** the ground at the bottom of the ocean, a river, or a lake **4** a special area of ground that has been prepared for plants to grow in: *rose beds* **5** a layer of something that forms a base on which other things are put: *potato salad on a bed of lettuce* **6 sb got up on the wrong side of the bed** SPOKEN said when someone is slightly angry or annoyed for no particular reason

**bed**[2] *v* **-dded, -dding**

**bed down** *phr v* [I] to make yourself comfortable and sleep in a place where you do not usually sleep: *I'll just bed down on the sofa.*

**bed and break·fast** /ˌ. . ˈ../ **B&B** *n* a small comfortable hotel like a house where you are served breakfast

**bed·clothes** /ˈbɛdklouz, -klouðz/ *n* [plural] ⇨ BEDDING

**bed·ding** /ˈbɛdɪŋ/ *n* [U] **1** the sheets, BLANKETs etc. that you put on a bed **2** material that an animal sleeps on

**bed·lam** /ˈbɛdləm/ *n* [singular, U] a lot of wild noisy activity in a place: *The classroom was bedlam.*

**bed·pan** /ˈbɛdpæn/ *n* a container used as a toilet by someone who has to stay in bed

**be·drag·gled** /bɪˈdɹæɡəld/ *adj* looking dirty, wet, and messy: *bedraggled hair*

**bed·rid·den** /ˈbɛdˌrɪdn/ *adj* unable to get out of bed because you are old or very sick

**bed·room** /ˈbɛdrum/ *n* a room with a bed in it, where you sleep

**bed·side** /ˈbɛdsaɪd/ *n* the area around a bed: *His family has been at his bedside all night.* | *a bedside table/lamp*

**bed·spread** /ˈbɛdsprɛd/ *n* a large piece of cloth that covers the top of a bed, including the PILLOWs

**bed·stead** /ˈbɛdstɛd/ *n* the frame of a bed

**bed·time** /ˈbɛdtaɪm/ *n* [C,U] the time when you usually go to bed: *It's way past your bedtime!*

**bee**

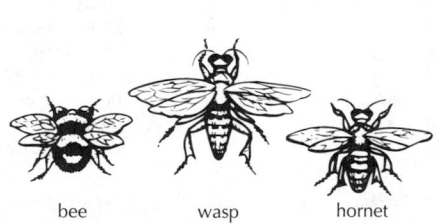

bee        wasp        hornet

**bee** /bi/ *n* a yellow and black insect that flies, makes HONEY, and can sting you – see also SPELLING BEE

**beech** /bitʃ/ *n* [C,U] a tree with smooth gray branches and dark green leaves, or the hard wood of this tree

**beef**[1] /bif/ *n* **1** [U] meat from a cow **2** INFORMAL a complaint: *The guy had a beef with the manager and yelled at him for about 15 minutes.* – see usage note at MEAT

**beef**[2] *v* [I] INFORMAL to complain: *The kids are beefing about their homework assignment.*

**beef** sth ↔ **up** *phr v* [T] INFORMAL to improve something, especially to make it stronger or more interesting: *Security around the White House has been beefed up since the attack.*

**beef·y** /ˈbifi/ *adj* a beefy man is big, strong, and usually fat

**bee·hive** /ˈbihaɪv/ *n* ⇨ HIVE

**bee·line** /ˈbilaɪn/ *n* **make a beeline for sth** INFORMAL to go quickly and directly toward someone or something: *The bear made a beeline for the woods.*

**been** /bɪn/ *v* **1** the PAST PARTICIPLE of BE **2 have/has been** used in order to say that someone has gone to a place and come back: *Sandy has just been to Japan.* | *Have you been to see Katrina's new house?* – see usage note at GO[1] – see picture at GO[1]

**beep** /bip/ *v* **1** [I] if a machine beeps, it makes a short high sound: *The computer beeps when you push the wrong key.* **2** [I,T] if a horn beeps or you beep it, it makes a loud sound **3** [T] to telephone someone who has a BEEPER – **beep** *n*

**beep·er** /ˈbipɚ/ *n* a small machine that you carry with you that makes a sound to tell you to telephone someone; PAGER

**beer** /bɪr/ *n* [C,U] an alcoholic drink made from grain, or a glass, can, or bottle of this drink – see also ROOT BEER

**bees·wax** /ˈbizwæks/ *n* [U] **1** a substance produced by BEEs, used in making CANDLEs and furniture polish **2 none of your beeswax** SPOKEN a way of telling someone that something is private and s/he does not have the right to know about it

**beet** /bit/ *n* a dark red round root that is cooked and eaten as a vegetable

**bee·tle** /ˈbitl/ *n* an insect with a hard round back that covers its wings

**be·fit** /bɪˈfɪt/ *v* **-tted, -tting** [T] FORMAL to be suitable or seem right for someone: *a funeral befitting a national hero* – **befitting** *adj*

**be·fore**[1] /bɪˈfɔr/ *prep* **1** earlier than something: *I usually shower before having breakfast.* | *Denise got there before me.* | *He arrived the day before yesterday.* (=two days ago) **2** ahead or in front of someone or something: *There were ten people before us in line.* | *The priest knelt before the altar.* **3** in a more important position than someone or something: *His wife and children come before* (=are more important than) *his job.* **4** at a particular distance in front of a place as you travel toward it: *Turn right just before the stop light.* **5** in a situation where something is being considered by someone so that a decision can be made: *The case is now before the Supreme Court.*

**before**[2] *adv* at an earlier time: *They'd met before, at one of Sandra's parties.*

**before**[3] *conjunction* **1** earlier than the time when something happens: *It will be several days before we know the results.* | *John wants to talk to you before you go.* **2** so that something bad does not happen: *You'd better lock your bike before it gets stolen.* **3 before you know it** SPOKEN used in order to say that something will happen very soon: *We'd better get going - it'll be dark before you know it.*

**be·fore·hand** /bɪˈfɔrˌhænd/ *adv* before something else happens or is done: *You should never eat a piece of fruit without washing it beforehand.*

**be·friend** /bɪˈfrɛnd/ *v* [T] FORMAL to become someone's friend, especially someone who needs your help

**be·fud·dled** /bɪˈfʌdld/ *adj* completely confused: *Annie looked a little befuddled.*

**beg** /bɛg/ *v* **-gged, -gging** **1** [I,T] to ask for something in an urgent or anxious way: *I begged him to stay, but he wouldn't.* | *He sank to his knees and begged for forgiveness.* **2** [I,T] to ask someone for food, money etc. because you are very poor: *homeless families begging for food* **3** [I] if an animal such as a dog begs, it asks for food **4 I beg your pardon** SPOKEN **a)** used in order to ask someone politely to repeat something: *"It's 7:00." "I beg your pardon?" "It's 7:00."* **b)** FORMAL used in order to say you are sorry: *Oh, I beg your pardon, did I hurt you?* **c)** FORMAL used in order to show that you strongly disagree with or disapprove of something someone has said: *"You never had to work hard in your life!" "I beg your pardon - I believe that I have!"*

**beg·gar** /ˈbɛgɚ/ *n* **1** someone who lives by asking people for food and money **2 beggars can't be choosers** SPOKEN used in order to say that if you need something, you have to accept what you are given, even if it is not what you would like

**be·gin** /bɪˈgɪn/ *v* **began, begun, beginning** **1** [I,T] to start doing or feeling something, or to start to happen or exist: *The meeting will begin at 10:00.* | *He began his career 30 years ago.* | *Let's begin with exercise 5.* | *I began to realize that he was lying.* ✗ DON'T SAY "I became to realize." ✗ **2 to begin with a)** used in order to introduce the first or most important point: *To begin with, photography is not really an art form at all.* **b)** used in order to say what something was like at the start: *If his hands weren't dirty to begin with, they certainly are now.* −see usage note at START[1]

**be·gin·ner** /bɪˈgɪnɚ/ *n* someone who has just started to do or learn something

**be·gin·ning** /bɪˈgɪnɪŋ/ *n* [C usually singular] the start or first part of something: *the beginning of the book* | *Placement tests are given at the beginning of the year.* | *The whole trip was a disaster from beginning to end.*

**be·gin·nings** /bɪˈgɪnɪŋz/ *n* [plural] the early part or early signs of something that later develops and becomes bigger or more important: *From its beginnings as a small rural shop, the store grew to be the US's second largest chain.*

**be·grudge** /bɪˈgrʌdʒ/ *v* [T] to feel upset or JEALOUS because of something that you think is unfair: *Honestly, I don't begrudge him his success.*

**be·guile** /bɪˈgaɪl/ *v* [T] to persuade or trick someone into doing something, especially by saying nice things to him/her

**be·gun** /bɪˈgʌn/ *v* the PAST PARTICIPLE of BEGIN

**be·half** /bɪˈhæf/ *n* **on behalf of sb/on sb's behalf** if you do something on behalf of someone, you do it for him/her or instead of him/her: *He agreed to speak on her behalf.*

**be·have** /bɪˈheɪv/ *v* **1** [I] to do or say things in a particular way: *Lions in a zoo do not behave like lions in the wild.* | *You behaved bravely in a very difficult situation.* **2** [I,T] to do or say things in a way that people think is good or correct: *Tom was quieter than his brother and knew how to behave.* | *If you behave yourself, you can stay up late.*

**be·hav·ior** /bɪˈheɪvyɚ/ *n* [U] **1** the way that a person or animal does or says things, or a particular example of this: *Can TV shows affect children's behavior?* | *Your behavior is not acceptable in my classroom!* **2** the things that an object, substance etc. normally does: *the behavior of cancer cells*

**be·head** /bɪˈhɛd/ *v* [T] to cut someone's head off

**be·hind**[1] /bɪˈhaɪnd/ *prep* **1** at or toward the back of something: *I was driving behind a truck on the freeway.* | *The liquor store is right behind* (=just behind) *the supermarket.* **2** not as successful or advanced as someone or something else: *The Lakers were four points behind the Celtics at half time.* | *Work on the new building is three months behind schedule.* **3** supporting a person, idea etc.: *Congress is behind the President on this issue.* **4** responsible for something, or causing something to happen: *The police believe a local gang is behind the killings.*

**behind**[2] *adv* **1** at or toward the back of something: *Several other runners followed close behind.* **2** in the place where someone or something was before: *I got there and realized I'd left the tickets behind.* | *Barb stayed behind to wait for Tina.* **3 be/get behind** to be late or slow in doing something: *I'm a little behind; I think I'll stay late and finish this.*

**behind**³ *n* INFORMAL the part of your body that you sit on

**be·hold** /bɪˈhoʊld/ *v* [T] LITERARY to see something −**beholder** *n*

**beige** /beɪʒ/ *n* [U] a pale yellow-gray color −**beige** *adj*

**be·ing** /ˈbiɪŋ/ *n* **1** a living thing, such as a person: *strange beings from outer space* **2 come into being** to begin to exist: *Their political system came into being in the early 1900s.*

**be·lat·ed** /bɪˈleɪtɪd/ *adj* happening or arriving late: *a belated birthday card*

**belch** /bɛltʃ/ *v* **1** [I] to let air from your stomach come out in a noisy way through your mouth **2** [T] to produce a lot of smoke, fire etc. from a particular area: *factories belching blue smoke*

**be·lie** /bɪˈlaɪ/ *v* [T] FORMAL to make someone have a false idea about something: *Her strong voice belied the horror of her story.*

**be·lief** /bəˈlif/ *n* **1** [singular, U] the feeling that something is definitely true or definitely exists: *the medieval belief that the sun went around the earth* | *a child's belief in Santa Claus* **2** [singular] the feeling that someone or something is good and can be trusted: *a strong belief in the importance of education* | **Contrary to popular belief** (=unlike what most people believe), *eating carrots does not improve your eyesight.* **3** [C usually plural] an idea that you think is true: *religious beliefs*

**be·liev·a·ble** /bəˈlivəbəl/ *adj* able to be believed: *a believable love story* −opposite UNBELIEVABLE

**be·lieve** /bəˈliv/ *v* **1** [T] to be sure that something is true or that someone is telling the truth: *Young children often believe (that) animals can understand them.* | *Believe me, I've been there, and it's not nice.* | *He said Chris started the fight, but no one believed him.* ✗ DON'T SAY "... no one believed in him." ✗ **2** [T] to think that something is true, although you are not completely sure: *I believe (that) she'll be back on Monday.* | *The jury believed him to be guilty.* **3** [I] to have religious faith

SPOKEN PHRASES

**4 can't/don't believe sth** said when you are very surprised or shocked: *I can't believe you lied to me!* **5 would you believe it** said when you are surprised or slightly angry about something: *Would you believe it, he even remembered my birthday!* **6 believe it or not** said when you are going to say something that is true but surprising: *Believe it or not, I kissed him.*

**believe in** *phr v* [T] **1** to be sure that something or someone definitely exists: *Do you believe in ghosts?* **2** to think that someone is good, or to trust him, her, or it: *He believes in the democratic system.* | *If you believe in yourself, you can do anything.*

**be·liev·er** /bəˈlivɚ/ *n* **1** someone who believes that a particular idea or thing is very good: *I'm a firm/great believer in healthy eating.* **2** someone who believes in a particular religion

**be·lit·tle** /bɪˈlɪtl/ *v* [T] FORMAL to say or do things that make someone or something seem less important: *I don't want to belittle her efforts, but it's not enough.*

**bell** /bɛl/ *n* **1** a hollow metal object shaped like a cup that makes a sound when it is hit by a piece of metal that hangs down inside it: *church bells* | *The bell rang for school to start.* **2** an electronic piece of equipment that makes a noise as a signal or warning: *We ran out of the classroom as soon as the bell rang.* **3 alarm/warning bells** something that makes you realize that there may be a problem with something you are doing −see also **ring a bell** (RING²)

**bell bot·toms** /ˈ. ˌ../ *n* [plural] a pair of pants with legs that are wide at the bottom

**bel·lig·er·ent** /bəˈlɪdʒərənt/ *adj* ready to fight or argue −**belligerence** *n* [U]

**bel·low** /ˈbɛloʊ/ *v* [I,T] to shout something in a very loud low voice

**bell pep·per** /ˌ. ˈ../ *n* ⇨ PEPPER¹

**bel·ly** /ˈbɛli/ *n* INFORMAL **1** your stomach, or the part of your body between your chest and the top of your legs **2 go belly up** to fail: *The store went belly up in 1969.*

**belly but·ton** /ˈ.. ˌ../ *n* INFORMAL the small hollow or raised place in the middle of your stomach −see picture at BODY

**be·long** /bɪˈlɔŋ/ *v* [I] **1** to be in the right place or situation: *Please put the chair back where it belongs.* | *Books like that don't belong in the classroom.* **2** to feel happy and comfortable in a place, or with a group of people: *I'm going back to Colorado where I belong.*

**belong to** *phr v* [T] **1** [belong to sth] to be a member of a group or organization: *Mary and her husband belong to the yacht club.* **2** [belong to sb] to be the property of someone: *Who does this umbrella belong to?*

**be·long·ings** /bɪˈlɔŋɪŋz/ *n* [plural] the things that you own, especially things that you are carrying with you

**be·loved** /bɪˈlʌvd, bɪˈlʌvɪd/ *adj* LITERARY loved very much −**beloved** *n* [singular]

**be·low**¹ /bɪˈloʊ/ *prep* **1** in a lower place or position than something, or on a lower level than something: *Can you read the writing below the picture?* | *A corporal is below a captain in rank.* **2** less than a particular number, amount etc.: *It was 20° below zero outside.* | *Sales for this year are well below last year's.* −compare UNDER¹

**be·low**² *adv* **1** in a lower place or position, or on a lower level: *Jake lives in the apartment be-*

*low.* **2** less than a particular number: *It was 10° below outside.* (=10° below zero in temperature) **3** on a later page, or lower on the same page: *For more information, see below.*

**belt**[1] /bɛlt/ *n* **1** a band of leather, cloth etc. that you wear around your waist **2** a circular band of material such as rubber that moves parts of a machine: *The car's fan belt is loose.* **3** a large area of land that has particular qualities: *the farm belt states* (=states with lots of farms) −see also SEAT BELT

**belt**[2] *v* [T] INFORMAL **1** to hit someone or something hard **2** also **belt** sth ↔ **out** to sing a song loudly

**belt·way** /'bɛlt⁀weɪ/ *n* **the Beltway a)** a road that goes around a city in order to keep traffic away from the center **b)** a group of people in large US cities, who are involved in government: *a discussion inside/outside the Beltway*

**be·mused** /bɪ'myuzd/ *adj* slightly confused

**bench**[1] /bɛntʃ/ *n* **1** a long seat for two or more people, for sitting on outdoors **2** **the bench a)** the job of a judge in a court: *He was appointed to the bench in 1974.* **b)** the place where a judge sits in a court

**bench**[2] *v* [T] to make a sports player stay out of a game for a period of time

**bench·mark** /'bɛntʃmɑrk/ *n* something used as a standard to measure another number, rate, level etc. against: *7.5% is the current benchmark set by banks for loan rates.*

**bend**[1] /bɛnd/ *v* bent, bent, bending [I,T] **1** to move a part of your body so that it is no longer straight or so that you are no longer standing upright: *He bent down/over to tie his shoelace. | Bend your knees slightly.* **2** to make something straight have a curved shape, or to become curved in shape: *Heavy rains had bent the wheat to the ground.* **3** **bend over backwards** to try very hard to help: *The neighbors bent over backwards to help when we moved into the house.* **4** **bend the rules** to allow someone to do something that is not normally allowed

**bend**[2] *n* a curve in something, especially a road or river: *The creek goes around a bend by the farm.*

**be·neath**[1] /bɪ'niθ/ *prep* FORMAL **1** under or below something: *the warm sand beneath her feet* **2** not good enough for someone: *She seemed to think that talking to us was beneath her.*

**beneath**[2] *adv* under or below something: *He stood on the bridge, looking at the water beneath.*

**ben·e·dic·tion** /ˌbɛnə'dɪkʃən/ *n* a prayer that asks God to protect and help someone

**ben·e·fac·tor** /'bɛnəˌfæktɚ/ *n* FORMAL someone who gives money to someone else or helps him/her

**ben·e·fi·cial** /ˌbɛnə'fɪʃəl/ *adj* good or useful: *The agreement will be **beneficial to** both groups.*

**ben·e·fi·ci·ar·y** /ˌbɛnə'fɪʃiˌɛri, -'fɪʃəri/ *n* FORMAL **1** someone who gets an advantage because of something: *Inner city residents will be the chief beneficiaries* (=will get the most advantages) *of this policy.* **2** someone who gets money when someone dies

**ben·e·fit**[1] /'bɛnəfɪt/ *n* **1** money or help that you get from something such as insurance or the government, or as part of your job: *The company provides medical benefits. | social security benefits* **2** [C,U] something that gives you an advantage, that helps you, or that has a good effect: *The aid program has brought lasting benefits to the area. | Liu Han translated what he had said for my benefit.* (=in order to help me) **3** a performance, concert etc. that is done in order to make money for a CHARITY (=organization that helps people) **4** **give sb the benefit of the doubt** to believe someone even though it is possible that s/he is lying

**benefit**[2] *v* -fited, -fiting, also -fitted, -fitting **1** [T] to help someone, or to be useful to him/her: *These policy changes mainly benefit cities in the South.* **2** [I] to get an advantage or help from something: *The whole nation **benefits by/ from** having skilled and educated workers.*

**be·nev·o·lent** /bə'nɛvələnt/ *adj* FORMAL kind, generous, and helpful

**be·nign** /bɪ'naɪn/ *adj* **1** TECHNICAL not likely to hurt you or cause CANCER: *a benign tumor* **2** FORMAL kind and unlikely to harm anyone −compare MALIGNANT

**bent**[1] /bɛnt/ *v* the past tense and PAST PARTICIPLE of BEND

**bent**[2] *adj* **1** **be bent on** to be determined to do something or have something: *Mendez was bent on getting a better job.* **2** curved and no longer flat or straight: *The grass was bent where he'd been lying on it.* **3** **bent out of shape** SPOKEN angry or annoyed: *Hey, don't get all bent out of shape!*

bent

**bent**[3] *n* [singular] a natural skill or ability: *Rebecca has an artistic bent.*

**be·queath** /bɪ'kwiθ, bɪ'kwið/ *v* [T] FORMAL to arrange for someone to get something that belongs to you after your death

**be·quest** /bɪ'kwɛst/ *n* FORMAL money or property that you BEQUEATH to someone

**be·rate** /bə'reɪt/ *v* [T] FORMAL to speak angrily to someone because s/he has done something wrong

**be·reaved**[1] /bə'rivd/ *adj* FORMAL having had someone you love die −**bereavement** *n* [C,U]

**bereaved**[2] *n* **the bereaved** the person or people whose friend or relative has died

**be·reft** /bə'rɛft/ *adj* FORMAL completely without something: *bereft of all hope*

**be·ret** /bə'reɪ/ *n* a soft round hat that is almost flat

**ber·ry** /'bɛri/ *n* one of several types of small soft fruits with very small seeds

**ber·serk** /bə'sɔk, -'zɔk/ *adj* **go berserk** INFORMAL to become very angry and violent in a crazy way. *The guy went berserk and started hitting Paul.*

**berth** /bɔθ/ *n* **1** a place to sleep on a train or boat **2** a place near land where a ship can be kept

**be·set** /bɪ'sɛt/ *v* beset, beset, besetting [T] FORMAL to make someone have a lot of trouble or problems: *The family was beset by financial difficulties.*

**be·side** /bɪ'saɪd/ *prep* **1** next to or very close to someone or something: *Gary sat down beside me.* | *a cabin beside the lake* **2** used in order to compare two people or things: *Pat looked big and clumsy beside her sister.* **3 be beside the point** to not be important compared to something else: *"I'm not hungry." "That's beside the point, you need to eat!"* **4 be beside yourself (with)** to feel a particular emotion very strongly: *The boy was beside himself with fear.*

**be·sides¹** /bɪ'saɪdz/ *adv* **1** SPOKEN said when giving another reason: *I wanted to help her out. Besides, I needed the money.* **2** in addition to: *Besides going to college, she works 15 hours a week.*

**besides²** *prep* in addition to something or someone: *Who's going to be there besides David and me?*

---

**USAGE NOTE besides and except**

Use **besides** to mean "in addition to someone or something": *Is there anything to drink besides coffee?* | *Who is coming besides your parents?* **Except** means that someone or something is not included: *I remembered to pack everything except my toothbrush.*

---

**be·siege** /bɪ'sidʒ/ *v* [T] FORMAL **1 besieged by** surrounded by a lot of people: *a rock star besieged by fans* **2** to send a lot of letters, ask a lot of questions, or annoy someone often: *The radio station was besieged by letters of complaint.* **3** to surround a place with an army

**best¹** /bɛst/ *adj* [the superlative of "good"] better in quality, skill etc. than anyone or anything else: *the best player on the team* | *What's the best way to get to El Paso?* | *It's one of the best books I've ever read.* | *my best friend* (=the one I know and like the most)

**best²** *adv* [the superlative of "well"] **1** to the greatest degree: *Helene knows him best.* | *Which song do you like best?* **2** in a way that is better

than any other: *It works best if you oil it thoroughly first.*

**best³** *n* [singular] **1** someone or something that is better than any others: *Which stereo is the best?* **2** a situation or result that is better than any other you could achieve: *All parents want the best for their children.* **3 do your best** to try very hard to achieve something: *I did my best, but I still didn't pass.* **4 at best** used in order to emphasize that something is not very good, even when you consider it in the best possible way: *At best, sales have been good but not great.* **5 at your/its best** performing as well or as effectively as you are able to: *The movie shows Hollywood at its best.* **6 make the best of sth** to accept a bad situation and do what you can to make it better: *It's not going to be fun, but we'll have to make the best of it.* **7 be for the best** to be the best thing to do or happen, although you do not like it: *She's upset that they broke up, but it's probably for the best.* —see study note on page 457

**best⁴** *v* [T] LITERARY to defeat someone

**bes·tial** /'bɛstʃəl, 'bis-/ *adj* behaving like an animal, especially in a cruel way —**bestiality** /ˌbɛstʃi'æləti, ˌbis-/ *n* [U]

**best man** /ˌ. './ *n* [singular] the man at a wedding who stands beside and helps the man who is getting married

**be·stow** /bɪ'stoʊ/ *v* [T] FORMAL to give someone something, especially something important

**best·sell·er** /ˌbɛst'sɛlə/ *n* a new book that a lot of people have bought —**best-selling** *adj*

**bet¹** /bɛt/ *v* bet, bet, betting [I,T] to risk money on the result of a race, game etc.: *Brad bet 50 bucks on the Bears to win.* | *Dad bet Mom ten dollars that I wouldn't pass my driver's test.*

SPOKEN PHRASES
**1 I/I'll bet a)** said when you think something is true or likely to happen: *I'll bet that made her mad!* | *I bet it will rain tomorrow.* **b)** said in order to show that you agree with someone or understand how s/he feels: *"I was furious." "I bet you were!"* **c)** said in order to show that you do not believe someone: *"I was really worried about you." "Yeah, I'll bet."* **2 you bet (your life)!** said in order to agree with someone, or to say that you are definitely going to do something: *"Are you coming along?" "You bet!"*

**bet²** *n* **1** an agreement to risk money on the result of a race, game etc.: *Higgins had a bet on the World Series.* **2** the money that you risk: *a $10 bet* **3 your best bet** SPOKEN said in order to give someone advice about the best thing to do: *Your best bet would be to take Highway 9.* **4 a good bet** something that is likely to be useful or successful: *The earrings seemed like a good bet for a birthday present.* **5 a safe bet** something that seems almost certain: *It's a pretty safe bet that the Arnolds will be at that party.*

**bet·cha** /ˈbɛtʃə/ SPOKEN NONSTANDARD a short form of "bet you": *I betcha I can run faster than you.*

**be·tray** /bɪˈtreɪ/ v [T] **1** to be disloyal to a friend, your country etc., for example by telling a secret: *Kaplan went to jail rather than betray his friends.* **2** to show an emotion you were trying to keep hidden: *Keith's voice betrayed his nervousness.*

**be·tray·al** /bɪˈtreɪəl/ n [C,U] the act of betraying your country, a friend etc.

**bet·ter**¹ /ˈbɛtɚ/ adj **1** [the comparative of "good"] higher in quality, or more useful, suitable, interesting etc. than something or someone else: *He's applying for a better job.* | *The weather is* **a lot better than** *it was last week.* | *The Mexican place across the street has* **much better** *food.* | *I'll* **feel better** *if I can talk to someone about this.* **2** [the comparative of "well"] **a)** less sick or painful than before: *He had the flu, but he's much better now.* | *I hope your sore throat* **gets better.** | *Dana's* **feeling** *a little* **better** *since he started taking the penicillin.* **b)** completely well again after being sick: *I don't think you should go swimming until you're better.* **3 get better** to improve: *Her tennis game is getting a lot better.* **4 have seen better days** INFORMAL to be in a bad condition: *The sofa had definitely seen better days.*

**bet·ter**² adv [the comparative of "well"] **1** to a higher degree; more: *Which one do you like better?* | *Marilyn knows New York a lot* **better than** *I do.* **2** in a better way: *Tina speaks French better than her sister.* **3 better late than never** used in order to say that it is better for something to happen late rather than not happen at all **4 the sooner/bigger etc., the better** used in order to emphasize that something should happen as soon as possible, that it should be as big as possible etc.: *She liked hot baths - the hotter the better.* –see study note on page 457

SPOKEN PHRASES

**5 had better (do sth) a)** used in order to say that you or someone else should do something: *It's getting late, you had better get changed.* **b)** said when threatening someone: *You'd better not tell Dad about this.* **6 be better (to do sth)** said when giving advice about what someone should do: *It's better if she doesn't stand for too long.*

–see also BETTER OFF

**bet·ter**³ n **1 get the better of sb a)** if a feeling gets the better of you, you do not control it when you should: *Finally, his curiosity got the better of him and he read Dee's letter.* **b)** to defeat someone: *Jack usually manages to get the better of his opponents.* **2 for the better** in a way that improves the situation: *Smaller classes are definitely* **a change for the better.**

**bet·ter**⁴ v [T] FORMAL to achieve something that is higher in quality, amount etc. than something else –**betterment** n [U]

**better off** /ˌ.. ˈ./ adj **1** more successful, richer, or having more advantages than you did before: *The more prepared you are, the better off you'll be.* | *Most businesses in the area are better off than they were 10 years ago.* **2 be better off doing sth** SPOKEN said when giving advice about what someone should do: *You're better off leaving early.* (=should leave early)

**be·tween**¹ /bɪˈtwin/ prep **1** in or into the space or time that separates two things, people, events etc.: *Jay was sitting between Kate and Lisa.* | *You know I don't want you to eat between meals.* –see also IN-BETWEEN **2** used in order to show a range of amounts, distances, times etc.: *Why don't you come over between seven and eight?* | *The project will cost between 10 and 12 million dollars.* ✗ DON'T SAY "between 10 to 12 million dollars." ✗ **3** used in order to show that something is divided or shared by two people, places, or things: *We had about two loads of laundry between us.* | *Linda and Dave split a milkshake between them.* **4** used in order to show a relationship between two people, things, events etc.: *What's the difference between the two computers?* | *Trade relations between the countries have improved.* **5** used in order to show how two places are connected: *the highway between Fresno and Visalia* **6 between you and me** SPOKEN said before you tell someone a secret or a private opinion: *Between you and me, I thought she looked ugly.*

USAGE NOTE **between** and **among**

Use **between** to talk about being in the middle of two people, things, times etc.: *They arrived between 2:30 and 3:00.* Use **among** to talk about being in the middle of three or more people, things etc.: *I found this old photo among her letters.*

**between**² adv in or into the space that separates two things, people etc., or in or into the time that separates two events: *two yards with a fence between* –see also IN-BETWEEN

**bev·eled** /ˈbɛvəld/ adj beveled glass or wood has edges that slope slightly

**bev·er·age** /ˈbɛvrɪdʒ, ˈbɛvərɪdʒ/ n FORMAL a drink: *alcoholic beverages*

**bev·y** /ˈbɛvi/ n **a bevy of** a large group, especially of people: *a bevy of artists*

**be·ware** /bɪˈwɛr/ v [I,T] used in order to warn someone to be careful: *Beware of the dog!*

**be·wil·dered** /bɪˈwɪldɚd/ adj very confused and not sure what to do or think –**bewilderment** n [U]

**be·wil·der·ing** /bɪˈwɪldərɪŋ/ adj making you feel very confused: *a bewildering number of choices*

**be·witched** /bɪ'wɪtʃt/ adj so interested in or attracted by someone or something that you cannot think clearly –**bewitching** adj

**be·yond**[1] /bɪ'yɑnd/ prep **1** on or to the farther side of something: *The ocean was beyond the dunes.* **2** not within someone's ability or skill: *an apple just beyond my reach | Chemistry was beyond my understanding.* **3** used when something is not possible: *In just six years, the town had changed beyond all recognition.* (=it could not be recognized) *| I think that this time the car is beyond repair.* (=it cannot be repaired) **4** more than a particular amount, level, or limit: *The population has grown beyond estimated levels.* **5** later than a particular time, date etc.: *The ban has been extended beyond 1998.* **6 it's beyond me why/what etc.** SPOKEN said when you do not understand something: *It's beyond me why they ever got married at all.* **7** besides: *Santa Fe doesn't have much industry beyond tourism.*

**beyond**[2] adv **1** on or to the farther side of something: *a view from the mountains with the plains beyond* **2** later than a particular time, date etc.: *planning for the year 2000 and beyond*

**bi·as** /'baɪəs/ n, plural **biases** /'baɪəsiz/ [C,U] an opinion about whether something is good or bad that influences how you deal with it: *We believe the court's decision reveals a bias against Hispanics.* –**bias** v [T]

**bi·ased** /'baɪəst/ adj **1** unfairly influenced by someone's opinion: *a biased report* **2** unfairly preferring one person or group over another: *My mother liked mine best, but of course she's biased!* –opposite UNBIASED

**bib** /bɪb/ n a piece of cloth that you tie under a baby's chin to protect his/her clothes while s/he eats

**bi·ble** /'baɪbəl/ n **1 the Bible** the holy book of the Christian religion **2** a copy of this book **3** a useful and important book on a particular subject: *This textbook is the medical student's bible.*

**bib·li·og·ra·phy** /ˌbɪbli'ɑgrəfi/ n a list of all the books and articles used in the preparation of another book, or a list of books and articles on a particular subject

**bi·cen·ten·ni·al** /ˌbaɪsɛn'tɛniəl/ n the day or year exactly 200 years after an important event: *The US had its bicentennial in 1976.*

**bi·ceps** /'baɪsɛps/ n, plural **biceps** the large muscle on the front of your upper arm

**bick·er** /'bɪkɚ/ v [I] to argue about something that is not very important: *The kids were bickering about/over who would sleep in the top bunk.*

**bi·cy·cle**[1] /'baɪsɪkəl/ n a vehicle with two wheels that you ride by pushing the PEDALs with your feet

**bicycle**[2] v [I] ⇨ BIKE[2]

**bid**[1] /bɪd/ n **1** an offer to do some work for someone at a particular price: *The company*

accepted the lowest **bid for** the project. **2** an attempt to achieve or gain something: *Clinton's successful bid for the presidency in 1992* **3** an offer to pay a particular price for something: *a bid of $50 for the plate*

**bid**[2] v **bid, bid, bidding 1** [I,T] to offer to pay a particular price for something: *Foreman bid $150,000 for an antique table.* **2** [I] to offer to do some work for someone at a particular price: *Four aerospace companies were invited to bid for the contract.*

**bid**[3] v **bade** or **bid, bid** or **bidden, bidding** [T] LITERARY **1 bid sb good morning/goodbye etc.** to say good morning etc. to someone **2** to tell someone to do something

**bid·ding** /'bɪdɪŋ/ n [U] **1** the activity of offering to pay a particular price for something, or offering to do some work **2 do sb's bidding** LITERARY to do what someone tells you to do

**bide** /baɪd/ v **bide your time** to wait until the right time to do something

**bi·en·ni·al** /baɪ'ɛniəl/ adj happening once every two years

**bi·fo·cals** /'baɪˌfoʊkəlz, baɪ'foʊkəlz/ n [plural] a pair of special glasses made so that you can look through the upper part to see things that are far away and through the lower part to see things that are close

**big** /bɪg/ adj **-gger, -ggest 1** of more than average size, amount etc.; large: *big baggy t-shirts | There's a big age difference between them. | That boy gets bigger every time I see him.* **2** important or serious: *The big game is on Friday. | The company lost a big contract this year.* **3** INFORMAL older: *This is my big sister.* **4** doing something to a large degree: *I've never been a big baseball fan. | Both the girls are big eaters.* (=they eat a lot) **5** successful or popular: *The song was a big hit. | Microsoft is big in the software market. | I knew I'd never make it big as a professional golfer.* **6 be big on** SPOKEN to like doing something very much or to be very interested in it: *Jenny's big on health food these days.*

> **USAGE NOTE big and large**
>
> Use **big** and **large** with countable nouns to describe size. **Big** is more informal than **large**: *She was wearing a really big hat. | a large company.* Use **large** to describe amounts: *a large amount of information* ✗ DON'T SAY "a big amount." ✗ Use **big** to describe how important something is: *a big problem/issue | I have big news!* ✗ DON'T SAY "a large problem." ✗

**big·a·my** /'bɪgəmi/ n [U] the crime of being married to two people at the same time –**bigamist** n –**bigamous** adj

**Big Ap·ple** /ˌ. '../ n INFORMAL New York City

**big broth·er** /ˌ. ˈ../ *n* any person, organization, or system that seems to control people's lives and restrict their freedom

**big busi·ness** /ˌ. ˈ../ *n* [U] very large companies that are considered as a group that influences the politics, the industry etc. of a country

**big deal** /ˌ. ˈ./ *n* SPOKEN **1** an important event or situation: *Marian hates cooking, so getting invited for dinner is a big deal!* **2** said when you do not think something is as important as someone else thinks it is: *His idea of a pay raise is giving me 50¢ more an hour - big deal!* **3 no big deal** said in order to show that you are not upset or angry about something that has just happened: *"I'm really sorry about all this!" "No big deal."*

**Big Dip·per** /ˌ. ˈ../ *n* a group of seven bright stars seen in the northern sky in the shape of a bowl with a long handle

**big·gie** /ˈbɪgi/ *n* **no biggie** SPOKEN ⇨ **no big deal** (BIG DEAL)

**big gov·ern·ment** /ˌ. ˈ.../ *n* [U] government, when people think it is controlling their lives too much

**big·head·ed** /ˈbɪghɛdɪd/ *adj* someone who is bigheaded thinks s/he is better than other people

**big-league** /ˈ. ˌ./ *adj* INFORMAL ⇨ MAJOR-LEAGUE

**big mouth** /ˈ. ˌ./ *n* INFORMAL someone who tells people things that should be secret

**big name** /ˌ. ˈ./ *n* a famous person, especially an actor, musician etc.: *a club where all the big names from Hollywood go* —**big name** *adj*: *big name Broadway entertainers*

**big·ot** /ˈbɪgət/ *n* someone who is BIGOTED

**big·ot·ed** /ˈbɪgətɪd/ *adj* having such strong opinions about race, religion, or politics that you are unwilling to listen to other people's opinions

**big·ot·ry** /ˈbɪgətri/ *n* [U] BIGOTED behavior or beliefs

**big shot** /ˈ. ˌ./ *n* INFORMAL someone who is very important or powerful in business or politics: *They could have hired one of the big shots, but they chose Miller because he works hard.*

**big-tick·et** /ˌ. ˈ../ *adj* very expensive: *Customers aren't buying big ticket items like CD players.*

**big time**[1] /ˈ. ˌ./ *adv* SPOKEN said in order to emphasize something that has just been said: *"So, I'm in trouble, huh?" "Yeah, big time!"*

**big time**[2] *n* **the big time** INFORMAL the position of being very famous or important, for example in politics or sports: *The coaches don't think he's ready for the big time yet.* —**big-time** *adj*: *big-time drug dealers*

**big·wig** /ˈ. ˌ./ *n* INFORMAL an important person: *one of the bigwigs in the movie business*

**bike**[1] /baɪk/ *n* INFORMAL **1** a bicycle: *kids riding their bikes in the street | We went for a bike ride around the lake today.* **2** a MOTORCYCLE

**bike**[2] *v* [I] to travel on a bicycle

**bik·er** /ˈbaɪkɚ/ *n* someone who rides a MOTORCYCLE, especially as part of a group

**bi·ki·ni** /bɪˈkini/ *n* a piece of clothing in two parts that women wear for swimming

**bi·lat·er·al** /baɪˈlætərəl/ *adj* **bilateral agreement/treaty etc.** an agreement etc. between two groups or countries: *bilateral Mideast peace talks* —**bilaterally** *adv*

**bile** /baɪl/ *n* [U] **1** a liquid produced by the LIVER to help the body DIGEST food **2** LITERARY strong anger and hate

**bi·lin·gual** /baɪˈlɪŋgwəl/ *adj* **1** able to speak two languages **2** containing or expressed in two languages: *a bilingual dictionary*

bill

beak

bill

**bill**[1] /bɪl/ *n* **1** a list of things you have bought or services you have used and the amount you have to pay for them: *I have to remember to pay the phone bill this week.* **2** a piece of paper money: *a ten-dollar bill* **3** a plan for a law, written down for a government to decide on: *a Senate tax bill* **4** a wide or long beak on a bird such as a duck —see also **foot the bill** (FOOT[2])

**bill**[2] *v* [T] **1** to send a bill to someone: *They've billed me for things I didn't buy.* **2 bill sth as** to advertise something in a particular way: *The boxing match was billed as "the fight of the century."*

**bill·board** /ˈbɪlbɔrd/ *n* a very large sign used for advertising, especially next to a road

**bill·fold** /ˈbɪlfould/ *n* ⇨ WALLET

**bil·liards** /ˈbɪlyɚdz/ *n* [plural] a game like POOL in which the balls go into the holes in a special order

**bil·lion** /ˈbɪlyən/ *number, plural* **billion** or **billions** 1,000,000,000: *$7 billion | Billions of dollars have been invested.* —**billionth** *number*

**bill of rights** /ˌ. . ˈ./ *n* **1** an official written list of the most important rights of the citizens of a country **2 the Bill of Rights** this document in the US

**bil·low** /ˈbɪlou/ *v* [I] to swell like a sail because of the wind: *clouds billowing overhead*

**billy goat** /ˈbɪli ˌgout/ *n* INFORMAL a word meaning a male goat, used especially when speaking to children

**bim·bo** /ˈbɪmbou/ *n* SLANG an insulting word meaning an attractive but stupid woman

**bi·month·ly** /baɪˈmʌnθli/ *adj, adv* happening or being done every two months, or twice each month: *a bimonthly magazine | The magazine is published bimonthly.*

**bin** /bɪn/ *n* a large container for storing things

**bi·na·ry** /'baɪˌnɛri, 'baɪnəri/ *adj* TECHNICAL
**1 the binary system** a system of counting, used in computers, in which only the numbers 0 and 1 are used **2** consisting of two things or parts

**bind**[1] /baɪnd/ **bound, bound, binding** *v* [T]
**1 a)** to tie someone so that s/he cannot move: *His legs were bound with rope.* **b)** to tie things firmly together or wrap something tightly with cloth, rope etc.: *sticks bound together with twine* **2** also **bind together** to form a strong relationship between two people, countries etc.: *Religious belief binds the community together.* **3** to make someone obey something such as a law or promise: *The countries are bound by the treaty to reduce the number of nuclear weapons.* **4** to fasten the pages of a book together and put them in a cover

**bind**[2] *n* an annoying or difficult situation: *I'm so mad at him for putting me in this bind!*

**bind·er** /'baɪndə/ *n* a cover for holding loose sheets of paper, magazines etc. together

**bind·ing**[1] /'baɪndɪŋ/ *adj* a contract, agreement etc. that is binding must be obeyed: *The contract isn't binding until you sign it.*

**binding**[2] *n* **1** the cover of a book **2** [U] material sewn along the edge of a piece of cloth for strength or decoration

**binge**[1] /bɪndʒ/ *n* INFORMAL a short period of time when you do too much of something: *He went on a drinking binge last week.* (=drank too much alcohol)

**binge**[2] *v* [I] to eat a lot of food in a very short time, especially as a result of an EATING DISORDER

**bin·go** /'bɪŋgoʊ/ *n* [U] a game in which you win if a set of numbers chosen by chance are the same as a line of numbers on your card

**bin·oc·u·lars** /bɪ'nɑkyələz, baɪ-/ *n* [plural] a pair of glasses like short TELESCOPEs used for looking at distant objects

**bi·o·chem·is·try** /ˌbaɪoʊ'kɛmɪstri/ *n* [U] the scientific study of the chemistry of living things **—biochemist** *n* **—biochemical** /ˌbaɪoʊ'kɛmɪkəl/ *adj*

**bi·o·de·grad·a·ble** /ˌbaɪoʊdɪ'greɪdəbəl/ *adj* a material, product etc. that is biodegradable is able to change or decay naturally so that it does not harm the environment: *Most plastic is not biodegradable.*

**bi·og·ra·pher** /baɪ'ɑgrəfə/ *n* someone who writes a BIOGRAPHY

**bi·og·ra·phy** /baɪ'ɑgrəfi/ *n* [C,U] a book about a particular person's life, or all books like this considered as a group

**bi·o·log·i·cal** /ˌbaɪə'lɑdʒɪkəl/ *adj* relating to BIOLOGY: *a biological process*

**biological war·fare** /...,... '../ *n* [U] methods of fighting a war in which living things such as BACTERIA are used in order to harm the enemy

**bi·ol·o·gy** /baɪ'ɑlədʒi/ *n* [U] the scientific study of living things **—biologist** *n*

**bi·o·pic** /'baɪoʊˌpɪk/ *n* a movie that tells the story of someone's life

**bi·op·sy** /'baɪˌɑpsi/ *n* the act of taking cells, skin etc. from someone who is sick, in order to learn more about his/her disease

**bi·o·tech·nol·o·gy** /ˌbaɪoʊtɛk'nɑlədʒi/ *n* [U] the use of living things such as cells and BACTERIA in science and industry to make drugs, chemicals etc.

**bi·par·ti·san** /baɪ'pɑrtəzən/ *adj* consisting of or representing two political parties: *a bipartisan committee in the Senate*

**bi·ped** /'baɪpɛd/ *n* TECHNICAL any animal with two legs, including humans

**bi·plane** /'baɪpleɪn/ *n* an old-fashioned type of plane with two sets of wings

**birch** /bətʃ/ *n* [C,U] a tree with BARK like paper that comes off easily, or the wood of this tree

**bird** /bəd/ *n* **1** an animal with wings and feathers that lays eggs and can usually fly **2 give/flip sb the bird** SLANG to put your middle finger up to make a very offensive sign at someone **3 sth is for the birds** SPOKEN said when you think something is useless or stupid: *Working in this heat is for the birds!* see also **early bird** (EARLY[1]) **kill two birds with one stone** (KILL[1])

**bird-brained** /'. ,./ *adj* INFORMAL silly or stupid

**bird·ie** /'bədi/ *n* INFORMAL ⇨ SHUTTLECOCK

**bird of prey** /ˌ. . './ *n* any bird that kills other birds and small animals for food

**bird·seed** /'bədsid/ *n* [U] a mixture of seeds for feeding birds

**bird's eye view** /ˌ. . './ *n* a view from a very high place: *From our hotel room, we had a bird's eye view over the city.*

**birth** /bəθ/ *n* **1 give birth (to)** if a woman gives birth, she produces a baby from her body: *Jo gave birth to a baby girl at 6:20 a.m.* **2** [C,U] the time when a baby comes out of its mother's body: *He died soon after the birth of their child. | The baby weighed 7 pounds at birth.* **3** [U] someone's family origin: *Her grandfather was French by birth.* **4 the birth of sth** the time when something begins to exist: *the birth of the new democracy*

**birth cer·tif·i·cate** /'. .,.../ *n* an official document that has information about your birth printed on it

**birth con·trol** /'. .,./ *n* [U] various methods of controlling the number of children you have

**birth·day** /'bəθdeɪ/ *n* the date on which someone was born, usually celebrated each year: *a birthday present/card | When is your birthday? |*

*Happy Birthday!* (=said to someone on his/her birthday)

**birth·mark** /ˈbɚθmɑrk/ *n* an unusual mark on someone's body at birth

**birth·rate** /ˈbɚθreɪt/ *n* the number of births for every 100 or 1000 people during a particular time

**bis·cuit** /ˈbɪskɪt/ *n* a type of bread that is baked in small round shapes

**bi·sect** /ˈbaɪsɛkt, baɪˈsɛkt/ *v* [T] TECHNICAL to divide something into two equal parts –**bisection** /ˈbaɪˌsɛkʃən, baɪˈsɛkʃən/ *n* [U]

**bi·sex·u·al**[1] /baɪˈsɛkʃuəl/ *adj* **1** sexually attracted to both men and women **2** having qualities or features of both sexes

**bisexual**[2] *n* someone who is sexually attracted to both men and women

**bish·op** /ˈbɪʃəp/ *n* a priest with a high rank who is in charge of the churches and priests in a large area

**bi·son** /ˈbaɪsən/ *n* TECHNICAL ⇨ BUFFALO

**bit**[1] /bɪt/ *n*
**1** **a (little) bit** slightly, but not very: *I'm a little bit tired.*
**2** **quite a bit** a fairly large amount: *He's willing to pay us quite a bit of money.*
**3** ▶SMALL PIECE◀ a small amount or piece of something: *The floor was covered in tiny bits of glass.*
**4** ▶COMPUTER◀ a unit for measuring the amount of information a computer can use
**5** **to bits** into small pieces: *I tore the letter to bits and burned it.*
**6** ▶TIME◀ a short amount of time: *We'll talk about the Civil War in just a bit.* | *I could see that she was learning, bit by bit.* (=gradually)
**7** **every bit as** just as: *Ray was every bit as good-looking as his brother.*
**8** ▶TOOL◀ a part of a tool for cutting or making holes
**9** ▶HORSE◀ a piece of metal that is put in the mouth of a horse to control its movements

**bit**[2] *v* the past tense of BITE

**bitch**[1] /bɪtʃ/ *n* **1** SPOKEN a rude word for a woman who you dislike: *You bitch!* **2** **be a bitch** SLANG to cause problems or be difficult: *I love this sweater but it's a bitch to wash.* **3** a female dog

**bitch**[2] *v* [I] IMPOLITE to complain or say unkind things about someone or something: *He's been bitching about the fact that Jimmy owes him money all day.*

**bitch·y** /ˈbɪtʃi/ *adj* SLANG tending to complain or say unkind things about people

**bite**[1] /baɪt/ *v* **bit, bitten, biting 1** [I,T] to cut or crush something with your teeth: *He bit a huge piece out of the cookie.* | *I had just bitten into the apple.* | *Be careful of the dog; he bites.* | *She bites her fingernails.* | *Marta got bitten by a snake.* **2** **bite sb's head off** SPOKEN

to speak to someone very angrily, especially when there is no good reason to do this: *I asked if she wanted help, and she bit my head off!* **3** **bite the dust** INFORMAL to die, fail, be defeated, or stop working: *My Chevy finally bit the dust last week.* **4** **bite the bullet** to decide to do something even though it is unpleasant: *We had to bite the bullet and buy a car we couldn't really afford.* **5** **bite off more than you can chew** to try to do more than you are able to do **6** [I] to have the effect that was intended, especially a bad effect: *The new tobacco taxes have begun to bite.* **7** if a fish bites, it takes food from a hook

bite

**bite**[2] *n* **1** the act of cutting or crushing something with your teeth, or the piece of food that is cut: *Can I have a bite of your steak?* | *He took a bite of the cheese.* **2** a wound made when an animal or insect bites you: *I'm covered in mosquito bites!* **3** **a bite (to eat)** INFORMAL a quick meal: *We can grab a bite at the airport before we go.* **4** an occasion when a fish takes the food from a hook

**bite-size** /ˈ. ˌ./ **bite-sized** *adj* the right size to fit in your mouth easily: *bite-size pieces of chicken*

**bit·ing** /ˈbaɪtɪŋ/ *adj* **1** a biting wind is cold and unpleasant **2** biting criticisms or remarks are very unkind

**bit·ten** /ˈbɪtⁿn/ *v* the PAST PARTICIPLE of BITE

**bit·ter** /ˈbɪtɚ/ *adj* **1** very angry because you feel something bad or unfair has happened to you: *Kyle's bitter voice showed how upset he was.* **2** having a strong taste, like coffee without sugar **3** air that is bitter is cold and unpleasant: *a bitter wind* –see usage note at TEMPERATURE **4** **to/until the bitter end** until the end, even though unpleasant things happen: *The UN stayed in the war zone until the bitter end.* –**bitterly** *adv* –**bitterness** *n* [U]

**bit·ter·sweet** /ˌbɪtɚˈswit◀/ *adj* pleasant, but sad too: *a bittersweet goodbye*

**bi·week·ly** /baɪˈwikli/ *adj, adv* **1** happening or being done every two weeks **2** twice each week: *a biweekly meeting* | *We now meet biweekly.*

**bi·zarre** /bɪˈzɑr/ *adj* very unusual and strange: *We had some very bizarre discussions last night.* | *a bizarre coincidence*

**blab** /blæb/ *v* **-bbed, -bbing** [I] SPOKEN to talk too much, especially when you say things you are not supposed to: *Marty will blab on and on if you let him.*

**blab·ber·mouth** /ˈblæbɚˌmaʊθ/ *n* SPOKEN a word meaning someone who BLABs, used especially by children

**black¹** /blæk/ *adj* **1** having a color that is darker than every other color, like the sky at night: *a black dress* | *The mountains looked black against the sky.* | *It was* **pitch black** (=completely dark)*, and I fell over the chair.* **2 Black** someone who is black has very dark skin, and is from a family that was originally from Africa: *Over half the students here are Black.* **3** black coffee does not have milk in it: *Do you take your coffee black?* **4 black sheep** someone who is different from the rest of a group or family, especially in a way that is considered to be bad – **blackness** *n* [U]

**black²** *n* **1** [U] a black color **2** also **Black** someone who has very dark skin, and whose family originally came from Africa **3 in black and white a)** in writing: *The rules are there in black and white for everybody to see.* **b)** in a very simple way, as if there are clear differences between good and bad: *Dad sees things in black and white, so for him, what we're doing is wrong.* **4 be in the black** to have more money than you owe: *We're in the black for the first time in 3 years.* –opposite **be in the red** (RED²)

---

**USAGE NOTE black**

Using **black** as a noun when talking about someone's race is usually offensive. However, it is acceptable in some situations, for example when you are comparing racial groups: *Relations between blacks and whites in the area are good.* Using **Black** as an adjective is less offensive: *a Black man.* However, **African** is usually the best choice of adjective: *an African-American woman.*

---

**black³** *v*
   **black out** *phr v* [I] to become unconscious: *Sharon blacked out while she was swimming.*

**black and blue** /ˌ. . './ *adj* skin that is black and blue has dark marks on it because it has been injured

**black belt** /'. ˌ./ *n* **1** a high rank in some types of Asian fighting sports, especially JUDO and KARATE **2** someone who has this rank

**black·ber·ry** /'blæk,bɛri/ *n* a very sweet black or dark purple BERRY

**black·bird** /'blækbɚd/ *n* a common American and European bird, the male of which is completely black

**black·board** /'blækbɔrd/ *n* a dark smooth surface on the wall, usually in a school, which you write on with CHALK

**black·en** /'blækən/ *v* [I,T] to become black, or to make something do this: *Smoke had blackened the kitchen walls.*

**black eye** /ˌ. './ *n* skin around someone's eye that becomes dark because it has been hit

**black·head** /'blækhɛd/ *n* a small spot on someone's skin that has a black center

**black hole** /ˌ. './ *n* TECHNICAL an area in outer space into which everything near it is pulled, including light

**black hu·mor** /ˌ. '../ *n* [U] jokes, funny stories etc. that deal with the unpleasant parts of human life

**black·jack** /'blækdʒæk/ *n* a card game, usually played for money, in which you try to get as close to 21 points as possible

**black·list** /'blæk,lɪst/ *v* to make a list of people, countries, products etc. that are not approved of, and should therefore be avoided: *Ritter is blacklisted in most of the nightclubs in Phoenix.* –**blacklist** *n*

**black mag·ic** /ˌ. '../ *n* [U] magic that is believed to use the power of the Devil for evil purposes

**black·mail** /'blækmeɪl/ *n* the practice of making someone do what you want by threatening to tell secrets about him/her –**blackmail** *v* [T] –**blackmailer** *n*

**black mar·ket** /ˌ. '..◂/ *n* the system by which people illegally buy and sell goods, foreign money etc. that are difficult to obtain: *The drug might be available* **on the black market.**

**black·out** /'blækaʊt/ *n* **1** a period of time when the lights do not work, because the electricity supply has failed: *The cause of the blackout in New York is not known yet.* **2** an occasion when you suddenly become unconscious: *He's suffered from blackouts since he came back from the war.* –see also **news blackout** (NEWS)

**black·smith** /'blæksmɪθ/ *n* someone who makes and repairs things made of iron, especially HORSESHOEs

**black-tie** /'. ˌ./ *adj* a party or social event that is black-tie is one at which you have to wear formal clothes

**black·top** /'blæktɑp/ *n* [C,U] the thick black substance used for covering roads

**blad·der** /'blædɚ/ *n* the organ in the body that stores waste liquid until it is ready to leave the body

**blade** /bleɪd/ *n* **1** the flat cutting part of a knife, tool, or weapon: *The blade needs to be kept sharp.* | *razor blades* **2** a leaf of grass or a similar plant **3** the flat wide part of an OAR, PROPELLER etc.

**blah¹** /blɑ/ *adj* SPOKEN **1** not having an interesting taste, appearance, character etc.: *The color of the walls is kind of blah.* **2** slightly sick or unhappy: *I feel really blah today.*

**blah²** *n* [U] blah, blah, blah SPOKEN said when you do not want to say or repeat something because it is boring: *Oh, you know Michelle; it's blah, blah, blah about her kids all the time.*

**blame¹** /bleɪm/ *v* [T] **1** to say or think that someone is responsible for something bad: *It's not fair to blame Charlie - he didn't know anything.* | *Mom* **blamed** *herself* **for** *Keith's problems.* | *Don't try to blame this* **on** *me!* **2** I

**don't blame you/them etc.** SPOKEN said when you think it was right or reasonable for someone to do what s/he did: *I don't blame her for not letting her kids see that movie!*

**blame**² *n* [U] responsibility for a mistake or for something bad: *Because she's the older child, she usually gets the blame.* | *You shouldn't have to take the blame* (=say it was your fault) *if Rader did it.*

**blame·less** /'bleɪmlɪs/ *adj* not guilty of anything bad: *blameless behavior*

**blanch** /blæntʃ/ *v* **1** [I] to become pale because you are afraid or shocked: *Nick blanched at the sight of blood.* **2** [T] to put vegetables, fruit, or nuts into boiling water for a short time

**bland** /blænd/ *adj* **1** without any excitement, strong opinions, or special character: *bland TV shows* **2** bland food has very little taste: *bland cheese*

**blank**¹ /blæŋk/ *adj* **1** without any writing, print, or recorded sound: *a blank sheet of paper* **2** go blank a) to be suddenly unable to remember something: *My mind went blank as I stood up to speak.* b) to stop showing any images, writing etc.: *The screen suddenly went blank.* **3** showing no expression, understanding, or interest: *a blank look*

**blank**² *n* **1** an empty space on a piece of paper, where you are supposed to write a word or letter: *Fill in the blanks on the application form.* **2** a CARTRIDGE (=container for a bullet in a gun) that has an explosive but no bullet: *The police were only firing blanks.* —**blankness** *n* [U]

**blank check** /ˌ. './ *n* [singular] **1** a check that has been signed but has not had the amount written on it **2** INFORMAL the authority to do whatever you want, without any limits

**blan·ket**¹ /'blæŋkɪt/ *n* **1** a heavy cover that keeps you warm in bed **2** LITERARY a thick covering of something: *a blanket of snow on the mountains*

**blanket**² *adj* **blanket statement** a statement that affects everyone or includes all possible cases: *You shouldn't make blanket statements about all single parents.*

**blank·ly** /'blæŋkli/ *adv* in a way that shows no expression, understanding, or interest: *When I walked in, he was staring blankly at the wall.*

**blank verse** /ˌ. './ *n* [U] poetry that does not RHYME

**blare** /blɛr/ *v* [I,T] to make a very loud unpleasant noise: *blaring horns* | *a radio blaring out music* —**blare** *n* [singular]

**bla·sé** /blɑˈzeɪ/ *adj* not worried or excited about things that most people think are important, impressive etc.: *The fans are more blasé about the playoffs this year than they were last year.*

**blas·phe·mous** /'blæsfəməs/ *adj* showing disrespect for God or people's religious beliefs: *a blasphemous book*

**blas·phe·my** /'blæsfəmi/ *n* [C,U] something you say or do that is insulting to God or to people's religious beliefs —**blaspheme** /blæsˈfim, 'blæsfim/ *v* [I,T]

**blast**¹ /blæst/ *n* **1** an explosion, or the very strong movement of air that it causes: *The blast knocked him forward.* **2** [singular] SPOKEN an enjoyable and exciting experience: *We had a blast at Mitch's party.* **3** full blast as strongly, loudly, or fast as possible: *When I got home, she had the TV on full blast.* **4** a sudden strong movement of wind or air: *a blast of icy air* **5** a sudden very loud noise: *a trumpet blast*

**blast**² *v* **1** [I,T] to break a large amount of rock into pieces using explosives: *Workers had to blast through the side of the mountain to build the road.* **2** [I,T] also **blast out** to produce a lot of loud noise, especially music: *How can you hear anything with the radio blasting?* **3** [T] to attack a place or person with bombs or large guns: *Two gunmen blasted their way into the building.* **4** [T] to criticize something very strongly: *The President's remarks were quickly blasted by Democratic leaders.*

**blast off** *phr v* [I] if a SPACECRAFT blasts off, it leaves the ground

**blast·ed** /'blæstɪd/ *adj* SPOKEN said in order to show you are annoyed: *Next year there'll be two of these blasted forms to fill out.*

**blast-off** /'. ./ *n* [U] the moment when a SPACECRAFT leaves the ground: *10 seconds till blast-off!*

**bla·tant** /'bleɪtⁿnt/ *adj* very noticeable and offensive: *blatant discrimination* —**blatantly** *adv*

**blaze**¹ /bleɪz/ *v* [I] to burn or shine very brightly and strongly: *a fire blazing in the fireplace* | *a Christmas tree blazing with lights*

**blaze**² *n* [singular] **1** a very bright light or color: *a blaze of sunshine* **2** the strong bright flames of a fire: *Fire officials continued searching for the cause of the blaze.* | *a cheerful blaze in the fireplace* **3** in a blaze of glory/publicity receiving a lot of praise or public attention: *In 1987, in a blaze of publicity, Maxwell launched a new newspaper.*

**blaz·er** /'bleɪzɚ/ *n* a suit JACKET (=piece of clothing like a short coat) without matching pants: *a wool blazer*

**blaz·ing** /'bleɪzɪŋ/ *adj* **1** extremely hot: *a blazing summer day* **2** very bright because of strong emotions: *blazing eyes*

**bleach**¹ /blitʃ/ *n* [U] a chemical used in order to make things white or to kill GERMs

**bleach**² *v* [T] to make something white by using chemicals or the light of the sun: *bleached hair*

**bleach·ers** /'blitʃɚz/ *n* [plural] a structure in a GYM or a park, that has several rows of seats where people sit to watch sports games —compare GRANDSTAND

**bleak** /blik/ *adj* **1** without anything to make you feel cheerful or hopeful: *Without a job, Carlo's future seemed bleak.* **2** cold and without any pleasant or comfortable features: *a bleak November day* –**bleakness** *n* [U]

**blear·y** /'blɪri/ *adj* unable to see clearly because you are tired: *Sam jumped up, looking bleary-eyed.* –**blearily** *adv*

**bleat** /blit/ *v* [I] to make the sound that a sheep, goat, or young cow makes –**bleat** *n*

**bleed** /blid/ *v* **bled** /bled/, **bled, bleeding**
**1** [I] to lose blood, especially from an injury: *The cut on his forehead was bleeding again.*
**2** [T] to make someone pay a lot of money for something, especially when s/he does not have much money: *Many poor countries are being bled dry by debt.* (=they have to pay all their money to repay debts)

**blem·ish** /'blemɪʃ/ *n* a small mark that spoils the appearance of something or someone: *a small blemish on her cheek* –**blemished** *adj*

**blend**[1] /blend/ *v* [I,T] **1** to thoroughly mix two or more foods together to form a single substance: *Blend the eggs with the sugar.* **2** to combine two different qualities, things etc. so that you cannot see the difference between them: *a story that blends fact and fiction* | *These immigrants did not blend easily into American society.*

**blend in** *phr v* [I] to be similar to other things or people: *Jessie never blended in with the other children at school.*

**blend**[2] *n* a combination: *the right blend of sunshine and soil for growing grapes*

**blend·er** /'blendɚ/ *n* a small electric machine that you use to mix liquids together, or to make soft foods more liquid

**bless** /bles/ *v* [T] **1 bless you** SPOKEN said when someone SNEEZES **2** to protect, help, and make good things happen to someone: *Thank you, and God bless you.* **3** to ask God to make something holy: *The priest blessed the bread and wine.* **4 bless him/her etc.** SPOKEN said in order to show that you like someone or are pleased by something s/he has done: *"Donna cleaned up." "Oh, bless her heart."* **5 be blessed with** to be lucky enough to have something, especially a good quality: *I'm blessed with good eyesight.*

**bless·ed** /'blesɪd/ *adj* holy, or loved by God

**bless·ing** /'blesɪŋ/ *n* **1** something that is good or helps you: *The rain was a real blessing after all that heat.* **2** [U] someone's approval or encouragement for a plan, activity etc.: *We want to get married, Dad, but we want your blessing first.* **3 a mixed blessing** something that is both good and bad: *The color printer is a mixed blessing - it looks good but takes too long to print.* **4 a blessing in disguise** something that seems to be bad but that you later realize is good: *He had a small heart attack which was a blessing in disguise because we hadn't known he had a heart problem.* **5** [singular, U] protection and help from God, or the prayer in which you ask for this

**blew** /blu/ *v* the past tense of BLOW

**blight** /blaɪt/ *n* [singular, U] something that damages or spoils something else, or the condition of being damaged or spoiled: *an area suffering from urban blight* (=severe problems that only a city has) –**blight** *v* [T]

**blight·ed** /'blaɪtɪd/ *adj* damaged or spoiled: *the blighted downtown area*

**blimp** /blɪmp/ *n* an aircraft without wings that looks like a very large BALLOON with an engine

**blind**[1] /blaɪnd/ *adj* **1** unable to see: *She was born blind.* | *People with the disease often go blind.* (=become blind) **2 the blind** people who cannot see **3** showing that you are not thinking carefully about something: *They have blind faith in the government.* (=they approve of it even when it is not good) **4** not noticing or realizing something: *The White House seems blind to the struggles of the middle class* **5 blind corner/bend/curve** a corner etc. that you cannot see around when you are driving **6 the blind leading the blind** a situation in which someone who does not know much about a subject is helping someone else who knows nothing about it **7 blind as a bat** HUMOROUS not able to see well –**blindly** *adv* –**blindness** *n* [U] –see also **turn a deaf ear/turn a blind eye** (TURN[1])

**blind**[2] *v* [T] **1** to make someone unable to see, either permanently or for a short time: *The deer was blinded by our headlights.* **2** to make someone unable to recognize the truth about something: *Being in love blinded me to his faults.*

**blind**[3] *n* a piece of cloth or other material that you pull down to cover a window –see also VENETIAN BLIND

**blind date** /ˌ. './ *n* an occasion when someone arranges for two people who have not met before to go on a DATE

**blind·fold** /'blaɪndfoʊld/ *n* a piece of cloth that you use to cover someone's eyes so that s/he cannot see –**blindfold** *v* [T]

**blind·side** /'blaɪndsaɪd/ *v* [T] to hit the side of a car with your car in an accident

**blind spot** /'. ˌ./ *n* **1 have a blind spot** to be unwilling to think about something, or pretend you cannot understand it: *He has a blind spot when it comes to his daughter's problems.* **2** the part of the road that you cannot see when you are driving a car: *The other car was right in my blind spot.*

**blink** /blɪŋk/ *v* **1** [I,T] to open and close your eyes quickly: *He blinked as he stepped out into the sunlight.* **2** if a light blinks, it goes on and off quickly and repeatedly: *The answering machine light was blinking.*

**blink·ers** /'blɪŋkəz/ n [plural] the small lights on a car that flash to show which direction you are turning

**blip** /blɪp/ n **1** a flashing light on a RADAR screen **2** INFORMAL a sudden and temporary change from the way something typically happens: *I think the loss of this game is just a blip - the team will continue to win.*

**bliss** /blɪs/ n [U] perfect happiness **–blissful** adj **–blissfully** adv

**blis·ter¹** /'blɪstə/ n **1** a painful swollen area on the skin containing a clear liquid, caused by a burn or by being rubbed too much **2** a slightly raised area on the surface of a metal, painted wood etc.

**blister²** v [I,T] to develop blisters or to make blisters form **–blistered** adj

**blis·ter·ing** /'blɪstərɪŋ/ adj criticizing someone very strongly: *Berkowski sent a blistering memo to his staff.*

**blithe** /blaɪð, blaɪθ/ adj LITERARY happy and not worried **–blithely** adv: *"I don't care!" she said blithely.*

**blitz** /blɪts/ n **1** a situation in football when a lot of football players attack the QUARTERBACK **2** a situation when you use a lot of effort to achieve something, often in a short time: *an advertising blitz* **3** a sudden military attack, especially from the air **–blitz** v [T]

**bliz·zard** /'blɪzəd/ n a long heavy storm with a lot of wind and snow **–see** usage note at WEATHER¹

**bloat·ed** /'bloʊtɪd/ adj looking or feeling larger than usual because of being too full of water, food, gas etc: *Sonny felt bloated with all the holiday food.*

**blob** /blɑb/ n a small drop of a thick liquid: *blobs of paint*

**bloc** /blɑk/ n a large group of people or countries with the same political aims, working together: *the liberal bloc in Congress*

**block¹** /blɑk/ n
**1** ►SOLID MATERIAL◄ a piece of a solid material with straight sides: *a block of concrete* | *children playing with wooden blocks*
**2** ►IN A CITY◄ a) the distance along a city street from where one street crosses it to the next: *We're just two blocks from the bus stop.* | *the sixteen hundred block of Glenwood Drive* (=where the buildings are numbered from 1600 to 1699) b) a square area of houses or buildings formed by four streets: *Let's walk around the block.* | *We were the first family on our block to get a swimming pool.*
**3** ►RELATED GROUP◄ a group of things of the same kind, that are related in some way: *Jason says he can get a block of seats* (=set of seats next to each other) *for the play.*
**4** ►AMOUNT◄ a continuous amount of something: *To delete a block of text, highlight it, then press Del.* | *a block of time to do homework*

**5** ►UNABLE TO THINK◄ [singular] a condition in which you are not able to think, learn, write etc. as you normally can: *After her first novel, she had writer's block for a year.*
**6** ►STOPPING MOVEMENT◄ something that stops things moving through or along something else: *Police put up a road block after the accident.*
**7** ►SPORTS◄ a movement in sports that stops an opponent going forward
**8** ►COMPUTER◄ a physical unit of stored information on a computer DISK

**block²** v [T] **1** also **block up** to prevent anything from moving through a narrow space by filling it: *My nose is blocked up.* | *It looks like the sink is blocked.* **2** to prevent anyone or anything from moving past a place: *Whose car is blocking the driveway?* **3** to stop something happening, developing, or succeeding: *The county council blocked the idea for a new shopping mall.* **4** to prevent someone from seeing a view, getting light etc.: *Could you move a little? You're blocking my view.*

**block** sth **↔ off** phr v [T] to completely close a road or path: *The freeway exit's blocked off.*

**block out** phr v **1** [T **block** sth **↔ out**] to stop light passing through something: *Witnesses said the black smoke blocked out the sun.* **2** [I,T **block** sth **↔ out**] to try to ignore something or stop yourself remembering a bad experience: *She had managed to block her childhood out completely.* **3** [T **block** sth **↔ out**] to decide that you will use a particular time only for a particular purpose: *I try to block out four hours a week for research.*

**block·ade** /blɑ'keɪd/ n the action of surrounding an area with soldiers or ships to stop people or supplies leaving or entering a place: *a naval blockade* **–blockade** v [T]

**block·age** /'blɑkɪdʒ/ n **1** something that is stopping movement in a narrow place: *a blockage in the drain* **2** [U] the state of being blocked or prevented from doing something: *the blockage of army movements*

**block·bust·er** /'blɑk,bʌstə/ n INFORMAL a book or movie that is very successful: *Spielberg's new blockbuster*

**block·head** /'blɑkhɛd/ n INFORMAL a very stupid person

**block par·ty** /'. ,../ n a party that is held in the street for all the people living in the area

**blond¹, blonde** /blɑnd/ adj **1** blond hair is pale or yellow **2** someone who is blond has blond hair

**blond², blonde** n INFORMAL someone with BLOND hair: *a good-looking blonde*

**blood** /blʌd/ n **1** [U] the red liquid that your heart pumps through your body: *Put pressure on the wound to stop the blood flow.* | *The Red Cross asks people to give/donate blood.* | *The doctor said she'd do a blood count/test.* (=see if anything is wrong with the blood) **2 in cold blood** in a deliberate way without any emotion: *a murder in cold blood* **3** [U] the family or race to which you belong: *You look like you've got some Irish blood.* | *a blood relative* (=related by birth, not by marriage) **4 new blood** new members in a group or organization who bring new ideas and energy: *We need some new blood in the department.* **5 bad blood** angry feelings between people about something bad that happened in the past: *There was some bad blood between Jose and Arriola over a woman.* **6 -blooded** having a particular type of blood: *Fish are cold-blooded.*

**blood-and-guts** /ˌ. . './ *adj* INFORMAL full of action and violence: *a blood-and-guts movie*

**blood bank** /'. ˌ./ *n* a supply of blood that people have given, to be used in hospitals for treating sick people

**blood·bath** /'blʌdbæθ/ *n* [singular] the violent killing of many people at the same time

**blood·cur·dling** /'blʌdˌkədl-ɪŋ/ *adj* extremely frightening: *a bloodcurdling scream*

**blood·hound** /'blʌdhaʊnd/ *n* a large dog with a very good sense of smell

**blood·less** /'blʌdlɪs/ *adj* **1** without killing or violence: *a bloodless revolution* **2** extremely pale: *bloodless cheeks*

**blood pres·sure** /'. ˌ../ *n* [U] the force with which blood travels through your body, that can be measured by a doctor: *a special diet for people with high/low blood pressure*

**blood·shed** /'blʌdʃɛd/ *n* [U] the killing of people, usually in fighting or a war

**blood·shot** /'blʌdʃɑt/ *adj* bloodshot eyes look slightly red

**blood·stain** /'blʌdsteɪn/ *n* a mark or spot of blood – **bloodstained** *adj*

**blood·stream** /'blʌdstrim/ *n* [singular] blood as it flows around the body: *Drugs were found in her bloodstream.*

**blood·thirst·y** /'blʌdˌθəsti/ *adj* showing that someone enjoys doing violent things or watching violence: *bloodthirsty attacks*

**blood type** /'. ./ *n* one of the groups into which human blood is divided, including A, B, AB, and O

**blood ves·sel** /'. ˌ../ *n* one of the tubes through which blood flows in your body

**blood·y** /'blʌdi/ *adj* **1** covered in blood, or losing blood: *a bloody nose* **2** with a lot of injuries or killing: *a bloody fight*

**bloom¹** /blum/ *n* [C,U] a flower or flowers: *lovely yellow blooms* | *roses in bloom* (=with flowers completely open)

**bloom²** *v* [I] **1** to open as flowers: *lilacs blooming in the spring* **2** to look happy and healthy or successful: *Sheila bloomed like a woman in love.*

**bloom·er** /'blumə/ *n* **late bloomer** INFORMAL

someone who grows or becomes successful at a later age than most people

**bloop·er** /'blupə/ *n* INFORMAL an embarrassing mistake made in front of other people

**blos·som¹** /'blɑsəm/ *n* [C,U] a small flower, or all the flowers on trees or bushes: *peach blossoms*

**blossom²** *v* [I] **1** if trees blossom, they produce flowers: *a blossoming plum tree* **2** to become happier, more beautiful, or successful: *By the end of the year she had blossomed into an excellent teacher.*

**blot¹** /blɑt/ *v* **-tted, -tting** [T] to press soft paper or cloth on to a wet spot or surface in order to dry it: *Blot wet hair with a towel, but don't rub it.*

**blot sth ↔ out** *phr v* [T] to hide or remove something completely: *He tried to blot out his memory of Marcia.* | *clouds blotting out the sun*

**blot²** *n* **1** a mark or spot that spoils something or makes it dirty: *ink blots* **2** a building, structure etc. that is ugly and spoils the appearance of a place: *a blot on the landscape*

**blotch** /blɑtʃ/ *n* a colored or dirty mark on something – **blotched** *adj*

**blotch·y** /'blɑtʃi/ *adj* blotchy skin is covered with pink or red marks

**blot·ter** /'blɑtə/ *n* a large piece of BLOTTING PAPER kept on the top of a desk

**blotting pa·per** /'.. ˌ../ *n* [U] soft thick paper used for drying wet ink on a page after writing

**blouse** /blaʊs/ *n* a shirt for women: *a summer blouse* – see picture at CLOTHES

**blow¹** /bloʊ/ *v* blew, blown, blowing

**1 ▶WIND MOVING◀** [I] if the wind or a current of air blows, it moves. *A cold wind was blowing from the east.*

**2 ▶WIND MOVING STH◀** [I,T] to move something, or to be moved, by the force of the wind or a current of air: *The wind must have blown the door shut/open.* | *curtains blowing in the breeze*

**3 ▶USING YOUR MOUTH◀ a)** [I,T] to send air out through your mouth: *Renée blew on her soup to cool it a little.* **b)** [T] to make or shape something by sending air out of your mouth and into a substance: *The kids are on the back porch blowing bubbles.* | *ornaments made of blown glass*

**4 blow your nose** to clean your nose by forcing air through it into a cloth or TISSUE (=piece of soft paper)

**5 ▶MAKE A SOUND◀** [I,T] to make a sound by sending air through a musical instrument or a horn: *Listen - can you hear the train whistle blowing?*

**6 ▶STOP WORKING◀** [I,T] also **blow out** if a piece of equipment blows or if something blows it, it suddenly stops working completely: *You're lucky you didn't blow the whole engine.*

**7 blow sth to bits/pieces** INFORMAL **a)** to destroy an idea, plan etc. by showing that it cannot work or be true: *The new data's blown their theory to pieces.* **b)** to completely destroy a building or structure with an explosion

**8 blow the whistle (on sb)** INFORMAL to tell the public or someone in authority about something wrong that someone has done

---

SPOKEN PHRASES

**9 ▶RUIN STH◀** [T] to ruin something, or lose a good opportunity, by making a mistake or being careless: *I blew it by talking too much in the interview.*

**10 ▶LEAVE◀** [T] to leave a place quickly: *Let's blow this joint.* (=leave this place)

**11 ▶SPEND MONEY◀** [T] to spend a lot of money at one time in a careless way: *He got a big insurance payment, but he blew it all on a new stereo.*

**12 blow your top/stack** to suddenly become extremely angry: *If you tell Dad about the car, he'll blow his top.*

**13 blow sb's mind** to make someone feel very surprised by something: *That's what really blew my mind about Michael.*

---

**blow away** *phr v* [T] **1** [**blow** sb **away**] SPOKEN to completely surprise someone; AMAZE: *It just blows me away to think how fast Graham has grown.* **2** [**blow** sb/sth ↔ **away**] INFORMAL to completely destroy something or kill someone with a weapon: *Stop or I'll blow you away.* **3** [**blow** sb ↔ **away**] INFORMAL to defeat someone completely, especially in a sports game: *The Giants blew away the Rams 31-0.*

**blow down** *phr v* [I,T **blow** sth ↔ **down**] if the wind blows something down, or if it blows down, the wind makes it fall: *A big tree had blown down and was blocking the road.*

**blow into** sth *phr v* [T] INFORMAL to arrive without warning: *Look who just blew into town!*

**blow off** *phr v* [T] **1** [**blow** sth ↔ **off**] to damage someone or something, or explode in a way that makes part of that person or thing come off: *a soldier whose leg was blown off by a land mine* **2** [**blow** sb/sth ↔ **off**] SPOKEN to treat someone or something as unimportant, for example by not doing what you were expected to do: *I blew off my 8 a.m. class again.*

**blow out** *phr v* [I,T **blow** sth ↔ **out**] to make a fire suddenly stop burning, or to stop burning: *Bobbi shut her eyes and blew out her birthday candles.*

**blow over** *phr v* **1** [I,T **blow** sth **over**] if the wind blows something over, or if it blows over, the wind makes it fall: *Our fence blew over during the storm.* **2** [I] to end, or no longer be important: *Matt was hoping the whole problem with Tim would blow over.*

**blow up** *phr v* **1** [I,T **blow** sth ↔ **up**] to destroy something, or to be destroyed, by an explosion: *A car was blown up near the embassy.* | *The Tatleys' gas boiler blew up last*

night. **2** [T **blow** sth ↔ **up**] to fill something with air or gas: *Come and help me blow up the balloons.* **3** [I] SPOKEN to shout angrily at someone: *I'm sorry I blew up at you earlier, Julie.* **4** [T **blow** sth ↔ **up**] to make a photograph larger: *I'd like to have this picture blown up.*

**blow²** *n* **1** a hard hit with a hand, tool, or weapon: *a blow to/in the stomach* **2** an event that makes you very unhappy or shocks you: *Not getting the job was a blow to Kate's confidence.* | *The death of their father was a terrible blow.* **3** the act of blowing: *Give the candles a good blow.* **4 come to blows** if two people come to blows, they get so angry that they start hitting each other

**blow-by-blow** /ˌ. . '.◂/ *adj* a blow-by-blow description, account etc. gives the details of an event as it happens

**blow dry** /'. ./ *v* [T] to dry hair using an electric machine that you hold in your hand: *blow dried hair*

**blown** /bloʊn/ *v* the PAST PARTICIPLE of BLOW

**blow·out** /'bloʊaʊt/ *n* INFORMAL **1** the sudden bursting of a TIRE **2** a big expensive meal or large party **3** an easy victory in a sports game

**blow·torch** /'bloʊˌtɔrtʃ/ *n* a piece of equipment that is held in the hand and produces a small, very hot flame, used for welding (WELD) metal

**blow-up** /'. ./ *n* **1** a photograph, or part of a photograph, that has been made larger **2** INFORMAL a sudden loud argument

**blub·ber¹** /'blʌbɚ/ *n* [U] the fat of sea animals, especially WHALEs

**blubber²** *v* [I] INFORMAL to cry in a noisy way: *Anna tried to talk but could only blubber.*

**blud·geon** /'blʌdʒən/ *v* [T] to hit someone many times with something heavy

**blue¹** /blu/ *adj* **1** having the same color as a clear sky during the day: *the blue lake water* | *a dark/light blue dress* **2** INFORMAL sad and without hope: *I've been feeling kind of blue lately.* **3 do sth till you're blue in the face** INFORMAL to do something a lot but without achieving what you want: *You can argue till you're blue in the face, but I won't change my mind.* —see also **once in a blue moon** (ONCE¹)

**blue²** *n* [U] **1** a blue color: *We're painting the bedroom blue.* **2 out of the blue** INFORMAL when you are not expecting something to happen: *The call from Judge Richey came out of the blue.* —see also BLUES

**blue·bell** /'blubɛl/ *n* a small plant with blue flowers that grows in the forest

**blue·ber·ry** /'bluˌbɛri/ *n* a small dark blue round BERRY: *blueberry muffins* —see picture on page 470

**blue·bird** /'blubɚd/ *n* a small North American wild bird that sings and has a blue back and wings

**blue-blood·ed** /ˌ. '..◂ / *adj* belonging to a royal or NOBLE family −**blue-blood** /'. ./ *n* [U]

**blue book** /'. ./ *n* **1** a book with a blue cover that is used in colleges for writing answers to test questions **2** a book with a list of prices that you should expect to pay for any used car

**blue cheese** /ˌ. './ *n* [C,U] a strong-tasting pale cheese with blue spots in it

**blue chip** /'. ˌ./ *adj* considered to be important, profitable, and unlikely to disappoint you: *a blue-chip investment* −**blue chip** *n*

**blue col·lar** /ˌ. '..◂ / *adj* blue collar workers do jobs such as repairing machines and working in factories −see usage note at CLASS¹

**blue·grass** /'blugræs/ *n* [U] a type of COUNTRY AND WESTERN music from the southern and western US, using string instruments such as the VIOLIN

**blue·jay** /'bludʒeɪ/ *n* a common North American wild bird that has blue, black, and white feathers

**blue jeans** /'. ./ *n* [plural] ⇨ JEANS

**blue law** /'. ./ *n* INFORMAL a law that limits the time when people can drink alcohol, work on Sundays etc.

**blue mov·ie** /ˌ. '../ *n* a movie showing sexual activity

**blue·print** /'bluˌprɪnt/ *n* **1** a plan for achieving something: *a blueprint for health care reform* **2** a print of a plan for a building, machine etc.

**blue rib·bon** /ˌ. '../ *n* a small piece of blue material given to someone who wins a competition

**blues** /bluz/ *n* [plural] **1** a slow sad style of music that came from the Afro-American culture: *a blues singer* **2 have/get the blues** INFORMAL to be or become sad

**bluff¹** /blʌf/ *v* [I,T] to pretend to be more confident that you are, or to pretend to know something that you do not know: *I could tell Sunderland was bluffing because he kept looking away.*

**bluff²** *n* [C,U] **1** the action of bluffing: *Grolsky's threat to resign is no more than a bluff.* **2 call sb's bluff** to tell someone to do what s/he threatens because you believe s/he has no intention of doing it: *If the general calls our bluff, we'd better have enough men in there to fight.* **3** a very steep cliff or slope: *Pine Bluff, Arkansas.*

**blun·der¹** /'blʌndɚ/ *n* a careless or stupid mistake: *a terrible political blunder*

**blunder²** *v* [I] **1** to make a careless or stupid mistake **2** to move in an unsteady way as if you cannot see well

**blunt¹** /blʌnt/ *adj* **1** not sharp or pointed: *blunt scissors | a blunt table knife* −compare DULL¹ −see picture at SHARP¹ **2** speaking in an honest way even if it upsets people: *Did you have to be so blunt?* −**bluntness** *n* [U]

**blunt²** *v* [T] to make something less sharp or

less strong: *a blunted axe | The whiskey had blunted his senses.*

**blunt·ly** /'blʌntˉli/ *adv* speaking in a direct, honest way that sometimes upsets people: *To put it bluntly, you're failing the class.*

**blur¹** /blɚ/ *n* [singular] **1** something that you cannot see clearly: *a blur of horses running past* **2** something that is difficult to remember: *The next day was all a blur.*

**blur²** *v* **-rred, -rring** [I,T] **1** to become difficult to see, or to make something difficult to see, because the edges are not clear, or to make something do this: *Tears blurred my vision.* **2** to make the difference between two things less clear: *Differences in social classes have been blurred.*

**blurb** /blɚb/ *n* a short description giving information about a book, new product etc.

**blurred** /blɚd/ *adj* **1** also **blur·ry** /'blɚi/ not clear in shape, or making it difficult to see shapes: *blurred vision | blurry photos* **2** difficult to understand or remember clearly: *blurred memories*

**blurt** /blɚt/ *v* [T] also **blurt out** to say something suddenly and without thinking, usually because you are nervous or excited: *"But I love you!" Ted blurted.*

**blush¹** /blʌʃ/ *v* [I] to become red in the face, usually because you are embarrassed: *She's so shy, she blushes when she talks.*

**blush²** *n* **1** the red color on your face that appears when you are embarrassed, confused, or ashamed **2** [U] cream or powder used for making your cheeks slightly red or pink

**blus·ter¹** /'blʌstɚ/ *v* [I] **1** to talk loudly and behave as if what you are doing is extremely important **2** if the wind blusters, it blows violently

**bluster²** *n* [U] noisy, proud talk

**blus·ter·y** /'blʌstəri/ *adj* blustery weather is very windy: *a blustery winter day*

**Blvd.** the written abbreviation of boulevard

**BO, B.O.** *n* [U] SLANG body odor; an unpleasant smell from someone's body

**boa con·strict·or** /ˌboʊə kən'strɪktɚ/ *n* a large tropical snake that kills animals for food by crushing them

**boar** /bɔr/ *n* **1** a male pig kept on a farm for breeding **2** a wild pig

**board¹** /bɔrd/ *n*

**1** ▶FOR DOING THINGS ON◀ a flat piece of wood, plastic etc. that you use for a particular purpose: *a cutting board | Where's the chess board?*

**2** ▶GROUP OF PEOPLE◀ a group of people in an organization who make the rules and important decisions: *the local school board | a board of directors*

**3** ▶FOR INFORMATION◀ a flat wide piece of wood, plastic etc. where information is written or shown: *Your vocabulary words for this week*

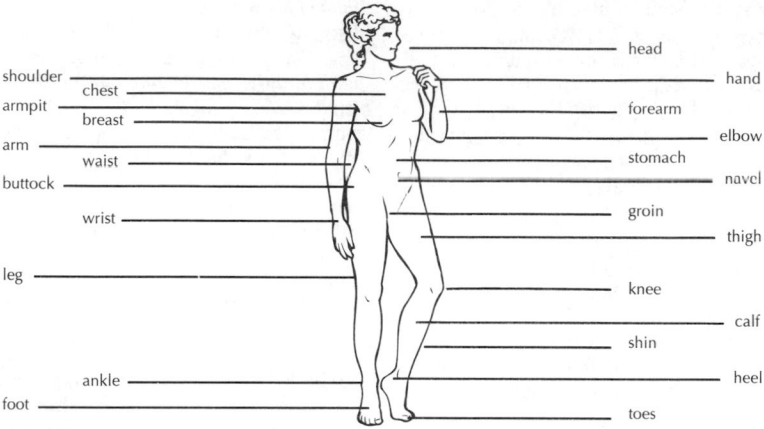

are on the board. —see also BLACKBOARD, BULLETIN BOARD

**4 ▶FOR BUILDING◀** a long thin flat piece of wood used for making floors, walls, fences etc.

**5 on board** on a plane, ship etc.: *No one on board was hurt.*

**6 take sth on board** to accept a suggestion, idea etc. and do something about it: *We'll try to take some of your points on board.*

**7 across the board** if something happens across the board, it affects everyone in a particular group: *increases in pay across the board*

**8 ▶MEALS◀** [U] the meals that are provided for you when you pay to stay somewhere: *Room and board is $3000 per semester.*

**board**[2] *v* [I,T] **1** to get on a plane, ship, train etc. in order to travel somewhere: *We invite our first class passengers to board the plane now.* **2** [I] to allow passengers onto a plane, ship, train etc.: *Flight 503 for Toronto is now boarding.*

**board** sth ↔ **up** *phr v* [T] to cover a window or door with wooden boards: *The house next door has been boarded up for months.*

**board·er** /'bɔrdɚ/ *n* someone who pays to live in another person's house with some or all of his/her meals provided

**board game** /'. ./ *n* an indoor game played with wooden or plastic pieces that you move on a specially designed board made of wood or thick CARDBOARD

**board·ing·house** /'bɔrdɪŋˌhaʊs/ *n* a private house where you pay to sleep and eat

**boarding school** /'.. ./ *n* a school where students live as well as study

**board·room** /'bɔrdrum/ *n* a room where the DIRECTORs of a company have meetings

**board·walk** /'bɔrdwɔk/ *n* a raised path made of wood, usually built next to the ocean

**boast**[1] /boʊst/ *v* **1** [I,T] to talk too proudly about your abilities, achievements etc. in order

to make people admire you; BRAG: *I don't want to sound like I'm boasting, but I'm sure I can do the job.* **2** [T] to have a good feature: *The new athletic center boasts an Olympic-sized swimming pool.* —**boastful** *adj*

**boast**[2] *n* something you like telling people because you are very proud of it

**boat** /boʊt/ *n* **1** a vehicle that travels across water: *fishing boats | You can only get to the island by boat.* —compare SHIP[1] **2 be in the same boat (as)** to be in the same unpleasant situation as someone else: *We're all in the same boat, so stop complaining.* —see also **miss the boat** (MISS[1]) **rock the boat** (ROCK[2])

**boat peo·ple** /'. ,../ *n* [plural] people who escape from bad conditions in their country in small boats

**bob**[1] /bab/ *v* **-bbed, -bbing 1** [I] to move up and down: *a boat bobbing up and down on the water* **2** [T] to cut someone's hair so that it is the same length all the way around his/her head

**bob**[2] *n* a way of cutting hair so that it is the same length all the way around your head

**bob·bin** /'babɪn/ *n* a small round object that you wind thread onto

**bob·cat** /'babkæt/ *n* a North American wild cat that has no tail

**bob·sled** /'babslɛd/, **bob·sleigh** /'babsleɪ/ *n* a small vehicle with two long thin metal blades that is used for racing down a special ice track —**bobsled** *v* [I]

**bode** /boʊd/ *v* **bode well/ill** LITERARY to be a good or bad sign for the future

**bod·ice** /'badɪs/ *n* the part of a woman's dress above her waist

**bod·i·ly**[1] /'badl-i/ *adj* relating to the human body: *bodily functions*

**bodily**[2] *adv* by moving all of your body or someone else's body: *She had to be carried bodily to bed.*

**bod·y** /'bɑdi/ *n*
**1** ▶PHYSICAL BODY◀ **a)** the physical structure of a person or animal: *a strong healthy body* **b)** the central part of a person or animal's body, not including the head, arms, legs or wings: *a short body and long legs* **c)** the body of a dead person: *They flew his body home to his parents.* ✗ DON'T SAY "his dead body." ✗ –see also pictures at HEAD and EYE
**2** ▶GROUP OF PEOPLE◀ a group of people who work together for a particular purpose: *the governing body of a university | the president of the student body* (=all the students in a school or college)
**3 a/the body of sth a)** a large amount or collection of something: *a body of literature* **b)** the main, central, or most important part of something: *the body of the report*
**4 -bodied a)** having a particular type of body: *thick-bodied men* **b)** having a particular amount of taste: *full-bodied red wine*
**5** ▶VEHICLE◀ the main structure of a vehicle, not including the engine, wheels etc.: *The body of the airplane was broken in two.*
**6 body and soul** with all your effort and attention: *devoting yourself body and soul to a cause*
**7 keep body and soul together** to manage to continue to live, although you may not have much money

**body build·ing** /'.. ,../ *n* [U] an activity in which you do hard physical exercise in order to develop big muscles –**body builder** *n*

**bod·y·guard** /'badi,gɑrd/ *n* a person or group of people whose job is to protect an important person

**body lan·guage** /'.. ,../ *n* [U] changes in your body position and movements that show what you are feeling or thinking

**body o·dor** /'.. ,../ *n* ⇨ BO

**bod·y·work** /'badi,wɚk/ *n* [U] work done to repair the frame of a vehicle, not including the engine, wheels etc.: *I know a garage that does good bodywork.*

**bog**[1] /bag, bɔg/ *n* [C,U] an area of wet muddy ground that you can sink into

**bog**[2] *v* **-gged, -gging be/get bogged down** to be or become too involved in dealing with something so that you cannot finish an activity that is more important: *The negotiations are getting bogged down in details.*

**bo·gey·man** /'bugi,mæn/ *n* ⇨ BOOGIE MAN

**bog·gle** /'bagəl/ *v* **the mind boggles/sth boggles the mind** INFORMAL used in order to say that something is difficult to believe or very confusing: *The paperwork you have to fill out just boggles the mind.*

**bo·gus** /'bougəs/ *adj* **1** INFORMAL not true or real, although someone tries to make you think it is; FAKE: *a bogus insurance claim* **2** SLANG completely worthless: *a bogus movie*

**bo·he·mi·an** /bou'himiən/ *adj* relating to a way of living in which someone does not accept society's rules of behavior –**bohemian** *n*

**boil**[1] /bɔil/ *v* **1** [I,T] if a liquid boils, it is hot enough for BUBBLEs to rise to the surface and for the liquid to change to gas: *Drop the noodles into boiling salted water.* | *Turn off the heat – the water has boiled.* **2** [I,T] if something containing liquid boils, the liquid inside it is boiling: *Ben, the kettle's boiling.* **3** also **boil up** [I,T] to cook food in boiling water: *Boil the vegetables for 10 minutes.*

**boil down to** sth *phr v* [T] **it (all) boils down to** used in order to say what the main cause or point of something is: *It all boils down to how much money you have.*

**boil over** *phr v* [I] if a liquid boils over, it flows over the side of a container because it is boiling

**boil**[2] *n* **1** [singular] the act or state of boiling: *Bring the soup to a boil and cook for 5 minutes.* **2** a painful infected swelling under the skin

**boil·er** /'bɔilɚ/ *n* a container for boiling water that is part of a steam engine, or that is used for providing heat in a house

**boil·ing** /'bɔiliŋ/ **boiling hot** *adj* too hot: *It's boiling hot in here!* –see usage note at TEMPERATURE

**boiling point** /'.. ,../ *n* **1** the temperature at which a liquid boils **2** a point at which people can no longer deal with a problem calmly: *Frustrations with the military government finally reached a boiling point.*

**bois·ter·ous** /'bɔistərəs/ *adj* noisy and cheerful: *boisterous children*

**bold** /bould/ *adj* **1** showing that you are confident and willing to take risks: *Yamamoto's plan was bold and original.* **2** writing, shapes, or colors that are bold are very clear and strong or bright: *wallpaper with bold stripes* –**boldly** *adv* –**boldness** *n* [U]

**bo·lo·gna** /bə'louni/ *n* a type of cooked meat often eaten in SANDWICHes

**bol·ster**[1] /'boulstɚ/ also **bolster up** *v* [T] **1** to improve someone's opinion about himself/herself: *Roy's promotion seems to have bolstered his confidence.* **2** to improve something by supporting it: *New reports have bolstered the committee's research.*

**bolster**[2] *n* a long firm PILLOW

**bolt**[1] /boult/ *n* **1** a piece of metal that you slide across a door or window to close or lock it **2** a screw with a flat head and no point, for fastening two pieces of metal together **3 bolt of lightning** LIGHTNING that appears as a white line in the sky –see also THUNDERBOLT **4** a large long roll of cloth

**bolt**[2] *v* **1** [I] **a)** to suddenly start to run very fast because you are frightened: *When the horse bolted, I fell off.* **2** [I,T] to close or lock a door or window with a bolt **3** [T] also **bolt down** to eat very quickly: *Kevin bolted his lunch and ran out the door.* **4** [I,T] to fasten two things together using a BOLT

**bolt**³ *adv* **sit/stand bolt upright** to sit or stand with your back very straight, because something has frightened you: *Suddenly Dennis sat bolt upright in bed.*

**bomb**¹ /bɑm/ *n* **1** a weapon made of material that will explode: *bombs dropping on the city* **2** **the bomb** ⇨ NUCLEAR WEAPON **3** a container in which insect poison, paint etc. is kept under pressure: *a flea bomb* (=used for killing FLEAS)

**bomb**² *v* **1** [T] to attack a place by exploding a bomb there, or by dropping a bomb by plane: *Terrorists threatened to bomb the building.* **2** [I,T] SPOKEN to fail a test very badly: *I bombed my history test.* **3** [I] if a play, movie, or joke bombs, it is not successful

**bom·bard** /bɑm'bɑrd/ *v* [T] **1** to attack a place by firing a lot of guns at it, or dropping bombs on it: *The town was bombarded from all sides.* **2** to continue to ask someone too many questions or give him/her too much information: *Teachers are continually bombarded with new materials.* –**bombardment** *n*

**bombed** /bɑmd/ *adj* SLANG drunk

**bomb·er** /'bɑmɚ/ *n* **1** a plane that carries and drops bombs **2** someone who puts a bomb somewhere

**bomb·shell** /'bɑmʃɛl/ *n* INFORMAL a shocking piece of news: *Last night she dropped the bombshell and told him she wouldn't marry him.*

**bo·na fide** /'boʊnə ˌfaɪd, 'bɑnə-/ *adj* real, true, and not pretending to be something else: *We need a bona fide expert on the subject.*

**bo·nan·za** /bə'nænzə, boʊ-/ *n* a lucky or successful situation in which people can make a lot of money: *a financial bonanza for the movie industry*

**bond**¹ /bɑnd/ *n* **1** a feeling or interest that unites two or more people or groups: *a strong bond of affection between the two women* **2** an official document promising that a government or company will pay back money that it has borrowed, often with INTEREST: *US savings bonds* –see also BONDS

**bond**² *v* [I] **1** to develop a special relationship with someone: *The two older children never really bonded.* **2** if two things bond to each other, they become firmly stuck together

**bond·age** /'bɑndɪdʒ/ *n* [U] the state of having your freedom limited or being prevented from doing what you want

**bond·ing** /'bɑndɪŋ/ *n* [U] OFTEN HUMOROUS a process in which a special relationship develops between two or more people: *The guys went away for the weekend to do some male bonding.* (=bonding between men)

**bonds** /bɑndz/ *n* [plural] LITERARY something that limits your freedom

**bone**¹ /boʊn/ *n* **1** one of the hard parts that form the frame of a human or animal body: *a broken bone in his arm | the thigh bone* **2** **make no bones about (doing) sth** to not feel nervous or ashamed about doing or saying something: *She makes no bones about her religious beliefs.* **3** **be chilled/frozen to the bone** to be extremely cold **4** **a bone of contention** something that causes arguments between people: *His smoking has been a bone of contention between us.*

**bone**² *v* [T] to remove the bones from fish or meat

**bone up on** sth *phr v* [T] INFORMAL to study something a lot for an examination: *I should bone up on my grammar before the test.*

**bone dry** /ˌ. './ *adj* completely dry

**bon·fire** /'bɑnˌfaɪɚ/ *n* a large outdoor fire either for burning waste, or for a celebration

**bon·gos** /'bɑŋgoʊz/, **bongo drums** /'bɑŋgoʊ ˌdrʌmz/ *n* a pair of small drums that you play with your hands

**bon·net** /'bɑnɪt/ *n* a warm hat for a baby that ties under his/her chin

**bo·nus** /'boʊnəs/ *n* **1** money added to someone's pay, especially as a reward for good work: *a Christmas bonus* **2** something good that you did not expect in a situation: *The fact that our house is so close to the school is a bonus.*

**bon·y** /'boʊni/ *adj* **1** very thin: *a bony hand* **2** full of bones: *bony fish*

**boo**¹ /bu/ *v* [I,T] to shout BOO to show that you do not like a person, performance etc.

**boo**² *n, interjection* **1** a noise made by people who do not like a person, performance etc. **2** a word you shout suddenly to someone to try to frighten him/her as a joke

**boob** /bub/ *n* SLANG a woman's breast

**boo-boo** /'bubu/ *n* a word meaning a silly mistake or a small injury, used when speaking to children

**boob tube** /'. ./ *n* SPOKEN ⇨ TV

**boo·by prize** /'bubi ˌpraɪz/ *n* a prize given as a joke to the person who is last in a competition

**booby trap** /'.. ˌ./ *n* a hidden bomb that explodes when you touch something else that is connected to it –**booby-trapped** *adj*

**boo·gie man** /'bʊgi ˌmæn/ *n* an imaginary man who frightens children

**book**¹ /bʊk/ *n* **1** a set of printed pages held together in a cover so that you can read them: *a book about/on photography | Have you read this book?* **2** a set of sheets of paper held together in a cover so that you can write on them: *an address book* –compare NOTEBOOK **3** a set of things such as stamps, tickets etc. held together inside a paper cover: *a book of matches* **4** **by the book** exactly according to rules or instructions: *Around here, we do everything by the* book, understand? −see also BOOKS **throw the book at sb** (THROW)

**book²** v **1** [T] to arrange for someone such as a speaker or singer to perform on a particular date: *They have a speaker booked for next Tuesday.* **2** [I,T] to arrange with a hotel to stay there at a particular time in the future: *I've booked a room for us at the Hilton.* **3** [T] to put someone's name officially in police records, with the charge made against him/her: *Ramey was booked on suspicion of murder.*

**book·case** /'bʊk-keɪs/ n a piece of furniture with shelves to hold books

**book·end** /'bʊkɛnd/ n one of a pair of objects that you put at each end of a row of books to prevent them from falling

**book·ie** /'bʊki/ n INFORMAL someone whose job is to collect money that people BET on a race, sport etc. and who pays them if they win

**book·ing** /'bʊkɪŋ/ n an arrangement in which a hotel, theater etc. agrees to let you have a particular room, seat etc. at a future time: *Cheaper prices are available on early bookings.*

**book·keep·ing** /'bʊk,kipɪŋ/ n [U] the job or activity of recording the financial accounts of an organization −**bookkeeper** n

**book·let** /'bʊklɪt/ n a very short book that contains information: *a booklet on AIDS*

**book·mak·er** /'bʊk,meɪkɚ/ n ⇨ BOOKIE

**book·mark** /'bʊkmɑrk/ n a piece of paper that you put in a book to show you the last page you have read

**books** /bʊks/ n [plural] written records of the financial accounts of a business

**book·shelf** /'bʊkʃɛlf/ n, plural **bookshelves** /-ʃɛlvz/ a shelf on a wall or a piece of furniture with shelves, used for holding books

**book·store** /'bʊkstɔr/ n a store that sells books

**book·worm** /'bʊkwɚm/ n INFORMAL someone who likes to read very much

**boom¹** /bum/ n **1** a rapid increase of activity or interest in something: *a boom in sales | the building boom in the 1980s | The fitness boom started in the 70s.* **2** a loud deep sound that you can hear for several seconds after it begins: *the boom of guns in the distance*

**boom²** v **1** [I] to make a loud deep sound: *Chris's voice boomed above the others.* **2** a sudden increase in activity, business, prices etc. −**booming** adj −see also **baby boom** (BABY)

**boom box** /'. ,./ n INFORMAL ⇨ GHETTO BLASTER

**boo·mer·ang** /'bumə,ræŋ/ n a curved stick that comes back to you when you throw it

**boom town** /'. ,./ n INFORMAL a city that suddenly becomes very successful because of new industry

**boon** /bun/ n LITERARY something that is very useful and makes your life a lot easier

**boon·docks** /'bundaks/, **boo·nies** /'buniz/ n [plural] INFORMAL **the boondocks/boonies** a place that is a long way from any town: *Ken's family live way out in the boondocks.*

**boor** /bʊr/ n someone who behaves in an unacceptable way in social situations −**boorish** adj

**boost¹** /bust/ n **1** [singular] something that helps someone be more successful and confident, or that helps something increase or improve: *Some women may need an extra boost from vitamins. | a real boost to the American fashion industry* **2 give sb a boost** to lift or push someone so s/he can get over or onto something high or tall: *Give your brother a boost.*

**boost²** v [T] **1** to increase something such as production, sales etc. because they are not as high as you want them to be: *The new facility will help boost oil production.* **2 boost sb's confidence/ego etc.** to make someone feel more confident and less worried: *I think Kathy's new job has boosted her ego.* **3** to help someone get over or onto something high or tall by lifting or pushing him/her up

**boost·er** /'bustɚ/ n **1** a small quantity of a drug that increases the effect of one that was given before: *a measles booster* **2 confidence/morale/ego etc. booster** something that BOOSTS someone's confidence etc.: *The letters from people at home are a great morale booster for the soldiers.* **3** someone who gives a lot of support to a person, organization, or idea: *The Williamstown High School Booster Club* **4** a ROCKET that provides more power for a SPACECRAFT

**boot¹** /but/ n **1** a type of shoe that covers your whole foot and the lower part of your leg: *hiking boots* **2 to boot** SPOKEN used at the end of a list of remarks to emphasize the last one: *Jack's tall, handsome, and rich to boot.*

**boot²** v **1** [I,T] also **boot up** to make a computer ready to be used by putting in its instructions **2** [T] INFORMAL to kick someone or something hard: *Joe booted the ball across the field.*

**boot camp** /'. ./ n a training camp for people who have joined the Army, Navy, or Marines

**boot·ee** /'buti/ n a sock that a baby wears instead of a shoe

**booth** /buθ/ n **1** a small, partly enclosed place where one person can do something privately: *a phone booth | a voting booth* **2** a partly enclosed place in a restaurant with a table between two long seats **3** a place at a market or FAIR where you can buy things, play games, or find information

**boot·leg** /'butlɛg/ adj bootleg products are made and sold illegally −**bootlegging** n [U] −**bootlegger** n

**boot·straps** /ˈbutstræps/ *n* **pull yourself up by your bootstraps** to get out of a difficult situation by your own effort

**boo·ty** /ˈbuṭi/ *n* LITERARY valuable things taken or won by the winners in a war, competition etc.

**booze**[1] /buz/ *n* [U] INFORMAL alcoholic drinks

**booze**[2] *v* [I] INFORMAL to drink a lot of alcohol −**boozer** *n*

**bop**[1] /bɑp/ *v* **-pped, -pping** [I] to hit someone gently

**bop**[2] *n* **1** a gentle hit **2** ⇨ BEBOP

**bor·der**[1] /ˈbɔrdɚ/ *n* **1** the official line that separates two countries: *the **border between** the US and Mexico* **2** a band along the edge of something such as a picture or piece of material: *a skirt with a red border*

**border**[2] *v* [T] **1** to share a border with another country: *Spain borders Portugal.* **2** to form a line around the edge of something: *willow trees bordering the river*

**border on** sth *phr v* [T] to be very close to reaching an extreme feeling or quality: *Jane's math skills **border on** genius.*

**bor·der·line**[1] /ˈbɔrdɚˌlaɪn/ *adj* very close to being unacceptable: *His grades are borderline; unless he works hard, he won't graduate.*

**borderline**[2] *n* **1** [singular] the point at which one quality, condition etc. ends and another begins: *the borderline between admiration and love* **2** a border between two countries

**bore**[1] /bɔr/ *v* **1** [T] to make someone feel bored, especially by talking too much: *I'm sorry to bore you with all the details.* **2** [I,T] to make a deep round hole in a hard surface **3** [I] if someone's eyes bore into you, s/he looks at you for a long time **4** the past tense of BEAR

**bore**[2] *n* **1** someone who talks too much about the same things: *Ralph is such a bore!* **2** [singular] something you have to do but do not like: *Ironing is a real bore.*

**bored** /bɔrd/ *adj* tired and impatient because you do not think something is interesting or because you have nothing to do: *George **got bored** with his job, so he quit.* | *Can't we do something else? I'm **bored stiff/bored to tears**.* (=extremely bored) | *I'm so bored!* ✗ DON'T SAY "I'm so boring." ✗

**bore·dom** /ˈbɔrdəm/ *n* [U] the feeling you have when you are bored

**bor·ing** /ˈbɔrɪŋ/ *adj* not interesting in any way: *I thought the book was boring.*

**born** /bɔrn/ *adj* **1 be born** when a person or animal is born, it comes out of its mother's body or out of an egg: *I was born in the South.* | *Lincoln was born on February 12.* | *She was **born into** a wealthy family.* **2 be born to do/be sth** to be very good at doing a particular job, activity etc.: *Mantle was born to play baseball.* **3 born leader/teacher etc.** someone who has a natural ability to lead, teach etc. **4** something that is born starts to exist: *Unions*

*were **born out of** (=started because of) a need for better working conditions.*

**born-a·gain** /ˈ. ., ./ *adj* **born-again Christian** someone who has become an EVANGELICAL Christian after having an important religious experience

**borne** /bɔrn/ *v* the PAST PARTICIPLE of BEAR

**bor·ough** /ˈbɚoʊ, ˈbʌroʊ/ *n* a town or part of a large city that is responsible for managing its own schools, hospitals, roads etc.

**borrow**

Jerry borrowed a CD from Sue.
Sue lent Jerry a CD.

Jerry gave it back later.

**bor·row** /ˈbɑroʊ, ˈbɔroʊ/ *v* [I,T] **1** to use something that belongs to someone else and give it back to him/her later: *Could I borrow your bike tomorrow?* | *We'll have to borrow money **from** the bank for the house.* −opposite LEND **2** to take or copy ideas or words: *English has borrowed many words from French.* −**borrower** *n* −see usage note at LEND

**bor·row·ings** /ˈbɑroʊɪŋz/ *n* [plural] the total amount of money that a person, company, or organization has borrowed, usually from a bank

**bos·om** /ˈbʊzəm/ *n* **1 bosom buddy** INFORMAL a very close friend **2** OLD-FASHIONED a woman's chest

**boss**[1] /bɔs/ *n* **1** the person who employs you or who is in charge of your work: *Our boss let us leave early today.* **2** [singular, U] the person who is the strongest in a relationship, who controls a situation etc.: *You have to **let them know who's boss**.* (=make sure you are in control)

**boss**[2] *v* [T] also **boss around** to tell people to do things, give them orders etc., especially when you have no authority to do it: *Stop bossing me around!*

**boss·y** /ˈbɔsi/ *adj* always telling other people what to do, in a way that is annoying: *Ruth's okay, but she can be bossy.*

**bot·a·ny** /ˈbɑt⁻n-i/ *n* [U] the scientific study of plants −**botanical** /bəˈtænɪkəl/ *adj*: *botanical gardens* −**botanist** /ˈbɑt⁻nɪst/ *n*

**botch** /bɑtʃ/ *v* [T] INFORMAL also **botch up** to do something badly because you were careless or did not have the skill to do it well: *She really botched my haircut this time.*

**both** /boʊθ/ *quantifier, pronoun* **1** used in order to talk about two people or things together: *They both have good jobs.* | *Hold it in both hands.* | *Both women are famous writers.* | *Both of my grandfathers are farmers.* **2 both...and...** used in order to emphasize that something is true of two people, things, situations etc.: *Dan plays both football and basketball.* –see usage note at EACH¹

**both·er¹** /'bɑðɚ/ *v* **1** [I,T] to make someone feel slightly annoyed or upset, especially by interrupting what s/he is doing: *"Why didn't you ask me for help?" "I didn't want to bother you."* **2** [I,T] to make the effort to do something: *I'll never get the job, so why bother applying?* **3 sorry to bother you** SPOKEN said in order to politely interrupt what someone is doing: *Sorry to bother you, but I have a few questions.* **4** [T] to upset or frighten someone by trying to hurt him/her, touch him/her sexually etc.: *If that man's bothering you, tell the police.*

**bother²** *n* someone or something that slightly annoys or upsets you: *"Thanks for your help." "That's okay; it's no bother at all."* (=it is not difficult to help) –**bothersome** *adj*

**bot·tle¹** /'bɑtl/ *n* **1** a container with a narrow top for keeping liquids in, usually made of glass or plastic: *a wine bottle* | *a baby's bottle* –see picture at CONTAINER **2** the amount of liquid that a bottle contains: *We drank the entire bottle.* **3 hit the bottle** to start drinking a lot of alcohol regularly

**bottle²** *v* [T] to put a liquid into a bottle after you have made it: *wine bottled in California*
**bottle** sth ↔ **up** *phr v* [T] to not allow yourself to show strong feelings or emotions: *You shouldn't bottle up your anger like that.*

**bottled** /'bɑtld/ *adj* **bottled water/beer etc.** water, beer etc. that is sold in a bottle

**bot·tle·neck** /'bɑtl,nɛk/ *n* **1** a place in a road where the traffic cannot pass easily, so that cars are delayed **2** a delay in part of a process that makes the whole process take longer: *a bottleneck in factory production*

**bot·tom¹** /'bɑtəm/ *n* **1** the lowest part of something: *The fruit at the bottom of the basket was spoiled.* **2** the flat surface on the lowest side of an object: *What's on the bottom of your shoe?* **3** the lowest position in an organization or company, or on a list etc.: *He started at the bottom, and now he manages the store.* **4** INFORMAL a word meaning the part of your body that you sit on, used especially when talking to children **5** the ground under an ocean, river etc., or the flat land in a valley: *The bottom of the river is rocky.* **6** the part of a set of clothes that you wear on the lower part of your body: *pajama bottoms* **7 get to the bottom of sth** INFORMAL to find the cause of a problem or

situation: *We've got to get to the bottom of this!* –compare TOP¹ –see also ROCK BOTTOM

**bottom²** *adj* in the lowest place or position: *The papers are in the bottom drawer.*

**bottom³** *v*
**bottom out** *phr v* [I] if a situation, price etc. bottoms out, it stops getting worse or lower, usually before it starts improving again. *The decrease in car sales has finally bottomed out.*

**bot·tom·less** /'bɑtəmlɪs/ *adj* **1** extemely deep **2** seeming to have no end: *a bottomless supply of money*

**bottom line** /ˌ.. './ *n* **the bottom line a)** the main fact about a situation that you must accept, even though you may not like it: *The bottom line is that we have to win this game.* **b)** the profit or the amount of money that a business makes or loses

**bough** /baʊ/ *n* LITERARY a main branch on a tree

**bought** /bɔt/ *v* the past tense and PAST PARTICIPLE of BUY

**boul·der** /'boʊldɚ/ *n* a large stone or piece of rock

**bou·le·vard** /'bʊləvɑrd, 'bu-/ *n* a wide road in a town or city

**bounce¹** /baʊns/ *v*
**1** [I,T] if a ball or other object bounces, it hits a surface and then immediately moves away from it, or you make it move in this way: *The ball bounced off the wall and hit Marie on the nose.* **2** [I] to move up and down, especially because you are walking or jumping on a surface that is made of rubber, has springs etc.: *Don't bounce on the bed.* **3** [I,T] if a check bounces or a bank bounces a check, the bank will not pay any money because there is not enough money in the account of the person who wrote it **4** [I] to walk quickly and with a lot of energy: *The kids came bouncing down the stairs.* **5 bounce ideas off sb** to ask someone for his/her opinion about an idea, plan etc. before you decide something: *Could I bounce a few ideas off you?*

bounce

**bounce back** *phr v* [I] to feel better quickly, or to become successful again after having a lot of problems: *Experts expect the economy to bounce back.*

**bounce²** *n* **1** [C,U] the quality that makes things able to BOUNCE, or an act of bouncing: *Catch the ball on the first bounce.* **2** [U] the ability to BOUNCE

**bounc·er** /'baʊnsɚ/ *n* someone whose job is to keep people who behave badly out of a club, BAR etc.

**bounc·ing** /'baʊnsɪŋ/ *adj* a word meaning healthy and active, used especially about babies: *a bouncing baby boy*

**bounc·y** /ˈbaʊnsi/ *adj* **1** able to BOUNCE or be bounced easily: *a bouncy ball* | *a bouncy bed* **2** happy and full of energy

**bound**[1] /baʊnd/ *v* the past tense and PAST PARTICIPLE of BIND

**bound**[2] *adj* **1 be bound to** to be certain to do something: *She's such a nice girl that she's bound to make friends.* **2** tied up and unable to move: *Their bodies were discovered bound and gagged.* **3** having a legal or moral duty to do something: *The company is bound by law to provide us with safety equipment.* **4 -bound** controlled or limited by something, so that you cannot do what you want: *a fog-bound airport* **5 bound and determined** determined to do or achieve something, even if it is difficult: *He's bound and determined to become one of baseball's premier players.* **6** intending to go in a particular direction or to a particular place: *a plane bound for Peru*

**bound**[3] *v* **1 be bounded by** if a place is bounded by another place or thing, its edges are marked by that place or thing: *The neighborhood is bounded by Decoto Road, Fremont Boulevard, and Interstate 880.* **2** [I] to move quickly and with a lot of energy: *George came bounding down the stairs.*

**bound**[4] *n* a long or high jump made with a lot of energy: *With one bound he had left his seat and was half way to the door.* —see also BOUNDS

**bound·a·ry** /ˈbaʊndəri, -dri/ *n* **1** the line that marks the edge of a surface, space, or area of land inside a country: *The Mississippi forms a natural boundary between Tennessee and Arkansas.* —compare BORDER[1] **2** the highest or most extreme limit that something can reach: *the boundaries of human knowledge*

**bound·less** /ˈbaʊndlɪs/ *adj* without any limits or end: *boundless optimism*

**bounds** /baʊndz/ *n* [plural] legal or social limits or rules: *His imagination knows no bounds.* (=has no limits) —see also OUT-OF-BOUNDS

**boun·ti·ful** /ˈbaʊnɪfəl/ *adj* LITERARY large or generous: *a bountiful harvest*

**boun·ty** /ˈbaʊnti/ *n* **1** [U] LITERARY a generous amount of something, especially food **2** money that is given as a reward for catching a criminal —**bountiful** *adj*: *a bountiful harvest*

**bou·quet** /boʊˈkeɪ, bu-/ *n* **1** a group of flowers given to someone as a present or carried at a formal occasion **2** [C,U] the smell of a wine: *a rich bouquet*

**bour·bon** /ˈbɚbən/ *n* [U] a type of American WHISKEY made from corn

**bour·geois** /bʊrˈʒwɑ, ˈbʊrʒwɑ/ *adj* DISAPPROVING too interested in having a lot of possessions and a high position in society

**bour·geoi·sie** /ˌbʊrʒwɑˈzi/ *n* **the bourgeoisie** ⇨ MIDDLE CLASS

**'bout** /baʊt/ SPOKEN NONSTANDARD ⇨ ABOUT

**bout** /baʊt/ *n* **1** a short period of time during which you do something a lot or suffer from a particular illness: *a bout of drinking* | *a bout of the flu* **2** a BOXING or WRESTLING competition

**bou·tique** /buˈtik/ *n* a small store that sells very fashionable clothes or decorations

**bo·vine** /ˈboʊvaɪn/ *adj* TECHNICAL relating to cows, or like a cow

**bow**[1] /baʊ/ *v* [I,T] to bend your head or the top part of your body forward, as a sign of respect or as a way of thanking an AUDIENCE after you perform

**bow down** *phr v* [I] to bend forward from your waist, especially when you are already kneeling, in order to pray

**bow out** *phr v* [I] to decide not to take part in something any longer: *Two more Republicans have bowed out of the presidential race.*

**bow to** sb/sth *phr v* [T] to finally agree to do something that other people want you to do, even though you do not want to: *Congress may bow to public pressure and reduce the gas tax.*

**bow**[2] /boʊ/ *n* **1** a knot of cloth or string with a curved part on each side: *a girl with a red bow in her hair* **2** a tool used for shooting ARROWS, made of a piece of wood held in a curve by a tight string **3** a long thin piece of wood with hair stretched tightly from one end to the other, used for playing STRING instruments

**bow**[3] /baʊ/ *n* **1** the act of bowing (BOW) **2 take a bow** to BOW at the end of a performance to receive APPLAUSE **3** the front part of a ship

**bow**[4] /boʊ/ *v* [I] to bend or curve

**bow·el** /ˈbaʊəl/ *n* [C usually plural] the part of the body below the stomach where food is made into solid waste material

**bowl**[1] /boʊl/ *n* **1** a wide round container that is open at the top, used for holding liquids, food etc.: *Mix the eggs and butter in a large bowl.* | *a soup bowl* **2** also **bowlful** the amount that a bowl will hold: *a bowl of rice* **3** the part of an object that is shaped like a bowl: *a toilet bowl* **4** also **Bowl** a special game played by two of the best football teams after the normal playing season: *the Rose Bowl*

**bowl**[2] *v* [I,T] to play the game of BOWLING

**bowl** sb ↔ **over** *phr v* [T] to surprise, please, or excite someone very much: *When Tony met Angela, he was completely bowled over.*

**bow-legged** /ˈboʊˌlɛgɪd, -ˌlɛgd/ *adj* having legs that curve out at the knee

**bowl·ing** /ˈboʊlɪŋ/ *n* [U] an indoor game in which you roll a heavy ball to try to knock down a group of objects shaped like bottles: *Let's go bowling!*

**bowl·ing al·ley** /ˈ.. ˌ../ *n* a building where you can go BOWLING

**bow tie** /ˈboʊ taɪ/ *n* a short piece of cloth tied in the shape of a BOW, which men wear around their necks

**box**[1] /bɑks/ *n* **1** a container for putting things in, especially one with four stiff straight sides: *a cardboard box* —see picture at CONTAINER **2** the amount that a box can hold: *a box of candy* **3** a small area in a larger space such as a theater or court: *the jury box* **4** a small square on an official form for people to write information in: *Write your name and address in the box at the top.* **5** ↳ P.O. BOX

**box**[2] *v* **1** [I,T] to fight someone with your hands as a sport while wearing big leather GLOVE*s* **2** [T] to put things in a box or in boxes **3** [T] to draw a box around something on a page

**box sb/sth** ↔ **in** *phr v* [T] **1** to enclose someone or something in a small space where it is not possible to move freely: *The Honda in the driveway has **boxed** my car **in**.* **2** **feel boxed in** to feel that you are limited in what you can do in a difficult situation

**box·car** /'bɑkskɑr/ *n* a railroad car with high sides and a roof that is used for carrying goods

**box·er** /'bɑksɚ/ *n* **1** someone who boxes, especially as a job: *a heavyweight boxer* **2** a dog with short light brown hair and a flat nose

**boxer shorts** /'.. ,./ *n* [plural] loose underwear for men

**box·ing** /'bɑksɪŋ/ *n* [U] the sport of fighting with your hands while wearing big leather GLOVE*s*

**box of·fice** /'. ,../ *n* a place in a theater, concert hall etc. where tickets are sold

**box spring** /'. ,./ *n* a base containing metal springs that you put under a MATTRESS to make a bed

**boy**[1] /bɔɪ/ *n* **1** a male child or young man: *a school for boys* **2** someone's son, especially a young one: *How old is your boy?* **3** **paper/delivery etc. boy** a young man who does a particular job **4** **city/local etc. boy** INFORMAL a man of any age from a particular place or social group: *I'm just a country boy.* **5** **the boys** INFORMAL a group of men who are friends and often go out together: *playing cards with the boys* **6** SPOKEN used when speaking to a male animal, such as a horse or a dog: *Good boy, Patches!*

**boy**[2], **oh boy** *interjection* said in order to emphasize a statement: *Boy, is he mad!*

**boy·cott** /'bɔɪkɑt/ *v* [T] to refuse to buy something, use something, or take part in something as a way of protesting: *We boycott all products tested on animals.* —**boycott** *n*

**boy·friend** /'bɔɪfrɛnd/ *n* a boy or man with whom you have a romantic relationship

**boy·hood** /'bɔɪhʊd/ *n* [U] LITERARY the time in a man's life when he is very young

**boy·ish** /'bɔɪ-ɪʃ/ *adj* looking or behaving like a boy: *his boyish laughter*

**Boy Scouts** /'. ,./ *n* an organization for boys that teaches them practical skills and helps develop their character —compare GIRL SCOUTS

**bo·zo** /'boʊzoʊ/ *n* INFORMAL someone who you think is stupid or silly

**bra** /brɑ/ *n* a piece of underwear that a woman wears to support her breasts

**brace**[1] /breɪs/ *v* [T] **1** to prepare for something unpleasant that is going to happen. ***Brace yourself for some bad news!*** **2** to prevent something from falling or moving by supporting it

**brace**[2] *n* something used or worn in order to support something: *Jill had to wear a neck brace for six weeks.* —see also BRACES

**brace·let** /'breɪslɪt/ *n* a band or chain that you wear around your wrist or arm as a decoration —see picture at JEWELRY

**brac·es** /'breɪsɪz/ *n* [plural] a connected set of wires that people, especially children, have to put on their teeth to make them straight

**brac·ing** /'breɪsɪŋ/ *adj* bracing air or weather is cold and makes you feel very awake and healthy

**brack·et**[1] /'brækɪt/ *n* **1** **income/tax/age etc. bracket** an income etc. that is inside a particular range: *Your new job puts you in the highest tax bracket.* **2** one of the pair of marks [ ] put around words to show that the rest of the writing can be read and understood without these words: *All grammar information is given **in brackets**.* **3** a piece of metal, wood, or plastic put in or on a wall to support something such as a shelf

**bracket**[2] *v* [T] to put BRACKET*s* around a written word, piece of information etc.

**brack·ish** /'brækɪʃ/ *adj* brackish water is not pure because it is slightly salty

**brag** /bræg/ *v* **-gged, -gging** [I,T] to talk too proudly about what you have done, what you own etc.: *Todd's always **bragging about** how smart he is.*

**brag·gart** /'brægɚt/ *n* someone who BRAG*s*

**braid**[1] /breɪd/ *n* [C,U] a length of hair or a narrow band of material that has been separated into three parts and then woven together: *a girl with her hair **in braids** \ a red jacket with gold braid* —**braided** *adj* —see picture at HAIRSTYLE

**braid**[2] *v* [T] to make a BRAID

**braille** /breɪl/ *n* [U] a form of printing with raised round marks that blind people can read by touching

**brain**[1] /breɪn/ *n* **1** [C,U] the organ inside your head that controls how you think, feel, and move: *Jorge suffered brain damage in the accident.* **2** the ability to think clearly and learn quickly: *She's nice, but she doesn't have much of a brain.* **3** INFORMAL someone who is very intelligent: *Some of the best brains in the country are here tonight.* **4** **have sth on the brain** INFORMAL to be always thinking about something:

*I have that song on the brain today.* —see also
NO-BRAINER

**brain**$^2$ *v* [T] OLD-FASHIONED to hit someone on the head very hard: *I'll brain you if you don't be quiet!*

**brain·child** /'breɪntʃaɪld/ *n* [singular] INFORMAL an idea, organization etc. that someone has thought of without any help from anyone else: *The personal computer was the brainchild of a man named Steve Jobs.*

**brain·less** /'breɪnlɪs/ *adj* INFORMAL silly and stupid: *You brainless idiot!*

**brains** /breɪnz/ *n* [plural] **1** the ability to think clearly and learn quickly: *If he had any brains he'd figure it out for himself.* | *Use your brains, Veronica.* **2 be the brains behind sth** to be the person who thought of and developed a particular plan, system, organization etc.: *Bill Gates is the brains behind Microsoft* —see also **pick sb's brain(s)** (PICK$^1$) **rack your brain(s)** (RACK$^2$)

**brain·storm** /'breɪnstɔrm/ *n* [singular] INFORMAL a sudden intelligent idea: *I've just had a brainstorm!*

**brain·storming** /'breɪn,stɔrmɪŋ/ *n* [U] the act of meeting with a group of people in order to try to develop ideas and think of ways to solve problems: *a brainstorming session*

**brain·wash** /'breɪnwɑʃ, -wɔʃ/ *v* [T] to make someone believe something that is not true by using force, confusing him/her, or continuously repeating it over a long period of time —**brainwashing** *n* [U]

**brain·y** /'breɪni/ *adj* INFORMAL able to think clearly and learn quickly: *Out of all of us, Richard was always the brainy one.*

**braise** /breɪz/ *v* [T] to cook meat or vegetables slowly in a small amount of liquid in a closed container

**brake**$^1$ /breɪk/ *n* **1** a piece of equipment that makes a vehicle go more slowly or stop: *My car needs new brakes.* —see picture on page 469 **2 put the brakes on sth** to stop something that is happening: *efforts to put the brakes on rising prices*

**brake**$^2$ *v* [I] to make a vehicle go more slowly or stop by using its BRAKE: *She had to brake suddenly to avoid a dog in the road.*

**bran** /bræn/ *n* [U] the crushed outer skin of wheat or a similar grain

**branch**$^1$ /bræntʃ/ *n* **1** part of a tree that grows out from the TRUNK (=main stem) and has leaves, fruit, or smaller branches growing from it **2** one part of something larger such as an organization, a subject of study, or a family: *The company has branches in Dallas and Toronto.* | *a branch of medicine* **3** a smaller, less important part of something that leads away from the larger, more important part of it: *a branch of the Missouri River*

**branch**$^2$ *v* [I] also **branch off** to divide into two or more smaller, narrower, or less important parts: *Turn off where the road branches to the right.*

**branch out** *phr v* [I] to do something new in addition to what you usually do: *The bookstore has decided to branch out into renting movies.*

**brand**$^1$ /brænd/ *n* **1** a type of product made by a particular company: *different brands of soap* **2 brand of humor/politics/religion etc.** a particular type of humor, politics etc.: *You know what I think of Jerry's brand of humor.* **3** a mark burned into an animal's skin that shows whom it belongs to

**brand**$^2$ *v* [T] **1** to make a mark on something such as an animal, in order to show whom it belongs to **2** to consider someone as a very bad type of person, often unfairly: *Pete got branded as a troublemaker when he was a kid.*

**bran·dish** /'brændɪʃ/ *v* [T] to wave something around in a dangerous and threatening way: *He burst into the store brandishing a knife.*

**brand name** /'. ,./ *n* the name a company gives to the goods it has produced: *brand names such as Jell-O and Coca-Cola*

**brand-new** /,bræn'nu◂/ *adj* new and not used: *a brand-new car*

**bran·dy** /'brændi/ *n* [C,U] a strong alcoholic drink made from wine, or a glass of this drink

**brash** /bræʃ/ *adj* behaving too confidently and speaking too loudly: *a brash young man*

**brass** /bræs/ *n* **1** [U] a very hard bright yellow metal that is a mixture of COPPER and ZINC **2 the brass (section)** the people in an ORCHESTRA or band who play musical instruments such as the TRUMPET or horn **3 get down to brass tacks** INFORMAL to start talking about the most important details or facts

**bras·siere** /brə'zɪr/ *n* ⇨ BRA

**brass knuck·les** /,. '../ *n* [plural] a set of metal rings worn over your KNUCKLEs, used as a weapon

**brass·y** /'bræsi/ *adj* **1** like BRASS in color **2** sounding loud and unpleasant **3** someone who is brassy talks loudly and behaves in a way that is too confident

**brat** /bræt/ *n* INFORMAL a badly behaved child: *Stop acting like a spoiled brat.*

**bra·va·do** /brə'vɑdoʊ/ *n* [U] behavior that is intended to show how brave you are, but is often unnecessary

**brave**$^1$ /breɪv/ *adj* dealing with danger, pain, or difficult situations with courage: *brave soldiers* | *her brave fight against cancer* —**bravely** *adv* —**bravery** *n* [U]

**brave**$^2$ *v* [T] to deal with a difficult, dangerous, or unpleasant situation: *15,000 people braved the hot sun to see Mandela.*

**brave**$^3$ *n* a young fighting man from a Native American tribe

**bread**

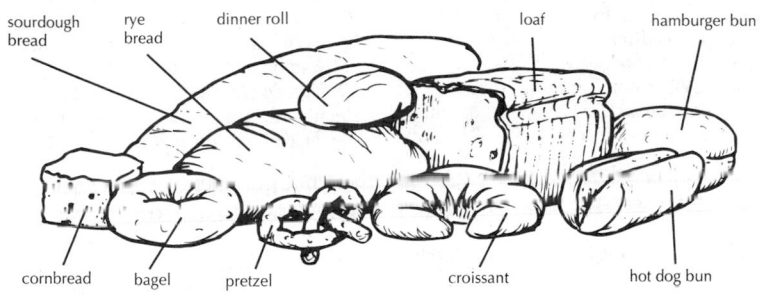

sourdough bread | rye bread | dinner roll | loaf | hamburger bun
cornbread | bagel | pretzel | croissant | hot dog bun

B

**bra·vo** /'brɑvou, brɑ'vou/ *interjection* said in order to show your approval when someone, especially a performer, has done well

**brawl¹** /brɔl/ *n* a noisy fight, especially in a public place

**brawl²** *v* [I] to fight in a noisy way, especially in a public place: *brawling in the street*

**brawn** /brɔn/ *n* [U] physical strength: *You have the brains, I have the brawn.* –**brawny** *adj*: *brawny arms*

**bray** /breɪ/ *v* [I] if a DONKEY brays, it makes a loud sound

**bra·zen¹** /'breɪzən/ *adj* showing that you do not feel ashamed about your behavior: *a brazen lie* –**brazenly** *adv*

**brazen²** *v*
   **brazen** sth ↔ **out** *phr v* [T] to deal with a difficult or embarrassing situation by appearing to be confident rather than ashamed

**bra·zier** /'breɪʒɚ/ *n* a metal pan that holds a fire

**breach** /britʃ/ *n* **1** [C,U] an act of breaking a law, rule, agreement etc.: *You are in breach of your contract.* **2** a hole or broken place in a wall or a similar structure, especially one made during a military attack –**breach** *v* [T]

**bread** /brɛd/ *n* [U] **1** a common food made from flour, water, and YEAST: *We need a loaf of bread.* (=large piece of bread that can be cut into pieces) | *bread and butter* **2** SLANG money **3** sb's bread and butter INFORMAL where the owner of a business gets most of his/her income from: *Tourists are our bread and butter.* **4** daily bread the money that you need in order to live **5** know which side your bread is buttered on INFORMAL to know who to be nice to in order to get advantages for yourself

**bread·bas·ket** /'brɛd,bæskɪt/ *n* **1** [singular] INFORMAL the part of a country or other large area that provides most of the food: *The midwest is the breadbasket of America.* **2** a basket for holding or serving bread

**bread·crumbs** /'brɛdkrʌmz/ *n* [plural] very small pieces of bread used in cooking

**bread·ed** /'brɛdɪd/ *adj* covered in BREAD-CRUMBS, then cooked: *breaded veal*

**breadth** /brɛdθ, brɛtθ/ *n* [U] **1** the distance from one side of something to the other, especially something very wide; width **2** a wide range or variety: *No one can match Dr. Brennan's breadth of knowledge.*

**bread·win·ner** /'brɛd,wɪnɚ/ *n* the member of a family who earns the money to support the others

**break¹** /breɪk/ *v* broke, broken, breaking
**1** ▶IN PIECES◀ [T] if something breaks or someone breaks it, it separates into two or more pieces, especially because it has been hit or dropped: *Careful, those glasses break easily.* | *I broke off a piece of the candy bar for Kathy.* | *They had to break the window to get into the house.*
**2** ▶BODY PART◀ [T] if you break a part of your body, the bone splits into two or more pieces: *Sharon broke her leg skiing.*
**3** ▶END STH◀ [I,T] to not continue, or to end something: *Dee's laugh broke the silence* | *I don't smoke anymore, but it was hard to break the habit.*
**4** ▶NOT WORK◀ [I,T] to damage something such as a machine so that it does not work, or to become damaged in this way: *You've broken the TV?* | *It just broke. I didn't even touch it!*
**5** ▶SURFACE/SKIN◀ [T] to damage the surface of something so that it splits or has a hole in it: *Do not use this product if the seal has been broken.*
**6** break loose/free to suddenly become free or able to move without any restrictions: *I broke free from him and ran.*
**7** break a law/rule to disobey a law or rule: *What's wrong? We're not breaking any rules.*
**8** break a promise/an agreement/your word to not do what you promised to do: *politicians who break their election promises*
**9** break your neck INFORMAL to hurt yourself very badly: *Get the ice off the sidewalk; we don't want people breaking their necks.*
**10** break for lunch/coffee etc. to stop working in order to eat or drink something: *We broke for lunch at about 12:30.*
**11** break a record to do something faster or better than it has ever been done before: *He decided he would retire if he broke the world rec-*

*ord.* (=beat the best one in the world)

**12 break the news to sb** to tell someone about something bad that has happened: *Freddy didn't want to break the news to Mom.*

**13 ▶NEWS/EVENT◀** if news about an important event breaks, it becomes known by everyone after having been secret: *The next morning, the news broke that Monroe was dead.*

**14 break even** to neither make a profit nor lose money: *We broke even in our first year of business.*

**15 ▶DAY◀** if day breaks, light begins to show in the sky as the sun rises

**16 ▶WAVE◀** if a wave breaks, it begins to look white on top because it is coming close to the shore –see also **break the ice** (ICE¹)

**break away** *phr v* [I] **1** to escape: *Nelson broke away from the policemen.* **2** to change what you have been doing because it limits your freedom, is boring etc.: *teenagers trying to break away from their parents*

**break down** *phr v* **1** [I] if a large machine breaks down, it stops working: *A truck had broken down in the middle of the intersection.* **2** [I] if a discussion, system, opinion etc. breaks down, it fails or stops existing: *The talks broke down completely in June 1982.* | *breaking down the divisions between racial groups* **3** [T **break** sth ↔ **down**] to hit something, such as a door, so hard that it falls down **4 break down and do sth** to finally do something that you did not want to do, because someone has persuaded or forced you: *He finally broke down and admitted he'd stolen it.* **5** [I,T] if a substance breaks down or is broken down, it is reduced or changed, usually as a result of a chemical process: *Wastes in the water are broken down using bacteria.* **6** [I] to be unable to stop yourself from crying: *She broke down several times during the funeral.* **7** [T **break** sth ↔ **down**] to make something such as a job, report, plan etc. simpler by dividing it into parts: *You can break the exam question down into three parts to make it easier.*

**break in** *phr v* **1** [I] to enter a building using force, in order to steal something: *They broke in through that window.* **2** [T **break** sb/sth ↔ **in**] to make a person or animal become used to the work she, he, or it has to do: *a training camp for breaking in new soldiers* **3** [I] to interrupt someone when s/he is speaking: *The operator broke in saying, "You need another 75¢ to continue the call."* **4** [I,T **break** sth ↔ **in**] if you break shoes or boots in, or they break in, they become more comfortable because you have been wearing them

**break into** sth *phr v* [T] **1** to enter a building using force in order to steal something: *We think he broke into the room through the back window.* **2 break into a run** to suddenly begin running **3** to become involved in a new activity, especially a business activity: *companies*

*trying to break into the Eastern European markets*

**break off** *phr v* **1** [T] to end a relationship, especially a political or romantic one: *They've broken off their engagement.* **2** [I, T] to suddenly stop doing something, especially talking to someone: *She broke off, forgetting what she wanted to say.*

**break out** *phr v* [I] **1** if something bad such as a disease, fire, or war breaks out, it begins to happen: *Last night fire broke out in the 12th Street warehouse.* **2** to change the way you live or behave, especially because you are bored: *You've got to break out of this rut!* (=stop doing the same things all the time) **3** to suddenly begin to have red spots on your skin, especially on your face: *Chocolate makes me break out.* **4 break out in a sweat** to start sweating (SWEAT) **5** to escape from prison

**break through** *phr v* **1** [T **break through** sth] to change or end a way of thinking: *It's difficult to break through cultural differences and meet people in a new country.* **2** [I,T] if the sun breaks through, you can see it through the clouds

**break up** *phr v* **1** [T **break** sth ↔ **up**] to separate something into smaller parts because it is too big, too long, or too boring: *Large companies were being broken up to encourage competition.* **2** [I] to end a marriage or romantic relationship, or to stop being together as a group: *Troy and I broke up last month.* | *When did the Beatles break up?* **3** [I,T] if a fight breaks up or someone breaks it up, the people stop fighting or are made to do this **4** [I] if a crowd or meeting breaks up, people start to leave **5** [I,T **break** sth ↔ **up**] to break, or break something into small pieces: *The ship broke up on the rocks.* | *We used shovels to break up the soil.*

**break with** sb/sth *phr v* [T] to leave a group or organization because you have had a disagreement with them: *The Socialists needed money after they broke with the Communists.*

**break²** *n*

**1 ▶A REST◀** a period of time when you stop working in order to rest, eat, or travel: *Matthews spoke for three hours without taking a break.* **lunch/coffee break** (=when you stop to eat lunch or drink coffee): *We needed a break, so we went up to the mountains for a few days.* | **Spring Break** (=spring vacation from college) *is at the end of March.* –see usage note at VACATION

**2 ▶STH STOPS◀** a period of time when something stops for a while and then starts again: *There was a break of two years between his last book and this one.* | *a break in the conversation*

**3 give sb a break** SPOKEN to stop annoying, criticizing, or being unkind to someone: *Give me a break, you guys! I can't get the money until Friday.*

**4 ►A CHANCE◄** a chance to do something that improves your job: *The band's big break came when they sang on a local TV show.*

**5 ►END/CHANGE◄** [singular] a situation when a relationship or something traditional ends suddenly or changes completely: *In a break with tradition, the city council decided not to have a parade.*

**6 ►A SPACE◄** a space between two things or in a group of things: *a break in the clouds*

**7 ►BONE◄** a place where a bone in someone's body has broken

**break·a·ble** /'breikəbəl/ *adj* made of material that breaks easily

**break·age** /'breikidʒ/ *n* FORMAL something that has been broken: *All breakages must be paid for.*

**break·a·way** /'breikə,wei/ *adj* **breakaway group/party/movement etc.** a group etc. that has been formed by people who left another group because of a disagreement

**break·down** /'breikdaun/ *n* **1** [C,U] the failure of a system or relationship: *a breakdown in the peace talks* **2** an occasion when a car or a piece of machinery stops working **3** ⇨ NERVOUS BREAKDOWN **4** a statement explaining the details of something such as a bill: *I'd like a breakdown of these figures, please.*

**break·fast** /'brɛkfəst/ *n* [C,U] the meal you have in the morning: *I had bacon and eggs for breakfast. | Did you have time to eat breakfast?* —see usage note at MEAL TIMES

**break-in** /'. ./ *n* an act of entering a building illegally using force

**break·ing point** /'.. ,./ *n* [U] the point at which someone or something is no longer able to work well or deal with problems: *He was at breaking point. I thought he was going to kill me.*

**break·neck** /'breiknɛk/ *adj* extremely and often dangerously fast: *She was driving at breakneck speed.*

**break·through** /'breikθru/ *n* an important new discovery in something you have been studying: *Scientists have made an important breakthrough in the treatment of heart disease.*

**break·up** /'breikʌp/ *n* [C,U] **1** the act of ending a marriage or other relationship **2** the separation of an organization, country etc. into smaller parts: *the breakup of Yugoslavia*

**break·wa·ter** /'breik,wɔtɚ, -,wɑtɚ/ *n* a strong wall built out into the sea to protect the shore from the force of the waves

**breast** /brɛst/ *n* **1** one of the two round raised parts on a woman's chest —see picture at BODY **2** [C,U] the part of the body, especially a bird's body, between the neck and the stomach, or the meat from this: *turkey breast*

**breast-feed** /'. ,./ *v* [I,T] if a woman breast feeds, she feeds a baby with milk from her breasts

**breast·stroke** /'brɛst/strouk/ *n* [U] a way of swimming in which you push your arms out from your chest and then bring them back to your side

**breath** /brɛθ/ *n* **1** [U] the air that comes out of your lungs when you breathe: *I can smell alcohol on your breath. | The cat has had bad breath.* (=it smells bad) **2** [C,U] the act of breathing air into your lungs, or the amount of air you breathe: *Take a big/deep breath* (=breathe in a lot of air once) *and try to calm down.* **3 be out of breath** to have difficulty breathing because you have just been running or exercising: *Lily was out of breath when she answered the phone.* **4 hold your breath a)** to breathe in and close your mouth to keep the air in your lungs: *I couldn't hold my breath anymore.* **b)** to wait anxiously to see what is going to happen: *We were all holding our breath, waiting for the winner to be announced.* **5 save your breath/don't waste your breath** SPOKEN used in order to tell someone that it is not worth saying anything: *Save your breath - he won't listen anyway.* **6 catch your breath** to begin breathing normally again after you have been running or exercising: *I had to sit down to catch my breath.* **7 a breath of fresh air** something that is different, exciting, and enjoyable: *Your happy face is like a breath of fresh air around here.* **8 take your breath away** to be extremely beautiful or exciting: *a view that will take your breath away* **9 under your breath** in a quiet voice: *"I hate you," he muttered under his breath.*

**breath·a·ble** /'briðəbəl/ *adj* **1** clothing that is breathable allows air to pass through it easily **2** able to be breathed: *breathable air*

**Breath·a·lyz·er** /'brɛθə,laizɚ/ *n* TRADEMARK a piece of equipment used by the police to see if a car driver has drunk too much alcohol —**breathalyze** *v* [T]

**breathe** /brið/ *v* **1** [I,T] to take air into your lungs and send it out again: *Relax and breathe deeply.* (=take in a lot of air) **2** [I,T] to blow air, smoke, or smells out of your mouth: *Stop breathing garlic all over me.* **3 breathe a sigh of relief** to stop being worried about something: *We all breathed a sigh of relief as he climbed off the roof.* **4 breathe down sb's neck** INFORMAL to watch what someone is doing so carefully that it makes him/her feel nervous or annoyed: *I can't work with you breathing down my neck.* **5 not breathe a word** to not tell anyone about a secret: *Promise not to breathe a word to anyone.* **6 breathe life into sth** to change a situation so that people feel more excited or interested: *Some new teachers might breathe a little life into this school.*

**breathe in** *phr v* [I,T **breathe sth ↔ in**] to take

air, smoke, a particular type of smell etc. into your lungs: *breathing in the fresh sea air*
**breathe out** *phr v* [I,T **breathe** sth ↔ **out**] [I] to send air, smoke, a particular type of smell etc. from your lungs: *OK, now breathe out slowly.*

**breath·er** /'briðə/ *n* INFORMAL a short period of rest from an activity: *OK, everybody, let's take a 20 minute breather.*

**breath·less** /'brɛθlɪs/ *adj* having difficulty breathing in a normal way —**breathlessly** *adv*

**breath·tak·ing** /'brɛθˌteɪkɪŋ/ *adj* extremely impressive, exciting, or surprising: *breathtaking scenery*

**breath·y** /'brɛθi/ *adj* if someone's voice is breathy, you can hear his/her breath when s/he speaks

**breed¹** /brid/ *v* **bred** /brɛd/, **bred, breeding**
**1** [I] if animals breed, they have babies: *Rats can breed every six weeks.* **2** [T] to keep animals or plants in order to produce babies, or to develop new animals or plants: *He breeds horses.* **3** [T] to cause a particular feeling or condition: *The crowded living conditions bred disease and crime.*

**breed²** *n* **1** a type of animal, especially one that people have kept to breed: *What breed is your dog?* **2** a particular type of person or type of thing: *the first in a new breed of home computers*

**breed·er** /'bridə/ *n* someone who breeds animals or plants

**breed·ing** /'bridɪŋ/ *n* [U] **1** the act or process of animals producing babies **2** the activity of keeping animals or plants in order to produce babies, or to develop new types **3** OLD-FASHIONED polite social behavior

**breeding ground** /'.. ,./ *n* a place or situation where something grows or develops: *Universities were a breeding ground for protests against the war.*

**breeze¹** /briz/ *n* **1** a light gentle wind —see usage note at WEATHER¹ **2** **be a breeze** SPOKEN to be very easy to do: *Learning to drive was a breeze.* —see also **shoot the breeze** (SHOOT¹)

**breeze²** *v* [I] INFORMAL to walk somewhere in a quick confident way: *She breezed into my office and sat down.*
**breeze through** sth *phr v* [T] INFORMAL to finish a piece of work or pass a test very easily: *Sherry breezed through her final exams.*

**breez·y** /'brizi/ *adj* **1** cheerful, confident, and relaxed: *his breezy manner* **2** breezy weather is when the wind blows in a fairly strong way

**breth·ren** /'brɛðrən/ *n* [plural] OLD-FASHIONED male members of an organization, especially a religious group

**brev·i·ty** /'brɛvəti/ *n* [U] FORMAL **1** the quality of expressing something in very few words: *We appreciated the speaker's brevity.* **2** shortness of time: *the brevity of the meeting*

**brew¹** /bru/ *v* **1** [I,T] if tea or coffee brews or you brew it, boiling water is poured over it to make it ready to drink **2** [I] if something unpleasant is brewing, it will happen soon: *There's a storm brewing.* **3** [T] to make beer

**brew²** *n* a drink that is brewed, such as tea, coffee, or beer

**brew·er** /'bruə/ *n* a person or company that makes beer

**brew·er·y** /'bruəri/ *n* a place where beer is made, or a company that makes beer

**bribe¹** /braɪb/ *n* money or gifts that you use to persuade someone to do something, usually something dishonest: *politicians accused of taking bribes*

**bribe²** *v* [T] to give someone a BRIBE: *They say he bribed the policeman to let him go.*

**brib·er·y** /'braɪbəri/ *n* [U] the act of giving or taking BRIBEs

**bric-a-brac** /'brɪk ə ˌbræk/ *n* [U] small inexpensive objects, used for decoration in a house

**brick¹** /brɪk/ *n* [C,U] a hard block of baked clay used for building walls, houses etc.

**brick²** *v*
**brick** sth ↔ **up** *phr v* [T] to fill or close a space by building a wall of bricks in it: *bricked up windows*

**brick·lay·er** /'brɪkˌleɪə/ *n* someone whose job is to build things with bricks —**bricklaying** *n* [U]

**bri·dal** /'braɪdl/ *adj* relating to a BRIDE or a wedding: *a bridal gown*

**bride** /braɪd/ *n* a woman at the time she gets married or just after she is married

**bride·groom** /'braɪdgrum/ *n* ⇨ GROOM²

**brides·maid** /'braɪdzmeɪd/ *n* a woman who helps the BRIDE and stands beside her during her wedding

**bridge¹** /brɪdʒ/ *n* **1** a structure built over a river, road etc., that allows people or vehicles to cross from one side to the other: *the Brooklyn Bridge* **2** something that provides a connection between two ideas or subjects: *His new book acts as a bridge between art and science.* **3 the bridge** the raised part of a ship from which it can be controlled **4** [U] a card game for four players who play in pairs **5 the bridge of your nose** the upper part of your nose between your eyes **6** a piece of metal for keeping a false tooth in place

**bridge²** *v* [T] **1 bridge the gap (between)** to reduce the difference between two things: *attempting to bridge the gap between rich and poor* **2** to build or form a bridge over something: *a log bridging the stream*

**bri·dle¹** /'braɪdl/ *n* a set of leather bands put on a horse's head to control its movements

**bridle²** *v* **1** [T] to put a BRIDLE on a horse **2** [I,T] to show anger, especially by making a proud upward movement of your chin: *Amy* ***bridled at*** *the insult.*

**brief**[1] /brif/ *adj* **1** continuing for a short time: *a brief look at the newspaper* **2** using only a few words and not describing things in detail: *I'll try to* ***be brief.*** *| a brief letter | Here is the news* ***in brief.*** **–briefly** *adv*

**brief**[2] *n* **1** a set of instructions about some one's duties or jobs: *My brief is to increase sales.* **2** a short statement giving facts about a law case

**brief**[3] *v* [T] to give someone all the information about a situation that s/he will need: *Before we go in, let me* ***brief*** *you* ***on*** *what to expect.* **–briefing** *n* [C,U]

**brief·case** /'brifkeis/ *n* a case used for carrying papers or documents

**briefs** /brifs/ *n* [plural] men's or women's underwear worn on the lower part of the body

**bri·gade** /brɪ'geɪd/ *n* **1** a large group of soldiers forming part of an army **2** USUALLY HUMOROUS a group of people who have similar qualities or beliefs: *the diaper brigade* (=a group of babies)

**brig·a·dier gen·er·al** /ˌbrɪgədɪr 'dʒɛnərəl/ **Brigadier General** *n* an officer who has a high rank in the Army, Air Force, or Marines

**bright** /braɪt/ *adj* **1** shining strongly or with plenty of light: *a bright sunny day | bright lights* **2** intelligent: *Vicky is a very bright child. | a bright idea* **3** bright colors are strong and easy to see: *Her pants were bright red.* **4** cheerful: *a bright smile* **5** likely to be successful: *You have a bright future ahead of you!* **6** **bright and early** SPOKEN very early in the morning: *I'll be here bright and early to pick you up.* **7** **look on the bright side** to see the good things about something that is bad in other ways: *Look on the bright side - at least you didn't lose your job.* **–brightly** *adv* **–brightness** *n* [U] –see also BRIGHTS

**bright·en** /'braɪtn/ **brighten up** *v* [I,T] **1** to become brighter or more pleasant, or to make something do this: *Flowers would brighten up this room. | The weather should brighten in the afternoon.* **2** to become more cheerful, or to make someone else feel like this: *She brightened up when she saw us coming.*

**brights** /braɪts/ *n* [plural] car HEADLIGHTs when they are on as brightly as possible

**bril·liant** /'brɪlyənt/ *adj* **1** brilliant light or color is very bright and strong **2** extremely intelligent: *a brilliant scientist* **–brilliance** *n* [U] **–brilliantly** *adv*

**brim**[1] /brɪm/ *n* **1** the part of a hat that sticks out to protect you from sun and rain **2** **the brim** the top of a container, such as a glass: *The glass was* ***full to the brim.***

**brim**[2] *v* **-mmed, -mming** [I] to be very full of something: *His eyes* ***brimmed with*** *tears.*

**brim over** *phr v* [I] to be full of an emotion or have a lot of ideas

**brine** /braɪn/ *n* [U] water that contains a lot of salt **–briny** *adj*

**bring** /brɪŋ/ *v* **brought, brought, bringing** [T] **1** to take someone or something to the place you are now, to the place you are going to, or to the person you are speaking to or about: *I brought these pictures to show you. | Can I bring a friend with me to the party? | Rob brought her a glass of water.* **2** to cause a particular type of result or reaction: *The article in the newspaper brought angry letters from readers. | The fishing industry brings lots of money into the area.* **3** to make someone come to a place: *"What brings you here?" "I need to discuss something with Mike."* **4** **not bring yourself to do sth** to not be able to do something, especially because you know it will upset or harm someone: *Brenda couldn't bring herself to tell him that Helen was dead.* **5** **bring sth to an end** to do something that shows that an event or situation is at an end: *The President's speech* ***brought*** *the Democratic Conference* ***to an end.*** **6** **bring sth to sb's attention** a phrase used especially in formal writing that means to tell someone something: *Thank you for bringing the problem to our attention.* **7** **bring sth to bear (on)** to use something in order to get the result you want: *Pressure had been brought to bear on the governor from state Democrats.*

**bring** sth ↔ **about** *phr v* [T] to make something happen: *"They say the bank is closing." "What brought that about?"*

**bring** sb/sth **around** *phr v* **1** **bring the conversation around to** to change the subject of a conversation gradually to something new: *Ginny tried to* ***bring*** *the conversation* ***around to*** *the subject of marriage.* **2** [T **bring** sb **around**] to make someone conscious again after s/he has been unconscious

**bring back** *phr v* **1** [T **bring** sth ↔ **back**] to start using something again that had been used in the past: *Many states have voted to* ***bring back*** *the death penalty.* **2** [T **bring back** sth] to make you remember something: *The smell of suntan lotion* ***brought back*** *memories of the summer.*

**bring** sb/sth **down** *phr v* [T] **1** to make something fall or come down: *We are taking action to* ***bring*** *inflation* ***down.*** **2** **bring down a government/president etc.** to force a government etc. to stop being in control of a country

**bring** sth ↔ **forth** *phr v* [T] FORMAL to make something happen, appear, or become available: *No evidence has been* ***brought forth*** *against Mr. Keele.*

**bring** sth ↔ **forward** *phr v* [T] **1** to change the date or time of something so that it happens sooner than it was originally planned to: *They had to* ***bring*** *the wedding* ***forward*** *because Lynn got a new job.* **2** to introduce or suggest a new plan or idea: *Many arguments were* **brought forward** *supporting the changes*.

**bring** sb/sth ↔ **in** *phr v* **1** [T **bring** sb ↔ **in**] to ask or persuade someone to become involved in a discussion, help with a problem etc.: *The police had to* **bring** *the FBI* **in** *to help with their search*. **2** [T **bring** sth ↔ **in**] to earn or produce a particular amount of money: *The painting should* **bring in** *at least a million dollars*. **3 bring in a verdict** if a court or JURY brings in a verdict, it says whether someone is guilty or not

**bring** sth **off** *phr v* [T] to succeed in doing something that is very difficult: *She'll get a promotion if she* **brings off** *the deal*.

**bring** sth ↔ **on** *phr v* [T] to make something bad or unpleasant happen or begin: *Her illness was* **brought on** *by working too much*.

**bring** sth ↔ **out** *phr v* [T] **1** to make something become easier to notice, see, taste etc.: *The red paint* **brings out** *the red in the curtains*. **2 bring out the best/worst in sb** to emphasize someone's best or worst qualities: *Becoming a father has* **brought out** *the best in Dan*. **3** to produce and begin to sell a new product, book, record etc.: *I heard that they're* **bringing out** *a new kind of home computer*.

**bring** sb ↔ **together** *phr v* [T] if an event brings a group of people together, it makes them care about each other more: *Stuart's death really* **brought** *the family* **together**.

**bring** sb/sth ↔ **up** *phr v* [T] **1** to start to talk about a particular subject or person: *Why do you always* **bring up** *your old girlfriends?* **2** to educate and care for a child until s/he is old enough to be independent: *She* **brought up** *three children by herself.* | *I* **was brought up** *a Catholic/Muslim etc*. (=taught to believe a particular religion) **3 bring sb up on charges** if the police bring someone up on charges, they say officially that they think s/he is guilty of a crime

**brink** /brɪŋk/ *n* **be on the brink of** to be about to begin a new or different situation: *Scientists say they're on the brink of a major discovery*.

**brisk** /brɪsk/ *adj* **1** quick and full of energy: *a brisk walk* **2** trade or business that is brisk is very busy **3** weather that is brisk is cold and clear – **briskly** *adv*

**bris·tle**[1] /'brɪsəl/ *n* [C,U] short stiff hair, wire etc.: *a brush with short bristles*

**bristle**[2] *v* [I] **1** to behave in a way that shows you are very angry or annoyed: *He bristled at my suggestion*. **2** if an animal's hair bristles, it stands up stiffly because the animal is afraid or angry

**bris·tly** /'brɪsəli, -sli/ *adj* **1** bristly hair is short and stiff **2** a bristly part of your body has short stiff hairs on it: *a bristly face*

**britch·es** /'brɪtʃɪz/ *n* INFORMAL **1 too big for your britches** too confident in a way that annoys other people **2** HUMOROUS pants

**Brit·ish**[1] /'brɪtɪʃ/ *adj* relating to or coming from Great Britain

**British**[2] *n* **the British** the people of Great Britain

**Brit·on** /'brɪt'n/ *n* someone from Great Britain

**brit·tle** /'brɪtl/ *adj* **1** hard but easily broken: *brittle glass* **2** a system, relationship etc. that is brittle is easily damaged or destroyed: *a brittle friendship* **3** showing no kind feelings: *his brittle nature*

**bro** /brou/ *n* SLANG ⇨ BROTHER[1]

**broach** /broutʃ/ *v* **broach the subject/question etc.** to introduce something as a subject of conversation: *It's often difficult to broach the subject of sex*.

**broad** /brɔd/ *adj* **1** very wide: *broad shoulders* **2** including many different kinds of things or people: *a movie that appeals to a broad range of people* **3** concerning only the main ideas or parts of something: *Could you give me a broad idea of your plans?* **4 in broad daylight** during the day when it is light: *He got stabbed in the street in broad daylight*.

**broad·cast**[1] /'brɔdkæst/ *n* a program on the radio or television: *a news broadcast*

**broadcast**[2] *v* **broadcast** *or* **broadcasted**, **broadcast** *or* **broadcasted**, **broadcasting** **1** [I,T] to send out a radio or television program: *Channel 5 will broadcast the game at 6 o'clock*. **2** [T] to tell something to a lot of people: *If I tell you, don't go broadcasting it all over the office*.

**broad·cast·er** /'brɔd,kæstɚ/ *n* someone who speaks on radio and television programs – compare NEWSCASTER

**broad·cast·ing** /'brɔd,kæstɪŋ/ *n* [U] the business of making radio and television programs

**broad·en** /'brɔdn/ *v* **1** [T] also **broaden out** to increase something such as your knowledge, experience, or number of activities: *Broaden your knowledge with reading*. **2** [I,T] also **broaden out** to make something wider, or to become wider: *The river broadens out here*. **3 broaden your mind** if something broadens your mind, it makes it easier for you to accept other people's beliefs, ways of doing things etc.: *Maybe traveling will broaden his mind*.

**broad·ly** /'brɔdli/ *adv* **1** in a general way: *I know broadly what to expect*. **2 smile/grin broadly** to have a big smile on your face

**broad·mind·ed** /,brɔd'maɪndɪd◂/ *adj* willing to respect opinions or behavior that are very different from your own

**broadside**[1] /,brɔd'saɪd◂/ *adv* with the longest side facing you: *He hit the car broadside*.

**broadside**[2] *v* [T] to crash into the side of another vehicle

**Broad·way** /'brɔdweɪ/ *n* a street in New York that is known as the center of American theater

**bro·cade** /broʊˈkeɪd/ *n* [U] thick heavy cloth that has a pattern of gold and silver threads

**broc·co·li** /ˈbrɑkəli/ *n* [U] a green vegetable with thick groups of small dark green flower-like parts −see picture on page 470

**bro·chure** /broʊˈʃʊr/ *n* a thin book that gives information or advertises something

**brogue** /broʊg/ *n* **1** a strong leather shoe, especially one with a pattern in the leather **2** an ACCENT, especially an Irish or Scottish one

**broil** /brɔɪl/ *v* [I,T] if you broil something, or if something broils, you cook it under or over direct heat: *broiled chicken*

**broil·er** /ˈbrɔɪlɚ/ *n* a special area of a STOVE used for cooking food under direct heat

**broke**¹ /broʊk/ *adj* **1** INFORMAL completely without money: *I'm flat broke*. **2 go broke** INFORMAL if a company or business goes broke, it can no longer operate because it has no money: *The record store went broke last year*. **3 go for broke** INFORMAL to take big risks trying to achieve something: *Let's go for broke and enter the race!*

**broke**² *v* the past tense of BREAK

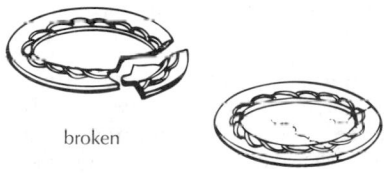

broken

broken

cracked

**bro·ken**¹ /ˈbroʊkən/ *adj* **1** not working correctly: *a broken clock | How did the lawn mower get broken?* **2** cracked or in pieces because of being hit, dropped etc.: *a broken leg | a broken plate* **3** not continuous: *a broken white line* **4** a broken relationship is one that has been destroyed by the separation of a husband and wife: *a broken marriage | Jenny comes from a broken home*. (=her parents separated) **5** extremely mentally or physically weak after suffering a lot: *a broken man* **6 broken agreement/promise etc.** a situation in which someone did not do what s/he promised to **7 broken English/French etc.** English, French etc. that is spoken very slowly, with a lot of mistakes

**broken**² *v* the PAST PARTICIPLE of BREAK

**broken-down** /ˌ.. ˈ.◂/ *adj* broken, old, and needing a lot of repair: *a broken-down trailer*

**broken-heart·ed** /ˌ.. ˈ..◂/ *adj* very sad, especially because someone you love has died or left you

**bro·ker**¹ /ˈbroʊkɚ/ *n* someone whose job is to buy and sell property, insurance, etc. for some-

one else: *a real estate broker* −see also STOCK-BROKER

**broker**² *v* [T] to arrange the details of a deal, plan etc. so that everyone can agree to it: *an agreement brokered by the UN*

**bro·ker·age** /ˈbroʊkərɪdʒ/ *n* [U] the business of being a BROKER

**bron·chi·tis** /brɑŋˈkaɪtɪs/ *n* [U] an illness that affects your breathing and makes you cough −**bronchitic** /brɑŋˈkɪtɪk/ *adj*

**bron·co** /ˈbrɑŋkoʊ/ *n* a wild horse

**bron·to·sau·rus** /ˌbrɑntəˈsɔrəs/ *n* a large DINOSAUR with a very long neck and body

**bronze**¹ /brɑnz/ *n* **1** [U] a hard metal that is a mixture of COPPER and TIN **2** [U] a dull red-brown color **3** a work of art made of bronze: *a bronze by Henry Moore*

**bronze**² *adj* **1** made of BRONZE **2** having the red-brown color of bronze

**bronze med·al** /ˌ. ˈ../ *n* a prize that is given to the person who finishes third in a race, competition etc., usually made of BRONZE

**brooch** /broʊtʃ, brutʃ/ *n* a piece of jewelry that you fasten to your clothes −see picture at JEWELRY

**brood**¹ /brud/ *v* [I] to think about something that you are worried, angry, or sad about for a long time: *Don't just sit there brooding about your problems*.

**brood**² *n* a family of young birds

**brook** /brʊk/ *n* a small stream

**broom** /brum, brʊm/ *n* a large brush with a long handle, used for sweeping floors −see picture at KITCHEN

**broom·stick** /ˈbrumˌstɪk, ˈbrʊm-/ *n* the long thin handle of a BROOM

**broth** /brɔθ/ *n* [U] a soup made by cooking meat or vegetables in water and then removing them: *beef broth*

**broth·el** /ˈbrɑθəl, ˈbrɔ-, -ðəl/ *n* a house where men pay to have sex with PROSTITUTEs

**broth·er**¹ /ˈbrʌðɚ/ *n* **1** a male who has the same parents as you: *Isn't that your big/little* (=older or younger) *brother?* −see picture at FAMILY **2** SPOKEN a word meaning a male friend, used especially by African Americans **3** a man who belongs to the same race, religion, organization etc. as you **4** ⇨ MONK: *Brother Francis* −**brotherly** *adv* −compare SISTER

**brother**² *interjection* **Oh brother!** said when you are annoyed or surprised

**broth·er·hood** /ˈbrʌðɚˌhʊd/ *n* **1** [U] OLD-FASHIONED a feeling of friendship between people: *peace and brotherhood* **2** OLD-FASHIONED a men's organization formed for a particular purpose

**brother-in-law** /ˈ.. . ˌ./ *n* **1** the brother of your husband or wife **2** the husband of your sister −see picture at FAMILY

**B**

**broth·er·ly** /ˈbrʌðəli/ *adj* showing helpfulness, love, loyalty etc., like a brother would: *brotherly love*

**brought** /brɔt/ *v* the past tense and PAST PARTICIPLE of BRING

**brou·ha·ha** /ˈbruhɑhɑ/ *n* [U] INFORMAL unnecessary noise and activity; COMMOTION: *a big brouhaha going on in the street*

**brow** /braʊ/ *n* **1** ⇨ FOREHEAD **2** ⇨ EYEBROW

**brow·beat** /ˈbraʊbit/ *v* [T] to force someone to do something by continuously asking him/her to do it, especially in a threatening way: *Don't let them **browbeat** you **into** doing anything.*

**brown**[1] /braʊn/ *adj* having the same color as earth, wood, or coffee: *brown shoes* – **brown** *n* [C,U]

**brown**[2] *v* [I,T] to become brown, or to make food do this: *brown the meat in hot oil*

**brown·ie** /ˈbraʊni/ *n* **1** a thick flat piece of chocolate cake **2 get/earn brownie points** INFORMAL if you do something to get brownie points, you do it to get praise

**Brown·ies** /ˈbraʊniz/ *n* the part of the GIRL SCOUTS that is for younger girls

**brown-nose** /ˈ. ˌ./ *v* [I,T] SLANG to try to make someone like you by being very nice to him/her – **brown-nose** *n*

**brown·stone** /ˈbraʊnstoʊn/ *n* **1** [U] a type of red-brown stone, often used for building in the eastern US **2** a house with a front made of this stone – see picture on page 471

**browse** /braʊz/ *v* [I] **1** to look at the goods in a store without wanting to buy anything: *"Can I help you?" "No thanks. I'm just browsing."* **2** to read only the most interesting parts of a book, magazine etc.: *I was **browsing** through the catalog, and I found this.*

**brows·er** /ˈbraʊzɚ/ *n* a computer program that lets you find and use information on the INTERNET

**bruise**[1] /bruz/ *n* a mark on the skin of a person or piece of fruit where it has been damaged by a hit or a fall: *That's a nasty bruise you've got.*

**bruise**[2] *v* [I,T] to become bruised, or to bruise a person or piece of fruit: *He fell and bruised his knee.* | *a bruised apple* – **bruising** *n* [U]

**brunch** /brʌntʃ/ *n* [C,U] a meal eaten in the late morning, as a combination of breakfast and LUNCH – see usage note at MEAL TIMES

**bru·nette** /bruˈnɛt/ *n* a woman with dark brown hair

**brunt** /brʌnt/ *n* **bear/take the brunt of sth** to have to deal with the worst part of something bad: *Women usually bear the brunt of caring for the ill.*

**brush**[1] /brʌʃ/ *n* **1** an object that you use for cleaning, painting etc., made with BRISTLEs, or thin pieces of plastic attached to a handle – see also HAIRBRUSH, PAINTBRUSH, TOOTHBRUSH **2** [singular] the movement of brushing some-

thing: *I'll just give my hair a quick brush.* **3** [U] small bushes and trees covering an open area of land: *a brush fire* **4 a brush with death/the law** an occasion when you just manage to avoid death or prison

**brush**[2] *v* **1** [T] to use a brush to clean something or to make it look smooth and neat: *Go brush your teeth.* | *He didn't brush his hair.* **2** [T] to remove something with a brush or your hand: *She **brushed** the crumbs **off** her lap.* **3** [I,T] to touch someone or something lightly by chance as you pass: *Her hair **brushed against** my arm.*

**brush** *n* brush

**brush** sb/sth ↔ **aside** *phr v* [T] to refuse to listen to someone or consider someone's opinion: *He **brushed** her objections **aside**.*

**brush** sth ↔ **off** *phr v* [T] to refuse to talk about something: *The President calmly **brushed off** their questions about his health.*

**brush up (on)** sth *phr v* [I] to quickly practice and improve your skills or knowledge of a subject: *I have to **brush up on** my French before I go to Paris.*

**brush-off** /ˈ. ./ *n* [singular] INFORMAL a clear refusal to accept someone's friendship, invitations etc.: *I thought she really liked me, but she gave me **the brush-off**.*

**brusque** /brʌsk/ *adj* using very few words in a way that seems impolite: *a brusque manner*

**brus·sels sprout** /ˈbrʌsəl ˌspraʊt/ *n* a small round green vegetable that has a slightly bitter taste

**bru·tal** /ˈbrutl/ *adj* **1** very cruel and violent: *a brutal attack* **2** not sensitive to people's feelings: *the brutal truth* – **brutally** *adv* – **brutality** /bruˈtæləti/ *n* [C,U]

**bru·tal·ize** /ˈbrutlˌaɪz/ *v* [T] to treat someone in a cruel and violent way

**brute**[1] /brut/ *n* **1** someone who is rough, cruel, and not sensitive: *Her husband is a real brute.* **2** an animal, especially a large one

**brute**[2] *adj* **brute force/strength** physical strength that is used rather than thought or intelligence

**brut·ish** /ˈbrutɪʃ/ *adj* very cruel: *brutish behavior*

**B.S.** *n* Bachelor of Science; a university degree in a subject such as chemistry or mathematics – compare B.A.

**BS, bs** *n* SPOKEN ⇨ BULLSHIT[1]

**bub** /bʌb/ *n* SPOKEN used in order to speak to a man or boy: *Hey bub, what are you up to?*

**bub·ble**[1] /ˈbʌbəl/ *n* **1** a ball of air in a liquid or solid substance: *soap bubbles* **2 burst sb's bubble** INFORMAL to destroy someone's beliefs or hopes about something: *I don't want to burst your bubble, but I don't think this will work.*

**bubble**[2] *v* [I] **1** to produce bubbles: *Heat the sauce until it starts to bubble.* **2** also **bubble over** to be full of a particular emotion: *The kids were **bubbling over with** excitement.*

**bubble**

**bubble gum** /'.. ,./ *n* [U] a type of CHEWING GUM that you can blow into a round shape

**bub·bly**[1] /'bʌbli/ *adj* **1** full of BUBBLES **2** cheerful and friendly: *a bubbly personality*

**bubbly**[2] *n* [U] INFORMAL ⇨ CHAMPAGNE

**buck**[1] /bʌk/ *n* **1** SPOKEN a dollar: *Could you lend me 20 bucks?* **2 pass the buck** to try to make someone else responsible for something that you should deal with: *You can't keep passing the buck!* **3 buck naked** SPOKEN wearing no clothes: *He was standing outside buck naked.* **4** the male of some animals, such as DEER, rabbits etc.

**buck**[2] *v* **1** [I] if a horse bucks, it kicks its back feet up in the air **2** [T] to throw a rider off by jumping in this way **3** [T] INFORMAL to oppose something: *He's finally realized he can't **buck the system**.* (=avoid the usual rules)

**buck·et** /'bʌkɪt/ *n* **1** an open container with a handle, used for carrying and holding things, especially liquids **2** the amount that a bucket will hold: *a **bucket of** water* –see also **a drop in the ocean/bucket** (DROP[2]) **kick the bucket** (KICK[1])

**buck·le**[1] /'bʌkəl/ *v* **1** [I,T] to fasten a buckle, or be fastened with a buckle: *The strap buckles at the side.* | *Tim **buckled up** his belt.* **2** [I] if your knees buckle, they become weak and bend **3** [I,T] to bend because of heat or pressure, or to make something do this

**buckle down** *phr v* [I ] INFORMAL to start working seriously: *You'd better **buckle down** or you'll never get your degree.*

**buckle up** *phr v* [I] to fasten your SEAT BELT in a car, aircraft etc.

**buckle**[2] *n* a metal fastener used for attaching the two ends of a belt or STRAP, for fastening a shoe, bag etc., or for decoration

**buck teeth** /,. './ *n* [plural] teeth that stick forward out of your mouth –**buck-toothed** /'bʌktuθt/ *adj*

**bud**[1] /bʌd/ *n* **1** SPOKEN ⇨ BUDDY **2** a young flower or leaf that is still tightly rolled up –see also **nip sth in the bud** (NIP[1])

**bud**[2] *v* **-dded, -dding** [I] to produce buds

**Bud·dhis·m** /'budɪzəm, 'bʊ-/ *n* [U] the belief and religion based on the teachings of Siddhartha Gautama Buddha –**Buddhist** *n* –**Buddhist** *adj*

**bud·ding** /'bʌdɪŋ/ *adj* beginning to develop: *a budding poet* | *a budding relationship*

**bud·dy** /'bʌdi/ *n* **1** SPOKEN used in order to speak to a man or boy: *Hey, buddy! Leave her alone!* | *Thanks, buddy!* **2** INFORMAL a friend: *We're good buddies.*

**budge** /bʌdʒ/ *v* [I,T] **1** to move, or to move someone or something from one place to another: *It's useless. The car won't budge.* | *Mark hasn't **budged from** his room all day.* **2** to make someone change his/her opinion: *The workers refused to **budge from** their demands.*

**budg·et**[1] /'bʌdʒɪt/ *n* a plan of how to spend the money that is available in a particular period in time, or the money itself: *a **budget of** $2 million for the project* | *We have to try to **cut/trim the budget**.* (=find ways to spend less) ***balance the budget*** (=make the money that goes out of the budget equal to the money that comes in) –**budgetary** /'b,dʒə,tɛri/ *adj*: *budgetary limits*

**budget**[2] *v* [I] to carefully plan and control how much you will spend: *I'm **budgeting for** a new computer.* (=planning to save enough money for one)

**budget**[3] *adj* very low in price: *a budget flight*

**buff**[1] /bʌf/ *n* **1 movie/jazz/computer etc. buff** someone who is interested in and knows a lot about movies, JAZZ etc. **2 in the buff** INFORMAL wearing no clothes

**buff**[2] *v* [T] to make a surface shine by polishing it with something soft

**buf·fa·lo** /'bʌfə,loʊ/ *n, plural* **buffalos, buffaloes,** *or* **buffalo** **1** a large animal like a cow with a very large head and thick hair on its neck and shoulders; BISON **2** an animal like a large black cow with long curved horns that lives in Africa and Asia

**buff·er** /'bʌfɚ/ *n* **1** something that protects one thing from being affected by another thing: *The walls are a **buffer against** noise from the airport.* | *Support from friends can provide a buffer against stress.* **2 buffer zone** a safe or quiet area where fighting or dangerous activity is not allowed to happen: *The armies have agreed to a 20 mile buffer zone in the north.* **3** a place in a computer's memory for storing information for a short time

**buf·fet**[1] /bə'feɪ, bʊ-/ *n* a meal in which people serve themselves at a table and then move away to eat

**buf·fet**[2] /'bʌfɪt/ *v* [T] to make someone or something move by hitting him, her, or it again and again: *boats buffeted by the wind and the rain*

**buf·foon** /bə'fun/ *n* someone who does silly things that make you laugh –**buffoonery** *n* [U]

**bug**[1] /bʌg/ *n* **1** INFORMAL any small insect, especially one you think is unpleasant: *a tiny little green bug* **2** INFORMAL a GERM (=very small creature) that causes an illness that is not very serious: *a flu bug* **3 the travel/skiing/**

writing etc. **bug** INFORMAL a sudden strong interest in doing something that usually only continues for a short time: *After going to India, I got the travel bug.*  **4** a small mistake in a computer program that stops it from working correctly  **5** a small piece of electronic equipment for listening secretly to other people's conversations

**bug**² *v* **-gged, -gging** [T]  **1** SPOKEN to annoy someone: *Stop bugging me!*  **2** to use a BUG in order to listen secretly to other people's conversations: *Are you sure this room isn't bugged?*

**bu·gle** /'byugəl/ *n* a musical instrument like a TRUMPET, which is used in the army to call soldiers

**build**¹ /bɪld/ *v* **built, built, building**  **1** [I,T] to make a structure such as a house, factory, ship etc.: *building a new bridge | More homes are being built near the lake.*  **2** [T] to make something develop or form: *working to build a more peaceful world*  **3** **confidence-building/ muscle-building/character-building etc** making someone's confidence, muscles etc. grow or develop

**build** sth ↔ **into** *phr v* [T]  **1** to make something a permanent part of a system, agreement etc.: *A completion date was **built into** the contract.*  **2** to make something so that it is a permanent part of a structure, machine etc.: *The alarm was small enough to be **built into** a watch.*

**build on** *phr v* [T **build on** sth] to use your achievements in order to develop: *We hope to **build on** the success of our products.*

**build up** *phr v*  **1** [I,T **build** sth ↔ **up**] if something builds up or you build it up, it gradually increases or grows: *You need to **build up** your strength. | They've **built up** a reputation as a reliable car dealer.*  **2** **build up sb's hopes** to make someone think that s/he will get something that s/he wants, often in a way that is unfair: *Don't **build up** the kids' hopes - they'll just be disappointed.*

**build up to** sth *phr v* [T] to gradually prepare for a particular moment or event: *All the activity was **building up to** something, but I didn't know what.*

**build**² *n* [singular, U] the shape and size of someone's body: *She has black hair and a slim build.*

**build·ing** /'bɪldɪŋ/ *n*  **1** a structure such as a house, church, or factory, that has a roof and walls: *I was surrounded by tall buildings.*  ✗ DON'T SAY "high buildings." ✗  **2** [U] the process or business of building things

**building block** /'.. ,./ *n*  **1** a block of wood or plastic for young children to build things with  **2** [plural] the pieces or parts that make it possible for something big or important to exist: *Reading and writing are the building blocks of our education.*

**build·up** /'bɪldʌp/ *n*  **1** [singular, U] a gradual increase: *The buildup of traffic on the roads is causing problems in the city.*  **2** a description of someone or something that says that he, she, or it is very special or important: *The magazine had a great buildup, but I don't like it much.*  **3** the length of time spent preparing for an event: *the long **buildup to** the opening of the new mall*

**built**¹ /bɪlt/ the past tense and PAST PARTICIPLE of BUILD

**built**² *adj* SLANG a word used by men to describe a woman with large breasts, considered offensive by many women

**built-in** /ˌ. '. ◂/ *adj* forming a part of something that cannot be separated from it: *built-in cupboards | Children have a built-in sense of survival.*

**bulb** /bʌlb/ *n*  **1** the glass part of an electric light, that the light shines from: *a 40 watt bulb*  **2** a root shaped like a ball that grows into a plant: *tulip bulbs*

**bul·bous** /'bʌlbəs/ *adj* fat and round: *a bulbous nose*

**bulge**¹ /bʌldʒ/ *n* a curved place on the surface of something, caused by something under or inside it: *Trent could see the bulge of a gun under the man's jacket.*

**bulge**² **bulge out** *v* [I] to stick out in a rounded shape: *His stomach bulged out.*

**bu·li·mia** /bə'limiə, bu-/ *n* [U] a mental illness that makes someone eat too much and then VOMIT because s/he is afraid of gaining weight  **–bulimic** /bə'limɪk/ *adj*

**bulk** /bʌlk/ *n*  **1 the bulk of sth** the main or largest part of something: *The bulk of the work has already been done.*  **2** [C,U] the large size of something or someone: *Greg squeezed his bulk into the car.*  **3 in bulk** in large quantities: *We buy our paper in bulk.*

**bulk·y** /'bʌlki/ *adj* big and heavy: *a bulky package*

**bull** /bʊl/ *n*  **1** a male cow, or the male of some other large animals, such as an ELEPHANT or WHALE  **2** [U] INFORMAL ⇨ BULLSHIT¹  **3 take the bull by the horns** INFORMAL to bravely or confidently deal with a difficult, dangerous, or unpleasant problem: *I just took the bull by the horns, hoping Sam wouldn't get mad.*

**bull·dog** /'bʊldɔg/ *n* a dog with a large head, a flat nose, a short neck, and short thick legs

**bull·doze** /'bʊldoʊz/ *v* [T] to move dirt and rocks, destroy buildings etc. with a BULLDOZER

**bull·doz·er** /'bʊlˌdoʊzɚ/ *n* a powerful vehicle with a broad metal blade, used for moving dirt and rocks, destroying buildings etc.

**bul·let** /'bʊlɪt/ *n* a small round piece of metal that is fired from a gun

**bul·le·tin** /'bʊlətn̩, 'bʊlətɪn/ *n*  **1** a short official news report or announcement that is made to tell people about something important: *a news bulletin*  **2** a letter or printed statement that a group or organization produces to tell people its news

**bulletin board** /'... ,./ *n* **1** a board on a wall that you put information or pictures on **2** a place in a system of computers where you can read messages or leave messages for anyone to read

**bull·fight** /'bʊlfaɪt/ *n* a type of entertainment in some countries, in which a man fights and kills a BULL –**bullfighter** *n* –**bullfighting** *n* [U]

**bull·horn** /'bʊlhɔrn/ *n* a piece of equipment that you hold up to your mouth when you talk, to make your voice louder

**bul·lion** /'bʊlyən/ *n* [U] blocks of gold or silver

**bull·ish** /'bʊlɪʃ/ *adj* relating to an increase in prices in the STOCK MARKET –compare BEARISH

**bull mar·ket** /ˌ. '../ *n* a situation in which the value of SHAREs in business increases –compare BEAR MARKET

**bull·pen** /'bʊlpɛn/ *n* the area in a baseball field in which PITCHERs practice throwing

**bull's-eye** /'. ./ *n* the center of a TARGET that you try to hit when shooting

**bull·shit**[1] /'bʊlʃɪt/ *interjection, n* SPOKEN a very impolite word meaning something that is stupid and completely untrue

**bullshit**[2] *v* [I,T] INFORMAL a very impolite word meaning to say something that is BULLSHIT –**bullshitter** *n*

**bul·ly** /'bʊli/ *v* [T] to threaten to hurt someone or frighten him/her, especially someone weaker or smaller than you –**bully** *n*

**bum**[1] /bʌm/ *n* INFORMAL **1** DISAPPROVING someone who has no home or job, and who usually asks people on the street for money **2** INFORMAL someone who is very lazy: *Get out of bed, you bum!* **3 beach/ski etc. bum** someone who spends all of his/her time on the beach, skiing (SKI) etc.

**bum**[2] *v* **-mmed, -mming** [T] SLANG to ask someone if you can borrow or have something: *Can I bum a cigarette?*

**bum around** *phr v* SLANG **1** [I,T] to spend time doing nothing, or in a very lazy way: *We were just bumming around at home yesterday.* **2** [T **bum around** sth] to travel around living very cheaply and having few plans: *bumming around Africa*

**bum**[3] *adj* INFORMAL bad and useless: *Andy gave me some bum advice about buying a car.*

**bum·ble·bee** /'bʌmbəl,bi/ *n* a large hairy BEE

**bum·bling** /'bʌmblɪŋ/ *adj* behaving in a careless way and making a lot of mistakes

**bummed** /bʌmd/ **bummed out** *adj* SPOKEN feeling disappointed: *I'm really bummed that we can't go!*

**bum·mer** /'bʌmɚ/ *n* [singular] SPOKEN a situation that is disappointing: *You can't go? What a bummer.*

**bump**[1] /bʌmp/ *v* **1** [I,T] to hit or knock against something, especially by accident: *It was so dark I bumped into a tree.* | *Don't bump your head!* **2** [I] to move up and down as you move forward, in a vehicle: *We bumped along the dirt road.*

**bump into** sb *phr v* [T] INFORMAL to meet someone when you were not expecting to: *Guess who I bumped into this morning?*

**bump** sb ‹› **off** *phr v* [T] INFORMAL to kill someone

**bump**[2] *n* **1** an area of skin that is swollen because you have hit it on something: *a bump on his head* **2** a small raised area on a surface: *a bump in the road* **3** a movement in which one thing hits against another thing, or the sound that this makes: *The elevator stopped with a bump.*

**bump·er**[1] /'bʌmpɚ/ *n* the part at the front and back of a car that protects it if it hits anything –see also picture on page 469

**bumper**
bumper

**bumper**[2] *adj* very large: *a bumper crop*

**bumper stick·er** /'.. ,../ *n* a small sign with a message on it on the BUMPER of a car

**bumper-to-bumper** /ˌ.. . '..‹ / *adj, adv* with a lot of cars that are very close together: *bumper-to-bumper traffic* | *driving bumper-to-bumper*

**bump·y** /'bʌmpi/ *adj* **1** a bumpy surface has a lot of raised parts on it: *a bumpy road* **2** a bumpy trip by car or plane is uncomfortable because of bad road or weather conditions

**bun** /bʌn/ *n* **1** a type of bread that is small and round: *a hamburger bun* –see picture at BREAD **2** a HAIRSTYLE in which a woman fastens her hair in a small round shape at the back of her head –see picture at HAIRSTYLE –see also BUNS

**bunch**[1] /bʌntʃ/ *n* [singular] a group or number of similar people or things, or a large amount of something: *The doctor asked me a bunch of questions.* | *a bunch of grapes* | *There are a whole bunch of little restaurants by the beach.*

**bunch**[2] *v* [I,T] **1** also **bunch together** to stay close together in a group, or to form a group: *The kids stood bunched together behind their mother.* **2** also **bunch up** to pull material together tightly in folds: *My skirt's all bunched up.*

**bun·dle**[1] /'bʌndl/ *n* **1** a group of things such as papers, clothes, or sticks that are fastened or tied together: *a bundle of newspapers* **2** SOFTWARE that is included with the computer you buy **3** [singular] INFORMAL a lot of money: *That car must have cost a bundle.* **4 be a**

**bundle of nerves/laughs etc.** INFORMAL to be very nervous, a lot of fun etc.

**bundle**[2] *v* [I,T] **1** also **bundle up** to make a bundle: *Bundle up those old clothes.* **2** also **bundle up** to dress warmly because it is cold **3** to move quickly in a particular direction or into a particular place, or to make someone or something do this: *The police bundled him into a car.*

**bun·ga·low** /'bʌŋgə,loʊ/ *n* a small house that has only one level

**bun·gle** /'bʌŋgəl/ *v* [T] to do something badly: *They bungled the job completely.* −**bungler** *n* −**bungling** *adj*

**bun·ion** /'bʌnyən/ *n* a painful sore on your big toe

**bunk** /bʌŋk/ *n* **1** a narrow bed that is attached to the wall, for example on a train or a ship **2** INFORMAL something that is not true or that does not mean anything

**bunk beds** /'. ./ *n* [plural] two beds that are attached together, one on top of the other

**bun·ker** /'bʌŋkɚ/ *n* a strongly built shelter for soldiers, usually under the ground

**bun·ny** /'bʌni/ **bunny rabbit** *n* a word meaning a rabbit, used especially by or to children

**buns** /bʌnz/ *n* [plural] SLANG your BUTTOCKS

**buoy**[1] /'bui, bɔɪ/ *n* an object that floats on the water, used for showing boats which parts of the water are safe or dangerous

**buoy**[2], **buoy up** *v* [T] **1** to make someone feel happier, more confident etc.: *Success buoyed his confidence.* **2** to keep profits, prices etc. at a high level

**buoy·ant** /'bɔɪənt/ *adj* **1** cheerful and confident: *a buoyant mood* **2** buoyant prices etc. tend not to fall **3** able to float −**buoyancy** *n* [U] −**buoyantly** *adv*

**bur·den**[1] /'bɚdn/ *n* FORMAL **1** something that is difficult, or that worries you because you are responsible for it: *I don't want to be a burden on my children when I'm old.* **2 the burden of proof** the duty to prove something **3** LITERARY something heavy that you have to carry

**burden**[2] *v* [T] **1** to make someone worry or cause trouble for him/her: *I won't burden you with my problems.* **2** to make someone carry something heavy

**bu·reau** /'byʊroʊ/ *n* **1** a government department or part of a government department: *the Federal Bureau of Investigation* **2** an office or organization that collects or provides information: *an employment bureau* **3** ⇨ CHEST OF DRAWERS

**bu·reauc·ra·cy** /byʊ'rɑkrəsi/ *n* **1** [U] an official system that is annoying or confusing because it has too many rules, long processes etc. **2** [C,U] the officials in a government or business who are employed rather than elected

**bu·reau·crat** /'byʊrə,kræt/ *n* someone who works in a BUREAUCRACY and follows official rules very carefully

**bu·reau·crat·ic** /,byʊrə'krætɪk/ *adj* involving a lot of complicated official rules and processes

**bur·geon·ing** /'bɚdʒənɪŋ/ *adj* growing, increasing, or developing very quickly: *the city's burgeoning population*

**burg·er** /'bɚgɚ/ *n* INFORMAL ⇨ HAMBURGER

**bur·glar** /'bɚglɚ/ *n* someone who goes into buildings, cars etc. in order to steal things −see usage note at THIEF

**bur·glar·ize** /'bɚglə,raɪz/ *v* [T] to go into a building, car etc. and steal things from it

**bur·gla·ry** /'bɚgləri/ *n* [C,U] the crime of going into a building, car etc. to steal things

**bur·i·al** /'bɛriəl/ *n* [C,U] the act or ceremony of putting a dead body into a grave

**bur·lap** /'bɚlæp/ *n* [U] a type of thick rough cloth

**bur·ly** /'bɚli/ *adj* a burly man is big and strong

**burn**[1] /bɚn/ *v* **burned, burned** *or* **burnt, burning** **1** [I,T] to damage something or hurt someone with fire or heat, or to be hurt or damaged in this way: *Ricky burned his hand on the stove.* | *My toast is burning!* | *I've burned the turkey to a crisp!* (=cooked it until it is black) **2** [I] to produce heat and flames: *Is the fire still burning?* **3 get burned** SPOKEN **a)** to be emotionally hurt by someone or something: *Sally's really afraid of getting burned in a relationship again.* **b)** to lose a lot of money, especially in a business deal **4** [I,T] if you burn a FUEL, or if it burns, it is used for producing power, heat, light etc.: *Cars burn gasoline.* **5** [I] also **burn up** to feel hot in an unpleasant way: *My face is burning up.* **6** [I] LITERARY if a light or lamp burns, it shines or produces light −**burned** *adj* −**burnt** *adj*

**burn** sth ↔ **down** *phr v* [I,T] if a building burns down or is burned down, it is destroyed by fire

**burn** sth ↔ **off** *phr v* [T] **burn off energy/fat/calories** to use energy etc. by doing physical exercise

**burn out** *phr v* **1** [I,T **burn** sth ↔ **out**] if a fire burns out or burns itself out, it stops burning because there is no coal, wood etc. left **2** [I,T **burn** sth ↔ **out**] if an engine or electric wire burns out or is burned out, it stops working because it has become too hot **3 be burned out a)** to feel very tired: *I was completely burned out after my finals.* **b)** if a building, car etc is burned out, the inside of it is destroyed by fire

**burn up** *phr v* **1** [I,T **burn** sth ↔ **up**] if something burns up or is burned up, it is completely destroyed by fire or great heat **2** [T **burn** sb **up**] INFORMAL to make someone angry: *The way she treats him really burns me up.*

**burn**[2] *n* an injury or mark caused by fire or heat: *a burn on her arm*

**burn·er** /'bɚnɚ/ *n* **1** the part of a STOVE that produces heat or a flame −see picture at KITCHEN **2 put sth on the back burner** INFORMAL to delay dealing with something until a later time

**burn·ing** /'bɚnɪŋ/ *adj* **1** on fire: *a burning house* **2** feeling very hot: *a burning fever* **3 burning ambition/need etc.** a very strong need etc. **4 burning question/issue** a very important question that must be answered quickly

**bur·nish** /'bɚnɪʃ/ *v* [T] to polish metal until it shines −**burnished** *adj*

**burnt**[1] /bɚnt/ *v* a past tense and PAST PARTICIPLE of BURN

**burnt**[2] *adj* having been burned: *burnt sugar*

**burp** /bɚp/ *v* INFORMAL **1** [I] if you burp, gas comes up from your stomach and makes a noise **2** [T] to help a baby get rid of stomach gas, especially by rubbing his/her back −**burp** *n*

**bur·ri·to** /bə'riṭou/ *n* a Mexican food made from a TORTILLA folded around meat or beans with cheese

**bur·row**[1] /'bɚou, 'bʌrou/ *v* [T] to make a hole or passage in the ground: *Gophers had burrowed under the wall.*

**burrow**[2] *n* a passage in the ground made by an animal such as a rabbit or a FOX

**bur·sar** /'bɚsɚ, -sar/ *n* someone at a college who is responsible for the money that is paid by students

**burst**[1] /bɚst/ *v* **burst, burst, bursting** **1** [I,T] to break open or apart suddenly and violently, or to make something do this: *a game in which kids sit on balloons to try to burst them* **2 be bursting** to be very full of something: *This town is bursting with tourists.* | *School classrooms are bursting at the seams.* (=are too full of students) **3** [I] to move suddenly, quickly, and often violently: *She burst through the door of my room.* **4 be bursting with pride/confidence/energy etc.** to be very proud, confident etc. −see also **burst sb's bubble** (BUBBLE[1])

**burst in on** sb/sth *phr v* [T] to interrupt something suddenly and noisily: *John's secretary burst in on the meeting with the news.*

**burst into** sth *phr v* [T] to suddenly start to do something: *Ellen burst into tears.* (=began crying) | *The car hit a tree and burst into flames.* (=began burning)

**burst out** *phr v* **1 burst out laughing/crying** to suddenly start to laugh or cry **2** [T] to suddenly say something forcefully: *"I don't believe it!" she burst out angrily.*

**burst**[2] *n* **1 a burst of sth** a short sudden period of increased activity, loud noise, or strong feeling: *A sudden burst of energy made her decide to clean the house.* **2** the action of

something bursting, or the place where it has burst: *a burst in the water pipes*

**bur·y** /'bɛri/ *v* [T] **1** to put a dead body into a grave: *Aunt Betty was buried in Woodlawn Cemetery.* **2** to cover something with something else so that it cannot be seen: *The dog buried a bone.* | *His glasses were buried under a pile of newspapers* **3** to ignore a feeling or memory and pretend that it does not exist

**bus**[1] /bʌs/ *n, plural* **buses** a large vehicle that people pay to travel on: *Are you going to drive or go by bus?* | *Five people got on the bus.* ✗ DON'T SAY "... get in the bus." ✗

**bus**[2] *v* **-sed, -sing** [T] **1** to take a group of people somewhere in a bus: *Many children are being bused to schools in other areas.* **2** to take away dirty dishes from the tables in a restaurant: *Frank has a job busing tables.*

**bus·boy** /'bʌsbɔɪ/ *n* a man whose job is to take away dirty dishes from the tables in a restaurant

**bush** /buʃ/ *n* **1** a short plant like a small tree with a lot of branches **2 the bush** wild country that has not been cleared in Australia or Africa −see also **beat around the bush** (BEAT[1])

**bushed** /buʃt/ *adj* INFORMAL very tired: *I'm bushed.*

**bush·el** /'buʃəl/ *n* a unit for measuring dry food, equal to 8 gallons or 36.4 liters

**bush·y** /'buʃi/ *adj* bushy hair or fur grows thickly: *a bushy tail*

**bus·i·ly** /'bɪzəli/ *adv* in a busy way

**busi·ness** /'bɪznɪs/ *n*
**1** ▶WORK DONE BY COMPANIES◀ [U] the activity of buying or selling goods or services: *We do a lot of business with people in Texas.*
**2** ▶YOUR JOB◀ [U] the work that you do as your job to earn money: *Al's gone to Japan on business.* (=because of his job)
**3 be in business** to be operating as a company: *He's in business for himself.* (=he owns a small company)
**4 go into business/go out of business** to begin or stop operating as a company
**5** ▶AMOUNT OF WORK◀ [U] the amount of work a company is doing, or the amount of money the company is making: *Our business is good/bad/slow during the winter.*
**6** ▶A COMPANY◀ an organization that produces or sells goods or services: *He runs a printing business in Chicago.*
**7** ▶PERSONAL LIFE◀ [U] something about your life that you do not think other people have the right to know: *It's none of your business how much I earn.* | *Why don't you just mind your own business!* (=used in order to tell someone rudely that you do not want his/her advice, help etc.)
**8** ▶SUBJECT/ACTIVITY◀ [singular] a subject, event, or activity that you have a particular opinion of: *Rock climbing can be a risky business.*

**9 get down to business** to start dealing with an important subject

**10 mean business** INFORMAL to be determined to do something: *I could tell from the look on his face that he meant business.*

**11 have no business doing sth** if someone has no business doing something, he or she should not do it: *He was drunk and had no business driving.* —see also BIG BUSINESS

**business card** /'.. ,./ *n* a card that shows your name, the name of your company, the company's address etc.

**busi·ness·like** /'bɪznɪs,laɪk/ *adj* effective and practical in the way you do things: *a businesslike attitude*

**busi·ness·man** /'bɪznɪs,mæn/ **busi·ness·wom·an** /'bɪznɪs,wʊmən/ *n* someone who works at a fairly high level in a company or has his/her own business

**bus·ing** /'bʌsɪŋ/ *n* [U] a system in which students ride buses to schools that are far from where they live, so that a school has students of different races

**bus lane** /'. ./ *n* a part of a wide street that only buses can use

**bus sta·tion** /'. ,../ *n* a place where buses start and finish their trips

**bus stop** /'. ./ *n* a place at the side of a road, marked with a sign, where buses stop for passengers

**bust**[1] /bʌst/ *v* [T] **1** NONSTANDARD to break something: *I busted my watch.* **2 bust sb (for sth)** INFORMAL if the police bust someone, they catch someone who has done something illegal **3 bust your butt/ass** SLANG an impolite phrase meaning to try very hard to do something: *Tim's been busting his ass to finish on time.*

**bust**[2] *n* **1** a woman's breasts, or the measurement around a woman's breasts and back: *a 34 inch bust* **2** INFORMAL a situation in which the police go into a place in order to catch people doing something illegal: *a drug bust* **3** a model of someone's head, shoulders, and upper chest: *a bust of Beethoven*

**bust**[3] *adj* **go bust** a business that goes bust stops operating because it does not have enough money

**bust·er** /'bʌstɚ/ *n* **1** INFORMAL something that ends a situation, or that stops a particular activity: *The storm should be a drought-buster.* **2** SPOKEN used when speaking to a man who is annoying you, or who you do not respect: *Keep your hands off me, buster!*

**bus·tle**[1] /'bʌsəl/ *n* [singular] busy and usually noisy activity: *the bustle of the big city* —**bustling** *adj*

**bustle**[2] *v* [I] to move around quickly, looking very busy: *Linda bustled around the kitchen.*

**bus·y**[1] /'bɪzi/ *adj* **1** spending time working or doing something, so that you do not have time to do other things: *I'm busy with a customer*

*right now - can I call you back?* | *He's busy studying for his finals.* | *a busy mother* **2** a busy place is full of people or vehicles, or has a lot happening in it: *a busy airport* **3** a telephone that is busy is being used **4** a pattern or design that is busy is full of too many details —**busily** *adv*

**busy**[2] *v* **busy yourself with** to do something in order to make time seem to go faster: *He busied himself with cleaning.*

**bus·y·bod·y** /'bɪzi,bɑdi, -,bʌdi/ *n* someone who is too interested in other people's private activities

**but**[1] /bət; *strong* bʌt/ *conjunction* **1** used before you say something that is different or the opposite from what you have just said: *Mom didn't like the movie, but Dad loved it.* | *Learning Chinese was difficult, but I got this job because of it.* **2** used before you give the reason why something did not happen or is not true: *Carla was supposed to come tonight, but her husband took the car.* **3** used in order to show surprise at what has just been said: *"I have to leave tomorrow." "But you only got here this morning!"*

---

SPOKEN PHRASES

**4** used in order to introduce a new subject: *That's why I've been so busy this week. But, how are you anyway?* **5 but then (again)...** used in order to show that what you have just said is not as surprising as it seems: *He doesn't have a strong French accent, but then he has lived in this country for 35 years.* **6** used after phrases such as "excuse me" and "I'm sorry": *I'm sorry, but you're not allowed to go in there.* | *Excuse me, but didn't you go to Laney High School?*

---

**but**[2] *prep* except for: *Joe can come any day but Monday.* | *There's nobody here but me.*

---

**USAGE NOTE but and except**

Use **but** and **except** to talk about someone or something that is not included in a particular group: *I'll eat anything except liver.* | *Everyone's here but Mary.* In formal and written English, only **but** can be used after words like "none," "all," "nobody," "anywhere," "everything," or after question words like "who," "where," and "what": *We looked everywhere but in the shed.* | *Who but John would do that?*

---

**butch** /bʊtʃ/ *adj* SLANG a woman who is butch looks, behaves, or dresses like a man

**butch·er**[1] /'bʊtʃɚ/ *n* someone who owns or works in a store that sells meat

**butcher**[2] *v* [T] **1** to kill animals and prepare them to be used as meat **2** to kill people in a cruel way —**butchery** *n* [U]

**but·ler** /'bʌtˡlɚ/ *n* the main male servant of a house

**butt**[1] /bʌt/ *n* **1** INFORMAL the part of your body that you sit on; BUTTOCKS: *Jody bruised her butt falling off the slide.* **2 get your butt in/out/ over etc.** SPOKEN used in order to rudely tell someone to go somewhere or do something: *Get your butt out of that bed!* **3 be the butt of** to be the person or thing that other people often make jokes about. *Poor John is always the butt of everyone's jokes.* **4** the end of a cigarette after most of it has been smoked **5** the end of the handle of a gun — see also **bust your butt/ ass** (BUST[1]) **a pain in the ass/butt** (PAIN[1])

**butt**[2] *v* [I,T] if a person or animal butts something or someone, it hits or pushes him, her, or it with its head

**butt in** *phr v* [I] INFORMAL to become involved in someone else's private situation or conversation

**butt out** *phr v* [I] INFORMAL used in order to tell someone to stop being involved in something private: *This has nothing to do with you, so just butt out!*

**butte** /byut/ *n* a large hill with steep sides and a flat top

**but·ter**[1] /'bʌtɚ/ *n* [U] a yellow food made from milk or cream that you spread on bread or use in cooking — **buttery** *adj*

**butter**[2] *v* [T] to spread butter on something

**butter** sb **up** *phr v* [T] INFORMAL to say nice things to someone so that s/he will do what you want

**but·ter·cup** /'bʌtɚ,kʌp/ *n* a small shiny yellow wild flower

**but·ter·fin·gers** /'bʌtɚ,fɪŋgɚz/ *n* [singular] INFORMAL someone who often drops things

**but·ter·fly** /'bʌtɚ,flaɪ/ *n* **1** an insect with large and usually colored wings **2 have butterflies (in your stomach)** INFORMAL to feel very nervous

**but·ter·milk** /'bʌtɚ,mɪlk/ *n* [U] the liquid that remains after butter has been made, used for drinking or cooking

**but·ter·scotch** /'bʌtɚ,skɑtʃ/ *n* [C,U] a type of candy made from butter and sugar boiled together

**but·tock** /'bʌtək/ *n* [C usually plural] FORMAL one of the soft parts of your body that you sit on — see picture at BODY

**but·ton**[1] /'bʌtˡn/ *n* **1** a small round flat object on your shirt, coat etc. that you pass through a hole to fasten it **2** a small round object on a machine that you press to make it work: *Push this button to make the machine stop.* **3** a small metal or plastic pin with a message or picture on it

**button**[2], **button up** *v* [I,T] to fasten something with buttons, or to be fastened with buttons: *Button up your coat.*

**but·ton·hole** /'bʌtˡn,houl/ *n* a hole for a

button to be put through to fasten a shirt, coat etc.

**but·tress**[1] /'bʌtrɪs/ *v* [T] FORMAL to do something to support a system, idea etc.: *the government's policy of buttressing democracy all over the world*

**buttress**[2] *n* a structure built to support a wall

**bux·om** /'bʌksəm/ *adj* a woman who is buxom has large breasts

**buy**[1] /baɪ/ *v* **bought, bought, buying 1** [I,T] to get something by paying money for it: *Did you buy Cheryl that book?* | *I bought my car from our neighbors.* | *He bought his house for $100,000.* **2** [T] INFORMAL to believe an explanation or reason for something: *If we tell the police it was an accident, do you think they'll buy it?* **3 buy time** INFORMAL to do something in order to get more time to finish something **4** [T] also **buy off** INFORMAL to pay money to someone in order to persuade him/her to do something dishonest: *They say the judge was bought.*

**buy into** sth *phr v* [T] **1** to buy part of a business or organization: *I used the money to buy into a computer company.* **2** to believe in an idea: *women who buy into the idea of having a "perfect body"*

**buy** sb/sth **out** *phr v* [T] to gain control of a business by buying all the SHAREs in it that you do not already own

**buy up** sth *phr v* [T] to quickly buy as much as you can of something: *He bought up all the copies of the magazine in the store.*

**buy**[2] *n* **be a good/bad buy** to be worth or not worth the price you paid: *These shoes were a good buy; they've really lasted well.*

**buy·er** /'baɪɚ/ *n* **1** someone who is buying or has bought something: *We've found a buyer for our boat.* **2** someone whose job is to choose and buy the goods that a store or company will sell

**buy·out** /'baɪaʊt/ *n* a situation in which someone gains control of a company by buying all of its SHAREs: *a management buyout*

**buzz**[1] /bʌz/ *v* **1** [I] to make a continuous noise like the sound of a BEE: *What's making that buzzing noise?* **2** [I] if a group of people or a place is buzzing, people are making a lot of noise because they are excited: *The room buzzed with excitement.* **3** [I,T] to call someone by pressing a buzzer: *Tina buzzed for her secretary.*

**buzz off** *phr v* [I] INFORMAL used in order to tell someone to go away in an impolite way

**buzz**[2] *n* **1** a continuous noise like the sound of a BEE **2** [singular] INFORMAL a strong feeling of excitement, pleasure, or success, especially one you get from alcohol or drugs: *A couple of glasses of that punch will give you a real buzz.*

**buz·zard** /'bʌzɚd/ *n* a large wild bird that eats dead animals

**buzz·er** /'bʌzɚ/ n a small thing like a button that makes a buzzing sound when you push it, for example on a door

**buzz·word** /'bʌzwɚd/ n a word or phrase relating to a particular subject, which is only popular for a limited time

**by**[1] /baɪ/ prep **1** used with PASSIVE forms of verbs to show who did something or what caused something: *a play (written) by Shakespeare | a film made by Steven Spielberg | Her money is controlled by her family.* **2** near: *He was standing by the window.* **3** past: *Two dogs ran by me.* **4** using or doing a particular thing: *Send the letter by airmail. | Carolyn earns extra money by babysitting. | We went from New York to Philadelphia by car/plane/train/bus.* —see usage note at TRANSPORTATION **5** no later than a particular time: *This report has to be done by 5:00.* **6 by mistake/accident** without intending to do something: *She locked the door by mistake.* **7** according to a particular way of doing things: *By law, cars cannot pass a school bus that has stopped.* **8** used in order to show which part of something that someone holds: *I picked up the pot by the handle. | She grabbed him by the arm.* **9** used in order to show a distance, amount, or rate: *The room is 24 feet by 36 feet. | Are you paid by the hour?* **10 by the way** SPOKEN used in order to begin talking about a subject that is not related to the one you were talking about: *Oh, by the way, Vicky called while you were out.* **11 (all) by yourself** completely alone: *They left the boy by himself for two days!* **12 day by day/little by little etc.** used in order to show that something happens gradually: *Little by little he began to understand the language.*

**by**[2] adv **1** past: *One or two cars went by, but nobody stopped. | Three hours went by before we heard any news.* **2 come/stop/go by** to visit or go to a place for a short time when you intend to go somewhere else afterward: *Come by (=come to my house, office etc.) any time tomorrow. | I had to stop by the supermarket on the way home.* **3 by and large** used when talking generally about something: *By and large, the more questions you ask now, the easier it will be.*

**bye** /baɪ/, **bye-bye** /ˌ. '., '. ./ interjection SPOKEN goodbye: *Bye, Sandy! See you later.*

**by·gone** /'baɪgɔn, -gɑn/ adj **bygone days/age/era etc.** an expression meaning a period in the past

**by·gones** /'baɪgɔnz, -gɑnz/ n **let bygones be bygones** INFORMAL to forgive someone for something bad that s/he has done to you

**by·law** /'baɪlɔ/ n a rule made by an organization

**by·line** /'baɪlaɪn/ n a line at the beginning of a newspaper or magazine article that gives the writer's name

**BYOB** adj Bring Your Own Bottle; used in order to describe a party or event that you bring your own alcoholic drinks to

**by·pass**[1] /'baɪpæs/ n **1** a road that goes around a town or other busy place rather than through it **2** a medical operation that repairs the system of arteries (ARTERY) around the heart

**bypass**[2] v [T] to avoid a place by going around it: *If we bypass the town, we'll save time.*

**by·prod·uct** /'. ˌ.../ n **1** a substance that is produced during the process of making something else: *Whey is a by-product of milk.* **2** an unexpected result of an event or of something you do: *The patient's ideas about men are a by-product of her relationship with her father.*

**by·stand·er** /'baɪˌstændɚ/ n someone who watches what is happening without taking part: *Several innocent bystanders were killed by the gunman.*

**byte** /baɪt/ n a unit for measuring the amount of information a computer can use, equal to 8 BITS

**by·way** /'baɪˌweɪ/ n a small road or path that is not used very much

**by·word** /'baɪwɚd/ n the name of someone or something that has become so well known for a particular quality, that it represents that quality: *His name has become a byword for honesty in the community.*

**C, c** /si/ **1** the third letter of the English alphabet **2** the ROMAN NUMERAL (=number) for 100

**C**[1] /si/ n **1** a grade given to a student's work to show that it is of average quality: *I got a C in biology.* **2** [C,U] the first note in the musical SCALE of C MAJOR, or the musical KEY based on this note

**C**[2] the written abbreviation of CELSIUS or CENTIGRADE

**c. 1** the written abbreviation of CENT **2** the written abbreviation of CIRCA

**C&W** n [U] ⇨ COUNTRY AND WESTERN

**CA** the written abbreviation of California

**cab** /kæb/ n **1** ⇨ TAXI **2** the part of a truck or train where the driver sits —see picture on page 469

**cab·a·ret** /ˌkæbə'reɪ/ n [C,U] entertainment such as music and dancing performed in a restaurant while customers eat and drink

**cab·bage** /'kæbɪdʒ/ n [C,U] a large round vegetable with thick green or purple leaves that can be cooked or eaten raw —see picture on page 470

**cab·bie, cabby** /'kæbi/ n INFORMAL someone who drives a CAB

**cab·in** /'kæbɪn/ n **1** a small house made of wood, usually in a forest or the mountains: *a log cabin* **2** a small room in which you sleep on a ship **3** the area inside a plane where the passengers sit

**cab·i·net** /'kæbənɪt/ n **1** a piece of furniture with doors and shelves or drawers, used for storing or showing things: *a filing cabinet | the kitchen cabinets* – see picture at KITCHEN **2** an important group of politicians who make decisions or advise the leader of a government

**ca·ble¹** /'keɪbəl/ n **1** [C,U] a plastic or rubber tube containing wires that carry electronic signals, telephone messages etc.: *an underground telephone cable* **2** [U] a system of broadcasting television by cable that is paid for by the person watching it: *I'll wait for the movie to come out on cable.* **3** [C,U] a thick strong metal rope used on ships, to support bridges etc. **4** ⇨ TELEGRAM

**cable²** v [I,T] to send a TELEGRAM

**cable car** /'.. ,./ n **1** a vehicle that is pulled by a CABLE along the road, used like a bus by people in a city **2** a vehicle that hangs from a CABLE and carries people up mountains

**cable tel·e·vi·sion** /,.. '..../ **cable TV** n [U] ⇨ CABLE¹

**ca·boose** /kə'bus/ n a small railroad car at the end of a train

**cache** /kæʃ/ n a group of things that are hidden, or the place where they are hidden: *Police found a cache of weapons in the house.*

**ca·chet** /kæ'ʃeɪ/ n [U] a quality that is good or desirable: *It's a great college, but it doesn't have the same cachet as Harvard.*

**cack·le** /'kækəl/ v [I] **1** to make the loud unpleasant noise a chicken makes **2** to laugh or talk in a loud rough voice – **cackle** n

**cac·tus** /'kæktəs/ n, plural **cacti** /'kæktaɪ/ or **cactuses** a desert plant with thick smooth stems and needles instead of leaves

**ca·dav·er** /kə'dævər/ n a dead human body

**cad·dy** /'kædi/ n someone who carries the equipment for someone who is playing GOLF

**ca·dence** /'keɪdns/ n a word meaning a regular pattern of sound, used especially to describe the way someone's voice gets louder or softer

**ca·det** /kə'dɛt/ n someone who is studying to become an officer in the military or the police

**ca·dre** /'kædri, 'ka-, -dreɪ/ n FORMAL a small group of specially trained people in a profession, political party, or military force: *a cadre of highly trained scientists*

**cae·sar·e·an** /sɪ'zɛriən/ n ⇨ CESAREAN

**ca·fe, café** /kæ'feɪ, kə-/ n a small restaurant

**caf·e·te·ri·a** /,kæfə'tɪriə/ n a restaurant where people get their own food and take it to a table to eat it: *the school cafeteria*

**caf·feine** /kæ'fin, 'kæfin/ n [U] a chemical substance in coffee, tea, and some other drinks that makes people feel more active: *a caffeine-free cola* (=one without caffeine)

**cage¹** /keɪdʒ/ n a structure of wires or BARs in which birds or animals can be kept

**cage²** v [T] to put an animal or bird in a CAGE **2 feel caged in** to feel uncomfortable and annoyed because you cannot go outside

**cag·ey** /'keɪdʒi/ adj INFORMAL not willing to talk about your plans or intentions: *The White House is being very cagey about the contents of the report.*

**ca·hoots** /kə'huts/ n INFORMAL **be in cahoots (with)** to be working secretly with others, usually to do something that is not honest: *Was Roger really in cahoots with the drug smugglers?*

**ca·jole** /kə'dʒoʊl/ v [T] to persuade someone to do something by praising him/her or making promises to him/her: *Mom and Dad would try to cajole us into eating our vegetables.*

**Ca·jun** /'keɪdʒən/ n a member of a group of people in southern Louisiana whose family originally came from the French-speaking part of Canada – **Cajun** adj

**cake¹** /keɪk/ n **1** [C,U] a sweet food made by baking flour, fat, sugar, and eggs: *a birthday cake | Do you want a piece of cake?* see picture at DESSERT **2** a small piece of something, made into a flat shape: *a cake of soap* **3 be a piece of cake** INFORMAL to be very easy: *Go on, jump off the high dive, Ben. It's a piece of cake!* **4 have your cake and eat it too** INFORMAL to have all the advantages of something without any of the disadvantages

**cake²** v **be caked in/with** to be covered with a thick layer of something: *Irene's boots were caked with mud.*

**ca·lam·i·ty** /kə'læməti/ n a very bad, unexpected event that causes a lot of damage or suffering: *Sudan suffered a number of calamities in the 1980s.* – **calamitous** adj

**cal·ci·um** /'kælsiəm/ n [U] a silver-white metal that is an ELEMENT and that helps form teeth, bones, and CHALK

**cal·cu·late** /'kælkyə,leɪt/ v [I,T] **1** to find out something or measure something using numbers: *These instruments calculate distances precisely.* **2 be calculated to do sth** to be intended to have a particular effect: *The ads are calculated to attract Hispanic buyers.*

**cal·cu·lat·ed** /'kælkyə,leɪtɪd/ adj **1 calculated risk/gamble** something you do after thinking carefully, although you know it may have bad results **2** deliberately and carefully planned to have a particular effect: *It was a calculated attempt to make the governor look silly.*

**cal·cu·lat·ing** /'kælkyə,leɪtɪŋ/ adj DISAPPROVING tending to make careful plans to get what you want, without caring about how it affects other people: *He's just another calculating politician.*

**cal·cu·la·tion** /ˌkælkyəˈleɪʃən/ *n* [C usually plural, U] the act of adding, multiplying, or dividing numbers to find out an amount, price etc.: *By their* **calculations**, *the debt will be paid off in four years.*

**cal·cu·la·tor** /ˈkælkyəˌleɪtə/ *n* a small machine that can add, multiply, divide etc. numbers

**cal·cu·lus** /ˈkælkyələs/ *n* [U] the part of mathematics that studies changing quantities, such as the speed of a falling stone or the slope of a curved line

**cal·en·dar** /ˈkæləndə/ *n* **1** a thing with pages that show the days and months of a year, that you usually hang on the wall **2** all the things that you plan to do in the next days, months etc.: *My calendar is full this week.* **3** a system that divides and measures time in a particular way: *the Jewish calendar* **4** **calendar year/month** a period of time that continues from the first day of the month or year until the last day of the month or year

**calf** /kæf/ *n, plural* **calves** /kævz/ **1** the part at the back of your leg between your knee and foot −see picture at BODY **2** the baby of a cow, or of some other large animals such as the ELEPHANT

**cal·i·ber** /ˈkæləbə/ *n* **1** the level of quality or ability that someone or something has achieved: *musicians of the highest caliber* **2** the width of a bullet or the inside part of a gun

**cal·i·brate** /ˈkæləˌbreɪt/ *v* [T] TECHNICAL to mark an instrument or tool so you can use it for measuring −**calibration** /ˌkæləˈbreɪʃən/ *n* [C,U]

**cal·i·co** /ˈkælɪˌkoʊ/ *n* [U] a light cotton cloth with a small pattern on it

**call¹** /kɔl/ *v*
**1** ▶TELEPHONE◀ [I,T] to telephone someone: *I called about six o'clock but no one was home.* | *He said he'd call me tomorrow.* −see usage note at TELEPHONE
**2** ▶DESCRIBE◀ [T] to describe someone or something in a particular way, or to say that s/he has a particular quality: *News reports have called it the worst disaster of this century.*
**3** ▶ASK/ORDER◀ [T] to ask or order someone to come to you: *Somebody call an ambulance!* | *I can hear Mom calling me; I'd better go.*
**4** ▶ARRANGE◀ [T] to arrange for something to happen at a particular time: *A meeting was called for 3 p.m. Wednesday.*
**5** ▶SAY/SHOUT◀ [I,T] to say or shout something because you want someone to hear you: *"I'm coming!" Paula called down the stairs.*
**6** **be called** to have a particular name: *What was that movie called again?*
**7** ▶NAME◀ [T] to give a person or pet a name: *They finally decided to call the dog "Torka."*
**8** **call the shots** INFORMAL to be the person who decides what to do in a situation: *I think it would be okay, but I'm not the one calling the shots around here.*
**9** **call it a day** SPOKEN said when you want to stop working, either because you are tired or because you have done enough: *Come on, guys, let's call it a day.*

**call back** *phr v* [I,T **call sb back**] to telephone someone again, or to telephone someone who tried to telephone you earlier: *Okay, I'll* **call back** *around three.* | *Ms. Brinston is on another line; can she* **call** *you* **back** *later?*

**call for** sb/sth *phr v* [T] **1** to demand or need something in a particular situation: *Representatives are* **calling for** *an investigation into the scandal.* | *a situation that* **calls for** *immediate action* **2** to say that a particular type of weather is likely to happen: *The forecast* **calls for** *more rain.*

**call in** *phr v* **1** [T **call sb ↔ in**] to ask or order someone to come and help you with a difficult situation: *The governor* **called in** *the National Guard to deal with the riots.* **2** [I] to telephone the place where you work, especially to report something: *Jan* **called in sick** *this morning.* (=telephoned to say that she was too sick to come to work) **3** to telephone a radio or television show to give your opinion or ask a question

**call** sb/sth ↔ **off** *phr v* [T] **1** to decide that a planned event will not happen: *The game had to be* **called off** *due to bad weather.* **2** to order a dog or person to stop attacking someone: *Call off your dog!*

**call on** sb/sth *phr v* [T] **1** to formally ask someone to do something: *The UN has* **called on** *both sides to start peace talks.* **2** to visit someone for a short time: *a salesman* **calling on** *customers*

**call out** *phr v* **1** [I,T **call sth ↔ out**] to say something loudly: *"Hey!" she* **called out** *to him as he got into his car.* **2** [T **call sb/sth ↔ out**] to ask or order someone to come and help you with a difficult situation: *"Where's Dr. Cook?" "She's been* **called out**.*"*

**call up** *phr v* **1** [I,T **call sb ↔ up**] to telephone someone: *Why don't you* **call** *Susie* **up** *and see if she wants to come?* **2** [T **call sth ↔ up**] to make information appear on a computer screen

**call²** *n* **1** an attempt to talk to someone by telephone: *She's expecting a call from the office soon.* | *I got a call yesterday from Teresa; she's fine.* | *Just give me a call from the airport when you arrive.* | *I have to* **make** *a telephone* **call**. | *Ask him to* **return my call** (=telephone me back) *when he comes home.* | *Can I make a* **local call**? (=a call made within the city or area where you are) −see usage note at TELEPHONE **2** **be**

**on call** ready to go to work if you are needed: *Heart surgeons are on call 24 hours a day.* **3** a shout or cry: *a call for help* **4 no call for sth/no call to do sth** SPOKEN used in order to tell someone that his/her behavior is wrong or that something is unnecessary: *She had no call to talk to you like that.* **5 a)** a decision made by someone in a sports game: *All the calls went against us.* **b)** a decision: *"Where should we eat tonight?" "I don't know, it's your call."* **6** a short visit for a particular reason. *We should* **pay** *Jerry and his wife* **a call** *since we're driving through Ohio.* **7** a request or demand for someone to do something: *Phillip said he'd received a call from God to preach.*

**call·er** /'kɔlɚ/ *n* someone who is making a telephone call: *Didn't the caller say who she was?*

**call girl** /'. ./ *n* ⇨ PROSTITUTE[1]

**cal·lig·ra·phy** /kə'lɪgrəfi/ *n* [U] the art of writing using special pens or brushes, or the beautiful writing produced in this way

**call-in** /'. ./ *n* a radio or television program in which people telephone to give their opinions or ask questions

**call·ing** /'kɔlɪŋ/ *n* a strong desire or feeling of duty to do a particular type of work, especially work that helps other people: *He felt a calling to become a teacher.*

**cal·lous** /'kæləs/ *adj* unkind and not caring that other people are suffering **–callousness** *n* [U] **–callously** *adv*

**cal·lus** /'kæləs/ *n* an area of hard rough skin. *Ron has calluses on his feet from walking so much.* **–callused** *adj*

**calm**[1] /kɑm/ **calm down** *v* [I,T] to become quiet after you have been angry, excited, or upset, or to make someone become quiet: *Calm down and tell me what happened.* | *It took a while to calm the kids down.* | *Matt was trying to calm the baby by singing to it.*

**calm**[2] *adj* **1** relaxed and not angry or upset: *The nurse was speaking in a calm and patient voice.* | *Please, everyone, try to* **keep/stay calm!** **2** completely still, or not moving very much: *the calm water of the lake* **3** not windy: *a calm clear beautiful day* **–calmly** *adv*

**calm**[3] *n* **1** [singular, U] a time that is quiet and peaceful **2 the calm before the storm** a peaceful situation just before a big problem or argument

**cal·o·rie** /'kæləri/ *n* **1** a unit for measuring the amount of ENERGY a particular food can produce: *An average potato has about 90 calories.* **2 count calories** to try to control your weight by calculating the number of calories you eat **3** TECHNICAL a unit for measuring heat

**calves** /kævz/ *n* the plural of CALF

**ca·ma·ra·der·ie** /kæm'rɑdəri, kɑm-/ *n* [U] a feeling of friendship that the people in a group have, especially when they work together: *the camaraderie of firefighters*

**cam·cord·er** /'kæm,kɔrdɚ/ *n* a small piece of equipment like a camera that you can hold in one hand to record pictures and sound on a VIDEO

**came** /keɪm/ *v* the past tense of COME

**cam·el** /'kæməl/ *n* a large animal with a long neck and one or two HUMPs (=large raised parts) on its back, that lives in the desert and carries goods or people

**ca·mel·lia** /kə'milyə/ *n* a large sweet-smelling red, pink, or white flower

**cam·e·o** /'kæmiou/ *n* **1** a small part in a movie or play acted by a famous actor: *Whoopi Goldberg makes a cameo appearance in the movie.* **2** a piece of jewelry with a raised shape, usually of a person's face, on a dark background: *a cameo brooch*

**cam·er·a** /'kæmrə, -ərə/ *n* a piece of equipment used for taking photographs, making films, or producing television pictures

**cam·er·a·man** /'kæmrə,mæn, -mən/, **cam·er·a·wom·an** /'kæmrə,wumən/ *n* someone who operates a camera for a television or film company

**cam·i·sole** /'kæmɪ,soul/ *n* a light piece of clothing that women wear on the top half of their bodies under other clothes

**cam·o·mile** /'kæmə,mil/ *n* [C,U] a plant with small white and yellow flowers, often used for making tea

**cam·ou·flage**[1] /'kæmə,flɑʒ, -,flɑdʒ/ *n* [C,U] the act of hiding something by making it look the same as the things around it, or the things you use to do this: *a soldier in camouflage* | *The Arctic fox's white fur is an excellent winter camouflage.*

camouflage

**cam·ou·flage**[2] /'kæməflɑʒ, -flɑdʒ/ *v* [T] to hide something by making it look like the things around it: *Hunters camouflage the traps with leaves and branches.*

**camp**[1] /kæmp/ *n* [C,U] **1** a place where people stay in tents in the mountains, forest etc. for a short time: *After hiking all morning, we returned to camp.* **2** a place where children go to stay for a short time and do special activities: *summer/scout/basketball camp* **3** a place where people are kept for a particular reason, when they do not want to be there: *a refugee/prison/labor camp* –see also DAY CAMP

**camp**[2] *v* [I] to set up a tent or shelter in a place and stay there for a short time: *Where should we camp tonight?* **–camping** *n* [U]: *We're going to* **go camping** *in Yellowstone Park this summer.*

**camp out** *phr v* [I] to sleep outdoors, usually in

a tent: *The kids like to **camp out** in the backyard.*

**cam·paign**[1] /kæm'peɪn/ *n* a series of actions that are intended to achieve a particular result, especially in business or politics: *Nixon's 1968 presidential campaign | a **campaign for/against** equal rights for homosexuals*

**campaign**[2] *v* [I] to do things publicly to try to achieve a particular result, especially in business or politics: *We're **campaigning for/against** the right to smoke in public places.*

**camp·er** /'kæmpɚ/ *n* **1** someone who is staying in a tent or shelter for a short time **2** a vehicle that has beds and cooking equipment so that you can stay in it while you are on vacation **3 happy camper** SPOKEN HUMOROUS someone who seems to be happy with his/her situation

**Camp·fire** /'kæmpfaɪɚ/ *n* an organization for girls and boys that teaches them practical skills and helps develop their character

**camp·ground** /'kæmpgraʊnd/ *n* a place where people who are on vacation can stay in tents, CAMPERs etc.

**camp·site** /'kæmpsaɪt/ *n* a place where you can camp: *We found a good campsite under a tree.*

**cam·pus** /'kæmpəs/ *n* the land or buildings of a college: *Many students live **on campus**.*

**can**[1] /kən; *strong* kæn/ *modal verb* **1** to be able to do something or know how to do something: *I can't (=cannot) swim! | Jean can speak French fluently. | We can't afford a vacation this year.* **2** to be allowed to do something: *You can go out when you've finished your homework. | In soccer, you can't touch the ball with your hands. (=it is against the rules)* **3** SPOKEN used in order to ask someone to do something or give you something: *Can I have a cookie? | Can you help me take the clothes off the line?* **4** used in order to show what is possible or likely: *It can't be Steve; he's in New York right now. | I still think the problem can be solved.* **5** used with the verbs "see," "hear," "feel," "smell," and "taste," and with verbs relating to thinking, to show that an action is happening: *Nancy can't understand why I'm so upset. | I can see Ralph coming now.* **6** used in order to show what often happens or how someone often behaves: *It can get pretty cold here at night.* —see also COULD —see study note on page 458

**USAGE NOTE can**

**Can** is used instead of the PRESENT CONTINUOUS with many verbs relating to physical or mental ability: *I can smell something burning. | Can you believe that?* ✗ DON'T SAY "I am smelling something burning" or "Are you believing that?" ✗

**can**[2] /kæn/ *n* **1** a metal container in which food or liquid is kept without air: *Soft drink cans may be recycled. | a can of tuna fish | a large can of paint* —see picture at CONTAINER **2 a (whole) can of worms** a complicated situation that causes a lot of problems when you start to deal with it **3** SLANG a toilet **4** OLD-FASHIONED SLANG BUTTOCKS **5** OLD-FASHIONED SLANG prison

**can**[3] /kæn/ *v* **1** to preserve food by putting it in a closed container without air: *My mother likes to can vegetables from the garden.* **2** SPOKEN to dismiss someone from their job **3 can it!** SPOKEN used in order to tell someone impolitely to stop talking or making a noise

**Ca·na·di·an**[1] /kən'eɪdiən/ *adj* relating to or coming from Canada

**Canadian**[2] *n* someone from Canada

**ca·nal** /kə'næl/ *n* a long narrow stream of water for ships or boats to travel along or to bring water from somewhere: *the Panama Canal*

**ca·nar·y** /kə'nɛri/ *n* a small yellow bird that sings and is often kept as a pet

**can·cel** /'kænsəl/ *v* [T] **1** to say or decide that something you have planned will not happen: *I had to cancel my trip.* **2** to tell someone that you no longer want something: *We're canceling our subscription to the magazine.* **cancel out** *phr v* [T] to have an equal but opposite effect on something, so that a situation does not change: *The big meal I ate **canceled out** the exercise I had done.*

**can·cel·la·tion** /ˌkænsə'leɪʃən/ *n* [C,U] a decision or statement that a planned activity or event will not happen: *The plane is full right now, but sometimes there are cancellations.*

**Can·cer** /'kænsɚ/ *n* **1** [singular] the fourth sign of the ZODIAC, represented by a CRAB **2** someone born between June 21 and July 22

**cancer** *n* [C,U] a serious disease in which the body's cells increase too fast, producing a growth that may lead to death: *breast/lung/bowel cancer | He died of cancer at the age of 63.* —**cancerous** *adj*

**can·did** /'kændɪd/ *adj* directly truthful, even when the truth may be unpleasant or embarrassing: *a candid article on birth control for teenagers* —**candidly** *adv*

**can·di·da·cy** /'kændədəsi/ *n* [C,U] the fact of being a CANDIDATE, usually for a political position: *She announced her candidacy at the convention.*

**can·di·date** /'kændə,deɪt, -dɪt/ *n* someone who applies for a job or is trying to be elected to a political position: *Which candidate are you voting for? | Sara seems to be a likely **candidate** for the job.*

**can·died** /'kændid/ *adj* cooked in or covered with sugar: *candied fruit*

**can·dle** /'kændl/ *n* a round stick of WAX with a piece of string through the middle that you burn to produce light

**can·dle·stick** /ˈkændlˌstɪk/ *n* a specially shaped metal or wooden object used for holding CANDLEs

**can·dor** /ˈkændɚ/ *n* [U] the quality of being honest and truthful

**can·dy** /ˈkændi/ *n* **1** [C,U] a sweet food made of sugar or chocolate, or a piece of this **2 mind/brain/eye etc. candy** INFORMAL something that is entertaining or pleasant to look at, but that does not make you think: *A lot of TV shows are just mind candy.*

**candy bar** /ˈ.. ˌ./ *n* a long narrow BAR of candy, usually covered with chocolate

**candy cane** /ˈ.. ˌ./ *n* a stick of hard sugar with a curved shape, colored red and white

**cane**[1] /keɪn/ *n* a long thin stick, usually with a curved handle, used for helping you walk

**cane**[2] *v* [T] to punish someone by hitting him/ her with a cane

**ca·nine** /ˈkeɪnaɪn/ *adj* relating to dogs

**can·is·ter** /ˈkænəstɚ/ *n* a metal container with a lid used for storing dry food or a gas: *a flour/sugar/salt canister*

**can·ker** /ˈkæŋkɚ/, **canker sore** /ˈ.. ˌ./ *n* [U] a sore area on the flesh of people or animals or on the wood of trees, caused by illness or a disease

**can·na·bis** /ˈkænəbɪs/ *n* [U] TECHNICAL ⇨ MARIJUANA

**canned** /kænd/ *adj* **1** preserved without air in a container: *canned tomatoes* **2 canned music/laughter/applause** music etc. that has been recorded and is used on television or radio programs

**can·ner·y** /ˈkænəri/ *n* a factory where food is put into cans

**can·ni·bal** /ˈkænəbəl/ *n* someone who eats human flesh **–cannibalism** *n* [U] **–cannibalistic** /ˌkænəbəˈlɪstɪk/ *adj*

**can·non** /ˈkænən/ *n* a large gun, fixed to the ground or on wheels, used in past times

**can·not** /ˈkænɑt, kəˈnɑt, kæ-/ *modal verb* the negative form of CAN: *I cannot accept your offer.*

**can·ny** /ˈkæni/ *adj* smart, careful, and showing that you understand a situation very well

**ca·noe** /kəˈnu/ *n* a long light narrow boat that is pointed at both ends, which you move using a PADDLE **–canoe** *v* [I]

**can·on** /ˈkænən/ *n* **1** FORMAL a generally accepted rule or standard for behaving or thinking **2** an established law of the Christian church

**can o·pen·er** /ˈ. ˌ.../ *n* a tool used for opening cans of food

**can·o·py** /ˈkænəpi/ *n* a cover attached above a bed or seat, used as a decoration or as a shelter **–canopied** *adj*

**can't** /kænt/ *modal verb* the short form of "cannot": *I can't go with you today.*

**can·ta·loupe** /ˈkæntəˌloʊp/ *n* [C,U] a type of MELON with a hard green skin and sweet orange flesh –see picture on page 470

**can·tan·ker·ous** /kænˈtæŋkərəs/ *adj* bad-tempered and complaining: *a cantankerous old man*

**can·teen** /kænˈtin/ *n* **1** a small container for carrying water or other drinks **2** a store or place where people in the military can buy things or go to be entertained

**can·ter** /ˈkæntɚ/ *v* [I,T] when a horse canters, it runs fast, but not as fast as possible –**canter** *n*

**Can·to·nese** /ˌkæntənˈiz/ *n* [U] a language used in Hong Kong and parts of southern China

**can·vas** /ˈkænvəs/ *n* **1** [U] a type of strong cloth that is used for making tents, sails, bags etc. **2** a piece of canvas on which a picture is painted

**can·vass** /ˈkænvəs/ *v* [I,T] to try to get information or support for a political party by going from place to place within an area and talking to people: *Someone was here canvassing for the Democrats.*

**can·yon** /ˈkænyən/ *n* a deep valley with very steep sides: *the Grand Canyon*

**cap**[1] /kæp/ *n* **1** a soft flat hat with a curved part sticking out at the front: *a baseball cap* **2** something that covers and protects the end or top of something: *a bottle cap | Put the cap back on that pen!* **3** a limit on the amount of money that someone can earn or spend: *There's a cap on the amount of money you can earn and still receive Social Security.*

**cap**[2] *v* [T] **1** to be the last and usually best thing that happens in a game, situation etc.: *Wilkes capped a perfect season by winning the 100 meter sprint.* **2** to cover the top of something: *All her front teeth are capped. | the snow-capped peaks of the Rocky Mountains* **3** to limit the amount of something, especially money, that can be used or spent: *The law caps the amount of interest that credit card companies can charge.*

**ca·pa·bil·i·ty** /ˌkeɪpəˈbɪləti/ *n* the ability of a machine, person, or organization to do something, especially something difficult: *The country has the **capability to** produce nuclear weapons. | What you can do depends on your computer's graphics capability.*

**ca·pa·ble** /ˈkeɪpəbəl/ *adj* [C,U] **1** having the power, skill, or other qualities that are needed to do something: *Do you think he is **capable of** murder?* –opposite INCAPABLE **2** skillful and effective: *Mary Beth is a capable lawyer.*

**ca·pac·i·ty** /kəˈpæsəti/ *n* **1** [singular, U] the amount that something can hold, produce, or carry: *My computer has a capacity of 400 mega-bytes. | The theater was **filled to capacity**.* (=completely full) **2** [singular, U] the ability to do or produce something: *Jan has a real capa-*

city for hard work. | *The factory is not yet work-ing* **at full capacity**. **3** [singular] someone's job, position, or duty: *She has traveled a lot in her capacity as a photojournalist.*

**cape** /keɪp/ *n* **1** a long loose piece of cloth-ing without SLEEVEs, that fastens around your neck and hangs from your shoulders: *Batman's black cape* **2** a large piece of land surrounded on three sides by water: *Cape Cod*

**ca·per**[1] /ˈkeɪpɚ/ *n* **1** a small dark green part of a flower used in cooking to give a sour taste to food **2** a planned activity, especially an il-legal or dangerous one

**caper**[2] *v* [I] to jump around and play in a happy excited way

**cap·il·lar·y** /ˈkæpəˌlɛri/ *n* a very small narrow tube that carries blood around your body −compare ARTERY, VEIN

**cap·i·tal**[1] /ˈkæpətl/ *n* **1** the city where a country or state's central government is: *The New York state capital is Albany.* −compare CAPITOL **2** ⇨ **capital letter** (CAPITAL[2]) **3** [singular, U] money or property you use to start a business or to make more money **4** a place that is important for a particular activity: *Hollywood is the capital of the movie industry.* −see study note on page 456

**capital**[2] *adj* **1** relating to money, machines, products, or property that can be used to create more wealth: *We need a bigger capital invest-ment to improve our schools.* **2** **capital letter** a letter of the alphabet that is printed in its large form, used at the beginning of a word or sentence **3** **capital offense/crime** a crime that is bad enough to be punished by death

**cap·i·tal·ism** /ˈkæpətlˌɪzəm/ *n* [U] an econo-mic and political system in which businesses be-long mostly to private owners, not to the government −compare COMMUNISM, SOCIALISM

**cap·i·tal·ist** /ˈkæpətl-ɪst/ *n* someone who supports or takes part in CAPITALISM −**capitalist** *adj*

**cap·i·tal·i·za·tion** /ˌkæpətl-əˈzeɪʃən/ *n* [U] the total value of a company, based on the value of its SHAREs

**cap·i·tal·ize** /ˈkæpətlˌaɪz/ *v* [T] **1** to write a letter of the alphabet using a CAPITAL letter **2** to supply a business with money so that it can operate

**capitalize on** sth *phr v* [T] to use something in order to gain an advantage: *The President should capitalize on his popularity and get that law passed.*

**capital pun·ish·ment** /ˌ... ˈ.../ *n* [U] the pun-ishment of legally killing someone for a crime s/he has done −see also DEATH PENALTY

**Cap·i·tol** /ˈkæpətl/ *n* **the Capitol** the building in which the people who make laws for the US or one of its 50 states meet −compare CAPITAL[1]

**Capitol Hill** /ˌ... ˈ./ *n* [singular] the US Con-gress: *The debate about gun control is continu-ing on Capitol Hill.*

**ca·pit·u·late** /kəˈpɪtʃəˌleɪt/ *v* [I] to stop fighting someone and accept his/her conditions or demands −**capitulation** /kəˌpɪtʃəˈleɪʃən/ *n* [C,U]

**cap·puc·ci·no** /ˌkæpəˈtʃinoʊ, ˌkɑ-/ *n* [C,U] a type of Italian coffee made with hot milk

**ca·price** /kəˈpris/ *n* [C,U] a sudden and unrea-sonable change in someone's opinion or beha-vior

**ca·pri·cious** /kəˈprɪʃəs/ *adj* likely to suddenly change decisions, emotions, conditions etc. without warning: *Helen's just as capricious as her mother was.* | *capricious spring weather* −**capriciously** *adv*

**Cap·ri·corn** /ˈkæprɪˌkɔrn/ *n* **1** [singular] the tenth sign of the ZODIAC, represented by a GOAT **2** someone born between December 22 and January 19

**cap·size** /ˈkæpsaɪz, kæpˈsaɪz/ *v* [I,T] if a boat capsizes or you capsize it, it turns over in the water

**cap·sule** /ˈkæpsəl/ *n* **1** a very small object with medicine inside that you swallow whole −see picture at MEDICINE **2** the part of a space vehicle in which people live and work

**cap·tain**[1] /ˈkæptən/ *n* **1** also **Captain** someone who commands a ship or aircraft **2** also **Captain** an officer who has a middle rank in the Army, Navy, Air Force, or Marines **3** someone who leads a team or group: *the football team captain*

**captain**[2] *v* [T] to lead a team or group of people as their CAPTAIN

**cap·tion** /ˈkæpʃən/ *n* words written above or below a picture that explain the picture

**cap·ti·vate** /ˈkæptəˌveɪt/ *v* [T] to attract and interest someone very much: *Alex was capti-vated by her beauty.* −**captivating** *adj*

**cap·tive**[1] /ˈkæptɪv/ *adj* **1** kept as a prisoner or in a small space: *captive animals* **2** **captive audience** a group of people who listen to or watch someone or something because they have to, not because they want to **3** **take/hold sb captive** to make someone become a prisoner, or to keep someone as a prisoner

**captive**[2] *n* someone who is kept as a prisoner, especially in a war

**cap·tiv·i·ty** /kæpˈtɪvəti/ *n* [U] the state of being kept as a prisoner or in a small space: *Many animals won't breed in captivity.*

**cap·tor** /ˈkæptɚ/ *n* FORMAL someone who keeps a person or animal as a prisoner or in a small space

**cap·ture**[1] /ˈkæptʃɚ/ *v* [T] **1** to catch some-one in order to keep him/her as a prisoner: *Lester was captured at the airport.* **2** to take control of something, often by using force: *They've captured a large share of the market.* | *a town captured by an enemy* **3** to catch an animal without killing it **4** to succeed in showing or describing something by using pictures or words: *His new book really captures what the 1920s were like.* **5 capture sb's imagination/attention** to make someone feel very interested in what you are saying or showing **6** TECHNICAL to put something in a form that a computer can use: *The data is captured by an optical scanner.*

**cap·ture**² *n* [U] **1** the act of catching someone in order to keep him/her as a prisoner, or of catching an animal: *Higgins avoided capture by hiding in the woods.* **2** the act of taking control of something, often by using force

**car** /kɑr/ *n* **1** a vehicle with four wheels and an engine, used for traveling from one place to another: *That's Lynn's new car.* | *Joe got in the car and buckled his seatbelt.* | *Wait for me here; don't get out of the car.* **2** one of the connected parts of a train: *I'll meet you in the dining/sleeping car.*

**ca·rafe** /kə'ræf/ *n* a glass bottle with a wide top, used for serving wine or water at meals

**car·a·mel** /'kærəməl, -ˌmɛl, 'kɑrməl/ *n* [C,U] candy made of cooked sugar, butter, and milk

**car·at** /'kærət/ *n* a unit for measuring the weight of jewels, equal to 200 MILLIGRAMS — see also KARAT

**car·a·van** /'kærəˌvæn/ *n* a group of people with animals or vehicles, who travel together

**car·bo·hy·drate** /ˌkɑrbou'haɪdreɪt, -drɪt, -bə-/ *n* [C,U] a substance in starchy foods that provides your body with heat and energy

**car·bon** /'kɑrbən/ *n* [U] a chemical that is an ELEMENT and that forms into DIAMONDs, and is in GASOLINE, coal etc.

**car·bon·at·ed** /'kɑrbəˌneɪtɪd/ *adj* carbonated drinks have a lot of BUBBLEs in them

**carbon cop·y** /ˌ.. '../ *n* **1** someone or something that is very similar to another person or thing: *The robbery is a carbon copy of one that took place last year.* **2** a copy of something made using CARBON PAPER

**carbon di·ox·ide** /ˌkɑrbən daɪ'ɑksaɪd/ *n* [U] the gas produced when animals breathe out, when CARBON is burned in air, or when animals and plants decay

**carbon mon·ox·ide** /ˌkɑrbən mə'nɑksaɪd/ *n* [U] a poisonous gas produced when engines burn gasoline

**carbon pap·er** /'.. ˌ../ *n* [C,U] thin paper with a blue or black substance on one side, that you put between two sheets of paper to make a copy of what you write on the top sheet

**car·bu·re·tor** /'kɑrbəˌreɪtə/ *n* the part of an engine that mixes the air and GASOLINE so they can burn in the engine to provide power

**car·cass** /'kɑrkəs/ *n* the body of a dead animal

**car·cin·o·gen** /kɑr'sɪnədʒən/ *n* TECHNICAL a substance that can cause CANCER —**carcinogenic** /ˌkɑrsɪnə'dʒɛnɪk/ *adj*

card

credit card

birthday card

playing cards

postcards

**card**¹ /kɑrd/ *n* **1** a small piece of plastic or stiff paper that shows information about someone or something: *a credit/library/business card* **2** a piece of folded stiff paper, usually with a picture on the front and a message inside, that you send to people on special occasions: *a birthday card* **3** one of a set of 52 small pieces of stiff paper with pictures or numbers on them, that are used for playing games — see also CARDS **4** ⇨ POSTCARD **5 play your cards right** INFORMAL to do the things that make you succeed in getting what you want **6 put/lay your cards on the table** INFORMAL to be completely honest about what your plans and intentions are **7** the flat piece of plastic inside a computer that has small electrical things attached to it, that allows the computer to do specific jobs

**card**² *v* [T] to ask someone to show a card proving that s/he is old enough to be in a particular place or to buy alcohol or cigarettes

**card·board** /'kɑrdbɔrd/ *n* [U] a thick material like stiff paper, used especially for making boxes

**card cat·a·log** /ˌ.. '.../ *n* a set of cards that contain information about something, especially books in a library, and are arranged in a particular order

**car·di·ac** /'kɑrdiˌæk/ *adj* TECHNICAL relating to the heart or to heart disease

**cardiac ar·rest** /ˌ... .'./ *n* TECHNICAL ⇨ HEART ATTACK

**car·di·gan** /'kɑrdəgən/ *n* a SWEATER that is fastened at the front with buttons

**car·di·nal**¹ /'kɑrdn-əl, -nəl/ *adj* very important or basic: *a cardinal rule*

**car·di·nal**² *n* **1** a common North American wild bird that is a bright red color **2** a priest of high rank in the Roman Catholic Church

**cardinal num·ber** /ˌ... '../ *n* any of the

numbers 1, 2, 3 etc. that show the quantity of something –compare ORDINAL NUMBER

**car·di·ol·o·gy** /ˌkɑrdiˈɑlədʒi/ *n* [U] the study or science of medical treatment of the heart

**cards** /kɑrdz/ *n* [plural] **1** a set of 52 small pieces of stiff paper with pictures or numbers on them, used for playing games: *a deck of cards* (=set of cards) **2** games played with such a set: *I'm going over to Herb's to play cards*.

**card ta·ble** /'. ˌ../ *n* a small light table that you can fold, on which you can play cards

**care¹** /kɛr/ *v* [I,T] to be concerned about or interested in someone or something: *He doesn't care about anybody but himself.|I don't care what you do.*

---
SPOKEN PHRASES

**1 who cares?** used in order to say in an impolite way that you do not care about something because you do not think it is important **2 I/he/they etc. couldn't care less** used in order to say in an impolite way that someone does not care at all about something **3 what do I/you/they etc. care?** used in order to say in an impolite way that someone does not care at all about something: *What does he care? He'll get his money whatever happens.* **4** FORMAL to like or want something: *Would you care to meet us after the show?|I don't really care for peanuts.*

---

**care for** sb/sth *phr v* [T] **1** to help someone when s/he is sick or not able to do things for himself/herself: *Angie cared for her mother after her stroke.* **2** to do things to keep something in good condition or working correctly: *instructions on caring for your new sofa*

**care²** *n*
**1** ▶HELP◀ [U] the process of helping someone who is sick or not able to do things for himself/herself: *Your father will need constant medical care.| the care of young children*
**2** ▶LOOKING AFTER STH◀ [U] the process of doing things to something so that it stays in good condition and works correctly: *With proper care, your washing machine should last years.*
**3 take care of a)** to watch and help someone: *Who's taking care of the baby?* **b)** to do things to keep something in good condition or working correctly: *Karl will take care of the house while we're on vacation.* **c)** to do the work or make the arrangements that are necessary for something to happen: *I'll take care of making the reservations.* **d)** to pay for something: *Don't worry about the bill, it's taken care of.*
**4** ▶CAREFULNESS◀ [U] carefulness to avoid damage, mistakes etc.: *Handle the package with care.|You'd better put more care into your work!*
**5** ▶WORRY◀ [C,U] feelings of worry, concern, or unhappiness: *Eddie doesn't have a care*

*in the world.* (=doesn't have any problems or worries)
**6 take care a)** SPOKEN used when saying goodbye to family or friends **b)** to be careful: *It's very icy, so take care driving home.*
**7 care of** used when sending letters to someone at someone else's address: *Just send the package to me care of my cousin.*

**ca·reen** /kəˈrin/ *v* [I] to move quickly forward in an uncontrolled way, making sudden sideways movements: *Morillo's truck careened down the embankment and burst into flames.*

**ca·reer¹** /kəˈrɪr/ *n* **1** a job or profession that you have been trained for and intend to do for a long time: *a career in law* **2** the period of time in your life that you spend working: *Will spent most of his career as a teacher.* –see usage note at JOB

**career²** *adj* intending to make a particular job your career: *a career soldier*

**care·free** /'kɛrfri/ *adj* without any problems or worries: *a carefree summer vacation*

**care·ful** /'kɛrfəl/ *adj* **1 (be) careful!** SPOKEN used in order to tell someone to think about what s/he is doing so that something bad does not happen **2** trying very hard to avoid doing anything wrong or damaging something: *a careful driver|Anna was careful not to upset Steven.| Be careful with that ladder!* **3** paying a lot of attention to detail: *Dr. Eng did a careful examination.* –**carefully** *adv* –**carefulness** *n* [U]

**care·giv·er** /'kɛrˌgɪvɚ/ *n* someone who takes care of a child or of someone who is old or sick

**care·less** /'kɛrlɪs/ *adj* **1** not paying enough attention to what you are doing: *It was very careless of you to leave your keys in the car.* **2** done without much effort or attention to detail: *This is very careless work - do it again!* –**carelessly** *adv* –**carelessness** *n* [U]

**care pack·age** /'. ˌ../ *n* a package of food, candy etc. that is sent to someone living away from home, especially a student at college

**carer** /'kɛrɚ/ *n* ⇨ CAREGIVER

**ca·ress** /kəˈrɛs/ *v* [T] to gently touch or kiss someone in a way that shows you love him/her –**caress** *n*

**care·tak·er** /'kɛrˌteɪkɚ/ *n* **1** someone whose job is to take care of a building or someone's land **2** someone such as a nurse who takes care of other people **3 caretaker government/administration** a government that has power only for a short time between the end of one government and the start of another

**car·go** /'kɑrgoʊ/ *n* -goes [C,U] the goods being carried in a ship, plane, TRUCK etc.: *a cargo of oil*

**Car·ib·be·an¹** /ˌkærɪˈbi-ən, kəˈrɪbi-ən/ *n* **the Caribbean** the Caribbean Sea (=sea east of Mexico), and the islands in it

**Caribbean**[2] *adj* relating to or coming from the Caribbean

**ca·ri·bou** /'kærəbu/ *n* a North American REINDEER

**car·i·ca·ture**[1] /'kærəkətʃə, -,tʃʊr/ *n* [C,U] a funny picture or description of someone that makes him/her look or seem more silly or amusing than s/he really is

**caricature**[2] *v* [T] to draw or describe someone in a way that makes him/her seem silly or amusing –**caricaturist** *n*

**car·ing** /'kɛrɪŋ/ *adj* providing care and support for others: *a warm and caring person*

**car·jack·ing** /'kar,dʒækɪŋ/ *n* [C,U] the crime of using a weapon to force the driver of a car to drive you somewhere or give you his/her car –**carjacker** *n* –**carjack** *v* [T]

**car·nage** /'karnɪdʒ/ *n* [U] FORMAL the killing and wounding of lots of people or animals, especially in a war

**car·nal** /'karnl/ *adj* FORMAL relating to the body or to sex: *carnal desires* –**carnally** *adv*

**car·na·tion** /kar'neɪʃən/ *n* a sweet-smelling white, pink, or red flower

**car·ni·val** /'karnəvəl/ *n* 1 [C,U] a public celebration with dancing, drinking, and entertainment, or the period when this takes place: *carnival time in Rio* 2 a noisy outdoor event where you can ride on special machines and play games for prizes

**car·ni·vore** /'karnə,vɔr/ *n* an animal that eats meat –**carnivorous** /kar'nɪvərəs/ *adj*

**car·ol**[1] /'kærəl/ *n* ⇨ CHRISTMAS CAROL

**carol**[2] *v* [I] to sing CHRISTMAS CAROLs

**ca·rouse** /kə'raʊz/ *v* [I] to drink a lot of alcohol, be noisy, and have fun

**car·ou·sel** /,kærə'sɛl/ *n* 1 the circular moving belt that you collect your bags and SUITCASEs from at an airport 2 ⇨ MERRY-GO-ROUND 3 a circular piece of equipment that you put photographic SLIDEs into for showing on a SLIDE PROJECTOR

**carp**[1] /karp/ *n* [C,U] a large fish that lives in lakes or rivers, or the meat from this fish

**carp**[2] *v* [I] to complain about something or criticize someone all the time

**car·pen·ter** /'karpəntə/ *n* someone whose job is making and repairing wooden objects

**car·pen·try** /'karpəntri/ *n* [U] the art or work of a carpenter

**car·pet**[1] /'karpɪt/ *n* 1 [C,U] a heavy woven material for covering all of a floor and stairs, or a piece of this material –compare RUG 2 **a carpet of leaves/flowers etc.** LITERARY a thick layer of leaves etc.

**carpet**[2] *v* [T] to cover something with a carpet

**car·pet·ing** /'karpətɪŋ/ *n* [U] ⇨ CARPET[1]

**car pool** /'. ./ *n* 1 a group of car owners who agree to drive everyone in the group to work, school etc. on different days, so that only one car is used at a time 2 a group of cars owned by a company or other organization so its members can use them

**car·port** /'karpɔrt/ *n* a shelter for a car that has a roof and is often built against the side of a house –compare GARAGE

**car·riage** /'kærɪdʒ/ *n* 1 a vehicle with wheels that is pulled by a horse 2 the movable part of a machine that supports another part: *a typewriter carriage* 3 [U] FORMAL the way someone walks and moves his/her head and body 4 ⇨ BABY CARRIAGE

**car·ri·er** /'kæriə/ *n* 1 a person or thing that moves goods or passengers from one place to another 2 someone who passes a disease to other people without having it himself/herself

**car·rot** /'kærət/ *n* a long thick orange root with a pointed end, eaten raw or cooked as a vegetable –see picture on page 470

**car·rou·sel** /,kærə'sɛl/ *n* another spelling of CAROUSEL

**car·ry** /'kæri/ *v*

1 ▶TAKE SOMEWHERE◀ [T] to take something somewhere by holding it, supporting it etc.: *Can you carry that suitcase for me?* | *The bus was carrying 25 passengers.* | *These pipes will* **carry** *oil* **across** *the desert.* –see picture on page 473

2 ▶INFORMATION/NEWS ETC.◀ [T] to contain a particular piece of information, story, advertisement etc.: *All the newspapers carried articles about the plane crash.*

3 ▶HAVE WITH YOU◀ [T] to have something with you in your pocket, on your belt, in your bag etc.: *Larry always carries a gun.*

4 ▶DISEASE◀ [T] to have a disease and pass it to others: *The disease was carried by rats.*

5 ▶AVAILABLE TO USE/BUY◀ [T] to have something that is available for people to use or buy: *All our products carry a 1 year guarantee.* | *I'm sorry, we don't carry that brand anymore.*

6 **be/get carried away** to be or become so excited that you are no longer in control of what you do or say: *I got carried away and bought three suits!*

7 ▶MOVE◀ to hold your body in a particular way as you move: *It was obvious by the way they* **carried themselves** *that they were soldiers.*

8 **carry weight** to have some influence over someone: *Lee's opinions carry a lot of weight with the boss.*

9 ▶RESULT◀ [T] to have something as a usual or necessary result: *Murder carries a life sentence in this state.* | *The job carries certain risks.*

10 **carry sth too far** to do or say too much about something: *It was funny at first, but you've carried the joke too far.*

11 ▶SUPPORT◀ [T] to support the weight of something else: *Those columns carry the whole roof.*

**12** ►TRAVEL/GO◄ [I] to be able to go as far as a particular place or a particular distance: *The boom carried as far as the lake.* | *These bullets carry for two miles.*

**13** ►ELECTION◄ [T] to win an election in a state or particular area: *Reagan carried California in 1980.*

**14** ►BEHAVE◄ [T] to behave in a particular way or have a particular quality: *Kevin always* **carries** *himself* **well.** (=stands and walks straight) | *Matthew's voice did not* **carry much** **conviction** (=he did not sound certain).

**15** **be carried** to be approved by a vote: *The motion has been carried.*

**16** **carry a tune** to sing correctly

**17** ►MATHEMATICS◄ [T] also **carry over** to move a total to the next row of figures for adding to other numbers

**carry** sth ↔ **forward** *phr v* [T] ⇨ **carry over**

**carry** sth ↔ **off** *phr v* [T] **1** to do something successfully: *I really don't know how I managed to* **carry** *that presentation* **off!** **2** to win a prize: *Fred* **carried off** *all the top awards at the banquet.*

**carry on** *phr v* **1** [I,T **carry on** sth] to continue doing something: *You'll get sick if you* **carry on** *working like that.* **2** [I] SPOKEN to behave in a silly or excited way: *We won't get anything done if you two don't stop* **carrying on!** **3** [I] OLD-FASHIONED to have a sexual relationship with someone when you should not

**carry** sth ↔ **out** *phr v* [T] **1** to do something that needs to be organized and planned: *Teenagers* **carried out** *a survey on attitudes to drugs.* **2** **carry out an order/threat etc.** to do something that you have said you will do or that someone has told you to do: *I'm supposed to* **carry out** *her instructions and report back.*

**carry** sth ↔ **over** *phr v* [T] to make an amount of something available to be used at a later time: *Can I* **carry over** *my vacation time to next year?*

**carry through** *phr v* [T] **1** [**carry** sth ↔ **through**] to complete or finish something successfully: *Once he starts a project, he always* **carries** *it* **through.** **2** [**carry** sb **through** (sth)] to help someone to manage during an illness or a difficult period: *Joe's courage* **carried** *him* **through** *Amanda's death.*

**car·ry·all** /'kæri,ɔl/ *n* a large soft bag, usually made of cloth

**carry-on** /'.. ,./ *adj, n* a bag that you can take on a plane with you

**car·ry·out** /'kæri,aut/ *n* ⇨ TAKEOUT

**car seat** /'. ./ *n* a special seat for babies or young children that you attach to the seat of a car

**car·sick** /'. ./ *adj* feeling sick because of the movement of traveling in a car −**carsickness** *n* [U]

**cart**[1] /kart/ *n* **1** a large wire basket on wheels used in a SUPERMARKET **2** a vehicle with two or four wheels: *a golf cart* | *a wooden cart*

*drawn* (=pulled) *by a horse* **3** a small table on wheels, used for moving and serving food

**4** **put the cart before the horse** to do things in the wrong order

**cart**[2] *v* [I,T] to carry or take something or someone somewhere: *Workers* **carted away** *several tons of trash.* | *The sheriff* **carted** *him* **off** *to jail.*

**car·tel** /kar'tɛl/ *n* [U] a group of companies that work together to control prices on a particular product

**car·ti·lage** /'kartl-ɪdʒ/ *n* [C,U] a strong substance that stretches and that is around the joints in your body

**car·tog·ra·phy** /kar'tagrəfi/ *n* [U] the skill or practice of making maps −**cartographer** *n*

**car·ton** /'kartn/ *n* a box made from stiff paper or plastic, used for holding food or drinks: *a milk carton* −see picture at CONTAINER

**car·toon** /kar'tun/ *n* **1** a funny short movie made using characters that are drawn and not real: *a Bugs Bunny cartoon* **2** a funny drawing, usually in a newspaper, that tells a joke or something humorous about the news −**cartoonist** *n*

**car·tridge** /'kartrɪdʒ/ *n* **1** a small piece of equipment that you put inside something to make it work: *computer game cartridges* **2** a tube containing explosive material and a bullet for a gun

**cart·wheel** /'kart wil/ *n* a movement in which you turn completely over by throwing yourself sideways onto your hands with your arms straight and bringing your legs straight over your head −**cartwheel** *v* [I]

cartwheel

**carve** /karv/ *v* **1** [T] to cut something, especially wood or stone, into a particular shape: *Their totem poles are carved from a single tree.* **2** [I,T] to cut cooked meat into smaller pieces with a large knife: *Dad always carves the turkey.* **3** [T] also **carve out** to become successful by working hard, especially in business: *She has* **carved** *a* **niche/place/career** *for herself in the competitive world of advertising.*

**carve** sth ↔ **up** *phr v* [T] DISAPPROVING to divide something into different parts: *The Assembly is* **carving up** *the area into new electoral districts.*

**carv·ing** /'karvɪŋ/ *n* **1** an object made by cutting wood, stone etc. **2** [U] the activity or skill of cutting wood, stone etc.

**car wash** /'. ./ *n* a place where you can take your car to be washed with special equipment

**cas·cade**[1] /kæ'skeɪd/ *n* **1** a stream of water that falls over rocks **2** something that seems to flow or hang down: *Her hair fell in a* **cascade of** *soft curls.*

**cascade**[2] *v* [I,T] to flow in large amounts

**case**[1] /keɪs/ *n*

**1** ▶SITUATION/EXAMPLE◀ [C usually singular] a particular situation that exists, or an example of that situation: *The action was a clear* **case** *of sexual harassment.* | *People working together can make a difference, and this certainly seems to* **be the case** *in Maria's neighborhood.* | *Some flowers can't survive the cold - impatiens are a* **case in point** (=a clear example) | *No one should be here after hours, but* **in your case** *I'll make an exception.*

**2** ▶COURT◀ a question that must be decided in a court of law: *a court case dealing with cruelty to animals*

**3** ▶POLICE◀ an event or set of events that the police deal with: *Sturgis is investigating a murder case.*

**4** ▶ARGUMENT◀ all the facts or reasons that support one side of an argument: *The prosecution's* **case against** *him is very strong.* | *There is a good* **case for** *changing the rule.*

**5** (just) in case a) used in order to say that someone should do something because something else might happen or be true: *Take your umbrella in case it rains.* b) used like "if": *In case you missed the program, here's a summary of the story.*

**6** ▶CONTAINER◀ a container for storing something: *a jewelry case* | *a* **case of** *wine*

**7** in case of if or when something happens: *In case of your death, your family will receive $50,000.*

**8** ▶DISEASE/ILLNESS◀ an example of a disease or illness, or the person suffering this disease or illness: *There have been ten* **cases of** *malaria in the village recently.* | *a bad* **case of** *sunburn*

**9** in that case SPOKEN used in order to describe what you will do or what will happen as a result of something: *"I'll be home late tonight." "Well, in that case, I won't cook dinner."*

**10** in any case used in order to say that a fact or situation remains the same even if other things change: *Sure we'll take you home - we're going that way in any case.*

**11** be on sb's case/get off sb's case SPOKEN to be criticizing someone a lot, or to stop criticizing him/her

**12** ▶GRAMMAR◀ [C,U] TECHNICAL the form of a word, usually a noun, that shows its relationship to other words in a sentence –see also LOWER CASE UPPER CASE

**case**[2] *v* **1** be cased in to be surrounded by a substance: *The building girders are cased in cement.* **2** case the joint/place SLANG to look around a place so that something can be stolen from it later

**case·load** /'keɪsloʊd/ *n* the number of people a doctor, lawyer etc. has to deal with

**case stud·y** /ˌ. '../ *n* a detailed study of a particular person, group, or situation over a long period of time

**case·work** /'keɪswɜːk/ *n* [U] work done to help particular people or families with their social problems –**caseworker** *n*

**cash**[1] /kæʃ/ *n* [U] **1** money in the form of coins and bills: *"Are you paying by credit card?" "No, I'll* **pay cash**." | *He had about $200* **in cash** *in his wallet.* **2** INFORMAL money in the bank: *I'm kind of short of cash at the moment.*

**cash**[2] *v* [T] to exchange a check for money: *Can I get this check cashed here?* –**cashable** *adj*

**cash in** *phr v* **1** [I] to gain advantages from a situation: *Brooks is* **cashing in on** *his new-found popularity.* **2** [T **cash sth ↔ in**] to exchange something for its value in money: *We decided to* **cash in** *our insurance policy early.*

**cash cow** /ˌ. './ *n* INFORMAL a business or product you can always depend on to make a profit

**cash crop** /ˌ. './ *n* a crop that is grown to be sold rather than to be used by the people growing it

**cash·ew** /'kæʃu, kæ'ʃu/ *n* a small curved nut that you can eat, or the tropical American tree on which these nuts grow

**cash flow** /'. ./ *n* [singular, U] the movement of money into and out of a company

**cash·ier** /kæ'ʃɪr/ *n* someone whose job is to receive and pay out money in a store

**cash·mere** /'kæʒmɪr, 'kæʃ-/ *n* [U] a type of fine soft wool. *an expensive cashmere sweater*

**cash on de·liv·er·y** /ˌ. . .'.../ *n* [singular] ⇨ C.O.D.

**cash reg·is·ter** /'. ,.../ *n* a machine used in stores to keep money in and to show how much customers have to pay

**cash-strapped** /'. ./ *adj* not having enough money: *a cash-strapped company*

**cas·ing** /'keɪsɪŋ/ *n* an outer layer of rubber, metal etc. that covers and protects something inside of it

**ca·si·no** /kə'sinoʊ/ *n* a place where people try to win money by playing games

**cask** /kæsk/ *n* a round wooden container used for holding wine, or the amount contained in this

**cas·ket** /'kæskɪt/ *n* ⇨ COFFIN

**cas·se·role** /'kæsəˌroʊl/ *n* [C,U] a mixture of meat and vegetables that are cooked together slowly, or the large dish that this food is served in

**cas·sette** /kə'sɛt/ *n* a small flat plastic case used for playing or recording sound or pictures; TAPE

**cast**[1] /kæst/ *v* cast, cast, casting [T]

**1** ▶MOVIE/TV◀ to give an actor a part in a movie, play etc.

**2** cast light on/onto a) to explain or give new information about something: *Can you cast any light on the meaning of these figures?*

**b)** LITERARY to send light onto a surface

**3 cast a shadow** LITERARY to make a shadow appear on something: *trees casting a shadow across the lawn*

**4 cast a spell on/over a)** to make someone feel very strongly attracted to something and keep his/her attention completely **b)** to say magic words to make something happen

**5 cast doubt on** to make someone feel less certain about something: *I didn't mean to cast doubt on Arthur's version of the story.*

**6 cast a vote** to vote in an election

**7 ▶ART◀** to make something by pouring metal or plastic into a specially shaped container: *a statue of Lincoln cast in bronze*

**8 ▶THROW◀** to throw something somewhere: *fishermen casting their nets into the sea*

**cast** sb/sth ↔ **aside** *phr v* [T] to get rid of something or someone in a careless way: *The new policy casts aside decades of work.*

**cast off** *phr v* **1** [I,T **cast off** sth] to untie the rope that keeps a boat on shore so that it can sail away **2** [T **cast** sb/sth ↔ **off**] LITERARY to get rid of something or someone: *a country that has cast off Communist rule*

**cast** sb/sth ↔ **out** *phr v* [T] LITERARY to make someone or something go away using force

**cast²** *n* **1** all of the actors in a movie: *an all-star cast* **2** a hard cover for a part of your body that supports a broken bone while it gets better: *a leg cast* **3** a container with a special shape into which you can pour metal or plastic to make a particular object **4** an act of throwing a fishing line

**cast·a·way** /'kæstə,weɪ/ *n* someone who is alone on an island after his/her ship has sunk

**caste** /kæst/ *n* [C,U] one of the social classes in India into which people are born, that cannot be changed

**cast·er** /'kæstɚ/ *n* a small wheel fixed to the bottom of a piece of furniture so it can be moved

**cas·ti·gate** /'kæstə,geɪt/ *v* [T] FORMAL to criticize or punish someone in a severe way –**castigation** /,kæstə'geɪʃən/ *n* [U]

**cast·ing** /'kæstɪŋ/ *n* [U] the act of choosing actors for a movie, play etc.: *a casting director*

**cast i·ron** /,. '../ *n* [U] a type of iron that is very hard but breaks easily

**cast-i·ron** /,. '../ *adj* **1** made of CAST IRON: *a cast-iron skillet* **2** INFORMAL very hard or strong: *a cast-iron stomach* (=one that does not get upset)

**cas·tle** /'kæsəl/ *n* a very large strong building built in past times to protect the people inside from attack

**cast-off** /'kæstɔf/ *n* INFORMAL something you no longer want, that you give to someone else who can use it –**cast-off** *adj*

**cas·trate** /'kæstreɪt/ *v* [T] to remove the sex-

ual organs of a male animal or a man –**castration** /kæ'streɪʃən/ *n* [C,U]

**cas·u·al** /'kæʒuəl, -ʒəl/ *adj* **1** not formal, or not for a formal situation: *casual clothes* | *a casual meal* **2** relaxed and not worried about things: *His casual attitude toward work really irritates me.* **3** without any clear aim or serious interest: *a casual glance at the newspapers* | *She wanted something more than a casual relationship.* **4** happening by chance without being planned: *a casual remark* **5** temporary, or used for only a short time: *casual workers* –**casually** *adv* –**casualness** *n* [U]

**cas·u·al·ty** /'kæʒəlti, -ʒuəlti,/ *n* **1** someone who is hurt in an accident or a battle: *The army suffered **heavy casualties**.* (=a lot of people were hurt or killed) **2 be a casualty of** to suffer because of a particular action: *The city library is the latest casualty of the cutbacks.*

**cat** /kæt/ *n* **1** a small animal with four legs that is often kept as a pet or used for catching mice (MOUSE) **2** a large animal that is related to this animal, such as a lion **3 let the cat out of the bag** INFORMAL to tell a secret without intending to

**cat·a·clysm** /'kætə,klɪzəm/ *n* LITERARY a sudden violent event or change, such as a big flood or EARTHQUAKE –**cataclysmic** /,kætə-'klɪzmɪk/ *adj*

**cat·a·log¹**, catalogue /'kætl,ɔg, -,ɑg/ *n* **1** a book with pictures and information about goods or services that you can buy: *the Sears catalog* **2** a list of the objects, paintings, books etc. in a place: *a museum catalog*

**catalog²** *v* [T] to put a list of things into a particular order and write it into a CATALOG

**cat·a·lyst** /'kætl-ɪst/ *n* **1** someone or something that makes an important event or change happen: *The women's movement became a catalyst for change in the workplace.* **2** a substance that makes a chemical reaction happen more quickly, without being changed itself

**cat·a·ma·ran** /,kætəmə'ræn/ *n* a SAILBOAT with two separate HULLs (=the part that goes in the water)

**cat·a·pult¹** /'kætə,pʌlt, -,pʊlt/ *v* [T] **1** to become famous or successful extremely suddenly: *The character of "Rocky" catapulted Stallone to stardom.* **2** to shoot something from a CATAPULT, or to throw something with the movement of a catapult

**catapult²** *n* a machine for throwing heavy stones or balls

**cat·a·ract** /'kætə,rækt/ *n* a change in the LENS of someone's eye that makes him/her slowly lose his/her sight

**ca·tas·tro·phe** /kə'tæstrəfi/ *n* [C,U] a terrible event that causes a lot of destruction or suffering: *catastrophes such as the Chernobyl explosion* –**catastrophic** /,kætə'strɑfɪk/ *adj*

**catch¹** /kætʃ/ *v* **caught, caught, catching**

**1** ▶HOLD◀ [I,T] to get hold of and stop something that is moving through the air: *Denise caught the bride's bouquet.* | *Here's your red ball, Sammy. Catch!*

catch

**2** ▶FIND SB STH◀ [T] to stop and hold someone or something after you have been chasing or hunting him, her, or it: *Look at all the fish we caught, Wes.*

**3** ▶SEE/SMELL◀ [T] to see or smell something for a moment: *I suddenly caught sight of Luisa in the crowd.* | *Yuck - did you catch a whiff of his aftershave?* (=did you smell it?)

**4** **catch sb's eye** to make someone notice someone or something: *A photograph on his desk caught my eye.*

**5** ▶GET SICK◀ [T] to get an illness: *Put your coat on! You don't want to catch (a) cold!*

**6** **catch (on) fire** to start burning, especially accidentally

**7** **catch your breath** to begin breathing normally again after you have been running or exercising

**8** ▶NOT BE TOO LATE◀ [T] to not be too late to do something, talk to someone etc.: *I'm catching the 7:30 bus.* | *If you hurry you might catch her before she leaves.*

**9** ▶FIND SB DOING STH◀ [T] to find someone doing something wrong or illegal: *I caught him sleeping with another woman.* | *A store detective caught him red-handed.* (=saw him stealing)

**10** ▶ATTACHED◀ [I,T] to become attached to or stuck on something, or to make something do this: *His shirt caught on the fence and tore.*

**11** **catch sb's interest/imagination** to make someone feel interested in something: *a story that will catch children's imaginations*

**12** **catch sb by surprise/catch sb off guard** to do something or happen in an unexpected way, so that someone is not ready to deal with it

**13** ▶STOP PROBLEM/DISEASE◀ [T] to discover a problem, especially a disease, and stop it from developing: *It's a type of cancer that can be cured, if it is caught early.*

---
SPOKEN PHRASES
---

**14** **not catch sth** to not hear or understand something clearly: *I'm sorry, I didn't catch your name.*

**15** **sb wouldn't be caught dead doing sth** said in order to emphasize that you would never do something: *I wouldn't be caught dead wearing a dress like that!*

**16** **you won't catch me doing sth** used in order to say you would never do something:

*You won't catch me ironing his shirts!*

**17** **Catch you later!** used in order to say goodbye

**catch on** *phr v* [I] **1** to begin to understand something: *Usually a couple of the children will catch on quickly and help the others.* **2** to become popular: *Rollerblades have sure caught on - you see them everywhere now.*

**catch up** *phr v* [I] **1** to come up from behind someone or something and reach the same point: *I had to run to catch up with her.* **2** to reach the same standard or level as someone or something else: *The US spent a lot of money trying to catch up with/to the Soviet Union in space exploration.*

**catch up on** sth *phr v* [T] to do something that needs to be done that you have not had time to do in the past: *I need to catch up on some work.*

**catch²** *n* **1** the act of catching something that has been thrown or hit: *That was a great catch!* **2** [U] a game in which two or more people throw a ball to each other: *Let's play catch.* **3** INFORMAL a hidden problem or difficulty: *The rent is so low there must be a catch.* **4** a quantity of something that has been caught, usually fish: *a large catch of tuna fish* **5** a hook for fastening something and holding it shut: *the catch on my necklace*

**Catch-22** /ˌkætʃ twɛnri 'tu/ *n* [singular, U] a situation that you cannot escape from because of something that is part of the situation itself: *You can't get a job without experience, and you can't get experience without a job. It's a Catch-22.*

**catch·er** /'kætʃɚ/ *n* the baseball player who SQUATs behind the plate where the BATTER stands, in order to catch missed balls —see picture on page 472

**catch·ing** /'kætʃɪŋ/ *adj* INFORMAL a disease or illness that is catching is infectious

**catch phrase** /'. ./ *n* a word or phrase that is easy to remember and is repeated by a political party, newspaper etc.

**catch·y** /'kætʃi/ *adj* pleasant and easy to remember: *a catchy song*

**cat·e·chism** /'kætə,kızəm/ *n* a set of questions and answers about the Christian religion that people learn before becoming members of the church

**cat·e·gor·i·cal** /ˌkætə'gɔrɪkəl, -'gɑr-/ *adj* clearly stating that something is true: *Foxe gave a categorical denial of his guilt.* —**categorically** *adv*

**cat·e·go·rize** /'kætəgə,raɪz/ *v* [T] to put people or things into groups according to what type they are; CLASSIFY: *We've categorized the wines by region.*

**cat·e·go·ry** /'kætə,gɔri/ *n* a group of people or things that have the same qualities: *Voters fall into (=belong to) one of three categories.*

**ca·ter** /'keɪtɚ/ v [I,T] to provide and serve food and drinks at a party: *Who's catering your daughter's wedding?* –**caterer** n

**cater to** sb phr v [T] to provide a particular group of people with something that they need or want: *newspapers that cater to business people*

**cat·er·pil·lar** /'kætɚˌpɪlɚ, 'kætə-/ n a small creature with a long rounded body and many legs, that eats leaves

**cat·fish** /'kætˈfɪʃ/ n [C,U] a common fish with long hairs around its mouth that lives mainly in rivers and lakes, or the meat from this fish

**ca·thar·tic** /kə'θɑrtɪk/ adj helping you to deal with difficult emotions and get rid of them: *Talking to a counselor can be a cathartic experience.* –**catharsis** /kə'θɑrsɪs/ n

**ca·the·dral** /kə'θidrəl/ n the main church in a particular area, that a BISHOP is responsible for

**cath·e·ter** /'kæθətɚ/ n a thin tube that is put into someone's body to take away liquids

**Cath·o·lic** /'kæθlɪk, -θəlɪk/ adj relating to the Roman Catholic Church –**Catholic** n –**Catholicism** /kə'θɑləˌsɪzəm/ n [U]

**catholic** adj FORMAL not limited to only a few things: *Susan has catholic tastes in music.*

**cat·nap** /'kætˈnæp/ n INFORMAL a short sleep during the day

**cat·nip** /'kætˈnɪp/ n [U] a type of grass with a pleasant smell that cats are attracted to

**cat·sup** /'kɛtʃəp, 'kæ-/ n [U] ⇨ KETCHUP

**cat·tail** /'kæt-teɪl/ n a plant that grows near water and has groups of brown flowers and seeds that look like the tail of a cat

**cat·tle** /'kætl/ n [plural] cows and BULLs kept on a farm

**cat·ty** /'kæti/ adj INFORMAL deliberately unkind in what you say about someone –**cattiness** n [U] –**cattily** adv

**cat·ty-cor·nered** /'.. ,../ adv ⇨ KITTY-CORNER

**cat·walk** /'kætˈwɔk/ n **1** a long raised path that MODELs walk on in a fashion show **2** a narrow structure built along something such as a bridge or above a stage, that is being built or repaired

**Cau·ca·sian** /kɔ'keɪʒən/ adj someone who is Caucasian belongs to the race that has pale skin –**Caucasian** n

**cau·cus** /'kɔkəs/ n a group of people in a political party, who meet to discuss and decide on political plans

**caught** /kɔt/ v the past tense and PAST PARTICIPLE of CATCH

**cau·li·flow·er** /'kɔliˌflaʊɚ, 'kɑ-/ n [C,U] a white vegetable with short firm stems and thick groups of small round flower-like parts –see picture on page 470

**'cause** /kəz/ conjunction SPOKEN because

**cause¹** /kɔz/ n **1** a person, event, or thing that makes something happen: *What was the*

*cause of the accident?* **2** [U] good reasons for feeling or behaving in a particular way: *She had no cause for complaint.* **3** a principle or aim that a group of people support or fight for: *I don't mind giving money if it's for a good cause.*

**cause²** v [T] to make something happen: *Heavy traffic is causing long delays on the freeway.| We still don't know what caused the computer to crash.*

**caus·tic** /'kɔstɪk/ adj **1 caustic remark/comment etc.** something you say that is extremely unkind or full of criticism **2** a caustic substance can burn through things by chemical action: *caustic soda*

**cau·tion¹** /'kɔʃən/ n [U] **1** the quality of doing something carefully, not taking risks, and avoiding danger: *Mulder moved with caution through the dark house.| You should use caution when driving at night.* **2 word/note of caution** a warning to be careful: *One note of caution: never try this trick at home.*

**caution²** v [T] FORMAL to warn someone that something might be dangerous or difficult: *The children were cautioned against talking to strangers.*

**cau·tion·ar·y** /'kɔʃəˌnɛri/ adj giving advice or warning: *a cautionary tale*

**cau·tious** /'kɔʃəs/ adj careful to avoid danger: *a cautious driver*

**cav·a·lier** /ˌkævə'lɪr/ adj not caring or thinking about other people: *The foreman had a cavalier attitude towards workers' safety.*

**cav·al·ry** /'kævəlri/ n soldiers who fight while riding on horses

**cave¹** /keɪv/ n a large natural hole in the side of a cliff or under the ground

**cave²** v

**cave in** phr v [I] **1** to fall down or inwards: *The roof of the old house had caved in.* **2** to stop opposing something because you have been persuaded or threatened: *Now is not the time to cave in to their demands.* –**cave-in** n

**cave·man** /'keɪvmæn/ n someone who lived in a CAVE many thousands of years ago

**cav·ern** /'kævɚn/ n a large deep CAVE –**cavernous** adj

**cav·i·ar** /'kæviˌɑr/ n [U] the salted eggs of various types of large fish, eaten as a special expensive food

**cav·i·ty** /'kævəti/ n **1** a hole in a tooth made by decay **2** a hole or space inside something solid

**ca·vort** /kə'vɔrt/ v [I] to jump or dance in a noisy, playful, or sexual way

**CB** n [C,U] Citizens Band; a radio on which people can speak to each other over short distances

**CBS** n Columbia Broadcasting System; one of the national companies that broadcasts television and radio programs in the US

**cc 1** the abbreviation of "cubic centimeter": *a 2000 cc engine* **2** the abbreviation of CARBON COPY; used at the end of a business letter to show that you are sending a copy to someone else

**CD** *n* **1** Compact Disc; a small circular piece of hard plastic on which recorded sound or information can be stored **2** ⇨ CERTIFICATE OF DEPOSIT

**CD play·er** /ˌ. ˈ. ˌ../ *n* a piece of equipment used for playing music CDs

**CD-ROM** /ˌsi di ˈrɑm/ *n* [C,U] Compact Disc Read-Only Memory; a CD on which large quantities of information can be stored to be used by a computer

**cease** /sis/ *v* [I,T] FORMAL to stop doing something or to make an activity stop happening: *By noon the rain had ceased.* | *He never ceases to amaze me.* (=I am always surprised by what he does)

**cease·fire** /ˌsisˈfaɪɚ, ˈsisfaɪɚ/ *adj* an agreement for both sides in a war to stop fighting for a period of time

**cease·less** /ˈsislɪs/ *adj* FORMAL continuing for a long time without stopping: *She was tired of her parents' ceaseless arguing.* **—ceaselessly** *adv*

**ce·dar** /ˈsidɚ/ *n* [C,U] a tall tree with leaves shaped like needles that do not fall off in winter, or the red sweet-smelling wood of this tree

**cede** /sid/ *v* [T] FORMAL to give something, usually land, to another country or person, often after losing a war

**ceil·ing** /ˈsilɪŋ/ *n* **1** the inside surface of the top part of a room **2** an official upper limit on things such as wages or rents

**cel·e·brate** /ˈsɛləˌbreɪt/ *v* **1** [I,T] to do something special because of a particular event or special occasion: *We should celebrate Dad's birthday at a restaurant.* **2** [T] FORMAL to praise someone or something in speech or writing

**cel·e·brat·ed** /ˈsɛləˌbreɪtɪd/ *adj* famous or talked about a lot: *Chicago is **celebrated** for its architecture.*

**cel·e·bra·tion** /ˌsɛləˈbreɪʃən/ *n* **1** an occasion or party when you celebrate something: *New Year's celebrations* **2** the act of celebrating: *There'll be a party **in celebration of** his promotion.*

**ce·leb·ri·ty** /səˈlɛbrəti/ *n* a famous person, especially someone in the entertainment business

**cel·er·y** /ˈsɛləri/ *n* [U] a vegetable with long firm pale green stems, often eaten raw —see picture on page 470

**ce·les·tial** /səˈlɛstʃəl/ *adj* LITERARY relating to the sky or heaven

**cel·i·bate** /ˈsɛləbɪt/ *adj* not having sex, especially for religious reasons **—celibacy** /ˈsɛləbəsi/ *n* [U]

**cell** /sɛl/ *n* **1** a small room in a police station or prison where prisoners are kept **2** the smallest part of an animal or plant that can exist on its own: *red blood cells*

**cel·lar** /ˈsɛlɚ/ *n* a room under a house or restaurant: *a wine cellar*

**cel·list** /ˈtʃɛlɪst/ *n* someone who plays the CELLO

**cel·lo** /ˈtʃɛloʊ/ *n* a large wooden musical instrument, shaped like a VIOLIN, that you hold between your knees and play by pulling a BOW (=special stick) across wire strings

**cel·lo·phane** /ˈsɛləˌfeɪn/ *n* TRADEMARK a thin transparent material used for wrapping food

**cel·lu·lar** /ˈsɛlyələɚ/ *adj* relating to the cells in a plant or animal

**cellular phone** /ˌ... ˈ./ *n* a telephone that you can carry with you, that works by using a network of radio stations to pass on signals

**cel·lu·lite** /ˈsɛlyəˌlaɪt/ *n* [U] fat that is just below someone's skin and that makes it look uneven and unattractive

**cel·lu·loid** /ˈsɛlyəˌlɔɪd/ *n* TRADEMARK a substance like plastic, used in past times to make film

**cel·lu·lose** /ˈsɛlyəˌloʊs/ *n* [U] the material that the cell walls of plants are made of and that is used for making plastics, paper etc.

**Cel·si·us** /ˈsɛlsiəs, -ʃəs/ *n* [U] a temperature scale in which water freezes at 0° and boils at 100°

**ce·ment¹** /sɪˈmɛnt/ *n* [U] **1** a gray powder used in building, that becomes hard when mixed with water and allowed to dry **2** a substance used to fill holes or as a glue

**cement²** *v* [T] **1** to cover something with CEMENT **2** to make a relationship stronger: *China has cemented its trade connections with the US.*

**cem·e·ter·y** /ˈsɛməˌtɛri/ *n* an area of land where dead people are buried

**cen·sor** /ˈsɛnsɚ/ *v* [T] to examine books, movies etc. in order to remove anything that is offensive, politically dangerous etc. **—censor** *n*

**cen·sor·ship** /ˈsɛnsɚˌʃɪp/ *n* [U] the practice or system of CENSORing something

**cen·sure** /ˈsɛnʃɚ/ *v* [T] FORMAL to officially criticize someone for something s/he has done wrong **—censure** *n*

**cen·sus** /ˈsɛnsəs/ *n* an official count of all the people in a country, including information about their ages, jobs etc.

**cent** /sɛnt/ *n* **1** a unit of money that is worth 1/100 of a dollar. Its sign is ¢. **2 put in your two cents' worth** INFORMAL to give your opinion about something

**cen·ten·ni·al** /sɛnˈtɛniəl/, **cen·ten·a·ry** /sɛnˈtɛnəri/ *n* the day or year exactly 100 years after an important event

**cen·ter¹** /ˈsɛntɚ/ *n* **1** the middle part or point of something: *I work in **the center of** the* city. | **the center of** the table **2** a place or building used for a particular purpose: *a shopping center* | *the Kennedy Space Center* **3** a place where most of the important things happen that relate to a business or activity: *the center of the country's music industry* | *a major banking center* **4 be the center of attention** to be the person to whom people are giving the most attention **5 the center** a position in politics that is not extreme **6** in basketball, the player who usually plays in the middle of the action – see picture on page 472 **7** in football, the player who starts the ball moving in each PLAY – see usage note at MIDDLE[1]

**center**[2] *v* [T] to move something to a position at the center of something else: *Stand back and tell me if the painting is centered.*

  **center around** sth *phr v* [I,T] if your thoughts, activities etc. center around something, it is the main thing you think is important: *Their whole life centers around that kid of theirs!*

  **center on** sth *phr v* [T] to pay more attention to one thing or person than anything or anyone else: *The discussion centered on gun control.*

**center field** /ˌ.. ˈ./ *n* [singular] the area in baseball in the center of the OUTFIELD

**cen·ter·fold** /ˈsɛntɚˌfoʊld/ *n* a picture of a woman with no clothes on that covers the two pages in the middle of a magazine

**center of grav·i·ty** /ˌ.. . ˈ.../ *n* the point on an object at which it will balance

**cen·ter·piece** /ˈsɛntɚˌpis/ *n* **1** a decoration in the middle of a table, usually made of flowers **2 the centerpiece of** the most important part of something: *the centerpiece of Canada's foreign policy*

**Cen·ti·grade** /ˈsɛntəˌgreɪd/ *n* ⇨ CELSIUS

**cen·ti·me·ter** /ˈsɛntəˌmitɚ/ written abbreviation **cm** *n* a unit for measuring length, equal to 1/100 of a meter or 0.39 inches

**cen·ti·pede** /ˈsɛntəˌpid/ *n* a very small creature with a long thin body and many legs

**cen·tral** /ˈsɛntrəl/ *adj* **1** in the middle of an object or area: *Central Asia* | *the central part of the house* **2** controlling or used by everyone or everything in a whole country or a large organization: *The computers are linked to a central database.* **3** the most important: *These questions have played a central role in the history of the US.* (=they have been very important) **4** convenient because of being near the center: *I want a hotel that's central.* –**centrally** *adv*

**Cen·tral Eu·rope** *n* ⇨ EASTERN EUROPE

**Central In·tel·li·gence A·gen·cy** /ˌ.. .ˈ... ,.../ *n* [singular] ⇨ CIA

**cen·tral·ize** /ˈsɛntrəˌlaɪz/ *v* [T] to change a government or organization so that it is controlled in one place, by one main group of people

**cen·tu·ry** /ˈsɛntʃəri/ *n* **1** one of the 100-year periods counted forward or backward from the

year of Christ's birth: *technology for the twenty-first century* | *My grandparents moved west at the turn of the century.* (=in or around the year 1900) **2** a period of time equal to 100 years

**CEO** *n* Chief Executive Officer; the person with the most authority in a large company

**ce·ram·ics** /səˈræmɪks/ *n* [plural, U] objects produced by shaping pieces of clay and baking them until they are hard, or the art of making them –**ceramic** *adj*

**ce·re·al** /ˈsɪriəl/ *n* **1** [C,U] breakfast food that is made from grain and usually eaten with milk **2** a plant grown to produce grain for foods, such as wheat, rice etc.

**ce·re·bral** /səˈribrəl, ˈsɛrə-/ *adj* TECHNICAL relating to or affecting the brain

**cer·e·mo·ni·al** /ˌsɛrəˈmoʊniəl/ *adj* used in a ceremony: *Native American ceremonial pipes* –**ceremonially** *adv*

**cer·e·mo·ny** /ˈsɛrəˌmoʊni/ *n* **1** a formal or traditional set of actions used at an important social or religious event: *The treaty was signed during a ceremony at the White House.* | *Pastor Hetland conducted/performed the marriage ceremony.* **2** [U] formal words and actions used on special occasions: *With great ceremony, the Mayor opened the new concert hall.*

**cer·tain**[1] /ˈsɚtn/ *determiner, pron* **1** a certain thing, person, idea etc. is a particular thing, person etc. that you are not naming or describing exactly: *The plant grows on a certain island in the South China Sea.* | *There are certain things I just can't talk about with her.* **2** some, but not a lot: *In certain ways he can be good to work for.* | *I had to spend a certain amount of time practicing, but it wasn't hard.* **3 to a certain extent** partly, but not completely: *I agree with you to a certain extent, but I think there are other problems too.*

**certain**[2] *adj* **1** completely sure and without any doubts: *I'm not certain (that) he's telling me the truth.* | *No one was certain what to expect.* | *Are you certain about that?* **2 know/ say for certain** to know something without any doubt: *I can't say for certain when her plane will arrive.* **3** something that is certain will definitely happen or is definitely true: *It's almost certain that the enemy will attack from the north.* | *He's certain to be offered the job.* **4 make certain (that)** to do something in order to be sure about a fact, about what to do etc.: *Employers are required to make certain that all employees are treated fairly.* –compare UNCERTAIN –see usage note at SURE[1]

**cer·tain·ly** /ˈsɚtnli/ *adv* without any doubt: *Diana certainly spends a lot of money on clothes.* | *"Can I borrow your notes?" "Certainly!"* (=yes, of course) –see usage note at SURE[1]

**cer·tain·ty** /'sət‾nti/ n **1** [U] the state of being completely sure about something: *We cannot say* **with** *complete* **certainty** *whether your wife will be all right.* **2** something that is definitely true or will definitely happen: *Ginny had to face the* **certainty that** *she was pregnant.*

**cer·ti·fi·a·ble** /ˌsəʔə'faɪəbəl/ adj INFORMAL crazy: *If you ask me, that guy is certifiable.*

**cer·tif·i·cate** /sə'tɪfəkɪt/ n an official document that states the facts about something or someone: *a birth/marriage/death certificate* (=giving details of someone's birth etc.) –see also GIFT CERTIFICATE

**certificate of de·pos·it** /.ˌ... . '.../ n TECHNICAL a bank account that you must leave a particular amount of money in for a particular amount of time in order to get INTEREST

**cer·ti·fied** /'səʔəfaɪd/ adj having successfully completed the training for a profession: *a certified nurse* –**certification** /ˌsəʔəfə'keɪʃən/ n [U]

**certified check** /ˌ... './ n a check that you get from a bank for a particular amount of money

**certified mail** /ˌ... './ n [U] a method of sending mail in which the person it is sent to must sign his/her name to prove s/he has received it

**certified pub·lic ac·count·ant** /ˌ... ˌ.. '.../ n ⇨ CPA

**cer·ti·fy** /'səʔəˌfaɪ/ v [T] **1** to officially state that something is true or that a document is correct: *Two doctors* **certified that** *the patient was dead.* **2** to give someone an official paper that states that s/he has completed a course of training: *He has been certified as a mechanic.*

**cer·vix** /'səvɪks/ n TECHNICAL the narrow opening into a woman's UTERUS –**cervical** /'səvɪkəl/ adj

**ce·sar·e·an** /sɪ'zɛriən/, **cesarean section** /.ˌ... '.../ n an operation in which a woman's body is cut open to take a baby out

**ces·sa·tion** /sɛ'seɪʃən/ n FORMAL the act of stopping something: *the cessation of nuclear tests*

**cess·pool** /'sɛspul/ n a container under the ground where waste water from a house is collected, especially SEWAGE

**CFC** n CHLOROFLUOROCARBON; one of the gases that are used in AEROSOLs, REFRIGERATORs etc., and in making some plastics

**chafe** /tʃeɪf/ v [I,T] **1** if a part of your body chafes or if something chafes it, it becomes sore because of something rubbing against it **2** also **chafe at** to be or become impatient or annoyed

**cha·grin** /ʃə'grɪn/ n [U] FORMAL a feeling of being disappointed and annoyed because something has not happened the way you hoped

**chagrin** v **be chagrined** FORMAL annoyed and disappointed

**chain** /tʃeɪn/ n **1** [C,U] a series of metal rings connected together in a line, used as je-

welry or for fastening things, supporting weights etc.: *a delicate gold chain* | *The snow is so bad, you'll probably need chains on the tires.* **2 chain of events** a connected series of events that lead to a particular result: *the chain of events that caused World War I* **3** a group of stores, hotels etc. that are owned by the same person or company **4** mountains, lakes, or islands that are close together in a line **in chains 5** prisoners in chains have heavy chains fastened around their legs or arms, to prevent them from escaping

chain

link

**chain**[2] v [T] to use a chain to fasten one thing or person to another: *a bicycle* **chained to** *a fence*

**chain let·ter** /ˌ. '../ n a letter that is sent to several people who send copies to more people

**chain of com·mand** /ˌ. . '.../ n a system in an organization by which decisions are made and passed from people at the top of the organization to people lower down

**chain re·ac·tion** /ˌ. '.., '. .ˌ../ n a series of events or chemical changes, each of which causes the next one

**chain·saw** /'tʃeɪnsɔ/ n [U] a tool used for cutting wood, consisting of a circular chain with sharp edges that is moved by a motor

**chain-smoke** /'. ., . './ v [I,T] to smoke cigarettes one after the other –**chain-smoker** n

**chair**[1] /tʃɛr/ n **1** a piece of furniture for one person to sit on, that has a back, a seat, and four legs, and that can be moved **2** someone who is in charge of a meeting, a committee, or a university department **3** [singular] INFORMAL ⇨ ELECTRIC CHAIR

**chair**[2] v [T] to be the CHAIRPERSON of a meeting or committee

**chair·per·son** /'tʃɛrˌpəsən/, **chair·man** /'tʃɛrmən/, **chair·wom·an** /'tʃɛrˌwʊmən/ n **1** someone who is in charge of a meeting or committee **2** someone who is in charge of a large organization

---

**USAGE NOTE chairman**

**Chairman** can be used for both men and women, but many people prefer to use **chairperson**, especially if the sex of the person is not known.

---

**cha·let** /ʃæ'leɪ, 'ʃæleɪ/ n a small wooden house with a steeply sloping roof

**chalk**[1] /tʃɔk/ n **1** [U] soft white rock **2** [C,U] small sticks of this substance used for writing or drawing –**chalky** adj

**chalk**[2] v [I,T] to write or draw with CHALK
**chalk sth ↔ up** phr v [T] INFORMAL to succeed in

winning or getting something: *Boston chalked up another win over Detroit last night.*

**chalk·board** /'tʃɔkbɔrd/ *n* ⇨ BLACKBOARD

**chalk·y** /'tʃɔki/ *adj* similar to CHALK, or containing CHALK

**chal·lenge**[1] /'tʃæləndʒ/ *n* [C,U] **1** something new, exciting, or difficult that needs a lot of skill and effort to do: *the challenge of a new job | Can American businesses* **meet the** *Japanese* **challenge?** (=can they do just as well?) | *The President* **faces a serious challenge to** *his leadership.* (=he must be ready to deal with it) **2** the act of questioning whether something is right, fair, or legal: *If I make any decisions myself, my boss thinks it's a* **direct challenge to** *her authority.* **3** an invitation from someone to compete or fight

**challenge**[2] *v* [T] **1** to question whether something is right, fair, or legal: *At meetings, she would often challenge the director's views.* **2** to invite someone to compete or fight against you: *We were* **challenged to** *a game of tennis.* **3** to test someone's skills and ability, or to encourage him/her to do this: *Nothing about school seems to challenge Brenda any more.* **−challenger** *n*

**chal·lenged** /'tʃæləndʒd/ *adj* **visually/ mentally/physically challenged** a phrase meaning that someone has difficulty with seeing, thinking, or doing things, used in order to be polite

**chal·leng·ing** /'tʃæləndʒɪŋ/ *adj* difficult in an interesting way: *a challenging new job*

**cham·ber** /'tʃeɪmbɚ/ *n* **1** a room used for a special purpose: *a gas/torture chamber* (=used for killing people by gas or for hurting them) | *the council's chamber in the Town Hall* **2** an enclosed space inside something, such as your body or a machine: *a gun with six chambers* **3** a group of people who make laws for a country, state etc.: *The Senate is the upper chamber of Congress.*

**chamber mu·sic** /'.. ,../ *n* [U] CLASSICAL MUSIC written for a small group of performers

**Chamber of Com·merce** /,... '../ *n* an organization of business people in a town or city whose aim is to encourage business

**chambers** /'tʃeɪmbɚz/ *n* the offices used by judges

**cha·me·leon** /kə'milyən, kə'miliən/ *n* **1** a small LIZARD (=type of animal) whose skin changes and becomes the same color as the things around it **2** someone who changes his/ her ideas, behavior etc. to fit different situations

**cham·o·mile** /'kæmə,mil/ *n* [U] ⇨ CAMOMILE

**champ** /tʃæmp/ *n* INFORMAL ⇨ CHAMPION[1]

**cham·pagne** /ʃæm'peɪn/ *n* [U] a French white wine that has a lot of BUBBLEs and is often drunk on special occasions

**cham·pi·on**[1] /'tʃæmpiən/ *n* **1** a person, team etc. that has won a competition, especially in sports: *the* **reigning** *national soccer* **champions** (=the champions right now) **2** **champion of** someone who publicly fights for and defends an aim, idea, group etc.: *a champion of the homeless*

**champion**[2] *v* [T] to publicly fight for an aim, idea, group etc: *people championing gay rights*

**cham·pi·on·ship** /'tʃæmpiən,ʃɪp/ *n* **1** a competition or series of competitions to find the best player or team in a particular sport: *the US basketball championships* **2** the position or period of being a champion: *Can she win the championship again?*

**chance**[1] /tʃæns/ *n* **1** a time or situation that you can use to do something that you want to do; opportunity: *Now I'll* **have/get a chance to** *find out what her husband looks like. | If you'll just* **give me a chance,** *I'll tell you what happened. | You should* **take the chance** (=use the opportunity) *to travel while you're young. | Mr. Yates has given us a* **second chance** *to pass the test.* (=another chance after you have failed the first time) **2** [C,U] how possible or likely it is that something is true or that someone will succeed: *What are Deirdre's* **chances of** *getting the job? |* **There's a chance** *she left her keys in the office. |* **Chances are** (=it is likely) *they're stuck in traffic.* **3** **by any chance** SPOKEN used in order to ask politely whether something is true: *Are you Ms. Hughes' daughter, by any chance?* **4** **fat chance!/not a chance!** SPOKEN said when you are sure that something could never happen: *"Maybe you'll win the lottery." "Sure, fat chance!"* **5** **take a chance** to do something that involves risk: *You take a chance investing money in stocks, but the gains can be huge.* **6** [U] the way things happen without being planned or caused: *We met* **by chance** *at a friend's party.* −see also **stand a chance (of doing sth)** (STAND[1])

---

**USAGE NOTE chance and opportunity**

Use these words to talk about something you are able to do because of luck: *I had the opportunity to visit Boston.* | *I had no chance to see him.* **Chance** can also mean a possibility: *There is a chance that I will see him.* ✗ DON'T SAY "There is an opportunity that I will see him." ✗

---

**chance**[2] *v* [T] INFORMAL to do something that involves a risk: *You could always ride the subway, if you're willing to* **chance it.**

**chance on/upon** sth *phr v* [T] LITERARY to meet someone or find something when you are not expecting to

**chance**[3] *adj* not planned; accidental: *a chance encounter* (=when you meet someone by accident)

**chan·cel·lor** /'tʃænsəlɚ/ *n* **1** the head of some universities: *the Chancellor of UCLA*

**2** the head of the government in some countries

**chanc·y** /'tʃænsi/ *adj* INFORMAL uncertain or involving risks: *The weather there can be chancy in the spring.*

**chan·de·lier** /ˌʃændə'lɪr/ *n* a large decoration that holds lights or CANDLEs, hangs from the ceiling, and is covered with small pieces of glass

**change**[1] /tʃeɪndʒ/ *v* **1** [I,T] to become different, or to make someone or something become different: *In the fall, its leaves change from green to gold.* | *Ed changed after Ricky died.* | *There are plans to change the voting system.* | *Let me know if you change your mind.* (=change your decision, plan, or opinion) **2** [I,T] to stop having or doing one thing and start something else instead: *You'll have to change in Denver.* (=get on a different plane) | *Would you mind changing places* (=exchanging positions) *with me?* **3** [I,T] to take off your clothes and put on different ones: *Go upstairs and change into your play clothes.* | *Eric went to get changed.* | *change the baby* (=put a clean DIAPER on the baby) **4** [T] **a)** to exchange a unit of money for smaller units that add up to the same value: *Can you change a $10 bill?* **b)** to exchange money from one country for money from another: *I want to change my dollars into pesos.* **5** **change the sheets** to put clean SHEETs on a bed **6** **change hands** to become someone else's property: *The house has changed hands twice in the last ten years.*

**change** sth ↔ **around** *phr v* [T] to move things into different positions: *The room looks bigger since we changed the furniture around.*

**change over** *phr v* [I] to stop doing or using one thing and start doing or using something different: *Will the US ever change over to the metric system?*

**change**[2] *n* **1** [C,U] the process or result when something or someone becomes different: *a change in the weather* | *a change of leadership* | *Grandpa's health has taken a change for the worse.* (=become worse) **2** a new or different thing or person used instead of something or someone else: *Take a change of clothes with you.* | *The car needs an oil change.* **3** [C usually singular] something that is interesting or enjoyable because it is different from what is usual: *Why don't we go out for a change?* **4** [U] the money that you get back when you pay for something with more money than it costs: *That's 32¢ change, ma'am.* **5** [U] money in the form of coins: *I have about a dollar in change.* **6** [U] coins or small bills that you give in exchange for the same amount of money in a larger unit: *Do you have change for a dollar?*

**change·a·ble** /'tʃeɪndʒəbəl/ *adj* likely to change, or changing often: *changeable weather*

**change·o·ver** /'tʃeɪnˌdʒoʊvɚ/ *n* a change from one activity or system to another

**chan·nel**[1] /'tʃænl/ *n* **1** a particular television station: *What's on channel 2?* **2** a long passage dug into the earth that water or other liquids can flow along **3** water that connects two seas: *the English Channel* **4** the deepest part of a river, sea etc. that ships can sail through **5** **channel hop/surf** INFORMAL to change from one television channel to another again and again

**channel**[2] *v* [T] **1** to use something such as money or energy for a particular purpose: *Wayne needs to channel his creativity into something useful.* **2** to cut a deep line or space into something

**channels** /'tʃænlz/ *n* [plural] ways of sending or obtaining information about a particular subject: *You'll have to go through official channels for help.*

**chant**[1] /tʃænt/ *v* [I,T] **1** to repeat a word or phrase again and again: *Crowds of chanting supporters filled the streets.* **2** to sing or say a religious song or prayer using only one note or TONE

**chant**[2] *n* **1** words or phrases that are repeated again and again: *The crowd responded with chants of "Resign! Resign!"* **2** a religious song with a regularly repeated tune

**Cha·nu·kah** /'hɑnəkə/ *n* [U] ⇨ HANUKKAH

**cha·os** /'keɪɑs/ *n* [U] a state of complete disorder and confusion: *After the earthquake, the city was in chaos.*

**cha·ot·ic** /keɪ'ɑtɪk/ *adj* a situation that is chaotic is very disorganized and confusing: *The lunchroom was chaotic, with kids shouting and throwing things.*

**chap·el** /'tʃæpəl/ *n* a small church or a room where Christians have religious services

**chap·e·rone**[1] /'ʃæpəˌroʊn/ *n* an older person who is responsible for young people on social occasions: *My parents are going to be chaperones at the dance on Friday.*

**chaperone**[2] *v* [T] to go somewhere with someone as his/her CHAPERONE

**chap·lain** /'tʃæplɪn/ *n* a minister who is responsible for the religious needs of people in a part of the army, a hospital, a prison etc.

**chapped** /tʃæpt/ *adj* skin that is chapped is sore and cracked as a result of cold weather or wind: *chapped lips* **−chap** *v* [T]

**chaps** /tʃæps/ *n* [plural] leather covers that protect your legs when you ride a horse

**chap·ter** /'tʃæptɚ/ *n* **1** one of the parts into which a book is divided **2** a particular period or event in someone's life or in history: *a sad chapter in our country's history* **3** the local members of a large organization or club: *the Boise chapter of the Sierra Club*

**char·ac·ter** /'kærɪktɚ/ *n* **1** [C,U] all of the qualities that make one person, place, or thing

different from another: *There's a very serious side to her character.* | *All these new buildings have really changed the character of this town.*
**2** [U] the good qualities that make someone or something special, interesting, valuable etc.: *an old house with a lot of character* **3** a person in a book, play, movie etc.: *I don't like the main character in the book.* **4** a person of a particular kind: *Dan's a strange character.* **5** an unusual and humorous person: *Charlie's such a character!* **6** a letter, mark, or sign used in writing, printing, or computing (COMPUTE): *Chinese characters*

**char·ac·ter·is·tic**[1] /ˌkærɪktə'rɪstɪk/ *n* a special quality or feature that someone or something has: *the characteristics of a good manager* | *Each wine has particular characteristics.*

**characteristic**[2] *adj* typical of a particular thing or person: *Mark, with characteristic kindness, offered to help.* –**characteristically** *adv*

**char·ac·ter·ize** /'kærɪktə,raɪz/ *v* [T] **1** to be typical of someone or something: *Alzheimer's disease is characterized by memory loss.*
**2** to describe the character of someone or something in a particular way: *His book characterizes Eisenhower as a natural leader.* –**characterization** /ˌkærɪktərə'zeɪʃən/ *n* [C,U]

**cha·rade** /ʃə'reɪd/ *n* a situation that seems to be true or serious, but that everyone knows is not: *Their happy marriage is just a charade.*

**cha·rades** /ʃə'reɪdz/ *n* [U] a game in which one person uses only actions to show the meaning of a word or phrase, and other people have to guess what it is

**char·coal** /'tʃɑrkoʊl/ *n* [U] a black substance made of burned wood, used for burning or drawing

**charge**[1] /tʃɑrdʒ/ *n*
**1** ▶MONEY◀ [C,U] the amount of money you have to pay for a particular thing: *There's a $70 charge for every extra piece of luggage.* | *We deliver free of charge.* (=at no cost)
**2 be in charge (of)** to be the person who controls or is responsible for someone or something: *Who is in charge of the department?*
**3 take charge (of)** to take control of someone or something: *Diane took charge of the business when her husband died.*
**4** ▶CRIME◀ an official statement saying that someone is guilty of a crime: *He's in court on charges of murder.* | *The charge against her was shoplifting.* | *They decided not to bring/press charges.* (=make official charges) | *Somebody else confessed, so the police had to drop the charges against him.* (=decide to stop making charges)
**5** ▶ELECTRICITY◀ [U] electricity that is put into a piece of electrical equipment: *The charge didn't last very long in the batteries.*
**6 get a charge out of sth** to enjoy something

very much: *I got a real charge out of seeing Jane win that prize.*
**7** ▶ATTACK◀ an attack in which people, animals etc. move forward quickly
**8** ▶EXPLOSIVE◀ an explosive material put into a gun or weapon

**charge**[2] *v* **1** [I,T] to ask for a particular amount of money for something you are selling: *How much do you charge for your eggs?*
**2** [T] to record the cost of something in someone's account, so that s/he can pay for it later: *Charge the room to my account.* | *"Would you like to pay cash?" "No, I'll charge it."* (=pay with a CREDIT CARD) **3** [T] to state officially that someone is guilty of a crime: *Ron's been charged with assault.* **4** [I,T] to put electricity into a piece of electrical equipment such as a BATTERY: *Leave the phone on its base to charge overnight.* **5** [I,T] to run very fast, often in order to attack someone or something

**charge ac·count** /'. .,./ *n* an account you have with a store that allows you to take goods away with you immediately and pay for them later

**charge card** /'. ./ *n* ⇨ CREDIT CARD

**char·i·ot** /'tʃæriət/ *n* a vehicle with two wheels pulled by a horse, used in ancient times in battles and races –**charioteer** /ˌʃæriə'tɪr/ *n*

**cha·ris·ma** /kə'rɪzmə/ *n* [U] the natural ability to attract other people and make them admire you –**charismatic** /ˌkærɪz'mætɪk/ *adj*

**char·i·ta·ble** /'tʃærətəbəl/ *adj* **1** relating to money or gifts given to people who need help, or organizations that give this type of help: *The money went to a charitable group.* **2** kind and generous –**charitably** *adv*

**char·i·ty** /'tʃærəti/ *n* **1** an organization that gives money or help to people who need it: *Several charities sent aid to the flood victims.*
**2** [U] charity organizations in general: *It's strange that poorer people donate more money to charity.* **3** [U] money or gifts given to people who need help: *She's too proud to accept charity.*

**char·la·tan** /'ʃɑrlətən/ *n* someone who pretends to have special skills or knowledge that s/he does not really have

**charm**[1] /tʃɑrm/ *n* **1** [C,U] the special quality someone or something has that makes people like him, her, or it: *This town has a charm you couldn't find in a big city.* **2** an object, phrase, or action believed to have special magic powers: *a lucky charm* **3 work like a charm** to happen exactly as you had hoped, or have the result you wanted

**charm**[2] *v* [T] to please someone or make him/her like you: *a story that has charmed youngsters for generations* –**charmer** *n*

**charmed** /tʃɑrmd/ *adj* lucky in a way that seems magical: *Until she was 18, Liz seemed to* *live a **charmed** life*. (=a life in which many good things happened)

**charm·ing** /'tʃɑrmɪŋ/ *adj* very pleasing or attractive: *What a charming house!* —**charmingly** *adv*

**charred** /tʃɑrd/ *adj* something that is charred is so burnt that it has become black —**char** *v* [I,T]

**chart**[1] /tʃɑrt/ *n* **1** information that is shown in the form of a picture, GRAPH etc.: *a weather chart* **2 the charts** a list of the most popular records: *That song was **top of the charts** for over 6 weeks.* **3** a detailed map of the sea or stars

**chart**[2] *v* [T] **1** to record information about a situation or set of events over a period of time: *a report charting the progress of the housing program* **2** to make a map of an area, or to draw lines on a map to show where you have traveled

**char·ter**[1] /'tʃɑrtɚ/ *n* **1** a statement of the principles, duties, and purposes of an organization: *the UN charter* **2** [C,U] the practice of paying money to a company to use their boats, aircraft etc., or the plane, boat etc. that is used in this way: *The airline is now primarily a charter service.*

**charter**[2] *v* [T] **1** to pay a company for the use of their boat, plane etc.: *We'll have to charter a bus.* **2** to say officially that a town, organization, or university exists and has special rights

**charter flight** /'.. ,./ *n* a plane trip that is arranged especially for a particular group or for a particular purpose

**charter mem·ber** /,.. '../ *n* an original member of a club or organization

**char·treuse** /ʃɑr'truz, -'trus/ *n* [U] a bright yellow-green color —**chartreuse** *adj*

**chase**[1] /tʃeɪs/ *v* **1** [I,T] to quickly follow someone or something in order to catch him, her, or it: *a cat **chasing after** a mouse | Cops **chased** the mugger **down** the street.* **2** [T] to make someone or something leave: *There was a racoon in the yard, but the dog **chased** it **away**.* **3** [I] to rush or hurry somewhere: *Those kids are always **chasing in and out!*** **4** [T] to try very hard to make someone like you in a romantic way: *Sherry's been chasing me for months.*

**chase**[2] *n* **1** the act of following someone or something quickly in order to catch him, her, or it: *The movie ended with a long car chase.* **2 give chase** LITERARY to chase someone or something **3 cut to the chase** INFORMAL to immediately begin to do or discuss the most important part of something

**chasm** /'kæzəm/ *n* **1** [singular] a big difference between ideas or groups of people: *the chasm between rich and poor people* **2** a very deep hole between two areas of rock or ice

**chas·sis** /'tʃæsi, 'ʃæ-/ *n, plural* **chassis** the frame on which the body, engine etc. of a vehicle is built

**chaste** /tʃeɪst/ *adj* OLD-FASHIONED not having sex with anyone, or not with anyone except the person you are married to

**chas·ten** /'tʃeɪsən/ *v* [T] FORMAL to make someone realize that his/her behavior is wrong, and that it must change

**chas·tise** /tʃæ'staɪz, 'tʃæstaɪz/ *v* [T] FORMAL to criticize or punish someone severely —**chas·tisement** *n* [C,U]

**chas·ti·ty** /'tʃæstəti/ *n* [U] the state of not having sex with anyone, or not with anyone except the person you are married to

**chat**[1] /tʃæt/ *v* **-tted, -tting** [I] to talk in a friendly and informal way

**chat**[2] *n* [C,U] a friendly informal conversation

**cha·teau** /ʃæ'tou/ *n, plural* **chateaux** /-'touz/ *or* **chateaus** a castle or large country house in France

**chat·ter**[1] /'tʃætɚ/ *v* [I] **1** to talk a lot about things that are not important **2** to make short high sounds: *monkeys chattering in the trees* **3** if your teeth chatter, they knock together because you are cold

**chatter**[2] *n* [U] **1** a conversation about something that is not important **2** a series of short high sounds or hard quick sounds: *the continuous chatter of machinery*

**chat·ter·box** /'tʃætɚ,bɑks/ *n* OLD-FASHIONED someone who talks too much

**chat·ty** /'tʃæti/ *adj* INFORMAL **1** liking to talk a lot **2** having a friendly informal style: *a chatty letter*

**chauf·feur**[1] /'ʃoufɚ, ʃou'fɚ/ *n* someone whose job is to drive a car for someone else

**chauffeur**[2] *v* [T] to drive a car for someone else, especially when it is your job or duty: *I spent all day chauffeuring my kids everywhere.*

**chau·vin·ism** /'ʃouvə,nɪzəm/ *n* [U] a strong belief that your sex or country is better than the other sex or other countries: *fears that ethnic chauvinism will lead to civil war*

**chau·vin·ist** /'ʃouvənɪst/ *n* someone who believes that his/her sex, country etc. is better than the other sex, other countries etc. —**chauvinist** *adj*: *Ernie's just a **male chauvinist pig**.* —**chauvinistic** /,ʃouvə'nɪstɪk/ *adj*

**cheap**[1] /tʃip/ *adj* **1** not expensive, or lower in price than you expected: *Their fruit is really cheap. | Those jeans are **dirt cheap**.* (=very low in price) **2** of bad quality: *Judy's shoes looked cheap to me.* **3** not liking to spend money: *He's so cheap we didn't even go out on my birthday.* **4** behaving in a way that is unkind or not respectful to other people, just because it is easy to do: *He made some **cheap shot** (=an unkind criticism) about her looks.* **5** behaving in a way that shows you do not respect or care about yourself, so that other people do not respect you: *He made me **feel cheap**.* **6 cheap thrill** excitement that does not take much effort to get —**cheaply** *adv* —**cheapness** *n* [U]

**cheap²** *adv* **1** at a low price: *I was lucky to get it so cheap.* | *Cars like that **don't come cheap**.* (=are expensive) | *Flights to Rio are going cheap.* (=selling for a lower price than usual) **2** INFORMAL in a way that makes someone difficult to respect: *I wish she wouldn't act so cheap.*

**cheap·en** /'tʃipən/ *v* **1** [T] to make someone or something seem to have less worth: *As an actress, I'd be **cheapening myself by** doing TV commercials.* **2** [I,T] to become lower in price or value, or to make something do this: *The dollar's rise in value has cheapened imports.*

**cheap·skate** /'tʃipskeɪt/ *n* INFORMAL someone who does not like spending money or giving gifts

cheat

Mike was cheating in the Spanish test.

**cheat¹** /tʃit/ *v* **1** [I] to behave in a dishonest way in order to win or gain something: *He always cheats when we play cards.* **2** [T] to trick or deceive someone: *The salesman **cheated** me **out of** $100.* **3** **feel cheated** to feel that you have been treated wrongly or unfairly – **cheating** *n* [U]

**cheat on** sb *phr v* [T] to be unfaithful to your husband, wife, or sexual partner by secretly having sex with someone else: *I think Dan's **cheating on** Debbie again.*

**cheat²** *n* someone who is dishonest and CHEATS: *You're a liar and a cheat!*

**check¹** /tʃɛk/ *v* **1** [I,T] to do something or look at something to find out if it is done, correct, in good condition etc.: *"Did Barry lock the back door?" "I don't know – I'll check."* | *I need to check the mailbox; I'm expecting a letter.* | *Make sure you **double check** (=check them twice) the spellings of these names.* **2** [I] to ask permission to do something or to ask whether something is correct or true: *Check with Jim to see if you can leave early.* | *Can you **check whether** we're still having a meeting?* **3** [T] to put someone's bags, coat etc. in a special place where they can be kept safe: *Can I check that for you, sir?* **4** [T] to try hard to stop yourself from doing something: *I had to check the urge to laugh out loud.* **5** [T] to stop something bad from getting worse: *The treatment checks the spread of the cancer.*

**check in** *phr v* [I,T] to go to the desk at a hotel, airport etc. and say that you have arrived: *Please **check in** at gate number 5.*

**check** sth ↔ **off** *phr v* [T] to make a mark (✓) next to an answer, something on a list etc. to show that it is correct, finished, or that you have noticed it: *Check their names off the list as they arrive.*

**check on** sb/sth *phr v* [T] to make sure that someone or something is doing what he, she, or it is supposed to be doing: *I have to go check on the roast.*

**check out** *phr v* **1** [T **check** sth ↔ **out**] INFORMAL to make sure that something is actually true, correct, or acceptable: *The police checked out his story with the other suspects.* | *We thought we'd check out this new restaurant Jim says is so good.* **2** [T **check** sb/sth ↔ **out**] SPOKEN to look at someone or something because he, she, or it is interesting or attractive: *Check it out, man! This place is great!* **3** [I] if something checks out, it is proven to be true, correct, or acceptable: *If your references check out, you can start the job on Monday.* **4** [I] to pay the bill and leave a hotel: *You must check out before 12 o'clock.* **5** [T **check** sth ↔ **out**] to borrow books from a library: *You can only check out 5 books at a time.*

**check** sth ↔ **over** *phr v* [T] to look carefully at someone or something to make sure that he, she, or it is in an acceptable condition: *Can you check over my paper for spelling mistakes?* | *The doctor checked her over and couldn't find anything wrong.*

**check up on** sb/sth *phr v* [T] to try to find out if someone is doing what s/he is supposed to be doing, or that something is correct: *Are you trying to check up on me, or what?*

**check²** *n*
**1** ▶EXAMINATION◀ an examination to find out if something is correct, true, or safe: *a security check* | *I want a **check on** the quality of all goods leaving the factory.* | *They're doing **spot checks** for drugs.* (=quick checks of one thing in a group of things, done without warning) | *I want you to **do/run a check on** this blood sample.* (=find out information about it)
**2** ▶MONEY◀ one of a set of printed pieces of paper that you can sign and use to pay for things: *a check for $50* | *Can I **pay by check**?*
**3** ▶CONTROL◀ [singular] something that controls something else: *The policy should act as a check on inflation.* | *We've **kept** the disease **in check** for over a year now.*
**4** ▶BILL◀ a list that you are given at a restaurant that shows what you have eaten and how much you must pay: *Can I have the check, please?*
**5** ▶MARK◀ a mark (✓) that you put next to an answer, something on a list etc. to show that it is correct, finished, or that you have noticed it
**6** **hat/coat check a)** a place in a restaurant, theater etc. where you can leave your coat, bag etc. **b)** a ticket that you are given so you can claim your things from this place

**7** ▶SQUARES◀ a pattern of squares on something: *a tablecloth with red and white checks*

**check·book** /'tʃɛkbʊk/ *n* a small book of checks that your bank gives you

**checked** /tʃɛkt/ *adj* having a regular pattern of different colored squares: *a checked skirt* −see picture at PATTERN

**check·ered** /'tʃɛkəd/ *adj* marked with squares of two different colors. *a checkered flag*

**chook·crs** /'tʃɛkəz/ *n* [U] a game for two players, using a set of 12 flat round pieces each and a special board with 64 squares

**check-in** /'. ./ *n* [U] the process of going to the desk at an airport, hotel etc. and saying that you have arrived: *Be at the check-in counter* (=place where you go to say that you have arrived) *an hour before your plane leaves.* −see also **check in** (CHECK¹)

**checking ac·count** /'.. .,./ *n* a bank account that you can take money out of at any time

**check·list** /'tʃɛk,lɪst/ *n* a list of things you have to do for a particular job or activity

**check·out coun·ter** /'tʃɛk-aʊt ,kaʊntə/ *n* the place in a SUPERMARKET where you pay for things

**check·point** /'tʃɛkpɔɪnt/ *n* a place where someone official, such as a police officer, stops people and cars to examine them

**check-up** /'tʃɛk-ʌp/ *n* an occasion when a doctor or DENTIST examines you to see if you are healthy: *Dentists recommend regular checkups to help prevent tooth decay.*

**ched·dar** /'tʃɛdə/ *n* [U] a firm smooth yellow or orange cheese

**cheek** /tʃik/ *n* **1** the soft round part of your face below your eyes: *He kissed her lightly on the cheek.* −see picture at HEAD¹ **2** SLANG ⇨ BUTTOCK

**cheek·bone** /'tʃikboʊn/ *n* the bone just below your eye

**cheep** /tʃip/ *v* [I] to make a high noise like a young bird −**cheep** *n*

**cheer¹** /tʃɪr/ *v* [I,T] to shout approval, encouragement etc: *The audience cheered as the band began to play.*

**cheer** sb **on** *phr v* [T] to encourage someone by cheering for him/her: *Hansen's family was there cheering him on.*

**cheer up** *phr v* **1** [T **cheer** sb **up**] to make someone feel happier: *I tried to cheer her up by taking her out to dinner.* **2** [I] to become happier: *Cheer up, Connie!*

**cheer²** *n* **1** a shout of approval and happiness: *The crowd gives a cheer as Griffey hits a home run!* **2 three cheers for sb** SPOKEN used in order to tell people to shout in order to praise someone

**cheer·ful** /'tʃɪrfəl/ *adj* **1** happy and feeling good: *Nancy gave me a cheerful grin.* **2** pleasant and making you feel happy: *a*

*cheerful kitchen* −**cheerfully** *adv* −**cheerfulness** *n* [U]

**cheer·lead·er** /'tʃɪr,lidə/ *n* someone who encourages a crowd to CHEER at a sports event

**cheer·y** /'tʃɪri/ *adj* smiling and cheerful: *a little boy with a cheery smile*

**cheese** /tʃiz/ *n* [C,U] **1** a solid food made from milk that is usually white or yellow **2 say cheese** SPOKEN said when you want people to smile as you take a photograph of them

**cheese·burg·er** /'tʃiz,bəgə/ *n* a HAMBURGER with cheese on it

**cheese·cake** /'tʃizkeɪk/ *n* [C,U] a sweet cake made with soft white cheese −see picture at DESSERT

**cheese·cloth** /'tʃizklɔθ/ *n* [U] a type of very thin cotton cloth, used in cooking

**chees·y** /'tʃizi/ *adj* INFORMAL cheap and not of good quality, or not sincere: *a really cheesy movie | a cheesy grin*

**chee·tah** /'tʃitə/ *n* an African wild cat that has black spots, long legs, and is able to run very fast

**chef** /ʃɛf/ *n* the chief cook in a restaurant

**chem·i·cal¹** /'kɛmɪkəl/ *adj* relating to substances used in chemistry, or involving the changes that happen when two substances combine: *a chemical reaction* −**chemically** *adv*

**chemical²** *n* a substance that is used in or produced by a chemical process: *chemicals used in agriculture*

**chem·ist** /'kɛmɪst/ *n* a scientist who has a special knowledge of chemistry: *a research chemist for a drug company*

**chem·is·try** /'kɛməstri/ *n* [U] **1** the science of studying substances and what happens to them when they change or combine with each other **2** the way substances combine in a particular process, thing, person etc.: *This drug causes changes to the body's chemistry.*

**che·mo·ther·a·py** /,kimoʊ'θɛrəpi/ *n* [U] the treatment of CANCER using special drugs

**cher·ish** /'tʃɛrɪʃ/ *v* [T] to love and take good care of someone or something: *He has been forced to sell cherished possessions to pay his debts.*

**cher·ry** /'tʃɛri/ *n* **1** a small round soft red fruit with a large seed −see picture on page 470 **2** [C,U] a tree that produces cherries, or the wood of this tree

**cher·ub** /'tʃɛrəb/ *n* an ANGEL shown in paintings as a small child with wings

**chess** /tʃɛs/ *n* [U] a game for two players, using a set of 16 pieces each and a special board with 64 squares

**chest** /tʃɛst/ *n* **1** the front part of your body between your neck and stomach: *a man with a hairy chest* −see picture at BODY **2** a large strong box with a lid, used for storing things:

*We keep our blankets in a cedar chest.* **3 get sth off your chest** to tell someone about something that you are worried about

**chest·nut** /'tʃɛsnʌt/ *n* **1** a smooth red-brown nut you can eat **2** [C,U] the tree on which these nuts grow, or the wood of this tree **3** [U] a dark red-brown color –**chestnut** *adj*

**chest of drawers** /ˌ. . './ *n* a piece of furniture with drawers that clothes can be kept in

**chew** /tʃu/ *v* [I,T] to crush food with your teeth before swallowing it: *We gave the dog a bone to chew on.* | *Come on, baby, chew it up,* (=chew it completely) *there's a good girl.*

**chew** sb **out** *phr v* [T] INFORMAL to talk angrily to someone who has done something you do not like: *Mom chewed me out for getting home late.*

**chewing gum** /'.. ,./ *n* [U] ⇨ GUM¹

**chew·y** /'tʃui/ *adj* needing to be chewed: *moist chewy brownies*

**chic** /ʃik/ *adj* fashionable and showing good judgment about style: *a chic clothes store*

**Chi·ca·no** /tʃɪ'kɑnoʊ/ *n* a US citizen whose family came from Mexico

**chick** /tʃɪk/ *n* **1** a baby bird, especially a baby chicken **2** INFORMAL a word meaning a young woman, that some people consider offensive

**chick·a·dee** /'tʃɪkə,di/ *n* a small North American wild bird with a black head

**chick·en¹** /'tʃɪkən/ *n* **1** a common farm bird that is kept for its meat and eggs **2** [U] the meat from this bird: *fried chicken* **3** INFORMAL someone who lacks courage: *"You won't jump? What a chicken!"*

**chicken²** *adj* INFORMAL having no courage: *He was too chicken to dive off the high board.*

**chicken³** *v*

**chicken out** *phr v* [I] INFORMAL to decide not to do something because you are afraid: *They chickened out at the last minute.*

**chick·en·feed** /'tʃɪkən,fid/ *n* [U] INFORMAL a small unimportant amount of money: *To a millionaire, $1000 is chickenfeed.*

**chicken pox, chickenpox** /'tʃɪkən ,pɑks/ *n* [U] a disease that children often get that causes ITCHY spots on the skin and a fever

**chide** /tʃaɪd/ *v* [I,T] LITERARY to speak in an angry way to someone who has done something wrong

**chief¹** /tʃif/ *n* the leader of a group or organization: *the chief of police*

**chief²** *adj* **1** most important: *The customers' chief complaint was the poor service.* **2** highest in rank: *the chief political reporter for the Washington Post*

**Chief Ex·ec·u·tive** /ˌ. .'..../ *n* the President of the United States

**chief ex·ec·u·tive of·fi·cer** /ˌ. .,... '.../ *n* ⇨ CEO

**chief jus·tice** /ˌ. '../ *n* the most important judge in a court of law, especially in the US Supreme Court

**chief·ly** /'tʃifli/ *adv* mainly: *They had borrowed a lot of money, chiefly from Dan's parents.*

**chief·tain** /'tʃiftən/ *n* the leader of a tribe

**chif·fon** /ʃɪ'fɑn/ *n* [U] a soft thin material used for make women's clothing, scarves (SCARF) etc.

**chi·hua·hua** /tʃɪ'wɑwə/ *n* a very small dog from Mexico with smooth short hair

**child** /tʃaɪld/ *n, plural* **children** /'tʃɪldrən/ **1** a young person who is not yet fully grown: *The children may start ballet lessons at the age of six.* **2** a son or daughter: *Dan has a child from a previous marriage.* | *Are you planning to have children?* (=give birth to children) –see picture at FAMILY **3 child's play** something that is very easy to do: *Stealing the money was child's play to him.*

**child·bear·ing** /'tʃaɪld,bɛrɪŋ/ *n* **1** [U] the process of being PREGNANT and then giving birth **2 childbearing age** the period of time during which a woman is old enough to give birth to a baby

**child·birth** /'tʃaɪldbɚθ/ *n* [U] the act of giving birth

**child·care** /'tʃaɪldkɛr/ *n* [U] an arrangement in which someone takes care of children while their parents are at work

**child·hood** /'tʃaɪldhʊd/ *n* [C,U] the time when you are a child: *happy childhood memories*

**child·ish** /'tʃaɪldɪʃ/ *adj* **1** typical of a child: *a childish game* **2** DISAPPROVING behaving in a way that makes you seem younger than you really are: *Stop being so childish.* –**childishly** *adv*

**child·less** /'tʃaɪldlɪs/ *adj* having no children: *childless couples* –**childlessness** *n* [U]

**child·like** /'tʃaɪldlaɪk/ *adj* APPROVING having the character, qualities etc. of a child: *childlike innocence*

**child·proof** /'tʃaɪldpruf/ *adj* designed to prevent a child from hurting something or being hurt: *a childproof cap on a pill bottle*

**chil·dren** /'tʃɪldrən/ the plural of CHILD –see picture at FAMILY

---

**USAGE NOTE children**

**Baby** and **infant** both mean "a very young child," but **infant** is more formal. A child who can walk and is under the age of 3 is a **toddler**. Children aged 13 to 19 are **teenagers**. Use the informal word **kids** to talk about all young people and children.

---

**child sup·port** /'. .,./ *n* [U] money that someone pays regularly to his/her former husband or wife in order to help support his/her children

**chil·i** /'tʃɪli/ *n, plural* **chilies** **1** [U] a dish made with beans and usually meat cooked with chilies **2** [C,U] a small thin type of red pepper with a very hot taste, often used in cooking −see picture on page 470

**chill**[1] /tʃɪl/ *v* **1** [I,T] to make something or someone very cold: *This wine should be chilled before serving .* **2** [I] also **chill out** to relax instead of feeling angry or nervous: *Chill out, Dave, it doesn't matter.* **3** [T] to make someone feel very cold: *The wind **chilled me to the bone**.*

**chill**[2] *n* **1** [singular] a feeling of coldness: *a chill in the early morning air* **2** a slight feeling of fear: *a horror movie that **sends chills through** the audience* (=makes them feel afraid) **3** a slight sickness with a fever: *I must have **caught a chill** from walking in the snow.*

**chill**[3] *adj* extremely cold: *a chill wind*

**chil·ling** /'tʃɪlɪŋ/ *adj* making you feel frightened because something is cruel, violent, or dangerous: *a chilling report on child abuse*

**chill·y** /'tʃɪli/ *adj* **1** cold enough to make you feel uncomfortable: *a chilly room* −see usage note at TEMPERATURE **2** unfriendly: *Relations between the two countries have been chilly since the incident.*

**chime**[1] /tʃaɪm/ *n* the ringing (RING) sound of a bell or clock: *the chime of the doorbell*

**chime**[2] *v* [I,T] to make a ringing (RING) sound, especially in order to show what time it is: *The clock chimed six.*

**chime in** *phr v* [I] to agree with what someone has just said, often by repeating it or adding to it slightly: *"Yes, the kids could go too," Maria **chimed in**.*

**chim·ney** /'tʃɪmni/ *n* a pipe inside a building for smoke from a fire to go out through the roof −see picture on page 471

**chim·pan·zee** /ˌtʃɪmpæn'zi/ **chimp** /tʃɪmp/ *n* a very intelligent small African APE (=animal like a monkey)

**chin** /tʃɪn/ *n* the front part of your face below your mouth −see picture at HEAD[1]

**chi·na** /'tʃaɪnə/ *n* [U] **1** a hard white substance made by baking a particular type of clay **2** plates, cups, and dishes made from this clay: *We were given a lot of china as wedding presents.*

**Chi·na·town** /'tʃaɪnəˌtaʊn/ *n* [C,U] an area in a city where there are Chinese restaurants and stores, and where a lot of Chinese people live

**Chi·nese**[1] /'tʃaɪniz/ *adj* **1** relating to or coming from China **2** relating to a Chinese language

**Chi·nese**[2] /tʃaɪ'niz/ *n* **1** [U] any of the languages that come from China, such as Mandarin or Cantonese **2** **the Chinese** the people of China

**chink** /tʃɪŋk/ *n* **1** a narrow crack or hole in something that lets light through: *a chink*

*in the wall* **2** a short ringing sound made by metal or glass objects hitting each other: *the chink of glassware*

**chi·nos** /'tʃinoʊz/ *n* [plural] loose pants made from heavy cotton

**chintz** /tʃɪnts/ *n* [U] smooth cotton cloth with brightly colored patterns on it: *chintz covers on the chairs*

**chin-up** /'. ./ *n* an exercise in which you hang on a BAR and pull yourself up until your chin is above the bar

a chipped plate

a silicon chip

potato chips

**chip**[1] /tʃɪp/ *n*

**1** ▶COMPUTER◀ a small piece of SILICON that has a set of electronic parts and their connections attached to it, used in computers

**2** ▶FOOD◀ a thin dry piece of FRIED potato or of a TORTILLA: *chips and salsa | barbecue flavor **potato chips***

**3** ▶CRACK/MARK◀ a crack or mark left when a small piece is broken off something: *This plate has a chip in it.*

**4** ▶SMALL PIECE◀ a small piece of wood, stone etc. that has broken off something: *Chips of wood can be used around plants to control weeds.*

**5** **bargaining chip** something that you can use or exchange in order to get something else you want: *The terrorists were using the hostages as bargaining chips to gain the release of the prisoners.*

**6** ▶GAME◀ a small flat colored piece of plastic used in games to represent money: *a gambling chip*

**7** **have a chip on your shoulder** INFORMAL to become angry easily about something because you think you have been treated unfairly in the past: *He's always had a chip on his shoulder about not going to college.*

**8** **be a chip off the old block** INFORMAL to be like one of your parents in the way you look or behave −see also BLUE CHIP

**chip**[2] *v* [I,T] to break a small piece off something accidentally, or to become broken in this way −**chipped** *adj*: *chipped fingernail polish*

**chip** sth ↔ **away** *phr v* [T] to break small pieces off something: *Sandy **chipped away** the plaster covering the tiles.*

**chip away at** sth *phr v* [T] to break small pieces off something to make it less effective or destroy it: *All this new paperwork is **chipping***

*away at* the time teachers can spend preparing for classes.

**chip in** *phr v* [I,T] to give help, money, advice etc. to add to what other people are giving: *Tanya's classmates have chipped in more than $100 to help her buy the special wheelchair.*

**chip·munk** /'tʃɪpmʌŋk/ *n* a small brown North American animal similar to a SQUIRREL, that has black and white lines on its fur

**chip·per** /'tʃɪpɚ/ *adj* happy and healthy: *Grandma's feeling pretty chipper again now that her back is better.*

**chi·ro·prac·tor** /'kaɪrə,præktɚ/ *n* a doctor who treats sickness by pressing on and moving the bones in your back

**chirp** /tʃɚp/ *n* the short high sound made by birds and some insects: *the chirp of crickets* −**chirp** *v* [I]

**chis·el** [1] /'tʃɪzəl/ *n* a metal tool with a sharp edge, used for cutting wood or stone

**chisel** [2] *v* [T] to cut or shape something with a CHISEL: *Small figures of deer, buffalo, and men have been chiseled into the sandstone.*

**chit** /tʃɪt/ *n* a short note that shows how much money someone owes or has paid

**chit-chat** /'tʃɪt-tʃæt/ *n* [U] INFORMAL informal conversation about unimportant things

**chiv·al·rous** /'ʃɪvəlrəs/ *adj* FORMAL showing polite and kind behavior toward women −**chivalry** /'ʃɪvəlri/ *n* [U]

**chives** /tʃaɪvz/ *n* [plural] a plant with long thin leaves that taste like onion, used in cooking

**chlo·ri·nate** /'klɔrə,neɪt/ *v* [T] to make water clean by putting CHLORINE in it to kill BACTERIA: *Public swimming pools have to be chlorinated.*

**chlo·rine** /'klɔrin, klɔ'rin/ *n* [U] a yellow-green gas that is an ELEMENT and is often used for keeping swimming pools clean

**chlo·ro·fluo·ro·car·bon** /,klɔrə,flʊroʊ-'karbən/ *n* TECHNICAL ⇨ CFC

**chlo·ro·form** /'klɔrə,fɔrm/ *n* [U] a colorless liquid with a strong smell that was used in medicine as an ANESTHETIC in past times

**chlo·ro·phyll** /'klɔrə,fɪl/ *n* [U] the green substance in the stems and leaves of plants

**chock-full** /,tʃɑk 'fʊl/ *adj* INFORMAL completely full: *a bus chock-full of people*

**choc·o·hol·ic, chocaholic** /,tʃɑkə'hɔlɪk/ *n* HUMOROUS someone who likes chocolate very much and eats a lot of it

**choco·late** /'tʃɑklɪt/ *n* **1** [U] a sweet hard brown food eaten for pleasure, or used for giving foods a special taste: *a chocolate bar | chocolate ice cream* **2** a candy covered with chocolate: *a box of chocolates*

**chocolate chip** /,.. './ *n* [C usually plural] a small piece of chocolate put in foods such as cookies and cakes

**choice** [1] /tʃɔɪs/ *n* **1** [singular, U] the right to choose or the chance to choose between two or

more things: *a choice between 31 flavors of ice cream | The bookstore has a wide choice of magazines. | If you had a choice* (=were able to choose), *where would you want to live? | He had no choice* (=it was the only thing he could do) *but to move back into his parents' house. | We were given a choice* (=allowed to choose) *between doing volleyball or basketball first in P.E.* **2** the act of choosing something: *The price of the car influenced our choice. | He left the choice of hotels to his wife. | Shea has had to make some hard choices about budgeting.* **3** one of several things that you can choose, or the range of things you can chose from: *The menu had several choices of soup. | You will have a choice of five questions on the test.* **4** [C usually singular] the person or thing that someone has chosen: *Going to Hawaii was our first choice, but we couldn't really afford it.* **5 the drug/treatment/magazine etc. of choice** the thing that a particular group of people prefer: *It is the treatment of choice for this particular disease.* **6 by choice** done because you want to: *Can anyone really believe that homeless people are homeless by choice?*

**choice** [2] *adj* having a high quality or standard: *choice fruit/vegetables/meat*

**choir** /kwaɪɚ/ *n* a group of people who sing together, especially in a church or school: *The school choir is putting on a concert Friday.*

**choke** [1] /tʃoʊk/ *v* **1** [I,T] to prevent someone from breathing, or to be prevented from breathing because something is blocking your throat or because there is not enough air: *Don't give her that fish - she'll choke on the bones. | The fumes were choking me.* **2** [T] to fill a space or passage with something that is harmful or not wanted: *The pipe was choked with leaves. | highways choked by pollution* **3** [I,T] if your voice is choked or choking with an emotion, it sounds strange and not very loud because the emotion is so strong: *Cranston read his statement in a voice choked with emotion.* **4** [I] SPOKEN to fail at doing something, especially a sport: *They were great all season, but choked in the playoffs.*

**choke** sth ↔ **back** *phr v* [T] to control a strong feeling so that you do not show it: *Annelise choked back tears as she tried to explain.*

**choke** sth ↔ **down** *phr v* [T] to eat something with difficulty, especially because you are ill or upset: *He managed to choke down a sandwich.*

**choke off** *phr v* [T] to prevent something from going where it was meant to go: *A blockade has choked off their main food supply.*

**choke up** *phr v* [I] **be choked up** to feel such strong emotions about something that you are almost crying: *He was so choked up about his award that he could hardly speak.*

**choke** [2] *n* **1** the act or sound of choking (CHOKE) **2** a piece of equipment that controls the amount of air going into a car engine

**choke chain** /'. ./ n a chain that is fastened around the neck of a dog to control it

**chok·er** /'tʃoʊkɚ/ n a piece of jewelry or narrow cloth that fits closely around your neck

**chol·er·a** /'kɑlərə/ n [U] a serious infectious disease that attacks the stomach and BOWELs

**cho·les·ter·ol** /kə'lɛstəˌrɔl, -ˌroʊl/ n [U] a substance in fat, blood, and other cells in your body, that can sometimes cause heart disease

**choose** /tʃuz/ v chose, chosen, choosing [I,T] **1** to decide which one of a number of things, possibilities, people etc. that you want: *Everything looks so good, I don't know what to choose.* | *They* **chose** *Roy* **to** *be the team captain.* | *You'll have to* **choose between** *taking French or Spanish.* | *a large selection of drinks to* **choose from 2** to decide or prefer to do something: *Donna* **chose** *to quit her job after she had the baby.* **3 there is little/nothing to choose between** used in order to say that two or more things are very much alike: *There's so little to choose between those two, I just don't know who to vote for.*

**choos·y** /'tʃuzi/ adj difficult to please: *Jean's very* **choosy about** *what she eats.*

**chop¹** /tʃɑp/ v **-pped, -pping 1** [T] also **chop up** to cut something, especially food, into small uneven pieces: *Chop up some onions.* | *Chop the tomatoes* **into** *fairly large pieces.* **2** [I,T] to cut something by hitting it many times with a heavy sharp tool such as an AXE: *Greta was out chopping wood for the fire.*

**chop** sth ↔ **down** phr v [T] to make a tree fall down by cutting it with a heavy sharp tool such as an AXE

**chop** sth ↔ **off** phr v [T] to remove something by cutting it with a heavy sharp tool so that it is no longer connected to something else: *Mitch's foot was* **chopped off** *in a horrible accident.*

**chop²** n **1** a small flat piece of meat on a bone: *a pork chop* **2** a quick hard hit with the side of your hand or with a heavy sharp tool: *a karate chop*

**chop·per** /'tʃɑpɚ/ n **1** INFORMAL ⇨ HELI-COPTER **2** a type of MOTORCYCLE on which the front wheel is far in front of the BARs you use to control the vehicle **3 choppers** SLANG teeth

**chop·py** /'tʃɑpi/ adj choppy water has many small waves **–choppiness** n [U]

**chop·sticks** /'tʃɑpstɪks/ n [plural] a pair of thin sticks used for eating food, especially by people in Asia

**cho·ral** /'kɔrəl/ adj intended to be sung by a CHOIR (=group of people that sing), or involving this type of singing: *choral music*

**chord** /kɔrd/ n **1** a combination of two or more musical notes played at the same time **2 strike a chord** to say or do something that people react well to because they feel it is familiar or true: *I think our campaign has* **struck a chord with** *the public.*

**chore** /tʃɔr/ n **1** a job that you have to do regularly, especially work that you do in a house or on a farm: *Do your chores before you go to school!* **2** something you have to do that is boring and unpleasant: *Grocery shopping is such a chore.*

**cho·re·og·ra·phy** /ˌkɔri'ɑgrəfi/ n [U] the art of arranging how dancers should move during a performance **–choreographer** n

**chor·tle** /'tʃɔrtl/ v [I] to laugh because something is funny or pleases you **–chortle** n

**cho·rus** /'kɔrəs/ n **1** the part of a song that is repeated after each VERSE (=main part of a song) **2** a group of people who sing together **3** a piece of music written to be sung by a large group of people: *the Hallelujah Chorus* **4** a group of singers and dancers in a show **5** something said or expressed by a lot of people at the same time: *a* **chorus of** *howls and whistles*

**chose** /tʃoʊz/ v the past tense of CHOOSE

**cho·sen** /'tʃoʊzən/ v the PAST PARTICIPLE of CHOOSE

**chow¹** /tʃaʊ/ n [U] SLANG food: *It's chow time!* (=time to eat)

**chow²** v

**chow down** phr v [I] SPOKEN to eat a lot of food: *We really* **chowed down** *at Larry's house last night.*

**chow·der** /'tʃaʊdɚ/ n [U] a thick soup made with milk, vegetables, and usually fish: *clam chowder*

**Christ¹** /kraɪst/ n ⇨ JESUS¹

**Christ²** interjection TABOO said when you are angry, annoyed, or surprised: *Christ! Can't you leave me alone?*

**chris·ten** /'krɪsən/ v [T] **1 be christened** to be given your name and be made a member of a Christian church at a religious ceremony soon after you are born: *She was christened Elizabeth Ann.* **2** to name a ship, airplane etc. at a special ceremony

**chris·ten·ing** /'krɪsənɪŋ/ n [C,U] a religious ceremony at which you are CHRISTENed

**Chris·tian** /'krɪstʃən, 'krɪʃtʃən/ adj based on Christianity, or believing in it: *Christian ministers* | *Christian values* **–Christian** n

**Chris·ti·an·i·ty** /ˌkrɪstʃi'ænəṭi/ n [U] the religion based on the life and teachings of Jesus Christ

**Christian Sci·ence** /ˌ.. '../ n [U] a church whose members believe that they can cure their own illnesses using their minds rather than with medical help **–Christian Scientist** n

**Christ·mas** /'krɪsməs/ n [C,U] **1** a Christian holiday on December 25 that celebrates the birth of Christ, when people give and receive gifts **2** the period of time just before and after this day: *What did you do over Christmas?*

**Christmas car·ol** /'.. ˌ../ n a Christian song sung at Christmas

**Christmas Day** /ˌ.. ˈ./ *n* [C,U] December 25

**Christmas Eve** /ˌ.. ˈ./ *n* [C,U] December 24, the day before Christmas

**Christmas tree** /ˈ.. ˌ./ *n* a real or artificial tree that you put inside your house and decorate for Christmas

**chrome** /kroʊm/, **chro·mi·um** /ˈkroʊmiəm/ *n* [U] a hard metal substance used for covering objects with a shiny protective surface. *chrome fenders on a car*

**chro·mo·some** /ˈkroʊməˌsoʊm, -ˌzoʊm/ *n* TECHNICAL a part of every living cell that controls the character, shape etc. that a plant or animal has

**chron·ic** /ˈkrɑnɪk/ *adj* **1** a chronic disease or illness is one that cannot be cured: *chronic arthritis* **2** a chronic problem, difficulty, or type of behavior is one that you cannot get rid of or that keeps happening again: *chronic unemployment* **–chronically** *adv*

**chron·i·cle** /ˈkrɑnɪkəl/ *n* a written record of historical events, arranged in the order in which they happened **–chronicle** *v* [T]

**chron·o·log·i·cal** /ˌkrɑnlˈɑdʒɪkəl/ *adj* arranged according to when something happened: *a list of World Series champions in chronological order* **–chronologically** *adv*

**chro·nol·o·gy** /krəˈnɑlədʒi/ *n* a list of events arranged according to when they happened: *a chronology of the 20th century*

**chrys·a·lis** /ˈkrɪsəlɪs/ *n* a MOTH or BUTTERFLY at the stage of development when it has a hard outer shell, before becoming a LARVA and then an adult **–compare** COCOON

**chry·san·the·mum** /krɪˈsænθəməm/ *n* a garden plant with large brightly colored flowers

**chub·by** /ˈtʃʌbi/ *adj* a word meaning slightly fat, used especially about children **–chubbiness** *n* [U] **–see** usage note at FAT[1]

**chuck** /tʃʌk/ *v* [T] INFORMAL to throw something in a careless or relaxed way: *Chuck that magazine over here, would you?*

**chuck** sth ↔ **away/out** *phr v* [T] INFORMAL to throw something away: *We had to chuck out a lot of stuff when we moved.*

**chuck** sb ↔ **out** *phr v* [T] INFORMAL to force someone to leave a place: *There was a fight, and some guys got chucked out of the bar.*

**chuck·le** /ˈtʃʌkəl/ *v* [I] to laugh quietly: *Terry chuckled to himself as he read his book.* **–chuckle** *n*

**chug** /tʃʌg/ *v* **-gged, -gging 1** [I] if a car, boat, or train chugs, it makes a repeated low sound while moving **2** [T] INFORMAL to drink all of something without stopping: *Chug that beer and let's go.* **–chug** *n* [C usually singular]

**chum** /tʃʌm/ *n* OLD-FASHIONED a good friend

**chump** /tʃʌmp/ *n* INFORMAL someone who is silly or stupid, and who can be easily deceived

**chunk** /tʃʌŋk/ *n* **1** a large piece of something: *a chunk of cheese* **2** a large part or

amount of something: *Having to get a new car took a big chunk out of her savings.*

**chunk·y** /ˈtʃʌŋki/ *adj* **1** thick and heavy: *chunky jewelry* **2** someone who is chunky has a broad heavy body

**church** /tʃɚtʃ/ *n* **1** a building where Christians go to have religious services **2** [U] the religious services in a church: *Come over after church.* **3** also **Church** one of the separate groups within the Christian religion: *the Catholic Church*

**churl·ish** /ˈtʃɚlɪʃ/ *adj* not polite or friendly

**churn[1]** /tʃɚn/ *n* a container in which milk is shaken until it forms butter

**churn[2]** *v* **1 make sb's stomach churn** to make someone feel sick because s/he is nervous or frightened **2** [T] to make butter using a CHURN **3** [I,T] also **churn up** if water churns or if it is churned, it moves around violently: *Buck tried to shout above the roar of the churning water.*

**churn** sth ↔ **out** *phr v* [T] INFORMAL to produce large quantities of something: *She churns out about three new books every year.*

**churn** sth ↔ **up** *phr v* [T] if something churns up the ground, water, dust etc., it makes the ground etc. turn over or move a lot: *Tractors had churned up the muddy fields.*

**chute** /ʃut/ *n* **1** a long narrow structure that slopes down, so that things or people can slide down it from one place to another: *a mail chute* **2** INFORMAL ⇨ PARACHUTE[1]

**chutz·pah** /ˈhʊtspə/ *n* [U] INFORMAL too much confidence, which is often considered to be rude: *Only Klinkman would have the chutzpah to say what he did.*

**CIA** *n* Central Intelligence Agency; the department of the US government that collects secret information about other countries

**ci·der** /ˈsaɪdɚ/ *n* [C,U] a drink made from apples

**ci·gar** /sɪˈgɑr/ *n* a thing that people smoke, that is made from tobacco leaves that have been rolled into a thick tube shape

**cig·a·rette** /ˌsɪgəˈrɛt, ˈsɪgəˌrɛt/ *n* a thing that people smoke, that is made from finely cut tobacco leaves that have been rolled inside a thin tube of paper

**cinch[1]** /sɪntʃ/ *n* **be a cinch** INFORMAL **a)** to be almost certain to happen: *The Cubs are a cinch to win the National League East.* **b)** to be very easy to do: *The written test was a cinch, but the oral one - well, I don't know.*

**cinch[2]** *v* [T] to pull a belt, STRAP etc. tightly around something

**cin·der** /ˈsɪndɚ/ *n* a very small piece of burned wood, coal etc.

**cin·e·ma** /ˈsɪnəmə/ *n* [singular U] **1** the art or business of making movies: *an important director in German cinema* **2** OLD-FASHIONED ⇨ MOVIE THEATER

**cin·e·ma·to·gra·phy** /ˌsɪnəmə'tɑgrəfi/ n [U] TECHNICAL the skill or study of making movies —**cinematographer** n

**cin·na·mon** /'sɪnəmən/ n [U] a sweet-smelling brown SPICE used especially in baking cakes and cookies

**ci·pher** /'saɪfɚ/ n a secret system of writing; CODE

**cir·ca** /'sɝkə/ written abbreviation **c,** prep FORMAL used with dates to show that something happened on nearly, but not exactly, that date: *He was born circa 1100.*

**cir·cle**[1] /'sɝkəl/ n a completely round shape —see picture at SHAPE[1] **1** a group of people or things forming the shape of a circle: *a circle of chairs* **2** a group of people who know each other or have a common interest: *a large circle of friends | Myers' new book has caused an uproar in literary circles.* **3 come full circle** to end in the same situation in which you began, even though there have been changes during the time in between: *After the experiments of the 1960s, education has come full circle in its methods of teaching reading.* **4 go around in circles** to think or argue about something a lot without deciding anything or making any progress

**circle**[2] v **1** [T] to draw a circle around something: *Circle the correct answer.* **2** [I,T] to move in a circle around something: *a plane circling an airport before landing.*

**cir·cuit** /'sɝkɪt/ n **1** [singular] all the places that are usually visited by someone who is doing a particular activity: *Hayes will get rich out of the lecture/talk show/cabaret circuit.* **2** the complete circle that an electric current travels

**circuit board** /'.. ˌ./ n a set of connections between points on a piece of electrical equipment that uses a thin line of metal to CONDUCT (=carry) the electricity

**circuit break·er** /'.. ˌ../ n a piece of equipment that stops an electric current if it becomes dangerous

**circuit court** /ˌ.. './ n a court of law in a US state that meets in different places within the area it is responsible for

**cir·cu·i·tous** /sɚ'kyuətəs/ adj FORMAL going from one place to another in a way that is longer than the most direct way: *the river's circuitous course*

**cir·cuit·ry** /'sɝkətri/ n [U] a system of electric CIRCUITS

**cir·cu·lar**[1] /'sɝkyələ/ adj **1** shaped like a circle **2** moving around in a circle: *a circular journey* **3 circular argument/discussion/logic etc.** an argument etc. in which you always return to the same statements or ideas that were expressed at the beginning —**circularity** /ˌsɝkyə'lærəti/ n [U]

**circular**[2] n a printed advertisement or notice that is sent to a lot of people at the same time:

*Did you see that circular from the new supermarket?*

**cir·cu·late** /'sɝkyəˌleɪt/ v **1** [I,T] to move around within a system, or to make something do this: *blood circulating around the body* **2** [I] if information, facts, or ideas circulate, they become known by many people: *There's a rumor circulating about Midori and Mr. Trenton.* **3** [T] to send or give information, facts, goods etc. to a group of people: *I'll circulate the report at the meeting.* **4** [I] to talk to a lot of different people in a group, especially at a party —**circulatory** /'sɝkyələˌtɔri/ adj

**cir·cu·la·tion** /ˌsɝkyə'leɪʃən/ n **1** [C,U] the movement of blood around your body: *Dick has bad circulation.* **2 in/out of circulation a)** used by a group or society and passing from one person to another, or no longer doing this: *The government has reduced the number of $100 bills in circulation.* **b)** INFORMAL having or not having an active social life: *Archie's out of circulation until after his operation.* **3** [singular] the average number of copies of a newspaper, magazine, or book that are usually sold over a particular period of time: *a magazine with a circulation of 400,000*

**cir·cum·cise** /'sɝkəmˌsaɪz/ v [T] **1** to cut off the skin at the end of the PENIS (=male sex organ) **2** to cut off a woman's CLITORIS (=part of her sex organs) —**circumcision** /ˌsɝkəm-'sɪʒən/ n [C,U]

**cir·cum·fer·ence** /sɚ'kʌmfrəns/ n [C,U] the distance around the outside of a circle or a round object: *The earth's circumference is nearly 25,000 miles.* —see picture at DIAMETER

**cir·cum·spect** /'sɝkəmˌspɛkt/ adj FORMAL thinking carefully about things before doing them; CAUTIOUS: *In politics you have to be more circumspect about what you say in public.*

**cir·cum·stance** /'sɝkəmˌstæns/ n [U] the combination of facts, events, and luck that influences your life, that you cannot control: *Circumstance played a large part in her getting the job.*

**cir·cum·stan·ces** /'sɝkəmˌstænsɪz/ n [plural] **1** the facts or conditions that affect a situation, action, event etc.: *You shouldn't judge him until you know the circumstances.* **2 under/in the circumstances** used in order to say that a particular situation makes an action, decision etc. necessary or acceptable: *Under the circumstances, I think we did the best we could.* **3 under/in no circumstances** used in order to emphasize that something must not happen: *Under no circumstances are you to leave this house!*

**cir·cum·stan·tial** /ˌsɝkəm'stænʃəl/ adj making you believe that something is true, because of the events or facts relating to it, but not able to be proved: *The circumstantial evidence strongly suggested that he was guilty.*

**cir·cum·vent** /ˌsɚkəm'vɛnt, 'sɚkəmˌvɛnt/ v [T] FORMAL to avoid something, especially a rule or law that restricts you: *The company has opened an office abroad in order to circumvent the tax laws.* –**circumvention** /ˌsɚkəm-'vɛnʃən/ n [U]

**cir·cus** /'sɚkəs/ n **1** a group of people and animals that travel to different places performing skillful tricks as entertainment, or a performance by these people and animals **2** [singular] INFORMAL a meeting, group of people etc. that is very noisy and uncontrolled: *Our office turns into a circus on Friday afternoons.*

**cir·rho·sis** /sɪ'roʊsɪs/ n [U] a serious disease of the LIVER, often caused by drinking too much alcohol

**cis·tern** /'sɪstɚn/ n a container in which water is stored inside a building

**ci·ta·tion** /saɪ'teɪʃən/ n **1** an official order for someone to appear in court or pay a FINE for doing something illegal: *a traffic citation* **2** a formal statement publicly praising someone's actions or achievements: *a citation for bravery* **3** [C,U] a line taken from a book, speech etc., or the act of using this line

**cite** /saɪt/ v [T] **1** to mention something as an example or proof of something else: *The mayor cited the latest crime figures as proof of the need for more police.* **2** LAW to order someone to appear before a court of law because s/he has done something wrong: *He was cited for speeding.* **3** to publicly praise someone: *Officer Johnson was cited for bravery.*

**cit·i·zen** /'sɪṭəzən/ n **1** someone who lives in a particular town, state, or country: *the citizens of Poland* **2** someone who legally belongs to a particular country, whether s/he lives there or not **3 second class citizen** someone who feels unimportant because of the way other people treat him/her

**citizens band** /'... ˌ./ n [U] ⇨ CB

**cit·i·zen·ship** /'sɪṭəzənˌʃɪp/ n [U] the legal right of belonging to a particular country

**cit·rus** /'sɪtrəs/ adj **1** a citrus fruit, such as an orange, has a thick skin, juicy flesh, and grows on a tree **2** a citrus tree grows this fruit

**cit·y** /'sɪṭi/ n **1** a large important town: *New York City* **2** the people who live in a city: *The city has been living in fear since last week's bombing.*

**city coun·cil** /ˌ.. '../ n the group of elected officials who are responsible for making a city's laws

**city hall** /ˌ.. './ n [C,U] the local government of a city, or the building it uses as its offices

**civ·ic** /'sɪvɪk/ adj relating to a city or its citizens: *It's your civic duty to vote.*

**civ·ics** /'sɪvɪks/ n [U] a school subject dealing with the rights and duties of citizens and the way government works

**civ·il** /'sɪvəl/ adj **1** relating to the people or things in a country that are not part of military or religious organizations: *We were married in a civil ceremony, not in church.* **2** relating to the laws concerning the private affairs of citizens, such as laws about business or property, rather than with crime: *a civil lawsuit* **3** relating to the people who live in a country: *The leaders must take care not to start new civil unrest.* **4** polite but not really very friendly: *At least try to be civil to him, even if you don't like him.* –**civilly** adv

**civil dis·o·be·di·ence** /ˌ.. ..'.../ n [U] actions done by a large group of people in order to protest against the government, but without being violent

**civil en·gi·neer·ing** /ˌ.. ..'../ n [U] the planning, building, and repair of roads, bridges, large buildings etc.

**ci·vil·ian** /sə'vɪlyən/ n anyone who is not a member of the military or the police: *Many innocent civilians were killed in the attack.* –**civilian** adj

**civ·i·li·za·tion** /ˌsɪvələ'zeɪʃən/ n **1** [C,U] a society that is well organized and developed: *modern American civilization | the ancient civilizations of Greece and Rome* **2** [U] all the societies in the world considered as a whole: *The book looks at the relationship between religion and civilization.*

**civ·i·lize** /'sɪvəˌlaɪz/ v [T] to improve a society so that it is more organized and developed: *The Romans hoped to civilize all the tribes of Europe.*

**civ·i·lized** /'sɪvəˌlaɪzd/ adj **1** well organized and developed socially: *Care for the disabled is essential in a civilized society.* **2** behaving in a polite and sensible way: *That's not the civilized way to deal with things.* –opposite UNCIVILIZED

**civil rights** /ˌ.. './ n [plural] the legal rights that every person in a particular country has. In the US, these include the right to have the same treatment whatever your race or religion is

**civil serv·ant** /ˌ.. '../ n someone who works in the civil service

**civil serv·ice** /ˌ.. '../ n **the civil service** the government departments that deal with all the work of the government except the military

**civil war** /ˌ.. './ n [C,U] a war in which opposing groups of people from the same country fight each other

**clack** /klæk/ v [I,T] if you clack something or if it clacks, it makes a continuous short hard sound: *We could hear Grandma's knitting needles clacking together.* –**clack** n [singular]

**clad** /klæd/ adj LITERARY wearing or covered in a particular thing: *a lady clad in silk and lace | an armor-clad ship*

**claim**[1] /kleɪm/ v **1** [T] to state that something is true, even if it has not been proved: *Scientists now claim that a cure can be* found. | *Ask Louie, he* **claims to be** *an expert.* | *She* **claims to have** *written the book herself.* **2** [I,T] to officially ask for money that you have a right to receive: *The damage is too slight to* **claim on** *insurance.* | *Congress intends to make welfare harder to claim.* ✗ DON'T SAY "harder to demand" ✗ **3** [T] to state that you have a right to something, or to take something that belongs to you: *Will whoever lost an earring please come to the front office to claim it.* **4** if something claims lives, people die because of it: *That year, plane crashes claimed 216 lives.*

**claim²** *n* **1** [C,U] an act of officially saying that you have a right to receive or own something, or the state of having this right: *The contract proves he has no* **claim on** *the house.* | *insurance claims* **2** a statement that something is true, even if it has not been proved: *Cardoza denied* **claims that** *he was involved in drug smuggling.* **3 claim to fame** a reason that someone or something ought to be famous: *Her chief/main claim to fame is the men she married.*

**clair·voy·ant** /klɛrˈvɔɪənt/ *n* someone who says s/he can see what will happen in the future —**clairvoyance** *n* [U] —**clairvoyant** *adj*

**clam¹** /klæm/ *n* **1** [C,U] a small sea animal that has a shell and lives in sand and mud, or the meat from this animal **2 as happy as a clam** INFORMAL very happy

**clam²** *v* -mmed, -mming

**clam up** *phr v* [I] INFORMAL to suddenly stop talking, especially when you are nervous or shy: *Lou always clams up if you ask him too many questions about his past.*

**clam·ber** /ˈklæmbɚ, ˈklæmɚ/ *v* [I] to climb something that is difficult to climb, using your hands and feet: *Jenny and I* **clambered up** *the side of the hill.*

**clam·my** /ˈklæmi/ *adj* wet, cold, and sticky in a way that is unpleasant: *clammy hands*

**clam·or¹** /ˈklæmɚ/ *n* [singular, U] **1** a very loud continuous noise: *a clamor of voices in the next room* **2** a complaint or a demand for something —**clamorous** *adj*

**clamor²** *v* [I,T] to complain about or demand something loudly: *All the kids were* **clamoring for** *attention at once.*

**clamp¹** /klæmp/ *v* [T] **1** to hold something tightly so that it does not move: *He* **clamped** *his hand* **over** *her mouth.* **2** to fasten or hold two things together with a CLAMP: *Clamp the boards* **together** *until the glue dries.*

**clamp down** *phr v* [I] to stop or limit an activity, especially a criminal activity: *The police are* **clamping down on** *drunk drivers.*

**clamp²** *n* a tool used for fastening or holding things together tightly

**clamp·down** /ˈklæmpdaʊn/ *n* a sudden action by the government, police etc. to stop a particular activity: *a clampdown on illegal immigration*

**clan** /klæn/ *n* INFORMAL a large family, especially one that is all together at once: *The whole clan will be coming over for Thanksgiving.*

**clan·des·tine** /klænˈdɛstɪn/ *adj* secret and often illegal: *a clandestine meeting*

**clang** /klæŋ/ *v* [I,T] to make a loud sound like metal being hit: *a bell clanging in the distance* —**clang** *n*

**clank** /klæŋk/ *v* [I,T] to make a short loud sound like metal objects hitting each other: *the clank of chains* —**clank** *n*

**clap¹** /klæp/ *v* **1** [I,T] **a)** to hit your hands together loudly and continuously to show that you approve of something: *The audience was clapping wildly as she sang the last words of the song.* **b)** to hit your hands together one or two times to get someone's attention: *The coach clapped his hands and yelled, "OK, listen up!"* **2 clap sb on the back/shoulder** to hit someone on the back or shoulder with your hand in a friendly way —**clapping** *n* [U]

**clap²** *n* **1 clap of thunder** a very loud sound made by THUNDER **2** the sound that you make when you hit your hands together **3 the clap** SLANG ⇨ GONORRHEA

**clap·board** /ˈklæbɚd, ˈklæpbɔrd/ *n* [C,U] a cover for the sides of a house made of many long thin boards, or one of these boards

**clap·per** /ˈklæpɚ/ *n* a piece of metal hung inside a bell that hits the bell to make it ring

**clar·i·fy** /ˈklærəˌfaɪ/ *v* [I,T] to make something easier to understand by explaining it in more detail: *His explanation did not clarify the matter for me.* —**clarification** /ˌklærəfəˈkeɪʃən/ *n* [C,U]

**clar·i·net** /ˌklærəˈnɛt/ *n* a wooden musical instrument shaped like a long black tube, that you play by blowing into it —**clarinetist** *n*

**clar·i·ty** /ˈklærəṭi/ *n* [U] **1** the quality of speaking, writing, or thinking in a clear way: *the clarity of Irving's writing style* | *I was amazed at his* **clarity of mind** (=how clearly he could think) *even at age 95.* **2** the ability to be seen or heard clearly: *the clarity of the TV picture*

**clash¹** /klæʃ/ *v* **1** [I] to fight or argue with someone: *Soldiers* **clashed with** *rebels near the border.* **2** [I] if two colors or patterns clash, they look very bad together: *That red tie* **clashes with** *your jacket.* **3** [I] if two events clash, they happen at the same time in a way that causes problems: *Unfortunately, the concert* **clashes with** *my evening class, so I can't go.* **4** [I,T] to make a loud sound by hitting two metal objects together

**clash²** *n* **1** a fight or argument between two people, armies etc.: *a* **clash between** *Democrats and Republicans in the Senate* **2** a loud sound made by two metal objects hitting together: *the clash of the cymbals*

**clasp¹** /klæsp/ *n* **1** a small metal object used for fastening a bag, belt, piece of jewelry etc. **2** [singular] a tight firm hold; GRIP

**clasp²** *v* [T] **1** to hold someone or something tightly in your hands or arms: *The President and the Prime Minister clasped hands.* (=shook each other's hands) **2** to fasten something with a CLASP

**class¹** /klæs/ *n*
**1** ▶GROUP OF STUDENTS◀ **a)** a group of students who are taught together: *a small class of ten people* **b)** a group of students who will finish college or HIGH SCHOOL in the same year: *Our class had its 30th reunion this year.* | *I was class of '96/'74/'88.* (=I finished in 1996, 1974 etc.)
**2** ▶TEACHING PERIOD◀ [C,U] a period of time during which students are taught: *When's your next class?* | *Bob wasn't in class today.*
**3** ▶SUBJECT◀ a set of lessons in which you study a particular subject: *a class in computer design* | *a Spanish/math/science class*
**4** ▶IN SOCIETY◀ **a)** a group of people in a society that earn a similar amount of money, have similar types of job etc.: *The Republicans are promising tax cuts for the middle class.* **b)** [U] the system in which people are divided into such groups: *the class system in Britain*
**5** ▶QUALITY◀ a group into which people or things are divided according to how good they are: *We can't afford to travel first class* (=the most expensive way) *on the plane.* | *As a tennis player, he's not in the same class as Sampras.* (=not as good as Sampras)
**6** ▶STYLE/SKILL◀ a particular style, skill, or way of doing something that makes people admire you: *I think she's one of the only actresses in Hollywood with class.*
**7** ▶PLANTS/ANIMALS◀ a group of plants, animals, words etc. that can be studied together because they are similar: *There are four main word classes: nouns, verbs, adjectives, and adverbs.*

---

**CULTURE NOTE** social classes

There are several phrases that are used when talking about the type of job that someone does and the money s/he earns. **Blue collar workers** do physical work that may or may not need a lot of skill, but that does not need a high level of education. Plumbers and electricians, and people who work in factories, restaurants, and stores are blue collar workers. **White collar workers** work in offices, banks, schools etc., and do work that involves information and needs a higher level of education. Managers, teachers, lawyers, and doctors are white collar workers. **Lower class** describes people's income rather than the kind of job they do. Both white collar and blue collar workers who do not earn a lot

of money, are not managers, or who do not own their own business or their own home, would consider themselves to be lower class. **Middle class** describes people who earn enough money to have a fairly comfortable life. They often own a small business or are managers or teachers. People in this class usually own their own home and have a high level of education. **Upper class** describes people who are not quite rich, but are very comfortable. They are usually managers with a high position, people who own very successful businesses, or are doctors or lawyers.

**class²** *v* [T] to decide that someone or something belongs in a particular group: *Heroin and cocaine are classed as hard drugs.*

**class-ac·tion** /ˌ. '../ *adj* a class-action LAW-SUIT is one that a group of people bring to a law court for themselves and all other people with the same problem –**class action** *n* [C,U]

**clas·sic¹** /'klæsɪk/ *adj* **1** a classic book, movie etc. is important and has been popular for a long time: *the classic rock music of the sixties* **2** a **classic example/case etc.** a typical or very good example etc.: *Forgetting to release the emergency brake is a classic mistake that many new drivers make.* **3** a classic style of dressing, art etc. is attractive in a simple or traditional way: *a classic blue suit*

**classic²** *n* **1** a book, movie etc. that is important and has been popular for a long time: *"Gone With The Wind" is a classic movie about the Civil War.* **2** something that is very good and one of the best examples of its kind: *The '65 Ford Mustang is a classic!*

**clas·si·cal** /'klæsɪkəl/ *adj* **1** based on a traditional set of ideas, especially in art or science: *classical Indian dance* **2** belonging to the CULTURE of ancient Greece and Rome: *classical architecture*

**classical mu·sic** /ˌ... '../ *n* [U] music that was written especially in Europe in past times by COMPOSERs such as Bach, Mozart, Beethoven etc.

**clas·sics** /'klæsɪks/ *n* [U] the study of the languages, literature, and history of ancient Greece and Rome

**clas·si·fi·ca·tion** /ˌklæsəfə'keɪʃən/ *n* **1** [U] the act of putting people or things into a group: *the classification of wines according to their region* **2** a group or class into which something is put: *Each college is given a classification according to its size.*

**clas·si·fied** /'klæsəˌfaɪd/ *adj* classified information, documents etc. are kept secret by the government or an organization

**classified ad** /ˌ... '../ *n* a small advertisement you put in a newspaper if you want to buy or sell something

classify

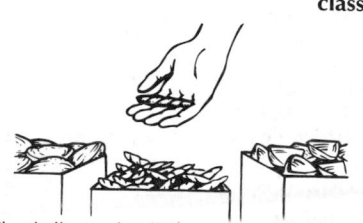

The shells are classified according to shape.

**clas·si·fy** /ˈklæsəˌfaɪ/ v [T] **1** to put animals, plants, books etc. into groups: *Whales are classified as mammals rather than fish.* **2** to make information or documents secret: *The military has classified the results of the weapons tests.*

**class·mate** /ˈklæsmeɪt/ n someone who is in the same class as you at school or college: *An old classmate of mine from high school is visiting.*

**class·room** /ˈklæsrum, -rʊm/ n **1** a room in a school where students are taught **2 in the classroom** in schools or classes in general: *Religion is rarely even discussed in the classroom.*

**class·work** /ˈklæswɚk/ n [U] school work that you do during class rather than at home —compare HOMEWORK

**class·y** /ˈklæsi/ adj INFORMAL stylish and fashionable: *a classy place to shop*

**clat·ter** /ˈklætɚ/ v **1** [I,T] to make a loud unpleasant noise by hitting hard objects together: *The pots clattered to the floor.* **2** [I] to move quickly and with a lot of noise: *a horse clattering down the street* —**clatter** n [singular, U]

**clause** /klɔz/ n **1** a part of a written law or legal document: *A clause in the contract states when payment must be made.* **2** TECHNICAL in grammar, a group of words that contains a subject and a verb, but which is usually only part of a sentence. In the sentence "Jim is the only one who knows the answer," "who knows the answer" is a clause

**claus·tro·pho·bi·a** /ˌklɔstrəˈfoʊbiə/ n [U] a feeling of fear or anxiety about being in a small enclosed place or in a crowd of people —**claustrophobic** /ˌklɔstrəˈfoʊbɪk/ adj

**claw¹** /klɔ/ n **1** a sharp curved hard part on the toe of an animal or bird **2** a curved part of the body on some insects and sea animals such as CRABs that is used for attacking and holding things

**claw²** v [I,T] to tear or pull at something using CLAWs: *Ow! Your kitten just clawed me!*

**clay** /kleɪ/ n [U] heavy soil that is soft and sticky when wet, but hard when dry or baked: *a clay pot*

**clean¹** /klin/ adj

**1** ▸NOT DIRTY◂ a) not dirty or messy: *Are your hands clean?* | *The kitchen looks cleaner than it did before.* b) not containing anything harmful or dirty: *clean water/air*

**2** ▸NO SEX/CRIME ETC.◂ not involving sex, drugs, or anything illegal: *kids having good clean fun* | *Billy's been clean* (=hasn't done anything illegal, especially take drugs) *for over a year now.*

**3** ▸HONEST◂ honest, fair, and not breaking any rules: *a clean fight*

**4 come clean** INFORMAL to tell the truth or admit that you have done something wrong: *Josh finally came clean about denting the car.*

**5 make a clean break** to leave a place or stop a relationship completely, so that you do not have any more connections with that place or person: *She wanted to make a clean break with the past.*

**6** ▸NOT USED◂ not yet used: *a clean sheet of paper*

**7** ▸SMOOTH◂ having a smooth edge: *a clean cut on his leg*

**8** ▸DESIGN◂ having a simple and attractive style or design: *the car's clean lines*

**9 a clean bill of health** something that says that a person, building etc. is healthy or safe: *Three months after the operation, Jim was given a clean bill of health.* —**cleanness** n [U]

**clean²** v **1** [I,T] to remove dirt from something: *I need to clean the bathtub.* | *He's been cleaning for hours!* **2** [T] to take out the inside parts of a fish, bird etc. so it can be cooked

**clean out** phr v [T] **1** |**clean** sth ↔ **out**] to make the inside of a car, room, house etc. clean, especially by removing things from it: *We cleaned out the garage Sunday.* **2** [**clean** sb/sth ↔ **out**] INFORMAL to steal everything from a place or from someone: *Two armed men cleaned out the computer store.* **3** [**clean** sb **out**] to spend all of your money on something so that you have none left: *The new refrigerator really cleaned me out.*

**clean up** phr v [I,T **clean** sb/sth ↔ **up**] **1** to make something or someone clean and neat: *Clean up your room - it's a mess!* **2** to remove dirt from something, especially your own body: *Go upstairs, get cleaned up, and then we can go.* **3 clean up your act** INFORMAL to begin to behave in a better way: *You'll have to clean up your act if you want to impress Diane's parents.* —see also CLEANUP

**clean³** adv completely: *I'm sorry, I clean forgot about your birthday.*

**clean-cut** /ˌ. ˈ.◂/ adj a man who is clean-cut dresses neatly in CONSERVATIVE clothes and has a short haircut

**clean·er** /ˈklinɚ/ n **1** someone whose job is to clean something **2** a machine or substance used for cleaning something: *a vacuum cleaner* **3 take sb to the cleaners** INFORMAL to get all of someone's money, especially in a way that is not honest: *The insurance company will take you to the cleaners if you're not careful.* —see also DRY CLEANERS

**clean·ing** /'klinɪŋ/ n [U] the process of making something clean and neat: *A woman comes twice a week to do the cleaning*.

**clean·li·ness** /'klɛnlinɪs/ n [U] the practice or state of being clean

**clean·ly** /'klinli/ adv quickly and smoothly in a neat way: *The doctor cut cleanly through the skin*.

**cleanse** /klɛnz/ v [T] to make something completely clean: *Cleanse the wound with alcohol*.

**cleans·er** /'klɛnzɚ/ n [C,U] a substance used for cleaning your skin or things like SINKs

**clean-shav·en** /ˌ. '..◂/ adj a man who is clean-shaven has cut off all the hair on his face

**clean·up** /'klinʌp/ n a process in which you clean something thoroughly: *The cleanup of the oil spill took months*. –**cleanup** adj

**clear¹** /klɪr/ adj

**1** ▸SIMPLE/EASY◂ easy to understand, hear, read, or see: *Are the instructions clear? | Most of the photographs were sharp and clear.*

**2** ▸CERTAIN◂ certain, and impossible to doubt, question or make a mistake about: *The newest tests make it clear that the drug is safe.*

**3** ▸SEE THROUGH◂ easy to see through rather than colored or dirty: *Clear glass bottles go in this box. | a clear mountain lake*

**4** ▸NOT BLOCKED◂ not blocked or covered: *a clear view of the harbor*

**5** ▸NO MARKS◂ not having marks, spots etc.: *smooth clear skin | a clear sky* (=with no clouds)

**6** **a clear head** the ability to think quickly and well: *Dee always has a clear head when things are stressful.*

**7** **(as) clear as mud** HUMOROUS used in order to say that something is difficult to understand: *As usual, the directions for putting the bed together were as clear as mud!*

**clear²** v

**1** ▸MAKE NEAT◂ [T] to make a place neat by removing things from it: *If you clear the table* (=take away the dishes, forks etc.)*, I'll make the coffee.*

**2** ▸REMOVE◂ [T] to remove something or someone from a place: *Trucks have just finished clearing the wreck from the road. | The area was cleared of workers as a safety precaution.*

**3** ▸LEGAL CHARGE◂ [T] to prove that someone is not guilty of something: *The jury cleared Johnson of the murder charge.*

**4** ▸WEATHER◂ [I] if the weather, sky etc. clears, it becomes better or there is more sun

**5** ▸PERMISSION◂ [T] to give or get official permission to do something: *Has the plane been cleared for landing?*

**6** ▸CHECK◂ [I,T] if a check clears, the bank allows the money to be paid into the account of the person who received the check

**7** **clear your throat** to cough so you can speak clearly or in order to get someone's attention

**8** **clear the air** to do something in order to end an argument or bad situation: *The White House*

*hopes that the investigation will clear the air.*

**9** ▸GO OVER◂ [T] to go over something without touching it: *The plane barely cleared the fence as it came down.*

**10** ▸DEBT◂ [T] to get rid of a debt by paying all the money you owe

**clear** sth ↔ **away** phr v [T] to make a place look neat by removing things or putting them where they belong: *Clear all these toys away before you go to bed.*

**clear out** phr v **1** [I,T **clear** sth ↔ **out**] to make a place neat by removing things from it: *I need to clear out that closet.* **2** [I] INFORMAL used in order to angrily tell someone to leave a place: *The campers were told to clear out by 9:00.*

**clear up** phr v **1** [T **clear** sth ↔ **up**] to explain something or make it easier to understand: *We have some facts that will clear up the mystery.* **2** [I] if the weather clears up, it gets better: *I hope it clears up by the weekend.* **3** [T **clear** sth ↔ **up**] to make a place look neat by putting things where they belong: *We should clear up the basement before your parents visit.* **4** [I] if an infection clears up, it gets better

**clear³** adv **1** away from something, or out of the way: *Firemen pulled the driver clear of the wreckage.* **2** **steer/stay clear of** to avoid someone or something because of possible danger or trouble: *Drivers should stay clear of Malta Bridge because of the ice.* **3** **clear to** sth all the way to a place or time that is distant: *You can see clear to the Rockies today.*

**clear⁴** n **in the clear** not guilty of something or not having difficulties because of something: *The debt is being paid off, but we're not in the clear yet.*

**clear·ance** /'klɪrəns/ n [C,U] **1** the process of getting official permission or approval to do something: *shipping and customs clearance* **2** the distance that is needed between one object and another one that is under or next to it, so that they do not touch each other: *the clearance between the bridge and the tops of trucks*

**clearance sale** /'.. ˌ./ n a sale in which goods are sold very cheaply to get rid of them

**clear·cut** /'klɪrkʌt/ n an area of forest in which all the trees have been cut down –**clearcut** v [T]

**clear-cut** /ˌ. '.◂/ adj impossible to be uncertain about; definite: *clear-cut goals*

**clear-head·ed** /ˌ. '..◂/ adj able to think in a clear and sensible way –**clear-headedness** n [U]

**clear·ing** /'klɪrɪŋ/ n a small area in a forest where there are no trees

**clear·ly** /'klɪrli/ adv **1** without any doubt: *Clearly, he felt he was to blame.* **2** in a way that is easy to see, understand, hear etc: *I clearly remember that time in my life.*

**clear-sight·ed** /ˌ. '..◂/ *adj* showing that someone is able to understand things easily and make good judgments: *a clear-sighted analysis of the problem*

**cleat** /klit/ *n* one of a set of pieces of metal or hard rubber attached to the bottom of a sports shoe to stop it from slipping on the ground

**cleats** /klits/ *n* [plural] a pair of shoes with cleats attached to them

**cleav·age** /'klivɪdʒ/ *n* [C,U] the space between a woman's breasts

**clea·ver** /'klivɚ/ *n* a large square knife used for cutting up large pieces of meat

**clef** /klɛf/ *n* a sign at the beginning of a line of written music to show the PITCH of the notes

**cleft**[1] /klɛft/ *n* a narrow crack in the ground or in rocks

**cleft**[2] *adj* partly split or divided: *a cleft chin*

**clem·en·cy** /'klɛmənsi/ *n* [U] FORMAL **grant/ give sb clemency** to forgive someone for a crime and make his/her punishment less severe

**clench** /klɛntʃ/ *v* [T] to close your hands or your mouth tightly, in order to hold something or because you feel angry or determined: *He had a cigar* **clenched between** *his teeth.* | *Raising clenched fists, the demonstrators sang the national anthem.* –**clench** *n*

**cler·gy** /'klɚdʒi/ *n* [plural] the official leaders of religious activities in organized religions, such as priests, RABBIs, and MULLAHs

**cler·gy·man** /'klɚdʒimən/, **cler·gy·wom·an** /'klɚdʒi,wumən/ *n* a male or female member of the CLERGY

**cler·ic** /'klɛrɪk/ *n* an official leader in an organized religion

**cler·i·cal** /'klɛrɪkəl/ *adj* **1** relating to office work: *a clerical worker* **2** relating to the CLERGY: *a clerical collar*

**clerk** /klɚk/ *n* **1** someone who deals with people arriving at a hotel: *Please return your keys to the desk clerk.* **2** someone whose job is to keep records, accounts etc. in an office –see also SALES CLERK

**clev·er** /'klɛvɚ/ *adj* **1** able to use your intelligence to do something, especially in a slightly dishonest way: *a lawyer's clever tricks* **2** able to learn things quickly **3** showing ability or skill, especially in making things: *Bill's very clever with his hands.* (=good at making things) –**cleverly** *adv* –**cleverness** *n* [U]

**cli·ché** /kli'ʃeɪ/ *n* DISAPPROVING an idea or phrase that has been used so much that it is no longer effective or does not have any meaning: *The cliché "better late than never" is true in this case.*

**click**[1] /klɪk/ *v* **1** [I,T] to make a short hard sound, or to make something produce this sound: *The dog's toenails clicked on the wooden floor.* | *clicking your heels together* **2** INFORMAL to suddenly understand something: *I was having a lot of trouble with algebra until one day it just*

clicked. **3** [I] INFORMAL to like someone and share his/her ideas, opinions etc.: *We clicked the first time we met.*

**click on** sth *phr v* [T] to press a button on a computer MOUSE in order to choose something from the screen that you want the computer to do

**click**[2] *n* a short hard sound: *the click of a key in the lock*

**cli·ent** /'klaɪənt/ *n* someone who pays for services or advice from a person or organization: *a lawyer with several important clients*

**cli·en·tele** /ˌklaɪən'tɛl, ˌkliɑn-/ *n* [singular] the people who regularly go to a store, restaurant etc: *a young clientele*

**cliff** /klɪf/ *n* a high rock or piece of land with a steep side

**cliff·hang·er** /'klɪf,hæŋɚ/ *n* INFORMAL a story or competition that is exciting because you do not know the result until the very end: *The show's writers have produced a real cliffhanger ending.*

**cli·mac·tic** /klaɪ'mæktɪk/ *adj* forming a very exciting or important part of a story or event, especially near the end of it: *the final climactic scene of the play*

**cli·mate** /'klaɪmɪt/ *n* **1** the typical weather conditions in a particular area: *a hot and humid climate* **2** the general feeling or situation in a place at a particular time: *the present economic climate*

**cli·max**[1] /'klaɪmæks/ *n* **1** the most important or exciting part of a book, movie, situation etc, that usually happens at the end: *Winning the gold medal was the climax of his sports career.* **2** ⇨ ORGASM

**climax**[2] *v* [I,T] to reach the most important or exciting part of something: *The strike climaxed two weeks of protests.*

**climb**[1] /klaɪm/ *v* [I,T]

climb

**1** to move up, down, or across something using your hands and feet, especially when this is difficult to do: *Kids like to climb trees.* | **Climbing down** *the ladder was harder than* **climbing up.** | *He tried to* **climb over** *the fence.* **2** [I] to move gradually to a higher position: *We watched as the plane* **climbed into** *the sky.* **3** [I] to increase in number, amount, or level: *The temperature was climbing steadily.* **4 climb the ladder** to move to a better position in your social or professional life: *women trying to climb the economic ladder* **5 be climbing the walls** SPOKEN to be very worried or impatient: *When he hadn't gotten back by midnight, I was climbing the walls.*

**climb²** *n* **1** a process in which you move up toward a place while using a lot of effort: *a tough* **climb to** *the top of the mountain* **2** an increase in value or amount: *a steady* **climb in** *house prices* **3** the process of improving your professional or social position: *a politician's* **climb to** *power*

**climb·er** /'klaɪmɚ/ *n* someone who climbs rocks, mountains etc. as a sport –see picture at CLIMB¹ –see also SOCIAL CLIMBER

**climb·ing** /'klaɪmɪŋ/ *n* [U] the sport of climbing mountains or rocks: *Let's* **go climbing** *this weekend.*

**clinch** /klɪntʃ/ *v* [T] INFORMAL to finally agree on something or get something after trying very hard: *A last-minute touchdown clinched the game for the Saints.* | *I think I know how we can clinch this deal.* –**clinch** *n*

**clinch·er** /'klɪntʃɚ/ *n* INFORMAL a fact or action that finally persuades someone to do something, or that ends an argument or competition: *The real clincher was her threat to sue the city.*

**cling** /klɪŋ/ *v* **clung, clung, clinging** [I] **1** to hold someone or something tightly, especially because you do not feel safe: *a climber* **clinging onto** *a rock* | *They* **clung to** *each other and cried.* **2** to stick to something: *The wet shirt* **clung to** *his body.*

**cling to** sth *phr v* [T] to continue to believe or do something, even though it may no longer be true or useful: *The villagers still* **clung to** *their traditions.*

**cling·ing** /'klɪŋɪŋ/ *adj* DISAPPROVING too dependent on another person: *a clinging child*

**cling·y** /'klɪŋi/ *adj* **1** fitting or sticking tightly to your body: *a clingy dress* **2** ⇨ CLINGING

**clin·ic** /'klɪnɪk/ *n* **1** a place where medical treatment is given to people who do not need to stay in a hospital: *a dental clinic* **2** a small hospital in an area far away from large cities: *a rural health clinic* **3** a meeting during which a professional person gives advice or help to people: *a marriage clinic*

**clin·i·cal** /'klɪnɪkəl/ *adj* **1** relating to treating or testing people who are sick: *The drug has undergone a number of clinical trials.* **2** considering only the facts and not influenced by emotions: *a cold clinical attitude toward the homeless* –**clinically** *adv*

**clin·i·cian** /klɪ'nɪʃən/ *n* a doctor who studies diseases by examining people

**clink** /klɪŋk/ *v* [I,T] if pieces of glass or metal clink or you clink them, they make a short ringing sound because they have been hit together –**clink** *n* [singular]

**clip¹** /klɪp/ *n* **1** a small metal or plastic object for holding things together: *a paper clip* **2** a short part of a movie or television program that is shown by itself, especially as an advertisement: *clips from Fox's new movie* **3** a container for bullets in a gun **4** **at a good/rapid/fast**

clip quickly: *Julie turned and headed down the beach at a fast clip.*

**clip²** *v* **-pped, -pping 1** [I,T] to put a CLIP on things to hold them together: *She'd* **clipped** *her business card* **to** *the letter.* **2** [T] to cut something out of a newspaper, magazine etc. in order to use it or save it: *Tara showed him an ad she'd* **clipped out of** *the Sunday paper.* **3** [T] to cut small amounts from something in order to make it look neater: *clipping a hedge*

**clip·board** /'klɪpbɔrd/ *n* a small flat board with a CLIP on the top that holds paper so that you can write on it

**clip-on** /'. ./ *adj* able to attach to something using a CLIP: *clip-on earrings*

**clip·pers** /'klɪpɚz/ *n* [plural] a tool for cutting something: *nail clippers*

**clip·ping** /'klɪpɪŋ/ *n* **1** an article or picture that you cut out of a newspaper or magazine **2** [C usually plural] a small piece cut from something bigger: *a pile of grass clippings*

**clique** /klik, klɪk/ *n* DISAPPROVING a small group of people that do not want others to join their group

**clit·o·ris** /'klɪtɚrɪs/ *n* a small part of a woman's outer sex organs, where she can feel sexual pleasure

**cloak¹** /kloʊk/ *n* a warm piece of clothing like a coat that hangs from your shoulders and does not have SLEEVEs

**cloak²** *v* [T] LITERARY to cover or hide something: *The early stages of the negotiations were* **cloaked in** *secrecy.*

**cloak-and-dag·ger** /ˌ. . '../ *adj* very secret and mysterious: *cloak-and-dagger methods of obtaining information*

**cloak·room** /'kloʊk-rum/ *n* a room in a school, MUSEUM etc. where you can leave your coat, bags etc. for a short time

**clob·ber** /'klɑbɚ/ *v* [T] INFORMAL **1** to hit someone hard: *Do it now or I'll clobber you!* **2** to defeat someone easily: *Our football team got clobbered again last Friday.*

**clock¹** /klɑk/ *n* **1** an instrument in a room or building that shows the time: *a big clock on the schoolroom wall* | *We left as the clock* **struck** *three.* (=made three loud noises to show the time) | *The kitchen* **clock is** *five minutes* **slow/ fast.** (=shows a time that is five minutes less or more than the right time) | *Don't forget to* **set your clocks back/ahead** *tonight.* (=change the time the clocks show to one hour earlier or later) **2** **turn/put/set the clock back** to go back to the ways things were done before, rather than trying new ideas or methods: *Women's groups warned that the law would turn the clock back fifty years.* **3** **around the clock** all day and all night without stopping: *We've been working around the clock to get done on time.* **4** **race/ work against the clock** to work quickly in order to finish something before a particular time: *"The harvest is a race against the clock to beat the winter rains,"* Johnson says. **5 watch the clock** to keep looking to see what time it is because you are bored or do not want to work −see also **punch a clock** (PUNCH¹)

**clock²** *v* [T] to measure how long it takes to travel a particular distance: *She clocked her best time in the 200-meter sprint.*

**clock in/out** *phr v* [I] to record on a special card the time when you begin or stop working: *I clocked in at 8:00 this morning.*

**clock up** sth *phr v* [T] to reach a particular number or amount: *We clocked up 125,000 miles on our old car.*

**clock ra·di·o** /ˌ. '.../ *n* a clock that you can set so that it turns on a radio to wake you up

**clock·wise** /ˈklɑk-waɪz/ *adv* moving in the same direction as the HANDs (=parts that point to the time) of a clock: *Turn the dial clockwise.* −**clockwise** *adj* −opposite COUNTERCLOCKWISE

**clock·work** /ˈklɑk-wɚk/ *n* [U] **1 like clockwork** a) INFORMAL easily and without problems: *Fortunately, production has been going like clockwork.* b) at the same time every day, week, or month: *At 6:30 every evening, like clockwork, Ari would milk the cows.* **2** machinery that you make work by turning a key around several times: *clockwork toy soldiers*

**clod** /klɑd/ *n* **1** a solid piece of clay or earth **2** INFORMAL someone who is not graceful and behaves in a stupid way

**clog** /klɑg/ **clog up** *v* -gged, -gging [I,T] to block something or become blocked: *potato peelings clogging up the drain | freeways clogged with heavy traffic*

**clogs** /klɑgz/ *n* shoes made of wood or with a wooden bottom

**clone¹** /kloʊn/ *n* TECHNICAL **1** an exact copy of a plant or animal that is made in an artificial way **2** a computer that can use SOFTWARE that was written for a different computer: *an IBM clone*

**clone²** *v* [T] to produce a plant or an animal that is a CLONE

**close¹** /kloʊz/ *v* [I,T] **1** to shut something or to become shut: *Rita walked over and closed the curtains. | The hinges creaked slightly as the door closed. | Close your eyes and go to sleep.* **2** to stop allowing the public to use a store, road, school etc. for a limited time: *What time does the mall close tonight? | Prentice Street has been closed to traffic.* **3** to end something, or to end: *the closing (=final) days of the Christmas shopping season | Professor Schmidt closed his speech with a quote from Tolstoy.* **4** also **close down** to stop all work at a business or factory: *Hundreds of timber mills have closed since World War II. | closing down local newspapers* −see usage note at OPEN²

**close in** *phr v* [I] to move closer in order to catch someone or something: *a tiger closing in for the kill*

**close²** /kloʊs/ *adj* **closer, closest**
**1** ▶NEAR◀ a) near in space; not far: *We live close to the school. | The victim was shot at close range.* (=from very near) b) near in time: *By the time we left it was close to midnight.*
**2** ▶ALMOST◀ almost at a particular level, in a particular state, like a particular thing, etc.: *They haven't reached an agreement yet, but they're close. | Inflation is now close to 6%. | Do you have any shoes that are closer in color to this scarf?*
**3** ▶CAREFUL◀ giving careful attention to details: *Take a closer look at the facts. | Scientists are keeping a close watch on the volcano. | The jury paid very close attention to the evidence.*
**4** ▶LIKING SB◀ liking or loving someone very much: *Are you very close to your sister? | We were pretty close friends in high school.*
**5** ▶AT WORK◀ working and talking together often: *Our job required close contact with the general manager.*
**6** ▶IN SPORTS◀ if a competition is close, the teams are not very far apart in points: *Right now it's too close to call.* (=no one can say who the winner will be)
**7** ▶ALMOST BAD◀ INFORMAL used when you just manage to avoid something bad, such as an accident: *I had a couple of close calls, but they weren't my fault.*
**8 close relation/relative** a member of your family, such as a parent, brother, or sister
**9** ▶WEATHER◀ too warm, and without any fresh air: *Further inland, the trees became denser and the air more close* −**closely** *adv* −**closeness** *n* [U]

**close³** /kloʊs/ *adv* **1** very near: *The woman held her baby close. | The grocery store is close by. | You're planting your tomatoes too close together.* **2 come close to (doing) sth** to almost do something: *I was so angry I came close to hitting him.* −see usage note at NEAR¹

**close⁴** /kloʊz/ *n* [singular] the end of an activity or period of time: *His retirement brought to a close a wonderful career. | Summer days finally drew to a close.*

**closed** /kloʊzd/ *adj* **1** shut, especially for a particular period of time: *Sorry, the store's closed on Sundays.* **2** restricted to a particular group of people: *a closed meeting between the mayor and community leaders* **3** not willing to accept new ideas or influences: *a closed society*

**closed cir·cuit tel·e·vi·sion** /ˌ. ˌ.. '.../ *n* [C,U] a system in which many cameras send pictures to a set of televisions that someone watches to see if any crimes are happening in a building or area

**closed shop** /ˌ. '.◂/ *n* a factory, store etc. where all the workers must belong to a particular UNION

**clothes**

jacket

coat

dress · skirt · pants · sweats

sweater · sweatshirt · shirt · blouse

**close-knit** /ˌkloʊs 'nɪt◂/ *adj* a close-knit group of people such as a family have good relationships with each other and care about each other

**close-set** /ˌkloʊs 'sɛt◂/ *adj* close-set eyes are very near to each other

**clos·et¹** /'klɑzɪt/ *n* **1** a tall cupboard that you keep your clothes in, built into the wall of a room **2 come out of the closet** INFORMAL to tell people that you are HOMOSEXUAL

**closet²** *adj* **closet liberal/homosexual etc.** someone who does not admit in public what s/he thinks or does in private

**close-up** /'kloʊs ʌp/ *n* a photograph that someone takes from very near: *a close-up of the children*

**clo·sure** /'kloʊʒɚ/ *n* [C,U] the act of permanently closing a building, factory, school etc: *We were surprised at the closure of the hospital.*

**clot¹** /klɑt/ *n* a place where blood or another liquid has become thick and almost solid: *a blood clot in his leg*

**clot²** *v* **-tted, -tting** [I,T] to become thicker and more solid, or to make a liquid do this: *a disease in which the blood does not clot* | *clotted cream*

**cloth** /klɔθ/ *n* **1** [singular, U] material that is made from cotton, wool etc. and used for making things such as clothes: *pants made from a hard-wearing cloth* **2** a piece of material that is used for a particular purpose: *Put the dough in a bowl, and cover it with a damp cloth.*

---

**USAGE NOTE cloth, fabric, and material**

Use **cloth** as an uncountable noun to talk about the cotton, wool etc. that is used for making clothes: *red silk cloth.* **Fabric** can be countable or uncountable, and can be used about things other than clothes: *What kind of fabric are your pants made of?* | *fine Italian fabrics.* When **material** is an uncountable noun, it means the same as

---

**fabric**: *There isn't enough material to make curtains.*

**clothe** /kloʊð/ *v* [T] **1** to provide clothes for someone: *They could barely keep the family fed and clothed.* **2** [I,T] to dress someone or be dressed in a particular way: *The kids were fast asleep, still fully clothed.*

**clothes** /kloʊz, kloʊðz/ *n* [plural] the things that people wear to cover their bodies or keep warm: *She likes casual clothes.*

**clothes·line** /'kloʊzlaɪn/ *n* a rope on which you hang clothes outside to dry

**clothes·pin** /'kloʊzpɪn/ *n* a small wooden or plastic object that you use for fastening clothes to a CLOTHESLINE −see picture at PIN¹

**cloth·ing** /'kloʊðɪŋ/ *n* [U] clothes that people wear: *The refugees needed food and clothing.*

**cloud¹** /klaʊd/ *n* **1** [C,U] a white or gray MASS floating in the sky that consists of very small drops of water: *Storm clouds moved closer overhead.* **2** a large amount of smoke or dust, or a large number of other things moving together: *They left a cloud of dust behind them.* | *clouds of flies* **3** something that makes you feel unhappy or afraid: *Ryder resigned under a cloud of suspicion.* **4 be on cloud nine** INFORMAL to be very happy: *When Caitlin was born, Adam was on cloud nine.*

**cloud²** *v* **1** [I,T] also **cloud up** to make something difficult to see through: *Steam clouded up the windows.* **2** [T] to make something less easy to understand or think about: *These unnecessary details are only clouding the issue.*

**cloud over** *phr v* [I] if the sky clouds over, it becomes dark and full of clouds

**cloud·burst** /'klaʊdbɚst/ *n* a sudden storm of rain

**cloud·y** /'klaʊdi/ *adj* **1** dark and full of clouds: *a cloudy day* **2** cloudy liquids are not clear or transparent

**clout** /klaʊt/ n [U] INFORMAL power or influence: *Several Christian groups have been gaining political clout in Washington.*

**clove** /kloʊv/ n one of the separate pieces that a GARLIC plant (=plant like a small onion) is made up of

**clo·ver** /'kloʊvɚ/ n a small plant with three round leaves on each stem

**clown**[1] /klaʊn/ n a performer who wears funny clothes and tries to make people laugh, especially in a CIRCUS

**clown**[2] v [I] to behave in a way that makes other people laugh: *A couple of boys were clowning around, trying to impress the girls.*

**club**[1] /klʌb/ n **1** a group of people who meet together to do something they are interested in: *the drama club* **2** ⇨ NIGHTCLUB **3** an organization for people who share a particular interest or enjoy similar activities, or the building where they meet: *It costs $600 a year to join the health club.* **4** a specially shaped stick for hitting a ball in some sports: *a golf club* **5** a playing card with one or more figures with three leaves on it: *the five of clubs* **6** a heavy stick that is used as a weapon

**club**[2] v **-bbed, -bbing** [T] to beat or hit someone with a club

**club·house** /'klʌbhaʊs/ n a building used by a club

**club sand·wich** /ˌ. '../ n three pieces of bread with meat and cheese between them

**club so·da** /ˌ. '../ n [C,U] water filled with BUBBLES that is often mixed with other drinks

**cluck** /klʌk/ v [I] to make a noise like a HEN **–cluck** n

**clue**[1] /klu/ n **1** an object, piece of information, reason etc. that helps you find an answer to a problem or solve a crime: *The police are searching for clues to the identity of the murderer.* **2 not have a clue** INFORMAL to not to have any idea about the answer to a question, how to do something, what a situation is etc.: *Brian doesn't have a clue about how she feels.* | *"Where's Jamie?" "I don't have a clue."*

**clue**[2]

**clue** sb ↔ **in** phr v [T] INFORMAL to give someone information about something: *He clued me in on how the washing machine works.*

**clump**[1] /klʌmp/ n a group of trees, bushes etc. growing close together

**clump**[2] v [I] to walk with slow noisy steps: *I could hear Grandpa clumping around in the basement.*

**clum·sy** /'klʌmzi/ adj **1** moving in an awkward way and tending to break things: *At 13, she was clumsy and shy.* | *a clumsy attempt to catch the ball* **2** a clumsy object is difficult to use and is often large and heavy **3** done carelessly or badly, without enough thought: *The clumsy solution pleased almost nobody.* **–clumsily** adv **–clumsiness** n [U]

**clung** /klʌŋ/ v the past tense and PAST PARTICIPLE of CLING

**clunk** /klʌŋk/ v [I,T] to make the loud sound of two heavy objects hitting each other **–clunk** n

**clunk·er** /'klʌŋkɚ/ n INFORMAL an old car or other machine that does not work very well

**clunk·y** /'klʌŋki/ adj heavy and awkward to wear or use: *clunky old boots*

**clus·ter**[1] /'klʌstɚ/ n a group of things of the same kind that are very close together: *a cluster of grapes*

**cluster**[2] v [I,T] to come together or be together in a group, or to be put together in a group: *The tulips were clustered around the fence.*

**clutch**[1] /klʌtʃ/ v [T] to hold something tightly: *Jamie stood there, clutching her purse.*

**clutch**[2] n **1** the PEDAL in a car that you press with your foot when you change GEARs **–see** picture on page 469 **2** an important but difficult situation, in which what you do can make the difference between success or failure: *Henderson came through in the clutch,* (=succeeded in the situation) *hitting a home run in the ninth inning.* **3 sb's clutches** OFTEN HUMOROUS the control that someone has over you

**clut·ter**[1] /'klʌtɚ/ v [T] to make something messy by filling it with things: *His desk is always cluttered with paper.*

**clutter**[2] n [U] a lot of things scattered in a messy way: *I can't stand all this clutter!*

**cm** n the written abbreviation of CENTIMETER

**CNN** n Cable News Network; an organization that broadcasts television news programs all over the world

**CO** the written abbreviation of Colorado

**Co.** /koʊ/ the abbreviation of COMPANY, which is usually written rather than spoken

**c/o** /ˌsi 'oʊ/ the written abbreviation of "in care of"; used when you are sending a letter for someone to another person who will keep it for him/her: *Send the letter to me c/o Anne Miller, 8 Brown St., Peoria, IL*

**coach**[1] /koʊtʃ/ n **1** someone who trains a person or team in a sport: *a basketball coach* **2** a less expensive type of seat on a plane or train: *Many business people have begun flying coach to save money.* **3** someone who gives private lessons in singing, acting etc.

**coach**[2] v [I,T] **1** to train a person or team in a sport: *He coaches our tennis team.* **2** to give someone private lessons in singing, acting etc.

**co·ag·u·late** /koʊ'ægyəˌleɪt/ v [I,T] to change from a liquid into a thicker substance or a solid: *Egg white coagulates when it is cooked.* **–coagulation** /koʊˌægyə'leɪʃən/ n [U]

**coal** /koʊl/ n [U] a black mineral that is dug from the earth and is burned for heat: *a coal fire* | *coal miners* **–see also** CHARCOAL, COALS

**co·a·lesce** /ˌkoʊəˈlɛs/ v [I] FORMAL to grow together or combine so as to form one group

**co·a·li·tion** /ˌkoʊəˈlɪʃən/ n a union of separate political parties or people for a special purpose, usually for a short time: *Italy's coalition government*

**coals** /koʊlz/ n [plural] burning pieces of coal —see also **rake sb over the coals** (RAKE)

**coarse** /kɔrs/ adj **1** rough and thick, not smooth or fine: *A coarse cloth was made from local wool.* **2** rude and offensive: *The guys were making coarse jokes about the women at the bar.* **—coarsely** adv **—coarseness** n [U]

**coars·en** /ˈkɔrsən/ v [I,T] to make something COARSE or to become coarse: *Washing dishes can coarsen your hands.*

**coast**[1] /koʊst/ n **1** the land next to the ocean: *the Pacific coast* —see usage note at SHORE **2 from coast to coast** across all of the US: *Their market now stretches from coast to coast.* **3 the coast is clear** INFORMAL used in order to say that there is no one who might see you or catch you: *Let's leave now while the coast is clear!* **—coastal** adj

**coast**[2] v [I] **1** to do something without using any effort: *Wilson coasted to victory in the election.* **2** to keep moving in a vehicle without using more power: *Andretti's car coasted to a stop.*

**coast·er** /ˈkoʊstɚ/ n a small round MAT you put under a glass or bottle to protect a table

**coast guard** /'. ./ n **the Coast Guard** the military organization whose job is to watch for ships in danger and prevent illegal activity at sea

**coast·line** /ˈkoʊstlaɪn/ n the edge of the coast: *a rocky coastline*

**coat**[1] /koʊt/ n **1** a piece of clothing with long SLEEVEs that you wear over your other clothes to protect them or to keep you warm: *her heavy winter coat | a lab coat* —see picture at CLOTHES **2** a layer of something that covers a surface: *a coat of paint* **3** an animal's fur, wool, or hair: *a dog with a black and brown coat*

**coat**[2] v [T] to cover a surface with a layer of something: *The books were thickly coated with dust.*

**coax** /koʊks/ v [T] to persuade someone to do something by talking gently and kindly: *The boy's mother coaxed him into eating a little.*

**cob** /kɑb/ n the long hard middle part of an EAR of corn: *corn on the cob*

**cob·bled** /ˈkɑbəld/ adj covered with round flat stones: *a cobbled street*

**cob·bler** /ˈkɑblɚ/ n **1** [C,U] cooked fruit covered with a mixture like sweet bread: *peach cobbler* **2** OLD-FASHIONED someone who makes shoes

**co·bra** /ˈkoʊbrə/ n an African or Asian poisonous snake

**cob·web** /ˈkɑbwɛb/ n a very fine network of sticky threads made by a SPIDER in order to catch insects

**Co·ca-Co·la** /ˌkoʊkə ˈkoʊlə/ **Coke** n [C,U] TRADEMARK a sweet brown SOFT DRINK

**co·caine** /koʊˈkeɪn, ˈkoʊkeɪn/ n [U] a drug used for preventing pain, or taken illegally for pleasure

**cock**[1] /kɑk/ n **1** SPOKEN TABOO ⇨ PENIS **2** ⇨ ROOSTER

**cock**[2] v [T] **1** to raise or move part of your head or face: *Jeremy cocked his head to one side and smiled.* **2** to pull back the part of a gun that hits the back of a bullet, so that you are ready to shoot **3** to put your hat on at an angle

**cock-a-doo·dle-doo** /ˌkɑk ə ˌdudl ˈdu/ the loud sound make by a ROOSTER

**cock·a·ma·mie** /ˈkɑkəˌmeɪmi/ adj INFORMAL silly and hard to believe: *a cockamamie excuse*

**cock·eyed** /ˈkɑkaɪd/ adj INFORMAL **1** not sensible or practical: *a cockeyed idea* **2** not straight or level: *His hat was on cockeyed.*

**cock·pit** /ˈkɑkˌpɪt/ n the part of a plane or racing car in which the pilot or driver sits —see picture at AIRPLANE

**cock·roach** /ˈkɑkroʊtʃ/ n a large black or brown insect that often lives where food is kept

**cock·sure** /ˌkɑkˈʃʊr/ adj INFORMAL too confident about what you know or what you can do

**cock·tail** /ˈkɑkteɪl/ n **1** an alcoholic drink made from a mixture of different drinks **2** a small dish of specially prepared food eaten at the start of a meal: *a shrimp cocktail*

**cocktail lounge** /'.. ,./ n a public room in a hotel or restaurant where people can buy alcoholic drinks

**cocktail par·ty** /'.. ,../ n a formal party where alcoholic drinks are served

**cock·y** /ˈkɑki/ adj INFORMAL too confident about yourself and what you can do: *Howitt was young and cocky.* **—cockiness** n [U]

**co·coa** /ˈkoʊkoʊ/ n **1** [U] a dark brown chocolate powder used in cooking to make cakes, cookies etc. **2** [C,U] a hot drink made from this powder, sugar, and milk or water: *a cup of cocoa*

**co·co·nut** /ˈkoʊkəˌnʌt/ n [C,U] a white fruit that has a hard brown shell and produces a liquid that looks like milk —see picture on page 470

**co·coon** /kəˈkun/ n **1** a bag of silky threads that some young insects make to cover and protect themselves while they are growing **2** a place where you feel comfortable and safe: *He needs to come out of his cocoon and have some sort of social life.* **—cocoon** v [T]

**C.O.D.** adv the abbreviation of "cash on delivery"; a system in which you pay for something when it is delivered: *Send the equipment C.O.D.*

**cod** /kɑd/ *n* [C,U] a large sea fish that lives in the North Atlantic, or the meat from this fish

**code**[1] /koʊd/ *n* **1** a set of rules or laws that tell people how to behave in their lives or in particular situations: *a strong **moral code** | The restaurant was fined for Health and Safety Code violations. | The school has a **dress code**.* (=set of rules about what kind of clothes people can wear) **2** [C,U] a system of words, letters, or signs that are used instead of ordinary writing in order to send secret messages: *Important reports were sent in code.* **3** a set of numbers, letters, or other marks that show what something is: *All products are marked with a bar code.* (=set of thick and thin black lines) −see also AREA CODE, ZIP CODE

**code**[2] *v* [T] to put a message into CODE −**coded** *adj*

**co-ed** /'koʊdɪd/ *adj* where students of both sexes study or live together: *co-ed dormitories*

**co·erce** /koʊ'ɚs/ *v* [T] FORMAL to force someone to do something by threatening him/her: *The women were **coerced into** hiding the drugs.*

**co·er·cion** /koʊ'ɚʃən, -ʒən/ *n* [U] the use of threats or authority to make someone do something s/he does not want to do: *Their confessions may have resulted from police coercion.* −**coercive** /koʊ'ɚsɪv/ *adj*

**co·ex·ist** /ˌkoʊɪg'zɪst/ *v* [I] to exist together in spite of having different opinions, needs, or political systems: *Can the two countries coexist after the war?* −**coexistence** *n* [U]

**cof·fee** /'kɔfi, 'kɑ-/ *n* [C,U] **1** a brown powder that is made by crushing the beans of the coffee tree **2** a hot brown drink made from this powder: *Do you want a cup of coffee?*

**coffee cake** /'.. ,./ *n* [C,U] a sweet heavy cake, usually eaten along with coffee

**coffee house** /'.. ,./ *n* a small restaurant where people go to talk and drink coffee

**coffee ma·chine** /'.. ,,./ *n* a machine that gives you a hot drink when you put money into it

**cof·fee·mak·er** /'. ,../ *n* an electric machine that makes a pot of coffee −see picture at KITCHEN

**coffee shop** /'.. ,./ *n* a small restaurant that serves cheap meals

**coffee ta·ble** /'.. ,../ *n* a small low table in a LIVING ROOM for putting drinks and magazines on

**cof·fin** /'kɔfɪn/ *n* the box in which a dead person is buried

**cog** /kɑg/ *n* **1** a tooth around the edge of a wheel that makes it move or be moved by another wheel in a machine **2 a cog in the machine/wheel** an unimportant worker in a large organization

**co·gent** /'koʊdʒənt/ *adj* a cogent reason or argument is clear, reasonable, and easy to believe −**cogently** *adv* −**cogency** *n* [U]

**co·gnac** /'kɑnyæk, 'kɔn-, 'koʊn-/ *n* a strong alcoholic drink made from wine

**co·hab·it** /ˌkoʊ'hæbɪt/ *v* [I] if two unmarried people cohabit, they live together as if they are married −**cohabitation** /koʊˌhæbə'teɪʃən/ *n* [U]

**co·her·ent** /koʊ'hɪrənt/ *adj* clear and easy to understand: *a coherent answer* −**coherently** *adv* −**coherence** *n* [U]

**co·he·sion** /koʊ'hiʒən/ *n* [U] the ability to fit together or stay together well: *Religious beliefs can provide cohesion among diverse groups of people.*

**coil**[1] /kɔɪl/ **coil up** *v* [I,T] to wind or twist into a round shape, or to wind or twist something in this way: *Dad coiled up the hose.*

**coil**[2] *n* **1** a length of wire, rope etc. that has been wound into a round shape **2** TECHNICAL a piece of wire that is wound into a continuous shape in order to carry an electrical current

**coin**[1] /kɔɪn/ *n* **1** a piece of money made of metal: *Uncle Henry collects foreign coins.* **2 toss/flip a coin** to choose or decide something by throwing a coin into the air and guessing which side will show when it falls

**coin**[2] *v* [T] **1** to invent a new word or phrase that many people start to use: *I wonder who coined the word "cyberpunk"?* **2** to make coins from metal

**co·in·cide** /ˌkoʊɪn'saɪd/ *v* [I] to happen at the same time: *Their wedding anniversary coincides with Thanksgiving.*

**co·in·ci·dence** /koʊ'ɪnsədəns/ *n* [C,U] a situation in which two things happen together by chance, in a surprising way: *By coincidence, my husband and my father have the same first name. | It's no coincidence that veterans are more likely to smoke than other people.* −**coincidental** /koʊˌɪnsə'dɛnɾl/ *adj* −**coincidentally** *adv*

**coke** /koʊk/ *n* **1 Coke** [C,U] TRADEMARK ⇨ COCA-COLA **2** [U] INFORMAL ⇨ COCAINE

**COLA** /'koʊlə/ *n* [singular] Cost of Living Adjustment; an increase in wages or SOCIAL SECURITY payments that is equal to the amount that prices, rents etc. have increased

**co·la** /'koʊlə/ *n* [C,U] a sweet brown SOFT DRINK, or a glass of this drink

**col·an·der** /'kɑləndɚ, 'kʌ-/ *n* a metal or plastic bowl with a lot of small holes in the bottom and sides, used for separating liquid from food

**cold**[1] /koʊld/ *adj*

**1** ▶TEMPERATURE◀ having a low temperature: *a cold clear day in March | It was cold in the car. | Let's go inside; I'm cold. | Your coffee's **getting cold**.* (=becoming cold) −see usage note at TEMPERATURE

**2** ▶FOOD◀ cold food has been cooked, but is not eaten while it is warm: *cold chicken*

**3** ▶UNFRIENDLY◀ without friendly feelings:

*a polite but cold greeting*
**4 leave sb cold** to not interest someone at all: *Shakespeare leaves me cold.*
**5 get/have cold feet** INFORMAL to suddenly feel that you are not brave enough to do something: *She was getting cold feet about getting married.*
**6 cold snap** a sudden short period of very cold weather
**7 cold spell** a period of several days or weeks of very cold weather
**8 give sb/sth the cold shoulder** to deliberately ignore a person or idea **–coldness** *n* [U]

**cold²** *n* **1** a common illness that makes it difficult to breathe through your nose and makes your throat hurt: *You sound like you **have a** cold.|Did you **catch a cold**?* (=get a cold) **2 the cold** a low temperature or cold weather: *She's not really dressed for the cold.* **3 out in the cold** not included: *The policy seems to **leave** many gay students **out in the cold**.*

**cold³** *adv* **1** suddenly and completely: *In the middle of his speech, he stopped cold.* **2 out cold** INFORMAL unconscious, especially because of being hit on the head

**cold-blood·ed** /ˌ. '..◂/ *adj* **1** not seeming to have any feelings: *a cold-blooded killer* **2** cold-blooded animals have a body temperature that changes with the air or ground temperature

**cold cuts** /'. ./ *n* [plural] thin pieces of different kinds of cold cooked meat

**cold-heart·ed** /ˌ. '..◂/ *adj* without sympathy or pity: *a cold-hearted man*

**cold·ly** /'kouldli/ *adv* without friendly feelings: *"I'm busy," said Sarah coldly.*

**cold sore** /'. ./ *n* a painful spot on the inside or outside of your mouth that you sometimes get when you are sick

**cold tur·key** /ˌ. '../ *n* [U] **go cold turkey** to suddenly stop a bad habit, such as taking drugs or smoking, without using any other drugs to help you do this

**cold war** /ˌ. '.◂/ *n* **1** an unfriendly political relationship between two countries that do not actually fight with each other **2 the Cold War** this type of relationship between the US and the Soviet Union, after World War II

**cole slaw** /'koul slɔ/ *n* [U] a SALAD made with thinly cut raw CABBAGE

**col·ic** /'kalɪk/ *n* [U] severe pain in the stomach and BOWELs of babies

**col·lab·o·rate** /kə'læbəˌreɪt/ *v* [I] **1** to work together for a special purpose: *The two authors **collaborated on** translating the novel.* **2** to help a country that your country is at war with: *He was accused of **collaborating with** the Nazis.* **–collaborator** *n*

**col·lab·o·ra·tion** /kəˌlæbə'reɪʃən/ *n* [U] **1** the act of working together to make or produce something: *Our departments worked **in**

*close collaboration** on the project.* **2** the act of helping an enemy during a war

**col·lage** /kə'laʒ, kou-/ *n* **1** a picture made by sticking various materials onto a surface **2** [U] the art of making pictures in this way

**col·lapse¹** /kə'læps/ *v* [I] **1** to fall down or inward suddenly: *Many buildings collapsed during the earthquake.* **2** to fall down and perhaps become unconscious: *She collapsed on hearing the news.* **3** to fail suddenly and completely: *a business venture that collapsed*

**collapse²** *n* [singular] **1** a sudden failure in the way something works: *the collapse of communism in Eastern Europe* **2** the act of falling down or inward: *Floods caused the collapse of the bridge.*

**col·laps·i·ble** /kə'læpsəbəl/ *adj* able to be folded up into a smaller size: *collapsible chairs*

**col·lar¹** /'kalɚ/ *n* **1** the part of a shirt, coat, dress etc. that fits around your neck **2** a band put around an animal's neck

**collar²** *v* [T] INFORMAL to catch and hold someone: *Two policemen collared the suspect near the scene.*

**col·lar·bone** /'kalɚˌboun/ *n* one of a pair of bones that go from the base of your neck to your shoulders

**col·late** /kə'leɪt, ka-, 'koulert, 'ka-/ *v* [T] to arrange things such as papers in the right order

**col·lat·er·al** /kə'lætərəl/ *n* [singular U] TECHNICAL property or money that you promise to give to someone if you cannot pay back a debt

**col·league** /'kalig/ *n* someone you work with, especially in a profession: *His colleagues described him as a man of great patience.*

**col·lect¹** /kə'lɛkt/ *v* **1** [T] to take things and put them together: *I'm still collecting data for my research paper.* **2** [T] to get and keep things of a particular kind that interest you: *A lot of boys collect baseball cards.* **3** [I,T] to get money from people: *kids **collecting for** charity|Does this ruling apply to taxes that have already been collected?* **4** [I] to come or gather together: *Dust had collected in the corners of the room.* **5** [T] to obtain something, especially because you have achieved something to get it: *"Beauty and the Beast" collected four Oscar nominations.*

**collect²** *adv* **1 call/phone someone collect** if you call someone collect, the person who gets the call pays for it **2 collect call** a telephone call that is paid for by the person who receives it

**col·lect·ed** /kə'lɛktɪd/ *adj* **1** put together in one book or as a COLLECTION: *the collected works of Emily Dickinson* **2** in control of yourself and your thoughts, feelings etc: *Jason seemed **calm and collected**.*

**col·lect·i·ble** /kə'lɛktəbəl/ *n* an object that you keep as part of a group of similar things: *a store that sells antiques and collectibles*

**col·lec·tion** /kəˈlɛkʃən/ n **1** a set of similar things that you keep or put together: *a stamp collection* | *a **collection of** toy soldiers* **2** [U] the act of bringing together things of the same type from different places: *the collection of reliable information* **3** several stories, poems, pieces of music etc. that are put together: *a collection of Jimi Hendrix songs* **4** [C,U] the act of taking something away from a place: *Garbage collection is on Fridays.* **5** [C,U] the act of asking for money from people for a particular purpose: *We're planning to **have a collection for** UNICEF.* | *tax collection*

**col·lec·tive** /kəˈlɛktɪv/ adj shared or done by all the members of a group together: *We had made a collective decision.* | *collective farms* **–collectively** adv

**collective bar·gain·ing** /..ˌ.. ˈ.../ n [U] talks between employers and unions about wages, working conditions etc.

**col·lec·tor** /kəˈlɛktɚ/ n **1** someone whose job is to collect things: *a tax collector* **2** someone who collects things for pleasure: *a rock collector*

**col·lege** /ˈkɑlɪdʒ/ n **1** [C,U] a large school where you can study after high school: *My oldest son is **in college**.* (=is a student at a college) **2** the part of a university that teaches a particular subject: *the college of fine arts*

**col·lide** /kəˈlaɪd/ v [I] **1** to crash violently into something: *His car **collided with** a bus.* **2** to strongly oppose someone: *The President **collided with** Congress over the proposed bill.*

**col·lie** /ˈkɑli/ n a middle-sized dog with long hair, kept as a pet or trained to look after sheep

**col·li·sion** /kəˈlɪʒən/ n [C,U] **1** a violent crash in which one vehicle hits another: *a **head-on collision*** (–between cars going in opposite directions) **2** a strong disagreement or fight: *a **collision between** police and demonstrators* **3** **be on a collision course** to be likely to have trouble because your aims are very different from someone else's: *Religion and politics are on a collision course over the issue.*

**col·lo·qui·al** /kəˈloʊkwiəl/ adj used in informal conversations: *colloquial expressions* **–colloquially** adv **–colloquialism** n

**col·lu·sion** /kəˈluʒən/ n [U] FORMAL the act of agreeing secretly with someone else to do something dishonest or illegal

**co·lon** /ˈkoʊlən/ n **1** the mark (:) used in writing to introduce a list, examples etc. **2** part of the large tube that takes waste matter down from your stomach

**colo·nel, Colonel** /ˈkɚnl/ n an officer who has a middle rank in the Army, Air Force, or Marines

**co·lo·ni·al** /kəˈloʊniəl/ adj **1** relating to the control of countries by a more powerful distant country: *the end of colonial rule in India* **2** also **Colonial** relating to the time when the

US was a COLONY of England: *a Colonial-style brick house* **–colonialism** n [U] **–colonialist** adj, n

**col·o·nize** /ˈkɑləˌnaɪz/ v [I,T] to control a country or area and send your own people to live there: *Austrialia was colonized in the 18th century.* **–colonization** /ˌkɑlənəˈzeɪʃən/ n [U]

**col·o·ny** /ˈkɑləni/ n **1** a country or area that is ruled by another country **2** a group of people from the same country or with the same interests, who live together: *an artists' colony* **3** a group of the same type of animals or plants living or growing together: *an ant colony*

**col·or¹** /ˈkʌlɚ/ n **1** red, blue, yellow, etc.: *the colors of the rainbow* | *houses painted bright colors* | *"What color is your new car?" "Blue."* ✗ DON'T SAY "What color does your new car have?" ✗ **2** [U] the quality of having colors: *These pages need more color.* | *color television* **3** [C,U] a paint, pencil, DYE etc. that has a color: *a big box of crayons, with 64 colors* | *The color is washing out of my shirt.* **4** [C,U] how dark or light someone's skin is: *You've got some color - have you been out in the sun?* **5** **people of color** people whose skin is brown, black etc.: *a conference of writers of color* **6** [U] the appearance of someone's skin, that shows how healthy s/he is: *Katie has a healthy color in her cheeks.* **–see also** COLORS

**color²** v **1** [T] to give color to something: *Do you color your hair?* **2** [I,T] to put color onto a drawing or picture, or to draw a picture using colored pencils or pens: *Give Grandma the picture you colored, Jenny.* **3** [T] to influence your opinion about something: *Personal feelings color his judgment.*

**color bar** /ˈ.. ˌ./ n ⇨ COLOR LINE

**col·or·blind** /ˈ.. ˌ./ adj **1** not able to see the difference between particular colors **2** treating all races of people fairly: *Equal rights laws are supposed to be colorblind.*

**color-co·or·di·nat·ed** /ˌ.. .ˈ..../ adj clothes or decorations that are color-coordinated have colors that look good together

**col·ored¹** /ˈkʌlɚd/ adj **1** having a color rather than being black or white: *brightly colored tropical birds* **2** OFFENSIVE having dark skin

**colored²** n OFFENSIVE someone who has dark skin

**color·fast** /ˈkʌlɚˌfæst/ adj colorfast clothing has a color that will not become lighter when you wash or wear it

**col·or·ful** /ˈkʌlɚfəl/ adj **1** having a lot of bright colors: *a colorful stained-glass window* **2** interesting and full of variety: *a colorful career* **–colorfully** adv

**col·or·ing** /ˈkʌlərɪŋ/ n **1** [U] the color of something, especially someone's hair, skin, eyes, etc.: *Mandy had her mother's dark color-*

*ing.* **2** [C,U] a substance used for giving a particular color to something, especially food

**coloring book** /'... ,./ *n* a book full of pictures that are drawn without color so that a child can color them in

**col·or·less** /'kʌlərlɪs/ *adj* **1** not having any color: *a colorless gas* **2** not interesting or exciting; boring

**color line** /'.. ,./ *n* a set of US laws in the past that did not let black people do the same things as white people

**col·ors** /'kʌlərz/ *n* [plural] the colors that are used as a sign to represent a team, school, club etc.: *UCLA's colors are blue and gold.*

**co·los·sal** /kə'lɑsəl/ *adj* very large: *a colossal building* | *They've run up colossal debts.*

**co·los·sus** /kə'lɑsəs/ *n* someone or something that is very large or very important

**colt** /koʊlt/ *n* a young male horse

**col·umn** /'kɑləm/ *n* **1** a tall thin round structure used as a support for part of a building or as a decoration **2** an article by a particular writer that appears regularly in a newspaper or magazine: *an advice column* **3** something with a long narrow shape: *a column of smoke* **4** one of the long narrow sets of printed lines that go down the page of a newspaper or book **5** a long moving line of people, vehicles etc.: *A column of tanks rolled through the streets.*

**col·um·nist** /'kɑləmnɪst, 'kɑləmɪst/ *n* someone who regularly writes an article for a newspaper or magazine

**co·ma** /'koʊmə/ *n* a state in which someone is not conscious for a long time, usually after an accident or illness: *Ben was in a coma for six days.*

**co·ma·tose** /'koʊmə,toʊs, 'kɑ-/ *adj* **1** TECHNICAL in a COMA **2** INFORMAL very tired or in a deep sleep: *Denny's usually comatose after he works nights.*

**comb¹** /koʊm/ *n* a flat piece of plastic or metal with a row of thin parts like teeth on one side, that you use to make your hair neat

**comb²** *v* [T] **1** to make your hair neat with a comb: *Go comb your hair.* **2** to search a place thoroughly: *Police combed the woods for the missing boy.*

**comb** sth ↔ **out** *phr v* [T] to make messy hair neat and smooth: *Let me comb out the tangles.*

**com·bat¹** /'kɑmbæt/ *n* [U] fighting during a war: *Her husband was killed in combat.* —**combat** *adj*

**com·bat²** /kəm'bæt, 'kɑmbæt/ *v* [T] **1** to try to stop something bad from happening or getting worse: *new measures to combat inflation* | *drugs to combat depression* **2** to fight against someone, especially in a war

**com·bat·ant** /kəm'bætⁿnt/ *n* someone who fights in a war

**com·ba·tive** /kəm'bætɪv/ *adj* showing eager-

ness to fight or argue: *Paul was in a combative mood.*

**com·bi·na·tion** /,kɑmbə'neɪʃən/ *n* **1** two or more different things, substances etc. that are used or put together: *A combination of factors led to the decision.* | *Vitamin C should be taken in combination with other vitamins for the best results.* **2** a particular arrangement or way of putting two or more things together: *She was dressed in an unusual combination of colors.* **3** a series of numbers or letters you need to open a COMBINATION LOCK **4** [U] used in order to show that something has more than one job or can do more than one thing: *a combination washer-dryer*

**combination lock** /,.... './ *n* a lock that is opened by using a special series of numbers or letters

**com·bine¹** /kəm'baɪn/ *v* **1** [I,T] if you combine two or more things, ideas, or qualities, or if they combine, they begin to work or exist together: *The two car makers combined to form a new company.* | *It was the heat combined with the jet lag that made her feel so tired.* | *The Dodge Viper combines speed with power.* **2** [I,T] if two or more substances combine or if you combine them, they mix together to produce a new substance: *Next, combine the flour with the milk and eggs.* **3** [T] to do two different activities at the same time: *It's hard to combine family life with a career.*

**com·bine²** /'kɑmbaɪn/ *n* **1** also **combine harvester** a large machine used on a farm to cut a crop and separate the grain at the same time **2** a group of people, businesses etc. that work together

**com·bo** /'kɑmboʊ/ *n* INFORMAL **1** a small group of musicians who play dance music **2** a combination of things, especially food at a restaurant: *I'll have the fish combo and a beer.*

**com·bus·ti·ble** /kəm'bʌstəbəl/ *adj* able to catch fire and burn easily: *Gasoline is highly combustible.* —**combustible** *n*

**com·bus·tion** /kəm'bʌstʃən/ *n* [U] the process of burning

**come** /kʌm/ *v* **came, come, coming** [I]

**1** ▶**MOVE TO**◀ to move to or toward the person who is speaking or the place that s/he is talking about: *She asked me to come and look at the report.* | *Come here, right now!* | *The car came slowly up the driveway.*

**2** ▶**ARRIVE**◀ to arrive somewhere: *When Bert came home from work, he looked tired.* | *The boxes will come later in the truck.*

**3** ▶**VISIT**◀ to visit somewhere: *She comes here every summer.*

**4** ▶**HAPPEN**◀ to begin to happen: *Spring came early that year.*

**5** ▶**LIST/COMPETITION ETC.**◀ to have a particular position in the order of something: *Jason came first/last in the 10K race.*

**6** ▶**LIGHT**◀ if light comes in or through something, you can see it in a particular place: *The morning sun came through the doorway.*

**7** ▶TRAVEL◀ to travel in a particular way or for a particular distance or time to get somewhere: *He had to come over the Bay Bridge, because of the traffic on the Golden Gate.*

**8 come open/loose/undone etc.** to become open, loose etc.: *Your shoe's come untied.*

**9 come in** to exist or be available: *People come in all shapes and sizes.* | *This shoe doesn't come in size 11.*

**10 come as a surprise to sb** to make someone feel surprised: *It didn't come as a surprise to learn she was pregnant.*

**11 sb/sth has come a long way** used in order to say that someone or something has achieved or developed a lot: *Jackie has come a long way since she first started teaching.*

**12** ▶LENGTH/HEIGHT◀ to reach a particular height or length: *The grass came up to our knees*

**13 come naturally/easily to sb** to be easy for someone to do: *Acting came naturally to Rae.*

**14 in the years/days to come** in the future

---

SPOKEN PHRASES

**15 how come?** used in order to ask someone why something happened or is true: *"She's moving to Alaska." "How come?"* | *So, how come we haven't met your boyfriend yet?*

**16 here comes sb** said when someone is about to arrive at the place where you are: *Here comes Karen now.*

**17 come to think of it** said when you have just realized or remembered something: *Come to think of it, Cooper did mention it to me.*

---

**come about** *phr v* [I] to happen or develop: *The rules have come about slowly, as a result of the way we work.*

**come across** *phr v* **1** [T **come across** sb/sth] to meet someone or discover something, usually by chance: *I had come across the article in a magazine.* **2** [I] to have a particular effect on people: *Brody comes across as being mean, but actually he's nice.* | *I thought his speech came across well/badly.*

**come along** *phr v* [I] **1** to happen, especially at a time that you do not expect: *Jobs like this don't come along very often!* **2** to develop or improve: *The corn crop is coming along fine this year.*

**come around** *phr v* [I] **1** to visit someone: *Why don't you come around at 10:00?* **2** if someone comes around, s/he decides to agree with you after disagreeing with you: *Alyssa finally came around and decided to help.* **3** if a regular event comes around, it happens as usual: *I can't believe his birthday is coming around already.*

**come at** sb *phr v* [T] to move toward someone in a threatening way

**come back** *phr v* [I] **1** to return from a place: *When is your sister coming back from Europe?* **2 come back to sb** to be remembered, especially suddenly: *Then, everything Williams had said came back to me.* —see also COMEBACK

**come between** sb *phr v* [T] to cause trouble between two or more people: *Don't let money come between you and David.*

**come by** sth *phr v* **1** [T] to visit someone for a short time before going somewhere else: *I'll come by about 6:00 to pick up the clothes.* **2 be hard to come by** to be difficult to get: *Good jobs are hard to come by right now.*

**come down** *phr v* [I] **1** to become lower in price, level etc.: *Wait until the price comes down to buy the computer.* **2** if something tall comes down, it falls or is pulled down

**come down on** sth *phr v* [T] **1** to punish someone severely: *The school came down hard on the students who were caught drinking.* **2 come down on the side of sth** to decide to support something: *The court came down on the side of the boy's father.*

**come down to** *phr v* [T] if a difficult or confusing situation comes down to one thing, that thing is the basic problem or the most important thing you have to do to solve it: *It comes down to this: How much time do we have left?*

**come down with** sth *phr v* [T] to become infected with a particular illness: *I think I'm coming down with the flu.*

**come forward** *phr v* [I] to offer to help someone in an official position with a crime or problem: *Several people came forward with information about the robbery.*

**come from** *phr v* [T] **1** to have been born in a particular place : *"Where do you come from?" "Texas."* **2** to have first existed, been made, or produced in a particular place, thing, or time: *Milk comes from cows.* | *The lines she read come from a Dickens novel.* **3** if a sound comes from a place, it begins there: *I heard a weird sound coming from the closet.*

**come in** *phr v* **1** [I] to arrive or be received: *Reports were coming in from Mexico about a huge earthquake.* **2** to enter a room or house: *I recognized him when he came in.* | *Please come in and take a seat.* **3 come in first/second etc.** to finish first, second etc. in a race or competition: *Trey came in second in the sack race.* **4** to become fashionable or popular: *Platform shoes came back in* (=were popular again) *in the 1990s.* —opposite go out (GO¹) **5** when the TIDE comes in, it rises —opposite go out (GO¹)

**come into** sth *phr v* [T] **1** to begin to be in a particular state or position: *As we turned the corner, the town came into view.* | *The new law comes into effect tomorrow.* **2 come into**

C

**money** to receive money because someone has died and given it to you

**come of** sth *phr v* [T] **1** to result from: *What good can **come of** getting so angry?* **2 come of age** to become a particular age, usually 18 or 21, when you are considered legally old enough to be responsible for your actions

**come off** *phr v* **1** [I,T **come off** sth] to no longer be on something, connected to it, or fastened to it: *A button **came off** my coat yesterday.* | *Ink had **come off** onto her hands.* **2** [I] to happen in a particular way: *The wedding **came off** as planned.* **3 Come off it!** SPOKEN said when you think someone is being stupid or unreasonable: *Oh, **come off** it! You're acting like a child.*

**come on** *phr v* [I] **1** if a light or machine comes on, it starts working: *The lights suddenly **came on** in the theater.* **2** if a television or radio program comes on, it starts: *What time does the show **come on**?* **3** if an illness comes on, you start to have it

---
SPOKEN PHRASES

**come on!** **a)** used in order to tell someone to hurry, or to come with you: *Come on, Sam! We have to go now.* | *Come on. I'll show you where it is.* **b)** said in order to encourage someone to do something: *Come on, it's not that hard.* **c)** used in order to say that you do not believe what someone has just said: *Oh, **come on**, don't lie to me!*

---

**come on to** sb *phr v* [T] INFORMAL to do or say something that makes it clear that you are sexually interested in someone

**come out** *phr v* [I]
**1** ▶BECOME KNOWN◀ to become known, after being hidden: *The news **came out** that the Mayor was very sick.*
**2** ▶TV/RADIO◀ if something you say comes out in a particular way, you say it in that way or it is understood by someone in that way: *When I try to explain, it **comes out** wrong, and she gets mad.*
**3** ▶SAY PUBLICLY◀ to say something publicly or directly: *Senator Peters has **come out against** abortion.* | *Why don't you just **come out and say** what you think?*
**4** ▶SELL◀ to begin to be sold: *When does his new book **come out**?*
**5** ▶DIRT◀ if dirt or a mark comes out of cloth, it can be washed out
**6 come out well/badly/ahead etc.** to finish an action or process in a particular way: *I can never get cakes to **come out** right.*
**7** ▶PHOTOGRAPH◀ if a photograph comes out, it looks the way it is supposed to
**8** ▶SUN/MOON◀ when the sun, moon, or stars come out, they appear in the sky

**come out with** sth *phr v* [T] to say something, especially in a way that is not expected: *Tanya **came out with** a really stupid remark.*

**come over** *phr v* **1** [I] to visit someone: *Can I **come over** and see the kitten tonight?* **2** [T **come over** sb] if an emotion or feeling comes over someone, s/he begins to feel it: *A wave of sleepiness **came over** her.*

**come through** sth *phr v* [T] to continue to live, exist, be strong, or succeed after a difficult or dangerous time: *Their house **came through** the storm without much damage.*

**come to** *phr v* **1 come to do sth** to begin to think or feel a particular way after knowing someone or doing something a long time: *Gabby was **coming to** hate all the rules at camp.* **2 come to** sb if an idea or memory comes to you, you suddenly realize or remember it: *Later that afternoon, the answer **came to** him.* **3 come to $20/$3 etc.** to add up to a total of $20, $3 etc.: *That **comes to** $24.67, ma'am.* **4 when it comes to sth** relating to a particular subject: *When it **comes to** fixing computers I know nothing.* **5** [I] to become conscious again after having been unconscious

**come under** sth *phr v* [T] **1 come under attack/fire/pressure etc.** to experience something unpleasant such as an attack, criticism etc.: *The future of the orchestra has **come under** threat.* **2** to be controlled or influenced by something such as a set of rules: *All doctors **come under** the same rules of professional conduct.*

**come up** *phr v* [I] **1** to be mentioned or suggested: *The subject didn't **come up** at the meeting.* **2 be coming up** to be happening soon: *Isn't your anniversary **coming up**?* **3** when the sun or moon comes up, it rises **4** if a problem comes up, it suddenly happens: *Something's **come up**, so I won't be able to go with you Thursday.*

**come up against** sb/sth *phr v* [T] to have to deal with difficult problems or people: *The novel's about a man who **comes up against** racism in a Midwest town.*

**come upon** sb/sth *phr v* [T] LITERARY to find or discover something by chance

**come up with** sth *phr v* [T] **1** to think of an idea, plan, reply etc: *I couldn't **come up with** a good excuse for being late.* **2** to be able to produce a particular amount of money: *I'll never be able to **come up with** $2000!*

**come·back** /ˈkʌmbæk/ *n* **1 make/stage a comeback a)** to become powerful, popular, or famous again after being unknown for a long time: *No one knew then that Tina Turner would make such a big comeback.* **b)** to play better in a sports competition after playing badly: *The Knicks made a remarkable comeback in the fourth quarter.* **2** a quick reply that is smart or funny: *I can never think of a good comeback when I need one.*

**co·me·di·an** /kəˈmidiən/, **co·me·di·enne** /kə-ˌmidiˈɛn/ *n* **1** a man or woman whose job is to tell jokes and make people laugh **2** INFORMAL

...cone who is amusing: *Dan was always trying to be the class comedian.*

**come·down** /'kʌmdaʊn/ *n* INFORMAL a situation that is not as good as one that you were in before: *From boxing champion to prison cook - what a comedown!*

**com·e·dy** /'kɑmədi/ *n* **1** [C,U] a funny movie, play etc. that makes people laugh: *a new Jim Carey comedy* **2** [U] the funny quality of something that makes you laugh

**come-on** /'kʌmɑn/ *n* INFORMAL **1** something that someone does to try to make someone else sexually interested in him/her: *I know a come-on when I see one.* **2** an attempt to get people to buy something using an advertisement: *We'll give you 20% off everything, and that's not a come-on!*

**com·et** /'kɑmɪt/ *n* an object in the sky like a very bright ball with a tail, that moves around the sun

**come·up·pance** /kʌm'ʌpəns/ *n* **get your comeuppance** INFORMAL to be punished or have something bad happen to you because you have done something bad: *I know he's treated you badly, but he'll get his comeuppance!*

**com·fort¹** /'kʌmfət/ *n* **1** [U] a feeling of being physically relaxed and satisfied: *These chairs are designed for comfort.* **2** [U] a way of living in which you have everything you need to be happy: *He envied the people living in comfort in those big houses.* **3** [U] a feeling of being calm or hopeful after having been worried or sad: *He can take comfort from the fact that his family will be with him.* **4** **(be) a comfort to sb** to help someone feel calm or less worried: *She was a great comfort to me while I was in the hospital.* **5** **be too close for comfort** something bad that is too close for comfort, worries or upsets you because it is too close in distance or time: *The lion in the safari park got a little too close for my comfort.* –opposite DISCOMFORT

**comfort²** *v* [T] to make someone feel less worried by being kind to him/her –**comforting** *adj* –**comfortingly** *adv*

**com·fort·a·ble** /'kʌmftəbəl, 'kʌmfətəbəl/ *adj* **1** feeling physically relaxed and satisfied: *Come in and make yourself comfortable.* **2** making you feel physically relaxed and satisfied: *a comfortable sofa* **3** not worried about what someone will do or about what will happen: *I feel very comfortable with him.* **4** having enough money to live on without worrying: *We're not rich, but we are comfortable.* –**comfortably** *adv* –opposite UNCOMFORTABLE

**com·fort·er** /'kʌmfətə/ *n* a thick cover for a bed

**com·fy** /'kʌmfi/ *adj* SPOKEN ⇨ COMFORTABLE

**com·ic¹** /'kɑmɪk/ *adj* funny or amusing: *a comic moment* (=short funny situation) | *At least*

*Marlene was there to give us comic relief.* (=make us laugh in a serious situation)

**comic²** *n* **1** ⇨ COMEDIAN **2** ⇨ COMIC BOOK –see also COMICS

**com·i·cal** /'kɑmɪkəl/ *adj* funny, especially in a strange or unexpected way: *men wearing comical hats* –**comically** *adv*

**comic book** /'.. ,./ *n* a magazine that tells a story using pictures that are drawn like COMIC STRIPs

**com·ics** /'kɑmɪks/ *n* [plural] the part of a newspaper that has COMIC STRIPs

**comic strip** /'.. ,./ *n* a series of pictures that are drawn that tell a short funny story

**com·ing¹** /'kʌmɪŋ/ *n* **1** **the coming of** the time when someone or something arrives or begins: *With the coming of the railroad, the population in the west grew quickly.* **2** **comings and goings** the things that people do during a particular time or in a particular place: *The camera records the comings and goings of the bank's customers.*

**coming²** *adj* happening soon: *preparing for the coming winter* –see also UP-AND-COMING

**com·ma** /'kɑmə/ *n* the mark (,) used in writing to show a short pause

**com·mand¹** /kə'mænd/ *n* **1** an order that must be obeyed: *The driver did not respond to a command to stop.* **2** [U] the total control of a group of people or a situation: *How many officers are under your command? | Who is in command here?* **3** **have a command of sth** to have knowledge of something, especially a language, or the ability to use something: *Fukiko has a good command of English.* **4** an instruction to a computer to do something **5** **be in command of yourself** to be able to control your emotions and thoughts

**command²** *v* **1** [I,T] to tell someone to do something, especially if you are a king, military leader etc.: *General Patton commanded the tank crews to attack.* –see usage note at ORDER² **2** [T] to get attention, respect etc. because you are important or popular: *He commands one of the highest fees in Hollywood.*

**com·man·dant** /'kɑmən,dɑnt/ *n* the chief officer in charge of a military organization

**com·man·deer** /,kɑmən'dɪr/ *v* [T] to take someone else's property for your own use: *The hotel was commandeered for use as a war hospital.*

**com·mand·er, Commander** /kə'mændə/ *n* an officer who has a middle rank in the Navy

**com·mand·ing** /kə'mændɪŋ/ *adj* **1** having the authority or confidence to give orders: *a commanding officer | a commanding voice* **2** from much higher or much farther ahead than is usual: *a commanding view | a commanding lead in the polls*

**com·mand·ment** /kə'mændmənt/ *n* **the**

**Ten Commandments** a set of rules in the Bible that tell people how they should behave

**com·man·do** /kə'mændoʊ/ *n* a soldier who is specially trained to make quick attacks into enemy areas

**com·mem·o·rate** /kə'mɛmə,reɪt/ *v* [T] to remember someone or something by a special action, ceremony, object etc.: *a plaque commemorating those who died during the war* –**commemoration** /kə,mɛmə'reɪʃən/ *n* [U] –**commemorative** /kə'mɛmərətɪv/ *adj*

**com·mence** /kə'mɛns/ *v* [I,T] FORMAL to begin or start something: *Work should commence on the new building immediately.*

**com·mence·ment** /kə'mɛnsmənt/ *n* **1** FORMAL [C,U] the beginning of something: *the commencement of the trial* **2** a ceremony at which students who have finished HIGH SCHOOL are given their DIPLOMAs

**com·mend** /kə'mɛnd/ *v* [T] FORMAL **1** to praise someone or something, especially in public: *The three firefighters were **commended for** their bravery.* **2** to tell someone that something is good; RECOMMEND

**com·mend·a·ble** /kə'mɛndəbəl/ *adj* FORMAL deserving praise –**commendably** *adv*

**com·men·da·tion** /,kamən'deɪʃən/ *n* FORMAL an honor or prize given to someone for being brave or successful

**com·men·su·rate** /kə'mɛnsərɪt, -ʃərɪt/ *adj* FORMAL matching something else in size, quality, or length of time: *a salary **commensurate with** your experience*

**com·ment**[1] /'kamɛnt/ *n* [C,U] **1** an opinion that you give about someone or something: *Do you want to **make** any **comments about** the proposal?* **2 no comment** SPOKEN said when you do not want to answer a question, especially in public

**comment**[2] *v* [I,T] to give an opinion about someone or something: *The police have refused to **comment on** the investigation until it is completed.*

**com·men·tar·y** /'kamən,tɛri/ *n* **1** a description of an event that is broadcast on the television or radio, or written in a newspaper: *an exciting **commentary on** the game* **2** [C,U] a book or article that explains or discusses something, or the explanation itself: *The article was an interesting **commentary on** life in a Chinese village.* **3 be a sad/tragic etc. commentary** to be a sign or example of how bad something is: *It's a sad commentary on our culture that we need constant entertainment.*

**com·men·tate** /'kamən,teɪt/ *v* [I] to describe an event as it is being broadcast on television or radio

**com·men·ta·tor** /'kamən,teɪtɚ/ *n* someone whose job is to COMMENTATE

**com·merce** /'kamɚs/ *n* [U] the buying and selling of goods and services: *interstate commerce* (=among US states)

**com·mer·cial**[1] /kə'mɚʃəl/ *adj* **1** relating to business and the buying and selling of things: *commercial activity* **2** relating to making money or a profit: *a movie that was a huge commercial success* –**commercially** *adv*

**commercial**[2] *n* an advertisement on television or radio: *There are too many commercials on TV these days.*

**commercial bank** /.,.. './ *n* TECHNICAL the type of bank that most people use, that provides services to both customers and businesses

**com·mer·cial·is·m** /kə'mɚʃə,lɪzəm/ *n* [U] the practice of being more concerned with making money that with the quality of what you sell

**com·mer·cial·ize** /kə'mɚʃə,laɪz/ *v* [T] to make money or profits, often in a way that people disapprove of: *Christmas is getting so commercialized!* –**commercialization** /kə,mɚʃələ'zeɪʃən/ *n* [U]

**com·mie** /'kami/ *n* INFORMAL ➪ COMMUNIST

**com·mis·e·rate** /kə'mɪzə,reɪt/ *v* [I] FORMAL to express your sympathy for someone who is unhappy about something –**commiseration** /kə,mɪzə'reɪʃən/ *n* [C,U]

**com·mis·sion**[1] /kə'mɪʃən/ *n* **1** [C,U] an amount of money paid to someone for selling something: *Salespeople earn a 30% **commission on/for** each new car.* **2** a group of people who have been given the official job of finding out about something or controlling something: *A commission is being set up to look at the welfare system.* **3** a piece of work that someone, especially an artist or a musician, is asked to do: *a commission for a new sculpture* **4 out of commission** a) not working correctly, or not able to be used: *I'm afraid the toilet's out of commission until the plumber gets here.* b) INFORMAL ill or injured **5** the official authority to be an officer in the military **6 the commission of a crime/felony etc.** FORMAL the act of doing something illegal

**commission**[2] *v* [T] to ask someone, especially an artist or musician, to do a piece of work for you: *John Williams has been **commissioned to** write another movie score.*

**com·mis·sion·er** /kə'mɪʃənɚ/ *n* someone who is officially in charge of a police department, sports organization etc.

**com·mit** /kə'mɪt/ *v* **-tted, -tting** [T] **1** to use all of the time and energy that you can in order to achieve something: *I don't think she's ready to **commit herself to** marriage. | His father's whole life was **committed to** education.* **2** to promise to use money, time, people etc. for a particular purpose: *They are unwilling to **commit** that many soldiers **to** the UN. | The city has **committed itself to** cleaning up the environment.* **3** to do something wrong or illegal: *Sto-*

*len cars are used by criminals to **commit** other crimes.*

**com·mit·ment** /kəˈmɪtˌmənt/ *n* **1** [C,U] a promise to do something or behave in a particular way: *Volunteers must be able to **make a commitment of** four hours a week.* | *a store's **commitment to** providing quality service* **2** [U] the hard work and loyalty that someone gives to an organization, activity, or person: *I'm impressed with Glen's deep **commitment to** coaching the kids.* **3** [C,U] the use of money, time, people etc. for a particular purpose: *a large **commitment of** resources **to** research and development*

**com·mit·ted** /kəˈmɪtɪd/ *adj* willing to work very hard at something: *a committed teacher*

**com·mit·tee** /kəˈmɪti/ *n* a group of people chosen to do a particular job, make decisions etc.: *I'm **on** the finance **committee**.*

**com·mod·i·ty** /kəˈmɑdəti/ *n* TECHNICAL a product that is bought and sold: *agricultural commodities*

**com·mo·dore, Commodore** /ˈkɑməˌdɔr/ *n* an officer who has a high rank in the Navy

**com·mon¹** /ˈkɑmən/ *adj* **1** existing in large numbers: *Foxes are very common around here.* **2** happening often and to many people, or in many places: *Heart disease is **common among** smokers.* | *It's **common for** new fathers **to** feel jealous of their babies.* ✗ DON'T SAY "It is common that." ✗ **3** belonging to, or shared by two or more people or things: *a common goal* | *problems that are **common to** all big cities* | *It's **common knowledge** (=something everyone knows) that Sam's an alcoholic.* **4 the common good** what is best for everyone in a society: *They truly believed they were acting for the **common good**.* **5 common ground** facts, opinions, and beliefs that a group of people can agree on, in a situation in which they are arguing about something: *Let's see if we can establish some **common ground**.* **6** ordinary and not special in any way: *They can put a man on the moon, but they can't cure the **common cold**.*

**common²** *n* **1 have sth in common (with sb)** to have the same qualities and interests as another person or group: *Terry and I have a lot **in common**.* **2** a word meaning a public park, used mostly in names: *walking on Boston Common*

**common-law** /ˈ.. ˌ./ *adj* **common-law marriage/husband/wife** a relationship that is considered in law to be a marriage because the man and woman have lived together a long time

**com·mon·ly** /ˈkɑmənli/ *adv* usually, or by most people: *a bird commonly found in Malaysia* | *the most commonly used computer*

**com·mon·place** /ˈkɑmənˌpleɪs/ *adj* very common or ordinary: *Expensive foreign cars are commonplace in this Chicago suburb.*

**common sense** /ˌ.. ˈ./ *n* [U] the ability to behave in a sensible way and make practical decisions: *Use your common sense for once!*

**com·mon·wealth** /ˈkɑmənˌwɛlθ/ *n* FORMAL a group of countries that are related politically or economically, for example the group of countries that have a strong relationship with Great Britain

**com·mo·tion** /kəˈmoʊʃən/ *n* [singular, U] sudden noisy activity or arguing: *Hicks **caused a commotion** by going next door and demanding to use the phone.*

**com·mu·nal** /kəˈmyunl/ *adj* shared by a group of people: *a communal bathroom*

**com·mune¹** /ˈkɑmyun/ *n* a group of people who live and work together and share their possessions: *Kyle belonged to a commune in the 1960s.*

**com·mune²** /kəˈmyun/ *v* [I] to try to communicate without using words: *I often walk on the beach to **commune with** nature.*

**com·mu·ni·ca·ble** /kəˈmyunɪkəbəl/ *adj* a communicable disease is infectious

**com·mu·ni·cate** /kəˈmyunəˌkeɪt/ *v* **1** [I] to express your thoughts and feelings so other people understand them: *Jack and I just can't communicate any more.* **2** [I,T] to exchange information or conversation with other people using words, signs, letters, telephones etc.: *We've **communicated** our offer **to** their director.* | *They managed to **communicate with** each other by using sign language.*

**com·mu·ni·ca·tion** /kəˌmyunəˈkeɪʃən/ *n* **1** [U] the process of speaking, writing etc., by which people exchange information: *The pilot was **in** constant **communication with** the control tower.* | *Radio and television are important **means of communication**.* (=ways of sending information somewhere) **2** [U] the way people express their thoughts and feelings or share information: *We have a real **communication problem** in this family!* (=we do not express our feelings well) **3** FORMAL a letter, message, or telephone call

**com·mu·ni·ca·tions** /kəˌmyunəˈkeɪʃənz/ *n* [plural] **1** the various ways of sending and receiving information, such as radio, telephone, television etc.: *global communications satellites/networks* | *The power failure disrupted communications at the airport.* **2** the study of using radio, TV, and film to communicate: *a degree in communications*

**com·mu·ni·ca·tive** /kəˈmyunɪkətɪv, -ˌkeɪtɪv/ *adj* willing or able to talk or give information: *Customers complained that the sales clerks were not very communicative.* –opposite UNCOMMUNICATIVE

**com·mun·ion** /kəˈmyunyən/ *n* [U] **1** FORMAL a special relationship with someone or something in which you feel that you understand him, her, or it very well: *Prayer is a form*

of **communion between** people and God.
**2 Communion** the Christian ceremony in which people eat bread and drink wine as signs of Christ's body and blood

**com·mu·ni·qué** /kəˈmyunə̩keɪ, -̩myunə-ˈkeɪ/ n an official report or announcement

**com·mu·nism** /ˈkɑmyə̩nɪzəm/ n [U] a political system in which the government controls all the production of food and goods and there is no privately owned property

**com·mu·nist** /ˈkɑmyənɪst/ n someone who supports or takes part in COMMUNISM —**communist** adj

**com·mu·ni·ty** /kəˈmyunə̩ṭi/ n **1** the people who live in the same area, town etc., or who have the same interests, religion, race etc.: They've done a lot for our local communities. | the Asian community **2 the community** society and the people in it: a plan to get young police officers out into the community

**community col·lege** /.̩... '../ n a college that people can go to for two years to learn a skill or prepare for a university

**community prop·er·ty** /.̩... '.../ n [U] LAW property that is considered to be owned equally by both a husband and wife

**community serv·ice** /.̩... '../ n [U] work that someone does to help other people without being paid, especially as punishment for a crime

**com·mute**[1] /kəˈmyut/ v **1** [I] to travel regularly in order to get to work: Jerry **commutes from** Scarsdale **to** New York every day. | I commute all the way **to** St. Louis from here. **2** [T] FORMAL to change the punishment given to a criminal to one that is less severe: Her sentence was **commuted** from death **to** life imprisonment.

**commute**[2] n [C usually singular] the trip made in commuting (COMMUTE): It's a long commute from Monroe to downtown.

**com·mut·er** /kəˈmyuṭɚ/ n someone who regularly travels in order to get to work

**com·pact**[1] /ˈkɑmpækt, kəmˈpækt/ adj **1** small, but designed well so that everything fits neatly into the available space: a compact computer | a new compact pickup truck **2** fitting closely into a small space: Look for plants with healthy leaves and a compact shape.

**com·pact**[2] /ˈkɑmpækt/ n **1** a small flat container with a mirror, containing powder for a woman's face **2** a small car **3** FORMAL an agreement between two or more people, countries etc.

**com·pact**[3] /kəmˈpækt/ v [T] to press something together so that it becomes smaller or more solid —**compacted** adj

**compact disc** /̩kɑmpækt ˈdɪsk/ n ⇨ CD

**com·pan·ion** /kəmˈpænyən/ n **1** someone whom you spend a lot of time with, especially someone who is a friend: He was my only companion during the war. **2** one of a pair of things that go together or can be used together: There used to be a **companion to** that ornament, but I broke it. **3** used in the title of books that explain something about a particular subject: The Fisherman's Companion

**com·pan·ion·a·ble** /kəmˈpænyənəbəl/ adj pleasantly friendly: They sat in a companionable silence.

**com·pan·ion·ship** /kəmˈpænyən̩ʃɪp/ n [U] a friendly relationship: When Stan died, I missed his companionship the most.

**com·pa·ny** /ˈkʌmpəni/ n **1** an organization that makes or sells goods or services: a bus company | What company do you work for? **2** [U] the act of being with someone so that s/he does not feel lonely: I wasn't much company for Aunt Margaret. | Why don't you come with me? I could use the company. | At least Carol had the dog to **keep her company**. (=to stay with her) **3** [U] one or more guests, or someone who is coming to see you: We're **having company** tonight, so be back home by five. **4** [singular, U] the group of people that you are friends with or spend time with: I don't like the company she keeps. **5 part company** to no longer work together or agree with each other: The show's writer and director have now parted company. **6** a group of about 120 soldiers who are usually part of a larger group

**com·pa·ra·ble** /ˈkɑmpərəbəl/ adj FORMAL similar to something else in size, number, quality etc.: Is the pay rate **comparable to** that of other companies?

**com·par·a·tive**[1] /kəmˈpærəṭɪv/ adj **1** showing what is different and similar between things of the same kind: a comparative study of European languages **2** measured or judged when compared with something of the same kind: the comparative wealth of Kuwait (= its wealth compared with the rest of the world)

**comparative**[2] n **the comparative** TECHNICAL in grammar, the form of an adjective or adverb that shows an increase in quality, quantity, degree etc. For example, "better" is the comparative of "good" —see study note on page 457

**com·par·a·tive·ly** /kəmˈpærəṭɪvli/ adv as compared to something else or to a previous state: The children were comparatively well-behaved today.

**com·pare**[1] /kəmˈpɛr/ v [T] **1** to examine or judge two or more things in order to show how they are similar to or different from each other: I'm healthy **compared to** most people. | **Compared with** our old house, this one's a lot bigger. | Compare these wines and tell us what you think. **2** to say that something or someone is like someone or something else, or that it is equally good, large etc.: Tammy has often been **compared to** Janet Jackson. | The oranges out here **don't compare with** (=are not as good as) the Florida ones. **3 compare notes (with sb)** INFORMAL to talk with someone in order to find out if his/her experience is the same as yours: *She and I both have allergies, and we are always comparing notes.*

**compare²** *n* **beyond/without compare** LITERARY a quality that is beyond compare is the best of its kind: *a beauty beyond compare*

**com·par·i·son** /kəm'pærəsən/ *n* **1** [U] the process of comparing two people or things: *In comparison with his older brother, he's a much better student.* | *My last job was so boring that this one seems great by comparison.* **2** a statement or examination of how similar two things, people etc. are: *a comparison of crime figures in Chicago and Detroit* | *You can't make a comparison between American and Japanese schools - they're too different.* | *Many writers have tried to draw comparisons* (=show similarities) *between the two presidents.* **3 there's no comparison** used when you think that someone or something is much better than someone or something else: *There's just no comparison between canned vegetables and fresh ones.*

**com·part·ment** /kəm'part˺mənt/ *n* a smaller enclosed space inside something larger: *a car's glove compartment* | *the luggage compartment on a plane*

**com·part·men·tal·ize** /kəm,part˺'mɛntəl-ˌaɪz/ *v* [T] to divide things into separate groups; CATEGORIZE

**com·pass** /'kʌmpəs/ *n* **1** an instrument that shows directions: *All I had was a map and a compass.* **2** an instrument with a sharp point, used for drawing circles or measuring distances on maps

compass

**com·pas·sion** /kəm-'pæʃən/ *n* [U] a strong feeling of sympathy for someone who is suffering: *She's really upset - can't you show a little compassion?* | *compassion for the poor*

**com·pas·sion·ate** /kəm'pæʃənɪt/ *adj* feeling sympathy for people who are suffering: *a caring compassionate man*

**com·pat·i·ble¹** /kəm'pætəbəl/ *adj* **1** able to exist or be used together without causing problems: *PC-compatible software* (=able to be used with personal computers) | *We wanted a trail that would be compatible with the rest of the park.* **2** two people who are compatible are able to have a good relationship, because they share interests, ideas etc. **–compatibility** /kəm,pætə'bɪləti/ *n* [U] **–**opposite INCOMPATIBLE

**compatible²** *n* a computer that can operate the same programs as a more famous type of computer: *programs for IBM PCs and compatibles*

**com·pa·tri·ot** /kəm'peɪtriət/ *n* someone who

was born in or is a citizen of the same country as someone else

**com·pel** /kəm'pɛl/ *v* **-lled, -lling** [T] to force someone to do something: *On Monday, Ozawa said he felt compelled to resign.* **–**see also COMPULSION

**com·pel·ling** /kəm'pɛlɪŋ/ *adj* so interesting or exciting that you have to pay attention: *It's a compelling story about one man's courage.*

**com·pen·di·um** /kəm'pɛndiəm/ *n* FORMAL a book that contains a complete collection of facts, drawings etc. on a particular subject: *a baseball compendium*

**com·pen·sate** /'kɑmpən,seɪt/ *v* **1** [I] to reduce or balance the bad effect of something: *Her intelligence more than compensates for her lack of experience.* | *A wet June doesn't compensate for a dry winter.* **2** [I,T] to pay someone money because s/he has suffered injury, loss, or damage: *Survivors were given $20,000 each to help compensate for their losses.* **–compensatory** /kəm'pɛnsə,tɔri/ *adj*

**com·pen·sa·tion** /,kɑmpən'seɪʃən/ *n* **1** [U] money paid to someone because s/he has suffered injury, loss, or damage: *Ralph still hasn't been paid compensation for his back injury.* | *They were each given $500 as/in compensation.* **2** [C,U] something that makes a bad situation seem better: *One of the few compensations of losing my job was seeing more of my family.*

**com·pete** /kəm'pit/ *v* [I] to try to win or gain something, or try to be better or more successful than someone else: *Kids start competing for college places as early as 10th grade.* | *We just can't compete with/against big companies like theirs.* | *How many runners will be competing in the race?*

**com·pe·tent** /'kɑmpətənt/ *adj* **1** having enough skill or knowledge to do something to a satisfactory standard: *Olive's a very competent teacher.* **2** satisfactory, but not especially good: *They did a competent job fixing the roof.* **–competence** *n* [U] **–competently** *adv* **–**opposite INCOMPETENT

**com·pe·ti·tion** /,kɑmpə'tɪʃən/ *n* **1** [U] a situation in which people or organizations COMPETE with each other: *The competition between the two sisters is obvious.* | *There's a lot of competition for the promotion.* | *Prices have gone down due to competition among the airlines.* | *Judy is in competition with* (=competing with) *four others for the role.* **2** [singular, U] the people or groups that are competing against you, especially in business: *trying to sell more than the competition* **3** an organized event in which people or teams COMPETE against each other: *a dancing competition* | *Teams from 10 different schools entered the competition.*

**com·pet·i·tive** /kəm'pɛtətɪv/ *adj* **1** determined to be more successful than other people or companies: *Steve's very competitive.* | *What* can we do to maintain our **competitive edge?** (=ability to be more successful) **2** relating to competition: *competitive sports* | *a competitive market* **3** competitive prices or wages are similar to the prices that are charged or the wages that are paid by other stores or companies –**competitiveness** *n* [U]

**com·pet·i·tor** /kəm'pɛtətər/ *n* a person, team, company etc. that is competing with another one: *Last year we sold twice as many computers as our competitors.*

**com·pi·la·tion** /ˌkɑmpə'leɪʃən/ *n* a book, list, record etc. that puts together many different pieces of information, music etc.: *a compilation of love songs*

**com·pile** /kəm'paɪl/ *v* [T] to make a book, list, record etc. using different pieces of information, music etc.: *The report is compiled from a survey of 5,000 households.*

**com·pla·cent** /kəm'pleɪsənt/ *adj* pleased with what you have achieved so that you stop trying to improve or change things: *Yes, we've been winning, but we're not going to get complacent.* –**complacency** *n* [U]

**com·plain** /kəm'pleɪn/ *v* [I,T] **1** to say that you are annoyed, not satisfied, or unhappy about something or someone: *Fred's always complaining about something.* | *Dee complained that she couldn't find a job anywhere.* | *I'm going to complain to the manager!* **2 I can't complain** SPOKEN said when you think a situation is satisfactory even though there may be a few problems: *I still don't feel too great, but I can't complain.*

**complain of** sth *phr v* [T] to say that you feel sick or have a pain in a part of your body: *Tom's been complaining of pain in his chest.*

**com·plaint** /kəm'pleɪnt/ *n* **1** [C,U] a statement in which someone complains about something: *a complaint against five police officers* | *I want to make a complaint!* (=complain formally to someone) | *I've had a lot of complaints about your work.* ✗ DON'T SAY "a complaint for something." ✗ **2** something that you complain about: *My only complaint is the high prices they charge.* **3** an illness that affects a particular part of your body: *a serious liver complaint*

**com·ple·ment¹** /'kɑmpləmənt/ *n* **1** someone or something that emphasizes the good qualities of another person or thing: *A fine wine is a complement to a good meal.* **2** the number or quantity needed to make a group complete: *The English department already has its full complement of teachers.* **3** TECHNICAL in grammar, a word or phrase that follows a verb and describes the subject of the verb. In the sentence "You look angry," "angry" is a complement –compare COMPLIMENT¹

**com·ple·ment²** /'kɑmplə,mɛnt/ *v* [T] to emphasize the good qualities of another person or thing, especially by adding something that was needed: *Terry and Jim really complement*

each other. –**complementary** /ˌkɑmplə'mɛntri, -mɛntəri/ *adj*: *complementary colors*

**com·plete¹** /kəm'plit/ *adj* **1** having all the parts, details, facts etc. that are necessary or usual: *You'll find complete cooking instructions on the cans.* | *the complete works of Shakespeare* | *a complete sentence* | *Christmas just didn't seem complete without Dad there.* –opposite INCOMPLETE **2** INFORMAL a word meaning in every way, used in order to emphasize what you are saying; total: *Bart's a complete idiot!* | *Their wedding announcement came as a complete surprise.* **3** finished: *Our research is nearly complete.* **4 complete with** including or containing something additional: *The house comes complete with a swimming pool.* –**completeness** *n* [U]

**complete²** *v* [T] **1** to finish doing or making something: *The book took five years to complete.* **2** to make something whole or perfect by adding what is missing: *I need one more stamp to complete my collection.*

**com·plete·ly** /kəm'plitˑli/ *adv* in every way; totally: *I completely forgot about your birthday.*

**com·ple·tion** /kəm'pliʃən/ *n* [U] the state of being finished, or the act of finishing something: *Repair work is scheduled for completion in April.* | *the completion of the $80 million project*

**com·plex¹** /kəm'plɛks, kɑm-, 'kɑmplɛks/ *adj* **1** consisting of many closely connected parts or processes: *There's a complex network of roads connecting the two cities.* **2** full of small details, and therefore difficult to understand or explain: "*This is a very complex issue,*" *Morrison said.*

**com·plex²** /'kɑmplɛks/ *n* **1** a group of buildings or one large building used for a particular purpose: *They're building a new shopping complex downtown.* **2** an emotional problem in which someone is too anxious about something or thinks too much about it: *Linda has a real complex about her appearance.*

**com·plex·ion** /kəm'plɛkʃən/ *n* the natural color and appearance of the skin on your face: *a pale/dark complexion*

**com·plex·i·ty** /kəm'plɛksəti/ *n* [U] the state or quality of being complicated and detailed: *the complexity of the book's plot*

**com·pli·ance** /kəm'plaɪəns/ *n* [U] FORMAL the act of obeying a rule or law: *Compliance with the law is expected of everyone.*

**com·pli·ant** /kəm'plaɪənt/ *adj* willing to obey or agree to other people's wishes and demands: *a compliant little girl* –**compliantly** *adv*

**com·pli·cate** /'kɑmplə,keɪt/ *v* [T] to make something difficult to understand or deal with: *It's a serious problem, complicated by the fact that we have no experience in this area.*

**com·pli·cat·ed** /'kɑmplə,keɪtɪd/ *adj* difficult to understand or deal with: *Don't ask me such* *complicated questions.* | *It's a complicated situation.* −opposite SIMPLE

**com·pli·ca·tion** /ˌkɑmpləˈkeɪʃən/ *n* **1** [C usually plural] a medical problem or illness that happens while someone is already ill: *Mrs. Potter died Thursday of complications following surgery.* **2** [C,U] a problem or situation that makes something more difficult to understand or deal with: *The drop in student numbers added further complications.*

**com·plic·i·ty** /kəmˈplɪsəti/ *n* [U] FORMAL the act of being involved in a crime with other people

**com·pli·ment**[1] /ˈkɑmpləmənt/ *n* something you say or do in order to praise someone or show that you admire or respect him/her: *"You look great." "Thanks for the compliment."* | *I took it as a compliment that Rickey even knew my name.* | *This is the highest compliment anyone has ever paid me.* −compare COMPLEMENT[1] −see also COMPLIMENTS

**com·pli·ment**[2] /ˈkɑmpləˌment/ *v* [T] to say something to someone that expresses praise, admiration, or respect: *That's the first time Bob has complimented me on my hair.*

**com·pli·men·ta·ry** /ˌkɑmpləˈmentri, -mentəri/ *adj* **1** expressing praise, admiration, or respect: *Your teacher made some very complimentary remarks about your work.* −opposite UNCOMPLIMENTARY **2** given free to people: *complimentary tickets*

**com·pli·ments** /ˈkɑmpləmənts/ *n* [plural] **1** praise, admiration, or good wishes: *Please give my compliments to the chef.* **2 with the compliments of/with sb's compliments** FORMAL used by a person or company when he, she, or it sends or gives something to you: *Please accept these tickets with our compliments.*

**com·ply** /kəmˈplaɪ/ *v* [I] FORMAL to do what you have to do or are asked to do: *Those who fail to comply with the law will be fined.*

**com·po·nent** /kəmˈpoʊnənt/ *n* one of several parts that make up a whole machine or system: *stereo components*

**com·pose** /kəmˈpoʊz/ *v* **1 be composed of** to be formed from a group of substances or parts: *Water is composed of hydrogen and oxygen.* −compare COMPRISE **2** [T] to combine together with other things or people to form something: *the letters that compose a word* **3** [I,T] to put sounds, words, colors or images together to form a piece of art: *Schumann was better at composing music than playing it.* −see usage note at COMPRISE

**com·posed** /kəmˈpoʊzd/ *adj* calm, rather than upset or angry

**com·pos·er** /kəmˈpoʊzɚ/ *n* someone who writes music

**com·pos·ite** /kəmˈpɑzɪt/ *adj* made up of different parts or materials: *a composite drawing* −composite *n*

**com·po·si·tion** /ˌkɑmpəˈzɪʃən/ *n* **1** [U] the way in which something is made up of different parts, members etc.: *the chemical composition of plants* **2** [C,U] a piece of music or a poem, or the art of writing one **3** [C,U] a short piece of writing about a particular subject that is done at school; ESSAY **4** [U] the way in which the different parts of a painting or photograph are arranged

**com·post** /ˈkɑmpoʊst/ *n* [U] a mixture of decayed leaves, plants etc. used for improving the quality of soil

**com·po·sure** /kəmˈpoʊʒɚ/ *n* [singular, U] a calm feeling that you have when you feel confident about dealing with a situation

**com·pound**[1] /ˈkɑmpaʊnd/ *n* **1** something that consists of a combination of two or more parts: *a chemical compound* **2** an area that contains a group of buildings and is surrounded by a fence or wall: *a prison compound* **3** TECHNICAL in grammar, a noun or adjective consisting of two or more words. The noun "ice cream" is a compound

**com·pound**[2] /kəmˈpaʊnd/ *v* [T] **1** to make a difficult situation worse by adding more problems: *Our difficulties were compounded by other people's mistakes.* **2** TECHNICAL to pay INTEREST that is calculated on both the sum of money and the INTEREST it is making

**com·pre·hend** /ˌkɑmprɪˈhend/ *v* [I,T] FORMAL to understand something: *The judge said it was difficult to fully comprehend* (=understand completely) *the actions of the police in this matter.*

**com·pre·hen·si·ble** /ˌkɑmprɪˈhensəbəl/ *adj* able to be understood: *A book like that is not comprehensible to the average student.* −opposite INCOMPREHENSIBLE

**com·pre·hen·sion** /ˌkɑmprɪˈhenʃən/ *n* [U] the ability to understand something, or knowledge about something: *Some politicians seem to have no real comprehension of what it's like to be poor.* | *a test of reading/listening comprehension* (=a student's ability to understand written or spoken language)

**com·pre·hen·sive** /ˌkɑmprɪˈhensɪv/ *adj* including everything that is necessary: *comprehensive health insurance*

**com·press** /kəmˈpres/ *v* [I,T] to press something or make it smaller so that it takes up less space: *The garlic is dried and compressed into a pill.* | *electronically compressing data* −compressed *adj* −compression /kəmˈpreʃən/ *n* [U]

**com·prise** /kəmˈpraɪz/ *v* FORMAL [linking verb] to consist of particular parts, groups etc.: *New York City comprises Manhattan, Queens, Brooklyn, The Bronx, and Staten Island.* ✗ DON'T SAY "is comprised of" ✗ [T] to form part of a larger group: *Women comprise over 75% of our staff.*

---

**USAGE NOTE** comprise, be composed of, consist of

Use these phrases to talk about the parts that things are made of, or the things that something contains. Each of the following sentences means the same thing, but the patterns are different: *The United States comprises 50 states.* | *The United States is composed of 50 states.* | *The United States consists of 50 states.* ✗ DON'T SAY "is comprised of" or "is consisted of." ✗

---

**com·pro·mise**[1] /'kɑmprə,maɪz/ *n* [C,U] an agreement that is achieved after everyone involved accepts less than what s/he wanted at first: *There is still hope that the warring sides will reach a compromise.* | *No one at the meeting was prepared to make compromises.*

**compromise**[2] *v* **1** [I] to end an argument by making an agreement in which everyone involved accepts less than what s/he wanted at first: *We managed to compromise on a price for the car.* | *Look, I'll compromise with you and pay half of the cost.* **2** [T] to do something in a way that does not match a legal or moral standard, for example in order to spend less money or get more power: *Safety has clearly been compromised in the building's construction.*

**com·pro·mis·ing** /'kɑmprə,maɪzɪŋ/ *adj* proving that you have done something morally wrong, or making it seem like you have done so: *a compromising photograph*

**comp time** /'kɑmp ,taɪm/ *n* [U] vacation time that you are given instead of money because you have worked more hours than you should have

**com·pul·sion** /kəm'pʌlʃən/ *n* **1** a strong unreasonable desire to do something: *Drinking is a compulsion with her.* **2** [singular, U] a force or influence that makes someone do something: *Remember that you are under no compulsion to sign the agreement.* –see also COMPEL

**com·pul·sive** /kəm'pʌlsɪv/ *adj* very difficult to stop or control: *compulsive eating* –**compulsively** *adv*

**com·pul·so·ry** /kəm'pʌlsəri/ *adj* having to be done because it is a rule or law: *Attendance is compulsory in all classes.*

**com·punc·tion** /kəm'pʌŋkʃən/ *n* [U] **have/feel no compunction about** FORMAL to not feel guilty or sorry about something although other people may think that it is wrong: *I have no compunction about saying what I think.*

**com·pute** /kəm'pyut/ *v* [I,T] FORMAL to calculate an answer, total, result etc. –**computation** /,kɑmpyə'teɪʃən/ *n* [C,U]

**com·put·er** /kəm'pyutɚ/ *n* an electronic machine that stores information and uses sets of instructions called PROGRAMS to help you find, organize, or change the information: *a personal computer* | *We do all our work on computer.*

**com·put·er·ize** /kəm'pyutə,raɪz/ *v* [T] to use a computer to control the way something is done, to store information etc. –**computerization** /kəm,pyutərə'zeɪʃən/ *n* [U]

**computer lit·er·ate** /.,.. '.../ *adj* able to use a computer

**com·put·ing** /kəm'pyutɪŋ/ *n* [U] the use of computers as a job, in a business etc.

**com·rade** /'kɑmræd/ *n* FORMAL a friend, especially someone who shares difficult work or the same aims as you –**comradeship** *n* [U]

**con**[1] /kɑn/ *v* [T] INFORMAL to trick someone, either to take his/her money or to get him/her to do something: *That guy tried to con me out of $20.*

**con**[2] *n* **1** INFORMAL a trick to get someone's money or make someone do something: *The ads you see in the paper are just a con.* **2** SLANG ⇨ CONVICT[2]

**con art·ist** /'. ,../ *n* INFORMAL someone who tricks people in order to get money from them

**con·cave** /,kɑn'keɪv◂/ *adj* TECHNICAL curved inward like a bowl: *a concave lens* –opposite CONVEX

**con·ceal** /kən'sil/ *v* [T] FORMAL to hide something carefully: *She tried to conceal her emotions from Ted.* –**concealment** *n* [U]

**con·cede** /kən'sid/ *v* **1** [T] to admit that something is true although you wish that it were not true: *Even the critics conceded that the movie was a success.* **2** [I,T] to admit that you are not going to win a game, argument, battle etc.: *Hawkins conceded defeat in the leadership election.* **3** [T] to let someone have something although you do not want to: *The Lakers conceded 12 points in a row to the Suns.*

**con·ceit** /kən'sit/ *n* [U] an attitude that shows that you have too much pride in your abilities, appearance etc.

**con·ceit·ed** /kən'sitɪd/ *adj* behaving in a way that shows too much pride in your abilities, appearance etc.: *I don't want to seem conceited, but I know I'll win.*

**con·ceiv·a·ble** /kən'sivəbəl/ *adj* able to be believed or imagined: *It is conceivable that the experts are wrong.* –**conceivably** *adv* –opposite INCONCEIVABLE

**con·ceive** /kən'siv/ *v* **1** [T] to imagine a situation or what something is like: *It is impossible to conceive of the size of the universe.* **2** [T] to think of a new idea or plan: *It was Dr. Salk who conceived the idea of a polio vaccine.* **3** [I,T] to become PREGNANT

**con·cen·trate**[1] /'kɑnsən,treɪt/ *v* **1** [I] to think very carefully about something you are doing: *With all this noise, it's hard to concentrate.* **2** to be present in large numbers or amounts in a particular place: *Most of New Zealand's population is concentrated in the north island.* **3** [T] to make a liquid stronger by removing most of the water from it

**concentrate on** sth ↔ *phr v* [T] to give most of your attention to one thing: *I want to concentrate on my career for a while before I have kids.*

**con·cen·trate²** *n* [C,U] a substance or liquid that has been made stronger by removing most of the water from it: *orange juice concentrate*

**con·cen·trat·ed** /ˈkɑnsənˌtreɪtɪd/ *adj* **1** showing a lot of determination or effort: *He made a concentrated effort to raise his grades.* **2** a substance that is concentrated has had some of the liquid removed from it

**con·cen·tra·tion** /ˌkɑnsənˈtreɪʃən/ *n* **1** [U] the ability to think very carefully about something for a long time: *Mendez has amazing* **powers** *of* **concentration.** **2** [C,U] a large amount of something in a particular place: *Tests show high* **concentrations** *of chemicals in the water.*

**concentration camp** /..ˈ.. ˌ./ *n* a prison for enemy soldiers or for people who are considered dangerous during a war

**con·cen·tric** /kənˈsɛntrɪk/ *adj* TECHNICAL having the same center: *concentric circles*

**con·cept** /ˈkɑnsɛpt/ *n* an idea of how something is, or how something should be done: *Jerry* **has no concept of** *how difficult being a parent is.*

**con·cep·tion** /kənˈsɛpʃən/ *n* **1** an idea about something, or a basic understanding of something: *One common* **conception** *of democracy is that it means "government by the people."* **2** [U] the process by which a woman or female animal becomes PREGNANT, or the time when this happens

**con·cep·tu·al** /kənˈsɛptʃuəl/ *adj* FORMAL dealing with CONCEPTs, or based on them: *plans that are in the conceptual stage* —**conceptually** *adv*

**con·cern¹** /kənˈsɚn/ *n* **1** [C,U] a feeling of worry about something important, or the thing that worries you: *There is growing* **concern** **about** *the rise in drug-related crimes.* | *Your father's health is* **giving** *the doctors* **cause for concern.** **2** [C,U] something important that worries you or involves you: *The destruction of the rainforest is* **of concern to** *us all.* | *Our main* **concern** *is* **for** *the children's safety.* **3** [singular, U] a feeling of wanting someone to be happy and safe: *Anne's* **concern for** *her elderly mother* **4 to whom it may concern** used at the beginning of a formal letter when you do not know the person you are writing to

**concern²** *v* [T] **1** to affect someone or involve him/her: *What we're planning doesn't*

concern you. **2** to make someone feel worried or upset: *My daughter's problems at school concern me greatly.* **3** to be about something or someone: *Many of Woody Allen's movies concern life in New York.* **4 concern yourself** to become involved in something that interests or worries you: *You don't need to* **concern yourself with** *this, Jan.*

**con·cerned** /kənˈsɚnd/ *adj* **1** involved in something or affected by it: *It was a shock for* **all concerned.** (=everyone involved) | *Everyone* **concerned with** *the car industry will be interested.* **2** worried about something important: *We're* **concerned about** *the results of the test.* **3** believing that something is important: *Some people are more* **concerned with** *just making money.* **4 as far as** sth **is concerned** used in order to show which subject or thing you are talking about: *As far as money is concerned, the club is doing fairly well.* **5 as far as** sb **is concerned** used in order to show what someone's opinion on a subject is: *As far as I'm concerned, the whole idea is crazy.* —see usage note at NERVOUS

**con·cern·ing** /kənˈsɚnɪŋ/ *prep* FORMAL about, or relating to: *We have questions concerning the report.*

**con·cert** /ˈkɑnsɚt/ *n* **1** a performance given by musicians or singers: *a rock/jazz/orchestra concert* **2 in concert (with)** a) playing or singing at a concert: *Live, tonight, in concert, it's Madonna!* b) FORMAL done together with someone else: *police working in concert with local authorities*

**con·cert·ed** /kənˈsɚtɪd/ *adj* **a concerted effort/attempt** etc. something that is done by people working together in a determined way: *Courtland County officials have* **made a concerted effort** *to raise the standards of education.*

**con·cer·to** /kənˈtʃɛrtoʊ/ *n* a piece of CLASSICAL MUSIC, usually for one instrument and an ORCHESTRA

**con·ces·sion** /kənˈsɛʃən/ *n* **1** something that you let someone have in order to end an argument: *Neither side is willing to* **make concessions on/about** *the issue of pay.* **2** a special right given to someone by the government, an employer etc.: *tax concessions for married people* **3** the right to have a business in a particular place, especially in a place owned by someone else

**concession stand** /.ˈ.. ˌ./ *n* a small business that sells food, drinks, and other things at sports events, theaters etc.

**con·ci·erge** /kɑnˈsyɛrʒ/ *n* someone in a hotel whose job is to help guests with problems, give advice about local places to go etc.

**con·cil·i·a·tion** /kənˌsɪliˈeɪʃən/ *n* [U] FORMAL the process of trying to end an argument between people —**conciliate** /kənˈsɪliˌeɪt/ *v* [T]

**con·cil·i·a·to·ry** /kənˈsɪliəˌtɔri/ *adj* FORMAL intended to make someone stop being angry with you or with someone else: *a conciliatory remark*

**con·cise** /kənˈsaɪs/ *adj* short and clear, without using too many words: *a concise answer* —**concisely** *adv* —**conciseness** *n* [U]

**con·clude** /kənˈklud/ *v* **1** [T] to decide something after considering all the information you have: *Doctors have concluded that sunburn can lead to skin cancer.* **2** [T] to complete something that you have been doing: *The study was concluded last month.* **3** [I,T] to end a meeting, speech, piece of writing etc. by doing or saying one final thing: *The carnival concluded with a fireworks display.* **4** [T] to successfully finish something or agree on something: *This lecture concludes the course.* —**concluding** *adj*: *concluding remarks*

**con·clu·sion** /kənˈkluʒən/ *n* **1** something that you decide after considering all the information you have: *I've come to the conclusion that she's lying.* | *It's hard to draw any conclusions without more data.* | *Megan, you're jumping to conclusions.* (=deciding something is true without knowing all the facts) **2** the end or final part of something: *Your essay's fine, but the conclusion needs more work.* **3** **in conclusion** FORMAL used in speech or a piece of writing to show that you are about to finish —see also FOREGONE CONCLUSION

**con·clu·sive** /kənˈklusɪv/ *adj* showing without any doubt that something is true: *There is no conclusive evidence connecting him with the crime.* —**conclusively** *adv*

**con·coct** /kənˈkɑkt/ *v* [T] **1** to invent a story, plan, or excuse, especially in order to deceive someone: *She concocted a story about her mother being sick.* **2** to make something unusual by mixing different things together: *Lou concocts wonderful things in the kitchen.* —**concoction** *n*

**con·course** /ˈkɑŋkɔrs/ *n* a large hall or open place in an airport, train station etc.

**con·crete**[1] /kɑnˈkrit, ˈkɑŋkrit/ *adj* **1** made of CONCRETE: *a concrete floor* **2** clearly based on facts, not on beliefs or guesses: *We need concrete evidence to prove that he did it.* —**concretely** *adv*

**con·crete**[2] /ˈkɑŋkrit/ *n* a substance used for building that is made by mixing sand, water, small stones, and CEMENT

**con·cur** /kənˈkɚ/ *v* **-rred, -rring** [I] FORMAL to agree with someone or have the same opinion: *Dr. Hastings concurs with the decision of the medical board.* —**concurrence** *n* [U]

**con·cur·rent** /kənˈkɚənt, -ˈkʌrənt/ *adj* FORMAL **1** existing or happening at the same time: *In 1992, di Gesu's work was displayed in three concurrent art exhibitions.* **2** FORMAL in

agreement: *concurrent opinions* —**concurrently** *adv*

**con·cus·sion** /kənˈkʌʃən/ *n* [C,U] a small amount of damage to the brain that makes you become unconscious or feel sick, caused by hitting your head

**con·demn** /kənˈdɛm/ *v* [T] **1** to say very strongly that you do not approve of someone or something: *Plans to dump nuclear waste here have been condemned by local residents.* **2** to give a severe punishment to someone who is guilty of a crime: *a murderer who was condemned to death* **3** to force someone to live in an unpleasant way or to suffer: *The orphans were condemned to a life of poverty.* **4** to say officially that a building is not safe enough to be lived in or used

**con·dem·na·tion** /ˌkɑndəmˈneɪʃən/ *n* [C,U] an expression of very strong disapproval: *Condemnation of the plans came from across the community.*

**con·den·sa·tion** /ˌkɑndənˈseɪʃən/ *n* [U] small drops of water that appear when steam or hot air touches something that is cool, such as a window

**con·dense** /kənˈdɛns/ *v* **1** [T] to make a speech or piece of writing shorter by using fewer words to say the same thing **2** [I,T] if gas or hot air condenses, it becomes a liquid as it becomes cooler **3** [T] to make a liquid thicker by removing some of the water from it: *condensed soup*

**con·de·scend** /ˌkɑndɪˈsɛnd/ *v* [I] **1** OFTEN HUMOROUS to agree to do something even though you think that you should not have to do it: *Do you think you can condescend to helping your sister?* **2** **condescend to sb** to behave as if you are better or more important than someone else —**condescension** /ˌkɑndəˈsɛnʃən/ *n* [U]

**con·de·scend·ing** /ˌkɑndɪˈsɛndɪŋ/ *adj* showing that you think you are better or more important than other people: *I can't stand his condescending attitude!*

**con·di·ment** /ˈkɑndəmənt/ *n* FORMAL something that you add to food when you are eating it to make it taste better

**con·di·tion**[1] /kənˈdɪʃən/ *n* [C,U] **1** the particular state that someone or something is in: *I'm not buying the car until I see what condition it's in.* | *The VCR is still in pretty good condition.* **2** something that must happen or be done before something else can happen or be done: *a set of conditions for getting into college* | *Grandma sent some money for Steve on condition that* (=if) *he save it.* **3** the state of health of a person or animal: *Molly is in no condition to return to work.* (=too sick or upset to work) | *a bad heart condition* (=that has affected you for a long time) —see also CONDITIONS

**condition**[2] *v* [T] **1** to make a person or animal behave in a particular way by training him, her, or it over a period of time: *Pavlov **conditioned** the dogs **to** expect food at the sound of a bell.* **2** to make your hair easy to comb by putting a special liquid on it

**con·di·tion·al** /kən'dɪʃənəl/ *adj* **1** if an offer, agreement etc. is conditional, it will only be done if something else happens: *Our buying the house is **conditional on** our loan approval.* **2** TECHNICAL a conditional sentence is one that usually begins with "if" or "unless," and states something that must be true or must happen before something else can be true or happen

**con·di·tion·er** /kən'dɪʃənə/ *n* a special liquid that you put on your hair after washing it to make it easier to comb

**con·di·tion·ing** /kən'dɪʃənɪŋ/ *n* [U] the process by which people or animals learn to behave in a particular way: *social conditioning*

**con·di·tions** /kən'dɪʃənz/ [plural] **1** the situation in which people live or work, especially the physical things that affect them: *Poor **living/working conditions** are part of their daily lives.* **2** the weather at a particular time: *Icy conditions on the roads are making driving dangerous.*

**con·do** /'kɑndoʊ/ *n* INFORMAL ⇨ CONDOMINIUM

**con·do·lence** /kən'doʊləns/ *n* [C usually plural, U] sympathy for someone when something very bad has happened: *My **condolences on** your mother's death.*

**con·dom** /'kɑndəm/ *n* a thin piece of rubber that a man wears over his PENIS during sex to stop a woman becoming PREGNANT, or to protect against disease

**con·do·min·i·um** /ˌkɑndə'mɪniəm/ *n* a building that consists of separate apartments, each of which is owned by the people living in it, or one of these apartments

**con·done** /kən'doʊn/ *v* [T] to approve of behavior that most people think is wrong: *I cannot condone the use of violence.*

**con·du·cive** /kən'dusɪv/ *adj* FORMAL **be conducive to** to provide conditions that make it easier to do something: *The sunny climate is conducive to outdoor activities.*

**con·duct¹** /kən'dʌkt/ *v* **1** [T] to do something in order to find out or prove something: *Dr. Hamilton is **conducting an experiment** for the class.* **2** [I,T] to stand in front of a group of musicians or singers and direct their playing or singing: *the Boston Pops Orchestra, **conducted** by John Williams.* **3** [T] if something conducts electricity or heat, it allows the electricity or heat to travel along or through it **4 conduct yourself** FORMAL to behave in a particular way: *He conducted himself well in the job interview.* **5** [T] to show someone a place as part of an official TOUR: *A guide will conduct us through the museum.*

**con·duct²** /'kɑndʌkt, -dəkt/ *n* [U] FORMAL **1** the way someone behaves **2** the way a bu-

siness or activity is organized and done: *The mayor was not satisfied with the conduct of the meeting.*

**con·duc·tor** /kən'dʌktə/ *n* **1** someone who CONDUCTs a group of musicians or singers **2** someone who is in charge of a train or the workers on it

cone

traffic cone     ice cream cone     pine cone

**cone** /koʊn/ *n* **1** a hollow or solid object with a round base and a point at the top: *an orange traffic cone* **2** ⇨ ICE CREAM CONE **3** the hard brown woody fruit of a PINE or FIR tree

**con·fed·er·a·cy** /kən'fɛdərəsi/ *n* **1 the Confederacy** the southern states that fought against northern states in the American Civil War **2** ⇨ CONFEDERATION **–confederate** /kən'fɛdərɪt/ *adj*

**con·fed·er·ate** /kən'fɛdərɪt/ *n* a soldier in the Confederacy

**con·fed·e·ra·tion** /kənˌfɛdə'reɪʃən/ *n* a group of people, political parties, or organizations that have united in order to achieve an aim: *a confederation of 47 insurance agencies* **–confederate** /kən'fɛdəˌreɪt/ *v* [I,T]

**con·fer** /kən'fə/ *v* **-rred, -rring 1** [I] to discuss something with other people so everyone can give his/her opinion: *The lawyers are **conferring on** this matter.* **2 confer a degree/honor etc. on sb** to give someone a degree etc. in order to reward him/her

**con·fer·ence** /'kɑnfrəns/ *n* [C,U] **1** a large formal meeting in which people exchange ideas about business, politics etc., especially for several days: *a sales conference | a conference room/center* **2** a private meeting in which a few people discuss something: *Ms. Chen is **in conference** at the moment.*

**conference call** /'.. ./ *n* a telephone conversation in which several people in different places can all talk to each other

**con·fess** /kən'fɛs/ *v* [I,T] **1** to admit that you have done something wrong or illegal: *It didn't take long for her to confess. | Jared wouldn't **confess to** the beating.* **2** to admit something that you feel embarrassed about: *Lyn **confessed that** she had fallen asleep in class.* **3** to tell a priest or God about the wrong things you have done **–confessed** *adj*

**con·fes·sion** /kən'fɛʃən/ *n* **1** a statement that you have done something wrong or illegal:

*He made a full **confession** at the police station.*
**2** [C,U] the act of CONFESSing to a priest

**con·fet·ti** /kənˈfɛti/ *n* [U] small pieces of colored paper thrown into the air at a wedding, party etc.

**con·fi·dant, confidante** /ˈkɑnfəˌdɑnt/ *n* someone to whom you tell secrets or personal information

**con·fide** /kənˈfaɪd/ *v* [T] to tell a secret to someone you trust: *Joel **confided to** her **that** he didn't want to study medicine.*

**confide in** sb *phr v* [T] to tell someone you trust about something that is very private: *I don't trust her enough to **confide in** her.*

**con·fi·dence** /ˈkɑnfədəns/ *n* **1** [U] belief in your own or someone else's ability to do things well: *She **has no confidence in** my driving ability.*| *Living in another country **gave** me more **confidence**.* **2** [U] the feeling that something is true, or that it will produce good results: *Young people today **have no confidence in** the future.*| *I **have confidence (that)** it will work.* **3** [U] a feeling of trust that someone will not tell your secrets to other people: *It took a long time to **gain** his **confidence**. (=make him feel he could trust me)* **4** a secret or a piece of information that is personal

**con·fi·dent** /ˈkɑnfədənt/ *adj* **1** sure that you can do something well: *We won't continue until you feel **confident about** using the equipment.*| *She seems very **confident of** winning.* ✗ DON'T SAY "She seems very confident of herself." ✗ —compare SELF-CONFIDENT **2** very sure that something is going to happen: *I'm **confident (that)** he'll help us out.* —**confidently** *adv*

**con·fi·den·tial** /ˌkɑnfəˈdɛnʃəl/ *adj* intended to be kept secret: *a confidential report* —**confidentially** *adv*

**con·fig·u·ra·tion** /kənˌfɪgyəˈreɪʃən/ *n* the way that the things in a place or the parts of something are arranged: *a table arranged in a U-shaped configuration*

**con·fine** /kənˈfaɪn/ *v* [T] **1** to happen in only one place or time, or affect only one group of people: *The fire was **confined to** one building.*| *This problem is not **confined to** the western world.* **2** to have to stay in a place, especially because you are ill: *Rachel is **confined to** her bed.* **3** to keep someone or something within the limits of a particular subject or activity: *Try to **confine yourself to** spending $120 a week.* **4** to make someone stay in a place s/he cannot leave, such as a prison

**con·fined** /kənˈfaɪnd/ *adj* a confined space or area is very small

**con·fine·ment** /kənˈfaɪnmənt/ *n* [U] the act of making someone stay in a room or area, or the state of being there: *Ellie hated the confinement of living in an apartment.* —see also SOLITARY CONFINEMENT

**con·fines** /ˈkɑnfaɪnz/ *n* [plural] the walls, limits or borders of something: *His son has only seen him **within the confines of** the prison.*

**con·firm** /kənˈfɚm/ *v* [T] **1** to say or prove that something is definitely true: *Dr. Martin confirmed the diagnosis of cancer.*| *Can you **confirm that** she really was there?* **2** to tell someone that a possible plan, arrangement etc. is now definite: *Please confirm your reservations 72 hours in advance.*

**con·fir·ma·tion** /ˌkɑnfɚˈmeɪʃən/ *n* [C,U] a statement or letter that says that something is definitely true, or the act of saying this: *We're waiting for confirmation of the report.*

**con·firmed** /kənˈfɚmd/ *adj* **a confirmed bachelor/alcoholic etc.** someone who seems completely happy with his/her way of life: *Charlie was a confirmed bachelor, until he met Helen.*

**con·fis·cate** /ˈkɑnfəˌskeɪt/ *v* [T] to officially take someone's property away from him/her, usually as a punishment: *The police confiscated his gun when they arrested him.* —**confiscation** /ˌkɑnfəˈskeɪʃən/ *n* [C,U]

**con·flict¹** /ˈkɑnˌflɪkt/ *n* [C,U] **1** disagreement between people, groups, countries etc.: *The two groups have been **in conflict with** each other for years.*| *a **conflict between** father and son*| ***conflicts over** who owns the land* **2** a situation in which you have to choose between opposing things: *In a **conflict between** work and family, I would always choose my family.* **3** a war or fight in which weapons are used

**con·flict²** /kənˈflɪkt/ *v* [I] if two ideas, beliefs, opinions etc. conflict, they cannot both be true: *What she just said **conflicts with** what she said before.*| *We have heard many **conflicting opinions** on the subject.*

**conflict of in·terest** /ˌ.. . ˈ../ *n* a situation in which you cannot legally be involved in one business activity, because you have connections with another business that would gain an unfair advantage from your involvement

**con·form** /kənˈfɔrm/ *v* [I] **1** to behave in the way that most people do: *There's always pressure on kids to conform.* **2** to obey or follow an established rule, pattern, etc.: *Seatbelts must **conform to** safety standards.* —**conformity** *n* [U]

**con·form·ist** /kənˈfɔrmɪst/ *n* someone who behaves or thinks too much like everyone else —opposite NONCONFORMIST

**con·found** /kənˈfaʊnd/ *v* [T] to be impossible to explain, often in a way that worries or surprises you: *Her illness confounded the doctors.*

**con·front** /kənˈfrʌnt/ *v* [T] **1** to try to make someone admit s/he has done something wrong: *I'm afraid to **confront** her **about** her drinking.* **2** to have to deal with something difficult or unpleasant, usually in a brave way: *Sooner or later you'll have to confront your problems.*

**3** to behave in a threatening way toward someone: *Security guards confronted us at the door.*

**con·fron·ta·tion** /ˌkɑnfrən'teɪʃən/ *n* [C,U] a situation in which there is a lot of angry disagreement: *Stan doesn't like confrontations.*

**con·fuse** /kən'fyuz/ *v* [T] **1** to make someone feel unable to think clearly or understand something: *His directions really confused me.* **2** to think wrongly that one person, thing, or idea is really someone or something else: *It's easy to confuse Sue with her sister. They look so much alike.*

**con·fused** /kən'fyuzd/ *adj* **1** unable to understand something clearly: *I'm totally confused.* | *If you're confused about anything, call me.* **2** not clear or not easy to understand: *a confused answer* | *confused instructions*

**con·fus·ing** /kən'fyuzɪŋ/ *adj* difficult to understand because there is no clear order or pattern: *The diagram is really confusing.*

**con·fu·sion** /kən'fyuʒən/ *n* **1** [C,U] a state of not understanding what is happening or what something means: *There's a lot of confusion about/over the new rules.* **2** [U] a situation in which there is a lot of activity that is difficult to understand or control: *After the explosion the airport was a scene of total confusion.*

**con·geal** /kən'dʒil/ *v* [I] if a liquid such as blood congeals, it becomes thick or solid

**con·ge·nial** /kən'dʒinyəl/ *adj* FORMAL pleasant in a comfortable and relaxed way: *a congenial host*

**con·gen·i·tal** /kən'dʒɛnəṭl/ *adj* TECHNICAL affecting someone from the time s/he is born: *a congenital heart problem*

**con·gest·ed** /kən'dʒɛstɪd/ *adj* **1** too full or blocked because of too many vehicles or people: *the problem of congested freeways* **2** a congested nose, chest etc. is filled with thick liquid that does not flow easily −**congestion** /kən'dʒɛstʃən/ *n* [U]

**con·glom·er·ate** /kən'glɑmərɪt/ *n* **1** a large company made up of many different smaller companies **2** a substance, such as rock, made up of many small pieces held together

**con·glom·er·a·tion** /kənˌglɑmə'reɪʃən/ *n* a group of many different things gathered together

**con·grats** /kən'græts/ *interjection* ⇨ CONGRATULATIONS

**con·grat·u·late** /kən'grætʃəˌleɪt/ *v* [T] to tell someone that you are happy because s/he has achieved something, or because something good has happened to him/her: *I want to congratulate you on a fine achievement.* −**congratulatory** /kən'grætʃələˌtɔri/ *adj*

**con·grat·u·la·tions** /kənˌgrætʃə'leɪʃənz/ *n* [plural] ESPECIALLY SPOKEN used in order to CONGRATULATE someone: *You won? Congratulations!* | *Congratulations on your engagement!*

**con·gre·gate** /'kɑŋgrəˌgeɪt/ *v* [I] to come together in a group: *Ducks congregate here in the fall.*

**con·gre·ga·tion** /ˌkɑŋgrə'geɪʃən/ *n* a group of people gathered in a church for a religious service, or the people who usually go to a particular church

**Con·gre·ga·tion·al** /ˌkɑŋgrə'geɪʃənl/ *adj* relating to a Protestant church in which each CONGREGATION makes its own decisions −**Congregationalist** *n, adj*

**con·gress** /'kɑŋgrɪs/ *n* **1 Congress** the group of people elected to make laws for the US, consisting of the Senate and the House of Representatives: *The bill has been approved by both houses of Congress.* | *an act of Congress* **2** a meeting of representatives of different groups, countries, etc. to exchange information and make decisions −**congressional** /kən'grɛʃənl/ *adj*

**con·gress·man** /'kɑŋgrɪsmən/, **con·gress·wom·an** /'kɑŋgrɪsˌwʊmən/ *n* someone who is elected to be in CONGRESS

**con·i·cal** /'kɑnɪkəl/ **con·ic** /'kɑnɪk/ *adj* shaped like a CONE, or relating to cones

**con·i·fer** /'kɑnəfə/ *n* any tree that makes CONES (=hard woody brown fruit) −**coniferous** /kə'nɪfərəs, koʊ–/ *adj*

**con·jec·ture** /kən'dʒɛktʃə/ *n* [C,U] FORMAL the act of guessing about things when you do not have enough information: *The report is based purely on conjecture.* −**conjecture** *v* [I,T]

**con·ju·gal** /'kɑndʒəgəl/ *adj* FORMAL relating to marriage or married people

**con·ju·gate** /'kɑndʒəˌgeɪt/ *v* [T] TECHNICAL to give all the parts of a verb in a fixed order: *Try conjugating these irregular verbs.* −**conjugation** /ˌkɑndʒə'geɪʃən/ *n* [C,U]

**con·junc·tion** /kən'dʒʌŋkʃən/ *n* **1 in conjunction with** working, happening, or being used with someone or something else: *There are worksheets for use in conjunction with the training video.* **2** TECHNICAL in grammar, a word such as "but," "and," or "while," that connects parts of sentences, phrases, or CLAUSES

**con·jure** /'kɑndʒə/ *v* [I,T] to make something appear using magic −**conjurer, conjuror** *n*
  **conjure sth** ↔ **up** *phr v* [T] **1** make an image, idea, memory etc. very clear and strong in someone's mind: *Maria conjured up the whole Mediterranean for us in her talk.* **2** to make something appear as if by magic: *Pete can conjure up a meal out of whatever is in the fridge.*

**con·man** /'kɑnˌmæn/ *n* INFORMAL someone who gets money or valuable things from people by tricking them

**con·nect** /kə'nɛkt/ *v* **1** [I,T] to attach two or more things together: *Next, you have to connect this bolt to the base.* | *I can't see how these hoses connect.* −*opposite* DISCONNECT **2** to realize that two facts, events, or people have a

relationship: *I never* **connected** *her* **with** *Sam.*
**3** [T] to attach something to a supply of electricity, gas, etc.: *Is the TV connected yet?*
−opposite DISCONNECT **4** [I] to be planned so that passengers can continue their trip on a different plane, train, bus, etc.: *a connecting flight to Omaha* **5** [T] to attach telephone lines so that people can speak −opposite DISCONNECT **6** [I] if people connect, they feel that they like and understand each other: *I really felt I* **connected with** *Jim's parents.*

**con·nect·ed** /kə'nɛktɪd/ *adj* **1** joined to or relating to something else: *Kai's problems are partly* **connected with** *drug abuse.* −opposite UNCONNECTED **2** **well-connected** having important or powerful friends or relatives: *a wealthy and well-connected lawyer*

**con·nec·tion** /kə'nɛkʃən/ *n* **1** [C,U] a relationship between things, people, ideas etc.: *What's the* **connection between** *the two events?* | *This has no* **connection with** *our conversation.* **2** [U] the joining together of two or more things, especially by electricity, telephone, computer etc.: *There must be a* **loose connection** *- I'm not getting any power.* **3** a plane, bus, or train that leaves at a time that allows passengers from an earlier plane, bus, or train to use it to continue their trip: *I barely* **made/ missed** *the* **connection** (=did or did not get the flight, train etc.) *to Boston.* **4** **in connection with** concerning something: *Police are questioning a man in connection with the crime.*

**con·nec·tions** /kə'nɛkʃənz/ *n* [plural] people who can help you because they have power: *Ramsey* **has connections** (=knows powerful people)*; maybe he can help you.*

**con·nive** /kə'naɪv/ *v* [I] to secretly work to achieve something wrong or illegal, or to allow something illegal to happen: *She's* **conniving with** *Tony* **to** *get Grandma's money.* −**connivance** *n* [C,U]

**con·nois·seur** /ˌkɑnə'sɚ, -'sʊɚ/ *n* someone who knows a lot about something such as art, good food, music etc.: *a true* **connoisseur of** *fine wines*

**con·no·ta·tion** /ˌkɑnə'teɪʃən/ *n* an idea or a feeling that a word makes you think of, rather than the actual meaning of the word: *a negative/positive connotation* −**connote** /kə-'noʊt/ *v* [T]

**con·quer** /'kɑŋkɚ/ *v* **1** [I,T] to win control of a land or country by attacking an enemy or fighting in a war: *Egypt was conquered by the Ottoman Empire in 1517.* **2** [T] to gain control over a feeling or a problem that you have: *I didn't think I'd ever conquer my fear of heights .* −**conqueror** *n*

**con·quest** /'kɑŋkwɛst/ *n* **1** [singular, U] the act of defeating or controlling a group of people: *the Spanish conquest of the Incas and the Aztecs* **2** HUMOROUS someone who is

persuaded to love or have sex with someone: *Jane was just another of his many conquests.*

**con·science** /'kɑnʃəns/ *n* [U] **1** the set of feelings that tell you whether what you are doing is morally right or wrong: *Pete acts like he* **has a guilty conscience**. (=as if he has done something wrong) | *At least my* **conscience** *is* **clear**. (=I know I have done nothing wrong) **2** **on sb's conscience** making someone feel guilty all the time for doing or not doing something: *Tim's suicide is always going to be on his mother's conscience.*

**con·sci·en·tious** /ˌkɑnʃi'ɛnʃəs/ *adj* showing a lot of care and attention: *a conscientious worker*

**con·scious** /'kɑnʃəs/ *adj* **1** noticing or realizing something; AWARE: *Jodie was very* **conscious of** *the fact that he was watching her.* **2** awake and able to understand what is happening around you: *Owen was still conscious when they arrived at the hospital.* **3** intended or planned: *Jenny* **made** *a* **conscious effort/ decision to** *smoke less.* −**consciously** *adv* −opposite UNCONSCIOUS[1]

**con·scious·ness** /'kɑnʃəsnɪs/ *n* [U] **1** the condition of being awake and understanding what is happening around you: *Charlie fell down the stairs and* **lost consciousness**. **2** the understanding that you or a group of people have about a situation: *a* **consciousness raising** *effort* (=effort to make people understand and care about a problem)

**cons·cript** /kən'skrɪpt/ *v* [T] FORMAL ⇨ DRAFT[2] −**conscription** /kən'skrɪpʃən/ *n* [U]

**con·se·crate** /'kɑnsə,kreɪt/ *v* [T] to have a special ceremony that makes a particular place or building holy: *consecrating a church*

**con·sec·u·tive** /kən'sɛkyətɪv/ *adj* consecutive numbers or periods of time happen one after the other: *It rained for three consecutive days.* −**consecutively** *adv*

**con·sen·sus** /kən'sɛnsəs/ *n* [singular, U] an agreement that everyone in a group reaches: *The consensus of opinion is that the military is not to blame.*

**con·sent**[1] /kən'sɛnt/ *n* [U] permission to do something: *We need your parents' written consent before you can join.*

**consent**[2] *v* [I] FORMAL to give your permission for something to happen: *Father will never* **consent to** *Jenny's marrying Tom.*

**con·se·quence** /'kɑnsə,kwɛns, -kwəns/ *n* **1** something that happens as a result of a particular action: *Think about the consequences if you drop out of college.* | *Much has happened* **as a consequence of** *my meeting with the board.* **2** FORMAL importance: *a matter* **of little/ no consequence**

**con·se·quent·ly** /'kɑnsə,kwɛntli, -kwənt-/ *adv* as a result: *Reports aren't trusted; conse-*

*quently, managers are refusing to believe the budget reports.*

**con·ser·va·tion** /ˌkɑnsɚ'veɪʃən/ *n* [U] **1** the protection of natural things such as wild animals, forests, or beaches from being harmed or destroyed **2** the controlled use of a limited amount of water, gas, electricity etc. to prevent the supply from being wasted **–conservationist** *n*

**con·serv·a·tism** /kən'sɚvə,tɪzəm/ *n* [U] the belief that any changes to the way things are done must happen slowly and have very good reasons: *political conservatism*

**con·serv·a·tive** /kən'sɚvətɪv/ *adj* **1** preferring to continue doing things the way they are being done or have been proven to work, rather than risking changes: *a very conservative attitude to education | a politically conservative family* **2** not very modern in style, taste etc.; traditional: *a conservative business suit* **3 a conservative estimate** a guess that is deliberately lower than the possible amount **–conservatively** *adv* **–conservative** *n*

**con·serv·a·tor** /kən'sɚvətɚ/ *n* LAW someone who is legally responsible for the property of a person who cannot take care of it himself/herself

**con·serv·a·to·ry** /kən'sɚvə,tɔri/ *n* **1** a school where students are trained in music or acting **2** ⇨ GREENHOUSE

**con·serve** /kən'sɚv/ *v* [T] to prevent something from being wasted, damaged, or destroyed: *Conserve water: fix any leaking pipes and faucets.*

**con·sid·er** /kən'sɪdɚ/ *v* [I,T] to think about something very carefully: *Has John ever considered applying for a loan?* ✗ DON'T SAY "considered to apply" ✗ **1** [T] to remember particular facts or details when making a judgment or decision about something: *If you consider how hard she studied, she really should have gotten higher grades.* **2** [T] to think of someone or something in a particular way: *Mrs. Greenwood was considered to be an excellent teacher. | We consider it important to get the Director's advice on this. | Greg should consider himself lucky* (=be glad) *he wasn't badly hurt.* **3** [T] to think about someone or his/her feelings, and try to avoid upsetting him/her: *It's all right for you, but have you considered the children?*

**con·sid·er·a·ble** /kən'sɪdərəbəl/ *adj* large enough to be noticeable or to have noticeable effects: *A considerable amount of time and money was spent on the project.* **–considerably** *adv: It's considerably colder tonight.*

**con·sid·er·ate** /kən'sɪdərɪt/ *adj* always thinking and caring about other people's feelings, wants, or needs etc.: *You really should be more considerate of your neighbors.* **–considerately** *adj* **–opposite** INCONSIDERATE

**con·sid·er·a·tion** /kənˌsɪdə'reɪʃən/ *n* **1** a particular fact or detail that you need to think about, especially when making a decision: *There are financial considerations to remember.* **2** [U] the quality of thinking and caring about other people's feelings, wants, or needs etc.: *Show a little consideration for the lady's feelings!* **3** [U] FORMAL careful thought and attention: *After further consideration, we decided not to sue.* **4 take sth into consideration** to remember a particular fact or detail when making a decision or judgment: *Of course, we'll take into consideration the fact that you were sick.*

**con·sid·ered** /kən'sɪdɚd/ *adj* **1 considered opinion/judgment** an opinion based on careful thought **2 all things considered** after thinking about all the facts: *All things considered, I think the meeting went pretty well.*

**con·sid·er·ing** /kən'sɪdərɪŋ/ *prep conjunction* used before stating a fact that you know has had an effect on a particular situation: *Considering we missed the bus, we're actually not too late.*

**con·sign** /kən'saɪn/ *v* [T] FORMAL **consign sb/sth to sth** *phr v* [T] to decide that someone or something is no longer important enough to pay attention to: *I'm not ready to be consigned to an old folks' home yet!*

**con·sign·ment** /kən'saɪnmənt/ *n* **1** a quantity of goods that is sent to someone in order to be sold **2 on consignment** goods that are on consignment are being sold by a store owner for someone else, for a share of the profit

**con·sist** /kən'sɪst/ *v* **consist of** sth *phr v* [T] to be made of or contain a number of different things: *The show at the Mexican Museum consists of over 30 paintings. | a sauce consisting of cream, onions, and herbs* **–see usage note at** COMPRISE

**con·sist·en·cy** /kən'sɪstənsi/ *n* **1** the quality of always being the same, or of always behaving in an expected way: *There's no consistency in the way they apply the rules.* **–opposite** INCONSISTENCY **2** [C,U] how thick or firm a substance is: *a dessert with a nice creamy consistency*

**con·sist·ent** /kən'sɪstənt/ *adj* **1** always happening in the same way or having the same attitudes, quality etc.: *I've tried to be consistent in applying the rules.* **2 be consistent with** to say the same thing or follow the same principles as something else: *His story is not consistent with the facts.* **–consistently** *adv: consistently high sales* **–opposite** INCONSISTENT

**con·so·la·tion** /ˌkɑnsə'leɪʃən/ *n* [C,U] someone or something that makes you feel better when you are sad or disappointed: *They were still together, and at least that was one consolation.*

**con·sole** /kən'soʊl/ v [T] to help someone who is sad or disappointed to feel better: *No one could console her when her first child died.* | *Danny consoled himself with the thought that Matt couldn't go either.*

**con·sol·i·date** /kən'sɑlə,deɪt/ v [I,T] **1** to combine two or more things such as organizations, duties, jobs, or large amounts of money to form a single thing that is more effective: *By consolidating their resources they could afford to buy new businesses.* **2** to make your power or level of success stronger so that it will continue: *Advertising helped them consolidate their leading position in Europe.* –**consolidation** /kən,sɑlə'deɪʃən/ n [C,U]

**con·som·mé** /,kɑnsə'meɪ/ n [U] a thin clear meat soup

**con·so·nant** /'kɑnsənənt/ n TECHNICAL any letter of the English alphabet except a, e, i, o, and u –compare VOWEL

**con·sort** /kən'sɔrt/ v FORMAL
**consort with** sb *phr v* [T] to spend time with a person or group that is morally bad

**con·sor·ti·um** /kən'sɔrʃiəm, -ṭiəm/ n a combination of several companies, organizations etc. working together: *a consortium of banks*

**con·spic·u·ous** /kən'spɪkyuəs/ adj very easy to notice because of being different: *There's still a very conspicuous burn mark on the seat.* –**conspicuously** adv –opposite INCONSPICUOUS

**con·spir·a·cy** /kən'spɪrəsi/ n [C,U] a secret plan made by two or more people to do something harmful or illegal

**con·spir·a·tor** /kən'spɪrəṭɚ/ n someone who is part of a group that secretly plans something harmful or illegal –**conspiratorial** /kən,spɪrə'tɔriəl/ adj

**con·spire** /kən'spaɪɚ/ v [I] **1** to secretly plan with other people to do something harmful or illegal: *a company conspiring with local stores to fix prices* **2** FORMAL to happen at the same time and cause a bad result: *Events conspired to ensure he lost the election.*

**con·stant** /'kɑnstənt/ adj **1** happening regularly or all the time: *The children must be kept under constant supervision.* **2** staying the same for a period of time: *driving at a constant speed* –**constancy** n [singular, U]

**con·stant·ly** /'kɑnstəntˉli/ adv always or regularly: *Marla is constantly on the phone!*

**con·stel·la·tion** /,kɑnstə'leɪʃən/ n a group of stars that forms a particular pattern and has a name

**con·ster·na·tion** /,kɑnstɚ'neɪʃən/ n [U] a feeling of shock or worry that makes it difficult for you to decide what to do

**con·sti·pa·tion** /,kɑnstə'peɪʃən/ n [U] the condition of someone being unable to empty his/her BOWELS –**constipated** /'kɑnstə,peɪṭɪd/ adj

**con·stit·u·en·cy** /kən'stɪtʃuənsi/ n an area of the country that has one or more elected officials, or all the people who live and vote there

**con·stit·u·ent** /kən'stɪtʃuənt/ n **1** someone who votes and lives in a particular area represented by one or more elected officials **2** one of the parts that forms something: *The FBI has found the constituents of a bomb inside the warehouse* –**constituent** adj

**con·sti·tute** /'kɑnstə,tut/ v [linking verb] FORMAL **1** if several parts constitute something, they form it together: *Students constituted the majority of the people in the bar.* **2** to be considered to be something: *According to Marx, money "constitutes true power."*

**con·sti·tu·tion** /,kɑnstə'tuʃən/ n **1** also **Constitution** a set of laws and principles that describes the power and the purpose of a particular government, organization etc.: *the Constitution of the United States* **2** [singular] the ability of your body to fight disease and illness: *a boy with a strong/weak constitution*

**con·sti·tu·tion·al** /,kɑnstə'tuʃənəl/ adj **1** officially allowed or restricted by the set of rules that a government or organization has: *a constitutional right to privacy* –opposite UNCONSTITUTIONAL **2** relating to a CONSTITUTION: *a constitutional amendment* (=change to the original set of laws) **3** relating to someone's health: *a constitutional weakness*

**con·strain** /kən'streɪn/ v [T] to limit what someone or something can do or become, by laws, rules, or by force: *They're constrained to work within very strict rules.*

**con·strained** /kən'streɪnd/ adj **1** prevented from developing, improving, or doing what you really want: *Victor felt more and more constrained by his father's firm.* **2** a constrained smile or manner seems too controlled and is not natural –opposite UNCONSTRAINED

**con·straint** /kən'streɪnt/ n something that restricts what you are doing: *working under time/ budget constraints*

**con·strict** /kən'strɪkt/ v [T] to make something smaller, tighter, or narrower: *Anna felt the tears coming, her throat constricting.* –**constriction** /kən'strɪkʃən/ n [C,U]: *constriction of the arteries*

**con·struct** /kən'strʌkt/ v [T] **1** to build something large such as a building, bridge etc.: *Right now they're constructing another runway.* **2** to join words, ideas etc. together to make a sentence, argument, or system: *Boyce has constructed a new theory of management.*

**con·struc·tion** /kən'strʌkʃən/ n [U] the process or method of building something large such as a house, road etc.: *Several new offices are under construction.* (=being built) | *a construction worker* –compare DESTRUCTION

**construction pa·per** /.'.. ,../ n [U] a thick

colored paper that is used especially by children at school

**con·struc·tive** /kən'strʌktɪv/ *adj* intended to be helpful, or likely to produce good results: *I'm always glad to hear constructive criticism.*

**con·strue** /kən'stru/ *v* [T] to understand something in a particular way: *What you think is friendly behavior might be construed as flirting.* −opposite MISCONSTRUE

**con·sul** /'kɑnsəl/ *n* an official who lives in a foreign city and whose job is to help citizens of his/her own country who also live or work there −**consular** *adj*

**con·sul·ate** /'kɑnsəlɪt/ *n* the official building where a CONSUL lives and works

**con·sult** /kən'sʌlt/ *v* [T] to ask or look for advice, information, etc. from someone or something that should have the answers: *Consult your physician if your symptoms persist.*

**consult with** sb *phr v* [T] to ask for someone's permission to do something before making a decision: *You may want to consult with your lawyer first.*

**con·sul·tan·cy** /kən'sʌltənsi/ *n* a company that gives advice and training in a particular area of business to people in other companies

**con·sult·ant** /kən'sʌltənt/ *n* someone with a lot of experience in a particular area of business whose job is to give advice about it· *a marketing consultant*

**con·sul·ta·tion** /ˌkɑnsəl'teɪʃən/ *n* [C,U]
**1** a discussion in which people who are affected by a decision can say what they think should be done: *The changes were made completely without consultation.* **2** a meeting in which you get advice from a professional, or the advice s/he gives: *The school counselor is always available for consultation.*

**con·sume** /kən'sum/ *v* [T] **1** to completely use time, energy, goods etc.: *His work seems to consume all his time these days.* **2** to eat or

drink something: *Americans in general consume a lot of beef.* **3 be consumed with passion/guilt/rage etc.** to have a very strong feeling that you cannot ignore **4** if a fire consumes something, it completely destroys it

**con·sum·er** /kən'sumɚ/ *n* **1** someone who buys or uses goods and services: *We received many calls from consumers saying they liked the old smell better.* **2** [singular] all the people who buy goods and services, considered as a group: *Our job is to make sure food is safe before it reaches the consumer.* | *consumer products* −compare CUSTOMER, PRODUCER

**con·sum·er·ism** /kən'sumə,rɪzəm/ *n* [U] the idea or belief that buying and selling things is the most important activity a person or society can do

**con·sum·mate¹** /'kɑnsəmɪt/ *adj* very skillful, or without any faults or weaknesses: *a consummate politician*

**con·sum·mate²** /'kɑnsə,meɪt/ *v* [T] FORMAL
**1** to make a marriage or a relationship complete by having sex **2** to make something such as an agreement complete −**consummation** /ˌkɑnsə'meɪʃən/ *n* [U]

**con·sump·tion** /kən'sʌmpʃən/ *n* [U] **1** the amount of electricity, gas etc. that is used: *We intend to reduce water consumption by up to 30% a year.* **2** FORMAL the act of eating or drinking: *The consumption of alcohol is not permitted on these premises.*

**con·tact¹** /'kɑntækt/ *n* **1** [U] communication with a person, organization, country etc.: *Have you kept/stayed in contact with any of your school friends?* | *We don't have much contact with other departments.* **2** [U] the state of touching or being close to someone or something: *Kids come in contact with all kinds of germs at school.* **3** someone you know who may be able to help you or give you advice: *I've got a few contacts in the movie industry.*

**container**

pack of cigarettes

packet of seeds

box of chocolates

carton of milk

tube of toothpaste

jar

bottle

can of soup

gas can

crate

pitcher

jug

pot

**4** ⇨ CONTACT LENS **5** an electrical part that completes a CIRCUIT when it touches another part

**contact²** *v* [T] to telephone or write to someone: *I've been trying to contact you for the past three days!* ✗ DON'T SAY "I've been trying to contact with you." ✗

**contact lens** /'.. ,., ,.. './ *n* a small round piece of plastic you put on your eye to help you see clearly —see picture at LENS

**con·ta·gious** /kən'teɪdʒəs/ *adj* **1** a disease that is contagious can be passed from person to person by touch or through the air **2** having a disease like this **3** a feeling, attitude, action etc. that is contagious is quickly felt or done by other people: *Jeannie's laughter was contagious.*

**con·tain** /kən'teɪn/ *v* [T] **1** to have something inside, or have something as a part: *We also found a wallet containing $43.72.* | *a report that contained some shocking information* **2** to control the emotions you feel: *Greg was so excited he could hardly contain himself.*

**con·tain·er** /kən'teɪnɚ/ *n* something such as a box, a bowl, a bottle etc. that can be filled with something: *an eight-gallon container*

**con·tain·ment** /kən'teɪnmənt/ *n* [U] the act of keeping something controlled, such as the cost of a plan or the power of an unfriendly country

**con·tam·i·nate** /kən'tæmə,neɪt/ *v* [T] **1** to spoil something by adding a dangerous or poisonous substance to it: *needles that have been contaminated with the herpes virus* **2** to influence someone or something in a way that has a bad effect: *Lack of trust will contaminate your whole relationship.* —**contamination** /kən,tæmə'neɪʃən/ *n* [U]

**contd** the written abbreviation of "continued"

**con·tem·plate** /'kɑntəm,pleɪt/ *v* [T] to think quietly and seriously for a long time about something you intend to do, or in order to understand something: *I can't even contemplate taking a vacation right now.* (=it is not possible, so it is not worth thinking about) —**contemplation** /,kɑntəm'pleɪʃən/ *n* [U]

**con·tem·pla·tive** /kən'templətɪv/ *adj* spending a lot of time thinking seriously and quietly

**con·tem·po·rar·y¹** /kən'tempə,reri/ *adj* **1** belonging to the present time; modern: *a museum of contemporary art* **2** happening or existing in the same period of time

**contemporary²** *n* someone who lives in the same period of time as a particular person or event: *Mozart was greatly admired by his contemporaries.*

**con·tempt** /kən'tempt/ *n* [U] **1** a feeling that someone or something does not deserve any respect: *Stephen's contempt for foreigners was well known.* **2** contempt of court not doing what a judge or court of law has told you to: *Cooper was fined $100 for contempt of court.*

**con·tempt·i·ble** /kən'temptəbəl/ *adj* not deserving any respect: *contemptible behavior* —**contemptibly** *adv*

**con·temp·tu·ous** /kən'temptʃuəs/ *adj* showing that you believe someone or something does not deserve any respect: *I hate her contemptuous attitude toward my mother.*

**con·tend** /kən'tend/ *v* [I] **1** to argue or claim that something is true: *Some critics contend that the changes will create even more problems.* **2** to compete for something: *Twelve teams are contending for the title.*
**contend with** sth *phr v* [T] to deal with a problem or difficult situation: *I have enough to contend with, without you yelling!*

**con·tend·er** /kən'tendɚ/ *n* someone who is involved in a competition

**con·tent¹** /'kɑntent/ *n* [singular] **1** the amount of a substance that something contains: *Peanut butter has a high fat content.* **2** the ideas, information, or opinions that are expressed in a speech, book etc.: *I like the content of the story but I don't think it's very well written.* —see also CONTENTS

**con·tent²** /kən'tent/ *adj* happy or satisfied because you have what you want or need: *Gary's content to sit at home in front of the TV all day.* | *I'd say she's pretty content with her job.* —**contentment** *n* [U]

**content³** *v* [T] **content yourself with** sth to do or have something that is not what you really want, but is still satisfactory: *Jack's driving, so he'll have to content himself with a soft drink.*

**content⁴** *n* [U] **do** sth **to your heart's content** to do something as much as you want: *For $8 you can eat to your heart's content at Big Al's Diner.*

**con·tent·ed** /kən'tentɪd/ *adj* satisfied or happy: *a contented cat curled up by the fire* —opposite DISCONTENTED

**con·ten·tion** /kən'tenʃən/ *n* **1** a belief or opinion that someone expresses: *It is my contention that bicycle helmets should be required.* **2** [U] a situation in which people or groups are competing: *Twenty teams are in contention for the NFL playoffs.* **3** [U] arguments and disagreement between people: *City planning has been a bone of contention* (=subject that people argue about) *for a long time.*

**con·ten·tious** /kən'tenʃəs/ *adj* likely to cause a lot of argument: *one of the most contentious issues in biotechnology* —**contentiously** *adv*

**con·tents** /'kɑntents/ *n* [plural] **1** the things that are in a box, bag, room etc.: *Customs officers searched through the contents of his luggage.* **2** the words or ideas that are written in a book, letter etc.: *The contents of the document are still unknown.* | *the table of contents*

(=a list at the beginning of a book that tells you what is in it)

**con·test**[1] /'kɑntɛst/ *n* **1** a competition, usually a small one: *a contest to see who can run the fastest | a pie-eating contest* **2** a struggle to win control or power: *the excitement of a political contest* **3** **no contest** INFORMAL used in order to say that a choice or a victory is not at all difficult: *In the end, it was no contest, with the Dolphins beating the Bengals 37-13.*

**con·test**[2] /kən'tɛst/ *v* [T] **1** to say formally that you do not think something is right or fair: *We intend to contest the judge's decision.* **2** to compete for something: *contesting a seat on the city council*

**con·test·ant** /kən'tɛstənt/ *n* someone who competes in a CONTEST

**con·text** /'kɑntɛkst/ *n* **1** the situation, events, or information that relate to something, and help you understand it better: *The events have to be considered in their historical context.* **2** the words and sentences that come before and after a word and that help you understand its meaning: *"Smart" can mean "intelligent" or "sarcastic," depending on the context.* **3** **take sth out of context** to repeat a sentence or phrase without describing the situation in which it was said, so that its meaning is not clear: *Journalists had taken his comments completely out of context.*

**con·tig·u·ous** /kən'tɪgyuəs/ *adj* FORMAL next to something, or sharing the same border: *the 48 contiguous States*

**con·ti·nent** /'kɑntənənt, 'kɑntⁿn-ənt/ *n* one of the main areas of land on the earth: *the continent of Africa*

**con·ti·nen·tal** /ˌkɑntən'ɛntl/ *adj* relating to a large area of land: *flights across the continental US*

**continental break·fast** /ˌ.... '../ *n* a breakfast consisting of coffee, juice, and a sweet ROLL (=type of bread)

**con·tin·gen·cy** /kən'tɪndʒənsi/ *n* an event or situation that might happen and could cause problems: *Of course there are contingency plans to cope with any computer failures.*

**con·tin·gent**[1] /kən'tɪndʒənt/ *adj* FORMAL dependent on something that may or may not happen in the future: *The purchase of the house is contingent on/upon a satisfactory inspection.*

**contingent**[2] *n* a group of people who have the same aims or are from the same area, and who are part of a larger group: *By late summer, a contingent of scientists had arrived.*

**con·tin·u·al** /kən'tɪnyuəl/ *adj* repeated often over a long period of time: *Their continual arguing really upset me.* **–continually** *adv*

USAGE NOTE **continual** and **continuous**

Use these words to talk about the way something happens and how long it con-

tinues. Use **continual** when something is repeated often over a long time: *The telephone has been ringing continually.* Use **continuous** when something continues without stopping: *The Salsa Club offers continuous music and entertainment from 5 pm to midnight.*

**con·tin·u·a·tion** /kənˌtɪnyu'eɪʃən/ *n* **1** something that follows after or is joined to something else and seems a part of it: *the continuation of our economic success* **2** [U] the act or state of continuing for a long time without stopping: *the continuation of family traditions*

**con·tin·ue** /kən'tɪnyu/ *v* **1** [I,T] to keep happening, existing, or doing something without stopping: *The city's population will continue to grow. | Do you plan on continuing with your education?* **2** [I,T] to start doing something again after a pause: *To be continued...* (=used at the end of a program to say that the story will be finished later) **3** [I] to go further in the same direction: *Route 66 continues on to Texas from here.*

**continuing ed·u·ca·tion** /ˌ.,... ..'../ *n* [U] classes for adults, often on subjects that relate to their jobs

**con·ti·nu·i·ty** /ˌkɑntə'nuəti/ *n* [U] the state of continuing over a long period of time without being interrupted or changing: *Changing doctors can affect the continuity of your treatment.*

**con·tin·u·ous**[1] /kən'tɪnyuəs/ *adj* **1** continuing to happen or exist without stopping or pausing: *These plants need a continuous supply of fresh water.* **2** without any spaces or holes in it: *a continuous line of cars* **–continuously** *adv* –see usage note at CONTINUAL

**continuous**[2] *n* **the continuous** TECHNICAL in grammar, the form of a verb that shows that an action or activity is continuing to happen, and is formed with "be" and the PRESENT PARTICIPLE. In the sentence "She is watching TV," "is watching" is in the continuous form

**con·tort** /kən'tɔrt/ *v* [I,T] to twist your face or body so that it does not have its normal shape **–contortion** /kən'tɔrʃən/ *n* [C,U]

**con·tour** /'kɑntʊr/ *n* the shape of the outer edges of something such as an area of land or someone's body

**con·tra·band** /'kɑntrəˌbænd/ *n* [U] goods that are brought into or taken out of a country illegally **–contraband** *adj*

**con·tra·cep·tion** /ˌkɑntrə'sɛpʃən/ *n* [U] the practice or methods of making it possible for a woman to have sex without becoming PREGNANT; BIRTH CONTROL

**con·tra·cep·tive** /ˌkɑntrə'sɛptɪv/ *n* [C] a drug, object, or method used so that a woman can have sex without becoming PREGNANT **–contraceptive** *adj*

**con·tract¹** /'kɑntrækt/ *n* **1** a legal written agreement between two people, companies etc. that says what each side must do for the other: *Stacy signed a three year contract with a small record company.* **2** INFORMAL an agreement to kill someone for money

**con·tract²** /kən'trækt/ *v* **1** [T] to get a CONTAGIOUS illness: *Just after high school, he contracted polio.* **2** [I] to become smaller or tighter: *Scientists say the universe will begin to contract.* –opposite EXPAND

**contract³** /'kɑntrækt/ *v* [T] to sign a contract to do something

**contract sth ↔ out** *phr v* [T] to arrange to have a job done by a person or company outside your own organization

**con·trac·tion** /kən'trækʃən/ *n* **1** TECHNICAL a very strong movement of a muscle in which it suddenly becomes tight, used especially about the muscles that become tight when a woman is going to give birth **2** [U] the process of becoming smaller or shorter **3** TECHNICAL a short form of a word or words, such as "don't" for "do not"

**con·trac·tor** /'kɑn,træktɚ, kən'træk-/ *n* a person or company that does work or supplies material for other companies

**con·trac·tu·al** /kən'træktʃuəl/ *adj* agreed in a contract: *contractual obligations*

**con·tra·dict** /,kɑntrə'dɪkt/ *v* **1** [T] if a statement, story, fact etc. contradicts another one, it is very different from or the opposite of the other one: *The witnesses' reports contradicted each other.* **2** [I,T] to say that what someone else has just said is wrong or not true: *You shouldn't contradict me in front of the kids.* **3** **contradict yourself** to say something that is the opposite of what you have said before –**contradictory** /,kɑntrə'dɪktəri/ *adj*

**con·tra·dic·tion** /,kɑntrə'dɪkʃən/ *n* **1** a difference between two stories, facts etc. that means they cannot both be true: *There's a contradiction between what they say and what they do.* **2** [U] the act of saying that what someone has just said is wrong or not true

**con·trap·tion** /kən'træpʃən/ *n* INFORMAL a piece of equipment that looks strange

**con·trar·y¹** /'kɑn,trɛri/ *n* FORMAL **1** **on the contrary** used in order to show that the opposite of what has just been said is actually true: *We didn't start the fire. On the contrary, we helped put it out.* **2** **to the contrary** showing that the opposite is true: *In spite of rumors to the contrary, their marriage is fine.*

**contrary²** *adj* **1** completely different or opposite: *Lying to her would be contrary to everything I believe in.* **2** **contrary to popular belief** used in order to show that something is true even though people may think the opposite: *Contrary to popular belief, gorillas are shy and gentle.*

**contrary³** /kan'trɛri/ *adj* deliberately doing or saying the opposite of what someone else wants: *Angela was an extremely contrary child.*

**con·trast¹** /'kɑntræst/ *n* **1** [C,U] a large difference between two people, situations, ideas etc. that are compared: *the contrast between the rich and poor in America* **2** **in contrast (to)** used when comparing objects or situations that are completely different from each other: *Claire is tall and dark, in sharp/marked contrast to her mother, who is short and fair.* **3** [U] the differences in color or in light and darkness on photographs, a television picture etc.

**con·trast²** /kən'træst/ *v* **1** [T] to compare two people, ideas, objects etc. to show how they are different from each other: *The lecture contrasted Chinese characters with the western alphabet.* **2** [I] if two things contrast, they are very different from each other: *His views on religion contrast sharply with my own.* –**contrasting** *adj*

**con·tra·vene** /,kɑntrə'vin/ *v* [T] FORMAL to do something that is not allowed by a law or a rule –**contravention** /,kɑntrə'vɛnʃən/ *n* [C,U]

**con·trib·ute** /kən'trɪbyut, -yət/ *v* **1** [I,T] to give money, help, or ideas to something that other people are also giving to: *We all contributed $5 toward his present.* **2** **contribute to sth** to help make something happen: *An electrical problem may have contributed to the crash.* **3** to write something for a newspaper or magazine –**contributor** *n* –**contributory** *adj*

**con·tri·bu·tion** /,kɑntrə'byuʃən/ *n* **1** something that is given or done to help something else be a success: *The Mayo Clinic has made important contributions to cancer research.* **2** an amount of money that is given to help pay for something: *Would you like to make a contribution to the Red Cross?* **3** a piece of writing that is printed in a newspaper or magazine

**con·trite** /kən'traɪt/ *adj* feeling guilty and sorry for something bad that you have done –**contrition** /kən'trɪʃən/ *n* [U]

**con·trive** /kən'traɪv/ *v* [T] to manage to do something difficult or to invent something by being very smart or dishonest: *Somehow she contrived to get herself invited to the governor's ball.*

**con·trived** /kən'traɪvd/ *adj* seeming false and not natural: *Alice spoke with a contrived southern accent.*

**con·trol¹** /kən'troʊl/ *n* **1** [U] the power or ability to make someone or something do what you want: *They don't have any control over their son.* | *The car went out of control* (=could not be controlled) *and hit a tree.* | *A military spokesman said the situation was now under control.* (=being controlled) | *These events are beyond our control.* (=not possible for us to control) **2** [U] the power to rule or govern a place, organization, or company: *Rioters took* *control of* the prison. | *The airport is now **under the control of** UN troops.* | *The government is no longer **in control** of the country.* **3** [C,U] the action or method of limiting the amount or growth of something: *After four hours firefighters **brought** the fire **under control**.* (=stopped it from getting worse) **4** [U] the ability to remain calm even when you are angry or excited: *I just **lost control** (=became unable to control my behavior) and punched him!* **5** something that you use to make a television, machine, vehicle etc. work —**controlled** *adj*

**control**[2] *v* **-lled, -lling** [T] **1** to make someone or something do what you want or work in a particular way: *If you can't **control** your dog you should put it on a leash.* **2** to limit the amount or growth of something: *It was impossible to control the flooding on the Ogallala River.* **3** to rule or govern a place, organization, or company, or to have more power than someone else: *Rebels **control** all the roads into the capital.* **4** to make yourself behave calmly, even if you feel angry, excited, or upset: *I was furious, but I managed to **control myself**.*

**control freak** /.'. ,./ *n* INFORMAL someone who is too concerned about controlling all the details in every situation s/he is involved in

**con·trol·ler** /kən'troʊlɚ/ *n* TECHNICAL someone whose job is to collect and pay money for a government or company department: *the state controller*

**control tow·er** /.'. ,../ *n* a building at an airport from which planes are watched and guided as they come down and go up

**con·tro·ver·sial** /ˌkɑntrə'vɚʃəl/ *adj* something that is controversial causes a lot of disagreement, because many people have strong opinions about it: *the controversial subject of abortion* —**controversially** *adv*

**con·tro·ver·sy** /'kɑntrəˌvɚsi/ *n* [C,U] a serious disagreement among many people over a plan, decision etc., over a long period of time: *There is a lot of **controversy over** the use of this drug.*

**con·va·lesce** /ˌkɑnvə'lɛs/ *v* [I] to spend time getting well after a serious illness —**convalescence** *n* [singular] —**convalescent** *n*

**con·va·les·cent** /ˌkɑnvə'lɛsənt/ *adj* **convalescent home/hospital** etc. a place where people stay when they need care from doctors and nurses but are not sick enough to be in a hospital

**con·vene** /kən'vin/ *v* [I,T] FORMAL if a group of people convenes, or if someone convenes them, they come together for a formal meeting

**con·ven·ience** /kən'vinyəns/ *n* **1** [U] the quality of being suitable or useful for a particular purpose, especially because it makes something easier: *I like the convenience of living near my work.* **2** [U] what is easiest and best for someone: *The package can be delivered **at your convenience**.* (=at a time that is best for

you) **3** a service, piece of equipment etc. that is useful because it saves you time or work: *modern conveniences* —opposite INCONVEN-IENCE[1]

**convenience store** /.'.. ,./ *n* a store where you can buy food, newspapers etc. and that is often open 24 hours each day

**con·ven·ient** /kən'vinyənt/ *adj* **1** useful to you because it makes something easier or saves you time: *It's more **convenient for** me to pay by credit card.* **2** near and easy to get to: *a convenient place to shop* —**conveniently** *adv* —opposite INCONVENIENT

**con·vent** /'kɑnvɛnt, -vənt/ *n* a place where NUNs (=religious women) live and work

**con·ven·tion** /kən'vɛnʃən/ *n* **1** a large formal meeting of people who belong to the same profession, organization etc.: *an astronomy convention* **2** [C,U] behavior and attitudes that most people in society think are normal and right: *We **broke with convention** (=did something unusual) and had our wedding at the beach.* **3** a formal agreement between countries: *the Geneva convention on human rights*

**con·ven·tion·al** /kən'vɛnʃənəl/ *adj* **1** always following the behavior and attitudes that most people in society think are normal and right, so that you seem boring: *My parents have very conventional attitudes about sex.* **2** a conventional method, product, practice etc. is one that has been used for a long time: *Acupuncture is one alternative to conventional medicine.* **3** conventional weapons and wars do not use NUCLEAR explosives —**conventionally** *adv*

**con·verge** /kən'vɚdʒ/ *v* [I] to move or come together from different directions to meet at the same point: *Thousands of fans **converged on** the stadium to watch the game.* —**convergence** *n* [C,U]

**con·ver·sant** /kən'vɚsənt/ *adj* FORMAL having knowledge or experience of something: *Are you **conversant with** word processors?*

**con·ver·sa·tion** /ˌkɑnvɚ'seɪʃən/ *n* [C,U] **1** a talk between two or more people in which people ask questions, exchange news etc.: *Don't interrupt while your mother and I are **having a conversation**.* | *The two women were deep **in conversation**.* (=they were concentrating on their conversation) | *He **struck up a conversation with** (=began to talk to) a man at the bus stop.* **2 make conversation** to talk to someone to be polite, not because you really want to —**conversational** *adj* —**conversationally** *adv*

**con·verse**[1] /kən'vɚs/ *v* [I] FORMAL to have a conversation with someone

**con·verse**[2] /'kɑnvɚs/ *n* [singular] **the converse** FORMAL the opposite of something: *The converse can also be true in some cases.* —**converse** /kən'vɚs, 'kɑnvɚs/ *adj* —**conversely** *adv*

**con·ver·sion** /kənˈvɚʒən, -ʃən/ n [C,U]
**1** the act or process of changing something
from one form, system, or purpose to another:
*Canada's* **conversion to** *the metric system* **2** a
change in which someone accepts a completely
new religion, belief etc.: *Tyson's* **conversion to**
*Islam surprised the media.*

**con·vert¹** /kənˈvɚt/ v [I,T] **1** to change or
make something change from one form, system,
or purpose to another: *We're going to* **convert**
*the garage* **into** *a workshop* **2** to accept or
make someone accept a completely new reli-
gion, belief etc.: *My wife has* **converted** *me* **to**
*aerobics.* (=persuaded me to do it so that I enjoy
it now)

**con·vert²** /ˈkɑnvɚt/ n someone who has
accepted a completely new religion, belief etc.

**con·vert·i·ble¹** /kənˈvɚtəbəl/ adj **1** something convertible is able to change or be
arranged so it becomes or can be used for something else: *a convertible couch* (=one that unfolds to become a bed) **2** TECHNICAL money that
is convertible can be exchanged for another type
of money

**convertible²** n a car with a roof that you can
fold back or remove −see picture on page 469

**con·vex** /ˌkɑnˈvɛks◂, kən-/ adj TECHNICAL
curved outwards, like the outside edge of a
circle: *a convex lens* −opposite CONCAVE

**con·vey** /kənˈveɪ/ v [T] FORMAL to communicate a message or information, with or without
using words: *Please* **convey** *my thanks* **to** *her.*

**con·vey·or belt** /.ˈ.. ˌ./ n a long continuous
moving band of rubber or metal, used in a place
such as a factory or airport to move things from
one place to another

**con·vict¹** /kənˈvɪkt/ v [T] to prove or
announce that someone is guilty of a crime after
a TRIAL in a court of law: *Both men were* **convicted of** *fraud.* −opposite ACQUIT

**con·vict²** /ˈkɑnvɪkt/ n someone who has been
proved to be guilty of a crime and sent to prison

**con·vic·tion** /kənˈvɪkʃən/ n [C,U] **1** a very
strong belief or opinion: *his firm religious con-
victions* **2** an official announcement in a court
of law that someone is guilty of a crime:
*Bradley's* **conviction for** *theft was no surprise.*
−opposite ACQUITTAL

**con·vince** /kənˈvɪns/ v [T] to make someone
feel certain that something is true: *The defense
lawyers failed to* **convince** *the jury* **that** *Booth
was innocent.* −compare PERSUADE

**con·vinced** /kənˈvɪnst/ adj **be convinced** to
feel certain that something is true: *Her folks
were convinced she was doing drugs.*

**con·vinc·ing** /kənˈvɪnsɪŋ/ adj making you
believe that something is true or right: *a convin-
cing argument* −**convincingly** adv

**con·viv·i·al** /kənˈvɪviəl/ adj FORMAL friendly
and pleasantly cheerful: *a convivial atmosphere*
−**conviviality** /kənˌvɪviˈæləti/ n [U]

**con·vo·lut·ed** /ˈkɑnvəˌlutɪd/ adj FORMAL complicated and difficult to understand: *convoluted
legal language*

**con·voy** /ˈkɑnvɔɪ/ n [C,U] a group of vehicles
or ships traveling together: *a convoy of army
trucks*

**con·vulse** /kənˈvʌls/ v **be convulsed with
laughter** to be laughing a lot

**con·vul·sion** /kənˈvʌlʃən/ n an occasion
when someone cannot control the violent movements of his/her body, because s/he is sick: *An
overdose of the drug can cause convulsions.*

**coo** /ku/ v **1** [I] to make a sound like the low
cry of a DOVE or a PIGEON **2** [I,T] to make soft
loving noises: *a mother cooing to her baby*

**cook¹** /kʊk/ v **1** [I,T] to prepare food for eating by using heat: *Whose turn is it to cook
supper tonight?* | *Grandma's cooking for the
whole family on Thanksgiving.* **2** [I] to be prepared for eating by using heat: *How long will it
take the stew to cook?* **3 be cooking with gas**
SPOKEN to be doing something in the correct or
best way, so that it is successful

**cook** sth ↔ **up** phr v [T] **1** INFORMAL to invent
an excuse, reason, plan etc. that is slightly dishonest or will not work: *She refused to be part
of a scheme that Lawrence had* **cooked up.**
**2** to prepare food, especially quickly: *The
oatmeal* **cooks up** *quickly in the microwave.*

**cook²** n someone who cooks and prepares food:
*Kevin works as a cook in an Italian restaur-
ant.* | *My cousin's a great cook.*

**cook·book** /ˈkʊkbʊk/ n a book that tells you
how to prepare and cook food

**cooked** /kʊkt/ adj ready for eating and not
raw: *cooked vegetables*

**cook·ie** /ˈkʊki/ n a small
flat sweet cake: *chocolate
chip cookies*

**cook·ing¹** /ˈkʊkɪŋ/ n [U]
**1** the act of making food
and cooking it: *I hate cooking.* **2** food made in a
particular way or by a
particular person: *Italian
cooking*

cookie

**cooking²** adj **1** suitable for cooking or used
in cooking: *cooking oil* **2** SLANG doing something very well: *The band is really cooking tonight.*

**cool¹** /kul/ adj **1** SPOKEN said in order to show
that you agree with something or that it does not
annoy you: *"Do you mind if I bring my sister?"
"No, that's cool."* **2** SPOKEN said in order to
show approval, especially of someone or something that is fashionable, attractive, or relaxed:
*He's a really cool guy.* **3** low in temperature
but not cold: *a cool summer evening* −see usage
note at TEMPERATURE **4** calm and not nervous
or excited: *a cool calculating politician*

**5** unfriendly: *a cool welcome* –**coolness** *n* [U]
–**coolly** /'kul-li/ *adv*

**cool²** *v* **1** [I,T] also **cool down** to make something slightly colder or to become slightly colder: *Allow the cake to cool before cutting it.* **2** [I] feelings or relationships that cool become less strong: *Their feelings for each other seem to be cooling.* **3 cool it** SPOKEN used to tell someone to stop being angry: *Will you stop shouting and just cool it!*

**cool down** *phr v* [I] **1** to become calm after being angry: *The long walk home helped me cool down.* **2** to do gentle physical exercises after doing more difficult exercises, so that you do not get injuries

**cool off** *phr v* [I] **1** to return to a normal temperature after being hot: *The kids cooled off by going for a swim.* **2** to become calm after being angry: *You need to cool off before trying to talk to her again.*

**cool³** *n* [U] **1 the cool** a temperature that is cool: *the cool of a spring morning* **2 keep your cool** to stay calm in a difficult situation: *He was starting to annoy her, but she kept her cool.* **3 lose your cool** to stop being calm in a difficult situation: *Nick lost his cool when Ryan yelled at him.*

**cool·er** /'kulɚ/ *n* a container in which you can keep food or drinks cool

**coop¹** /kup/ *n* a cage for hens

**coop²** *v*

**coop sb up** *phr v* [T] to make someone stay indoors, or in a small space: *After being cooped up all morning, we were happy to go outside.*

**co·op·er·ate** /kou'apə,reɪt/ *v* [I] **1** to work with someone else to achieve something that you both want: *The local police are cooperating with the FBI in the search for the killers* **2** to do what someone asks you to do: *We can deal with this problem, if you're willing to cooperate.*

**co·op·er·a·tion** /kou,apə'reɪʃən/ *n* [U] **1** the act of working with someone else to achieve what you both want: *The sales team will be working in cooperation with other departments.* **2** willingness to work with other people, or to do what they ask you to do: *I'd like to thank you for your cooperation.*

**co·op·er·a·tive¹** /kou'aprətɪv/ *adj* **1** willing to help: *I've always found her very cooperative.* **2** made, done, or owned by people working together: *a cooperative farm venture* –**cooperatively** *adv*

**cooperative²** *n* a company, farm etc. that is owned and operated by people working together: *They turned their business into a cooperative.*

**co-opt** /kou'apt/ *v* [T] DISAPPROVING to use something that was not originally yours to help you do something, or to persuade someone to help you: *Conservative Christians have been accused of co-opting the Republican party.*

**co·or·di·nate** /kou'ɔrdn,eɪt/ *v* [T] **1** to organize people or things so that they work together well: *Liza is coordinating our sales effort.* **2** to make the parts of your body work together well: *Her movements were perfectly coordinated.*

**co·or·di·na·tion** /kou,ɔrdn'eɪʃən/ *n* [U] **1** the organization of people or things so that they work together well: *the coordination of research teams* **2** the way that the parts of your body work together to do something: *Skating in pairs takes good coordination.*

**co·or·di·na·tor** /kou'ɔrdn,eɪtɚ/ *n* someone who organizes the way people work together

**coo·ties** /'kutiz/ *n* [plural] a word meaning lice (LOUSE), used by children as an insult when they do not want to play with or sit with another child: *Jenny has cooties.*

**cop** /kap/ *n* INFORMAL a police officer

**cope** /koup/ *v* [I] to deal successfully with something: *How do you cope with all this work?*

**cop·i·er** /'kapiɚ/ *n* a machine that quickly copies documents onto paper by photographing them

**co-pi·lot** /'kou ,paɪlət/ *n* a pilot who helps the main pilot fly an airplane

**co·pi·ous** /'koupiəs/ *adj* produced in large amounts: *He always takes copious notes.* –**copiously** *adv*

**cop-out** /'. ./ *n* INFORMAL something you do or say in order to avoid doing something: *Blaming failing grades on TV is a cop-out.* –**cop out** *v*

**cop·per** /'kapɚ/ *n* [U] an orange brown metal that is an ELEMENT and is often used to make wire –**copper** *adj*

**cop·ter** /'kaptɚ/ *n* INFORMAL ⇨ HELICOPTER

**cop·u·late** /'kapyə,leɪt/ *v* [I] FORMAL to have sex –**copulation** /,kapyə'leɪʃən/ *n* [U]

**cop·y¹** /'kapi/ *n* **1** something that is made to look exactly like something else: *Please make me a copy of the report.* | *a very good copy of Van Gogh's famous painting* **2** one of many books, magazines etc. that are exactly the same: *a copy of Irving's new novel* **3** [U] TECHNICAL something written to be printed, especially for an advertisement: *We need someone who can write good copy.*

**copy²** *v* **1** [T] to make a thing that is exactly like something else: *Could you copy this tape for me?* **2** [T] to do something that someone else has done, or behave like someone else: *The system has been copied by other organizations, and has worked well.* **3** [I,T] to write exactly what someone else has written: *He copied his friend's answers during the test.*

**cop·y·cat** /'kapi,kæt/ *n* INFORMAL **1** a word used by children to criticize someone who copies other people's clothes, behavior etc. **2 copycat crime/murder etc.** a crime, murder etc. that someone has copied from another person

**cop·y·right** /'kɑpi,raɪt/ n [C,U] the legal right to produce and sell a book, play, movie, or record

**cor·al** /'kɔrəl, 'kɑrəl/ n [U] a hard colored substance that grows in warm sea water

**cord** /kɔrd/ n [C,U] **1** a piece of wire covered with plastic for connecting electrical equipment to the supply of electricity: *an extension cord for the TV* **2** a piece of thick string or thin rope

**cor·dial** /'kɔrdʒəl/ adj friendly and polite but formal: *a cordial greeting* –**cordiality** /,kɔrdʒi'æləti/ n [U] –**cordially** /'kɔrdʒəli/ adv

**cord·less** /'kɔrdlɪs/ adj a cordless piece of equipment uses a BATTERY instead of a CORD: *a cordless telephone*

**cor·don**[1] /'kɔrdn/ n a line of police, soldiers, or vehicles that are put around an area to protect or enclose it: *Several protesters tried to push through the police cordon.*

**cordon**[2] v
**cordon** sth ↔ **off** phr v [T] to surround and protect an area with police officers, soldiers, or vehicles: *Police have **cordoned off** the building where the bomb was found.*

**cords** /kɔrdz/ n [plural] INFORMAL CORDUROY pants

**cor·du·roy** /'kɔrdə,rɔɪ/ n [U] thick strong cotton cloth with raised lines on one side: *a corduroy jacket*

**core**[1] /kɔr/ n **1** the central or most important part of something: *The city is the core of a large industrial area.* **2** the hard central part of an apple or PEAR **3** the central part of the earth or any other PLANET **4** a group of people who do important work in an organization: *The department has a small core of experienced staff.* **5** the central part of a NUCLEAR REACTOR –see also HARDCORE

**core**[2] v [T] to remove the hard center of a piece of fruit

**cork**[1] /kɔrk/ n **1** [U] the light outer part of a particular type of tree that is used for making things: *cork mats* **2** a round piece of this material that is put into the top of a bottle to keep liquid inside

**cork**[2] v [T] to close a bottle tightly by putting a CORK in it

**cork·screw** /'kɔrkskru/ n a tool used for pulling CORKs out of bottles

**corn** /kɔrn/ n [U] **1** a tall plant with yellow seeds that are cooked and eaten as a vegetable: *an **ear of corn** (=the top part of a corn plant on which these yellow seeds grow) | steak and **corn on the cob** (=an ear of corn that is boiled and eaten as a vegetable) –see picture on page 470 **2** a thick, hard, and painful area of skin on your foot

**corn·bread** /'kɔrnbrɛd/ n [U] bread that is made from CORNMEAL –see picture at BREAD

**cor·ne·a** /'kɔrniə/ n the strong transparent covering on the outer surface of your eye –**corneal** adj

**corned beef** /,kɔrn'bif◂/ n [U] BEEF that has been preserved in salt water and SPICEs

**cor·ner**[1] /'kɔrnɚ/ n **1** the point at which two lines, surfaces, or edges meet: *a table **in the corner** of the room | a calendar **on the corner** of her desk* –see picture at EDGE[1] **2** the place where two roads, streets, or paths meet: *Meet me **on the corner** of 72nd and Central Park. | We went to a place **around the corner** for coffee. | When you **turn the corner** (=go around the corner) you'll see a video store.* **3** a distant part of the world: *You can hear Voice of America in almost every corner of the world.* **4 see sth out of the corner of your eye** to notice something without turning your head –see also **cut corners** (CUT[1])

**corner**[2] v [T] **1** to move closer to a person or an animal so that he, she, or it cannot escape: *Gibbs cornered Cassetti after the meeting and asked for his decision.* **2 corner the market** to sell or produce all of a particular type of goods

**cor·ner·stone** /'kɔrnɚ,stoʊn/ n **1** a stone set at one of the bottom corners of a building, often as part of a special ceremony **2** something that is very important because everything else depends on it: *Free speech is **the cornerstone** of democracy.*

**cor·net** /kɔr'nɛt/ n a small musical instrument like a TRUMPET

**corn·flakes** /'kɔrnfleɪks/ n [plural] a type of breakfast food made from corn

**corn·meal** /'kɔrnmil/ n [U] a rough type of flour made from crushed dried corn

**corn·starch** /'kɔrnstɑrtʃ/ n [U] a fine white flour made from corn, used in cooking to make liquids thicker

**corn·y** /'kɔrni/ adj INFORMAL old, silly, and too familiar to be interesting: *a corny song from the '40s*

**cor·o·na·ry**[1] /'kɔrə,nɛri/ adj concerning or relating to the heart: *coronary disease*

**coronary**[2] n ⇨ HEART ATTACK

**cor·o·na·tion** /,kɔrə'neɪʃən/ n a ceremony in which someone officially becomes a king or queen

**cor·o·ner** /'kɔrənɚ/ n an official whose job is to discover the cause of someone's death, if it is sudden or unexpected, especially by examining his/her body

**cor·po·ral, Corporal** /'kɔrpərəl/ n the lowest rank in the Army or Marines, or someone who has this rank

**cor·po·ral pun·ish·ment** /,... '.../ n [U] the punishment of someone by hitting him/her

**cor·po·rate** /'kɔrpərɪt/ adj belonging to or relating to a CORPORATION: *They're building new corporate headquarters.* –**corporately** adv

**cor·po·ra·tion** /ˌkɔrpəˈreɪʃən/ n a large business organization that is owned by SHARE-HOLDERs: *an executive position in a large corporation*

**corps** /kɔr/ n [singular] TECHNICAL **1** a trained group of people with special duties in the military: *the Naval Air Corps* **2** a group of people who do a particular job: *the press corps*

**corpse** /kɔrps/ n a dead body

**cor·pu·lent** /ˈkɔrpyələnt/ adj FORMAL very fat

**cor·pus·cle** /ˈkɔrˌpʌsəl/ n a red or white blood cell in your body

**cor·ral**[1] /kəˈræl/ n an enclosed area where cattle, horses etc. are kept

**corral**[2] v [T] to put animals into a CORRAL

**cor·rect**[1] /kəˈrɛkt/ adj **1** right or without any mistakes: *the correct answers* | *"Your name is Ives?" "Yes, that's correct."* **2** suitable for a particular occasion or use: *the correct procedure for making an application* –**correctly** adv –**correctness** n [U] –opposite INCORRECT

**correct**[2] v [T] to make something right or better: *Your eyesight can be corrected with better glasses.* | *Teachers spend hours correcting papers.*

**cor·rec·tion** /kəˈrɛkʃən/ n a change in something that makes it right or better: *Johnson made a few corrections to the article before allowing it to be printed.*

**cor·rec·tive** /kəˈrɛktɪv/ adj FORMAL intended to make something right or better, after being wrong or not working correctly: *corrective lenses for the eyes*

**cor·re·la·tion** /ˌkɔrəˈleɪʃən, ˌkɑr-/ n [C,U] a relationship in which two things happen together and may have an effect on each other: *There's a high correlation between hot weather and this type of illness.* –**correlate** /ˈkɔrəˌleɪt/ v [I,T]

**cor·re·spond** /ˌkɔrəˈspɑnd, ˌkɑr-/ v [I] **1** if two things correspond, they are like each other or relate to each other: *The name on the envelope doesn't correspond with the one on the letter.* | *His salary doesn't correspond to his responsibilities.* **2** if two people correspond, they write letters to each other: *They've been corresponding for years.*

**cor·re·spond·ence** /ˌkɔrəˈspɑndəns, ˌkɑr-/ n [U] **1** letters that people write: *I try to type all my correspondence.* **2** the activity of writing letters: *His correspondence with Hemingway continued until his death.*

**correspondence course** /..ˈ.. ./ n a course of lessons that you receive by mail and do at home

**cor·re·spond·ent** /ˌkɔrəˈspɑndənt, ˌkɑr-/ n **1** someone whose job is to report news from a distant area or about a particular subject to a newspaper or television: *the White House correspondent* | *the London correspondent for the Los Angeles Times* **2** someone who writes to

another person regularly: *I like getting her letters; she's a good correspondent.*

**cor·re·spond·ing** /ˌkɔrəˈspɑndɪŋ, ˌkɑr-/ adj similar or matching: *a promotion and a corresponding increase in salary* –**correspondingly** adv

**cor·ri·dor** /ˈkɔrədɚ, -ˌdɔr, ˈkɑr-/ n **1** a passage between two rows of rooms: *The elevator's at the end of the corridor.* **2** a narrow area of land within a large area, especially one used for traveling from one place to another: *the New York - Washington DC corridor*

**cor·rob·o·rate** /kəˈrɑbəˌreɪt/ v [T] FORMAL to support an opinion or claim with new information or proof: *Can you corroborate his story?* –**corroboration** /kəˌrɑbəˈreɪʃən/ n [U] –**corroborative** /kəˈrɑbərətɪv/ adj: *corroborative evidence*

**cor·rode** /kəˈroʊd/ v [I,T] to destroy something slowly or be destroyed slowly, especially by chemicals: *metal doors corroded by rust*

**cor·ro·sion** /kəˈroʊʒən/ n [U] **1** the process of becoming slowly destroyed by chemicals **2** a substance such as RUST (=weak red metal) that is produced by this process –**corrosive** /kəˈroʊsɪv/ adj

**cor·ru·gat·ed** /ˈkɔrəˌgeɪtɪd, ˈkɑr-/ adj formed in rows of folds that look like waves: *corrugated cardboard*

**cor·rupt**[1] /kəˈrʌpt/ adj **1** dishonest and ready to accept money to do something illegal: *a corrupt judge who took a bribe* **2** very bad morally: *a corrupt society* –**corruptly** adv

**corrupt**[2] v [T] **1** to make someone dishonest or immoral: *Bakker's Christian ministry was corrupted by greed.* **2** to change or spoil something so that it is not as good: *a traditional culture corrupted by outside influences* **3** to change the information in a computer so that it does not work correctly –**corruptible** adj

**cor·rup·tion** /kəˈrʌpʃən/ n [U] **1** dishonest or immoral behavior: *We must fight against corruption in city politics.* **2** the act or process of making someone dishonest or immoral: *the corruption of today's youth by drugs*

**cor·sage** /kɔrˈsɑʒ/ n a small group of flowers that a woman wears on her dress for special occasions

**cor·set** /ˈkɔrsɪt/ n a type of underwear that fits very tightly, that women in past times wore in order to look thinner

**cor·tege** /kɔrˈtɛʒ/ n FORMAL a line of people, cars etc. that move slowly in a funeral

**cos·met·ic** /kazˈmɛtɪk/ adj **1** intended to make your skin or body more beautiful: *cosmetic surgery* **2** dealing only with the appearance of something: *cosmetic changes to the policy* –**cosmetically** adv

**cos·me·ti·cian** /ˌkɑzməˈtɪʃən/ n someone who is trained to put COSMETICS on other people

**cos·met·ics** /kɑz'mɛtɪks/ n [plural] substances such as creams or powders that are used in order to make your face and skin more attractive

**cos·mic** /'kɑzmɪk/ adj **1** relating to the whole universe, or happening in, or coming from space: *cosmic radiation* **2** INFORMAL relating to the meaning of the universe: *philosophers asking cosmic questions* —**cosmically** adv

**cos·mo·naut** /'kɑzmə,nɔt/ n an ASTRONAUT from Russia or the former Soviet Union

**cos·mo·pol·i·tan** /,kɑzmə'pɑlətn, -lət⌐n/ adj **1** consisting of people from many different parts of the world: *a cosmopolitan city like New York* **2** showing wide experience of different people and places: *a cosmopolitan outlook*

**cos·mos** /'kɑzmoʊs, -məs/ n **the cosmos** the universe considered as a whole system

**cost¹** /kɔst/ n **1** [C,U] the amount of money you must pay in order to buy, do, or produce something: *Will $100 **cover the cost** of books?* (=be enough to pay for them)\ *the **high/low cost** of educating children* —compare PRICE¹ **2** [singular] something that you must give or lose in order to get something else: *War is never worth its cost in human life.*\ *He saved his family, **at the cost of** his own life.* **3 at all costs/at any cost** whatever happens, or whatever effort is needed: *We need to get that contract, at any cost.* **4 at cost** for the same price that you paid: *We had to sell the van at cost.* —see also COSTS

---

**USAGE NOTE cost**

Use **cost** to talk about how much you have to pay for something: *How much does this CD cost?* \ *the cost of having the TV repaired.* Use **price** only to talk about the amount of money you have to pay to buy something in a store, restaurant etc.: *Their prices seem pretty high.* Use **charge** to talk about the amount of money someone makes you pay: *They charged me $35 to deliver the couch.* Use **value** to talk about how much something such as jewelry or furniture is worth: *He sold the house for less than its real value.* Use **expense** to talk about a very large amount of money: *the expense of health care.*

---

**cost²** v [T] **1** to have a particular price: *This dress cost $75.*\ *It'll cost you less to drive than to take the train.* **2** to make someone lose something: *Your mistake cost us the deal.* **3 cost an arm and a leg** INFORMAL to be extremely expensive: *I love these boots, but they cost an arm and a leg.*

**cost³** v **costed, costed, costing** to calculate the price to be charged for a job, someone's time etc: *The electrician **costed** the job **at** $400.*

**co-star¹** /'koʊ stɑr/ n one of two or more famous actors who work together in a movie or play

**co-star²** v [I] to be working in a movie or play with other famous actors

**cost ef·fec·tive** /'. .,../ adj producing the best profits or advantages at the lowest cost: *It's more cost-effective to take public transportation.*

**cost·ly** /'kɔstli/ adj **1** costing a lot of money: *a costly vacation* **2** causing a lot of problems or making you lose something important: *The Vietnam War was costly in terms of both human life and American pride.*

**cost of liv·ing** /,. . '../ n [singular] the average amount that people spend to buy food, pay bills, own a home etc. in a particular area: *The cost of living is much higher in California than in Iowa.*

**costs** /kɔsts/ n [plural] **1** the money that you must regularly spend in a business, or on your home, car etc: *We're trying to **cut costs** (=spend less money) by driving a smaller car.* **2** the money that you must pay to lawyers if you are involved in a legal case: *Burdell lost the case and was ordered to pay the defense's costs.*

**cos·tume** /'kɑstum/ n [C,U] **1** clothes worn to make you look like someone in a particular job or something such as an animal, GHOST etc.: *a prize for the best Halloween costume* **2** the clothes that were typical of a particular period of time, a country, an activity etc.

**costume jew·el·ry** /'.. ,..., ,.. '.../ n [U] cheap jewelry that looks expensive

**cot** /kɑt/ n a light narrow bed that folds up

**cot·tage** /'kɑtɪdʒ/ n a small house, especially in the country

**cottage cheese** /,.. '.◂ / n [U] a type of soft wet white cheese

**cot·ton** /'kɑt⌐n/ n [C,U] **1** cloth made from the cotton plant: *a cotton shirt* **2** a plant that produces seeds covered in soft white hair that is used for making thread and cloth

**cotton ball** /'.. ,./ n a small soft ball made from cotton, used for cleaning skin

**cotton can·dy** /,.. '../ n [U] a type of sticky pink candy that looks like cotton

**cot·ton·wood** /'kɑt⌐n,wʊd/ n a North American tree with seeds that look like cotton

**couch¹** /kaʊtʃ/ n a comfortable piece of furniture, usually with a back and arms, on which more than one person can sit

**couch²** v **be couched in sth** FORMAL to be expressed in a particular way in order to be polite or not offend someone: *His refusal was couched in polite terms.*

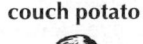
couch potato

**couch po·ta·to** /'. .,../ n INFORMAL someone who spends a lot of time sitting and watching television

**cou·gar** /'kugɚ/ *n* a large pale brown wild cat from the mountains of western North and South America

**cough**[1] /kɔf/ *v* [I] to push air out of your throat with a sudden rough sound, especially because you are sick: *He's been coughing and sneezing all day.*

  **cough up** *phr v* **1** [I,T **cough** sth ↔ **up**] INFORMAL to unwillingly give someone money, information etc: *I'm trying to get my Dad to cough up some money for a motorcycle.* **2** [T **cough up** sth] to get something out of your throat or lungs by coughing: *We got worried when she started coughing up blood.*

**cough**[2] *n* **1** the sound made when you cough: *She gave a nervous cough before speaking.* **2** **have a cough** to have an illness in which you cough a lot: *I have a terrible cough and a headache.*

**cough drop** /'. ./ *n* a type of medicine like a piece of candy that you suck when you have a cough

**cough syr·up** /'. ,../ *n* [U] a thick liquid medicine that you take when you have a cough

**could** /kəd; *strong* kʊd/ *modal verb* **1** used in order to talk about what you were able to do: *Could you hear that all right?* | *I looked everywhere, but I couldn't* (=could not) *find it.* **2** used in order to show that something might be possible or might happen: *Most accidents in the home could easily be prevented.* | *It could be weeks before they're finished.* **3** used instead of "can" when reporting what someone said: *He said we could smoke if we wanted.* **4** used in order to politely ask if someone is allowed to do something: *Could I ask you a couple of questions?* **5** used in order to politely ask someone to do something: *Could you deposit this check at the bank for me?* **6** **I couldn't believe sth** used when you are very surprised about something: *I couldn't believe how easy it was.* −see also CAN[1] −see study note on page 458

SPOKEN PHRASES
**7** said when you are annoyed because you think someone should have done something: *You could have told me you were going to be late!* **8** **I could have strangled/hit/killed etc. sb** used in order to emphasize that you were very angry with someone: *I could have murdered Kerry for telling Jason that!* **9** **I couldn't care less** used when you are not at all interested in something: *I couldn't care less what he says - I'm not going!* **10** used in order to suggest doing something: *We could always stop and ask directions.*

**could·n't** /'kʊdnt/ *modal verb* the short form of "could not": *We just couldn't stop laughing.*

**coun·cil** /'kaʊnsəl/ *n* **1** a group of people who are elected as part of a town or city government **2** a group of people who make decisions for a church, organization etc., or who give advice: *the UN Security Council*

**coun·cil·man** /'kaʊnsəlmən/, **coun·cil·wom·an** /'kaʊnsəl,wʊmən/ *n* a COUNCILOR

**coun·cil·or** /'kaʊnsələ/ *n* a member of a COUNCIL

**coun·sel**[1] /'kaʊnsəl/ *n* [U] **1** LAW a lawyer or group of lawyers who speak for someone in a court of law: *The counsel for the defense gave her opening statement.* **2** **keep your own counsel** to not talk about your private thoughts and opinions **3** FORMAL advice

**counsel**[2] *v* [T] FORMAL to listen to and advise someone: *Tyrone got a job counseling teenagers about drugs.*

**coun·sel·ing** /'kaʊnsəlɪŋ/ *n* [U] advice given to people about their personal problems or difficult decisions: *She's been getting career counseling.*

**coun·sel·or** /'kaʊnsələ/ *n* **1** someone whose job is to help people with their personal problems or with difficult decisions: *a marriage counselor* **2** also **Counselor** a name used when speaking to a lawyer in court **3** someone who takes care of a group of children at a CAMP

**count**[1] /kaʊnt/ *v* **1** [T] also **count up** to calculate the total number of things in a group: *The nurses counted the bottles of medicine as they put them away.* **2** [I,T] also **count up** to say numbers in order, one by one or in groups: *My daughter is learning to count in French.* | *He's only three, but he can count to ten.* **3** [I] to be officially allowed or accepted: *"I won!" "You cheated, so it doesn't count."* **4** [T] to include someone or something in a total: *There are five in our family, counting me.* **5** [T] to consider something or someone in a particular way: *I count her as one of my best friends.* | *You should count yourself lucky that you weren't badly hurt.* **6** [I] to be important or valuable: *I felt my opinion didn't count for much.* **7** **be able to count sth on one hand** SPOKEN used in order to emphasize how small the number of something is: *I can count on one hand the number of times he's come to visit me.*

  **count down** *phr v* [I,T **count** sth ↔ **down**] to count the number of days, minutes etc. left until a particular moment or event: *Okay, get ready to count down to midnight.* (=on New Year's Eve)

  **count** sb **in** *phr v* [T] INFORMAL to include someone or something in an activity: *If you're going dancing, count me in.*

  **count on** sb/sth *phr v* [T] **1** to depend on someone or something: *You can always count on him to help.* **2** to expect someone to do something, or something to happen: *We didn't count on this many people coming.*

  **count out** *phr v* [T] **1** [**count** sb **out**] INFORMAL to not include someone or something in an activity: *If you're looking for a fight, count me out.* **2** [**count out** sth] to lay things down one by one as you count them: *Jamie* **counted out** *the number of spoons needed.*

**count**[2] *n* **1** [C usually singular] the process of counting, or the total that you get when you count things: *The final count showed that Gary had won by 110 votes to 86.* | **At the last/latest count** (=the last time you counted), *46 students were interested in the trip.* **2** [C usually singular] a measurement that shows the total number of things in a particular group. *The pollen count is high today.* (=the amount of plant material in the air is high) **3 keep count** to know the total of something: *Are you keeping count of the people you've invited?* **4 lose count** to forget the total number of something: *I've lost count of how many times she's been married.* **5** LAW one of the crimes that the police say someone has done: *He's guilty on two counts of robbery.*

**count·a·ble** /'kaʊntəbəl/ *adj* **countable noun** a noun such as "book," that has a singular and a plural form −opposite UNCOUNTABLE −see study note on page 466

**count·down** /'kaʊntˌdaʊn/ *n* the act of counting backward to zero before something happens, especially before a space vehicle is sent into the sky: *The countdown has begun at Cape Canaveral.*

**coun·te·nance**[1] /'kaʊntənəns/ *n* LITERARY your face or your expression

**countenance**[2] *v* [T] FORMAL to support or approve of something: *We cannot countenance violent behavior.*

**coun·ter**[1] /'kaʊntɚ/ *n* **1** a flat surface in the kitchen where you work, prepare food etc. **2** a narrow table or flat surface in a store or bank where you go to be served: *the checkout counter in a supermarket* **3 over the counter** over the counter medicines can be bought without a PRESCRIPTION from your doctor **4 under the counter** secretly and not legally: *They pay her under the counter for her dishwashing job.*

**counter**[2] *v* [I,T] to react to an action, criticism, argument etc. by doing or saying something that will have an opposite effect: *Bradshaw countered the protests by saying that the plan had been approved by school officials.*

**counter**[3] *adv* in a way that is opposite to someone else's opinion, ideas etc.: *His ideas always* **run counter to** *my own.* −**counter** *adj*

**coun·ter·act** /ˌkaʊntɚˈækt/ *v* [T] to reduce or prevent the bad effect of something by doing something that has the opposite effect

**coun·ter·at·tack** /'kaʊntɚəˌtæk/ *n* an attack on an enemy that has attacked you −**counterattack** /ˌ...'.../ *v* [I,T]

**coun·ter·bal·ance** /'kaʊntɚˌbæləns/ *v* [T] to have an effect that is the opposite of the effect of something else: *Good sales in Europe have counterbalanced the weak sales in the US.* −**counterbalance** *n*

**coun·ter·clock·wise** /ˌkaʊntɚˈklɑk-waɪz/ *adj, adv* moving in the opposite direction to the HANDs (=parts that point to the time) on a clock −opposite CLOCKWISE

**coun·ter·feit**[1] /'kaʊntɚˌfɪt/ *adj* made to look exactly like something else in order to deceive people: *counterfeit money*

**counterfeit**[2] *v* [T] to copy something exactly in order to deceive people −**counterfeiter** *n*

**coun·ter·part** /'kaʊntɚˌpart/ *n* a person or thing that has the same job or purpose as someone or something else in a different place: *a meeting between the US president and his French counterpart*

**coun·ter·pro·duc·tive** /ˌkaʊntɚprəˈdʌktɪv/ *adj* achieving the opposite result to the one you want: *Punishing children too harshly can be counterproductive.*

**coun·ter·sign** /'kaʊntɚˌsaɪn/ *v* [T] to sign something that someone else has already signed: *My boss will countersign the check.*

**count·less** /'kaʊntˈlɪs/ *adj* too many to be counted: *She spent countless hours making that clock.*

**coun·try**[1] /'kʌntri/ *n* **1** a nation or state with its land and people: *Bahrain became an independent country in 1971.* **2** the people of a nation or state: *a peace-loving country* **3 the country** the land that is outside cities or towns, especially land that is used for farming

**country**[2] *adj* in the area outside cities, or relating to this area: *clean country air*

**country and west·ern** /ˌ... '../, **country** *n* [U] a type of popular music from the southern and western US

**country club** /'.. ˌ./ *n* a sports and social club, especially for rich people

**coun·try·man** /'kʌntrimən/ *n* OLD-FASHIONED someone from your own country

**coun·try·side** /'kʌntriˌsaɪd/ *n* [U] a word meaning the area outside cities and towns, used especially when you are talking about its beauty: *the peaceful countryside* −compare COUNTRY[1]

**coun·ty** /'kaʊnti/ *n* a large area of land within a state or country that has its own government to deal with local matters

**county fair** /ˌ... './ *n* an event that happens each year in a particular COUNTY, with games, competitions for the best farm animals, for the best cooking etc.

**coup** /ku/ *n* **1** also **coup d'état** /ˌku deɪˈta/ an act in which citizens or the army suddenly take control of the government by force: *President Aristide fled from a military coup in Haiti.* **2** something you do that is successful: *Getting that job was quite a coup.*

**cou·ple**[1] /'kʌpəl/ *n* **1 a couple of** INFORMAL **a)** a small number of things: *We leave in a couple of days.* | *I need to make a couple (of) phone calls.* **b)** two things or people of the same kind: *I think they have a couple (of) kids* *now.* **2** two people who are married or who have a romantic relationship: *the young couple next door*

---

**USAGE NOTE** couple

Use **couple** to talk about any two things of the same kind: *There are a couple of cars parked outside.* Use **pair** to talk about something that has two main parts of a similar shape that are joined together: *a pair of pants | a pair of scissors.* **Pair** is also used to talk about two things that are used together as a set: *a pair of shoes.*

---

**couple²** *v* FORMAL [T] to join two things together, especially two vehicles
  **coupled with** *phr v* [T] to happen, exist, or be used together: *Technology coupled with better health care means people live longer.*

**cou·pon** /'kupɑn, 'kyu-/ *n* **1** a small piece of paper that you can use to pay less money for something or get it free: *a coupon for fifty cents off a jar of coffee* **2** a printed form used when you order something, enter a competition etc.

**cour·age** /'kɝɪdʒ, 'kʌr-/ *n* [U] the ability to be brave when you are in danger, a difficult situation etc.: *It must have taken a lot of courage for him to drive again after the accident.*

**cou·ra·geous** /kə'reɪdʒəs/ *adj* brave and not afraid: *a courageous hero* —**courageously** *adv*

**cou·ri·er** /'kʊriɚ, 'kɚ-/ *n* someone who delivers messages

**course¹** /kɔrs/ *n*

**1 of course a)** used when what you or someone else has just said is not surprising: *The insurance has to be renewed every year, of course.* **b)** SPOKEN used in order to agree with someone or to give permission to someone: *"Can I borrow your notes?" "Of course you can."* **c)** SPOKEN said in order to emphasize that what you are saying is true or correct: *"You'll tell her?" "Of course!"*

**2 of course not** SPOKEN said in order to emphasize that you are saying no to something, or that something is not true or correct: *"Do you mind if I come a little late?" "Of course not."*

**3 course of action** an action you can take in a particular situation: *The best course of action is to speak to her alone.*

**4** ▶SPORTS◀ an area of land or water on which a race is held or a particular type of sport is played: *a race course | a golf course*

**5** ▶DIRECTION◀ the direction of movement that someone or something takes: *During the flight we had to change course.*

**6** ▶SCHOOL◀ a class in a particular subject: *I'm taking an evening course in math.*

**7 in/during the course of** FORMAL during a process or period: *During the course of our conversation, I found out that he had worked in France.*

**8** ▶WAY STH DEVELOPS◀ the usual or natural way that something happens, develops etc: *a major event that changed the course of history*

**9** ▶MEAL◀ the parts of a meal: *Fish is often our main course.*

**course²** *v* [I] LITERARY if a liquid courses somewhere, it flows rapidly

**court¹** /kɔrt/ *n* **1** [C,U] a room or building in which a judge, lawyers, and other people officially decide whether someone is guilty of a crime and what the punishment should be: *He had to appear in court as a witness. | We decided to take them to court* (=make them be judged in a court) *to get our money back. | The case should go to court* (=start being judged in a court) *in August. | The insurance company settled out of court.* (=they made an agreement without going to a court) **2 the court** the judge, lawyers, and other people who officially decide whether someone is guilty of a crime and what the punishment should be: *The court decided he wasn't guilty.* **3** [C,U] an area that has been made specially for playing some types of sports: *a tennis court* **4** the official place where a king or queen lives and works

**court²** *v* **1** [T] to pay attention to someone important so that s/he will like or help you in some way: *Politicans are courting voters before the elections.* **2 court disaster/danger etc.** to do something that makes a problem or failure more likely: *The Hamiltons are courting disaster if they invite both Jim and Lynne to the party.* **3** [I,T] OLD-FASHIONED to have a romantic relationship with someone, especially someone you are likely to marry

**cour·te·ous** /'kɝtiəs/ *adj* FORMAL polite and respectful: *a courteous reply* —**courteously** *adv*

**cour·te·sy** /'kɝtəsi/ *n* **1** [U] polite and respectful behavior to other people: *She didn't have the courtesy to apologize.* **2** a polite action or remark: *As a courtesy to your hosts, you should reply quickly to invitations.*

**court·house** /'kɔrthaʊs/ *n* a building containing courts of law and government offices

**court-mar·tial** /'. ,../ *n, plural* **courts-martial** *or* **court-martials 1** a military court that deals with people who break military law **2** an occasion when someone is judged by a military court: *He'll face a court-martial on drug charges.* —**court-martial** *v* [T]

**court·room** /'kɔrtˈrum/ *n* the room where a CASE is judged by a court of law

**court·ship** /'kɔrtˈʃɪp/ *n* [C,U] OLD-FASHIONED the time when a man and a woman have a romantic relationship before getting married

**court·yard** /'kɔrtˈyɑrd/ *n* an open space that is surrounded by walls or buildings

**cous·in** /'kʌzən/ *n* the child of your AUNT or UNCLE —see picture at FAMILY

**cove** /koʊv/ *n* a small area on the coast that is

partly surrounded by land and is protected from the wind

**cov·e·nant** /ˈkʌvənənt/ *n* a formal agreement between two or more people or groups

**cov·er¹** /ˈkʌvɚ/ *v* [T]

**1** ▶PUT STH OVER STH◀ also **cover up** to put something over the top of something else in order to hide or protect it: *Cover the pan and simmer the beans for two hours.*

**2** ▶BE OVER STH◀ to be on top of something or spread over something: *His bedroom walls are* **covered with** *posters.*

**3** ▶INCLUDE◀ to include or deal with something: *The class covers twentieth century American poetry.*

**4** ▶NEWS◀ to report the details of an event for a newspaper or a television or radio program: *Scully will be covering the World Series this year.*

**5** ▶PAY FOR STH◀ to be enough money to pay for something: *That should be enough to cover the tip too.*

**6** ▶INSURANCE◀ to protect someone from loss, especially through insurance: *a policy that covers medical expenses*

**7** ▶DISTANCE◀ to travel a particular distance: *We should cover another 50 miles before lunch.*

**8 a) cover for sb** to do the work that someone else usually does, but that s/he cannot do because s/he is sick or not present: *Will you cover for Ruth again today?* **b)** to prevent someone from getting into trouble by lying about where s/he is: *Can you cover for me? Just say I had an appointment.*

**9** ▶GUN◀ to aim a gun at a person or a place in order to protect someone from being attacked or to prevent someone from escaping: *We'll cover you while you run for it.* | *The police covered the back entrance.*

**10 cover (all) the bases** INFORMAL to make sure that you can deal with any situation or problem

**cover** sth ↔ **up** *phr v* [T] to prevent mistakes or unpleasant facts from being known: *A lot of people tried to* **cover up** *the Watergate affair.*

**cover up for** sb *phr v* [T] to protect someone by hiding unpleasant facts about him/her: *The mayor's friends tried to* **cover up** *for him.*

**cover²** *n* **1** something that protects something else by covering it: *a plastic cover over the bowl* **2** the outside of a book, magazine etc.: *Rolling Stone magazine always has interesting covers.* **3** [U] shelter or protection from bad weather or attack: *The soldiers* **ran for cover** *when the shooting started.* | *We* **took cover** *from the rain under a tree.* **4** something that hides something or keeps it secret: *The company is just* **a cover for** *the Mafia.* **5** [U] insurance against loss, injury, or damage: *We'll need cover for theft.* **6 under cover** pretending to be someone else in order to do something without being noticed: *Policemen working under cover*

*arrested several drug dealers.* **7 cover your tracks** to be careful not to leave any signs that could let people know where you have been or what you have done —see also COVERS

**cov·er·age** /ˈkʌvrɪdʒ/ *n* [U] **1** the amount of time and space given on television or by a newspaper to report something: *excellent news coverage of the elections* **2** things that are included in insurance: *Make sure your policy will give you accident coverage.*

**cov·er·alls** /ˈkʌvɚˌɔlz/ *n* [plural] a piece of clothing that covers your upper and lower body, usually worn over your clothes to keep them clean while you work —see picture at OVERALLS

**cover charge** /ˈ.. ˌ./ *n* money that you have to pay in a restaurant in addition to the cost of food and drinks

**cov·er·ing** /ˈkʌvrɪŋ, -ərɪŋ/ *n* something that covers or hides something else: *a light covering of snow*

**cover let·ter** /ˈ.. ˌ../ *n* a letter that you send with another letter or a package to explain what it is or give more information: *Always include a typed cover letter with your résumé*

**cov·ers** /ˈkʌvɚz/ *n* [plural] BLANKETs, SHEETs (=large pieces of cloth) etc. that cover you in bed

**co·vert** /ˈkoʊvɚt, ˈkʌ-, koʊˈvɚt/ *adj* secret or hidden: *the covert actions of spies* —**covertly** *adv*

**cover-up** /ˈ.. ˌ./ *n* an attempt to prevent people knowing about something shameful or illegal: *CIA officials denied there had been a cover-up.*

**cov·et** /ˈkʌvɪt/ *v* [T] LITERARY to have a strong desire to possess something that someone else has —**covetous** *adj*

**cow¹** /kaʊ/ *n* **1** an adult female farm animal that is kept for its milk and meat —compare BULL, STEER² **2 have a cow** SPOKEN to be very angry or surprised about something: *It was just an accident. Don't have a cow!* **3** the female of some large land and sea animals, such as the ELEPHANT or the WHALE

**cow²** *v* [T] to make someone afraid or control him/her by using violence or threats: *The children were* **cowed into** *obedience.*

**cow·ard** /ˈkaʊɚd/ *n* DISAPPROVING someone who is not brave in dangerous situations —**cowardly** *adj*

**cow·ard·ice** /ˈkaʊɚdɪs/ *n* [U] a lack of courage

**cow·boy** /ˈkaʊbɔɪ/ *n* a man whose job is to take care of cattle

**cow·er** /ˈkaʊɚ/ *v* [I] to bend low and move back because you are afraid: *The hostages were cowering in a corner.*

**cow·girl** /ˈkaʊgɚl/ *n* a woman whose job is to take care of cattle

**co-work·er** /ˈkoʊˌwɚkɚ/ *n* someone who works with you

**coy** /kɔɪ/ *adj* a person or action that is coy seems quiet or shy but is really trying to attract attention: *a coy smile* **–coyly** *adv*

**coy·ote** /kaɪ'outi, 'kaɪ-out/ *n* a wild animal like a dog that lives in western North America and Mexico

**co·zy** /'kouzi/ *adj* small, comfortable, and warm: *a cozy cabin in the woods* **–cozily** *adv* **–coziness** *n* [U]

**CPA** *n* Certified Public Accountant; an ACCOUNTANT who has passed all of his/her examinations

**CPR** *n* cardiopulmonary resuscitation; a set of actions that you do to help someone who has stopped breathing or whose heart has stopped beating

**CPU** *n* Central Processing Unit; the part of a computer that controls and organizes what the computer does

**crab** /kræb/ *n* [C,U] a sea animal with a round flat shell and its two large CLAWs on front legs, or the meat from this animal

**crab·by** /'kræbi/ *adj* easily annoyed or upset: *Mom gets really crabby right before dinner.*

**crack**[1] /kræk/ *v*

**1** ▶BREAK◀ [I,T] to break something so that lines appear on its surface, or to break in this way: *Two of my best plates cracked in the dishwasher.*

**2** ▶NOISE OF BREAKING◀ [I,T] to make a loud sudden noise that sounds like something breaking, or to make something do this: *A stick cracked under his foot.*

**3** ▶HIT STH◀ [I,T] to accidentally hit something very hard: *Carly tripped and cracked her head on the sidewalk.*

**4** ▶LOSE CONTROL◀ [I] to lose control of your emotions or tell a secret because someone or something is making you feel extremely anxious: *a spy who never cracked under questioning*

**5** ▶EGG/NUT◀ [T] to break the shell of an egg, nut etc. in order to get the food inside it

**6** ▶VOICE◀ [I] if your voice cracks, it suddenly get softer or louder because you feel a strong emotion

**7** ▶SOLVE◀ [T] to solve a problem or a CODE

**8 crack a joke** INFORMAL to tell a joke: *John keeps cracking jokes about my hair.*

**9 not be all sth is cracked up to be** INFORMAL not as good as people say it is: *Life as a model isn't all it's cracked up to be.*

**crack down** *phr v* [I] to become more strict when dealing with someone's bad behavior or an illegal activity: *Police are cracking down on drunk drivers.* **–crackdown** *n*

**crack up** *phr v* INFORMAL **1** [I,T] to laugh a lot at something, or to make someone laugh a lot: *Sue just cracks me up!* **2** [I] to become unable to think clearly or behave normally because you are tired, worried, too busy etc.

**crack**[2] *n* **1** a very narrow space between two things: *Can you open the window a crack?* **2** a thin line on the surface of something that is damaged: *These cracks on the wall are from last year's earthquake.* **3** INFORMAL a cruel joke or remark: *Stop making cracks about my sister!* **4 a crack at** INFORMAL an attempt to do or use something: *Okay, Dave, let's take/have a crack at fixing this bike.* **5** a sudden loud noise that sounds like a stick breaking: *the cracks of the fireworks* **6** a pure form of the drug COCAINE that some people take illegally for pleasure **7 the crack of dawn** the very early time in the morning when the sun appears

**crack**[3] *adj* having a lot of skill: *a crack shot* (=someone who is very good at shooting)

**crack·down** /'. ./ *n* [C usually singular] an effort to stop bad or illegal behavior by being strict and determined: *a national crackdown on illegal immigrants*

**cracked** /krækt/ *adj* something that is cracked has thin lines on its surface because it is damaged **–see picture at** BROKEN[1]

**crack·er** /'krækɚ/ *n* a type of hard dry bread that is thin and flat: *cheese and crackers*

**crack·le** /'krækəl/ *v* [I] to make a lot of short noises that sound like something burning in a fire: *a log fire crackling in the fireplace* | *a radio program crackling with static* **–crackle** *n*

**crack·pot** /'krækpɑt/ *adj* slightly crazy or strange: *a crackpot idea* **–crackpot** *n*

**cra·dle**[1] /'kreɪdl/ *n* **1** a small bed for a baby, that can swing gently from side to side **2 the cradle of** the place where something important began: *Some say Athens was the cradle of democracy.*

**cradle**[2] *v* [T] to gently hold someone or something: *Tony cradled his baby daughter in his arms.*

**craft** /kræft/ *n* **1** a job or activity that you need to have a lot of skill to do, especially one in which you make things: *a craft such as knitting* **2** *plural* **craft** a boat, ship, or plane

**crafts·man** /'kræftsmən/ *n* someone who has a lot of skill in a particular craft: *furniture made by the finest craftsmen* **–craftsmanship** *n* [U]

**craft·y** /'kræfti/ *adj* good at deceiving people in order to get what you want **–craftily** *adv*

**crag·gy** /'krægi/ *adj* a craggy mountain or cliff is very steep and is covered with large sharp rocks

**cram** /kræm/ *v* **-mmed, -mming 1** [T] to force something into a small space: *You should see how many clothes we crammed into that suitcase!* **2** [T] to fill an area with too many people: *The mall was totally crammed with Christmas shoppers.* **3** [I] to prepare yourself for a test by studying a lot of information very quickly: *Julia stayed up all night cramming for her math final.* **–crammed** *adj*

**cramp** /kræmp/ *n* a severe pain that you get when a muscle becomes very tight: *I have a cramp in my wrist from writing all day.* −**cramping** *n* [U]

**cramped** /kræmpt/ *adj* uncomfortable because there is not enough space: *I can never sleep on planes because I always feel so cramped.*

**cramps** /kræmps/ *n* [plural] pain that women get during MENSTRUATION

**cran·ber·ry** /'kræn,bɛri/ *n* a small sour red BERRY: *cranberry sauce*

**crane**[1] /kreɪn/ *n* **1** a large machine with a thick strong wire that builders use to lift heavy things **2** a tall water bird with very long legs

**crane**[2] *v* [I,T] to look around or over something by stretching or leaning: *All the kids craned their necks to see who Mrs. Miller was talking to.*

**cra·ni·um** /'kreɪniəm/ *n* TECHNICAL the bones in an animal's or person's head that cover the brain

**crank**[1] /kræŋk/ *n* **1 crank call** INFORMAL a telephone call intended as a joke or made in order to frighten, annoy, or upset someone **2** INFORMAL someone who easily becomes angry or annoyed **3** a handle on a piece of equipment that you turn in order to move something

**crank**[2] *v* INFORMAL

**crank sth out** *phr v* [T] to produce a lot of something very quickly: *He cranks out novels at the rate of one a year.*

**crank sth ↔ up** *phr v* [T] to make the sound from a radio etc. a lot louder: *Hey, Vince, crank up the stereo!*

**crank·y** /'kræŋki/ *adj* very easily annoyed or made angry, especially because you are tired: *Steve woke up cranky this morning.*

**crap** /kræp/ *n* [U] INFORMAL **1** an impolite word for something that you think is very bad, wrong, or untrue: *That movie was crap.* **2** an impolite word for things that you do not need or want: *What's all this crap doing on my desk?* −**crappy** *adj*

**craps** /kræps/ *n* [U] a game played for money in which you throw two DICE

**crash**[1] /kræʃ/ *v* **1** [I,T] to have an accident in which a car, plane etc. hits something and is badly damaged: *We crashed straight into the car ahead of us.* **2** [I,T] if a computer crashes or you crash it, it suddenly stops working **3** [I] SPOKEN **a)** also **crash out** to go to sleep very quickly because you are very tired: *I crashed out on the sofa watching TV.* **b)** to stay at someone's house for the night: *You can crash at our place if you can't get a ride home.* **4** [I,T] to make a sudden loud noise, especially by hitting or breaking something: *A baseball crashed into/through our living room window.* **5** [I] if the STOCK MARKET crashes, STOCKs suddenly become worth less money than before

**6** [T] if you crash a party or event, you go to it although you have not been invited

**crash**[2] *n* **1** a very bad accident involving cars, planes etc. that have hit something: *Both the passenger and the driver were killed in the crash.* **2** an occasion when a computer suddenly stops working **3** a sudden loud noise that sounds like something breaking or hitting something else: *a crash of plates falling on the floor* **4** an occasion when a business or a financial system suddenly fails and STOCKs become worth much less money than before: *the crash of the New York Stock Exchange*

**crash course** /ˌ. './ *n* a course in which you try to learn a particular subject very quickly

**crash di·et** /ˌ. '../ *n* an attempt to make yourself thinner quickly by strictly limiting how much you eat

**crash hel·met** /'. ˌ../ *n* a very strong hat that covers and protects someone's whole head, worn by people who drive race cars, MOTORCYCLEs, etc.

**crash land·ing** /ˌ. '../ *n* **make a crash landing** to try to fly a damaged plane to the ground in a way that will not damage it more

**crass** /kræs/ *adj* offensive or rude: *Dick made a crass remark about her weight.*

**crate** /kreɪt/ *n* a large wooden or plastic box used for sending things a long distance: *a crate of wine* −see picture at CONTAINER

**cra·ter** /'kreɪtɚ/ *n* **1** a round hole in the ground made by something that has fallen on it or exploded on it: *a bomb crater | craters on the moon's surface* **2** the round open top of a VOLCANO

**crave** /kreɪv/ *v* [T] to have a very strong desire for something: *Most little kids crave attention.*

**crav·ing** /'kreɪvɪŋ/ *n* a very strong desire for something: *I have a major craving for chocolate chip cookies.*

**craw·dad** /'krɔdæd/, **craw·fish** /'krɔˌfɪʃ/ *n* ⇨ CRAYFISH

**crawl**[1] /krɔl/ *v* [I] **1** to move on your hands and knees or with your body close to the ground: *When did your baby start crawling? | There's a bee crawling on your arm!* **2** to move very slowly: *We got stuck behind a truck crawling along at 25 mph.*

crawl

**3 be crawling with** to be completely covered with insects, people etc.: *Oh gross! Nibby's dog dish is crawling with ants!*

**crawl**[2] *n* **1** a very slow speed: *Traffic has slowed to a crawl.* **2** a fast way of swimming in which you lie on your stomach and move one arm and then the other over your head

**cray·fish** /'kreɪˌfɪʃ/ *n* [C,U] a small animal

that is similar to a LOBSTER and lives in rivers and streams, or the meat from this animal

**cray·on** /'kreɪɑn, -ən/ n a stick of colored WAX that children use to draw pictures

**craze** /kreɪz/ n a fashion, game, type of music etc. that becomes very popular for a short amount of time: *the latest teenage craze*

**crazed** /kreɪzd/ adj wild, strange, or crazy: *a crazed evil laugh*

**cra·zy** /'kreɪzi/ adj INFORMAL **1** very strange or not very sensible: *You must be crazy to drive in that snow! | Whose crazy idea was it to go hiking in November?* **2 be crazy about sb/ sth** to like someone or something very much: *Lee and John are crazy about skiing.* **3** angry or annoyed: *Shut up! You're driving me crazy!* (=really annoying me) | *Dad's going to go crazy* (=be very angry) *when he hears that I flunked math.* **4 like crazy** very much or very quickly: *These mosquito bites on my leg are itching like crazy. | We ran like crazy to the bus stop.* **5** mentally ill: *I feel so alone, sometimes I wonder if I'm going crazy.* –**crazily** adv –**craziness** n [U]

**creak** /krik/ v [I] if something such as a door, wooden floor, or old bed creaks, it makes a long high noise when you push it, step on it, or sit on it –**creak** n –**creaky** adj

**cream**¹ /krim/ n **1** [U] a thick yellow-white liquid that can be separated from milk: *Do you take cream and sugar in your coffee?* **2** [U] a pale yellow-white color **3** [C,U] a food containing cream or something similar to it: *banana cream pie | cream of mushroom soup* **4** [C,U] a thick smooth substance that you put on your skin to make it feel soft, treat a medical condition etc.: *The doctor recommended a cream to put on my sunburn.* **5 the cream of the crop** the best of a particular group: *"We're unable to get the cream of the crop," admitted the athletic director.* –**creamy, cream** adj

**cream**² v [T] **1** to mix foods together until they become a thick creamy mixture: *Next, cream the butter and sugar.* **2 cream sb** INFORMAL to hit someone very hard or easily defeat someone in a game, competition etc.: *We got creamed 25 runs to 2.*

**cream cheese** /ˌ. './ n [U] a type of soft white smooth cheese

**cream·er** /'krimɚ/ n [U] a substance you can use instead of milk or cream in coffee or tea

**crease**¹ /kris/ n **1** a line on a piece of cloth, paper etc. where it has been folded or IRONed: *pants with creases down the front* **2** a fold in someone's skin: WRINKLE

**crease**² v [T] to make a line appear on a piece of cloth, paper etc. by folding or crushing it –**creased** adj

**cre·ate** /kri'eɪt/ v [T] **1** to make something exist: *Scientists believe the universe was created by a big explosion. | Why do you want to create*

problems for everyone? **2** to invent something new: *Janet created a wonderful chocolate dessert for the party.*

**cre·a·tion** /kri'eɪʃən/ n **1** [U] the act of creating (CREATE) something: *the creation of 300 new jobs* **2** [U] the whole universe and all living things **3** something that has been created: *this year's fashion creations* **4 the Creation** the act by God of making the universe and everything in it, according to the Bible

**cre·a·tive** /kri'eɪtɪv/ adj **1** producing or using new and effective ideas: *a creative solution to our problems* **2** good at using your imagination and skills: *a creative young author* –**creatively** adv

**cre·a·tiv·i·ty** /ˌkrieɪ'tɪvɪti/ n [U] the ability to use your imagination to produce or use new ideas, make things etc.

**cre·a·tor** /kri'eɪtɚ/ n **1** someone who CREATEs something: *Walt Disney, the creator of Mickey Mouse* **2 the Creator** God

**crea·ture** /'kritʃɚ/ n **1** any living thing such as an animal, fish, or insect, except plants: *Native Americans believe that all living creatures should be respected.* **2** an imaginary animal or person, or one that is very strange: *creatures from outer space* **3 a creature of sth** someone who is a creature of something is influenced by it a lot or has a quality produced by it: *Today's kids are creatures of television.* **4 creature comforts** things that people need to feel comfortable, such as warmth, good food, comfortable furniture etc. **5 creature of habit** someone who always does things in the same way or at the same time

**cre·dence** /'kridns/ n [U] FORMAL the acceptance of something as true: *His ideas quickly gained credence* (=started to be believed) *among economists.*

**cre·den·tials** /krə'dɛnʃəlz/ n [plural] someone's education, achievements, experience etc., that prove that s/he has the ability to do something

**cred·i·bil·i·ty** /ˌkrɛdə'bɪləti/ n [U] the quality of being CREDIBLE: *The scandal has ruined his credibility as a leader.*

**cred·i·ble** /'krɛdəbəl/ adj deserving to be believed, or able to be trusted: *a credible witness* –**credibly** adv

**cred·it**¹ /'krɛdɪt/ n **1** [U] an arrangement with a bank, store etc. that allows you to buy something and pay for it later: *We bought a new stove on credit. | six months of interest-free credit* (=credit with no additional charge) **2** [U] approval or praise for doing something good: *They never give Jess any credit for all the extra work he does. | I can't take all the credit; Nicky helped a lot too! | Much to Todd's credit, the dance was a great success.* (=Todd deserves praise for organizing it) **3 be in credit** to have money in your bank account **4 be a credit to**

**sb/sth** to be so successful or good that everyone who is connected with you can be proud of you: *Jo's a credit to her family.* **5** a unit that shows you have completed part of a college course: *a 5-credit class* **6 have sth to your credit** to have achieved something: *She already has two best-selling novels to her credit.* **7** [U] the belief that something is true or correct: *The witness's story is gaining credit with the jury* —see also CREDITS

**credit²** *v* [T] **1** to add money to a bank account: *For some reason the bank has credited my account with an extra $237.* —opposite DEBIT² **2 credit sb/sth with sth** to believe or admit that someone or something has a particular quality: *I wouldn't have credited him with that much intelligence.*

**cred·it·a·ble** /ˈkrɛdɪt̬əbəl/ *adj* deserving praise or approval: *a creditable piece of scientific research* —**creditably** *adv*

**credit card** /ˈ.. ˌ./ *n* a small plastic card that you use to buy goods or services and pay for them later —see picture at CARD¹

**credit lim·it** /ˈ.. ˌ./ *n* the amount of money that you are allowed to borrow or spend using your CREDIT CARD

**cred·i·tor** /ˈkrɛdət̬ɚ/ *n* a person, bank, or company that you owe money to —compare DEBTOR

**credit rat·ing** /ˈ.. ˌ./ *n* a judgment made by a bank or other company about how likely a person or a business is to pay debts

**cred·its** /ˈkrɛdɪts/ *n* **the credits** a list of all the people involved in making a television program or movie

**cre·do** /ˈkridoʊ/ *n* a short statement that expresses a belief or rule that a particular person or group has: *Dad's credo has always been, "Never give up!"*

**creed** /krid/ *n* a set of beliefs or principles, especially religious ones

**creek** /krik, krɪk/ *n* **1** a small narrow stream or river **2 be up the creek** SPOKEN to be in a difficult situation: *I'll really be up the creek if I don't pay my bills by Friday.*

**creep¹** /krip/ *v* **crept, crept, creeping** [I] **1** to move very carefully and quietly so that no one will notice you: *She crept down the hall, trying not to wake up her mom.* **2** to move very slowly: *a tractor creeping along the road at 15 mph* **3** to gradually begin to appear: *Bitterness crept into his voice.*

**creep²** *n* **1** someone you dislike a lot, especially because s/he annoys you or frightens you a little: *Get lost, you little creep!* **2 give sb the creeps** a person or place that gives you the creeps makes you feel nervous and slightly frightened: *That house gives me the creeps.* —**creepy** *adj*

**cre·mate** /ˈkrimeɪt, krɪˈmeɪt/ *v* [T] to burn

the body of a dead person —**cremation** /krɪˈmeɪʃən/ *n* [U]

**cre·ma·to·ri·um** /ˌkriməˈtɔriəm/ *n, plural* **crematoriums, crematoria** a building in which the bodies of dead people are CREMATEd

**cre·ole** /ˈkrioʊl/ *n* **1** [C,U] a language that is a combination of a European language and one or more others **2 Creole a)** someone whose family was originally from both Europe and Africa **b)** someone whose family were originally French SETTLERs in the southern US —**creole** *adj*

**crepe, crêpe** /kreɪp/ *n* **1** [U] thin light cloth with very small folded lines on its surface, made from cotton, silk, wool etc. **2** a very thin PANCAKE

**crepe pa·per** /ˈ. ˌ../ *n* [U] thin brightly colored paper with small folded lines on its surface, used as a decoration at parties

**crept** /krɛpt/ the past tense and PAST PARTICIPLE of CREEP

**cre·scen·do** /krəˈʃɛndoʊ/ *n* a sound or a part of a piece of music that becomes gradually louder

**cres·cent** /ˈkrɛsənt/ *n* a curved shape that is wider in the middle and pointed on the ends: *a crescent moon*

**crest** /krɛst/ *n* **1** [C usually singular] the top of something such as a mountain, hill, or wave **2** a pointed group of feathers on top of a bird's head

**crest·fall·en** /ˈkrɛstˌfɔlən/ *adj* disappointed and sad

**cre·vasse** /krəˈvæs/ *n* a deep wide crack, especially in thick ice

**crev·ice** /ˈkrɛvɪs/ *n* a narrow crack, especially in rock

**crew** /kru/ *n* **1** all the people that work together on a ship, plane etc. **2** a group of people with special skills who work together on something: *the movie's cast and crew*

**crew cut** /ˈ. ./ *n* a very short hair style for men

**crib** /krɪb/ *n* **1** a baby's bed with BARs around the sides **2** SLANG the place where someone lives

**crib death** /ˈ. ./ *n* the unexpected death of a healthy baby while s/he is asleep

**crib sheet** /ˈ. ./ *n* INFORMAL something on which answers to questions are written, usually used in order to cheat on a test

**crick** /krɪk/ *n* a sudden stiff feeling in a muscle in your neck or back

**crick·et** /ˈkrɪkɪt/ *n* **1** a small brown insect that makes a short loud noise by rubbing its wings together **2** [U] a game in which two teams try to get points by hitting a ball and running between two sets of special sticks

**crime** /kraɪm/ *n* **1** [U] illegal activity in general: *There's some petty crime* (=crime that is not serious) *in our neighborhood, but not much*

**serious crime**. (=crime that is more violent) | *methods of crime prevention* (=ways to stop crime) **2** an illegal action that can be punished by law: *crimes against the elderly | She committed a number of crimes in the area.* ✗ DON'T SAY "do a crime." ✗ **3 it's a crime** SPOKEN said when you think something is wrong: *It's a crime to throw away all that food.*

**crim·i·nal**[1] /'krɪmənəl/ *adj* **1** relating to crime. *a criminal record* (=an official record of crimes someone has done) **2** INFORMAL wrong but not illegal: *It's criminal to charge so much for popcorn at the movies!* —**criminally** *adv*

**criminal**[2] *n* someone who is proved guilty of a crime

**crimp**[1] /krɪmp/ *n* **put a crimp in/on** to reduce or restrict something, so that it is difficult to do something else: *Falling wheat prices have put a crimp on farm incomes.*

**crimp**[2] *v* [T] to restrict the development, use, or growth of something: *The lack of effective advertising has crimped sales.*

**crim·son** /'krɪmzən/ *n* [U] a dark slightly purple red color —**crimson** *adj*

**cringe** /krɪndʒ/ *v* [I] **1** to move back or away from someone or something because you are afraid: *a dog cringing in the corner* **2** to feel embarrassed by something: *Paul cringed at the thought of having to speak in public.* —**cringe** *n*

**crin·kle** /'krɪŋkəl/ **crinkle up** *v* [I,T] to become covered with very small folds, or to make something do this: *Mandy crinkled up her nose in disgust.* —**crinkled** *adj* —**crinkly** *adv*

**crip·ple**[1] /'krɪpəl/ *n* **1** OFFENSIVE someone who cannot walk **2 emotional cripple** DISAPPROVING someone who is not able to deal with his/her own or other people's feelings

**cripple**[2] *v* [T] **1** to injure someone so s/he cannot walk or use his/her arms **2** to make something very weak or damage it: *The country's economy has been crippled by drought.* —**crippled** *adj* —**crippling** *adj*

**cri·sis** /'kraɪsɪs/ *n, plural* **crises** /'kraɪsiz/ [C,U] **1** a very bad or dangerous situation that might get worse, especially in politics or ECONOMICS: *the worst budget crisis in a decade | the hostage crisis* **2** a time when an emotional problem or illness is at its worst: *I had reached a crisis in my personal life.*

**crisp** /krɪsp/ *adj* **1** APPROVING dry and hard enough to be broken easily: *nice crisp pastry* **2** fruit and vegetables that are crisp are firm and fresh **3** paper or clothes that are crisp are fresh, clean, and stiff: *a crisp $20 bill* **4** weather that is crisp is cold and dry: *a crisp winter morning* —**crisply** *adv*

**crisp·y** /'krɪspi/ *adj* CRISP and good to eat: *crispy bacon*

**criss·cross** /'krɪskrɔs/ *v* [I,T] **1** to travel many times from one side of an area to the other: *crisscrossing the country by plane* **2** to make a pattern of straight lines that cross over each other —**crisscross** *n*

**cri·te·ri·a** /kraɪ'tɪriə/ *n, singular* **criterion** /-'tɪriən/ [plural] facts or standards used in order to help you judge or decide something: *What are the main criteria for awarding the prize?*

**crit·ic** /'krɪtɪk/ *n* **1** someone whose job is to judge whether a movie, book etc. is good or bad: *a literary critic for The Times* **2** someone who severely judges a person, idea etc.: *a critic of the plans for developing Yosemite*

**crit·i·cal** /'krɪtɪkəl/ *adj* **1** severely judging people or things, sometimes in an unfair way: *Darren was critical of the plan to reorganize the company.* **2** very important, because what happens in the future depends on it: *This next phase is critical to the project's success.* **3** very serious or dangerous, because a situation could get better or worse: *Seth is at a critical stage in his recovery from his operation.* **4** making judgments about whether someone or something is good or bad: *a critical analysis of the play* —**critically** *adv*

**crit·i·cism** /'krɪtə,sɪzəm/ *n* [C,U] **1** the act of judging whether someone or something is good or bad: *I'm always willing to hear constructive criticism.* (−helpful advice) **2** written or spoken remarks that show that you do not approve of someone or something: *There is growing criticism of the President's decision.*

**crit·i·cize** /'krɪtə,saɪz/ *v* **1** [I,T] to judge someone or something severely: *Journalists criticized the White House for cutting the Social Security budget.* **2** [T] ⟶ CRITIQUE[2]

**cri·tique**[1] /krɪ'tik/ *n* [C,U] an article, book etc. that makes judgments about the good and bad qualities of someone or something

**critique**[2] *v* [T] to judge whether someone or something is good or bad: *a group of artists meeting to critique each others' work*

**crit·ter** /'krɪtə/ *n* INFORMAL an animal, fish, or insect; creature

**croak**[1] /krouk/ *v* **1** [I] to make a deep low sound like the sound a FROG makes **2** [I,T] to speak in a low deep voice as if you have a sore throat **3** [I] SLANG to die

**croak**[2] *n* a low deep sound made in the throat, like the sound a FROG makes

**cro·chet** /krou'ʃeɪ/ *v* [I,T] to make clothes, hats etc. using a special needle with a hook at one end —**crochet** *n* [U]

**crock** /krɑk/ *n* **sth is a crock** SPOKEN an impolite expression used in order to say that something is not true or that you do not believe someone

**crock·er·y** /'krɑkəri/ *n* [U] dishes made from clay

**croc·o·dile** /'krɑkə,daɪl/ *n* a large REPTILE (=type of animal) that has a long body and a long mouth with sharp teeth, and lives in hot wet areas

**cro·cus** /ˈkroʊkəs/ *n* a small purple, yellow, or white flower that appears in early spring

**crois·sant** /krwɑˈsɑnt/ *n* a soft bread ROLL shaped in a curve —see picture at BREAD

**cro·ny** /ˈkroʊni/ *n* INFORMAL someone that you spend a lot of time with, especially someone you help unfairly by using your power or authority

**crook**[1] /krʊk/ *n* **1** INFORMAL someone who is not honest: *Politicians are just* **a bunch of crooks**. **2 the crook of your arm** the inside part of your arm where it bends at the elbow

**crook**[2] *v* [I,T] to bend something, especially your finger or arm

**crook·ed** /ˈkrʊkɪd/ *adj* **1** twisted or not straight: *crooked country roads* **2** INFORMAL not honest: *a crooked cop* —**crookedly** *adv*

**croon** /krun/ *v* [I,T] to sing or speak in a soft gentle voice: *crooning love songs* —**crooner** *n*

**crop**[1] /krɑp/ *n* **1** a plant such as corn, wheat etc. that is grown by a farmer and used as food **2** the amount of corn, wheat etc. that is produced in a single season: *a* **bumper crop** (=a very large amount) *of barley* **3 a crop of** INFORMAL a group of people, problems etc. that arrive at the same time: *this year's crop of college freshmen*

**crop**[2] *v* **-pped, -pping** [T] **1** to make something smaller or shorter by cutting it: *cropped hair* **2** if an animal crops grass, it makes it shorter by eating the top part

**crop up** *phr v* [I] to happen or appear suddenly in an unexpected way: *Several problems cropped up soon after we bought the car.*

**cro·quet** /kroʊˈkeɪ/ *n* [U] an outdoor game in which you hit heavy balls under curved wires using a wooden hammer

**cross**[1] /krɔs/ *v* **1** [I,T] to go from one side of a road, river, place etc. to the other side: *Look both ways before crossing the street!* **2** [T] if two or more roads, lines etc. cross, they go across each other: *There's a post office where Main Street crosses Elm.* **3** [T] if you cross your arms or legs, you put one on top of the other: *a big man standing at the door with his arms crossed* **4 cross your mind** if something crosses your mind, you think about it: *It never crossed my mind that she might be sick.* **5** [T] to mix two or more breeds of animal or plant to form a new breed: *crossing a horse with a donkey to get a mule* **6 cross my heart (and hope to die)** SPOKEN a phrase used especially by children to promise that what you have said is true **7 cross yourself** to move your hand across your chest in the shape of a cross, as a sign of Christian faith

**cross** sth ↔ **off** *phr v* [I,T] to draw a line through something on a list to show that it is not needed or that it has been done: *Cross off their names as they arrive.*

**cross** sth ↔ **out** *phr v* [T] to draw a line through something that you have written or drawn, especially to show that it is wrong: *a handwritten letter with a few words* **crossed out**

**cross**[2] *n* **1** a wooden post with another post crossing it near the top, that people were NAILed to as a punishment in ancient times **2** an object in the shape of a cross that is used as a decoration or as a sign of the Christian faith: *She wore a tiny gold cross around her neck.* **3** a mixture of two or more things, breeds, qualities etc.: *His dog is a* **cross between** *a retriever and a collie.*

**cross**[3] *adj* OLD-FASHIONED annoyed and angry

**cross·bow** /ˈkrɔsboʊ/ *n* a weapon used in past times to shoot ARROWs with a lot of force

**cross·check** /ˌkrɔsˈtʃɛk, ˈkrɔstʃɛk/ *v* [T] to make sure that something is correct by using a different method to calculate it again

**cross-coun·try** /ˌ. ˈ.../ *adj* **1** across fields and not along roads: *cross-country running* **2** from one side of a country to the other side: *a cross-country flight*

**cross-cul·tur·al** /ˌ. ˈ.../ *adj* belonging to or involving two or more societies, countries, or CULTUREs

**cross-dress** /ˈ. ./ *v* [I] to wear the clothes of the opposite sex, especially for sexual pleasure —**cross-dressing** *n* [U]

**cross-ex·am·ine** /ˌ. .ˈ.../ *v* [I,T] to ask someone questions about something s/he has just said to see if s/he is telling the truth, especially in a court of law —**cross-examination** /ˌ. ...ˈ.../ *n* [C,U]

**cross-eyed** /ˈ. ./ *adj* having eyes that look inward toward the nose

**cross·fire** /ˈkrɔsfaɪr/ *n* [U] **1 be caught in the crossfire** to be involved in a situation in which other people are arguing **2** bullets from two or more different directions that pass through the same area

**cross·ing** /ˈkrɔsɪŋ/ *n* **1** a marked place where you can safely cross a road, railroad, river etc. **2** a place where two roads, lines etc. cross **3** a trip across the ocean

**cross-legged**

Tony is sitting cross-legged.

Kara is sitting with her legs crossed.

**cross-leg·ged** /ˈkrɔs ˌlɛgɪd, -lɛgd/ *adv* in a sitting position with your knees wide apart and your feet crossed: *children sitting cross-legged on the floor* —**cross-legged** *adj*

**cross·o·ver** /ˈkrɔsˌoʊvɚ/ adj moving or changing from one type of group, style, period etc. to another: *the band's crossover move from jazz into pop music*

**cross-pur·pos·es** /ˌ. ˈ.../ n [plural] **be at cross-purposes** if two people are at cross-purposes, they do not understand each other because they do not know that they want, or are talking about different things

**cross-ref·er·ence** /ˈ ˌ . ˌ . ˈ.../ n a note in a book that directs you to look in a different place in the same book for more information

**cross·roads** /ˈkrɔsroʊdz/ n, plural **cross-roads** 1 a place where two roads meet and cross each other 2 a time in your life when you have to make an important decision that will affect your future: *Neale's career was at a crossroads.*

**cross sec·tion, cross-section** /ˈ. ˌ../ n 1 something that has been cut in half so that you can look at the inside, or a drawing of this: *a cross section of the brain* 2 a group of people or things that is typical of a larger group: *a cross-section of the American public*

**cross street** /ˈ. ./ n a street that crosses another street: *The nearest cross streets are Victory and Reseda Blvd.*

**cross·walk** /ˈkrɔswɔk/ n a specially marked place for people to walk across a street

**cross·word puz·zle** /ˈkrɔswɚd ˌpʌzəl/ **crossword** n a game in which you write the words that are the answers to questions in a special pattern of squares with numbers in their corners

**crotch** /krɑtʃ/ n the part of your body between the tops of your legs, or the part of a piece of clothing that covers this

**crotch·et·y** /ˈkrɑtʃəti/ adj INFORMAL easily annoyed or made angry: *a crotchety old man*

**crouch** /kraʊtʃ/ **crouch down** v [I] to lower your body close to the ground by bending your knees and back: *We crouched down behind your wall to hide.* —see picture on page 473

**crow**[1] /kroʊ/ n 1 a large shiny black bird that makes a loud sound 2 [singular] the loud sound that a ROOSTER makes 3 **as the crow flies** measured in a straight line: *My house is ten miles from here as the crow flies.*

**crow**[2] v [I] to make the loud sound of a ROOSTER

**crow·bar** /ˈkroʊbɑr/ n a strong iron BAR used for lifting or opening things

**crowd**[1] /kraʊd/ n 1 a large group of people in a particular place: *A crowd gathered to watch the parade.* 2 a group of people who are friends, work together etc: *I guess the usual crowd will be at the party.*

**crowd**[2] v 1 [I,T] if people crowd somewhere or around something, they gather together in large numbers, filling a particular place: *People crowded around the scene of the accident.*

2 [T] to make someone angry by moving too close to him/her or by asking him/her to do too much for you: *Stop crowding me!*

**crowd sb/sth** ↔ **out** phr v [T] to force someone or something out of a place or situation: *The big supermarkets have been crowding out small grocery stores for years.*

**crowd·ed** /ˈkraʊdɪd/ adj too full of people or things: *a crowded room*

**crown**[1] /kraʊn/ n 1 a circle made of gold that a king or queen wears on his/her head 2 the top part of a hat, head, or hill: *a hat with a high crown* 3 an artificial top for a damaged tooth 4 the position you have if you have won a sports competition: *He lost the heavyweight boxing crown in 1972.* 5 **the crown** the position of being king or queen

**crown**[2] v [T] 1 to put a CROWN on someone's head, so that s/he officially becomes king or queen: *He was crowned at the age of six.* 2 to do something or get something that is the best and usually last thing in a series of things you have done or gotten: *His successful career was crowned by the best actor award.* 3 to put a protective top on a damaged tooth

**crown·ing** /ˈkraʊnɪŋ/ adj being the best and usually last of a series of things: *Winning a fourth championship was her crowning achievement.*

**crown prince** /ˌ. ˈ. /, **crown prin·cess** /ˌ. ˈ..ɪ/ n the child of a king or queen, who will be the next king or queen

**cru·cial** /ˈkruʃəl/ adj extremely important: *crucial decisions involving millions of dollars* —**crucially** adv

**cru·ci·fix** /ˈkrusəˌfɪks/ n a CROSS with a figure of Christ on it

**cru·ci·fix·ion** /ˌkrusəˈfɪkʃən/ n 1 [C,U] the act of killing someone by fastening him/her to a CROSS and leaving him/her to die 2 **the Crucifixion** the death of Christ in this way, or a picture or object that represents it

**cru·ci·fy** /ˈkrusəˌfaɪ/ v [T] 1 to kill someone by fastening him/her to a CROSS and leaving him/her to die 2 to criticize someone severely and cruelly, especially in public: *Gardner was crucified by the press for his offensive comments.*

**crud** /krʌd/ n [U] INFORMAL something that is very unpleasant to look at, taste, smell etc.: *I can't get this crud off my shoe.* —**cruddy** adj

**crude** /krud/ adj 1 offensive or rude, especially in a sexual way: *One of the young men yelled something crude at her.* 2 in a natural or raw condition: *crude oil* 3 not developed to a high standard, or made with little skill: *a crude shelter in the forest* —**crudely** adv

**cru·el** /ˈkruəl/ adj 1 deliberately hurting people or animals or making them feel unhappy: *Children can be very cruel to each other.* | *Keeping animals in cages seems cruel.*

**2** making someone feel very unhappy: *Her father's death was a cruel blow.* (=a sudden event that seems unfair and makes you unhappy) —**cruelly** *adv*

**cru·el·ty** /ˈkruəlti/ *n* **1** [U] behavior that is cruel: *cruelty to animals* **2** a cruel action

**cruise**[1] /kruz/ *v* **1** [I] to sail along slowly: *boats cruising on Lake Michigan* **2** [I] to move at a steady speed in a car, plane etc.: *We cruised along at 65 miles per hour.* **3** INFORMAL [I,T] to drive a car without going to any particular place: *Terry and I were out cruising Friday night .* **4** [I,T] SLANG to look for a sexual partner in a public place

**cruise**[2] *n* a vacation in which you travel on a large boat: *a Caribbean cruise*

**cruis·er** /ˈkruzɚ/ *n* a large fast WARSHIP: *a battle cruiser*

**cruise ship** /ˈ. ./ *n* a large ship with restaurants, BARs, etc. that people travel on for a vacation

**crumb** /krʌm/ *n* **1** a very small piece of dry food, especially bread or cake **2** a very small amount of something: *a few crumbs of information*

**crum·ble** /ˈkrʌmbəl/ *v* **1** [I,T] to break apart into small pieces, or make something do this: *an old stone wall, crumbling with age* **2** [I] to lose power, become weak, or fail: *the crumbling Roman empire*

**crum·my** /ˈkrʌmi/ *adj* SPOKEN bad or unpleasant: *What a crummy movie!*

**crum·ple** /ˈkrʌmpəl/ *v* [I,T] to crush something so that it becomes smaller and bent, or to be crushed in this way: *The front of the car crumpled from the impact.*

**crunch**[1] /krʌntʃ/ *v* **1** [I] to make a sound like something being crushed: *Our feet crunched on the frozen snow.* **2** [I,T] to eat hard food in a way that makes a noise: *The dog was crunching on a bone.* —**crunchy** *adj*

**crunch**[2] *n* **1** [singular] a noise like the sound of something being crushed: *I could hear the crunch of their footsteps on the gravel.* **2 the crunch** INFORMAL **a)** a difficult situation caused by a lack of something, especially money or time: *We're all feeling the crunch these days.* **b)** also **crunch time** a period when you have to make the most effort to make sure you achieve something

**cru·sade**[1] /kruˈseɪd/ *n* a determined attempt to change something because you think you are right: *a crusade for better schools*

**crusade**[2] *v* [I] to take part in a CRUSADE: *students crusading against nuclear weapons* —**crusader** *n*

**crush**[1] /krʌʃ/ *v* [T] **1** to press something so hard that it breaks or is damaged, or to injure someone seriously this way: *crushing grapes to make wine | people crushed beneath a collapsing building* **2** to completely defeat someone or

something: *The uprising was crushed by the military.* **3** to make someone feel extremely upset, shocked, sad etc.: *If I discover I've hurt someone's feelings, I'm crushed.*

**crush**[2] *n* **1** INFORMAL a feeling of romantic love for someone, especially someone older than you are: *Ben has a crush on his teacher.* **2** [singular] a crowd of people pressed so close together that it is difficult for them to move

**crust** /krʌst/ *n* [C,U] **1** the hard brown outer surface of bread **2** the baked outer part of foods such as PIEs **3** a thin hard covering on the surface of something: *the earth's crust*

**crus·ta·cean** /krʌˈsteɪʃən/ *n* TECHNICAL one of a group of animals such as a CRAB that have a hard outer shell and several pairs of legs, and that usually live in water —**crustacean** *adj*

**crust·y** /ˈkrʌsti/ *adj* **1** having a hard CRUST: *crusty bread* **2** INFORMAL easily annoyed and not patient: *a crusty old man*

**crutch** /krʌtʃ/ *n* **1** [C usually plural] a special stick that you put under your arm to help you walk when you have hurt your leg **2** DISAPPROVING something that gives you support or help: *Tom uses those pills as a crutch.*

**crux** /krʌks/ *n* **the crux** the most important part of a problem, question, argument etc.: *The crux of the matter is whether she intended to commit murder.*

**cry**[1] /kraɪ/ *v* **cried, cried, crying** **1** [I] to produce tears from your eyes, usually because you are unhappy or hurt: *The baby was crying upstairs. | I always cry at sad movies.* **2** [T] to shout something loudly: *"Stop!" she cried.* **3 for crying out loud** SPOKEN said when you feel annoyed with someone: *For crying out loud, will you shut up!* **4 cry over spilled milk** INFORMAL to waste time worrying about something that cannot be changed **5** [I] if animals and birds cry, they make a loud sound: *Listen to the gulls crying.* **6 cry wolf** to often ask for help when you do not need it, so that people do not believe you when you really need help

**cry out** *phr v* **1** [I,T] to make a loud sound or shout something loudly: *He cried out in pain.* **2 be crying out for sth** to need something urgently: *The health care system is crying out for reform.*

**cry**[2] *n, plural* **cries** **1** a loud sound showing fear, pain, shock etc.: *a baby's cry* **2** a loud shout: *Miller heard a cry of "Stop, thief!"* **3** a sound made by a particular animal or bird: *the cry of the eagle* **4** [singular] a period of time during which you cry: *You'll feel better after you've had a good cry.* **5** a phrase used in order to unite people in support of a particular action or idea: *a war/battle cry*

**cry·ba·by** /ˈkraɪˌbeɪbi/ *n* INFORMAL someone who cries or complains too much

**cry·ing** /'kraɪ-ɪŋ/ *adj* **1 a crying need for sth** a serious need for something: *There's a crying need for better housing.* **2 it's a crying shame** SPOKEN used in order to say that you are angry and upset about something: *It's a crying shame the way she treats that child.*

**crypt** /krɪpt/ *n* a room under a church, used in past times for burying people

**cryp·tic** /'krɪptɪk/ *adj* having a hidden meaning that is not easy to understand: *a cryptic message* **–cryptically** *adv*

**crys·tal** /'krɪstəl/ *n* **1** [C,U] rock that is clear like ice, or a piece of this **2** [U] clear glass that is of very high quality: *crystal wine glasses* **3** a small piece of a substance with a particular shape, formed naturally when this substance becomes solid: *sugar and salt crystals* **4** the clear plastic or glass cover on a clock or watch

**crystal ball** /ˌ.. './ *n* a magic glass ball that you look into in order to see the future

**crystal clear** /ˌ.. './ *adj* **1** very clearly stated and easy to understand: *I made it crystal clear that you weren't allowed to go!* **2** completely clean and clear: *The lake was crystal clear.*

**crys·tal·lize** /'krɪstəˌlaɪz/ *v* [I,T] **1** to make a substance form CRYSTALs: *At what temperature does sugar crystallize?* **2** to make an idea, plan etc. become clear in your mind: *The team had several ideas that gradually crystallized into a plan.* **–crystallization** /ˌkrɪstələ'zeɪʃən/ *n* [U]

**c-sec·tion** /'si ˌsɛkʃən/ *n* ⇨ CESAREAN

**CT** the written abbreviation of Connecticut

**cub** /kʌb/ *n* the baby of a wild animal such as a lion or bear

**cub·by·hole** /'kʌbi ˌhoʊl/ *n* a small space or a small room for working or storing things in

**cube¹** /kyub/ *n* **1** a solid object with six equal square sides: *a sugar cube* **2 the cube of sth** the number you get when you multiply a number by itself twice: *The cube of 3 is 27.*

**cube²** *v* [T] **1** to multiply a number by itself twice: *3 cubed is 27.* **2** to cut something into CUBEs

**cu·bic** /'kyubɪk/ *adj* **cubic inch/centimeter/yard etc.** a measurement of space in which the length, width, and height are all equal

**cu·bi·cle** /'kyubɪkəl/ *n* a small enclosed part of a room: *cubicles in the library for studying in*

**Cub Scouts** /'. ./ *n* the part of the BOY SCOUTS that is for younger boys

**cuck·oo¹** /'kuku/ *adj* INFORMAL crazy or silly

**cuckoo²** *n* a gray European bird that puts its eggs in other birds' NESTs and that has a call that sounds like its name

**cu·cum·ber** /'kyuˌkʌmbɚ/ *n* a long thin rounded vegetable with a dark green skin, usually eaten raw –see picture on page 470

**cud·dle¹** /'kʌdl/ *v* [I,T] to hold someone or something very close to you with your arms

around him, her, or it: *Chris cuddled her new puppy.*

**cuddle up** *phr v* [I] to lie or sit very close to someone or something: *The children cuddled up to each other in the dark.*

**cuddle²** *n* [singular] an act of cuddling (CUDDLE): *Give me a cuddle.*

**cud·dly** /'kʌdli/ *adj* someone or something that is cuddly makes you want to CUDDLE him, her, or it: *a cuddly baby*

**cue** /kyu/ *n* **1** a word or action that is a signal for someone to speak or act in a play, movie etc.: *Tony stood by the stage, waiting for his cue.* **2** an action or event that is a signal for something else to happen: *a cue for prices to rise again* **3 (right) on cue** happening or done at exactly the right moment: *I was just asking where you were when you walked in, right on cue.* **4 take your cue from sb** to do something similar to what someone else does, especially in order to behave in the right way: *Wayne took his cue about which fork to use from the guy sitting next to him.* **5** a long straight wooden stick used for hitting the ball in games such as POOL

**cuff¹** /kʌf/ *n* **1** the end part of a SLEEVE (=the arm of a shirt, dress etc.) **2** a narrow band of cloth turned up at the bottom of your pants **3 off-the-cuff** without previous thought or preparation: *an off-the-cuff remark* –see also CUFFS

**cuff²** *v* [T] to put HANDCUFFS on someone: *Cuff him and take him to the station.*

**cuff link** /'. ./ *n* a small piece of jewelry that a man uses instead of a button to hold the CUFF on his shirt together

**cuffs** /kʌfs/ *n* [plural] INFORMAL ⇨ HANDCUFFS

**Cui·sin·art** /'kwizɪnˌɑrt/ *n* TRADEMARK ⇨ FOOD PROCESSOR

**cui·sine** /kwɪ'zin/ *n* [U] a particular style of cooking: *French cuisine*

**cul-de-sac** /ˌkʌl də 'sæk, ˌkʊl-/ *n* a street that is closed at one end

**cu·li·nar·y** /'kʌləˌnɛri, 'kyu-/ *adj* FORMAL relating to cooking

**cull** /kʌl/ *v* FORMAL **1** [T] to find or choose information from many different places: *data culled from various sources* **2** [I,T] to kill the weakest animals in a group –**cull** *n*

**cul·mi·nate** /'kʌlməˌneɪt/ *v* [T] FORMAL **culminate in sth** to result in something: *a series of arguments that culminated in a divorce*

**cul·mi·na·tion** /ˌkʌlmə'neɪʃən/ *n* [singular, U] the final or highest point of something, especially after a long period of effort or development: *That discovery was the culmination of his life's work.*

**cu·lottes** /ku'lɑts, 'kulɑts/ *n* [plural] women's pants that stop at the knee and are shaped to look like a skirt

**cul·pa·ble** /'kʌlpəbəl/ *adj* FORMAL deserving blame; guilty −**culpability** /ˌkʌlpə'bɪləti/ *n* [U]

**cul·prit** /'kʌlprɪt/ *n* **1** someone who is guilty of a crime or of doing something wrong **2** INFORMAL the reason for a particular problem or difficulty: *High labor costs are the main culprit for the rise in prices.*

**cult** /kʌlt/ *n* **1** an extreme religious group that is not part of an established religion **2** a particular fashion, style, movie, group etc. that has become very popular among a small number of people: *a cult movie*

**cul·ti·vate** /'kʌltəˌveɪt/ *v* [T] **1** to prepare and use land for growing crops **2** to develop a particular skill or quality in yourself: *cultivating a knowledge of art* **3** to develop a friendship with someone, especially someone who can help you

**cul·ti·vat·ed** /'kʌltəˌveɪtɪd/ *adj* **1** intelligent and extremely polite in social situations: *a cultivated gentleman* **2** used for growing crops: *cultivated fields*

**cul·ti·va·tion** /ˌkʌltə'veɪʃən/ *n* [U] **1** the preparation and use of land for growing crops: *These fields have been under cultivation (=used for growing crops) for over 50 years.* **2** the deliberate development of a particular skill or quality

**cul·tur·al** /'kʌltʃərəl/ *adj* **1** relating to a particular society and its way of life: *England has a rich cultural heritage.* **2** relating to art, literature, music etc.: *The city is trying to promote cultural activities.* −**culturally** *adv*

**cul·ture** /'kʌltʃɚ/ *n* **1** [C,U] the art, beliefs, behavior, ideas etc. of a particular society or group of people: *the culture of ancient Greece | youth culture | students learning about American culture* ✗ DON'T SAY "the American culture" ✗ **2** [U] activities relating to art, literature, music etc.: *Boston is a good place for anyone who is interested in culture.* **3 culture shock** the strange feelings that someone has when s/he visits a foreign country or a new place for the first time **4** [C,U] the process of growing BACTERIA for scientific use, or the bacteria produced by this

**cul·tured** /'kʌltʃɚd/ *adj* intelligent, polite, and interested in art and music: *a handsome cultured man*

**cum·ber·some** /'kʌmbɚsəm/ *adj* **1** slow and difficult: *Getting a passport can be a cumbersome process.* **2** heavy and difficult to move or use: *cumbersome equipment*

**cu·mu·la·tive** /'kyumyələtɪv, -ˌleɪ-/ *adj* increasing gradually as more of something is added or happens: *the cumulative effect of air pollution* −**cumulatively** *adv*

**cun·ning** /'kʌnɪŋ/ *adj* good at deceiving people: *a cunning criminal* −**cunning** *n* [U] −**cunningly** *adv*

**cunt** /kʌnt/ *n* TABOO **1** a very offensive word for a woman **2** a woman's sexual organs

**cup¹** /kʌp/ *n* **1** a small round container with a handle, used for drinking from, or the liquid it contains: *a cup and saucer | a cup of coffee* **2** a unit for measuring liquids or dry foods, equal to half a PINT: *Stir in a cup of flour.* **3** a specially shaped container that is given as a prize in a competition **4** something round and hollow that is shaped like a cup: *the cup of a flower*

**cup²** *v* **-pped, -pping** [T] to form your hands into the shape of a cup: *Greta cupped her hands around the mug.*

**cup·board** /'kʌbɚd/ *n* a piece of furniture for storing clothes, plates, food etc., that is usually attached to a wall and has shelves and a door

**cup·cake** /'kʌpkeɪk/ *n* a small round cake

**cur·a·ble** /'kyurəbəl/ *adj* able to be cured: *a curable disease* −opposite INCURABLE

**cu·ra·tor** /'kyuˌreɪtɚ, -ətɚ, kyu'reɪtɚ/ *n* someone who is in charge of a MUSEUM

**curb¹** /kɚb/ *n* the edge of a street between where cars can drive and where people can walk: *Larry tripped on the curb.*

curb
curb
drain

**curb²** *v* [T] to control or limit something: *Doctors are trying to curb the spread of the disease.*

**curd** /kɚd/ *n* [C usually plural] the thick substance that forms in milk when it becomes sour

**cur·dle** /'kɚdl/ *v* [I,T] to become thicker or form CURDs, or to make a liquid do this: *The milk got too warm and curdled.*

**cure¹** /kyuɚ/ *v* [T] **1** to make an injury or illness better, so that the person who was sick is well: *Penicillin will cure most infections.* −compare HEAL **2** to solve a problem or improve a bad situation: *No one can completely cure unemployment.* **3** to preserve food, leather etc. by drying it, hanging it in smoke, or covering it with salt

**cure²** *n* **1** a medicine or medical treatment that can cure an illness or disease: *a cure for cancer* **2** something that solves a problem or improves a bad situation: *There's no easy cure for poverty.*

**cur·few** /'kɚfyu/ *n* a time during which everyone must stay indoors: *The government imposed a curfew from sunset to sunrise.*

**cu·ri·o** /'kyuriˌou/ *n* a small object that is valuable because it is old, beautiful, or rare

**cu·ri·os·i·ty** /ˌkyuri'asəti/ *n* [singular, U] the desire to know something or to learn about something: *Children have a natural curiosity about the world around them. | Just out of curiosity, how old are you? | I just had to satisfy my curiosity, so I opened the box.*

**cu·ri·ous** /'kyʊriəs/ *adj* **1** wanting to know or learn about something: *We were* **curious about** *what was going on next door.* | *I was* **curious to** *see how it worked.* **2** strange or unusual in a way that makes you interested: *a curious noise* | *Joe's remark had a curious effect on Peter.* —**curiously** *adv*

**curl¹** /kɔl/ *n* **1** a small piece of hair that hangs down in a curved shape: *a little girl with blonde curls* **2** something that forms a curved shape: *chocolate curls* —**curly** *adj*

**curl²** *v* [I,T] **1** to form a curved shape, or to make something do this: *I don't know if I should curl my hair or leave it straight.* **2** to move while forming a curved shape, or to make something do this: *Thick smoke curled from the chimney.*

 **curl up** *phr v* [I] **1** to lie or sit with your arms and legs bent close to your body: *Pepe* **curled up** *on the couch to watch some TV.* **2** if paper, leaves etc. curl up, their edges become curved and point up: *The old photos had begun to* **curl up** *and turn yellow.*

**curl·er** /'kɔlɔ/ *n* [C usually plural] a small metal or plastic tube that hair is wound around in order to curl it

**curl·ing i·ron** /'kɔlɪŋ ˌaɪɔn/ *n* a piece of electrical equipment that you heat and use to curl your hair

**cur·rant** /'kɔɔnt, 'kʌr-/ *n* a small round red or black BERRY, usually dried

**cur·ren·cy** /'kɔɔnsi, 'kʌr-/ *n* **1** [C,U] the particular type of money that a country uses: *Polish currency* **2** [U] the state of being generally accepted or used: *Some of the songs had been* **in currency** *for a hundred years.*

**cur·rent¹** /'kɔɔnt, 'kʌr-/ *adj* happening or being used right now, but not likely to last a long time: *Sales for the* **current** *year (=this year) are low.* | *Denise's current boyfriend* —see usage note at NEW

**current²** *n* **1** a continuous movement of water or air in a particular direction: *There's a strong current in the river.* **2** a flow of electricity through a wire: *Turn off the electric current before changing that fuse.*

**cur·rent·ly** /'kɔɔntli/ *adv* at the present time: *She's currently studying in Japan.*

**cur·ric·u·lum** /kə'rɪkyələm/ *n, plural* **curricula** /-kyələ/ *or* **curriculums** all of the subjects that are taught at a school, college etc.

**cur·ry** /'kɔi, 'kʌri/ *n* [C,U] a mixture of SPICEs that is used for giving food a hot taste

**curse¹** /kɔs/ *v* **1** [I] to swear because you are very angry: *We heard him* **cursing at** *the lawn mower because it wouldn't start.* **2** [T] to say or think bad things about someone or something: *I* **cursed** *myself* **for** *not buying the car insurance sooner.* **3** to ask God or a magical power to do something bad to someone

**curse²** *n* **1** a swear word, or words, that you say because you are very angry **2** a word or sentence that asks God or a magical power to do something bad to someone: *If feels like someone has* **put a curse on** *my career.*

**cursed** /kɔst/ *adj* **be cursed with** to suffer because of a problem that you have and cannot get rid of: *Randy's cursed with a bad back.*

**cur·sor** /'kɔsɔ/ *n* a mark that you can move on a computer screen that shows you where you are writing

**cur·so·ry** /'kɔsəri/ *adj* done quickly without much attention to detail: *After a* **cursory** *glance/look at the menu, Grant ordered coffee.*

**curt** /kɔt/ *adj* using very few words when you speak to someone, in a way that seems rude —**curtly** *adv*

**cur·tail** /kɔ'teɪl/ *v* [T] FORMAL to reduce or limit something: *new laws to curtail immigration* —**curtailment** *n* [U]

**cur·tain** /'kɔt⁻n/ *n* a large piece of hanging cloth that can be pulled across a window, stage, or SHOWER: *Can you* **pull/draw the curtains** *for me?* (=close the curtains)

**curt·sy, curtsey** /'kɔtsi/ *v* [I] if a woman curtsies to someone, she bends her knees and puts one foot forward as a sign of respect —**curtsy** *n*

**curve¹** /kɔv/ *n* **1** a line that bends like part of circle: *a sharp curve in the road* **2** a method of giving grades based on how a student's work compares with other students' work

**curve²** *v* [I,T] to bend or move in the shape of a curve, or to make something do this: *a golf ball curving through the air* —**curved** *adj* –**curvy** *adj*

**cush·ion¹** /'kʊʃən/ *n* **1** a soft, usually square PILLOW that you put on a chair, floor etc. so you can sit or lie on it to make yourself more comfortable **2** something, especially money, that prevents you from being affected by a situation immediately: *If I lose my job, my savings will provide a cushion for a while.*

**cushion²** *v* [T] to reduce the effects of something unpleasant: *This time, James wasn't there to* **cushion the blow.** (=help make a bad situation less bad)

**cuss** /kʌs/ *v* [I] INFORMAL to use offensive language; swear

 **cuss** sb **out** *phr v* [T] INFORMAL to swear and shout at someone because you are very angry

**cus·tard** /'kʌstɔd/ *n* a soft baked mixture of milk, eggs, and sugar

**cus·to·di·an** /kə'stoʊdiən/ *n* someone who takes care of a public building

**cus·to·dy** /'kʌstədi/ *n* [U] **1** the right to take care of a child, given by a court when the child's parents are legally separated: *My ex-wife has custody of the kids.* | *The judge awarded us* **joint custody**. (=both parents will take care of the child) **2 in custody** being kept in prison by the police until going to court: *Two robbery suspects are being* **held in custody**. *—custodial* /kəˈstoʊdiəl/ *adj*

**cus·tom** /ˈkʌstəm/ *n* [C,U] something that is done by people in a particular society because it is traditional: *the custom of throwing rice at weddings* | *Chinese customs and culture* —see also CUSTOMS —compare HABIT —see usage note at HABIT

**cus·tom·ar·y** /ˈkʌstəˌmɛri/ *adj* something that is customary is normal because it is the way it is usually done: *It is customary for a local band to lead the parade.* **—customarily** /ˌkʌstəˈmɛrəli/ *adv*

**custom-built** /ˌ.. ˈ.◁/ *adj* a custom-built car, machine etc. is built specially for the person buying it

**cus·tom·er** /ˈkʌstəmɚ/ *n* someone who buys goods or services from a store, company etc.: *Dow is one of our biggest customers.*

> **USAGE NOTE** customer
>
> When you go out to buy things, you are a **shopper**; but when you buy goods from a particular store, you are that store's **customer**: *The mall is full of shoppers.* | *We don't get many customers in the evenings.* If you are paying someone such as a lawyer for professional services, you are a **client**, but if you are seeing a doctor you are a **patient**. If you are staying in a hotel, you are a **guest**.

**cus·tom·ize** /ˈkʌstəˌmaɪz/ *v* [T] to change something to make it more useful for you, or to make it look special or unusual: *a customized software package*

**custom-made** /ˌ.. ˈ.◁/ *adj* a custom-made shirt, pair of shoes, etc. is made specially for the person buying it

**cus·toms** /ˈkʌstəmz/ *n* [plural] the place where your bags are checked for illegal goods when you go into a country: *It shouldn't take too long to* **clear customs**. (=be allowed into a country after being checked)

**cut¹** /kʌt/ *v* **cut, cut, cutting**
**1** ►USE KNIFE/SCISSORS◄ [I,T] to use a knife, scissors etc. to divide something into pieces, remove a piece from something, open something etc.: *Abby, go cut Grandpa a piece of pie.* | *Cut some cheese into cubes and add them to the salad.* | *Uncle Bert used a saw to* **cut a hole in** *the ice.*
**2** ►REDUCE◄ [T] to reduce the amount of something, especially something such as time or money: *The company had to close several factories to* **cut costs**. | *The number of soldiers had to be* **cut in half**.
**3** ►MAKE SHORTER◄ [T] to make something shorter using a knife, scissors etc.: *A neighbor boy cuts our grass once a week.* | *Where did you*

get *your hair cut?*
**4** ►INJURE◄ [T] to injure yourself or someone else using a sharp object such as a knife, so that you start bleeding: *He* **cut** *his finger* **on** *a piece of broken glass.* | *Sarah says her head got* **cut open** *when she fell.*
**5** **cut sb free/loose** to cut something such as a rope or metal in order to let someone escape: *Firemen were carefully cutting the driver free from the wreckage.*
**6** **cut class/school** to not go to a class or to school when you ought to
**7** **cut corners** to do something in a way that is not as good as it should be, in order to save time, effort, or money: *Parents are worried that the city is cutting corners in education.*
**8** **cut sth short** to end something earlier than you had planned to end it: *His career was cut short by a back injury.*
**9** **cut a record/CD/album** to record music to be sold to the public

| SPOKEN PHRASES |
|---|
| **10** **cut it/that out!** used in order to tell someone to stop doing something that is annoying you: *Cut that out, you two, or you'll go to your rooms.* **11** **cut sb some slack** to allow someone to do something without criticizing him/her or making it more difficult: *He's only been here two weeks! Cut him some slack - he'll learn.* **12** **cut the crap** an impolite way of telling someone to talk only about what is important, instead of wasting time on other things: *Cut the crap and tell me what you really mean, Nicholas.* **13** **not cut it** to not be good enough: *Barry's just not cutting it as a journalist.* **14** **cut it close** to leave yourself only just enough time or money to do something: *He cut it pretty close but he made it to the airport all right.* |

**cut across** sth *phr v* [T] **1** to go across an area rather than around it: *Sherman cut across three lanes of traffic to the exit.* **2** if a problem or feeling cuts across different groups of people, they are all affected by it

**cut back** *phr v* [I,T **cut** sth ↔ **back**] to reduce the amount, size, cost etc. of something: *The company is attempting to* **cut back on** *expenses.*

**cut down** *phr v* **1** [I,T **cut** sth ↔ **down**] to reduce the amount of something, especially something you do, eat, buy etc.: *I'm trying to* **cut down on** *my drinking.* **2** [T **cut** sth ↔ **down**] to cut the main stem of a tree so that it falls to the ground: *Beautiful old oaks had been* **cut down** *to build houses.*

**cut in** *phr v* [I] **cut in front/cut in line** to unfairly go in front of other people who are waiting to do something: *Some idiot* **cut in** *front of me on the freeway and almost caused an accident.*

**cut off** *phr v* [T] **1** [cut sth ↔ off] to remove a piece from something using a sharp tool such as a knife: *Cut the top off a large ripe pineapple.* **2** [cut sth ↔ off] to stop the supply of something: *They're going to cut off our electricity if you don't pay that bill.* **3** be/get cut off to be unable to finish talking to someone because something is wrong with the telephone connection **4** [cut sb/sth ↔ off] to separate someone or something from other people or things, or to prevent them from going somewhere: *A heavy snowfall cut us off from the town.* **5** [cut sb off] to interrupt someone: *He cut her off in mid-sentence.*

**cut out** *phr v* **1** [T cut sth ↔ out] to remove a piece from something using a sharp tool such as a knife or scissors: *The children can cut star shapes out of colored paper.* **2** [I] if a motor cuts out, it stops working suddenly **3** not be cut out for/not be cut out to be to not have the particular job or activity: *I decided I wasn't really cut out to be a teacher.*

**cut** sth ↔ **up** *phr v* [T] to cut something into smaller pieces: *Cut up two carrots and three potatoes.*

**cut²** *n* **1** a wound that you get if a sharp object cuts your skin: *Luckily, I only got a few cuts and bruises.* **2** a reduction in the size, number, or amount of something: *Workers were forced to take a cut in pay.* | *the promise of new tax cuts* **3** INFORMAL ⇨ HAIRCUT **4** INFORMAL someone's share of something, especially money: *Everyone's taking a cut of the profits.* **5** a piece of meat that is cut so you can cook it: *tender cuts of beef* **6** the shape or style of your clothes: *a well-cut suit* **7** be a cut above (the rest) to be better than someone or something else: *The movie is a cut above most made-for-TV films.*

**cut and dried** /ˌ. . '.ˌ/ *adj* a situation that is cut and dried is certain to happen because it has already been planned or decided, and nothing can be done to change it: *The outcome of the election is already cut and dried.*

**cut·back** /ˈkʌtbæk/ *n* a reduction that is made in something such as the number of people in an organization or the amount of money spent by the government: *a number of cutbacks in funding for public libraries*

**cute** /kyut/ *adj* **1** cute people are attractive in the way they look or behave: *What a cute little baby!* | *Tim is so cute.* **2** cute things are attractive and pretty: *That's a cute skirt.* **3** smart in a way that can be rude: *Don't pay any attention to him; he's just trying to be cute.* –**cutely** *adv* –**cuteness** *n* [U] –see usage note at BEAUTIFUL

**cute·sy, cutesie** /ˈkyutsi/ *adj* INFORMAL too pretty or smart in a way that is annoying: *a cutesy dress with a lot of frills*

**cu·ti·cle** /ˈkyutɪkəl/ *n* the hard thin skin at the bottom of your FINGERNAILS

**cut·ler·y** /ˈkʌtˌləri/ *n* [U] knives, forks, and spoons

**cut·let** /ˈkʌtˌlɪt/ *n* a small piece of meat

**cut·off** /ˈkʌtɔf/ *n* a limit or level at which you must stop doing something: *The cutoff date for applying was June 3rd.*

**cut·offs** /ˈkʌtɔfs/ *n* [plural] a pair of SHORTS that you make by cutting off the legs of an old pair of pants

**cut-rate** /ˌ. '.ˌ/ *cut-price adj* cheaper than the normal price: *cut-rate insurance*

**cut·ter** /ˈkʌtɚ/ *n* a tool that cuts things: *wire cutters* | *a cookie cutter*

**cut·throat** /ˈkʌtθroʊt/ *adj* willing to do anything to succeed: *the cutthroat competition of software companies*

**cut·ting** /ˈkʌtɪŋ/ *adj* unkind and intended to upset someone: *a cutting remark*

**cutting edge** /ˌ.. '.ˌ/ *n* be at/on the cutting edge to be working on the most advanced stage or development of something: *Her designs are at the cutting edge of fashion.*

**cy·a·nide** /ˈsaɪəˌnaɪd/ *n* [U] a very strong poison

**cy·ber·punk** /ˈsaɪbɚˌpʌŋk/ *n* [U] a character in stories about life in a future society in which computers are very important

**cy·ber·space** /ˈsaɪbɚˌspɛrs/ *n* [U] all the connections between computers in different places, considered as a real place where information, messages, pictures etc. exist

**cy·cle** /ˈsaɪkəl/ *n* a number of related events that happen again and again in the same order: *the life cycle of flowering plants*

**cy·clic** /ˈsaɪklɪk, ˈsɪ-/, **cy·cli·cal** /ˈsaɪklɪkəl, ˈsɪ-/ *adj* happening again and again in a regular pattern –**cyclically** *adv*

**cy·clone** /ˈsaɪkloʊn/ *n* a strong wind that moves in a circle –see usage note at WEATHER

**cyl·in·der** /ˈsɪləndɚ/ *n* **1** a shape, object, or container with circular ends and straight sides, such as a can **2** the hollow part of a car engine in which the PISTON moves up and down: *a six-cylinder engine*

**cy·lin·dri·cal** /səˈlɪndrɪkəl/ *adj* in the shape of a CYLINDER

**cym·bal** /ˈsɪmbəl/ *n* a musical instrument made of a round metal plate, played by hitting it with a stick or hitting two of them together

**cyn·ic** /ˈsɪnɪk/ *n* someone who believes that people do things only to help themselves and not to help other people: *Working in politics has made Sheila a cynic.* –**cynicism** /ˈsɪnəˌsɪzəm/ *n* [U]

**cyn·i·cal** /ˈsɪnɪkəl/ *adj* unwilling to believe that someone has good or honest reasons for doing something: *Since her divorce she's become very cynical about men.* –**cynically** *adv*

**cyst** /sɪst/ *n* a small LUMP in someone's body that grows and fills with liquid

**czar** /zɑr/ *n* **1** INFORMAL a government official who is responsible for important decisions in a particular area: *the President's drugs czar* **2** a male ruler of Russia before 1917

# D

**D, d** /di/ **1** the fourth letter of the English alphabet **2** the number 500 in the system of ROMAN NUMERALs

**D** /di/ *n* **1** a low grade on a test or piece of school work: *a D in chemistry* **2** [C.U] the second note in the musical SCALE of C, or the musical KEY based on this note

**d** the abbreviation of died: *d.1937*

**d** /d/ **1** the short form of WOULD: *Ask her if she'd* (=she would) *like to go with us.* **2** the short form of HAD: *If I'd* (=I had) *only known you were there!*

**D.A** *n* the abbreviation of DISTRICT ATTORNEY

**dab**[1] /dæb/ *n* a small amount of a substance: *a dab of butter*

**dab**[2] *v* **-bbed, -bbing** [I,T] **1** to quickly and lightly touch something several times in order to dry it: *Emily dabbed at her eyes with a handkerchief.* **2** [T] to quickly put a small amount of a substance onto something: *She dabbed some suntan lotion onto her cheeks.*

dab

**dab·ble** /'dæbəl/ *v* [I] to do something or be involved in something in a way that is not serious: *My husband dabbles in art.*

**dachs·hund** /'dɑkshʊnt, -hʊnd/ *n* a small dog with short legs and a long body

**dad** /dæd/, **dad·dy** /'dædi/ *n* INFORMAL father

**daf·fo·dil** /'dæfə‚dɪl/ *n* a tall yellow flower that appears in early spring

**dag·ger** /'dægɚ/ *n* a short pointed knife used as a weapon

**dai·ly** /'deɪli/ *adj* **1** happening, done, or produced every day: *daily flights to Miami* | *a daily newspaper* **2** relating to a single day: *a daily rate of pay* **3** **daily life** the things you do every day: *the weather and its effect on daily life* —**daily** *adv*

**dain·ty** /'deɪnti/ *adj* small, pretty, and delicate: *a dainty china doll* —**daintily** *adv*

**dair·y** /'dɛri/ *n* **1** a place on a farm where milk is kept and butter and cheese are made **2** a company that buys and sells milk, butter etc. **3** **dairy products** milk and foods made from milk, such as butter, cheese, or YOGURT

**dai·sy** /'deɪzi/ *n* a white flower with a bright yellow center

**dal·ly** /'dæli/ *v* [I] OLD-FASHIONED to move slowly or waste time: *children dallying on their way to school*

**dal·ma·tian** /dæl'meɪʃən/ a dog with white fur and small black spots

**dam**[1] /dæm/ *n* a wall built across a river in order to make a lake behind it or to produce electricity

**dam**[2] *v* **-mmed, -mming** [T] to build a dam across a river

**dam sth ↔ up** *phr v* [T] to stop the flow of a stream, river etc.: *Falling rocks have dammed up the creek.*

**dam·age**[1] /'dæmɪdʒ/ *n* [U] **1** physical harm done to something, so that it is broken or injured: *The tests show some brain/liver damage.* | *Was there any damage to your car ?* | *The earthquake caused serious/severe damage to the freeway system.* | *Don't worry, the kids can't do any damage.* **2** a bad effect on someone or something: *the damage to Symon's reputation* —see also DAMAGES

**dam·age**[2] *v* [T] **1** to physically harm someone or something: *The storm damaged the tobacco crop.* **2** to have a bad effect on someone or something: *The scandal has badly damaged his ability to control Congress.* —**damaging** *adj*

**dam·ag·es** /'dæmɪdʒɪz/ *n* [plural] LAW money that someone must pay to someone else for harming that person or his/her property: *The court ordered her to pay $2000 in damages.*

**dame** /deɪm/ *n* OLD-FASHIONED a woman

**dam·mit** /'dæmɪt/ *interjection* NONSTANDARD said when you are annoyed or angry: *Hurry up, dammit!*

**damn**[1] /dæm/ *adj* SPOKEN OFFENSIVE said when you are angry or annoyed about something: *Turn off that damn TV!*

**damn**[2] *adv* SPOKEN OFFENSIVE **1** used in order to emphasize something: *We're damn lucky we got here ahead of the storm.* **2** **damn well** used in order to emphasize how determined or sure you are about something: *He knows damn well he shouldn't drive my car.*

**damn**[3] *interjection* SPOKEN OFFENSIVE said when you are annoyed or disappointed: *Damn! I forgot my wallet!*

**damn**[4] *n* SPOKEN OFFENSIVE **not give a damn** said in order to emphasize that you do not care at all about something: *I don't give a damn if he's sorry!*

**damn**[5] *v* [T] **damn it/you/sb etc.** SPOKEN OFFENSIVE said when you are very angry: *Damn it! This is the third time those kids have broken the window.*

**damned**[1] /dæmnd/ *adj* SPOKEN OFFENSIVE **1** ⇨ DAMN[1] **2** **I'll be damned** said when you are surprised: *Well, I'll be damned! When did you get here, Tom?* **3** **damned if** used in order to emphasize that you do not want something to happen, or that you do not know something: *I'll be damned if I'll sleep on the floor! | Damned if I know!* (=I don't know) **4 damned if you do, damned if you don't** used in a situation where the result will be bad whether or not you do something **5 be damned** to be punished by God after your death by being sent to HELL

**damned**[2] *adv* SPOKEN ⇨ DAMN[1]

**damned·est, damn·dest** /'dæmdɪst/ *adj* SPOKEN **1** said when you think something is very surprising or strange: *It was the damnedest thing I ever saw!* **2 do your damnedest** to try as hard as you can to achieve something

**damn·ing** /'dæmɪŋ/ *adj* proving or showing that something is very bad or wrong: *a damning article about pollution*

**damp** /dæmp/ *adj* slightly wet, usually in a cold and unpleasant way: *My swimsuit is still damp.* —**dampness** *n* [U]

**damp·en** /'dæmpən/ *v* [T] **1** to make something slightly wet: *Dampen the clothes before ironing them.* **2 dampen sb's enthusiasm/ spirits** to make someone feel less excited or interested about something

**damp·er** /'dæmpɚ/ *n* **put a damper on sth** to stop something from being enjoyable

**dam·sel** /'dæmzəl/ *n* **damsel in distress** HUMOROUS a young woman who needs help

**dance**[1] /dæns/ *v* **1** [I] to move your feet, body, and arms to match the style and speed of music: *Juan and Roberta danced to the radio.* **2 dance the waltz/tango etc.** to do a particular type of dance —**dancing** *n* [U]: *We used to go dancing pretty regularly.*

**dance**[2] *n* **1** a party for dancing: *a school dance* **2** an act of dancing: *May I have this dance?* (=will you dance with me?) **3** a particular set of movements that you perform with music: *The only dance I know is the fox-trot.* **4** [U] the art or activity of dancing: *dance lessons*

**danc·er** /'dænsɚ/ *n* someone who dances, especially as a job

**dan·de·li·on** /'dændə,laɪən/ *n* a small bright yellow wild flower that becomes a white ball of seeds when it dies

**dan·druff** /'dændrəf/ *n* [U] small white pieces of dead skin from your head that show in your hair or on your clothes

**dan·dy** /'dændi/ *adj* HUMOROUS very good: *This gadget makes a dandy present for a cook.*

**dang** /dæŋ/ *interjection* SPOKEN a word meaning DAMN that people consider less offensive

**dan·ger** /'deɪndʒɚ/ *n* **1** [U] the possibility that someone or something will be harmed: *Is there any danger of infection? | The UN wants to move civilians who are in danger.* (=in a dangerous situation) **2** something or someone that may harm you: *What are the dangers of scuba diving?* **3** [C,U] the possibility that

something unpleasant will happen: *Margie is in danger of losing her job.*

**dan·ger·ous** /'deɪndʒərəs/ *adj* **1** able or likely to harm you: *a dangerous criminal | It's dangerous for women to walk alone at night.* **2** likely to cause problems or involving a lot of risk: *The company is in a dangerous financial position.* —**dangerously** *adv*

**dan·gle** /'dæŋgəl/ *v* [I,T] to hang or swing loosely, or to make something do this: *keys dangling from a chain*

**da·nish** /'deɪnɪʃ/, **Danish pas·try** /ˌ.. '../ *n* a round slightly flat sweet bread, usually with fruit in the middle

**dank** /dæŋk/ *adj* a dank place is wet and cold in an unpleasant way

**dap·per** /'dæpɚ/ *adj* a dapper man is neatly dressed

**dare**[1] /dɛr/ *v* **1** [T] to try to persuade someone to do something dangerous: *I dare you to jump!* **2** [I] to be brave enough to do something, used especially in negative sentences: *Robbins wouldn't dare tell the boss he's wrong.* **3 don't you dare** SPOKEN said in order to warn someone against doing something: *Don't you dare tell!* **4 how dare you/he etc.** SPOKEN said when you are very upset about what someone has said or done: *How dare you say that!*

**dare**[2] *n* a suggestion that someone should do something dangerous to prove that s/he is not afraid

**dare·dev·il** /'dɛr,dɛvəl/ *n* someone who likes doing dangerous things —**daredevil** *adj*

**dar·ing**[1] /'dɛrɪŋ/ *adj* **1** willing to do things that might be dangerous, or involving danger: *a daring adventure* **2** new or unusual in a way that is sometimes shocking: *a daring movie*

**daring**[2] *n* [U] courage to do dangerous things

**dark**[1] /dɑrk/ *adj* **1** with very little or no light: *Turn on the light; it's dark in here.* **2** closer to black than to white in color: *a dark blue tie | Lewis has dark hair.* —compare LIGHT[2] **3 get dark** to become night: *We'd better go home, it's getting dark.* **4** a dark person has brown skin, hair, or eyes: *a small dark woman* **5** threatening, mysterious, or frightening: *a dark side to his character* **6** LITERARY unhappy or without hope: *the dark days of the war*

**dark**[2] *n* **1 the dark** a situation in which there is no light: *My son is afraid of the dark.* **2 after dark** at night: *Don't go out after dark.* **3 before dark** before night has begun: *Mom wants us home before dark.* **4 in the dark** INFORMAL knowing nothing about something important because no one has told you about it: *Employees were kept in the dark* (=not told) *about the possible layoffs.*

**dark·en** /'dɑrkən/ *v* [I,T] to make something dark, or to become dark: *The sky darkened before the storm.*

D

**dark horse** /ˌ. './ *n* someone who is not well known and who surprises people by winning a competition

**dark·ly** /'dɑrkli/ *adv* in an unpleasant or threatening way: *scientists speaking darkly about the future*

**dark·ness** /'dɑrknɪs/ *n* [U] a place or time when there is no light, or the lack of light: *the darkness of a winter morning* | *The whole room was in darkness.*

**dark·room** /'dɑrkrum/ *n* a special room with a red light or no light, where film is taken out of a camera and made into a photograph

**dar·ling**[1] /'dɑrlɪŋ/ *n* SPOKEN used when speaking to someone you love: *Come here, darling.*

**darling**[2] *adj* much loved: *my darling child*

**darn**[1] /dɑrn/ *v* [T] **1 darn it!** SPOKEN said when you are annoyed about something: *Darn it! I broke my shoelace.* −see also DAMMIT **2 I'll be darned** SPOKEN said when you are surprised about something **3** to repair a hole in clothes by sewing thread through it many times: *darning socks*

**darn**[2] also **darned** *adv* SPOKEN said in order to emphasize how bad or good someone or something is: *a darned good movie*

**darn**[3] also **darned** *adj* SPOKEN said in order to emphasize how bad, stupid etc. someone or something is, especially when you are annoyed: *The darn fool got lost.* −see also DAMN[1]

**dart**[1] /dɑrt/ *n* **1** a small object with a sharp point that you can throw or shoot as a weapon or in games: *a poisoned dart* **2** a small fold stitched into a piece of clothing to make it fit better −see also DARTS

**dart**[2] *v* [I] to move suddenly and quickly in a particular direction: *The dog darted into the street.*

**darts** /dɑrts/ *n* [U] a game in which you throw DARTS at a circular board

**dash**[1] /dæʃ/ *v* **1** [I] to run somewhere very quickly: *She dashed into the room just before the boss arrived.* **2 dash sb's hopes** to ruin someone's hopes completely: *Her hopes of running in the Olympics were dashed after the accident.* **3** [T] to make something hit violently against something else, usually so that it breaks: *The ship was dashed against the rocks.*

**dash off** *phr v* [I] to leave somewhere very quickly: *Tim dashed off after class.*

**dash**[2] *n* **1 make a dash for** to run a short distance very quickly: *I made a dash for the house to get my umbrella.* **2** a small amount of something: *a dash of lemon* **3** a mark (-) used in writing to separate thoughts in a sentence **4** ⇨ DASHBOARD

**dash·board** /'dæʃbɔrd/ *n* the board at the front of a car that has the controls on it −see picture on page 469

**DAT** *n* [U] digital audio tape; a type of TAPE used in order to record music, sound, or information in DIGITAL form

**da·ta** /'deɪtə, 'dætə/ *n* [U, plural] information or facts: *He's collecting data for his report.*

**data·base** /'deɪtəˌbeɪs/ *n* a large amount of DATA stored in a computer system so that you can find and use it easily

**da·ta pro·cess·ing** /'.. ,.../ *n* [U] the use of computers to store and organize information, especially in business

**date**[1] /deɪt/ *n* **1** a particular day of the month or of the year, shown by a number: *"What's today's date?" "It's August 11th."* | *Have you set a date* (=chosen a day) *for the wedding?* **2** an arrangement to meet someone you like in a romantic way: *Mike's going (out) on a date on Friday.* **3** an arrangement to meet at a particular time or place: *Let's make a date to see that new movie.* **4** someone you have a date with: *My date's taking me out to dinner.* **5 to date** up to now: *This is the best research on the subject to date.* **6 at a later date** at some time in the future: *This will be discussed at a later date.* **7** a small sweet sticky brown fruit with a single long seed −see also OUT-OF-DATE, UP-TO-DATE

**date**[2] *v* **1** [I,T] to have a romantic relationship with someone: *How long have you been dating Mona?* **2** [T] to write the date on something: *a letter dated May 1, 1998* **3** [T] to find out when something old was made or how long it has existed: *Geologists date these rocks to 30 million years ago.*

**date from/ date back to** *phr v* [I] to have existed or been made at a particular time: *Independence Hall dates from the 17th century.*

**dat·ed** /'deɪtɪd/ *adj* no longer fashionable: *These shoes are really dated.*

**date rape** /'. ./ *n* [C,U] a RAPE that happens on a date

**daub** /dɔb/ *v* [T] to paint something in a careless way

**daugh·ter** /'dɔtər/ *n* your female child −see picture at FAMILY

**daughter-in-law** /'.. . ,./ *n, plural* **daughters-in-law** the wife of your son −see picture at FAMILY

**daunt** /dɔnt, dɑnt/ *v* [T] to make someone afraid or less confident: *Cooper is feeling daunted by his new responsibilities.*

**daunt·ing** /'dɔntɪŋ/ *adj* frightening in a way that makes you feel less confident: *a daunting task*

**da·ven·port** /'dævənˌpɔrt/ *n* a large SOFA

**daw·dle** /'dɔdl/ *v* [I] INFORMAL to waste time by doing things too slowly: *Stop dawdling; we'll be late.*

**dawn**[1] /dɔn/ *n* [C,U] **1** the time of day when light first appears: *We talked until dawn.* | *The boat left at the crack of dawn.* (=very early in the morning) **2 the dawn of** the time when something is just beginning to develop: *the dawn of civilization*

**dawn**[2] *v* [I] if a day or morning dawns, it begins: *The morning dawned cool and clear.*

**dawn on** sb *phr v* [T] to realize something: *It suddenly dawned on me that he was right.*

**day** /deɪ/ *n*

**1 ▶24 HOURS◀** a period of time equal to 24 hours: *I'll be back in ten days.* | *We're leaving for Arizona* **the day after tomorrow.** | *I saw Margo downtown* **the day before yesterday.** ✗ DON'T SAY "We're leaving for Arizona after tomorrow." or "I saw Margo before yesterday." ✗

**2 ▶MORNING UNTIL NIGHT◀** [C,U] the period of time between when it becomes light in the morning and when it becomes dark in the evening, when most people are awake: *The days begin to get longer in the spring.* | *a beautiful summer day*

**3 ▶WORK◀** a period of work within a 24 hour period: *Jean works an eight-hour day.* | *I need a* **day off** (=a day when you do not have to work). | *It's been a* **long day** (=a day when you had to get up early and were busy all day). | *Jan's been studying* **all day.** (=for the whole day) | *Jim had a really* **bad/good day** *at work.* | *I have Spanish class* **every day.**

**4 ▶POINT IN TIME◀** a period or point in time: **back in the days** *before the war* | *It's not safe to walk the streets* **these days.** (=now, as opposed to the past) | *Things were different* **in my day.** (=when I was young) | *We'll buy our dream home* **one/some day.** (=at some time in the future) | **To this day** (=until now) *we haven't heard the whole story.* | *Grandpa was telling stories about* **the good old days.** (=a time in the past that was better than the present)

**5 the other day** INFORMAL within the last few days: *I saw Randy the other day.*

**6 make someone's day** INFORMAL to make someone very pleased or happy: *That card made my day.*

**7 (has) had its day** no longer popular or successful: *The old steam trains were something to see, but they've had their day.*

**8 those were the days** SPOKEN used in order to say that a time in the past was better than the present time

**9 day after day/day in day out** continuously: *I drive the same route to work day in day out.*

**10 from day to day/day by day** from each day to the next: *You change your mind from day to day.* —see also DAYS[2], DAILY, **call it a day** (CALL[1])

**day·break** /'deɪbreɪk/ *n* [U] the time of day when light first appears: *We broke camp* **at daybreak.**

**day camp** /'. ./ *n* a CAMP where children do activities, sports etc. during the day, but go home at night

**day·care** /'deɪkɛr/ *n* [U] the care of children while their parents are at work: *a daycare center* | *My youngest is* **in daycare.**

**day·dream**[1] /'deɪdrim/ *v* [I] to think about pleasant things so that you forget what you should be doing: *Joan sat at her desk, daydreaming about Tom.* —**daydreamer** *n*

**daydream**[2] *n* the pleasant thoughts you have which you DAYDREAM

**Day-Glo** /'deɪɡloʊ/ *adj* TRADEMARK having a very bright orange, green, yellow, or pink color

**day·light** /'deɪlaɪt/ *n* [U] the light produced by the sun during the day: *There's more daylight in summer.* | *She was attacked* **in broad daylight.** (=during the day when everyone could see)

**day·lights** /'deɪlaɪts/ *n* [plural] INFORMAL **1 scare/frighten the living daylights out of** sb to frighten someone a lot **2 beat the living daylights out of** sb to hit someone many times and hurt him/her

**daylight sav·ing time** /,.. '.. ,./ **daylight savings** *n* [U] the time in the spring when clocks are set one hour ahead of standard time

**days**[1] /deɪz/ *n* LITERARY life: *He began his days in a small town.*

**days**[2] *adv* during each day: *This week I work days; next week it's nights.*

**day·time** /'deɪtaɪm/ *n* the time between when it gets light in the morning and when it gets dark in the evening: *I've never been here* **in/during the daytime.**

**day-to-day** /,. . '.◀/ *adj* happening every day as a regular part of life: *our day-to-day routine at work*

**daze** /deɪz/ *n* **in a daze** unable to think clearly

**dazed** /deɪzd/ *adj* unable to think clearly, usually because you are shocked, have been hurt etc.: *dazed victims of the bombing*

**daz·zle** /'dæzəl/ *v* [T] **1** to make someone unable to see by shining a strong light in his/her eyes: *deer dazzled by our headlights* **2** to make someone admire someone or something a lot: *We were all dazzled by her talent and charm.*

**daz·zling** /'dæzlɪŋ/ *adj* very impressive, exciting, or interesting: *a dazzling performance*

**D.C.** District of Columbia; the area containing the city of Washington, the CAPITAL of the US

**DC** *n* [U] direct current; the type of electric current that comes from batteries (BATTERY) —compare AC

**DDT** *n* [U] a chemical used in order to kill insects, that is now illegal

**DE** the written abbreviation of Delaware

**dea·con** /'dikən/, **dea·con·ess** /'dikə,nɛs/ *n* an official in some Christian churches

**dead**[1] /dɛd/ *adj*

**1 ▶NOT ALIVE◀** no longer alive: *Her mom's been dead for two years.* | *Two boys found a* **dead body** (=a dead person) *by the train tracks.*

**2 ▶NOT WORKING◀** not working, especially because there is no power: *Is the battery dead?* | *The phones went dead during the storm.*
**3 ▶PLACE◀** a place that is dead does not have anything interesting happening in it: *The bar is usually dead until around 10:00.*
**4 ▶NOT USED◀** no longer used or no longer able to be used: *a dead language*
**5 ▶TIRED◀** INFORMAL very tired: *I think I'll go to bed early, I'm absolutely dead.*
**6 ▶PART OF BODY◀** a part of your body that is dead has no feeling in it for a short time: *I'd been sitting so long my legs went dead.*
**7 over my dead body** SPOKEN used when you are determined not to allow something to happen: *You'll marry him over my dead body!*
**8** SPOKEN also **dead meat** in serious trouble: *If anything happens to the car, you're dead!* —see also **sb wouldn't be caught dead doing sth** (CATCH¹)

---

**USAGE NOTE** dead and died

Use **dead** as an adjective to talk about things or people that are no longer alive: *I think this plant is dead.* **Died** is the past tense and past participle of "die": *She died of a heart attack.*

---

**dead²** *adv* **1** INFORMAL completely or extremely: *Paula stopped dead when she saw us.* | *The baby was up all night; I'm dead tired.* **2** INFORMAL directly or exactly: *You can't miss it; it's dead ahead.*

**dead³** *n* **1 in the dead of winter/night** in the middle of winter or the night when everything is quiet **2 the dead** people who have died

**dead·en** /'dɛdn/ *v* [T] to make a feeling or sound less strong: *a drug to deaden the pain*

**dead end** /ˌ. './ *n* **1** a street with no way out at one end **2** a job or situation from which no more progress is possible

**dead·line** /'dɛdlaɪn/ *n* a time by which you must finish something: *Can you meet the 5:00 deadline?*

**dead·lock** /'dɛdlɑk/ *n* [C,U] a situation in which a disagreement cannot be settled: *the UN's attempt to break the deadlock* (=end it) *in the region.*

**dead·ly** /'dɛdli/ *adj* **1** very dangerous and likely to cause death: *a deadly virus* **2** complete or total, often in an unpleasant or frightening way: *Brian hit the target with deadly accuracy.*

**dead·pan** /'dɛdpæn/ *adj* sounding and looking like you are completely serious when you are not: *a deadpan expression*

**deaf** /dɛf/ *adj* **1** unable to hear: *I'm deaf in my right ear.* **2 the deaf** people who are deaf **3 deaf to sth** unwilling to listen to something: *The guards were deaf to the prisoners' complaints.* **4 fall on deaf ears** to not be listened

to: *My warning fell on deaf ears.* —**deafness** *n* [U]

**deaf·en** /'dɛfən/ *v* [T] to make it difficult for you to hear anything —**deafening** *adj*: *deafening music*

**deal¹** /dil/ *n* **1** an agreement or arrangement, especially in business or politics: *They've just signed a new deal with their record company.* | *You can get some good deals at the new travel agency.* (=buy something at a good price.) **2 it's a deal** SPOKEN used in order to say that you agree to something, especially when you get something in return: *"I'll give you $100." "It's a deal."* **3 a great/good deal** a large quantity of something: *He knows a great deal more* (=a lot more) *than I do about computers.* **4** the way someone is treated in a particular situation: *Women often get a raw deal* (=unfair treatment) *from their employers.* **5 what's the deal?** SPOKEN used when you want to know what is happening: *So what's the deal? Why is he so mad?* **6** someone's turn to give out playing cards in a game: *It's your deal.* —see also BIG DEAL

**deal²** *v* dealt, dealt /dɛlt/, dealing **1** [I,T] also **deal out** to give out playing cards to players in a game: *Whose turn is it to deal?* **2** [I,T] to buy and sell illegal drugs: *He was arrested for dealing cocaine.*

**deal with** sb/sth *phr v* [T] **1** to take the correct action for a problem, piece of work etc.: *Who's dealing with the new account?* **2** to not lose confidence or to not become too upset in a difficult situation: *I can't deal with any more crying children today.* **3** to do business with someone or have a business connection with someone: *We've been dealing with their company for ten years.* **4** to be about a particular subject: *a book dealing with 20th century art*

**deal in** sth *phr v* [T] to buy and sell a particular type of product: *a business dealing in medical equipment*

**deal·er** /'dilɚ/ *n* **1** someone who buys and sells a particular product: *a car dealer* **2** someone who gives out the playing cards in a game

**deal·er·ship** /'dilɚˌʃɪp/ *n* a business that sells the products of a particular company, especially cars: *a Ford dealership*

**deal·ing** /'dilɪŋ/ *n* [U] the buying and selling of things: *problems with drug dealing in the school*

**deal·ings** /'dilɪŋz/ *n* [plural] personal or business relations with someone: *Have you had any dealings with IBM?*

**dean** /din/ *n* an official with a high rank in some universities: *Dean of Arts*

**dear¹** /dɪr/ *interjection* said when you are surprised, annoyed, or upset: *Oh dear! I forgot to phone Jill.*

D

**dear**[2] *n* SPOKEN used when speaking to someone you like or love: *How was your day, dear?*

**dear**[3] *adj* **1** used before a name or title at the beginning of a letter: *Dear Sue, ... | Dear Dr. Ward, ...* **2** much loved and very important to you: *She's a dear friend.*

**dear·ly** /'dɪrli/ *adj* very much: *I'd dearly love to go to Hawaii.*

**dearth** /dɚθ/ *n* FORMAL a lack of something

**death** /dɛθ/ *n* **1** [C,U] the end of a person or animal's life: *Maretti lived in Miami until his death. | The number of deaths from AIDS is increasing. | He choked to death* (=choked until he died) *on a fish bone.* **2 bored/scared to death** INFORMAL very bored or afraid **3** the end of something: *the death of Communism* –see also **be sick (and tired) of, be sick to death of** (SICK[1])

**death·bed** /'dɛθbɛd/ *n* **sb's deathbed** the point in time when someone is dying and will be dead very soon: *Marquez flew home to be with his mother, who was on her deathbed.*

**death pen·al·ty** /'. ,.../ *n* the legal punishment of being killed for a serious crime: *Gilmore was given the death penalty for murder.* –see also CAPITAL PUNISHMENT

**death row** /,. './ *n* [U] the part of a prison where prisoners are kept while they wait to be punished by being killed: *He's been on death row for three years.*

**death trap** /'. ./ *n* INFORMAL a vehicle or building that is in such bad condition that it is dangerous

**de·base** /dɪ'beɪs/ *v* [T] to reduce the quality or value of something –**debasement** *n* [C,U]

**de·bat·a·ble** /dɪ'beɪt̬əbəl/ *adj* an idea or problem that is debatable is one for which two or more different opinions or answers could be true or right

**de·bate**[1] /dɪ'beɪt/ *n* **1** a discussion or argument on a subject that people express different opinions about: *a debate on/about equal pay* **2** [U] the process of discussing a subject or question: *After much debate, the committee decided to raise the fees.*

**debate**[2] *v* **1** [I,T] to discuss a subject formally with someone so that you can make a decision or solve a problem: *The Senate is debating the future of health care. | We were debating which person to hire.* **2** [T] to seriously consider something: *I was debating whether to go to work.*

**de·bauched** /dɪ'bɔʃt/ *adj* someone who is debauched drinks too much alcohol, takes drugs, or has an immoral attitude about sex –**debauchery** *n* [U]

**de·bil·i·tate** /dɪ'bɪlə,teɪt/ *v* [T] to make someone weak, especially from sickness, heat, or lack of food: *debilitated by disease* –**debilitating** *adj* –**debility** *n*

**deb·it**[1] /'dɛbɪt/ *n* a record of the money that you have taken out of your bank account

**debit**[2] *v* [T] to take money out of a bank account: *The sum of $50 has been debited from your account.* –opposite CREDIT[2]

**deb·o·nair** /,dɛbə'nɛr/ *adj* a man who is debonair is fashionable and behaves in a confident way

**de·brief** /di'brif/ *v* [T] to ask someone such as a soldier to give a report of a job that s/he has done –**debriefing** *n*

**de·bris** /dɪ'bri/ *n* [U] the pieces of something that are left after it has been destroyed: *The street was full of debris after the explosion.*

**debt** /dɛt/ *n* **1** money that you owe to someone: *Gordon can finally pay off his debts.* **2** [U] the state of owing money to someone: *a company heavily in debt* (=owing a lot of money) **3 be in sb's debt** to be very grateful to someone for what s/he has done for you

**debt·or** /'dɛt̬ɚ/ *n* a person, group, or organization that owes money

**de·bug** /di'bʌg/ *v* [T] to take the mistakes out of a computer PROGRAM

**de·bunk** /di'bʌŋk/ *v* [T] to show that an idea or belief is false: *She set out to debunk the myth that French cooking is difficult.*

**de·but** /deɪ'byu, 'deɪbyu/ *n* the first time that a performer or sports player performs in public, or the first time something is available to the public: *the band's debut album | Foster made her debut in movies at a young age.*

**deb·u·tante** /'dɛbyu,tɑnt/ *n* a girl who has just formally begun going to parties etc. in rich people's society

**dec·ade** /'dɛkeɪd/ *n* a period of time equal to 10 years

**dec·a·dent** /'dɛkədənt/ *adj* more interested in pleasure than anything else: *decadent behavior* –**decadence** *n* [U]

**de·caf** /'dikæf/ *n* [U] DECAFFEINATED coffee

**de·caf·fein·at·ed** /di'kæfə,neɪt̬ɪd/ *adj* coffee, tea, or COLA that is decaffeinated has had the CAFFEINE removed

**de·cal** /'dikæl/ *n* a piece of paper with a picture on it that you stick onto a surface

**de·cant·er** /dɪ'kænt̬ɚ/ *n* a glass container for alcoholic drinks

**dec·ath·lon** /dɪ'kæθlɑn, -lən/ *n* [singular] a competition with ten running, jumping, and throwing events

**de·cay**[1] /dɪ'keɪ/ *n* [U] the process, state, or result of decaying: *The building has fallen into decay over the last few years. | the decay of the country's morals*

**decay**[2] *v* **1** [I,T] to be slowly destroyed by natural chemical processes, or to destroy something in this way: *The dead animal had started to decay. | Sugar decays teeth.* **2** [I] to become weaker or less important, or to no longer be in

*D*

good condition, because of not being taken care of: *the decaying downtown area*

**de·ceased** /dɪˈsist/ *n* FORMAL **the deceased** someone who has died –**deceased** *adj*

**de·ceit** /dɪˈsit/ *n* [U] behavior that is intended to make someone believe something that is not true: *the government's history of deceit and prejudice in its dealings with Native Americans*

**de·ceit·ful** /dɪˈsitfəl/ *adj* intending to make someone believe something that is not true

**de·ceive** /dɪˈsiv/ *v* [T] **1** to make someone believe something that is not true: *Cusack tried to deceive the police.* **2 deceive yourself** to pretend to yourself that something is not true, though you know that it is true: *Stop deceiving yourself! She's never coming back!*

**De·cem·ber** /dɪˈsɛmbɚ/ written abbreviation **Dec.** *n* the twelfth month of the year –see usage note at JANUARY

**de·cen·cy** /ˈdisənsi/ *n* [U] the quality of being honest and polite, and respecting other people: *You could at least* **have the decency to** *call if you know you're late.*

**de·cent** /ˈdisənt/ *adj* **1** acceptable and good enough: *Don't you have a decent pair of shoes?* **2** honest and good: *Dr. Green was a decent man.* **3** wearing enough clothes to not show too much of your body: *Don't come in, I'm not decent.* –**decently** *adv*

**de·cen·tral·ize** /diˈsɛntrəˌlaɪz/ *v* [T] to move parts of a government, organization etc. from one central place to several smaller ones –**decentralization** /diˌsɛntrələˈzeɪʃən, ˌdisɛn-/ *n* [U]

**de·cep·tion** /dɪˈsɛpʃən/ *n* [C,U] the act of deliberately making someone believe something that is not true: *People were outraged when they learned of the deception.*

**de·cep·tive** /dɪˈsɛptɪv/ *adj* able to make someone believe something that is not true: *deceptive advertising* –**deceptively** *adj*

**dec·i·bel** /ˈdɛsəˌbɛl, -bəl/ *n* TECHNICAL a unit for measuring how loud a sound is

**de·cide** /dɪˈsaɪd/ *v* **1** [I,T] to make a choice or judgment about something: *I've* **decided to** *stay at home.* | *Jane* **decided against** *going to Washington on vacation.* | *Ted* **decided (that)** *the car would cost too much.* | *I can't* **decide whether/if** *I want fish or chicken.* **2 deciding factor** a very strong reason that forces you to make a particular decision **3** [T] to influence the result of a game, competition etc.: *One punch decided the fight.*

**decide on** sth *phr v* [T] to choose one thing from many possible choices: *Have you* **decided on** *a name for the baby?*

**de·cid·ed** /dɪˈsaɪdɪd/ *adj* definite and easy to notice: *a decided change for the worse* –**decidedly** *adv*

**de·cid·u·ous** /dɪˈsɪdʒuəs/ *adj* deciduous trees

have leaves that fall off in autumn –compare EVERGREEN

**dec·i·mal**[1] /ˈdɛsəməl/ *adj* based on the number ten: *a decimal system*

**decimal**[2] *n* TECHNICAL a number less than one that is shown by a mark (.) followed by the number of TENTHs, then the number of HUNDREDTHs etc.: *The decimal .37 is equal to the fraction 37/100.*

**decimal point** /ˈ... ˌ./ *n* the mark (.) in a DECIMAL, used in order to separate whole numbers from TENTHs, HUNDREDTHs etc.

**dec·i·mate** /ˈdɛsəˌmeɪt/ *v* [T] to destroy a large part of something: *Disease decimated the population.*

**de·ci·pher** /dɪˈsaɪfɚ/ *v* [T] to find the meaning of something that is difficult to read or understand: *deciphering a code* | *I can't decipher his handwriting.*

**de·ci·sion** /dɪˈsɪʒən/ *n* **1** a choice or judgment that you make: *We'll* **make a decision** *by Friday.* | *Gina's* **decision to** *go to college* | *Do you expect to* **reach a decision** *soon?* | *a decision about where to go on vacation* **2** [U] the ability to make choices or judgments quickly

**decision-mak·ing** /ˈ... ˌ../ *n* [U] the action of deciding on something, or the ability to decide something: *Most of the decision-making is done by elected officials.*

**de·ci·sive** /dɪˈsaɪsɪv/ *adj* **1** having a great effect on the result of something: *a decisive moment in his career* **2** good at making decisions quickly: *We need a strong decisive leader.* **3** definite and not able to be doubted: *a decisive advantage* –**decisively** *adv*

**deck**[1] /dɛk/ *n* **1** a wooden floor outside the back of a house, used for relaxing on **2** a set of playing cards: *Take one from the top of the deck.* **3** the outside top level of a ship that you can walk on, or any of the levels on a ship, plane, or bus: *Let's go up* **on deck.**

**deck**

**deck**[2] *v* [T] **1** also **deck** sb/sth ↔ **out** to make someone or something more attractive, especially for a special occasion: *The street was* **decked out with** *flags for the big parade.* **2** SLANG to hit someone so hard that s/he falls over

**dec·la·ra·tion** /ˌdɛkləˈreɪʃən/ *n* [C,U] **1** a statement saying that something has officially begun or happened: *a declaration of war* **2** an official statement that gives information

**de·clare** /dɪˈklɛr/ *v* [T] **1** to state officially and publicly that something is happening or that something is true: *The US* **declared war on** *England in 1812.* | *The doctor* **declared that** *she was dead.* | *The bridge has been* **declared un-**

*safe.* | *Jones was declared the winner.* **2** to say clearly and publicly what you think or feel: *Parson declared (that) he would never go back there.* **3** to make an official statement saying how much money you have earned, what property you own etc.: *You must declare your full income.*

**de·cline**[1] /dɪˈklaɪn/ *v* **1** [I] to decrease in quality, quantity, importance etc : *As his health has declined, so has his influence.* **2** [I,T] to refuse something, usually politely: *We asked them to come, but they declined.* | *The senator declined to make a statement.* —see usage note at REFUSE[1]

**decline**[2] *n* [singular, U] a gradual decrease in the quality, quantity, or importance of something: *New car sales are on the decline.* | *a decline in profits*

**de·code** /diˈkoʊd/ *v* [T] to discover the meaning of a secret or complicated message

**de·com·pose** /ˌdikəmˈpoʊz/ *v* [I,T] to decay or to make something do this —**decomposition** /ˌdikɑmpəˈzɪʃən/ *n* [U]

**de·cor** /ˈdeɪkɔr, deɪˈkɔr/ *n* [C,U] the furniture and decoration of a place

**dec·o·rate** /ˈdɛkəˌreɪt/ *v* [T] **1** to make something look more attractive by adding pretty things to it: *This year we're decorating the Christmas tree with big red bows.* **2** to give someone an official sign of honor, such as a MEDAL: *He was decorated for bravery in the war.*

**dec·o·ra·tion** /ˌdɛkəˈreɪʃən/ *n* **1** something pretty that you add in order to make something look more attractive: *Christmas decorations* **2** [U] the way in which something is decorated: *the tasteful decoration of their living room* **3** an official sign of honor, such as a MEDAL, that is given to someone

**dec·o·ra·tive** /ˈdɛkərətɪv/ *adj* pretty or attractive: *a decorative pot*

**dec·o·ra·tor** /ˈdɛkəˌreɪtər/ *n* someone who chooses furniture, paint, curtains etc. for houses, offices etc. as his/her job

**de·cor·um** /dɪˈkɔrəm/ *n* [U] behavior that is respectful and correct for a particular occasion —**decorous** /ˈdɛkərəs/ *adj*

**de·coy** /ˈdikɔɪ/ *n* something that is used in order to lead a person or a bird into a trap —**decoy** *v* [T]

**de·crease**[1] /dɪˈkris, ˈdikris/ *v* [I,T] to become less in size, number, or amount, or to make something do this: *The company's profits decreased in 1992.* —opposite INCREASE[1]

**de·crease**[2] /ˈdikris, dɪˈkris/ *n* [C,U] the process of reducing something, or the amount by which it is reduced: *a decrease in sales*

**de·cree**[1] /dɪˈkri/ *n* an official command or decision

**decree**[2] *v* [T] to make a DECREE

**de·crep·it** /dɪˈkrɛpɪt/ *adj* old and in bad condition

**de·crim·i·nal·ize** /diˈkrɪmənəˌlaɪz/ *v* [T] to state officially that something is no longer illegal —**decriminalization** /diˌkrɪmɪnələˈzeɪʃən/ *n* [U]

**de·cry** /dɪˈkraɪ/ *v* [T] FORMAL to state publicly that you do not approve of something

**ded·i·cate** /ˈdɛdəˌkeɪt/ *v* [T] **1** to say that something such as a book, movie, song etc. has been written, made, or sung in honor of someone: *The book is dedicated to his mother.* **2** **dedicate yourself/your life to sth** to use all your energy, time, effort etc. for one particular thing: *I've dedicated my life to my work.* **3** to state in an official ceremony that something such as a building or bridge will be given someone's name: *a chapel dedicated to Saint Paul*

**ded·i·cat·ed** /ˈdɛdəˌkeɪtɪd/ *adj* working very hard for a particular purpose: *She's very dedicated to her job.*

**ded·i·ca·tion** /ˌdɛdɪˈkeɪʃən/ *n* **1** [U] the hard work or effort that someone puts into a particular activity: *He shows great dedication to his work.* **2** the act or ceremony of dedicating (DEDICATE) something to someone **3** the words used in dedicating a book

**de·duce** /dɪˈdus/ *v* [T] FORMAL to make a judgment based on the information that you have

**de·duct** /dɪˈdʌkt/ *v* [T] to take away an amount or a part from a total: *Taxes are deducted from your pay.* —**deductible** *adj*

**de·duct·i·ble** /dɪˈdʌktəbəl/ *n* the part of a bill you must pay before the insurance company will pay the rest

**de·duc·tion** /dɪˈdʌkʃən/ *n* [C,U] **1** the process of taking away an amount from a total, or the amount that is taken away: *You can receive a tax deduction for giving money to charity.* (=you can pay less tax if you give money to CHARITY) **2** the process of making a judgment about something, based on the information that you have: *a game that teaches logic and deduction*

**deed** /did/ *n* **1** LITERARY an action: *good deeds* **2** LAW an official paper that is a record of an agreement, especially one that says who owns property

**deem** /dim/ *v* [T] FORMAL to consider something in a particular way: *The judge deemed several of the questions inappropriate.*

**deep**[1] /dip/ *adj*
**1 ▸GO FAR IN/DOWN◂** going far down or far in from the top, the front, or the surface of something: *The water's not very deep here.* | *Terry had a deep cut in his forehead.* | *a shelf 3 feet long and 8 inches deep*

**deep**

deep    shallow

**2** ►FEELING/BELIEF◄ a deep feeling or belief is very strong and sincere: *deep feelings of hatred*

**3** ►SOUND◄ a deep sound is very low: *a deep voice*

**4** ►COLOR◄ a deep color is dark and strong: *a deep blue sky*

**5** ►SERIOUS◄ serious and often difficult to understand: *a deep conversation about the meaning of life*

**6 deep sleep** a sleep that is difficult to wake up from

**7 take a deep breath** to breathe in a lot of air at once, especially in order to do something difficult or frightening: *I took a deep breath and plunged into the water.*

**8 be in deep trouble/water** INFORMAL to be in serious trouble or in an extremely difficult situation: *If mom sees you doing that, you'll be in deep trouble!*

**9 deep in debt** owing a lot of money

**10 deep in thought/conversation** thinking so hard or talking so much that you do not notice anything else: *Martin sat at his desk, deep in thought.*

**11 go off the deep end** INFORMAL to suddenly become angry or violent – see also DEPTH

**deep**² *adv* **1** far into something: *He stepped deep into the mud.* **2 deep down** a) if you feel or know something deep down, then you are sure about it even though you may not admit it: *Deep down, I knew she was gone forever.* b) if someone is good, evil etc. deep down, that is what s/he is really like even though s/he hides it: *He seems mean, but deep down he's really very nice.* **3 two/three etc. deep** in two, three etc. rows or layers – see also **run deep** (RUN)

**deep·en** /ˈdipən/ *v* [I,T] to make something deeper or to become deeper

**deep freeze** /ˌ. ˈ./ *n* ⇨ FREEZER

**deep fried** /ˌ. ˈ.◄/ *adj* cooked in a lot of hot oil –**deep fry** *v* [T]

**deep·ly** /ˈdipli/ *adv* extremely or very much: *The Americans did not want to get **deeply involved** in a European war.*

**deep-seat·ed** /ˌ. ˈ..◄/, **deep-rooted** *adj* a deep-seated feeling or idea is strong and very difficult to change

**deer** /dɪr/ *n, plural* **deer** a large wild animal that lives in forests, the male of which has long horns that look like tree branches

**de·face** /dɪˈfeɪs/ *v* [T] to spoil the appearance of something, especially by writing or making marks on it: *walls defaced by graffiti*

**de·fame** /dɪˈfeɪm/ *v* [T] FORMAL to write or say something that makes people have a bad opinion of someone –**defamation** /ˌdɛfəˈmeɪʃən/ *n* [U] –**defamatory** /dɪˈfæməˌtɔri/ *adj*

**de·fault**¹ /dɪˈfɔlt/ *v* [I] to not do something

that you are legally supposed to: *He defaulted on his loan payments.*

**default**² *n* **1** [U] failure to do something that you are supposed to do: *a **default on** his mortgage payments* | *The other team never arrived, so we won **by default**.* (=because they failed to arrive) **2** [C usually singular] the way in which things will be arranged on a computer screen unless you change them

**de·feat**¹ /dɪˈfit/ *v* [T] **1** to win a victory over someone: *Michigan defeated USC in Saturday's game.* **2** to make something fail: *The plan was defeated by a lack of money.*

**defeat**² *n* **1** [C,U] failure to win or succeed: *He'll never **admit defeat**.* (=admit that he has failed) | *The vote resulted in a **serious defeat** for the governor.* **2** [singular] victory over someone or something: *The defeat of racism is our main goal.*

**de·feat·ist** /dɪˈfitɪst/ *n* someone who expects to fail

**def·e·cate** /ˈdɛfəˌkeɪt/ *v* [I] FORMAL to get rid of waste matter from your BOWELs –**defecation** /ˌdɛfəˈkeɪʃən/ *n* [U]

**de·fect**¹ /ˈdifɛkt, dɪˈfɛkt/ *n* a fault or a lack of something that makes something not perfect: *The cars are tested for any defects before being sold.* | *a birth defect* (=something that makes a baby not normal)

**de·fect**² /dɪˈfɛkt/ *v* [I] to leave your own country or a group and join or go to an opposing one –**defection** /dɪˈfɛkʃən/ *n* [C,U] –**defector** /dɪˈfɛktər/ *n*

**de·fec·tive** /dɪˈfɛktɪv/ *adj* not made correctly or not working correctly: *defective machinery*

**de·fend** /dɪˈfɛnd/ *v* **1** [T] to protect someone or something from being attacked or taken away: *You should learn to **defend** yourself.* | *Soldiers **defended** the fort **from** attack.* **2** [T] to use arguments to protect something or someone from criticism: *How can you defend the use of animals for cosmetics testing?* | *He had to **defend himself against** their charges.* **3** [I,T] to protect your GOAL in a game, and prevent your opponents from getting points **4** [T] to be a lawyer for someone who is said to be guilty of a crime –**defender** *n* –**defensible** /dɪˈfɛnsəbəl/ *adj*

**de·fend·ant** /dɪˈfɛndənt/ *n* LAW the person in a court of law who has been charged with doing something illegal –compare PLAINTIFF

**de·fense**¹ /dɪˈfɛns/ *n* **1** [U] the act of protecting someone or something from attack or criticism: *Senator Stevens spoke today **in defense** of the bill to make handguns illegal.* **2** [U] the weapons and people that a country uses to protect itself from attack: *the country's military defense* | *Defense spending* (=spending money on weapons etc.) *has increased.* **3** something that is used for protection against something else: *Vitamin C is my **defense against***

colds. **4** the things that are said in a court of law to prove that someone is not guilty of a crime: *Our defense is pretty weak.* **5 the defense** the people in a court of law who are trying to show that someone is not guilty of a crime: *Is the defense ready to call their first witness?*

**de·fense**[2] /'difɛns/ *n* [U] the players in a game such as football whose main job is to try to prevent the other team from getting points —see picture on page 472

**de·fense·less** /dɪ'fɛnslɪs/ *adj* unable to protect yourself from being hurt or criticized

**defense mech·a·nism** /.'. ,..../ *n* **1** a process in your brain that makes you forget things that are too unpleasant or painful to think about **2** a natural reaction in your body that protects you from illness or danger

**de·fen·sive**[1] /dɪ'fɛnsɪv/ *adj* **1** used or intended for protection against attack: *defensive weapons* **2** behaving in a way that shows you think someone is criticizing or attacking you: *She got really defensive when I asked her why she hadn't finished.* **3** relating to the DEFENSE in sports such as football: *a defensive play* —defensively *adv* —defensiveness *n* [U]

**defensive**[2] *n* **on the defensive** having to react to criticism or an attack: *Danton was on the defensive after Roberts disagreed with him.*

**de·fer** /dɪ'fɚ/ *v* **-rred, -rring** [T] to delay something until a later date: *His military service was deferred until he finished college.*

**defer to** sb/sth *phr v* [T] FORMAL to accept someone's opinion or decision because you have respect for that person: *She had more experience, so I deferred to her suggestions.*

**def·er·ence** /'dɛfərəns/ *n* [U] FORMAL behavior that shows you respect someone and are willing to accept his/her opinions or judgment —deferential /ˌdɛfə'rɛnʃəl/ *adj*

**de·fi·ant** /dɪ'faɪənt/ *adj* refusing to do what someone tells you to do because you do not respect him/her —defiance *n* [U] —defiantly *adv*

**de·fi·cien·cy** /dɪ'fɪʃənsi/ *n* [C,U] **1** a lack of something that is needed: *a vitamin deficiency* **2** a condition of not being good enough: *the deficiencies of the public transportation system*

**de·fi·cient** /dɪ'fɪʃənt/ *adj* **1** not having or containing enough of something: *food deficient in iron* **2** not good enough

**def·i·cit** /'dɛfəsɪt/ *n* the difference between the amount of money that a company or country has and the higher amount that it needs: *Our records show a deficit of $2.5 million.*

**de·file** /dɪ'faɪl/ *v* [T] FORMAL to make something less pure, good, or holy: *graves defiled by Nazi symbols*

**de·fine** /dɪ'faɪn/ *v* [T] **1** to show or describe what something is or means: *Some words are hard to define.* **2** to clearly show the limits or

shape of something: *The footprints were sharply defined in the snow.* —definable *adj*

**def·i·nite** /'dɛfənɪt/ *adj* clearly known, seen, or stated, and completely certain: *They want to leave Monday; John was very definite about it.* | *We don't have a definite arrangement yet.* —opposite INDEFINITE

**definite ar·ti·cle** /ˌ... '.../ *n* ⇨ ARTICLE

**def·i·nite·ly** /'dɛfənɪtli/ *adv* certainly and without any doubt: *That was definitely the best movie I've seen all year.* | *It's definitely not the right time to tell her.*

**def·i·ni·tion** /ˌdɛfə'nɪʃən/ *n* **1** a phrase or sentence that says exactly what a word, phrase, or idea means **2** [U] the clearness of something such as a picture or sound: *The photograph lacks definition.*

**de·fin·i·tive** /dɪ'fɪnətɪv/ *adj* **1** a definitive book, description etc. is considered to be the best and cannot be improved: *Wasserman's definitive book on wine* **2** a definitive statement, answer etc. cannot be doubted or changed: *The group has taken a definitive stand against pornography.* —definitively *adv*

**de·flate** /dɪ'fleɪt, di-/ *v* **1** [I,T] if something deflates or if you deflate it, it becomes smaller because the air or gas inside it comes out —opposite INFLATE **2** [T] to make someone feel less important or confident: *I'd love to deflate that ego of his!* **3** [T] TECHNICAL to change the economic rules or conditions in a country so that prices become lower or stop rising —deflation /di'fleɪʃən/ *n* [U]

**de·flect** /dɪ'flɛkt/ *v* **1** [I,T] to turn something in a different direction by hitting it, or to be turned in this way: *The ball was deflected into the crowd.* **2 deflect attention/criticism/anger etc.** to stop people paying attention to something, criticizing it etc. —deflection /dɪ'flɛkʃən/ *n* [C,U]

**de·form** /dɪ'fɔrm/ *v* [T] to change the usual shape of something so that its usefulness or appearance is spoiled: *The disease had deformed his left hand.* —deformed *adj* —deformation /ˌdifɔr'meɪʃən/ *n* [C,U]

**de·form·i·ty** /dɪ'fɔrməti/ *n* [C,U] a condition in which part of someone's body is not the normal shape

**de·fraud** /dɪ'frɔd/ *v* [T] to deceive a person or organization in order to get money from him, her, or it

**de·frost** /dɪ'frɔst/ *v* **1** [I,T] if frozen food defrosts, or if you defrost it, it gets warmer until it is not frozen **2** [I,T] if a FREEZER or REFRIGERATOR defrosts, or if you defrost it, it is turned off so that the ice inside it melts **3** [T] to remove ice or steam from the windows of a car by blowing warm air onto them

**deft** /dɛft/ *adj* quick and skillful: *a deft catch* —deftly *adv*

D

**de·funct** /dɪ'fʌŋkt/ *adj* FORMAL no longer existing or useful

**de·fuse** /di'fyuz/ *v* [T] **1** to stop a bomb from exploding **2** to improve a difficult situation: *Tim tried to defuse the tension.*

**de·fy** /dɪ'faɪ/ *v* [T] **1** to refuse to obey someone or something: *He defied his father's wishes and joined the army.* **2 defy description/ analysis/imagination etc.** to be almost impossible to describe or understand: *The place just defies description.*

**de·gen·er·ate**[1] /dɪ'dʒenə,reɪt/ *v* [I] to become worse: *The party soon degenerated into a drunken brawl.* −**degeneration** /dɪ,dʒenə-'reɪʃən/ *n* [U]

**de·gen·e·rate**[2] /dɪ'dʒenərɪt/ *adj* **1** worse than before in quality **2** having very low moral standards −**degenerate** *n*

**de·grade** /dɪ'greɪd, di-/ *v* [T] **1** to treat someone without respect, or to make people lose their respect for someone: *Don't degrade yourself by arguing with him.* | *Pornography degrades women.* **2** FORMAL to make a situation or condition worse: *The proposed law could degrade safety standards.* −**degradation** /,degrə-'deɪʃən/ *n* [U]

**de·grad·ing** /dɪ'greɪdɪŋ/ *adj* making people lose their respect for someone, or making you feel that other people have lost respect for you: *She treats her children in a degrading way.*

**de·gree** /dɪ'gri/ *n* **1** a unit for measuring temperature or the size of an angle **2** [C,U] the level or amount of something, especially of ability or progress: *students with different degrees of ability* | *To what degree can he be trusted?* **3** a course of study at a university, or the QUALIFICATION given to someone who has successfully completed this: *a law degree* | *a degree in history*

**de·hy·drate** /di'haɪdreɪt/ *v* **1** [T] to remove all the water from something **2** [I] to lose too much water from your body −**dehydrated** *adj* −**dehydration** /,dihaɪ'dreɪʃən/ *n* [U]

**deign** /deɪn/ *v* **deign to do sth** HUMOROUS to agree to do something that you think you are too important to do: *She finally deigned to join us for lunch.*

**de·i·ty** /'diəti, 'deɪ-/ *n* a god or GODDESS

**dé·jà vu** /,deɪʒɑ 'vu/ *n* [U] the feeling that what is happening now has happened before in exactly the same way

**de·ject·ed** /dɪ'dʒektɪd/ *adj* sad and disappointed: *a dejected look* −**dejectedly** *adv* −**dejection** /dɪ'dʒekʃən/ *n* [U]

**de·lay**[1] /dɪ'leɪ/ *v* **1** [I,T] to wait until a later time to do something: *We've decided to delay the trip until next month.* | *Don't delay, call us today!* **2** [T] to make someone or something late: *Our flight was delayed by bad weather.* −**delayed** *adj*

**de·lay**[2] *n* [C,U] a situation in which someone or something is made to wait, or the length of the waiting time: *There are severe delays on Route 95 because of an accident.* | *Delays of two hours or more are common.* | *Do it without delay!*

**de·lec·ta·ble** /dɪ'lektəbəl/ *adj* FORMAL very pleasant to taste, smell etc.

**del·e·gate**[1] /'deləgɪt/ *n* someone who is chosen to speak, vote, and make decisions for a group: *Delegates from 50 colleges met to discuss the issue.*

**del·e·gate**[2] /'delə,geɪt/ *v* [I,T] to give part of your work or the things you are responsible for to someone in a lower position than you: *Smaller jobs should be delegated to your assistant.*

**del·e·ga·tion** /,delə'geɪʃən/ *n* **1** a small group of people who are chosen to speak, vote, and make decisions for a larger group or organization: *A UN delegation was sent to the peace talks.* **2** [U] the process of delegating (DELEGATE) work: *the delegation of authority*

**de·lete** /dɪ'lit/ *v* [T] **1** to remove a letter, word etc. from a piece of writing **2** to remove a piece of information from a computer's MEMORY −**deletion** /dɪ'liʃən/ *n*

**del·i** /'deli/ *n* INFORMAL a small store that sells cheese, cooked meat, SALADs, breads etc.

**de·lib·er·ate**[1] /dɪ'lɪbrɪt, -bərɪt/ *adj* **1** intended or planned: *I'm sure her story was a deliberate attempt to confuse us.* **2** deliberate speech, thought, or movement is slow and careful

**de·lib·e·rate**[2] /dɪ'lɪbə,reɪt/ *v* [I,T] to think about something very carefully, especially a TRIAL: *The jury deliberated for 3 days before finding him guilty.*

**de·lib·er·ate·ly** /dɪ'lɪbrɪt⌐li/ *adv* not happening by accident; planned: *She deliberately spilled coffee on my dress!*

**de·lib·er·a·tion** /dɪ,lɪbə'reɪʃən/ *n* [C,U] careful thought or discussion about a problem: *The committee will finish its deliberations today.*

**del·i·ca·cy** /'delɪkəsi/ *n* **1** [U] the quality of being delicate: *the delicacy of the clock's machinery* | *The delicacy of the situation means we have to be very careful about what we say.* **2** a particular food that tastes very good or that is expensive and rare: *In France, snails are considered a delicacy.*

**del·i·cate** /'delɪkɪt/ *adj* **1** made in a way that is not solid or is weak and therefore easily damaged: *a delicate piece of lace* **2** needing to be done very carefully in order to avoid causing problems: *doctors performing a delicate operation on her eye* **3** a part of the body that is delicate is attractive and graceful: *long delicate fingers* −**delicately** *adv*

**del·i·ca·tes·sen** /,delɪkə'tesən/ *n* ⇨ DELI

**de·li·cious** /dɪˈlɪʃəs/ *adj* having a very enjoyable taste or smell: *That chocolate cake was delicious!*

**de·light¹** /dɪˈlaɪt/ *n* **1** [U] a feeling of great pleasure or satisfaction: *Krystal laughed with delight.* **2** something that makes you feel very happy or satisfied: *the delights of owning your own home*

**delight²** *v* [T] to give someone a feeling of satisfaction and enjoyment: *This movie classic will delight the whole family.*

**delight in** sth *phr v* [T] to enjoy something very much, especially something unpleasant: *twins who delight in confusing people*

**de·light·ed** /dɪˈlaɪtɪd/ *adj* very happy or satisfied: *We were delighted to hear their good news.*

**de·light·ful** /dɪˈlaɪtˈfəl/ *adj* very nice or enjoyable: *a delightful book for children*

**de·lin·e·ate** /dɪˈlɪniˌeɪt/ *v* [T] to describe something carefully so that it is easy to understand

**de·lin·quen·cy** /dɪˈlɪŋkwənsi/ *n* [U] behavior that is illegal or socially unacceptable: *the problem of juvenile delinquency* (=crime done by young people)

**de·lin·quent** /dɪˈlɪŋkwənt/ *adj* **1** late in paying the money you owe: *delinquent loans* **2** young people who are delinquent do illegal things —**delinquent** *n*

**de·lir·i·ous** /dɪˈlɪriəs/ *adj* **1** confused, anxious, and excited because you are very sick **2** extremely happy and excited: *people delirious with joy* —**delirium** /dəˈlɪriəm/ *n* [C,U]

**de·liv·er** /dɪˈlɪvɚ/ *v* **1** [I,T] to take a letter, package, goods etc. to a particular place: *I used to deliver newspapers when I was a kid.* | *I'm having some flowers delivered for her birthday.* **2** [T] to make a speech to a lot of people: *Rev. Whitman delivered a powerful sermon about love and forgiveness.* **3** [I,T] to do the things that you have promised: *Voters are angry that politicians haven't delivered on their promises yet.* **4 deliver a baby** to help a woman with the birth of her baby **5** [T] to get votes or support from a particular group of people: *We're expecting Rigby to deliver the blue collar vote.*

**de·liv·er·y** /dɪˈlɪvəri/ *n* **1** [C,U] the act of taking something to someone's house, work etc.: *Pizza Mondo offers free delivery for any pizza over $10.* **2** the process of a baby being born: *Mrs. Haims was rushed into the delivery room* (=hospital room where a baby is born) *at 7:42 p.m.* **3** [singular] the way that someone speaks or performs in public: *Your speech is good, but you'll have to improve your delivery.*

**del·ta** /ˈdɛltə/ *n* a low area of land where a river separates into many smaller rivers flowing toward an ocean: *the Mississippi Delta*

**de·lude** /dɪˈlud/ *v* [T] to make someone believe something that is not true; deceive: *Don't*

**delude yourself** - *Jerry won't change his mind.* —**deluded** *adj*

**del·uge¹** /ˈdɛlyudʒ/ *n* **1** a large flood, or a period of time when it rains continuously **2** a large amount of something such as letters, questions etc. that someone gets at the same time

**deluge²** *v* [T] **1** to send a lot of letters, questions etc. to someone at the same time: *The radio station was deluged with complaints.* **2** LITERARY to completely cover something with water

**de·lu·sion** /dɪˈluʒən/ *n* [C,U] a false belief about something that you wish were true: *Walter's still under the delusion that his wife loves him.*

**de·luxe** /dɪˈlʌks/ *adj* having a better quality and more expensive price than other similar things: *a deluxe queen-sized bed*

**delve** /dɛlv/ *v*

**delve into** *phr v* [T] to search for more information about someone or something: *Reporters are always delving into actors' personal lives.*

**dem·a·gogue** /ˈdɛməˌgɑg/ *n* DISAPPROVING a political leader who tries to make people feel strong emotions in order to influence their opinions —**demagogic** /ˌdɛməˈgɑgɪk, -ˈgɑdʒɪk/ *adj*

**de·mand¹** /dɪˈmænd/ *n* **1** [singular, U] the need or desire that people have for particular goods or services: *There isn't any demand for leaded gas anymore.* **2** a strong request that shows you believe you have the right to get what you ask for: *Union members will strike until the company agrees to their demands.* **3 be in demand** to be wanted by a lot of people: *She's been in great demand ever since her book was published.* —see also DEMANDS

**demand²** *v* **1** [T] to ask strongly for something, especially because you think you have a right to do this: *The President demanded the release of all the hostages.* | *Horrocks was demanding that he give the checks to her.* **2** [I,T] to order someone to tell you something: *"What are you doing here?" she demanded.* **3** [T] something that demands your time, skill, attention etc. makes you use a lot of your time, skill etc.: *The baby demands most of her time.* —see usage notes at ASK, RECOMMEND

**de·mand·ing** /dɪˈmændɪŋ/ *adj* making you use a lot of your time, skill, attention etc.: *a very demanding job*

**de·mands** /dɪˈmændz/ *n* [plural] the difficult or annoying things that a job, situation etc. forces you to do: *women dealing with the demands of family and career* | *The school makes heavy demands on its teachers.*

**de·mean** /dɪˈmin/ *v* [T] to treat someone without respect, or to make people lose respect for someone

D

**de·mean·ing** /dɪ'minɪŋ/ *adj* making someone feel very embarrassed or ashamed: *a demeaning job*

**de·mean·or** /dɪ'minɚ/ *n* [singular, U] FORMAL the way someone behaves, dresses, speaks etc., that shows what his or her character is like

**de·ment·ed** /dɪ'mɛntɪd/ *adj* behaving in a way that is crazy or very strange

**de·mer·it** /dɪ'mɛrɪt/ *n* a mark that is given to a student to warn him/her not to cause any more trouble at school

**de·mise** /dɪ'maɪz/ *n* [U] **1** the failure of someone or something that used to be successful: *the demise of the steel industry* **2** FORMAL the death of a person

**dem·o** /'dɛmoʊ/ *n* INFORMAL an example of a piece of recorded music, SOFTWARE etc. that you play or show to someone who you hope will buy more: *a demo tape*

**de·moc·ra·cy** /dɪ'mɑkrəsi/ *n* **1** [U] a system of government in which everyone in a country can vote to elect its leaders **2** a country that allows its people to elect its government officials **3** [U] a situation or society in which everyone is socially equal and has the same right to vote, speak etc.

**dem·o·crat** /'dɛmə,kræt/ *n* **1** Democrat someone who supports or is a member of the DEMOCRATIC PARTY in the US **2** someone who believes in or works to achieve DEMOCRACY —compare REPUBLICAN[2]

**dem·o·crat·ic** /,dɛmə'krætɪk/ *adj* **1** organized by a system in which everyone has the same right to vote, speak etc.: *a democratic way of making decisions* **2** controlled by leaders who are elected by the people of a country: *a democratic government*

**Democratic Par·ty** /,...,.. '../ *n* [singular] one of the two main political parties of the US —see culture note at PARTY[1]

**dem·o·graph·ics** /,dɛmə'græfɪks/ *n* [plural] the changes in the number of people or types of people that live in an area

**de·mol·ish** /dɪ'mɑlɪʃ/ *v* [T] **1** to completely destroy a building: *Several old houses were demolished to make space for a new park.* **2** to prove that an idea or opinion is completely wrong: *Every one of his arguments was demolished by the defense lawyer.*

**dem·o·li·tion** /,dɛmə'lɪʃən/ *n* [C,U] the act or process of completely destroying a building

**de·mon** /'dimən/ *n* an evil spirit —**demonic** /dɪ'mɑnɪk/ *adj*

**dem·on·strate** /'dɛmən,streɪt/ *v* [T] **1** to prove something clearly: *Our studies demonstrate that fewer college graduates are finding jobs.* **2** to show or describe how to use or do something: *Our aerobics instructor always demonstrates each new movement first.* **3** to show that you have a particular skill, quality, or ability: *The contest gave her a chance to demon-*

*strate her ability.* **4** to meet with other people in order to protest or support something in public

**dem·on·stra·tion** /,dɛmən'streɪʃən/ *n* **1** an event at which a lot of people meet to protest or support something in public: *Students staged/held a demonstration against the war.* **2** [C,U] the act of showing and explaining how to do something: *She gave a demonstration on how to use the electronic dictionary.* **3** proof that someone or something has a particular quality, ability, emotion etc.: *People gathered around the school in a demonstration of support for the missing children.*

**de·mon·stra·tive** /dɪ'mɑnstrətɪv/ *adj* willing to show how much you care about someone: *He loves me, but he's not very demonstrative.*

**dem·on·strat·or** /'dɛmən,streɪtɚ/ *n* someone who meets with other people in order to protest or support something in public

**de·mor·al·ize** /dɪ'mɔrə,laɪz, di-, -'mɑr-/ *v* [T] to make someone lose his or her confidence or courage: *The soldiers were demoralized by the defeat.* —**demoralizing** *adj*

**de·mote** /dɪ'moʊt, di-/ *v* [T] to make someone have a lower rank or less important position —**demotion** /dɪ'moʊʃən/ *n* [,C,U] —opposite PROMOTE

**de·mure** /dɪ'myʊr/ *adj* a girl or woman who is demure is shy, quiet, and always behaves well

**den** /dɛn/ *n* **1** a room in a house where people relax, read, watch television etc. **2** the home of some types of animals such as lions and foxes (FOX)

**de·ni·al** /dɪ'naɪəl/ *n* **1** [C,U] a statement saying that something is not true: *Diaz made a public denial of the rumor.* **2** [U] a condition in which you refuse to admit or believe that something bad exists or has happened: *She went through a phase of denial after her child's death.* **3** FORMAL the act of refusing to allow someone to do or do something: *the denial of basic human rights* —see also DENY

**den·i·grate** /'dɛnɪ,greɪt/ *v* [T] to do or say things in order to make someone or something seem less important or good

**den·im** /'dɛnəm/ *n* [U] a type of strong cotton cloth used for making JEANS

**de·nom·i·na·tion** /dɪ,nɑmə'neɪʃən/ *n* **1** a religious group that is part of a larger religious organization **2** the value of coins, BILLS, BONDs etc.: *bills in denominations of $1 and $5*

**de·note** /dɪ'noʊt/ *v* [T] to represent or mean something: *Each X on the map denotes 500 people.*

**de·nounce** /dɪ'naʊns/ *v* [T] to publicly express disapproval of someone or something: *The bishop denounced the film as being immoral.*

**dense** /dɛns/ *adj* **1** made of or containing a lot of things or people that are very close together: *the city's dense population | dense forests of pine trees* **2** difficult to see through or breathe in: *dense clouds of smoke* **3** INFORMAL stupid —**densely** *adv*

**den·si·ty** /'dɛnsəti/ *n* [U] **1** how crowded something is: *a high density neighborhood* (=very crowded neighborhood) **2** TECHNICAL the relationship between an object's weight and the amount of space it fills

**dent**[1] /dɛnt/ *n* **1** a mark made when you hit or press something so that its surface is bent: *a big dent in the car* **2** **make a dent in sth** INFORMAL to reduce the amount of something: *I haven't made a dent in the money I have to pay back on my loan.*

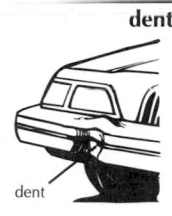

dent

dent

**dent**[2] *v* [T] to hit or press something so that its surface is bent and marked: *Some idiot dented my car door last night.* —**dented** *adj*

**den·tal** /'dɛntəl/ *adj* relating to your teeth: *dental care*

**dental floss** /'.. ,./ *n* [U] a thin string that you use to clean between your teeth

**den·tist** /'dɛntɪst/ *n* someone whose job is to treat people's teeth —see usage note at DOCTOR[1]

**den·tures** /'dɛntʃɚz/ *n* [plural] artificial teeth worn to replace the natural ones that someone has lost; FALSE TEETH

**de·nun·ci·a·tion** /dɪˌnʌnsi'eɪʃən/ *n* a public statement in which you criticize someone or something

**de·ny** /dɪ'naɪ/ *v* [T] **1** to say that something is not true: *Simmons denied that he had murdered his wife.* **2** to refuse to allow someone to have or do something: *They denied him entry into the country.* —see also DENIAL

**de·o·dor·ant** /di'oʊdərənt/ *n* [C,U] a substance that you put on the skin under your arms to stop you from smelling bad

**de·o·dor·ize** /di'oʊdə,raɪz/ *v* [T] to remove an unpleasant smell or to make it less noticeable

**de·part** /dɪ'pɑrt/ *v* [I] to leave: *All passengers departing for New York on flight UA179 should go to Gate 7. | The train will depart from platform 7.*
**depart from** sth *phr v* [T] FORMAL to start to use new ideas or do something in an unusual or unexpected way: *a treatment for cancer that departs from the usual methods*

**de·part·ment** /dɪ'pɑrtˀmənt/ *n* **1** any of the groups of people that form a part of a large organization such as a college, government, or business: *the design department in a large advertising company | the English department* **2** a specific area in a large store where a particular type of product is sold: *the men's department* (=sells clothes for men)

**department store** /.'.. ,./ *n* a large store that sells many different products such as clothes, kitchen equipment etc.

**de·par·ture** /dɪ'pɑrtʃɚ/ *n* **1** [C,U] the action of leaving a place, especially to travel in a plane, car, etc.: *Check in at the airport an hour before departure.* **2** FORMAL a change from what is usual or expected

**de·pend** /dɪ'pɛnd/ *v* **it/that depends** SPOKEN used in order to say that because you do not know what will happen yet, you cannot decide: *"Are you coming to my house later?" "It depends. I might have to work."*
**depend on/upon** *phr v* [T] **1** to need the help, support, or existence of someone or something else: *Children depend on their parents for almost everything.* **2** to change because of other things that happen or change: *The amount you spend depends on how/where you live.* **3** to trust someone or something: *Sometimes I think you're the only person I can depend on.*

**de·pend·a·ble** /dɪ'pɛndəbəl/ *adj* able to be trusted: *a dependable employee*

**de·pend·ent**[1] /dɪ'pɛndənt/ *adj* **1** needing someone or something else in order to exist, be successful etc.: *dependent children* **2** **be dependent on/upon** FORMAL to change because of other things that happen or change: *Your success is dependent on how hard you work.* —opposite INDEPENDENT

**dependent**[2] *n* someone, especially a child, who needs someone else to provide him/her with food, money, clothing etc.

**de·pict** /dɪ'pɪkt/ *v* [T] to clearly describe a character, situation, or event in a story or by using pictures: *The painting depicts the Fall of Rome.*

**de·plete** /dɪ'plit/ *v* [T] to reduce the amount of something: *Many of our forests have been depleted by the paper industry.*

**de·plor·a·ble** /dɪ'plɔrəbəl/ *adj* FORMAL deserving strong disapproval: *the deplorable act of illegally polluting our rivers*

**de·plore** /dɪ'plɔr/ *v* [T] FORMAL to severely criticize something that you disapprove of: *a statement deploring the use of chemical weapons*

**de·ploy** /dɪ'plɔɪ/ *v* [T] to organize the soldiers, military equipment etc. that may be used in an attack: *Nuclear missiles were being deployed in Europe.*

**de·port** /dɪ'pɔrt/ *v* [T] to force a foreigner to return to the country s/he came from —**deportation** /ˌdipɔr'teɪʃən/ *n* [C,U]

**de·pos·it**[1] /dɪ'pɑzɪt/ *n* **1** part of the price of a house, car etc. that you pay first so that it will not be sold or given to anyone else: *We put down a deposit on the house yesterday.* **2** an amount of money that is added to someone's bank account: *I'd like to make a deposit please.* **3** an amount or layer of a substance in a particular place: *rich deposits of gold in the hills*

D

**deposit**[2] *v* [T] **1** to put money into a bank account **2** LITERARY to put something down, especially in a particular place

**de·pot** /'dipoʊ/ *n* **1** a small train or bus station **2** a place where goods are stored

**de·praved** /dɪ'preɪvd/ *adj* morally unacceptable and evil: *a depraved murderer* **–depravity** /dɪ'prævəti/ *n* [U]

**de·pre·ci·ate** /dɪ'priʃi,eɪt/ *v* [I] to become less valuable: *A new car depreciates as soon as it is driven.*

**de·press** /dɪ'prɛs/ *v* [T] **1** to make someone feel very sad: *The news depressed my father.* **2** to reduce the amount or value of something: *The value of the peso fell, depressing the nation's economy.*

**de·pressed** /dɪ'prɛst/ *adj* **1** very sad: *I got really depressed just thinking about her.* **2** not having enough jobs or business activity to make an area, industry etc. successful: *a depressed economy*

**de·press·ing** /dɪ'prɛsɪŋ/ *adj* making you feel sad: *It's so depressing - we should have won.*

**de·pres·sion** /dɪ'prɛʃən/ *n* **1** [C,U] a feeling of sadness and a loss of hope: *The patient is suffering from depression.* **2** [C,U] a long period when businesses are not very active and many people do not have jobs: *the Great Depression of the 1930s* **3** an area of a surface that is lower than the other parts

**de·prive** /dɪ'praɪv/ *v*
**deprive sb of sth** *phr v* [T] to take something that someone needs away from him/her: *The troops had been deprived of food, water, and electricity.*

**de·prived** /dɪ'praɪvd/ *adj* not having or giving someone the things that are considered to be necessary for a comfortable or happy life: *a deprived childhood*

**dept** the written abbreviation of DEPARTMENT

**depth** /dɛpθ/ *n* **1** [C usually singular] **a)** the distance from the top of something to the bottom of it: *a lake with a depth of 30 feet* **b)** the distance from the front of an object to the back of it: *the depth of the shelves* **2** [U] how serious and important someone's feelings, conversations etc. are: *the depth of their friendship* **3 in depth** including all the details: *He gave us an in depth report on the problem.*

**dep·u·ty** /'dɛpyəti/ *n* **1** someone who has the second most powerful position in an organization: *the deputy vice president of the Foundation* **2** someone whose job is to help a SHERIFF

**de·rail** /dɪ'reɪl, di-/ *v* [I,T] to make a train come off a railroad track

**de·ranged** /dɪ'reɪndʒd/ *adj* behaving in a crazy or dangerous way: *a deranged criminal*

**der·by** /'dɚbi/ *n* **1** a type of horse race: *the Kentucky Derby* **2** a stiff round hat for men worn in past times

**der·e·lict**[1] /'dɛrə,lɪkt/ *adj* a building, boat etc. that is derelict is in bad condition because no one uses it

**der·e·lict**[2] *n* OFFENSIVE someone who has no home or money

**de·ride** /dɪ'raɪd/ *v* [T] FORMAL to say something that shows you think something is silly or has no value **–derision** /dɪ'rɪʒən/ *n* [U] **–derisory** /dɪ'raɪsəri/ *adj*

**der·i·va·tion** /,dɛrə'veɪʃən/ *n* **1** [C,U] the origin of something, especially a word or phrase **2** a word that comes from another word or language

**de·riv·a·tive** /dɪ'rɪvətɪv/ *adj* developing or coming from something else, and often not as good **–derivative** *n*

**de·rive** /dɪ'raɪv/ *v* **1** [T] to get something such as happiness, strength, or satisfaction from someone or something: *He derives a lot of pleasure from meeting people.* **2** [I] to develop or come from something else: *This word is derived from Latin.*

**der·ma·ti·tis** /,dɚmə'taɪtɪs/ *n* [U] a disease of the skin that makes it swell, become red, and be painful

**de·rog·a·to·ry** /dɪ'rɑgə,tɔri/ *adj* insulting or criticizing someone or something: *"Bitch" is a derogatory term for a woman.*

**der·rick** /'dɛrɪk/ *n* the tall tower over an oil well that holds the DRILL

**de·scend** /dɪ'sɛnd/ *v* [I,T] FORMAL to go down or move from a higher level to a lower one: *a plane descending to the airport* –opposite ASCEND
**descend from sb** *phr v* [T] **be descended from sb** to be related to someone who lived a long time ago: *My father's family is descended from the Pilgrims.*
**descend on/upon sb** *phr v* [T] INFORMAL if a lot of people descend on a place or on you, they arrive at a place or at your house: *Thousands of tourists descend on Athens each year.*

**de·scend·ant** /dɪ'sɛndənt/ *n* someone who is related to a person who lived a long time ago: *a descendant of African slaves* –compare ANCESTOR

**de·scent** /dɪ'sɛnt/ *n* **1** [C,U] a movement down, or the process of going down: *a plane beginning its descent* –opposite ASCENT **2** [U] your family origins, especially the country that you came from: *We're Irish by descent.*

**de·scribe** /dɪ'skraɪb/ *v* [T] to say what someone or something is like by giving details: *Can you describe the man?* | *It's hard to describe how I feel.* | *Would you describe Jim as a good worker?*

**de·scrip·tion** /dɪ'skrɪpʃən/ *n* [C,U] a piece of writing or a speech that gives details about what someone or something is like: *Police have a detailed description of the missing child.* | *You* *fit the description of* (=look like) *a man seen running from the scene.*

**de·scrip·tive** /dɪˈskrɪptɪv/ *adj* giving a description of something using words or pictures

**des·e·crate** /ˈdɛsəˌkreɪt/ *v* [T] to damage something holy –**desecration** /ˌdɛsəˈkreɪʃən/ *n* [U]

**de·seg·re·gate** /diˈsɛgrəˌgeɪt/ *v* [T] to end a system in which people of different races are kept separate: *an attempt to desegregate the schools* –**desegregation** /ˌdisɛgrəˈgeɪʃən/ *n* [U] –**desegregated** /diˈsɛgrəˌgeɪtɪd/ *adj*

**des·ert**[1] /ˈdɛzɚt/ *n* [C,U] a very large area of land where it is always hot and dry: *the Sahara desert*

**de·sert**[2] /dɪˈzɚt/ *v* **1** [T] to leave someone alone and not help him/her any more: *My boyfriend deserted me when I got pregnant.* **2** [T] to leave a place so that it is empty: *Everyone deserted the village and fled to the hills.* **3** [I] to leave the army without permission –**desertion** /dɪˈzɚʃən/ *n* [C,U]

**de·sert·ed** /dɪˈzɚtɪd/ *adj* empty and quiet, especially because the people who are usually there have left: *At night the streets are deserted.*

**de·sert·er** /dɪˈzɚtɚ/ *n* a soldier who leaves the army without permission

**de·serve** /dɪˈzɚv/ *v* if someone deserves something, s/he should get it because of the way s/he has behaved: *After all that work you deserve a rest!* | *Migrant workers deserve to make more than $3 an hour.* | *The drug dealer got what he deserved.* (=received the right punishment) –**deserved** *adj*

**de·sign**[1] /dɪˈzaɪn/ *n* **1** [U] the way that something has been planned or made: *We're working to improve the design of the computer.* **2** a pattern used for decorating something: *curtains with a floral design* **3** a drawing or plan that shows how something will be made or what it will look like: *Have you seen the designs for the new store?* **4** [U] the art or process of making drawings or plans for something: *Vicky studied graphic design at college.* **5** **have designs on sth** to want something and be planning a way to get it

**design**[2] *v* **1** [I,T] to make a drawing or plan of something that will be made or built: *Armani is designing some exciting new suits for the fall.* **2** [T] to plan or develop something for a particular purpose: *an engine designed to give more power* | *a video game designed for children*

**des·ig·nate** /ˈdɛzɪgˌneɪt/ *v* [T] to choose someone or something for a particular job or purpose: *a check-out line designated for shoppers who will pay cash*

**des·ig·nat·ed driv·er** /ˌ.... '../ *n* someone who drives his/her friends to a party, BAR etc. and agrees not to drink alcohol

**des·ig·na·tion** /ˌdɛzɪgˈneɪʃən/ *n* [C,U] **1** the act or state of designating (DESIGNATE) something: *the designation of 100 acres around the lake as a protected area for wildlife* **2** the description or title that someone or something is given: *Any beef with the designation "extra lean" must only have 5% of its weight in fat.*

**de·sign·er** /dɪˈzaɪnɚ/ *n* someone whose job is to make plans or patterns for clothes, jewelry etc.

**de·sir·a·ble** /dɪˈzaɪrəbəl/ *adj* FORMAL **1** worth having or doing because it is useful or popular: *a desirable job with a big law firm* **2** someone who is desirable is sexually attractive –**desirability** /dɪˌzaɪrəˈbɪləti/ *n* [U]

**de·sire**[1] /dɪˈzaɪɚ/ *n* **1** a strong hope or wish: *students with strong desire for knowledge* | *I have no desire to meet her.* **2** FORMAL a strong wish to have sex with someone

**desire**[2] *v* [T] **1** **leave a lot to be desired** said when something is not as good as it should be: *This coffee leaves a lot to be desired!* **2** FORMAL to want or hope for something very much: *All those desiring to vote must come to the meeting.* **3** FORMAL to want to have sex with someone

**USAGE NOTE desire, want, and wish**

Use **want** to talk about things you would like to do or have: *He wants to talk to you.* Use **desire** and **wish** only in very formal writing or in literature: *He wishes to speak with you.* | *She has everything her heart desires.* ✗ DON'T SAY "desire to do something." ✗

**de·sir·ous** /dɪˈzaɪrəs/ *adj* FORMAL wanting someone or something very much

**de·sist** /dɪˈzɪst, dɪˈsɪst/ *v* [I] FORMAL to stop doing something

**desk** /dɛsk/ *n* **1** a piece of furniture like a table that you sit at to write and work **2** a place where you can get information at a hotel, airport etc.: *You should check in at the hotel desk first.*

**desk·top com·put·er** /ˌdɛsktɑp kəmˈpyutɚ/ *n* a computer that is small enough to be used on a desk –compare LAPTOP

**desk·top pub·lish·ing** /ˌ.. '.../ **DTP** *n* [U] the work of producing magazines, books etc. using a DESKTOP COMPUTER

**des·o·late** /ˈdɛsəlɪt/ *adj* **1** empty and not attractive: *the desolate terrain of the Moon* **2** feeling very sad and lonely: *He was desolate when his wife died.* –**desolation** /ˌdɛsəˈleɪʃən/ *n* [U]

**de·spair**[1] /dɪˈspɛr/ *n* [U] a feeling of being very unhappy and having no hope at all: *Nancy's suicide left him in deep despair.*

**despair**[2] *v* [I] to feel that there is no hope at all: *The trapped miners despaired of ever being found alive.*

**des·per·ate** /'dɛsprɪt, -pərɪt/ *adj* **1** willing to do anything to change a very bad situation, and not caring about danger: *prisoners making a **desperate attempt** to escape* **2** needing or wanting something very much: *By then I was so broke I was **desperate for** a job.* **3** a desperate situation is very bad, serious, or dangerous: *There is a desperate shortage of food in the city.* —**desperately** *adv*

**des·per·a·tion** /,dɛspə'reɪʃən/ *n* [U] a strong feeling that you will do anything to change a very bad situation: *The drowning man grabbed at the life raft **in desperation**.*

**de·spic·a·ble** /dɪ'spɪkəbəl/ *adj* extremely unpleasant or cruel

**de·spise** /dɪ'spaɪz/ *v* [T] to dislike someone or something very much: *He despised her from the moment they met.*

**de·spite** /dɪ'spaɪt/ *prep* in spite of something: *Despite the doctors' efforts, the patient died.*

**de·spond·ent** /dɪ'spandənt/ *adj* unhappy and without hope —**despondency** *n* [U] —**despondently** *adv*

**des·pot** /'dɛspət, -pat/ *n* someone, especially the ruler of a country, who uses power in a cruel and unfair way —**despotic** /dɛ'spatɪk/ *adj*

---

dessert

cake     pie     cheesecake

sundae     Jell-o

**des·sert** /dɪ'zɚt/ *n* [C,U] sweet food served after the main part of a meal

**des·ti·na·tion** /,dɛstə'neɪʃən/ *n* the place that someone or something is going to: *The Alamo is a popular tourist destination in Texas.*

**des·tined** /'dɛstnd/ *adj* seeming certain to happen at some time in the future, because of FATE: *She seemed **destined for** an acting career.*

**des·ti·ny** /'dɛstəni/ *n* [C,U] the things that will happen to someone in the future, or the power that controls this; FATE: *a nation fighting to control its destiny*

**des·ti·tute** /'dɛstə,tut/ *adj* having no money, no place to live, no food etc.: *The floods left thousands of people destitute.* —**destitution** /,dɛstə'tuʃən/ *n* [U]

**de·stroy** /dɪ'strɔɪ/ *v* [T] to damage something very badly, so that it cannot be used or no longer exists: *a building completely destroyed by fire*

**de·struc·tion** /dɪ'strʌkʃən/ *n* [U] the act or process of destroying something: *Scientists are trying to stop the **destruction of** the ozone layer.* —**destructive** /dɪ'strʌktɪv/ *adj*

**de·tach** /dɪ'tætʃ/ *v* [T] to remove part of something that is designed to be removed: *Unsnap the buttons to **detach** the hood **from** the jacket.* —**detachable** *adj*

**de·tached** /dɪ'tætʃt/ *adj* not reacting to something in an emotional way: *Rescue workers must remain detached to do their jobs well.* —**detachment** *n* [U]

**de·tail** /'diteɪl, dɪ'teɪl/ *n* [C,U] a single fact or piece of information about something: *Dad planned our vacation down to the smallest detail.* | *Dr. Blount described the process **in detail**.* (=using lots of details) | *There's no need to **go into detail*** (=give a lot of details) *about the contract at this early stage.*

**de·tailed** /dɪ'teɪld, 'diteɪld/ *adj* containing or using a lot of information or facts: *a detailed examination of the body*

**de·tain** /dɪ'teɪn/ *v* [T] to officially stop someone from leaving a place: *The police detained two suspects for questioning.*

**de·tect** /dɪ'tɛkt/ *v* [T] to notice or discover something, especially something that is not easy to see, hear etc.: *I detected the faint smell of perfume in the air.* —**detectable** *adj* —**detection** /dɪ'tɛkʃən/ *n* [U]

**de·tec·tive** /dɪ'tɛktɪv/ *n* a police officer whose job is to discover information about crimes and to catch criminals

**de·tect·or** /dɪ'tɛktɚ/ *n* a machine or piece of equipment that finds or measures something: *the metal detectors at the airport*

**dé·tente** /deɪ'tant/ *n* [C,U] FORMAL a state in which two countries that are not friendly toward each other agree to behave in a more friendly way

**de·ten·tion** /dɪ'tɛnʃən/ *n* **1** [U] the state of being kept in prison: *a political prisoner who was released after five years of detention* **2** [C,U] a punishment in which students who have behaved badly must stay at school for a short time after other students have left

**de·ter** /dɪ'tɚ/ *v* **-rred, -rring** [T] to make someone not want to do something by making it difficult, or by threatening him/her with a punishment: *a new program to deter crime in the inner cities*

**de·ter·gent** /dɪ'tɚdʒənt/ *n* [C,U] a liquid or powder containing soap, used for washing clothes, dishes etc.

**de·te·ri·o·rate** /dɪ'tɪriə,reɪt/ *v* [I] to become worse: *My grandmother's health is deteriorating quickly.* —**deterioration** /dɪ,tɪriə'reɪʃən/ *n* [U]

**de·ter·mi·na·tion** /dɪ,tɚmə'neɪʃən/ *n* [U] the quality of continuing to try to do something even when it is difficult: *Marco has **shown** great **determination to** learn English.*

**de·ter·mine** /dɪ'tɚmɪn/ *v* [T] **1** FORMAL to find out the facts about something: *Using sonar, they determined exactly where the ship had sunk.* **2** to decide something, or to influence a decision about something: *The number of incoming students will determine the size of the classes.*

**de·ter·mined** /dɪ'tɚmɪnd/ *adj* having a strong desire to continue to do something even when it is difficult: *She's a very determined woman.*

**de·ter·min·er** /dɪ'tɚmənɚ/ *n* TECHNICAL in grammar, a word that is used before an adjective or a noun in order to show which thing you mean. In the phrases "the car" and "some cars," "the" and "some" are determiners

**de·ter·rent** /dɪ'tɚənt/ *n* something that makes someone not want to do something: *Car alarms can be an effective **deterrent to** burglars.* −**deterrence** *n* [U]

**de·test** /dɪ'tɛst/ *v* [T] to hate someone or something very much: *I detest drivers who follow too closely!*

**det·o·nate** /'dɛt⁻n,eɪt, -tə,neɪt/ *v* [I,T] to explode, or to make something do this: *Nuclear bombs were detonated in tests in the desert.* −**detonation** /,dɛt⁻n'eɪʃən/ *n* [C,U]

**det·o·na·tor** /'dɛt⁻n,eɪtɚ, -tə,neɪtɚ/ *n* a small object used in order to make a bomb explode

**de·tour¹** /'ditʊr/ *n* a way of going from one place to another that is longer than the usual way, because you want to avoid traffic, go somewhere special etc.: *We **made a detour** to avoid the street repairs.*

**detour²** *v* [I,T] to make a DETOUR

**de·tox** /'ditɑks/ *n* [U] INFORMAL a special treatment to help people stop drinking alcohol or taking drugs

**de·tract** /dɪ'trækt/ *v*
**detract from** sth *phr v* [T] to make something seem less good than it really is: *The billboards lining the streets **detract from** the city's beauty.*

**det·ri·ment** /'dɛtrəmənt/ *n* [U] FORMAL harm or damage that is done to something: *He works long hours, **to the detriment of** his marriage.* −**detrimental** /,dɛtrə'mɛntl/ *adj*

**de·val·ue** /di'vælyu/ *v* **1** [I,T] TECHNICAL to reduce the value of a country's money, especially in relation to the value of another country's money **2** [T] to make someone or something seem less important or valuable −**devaluation** /di,vælyu'eɪʃən/ *n* [C,U]

**dev·as·tate** /'dɛvə,steɪt/ *v* [T] **1** to make someone feel extremely sad or shocked: *Hannah was devastated by the sudden death of her mother.* **2** to damage something, or to destroy something completely: *Bombing raids devastated the city of Dresden.* −**devastation** /,dɛvə'steɪʃən/ *n* [U]

**dev·as·tat·ing** /'dɛvə,steɪtɪŋ/ *adj* **1** badly damaging or destroying something: *The drought has had a **devastating effect** on crops.* **2** making someone feel extremely sad or shocked: *the devastating news of her sister's death*

**de·vel·op** /dɪ'vɛləp/ *v* **1** [I,T] to grow or change into something bigger or more advanced, or to make someone or something do this: *It's hard to believe that a tree can **develop from** a small seed. | plans to develop the local economy* **2** [T] to make a new idea or product successful by working on it for a long time: *scientists developing new drugs to fight AIDS* **3** [T] to begin to have a quality or illness: *Her baby developed a fever during the night.* **4** [I] to begin to happen, exist, or be noticed: *Clouds are developing over the mountains.* **5** [T] to use land to build things that people need: *This area will be developed over the next five years.* **6** [T] to make pictures out of film from a camera: *I have three rolls of film to develop.*

**de·vel·oped** /dɪ'vɛləpt/ *adj* **1** larger, more advanced, or stronger: *a child with **fully developed** social skills | **well developed** muscles* **2 developed countries/nations** rich countries that have many industries, comfortable living for most people, and usually elected governments

**de·vel·op·er** /dɪ'vɛləpɚ/ *n* someone who makes money by buying land and then building houses, factories etc. on it

**de·vel·op·ing** /dɪ'vɛləpɪŋ/ *adj* **1** growing or changing: *a developing child* **2 developing countries/nations** countries without much money or industry, but that are working to improve life for their people

**de·vel·op·ment** /dɪ'vɛləpmənt/ *n* **1** [U] the process of becoming bigger, stronger, or more advanced: *the development of skin cancer | economic/industrial development* **2** a new event that changes a situation: *Our reporter in Denver has the latest developments.* **3** a change that makes a product, plan, idea etc. better: *new developments in computer technology* **4** [U] the process of planning and building new streets, buildings etc. on land: *100 acres ready for development* **5** land that has buildings on it that were all planned together: *a housing development*

**de·vi·ant** /'diviənt/, **de·vi·ate** /,diviɪt/ *adj* FORMAL different, in a bad way, from what is normal: *deviant behavior* −**deviant** *n*

**de·vi·ate** /'divi,eɪt/ *v* [I] FORMAL to be or become different from what is normal or acceptable: *The results of this study **deviate from** the earlier study.* −**deviate** /'diviɪt/ *n*

**de·vi·a·tion** /,divi'eɪʃən/ *n* [C,U] FORMAL a noticeable difference from what is expected or normal, especially in behavior: *The school does not allow **deviation from** the rules.*

**de·vice** /dɪ'vaɪs/ *n* **1** a machine or tool that is usually small and usually electronic, that does a special job: *a **device for** separating metal from garbage* **2** a way of achieving a particular purpose: *a language learning device* −see usage note at MACHINE¹

**dev·il** /ˈdɛvəl/ n **1 the Devil** the most power-ful evil spirit; Satan **2** any evil spirit

**dev·il·ish** /ˈdɛvəlɪʃ/ adj OLD-FASHIONED very bad, difficult, or unpleasant **–devilishly** adv

**dev·il's ad·vo·cate** /ˌ.. ˈ...ˌ./ n someone who pretends to disagree with you in order to have a good discussion about something: Let me **play devil's advocate** and say that you should take the job even though the pay is less.

**de·vi·ous** /ˈdiviəs/ adj using tricks or lies to get what you want: a devious way of not paying taxes

**de·vise** /dɪˈvaɪz/ v [T] to plan or invent a way of doing something: A teacher devised the game as a way of making math fun.

**de·void** /dɪˈvɔɪd/ adj **devoid of sth** not having a particular quality at all: The food is **completely devoid** of taste.

**de·vote** /dɪˈvoʊt/ v [T] **1 devote time/ money/attention to sth** to give your time, money etc. to something: She devotes her time on the weekends to her family. **2 devote yourself to sth** to do everything that you can to achieve something or help someone: He has de-voted himself to finding out who killed his son.

**de·vot·ed** /dɪˈvoʊtɪd/ adj giving someone or something a lot of love, concern, and attention: a devoted wife/father **–devotedly** adv

**dev·o·tee** /ˌdɛvəˈti, -ˈteɪ, -voʊ-/ n someone who enjoys or admires someone or something very much: a video game devotee

**de·vo·tion** /dɪˈvoʊʃən/ n [U] **1** a strong feeling of love that you show by paying a lot of attention to someone or something: He should be admired for his **devotion to** duty. **2** strong religious feeling

**de·vour** /dɪˈvaʊɚ/ v [T] **1** to eat something quickly because you are very hungry **2** if you devour information, books etc. you read a lot very quickly

**de·vout** /dɪˈvaʊt/ adj having very strong reli-gious beliefs: a devout Jew/Muslim **–devoutly** adv

**dew** /du/ n [U] small drops of water that form on outdoor surfaces during the night

**dex·ter·i·ty** /dɛkˈstɛrəti/ n [U] skill in using your hands to do things **–dexterous, dextrous** /ˈdɛkstrəs/ adj

**di·a·be·tes** /ˌdaɪəˈbitiz, -ˈbitɪs/ n [U] a dis-ease in which there is too much sugar in the blood

**di·a·bet·ic** /ˌdaɪəˈbɛtɪk/ n someone who has DIABETES **–diabetic** adj

**di·a·bol·i·cal** /ˌdaɪəˈbɑlɪkəl/ adj very bad, evil, or cruel: a diabolical killer

**di·ag·nose** /ˌdaɪəgˈnoʊs, ˈdaɪəgˌnoʊs/ v [T] to find out what illness a person has or what is wrong with something: Her doctor diagnosed cancer. | He was **diagnosed as having** hepatitis.

**di·ag·no·sis** /ˌdaɪəgˈnoʊsɪs/ n, plural **diag-noses** [C,U] the result of diagnosing (DIAGNOSE) someone or something: The doctor **gave/made a diagnosis of** pneumonia. **–diagnostic** /ˌdaɪəg-ˈnɑstɪk/ adj

**di·ag·o·nal** /daɪˈægənəl/ adj **1** a diagonal line is straight and sloping: a **diagonal line** across the field | diagonal parking spaces **2** going from one corner of a square shape to the opposite corner **–diagonal** n **–diagonally** adv **–see picture at** VERTICAL

**di·a·gram** /ˈdaɪəˌgræm/ n a drawing that shows how something works, where something is, what something looks like etc.: a diagram of a car engine

**di·al¹** /ˈdaɪəl/ v [I,T] to turn the wheel with numbers on a telephone, or to press the buttons on a telephone: Dial 911 - there's been an acci-dent. | Put the money in before you dial. **–see usage note at** TELEPHONE

**dial²** n **1** the round part of a clock, watch, machine etc. that has numbers that show you the time or a measurement **2** the part of a radio or television that you turn to find different stations, or that shows which station you are listening to **3** the wheel with holes for fingers on some telephones

**di·a·lect** /ˈdaɪəˌlɛkt/ n [C,U] a form of a language that is spoken in one area in a different way than it is spoken in other areas: a dialect of Arabic | The children speak only **in** the local **dialect**.

**di·a·logue, dialog** /ˈdaɪəˌlɔg, -ˌlɑg/ n [C,U] **1** a conversation in a book, play, or film: The dialogue in the movie didn't seem natural. **2** a formal discussion between countries or groups in order to solve problems: an opportunity for **dialogue between** the fighting countries

**dial tone** /ˈ.. ./ n the sound that you hear when you pick up a telephone

**di·am·e·ter** /daɪˈæmətɚ/ n a line or measurement from one side of a circle to the other that passes through the center: a wheel two feet **in diameter**

diameter
circumference
radius
diameter

**di·a·met·ri·cal·ly** /ˌdaɪə-ˈmɛtrɪkli/ adv **diametric-ally opposed** completely different or opposite: The women hold diametrically opposed views on abortion.

**di·a·mond** /ˈdaɪmənd, ˈdaɪə-/ n [C,U] **1** a clear, very hard, valuable stone, used in jewelry and in industry: a diamond ring **2** a shape with four straight points that stands on one of its points **–see picture at** SHAPE¹ **3** a playing card with red diamond shapes on it

**di·a·per** /ˈdaɪpɚ, -ˈdaɪə-/ n a piece of material that is put between a baby's legs and fastened around its waist: I think we need to **change the baby's diaper**. (=put on a new one)

**di·a·phragm** /'daɪə,fræm/ n **1** the muscle between your lungs and your stomach that controls your breathing **2** a small round rubber object that a woman can put inside her body to stop her from getting PREGNANT

**di·ar·rhe·a** /,daɪə'riə/ n [U] an illness in which waste from the BOWELs is watery and comes out often

**di·a·ry** /'daɪəri/ n a book in which you write down important or interesting things that happen in your life: *I'm going to keep a diary* (=write in it regularly) *this summer.*

**dice¹** /daɪs/ n, *plural* **dice 1** a small block of wood or plastic with a different number of spots on each side, used in games: *Jeanie rolled the dice.* **2 no dice** SPOKEN said when you refuse to do something: *I asked if I could borrow the car but she said no dice.*

**dice²** v [T] to cut food into small square pieces: *Dice the carrots.*

**dic·ey** /'daɪsi/ adj INFORMAL risky and possibly dangerous: *a dicey situation*

**di·chot·o·my** /daɪ'kɑtəmi/ n FORMAL the difference between two things or ideas that are not like each other: *a dichotomy between what he says and what he does*

**dick** /dɪk/ n SPOKEN OFFENSIVE **1** ⇨ PENIS **2** a stupid annoying person, especially a man

**dic·tate** /'dɪkteɪt, dɪk'teɪt/ v **1** [I,T] to say words for someone else to write down: *She dictated a letter to her secretary.* **2** [I,T] to tell someone exactly what s/he must do: *You can't dictate how I should live my life!* **3** [T] to influence or control something: *The weather will dictate whether we can go or not.*

**dic·ta·tion** /dɪk'teɪʃən/ n **1** [U] the act of saying words for someone to write down **2** sentences that a teacher reads out to test your ability to understand and write a language correctly: *Dictations are the hardest part of learning French.*

**dic·ta·tor** /'dɪkteɪtɚ/ n a leader of a country who controls everything, and who people usually do not like and are afraid of **–dictatorial** /,dɪktə'tɔriəl/ adj

**dic·ta·tor·ship** /dɪk'teɪtɚ,ʃɪp, 'dɪkteɪtɚ-/ n **1** [U] government by a DICTATOR **2** a country under the control of a DICTATOR

**dic·tion** /'dɪkʃən/ n [U] the way in which someone pronounces words

**dic·tion·ar·y** /'dɪkʃə,nɛri/ n a book that gives a list of words in ALPHABETICAL order, with their meanings in the same or another language

**did** /dɪd, d; *weak* dəd/ v the past tense of DO

**di·dac·tic** /daɪ'dæktɪk/ adj FORMAL speech or writing that is didactic is intended to teach people a lesson

**did·n't** /'dɪdnt/ v the short form of "did not": *He didn't say anything to me.*

**die** /daɪ/ v **died, died, dying** [I] **1** to stop living: *Hector's upset because his dog died.* | *Mrs.*

*Chen died of/from* (=because of) *heart disease.* **2** to disappear or stop existing: *Her hope of returning home never died.* **3** INFORMAL if a machine or motor dies, it stops working: *My car died when I was stopped at a red light.*

---

SPOKEN PHRASES

**4 be dying to do something** to want to do something very much: *I'm dying to meet her brother.* **5 be to die for** something that is to die for is extremely good: *Max's chocolate cake is to die for!* **6 die laughing** to laugh a lot: *I nearly died laughing when Jerry fell in the swimming pool.* **7 I could have died** said when you are very surprised or embarrassed: *I could've died when I realized there was a hole in the back of my skirt.*

---

—see usage note at DEAD¹

**die away** phr v [T] if a sound dies away it becomes weaker and then stops

**die down** phr v [I] to become less strong or violent: *The wind finally died down this morning.*

**die off** phr v [I] to die one at a time until none is left: *All the elm trees are dying off.*

**die out** phr v [I] to disappear completely so that no one or no part is left: *The last bears in this area died out 100 years ago.*

**die·hard** /'daɪhɑrd/ adj INFORMAL unwilling to stop doing something or stop supporting someone even though other people have: *a diehard group of Grateful Dead fans*

**die·sel en·gine** /,dizəl 'ɛndʒɪn, -səl-/, **diesel** n an engine used in buses, TRUCKs, and some cars that uses DIESEL FUEL

**diesel fu·el** /,.. '.., '.. ,../, **diesel** n [U] a type of fuel that only burns under extreme pressure, and is cheaper than GASOLINE

**di·et¹** /'daɪət/ n **1** [C,U] the type of food that you eat each day: *A healthy diet and exercise are important for good health.* **2** a plan to eat only particular kinds or amounts of food: *a low-fat diet* | *No dessert for me - I'm on a diet.* (=trying to become thinner)

**diet²** v [I] to eat less or eat only particular foods in order to lose weight: *Jill's always dieting.*

**dif·fer** /'dɪfɚ/ v [I] **1** to be different: *The students differ in their ability to understand English.* | *His views differ from mine.* **2** FORMAL to have different opinions: *The two groups differ on/about/over where to have the meeting.*

**dif·fer·ence** /'dɪfrəns/ n **1** a way in which two or more things are not like each other: *There are many differences between public and private schools.* **2** [singular, U] the fact of not being the same as something else, or an amount by which one thing is not the same as another: *What's the difference in price?* | *There's an age difference of 4 years between the two children.* | *Can you tell the difference between the twins?* (=recognize that they are different) **3 make a difference/make all the difference**

to have a good effect on a situation or person: *Swimming twice a week can make a big difference in the way you feel.* **4 make no difference** to have no effect on a situation or person: *It makes no difference to me what you do.* **5 have your differences** to have disagreements with or different opinions from someone: *We've had our differences, but we're still friends.* **6 difference of opinion** a disagreement: *Perkins left his job because of a difference of opinion with his boss.*

**dif·fer·ent** /'dɪfrənt/ *adj* **1** not like something or someone else, or not the same as before: *Have you had a haircut? You look different.* | *New York and Chicago are very **different** from each other.* | *My new job's **different than** anything I've done before.* **2** separate: *The bookstore has a lot of different books about Kennedy.* **3** SPOKEN unusual, often in a way that you do not like: *"How do you like my shirt?"* *"Well, it's different."* —**differently** *adv*

> **USAGE NOTE different**
>
> We use both **different from** and **different than** to talk about two things that are not the same: *My new school is different from/than my old one.* However, most teachers prefer **different from**.

**dif·fer·en·ti·ate** /ˌdɪfə'rɛnʃiˌeɪt/ *v* **1** [I,T] to recognize or express the difference between things or people: *Most people couldn't **differentiate between** the two types of soft drink.* **2** [T] to make one thing different from another: *Our company tries to **differentiate** its products from the competitors.* —**differentiation** /ˌdɪfəˌrɛnʃi'eɪʃən/ *n* [U]

**dif·fi·cult** /'dɪfəˌkʌlt/ *adj* **1** not easy to do or understand: *She sometimes finds math **difficult**.* **2** involving a lot of problems and causing trouble: *His home life is difficult right now.* | *The bus strike is **making life difficult for** commuters.* **3** someone who is difficult is never satisfied, friendly, or pleased

**dif·fi·cul·ty** /'dɪfɪˌkʌlti/ *n* **1** [U] the state of being hard to do: *David's **having difficulty (in)** finding a job.* | *She spoke **with difficulty**.* | *Their business is **in** financial **difficulty**.* **2** [usually plural] a problem or something that causes trouble: *a country with economic difficulties* | *We **ran into difficulties** (=had trouble) buying the house.* **3** [U] how hard something is to understand: *The books vary in level of difficulty.*

**dif·fuse¹** /dɪ'fyus/ *adj* FORMAL **1** spread over a large area or in many places: *a large and diffuse organization* **2** using too many words and not expressing ideas clearly: *a diffuse and complicated book*

**dif·fuse²** /dɪ'fyuz/ *v* [I,T] FORMAL **1** to make ideas, information etc. available to many people: *a policy diffused throughout the company* **2** to make a bad feeling less strong: *Mara tried tell-*

*ing jokes to diffuse the tension.* **3** to make heat, a gas, light etc. spread over a larger area

**dig¹** /dɪg/ *v* **dug, dug, digging** **1** [I,T] to break up and move earth with a tool, your hands, or a machine: *The kids enjoyed digging in the sand.* | *Dig a large hole.* **2** [I,T] to get something by digging: *dig coal* | *dig for gold* **3 dig your own grave** INFORMAL to do something that will make you have problems later **4** [T] SPOKEN to like something or someone: *You really dig her, don't you?*

dig
shovel

**dig in** *phr v* [I] SPOKEN to start eating food that is in front of you: *Come on everyone - **dig in**!*

**dig into** *phr v* [I,T **dig** sth **into** sth] to push hard into something, or to make something do this: *She **dug** her fingernails **into** my arm.*

**dig** sth ↔ **up** *phr v* [T] **1** to remove something from under the earth with a tool or your hands: *Beth was **digging up** weeds.* **2** INFORMAL to find hidden or forgotten information by careful searching: *See what you can **dig up** on the guy.*

**dig** sth ↔ **out** *phr v* [T] **1** to get something out of a place using a tool or your hands: *We had to **dig** our car **out** of the snow.* **2** to find something that you have not seen for a long time, or that is not easy to find: *Mom **dug** her wedding dress **out** of the closet.*

**dig²** *n* **1** an unkind thing you say to annoy someone: *Sally keeps **making digs** about my work.* **2** a small quick push that you give someone with your finger or elbow: *a dig in the ribs* **3** the process of digging in a place in order to find ancient objects to study

**di·gest¹** /daɪ'dʒɛst, dɪ-/ *v* [T] **1** to change food in the stomach into a form your body can use: *Some babies can't digest cow's milk.* **2** to understand something after thinking about it carefully: *It took a while to digest the theory.*

**di·gest²** /'daɪdʒɛst/ *n* a short piece of writing that gives the most important facts from a book, report etc.

**di·ges·tion** /daɪ'dʒɛstʃən, dɪ-/ *n* [C,U] the process or ability to DIGEST food: *I've always had good digestion.* —**digestive** *adj*

**dig·it** /'dɪdʒɪt/ *n* **1** any of the numbers from 0 to 9: *a seven-digit phone number* **2** TECHNICAL a finger or toe

**dig·i·tal** /'dɪdʒɪt̬l/ *adj* **1** giving information in the form of numbers: *a digital clock* **2** using a system in which information is represented in the form of changing electrical signals: *It's a digital recording of the concert.*

**dig·ni·fied** /'dɪgnəˌfaɪd/ *adj* calm, serious, proud, and making people feel respect: *a dignified leader* —opposite UNDIGNIFIED

**dig·ni·tar·y** /'dɪgnə,tɛri/ *n* someone who has an important official position: *foreign dignitaries*

**dig·ni·ty** /'dɪgnəṭi/ *n* [U] **1** calm serious behavior, even in difficult situations, that makes people respect you: *a woman of compassion and dignity* **2** the quality of being serious and formal: *Lawyers must respect the dignity of the court.*

**di·gress** /daɪ'grɛs, dɪ-/ *v* [I] FORMAL to begin talking about something that is not related to the subject you were talking about –**digression** /daɪ'grɛʃən/ *n* [C,U]

**di·lap·i·dat·ed** /də'læpə,deɪṭɪd/ *adj* old, broken, and in very bad condition: *a dilapidated old house* –**dilapidation** /dɪ,læpə'deɪʃən/ *n* [U]

**di·late** /daɪ'leɪt, 'daɪleɪt/ *v* [I,T] to become wider or more open: *Her eyes were dilated.* –**dilation** /daɪ'leɪʃən/ *n* [U]

**di·lem·ma** /də'lɛmə/ *n* a situation in which you have to make a difficult choice between two actions: *We're in a dilemma about whether to move or not.*

**dil·i·gent** /'dɪlədʒənt/ *adj* someone who is diligent always works hard and carefully: *a diligent student* –**diligently** *adv* –**diligence** *n* [U]

**dill** /dɪl/ *n* [U] a plant whose seeds and leaves are used in cooking

**dill pick·le** /,. '../ *n* a CUCUMBER that is preserved in VINEGAR (=a sour-tasting liquid)

**di·lute** /dɪ'lut, daɪ-/ *v* [T] to make a liquid weaker or thinner by mixing another liquid with it: *diluted fruit juice* | **Dilute** *the paint with oil.* –**dilute** *adj* –**dilution** /daɪ'luʃən, dɪ-/ *n* [C,U]

**dim**[1] /dɪm/ *adj* **1** not bright or easy to see well: *a dim room with a tiny window* | *the dim outline of a building* **2** **dim recollection/ awareness etc.** something that is difficult for someone to remember, understand etc.: *a dim memory of her old house* **3** **take a dim view of** to disapprove of something –**dimly** *adv*

**dim**[2] *v* **-mmed, -mming** [I,T] **1** to become less bright, or to make something do this: *Can you dim the lights?* **2** if a feeling or quality dims, it grows weaker: *The painful memory began to dim.*

**dime** /daɪm/ *n* **1** a coin worth 10 cents (=10/ 100 of a dollar), used in the US and Canada **2** **a dime a dozen** INFORMAL very common and not valuable: *Jobs like his are a dime a dozen.* **3** **on a dime** within a small area: *He can park on a dime.*

**di·men·sion** /dɪ'mɛnʃən, daɪ-/ *n* **1** a part of a situation that affects the way you think about it: *The baby added a new dimension to our life at home.* **2** a measurement of space in a particular direction, such as length, height, or width

**di·men·sions** /dɪ'mɛnʃənz/ *n* [plural] **1** the measurement or size of something: *What are the dimensions of the room?* **2** the seriousness of a

problem: *They didn't realize the true dimensions of the crisis.*

**dime store** /'. ./ *n* a store that sells different types of inexpensive things

**di·min·ish** /dɪ'mɪnɪʃ/ *v* [I,T] to become smaller or less important, or to make something do this: *the country's diminishing political influence*

**di·min·u·tive** /dɪ'mɪnyəṭɪv/ *adj* FORMAL very small: *a diminutive man*

**dim·ple** /'dɪmpəl/ *n* a small hollow place on your cheek or chin, especially one that forms when you smile –**dimpled** *adj* –see picture at HEAD[1]

**din** /dɪn/ *n* a loud, continuous, and unpleasant noise

**dine** /daɪn/ *v* [I] FORMAL to eat dinner

**dine on** *phr v* [T] FORMAL to eat a particular type of food for dinner, especially expensive food: *We dined on lobster.*

**dine out** *phr v* [I] FORMAL to eat in a restaurant

**din·er** /'daɪnɚ/ *n* **1** a small restaurant that serves inexpensive meals **2** someone who is eating in a restaurant

**ding-dong** /'dɪŋ dɔŋ, -dɑŋ/ *n* [U] the noise made by a bell

**din·ghy** /'dɪŋi/ *n* a small open boat usually used for taking people between a ship and the shore

**din·gy** /'dɪndʒi/ *adj* dirty and in bad condition: *a dingy room*

**dining room** /'.. ,./ *n* a room where you eat meals in a house or hotel

**din·ner** /'dɪnɚ/ *n* **1** [C,U] the main meal of the day, usually eaten in the evening: *We had fish for dinner.* | *Grandma had everyone over for Thanksgiving dinner.* **2** a formal occasion when an evening meal is eaten, often to celebrate something: *There was a dinner in honor of his retirement.* –see usage note at MEAL TIMES

**din·ner·time** /'dɪnɚ,taɪm/ *n* [U] the time in the early evening when people eat dinner, usually between 5 and 7 o'clock

**di·no·saur** /'daɪnə,sɔr/ *n* one of many types of animal that lived in ancient times and no longer exist

**dip**[1] /dɪp/ **-pped, -pping** *v* **1** [T] to put something into a liquid and quickly lift it out again: *Janet dipped her feet into the water.* **2** INFORMAL to go down or become lower: *Nighttime temperatures dipped below freezing.*

**dip into** sth *phr v* [T] to use some of an amount of money that you have: *Medical bills forced her to dip into her savings.*

**dip**[2] *n* **1** [C,U] a thick mixture that you can DIP food into before you eat it: *a sour cream dip for the potato chips* **2** an occasion when the level or amount of something becomes lower: *a dip in prices* **3** a place where the surface of something is lower than the rest of the area: *a dip in* the road **4** INFORMAL a quick swim: *Is there time for a dip before lunch?*

**diph·the·ri·a** /dɪf'θɪriə, dɪp-/ *n* [U] a serious infectious disease of the throat that makes breathing difficult

**di·plo·ma** /dɪ'ploumə/ *n* an official paper showing that someone has successfully finished a course of study: *a high school diploma*

**di·plo·ma·cy** /dɪ'plouməsi/ *n* [U] **1** the management of political relations between countries: *an expert at international diplomacy* **2** skill in dealing with people and difficult situations successfully: *Bill handles personnel problems with diplomacy.*

**dip·lo·mat** /'dɪplə,mæt/ *n* someone who officially represents his/her country in a foreign country

**dip·lo·mat·ic** /,dɪplə'mætɪk/ *adj* **1** relating to the management of political relations between countries: *Feingold plans to join the diplomatic service.* **2** good at dealing with people in a way that causes no bad feelings: *Try to be diplomatic when you criticize his work.* –**diplomatically** *adv*

**dip·stick** /'dɪpstɪk/ *n* a stick used for measuring the amount of liquid in a container, such as oil in a car's engine

**dire** /daɪr/ *adj* **1** extremely serious or terrible: *Max is in dire trouble with the tax office.* | *a family in dire poverty/need* **2** **be in dire straits** to be in an extremely difficult or serious situation

**di·rect¹** /də'rɛkt, daɪ-/ *adj* **1** saying exactly what you mean in an honest way: *It's better to be direct when talking with the management.* **2** done without involving any people, actions, processes etc. that are not necessary: *direct government help for the unemployed* **3** going straight from one place to another without stopping or changing direction: *We got a direct flight to Cairo.* **4** likely to change something immediately: *new laws that have a direct impact on health care* **5** exact or total: *a direct translation from French* –**directness** *n* [U] –opposite INDIRECT

**di·rect²** *v* [T] **1** to give attention, money, information etc. to a particular person, group etc.: *My remark was directed at Tom, not at you.* | *money directed towards community projects* **2** to aim something in a particular direc-

**direct**

I'm flying direct from New York to San Francisco, but coming back via Chicago.

tion: *He directed the light towards the house.* **3** to be in charge of something: *Hanley was asked to direct the investigation.* **4** to give actors in a play, movie etc. instructions about what to do: *Who's directing the school play this year?* **5** FORMAL to tell someone the way to a place: *He directed me to the airport.* –see usage note at LEAD¹

**direct³** *adv* **1** without stopping or changing direction: *You can fly direct from London to Nashville.* **2** without dealing with anyone else first: *You'll have to contact the manager direct.*

**di·rec·tion** /də'rɛkʃən, daɪ-/ *n* **1** the way that someone or something is moving, facing, or aimed: *We took a walk in the opposite direction from the hotel.* | *Brian drove off in the direction of the party.* (=toward the party) **2** the general way in which someone or something changes or develops: *Suddenly the conversation changed direction.* **3** [U] control, guidance, or advice: *The company's been successful under Martini's direction.* **4** [U] a general purpose or aim: *Sometimes I feel that my life lacks direction.* **5** **sense of direction** the ability to know which way to go in a place you do not know well: *Matt's always getting lost; he has no sense of direction.* **6** [U] the instructions given to actors and other people in a play, movie etc.

**di·rec·tions** /də'rɛkʃənz, daɪ-/ *n* [plural] instructions about how to go from one place to another, or about how to do something: *Could you give me directions to the theater?* | *Read the directions at the top of the page.*

**di·rec·tive** /də'rɛktɪv/ *n* an official order or instruction to do something

**di·rect·ly** /də'rɛktli, daɪ-/ *adv* **1** only involving people or actions that are necessary: *programs aimed directly at people on welfare* **2** exactly: *Lucas sat directly behind us.*

**direct ob·ject** *n* /.,. '../ ⇨ OBJECT¹

**di·rec·tor** /də'rɛktər, daɪ-/ *n* **1** someone who controls or manages a company, organization, or activity: *Her new job is marketing director of Sun Life.* **2** someone who gives instructions to actors and other people in a movie or play

**di·rec·to·ry** /də'rɛktəri, daɪ-/ *n* a book or list of names, facts, events etc., arranged in ALPHABETICAL order

**dirt** /dərt/ *n* **1** earth or soil: *a dirt road* **2** any substance, such as dust or mud, that makes things not clean: *The floor was covered with dirt!* **3** INFORMAL information about someone's private life or activities that might give people a bad opinion about him/her

**dirt cheap** /,. './ *adj, adv* INFORMAL extremely cheap: *We got this chair dirt cheap at a sale.*

**dirt·y¹** /'dərti/ *adj* **1** not clean: *dirty dishes in the sink* **2** concerned with sex in a way that is considered immoral: *dirty jokes* **3** unfair or dishonest: *a dirty fighter* **4** **do sb's dirty work**

to do an unpleasant or dishonest job for someone: *I told them to do their own dirty work.*

**dirty²** *v* [T] to make something not clean

**dis** /dɪs/ *v* [T] SLANG to make unfair and unkind remarks about someone

**dis·a·bil·i·ty** /ˌdɪsəˈbɪləti/ *n* **1** a physical or mental condition that makes it difficult for someone to do the things most people are able to do: *Her disability doesn't keep her from working.* **2** [U] the state of having a disability: *learning to live with disability*

**dis·a·bled** /dɪsˈeɪbəld/ *adj* **1** someone who is disabled cannot use a part of his/her body properly: *a disabled worker* **2 the disabled** people who are disabled: *The bank has an entrance for the disabled.* –**disablement** *n* [U]

**dis·ad·van·tage** /ˌdɪsədˈvænʧɪdʒ/ *n* **1** something that may make someone less successful than other people: *Your main disadvantage is lack of experience.* | *I was at a disadvantage because I didn't speak Spanish.* **2** something that is not good or causes problems: *The only disadvantage of the job is the traveling.* –**disadvantageous** /ˌdɪsædvənˈteɪdʒəs, -væn-/ *adj*

**dis·ad·van·taged** /ˌdɪsədˈvænʧɪdʒd/ *adj* having social DISADVANTAGES such as a lack of money or education, that make it difficult for someone to succeed: *disadvantaged members of society*

**dis·af·fect·ed** /ˌdɪsəˈfɛktɪd◂/ *adj* no longer loyal because you are not satisfied with your leader, ruler etc.: *Candidates are trying to attract disaffected voters.* –**disaffection** *n* /ˌdɪsəˈfɛkʃən/ [U]

**dis·a·gree** /ˌdɪsəˈgri/ *v* [I] **1** to have or express a different opinion from someone else: *Roth doesn't like anybody who disagrees with him.* | *We disagree about the best way to solve the problem.* **2** if statements or reports about the same thing disagree, they are different from each other

**disagree with** *phr v* [T] to make you feel sick: *Crab meat disagrees with me.*

**dis·a·gree·a·ble** /ˌdɪsəˈgriəbəl/ *adj* **1** not enjoyable or pleasant: *a disagreeable experience* **2** unfriendly and having a bad temper: *a disagreeable person*

**dis·a·gree·ment** /ˌdɪsəˈgrimənt/ *n* **1** [C, U] the state of having a different opinion from someone: *She had a disagreement with the store's manager.* | *There was a slight disagreement over who should pay the bill.* **2** [U] differences between two statements, reports etc. that should be similar: *There was major disagreement between the witnesses' statements.*

**dis·al·low** /ˌdɪsəˈlaʊ/ *v* [T] FORMAL to officially refuse to allow something because a rule has been broken: *The referee disallowed the goal.*

**dis·ap·pear** /ˌdɪsəˈpɪr/ *v* [I] **1** to become impossible to see or find: *The cat had dis-*

*appeared under the couch.* | *a plane disappearing behind the clouds* **2** to stop existing: *Many species of plants and animals disappear every year.* **3 to disappear into thin air** to suddenly become impossible to find with no explanation –**disappearance** *n* [C,U] –see usage note at LOSE

**dis·ap·point** /ˌdɪsəˈpɔɪnt/ *v* [T] to make someone unhappy because something s/he hoped for does not happen or is not as good as s/he expected: *I'm sorry to disappoint you, but the trip is canceled.*

**dis·ap·point·ed** /ˌdɪsəˈpɔɪntɪd/ *adj* unhappy because something did not happen, or because something or someone is not as good as you hoped it would be: *Are you disappointed (that) you didn't get an invitation?* | *We were disappointed with the election results.* | *I've been disappointed in his work.*

**dis·ap·point·ing** /ˌdɪsəˈpɔɪntɪŋ/ *adj* not as good as you expected or hoped something would be: *disappointing test scores* –**disappointingly** *adv*

**dis·ap·point·ment** /ˌdɪsəˈpɔɪntˀmənt/ *n* **1** [U] a feeling of sadness because something is not as good as you expected or has not happened: *his disappointment at not being chosen for the job* **2** someone or something that is not as good as you hoped or expected: *What a disappointment that movie was!* | *Kate feels like she's a disappointment to her family.*

**dis·ap·prov·al** /ˌdɪsəˈpruvəl/ *n* [U] a feeling or opinion that someone else is behaving badly: *public disapproval of the war* | *People were looking with disapproval at our clothes.* | *Marion shook her head in disapproval.*

**dis·ap·prove** /ˌdɪsəˈpruv/ *v* [I] to think that something is bad, wrong etc.: *Her parents disapprove of her lifestyle.*

**dis·arm** /dɪsˈɑrm/ *v* **1** [I] to reduce the size of the army, navy etc. and the number of weapons: *Both sides must disarm before the peace talks.* **2** [T] to take away someone's weapons: *Police disarmed the two men.* **3** [T] to make someone less angry and more friendly: *Susie's reply disarmed him.*

**dis·ar·ma·ment** /dɪsˈɑrməmənt/ *n* [U] the reduction in numbers or size of a country's weapons, army, navy etc.: *plans for nuclear disarmament*

**dis·arm·ing** /dɪsˈɑrmɪŋ/ *adj* making you feel less angry and more friendly or trusting: *a disarming smile*

**dis·ar·ray** /ˌdɪsəˈreɪ/ *n* [U] FORMAL the state of being messy or not organized: *papers in disarray on the desk*

**dis·as·ter** /dɪˈzæstə/ *n* [C,U] **1** a sudden event such as an accident, flood, or storm that causes great harm or damage: *an air disaster in which 329 people died* **2 natural disaster** a disaster caused by nature: *The 1994 flood of the*

*Mississippi was a terrible natural disaster.* **3** a complete failure: *What a disaster that party was!*

**dis·as·trous** /dɪˈzæstrəs/ *adj* very bad or ending in failure: *The whole evening was disastrous.* –**disastrously** *adv*

**dis·a·vow** /ˌdɪsəˈvaʊ/ *v* [T] FORMAL to state that you are not responsible for something, or that you do not know about it: *The President has disavowed any knowledge of the affair.* –**disavowal** *n* [C,U]

**dis·band** /dɪsˈbænd/ *v* [I,T] FORMAL to stop existing as an organization

**dis·be·lief** /ˌdɪsbəˈlif/ *n* [U] a feeling that something is not true or does not exist: *I looked at him in disbelief.* –**disbelieve** /ˌdɪsbəˈliv/ *v* [T] –**disbelieving** *adj*

**disc** /dɪsk/ *n* ⇨ DISK

**dis·card** /dɪˈskɑrd/ *v* [T] to get rid of something: *discarding old clothes* –**discard** /ˈdɪskɑrd/ *n*

**dis·cern** /dɪˈsɚn, dɪˈzɚn/ *v* [T] FORMAL to see, notice, or understand something by looking at it or thinking about it carefully: *Walters couldn't discern any difference between the two plants.* –**discernible** *adj* –**discernibly** *adv*

**dis·cern·ing** /dɪˈsɚnɪŋ, -ˈzɚ-/ *adj* able to make good judgments about people, styles, and things: *the discerning traveler's guide to the Southeast*

**dis·charge¹** /dɪsˈtʃɑrdʒ/ *v* **1** [T] to allow someone to go or to send him/her away from a place: *Blanton was discharged from the hospital last night.* **2** [I,T] to send, pour, or let out something from something else, especially a liquid or gas: *Sewage was discharged into the ocean.* | *The gun accidentally discharged.* (=it shot a bullet) **3** [T] FORMAL to perform a duty or promise

**dis·charge²** /ˈdɪstʃɑrdʒ/ *n* **1** [U] the action of sending someone or something away: *After his discharge from the army, he got married.* **2** [C,U] a substance that comes out of something, especially a wound or part of your body: *infected discharge from the cut on her leg*

**dis·ci·ple** /dɪˈsaɪpəl/ *n* **1** a follower of a religious teacher, especially one of the 12 original followers of Christ **2** a follower of any great leader or teacher

**dis·ci·pli·nar·i·an** /ˌdɪsəpləˈnɛriən/ *n* someone who believes that people should obey rules and who makes them do this: *Sam's father is a strict disciplinarian.*

**dis·ci·pline¹** /ˈdɪsəplɪn/ *n* **1** [C,U] a way of training your mind and body so that you control your actions and obey rules: *It takes a lot of self discipline to study so hard.* | *military discipline* **2** [U] the result of such training: *maintaining discipline in the classroom* **3** [U] punishment for not obeying rules: *That child needs disci-*

*pline.* **4** FORMAL an area of knowledge or teaching

**discipline²** *v* [T] **1** to train someone to behave or act in a particular way: *sergeants disciplining the soldiers* **2** to punish someone: *The staff members were disciplined for their carelessness.*

**dis·claim** /dɪsˈkleɪm/ *v* [T] FORMAL to say that you are not responsible for or do not know anything about something: *The group has disclaimed any involvement in the attack.*

**dis·claim·er** /dɪsˈkleɪmɚ/ *n* FORMAL a statement that you are not responsible for or do not know about something, often used in advertising

**dis·close** /dɪsˈkloʊz/ *v* [T] to make something known publicly: *GM did not disclose details of the agreement.*

**dis·clo·sure** /dɪsˈkloʊʒɚ/ *n* [C,U] a secret that someone tells people, or the act of telling this secret: *the disclosure of corruption in the mayor's office*

**dis·co** /ˈdɪskoʊ/ *n* **1** [U] a type of dance music with a strong repeating beat that was first popular in the 1970s **2** a place where people dance to recorded popular music

**dis·col·or** /dɪsˈkʌlɚ/ *v* [I,T] to change color, or to make something change color, so that it looks unattractive: *His teeth were discolored from smoking.* –**discoloration** /dɪsˌkʌləˈreɪʃən/ *n* [C,U]

**dis·com·fort** /dɪsˈkʌmfɚt/ *n* **1** [U] slight pain or an unpleasant feeling: *Your injury isn't serious, but it may cause some discomfort.* **2** something that makes you uncomfortable: *the discomforts of long distance travel*

**dis·con·cert·ing** /ˌdɪskənˈsɚtɪŋ/ *adj* making someone feel slightly embarrassed, confused, or worried: *It was disconcerting to be watched while I worked.* –**disconcerted** *adj*

**dis·con·nect** /ˌdɪskəˈnɛkt/ *v* [T] **1** to take out the wire, pipe etc. that connects a machine or piece of equipment to something: *Disconnect the cables before you move the computer.* **2** to remove the supply of power to something such as a telephone line or a building: *I tried to call, but the phone had been disconnected.* –**disconnection** /ˌdɪskəˈnɛkʃən/ *n* [C,U]

**dis·con·tent** /ˌdɪskənˈtɛnt/ *n* [U] a feeling of not being happy or satisfied

**dis·con·tent·ed** /ˌdɪskənˈtɛntɪd/ *adj* unhappy or not satisfied: *After two years, I began to get discontented with my job.*

**dis·con·tin·ue** /ˌdɪskənˈtɪnyu/ *v* [T] to stop doing or providing something: *Five bus routes will be discontinued.* –**discontinuation** /ˌdɪskənˌtɪnyuˈeɪʃən/ *n* [U]

**dis·cord** /ˈdɪskɔrd/ *n* **1** [U] FORMAL disagreement between people: *fears that the law will increase racial discord* **2** [C,U] an unpleasant sound produced by musical notes that do not go together well – **discordant** adj

**dis·count**[1] /ˈdɪskaʊnt/ n a reduction in the usual price of something: I got this jacket **at a huge discount**.

**dis·count**[2] /dɪsˈkaʊnt/ v [T] **1** to reduce the price of something: a good wine, discounted to $3.99 **2** to regard something as unlikely to be true or important: Scientists discounted his method of predicting earthquakes.

**dis·cour·age** /dɪˈskɜːrɪdʒ, -ˈskʌr-/ v [T] **1** to persuade someone not to do something, especially by making it seem difficult or unpleasant: Keith's mother tried to **discourage** him **from** joining the navy. **2** to make someone less confident or less willing to do something: Her failure on the first two attempts had discouraged her. **3** to make something become less likely to happen: Put the plant in a cold room to discourage growth. –opposite ENCOURAGE

**dis·cour·aged** /dɪˈskɜːrɪdʒd, -ˈskʌr-/ adj no longer having the confidence you need to continue doing something: Children may **get discouraged** if they are criticized too often.

**dis·cour·age·ment** /dɪˈskɜːrɪdʒmənt, -ˈskʌr-/ n **1** [C,U] a feeling of being DISCOURAGED **2** [U] the act of trying to DISCOURAGE someone from doing something

**dis·cour·ag·ing** /dɪˈskɜːrɪdʒɪŋ, -ˈskʌr-/ adj making you lose the confidence you need to continue doing something: It was very discouraging to see my sister do it so easily.

**dis·course** /ˈdɪskɔrs/ n **1** a serious speech or piece of writing on a particular subject: a discourse on the history of Indian society **2** [U] serious conversation between people: a chance for meaningful discourse between the two leaders

**dis·cour·te·ous** /dɪsˈkɜːtiəs/ adj FORMAL not polite –**discourtesy** n [C,U]

**dis·cov·er** /dɪˈskʌvɚ/ v **1** [T] to find something that was hidden or that people did not know about before: Benjamin Franklin discovered electricity. **2** [I,T] to find out something that is a fact, or the answer to a question: Did you ever **discover who** sent you the flowers? –**discoverer** n

**dis·cov·er·y** /dɪˈskʌvri, -vəri/ n **1** a fact, thing, or answer to a question that someone discovers: Einstein **made an** important scientific **discovery**. **2** [U] the act of finding something that was hidden or not known before: the discovery of oil in Texas

**dis·cred·it** /dɪsˈkrɛdɪt/ v [T] to make people stop trusting or having respect for someone or something: the newspaper's attempt to discredit the senator –**discredit** n [U]

**dis·creet** /dɪˈskrit/ adj careful about what you say or do so that you do not upset or embarrass

people: a discreet romance between co-workers –**discreetly** adv

**dis·crep·an·cy** /dɪˈskrɛpənsi/ n [C,U] a difference between two amounts, details etc. that should be the same: How do you explain the **discrepancies in** these totals?

**dis·cre·tion** /dɪˈskrɛʃən/ n [U] **1** the ability to be careful about what you say or do in a particular situation, so that you do not upset or embarrass people: This situation must be handled with discretion. **2** the ability to decide what is the right thing to do in a situation: Pay raises are left to the manager's discretion. –**discretionary** adj

**dis·crim·i·nate** /dɪˈskrɪməˌneɪt/ v **1** [I] to treat a person or group differently from another in an unfair way: a law that **discriminates against** immigrants **2** [I,T] to recognize a difference between things: You must learn to **discriminate between** facts and opinions.

**dis·crim·i·nat·ing** /dɪˈskrɪməˌneɪtɪŋ/ adj able to judge what is of good quality and what is not: fine food for those with discriminating taste

**dis·crim·i·na·tion** /dɪˌskrɪməˈneɪʃən/ n [U] **1** the practice of treating one group of people differently from another in an unfair way: sex discrimination | working to stop **discrimination against** the disabled **2** the ability to judge what is of good quality and what is not

**dis·cus** /ˈdɪskəs/ n [singular] a sport in which you throw a heavy plate-shaped object as far as you can

**dis·cuss** /dɪˈskʌs/ v [T] to talk about something with someone in order to exchange ideas or decide something: I wanted to **discuss** my plans **with** my father.

**dis·cus·sion** /dɪˈskʌʃən/ n [C,U] the act of discussing something, or a conversation in which people discuss something: I want to **have a discussion about** your behavior in class. | The subject now **under discussion** (=being discussed) is the Vietnam War.

**dis·dain**[1] /dɪsˈdeɪn/ n [U] FORMAL a lack of respect for someone or something, because you think he, she, or it is not important or not good enough: Mason's **disdain for** people without education –**disdainful** adj

**disdain**[2] v [T] FORMAL to feel DISDAIN for someone

**dis·ease** /dɪˈziz/ n [C,U] an illness or unhealthy condition that can be named: My uncle has heart disease. | Tina **suffers from** a rare brain **disease**. | Lack of clean water can **cause disease**. –**diseased** adj

---

**USAGE NOTE  disease, illness, and sickness**

Although we often use **disease** and **illness** to mean the same thing, it is a **disease** that actually makes you sick: He suffers from heart disease. **Illness** is the state of being sick: *Janey missed a lot of school because of illness.* **Sickness** is a particular type of illness: *radiation sickness | motion sickness.*

**dis·em·bark** /ˌdɪsɪmˈbark/ v [I,T] to get off or be taken off a ship or plane —**disembarkation** /ˌdɪsɛmbarˈkeɪʃən/ n [U]

**dis·em·bod·ied** /ˌdɪsɪmˈbadid/ adj **1** a disembodied sound or voice comes from someone who cannot be seen **2** without a body: *disembodied spirits*

**dis·en·chant·ed** /ˌdɪsɪnˈtʃænt̬ɪd/ adj no longer liking or believing in the value of someone or something: *She was becoming disenchanted with her marriage.* —**disenchantment** n [U]

**dis·en·fran·chised** /ˌdɪsɪnˈfræntʃaɪzd/ adj not having any rights, especially the right to vote, and not feeling part of society —**disenfranchise** v [T]

**dis·en·gage** /ˌdɪsɪnˈgeɪdʒ/ v [I,T] to separate something from something else that was holding it or connected to it: *Disengage the gears when you park the car.* —**disengagement** n [U]

**dis·en·tan·gle** /ˌdɪsɪnˈtæŋgəl/ v [T] to separate different ideas or pieces of information that have become confused together: *Investigators had to disentangle Maxwell's complicated financial affairs.*

**dis·fa·vor** /dɪsˈfeɪvɚ/ n [U] FORMAL a feeling of dislike or disapproval

**dis·fig·ure** /dɪsˈfɪgyɚ/ v [T] to spoil the appearance of someone or something: *His face was badly disfigured in the accident.* —**disfigurement** n [C,U]

**dis·grace[1]** /dɪsˈgreɪs, dɪˈskreɪs/ n [singular, U] **1** something that makes people feel disapproving or ashamed: *That old suit of yours is a disgrace.|Doctors like you are a disgrace to our hospital.* **2 be in disgrace** to be regarded with disapproval because of something you have done: *Harry left the school in disgrace.*

**disgrace[2]** v [T] to do something so bad that people lose respect for you: *Peter disgraced himself last night by getting drunk and starting a fight.*

**dis·grace·ful** /dɪsˈgreɪsfəl/ adj completely unacceptable: *Your manners are disgraceful!*

**dis·grun·tled** /dɪsˈgrʌnt̬ld/ adj annoyed, disappointed, and not satisfied: *disgruntled employees*

**dis·guise[1]** /dɪsˈgaɪz, dɪˈskaɪz/ v [T] **1** to change the usual appearance, sound etc. of someone or something: *She disguised herself as a man.* **2** to hide something so that people will not notice it: *We can't disguise the fact that the business is losing money.*

**disguise[2]** n [C,U] something that you wear to change your appearance and hide who you really are, or the act of wearing this: *He traveled to Russia in disguise.*

**dis·gust[1]** /dɪsˈgʌst, dɪˈskʌst/ n [U] a strong feeling of dislike and disapproval: *Joe was filthy, and everyone was looking at him with disgust.|We waited an hour before leaving in disgust.*

**disgust[2]** v [T] to make someone feel strong dislike and disapproval: *The dirt and smells of the city disgusted him.*

**dis·gust·ed** /dɪsˈgʌstɪd/ adj feeling or showing DISGUST: *I felt sorry for Al, but Mike just looked disgusted and told him to get a job.*

**dis·gust·ing** /dɪsˈgʌstɪŋ/ adj very unpleasant or unacceptable: *The smell in there is disgusting!|Fifteen dollars for a salad is disgusting!* —**disgustingly** adv

**dish[1]** /dɪʃ/ n **1** a round container with low sides, used for holding food: *a serving dish* **2** food cooked or prepared in a particular way: *a wonderful pasta dish* —see also DISHES

**dish[2]** v

**dish** sth ↔ **out** phr v [T] INFORMAL **1** to give something to people: *He's always dishing out unwanted advice.* **2** to serve food to people: *Dad dished out the barbecued steaks.* **3 sb can dish it out but s/he can't take it** INFORMAL used in order to say that someone criticizes others but does not like to be criticized

**dish** sth ↔ **up** phr v [I,T] to put the food for a meal onto plates: *Will you help me dish up dinner?*

**dis·heart·ened** /dɪsˈhartˌnd/ adj feeling disappointed and without hope and confidence —**dishearten** v [T]

**dis·heart·en·ing** /dɪsˈhartˌn-ɪŋ/ adj making you lose hope and confidence: *It was disheartening to see that the changes we made didn't help.* —**dishearteningly** adv

**dish·es** /ˈdɪʃɪz/ n [plural] all the plates, cups, bowls etc. that are used during a meal: *The dishes go in the cupboard near the stove.|It's your turn to do the dishes.* (=wash the dishes)

**di·shev·eled** /dɪˈʃɛvəld/ adj very messy: *She looked tired and disheveled.*

**dis·hon·est** /dɪsˈanɪst/ adj not honest: *a dishonest politician* —**dishonestly** adv

**dis·hon·est·y** /dɪsˈanɪsti/ n [U] dishonest behavior

**dis·hon·or[1]** /dɪsˈanɚ/ n [U] FORMAL a state in which people no longer respect you or approve of you: *His behavior brought dishonor on the family.*

**dishonor[2]** v [T] FORMAL to do something bad that makes people stop respecting you

**dis·hon·or·a·ble** /dɪsˈanərəbəl/ adj not morally correct or acceptable: *a dishonorable man* —**dishonorably** adv

**dish rack** /ˈ. ./ n a thing in which you put dishes to dry —see picture at KITCHEN

**dish·tow·el** /'dɪʃtauəl/ *n* a cloth used for drying dishes

**dish·wash·er** /'dɪʃ‚waʃɚ/ *n* a machine that washes dishes –see picture at KITCHEN

**dis·il·lu·sion** /‚dɪsə'luʒən/ *v* [T] to make someone realize that something s/he thought was true or good is not really true or good: *I hate to disillusion you, but she won't pay you.* –**disillusionment** *n* [U]

**dis·il·lu·sioned** /‚dɪsə'luʒənd/ *adj* disappointed because you have lost your belief that someone or something is good or right

**dis·in·fect** /‚dɪsɪn'fɛkt/ *v* [T] to clean something with a chemical that destroys BACTERIA

**dis·in·fect·ant** /‚dɪsɪn'fɛktənt/ *n* [C,U] a chemical that destroys BACTERIA

**dis·in·her·it** /‚dɪsɪn'hɛrɪt/ *v* [T] to prevent someone from receiving any of your money or property after your death: *Crowley disinherited his son.*

**dis·in·te·grate** /dɪs'ɪntə‚greɪt/ *v* [I] **1** to break up into small pieces: *The heat had made the foam rubber disintegrate.* **2** to become weaker and be gradually destroyed: *The whole project just disintegrated through lack of interest.* –**disintegration** /dɪs‚ɪntə'greɪʃən/ *n* [U]

**dis·in·terest·ed** /dɪs'ɪntrɪstɪd, -'ɪntə‚rɛstɪd/ *adj* **1** able to judge a situation fairly because you will not gain an advantage from it: *a disinterested observer of the voting process* **2** NONSTANDARD not interested –**disinterest** *n* [U]

> **USAGE NOTE** disinterested
>
> We often use **disinterested** to mean "not interested." However, many teachers think this is incorrect. If you want to say that someone is "not interested," use **uninterested**: *She seemed uninterested in the details.*

**dis·joint·ed** /dɪs'dʒɔɪntɪd/ *adj* disjointed speaking or writing is not easy to understand because the words or ideas are not arranged in a reasonable order

**disk** /dɪsk/ *n* **1** a small flat piece of plastic or metal used for storing information in a computer –see also HARD DISK **2** ⇨ DISKETTE **3** a flat object in the shape of a circle: *a metal disk* **4** a flat piece of CARTILAGE (=a strong substance that stretches) between the bones of your back

**disk drive** /'. ./ *n* a piece of equipment in a computer that is used in order to get information from a DISK or to store information on one

**disk·ette** /dɪ'skɛt/ *n* a small square plastic object that you put into a computer, that is used for storing information

**disk jock·ey** /'. ‚../ *n* ⇨ DJ

**dis·like¹** /dɪs'laɪk/ *v* [T] to not like someone or something: *Why do you dislike her so much?*

**dislike²** *n* [C,U] a feeling of not liking someone or something: *She shared her mother's dislike of housework.*

**dis·lo·cate** /dɪs'loukeɪt, 'dɪslou‚keɪt/ *v* [T] to put a bone out of its normal place: *I dislocated my shoulder playing football.* –**dislocation** /‚dɪslou'keɪʃən/ *n* [C,U]

**dis·lodge** /dɪs'lɑdʒ/ *v* [T] to force or knock something out of its position: *Lee dislodged a stone as he climbed over the old wall.*

**dis·loy·al** /dɪs'lɔɪəl/ *adj* not loyal: *He was accused of being disloyal to his country.* –**disloyalty** /dɪs'lɔɪəlti/ *n* [C,U]

**dis·mal** /'dɪzməl/ *adj* very bad, and making you feel unhappy and without hope: *dismal weather | the team's dismal record in the past month* –**dismally** *adv*

**dis·man·tle** /dɪs'mæntəl/ *v* [I,T] **1** to take something apart so that it is in separate pieces: *I'll have to dismantle the engine.* **2** to gradually get rid of a system or organization: *plans to dismantle the existing tax laws*

**dis·may¹** /dɪs'meɪ/ *n* [U] a strong feeling of being disappointed and unhappy: *Jan read the news of the disaster with dismay.*

**dismay²** *v* [T] to make someone feel worried, disappointed, and upset: *I was dismayed to hear that you were moving.*

**dis·mem·ber** /dɪs'mɛmbɚ/ *v* [T] FORMAL to cut or tear a body into pieces

**dis·miss** /dɪs'mɪs/ *v* [T] **1** to refuse to consider someone's idea, opinion etc.: *He dismissed the idea as impossible.* **2** FORMAL to remove someone from his/her job: *If you're late again you'll be dismissed!* **3** to send someone away or allow him/her to go: *Class is dismissed.* –**dismissal** *n* [C,U]

**dis·mis·sive** /dɪs'mɪsɪv/ *adj* refusing to consider someone or something seriously: *Freud was much too dismissive of religion.*

**dis·mount** /dɪs'maunt/ *v* [I] to get off a horse, bicycle, or MOTORCYCLE

**dis·o·be·di·ent** /‚dɪsə'bidiənt/ *adj* deliberately not doing what you are told to do: *a disobedient child* –**disobedience** *n* [U]

**dis·o·bey** /‚dɪsə'beɪ/ *v* [I,T] to refuse to do what you are told to do, or to refuse to obey a rule or law: *Drivers who disobey the speed limit will be fined.*

**dis·or·der** /dɪs'ɔrdɚ/ *n* **1** [U] a situation in which things or people are very messy or not organized: *The house was in a state of complete disorder.* **2** civil/public disorder a situation in which many people disobey the law and are difficult to control **3** a disease or illness that prevents part of your body from working correctly: *a rare liver disorder*

**dis·or·der·ly** /dɪs'ɔrdɚli/ *adj* **1** messy: *clothes left in a disorderly heap* **2** noisy or violent in public: *Jerry was charged with being drunk and disorderly.*

D

**dis·or·ga·nized** /dɪsˈɔrgəˌnaɪzd/ *adj* not arranged or planned in a clear order, or not planned at all: *The meeting was disorganized and too long.* —**disorganization** /dɪsˌɔrgənəˈzeɪʃən/ *n* [U]

**dis·o·ri·ent·ed** /dɪsˈɔriɛnʈɪd/ *adj* confused and not really able to understand what is happening: *You'll feel disoriented for a while after the operation.* —**disorientation** /dɪsˌɔriən-ˈteɪʃən/ *n* [U]

**dis·own** /dɪsˈoʊn/ *v* [T] to say that you no longer want to have any connection with someone or something: *Her family disowned her for marrying him.*

**dis·par·age** /dɪˈspærɪdʒ/ *v* [T] FORMAL to criticize someone or something in a way that shows you do not think he, she, or it is very good or important: *Clay's humor tends to disparage women and gays.*

**dis·par·a·ging** /dɪˈspærədʒɪŋ/ *adj* showing that you think someone or something is not very good or important: *disparaging remarks/comments*

**dis·par·ate** /ˈdɪsпərɪt/ *adj* FORMAL very different and not related to each other: *The project brought together several disparate groups to work on a common problem.* —**disparately** *adv*

**dis·par·i·ty** /dɪˈspærəti/ *n* [C,U] FORMAL a difference between things, especially an unfair difference: *a huge disparity between our salaries*

**dis·pas·sion·ate** /dɪsˈpæʃənɪt/ *adj* not easily influenced by personal feelings: *a dispassionate opinion* —**dispassionately** *adv*

**dis·patch¹** /dɪˈspætʃ/ *v* [T] to send someone or something away: *The packages were dispatched yesterday.*

**dispatch²** *n* a message sent between government or military officials, or sent to a newspaper by one of its writers

**dis·pel** /dɪˈspɛl/ *v* **-lled, -lling** [T] FORMAL to stop someone believing or feeling something: *Mark's calm words dispelled our fears.*

**dis·pen·sa·ry** /dɪˈspɛnsəri/ *n* a place where medicines are prepared and given out in a hospital

**dis·pen·sa·tion** /ˌdɪspən'seɪʃən, -pɛn-/ *n* [C,U] special permission to do something that is not usually allowed

**dis·pense** /dɪˈspɛns/ *v* [T] FORMAL **1** to give something to people, especially a particular amount of something: *The soldiers helped to dispense supplies.* **2** to give or provide people with advice, information etc.: *a clinic dispensing advice on family planning*

**dispense with** sth *phr v* [T] FORMAL to not use or do something that you usually use or do, because it is no longer necessary

**dis·pens·er** /dɪˈspɛnsɚ/ *n* a machine that gives you things such as drinks or money when you press a button

**dis·perse** /dɪˈspɚs/ *v* [I,T] to scatter in different directions, or to make something do this: *The police used tear gas to disperse the crowd.* —**dispersal** *n* [U]

**dis·pir·it·ed** /dɪˈspɪrɪʈɪd/ *adj* LITERARY sad and without hope

**dis·place** /dɪsˈpleɪs/ *v* [T] **1** to take the place of someone or something by becoming more important or useful: *Coal is being displaced by natural gas as a major source of energy.* **2** to make a group of people or animals leave the place where they normally live —**displacement** *n* [U]

**dis·play¹** /dɪˈspleɪ/ *n* **1** [C,U] an arrangement of things for people to look at: *a display of African masks* **2** a show or performance intended to entertain people: *a fireworks display* **3 be on display** something that is on display is in a public place where people can look at it **4** the act of clearly showing a feeling, attitude, or quality: *Displays of affection* (=showing loving feelings for someone) *are disapproved of in many cultures.*

**display²** *v* [T] **1** to put things where people can see them easily: *tables displaying pottery and other crafts* **2** to clearly show a feeling, attitude, or quality: *He displayed no emotion at Helen's funeral.*

**dis·pleased** /dɪsˈplizd/ *adj* FORMAL annoyed and not satisfied: *Many employees were displeased with the decision.* —**displease** *v* [T]

**dis·pleas·ure** /dɪsˈplɛʒɚ/ *n* [U] FORMAL the state of being DISPLEASED: *The audience showed their displeasure by leaving as the orchestra played.*

**dis·pos·a·ble** /dɪˈspoʊzəbəl/ *adj* intended to be used once or for a short time and then thrown away: *disposable razors*

**disposable in·come** /.ˌ... ˈ.../ *n* the amount of money you have after paying all your bills, taxes etc., that you can spend on things you want

**dis·pos·al** /dɪˈspoʊzəl/ *n* **1** [U] the act of getting rid of something: *the safe disposal of radioactive waste* **2 at sb's disposal** available for someone to use: *My car and driver are at your disposal.* **3** ⇨ GARBAGE DISPOSAL

**dis·pose** /dɪˈspoʊz/ *v*

**dispose of** sth *phr v* [T] **1** to get rid of something: *How did the killer dispose of his victims' bodies?* **2** to deal with something such as a problem or question successfully: *The court quickly disposed of the case.*

**dis·posed** /dɪˈspoʊzd/ *adj* FORMAL **1 be disposed to do sth** to feel willing to do something or behave in a particular way: *I don't feel disposed to interfere.* **2 well/favorably disposed (to)** liking or approving of something: *The countries seem favorably disposed to a conference.* (=they want one)

**dis·po·si·tion** /ˌdɪspə'zɪʃən/ *n* FORMAL the

way someone tends to behave: *a nervous disposition*

**dis·pos·sess** /ˌdɪspəˈzɛs/ *v* [T] FORMAL to take property or land away from someone –**dispossession** /ˌdɪspəˈzɛʃən/ *n* [U]

**dis·pro·por·tion·ate** /ˌdɪsprəˈpɔrʃənɪt/ *adj* too much or too little in relation to something else: *the disproportionate amount of money being spent on defense projects* –**disproportionately** *adv*

**dis·prove** /dɪsˈpruv/ *v* [T] to prove that something is false: *Evidence that disproves Lane's claim.*

**dis·pute**[1] /dɪˈspyut/ *n* [C,U] **1** a serious argument or disagreement: *a pay dispute* | *The land's ownership is **in dispute**.* (=being argued about) | *The bus drivers are still **in dispute with** (=having an argument with) their employers over pay.* **2 be beyond dispute** to clearly be true, so that no one can question it or argue about it: *The facts are beyond dispute.* **3 be open to dispute** to not be completely certain, so that people can question it or argue about it: *The results of this research are still open to dispute.*

**dispute**[2] *v* [I,T] to argue or disagree with someone, especially about whether something is true: *The question was **hotly disputed** (=argued about with strong feelings) in the Senate.*

**dis·qual·i·fy** /dɪsˈkwɑləˌfaɪ/ *v* [T] to stop someone from taking part in an activity or competition, usually because s/he has done something wrong: *Dennis was **disqualified from** the competition for cheating.* –**disqualification** /dɪsˌkwɑləfəˈkeɪʃən/ *n* [C,U]

**dis·re·gard**[1] /ˌdɪsrɪˈgɑrd/ *v* [T] to ignore something: *The judge ordered us to disregard the lawyer's last statement.*

**disregard**[2] *n* [U] the act of ignoring something, especially something important: *Thomas' actions show a total **disregard for** the law.*

**dis·re·pair** /ˌdɪsrɪˈpɛr/ *n* [U] the state of being in a bad condition and needing to be repaired: *The old house has been allowed to **fall into disrepair**.*

**dis·rep·u·ta·ble** /dɪsˈrɛpyəˌtəbəl/ *adj* not respected and thought to be involved in dishonest activities: *your disreputable friends*

**dis·re·pute** /ˌdɪsrəˈpyut/ *n* [U] FORMAL **bring sb/sth into disrepute** to make people stop trusting or having respect for someone or something: *Your behavior has brought the whole school into disrepute.*

**dis·re·spect** /ˌdɪsrɪˈspɛkt/ *n* [U] lack of respect or politeness –**disrespectful** *adj* –**disrespectfully** *adv*

**dis·rupt** /dɪsˈrʌpt/ *v* [T] to stop a situation, event etc. from continuing in its usual way: *A crowd of protesters tried to disrupt the meeting.* –**disruption** /dɪsˈrʌpʃən/ *n* [C,U] –**disruptive** /dɪsˈrʌptɪv/ *adj*

**dis·sat·is·fac·tion** /dɪˌsætɪsˈfækʃən, dɪsˌsæ-/ *n* [U] a feeling of not being satisfied: *The poll shows voters' **dissatisfaction with** politicians.*

**dis·sat·is·fied** /dɪˈsætɪsˌfaɪd/ *adj* not satisfied because something is not as good as you had expected: *If you are **dissatisfied with** this product, please return it for a full refund.*

**dis·sect** /dɪˈsɛkt, daɪ-/ *v* [T] **1** to cut up the body of a plant or animal in order to study it **2** to examine something in great detail: *The book dissects historical data to show how Napoleon ran his army.* –**dissection** /dɪˈsɛkʃən/ *n* [C,U]

**dis·sem·i·nate** /dɪˈsɛməˌneɪt/ *v* [T] FORMAL to spread information, ideas etc. to as many people as possible: *a Web site that disseminates health information* –**dissemination** /dɪˌsɛməˈneɪʃən/ *n* [U]

**dis·sen·sion** /dɪˈsɛnʃən/ *n* [C,U] disagreement that often leads to argument

**dis·sent**[1] /dɪˈsɛnt/ *n* [U] refusal to accept an opinion that most people accept: *political dissent*

**dissent**[2] *v* [I] to say that you refuse to accept an opinion that most people accept: *Two of the court's nine judges dissented from the opinion.* –**dissenter** *n* –opposite ASSENT

**dis·ser·ta·tion** /ˌdɪsəˈteɪʃən/ *n* a long piece of writing about a subject, especially one that you write at a university to get a PH.D.

**dis·serv·ice** /dɪˈsəvɪs, dɪsˈsə-/ *n* [singular, U] something that harms someone or something: *The players' actions have **done a** great **disservice** to the game.*

**dis·si·dent** /ˈdɪsədənt/ *n* someone who publicly criticizes an opinion, group, government etc. –**dissidence** *n* [U] –**dissident** *adj*

**dis·sim·i·lar** /dɪˈsɪmələ, dɪsˈsɪ-/ *adj* not the same: *countries with dissimilar legal systems* –**dissimilarity** /dɪˌsɪməˈlærəti/ *n* [C,U]

**dis·si·pate** /ˈdɪsəˌpeɪt/ *v* FORMAL [I,T] to gradually disappear, or to make something do this: *The smoke gradually dissipated.*

**dis·so·ci·ate** /dɪˈsoʊʃiˌeɪt, -siˌeɪt/ *v* [T] FORMAL to believe or claim that one thing or person has no relation to another: *We have **dissociated ourselves from** any kind of terrorist activity.* –**dissociation** /dɪˌsoʊsiˈeɪʃən, -ˌsoʊʃi-/ *n* [U]

**dis·so·lute** /ˈdɪsəˌlut/ *adj* FORMAL having bad or immoral habits: *a dissolute life*

**dis·so·lu·tion** /ˌdɪsəˈluʃən/ *n* [U] FORMAL the act of ending a marriage, business arrangement etc.

**dis·solve** /dɪˈzɑlv/ *v* **1** [I,T] to mix with a liquid and become part of it, or to make something do this: ***Dissolve** the tablets **in** warm water.* | *The aspirin dissolves quickly.* **2** [T] to end a marriage, business arrangement etc. **3** [I] to become weaker and disappear: *Our fears gradually dissolved.*

**dis·suade** /dɪˈsweɪd/ v [T] FORMAL to persuade someone not to do something: *a program to dissuade teenagers from drinking*

**dis·tance**[1] /ˈdɪstəns/ n **1** [C,U] the amount of space between two places or things: *What's the distance from Louisville to Memphis?* | *The church is still some distance* (=a fairly long distance) *away.* **2** [singular] a point or place that is far away, but close enough to be seen or heard: *The ruins look very impressive from a distance.* | *That's Long Island in the distance over there.* | *The Empire State Building is visible at a distance of several miles.* **3** within walking/driving distance near enough to walk or drive to: *The lake is within driving distance of my house.* **4** keep your distance to stay far away from someone or something: *Mark could see that the guy was drunk, so he kept his distance.* **5** keep sb at a distance to avoid telling someone your private thoughts or feelings: *We've known each other for years, but I've always felt she keeps me at a distance.* **6** [U] an amount of time between two events

**distance**[2] v distance yourself to say that you are not involved with someone or something, or to try to become less involved with someone or something: *Tony tried to distance himself from the company's position.*

**dis·tant** /ˈdɪstənt/ adj **1** far away from where you are now, or at a much different time than now: *the distant hills* | *the distant past* **2** unfriendly and showing no emotion: *Jeff's been kind of distant lately.* **3** not very closely related: *a distant cousin*

**dis·taste** /dɪsˈteɪst/ n [singular, U] a feeling of dislike for someone or something: *a distaste for office work*

**dis·taste·ful** /dɪsˈteɪstfəl/ adj very unpleasant or offensive: *I just want to forget the whole distasteful affair.* —distastefully adv

**dis·tend** /dɪˈstɛnd/ v [I,T] FORMAL to swell because of pressure from inside, or to make something do this: *His stomach was distended from lack of food.* —distension /dɪˈstɛnʃən/ n [U]

**dis·till** /dɪˈstɪl/ v [T] to heat a liquid so that it becomes a gas and then let it cool so that it becomes liquid again, in order to make it more pure or in order to make a strong alcoholic drink: *distilled water* —distillation /ˌdɪstəˈleɪʃən/ n [C,U]

**dis·till·er·y** /dɪˈstɪləri/ n a factory where alcoholic drinks are produced by DISTILLing

**dis·tinct** /dɪˈstɪŋkt/ adj **1** clearly different or separate: *The two types of monkeys are quite distinct from each other.* **2** clearly seen, heard, understood etc.: *There's a distinct possibility that we'll all lose our jobs.* —distinctly adv

**dis·tinc·tion** /dɪˈstɪŋkʃən/ n **1** a clear difference between things: *The school makes no distinction between male and female students.* (=the school does not treat male and female students differently) **2** a special honor given to someone: *Neil Armstrong had the distinction of being the first man on the moon.* **3** [U] the quality of being unusually good: *a poet of distinction*

**dis·tinc·tive** /dɪˈstɪŋktɪv/ adj clearly marking a person or thing as different from others: *Chris has a very distinctive laugh.* —distinctively adv —distinctiveness n [U]

**dis·tin·guish** /dɪˈstɪŋgwɪʃ/ v **1** [I,T] to recognize or understand the difference between two similar things, people etc.: *Young children often can't distinguish between TV programs and commercials.* **2** [T] to be able to see, hear, or taste something, even if it is difficult: *It was so noisy it was difficult to distinguish what he was saying.* **3** [T] to be the thing that makes someone or something different from other people or things: *The bright feathers distinguish the male peacock from the female.* **4** distinguish yourself to do something so well that people notice you, praise you, or remember you: *Eastwood distinguished himself as an actor before becoming a director.* —distinguishable adj

**dis·tin·guished** /dɪˈstɪŋgwɪʃt/ adj **1** very successful and therefore admired or respected: *a distinguished medical career* **2** looking important and successful: *a distinguished looking man* —opposite UNDISTINGUISHED

**dis·tort** /dɪˈstɔrt/ v [T] **1** to explain a fact, statement etc. so that it seems to mean something different from what it really means: *a reporter accused of distorting the facts* **2** to change the shape or sound of something so it is strange or unclear: *Bruno's face was distorted with rage.* —distorted adj —distortion /dɪˈstɔrʃən/ n [C,U]

**dis·tract** /dɪˈstrækt/ v [T] to make someone look at or listen to something when s/he should be giving attention to something else: *Don't distract me while I'm driving!*

**dis·tract·ed** /dɪˈstræktɪd/ adj anxious and not able to think clearly: *Laura seems distracted - she must be worried about her finals.*

**dis·trac·tion** /dɪˈstrækʃən/ n [C,U] something that takes your attention away from what you are doing: *I study in the library; there are too many distractions at home.*

**dis·traught** /dɪˈstrɔt/ adj extremely anxious or upset: *A policewoman was trying to calm the boy's distraught mother.*

**dis·tress**[1] /dɪˈstrɛs/ n [U] **1** a feeling of extreme worry and sadness: *Children suffer emotional distress when their parents divorce.* **2** a situation in which someone suffers because s/he does not have any money, food etc.: *money to help families in distress* **3** be in distress if a ship, plane etc. is in distress, it is in danger of sinking or crashing —distressed adj

**distress**² *v* [T] to make someone feel very worried or upset: *We were shocked and distressed to learn of Thomas's death.*

**dis·tress·ing** /dɪ'strɛsɪŋ/ *adj* making someone feel very worried or upset

**dis·trib·ute** /dɪ'strɪbyət/ *v* [T] **1** to give something such as food or medicine to each person in a large group: *The Red Cross is distributing food and clothing to the refugees.* **2** to supply goods to stores, companies etc. in a particular area. *Most of the steel is distributed by rail.*

**dis·tri·bu·tion** /ˌdɪstrə'byuʃən/ *n* [U] the act of giving something to each person in a large group, or supplying goods to stores, companies etc.: *the distribution of tickets for the concert*

**dis·tri·bu·tor** /dɪ'strɪbyətɚ/ *n* **1** a company or person that supplies goods to stores or other companies **2** a part of a car's engine that sends an electric current to the SPARK PLUGs

**dis·trict** /'dɪstrɪkt/ *n* a particular area of a city, country etc., especially an area officially divided from others: *the manufacturing district*

**district at·tor·ney** /ˌ.. .'../, **D.A.** *n* a lawyer who works for the government in a particular DISTRICT and brings criminals to court

**district court** /ˌ.. '../ *n* a court where people are judged in cases involving national rather than state law

**dis·trust**¹ /dɪs'trʌst/ *n* [U] a feeling that you cannot trust someone: *Many people regard politicians with distrust.* **–distrustful** *adj* **–distrustfully** *adv*

**distrust**² *v* [T] to not trust someone or something: *Do you have any reason to distrust Arnold?*

**dis·turb** /dɪ'stɚb/ *v* [T] **1** to interrupt what someone is doing by making a noise, asking a question etc.: *Try not to disturb other users of the library.* **2** to make someone feel worried or upset: *I was disturbed to hear that Don and Betty were getting divorced.*

**dis·turb·ance** /dɪ'stɚbəns/ *n* **1** [C,U] something that interrupts you so that you cannot continue what you are doing: *People are complaining about the disturbance caused by the work on the roads.* **2** a situation in which people fight or behave violently in public: *The police arrested three men for creating a disturbance at the bar.*

**dis·turbed** /dɪ'stɚbd/ *adj* not behaving in a normal way because of mental or emotional problems

**ditch**¹ /dɪtʃ/ *n* a long narrow hole in the ground for water to flow through, usually at the side of a field, road etc.

**ditch**² *v* [T] INFORMAL to get rid of something because you do not need it: *The bank robbers ditched the stolen car as soon as they could.*

**dith·er** /'dɪðɚ/ *v* [I] to be unable to make a decision: *He's been dithering about what to do.*

**dit·to**¹ /'dɪtoʊ/ *interjection* INFORMAL said when you agree with someone about something, or when something is the same as something else: *"I love pepperoni pizza!" "Ditto!"*

**ditto**² *n* a mark (") that you write beneath a word in a list so that you do not have to write the same word again

**dit·ty** /'dɪti/ *n* HUMOROUS a short simple song or poem

**dive**¹ /daɪv/ *v* **dived** *or* **dove, dived, diving** [I] **1** to jump into the water with your head and arms going in first: *Harry dived into the swimming pool.* **2** to swim under water using special equipment to help you breathe: *treasure hunters diving to look at the old shipwreck* **3** to go down through the air or water very quickly and suddenly: *birds swooping and diving in the air* **4** to jump forward or sideways quickly to catch something or to avoid something: *Ripken dived to his left and caught the ball.*

dive

**dive**² *n* **1** a jump into the water with your head and arms going in first **2** INFORMAL a place such as a BAR or a hotel that is cheap and dirty: *We ate at a dive out by the airport.*

**div·er** /'daɪvɚ/ *n* **1** someone who swims under water using special equipment to help him/her breathe: *a scuba diver* **2** someone who DIVEs into the water

**di·verge** /də'vɚdʒ, daɪ-/ *v* [I] to become separate or different, or to go in two different directions: *The new plan diverges considerably from the original one.* **–divergence** *n* [C,U] **–divergent** *adj* –opposite CONVERGE

**di·verse** /də'vɚs, daɪ-/ *adj* very different from each other: *New York is one of the most culturally diverse cities in the world.*

**di·ver·si·fy** /də'vɚsə,faɪ, daɪ-/ *v* [I,T] if a company diversifies, it begins to make new products or to become involved in new types of business in addition to what it already does: *They started as a computer company and then diversified into software.* **–diversification** /də,vɚsəfə'keɪʃən/ *n* [U]

**di·ver·sion** /də'vɚʒən, daɪ-/ *n* **1** [C,U] a change in the direction or purpose of something: *the illegal diversion of money from the project* **2** something that takes your attention away from what someone else is trying to do: *The prisoners created a diversion to allow the others time to escape.* **3** FORMAL an activity that you do for pleasure or amusement: *Fishing is a pleasant diversion.*

**di·ver·si·ty** /də'vɚsɪti, daɪ-/ *n* [C,U] a range of different people or things; variety: *the religious diversity of the US*

D

**di·vert** /dəˈvɚt, daɪ-/ v [T] **1** to change the direction or purpose of something: *Traffic is being diverted to avoid the accident.* **2 divert (sb's) attention from sth** to stop someone from paying attention to something: *The tragedy has diverted attention from the country's political problems.* **3** FORMAL to amuse or entertain someone: *a game to divert the children*

**di·vest** /dɪˈvɛst, daɪ-/ v

**divest** sb **of** sth phr v [T] FORMAL to take something away from someone

**di·vide** /dəˈvaɪd/ v **1** [I,T] to separate something, or to become separated, into two or more parts: *The class divided into groups.* | *Brenda's trying to divide her time between work and school.* **2** [T] to keep two areas separate from each other: *the long border dividing America from Canada* **3** [T] also **divide up** to separate something into two or more parts and share it among two or more people: *The money will be divided equally among his children.* **4** [I,T] to calculate how many times one number is contained in a larger number: *15 divided by 3 is 5.* **5** [T] to make people disagree and form groups with different opinions: *Congress is divided over whether to raise taxes or cut spending.*

**div·i·dend** /ˈdɪvəˌdɛnd, -dənd/ n **1** a part of a company's profit that is paid to people who have SHARES in the company **2 pay dividends** to get an advantage at a later time from something that you are doing now: *Studying hard at school will pay dividends when you apply for college.*

**di·vid·er** /dəˈvaɪdɚ/ n **1** something that divides something else into two or more parts: *the center divider on a road* **2** a stiff piece of paper used in order to keep other papers separate

**di·vine** /dəˈvaɪn/ adj having the qualities of God, or coming from God

**div·ing** /ˈdaɪvɪŋ/ n [U] the activity of jumping into water with your head and arms first

**diving board** /ˈ.. ˌ./ n a board above a SWIMMING POOL from which you can jump into the water

**di·vin·i·ty** /dəˈvɪnəti/ n **1** [U] the study of God and religious beliefs; THEOLOGY **2** [U] the quality of being like God **3** a male or female god

**di·vis·i·ble** /dəˈvɪzəbəl/ adj able to be divided, especially by another number: *15 is divisible by 3 and 5.*

**di·vi·sion** /dəˈvɪʒən/ n **1** [C,U] the act of dividing something into two or more parts or groups, or the way that it is divided: *the division of the students into groups for discussion* | *the division of the money between the government departments* **2** [C,U] a disagreement among members of a group: *strong divisions in the Republican party* **3** [U] the process of calculating how many times a small number will go into a larger number —compare MULTIPLICATION **4** a

group within a large company, army, organization etc.: *the finance division of the company*

**di·vi·sive** /dəˈvaɪsɪv, -ˈvɪs-/ adj causing a lot of disagreement among people: *Abortion is one of the most divisive issues in America.*

**di·vorce¹** /dəˈvɔrs/ n [C,U] the legal ending of a marriage: *She finally got a divorce after six years of unhappiness.* —divorced adj

**divorce²** v **1** [I,T] to legally end a marriage: *My parents got divorced when I was ten.* **2** to separate two ideas, values, organizations etc.: *Some of his ideas are completely divorced from reality.* (=not based on real experience or sensible thinking)

**di·vor·cée** /dəˌvɔrˈseɪ, -ˈsi/ n a woman who has legally ended her marriage

**di·vulge** /dəˈvʌldʒ, daɪ-/ v [T] to give someone information, especially about something that was secret: *Wolf refused to divulge the names of those who helped.*

**Dix·ie** /ˈdɪksi/ n INFORMAL the southern states of the US

**diz·zy** /ˈdɪzi/ adj **1** having a feeling of not being able to balance yourself, especially after spinning around or because you feel sick **2** HUMOROUS someone who is dizzy is silly or stupid —dizziness n [U]

**DJ** /ˈdi dʒeɪ/ n DISK JOCKEY; someone whose job is to play the music on a radio show or in a club where you can dance

**DNA** n [U] TECHNICAL deoxyribonucleic acid; an acid that carries GENETIC information in a cell

**do¹** /də; *strong* du/ *auxiliary verb*

| PRESENT TENSE | |
|---|---|
| singular | plural |
| I **do** | we **do** |
| you **do** | you **do** |
| he/she/it **does** | they **do** |

| PAST TENSE | |
|---|---|
| singular | plural |
| I **did** | we **did** |
| you **did** | you **did** |
| he/she/it **did** | they **did** |

| PAST PARTICIPLE | **done** |
|---|---|
| PRESENT PARTICIPLE | **doing** |
| NEGATIVE *short forms* | **don't, doesn't, didn't** |

**1** used with another verb to form questions or negatives: *Do you have a VCR?* | *What time does Linda usually go to bed?* | *Mark doesn't think he's going to get that job he applied for.* **2** SPOKEN used at the end of a sentence to make a question or to ask someone to agree with it: *That dress looks really nice on her, doesn't it?* **3** used in order to emphasize the main verb: *He hasn't been here in a while, but he does come to visit us most weekends.* **4** used in order to avoid repeating another verb: *"Go* *clean up your room." "I already did!" | "Craig really likes Thai food." "So do I." | "I didn't like the movie." "Neither did I." | Emilio speaks much better English than he did a year ago.*

**do²** /du/ *v* **1** [T] to perform an action or job: *Have you done your homework yet? | It's Jim's turn to do the dishes. | "What are you doing?" "Making cookies."* **2** [I] to make progress or be successful: *How is Jayne doing in her new job? | Neil has done well this year in his chemistry class.* **3** [T] to have a particular effect on something or someone: *The new car factory has done a lot for* (=had a good effect on) *the local economy. | Let's go to the beach. Come on, it will do you good.* (=make you feel better or happier) **4 do your hair/nails/makeup etc.** to spend time making your hair, nails etc. look good **5** [T] to travel at a particular speed or to travel a particular distance: *This car will do 0 to 60 miles per hour in six seconds.* **6** [I,T] to be suitable: *The recipe calls for butter, but margarine will do. | I wanted to get a new dress for the wedding, but my blue one will have to do.* (=be good enough, even though you would like something better) **7 what do you do (for a living)?** SPOKEN used in order to ask someone what his/her job is —see also **How are you (doing)?/How's it going?** (HOW), **how do you do?** (HOW) —see usage note at MAKE¹

**do away with** *phr v* [T] INFORMAL **1** [do away with sth] to get rid of something: *Some senators would like to do away with affirmative action laws.* **2** [do away with sb] to kill someone

**do** sb **in** *phr v* [T] INFORMAL **1** to make someone feel very tired: *That long walk did me in.* **2** to kill someone

**do** sth **over** *phr v* [T] to do something again, especially because you did it wrong the first time: *If there are mistakes, the teacher makes you do it over.*

**do with** sth *phr v* [T] **have/be to do with** to be about something, related to something, or involved in something: *The book has to do with new theories in physics. | Diane wanted nothing to do with the party for Sara.* (=she did not want to be involved at all) | *Jack's job is something to do with marketing.* (=related to marketing, but you are not sure exactly how)

---
SPOKEN PHRASES
---

**1 what has sb done with sth?** used in order to ask where someone has put something: *What have you done with the scissors?* **2 what sb does with himself/herself** the activities that someone does as a regular part of his/her life: *What is your dad doing with himself since he retired?* **3 what is sb doing with sth?** used in order to ask why someone has something: *What are you doing with my wallet?*

—see also **make do** (MAKE¹)

**do without** *phr v* **1** [I,T **do without** sth] to manage to continue living or doing something without having a particular thing: *It's almost impossible to do without a car in Los Angeles.* **2 can do without** SPOKEN used in order to say that something is annoying you or making it difficult for you: *I could do without all this hassle at work.*

---
**USAGE NOTE do**

If someone asks what you have **done to** something, you have probably changed it in some way: *What did you do to your hair?* However, if someone asks what you have **done with** something, s/he wants to know where it is: *What did you do with my book?* If someone asks what you **do**, s/he wants to know what kind of work you do: *"What do you do, Sally?" "I'm a doctor."* However, if s/he asks what you **are doing**, s/he wants to know what activity you are doing at that particular moment: *"What are you doing, Sally? "I'm making lunch."*

---

**do³** *n* **dos and don'ts** things that you should or should not do in a particular situation: *I'm still learning all the dos and don'ts of the job.*

**d.o.b.** the written abbreviation for date of birth (=the day you were born)

**do·ber·man pin·scher** /ˌdoubəʳmən ˈpɪntʃəʳ/, **doberman** *n* a large black and brown dog with very short hair, often used in order to guard property

**doc** /dɑk/ *n* SPOKEN ⇨ DOCTOR¹

**doc·ile** /ˈdɑsəl/ *adj* quiet and easy to control: *a docile animal*

**dock¹** /dɑk/ *n* a place where goods are put onto or taken off of ships or trucks

**dock²** *v* **1** if a ship docks or you dock it, you sail it into a DOCK **2 dock sb's pay** to reduce the amount of money that you pay someone: *If you come in late one more time, we'll have to dock your pay.*

**dock·et** /ˈdɑkɪt/ *n* **1** LAW a list of legal cases that will take place in a particular court **2** TECHNICAL a short document that shows what is in a package or describes goods that are being delivered

**doc·tor¹** /ˈdɑktəʳ/ *n* **1** someone whose job is to treat people who are sick: *You really should see a doctor about that cough.* **2** someone who has the highest level of degree given by a university: *a Doctor of Philosophy*

---
**USAGE NOTE doctor**

Use **Doctor** for both doctors and DENTISTs. **Physician** is a formal word for a medical doctor, while a **surgeon** is a medical doctor who can operate on you.

---

D

**doctor**[2] *v* [T] to change something, especially in a way that is not honest: *The police may have doctored the evidence.*

**doc·trine** /'daktrɪn/ *n* a belief or set of beliefs, especially religious or political beliefs: *the Christian* **doctrine** *of the Holy Trinity* −**doctrinal** *adj*

**doc·u·dra·ma** /'dakyə,dramə/ *n* a movie, usually for television, that is based on a true story

**doc·u·ment**[1] /'dakyəmənt/ *n* **1** a piece of paper that has official information written on it: *You'll need to sign a few legal documents.* **2** a piece of work that you write on a computer −**documentary** /,dakyə'mɛnʧəri, -'mɛntri/ *adj*

**doc·u·ment**[2] /'dakyə,mɛnt/ *v* [T] to write about something, photograph it etc. in order to have information that you can keep: *a TV program documenting the daily life of a teenage mother*

**doc·u·men·ta·ry** /,dakyə'mɛntri, -'mɛnʧəri/ *n* a movie or television program that gives facts and information on something: *a documentary about alcoholism*

**doc·u·men·ta·tion** /,dakyəmən'teɪʃən/ *n* [U] official documents that are used in order to prove that something is true or correct

**dodge**[1] /dadʒ/ *v* **1** [I,T] to move quickly in order to avoid someone or something: *dogs dodging in and out of city traffic* **2** [T] to avoid talking about something or doing something that you do not want to do: *Senator O'Brian skillfully dodged the reporter's question.*

**dodge**[2] *n* something dishonest you do in order to avoid a responsibility or law: *a tax dodge*

**doe** /doʊ/ *n* a female DEER

**does** /dəz, z, s; *strong* dʌz/ *v* the third person singular of the present tense of DO

**does·n't** /'dʌzənt/ *v* the short form of "does not": *The plant doesn't look healthy.*

**dog**[1] /dɔg/ *n* **1** a very common animal with four legs that is often kept as a pet or used for guarding buildings **2** OFFENSIVE an ugly woman **3** something that is not of good quality: *It was a dog of a movie.* **4** **dog eat dog** used when describing a situation in which people do anything they can to get what they want: *Advertising is a dog-eat-dog business.* −see also **top dog** (TOP[2])

**dog**[2] *v* **-gged**, **-gging** [T] if a problem or bad luck dogs you, it causes trouble for a long time: *Bad luck has dogged the team for the whole season.*

**dog-eared** /'. ./ *adj* dog-eared books have the corners of their pages folded or torn

**dog·ged** /'dɔgɪd/ *adj* determined to do something even though it is difficult: *Barry's dogged efforts to learn Greek.* −**doggedly** *adv*

**dog·gone** /,dɔ'gɔn‹/, **doggone it** *interjection* OLD-FASHIONED said when you are annoyed: *Doggone it, I said leave that alone!* −**doggone** *adj*

**dog·gy, doggie** /'dɔgi/ *n* a word meaning dog, used by or when speaking to young children

**doggy bag** /'.. ,./ *n* a small bag for taking home the food you did not eat from a meal at a restaurant

**doggy paddle** /'.. ,../ *n* ⇨ DOG PADDLE

**dog·house** /'dɔghaʊs/ *n* **1** **be in the doghouse** INFORMAL to be in a situation in which someone is angry or annoyed with you: *If Andy finds out I spent that money, I'll be in the doghouse.* **2** a little building for a dog to sleep in

**dog·ma** /'dɔgmə, 'dagmə/ *n* [C,U] an important belief or set of beliefs that people are supposed to accept without doubting them: *church dogma* | *political dogmas*

**dog·mat·ic** /dɔg'mæṭɪk, dag-/ *adj* having beliefs or ideas that you will not change and that you think other people should accept −**dogmatically** *adv*

**do-good·er** /'du ,gʊdɚ/ *n* INFORMAL someone who does things to help people who have less than s/he does, but who sometimes gets involved when s/he is not wanted

**dog pad·dle** /'. ,../ *n* [singular] INFORMAL a simple way of swimming that you do by moving your arms and legs like a swimming dog

**dog tag** /'. ./ *n* small piece of metal a soldier wears on a chain around his/her neck, with his/her name, blood type, and official number written on it

**dog·wood** /'dɔgwʊd/ *n* an eastern North American tree or bush with flat white or pink flowers

**do·ing** /'duɪŋ/ *n* **1** **be sb's (own) doing** to be someone's fault: *His bad luck was all his own doing.* **2** **take some doing** to be hard work: *Getting this old car to run is going to take some doing.*

**dol·drums** /'doʊldrəmz, 'dal-/ *n* [plural] INFORMAL **1** a state in which something is not improving or developing: *The building industry is temporarily in* **the doldrums**. **2** [plural] a state in which you feel sad; DEPRESSION: *Beat the post-Christmas doldrums - visit the Children's Museum.*

**dole** /doʊl/ *v*

**dole** sth ↔ **out** *phr v* [T] to give something such as money, food, advice etc. in small amounts to a lot of people: *people doling out candy on Halloween*

**dole·ful** /'doʊlfəl/ *adj* very sad: *She had such a doleful expression on her face.*

**doll** /dal/ *n* a child's toy that looks like a small person

**dol·lar** /'dalɚ/ *n* **1** the standard of money used in the US, Canada, Australia, New Zealand etc. Its sign is $ and it is worth 100 cents: *The company has a $7 million debt.* **2** a piece of paper money or a coin of this value

**dol·lop** /ˈdɑləp/ n a small amount of soft food, usually dropped from a spoon: *a dollop of whipped cream*

**dol·ly** /ˈdɑli/ n **1** SPOKEN a word meaning a DOLL, used when speaking to children **2** a flat frame on wheels, used for moving heavy objects

**dol·phin** /ˈdɑlfɪn, ˈdɔl-/ n a sea animal like a large gray fish with a long pointed nose

**do·main** /douˈmeɪn, də-/ n **1** the range of things that are included in a particular subject, type of art, or activity: *the domain of science fiction* **2** a particular place or activity that is controlled by one person or government: *In the past, politics has been mainly a male domain.*

**dome** /doum/ n a round curved roof on a building or room −**domed** adj

**dome**

**do·mes·tic** /dəˈmɛstɪk/ adj **1** happening within one country and not involving any other countries: *Canada's domestic affairs* **2** relating to family relationships and life at home: *a victim of **domestic violence*** (=violence between members of the same family) **3** someone who is domestic enjoys spending time at home and is good at cooking, cleaning etc.

**do·mes·ti·cat·ed** /dəˈmɛstɪˌkeɪṭɪd/ adj domesticated animals live with people as pets or work for them on a farm −**domesticate** v [T] −**domestication** /dəˌmɛstəˈkeɪʃən/ n [U] −compare TAME¹

**do·mes·tic·i·ty** /ˌdoumɛˈstɪsəṭi/ n [U] life at home with your family, or the state of enjoying this life

**dom·i·cile** /ˈdɑməˌsaɪl, ˈdou-/ n LAW the place where someone officially lives

**dom·i·nance** /ˈdɑmənəns/ n [U] great power, control, or importance: *the Soviet Union's past **dominance over/in** Eastern Europe*

**dom·i·nant** /ˈdɑmənənt/ adj **1** strongest, most important, or most noticeable: *TV news is the **dominant source** of information in our society.* **2** controlling other people or things, or showing this quality: *her husband's dominant behavior*

**dom·i·nate** /ˈdɑməˌneɪt/ v **1** [I,T] to have power and control over someone or something: *For sixty years France had dominated Europe.* **2** [I,T] to be the most important feature of something: *The murder trial has been dominating the news this week.* **3** [T] to be larger or more noticeable than anything else in a place or

situation: *A large wooden desk dominates the room.* | *Nursing used to be a profession dominated by women.* −**domination** /ˌdɑmə-ˈneɪʃən/ n [U]

**dom·i·neer·ing** /ˌdɑməˈnɪrɪŋ/ adj trying to control other people without considering how they feel or what they want: *his domineering father*

**do·min·ion** /dəˈmɪnyən/ n [U] the power or right to rule people

**dom·i·no** /ˈdɑməˌnou/ n, plural **dominoes** **1** a small piece of wood, plastic etc. with a different number of spots on each half of its top side, used in playing a game **2 the domino effect** a situation in which one event or action causes several other things to happen, one after the other

**dom·i·noes** /ˈdɑməˌnouz/ n [U] the game played using dominoes (DOMINO)

**do·nate** /ˈdouneɪt, douˈneɪt/ v [I,T] **1** to give something useful to a person or organization that needs help: *Our school **donated** $500 **to** the Red Cross.* **2 donate blood/organs etc.** to allow some of your blood or a part of your body to be used for medical purposes

**do·na·tion** /douˈneɪʃən/ n [C,U] something, especially money, that you give to help a person or organization: *Please **make a donation** to UNICEF.*

**done¹** /dʌn/ v the PAST PARTICIPLE of DO −see usage note at DO¹

**done²** adj **1** finished or completed: *The job's almost done.* **2** cooked enough to be eaten: *I think the hamburgers are done.* **3 done!** SPOKEN said in order to accept a deal that someone offers you: *"I'll give you $50 for it and that's my final offer." "Done!"* **4 be done for** INFORMAL to be in serious trouble or likely to fail: *If we get caught, we're done for.*

**don·key** /ˈdɑŋki, ˈdʌŋ-, ˈdɔŋ-/ n a gray or brown animal like a horse, but smaller and with longer ears

**do·nor** /ˈdounɚ/ n **1** a person, group etc. that gives something, especially money, in order to help an organization: *The Museum received $10,000 from an anonymous donor.* **2** someone who allows some of his/her blood or part of his/her body to be used for medical purposes

**don't** /dount/ v the short form of "do not": *I don't know how to ski.*

**do·nut** /ˈdounʌt/ n ⇨ DOUGHNUT

**doo·dad** /ˈdudæd/, **doo·hick·ey** /ˈduˌhɪki/ n INFORMAL a small object whose name you have forgotten or do not know: *What's this doodad for?*

**doo·dle** /ˈdudl/ v [I,T] to draw lines, shapes etc. without really thinking about what you are doing: *Stein was doodling on a napkin.* −**doodle** n

D

**doom**[1] /dum/ *n* [U] **1** destruction, death, or failure that you are unable to avoid: *a terrible sense of doom* **2 doom and gloom** HUMOROUS a state or attitude in which there is no hope for the future: *Chloe's always full of doom and gloom.*

**doom**[2] *v* [T] to make someone or something certain to fail, be destroyed, or die: *He was doomed to repeat the same mistakes his parents made.* **–doomed** *adj*

**dooms·day** /'dumzdeɪ/ *n* ⇨ JUDGMENT DAY

**door** /dɔr/ *n* **1** a large tall flat piece of wood, glass etc. that you push or pull in order to go into a building, room, car etc., or to open a piece of furniture: *Could someone please open/close/shut the door for me?* | *Don't forget to lock the front/back/side door.* | *How many times do I have to tell you not to slam the door?* (=shut it very hard) | *Did you hear someone knock on/at the door?* **2** the space made by an open door: *You just go out/through this door and turn right.* **3 next door** in the room, house etc. next to where you are: *the people who live next door* **4 at the door** if someone is at the door, s/he is waiting for you to open it **5 answer/get the door** to open the door to see who is there: *Mary, would you get the door?* **6 two/three etc. doors down** a particular number of rooms, houses etc. away from where you are: *Her office is just two doors down.* **7 show/see sb to the door** to walk with someone to the main door of a building **8 (from) door to door a)** between one place and another: *If you drive it should only take you 20 minutes door to door.* **b)** going to each house on a street to sell something, collect money etc.: *We went door to door asking people to sponsor us in the race.*

**door·bell** /'dɔrbɛl/ *n* a button by the door of a house that you press to make a sound so that the people inside know you are there

**door·knob** /'dɔrnɑb/ *n* a round handle that you turn to open a door

**door·man** /'dɔrmæn, -mən/ *n* a man who works in a hotel or apartment building watching the door, helping people find taxis etc.

**door·mat** /'dɔrmæt/ *n* **1** a thick piece of material just outside a door for you to clean your shoes on **2** INFORMAL someone who lets other people treat him/her badly and never complains

**door prize** /'. ./ *n* a prize given to someone who has the winning number on his/her ticket for a show, dance etc.

**door·step** /'dɔrstɛp/ *n* **1** a step just outside a door to a building **2 on your doorstep** very near to where you live or are staying: *Wow! You have the beach right on your doorstep!*

**door·stop** /'dɔrstɑp/ *n* something you put under or against a door to keep it open

**door·way** /'dɔrweɪ/ *n* the space where the door opens into a room or building

**dope**[1] /doʊp/ *n* INFORMAL **1** [U] a drug that is taken illegally for pleasure **2** a stupid person

**dope**[2], **dope up** *v* [I,T] INFORMAL to give a drug to a person or animal to make him, her, or it sleep, feel better, or work better: *athletes doping up to improve their performance* **–doping** *n* [U]

**dork** /dɔrk/ *n* INFORMAL someone who you think is silly or stupid because s/he behaves strangely or wears strange clothes: *I look like such a dork in that picture.* **–dorky** *adj*

**dorm** /dɔrm/ *n* INFORMAL a large building at a school or college where students live

**dor·mant** /'dɔrmənt/ *adj* not active or not producing any effects at the present time: *a dormant volcano* **–dormancy** /'dɔrmənsi/ *n* [U]

**dor·mi·to·ry** /'dɔrmə,tɔri/ *n* **1** a large room in a HOSTEL, CONVENT etc. with many beds in it **2** ⇨ DORM

**dor·sal** /'dɔrsəl/ *adj* TECHNICAL on or relating to the back of a fish or animal: *a whale's dorsal fin*

**DOS** /dɑs, dɔs/ *n* [U] TRADEMARK Disk Operating System; SOFTWARE used in a computer system to make all the different parts work together

**dose** /doʊs/ *n* **1** also **do·sage** /'doʊsɪdʒ/ a measured amount of medicine: *The average adult dose is 300 mg daily.* **2** the amount of something that you experience at one time: *I can only handle Jason in small doses.* (=for short amounts of time)

**dos·si·er** /'dɑsi,eɪ, 'dɔ-/ *n* a set of papers that include detailed information about someone or something: *The police keep dossiers on all their prisoners.*

**dot**[1] /dɑt/ *n* **1** a small round mark or spot: *The stars look like small dots of light in the sky.* **2 on the dot** exactly at a particular time: *Parry arrived at nine o'clock on the dot.*

**dot**[2] *v* **-tted, -tting** [T] **1** to mark something by putting a DOT on it or above it: *She never dots her "i's."* **2** to spread things over a wide area and fairly far apart: *We have over 20 stores dotted around the state.*

**dote** /doʊt/ *v*

**dote on** sb/sth *phr v* [T] to love and care about someone more than other people think you should: *Steve just dotes on his little grandson.* **–doting** *adj*

**dot·ted line** /,.. './ *n* a printed or drawn line made of a lot of DOTs: *Please sign on the dotted line.*

**dou·ble**[1] /'dʌbəl/ *adj* **1** twice the usual amount or size: *I'll have a double whiskey.* **2** having two parts that are exactly the same: *a double line* | *double doors* **3** intended to be used by two people: *a double room/bed* **–compare** SINGLE[1] **4 double meaning/nature etc.** two very different or opposite meanings, qualities, etc. that one thing has at the same time: *For years Jack had led a double life.* (=one part of his life was very different from the other)

**double**[2] *v* **1** [I] to become twice as large or twice as much: *Our house has **doubled in** value since we bought it.* **2** [T] to make something be twice as large or twice as much: *The new job will double my salary.*

**double as** sb/sth *phr v* [T] to have a second use, job, or purpose: *The sofa **doubles as** a bed.*

**double back** *phr v* [I] to turn around and go back in the direction you just came from: *I doubled back and headed south to Houston.*

**double up, double over** *phr v* [I] to suddenly bend at the waist because you are laughing too much or are in pain: *Greene **doubled over** from a kick to his stomach.*

**double**[3] *n* **1** [C,U] something that is twice the size, quantity, value, or strength of something else: *I'll have a whiskey please - make it a double.* **2** sb's **double** someone who looks very similar to someone else **3** on the **double** INFORMAL very soon or immediately: *I want that report here on the double!* –see also DOUBLES

**double**[4] *adv* **see double** to have a problem with your eyes so that you see two things instead of one

**double**[5] *determiner* twice as much or twice as many: *The car is worth double the amount we paid for it.*

**double bass** /ˌdʌbəl ˈbeɪs/ *n* a very large wooden musical instrument, shaped like a VIOLIN, that you play while standing up by pulling a special stick across wire strings

**double boil·er** /ˌ.. ˈ../ *n* a pot for cooking food, made of one pot resting on top of another pot that has hot water in it

**double-breast·ed** /ˌ.. ˈ..◂/ *adj* a double-breasted JACKET (=coat that has two rows of buttons on the front)

**double-check** /ˌ..ˈ./ *v* [T] to check something again to find out if it is safe, ready, correct etc.: *I think I turned off the oven, but let me go double check.*

**double chin** /ˌ.. ˈ./ *n* an additional fold of skin under someone's chin that looks like a second chin

**double-cross** /ˌ.. ˈ./ *v* [T] to cheat someone whom you have encouraged to trust you: *He was killed for double-crossing his Mob bosses.* –**double cross** *n*

**double date** /ˌ.. ˈ./ *n* an occasion in which two COUPLES meet to go to a movie, restaurant etc. together –**double-date** *v* [I,T]

**double du·ty** /ˌ.. ˈ../ *n* **do double duty** to do more than one job or be used for more than one purpose at the same time: *The lids on the pots do double duty as plates when we're camping.*

**double fea·ture** /ˌ.. ˈ../ *n* two movies that you watch for the price of a single ticket

**double-head·er** /ˌ.. ˈ../ *n* two baseball games that are played one after the other

**double-joint·ed** /ˌ.. ˈ..◂/ *adj* able to move the joints in your arms, fingers etc. backward as well as forward

**double-park** /ˌ.. ˈ./ *v* [I,T] to leave a car on the road beside another car that is already parked there: *I got a ticket for double-parking.* –**double-parking** *n* [U]

**dou·bles** /ˈdʌbəlz/ *n* [U] a tennis game played by two pairs of players

**double-spaced** /ˌ.. ˈ.◂/ *adj* a piece of writing that is double-spaced has a line of space between every line of writing

**double stand·ard** /ˌ.. ˈ../ *n* a rule or principle that is unfair because it treats one group or type of people more severely than another in the same situation: *There is a double standard that says men can want sex but women aren't supposed to.*

**double take** /ˈ.. ˌ./ *n* **do a double take** to suddenly look at someone or something again because you are surprised by what you originally saw or heard

**double talk** /ˈ.. ˌ./ *n* [U] INFORMAL speech that seems to be serious and sincere, but actually has another meaning or no meaning: *Don't be fooled by the double talk you'll get from the salesmen.*

**double vi·sion** /ˌ.. ˈ../ *n* [U] a medical condition in which you see two of everything

**double wham·my** /ˌdʌbəl ˈwæmi/ *n* INFORMAL two bad things that happen at the same time or one after the other

**dou·bly** /ˈdʌbli/ *adv* **1** twice as much: *doubly painful* **2** in two ways: *Rita was doubly distrusted, as a woman and as a foreigner.*

**doubt**[1] /daʊt/ *n* **1** the feeling of being unable to trust or believe in someone or something: *Dad's always **had** serious **doubts about** Meg's boyfriend.|He was **in doubt** about what he should do.|I have **no doubt that** (=I believe that) Marshall was speaking the truth.* **2** **no doubt** used when emphasizing that you think something is probably true: *No doubt he's married and has three kids by now.* **3** **without/beyond doubt** used in order to emphasize what you think is true: *Your mom is without a doubt the best cook this side of Texas!*

---

**USAGE NOTE** doubt

When you use the verb **doubt** in a simple statement, it can be followed by "that", "if," or "whether": *I doubt that the mail has arrived.* | *I doubt if/whether he's coming.* However, if the statement is negative, it can only be followed by "that": *We don't doubt that she can finish on time.* (=we know that she can do it) When you use the noun **doubt** after "no" or "not," it is always followed by "that": *There is no doubt that she is guilty.*

**doubt**² *v* [T] **1** to think that something may not be true or that it is unlikely: *I doubt (that) anyone was really paying attention.* **2** to not trust or believe in someone or something: *We doubted her willingness to help the group.*

**doubt·ful** /'daʊtˌfəl/ *adj* **1** probably not true or not likely to happen: *It's doubtful that we'll get to take a vacation this summer.* **2** unable to be trusted or believed. *his doubtful character* **3** feeling doubt: *Corrine believed him, but Henry was doubtful.* —**doubtfully** *adv*

**doubt·less** /'daʊtˌlɪs/ *adv* very likely: *Jim doubtless knew that he was going to be fired.*

**dough** /doʊ/ *n* [U] **1** a soft mixture of flour and water etc. that you bake to make bread or cookies **2** INFORMAL money

**dough·nut** /'doʊnʌt/ *n* a small round cake that is usually shaped like a ring

**dour** /'daʊɚ, dʊɚ/ *adj* very severe and not smiling: *a dour expression*

**douse** /daʊs/ *v* [T] to stop something burning by throwing water on it: *20 firefighters quickly doused the blaze.*

**dove**¹ /dʌv/ *n* a type of small white PIGEON (=bird) often used as a sign of peace

**dove**² /doʊv/ *v* a past tense of DIVE

**dow·dy** /'daʊdi/ *adj* a dowdy woman wears clothes that are old-fashioned or that are not attractive

**down**¹ /daʊn/ *adv* **1** from above a place or position toward a lower place or position: *She looked down at the street from her window.* | *The sun goes down about 5:00 in the winter.* **2** from a position in which someone or something is standing up to a position in which he, she, or it is lying flat or sitting: *Come in and sit down.* | *trees blown down by the big storm* **3** toward or in the south: *Gail drove down to North Carolina to see her brother.* **4** in a direction away from the person speaking: *Could you go down to the store and get some bread?* **5** SPOKEN used in order to emphasize where something is when it is in a different place from the person who is speaking: *I saw her earlier today down on Main Street.* **6** to a lower level of noise, strength, activity etc: *Can you turn the TV down? I'm on the phone.* | *Slow down! You're going too fast.* **7** to a level, state, or condition that is lower or worse than before: *Exports are down this year by 10%.* | *Everything in the store has been marked down.* (=given a lower price) **8** on paper, or in writing: *When you know the answer, write it down in the blank.* | *I have his number down somewhere.* **9** in a low place: *The cows are down in the valley.* —see also **come down with** (COME¹)

**down**² *adj* **1** sad: *I've never seen Bret looking so down.* **2** behind in a game by a particular number of points: *We were down by 6 points at half-time.* **3** not working or operating: *The computers were down this afternoon.* **4** SPOKEN

used in order to say that a particular number of things in a list are finished: *That's two down. Only two more to do.* **5** **be down on** SPOKEN to have a bad opinion of someone or something: *Why is Jerome so down on work?*

**down**³ *prep* **1** toward the ground or a lower point, or in a lower position: *The bathroom is down those stairs.* **2** along or toward the far end of something: *We walked down the beach as the sun rose.* | *They live down the road from us.* **3** **down the road/line** SPOKEN at some time in the future: *We'd like to have children sometime down the line.*

**down**⁴ *v* [T] to drink something very quickly: *Matt downed his coffee and left for work.*

**down**⁵ *n* [U] thin soft feathers or hair

**down-and-out** /ˌ. . '.◂/ *adj* having no luck or money

**down·cast** /'daʊnkæst/ *adj* sad or upset because something bad has happened: *Jason looked downcast as his mother left.*

**down·er** /'daʊnɚ/ *n* **1** [singular] SPOKEN an experience that makes you feel unhappy: *Failing my last exam was a real downer.* **2** INFORMAL a drug that makes you feel very relaxed or sleepy

**down·fall** /'daʊnfɔl/ *n* a sudden loss of money, power, social position etc., or something that leads to this: *Greed will be his downfall.*

**down·grade** /'daʊngreɪd/ *v* [T] to give someone a less important job, or to make something seem less important: *He may be downgraded to assistant manager.*

**down·heart·ed** /ˌdaʊn'hɑrtɪd◂/ *adj* be **downhearted** to feel sad about something

**down·hill**¹ /ˌdaʊn'hɪl/ *adv* **1** toward the bottom of a hill or toward lower land: *The truck's brakes failed, and it rolled downhill.* **2** **go downhill** to become worse: *After he lost his job, things went downhill.*

**downhill**² *adj* **1** on a slope that goes down to a lower point: *downhill skiing* **2** **be (all) downhill** to get worse : *We got three runs in the first inning, but it was all downhill from there.*

**down·load** /'daʊnloʊd/ *v* [T] to move information from one part of a computer system to another, or from one computer to another using a MODEM

**down pay·ment** /ˌ. '../ *n* the first payment you make on something expensive that you will pay for over a longer period: *a down payment on a car*

**down·play** /'daʊnpleɪ/ *v* [T] to make something seem less important than it really is: *Fred downplayed the seriousness of his illness.*

**down·pour** /'daʊnpɔr/ *n* a lot of rain that falls in a short time

**down·right** /'daʊnraɪt/ *adv* INFORMAL thoroughly and completely: *You're just downright lazy.*

**down·riv·er** /ˌdaʊn'rɪvɚ/ *adv* ⇨ DOWNSTREAM

**down·side** /'daʊnsaɪd/ *n* **the downside** the negative side of something: *The downside of the plan is the cost.*

**down·size** /'daʊnsaɪz/ *v* [I,T] to make a company smaller by reducing the number of people who work there —**downsizing** *n* [U]

**down·spout** /'daʊnspaʊt/ *n* a pipe that carries rain water away from the roof of a building —see picture on page 471

**Down's Syn·drome** /'. ,../ *n* [U] a condition that someone is born with that stops him/her from developing normally both mentally and physically

**down·stairs** /,daʊn'stɛrz/ *adv* **1** on or going toward a lower floor of a building, especially a house: *Run downstairs and answer the door.* **2 the downstairs** the rooms on the ground floor of a house: *Let's paint the downstairs blue.* —**downstairs** /'daʊnstɛrz/ *adj*: *the downstairs rooms* —opposite UPSTAIRS¹

**down·state** /,daʊn'steɪt‹/ *adj, adv* in or toward the southern part of a state: *He lives downstate, near the city.*

**down·stream** /,daʊn'strim/ *adv* in the direction the water in a river or stream flows —opposite UPSTREAM

**down·time** /'daʊntaɪm/ *n* [U] **1** the time when a computer is not working **2** INFORMAL time spent relaxing

**down-to-earth** /,. . '.‹ / *adj* practical and honest: *He liked her down-to-earth way of talking*

**down·town¹** /,daʊn'taʊn/ *n* [U] the business center of a city or town: *The university is 20 minutes from downtown.* | *downtown Phoenix* —**downtown** /'daʊntaʊn/ *adj*: *a downtown hotel*

**downtown²** *adv* to or in the business center of a city or town: *Do you work downtown?* | *We went downtown to eat and see a movie.*

**down·trod·den** /'daʊn,trɑdn/ *adj* LITERARY treated badly or without respect by people in positions of power

**down·turn** /'daʊntɚn/ *n* a time during which business activity is reduced and conditions become worse: *an economic downturn* | *a downturn in the number of product orders* —opposite UPTURN

**down·ward¹** /'daʊnwɚd/ **downwards** *adv* from a higher place or position to a lower one: *Tim pointed downward at his shoes.* —opposite UPWARD²

**downward²** *adj* going or moving down to a lower level or place: *a quick downward movement*

**down·wind** /,daʊn'wɪnd‹ / *adj, adv* in the same direction that the wind is moving

**down·y** /'daʊni/ *adj* having thin soft feathers or hair: *the baby's downy head*

**dow·ry** /'daʊri/ *n* money or property that women in some societies bring to their new husband from their families

**doze** /doʊz/ *v* [I] to sleep for a short time: *He dozed for an hour.*

**doze off** *phr v* [I] to fall asleep when you do not intend to do so: *I usually doze off watching TV.*

**doz·en** /'dʌzən/ *n* [determiner, n] **1** a group of 12 things: *a dozen eggs* **2 dozens (of)** INFORMAL a lot of something: *We looked at dozens of houses before we found this one.*

**Dr.** /'dɑktɚ/ the written abbreviation of Doctor

**drab** /dræb/ *adj* not bright in color, or not interesting: *a drab coat*

**dra·co·ni·an** /dræ'koʊniən/ *adj* FORMAL very strict and severe: *draconian laws*

**draft¹** /dræft/ *n* **1** a piece of writing, drawing etc. that is not yet in its finished form: *Make a draft of your paper first.* | *This is only a first draft.* **2 the draft** a system in which people must fight for their country when it is in a war **3** a current of air: *a draft coming through a crack in the walls* **4** a system in American sports in which PROFESSIONAL teams choose players from colleges for their teams: *He was chosen in the third round of the NFL draft this year.* **5** a written order for money to be paid by a bank

**draft²** *v* [T] **1** to write a plan, letter, report etc. that you will need to change before it is finished: *The House plans to draft a bill on education.* **2** to order someone to fight for his/her country during a war: *Jim was drafted into the army.*

**draft³** *adj* **1** not finished: *the draft treaty* **2** used for pulling loads: *a draft horse*

**draft beer** /,. './ beer that is fresh because it has not been kept in cans or bottles

**draft dodg·er** /'. ,../ *n* someone who illegally avoids joining the military service

**drafts·man** /'dræftsmən/, **drafts·wom·an** /'dræfts,wʊmən/ *n* someone whose job is to make detailed drawings of a building, machine etc.

**draft·y** /'dræfti/ *adj* with currents of air flowing through: *a drafty room*

**drag¹** /dræg/ *v* **-gged, -gging**

**drag**

**1** ▶PULL◀ [T] to pull someone or something heavy along the ground or away from somewhere: *Ben dragged his sled through the snow.* | *protestors dragged away by police*

**2** ▶GO SOMEWHERE◀ [T] to make someone go somewhere that s/he does not want to go: *Mom dragged us to a concert last night.*

**3 drag yourself away (from)** to stop doing something, although you do not want to: *Drag yourself away from the TV and come for a swim.*

**4** ▶BORING◀ [I] if time or an event drags, it is boring and seems to go very slowly: *Friday* *afternoons really drag.*

**5 ▶COMPUTER◀** [T] to move something on a computer screen by pulling it along with the MOUSE

**6 ▶TOUCHING GROUND◀** [I] if something is dragging along the ground, part of it is touching the ground as you move

**7 drag your feet** INFORMAL to take too much time to do something because you do not want to do it: *The police are being accused of dragging their feet on this case.*

**8 drag yourself up/over/along etc.** to move somewhere when it is difficult: *I dragged myself out of bed to call the doctor.*

**drag** sb/sth ↔ **into** *phr v* [T] to make someone get involved in a situation even though s/he does not want to: *I'm sorry to **drag** you **into** this mess.*

**drag on** *phr v* [I] to continue for too long: *The meeting **dragged on** all afternoon.*

**drag** sth ↔ **out** *phr v* [T] to make a situation or event last longer than necessary: *How long are you going to **drag** this discussion **out**?*

**drag²** *n* **1 a drag** INFORMAL something or someone that is boring or uninteresting: *"I have to stay home tonight." "What a drag."* **2 a drag on sth** someone or something that prevents someone from making progress: *Marriage would **be a drag on** my career.* **3** the act of breathing in smoke from your cigarette: *Al took **a drag on** his cigarette.* **4 in drag** INFORMAL a man who is in drag is wearing women's clothes

**drag·on** /ˈdrægən/ *n* a large imaginary animal that has wings, a long tail, and can breathe out fire

**drag·on·fly** /ˈdrægənˌflaɪ/ *n* a flying insect with a long brightly colored body

**drag race** /ˈ. ./ *n* a car race over a short distance

**drain¹** /dreɪn/ *v* **1 a)** [T] also **drain off** to make a liquid flow away from something: *They drained the water out of the lake.* | *Drain off the fat from the meat.* **b)** [I] if something drains, the liquid in it or on it flows away: *Let the pasta drain well.* **2** [T] to make someone feel very tired: *The argument drained me completely.* **3** [I] if the color drains from your face, you suddenly become pale **4** [T] to drink all the liquid in a glass, cup etc.: *Lori quickly drained her cup.*

**drain²** *n* **1** a pipe or hole that dirty water or other waste liquids DRAIN into: *The drain in the sink is blocked.* —see picture at CURB¹ **2 be a drain on sth** to use too much time, money etc.: *Doing a graduate degree has been a drain on Fran's savings.* **3 down the drain** INFORMAL wasted or having no result: *There's another $50 down the drain.*

**drain·age** /ˈdreɪnɪdʒ/ *n* [U] **1** a system of pipes or passages in the ground for carrying water or waste liquids: *drainage ditches* **2** the

process by which water or waste liquids flow through this system

**drained** /dreɪnd/ *adj* very tired: *I felt so drained after my parents left.*

**drain·er** /ˈdreɪnɚ/, **drain·board** /ˈdreɪnbɔrd/ *n* a flat area next to a SINK where you put dishes to dry

**dra·ma** /ˈdrɑmə, ˈdræmə/ *n* **1** a play for the theater, television, radio etc. **2** [U] the study of drama: *drama classes* **3** [C,U] an exciting and unusual situation or event: *the drama of a sea rescue*

**dra·mat·ic** /drəˈmætɪk/ *adj* **1** sudden and noticeable: *a dramatic change in temperature* **2** exciting and impressive: *a dramatic speech about the dangers of drugs* **3** related to the theater or plays: *Miller's dramatic works* **4** showing feelings in a way that makes other people notice you: *Don't be so dramatic.* —**dramatically** *adv*

**dra·mat·ics** /drəˈmætɪks/ *n* **1** [plural] behavior that shows a lot of feeling but is not sincere: *I'm really tired of your dramatics.* **2** [U] the study or practice of skills used in DRAMA, such as acting

**dram·a·tist** /ˈdræmətɪst, ˈdrɑ-/ *n* someone who writes plays, especially serious ones

**dram·a·tize** /ˈdræməˌtaɪz, ˈdrɑ-/ *v* **1** to make a book or event into a play: *a dramatized children's story* **2** to make an event seem more exciting than it really is: *The incident was dramatized by the newspaper.* —**dramatization** /ˌdræmətəˈzeɪʃən/ *n*

**drank** /dræŋk/ *v* the past tense of DRINK

**drape** /dreɪp/ *v* [T] to let something, especially cloth, hang or lie somewhere loosely: *a scarf draped over her shoulders* —see also DRAPES

**drap·er·y** /ˈdreɪpəri/ *n* [C,U] cloth or clothing that is arranged in folds over something

**drapes** /dreɪps/ *n* [plural] heavy curtains: *We need new drapes for the living room.*

**dras·tic** /ˈdræstɪk/ *adj* extreme, sudden, and often violent or severe: *The President promised drastic changes in health care.* —**drastically** *adv*

**draw¹** /drɔ/ *v* **drew, drawn, drawing** **1 ▶PICTURE◀** [I,T] to make a picture of something with a pencil or a pen: *Could you draw me a map?* | *He drew an elephant on the paper.* **2 draw (sb's) attention** to make someone notice something: *Because she's tall, Roz draws attention in a crowd.* | *I'd like to **draw** your **attention to** the six exit doors in the plane.* **3 draw a conclusion** to decide that something is true after thinking carefully about it: *It's difficult to **draw conclusions from** so little data.* **4 draw a distinction/comparison** to make someone understand that two things are different from or similar to each other: *We have to **draw**

*a distinction between* what is right and wrong for our children.

**5** ▶PULL SB/STH◀ [T] to make someone or something move by pulling him/her or it gently: *Grant drew me aside to tell me the news.*

**6 draw the curtains** to open or close the curtains

**7** ▶ATTRACT/INTEREST◀ [T] to attract or interest people: *"Batman Forever" drew large crowds on the first day. | What could have drawn Alex to drugs?*

**8** ▶TAKE CARD ETC.◀ [T] to take a playing card, piece of paper, number etc. from a group of other cards or papers: *Lotto numbers are drawn on Saturdays.*

**9 draw a blank** INFORMAL to be unable to think or remember something: *I drew a blank when I tried to remember the number.*

**10 drawn the line (at)** to refuse to do something because you do not approve of it: *I don't mind helping you, but I draw the line at telling lies.*

**11** ▶TAKE OUT◀ to remove something from its place or container: *Suddenly Ed drew a gun/knife. | She drew $50 out of the bank.*

**12 draw fire/criticism** to be criticized: *The company drew criticism for putting chemicals into the river.*

**13** ▶RECEIVE MONEY◀ [T] to receive an amount of money regularly from the government: *people drawing unemployment benefits*

**14 draw up/along/beside etc.** if a vehicle draws up etc., it moves near you: *A police car drew up behind me.*

**15 draw a check (on sth)** to write a check for taking money out of a bank: *a check drawn on a British bank*

**16** ▶LIQUID◀ [T] to take liquid from the place where it is contained, especially water, beer, or blood

**17 draw near/close** LITERARY to move closer in time or space: *Summer vacation is drawing near.*

**18** ▶PULL VEHICLE◀ [T] to pull a vehicle using an animal: *a carriage drawn by six horses*

**draw back** *phr v* [I] to move back from something: *The crowd drew back to let the police by.*

**draw sb ↔ into** *phr v* [T] to make someone become involved in something: *I let myself be drawn into the argument. | Keith refused to be drawn in during the argument.*

**draw on** *phr v* to use your money, experiences etc. to help you do something: *A good writer draws on his or her own experience.*

**draw up** *phr v* [T] to prepare a written document: *We drew up some guidelines for the new committee.*

**draw²** *n* **1** the act of taking a playing card, number etc.: *Come on, Doug, it's your draw. | the lottery draw* **2** something or someone that a lot of people are willing to pay to see: *The Lakers are always a big draw.* **3** ⇨ TIE²

**draw·back** /'drɔbæk/ *n* something that can cause trouble: *The big drawback to the plan is that it takes a long time.*

**draw·bridge** /'drɔbrɪdʒ/ *n* a bridge that can be pulled up to let ships go under it

**drawer** /drɔr/ *n* a part of a piece of furniture that slides in and out and is used for keeping things in: *The pens are in the top drawer of my desk.*

**draw·ing** /'drɔ-ɪŋ/ *n* **1** a picture you make with a pen, pencil etc.: *She showed us a drawing of the house.* **2** [U] the art or skill of making pictures with a pen, pencil etc.: *I've never been good at drawing.*

**drawing board** /'.. ,./ *n* **back to the drawing board** to start working on a plan or idea again after an idea you have tried has failed: *They rejected our proposal, so it's back to the drawing board.*

**drawl** /drɔl/ *n* [U] a way of speaking with vowels that are longer: *a Southern drawl* **–drawl** *v* [I,T]

**drawn¹** /drɔn/ *v* the PAST PARTICIPLE of DRAW

**drawn²** *adj* someone who is drawn has a thin pale face because s/he is sick or worried

**drawn-out** /ˌ. '.◂/ *adj* seeming to pass very slowly: *a long drawn-out speech*

**draw·string** /'drɔstrɪŋ/ *n* a string through the top of a bag, piece of clothing etc. that you can pull tight or make loose

**dread¹** /drɛd/ *v* [T] to feel very worried about something: *Jill's really dreading her interview. | I dread going to the dentist tomorrow.*

**dread²** *n* [U] a strong fear of something that may or will happen

**dread·ful** /'drɛdfəl/ *adj* very bad: *a dreadful movie* **–dreadfully** *adv*

**dread·locks** /'drɛdlɑks/ *n* [plural] a way of arranging your hair in which it hangs in lots of thick pieces that look like rope

**dream¹** /drim/ *n* **1** a series of thoughts, pictures, and feelings you have when you are asleep: *I had a funny dream last night.* **2 beyond your wildest dreams** better than anything you imagined or hoped for **3 a dream come true** something that you have wanted to happen for a long time: *Owning this boat is a dream come true.*

**dream²** *v* **dreamed** *or* **dreamt** /drɛmt/, **dreamed** *or* **dreamt, dreaming** **1** [I,T] to think about something that you would like to happen: *She dreamed about/of becoming a pilot.* **2** [I,T] to have a dream while you are asleep: *I often dream that I'm falling.* **3 dream on** SPOKEN said when you think that what someone is hoping for will not happen: *You really believe we'll win? Dream on!*

**dream sth ↔ up** *phr v* [T] to think of a plan or idea, especially an unusual one: *Who dreams up these TV commercials?*

**dream³** *adj* the best you can imagine: *A Porsche is my dream car.*

**dream·er** /'drimɚ/ *n* someone who has plans that are not practical

**dream·y** /'drimi/ *adj* **1** someone who is dreamy likes to imagine things **2** like something in a dream, or like you are imagining something: *a dreamy look* **3** pleasant, peaceful, and relaxing: *dreamy music* **–dreamily** *adv*

**drear·y** /'drɪri/ *adj* dull and uninteresting: *a dreary afternoon of rain* **–drearily** *adv* **–dreariness** *n* [U]

**dredge** /drɛdʒ/ *v* [I,T] to remove mud or sand from the bottom of a river

**dredge** sth ↔ **up** *phr v* [T] INFORMAL **1** to start talking about something that happened a long time ago: *Why do the papers have to **dredge up** that old story?* **2** to pull something up from the bottom of a river

**dredg·er** /'drɛdʒɚ/ **dredge** *n* a machine or ship used for removing mud or sand from the bottom of a river, lake etc.

**dregs** /drɛgz/ *n* [plural] **1** small solid pieces in a liquid, that sink to the bottom: *coffee dregs* **2 the dregs of society** OFFENSIVE people that you think are the least important or useful

**drench** /drɛntʃ/ *v* [T] to make something completely wet: *I forgot my umbrella and got drenched.*

**dress¹** /drɛs/ *v* **1** [I,T] to put clothes on someone or yourself: *Hurry up and get dressed! | Can you dress the kids while I make breakfast?* **2** [I] to wear a particular type of clothes: *Dress warmly; it's cold out. | teenagers **dressed in** black* **3 dress a wound/cut etc.** to clean and cover a wound to protect it

Sarah's going trick or treating dressed up as a witch.

**dress down** *phr v* [I] to wear clothes that are more informal than you usually wear

**dress up** *phr v* **1** [I] to wear clothes that are more formal than you usually wear: *Should we **dress up** to go to the club?* **2** [I,T **dress** sb ↔ **up**] to wear special clothes, shoes etc. for fun: *She **dressed up** as a witch for Halloween. | old clothes for the kids to **dress up** in*

---

**USAGE NOTE dress, put on, and wear**

Use **dress** to mean "put on clothes" or "wear a particular type of clothes": *David dressed quickly. | She always dresses fashionably.* If you **put on** a piece of clothing, you dress yourself in that thing: *You'd better put on your sweater before going out.* Use **wear** to mean that you have something on your body: *Is that a new shirt you're wearing?*

---

**dress²** *n* **1** a piece of clothing worn by a woman or girl, that covers the top of her body and some or all of her legs: *Do you like my new dress?* –see picture at CLOTHES **2 casual/informal dress** clothes that are not formal in style: *It's casual dress for dinner tonight.* **3 evening/national etc. dress** special clothes that you wear for a particular occasion

**dress³** *adj* used for formal occasions: *a dress shirt*

**dress code** /'. ./ *n* a standard of what you should wear for a particular situation: *The company has a strict dress code.*

**dress·er** /'drɛsɚ/ *n* ⇨ CHEST OF DRAWERS

**dress·ing** /'drɛsɪŋ/ *n* **1** [C,U] a mixture of liquids that you can pour over food: *salad dressing* **2** [C,U] ⇨ STUFFING **3** a special piece of material used for covering and protecting a wound: *a clean dressing for the cut*

**dressing room** /'.. ˌ./ *n* a room where an actor gets ready to act on stage, on TV etc.

**dress·mak·er** /'drɛsˌmeɪkɚ/ *n* ⇨ SEAMSTRESS

**dress re·hear·sal** /'. .ˌ../ *n* the last time actors practice a play, using all the clothes, objects etc. that will be used in the real performance

**dress sense** /'. ./ *n* [U] the ability to choose clothes that make you look attractive

**dress·y** /'drɛsi/ *adj* suitable for formal occasions: *a dressy skirt*

**drew** /dru/ *v* the past tense of DRAW

**drib·ble** /'drɪbəl/ *v* **1** [I] if liquid dribbles, it comes out of something in a thin irregular stream: *Ice cream **dribbled from** his mouth.* **2** [T] to move a ball forward by bouncing (BOUNCE) or kicking it again and again **–dribble** *n*

**dribs and drabs** /ˌdrɪbz ən 'dræbs/ *n* [plural] **in dribs and drabs** in small irregular amounts over a period of time: *News is coming in dribs and drabs.*

**dried¹** /draɪd/ *v* the past tense and PAST PARTICIPLE of DRY

**dried²** *adj* dried food or flowers have had all the water removed from them

**drift¹** /drɪft/ *v* [I] **1** to move very slowly through the air or on the surface of water: *We watched their boat drift along the shore.* **2** to move or go somewhere without any plan or purpose: *Julie stood up and drifted towards the window.* **3** to gradually change from being in one condition, situation etc. into another: *During the ambulance ride he drifted in and out of consciousness.* **4** snow or sand that drifts is moved into a large pile by the wind

**drift apart** *phr v* [I] if people drift apart, they gradually stop having a relationship: *Over the years my college friends and I have **drifted apart**.*

**drift**[2] *n* **1** a large pile of snow, sand etc. that has been blown by the wind: *All the roads in Lake Tahoe were blocked with snow drifts.* **2 catch/get sb's drift** to understand the general meaning of what someone says: *I don't speak Spanish very well but I think I got her drift.* **3** a gradual change or development in a situation, people's opinion etc.: *a long downward drift in the birth rate* **4** a very slow movement: *the drift of the continents away from each other*

**drift·er** /'drɪftɚ/ *n* someone who is always moving to a different place or doing different jobs

**drift·wood** /'drɪftwʊd/ *n* [U] wood floating in the ocean or left on the shore

**drill**[1] /drɪl/ *n* **1** a tool or machine used for making holes in something hard: *an electric drill* | *a dentist's drill* **2** [C,U] a method of teaching something by making students or soldiers repeat the same lesson, exercise etc. many times: *a spelling drill* **3 fire/ emergency etc. drill** an occasion when you practice what you should do during a dangerous situation: *We had a tornado drill at school yesterday.*

**drill**[2] *v* **1** [I,T] to make a hole with a drill: *We'll have to drill some holes in the wall to put up the shelves.* | *drilling for oil in Texas* **2** [T] to teach soldiers or students something by repeating the same exercise, lesson etc. many times

**drill** sth **into** sb *phr v* [T] to continue telling something to someone until s/he knows it very well: *Momma* **drilled into** *my head that I should never talk to strangers.*

**dri·ly** /'draɪli/ *adv* ⇨ DRYLY

**drink**[1] /drɪŋk/ *n* **1** [C,U] liquid that you can drink, or an amount of liquid that you drink: *Could I have a drink of water please?* | *food and drink* **2** an alcoholic drink: *Let's go find a quiet bar and have a drink.*

**drink**[2] *v* **drank, drunk, drunking** **1** [I,T] to pour a liquid into your mouth and swallow it: *What would you like to drink?* | *Charlie drinks way too much coffee.* **2** [I] to drink alcohol, especially too much or too often: *"Whiskey?" "No, thanks, I don't drink."*

**drink** sth ↔ **in** *phr v* [T] to listen, look at, feel, or smell something in order to enjoy it: *We spent the day* **drinking in** *the sights and sounds of Paris.*

**drink to** sth *phr v* [T] to wish someone success, good health etc. before having an alcoholic drink: *Let's all* **drink to** *their happiness as a married couple!*

**drink·er** /'drɪŋkɚ/ *n* someone who often drinks alcohol: *Greg's always been a* **heavy drinker.** (=has always drunk a lot)

**drink·ing foun·tain** /'.. ,../ *n* a piece of equip-ment in a public place that produces a stream of water for you to drink from

**drinking prob·lem** /'.. ,../ *n* [singular] some-one who has a drinking problem drinks too much alcohol

**drip**[1] /drɪp/ *v* **-pped, -pping** **1** [I] to produce small drops of liquid: *Did you turn off the faucet? It sounds like it's still drip-ping.* | *a brush* **dripping with** *paint* **2** [I,T] to fall in the shape of a small drop, or have something falling in small drops: *Sweat was dripping off his arms.* | *Her finger was dripping blood.*

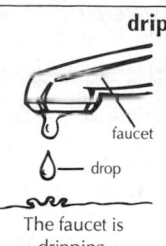
drip

faucet
drop

The faucet is dripping.

D

**drip**[2] *n* **1** one of the small drops of liquid that falls from something **2** [singular, U] the action or sound of a liquid falling in small drops: *the drip of rain from the roof* **3** INFORMAL someone who is boring and annoying

**drip-dry** /,. '../ *adj* clothes that are drip-dry do not need to be IRONed

**drive**[1] /draɪv/ *v* **drove, driven, driving** **1** [I,T] to make a car, bus etc. move and con-trol where it goes: *I can't drive.* | *Farrah drives a red Porsche.* **2** [I,T] to travel in a car or take someone somewhere by car: *We're* **driving up/ down** *to Washington this weekend.* | *Would you mind driving me to the airport?* **3** [T] to make people, animals, or an activity move some-where: *Our party was driven indoors by the heavy rain.* | *The gang activity drove business away from the town.* **4** [T] to strongly in-fluence someone to do something:* **Driven by** *jealousy, Mel decided to read his girlfriend's diary.* **5 drive sb crazy/nuts/insane etc.** to make someone feel very annoyed and angry: *The kids are driving me crazy!* **6 drive sb up the wall** SPOKEN to make someone extremely annoyed: *All the barking is driving me up the wall!* **7** [T] to hit something very hard: *driving a nail into the wall*

**drive** sb ↔ **away** *phr v* [T] to behave in a way that makes someone want to leave you: *If you keep on drinking I guarantee you'll* **drive** *her* **away.**

**drive off** *phr v* **1** [I] if a driver or a car drives off then he, she, or it leaves **2** [I,T **drive** sb ↔ **off**] to force someone or something to go away from you: *The army used tear gas to* **drive off** *the rioting crowds.*

**drive** sth ↔ **up** *phr v* [T] to make prices, costs etc. increase: *The price of gasoline was* **driven up** *by at least 5% during the Gulf War.*

**drive**[2] *n* **1** a trip in a car: *Let's* **go for a drive.** | *Our house is just a twenty minute drive from the city.* **2** a strong natural need, such as hunger, that people or animals must satisfy: *the* **male sex drive** **3** a planned effort by an orga-nization to achieve a particular result: *an*

**D**

*economy/efficiency drive* **4** [U] a determination to succeed: *I've never met anyone who has as much drive as he has.* **5** the power from an engine that makes the wheels of a car, bus etc. turn: *a four-wheel drive pickup*

**drive-by** /'. ./ *adj* **drive-by shooting/killing** the act of shooting someone from a moving car

**drive-in**[1] /'. ./ *n* a place where you can watch movies outdoors while sitting in your car

**drive-in**[2] *adj* **drive-in restaurant/bank/movie** a restaurant etc. where you stay in your car to be served

**driv·el** /'drɪvəl/ *n* [U] something written or said that is silly or does not mean anything: *Walter was **talking** complete **drivel**.*

**driv·en** /'drɪvən/ the PAST PARTICIPLE of DRIVE

**driv·er** /'draɪvɚ/ *n* someone who drives

**driver's li·cense** /'.. ,../ *n* a official card with your name, picture etc. on it that says you are legally allowed to drive

**drive-through** /'. ./ *adj* a drive-through restaurant, bank etc. can be used without getting out of your car: *We ordered food at the drive-through window.*

**drive·way** /'draɪvweɪ/ *n* the road or area for cars between a house and the street – see picture on page 471

**driz·zle**[1] /'drɪzəl/ *n* [singular, U] weather that is a combination of mist and light rain – see usage note at WEATHER

**drizzle**[2] *v* **it drizzles** if it drizzles, mist and light rain come out of the sky: *It started to drizzle.*

**droll** /droʊl/ *adj* OLD-FASHIONED unusual and slightly funny

**drone**[1] /droʊn/ *v* [I] to make a continuous low noise: *An airplane droned overhead.*

 **drone on** *phr v* [I] to talk in a boring way for a long time: *The Principal **droned on** about his plans for our school.*

**drone**[2] *n* a low continuous noise: *the drone of the lawnmower*

**drool** /drul/ *v* [I] **1** to have SALIVA (=the liquid in your mouth) flow from your mouth: *At the sight of food the dog began to drool.* **2** to show in a silly way that you like someone or something a lot: *Sarah was **drooling over** the lead singer through the whole concert!*

**droop** /drup/ *v* [I] to hang or bend down: *Can you water the plants - they're starting to droop.*

**drop**[1] /drɑp/ *v* **-pped, -pping**

**1** ▶LET GO◀ [T] to suddenly or accidentally let go of something you are holding or carrying, so that it falls: *One of the waiters tripped and dropped a tray full of food.*

**2** ▶FALL◀ [I] to fall: *The bottle rolled off the table and dropped onto the floor.* | *He dropped into his chair with a sigh.*

**3** ▶TAKE IN A CAR◀ [T] also **drop off** to take someone or something to a place in a car, when you are going on to somewhere else: *I'll drop you at the corner, okay?* | *She drops the kids off at school on her way to work.*

**4 drop by/in** to visit someone when you have not arranged to come at a particular time: *Doris and Ed dropped by on Saturday.*

**5** ▶DECREASE◀ [I] to decrease to a lower level or amount: *The price of wheat dropped steadily during the late 1920s.*

**6** ▶STOP DOING STH◀ [T] to stop doing something or stop planning to do something: *We've **dropped the idea** of going by plane.* | *At the sound of the alarm, the men **dropped everything** (=stopped everything they were doing) and ran for safety.* | *I wasn't doing very well, so I decided to **drop French**.* (=stop studying French)

**7** ▶STOP INCLUDING◀ [T] to decide not to include someone or something: *Morris has been dropped from the team.*

**8** ▶STOP TALKING◀ [T] to stop talking about something, especially because it is upsetting someone: *She didn't understand, so I **let it drop**.* | ***Drop it**, man, it's just a rumor.*

**9** ▶STOP RELATIONSHIP◀ [T] to stop having a relationship with someone, especially suddenly: *Marian has dropped all her old friends since she started college.*

**10 drop dead a)** to die suddenly and unexpectedly **b)** SPOKEN used in order to tell someone to be quiet, stop annoying you etc., in an angry way

**11 work/run etc. until you drop** INFORMAL to do something until you are extremely tired

**12 drop sb a line** INFORMAL to write to someone: *Drop us a line sometime.*

**13 drop a hint** to say something in a way that is not direct: *I've dropped a few hints about what I want for my birthday.*

**14 be dropping like flies** INFORMAL used in order to say that a lot of people are getting sick with the same illness – see also **drop/lower your eyes** (EYE[1])

 **drop off** *phr v* [I] **1** to begin to sleep: *The baby **dropped off** to sleep in the car.* **2** to become less in level or amount: *The demand for leaded fuel **dropped off** in the late 1970s.*

 **drop out** *phr v* [I] to stop going to school or stop an activity before you have finished it: *teenagers **dropping out** of high school* | *The injury forced him to **drop out** of the race.*

**drop**[2] *n* **1** a very small amount of liquid that falls in a round shape: *Big drops of rain splashed on the sidewalk.* | *a tear drop* – see picture at DRIP[1] **2** a small amount of a liquid: *Add a couple drops of lemon juice.* **3** [singular] a distance from something down to the ground: *It's a twenty-five foot drop from this cliff.* **4** [singular] a decrease in the amount, level, or number of something: *a drop from 72% to 34%* **5 a drop in the ocean/bucket** an amount of something that is too small to have any effect – see also DROPS

**drop·out** /ˈdrɑp-aʊt/ *n* someone who leaves school or college without finishing it

**drop·per** /ˈdrɑpɚ/ *n* a short glass tube with a hollow rubber part at one end, used for measuring liquid in drops

**drop·pings** /ˈdrɑpɪŋz/ *n* [plural] solid waste from animals or birds

**drops** /drɑps/ *n* [plural] **eye/ear/nose drops** medicine that you put in your eye etc. in drops

**drought** /draʊt/ *n* a long period of dry weather when there is not enough water: *In the sixth year of drought more than half the corn crop was lost.* −see usage note at WEATHER

**drove¹** /droʊv/ the past tense of DRIVE

**drove²** *n* a large group of animals or people that move or are moved together: *Tourists come in droves to see the White House.* | *a drove of cattle*

**drown** /draʊn/ *v* **1** [I,T] to die by being under water too long, or to kill someone in this way: *Two surfers drowned near Santa Cruz yesterday.* | *Five people were drowned in the flood.* **2** [T] also **drown out** to prevent a sound from being heard by making a louder noise: *We put on some music to drown out their yelling.* **3** [T] to completely cover something with liquid: *Dad always drowns his pancakes in/with maple syrup.* **4 drown your sorrows** to drink a lot of alcohol in order to forget your problems

**drown·ing** /ˈdraʊnɪŋ/ *n* [C,U] death caused by staying under water too long: *a fear of drowning* | *accidental drowning*

**drows·y** /ˈdraʊzi/ *adj* tired and almost asleep: *The doctor said the pills might make me feel drowsy.* −**drowsiness** *n* [U]

**drudge** /drʌdʒ/ *n* someone who does difficult boring work −**drudge** *v* [I]

**drudg·er·y** /ˈdrʌdʒəri/ *n* [U] difficult boring work

**drug¹** /drʌg/ *n* **1** an illegal substance that people smoke, INJECT etc. for pleasure: *Bill was accused of taking/using drugs.* | *My mom thinks I'm on drugs.* (=using drugs regularly) | *Dave's been doing drugs* (=using drugs regularly) *since he was thirteen.* | *the problem of drug abuse* (=the use of illegal drugs) | *drug dealing* (=selling illegal drugs) *in the neighborhood* | *He was sent to prison for selling hard drugs.* (=dangerous illegal drugs such as HEROIN and COCAINE) **2** a medicine or a substance for making medicines: *She's on some kind of drug for her depression.*

**drug²** *v* **-gged, -gging** [T] to put drugs into someone's body, usually to prevent him/her from moving or from feeling pain: *A man has been arrested for drugging and strangling 14 victims.*

**drug·store** /ˈdrʌgstɔr/ *n* a store where you can buy medicines, beauty products etc.; PHARMACY

**drum¹** /drʌm/ *n* **1** a musical instrument made of skin stretched over a circular frame, which you play by hitting it with your hand or a stick: *Fred plays guitar and I play the drums.* (=a set of drums) **2** something that looks like a drum, especially part of a machine **3** a large round container for storing liquids such as oil, chemicals etc.

**drum²** *v* **-mmed, -mming** [I,T] to hit the surface of something again and again in a way that sounds like drums: *He drummed his fingers on the table.* | *rain drumming on the roof*

**drum sth into sb** *phr v* [T] to say something to someone so often that s/he cannot forget it: *Patriotism was drummed into us at school.*

**drum sb out of sth** *phr v* [T] to force someone to leave an organization: *soldiers drummed out of the military*

**drum sth ↔ up** *phr v* [T] to obtain help, money etc. by asking a lot of people: *a group drumming up support for the "Save the Whales" campaign*

**drum·mer** /ˈdrʌmɚ/ *n* someone who plays the drums

**drum·stick** /ˈdrʌmˌstɪk/ *n* **1** the leg of a chicken, TURKEY etc., cooked as food **2** a stick that you use to hit a drum

**drunk¹** /drʌŋk/ *adj* unable to control your behavior, speech etc. because you have drunk too much alcohol: *We got totally drunk at Sue's party.*

**drunk²** the PAST PARTICIPLE of DRINK

**drunk³, drunk·ard** /ˈdrʌŋkɚd/ *n* DISAPPROVING someone who is drunk or often gets drunk

**drunk·en** /ˈdrʌŋkən/ *adj* **1** drunk: *a drunken crowd* **2** resulting from or related to drinking too much alcohol: *drunken shouting* −**drunkenness** *n* [U] −**drunkenly** *adv*

**dry¹** /draɪ/ *adj* **1** having no water or other liquid inside or on the surface; not wet: *Can you check and see if the laundry's dry yet?* | *dry dusty ground* **2** dry weather does not have much rain or MOISTURE: *The weather tomorrow will be cold, dry, and sunny.* | *March was a really dry month.* **3** if your mouth, throat, or skin is dry, it does not have enough of the natural liquid that is usually in it: *Do you have any lotion? My skin's really dry.* **4 dry wine/champagne etc.** wine etc. that is not sweet: *a glass of dry white wine* **5** humor or a voice that is dry says funny things in a serious way

**dry²** *v* **dried, dried, drying** [I,T] to become dry, or to make something do this: *It'll only take me a few minutes to dry my hair.*

**dry off** *phr v* [I,T] to become dry, or to make the surface of something dry: *The kids played in the ocean and then dried off in the sun.*

**dry out** *phr v* [I,T **dry sth ↔ out**] to dry completely, or to dry something completely: *Keep the dough covered so that it doesn't dry out.*

D

**dry up** *phr v* **1** [I,T] a river, lake, or area of land that dries up has no more water in it: *During the drought all the reservoirs dried up.* **2** [I] if a supply of something dries up, there is no more of it: *Our research project was canceled when the money dried up.*

**dry clean** /'. ./ *v* [T] to clean clothes with chemicals instead of water

**dry clean·ers** /ˌ. '.., ˌ. ˌ../ *n* a place where you take clothes to be DRY CLEANed

**dry·er** /'draɪɚ/ *n* a machine that dries things, especially clothes or hair

**dry goods** /'. ./ *n* [plural] things that are made from cloth, such as clothes, sheets, and curtains

**dry ice** /ˌ. './ *n* [U] CARBON DIOXIDE in a solid state, often used for keeping food and other things cold

**dry·ly** /'draɪli/ *adv* speaking in a serious way, although you are actually joking

**dry run** /ˌ. './ *n* an occasion when you practice for an important event

**du·al** /'duəl/ *adj* having two of something, or two parts: *My wife has dual nationality; her parents are Brazilian but she was born in the States.*

**dub** /dʌb/ *v* **-bbed, -bbing** [T] **1** to replace the original sound recording of a film, television show etc. with another sound recording: *They're showing an Italian movie that's been dubbed into English.* **2** to give someone or something a humorous name that describes his, her, or its character: *We dubbed our star quarterback "The King."*

**du·bi·ous** /'dubiəs/ *adj* **1** be dubious to have doubts about whether something is good, true etc.: *Your father and I are a little dubious about your getting married so young.* **2** not seeming honest, safe, valuable etc.: *a dubious partnership*

**duch·ess** /'dʌtʃɪs/ *n* a woman with the highest social rank below a PRINCESS, or the wife of a DUKE

**duck¹** /dʌk/ *n* **1** a common water bird with short legs and a wide beak that is used for its meat, eggs, and soft feathers **2** [U] the meat from this bird: *roast duck*

**duck²** *v* **1** [I,T] to lower your body or head very quickly, especially to avoid being hit or seen: *She had to duck her head to get through the doorway.* **2** [T] INFORMAL to avoid something that is difficult or unpleasant: *His campaign speech ducked all the major issues.* **3** [T] to push someone or something under water: *Doug ducked his head in the stream to cool off.*

**duck·ling** /'dʌklɪŋ/ *n* a young duck

**duct** /dʌkt/ *n* **1** a pipe or tube in a building that liquid, air, electric CABLEs etc. go through **2** a thin narrow tube inside your body, a plant etc. that liquid, air etc. goes through: *a tear duct*

**dud** /dʌd/ *adj* INFORMAL not working or useless: *a couple of dud batteries* **–dud** *n* –see also DUDS

**dude** /dud/ *n* SLANG used when talking to a man or a group of people, male or female: *Hey, dudes, how's it going?*

**dude ranch** /'. ./ *n* a vacation place where you can ride horses and live like a COWBOY

**duds** /dʌdz/ *n* [plural] HUMOROUS clothes

**due¹** /du/ *adj* **1** be due to be expected to happen or arrive at a particular time: *The flight from Chicago is due at 7:48 p.m.* | *My library books are due back tomorrow.* | *The movie isn't due to start until 10:30.* **2** due to because of: *Our bus was late due to heavy traffic.* | *His success is due to hard work.* **3** needing to be paid: *The first installment of $250 is now due.* **4** deserved by someone or owed to someone: *He never got the recognition he was due for his help.* | *Much of the credit is due to our backup team.* **5** in due course/time at a more suitable time in the future: *The committee will answer your complaints in due course.*

**due²** *adv* **due north/south/east/west** directly or exactly north etc.

**due³** *n* **give sb his/her due** to admit that someone has good qualities even though you are criticizing him/her: *Mr. Johnston was a bad teacher, but to give him his due, he did try hard.* –see also DUES

**du·el** /'duəl/ *n* a fight in past times between two people with guns or swords **–duel** *v* [I]

**due proc·ess** /ˌ. '../, **due process of law** /ˌ. ˌ.. . './ *n* [U] LAW a set of laws that must be obeyed to protect someone's legal rights when s/he goes to court

**dues** /duz/ *n* [plural] the money that you pay to be a member of an organization

**du·et** /du'ɛt/ *n* a piece of music written for two performers

**duf·fel bag** /'dʌfəl ˌbæg/ *n* a cloth bag with a round bottom and a string around the top to tie it closed

**dug** /dʌg/ *v* the past tense and PAST PARTICIPLE of DIG

**dug·out** /'dʌgaʊt/ *n* a low shelter at the side of a sports field, where players and team officials sit

**duke** /duk/ *n* a man with the highest social rank below a PRINCE

**dull¹** /dʌl/ *adj* **1** not interesting or exciting: *What a dull party.* **2** not bright or shiny: *a dull gray sky* **3** a dull sound is not clear or loud: *I heard a dull thud from upstairs.* **4** a dull pain is not severe: *a dull ache in my shoulder* **5** not sharp; BLUNT: *a dull knife* **6** not able to think quickly or understand things easily: *a dull student* **–dully** *adv* **–dullness** *n* [U]

**dull²** *v* [T] to make something become less sharp, less clear etc.: *a drug to dull the pain*

D

**du·ly** /'duli/ *adv* FORMAL at the correct time or in the correct way: *Your suggestion has been duly noted.*

**dumb** /dʌm/ *adj* **1** INFORMAL stupid: *What a dumb idea.* **2** OLD-FASHIONED unable to speak; MUTE

**dumb·bell** /'dʌmbɛl/ *n* **1** two weights connected by a short piece of metal that you lift for exercise **2** INFORMAL someone who is stupid

**dumb·found·ed** /ˌdʌmˈfaʊndɪd◂/ *adj* so surprised that you cannot speak: *He stared at me, dumbfounded.*

**dum·my¹** /'dʌmi/ *n* **1** INFORMAL someone who is stupid **2** a figure made to look like a person

**dummy²** *adj* a dummy tool, weapon etc. looks like a real one but does not work: *a dummy rifle*

**dump¹** /dʌmp/ *v* [T] **1** to drop or put something somewhere in a careless way, sometimes in order to get rid of it: *illegal chemicals dumped in the river|They dumped their bags on the floor and left.* **2** to suddenly end a relationship: *Tammy dumped her boyfriend.*

**dump²** *n* **1** a place where unwanted waste is taken and left: *I'm going to take those boxes down to the dump.* **2** INFORMAL a place that is unpleasant because it is dirty, ugly, or boring: *This town's a real dump.* **3 be down in the dumps** INFORMAL to feel very sad

**dump·ster** /'dʌmpstɚ/ *n* TRADEMARK a large metal container used for holding waste

**dump truck** /'. ./ *n* a vehicle with a large open container at the back that can pour sand, soil etc. onto the ground

**dump·y** /'dʌmpi/ *adj* INFORMAL short and fat: *a dumpy little man*

**dunce** /dʌns/ *n* INFORMAL OFFENSIVE someone who is slow at learning things

**dune** /dun/ *n* a hill made of sand near the ocean or in the desert

**dung** /dʌŋ/ *n* [U] solid waste from animals, especially large ones

**dun·geon** /'dʌndʒən/ *n* a prison under the ground, used in past times

**dunk** /dʌŋk/ *v* [T] **1** to quickly put something that you are eating into coffee, milk etc., and take it out again **2** to push someone under water for a short time as a joke **3** to jump up toward the basket in a game of basketball and throw the ball down into it –see picture on page 472 –**dunk** *n*

**dun·no** /də'noʊ/ SPOKEN NONSTANDARD **I dunno** a short form of "I do not know"

**du·o** /'duoʊ/ *n* two people who do something together, especially play music or sing

**dupe** /dup/ *v* [T] to trick or deceive someone: *Many older people were duped into buying worthless insurance.* –**dupe** *n*

**du·plex** /'duplɛks/ *n* a type of house that is divided so that it has two separate homes in it

**du·pli·cate¹** /'dupləkɪt/ *n* an exact copy of something that you can use in the same way: *We'd better make a duplicate of that key.*

**du·pli·cate²** /'dupləˌkeɪt/ *v* [T] to copy something exactly: *a machine that duplicates the movements of the human hand* –**duplication** /ˌdupləˈkeɪʃən/ *n* [U]

**du·plic·i·ty** /du'plɪsəti/ *n* [U] FORMAL dishonest behavior that is intended to deceive someone

**dur·a·ble** /'dʊrəbəl/ *adj* **1** staying in good condition for a long time: *durable clothing* **2** FORMAL continuing for a long time: *a durable peace* –**durability** /ˌdʊrəˈbɪləti/ *n* [U]

**du·ra·tion** /dʊ'reɪʃən/ *n* [U] FORMAL the length of time that something continues: *Food was rationed for the duration of the war*

**du·ress** /dʊ'rɛs/ *n* [U] FORMAL **under duress** as a result of using illegal or unfair threats: *Her confession was made under duress.*

**dur·ing** /'dʊrɪŋ/ *prep* **1** all through a particular period of time: *I try to swim every day during the summer.* **2** at some point in a period of time: *Henry died during the night.*

---

**USAGE NOTE during and for**

**During** answers the question "when?": *She learned Italian during her stay in Milan.* **For** answers the question "how long?": *He studied in the US for five years.*

---

**dusk** /dʌsk/ *n* [U] the time before it gets dark when the sky is becoming darker

**dust¹** /dʌst/ *n* [U] extremely small pieces of dirt, sand etc. that are like a dry powder: *The truck drove off in a cloud of dust|a thick layer of dust on the table*

**dust²** *v* **1** [I,T] to clean the dust from something: *I just dusted the living room.* **2** [T] to cover something with a fine powder: *Lightly dust the cakes with sugar.*

**dust sth ↔ off** *phr v* [T] to clean something using a dry cloth or your hand: *She dusted the snow off Billy's coat.*

**dust jack·et** /'. ../ *n* a thick folded piece of paper that fits over the cover of a book

**dust·pan** /'dʌstpæn/ *n* a flat container with a handle that you use with a brush to remove dust and waste from the floor

**dust·y** /'dʌsti/ *adj* covered or filled with dust: *a dusty room*

**Dutch¹** /dʌtʃ/ *adj* **1** relating to or coming from the Netherlands **2** relating to the Dutch language

**Dutch²** *n* **1** [U] the language used in the Netherlands **2 the Dutch** the people of the Netherlands

**dutch** *adj* **go dutch (with sb)** to share the cost of something such as a meal in a restaurant

**du·ti·ful** /'dutɪfəl/ *adj* always obeying other people, doing what you are supposed to do, and behaving in a loyal way –**dutifully** *adv*

**du·ty** /ˈduti/ n **1** [C,U] something that you have to do because you think it is right: *I feel it's my* **duty** *to help you.* | *The government* **has a** **duty** *to provide education.* | *jury duty* **2** [C,U] something that you have to do because it is part of your job: *The soldiers were expected to do their* **duty.** | *Please* **report for duty** *tomorrow morning.* | *his duties at the airport* **3** **be on/off duty** to be working or not working at a particular time: *Is she the nurse who was on duty last night?* **4** a tax you pay on something, especially on goods you bought in another country

**duty-free** /ˌ.. ˈ.◂/ adj duty-free goods can be brought into a country without paying tax on them –**duty-free** adv

**DVD** n digital versatile disc; special kind of CD that can store large amounts of music, VIDEOs, and computer information

**dwarf¹** /dwɔrf/ n **1** an imaginary creature that looks like a small man: *Snow White and the Seven Dwarfs* **2** a person, animal, or plant that does not grow to the normal height

**dwarf²** v [T] to be so big that other things seem very small: *The church is dwarfed by the surrounding office buildings.*

**dweeb** /dwib/ n SLANG a weak, slightly strange person who is not popular or fashionable

**dwell** /dwɛl/ v **dwelt** or **dwelled, dwelt** or **dwelled, dwelling** [I] LITERARY to live in a particular place: *They dwelt on an island.*

**dwell on/upon** sth phr v [T] to think or talk for too long about something, especially something unpleasant: *There's no point in* **dwelling on** *the past.*

**dwell·er** /ˈdwɛlɚ/ n **city/town/cave dweller etc.** a person or animal that lives in a city, town etc.

**dwell·ing** /ˈdwɛlɪŋ/ n FORMAL a house, apartment etc. where people live

**dwelt** /dwɛlt/ v the past tense and PAST PARTICIPLE of DWELL

**dwin·dle** /ˈdwɪndl/ v [I] to gradually become fewer or smaller: *Their supplies have* **dwindled away to** *almost* **nothing.** –**dwindling** adj

**dye¹** /daɪ/ n [C,U] a substance you use to change the color of your hair, clothes etc.

**dye²** v [T] to give something a different color using a DYE: *Brian dyed his hair green.*

**dyed-in-the-wool** /ˌ. . . ˈ.◂/ adj having strong beliefs or opinions that will never change: *a dyed-in-the-wool Republican*

**dy·ing** /ˈdaɪ-ɪŋ/ v the PRESENT PARTICIPLE of DIE

**dyke** /daɪk/ n OFFENSIVE ⇨ LESBIAN

**dy·nam·ic** /daɪˈnæmɪk/ adj **1** interesting, exciting, and full of energy: *a dynamic young man* **2** continuously moving or changing: *a dynamic society* **3** TECHNICAL relating to a force or power that causes movement: *dynamic energy*

**dy·nam·ics** /daɪˈnæmɪks/ n [U] **1** the way in which systems or people behave, react, and affect each other: *family dynamics* | *the dynamics of power in large businesses* **2** the science concerned with the movement of objects and with the forces related to movement

**dy·na·mism** /ˈdaɪnəˌmɪzəm/ n [U] the quality of being DYNAMIC

**dy·na·mite¹** /ˈdaɪnəˌmaɪt/ n [U] a powerful explosive

**dynamite²** v [T] to damage or destroy something with DYNAMITE

**dy·na·mo** /ˈdaɪnəˌmoʊ/ n **1** INFORMAL someone who has a lot of energy and is very excited about what s/he does **2** a machine that changes some other form of power into electricity

**dy·nas·ty** /ˈdaɪnəsti/ n a family of kings or other rulers who have ruled a country for a long time, or the period of time during which this family rules: *the Ming dynasty* –**dynastic** /daɪˈnæstɪk/ adj

**dys·en·ter·y** /ˈdɪsənˌtɛri/ n [U] a serious disease of the BOWELs that makes someone pass much more waste than usual

**dys·func·tion·al** /dɪsˈfʌŋkʃənl/ adj not working normally or not showing normal social behavior: *dysfunctional relationships within the family*

**dys·lex·i·a** /dɪsˈlɛksiə/ n [U] a condition that makes it difficult for someone to read –**dyslexic** /dɪsˈlɛksɪk/ adj

**E, e** /i/ the fifth letter of the English alphabet

**E¹** /i/ n [C,U] the third note in the musical SCALE of C, or the musical KEY based on this note

**E²** **1** the written abbreviation of EAST or EASTERN **2** SLANG the abbreviation of ECSTASY, an illegal drug

**each¹** /itʃ/ determiner, pronoun every single one of two or more things, considered separately: *Each student will be given a book.* | *I gave a piece of candy to* **each of** *the children.*

---

**USAGE NOTE each, every, all, and both**

Use **each** with a singular countable noun to mean "every person or thing in a group, considered separately": *Each child at the party will get a balloon.* Use **every** with a singular countable noun to mean "every person or thing in a group, considered together": *Every child in the class passed the test.* Use **all** with a plural countable noun to mean "every one of a group of things or people": *All of the children enjoyed the* *trip.* Use **both** with a plural countable noun to mean "two people or things in a group, considered together": *Both of our children are in college.*

**each**[2] *adv* for or to every one: *The tickets are $5 each.* | *You kids can have two cookies each.*

**each oth·er** /ˌ. '../ *pron* used in order to show that each of two people does something to the other person, or that each of several people does something to each of the others: *Susan and Robert kissed each other.* | *The two kids played with each other all morning.* | *It's normal for people to ignore each other in an elevator.*

---

**USAGE NOTE each other and one another**

Some teachers prefer to use **each other** when talking about two people or things, and **one another** when talking about many people or things: *The two leaders shook hands with each other.* | *All the leaders shook hands with one another.* **One another** is also more formal than **each other**.

---

**ea·ger** /ˈigɚ/ *adj* **1** having a strong desire to do something or a strong interest in something: *I've been eager to meet you.* | *a young woman eager for success* **2 eager to please** willing to do anything that people want —**eagerly** *adv* —**eagerness** *n* [U]

**ea·gle** /ˈigəl/ *n* a large wild bird with a beak like a hook, that eats small animals, birds etc.

**eagle-eyed** /ˈ.. ˌ./ *adj* very good at seeing or noticing things: *an eagle-eyed teacher*

**ear** /ɪr/ *n* **1** the part of your body that you hear with: *Stop shouting in my ear!* —see picture at HEAD[1] **2** [U] the ability to hear, recognize, or copy sounds, especially in music and languages: *Joel has a good ear for music.* **3** the top part of plants that produce grain: *an ear of corn* **4 be up to your ears in sth** INFORMAL to be very busy with something: *I'm up to my ears in work.* **5 go in one ear and out the other** INFORMAL to be heard and then forgotten immediately **6 be all ears** INFORMAL to be very interested in listening to someone: *Go ahead, I'm all ears.* **7 be out on your ear** INFORMAL to be forced to leave a place because of something you have done wrong: *If you come to work that late again, you'll be out on your ear!* —see also **play it by ear** (PLAY[1]) **wet behind the ears** (WET[1])

**ear·drum** /ˈɪrdrʌm/ *n* a tight thin MEMBRANE (=layer like skin) over the inside of your ear that allows you to hear sound

**ear·lobe** /ˈɪrloʊb/ *n* the soft piece of flesh at the bottom of your ear

**ear·ly**[1] /ˈɚli/ *adj* **1** near to the beginning of a day, year, someone's life etc.: *She woke in the early morning.* | *a man in his early twenties*

**2** before the usual or expected time: *The train was ten minutes early.* **3** existing before other people, events, machines etc. of the same kind: *early settlers in New England* **4 at the earliest** used in order to say that a particular time is the soonest that something can happen: *He'll arrive on Monday at the earliest.* **5 the early hours** the time between MIDNIGHT and morning **6 the early days** the time when something had just started to be done or to exist: *the early days of television* **7 early bird** someone who gets up early or arrives early —opposite LATE[1]

**early**[2] *adv* **1** before the usual, arranged, or expected time: *You should arrive early if you want a good seat.* **2** near the beginning of a particular period of time: *These flowers were planted early in the spring.* | *I'll have to leave early tomorrow morning.* **3** near the beginning of an event, story, process etc.: *I realized early on that this relationship wasn't going to work.* —opposite LATE[2]

**ear·mark** /ˈɪrmɑrk/ *v* [T] to save something to be used for a particular purpose: *We've earmarked funds for the new bridge.*

**ear·muffs** /ˈɪrmʌfs/ *n* [plural] two pieces of material attached to the ends of a band, that you wear to keep your ears warm

**earn** /ɚn/ *v* [T] **1** to get money by working: *Alan earns $30,000 a year.* **2** to make a profit from business, or from putting money in a bank, lending it etc.: *I earned $5000 from my investments last year.* **3** to get something that you deserve: *She earned her place on the team by practicing hard.* **4 earn a living** to work to get enough money to pay for the things you need: *He earned his living as a writer.* —see usage note at GAIN[1]

**ear·nest**[1] /ˈɚnɪst/ *adj* serious and sincere: *an earnest young man* —**earnestly** *adv* —**earnestness** *n* [U]

**earnest**[2] *n* **1 in earnest** happening more seriously or with greater effort than before: *Soon they were talking in earnest about business plans.* **2 be in earnest** to be serious about what you are saying: *I'm sure he was in earnest when he said he was going to quit.*

**earn·ings** /ˈɚnɪŋz/ *n* [plural] **1** the money that you earn by working **2** the profit that a company makes

**ear·phones** /ˈɪrfoʊnz/ *n* [plural] electrical equipment that you put over or into your ears to listen to a radio, TAPE DECK etc.

**ear·plug** /ˈɪrplʌg/ *n* [C usually plural] a small piece of rubber that you put into your ear to keep out noise or water

**ear·ring** /ˈɪrɪŋ/ *n* [C usually plural] a piece of jewelry that you fasten to your ear —see picture at JEWELRY

**ear·shot** /ˈɪrʃɑt/ *n* **within earshot/out of earshot** near enough or not near enough to hear what someone is saying

E

**ear-split·ting** /'. ͵../ *adj* very loud: *an ear-splitting scream*

**earth** /ɚθ/ *n* **1** [singular] also **Earth** the world that we live in, especially considered as a PLANET: *The Earth moves around the sun.* | *The space shuttle is returning to the earth.* | *the most beautiful woman on earth* —compare WORLD —see pictures at ORBIT¹ and GREENHOUSE EFFECT **2** [U] the substance that plants, trees etc. grow in; dirt: *footprints in the wet earth* **3 what/why/how etc. on earth...?** SPOKEN said when you are asking a question about something that you are very surprised or annoyed about: *What on earth did you do to your hair?* —see also DOWN-TO-EARTH

---

**USAGE NOTE** earth, world, and land

The **earth** is the planet we live on: *The earth moves around the sun every 365 days.* The **world** is a place with people, countries etc.: *It's one of the largest countries in the world.* You can also use **earth** to mean "the world": *It's the highest mountain on earth.* ✗ DON'T SAY "in earth" or "on the world." ✗ When you compare the earth's surface to the ocean, use **land**: *After weeks at sea, the sailors saw land.* When you compare it to the sky, use **earth**: *The spacecraft returned to earth safely.*

---

**earth·ly** /'ɚθli/ *adj* **1 no earthly reason/use/chance etc.** no reason, use etc. at all: *There's no earthly reason for me to go.* **2** LITERARY relating to life on Earth rather than in heaven: *all my earthly possessions*

**earth·quake** /'ɚθkweɪk/ *n* a sudden shaking of the earth's surface that often causes a lot of damage

**earth-shat·ter·ing** /'. ͵.../, **earth-shak·ing** /'. ͵../ *adj* surprising or shocking and very important: *It's interesting, but not earth-shattering.*

**earth·worm** /'ɚθwɚm/ *n* ⇨ WORM¹

**earth·y** /'ɚθi/ *adj* **1** talking about sex and the human body in a direct and impolite way: *Jimmy has an earthy sense of humor.* **2** tasting, smelling, or looking like earth or soil: *mushrooms with an earthy flavor* —**earthiness** *n* [U]

**ease¹** /iz/ *n* [U] **1 with ease** if you do something with ease, it is very easy for you to do it: *Randy climbed the ladder with ease.* **2 at ease a)** feeling comfortable and confident: *She tried to make the new students feel at ease.* | *You always look ill at ease* (=not relaxed) *in a suit.* **b)** SPOKEN used in order to tell soldiers to stand in a relaxed way with their feet apart **3** the ability to feel or behave in a natural or relaxed way: *He had a natural ease which made him very popular.* **4 a life of ease** a comfortable life, without problems or worries

**ease²** *v* **1** [I,T] to make something less severe or difficult, or to become less severe or difficult: *He was given drugs to ease the pain.* | *Tensions in the region have eased slightly.* **2** [T] to move something slowly and carefully into another place: *Ease the patient onto the bed.*

**ease up** *phr v* [I] **1** also **ease off** if something, especially something that annoys you, eases off or eases up, it becomes less or gets better: *The rain is starting to ease up.* **2** to stop being unpleasant to someone: *Ease up on Roger, will you; he's doing all right.* **3** to do something more slowly or less often than before: *I think it's time you eased up on the cigarettes.*

**ea·sel** /'izəl/ *n* a frame that you put a painting on while you paint it

**eas·i·ly** /'izəli/ *adv* **1** without difficulty: *I can easily finish it today.* **2** without doubt; definitely: *She is easily the most intelligent girl in the class.*

**east¹, East** /ist/ *n* **1** [singular, U] the direction from which the sun rises: *Which way is east?* **2 the east** the eastern part of a country, state etc.: *Rain will spread to the east later today.* **3 the East a)** the countries in Asia, especially China, Japan, and Korea **b)** the countries in the eastern part of Europe, especially the ones that had Communist governments **c)** the part of the US east of the Mississippi River, especially the states north of Washington, D.C. **4 back East** in the East, or to the East of the US: *My son goes to college back East.* —see usage note at NORTH³

**east²** *adj* **1** in, to, or facing east: *12 miles east of Portland* | *the east coast of the island* **2 east wind** a wind coming from the east

**east³** *adv* toward the east: *Go east on I-80 to Omaha.* | *The window faces east.*

**east·bound** /'istbaʊnd/ *adj* traveling or leading toward the east: *eastbound traffic* | *the eastbound lanes of the freeway*

**Eas·ter** /'istɚ/ *n* [C,U] **1** a Christian holiday on a Sunday in March or April to celebrate Christ's return to life after his death **2** the period of time just before and after this day: *We went skiing in Vermont at Easter.*

**Easter Bun·ny** /'.. ͵../ *n* [singular] an imaginary rabbit that children believe brings colored eggs and chocolate at Easter

**Easter egg** /'.. ͵./ *n* an egg that has been colored and decorated

**east·er·ly** /'istɚli/ *adj* **1** in or toward the east: *sailing in an easterly direction* **2** easterly winds come from the east

**east·ern** /'istɚn/ *adj* **1** in or from the east part of an area, country, state etc.: *eastern Oregon* **2 Eastern** in or from the countries in Asia, especially China, Japan, and Korea: *Eastern religions* **3** in or from the countries in the eastern part of Europe, especially the ones that used to have Communist governments – see usage note at NORTH³

**east·ern·er, Easterner** /'istənɚ/ n someone who comes from the EASTERN part of a country or the eastern HEMISPHERE

**Eastern Eu·rope** /ˌ.. '../ n the eastern part of Europe, including places such as Poland and part of Russia – **Eastern European** adj

**east·ern·most** /'istənmoust/ adj farthest east: *the easternmost part of the island*

**east·ward** /'istwɚd/ adj, adv toward the east

**eas·y¹** /'izi/ adj **1** not difficult: *Making brownies is easy.| I want a book that's easy to read.| Having a computer will definitely make things a lot easier.* **2** comfortable and not feeling worried or anxious: *I imagine Paul has a very easy life.* **3** I'm easy SPOKEN used in order to show that you do not mind what choice is made: *"Do you want to go to the movies or out to eat?" "Oh, I'm easy."* **4** easy money INFORMAL money that you do not have to work hard to get **5** INFORMAL DISAPPROVING someone who is easy has a lot of sexual partners **6** eggs over easy eggs cooked on a hot surface and turned over quickly before serving, so that the YOLKs (=yellow part) are not completely cooked

**easy²** adv **1** take it easy a) to relax and not do very much: *I'm going to take it easy this weekend.* b) SPOKEN used in order to tell someone to become less upset or angry **2** go easy on/with sth INFORMAL to not use too much of something: *My doctor said that I should go easy on the salt.* **3** go easy on sb INFORMAL to be more gentle and less strict or angry with someone: *Go easy on Peter - he's having a hard time at school* **4** rest/sleep easy to be able to relax because you are not worried or anxious: *I won't rest easy until I know she's safe.* **5** easy does it SPOKEN used in order to tell someone to be careful, especially when s/he is moving something **6** easier said than done SPOKEN used when it would be difficult to actually do what someone has suggested: *I should just tell her to go away, but that's easier said than done.*

**easy chair** /'.. ˌ./ n a large comfortable chair

**eas·y·go·ing** /ˌizi'gouɪŋ◄/ adj not easily worried or annoyed: *Phil's a pretty easygoing person.*

**easy lis·ten·ing** /ˌ.. '../ n [U] music that is relaxing to listen to

**eat** /it/ v ate, eaten /'it⁻n/, eating **1** [I,T] to put food in your mouth and swallow it: *Eat your dinner!* | **eat like a horse/bird** (=eat a lot or eat very little) | **eat right** (=eat food that keeps you healthy) **2** [I] to have a meal: *What time do we eat?* **3** eat sb alive/eat sb for breakfast INFORMAL to be very angry with someone **4** eat your heart out INFORMAL used in order to say that someone should be sad or JEALOUS: *Yeah, I just bought a new convertible. Eat your heart out, Jay.* **5** what's eating him/her/you? SPOKEN said in order to ask why someone seems annoyed or upset **6** eat your words INFORMAL to admit that what you said was wrong: *I had to eat my words when he turned up on time after all.* **7** eat crow/eat humble pie INFORMAL to be forced to admit that you were wrong and say that you are sorry **8** [T] also eat up SPOKEN to use all of something until it is gone: *That car of mine just eats money.*

**eat** sth ↔ **away, eat away at** sth phr v [T] to gradually remove or reduce the amount of something: *Rust had eaten away at the metal frame.*

**eat into** sth phr v [T] **1** to gradually reduce the amount of time, money etc. that is available: *All these car expenses are really eating into our savings.* **2** to damage or destroy something: *This acid will eat into the surface of the metal.*

**eat out** phr v [I] to eat in a restaurant: *I don't feel like cooking. Let's eat out tonight.*

**eat** sth ↔ **up** phr v [I,T] SPOKEN to eat all of something: *Come on, Kaylee, eat up!*

**eat·er** /'itɚ/ n big/light/fussy etc. eater someone who eats a lot, not much, only particular things etc.

**eat·ing dis·or·der** /'.. ˌ.../ n a medical condition in which you do not eat normal amounts of food or do not eat regularly – see also ANOREXIA, BULIMIA

**eaves** /ivz/ n [plural] the edges of a roof that stick out beyond the walls: *birds nesting under the eaves*

**eaves·drop** /'ivzdrɑp/ v -pped, -pping [I] to listen secretly to other people's conversations – **eaves·dropper** n – compare OVERHEAR

eavesdrop

**ebb¹** /ɛb/ n **1** ebb and flow a situation or state in which something increases and decreases in a type of pattern: *the ebb and flow of consumer demand* **2** be at a low ebb to be in a bad state or condition: *By March 1933, the economy was at its lowest ebb.* **3** [singular, U] the flow of the sea away from the shore, when the TIDE goes out

**ebb²** v [I] **1** LITERARY to gradually decrease: *His courage slowly ebbed away.* **2** if the TIDE ebbs, it flows away from the shore

**eb·o·ny** /'ɛbəni/ n **1** [C,U] a tree with dark hard wood, or the wood itself **2** [U] LITERARY a black color – **ebony** adj

**e·bul·lient** /ɪ'bʌlyənt, ɪ'bʊl-/ adj FORMAL very happy and excited: *an ebullient mood* – **ebullience** n [U]

**ec·cen·tric¹** /ɪk'sɛntrɪk/ adj behaving in a way that is unusual and strange: *That old lady has some eccentric habits.* – **eccentricity** /ˌɛksɛn'trɪsəti/ n [C,U]

**eccentric²** n an unusual and strange person

E

**ec·cle·si·as·ti·cal** /ɪˌklizi'æstɪkəl/ *adj* relating to the Christian church: *ecclesiastical history*

**ech·o¹** /'ɛkoʊ/ *n, plural* **echoes** a sound that you hear again because it was made near something such as a wall or a hill

**echo²** *v* **echoed, echoed, echoing 1** [I] if a sound echoes, it is heard again because it was made near something such as a wall or a hill: *voices echoing around the cave* **2 echo with** to be full of a sound: *The theater echoed with laughter and applause.* **3** [T] to repeat what someone else has said: *This report simply echoes what I said two weeks ago.*

**é·clair** /eɪ'klɛr, ɪ-/ *n* a long cake covered with chocolate and filled with cream

**e·clipse¹** /ɪ'klɪps/ *n* a short time when you cannot see the sun because the moon is in front of it, or when you cannot see the moon because it is covered by the earth's shadow

**eclipse²** *v* [T] **1** to become more powerful, famous, important etc. than someone or something else: *a 100-meter record that was eclipsed only ten days after it was set* **2** to make the sun or moon disappear in an ECLIPSE

**e·co·log·i·cal** /ˌikə'lɑdʒɪkəl, ˌɛ-/ *adj* **1** relating to the way that plants, animals, and people are related to each other and to their environment: *ecological problems caused by the huge oil spill* **2** concerned with making or keeping the environment healthy: *an ecological study* –**ecologically** *adv*

**e·col·o·gy** /ɪ'kɑlədʒi/ *n* [singular, U] the way in which plants, animals, and people are related to each other and to their environment, or the study of this –**ecologist** *n*

**ec·o·nom·ic** /ˌɛkə'nɑmɪk, ˌi-/ *adj* relating to business, industry, and managing money: *economic development* –**economically** *adv*

**ec·o·nom·i·cal** /ˌɛkə'nɑmɪkəl, ˌi-/ *adj* using time, money, products, etc. without wasting any: *an economical way to produce energy* –**economically** *adv*

**ec·o·nom·ics** /ˌɛkə'nɑmɪks, ˌi-/ *n* [U] the study of the way in which money, goods, and services are produced and used

**e·con·o·mist** /ɪ'kɑnəmɪst/ *n* someone who studies ECONOMICS

**e·con·o·mize** /ɪ'kɑnəˌmaɪz/ *v* [I] to save something such as money, time, effort, etc. by using it carefully and not wasting it: *We're trying to economize on food costs.*

**e·con·o·my¹** /ɪ'kɑnəmi/ *n* **1** the way that money, businesses, and products are organized in a particular country, area etc.: *A new factory would help the local economy.* (=in a particular town or city) | *the growing economies of southeast Asia* **2** [U] the careful use of money, time, products etc. so that nothing is wasted

**economy²** *adj* **economy size/package etc.** the biggest container that a product is sold in

**economy class** /.'... ˌ./, **economy** *n* [U] the cheapest way to travel on a plane

**e·co·sys·tem** /'ikoʊˌsɪstəm/ *n* all the animals and plants in a particular area, and the way in which they are related to each other and to their environment

**ec·sta·sy** /'ɛkstəsi/ *n* **1** [C,U] a feeling of extreme happiness: *Fans sang along, in ecstasy at hearing their old favorites.* **2 Ecstasy** [U] an illegal drug used especially by young people to give a feeling of happiness and energy

**ec·stat·ic** /ɪk'stætɪk, ɛk-/ *adj* feeling extremely happy and excited: *Luke is ecstatic about being accepted at Harvard.*

**ec·u·men·i·cal** /ˌɛkyə'mɛnɪkəl/ *adj* bringing together different Christian churches, or supporting this

**ec·ze·ma** /'ɛksəmə, 'ɛgzəmə, ɪg'zimə/ *n* [U] a condition in which skin becomes dry and red, and begins to ITCH

**ed.** *n* [singular, U] INFORMAL the abbreviation of EDUCATION: *the adult ed. department*

**ed·dy** /'ɛdi/ *n* a circular movement of water, wind, dust etc. –**eddy** *v* [I]

**edge¹** /ɛdʒ/ *n* **1** the part of something that is farthest from the center: *She had sewn ribbon on the edge of the cloth.* | *a lake with houses around the edge* **2** the thin sharp part of a tool used for cutting **3** an advantage in a competition, game, or fight: *This new software should give our company an edge in the market.* **4 be on edge** to feel nervous because you are expecting something bad to happen: *Rudy was on edge all night.*

edge
corner edge
edge
edge

**edge²** *v* **1** [I,T] to move slowly and gradually, or to make something do this: *Ramon edged the gun toward my hand.* | *Witnesses edged away from the scene.* **2** [T] to put something on the edge or border of something else: *sleeves edged with gold thread* **3** [I,T] to develop or increase slowly and gradually, or to make something do this: *The price of gasoline is edging up.*

**edge·wise** /'ɛdʒwaɪz/ *adv* **1 not get a word in edgewise** to not be able to say something in a conversation because someone else is talking too much: *When Ann's mother is here I can't get a word in edgewise.* **2** with the edge or thinnest part forward: *Slide the table in edgewise.*

**edg·y** /'ɛdʒi/ *adj* nervous and easy to upset: *Bill was edgy after a hard day at work.*

**ed·i·ble** /'ɛdəbəl/ *adj* something that is edible is safe or acceptable to eat –opposite INEDIBLE

**e·dict** /'idɪkt/ *n* FORMAL an official public order made by someone in a position of power

**ed·i·fice** /'ɛdəfɪs/ *n* FORMAL a large building

**ed·i·fy** /'ɛdə,faɪ/ v [T] FORMAL to improve someone's mind or character by teaching him/ her something –**edification** /,ɛdəfə'keɪʃən/ n [U]

**ed·it** /'ɛdɪt/ v [T] to prepare a book, movie, article etc. for people to read or see by arranging the parts, correcting mistakes, and deciding which parts to keep

**e·di·tion** /ɪ'dɪʃən/ n the form that a book is printed in, or the total numbers of a particular book produced at one time: *the newest edition of a dictionary*

**ed·i·tor** /'ɛdətɚ/ n **1** the person who decides what should be included in a newspaper, magazine etc. **2** someone who prepares a book, movie etc. for printing or broadcasting by deciding what to include and checking for any mistakes –**editorial** /,ɛdə'tɔriəl/ adj

**ed·i·to·ri·al** /,ɛdə'tɔriəl/ n a piece of writing in a newspaper that gives the opinion of the writer rather than reporting facts: *an editorial on* (=about) *gun control laws*

**ed·u·cate** /'ɛdʒə,keɪt/ v [T] to teach someone, especially in a school or college: *Most Americans are educated in public schools.* | *We need to educate ourselves about environmental issues.* –**educator** n

**ed·u·cat·ed** /'ɛdʒə,keɪtɪd/ adj **1** having knowledge as a result of studying or being taught; *Frank comes from a well-educated family.* **2 educated guess** a guess that is likely to be correct because you know something about the subject

**ed·u·ca·tion** /,ɛdʒə'keɪʃən/ n [singular, U] **1** the process of learning in a school or other program of study: *parents saving for their kids' college education* **2** the work of teaching in schools and colleges: *jobs in higher education* (=colleges)

**ed·u·ca·tion·al** /,ɛdʒə'keɪʃənəl/ adj **1** relating to teaching and learning: *educational opportunities for high school graduates* **2** teaching you something that you did not know: *It was really educational, one of the best jobs I've had.* –**educationally** adv

**ed·u·tain·ment** /,ɛdʒu'teɪnmənt/ n [U] movies, television programs, or computer SOFTWARE that both educate and entertain children

**eel** /il/ n a long thin fish that looks like a snake

**ee·rie** /'ɪri/ adj strange and frightening: *an eerie light* –**eerily** adv

**ef·fect¹** /ɪ'fɛkt/ n **1** [C,U] a result, or a reaction to something or someone: *the effects of a long illness* | *Seeing him so upset really had an effect on Mom.* | *Red has the effect of making the room seem warmer.* **2 put sth into effect** to make a plan or idea happen: *Nothing had been done to put the changes into effect.* **3 come/go into effect** to start officially: *The new tax laws come into effect January 1st.* **4 take effect** to start to have results, or to start

being used: *The drug should take effect in about ten minutes.* **5 in effect** used when you are describing what the real situation is, instead of what it seems to be: *Ellie is his secretary, but in effect she's the manager.* –compare AFFECT, EFFECTS

**effect²** v [T] FORMAL to make something happen

**ef·fec·tive** /ɪ'fɛktɪv/ adj **1** producing the result that was wanted or intended: *a very effective medicine for headaches* – opposite INEFFECTIVE **2** done with skill, or having a skillful way of doing things: *an effective politician/speech* –opposite INEFFECTIVE **3 be/become effective** to be in use, or to start to be in use officially: *These prices are effective from April 1.* –**effectiveness** n [U]

**ef·fec·tive·ly** /ɪ'fɛktɪvli/ adv **1** in a way that produces the result you wanted: *He didn't deal with the problem very effectively.* **2** actually; really: *By parking here you effectively prevented everyone from leaving.*

**ef·fects** /ɪ'fɛkts/ n [plural] FORMAL the things that someone owns; BELONGINGS –see also SPECIAL EFFECTS

**ef·fem·i·nate** /ɪ'fɛmənɪt/ adj a man or boy who is effeminate behaves like a woman or girl

**ef·fer·ves·cent** /,ɛfɚ'vɛsənt/ adj **1** TECHNICAL a liquid that is effervescent has BUBBLES of gas rising in it **2** someone who is effervescent is very active and cheerful –**effervescence** n [U]

**ef·fi·cient** /ɪ'fɪʃənt/ adj working well, quickly, and without wasting time, energy, or effort: *a very efficient secretary/organization* –**efficiency** n [U ] –**efficiently** adv –opposite INEFFICIENT

**ef·fi·gy** /'ɛfədʒi/ n a figure of a particular person that is usually burned in order to show that the person is not liked

**ef·flu·ent** /'ɛfluənt/ n [C,U] FORMAL liquid waste that flows out of a place

**ef·fort** /'ɛfɚt/ n **1** [U] the physical or mental energy needed to do something: *Kenny's teacher wants him to put more effort into his work.* | *I'm so tired, I can't do anything that takes any effort.* | *Is it really worth the effort to move these boxes?* **2** [C,U] an attempt to do something that may be difficult: *Sheila's very nice when you make the effort to know her better.* | *This is an effort to help the homeless.* | *Tom will do anything in his efforts to* (=in order to) *please his wife.*

**ef·fort·less** /'ɛfɚt˺lɪs/ adj done skillfully in a way that seems easy: *Brad's seemingly effortless skiing* –**effortlessly** adv

**ef·fu·sive** /ɪ'fyusɪv/ adj showing strong, excited feelings: *effusive greetings* –**effusively** adv

**EFL** English as a Foreign Language; the methods used for teaching English to people whose first language is not English, and who do not live in an English-speaking country

**e.g.** /ˌi ˈdʒi/ a written abbreviation that means "for example": *the Gulf States, e.g. Texas, Louisiana, and Mississippi*

**e·gal·i·tar·i·an** /ɪˌgæləˈtɛriən/ *adj* believing that everyone should have the same rights and opportunities – **egalitarianism** *n* [U]

**egg**[1] /ɛg/ *n* **1** a slightly round object with a hard surface that contains a baby bird, insect, snake etc.: *We saw two eggs in the bluebird's nest.* **2** an egg from a chicken, used as food **3** a cell produced inside a female that can develop into a new animal or person when it joins with a SPERM

**egg**[2] *v*

**egg** sb ↔ **on** *phr v* [T] to encourage someone to do something that is not wise for him/her to do: *He wouldn't have dived off the bridge if people hadn't egged him on.*

**egg·head** /ˈɛghɛd/ *n* INFORMAL someone who is very educated but not very practical

**egg·plant** /ˈɛgplænt/ *n* [C,U] a large shiny dark purple fruit that is cooked and eaten as a vegetable – see picture on page 470

**egg·shell** /ˈɛgʃɛl/ *n* [C,U] the hard outside part of a bird's egg

**e·go** /ˈigoʊ/ *n* **1** the opinion that you have about yourself: *Her boyfriend has a big ego.* (=thinks he is very interesting or important) **2 ego trip** INFORMAL something that someone does for himself/herself because it makes him/her feel good or important

**e·go·tism** /ˈigəˌtɪzəm/, **e·go·ism** /ˈigoʊɪzəm/ *n* the belief that you are more interesting or important than other people, or behavior that shows this – **egotistical** /ˌigəˈtɪstɪkəl/ *adj* – **egotist** /ˈigətɪst/ *n*

**e·gre·gious** /ɪˈgridʒəs/ *adj* FORMAL an egregious ERROR (=mistake), failure etc. is extremely bad and noticeable – **egregiously** *adv*

**eight** /eɪt/ *number* **1** 8 **2** eight o'clock: *Dinner will be at eight.*

**eight·een** /ˌeɪˈtin◂/ *number* 18 – **eighteenth** *number*

**eighth** /eɪtθ/ *number* **1** 8th **2** 1/8

**eight·y** /ˈeɪti/ *number* **1** 80 **2 the eighties a)** the years between 1980 and 1989 **b)** the numbers between 80 and 89, especially when used in measuring temperature – **eightieth** /ˈeɪtiɪθ/ *number*

**ei·ther**[1] /ˈiðɚ, ˈaɪ-/ *conjunction* used in order to begin a list of possibilities separated by "or": *There's either coffee or tea to drink.* | *Either say you're sorry, or get out!*

> **USAGE NOTE** either...or and neither...nor
>
> When you use these phrases in formal speech or writing, use a singular verb if the second noun is singular: *If either Doris or*

Meg calls, please take a message. | *Neither Theo nor Garth is very tall.* If the second noun is plural, use a plural verb: *If either my sister or my parents come, please let them in.* In informal speech, the verb is usually plural.

**either**[2] *determiner, pronoun* **1** one or the other of two: *I've lived in New York and Chicago, but I don't like either city very much.* | *"Do you want to meet, or just talk on the phone?" "Either way is fine."* **2** one and the other of two things; each: *He was standing there with a policeman on either side of him.* – compare BOTH

> **USAGE NOTE** either, neither, none, and any
>
> In formal speech and writing, use these pronouns with a singular verb: *None/neither of us has seen the exhibit.* | *Is any of the paintings for sale?* In informal speech, you can use a plural verb: *Have either of you ever been to Dallas?*

**either**[3] *adv* **1** used in negative sentences to mean also: *"I haven't seen 'Batman' yet." "I haven't either."* **2 me either** SPOKEN NONSTANDARD used in order to say that something is also true about you: *"I don't like broccoli." "Me either."*

**e·jac·u·late** /ɪˈdʒækyəˌleɪt/ *v* [I,T] when a male ejaculates, SPERM comes out of his PENIS – **ejaculation** /ɪˌdʒækyəˈleɪʃən/ *n* [C,U]

**e·ject** /ɪˈdʒɛkt/ *v* **1** [T] to push or throw out with force: *The plane had to eject most of its fuel as it went down.* **2** [I] to jump out of a plane that is going to crash **3** [T] to make something come out of a machine by pressing a button: *Rewind and eject the tape.* – **ejection** /ɪˈdʒɛkʃən/ *n* [C,U]

**eke** /ik/ *v*

**eke** sth ↔ **out** *phr v* [T] LITERARY **1** to make something such as food or money last a long time by using small amounts of it, or by adding something else **2 eke out a living/existence** to get just enough food or money to live on

**e·lab·o·rate**[1] /ɪˈlæbrɪt/ *adj* having a lot of small details or parts that are connected together in a complicated way: *The Nelsons are planning an elaborate Thanksgiving dinner.* | *wallpaper with an elaborate design* – **elaborately** *adv*

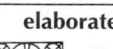
an elaborate pattern

a simple pattern

**e·lab·o·rate**[2] /ɪˈlæbəˌreɪt/ *v* [I,T] to give more details about something you have said or written: *Would you please elaborate on your earlier statement?* – **elaboration** /ɪˌlæbəˈreɪʃən/ *n* [U]

**e·lapse** /ɪ'læps/ *v* [I] FORMAL if a period of time elapses, it passes

**e·las·tic** /ɪ'læstɪk/ *adj* able to stretch and then go back to its usual shape or size: *an elastic waistband* −**elasticity** /ɪ,læs'tɪsəti/ *n* [U] −**elastic** /ɪ'læstɪk/ *n*

**e·lat·ed** /ɪ'leɪt̬ɪd/ *adj* extremely happy and excited: *I was elated when Mary told me she was pregnant.* −**elation** /ɪ'leɪʃən/ *n* [U]

**el·bow¹** /'ɛlboʊ/ *n* **1** the joint where your arm bends −see picture at BODY **2 elbow room** INFORMAL enough space, so that you can move easily: *Let's sit in a booth. There's more elbow room.* **3 elbow grease** INFORMAL hard physical effort: *All it needs is a little elbow grease to get the cabin cleaned up.*

**elbow²** *v* [T] to push someone with your elbows, especially in order to move past him/her: *She elbowed her way through the crowd.*

**el·der¹** /'ɛldɚ/ *adj* **elder brother/sister** an older brother or sister in a family: *My elder sister is a nurse.*

> ### USAGE NOTE elder and older
>
> Use **elder** to talk about the members of a family: *Nick is my elder brother.* Use **older** to compare the age of people or things: *My sister is two years older than I am.* ✗ DON'T SAY "elder than." ✗

**elder²** *n* **1** [C usually plural] someone who is older than you are: *Young people should have respect for their elders.* **2** an older person who is important and respected: *the town elders*

**el·der·ly** /'ɛldɚli/ *adj* **1** a word meaning old, used in order to be polite: *an elderly woman with white hair* **2 the elderly** people who are old: *a home that provides care for the elderly* −compare OLD ANCIENT −see usage note at OLD

**el·dest** /'ɛldɪst/ *adj* **eldest son/daughter/ brother/sister** the oldest son etc. in a family

**e·lect¹** /ɪ'lɛkt/ *v* [T] **1** to choose someone for an official position by voting: *Clinton was elected President in 1992.* **2 elect to do sth** FORMAL to choose to do something: *Hanley elected to take early retirement.*

**elect²** *adj* **president-elect/senator-elect** etc. the person who has been elected but has not officially started his/her job

**e·lec·tion** /ɪ'lɛkʃən/ *n* an occasion when you vote in order to choose someone for an official position: *The election results are still coming in.* −**electoral** /ɪ'lɛktərəl/ *adj*

> ### CULTURE NOTE elections
>
> In the US, there are elections to choose a President and Vice-President every four years. Every two years, all of the members of the House of Representatives and one-third of the Senators are elected. The

period of office for a Senator is six years; for a President it is four years; and for a Representative it is two years. A President can only serve for eight years.

**e·lec·tive¹** /ɪ'lɛktɪv/ *n* a subject that a student chooses to study, but that s/he does not have to study in order to GRADUATE

**elective²** *adj* an elective office, position etc. is one for which there is an election

**e·lec·to·ral col·lege** /ɪ,... '../ *n* [singular] a group of people chosen by the votes of the people in each US state, who come together to elect the president

**e·lec·tor·ate** /ɪ'lɛktərɪt/ *n* [singular] all the people who are allowed to vote in an election

**e·lec·tric** /ɪ'lɛktrɪk/ *adj* **1** needing electricity in order to work: *an electric oven | an electric guitar* **2** making people feel very excited: *The atmosphere at the concert was electric.*

> ### USAGE NOTE electric and electrical
>
> Use **electric** as an adjective before the names of things that need electricity in order to work: *an electric clock | electric lights.* Use **electrical** as a more general word to talk about power and their work, or about things that use or produce electricity: *an electrical engineer | My dad's company imports electrical goods.*

**e·lec·tri·cal** /ɪ'lɛktrɪkəl/ *adj* relating to or using electricity: *an electrical fault | electrical goods* −see usage note at ELECTRIC

**electric chair** /ɪ'.. ,./ *n* **the electric chair** a chair in which criminals are killed using electricity

**e·lec·tri·cian** /ɪ,lɛk'trɪʃən, i-/ *n* someone whose job is to fit and repair electrical equipment

**e·lec·tric·i·ty** /ɪ,lɛk'trɪsəti, i-/ *n* [U] **1** the power that is carried by wires and used in order to provide heat or light, to make machines work etc.: *The electricity went out (=stopped working) during the storm.* **2** a feeling of excitement: *You could feel the electricity in the air!*

**e·lec·tri·fy** /ɪ'lɛktrə,faɪ/ *v* [T] **1** to make people feel very excited or interested: *Guns 'n' Roses electrified the crowd.* **2** to make electricity available in a particular area −**electrified** *adj* −**electrifying** *adj*

**e·lec·tro·cute** /ɪ'lɛktrə,kyut/ *v* [T] to kill someone by passing electricity through his/her body −**electrocution** /ɪ,lɛktrə'kyuʃən/ *n* [U]

**e·lec·trode** /ɪ'lɛktroʊd/ *n* the point at which electricity enters or leaves something such as a BATTERY

**e·lec·trol·y·sis** /ɪ,lɛk'trɑlɪsɪs/ *n* [U] the process of using electricity to remove hair from your face, legs etc.

E

**e·lec·tron** /ɪˈlɛktrɑn/ *n* a very small piece of matter that moves around the NUCLEUS (=central part) of an atom −compare NEUTRON, PROTON

**e·lec·tron·ic** /ɪˌlɛkˈtrɑnɪk/ *adj* **1** electronic equipment, such as computers or televisions, that uses electricity in special ways **2** using electronic equipment: *electronic banking* −**electronically** *adv*

**e·lec·tron·ics** /ɪˌlɛkˈtrɑnɪks/ *n* [U] the study of making equipment, such as computers or televisions, that uses electricity in special ways

**el·e·gant** /ˈɛləgənt/ *adj* very beautiful and graceful: *a tall elegant woman* −**elegance** *n* [U] −**elegantly** *adv*

**el·e·gy** /ˈɛlədʒi/ *n* a poem or song that shows that you are sad for someone who has died, or sad about something in the past

**el·e·ment** /ˈɛləmənt/ *n* **1** a simple chemical substance such as oxygen or gold, that is made of only one type of atom −compare COMPOUND **2** **an element of danger/truth/risk etc.** a small amount of danger, truth, risk etc.: *There's an element of truth in what he says.* **3** one part of a plan, system, piece of writing etc.: *a movie with all the elements of a great love story* **4** **be in your element** to be in a situation that you enjoy, because you are good at it: *When talking about wine, Glenn is really in his element.* −see also ELEMENTS

**el·e·men·tal** /ˌɛləˈmɛntəl/ *adj* an elemental feeling is simple, basic, and strong

**el·e·men·ta·ry** /ˌɛləˈmɛntri, -ˈmɛntəri/ *adj* **1** relating to the first and easiest part of a subject: *a book of elementary math exercises* **2** simple or basic: *the elementary human need for food* **3** relating to an ELEMENTARY SCHOOL

**elementary school** /..ˈ.. ˌ../ *n* a school in the US for the first six or eight years of a child's education; GRADE SCHOOL

**el·e·ments** /ˈɛləmənts/ *n* [plural] weather, especially bad weather: *A tent provided shelter from the elements.*

**el·e·phant** /ˈɛləfənt/ *n* a very large gray animal with two TUSKs (=long curved teeth), big ears, and a TRUNK (=a long nose) that it can use to pick things up

**el·e·vate** /ˈɛləˌveɪt/ *v* [T] FORMAL **1** to make someone more important, or to make something better: *Sloane was elevated to the rank of captain.* **2** to raise someone or something to a higher position or level: *This drug tends to elevate body temperature.*

**el·e·va·tion** /ˌɛləˈveɪʃən/ *n* **1** a height above the level of the sea: *We camped at an elevation of 10,000 feet.* **2** [U] FORMAL the act of making someone more important: *the judge's elevation to the Supreme Court* **3** [C,U] FORMAL an increase in the quantity or level of something: *Elevation of blood pressure can cause headaches.*

**el·e·va·tor** /ˈɛləˌveɪtɚ/ *n* a machine in a building that takes people from one level to another

**e·lev·en** /ɪˈlɛvən/ *number* **1** 11 **2** eleven o'clock: *an appointment at eleven*

**e·lev·enth** /ɪˈlɛvənθ/ *number* **1** 11th **2** 1/11 **3** **eleventh hour** the latest possible time: *the eleventh hour cancellation of her wedding*

**elf** /ɛlf/ *n, plural* **elves** a small imaginary person with pointed ears −**elfin** /ˈɛlfɪn/ *adj*

**e·lic·it** /ɪˈlɪsɪt/ *v* [T] FORMAL to get information, a reaction etc. from someone, when this is difficult: *Short questions are more likely to elicit a response.*

**el·i·gi·ble** /ˈɛlədʒəbəl/ *adj* **1** able or allowed to do something: *In the US you're eligible to vote at the age of 18.* **2** an eligible man or woman would be good to marry because s/he is rich, attractive etc. −**eligibility** /ˌɛlədʒəˈbɪləti/ *n* [U]

**e·lim·i·nate** /ɪˈlɪməˌneɪt/ *v* [T] **1** to get rid of something completely: *a plan to eliminate all nuclear weapons* **2** **be eliminated** to be defeated in a sports competition, so that you can no longer take part in it

**e·lim·i·na·tion** /ɪˌlɪməˈneɪʃən/ *n* [U] **1** the removal or destruction of something: *The elimination of unemployment is still our goal.* **2** **process of elimination** a way of finding out the answer to something by getting rid of other answers that are not correct until only one is left

**e·lite** /eɪˈlit, ɪ-/ *n* a small group of people who are powerful or important because they have money, knowledge, special skills etc.

**e·lit·ist** /eɪˈlitɪst, ɪ-/ *adj* DISAPPROVING an elitist system, government etc. is one in which a small group of people have much more power than other people −**elitism** *n* [U]

**elk** /ɛlk/ *n* a large DEER with a lot of hair around its neck

**el·lip·ti·cal** /ɪˈlɪptɪkəl/, **el·lip·tic** /ɪˈlɪptɪk/ *adj* shaped like a circle but with slightly flat sides; OVAL: *the elliptical orbit of the planets*

**elm** /ɛlm/ *n* [C,U] a large tall tree with broad leaves, or the wood of this tree

**e·lon·gat·ed** /ɪˈlɔŋgeɪtɪd/ *adj* long and thin: *elongated shadows* −**elongate** *v* [I,T]

**e·lope** /ɪˈloʊp/ *v* [I] to go away secretly with someone to get married −**elopement** *n* [C,U]

**el·o·quent** /ˈɛləkwənt/ *adj* able to express your ideas, opinions, or feelings clearly, in a way that influences other people: *He gave an eloquent speech after dinner.* −**eloquently** *adv* −**eloquence** *n* [U]

**else** /ɛls/ *adv* **1** a word meaning "in addition," used after words beginning with "any-," "no-," "some-," and after question words: *Clayton needs someone else to help him.* | *There's nothing else to do.* | *What else can I get you?* **2** a word meaning "different," used after words beginning with "any-," "no-," "some-," and after question words: *Is there anything else to* *eat?* | *She was wearing someone else's coat.* (=not her own coat) | *Well, what else can I do?* **3 or else** used when saying what the result of not doing something will be: *They said she'd have to pay, or else she'd go to jail.* **4 if nothing else** used when a situation gives you one opportunity, or has one good result, even though there are no others: *It's boring, but if nothing else, I can get my homework done.*

**else·where** /'ɛlswɛr/ *adv* in or to another place: *Most of the city's residents were born elsewhere.*

**e·lu·ci·date** /ɪ'lusə,deɪt/ *v* [I,T] FORMAL to explain very clearly something that is difficult to understand

**e·lude** /ɪ'lud/ *v* [T] **1** to avoid being found or caught by someone, especially by tricking him/her: *Jones eluded the police for six weeks.* **2** if something that you want eludes you, you do not find it or achieve it: *Success has eluded him so far.* **3** if a fact, someone's name etc. eludes you, you cannot remember it: *Her name eludes me at the moment.*

**e·lu·sive** /ɪ'lusɪv/ *adj* difficult to find, or difficult to remember: *The fox is a sly elusive animal.*

**elves** /ɛlvz/ *n* the plural of ELF

**em** /əm/ *pron* SPOKEN NONSTANDARD them: *Tell the kids I'll pick 'em up after school.*

**e·ma·ci·at·ed** /ɪ'meɪʃi,eɪt̬ɪd/ *adj* extremely thin because of illness or lack of food −see usage note at THIN[1]

**e-mail, email** /'i meɪl/ *n* [U] electronic mail; a system in which you can quickly send letters, information, reports etc. from your computer to someone else who is using a computer −**e-mail, email** *v* [T] −see culture note at INTERNET

**em·a·nate** /'ɛmə,neɪt/ *v*
**emanate from** sth *phr v* [T] to come from or out of something: *Wonderful smells were emanating from the kitchen.*

**e·man·ci·pate** /ɪ'mænsə,peɪt/ *v* [T] FORMAL to make someone free from social, political, or legal rules that limit what s/he can do −**emancipated** *adj* −**emancipation** /ɪ,mænsə'peɪʃən/ *n* [U]

**em·balm** /ɪm'bɑm/ *v* [T] to use chemicals to prevent a dead body from decaying

**em·bank·ment** /ɪm'bæŋkmənt/ *n* a wide wall of earth or stones built to stop water from flooding an area, or to support a road or railroad

**em·bar·go**[1] /ɪm'bɑrgoʊ/ *n* **embargoes** an official order to stop trade with another country: *The UN imposed an arms embargo on the country.*

**embargo**[2] *v* **embargoed, embargoed, embargoing** [T] to officially stop particular goods from being traded with another country

**em·bark** /ɪm'bɑrk/ *v* [I] to go onto a ship or plane −opposite DISEMBARK

**embark on/upon** sth *phr v* [T] to start something new, difficult, or exciting: *Hal is embarking on a new career.*

**em·bar·rass** /ɪm'bærəs/ *v* [T] to make someone feel EMBARRASSED: *I hope I didn't embarrass you in front of your friends.*

**em·bar·rassed** /ɪm'bærəst/ *adj* ashamed, anxious, or nervous, especially in front of other people: *I felt embarrassed about how dirty my house was.* −see usage note at GUILTY

**em·bar·ras·sing** /ɪm'bærəsɪŋ/ *adj* making you feel EMBARRASSED: *He asked a lot of embarrassing questions.*

**em·bar·rass·ment** /ɪm'bærəsmənt/ *n* [U] the feeling that you have when you are EMBARRASSED: *Billy looked down and tried to hide his embarrassment.*

**em·bas·sy** /'ɛmbəsi/ *n* a group of officials who represent their country in a foreign country, or the building they work in

**em·bat·tled** /ɪm'bæt̬ld/ *adj* FORMAL **1** surrounded by enemies, especially in a war: *the embattled city* **2** an embattled person, company etc. has many problems or difficulties

**em·bed** /ɪm'bɛd/ *v* **-dded, -dding** [T] **1** to put something firmly and deeply into something else: *A piece of glass was embedded in his hand.* **2** if your ideas, feelings, or attitudes are embedded, you believe them very strongly: *The idea of freedom is deeply embedded in America's values.*

**em·bel·lish** /ɪm'bɛlɪʃ/ *v* [T] **1** to make something more beautiful by adding decorations to it: *a crown embellished with gold stars* **2** to make a story or statement more interesting by adding details to it that are not true: *Larry couldn't help embellishing the story.* −**embellishment** *n* [C,U]

**em·ber** /'ɛmbɚ/ *n* a piece of wood or coal that stays red and very hot after a fire has stopped burning

**em·bez·zle** /ɪm'bɛzəl/ *v* [I,T] to steal money from the place where you work −**embezzlement** *n* [U] −**embezzler** *n*

**em·bit·tered** /ɪm'bɪt̬ɚd/ *adj* feeling anger, sadness, or hatred because of unpleasant or unfair things that have happened to you −**embitter** *v* [T]

**em·bla·zon** /ɪm'bleɪzən/ *v* [T] to put a name, design etc. on something such as a piece of clothing so that it can be seen clearly

**em·blem** /'ɛmbləm/ *n* a picture, shape, or object that represents a country, company, idea etc.: *The bald eagle is the national emblem of the US.*

**em·bod·y** /ɪm'bɑdi/ *v* [T] to be the best example of an idea or quality: *Mrs. Miller embodies everything I admire in a teacher.* −**embodiment** *n* [U]

**em·boss** /ɪm'bɔs, ɪm'bɑs/ *v* [T] to decorate the surface of metal, leather, paper etc. with a raised pattern **–embossed** *adj: embossed stationery*

**em·brace** /ɪmˈbreɪs/ *v* [T] **1** to put your arms around someone and hold him/her in a caring way: *Rob reached out to embrace her.* **2** FORMAL to eagerly accept ideas, opinions, religions etc.: *young men who are embracing Islam* **–embrace** *n: a tender embrace*

**em·broi·der** /ɪmˈbrɔɪdɚ/ *v* **1** [I,T] to decorate cloth by sewing a picture or pattern on it with colored threads **2** [T] to add untrue details to a story to make it more interesting or exciting **–embroidery** *n* [U]

**em·broil** /ɪmˈbrɔɪl/ *v* [T] **be embroiled in** to be involved in a difficult situation: *Soon the whole group was embroiled in a fierce argument.*

**em·bry·o** /ˈɛmbriˌoʊ/ *n* an animal or human that has not yet been born and has just begun to develop **–compare** FETUS

**em·bry·on·ic** /ˌɛmbriˈɑnɪk/ *adj* not fully developed: *the country's embryonic nuclear weapons program*

**em·cee** /ˌɛmˈsi/ *n* master of ceremonies; someone who introduces the performers on a television program or at a social event **–emcee** *v* [I,T]

**em·er·ald** /ˈɛmərəld/ *n* a valuable bright green jewel

**e·merge** /ɪˈmɚdʒ/ *v* [I] **1** to appear after being hidden: *The sun emerged from behind the clouds.* | *New evidence has emerged during the trial.* **2** to have a particular quality or position after experiencing a difficult situation: *She emerged from the divorce a stronger person.* **–emergence** *n* [U]

**e·mer·gen·cy** /ɪˈmɚdʒənsi/ *n* an unexpected and dangerous situation that you must deal with immediately: *Call an ambulance! This is an emergency!* **–emergency** *adj: an emergency exit*

**emergency room** /.ˈ... ˌ./ *n* the part of a hospital that immediately treats people who have been hurt in a serious accident

**e·mer·gent** /ɪˈmɚdʒənt/ *adj* beginning to develop and be noticeable: *the emergent nations of Eastern Europe and Africa*

**e·mer·i·tus** /ɪˈmɛrətəs/ *adj* a PROFESSOR emeritus is no longer working but still has an official title

**em·er·y board** /ˈɛmri ˌbɔrd/ *n* a NAIL FILE made from thick card covered with a mineral powder

**em·i·grant** /ˈɛməgrənt/ *n* someone who leaves his/her own country to live in another: *an emigrant to the United States* **–compare** IMMIGRANT

**em·i·grate** /ˈɛməˌgreɪt/ *v* [I] to leave your own country in order to live in another: *Maria emigrated from Canada three years ago.*

**–emigration** /ˌɛməˈgreɪʃən/ *n* [C,U] **–compare** IMMIGRATION

**em·i·nent** /ˈɛmənənt/ *adj* famous and admired by many people: *an eminent professor of medicine*

**eminent do·main** /ˌ... .ˈ./ *n* LAW the right of the US government to pay for and take someone's private land so it can be used for a public purpose

**em·i·nent·ly** /ˈɛmənəntˈli/ *adv* FORMAL completely, and without any doubt: *He's eminently qualified to do the job.*

**e·mir** /ɛˈmɪr, i-/ *n* a Muslim ruler, especially in Asia and parts of Africa

**e·mir·ate** /ˈɛmərɪt/ *n* the country ruled by an EMIR

**em·is·sar·y** /ˈɛməˌsɛri/ *n* someone who is sent with an official message, or who must do other official work: *an emissary from the Italian government*

**e·mis·sion** /ɪˈmɪʃən/ *n* [C,U] the sending out of gas, heat, light, sound etc., or the gas etc. that is sent out: *an emissions test* (=a test to make sure the gases your car sends out are at the right level)

**e·mit** /ɪˈmɪt/ *v* **-tted, -tting** [T] FORMAL to send out gas, heat, light, sound etc.: *The kettle emitted a shrill whistle.*

**Em·my** /ˈɛmi/ *n* a prize given every year to the best program, actor etc. on US television

**e·mo·tion** /ɪˈmoʊʃən/ *n* [C,U] a strong human feeling such as love or hate: *David doesn't usually show his true emotions.* | *Her voice was full of emotion.*

**e·mo·tion·al** /ɪˈmoʊʃənəl/ *adj* **1** making people have strong feelings: *The end of the movie was really emotional.* **2** showing your emotions to other people, especially by crying: *Please don't get all emotional.* **3** relating to your feelings or how they are controlled: *the emotional development of children* **4** influenced by what you feel rather than what you know: *an emotional response to the problem* **–emotionally** *adv*

**e·mo·tive** /ɪˈmoʊtɪv/ *adj* making people have strong feelings: *an emotive speech about the effects of war*

**em·pa·thy** /'ɛmpəθi/ *n* [U] the ability to understand someone else's feelings and problems –**empathize** *v* [I] –compare SYMPATHY

**em·per·or** /'ɛmpərɚ/ *n* the ruler of an EMPIRE

**em·pha·sis** /'ɛmfəsɪs/ *n, plural* **emphases** /'ɛmfəsiz/ [C,U] special importance: *Jamieson's report* **puts/places an emphasis on** *the need for better working conditions.*

**em·pha·size** /'ɛmfə,saɪz/ *v* [T] to show that an opinion, idea, quality etc. is important: *My teacher emphasized the importance of grammar.* ✗ DON'T SAY "...emphasize on." ✗

**em·phat·ic** /ɪm'fætɪk/ *adj* done or said in a way that shows something is important or should be believed: *Dale's answer was an emphatic "No!"* –**emphatically** *adv*

**em·phy·se·ma** /,ɛmfə'zimə, -'si-/ *n* [U] a serious disease that affects the lungs, making it difficult to breathe

**em·pire** /'ɛmpaɪɚ/ *n* **1** a group of countries that are all controlled by one ruler or government **2** a group of organizations that are all controlled by one person or company: *a media empire*

**em·pir·i·cal** /ɪm'pɪrɪkəl, ɛm-/ *adj* based on practical experience rather than on ideas: *an empirical approach to studying sociology*

**em·ploy** /ɪm'plɔɪ/ *v* [T] **1** to pay someone to work for you: *The factory employs over 2000 people.* **2** to use a particular object, method, or skill in order to achieve something: *research methods employed by scientists*

**em·ploy·ee** /ɪm'plɔɪ-i, ,ɪmplɔɪ'i, ,ɛm-/ *n* someone who is paid to work for a person, organization, or company: *a government employee*

**em·ploy·er** /ɪm'plɔɪɚ/ *n* a person, company, or organization that employs people: *The shoe factory is the largest employer in this area.*

**em·ploy·ment** /ɪm'plɔɪmənt/ *n* [U] **1** work that you do to earn money: *Steve's still looking for employment.* **2** the use of an object, method, skill etc. to achieve something: *the employment of weapons to gain control of the area* –compare UNEMPLOYMENT

**em·po·ri·um** /ɪm'pɔriəm/ *n* a word meaning a large store, used in the names of stores

**em·pow·er** /ɪm'paʊɚ/ *v* [T] to give someone the confidence, power, or right to do something: *Our aim is to* **empower** *women* **to defend themselves.**

**em·press** /'ɛmprɪs/ *n* the female ruler of an EMPIRE, or the wife of an EMPEROR

**emp·ty**[1] /'ɛmpti/ *adj* **1** having nothing inside: *Your glass is empty - would you like some more wine?* | *an empty box* **2** not filled with people, or not being used by any-

**empty**

empty

full

one: *Is this seat empty?* | *an empty restaurant* **3** unhappy because nothing seems interesting, important, or worth doing: *After the divorce, my life felt empty.* **4 empty words/promises/gestures etc.** words etc. that are not sincere and therefore have no meaning **5 on an empty stomach** without having eaten anything first: *You shouldn't go to school on an empty stomach.* **6 empty nest (syndrome)** a situation in which parents become sad because their children have grown up and left home

**empty**[2] *v* **1** [T] also **empty out** to remove everything that is inside of something else: *I found my umbrella when I was emptying out the closet.* | *Troy, please empty the dishwasher.* **2** [T] to pour the things that are in a container into or onto something else: *Empty the contents of one pudding package* **into** *a large bowl.* **3** [I,T] to leave a place, vehicle etc., or to make someone do this: *Judge Sinclair ordered the courtroom to be emptied.* **4** [I] to flow into a large area of water: *the place where Waddell Creek* **empties into** *the ocean*

**empty-hand·ed** /,.. '../ *adj* without gaining or getting anything: *The thieves fled the building empty-handed.*

**em·u·late** /'ɛmyə,leɪt/ *v* [T] FORMAL to try to do something or behave in the same way as someone; copy: *Children emulate their parents' behavior.*

**en·a·ble** /ɪ'neɪbəl/ *v* [T] to make someone or something able to do something: *The new plastic enables us to make our products more cheaply.*

**en·act** /ɪ'nækt/ *v* [T] to make something a law: *The measure was enacted to prevent tax abuses.*

**en·am·el** /ɪ'næməl/ *n* [U] **1** a substance like glass that is put on metal, clay etc. for decoration or for protection **2** the hard smooth outer surface of your teeth

**en·am·ored** /ɪ'næmɚd/ *adj* FORMAL **be enamored of** to like and admire someone or something very much: *Not everyone in town is quite so enamored of the new building.*

**en·case** /ɪn'keɪs/ *v* [T] to cover or surround something completely: *art objects* **encased in** *a glass box*

**en·chant·ed** /ɪn'tʃæntɪd/ *adj* something that is enchanted has been changed by magic so that it has special powers: *an enchanted forest*

**en·chant·ing** /ɪn'tʃæntɪŋ/ *adj* very pleasant in a way that makes you feel very interested, happy, or excited: *an enchanting movie about young love*

**en·chi·la·da** /,ɛntʃə'lɑdə/ *n* a Mexican food made from a corn TORTILLA rolled around meat or beans and covered with a hot-tasting liquid

**en·clave** /'ɛnkleɪv, 'ɑŋ-/ *n* a place or group of people that is surrounded by areas or groups of

E

people that are different from it: *the Italian-American enclave in New York*

**en·close** /ɪnˈkloʊz/ v [T] **1** to put something inside an envelope with a letter: *A copy of the article is enclosed.* **2** to surround an area, especially with a fence or wall: *A high wall enclosed the yard.* —**enclosed** *adj*

**en·clo·sure** /ɪnˈkloʊʒɚ/ n **1** an area that is surrounded by something such as a wall or fence: *The animals are kept in a large enclosure.* **2** things such as documents, photographs, money etc. that you send with a letter

**en·com·pass** /ɪnˈkʌmpəs/ v [T] **1** to include a range of ideas, subjects etc.: *Crosby's career encompassed radio, records, TV, and movies.* **2** to completely cover or surround an area: *a national park encompassing 400 square miles*

**en·core** /ˈɑŋkɔr/ n an additional performance that is performed because the people listening want to hear more

**en·coun·ter**[1] /ɪnˈkaʊntɚ/ v [T] **1** to experience something bad that you have to deal with: *She encountered a lot of difficulties trying to get her article published.* **2** FORMAL to see someone or something that you were not expecting to see

**encounter**[2] n **1** a dangerous or unpleasant meeting between two people or groups: *one of the bloodiest encounters of the Civil War* **2** an occasion when you meet someone without planning to: *I had an encounter with my ex-boyfriend the other day.*

**en·cour·age** /ɪnˈkɚɪdʒ, -ˈkʌr-/ v [T] **1** to help someone become confident or brave enough to do something: *My drama teacher encouraged me to try out for the school play.* **2** to make something become more likely to happen: *a plant food that encourages growth* —**encouragement** n [C,U] —opposite DISCOURAGE

**en·cour·ag·ing** /ɪnˈkɚɪdʒɪŋ/ adj giving you hope and confidence: *This time, the news is more encouraging.* —**encouragingly** adv

**en·croach** /ɪnˈkroʊtʃ/ v [T] **1** to cover more and more land in a way that affects or changes that land: *The forest fire is now encroaching on the town of Bridgeway.* **2** to take away more and more of someone's time, rights etc.: *Recent court decisions have allowed the government to encroach on people's lives.*

**en·crust·ed** /ɪnˈkrʌstɪd/ adj covered with something hard and sharp, such as jewels, ice, or dried mud

**en·cum·ber** /ɪnˈkʌmbɚ/ v [T] FORMAL to make someone have difficulty moving or doing something —**encumbrance** /ɪnˈkʌmbrəns/ n

**en·cy·clo·pe·di·a** /ɪnˌsaɪkləˈpidiə/ n a book, set of books, or CD that contains facts about many subjects or about one particular subject

**end**[1] /ɛnd/ n

**1** ▶LAST PART◀ the last part of something

such as a period of time, activity, book, or movie: *Of course, the hero died at the end of the story.* | *Rob's moving to Maine at the end of September.*

**2** ▶FARTHEST POINT◀ the farthest point of a place or thing: *Mr. Williams sent us to the end of the line.* | *the **deep/shallow end** of the pool* | *the **north/south end** of the lake*

**3** ▶OF A SITUATION◀ a situation in which something is finished or no longer exists: *Their relationship had **come to an end**.* (=had finished) | *the UN's latest plan to **put an end to** (=stop) the war*

**4 in the end** after a lot of thinking or discussion; finally: *In the end, we decided to go to Florida.*

**5 make ends meet** to have just enough money to buy what you need: *It's been hard to make ends meet since Ray got laid off.*

**6 it's not the end of the world** SPOKEN used in order to say that a problem is not too serious or bad: *If you don't get the job, it's not the end of the world.*

**7** ▶RESULT◀ FORMAL the result that you hope to achieve: *Stalin wanted a weak China, and worked **to that end**.* (=to achieve that result)

**8 at the end of your rope** extremely annoyed, upset, and impatient because you cannot control, change, or achieve something

**9 end to end** with the end of something next to the end of something else: *cars parked end to end*

**10** ▶IN SPORTS◀ in football, one of two players who play on the outside of the TACKLEs and try to catch the ball —see also **go off the deep end** (DEEP[1])

**end**[2] v [I,T] to finish or stop, or to make something do this: *World War II ended in 1945.* | *Janet's party didn't end until 4 o'clock in the morning.* | *Lucy decided to end her relationship with Jeff.*

**end in** sth phr v [T] to have a particular result or to finish in a particular way: *The meeting **ended in** a huge argument.*

**end up** phr v [I] to come to be in a place, situation, or condition that you did not expect or intend: *Whenever we go out to dinner I always **end up** paying the bill.*

**en·dan·ger** /ɪnˈdeɪndʒɚ/ v [T] to put someone or something in a dangerous or harmful situation: *Smoking seriously endangers your health.*

**en·dan·gered spe·cies** /ɪˌ.. ˈ../ n a type of animal or plant that soon might not exist

**en·dear** /ɪnˈdɪr/ v

**endear** sb **to** sb phr v [T] to make someone be liked by other people: *His speech did not **endear** him to the voters.*

**en·dear·ing** /ɪnˈdɪrɪŋ/ adj making someone like or love you: *an endearing smile*

**en·dear·ment** /ɪnˈdɪrmənt/ n something you say that shows your love for someone

**en·deav·or**[1] /ɪnˈdɛvɚ/ n [C,U] an attempt or effort to do something new or different: *The artist fails in his* **endeavor to** *create a new style.*

**endeavor**[2] v [I] FORMAL to try very hard: *One must always* **endeavor to** *do one's best.*

**en·dem·ic** /ɛnˈdɛmɪk, ɪn-/ adj regularly happening in a particular place or among a particular group of people: *Violent crime is now endemic in parts of the city.*

**end·ing** /ˈɛndɪŋ/ n the end of a story, movie, play etc.: *a happy ending*

**en·dive** /ˈɛndaɪv/ n [C,U] a vegetable with bitter-tasting leaves that are eaten raw in SALADs

**end·less** /ˈɛndlɪs/ adj continuing for a very long time, especially in a way that is annoying: *his endless complaining*

**en·dorse** /ɪnˈdɔrs/ v [T] **1** to officially say that you support or approve of someone or something: *The company endorses a policy of equal pay for women.* **2** to sign your name on the back of a check **–endorsement** n [C,U]

**en·dow** /ɪnˈdaʊ/ v [T] **1** to give an ENDOWMENT to a college, hospital etc. **2 be endowed with talent/resources/rights etc.** FORMAL to have or be given a good quality, feature, or ability

**en·dow·ment** /ɪnˈdaʊmənt/ n [C,U] a large amount of money or property that is given to a college, hospital etc. so that it has an income

**en·dur·ance** /ɪnˈdʊrəns/ n [U] the ability to remain strong and patient even though you feel pain or have problems: *Jogging will help increase your endurance.*

**en·dure** /ɪnˈdʊr/ v [T] to suffer pain or deal with a very difficult situation for a long time: *People in the war-torn country have endured months of fighting.*

**en·dur·ing** /ɪnˈdʊrɪŋ/ adj continuing to exist in spite of difficulties: *an enduring relationship*

**end zone** /ˈ. ./ n the end of a football field to which you carry or catch a ball to win points –see picture on page 472

**en·e·my** /ˈɛnəmi/ n **1** someone who hates you and wants to harm you or prevent you from being successful: *Judge Lonza has* **made a lot of enemies** *during her career.* **2** the person or group of people that you are fighting in a war: *a surprise attack on* **the enemy**

**en·er·get·ic** /ˌɛnɚˈdʒɛtɪk/ adj very active: *Sam's kids are really energetic.* **–energetically** adv

**en·er·gy** /ˈɛnɚdʒi/ n [C,U] **1** the ability to be active and do a lot of work or activities without being tired: *I'm finally getting my energy back after my surgery.* **2** power from burning oil, coal etc. that produces heat and makes machines work: *atomic energy | the world's energy resources*

**en·force** /ɪnˈfɔrs/ v [T] to make people obey a rule or law: *They're strict here about enforcing*

the speed limit. **–enforcement** n [U] **–enforceable** adj

**en·fran·chise** /ɪnˈfræn̩tʃaɪz/ v [T] FORMAL to give a group of people rights, especially the right to vote –opposite DISENFRANCHISE

**en·gage** /ɪnˈgeɪdʒ/ v [T] FORMAL **1** to make someone remain interested in something: *a storyteller able to* **engage** *the children's imaginations* **2** to employ someone: *I suggest that you* **engage** *a good accountant.*

**engage in** phr v [T] **1** involve yourself in an activity: *They're* **engaging in** *a price war with three other companies* **2** FORMAL **engage sb in (a) conversation** to begin talking to someone

**en·gaged** /ɪnˈgeɪdʒd/ adj two people who are engaged have agreed to marry each other: *Viv and Tyrell* **got engaged** *last month. | Sheri's* **engaged to** *a guy in the Army.* ✗ DON'T SAY "engaged with someone." ✗

**en·gage·ment** /ɪnˈgeɪdʒmənt/ n **1** an agreement to marry someone: *Charlene and I have* **broken off** *our* **engagement.** (=decided to end it) **2** FORMAL an arrangement to do something or meet someone: *an engagement calendar*

**en·gag·ing** /ɪnˈgeɪdʒɪŋ/ adj attracting people's attention and interest: *an engaging personality*

**en·gen·der** /ɪnˈdʒɛndɚ/ v [T] FORMAL to be the cause of something such as a situation, action, or emotion

**en·gine** /ˈɛndʒɪn/ n **1** a piece of machinery that produces power from oil, steam, electricity etc. and uses it to make something move: *the engine of a car | a jet engine* **2** the part of a train that pulls the other CARs along a railroad

**en·gi·neer**[1] /ˌɛndʒəˈnɪr/ n **1** someone who designs the way roads, bridges, machines etc. are built: *a software engineer* **2** someone who controls the engines on a ship, plane, or train

**engineer**[2] v [T] to secretly and effectively arrange something: *He had powerful enemies who engineered his downfall.*

**en·gi·neer·ing** /ˌɛndʒəˈnɪrɪŋ/ n [U] the profession or activity of designing the way roads, bridges, machines etc. are built

**En·glish**[1] /ˈɪŋglɪʃ/ n **1** [U] the language used in places such as the US, Canada, and Great Britain **2 the English** [plural] the people of England

**English**[2] adj **1** relating to the English language **2** relating to or coming from England

**en·grave** /ɪnˈgreɪv/ v [T] to cut words or pictures onto the surface of metal, wood, glass etc.: *an engraved trophy*

**en·grav·ing** /ɪnˈgreɪvɪŋ/ n [T] a picture printed from an ENGRAVEd piece of metal or wood

**en·grossed** /ɪnˈgroʊst/ adj so interested in something that you do not notice anything else:

*Kit was in a corner, completely **engrossed in** a book.*

**en·gross·ing** /ɪnˈgroʊsɪŋ/ *adj* so interesting that you do not notice anything else: *an engrossing story*

**en·gulf** /ɪnˈgʌlf/ *v* [T] **1** to suddenly affect someone so strongly that s/he feels nothing else: *Fear engulfed him as he approached the stage.* **2** to completely surround or cover something: *a home **engulfed in** flames*

**en·hance** /ɪnˈhæns/ *v* [T] to make something such as a taste, feeling, or ability better: *Adding lemon juice will enhance the flavor.* —**enhancement** *n* [C,U]

**e·nig·ma** /ɪˈnɪgmə/ *n* a person, thing, or event that is strange, mysterious, and difficult to understand: *That man will always be an enigma to me.* —**enigmatic** /ˌɛnɪgˈmætɪk/ *adj*

**en·joy** /ɪnˈdʒɔɪ/ *v* [T] **1** if you enjoy something, it gives you pleasure: *Did you enjoy the movie? | I really enjoy walking the dog.* ✗ DON'T SAY "I enjoy to walk the dog." ✗ **2 enjoy yourself** to be happy and have fun in a particular situation: *She was determined to enjoy herself at the prom even though she was by herself.* **3** to have a particular ability, advantage, or success: *The team has enjoyed some success this season.* —**enjoyment** *n* [U]

**en·joy·a·ble** /ɪnˈdʒɔɪəbəl/ *adj* giving you pleasure: *an enjoyable afternoon/concert/book*

**en·large** /ɪnˈlɑrdʒ/ *v* [T] to become bigger, or to make something become bigger: *I'm going to get some of these pictures enlarged.*

**en·large·ment** /ɪnˈlɑrdʒmənt/ *n* a photograph that has been printed again in a larger size

**en·light·en** /ɪnˈlaɪtˈn/ *v* [T] FORMAL to explain something to someone so that s/he finally understands it —**enlightening** *adj*: *an enlightening experience*

**en·light·ened** /ɪnˈlaɪtˈnd/ *adj* wise, fair, and sensible because you know what is true and what is false: *an enlightened progressive company that treats its employees well*

**en·list** /ɪnˈlɪst/ *v* **1** [T] to persuade someone to help you, do a job for you etc.: *Moore **enlisted the help of** four friends to move the piano.* **2** [I] to join the army, navy etc.: *My grandfather enlisted when he was 18.* —**enlistment** *n* [C,U]

**en·liv·en** /ɪnˈlaɪvən/ *v* [T] to make something more interesting or exciting

**en masse** /ɑn ˈmæs, -ˈmɑs, ɛn-/ *adv* together as one group: *City councilors threatened to resign en masse.*

**en·mi·ty** /ˈɛnməti/ *n* [U] feelings of hatred and anger; ANIMOSITY

**e·nor·mi·ty** /ɪˈnɔrməti/ *n* [singular, U] the fact of being very large or serious: *He could not understand the enormity of his crime.*

**e·nor·mous** /ɪˈnɔrməs/ *adj* extremely large in size or amount: *You should see their house - it's*

enormous! | *an enormous amount of work to finish*

**e·nor·mous·ly** /ɪˈnɔrməsli/ *adv* extremely or very much: *an enormously popular writer*

**e·nough¹** /ɪˈnʌf/ *adv* **1** as big, as well, as far, as much etc. as necessary: *This bag isn't big enough to hold all my stuff. | I couldn't see well enough to read the sign.* **2** not very, but in an acceptable way: *She's nice enough, but I don't think she likes me.*

enough

Her bag isn't big enough.

**3 sth is bad enough...** SPOKEN said when one thing is bad, but another thing is worse: *It's bad enough that I have to work late - then you make jokes about it!* **4 strangely/oddly/funnily enough** SPOKEN said when what you have just said or are about to say is strange: *Funnily enough, I met him today after not having seen him for months.* —see also **sure enough** (SURE²) —see usage note at TOO

> **USAGE NOTE** using **enough** in sentences
>
> **Enough** is used after adjectives or adverbs, but it is usually used before a noun: *They're rich enough to have three cars. | I can't walk fast enough to keep up with you. | Do we have enough money for the tickets?* In sentences with "there" as the subject, **enough** can also be used after a noun: *There's room enough for everyone.*

**enough²** *determiner, pronoun* **1** as much or as many as necessary: *Do we have enough food for everybody? | I think we've done enough for one day. | He doesn't earn **enough** to pay the rent.* **2 have had enough (of)** to be very annoyed with someone or something: *I'd had enough of the neighbors' noise, so I called the police.*

**en·rage** /ɪnˈreɪdʒ/ *v* [T] to make someone very angry: *Ed was **enraged at/by** what Dee said to me.* —**enraged** *adj*

**en·rich** /ɪnˈrɪtʃ/ *v* [T] to improve the quality of something: *activities to enrich your language ability | vitamin-enriched flour* —**enrichment** *n* [U]

**en·roll, enrol** /ɪnˈrol/ *v* [I,T] to make yourself or another person officially a member of a course, school etc.: *More students are enrolling in special education classes.*

**en·roll·ment** /ɪnˈrolmənt/ *n* [C,U] the number of students who are ENROLLed in a course or class, or the process of enrolling them: *Enrollment was high this year.*

**en route** /ɑn ˈrut, ɛn-/ *adv* on the way: *Dinner will be served **en route to** Dallas.*

**en·sconce** /ɪnˈskɑns/ *v* [T] FORMAL OR HUMOROUS to put someone in a safe and comfortable place: *Martha **ensconced herself in** the biggest chair.*

**en·sem·ble** /ɑn'sɑmbəl/ *n* a small group of musicians who play together regularly

**en·shrine** /ɪn'ʃraɪn/ *v* [T] FORMAL to put something in a special place so that people can see it and remember it: *civil rights **enshrined in** the Constitution*

**en·sign** /'ɛnsən/ *n* **1** also **Ensign** an officer who has a low rank in the Navy or Coast Guard **2** a flag on a ship that shows what country the ship belongs to

**en·slave** /ɪn'sleɪv/ *v* [T] FORMAL **1** to put someone into a situation that is difficult to escape from **2** to make someone a SLAVE

**en·sue** /ɪn'su/ *v* [I] FORMAL to happen after something, often as a result of it: *They received the report, and a long discussion ensued.* **–ensuing** *adj: The ensuing battle was fierce.*

**en·sure** /ɪn'ʃʊr/ *v* [T] to do something to be certain of a particular result: *We must **ensure that** standards are maintained.*

**en·tail** /ɪn'teɪl/ *v* [T] to make something necessary, or have something as a necessary part: *Does your new job entail much traveling?*

**en·tan·gle** /ɪn'tæŋgəl/ *v* [T] **1** be **entangled in/with** to make someone be involved with someone or something bad: *He became **entangled with** dishonest business partners.* **2** to make something be twisted or caught in something else: *a fish **entangled in** the net* **–entanglement** *n* [C,U]

**en·ter** /'ɛntər/ *v* **1** [I,T] to go or come into a place: *When the President entered, we stood up.* | *Army tanks entered the capital.* **2** [T] to go inside something: *The infection hasn't entered her bloodstream.* **3** [T] to start working in a particular profession, or studying at a particular university, school etc.: *Julia's planning to enter the Navy.* | *Many older students are now entering university.* **4** [T] to start to take part in an activity: *There was a great feeling of national pride after we entered the war.* **5** [I,T] to take part in something such as a competition or to arrange for someone else to do this: *She entered the competition and won.* | *Mary entered her son in the race.* **6** [T] to put information into a computer by pressing the keys, or to write information on a form, document etc.: *Enter your name on the form.* **7** [T] to begin a period of time: *The economy is entering a period of growth.*

**enter into sth** *phr v* [T] **1** to start doing something, discussing something etc.: *Both sides must **enter into** negotiations.* **2** to be considered as a reason for something: *Money didn't **enter into** my decision to leave.* **3 enter into an agreement/contract etc.** FORMAL to officially make an agreement

**en·ter·prise** /'ɛntər,praɪz/ *n* **1** a company, organization, or business, especially a new one:

*The store is a family enterprise.* (=owned by one family) **2** a large and complicated plan or process that you work on with other people: *The show is a huge enterprise that takes a year to plan.* **3** [U] the ability to work hard and think of new ideas, especially in business: *We have a great product due to the enterprise and energy of this team.* **4** [U] the activity of starting and running businesses: *private enterprise* –see also FREE ENTERPRISE

**en·ter·pris·ing** /'ɛntər,praɪzɪŋ/ *adj* able and willing to do things that are new or difficult: *an enterprising law student*

**en·ter·tain** /,ɛntər'teɪn/ *v* **1** [T] to do something that interests and amuses people: *He spent the next hour **entertaining** us **with** jokes.* **2** [I,T] to treat someone as a guest by providing food and drink for him/her: *Mike's entertaining clients at JoJo's restaurant.* **3** [T] FORMAL to consider or think about an idea, doubt, suggestion etc.

**en·ter·tain·er** /,ɛntər'teɪnər/ *n* someone whose job is to amuse people and make them laugh: *a circus entertainer*

**en·ter·tain·ing** /,ɛntər'teɪnɪŋ/ *adj* amusing and interesting: *an entertaining movie/book* | *an entertaining evening*

**en·ter·tain·ment** /,ɛntər'teɪnmənt/ *n* [U] things such as television, movies etc. that amuse or interest people: *the entertainment industry* | *What do people **do for entertainment** in this town?*

**en·thrall** /ɪn'θrɔl/ *v* [T] to completely hold someone's attention and interest: *We were enthralled by the new play.* **–enthralling** *adj*

**en·thuse** /ɪn'θuz/ *v* [I] to talk about something with excitement and admiration: *Jeff showed us pictures and enthused about his trip to Africa.*

**en·thu·si·as·m** /ɪn'θuzi,æzəm/ *n* [U] a strong feeling of interest, excitement, or admiration about something: *He sang **with enthusiasm**.* | *A few of the kids showed **enthusiasm for** art.* **–enthusiast** /ɪn'θuziəst/ *n*

**en·thu·si·as·tic** /ɪn,θuzi'æstɪk/ *adj* showing a lot of interest and excitement about something: *I was really **enthusiastic about** going to the party.* **–enthusiastically** *adv*

**en·tice** /ɪn'taɪs/ *v* [T] to persuade someone to do something by offering him/her something nice: *another ad trying to **entice** people **into** buying a new car* **–enticing** *adj: enticing smells from the kitchen* **–enticement** *n* [C,U]

**en·tire** /ɪn'taɪr/ *adj* a word meaning whole or complete, used in order to emphasize what you are saying: *I've spent my entire day cooking.* | *The entire wheat crop was lost to bad weather.*

**en·tire·ly** /ɪn'taɪrli/ *adv* completely: *Things are entirely different now.* | *The decision is entirely yours.*

**en·tire·ty** /ɪn'taɪəti, -'taɪrəti/ *n* [U] **in sth's entirety** using or affecting all of something: *The speech is published in its entirety.*

**en·ti·tle** /ɪn'taɪtl/ *v* [T] **1** to give someone the right to have or do something: *This coupon entitles you to 50¢ off a box of cornflakes.* **2** to give a title to a book, play etc., or to have a particular title: *a book entitled "The Stone Diaries"*

**en·ti·tle·ment** /ɪn'taɪtlmənt/ *n* [C,U] the official right to have or receive something, or the amount you receive: *an employee's entitlement to free medical care*

**en·ti·ty** /'ɛnɾəti/ *n* FORMAL something that exists as a single and complete unit: *The treaty made East and West Germany a single economic entity.*

**en·to·mol·o·gy** /ˌɛntə'malədʒi/ *n* [U] the scientific study of insects −**entomologist** *n*

**en·tou·rage** /ˌɑntʊ'rɑʒ/ *n* a group of people who travel with an important person: *the President's entourage*

**en·trails** /'ɛntreɪlz/ *n* [plural] the inside parts of a person or animal, especially the BOWELs

**en·trance** /'ɛntrəns/ *n* **1** a door, gate, or other opening that you go through to enter a place: *Meet us at the main entrance to the school.* **2** [U] the right or opportunity to enter a place, become a member of a profession, university etc.: *Entrance will be denied to those without tickets.* | *There will be an entrance fee of $30.* **3 make an entrance** to come into a place in a way that makes people notice you: *She loves to make an entrance at a party.* −compare ENTRY

**en·tranced** /ɪn'trænst/ *adj* very interested in and pleased with something: *The children were entranced by the performance.* −**entrance** *v* [T]

**en·trant** /'ɛntrənt/ *n* FORMAL someone who enters a competition

**en·trap** /ɪn'træp/ *v* -**pped**, -**pping** [T] FORMAL to deceive someone so that s/he is caught doing something illegal −**entrapment** *n* [U]

**en·treat** /ɪn'trit/ *v* [T] FORMAL to ask someone, with a lot of emotion, to do something −**entreaty** *n* [C,U]

**en·trée** /'ɑntreɪ/ *n* the main dish of a meal

**en·trenched** /ɪn'trɛntʃt/ *adj* strongly established and not likely to change: *entrenched values and attitudes*

**en·tre·pre·neur** /ˌɑntrəprə'nɚ, -'nʊr/ *n* someone who starts a company, arranges business deals, and takes risks in order to make a profit −**entrepreneurial** /ˌɑntrəprə'nʊriəl/ *adj*

**en·trust** /ɪn'trʌst/ *v* [T] to give someone something to be responsible for: *Bergen was entrusted with delivering the documents.*

**en·try** /'ɛntri/ *n* **1** the act of coming or going into a place: *What was your point of entry into the United States?* **2** [U] the right or opportun-ity to enter a place or become a member of a group: *the entry of new firms into the market* **3** also **entryway** a door, gate, or passage that you go through to go into a place **4** something written or printed in a book, list etc.: *a dictionary entry* **5** [U] the act of recording information on paper or in a computer: *data entry* **6** a person or thing in a competition, race etc.: *the winning entry* **7** the act of entering a competition, race etc.: *Entry is open to anyone over 18.*

**en·twine** /ɪn'twaɪn/ *v* [T] **1 be entwined** to be closely connected with each other in a complicated way: *The two sisters' lives were deeply entwined.* **2** to twist something around something else: *flowers entwined in her hair*

**e·nu·mer·ate** /ɪ'numə,reɪt/ *v* [T] FORMAL to name a list of things, one by one

**e·nun·ci·ate** /ɪ'nʌnsi,eɪt/ *v* FORMAL **1** [I,T] to pronounce words or sounds clearly **2** [T] to express ideas or principles clearly and firmly −**enunciation** /ɪ,nʌnsi'eɪʃən/ *n* [C,U]

**en·vel·op** /ɪn'vɛləp/ *v* [T] to cover something completely: *a building enveloped in flames* −**enveloping** *adj*

**en·ve·lope** /'ɛnvə,loʊp, 'ɑn-/ *n* the paper cover in which you put a letter

envelope

**en·vi·a·ble** /'ɛnviəbəl/ *adj* making you wish you had something or could do something: *an enviable position in the company* −**enviably** *adv*

envelope

**en·vi·ous** /'ɛnviəs/ *adj* wishing that you had someone else's qualities or things: *Jackie was envious of Sylvia's success.* −**enviously** *adv* −see usage note at JEALOUS

**en·vi·ron·ment** /ɪn'vaɪərnmənt/ *n* **1 the environment** the land, water, and air in which people, animals, and plants live: *laws to protect the environment* **2** [C,U] the situations, people etc. that influence the way in which people live and work: *a pleasant work environment*

**en·vi·ron·men·tal** /ɪn,vaɪərn'mɛntl/ *adj* relating to or affecting the air, land, or water on Earth: *environmental damage caused by oil spills* −**environmentally** *adv*

**en·vi·ron·men·tal·ist** /ɪn,vaɪərn'mɛntl-ɪst/ *n* someone who is concerned about protecting the environment

**en·vi·rons** /ɪn'vaɪrənz, ɛn-/ *n* [plural] FORMAL the area surrounding a place

**en·vi·sion** /ɪn'vɪʒən/, **en·vis·age** /ɪn'vɪzɪdʒ/ *v* [T] to imagine something as a future possibility: *Eve had envisioned a career as a diplomat.*

**en·voy** /'ɛnvɔɪ, 'ɑn-/ *n* someone who is sent to another country as an official representative

**en·vy**[1] /'ɛnvi/ *n* [U] **1** the feeling of wanting to have the qualities or things that someone else has: *She was looking* **with envy** *at Pat's new shoes.* **2** **be the envy of** to be something that other people admire and want: *Our social programs are the envy of other cities.*

**envy**[2] *v* [T] to wish you had the qualities or things that someone else has: *I envy Nina - she gets to travel all over the world in her job! | I envy you your house." ✗* DON'T SAY "I envy your house." ✗

**en·zyme** /'ɛnzaɪm/ *n* TECHNICAL a chemical substance produced by living cells in plants and animals, that causes changes in other chemical substances

**ep·au·let** /ˌɛpə'lɛt, 'ɛpəˌlɛt/ *n* a shoulder decoration on a military uniform

**e·phem·er·al** /ɪ'fɛmərəl/ *adj* existing only for a short time

**ep·ic**[1] /'ɛpɪk/ *adj* **1** full of brave action and excitement: *an epic journey* **2** very big, long, or impressive: *an epic movie*

**epic**[2] *n* **1** a book or movie that tells a long story: *"Gone with the Wind," an epic about the Civil War* **2** a long poem about what gods or important people did in past times: *Homer's epic "The Odyssey"*

**ep·i·cen·ter** /'ɛpəˌsɛntɚ/ *n* TECHNICAL the place on the Earth's surface above the point where an EARTHQUAKE begins

**ep·i·dem·ic** /ˌɛpə'dɛmɪk/ *n* **1** the rapid spread of an infectious disease among many people in the same area: *a typhoid epidemic* **2** something bad that develops and spreads quickly: *an epidemic of crime* –**epidemic** *adj*

**ep·i·gram** /'ɛpəˌgræm/ *n* a short amusing poem or saying that expresses a wise idea

**ep·i·lep·sy** /'ɛpəˌlɛpsi/ *n* [U] a disease of the brain that causes someone to become unconscious, and often move his/her body in a violent uncontrolled way

**ep·i·lep·tic** /ˌɛpə'lɛptɪk/ *n* someone who has EPILEPSY –**epileptic** *adj*

**ep·i·logue** /'ɛpəˌlɔg, -ˌlag/ *n* a speech or piece of writing added to the end of a book, movie, or play

**E·pis·co·pal** /ɪ'pɪskəpəl/ *adj* relating to the Protestant church in America that developed from the Church of England –**Episcopalian** /ɪˌpɪskə'peɪliən/ *adj*

**ep·i·sode** /'ɛpəˌsoʊd/ *n* **1** a television or radio program that is one of a series of programs that tell a story: *The final episode will be broadcast next week.* **2** an event, or a short time that is different from the time around it: *She's had several episodes of depression lately.* –**episodic** /ˌɛpə'sadɪk/ *adj*

**e·pis·tle** /ɪ'pɪsəl/ *n* FORMAL OR HUMOROUS a long and important letter

**ep·i·taph** /'ɛpəˌtæf/ *n* a statement about a dead person, on the stone over his/her grave

**ep·i·thet** /'ɛpəˌθɛt/ *n* an adjective or short phrase used for describing someone

**e·pit·o·me** /ɪ'pɪtəmi/ *n* **the epitome of** the perfect example of something: *He was the epitome of a good doctor - caring and knowledgeable.*

**e·pit·o·mize** /ɪ'pɪtəˌmaɪz/ *v* [T] to be the perfect or most typical example of something: *Chicago's busy liveliness seemed to epitomize the US.*

**ep·och** /'ɛpək/ *n* a period in history during which important events or developments happened

**e·qual**[1] /'ikwəl/ *adj* **1** the same in size, value, amount etc.: *Divide the dough into three equal parts. | The country's population growth is* **equal to** *2% a year.* **2** having the same rights, chances etc. as everyone else, or giving everyone the same rights, chances etc.: *The Constitution says that all people are created equal. | We are equal partners in the business.* **3** **on equal footing/terms** with neither side having any advantages over the other: *The contest was fair, with the two sides starting on equal footing.*

**equal**[2] *v* **1** [linking verb] to be the same as something else in size, number, amount etc.: *Four plus four equals eight.* **2** [T] to be as good as something or someone else: *He has equalled the Olympic record!*

**equal**[3] *n* someone who is as important, intelligent etc. as you are, or who has the same rights and opportunities as you do: *My boss treats her employees as equals. | Rembrandt was an artist* **without equal**. (=no one was as good as he)

**e·qual·i·ty** /ɪ'kwaləti/ *n* [U] the state of having the same conditions, opportunities, and rights as everyone else: *Women haven't achieved equality in the work force.* –opposite INEQUALITY

**e·qual·ize** /'ikwəˌlaɪz/ *v* [T] to make two or more things equal in size, value etc.: *equalizing pay rates in the steel industry*

**e·qual·ly** /'ikwəli/ *adv* **1** to the same degree or limit: *The candidates are equally qualified for the job.* **2** in parts that are the same size: *We'll divide the work equally.*

**equal sign** /'.. ˌ./ *n* the sign (=), used in mathematics to show that two amounts or numbers are the same

**e·qua·nim·i·ty** /ˌikwə'nɪməti, ˌɛk-/ *n* [U] FORMAL calmness in a difficult situation

**e·quate** /ɪ'kweɪt/ *v* [T] FORMAL to consider that one thing is the same as something else: *Don't equate criticism with blame.*

**e·qua·tion** /ɪ'kweɪʒən/ *n* a statement in mathematics showing that two quantities are equal, for example $2x + 4 = 10$

**e·qua·tor** /ɪ'kweɪtɚ/ *n* [singular, U] **the equator** an imaginary circle around the Earth, that divides it equally into its northern and southern halves –**equatorial** /ˌɛkwə'tɔriəl/ *adj*

**E**

**e·ques·tri·an** /ɪˈkwɛstriən/ *adj* relating to horse riding

**e·qui·lat·er·al** /ˌikwəˈlætərəl/ *adj* having all sides equal: *an equilateral triangle*

**e·qui·lib·ri·um** /ˌikwəˈlɪbriəm/ *n* [U] **1** a balance between opposing forces, influences etc.: *The supply and the demand for money must be kept in equilibrium.* **2** a calm emotional state

**e·quine** /ˈikwaɪn, ˈɛ-/ *adj* relating to horses, or looking like a horse

**e·qui·nox** /ˈikwəˌnɑks, ˈɛ-/ *n* one of the two times each year when day and night are equal in length everywhere

**e·quip** /ɪˈkwɪp/ *v* -pped, -pping [T] **1** to provide a person, group, building etc. with the things that are needed for a particular purpose: *The new school will be equipped with computers.* **2** to prepare someone for a particular purpose: *Your education should equip you for a good job.* —**equipped** *adj*

**e·quip·ment** /ɪˈkwɪpmənt/ *n* [U] the tools, machines etc. that you need for a particular activity: *camera equipment* | *We bought several new pieces of equipment for the chemistry lab.*

**eq·ui·ta·ble** /ˈɛkwətəbəl/ *adj* FORMAL fair and equal to everyone involved: *We'll find an equitable solution to the problem.*

**eq·ui·ty** /ˈɛkwəti/ *n* [U] **1** FORMAL a situation in which everyone is fairly treated **2** TECHNICAL the value of something you own, such as a house or SHAREs, after you have taken away the amount of money you still owe on it

**e·quiv·a·lent**[1] /ɪˈkwɪvələnt/ *adj* equal in value, purpose, rank etc. to something or someone else: *The atomic bomb has power equivalent to 10,000 tons of dynamite.*

**equivalent**[2] *n* something that has the same value, size, etc. as something else: *Some French words have no equivalents in English.*

**e·quiv·o·cal** /ɪˈkwɪvəkəl/ *adj* **1** deliberately not clear or definite in meaning: *an equivocal answer* **2** difficult to understand or explain: *The results of the test were equivocal.* —opposite UNEQUIVOCAL

**ER** *n* ⇨ EMERGENCY ROOM

**e·ra** /ˈɪrə, ˈɛrə/ *n* a long period of time that begins with a particular date or event: *the Reagan era*

**e·rad·i·cate** /ɪˈrædəˌkeɪt/ *v* [T] to completely destroy something: *Smallpox has been eradicated.* —**eradication** /ɪˌrædəˈkeɪʃən/ *n* [U]

**e·rase** /ɪˈreɪs/ *v* [T] to completely remove written or recorded information so that it cannot be seen or heard: *Erase any incorrect answers.* | *Ben erased one of my favorite tapes.*

erase

eraser

**e·ras·er** /ɪˈreɪsɚ/ *n* **1** a piece of rubber used for erasing (ERASE) pencil marks from paper —see picture at ERASE **2** an object used for cleaning marks from a BLACKBOARD

**e·rect**[1] /ɪˈrɛkt/ *adj, adv* in a straight upright position: *standing erect*

**erect**[2] *v* [T] **1** FORMAL to build something: *a statue erected in honor of Lincoln* **2** to put something in an upright position: *The tents for the fair were erected overnight.*

**e·rec·tion** /ɪˈrɛkʃən/ *n* **1** the swelling of a man's PENIS during sexual excitement **2** [U] the act of ERECTing something: *the erection of a new church*

**e·rode** /ɪˈroʊd/ *v* **1** [I,T] to destroy something gradually by the action of wind, rain, or acid, or to be destroyed in this way: *The cliffs had been eroded by the sea.* **2** [T] to gradually destroy someone's power, authority etc., or be destroyed: *Congress reversed a series of Supreme Court decisions that had eroded civil rights.*

**e·ro·sion** /ɪˈroʊʒən/ *n* [U] the process of eroding (ERODE) something: *soil erosion* | *the erosion of society's values*

**e·rot·ic** /ɪˈrɑtɪk/ *adj* relating to sexual love and desire: *erotic pictures* —**erotically** *adv* —**eroticism** /ɪˈrɑtəsɪzəm/ *n* [U]

**err** /ɛr, ɚ/ *v* [I] **1 err on the side of caution/mercy etc.** to be too careful, too kind etc. rather than risk making mistakes: *Doctors would prefer to err on the side of caution, by keeping newborns in the hospital longer.* **2** FORMAL to make a mistake

**er·rand** /ˈɛrənd/ *n* a short trip that you make to take a message or buy something: *I have errands to do downtown.* | *Could you run an errand for Grandma?*

**er·rant** /ˈɛrənt/ *adj* **1** FORMAL going in the wrong direction: *Rainer caught the errant pass.* **2** HUMOROUS behaving in a bad or irresponsible way: *an errant husband*

**er·rat·ic** /ɪˈrætɪk/ *adj* changing often or moving in an irregular way, without any reason: *erratic eating habits* —**erratically** *adv*

**er·ro·ne·ous** /ɪˈroʊniəs/ *adj* FORMAL incorrect: *erroneous statements* —**erroneously** *adv*

**er·ror** /ˈɛrɚ/ *n* [C,U] a mistake that causes problems: *an accident caused by human error* (=by a person rather than a machine) | *The company admitted it was in error.* (=made a mistake) | *Kovitz apologized yesterday for his error in/of judgment.* (=a decision that was a mistake)

---

**USAGE NOTE error and mistake**

A **mistake** is something that you do by accident, or that is the result of a bad judgment: *I'm sorry; I took your pen by mistake.* | *We made a mistake in buying this car.* An **error** is a mistake that you do not realize that you are making, that can cause problems: *You've made a serious error in calculating your taxes.*

**er·u·dite** /'ɛryə,daɪt, 'ɛrə-/ *adj* FORMAL showing a lot of knowledge: *an erudite speech* **–erudition** /,ɛryə'dɪʃən/ *n* [U]

**e·rupt** /ɪ'rʌpt/ *v* [I] **1** to happen suddenly: *Violence erupted after the demonstrations.* **2** if a VOLCANO erupts, it sends out smoke, fire, and rock into the sky **3** to appear suddenly on the skin: *A rash erupted on his arms.*

**es·ca·late** /'ɛskə,leɪt/ *v* **1** [I,T] if violence or a war escalates or is escalated, it becomes more serious: *Fighting has escalated in several areas.* **2** [I] to become higher or increase: *Housing prices escalated recently.* **–escalation** /,ɛskə'leɪʃən/ *n* [C,U]

**es·ca·la·tor** /'ɛskə,leɪtɚ/ *n* a set of stairs that move and carry people from one level of a building to another

**es·ca·pade** /'ɛskə,peɪd/ *n* an exciting adventure or series of events that may be dangerous

**es·cape¹** /ɪ'skeɪp/ *v* **1** [I,T] to leave a dangerous place, especially when someone is trying to catch you or stop you from leaving: *Many people were killed trying to **escape** (**from**) the war zone.*|*Most passengers escaped the fire.* **2** [I,T] to stop thinking about an unpleasant situation: *Children use TV to **escape** (**from**) reality.* **3** [T] to not be noticed by someone: *Nothing escapes Bill's attention.* **–escaped** *adj*

escape

The dog escaped through a gap in the fence.

**escape²** *n* **1** [C,U] the act of escaping: *There's no chance of escape.*|*He **made** a daring **escape from** jail.* **2** [U] a way to forget about an unpleasant situation: *Books are a good form of escape.*

**es·cap·ism** /ɪ'skeɪp,ɪzəm/ *n* [U] a way of forgetting about an unpleasant situation and think of pleasant things: *The world looks to Hollywood for escapism.* **–escapist** *adj*

**es·chew** /ɛs'tʃu/ *v* [T] FORMAL to deliberately avoid doing, using, or having something: *a man who eschews violence*

**es·cort¹** /ɪ'skɔrt, 'ɛskɔrt/ *v* [T] **1** to go somewhere with someone, especially in order to protect him/her: *Armed guards escorted the prisoners into the courthouse.* **2** to go with someone of the opposite sex to a social event: *The princess was escorted by her cousin.*

**es·cort²** /'ɛskɔrt/ *n* the person or people who ESCORT someone: *The Governor travels with a police **escort**.*|*prisoners transported **under escort** (=with an escort)*

**Es·ki·mo** /'ɛskə,moʊ/ *n* a word meaning a member of one of the Native American tribes in

Alaska or northern Canada, that some people consider offensive –compare INUIT

**ESL** *n* English as a Second Language; the methods used for teaching English to people whose first language is not English, who are living in an English-speaking country

**e·soph·a·gus** /ɪ'safəgəs/ *n* the tube that goes from the mouth to the stomach

**es·o·ter·ic** /,ɛsə'tɛrɪk/ *adj* known and understood only by a few people: *esoteric teachings*

**ESP** *n* extrasensory perception; knowledge of other people's thoughts, of GHOSTs etc. that is gained not by seeing or hearing things, but in a way that cannot be explained

**es·pe·cial·ly** /ɪ'spɛʃəli/ *adv* **1** used in order to emphasize that something is more important, or happens more with one thing than with others: *Everyone's excited about the trip, especially Doug.*|*Drive carefully, especially at night.* **2** to a particularly high degree, or more than usual: *I'm especially looking forward to seeing the new baby.* **3** for a particular purpose, reason etc.: *These flowers are especially for you.* –compare SPECIALLY

**es·pi·o·nage** /'ɛspiə,naʒ/ *n* [U] the activity of finding out secret information and giving it to a country's enemies or a company's competitors

**ESPN** *n* a CABLE TELEVISION company that broadcasts sports programs in the US

**es·pouse** /ɛ'spaʊz, ɪ-/ *v* [T] FORMAL to believe in and support an idea, especially a political one: *anti-drug policies espoused by the government*

**es·pres·so** /ɛ'sprɛsoʊ/ *n* [C,U] very strong coffee that you drink in small cups

**es·say** /'ɛseɪ/ *n* a short piece of writing about a particular subject, especially as part of a course of study

**es·sence** /'ɛsəns/ *n* **1** [singular] the most basic and important quality of something: *The essence of his argument is that we shouldn't use cars when we can walk.*| **In essence,** (=the most basic thing, said in a shortened form) *he said we should send more food aid.* **2** [U] a liquid that has a strong smell or taste and is obtained from a plant, flower etc.: *vanilla essence*

**es·sen·tial¹** /ɪ'sɛnʃəl/ *adj* **1** important and necessary: *Good food is **essential for** your health.* **2** the essential parts, qualities, or features of something are the ones that are most important, typical, or easily noticed: *What is the essential difference between these two books?*

**essential²** *n* [C usually plural] something that is important and necessary: *We provide people with the **bare essentials** (=the most necessary things) such as food and clothing.*

**es·sen·tial·ly** /ɪ'sɛnʃəli/ *adv* relating to the most important or basic qualities of something: *Your argument is essentially correct.*

**es·tab·lish** /ɪ'stæblɪʃ/ *v* [T] **1** to start something such as a company, system, situation etc., especially one that will exist for a long time:

*The school was established in 1922.* **2** to begin a relationship, conversation etc. with someone: *The group has established contacts with other groups overseas.* **3** to get yourself a position or to be respected because of something you have done or a quality you have: *He's* **established** *himself as the most powerful man in the state.* **4** to find out facts that will prove that something is true: *His lawyer* **established** *that Shea did not know the victim.*

**es·tab·lish·ment** /ɪˈstæblɪʃmənt/ *n* **1** FORMAL an institution, especially a business, store, hotel etc.: *an educational establishment* **2** the **Establishment** the organizations and people in a society who have a lot of power and who often are opposed to change or new ideas **3** [U] the act of starting something such as a company, organization, system etc.: *the establishment of new laws protecting children*

**es·tate** /ɪˈsteɪt/ *n* **1** a large area of land in the country, usually with one large house on it **2** [singular] LAW all of someone's property and money, especially everything that is left after s/he dies: *She left her entire estate to my mother.*

**es·teem**[1] /ɪˈstim/ *n* [U] FORMAL a feeling of respect and admiration for someone: *She was* **held in high esteem** *by everyone on the team.* −see also SELF-ESTEEM

**esteem**[2] *v* [T] FORMAL to respect and admire someone: *a* **highly esteemed** (=greatly respected) *artist*

**es·thet·ic** /ɛsˈθɛṭɪk/ *adj* relating to beauty and the study of beauty: *an esthetic point of view* −**esthetically** *adv*

**es·thet·ics** /ɛsˈθɛṭɪks/ *n* [U] the study of beauty, especially beauty in art

**es·ti·ma·ble** /ˈɛstəməbəl/ *adj* FORMAL deserving respect and admiration

**es·ti·mate**[1] /ˈɛstəˌmeɪt/ *v* [T] to judge the value, size etc. of something: *It is* **estimated that** *75% of our customers are adult men.* −**estimated** *adj*

**es·ti·mate**[2] /ˈɛstəmɪt/ *n* **1** a calculation or judgment of the value, size etc. of something: *I'd say it's about 200 miles to the mountains, but that's just a* **rough estimate**. (=a calculation that is not very exact) **2** a statement of how much it will probably cost to build or repair something: *I got three estimates so I could pick the cheapest.*

**es·ti·ma·tion** /ˌɛstəˈmeɪʃən/ *n* [U] your judgment or opinion of the value of someone or something: *In my estimation, McEnery has been a great mayor.*

**es·tranged** /ɪˈstreɪndʒd/ *adj* **1** no longer living with your husband or wife **2** no longer having any relationship with a relative or friend: *Molly is* **estranged from** *her son.* −**estrangement** *n* [C,U] FORMAL

**es·tro·gen** /ˈɛstrədʒən/ *n* [U] TECHNICAL a

HORMONE (=chemical substance) that is produced by a woman's body

**es·tu·ar·y** /ˈɛstʃuˌɛri/ *n* the wide part of a river where it goes into the ocean

**et al.** /ˌɛt ˈɑl, -ˈæl/ *adv* FORMAL used after a list of names to mean that other people, who are not named, are also involved in something: *"The Human Embryo" by Brodsky, Rosenblum et al.*

**etc.** /ɛt ˈsɛtrə, -ṭərə/ *adv* the written abbreviation of "et cetera"; used after a list to show that there are many other similar things or people that could be added: *cars, ships, planes etc.*

**etch** /ɛtʃ/ *v* [I,T] to cut lines on a metal plate, piece of glass, stone etc. to form a picture

**e·ter·nal** /ɪˈtɚnl/ *adj* continuing for ever: *eternal life* −**eternally** *adv*

**e·ter·ni·ty** /ɪˈtɚnəti/ *n* **1** an eternity a period of time that seems long because you are annoyed, anxious etc.: *We waited for what seemed like an eternity.* **2** [U] time without any end, especially the time after death that some people believe continues for ever

**e·ther** /ˈiθɚ/ *n* [U] a clear liquid, used in past times to make people sleep during a medical operation

**e·the·re·al** /ɪˈθɪriəl/ *adj* very delicate and light, in a way that does not seem real

**eth·ic** /ˈɛθɪk/ *n* an idea or belief that influences people's behavior and attitudes: *the Christian ethic* −see also ETHICS

**eth·i·cal** /ˈɛθɪkəl/ *adj* **1** relating to principles of what is right and wrong: *The use of animals in scientific tests raises some difficult ethical questions.* **2** morally good and correct: *Is it ethical to use drugs to control unacceptable behavior?* −**ethically** *adv*

**eth·ics** /ˈɛθɪks/ *n* **1** [plural] moral rules or principles of behavior for deciding what is right and wrong **2** [U] the study of moral rules and behavior

**eth·nic** /ˈɛθnɪk/ *adj* relating to a particular race, nation, tribe etc.: *ethnic food*

**e·thos** /ˈiθɑs/ *n* [singular] the set of ideas and moral attitudes belonging to a person or group: *the competitive spirit in the American ethos*

**et·i·quette** /ˈɛṭɪkɪt/ *n* [U] the formal rules for polite behavior in society or in a particular group

**et·y·mol·o·gy** /ˌɛṭəˈmɑlədʒi/ *n* [U] the study of the origins, history, and meanings of words −**etymological** /ˌɛṭəməˈlɑdʒɪkəl/ *adj*

**Eu·cha·rist** /ˈyukərɪst/ *n* **the Eucharist** the bread and wine that represent Christ's body and blood and are used during a Christian ceremony, or the ceremony itself

**eu·lo·gize** /ˈyuləˌdʒaɪz/ *v* [T] FORMAL to praise someone or something very much

**eu·lo·gy** /ˈyulədʒi/ *n* [C,U] FORMAL a speech or piece of writing that praises someone or something very much, especially at a funeral

**eu·nuch** /'yunɪk/ *n* a man who has had his TESTICLEs removed

**eu·phe·mism** /'yufə,mɪzəm/ *n* a polite word or expression that you use instead of a more direct one to avoid shocking or upsetting someone –**euphemistic** /,yufə'mɪstɪk/ *adj* –**euphemistically** *adv*

**eu·pho·ri·a** /yu'fɔriə/ *n* [U] a feeling of extreme happiness and excitement –**euphoric** /yu'fɔrɪk/ *adj*

**Eu·rope** /'yurəp/ *n* one of the seven CONTINENTs, that includes land north of the Mediterranean Sea and west of the Ural mountains

**Eu·ro·pe·an**[1] /,yurə'piən/ *adj* relating to or coming from Europe

**European**[2] *n* someone from Europe

**eu·tha·na·sia** /,yuθə'neɪʒə/ *n* [U] the painless killing of people who are very ill or very old in order to stop them suffering

**e·vac·u·ate** /ɪ'vækyu,eɪt/ *v* [T] to move people from a dangerous place to a safer place: *During the flood, we were all evacuated to higher ground.* –**evacuation** /ɪ,vækyu'eɪʃən/ *n* [C,U]

**e·vac·u·ee** /ɪ,vækyu'i/ *n* someone who has been EVACUATEd

**e·vade** /ɪ'veɪd/ *v* [T] **1** to avoid doing something you should do, or avoid talking about something: *If you try to evade paying taxes you risk going to prison.* | *Briggs was evading the issue.* **2** to avoid being caught by someone who is trying to catch you: *He evaded capture by hiding in a cave.*

**e·val·u·ate** /ɪ'vælyu,eɪt/ *v* [T] FORMAL to carefully consider something or someone in order to judge him, her, or it: *Our work is evaluated regularly.*

**e·val·u·a·tion** /ɪ,vælyu'eɪʃən/ *n* [C,U] the act of considering and judging something or someone, or a document in which this is done: *an evaluation of new surgical techniques*

**e·van·gel·i·cal** /,ivæn'dʒɛlɪkəl, ,ɛvən-/ *adj* believing that religious ceremonies are not as important as Christian faith and studying the Bible, and trying to persuade other people to accept these beliefs

**e·van·ge·list** /ɪ'vændʒəlɪst/ *n* someone who travels from place to place in order to try to persuade people to become Christians –**evangelism** *n* [U] –**evangelistic** /ɪ,vændʒə-'lɪstɪk/ *adj*

**e·vap·o·rate** /ɪ'væpə,reɪt/ *v* **1** [I,T] if a liquid evaporates or if something evaporates it, it changes into steam **2** [I] to slowly disappear: *Support for the idea has evaporated.* –**evaporation** /ɪ,væpə'reɪʃən/ *n* [U]

**e·va·sion** /ɪ'veɪʒən/ *n* [C,U] **1** the act of avoiding doing something you should do: *tax evasion* **2** the act of deliberately avoiding talking about something or dealing with something: *a speech full of lies and evasions*

**e·va·sive** /ɪ'veɪsɪv/ *adj* **1** not willing to answer questions directly: *an evasive answer* **2 evasive action** an action someone does to avoid being injured or harmed

**eve** /iv/ *n* **1** [C usually singular] the night or day before a religious day or a holiday: *a party on New Year's Eve* **2 the eve of** the time just before an important event: *on the eve of the election*

**e·ven**[1] /'ivən/ *adv* **1** used in order to emphasize that something is surprising or unexpected: *Even Arnie was bored by the game, and he loves baseball.* | *Carrie doesn't even like cookies!* **2** used in order to make a comparison stronger: *I know even less about calculus than my son does.* **3 even if** used in order to show that what you have just said will not change for any reason: *I wouldn't go into that place, even if you paid me!* **4 even though** used in order to emphasize that although one thing happens or is true, something else also happens or is true: *She wouldn't go onto the ski slope, even though Tom offered to help her.* **5 even so** although that is true: *They made lots of money that year, but even so the business failed.*

**even**[2] *adj* **1** flat, level, or smooth: *The floor has to be even before we put the boards down.* **2** an even rate, temperature etc. does not change much: *Store the chemicals at an even temperature.* **3** separated by equal spaces: *his even white teeth* **4 be even** INFORMAL to no longer owe someone money: *If you give me $5, we'll be even.* **5** an even number can be divided by 2: *2, 4, 6, 8 etc. are even numbers.* –opposite ODD **6 get even** INFORMAL to harm someone just as much as s/he has harmed you: *No matter how long it takes, I'll get even with him one day.* –**evenness** *n* [U] –see also **break even** (BREAK[1]) –opposite UNEVEN

**even**[3] *v*

**even out** *phr v* [I,T **even** sth ↔ **out**] to become equal or level, or to make something do this: *Some students are being bused in order to even out enrollment at the two schools.*

**even up** *phr v* [I,T **even** sth ↔ **up**] to become equal or the same, or to make something do this: *O'Malley hit a home run to even up the score.*

**even·hand·ed** /,.. '..◂/ *adj* giving fair and equal treatment to everyone: *Justice must be even-handed.*

**eve·ning** /'ivnɪŋ/ *n* **1** [C,U] the end of the day and the early part of the night: *I have a class on Thursday evenings.* **2 (Good) Evening** SPOKEN said in order to greet someone when you meet him/her in the evening: *Evening, Rick.*

**evening wear**

**evening gown** /'.. ,./, **evening dress** *n* a dress worn by women for formal occasions in the evening

**evening wear** /'.. ,./ *n* [U] special clothes worn for formal occasions in the evening

**e·ven·ly** /'ivənli/ *adv* **1** with equal amounts or numbers of something spread all through an area or divided among a group of people: *We divided the money evenly.* | *He spread the butter evenly on his toast.* **2** in a steady or regular way: *I could hear the baby breathing evenly in her crib.* | *evenly spaced rows of young trees* **3** if two teams are evenly matched, they have an equal chance of winning

**e·vent** /ɪ'vɛnt/ *n* **1** something that happens, especially something important, interesting, or unusual: *the most important events of the 1990s* **2** a performance, sports competition, party etc. that has been arranged for a particular date and time: *"Which event are you entered in?" "The long jump."* **3 in any event** whatever happens or whatever situation: *My career, after this trial, is probably over in any event.* **4 in the event of rain/fire/an accident etc.** used in order to tell people what they should do or what will happen if something else happens: *Britain agreed to support the US in the event of war.*

**e·vent·ful** /ɪ'vɛntˈfəl/ *adj* full of interesting or important events: *an eventful meeting*

**e·ven·tu·al** /ɪ'vɛntʃuəl/ *adj* happening at the end of a process: *China's eventual control of Hong Kong*

**e·ven·tu·al·i·ty** /ɪ,vɛntʃu'æləti/ *n* FORMAL a possible event or result, especially an unpleasant one

**e·ven·tu·al·ly** /ɪ'vɛntʃəli, -tʃuəli/ *adv* after a long time: *He worked so hard that eventually he made himself sick.*

**ev·er** /'ɛvɚ/ *adv* **1** a word meaning at any time, used mostly in questions, negatives, comparisons, or sentences with "if": *Nothing ever makes Paula angry.* | **Have you ever** *eaten snails?* | *If you're ever in Wilmington, give us a call.* | *That was one of the best meals I've ever had.* | *Jim's parents* **hardly ever** (=almost never) *watch TV.* **2 ever since** continuously since: *He started teaching here when he was 20, and he's been here ever since.* **3 ever-growing/ ever-increasing etc.** continuously becoming longer etc.: *the ever-growing population problem*

**ev·er·green** /'ɛvɚ,grin/ *adj* evergreen trees have leaves that do not fall off in winter —**evergreen** *n* —compare DECIDUOUS

**ev·er·last·ing** /,ɛvɚ'læstɪŋ‹/ *adj* continuing for ever: *everlasting peace*

**ev·er·more** /,ɛvɚ'mɔr/ *adv* LITERARY always; FOREVER

**ev·er·y** /'ɛvri/ *determiner* **1** each one of a group of people or things: *Every student will take the test.* | *He told Jan* **every single** *thing* (=all the things) *I said.* **2** used in order to show how often something happens: *We get the newspaper every day.* | *Change the oil in the car*

*every 5000 miles.* | *He came to see us* **every other day.** (=every two days) | *I still see her* **every now and then/every so often.** (=sometimes but not often) **3 one in every 100/3 in every 5 etc.** used in order to show how often something affects a particular group of people or things: *One in every three couples live together without being married.* **4 every which way** INFORMAL in every direction: *People were running every which way.* —see usage note at EACH[1]

---

**USAGE NOTE every one and everyone**

Use **every one** to mean "each single person or thing in a group": *Every one of the books had a torn page.* Use **everyone** to mean "all the people in a group": *Everyone is waiting for you.*

---

**ev·er·y·bod·y** /'ɛvri,bɑdi, -,bʌdi/ *pron* ⇨ EVERYONE

**ev·er·y·day** /'ɛvri,deɪ/ *adj* ordinary, usual, or happening every day: *Stress is just part of* **everyday life.**

**ev·er·y·one** /'ɛvri,wʌn/, **everybody** *pron* **1** every person involved in a particular activity or in a particular place: *Is everyone ready to go?* | *They gave a small prize to everyone who ran in the race.* | *Where is everybody?* (=where are the people that are usually here) | *I was still awake but* **everybody else** (=all the other people) *had gone to bed.* | *Everyone but* (=all the people except) *Lisa went home.* **2** all people in general: *Everyone has bad days.* —see usage notes at EVERY, PRONOUN

**ev·er·y·place** /'ɛvri,pleɪs/ *adv* SPOKEN ⇨ EVERYWHERE

**ev·er·y·thing** /'ɛvri,θɪŋ/ *pron* **1** each thing or all things: *I think everything is ready for the party.* | *I've forgotten everything I learned about math in school.* | *There's only bread left. They've eaten* **everything else.** (=all other things) **2** used when you are talking in general about your life or about a situation: *"How's everything at work these days?" "It's been really busy!"* **3 be/mean everything** to be the thing that matters most: *Money isn't everything.* **4 and everything** SPOKEN a phrase meaning all the things related to what you have just said: *She's at the hospital having tests and everything, but they don't know what's wrong.* —compare NOTHING[1]

**ev·er·y·where** /'ɛvri,wɛr/ *adv* in or to every place: *The dog follows me everywhere.* | *I've looked everywhere for my keys.* —compare NOWHERE

**e·vict** /ɪ'vɪkt/ *v* [T] to legally force someone to leave the house s/he is renting from you: *Carl was evicted when he didn't pay his rent.* —**eviction** /ɪ'vɪkʃən/ *n* [C,U]

**ev·i·dence** /'ɛvədəns/ *n* **1** [U] facts, objects, or signs that make you believe that something exists or is true: *The police **have evidence that** the killer was a woman.* | *scientists looking for evidence of life on other planets* | *I had to **give evidence** (=tell the facts) in my brother's trial.* **2 be in evidence** FORMAL to be easily seen or noticed: *The police were very much in evidence at the march.*

**ev·i·dent** /'ɛvədənt/ *adj* easily noticed or understood: *It's evident that you've been drinking again.* **evidently** *adv*

**e·vil¹** /'ivəl/ *adj* deliberately cruel or harmful: *an evil dictator responsible for the death of millions of people*

**evil²** *n* FORMAL **1** [U] actions and behavior that are morally wrong and cruel: *the battle between good and evil* **2** something that has a very cruel, harmful, or unpleasant effect: *the evils of alcohol*

**e·voc·a·tive** /ɪ'vɑkətɪv/ *adj* making people remember something by reminding them of a feeling or memory: *The scent of bread baking **is evocative of** my childhood.*

**e·voke** /ɪ'voʊk/ *v* [T] to produce a strong feeling or memory in someone: *Hitchcock's movies can evoke a sense of terror.* **−evocation** /ˌɛvə'keɪʃən, ˌivoʊ-/ *n* [C,U]

**ev·o·lu·tion** /ˌɛvə'luʃən/ *n* [U] **1** the scientific idea that plants and animals develop gradually from simpler to more complicated forms **2** the gradual change and development of an idea, situation, or object: *the evolution of the home computer* **−evolutionary** *adj*

**e·volve** /ɪ'vɑlv/ *v* [I,T] to develop by gradually changing or to make something do this: *Did man **evolve from** apes?*

**ewe** /yu/ *n* a female sheep

**ex** /ɛks/ *n* [C usually singular] INFORMAL someone's former wife, husband, GIRLFRIEND, or BOYFRIEND

**ex·ac·er·bate** /ɪg'zæsəˌbeɪt/ *v* [T] FORMAL to make a bad situation worse: *The drugs they gave her only exacerbated the pain.* **−exacerbation** /ɪgˌzæsə'beɪʃən/ *n* [U]

**ex·act¹** /ɪg'zækt/ *adj* correct and including all the necessary details: *The exact time is 2:47.* | *It has been nine months, **to be exact**.*

**exact²** *v* [T] FORMAL to demand and get something from someone by using threats, force etc.: *the penalty exacted for breaking the rules*

**ex·act·ing** /ɪg'zæktɪŋ/ *adj* demanding a lot of care, effort, and attention: *an exacting piece of work*

**ex·act·ly** /ɪg'zæktli/ *adv* **1** used in order to emphasize that a particular number, amount, or piece of information is completely correct: *We got home at exactly six o'clock.* | *I don't know **exactly where** she lives.* **2** SPOKEN said in order to emphasize a statement or question: *That's **exactly what** I've been trying to tell you!* **3** SPOKEN said when you agree with what some-

one is saying: *"So we should spend more on education?" "Exactly!"*

**ex·ag·ger·ate** /ɪg'zædʒəˌreɪt/ *v* [I,T] to make something seem better, larger, worse etc. than it really is: *Charlie says that everyone in New York has a gun, but I'm sure he's exaggerating.* **−exaggerated** *adv* **−exaggeration** /ɪgˌzædʒə'reɪʃən/ *n* [C,U]

**ex·alt** /ɪg'zɔlt/ *v* [T] FORMAL to praise someone

**ex·al·ta·tion** /ˌɛgzɔl'teɪʃən, ˌɛksɔl-/ *n* [C,U] FORMAL a very strong feeling of happiness

**ex·alt·ed** /ɪg'zɔltɪd/ *adj* FORMAL **1** having a very high rank and highly respected **2** filled with a feeling of great happiness

**ex·am** /ɪg'zæm/ *n* **1** an official test of knowledge or ability in a particular subject: *a chemistry exam* | *When do you **take/have** your final exams?* **2** a set of medical tests: *an eye exam*

**ex·am·i·na·tion** /ɪgˌzæmə'neɪʃən/ *n* **1** the process of looking at something carefully in order to see what it is like or find out something: *a detailed examination of the photographs* **2** FORMAL ⇨ EXAM

**ex·am·ine** /ɪg'zæmɪn/ *v* [T] **1** to look at something carefully in order to make a decision, find out something etc.: *The doctor examined me thoroughly.* | *The police **examined** the room for fingerprints.* **2** FORMAL to ask someone questions to get information or to test his/her knowledge about something: *On Friday, you will be **examined on** American history.* **−examiner** *n*

**ex·am·ple** /ɪg'zæmpəl/ *n* **1** someone or something that you mention to show what you mean, show that something is true, or show what something is like: *This church is a good example of Gothic architecture.* | *Can anyone **give** me **an example** of a transitive verb?* | *Everything costs too much. The price of meat, **for example**, (=as an example) has doubled since April.* **2** someone whose behavior is very good and should be copied by other people: *Parents should **set an example for** their children.* (=parents should behave in a good way so their children will behave in a good way) **3 make an example of sb** to punish someone for doing something so that other people will be afraid to do the same thing

**ex·as·per·ate** /ɪg'zæspəˌreɪt/ *v* [T] to make someone feel very annoyed by continuing to do something that upsets him/her: *His refusal to agree has exasperated his lawyers.* **−exasperating** *adj* **−exasperation** /ɪgˌzæspə'reɪʃən/ *n* [U]

**ex·as·per·at·ed** /ɪg'zæspəˌreɪtɪd/ *adj* feeling annoyed because someone is continuing to do something that upsets you

**ex·ca·vate** /'ɛkskəˌveɪt/ *v* [I,T] **1** to dig a hole in the ground **2** to dig up the ground in order to find something that was buried there in an earlier time: *archeologists excavating an*

E

*ancient city* −**excavation** /ˌɛkskəˈveɪʃən/ *n* [C,U]

**ex·ceed** /ɪkˈsid/ *v* [T] FORMAL **1** to be more than a particular number or amount: *The cost must not exceed $150.* **2** to go beyond an official or legal limit: *a fine for exceeding the speed limit*

**ex·ceed·ing·ly** /ɪkˈsidɪŋli/ *adv* FORMAL extremely: *The show has done exceedingly well.*

**ex·cel** /ɪkˈsɛl/ *v* -**lled, -lling** [I] FORMAL to do something very well, or much better than most people: *I've never excelled at math.* | *That was a great meal! You've really excelled yourself* (=done even better than usual) *this time.*

**ex·cel·lence** /ˈɛksələns/ *n* [U] the quality of being excellent: *an honor given for academic excellence*

**ex·cel·lent** /ˈɛksələnt/ *adj* **1** extremely good or of very high quality: *Jim's in excellent health.* | *That was an excellent meal.* **2** SPOKEN said when you approve of something: *"There's a party at Becky's house tonight." "Excellent!"* −**excellently** *adv*

**ex·cept¹** /ɪkˈsɛpt/ *prep* **except (for)** used in order to show the things or people who are not included in a statement: *Everyone went to the show, except for Scott and Danny.* | *We're open every day except Monday.* | *I don't know anything about it, except what I've read in the newspaper.* −see usage note at BESIDES²

**except²** *conjunction* **except (that)** used in order to show that the statement you have just made is not true or not completely true: *It is like all the other houses, except that it's painted bright blue.* | *I have earrings just like those, except they're silver.* | *I'd go, except it's too far.* −see usage note at BUT¹

**except³** *v* [T] FORMAL to not include something

**ex·cept·ed** /ɪkˈsɛptɪd/ *adj* not included: *He's not interested in anything, politics excepted.*

**ex·cept·ing** /ɪkˈsɛptɪŋ/ *prep* FORMAL not including

**ex·cep·tion** /ɪkˈsɛpʃən/ *n* [C,U] **1** someone or something that is not included in something: *It's been very cold, but today's an exception.* | *We don't usually take credit cards, but for you we'll make an exception.* (=not include you in this rule) | *Everyone has improved, with the possible exception of Simon.* (=everyone has improved except Simon) **2** **be no exception** used in order to say that something is not different than before or than the other things mentioned: *March weather is usually changeable and this year was no exception.* **3** **without exception** FORMAL used in order to say that something is true of all the people or things in a group: *Almost without exception, teachers said that students do not work hard enough.*

**ex·cep·tion·al** /ɪkˈsɛpʃənəl/ *adj* **1** unusually good: *an exceptional student* **2** unusual and not likely to happen often: *The teachers*

*were doing their best under exceptional circumstances.* −**exceptionally** *adv*

**ex·cerpt** /ˈɛksɚpt/ *n* a short piece of writing or music taken from a longer book, poem etc.

**ex·cess¹** /ˈɛksɛs, ɪkˈsɛs/ *n* **1** [singular, U] a larger amount of something than is needed, usual, or allowed: *There is an excess of alcohol in his blood.* **2** **in excess of** more than a particular amount: *Our profits were in excess of $5 million.* **3** **do sth to excess** to do something too much or too often: *He drinks to excess.* −see also EXCESSES

**excess²** *adj* additional and more than is needed or allowed: *a charge of $75 for excess baggage*

**ex·cess·es** /ɪkˈsɛsɪz, ˈɛksɛsɪz/ *n* [plural] actions that are socially or morally unacceptable: *the army's excesses during the last war*

**ex·ces·sive** /ɪkˈsɛsɪv/ *adj* much more than is reasonable or necessary: *Don's wife left him because of his excessive gambling.* −**excessively** *adv*

**ex·change¹** /ɪksˈtʃeɪndʒ/ *n* **1** [C,U] the act of exchanging one thing for another, or the act of doing something to someone at the same time as s/he does it to you: *an exchange of political prisoners* | *I gave Larry my bike in exchange for some video games.* (=I gave him my bike, and he gave me some video games) **2** an angry argument between two people or groups **3** an arrangement in which a student, teacher etc., visits another country to work or study **4** ⇨ STOCK EXCHANGE

**exchange²** *v* [T] to give something to someone who gives you something else: *This shirt is too big. Can I exchange it for a smaller one?* −**exchangeable** *adj*

**exchange rate** /.ˈ. ˌ./ *n* the value of the money of one country compared to the money of another country

**ex·cise¹** /ˈɛksaɪz, -saɪs/ *n* [C,U] the government tax on particular goods produced and used inside a country

**ex·cise²** /ɪkˈsaɪz/ *v* [T] FORMAL to remove something completely by cutting it out: *Doctors excised the tumor.* −**excision** /ɪkˈsɪʒən/ *n* [C,U]

**ex·cit·a·ble** /ɪkˈsaɪtəbəl/ *adj* easily excited

**ex·cite** /ɪkˈsaɪt/ *v* [T] **1** to make someone feel happy, eager, or nervous: *That movie was good, but it didn't really excite me very much.* **2** to make someone have strong feelings: *The murder trial has excited a lot of public interest.*

**ex·cit·ed** /ɪkˈsaɪtɪd/ *adj* happy, interested, or hopeful because something good has happened or will happen: *The kids are really excited about our trip to California.* −**excitedly** *adv*

**ex·cite·ment** /ɪkˈsaɪtᵊmənt/ *n* [U] the feeling of being excited: *Ann couldn't hide her excitement at the possibility of meeting the Senator.*

**ex·cit·ing** /ɪkˈsaɪṭɪŋ/ *adj* making you feel happy or interested in something: *an exciting story*

**ex·claim** /ɪkˈskleɪm/ *v* [I,T] to say something suddenly because you are surprised, excited, or angry: *"Wow!" exclaimed Bobby, "Look at that car!"* —**exclamation** /ˌɛksklaˈmeɪʃən/ *n*

**exclamation point** /..ˈ.. ˌ./, **exclamation mark** *n* the mark (!) used in writing after a sentence or word that expresses surprise, excitement, or anger

**ex·clude** /ɪkˈsklud/ *v* [T] **1** to not allow someone to enter a place, or to do something: *In the Army, women usually are* **excluded from** *fighting.* **2** to deliberately not include something: *Some of the data was* **excluded from** *the report.*

**ex·clud·ing** /ɪkˈskludɪŋ/ *prep* not including: *The trip costs $1300, excluding airfare.*

**ex·clu·sion** /ɪkˈskluʒən/ *n* [U] **1** a situation in which someone is not allowed to do something or something is not used: *the former exclusion of professional athletes from the Olympics* **2 do sth to the exclusion of** to do something so much that you do not do, consider, or have time for something else: *He works constantly, to the exclusion of everything else.*

**ex·clu·sive¹** /ɪkˈsklusɪv, -zɪv/ *adj* **1** exclusive places, organizations etc. are for people who have a lot of money, or who belong to a high social class: *an exclusive Manhattan hotel* **2** used by only one person or group, and not shared: *a car for the exclusive use of the Pope* **3 exclusive of** not including: *The trip cost $450, exclusive of meals.*

**exclusive²** *n* an important news story that is in only one newspaper, magazine, television news program etc.

**ex·clu·sive·ly** /ɪkˈsklusɪvli, -zɪv-/ *adv* only: *This offer is available exclusively to those who call now.*

**ex·com·mu·ni·cate** /ˌɛkskəˈmyunəˌkeɪt/ *v* [T] to punish someone by not allowing him/her to continue to be a member of a church —**excommunication** /ˌɛkskəˌmyunəˈkeɪʃən/ *n* [C,U]

**ex·cre·ment** /ˈɛkskrəmənt/ *n* [U] FORMAL the solid waste from a person's or animal's body

**ex·crete** /ɪkˈskrit/ *v* [I,T] FORMAL to get rid of waste from the body through the BOWELs, or to get rid of waste liquid through the skin

**ex·cru·ci·at·ing** /ɪkˈskruʃiˌeɪtɪŋ/ *adj* extremely painful: *The pain in my knee was excruciating.* —**excruciatingly** *adv*

**ex·cur·sion** /ɪkˈskɚʒən/ *n* a short trip, usually made by a group of people: *an excursion to Sea World*

**ex·cus·a·ble** /ɪkˈskyuzəbəl/ *adj* behavior or words that are excusable are easy to forgive —opposite INEXCUSABLE

**ex·cuse¹** /ɪkˈskyuz/ *v* [T] **1 excuse me** SPOKEN **a)** said when you want to politely get someone's attention in order to ask a question: *Excuse me, is this the right bus for the airport?* **b)** used in order to say you are sorry when you have done something that is embarrassing or rude: *Oh, excuse me, I didn't mean to step on your foot.* **c)** used in order to politely tell someone that you are leaving a place: *Excuse me, I'll be right back.* **d)** used in order to ask someone to repeat what s/he has just said: *"What time is it?" "Excuse me?" "I asked what time it is."* **e)** used in order to ask someone to move so you can go past him/her: *Excuse me, I need to get through.* **2** to forgive someone, usually for something not very serious: *Please excuse my bad handwriting.* **3** to not make someone do something that s/he is supposed to do: *You are excused from doing the dishes tonight.* —see usage note at APOLOGIZING

**ex·cuse²** /ɪkˈskyus/ *n* **1** a reason that you give to explain why you did something wrong: *His excuse for being late wasn't very good.* **2** a false reason that you give to explain why you are or are not doing something: *I'll make an excuse and get away from the party early.*

---

**USAGE NOTE excuse and reason**

An **excuse** is the explanation that you give when you have not done something that you should have done, or when you have done something wrong: *What's your excuse for not doing your homework?* A **reason** is a fact that explains why something happens, exists, or is true: *The reason I'm tired is that the neighbors had a noisy party.*

---

**ex·ec** /ɪgˈzɛk/ *n* INFORMAL a business EXECUTIVE

**ex·e·cute** /ˈɛksɪˌkyut/ *v* [T] **1** to kill someone, especially as a legal punishment for a crime **2** FORMAL to do something that you have planned: *These ideas require money and materials to execute.*

**ex·e·cu·tion** /ˌɛksɪˈkyuʃən/ *n* **1** [C,U] the act of killing someone, especially as a legal punishment for a crime: *An hour before the execution, a crowd gathered outside the jail.* **2** [U] FORMAL a process in which you do something that you have planned to do: *the planning and execution of urban policy*

**ex·e·cu·tion·er** /ˌɛksɪˈkyuʃənɚ/ *n* someone whose job is to kill someone else as a legal punishment for a crime

**ex·ec·u·tive¹** /ɪgˈzɛkyəṭɪv/ *n* someone whose job is to decide what a company or business will do

**executive²** *adj* **1** relating to making decisions, especially in a company or business: *an executive committee* **2 executive branch** the part of a government that approves decisions and laws and organizes how they will work —compare JUDICIARY, LEGISLATURE

**ex·ec·u·tor** /ɪgˈzɛkyətɚ/ *n* LAW someone who deals with the instructions in a WILL

**ex·em·pla·ry** /ɪgˈzɛmpləri/ *adj* FORMAL
**1** excellent and extremely good, and used as an example: *the students' exemplary behavior* **2** severe and used as a warning: *an exemplary punishment*

**ex·em·pli·fy** /ɪgˈzɛmpləˌfaɪ/ *v* [T] FORMAL to be a very typical example of something, or to give an example like this: *Stuart exemplifies the kind of student we like at our school.*

**ex·empt**[1] /ɪgˈzɛmpt/ *adj* having special permission not to do a duty, pay for something etc., that you would usually have to do: *The money is exempt from state taxes.*

**exempt**[2] *v* [T] to give someone special permission not to do something, pay for something etc., that s/he would usually have to do: *Children are exempted from this rule.*

**ex·emp·tion** /ɪgˈzɛmpʃən/ *n* **1** an amount of money that you do not have to pay tax on in a particular year: *a tax exemption for gifts to charity* **2** [C,U] permission not to do something, pay for something etc., that you would usually have to do: *an exemption from military service*

**ex·er·cise**[1] /ˈɛksɚˌsaɪz/ *n* **1** [C,U] physical activity that you do regularly in order to stay strong and healthy: *stretching exercises for the back* | *Have you done your stomach exercises today?* **2** a set of written questions that test your skill or knowledge: *For homework, do exercises 1 and 2.* **3** a set of military actions that are not part of a war, but that allow soldiers to practice their skills **4** FORMAL the use of power, a right etc. in order to make something happen: *laws that protect the exercise of our freedom of speech*

**exercise**[2] *v* [I,T] **1** to do physical activities regularly so that you stay strong and healthy: *Hilary exercises by walking to work.* **2** FORMAL to use power, a right etc. to make something happen: *She exercised her influence to get Rigby the position.*

**exercise bike** /ˈ... ˌ./ *n* a bicycle that does not move and is used indoors for exercise

**ex·ert** /ɪgˈzɚt/ *v* [T] **1 exert authority/pressure etc.** to use your authority etc. to make something happen: *The UN is exerting pressure on the countries to stop the war.* **2 exert yourself** to make a strong physical or mental effort

**ex·er·tion** /ɪgˈzɚʃən/ *n* [C,U] strong physical or mental effort: *Paul's face was red with exertion.*

**ex·hale** /ɛksˈheɪl, ɛkˈseɪl/ *v* [I,T] to breathe air, smoke etc. out of your mouth: *Take a deep breath, then exhale slowly.* –opposite INHALE

**ex·haust**[1] /ɪgˈzɔst/ *v* [T] **1** to make someone very tired: *The trip totally exhausted us.* **2** to use all of something: *We are in danger of exhausting the world's oil supply.*

**exhaust**[2] *n* **1** [U] the gas that is produced when a machine is working: *Car exhaust is the main reason for pollution in the city.* **2** also **exhaust pipe** a pipe on a car or machine that exhaust comes out of –see picture on page 469

**ex·haust·ed** /ɪgˈzɔstɪd/ *adj* extremely tired: *Ron was exhausted from lack of sleep.*

**ex·haust·ing** /ɪgˈzɔstɪŋ/ *adj* making you feel extremely tired: *an exhausting trip*

**ex·haus·tion** /ɪgˈzɔstʃən/ *n* [U] the state of being extremely tired: *Neil is suffering from mental exhaustion.*

**ex·haus·tive** /ɪgˈzɔstɪv/ *adj* extremely thorough: *The rescue team made an exhaustive search of the area.* –**exhaustively** *adv*

**ex·hib·it**[1] /ɪgˈzɪbɪt/ *v* **1** [I,T] to put something in a public place so people can see it: *The art gallery will exhibit some of Dali's paintings.* **2** [T] FORMAL to show a quality, sign, emotion etc. in a way that people easily notice: *The patient exhibited symptoms of heart disease.*

**exhibit**[2] *n* **1** something that is put in a public place so people can see it: *a new sculpture exhibit at the museum* **2** something that is shown in a court of law to prove that someone is guilty or not guilty

**ex·hi·bi·tion** /ˌɛksəˈbɪʃən/ *n* [C,U] a public show where you put something so people can see it: *A collection of rare books is on exhibition at the city library.* | *an exhibition of historical photographs*

**ex·hi·bi·tion·ism** /ˌɛksəˈbɪʃəˌnɪzəm/ *n* [U] **1** behavior that makes people notice you, but that most people think is not acceptable **2** a mental problem in which someone likes to show his/her sexual organs to other people in public places –**exhibitionist** *n*

**ex·hil·a·rat·ed** /ɪgˈzɪləˌreɪtɪd/ *adj* feeling extremely happy and excited: *Rita was exhilarated when she first saw the ocean.*

**ex·hil·a·rat·ing** /ɪgˈzɪləˌreɪtɪŋ/ *adj* making you feel extremely happy and excited: *The balloon ride was exhilarating.*

**ex·hil·a·ra·tion** /ɪgˌzɪləˈreɪʃən/ *n* [U] a feeling of being extremely happy and excited –**exhilarate** /ɪgˈzɪləˌreɪt/ *v* [T]

**ex·hort** /ɪgˈzɔrt/ *v* [T] FORMAL to try to persuade someone to do something –**exhortation** /ˌɛksɔrˈteɪʃən, ˌɛgzɔr-/ *n* [C,U]

**ex·hume** /ɪgˈzum, ɛksˈhyum/ *v* [T] FORMAL to remove a dead body from the ground after it has been buried –**exhumation** /ˌɛksyuˈmeɪʃən/ *n* [C,U]

**ex·ile**[1] /ˈɛgzaɪl, ˈɛksaɪl/ *v* [T] to force someone to leave his/her country and live in another country, usually for political reasons –**exiled** *adj*

**exile**[2] *n* **1** [U] a situation in which someone is EXILED: *a writer who lives in exile in Britain* **2** someone who has been EXILED

**ex·ist** /ɪgˈzɪst/ v [I] **1** to be real or alive: *Do ghosts really exist?* ✗ DON'T SAY "It is existing/they are existing." ✗ **2** to stay alive, especially in difficult conditions: *Poor families in our city are barely able to exist in the winter.*

**ex·ist·ence** /ɪgˈzɪstəns/ n **1** [U] the state of existing: *Do you believe in the existence of God?* | *laws that are already in existence* **2** the type of life that someone has, especially when it is difficult: *a terrible existence*

**ex·ist·ing** /ɪgˈzɪstɪŋ/ adj present now and available to be used: *We need new computers to replace the existing ones.*

**ex·it**[1] /ˈɛgzɪt, ˈɛksɪt/ n **1** a door through which you can leave a room, building etc.: *There are two exits at the back of the plane.* **2** the act of leaving a room, theater stage etc.: *The President made a quick exit after his speech.* **3** a small road that you can drive on to leave a larger road: *Take exit 23 into the city.*

**exit**[2] v **1** [I] to leave a place: *The band exited through a door behind the stage.* **2** [I,T] to stop using a computer or computer program

**ex·o·dus** /ˈɛksədəs/ n [singular] a situation in which a lot of people leave a particular place at the same time: *the exodus of Russian scientists to America*

**ex·on·er·ate** /ɪgˈzɑnəˌreɪt/ v [T] FORMAL to officially say that someone who has been blamed for something is not guilty: *Ross was exonerated from all charges of child abuse.* −**exoneration** /ɪgˌzɑnəˈreɪʃən/ n [U]

**ex·or·bi·tant** /ɪgˈzɔrbətənt/ adj an exorbitant price, demand etc. is much higher or greater than it should be: *It's a nice hotel but the prices are exorbitant!*

**ex·or·cize** /ˈɛksɔrˌsaɪz, -sə-/ v [T] to force evil spirits to leave a place or someone's body by using special words and ceremonies −**exorcism** /ˈɛksɔrˌsɪzəm, -sə-/ n [C,U] −**exorcist** /ˈɛksɔrsɪst/ n

**ex·ot·ic** /ɪgˈzɑt̬ɪk/ adj unusual and exciting because of a connection with a foreign country: *an exotic flower from Africa* −**exotically** adv

**ex·pand** /ɪkˈspænd/ v [I,T] to become larger in size, area, activity, or number, or to make something become larger: *The population of Texas expanded rapidly in the '60s.* | *McDonalds is beginning to expand* (=open new stores) *in Asia.* −**expandable** adj −compare CONTRACT[2]

**expand on/upon** sth phr v [T] FORMAL to add more details or information to something that you have already said

**ex·panse** /ɪkˈspæns/ n a very large area of water, sky, land etc.: *the vast expanse of the Pacific Ocean*

**ex·pan·sion** /ɪkˈspænʃən/ n [U] the process of increasing in size, number, or amount: *a period of economic expansion* −**expansionist** adj

**ex·pan·sive** /ɪkˈspænsɪv/ adj **1** very friendly and willing to talk a lot: *After dinner, Mr. Woods relaxed and became more expansive.* **2** very large and wide in area: *a window with an expansive view of the beach*

**ex·pa·tri·ate** /ɛksˈpeɪtriɪt/ n someone who lives in a foreign country −**expatriate** adj

**ex·pect** /ɪkˈspɛkt/ v [T] **1** to think that something will happen: *The hotel bill was more than we expected it to be.* | *We expect her to arrive any day.* | *I expect (that) Beth will do well on the test.* **2** to demand that someone do something because it is his/her duty: *You are expected to return all books by Monday.* | *Wanda's parents expect too much of her.* (=think she can do more than she really can) **3 be expecting** if a woman is expecting, she is going to have a baby soon −see usage note at WAIT[1]

**ex·pect·an·cy** /ɪkˈspɛktənsi/ n [U] the feeling that something exciting or interesting is about to happen: *a look of expectancy in her eyes* −see also LIFE EXPECTANCY

**ex·pect·ant** /ɪkˈspɛktənt/ adj **1** hopeful that something good or exciting will happen: *An expectant crowd gathered at the movie premiere.* **2 expectant mother/father** someone whose baby will be born soon −**expectantly** adv

**ex·pec·ta·tion** /ˌɛkspɛkˈteɪʃən/ n **1** [C,U] the belief or hope that something will happen: *Sales of the car have exceeded expectations.* (=have been better than expected) | *expectations that the dollar will drop in value* **2** [C usually plural] a feeling or belief about the way something should be or how someone should behave: *The movie did not live up to our expectations.* (=was not as good as we thought it would be) | *My parents have high expectations* (=believe I should succeed) *about my future.*

**ex·pe·di·en·cy** /ɪkˈspidiənsi/ also **expe·dience** /ɪkˈspidiəns/ n [C,U] what is useful, easy, or necessary to do in a particular situation, even if it is morally wrong: *The governor vetoed the bill as an act of political expediency.*

**ex·pe·di·ent** /ɪkˈspidiənt/ adj helpful or useful, sometimes in a way that is morally wrong: *We thought it would be expedient to consult a lawyer.* −**expedient** n

**ex·pe·dite** /ˈɛkspəˌdaɪt/ v [T] to make a process, action etc. happen more quickly: *More money would, of course, expedite things.*

**ex·pe·di·tion** /ˌɛkspəˈdɪʃən/ n **1** a long and carefully organized trip, especially to a dangerous place: *an expedition to the North Pole* **2** a short trip, usually made for a particular purpose: *a shopping expedition*

**ex·pel** /ɪkˈspɛl/ v **-lled, -lling** [T] **1** to officially make someone leave a school, organization, or country: *Larry was expelled from school for*

E

*smoking.* **2** to force air, water, or gas out of something

**ex·pend** /ɪk'spɛnd/ *v* [T] FORMAL to use money, time, energy etc. to do something: *A lot of effort has been expended on this research project.*

**ex·pend·a·ble** /ɪk'spɛndəbəl/ *adj* not needed enough to be kept or saved: *Health clinics for the poor are not expendable.*

**ex·pend·i·ture** /ɪk'spɛndətʃɚ/ *n* FORMAL **1** [C,U] the total amount of money that a person or organization spends: *US expenditure on welfare programs went down by 5%.* **2** [U] the action of spending or using time, money, effort etc.

**ex·pense** /ɪk'spɛns/ *n* [C,U] **1** the amount of money you spend on something: *Sally's parents **spared no expense** (=spent all the money necessary to buy the best things) for her wedding.* **2 at the expense of** achieved by harming someone or something else: *The cars were produced quickly, at the expense of safety.* **3 at sb's expense** achieved by someone else paying for something, being harmed by something etc.: *Education is provided at the public's expense.* −see also EXPENSES

**expense ac·count** /.'. .,./ *n* money that is available to someone who works for a company so that s/he can pay for hotels, meals etc. when traveling for work

**ex·pens·es** /ɪk'spɛnsɪz/ *n* [plural] **1** money that you spend on travel, hotels, meals etc. when you are working, and that your employer gives back to you later **2 all expenses paid** having all of your costs for hotels, travel, meals etc. paid for by someone else: *The prize is an all expenses paid trip to Hawaii.*

**ex·pen·sive** /ɪk'spɛnsɪv/ *adj* costing a lot of money: *an expensive piece of jewelry* −opposite INEXPENSIVE

**ex·pe·ri·ence¹** /ɪk'spɪriəns/ *n* **1** [U] knowledge or skill that you gain from doing a job or activity: *Do you **have** any **experience** in the publishing business?* **2** [U] knowledge that you gain about life and the world by being in different situations and meeting different people: *In my experience, a credit card is always useful.* **3** something that happens to you and has an effect on how you feel or what you think: *Visiting Paris was a wonderful experience.* | *People often say they have **had** similar **experiences**.*

**experience²** *v* [T] to be influenced or affected by something that happens to you or by emotions, pain etc.: *The company is experiencing problems with its computer system.* | *The patient is experiencing a lot of pain.*

**ex·pe·ri·enced** /ɪk'spɪriənst/ *adj* having particular skills or knowledge because you have done something often or for a long time: *an experienced pilot* −opposite INEXPERIENCED

**ex·per·i·ment¹** /ɪk'spɛrəmənt/ *n* **1** a scientific test done to show how something will react in a particular situation, or to prove that an idea is true: *They **performed/did experiments on** rats to test the drug.* **2** a process in which you try a new idea, method etc. in order to find out if it is effective: *St. Mary's School is an **experiment in** bilingual education.*

**ex·per·i·ment²** /ɪk'spɛrə,mɛnt/ *v* [I] **1** to try using various ideas, methods, materials etc. in order to find out how effective or good they are: *Many teenagers **experiment with** drugs.* **2** to do a scientific test in order to find out if a particular idea is true or to obtain more information: *Scientists often **experiment on** animals when testing new products.* −experimentation /ɪk,spɛrəmən'teɪʃən/ *n* [U]

**ex·per·i·men·tal** /ɪk,spɛrə'mɛntəl/ *adj* **1** used for or related to EXPERIMENTS: *experimental research* **2** using or testing new ideas: *an experimental theater group* −experimentally *adv*

**ex·pert** /'ɛkspɚt/ *n* someone with special skills or knowledge of a subject, gained as a result of training or experience: *an **expert on/in** ancient Egyptian art* −expert *adj* −expertly *adv*

**ex·per·tise** /,ɛkspɚ'tiz/ *n* [U] a special skill or knowledge that you learn by experience or training: *We should use his medical expertise to our advantage.*

**ex·pi·ra·tion** /,ɛkspə'reɪʃən/ *n* [U] the end of a period of time during which an official document or agreement is allowed to be used: *the expiration of the treaty*

**expiration date** /..'.. .,./ *n* the date when something stops being safe to eat or to use: *The milk is past its expiration date.*

**ex·pire** /ɪk'spaɪɚ/ *v* [I] **1** if a document expires, you cannot legally continue to use it beyond a particular date: *My driver's license expires in September.* **2** LITERARY to die

**ex·plain** /ɪk'spleɪn/ *v* [I,T] **1** to say or write something so that it is easy to understand: *Could you **explain** the rules **to** me?* ✗ DON'T SAY *"explain me the rules."* ✗ | *Can someone **explain how** this thing works?* ✗ DON'T SAY *"explain me how it works."* ✗ **2** to give or be the reason for something: *Brad never **explained why** he was late.*

**explain** sth ↔ **away** *phr v* [T] to make something seem to be less important or not your fault: *Claire tried to **explain away** the bruises on her arm.*

**ex·pla·na·tion** /,ɛksplə'neɪʃən/ *n* **1** what you say or write to make something easier to understand: *a detailed explanation of how to write a proposal* **2** [C,U] the reason something happened or why you did something: *Smith could not **give an explanation for** the blood on his jacket.*

**ex·plan·a·to·ry** /ɪkˈsplænəˌtɔri/ *adj* giving information about something or describing how something works: *an explanatory booklet* –see also SELF-EXPLANATORY

**ex·ple·tive** /ˈɛksplətɪv/ *n* FORMAL a rude word that you use when you are angry or in pain

**ex·pli·ca·ble** /ɪkˈsplɪkəbəl, ˈɛksplɪ-/ *adj* able to be easily understood or explained –opposite INEXPLICABLE

**ex·plic·it** /ɪkˈsplɪsɪt/ *adj* **1** expressed in a way that is very clear: *The workers were given explicit instructions.* **2** language or pictures that are explicit describe or show a lot of sex or violence –**explicitly** *adv*

**ex·plode** /ɪkˈsploʊd/ *v* **1** [I,T] to burst into small pieces, making a loud noise and causing damage, or to make something do this: *The car bomb exploded at 6:16.* | *In 1949 the USSR exploded its first atomic bomb.* **2** [I] to suddenly become very angry: *Susie exploded when I told her I'd wrecked her car.* **3** [I] if the population explodes, it suddenly increases

**ex·ploit**[1] /ɪkˈsplɔɪt/ *v* [T] **1** to treat someone unfairly in order to gain what you want: *Children were exploited in factories in the 19th century.* **2** to use something effectively and completely: *The country must exploit its resources more effectively.* –**exploitation** /ˌɛksplɔɪˈteɪʃən/ *n* [U]

**ex·ploit**[2] /ˈɛksplɔɪt/ *n* [C usually plural] a brave, exciting, and interesting action: *a book about Annie Oakley's exploits*

**ex·plo·ra·tion** /ˌɛkspləˈreɪʃən/ *n* [C,U] **1** a trip to a place you have not been, or a place where you are looking for something: *exploration for oil* | *space exploration* **2** an examination or discussion about something to find out more about it: *an exploration of spiritual issues*

**ex·plo·ra·to·ry** /ɪkˈsplɔrəˌtɔri/ *adj* done in order to find out more about something: *exploratory surgery on his knee*

**ex·plore** /ɪkˈsplɔr/ *v* **1** [I,T] to travel through an unfamiliar area in order to find out what it is like: *We spent a week exploring the Oregon coastline.* **2** [T] to discuss, examine, or think about something carefully: *We're exploring new solutions to the problem.*

**ex·plor·er** /ɪkˈsplɔrə/ *n* someone who travels to places that have not been visited before

**ex·plo·sion** /ɪkˈsploʊʒən/ *n* **1** [C,U] the action of something exploding, or a loud noise that sounds like something exploding: *a nuclear explosion* | *an explosion of thunder* **2** a sudden or quick increase in number or amount: *the population explosion*

**ex·plo·sive**[1] /ɪkˈsploʊsɪv/ *n* a substance that can cause an explosion

**explosive**[2] *adj* **1** able or likely to explode: *Dynamite is highly explosive.* **2** likely to suddenly become violent and angry: *the teenager's explosive behavior* **3** able to make

people argue and become angry: *the explosive issue of abortion*

**ex·po** /ˈɛkspoʊ/ *n* ⇨ EXPOSITION

**ex·po·nent** /ɪkˈspoʊnənt, ˈɛkspoʊ-/ *n* someone who supports a particular idea, belief etc. and tries to persuade others to accept it: *an exponent of socialism*

**ex·port**[1] /ˈɛkspɔrt/ *n* [C,U] the business of selling and sending products to another country, or the products that are sold: *The Government has banned the export of lumber.* | *Wheat is one of our country's chief exports.* –compare IMPORT[1]

**ex·port**[2] /ɪkˈspɔrt/ *v* [I,T] to send and sell goods to another country –**exporter** *n* –**exportation** /ˌɛkspɔrˈteɪʃən/ *n* [U] –compare IMPORT[2]

**ex·pose** /ɪkˈspoʊz/ *v* [T] **1** to show something that is usually covered or not able to be seen: *Her skin has never been exposed to the sun.* **2** to put someone in a situation, place etc. that could be harmful or dangerous: *Smoking exposes people to the risk of lung cancer.* **3** to help someone experience new ideas, TRADITIONS etc.: *The Shinsekis exposed me to Japanese art.* **4** to tell people the truth about a dishonest person, event, or situation: *We threatened to expose him to the police.* **5** to allow light onto a piece of film in a camera in order to produce a photograph

**ex·po·sé** /ˌɛkspoʊˈzeɪ/ *n* a television or newspaper story that tells people about a dishonest person, event, or situation

**ex·posed** /ɪkˈspoʊzd/ *adj* not protected or covered: *tiny plants growing out of the exposed rocks*

**ex·po·si·tion** /ˌɛkspəˈzɪʃən/ *n* **1** [C,U] a detailed explanation that is easy to understand **2** a large public event at which you show and sell a particular type of product

**ex·po·sure** /ɪkˈspoʊʒə/ *n* **1** [C,U] the state of being put into a harmful situation without any protection: *Skin cancer is often caused by too much exposure to the sun.* **2** [U] an opportunity to experience new ideas, events, methods etc.: *My first exposure to classical music was at college.* **3** **get/receive exposure** to be written or talked about in newspapers or on television: *The issue has received a lot of exposure in the press.* **4** [C,U] the action of telling people about a dishonest person, event, or situation: *We threatened him with public exposure.* **5** [U] the harmful effects of staying outside for a long time when the weather is extremely cold: *Three climbers died of exposure in the Himalayas.* **6** the part of a film in a camera that is used for producing a photograph: *This roll has 36 exposures.*

**ex·press**[1] /ɪkˈsprɛs/ *v* [T] **1** to use words or actions in order to let people know what you are thinking or feeling: *A number of people*

E

*expressed the fear that they would never get another job.* | *It's hard sometimes for children to* **express themselves.** **2 express an interest in sth** to say that you are interested in something: *She expressed an interest in seeing the old map.*

**express²** *adj* **1** specific, deliberate, or exact: *It was her* **express wish** *that you inherit her house.* **2 express train/bus** a train or bus that travels quickly and does not stop in many places

**ex·pres·sion** /ɪk'sprɛʃən/ *n* **1** a word or phrase that has a particular meaning: *You use the expression "break a leg" to wish an actor good luck.* **2** a look on someone's face that shows what s/he is thinking or feeling: *a cheerful expression* **3** [C,U] something that you say, do, or write that shows what you think or feel: *I'm sending these flowers as an* **expression of** *my thanks.*

**ex·pres·sion·less** /ɪk'sprɛʃənlɪs/ *adj* an expressionless face or voice does not show what someone feels or thinks

**ex·pres·sive** /ɪk'sprɛsɪv/ *adj* showing what someone thinks or feels: *He has really expressive eyes.*

**ex·press·ly** /ɪk'sprɛsli/ *adv* FORMAL in a detailed or exact way: *Mr. Samson expressly asked you to leave.*

**ex·press·way** /ɪk'sprɛs,weɪ/ *n* a very wide road in a city on which cars can travel at a fast speed

**ex·pro·pri·ate** /ɛks'proʊpri,eɪt/ *v* [T] FORMAL to take away someone's private property for public use —**expropriation** /ɛks,proʊpri-'eɪʃən/ *n* [C,U]

**ex·pul·sion** /ɪk'spʌlʃən/ *n* [C,U] the official act of making someone leave a country, school, or organization: *the expulsion of Communists from the government*

**ex·quis·ite** /ɪk'skwɪzɪt, 'ɛkskwɪ-/ *adj* extremely beautiful and delicate, and seeming to be perfect: *an exquisite piece of jewelry* —**exquisitely** *adv*

**ex·tem·po·ra·ne·ous** /ɪk,stɛmpə'reɪniəs, ɛk-/ *adj* spoken or done without any preparation or practice: *an extemporaneous speech*

**ex·tend** /ɪk'stɛnd/ *v* **1** [I] to continue, reach, or stretch: *The river* **extends for** *more than 200 miles* **through** *the Grand Canyon.* | *The 90° weather extended into late September.* **2** [T] to increase something in size or amount of time: *Immigration is extending her visa by another six months.* **3** [I,T] to be able to be used in more than one way or by more than one person or group: *My insurance policy can be extended to cover my family too.* **4** [T] FORMAL to offer someone help, thanks, sympathy etc.: *We'd like to* **extend a welcome/greeting** *to all our new members.* **5** [T] to stretch out a part of your body

**ex·tend·ed fam·i·ly** /.,.. '../ *n* a family that in-

cludes parents, children, grandparents, AUNTs etc. —compare NUCLEAR FAMILY

**ex·ten·sion** /ɪk'stɛnʃən/ *n* **1 a)** the set of additional numbers for a particular telephone line in a large building: *Hello, I'd like extension 1334, please.* **b)** one of the telephones in a house, that all have the same number **2** [C usually singular] an additional period of time that someone is given to finish a job, pay money that s/he owes etc.: *The professor gave me a two-week extension on my paper.* **3** [C,U] the process of making something bigger or longer, or the part that is added in this process: *The city is building an extension to the subway line.* **4** [singular, U] the process of increasing something that is already there: *the extension of Soviet power in Eastern Europe*

**extension cord** /.'.. ,./ *n* an additional piece of electric wire that you attach to another wire in order to make it longer

**ex·ten·sive** /ɪk'stɛnsɪv/ *adj* **1** containing a lot of information, details, work etc.: *Doctors have done extensive research into the effects of stress.* **2** very large in the size, amount, or degree of something: *Forests were destroyed due to extensive logging.*

**ex·tent** /ɪk'stɛnt/ *n* **1** [U] the limit, size, or degree of something: *What's the extent of the damage?* **2 to some extent/to a certain extent/to a large extent** used when saying that something is partly but not completely true: *To some extent, you're right.* **3 to such an extent that/to the extent that/to the extent of** used when saying that something is affected or influenced so much that something else happens: *The building was damaged to such an extent that it had to be knocked down.*

**ex·te·ri·or¹** /ɪk'stɪriɚ/ *n* the appearance or outside surface of something: *the exterior of the house* | *Her calm exterior hid her intense anger.* —opposite INTERIOR¹

**exterior²** *adj* on the outside or outside surface of something: *the exterior walls of the church* —opposite INTERIOR²

**ex·ter·mi·nate** /ɪk'stɚmə,neɪt/ *v* [T] to kill most or all members of a particular group of people, animals, or insects —**exterminator** *n* —**extermination** /ɪk,stɚmə'neɪʃən/ *n* [C,U]

**ex·ter·nal** /ɪk'stɚnl/ *adj* **1** coming from outside something: *The plant must live in constantly changing external conditions.* **2** relating to the outside of something: *This medicine is* **for external use only.** —opposite INTERNAL

**ex·tinct** /ɪk'stɪŋkt/ *adj* an extinct plant, animal, or language no longer exists

**ex·tinc·tion** /ɪk'stɪŋkʃən/ *n* [U] the state of being EXTINCT: *Greenpeace believes that whales are in danger of extinction.*

**ex·tin·guish** /ɪk'stɪŋgwɪʃ/ *v* [T] **1** to make a fire or light stop burning or shining: *Please* *extinguish all cigarettes.* **2** LITERARY to destroy an idea or feeling: *The news extinguished all hope of his return.*

**ex·tin·guish·er** /ɪkˈstɪŋgwɪʃɚ/ *n* ⇨ FIRE EXTINGUISHER

**ex·tol** /ɪkˈstoʊl/ *v* **-lled, -lling** [T] to praise something very much: *Jaime was **extolling the virtues of** being vegetarian.*

**ex·tort** /ɪkˈstɔrt/ *v* [T] to force someone to give you money by threatening him/her: *The policemen were actually **extorting** money from drug dealers.* –**extortion** /ɪkˈstɔrʃən/ *n* [U]

**ex·tor·tion·ate** /ɪkˈstɔrʃənɪt/ *adj* too expensive or unfair: *an extortionate price for a hotel room*

**ex·tra¹** /ˈɛkstrə/ *adj* more than the usual or standard amount of something: *a large mushroom pizza with extra cheese*

**extra²** *adv* **1** being more money than the usual amount: *You have to pay extra if you want to travel first class.* **2** used when emphasizing an adjective or adverb: *If you're extra good I'll buy you an ice cream.*

**extra³** *n* **1** something that is added to a product or service and that usually costs more: *a car with extras such as a sun roof and CD player* **2** an actor who is not a main character in a movie but pretends to be part of a crowd

**ex·tract¹** /ɪkˈstrækt/ *v* [T] **1** to remove an object or substance from the place where it belongs or comes from: *I'm having my wisdom teeth extracted.* | *Olive oil is **extracted** from green olives.* **2** to make someone give you information, money etc. that s/he does not want to give: *The police couldn't extract any information from him.*

**ex·tract²** /ˈɛkstrækt/ *n* **1** a small part of a story, poem, song etc.: *an **extract from** "A Midsummer Night's Dream"* **2** [C,U] a substance that is removed from a root, flower etc. by a special process: *vanilla extract*

**ex·trac·tion** /ɪkˈstrækʃən/ *n* **1** [C,U] the process of removing an object or substance from something else: *the extraction of coal and other natural resources* **2 of French/Irish etc. extraction** having family members who come from France etc. even though you were born in another country

**ex·tra·cur·ric·u·lar** /ˌɛkstrəkəˈrɪkyələ/ *adj* extracurricular activities are sports, classes etc. that you do for fun and are not part of the usual work you do for school

**ex·tra·dite** /ˈɛkstrəˌdaɪt/ *v* [T] to send someone who may be guilty of a crime back to the country where the crime happened –**extradition** /ˌɛkstrəˈdɪʃən/ *n* [C,U]

**ex·tra·ne·ous** /ɪkˈstreɪniəs/ *adj* FORMAL not directly related to a particular subject or problem: *His report contains too many extraneous details.*

**ex·traor·di·nar·y** /ɪkˈstrɔrdnˌɛri/ *adj* very unusual, special, or surprising: *Ellington had an extraordinary musical talent.*

**ex·trap·o·late** /ɪkˈstræpəˌleɪt/ *v* [I,T] FORMAL to use the information you already know in order to guess what will happen

**ex·tra·ter·res·tri·al** /ˌɛkstrətəˈrɛstriəl/ *n* a living creature that people think may live on another PLANET –**extraterrestrial** *adj*

**ex·trav·a·gant** /ɪkˈstrævəgənt/ *adj* **1** spending a lot of money on things that are not necessary, or costing a lot of money: *the extravagant lifestyles of movie stars* | *extravagant parties* **2** unusual and exciting, but not practical or reasonable: *extravagant claims that the drug cures AIDS* –**extravagantly** *adv* –**extravagance** *n* [C,U]

**ex·treme¹** /ɪkˈstrim/ *adj* **1** very great: *Mountain climbers face extreme danger.* **2** extreme opinions, actions, conditions etc. are not acceptable because they are very unusual or unreasonable: *Mr. Wong uses extreme methods to discipline his students.* **3 extreme example/case** the strangest, most unusual, or most unlikely possibility: *In an extreme case, pregnant women who use this drug may harm the baby.*

**extreme²** *n* **1** one of the limits to a range of things, such as temperatures, actions, or emotions: *Seals can survive extremes of hot summers and very cold winters.* | *between the extremes of joy and depression* **2 in the extreme** to a very great degree or amount

**ex·treme·ly** /ɪkˈstrimli/ *adv* to a very great degree: *Wilma's little girl is extremely pretty.*

**ex·trem·ist** /ɪkˈstrimɪst/ *n* someone who has extreme political aims, and who is willing to do unusual or illegal things to achieve them –**extremist** *adj* –**extremism** *n* [U]

**ex·trem·i·ties** /ɪkˈstrɛmətiz/ *n* [plural] your hands, feet, legs, or arms

**ex·trem·i·ty** /ɪkˈstrɛməti/ *n* the area farthest from something: *the city's northern extremity*

**ex·tri·cate** /ˈɛkstrəˌkeɪt/ *v* [T] to get someone out of a place or a difficult situation: *They couldn't **extricate themselves from** the huge crowd of people.*

**ex·tro·vert·ed** /ˈɛkstrəˌvɚtɪd/ *n* confident and enjoying being with other people –**extrovert** *n* –compare INTROVERTED

**ex·u·ber·ant** /ɪgˈzubərənt/ *adj* very happy, excited, and full of energy: *the exuberant bride* –**exuberance** *n* [U]

**ex·ude** /ɪgˈzud, ɪkˈsud/ *v* **1** [T] to show that you have a lot of a particular feeling: *new students exuding excitement* **2** [I,T] to flow out slowly and steadily, or to make liquid do this

**ex·ult** /ɪgˈzʌlt/ *v* [I] to be very happy and proud because you have achieved something: *The people **exulted over** the defeat of their en-*

*emy.* **−exultant** *adj* **−exultation** /ˌɛgzʌl-ˈteɪʃən, ˌɛksʌl-/ *n* [U]

**eye**

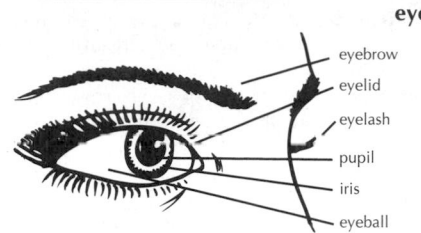

eyebrow
eyelid
eyelash
pupil
iris
eyeball

**eye¹** /aɪ/ *n*

**1** ▶SEE◀ one of the two parts of your body that you see with: *Gina has blue eyes. | My eyes are going bad; I think I need glasses.* −see picture at HEAD¹

**2 keep an eye on sb/sth** INFORMAL to watch what someone or something does in order to prevent something bad from happening: *Can you keep an eye on the baby while I go to the store?*

**3 lay/set eyes on sb/sth** SPOKEN a phrase meaning to see someone or something: *The first time I laid eyes on him I knew I liked him.*

**4 cannot take your eyes off sb/sth** to be unable to stop looking at someone or something because s/he or it is so attractive or interesting: *You looked so pretty I just couldn't take my eyes off you.*

**5 make eye contact** to look directly at someone while s/he is looking at you: *We made eye contact on the bus.*

**6 keep an eye out for sb/sth** to look around in order to find someone or something, even though you are doing other things at the same time: *Keep an eye out for Rick's car.*

**7 in the eyes of the law/world/police etc.** in the opinion or the judgment of the law, world, etc.: *Divorce is a sin in the eyes of the Catholic Church.*

**8 have your eye on sb** to notice someone that you think is so attractive or interesting that you want to meet him/her: *Mark really has his eye on Yvonne.*

**9 have your eye on sth** to have noticed something that you want to buy or have: *Harris has his eye on a two-storey house in Woodside.*

**10 drop/lower your eyes** to look down, especially because you are shy, embarrassed, or ashamed: *She looked up, saw him staring at her, and lowered her eyes again.*

**11 blue-eyed/one-eyed/bright-eyed etc.** having blue eyes, one eye, bright eyes etc.

**12** ▶NEEDLE◀ the hole in a needle that you put thread through

**13** ▶STORM◀ the calm center of a storm such as a CYCLONE or HURRICANE −see also **catch sb's eye** (CATCH¹) **look sb in the eye** (LOOK¹)

**eye²** *v* **eyed, eyed, eyeing** *or* **eying** [T] to look at someone in a way that shows you think s/he

is sexually attractive: *Sarah kept eyeing my boyfriend all night.*

**eye·ball** /ˈaɪbɔl/ *n* the whole of your eye, including the part that is inside your head −see picture at EYE¹

**eye·brow** /ˈaɪbraʊ/ *n* the line of short hairs above your eye −see pictures at EYE¹ and HEAD¹

**eye·catch·ing** /ˈ. ˌ../ *adj* something that is eye-catching is so unusual or attractive that you notice it: *an eye-catching dress*

**eye·lash** /ˈaɪlæʃ/ *n* one of the small hairs that grow on the edge of your EYELID −see picture at EYE¹

**eye·lid** /ˈaɪˌlɪd/ *n* the piece of skin that covers your eye when it is closed −see picture at EYE¹

**eye·o·pen·er** /ˈ. ˌ../ *n* [singular] an event, situation etc. that makes you learn something surprising: *The documentary about runaway children was a real eye-opener for me.*

**eye·shad·ow** /ˈaɪˌʃædoʊ/ *n* [U] a colored powder women put over their eyes to make them look attractive

**eye·sight** /ˈaɪsaɪt/ *n* [U] the ability to see: *Grandma is slowly losing her eyesight.*

**eye·sore** /ˈaɪsɔr/ *n* something ugly in a place that makes an area look less nice: *The old mall has become an eyesore.*

**eye·wit·ness** /ˌaɪˈwɪtˈnɪs, ˈaɪˌwɪtˈnɪs/ *n* someone who has seen a crime, important event etc.: *According to an eyewitness, the bomb exploded at exactly 3:00 p.m.*

# F

**F, f** /ɛf/ the sixth letter of the English alphabet

**F¹** /ɛf/ *n* **1** a failing grade on a test or piece of school work **2** [C,U] the fourth note in the musical SCALE of C, or the musical KEY based on this note

**F²** **1** the written abbreviation of FAHRENHEIT: *Water boils at 212° F.* **2** the written abbreviation of FEMALE **3** the written abbreviation of FALSE

**fa·ble** /ˈfeɪbəl/ *n* a short story, often about animals, that teaches a moral lesson

**fab·ric** /ˈfæbrɪk/ *n* **1** [C,U] cloth used for making clothes, curtains etc. **2** the basic structure of something such as a society, system etc. −see usage note at CLOTH

**fab·ri·cate** /ˈfæbrəˌkeɪt/ *v* [T] to make up a story, piece of information etc. in order to deceive someone; lie **−fabrication** /ˌfæbrəˈkeɪʃən/ *n* [C,U]

**fab·u·lous** /ˈfæbyələs/ *adj* **1** extremely good or impressive: *You look fabulous!* **2** unusually large in amount or size: *a fabulous sum of money* **−fabulously** *adv*

**fa·cade, façade** /fə'sɑd/ n **1** a way of behaving that hides your real feelings or character: *Behind that cheerful facade she's really a lonely person.* **2** the front of a building

**face¹** /feɪs/ n

**1** ▶FRONT OF YOUR HEAD◀ the front part of your head, where your eyes, nose, and mouth are: *Jodi has such a pretty face.* | *He had a surprised look on his face.* —see picture at HEAD¹

**2** ▶EXPRESSION◀ an expression on someone's face: *Carl was making faces at Lisa all morning.* (=using his face to try to make her laugh, or to annoy her) | *I just couldn't keep a straight face.* (=avoid laughing)

**3 in the face of** when dealing with difficult situations or danger: *cities that did well, even in the face of budget cuts*

**4 face to face** if you are face to face with someone, you are looking directly at him/her: *I've never met her face to face. We've only talked on the phone.*

**5** ▶SURFACE◀ an outside surface of an object, usually on its front: *a clock face* | *the north face of Mount Rainier*

**6 come/be face to face with sth** to have to deal with something unpleasant: *It was the first time he'd ever come face to face with death.*

**7 on the face of it** when you first consider something, before you know the details: *On the face of it, the data is not very helpful.*

**8 lose/save face** to lose or avoid losing the respect of other people: *If I win, Mosad will lose face and hate me even more.*

**9 say sth to sb's face** to say something to someone directly: *I'd never say it to his face, but his breath stinks.*

**10 what's-his-face/what's-her-face** SPOKEN used instead of someone's name when you cannot remember it: *There's a letter from what's-his-face for Troy.*

**11 in your face** INFORMAL behavior, remarks etc. that are in your face are very direct and make people feel uncomfortable

**12 get out of my face** SPOKEN used in order to tell someone rudely to go away because s/he is annoying you

**face²** v [T] **1** also **face up to** to accept that a difficult situation or problem exists, and to be willing to deal with it: *I hope that's the worst problem we'll have to face.* | *Randy refuses to face the fact that he needs help.* **2** to be turned or pointed in a particular direction or toward someone or something: *Dean turned to face me.* | *a north-facing window* | *apartments that face the ocean* **3 be faced with sth** to be in a situation where you have to deal with something difficult: *She's faced with some very tough choices.* **4** to deal with someone, or talk to someone, when this is difficult: *You're going to have to face him sooner or later.* **5** to play against an opponent or team in a game or

competition: *The Jets face the Dolphins in two weeks.*

**face** sb ↔ **down** phr v [T] to deal in a strong and confident way with someone who opposes you: *Yeltsin faced down a coup.*

**face off** phr v [I] to get in a position in which you are ready to fight, argue, or COMPETE with someone: *The two candidates will face off in the election in November.*

**face·less** /'feɪslɪs/ adj a faceless person, organization etc. is boring or is not easily noticed

**face·lift** /'feɪslɪft/ n **1** a medical operation in which doctors remove loose skin on someone's face in order to make him/her look younger **2 give sth a facelift** to make something look newer or better by working on it or repairing it

**fac·et** /'fæsɪt/ n **1** one of several parts of someone's character, a situation etc.: *You've only seen one facet of his personality.* **2** one of the flat sides of a cut jewel

**fa·ce·tious** /fə'siʃəs/ adj intended to be funny, but annoying or not suitable instead —**facetiously** adv

**face val·ue** /'. ,../ n [U] **1** the value that is written on something such as a coin, STOCK etc., but that may not actually be what the coin etc. is worth: *A Treasury note with a face value of $10,000 was sold for $9998.* **2 take sth at face value** to accept something without thinking that it might not be as good or true as it seems: *Don't take anything Burgess tells you at face value.*

**fa·cial¹** /'feɪʃəl/ adj on the face, or relating to the face: *facial hair*

**facial²** n a process in which your face is specially cleaned

**fac·ile** /'fæsəl/ adj too simple and showing a lack of careful thought or understanding: *a facile argument against abortion*

**fa·cil·i·tate** /fə'sɪlə,teɪt/ v [T] FORMAL to make it easier for something to happen: *We've hired more people to facilitate the enrollment of new students.*

**fa·cil·i·ties** /fə'sɪlətiz/ n [plural] rooms, equipment, or services that are provided for a particular purpose: *The college has excellent research facilities.*

**fa·cil·i·ty** /fə'sɪləti/ n **1** a place or building used for a particular purpose: *a sports facility* **2** [singular] an ability to do or learn something easily: *a facility for languages*

**fac·sim·i·le** /fæk'sɪməli/ n **1** an exact copy of a picture, piece of writing etc. **2** ⇨ FAX

**fact** /fækt/ n **1** something that is known to be true, or that has definitely happened: *What are the facts of/in this case?* | *interesting facts about plants* | *I appreciate the fact that you're willing to help.* **2 in fact/as a matter of fact** a) used in order to add information: *I know her really well, in fact I had dinner with her last week.* b) used in order to emphasize that something is true, especially when it is surprising: *It's cheaper to fly, as a matter of fact.* **3 sth is a fact of life** used in order to say that a situation exists and must be accepted: *Violent crime seems to have become a fact of life.* **4 the facts of life a)** the details about sex and how babies are born **b)** the way life really is, with all its problems and difficulties

**fac·tion** /'fækʃən/ *n* a small group of people within a larger group, who have different ideas from the other members **–factional** *adj*

**fac·tor** /'fæktɚ/ *n* **1** one of several things that influence or cause a situation: *The weather could be an important factor in tomorrow's game.* **2** TECHNICAL a number that divides into another number exactly: *3 is a factor of 15.*

**fac·to·ry** /'fæktəri/ *n* a building or group of buildings where goods are produced in large quantities: *a shoe factory*

**fac·tu·al** /'fæktʃuəl/ *adj* based on facts **–factually** *adv*

**fac·ul·ty** /'fækəlti/ *n* **1 the faculty a)** all the teachers in a particular school or college: *a faculty meeting* **b)** the teachers in a particular department of a school or college: *the history faculty* **2** FORMAL a natural ability, such as the ability to see or think: *the faculty of hearing*

**fad** /fæd/ *n* something that someone likes or does for a short time, or that is fashionable for a short time: *a fad for big baggy t-shirts*

**fade** /feɪd/ *v* **1** [I] also **fade away** to gradually disappear or become weaker: *Hopes of a peace settlement are beginning to fade.* **2** [I,T] to lose color or brightness, or to make something do this: *faded jeans*
   **fade out** *phr v* [I,T **fade** sth ↔ **out**] to disappear slowly or become quieter, or to make a picture or sound do this

**fag** /fæg/, **fag·got** /'fægət/ *n* SLANG a very offensive word for a HOMOSEXUAL man **–compare** GAY²

**Fahr·en·heit** /'færən,haɪt/ *n* [U] a scale of temperature in which water freezes at 32° and boils at 212°

**fail¹** /feɪl/ *v* **1** [I,T] to be unsuccessful in doing something: *Doctors failed to save the girl's life.|I failed my math test.* **2** [I] to not do what is expected or needed: *Larry failed to present his proposal on time.|The wheat crop failed* (=did not grow) *due to drought.* **3 I fail to see/understand** used in order to show that you are annoyed by something that you do not accept or understand: *I fail to see the humor in this situation.* **4** [I] if a bank, company etc. fails, it has to stop operating because of a lack of money **5** [I] to stop working correctly or at all: *The engine failed just after the plane took off.* **6 your courage/nerve fails** if your courage fails, you do not have it when you need it **7 failing sight/health** sight or health that is becoming worse

**fail²** *n* **without fail** FORMAL **a)** if you do something without fail, you always do it: *Barry comes over every Friday without fail.* **b)** used when telling someone that s/he must do something: *I want that work finished by tomorrow, without fail!*

**fail·ing¹** /'feɪlɪŋ/ *n* a fault or weakness: *He loved her in spite of her failings.*

**failing²** *prep* used in order to say that if one thing is not possible or available, there is another one you could try: *You could try calling, but failing that a letter only takes a few days.*

**fail-safe** /'. ./ *adj* **1** a fail-safe machine, piece of equipment etc. will stop working if one part of it breaks or stops working correctly **2** a fail-safe plan is certain to succeed

**fail·ure** /'feɪlyɚ/ *n* **1** [C,U] a lack of success in achieving or doing something: *The recession has caused the failure of many small businesses.|Are teachers to blame for students' failure to learn?|The whole project ended in failure.* **2** someone or something that is not successful: *I feel like such a failure.* **3** an occasion when a machine or part of your body stops working in the correct way: *He died of heart failure.|the failure of the computer system* **4** the act of not doing something you should do or are expected to do: *We were worried about his failure to contact us.*

**faint¹** /feɪnt/ *adj* **1** difficult to see, hear, smell etc.: *a faint sound* **2 a faint possibility/ chance etc.** a very small or slight possibility etc.: *There's still a faint hope that they might be alive.* **3** feeling weak and as if you are about to become unconscious: *He was faint with hunger* **4 not have the faintest idea** to not know anything at all about something: *I don't have the faintest idea what you are talking about.* **–faintly** *adv*

**faint²** *v* [I] to become unconscious for a short time **–faint** *n*

**fair¹** /fɛr/ *adj*
**1** ▶REASONABLE◀ reasonable and acceptable according to what people normally accept as being right: *That's not fair! You went last time - I want to go.|What do you think is the fairest solution?*
**2** ▶EQUAL◀ treating everyone in an equal way: *That law isn't fair to women.*
**3** ▶AVERAGE◀ neither particularly good nor particularly bad: *Her written work is excellent but her practical work is only fair.*
**4** ▶ACCORDING TO RULES◀ played or done according to the rules: *free and fair elections*
**5 fair share** a reasonable and acceptable amount of something: *Tim's had more than his fair share of bad luck this year.*
**6** ▶HAIR/SKIN◀ light in color
**7** ▶WEATHER◀ sunny
**8 fair game** someone or something that you can criticize or try to get: *Reporters seem to think movie stars are fair game just because*

*they are public figures.*

**9 give/get a fair shake** to treat someone, or to be treated, fairly, so that everyone has the same chance: *Women don't always get a fair shake in business.*

**10** ►BEAUTY◄ LITERARY beautiful —**fairness** *n* [U]

**fair**[2] *adv* **1 fair and square** in a fair and honest way: *They won fair and square* **2 play fair** to play or behave in a fair and honest way

**fair**[3] *n* **1** an outdoor event, at which there are large machines to ride on, games to play, and sometimes farm animals being judged and sold **2** a regular event where companies show and advertise their products: *a trade fair*

**fair·ground** /'fɛrgraʊnd/ *n* an open space on which a FAIR takes place

**fair·ly** /'fɛrli/ *adv* **1** more than a little, but much less than very: *She speaks English fairly well.* **2** in a way that is honest or reasonable: *I felt that I hadn't been treated fairly.*

**fair·y** /'fɛri/ *n* **1** SLANG an offensive word for a HOMOSEXUAL man **2** a very small imaginary creature with magic powers, that looks like a person with wings

**fairy tale** /'.. ,./ *n* a story for children in which magical things happen

**fait ac·com·pli** /ˌfeɪt əkɑm'pli, ˌfɛt ækɔm'pli/ *n* [singular] something that has already happened and cannot be changed

**faith** /feɪθ/ *n* **1** [U] a strong belief that someone or something can be trusted to be right or to do the right thing: *I have great faith in her ability to succeed.* **2** [U] belief and trust in God: *a strong faith in God's power to heal* **3 in good faith** with honest and sincere intentions: *The guy who sold me the car claimed he had acted in good faith.* **4** a religion: *the Jewish faith*

**faith·ful** /'feɪθfəl/ *adj* **1** showing loyalty and giving continuous support to someone or something: *a faithful friend* **2** describing an event or copying an image exactly: *a faithful reproduction of the original picture* **3** loyal to your wife, BOYFRIEND etc. by not having a sexual relationship with anyone else —**faithfulness** *n* [U]

**faith·ful·ly** /'feɪθfəli/ *adv* in a faithful way: *He visited his aunt faithfully.*

**faith·less** /'feɪθlɪs/ *adj* FORMAL not able to be trusted: *a faithless friend*

**fake**[1] /feɪk/ *n* **1** a copy of a valuable object, painting etc. that is intended to deceive people: *We thought it was a Picasso, but it was a fake.* **2** someone who does not really have the knowledge, skills etc. that s/he claims to have: *It turned out her doctor was a fake.*

**fake**[2] *adj* made to look like a real material or object in order to deceive people: *fake fur*

**fake**[3] *v* **1** [T] to make an exact copy of something, or to make up figures or results, in order to deceive people: *He faked his uncle's signature on the check.* **2** [I,T] to pretend to be

sick, or to be interested, pleased etc. when you are not: *I thought he was really hurt but he was just faking it.* **3** to pretend to move in one direction, but then move in another, especially when playing a sport: *Everett faked a pass and ran with the ball.*

**fake** sb **out** *phr v* [T] to deceive someone by making him/her think you are planning to do one thing when you are really planning something else

**fal·con** /'fælkən, 'fɔl-/ *n* a large bird that is often trained to hunt small animals

**fall**[1] /fɔl/ *v* **fell, fallen, falling** [I]

**1** ►THINGS FALLING◄ to move or drop down toward the ground: *as the rain/snow began to fall* | *Some of the big trees fell over in the storm.* | *apples that had fallen from the trees*

fall

**2** ►PERSON FALLING◄ to accidentally fall onto the ground when you are standing, walking, running etc.: *Don't worry, I'll catch you if you fall.* | *I slipped and fell down the stairs.*

**3** ►LOWER LEVEL/AMOUNT◄ to become lower in level, degree, quantity, or quality: *Temperatures should fall below zero tonight.* | *The number of traffic deaths fell by 10% last year.*

**4 fall asleep/ill etc.** to start to sleep, be sick etc.: *I fell asleep at 8:30.* | *Everyone fell silent as Beth walked in.*

**5 fall in love** to begin to love someone: *Your father and I fell in love during the war.*

**6** ►GROUP/PATTERN◄ to be part of a particular group, pattern, or range: *These substances fall into two categories.*

**7 fall into place** to become organized or easy to understand: *If you have a good outline for your paper, the rest just falls into place.*

**8** ►HAPPEN◄ to happen, especially at a particular time: *Christmas falls on a Monday this year.*

**9** ►LIGHT/DARKNESS◄ if light or darkness falls, it makes something brighter or darker: *A shadow fell across his face, hiding his expression.* | *The lights came on as darkness/night fell on the city.*

**10** ►HANG DOWN◄ to hang loosely: *Maria's hair fell over her shoulders.*

**11 fall short (of)** to fail to achieve the result or standard you wanted: *Her newest book fell short of my expectations.*

**12** ►FACE◄ if your face falls, you suddenly look sad or disappointed

**13 fall flat** to fail to produce the effect you wanted: *Your joke about the nuns really fell flat, didn't it?*

**14 fall into poverty/despair etc.** to start being poor, sad etc.: *an old house allowed to fall*

F

*into disrepair*

**15** ▶DIE◀ to be killed or destroyed in a war: *The first man to fall in battle was only 18.*

**16** ▶LOSE POWER◀ to fail or lose power: *After World War II, the British Empire fell.*

**fall apart** *phr v* [I] **1** to separate into small pieces: *The old book **fell apart** in my hands.* **2** to stop working effectively: *The country's economy was **falling apart**.* **3** to start having problems dealing with life or your emotions: *When Pam left, I thought I was going to **fall apart**.*

**fall back on** sth *phr v* [T] to use something that is familiar or easy after something new or difficult has failed to work: *Theaters are **falling back on** old favorites rather than risking money on new plays.*

**fall behind** *phr v* [I,T] to not finish something by the time you were supposed to: *The manufacturers have **fallen behind** schedule.*

**fall for** *phr v* [T] **1** [**fall for** sth] to be tricked into believing something that is not true: *We told him we were Italian and he **fell for** it!* **2** [**fall for** sb] to suddenly feel romantic love for someone: *Samantha **fell for** a man half her age.*

**fall off** *phr v* [I] to become less in quality, amount etc.: *Demand for records has **fallen off** recently.*

**fall out** *phr v* [I] if a tooth or your hair falls out, it drops out of the place where it grows

**fall through** *phr v* [I] to fail to happen or be completed: *The deal **fell through** at the last minute.*

**fall²** *n* **1** the season between summer and winter, when the weather becomes cooler; AUTUMN: *Brad's going to Georgia Tech **in the fall**.* | *Dad's going to retire **this fall**.* | *last/next fall* (=the fall before or after this one) **2** a decrease in the level, quantity, price etc. of something: *a sudden **fall in** temperature* —opposite

RISE² **3** the act of falling: *He had a bad fall from a ladder.* **4** [singular] a situation when someone or something is defeated or loses power: *the fall of Rome* —see also FALLS

**fal·la·cious** /fə'leɪʃəs/ *adj* FORMAL containing or based on false ideas: *a fallacious argument* —**fallaciously** *adv*

**fal·la·cy** /'fæləsi/ *n* a false idea or belief: *the fallacy that money brings happiness*

**fall·en** /'fɔlən/ the past participle of fall

**fall guy** /'. ./ *n* INFORMAL someone who is punished for someone else's crime or mistake

**fal·li·ble** /'fæləbəl/ *adj* able to make a mistake —**fallibility** /ˌfælə'bɪləti/ *n* [U] —opposite INFALLIBLE

**fall·out** /'fɔlaʊt/ *n* [U] **1** the dangerous RADIOACTIVE dust that is left in the air after a NUCLEAR explosion **2** the bad results or effects of an event: *The fallout from the scandal cost him his job.*

**falls** /fɔlz/ *n* [plural] ⇨ WATERFALL

**false** /fɔls/ *adj* **1** not true or correct: *He gave the police false information.* **2** not real, but intended to seem real: *false eyelashes* **3** not sincere or honest: *Her smile and welcome seemed false.* **4** **false alarm** a warning of something bad that does not happen: *We thought there was a fire, but it was a false alarm.* **5** **false start** an unsuccessful attempt to begin a process or event: *After several false starts, the show finally began.* **6** **under false pretenses** if you get something under false pretenses, you get it by deceiving people —**falsely** *adv* —**falsity** *n* [U]

**false·hood** /'fɔlshʊd/ *n* FORMAL a statement that is not true

**false teeth** /ˌ. './ *n* [plural] ⇨ DENTURES

**fal·set·to** /fɔl'sɛtoʊ/ *n* a very high male voice —**falsetto** *adj, adv*

**family**

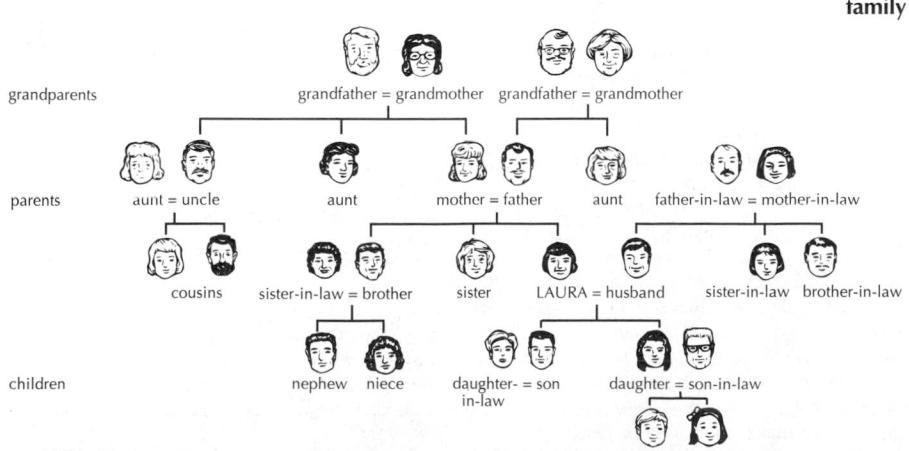

| grandparents | grandfather = grandmother | grandfather = grandmother |
| --- | --- | --- |
| parents | aunt = uncle      aunt      mother = father      aunt | father-in-law = mother-in-law |
| | cousins   sister-in-law = brother   sister   LAURA = husband   sister-in-law   brother-in-law |
| children | nephew  niece   daughter-  = son   daughter = son-in-law |
| | in-law |
| grandchildren | grandson  granddaughter |

**fal·si·fy** /ˈfɔlsəˌfaɪ/ v [T] to change information and make it untrue: *He was accused of falsifying the company's records.* **–falsification** /ˌfɔlsəfəˈkeɪʃən/ n [C,U]

**fal·ter** /ˈfɔltər/ v [I] **1** to become weaker, less determined etc.: *The economy is faltering.* **2** to speak or move in a way that seems weak or uncertain: *She faltered for a moment.*

**fame** /feɪm/ n [U] the state of being known about by a lot of people because of your achievements: *Elizabeth Taylor's rise to fame came in the movie "National Velvet."* –see also **claim to fame** (CLAIM²)

**famed** /feɪmd/ adj known about by a lot of people: *mountains famed for their beauty*

**fa·mil·iar** /fəˈmɪlyər/ adj **1** someone or something that is familiar is easy to recognize because you have seen or heard him, her, or it before: *Your face looks familiar to me.* | *the familiar sounds of the classroom* **2** be familiar with to have a good knowledge of something: *Are you familiar with his books?* **3** friendly and informal in speech, writing etc.: *Vic has an easy familiar style of writing.*

**fa·mil·iar·i·ty** /fəˌmɪlˈyærəti, -ˌmɪliˈær-/ n [U] **1** a good knowledge of something: *a familiarity with Russian poetry* **2** relaxed and friendly behavior

**fa·mil·iar·ize** /fəˈmɪlyəˌraɪz/ v **1** familiarize yourself with sth to learn about something so that you understand it: *I spent the first few weeks familiarizing myself with the new job.* **2** [T] to teach someone about something so that s/he understands it: *We'd like to familiarize you with the new regulations.* **–familiarization** /fəˌmɪlyərəˈzeɪʃən/ n [U]

**fa·mil·iar·ly** /fəˈmɪlyərli/ adv in an informal or friendly way

**fam·i·ly** /ˈfæmli, -məli/ n **1** [C,U] any group of people who are related to each other, especially a mother, father, and their children: *Do you know the family next door?* | *a car that will comfortably seat a family of five* (=a family with five people in it) | *Heart disease runs in our family.* (=is common in our family) | *Terry wants to work in the family business.* (=a small business owned by one family) **2** children: *Steve and Linda want to start a family* (=have children) *next year.* | *the problems of raising a family* (=educating and caring for your children) **3** a group of related animals, plants, languages etc.: *tigers and other members of the cat family*

**family plan·ning** /ˌ.. ˈ../ n [U] the practice of controlling the number of children that are born by using CONTRACEPTIVES

**family room** /ˈ.. ˌ./ n a room in a house where the family can play games, watch television etc.

**family tree** /ˌ.. ˈ./ n a drawing that gives the names of all the members of a family and shows how they are related to each other

**fam·ine** /ˈfæmɪn/ n [C,U] a situation in which a large number of people have little or no food for a long time

**fam·ished** /ˈfæmɪʃt/ adj INFORMAL very hungry: *What's for dinner? I'm famished.*

**fa·mous** /ˈfeɪməs/ adj known about or recognized by a lot of people: *a famous actor* | *France is famous for its food and wine.* | *Da Vinci's world-famous* (=recognized by everyone) *portrait of the Mona Lisa* **–famously** adv

**fan¹** /fæn/ n **1** someone who likes a particular sport, type of music etc. very much, or who admires a famous person: *He was a big fan of Elvis Presley.* **2** a machine, or a thing that you wave with your hand, that makes the air move so that you become cooler: *a ceiling fan*

fan

**fan²** v **-nned, -nning** [T] to make air move around near something by waving a FAN, piece of paper etc.: *She fanned her face with a newspaper.*

**fan out** phr v [I,T **fan** sth ↔ **out**] to spread out from a central point, or to make something do this: *The soldiers fanned out and walked into the jungle.*

**fa·nat·ic** /fəˈnætɪk/ n someone whose beliefs and behavior are extreme, especially concerning religion or politics **–fanatical** adj **–fanaticism** /fəˈnætəˌsɪzəm/ n [U]

**fan·ci·ful** /ˈfænsɪfəl/ adj imagined rather than based on facts: *fanciful ideas*

**fan club** /ˈ. ./ n an organization for FANs of a particular team, famous person etc.

**fan·cy¹** /ˈfænsi/ adj **1** expensive and not simple or ordinary: *a fancy hotel* **2** having a lot of decorations: *I'd just like plain brown shoes, nothing fancy.* **3** needing technical skill: *fancy skiing* **4** high quality: *fancy eggs* **–fancily** adv

**fan·cy²** n [singular] OLD-FASHIONED a feeling that you like something or someone: *Grant's taken a fancy to you!*

**fan·cy³** v [T] **1** to consider that something is true: *Hiram fancies himself a good writer.* **2** OLD-FASHIONED to like or want something

**fan·fare** /ˈfænfɛr/ n a short piece of music played on a TRUMPET to introduce an important person or event

**fang** /fæŋ/ n a long sharp tooth of an animal such as a snake or dog

**fan mail** /ˈ. ./ n [U] letters sent to famous people by their FANs

**fan·ny** /ˈfæni/ n INFORMAL the part of your body that you sit on; BOTTOM

**fan·ta·size** /ˈfæntəˌsaɪz/ v [I,T] to imagine

something strange or pleasant happening to you: *I used to fantasize that I was a famous dancer.*

**fan·tas·tic** /fæn'tæstɪk/ *adj* **1** extremely good, attractive, enjoyable etc.: *You look fantastic! | We had a fantastic trip to New Orleans.* **2** | SPOKEN used when someone has just told you something good: *"Hey Mom, I passed my math test!" "Fantastic!"* **3** very large: *She spends fantastic amounts of money on clothes.* **4** strange or unreal: *a fantastic dream* —**fantastically** *adv*

**fan·ta·sy** /'fænṱəsi, -zi/ *n* [C,U] imagined situations that are not related to the real world: *When I was young, I had fantasies about becoming a race car driver.*

**far**[1] /fɑr/ *adv* **farther, farthest,** *or* **further, furthest**
**1** ▶DISTANCE◀ moving over a long distance: *I don't want to drive very far. | The boat had moved farther away from the dock. | Let's see who can swim the farthest.* ✗ DON'T SAY "I walked far." SAY "I walked a long way." ✗
**2** ▶AMOUNT/DEGREE◀ very much or to a great degree: *Our new car is far better than the old one. | a plane flying far above the clouds*
**3** **so far** until a particular time, point, degree etc.: *We haven't had any problems so far.*
**4** **how far have you gotten (with sth)?** used when asking how much of something someone has done or achieved: *How far have you gotten with painting the kitchen?*
**5** **sb will/should go far** used in order to say that you think someone will be successful: *She's a good dancer and should go far.*
**6** **as far as possible** as much as possible: *We try to buy from local stores as far as possible.*
**7** **go so far as to do sth** to behave in a way that seems surprising or extreme: *He even went so far as to call her a liar.*
**8** **go too far** to do something too much or in an extreme way so that people are angry: *He's always been a little rude, but this time he went too far.*
**9** **not go far** if something does not go far, there is not enough of it to do what you need it to do: *A dollar doesn't go far anymore.* (=it does not buy enough)

---
SPOKEN PHRASES
**10** **as far as I know/as far as I can remember** said when you think that something is true, although you do not know or cannot remember all the facts: *Cole wasn't even there, as far as I can remember.*
**11** **so far so good** said when things have been happening successfully until now: *"How's your new job?" "So far so good."*
---

—see also **as far as sb's concerned** (CONCERNED)

**far**[2] *adj* **farther, farthest,** *or* **further, furthest**
**1** if something is far, it is a long distance from something else: *We can walk if it's not*

far. | *Denver's farther away than I thought. | Aim at the target that's farthest from you.* **2** most distant from where you are: *The parking lot is on the far side of the building.* **3** **how far** used when asking the distance between two places or the distance someone has traveled: *How far is Boston from here?* **4** **the far left/right** people who have political opinions that are much more extreme than those of most people **5** **be a far cry from** to be very different from something else: *Europe was a far cry from what Tom had expected.*

**far·a·way** /'fɑrə,weɪ/ *adj* **1** LITERARY distant: *faraway cities* **2** **faraway look** an expression on your face that shows that you are not thinking about what is around you

**farce** /fɑrs/ *n* **1** [singular] an event or situation that is badly organized and does not happen the way it should: *I'm telling you, the trial was a total farce.* **2** a humorous play in which a lot of silly things happen —**farcical** *adj*

**fare**[1] /fɛr/ *n* **1** the price you pay to travel by train, plane, bus etc.: *Air fares are going up again.* **2** a passenger in a taxi

**fare**[2] *v* [I] FORMAL to succeed in a particular situation: *Women are now faring better in politics.*

**Far East** /ˌ. './ *n* **the Far East** the part of Asia that is the farthest east, including areas such as Hong Kong and Japan

**fare·well** /ˌfɛr'wɛl/ *n interjection* **1** FORMAL goodbye: *It is time to bid farewell to our friends.* (=say goodbye to them) **2** **farewell party/drink** a party or drink that you have with someone who is leaving

**far-fetched** /ˌ. '.◂/ *adj* unlikely to be true: *I thought her story was pretty far-fetched.*

**far-flung** /ˌ. '.◂/ *adj* very far away or spread over a wide area: *the far-flung cities of the world*

**far gone** /ˌ. './ *adj* INFORMAL very ill, drunk, crazy etc.: *She's too far gone to understand what's happening.*

**farm**[1] /fɑrm/ *n* an area of land used for raising animals or growing food

**farm**[2] *v* [I,T] to use land for growing crops, raising animals etc.: *Our family has farmed here for years.*
**farm sth** ↔ **out** *phr v* [T] to send work to other people instead of doing it yourself: *Most of the editing is farmed out.*

**farm·er** /'fɑrmɚ/ *n* someone who owns or manages a farm

**farm·hand** /'fɑrmhænd/ *n* someone who is employed to work on a farm

**farm·ing** /'fɑrmɪŋ/ *n* [U] the practice or business of raising animals or growing crops on a farm

**farm·yard** /'fɑrmyɑrd/ *n* the area next to or around farm buildings

**far-off** /ˌ. '.◂/ *adj* LITERARY distant in time or space: *a far-off land*

**far-out** /ˌ. ˈ.◂/ *adj* INFORMAL unusual or strange: *far-out clothes*

**far-reach·ing** /ˌ. ˈ..◂/ *adj* having a big influence or effect: *This will be the most far-reaching tax reform in our history.*

**far·sight·ed** /ˈfɑrˌsaɪtɪd/ *adj* **1** able to see distant things more clearly than close ones **2** APPROVING considering what will happen in the future: *a farsighted economic plan*

**fart** /fɑrt/ *v* [I] INFORMAL an impolite word meaning to make air come out of your BOWELs —**fart** *n*

**fart around** *phr v* [I] INFORMAL an impolite phrase meaning to waste time not doing very much: *Stop **farting around** and help me out.*

**far·ther** /ˈfɑrðɚ/ *adj, adv* the COMPARATIVE of FAR —compare FURTHER¹

---

**USAGE NOTE** farther and further

Use **farther** to talk about distance: *The bar's just a little farther down the street.* Use **further** to talk about time, quantities, or degrees: *House prices will probably drop further next year.* | *I don't want to discuss this any further.* We also use **further** to talk about distance, but many teachers think this is incorrect.

---

**far·thest** /ˈfɑrðɪst/ *adj, adv* the SUPERLATIVE of FAR

**fas·ci·nate** /ˈfæsəˌneɪt/ *v* [T] to attract or interest someone very much: *Mechanical things fascinate me.*

**fas·ci·nat·ing** /ˈfæsəˌneɪt̬ɪŋ/ *adj* extremely interesting, especially because you are learning something new: *a fascinating subject/film/woman*

**fas·ci·na·tion** /ˌfæsəˈneɪʃən/ *n* [singular, U] the state of being very interested in something: *Jan **had a fascination with/for** movie stars.*

**fas·cism** /ˈfæʃɪzəm/ *n* [U] an extreme political system in which people's lives are completely controlled by the state

**fas·cist** /ˈfæʃɪst/ *n* **1** someone who supports FACISM **2** someone who is cruel and unfair —**fascist** *adj*

**fash·ion¹** /ˈfæʃən/ *n* **1** [C,U] the popular style of clothes, hair, behavior etc. at a particular time: *Hats are now **in fashion** again.* | *Shoes like that **went out of fashion** years ago.* | *She always buys the **latest fashions**.* **2** [U] the business or study of making or selling clothes: *the assistant fashion editor at Vogue* **3 in a …** **fashion** FORMAL in a particular way: *Albert smiled in a tired fashion.*

**fashion²** *v* [T] FORMAL **1** to shape or make something with your hands or a few tools: *fashioning a dress out of old curtains* **2** to influence and form someone's ideas and opinions: *Our attitudes to politics are often fashioned by the media.*

**fash·ion·a·ble** /ˈfæʃənəbəl/ *adj* popular, especially for a short time: *Long skirts are fashionable now.* | *a fashionable restaurant* —opposite UNFASHIONABLE

**fashion show** /ˈ.. ˌ./ *n* an event at which new styles of clothes are shown to the public

**fast¹** /fæst/ *adj*
**1** ▶MOVING QUICKLY◀ moving, or able to move quickly: *a fast runner* | *a fast car*
**2** ▶DONE QUICKLY◀ doing something or happening in a short time: *The subway is the fastest way to get downtown.* | *a fast reader*
**3** ▶CLOCK/WATCH◀ showing time that is later than the true time: *Is it really 5:00, or is my watch fast?*
**4 pull a fast one** INFORMAL to trick someone: *Don't try and pull a fast one on me.*
**5 fast track** a way of achieving something more quickly than it is normally done: *young professionals **on the fast track for** promotion*
**6 the fast lane** an exciting way of living that involves dangerous or expensive activities: *living life in the fast lane*
**7 make sth fast** to tie something such as a boat or tent firmly to something else
**8** ▶COLOR◀ ⇨ COLORFAST

**fast²** *adv* **1** moving quickly: *He likes driving fast.* **2** in a short time: *You're learning fast.* **3 fast asleep** sleeping very deeply: *The baby's fast asleep.* **4** firmly or tightly: *The boat's **stuck fast** in the mud.* | *Walter began to fall, but the rope **held** him **fast**.* **5 hold fast to** to continue to believe in or support an idea, principle etc.: *In spite of everything, her father held fast to his religion.* **6 not so fast** SPOKEN said when telling someone to do something more slowly or carefully: *Not so fast! You'll scrape the paint.*

**fast³** *n* a period of time during which someone eats very little or nothing, usually for religious reasons —**fast** *v* [I]

**fas·ten** /ˈfæsən/ *v* **1** [I,T] to join together the two sides of something so that it is closed, or to become joined in this way: *Fasten your seat belts.* | *I'm too fat. My skirt won't fasten.* **2** [T] to firmly close a window, gate etc. so it will not open **3** [T] to attach something firmly to another object: *Jill **fastened** a flower **onto** her dress.*

**fas·ten·ing** /ˈfæsənɪŋ/ *n* something you use to hold another thing shut or in the right position

**fast food** /ˌ. ˈ./ *n* [U] inexpensive food, for example, HAMBURGERs, that is prepared and served quickly in a restaurant

**fast for·ward** /ˌ. ˈ../ *n* [singular] the button that you push on a machine to make a TAPE wind more quickly

**fas·tid·i·ous** /fæˈstɪdiəs, fə-/ *adj* very careful about small details in your appearance, work etc. —**fastidiously** *adv*

**fat¹** /fæt/ *adj* **1** weighing too much: *Chris is worried about getting fat.* **2** thick or wide: *a*

**F**

big fat letter from Grandma **3** INFORMAL containing or worth a lot of money: *I should get a nice fat check at the end of the month.* **4 fat chance** SPOKEN said when something is very unlikely to happen: *What, Max get a job? Fat chance!*

---

**USAGE NOTE fat**

**Fat** means that someone weighs too much, but this word is not very polite. Use **plump** in order to be polite: *Grandma was always fairly plump.* Use **chubby** to describe babies or young children. **Overweight** means that someone weighs too much, and is often used by doctors or people who are worried about their weight. **Obese** means that someone is extremely fat in a way that is dangerous to his/her health.

---

**fat²** *n* **1** [U] a substance that is under the skin of people and animals, that helps keep them warm: *Take two chicken breasts, and cut off all the fat.* **2** [C,U] an oily substance in some foods: *food that is **low/high in fat*** **3** [C,U] a thick oily substance taken from animals or plants and used in cooking: *Fry the potatoes in oil or melted fat.*

**fa·tal** /ˈfeɪtl/ *adj* **1** resulting in someone's death: *a fatal accident/injury* | *a disease that **proved fatal*** (=killed someone) **2** having a very bad effect: *Her **fatal mistake** was to marry too young.* | *There's a **fatal flaw** (=serious weakness) in his argument.* **—fatally** *adv*

**fa·tal·ism** /ˈfeɪtlˌɪzəm/ *n* [U] the belief that there is nothing you can do to prevent events from happening **—fatalistic** /ˌfeɪtlˈɪstɪk/ *adj*

**fa·tal·i·ty** /feɪˈtæləti, fə-/ *n* a death in an accident or violent attack: *This year there have been fewer traffic fatalities.*

**fate** /feɪt/ *n* **1** the things that happen to someone: *No one knows what the fate of the refugees will be.* | *Their **fate is sealed.*** (=something unpleasant is certain to happen) **2** [U] a power that is believed to control what happens in people's lives: *Fate brought us together.* | *By a lucky **twist of fate**, we were on the same plane.* **3 a fate worse than death** HUMOROUS an experience that seems like the worst thing that could happen to you

**fat·ed** /ˈfeɪtɪd/ *adj* **be fated to** certain to happen or to do something because a mysterious force is controlling events: *We were fated to meet.*

**fate·ful** /ˈfeɪtfəl/ *adj* having an important, usually bad effect on future events: *a fateful decision*

**fat farm** /ˈ. ./ *n* INFORMAL a place where people who are fat can go to lose weight and improve their health

**fat-free** /ˌ. ˈ.◂/ *adj* food that is fat-free does not have any fat in it: *fat-free yogurt*

**fa·ther¹** /ˈfɑðɚ/ *n* **1** your male parent —see picture at FAMILY **2 Father** a priest, especially in the Roman Catholic Church: *Do you know Father Vernon?* **3 the father of sth** the man who was responsible for starting something: *George Washington is the father of our country.*

**father²** *v* [T] to become a male parent: *his desire to father a child*

**fa·ther·hood** /ˈfɑðɚˌhʊd/ *n* [U] the state of being a father

**father-in-law** /ˈ.. . ˌ./ *n* the father of your husband or wife —see picture at FAMILY

**fa·ther·ly** /ˈfɑðɚli/ *adj* typical of a kind or concerned father: *talking in a fatherly way*

**Father's Day** /ˈ.. ˌ./ *n* a holiday in the US and Canada on the third Sunday of June in honor of fathers

**fath·om¹** /ˈfæðəm/ *v* [T] to understand what something means after thinking about it carefully

**fathom²** *n* a unit for measuring how deep water is, equal to 6 feet or 1.83 meters

**fa·tigue** /fəˈtig/ *n* [U] **1** extreme tiredness: *They were cold, and weak with fatigue, but not hurt.* **2** TECHNICAL weakness in a substance such as metal, that may cause it to break **—fatigue** *v* [T]

**fa·tigues** /fəˈtigz/ *n* [plural] army clothes that fit loosely

**fat·ten** /ˈfætˀn/ *v* [I,T] to make an animal become fatter so that it is ready to eat, or to become fat and ready to eat: *fattened pigs*

**fatten** sb/sth **up** *phr v* [T] OFTEN HUMOROUS to make a thin person or animal fatter: *Grandma always thinks she needs to **fatten me up**.*

**fat·ten·ing** /ˈfætˀn-ɪŋ/ *adj* likely to make you fat: *I wish pizza weren't so fattening!*

**fat·ty** /ˈfæti/ *adj* containing a lot of fat: *fatty foods*

**fat·u·ous** /ˈfætʃuəs/ *adj* very silly or stupid: *a fatuous remark*

**fau·cet** /ˈfɔsɪt/ *n* a piece of equipment that you turn on and off to control the flow of water from a pipe —see picture at DRIP¹

**fault¹** /fɔlt/ *n*

**1** ▶BLAME◀ responsibility for a mistake: *It's not my fault we missed the bus.*

**2 at fault** the state of being responsible for something bad that has happened: *It was the other driver who was at fault.*

**3** ▶PROBLEM◀ a problem with something that stops it working correctly: *a fault in the electrical system*

**4 find fault with** to criticize something or someone and complain about him, her, or it: *Why do you always have to find fault with my work?*

**5 through no fault of sb's own** used in order to say that something bad that happened to

someone was not caused by him/her: *Through no fault of their own, some students have trouble learning.*
**6 ▶NOT PERFECT◀** something that is wrong or not perfect: *For all her faults* (=in spite of her faults) *I still love her.*
**7 ▶CRACK◀** a large crack in the rocks that form the Earth's surface: *the San Andreas fault*
**8 to a fault** to a degree that is unnecessary or bad: *Mr. Blackburn is generous to a fault.*

**fault²** *v* [T] to find a mistake in something: *We couldn't fault her singing.*

**fault·less** /ˈfɔltlɪs/ *adj* having no mistakes; perfect: *a faultless performance*

**fault·y** /ˈfɔlti/ *adj* **1** not working correctly: *faulty wires* **2** not correct: *faulty reasoning*

**fau·na** /ˈfɔnə/ *n* [U] TECHNICAL all the animals that live in a particular place or at a particular time in history —compare FLORA

**faux pas** /ˌfoʊ ˈpɑ/ *n* an embarrassing mistake in a social situation: *The other day I made a terrible faux pas.*

**fa·vor¹** /ˈfeɪvɚ/ *n* **1** something you do for someone to help or be kind to him/her: *Could you do me a favor and watch the baby for half an hour?* | *Can I ask you a favor?* **2 in favor of** choosing one plan, idea, or system instead of another: *Plans for a tunnel were rejected in favor of the bridge.* **3** [U] support or approval for a plan, idea, or system: *All the board members were in favor of the idea.* **4 in sb's favor** to someone's advantage: *The vote was 60−59 in his favor.* **5 in favor/out of favor** liked and approved of, or no longer liked and approved of: *Although he's out of favor, some people still read his books.* **6** a small gift that is given to guests at a party

**favor²** *v* [T] **1** to prefer something more than other choices: *Blyth favors gun control laws.* **2** to unfairly treat one person or group better than another: *tax cuts that favor the rich* **3** to provide the right conditions for something to happen: *wind conditions that favor sailing*

**fa·vor·able** /ˈfeɪvərəbəl/ *adj* **1** making people like or approve of someone or something: *Try to make a favorable impression.* **2** saying or showing that you approve of something or someone: *I've heard favorable reports about your work.* **3** likely to make something happen or succeed: *a favorable economic environment* —**favorably** *adv* —opposite UNFAVORABLE

**fa·vor·ite¹** /ˈfeɪvrɪt, -vərɪt/ *adj* liked more than others of the same kind: *Who's your favorite actor?* ✗ DON'T SAY "most favorite." ✗

**favorite²** *n* **1** someone or something that you like more than any other one of its kind: *I like all her books, but this one is my favorite.* **2** someone who receives more attention and approval than is fair: *Teachers shouldn't have favorites.* **3** the team, person etc. that is

expected to win a competition: *The Yankees are favorites to win the World Series.*

**fa·vor·it·ism** /ˈfeɪvrəˌtɪzəm/ *n* [U] the act of unfairly treating one person or group better than another

**fawn¹** /fɔn/ *v*
**fawn on/over** sb *phr v* [T] to praise someone and be friendly to him/her because you want something: *All those people are fawning over her as if she's someone special!*

**fawn²** *n* a young DEER

**fax** /fæks/ *n* **1 a)** a document that is sent in electronic form down a telephone line and then printed using a special machine: *Did you get my fax?* **b)** [U] the system of sending documents this way: *a letter sent by fax* **2** also **fax machine** a machine used for sending and receiving faxes: *What's your fax number?* —**fax** *v* [T]

**faze** /feɪz/ *v* [T] INFORMAL to make someone feel nervous or confused: *Nothing ever seemed to faze Rosie.* —**fazed** *adj*

**FBI** *n* **the FBI** the Federal Bureau of Investigation; the US police department that is controlled by the government and is concerned with FEDERAL law rather than state law

**fear¹** /fɪr/ *n* **1** [C,U] the feeling you get when you are afraid or worried that something bad will happen: *a fear of heights/flying/spiders* | *Here, refugees live in fear of being sent back.* | *the fear that the guy next to you will have a gun* | *parents' fears for their children's safety* **2 for fear of/for fear that** because you are worried that something will happen: *She kept quiet, for fear of saying the wrong thing.*

**fear²** *v* [T] **1** to feel afraid or worried that something bad will happen: *Fearing a snowstorm, many people stayed home.* **2 fear the worst** to think that the worst possible thing has happened or will happen: *When they heard about Heidi's car crash, they feared the worst.* **3** to be afraid of someone because s/he is very powerful: *a dictator feared by his country* **4 fear for sb** to be worried about someone who may be in danger: *Obviously, they left because they feared for their lives.*

**fear·ful** /ˈfɪrfəl/ *adj* FORMAL **1** afraid: *Even doctors are fearful of getting the disease.* **2** causing fear: *a fearful noise* —**fearfully** *adv*

**fear·less** /ˈfɪrlɪs/ *adj* not afraid of anything: *a fearless soldier* —**fearlessness** *n* [U]

**fear·some** /ˈfɪrsəm/ *adj* very frightening: *a fearsome sight*

**fea·si·ble** /ˈfizəbəl/ *adj* possible, and likely to work: *a feasible plan*

**feast¹** /fist/ *n* **1** a large meal for many people to celebrate a special occasion: *a wedding feast* **2** a very good large meal: *That was a real feast!* **3** a religious holiday

**feast²** *v* **1** [I] to eat and drink a lot to celebrate something **2 feast your eyes on** to look at

something for a long time because you like it
**3 feast on sth** to eat a lot of a particular food with great enjoyment: *feasting on fresh corn on the cob*

**feat** /fit/ *n* something that someone does that shows strength, skill etc.: *an amazing feat of engineering* | *Getting your doctorate is no mean feat*. (=difficult to do)

**feath·er**[1] /'fɛðɚ/ *n* one of the light soft things that cover a bird's body

**feather**[2] *v* [T] **feather your nest** to make yourself rich by dishonest methods

**feath·er·y** /'fɛðəri/ *adj* **1** covered with feathers **2** soft and light: *feathery snow*

**fea·ture**[1] /'fitʃɚ/ *n* **1** a part of something that you notice because it seems important, interesting, or typical: *a report that compares the safety features of new cars* **2** a special newspaper or magazine article, or a special treatment of a subject on radio or television: *a feature on Johnny Depp in Sunday's paper* **3** a part of someone's face: *Her eyes are her best feature.* **4** a movie: *There's a double feature* (=two movies the same evening) *playing at the mall theater.*

**feature**[2] *v* **1** [T] to show a particular person or thing in a film, magazine, show etc.: *a new movie featuring Meryl Streep* **2** [I] to be an important part of something: *Violence features too strongly in many TV shows.* **3** [T] to advertise a particular product: *The supermarket's featuring a new ice cream.*

**Feb·ru·ar·y** /'fɛbyu,ɛri, 'fɛbru,ɛri/ written abbreviation **Feb.** *n* the second month of the year — see usage note at JANUARY

**fe·ces** /'fisiz/ *n* [plural] FORMAL solid waste material from the BOWELs —**fecal** /'fikəl/ *adj*

**Fed** /fɛd/ *n* **the Fed** INFORMAL ⇨ FEDERAL RESERVE SYSTEM

**fed**[1] *v* the past tense and PAST PARTICIPLE of FEED

**fed**[2] *n* INFORMAL a police officer in the FBI

**fed·er·al** /'fɛdərəl/ *adj* **1** relating to the central government of a country: *federal and state taxes* **2** consisting of a group of states that control their own affairs but are controlled by a central government: *the Federal Republic of Germany*

**Federal Bu·reau of In·ves·ti·ga·tion** /,... ,.. . ...'.../ *n* [singular] ⇨ FBI

**fed·er·al·ism** /'fɛdərə,lɪzəm/ *n* [U] belief in or support for a FEDERAL system of government —**federalist** *n, adj*

**Federal Re·serve Sys·tem** /,... .'. ,../ *n* [singular] the main system of banks in the US, in which a group of 7 officials and 12 banks control the way the country's banks work

**fed·er·a·tion** /,fɛdə'reɪʃən/ *n* a group of countries, organizations, clubs, or people that have joined together to form a single group: *the*

American Federation of Teachers —**federate** /'fɛdə,reɪt/ *v* [I]

**fed up** /, '. './ *adj* INFORMAL annoyed or bored, and wanting something to change: *I'm really fed up with these boring business dinners.*

**fee** /fi/ *n* **1** an amount of money that you pay for professional services: *medical fees* | *college fees* **2** an amount of money that you pay to do something: *video rental fees*

**fee·ble** /'fibəl/ *adj* **1** extremely weak: *His voice sounded feeble.* **2** a feeble joke, excuse, argument etc. is not very good

**feeble-mind·ed** /'.. ,../ *adj* unable to think clearly and decide what to do, or showing this quality

**feed**[1] /fid/ *v* **fed, fed, feeding 1** [T] to give food to a person or animal: *Jimmy likes feeding acorns to the squirrels.* **2** [T] to provide enough food for a group of people: *How can you feed a family on $50 a week?* **3** [T] to give a special substance to a plant to make it grow: *Feed your violets once a month.* **4** [T] to put something slowly and continuously into something else: *The tube was fed into the patient's stomach.* **5** to give someone information or ideas: *She's been fed a lot of lies by her friends at school.* **6 well-fed/under-fed/poorly-fed** etc. having plenty of food or not enough food **7** [I] a word meaning to eat, used about animals or babies: *Frogs feed at night.*

**feed on** sth *phr v* [T] if an animal feeds on a particular food, it usually eats that food: *Cows feed on grass.*

**feed**[2] *n* [U] food for animals: *cattle feed*

**feed·back** /'fidbæk/ *n* [U] advice, criticism etc. about how good or useful something is: *The teacher's been giving us helpful feedback.* | *Can I get some feedback on this artwork?*

**feed·bag** /'fidbæg/ *n* a bag put around a horse's head, containing food

**feed·ing** /'fidɪŋ/ *n* a meal eaten by a baby: *It's time for her noon feeding.*

**feel**[1] /fil/ *v* **felt, felt, feeling**

**1 ▶EMOTIONS◀** [linking verb, I] to experience a particular feeling or emotion: *We felt guilty for not asking her to come with us.* | *They didn't make us feel very welcome.* | *I walked through the door, and I felt as if/as though I was walking into a foreign country.* | *The Lees made me feel like their own son.*

**2 ▶PHYSICAL◀** [linking verb] to have a particular physical feeling: *I feel better today.* | *Do you feel cold?* | *The ground still feels damp.*

**3 ▶OPINION◀** [I,T] to have an opinion based on your feeling rather than on facts: *How do you feel about your new stepfather?*

**4 ▶TOUCH◀** [T] to touch something with your fingers to find out about it: *Feel my forehead. Does it seem hot?*

**5 ▶NOTICE STH◀** [T] to notice something

physical that is happening to you: *She felt a bug crawling up her leg.* | *Just feel that fresh sea air!*

**6 feel the effects/benefits etc. of sth** to experience the good or bad results of something: *We've started to feel the effects of the recession.*

**7 feel your way** to move carefully with your hands out in front of you because you cannot see well

**8 feel the pinch** to have problems because of lack of money: *Small businesses are feeling the pinch of the recession.*

---
SPOKEN PHRASES
---

**9 feel like** to want to have something or do something: *Do you feel like ordering a pizza?* | *I feel like a cigarette.* (=feel like having a cigarette)

**10 feel free** used in order to say that you are happy if someone wants to do something: *Please feel free to come by my office.*

**11 I know how you feel** said in order to show your sympathy with someone: *"I can't seem to do anything right today." "I know exactly how you feel."*

**feel for** sb *phr v* [T] to feel sympathy for someone: *I really **feel for** you, Joel, but I don't know what to suggest.*

**feel** sb ↔ **out** *phr v* [T] INFORMAL to find out what someone's opinions or feelings are without asking him/her directly: *Well, I could **feel** my Dad **out about** using the cabin.*

**feel** sb ↔ **up** *phr v* [T] SLANG to touch someone sexually

**feel up to** sth *phr v* [T] INFORMAL to feel you can do a particular job: *I don't really **feel up to** going out tonight.*

**feel²** *n* [singular] **1** the way something feels when you touch it: *the feel of the sand under our feet* | *Wet soap has a greasy feel.* **2** a quality that something has that makes you feel a particular way about it: *The beach has a kind of lonely feel.* | *The house had a nice **feel about it**.* **3 have a feel for** INFORMAL to have a natural understanding of something and skill in doing it: *Pete has a real feel for music.* **4 get the feel of** to become comfortable with something: *You'll soon get the feel of the car.*

**feel·er** /'filɚ/ *n* **1 put out feelers** to start to try to discover what people think about something that you want to do: *I'm putting out feelers to see if they have any jobs open.* **2** INFORMAL one of the two long things on an insect's head that it uses to feel or touch things

**feel·ing** /'filɪŋ/ *n* **1** something that you feel such as anger, sadness, or happiness: *There's no reason for you to have these guilt feelings.* | *a feeling of* confidence –see also **hurt sb's feelings** (FEELINGS) **2** a belief or opinion about something: *What are your **feelings on** the drug problem?* | *I **have a feeling** she's lying to us.* | *Mothers sometimes **have mixed feelings** about going to work.* (=are not sure what they

feel or think) **3** [singular, U] a general attitude among a group of people about a subject: *a strong anti-war feeling* **4** [C,U] something that you feel in your body such as pain, heat, cold etc., or your ability to feel this: *I have this funny feeling* (=a strange feeling) *in my neck.* | *He has no feeling in his legs.* **5 with feeling** in a way that shows you understand or care very much about something: *She plays the violin with great feeling* | *He spoke with deep feeling about the war.* **6 bad/ill feeling** anger, lack of trust etc. between people: *The divorce caused a lot of bad feeling between them.* **7 I know the feeling** SPOKEN said when you understand how someone feels because you have had the same feeling: *"I'm too tired to work today." "I know the feeling."*

**feel·ings** /'filɪŋz/ *n* **hurt sb's feelings** to upset or offend someone, especially by saying something unfair or untrue about him/her: *Don't say things like that! You really hurt her feelings.*

**feet** /fit/ *n* the plural of FOOT

**feign** /feɪn/ *v* [T] FORMAL to pretend to have a particular feeling or to be ill, asleep etc.: *We feigned interest in Mr. Dixon's stamp collection.*

**feint** /feɪnt/ *n* a movement or an attack that is intended to deceive an opponent

**feist·y** /'faɪsti/ *adj* APPROVING having a lot of energy and liking to argue: *a feisty 8-year old girl*

**fe·line** /'filaɪn/ *n* TECHNICAL a cat or a member of the cat family –**feline** *adj*

**fell¹** /fɛl/ *v* the past tense of FALL

**fell²** *v* [T] **1** to cut down a tree **2** to knock someone down with a lot of force

**fel·low¹** /'fɛloʊ/ *n* **1** INFORMAL a man: *I have a fellow who cuts my grass.* **2** a GRADUATE student who has a FELLOWSHIP in a university **3** a member of a society in a school or university

**fellow²** *adj* relating to people who do the same thing you do: *He traveled with some of his fellow workers/students.*

**fel·low·ship** /'fɛloʊˌʃɪp, -lə-/ *n* **1** money given to a student to allow him/her to continue his/her studies: *a graduate fellowship* **2** a group with similar interests or beliefs: *a Christian youth fellowship* **3** [U] a feeling of friendship resulting from shared interests or experiences

**fel·on** /'fɛlən/ *n* a criminal who has COMMITted a serious crime: *a **convicted felon*** (=a criminal who is sent to prison)

**fel·o·ny** /'fɛləni/ *n* LAW a serious crime such as murder

**felt¹** /fɛlt/ *v* the past tense and PAST PARTICIPLE of FEEL

**felt²** *n* [U] a thick soft material made of wool, hair, or fur that has been pressed flat

**felt tip pen** /ˌ. . . '. / *n* a pen that has a hard piece of felt at the end that the ink comes through

F

**fe·male**[1] /'fimeɪl/ n a person or animal that belongs to the sex that can have babies or produce eggs

**female**[2] adj **1** belonging to the sex that can have babies or produce eggs: *a female horse* **2** a female plant or flower produces fruit –see usage note at MASCULINE

**fem·i·nine** /'fɛmənɪn/ adj **1** having qualities that are considered to be typical of women: *feminine clothes* **2** TECHNICAL in grammar, a feminine noun or PRONOUN has a special form that means it relates to a female, such as "actress" or "her" –compare MASCULINE

**fem·i·nin·i·ty** /ˌfɛmə'nɪnəti/ n [U] qualities that are considered to be typical of women –compare MASCULINITY

**fem·i·nism** /'fɛməˌnɪzəm/ n [U] the belief that women should have the same rights and opportunities as men –**feminist** n, adj

**fence**[1] /fɛns/ n **1** a structure made of wood, metal etc. that surrounds a piece of land **2 on the fence** not having decided something: *54 senators were in favor, 29 were opposed, and 17 were still sitting on the fence.* **3** someone who buys and sells stolen goods

**fence**[2] v **1** [T] to put a fence around something **2** [I] to fight with a sword as a sport
**fence** sth ↔ **in** phr v [T] to surround a place with a fence –**fenced-in** /ˌfɛnst 'ɪn◂/ adj
**fence** sb/sth ↔ **off** phr v [T] to separate one area from another with a fence: *We fenced off part of the backyard.*

**fenc·ing** /'fɛnsɪŋ/ n [U] **1** the sport of fighting with a long thin sword **2** fences, or the material used for making them

**fend** /fɛnd/ v **fend for yourself** to take care of yourself without help from other people: *Now that the kids are old enough to fend for themselves, we're free to travel more.*
**fend** sb/sth ↔ **off** phr v [T] to defend yourself from something such as competition, an attack, or things you do not want to deal with: *Mrs. Spector tried to fend off the other mugger.* | *Henry did his best to fend off the journalists.*

**fend·er** /'fɛndɚ/ n **1** the part of a car that covers the wheels –see picture on page 469 **2** a curved piece of metal that covers the wheel on a bicycle

**fer·ment**[1] /fɚ'mɛnt/ v [I,T] if fruit, beer, or wine ferments, the sugar in it changes to alcohol –**fermentation** /ˌfɚmən'teɪʃən/ n [U] –**fermented** /fɚ'mɛnɪd/ adj

**fer·ment**[2] /'fɚmɛnt/ n [U] a situation of excitement or trouble in a country, especially caused by political change

**fern** /fɚn/ n a plant with green leaves shaped like large feathers, but no flowers

**fe·ro·cious** /fə'roʊʃəs/ adj extremely violent or severe: *There was a big ferocious dog chained inside the gate.* | *a ferocious Atlantic storm* –**ferociously** adv

**fe·roc·i·ty** /fə'rɑsəti/ n [U] the state of being extremely violent or severe: *Felipe was shocked by the ferocity of her anger.*

**fer·ret**[1] /'fɛrɪt/ v [I] INFORMAL to search for something, especially inside a box, drawer etc.: *Andy ferreted around in his desk for a pen.*
**ferret** sth ↔ **out** phr v [T] INFORMAL to succeed in finding something, especially information: *It took years of research to ferret out the truth.*

**ferret**[2] n a small animal with soft fur, used for hunting rats and rabbits

**fer·ris wheel** /'fɛrɪs ˌwil/ n a very large wheel with seats on it for people to ride on in an AMUSEMENT PARK

**fer·rous** /'fɛrəs/ adj TECHNICAL containing iron, or relating to iron: *ferrous metals*

**fer·ry**[1] /'fɛri/ n a boat that carries people, often with their cars, across a narrow area of water such as a river

**ferry**[2] v [T] to carry people or goods a short distance from one place to another: *a bus that ferries tourists from the hotel to the beach*

**fer·tile** /'fɚtl/ adj **1** fertile land or soil is able to produce a lot of plants –opposite INFERTILE **2** fertile people or animals are able to produce babies –opposite INFERTILE **3 fertile imagination** an imagination that is able to produce a lot of unusual ideas –**fertility** /fɚ'tɪləti/ n [U]

**fer·til·ize** /'fɚtlˌaɪz/ v [T] **1** to put FERTILIZER on the soil to help plants grow **2** to make new animal or plant life begin to develop: *a fertilized egg* –**fertilization** /ˌfɚtlə'zeɪʃən/ n [U]

**fer·til·iz·er** /'fɚtlˌaɪzɚ/ n [C,U] a substance that is put on the soil to help plants grow

**fer·vent** /'fɚvənt/ adj believing or feeling something very strongly: *Marion's a fervent believer in working hard.* –**fervently** adv

**fer·vor** /'fɚvɚ/ n [U] very strong belief or feeling: *religious fervor*

**fess** /fɛs/ v
**fess up** phr v [I] SPOKEN to admit that you have done something wrong, although it is not serious: *Come on, fess up! Who drank all the milk?*

**fest** /fɛst/ n **beer/song/food fest etc.** an informal occasion when a lot of people do a fun activity together

**fes·ter** /'fɛstɚ/ v [I] **1** if a bad situation or a problem festers, it continues for too long because is has not been dealt with: *Letting your anger fester will only make things worse.* **2** if a wound festers, it becomes infected

**fes·ti·val** /'fɛstəvəl/ n **1** an organized set of events such as musical performances or movies: *the Cannes film festival* **2** a time of public celebration, especially for a religious event

**fes·tive** /'fɛstɪv/ adj happy or cheerful in a way that is suitable for celebrating something: *Hollie was in a festive mood at the office party.*

**fes·tiv·i·ties** /fɛˈstɪvətiz/ [plural] things such as dancing, eating etc. that are done to celebrate a special occasion

**fes·toon** /fɛˈstun/ v [T] to cover something with cloth, flowers etc., especially as a decoration

**fe·tal** /ˈfitl/ adj relating to a FETUS: *an instrument to measure fetal growth*

**fetal po·si·tion** /ˌ.. ˌ.../ n a body position in which your body is curled up, and your arms and legs are pulled up against your chest

**fetch** /fɛtʃ/ v [T] INFORMAL **1** to be sold for a particular amount of money: *The tractor should fetch over $10,000 at public auction.* **2** to go and get something, and bring it back: *Would you fetch me a glass of water from the kitchen?*

**fetch·ing** /ˈfɛtʃɪŋ/ adj OLD-FASHIONED attractive

**fete¹** /feɪt/ v [T] to honor someone by having a public celebration for him/her: *The champions were feted from coast to coast.*

**fete²** n a special occasion to celebrate something

**fet·id** /ˈfɛtɪd/ adj FORMAL having a very bad smell: *the black fetid water*

**fet·ish** /ˈfɛtɪʃ/ n **1** an unusual object or activity that gives someone sexual pleasure: *a leather fetish* **2** something that you are always thinking about, or spending too much time doing: *McBride has a real fetish about exercising every day.* **3** an object that is thought to have magical powers

**fet·ter** /ˈfɛtɚ/ v [T] FORMAL to prevent someone from doing what s/he wants to do: *managers fettered by rules and regulations*

**fet·ters** /ˈfɛtɚz/ n [plural] **1** FORMAL things that prevent someone from doing what s/he wants to do **2** OLD-FASHIONED chains that are put around a prisoner's feet

**fe·tus** /ˈfitəs/ n TECHNICAL a young human or animal before birth —compare EMBRYO

**feud** /fyud/ n an angry quarrel between two people or groups that continues for a long time: *a bitter feud between the two neighbors* —**feud** v [I]

**feu·dal·is·m** /ˈfyudəˌlɪzəm/ n [U] a social system in the Middle Ages, in which people received land and protection from someone of higher rank when they worked and fought for him —**feudal** adj

**fe·ver** /ˈfivɚ/ n **1** [C,U] an illness in which you have a very high temperature: *Drink a lot of fluids, it'll help your fever go down.* **2** [U] a state in which a lot of people are excited about something in a crazy way: *lottery fever* (=excitement about winning money) | *When the TV crews arrived, the demonstration reached fever pitch.* (=an extreme level of excitement) —**fevered** adj

**fe·ver·ish** /ˈfivərɪʃ/ adj **1** suffering from a fever **2** done extremely quickly by people who are very excited or worried: *working at a feverish pace* —**feverishly** adv

**few** /fyu/ quantifier n [plural] **1** a few/the few a small number of something: *I've seen a few of those new cars around.* | *Let's wait a few minutes and see if Carrie gets here.* | *Don has seemed really happy these last few weeks.* (=the weeks just before this) | *You'll have to work hard over the next few months.* (=the months just after this time) | *There are a few more things I'd like to talk about before we go.* | *I've read a few of her books.* | *Grant's one of the few people I know who can tell stories well.* **2** quite a few a fairly large number of things or people: *Quite a few people came to the meeting.* **3** not many: *There are few events that are as exciting as having a baby.* **4** be few and far between to be rare: *Good jobs are few and far between these days.* —see usage note at LESS¹

> **USAGE NOTE** few, a few, little, and a little
>
> Use **few** with plural countable nouns to mean "not many": *Few people said they'd help.* Use **a few** with plural countable nouns to mean "some": *A few people arrived late.* Use **little** with uncountable nouns to mean "not much": *There's usually little traffic early in the morning.* Use **a little** with uncountable nouns to mean "a small amount of something": *There was only a little ice cream left.*

**fez** /fɛz/ n a small round red hat with a flat top

**fi·an·cé** /ˌfiɑnˈseɪ, fiˈɑnseɪ/ n the man whom you are going to marry

**fi·an·cée** /ˌfiɑnˈseɪ, fiˈɑnseɪ/ n the woman whom you are going to marry

**fi·as·co** /fiˈæskoʊ/ n, plural **fiascoes** or **fiascos** [C,U] something that is done that is completely unsuccessful: *Their attempt to compete in the software market has been a total fiasco.*

**fi·at** /ˈfiæt, -ɑt, -ət/ n [C,U] FORMAL a command that is given by someone in authority without considering what other people want: *Too often he governed by fiat rather than by the law.*

**fib¹** /fɪb/ n INFORMAL a small, unimportant lie: *You shouldn't tell fibs. It's not nice.*

**fib²** v [I] SPOKEN to tell a small, unimportant lie —**fibber** n

**fi·ber** /ˈfaɪbɚ/ n **1** [U] parts of plants that you eat but do not DIGEST, that help food to move through your body: *The doctor said I need more fiber in my diet.* **2** [U] the woody part of some plants that is used for making materials such as rope or cloth **3** a natural or artificial thread used for making cloth: *cotton fibers* | *polyester fibers* —**fibrous** /ˈfaɪbrəs/ adj

**fi·ber·glass** /ˈfaɪbɚˌglæs/ n [U] a light material made from small FIBERs of glass, used for making racing cars, small boats etc.

**fiber op·tics** /ˌ.. '../ *n* [U] the use of long thin threads of glass to carry information in the form of light, especially on telephone lines – **fiber optic** *adj*

**fick·le** /'fɪkəl/ *adj* **1** someone who is fickle always changes his/her opinions or feelings about what s/he wants or likes: *Every politician knows that voters are fickle.* **2** something that is fickle, such as the weather, often changes suddenly

**fic·tion** /'fɪkʃən/ *n* **1** [U] books and stories about people and things that are imaginary: *A. A. Milne was a popular writer of children's fiction.* –compare NONFICTION **2** something that someone wants you to believe is true, but that is not true: *The newspaper story turned out to be a complete fiction.*

**fic·tion·al** /'fɪkʃənəl/ *adj* fictional people or events are from a book or story, and are not real

**fic·tion·al·ize** /'fɪkʃənə,laɪz/ *v* [T] to tell the story of a real event, changing some details and adding imaginary characters

**fic·ti·tious** /fɪk'tɪʃəs/ *adj* not true, or not real: *Evans uses a fictitious name when he writes articles for the magazine.*

**fid·dle**[1] /'fɪdl/ *v*
**fiddle around** *phr v* [I] to waste time by doing things that are not important: *If you keep fiddling around we're going to be late!*
**fiddle around with** sth *phr v* [T] to keep making changes to something in a way that annoys people: *Why can't they stop fiddling around with the Social Security system?*
**fiddle with** sth *phr v* [I] to keep moving something or touching something with your fingers because you are bored, nervous, or want to change something: *Stop fiddling with your hair! | Joshua's been fiddling with the TV controls again.*

**fiddle**[2] *n* ⇨ VIOLIN –see also **play second fiddle** (PLAY)

**fid·dler** /'fɪdlɚ/ *n* someone who plays the VIOLIN

**fi·del·i·ty** /fə'dɛləti, faɪ-/ *n* [U] **1** loyalty to a person, organization, set of beliefs etc.: *Joan's fidelity to her husband has never been doubted.* –opposite INFIDELITY **2** FORMAL the quality of not changing something when you copy, record, or translate it

**fidg·et** /'fɪdʒɪt/ *v* [I] to keep moving your hands or feet, especially because you are bored or nervous: *children fidgeting in their seats* –**fidgety** *adj*

**field**[1] /fild/ *n* **1** an area of land that is used for a special purpose, or that is covered with the same plants or substances: *a corn field* (=where corn is grown) | *a football/baseball/soccer field* (=for playing football etc.) | *an oil/coal/gas field* (=where oil etc. has been found) | *a snow/ice field* (=area covered with snow or ice) **2** a particular subject that people study: *Professor* *Kramer is an expert in the field of ancient history.* **3 the field** all the competitors, companies etc. that are involved in a particular activity: *They now lead the field* (=are the most successful company) *in making powerful computer chips.* **4 field of view/vision** the area that you can see when looking through something, such as a camera **5 magnetic/gravitational/force field** an area where a strong natural force is felt or has an effect on things

**field**[2] *v* [T] **1** if you field a ball, you catch it after it has been hit **2 field a question** to answer a difficult question: *The Mayor fielded a lot of tricky questions from the reporters.*

**field day** /'. ./ *n* **1 have a field day** to have a chance to do something you want, especially a chance to criticize someone or something: *Any time there's a scandal in politics, the media have a field day with it.* **2** a day when students have outdoor sports competitions at school

**field·er** /'fildɚ/ *n* one of the players who tries to catch the ball in baseball

**field e·vent** /'. .,./ *n* a sports activity such as jumping over BARs or throwing heavy things, that is part of an outdoor competition

**field glass·es** /'. ,../ *n* [plural] ⇨ BINOCULARS

**field goal** /'. ./ *n* the action of kicking the ball over the BAR of the GOAL for three points in football

**field hock·ey** /'. ,../ *n* [U] an outdoor game in which two teams of eleven players try to hit a ball with special sticks into their opponents' GOAL

**field house** /'. ./ *n* a large building used for indoor sports events such as basketball

**field test** /'. ./ *n* a test of a new product or system that is done outside the LABORATORY in real conditions: *Vegetables that can resist insects are doing well in field tests.* –**field-test** *v* [T]

**field trip** /'. ./ *n* an occasion when students go somewhere to learn about a particular subject: *We're going on a field trip to the Science Museum.*

**field·work** /'fildwɚk/ *n* [U] the study of scientific or social subjects that is done outside the school or LABORATORY: *I'll be doing archeological fieldwork over the summer.*

**fiend** /find/ *n* **1 sports/television etc. fiend** INFORMAL someone who likes doing something much more than other people do: *Isaac turns into a football fiend during the Super Bowl.* **2** LITERARY an evil spirit, or someone who is very cruel

**fiend·ish** /'findɪʃ/ *adj* **1** LITERARY very bad in a way that seems evil: *a fiendish temper/plot* **2** FORMAL very difficult: *a fiendish puzzle*

**fierce** /fɪrs/ *adj* **1** very angry, violent, and ready to attack: *fierce dogs* **2** done with a lot of energy and strong feelings: *a fierce debate* between the political parties **3** fierce heat, cold, weather etc. is much more extreme than usual –**fiercely** adv

**fi·er·y** /ˈfaɪəri/ adj **1** involving fire, or on fire: the fiery launch of the space shuttle **2** making people feel strong emotions such as anger, or showing these types of emotions: a fiery speech | a fiery temper

**fi·es·ta** /fiˈɛstə/ n a religious holiday in Spain or Latin America, with dancing, music etc.

**fif·teen** /ˌfɪfˈtin◂/ number 15 –**fifteenth** number

**fifth**[1] /fɪfθ/ number **1** 5th **2** 1/5 **3 feel like a fifth wheel** to feel that the people you are with do not want you to be there: I felt like a fifth wheel with all those couples.

**fifth**[2] n an amount of alcoholic drink equal to 1/5 of a gallon, sold in bottles

**fif·ty**[1] /ˈfɪfti/ number **1** 50 **2 the fifties a)** the years between 1950 and 1959 **b)** the numbers between 50 and 59, especially when used for measuring temperature –**fiftieth** /ˈfɪftiəθ/ number

**fifty**[2] n a piece of paper money worth $50

**fifty-fifty** /ˌ.. ˈ..◂/ adj, adv SPOKEN **1** divided or shared equally between two people: We should divide the profits fifty-fifty. **2 a fifty-fifty chance** an equal chance that something will happen or not happen: I think we have a fifty-fifty chance of winning.

**fig** /fɪg/ n a small soft sweet fruit, often eaten dried, or the tree on which this grows

**fig.** the written abbreviation of FIGURE

**fight**[1] /faɪt/ v fought, fought, fighting **1** [I,T] to use violence, guns, weapons etc. against someone or something: Did your uncle fight in the war? | The country fought a three-year civil war. | dogs fighting over a bone **2** [I] to argue: Are the kids fighting again? **3** [I,T] to try hard to get, change, or prevent something: He had to fight for the leadership. | Senator Redkin is fighting the proposal. **4** [I,T] ⇨ BOX[2] **5** [T] also **fight back** to try very hard not to show your feelings or not to do something you want to do: He fought the impulse to yell at her. **6 fight your way** to move through a group of people by pushing past them: We had to fight our way through the crowd. **7 a fighting chance** a chance to achieve something by working very hard: We still have a fighting chance of winning.

**fight back** phr v [I] to use violence or arguments against someone who has attacked you or argued with you

**fight** sb/sth ↔ **off** phr v [T] **1** to use violence to keep someone or something away: They managed to fight off their attackers. **2** to try hard to get rid of a feeling or illness: I've been fighting off a cold for days.

**fight** sth **out** phr v [T] to argue or use violence

until a disagreement is settled: We left them alone to fight it out themselves.

**fight**[2] n **1** an act of fighting between two people or groups: He's always getting into fights at school. | Who picked the fight? (=started it) **2** a battle between two armies: a fight for control of the islands **3** an argument: They've had a fight with the neighbors. **4** [singular] the process of trying to achieve something difficult or prevent something: the union's fight for better working conditions.

**fight·er** /ˈfaɪtɚ/ n **1** someone who continues to try to do something although it is difficult **2** ⇨ BOXER **3** also **fighter plane** a small, fast military plane that can destroy other planes

**fig·ment** /ˈfɪgmənt/ n **a figment of sb's imagination** something you imagine to be real, but does not exist: The "friend" that the boy talks about is just a figment of his imagination.

**fig·u·ra·tive** /ˈfɪgyərətɪv/ adj a figurative word or expression is used in a different way from the usual one, to give you a picture in your mind –**figuratively** adv –compare LITERAL

**fig·ure**[1] /ˈfɪgyɚ/ n **1** a number that represents an amount, especially an officially printed number: population figures **2** the shape of a woman's body, used when describing how attractive it is: She has a great figure. **3** a particular amount of money: a six-figure income (=over $100,000) **4** a number from 0 to 9, written as a sign rather than spelled with letters **5** someone with a particular type of character, position, appearance etc.: an important political figure | a sad figure dressed in old clothes **6** a drawing in a book that has a number on it to show what part of the book it relates to **7** a shape in mathematics: a six-sided figure

**figure**[2] v [I] to be important or included in something: The Kennedys figure in her recent book.

SPOKEN PHRASES
**1** [T] to have a particular opinion after thinking about a situation: I figured (that) you'd need help moving, so I came over. **2 that figures/it figures** said when you are annoyed because something bad you expected to happen does happen: "I forgot to bring my checkbook again." "That figures." **3 go figure** said in order to show that you cannot believe something because it seems so strange

**figure on** sth phr v [T] SPOKEN to include something in your plans: With traffic so heavy, we'd better figure on an extra hour.

**figure** sb/sth ↔ **out** phr v [T] to understand someone or something after thinking about him, her, or it: I can't figure Betty out.

**figure eight** /ˌ.. ˈ./ n the pattern of the number 8, for example, in a dance

**fig·ure·head** /ˈfɪgyɚˌhɛd/ *n* a leader who has no real power

**figure of speech** /ˌ.. . ˈ./ *n* a word or expression that is used in a different way from the usual one, to give you a picture in your mind: *"We died laughing" is a figure of speech.*

**figure skat·ing** /ˈ.. ˌ../ *n* a type of skating (SKATE) in which you move in patterns on the ice

**fil·a·ment** /ˈfɪləmənt/ *n* a very thin thread, especially the thin wire in a LIGHT BULB

**filch** /fɪltʃ/ *v* [T] INFORMAL to steal something small

**file¹** /faɪl/ *n* **1** a box or folded piece of heavy paper that is used in order to keep papers organized or separate from other papers: *a desk cluttered with files* **2** a collection of information about a particular person or thing: *The school keeps files on each student.* **3** a collection of information in a computer that is kept under a particular name **4 on file a)** kept in a file so that it can be used later: *We'll keep your application on file for six months.* **b)** officially recorded: *Your insurance claim has to be on file by April 1.* **5** a metal tool with a rough surface that is used for making other surfaces smooth

**file²** *v* **1** [T] LAW to officially record something such as a complaint, law case etc.: *Some employees are filing a claim against the department.* **2** [T] to keep papers with information on them in a particular place: *File the contracts alphabetically.* **3** [I] to walk in a line of people, one behind the other: *The jury filed into the courtroom.* **4** [T] to rub something with a metal tool to make it smooth or cut it

**file cab·i·net** /ˈ. ˌ.../ *n* ⇨ FILING CABINET

**fil·et, fillet** /fɪˈleɪ/ *n* a piece of meat or fish without bones

**fil·i·bus·ter** /ˈfɪləˌbʌstɚ/ *v* [I] to try to delay action in Congress by making very long speeches –**filibuster** *n*

**fil·i·gree** /ˈfɪləˌgri/ *n* [U] delicate decoration made of gold or silver wire

**filing cab·i·net** /ˈ.. ˌ.../ *n* a piece of office furniture with drawers for keeping reports, letters etc.

**fil·ings** /ˈfaɪlɪŋz/ *n* [plural] very small pieces that come off a piece of metal when it is FILEd

**fill¹** /fɪl/ *v* **1** [I,T] also **fill up** to become full of something, or to make something full: *The audience soon filled the theater.* | *The bedroom was filled with smoke.* **2** [T] also **fill in** to put something in a hole or crack in order to make a smooth surface **3** [T] if a sound, smell, or light fills a place or space, you notice it because it is loud or strong: *The smell of fresh bread filled the kitchen.* **4 fill a**

**fill out**

**need/demand etc.** to give people something they want or need: *Daycare centers fill a need for working parents.* **5 fill a job/position etc.** to find someone to do a job: *Anderson says he hopes to fill the position by spring.* **6** [T] if an emotion fills you, you feel it strongly **7 fill sb's shoes** to be able to do a job as well as the person who had it before you: *It will be difficult to fill Ms. Brower's shoes, but I'll try.*

**fill in** *phr v* **1** [T **fill** sth ↔ **in**] to write all the necessary information in special spaces on a document: *In the next part of the test, fill in the blanks with the correct answers.* **2** [T **fill** sb ↔ **in**] to tell someone about things that have happened recently: *I'll fill you in on all the news later.* **3** [I] to do someone's job or work because s/he is unable to do it: *Could you fill in for Bob while he's sick?*

**fill** ↔ **out** *phr v* [T] to write all the necessary information in special spaces on a document: *Fill out the application form by Oct. 1.*

**fill up** *phr v* **1** [T **fill** sth ↔ **up**] to put enough of a liquid or substance in a container to make it full: *Can I fill up your glass?* **2** [I] to gradually become full of people, things, etc.: *After school, the swimming pool starts filling up with kids.*

**fill²** *n* **have/eat your fill** to have or eat as much of something as you want or can deal with: *I've had my fill of screaming kids today!*

**fil·let¹** /fɪˈleɪ/ *v* [T] to remove the bones from a piece of meat or fish

**fillet²** *n* ⇨ FILET

**fill·ing¹** /ˈfɪlɪŋ/ *n* **1** a small amount of metal that is put into a hole in your tooth to preserve the tooth **2** [C,U] the food that is put inside food such as a PIE or SANDWICH: *apple pie filling*

**filling²** *adj* food that is filling makes your stomach feel full

**fil·ly** /ˈfɪli/ *n* a young female horse

**film¹** /fɪlm/ *n* **1** [U] the material used in a camera for taking photographs or recording moving pictures: *I don't have any film for my camera.* | *The coach has the game on film.* (=we made a movie of the game) **2** ⇨ MOVIE **3** [U] the art or business of making movies: *the film industry* **4** [singular, U] a very thin layer of something on the surface of something else: *a film of oil on the lake*

**film²** *v* [I,T] to use a camera to make a movie: *The movie was filmed in China.* –compare RECORD²

**film·mak·er** /ˈfɪlmˌmeɪkɚ/ *n* someone who makes movies

**film·strip** /ˈfɪlmˌstrɪp/ *n* a short film that shows photographs, drawings etc. one at a time

**film·y** /ˈfɪlmi/ *adj* fine and thin: *a filmy skirt*

**fil·ter¹** /ˈfɪltɚ/ *n* something that gas or liquid is put through to remove unwanted substances: *a water filter*

**filter**[2] v **1** [T] to clean a liquid or gas using a FILTER: *filtered drinking water* **2** [I] if people filter somewhere, they gradually move in that direction through a door, hall etc.: *The audience began to **filter into** the hall.* **3** [I] if information filters somewhere, people gradually hear about it: *The news slowly **filtered through to** everyone in the office.* **4** [I] if light or sound filters into a place, it can be seen or heard only slightly: *Sunshine **filtered through** the curtains.*

**filter** sth ⟷ **out** *phr v* [T] to remove something by using a FILTER

**filth** /fɪlθ/ n [U] **1** an extremely dirty substance: *Wash that filth off your shoes.* **2** very rude or offensive language, stories etc. about sex

**filth·y**[1] /'fɪlθi/ adj **1** extremely dirty: *Doesn't he ever wash that jacket? It's filthy.* **2** showing or describing sexual acts in a very rude or offensive way: *a filthy joke*

**filthy**[2] adv **1** **filthy dirty** INFORMAL very dirty **2** **filthy rich** DISAPPROVING extremely rich

**fin** /fɪn/ n **1** one of the thin body parts that a fish uses to swim **2** a part shaped like this on a plane or car –see picture at AIRPLANE

**fi·na·gle** /fə'neɪgəl/ v [T] INFORMAL to get something that is difficult to get, by using unusual methods: *He managed to finagle himself a job.*

**fi·nal**[1] /'faɪnl/ adj **1** last in a series of actions, events, or parts of something: *the final chapter of the book* **2** unable to be changed or doubted: *Is that your final decision? | No more cookies, and that's final!*

**final**[2] n **1** the last and most important game, race or set of games etc. in a competition: *She skated very well in the final. | the NBA finals* **2** an important test that students take at the end of each class in HIGH SCHOOL or college: *How did your finals go?*

**fi·nal·e** /fɪ'næli, -'nɑ-/ n the last part of a piece of music or a performance: *the grand finale* (=very impressive end) *of a Broadway musical*

**fi·nal·ist** /'faɪnl-ɪst/ n one of the people or teams that reaches the last competition in a series of competitions

**fi·nal·i·ty** /faɪ'næləti, fə-/ n [U] the feeling or idea that something is finished and cannot be changed: *the finality of death*

**fi·nal·ize** /'faɪnl,aɪz/ v [T] to finish the last part of a plan, business deal etc.: *Can we finalize the details tomorrow?*

**fi·nal·ly** /'faɪnl-i/ adv **1** after a long time: *After several delays, the plane finally took off at 6:00.* **2** as the last of a series of things: *And finally, I'd like to thank my teachers.* **3** in a way that does not allow further change: *It's not finally settled yet.*

**fi·nance**[1] /fə'næns, 'faɪnæns/ n [U] the management of money, especially for a company or a government: *She's an accountant in the Finance Department.*

**finance**[2] v [T] to provide money for something: *publicly financed services*

**fi·nanc·es** /fə'nænsɪz, 'faɪnænsɪz/ n [plural] **1** the money that a person, company etc. has: *The school's finances are limited.* **2** the way a person, company etc. manages money: *My finances are a mess.*

**fi·nan·cial** /fə'nænʃəl, faɪ-/ adj relating to money or the management of money: *a financial adviser* –**financially** adv

**financial aid** /.,.. './ n [U] money that is given or lent to students at college to pay for their education

**fin·an·cier** /,faɪnæn'sɪr, fə,næn-, ,fɪnən-/ n someone who controls or lends large sums of money

**fi·nanc·ing** /'faɪnænsɪŋ/ n [U] money provided by a bank to help a person or business

**finch** /fɪntʃ/ n a small wild bird with a short beak

**find**[1] /faɪnd/ v **found, found, finding** [T] **1** ▶DISCOVER◀ to discover or see something, either by searching for it or by chance: *I can't find my keys. | Scientists are trying to find a cure for AIDS. | I found a $20 bill today!* **2** ▶REALIZE◀ to discover or realize something, especially something you did not expect: *We got home and found that the basement had flooded. | I found it difficult/easy to understand her.* **3** ▶FEEL◀ to have a particular feeling or idea about something: *I don't find any of this funny.* **4** ▶LEARN◀ to learn or know something by experience: *I tried using oil, but I've found that butter works best.* **5** **be found** to live or exist somewhere: *This type of grass is found only in the swamp.* **6** ▶TIME/MONEY/ENERGY◀ to have enough of something to be able to do what you want to do: *When do you find the time to read?* **7** ▶ARRIVE◀ to arrive in a place by discovering the way to get there: *Can you find your way, or do you need a map?* **8** **find yourself somewhere** to realize that you are doing something or have arrived somewhere without intending to: *Suddenly I found myself back at the hotel.* **9** **find sb** to meet someone that you can begin a romantic relationship with: *Rob needs to find somebody to make him happy.* **10** **find sb guilty/find sb not guilty** LAW to officially decide that someone is guilty or not guilty of a crime

**find out** *phr v* **1** [I,T **find** sth ↔ **out**] to learn information after trying to discover it, or by chance: *We should find out more about the show before we reserve tickets.* **2** [T **find** sb ↔ **out**] INFORMAL to discover that someone has done something wrong: *What happens if we get found out?*

**find**[2] n something very good or valuable that

you discover by chance: *That antique carpet of Janine's was a real find.*

**find·ing** /'faɪndɪŋ/ *n* [C usually plural] the information that someone has learned as a result of studies, work etc.: *the newest research findings*

**fine**[1] /faɪn/ *adj* **1** expensive or of a very high quality: *fine clothes | Dickinson's finest poems* **2** very thin, or in small pieces or drops: *a fine layer of dust | fine rain* **3** involving differences, changes, or details that are difficult to notice: *the fine tuning on the radio* **4 a fine woman/man/person** a good person that you have respect for **5 a fine line** a point at which one thing can easily become a very different thing: *There's a fine line between genius and madness.*

---
SPOKEN PHRASES

**6 a)** good enough; all right: *"What do you want for lunch?" "A sandwich is fine." | "More coffee?" "No, I'm fine, thanks."* **b)** healthy: *"How are you?" "Fine, thanks."* **7 that's/it's fine** said when you agree to something: *"How about seeing a movie?" "That's fine by me."* **8** said when you are angry with someone because s/he is not being reasonable: *Fine then, I'll do it myself.* **9** used when you think someone is attractive: *There are a bunch of fine ladies out there.*

---

**fine**[2] *adv* SPOKEN **1** in a way that is satisfactory: *"How's everything going?" "Fine." | The washer's working fine now.* **2 do fine** to be good enough or to do something well enough: *"I can't paint." "Come on, you're doing fine."*

**fine**[3] *n* money that you have to pay as a punishment: *a library fine for returning books late*

**fine**[4] *v* [T] to make someone pay money as a punishment: *He was fined $50 for speeding.*

**fine arts** /ˌ. './ *n* **the fine arts** activities such as painting, music etc. that are concerned with making beautiful things

**fine·ly** /'faɪnli/ *adv* **1** in very thin or small pieces: *finely chopped onion* **2** to a very exact degree: *finely tuned instruments*

**fine print** /ˌ. './ *n* [U] the part of a contract or other document that has important information, often written in small print

**fi·nesse** /fɪˈnɛs/ *n* [U] delicate and impressive skill: *dancers performing with finesse*

**fin·ger**[1] /'fɪŋgɚ/ *n* **1** one of the four long thin parts at the end of your hand —see picture at HAND[1] **2 not lift/raise a finger** to not make any effort to help someone with his/her work: *I do all the work - Frank never lifts a finger.* **3 keep/have your fingers crossed** SPOKEN said when you hope that something will happen the way you want: *I had a job interview today. Keep your fingers crossed!* **4 not put your**

**finger on sth** INFORMAL to be unable to realize exactly what is wrong, different, or unusual about a situation: *Something's different here, but I can't put my finger on what it is.* **5 give sb the finger** SLANG to make a very rude sign at someone by holding up your middle finger

**finger**[2] *v* [T] to touch or handle something with your fingers

**fin·ger·nail** /'fɪŋgɚˌneɪl/ *n* the hard flat part that covers the top end of your finger

**fin·ger·print** /'fɪŋgɚˌprɪnt/ *n* the mark made by the pattern of lines at the end of someone's finger

**fin·ger·tip** /'fɪŋgɚˌtɪp/ *n* **1** the end of a finger **2 have something at your fingertips** to have something easily available, especially knowledge or information

**fin·ick·y** /'fɪnɪki/ *adj* someone who is finicky only likes a few kinds of food, clothes, music etc. and is difficult to please: *a finicky eater*

**fin·ish**[1] /'fɪnɪʃ/ *v* **1** [I,T] to come to the end of doing or making something, so it is complete: *I'll just finish this, and then we'll go. | Are you almost finished? | One more point, then I'll finish.* –opposite START[1] **2** [T] to eat or drink all the rest of something: *Finish your dinner, or there's no dessert.* **3** [I,T] to be in a particular position at the end of a race, competition etc.: *She finished second in the marathon.* **4** [T] to give the surface of something a smooth appearance by painting, polishing etc.

**finish off** *phr v* **1** [T **finish** sth ↔ **off**] to use or eat all of something: *Who finished off the cake?* **2** [T **finish** sb/sth ↔ **off**] to kill a person or animal when he, she, or it is weak or wounded

**finish up** *phr v* **1** [I,T **finish** sth ↔ **up**] to eat or drink all the rest of something: *Why don't you finish up the pie?* **2** [I,T **finish** sth ↔ **up**] to end an event, situation etc. by doing one final thing: *Let me finish up the dishes first.*

**finish with** sb/sth *phr v* [T] **be finished with** to no longer need something that you are using: *Are you finished with the scissors?*

**finish**[2] *n* **1** the end or last part of something: *It was a close finish (=a race in which competitors are very close at the end), but Jarrett won.* **2** [C,U] the appearance of the surface of an object after it has been painted, polished etc.: *a table with a glossy finish*

**fin·ished** /'fɪnɪʃt/ *adj* **1** at the end of an activity: *I'm not quite finished.* **2** completed: *the finished product* **3** no longer able to do something successfully: *If the bank doesn't loan us the money, we're finished.*

**finish line** /'.. ˌ./ *n* the line at the end of a race that a competitor must cross first in order to win

**fi·nite** /'faɪnaɪt/ *adj* having an end or a limit: *the Earth's finite resources*

**fir** /fɚ/ *n* a tree with leaves shaped like needles that do not fall off in winter

Nancy lit the candles.

The newspapers caught fire.

**fire**¹ /faɪɚ/ n **1** [U] the flames, light, and heat produced when something burns: *Fire destroyed part of the building.* | *The house is on fire!* (=burning) | *Some other buildings caught fire.* (=started to burn) | *Rioters set fire to cars and stores.* (=deliberately made them burn) **2** uncontrolled burning that destroys things: *a forest fire* | *Police are trying to find out who started the fire.* (=deliberately made it start) | *It took firefighters two days to put out the fire.* (=stop it burning) **3** burning wood or coal that provides heat. *Let's light a fire in the fireplace.* **4** [U] shooting by guns: *Our camp was under fire.* (=being shot at) | *Troops opened fire on* (=started shooting) *the rebels.* **5** be/come under fire to be criticized very strongly for something you have done: *The school district has come under fire for its sex education policy.*

**fire**² v **1** [T] to make someone leave his/her job **2** [I,T] to shoot bullets from a gun: *He fired the gun by mistake.* | *Don't fire until I tell you.* **3** [T] also **fire up** to make someone very excited or interested in something: *Jo's imagination was fired by her grandmother's stories.* **4** fire away! SPOKEN said in order to show that you are ready to answer someone's questions

**fire a·larm** /'. .,./ n a thing that makes a loud noise to warn people of a fire in a building

**fire·arm** /'faɪɚɑrm/ n a gun that can be carried

**fire·brand** /'faɪɚbrænd/ n someone who tries to make people angry enough about a law, government etc. to change it

**fire·crack·er** /'faɪɚ,krækɚ/ n a small explosive that explodes loudly, usually used when celebrating a special day

**fire de·part·ment** /'. .,../ n an organization that works to prevent fires and stop them burning

**fire drill** /'. ./ n the act of practicing what to do in order to leave a burning building safely

**fire en·gine** /'. ,../ n a special large vehicle that carries people and equipment to stop fires burning

**fire es·cape** /'. .,./ n metal stairs on the outside of a building, that people can use in order to escape if there is a fire

**fire ex·tin·guish·er** /'. .,.../ n a metal container with water or chemicals in it, used for stopping fires

**fire·fight·er** /'faɪɚ,faɪtɚ/ n someone whose job is to stop fires

**fire·fly** /'faɪɚflaɪ/ n a flying insect that produces a bright light at night

**fire hy·drant** /'. ,../ n a water pipe in a street, used for getting water to stop fires

**fire·man** /'faɪɚmən/ n a man whose job is to stop fires

**fire·place** /'faɪɚpleɪs/ n the open place in a wall of a room where you can burn wood etc. to heat the room

**fire·proof** /'faɪɚpruf/ adj a building, piece of cloth etc. that is fireproof cannot be damaged very much by fire —**fireproof** v [T]

**fire·side** /'faɪɚsaɪd/ n the area close to a FIRE-PLACE or around a small fire: *We were sitting by the fireside.*

**fire sta·tion** /'. ,../ n a building where FIRE-FIGHTERs and their equipment stay until they are needed for stopping fires

**fire truck** /'. ./ n ⇨ FIRE ENGINE

**fire·wall** /'faɪɚwɔl/ n **1** a wall that stops a fire from spreading into another room **2** a system to stop people from looking at particular information on the INTERNET

**fire·wood** /'faɪɚwʊd/ n [U] wood that is cut to be used on fires

**fire·works** /'faɪɚwɚks/ n [plural] colorful explosives that people burn when celebrating a special day: *a Fourth of July fireworks display*

**fir·ing line** /'.. ,./ n be on the firing line to be in a position or situation in which you can be attacked or criticized: *As Communications Director, Harris is constantly on the firing line.*

**fir·ing squad** /'.. ,./ n a group of soldiers whose duty is to punish prisoners by shooting and killing them

**firm**¹ /fɚm/ n a business or small company: *I'm supposed to work at my uncle's law firm this summer.*

**firm**² adj **1** not completely hard, but not soft and not easy to bend or press: *a bed with a firm mattress* | *Choose the ripest firmest tomatoes.* **2** a firm grip/grasp/hold a tight, strong hold on something: *Roger took her hand in his firm grip.* **3** not likely to change: *East Germany was the Soviet Union's firmest ally in Eastern Europe.* **4** showing that you are strong and have control: *You'll just have to be firmer with him.*

**firm**³ v

**firm** sth ↔ **up** phr v [T] to make arrangements, ideas, or plans more definite and exact: *We hope to firm up the deal later this month.*

**first**[1] /fɚst/ *determiner, adj* **1** before anyone or anything else: *Who would like to go first? | Just try a little first to see if you like it.* **2** **at first** in the beginning: *At first I thought he was weird, but now I really like him.* **3** **first (of all) a)** used when telling someone the first or most important thing in a series of statements: *First of all, I need my car back so we can drive to Renee's.* **b)** before doing anything else: *First, let's look at the sales reports.* **4** **in the first place** before something happens that cannot be changed: *If you'd done things right in the first place, we wouldn't have problems now.* **5** **first thing** SPOKEN as soon as you wake up or start work in the morning: *I'll call you first thing tomorrow, okay?* **6** **first come, first served** used in order to say that only the first people to arrive, ask for something etc. will be given something: *Free movie tickets are being given away on a first come, first served basis.* **7** **first things first** used in order to say that something is important and must be dealt with before other things: *First things first: who is going to pick up Ryder from the airport?* —see also **first/second/third string** (STRING[1]) **in the first/second/third place** (PLACE[1])

> **USAGE NOTE** first, first of all, and at first
>
> Use **first** and **first of all** at the beginning of a sentence to talk about the first or most important thing in a series of things: *First, chop the onions. | First of all, I'd like to thank everyone for coming today.* Use **at first** to talk about what happened at the beginning of an event or situation: *We really liked the hotel at first, but then we saw the roaches.*

**first**[2] *n, pron* **1** 1st; someone or something that is before anyone or anything else: *Who's first in line? | My uncle was the first in my family to go to college. | the 1st of June* (=first day of June) **2** **that's a first** SPOKEN said when you are surprised that something different or unusual has happened: *"Dad actually washed the dishes tonight." "That's a first."* **3** **come (in) first** to win a race or competition: *Bill came in first in the 100-yard dash.*

**first aid** /ˌ. './ *n* [U] simple medical treatment that you give to someone who is injured until a doctor can help

**first base** /ˌ. './ *n* [singular] **1** in baseball, the first place a player must touch before s/he can gain a point —see picture on page 472 **2** **get to first base** SPOKEN an expression meaning to HUG or kiss someone in a sexual way, used especially by young people

**first class**[1] /ˌ. '.◂/ *n* [U] the best and most expensive place to sit on a plane, train, or ship: *In first class they get free champagne.*

**first-class**[2] *adj* **1** much better than other things of the same type: *a first-class educational system* **2** using the FIRST CLASS on a plane, train, or ship: *two first-class tickets to Hawaii* —**first class** *adv*: *flying first class*

**first floor** /ˌ. '.◂/ *n* the floor of a building that is at ground level; GROUND FLOOR —see picture at ATTIC

**first gear** /ˌ. './ *n* [singular] the lowest GEAR in a car, bicycle, vehicle etc.: *Put it in first gear and try again.*

**first·hand** /ˌfɚst'hænd◂/ *adj, adv* from your own experience: *Garner knows firsthand how the media work. | firsthand knowledge*

**first la·dy** /ˌ. '../ *n* the wife of the President of the US

**first·ly** /'fɚstli/ *adv* ⇨ **first (of all)** (FIRST[1])

**first name** /'. ./ *n* the name that is your own name, and that in English comes before your family's name: *My teacher's first name is Caroline.* —compare LAST NAME, MIDDLE NAME —see usage note at NAMES

> **USAGE NOTE** first name
>
> Your **first name** is your own name, used by people who know you when they are speaking to you. Your **last name** is the one you share with all the members of your family. Some people also have a **middle name** that comes between their other two names. This name is usually used only on official documents.

**first per·son** /ˌ. '..◂/ *n* [singular] TECHNICAL in grammar, a form of a verb or PRONOUN that you use to show that you are the speaker. "I," "we," "me," and "us" are all first person pronouns, and "I am" is the first person singular of the verb "to be"

**first-rate** /ˌ. '.◂/ *adj* extremely good: *a first-rate performance by the San Francisco Ballet*

**fis·cal** /'fɪskəl/ *adj* **1** relating to government taxes, debts and spending: *the city's social and fiscal policies* **2** **fiscal year** a period of 12 months, used by a government or business to calculate its accounts

**fish**[1] /fɪʃ/ *n, plural* **fish** *or* **fishes** [C,U] an animal that lives in water and uses its FINs and tail to swim: *How many fish did you catch? | We're having fish for supper tonight.*

**fish**[2] *v* **1** [I] to try to catch fish: *Dad's fishing for salmon.* **2** [I,T] to search for something in a bag, pocket etc.: *Sally fished her keys out of her purse and unlocked the door. | Then he started fishing around in his pocket for a quarter.* **3** **be fishing for compliments** to be trying to make someone say nice things about you

**fish·bowl** /'fɪʃboʊl/ *n* **1** a glass container that pet fish are kept in **2** a situation in which everyone else can see what you are doing: *The* *president's entire family is forced to live in a fishbowl.*

**fish·er·man** /'fɪʃəmən/ n a man who catches fish as a job or a sport

**fish·er·y** /'fɪʃəri/ n a part of the ocean that is used for catching fish as a business

**fish·ing** /'fɪʃɪŋ/ n [U] the sport or job of catching fish: *Do you want to go fishing?* –**fishing** *adj*

**fishing pole** /'.. ,./, **fishing rod** n a long thin pole with a long string and a hook tied to it, used for catching fish

**fish·net** /'fɪʃnɛt/ n [U] a material with a pattern of threads and small holes like a net: *fishnet stockings*

**fish·tail** /'fɪʃteɪl/ v [I] if a vehicle fishtails, it slides from side to side on the road, especially because the road is wet

**fish·y** /'fɪʃi/ adj **1** INFORMAL seeming bad or dishonest: *I bet Mark's up to something fishy.* (=doing something bad or dishonest) **2** tasting or smelling like fish

**fis·sion** /'fɪʃən/ n [U] TECHNICAL the process of splitting an atom to produce large amounts of energy or an explosion –compare FUSION

**fis·sure** /'fɪʃə/ n a deep crack in rock or the ground

**fist** /fɪst/ n a hand with all the fingers bent tightly in toward the PALM: *She clenched her fist and screamed, "I hate you!"*

**fit¹** /fɪt/ **fit** or **fitted, fitted, fitting** v **1** [I,T] to be the right size and shape for someone: *The pants fit fine, but the jacket's too tight.* | *I wonder if my wedding dress still fits me?* **2** [I] to be the right size, shape, or amount for a particular space, and not be too big or too much: *You can't move the table there. It won't fit through the door.* | *Sorry, you can't all fit in the car.* | *I'm looking for the puzzle piece that fits here.* **3** [T] to have enough space for people or things, or to put something in a place that has enough space: *Are you sure your truck will fit all this gear?* | *I can't fit any more stuff into this suitcase.* **4** [I,T] to be suitable or to seem to have the right qualities for something: *We wanted an experienced journalist, and Watts fit the bill.* (=had the right experience) | *A man fitting the police description* (=looking like it) *was seen running from the park.*

Jim's shirt doesn't fit him anymore.

**fit in** phr v **1** [I] to be accepted by other people in a group because you have similar interests and attitudes: *The new students all had a hard time fitting in.* **2** [T **fit** sb/sth ↔ **in**] to manage to do something during a very busy time: *Dr. Tyler can fit you in on Monday at 3:30 p.m.*

**fit²** n [singular] **1 have/throw a fit** SPOKEN to become very angry and shout a lot: *Mom's going to have a fit when she sees what you've done.* **2** a short period of time when someone stops being conscious and cannot control his/her body: *an epileptic fit* **3** a very strong emotion that you cannot control: *a fit of rage* **4** the way that something fits or is suitable for a particular person, space etc.: *I thought they'd be too big, but the shelves are a perfect fit.*

**fit³** adj **1** having the qualities that are suitable for something: *You're in no fit state to drive.* –opposite UNFIT **2 see fit to do sth** to decide that it is suitable to do something, even though most people disagree: *The government has seen fit to start testing more nuclear weapons.* **3** healthy and strong: *physically fit*

**fit·ful** /'fɪtfəl/ adj happening for short and irregular periods of time: *a fitful sleep*

**fit·ness** /'fɪt⁻nɪs/ n [U] **1** the condition of being healthy or strong enough to do hard work or sports: *Join a health club to improve your fitness.* **2** the quality of being suitable for something, especially a job: *He felt unsure of his fitness for the priesthood.*

**fit·ted** /'fɪtɪd/ adj fitted clothes are designed so that they fit closely to someone's body: *a fitted jacket*

**fit·ting¹** /'fɪtɪŋ/ adj FORMAL right or suitable: *It seemed fitting that it rained the day of his funeral.*

**fitting²** n an occasion when you put on clothes that are being made for you to find out if they fit

**five¹** /faɪv/ number **1** 5 **2** five o'clock: *I get off work at five.*

**five²** n a piece of paper money worth $5

**five and ten** /,. . './, **five and dime** n OLD-FASHIONED ⇨ DIME STORE

**fix¹** /fɪks/ v [T]

**1** ▶REPAIR◀ to repair something that is broken or not working: *Do you know anyone who can fix the sewing machine?*

**2** ▶PREPARE◀ to prepare a meal or drinks: *Can you set the table while I finish fixing dinner?*

**3** ▶ARRANGE◀ to make arrangements for something: *Let's fix a day to go to the gallery together.*

**4** ▶HAIR/FACE◀ to make your hair or MAKEUP look neat and attractive: *Let me fix my hair first and then we can go.*

**5** ▶CAT/DOG◀ INFORMAL to do a medical operation on a cat or dog so that it cannot have babies

**6** ▶RESULT◀ to make dishonest arrangements

so that an election, competition etc. has the results that you want: *If you ask me, the game was fixed.*

**7 ▶INJURY◀** INFORMAL to treat an injury on your body so that it is completely better: *The doctors don't know if they can fix my kneecap.*

**8 ▶PUNISH◀** SPOKEN to harm or punish someone because s/he has done something you do not like: *I'll fix him! Just you wait!*

**fix up** *phr v* [T] **1** [**fix** sth ↔ **up**] to make a place look attractive by doing small repairs, decorating it again, etc.: *We're trying to get the house fixed up before Grandpa and Grandma come to visit.* **2** [**fix** sb ↔ **up**] INFORMAL to find a romantic partner for someone: *Rachel keeps trying to fix me up with her brother.*

**fix²** *n* **1** [singular] SLANG an amount of something, such as an illegal drug, that you think you need and want to use: *I have to have my coffee fix in the morning!* **2 be in a fix** to have a problem that is difficult to solve: *We're going to be in a real fix if we miss the last bus.*

**fix·a·tion** /fɪkˈseɪʃən/ *n* an unnaturally strong interest in or love for someone or something: *Brian has a fixation with/about motorcycles.* **–fixated** /ˈfɪkseɪtɪd/ *adj*

**fixed** /fɪkst/ *adj* **1** not changing or moving: *A fixed number of tickets will be on sale the day of the show.\a fixed smile* **2 have fixed ideas/ opinions** to have very strong opinions or ideas that often do not seem reasonable: *Lloyd has fixed ideas about religion.*

**fix·ed·ly** /ˈfɪksɪdli/ *adv* without looking at or thinking about anything else: *Grover was staring fixedly at the boat.*

**fix·ture** /ˈfɪkstʃɚ/ *n* **1** [C usually plural] a piece of equipment that is attached inside a house, such as an electric light or a FAUCET **2 be a (permanent) fixture** to always be present, and unlikely to move or go away: *Goldie's Bar has been a fixture on University Avenue for nine years.*

**fizz** /fɪz/ *n* [singular] the BUBBLEs of gas in some types of drinks, or the sound they make: *The soda in the fridge has lost its fizz.* **–fizz** *v* [I] **–fizzy** *adj*

**fiz·zle** /ˈfɪzəl/ *v*

**fizzle out** *phr v* [I] to gradually stop being interesting, and therefore stop happening: *The party fizzled out before midnight.*

**fjord** /fyɔrd/ *n* a long narrow area of sea between high cliffs

**FL** the written abbreviation of Florida

**flab** /flæb/ *n* [U] INFORMAL soft loose fat on a person's body: *I need to get rid of some of this flab!*

**flab·ber·gast·ed** /ˈflæbɚˌgæstɪd/ *adj* INFORMAL extremely shocked or surprised

**flab·by** /ˈflæbi/ *adj* INFORMAL having too much soft loose fat instead of strong muscles: *Since*

*I've stopped swimming my arms have gotten flabby.*

**flac·cid** /ˈflæsɪd/ *adj* TECHNICAL soft and weak instead of firm: *flaccid muscles*

**flag¹** /flæg/ *n* **1** a piece of cloth with a colored picture or pattern on it that represents a particular country or organization: *The crowd was cheering, waving Canadian flags.* **2** a colored piece of cloth used as a signal: *The flag went down, and the race began.*

**flag²** *v* **-gged, -gging** [I] to become tired, weak, or less interested in something: *After fighting for four years, the soldier's morale was beginning to flag.* **–flagging** *adj*

**flag** sb/sth ↔ **down** *phr v* [T] to make the driver of a car, bus etc. stop by waving at him/her: *Rhoda flagged down a cab.*

**flag·pole** /ˈflægpoʊl/ *n* a tall pole used for hanging flags

**fla·grant** /ˈfleɪgrənt/ *adj* shocking and not showing any respect for laws, truth, someone's feelings etc.: *The arrests are a flagrant violation of human rights.* **–flagrantly** *adv*

**flag·ship** /ˈflægˌʃɪp/ *n* the most important ship in a group of Navy ships, on which the ADMIRAL sails

**flag·stone** /ˈflægstoʊn/ *n* a smooth flat piece of stone used for floors, paths etc.

**flail** /fleɪl/ *v* [I,T] to wave your arms and legs in a fast but uncontrolled way

**flair** /flɛr/ *n* [singular, U] a natural ability to do something very well or to use your imagination: *Carla's always had a flair for advertising.*

**flak** /flæk/ *n* [U] INFORMAL strong criticism: *Melissa knew she'd get/take a lot of flak for dating her boss.*

**flake¹** /fleɪk/ *v* [I] to break or come off in small thin pieces: *The paint on the door is starting to flake off.*

**flake out** *phr v* [I] SPOKEN **1** do something strange or forgetful: *Kathy kind of flaked out on us today.* **2** to fall asleep: *Karl was flaked out on the sofa.*

**flake²** *n* **1** SPOKEN someone who easily forgets things or who does strange things: *Sometimes I'm such a flake.* **2** a small flat thin piece that breaks off of something: *chocolate flakes on a cake* **–flaky** *adj*

**flam·boy·ant** /flæmˈbɔɪənt/ *adj* **1** behaving in a loud, confident, or surprising way so that people notice you: *flamboyant gestures* **2** noticeable because of being brightly colored, expensive, big etc.: *a flamboyant red sequined dress* **–flamboyance** *n* [U]

**flame¹** /fleɪm/ *n* [C,U] **1** hot bright burning gas that you see when something is on fire: *a candle flame* **2 in flames** burning strongly: *By the time the firemen arrived, the house was in flames.*

**flame²** *v* [I] **1** LITERARY to suddenly become red or bright: *Her cheeks were flaming with* *embarrassment.* **2** SLANG to send someone a message on the INTERNET that is insulting, or that shows you are angry by being written only in CAPITALS

**fla·men·co** /fləˈmɛŋkoʊ/ *n* [C,U] a very fast and exciting Spanish dance, or the music for this dance

**flam·ing** /ˈfleɪmɪŋ/ *adj* very bright: *flaming red hair*

**fla·min·go** /fləˈmɪŋgoʊ/ *n* a tall tropical water bird with long thin legs, pink feathers, and a long neck

**flam·ma·ble** /ˈflæməbəl/ *adj* something that is flammable burns very easily —opposite NON-FLAMMABLE —compare INFLAMMABLE

**USAGE NOTE flammable, inflammable**

Both of these words mean the same thing, but we usually use **flammable**. The negative of both of these words is **nonflammable**.

**flank¹** /flæŋk/ *n* **1** the side of a person's or animal's body between the RIBS and the HIP **2** the side of an army in a battle: *The enemy attacked us on our left flank.*

**flank²** *v* be flanked by to have one person or thing standing on one side, and one on the other side: *The President stepped onto the plane, flanked by bodyguards.*

**flan·nel** /ˈflænl/ *n* [U] soft light cotton or wool cloth that is used for making warm clothes: *a flannel shirt*

**flap¹** /flæp/ *v* **-pped, -pping 1** [T] if a bird flaps its wings, it moves them up and down **2** [I] if a piece of cloth, paper etc. flaps, it moves around quickly and makes a noise: *The ship's sails flapped in the wind.*

**flap²** *n* a piece of cloth or paper that is used in order to cover the opening of a pocket, envelope, or TENT

**flap·jack** /ˈflæpdʒæk/ *n* ⇨ PANCAKE

**flare¹** /flɛr/ *v* **1** [I] also **flare up** to suddenly begin to burn very brightly: *rockets flaring above Cape Canaveral* **2** [I] also **flare up** to suddenly become very angry or violent: *Maddie's temper flared.* **3** [I,T] to become wider at the bottom edge, or to make something do this: *a skirt that flares out*

**flare²** *n* a very bright light used outdoors as a signal to show people where you are, especially because you need help

**flare-up** /ˈ. ./ *n* a situation in which something bad becomes a problem again, after not being a problem for a while: *a flare-up of her arthritis*

**flash¹** /flæʃ/ *v* **1** [I,T] to suddenly shine brightly for a short time, or to make something do this: *Why did that guy flash his headlights at me?* **2** [I] to move very quickly: *An ambulance flashed by/past.* **3** [T] to show something suddenly and for a very short amount of

time: *Sergeant Wicks flashed his badge.* **4** [I] if images, thoughts etc. flash through your mind, you suddenly remember or think about them: *Memories of Hawaii flashed through/across my mind.* **5** flash a smile/glance/look to smile or look at someone quickly **6** [I,T] INFORMAL if a man flashes, he suddenly shows his sex organs in public to a woman

**flash sth around** *phr v* [T] to show a lot of people something that you have, in order to try to make them admire you: *Smythe was there, flashing his cash around.*

**flash²** *n* **1** a sudden quick bright light: *a flash of lightning* **2** [C,U] a small light on a camera that you use when taking photographs when it is dark: *Did the flash go off?* **3** in/like a flash very quickly: *Wait right here. I'll be back in a flash.*

**flash·back** /ˈflæʃbæk/ *n* a sudden memory of an event that you or a character in a book, play etc. experienced in the past

**flash·card** /ˈflæʃkɑrd/ *n* a card with a word or picture on it, used in teaching

**flash·er** /ˈflæʃɚ/ *n* INFORMAL a man who shows his sex organs to women in public

**flash·light** /ˈflæʃlaɪt/ *n* a small electric light that you carry in your hand

**flash·y** /ˈflæʃi/ *adj* intended to be impressive: *a flashy new sports car*

**flask** /flæsk/ *n* **1** a small flat container used for carrying alcohol in your pocket **2** a glass bottle with a narrow top used by scientists

**flat¹** /flæt/ *adj* **1** smooth and level, without any hollow or raised areas: *The highway stays flat for the next 50 miles.* | *a flat roof* **2** a tire or ball that is flat does not have enough air inside it **3** a drink that is flat does not taste fresh because it has no more BUBBLES or gas **4** a musical note that is flat is played or sung slightly lower than it should be —compare SHARP¹ **5** flat rate/fee etc. an amount of money that is paid and that does not increase or decrease

**flat²** *adv* **1** in a straight position or stretched against a flat surface: *I have to lie flat on my back when I sleep.* **2** 10 seconds/two minutes etc. flat INFORMAL in exactly 10 seconds, two minutes etc.: *I was out of the house in ten minutes flat.* **3** fall flat to not have the result that you hoped or expected: *All of her jokes/plans fell flat.* **4** slightly lower than a musical note should be sung or played **5** flat out INFORMAL in a direct way, or completely: *Dolly flat out refused to go.* **6** go/work/move etc. flat out to go etc. as fast as possible: *We worked flat out to finish on time*

**flat³** *n* **1** INFORMAL a TIRE that does not have enough air inside it **2** a musical note that is one half STEP lower than a particular note, represented by the sign (♭) in written music

**flat·ly** /ˈflætli/ *adv* **1** said in a definite way that is not likely to change: *They flatly refused* *to help me.* **2** without showing any emotion: *"It's hopeless," he said flatly.*

**flats** /flæts/ *n* [plural] a type of women's shoes with very low heels −see picture at SHOE¹

**flat·ten** /'flæt⁻n/ *v* [I,T] to make something flat or to become flat: *The hills **flatten out** near the coast.*

**flat·ter** /'flæt̬ɚ/ *v* **1 be flattered** to be pleased because someone has shown you that s/he likes or admires you: *I was flattered to be considered for the job.* **2** [T] to praise someone in order to please him/her, even though you do not really mean it: *Don't try to flatter me!* **3** [T] to make someone look more attractive, younger etc. than s/he really is: *It's not a very flattering photograph.* **4 flatter yourself** to let yourself believe that something good about yourself is true, although it is not: *"I think you like me more than you'll admit." "Don't flatter yourself."* −**flatterer** *n*

**flat·ter·y** /'flæt̬əri/ *n* [U] praise that you do not really mean: *Flattery will get you nowhere!* (=will not help you get what you want)

**flat·u·lence** /'flætʃələns/ *n* [U] FORMAL the condition of having too much gas in your stomach

**flaunt** /flɔnt, flɑnt/ *v* [T] to show your money, success, beauty etc. in order to make other people notice it: *Pam was flaunting her diamonds at Gary's party.*

**fla·vor¹** /'fleɪvɚ/ *n* **1** the particular taste of a food or a drink: *We have 21 flavors of ice cream.* **2** [U] the quality of tasting good: *For extra flavor, add some red wine to the stew.* **3** [singular] a particular quality or the typical qualities of something: *His book gives us the flavor of life on a midwestern farm.*

**flavor²** *v* [T] to give something a particular taste or more taste

**fla·vored** /'fleɪvɚd/ *adj* **strawberry-flavored/chocolate-flavored etc.** tasting like a STRAWBERRY, chocolate etc.: *almond-flavored cookies*

**fla·vor·ing** /'fleɪvərɪŋ/ *n* [C,U] a substance used for giving something a particular FLAVOR

**flaw** /flɔ/ *n* **1** a mark, or weakness that makes something not perfect: *a flaw in the table's surface* **2** a mistake in an argument, plan etc.: *The design has a major flaw.*

**flawed** /flɔd/ *adj* spoiled by having mistakes, weaknesses, or damage: *The whole system is flawed.*

**flaw·less** /'flɔlɪs/ *adj* perfect, with no mistakes, marks, or weaknesses: *Burton's flawless performance as Hamlet | Lena has flawless skin.* −**flawlessly** *adv*

**flea** /fli/ *n* a very small jumping insect that bites animals to drink their blood

**flea·bag** /'flibæg/ *adj* INFORMAL cheap and dirty: *a fleabag hotel*

**flea col·lar** /'. ˌ../ *n* a collar, worn by dogs or cats, that contains chemicals to keep FLEAs away from them

**flea mar·ket** /'. ˌ../ *n* a market, usually in the street, where old or used goods are sold

**fleck** /flɛk/ *n* a small mark or spot: *brown cloth with flecks of red*

**flecked** /flɛkt/ *adj* having small marks or spots: *red cloth flecked with white*

**fledg·ling** /'flɛdʒlɪŋ/ *adj* a fledgling country, organization etc. has only recently been formed: *a fledgling republic*

**flee** /fli/ *v* **fled** /flɛd/, **fled, fleeing** [I,T] to leave somewhere very quickly in order to escape from danger: *The president was forced to flee the country after the revolution. | thousands of people fleeing from the fighting*

**fleece¹** /flis/ *n* **1** the wool of a sheep **2** an artificial soft material used for making warm coats −**fleecy** *adj*

**fleece²** *v* [T] INFORMAL to charge someone too much money for something, usually by tricking him/her

**fleet** /flit/ *n* **1** a group of ships, or all the ships in a navy **2** a group of vehicles that are controlled or owned by one company: *a fleet of trucks*

**fleet·ing** /'flitɪŋ/ *adj* continuing for only a short time: *a fleeting glance*

**flesh¹** /flɛʃ/ *n* [U] **1** the soft part of the body of a person or animal between the skin and the bones **2** the soft part of a fruit or vegetable that you eat **3 see/meet sb in the flesh** if you see or meet someone in the flesh, you see or meet someone who you previously had only seen in pictures, in movies, etc.: *He's more handsome in the flesh than on television.* **4 flesh and blood** someone who is part of your family: *He raised those kids like they were his own flesh and blood.*

**flesh²** *v*

**flesh sth ↔ out** *phr v* [T] to add more details to something in order to improve it: *Try to flesh your essay out with a few more examples.*

**flesh·y** /'flɛʃi/ *adj* **1** having a lot of flesh: *a round fleshy face* **2** having a soft thick inner part: *a plant with green fleshy leaves*

**flew** /flu/ *v* the past tense of FLY

**flex** /flɛks/ *v* [T] to bend and move part of your body so that your muscles become tight

**flex·i·ble** /'flɛksəbəl/ *adj* **1** a person, plan etc. that is flexible can change or be changed easily to suit any new situation: *a flexible style of management* **2** something that is flexible can bend or be bent easily: *flexible plastic* −**flexibility** /ˌflɛksə'bɪlət̬i/ *n* [U] −opposite INFLEXIBLE

**flex·time** /'flɛks-taɪm/ *n* [U] a system in which people can change the times at which they start and finish working

**flick**[1] /flɪk/ *v* [T]  **1** to make something move by hitting or pushing it quickly, especially with your thumb and finger: *Barry **flicked** the ash **from** his cigarette.*  **2** to shake something such as a whip or rope so that the end moves quickly away from you

**flick**[2] *n*  **1** SPOKEN a movie: *That was a great flick!*  **2** a short, light, sudden movement or hit with your hand, a whip etc.

**flick·er**[1] /'flɪkə/ *v* [I]  **1** to burn or move in a quick and unsteady way: *flickering candles*  **2** if an emotion or expression flickers on someone's face, it is there for only a short time: *A look of anger flickered across Andrea's face.*

**flicker**[2] *n*  **1** [singular] an unsteady light or movement: *the **flicker** of the old gas lamp*  **2** **a flicker of interest/guilt etc.** a feeling or an expression on your face that only continues for a short time: *Not even a flicker of emotion showed on his face.*

**fli·er** /'flaɪə/ *n*  **1** a sheet of paper advertising something: *People from the theater are passing out fliers in the street.*  **2** INFORMAL a pilot or someone who travels on a plane – see also FREQUENT FLIER

**flight** /flaɪt/ *n*  **1** a trip in a plane or space vehicle, or a plane making a particular trip: *What time is the next flight to Miami?* | *I'm coming in on Flight 255 from Chicago.*  **2** [U] the act of flying through the air: *a bird **in flight***  **3** a set of stairs between one floor and the next: *She fell down a whole **flight of stairs**.*  **4** [U] the act of avoiding a difficult situation by leaving or escaping: *The movie ends with the family's **flight from** Austria in World War II.*

**flight at·tend·ant** /'. .,../ *n* someone who is responsible for the comfort and safety of the passengers on a plane

**flight deck** /'. ,./ *n* the place where the pilot sits to control the plane

**flight·less** /'flaɪtlɪs/ *adj* a bird that is flightless is unable to fly

**flight·y** /'flaɪti/ *adj* someone who is flighty changes his/her ideas or activities a lot without finishing them or being serious about them

**flim·sy** /'flɪmzi/ *adj*  **1** thin, light, and not strong: *flimsy cloth*  **2** weak and not made very well: *a flimsy table*  **3** a flimsy argument, excuse etc. is hard to believe: *The evidence against him is very flimsy.*

**flinch** /flɪntʃ/ *v* [I]  **1** to make a sudden small backward movement when you are hurt or afraid of something: *He raised his hand, and the child flinched.*  **2** to avoid doing something because you dislike it or are afraid of it: *Ann told us, **without flinching**, exactly what she thought.*

**fling**[1] /flɪŋ/ *v* flung, flung, flinging [T]  **1** to throw or move something quickly with a lot of force: *She **flung** her coat **onto** the bed and sat down.* | *Sister Margaret marched across the room and **flung** the windows **open**.*  **2** to move

yourself or part of your body suddenly and with a lot of force: *Val **flung her arms around** my neck.* | *"I'm bored," said Wade, **flinging himself** on the couch.*

**fling**[2] *n* a short and not very serious sexual relationship: *I've **had** a few **flings** since Tom and I split up, but nothing serious.*

**flint** /flɪnt/ *n* [C,U] a type of very hard black or gray stone that makes a small flame when you strike it with steel

**flip**[1] /flɪp/ *v* -pped, -pping [T]  **1** to turn something over or put it into a different position with a quick sudden movement: *Could you flip the lid of that box open for me?* | *You just **flip a switch** and the machine does everything for you.*  **2** to throw something flat such as a coin up so that it turns over in the air  **3** also **flip out** [I] INFORMAL to suddenly become very angry or upset, or start behaving in a crazy way: *Harry flipped out when he found out that I wrecked his motorcycle.*

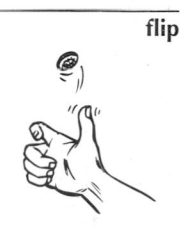
flip

**flip for** sb *phr v* [T] INFORMAL to suddenly begin to like someone very much: *Ben has really **flipped for** Amanda.*

**flip** sb ↔ **off** *phr v* [T] SLANG to make a rude sign at someone by holding up your middle finger

**flip through** sth *phr v* [T] to look at a book, magazine etc. quickly

**flip**[2] *n* a movement in which you jump up and turn over in the air, so that your feet go over your head

**flip**[3] *adj* INFORMAL ⇨ FLIPPANT

**flip-flop** /'. ./ *n* an occasion when someone changes his/her decision

**flip·pant** /'flɪpənt/ *adj* not serious about something that other people think you should be serious about: *a flippant answer to her question*

**flip·per** /'flɪpə/ *n*  **1** a flat part on the body of some large sea animals, used for pushing themselves through water  **2** a large flat rubber shoe that you use in order to help you swim faster

**flip side** /'. ./ *n* [singular]  **1** INFORMAL used when you describe the bad effects of something, after you have just described the good effects: *The flip side is that the medicine may cause hair loss.*  **2** the other side of a popular record

**flirt**[1] /flət/ *v* [I] to behave toward someone as though you are sexually attracted to him/her, but not in a very serious way: *He's always **flirting with** the women in the office.*

**flirt with** sth *phr v* [T]  **1** to consider doing something, but not be very serious about it: *I've been **flirting with** the idea of moving to Greece.*  **2** **flirt with danger/disaster etc.** to take an unnecessary risk and not be worried about it:

F

*You're **flirting with** disaster if you don't get this car fixed.*

**flirt²** *n* someone who likes to FLIRT: *Dave is such a flirt!*

**flir·ta·tion** /fləˈteɪʃən/ *n* **1** a short period of time during which you are interested in someone or something: *the artist's brief **flirtation with** photography* **2** [U] behavior that shows you are sexually attracted to someone, though not in a serious way

**flir·ta·tious** /fləˈteɪʃəs/ *adj* behaving in a way that tries to attract sexual attention, but not in a serious way

**flit** /flɪt/ *v* **-tted, -tting** [I] to move lightly or quickly from one place to another: *birds flitting from branch to branch*

**float¹** /floʊt/ *v* **1** [I] to stay or move on the surface of a liquid or up in the air without sinking: *Boats floated down the river.* | *I watched a balloon float up into the sky.* **2** [T] to make something float **3** [T] to sell SHAREs in a company or business to the public for the first time **4 float sb a loan** INFORMAL to allow someone to borrow money from you: *I could float you a small loan.*

float

**float²** *n* **1** a large vehicle that is decorated to be part of a PARADE **2** a SOFT DRINK that has ICE CREAM floating in it

**flock¹** /flɑk/ *n* **1** a group of sheep, goats, or birds: *a flock of geese* **2** a large group of the same type of people, or a group of people who regularly attend the same church: *a flock of tourists*

**flock²** *v* [I] if people flock to a place, a lot of them go there: *People are flocking to that new Thai restaurant.*

**flog** /flɑg, flɔg/ *v* [T] to beat a person or animal with a whip or stick as a punishment –**flogging** *n*

**flood¹** /flʌd/ *v* **1** [I,T] to fill a place with water, or to become filled with water: *The river floods the valley every spring.* | *The basement flooded and everything got soaked.* **2** [I,T] to arrive or go somewhere in large numbers or amounts: *Letters came flooding in.* | *We've been flooded with phone calls since her new book came out.* **3 flood the market** to sell something in very large numbers or amounts: *The company is flooding the market with cheap imports.*

**flood²** *n* **1** a very large amount of water that covers an area that is usually dry: *The town was destroyed by floods.* –see usage note at WEATHER **2 flood of** a very large number of things or people that arrive at the same time: *a flood of complaints about last night's TV show*

**flood·gate** /ˈflʌdgeɪt/ *n* **1 open the floodgates** to suddenly make it possible for a lot of people to do something: *The new laws opened the floodgates to increased immigration.* **2** a gate used in order to control the flow of water from a large lake, river etc.

**flood·light** /ˈflʌdlaɪt/ *n* a very bright light, used at night to light the outside of buildings, sports fields etc.

**flood·lit** /ˈflʌdˌlɪt/ *adj* lit at night by FLOOD-LIGHTs

**floor¹** /flɔr/ *n* **1** the flat surface on which you stand indoors: *Ernie spilled his milk on the floor.* **2** one of the levels in a building: *My office is on the third floor.* –see picture at ATTIC **3 ocean/forest floor** the ground at the bottom of the ocean or in a forest **4 the floor a)** the part of a public or government building where people discuss things: *an argument on the Senate floor* **b)** the people attending a public meeting: *Are there any questions from the floor?*

**floor²** *v* [T] **1** to surprise or shock someone so much that s/he does not know what to say or do: *I was totally floored when I heard about her death.* **2** to make a car go very fast by pressing the PEDAL all the way down

**floor·board** /ˈflɔrbɔrd/ *n* **1** a board in a wooden floor **2** the floor in a car

**floor·ing** /ˈflɔrɪŋ/ *n* [U] a substance used for making or covering floors

**floor lamp** /ˈ. ./ *n* a lamp on the top of a tall pole that stands on the floor –see picture at LAMP

**floor-length** /ˈ. ./ *adj* long enough to reach the floor: *a floor-length skirt*

**floor plan** /ˈ. ./ *n* a drawing that shows the shape of a room or rooms in a building and the positions of things in it, as seen from above

**floo·zy** /ˈfluzi/ *n* INFORMAL DISAPPROVING a woman whose sexual behavior is considered to be immoral

**flop¹** /flɑp/ *v* **-pped, -pping** [I] **1** to move or fall in a heavy or awkward way: *Jan flopped onto the bed.* **2** INFORMAL if something such as a product, play, or plan flops, it is not successful: *The musical flopped after its first week on Broadway.*

**flop²** *n* **1** INFORMAL a film, play, plan etc. that is not successful: *Dean's party was a flop.* **2** a heavy falling movement or the noise that it makes: *He fell with a flop into the water.*

**flop·house** /ˈflɑphaʊs/ *n* SLANG a cheap hotel, especially one that has many beds in one room

**flop·py** /ˈflɑpi/ *adj* soft and hanging loosely down: *a floppy hat*

**floppy disk** /ˌ.. ˈ./, **floppy** *n* ⇨ DISKETTE

**flo·ra** /ˈflɔrə/ *n* [U] TECHNICAL all the plants in a particular place or of a particular period of time –compare FAUNA

**flo·ral** /ˈflɔrəl/ *adj* made of or decorated with flowers: *floral curtains*

**flor·id** /'flɔrɪd, 'flɑrɪd/ *adj* **1** LITERARY skin that is florid is red: *florid cheeks* **2** having too much decoration or detail: *florid language*

**flo·rist** /'flɔrɪst, 'flɑr-/ *n* someone who owns or works in a store that sells flowers

**floss**¹ /flɔs, flɑs/ *n* [U] ⇨ DENTAL FLOSS

**floss**² *v* [T] to clean between your teeth with DENTAL FLOSS

**flo·til·la** /flou'tɪlə/ *n* a group of small ships

**flounce** /flauns/ *v* [I] to walk in a way that shows you are angry: *She frowned and flounced out of the room.*

**floun·der**¹ /'flaundɚ/ *v* [I] **1** to have great difficulty saying or doing something: *The team was floundering in the first half of the season.* **2** to move awkwardly or with difficulty, especially in water, mud etc.

**flounder**² *n* [C,U] a flat ocean fish, or the meat from this fish

**flour** /flauɚ/ *n* [U] a powder made from grain, usually wheat, that is used for making bread, cakes etc.

**flour·ish**¹ /'flɚɪʃ, 'flʌrɪʃ/ *v* **1** [I] to grow or develop well: *The plants flourished in the warm sun.* | *The company has flourished since we moved the factory.* **2** [T] to wave something in your hand in order to make people notice it: *Eve ran in, flourishing her acceptance letter.*

**flourish**² *n* **with a flourish** with a large confident movement that makes people notice you: *He opened the door with a flourish.*

**flout** /flaut/ *v* [T] FORMAL to deliberately disobey a rule or law

**flow**¹ /flou/ *v* [I] **1** if a liquid flows, it moves in a steady continuous stream: *The river flows past our cabin.* **2** to move easily, smoothly, and continuously from one place to another: *The cars flowed in a steady stream.* **3** if conversation or ideas flow, people talk or have ideas without being interrupted **4** if clothing, hair etc. flows, it hangs loosely and gracefully

**flow**² *n* **1** [C usually singular] a smooth steady movement of liquid: *the body's flow of blood* **2** [C usually singular] a continuous movement of something from one place to another: *the constant flow of traffic in the street* **3** [U] actions, words or ideas that are produced continuously: *I had interrupted the flow of their conversation.* **4** **go with the flow** SPOKEN to do what is easiest in your situation, and not try to do something difficult

**flow chart** /'. ./, **flow di·a·gram** /'. ,.../ *n* a drawing that uses shapes and ARROWs to show how a series of actions or parts of a system are connected with each other

**flow·er**¹ /'flauɚ/ *n* **1** the colored part of a plant or tree that produces the seeds or fruit: *a bunch of flowers* **2** a plant that is grown for the beauty of this part: *a yard full of flowers*

**flower**² *v* [I] to produce flowers

**flow·er·bed** /'flauɚˌbɛd/ *n* an area of ground in which flowers are grown

**flow·ered** /'flauɚd/ *adj* decorated with pictures of flowers: *a flowered dress*

**flow·er·pot** /'flauɚˌpɑt/ *n* a pot in which you grow plants

**flow·er·y** /'flauɚi/ *adj* **1** decorated with pictures of flowers: *a flowery pattern* **2** flowery speech or writing uses complicated and rare words instead of simple clear language

**flown** /floun/ the PAST PARTICIPLE of FLY

**flu** /flu/ *n* **the flu** a common disease that is like a bad cold but is more serious

**flub** /flʌb/ *v* **-bbed, -bbing** [I,T] SPOKEN to make a mistake or do something badly: *I flubbed the geography test.*

**fluc·tu·ate** /'flʌktʃuˌeɪt/ *v* [I] to change very often, especially from a high level to a low one and back again: *Our output fluctuates between 20 and 30 units per week.*

**fluc·tu·a·tion** /ˌflʌktʃu'eɪʃən/ *n* the act of fluctuating (FLUCTUATE): *These plants are affected by fluctuations in temperature.*

**flue** /flu/ *n* a pipe through which smoke or heat from a fire can pass out of a building

**flu·en·cy** /'fluənsi/ *n* [U] the ability to speak or write a language well: *I wanted to gain fluency in English*

**flu·ent** /'fluənt/ *adj* **1** able to speak or write a language very well: *Ted's fluent in six languages.* **2** speaking, writing, or playing a musical instrument confidently and without long pauses **–fluently** *adv*: *She speaks Spanish fluently.*

**fluff**¹ /flʌf/ *n* [U] **1** soft light pieces of thread or wool that have come from wool, cotton, or other materials **2** very soft fur or feathers, especially from a young animal or bird

**fluff**² *v* [T] **1** also **fluff up/out** to make something soft appear larger by shaking or brushing it: *a bird fluffing out its feathers* **2** INFORMAL to make a mistake or do something badly: *Ricky fluffed the catch and we lost the game.*

**fluff·y** /'flʌfi/ *adj* made of or covered with something soft and light: *a fluffy kitten*

**flu·id**¹ /'fluɪd/ *n* [C,U] a liquid: *It is a clear fluid that smells of alcohol.* –see also FLUIDS

**fluid**² *adj* **1** having a moving, flowing quality like a liquid or gas: *fluid movements* **2** likely to change or able to change: *Our plans for the project are still fluid.* **–fluidity** /flu'ɪdəti/ *n* [U]

**fluid ounce** /ˌ.. './ written abbreviation **fl. oz.** *n* a unit for measuring liquid, equal to $\frac{1}{16}$ of a PINT or 0.0296 liters

**flu·ids** /'fluɪdz/ *n* [plural] TECHNICAL water, juice, and other things you drink: *Rest in bed, and drink lots of fluids.*

**fluke** /fluk/ *n* INFORMAL something that only happens because of chance or luck: *It was just a*

F

*fluke that we both were in St. Louis at the same time.*

**flung** /flʌŋ/ v the past tense and PAST PARTICIPLE of FLING

**flunk** /flʌŋk/ v [I,T] INFORMAL to fail a test or course, or to give someone a low grade so s/he does this: *I flunked the history exam.* | *Mrs. Harris flunked me in English.*

**flunk out** phr v [I] INFORMAL to be forced to leave a school or college because your work is not good enough: *Tim flunked out of Yale.*

**flun·ky,** **flunkey** /'flʌŋki/ n INFORMAL DISAPPROVING someone who is always with an important person and treats him/her with too much respect

**flu·o·res·cent** /flʊˈrɛsənt, flɔ-/ adj 1 a fluorescent light is a very bright electric light in the form of a tube 2 fluorescent colors shine very brightly

**fluor·ide** /'flɔraɪd/ n [U] a chemical that helps to protect teeth against decay

**flur·ries** /'fləʳiz, 'flʌriz/ n [plural] a small amount of snow that falls: *Colder temperatures and flurries are expected tonight.*

**flur·ry** /'fləʳi, 'flʌri/ n [singular] an occasion when there is suddenly a lot of activity for a short time: *His arrival produced a flurry of excitement.* —see also FLURRIES

**flush¹** /flʌʃ/ v 1 [I,T] if you flush a toilet or it flushes, you make water go through it to clean it 2 [I] to become red in the face, especially because you are embarrassed or angry: *Billy flushed and looked down.* —see also FLUSHED 3 [T] also **flush out** to clean an area or place by forcing water or another liquid through it

**flush** sb ↔ **out** phr v [T] to make someone leave the place where s/he is hiding: *The animals were flushed out and captured.*

**flush²** n 1 [singular] the red color that appears on your face when you FLUSH 2 **a flush of pride/embarrassment/happiness** etc. a sudden feeling of pride, embarrassment etc.: *He felt a strong flush of pride as he watched his daughter on stage.*

**flush³** adj 1 if two surfaces are flush, they are at exactly the same level, so that the place where they meet is flat: *Is that cupboard flush with the wall?* 2 INFORMAL if someone is flush, s/he has plenty of money: *I'll buy dinner. I'm feeling flush right now.*

**flush⁴** adv fitting together so that the place where two surfaces meet is flat: *Make sure that door fits flush into its frame.*

**flushed** /flʌʃt/ adj 1 red in the face: *You look a little flushed.* 2 **flushed with excitement/success** excited or pleased in a way that is easy to notice: *Jill ran in, flushed with excitement.*

**flus·tered** /'flʌstəd/ adj feeling nervous and confused: *Jay got flustered and forgot what he was supposed to say.*

**flute** /flut/ n a musical instrument shaped like a pipe, that you play by holding it across your lips and blowing into it

**flut·ist** /'flutɪst/ n someone who plays the FLUTE

**flut·ter¹** /'flʌtə/ v 1 [I,T] if a bird or insect flutters, or flutters its wings, its wings move quickly and lightly up and down: *moths fluttering around the light* 2 [I] to wave or move gently in the air: *flags fluttering in the wind* 3 [I] if your heart or your stomach flutters, you feel very excited or nervous

**flut·ter²** n [singular] a FLUTTERing movement: *a flutter of wings in the trees*

**flux** /flʌks/ n **be in (a state of) flux** to be changing a lot so that you cannot be sure what will happen: *The economy is in flux at the moment.*

**fly¹** /flaɪ/ v flew, flown, flying
1 ▶THROUGH AIR◀ [I,T] to move through the air, or to make something do this: *We watched the birds flying overhead.* | *flying a kite* | *The planes fly right over our house.*
2 ▶TRAVEL◀ [I,T] to travel by plane, or to make a person or thing go somewhere by plane: *Fran flew to Paris last week.* | *Food and medicine are being flown into the area.*
3 ▶BE A PILOT◀ [I,T] to be the pilot of a plane: *Bill's learning to fly.* | *He flew helicopters in Vietnam.*
4 ▶MOVE◀ [I] to move very quickly and often unexpectedly: *Timmy flew down the stairs and out the door.* | *The door suddenly flew open.*
5 ▶TIME◀ [I] INFORMAL if time flies, it seems to pass quickly: *Is it 5:30 already? Boy, time sure does fly !* | *Last week just flew by.*
6 **fly off the handle** INFORMAL to become angry suddenly and unexpectedly: *I've never seen her fly off the handle like that before.*
7 ▶FLY OVER STH◀ [T] to fly a plane over a large area: *the first woman to fly the Atlantic*
8 **fly into a temper/rage** to suddenly become very angry

**fly²** n 1 a small flying insect with two wings: *There were flies all over the food.* 2 the part at the front of a pair of pants that you can open: *Your fly is unzipped.* 3 a hook that is made to look like a fly, used for catching fish —see also **be dropping like flies** (DROP¹)

**fly-by-night** /'. . ˌ./ adj INFORMAL a fly-by-night organization cannot be trusted and is not likely to exist very long: *a fly-by-night insurance company*

**fly·er** /'flaɪə/ n ⇨ FLIER

**fly·ing¹** /'flaɪ-ɪŋ/ n [U] the activity of traveling by plane or of being a pilot: *My brother-in-law enjoys flying.*

**flying²** adj 1 able to fly: *a type of flying insect* 2 **with flying colors** if you pass a test with flying colors, you are very successful on it 3 **get off to a flying start** to begin something such as a job or a race very well

**flying sau·cer** /ˌ..'../ *n* a space vehicle shaped like a plate, that some people believe carries creatures from another world; UFO

**fly·swat·ter** /'flaɪˌswɑtɚ/ *n* a plastic square attached to a long handle, used for killing flies

**FM** *n* [U] frequency modulation; a system of broadcasting radio programs in which the rate of the radio wave varies −compare AM

**foal** /foʊl/ *n* a very young horse

**foam**[1] /foʊm/ *n* [U] **1** a lot of very small BUBBLES on the surface of something: *white foam on the tops of the waves* **2** a thick substance made of very small BUBBLES of something; FOAM PACKAGING −**foamy** *adj*

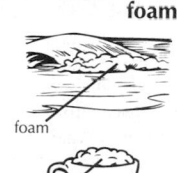

foam

foam

foam

**foam**[2] *v* [I] **1** to produce foam **2 foam at the mouth** to be very angry

**foam rub·ber** /ˌ. '../ *n* [U] soft rubber full of air BUBBLES that is used, for example, to fill PILLOWS

**fo·cal point** /'foʊkəl ˌpɔɪnt/ *n* someone or something that you pay the most attention to: *Television has become **the focal point of** most American homes.*

**fo·cus**[1] /'foʊkəs/ *v* **1** [I,T] to pay special attention to a particular person or thing instead of others: *Their attention was again focused on the strange noise.* **2** [T] to change the position of the LENS on a camera, TELESCOPE etc., so you can see something clearly **3** [I,T] if you focus your eyes or if your eyes focus, you are able to see something clearly

**focus**[2] *n, plural* **focuses** *or* **foci** /'foʊsaɪ/ **1** [singular] a situation or subject that people are interested in because it is important: *The war has become the **focus of** worldwide **attention**.* **2** special attention that you give to a particular person or subject: *Our language school puts a special **focus on** speaking English as well as writing it.* **3 in focus/out of focus** if a photograph, camera etc. is in focus, the edges of the things you see are clear; if it is out of focus the edges are not clear −**focused** *adj*

**fod·der** /'fɑdɚ/ *n* [C,U] food for farm animals

**foe** /foʊ/ *n* LITERARY an enemy

**fog**[1] /fɑg, fɔg/ *n* [C,U] **1** thick cloudy air that is difficult for you to see through **2 be in a fog** INFORMAL to be confused and unable to think clearly

**fog**[2] **fog up** *v* **-gged, -gging** [I,T] if glass fogs or becomes fogged, it becomes covered with very small drops of water so you cannot see through it

**fog·bound** /'fɑgbaʊnd, 'fɔg-/ *adj* prevented from traveling or working because of thick FOG: *Kennedy airport was fogbound on Monday.*

**fo·gey, fogy** /'foʊgi/ *n, plural* **fogeys** *or* **fogies** INFORMAL someone who is old-fashioned and who does not like change: *Don't listen to Mr. Dee; he's just an old fogey.*

**fog·gy** /'fɑgi, 'fɔgi/ *adj* **1** not clear because of FOG: *a damp and foggy morning* **2 I don't have the foggiest (idea)** SPOKEN said in order to emphasize that you do not know something: *"When's Barry coming back?" "I don't have the foggiest."* −**fogginess** *n* [U]

**fog·horn** /'fɑghɔrn, 'fɔg-/ *n* a loud horn used by ships in a FOG to warn other ships of their position

**foi·ble** /'fɔɪbəl/ *n* FORMAL a habit that someone has that is slightly strange or silly

**foil**[1] /fɔɪl/ *n* **1** [U] metal sheets that are thin like paper, used for wrapping food **2 (be) a foil to** to make the good qualities of someone or something more noticeable: *Newman's low singing voice is the perfect foil to Allen's tenor.*

**foil**[2] *v* [T] if you foil someone's plans, you stop him/her from doing something

**foist** /fɔɪst/ *v*

**foist sth on/upon sb** *phr v* [T] to make someone accept something that s/he does not want: *Marie is always trying to **foist** her religious beliefs **on** everyone.*

**fold**[1] /foʊld/ *v* **1** [T] to bend a piece of paper, cloth etc. so that one part covers another part: *Slide the omelet toward the edge of the pan and fold it in half.* −opposite UNFOLD **2** [I,T] if something such as furniture folds or you fold it, you make it smaller by bending it or closing it: *Be sure to **fold up** the ironing board when you're finished.* **3 fold your arms** to bend your arms so they are resting across your chest **4** [I] also **fold up** if a business folds, it fails and is not able to continue

**fold sth in** *phr v* [T] to gently mix another substance into a mixture when you are preparing food

**fold**[2] *n* **1** a line made in paper, cloth etc. when you fold one part of it over another **2** [C usually plural] the folds in material, skin etc. are the loose parts that hang over other parts of it **3 the fold** the group of people you belong to or have the same beliefs as: *Democrats have to find some way to make voters **return to the fold**.* (=vote Democrat again) **4** a small area where sheep are kept for safety

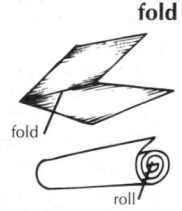

fold

fold

roll

**fold·er** /'foʊldɚ/ *n* **1** a large folded piece of hard paper, in which you keep loose papers **2** a picture on a computer screen that shows you where a FILE is kept

**fo·li·age** /'foʊliɪdʒ/ *n* [U] the leaves of a plant

**folk**[1] /foʊk/ *adj* folk art, dance, knowledge etc. is traditional and typical of the ordinary people who live in a particular area

**folk**² *n* [U] ⇨ FOLK MUSIC

**folk·lore** /ˈfoʊk-lɔr/ *n* [U] the traditional stories, customs etc. of the ordinary people of a particular area

**folk mu·sic** /ˈ. ˌ../ *n* [U] traditional music that is played by the ordinary people of a particular area

**folks** /foʊks/ *n* **1** [plural] your parents or family: *I need to call my folks sometime this weekend.* **2** SPOKEN said when you are talking to a group of people in a friendly way: *Howdy folks, it's good to see everyone here tonight!* **3** people: *Most folks around here are very friendly.*

**folk·sy** /ˈfoʊksi/ *adj* INFORMAL **1** friendly and informal: *As a town, Colville has a folksy charm.* **2** in a style that is typical of country speech and customs: *a funny folksy radio show*

**fol·li·cle** /ˈfɑlɪkəl/ *n* one of the small holes in the skin that hair grows from

**fol·low** /ˈfɑloʊ/ *v*

**1** ▶COME BEHIND◀ [I,T] to walk, drive etc. behind or after someone else: *If you follow me, I'll show you to your room. | Go on ahead - Dan will follow later.*

**2** ▶IN ORDER TO WATCH SB◀ [T] to go closely behind someone else in order to find out where s/he is going: *Marlowe looked over his shoulder to make sure no one was following him.*

**3** ▶HAPPEN AFTER◀ [I,T] to happen or come immediately after something else: *There was a shout from the garage followed by a loud crash. | In the days/weeks/months that followed, Angie tried to forget about Sam.*

**4 follow the instructions/rules/signs etc.** to do something according to how the instructions, rules etc. say it should be done: *Did you follow the instructions on the box?*

**5** ▶GO IN A DIRECTION◀ [T] to go in the same direction as something else: *The road follows the river for the next six miles.*

**6 follow suit** to do the same thing as someone else: *When Allied Stores reduced prices, other companies were forced to follow suit.*

**7 follow sb's example/lead etc.** to do the same type of thing as someone else: *Don't be nervous; just follow my lead and you'll be fine.*

**8** ▶BE INTERESTED◀ [T] to be interested in something, and pay attention to it: *Do you follow baseball at all?*

**9 follow (in) sb's footsteps** to do something that someone else did before you: *Toshi followed in his father's footsteps and started his own business.*

**10 as follows** used in order to introduce a list of names, instructions etc.: *The winners are as follows: first place, Tony Gwynn; second place, ...*

**11** ▶UNDERSTAND◀ [I,T] SPOKEN to understand something such as an explanation or story: *Sorry, I don't follow you.*

**12 it follows that** used in order to show that something must be true as a result of something else that is true: *Of course she drinks, but it doesn't follow that she's an alcoholic.*

**13** ▶BELIEVE/OBEY◀ [T] to believe in or obey a particular set of religious or political ideas: *They still follow the teachings of Gandhi.*

**follow** sb **around** *phr v* [T] to keep following someone everywhere s/he goes: *My little brother is always following me around.*

**follow** sth ↔ **through** *phr v* [I,T] to do what needs to be done to complete something or make it successful: *Harry was trained as an actor, but he never followed through with it.*

**follow** sth ↔ **up** *phr v* [I,T] to find out more about something, or to do more about something: *Did Jay ever follow up on that job possibility in Tucson?*

**fol·low·er** /ˈfɑloʊɚ/ *n* someone who believes in or supports a particular leader or set of ideas

**fol·low·ing**¹ /ˈfɑloʊɪŋ/ *adj* **the following day/year/chapter etc.** the day, year etc. after the one you have just mentioned: *Neil arrived on Friday, and his wife came the following day.*

**following**² *n* **1** a group of people who support or admire someone such as a performer: *I was playing in clubs and I'd gotten a following there.* **2 the following** the people or things that you are going to mention next: *Typical examples of opposites include the following: small and large, cold and hot ...*

**following**³ *prep* immediately after: *There will be time for questions following the lecture.*

**follow-up** /ˈ.. ˌ./ *adj* done in order to find out more or do more about something: *He's on drug treatments, with monthly follow-up visits.* **–follow-up** *n* [U]

**fol·ly** /ˈfɑli/ *n* [C,U] FORMAL a very stupid thing to do: *It would be sheer folly to buy another car at this point.*

**fo·ment** /ˈfoʊmɛnt, foʊˈmɛnt/ *v* [T] FORMAL **foment war/revolution/trouble etc.** to make people do something that causes a lot of trouble in a society

**fond** /fɑnd/ *adj* **1 be fond of** to like someone or something very much: *Mrs. Winters is very fond of her grandchildren.* **2 fond memory** a memory that makes you happy when you think of it: *"I really have fond memories of those times," Bentley said.* **3 be fond of doing sth** to enjoy doing something, and to do it often: *There's a story the old lady is fond of telling.* **4** a fond look, smile etc. is a kind, gentle one that shows that you like someone very much **–fondness** *n* [U]

**fon·dle** /ˈfɑndl/ *v* [T] **1** to touch someone or something in a gentle way: *a little girl fondling her cat* **2** to touch someone's body in a sexual way: *She accused Harper of fondling her in the elevator.*

**fond·ly** /'fɑndli/ *adv* **1** in a way that shows you like someone or something very much: *Greta smiled fondly at him from across the room.* **2 fondly remember/recall** to feel happy when you remember what you liked about a person or place: *Mrs. Vance fondly remembers when Sunnyvale was a city of gardens.*

**font** /fɑnt/ *n* **1** TECHNICAL a set of printed letters that is a particular size and shape **2** a container for the water used in the ceremony of BAPTISM

**food** /fud/ *n* **1** [U] things that people and animals eat: *What kind of food are you in the mood for tonight?* **2** [C,U] a particular type of food: *All he ever eats is junk food.* | *a health food store* **3 give sb food for thought** to make someone think carefully about something

**food bank** /'. ./ *n* a place that gives food to people who need it

**food chain** /'. ./ *n* [singular] animals and plants considered as a group in which one animal is eaten by another animal, which is eaten by another etc.

**food poi·son·ing** /'. ,.../ *n* [U] an illness caused by eating food that contains harmful BACTERIA

**food pro·ces·sor** /'. ,.../ *n* a piece of electrical equipment for preparing food, that cuts or mixes it very quickly –see picture at KITCHEN

**food stamp** /'. ./ *n* [C usually plural] an official piece of paper that poor people can use instead of money to buy food

**fool¹** /ful/ *n* **1** a stupid person: *I felt like a fool, locking my keys in the car like that.* **2 make a fool of yourself** to do something embarrassing in front of other people: *You're drunk, and you're making a fool of yourself.*

**fool²** *v* **1** [T] to trick or deceive someone: *Don't be fooled into buying more insurance than you need.* **2 you could have fooled me** SPOKEN said when you do not believe what someone has told you: *"Your dad's upset about this too, you know." "Well, you could have fooled me!"*

**fool around** *phr v* [I] **1** to spend time doing something that you enjoy: *We spent the day fooling around at the beach.* **2** to behave in a silly way: *Stop fooling around with those scissors before you hurt yourself!* **3** to have a sexual relationship with someone else: *Matt thinks his wife is fooling around with someone.*

**fool with** sb/sth *phr v* [T] INFORMAL to do something that could be dangerous or could ruin something: *A hacker had been fooling with the hospital computers.*

**fool·har·dy** /'ful,hɑrdi/ *adj* taking risks that are not necessary

**fool·ish** /'fulɪʃ/ *adj* **1** not sensible or wise: *It would be foolish of them to start fighting over this.* **2** silly or stupid: *a foolish young man* –**foolishly** *adv* –**foolishness** *n* [U]

**fool·proof** /'fulpruf/ *adj* a foolproof plan, method etc. is certain to be successful

**foot¹** /fut/ *n*
**1** ▶BODY PART◄ *plural* **feet** the part of your body that you stand on and walk on –see picture at BODY
**2** ▶MEASUREMENT◄ written abbreviation **ft.**, *plural* **feet** *or* **foot** a unit for measuring length, equal to 12 INCHes or 0.3048 meters
**3 on foot** if you go somewhere on foot, you walk there: *We set out on foot to explore the city.*
**4 the foot of** the lowest part of something such as a mountain or tree, or the end of something such as a bed
**5 be on your feet a)** to be standing for a long time without sitting down: *Waitresses are on their feet all day.* **b)** to be healthy again after being sick: *It's good to see you on your feet again!*
**6 get/rise/jump etc. to your feet** to stand up after you have been sitting: *The fans cheered and rose to their feet.*
**7 set foot in** to go into a place: *If that woman ever sets foot in this house, I'm leaving!*
**8 put your foot down a)** to say very firmly what someone must do or not do: *Brett didn't want to go to the doctor, but Dad put his foot down.* **b)** to make a car go faster
**9 put your feet up** to relax and rest, especially by having your feet supported on something
**10 put your foot in your mouth** to say something that is embarrassing, or that upsets someone
**11 have/keep both feet on the ground** to be sensible and practical in the way you do things
**12 get your foot in the door** to get your first opportunity to work in a particular organization or industry
**13 have one foot in the grave** HUMOROUS to be old
**14 -footed** having a particular number or type of feet: *a four-footed animal* | *a flat-footed man*
**15 -footer** being a particular number of feet in length: *Our sailboat's a twenty-footer.*

**foot²** *v* **foot the bill** INFORMAL to pay for something: *The insurance company should foot the bill for the damage.*

**foot·age** /'futɪdʒ/ *n* [U] film that shows a particular event: *black-and-white footage of the 1936 Olympics*

**foot·ball** /'fut¯bɔl/ *n* **1** [U] a game in which two teams of eleven players carry, kick, or throw a ball into an area at the end of a field to win points –see picture on page 472 **2** the ball used in this game –see also SOCCER

**foot·bridge** /'fut,brɪdʒ/ *n* a narrow bridge for people to walk over

**foot·fall** /'futfɔl/ *n* LITERARY FOOTSTEP

**foot·hill** /'fut,hɪl/ *n* [C usually plural] one of the low hills at the bottom of a group of mountains: *the foothills of the Rockies*

**foot·hold** /'fʊthoʊld/ *n* **1** a position from which you can start trying to get what you want: *The Republicans **gained a foothold** during the last elections.* **2** a space where you can safely put your foot when climbing a rock

**foot·ing** /'fʊtɪŋ/ *n* [U] **1** the conditions or arrangements under which something exists or operates: *Most of all, the city needs to get on a firm financial **footing**. | Talks were held in Geneva so that the two sides were **on an equal footing**.* (=had the same advantages and disadvantages) **2** a firm hold with your feet on a surface: *A local boy **lost** his **footing** and fell 200 feet down a steep bank.*

**foot·lights** /'fʊtlaɪts/ *n* [plural] a row of lights along the front of the stage in a theater

**foot lock·er** /'. ˌ../ *n* a large strong plain box for keeping your possessions in

**foot·loose** /'fʊtlus/ *adj* **footloose and fancy free** able to do what you want and enjoy yourself because you are not responsible for anyone or anything: *No, I'm not married - still footloose and fancy free.*

**foot·note** /'fʊt˺noʊt/ *n* a note at the bottom of the page in a book, that gives more information about something on that page

**foot·path** /'fʊtpæθ/ *n* a narrow path for people to walk along, especially in the country; TRAIL

**foot·print** /'fʊtˌprɪnt/ *n* a mark made by a foot or shoe: *a deer's footprints in the snow*

**foot·rest** /'fʊt˺rɛst/ *n* a part of a chair that you can raise or lower in order to support your feet when you are sitting down

**foot·sie** /'fʊtsi/ *n* **play footsie** INFORMAL to secretly touch someone's feet with your feet under a table, to show that you think s/he is sexually attractive

**foot·step** /'fʊtstɛp/ *n* the sound of each step when someone is walking: *He heard someone's footsteps in the hall.* —see also **follow (in) sb's footsteps** (FOLLOW)

**foot·stool** /'fʊtstul/ *n* a low piece of furniture used for supporting your feet when you are sitting down

**foot·wear** /'fʊt˺wɛr/ *n* [U] things you wear on your feet, such as shoes or boots

**foot·work** /'fʊt˺wɚk/ *n* [U] skillful use of your feet when dancing or playing a sport

**for**[1] /fɚ; *strong* fɔr/ *prep* **1** ▶MEANT FOR SB◀ intended to be given to or used by a particular person or group: *Save a piece of cake for Noah. | I've got some good news for you. | Leave those chairs out - they're for the concert.* **2** ▶PURPOSE◀ used in order to show the purpose of an object action, etc.: *a knife for cutting bread | **What** did you **do** that **for**?* (=why did you do it?) *| **What's** this gadget **for**?* (=what is its purpose?) *| a space just large enough for the bed to fit into | The house is for*

*sale.* (=available to be sold) **3** ▶SB WANTS TO GET/DO STH◀ in order to get or do something: *Alison is looking for a job. | We were waiting for the bus. | Let's **go for** a walk. | **For more information**, write to this address.* **4** ▶PLANNED TIME◀ used in order to show the time when something is planned to happen: *an appointment for 3:00 | **It's time for** dinner.* (=we're going to have dinner now) **5** ▶HELP◀ in order to help someone: *Let me lift that box for you. | **What can I do for you**?* (=can I help you?) **6** ▶PERIOD OF TIME◀ used in order to express a length of time: *I've known Kim for a long time. | Bake the cake for 40 minutes.* —see usage note at SINCE[2] **7** ▶REASON◀ because of or as a result of: *I got a ticket for going through a red light. | The award for the highest sales goes to Pete McGregor.* **8** ▶DIRECTION◀ used in order to show where a person, vehicle etc. is going: *The plane for Las Vegas took off an hour late. | I was just leaving for church when the phone rang.* **9** ▶DISTANCE◀ used in order to express a distance: *We walked for miles.* **10** ▶AMOUNT/PRICE◀ used in order to show a price or amount: *a check for $100 | an order for 200 copies | I'm not working **for nothing/for free**.* (=without being paid) **11 for breakfast/lunch/dinner** used in order to say what you ate or will eat at breakfast, LUNCH etc.: *"What's **for lunch**?" "Hamburgers." | We **had** steak **for dinner** last night.* **12 for sb/sth to do sth** used when discussing what is happening, what may happen, or what can happen: *It's unusual for it to be this cold in June. | The plan is for us to leave on Friday morning and pick up Joe. | The cat's too high up the tree for me to reach her.* **13** ▶FEELING TOWARD SOMEONE◀ used in order to show which person a feeling relates to: *I'm really happy for you. | He has a lot of respect for his teachers.* **14 for now** used in order to say that a situation can be changed later: *Just put the pictures in a box for now.* **15 work for/play for etc.** to play a sport on a particular team, work at a particular company etc.: *She worked for Exxon until last year. | He plays for the Boston Red Sox.* **16** ▶SUPPORT/AGREE◀ in favor of, supporting, or agreeing with someone or something: *How many people voted for Mulhoney? | I'm for getting a pizza, what about you?* **17 for all a)** considering how little: *For all the good I did, I shouldn't have tried to help.* **b)** considering how much or many: *For all the plays she's seen, she's never seen Hamlet.* **18 for all I know/care** SPOKEN used in order to say that you really do not know or care: *He could be in Canada by now for all I know.*

**19 for Christmas/for sb's birthday etc.** in order to celebrate Christmas, someone's BIRTHDAY etc.: *What did you get for your birthday?* | *We went to my grandmother's for Thanksgiving last year.*
**20 ▶MEANING◀** meaning or representing: *What's the Spanish word for oil?*
**21 ▶COMPARING◀** when you consider a particular fact: *Libby's very tall for her age.*
**22 if it hadn't been for/if it weren't for** if something had not happened, or if a situation were different: *If it weren't for Missy's help, we'd never get this job done.* —see usage note at AGO

### USAGE NOTE for

Use verbs like "buy" or "make" without **for** only to talk about buying or making something for a person or animal: *He bought a new dish for his dog.* or *He bought his dog a new dish.* | *She made a dress for her daughter.* or *She made her daughter a dress.* If you talk about buying or making something for an object, you must use **for**: *I bought a new tablecloth for the table.* ✗ DON'T SAY "I bought the table a new tablecloth." ✗

**for²** *conjunction* LITERARY because

**for·age** /ˈfɔrɪdʒ, ˈfɑr-/ *v* [I] to go around searching for food or other supplies: *animals foraging for food*

**for·ay** /ˈfɔreɪ, ˈfɑreɪ/ *n* **1** a short attempt at doing a particular job or activity: *a brief foray into politics* **2** a short sudden attack by a group of soldiers: *nightly forays into enemy territory*

**for·bade** /fɚˈbæd/ *v* the past tense of FORBID

**for·bear** /fɔrˈbɛr, fɚ-/ *v* forbore /-ˈbɔr/, forborne /-ˈbɔrn/ [I] FORMAL to not do something that you could do because you think it is wiser not to do it: *They were silly games, which Thornton forbore to join.*

**for·bear·ance** /fɔrˈbɛrəns, fɚ-/ *n* [U] FORMAL the quality of being patient, having control over your emotions, and being willing to forgive someone: *I know what forbearance you have shown him.*

**for·bid** /fɚˈbɪd/ *v* forbade *or* forbid, forbid *or* forbidden, forbidding [T] **1** to order someone not to do something: *I forbid you to see that man again.* **2 God/Heaven forbid** SPOKEN said in order to emphasize that you hope that something will not happen: *God forbid you should have an accident.*

**for·bid·den** /fɚˈbɪdn/ *adj* **1** not allowed, especially because of an official rule: *It's forbidden to smoke in the hospital.* **2** a forbidden place is one that you are not allowed to go to: *This is a forbidden area to everyone but the army.*

**for·bid·ding** /fɚˈbɪdɪŋ/ *adj* looking frightening, unfriendly, or dangerous: *The mountains looked more forbidding as we got closer.*

**force¹** /fɔrs/ *n*
**1 ▶TRAINED GROUP◀** a group of people who have been trained to do military or police work: *the Air Force* | *forces that are loyal to the rebels* | *Both of her sons are in the forces.* (=a country's military)
**2 ▶MILITARY ACTION◀** [U] military action used as a way of achieving your aims: *The UN tries to limit the use of force in conflicts.*
**3 ▶VIOLENT ACTION◀** [U] violent physical action used in order to get what you want: *The police used force to break up the demonstration.*
**4 ▶NATURAL POWER◀ a)** [U] the natural power that is used or produced when one thing moves or hits another thing: *Waves were hitting the rocks with great force.* | *The force of the explosion threw her backwards.* **b)** [C,U] a natural power that produces movement in another object: *natural forces, such as gravity*
**5 ▶SB/STH THAT INFLUENCES◀** something or someone that has a strong influence or a lot of power: *Mandela was the driving force behind the changes.* (=the one who made them happen) | *a powerful force for peace/change* (=one that makes peace or change more likely to happen)
**6 ▶STRONG EFFECT◀** [U] the powerful effect of someone or something: *The force of public opinion stopped the new highway project.*
**7 join/combine forces** to work together to do something: *Workers are joining forces with the students to protest the new bill.*
**8 in force a)** in a large group: *The mosquitoes are going to be out in force tonight!* **b)** if a law or rule is in force, it must be obeyed
**9 by/from force of habit** because you have always done a particular thing: *Ken puts salt on everything by force of habit.*

### USAGE NOTE force, power, strength

**Force** is the natural power that something has: *The force of the wind knocked the fence down.* **Power** is the ability and authority that you have to do something, or the energy that is used in order to make something work: *Congress has the power to make laws.* | *Their home is heated by solar power.* **Strength** is the physical quality that makes you strong: *I don't have the strength to lift this.*

**force²** *v* [T] **1** to make someone do something s/he does not want to do: *Nobody's forcing you to come, you know.* | *I had to force myself to get up this morning.* | *Bad health forced him into early retirement.* | *A truck driver forced her off the road yesterday.* **2** to use physical strength to move something: *Firefighters had to force the door.* (=open it using force) | *Burglars had* *forced their way into the garage.* **3 force the issue** to do something that makes it necessary for someone to make decisions or take action: *Don't force the issue; give them time to decide.*

**forced** /fɔrst/ *adj* **1** done because you must do something, not because of any sincere feeling: *"It looks nice," he said with forced cheerfulness.* **2** done suddenly and quickly because a situation makes it necessary: *The plane had to make a forced landing in a field.*

**force-feed** /'. ./ *v* [T] to force someone to eat by putting food or liquid down his/her throat

**force-ful** /'fɔrsfəl/ *adj* powerful and strong: *a forceful personality | a forceful argument* **–forcefully** *adv*

**for-ceps** /'fɔrsəps, -sɛps/ *n* [plural] a medical tool used for picking up, holding, or pulling things

**forc-i-ble** /'fɔrsəbəl/ *adj* done using physical force: *There aren't any signs of **forcible entry** into the building.* **–forcibly** *adv*: *The demonstrators were **forcibly removed** from the embassy.*

**ford**[1] /fɔrd/ *n* a place in a river that is not deep, so that you can walk or drive across it

**ford**[2] *v* [T] to walk or drive across a river at a place where it is not too deep

**fore** /fɔr/ *n* **come to the fore** to become important or begin to have influence: *Environmental issues came to the fore in the 1980s.*

**fore-arm** /'fɔrɑrm/ *n* the lower part of the arm between the hand and the elbow –see picture at BODY

**fore-bod-ing** /fɔr'boʊdɪŋ/ *n* [U] a feeling that something bad will happen soon: *We waited for news of the men with a **sense of foreboding**.*

**fore-cast**[1] /'fɔrkæst/ *n* a description of what is likely to happen in the future, based on information you have now: *the weather forecast | the company's sales forecast*

**forecast**[2] **forecast** *or* **forecasted, forecast** *or* **forecasted, forecasting** *v* [T] to say what is likely to happen in the future, based on information you have now: *Warm weather has been forecast for this weekend.*

**fore-cast-er** /'fɔrkæstɚ/ *n* someone who says what is likely to happen in the future, especially the person on television who explains the weather

**fore-close** /fɔr'kloʊz/ *v* [I] TECHNICAL to take away someone's property because s/he cannot pay back the money that s/he has borrowed to buy it **–foreclosure** /fɔr'kloʊʒɚ/ *n* [U]

**fore-fa-thers** /'fɔr,fɑðɚz/ *n* [plural] the people who were part of your family a long time ago; ANCESTORs

**fore-fin-ger** /'fɔr,fɪŋgɚ/ *n* ⇨ INDEX FINGER

**fore-front** /'fɔrfrʌnt/ *n* **in/at/to the forefront** in the main or most important position: *Today, violence has come to the forefront of society's concerns.*

**fore-gone con-clu-sion** /,fɔrgɔn kən-'kluʒən/ *n* **be a foregone conclusion** to be certain to have a particular result: *The last three elections were all foregone conclusions.*

**fore-ground** /'fɔrgraʊnd/ *n* **the foreground** the nearest part of a scene in a picture or photograph –opposite BACKGROUND

**fore-head** /'fɔrhɛd, 'fɔrɪd, 'fɑrɪd/ *n* the part of the face above the eyes and below the hair –see picture at HEAD[1]

**for-eign** /'fɑrɪn, 'fɔrɪn/ *adj* **1** not from your own country: *a foreign accent | the foreign languages department | I don't like foreign cars.* **2** involving or dealing with other countries: *the Senate Foreign Relations Committee | foreign aid workers* **3 foreign to** not familiar, or not typical: *Their way of life was completely foreign to her.* **4 foreign body/matter** TECHNICAL something that has come into a place where it does not belong: *foreign matter in someone's eye*

**for-eign-er** /'fɑrənɚ, 'fɔr-/ *n* someone who is from a country that is not your own

---

**USAGE NOTE foreigner**

It is not polite to call someone from another country a **foreigner** because this can sometimes mean that s/he is strange or different in a way that we do not like. You should say that someone is "from Canada/Japan/Russia etc." instead.

---

**fore-leg** /'fɔrlɛg/ *n* one of the two front legs of an animal that has four legs

**fore-lock** /'fɔrlɑk/ *n* a piece of hair that falls over an animal's or person's FOREHEAD

**fore-man** /'fɔrmən/ *n* **1** someone who is the leader of a group of workers, for example, in a factory **2** the leader of a JURY

**fore-most** /'fɔrmoʊst/ *adj* the most famous or important: *the foremost writer of her time*

**fo-ren-sic** /fə'rɛnsɪk, -zɪk/ *adj* **1** relating to methods for finding out about a crime: *a specialist in forensic science* **2** relating to arguments about the law: *politician's forensic skill* **–forensics** *n* [singular]

**fore-play** /'fɔrpleɪ/ *n* [U] sexual activity such as touching the sexual organs and kissing, before having sex

**fore-run-ner** /'fɔr,rʌnɚ/ *n* someone or something that is an early example or a sign of something that comes later: *a race that was the forerunner of the Grand Prix*

**fore-see** /fɔr'si/ *v* [T] to know that something will happen before it happens: *No one could have foreseen such a disaster.*

**fore-see-a-ble** /fɔr'siəbəl/ *adj* **1 for/in the foreseeable future** for as long as anyone can know about, or in a period of time anyone can know about: *Leila will be staying here for the foreseeable future. | House prices will not rise in* the foreseeable future. **2** relating to what you can expect to happen: *foreseeable problems*

**fore·shad·ow** /fɔr'ʃædoʊ/ *v* [T] LITERARY to be a sign of something that will happen in the future

**fore·sight** /'fɔrsaɪt/ *n* [singular, U] the ability to imagine what will probably happen, and to consider this in your plans for the future: *City planners were criticized for not having the foresight to build bus lanes.* —compare HINDSIGHT

**fore·skin** /'fɔrˌskɪn/ *n* a loose fold of skin covering the end of a man's PENIS

**for·est** /'fɔrɪst, 'fɑr-/ *n* [C,U] a very large number of trees, covering a large area of land: *We'll keep fighting to save our ancient forests.*

**fore·stall** /fɔr'stɔl/ *v* [T] to prevent an action or situation by doing something first: *The National Guard was sent in, to forestall trouble.*

**forest rang·er** /'.. ˌ../ *n* someone whose job is to protect or manage part of a public forest

**for·est·ry** /'fɔrəstri, 'fɑr-/ *n* [U] the science and practice of planting and taking care of forests

**fore·taste** /'fɔrteɪst/ *n* **be a foretaste of** FORMAL to be a sign of something that is likely to happen in the future: *The latest violence is only a foretaste of what might come.*

**fore·tell** /fɔr'tɛl/ *v* [T] to say what will happen in the future, especially by using special magic powers

**fore·thought** /'fɔrθɔt/ *n* [U] careful thought or planning before you do something: *A long hiking trip will require more forethought.*

**for·ev·er** /fə'rɛvɚ, fɔ-/ *adv* **1** for all future time; always: *I'll remember you forever. | You can't avoid him forever.* **2** SPOKEN for a very long time: *Greg will probably be a student forever. | With traffic this slow, it'll* **take forever** (=take a long time) *to get to Helen's.* **3** **be forever doing sth** SPOKEN to do something many times, especially something that annoys people: *You're forever losing those gloves!* **4** **go on forever** to be extremely long or large: *The train just seemed to go on forever.*

**fore·warn** /fɔr'wɔrn/ *v* [T] **1** to warn someone about something dangerous or unpleasant that will happen: *We'd been forewarned about the dangers of traveling at night.* **2** **forewarned is forearmed** used in order to say that if you know about something before it happens, you can be prepared for it

**fore·wom·an** /'fɔrˌwʊmən/ *n* **1** a woman who is the leader of a group of workers, for example in a factory **2** a woman who is the leader of a JURY

**fore·word** /'fɔrwɚd/ *n* a short piece of writing at the beginning of a book that introduces the book or the person who wrote it

**for·feit¹** /'fɔrfɪt/ *v* [T] to give something up or have it taken away from you, because of a rule

or law: *Students will have to live with their parents or forfeit their benefits.*

**forfeit²** *n* something that is taken away from you or something that you have to do as a punishment or because you have broken a rule or law

**for·gave** /fɚ'geɪv/ *v* the past tense of FORGIVE

**forge¹** /fɔrdʒ/ *v* [T] **1** to illegally copy something such as a document, a painting, or money in order to make people think it is real: *Most experts thought the picture had been forged.* **2** to develop a strong relationship with other people or groups: *A special alliance has been forged between the US and Canada.* **3** to make something from a piece of metal by heating and shaping it

**forge ahead** *phr v* [I] to make progress quickly: *A small number of people who take risks are* **forging ahead** *in business.*

**forge²** *n* a large piece of equipment that is used for heating and shaping metal objects, or the building where this is done

**forg·er** /'fɔrdʒɚ/ *n* someone who illegally copies documents, money, paintings etc. and tries to make people think they are real

**for·ger·y** /'fɔrdʒəri/ *n* **1** a document, painting, or piece of paper money that has been illegally copied; FAKE **2** [U] the crime of illegally copying something

**for·get** /fə'gɛt/ *v* **forgot, forgotten, forgetting 1** [I,T] to be unable to remember facts, information, or something that happened: *I've forgotten what her name is. | Don't* **forget (that)** *Linda's birthday is Friday. | I'd* **forgotten all about** *our bet until Bill reminded me.* ✗ DON'T SAY "I am forgetting." ✗ **2** [I,T] to not remember to do something that you should do: *Who* **forgot** *to turn off the lights? | David* **forgot (that)** *we had a meeting today. | Oh, I forgot the book.* (=I did not remember to bring it) **3** [I,T] to stop thinking or worrying about someone or something: *You'll* **forget (that)** *you're wearing contact lenses after a while. | I can't just* **forget about** *her. We were married for six years.* **4** [I,T] to stop planning to do or get something, because it is no longer possible: *If you don't finish your homework, you can* **forget about** *going skiing this weekend.*

SPOKEN PHRASES

**5 forget it a)** used in order to tell someone that something is not important: *"I'm sorry I broke your mug." "Forget it." | "Did you say something?" "No, forget it."* **b)** used in order to tell someone to stop asking or talking about something because it is annoying you: *I'm not buying you that bike, so just forget it.* **6 I forget** NONSTANDARD said instead of "I have forgotten": *You know the guy we saw last week - I forget his name.* **7 forget it/you!** an impolite expression that is used in order to refuse to do something, or to say that something is impossible: *Drive to the airport in this snow? Forget it.* | *Forget you! I took out the garbage last week.* **8 ...and don't you forget it!** said in order to remind someone angrily about something important that should make him/her behave differently: *I'm your father, and don't you forget it!*

—see usage note at LEAVE¹

**for·get·ful** /fɚˈgɛtfəl/ *adj* often forgetting things: *Papa's getting forgetful in his old age!* —**forgetfulness** *n* [U]

**forget-me-not** /.'. . ‚./ *n* a plant with small blue flowers

**for·give** /fɚˈgɪv/ *v* **forgave, forgiven** /fɚˈgɪvən/, **forgiving** [I,T] **1** to decide not to blame someone or be angry at him/her, although s/he has done something wrong: *Can you ever forgive me?* | *If you tell Laurie, I'll never forgive you for it!* | *"I'm sorry." "That's OK - you're forgiven."* (=I forgive you) | *If anything happened to the kids, I'd never forgive myself.* | *Maybe you can forgive and forget, but I can't.* (=forgive someone and behave as if s/he had never done anything wrong) **2 forgive me** SPOKEN said when you are going to say or ask something that might seem rude or offensive: *Forgive me for saying so, but yellow doesn't look good on you.* **3 forgive a loan/debt** if a country forgives a LOAN, it says that the country that borrowed the money does not have to repay it

**for·give·ness** /fɚˈgɪvnɪs/ *n* [U] FORMAL the act of forgiving someone

**for·giv·ing** /fɚˈgɪvɪŋ/ *adj* willing to forgive: *a forgiving person*

**for·go** /fɔrˈgoʊ/ *v* [T] FORMAL to decide not to do or have something: *Johnson was not likely to forgo his executive privileges.*

**for·got** /fɚˈgɑt/ *v* the past tense of FORGET

**for·got·ten** /fɚˈgɑt⌐n/ *v* the PAST PARTICIPLE of FORGET

**fork¹** /fɔrk/ *n* **1** a tool used for picking up and eating food, with a handle and three or four points: *knives, forks, and spoons* **2** a place where a road or river divides into two parts: *Turn left at the fork in the road.* **3** ⇨ PITCHFORK

**fork²** *v* **1** [I] if a road or river forks, it divides into two parts **2** [T] to pick up, carry, or turn something over using a fork: *Anna forked more potatoes onto her plate.*

**fork** sth **over/out/up** *phr v* [T] INFORMAL to spend a lot of money on something because you have to: *I had to fork over $150 for two front-row seats.*

**forked** /fɔrkt/ *adj* with one end divided into two or more parts: *a snake's forked tongue*

**fork·lift** /ˈfɔrkˌlɪft/ *n* a vehicle with special

equipment on the front for lifting and moving heavy things, for example, in a factory

**for·lorn** /fɚˈlɔrn, fɔr-/ *adj* LITERARY sad and lonely: *a forlorn line of refugees at the station*

**form¹** /fɔrm/ *n* **1** one type of something, that exists in many different types; KIND: *Ryan likes movies and other forms of entertainment.* | *Felicia died of the same form of cancer as her mother.* **2** [C,U] the way in which something exists, is presented, or appears: *You can get the vitamin C in tablet or liquid form.* | *notes written in outline form* | *Language practice can take the form of drills or exercises.* **3** an official document with spaces where you have to provide information: *an application form for college* | *Please fill in the form clearly.* **4** a shape, especially of something you cannot see clearly: *dark forms behind the trees* **5** TECHNICAL in grammar, a way of writing or saying a word that shows its number, tense etc. For example, "was" is a past form of the verb "to be"

**form²** *v* **1** [I,T] to start to exist, or to make something start to exist; develop: *Ice was already forming on the roads.* | *the cloud of dust and gas that formed the universe* | *Reporters had already formed the impression* (=begun to think) *that Myers was guilty.* **2** [I,T] to come together in a particular shape or a line, or to make something have a particular shape: *Form the dough into a circle, then roll it out.* | *The line forms to the right.* | *Our house and the barn form a big "L."* **3** [T] to start a new organization, committee, relationship etc.: *They're forming a computer club at Joan's high school.* | *Everett seemed unable to form close friendships.* **4** [T] to make something by combining two or more parts: *One way to form nouns is to add the suffix "-ness."* **5** [linking verb] to be the thing, or one of the things, that makes up something else: *Rice forms a basic part of their diet.* | *The Rio Grande forms the boundary between Texas and Mexico.*

**for·mal¹** /ˈfɔrməl/ *adj* **1** formal language, behavior, or clothes are used for official or serious situations, or for when you do not know the people you are with very well: *a formal letter* | *Jack won't wear a tie, even on formal occasions.* | *Please, call me Sam. There's no need to be formal.* | *men's formal wear* (=clothes for important events, parties etc.) **2** official or public: *a formal announcement* | *The council never took a formal position on the issue.* **3 formal education/training/qualifications** education in a subject or skill that you get in school rather than by practical experience: *Most priests have no formal training in counseling.* —**formally** *adv* —opposite INFORMAL

**formal²** *n* **1** a dance at which you have to wear formal clothes **2** an expensive and usually long dress that women wear on formal occasions

**for·mal·de·hyde** /fɚˈmældə,haɪd, fɔr-/ *n* [U] a strong-smelling liquid that can be mixed with water and used for preserving things such as parts of a body

**for·mal·i·ty** /fɔrˈmæləti/ *n* **1** [C usually plural] something formal or official that you must do as part of an activity or process, although it may not be important: *I'm just waiting for some legal formalities before moving out.* | *Ms. Cox has to interview you, but it's just a formality.* **2** [U] careful attention to the right behavior or language in formal situations

**for·mal·ize** /ˈfɔrmə,laɪz/ *v* [T] to make a plan or decision official and describe all its details: *The contracts must be formalized within one month.*

**for·mat**[1] /ˈfɔrmæt/ *n* **1** the way something such as a computer document, television show, or meeting is organized or arranged: *The interview was written in a question and answer format.* **2** the size, shape, design etc. in which something such as a book, magazine, or VIDEO is produced

**format**[2] *v* **-tted, -tting** [T] **1** TECHNICAL to organize the space on a computer DISK so that information can be stored on it **2** to arrange a book, document, page etc. according to a particular design or plan **–formatting** *n* [U] **–formatted** *adj*

**for·ma·tion** /fɔrˈmeɪʃən/ *n* **1** [U] the process by which something develops into a particular thing or shape: *rules for the formation of the past tense* | *the formation of the solar system* **2** [U] the process of starting a new organization or group: *the formation of a democratic government* **3** [C,U] something that is formed in a particular shape, or the shape in which it is formed: *rock formations* | *ducks flying in a "V" formation* | *soldiers marching in formation* (=in a special order)

**form·a·tive** /ˈfɔrmətɪv/ *adj* having an important influence on the way something develops: *a formative stage of his career* | *a child's formative years* (=when his/her character develops)

**for·mer**[1] /ˈfɔrmɚ/ *adj* having a particular position before, but not now: *a reunion of former baseball players* | *our former president*

**former**[2] *n* **the former** FORMAL the first of two people or things that are mentioned: *The former seems more likely as a possibility.* –compare LATTER[1]

**for·mer·ly** /ˈfɔrmɚli/ *adv* in earlier times: *New York was formerly New Amsterdam.*

**for·mi·da·ble** /ˈfɔrmədəbəl, fɔrˈmɪdə-/ *adj* **1** very powerful or impressive: *her formidable debating skills* | *a formidable opponent* **2** difficult to deal with and needing a lot of skill: *the formidable task of working out a peace plan* **–formidably** *adv*

**form·less** /ˈfɔrmlɪs/ *adj* without a definite shape; not clear

**form let·ter** /'. ,../ *n* a standard letter that is sent to many people, without any personal details in it

**for·mu·la** /ˈfɔrmyələ/ *n, plural* **formulas** *or* **formulae** /ˈfɔrmyəli/ **1** a method or set of principles that you use in order to solve a problem or to make sure that something is successful: *a formula for peace* | *There's no magic formula for a happy marriage.* **2** a series of numbers or letters that represent a mathematical or scientific rule **3** a list of substances used in order to make something, showing the amounts of each substance to use **4** [C,U] a liquid food for babies that is similar to a woman's breast milk

**for·mu·late** /ˈfɔrmyə,leɪt/ *v* [T] **1** to develop something such as a plan or set of rules and decide all the details of how it will be followed: *Local governments will be able to formulate their own policies.* **2** to think carefully about what you want to say, and say it clearly: *Ricardo asked for time to formulate a reply.* **–formulation** /,fɔrmyəˈleɪʃən/ *n* [C,U]

**for·ni·cate** /ˈfɔrnə,keɪt/ *v* [I] OLD-FASHIONED DISAPPROVING to have sex with someone you are not married to **–fornication** /,fɔrnəˈkeɪʃən/ *n* [U]

**for·sake** /fɚˈseɪk, fɔr-/ *v* **forsook** /-ˈsʊk/, **forsaken** /-ˈseɪkən/, **forsaking** [T] FORMAL to leave someone, especially when s/he needs you

**for·swear** /fɔrˈswɛr/ *v* [T] LITERARY to stop doing something, or to promise that you will stop doing something

**fort** /fɔrt/ *n* a strong building or group of buildings used by soldiers or an army for defending an important place

**forte** /fɔrt, ˈfɔrteɪ/ *n* **be sb's forte** to be something that someone is good at doing: *Cooking isn't my forte.*

**forth** /fɔrθ/ *adv* **go forth** LITERARY to go out or away from where you are –see also **back and forth** (BACK[2]) **and so on/forth** (SO[1])

**forth·com·ing** /,fɔrθˈkʌmɪŋ◂/ *adj* FORMAL **1** happening or coming soon: *their forthcoming marriage* **2** given or offered when needed: *If more money is not forthcoming, we'll have to close the theater.* **3** willing to give information about something: *Jerry's not the type to be forthcoming about his problems.*

**forth·right** /ˈfɔrθraɪt/ *adj* saying honestly what you think, in a way that may seem rude: *a forthright answer*

**for·ti·eth** /ˈfɔrtiɪθ/ *number* 40th

**for·ti·fi·ca·tion** /,fɔrtəfəˈkeɪʃən/ *n* [U] the process of making something stronger

**for·ti·fi·ca·tions** /,fɔrtəfəˈkeɪʃənz/ *n* [plural] towers, walls etc. built around a place in order to protect it

**for·ti·fy** /ˈfɔrtəˌfaɪ/ *v* [T] **1** to build towers, walls etc. around a place in order to defend it: *a fortified city* **2** FORMAL OR HUMOROUS to make someone feel physically or mentally stronger: *We fortified ourselves with a beer before we started.* **3** to make food or drinks more healthy by adding VITAMINs to them: *vitamin D fortified milk*

**for·ti·tude** /ˈfɔrtəˌtud/ *n* [U] courage shown when you are in pain or having a lot of trouble

**for·tress** /ˈfɔrtrɪs/ *n* a large, strong building used for defending an important place

**for·tu·i·tous** /fɔrˈtuətəs/ *adj* FORMAL lucky and happening by chance: *a fortuitous discovery*

**for·tu·nate** /ˈfɔrtʃənɪt/ *adj* lucky: *We were fortunate enough to get tickets for the last show.* | *It was fortunate that the ambulance arrived so quickly.* –opposite UNFORTUNATE

**for·tu·nate·ly** /ˈfɔrtʃənɪtli/ *adv* happening because of good luck: *We were late getting to the airport, but fortunately our plane was delayed.*

**for·tune** /ˈfɔrtʃən/ *n* **1** a very large amount of money: *Julia must've spent a fortune on her wedding dress.* **2** **make a fortune** to gain a very large amount of money doing something: *Someday he's going to make a fortune in the music business.* **3** [U] luck: *I had the good fortune to have Mrs. Dawson as my instructor.* **4** **tell sb's fortune** to use special cards or look at someone's hand in order to tell them what will happen to him/her in the future

**fortune cook·ie** /ˈ.. ˌ../ *n* a Chinese-American cookie with a piece of paper inside it that tells you what will happen in your future

**fortune tell·er** /ˈ.. ˌ../ *n* someone who tells you what is going to happen to you in the future

**for·ty** /ˈfɔrt̬i/ *number* **1** 40 **2** **the forties a)** the years between 1940 and 1949 **b)** the numbers between 40 and 49, especially when used for measuring temperature –**fortieth** *number*

**fo·rum** /ˈfɔrəm/ *n* an organization, meeting, report etc. in which people have a chance to publicly discuss an important subject: *a neighborhood forum for dealing with gang problems*

**for·ward¹** /ˈfɔrwəd/ *adv* **1** also **forwards** toward a place or position that is in front of you: *The truck was moving forward into the road.* | *He leaned forwards to hear what they were saying.* **2** toward more progress, improvement, or development: *NASA's space project cannot go forward without more money.* **3** toward the future: *The company must look forward* (=make plans for the future) *and use the newest technology.* –see also FAST FORWARD, **look forward to** (LOOK¹) –opposite BACKWARD¹

**forward²** *adj* **1** **forward progress/planning/thinking etc.** progress, plans, ideas etc. that are helpful in a way that prepares you

for the future **2** closer to a person, place etc. that is in front of you: *Troops were moved to a forward position on the battlefield.* **3** at the front part of a ship, car, plane etc.: *the forward cabin*

**forward³** *v* [T] to send a message or letter that you have received to the person it was intended for, usually at his/her new address: *The Post Office should be forwarding all my mail.*

**forward⁴** *n* in basketball, one of two players whose main job is to SHOOT the ball at the other team's BASKET –see picture on page 472

**for·ward·ing ad·dress** /ˌ... ˈ.., ˌ... .ˈ./ *n* an address you give to someone when you move so that s/he can send your mail to you

**forward-look·ing** /ˈ.. ˌ../, **forward-thinking** *adj* thinking about and planning for the future in a positive way, especially by being willing to try new ideas: *Forward-looking businessmen are already trying this new method.*

**fos·sil** /ˈfɑsəl/ *n* part of an animal or plant that lived millions of years ago, or the shape of one of these plants or animals that is now preserved in rock –**fossil** *adj*

**fossil fu·el** /ˌ.. ˈ../ *n* [C,U] a FUEL such as gas or oil that has been formed from plants and animals that lived millions of years ago

**fos·sil·ize** /ˈfɑsəˌlaɪz/ *v* [I,T] to become a FOSSIL by being preserved in rock, or to make something do this

**fos·ter¹** /ˈfɑstɚ, ˈfɔ-/ *v* [T] **1** to help to develop an idea, skill, feeling etc.: *Keely's interested in art, and we want to foster that somehow.* **2** to take care of someone else's child for a period of time without becoming his/her legal parent –compare ADOPT

**foster²** *adj* **1** **foster mother/father/parents/family** the person or people who FOSTER a child **2** **foster child** a child who is fostered **3** **foster home** a person's or family's home where a child is fostered

**fought** /fɔt/ the past tense and PAST PARTICIPLE of FIGHT

**foul¹** /faʊl/ *v* **1** [I,T] if a sports player fouls or is fouled, s/he does something in a sport that is against the rules: *Johnson was fouled trying to get to the basket.* **2** [T] to make something very dirty: *Clouds of orange smog are fouling the city's air.*

**foul sth ↔ up** *phr v* [I,T] INFORMAL to do something wrong or to ruin something by making a mistake: *She's suing her doctor for fouling up her operation.*

**foul²** *adj* **1** very dirty or not having a pleasant smell: *a pile of foul-smelling rotting garbage* **2** **foul language** rude and offensive words **3** LITERARY evil or cruel

**foul³** *n* an action in a sport that is against the rules

**foul play** /ˌ. ˈ./ *n* [C,U] an activity that is dishonest and unfair, especially when it is violent or illegal: *They think that there was some kind of foul play involved in the man's death.*

**found**[1] /faʊnd/ the past tense and PAST PARTICIPLE of FIND

**found**[2] *v* [T] **1** to start an organization, town, or institution that is intended to continue for a long time: *The college was founded in 1701.* **2 be founded on/upon** to base your ideas, beliefs etc. on something: *The US was founded on the idea of religious freedom.*

**foun·da·tion** /faʊn'deɪʃən/ *n* **1** an idea, fact, or system from which a religion, way of life etc. develops: *The Constitution provided/laid the foundation for the American government.* **2** an organization that collects money to be used for special purposes: *the National Foundation for the Arts* **3** the solid base that is built underground to support a building **4** [C,U] the action of establishing an organization, city, or institution **5 without foundation** not true, reasonable, or able to be proved: *Luckily my fears were without foundation.*

**found·er** /'faʊndɚ/ *n* someone who establishes a business, organization, school etc.: *the founders of Brandon College*

**found·ing fa·ther** /ˌ.. '../ *n* **the Founding Fathers** the men who started the government of the US by writing the Constitution and the Bill of Rights

**found·ry** /'faʊndri/ *n* a place where metals are melted and made into new parts for machines

**foun·tain** /'faʊntⁿn/ *n* a structure that sends water straight up into the air, built for decoration: *Children were splashing and playing in the park fountain.* –see also DRINKING FOUNTAIN

**four** /fɔr/ *number, n* **1** 4 **2** four o'clock: *I'll meet you at four.* **3 on all fours** on your hands and knees: *I came in and found Andy crawling around on all fours looking for something.*

**four-leaf clo·ver** /ˌ. . '../ *n* a CLOVER plant with four leaves instead of the usual three, that is considered to be lucky

**four·teen** /ˌfɔr'tin◂/ *number* 14 –**fourteenth** *number*

**fourth** /fɔrθ/ *number, n* **1** 4th **2** ¼; quarter: 5¾ (=said as "five and three fourths" or "five and three quarters") **3** [singular] also **fourth gear** a high GEAR in a car, bicycle, vehicle etc.: *Suddenly I realized I was still in fourth.*

**Fourth of Ju·ly** /ˌ. . .'./ *n* [singular] a US national holiday to celebrate the beginning of the United States as an independent nation

**fowl** /faʊl/ *n* a bird, especially one such as a chicken that is kept for its meat and eggs

**FOX** /faks/ *n* one of the main companies that broadcasts television programs in the US

**fox** /faks/ *n* **1** a wild animal like a small dog with dark red fur, a pointed face and a thick tail **2** SPOKEN an attractive person: *He is such a fox!*

**fox·trot** /'fakstrat/ *n* a type of formal dancing

with quick movements, or the music for this dance

**fox·y** /'faksi/ *adj* INFORMAL someone who is foxy is sexually attractive

**foy·er** /'fɔɪɚ/ *n* a room or hall at the entrance of a house, hotel, theater etc.

**fra·cas** /'freɪkəs, 'freɪ-/ *n* a short noisy fight involving a lot of people: *She was arrested after the fracas at the bowling alley.*

**frac·tion** /'frækʃən/ *n* **1** a very small amount of something: *At Mo's Motors we're selling cars for a fraction of the manufacturer's price!* **2** a number that is smaller than 1; ¾ and ¼ are fractions –**fractional** *adj* –**fractionally** *adv*

**frac·tious** /'frækʃəs/ *adj* someone who is fractious gets angry very easily and tends to start fights

**frac·ture**[1] /'fræktʃɚ/ *n* TECHNICAL a crack or break in something hard such as a bone or rock

**fracture**[2] *v* [I,T] TECHNICAL to crack or break something hard such as a bone or rock: *He fractured his arm when he fell.*

**frag·ile** /'frædʒəl/ *adj* **1** easily broken, damaged, or ruined: *Be careful with that vase - it's very fragile.* **2** able to be harmed easily: *Remember that chicks are fragile creatures and need to be treated with care.* –**fragility** /frə'dʒɪləti/ *n* [U]

**frag·ment** /'frægmənt/ *n* **1** a part of something, or a small piece that has broken off of something: *Only fragments of the text have survived.* | *fragments of glass* **2** also **sentence fragment** a sentence that is not complete, often because it does not have a verb –**fragment** /fræg'mɛnt/ *v* [T]

**frag·ment·ed** /'fræg,mɛntɪd/ *adj* separated into many parts, groups, or events and not seeming to have a main purpose: *Our society seems to be becoming more fragmented.*

**fra·grance** /'freɪgrəns/ *n* [C,U] a pleasant smell: *the sweet, spicy fragrance of the flowers* –see usage note at SMELL[2]

**fra·grant** /'freɪgrənt/ *adj* having a pleasant smell: *a fragrant bouquet of red roses*

**frail** /'freɪl/ *adj* thin and weak, especially because of being old: *Grandpa looked tiny and frail in the hospital bed.*

**frail·ty** /'freɪlti/ *n* [C,U] FORMAL the lack of strength, determination, or confidence: *human frailties*

**frame**[1] /freɪm/ *n* **1** a firm structure that holds or surrounds something such as a picture, door, or window: *I should put this graduation picture in a frame.* | *Wes leaned against the door frame.* **2** the main structure that supports something such as a house, piece of furniture, or vehicle: *a bicycle frame* | *a frame house* (=with a wooden frame) **3** LITERARY someone's body: *her slender frame* **4 frame of mind** a particular attitude or feeling that you have: *Melissa was in a good* *frame of mind* when we visited. **5 frame of reference** all your knowledge, experiences etc. that influence the way you think

**frame²** *v* [T] **1** to put a structure around something to support or hold it firmly: *I have a Monet print that I want to get framed.* **2** to try to make someone seem guilty of a crime by deliberately giving false information: *Murphy claims he was framed by his partner.* **3** FORMAL to organize the way you are going to say a question or statement: *Frank thought carefully, framing his response.*

**frames** /freɪmz/ *n* [plural] the metal or plastic part of a pair of GLASSES that surrounds each LENS −see picture at GLASSES

**frame·work** /'freɪmwɚk/ *n* **1** a set of rules, beliefs, knowledge etc. that people use when making a decision or planning something: *We were working within the framework of our financial aims.* **2** the main structure that supports a large thing such as a building or vehicle

**fran·chise** /'fræntʃaɪz/ *n* permission that a company gives to a person or group so that she, he, or it can sell the company's products or services

**frank** /fræŋk/ *adj* honest and direct in the way that you speak: *Jane and I have always been frank with each other about our feelings.*

**frank·fur·ter** /'fræŋkˌfɚtɚ/, **frank** /fræŋk/ *n* a long rounded piece of cooked meat, often eaten in a long round piece of bread; HOT DOG

**frank·ly** /'fræŋkli/ *adv* **1** used in order to show that you are saying what you really think about something: *Frankly, I don't want to be near her if she's going to be moody.* **2** honestly and directly: *Alphonso frankly told us his concerns.*

**fran·tic** /'fræntɪk/ *adj* **1** extremely hurried and not very organized: *The mall was full of frantic Christmas shoppers.* **2** very worried, frightened, or anxious: *The police tried to calm the boy's frantic mother.* −**frantically** *adv*

**frat¹** /fræt/ *adj* INFORMAL belonging or relating to a FRATERNITY: *a frat house*

**frat²** *n* INFORMAL ⇨ FRATERNITY

**fra·ter·nal** /frə'tɚnl/ *adj* **1** friendly because you share the same interests with someone: *a fraternal organization* **2** relating to brothers: *fraternal love*

**fra·ter·ni·ty** /frə'tɚnəti/ *n* **1** also **fraternity house** /.'... ,../ a club at a college or university that has only male members −compare SORORITY **2** [U] a feeling of friendship among people who have the same interests, job, or nationality

**frat·er·nize** /'frætɚˌnaɪz/ *v* [I] to be friendly with someone who is not allowed to be your friend: *Soldiers who fraternize with the enemy will be shot.*

**fraud** /frɔd/ *n* **1** [C,U] the illegal action of deceiving people in order to gain money: *The police arrested him for tax fraud.* **2** someone

who pretends to be someone else in order to gain money, friendship etc.

**fraud·u·lent** /'frɔdʒələnt/ *adj* intended to deceive people: *the sale of fraudulent bonds\fraudulent statements* −**fraudulently** *adv*

**fraught** /frɔt/ *adj* **fraught with problems/danger/pain etc.** full of problems, danger, pain etc.: *"I'm so sorry," he said in a voice fraught with emotion.*

**fray¹** /freɪ/ *v* [I] if a cloth or rope frays, its threads become loose because it is old or torn

**fray²** *n* **the fray** a fight or argument: *Then, two junior congressmen joined/entered the fray.*

**fraz·zled** /'fræzəld/ *adj* INFORMAL confused, tired, and worried

**freak¹** /frik/ **1 bike/movie/health etc. freak** someone who is so interested in bikes, movies etc. that other people think s/he is strange: *Pat is turning into a health freak.* (=she's become very interested in being healthy) **2** someone or something that looks very strange or behaves in an unusual way: *He looked at me as if I were some kind of freak.* **3 by some freak (of nature)** happening without any reason: *By some strange freak it started snowing in August.*

**freak²** *adj* **freak accident/storm etc.** a very unusual accident, storm etc.

**freak³** *v* [I,T] SPOKEN also **freak out** to suddenly become very angry, frightened, or anxious, or to make someone do this: *Mom totally freaked when Dad wasn't home on time.\Horror films always freak me out.*

**freak·y** /'friki/ *adj* SPOKEN strange and slightly frightening: *That was a freaky movie!*

**freck·le** /'frɛkəl/ *n* [C usually plural] a small brown spot on someone's skin, especially the face: *a little girl with red hair and freckles* −**freckled** *adj*

**free¹** /fri/ *adj*

**1 ▶NOT RESTRICTED◀** allowed to live, exist, or happen without being controlled or restricted: *People should be free to choose their own religion.\This is the country's first free election* (=not controlled by the government) *in 30 years.*

**2 ▶NO COST◀** not costing any money: *I won free tickets for tonight's concert.*

**3** not having any of a particular substance: *sugar-free bubble gum*

**4 ▶NOT BUSY◀** not busy doing other things: *If you're free next weekend do you want to go see a movie?*

**5 ▶NOT BEING USED◀** not being used at this time: *Excuse me, is this seat free?*

**6 feel free** SPOKEN used in order to tell someone that s/he is allowed to do something: *Feel free to ask me any questions after the class.*

**7 ▶NOT A PRISONER◀** not a prisoner or SLAVE: *The UN demanded that the three American hostages be set free.* (=be given their freedom)

**8 free of/from sth** without something, especially something bad or unpleasant: *free of danger | free from disease*

**free**[2] *v* [T] **1** to allow someone to leave a place where s/he has been forced to stay, such as a prison: *Nelson Mandela was freed in 1990.* **2** to move someone or something that is trapped or stuck, or to make something loose: *Firefighters helped free two men trapped in the burning car.* **3** to help someone by removing something that is bad or unpleasant: *The scholarship has freed her from having to work while she studies.* **4** also **free up** to help someone be able to do something or to make something be able to be used: *Hiring an assistant will free up your time to do other tasks.*

**free**[3] *adv* **1** without having to pay any money: *Students can visit the museum free of charge. | Kyle is fixing my car for free.* **2** not being restricted or controlled by someone: *Lucille finally broke free* (=left a person, place, or situation that restricted her) *and started a new life in Oregon.* **3** not stuck or held in a particular place or position: *He grabbed my wrist but I managed to struggle/pull free.* (=move to become free)

**free·bie, freebee** /ˈfribi/ *n* INFORMAL something that you are given by that you do not have to pay form, especially by a business, store etc.

**free·dom** /ˈfridəm/ *n* **1** [C,U] the right to do whatever you want without being restricted or controlled by someone else: *freedom of speech/religion etc.* (=the legal right to say what you want, choose your own religion etc.) *| The government must respect our basic freedoms.* **2** [U] the state of being free and allowed to do what you want: *My father thinks that kids have too much freedom these days.* **3 freedom from sth** the state of not being hurt or affected by something: *freedom from hunger*

**freedom fight·er** /ˈ.. ˌ../ *n* someone who fights in a war against a dishonest government, army etc.

**free en·ter·prise** /ˌ. ˈ.../ *n* [U] the freedom for companies to control their own business without being limited by the government very much

**free-for-all** /ˈ. . ˌ./ *n* INFORMAL a fight or noisy argument that a lot of people join: *The argument in the bar turned into a free-for-all.*

**free·hand** /ˈfrihænd/ *adj* drawn without any special tools, by using just your hands and a pen or pencil

**free·lance** /ˈfrilæns/ *adj, adv* doing work for a company without being one of its regular workers: *She worked as a freelance journalist for 15 years.* –**freelancer** *n* –**freelance** *v* [I]

**free·load** /ˈfriloʊd/ *v* [I] INFORMAL to eat other people's food, use their money etc. without giving them anything in return –**freeloader** *n*

**free·ly** /ˈfrili/ *adv* **1** in a way that shows you are not afraid to express what you believe: *We encourage our students to speak freely.* **2** without any restrictions: *People can now travel freely across the border.* **3 freely admit/acknowledge** to say that something is true, even though this is difficult: *I freely admit I made a bad choice.* **4** generously or in large amounts: *a company that gives freely to local charities*

**free mar·ket** /ˌ. ˈ../ *n* [singular] a situation in which prices are not controlled by the government or any other powerful group

**free speech** /ˌ. ˈ./ *n* [U] the act of saying or right to say anything you want to: *We are guaranteed the right to free speech in the US Constitution.*

**free·think·er** /ˌfriˈθɪŋkɚ/ *n* someone who does not accept official opinions or ideas, especially about religion –**free-thinking** *adj*

**free throw** /ˈ. ./ *n* an occasion in the game of basketball when a player is allowed to throw the ball without any opposition, because another player has FOULed him/her

**free·way** /ˈfriweɪ/ *n* a very wide road in a city on which cars can travel at a fast speed

**free·wheel·ing** /ˌfriˈwilɪŋ/ *adj* INFORMAL having the quality of not worrying about rules or being responsible for something: *a freewheeling lifestyle*

**free will** /ˌ. ˈ./ *n* **do sth of your own free will** to do something because you want to and not because someone forces you to: *She's offered to go of her own free will.*

**freeze**[1] /friz/ *v* froze, frozen, freezing **1** [I,T] if a liquid or thing freezes or something freezes it, it becomes solid and hard because it is so cold: *Last winter it was so cold that the water pipes froze.* **2** [I,T] to preserve food for a long time by keeping it very cold in a FREEZER: *Do you want to freeze some of these pies?* **3 it's freezing** SPOKEN said when the temperature is extremely cold **4 be freezing** SPOKEN to feel very cold: *Man, we were freezing out there in the car.* –see usage note at TEMPERATURE **5** [I] to suddenly stop moving and stay very quiet and still: *Officer Greer shouted, "Freeze!"* **6** [T] to officially prevent money from being spent, or prevent prices, wages etc. from being increased

**freeze up** *phr v* [I] to be unable to move, speak, or do anything because you are so nervous or frightened: *He freezes up whenever she asks him a question.*

**freeze**[2] *n* **1 price/wage freeze** an occasion when prices or wages are not allowed to be increased **2** a short period of time, especially at night, when the temperature is very low

**freeze-dried** /ˈ. ./ *adj* freeze-dried food or drinks are preserved by being frozen and then dried very quickly: *freeze-dried coffee*

F

**freez·er** /'frizɚ/ n a large piece of electrical equipment that is usually part of a REFRIGERATOR and is used for storing food at a very low temperature for a long time —see picture at KITCHEN

**freez·ing** /'frizɪŋ/ n [U] **above/below freezing** above or below 32°F or 0°C, the temperature at which water freezes

**freezing point** /'.. ,./ n TECHNICAL the temperature at which a liquid freezes

**freight** /freɪt/ n [U] **1** goods that are carried by train, plane, or ship **2** ⇨ FREIGHT TRAIN

**freight·er** /'freɪtɚ/ n a plane or ship that carries goods

**freight train** /'. ./ n a train that carries goods

**French¹** /frɛntʃ/ adj **1** relating to or coming from France **2** relating to the French language

**French²** n **1** [U] the language used in France **2 the French** [plural] the people of France

**French bread** /, './ n [U] white bread that is shaped like a long stick

**French fry** /'. ./ n [C usually plural] ⇨ FRIES

**French toast** /, './ n [U] pieces of bread that are put into a mixture of egg and milk, then cooked in hot oil

**fre·net·ic** /frə'nɛtɪk/ adj frenetic activity happens in a way that is fast, exciting, and not very organized: the frenetic pace of life in the city

**fren·zied** /'frɛnzid/ adj frenzied activity is completely uncontrolled: a frenzied attack

**fren·zy** /'frɛnzi/ n [singular,U] **1** the state of being very anxious, excited, and unable to control your behavior: In a frenzy of frustration, Matt threw rocks at the window. **2 a frenzy of activity/preparation etc.** a period in which people do a lot of things very quickly: The house was a frenzy of activity as we got ready for the party.

**fre·quen·cy** /'frikwənsi/ n **1** [U] the number of times that something happens within a particular period, or the fact that it happens a lot: We want to reduce the frequency of these bacterial infections in AIDS patients. **2** [C,U] the rate at which a sound or light WAVE pattern is repeated

**fre·quent¹** /'frikwənt/ adj happening very often: Her teacher is worried about her frequent absences from class. —opposite INFREQUENT

**fre·quent²** /fri'kwɛnt, 'frikwənt/ v [T] to go to a particular place very often: a restaurant frequented by students

**frequent fli·er** /,.. '../ n someone who travels on planes very often, especially on a particular AIRLINE's planes —**frequent-flier** adj

**fre·quent·ly** /'frikwəntˈli/ adv very often: She has frequently promised to help me, but she hasn't yet.

**fresh** /frɛʃ/ adj **1 ▶ADDED/REPLACING◀** an amount or a thing that is fresh is added to or replaces what

was there before: Do you want some fresh coffee? | fresh sheets for the bed

**2 ▶RECENT◀** recently done, made, or learned: fresh news/information/data | a fresh attempt/approach/idea (=a new way of doing something)

**3 ▶FOOD◀** fresh food or flowers are in good condition because they have recently been produced, picked, or prepared: I bought some fresh strawberries for dessert.

**4 ▶CLEAN◀** looking, feeling, smelling, or tasting clean, cool, and nice: a fresh breeze | a fresh minty taste

**5 fresh air** air from outside, especially away from a city where the air is cleaner: It's nice to get some fresh air.

**6 be fresh out of sth** SPOKEN used in order to say that you have just used or given away the last supply of something: I'm sorry, we're fresh out of bagels. Would you like a muffin instead?

**7 fresh-made/fresh-cut etc.** having just been made, cut etc.: fresh-squeezed orange juice

**8 ▶WATER◀** fresh water has no salt and comes from rivers and lakes

**9 make a fresh start** to try doing something again by using a completely different method, especially because you want to succeed, be happy etc.: My mother and I left Chicago to try to make a fresh start (=start a new life) in California.

**10 fresh in your mind/memory etc.** recent enough to be remembered: You might want to write about your trip while it's still fresh in your mind.

**fresh·en** /'frɛʃən/ v

**freshen up** phr v [I,T **freshen yourself up**] to wash your hands and face in order to feel comfortable: Would you like to **freshen up** before dinner?

**fresh·ly** /'frɛʃli/ adv very recently: freshly mown grass

**fresh·man** /'frɛʃmən/ n a student in the first year of HIGH SCHOOL or college

**fresh·wa·ter** /'frɛʃˌwɔtɚ, -ˌwɑtɚ/ adj relating to rivers or lakes rather than the ocean: freshwater fish

**fret¹** /frɛt/ v [I,T] OLD-FASHIONED to worry about small or unimportant things, or to make someone do this

**fret²** n one of the raised lines on the long straight part of a GUITAR or similar instruments

**fret·ful** /'frɛtfəl/ adj OLD-FASHIONED worried and complaining about small things: a fretful child

**Freud·i·an** /'frɔɪdiən/ adj **1** relating to Sigmund Freud's ideas about the way the mind works **2 Freudian slip** something you say by mistake that shows a thought or feeling you did not mean to show, or did not know you had

**fri·ar** /'fraɪɚ/ n a man who belongs to a Roman Catholic group, whose members in past times traveled around teaching about religion and who were very poor

**fric·tion** /'frɪkʃən/ n [U] **1** disagreement, angry feelings, or unfriendliness between people: *The way housework is shared has been a source of friction between Cathy and Jerry.* **2** the rubbing of one surface against another: *friction between tires and the road*

**Fri·day** /'fraɪdi, -deɪ/ written abbreviation **Fri.** n the sixth day of the week —see usage note AT SUNDAY

**fridge** /frɪdʒ/ n INFORMAL ⇨ REFRIGERATOR

**fried**[1] /fraɪd/ adj **1** cooked in hot fat: *a fried egg* **2** SLANG very tired: *My brain is fried today.*

**fried**[2] v the past tense and PAST PARTICIPLE of FRY

**friend** /frɛnd/ n **1** someone whom you like very much and enjoy spending time with: *I'm meeting a friend for lunch.* | *Tony's her best friend.* (=the friend she likes best) | *Lee's an old friend.* (=one you have known a long time) **2** make/be friends (with) to have someone as your friend: *We made friends with our neighbors right away.* | *They've been friends with the Wilsons for years.* **3** someone who supports a theater, MUSEUM etc. by giving money or help: *You can become a friend of the art gallery for $100 a year.* **4** have friends in high places to know important people who can help you

**friend·ly** /'frɛndli/ adj **1** showing that you like someone and are ready to talk to him/her: *Diane's friendly to/with everyone.* | *a friendly smile* —opposite UNFRIENDLY **2** -friendly **a)** easy for people to use or be comfortable with: *user-friendly computers* | *a kid friendly house* **b)** not damaging or harming something: *environmentally friendly detergent* **3** friendly fire bombs, bullets etc. that accidentally kill people who are fighting on the same side —friendliness n [U]

**friend·ship** /'frɛndʃɪp/ n **1** a relationship between friends: *Their friendship began in college.* | *Our children have formed/developed a friendship with the Websters.* | *a close friendship* **2** [U] the feelings that exist between friends, and the way they behave with each other: *I was grateful for her friendship and support.*

**fries** /fraɪz/ n [plural] potatoes cut into long thin pieces and cooked in hot oil

**frieze** /friz/ n a thin border along the top of a wall, usually decorated with pictures, patterns etc.

**frig·ate** /'frɪgɪt/ n a small fast ship used especially for protecting other ships in a war

**frig·ging** /'frɪgɪŋ/ adj, adv SLANG used in order to emphasize something, or to show that you are annoyed: *I can't get this frigging car to start.*

**fright** /fraɪt/ n [singular, U] a sudden fear: *People screamed and ran away in fright.*

**fright·en** /'fraɪtⁿn/ v [T] **1** to make someone feel afraid: *Libby was frightened by the loud thunder.* **2** frighten sb into sth/frighten sb out of sth to force someone to do something or not to do something by making him/her afraid: *At least the heart attack has frightened him out of smoking.*

**frighten** sb/sth ↔ **away** phr v [T] to make a person or animal go away by making him, her, or it afraid: *Be quiet or you'll frighten away the birds.*

**frighten** sb ↔ **off** phr v [T] to make someone so nervous or afraid that s/he goes away and does not do something s/he was going to do: *A car alarm is usually enough to frighten off a burglar.*

**fright·ened** /'fraɪtⁿnd/ adj feeling afraid: *a frightened child* | *He's still too frightened to be able to sleep.*

**fright·en·ing** /'fraɪtⁿnɪŋ/ adj making you feel afraid or nervous: *a frightening experience* —frighteningly adv

**frig·id** /'frɪdʒɪd/ adj **1** a woman who is frigid does not like having sex **2** LITERARY not friendly: *She gave me a frigid look.* **3** a place that is frigid is very cold —frigidity /frɪ'dʒɪdəṭi/ n [U]

**frill** /frɪl/ n **1** a decoration on the edge of a piece of cloth, made of another piece of cloth with many small folds in it **2** additional features that are nice but not necessary. *Southwest Airlines offers few frills.* —see also NO-FRILLS

**frill·y** /'frɪli/ adj with many FRILLs: *a frilly blouse*

**fringe**[1] /frɪndʒ/ n **1** the political/radical/lunatic etc. fringe a small number of people whose ideas are more unusual or extreme than those of most other people: *the environmental fringe* **2** on the fringes of sth not completely involved in or accepted by a particular group: *Cato lived on the fringes of society.* **3** [C,U] a decoration on a curtain, piece of clothing etc., made of hanging threads: *a cowboy jacket with leather fringe* **4** the area along the edge of a place: *the eastern fringes of downtown Vancouver*

**fringe**[2] adj not representing or involving many people, and expressing unusual ideas: *a fringe group of political extremists* | *a fringe presidential candidate*

**fringe ben·e·fit** /'. ,.../ n [usually plural] a service or advantage that you are given with your job in addition to pay: *Fringe benefits include a company car and health club membership.*

**fringed** /frɪndʒd/ adj **1** decorated with a FRINGE: *a large fringed shawl* **2** having something on the edge: *a palm-fringed beach*

**Fris·bee** /'frɪzbi/ n [C,U] TRADEMARK a piece of

plastic shaped like a plate, that people throw and catch as a game

**frisk** /frɪsk/ v [T] to search someone for hidden weapons, drugs etc. by passing your hands over his/her body

**frisk·y** /'frɪski/ adj full of energy, happiness, and fun: *a frisky little boy*

**frit·ter¹** /'frɪtɚ/ n a thin piece of fruit, vegetable, or meat covered with a mixture of eggs and flour and cooked in oil: *corn fritters*

**fritter²**

**fritter** sth ↔ **away** phr v [T] to waste time, money, or effort on something that is not important: *They **fritter away** their days hanging around at the mall.*

**fritz** /frɪts/ n INFORMAL **be on the fritz** if something electrical is on the fritz, it is not working correctly: *It could be that your printer's on the fritz.*

**fri·vol·i·ty** /frɪ'valəti/ n [C,U] behavior or activities that are not serious or sensible: *childish frivolity*

**friv·o·lous** /'frɪvələs/ adj **1** not sensible: *pretty, frivolous clothes* **2** not important or necessary: *a frivolous request*

**frizz** /frɪz/ v [T] INFORMAL to make your hair curl very tightly

**frizz·y** /'frɪzi/ adj frizzy hair is very tightly curled

**fro** /froʊ/ adv ⇨ TO AND FRO

**frog** /frɔg, frag/ n **1** a small animal with smooth skin that lives in or near water, makes a deep sound, and has long legs for jumping −compare TOAD **2** **have a frog in your throat** INFORMAL to have difficulty in speaking because your throat is dry

**frol·ic** /'fralɪk/ v [I] to play in an active, happy way −**frolic** n

**from** /frəm; strong frʌm/ prep
**1** ▶WHERE SB/STH STARTS◄ starting at a particular place, position, or condition: *He drove all the way from Colorado.* | *I liked him from the first time I met him.* | *prices ranging from $80 to $250*
**2** ▶ORIGIN◄ **a)** used in order to show the origin of someone or something: *I took the lines from a play.* | *a doll made from grass* | *Our speaker today is from the University of Montana.* | *"Where do you **come from**?" "I'm from Norway."* **b)** sent or given by someone: *Who is the present from?* | *I got a phone call from Ernie today.*
**3** ▶MOVED/SEPARATED◄ used in order to show that things or people are moved, separated, or taken away: *He pulled his shoes out from under the bed.* | *I'll **take** that **away from** you if you hit me with it again!* | *She needs some time **away from** the kids.* (=time when she is not with them) | *Subtract $40 from the total.*
**4** ▶DISTANCE/TIME◄ used in order to show distance or time: *We live about 3 miles from Des*

Moines. | *It'll cost $400 to fly **from** Albuquerque to Atlanta.* | *The morning class is **from** 9:00 **to** 11:00.*
**5** ▶POSITION◄ used in order to show where you are when you see, watch, or do something: *There's a man watching us from behind that fence.* | *We could see the house from the road.*
**6** ▶RESULT◄ because of, or as a result of: *I got this cold from walking in the rain all day Sunday.* | *We could tell what he was thinking from the expression on his face.*
**7** **a week/2 months/5 years from now** one week, 2 months etc. after the time when you are speaking: *One month from now we'll be in Mexico!*
**8** **from now on** starting now and continuing into the future: *From now on, Richard will be working in the Sales Department.*
**9** ▶STOP SOMETHING HAPPENING◄ used with verbs such as "keep," "stop," "protect," and "prevent" in order to show the action that is stopped or avoided: *Winston's bad eyesight prevented him from driving.*
**10** ▶COMPARING◄ used when comparing things: *Frieda is very different from her sister.*

**frond** /frand/ n a leaf of a FERN or PALM TREE

**front**

Amy walked in front of the bus.

Vicky got in the front seat of the car.

**front¹** /frʌnt/ n
**1** **the front a)** the most forward part of something: *Let's sit at the front of the bus.* | *I can't remember the page number, but it's near the front of the book.* **b)** the side or surface of something that is in the direction that it faces or moves: *Go in at the front of the building.* | *There's a dent in the front of my bike.* **c)** the most important side or surface of something, that you look at first: *On the front of the postcard was a picture of the Golden Gate Bridge.* −opposite BACK¹
**2** **in front of sth a)** near the side of something that is in the direction it faces or moves: *a tree in front of the house* | *A car suddenly pulled out in front of my van.* **b)** near the entrance of a building: *Park in front of the theater.* −opposite BEHIND¹

**3 in front of sb a)** ahead of someone, in the direction that s/he is facing or moving: *There are about 50 people in front of us in line.* **b)** facing a person or group: *Come up here in front of the class.* **c)** where someone can see or hear you: *Don't say anything in front of the children.*

**4 in (the) front a)** in the most forward or leading position; ahead: *Watch the car in front!* **b)** in the area nearest to the most forward part of something, or nearest to the entrance to a building: *The club has two bars, one in the front and one in the back.*

**5 out front** in the area near the entrance to the building that you are in: *Jim's waiting out front.*

**6 in (the) front** in the part of a car where the driver sits: *Can I sit in front with you?*

**7 ▶WEATHER◀** TECHNICAL the place where two areas of air that have different temperatures meet each other: *The weather report says a warm/cold front is coming.*

**8 on the publicity/money/health etc. front** in a particular area of activity: *We've had some new developments on the economic front.*

**9 up front** INFORMAL **a)** money that is paid up front is paid before work is done or goods are supplied: *We need the money up front before we can do anything.* **b)** directly and clearly from the start: *She told him up front she wasn't interested in marriage.*

**10 ▶ON YOUR BODY◀** INFORMAL someone's chest, or the part of the body that faces forward: *Oh, I've just spilled milk down my front!*

**11 ▶BEHAVIOR◀** a way of behaving that shows what you want people to see, rather than what you may feel: *Parents should always present a united front (=seem to agree with each other) to their children.*

**12 ▶POLITICAL PARTY◀** used in the names of political parties or unofficial military organizations: *the Quebec Liberation Front*

**13 ▶WAR◀** a line along which fighting takes place during a war

**front²** *adj* **1** at, on, or in the front of something: *the front door | tickets for front row seats* **2** legally doing business as a way of hiding a secret or illegal activity: *a front organization for drug dealing*

**front³** *v* **1** [I,T] to face something: *a building fronting Lake Michigan* **2** [T] to lead something such as a musical group by being the person that the public sees most: *He's now fronting his own band.*

**front for** sb/sth *phr v* [T] to be the person or organization used for hiding the real nature of a secret or illegal activity: *The FBI suspected him of fronting for a smuggling ring.*

**front·age** /ˈfrʌntɪdʒ/ *n* the part of a building or piece of land that is along a road, river etc.

**fron·tal** /ˈfrʌntəl/ *adj* **1** toward the front of something: *a frontal attack* **2** at the front part of something: *the frontal lobe of the brain*

**fron·tier** /frʌnˈtɪr/ *n* **1 the frontier** the area beyond the places that people know well, especially in the western US in the 19th century: *the settlement of the Oklahoma frontier* **2** the limit of what is known about something: *the frontiers of science* **3** the border of a country, or the area near the border

**front man** /ˈ. ./ *n* **1** someone who speaks for an organization, often an illegal one, but is not the leader of it **2** the leader of a JAZZ or ROCK band

**front·run·ner** /ˈfrʌntˌrʌnɚ-/ *n* the person or thing that is most likely to succeed in a competition: *the frontrunner in the race for the Republican nomination*

**frost¹** /frɔst/ *n* **1** [U] ice that looks white and powdery and covers things that are outside when the temperature is very cold: *trees covered with frost* **2** very cold weather, when water freezes: *an early frost*

**frost²** *v* [T] **1** to cover a cake with FROSTING **2** to cover something with FROST, or to become covered with frost

**frost·bite** /ˈfrɔstbaɪt/ *n* [U] a condition that is caused by extreme cold, that makes your fingers, toes etc. swell, become darker, and sometimes drop off —**frostbitten** /ˈfrɔstˌbɪtⁿn/ *adj*

**frost·ing** /ˈfrɔstɪŋ/ *n* [U] a sweet substance that you put on cakes, made from sugar and liquid

**frost·y** /ˈfrɔsti/ *adj* **1** very cold or covered with FROST: *a frosty morning | frosty ground* **2** unfriendly: *a frosty greeting*

**froth¹** /frɔθ/ *n* [singular, U] a lot of BUBBLEs formed on top of a liquid

**froth²** *v* [I] to make FROTH: *When you open the bottle, the beer will froth for a few seconds.*

**froth·y** /ˈfrɔθi, -ði/ *adj* full of FROTH or covered with froth: *frothy beer*

**frown¹** /fraʊn/ *v* [I] to make an angry or unhappy expression by moving your EYEBROWs together, so that lines appear on your FOREHEAD: *Mel frowned and pretended to ignore me.*

**frown on/upon** sth *phr v* [T] to disapprove of something: *Even though divorce is legal, it's often frowned upon.*

**frown²** *n* the expression on your face when you frown: *Marty looked at his grades with a frown.*

**froze** /froʊz/ *v* the past tense of FREEZE

**fro·zen¹** /ˈfroʊzən/ *v* the PAST PARTICIPLE of FREEZE

**frozen²** *adj* **1** preserved by being kept at a very low temperature: *frozen peas* **2 be frozen (stiff)** SPOKEN to feel very cold: *Can you turn up the heat? I'm frozen!* **3** made very hard or turned to ice because of the cold: *frozen ground | the frozen lake* **4 be frozen with fear/terror/fright** to be so afraid, shocked etc. that you cannot move: *The dog was under the* *bed, frozen with terror, throughout the thunder storm.*

**fru·gal** /ˈfrugəl/ *adj* **1** careful to only buy what is necessary: *Dan's a very frugal young man.* **2** small in quantity and cost: *a frugal lunch of cheese and bread* —**frugally** *adv* —**frugality** /fruˈgæləti/ *n* [U]

**fruit** /frut/ *n, plural* **fruit** or **fruits** **1** [C,U] the part of a plant, tree, or bush that contains seeds and is often eaten as food: *Apples and bananas are Nancy's favorite fruits.* | *Would you like a piece of fruit?* | *You should eat more fruit.* **2 the fruits of sth** the good results that you have from something you have worked hard at: *It's nice to see Barry enjoying the fruits of all his hard work.* —see also **bear fruit** (BEAR¹)

**fruit·cake** /ˈfrutˌkeɪk/ *n* **1** [C,U] a cake that has dried fruit in it **2** INFORMAL someone who seems to be mentally ill or behaves in a strange way

**fruit fly** /ˈ. ./ *n* a small fly that eats and lays eggs on fruit

**fruit·ful** /ˈfrutfəl/ *adj* producing good results: *a fruitful meeting*

**fru·i·tion** /fruˈɪʃən/ *n* [U] FORMAL the successful result of a plan, idea etc.: *After three years, many of the president's plans have finally come to fruition.*

**fruit·less** /ˈfrutlɪs/ *adj* failing to produce good results, especially after much effort: *a fruitless attempt to end the fighting* —**fruitlessly** *adv*

**fruit·y** /ˈfruti/ *adj* tasting or smelling strongly of fruit: *a fruity wine*

**frump·y** /ˈfrʌmpi/ *adj* someone, especially a woman, who is frumpy wears old-fashioned clothes and looks unattractive

**frus·trate** /ˈfrʌstreɪt/ *v* [T] **1** if something frustrates you, it makes you feel annoyed or angry because you are unable to do what you want: *It's the lack of money that really frustrates me.* **2** to prevent someone's plans, efforts, or attempts from succeeding: *His attempts to escape were frustrated by an alert guard.*

**frus·trat·ed** /ˈfrʌstreɪtɪd/ *adj* feeling annoyed or angry because you are unable to do what you want to do: *Don't get so frustrated; learning a language takes time.*

**frus·trat·ing** /ˈfrʌstreɪtɪŋ/ *adj* making you feel annoyed or angry because you cannot do what you want to do: *They keep sending me the wrong forms - it's really frustrating.*

**frus·tra·tion** /frʌˈstreɪʃən/ *n* [C,U] the feeling of being annoyed or angry because you are unable to do what you want to do: *A toddler was kicking the ground in frustration.*

**fry** /fraɪ/ *v* **fried, fried, frying** [I,T] to cook something in hot fat or oil, or to be cooked in hot fat or oil: *Do you want me to fry some eggs?*

**fry·ing pan** /ˈ.. ./ *n* a round pan with a flat handle, used for FRYing food —see picture at PAN¹

**ft.** the written abbreviation of FOOT

**fuck¹** /fʌk/ *v* SPOKEN TABOO **1** [I,T] used in very offensive phrases to show that you strongly dislike someone or something or are very annoyed **2** [I,T] to have sex with someone —**fucking** *adj* —**fucker** *n*

**fuck up** *phr v* SPOKEN TABOO [I,T **fuck** sth ↔ **up**] to make a mistake or do something badly

**fuck²** *n* SPOKEN TABOO **1** the act of having sex **2 the fuck** used in order to emphasize what you are saying when you are angry: *What the fuck do you think you're doing?*

**fucked up** /ˌ. ˈ. ./ *adj* SPOKEN TABOO **1** very unhappy and unable to control your life **2** having drunk too much alcohol or taken illegal drugs

**fudge¹** /fʌdʒ/ *n* [U] a soft creamy sweet food, usually made with chocolate

**fudge²** *v* [T] to avoid giving exact figures or facts, in order to deceive people: *I knew that the only way I could get the job was to fudge on my experience.*

**fu·el¹** /ˈfyuəl, fyul/ *n* [C,U] a substance such as coal, gas, or oil that can be burned to produce heat or energy

**fuel²** *v* **1** [T] to make a situation worse or to make someone's feelings stronger: *The attempts to end the strike only fueled tensions on both sides.* **2** [I,T] also **fuel up** to take fuel into a vehicle, or to provide a vehicle with fuel

**fu·gi·tive** /ˈfyudʒətɪv/ *n* someone who is trying to avoid being caught, especially by the police: *a fugitive from justice*

**ful·crum** /ˈfʊlkrəm, ˈfʌl-/ *n* the point on which a BAR that is being used for lifting something turns or is supported

**ful·fill** /fʊlˈfɪl/ *v* [T] **1** if a hope, promise, wish etc. is fulfilled, the thing that you had hoped etc. happens or is done: *The president finally fulfilled his election promise to cut taxes.* **2** if a need, demand, or condition is fulfilled, you get what you need or want: *Do you know enough about computers to fulfill our requirements?* **3** to make something become true or cause something to happen: *If Terry doesn't work harder, he'll never fulfill his ambition to be a doctor.* **4 fulfill yourself** to feel satisfied because you are using all your skills and qualities: *She fulfilled herself both as a mother and as a successful writer.*

**ful·filled** /fʊlˈfɪld/ *adj* satisfied with your life, job etc. because you feel that it is interesting, or useful and you are using all your skills: *I just don't feel fulfilled.*

**ful·fill·ing** /fʊlˈfɪlɪŋ/ *adj* a job, relationship etc. that is fulfilling makes you feel satisfied because it allows you to use all your skills and qualities

**ful·fill·ment** /fʊlˈfɪlmənt/ *n* [U] **1** the feeling of being satisfied after a successful effort: *Ann's work gives her a real sense of fulfillment.* **2** the act or state of meeting a need, demand, or condition: *The offer of this contract depends upon the fulfillment of certain conditions.*

**full**[1] /fʊl/ *adj*
**1 ▸CONTAINER/ROOM/PLACE ETC.◂** holding or containing as much of something, or as many things or people as possible: *Is your glass full?* | *a box **full of** paper* –see picture at EMPTY[1]
**2 ▸COMPLETE◂ a)** including all parts or details; complete: *Please write down your full name and address.* | *Because it was slightly damaged, I didn't have to pay the **full price** for it.* **b)** being the highest level or greatest amount of something: *You have our **full support** in whatever you decide to do.*
**3 be full of a)** to contain many things of the same kind: *Eric's essay is full of mistakes.* **b)** to feel or express a strong emotion: *Cathy is full of guilt about the death of her mother.* **c)** to think or talk about only one subject all the time: *Tim is just so **full of himself** - he really makes me mad!*
**4 ▸FOOD◂** having eaten so much food that you cannot eat any more: *"Would you like some more soup?" "No thanks. I'm full."*
**5 ▸SPEED/HEIGHT ETC.◂** as large, fast, strong etc. as possible: *running **at full speed***
**6 be full of it/crap/shit** SPOKEN OFFENSIVE said when you think what someone is saying is wrong or stupid: *Don't listen to him. He's full of shit.*
**7 ▸CLOTHING◂** a full skirt, pair of pants etc. is made with a lot of material and fits loosely
**8 ▸BODY◂** a full face, body etc. is rounded or large: *clothes for the fuller figure*
**9 ▸TASTE/SOUND ETC.◂** a full taste, sound, color etc. is strong and pleasant: *a **full bodied** wine*

**full**[2] *n* **1 in full** if you pay an amount of money in full, you pay the whole amount: *The bill was marked "paid in full."* **2 to the full** in the best or most complete way: *Ronnie lived his life to the full.*

**full**[3] *adv* LITERARY directly: *The sun shone **full on** her face.*

**full-blown** /ˌ. ˈ.◂/ *adj* fully developed: *full-blown AIDS*

**full-fledged** /ˌfʊl ˈflɛdʒd◂/ *adj* completely developed, trained, or established: *a full-fledged lawyer*

**full-grown** /ˌ. ˈ.◂/ *adj* a full-grown animal, plant, or person has developed to his, her, or its full size and will not grow any bigger

**full house** /ˌ. ˈ./ *n* an occasion at a concert hall, sports field etc. when every seat has someone sitting in it

**full-length** /ˌ. ˈ.◂/ *adj* **1 full-length mirror/photograph etc.** a mirror etc. that shows all of a person, from his/her head to his/her feet **2 full-length skirt/dress** a skirt etc. that reaches the ground **3 full-length play/book etc.** a play etc. of the normal length

**full moon** /ˌ. ˈ./ *n* [singular] the moon when it looks completely round

**full·ness** /ˈfʊlnɪs/ *n* [U] **in the fullness of time** FORMAL when the right time comes: *I'm sure he'll tell us everything in the fullness of time.*

**full-scale** /ˌ. ˈ.◂/ *adj* **1** using all possible powers or forces: *a full-scale inquiry into the disaster* **2** a full-scale model, copy, picture etc. is the same size as the thing it represents

**full-time** /ˌ. ˈ.◂/ *adj, adv* working or studying for the number of hours that work is usually done: *Until she had a baby, Andrea worked full-time for an insurance company.* | *a full-time job* –compare PART-TIME

**ful·ly** /ˈfʊli/ *adv* completely: *a fully trained nurse*

**fum·ble** /ˈfʌmbəl/ *v* **1** [I,T] to drop the ball in a game of football **2** [I] to move your fingers or hands awkwardly when you are looking for something or trying to do something: *Gary **fumbled for** the light switch in the dark.* –**fumble** *n*

**fume** /fyum/ *v* [I] to show that you are very angry, usually without saying anything: *"Was he angry?" "Yeah, he was really fuming."*

**fumes** /fyumz/ *n* [plural] strong-smelling gas or smoke that is unpleasant to breathe in: *gasoline fumes*

**fu·mi·gate** /ˈfyuməˌgeɪt/ *v* [T] to remove disease, BACTERIA, insects etc. from somewhere using chemical smoke or gas –**fumigation** /ˌfyuməˈgeɪʃən/ *n* [U]

**fun**[1] /fʌn/ *n* [U] **1** pleasure, amusement, and enjoyment, or something that causes these: *Swimming is fun.* | *Did you **have fun** at Phil's party?* | *He's learning to speak Spanish, just **for fun**.* (=because he enjoys it) | *It's **no fun*** (=not fun) *to be sick.* **2 make fun of sb/sth** to make unkind jokes about someone or something: *All the kids at school are making fun of Billy because he can't read.* **3 in fun** if you make a joke or say something about someone in fun, you do not intend it to be insulting: *I'm sorry, I only said it in fun.*

**USAGE NOTE fun and funny**

Use **fun** as a noun to talk about events and activities that are enjoyable, such as games and parties: *Let's go to the beach and have some fun!* Use **fun** as an adjective to say that something was enjoyable: *Going to the beach was fun.* **Funny** is an adjective that describes someone or something that makes us laugh: *Bob's jokes are really funny.* ✗ DON'T SAY "Going to the beach was funny." ✗

**fun**[2] *adj* **1** a fun activity or experience is enjoyable: *It'll be a fun thing to do.* **2** a fun

F

person is enjoyable to be with: *Terry is always fun to be with.*

**func·tion**[1] /'fʌŋkʃən/ *n* **1** the usual purpose of a thing, or the job that someone usually does: *What's the exact function of this program? | A manager has to perform many different functions.* **2** a large party or ceremonial event, especially for an important or official occasion: *The mayor has to attend all kinds of official functions.*

**function**[2] *v* [I] to work in a particular way or in the correct way: *Can you explain exactly how this new system will function?*

 **function as** sth *phr v* [T] to be used or work as something: *The new space station will function as a laboratory in space.*

**func·tion·al** /'fʌŋkʃənəl/ *adj* designed to be useful rather than attractive: *functional furniture* −**functionally** *adv*

**function key** /'.. ,./ *n* TECHNICAL a key on the KEYBOARD of a computer that tells it to do something

**fund**[1] /fʌnd/ *n* an amount of money that is kept for a particular purpose: *the school sports fund* −see also FUNDS

**fund**[2] *v* [T] to provide money for an activity, organization, event etc.: *How are you going to fund this project?*

**fun·da·men·tal**[1] /ˌfʌndə'mɛntəl/ *adj* **1** relating to the most basic and important parts of something: *He's promised to make some fundamental changes in the tax laws.* **2** necessary for something to exist or develop: *Water is fundamental to life.* −**fundamentally** *adv*: *two fundamentally different approaches to solving the problem*

**fundamental**[2] *n* **the fundamentals of sth** the most important ideas, rules etc. that something is based on: *a class in the fundamentals of computer programming*

**fun·da·men·tal·ist** /ˌfʌndə'mɛntəlɪst/ *n* someone who follows the rules of his/her religion very exactly and believes that no other religion is true −**fundamentalist** *adj* −**fundamentalism** *n* [U]

**fund·ing** /'fʌndɪŋ/ *n* [U] an amount of money used for a special purpose

**fund-rais·ing** /'. ,../ *adj* fund-raising events collect money for a specific purpose

**funds** /fʌndz/ *n* [plural] the money needed to do something: *It's a good idea, but we don't have the funds to do it.*

**fu·ner·al** /'fyunərəl/ *n* a ceremony, usually religious, for burying or burning a dead person: *The funeral will be held on Thursday at St. Patrick's church.*

**funeral home** /'... ,./, **funeral par·lor** /'... ,../ *n* the place where a body is kept before a funeral and where sometimes the funeral is held

**fun·gus** /'fʌŋgəs/ *n, plural* **fungi** /'fʌndʒaɪ, -gaɪ/ *or* **funguses** **1** [C,U] a simple plant without leaves, such as MUSHROOMs and MOLD, that grows in dark warm slightly wet places **2** [U] this type of plant, especially considered as a disease −**fungal** /'fʌŋgəl/ *adj*

**funk** /fʌŋk/ *n* [U] a type of popular music with a strong beat that is based on JAZZ and African music

**funk·y** /'fʌŋki/ *adj* INFORMAL **1** modern, fashionable, and interesting: *Where did you get those funky boots?* **2** relating to the strong RHYTHM of FUNK music

**fun·nel**[1] /'fʌnl/ *n* a tube with a wide top and a narrow bottom, used for pouring liquids or powders into a container

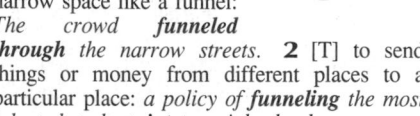
funnel

**funnel**[2] *v* **1** [I,T] to pass or to put something through a funnel or a narrow space like a funnel: *The crowd funneled through the narrow streets.* **2** [T] to send things or money from different places to a particular place: *a policy of funneling the most talented students into special schools*

**fun·nies** /'fʌniz/ *n* **the funnies** a number of different CARTOONs (=funny pictures) printed together in newspapers or magazines

**fun·ni·ly** /'fʌnəli/ *adv* ⇨ **oddly/funnily enough** (ENOUGH[1])

**funny**[1] /'fʌni/ *adj* **1** amusing you and making you laugh: *I have to tell you what she said. It was so funny. | You'd enjoy that book, it's really funny. | a funny joke* **2** strange or unexpected, and difficult to understand or explain: *What's that funny noise coming from upstairs?* **3** slightly ill: *I've felt a little funny all week, so I thought I'd take the day off.*

| SPOKEN PHRASES |
|---|
| **4 it's funny** used in order to say that you do not understand something that seems strange or unexpected: *It's funny - he looks so healthy but he's always getting sick.* **5 that's funny** said when you are surprised by something that has happened, that you cannot explain: *That's funny! She was here just a minute ago.* **6 the funny thing is** used in order to say what the strangest or most amusing part of a story or situation is: *The funny thing is, I knew what was going to happen before I even got to the meeting.* **7 very funny!** said when someone is laughing at you or making a joke that you do not think is funny |

−see usage note at FUN[1]

**funny**[2] *adv* in a strange or unusual way: *Judy's been acting kind of funny lately.*

**funny bone** /'.. ,./ *n* [singular] the soft part of your elbow that hurts a lot when you hit it against something

**fur** /fɚ/ n **1** [U] the thick soft hair that covers the bodies of some animals such as dogs and cats **2** [C,U] the fur-covered skin of an animal, used especially for making clothes, or a piece of clothing made from fur: *Several valuable furs were stolen last night.* | *a fur coat*

**fu·ri·ous** /'fyʊriəs/ adj **1** very angry: *Jim'll be furious with me if I'm late.* **2** done with a lot of uncontrolled energy or anger: *He woke up to a furious pounding at the door.* –**furiously** adv

**furl** /fɚl/ v [T] to roll or fold something such as a flag or sail –see also UNFURL

**fur·long** /'fɚlɔŋ/ n OLD-FASHIONED a unit for measuring length, equal to ⅛ of a mile or 201 meters

**fur·nace** /'fɚnɪs/ n a large container with a hot fire inside it, used for producing power or heat, or to melt metals and other materials

**fur·nish** /'fɚnɪʃ/ v [T] **1** to put furniture and other things into a house or room: *a room furnished with two beds* **2** to supply something that is necessary for a special purpose: *The company furnished us with a free copy of their catalog.* –**furnished** adj: *a furnished apartment*

**fur·nished** /'fɚnɪʃt/ adj a room, house, etc. that is furnished, has furniture in it: *a beautifully furnished room* | *We got a furnished apartment for $400 a month!* –opposite UNFURNISHED

**fur·nish·ings** /'fɚnɪʃɪŋz/ n [plural] the furniture and other things in a room, such as curtains, decorations etc.

**fur·ni·ture** /'fɚnɪtʃɚ/ n [U] large movable objects such as chairs, tables, and beds, that you use in a room, office etc.: *Aunt Sarah has a lot of antique furniture.* | *office furniture*

**fu·ror** /'fyʊrɔr/ n [singular] a sudden expression of anger or excitement among a large group of people: *His decision to resign caused quite a furor.*

**fur·row**[1] /'fɚou, 'fʌrou/ n a long deep fold or cut in the surface of something such as skin or the ground: *The deep furrows made it hard to walk across the field.*

**furrow**[2] v [T] to make a long deep fold or cut in the surface of something such as skin or the ground: *Saks furrowed his brow.* –**furrowed** adj

**fur·ry** /'fɚi/ adj covered with fur, or looking or feeling as if covered with fur: *furry material* | *a furry little rabbit*

**fur·ther**[1] /'fɚðɚ/ adv **1** more than before: *I have nothing further to say.* **2** a longer way in time or space: *The records don't go any further back than 1960.* | *Their home is further down the street.* **3** take sth further to do something at a more serious or higher level: *Hallas decided not to take the court case any further.* **4** FORMAL ⇨ FURTHERMORE –see usage note at FARTHER

**further**[2] adj additional: *Are there any further questions?*

**further**[3] v [T] FORMAL to help something to succeed: *They hope that the strike will further their cause.* (=help them to succeed)

**fur·ther·more** /'fɚðɚˌmɔr/ adv FORMAL in addition to what has already been written or said: *The house is far too small for us. Furthermore, it's not close enough to the city.*

**fur·thest** /'fɚðɪst/ adj, adv **1** to the greatest degree or amount, or more than before: *Smith's book has probably gone the furthest* (=done the most) *in trying to explain the causes of war.* **2** as far away as possible from a particular point in time, or from a particular place: *the houses furthest from the town center*

**fur·tive** /'fɚtɪv/ adj behaving as if you want to keep something secret: *a furtive glance* –**furtively** adv

**fu·ry** /'fyʊri/ n **1** [C,U] a state or feeling of extreme anger: *She was filled with fury.* | *Hank left the meeting in a fury.* **2** the fury of the wind/sea/storm etc. used in order to describe very bad weather: *After three hours, the fury of the storm began to pass.* **3** a fury of a state of great activity or strong feeling: *After the interview, Joe went home in a fury of frustration.*

**fuse**[1] /fyuz/ n **1** a short wire inside a piece of electrical equipment that melts if too much electricity passes through it: *The lights in the kitchen are all out. I think we must have blown a fuse.* (=melted the wire) **2** a thing such as a string that is connected to a bomb and used for making it explode **3** used in expressions relating to someone's temper: *Randy finally blew a fuse* (=got angry very suddenly) *and screamed at us.* | *I think Martina has a short fuse* (=gets angry easily) *when she's dealing with kids.*

**fuse**[2] v [I,T] **1** to join together and become one thing, or to join two things together: *His novel fuses historical information with a romantic story.* **2** TECHNICAL if metals, rocks etc. fuse together, they become melted and are joined together

**fuse·box** /'fyuzbɑks/ n a metal box that contains the FUSEs for the electrical system in a building

**fu·se·lage** /'fyusəˌlɑʒ, -lɪdʒ, -zə-/ n the main part of a plane, in which people sit or goods are carried –see picture at AIRPLANE

**fu·sion** /'fyuʒən/ n [C,U] **1** the action of combining things such as metals by heating them **2** the combination of separate things, groups, or ideas, or the action of joining them: *jazz-funk fusion* –compare FISSION

**fuss**[1] /fʌs/ n **1** [singular, U] attention or excitement that makes something seem more serious or important than it is: *Hey, what's all the fuss about?* (=why are people so excited, angry, busy etc.) **2** make a fuss/kick up a fuss to complain or become angry about something that other people do not think is important: *Cory made a fuss in the restaurant because her meat*

F

*was burned.* **3 make a fuss over sb/sth** to pay too much attention to someone or something that you like: *You always make a fuss over Kenny - it's really embarrassing!*

**fuss**[2] *v* [I] to complain or become upset: *Stop fussing! We'll be home soon!*

**fuss over** sb/sth *phr v* [T] to pay too much attention to someone or something that you like: *Grandma's always fussing over the kids.*

**fuss with** sth *phr v* [T] to move or touch something again and again in a nervous way: *Stop fussing with your hair!*

**fuss·y** /'fʌsi/ *adj* too concerned or worried about things that are not very important: *Kids are often fussy eaters*

**fu·tile** /'fyutl/ *adj* not effective or successful: *Janet ran after the thief in a futile attempt/effort to get her purse back.* –**futility** /fyu'tɪləti/ *n* [U]

**fu·ton** /'futɑn/ *n* a soft flat MATTRESS that can be used as a bed or folded into a chair

**fu·ture**[1] /'fyutʃɚ/ *n* **1 the future** the time that will happen after the present: *Do you have any plans for the future?* **2 in the future a)** at some time in the future: *I'm hoping to go to Atlanta in the near/immediate future.* (=soon) **b)** the next time you do the same activity: *In the future I'll be sure to reserve tickets.* **3** what will happen to someone or something: *My parents have already planned out my whole future.* **4** [singular, U] the possibility of being or becoming successful: *Pickford feels confident about the company's future.* **5 in future** used in order to warn someone or announce something about the future: *In future, you will need a note from your parents in order to leave campus for lunch.* **6 the future** TECHNICAL in grammar, the tense of a verb that shows that an action or state will happen or exist at a later time. It is often shown in English by the MODAL VERB "will" followed by a verb. In the sentence, "We will leave tomorrow," "will leave" is in the future tense

**future**[2] *adj* **1** likely to happen or exist during the time after the present: *I'd like you to meet Pam, my future wife/mother-in-law etc.* (=someone who will be your wife etc.) | *We'll discuss that in future contract talks.* **2** TECHNICAL in grammar, being a tense of a verb that shows a future action or state: *the future tense* **3 for future reference** kept or remembered in order to be used again at a later time: *Can I keep that article for future reference?*

**future per·fect** /ˌ.. '../ *n* **the future perfect** TECHNICAL in grammar, the tense of a verb that shows that an action will be completed before a particular time in the future. It is shown by the AUXILIARY VERBs "will have" followed by a PAST PARTICIPLE. In the sentence "I will have finished my finals by next Friday," "will have finished" is in the future perfect

**fu·tur·is·tic** /ˌfyutʃə'rɪstɪk/ *adj* futuristic ideas, books, movies etc. describe what might happen in the future, especially because of scientific developments

**fuzz** /fʌz/ *n* [U] INFORMAL small soft thin hairs, or a similar material on fruit such as PEACHes: *Kelly's baby has a light fuzz of black hair on her head.*

**fuzz·y** /'fʌzi/ *adj* **1** not easy to understand or not having very clear details: *Unfortunately all the photographs are a little fuzzy.* | *I only have a fuzzy idea of what she looks like.* **2** having a lot of very small thin hairs, fur etc. that look very soft: *a fuzzy sweater*

**fwy** the written abbreviation of FREEWAY

**FYI** the abbreviation of "for your information," used especially on MEMOs (=short business notes)

**G, g** /dʒi/ the seventh letter of the English alphabet

**G**[1] /dʒi/ *n* **1** [C,U] the fifth note in the musical SCALE of C, or the musical KEY based on this note **2** TECHNICAL an amount of force that is equal to the Earth's GRAVITY

**G**[2] *adj* the abbreviation of "general audience," used in order to show that a movie has been officially approved for people of all ages

**GA** the written abbreviation of Georgia

**gab** /gæb/ *v* **-bbed, -bbing** [I] INFORMAL to talk continuously, usually about things that are not important –**gabby** *adj*

**ga·ble** /'geɪbəl/ *n* the top part of a wall of a house where it joins with a pointed roof, making a shape like a TRIANGLE

**gadg·et** /'gædʒɪt/ *n* a small tool or machine that makes a particular job easier: *an interesting little gadget for cutting tomatoes* –see usage note at MACHINE[1]

**gaffe** /gæf/ *n* an embarrassing mistake made in a social situation

**gag**[1] /gæg/ *v* **-gged, -gging** **1** [I] to feel sick in a way that makes food come up from your stomach to your throat without coming out: *The smell from the garbage made me gag.* **2** [T] to tie someone's mouth with a piece of cloth so that s/he cannot make any noise

**gag**[2] *n* **1** INFORMAL a joke or funny story **2** a piece of cloth used in order to GAG someone

**gagged** /gægd/ *adj* having your mouth tied with a piece of cloth so that you cannot make any noise

**gag·gle** /'gægəl/ *n* a group of geese (GOOSE), or a noisy group of people

**gag o·rder** /ˈ. ͵../ *n* an order given by a court of law to prevent any public reporting of a case that is still being considered in the court

**gai·e·ty** /ˈgeɪəti/ *n* [U] OLD-FASHIONED the state of having fun and being cheerful

**gai·ly** /ˈgeɪli/ *adv* OLD-FASHIONED in a happy cheerful way

**gain¹** /geɪn/ *v* **1** [I,T] to get, win, or achieve something that is important, useful, or valuable: *You can gain a lot of computer experience doing this job.│A small army gained control of enemy territory.* –opposite LOSE **2 gain weight/ speed** to increase in weight or speed: *Bea has gained a lot of weight since Christmas.* **3 gain access a)** to be able to enter a room or building: *Somehow the thief had gained access to his apartment.* **b)** to be allowed to see or use something: *Marston had difficulty gaining access to official documents.*

**gain on** sb/sth *phr v* [T] to start getting closer to the person, car etc. that you are chasing: *Hurry up! They're gaining on us!*

---

**USAGE NOTE** gain, earn, and win

Use **gain** to talk about gradually getting more of something, such as an ability or quality: *You'll gain a lot of experience working here.* Use **earn** to talk about getting money by working: *She earns about $50,000 a year.* Use **win** to say that someone has gotten a prize in a competiton: *Brian won first prize in the skating competition.*

---

**gain²** *n* **1** [C,U] an increase in the amount or level of something: *We were delighted by their recent gain in popularity.│weight gain* **2** an advantage or an improvement: *gains in medical science*

**gait** /geɪt/ *n* [U] the way that someone walks

**gal** /gæl/ *n* INFORMAL a girl or woman

**ga·la** /ˈgælə, ˈgeɪlə/ *n* an event at which a lot of people are entertained and celebrate a special occasion –**gala** *adj*

**ga·lac·tic** /gəˈlæktɪk/ *adj* relating to the GAL-AXY

**gal·ax·y** /ˈgæləksi/ *n* any of the large groups of stars that are in the universe

**gale** /geɪl/ *n* a very strong wind: *Our back fence was blown down in the gale.* –see usage note at WEATHER

**gall** /gɔl/ *n* **have the gall to do sth** to do something without caring that other people think you are being rude or unreasonable: *She had the gall to say that I looked fat!*

**gal·lant** /ˈgælənt/ *adj* OLD-FASHIONED brave and kind: *a gallant soldier* –**gallantly** *adv* –**gallant·ry** *n* [U]

**gall blad·der** /ˈ. ͵../ *n* the organ in your body that stores BILE

**gal·ler·y** /ˈgæləri/ *n* **1** a room, hall, or building where people can look at famous paintings and other types of art: *I took Monique to the little art gallery on Ridge Street.* **2** a small expensive store where people can look at and buy art **3** an upper floor like a BALCONY inside a hall, church, or theater, where people can sit

**gal·ley** /ˈgæli/ *n* **1** a kitchen on a ship or a plane **2** a long Greek or Roman ship that was rowed by SLAVEs

**gal·li·vant** /ˈgælə͵vænt/ *v* [I] INFORMAL OR HUMOROUS to go from place to place enjoying yourself: *Oh, he's out **gallivanting around town**.*

**gal·lon** /ˈgælən/ *n* a unit for measuring liquid, equal to 4 QUARTs or 3.785 liters

**gal·lop¹** /ˈgæləp/ *v* [I] if a horse gallops it runs as fast as it can

**gallop²** *n* [singular] the fastest speed that a horse can go, or the movement of a horse at this speed: *riding at a gallop*

**gal·lop·ing** /ˈgæləpɪŋ/ *adj* increasing or developing very quickly: *galloping prices*

**gal·lows** /ˈgæloʊz/ *n, plural* **gallows** a structure that is used for killing criminals by hanging them

**ga·lore** /gəˈlɔr/ *adj* in large amounts or numbers: *He had toys and clothes galore.* ✗ DON'T SAY "He had galore clothes." ✗

**ga·losh·es** /gəˈlɑʃɪz/ *n* [plural] OLD-FASHIONED rubber shoes you wear over your normal shoes when it rains or snows

**gal·va·nize** /ˈgælvə͵naɪz/ *v* [T] to shock someone so much that s/he realizes s/he needs to do something to solve a problem or improve the situation: *News of the captain's death galvanized the soldiers into action.*

**gal·va·nized** /ˈgælvə͵naɪzd/ *adj* galvanized metal has been treated in a special way so that it does not RUST

**gam·bit** /ˈgæmbɪt/ *n* something you do or say in order to gain control in an argument, conversation, or meeting

**gam·ble¹** /ˈgæmbəl/ *v* **1** [I] to risk money or possessions because you might win a lot more if a card game, race etc. has the result you want: *Jack won $700 gambling in Las Vegas.* **2** [I,T] to do something risky because you hope a particular result will happen: *We're **gambling on** the weather being nice for our outdoor wedding.*

**gamble** sth ↔ **away** *phr v* [T] to lose money or possessions by gambling: *Tom's wife **gambled away** their car.*

**gamble²** *n* [singular] an action or plan that is risky because it might not be successful: *Buying an old car is a real gamble, you know.*

**gam·bler** /ˈgæmblɚ/ *n* someone who GAMBLEs, especially as a habit

**gam·bling** /ˈgæmblɪŋ/ *n* [U] the activity of risking money and possessions because you might win a lot more if a card game, race etc. has the result you want: *My parents think gambling should be illegal.*

**game**[1] /geɪm/ *n* **1** an activity or sport that people play for fun or in a competition: *Do you know any good card games?* **2** a particular occasion when you play a sport or activity: *Who won the football game last night?* **3** one of the parts of a competition, such as in tennis or BRIDGE **4** **play games** to behave in a dishonest or unfair way because you want to annoy or trick someone: *Stop playing games with me and tell me the truth!* **5** **be (just) a game** if something is just a game to you, you do not consider how serious or important it is: *Marriage is just a game to you, isn't it?* **6** [U] wild animals and birds that are hunted for food and as a sport —see also GAMES —see usage note at SPORT

**game**[2] *adj* willing to do something dangerous, new, or difficult: *I'm game if you are.* | *Who's game for trying bungee jumping?*

**game plan** /'. ./ *n* a plan for achieving success, especially in business: *What's the game plan for next year?*

**games** /geɪmz/ *n* [plural] a variety of sports played at one large event: *the Olympic Games*

**game show** /'. ./ *n* a television program in which people play games or answer questions in order to win money and prizes

**gam·ut** /'gæmət/ *n* [singular] a complete range of possibilities: *Riesling wines run the gamut from dry to sweet.* (=they include all the possibilities between two extremes) | *She had experienced the whole/full gamut of emotions in the weeks before she left home.*

**gan·der** /'gændɚ/ *n* **1** a male GOOSE **2** **have/take a gander at** INFORMAL to look at something: *Come here and have a gander at this!*

**gang**[1] /gæŋ/ *n* **1** a group of young people who often cause trouble and fight other similar groups: *Two members from their gang were shot.* **2** a group of people such as young criminals or prisoners who work together: *a gang of drug dealers*

**gang**[2] *v*
**gang up on** sb *phr v* [T] to join a group in order to criticize or attack someone: *Mommy! Tell Ricky and Paula to stop ganging up on me!*

**gang·bust·ers** /'gæŋˌbʌstɚz/ *n* **like gang-busters** INFORMAL very quickly and successfully: *The town is growing like gangbusters.*

**gang·land** /'gæŋlænd/ *adj* **a gangland killing/shooting/murder** a violent action that happens because of organized crime

**gan·gling** /'gæŋglɪŋ/, **gan·gly** /'gæŋgli/ *adj* unusually tall and thin and unable to move gracefully: *a gangly teenager*

**gang·plank** /'gæŋplæŋk/ *n* a board you walk on between a ship and the shore, or between two ships

**gan·grene** /'gæŋgrin, gæŋˈgrin/ *n* [U] the decay of the flesh on part of someone's body that happens when blood stops flowing to that area

**gang·ster** /'gæŋstɚ/ *n* a member of a group of violent criminals

**gang·way** /'gæŋweɪ/ *n* a large GANGPLANK

**gap** /gæp/ *n* **1** an empty space between two things or two parts of something: *Dana has a really big gap between her two front teeth.* | *a gap in the fence* —see picture at ESCAPE[1] **2** a difference between two situations, groups, amounts etc.: *a group trying to bridge the gap between college students and the local citizens* (=reduce the importance of the differences between them) | *a large age gap between Jorge and his sister* **3** something that is missing that stops something else from being good or complete: *No new producers have yet filled the gap in the market.* | *His death left a gap in my life.* | *a gap in her memory* **4** a period of time in which nothing happens or nothing is said: *an uncomfortable gap in the conversation* **5** a low place between two higher parts of a mountain

**gape** /geɪp/ *v* [I] **1** to look at something for a long time, usually with your mouth open, because you are very shocked: *Mother cried out and gaped at him in horror.* **2** also **gape open** to come apart or open widely

**gap·ing** /'geɪpɪŋ/ *adj* a gaping hole, wound, or mouth is very wide and open

**ga·rage** /gəˈrɑʒ, gəˈrɑdʒ/ *n* **1** a building, usually connected to your house, where you keep your car —see picture on page 471 **2** a place where cars are repaired

**garage sale** /.'. ,./ *n* a sale of used clothes, furniture, toys etc. from people's houses, usually held in someone's garage

**garb** /gɑrb/ *n* [U] LITERARY a particular style of clothing

**gar·bage** /'gɑrbɪdʒ/ *n* **1** [singular, U] waste material such as old food, dirty paper, and empty bags, or the container this is put in: *Can somebody take out the garbage?* | *Stop leaving garbage all over the house!* **2** INFORMAL statements or ideas that are silly or wrong; nonsense: *You didn't believe that garbage about him being in love, did you?*

**garbage can** /'.. ,./ *n* a large container with a lid in which you put waste materials, usually kept outside; TRASH CAN —see picture on page 471

**garbage col·lec·tor** /'.. .,../ *n* someone whose job is to remove waste from GARBAGE CANS

**garbage dis·pos·al** /'.. .,../ *n* a small machine in a kitchen SINK that cuts food waste into small pieces

**garbage man** /'.. ,./ *n* ⇨ GARBAGE COLLECTOR

**garbage truck** /'.. ˌ./ *n* a large vehicle used for carrying waste that is removed from people's GARBAGE CANs

**gar·bled** /'gɑrbəld/ *adj* confusing and not giving correct information: *The newspapers gave a garbled version of the story.*

**gar·den** /'gɑrdn/ *n* the part of someone's land used for growing flowers or vegetable and fruit plants: *Mom's planting a rose garden in the back yard.* –see also GARDENS

**gar·den·er** /'gɑrdnɚ/ *n* someone who does gardening as a job

**gar·den·ing** /'gɑrdn-ɪŋ/ *n* [U] the activity or job of making a garden, yard etc. look pretty by growing flowers, removing WEEDs etc.: *I'm hoping to do some gardening this weekend.*

**gar·dens** /'gɑrdnz/ *n* [plural] a public park where a lot of flowers and unusual plants are grown: *the Japanese Tea Gardens in Golden Gate park*

**gar·gan·tu·an** /gɑr'gæntʃuən/ *adj* extremely large: *a gargantuan bed*

**gar·gle** /'gɑrgəl/ *v* [I] to move medicine or liquid around in your throat in order to make it stop feeling sore, or to clean the inside of your mouth –**gargle** *n* [C,U]

**gar·goyle** /'gɑrgɔɪl/ *n* a stone figure shaped like the face of a strange creature, usually on the roofs of old buildings

**gar·ish** /'gærɪʃ, 'gɛr-/ *adj* very brightly colored and unpleasant to look at: *the garish carpet in the hotel lobby*

**gar·land** /'gɑrlənd/ *n* a ring of flowers or leaves, worn for decoration or in special ceremonies

**gar·lic** /'gɑrlɪk/ *n* [U] a small plant like an onion with a very strong taste, used in cooking –see picture on page 470

**gar·ment** /'gɑrmənt/ *n* FORMAL a piece of clothing

**gar·net** /'gɑrnɪt/ *n* a dark red stone used in jewelry

**gar·nish**¹ /'gɑrnɪʃ/ *v* [T] **1** to decorate food with a small piece of a fruit or vegetable **2** TECHNICAL also **gar·nish·ee** /'gɑrnə'ʃi/ to take money from someone's wages because s/he has not paid his/her debts

**garnish**² *n* a small piece of a fruit or vegetable that you use to decorate food

**gar·ret** /'gærɪt/ *n* LITERARY a small room at the top of a house

**gar·ri·son** /'gærəsən/ *n* a group of soldiers who live in a particular area in order to defend it –**garrison** *v* [T]

**gar·ru·lous** /'gærələs/ *adj* always talking too much

**gar·ter** /'gɑrtɚ/ *n* **1** an ELASTIC (=material that stretches) band that is used for holding socks or STOCKINGs up **2** a band worn for decoration on the upper part of a woman's leg

**garter snake** /'.. ˌ./ *n* a harmless American snake with colored lines along its back

**gas**¹ /gæs/ *n* **1** [U] also **gasoline** a liquid made from PETROLEUM, used for producing power in the engines of cars, planes etc.: *We need to **stop for gas** (=buy gas) before we drive into the city.* **2** [C,U] a substance like air that is not liquid or solid, and usually cannot be seen: *hydrogen gas* **3** [U] a clear substance like air that is burned and used for cooking and heating: *a gas stove* **4** [U] INFORMAL the condition of having air or gas in your stomach: *Eating too much fried food gives me gas.* **5** **the gas** also **gas pedal** the part of a car that you press with your foot in order to make the car move faster; ACCELERATOR

**gas**² *v* [T] to poison or kill someone with gas

**gas cham·ber** /'. ˌ../ *n* a room that is filled with poisonous gas, used for killing people or animals

**gas·e·ous** /'gæsiəs, 'gæʃəs/ *adj* like gas or in the form of gas

**gash** /gæʃ/ *n* a large deep cut in something –**gash** *v* [T]

**gas·ket** /'gæskɪt/ *n* a flat piece of rubber between two surfaces of a machine that prevents steam, oil etc. from escaping

**gas mask** /'. ./ *n* a piece of equipment worn over your face that protects you from breathing poisonous gases

**gas·o·line** /ˌgæsə'lin, 'gæsəˌlin/ *n* [U] ⇨ GAS¹

**gasp** /gæsp/ *v* [I] **1** to quickly breathe in a lot of air because you are having difficulty breathing normally: *Kim crawled out of the pool, gasping for air/breath.* **2** to make a short sudden noise when you breathe in, usually because you are surprised or shocked: *"Oh no!" she gasped.* –**gasp** *n*

**gas sta·tion** /'. ˌ../ *n* a place where you can buy gas for your car

**gas·sy** /'gæsi/ *adj* uncomfortable because you have too much gas in your stomach

**gas·tric** /'gæstrɪk/ *adj* TECHNICAL **1** relating to the stomach: *gastric ulcers* **2** **gastric juices** the acids in the stomach that break food into smaller parts

**gas·tro·nom·ic** /ˌgæstrə'nɑmɪk/ *adj* relating to cooking good food, or the pleasure of eating it: *the gastronomic delights of Chinatown*

**gas·works** /'gæswɚks/ *n* a factory that produces the gas used for heating and cooking

**gate** /geɪt/ *n* **1** the part of a fence or outside wall that you can open and close like a door: *Who left the gate open?* **2** the part of an airport that passengers walk through

**gate**

when getting onto a plane: *Flight 207 to Chicago will be leaving from gate 16.*

**gate·crash** /'geɪt˺kræʃ/ *v* [I,T] to go to a party or event that you have not been invited to –**gatecrasher** *n*

**gate·way** /'geɪt˺weɪ/ *n* **1** an opening in a fence or outside wall that can be closed with a gate **2 the gateway to** a place such as a city that you go through in order to reach a much larger place: *St. Louis was once the gateway to the West.* **3** a connection between two different computer NETWORKs that helps them to work together

**gath·er** /'gæðɚ/ *v* **1** [I] to come together and form a group: *A crowd gathered around to watch the fight.* **2** [T] to believe that something is true based on what you have already seen or heard: *From what I can gather/As far as I can gather* (=I think it is true that) *he never intended to sell the house.* **3** [T] to gradually obtain information, ideas etc.: *I'm currently trying to gather new ideas for my next novel.* **4 gather force/speed/intensity etc.** to become stronger, faster, more INTENSE etc.: *The car gathered speed quickly as it rolled down the hill.* **5** [T] also **gather up** to collect or move similar things into one pile or place: *"Wait for me," said Anna, gathering up her books.*

**gath·ered** /'gæðɚd/ *adj* having small folds produced by pulling the edge of a piece of cloth together: *a gathered skirt* –**gathers** *n* [plural]

**gath·er·ing** /'gæðərɪŋ/ *n* a group of people meeting together for a particular purpose: *a large gathering of Vietnam veterans*

**gauche** /goʊʃ/ *adj* awkward and uncomfortable with other people, and always saying or doing the wrong thing

**gaud·y** /'gɔdi/ *adj* clothes, decorations etc. that are gaudy are too bright and look cheap

**gauge¹** /geɪdʒ/ *n* **1** an instrument that measures the amount or size of something: *a car's gas gauge | a depth gauge* –see picture on page 469 **2** a standard by which something else is measured: *The amount of money you make is not the only gauge of your success.* **3** the width or thickness of something such as a wire, a piece of metal, or the BARREL of a gun: *a twelve-gauge shotgun*

**gauge²** *v* [T] **1** to judge what someone's feelings, intentions etc. are: *It's difficult to gauge exactly how he's going to respond.* **2** to measure or judge something using a particular instrument or method: *Grades are still the best way to gauge a student's success.*

**gaunt** /gɔnt, gant/ *adj* very thin and pale, especially because of illness or worry

**gaunt·let** /'gɔnt˺lɪt, 'gant˺-/ *n* **1 run the gauntlet** to be criticized or attacked by a lot of people: *There was no way to avoid running the gauntlet of media attention.* **2 throw down the gauntlet** to invite someone to argue or

compete with you **3** a thick long GLOVE worn for protection

**gauze** /gɔz/ *n* [U] a very thin light cloth used for covering wounds and making clothes –**gauzy** *adj*

**gave** /geɪv/ *v* the past tense of GIVE

**gav·el** /'gævəl/ *n* a small hammer that someone in charge of a law court, meeting etc. hits on a table to get people's attention

**gawk** /gɔk/ *v* [I] to look at someone or something in a way that is rude, stupid, or annoying: *Lenny couldn't stop gawking at the car accident.*

**gawk·y** /'gɔki/ *adj* awkward in the way you move: *a tall gawky teenager*

**gay¹** /geɪ/ *adj* **1** sexually attracted to people of the same sex; HOMOSEXUAL: *Did you know that Ken is gay?* –compare LESBIAN **2** OLD-FASHIONED bright and attractive: *a room painted in gay colors* **3** OLD-FASHIONED happy and cheerful: *gay laughter*

**gay²** *n* someone, especially a man, who is sexually attracted to people of the same sex; HOMOSEXUAL: *a parade organized by gays and lesbians*

**gaze¹** /geɪz/ *v* [I] to look at someone or something for a long time: *He sat for hours just gazing out the window.*

**gaze²** *n* [singular] a long steady look: *Molly felt uncomfortable under the teacher's steady gaze.*

**ga·ze·bo** /gə'zibou/ *n* a small shelter in a garden or park that you can sit in

**ga·zelle** /gə'zɛl/ *n* an animal like a small DEER that moves very quickly and gracefully

**ga·zette** /gə'zɛt/ *n* a newspaper or magazine

**gear¹** /gɪr/ *n* **1** [C,U] the machinery in a vehicle that turns power from the engine into movement: *There's a weird noise every time I change gears.* (=go from one gear to another one) **2** [U] special equipment, clothing etc. that you need for a particular activity: *camping gear* **3** [U] a piece of machinery that does a particular job: *the landing gear on a plane*

**gear²** *v* [T] **1 be geared to** to be organized in order to achieve a particular purpose: *All his training was geared to winning an Olympic gold medal.* **2 be geared up** to be prepared to do a particular activity: *The factory's geared up to make 300 cars a day.*

**gear·box** /'gɪrbaks/ *n* a metal box that contains the GEARs of a vehicle

**gear shift** /'. ./ *n* a long stick with a handle that you move to change GEARs in a vehicle –see picture on page 469

**GED** *n* **the GED** General Equivalency Diploma; a DIPLOMA that can be studied for at any time by people who left HIGH SCHOOL without finishing

**gee** /dʒi/ *interjection* OLD-FASHIONED said when you are surprised or annoyed: *Aw, gee, Mom, I'm not ready to go to bed.*

G

**geek** /gik/ *n* SLANG someone who is not popular because s/he wears strange clothes or does strange things – **geeky** *adj*

**geese** /gis/ *n* the plural of GOOSE

**geez** /dʒiz/ *interjection* ⇨ JEEZ

**gee·zer** /'gizɚ/ *n* SLANG an impolite word meaning an old man

**Gei·ger count·er** /'gaɪgɚ ˌkaʊntɚ/ *n* an instrument that finds and measures RADIOACTIVITY

**gei·sha** /'geɪʃə, 'giʃə/ *n* a Japanese woman who is trained to dance, play music, and entertain men

**gel**[1] /dʒɛl/ *n* [C,U] a thick wet substance like JELLY, used in beauty or cleaning products: *hair gel*

**gel**[2] *v* **-lled, -lling** [I] **1** if a liquid gels, it becomes thicker **2** if an idea or plan gels, it becomes clearer or more definite: *They were going to make a movie together, but the project never gelled.* **3** if people gel, they begin to work together well as a group

**gel·a·tin** /'dʒɛlətən, -lət⁻n/ *n* [U] a clear substance from boiled animal bones, used for making liquid food more solid

**geld·ing** /'gɛldɪŋ/ *n* a male horse that has had its TESTICLEs removed

**gem** /dʒɛm/ *n* a jewel that is cut into a particular shape

**Gem·i·ni** /'dʒɛməˌnaɪ/ *n* **1** [singular] the third sign of the ZODIAC, represented by TWINs **2** someone born between May 21 and June 21

**gen·der** /'dʒɛndɚ/ *n* **1** [C,U] FORMAL the fact of being male or female: *A person cannot be denied a job because of age, race, or gender.* **2** [U] TECHNICAL a system in some languages for separating words into special groups of grammar

**gene** /dʒin/ *n* a part of a cell that controls the development of a quality that is passed on to a living thing from its parents

**ge·ne·al·o·gy** /ˌdʒiniˈɑlədʒi/ *n* [C,U] the history of a family, or the study of family histories – **genealogical** /ˌdʒiniəˈlɑdʒɪkəl/ *adj* – **genealogist** /ˌdʒiniˈɑlədʒɪst/ *n*

**gen·er·al**[1] /'dʒɛnərəl/ *adj*
**1** ▶NOT DETAILED◀ describing only the main features of something, not the details: *a general introduction to computers | I think I've got the general idea now.* (=I understand the main points)
**2 in general a)** usually, or in most situations: *In general, the Republicans favor tax cuts.* **b)** as a whole: *I think people in general are against nuclear weapons.*
**3** ▶AS A WHOLE◀ considering the whole of a thing, group, or situation, rather than its parts; OVERALL: *The general condition of the car is good, but it does need new tires. | The general standard of the students isn't very high.*
**4** ▶FOR MOST PEOPLE◀ affecting or shared by everyone or most people: *How soon will the drug be available for general use?*

**5** ▶NOT LIMITED◀ not limited to one subject, service, product etc.: *a general education* – opposite SPECIALIZED
**6 as a general rule** usually, or in most situations: *As a general rule, you should call before visiting someone.*
**7 the general public** the ordinary people in a society: *The AIDS ad is designed to educate the general public.*

**general**[2] **General** *n* an officer with a very high rank in the Army, Air Force, or Marines

**general e·lec·tion** /ˌ... .'../ *n* an election in which all the people in a country elect a government

**gen·er·al·i·ty** /ˌdʒɛnəˈrælət̬i/ *n* a statement that does not mention facts, details etc.: *Can we stop talking in generalities and get to the point?*

**gen·er·al·i·za·tion** /ˌdʒɛnərələˈzeɪʃən/ *n* a statement that may be true in most situations, but is not true all of the time: *You shouldn't make sweeping generalizations* (=say something is always true) *about other countries.*

**gen·er·al·ize** /'dʒɛnərəˌlaɪz/ *v* [I] **1** to make a statement about people, events, or facts without mentioning any details: *It's difficult to generalize about a subject as big as American history.* **2** to form an opinion about something after considering only a few examples of it: *It's not fair to generalize from a few cases that all politicians are dishonest.*

**gen·er·al·ly** /'dʒɛnərəli/ *adv* **1** considering something as a whole: *Her school work is generally very good.* **2** by or to most people: *It's generally believed that the story is true. | an agreement that is generally acceptable* **3** usually, or most of the time: *Megan generally works late on Fridays.* **4 generally speaking** used in order to introduce a statement that is true most of the time, but not always: *Generally speaking, movie audiences like happy endings.*

**general store** /ˌ... './ *n* a store that sells a lot of different things, especially in a small town

**gen·er·ate** /'dʒɛnəˌreɪt/ *v* [T] **1** to produce or make something: *Our discussion generated a lot of new ideas.* **2** to produce energy such as heat or electricity

**gen·er·a·tion** /ˌdʒɛnəˈreɪʃən/ *n* **1** all the people who are about the same age, especially in a family: *Three generations of Monroes have lived in this house. | the younger/older generation* **2** the average period of time between someone's birth and the birth of his/her children: *A generation ago, no one had home computers.* **3** a group of machines, products etc. at a similar stage of development: *the next generation of TV technology* **4** [U] the process of producing something, or making something happen: *the generation of electricity*

**generation gap** /ˌ..'.. ˌ./ *n* [singular] the lack

G

of understanding between GENERATIONs, caused by their different attitudes and experiences

**Generation X** /ˌ...ˌ.. '.../ *n* [U] INFORMAL the group of people who were born during the late 1960s and the early 1970s in the US

**gen·er·a·tor** /'dʒɛnəˌreɪtɚ/ *n* a machine that produces electricity

**ge·ner·ic** /dʒə'nɛrɪk/ *adj* **1** a generic product does not have a special name to show that it is made by a particular company: *generic drugs* **2** relating to a whole group of things, rather than to one in particular: *Fine Arts is a generic term for subjects such as painting, music, and sculpture.* –**generically** *adv*

**gen·er·os·i·ty** /ˌdʒɛnə'rɑsəṭi/ *n* [C,U] willingness to give money, time etc. to help someone, or something you do that shows this: *Thank you for your generosity.*

**gen·er·ous** /'dʒɛnərəs/ *adj* **1** willing to give more money, time etc. to help someone than is expected: *It is very generous of you to help.* **2** larger than the usual amount: *a generous slice of cake*

**gen·e·sis** /'dʒɛnəsɪs/ *n* [singular] FORMAL the beginning of something

**gene ther·a·py** /ˌ. '.../ *n* [U] a way of using GENEs to treat diseases

**ge·net·ic** /dʒə'nɛṭɪk/ *adj* relating to GENEs or GENETICS –**genetically** *adv*

**genetic en·gi·neer·ing** /.ˌ.. ..'../ *n* [U] the science of changing the GENEs of a plant or animal to make it stronger or more healthy

**ge·net·ics** /dʒə'nɛṭɪks/ *n* [plural] the study of how the qualities of living things are passed on through the GENEs –**geneticist** *n*

**ge·nial** /'dʒinyəl, -niəl/ *adj* cheerful, kind, and friendly

**ge·nie** /'dʒini/ *n* a magical spirit in old Arabian stories

**gen·i·tals** /'dʒɛnəṭlz/, **genitalia** /ˌdʒɛnə-'teɪlyə/ *n* [plural] TECHNICAL the outer sex organs –**genital** *adj*

**ge·nius** /'dʒinyəs/ *n* [C,U] a very high level of intelligence or ability, or someone who has this: *Sandra's a genius at crossword puzzles.* | *Even the movie's title was a stroke of genius* (=a very smart idea)

**gen·o·cide** /'dʒɛnəˌsaɪd/ *n* [U] the deliberate murder of a race of people: *What the army did there was an act of genocide.* –**genocidal** /ˌdʒɛnə'saɪdl/ *adj*

**gen·re** /'ʒɑnrə/ *n* FORMAL a type of art, music, literature etc. that has a particular style or subject: *the science fiction genre*

**gent** /dʒɛnt/ *n* INFORMAL ⇨ GENTLEMAN

**gen·teel** /dʒɛn'til/ *adj* extremely polite because you belong to a high social class –**gentility** /dʒɛn'tɪləṭi/ *n* [U]

**gen·tile** /'dʒɛntaɪl/ *n* someone who is not Jewish –**gentile** *adj*

**gen·tle** /'dʒɛnṭl/ *adj* **1** careful in the way you behave, so that you do not hurt or damage anyone or anything: *Be gentle with the baby, Michael.* | *Mia's such a gentle person!* **2** not strong, loud, or forceful: *a gentle voice* **3** a gentle wind or rain is soft and light **4** a gentle hill or slope is not very steep –**gentleness** *n* [U] –**gently** *adv*

**gen·tle·man** /'dʒɛnṭlmən/ *n, plural* **gentlemen** **1** a man who is polite and behaves well toward other people: *Roland was a perfect gentleman last night.* **2** a polite word meaning a man whose name you do not know: *Can you show this gentleman to his seat?* –**gentlemanly** *adj*

**gen·tri·fi·ca·tion** /ˌdʒɛntrəfə'keɪʃən/ *n* [U] the change that happens when people with more money go to live in an area where poor people have lived

**gen·try** /'dʒɛntri/, **the gentry** *n* OLD-FASHIONED people who belong to a high social class

**gen·u·flect** /'dʒɛnyəˌflɛkt/ *v* [I] to bend one knee when in a church or a holy place, as a sign of respect

**gen·u·ine** /'dʒɛnyuɪn/ *adj* **1** a genuine feeling or desire is one that you really have, not one that you only pretend to have; sincere: *Mrs. Liu showed a genuine concern for Lisa's well-being.* **2** something genuine really is what it seems to be; real: *a genuine diamond* –**genuinely** *adv*

**ge·nus** /'dʒinəs/ *n, plural* **genera** /'dʒɛnərə/ TECHNICAL a group of animals or plants that are closely related, but cannot BREED with each other

**ge·o·gra·phi·cal** /ˌdʒiə'græfɪkəl/, **ge·o·graph·ic** /ˌdʒiə'græfɪk/ *adj* relating to GEOGRAPHY: *geographical maps of the area*

**ge·og·ra·phy** /dʒi'ɑgrəfi/ *n* [U] the study of the countries of the world, including such things as oceans, rivers, mountains, cities, population, and weather –**geographer** *n*

**ge·ol·o·gy** /dʒi'ɑlədʒi/ *n* [U] the study of materials such as rocks, soil, and minerals, and the way they have changed since the Earth was formed –**geological** /ˌdʒiə'lɑdʒɪkəl/ **geologic** /ˌdʒiə'lɑdʒɪk/ *adj* –**geologist** /dʒi'ɑlədʒɪst/ *n*

**ge·o·met·ric** /ˌdʒiə'mɛtrɪk/, **ge·o·met·ric·al** /ˌdʒiə'mɛtrɪkəl/ *adj* **1** a GEOMETRIC shape or pattern has straight lines that form squares, circles etc. **2** relating to GEOMETRY

**ge·om·e·try** /dʒi'ɑmətri/ *n* [U] the study in mathematics of the form and relationships of angles, lines, curves, shapes, and solid objects

**ge·ra·ni·um** /dʒə'reɪniəm/ *n* a common house plant with colorful flowers and large round leaves

**ger·bil** /'dʒɚbəl/ *n* a small animal with soft fur and a long tail, that is often kept as a pet

**ger·i·at·ric** /ˌdʒɛri'ætrɪk/ *adj* **1** relating to GERIATRICS: *a geriatric hospital* **2** INFORMAL too old or too weak to work well: *A geriatric truck had stalled near the highway.*

**ger·i·at·rics** /ˌdʒɛriˈætrɪks/ *n* [U] the medical treatment and care of older people

**germ** /dʒɚm/ *n* **1** a very small living thing that can make you ill: *Cover your mouth when you cough so you won't spread germs.* **2 the germ of an idea/hope etc.** the beginning of an idea etc. that may develop into something else

**Ger·man¹** /ˈdʒɚmən/ *adj* **1** relating to or coming from Germany **2** relating to the German language

**German²** *n* **1** [U] the language used in Germany **2** someone from Germany

**German mea·sles** /ˌ.. ˈ../ *n* [plural] a disease that causes red spots on the body

**German shep·herd** /ˌ.. ˈ../ *n* a large dog that looks like a WOLF, often used by the police and for guarding property

**ger·mi·nate** /ˈdʒɚməˌneɪt/ *v* [I,T] if a seed germinates or is germinated, it begins to grow –**germination** /ˌdʒɚməˈneɪʃən/ *n* [U]

**ger·ry·man·der·ing** /ˈdʒɛriˌmændərɪŋ/ *n* [U] the action of changing the borders of an area before an election, so that one person or party has an unfair advantage –**gerrymander** *v* [I,T]

**ger·und** /ˈdʒɛrənd/ *n* TECHNICAL in grammar, a noun formed from the PRESENT PARTICIPLE of a verb, such as "reading" in the sentence "He enjoys reading"

**ges·ta·tion** /dʒɛˈsteɪʃən/ *n* TECHNICAL [U] the process of a baby developing inside its mother's body, or the period when this happens: *a nine-month gestation period*

**ges·tic·u·late** /dʒɛˈstɪkyəˌleɪt/ *v* [I] to move your arms and hands to express something, especially while you are speaking

**ges·ture¹** /ˈdʒɛstʃɚ, ˈdʒɛstʃɚ/ *n* **1** [C,U] a movement of your head, arm, or hand that shows what you mean or how you feel: *a rude gesture* **2** something you do or say to show that you care about someone or something: *a gesture of friendship/support*

**gesture²** *v* [I] to tell someone something by moving your arms, hands, or head: *Tom gestured for me to move out of the way.*

**get** /gɛt/ *v* **got, gotten, getting**
**1** ▶BUY/OBTAIN◀ [T] to buy or obtain something: *Could you get me some coffee from the machine?* | *My mom got these earrings for a dollar.* | *Jill knows a woman who can get the material for you.*
**2** ▶RECEIVE◀ [T] to receive or be given something: *How much money did you get from Grandma?* | *We haven't gotten any mail for three days.* | *Did you get the job?*
**3 have got** ⇨ HAVE²: *I've got a lot of work to do.*
**4** ▶BECOME◀ [linking verb] to change from one state, feeling etc. to another; become: *Vicky got really mad at him.* | *If I wear wool, my skin*

gets all red. | *The weather had suddenly gotten cold.* | *Mom told you that you'd get hurt if you did that!* –see usage note at BECOME
**5** ▶CHANGE POSITION/STATE◀ [I,T] to change or move from one place, position, or state to another, or to make something do this: *How did the guy get into their house?* | *I can't get the milk open.* | *Everybody get down on the floor!* | *Can you get the bags out of the car for me?*
**6** ▶REACH A PLACE◀ [I] to reach a particular place or position: *She got downstairs, and found that the room was full of smoke.* | *You might be disappointed when you get to the end of the book.*
**7** ▶BRING/TAKE◀ [T] to bring someone or something back from somewhere, or take something from somewhere: *Carrie, can you go upstairs and get me that book, please?* | *She got some money out of her purse.*
**8 get sb/sth to do sth** to make someone or something do something, or persuade someone to do something: *Bert couldn't get the light to work.* | *I tried to get Jill to come out tonight, but she was too tired.*
**9 get to do sth** to have an opportunity to do something: *Tom got to drive a Porsche today.* | *I'm so tired. I didn't get to sit down all day.*
**10 get sth fixed/done etc.** to fix something, finish something etc., or have someone else do this: *I have to get the paper done by 9:00 tomorrow morning.* | *We'll have to get this room painted before they move in.*
**11** ▶ILLNESS◀ [T] to have an illness: *I got the flu when we were on vacation.*
**12 get the feeling/idea etc.** to start to feel, think etc. something: *I get the feeling you don't like her.*
**13** ▶MONEY◀ [T] to earn a particular amount of money, or receive a particular amount of money by selling something: *How much can you get for a house this size?*
**14 get the bus/a flight etc.** to travel somewhere on a bus, plane etc.: *She managed to get a flight into Detroit.*
**15 you/we/they get sth** SPOKEN used in order to say that something happens or exists: *We get a lot of rain around here in the summer.*
**16** ▶UNDERSTAND◀ INFORMAL [T] to understand something: *Tracey didn't get the joke.* | *Oh, I get it now - you have to divide 489 by 3.*
**17 get going/moving** SPOKEN to make yourself do something more quickly: *We have to get going, or we'll be late!*
**18 get to know/like etc.** to gradually begin to know, like etc. someone or something: *As you get to know the city, I'm sure you'll like it better.*
**19 get the door/phone** SPOKEN to go to the door to see who is there, or answer the telephone: *Val, can you get the phone, please - I'm making dinner.*

G

**20** ▸RADIO/TV◂ [T] to be able to receive a particular radio signal or television station: *Her TV doesn't get channel 24.* –see also HAVE TO –see usage note at BECOME

**get** sth ↔ **across** *phr v* [T] to be able to make someone understand an idea or piece of information: *It was difficult to get my idea across to the committee.*

**gct along** *phr v* [I] **1** to have a friendly relationship with someone or a group of people: *Rachel doesn't get along with Cy at all.* **2 get along without sb/sth** to be able to continue doing something without having someone or something to help: *We'll have to get along without the car until the new part arrives.*

**get around** *phr v* **1** [T **get around** sth] to find a way of dealing with a problem, usually by avoiding it: *businesses looking for ways to get around the tax laws* **2** [I] to move or travel to different places: *His new wheelchair lets him get around more easily.* **3** [I] if news or information gets around, a lot of people hear about it: *If this news gets around, we'll have reporters calling us all day.* **4** [T **get around** sb/sth] to solve a problem in an unusual and intelligent way: *We have to find some way to get around these difficulties.* **5 sb gets around** SPOKEN used in order to say that someone has had sex with a lot of people

**get around to** sth *phr v* [T] to do something you have been intending to do for a long time: *I meant to go to the bookstore, but I never got around to it.*

**get at** sth *phr v* [T] **1** to try to explain something, especially something difficult: *Did you understand what he was getting at?* **2 get at the meaning/facts etc.** to discover the meaning of something, the facts about something or someone etc.: *The judge asked a few questions to try to get at the truth.* **3** to be able to reach or find something easily: *I could see the ring stuck under there, but I couldn't get at it.*

**get away** *phr v* [I] **1** to leave a place, especially when this is difficult: *Barney had to work late, and couldn't get away until 9:00.* **2** to escape from someone who is chasing you: *The two men got away in a blue pickup truck.* **3** to go on vacation: *Are you going to be able to get away this summer?*

**get away with** sth *phr v* [T] to not be noticed or punished when you have done something wrong: *The kid was kicking me, and his mother just let him get away with it!*

**get** sb **back** *phr v* [T] also **get back at** sb to do something to hurt or embarrass someone who has hurt or embarrassed you: *Jerry's trying to think of ways to get back at her for leaving him.*

**get back to** sth *phr v* [T] **1** to start doing something again after not doing it for a while: *She found it hard to get back to work after her vacation.* **2** to talk or write to someone at a later time because you are busy, or do not know how to answer his/her question: *I'll try to get back to you later today.*

**get behind** *phr v* [I] to not do or pay as much of something as you should have by a particular time: *They made people pay extra if they got behind on their rent.*

**get by** *phr v* [I] **1** to have enough money to buy the things you need, but not more: *He only earns just enough to get by.* **2 get by on $10/$200 etc.** to manage to spend only $10, $200 etc. during a particular amount of time: *families trying to get by on $800 a month*

**get down** *phr v* **1** [T **get** sth ↔ **down**] to write something down on paper, especially quickly: *Let me get your number down before I forget it.* **2** [T **get** sb **down**] INFORMAL to make someone feel unhappy: *You can't let the illness get you down, or you won't get better.* **3** [T **get** sth ↔ **down**] to be able to swallow food or drink

**get down to** sth *phr v* [T] to finally start doing something that will take a lot of time or effort: *By the time we finally got down to work, it was already 10:00.*

**get in** *phr v* **1** [I] to be allowed or able to enter a place: *You can't get in to the club without an I.D. card.* **2** [I] to arrive at a particular time or in a particular place: *What time does the plane/bus get in? | Steve just got in a few minutes ago.* **3** [T **get** sth **in**] to send or give something to a particular person, company etc.: *Make sure you get your homework in by Thursday.*

**get in on** sth *phr v* [T] INFORMAL to become involved in something that other people are doing: *The kids saw us playing ball and wanted to get in on the game.*

**get into** sth *phr v* [T] **1** to be accepted by a college or university: *Liz got into the graduate program at Berkeley.* **2** INFORMAL to begin to be interested in an activity or subject: *When I was in high school I got into rap music.* **3** INFORMAL to begin to have a discussion about something: *Let's not get into it right now. I'm tired.*

**get off** *phr v* **1** [I,T] to finish working: *What time do you get off (work)?* **2** [I,T **get** sb **off**] to get little or no punishment for a crime, or to help someone escape punishment: *I can't believe his lawyers managed to get him off.* **3 where does** sb **get off doing** sth SPOKEN said when you think someone has done something to you that s/he does not have a right to do: *Where does he get off telling me how to live my life?*

**get off on** sth *phr v* [T] SLANG to be excited by someone or something, especially sexually

**get on** *phr v* **1 get on with** sth to continue doing something after you have stopped doing it for a while: *Can't we just get on with the job, so we can go home on time?* **2 be getting on (in years)** to be old

**get onto** sth *phr v* [T] to start talking about a

particular subject: *Then, we **got onto** the subject of women, and Craig wouldn't shut up.*

**get out** *phr v* **1** [I] to escape from a place: *How did the dog **get out** of the yard?* **2** [T **get** sth ↔ **out**] to produce or publish something: *We have to **get** the book **out** next month.*

**get out of** sth *phr v* [T] **1** to not do something you have promised to do or are supposed to do: *She couldn't **get out of** the meeting, so she canceled our dinner.* **2 get pleasure/ satisfaction out of** sth to feel happy or satisfied because of doing something: *She **gets** a lot of pleasure **out of** acting.*

**get over** *phr v* **1** [T] to become healthy again after being sick, or to feel better after an upsetting experience: *The doctor said it will take a couple weeks to **get over** the infection.* **2 get** sth **over with** to finish something you do not like doing as quickly as possible: *"It should only hurt a little." "OK. Just **get** it **over with**."* **3 sb can't/couldn't get over** SPOKEN said when you are surprised, shocked, or amused by something: *I can't **get over** the way you look. You're so thin!*

**get through** *phr v* **1** [T] to manage to deal with an unpleasant experience until it ends: *I was so embarrassed. I don't know how I **got through** the rest of the dinner.* **2** [I] to be able to talk to someone on the telephone without any problems: *When she finally **got through**, the department manager wasn't there.* **3** [I,T] if a law gets through Congress, it is officially accepted

**get through to** sb *phr v* [T] to be able to make someone understand something difficult: *Ben tried to apologize a few times, but he couldn't **get through to** her.*

**get to** sb *phr v* [T] INFORMAL to upset or annoy someone: *Don't let him **get to** you, honey. He's just teasing you.*

**get together** *phr v* [I] **1** to meet with someone or with a group of people: *Every time he **got together** with Murphy they argued.* **2** to start a romantic relationship with someone **3 get yourself together/get it together** to begin to be in control of your life and your emotions: *It took a year for me to **get** myself **together** after she left.*

**get up** *phr v* **1** [I,T **get** sb **up**] to wake up and get out of your bed, especially in the morning, or to make someone do this: *I have to **get up** at 6:00 tomorrow. | Could you **get** me **up** at 8:00?* **2** [I] to stand up: *Corrinne **got up** slowly and went to the window.* **3 get it up** SLANG to be able to have an ERECTION

**get·a·way** /'gɛtə,weɪ/ *n* **make a getaway** to escape from a place or a bad situation, especially after doing something illegal

**get-to·geth·er** /'. .,../ *n* a friendly informal meeting or party: *a small **get-together** with some friends*

**get·up** /'gɛtʌp/ *n* INFORMAL strange or unusual clothes that someone is wearing

**get-up-and-go** /,. . . './ *n* [U] INFORMAL energy and determination: *He's lost a lot of his get-up-and-go.*

**gey·ser** /'gaɪzɚ/ *n* hot water and steam that suddenly rises into the air from a natural hole in the ground

**ghast·ly** /'qæstli/ *adj* extremely bad or unpleasant

**ghet·to** /'gɛtoʊ/ *n, plural* **ghettos** *or* **ghettoes** a crowded and poor part of a city

**ghetto blast·er** /'.. ,../ *n* INFORMAL a large radio and TAPE DECK that you can carry around

**ghost** /goʊst/ *n* the spirit of a dead person that some people believe they can see or feel: *They say the captain's ghost still haunts the waterfront.* **–ghostly** *adj*

**ghost sto·ry** /'. ,../ *n* a story you tell people late at night in order to frighten them

**ghost town** /'. ./ *n* a town that is empty because most of its people have left

**ghoul** /gul/ *n* an evil spirit in stories that eats dead bodies that it steals from graves **–ghoulish** *adj*

**GI** /,dʒi 'aɪ/ *n* Government Issue; a soldier in the US army

**gi·ant¹** /'dʒaɪənt/ **giant-sized** /'. ./ *adj* extremely large and much bigger than other things of the same type: *a giant TV screen*

**giant²** *n* **1** an extremely tall strong man in children's stories **2** a very successful or important person or company: *one of the giants of the music industry*

**gib·ber·ish** /'dʒɪbərɪʃ/ *n* [U] things you say or write that have no meaning

**gibe** /dʒaɪb/ *n* an unkind remark intended to make someone seem silly

**gib·lets** /'dʒɪblɪts/ *n* [plural] organs such as the heart and LIVER that you remove from a bird before cooking it

**gid·dy** /'gɪdi/ *adj* **1** behaving in a silly, happy, excited way: *Drinking champagne always makes me giddy.* **2** ⇨ DIZZY

**gift** /gɪft/ *n* **1** something that you give to someone you like or want to thank; PRESENT: *You didn't have to buy me a gift for my birthday!* **2** a natural ability to do something: *Gary sure has a gift for telling stories!*

### CULTURE NOTE  giving gifts

In the US and Canada, gifts are given to family members and close friends on special occasions such as Christmas and birthdays. If you are invited to someone's home as a guest, you should also bring a gift, such as flowers, a bottle of wine, or a box of candy. If you are invited to the home of a good friend, you can ask if s/he would like you to bring something for dinner, such as a dessert. Gifts are usually opened immediately and the person who gives the gift is thanked. It is polite to say how much you like the gift. If you receive a gift through the mail, it is polite to send a note to thank the person who gave it.

**gift cer·tif·i·cate** /'. .,.../ *n* a special piece of paper that is worth a specific amount of money when it is exchanged at a store for goods

**gift·ed** /'gɪftɪd/ *adj* **1** having the natural ability to do something very well: *a gifted poet* **2** very intelligent: *a special class for gifted children*

**gift wrap**[1] /'. ./ *n* attractive colored paper for wrapping presents in

**gift wrap**[2] *v* [T] to wrap a present with GIFT WRAP: *Would you like this gift wrapped?*

**gig** /gɪg/ *n* INFORMAL a musical performance that is played for money to a small group of people: *Tom's band has a gig at the Blues Bar next week.*

**gig·a·byte** /'gɪgə,baɪt/ *n* TECHNICAL one BILLION BYTES

**gi·gan·tic** /dʒaɪˈgænt̬ɪk/ *adj* extremely large: *The company is gigantic and has offices all over the world.*

**gig·gle** /'gɪgəl/ *v* [I] to laugh quietly because you think something is very funny, or because you are nervous: *I can't stop giggling!* **–giggle** *n*

**gild** /gɪld/ *v* [T] to cover the surface of something with a thin layer of gold or gold paint

**gill** /gɪl/ *n* one of the organs on the side of a fish through which it breathes

**gilt** /gɪlt/ *adj* covered with a thin layer of gold or gold-colored paint **–gilt** *n* [U]

**gim·me** /'gɪmi/ SPOKEN NONSTANDARD a short form of "give me": *Gimme that ball back!*

**gim·mick** /'gɪmɪk/ *n* INFORMAL a trick or something unusual that you use or do in order to make people notice someone or something: *advertising gimmicks* **–gimmicky** *adj*

**gin** /dʒɪn/ *n* [U] a strong alcoholic drink made from grain

**gin·ger** /'dʒɪndʒɚ/ *n* [U] a hot-tasting light brown root, or the powder made from this root, used in cooking

**ginger ale** /'.. ,., ,.. './ *n* [U] a SOFT DRINK with a GINGER taste

**gin·ger·bread** /'dʒɪndʒɚ,brɛd/ *n* [U] a type of cookie with GINGER and sweet SPICEs in it: *a gingerbread house/man* (=made into the shape of a house or person)

**gin·ger·ly** /'dʒɪndʒɚli/ *adv* very slowly, carefully, and gently: *Gingerly, she cleaned the wound on her arm.*

**ging·ham** /'gɪŋəm/ *n* [U] cotton cloth that has a pattern of small white and colored squares on it

**gi·raffe** /dʒəˈræf/ *n* a tall animal that has a

very long neck and dark spots on its fur, and that lives in Africa

**gird·er** /'gɚdɚ/ *n* a strong beam made of iron or steel, used for supporting a roof, floor, or bridge

**gir·dle** /'gɚdl/ *n* a type of underwear that a woman wears to make her look thinner

**girl** /gɚl/ *n* **1** a female child: *She's tall for a girl of her age.* **2** a daughter: *Karen has a little baby girl.* **3** a word meaning "woman", considered offensive by some women: *A nice girl like you needs a boyfriend.* **4 the girls** INFORMAL a woman's female friends: *I'm going to the movies with the girls from work.* **5** SPOKEN a way of speaking to a female animal, such as a horse or a dog: *Come here, girl!*

**girl·friend** /'gɚlfrɛnd/ *n* **1** a girl or woman with whom you have a romantic relationship: *Seth is bringing his new girlfriend to Heidi's party.* **2** a woman's female friend

**girl·hood** /'gɚlhʊd/ *n* [U] the time in a woman's life when she is very young

**Girl Scouts** /'. ./ *n* an organization for girls that teaches them practical skills and helps develop their character **–compare** BOY SCOUTS

**girth** /gɚθ/ *n* [C,U] the distance around the middle of something: *the girth of the tree's trunk*

**gist** /dʒɪst/ *n* **the gist** the main idea or meaning of what someone had said or written: *Don't worry about all the details, just get the gist of it.* (=understand the main ideas)

**give**[1] /gɪv/ *v* gave, given, giving
**1** ▶PROVIDE◀ [T] to provide someone with something, or let someone have or do something: *Dan gave me/him/her a ride to work.* | *They gave the job to that guy from Texas.* | *I was never given a chance to explain.*
**2** ▶IN SB'S HAND◀ [T] to put something in someone's hand or near him/her so that s/he can use it, hold it etc.: *He gave the books to Carl.* | *Here, give me your coat. I'll hang it up for you.*
**3** ▶PRESENT◀ [T] to provide someone with something as a present: *She gave Jen a CD for Christmas.*
**4** ▶TELL SB STH◀ [T] to tell someone information or details about something: *Would you give Kim a message for me?* | *The police will ask him to give a description of the man.* | *Let me give you some advice.*
**5** ▶PERFORM AN ACTION◀ [T] a word used before some words that show action, meaning to do the action: *The boy gave Lydia a big smile.* | *Yo Yo Ma gave a performance of pieces by Bach.* | *Give me a call* (=telephone me) *at 8:00.* | *Come on, give your Grandpa a hug.*
**6 give sb trouble/problems etc.** to cause problems or make a situation difficult: *The machines in the lab are giving us trouble.* | *Stop giving me a hard time!* (=stop criticizing me)
**7** ▶ILLNESS◀ [T] to infect someone with an

illness, or make someone feel a particular way: *My husband gave me this cold.* | *The noise is giving me a headache.*
**8 give sb/sth time** to allow a person or situation to have time to think, act, or develop: *Give her some time. She'll make the right decision.*
**9 ▶QUALITY/SHAPE ETC.◀** [T] to make someone or something have a particular quality, shape, look etc.. *The color of the room gives it a warm cozy feeling.*
**10 give the impression/feeling** to make someone have a particular idea or feeling about someone or something: *He gave us the impression that the last few years had been hard for him.*
**11 ▶MONEY◀** [T] to be willing to pay a particular amount of money for something: *I'll give you $75 for the oak desk.*
**12 ▶BEND/STRETCH◀** [I] to bend, stretch, or break because of weight or pressure: *The leather will give slightly when you wear the boots.*
**13 give or take** used in order to show that a number or amount is not exact: *The show lasts about an hour, give or take five minutes.*
**14 give a party** to be the person who organizes a party

---

SPOKEN PHRASES
**15 not give a damn/shit etc.** an impolite phrase used in order to say that you do not care about something: *I don't give a damn what you think!*
**16 sb would give anything** said in order to emphasize that you want something very much: *I'd give anything to be able to get tickets to the R.E.M. concert.*
**17 don't give me that!** said when someone has just said something that you know is not true: *"I'm too tired." "Oh, don't give me that. You just don't want to come."*

---

—see also GIVE AND TAKE, **give sb a (big) hand** (HAND¹)
**give away** *phr v* **1** [T **give** sth ↔ **away**] to give someone something instead of selling it: *The store is **giving away** a toaster to the first 50 customers.* | *I **gave** my old clothes **away** to the Salvation Army.* **2** [T **give** sb/sth ↔ **away**] to do or say something that shows thoughts or feelings that should be secret: *He said he hadn't told her, but his face **gave** him **away**.* (=showed that he had told her) | *I was afraid that the kids would **give the game away**.* (=tell the secret) —see also GIVEAWAY
**give** sth ↔ **back** *phr v* [T] to return something to the person who owns it or who owned it before you: *Give me **back** my popcorn!* | *Will you **give** the money **back to** Rich for me?* —see picture at BORROW
**give in** *phr v* [I] to agree to something you were unwilling to agree to before, especially after a long argument: *Randy had been asking her out for months, so she finally **gave in**.*

**give in to** sth *phr v* [T] to stop being able to control a strong need or desire: *If you feel the need for a cigarette, don't **give in to** it.*
**give off** *phr v* [T] to produce a smell, light, heat, a sound etc.: *People complain about the terrible smell that the factory **gives off**.*
**give out** *phr v* **1** [T **give** sth ↔ **out**] to give something to each of several people: *She **gave** copies of the report **out** to the committee before the meeting.* **2** [I] to stop working correctly: *My voice **gave out** half way through the song.*
**give up** *phr v* **1** [I,T **give** sth ↔ **up**] to stop trying to do something or working at something: *I looked everywhere for the keys - finally, I just **gave up**.* | *Vladimir has **given up** trying to teach her Russian.* **2** [T **give** sth ↔ **up**] to stop doing or having something: *She **gave up** her job, and started writing full time.* **3** [T **give** sb **up**] to allow yourself or someone else to be caught by the police or enemy soldiers
**give up on** sb *phr v* [T] to stop hoping that someone will change his/her behavior: *I'd been in trouble so many times that my parents had **given up on** me.*
**give²** *n* [U] the ability of a material to bend or stretch when it is under pressure
**give and take** /ˌ. . './ *n* [U] a situation in which two people or groups are each willing to let the other have or do some of the things they want: *In every successful marriage there is a certain amount of give and take.*
**give·a·way** /ˈɡɪvəˌweɪ/ *n* **1 be a dead give-away** to make it very easy for someone to guess something: *Vince was lying. His red face was a dead giveaway.* **2** a product, prize etc. that a store or company gives to its customers for free —**giveaway** *adj*: *giveaway prices*
**giv·en¹** /ˈɡɪvən/ *adj* **1 any/a given ...** any particular time, idea, or thing that is being used as an example: *In any given year, over half of all accidents happen in the home.* **2** a given time, date etc. is one that has been fixed or agreed on: *How much electricity is used in any given period?*
**given²** *prep* if you consider: *Given the number of people we invited, I'm surprised that so few came.*
**given³** *v* the PAST PARTICIPLE of GIVE
**given⁴** *n* **a given** a basic fact that you accept as the truth
**given name** /'.. ˌ./ *n* ⇨ FIRST NAME
**giz·mo** /ˈɡɪzmoʊ/ *n* ⇨ GADGET
**giz·zard** /ˈɡɪzɚd/ *n* an organ near a bird's stomach that helps it break down food
**gla·cial** /ˈɡleɪʃəl/ *adj* relating to ice or GLACIERs, or formed by glaciers: *glacial streams*
**gla·cier** /ˈɡleɪʃɚ/ *n* a large area of ice that moves slowly over an area of land
**glad** /ɡlæd/ *adj* **1** happy or satisfied about something good that has happened: *Mom's really glad (that) you could come home for Christ-*

*mas.* ✗ DON'T SAY "She's a really glad person." ✗ **2 be glad to do sth** to be willing to do something: *He said he'd be glad to help me.*

**glade** /gleɪd/ *n* LITERARY an area with very few trees inside a forest

**glad·i·a·tor** /ˈɡlædiˌeɪtɚ/ *n* a strong man who fought other men or animals as a public event in ancient Rome

**glad·ly** /ˈɡlædli/ *adv* willingly or eagerly: *"Would you drive Jenny to school today?" "Gladly."*

**glam·or** /ˈɡlæmɚ/ *n* [U] the quality of being attractive, exciting, rich, and successful: *the glamor of Hollywood*

**glam·or·ize** /ˈɡlæməˌraɪz/ *v* [T] to make something seem more attractive or exciting than it really is

**glam·or·ous** /ˈɡlæmərəs/ *adj* attractive, exciting, and relating to wealth and success: *On television she looked so beautiful and glamorous.*

**glance**[1] /ɡlæns/ *v* [I] **1** to quickly look at someone or something: *He glanced at his watch.* **2** to read something very quickly: *Paul glanced through/at the menu and ordered a ham sandwich.*

**glance**[2] *n* **1** a quick look that you give someone or something: *She took/shot/threw a glance at the man behind her.* **2 at a glance** immediately: *I knew at a glance that something was wrong.* **3 at first glance** when you see or think about something for the first time: *At first glance, the place seemed completely empty.*

**gland** /ɡlænd/ *n* an organ in the body that produces a liquid substance that the body needs, such as SWEAT or SALIVA –**glandular** /ˈɡlændʒələ/ *adj*

**glare** /ɡlɛr/ *v* [I] **1** to angrily look at someone or something for a long time: *What's wrong with Kathy? She's been glaring at me all day.* **2** to shine with such a bright light that it hurts your eyes: *Sunlight was glaring off the shiny hood of the car.*

**glar·ing** /ˈɡlɛrɪŋ/ *adj* **1** shining a light that is too bright to look at: *the glaring white light from the explosion* **2** very bad and very noticeable: *glaring mistakes*

**glass** /ɡlæs/ *n* **1** [U] a transparent material that is usually used for making windows and bottles: *Be careful! Don't cut yourself on the broken glass!* **2** a glass container without a handle that you use for drinking liquids: *Did you put the wine glasses on the table?* **3** the amount of a drink contained in a glass: *Would you like a glass of milk?* **4** [U] objects made of glass: *an impressive collection of Venetian glass* –see also GLASSES

glass

stem    straw

**glass ceil·ing** /ˌ. ˈ../ *n* the attitudes and practices that prevent women or people from MINORITY groups from getting high level jobs

**glassed-in** /ˌɡlæst ˈɪn/ *adj* surrounded by a glass structure: *a glassed-in porch*

**glass·es** /ˈɡlæsɪz/ *n* [plural] two round pieces of glass in a FRAME that you wear in front of your eyes in order to see better: *I need to buy a new pair of glasses.*

glasses

lens    frame

**glass·ware** /ˈɡlæswɛr/ *n* [U] glass containers that you drink from

**glass·y** /ˈɡlæsi/ *adj* **1** smooth and shiny, like glass: *the glassy surface of the lake* **2** glassy eyes are shiny, do not move, and do not show any expression

**glaze**[1] /ɡleɪz/ *v* **1** [I] also **glaze over** if your eyes glaze, they stop showing any expression because you are bored or tired **2** [T] to cover clay pots, bowls etc. with a thin liquid in order to give them a shiny surface **3** [T] to put a liquid on fruit, cake, or meat so that it has a shiny attractive surface **4** [T] to put glass into a window frame –**glazed** *adj*

**glaze**[2] *n* **1** a thin liquid paint that is put on clay pots, bowls etc. to give them a shiny surface **2** [U] a liquid put on fruit, cake, or meat to give it an attractive shiny surface

**gleam**[1] /ɡlim/ *v* [I] to shine, especially after being cleaned: *Grandpa polished his shoes until they gleamed.*

**gleam**[2] *n* **1** the slightly shiny quality that something that is polished has when light shines on it **2 with a gleam in your eye** showing that you are amused, or that you are not telling someone something secret: *"I bet you want to know what your birthday present is!" he said with a gleam in his eye.*

**glean** /ɡlin/ *v* [T] to find out information, even though this is difficult and takes time: *Several lessons can be gleaned from our experience so far.*

**glee** /ɡli/ *n* [U] a feeling of happy excitement and satisfaction: *The kids shouted with glee when they saw Santa.* –**gleefully** *adv*

**glen** /ɡlɛn/ *n* a deep narrow valley

**glib** /ɡlɪb/ *adj* **1** said without thinking about all the problems in something, or about how your remarks will affect someone: *The doctor made some glib remark, saying my headaches were just "stress."* **2** able to persuade people that what you are saying is true: *a glib talker* –**glibly** *adv*

**glide** /ɡlaɪd/ *v* [I] to move smoothly and quietly, as if no effort were being made: *We watched the sailboats glide across the lake.* –**glide** *n*

**glid·er** /ˈɡlaɪdɚ/ *n* a plane without an engine

**glid·ing** /'glaɪdɪŋ/ *n* the sport of flying a GLIDER

**glim·mer**[1] /'glɪmɚ/ *n* **1 a glimmer of hope/doubt etc.** a small amount of hope, doubt etc. **2** a light that does not shine very brightly

**glimmer**[2] *v* [I] to shine weakly with a pale light

**glimpse**[1] /glɪmps/ *n* **1** a look at someone or something that is quicker than you want it to be: *Dad only got/caught a glimpse of the guy who stole our car.* **2** a short experience of something that helps you begin to understand it: *a glimpse into the future*

**glimpse**[2] *v* [T] to quickly look at someone or something: *Glimpsing Joe behind him, he turned around to say "hello."*

**glint**[1] /glɪnt/ *v* [I] if something that is shiny or smooth glints, it flashes with a very small amount of light: *Her teeth glinted as she smiled.*

**glint**[2] *n* a small flash of light that shines off something smooth or shiny: *the glint of his gold watch*

**glis·ten** /'glɪsən/ *v* [I] to shine because of being wet or oily: *His back was glistening with sweat.* —**glistening** *adj*

**glitch** /glɪtʃ/ *n* a small problem that prevents something from working correctly: *Company records were lost due to a computer glitch.*

**glit·ter**[1] /'glɪtɚ/ *v* [I] to shine with a lot of small flashes of light: *Fresh snow was glittering outside in the morning light* —**glittering** *adj*

**glitter**[2] *n* **1** [singular] a lot of small flashes of light: *the glitter of her diamond ring* **2** [U] very small pieces of shiny plastic or metal that you glue onto paper, cards etc. for decoration

**gloat** /gloʊt/ *v* [I] to behave in an annoying way because you are proud of your success, or happy about someone else's failure: *The baseball team was gloating over its victory.*

**glob** /glɑb/ *n* INFORMAL a small amount of a soft substance or thick liquid: *a glob of ketchup*

**glob·al** /'gloʊbəl/ *adj* **1** affecting the whole world, or relating to the whole world: *the global problems of pollution, disease, and overpopulation* **2** considering all the parts of a problem or a situation: *a global study on the company's weaknesses* —**globally** *adv*

**global warm·ing** /ˌ.. '../ *n* [U] an increase in the world's temperature, caused by an increase of CARBON DIOXIDE around the earth

**globe** /gloʊb/ *n* **1 the globe** the world: *Our company has offices all over the globe.* **2** an object shaped like a ball **3** a round object that has a map of the earth painted on it

**glob·u·lar** /'glɑbyələ/ *adj* shaped like a ball or a drop of liquid

**glob·ule** /'glɑbyul/ *n* a small drop of liquid or a melted substance

**gloom** /glum/ *n* [singular, U] **1** darkness that you can hardly see through: *A man was sitting alone in the gloom.* **2** a feeling of sadness, or having no hope

**gloom·y** /'glumi/ *adj* **1** feeling sad because you do not have a lot of hope, or making you feel sad: *a gloomy movie about a girl who dies of cancer* **2** dark in a way that makes you feel sad: *the cold gloomy weather* —**gloomily** *adv*

**glo·ri·fied** /'glɔrəˌfaɪd/ *adj* made to seem like something more important: *My title is "Editorial Assistant," but I'm just a glorified secretary.*

**glo·ri·fy** /'glɔrəˌfaɪ/ *v* [T] **1** to make someone or something seem more important or better than he, she, or it is: *We must avoid glorifying the war.* **2** to praise someone or something important, especially God —**glorification** /ˌglɔrəfə'keɪʃən/ *n* [U]

**glo·ri·ous** /'glɔriəs/ *adj* **1** deserving praise or honor: *a glorious achievement* **2** beautiful or extremely nice; WONDERFUL: *It was a glorious day!* (=beautiful sunny weather) —**gloriously** *adv*

**glo·ry**[1] /'glɔri/ *n* **1** the importance, praise, and honor that people give someone they admire: *At 19 he won glory as an Olympic champion.* | *Someone in the church shouted out "glory to God!"* **2** an achievement that you are proud of: *Becoming a Supreme Court judge was the crowning glory* (=the final, most successful part) *of her legal career.* **3** [C,U] a beautiful and impressive appearance: *They spent $10 million on restoring the Grand Theater to its former glory.*

**glory**[2] *v*

**glory in** sth *phr v* [T] to enjoy or be proud of the praise, attention, and success that you get: *The new mayor gloried in his victory.*

**gloss**[1] /glɔs, glɑs/ *n* **1** [singular, U] a shiny attractive surface: *a new hair gel that adds gloss to even the dullest hair* **2** an explanation of a written word or expression

**gloss**[2] *v* [T] to provide an explanation for something that is written in a book

**gloss over** sth *phr v* to deliberately avoid talking about the details of a situation, fact etc.: *The report glossed over the company's recent profit losses.*

**glos·sa·ry** /'glɑsəri, 'glɔ-/ *n* a list of special words and explanations of what they mean, written at the end of a book

**gloss·y** /'glɔsi, 'glɑsi/ *adj* **1** shiny and smooth: *glossy healthy hair* **2** a glossy magazine, book, or photograph is printed on shiny, good quality paper

**glove** /glʌv/ *n* a piece of clothing worn on your hand, with separate parts to cover the thumb and each finger

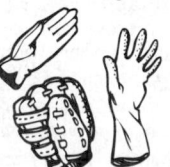

glove

**glove com·part·ment** /ˈ. .ˌ.ˌ./, **glove box** /ˈ. ./ *n* a place like a small cupboard in front of the passenger

seat of a car, often used for storing road maps
—see picture on page 469

**glow¹** /gloʊ/ *v* [I] **1** to shine with a gentle
steady light: *The church walls glowed in the
candlelight.* **2** to produce a red light and heat
without flames: *A log fire was glowing in the
fireplace.* **3** to look very happy and healthy:
*Jodie was glowing with pride as she looked at
the baby.*

**glow²** *n* [singular] **1** a gentle steady light,
especially from something that is burning without flames: *The sky was filled with an orange
glow.* **2** the slightly red appearance your face
or body has when you exercise or feel very happy: *the healthy glow in her cheeks*

**glow·er** /ˈglaʊɚ/ *v* [I] to look at someone in an
angry way: *Donna glowered at her husband but
said nothing.* —**glowering** *adj*

**glow·ing** /ˈgloʊɪŋ/ *adj* **1 glowing report/
description etc.** a report etc. that is full of
praise for someone or something **2** looking
very healthy and attractive —**glowingly** *adv*

**glow·worm** /ˈgloʊwɚm/ *n* an insect that gives
out light from its body

**glu·cose** /ˈglukoʊs/ *n* [U] a natural form of
sugar that is in fruits

**glue¹** /glu/ *n* [C,U] a sticky substance used for
joining things together

**glue²** *v* **glued, gluing** *or* **glueing** [T] **1** to join
two things together using glue **2 be glued to
sth** to look at something with all your attention:
*The kids are glued to the TV set all day long!*

**glum** /glʌm/ *adj* sad and quiet

**glut¹** /glʌt/ *n* a large supply of something that
is more than you need: *a glut of oil on the
market*

**glut²** *v* **-tted, -tting** [T] **be glutted with** to be
supplied with too much of something: *an area
glutted with half-empty office buildings*

**glut·ton** /ˈglʌt⁻n/ *n* **1** someone who eats too
much food **2 a glutton for punishment**
someone who seems to enjoy working very hard
or doing something unpleasant

**glut·ton·y** /ˈglʌt⁻n-i/ *n* [U] the bad habit of
eating and drinking too much

**glyc·er·in** /ˈglɪsərɪn/ *n* [U] a sticky colorless
liquid used in making soap, medicine, and
EXPLOSIVEs

**gm.** the written abbreviation of GRAM

**gnarled** /nɑrld/ *adj* rough and twisted: *a
gnarled branch | gnarled fingers*

**gnash** /næʃ/ *v* [T] **gnash your teeth** LITERARY
to move your teeth against each other because
you are angry or unhappy

**gnat** /næt/ *n* a small flying insect that bites

**gnaw** /nɔ/ *v* [I,T] to keep biting something: *a
dog gnawing on a bone*

  **gnaw at** sb *phr v* [T] to make someone feel
worried or anxious: *Fear had been gnawing at
him all day.*

**gnaw·ing** /ˈnɔ-ɪŋ/ *adj* worrying or painful,
usually for a long time: *a gnawing fear/pain*

**gnome** /noʊm/ *n* a creature in children's stories like a little old man, who lives under the
ground

**GNP** *n* **the GNP** Gross National Product; the total value of the goods and services produced in a
country, including income from abroad

go

Lucia has gone to Paris.

Lucia has been to Paris.

**go¹** /goʊ/ *v* **went, gone, going,** *third person
singular* **goes**

**1** ▶**LEAVE**◀ [I] to leave the place where the
speaker is in order to go somewhere else: *I
wanted to go, but Craig wanted to stay. | It's late
- we should be/get going.* —compare COME

**2** ▶**VISIT**◀ *past participle* also **been** [I] to
visit a place and then leave it: *Lucia has gone to
Paris.* (=she is in Paris now) | *Lucia has been to
Paris.* (=she has visited Paris in the past) | *The
doctor hasn't been here yet.* | *Are you going to
the game on Saturday?*

**3** ▶**TRAVEL/MOVE**◀ [I] to travel or move in a
particular way, to a particular place, or for a
particular distance: *We can go by bus. | We went
home to eat dinner. | Where are you going?*

**4 be going to do sth** used in order to say that
something will happen, or is supposed to happen
in the future: *It looks like it's going to rain.*
—compare GONNA —see usage note at GONNA

**5 go shopping/swimming etc.** to go somewhere in order to buy things, swim etc.: *Let's go
running tomorrow morning.*

**6 go for a walk/swim etc.** to spend some time
walking, swimming etc.: *We went for a ride in
the car after lunch.*

**7** ▶**REACH**◀ [I] to reach as far as a particular
place, or lead to a particular place: *The roots of
the tree go very deep.*

**8** ▶**BELONG**◀ [I] to belong or fit in a
particular place or position: *"Where do the
plates go?" "On the shelf."*

**9** ▶**BECOME**◀ [linking verb] to become: *My
hair's going gray.* —see usage note at BECOME

**10** ▶**BE IN A STATE**◀ [linking verb] to be or

remain in a particular state: *The mother bird will* **go** *hungry to keep the babies alive.*

**11 go to church/school etc.** to regularly go to a church, school etc.: *Is Brett going to college next year?*

**12 ►GET RID OF◄** [I] to be bad enough to be made to leave or be thrown away: *They knew that Parker **had to go**.│"Do you want all these magazines?" "No, they **can go**."*

**13 ►SPEND◄** [I] if money or time goes, it is spent: *The money **goes to** local charities.│I just don't know where the time **goes!***

**14 ►WORK CORRECTLY◄** [I] INFORMAL if a machine goes, it works in the way that it should: *I can't get the car to **go**.*

**15 ►BE SOLD◄** [I] to be sold: *The painting should **go for** $2000.*

**16 ►NO LONGER WORK◄** [I] to become weak and not work correctly: *He's old, and his hearing is going.*

**17 ►SOUND/SONG◄** [T] to make a particular sound, or have particular words or music: *Ducks **go** "quack."│How does the song **go**?*

**18 ►HAPPEN◄** [I] to happen or develop in a particular way: *The play **went well/fine** (=happened in the way it was intended to) until the last ten minutes.│Then everything **went wrong.*** (=happened in the wrong way)

**19 ►MATCH◄** [I] to look or taste good together: *Those colors don't **go together** very well.│Does red wine **go with** chicken?*

**20 get going** INFORMAL to start doing something: *It's time to **get going on** the cleaning.*

**21 ready to go** ready to start doing something: *The builders are ready to **go**, but their equipment isn't here yet.*

**22 to go a)** remaining before something happens: *Only two weeks **to go** before we leave for South America!* **b)** food that is to go is bought from a restaurant and taken away to be eaten: *I'll have a large order of fries **to go**, please.*

**23 it (just) goes to show** used in order to emphasize what something proves or shows: *It just **goes to show** that anything can happen in America.*

─────── SPOKEN PHRASES ───────

**24 How's it going?** said in order to ask someone how s/he is: *"Hey, Jimmy, how's it going?" "All right, I guess."*

**25 go and do sth** to go somewhere in order to do something: *I'll **go and** pick up the car for you.*

**26** [I] to make a particular movement: *He **went like this** and knocked the lamp over.*

**27** [T] NONSTANDARD said when telling someone what someone else has said: *I asked her how she was, and she **goes**, "Do you really care?"*

**28** [I] to pass liquid or solid waste from your body: *Mommy, I have to **go**!*

**go about** sth *phr v* [T] to do something or begin doing something: *I don't know how to **go about** this.*

**go after** sb/sth *phr v* [T] to try to get or catch someone: ***Go after** him and tell him he has to be home by 6:00.*

**go against** sb/sth *phr v* [T] to do the opposite of what someone wants you to do, or be the opposite of what you want or believe in: *He would never force her to **go against** her principles.*

**go ahead** *phr v* [I] **1** SPOKEN said in order to politely let someone move in front of you, or to speak before you: *You can **go ahead of** me - I'm waiting for someone.* **2 go ahead and do sth** SPOKEN said when something you were possibly going to do is now definite: *Okay, I'll **go ahead** and call her today.* **3** to begin or continue: *Work on the new church will **go ahead** in May.*

**go along** *phr v* [I] **1** to continue: *I **went along** making the same mistakes for weeks.* **2** to agree with or support something: *You'll never get Mom to **go along with** it.*

**go around** *phr v* [I] **1 go around doing sth** to do something that other people do not approve of: *You can't **go around** lying to people all the time!* **2** if an illness goes around, many people get it **3** to be enough for everyone: *Are there enough glasses to **go around**?*

**go at** sb/sth *phr v* [T] to start to do something, especially fighting or arguing, with a lot of energy: *The dogs **went at** each other as soon as we let go.*

**go away** *phr v* [I] **1** to leave a place or a person: ***Go away!** Leave me alone!* **2** to spend some time away from home: *We're **going away** for two weeks in June.* **3** to disappear or not happen any longer: *My headache hasn't **gone away**.*

**go back on** sth *phr v* [T] if you go back on a promise or agreement, you do not do what you promised to do

**go back to** sth *phr v* [T] **1** to do something again after having stopped doing it: *I can't study any more. I'll **go back to** it later.* **2** to have been started or made at a particular time in the past: *His family history **goes back to** the 16th century.*

**go by** *phr v* **1** [I] to pass: *Two months **went by** before Winton called.* **2** [I,T **go by** sth] to go to a place for a short time on your way to somewhere else: *We **went by** Greg's house before we came here.* **3** [T **go by** sth] to use information, rules etc. to help you decide what to do: *Don't **go by** that map. It's really old.*

**go down** *phr v* [I]

**1 ►FOR A PURPOSE◄** SPOKEN to go to a place for a particular purpose: *We **went down** to Hudson's to buy a camera.*

**2 ►GO LOWER◄** to go to a lower floor of a building: ***Go down** and see who's at the door.*

**3 ►BECOME LESS◄** to become lower or less in

G

level, amount, size, quality etc.: *The temperature* **went down** *to freezing last night.* | *The swelling in her knee didn't* **go down** *for days.*
**4** ▶GO UNDER◀ to sink below the level of a surface: *He watched the sun* **go down** *over the ocean.*
**5** ▶GO SOUTH◀ to go south from the place where you are: *We're* **going down** *to Florida for spring break.*
**6** ▶REMEMBER◀ to be remembered or recorded in a particular way: *This day will* **go down in history**. (=be remembered always)
**7 go down well/badly etc.** to be liked, not liked etc.: *Robbie's jokes didn't* **go down** *very well with her parents.*

**go for** sb/sth *phr v* [T] **1 I could/would go for sth** SPOKEN to want or like something: *I could really* **go for** *a taco right now.* **2** [**go for** sb/sth] SPOKEN to choose a particular thing, or like a particular type of person: *I think you should* **go for** *the gray suit.* **3 go for it** SPOKEN said when you think someone should do or try something: *Well, if you're sure you want to,* **go for it!** **4** [**go for** sth] to try to get or win something: *a swimmer* **going for** *an Olympic record*

**go into** sth *phr v* [T] **1** to start working in a particular profession or type of business: *Vivian wants to* **go into** *politics.* **2** to be used in order to make something work or happen: *A lot of money has* **gone into** *building this house.* **3** to describe or explain something thoroughly: *I don't want to* **go into details** *right now, but it was horrible.* **4** if one number goes into another, it can divide it: *12* **goes into** *60 five times.*

**go off** *phr v* [I] **1** to explode: *Fireworks* **went off** *all over the city that night.* **2** to make a loud noise: *My alarm clock didn't* **go off**. **3** if a machine or light goes off, it stops working or stops shining

**go on** *phr v* [I] **1** to continue without stopping or changing: *We can't* **go on** *fighting like this!* | *This guy* **went on and on** (=talked for a long time) *about himself all night.* **2** to happen: *What's* **going on** *down there? Did something break?* **3** to do something new when you have finished something else: *Go on to question number 5 when you're done.* **4** if a machine or light goes on, it starts working or starts shining **5** to continue talking or explaining something, after you have stopped for a while: *Go on, I'm listening.* | *After a minute, she stopped crying and* **went on with** *the story.* **6** if time goes on, it passes: *As time* **went on**, *he became more friendly.* **7** SPOKEN said in order to encourage someone to do something: *Go on, have another drink.*

**go out** *phr v* [I] **1** to leave your house, especially in order to do something you enjoy: *Are you* **going out** *tonight?* | *We* **went out** *for dinner/lunch on Saturday.* | *Can I* **go out and** *play now?* **2** to have a romantic relationship

with someone: *Leah used to* **go out with** *Dan's brother.* **3** if a light or fire goes out, it stops shining or burning **4** to travel to a place that is far away, in order to live there: *They've* **gone out** *to Malaysia to live.*

**go over** *phr v* **1** [T] to look at something or think about something carefully: *Jake* **went over** *his notes again before the test.* **2** [T] to search a place thoroughly. *The police will* **go over** *the area in the morning.* **3 go down well/badly etc.** (GO¹)

**go through** *phr v* **1** [T **go through** sth] to have a very upsetting experience or a period of time when a lot of bad things happen: *She's just* **been through** *a divorce.* **2** [T **go through** sth] to use all of something: *Jeremy* **goes through** *at least a quart of milk every day!* **3** [I,T **go through** sth] if a deal, agreement, or law goes through, it is officially accepted: *My car loan has finally* **gone through**. | *a law* **going through** *Congress* **4** [T **go through** sth] to practice something from the beginning to the end: *Let's* **go through** *the song one more time.* **5** [T **go through** sth] to look at something carefully, especially because you are looking for something: *She had to* **go through** *all her uncle's papers after he died.*

**go to** sth *phr v* [T] **1 go to a lot of trouble** to use a lot of effort to do something, especially for someone else: *Suki* **went to** *a lot of trouble to get us the tickets.* **2 go to sleep/war etc.** to begin sleeping, fighting a war etc.

**go together** *phr v* [I] to have a romantic relationship: *Are Lizzie and Bud* **going together**?

**go under** *phr v* [I] if a business goes under, it has serious problems and fails

**go up** *phr v* [I] **1 go up to** SPOKEN to walk toward someone or something until you are standing in front of him, her, or it: *Andrea* **went up to** *him and asked him for directions.* **2** to increase in number or amount: *Housing prices* **went up** *again last quarter.* **3** to be built: *All of those houses have* **gone up** *in the past six months.* **4** to explode or be destroyed by fire: *The factory* **went up in flames** *before the firemen got there.*

**go with** sb/sth *phr v* [T] **1** to be included as part of something: *The car* **goes with** *the job.* **2** to choose something: *I'd* **go with** *the green tie if I were you.*

**go without** *phr v* **1** [I,T **go without** sth] to not have something you need or want: *We can* **go without** *a car in the city.* **2 it goes without saying (that)** used in order to say that something should be clear without needing to be said: *It* **goes without saying** *that artists should have the right of freedom of expression.*

---

**USAGE NOTE** go, gone, and been

Use **gone** as the usual past participle of **go**: *George has* **gone** *to Denver.* (=he is there now). Use **been** as the past participle with the sense of **go** that means "visit": *George has been to Denver.* (=he has visited Denver before, but is not there now)

**go²** *n* **1 make a go of sth** to try to make something such as a business or marriage successful **2 on the go** very busy or working all the time

**goad** /goʊd/ *v* [T] to make someone do something by annoying him/her until s/he does it: *Troy's friends goaded him into asking Susan for a date.*

**go·a·head** /'. .,./ *n* **give sb the go-ahead** INFORMAL to give someone permission to start doing something

**goal** /goʊl/ *n* **1** something that you hope to achieve in the future: *The company achieved its sales goal for the month.* **2** the action in a game or sport of making the ball go into a particular area to win a point, or the point won by doing this: *Ramos scored two goals for the US.* **3** the area into which a player tries to put the ball in order to win a point

**goal·ie** /'goʊli/ *n* INFORMAL ⇨ GOALKEEPER

**goal·keep·er** /'goʊl,kipɚ/, **goal·tend·er** /'goʊl,tɛndɚ/ *n* the player on a sports team who tries to stop the ball from going into the GOAL

**goal·post** /'goʊlpoʊst/ *n* one of the two upright BARS, with another bar along the top or across the middle, that form the GOAL in games like SOCCER and football – see picture on page 472

**goat** /goʊt/ *n* **1** a common farm animal with horns and with long hair under its chin **2 get sb's goat** INFORMAL to make someone very angry or annoyed

**goat·ee** /goʊ'ti/ *n* a small BEARD on the end of a man's chin

**gob·ble** /'gɑbəl/ *v* INFORMAL **1** [T] also **gobble up** to eat something very quickly **2** [T] also **gobble up** to use a supply of something quickly: *Taxes gobble up 25% of my income.* **3** [I] to make a sound like a TURKEY

**gob·ble·dy·gook**, gobbledegook /'gɑbəldi-,gʊk/ *n* [U] INFORMAL complicated language, especially in official letters, that you do not understand

**go-be·tween** /'. .,./ *n* someone who takes messages from one person or group to another, because the two sides do not want to meet or cannot meet: *The lawyer will act as a go-between for the couple.*

**gob·let** /'gɑblɪt/ *n* a cup with a base and long stem but no handles

**gob·lin** /'gɑblɪn/ *n* a small and ugly creature in children's stories who likes to trick people

**gobs** /gɑbz/ *n* [plural] INFORMAL a large amount of something: *I'm sure old Mr. Kratten has gobs of money hidden in his house.*

**go-cart** /'. ./ *n* a small car made of an open frame on four wheels, that people race for fun

**God** /gɑd/ *n* [singular] **1** the spirit or BEING whom Christians, Jews, and Muslims pray to **2 play God** to behave as if you have the power to do whatever you want **3 a God-given duty/right/talent etc.** a duty etc. received from God

SPOKEN PHRASES

**4 God/oh God/my God** a phrase said in order to add force to what you are saying when you are surprised, angry etc., that some people consider offensive **5 I swear/hope/wish etc. to God** said in order to emphasize that you promise, hope etc. that something is true **6 God (only) knows** said in order to show that you are annoyed because you do not know something or understand something: *God only knows where those kids are now!* **7 what/how/where/who in God's name** said in order to add force to a question when you are surprised or angry: *Where in God's name have you been?* **8 honest to God** said in order to emphasize that you are not lying or joking **9 God bless** said in order to show that you hope someone will be safe and happy: *Good night, and God bless.*

**god** *n* **1** a male spirit or BEING who is believed to control the world, or a part of it **2** someone or something that is given too much importance or respect – see also GODDESS

**god-aw·ful** /,. '../ *adj* INFORMAL very bad or unpleasant: *What is that god-awful smell?*

**god·child** /'gɑdtʃaɪld/ *n, plural* **godchildren** a child that a GODPARENT promises to help, usually by teaching him/her religious values

**god·dam·mit** /,gɑd'dæmɪt/ *interjection* OFFENSIVE ⇨ DAMMIT

**god·damn** /,gɑd'dæm‹/, **god·damned** /,gɑd-'dæmd‹/ *adj* SPOKEN OFFENSIVE ⇨ DAMN¹

**god·dess** /'gɑdɪs/ *n* **1** a female spirit or BEING who is believed to control the world, or part of it **2** a woman who is very beautiful or sexually attractive: *Hollywood movie goddess Marilyn Monroe*

**god·fa·ther** /'gɑd,fɑðɚ/ *n* **1** a male GODPARENT **2** SLANG the leader of a criminal organization

**god·fear·ing** /'. ,../ *adj* OLD-FASHIONED behaving according to the moral rules of a religion

**god·for·sak·en** /'gɑdfɚ,seɪkən/ *adj* a godforsaken place is far away from where people live, and does not have anything interesting or cheerful in it

**god·less** /'gɑdlɪs/ *adj* not showing respect for God or a god, or belief in God or a god

**god·like**, Godlike /'gɑdlaɪk/ *adj* having a quality like God or a god

**god·ly** /'gɑdli/ *adj* OLD-FASHIONED showing that you obey God by behaving according to the moral rules of a religion

**god·moth·er** /ˈgɑdˌmʌðɚ/ *n* a female GODPARENT

**god·par·ent** /ˈgɑdˌpɛrənt/ *n* someone who promises to help a child, usually by teaching him/her religious values

**god·send** /ˈgɑdsɛnd/ *n* [singular] something good that happens to you at a time when you really need it

**go·fer** /ˈgoʊfɚ/ *n* INFORMAL someone whose job is to get and carry things for other people

**go-get·ter** /ˌ. ˈ../ *n* INFORMAL someone who is very determined to succeed

**gog·gle-eyed** /ˈgɑgəl ˌaɪd/ *adj* INFORMAL with your eyes wide open and looking at something that surprises you

**gog·gles** /ˈgɑgəlz/ *n* [plural] something that protects your eyes, made of two large round pieces of glass or plastic with an edge that fits against your skin: *skiing goggles*

**go·ing**[1] /ˈgoʊɪŋ/ *n* [U] **1** the act of leaving a place: *His going will be a great loss to the company.* **2** the speed at which you travel or work: *We made the trip in four hours, which is not bad going.*

**going**[2] *adj* **1 the going rate** the usual cost of a service, or the usual pay for a job **2** available, or able to be found: *We think we make the best computers going.* **3 a going concern** a successful business

**going-o·ver** /ˌ.. ˈ../ *n* a thorough examination of something: *My car needs a good going-over.*

**goings-on** /ˌ.. ˈ./ *n* [plural] INFORMAL activities or events that you think are strange or interesting

**gold**[1] /goʊld/ *n* **1** [U] a valuable soft yellow metal that is used for making jewelry, coins etc. **2** [C,U] a bright shiny yellow color

**gold**[2] *adj* **1** made of gold: *a gold necklace* **2** having the color of gold: *a gold dress*

**gold dig·ger** /ˈ. ˌ../ *n* INFORMAL someone who marries someone else only for his/her money

**gold·en** /ˈgoʊldən/ *adj* **1** having a bright shiny yellow color: *golden hair* **2** made of gold: *a golden crown* **3 golden age** the time when something was at its best: *the golden age of television* **4 a golden opportunity** a good chance to get something valuable, or to be very successful **5 golden years** old age: *I want to enjoy my golden years.*

**gold·fish** /ˈgoʊldˌfɪʃ/ *n* a small shiny orange fish often kept as a pet

**gold med·al** /ˌ. ˈ../ *n* a prize that is given to the winner of a race, competition etc., and that is usually made of gold

**gold·mine** /ˈgoʊldmaɪn/ *n* **1** a business or activity that produces a lot of money **2** a hole under the ground from which gold is taken

**golf** /gɑlf, gɔlf/ *n* [U] a game in which you hit a small white ball into a hole in the ground with a golf club, using as few hits as possible —**golfer** *n*

**golf club** /ˈ. ./ *n* **1** a long wooden or metal stick used for hitting the ball in golf **2** a group of people who pay to play golf at a particular place, or the land and buildings they use

**golf course** /ˈ. ./ *n* an area of land on which you play golf

**gol·ly** /ˈgɑli/ *interjection* OLD-FASHIONED said when you are surprised

**gon·do·la** /ˈgɑndələ, gɑnˈdoʊlə/ *n* a long narrow boat, used on the CANALS of Venice

**gon·do·lier** /ˌgɑndəˈlɪɚ/ *n* someone who rows a GONDOLA

**gone** /gɔn, gɑn/ *v* the PAST PARTICIPLE of GO —see usage note at GO[1]

**gon·er** /ˈgɔnɚ/ *n* INFORMAL **be a goner** SPOKEN to be about to die, or in a lot of danger: *The car kept spinning, and I thought we were goners.*

**gong** /gɔŋ, gɑŋ/ *n* a round piece of metal that hangs in a frame and is hit with a stick to make a loud sound as a signal

**gon·na** /ˈgɔnə, gənə/ SPOKEN NONSTANDARD a short form of "going to," used when talking about the future: *I'm gonna talk to her about it tomorrow.*

---

**USAGE NOTE gonna and going to**

Use **going to** in front of another verb to talk about something that will happen in the future: *I'm going to buy it later.* In informal speech, we often pronounce this as **gonna**: *I'm gonna buy it later.* Use **going to** to talk about a place you are traveling to: *I'm going to Montreal for the weekend.* ✗ DON'T SAY "I'm gonna Montreal for the weekend." ✗

---

**gon·or·rhe·a** /ˌgɑnəˈriə/ *n* [U] a disease of the sex organs that is passed from one person to another during sex; VD

**goo** /gu/ *n* [U] ⇨ GOOP

**good**[1] /gʊd/ *adj* **better, best**

**1** ▶HIGH IN QUALITY◀ of a high standard: *His score on the test was **very good**.* | *Thanks, Maria, you **did a good job**.* ✗ DON'T SAY "You did good." SAY "You did well." ✗

**2** ▶SUITABLE◀ **a)** useful or suitable for a particular purpose: *It's a good day for going to the beach.*

**3** ▶SKILLFUL◀ smart or skillful: *Andrea is very **good at** Cajun cooking.*

**4 no good/not any good a)** not likely to be useful or successful: *It's no good trying to explain it to her, she won't listen!* **b)** bad: *That movie isn't any good.*

**5** ▶NICE◀ enjoyable and pleasant: *good weather* | *It's **good to** see you again.*

**6** ▶HEALTHY◀ **a)** useful for your health or character: *Watching so much TV isn't **good for you**.* **b)** healthy: *"How do you feel today?" "Better, thanks."*

**7** ▶ABLE TO BE USED◀ in a satisfactory con-

G

dition for use; not broken, damaged etc.: *There now, your dress is **as good as new**.* (=fixed so that it looks new again) | *The product guarantee is **good for*** (=can be used for) *three years.*

**8** ▶**WELL-BEHAVED**◀ a word meaning well-behaved, used especially about children: *Sit here and be a good girl.*

**9** ▶**KIND**◀ kind and helpful: *It's **good of** you to come on such short notice.*

**10 as good as** almost. *The work is as good as finished.*

**11 a good deal (of sth)** a lot: *I spent a good deal of time preparing for this test.*

**12** ▶**RIGHT**◀ morally right: *Billy Amos led a good life.*

**13** ▶**LARGE/LONG**◀ large in amount, size etc.: *a good-sized car* | *They've been gone **a good while**.* (=a long time)

**14** complete; thorough: *The car needs a good wash.*

**15 be in sb's good graces** to be liked and approved of by someone at a particular time

---

SPOKEN PHRASES

**16 good/oh good** said when you are pleased that something has happened or has been done: *"I've finished." "Good, put your papers in the box."*

**17 that's/it's not good enough** said when you are not satisfied with someone or something

**18 good luck** used in order to say that you hope that someone is successful, or that something good will happen to him/her

**19 good God/grief/heavens etc.** said in order to express anger, surprise, or other strong feelings. Saying "God" in this way is offensive to some people: *Good grief! Is it that late?*

**20 it's a good thing** said when you are glad that something has happened: *It's a good thing you remembered to bring napkins.*

**21 Good for you!** said when you are pleased with something someone has done

---

**USAGE NOTE good and well**

Use **good** as an adjective to talk about the quality of someone or something: *She's a good singer.* Use **well** as an adverb to talk about the way that something is done: *She sings very well.*

---

**good²** *n* [U] **1** something that improves a situation or gives you an advantage: *It'll **do** you **a world of good*** (=make you feel better) *to take a vacation.* **2 do no good** to not be of any use, or to have no effect on something: *You can talk to her all you want, but it won't do any good.* **3 make good on a promise/threat/claim etc.** to succeed in doing what you have said you would do: *They're asking for more*

time to make good on their debts. **4** behavior or actions that are morally right or follow religious principles: *the battle between good and evil* **5 for good** permanently: *Is he really gone for good?* **6 be up to no good** INFORMAL to be doing or planning to do something that is wrong or bad –see also GOODS

**good af·ter·noon** /. ˌ..'./ *interjection* used in order to say hello to someone in the afternoon

**good·bye** /gʊd'baɪ, gəd'baɪ/ *interjection* said when you are leaving or being left by someone: *Goodbye, Mrs. Anderson.* | *I just have to **say goodbye to** Erica.*

**good eve·ning** /. '../ *interjection* used in order to say hello to someone in the evening: *Good evening, ladies and gentlemen!* –compare GOOD NIGHT

**good-for-noth·ing** /'. . ˌ../ *n, adj* someone who is lazy or has no skills: *He's a lazy good-for-nothing.*

**Good Fri·day** /ˌ. '../ *n* [C,U] the Friday before EASTER

**good-hu·mored** /ˌ. '..◂/ *adj* naturally cheerful and friendly

**good-look·ing** /ˌ. '..◂/ *adj* someone who is good-looking is attractive –see usage note at BEAUTIFUL

**good morn·ing** /. '../ *interjection* used in order to say hello to someone in the morning: *Good morning! Did you sleep well?*

**good-na·tured** /ˌ. '..◂/ *adj* naturally kind and helpful, and not easily made angry –**good-naturedly** *adv*

**good·ness** /'gʊdnɪs/ *n* [U] **1** SPOKEN said when you are surprised or annoyed: *My goodness, you've lost a lot of weight!* | *For goodness' sake, will you be quiet!* **2** the quality of being good: *Anne believed in the basic goodness of people.* **3** the best part of food that is good for your health: *All the goodness has been boiled out of these carrots.*

**good night** /. './ *interjection* said when you are leaving or being left by someone at night, especially late at night: *Good night, Sandy. Be careful driving home!* –compare GOOD EVENING

**goods** /gʊdz/ *n* [plural] **1** things that are produced in order to be sold: *electrical goods* –see also DRY GOODS **2** possessions that can be moved, as opposed to houses, land etc.; BELONGINGS

**good·will** /gʊd'wɪl/ *n* [U] kind feelings toward or between people: *The company gave our Little League team $1000 as a **goodwill gesture**.* (=something you do to show you are kind)

**good·y¹** /'gʊdi/ *n* [C usually plural] INFORMAL something that is attractive, pleasant, or desirable, especially something good to eat: *We brought lots of goodies for the picnic.*

**goody²** *interjection* said especially by children when they are excited or happy: *Oh goody - we're having ice cream!*

**goody-good·y** /'.. ,..., ,.. '../, **goody-two-shoes** /,.. '. ./ *n* DISAPPROVING someone who likes to seem very good and helpful in order to please his/her parents, teachers etc.

**goo·ey** /'gui/ *adj* INFORMAL **1** sticky, soft, and usually sweet: *gooey caramel* **2** expressing your love for someone in a way that other people think is silly: *I hate gooey romantic movies!*

**goof**[1] /guf/ *v* [I] INFORMAL to make a silly mistake: *Oops! I goofed.*

**goof around** *phr v* [I] INFORMAL to spend time doing silly things: *We were just goofing around at the mall.*

**goof off** *phr v* [I] INFORMAL to waste time or avoid doing any work: *Jason's been goofing off in class lately.* –**goof-off** /'. ./ *n*

**goof**[2] *n* INFORMAL **1** a silly mistake **2** someone who is silly: *You big goof!*

**goof·y** /'gufi/ *adj* INFORMAL stupid or silly: *a goofy smile*

**gook** /guk/ *n* SPOKEN TABOO an extremely offensive word for someone from a country in the Far East

**goon** /gun/ *n* INFORMAL **1** a violent criminal who is paid to frighten or attack people **2** a silly or stupid person

**goop** /gup/ *n* [U] INFORMAL a thick, slightly sticky substance: *What's that goop in your hair?*

**goose** /gus/ *n, plural* **geese** **1** a common water bird that is similar to a duck but larger, and makes loud noises **2** [U] the meat from this bird

**goose·bumps** /'gusbʌmps/, **goose pim·ples** /'. ,../ *n* [plural] a condition in which your skin is raised up in small points because you are cold or afraid

**GOP** *n* **the GOP** Grand Old Party; another name for the Republican party in US politics

**go·pher** /'goufɚ/ *n* a North and Central American animal like a SQUIRREL with a short tail, that lives in holes in the ground

**gore**[1] /gɔr/ *v* [T] if an animal gores someone, it wounds him/her with its horns

**gore**[2] *n* [U] blood that has flowed from a wound and become thicker and darker

**gorge**[1] /gɔrdʒ/ *n* a deep narrow valley with steep sides

**gorge**[2] *v* **gorge yourself on/with sth** to eat until you are too full: *We were gorging ourselves on popcorn and hot dogs at the game.*

**gor·geous** /'gɔrdʒəs/ *adj* very beautiful or pleasant: *What a gorgeous sunny day!* | *I think Lizzie is gorgeous.*

**go·ril·la** /gə'rɪlə/ *n* the largest type of APE (=animal like a monkey)

**gor·y** /'gɔri/ *adj* clearly describing or showing violence, blood, and killing: *a gory movie*

**gosh** /gɑʃ/ *interjection* said when you are surprised: *Gosh! I never knew that!*

**gos·ling** /'gɑzlɪŋ/ *n* a baby GOOSE

**gos·pel** /'gɑspəl/ *n* **1** also **Gospel** one of the four stories of Christ's life in the Bible **2** [U] also **gospel truth** /,.. './ something that is completely true: *Don't take what Ellen says as gospel.* (=believe it to be completely true) **3** [U] also **gospel mu·sic** /'.. ,../ a type of Christian music, performed especially in African-American churches

**gos·sip**[1] /'gɑsəp/ *n* **1** [C,U] conversation or information about other people's behavior and private lives, often including unkind or untrue remarks: *People love hearing gossip about movie stars.* **2** someone who likes talking about other people's private lives

**gossip**[2] *v* [I] to talk or write gossip about someone or something: *What are you gossiping about?*

**got** /gɑt/ *v* **1** the past tense of GET **2** a PAST PARTICIPLE of GET

---

**USAGE NOTE got, gotten, have got, and have**

Use **gotten** as the past participle of **get**: *He'd gotten up early that day.* | *Kim has gotten engaged!* ✗ DON'T SAY "Kim has got engaged!" ✗  You can use **got** as a past tense instead of "became": *Kim just got engaged!* You can use **have got** to mean "possess": *I've got a new bicycle.* Usually, however, we use **have**: *I have a new bicycle.*

---

**got·cha** /'gɑtʃə/ *interjection* SPOKEN NONSTANDARD **1** a short form of "I've got you," said when you catch someone, or you have gained an advantage over him/her: *Gotcha, Pete! You're it now.* (=you're the person who chases other people in a game) **2** a word meaning "I understand" or "all right": *"First put this one here, and then tie them like this, OK?" "Gotcha."*

**got·ta** /'gɑtə/ *v* SPOKEN NONSTANDARD a short form of "got to," used alone or with "have": *I gotta go now.* | *You've gotta admit he plays really well.* –see usage note at HAVE TO

**got·ten** /'gɑt⁻n/ *v* the usual PAST PARTICIPLE of GET –see usage note at GOT

**gouge** /gaudʒ/ *v* [T] **1** to make a deep hole or cut in the surface of something **2** INFORMAL to charge someone too much money for something: *Hotels are ready to gouge Olympic visitors by raising their prices.* –**gouge** *n*

**gouge sth ↔ out** *phr v* [T] to make a hole in something by removing material that is on its surface

**gou·lash** /'gulɑʃ, -læʃ/ *n* [C,U] a dish made of meat cooked in liquid with a hot tasting pepper

**gourd** /gɔrd, gurd/ *n* a large fruit with a hard shell that is sometimes used as a container

**gour·met**[1] /gʊr'meɪ, 'gʊrmeɪ/ *adj* relating to very good food and drink: *a gourmet restaurant* | *gourmet food*

**gourmet**[2] *n* someone who knows a lot about good food and drink, and who enjoys them

**gout** /gaʊt/ *n* [U] a disease that makes your toes, knees, and fingers hurt and swell

**gov·ern** /'gʌvən/ *v* **1** [I,T] to officially control a country, state etc. and make all the decisions about things such as taxes and laws: *The same party governed for thirty years.* | *The Socialists have governed the country well.* **2** [T] to control the way a system or situation works: *new rules governing immigration*

**gov·ern·ess** /'gʌvənɪs/ *n* a female teacher who lives with a family and teaches their children at home

**gov·ern·ment** /'gʌvəmənt, 'gʌvənmənt/ *n* **1** also **Government** the group of people who govern a country, state etc.: *The government will send aid to the disaster area.* **2** [U] the process of governing, or the system used for governing: *a democratic government* –**governmental** /ˌgʌvən'mɛntl/ *adj*

**gov·er·nor**, **Governor** /'gʌvənə, -və-/ *n* the person in charge of governing a US state: *the Governor of California* –**governorship** *n* [U]

**gown** /gaʊn/ *n* **1** a long dress worn by a woman on formal occasions: *a silk evening gown* **2** a long loose piece of clothing worn for a special reason, for example by doctors, or by students at GRADUATION: *a hospital gown* (–worn by someone who is sick in the hospital)

**GPA** *n* grade point average; the average score that a student earns based on all of his/her grades, in which an A is 4 points, a B is 3, a C is 2, a D is 1, and an F is 0: *To be on the Honor Roll, students must have a GPA of at least 3.5.*

**grab**[1] /græb/ *v* **-bbed, -bbing** [T] **1** to take hold of someone or something with a sudden or violent movement: *He grabbed my bag and ran off.* **2** INFORMAL to do something such as eat or sleep for a very short time: *I'll just grab a sandwich for lunch.* **3** INFORMAL to quickly take an opportunity to do something: *Try to get there early and grab a seat.* | *Sylvia grabbed the chance to work in Italy.* **4 how does sth grab you?** SPOKEN used in order to ask if someone would be interested in doing a particular thing: *How does the idea of a trip to Hawaii grab you?*
**grab at** *phr v* [T] to quickly and suddenly put out your hand in order to take hold of something

**grab**[2] *n* **1 make a grab for/at** to suddenly try to take hold of something: *Parker made a grab for the knife.* **2 be up for grabs** INFORMAL if a job, prize, opportunity etc. is up for grabs, it is available for anyone who wants to try to get it: *There are still four tickets up for grabs for tonight's show.*

**grace**[1] /greɪs/ *n* **1** [U] a smooth way of moving that appears natural, relaxed, and attractive: *She moved with the grace of a dancer.* **2** [U] polite and pleasant behavior: *At least he had the grace to admit he was wrong.* **3** [U] also **grace period** more time that is added to the period you are allowed for finishing a piece of work, paying a debt etc.: *The bill was supposed to be paid by Friday, but they're giving me a week's grace.* **4 with good/bad grace** willingly and cheerfully, or in an unwilling and angry way: *Kevin smiled and accepted his defeat with good grace.* **5 the grace of God** the kindness shown to people by God: *It was only by the grace of God that we weren't killed.* **6** [C,U] a prayer thanking God that you say before a meal: *Who would like to say grace?* –see also **be in sb's good graces** (GOOD[1])

**grace**[2] *v* [T] **1 grace sb/sth with your presence** HUMOROUS said when someone arrives late, or when someone who does not often come to meetings or events arrives: *I'm so glad you've decided to grace us with your presence!* **2** FORMAL to make a place or an object look more beautiful or attractive: *His new painting now graces the wall of the dining room.*

**grace·ful** /'greɪsfəl/ *adj* **1** moving in a smooth and attractive way, or having an attractive shape: *a graceful dancer* | *graceful arched windows* **2** polite and exactly right for a situation: *a graceful apology* –**gracefully** *adv* –compare GRACIOUS

**gra·cious** /'greɪʃəs/ *adj* **1** behaving in a polite, kind, and generous way: *a gracious host* **2** having the type of expensive style, comfort, and beauty that only wealthy people can afford: *gracious living* **3 (goodness) gracious!** SPOKEN OLD-FASHIONED used in order to express surprise or to emphasize "yes" or "no" –**graciously** *adv*

**grad** /græd/ *n* SPOKEN ⇨ GRADUATE[1]

**gra·da·tion** /greɪ'deɪʃən, grə-/ *n* FORMAL a small change in a set of changes, or one level in a number of levels of development: *gradations of color from dark red to pink*

**grade**[1] /greɪd/ *n* **1** a) one of the 12 years you are in school in the US, or the students in a particular year: *He's just finished third/fourth etc. grade.* | *What grade are you in?* **2** [C,U] a particular standard or level of quality that a product, material etc. has: *Grade A milk/eggs/beef* **3** a number or letter that shows how well you have done at school, college etc: *Betsy always gets good grades.* **4 make the grade** to succeed or reach the necessary standard: *Only a few athletes make the grade in professional sports.* **5** ⇨ GRADIENT

**grade**[2] *v* [T] **1** to separate things, or arrange them in order according to their quality or rank: *eggs graded according to size* **2** to give a grade to an examination paper or to a piece of school work: *I spent the weekend grading tests.*

**grade point av·er·age** /'. . ,..' / *n* ⇨ GPA

**-grad·er** /'greɪdə/ *n* a child in a particular grade: *a cute little first-grader*

**grade school** /'. ./ *n* ⇨ ELEMENTARY SCHOOL

**gra·di·ent** /'greɪdiənt/ *n* a degree of slope, especially in a road or railroad: *a steep gradient*

**grad school** /'. ./ *n* INFORMAL ⇨ GRADUATE SCHOOL

**grad·u·al** /'grædʒuəl/ *adj* **1** happening, developing, or changing slowly over a long time: *gradual changes* –see picture at INCREASE² **2** a gradual slope is not steep

**grad·u·al·ly** /'grædʒuəli, -dʒəli/ *adv* in a way that happens or develops slowly over time: *Gradually, their marriage got better.*

**grad·u·ate¹** /'grædʒuɪt/ *n* someone who has completed a course at a school, college, or university: *a **graduate** of UCLA* –**graduate** *adj*

**grad·u·ate²** /'grædʒu,eɪt/ *v* [I] to obtain a degree from a college or university, or to complete your education at HIGH SCHOOL: *Ruth has just **graduated from** Princeton.*

**grad·u·at·ed** /'grædʒu,eɪtɪd/ *adj* divided into different levels or sizes from lower to higher amounts or degrees: *graduated rates of income tax | graduated measuring cups*

**graduate school** /'... ,./ *n* [C,U] a college or university where you can study for a MASTER'S DEGREE or a PH.D., or the period of time when you do this

**grad·u·a·tion** /,grædʒu'eɪʃən/ *n* **1** [U] the time when you complete a university degree or HIGH SCHOOL education: *After graduation, Jayne went to nursing school.* **2** [U] a ceremony at which you receive a degree or DIPLOMA: *graduation speeches*

**graf·fi·ti** /grə'fiʈi/ *n* [U] rude, humorous, or political writing and pictures on the walls of buildings

**graft¹** /græft/ *n* **1** [U] the practice of dishonestly using your position to get money or advantages: *politicians accused of graft* **2** a piece of healthy skin or bone taken from someone's body and put on a damaged part of his/her body **3** a piece cut from one plant and joined to another plant so that it grows where it is joined

**graft²** *v* [I,T] **1** to put a piece of skin or bone from one part of someone's body onto another part that has been damaged: *Doctors **grafted** skin from Mike's arm **onto** his face where it was burned.* **2** to join a part of a flower, plant, or tree onto another flower, plant, or tree

**grain** /greɪn/ *n* **1 a)** [C,U] a seed or seeds of crops such as corn, wheat, or rice that are used for food, or the crops themselves: *five-grain cereal | fields of grain* **2** a single, very small piece of something such as sand, salt etc. **3 the grain** the lines or patterns you can see in things such as wood or rock: *Split the wood along the grain.* **4 go against the grain** if something that you must do goes against the grain, you do not like doing it because it is not what you would naturally do **5 a grain of**

truth/doubt etc. a small amount of truth etc.: *There's not a grain of truth in what she said.* **6 take sth with a grain of salt** to not completely believe what someone tells you, because you know that s/he often lies or is wrong

grainy　　　sharp

**grain·y** /'greɪni/ *adj* a photograph that is grainy has a rough appearance, as if the images are made up of spots

**gram** /græm/ *n, written abbreviation* **gm.** a unit for measuring weight, equal to 1/1000 of a kilogram or 0.035 OUNCES

**gram·mar** /'græmɚ/ *n* **1** [U] the rules by which words change their form and are combined into sentences, or the study or use of these rules: *Mr. Watson, will you correct the grammar in my essay?* **2** a particular description of grammar, or a book that describes grammar rules: *a good English grammar*

**gram·mat·i·cal** /grə'mæṭɪkəl/ *adj* **1** relating to the use of grammar: *You're still making grammatical errors.* ✗ DON'T SAY "You're still making errors that are grammatical." ✗ **2** correct according to the rules of grammar: *a grammatical sentence* –**grammatically** *adv* –opposite UNGRAMMATICAL

**Gram·my** /'græmi/ *n* a prize given in the US every year to the best song, the best singer etc. in the music industry

**grand¹** /grænd/ *adj* **1** higher in rank than others of the same kind: *the grand prize* **2 grand total** the final total you get when you add up several numbers or amounts **3** OLD-FASHIONED very good or impressive: *a grand old house* –**grandly** *adv*

**grand²** *n* INFORMAL **1** [plural] **grand** 1000 dollars: *Bill only paid five grand for that car.* **2** ⇨ GRAND PIANO

**grand·child** /'græntʃaɪld/ *n* the child of your son or daughter –see picture at FAMILY

**grand·dad** /'grændæd/ *n* INFORMAL ⇨ GRAND-FATHER

**grand·daugh·ter** /'græn,dɔṭɚ/ *n* the daughter of your son or daughter –see picture at FA-MILY

**gran·deur** /'grændʒɚ, -dʒʊr/ *n* [U] impressive beauty, power, or size: *the grandeur of the Pacific Ocean*

**grand·fa·ther** /'grænd,fɑðɚ/ *n* the father of your mother or father –see picture at FAMILY

**grandfather clock** /'... ,./ *n* a tall clock in a wooden case that stands on the floor

**gran·di·ose** /'grændi,ous, ,grændi'ous/ *adj* DISAPPROVING grandiose plans sound very important but are really not practical

**grand ju·ry** /, '../ *n* a group of people who decide whether someone who may be guilty of a crime should be judged in a court of law

**grand·ma** /'grændmɑ, 'græmɑ/ *n* INFORMAL ⇨ GRANDMOTHER

**grand·moth·er** /'grænd,mʌðɚ/ *n* the mother of your mother or father −see picture at FAMILY

**grand·pa** /'grændpɑ, 'græmpɑ/ *n* INFORMAL ⇨ GRANDFATHER

**grand·par·ent** /'grænd,pɛrənt/ *n* the parent of your mother or father −see picture at FAMILY

**grand pi·an·o** /, .'../ *n* the type of large piano often used at concerts

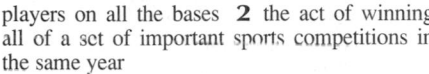
grand piano

**grand prix** /,grɑn 'pri/ *n* one of a set of international races, especially a car race

**grand slam** /, '.'./ *n* **1** a hit in baseball that gets four points because it is a HOME RUN and there are players on all the bases **2** the act of winning all of a set of important sports competitions in the same year

**grand·son** /'grændsʌn/ *n* the son of your son or daughter −see picture at FAMILY

**grand·stand** /'grændstænd/ *n* a large structure that has many rows of seats and a roof, where people sit to watch sports competitions or races −compare BLEACHERS

**gran·ite** /'grænɪt/ *n* a very hard gray rock, often used in buildings

**gran·ny** /'græni/ *n* INFORMAL ⇨ GRANDMOTHER

**gra·no·la** /grə'noulə/ *n* [U] a breakfast food made from nuts, OATS, and seeds

**grant¹** /grænt/ *n* an amount of money given to someone by the government for a particular purpose: *a research grant for cancer treatment*

**grant²** *v* **1 take it for granted (that)** to believe that something is true without making sure; ASSUME: *You shouldn't take it for granted that your parents will pay for college.* **2 take sb for granted** to expect that someone will always support you, and never thank him/her: *He's so busy with his work that he takes his family for granted.* **3** [T] FORMAL to give someone something that s/he has asked for or earned, especially official permission to do something: *Ms. Chung was granted American citizenship last year.* **4 granted (that)** used in order to say that something is true, before you say something else about it: *Granted, he didn't practice much, but he played well anyway.*

**gran·u·lat·ed** /'grænyə,leɪṭɪd/ *adj* granulated sugar is in the form of small white grains

**gran·ule** /'grænyul/ *n* a very small hard piece of something: *instant coffee granules* −**granular** /'grænyələ/ *adj*

**grape** /greɪp/ *n* a small round green or purple fruit that grows on a VINE and is often used for making wine −see picture on page 470

**grape·fruit** /'greɪpfrut/ *n* a yellow bitter-tasting fruit, with thick skin like an orange −see picture on page 470

**grape·vine** /'greɪpvaɪn/ *n* **1 hear sth on/through the grapevine** to hear news because it has been passed from one person to another in conversation: *Sarah had heard through the grapevine that Larry was getting the job.* **2** a plant that produces GRAPES

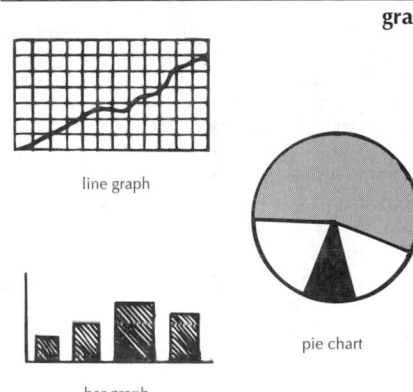
graph

line graph

bar graph

pie chart

**graph** /græf/ *n* a drawing that shows how two or more sets of measurements are related to each other: *a graph showing population growth over 50 years*

**graph·ic** /'græfɪk/ *adj* **1** relating to drawing or printing: *graphic illustrations* **2 a graphic account/description etc.** a very clear description of an event that gives a lot of details −see also GRAPHICS

**graph·i·cally** /'græfɪkli/ *adv* **1** clearly and with a lot of detail: *She described the scene so graphically that we felt we were there.* **2** FORMAL using a graph: *temperature changes shown graphically*

**graphic de·sign** /,.. .'./ *n* [U] the art of combining pictures, words, and decoration in the production of books, magazines etc.

**graph·ics** /'græfɪks/ *n* [plural, U] the activity of drawing pictures or designs, or the designs or pictures themselves: *a graphics program for the computer | a magazine with strong graphics*

**graph·ite** /'græfaɪt/ *n* [U] a soft black substance that is a type of CARBON and is used in pencils

**grap·ple** /'græpəl/ *v* [I] to fight or struggle with someone, holding him/her tightly: *A young man was grappling with the guard.*

**grapple with** sth *phr v* [T] to try hard to solve a difficult problem: *He'd never grappled with the issues that most principals deal with.*

**grasp**[1] /græsp/ *v* [T] **1** to take and hold something firmly: *He stumbled a little and grasped Tanya's arm.* **2** to completely understand something, especially a complicated fact or idea: *They couldn't quite grasp the significance of the problem.*

**grasp at** sth *phr v* [T] **1 sb is grasping at straws** used when someone keeps trying to stop a bad thing from happening, even though nothing s/he does will stop it **2** to eagerly try to reach something or to use an opportunity: *The public is grasping at these reforms because they believe schools have failed to do their job.*

**grasp**[2] *n* [singular] **1** the ability to understand a complicated idea or situation: *a good grasp of world politics | ideas that are beyond their grasp* (=too difficult to understand) **2** the possibility of being able to achieve or gain something: *Control over the whole program was now within her grasp.* **3** a hold on something, or your ability to hold it: *a firm grasp*

**grasp·ing** /'græspɪŋ/ *adj* too eager to get money: *a grasping man*

**grass** /græs/ *n* **1** [U] a very common plant with thin green leaves that grows across fields, parks, hills, and yards: *Please keep off the grass. | a blade of grass* **2** [C,U] a particular type of grass: *mountain grasses* **3** [U] SLANG ⇨ MARIJUANA

**grass·hop·per** /'græs,hɑpɚ/ *n* an insect that jumps with its long back legs and makes short loud noises

**grass·land** /'græslænd/ *n* [U] a large area of land covered with wild grass

**grass roots** /ˌ. './ *n* **the grass roots** the ordinary people in an organization rather than the leaders —**grass-roots** *adj*: *a grass-roots campaign/movement*

**gras·sy** /'græsi/ *adj* covered with grass: *a grassy hill*

**grate**[1] /greɪt/ *v* **1** [T] to rub food such as cheese against a rough surface in order to break it into small pieces **2** [I] to make an unpleasant sound by rubbing against something else: *chalk grating against the blackboard* **3 grate on sb's nerves** INFORMAL to annoy someone often: *She really grates on my nerves.*

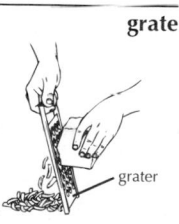

grate

grater

**grate**[2] *n* the metal BARs or frame that holds wood, coal etc. in a FIREPLACE

**grate·ful** /'greɪtfəl/ *adj* **1** feeling that you want to thank someone because of something kind that s/he has done: *Mona was grateful to Lorenzo for his support.* —opposite UNGRATE-

FUL **2 I/we would be grateful if ...** used in formal situations or letters to make a request: *I would be grateful if you would allow me to visit your school.*

**grat·er** /'greɪtɚ/ *n* a kitchen tool used for grating (GRATE) food —see picture at GRATE[1]

**grat·i·fy** /'grætə,faɪ/ *v* [T] FORMAL **1** be gratified to feel pleased and satisfied: *I was gratified to hear/know that they like my work.* **2 gratify a desire/need etc.** to do something so that you learn or get what you want —**gratification** /ˌgrætəfə'keɪʃən/ *n* [U]

**grat·i·fy·ing** /'grætə,faɪ-ɪŋ/ *adj* FORMAL pleasing and satisfying: *It's gratifying to know that we helped Matt get his job.*

**grat·ing**[1] /'greɪtɪŋ/ *n* a metal frame with BARs across it, used for covering a window or a hole in the ground

**grating**[2] *adj* a grating sound is unpleasant and annoying: *a grating voice*

**gra·tis** /'grætɪs, 'grɑ-/ *adj, adv* FORMAL provided without payment; free

**grat·i·tude** /'grætə,tud/ *n* [U] the feeling of being grateful: *I would like to express my gratitude to everyone who helped us.* —opposite INGRATITUDE

**gra·tu·i·tous** /grə'tuətəs/ *adj* said or done without a good reason in a way that offends someone: *The gratuitous killing of dolphins must be stopped.*

**gra·tu·i·ty** /grə'tuəti/ *n* FORMAL ⇨ TIP[1]

**grave**[1] /greɪv/ *n* **1** the place where a dead body is buried **2 sb would turn/roll over in the grave** used in order to say that someone who is dead would strongly disapprove of something that is happening now: *Mozart would roll over in his grave if he heard this music.* **3 the grave** LITERARY death —see also **dig your own grave** (DIG[1])

**grave**[2] *adj* **1** very serious and worrying: *I have grave doubts about his ability.* **2** looking or sounding very serious: *Dr. Fromm looked grave. "I have some bad news," he said.* —**gravely** *adv*

**grav·el** /'grævəl/ *n* [U] small stones used in order to make a surface for paths or roads —**graveled** *adj*: *a graveled driveway*

**grav·el·ly** /'grævəli/ *adj* **1** a gravelly voice sounds low and rough **2** covered or mixed with GRAVEL

**grave·side** /'greɪvsaɪd/ *n* **at the graveside** beside a grave, especially when someone is being buried there

**grave·stone** /'greɪvstoun/ *n* a stone on a grave that shows the name of the dead person and the dates of his/her birth and death

**grave·yard** /'greɪvyɑrd/ *n* an area of ground where people are buried, often near a church —compare CEMETERY

**grav·i·tate** /'grævə,teɪt/ *v* [I] **gravitate to/toward** to be attracted to something and move toward it, or become involved with it: *Different types of students gravitate toward different subjects.*

**grav·i·ta·tion** /ˌɡrævəˈteɪʃən/ *n* [U] TECHNICAL the force that makes two objects, such as PLANETs, move toward each other because of their MASS

**grav·i·ta·tion·al** /ˌɡrævəˈteɪʃənl/ *adj* TECHNICAL related to GRAVITY: *the Earth's gravitational pull*

**grav·i·ty** /ˈɡrævəti/ *n* [U] **1** TECHNICAL the force that makes objects fall to the ground: *the laws of gravity* **2** FORMAL the seriousness or importance of an event, situation etc.

**gra·vy** /ˈɡreɪvi/ *n* [U] **1** SAUCE made from the juice of cooked meat, flour, and milk **2** INFORMAL something good that is more than you expected to get: *Once you've paid your debts, the rest is gravy.*

**gray¹** /ɡreɪ/ *adj* **1** having a color of black mixed with white, like rain clouds **2** having gray hair: *Ryan turned gray when he was only 30.* **3** if the weather is gray, the sky is full of clouds **4 a gray area** a subject that is hard to deal with or understand because it does not have clear rules or limits

**gray²** *n* [U] a color made from black mixed with white: *The suit comes in gray or red.*

**gray³** *v* [I] if someone grays, his/her hair becomes gray

**gray mat·ter** /ˌ. ˈ../ *n* [U] INFORMAL your intelligence

**graze** /ɡreɪz/ *v* **1** [I,T] if an animal grazes or you graze it, it eats grass: *cattle grazing in the field* **2** [T] to touch something lightly while passing it, sometimes damaging it: *A bullet grazed his arm.* **3** [T] to injure yourself by accidentally rubbing against something rough: *Billy grazed his knee on the sidewalk when he fell.* **–graze** *n*

**grease¹** /ɡris/ *n* [U] **1** a thick oily substance that is put on the moving parts of a car or machine to make it run smoothly **2** soft fat from animals or vegetables

**grease²** *v* [T] to put GREASE on something

**greas·y** /ˈɡrisi, -zi/ *adj* covered in GREASE or oil, or full of grease: *greasy food* | *greasy hair*

**greasy spoon** /ˌ.. ˈ./ *n* INFORMAL an old, slightly dirty restaurant that serves cheap food that is mainly fried (FRY)

**great** /ɡreɪt/ *adj*
**1** ▶USEFUL◀ INFORMAL very useful or suitable for something: *This stuff's great for getting stains out of clothes.*
**2** ▶LARGE◀ very large in size, amount, or degree: *Willis caught a great big fish!* | *A great many people died.*
**3** ▶IMPORTANT◀ very important, successful, or famous: *the great civilizations of the past* | *the greatest movie star of all time*
**4 a great deal** a lot: *He's traveled a great deal.*

**5 (the) Great** used in names to mean large or important: *Alexander the Great* | *the Great Lakes*
**6 great-grandmother/great-uncle** etc. the grandmother etc. of one of your parents
**7 great-granddaughter / great-nephew** etc. the GRANDDAUGHTER etc. of your child
**8 Greater** used before the name of a city to mean the city and its outer areas: *Greater Seattle*

SPOKEN PHRASES
**9** very good; excellent: *It's great to see you again!* | *We had a great time.*
**10** said when you are annoyed and think that something is not good at all: *"Your car won't be ready until next week." "Oh, great!"*

**–greatness** *n* [U]

**great·ly** /ˈɡreɪtli/ *adv* FORMAL extremely or very much: *The money you lent us was greatly appreciated.* ✗ DON'T SAY "The money was appreciated greatly." ✗

**greed** /ɡrid/ *n* [U] a strong desire to have more money, food, power etc. than you need

**greed·y** /ˈɡridi/ *adj* wanting more money, food, power etc. than you need: *Don't be so greedy - leave some cake for the rest of us!* **–greedily** *adv* **–greediness** *n* [U]

**Greek¹** /ɡrik/ *adj* **1** relating to or coming from Greece **2** relating to the Greek language

**Greek²** *n* **1** [U] the language used in Greece **2** someone from Greece

**green¹** /ɡrin/ *adj* **1** having the color of grass: *green eyes* | *Go on - the light's green.* **2** covered with grass, trees, bushes etc.: *green fields* **3** fruit that is green is not yet ready to be eaten: *green bananas* **4** relating to the environment: *green issues* **5 be green with envy** to be very JEALOUS **6 give sb/sth the green light** to allow a PROJECT, plan etc. to begin: *The board just gave us the green light to begin research.* **7** INFORMAL young and lacking experience in a job: *The trainees are still pretty green.* **8 have a green thumb** to be good at making plants grow

**green²** *n* **1** [C,U] the color of grass and leaves **2** the smooth flat area of grass around a hole on a GOLF COURSE –see also GREENS

**green·back** /ˈɡrinbæk/ *n* INFORMAL a dollar BILL

**green bean** /ˈ. ., ˌ. ˈ./ *n* a long thin green vegetable that is picked and eaten before the beans inside it grow –see picture on page 470

**green card** /ˈ. ./ *n* a document that shows that a foreigner can live and work in the US. The card itself is no longer green

**green·er·y** /ˈɡrinəri/ *n* [U] green leaves and plants, often used as a decoration

**green·horn** /ˈɡrinhɔrn/ *n* INFORMAL someone who lacks experience in a job and can be easily deceived

**green·house** /'grinhaʊs/ *n* a glass building in which you grow plants that need to be protected from the weather

**greenhouse ef·fect** /'.. ..,./ *n* **the greenhouse effect** the gradual warming of the air around the Earth as a result of the sun's heat being trapped by POLLUTION

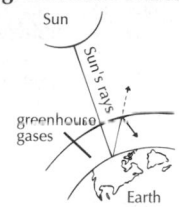

greenhouse effect

Sun

Sun's rays

greenhouse gases

Earth

**green on·ion** /,. '../ *n* [C,U] a small white onion with long thin green leaves that you eat raw

**greens** /grinz/ *n* [plural] **1** vegetables with large green leaves: *Eat your greens, they're good for you.* **2** leaves and branches used for decoration, especially at Christmas

**greet** /grit/ *v* [T] **1** to say hello to someone or welcome him/her: *Roz's mother greeted her with hugs and kisses.* **2** to react to something in a particular way: *The first speech was greeted with cheers and laughter.*

**greet·ing** /'gritɪŋ/ *n* **1** something that you say or do when you meet someone: *The two men exchanged greetings.* (=said hello to each other) **2** birthday/Christmas etc. greetings a message saying that you hope someone will be happy and healthy on his/her BIRTHDAY, at Christmas etc.

---

**USAGE NOTE** greetings

When you see someone you know, you can greet him/her informally by saying "Hi, how are you?" or more formally by saying "Hello, how are you?" You usually answer by saying "Fine, thanks, and you?" Asking "How are you?" is just a greeting. Do not answer this question by talking about your health or any problems you might have, unless you are talking to a good friend.

---

**greeting card** /'.. ,./ *n* a card that you send to someone on his/her BIRTHDAY, at Christmas etc.

**gre·gar·i·ous** /grɪ'gɛriəs/ *adj* someone who is gregarious is friendly and enjoys being with other people; SOCIABLE: *Kim's very gregarious.*

**grem·lin** /'grɛmlən/ *n* an imaginary evil spirit that is blamed for problems in machinery

**gre·nade** /grə'neɪd/ *n* a small bomb that can be thrown by hand or fired from a gun

**grew** /gru/ *v* the past tense of GROW

**grey** /greɪ/ *adj* ⇨ GRAY¹

**grey·hound** /'greɪhaʊnd/ *n* a thin dog with long legs that can run very fast, often used in races

**grid** /grɪd/ *n* **1** a pattern of straight lines that cross each other and form squares: *streets organized in a grid system* **2** the system of squares with numbers on them that are printed on a map so the exact position of any place can be found

**grid·dle** /'grɪdl/ *n* an iron plate used for cooking food on top of a STOVE

**grid·i·ron** /'grɪdaɪən/ *n* INFORMAL a football field

**grid·lock** /'grɪdlɑk/ *n* [U] a situation in which the streets are so full of cars that the cars cannot move

**grief** /grif/ *n* [U] **1** extreme sadness, especially because someone you love has died: *His grief was obvious from the way he spoke.* **2** give sb grief INFORMAL to say something that annoys or causes trouble for someone: *My mom's been giving me grief about not helping with my little sister.* **3** come to grief to not be successful, or to be harmed in an accident –see also **good grief** (GOOD)

**griev·ance** /'grivəns/ *n* [C,U] something that you complain about because you think it is unfair: *You ought to follow the correct grievance procedure.* (=the official way to make a complaint)

**grieve** /griv/ *v* **1** [I,T] to feel extremely sad, especially because someone you love has died **2** [T] FORMAL to make someone feel very unhappy: *It grieves me to see him wasting his talents.*

**griev·ous** /'grivəs/ *adj* FORMAL very serious and likely to be harmful; severe: *a grievous error* –**grievously** *adv*

**grill¹** /grɪl/ *v* **1** [I,T] if you grill something, or if something grills, you cook it over a fire –compare BROIL **2** [T] INFORMAL to ask someone a lot of difficult questions for a long period of time: *Police are grilling the suspect now.*

**grill²** *n* **1** a flat metal frame with BARs across it that can be put over a fire so that food can be cooked on it **2** also **grille** a frame of metal bars used for protecting something such as a window or the front of a car

**grim** /grɪm/ *adj* **1** making you feel worried and unhappy: *grim news | We were running out of money and things were looking pretty grim.* **2** very serious, not smiling: *a grim-faced judge | their grim determination to reach the mountain top* (=determination in spite of difficulties or danger) **3** a place that is grim is unattractive and unpleasant –**grimly** *adv*

**grim·ace** /'grɪməs/ *v* [I] to twist your face in an ugly way because you feel pain, do not like something, or are trying to be funny: *Theo rolled around on the field grimacing with pain.* –**grimace** *n*

**grime** /graɪm/ *n* [U] thick black dirt that forms a layer on surfaces

**grim·y** /'graɪmi/ *adj* covered in thick black dirt

**grin¹** /grɪn/ *v* **-nned, -nning** [I] **1** to smile continuously with a very big smile: *Sally was grinning at Martin from across the room.* **2** grin and bear it INFORMAL to accept a difficult situation without complaining because you cannot change it: *It won't be fun, but we'll have to grin and bear it.*

**grin²** *n* a wide smile

**grind¹** /graɪnd/ *v* **ground, ground, grinding** [T] **1** to crush something such as coffee beans into small pieces or powder, either in a machine or between two hard surfaces **2** to cut food such as raw meat into small pieces by using a machine **3** to rub two hard surfaces against each other, especially to make one of them sharper or smoother: *Sam grinds his teeth at night.* | *grinding knives* **4 grind to a halt** if something grinds to a halt, it slowly stops moving or stops being successful: *Traffic slowly ground to a halt.* | *Production ground to a halt at five of the factories.*

grind

pepper mill

**grind²** *n* [singular] INFORMAL work that makes you tired because it is physically hard or boring: *It's Monday again - back to the grind.*

**grind·er** /ˈgraɪndɚ/ *n* a machine for GRINDing something: *a coffee grinder* | *a knife grinder*

**grind·ing** /ˈgraɪndɪŋ/ *adj* **grinding poverty** the state of being extremely poor

**grind·stone** /ˈgraɪndstoʊn/ *n* a large round stone that is turned like a wheel and is used for making tools sharp —see also **keep your nose to the grindstone** (NOSE¹)

**grip¹** /grɪp/ *n* **1** [singular] a tight hold on something, or your ability to hold it: *Get a firm grip on the rope, then pull.* **2** [singular] power and control over a person, a situation, or your emotions: *Come on, Dee, get a grip on yourself!* (=make an effort to control your emotions) **3 come/get to grips with** to understand and deal with a difficult problem or situation: *Eric still hasn't come to grips with his drug problem.* **4 be in the grip of** to be experiencing a very unpleasant situation: *a country in the grip of a bad winter*

**grip²** *v* **-pped, -pping 1** [I,T] to hold something very tightly **2** [T] to have a strong effect on someone or something: *Unusually cold weather has gripped the northwest.* **3** [T] if something grips a surface, it stays on without slipping: *tires that grip the road*

**gripe¹** /graɪp/ *v* [I] INFORMAL to complain about something continuously and in an annoying way: *Now what's Pete griping about?*

**gripe²** *n* something that you keep complaining about: *The students' main gripe is the dorm food.*

**grip·ping** /ˈgrɪpɪŋ/ *adj* very exciting and interesting: *a gripping story*

**gris·ly** /ˈgrɪzli/ *adj* extremely unpleasant because death or violence is involved: *a grisly murder*

**grist** /grɪst/ *n* **grist for the mill** something that is useful in a particular situation: *a baseball player whose love life is grist for the gossip mill* (=it gives people something to talk about)

**gris·tle** /ˈgrɪsəl/ *n* [U] the part of a piece of meat that is not soft enough to eat

**grit¹** /grɪt/ *n* [U] **1** very small pieces of stone **2** INFORMAL determination and courage: *He's a guy who plays ball with a lot of grit.* —**gritty** *adj*

**grit²** *v* **grit your teeth** to use all your determination to continue doing something in spite of pain or difficulties: *Just grit your teeth; the worst is almost over.*

**grits** /grɪts/ *n* [plural] crushed grain that is cooked and often eaten for breakfast

**griz·zly bear** /ˈgrɪzli bɛr/ **grizzly** *n* a large brown bear that lives in the northwest of North America

**groan** /groʊn/ *v* [I] **1** to make a long deep sound because you are in pain, or are not happy about something: *Captain Marsh was holding his arm and groaning.* | *Scott told a terrible joke, and everyone groaned.* **2** to bend from carrying a heavy load: *shelves groaning under hundreds of books* —**groan** *n*: *Loud groans came from the crowd.*

**gro·cer** /ˈgroʊsɚ, -sɚ/ *n* someone who owns a GROCERY STORE or is in charge of one

**gro·cer·ies** /ˈgroʊsəriz, ˈgroʊʃriz/ *n* [plural] the food or other goods sold in a GROCERY STORE

**gro·cer·y store** /ˈgroʊsri ˌstɔr, -ʃri-/, **grocery** *n* a store that sells food and other things used in the home

**grog·gy** /ˈgrɑgi/ *adj* weak and unable to think clearly, because you are ill or tired: *Bill was groggy after studying all night.*

**groin** /grɔɪn/ *n* the part of your body where your legs join at the front —see picture at BODY

**groom¹** /grum/ *v* **1** [I,T] to take care of your appearance by keeping your hair and clothes clean and neat: *a well-groomed/badly-groomed young man* **2** [T] to prepare someone for an important job or position by training him/her: *Sharon's being groomed to take over the business.* **3** [T] to take care of animals by cleaning and brushing them —**grooming** *n* [U]

**groom²** *n* **1** a man at the time he gets married, or just after he is married **2** someone whose job is to take care of horses

**groove** /gruv/ *n* **1** a thick line cut into a surface to hold something, or to make something move or flow where you want it to: *Plant the seeds in grooves about a foot apart.* **2** [singular] INFORMAL the way things should be done, so that it seems easy and natural: *It will take the players a while to get back in the groove.*

**groov·y** /ˈgruvi/ *adj* INFORMAL a word meaning very good, fashionable, or fun, used especially in the 1960s

G

**grope** /group/ v **1** [I] to try to find something you cannot see, using your hands: *She groped in the dark for the flashlight.* **2 grope your way along/across** etc. to go somewhere by feeling the way with your hands because you cannot see **3 grope for sth** to try hard to find the right words to say, or the right solution to a problem **4** [T] INFORMAL to touch someone's body in a sexual way −**grope** n

**gross¹** /grous/ adj **1** SPOKEN very unpleasant to look at or think about: *There was one really gross part in the movie.* | *"Yesterday the dog threw up on the rug." "Oh, gross."* **2** a gross amount of money is the total amount before any tax or costs have been taken away: *gross income/sales* −compare NET³ **3** a gross weight is the total weight of something, including its wrapping **4** wrong and unacceptable: *gross inequalities in pay* −**grossly** adv

**gross²** v [T] to earn an amount as a total profit or as wages, before tax has been taken away: *the year's biggest grossing movie*

**gross** sb ↔ **out** phr v [T] SPOKEN to make someone feel sick because of something you say or do: *Don't talk about your operation! It grosses me out.*

**gross na·tion·al prod·uct** /ˌ. ˌ... ˈ../ n [singular] ⇨ GNP

**gro·tesque** /grouˈtɛsk/ adj ugly or strange in a way that is not natural or makes you uncomfortable: *drawings of grotesque monsters* −**grotesquely** adv

**grot·to** /ˈgrɑtou/ n a small natural CAVE, or one that someone has made

**grouch¹** /grautʃ/ n INFORMAL someone who is always complaining

**grouch²** v [I] INFORMAL to complain in a slightly angry way

**grouch·y** /ˈgrautʃi/ adj feeling annoyed and complaining a lot, especially because you are tired

**ground¹** /graund/ n **the ground a)** the surface of the earth: *The ground is too wet to sit on.* **b)** the soil on and under the surface of the earth: *The ground's too hard to plant trees now.* **1** ▶KNOWLEDGE◀ [U] an area of knowledge, ideas, experience etc.: *Scientists are breaking new ground* (=discovering new ideas) *in cancer research.* **2** ▶OPINIONS◀ [U] the opinions you have about something that people disagree about: *There has to be a way we can find some common ground.* (=something that everyone can agree about) | *It isn't likely that the Mayor will give ground.* (=change his/her opinions) **3 parade/sports/hunting** etc. **ground** a piece of land used for a special purpose **4 get off the ground** to start being successful: *His company hasn't really gotten off the ground yet.* **5 gain/lose ground** to become more or less

successful or popular: *Republicans have been gaining ground in recent months.* **6 hold/stand your ground** to refuse to change your opinion in spite of opposition **7** ▶WIRE◀ [singular] a wire that connects a piece of electrical equipment to the ground for safety −see also GROUNDS, UNDERGROUND

---

**USAGE NOTE ground**

Use **on the ground** to say where something is: *Sue's dropped her glove on the ground.* Use **to the ground** to talk about downward movement: *Eddie was knocked to the ground.*

---

**ground²** v [T] **1** to stop an aircraft or pilot from flying: *All planes are grounded due to snow.* **2 be grounded in** to be based on something: *a way of life grounded in your beliefs* **3** INFORMAL to stop a child from going out with his/her friends as a punishment for doing something wrong: *If you stay out that late again, you'll be grounded for a week.* **4** to make a piece of electrical equipment safe by connecting it to the ground with a wire

**ground³** adj ground coffee, pepper etc. has been crushed into small pieces

**ground⁴** v the past tense and PAST PARTICIPLE of GRIND

**ground beef** /ˌ. ˈ./ n ⇨ HAMBURGER

**ground·break·ing** /ˈ. ˌ../ adj involving new discoveries or new methods: *groundbreaking research in physics*

**ground crew** /ˈ. ./ n the group of people who work at an airport taking care of aircraft

**ground floor** /ˌ. ˈ.◀/ n **1** the part of a building that is on the same level as the ground −see picture at ATTIC **2 be/get in on the ground floor** to become involved in a plan or business activity from the beginning

**ground·hog** /ˈgraund-ˌhɔg/ n a small North American animal that has thick brown fur and lives in holes in the ground; WOODCHUCK

**groundhog**

**Groundhog Day** /ˈ.. ˌ./ n February 2; according to American stories, the first day of the year that a GROUNDHOG comes out of its hole. If it sees its shadow, there will be six more weeks of winter; if it does not, good weather will come early

**ground·less** /ˈgraundlɪs/ adj without any reason: *groundless fears* −**groundlessly** adv

**ground rule** /ˈ. ./ n a rule or principle on which future action or behavior should be based: *First, they had to set the ground rules for the debate.*

**grounds** /graundz/ n [plural] **1** a large area of land or sea that is used for a particular purpose: *burial grounds | fishing grounds* **2** the land or gardens around a building **3** reasons for thinking that something is true or for doing something: *Mark's drinking was grounds for divorce.* **4** the small pieces of something that sink to the bottom of a liquid: *coffee grounds*

**ground·swell** /'graʊndswel/ *n* **1 a groundswell of support/enthusiasm** a sudden increase in how strongly people feel about something **2** [singular, U] the strong movement of the sea that continues after a storm or strong winds

**ground·work** /'graʊndwɜrk/ *n* [U] important work that has to take place before another activity can be successful: *The groundwork for next year's conference will start soon.*

**group¹** /grup/ *n* **1** several people or things that are all together in the same place: *Everyone please get into groups of four.* **2** several people or things that are connected with each other in some way: *a group of Native American writers | One woman in our group goes to night school.* ✗ DON'T SAY "One woman of our group." ✗ **3** several companies that all have the same owner: *a book publishing group* **4** a number of musicians or singers who perform together, usually playing popular music: *a rock group*

**group²** *v* [I,T] to come together to make a group, or to arrange people or things in a group: *The visitors grouped themselves around the statue. | Birds can be grouped into several types.*

**group·ie** /'grupi/ *n* INFORMAL someone who follows ROCK musicians to their concerts, hoping to meet them

**group·ing** /'grupɪŋ/ *n* a set of people, things, or organizations that have the same interests, qualities, or features: *social groupings*

**group ther·a·py** /ˌ. '.../ *n* [U] a method of treating people with emotional or PSYCHOLOGICAL problems by bringing them together in groups to talk about their problems

**grouse¹** /graʊs/ *v* [I] INFORMAL to complain: *Tourists were grousing about the long lines.*

**grouse²** *n* [C,U] a small fat bird that is hunted for food and sport, or the meat from this bird

**grove** /groʊv/ *n* **1** an area of land planted with a particular type of tree: *a lemon grove* **2** a small group of trees

**grov·el** /'grɑvəl, 'grʌ-/ *v* [I] **1** to behave with too much respect toward someone because you want him/her to help or forgive you: *I've apologized, I've even groveled to him.* **2** to lie or move flat on the ground because you are afraid of someone, or as a way of obeying: *a dog groveling in front of its owner*

**grow** /groʊ/ *v* grew, grown, growing [I] **1** ▶DEVELOP◀ to develop and become bigger or longer over time, or to make something do this: *Jamie's grown two inches this year. | Are you growing a beard? | Your hair's grown really*

long.
**2** ▶PLANTS◀ [I,T] to exist and develop in a natural way, or to help plants do this: *Not many plants can grow in the far north. | We're trying to grow roses this year.*
**3** ▶INCREASE◀ [I] to increase in amount, size, or degree: *A growing number of students are dropping out of college. | a growing business*
**4** ▶BECOME◀ [linking verb] to become old, hot, worse etc. over a period of time: *We're growing older, Margaret.*
**5 grow to like/fear/respect etc.** to gradually start to have an opinion or feeling about someone or something: *I'm growing to like Dallas more.*
**6** ▶IMPROVE◀ [I] to improve in ability or character: *Beth's really growing as a singer.*
**7** ▶BUSINESS◀ [T] to make part of a business become larger or more successful

**grow apart** *phr v* [I] if two people grow apart, their relationship becomes less close

**grow into** sb/sth *v* [T] **1** to develop over time and become a particular type of person or thing: *Gene's grown into a handsome young man.* **2** if a child grows into clothes, s/he becomes big enough to wear them

**grow on** sb *phr v* [T] to gradually become more liked by someone: *Their music's strange, but after a while it grows on you.*

**grow out of** sth *phr v* [T] **1** to become too big to wear your old clothes **2** to stop doing something as you get older: *Sarah still sucks her thumb, but she'll grow out of it.*

**grow up** *phr v* [I] **1** to develop from being a child to being an adult: *I grew up in San Diego.* **2 grow up!** SPOKEN said in order to tell someone to behave more like an adult

**grow·er** /'groʊə/ *n* a person or company that grows fruit, vegetables etc. in order to sell them

**grow·ing pains** /'.. ˌ./ *n* [plural] problems and difficulties that start at the beginning of a new activity, for example starting a business

**growl** /graʊl/ *v* **1** [I] to make a deep angry sound: *dogs growling at a visitor* **2** [I,T] to say something in a low angry voice: *"Go away!" he growled.* **–growl** *n*

**grown¹** /groʊn/ *adj* **grown man/woman** a phrase meaning an adult, used when you think someone is not behaving in an adult way: *I've never seen a grown man act like that!*

**grown²** *v* the PAST PARTICIPLE of GROW

**grown-up¹** /'. ./ *n* a word meaning an adult, used especially by or to children: *Ask a grown-up to help you.*

**grown-up²** *adj* fully developed as an adult: *a grown-up son*

**growth** /groʊθ/ *n* **1** [singular, U] an increase or development in size, quality, amount, or importance: *Vitamins are necessary for healthy growth. | the growth of modern technology | population growth | There's a growth of interest in African music.* **2** [U] the development of someone's character, intelligence, or emotions: *a job that provides opportunities for personal growth* **3** something that grows in your body or on your skin, caused by a disease **4** [C,U] something that is growing: *New growth is showing on the plants.*

**grub**[1] /grʌb/ *n* **1** [U] INFORMAL food **2** an insect when it is in the form of a soft white WORM

**grub**[2] *v* -bbed, -bbing [I] INFORMAL to dig in order to get something: *pigs grubbing for roots*

**grub·by** /'grʌbi/ *adj* dirty: *grubby hands*

**grudge**[1] /grʌdʒ/ *n* a feeling of anger or dislike you have for someone who has harmed you: *Diane doesn't hold grudges.* (=stay angry with people) | *Aunt Alice bore a grudge against him for 25 years.*

**grudge**[2] *v* [T] ⇨ BEGRUDGE

**grudg·ing** /'grʌdʒɪŋ/ *adj* done or given without wanting to do so: *their grudging acceptance of the changes*

**gru·el** /'gruəl/ *n* [U] thin OATMEAL that was eaten in past times by poor or sick people

**gru·el·ing** /'gruəlɪŋ/ *adj* very tiring: *a grueling climb*

**grue·some** /'grusəm/ *adj* very unpleasant to look at, and usually involving death or injury: *a gruesome accident*

**gruff** /grʌf/ *adj* unfriendly or annoyed: *a gruff answer* **—gruffly** *adv*

**grum·ble** /'grʌmbəl/ *v* [I] to complain in a quiet but slightly angry way: *Their school bus driver used to grumble about the noise.*

**grump·y** /'grʌmpi/ *adj* having a bad temper and tending to complain **—grumpily** *adv*

**grunge** /grʌndʒ/ *n* **1** INFORMAL dirt and GREASE; GRIME: *What's all this grunge in the bathtub?* **2** a style of music and fashion popular with young people in the early 1990s

**grun·gy** /'grʌndʒi/ *adj* INFORMAL dirty and sometimes smelling bad

**grunt** /grʌnt/ *v* **1** [I,T] to make short sounds or say only a few words, when you do not want to talk: *He just grunted hello and kept walking.* **2** [I] to make short low sounds deep in your throat, like the sounds a pig makes **—grunt** *n*

**G-string** /'. ./ *n* very small underwear that does not cover the BUTTOCKs

**gua·ca·mo·le** /ˌgwɑkə'mouleɪ/ *n* [U] a Mexican dish made with crushed AVOCADOs

**guar·an·tee**[1] /ˌgærən'ti/ *v* [T] **1** to promise that something will happen or be done: *We guarantee to provide you with the most up-to-date market information.* **2** to make a formal written promise to repair or replace a product if it has a problem within a specific time: *All stereo parts are guaranteed against failure for a year.* **3** to make it certain that something will happen: *An education doesn't guarantee a good job.* **4** be guaranteed to do sth to be certain to behave, work, or happen in a

particular way: *Buying something new is guaranteed to make you feel better.*

**guarantee**[2] *n* **1** a formal written promise to repair or replace a product without charging, if it has a problem within a specific time after you buy it: *a two-year guarantee* | *Is the microwave still under guarantee?* (=protected by a guarantee) **2** a formal promise that something will be done or will happen: *There's no guarantee that the books will be delivered this week.* (=it is not at all sure to happen)

**guar·an·tor** /ˌgærən'tɔr, 'gærəntɚ/ *n* LAW someone who promises that s/he will pay for something if the person who should pay for it does not

**guar·an·ty** /'gærənti/ *n* LAW a formal promise, especially of payment

**guard**[1] /gɑrd/ *n*
**1** ▶PROTECTOR◀ someone whose job is to guard people, places, or objects so that they are not attacked or stolen: *security guards at the bank*
**2** ▶IN A PRISON◀ someone whose job is to prevent prisoners from escaping
**3** be on guard/stand guard to be responsible for guarding a place or person for a specific time: *Hogan was on guard until midnight.*
**4** catch/take sb off guard to surprise someone by doing something that s/he is not ready to deal with: *The question caught the senator off guard.*
**5** ▶EQUIPMENT◀ something that covers and protects someone or something: *a hockey player's face guard*
**6** be under (armed) guard to be guarded by a group of people with weapons
**7** sb's guard the state of being ready to defend yourself against an attack: *She's not going to let her guard down.* (=relax because a threat is gone)
**8** ▶SPORTS◀ a) one of two players in basketball whose main job is to defend his/her BASKET —see picture on page 472 b) one of two football players who play on either side of the CENTER

**guard**[2] *v* [T] to protect someone or something from being attacked or stolen, or to prevent a prisoner from escaping: *They have a dog to guard their house.*
**guard against** sth *phr v* [T] to try to prevent something from happening by being careful: *Exercise can help guard against a number of serious illnesses.*

**guard·ed** /'gɑrdɪd/ *adj* careful not to say too much: *a guarded answer*

**guard·i·an** /'gɑrdiən/ *n* **1** someone who is legally responsible for someone else, especially a child **2** FORMAL a person or organization that tries to protect laws, moral principles, traditional ways of doing things etc. **—guardianship** *n* [U]

**guardian an·gel** /ˌ... '../ *n* an imaginary good spirit who protects a person

G

**guard·rail** /ˈgɑrd-reɪl/ *n* a long metal BAR that keeps cars or people from falling over the edge of a road, boat, or high structure

**gua·va** /ˈgwɑvə/ *n* a small tropical fruit with pink flesh and many seeds inside

**gu·ber·na·to·ri·al** /ˌgubənəˈtɔriəl/ *adj* FORMAL relating to the position of being a GOVERNOR

**guer·ril·la**, **guerilla** /gəˈrɪlə/ *n* a member of an independent fighting group that fights for political reasons and attacks the enemy in small groups: *guerrilla warfare*

**guess¹** /gɛs/ *v* **1** [I,T] **a)** to try to answer a question or make a judgment without knowing all the facts: *"How old is Ginny's son?" "I'd say 25, but I'm just guessing."* **b)** to get the right answer to something in this way: *"Don't tell me; you got the job." "How did you guess?"* **2 keep sb guessing** to not tell someone what is going to happen next

SPOKEN PHRASES

**3 I guess a)** said when you suppose that something is true or likely: *His light's on, so I guess he's still up.* **b)** used in order to show that you know about a situation because someone else has told you about it: *I wasn't there, but I guess Mr. Radkin yelled at Jeannie.* **4 I guess so/not** used in order to say yes or no when you are not very sure: *"She wasn't happy?" "I guess not."* **5 guess what/you'll never guess** said when you are about to tell someone something that will surprise him/her: *You'll never guess what I bought!*

**guess²** *n* **1** an attempt to guess something: *Just take a guess.* **2** an opinion you get by guessing: *My guess is (that) Don won't come.* **3 be anybody's guess** to be something that no one knows: *Where he disappeared to was anybody's guess.* **4 your guess is as good as mine** SPOKEN said in order to tell someone that you do not know any more than s/he does about something

**guess·ti·mate** /ˈgɛstəmɪt/ *n* INFORMAL an attempt to judge a quantity by guessing it –**guesstimate** /ˈgɛstəˌmeɪt/ *v* [I,T]

**guess·work** /ˈgɛswɚk/ *n* [U] a way of trying to find the answer to something by guessing: *Many of Carey's price estimates are based on guesswork.*

**guest¹** /gɛst/ *n* **1** someone who is visiting or staying in someone else's home because s/he has been invited: *We're having guests this weekend.* | *a dinner guest* **2** someone who is paying to stay in a hotel **3** someone who is invited to a restaurant, theater, club etc. by someone else who pays for him/her: *Now, you and Anna are our guests this evening, all right?* **4 be my guest** SPOKEN said when giving someone permission to do what s/he has asked to do: *"Could I use your phone?" "Be my guest."*

**guest²** *adj* **1 guest speaker/artist/star** someone famous who is invited to speak on a subject or take part in a performance **2** for guests to use: *the guest room* | *guest towels*

**guff** /gʌf/ *n* [U] SPOKEN stupid or annoying behavior or talk: *Don't take any guff from those guys.*

**guf·faw** /gəˈfɔ/ *v* [I] to laugh loudly –**guffaw** *n*

**guid·ance** /ˈgaɪdns/ *n* [U] helpful advice about work, education etc.: *Francis had worked at a magazine, and gave me some guidance.*

**guidance coun·sel·or** /ˈ.. ˌ.../ *n* someone who works in a school to give advice to students about what subjects to study, and to help them with personal problems

**guide¹** /gaɪd/ *n* **1** someone who shows you the way to a place, especially someone whose job is to show a place to tourists: *a tour guide* **2** a book that provides information about a particular subject or explains how to do something: *a guide for new parents* **3** something or someone that helps you decide what to do or how to do it: *A friend's experience isn't always the best guide for you.*

**guide²** *v* [T] **1** to take someone to a place that you know very well and show it to him/her: *He offered to guide us around/through the city* **2** to help someone go somewhere or do something correctly: *The pilot guided the plane to a safe landing.* **3** to strongly influence someone: *We hope you'll be guided by our advice.* –see usage note at LEAD¹

**guide·book** /ˈgaɪdbʊk/ *n* a special book about a city or country that gives details about the place and its history

**guide·lines** /ˈgaɪdlaɪnz/ *n* [plural] rules or instructions about the best way to do something

**guild** /gɪld/ *n* an organization of people who share the same interests, skills, or profession: *the writers' guild*

**guile** /gaɪl/ *n* [U] FORMAL the use of smart but dishonest methods to deceive someone

**guile·less** /ˈgaɪl-lɪs/ *adj* behaving in an honest way, without trying to deceive people

**guil·lo·tine** /ˈgɪləˌtin, ˈgiə-, ˌgɪəˈtin/ *n* a piece of equipment that was used in past times to cut off the heads of criminals –**guillotine** *v* [T]

**guilt** /gɪlt/ *n* [U] **1** a strong feeling of shame and sadness that you have when you know or believe you have done something wrong: *Marta felt a sense of guilt about leaving home.* **2 guilt trip** INFORMAL a feeling of guilt about something, when this is unreasonable: *I wish my parents would stop laying a guilt trip on me about not going to college.* (=making me feel guilty) **3** the fact of having broken an official law or moral rule: *The jury was sure of the defendant's guilt.* **4** the state of being responsible for something bad that has happened; FAULT:

*Ron admitted that the guilt was his.* −opposite INNOCENCE

**guilt·rid·den** /'. ,../ *adj* feeling so guilty about something that you cannot think about anything else

**guilt·y** /'gɪlti/ *adj* **1** ashamed and sad because you have done something that you know is wrong: *I feel guilty about not inviting her to the party.* **2** having done something that is a crime: *He was found guilty of fraud.* −**guiltily** *adv* −**guiltiness** *n* [U] −opposite INNOCENT

---

**USAGE NOTE** guilty, ashamed, and embarrassed

Use **guilty** to say that someone is unhappy because s/he has done something that has harmed someone else: *He felt guilty about always working so late.* Use **ashamed** to say that someone feels disappointed with himself/herself about doing something that is wrong or unacceptable: *She was ashamed of having told her mother a lie.* Use **embarrassed** to say that someone is upset because s/he has done something that makes him/her seem silly: *He was embarrassed about the way he acted at the party.*

---

**guin·ea pig** /'gɪni ˌpɪg/ *n* **1** a small animal like a rat with fur, short ears, and no tail, that is often kept as a pet **2** INFORMAL someone who is used in a test to see how successful or safe a new product, system etc. is

**guise** /gaɪz/ *n* FORMAL the way someone or something seems to be, which is meant to hide the truth: *In/under the guise of being protectors, the army took over the government.*

**gui·tar** /gɪ'tɑr/ *n* a musical instrument with six strings, a long neck, and a wooden body, which you play by PLUCKing the strings −**guitarist** *n*

**gulch** /gʌltʃ/ *n* a narrow deep valley formed by flowing water, but usually dry

**gulf** /gʌlf/ *n* **1** a large area of ocean partly enclosed by land: *the Gulf of Mexico* **2** a great difference and lack of understanding between two groups of people: *the wide gulf between the rich and the poor* **3** a deep hollow place in the Earth's surface

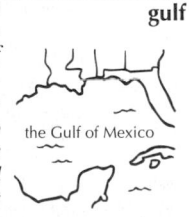

gulf

the Gulf of Mexico

**gull** /gʌl/ *n* ⇨ SEAGULL

**gul·let** /'gʌlɪt/ *n* INFORMAL ⇨ ESOPHAGUS

**gul·li·ble** /'gʌləbəl/ *adj* too ready to believe what other people say, and therefore easy to trick −**gullibility** /ˌgʌlə'bɪləti/ *n* [U]

**gul·ly** /'gʌli/ *n* **1** a small narrow valley, formed by a lot of rain flowing down the side of a hill **2** a deep DITCH

**gulp¹** /gʌlp/ *v* **1** [T] also **gulp down** to swallow something quickly: *She gulped her tea and ran to catch the bus.* **2** [T] also **gulp in** to quickly take in large breaths of air: *Steve leaned on the car and gulped in the night air.* **3** [I] to swallow suddenly because you are surprised or nervous: *Shula read the test questions, and gulped.*

**gulp** sth ↔ **back** *phr v* [T] to stop yourself from expressing your feelings: *The boy was trying to gulp back his tears.*

**gulp²** *n* an act of swallowing something quickly: *He drank his beer in one gulp.*

**gum¹** /gʌm/ *n* **1** a sweet substance that you CHEW for a long time but do not swallow **2** [C usually plural] the pink part inside your mouth that holds your teeth **3** [U] a sticky substance in the stems of some trees −**gummy** *adj*

**gum²** *v*

**gum** sth ↔ **up** *phr v* [T] INFORMAL to prevent something from working correctly by covering it with a sticky substance: *How did this lock get so gummed up?*

**gum·bo** /'gʌmboʊ/ *n* [U] a thick soup made with meat, fish, and particular vegetables

**gum·drop** /'gʌmdrɑp/ *n* a small CHEWY candy

**gump·tion** /'gʌmpʃən/ *n* [U] INFORMAL the ability and determination to decide what needs to be done and to do it: *At least Kathy has the gumption to get what she wants.*

**gun¹** /gʌn/ *n* **1** a weapon from which bullets or SHELLs (=large metal objects) are fired **2 be/go gunning for sb** to look for someone in order to criticize or harm him/her: *After the meeting, Ken went gunning for Mike.* **3 big/top gun** INFORMAL someone who controls an organization, or who is the most successful person in a group **4** a tool used in order to send out a liquid by pressure: *a spray gun* **5 hired gun** INFORMAL someone who is paid to shoot someone else or to protect someone −see also **jump the gun** (JUMP¹) **stick to your guns** (STICK¹)

**gun²** *v* [T] INFORMAL to make the engine of a car go very fast by pressing the ACCELERATOR very hard

**gun** sb ↔ **down** *phr v* [T] to shoot someone who cannot defend himself/herself: *Bobby Kennedy was gunned down in a hotel.*

**gun·boat** /'gʌnboʊt/ *n* a small military ship that is used near the coast

**gun·fire** /'gʌnfaɪɚ/ *n* [U] the repeated firing of guns, or the noise made by this

**gung-ho** /ˌgʌŋ'hoʊ/ *adj* INFORMAL very eager, or too eager: *a gung-ho attitude*

**gunk** /gʌŋk/ *n* INFORMAL a substance that is thick and dirty: *There's a bunch of gunk clogging the drain.*

**gun·man** /'gʌnmən/ *n* a criminal who uses a gun

**gun·ner** /ˈgʌnɚ/ n a soldier, sailor etc. whose job is to aim or fire a large gun

**gun·nysack** /ˈgʌniˌsæk/ n a large BURLAP bag used for storing and sending grain, coffee etc.

**gun·point** /ˈgʌnpɔɪnt/ n **at gunpoint** while threatening people with a gun, or being threatened with a gun: *a bank robbed at gunpoint*

**gun·pow·der** /ˈgʌnˌpaʊdɚ/ n [U] an explosive substance in the form of powder

**gun·run·ning** /ˈgʌnˌrʌnɪŋ/ n [U] the activity of taking guns into a country secretly and illegally —**gunrunner** n

**gun·shot** /ˈgʌnʃɑt/ n **1** the sound made when a gun is fired **2** [U] the bullets fired from a gun: *a gunshot wound*

**gup·py** /ˈgʌpi/ n a small brightly colored tropical fish

**gur·gle** /ˈgɚgəl/ v [I] to make a sound like flowing water: *a baby gurgling in her crib* —**gurgling** adj —**gurgle** n

**gu·ru** /ˈguru, ˈgʊru/ n **1** INFORMAL someone who knows a lot about a particular subject, and to whom people go for advice: *a computer guru* **2** a Hindu religious teacher or leader

**gush¹** /gʌʃ/ v [I,T] **1** to flow or pour out quickly in large quantities: *water **gushing out** of a pipe | a wound gushing blood* **2** to express praise so strongly that people think you are not sincere

**gush²** n **1** a large quantity of liquid that suddenly flows from somewhere: *a gush of oil* **2 a gush of relief/anxiety etc.** a sudden feeling or expression of emotion

**gush·er** /ˈgʌʃɚ/ n INFORMAL an oil WELL where the flow of oil is suddenly so strong that it shoots into the air

**gush·y** /ˈgʌʃi/ adj too full of praise for someone or something, so that people think you are not sincere

**gust¹** /gʌst/ n a sudden strong movement of wind, air, snow etc.: *A gust of wind blew our tent over.* —**gusty** adj —see usage note at WEATHER

**gust²** v [I] if wind gusts, it blows strongly with sudden short movements

**gus·to** /ˈgʌstoʊ/ n [U] **with gusto** with eager enjoyment: *a band playing with gusto*

**gut¹** /gʌt/ n INFORMAL **1 gut reaction/feeling etc.** a reaction or feeling that you are sure is right, although you cannot give a reason for it: *My gut reaction is that it's a bad idea.* **2** the tube through which food passes from your stomach —see also GUTS

**gut²** v -tted, -tting [T] **1** to completely destroy the inside of a building, especially by fire **2** to remove the organs from inside a fish or animal in order to prepare it for cooking

**guts** /gʌts/ n [plural] INFORMAL **1** the courage and determination you need to do something difficult or unpleasant: *Dickie didn't **have the**

**guts to** say what he really thought.* **2** the organs inside your body **3 hate sb's guts** to hate someone very much

**gut·sy** /ˈgʌtsi/ adj INFORMAL brave and determined: *a gutsy speech*

**gut·ter** /ˈgʌtɚ/ n **1** the low place along the edge of a road, where water collects and flows away **2** an open pipe at the edge of a roof for collecting and carrying away rain water **3 the gutter** the bad social conditions of the lowest and poorest people in society

**gut·ter·al** /ˈgʌtərəl/ adj a gutteral sound is produced deep in the throat

**guy** /gaɪ/ n **1** INFORMAL a man: *I'm going out with a few guys from work tonight. | Some guy wanted to talk to you.* **2 you guys/those guys** SPOKEN said when talking to or about two or more people, both men and women: *We'll see you guys Sunday, okay?* —compare Y'ALL

**guz·zle** /ˈgʌzəl/ v [I,T] INFORMAL to drink a lot of something eagerly and quickly: *Marge was guzzling martinis because they were free.*

**guz·zler** /ˈgʌzlɚ/ n INFORMAL **gas guzzler** a car that uses too much gas

**gym** /dʒɪm/ n **1** a special hall or room that has equipment for doing physical exercise **2** [U] sports and exercises done indoors, especially as a school subject: *gym class*

**gym·na·si·um** /dʒɪmˈneɪziəm/ n ⇨ GYM

**gym·nast** /ˈdʒɪmnæst, -nəst/ n someone who does GYMNASTICS as a sport

**gym·nas·tics** /dʒɪmˈnæstɪks/ n [plural] **1** a sport involving physical exercises and movements that need skill and control, and that are often performed in competitions **2 mental/intellectual gymnastics** very quick or skillful thinking

**gy·ne·col·o·gy** /ˌgaɪnəˈkɑlədʒi/ n [U] the study and treatment of medical conditions and illnesses affecting only women —**gynecologist** n —**gynecological** /ˌgaɪnəkəˈlɑdʒɪkəl/ adj

**gyp** /dʒɪp/ v -pped, -pping [T] SPOKEN to trick or cheat someone: *I got gypped out of $50!*

**gyp·sy** /ˈdʒɪpsi/ n **1** a member of a group of people originally from northern India, who usually live and travel around in CARAVANS **2** someone who does not like to stay in the same place for a long time

**gy·rate** /ˈdʒaɪreɪt/ v [I] to turn around fast in circles: *dancers gyrating wildly* —**gyration** /dʒaɪˈreɪʃən/ n [C,U]

**gy·ro·scope** /ˈdʒaɪrəˌskoʊp/, **gy·ro** /ˈdʒaɪroʊ/ n a heavy wheel that spins inside a frame, and is used for keeping ships and aircraft steady

G

# H

**H, h** /eɪtʃ/ the eighth letter of the English alphabet

**ha** /hɑ/ *interjection* said when you have discovered something, or are proud of yourself: *Ha! I knew I was right.* –see also HA HA –compare HUH

**hab·er·dash·er·y** /ˈhæbəˌdæʃəri/ *n* [C,U] OLD-FASHIONED a store or part of a store that sells men's clothing, or the clothes and hats sold there

**hab·it** /ˈhæbɪt/ *n* **1** [C,U] something that you do regularly, and usually without thinking: *Jen had developed a/the habit of asking her sister for advice.*|*After he moved out, I was still cleaning his room out of habit.* (=because it was a habit)|*I've gotten in the habit of running every morning.* (=I've started running regularly)|*Dad needs to change his eating/drinking habits.* (=what he eats or drinks, and when he does it) –compare CUSTOM **2** something you do regularly that annoys other people: *He has a habit of being late.*|*I admit smoking is a bad habit of mine.* **3 make a habit of doing sth** to start doing something very often: *Don't make a habit of staying up late studying!* **4 kick/ break the habit** to stop doing something that is bad for your health, such as regularly taking drugs **5** a set of long loose clothes worn by members of some religious groups

> **USAGE NOTE habit, custom, tradition**
>
> A **habit** is something that someone does often, and usually without thinking about it: *Smoking is a dangerous habit.* A **custom** is a way of doing something that people in a particular society think is normal, and that everyone does: *The custom here is to shake hands when you meet.* A **tradition** is a belief or a way of doing something that a particular group or society has followed for a very long time: *It's a family tradition to put real candles on the Christmas tree.*

**hab·it·a·ble** /ˈhæbətəbəl/ *adj* suitable for people to live in –opposite UNINHABITABLE

**hab·i·tat** /ˈhæbəˌtæt/ *n* the natural environment in which a plant or animal lives

**hab·i·ta·tion** /ˌhæbəˈteɪʃən/ *n* FORMAL **1** [U] the act of living in a place: *There was no sign of habitation on the island.* **2** a house or place to live in

**ha·bit·u·al** /həˈbɪtʃuəl/ *adj* **1** happening as a habit, or often doing something because it is a habit: *his habitual smoking*|*a habitual smoker*

**2** usual or typical: *her habitual bad temper*
–**habitually** *adv*

**hack**[1] /hæk/ *v* **1** [I,T] to violently cut something into pieces: *All of the murder victims had been hacked to death.* **2** [I] to cough very loudly and painfully: *She started hacking and gasping.* **3 sb can't hack it** INFORMAL used in order to say that someone cannot continue to do something difficult or boring

**hack into** sth *phr v* [T] to use a computer to enter someone else's computer system: *Morris managed to hack into a federal computer network.*

**hack**[2] *n* someone who writes low quality books, articles etc.

**hack·er** /ˈhækɚ/ *n* INFORMAL someone who uses computers a lot, especially in order to secretly use or change the information in another person's computer system –**hacking** *n* [U]

**hack·neyed** /ˈhæknid/ *adj* a hackneyed phrase or statement is no longer interesting because it has been used too often

**hack·saw** /ˈhæksɔ/ *n* a small SAW (=cutting tool) used especially to cut metal

**had** /d, əd, həd; *strong* hæd/ *v* **1** the past tense and PAST PARTICIPLE of HAVE **2 be had** to be tricked or made to look stupid: *She had the feeling she'd been had.*

**had·dock** /ˈhædək/ *n* [C,U] a common fish that lives in northern oceans, or the meat from this fish

**had·n't** /ˈhædnt/ *v* the short form of "had not": *We hadn't been there long.*

**hag** /hæg/ *n* an impolite word meaning an ugly or old woman

**hag·gard** /ˈhægɚd/ *adj* having lines on your face and dark marks around your eyes because you are tired, sick, or worried: *He was thin and haggard.*

**hag·gle** /ˈhægəl/ *v* [I] to argue, especially about the amount of money you will pay for something: *The car dealer and I were haggling over the price for an hour.*

**hah** /hɑ/ *interjection* ⇨ HA

**ha ha** /hɑ ˈhɑ/ *interjection* **1** used in writing to represent laughter **2** SPOKEN said in order to show that you are annoyed and do not think something is funny: *Very funny, Tyrell, ha ha.*

**hail**[1] /heɪl/ *v* **1** [T] to call out to someone in order to get his/her attention or to greet him/her: *He tried hailing a taxi/cab, but it drove by.* **2** [I] if it hails, frozen rain falls from the sky

**hail** sb/sth **as** sth *phr v* [T] to publicly state how good someone or something is: *Their discovery was hailed as the most important event of the century.*

**hail from** *phr v* [I] to come from a particular place: *The professor hailed from Massachusetts.*

**hail**[2] *n* **1** [U] small hard drops of frozen rain that fall from the sky –see usage note at WEATHER **2 a hail of bullets/stones etc.** a lot of bullets, stones etc. that are shot or thrown at someone

**hail·stone** /'heɪlstoʊn/ *n* a small drop of hard frozen rain

**hail·storm** /'heɪlstɔrm/ *n* a storm when a lot of HAIL falls

**hair** /hɛr/ *n* **1** [U] the things like thin threads that grow on your head: *Mike's the guy with the blond curly hair* | *She's tall and she has dark brown hair.* | *I used to have/wear my hair very long.* **2** [C,U] the things like thin threads that grow on a person's or animal's skin: *an old blanket covered with cat hair* —compare FUR **3 let your hair down** INFORMAL to stop being serious and enjoy yourself **4 -haired** having a particular type of hair or fur: *a long-haired cat* **5** SPOKEN a very small amount or distance: *"Is this picture straight?" "Raise the right side just a hair."*

**hair·brush** /'hɛrbrʌʃ/ *n* a brush you use on your hair to make it look neat

**hair·cut** /'hɛrkʌt/ *n* **1** the act of having your hair cut by someone: *I'm getting a haircut tomorrow.* **2** the style your hair has when it is cut: *They gave her a really short haircut.*

**hair·do** /'hɛrdu/ *n, plural* **hairdos** INFORMAL a woman's HAIRSTYLE

**hair·dress·er** /'hɛr,drɛsɚ/ *n* someone who washes, cuts, and arranges people's hair

**hair·dryer** /'hɛr,draɪɚ/ *n* a machine that you sit under that blows out hot air, used for drying hair

**hair·line** /'hɛrlaɪn/ *n* **1** the area around the top of your face where your hair starts growing **2 a hairline crack/fracture** a very thin crack in something hard such as a glass or bone

**hair·net** /'hɛrnɛt/ *n* a thin net worn over your hair in order to keep it in place

**hair·rais·ing** /'. ,../ *adj* frightening in an exciting way: *a hair-raising adventure*

**hair·split·ting** /'hɛr,splɪtɪŋ/ *n* [U] the act of paying too much attention to unimportant details and differences

**hair spray** /'. ./ *n* [C,U] a sticky liquid that you put onto your hair in order to make it stay in place

**hair·style** /'hɛrstaɪl/ *n* the particular style your hair has when it is cut, brushed, or arranged

**hair·y** /'hɛri/ *adj* **1** having a lot of body hair: *His arms and chest are really hairy.* | *a hairy man* **2** INFORMAL a hairy situation makes people feel angry, worried, excited, or frightened: *Tom and Linda are in a really hairy lawsuit right now.*

**hal·cy·on** /'hælsiən/ *adj* LITERARY **halcyon days/years/season** etc. the happiest, most peaceful time of someone's life, or a company's most successful time

**hale** /heɪl/ *adj* **hale and hearty** HUMOROUS healthy and full of energy

**half¹** /hæf/ *determiner adj* **1** ½ of an amount, time, distance, number etc.: *The wall is half a mile long.* | *At least half the time was spent deciding what to do.* | *Cyndi was more than half an hour late.* **2 half the fun/time** etc. a lot of the fun, a lot of times etc.: *Half the time she makes me so mad that I want to hit her.* **3 half a second/minute** a very short time: *If you can wait half a second, I'll be ready to go.*

**half²** *number* ½: *five and a half* (=5½)

**half³** *n, plural* **halves 1** one of two equal parts of something: *Half of 10 is 5.* | *Do you want the sandwich cut in half?* (=in two equal pieces) | *Half of the rooms have double beds in them.* ✗ DON'T SAY "the half of the rooms." ✗ | *Our profits increased in the second half of the year.* | *"How old is your daughter?" "She's two and a half."* ✗ DON'T SAY "two and one half." ✗ **2** one of two parts into which a sports event is divided: *The score was 21 to 10 at the end of the second half.*

**half⁴** *adv* **1** partly but not completely: *He shouldn't be allowed to drive. He's half blind!* | *I half expected her to yell at me, but she laughed instead.* | *There were several half-empty coffee cups on the table.* **2 half French/American** etc. having one parent who is French, American etc. **3 not half bad** said when something that you expected to be bad is actually good: *Murray told us he couldn't cook, but the dinner wasn't half bad.* **4 half and half** partly one thing and partly something else: *"Do you make it with milk or water?" "Half and half."*

**half a doz·en** /,. . '../ *number* **1** also **a half dozen** six: *half a dozen donuts* | *a half dozen eggs* **2** several: *"Where's Tom?" "I've already told you half a dozen times!"*

**half-and-half** /,. . './ *n* [U] a mixture of milk and cream, used in coffee

**half-assed** /,hæf 'æst◂/ *adj* SLANG an impolite expression meaning done or made without enough attention, used when you are annoyed:

**hairstyles**

mustache

bun

beard

bangs

braid

pigtails

ponytail

*Marty only did a half-assed job of cleaning out the garage.*

**half-baked** /ˌ. '.◂/ *adj* INFORMAL a half-baked idea, plan, or suggestion is not sensible or intelligent enough to be successful

**half-broth·er** /'. ˌ../ *n* a brother who is the child of only one of your parents

**half-heart·ed** /ˌ. '..◂/ *adj* a half-hearted attempt is something that you do without really trying or wanting to be successful

**half-life** /'. ./ *n* the amount of time it takes for a RADIOACTIVE substance to lose half of its RADIO-ACTIVITY

**half-mast** /ˌ. './ *adj* **fly/be at half-mast** if a flag flies or is at half-mast, it is lowered to the middle of its pole because someone important has died

**half note** /'. ./ *n* a musical note equal to two QUARTER NOTES

**half-sis·ter** /'. ˌ../ *n* a sister who is the child of only one of your parents

**half time** /'. ./ *n* [U] a period of rest between two parts of a game such as football or basketball

**half·way** /ˌhæf'weɪ◂/ *adj, adv* **1** at the middle point between two places or two points: *Their boat was halfway across the lake when it started to rain.* | *We had reached the halfway mark/point of the trail.* **2** in the middle of a period of time or an event: *I fell asleep halfway through the concert.* –see also **meet (sb) halfway** (MEET[1])

**hal·i·but** /'hæləbət/ *n* [C,U] a large flat sea fish, or the meat from this fish

**hall** /hɔl/ *n* **1** a passage in a house or building that leads to other rooms: *The bathroom's just down the hall.* **2** a public building or large room that is used for important events such as meetings, concerts, and formal parties: *Carnegie Hall*

**hal·le·lu·jah** /ˌhælə'luyə/ *interjection* said in order to express thanks, or praise to God

**hall·mark** /'hɔlmɑrk/ *n* **1** a quality, idea, or method that is typical of a particular person or thing: *Discipline is the hallmark of this institution.* **2** an official mark put on silver, gold, or PLATINUM to prove that it is real

**Hall of Fame** /ˌ. . './ *n* a list of famous sports players, or the building where their uniforms, sports equipment, and information about them are all shown

**hal·lowed** /'hæloʊd/ *adj* **1** made holy: *hallowed ground* **2** respected, honored, and important: *the hallowed memories of our war heroes*

**Hal·low·een** /ˌhælə'win, ˌhɑ-/ *n* [U] a holiday on the night of October 31, when children wear COSTUMES, play tricks, and walk from house to house in order to get candy

**hal·lu·ci·nate** /hə'lusəˌneɪt/ *v* [I] to see, feel, or hear something that is not really there

**hal·lu·ci·na·tion** /həˌlusə'neɪʃən/ *n* [C,U] something you see, feel, or hear that is not really there, or the experience of this, usually caused by a drug or mental illness –**hallucinatory** /hə'lusənəˌtɔri/ *adj*

**hal·lu·ci·no·gen·ic** /həˌlusənə'dʒɛnɪk/ *adj* causing HALLUCINATIONS

**hall·way** /'hɔlweɪ/ *n* ⇨ HALL

**ha·lo** /'heɪloʊ/ *n, plural* **halos** a golden circle that is painted above the head of a holy person in a religious painting

**halt[1]** /hɔlt/ *v* [I,T] to stop or make something stop: *The city council had halted repair work on the subway.*

**halt[2]** *n* a stop or pause: *Traffic suddenly came/ground to a halt.* (=stopped) | *The project was brought to a halt* (=ended) *due to lack of money.*

**hal·ter** /'hɔltɚ/ *n* **1** also **halter top** a piece of women's clothing that ties behind the neck and does not cover the arms or back **2** a rope or leather band fastened around a horse's head in order to lead it

**halt·ing** /'hɔltɪŋ/ *adj* stopping a lot when you move or speak, especially because you are nervous: *her halting voice*

**halve** /hæv/ *v* [T] **1** to reduce the amount of something by half: *Food production was almost halved during the war.* **2** to cut something into two equal parts: *Wash and halve the mushrooms.*

**halves** /hævz/ *n* the plural of HALF

**ham[1]** /hæm/ *n* **1** [C,U] meat from the upper part of a pig's leg that is preserved with salt or smoke: *a ham sandwich* –see usage note at MEAT **2** INFORMAL someone who behaves in a silly way in order to get a lot of attention: *Your nephew's such a ham!*

**ham[2]** *v* INFORMAL **ham it up** to perform or behave with too much false emotion

**ham·burg·er** /'hæmˌbɚgɚ/ *n* **1** [U] BEEF that is ground (GRIND) into very small pieces: *a pound of hamburger* **2** this type of beef cooked in a flat round shape and eaten between pieces of round bread

**ham·let** /'hæmlɪt/ *n* a very small village

**ham·mer[1]** /'hæmɚ/ *n* a tool with a heavy metal part on a straight handle, used for hitting nails into wood

**ham·mer[2]** *v* **1** [I,T] to hit something with a hammer **2** [I] to hit something again and again, making a lot of noise: *They hammered on the door until I opened it.*

**hammer sth in/into** *phr v* [T] also **hammer sth home** to continue repeating something until people completely understand it: *Mom hammered the message into us: don't talk to strangers!*

**hammer out** sth *phr v* [T] to finally agree on a solution, contract etc. after arguing about details for a long time: *It took several days to **hammer out** an agreement.*

**ham·mock** /ˈhæmək/ *n* a large piece of material or a net you can sleep on that hangs between two trees or poles

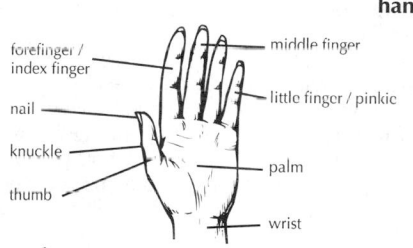
hammock

**ham·per**¹ /ˈhæmpɚ/ *v* [T] to make someone have difficulty moving, doing something, or achieving something: *The searches for the missing girl were hampered by the bad weather.*

**hamper**² *n* **1** a large basket with a lid, used for holding dirty clothes until they can be washed **2** a basket with a lid, used for carrying food

**ham ra·di·o** /ˌ. ˈ.../ *n* [U] a legal method of sending and receiving messages by radio for fun, rather than officially

**ham·ster** /ˈhæmstɚ/ *n* a small animal with soft fur and no tail that is often kept as a pet

**ham·string**¹ /ˈhæmˌstrɪŋ/ *n* a TENDON behind your knee

**hamstring**² *v* [T] to make a person or group have difficulty doing or achieving something: *a government hamstrung by student protests*

---

**hand**

forefinger / index finger — middle finger
nail — little finger / pinkie
knuckle — palm
thumb — wrist

**hand**¹ /hænd/ *n*
**1** ▶**BODY PART**◀ the body part at the end of a person's arm that includes the fingers and thumb, used for picking up, holding, and touching things: *I write with my **right/left hand**. | **Hold hands with** your sister while we cross the street. | I **took her hand** and helped her down the stairs. | **Raise your hand** (=lift it up) if you know the answer.* –see picture at BODY
**2** **right-handed/left-handed** always using the right hand to do important things such as writing, using tools, holding things etc., or always using the left hand to do things
**3** **on the one hand... on the other hand** used when comparing two different or opposite facts or ideas: *The movie was scary, but on the other hand it made me laugh. | On the one hand, they work slowly, but on the other hand they always finish the job.*
**4** **on hand** close and ready to be used when needed: *Keep a supply of candles on hand in case of power cuts.*
**5** **at hand** FORMAL **a)** near in time or space:

*Nurses are always **close at hand** in case of emergency.* **b)** needing to be dealt with now: *Let's discuss the case at hand, shall we?*
**6** **by hand a)** by a person and not by a machine: *Each porcelain doll was decorated by hand.* **b)** delivered from one person to another, not through the mail
**7** **a hand** help: *Can you **give/lend me a hand** with this box? It's really heavy. | Do you **need a hand** with the cooking?*
**8** **have a hand in** to be involved in doing or making something: *Eddie has had a hand in the operation of the club.*
**9** **in sb's hands/in the hands of** controlled by someone or taken care of by someone: *The schedule will be entirely in your hands.*
**10** **get/lay your hands on sth** to find or obtain something: *I read every book I could get my hands on at school.*
**11** **get out of hand** to become impossible to control: *The party was getting out of hand so someone called the police.*
**12** **hand in hand** holding each other's hands
**13** **in hand** being dealt with now: *We need to solve **the matter in hand** before we can solve other problems.*
**14** **have your hands full** to be very busy or too busy: *You're going to have your hands full once you have the baby!*
**15** **give sb a (big) hand** to CLAP loudly for a performer or speaker
**16** ▶**WORKER**◀ OLD-FASHIONED someone who works with his/her hands
**17** ▶**CLOCK**◀ one of the long things that point to the numbers on a clock
**18** ▶**CARDS**◀ the cards that you are holding in a game –see also FIRSTHAND, LEFT-HAND, RIGHT-HAND, SECONDHAND, **shake hands (with sb)** (SHAKE¹) **wait on sb hand and foot** (WAIT¹)

**hand**² *v* [T] **1** to pass something to someone else: *Can you hand me a towel?* **2** **you have to hand it to sb** SPOKEN said when you are admiring something that someone has done: *I have to hand it to you, Claire: you sure know how to cook!*

**hand** sth ↔ **back** *phr v* [T] to give something back to the person it belongs to, or to the person who just gave it to you: *Mr. Evans **handed back** our essays today.*

**hand** sth ↔ **down** *phr v* [T] **1** to give something to a younger relative, or to people who live after you: *traditions that were **handed down** from generation to generation* **2** if a court of law hands down a decision or sentence, it officially announces a decision or punishment

**hand** sth ↔ **in** *phr v* [T] to give something to someone in a position of authority: *Please **hand in** your application by September 30.*

**hand** sth ↔ **out** *phr v* [T] to give something to everyone who is part of a group or in a particular place: *They were **handing out** free t-shirts at the club.*

**hand over** *phr v* **1** [T **hand** sb/sth ↔ **over**] to give someone or something to the person who wants to control him, her, or it: *The thief was caught and **handed over** to the police.* **2** [I,T **hand** sth ↔ **over**] to give power or duties to someone else: *Cirallo will be **handing over** the chairmanship in June.*

**hand·bag** /'hændbæg/ *n* ⇨ PURSE¹

**hand·book** /'hændbʊk/ *n* a small book with instructions and information about a particular subject: *an employee handbook*

**hand·cuff** /'hændkʌf/ *v* [T] to put HANDCUFFs on someone

**hand·cuffs** /'hændkʌfs/ *n* [plural] two metal rings joined by a chain, used for holding a prisoner's wrists together

**hand·ful** /'hændfʊl/ *n* **1** an amount that you can hold in your hand: *We were eating popcorn **by the handful**.* **2 a handful of** a small number of people or things: *Only a handful of people showed up.* **3 a handful** INFORMAL someone, especially a child, who is difficult to control: *She's a real handful!*

**hand·gun** /'hændgʌn/ *n* a small gun you hold in one hand when you shoot

**hand·i·cap** /'hændi,kæp/ *n* **1** a condition in which you cannot use a part of your body or mind because it is damaged **2** something that makes a race or competition more difficult for stronger or more skillful competitors, so the players who are not so good have a better chance of winning

**hand·i·capped** /'hændi,kæpt/ *adj* **1** not able to use a part of your body or mind normally because it has been damaged: *schools for **mentally/physically handicapped** children* **2 the handicapped** people who are mentally or physically handicapped **3 be handicapped by** to have difficulties that are caused by a particular problem: *Firefighters were handicapped by the strength of the wind.*

---

**USAGE NOTE handicapped**

Using the word **handicapped** to talk about someone who cannot use a part of her/his body or mind normally may be considered offensive by some people. The word **disabled** is used by many people, but it is most polite to say **challenged** or **impaired:** *a special library entrance for the disabled | physically challenged | hearing impaired.*

---

**hand·i·work** /'hændi,wɚk/ *n* [U] **1** something that someone does or makes: *The documentary is the handiwork of a respected director.* **2** skillful work that you do with your hands

**hand·ker·chief** /'hæŋkɚtʃɪf, -,tʃif/ *n* a piece of cloth that you use for drying your nose or eyes

**han·dle¹** /'hændl/ *v* [T] **1** to deal with someone or something: *She couldn't handle the responsibility of being a doctor.* | *How did he **handle himself** (=behave) at the meeting?* **2** to pick up, hold, or touch something: *Please handle this package **with care**.* **3** to organize or be in charge of something: *Ms. Lee handled all of our travel arrangements.* **4** to buy, sell, or deal with particular products or services: *Upton was charged with handling stolen goods.*

**handle²** *n* **1** the part of a door, window, etc. that you hold in order to open it **2** the part of a tool, knife, pot etc. that you can hold to use or carry it

**handle**

**han·dle·bars** /'hændl,bɑrz/ *n* [plural] the metal BARs above the front wheel of a bicycle or MOTOR-CYCLE, that you turn to control the direction you go in

**han·dler** /'hændlɚ/ *n* someone who trains animals, especially dogs

**hand lug·gage** /'. ,../ *n* [U] small bags that you carry with you when you travel, especially on a plane

**hand·made** /,hænd'meɪd◂/ *adj* made by a person and not a machine

**hand-me-down** /'. . ,./ *n* a piece of clothing that has been worn by someone and then given to his/her younger relative –**hand-me-down** *adj*

**hand·out** /'hændaʊt/ *n* **1** money or food that is given to someone, usually because s/he is poor **2** a piece of paper with printed or copied information, that is given to people in a class, meeting etc.

**hand·picked** /,hænd'pɪkt/ *adj* someone who is handpicked has been carefully chosen for a particular purpose

**hand·shake** /'hændʃeɪk/ *n* the action of taking someone's right hand and shaking it, usually done when people meet or leave each other

**hands off** /,. './ *interjection* said when warning someone not to touch something that is yours: *Hands off my cookies!*

**hand·some** /'hænsəm/ *adj* **1 a)** a man who is handsome is attractive **b)** a woman who is handsome looks healthy and strong in an attractive way –see usage note at BEAUTIFUL **2 a handsome gift/reward/profit** a gift etc. that is valuable or is a lot of money

**hands-on** /,. './ *adj* **hands-on experience/training etc.** experience, training etc. that you get by doing something

**hand·stand** /'hændstænd/ *n* a movement in which you kick your legs up into the air so that you are upside down and supporting yourself on your hands

**hands up** /ˌ. './ *interjection* **1** used when telling people to raise an arm if they can answer a question, want something etc.: *Hands up if you know the answer.* **2** said when threatening someone with a gun

**hand·writ·ing** /ˈhændˌraɪt̬ɪŋ/ *n* [U] the way someone writes with his/her hand: *His handwriting is so messy, I can hardly read it.*

**hand·y** /ˈhændi/ *adj* **1** useful, or simple to use: *The extra key may* **come in handy**. (=be useful in the future) **2** INFORMAL near and easy to reach: *You should always* **keep** *a first aid kit* **handy**. **3 be handy with sth** to be good at using something, especially a tool: *Terry's very handy with a needle and thread.*

**hand·y·man** /ˈhændiˌmæn/ *n* someone who is good at making and repairing things

---

**hang up**

**hang¹** /hæŋ/ *v* hung, hung, hanging **1** [I,T] to put something somewhere so that its top part is fixed but its bottom part is free to move, or to be in this position: *You can hang your coat in the closet.* | *paintings* **hanging on** *the wall* | *Thick curtains were* **hung at** *the windows.* **2 hang in there** INFORMAL to remain determined to succeed in a difficult situation: *Just hang in there, Midori, things will get better.* **3 hang in the balance** to be in a situation in which the result is not certain, and something bad may happen: *The whole future of the airline is hanging in the balance.* **4 leave sb/sth hanging** to fail to finish something, or tell someone your decision about something: *The investigation should not be left hanging.* **5 hang a right/left** SPOKEN said in order to tell the driver of a car to turn right or left **6** to stay in the air in the same place for a long time: *Dark clouds hung over the valley.*

**hang around** *phr v* [I,T] INFORMAL **1** to stay in one place without doing very much, often because you are waiting for someone: *I* **hung around** *for about an hour and then left.* **2 hang around with sb** to spend a lot of time with someone

**hang back** *phr v* [I] to be unwilling to say or do something, often because you are shy

**hang on** *phr v* [I] **1** INFORMAL to hold something tightly: *Hang on, everybody, the road's pretty bumpy.* **2 hang on!** SPOKEN said in order to tell someone to wait for you: *Hang on, I'll be with you in a minute!*

**hang onto** sb/sth *phr v* [T] SPOKEN to keep something: *I'd* **hang onto** *that letter. You might need it later.*

**hang out** *phr v* [I] INFORMAL to spend a lot of time at a particular place or with particular people: *kids* **hanging out** *at the mall*

**hang up** *phr v* **1** [I] to finish a telephone conversation by putting the telephone down: *She got mad and* **hung up** *on me.* (=put the phone down before I was finished speaking) **2** [T **hang** sth ↔ **up**] to put something such as clothes on a hook or HANGER

**hang²** *v* [I,T] to kill someone by dropping him/her with a rope around his/her neck, or to die in this way: *Clayton* **hanged himself** *in his prison cell.*

**hang³** *n* **get the hang of sth** INFORMAL to learn how to do something: *Driving a car is hard at first, but you'll get the hang of it.*

**hang·ar** /ˈhæŋɚ, ˈhæŋɡɚ/ *n* a very large building where aircraft are kept

**hang·er** /ˈhæŋɚ/ *n* a thing for hanging clothes on, made of a curved piece of metal, wood, or plastic with a hook on it

**hanger-on** /ˌ.. './ *n, plural* **hangers-on** someone who tries to spend a lot of time with important people for his/her own advantage

**hang glid·ing** /ˈ. ˌ../ *n* [U] the sport of flying using a large frame covered with cloth that you hold on to −**hang glider** *n*

**hang·ing** /ˈhæŋɪŋ/ *n* [C,U] the action of killing someone by dropping him/her with a rope around his/her neck as a punishment

**hang·man** /ˈhæŋmən/ *n* someone whose job is to kill criminals by hanging them

**hang·nail** /ˈhæŋneɪl/ *n* a piece of dead skin that has become loose near the bottom of your FINGERNAIL

**hang·out** /ˈhæŋaʊt/ *n* INFORMAL a place that you like to go to often, such as a BAR

**hang·o·ver** /ˈhæŋˌoʊvɚ/ *n* the feeling of sickness that someone has the day after s/he has drunk too much alcohol

**hang·up** /ˈhæŋʌp/ *n* INFORMAL **have a hangup about sth** to feel worried or embarrassed about something in an unreasonable way: *Cindy has a hangup about her nose.*

**hank·er** /ˈhæŋkɚ/ *v* INFORMAL
**hanker after/for** sth *phr v* [T] to have a very strong desire for something over a period of time: *Julie's been* **hankering for** *some carrot cake.* −**hankering** *n*

**han·kie, hanky** /ˈhæŋki/ *n* INFORMAL ⇨ HANDKERCHIEF

**han·ky-pan·ky** /ˌhæŋki ˈpæŋki/ *n* [U] INFORMAL sexual or criminal behavior that is not very serious

**Ha·nuk·kah** /ˈhɑnəkə/ *n* an eight-day Jewish holiday in December

**hap·haz·ard** /ˌhæpˈhæzɚd/ *adj* happening or

**H**

done in a way that is not organized or planned
–**haphazardly** adv

**hap·less** /ˈhæplɪs/ adj LITERARY unlucky

**hap·pen** /ˈhæpən/ v [I] **1** if an event or
situation happens, it starts, exists, and continues
for a period of time, usually without being
planned: *It's impossible to say what will happen
next year.* | *What happened last night, Roger?* |
*When did the accident happen?* **2** to be caused
as the result of an event or action: **What happens if** *your parents find out?* (=what will they
do as a result?) | *Look, when I try to turn on the
motor, nothing happens.* | *Let's wait and* **see
what happens.** (=find out what the result is)
**3** to do or to have something by chance: *I happened to see Hannah at the store today.* **4 sb/
sth happens to be** SPOKEN said when you are angry or annoyed, to add force to what you are
saying: *That happens to be my foot that you just
stepped on!* **5 it (just) so happens** SPOKEN said
when the thing you are about to say is slightly
surprising, because it is related to what someone
else has said: *"We visited Miami last week."
"Really? It just so happens our son lives in Miami."*

**happen on/upon** sb/sth phr v [T] to find something or meet someone by chance: *We just* **happened on** *the cabin when we were hiking one
day.*

**happen to** sb/sth phr v [T] **1** to be affected
by something: *I don't know what I'd do if anything* **happened to** *Jane.* (=if something hurt her,
or she died) **2 what/whatever happened to
...?** used in order to ask where something is or
what someone is doing now: *What* **happened to**
*my blue sweater?* | *Whatever* **happened to** *Jenny
Beale?*

> **USAGE NOTE happen, occur, take
> place, and happen to**
>
> Use **happen** especially to talk about past or
> future events that are accidents or that
> cannot be planned: *A funny thing hap-
> pened on my way to school.* | *What will
> happen if you have to change jobs?* **Occur**
> is more formal, and is used in order to talk
> about a specific event that has already hap-
> pened: *The explosion occurred about 5:30
> a.m.* Use **take place** to talk about a
> planned event: *Their wedding will take
> place on Saturday.* Use **happen to** to say
> that a person or thing is affected by an
> event: *What happened to your car?* | *This
> is the second time this has happened to
> him.*

**hap·pen·ing¹** /ˈhæpənɪŋ/ adj SLANG fashionable and exciting: *a happening club*

**happening²** n something that happens, especially a strange event

**hap·pi·ly** /ˈhæpəli/ adv **1** in a happy way:
*children playing happily in the pool*

**2** fortunately: *Happily no one was hurt in the
fire.* **3** very willingly: *I'll happily watch the
kids for you while you're gone.*

**hap·pi·ness** /ˈhæpinɪs/ n [U] the state of
being happy

**hap·py** /ˈhæpi/ adj **1** having feelings of pleasure, often because something good has happened to you: *You look happier today than
yesterday.* | *I am very* **happy for** *both of you.*
–opposite UNHAPPY **2 be happy to do sth** to
be willing to do something, especially to help
someone else: *I'll be happy to answer questions
later.* **3** a happy time, place etc. is one that
makes you feel pleased: *Those were the happiest
years of my life.* **4** satisfied or not worried:
*Amy was not very* **happy with** *their decision.*
**5 Happy Birthday/New Year etc.** used as a
greeting, or to wish someone good luck on his/
her BIRTHDAY or a special occasion

> **USAGE NOTE happy**
>
> We use several different words when we
> talk about being **happy**. If you are **content**,
> you are feeling happy because you are sa-
> tisfied: *They're content to lead a simple
> life.* If you are **glad**, you are pleased about
> something that has happened: *I'm so glad
> you were able to come.* If you feel excited
> as well as happy, you are **ecstatic** or
> **elated**: *The kids were ecstatic when
> summer vacation began.*

**happy-go-luck·y** /ˌ.. . ˈ..◂/ adj not caring or
worrying about what happens

**happy hour** /ˈ.. ˌ./ n [singular] a special time
when a BAR sells drinks at a lower price

**ha·rangue** /həˈræŋ/ v [T] to speak in an angry
way, often for a long time, to try to persuade
someone that you are right –**harangue** n

**ha·rass** /həˈræs, ˈhærəs/ v [T] to annoy or
threaten someone again and again: *The police
are accused of harassing Asian families.* | *Stop
harassing me! I'll get it done!*

**ha·rassed** /həˈræst, ˈhærəst/ adj anxious and
tired because you have too many problems or
too much to do

**ha·rass·ment** /həˈræsmənt, ˈhærəs-/ n [U]
behavior that is threatening or offensive to other
people: *Tina accused her boss of* **sexual harass-
ment.** (=offensive sexual behavior)

**har·bor¹** /ˈhɑrbɚ/ n [C,U] an area of water
next to the land where the water is calm, so that
ships are safe when they are inside it, and can be
left there

**harbor²** v [T] **1** to protect someone by hiding
him/her from the police **2** to keep hopes, bad
thoughts, or fears in your mind for a long time:
*Some parents still harbor suspicions about the
principal.*

**hard¹** /hɑrd/ adj

**1** ▶FIRM TO TOUCH◄ firm and stiff, and

difficult to cut, press down, or break: *I can't sleep on a hard mattress.* | *hard candy* | *The plums are still too hard to eat.* −opposite SOFT

**2 ▶DIFFICULT◀** difficult to do or understand: *It was the hardest class he'd ever had.* | *It's **hard to say** (=difficult to know) when Glenn will be back.* | *It is **hard for** me to understand why this happened.* −opposite EASY¹

**3 ▶A LOT OF EFFORT◀** involving a lot of physical or mental effort: *I had a **hard day** at work.* | *Mowing the lawn is hard work.*

**4 ▶NOT KIND◀** showing no kindness or sympathy: *Mr. Katz is a hard man to work for, but he's fair.*

**5 be hard on sb** INFORMAL **a)** to treat someone in a way that is unfair or too strict: *Don't be too hard on the children - they were only playing.* **b)** to cause someone a lot of problems: *It's hard on her, having her husband in the hospital.*

**6 be hard on sth** INFORMAL to have a bad effect on something: *Those pills are pretty hard on your stomach.*

**7 give sb a hard time** INFORMAL **a)** to make someone feel embarrassed or uncomfortable, often by making jokes about him/her: *The guys were giving him a hard time about missing the ball.* **b)** to criticize someone a lot

**8 find sth hard to believe** to think that something is probably not true: *I find it hard to believe that no one saw the accident.*

**9 ▶PROBLEMS◀** full of problems: *Poor Mary, she's had a hard life.*

**10 do/learn sth the hard way** to make a lot of mistakes or have a lot of difficulty before learning something: *Darcy said she had learned the hard way to watch what she said around reporters.*

**11 no hard feelings** SPOKEN used in order to tell someone that you no longer feel angry with him/her

**12 ▶WATER◀** hard water has a lot of MINERALs in it −compare SOFT −**hardness** *n* [U]

**hard²** *adv* **1** using a lot of effort: *She's working very hard.* | *You're not trying hard enough.* | *Come on, push harder!* **2** with a lot of force: *It's raining hard outside.* **3 be hard pressed/ put/pushed to do sth** to have difficulty doing something: *The painters will be hard pressed to finish by 6 o'clock.* **4 take sth hard** to feel very upset about something: *I didn't know that Joe would take the news so hard.* **5 laugh/cry hard etc.** to laugh, cry etc. a lot: *We were laughing so hard we couldn't breathe.*

---

**USAGE NOTE hard and hardly**

Use **hard** as an adverb to say that something is done using a lot of effort or force: *We studied hard for two weeks.* | *You have to push hard or it won't open.* Use **hardly** to mean "almost not": *I could hardly believe what she said.* | *I hardly know the guy.* | *There's hardly any difference*

between them. ✗DON'T USE "hardly" with "not" or "no." ✗

**hard-and-fast** /ˌ. . '.◂/ *adj* **hard-and-fast rules/regulations** rules that cannot be changed

**hard·back** /'hɑrdbæk/ *n* a book that has a strong stiff cover −compare PAPERBACK

**hard·ball** /'hɑrdbɔl/ *n* [C,U] **play hardball** INFORMAL to do everything you can to prevent someone from succeeding

**hard-boiled** /ˌ. '.◂/ *adj* **1** a hard-boiled egg has been boiled until it becomes solid **2** INFORMAL not showing your emotions, and not influenced by them in what you do

**hard cash** /ˌ. './ *n* [U] coins and bills

**hard cop·y** /ˌ. '../ *n* [U] information from a computer that is printed onto paper

**hard·core** /ˌhɑrd'kɔr◂/ *adj* extreme, and unlikely to change: *hardcore opposition to abortion* | *a hardcore drug addict*

**hard cur·ren·cy** /ˌ. '.../ *n* [C,U] money that can be used in any country because it is from a country that has a strong ECONOMY

**hard disk** /ˌ. './, **hard drive** *n* a part that is fixed inside a computer, used for permanently keeping information

**hard drugs** /ˌ. './ *n* [plural] very strong illegal drugs such as COCAINE

**hard·en** /'hɑrdn/ *v* **1** [I,T] to become firm or stiff, or to make something do this: *The pottery has to harden before it's painted.* **2** [I,T] to become less kind, less afraid, and more determined, or to make someone become this way: *Leslie's face hardened, and she turned away from him.* | *a hardened criminal*

**hard hat** /'. ./ *n* a protective hat, worn by workers in places where buildings are being built

**hard-head·ed** /ˌ. '..◂/ *adj* able to make difficult decisions without being influenced by your emotions

**hard-heart·ed** /ˌ. '..◂/ *adj* not caring about other people's feelings

**hard-hit·ting** /ˌ. '..◂/ *adj* criticizing someone or something in a strong and effective way

**hard·line** /ˌhɑrd'laɪn◂/ *adj* unwilling to change your extreme political opinions: *hardline conservatives* −**hardliner** *n*

**hard liq·uor** /ˌ. '../ *n* [U] strong alcohol such as WHISKEY

**hard·ly** /'hɑrdli/ *adv* **1** almost not: *I hardly know the people I'm working with.* (=don't know them very well) | *I remember how we could hardly wait for Christmas when we were kids.* | *Hardly anyone* (=very few people) *goes to the old theater anymore.* | *Katy is hardly ever* (=almost never) *at home.* **2** FORMAL used in order to say that something is not at all true, possible, surprising etc.: *This is hardly the ideal time to buy a house.* −compare BARELY −see usage note at HARD²

H

**hard-nosed** /ˌ. '.◂ / *adj* not affected by emotions, and determined to get what you want: *a hard-nosed negotiator*

**hard of hear·ing** /ˌ. . '../ *adj* unable to hear well

**hard-pressed** /ˌ. '.◂ / *adj* **1** sb will/would be hard-pressed to do sth used in order to say that it will or would be difficult for someone to do something: *I think he'll be hard-pressed to repay the money.* **2** having a lot of money problems: *help for hard-pressed families with young children*

**hard rock** /ˌ. './ *n* [U] extremely loud ROCK music that uses a lot of electric instruments

**hard sell** /ˌ. './ *n* [singular] a way of selling something in which you try very hard to persuade someone to buy it

**hard·ship** /'hɑrdˌʃɪp/ *n* [C,U] something that makes your life difficult, especially the condition of having very little money: *Many families were suffering economic hardship.| the hardships of daily life*

**hard up** /ˌ. '.◂ / *adj* INFORMAL not having something that you want or need, especially money or sex: *Scott was pretty hard up, so I gave him $20.*

**hard·ware** /'hɑrdwɛr/ *n* [U] **1** computer machinery and equipment –compare SOFTWARE **2** equipment and tools you use in your home and yard: *a **hardware store** (=where you can buy these things)*

**hard·wood** /'hɑrdwʊd/ *n* [C,U] strong heavy wood used for making furniture, or a type of tree that produces this kind of wood

**hard-work·ing** /ˌ. '..◂ / *adj* working seriously with a lot of effort, and not wasting time; DILIGENT: *a hard-working student*

**har·dy** /'hɑrdi/ *adj* strong and healthy and able to bear difficult conditions: *hardy plants*

**hare** /hɛr/ *n* an animal like a rabbit, but larger, with longer ears and longer back legs

**hare·brained** /'hɛrbreɪnd/ *adj* not sensible or practical: *a harebrained scheme*

**hare·lip** /'hɛrˌlɪp/ *n* [singular, U] the condition of having a top lip that is divided into two parts

**har·em** /'hɛrəm, 'hærəm/ *n* **1** the rooms in a Muslim home where the women live **2** the group of wives or women who lived with a rich or powerful man in some Muslim societies in past times

**hark** /hɑrk/ *v*

**hark back to** *phr v* [I] to remember or to remind people of things that happened in the past: *His writing style **harks back to** Fitzgerald.*

**har·lot** /'hɑrlət/ *n* LITERARY a PROSTITUTE

**harm**[1] /hɑrm/ *n* [U] **1** damage, injury, or trouble caused by someone's actions or by an event: *chemicals that **cause harm** to the environment| I don't think a little wine **does** you any **harm**.| Trying to lose weight can **do** more **harm than good**. (=cause problems)* **2** there's no

**harm in doing sth** used in order to suggest that doing something may be helpful or useful: *There's no harm in asking.* **3** not mean any harm to have no intention of hurting or upsetting anyone: *I was just kidding; I didn't mean any harm.* **4** no harm done SPOKEN said in order to tell someone that you are not upset by what s/he has done or said: *"I'm sorry." "That's OK; no harm done."*

**harm**[2] *v* [T] to damage or hurt something: *Too much sun will harm your skin.*

**harm·ful** /'hɑrmfəl/ *adj* causing harm, or likely to cause harm: *the harmful effects of pollution*

**harm·less** /'hɑrmlɪs/ *adj* **1** unable or unlikely to hurt anyone or cause damage: *Don't worry, the dog is harmless.* **2** not likely to upset or offend anyone: *harmless fun* –**harmlessly** *adv*

**har·mon·i·ca** /hɑr'mɑnɪkə/ *n* a small musical instrument that you play by blowing into it and moving it from side to side

**har·mo·nize** /'hɑrməˌnaɪz/ *v* [I] **1** to work well or look good together: *clothes that **harmonize** with her coloring* **2** to sing or play music in HARMONY

**har·mo·ny** /'hɑrməni/ *n* **1** [U] a situation in which people are friendly and peaceful, and agree with each other: *a city that **lives/works in** racial **harmony*** **2** [C,U] combinations of musical notes that sound good together: *four-part harmony* –**harmonious** /hɑr'moʊniəs/ *adj*

**har·ness**[1] /'hɑrnɪs/ *n* **1** [C,U] a set of leather bands fastened with metal that is used in order to control a horse and attach it to a vehicle that it pulls **2** a set of bands that is used to hold someone in a place, or to stop him/her from falling: *a safety harness*

**harness**[2] *v* [T] **1** to control and use the natural force or power of something: *water harnessed to generate electricity* **2** to fasten two animals together, or to fasten an animal to something using a HARNESS

**harp**[1] /hɑrp/ *n* a large musical instrument with strings stretched on a frame with three corners –**harpist** *n*

**harp**[2] *v*

**harp on** *phr v* [T] INFORMAL to talk about something again and again, in a way that is annoying or boring: *They kept **harping on** the fact that she'd left her daughter alone.*

**har·poon** /hɑr'pun/ *n* a weapon used for hunting WHALES

**harp·si·chord** /'hɑrpsɪˌkɔrd/ *n* a musical instrument like a piano, used especially in CLASSICAL MUSIC

**har·row·ing** /'hæroʊɪŋ/ *adj* a harrowing sight or experience is one that frightens, shocks, or upsets you very much

**harsh** /hɑrʃ/ *adj* **1** harsh conditions are difficult to live in and very uncomfortable: *harsh Canadian winters* **2** unpleasant and too loud or too bright: *a harsh voice| the harsh* *street lights* **3** unkind, cruel, or strict: *harsh criticism* | *harsh unfair laws* −**harshly** *adv* −**harshness** *n* [U]

**har·vest**[1] /ˈhɑrvɪst/ *n* [C,U] **1** the time when crops are gathered from the fields, or the act of gathering them: *It was harvest time.* | *the wheat harvest* **2** the size or quality of the crops: *a good harvest*

**harvest**[2] *v* [T] to gather crops from the fields

**has** /z, s, həz, həz; *strong* hæz/ *v* the third person singular of the present tense of HAVE

**has-been** /ˈ. ./ *n* INFORMAL someone who was important or popular, but who has been forgotten

**hash**[1] /hæʃ/ *n* **1** [C,U] a dish made with cooked meat and potatoes **2** INFORMAL a drug similar to MARIJUANA, made from the HEMP plant

**hash**[2] *v*

**hash** sth ↔ **out** *phr v* [T] to discuss something very thoroughly and carefully: *Look, let's get together and hash this thing out.*

**hash browns** /ˈ. ./ *n* [plural] potatoes that are cut into very small pieces, pressed together, and cooked in oil

**has·n't** /ˈhæzənt/ *v* the short form of "has not": *She hasn't seen Bruce in seven years.*

**has·sle**[1] /ˈhæsəl/ *n* **1** [C,U] something that is annoying because it causes problems, or is difficult to do: *Driving downtown is just too much hassle.* **2** an argument: *We always have this big hassle about who's going to pay.*

**hassle**[2] *v* INFORMAL [T] to ask someone again and again to do something, in a way that is annoying: *Just stop hassling me, will you?*

**haste** /heɪst/ *n* [U] **1** great speed in doing something, especially because you do not have enough time: *In her haste to get to the airport, Pam forgot the tickets.* **2** in **haste** quickly or in a hurry

**has·ten** /ˈheɪsən/ *v* **1** [T] to make something happen faster or sooner: *The popularity of radio hastened the end of silent movies.* **2** **hasten to do sth** to do or say something quickly or without delay

**hast·y** /ˈheɪsti/ *adj* done in a hurry, especially with bad results: *a hasty decision* −**hastily** *adv*: *a hastily written speech*

**hat** /hæt/ *n* **1** a piece of clothing that you wear on your head: *a big straw hat* **2** **keep sth under your hat** INFORMAL to keep information secret **3** **hats off to sb** INFORMAL used in order to praise someone: *"Jane played great. Hats off to her," Sheehan said.*

**hatch**[1] /hætʃ/ *v* [I,T] **1** if an egg hatches or is hatched, it breaks and a baby bird, fish, or insect is born **2** also **hatch out** to break though an egg in order to be born

**hatch**[2] *n* a hole in a ship or aircraft, used for loading goods, or the door that covers it −see picture at AIRPLANE

**hatch·back** /ˈhætʃbæk/ *n* a car with a door at the back that opens up −see picture on page 469

**hatch·et** /ˈhætʃɪt/ *n* **1** a small AXE with a short handle **2** **do a hatchet job on sb** INFORMAL to criticize someone severely and unfairly in a newspaper or on television

**hate**[1] /heɪt/ *v* [T] **1** to dislike someone or something very much: *She hated Eddie when he was drunk.* | *Tony hates it when people are late.* **2** **I hate to think what/how** SPOKEN used when you feel sure that something would have a bad result: *I hate to think what would happen if Joe got lost.* −**hated** *adj* −see also **hate sb's guts** (GUTS)

**hate**[2] *n* [U] an angry feeling of wanting to harm someone you dislike: *a look of hate*

**hate·ful** /ˈheɪtfəl/ *adj* very bad, unpleasant, or unkind: *a hateful thought*

**ha·tred** /ˈheɪtrɪd/ *n* [U] FORMAL hate: *eyes full of hatred*

**haugh·ty** /ˈhɔti/ *adj* proud and unfriendly −**haughtily** *adv*

**haul**[1] /hɔl/ *v* **1** to carry or pull something heavy: *trucks hauling cement* **2** **haul ass** SLANG to hurry

**haul off** *phr v* [I] INFORMAL to take someone somewhere s/he does not want to go: *getting hauled off to jail*

**haul**[2] *n* **1** a large amount of illegal or stolen goods that are found by the police: *a big drugs haul* **2** **the long haul** the long time that it takes to achieve something difficult: *"We're in this for the long haul," said a government source.* **3** **a long haul** a long distance to travel: *It's a long haul, driving from here to Phoenix.*

**haunch·es** /ˈhɔntʃɪz, ˈhɑntʃɪz/ *n* [plural] the part of your body at the back between your waist and legs: *They squatted on their haunches playing dice.*

**haunt**[1] /hɔnt, hɑnt/ *v* [T] **1** if the spirit of a dead person haunts a place, it appears there often: *a ship haunted by ghosts of sea captains* **2** if something haunts you, you keep remembering it or being affected by it, although you do not want this: *It's the kind of decision that comes back to haunt you later.*

**haunt**[2] *n* a place that someone likes to go to often: *Dan went back to visit his favorite old haunts.*

**haunt·ed** /ˈhɔntɪd, ˈhɑn-/ *adj* a place that is haunted is one where the spirits of dead people are believed to live: *a haunted house*

**haunt·ing** /ˈhɔntɪŋ, ˈhɑn-/ *adj* sad, beautiful, and staying in your thoughts for a long time: *a haunting memory* −**hauntingly** *adv*

**have**[1] /v, əv, həv; *strong* hæv/ *auxiliary verb* PRESENT TENSE

| singular | plural |
| --- | --- |
| I **have**, I've | we **have**, we've |
| you **have**, you've | you **have**, you've |

| he/she/it **has**, he's/she's/it's | they **have**, they've |
|---|---|

PAST TENSE

| singular | plural |
|---|---|
| I **had**, I'd | we **had**, we'd |
| you **had**, you'd | you **had**, you'd |
| he/she/it **had**, he'd/she'd/it'd | they **had**, they'd |

| PAST PARTICIPLE | **had** |
|---|---|
| PRESENT PARTICIPLE | **having** |

NEGATIVE *short forms* **haven't, hasn't, hadn't**

**1** used with the PAST PARTICIPLE of a verb to make the perfect tenses: *Yes, I've read the book.* | *Have you seen the new Disney movie?* | *She had lived in Peru for 30 years.* | *Rick has not been honest with us.* **2** used with some MODAL VERBS and a PAST PARTICIPLE to make a past modal: *Carrie should have been nicer.* | *I must've left my wallet at home.* **3** **had better** used in order to give advice, or to say what is the best thing to do: *You'd better take the popcorn off the stove or it'll burn.* | *I'd better not go out tonight - I'm too tired.* **4** **have had it** SPOKEN **a)** said when someone or something is old, broken, or not good any longer: *I think the car has had it. It wouldn't start this morning.* **b)** **I've had it with** said when you are so annoyed by someone or something that you do not want to deal with him, her, or it any longer: *I've had it with the noise here. I want to move!*

**have**² *v* [T not in passive]

**1** ►FEATURES/QUALITIES◄ used when saying what someone or something looks like, or what qualities or features he, she, or it possesses: *Rudy has brown eyes and dark hair.* | *The stereo doesn't have a tape deck.* | *Japan has a population of over 120 million.*

**2** ►OWN OR USE◄ to own something, or be able to use something: *Kurt had a nice bike, but it got stolen.* | *The school doesn't have room for any more students.* | *We don't have enough money for a washing machine.* | *Dad, can I have the car tonight?*

**3** **have got** used instead of "have" to mean "possess": *I've got four tickets to the opera.*

**4** ►EAT/DRINK◄ to eat, drink, or smoke something: *Do you want to come have a beer with us?* | *We're having steak for dinner tonight.* | *What time do you usually have lunch/breakfast/dinner?*

**5** ►EXPERIENCE/DO◄ to experience or do something: *I have a meeting in 15 minutes.* | *The kids will have fun at the circus.* | *Her secretary had trouble/problems with the copy machine.*

**6** ►RECEIVE◄ to receive something: *Jenny! You have a phone call!* | *I'm sure he had help from his father on his homework.*

**7** ►IN A POSITION/STATE◄ to put or keep something in a particular position or state: *He had his eyes closed.* | *Why do you always have the TV on so loud?*

**8** **may I have/can I have/I'll have** SPOKEN said when you are asking for something: *I'll have two hot dogs to go, please.* | *Could I have that pencil, please?*

**9** ►SELL/MAKE AVAILABLE◄ to sell something, or make it available for people to use: *Do they have lawn mowers at Sears?* | *The other pool has a water slide.*

**10** ►FAMILY/FRIENDS ETC◄ to know or be related to someone: *She has six brothers.* | *Chris has a friend who lives in Malta.*

**11** ►AMOUNT OF TIME◄ also **have got** to be allowed a particular amount of time to do something: *You have 30 minutes to finish the test.*

**12** **have time** if you have time to do something, there is nothing else that you must do at that particular time: *Do you have time to come and have a cup of coffee with us?*

**13** ►BE SICK/INJURED◄ to become sick with a particular illness, or be injured in a particular way: *Sheila had the flu for a week.* | *He has a broken leg.*

**14** ►CARRY WITH YOU◄ to be carrying something with you: *Do you have your knife?* | *How much money do you have on you?*

**15** ►IDEA/THOUGHT◄ to think of something, or realize something: *Listen, I have an idea.*

**16** **have sth ready/done etc.** to make something ready, or finish something: *They promised to have it done by Friday.*

**17** ►GIVE BIRTH◄ to give birth: *Sasha had twins!*

**18** **have your hair cut/have your house painted etc.** to employ someone to cut your hair, paint your house etc.

**19** ►GUESTS◄ to be with someone, or be visited by someone: *Sorry, I didn't realize you had guests.* | *Barry had an Australian guy with him.*

**20** **have an influence/effect etc.** to influence someone or something, or cause a particular effect: *Hungarian folk songs had a great influence on Bartok's music.*

**21** **have nothing against** used in order to say that you do not dislike someone or something: *I have nothing against hard work, but 80 hours a week is too much.* –see also **be had** (HAD) –see usage note at GOT

**have on** *phr v* [T] **1** [**have** sth **on**] to be wearing something: *Marty had a blue shirt on.* **2** [**have** sth **on** sb] to know about something bad someone has done: *Do the police have anything on him?*

**ha·ven** /'heɪvən/ *n* [C,U] a place where people go to be safe: *a haven for refugees*

**have·n't** /'hævənt/ *v* the short form of "have not": *We haven't tried Indian food yet.* ✗ DON'T SAY "haven't to." ✗

**have to** /'hæftə; *strong* 'hæftu/, **have got to** /v 'gʌtə, əv-, həv-/ *modal verb* **1** to be forced to do something because someone makes you do it, or because a situation makes it necessary: *We don't have to answer their questions.* | *Susan hates having to get up early.* | *I've got to go now. I'm already late!* **2** used when saying that it is important that something happens: *You'll have to be nice to Aunt Lynn.* **3** used when telling someone how to do something: *First you have to take the wheel off.* **4** used when saying that you are sure that something will happen or is true: *He has to be stuck in traffic - he wouldn't be late otherwise.* –see study note on page 458

---

**USAGE NOTE have to, have got to and must**

Use all of these phrases to talk about what it is necessary to do. Use **have to** to say that something is necessary, and you do not have a choice about it: *I have to study for my test.* | *We have to visit Grandma on Sunday.* Use **must** to say that something is necessary, and that you know it is a good idea: *I really must study harder.* | *We must visit Grandma sometime soon.* Use **have got** instead of **have to** or **must** in order to emphasize how important something is: *I've got to talk to him.* In informal speech, we often say **gotta** instead of **have got to**: *I gotta talk to him.* ✗ DON'T USE "gotta" in written or formal English. ✗ The past tense of **have to**, **have got to**, and **must** is **had to**: *I had to talk to him.*

---

**hav·oc** /ˈhævək/ *n* [U] a situation in which there is a lot of confusion and damage: *a bus strike that **caused/created havoc** in the city's streets* | *The war will **wreak havoc on** the country's economy.*

**hawk¹** /hɔk/ *v* [T] to try to sell goods by carrying them around and talking about them –**hawker** *n*

**hawk²** *n* a large wild bird that eats small birds and animals

**hay** /heɪ/ *n* [U] a type of long grass that has been cut and dried, used as food for horses

**hay fe·ver** /ˈ. ,../ *n* [U] a medical condition like a bad COLD, caused by breathing in POLLEN (=dust from plants)

**hay·ride** /ˈheɪraɪd/ *n* an organized ride in a CART filled with HAY, usually as part of a social event

**hay·stack** /ˈheɪstæk/ *n* a large, firmly built pile of HAY

**hay·wire** /ˈheɪwaɪɚ/ *adj* **go haywire** INFORMAL to start working in completely the wrong way: *My computer's going haywire again.*

**haz·ard¹** /ˈhæzɚd/ *n* **1** something that may be dangerous or cause accidents, problems etc.: *a health hazard* | *the hazards of starting your own business* **2 occupational hazard** a problem or risk that cannot be avoided in the job

that you do –**hazardous** *adj*: *hazardous waste from factories*

**hazard²** *v* [T] to say something that is only a suggestion or guess: *I don't know, but I could **hazard a guess**.*

**haze** /heɪz/ *n* [U] smoke, dust etc. in the air that is difficult to see through: *a gray haze of smoke over the mountains*

**ha·zel** /ˈheɪzəl/ *adj* eyes that are hazel are green-brown

**ha·zel·nut** /ˈheɪzəl,nʌt/ *n* a sweet round nut

**haz·ing** /ˈheɪzɪŋ/ *n* [C,U] the activity of making people who want to join a club or FRATERNITY do silly or dangerous things before they can join

**haz·y** /ˈheɪzi/ *adj* **1** air that is hazy is not clear because there is a lot of smoke, dust, or mist in it: *a hazy sky* **2** an idea, memory etc. that is hazy is not clear: *My memories of that night are a little hazy.*

**H-bomb** /ˈeɪtʃ bɑm/ *n* ⇨ HYDROGEN BOMB

**he** /i; *strong* hi/ *pron* a male person or animal that has already been mentioned or is already known about: *"Does Josh still live in New York?" "No, he lives in Ohio now."* | *How old is he?* | *He's (=he is) my brother.*

**head**

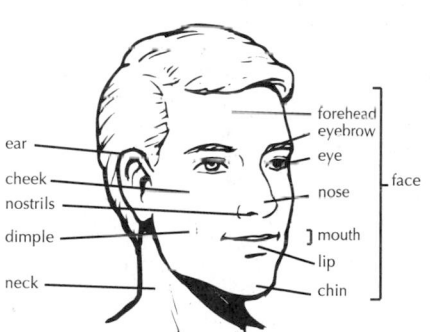

ear
cheek
nostrils
dimple
neck

forehead
eyebrow
eye
nose
face
mouth
lip
chin

H

**head¹** /hɛd/ *n*
**1** ▶TOP OF BODY◀ the top part of your body that has your eyes, mouth etc. in it: *He turned his head to kiss her.* –see also picture at BODY
**2** ▶MIND◀ your mind: *Troy's head is filled with ideas.* | *a good head for math*
**3** ▶LEADER◀ the leader or most important person in a group or organization: *the head of the biology department* | *the head waiter*
**4** ▶POSITION◀ [singular] the top or front of something, or the most important part of it: *Edgar sat proudly **at the head of the table**.* (=the end where the important people sit)
**5** ▶ON A TOOL◀ the widest or top part of something such as a piece of equipment or a tool: *a shower head*
**6** ▶PLANT◀ the top part of a plant with a lot of leaves: *a head of lettuce/cabbage*

**7 use your head** INFORMAL to think about something in a sensible way: *You're not using your head!*

**8 put your heads together** INFORMAL to discuss a difficult problem together: *If we put our heads together we'll think of a way.*

**9 go over sb's head** a) to be too difficult for someone to understand: *I could see that the discussion was going over their heads* b) to ask a more important person to deal with something than the person you would normally ask

**10 get sth into your head** INFORMAL to understand and realize something: *I wish he'd get it into his head that school is important.*

**11 keep/lose your head** to behave reasonably or stupidly in a difficult situation

**12 go to sb's head** a) to make someone feel more important than s/he really is: *It's too bad Dave let his promotion go to his head.* b) to make someone quickly feel slightly drunk: *That beer went right to my head.*

**13 come to a head** if a problem comes to a head, it becomes worse and you have to do something about it immediately: *The situation came to a head when the workers went on strike.*

**14 heads up!** SPOKEN used in order to warn people that something is falling from above, or that something is being thrown to them

**15 keep your head above water** to only just be able to live or keep your business working when you have money problems

**16 laugh/scream/shout your head off** INFORMAL to laugh, scream etc. very much

**17 head over heels in love** loving someone very much –see also BIGHEADED, REDHEAD

**head²** *v* **1** [I,T] to go or make something go in a particular direction: *Where are you guys headed?* | *a boat **heading** toward/for the shore* | *Roz headed the car down the hill.* **2** [T] to be in charge of a government, organization, or group: *The commission was headed by Barry Kerr.* | *Most single-parent families are headed by women.* **3 be heading/headed for** if you are heading for a situation, it is likely to happen: *They're heading for trouble.* **4** [T] to be at the top of a list, a page, or a group of words: *The longest list was headed "Problems."*

**head** sb/sth ↔ **off** *phr v* [T] to stop someone moving in a particular direction by moving in front of him/her: *The police **headed** them **off** at the cross street.*

**head·ache** /'hɛdeɪk/ *n* **1** a pain in your head: *I **have** a bad **headache**.* **2** INFORMAL an annoying or worrying problem: *Balancing the checkbook is always a headache.*

**head·band** /'hɛdbænd/ *n* a band that you wear around your head to keep your hair off your face

**head count** /'. ./ *n* the exact number of people who work somewhere or are attending a meeting, party etc., or the process of counting them

**head·dress** /'hɛd-drɛs/ *n* something that someone wears on his/her head for decoration on a special occasion: *a feathered headdress*

**head·first** /,hɛd'fɚst/ *adv* moving or falling forward with your head going first: *He fell down the stairs headfirst.*

**head·gear** /'hɛdgɪr/ *n* [U] hats and similar things that you wear on your head

**head·hunt·er** /'hɛd,hʌntɚ/ *n* someone who finds people with the right skills and experience to do a particular job

**head·ing** /'hɛdɪŋ/ *n* the title written at the top of a piece of writing

**head·land** /'hɛdlənd, -lænd/ *n* an area of land that sticks out from the coast into the ocean

**head·light** /'hɛdlaɪt/ *n* one of the large lights at the front of a vehicle –see picture on page 469

**head·line** /'hɛdlaɪn/ *n* **1** the title of a newspaper article, printed in large letters above the article **2 make headlines** to do something important, shocking, or new, so that newspapers, television shows etc. talk about you: *Johnson's announcement that he had AIDS made headlines.*

**head·long** /'hɛdlɔŋ, ,hɛd'lɔŋ/ *adv* **1** without thinking carefully: *They **rushed headlong into** marriage.* **2** falling with your head going first: *tumbling headlong down the slope*

**head·mas·ter** /'hɛd,mæstɚ/, **head·mis·tress** /'hɛd,mɪstrɪs/ *n* a PRINCIPAL in a private school

**head-on** /,. '.√/ *adv* **1 meet/hit head-on** if two vehicles meet or hit head-on, the front part of one vehicle comes toward or hits the front part of the other vehicle **2** to deal with someone or something in a direct and determined way: *She intended to **face** her difficulties **head-on**.* –**head-on** *adj*: *a head-on collision*

**head·phones** /'hɛdfoʊnz/ *n* [plural] a piece of equipment that you wear over your ears to listen to a radio or recording

**head·quar·ters** /'hɛd,kwɔtɚz/ *n* [plural] **1** a building or office that is the center of a large organization, or the center of a particular activity: *Republican Party headquarters* **2** also **HQ** the place from which military operations are controlled

**head·rest** /'hɛdrɛst/ *n* the top part of a chair or seat that supports the back of your head

**head·room** /'hɛd-rum/ *n* [U] the amount of space above your head inside a car

**heads** /hɛdz/ *n* [plural] the side of a coin that has a picture of a head on it –opposite TAILS

**head start** /,. './ *n* the advantage you gain in a particular activity by starting before other people: *The younger children were given a head start in the race.*

**head·stone** /'hɛdstoʊn/ *n* ⇨ GRAVESTONE

**head·strong** /'hɛdstrɔŋ/ *adj* very determined

to do what you want, even when other people advise you not to do it: *a headstrong child*

**head-to-head** /ˌ. . '.◂/ *adj, adv* directly competing with another person or group: *Courier companies are **going head-to-head** with the Post Office.* | *head-to-head competition*

**head·way** /'hedweɪ/ *n* **make headway** **a)** to make progress toward achieving something even when you have difficulties: *They have made little headway in the peace talks.* **b)** to move forward: *a ship making headway through the channel*

**head·wind** /'hedˌwɪnd/ *n* a wind that blows directly toward you when you are moving

**head·y** /'hedi/ *adj* exciting in a way that makes you feel you can do anything: *the heady days of our youth*

**heal** /hil/ *v* **1** [I] if a wound or broken bone heals, it becomes healthy again: *The scratch on her finger healed quickly.* **2** [T] to cure someone who is ill, or make a wound heal —**healer** *n*

**health** /hɛlθ/ *n* [U] **1** the general condition of your body, and how healthy you are: *You should take better care of your health.* | *She's not **in the best of health**.* | *a 68-year-old man **in good health*** **2** the state of being without illness or disease: *I wish you health and happiness.* **3** how successful an ECONOMY, business, or organization is

**health care** /'. ˌ./ *n* [U] the service of taking care of the health of all the people in a country or area: *a health care plan*

**health club** /'. ./ *n* a place where people go to exercise, that you have to pay to use

**health food** /'. ./ *n* [C,U] food that contains only natural substances

**health·ful** /'hɛlθfəl/ *adj* likely to make you healthy

**health·y** /'hɛlθi/ *adj* **1** physically strong and not likely to become ill: *a healthy baby girl* —opposite UNHEALTHY **2** good for your body or your mind: *a healthy diet/lifestyle* | *It's not healthy for her to depend on him like that.* | *We all have the right to a healthy workplace.* **3** successful and likely to stay that way: *a healthy economy/business/relationship* **4** INFORMAL fairly large or noticeable: *She seems to have a healthy appetite.* | *a healthy increase in sales* | *Reed has a healthy respect for rattlesnakes.* **5** showing that you are healthy: *healthy skin* —**healthiness** *n* [U]

**heap¹** /hip/ *n* **1** a large messy pile of things: *a **heap of** newspapers* | *His clothes lay **in a heap** by the bed.* **2** INFORMAL an old car that is in bad condition

**heap²** *v* [T] **1** to put a lot of things on top of each other in a messy way: *magazines heaped on the table* **2** **be heaped with** to have a lot of things on top of something: *a plate heaped with food*

**heap·ing** /'hipɪŋ/ *adj* a heaping measurement of food is slightly more than the tool it is being measured with can hold

**hear**

Mike didn't hear the phone because he was listening to music.

**hear** /hɪr/ *v* **heard, heard** /hɜrd/, **hearing** **1** [I,T] to know that a sound is being made, using your ears: *I love to hear the baby laugh like that.* | *Didn't you hear when I called you?* **2** [T] to listen to music that is being played, what someone is saying etc.: *I heard a great song on the radio.* | *You should at least hear what she has to say.* **3** [I,T] to be told or find out a piece of information: *Have you **heard about** the new project?* | *"Mark's going to law school." "So I've heard."* (=said when you already know about something) **4** **hear a case** to listen to what is said in a court of law, and make a decision: *The case will be heard on July 16.* **5** **(do) you hear (me)?** SPOKEN said when you are giving someone an order and want to be certain that s/he will obey you: *Be home by ten, you hear?* —see usage note at LISTEN

**hear from** sb *phr v* [T] to get news or information from someone, usually by letter: *Have you heard from Jane yet?*

**hear of** sb/sth *phr v* [T] **have heard of** to know that someone or something exists because you have been told about him, her, or it: *"Do you know a guy named Phil Merton?" "I've never **heard of** him."*

**hear** sb **out** *phr v* [T] to listen to all of someone's explanation for something, without interrupting: *Look, I know you're mad, but at least hear me out.*

**hear·ing** /'hɪrɪŋ/ *n* **1** [U] the sense that you use to hear sounds: *My hearing's not as good as it used to be.* **2** a meeting of a court or special committee to find out the facts about a case

**hearing aid** /'.. ˌ./ *n* a small thing that makes sounds louder, that you put in your ear if you cannot hear well

**hearing im·paired** /'.. .ˌ./ *adj* unable to hear well or hear at all

**hear·say** /'hɪrseɪ/ *n* [U] something that you have heard about from other people but do not know to be true: *This witness's testimony is based only on hearsay.*

**hearse** /hɜrs/ *n* a large car for carrying a dead body in a COFFIN at a funeral

**heart** /hart/ *n*

**1** ▶BODY◀ the organ inside a person's or animal's chest that pumps blood through the body:

*He could feel his heart beating faster.*

**2** ▶EMOTIONS◀ [C,U] the part of you that is able to feel strong emotions such as love: *I knew in my heart that I wouldn't see her again.* | *I was hoping with all my heart that you would win.*

**3** ▶SHAPE◀ a shape used for representing love −see picture at SHAPE

**4 the heart of sth a)** the main or most important part of something: *We talked for hours before we got to the heart of the problem/matter.* **b)** [singular] the middle or the busiest part of an area: *a big hotel in the heart of the city*

**5 at heart** if you are a particular type of person at heart, that is the type of person you really are: *I guess I'm just a kid at heart.*

**6 know/learn sth by heart** to correctly remember all of something that you have been taught

**7** ▶GAME◀ a playing card with one or more red heart shapes on it

**8 sb's heart sank** used in order to say that someone suddenly became very sad or disappointed: *Bert's heart sank when he saw the mess in the house.*

**9 do sth to your heart's content** to do something as much as you want to: *Finish your homework, and then you can play video games to your heart's content.*

**10 -hearted** having a particular type of character: *a kind-hearted man*

**11 take/lose heart** to begin to have more hope, or to stop having hope

---
SPOKEN PHRASES
---

**12 not have the heart to do sth** to be unable to do something because you do not want to upset someone: *I didn't have the heart to tell her she was wrong.*

**13 my/her etc. heart isn't in it** if you do something when your heart isn't in it, you do not care about what you are doing

**14 have a heart** said when you want someone to be kinder or more helpful: *Have a heart - don't leave your dog in the car on a hot day.*

**15 a man/woman after my own heart** SPOKEN said when you like someone because s/he is similar to you: *"Jill only drinks whiskey." "A woman after my own heart!"*

**16 my heart goes out to sb** used in order to say that you feel sympathy for someone

−see also **cross my heart (and hope to die)** (CROSS¹)

**heart·ache** /'hɑrteɪk/ *n* [U] a strong feeling of sadness

**heart at·tack** /'. .,./ *n* a serious medical condition in which a person's heart suddenly stops working

**heart·beat** /'hɑrtˌbit/ *n* the action or the sound of a heart pumping blood through the body: *The doctor listened to my heartbeat.*

**heart·break** /'hɑrtˌbreɪk/ *n* [U] a strong feeling of sadness and disappointment

**heart·break·ing** /'hɑrtˌbreɪkɪŋ/ *adj* making you feel very upset: *the heartbreaking sound of an animal in pain*

**heart·bro·ken** /'hɑrtˌbroʊkən/ *adj* very sad because someone or something has disappointed you: *The kid was heartbroken.*

**heart·burn** /'hɑrtˌbɚn/ *n* [U] a slightly painful burning feeling in your stomach or chest caused by INDIGESTION

**heart di·sease** /'. .,./ *n* [U] a medical condition in which a person's heart has difficulty pumping blood

**heart·ened** /'hɑrtˌnd/ *adj* feeling happier and more hopeful −**hearten** *v* [T] −opposite DISHEARTENED

**heart·en·ing** /'hɑrtˌn-ɪŋ/ *adj* making you feel happier and full of hope: *heartening news* −opposite DISHEARTENING

**heart fail·ure** /'. ,../ *n* [U] the failure of the heart to continue working, which causes death

**heart·felt** /'hɑrtfɛlt/ *adj* felt very strongly and sincerely: *heartfelt thanks*

**hearth** /hɑrθ/ *n* the part of the floor around a FIREPLACE

**heart·i·ly** /'hɑrtl-i/ *adv* **1** loudly and cheerfully: *He laughed heartily.* **2** very much or completely: *I heartily agree with you.*

**heart·land** /'hɑrtlænd/ *n* **the heartland** the part of a country where most of the food is produced and where people live in a way that represents the basic values of that country

**heart·less** /'hɑrtlɪs/ *adj* cruel or not feeling any pity

**heart·rend·ing** /'hɑrtˌrɛndɪŋ/ *adj* making you feel great pity: *heartrending sobs*

**heart·strings** /'hɑrtˌstrɪŋz/ *n* **tug/pull on sb's heartstrings** to make someone feel a lot of pity or love

**heart·throb** /'hɑrtθrɑb/ *n* a famous person who many young people feel romantic love for: *1950s heartthrob and movie star - James Dean*

**heart-to-heart** /ˌ. . '.◀/ *n* a conversation in which two people honestly express their feelings or opinions about something −**heart-to-heart** *adj*

**heart·warm·ing** /'hɑrtˌwɔrmɪŋ/ *adj* making you feel happy, calm, and hopeful: *a heart-warming story*

**heart·y** /'hɑrti/ *adj* **1** very cheerful and friendly: *We were given a hearty welcome.* **2** a hearty meal or APPETITE is very large

**heat¹** /hit/ *n* **1** [U] warmth or hotness: *heat generated by the sun* **2 the heat a)** very hot weather: *Cindy was constantly complaining about the heat.* **b)** the system in a house that keeps it warm: *Can you turn the heat on/off?*

c) the heat that comes from this type of system, or from an OVEN or STOVE: *Lower the heat to 250°.* **3 the heat of the moment/argument etc.** the period in a situation, argument etc. when you feel extremely angry or excited: *In the heat of the moment, I said some things I didn't mean.* **4 take the heat** to deal with difficulties in a situation, especially by saying that you are responsible for them: *Coach Brown took the heat for the team's loss.* **5** one of the parts of a sports competition from which the winners are chosen to go on to the next part **6 in heat** if a female animal is in heat, she is able to become PREGNANT

**heat²** *v* [I,T] also **heat up** to become warm or hot, or to make something warm or hot: *We could heat up some soup for dinner.*

**heat up** *phr v* [I] if a situation, argument etc. heats up, the people involved in it become angrier and more excited

**heat·ed** /ˈhiṭɪd/ *adj* **1** kept warm by a HEATER: *a heated swimming pool* **2 heated argument/discussion etc.** an argument etc. in which people become very angry and excited

**heat·er** /ˈhiṭɚ/ *n* a machine used for heating air or water

**hea·then** /ˈhiðən/ *n* OLD-FASHIONED DISAPPROVING someone who does not belong to your religion −**heathen** *adj*

**heat wave** /ˈ. ./ *n* a period of unusually hot weather

**heave¹** /hiv/ *v* **1** [I,T] to pull, throw, or lift something with a lot of effort: *She heaved the box onto the back of the truck.* **2 heave a sigh** to breathe out loudly, especially because you have stopped worrying about something: *We all heaved a sigh of relief when it was over.* **3** [I] if your chest heaves, it moves up and down quickly because it is difficult to breathe **4** [I] INFORMAL ⇨ VOMIT¹

**heave²** *n* a strong pulling, pushing, or throwing movement

**heav·en** /ˈhɛvən/ *n* **1** [U] also **Heaven** the place where God or the gods are believed to live, and where good people go after they die −compare HELL **2** [U] INFORMAL a very good thing, situation, or place: *"How was your vacation?" "Oh, it was heaven!"* **3 for heaven's sake** SPOKEN said when you are annoyed or angry: *For heaven's sake, just shut up!* **4 heaven forbid** SPOKEN said in order to emphasize that you hope something will not happen: *And if - heaven forbid - he has an accident, what do I do then?*

**heav·en·ly** /ˈhɛvənli/ *adj* **1** relating to heaven **2** very good or pleasing: *a heavenly dessert*

**heavenly bod·y** /ˌ... ˈ../ *n* a star, PLANET, or moon

**heav·ens** /ˈhɛvənz/ *n* **1 (Good) Heavens!** SPOKEN said when you are surprised or slightly

annoyed: *Good Heavens! Where have you been?* **2 the heavens** LITERARY the sky

**heav·i·ly** /ˈhɛvəli/ *adv* **1** in very large amounts: *He's been drinking heavily recently.* **2** very or very much: *The building was heavily damaged by the fire.* | *Our work is heavily dependent on computers.* **3** someone who breathes heavily is breathing very loudly and slowly

*heavy*

heavy bags                                      heavy traffic

**heav·y** /ˈhɛvi/ *adj*
**1** ▸THINGS◂ weighing a lot: *Be careful lifting that box - it's really heavy.* | *The suitcase feels heavier than before.*
**2** ▸PEOPLE◂ used in order to politely describe someone who is fat: *He's gotten very heavy since we saw him last.*
**3** ▸AMOUNT◂ unusually large in amount or quantity: *Roads were closed due to heavy rains/snow.* | *Traffic is heavy on the 405 freeway.*
**4** ▸BUSY◂ very busy and full of activities: *a heavy day/schedule*
**5 heavy sleeper** someone who does not wake up very easily
**6 a heavy smoker/drinker** someone who smokes a lot or drinks a lot of alcohol
**7** ▸SERIOUS◂ very complicated or serious and involving a lot of mental effort: *a heavy discussion* | *For a comedy that movie was heavy going.*
**8 heavy breathing** breathing that is slow and loud
**9 be heavy into sth** SPOKEN NONSTANDARD to be very involved in an activity, especially one that is not good for you: *Eric was real heavy into drugs.*
**10 a heavy load/burden** a problem or situation that is large or too difficult to deal with: *Three jobs! That's a heavy load for just one person.*
**11 with a heavy heart** LITERARY feeling very sad −**heaviness** *n* [U] −compare LIGHT²

**heavy-du·ty** /ˌ.. ˈ..◂/ *adj* **1** strong enough to be used often or for hard work without being damaged: *heavy-duty plastic gloves* **2** SLANG said when you want to emphasize how complicated, serious etc. someone or something is: *That was a heavy-duty conversation!*

**heavy-hand·ed** /ˌ.. ˈ..◂ / *adj* strict, unfair, and not considering other people's feelings: *heavy-handed demands*

H

**heavy in·dus·try** /ˌ.. '.../ *n* [U] industry that produces goods such as coal, steel, or chemicals, or large goods such as cars and machines

**heavy met·al** /ˌ.. '../ *n* [U] a type of ROCK music with a strong beat that is played very loudly on electric GUITARs

**heav·y·weight** /ˈhɛviˌweɪt/ *n* **1** someone who BOXes or WRESTLEs, and is in the heaviest weight group **2** someone who has a lot of power and experience in a particular business or job: *a debate between political heavyweights*

**He·brew** /ˈhibru/ *n* [U] the official language of Israel, also used in many other places by Jewish people –**Hebrew, Hebraic** /hɪˈbreɪ-ɪk/ *adj*

**heck** /hɛk/ *interjection* **1** said in order to emphasize a question, or when you are annoyed: *Who/what/where etc. the heck is that?* | *Ah, heck! I've lost my glasses.* **2 What the heck!** said when you do something that you should not do: *"Want another piece of pie?" "Yeah, what the heck!"* –see also HELL

**heck·le** /ˈhɛkəl/ *v* [T] to interrupt and try to embarrass someone who is speaking or performing –**heckler** *n* –**heckling** *n* [U]

**hec·tare** /ˈhɛktɛr/ *n* a unit for measuring an area of land, equal to 10,000 square meters or 2.471 ACRES

**hec·tic** /ˈhɛktɪk/ *adj* very busy, hurried, and slightly exciting: *It's been a really hectic week.*

**he'd** /ɪd; *strong* hid/ **1** the short form of "he would": *I'm sure he'd drive you there.* **2** the short form of "he had": *He'd never been a good dancer.*

**hedge**[1] /hɛdʒ/ *n* **1** a row of bushes used as a border around a yard or between two yards **2 hedge against disaster/inflation etc.** something that helps avoid problems, losing a lot of money etc.: *a hedge against financial risk*

**hedge**[2] *v* **1** to avoid giving a direct answer to a question: *I got the feeling he was hedging.* **2 hedge your bets** to reduce your chances of failing by trying several different possibilities instead of one

**hedge against** sth *phr v* [T] to protect yourself from having problems, losing a lot of money etc.: *A well-managed business will hedge against financial loss.*

**he·do·nism** /ˈhidnˌɪzəm/ *n* [U] the belief that pleasure is the most important thing in life –**hedonist** *n* –**hedonistic** /ˌhidnˈɪstɪk/ *adj*

**heed**[1] /hid/ *v* [T] FORMAL to pay attention to someone's advice or warning

**heed**[2] *n* [U] FORMAL **take heed of/pay heed to** to pay attention to something and think about it seriously

**heed·less** /ˈhidlɪs/ *adj* LITERARY not paying attention to something important

**heel**[1] /hil/ *n* **1** the back part of your foot –see picture at BODY **2** the back raised part of a shoe, or the back part of a sock that is under your heel **3 -heeled** having a particular type of heel: *a high-heeled shoe* **4 on the heels of** very soon after something: *Christmas vacation came on the heels of our finals.* **5** the raised part of your hand near your wrist

**heel**[2] *v* **heel!** used in order to tell your dog to stay near you

**heels** /hilz/ *n* [plural] ⇨ HIGH HEELS

**heft·y** /ˈhɛfti/ *adj* **1** big or strong: *a hefty man* **2 a hefty price/sum etc.** a large amount of money

**heif·er** /ˈhɛfɚ/ *n* a young female cow that has not yet given birth to a CALF (=baby cow)

**height** /haɪt/ *n* **1** [C,U] how tall someone or something is: *Howard and Ben are about the same height.* | *Sunflowers can grow to a height of 15 feet.* **2** a particular distance above the ground: *The shelves were installed at the wrong height.*

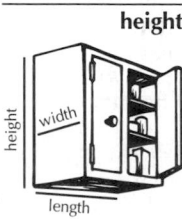
height

**3 the height of a)** the period when something is the strongest, most intense, best etc. it can ever be: *the height of the oil crisis* **b)** the greatest degree or amount of something: *rich people living in the height of luxury* –see also HEIGHTS

**height·en** /ˈhaɪtn/ *v* [I,T] to increase or make something become increased: *Taking the class has heightened my appreciation of modern art.*

**heights** /haɪts/ *n* [plural] **1** a high position or place: *I'm afraid of heights.* **2 to new heights** to an increased or more successful level: *Prices jumped to new heights on Wednesday.*

**hei·nous** /ˈheɪnəs/ *adj* extremely bad: *a heinous crime*

**heir** /ɛr/ *n* someone who will legally receive all of the money, property etc. of a person who has died

**heir·loom** /ˈɛrlum/ *n* a valuable object that a family owns for many years

**heist** /haɪst/ *n* a BURGLARY

**held** /hɛld/ the past tense and PAST PARTICIPLE of hold

**hel·i·cop·ter** /ˈhɛliˌkɑptɚ/ *n* a type of aircraft with metal blades on top of it that spin very fast

helicopter

**hel·i·port** /ˈhɛləˌpɔrt/ *n* an airport for HELICOPTERs

**he·li·um** /ˈhiliəm/ *n* [U] a gas that is an ELEMENT and that is lighter than air, often used in order to make BALLOONs float

**he'll** /ɪl, il, hɪl; *strong* hil/ **1** the short form of "he will": *He'll be arriving later tonight.* | *The law says he'll be punished for his crimes.* **2** the short form of "he shall"

**hell** /hɛl/ *n* **1** [singular] also **Hell** the place where bad people will be punished after they die, according to the Christian and Muslim religions **2 be hell** to be very bad: *Traffic was hell all the way home.*

SPOKEN PHRASES

**3** an impolite way to emphasize a question or statement: *What the hell are you doing?* | *"Are you working late tonight?" "Hell, no!"* | *Get the hell out of here!* | *It's hard as* **hell** *to hear anything in there.* | *He's a* **hell** *of a salesman.* (=he's a good salesman) **4 go to hell** an impolite phrase said when you are very angry with someone **5 for the hell of it** for no particular reason or purpose: *We just decided to drive up to Montreal for the hell of it.* **6 to hell with sb/ sth** an impolite way of saying that you do not care about someone or something any longer **7 from hell** said when you think something is the worst it could be: *It was the vacation from hell.* **8 give sb hell** an impolite phrase meaning to tell someone angrily that s/he should not have done something **9 like hell** used for emphasizing what you are saying: *I'd been really sick, and I looked like hell.* (=looked terrible) | *We're going to have to work like hell to get this done.* (=work very hard) **10 go through hell/put sb through hell** to experience a situation that is extremely bad, or to make someone do this: *My father's drinking problem must have put my mother through hell.* **11 raise hell** an impolite phrase meaning to have fun in a loud and annoying way: *kids raising hell at 3:00 a.m.* **12 all hell breaks loose** used in order to say that a situation suddenly becomes very bad, disorganized, or violent

**hel·lo** /həˈloʊ, hɛˈloʊ, ˈhɛloʊ/ *interjection* **1** used when meeting someone or greeting someone: *Hello, my name is Betty.* **2** said when answering the telephone or when starting a telephone conversation: *"Hello?" "Hello, is Chad there?"* **3** said when trying to get someone's attention: *Hello? Is anybody here?* **4 say hello** to have a quick conversation with someone: *I'll drop by later and say hello.*

**helm** /hɛlm/ *n* **1 at the helm** controlling a group or organization: *With Ms. Mathis at the helm, the company has grown by 20%.* **2** a wheel used for guiding a ship's direction

**hel·met** /ˈhɛlmɪt/ *n* a hard hat that covers and protects your head: *a motorcycle helmet* –see picture at MASK¹

**help¹** /hɛlp/ *v* **1** [I,T] to make someone be able to do something more easily: *Do you want me to help you move that table?* | *Mom, can you* **help** *me with my homework?* | *Is there anything I can do to help?* **2** [I,T] to make it possible for something to become better, easier, or more

developed: *It might* **help to** *talk to someone about your problems.* | *Brushing your teeth helps prevent cavities.*

SPOKEN PHRASES

**3 can't/couldn't help** said when you are unable to stop doing something: *I just couldn't help laughing.* **4 I can't help it** said when you think something is not your fault: *I can't help it if she lost the stupid book!* **5 help yourself** used when telling someone to take as much food or drink as s/he wants: **Help yourself to** *anything in the fridge.* **6 help!** said when you need someone to help you, especially because you are in danger

**help out** *phr v* [I,T **help** sb ↔ **out**] to help someone because s/he is very busy, has a lot of problems etc.: *They did everything they could to* **help us out.**

**USAGE NOTE** help and assist

**Assist** is more formal than **help**. Use **help** to mean "make it easier for someone to do something": *Could you help me move this desk?* Use **assist** when someone has special skills to help someone do something: *Dr. Taylor assisted in the research of this article.*

**help²** *n* [U] **1** the action of helping someone: *Do you need any help washing the dishes?* **2** the quality of being useful: *Unfortunately the instructions* **weren't a lot of help.** **3** advice, treatment, money etc. that someone gives you in order to help you: *Go get help, quickly!*

**help·er** /ˈhɛlpɚ/ *n* someone who helps another person

**help·ful** /ˈhɛlpfəl/ *adj* **1** useful: *The map was really helpful.* **2** willing to help: *Everyone was so helpful and friendly.* – **helpfully** *adv*

**help·ing¹** /ˈhɛlpɪŋ/ *n* the amount of food you are given or that you take: *Who wants another helping of apple pie?*

**helping²** *adj* **lend/give a helping hand** to help someone

**helping verb** /ˈ.. ˌ./ *n* TECHNICAL ⇨ AUXILIARY VERB

**help·less** /ˈhɛlplɪs/ *adj* unable to take care of yourself or protect yourself: *The man lay helpless in the street.* – **helplessness** *n* [U] – **helplessly** *adv*

**hel·ter-skel·ter** /ˌhɛltɚˈskɛltɚ/ *adv* done in a disorganized, confusing, and hurried way

**hem¹** /hɛm/ *n* the folded and sewn edge of a piece of clothing

**hem²** *v* **-mmed, -mming** [T] to fold and sew the edge of a piece of clothing

**hem** sb ↔ **in** *v* [T] to surround someone so that s/he cannot move where s/he wants: *It was real-*

H

ly scary - I *was hemmed in by two cars and a big truck on the freeway.*

**hem·i·sphere** /ˈhɛməˌsfɪr/ *n* one of the halves of the earth, especially the northern or southern parts above and below the EQUATOR

**hem·line** /ˈhɛmlaɪn/ *n* the length of a dress, skirt, or pants

**hem·lock** /ˈhɛmlɑk/ *n* [C,U] a very poisonous plant, or the poison of this plant

**he·mo·glo·bin** /ˈhiməˌgloʊbɪn/ *n* [U] a red substance in the blood that carries oxygen and iron

**he·mo·phil·i·a** /ˌhiməˈfɪliə, -ˈfilyə/ *n* [U] a serious disease that usually affects only men, in which the blood does not become thick, so that they lose too much blood after being cut or wounded –**hemophiliac** /ˌhiməˈfɪliˌæk/ *n*

**hem·or·rhage** /ˈhɛmərɪdʒ/ *n* a serious medical condition in which an area in someone's body loses too much blood

**hem·or·rhoids** /ˈhɛməˌrɔɪdz/ *n* [plural] painfully swollen BLOOD VESSELs at the ANUS

**hemp** /hɛmp/ *n* [U] a plant used for making strong rope, a rough cloth, and the drug CANNABIS

**hen** /hɛn/ *n* a fully grown female bird, especially a female chicken

**hence** /hɛns/ *adv* FORMAL for this reason: *The sugar from the grapes remains in the wine, hence the sweet taste.*

**hence·forth** /ˈhɛnsfɔrθ, ˌhɛnsˈfɔrθ/, **hence·for·ward** /hɛnsˈfɔrwərd/ *adv* FORMAL from this time on: *Henceforth in this book, these people will be called "The Islanders."*

**hench·man** /ˈhɛntʃmən/ *n* someone who faithfully obeys a powerful person such as a politician or a criminal

**hep·a·ti·tis** /ˌhɛpəˈtaɪtɪs/ *n* [U] a serious disease of the LIVER

**her**[1] /ɚ, hɚ; *strong* hɚ/ *posessive adj* **1** belonging to or relating to a female person or animal that has been mentioned or is known about: *Maura wants to know where her yellow sweater is.* | *That's her new car.* **2** used when talking about a country, car, ship etc. that has been mentioned: *Her top speed is 110 miles per hour.*

**her**[2] *pron* **1** the object form of "she": *I've never seen your boss. Is that her?* | *I gave her $20.* –see usage note at ME **2** a country, ship, car etc. that has been mentioned

**her·ald** /ˈhɛrəld/ *v* [T] **1** to publicly praise someone or something: *He was **heralded** as the poet of his generation.* **2** to be a sign that something is going to come or happen soon: *The development of the computer chip heralded a new age of technology.*

**herb** /ɚb/ *n* a plant used in cooking to give food more taste, or to make medicine

**herb·al** /ˈɚbəl/ *adj* relating to HERBs: *herbal medicine*

**herb·i·vore** /ˈhɚbəˌvɔr, ˈɚbə-/ *n* an animal that only eats plants –compare CARNIVORE

**herd**[1] /hɚd/ *n* a group of a particular type of animal that lives together: *a herd of cattle*

**herd**[2] *v* [I,T] to form a group, or to make people or animals move together as a group: *The tour guide herded us onto the bus.*

**here**[1] /hɪr/ *adv* **1** in or to this place: *I'm going to stay here with Kim.* | *How far is Canada from here?* | *Remember, we came here on Dad's birthday.* | *It's so dark **out here**.* **2** if a period of time is here, it has begun: *Spring is here!* **3** at this point in a discussion or piece of writing: *The subject is too difficult to explain here, but I'll give you some books that will help you.*

---

SPOKEN PHRASES

**4 here you are/go** said when you give someone something s/he has asked for: *"Could you bring me a glass of water, please?" "Here you are, sir."* **5 here's....** also **here he/she/it is** used in order to say that you have arrived somewhere, or that someone you have been waiting or looking for has arrived: *Here's the restaurant I was telling you about.* | *Here you are - we've been looking everywhere for you.* **6 here comes...** said as the person or vehicle you have been waiting for is arriving: *Oh, here comes Sam now.* | *Here comes the bus.* **7 here goes** said before you do something exciting, dangerous, or new: *Are you ready? OK, here goes.* **8 here's to sb/sth** said when you are praising or thanking someone or something: *Here's to Jane for all her hard work!*

---

**here**[2] *interjection* said when you offer something to someone: *Here, use my pen.*

**here·a·bouts** /ˈhɪrəˌbaʊts, ˌhɪrəˈbaʊts/ *adv* around or near the place where you are: *Everyone hereabouts thinks he's guilty.*

**here·af·ter**[1] /ˌhɪrˈæftɚ/ *adv* FORMAL from this time or in the future

**hereafter**[2] *n* **the hereafter** life after you die: *Do you believe in the hereafter?*

**here·by** /ˌhɪrˈbaɪ, ˈhɪrbaɪ/ *adv* FORMAL as a result of this statement: *I hereby pronounce you man and wife.*

**he·red·i·tar·y** /həˈrɛdəˌtɛri/ *adj* if a mental or physical quality, or a disease is hereditary, it is passed to a child from the GENEs of his/her parents: *Heart disease is often hereditary.*

**he·red·i·ty** /həˈrɛdəti/ *n* [U] the process of passing on a mental or physical quality from a parent's GENEs to a child

**here·in** /ˌhɪrˈɪn/ *adv* FORMAL in this place, situation, or piece of writing

**her·e·sy** /ˈhɛrəsi/ *n* [C,U] a belief that a religious, political, or social group considers to be wrong or evil

**her·e·tic** /'hɛrə,tɪk/ *n* someone whose beliefs are considered to be wrong or evil –**heretical** /hə'rɛtɪkəl/ *adj*

**here·with** /,hɪr'wɪθ, -'wɪð/ *adv* FORMAL with this letter or document

**her·it·age** /'hɛrətɪdʒ/ *n* [C,U] the traditional beliefs, values, customs etc. of a family or country: *Ireland's musical heritage*

**her·met·i·cal·ly** /hə'mɛtɪkli/ *adv* TECHNICAL **hermetically sealed** very tightly closed so that no air can get in or out –**hermetic** *adj*

**her·mit** /'hə·mɪt/ *n* someone who prefers to live far away from other people

**her·ni·a** /'hə·niə/ *n* [C,U] a medical condition in which an organ pushes through the skin or muscle that covers it; RUPTURE

**he·ro** /'hɪroʊ/ *n, plural* **heroes 1** someone who is admired for doing something very brave or good: *He became a local hero for saving the child's life.* **2** someone, especially a man or boy, who is the main character of a book, play, or movie **3** also **hero sandwich** ⇨ SUB –see also HEROINE

**he·ro·ic** /hɪ'roʊɪk/ *adj* **1** admired for being brave, strong, and determined: *the people's heroic efforts in the fight for independence* **2** a heroic story, poem etc. has a HERO in it

**he·ro·ics** /hɪ'roʊɪks/ *n* [plural] brave or impressive actions or words that someone does in order to seem impressive to other people

**her·o·in** /'hɛroʊɪn/ *n* [U] a strong illegal drug made from MORPHINE

**her·o·ine** /'hɛroʊɪn/ *n* a female HERO

**her·o·ism** /'hɛroʊ,ɪzəm/ *n* [U] very great courage: *Firefighters were praised for their heroism.*

**her·on** /'hɛrən/ *n* a large wild bird with very long legs and a long beak, that lives near water

**her·pes** /'hə·piz/ *n* [U] a very infectious disease that causes spots on the skin, especially on the face or GENITALS

**her·ring** /'hɛrɪŋ/ *n* [C,U] a long thin silver sea fish, or the meat from this fish

**hers** /hə·z/ *possessive pron* the thing or things belonging to or relating to a female person or animal that has been mentioned or is known about: *That's my car. This is hers.|Angela is a friend of hers.|My boots are black. Hers are brown.*

**her·self** /ə·'sɛlf; *strong* hə·'sɛlf/ *pron* **1** the REFLEXIVE form of "she": *Carol hurt herself.|She made herself a cup of coffee.* **2** the strong form of "she," used in order to emphasize the subject or object of a sentence: *She went to the library herself to get the information.|It's true! Vicky told me herself.* **3 (all) by herself a)** without help: *My daughter made dinner all by herself.* **b)** alone: *She went to the concert by herself.* **4 (all) to herself** for her own use: *Alison had the whole house to herself that night.* **5 not be herself**

SPOKEN if someone is not herself, she is not behaving or feeling the way she usually does, because she is sick or upset: *Mom hasn't been herself lately.*

**hertz** /hə·ts/ *written abbreviation* **Hz** *n, plural* **hertz** a unit for measuring sound WAVES

**he's** /iz; *strong* hiz/ **1** the short form of "he is": *He's my brother.* **2** the short form of "he has": *He's lost his keys.*

**hes·i·tant** /'hɛzətənt/ *adj* not willing to do or say something because you are uncertain or worried: *He was hesitant about admitting he was wrong.*

**hes·i·tate** /'hɛzə,teɪt/ *v* [I] **1** to pause before doing or saying something because you are uncertain: *She hesitated before answering his question.* **2 do not hesitate to do sth** SPOKEN FORMAL used in order to tell someone not to worry about doing something: *Don't hesitate to call me if you need any help.*

**hes·i·ta·tion** /,hɛzə'teɪʃən/ *n* [U] the action of hesitating (HESITATE): *Without hesitation he said, "Yes!"*

**het·er·o·ge·ne·ous** /,hɛtərə'dʒiniəs, -nyəs/ **heterogenous** *adj* FORMAL consisting of parts or members that are very different from each other: *a heterogeneous population* –**heterogeneity** /,hɛtəroʊdʒə'niəti/ *n* [U] –compare HOMOGENEOUS

**het·er·o·sex·u·al** /,hɛtərə'sɛkʃuəl/ *n* someone who is sexually attracted to people of the opposite sex –**heterosexual** *adj* –**heterosexuality** /,hɛtərə,sɛkʃu'æləti/ *n* [U] –compare BISEXUAL², HOMOSEXUAL

**hew** /hyu/ *v* **hewed**, **hewed** or **hewn** /hyun/, **hewing** [I,T] LITERARY to cut something with a cutting tool

**hew to** sth *phr v* [T] to obey someone or do something according to the rules or instructions: *a country that hews to socialist principles*

**hex·a·gon** /'hɛksə,gɑn/ *n* a flat shape with six sides –**hexagonal** /hɛk'sægənl/ *adj*

**hey** /heɪ/ *interjection* said in order to get someone's attention, or to show someone you are surprised or annoyed: *Hey, you! What are you doing?*

**hey·day** /'heɪdeɪ/ *n* the time when someone or something was most popular, successful, or powerful: *the heyday of silent movies*

**HI** the written abbreviation of Hawaii

**hi** /haɪ/ *interjection* INFORMAL hello: *Hi! How are you?*

**hi·a·tus** /haɪ'eɪtəs/ *n* [C usually singular] FORMAL a pause in an activity

**hi·ber·nate** /'haɪbə·,neɪt/ *v* [I] if an animal hibernates, it sleeps all the time during the winter –**hibernation** /,haɪbə·'neɪʃən/ *n* [U]

**hic·cup¹** /'hɪkʌp/ *n* **1** a sudden repeated stopping of the breath, usually caused by eating or drinking too fast: *I have the hiccups.* **2** a

**H**

small problem or delay: *There's a slight hiccup in the schedule for today.*

**hiccup²** *v* **-pped, -pping** [I] to have HICCUPS

**hick** /hɪk/ *n* DISAPPROVING someone who lives in the country and is thought to be uneducated or stupid

**hick·ey** /'hɪki/ *n* [] INFORMAL a slight BRUISE (=dark mark on your skin) from being kissed too hard

**hIck·o·ry** /'hɪkəri/ *n* a North American tree that produces nuts, or the hard wood from this tree

**hid** /hɪd/ *v* the past tense of HIDE

**hid·den¹** /'hɪdn/ *v* the PAST PARTICIPLE of HIDE

**hidden²** *adj* **1** difficult to see or find: *Marcia kept her letters hidden in a box.* **2** not easy to notice or discover: *There may have been a hidden meaning in what he said.*

**hide¹** /haɪd/ **hid, hid, hidden** *v* **1** [T] to put something in a place where no one else can see or find it: *Jane hid the Christmas presents in the closet.* **2** [I] to go to or stay in a place where no one can see or find you: *I'll hide behind the tree.* **3** [T] to not show your feelings to people, or to not tell someone about something: *Lee was heartbroken, but hid her feelings.* **4** to not tell someone about something: *I'll talk to the police - I have nothing to hide.* (=I have not done anything wrong that I do not want to talk about)

**hide²** *n* an animal's skin, especially when it is removed to be used for leather

**hide-and-seek** /ˌ. . '. / *n* [U] a children's game in which one child shuts his/her eyes while the other children hide, and then tries to find them

**hide·a·way** /'haɪdəˌweɪ/ *n* a place where you can go to hide or be alone

**hid·e·ous** /'hɪdiəs/ *adj* extremely ugly or unpleasant: *a hideous monster* **–hideously** *adv*

**hide·out** /'haɪdaʊt/ *n* a place where you can hide

**hid·ing** /'haɪdɪŋ/ *n* **go into hiding** to hide yourself, often because you have done something illegal or you are in danger

**hi·er·ar·chy** /'haɪəˌrɑrki/ *n* **1** [C,U] a system of organization in which people have higher and lower ranks **2** the most powerful members of an organization **–hierarchical** /haɪə'rɑrkɪkəl/ *adj*

**hi·er·o·glyph·ics** /ˌhaɪrə'glɪfɪks/ *n* [U] a system of writing that uses pictures to represent words **–hieroglyphic** *adj*

**hi-fi** /ˌhaɪ 'faɪ/ *adj* OLD-FASHIONED hi-fi equipment produces very clear sound **–hi-fi** *n*

**high¹** /haɪ/ *adj*

**1** ▶TALL◀ having a top that is a long distance from its bottom: *Pike's Peak is the highest mountain in Colorado.* | *a high wall* **–opposite** LOW¹ **–compare** TALL

**2** ▶ABOVE GROUND◀ being a long way

above the ground: *We were looking down from a high window.*

**high**

a high shelf         a tall tree

**3** ▶MORE THAN USUAL◀ a high amount, number, or level is greater than usual: *clothes selling at high prices* (=expensive prices) | *achieving a higher level of productivity*

**4** ▶RANK/POSITION◀ having an important or powerful position or rank: *She was elected to high office last November.* | *the highest levels of management*

**5** ▶GOOD◀ very good: *The boss has a high opinion of my work.* (=thinks my work is very good) | *Insist on high standards of quality and efficiency.*

**6** ▶DRUGS◀ under the effects of drugs or alcohol: *He was so high on drugs that he didn't know what he was doing.* | *kids getting high on marijuana*

**7** ▶CONTAINING A LOT◀ containing a lot of a particular substance or quality: *Most candy bars are high in calories.*

**8** ▶SOUND/VOICE◀ near the top of the range of sounds that humans can hear: *singing the high notes*

**9** **-high** having a particular height: *The grass was knee-high.*

**10** **high noon** exactly 12 o'clock in the day

**high²** *adv* **1** at or to a level high above the ground: *kites flying high in the sky* **2** at or to a high value, amount, rank etc.: *Jenkins has risen high in the company.* | *Ribas advised the graduating students to "aim high."* (=try to be successful) **3** **look/search high and low** to look everywhere for someone or something: *I searched high and low for the car keys.* **4** **be left high and dry** INFORMAL to be left without any help in a difficult situation

**high³** *n* **1** the highest level, number, temperature etc. that has been recorded in a particular time period: *The price of gold reached a new high yesterday.* | *a high* (=high temperature) *in the mid 90s* **2** a feeling of great excitement caused by success, drugs, alcohol etc.

**high·brow** /'haɪbraʊ/ *adj* a highbrow book, movie etc. is very serious and may be difficult to understand **–compare** LOWBROW

**high chair** /'. ./ *n* a tall chair that a baby sits in to eat

**high-class** /ˌ. '.◀/ *adj* of good quality and

style, and usually expensive: *a high-class restaurant*

**higher ed·u·ca·tion** /ˌ... ..'../ *n* [U] education at a college or university

**high fi·del·i·ty** /ˌ. .'.../ *adj* ⇨ HI-FI

**high-grade** /ˌ. '.◂/ *adj* of high quality: *high-grade motor oil*

**high-hand·ed** /ˌ. '.◂/ *adj* DISAPPROVING using your authority in a way that is not reasonable

**high heels** /ˌ. './ *n* [plural] women's shoes with a high HEEL (=raised part at the back) –**high-heeled** *adj* –see picture at SHOE¹

**high jinks** /'. ./ *n* [U] OLD-FASHIONED noisy or excited behavior when people are having fun

**high jump** /'. ./ *n* **the high jump** a sport in which you run and jump over a BAR that is raised higher after each successful jump –**high jumper** *n*

**high·lands** /'haɪləndz/ *n* [plural] an area with a lot of mountains

**high-lev·el** /ˌ. '..◂/ *adj* involving important people, especially in the government: *High-level peace talks began this week.*

**high·light¹** /'haɪlaɪt/ *v* [T] **1** to make a problem, subject etc. easy to notice so people will pay attention to it: *The report highlights the problem of inner-city crime.* **2** to mark written words with a pen or on a computer so you can see them more easily

**highlight²** *n* the most important or exciting part of a movie, sports event etc.: *a video of football highlights*

**high·light·er** /'haɪlaɪtɚ/ *n* a special pen that you use to mark written words so that you can see them more easily

**high·ly** /'haɪli/ *adv* **1** very: *We had a highly successful meeting.* **2** to a high level or degree: *a highly paid attorney*

**high-mind·ed** /ˌ. '..◂/ *adj* having high moral standards or principles

**High·ness** /'haɪnɪs/ *n* **Your/His etc. Highness** a royal title used when speaking to a king, queen etc.

**high-pitched** /ˌ. '.◂/ *adj* a high-pitched song or voice is higher than most sounds or voices

**high-pow·ered** /ˌ. '..◂/ *adj* **1** very powerful: *a high-powered speedboat* **2** very important or successful: *a high-powered businessman*

**high-pres·sure** /ˌ. '..◂/ *adj* **1** a high-pressure job or situation is one in which you need to work very hard to be successful **2** having or using a lot of pressure: *a high-pressure hose*

**high-pro·file** /ˌ. '..◂/ *adj* attracting a lot of attention from people: *a high-profile court case*

**high-rise** /'. ./ *n* a tall building –**high-rise** *adj*

**high roll·er** /ˌ. '../ *n* INFORMAL someone who spends a lot of money, especially by BETTing on games, races etc.

**high school** /'. ./ *n* [C,U] a school in the US and Canada for students over the age of 14

**high-spir·it·ed** /ˌ. '...◂/ *adj* having a lot of energy and liking to have fun: *a high-spirited four-year-old boy*

**high-strung** /ˌ. '.◂/ *adj* nervous, and easily upset or excited: *a high-strung horse*

**high-tech** /ˌ. '.◂/ *adj* using the most modern information, machines etc.: *a new high-tech camera*

**high tide** /ˌ. './ *n* [C,U] the time when the sea is at its highest level

**high·way** /'haɪweɪ/ *n* a wide fast road that connects cities or towns

**hi·jack** /'haɪdʒæk/ *v* [T] **1** to take control of a plane, vehicle etc. illegally **2** to take control of something: *The protesters tried to hijack the meeting.* –**hijacker** *n* –**hijacking** *n* [C,U]

**hike¹** /haɪk/ *n* **1** a long walk in the country, mountains etc. **2** INFORMAL a large increase in something: *a huge tax hike* **3** **take a hike** SPOKEN a rude way of telling someone to go away

**hike²** *v* **1** [I,T] to take a long walk in the country, mountains etc. **2** [T] also **hike** sth ‹› **up** to increase the price of something by a large amount: *Gas stations hiked prices in response to the Gulf War.*

**hik·ing** /'haɪkɪŋ/ *n* [U] an outdoor activity in which you take long walks in the mountains or country

**hi·lar·i·ous** /hɪ'lɛriəs, -'lær-/ *adj* extremely funny: *I thought the movie was hilarious!* –**hilariously** *adv* –**hilarity** /hɪ'lærəti/ *n* [U]

**hill** /hɪl/ *n* **1** an area of high land, like a small mountain: *the hills in upstate New York* | *driving up a steep hill* **2** **over the hill** INFORMAL no longer young, or too old to do a job well: *Larry can still play football - he's not over the hill yet.* **3** **the Hill** ⇨ CAPITOL HILL –**hilly** *adj*

**hill·bil·ly** /'hɪlˌbɪli/ *n* someone who lives in the mountains and is thought to be uneducated or stupid

**hill·side** /'hɪlsaɪd/ *n* the side of a hill

**hilt** /hɪlt/ *n* **1** **to the hilt** completely or extremely: *a warship armed to the hilt* **2** the handle of a sword or a large knife

**him** /ɪm; *strong* hɪm/ *pron* the object form of "he": *Why don't you just ask him yourself?* | *The cop ordered him out of the car.* –see usage note at ME

**him·self** /ɪm'sɛlf; *strong* hɪm'sɛlf/ *pron* **1** the REFLEXIVE form of "he": *Bill looked at himself in the mirror.* **2** the strong form of "he," used in order to emphasize the subject or object of a sentence: *It's true! He told me himself.* **3** **(all) by himself a)** without help: *He tried to fix the car by himself.* **b)** alone: *Sam was all by himself on the mountain trail.* **4** **(all) to himself** SPOKEN for his own use: *Ben had the house to himself for a week.* **5** **not be himself** if someone is not himself, he is not behaving or feeling as he usually does, because he is sick or upset: *Andy hasn't been himself lately.*

**hind** /haɪnd/ *adj* **hind legs/feet** the back legs or feet of an animal

**hin·der** /'hɪndɚ/ *v* [T] to make it difficult for someone to do something: *The bad weather is hindering rescue efforts.*

**Hin·di** /'hɪndi/ *n* [U] a language used in India

**hind·quar·ters** /'haɪnd,kwɔrtɚz/ *n* [plural] the back part of an animal

**hin·drance** /'hɪndrəns/ *n* someone or something that makes it difficult for you to do something: *He feels marriage would be a hindrance to his career.*

**hind·sight** /'haɪndsaɪt/ *n* [U] the ability to understand something after it has happened: *In hindsight, I think it was a terrible mistake.*

**Hin·du** /'hɪndu/ *n* someone who believes in Hinduism

**Hin·du·ism** /'hɪndu,ɪzəm/ *n* [U] the main religion in India, which includes belief in many gods and in REINCARNATION

**hinge¹** /hɪndʒ/ *n* a metal part that joins two things together, such as a door and a frame, so that one part can swing open and shut –**hinged** *adj*

**hinge²** *v*

**hinge on/upon** sth *phr v* [T] to depend on something: *The success of the team hinges on how well Ripken plays.*

**hint¹** /hɪnt/ *n* **1** something that you say or do that helps someone guess what you really want: *I don't know the answer, can you give me a hint?* | *Sue has been dropping hints* (=giving hints) *about what she wants for her birthday.* **2 a hint of** sth a small amount of something: *There was a hint of perfume in the air.* **3** a useful piece of advice on how to do something: *a book full of hints on gardening*

**hint²** *v* [I,T] to say something that helps someone guess what you want, or what will happen: *Archie hinted at the possibility that he was going to retire.*

**hin·ter·land** /'hɪntɚ,lænd/ *n* [singular] **the hinterland** the inner part of a country, usually away from cities or the coast

**hip¹** /hɪp/ *n* one of the two parts on either side of your body, where your legs join your body

**hip²** *adj* INFORMAL modern and fashionable: *a hip new comedy on NBC*

**hip·pie, hippy** /'hɪpi/ *n* someone, especially in the 1960s and 1970s, who usually had long hair, opposed the standards of society, and took drugs for pleasure

**hip·po·pot·a·mus** /,hɪpə'pɑtəməs/, **hip·po** /'hɪpoʊ/ *n, plural* **hippopotamuses, hippopotami** /-'pɑtəmaɪ/ a large African animal with a big head, fat body, and thick gray skin, that lives in and near water

**hire** /haɪɚ/ *v* [T] to employ someone to work for you: *Peter got hired at the new factory.*

**his¹** /ɪz; *strong* hɪz/ *possessive adj* belonging to or relating to a male person or animal that has been mentioned or is known about: *Leo hates cleaning his room.*

**his²** *possessive pron* the thing or things belonging to or relating to a male person or animal that has been mentioned or is known about: *I think he has my suitcase, and I have his.* | *Dave is a friend of his.* | *My boots are black. His are brown.*

**His·pan·ic** /hɪ'spænɪk/ *adj* from or relating to a country where Spanish or Portuguese is spoken –**Hispanic** *n*

**hiss** /hɪs/ *v* [I] to make a noise that sounds like "ssss": *I could hear steam hissing from the pipe.* –**hiss** *n*

**his·to·ri·an** /hɪ'stɔriən/ *n* someone who studies or writes about history

**his·tor·ic** /hɪ'stɔrɪk, -'stɑr-/ *adj* a historic place or event is important as a part of history

**his·tor·i·cal** /hɪ'stɔrɪkəl, -'stɑr-/ *adj* **1** relating to the study of history: *a collection of historical documents* **2** historical events, people etc. really happened or existed in the past: *Jesus is a historical figure.*

**his·to·ry** /'hɪstəri/ *n* **1** [U] all the things that happened in the past: *All through human history, wars have been fought over religion.* **2** the study of history, especially the political, social, or economic development of a particular country: *a class in European history* **3** a book about events that happened in the past: *a history of the Roman empire* **4 have a history of** sth to have had illness, problems etc. in the past: *Paul has a history of heart disease.* **5 make history/go down in history** to do something important that will be remembered

**his·tri·on·ics** /,hɪstri'ɑnɪks/ *n* [plural] DISAPPROVING behavior that is very emotional but is not sincere –**histrionic** *adj*

**hit¹** /hɪt/ *v* **hit, hit, hitting** [T]

**1** ▶STRIKE◀ to swing your hand, or something held in your hand, hard against someone or something: *He hit the boy on the nose.* | *She swung the bat and hit the ball.*

hit

**2** ▶CRASH◀ to crash into someone or something quickly and hard: *The car was totalled after hitting a wall.* | *I hit my head on the table.*

**3** ▶BAD EFFECT◀ to have a bad effect on someone or something: *The economy has been hard hit by inflation.*

**4** ▶BULLET/BOMB◀ to wound someone or damage something with a bullet or bomb: *A bullet hit her in the thigh.*

**5** ►REACH STH◄ to reach a particular level, number, position etc.: *Unemployment has hit a new high, at 11.3%.* | *We'll hit the exit in three miles.*
**6 hit it off (with sb)** INFORMAL to like someone as soon as you meet him/her
**7** ►THINK OF◄ if an idea, thought etc. hits you, you suddenly think of it: *It suddenly hit me that he was just lonely.*
**8 hit the roof/ceiling** INFORMAL to become very angry: *Dad's going to hit the roof when he sees this mess!*
**9 hit the road** INFORMAL to start on a trip
**10 hit the hay/sack** SPOKEN to go to bed
**11 hit the spot** SPOKEN if a food or drink hits the spot, it tastes good and is exactly what you want –see also **hit the bottle** (BOTTLE¹)
**hit back** *phr v* [I] to attack or criticize someone who is attacking or criticizing you: *Today the President hit back at his critics.*
**hit on** *phr v* [T] **1** [hit on sth] to have a good idea about something, often by chance: *I think Turner may have hit on a solution there.* **2** [hit on sb] INFORMAL to try to talk to someone who you are sexually interested in: *Men are always trying to hit on me at parties.*
**hit sb up for** sth *phr v* [T] SPOKEN to ask someone for something: *Mitch will probably try to hit you up for a loan.*

---

**USAGE NOTE** hit, strike, and beat

Use **hit** as a general word to talk about most kinds of hitting: *Dave hit Peter.* | *The van hit the car in front of it.* **Strike** is more formal and means "to hit very hard": *She had been struck on the side of the head.* | *A car ran off the highway and struck a telephone pole.* **Beat** means "to hit someone or something many times": *The man was robbed and beaten.* You can **hit** or **strike** someone or something accidentally or deliberately, but you **beat** someone or something deliberately.

---

**hit²** *n* [C usually singular] **1** a movie, song, play etc. that is very successful: *Her first novel was a **big hit**.* **2** the action of successfully striking something you are aiming at: *The missile scored a **direct hit**.* **3 be a hit (with sb)** to be liked very much by someone: *These brownies are always a hit with my guests.* **4** a quick hard blow with your hand, or something in your hand
**hit-and-miss** /ˌ. . ˈ.◄/, **hit-or-miss** *adj* INFORMAL done in a way that is not planned or organized well
**hit-and-run** /ˌ. . ˈ.◄/ *adj* a hit-and-run accident is one in which the driver of a car hits someone and then drives away without stopping to help
**hitch¹** /hɪtʃ/ *v* **1** [I,T] INFORMAL to travel by asking for free rides in other people's cars; HITCHHIKE: *We hitched a ride with a couple*

*from Florida.* **2** [T] to fasten something to something else: *Dad finished hitching the trailer on to the car.* **3 get hitched** INFORMAL to get married
**hitch** sth **up** *phr v* [T] to pull a piece of clothing up: *Bill hitched up his pants.*
**hitch²** *n* a small problem that causes a delay: *The performance went off **without a hitch**.* (=with no problems)
**hitch·hike** /ˈhɪtʃhaɪk/ *v* [I] to travel by asking for free rides in other people's cars –**hitchhiker** *n* –**hitchhiking** *n* [U]
**hith·er** /ˈhɪðɚ/ *adv* LITERARY **1** OLD-FASHIONED here, to this place: *Come hither!* **2 hither and thither/yon** in many directions
**hith·er·to** /ˌhɪðɚˈtu, ˈhɪðɚˌtu/ *adv* FORMAL up until now: *The Pilgrims were sailing to a hitherto unexplored land.*
**hit man** /ˈ. ./ *n* INFORMAL a criminal whose job is to kill someone
**HIV** *n* [U] Human Immunodeficiency Virus; a type of VIRUS that enters the body through the blood or sexual activity, and can cause AIDS: *Brad tested **HIV positive**.* (=has HIV)
**hive** /haɪv/ beehive *n* a place where BEES live
**hives** /haɪvz/ *n* [U] a condition in which someone's skin swells and becomes red, usually because s/he is ALLERGIC to something
**h'm, hmm** /hm, hmh/ *interjection* a sound that you make to express doubt or disagreement
**hoard¹** /hɔrd/ **hoard up** *v* [T] to collect things in large amounts and keep them in a secret place: *Fearful citizens were hoarding food in case of war.* –**hoarder** *n*
**hoard²** *n* a group of valuable things that someone has hidden to keep it safe: *a hoard of gold*
**hoarse** /hɔrs/ *adj* someone who is hoarse has a voice that sounds rough, often because of a sore throat
**hoax** /hoʊks/ *n* a trick that makes someone believe something that is not true: *The bomb threat turned out to be a hoax.* –**hoax** *v* [T]
**hob·ble** /ˈhɑbəl/ *v* [I] to walk with difficulty, taking small steps, usually because you are injured
**hob·by** /ˈhɑbi/ *n* an activity that you enjoy doing in your free time: *Do you **have a hobby**?* | *I started painting **as a hobby**.* –see usage note at SPORT
**hob·nob** /ˈhɑbnɑb/ *v* **-bbed, -bbing** [I] INFORMAL to spend time talking to people who are more famous or more important than you: *Jeremy is always **hobnobbing with** the bosses.*
**ho·bo** /ˈhoʊboʊ/ *n, plural* **hoboes, hobos** INFORMAL someone who travels around and has no home or regular job; TRAMP
**hock¹** /hɑk/ *n* **be in hock** INFORMAL to be in debt
**hock²** *v* [T] INFORMAL ⇨ PAWN²

**hock·ey** /'hɑki/ n [U] **1** also **ice hockey** a sport played on ice in which players use long curved sticks to try to hit a hard flat round object into a GOAL **2** ⇨ FIELD HOCKEY

**hodge·podge** /'hɑdʒpɑdʒ/ n [singular] a lot of things put together with no order or arrangement: *a hodgepodge of old toys*

**hoe** /hoʊ/ n a garden tool with a long handle, used for making the soil loose and for removing wild plants –**hoe** v [I,T]

**hog**[1] /hɔg, hɑg/ n **1** a large pig that is kept for its meat **2** INFORMAL someone who keeps or uses all of something for himself/herself **3** **go (the) whole hog** INFORMAL to do something thoroughly or completely

**hog**[2] v **-gged, -gging** [T] INFORMAL to keep or use all of something for yourself: *Look at that guy **hogging the road**.* (=driving so that no one can pass)

**ho-hum** /ˌhoʊ 'hʌm/ adj INFORMAL disappointing or boring: *The food was ho-hum.*

**hoist**[1] /hɔist/ v [T] to raise or lift something, especially using ropes or a special machine

**hoist**[2] n a piece of equipment used for lifting heavy things

**ho·key** /'hoʊki/ adj INFORMAL expressing emotions in a way that seems old-fashioned, silly, or too simple: *a hokey love song*

**hold**

hold your hand out      hold hands

**hold**[1] /hoʊld/ v **held, held, holding**
**1** ▶**IN YOUR HANDS/ARMS**◀ [T] to have something firmly in your hands or arms: *Hold my purse for a minute.* | *She was crying, and I held her tight.* –see also picture on page 473
**2** ▶**KEEP STH IN POSITION**◀ [T] to hold or keep something in a particular position: *She **held** the piece of paper **up** so we could see it.* | ***Hold** your hand **out**, and I'll give you a present.* | ***Hold still** (=don't move) so I can cut your hair!*
**3** ▶**HAVE SPACE FOR**◀ [T] to have space for a particular amount of something: *The jug holds two gallons of liquid.*
**4** ▶**KEEP/CONTAIN**◀ [T] to keep or contain something: *All our files are now held on computer.* | *the closet that held our winter clothes*
**5** ▶**POSITION/RANK/JOB**◀ [T] to have a particular position, job, or level of achievement: *Dr. Werner holds a degree in Political Science.*
**6** ▶**ARRANGE TIME/PLACE**◀ [T] to have a meeting, party etc. in a particular place or at a

particular time: *The conference will be held in Las Vegas.*
**7** **hold hands** if two people hold hands, they hold each other's hands: *a couple walking on the beach, holding hands*
**8** ▶**CONTINUE/NOT CHANGE**◀ [I,T] to continue at a particular level, rate, or number, or to make something do this: ***Hold** your speed **at** fifty.* | *Housing prices have held at the current level for three months.*
**9** **hold it!** SPOKEN used in order to tell someone to wait, or to stop doing something: *Hold it a minute! I'm trying to explain it to you.*
**10** ▶**TELEPHONE**◀ [I] to wait until the person you have telephoned is ready to answer: *Mr. Penrose is on the other line. Can you hold?*
**11** **hold sb's interest/attention** to keep someone interested: *She knows how to hold her students' interest.*
**12** **hold sb responsible** to think that someone is responsible for something bad that has happened: *Parents may be **held responsible for** their children's crimes.*
**13** **hold your own** to succeed in a difficult situation, or to be good enough when compared to similar things: *Tanner's art can hold its own alongside other American artists of his time.*
**14** ▶**HAVE A QUALITY**◀ [T] to have a particular quality: *This new industry holds great promise for the future.*
**15** ▶**CAGE/PRISONER**◀ [T] to keep a person or animal in a place where he, she, or it cannot leave: *Virginia Piper was kidnapped and held for two days.* | *tigers held in cages*
**16** ▶**SUPPORT WEIGHT**◀ [I,T] to support the weight of something: *The branch held, and Nick climbed higher up the tree.*
**17** ▶**THINK/BELIEVE**◀ FORMAL to think or believe something: *My grandfather **held the belief** that women should not speak too often.* | *Pythagoras **held that** planets have souls.*
**18** **be left holding the bag** to have to deal with problems that someone else has started: *Rogers went on vacation and left us holding the bag.*
**19** **hold true/good** FORMAL to be true in particular situations: *I think her statement **holds true for** older women.* (=is true about them) –see also **hold your breath** (BREATH) **hold your horses!** (HORSE[1]) **bite/hold your tongue** (TONGUE)

**hold** sth **against** sb phr v [T] to blame someone for something s/he has done: *If the economy worsens, voters are likely to **hold** it **against** him when they vote in November.*

**hold back** phr v **1** [T **hold** sth ↔ **back**] to control something or make it stay in one place: *The police couldn't **hold** the crowds **back**.* **2** [I,T **hold back** sth] to stop yourself from showing a particular feeling or saying something: *He didn't **hold back**. He yelled at me for at least ten minutes.* | *I couldn't **hold** my laugh-*

ter *back* any longer.   **3** [T **hold** sb ↔ **back**] to prevent someone from developing or improving: *Your son's reading is **holding** him **back**.*

**hold** sth **down** *phr v* [T]   **1** to keep something at a low level: *We're going to **hold down** these prices until the New Year.*   **2 hold down a job** to keep your job: *We can't hire a guy who's never been able to **hold down** a job.*

**hold forth** *phr v* [I] to say what you think about something, loudly and for a long time: *A guy at the bar was **holding forth on** why movies aren't as good as they used to be.*

**hold off** *phr v* [I] to delay doing something: *We **held off** making the decision for a month.*

**hold on** *phr v*   **1** SPOKEN said when you want someone to wait or stop talking, for example during a telephone call: *Yeah, **hold on**, Mike is right here.* | ***Hold on a minute/second.** Let me put this in the car.*   **2** to hold something tightly with your hand or arms: *I was so scared, I **held on to** the reins as tightly as I could.*   **3** to continue to do something difficult until it gets better: *The Rangers **held on** to win the game in the final period.*

**hold on to** sth *phr v* [T] to keep something, especially something that someone else wants: *I think you should **hold on to** it. After all, your mother gave it to you.*

**hold out** *phr v* [I]   **1** if a supply of something holds out, there is still some of it left: *We talked for as long as the wine **held out**.*   **2** to continue to defend yourself, or keep on refusing to do something: *The rebels are **holding out** in the south.*   **3 hold out hope/the prospect etc.** to say that something may happen: *The doctors don't **hold out** much hope that she will live.*

**hold out for** sth *phr v* [T] to refuse to accept less than you have asked for: *We expected him to **hold out for** more money, but he just signed the contract.*

**hold out on** sb *phr v* [T] to refuse to tell someone something s/he wants or needs to know: *You should have told me, instead of **holding out on** me for so long!*

**hold over** *phr v*   **1 be held over** if a concert, play, or movie is held over, it is shown for longer than was planned because it is very good: *Come see "Pulp Fiction." **Held over** for the fifth week.*   **2** [T **hold** sth **over** sb] to use something bad that you know about someone to control or threaten him/her: *My brother **held** that secret over me until I was 30 years old.*

**hold** sb **to** sth *phr v* [T] to make someone do what s/he has promised to do: *"He said he would do it." "Well, you'd better **hold** him **to** it."*

**hold together** *phr v*   **1** [I,T **hold** sth **together**] if a group, family, organization etc. holds together or something holds it together, it stays together: *The children are the only thing **holding** their marriage **together**.*   **2** [I] to re-

main whole, without breaking: *I hope this bus **holds together** long enough to get us to Fresno.*

**hold up** *phr v*   **1** [T **hold** sb/sth ↔ **up**] to make someone or something late: *Sorry, I didn't mean to **hold** everybody **up**.*   **2** [T **hold up** sth] to try to steal money from a store, bank etc. using a gun: *Brad's in jail for **holding up** a convenience store.*   **3** [I] to remain physically or emotionally strong: *Nancy **held up** really well through all her family troubles.*

**hold²** *n*   **1** [singular] the action of holding something: *Take **hold of** the rope and we'll pull you up.*   **2 get (a) hold of** to find someone or something for a particular purpose: *I need to get **hold of** Mark to ask him if he's coming to the party.* | *The kids don't seem to have a problem getting a **hold of** drugs.*   **3 on hold** waiting on the telephone before speaking to someone: *I will have to put you **on hold**.*   **4 have a hold over/on** sb to have power or control over someone   **5 take hold** to start to have an effect on someone or something: *These new ideas are taking **hold** across the country.*   **6** the part of a ship where goods are stored

**hold·er** /'houldɚ/ *n*   **1** someone who has control of or owns a place, position, or thing: *Only **ticket holders** will be admitted.*   **2** something that holds or contains something else: *a red candle holder*

**hold·ing** /'houldɪŋ/ *n* something that you own or rent, especially land or part of a company

**hold·o·ver** /'hould,ouvɚ/ *n* a feeling, idea, fashion etc. from the past that has continued to the present: *styles that are a holdover from the 60s*

**hold·up** /'houldʌp/ *n*   **1** a delay, especially one caused by traffic   **2** an attempt to rob someone, especially using a gun

**hole¹** /houl/ *n*   **1** an empty or open space in something solid: *We saw the dog digging a **hole** in the yard.* | *I have a **hole** in my sock.*   **2** the home of a small animal: *a rabbit hole*   **3** one of the small holes in the ground that you try to hit the ball into in the game of GOLF   **4** a problem or fault in an idea, plan, or story, so that it can be proved wrong or does not make sense: *The witness's testimony was **full of holes**.*   **5** INFORMAL an unpleasant place to live in, work in etc.: *I have to get out of this hole.*   **6 be in the hole** SPOKEN to owe money: *We're still $600 in the hole.*

**hole²** *v*

**hole up** *phr v* [I] to hide somewhere, or find shelter somewhere: *The rebels are still **holed up** in an army building.*

**hol·i·day** /'halə,deɪ/ *n* a day when you do not have to go to work, school etc.: *Labor Day is a **national holiday** in America.* —see usage note at VACATION

**ho·li·ness** /'houlinɪs/ *n*   **1** [U] the quality of being pure and holy   **2 Your/His Holiness** a title used for talking to or about some religious leaders, especially the Pope

**ho·lis·tic** /hoʊˈlɪstɪk/ *adj* concerning the whole of something rather than its parts: *a doctor interested in* **holistic medicine** (=medicine that treats the whole person, not just the illness)

**hol·ler** /ˈhɑlɚ/ *v* [I,T] INFORMAL to shout loudly: *Dad* **hollered** *at me to hurry up.* –**holler** *n*

**hol·low**[1] /ˈhɑloʊ/ *adj* **1** having an empty space inside: *a hollow tree* **2** feelings or words that are hollow are not sincere: *His promises* **ring hollow**. (=seem not sincere) **3** **hollow cheeks/eyes etc.** cheeks, eyes etc. where the skin has sunk inward

**hollow**[2] *n* **1** a hole in something, especially the ground, that is not very deep **2** a small valley: *cows grazing in the hollow*

**hollow**[3] *v*
**hollow** sth ↔ **out** *phr v* [T] to remove the inside of something

**hol·ly** /ˈhɑli/ *n* [U] a small tree with dark shiny pointed green leaves and red berries (BERRY), often used as a decoration at Christmas

**Hol·ly·wood** /ˈhɑliˌwʊd/ *n* [singular] a city in California near Los Angeles, known as the center of the American movie industry

**hol·o·caust** /ˈhɑlaˌkɔst, ˈhoʊ-/ *n* **1** an event that kills many people and destroys many things: *a nuclear holocaust* **2** **the Holocaust** the killing of millions of Jews by the Nazis in World War II

**hol·o·gram** /ˈhoʊlaˌgræm, ˈhɑ-/ *n* a special picture made with a LASER that looks as if it is not flat

**hol·ster** /ˈhoʊlstɚ/ *n* a leather object that you use for carrying a gun

**ho·ly** /ˈhoʊli/ *adj* **1** relating to God or religion; SACRED: *the holy city of Jerusalem* **2** very religious and morally pure: *a holy man*

**Holy Land** /ˈ.. ˌ./ *n* [singular] the parts of the Middle East where the events in the Bible happened

**hom·age** /ˈhɑmɪdʒ, ˈɑ-/ *n* [singular, U] FORMAL something that you say or do to show respect for an important person: *The visitors* **paid homage to** *the Queen.*

**home**[1] /hoʊm/ *n* **1** [C,U] the place where you usually live, especially with your family: *I'm sorry, Lisa is not* **at home** *now.* | *I've been* **living at home/living away from home** *for the past two years.* (=living with my parents/living in a different house from my parents) | *Neil is determined to* **leave home** *as soon as he is 18.* (=stop living with his parents) **2** **be/feel at home** to feel comfortable somewhere, or confident doing something: *It's hard to feel at home in a new place.* **3** **the home of sth/be home to** the place where something lives or comes from: *Australia is the home of the kangaroo.* **4** **make yourself at home** SPOKEN said in order

to tell someone who is visiting that s/he should relax **5** a place where people live who cannot take care of themselves, because they are very old, sick etc. **6** also **home plate** the base that players must touch in baseball to gain a point –see picture on page 472

**home**[2] *adv* **1** to or at the place where you live: *Hi, honey,* **I'm home.** | *When does Mike* **get home**? (=arrive at home) | *What time did you* **go home**? (=go to your house) ✗ DON'T SAY "go/get/arrive at home." ✗ **2** **take home** to earn a particular amount of money after tax has been taken away: *I take home about $200 a week.* **3** **hit/drive sth home** to make someone understand what you mean by saying it in a very clear and determined way: *The teacher* **drove the point home** *by doing an experiment.*

**home**[3] *adj* **1** relating to or belonging to your home or family: *My* **home town** *is Matamata.* | *What's your* **home address**? | *I'm looking forward to some* **home cooking** (=meals cooked by your family) *over Christmas.* **2** playing on your own sports field rather than an opponent's field: *The* **home team** *is ahead by four runs.* –opposite AWAY[2]

**home**[4] *v*
**home in on** *phr v* [T] to aim exactly at something and move directly toward it

**home·boy** /ˈhoʊmbɔɪ/ *n* SLANG ⇨ HOMEY[2]

**home·com·ing** /ˈhoʊmˌkʌmɪŋ/ *n* **1** an occasion when someone comes back to his/her home after being away for a long time **2** an occasion when former students return to their school or college

**home·land** /ˈhoʊmlænd/ *n* the country where you were born

**home·less** /ˈhoʊmlɪs/ *adj* **1** **the homeless** people who do not have a place to live, and who often live in the streets **2** without a home: *The war left a lot of people homeless.* –**homelessness** *n* [U]

**home·ly** /ˈhoʊmli/ *adj* a homely person is not very attractive –**homeliness** *n* [U]

**home·made** /ˌhoʊmˈeɪd◂/ *adj* made at home and not bought from a store: *homemade jam*

**home·mak·er** /ˈhoʊmˌmeɪkɚ/ *n* someone who works at home cooking and cleaning, and does not have another job

**home of·fice** /ˌ. ˈ../ *n* an office you have in your house so that you can do your job at home

**ho·me·op·a·thy** /ˌhoʊmiˈɑpəθi/ *n* [U] a system of medicine in which someone who is sick is given very small amounts of a substance that has the same effects as the disease –**homeopathic** /ˌhoʊmiəˈpæθɪk/ *adj*

**home·page** /ˈhoʊmpeɪdʒ/ *n* a place on the INTERNET where you can find information about a particular person, company etc.

**hom·er** /ˈhoʊmɚ/ *n* ⇨ HOME RUN –**homer** *v* [I]

**home·room** /ˈhoʊmrum/ *n* the room where students go at the beginning of the school day, or at the beginning of each SEMESTER

**home run** /ˌ. ˈ./ *n* a long hit in baseball that lets the player run around all the bases and get a point

**home·sick** /ˈhoʊmˌsɪk/ *adj* feeling sad because you are away from your home: *On her first night at camp, Sheila felt very* **homesick for** *her family.* −**homesickness** *n* [U]

**home·stead** /ˈhoʊmstɛd/ *n* a farm and the area of land and buildings around it, especially one that was originally given to someone by the government

**home·ward** /ˈhoʊmwɚd/ *adj* going towards home: *my homeward trip* −**homeward** *adv*

**home·work** /ˈhoʊmwɚk/ *n* [U] **1** work for school that a student does at home **2 sb has done his/her homework** someone has prepared well for something −compare HOUSEWORK

**hom·ey**[1] /ˈhoʊmi/ *adj* comfortable and pleasant, like home: *The restaurant had a nice homey atmosphere.*

**homey**[2] *n* SLANG a friend, or someone who comes from your area or GANG

**hom·i·ci·dal** /ˌhɑməˈsaɪdl̩ˌ ˌhoʊ-/ *adj* likely to murder someone

**hom·i·cide** /ˈhɑməˌsaɪd, ˈhoʊ-/ *n* [C,U] the crime of murder

**ho·mo·ge·ne·ous** /ˌhoʊməˈdʒiniəs, -nyəs/, **ho·mog·e·nous** /həˈmɑdʒənəs/ *adj* FORMAL consisting of parts or members that are all the same −**homogeneity** /ˌhoʊmoʊdʒəˈniəti, -ˈneɪti/ *n* [U] −compare HETEROGENEOUS

**ho·mo·ge·nize** /həˈmɑdʒəˌnaɪz/ *v* [T] FORMAL to change something so that its parts become more similar, or the whole of it is the same

**ho·mo·gen·ized** /həˈmɑdʒəˌnaɪzd/ *adj* homogenized milk has had its cream mixed in with the milk

**hom·o·nym** /ˈhɑməˌnɪm/ *n* a word that sounds the same and is spelled the same as another word, but has a different meaning, for example, the noun "bear" and the verb "bear"

**ho·mo·pho·bi·a** /ˌhoʊməˈfoʊbiə/ *n* [U] hatred and fear of HOMOSEXUALs −**homophobic** *adj*

**hom·o·phone** /ˈhɑməˌfoʊn, ˈhoʊ-/ *n* a word that sounds like another word, but is different in spelling or meaning, for example, "pair" and "pear"

**ho·mo·sex·u·al** /ˌhoʊməˈsɛkʃuəl/ *adj* sexually attracted to people of the same sex −**homosexual** *n* −**homosexuality** /ˌhoʊməˌsɛkʃuˈæləti/ *n* [U] −compare BISEXUAL[1], GAY[1], HETEROSEXUAL

**hon·cho** /ˈhɑntʃoʊ/ *n* INFORMAL an important person who controls something: *The company's* **head honchos** *are meeting next week.*

**hone** /hoʊn/ *v* [T] **1** to improve a skill: *players honing their skills* **2** to make a knife, sword etc. sharp

**hon·est** /ˈɑnɪst/ *adj* **1** someone who is honest does not lie, cheat, or steal −opposite DISHONEST **2** truthful and sincere: *Give me an honest answer.* **3 honest/to be honest** SPOKEN said to emphasize that what you are saying is true: *We didn't think to do that, to be honest with you.*

**hon·est·ly** /ˈɑnɪstli/ *adv* **1** SPOKEN said when you want to make someone believe what you have just said: *I honestly don't know what's the best thing to do.* **2** in an honest way: *Walters spoke honestly about her problems.*

**hon·es·ty** /ˈɑnəsti/ *n* [U] **1** the quality of being honest: *We never doubted Frank's honesty.* **2 in all honesty** SPOKEN said when you tell someone what you really think: *In all honesty, we made a lot of mistakes.*

**hon·ey** /ˈhʌni/ *n* [U] **1** a sweet sticky substance made by BEEs, used as food **2** SPOKEN a name that you call someone you love

**hon·ey·comb** /ˈhʌniˌkoʊm/ *n* a structure made by BEEs to store HONEY in

**hon·ey·moon** /ˈhʌniˌmun/ *n* a vacation taken by two people who have just been married: *Jen and Dave are going to Alaska* **on their honeymoon.** −**honeymooner** *n*

**hon·ey·suck·le** /ˈhʌniˌsʌkəl/ *n* a climbing plant with yellow or pink flowers that smell sweet

**honk** /hɑŋk, hɔŋk/ *v* [I,T] to make a loud noise like a car horn or a GOOSE −**honk** *n*

**hon·or**[1] /ˈɑnɚ/ *n* **1** [U] the respect that someone or something receives from other people: *a ceremony* **in honor of** (=to show respect to) *the soldiers who died* **2** [singular] something that makes you feel proud and glad: *It's an honor to meet you.* **3** [U] strong moral beliefs and standards of behavior that make people respect and trust you: *He's a* **man of honor.** **4** something that is given to someone to show him/her that people respect and admire what s/he has done **5 Your Honor** used when speaking to a judge −compare DISHONOR[1]

**honor**[2] *v* [T] **1** to treat someone with special respect: *Morgan was honored at a retirement dinner.* **2** to feel very proud and glad: *I'm honored to meet you.* **3 honor a contract/agreement etc.** to do what you have agreed to do in a contract etc. **4 honor a check** to accept a check as payment

**hon·or·a·ble** /ˈɑnərəbəl/ *adj* morally correct, and deserving respect and admiration: *an honorable man/action* −**honorably** *adv* −opposite DISHONORABLE

**hon·or·a·ry** /ˈɑnəˌrɛri/ *adj* **1** given to someone as an honor: *an honorary degree* **2** someone who has an honorary position does not receive payment for his/her work

H

**honor roll** /'.. ,./ n a list of the best students in a school: *Did you **make the honor roll**?*

**hon·ors** /'anɚz/ n [plural] **with honors** if you finish high school or college with honors, you get one of the highest grades

**hood** /hʊd/ n **1** the part of a coat that you pull up to cover your head **2** the metal cover over the engine on a car –see picture on page 469 **3** SLANG ⇨ NEIGHBORHOOD **4** INFORMAL ⇨ HOODLUM

**hood·ed** /'hʊdɪd/ adj having a HOOD or wearing a hood: *a hooded jacket*

**hood·lum** /'hudləm, 'hʊd-/ n OLD-FASHIONED a young person who does bad, often illegal things

**hoof** /hʊf/ n, plural **hoofs** or **hooves** the hard foot of an animal such as a horse

**hook¹** /hʊk/ n **1** a curved object that you hang things on: *a coat hook* **2** a curved piece of metal with a sharp point that you use for catching fish **3** **let sb off the hook** to decide not to punish someone for something s/he did wrong: *I'll let you off the hook today, but don't be late again.* **4** **off the hook** if a telephone is off the hook, the part of the telephone that you speak into is not on its base, so no one can call you

**hook²** v [T] **1** to fasten or hang something onto something else: ***Hook** the rope **over** the nail.* **2** INFORMAL to catch a fish with a hook: *Ben hooked a four-pound bass.*

**hook** sth ↔ **up** phr v [T] to connect a piece of electronic equipment to another piece of equipment: *Are the speakers **hooked up**?*

**hooked** /hʊkt/ adj **1** shaped like a hook: *a hooked nose* **2** **be hooked on** INFORMAL **a)** to be unable to stop taking a drug; ADDICTED **b)** to like something a lot: *Gina's hooked on old movies.*

**hook·er** /'hʊkɚ/ n INFORMAL ⇨ PROSTITUTE¹

**hook·y** /'hʊki/ n INFORMAL **play hooky** to stay away from school without permission: *The kids were caught playing hooky at the mall.*

**hoo·li·gan** /'hulɪgən/ n a noisy violent person who tries to make people fight and deliberately damages things

**hoop** /hup/ n a circular piece of wood, metal, plastic etc.: *hoop earrings | a basketball hoop* (=what you throw the ball through) –see picture at NET¹

**hoops** /hups/ n [U] INFORMAL basketball: *The guys are out **shooting hoops**.* (=playing basketball)

**hoo·ray** /hʊ'reɪ/ interjection shouted when you are very excited and happy about something

**hoot¹** /hut/ n **1** the sound made by an OWL or a ship's horn **2** **be a hoot** SPOKEN to be a lot of fun: *The show was a hoot!* **3** **not give a hoot** SPOKEN to not care or be interested in something: *I don't give a hoot what they think.*

**hoot²** v [I,T] **1** if an OWL or a ship's horn hoots, it makes a loud clear noise **2** to shout or

laugh loudly because you think something is funny or stupid: *The crowd was hooting and whistling.*

**hooves** /huvz, hʊvz/ n the plural of HOOF

**hop¹** /hap/ v **-pped, -pping** [I] **1** to move by making short quick jumps: *rabbits hopping along* **2** INFORMAL to get into, onto, or out of something, such as a vehicle: ***Hop in** and I'll give you a ride. | Richie hopped on his bike.*

**hop²** n **1** a short jump **2** **short hop** INFORMAL a short trip by plane

**hope¹** /houp/ v [I,T] to want something to happen or be true: *I **hope (that)** you feel better soon. | He's **hoping to** take a trip to Africa next year. | "Will Grandma be there?" "I hope so."* (=I hope this will happen) | *"Do you think it's going to rain?" "I hope not!"* (=I hope this will not happen)

---

**USAGE NOTE** hope to and hope that

Use **hope to** to talk about something that you or someone else wants to do, and **hope that** to talk about what you hope will happen: *Michelle hopes to go to college. | I hope that Michelle can go to college.*

---

**hope²** n **1** [singular, U] the feeling that good things can or will happen: *a new treatment that gives **hope to** cancer patients* (=makes them have hope) **2** something that you hope will happen: *Andy **had hopes of** competing in the Olympics.* **3** **in the hope that/of** if you do something in the hope that you will get a particular result, you do it even though you cannot be sure of this result **4** **don't get your hopes up** SPOKEN used in order to tell someone that something s/he is hoping for is not likely to happen **5** [C,U] a chance that something good will happen: *There was no **hope of** escape.*

**hope·ful** /'houpfəl/ adj **1** believing that what you want is likely to happen: *We're **hopeful about** our chances of winning.* **2** making you feel that what you want is likely to happen: *There are hopeful signs that an agreement will be reached.* **–hopefulness** n [U]

**hope·ful·ly** /'houpfəli/ adv **1** a word used at the beginning of a sentence when saying what you hope will happen, which some people consider nonstandard: *Hopefully the letter will come Monday.* **2** in a hopeful way: *"Can we go to the zoo tomorrow?" he asked hopefully.*

**hope·less** /'houp-lɪs/ adj **1** without any chance of success or improvement: *a hopeless situation* **2** INFORMAL unable or unwilling to do something correctly: *He's hopeless at fixing stuff.* **3** feeling no hope, or showing this: *a hopeless look on her face* **–hopelessly** adv **–hopelessness** n [U]

**hop·scotch** /'hapskatʃ/ n [U] a game in which children jump on squares drawn on the ground

**horde** /hɔrd/ *n* a large crowd moving in a noisy uncontrolled way: *hordes of tourists*

**ho·ri·zon** /həˈraɪzən/ *n* **the horizon** the place where the land or ocean seems to meet the sky: *a ship on the horizon*

**horizons** /həˈraɪzənz/ *n* [plural] the limit of your ideas, knowledge, and experience: *I took an evening class to broaden my horizons.*

**hor·i·zon·tal** /ˌhɔrəˈzɑntəl, ˌhɑr-/ *adj* flat and level: *a horizontal surface* –**horizontally** *adv* –compare VERTICAL –see picture at VERTICAL

**hor·mone** /ˈhɔrmoʊn/ *n* a substance in the body that influences its growth, development, and condition –**hormonal** /hɔrˈmoʊnl/ *adj*

**horn**

horn

sound the horn

**horn** /hɔrn/ *n* **1** a hard pointed part that grows on the heads of cows, goats etc., or the substance this is made of **2** the thing in a car, truck etc. that you push to make a sound as a warning: *Ernie blew his horn* (=made a noise with his horn) *at the boys in the street.* –see picture on page 469 **3 a)** a metal musical instrument that is wide at one end, which you play by blowing: *the French horn* **b)** INFORMAL ⇨ TRUMPET[1]

**hor·net** /ˈhɔrnɪt/ *n* a large black and yellow insect that can sting you –see picture at BEE

**horn·y** /ˈhɔrni/ *adj* SLANG sexually excited

**hor·o·scope** /ˈhɔrəˌskoʊp, ˈhɑr-/ *n* a description of your character and things that will happen to you, based on the position of the stars and PLANETs when you were born

**hor·ren·dous** /həˈrɛndəs, hɔ-/ *adj* **1** frightening and terrible: *a horrendous experience* **2** extremely bad: *a horrendous meal*

**hor·ri·ble** /ˈhɔrəbəl, ˈhɑr-/ *adj* **1** very unpleasant and often frightening: *a horrible accident* **2** very bad, unpleasant, or rude: *horrible manners* –**horribly** *adv*

**hor·rid** /ˈhɔrɪd, ˈhɑrɪd/ *adj* ⇨ HORRIBLE

**hor·rif·ic** /həˈrɪfɪk, hɔ-/ *adj* very frightening and upsetting: *horrific violence*

**hor·ri·fied** /ˈhɔrəˌfaɪd, ˈhɑr-/ *adj* feeling shocked or upset: *We were horrified to see how sick he looked.* –**horrifying** *adj* –**horrify** *v* [T]

**hor·ror** /ˈhɔrɚ, ˈhɑrɚ/ *n* [C,U] a strong feeling of shock and fear, or someone or something that makes you feel this: *I watched in horror as Ramsey hit her.* | *the horrors of war*

**hors d'oeu·vre** /ɔr ˈdɚv/ *n* a small amount of food that is served before people sit down at the table for the main meal

**horse¹** /hɔrs/ *n* **1** a large strong animal that people ride on and use for pulling heavy things **2 hold your horses!** SPOKEN said when you want someone to wait or to stop doing something

**horse²** *v*

**horse around** *phr v* [I] INFORMAL to play in a rough and silly way: *Stop horsing around and get back to work!*

**horse·back** /ˈhɔrsbæk/ *n* **1** horseback riding the activity of riding a horse for pleasure **2 on horseback** riding a horse

**horse·play** /ˈhɔrs-pleɪ/ *n* [U] rough noisy play, usually involving more than one child

**horse·pow·er** /ˈhɔrsˌpaʊɚ/ *n, plural* **horsepower** written abbreviation **hp** a unit for measuring the power of an engine

**horse·shoe** /ˈhɔrʃ-ʃu, ˈhɔrs-/ *n* a curved piece of iron that is attached to the bottom of a horse's foot to protect it

**hor·ti·cul·ture** /ˈhɔrtəˌkʌltʃɚ/ *n* [U] the practice or science of growing plants –**horticultural** /ˌhɔrtəˈkʌltʃərəl/ *adj*

**hose¹** /hoʊz/ *n* **1** [C,U] a long tube that can bend, used for putting water onto a garden, allowing liquids or air to flow through an engine etc. **2** [plural] ⇨ PANTYHOSE

**hose²** *v*

**hose** sth ↔ **down** *phr v* [T] to use a HOSE to put water on something, for example in order to clean it

**ho·sier·y** /ˈhoʊʒəri/ *n* [U] clothing such as socks and STOCKINGs

**hos·pice** /ˈhɑspɪs/ *n* a special hospital where people who are dying are cared for

**hos·pi·ta·ble** /hɑˈspɪtəbəl, ˈhɑspɪ-/ *adj* friendly, welcoming, and generous to visitors: *The local people were really hospitable to us.* –compare INHOSPITABLE

**hos·pi·tal** /ˈhɑspɪtl/ *n* [C,U] a building where sick or injured people receive medical treatment: *Rick's dad is still in the hospital.* (=being cared for in a hospital)

**hos·pi·tal·i·ty** /ˌhɑspəˈtæləti/ *n* [U] friendly behavior toward visitors: *the hospitality of the inn's owners*

**hos·pi·tal·ize** /ˈhɑspɪtlˌaɪz/ *v* [T] to put someone into a hospital for medical treatment: *Two people were hospitalized with stab wounds.* –**hospitalization** /ˌhɑspɪtl-əˈzeɪʃən/ *n* [U]

**host¹** /hoʊst/ *n* **1** the person at a party who invited the guests and organized the party **2** someone who introduces the guests on a television or radio show: *a game show host* **3** a country or organization that provides the space, equipment etc. for a special event: *the host city for the next Olympic Games* **4 a (whole) host of** a large number of: *a host of possibilities*

H

**host**² *v* [T] to be the HOST of an event: *What country is hosting the next World Cup?*

**hos·tage** /ˈhɑstɪdʒ/ *n* someone who is kept as a prisoner by an enemy, so that the other side will do what the enemy demands: *Three nurses were **taken/held hostage** (=caught and used as hostages) by the terrorists.*

**hos·tel** /ˈhɑstl/ *n* a cheap place for young people to stay when they are away from home

**host·ess** /ˈhoustɪs/ *n* **1** the woman at a party who invited the guests and organized the party **2** a woman who takes people to their seats in a restaurant

**hos·tile** /ˈhɑstl, ˈhɑstaɪl/ *adj* **1** very unfriendly and ready to fight or argue with someone: *a hostile crowd throwing rocks* **2** opposing a plan or idea very strongly: *One senator was **hostile to** the proposed law.* **3** belonging to an enemy: *hostile territory*

**hostile take·over** /ˌ.. ˈ.../ *n* a situation in which a company starts to control a smaller one because the smaller one does not have enough power or money to stop it

**hos·til·i·ties** /hɑˈstɪlətiz/ *n* [plural] FORMAL acts of fighting: *efforts to end the hostilities in the region*

**hos·til·i·ty** /hɑˈstɪləti/ *n* [U] **1** unfriendly and angry feelings or behavior: *Jessie has so much **hostility toward** men!* **2** strong opposition to a plan or idea: *There's too much **hostility to** the changes for us to go ahead.*

**hot** /hɑt/ *adj* **-tter, -ttest 1** high in temperature: *The soup's really hot.* | *the hottest day of the year* | *Your forehead feels hot.* –see usage note at TEMPERATURE **2** having a burning taste; SPICY: *hot salsa* **3** INFORMAL very good, popular, or exciting: *a hot new singer* | *the **hottest item** (=thing that sold the most) at the software exposition* **4** likely to cause trouble or arguments: *Studio bosses decided her video was **too hot to handle**. (=too much trouble to deal with)* | *Fishing rights have become a **hot topic/issue** (=subject that people are arguing about) in the race for Governor.* **5** **not so hot** SPOKEN not very good: *I'm not feeling so hot.* **6** SLANG goods that are hot have been stolen: *a hot car* **7 be hot at sth** to be very good at doing something: *I wasn't too hot at math.*

**hot air** /ˌ. ˈ./ *n* [U] INFORMAL things someone says that sound important, but really are not

**hot air bal·loon** /ˌ. ˈ. ˌ./ *n* a very large BALLOON made of cloth and filled with hot air, used for carrying people in the air

**hot·bed** /ˈhɑtˌbɛd/ *n* a place where a lot of a particular type of activity happens: *colleges that were hotbeds of dissent during the 1960s*

**hot but·ton** /ˈ. ˌ./ *n* something that makes people react with strong opinions: *An issue such as abortion pushes all the hot buttons.*

**hot·cake** /ˈhɑtˌkeɪk/ *n* **1 sell/go like**

**hotcakes** SPOKEN to sell very quickly and in large amounts **2** ⇨ PANCAKE

**hot dog** /ˈ. ./ *n* a long SAUSAGE (=tube-shaped piece of cooked meat), eaten in a long BUN (=type of bread)

hot dog

**ho·tel** /houˈtɛl/ *n* a large building where people pay to stay for a short time

**hot flash** /ˌ. ˈ./, **hot flush** *n* a sudden hot feeling that women have during MENOPAUSE

**hot·head·ed** /ˌhɑtˈhɛdɪd◂/ *adj* getting angry or excited easily and doing things too quickly, without thinking –**hothead** /ˈhɑthɛd/ *n*

**hot·line** /ˈhɑtˌlaɪn/ *n* a special telephone number that people can call for quick help with questions or problems: *a suicide hotline*

**hot·ly** /ˈhɑtli/ *adv* **1 hotly debated/disputed** etc. discussed or argued about very angrily: *a hotly debated issue* **2 hotly contested/fought** fought or COMPETEd for in an extremely strong way: *the hotly contested race for Governor*

**hot plate** /ˈ. ./ *n* a small piece of equipment with a flat heated top, used for cooking food

**hot po·ta·to** /ˌ. .ˈ../ *n* INFORMAL a subject or problem that no one wants to deal with, because any decision would make a lot of people angry: *The issue of prayer in schools became a political hot potato in the 1980s.*

**hot rod** /ˈ. ./ *n* INFORMAL a car that you have put a powerful engine into

**hot seat** /ˈ. ./ *n* INFORMAL **be in the hot seat** to be forced to deal with a difficult or unpleasant situation, especially in politics

**hot·shot** /ˈhɑtˌʃɑt/ *n* INFORMAL someone who is very successful and confident –**hotshot** *adj*: *a hotshot lawyer*

**hot spot** /ˈ. ./ *n* **1** a place where there is likely to be trouble, fighting etc.: *Soldiers were moved to hot spots along the border.* **2** an area on a computer screen that you CLICK on in order to make other pictures, words etc. appear

**hot-tem·pered** /ˌ. ˈ..◂/ *adj* tending to become angry very easily

**hot tub** /ˈ. ./ *n* a heated bathtub that several people can sit in

**hot-wa·ter bot·tle** /ˌ. ˈ.. ˌ../ *n* a rubber container filled with hot water, used for keeping part of your body warm

**hot-wire** /ˈhɑtˌwaɪɚ/ *v* [T] INFORMAL to start the engine of a vehicle without a key, by using the wires of the IGNITION system

**hound**¹ /haʊnd/ *v* [T] to keep following someone and asking him/her questions in an annoying or threatening way: *She's constantly hounded by reporters.*

**hound**² *n* a dog used for hunting

**hour** /aʊɚ/ n **1** a period of 60 minutes: *It takes two **hours** to get here from the city.* | *I'll be home in an hour.* | *a ten-hour trip* (=one that is ten hours long) ✗ DON'T SAY "a ten hours trip." ✗ **2** the distance you can travel in an hour: *The lake is **an hour from** Hartford.* **3** [singular] a time of day when a new hour starts: *Classes begin **on the hour**.* (=exactly at 1 o'clock, 2 o'clock etc.) **4** a period of time in the day when a particular activity always happens: *Opening hours are from 9:00 a.m. to 8:00 p.m.* | *I'll go to the store **on my lunch hour**.* **5** a particular time of the day or night: *The subway doesn't run **at this hour** of the night.* **6** an important time in history or in your life: *You were there **in my hour of need**.* (=when I needed help) −see also HOURS

**hour·glass** /'aʊɚglæs/ n a glass container for measuring time, in which sand moves from the top half to the bottom in exactly one hour

**hour·ly** /'aʊɚli/ adj, adv **1** happening or done every hour or once an hour: *Trains from Boston arrive hourly.* | *an hourly news bulletin* **2** **hourly pay/fees** etc. the amount you earn or charge for every hour you work

**hours** /aʊɚz/ n [plural] **1** the period of time when a store or business is open: *The mall's **opening hours** are from 9 a.m. till 9 p.m.* | ***visiting hours*** (=the time when you can visit) *at the hospital* | *The inventory will be done **after hours**.* (=when the store is closed) **2 hours before/ earlier/after/later** two or more hours before or after something happens: *A bomb exploded in the airport just hours before the President's arrival.* **3** INFORMAL a long time: *She spends hours on the phone.* **4 at all hours** at any time during the day and night: *They're up with that baby at all hours.*

**house¹** /haʊs/ n, plural **houses** /'haʊzɪz/ **1** a building that you live in, especially one that is intended to be used by one family: *I'm going over to Dean's house.* **2** all the people who live in a house: *Be quiet, or you'll wake the whole house!* **3** a building used for a particular purpose or to keep a particular thing in: *the Opera House* | *a hen house* **4 a)** one of the groups of people who make the laws of a state or country: *The President will speak to both houses of Congress on Thursday.* **b) the House** ⇨ HOUSE OF REPRESENTATIVES **5 publishing/fashion house** a company that produces books or designs clothes **6** the part of a theater where people sit, or the people in it: *We had a full house for the play.* **7 be on the house** SPOKEN if drinks or meals in a restaurant are on the house, they are free

**house²** /haʊz/ v [T] **1** to provide someone with a place to live: *a program to house the homeless* **2** if a building houses something, it is kept there: *The new building will house the college's art collection.*

**house ar·rest** /ˌ. .ˈ./ n **be under house arrest** to not be allowed to leave your house by the government

**house·boat** /'haʊsboʊt/ n a special boat that you can live in

**house·bound** /'haʊsbaʊnd/ adj unable to leave your house, especially because you are sick or old

**house·bro·ken** /'haʊsˌbroʊkən/ adj an animal that is housebroken has been trained not to empty its BOWELS or BLADDER in the house

**house·hold¹** /'haʊshoʊld, 'haʊsoʊld/ adj **1** relating to a house and the people in it: *household chores* **2 be a household name/ word** to be famous or known about by many people

**household²** n all the people who live together in one house

**house hus·band** /'. ˌ../ n a married man who works at home doing the cooking, cleaning etc.

**house·keep·er** /'haʊsˌkipɚ/ n someone whose job is to do the cooking, cleaning etc. in a house or hotel

**house·keep·ing** /'haʊsˌkipɪŋ/ n [U] the work that you do at home, such as cooking and cleaning

**House of Rep·re·sent·a·tives** /ˌ. . .ˈ.ˌ.../ n [singular] the larger of the two groups of people who are part of the government and who make the laws in countries such as the US and Australia −compare SENATE

**house·plant** /'haʊsplænt/ n a plant that is grown indoors for decoration

**house-sit** /'. ./ v [I] to take care of someone's house while s/he is away −**house sitter** n

**house·wares** /'haʊswɛrz/ n things used in the home, such as plates and lamps

**house·warm·ing** /'haʊsˌwɔrmɪŋ/ n a party that you give to celebrate moving into a new house

**house·wife** /'haʊswaɪf/ n, plural **housewives** /-waɪvz/ a married woman who works at home doing the cooking, cleaning etc. −see also HOMEMAKER

**house·work** /'haʊswɚk/ n [U] the work that you do to take care of a house −compare HOMEWORK

**hous·ing** /'haʊzɪŋ/ n **1** [U] buildings that people live in: *a shortage of good housing* **2** [U] the work of providing houses for people to live in: *a housing program* **3** a protective cover for a machine: *the engine housing*

**housing de·vel·op·ment** /'.. .ˌ.../ n a number of houses built in the same area

**housing proj·ect** /'.. ˌ../ n a group of houses or apartments for poor families, usually built with money from the government

**hov·el** /'hʌvəl, 'hɑ-/ n a small dirty place where someone lives

H

**hov·er** /ˈhʌvɚ/ v [I] **1** to stay in one place in the air while flying: *A helicopter hovered above the crowd.* **2** to stay around one place, especially because you are waiting for something: *Richard was hovering by the door, hoping to talk to me.*

**how** /haʊ/ adv conjunction **1** used in order to ask about or explain the way to do something, or the way something happened: *How do you spell your name?* | *How do I get to K-Mart from here?* | *The advisor can show you how to apply for the loan.* **2** used in order to ask about the amount, size, or degree of something: *How old is Debbie?* | *How tall do you think Mario is?* | *How much is that car?* (=what does it cost?) **3** used in order to ask about someone's health: *How is your mother doing?* **4** used in order to ask someone his/her opinion, or about his/her experience of something: *"How do I look?" "Great!"* | *How was your vacation?* **5** used in order to ask what someone or something looks like, behaves like, or the way something is expressed: *How does that song go?* | *How does she act with other children?* **6** used before an adjective or adverb to emphasize it: *I can't even remember how many times I've seen "Star Wars."* | *Did he tell you how boring it was?*

---

SPOKEN PHRASES

**7 How are you?/How's it going?** used when asking if someone is well and happy: *"Hi, Kelly. How are you doing?" "Fine, thanks."* | *So, how's it going at work?* **8 how about...?** used when making a suggestion about what to do: *I'm busy tonight, but how about tomorrow?* **9 how come?** used when asking why something has happened: *"I can't come to the dance." "How come?"* **10 how do you know?** used when asking why someone is sure about something: *"I'm sure she's nice." "How do you know? You haven't met her."* **11 how can sb do sth** said when you are surprised, shocked, or angry, or when you disapprove of something: *How could you say a mean thing like that to her?* **12 how do you do?** FORMAL said when you meet someone for the first time

---

**how·dy** /ˈhaʊdi/ SPOKEN used in order to say "hello" in an informal, usually humorous way

**how·ev·er¹** /haʊˈɛvɚ/ adv **1** used in order to add an idea or fact that is surprising or seems like the opposite of what you have just said: *The clouds were very thick; however, we managed to land the plane smoothly.* | *I love tomatoes. I don't, however, like tomato soup.* **2 however long/serious/slowly etc.** used before adjectives and adverbs to show that it does not matter how long, serious etc. something is or how slowly etc. it happens: *We'll have to keep working,*

*however difficult the job gets.* | *I want that car, however much it costs.*

**however²** conjunction in whatever way: *However you do it, I'm sure it will be good.*

**howl** /haʊl/ v [I] **1** to make a long loud crying sound like a dog or a WOLF **2** if the wind howls, it makes a loud high sound as it blows **3** to make a loud shouting or crying sound: *an audience howling with laughter* **–howl** n

**HQ** n the abbreviation of HEADQUARTERS

**hr.** n, plural **hrs.** the written abbreviation of HOUR

**hub** /hʌb/ n **1** the central part of an area, system etc. that all the other parts are connected to: *the hub of a transit system* **2** the central part of a wheel

**hub·bub** /ˈhʌbʌb/ n [singular, U] INFORMAL many noises heard at the same time: *the hubbub of the crowd*

**hub·cap** /ˈhʌbkæp/ n a metal cover for the center of a wheel on a vehicle –see picture on page 469

**hud·dle¹** /ˈhʌdl/ **huddle together/up** v [I,T] if a group of people huddle together, they gather very closely together: *homeless people huddled around/over fires*

**huddle²** n a group of people or things that are HUDDLEd

**hue** /hyu/ n LITERARY a color or type of color: *a golden hue*

**huff¹** /hʌf/ n **in a huff** feeling angry: *Ray got mad and left in a huff.*

**huff²** v INFORMAL **huff and puff** to breathe out in a noisy way, especially because you are tired: *At the end of the hike, we were all huffing and puffing.*

**huff·y** /ˈhʌfi/ adj INFORMAL in a bad temper: *Don't get huffy with me.*

**hug¹** /hʌg/ v **-gged, -gging** [T] **1** to put your arms around someone and hold him/her tightly to show love or friendship **2** to move along the side, edge, top etc. of something, staying very close to it: *a boat hugging the coast*

hug

**hug²** n the act of hugging (HUG) someone: *Give me a hug before you go.*

**huge** /hyudʒ/ adj very big: *a huge house* **–hugely** adv

**huh** /hʌ/ interjection **1** said when you have not heard or understood a question: *"What do you think, Bob?" "Huh?"* **2** said at the end of a question to ask for agreement: *Not a bad restaurant, huh?*

**hulk** /hʌlk/ n **1** an old ship, plane, or vehicle that is no longer used **2** a large heavy person or thing

**hull¹** /hʌl/ n the main part of a ship

**hull**[2] *v* [T] to take off the outer part of rice, grain, seeds etc.

**hul·la·ba·loo** /ˈhʌləbəˌlu, ˌhʌləbəˈlu/ *n* INFORMAL excited talk, newspaper stories etc., especially about something surprising or shocking: *a huge hullabaloo over his new book*

**hum** /hʌm/ *v* **-mmed, -mming 1** [I,T] to sing a tune by making a continuous sound with your lips closed: *If you don't know the words, just hum it.* **2** [I] to make a low continuous sound: *What's making that humming noise?* **3** [I] if a place is humming, it is very busy and full of activity **–hum** *n* [singular]

**hu·man**[1] /ˈhyumən/ *adj* **1** belonging to or relating to people: *the human voice | NASA said the accident was a result of **human error**.* (=a mistake made by a person not a machine) **2** human weaknesses, emotions etc. are typical of ordinary people: ***human nature*** (=the good and bad qualities that are typical of people) **3 sb is only human** used in order to say that someone should not be blamed for what s/he has done **–compare** INHUMAN

**human**[2], **human be·ing** /ˌ.. ˈ../ *n* a man, woman, or child

**hu·mane** /hyuˈmeɪn/ *adj* treating people or animals in a way that is kind, not cruel **–humanely** *adv* **–opposite** INHUMANE

**hu·man·ism** /ˈhyuməˌnɪzəm/ *n* [U] a system of beliefs that tries to solve human problems through science rather than religion **–humanistic** /ˌhyuməˈnɪstɪk/ *adj* **–humanist** /ˈhyumənɪst/ *n*

**hu·man·i·tar·i·an** /hyuˌmænəˈtɛriən/ *adj* concerned with improving bad living conditions and preventing unfair treatment of people **–humanitarianism** *n* [U] **–humanitarian** *n*

**hu·man·i·ties** /hyuˈmænətiz/ *n* **the humanities** subjects you study that are related to literature, history, art etc. rather than mathematics or science

**hu·man·i·ty** /hyuˈmænəti/ *n* [U] **1** kindness, respect, and sympathy toward other people: *a man of great humanity* **–opposite** INHUMANITY **2** people in general: *the danger pollution poses to humanity* **–see also** HUMANKIND **3** the state of being human

**hu·man·ize** /ˈhyuməˌnaɪz/ *v* [T] to make a system more pleasant for people: *attempts to humanize the prison*

**hu·man·kind** /ˈhyumənˌkaɪnd/ *n* [U] people in general **–see also** HUMANITY **–see usage note at** MAN[1]

**hu·man·ly** /ˈhyumənli/ *adv* **humanly possible** able to be done using all your skills, knowledge, time etc.: *It's **not humanly possible** (=impossible) to finish the building by next week. | We **did everything humanly possible** to save people from the fire.*

**human race** /ˌ.. ˈ./ *n* **the human race** all people, considered as a single group

**human re·sourc·es** /ˌ.. ˈ.../ *n* [plural] the department in a company that deals with employing, training, and helping people

**human rights** /ˌ.. ˈ./ *n* [plural] the basic rights that every person has to be treated in a fair, equal way without cruelty, especially by his/her government

**hum·ble**[1] /ˈhʌmbəl/ *adj* **1** APPROVING not considering yourself or your ideas to be as important as other people's **2** relating to a low social class or position: *the senator's humble beginnings on a farm in Iowa* **–humbly** *adv*

**humble**[2] *v* [T] to make someone realize that s/he is not as important, good, kind etc. as s/he thought: *I felt humbled after the interview.* **–humbling** *adj*

**hum·drum** /ˈhʌmdrʌm/ *adj* boring, ordinary, and having very little variety: *a humdrum job*

**hu·mid** /ˈhyumɪd/ *adj* air that is humid feels warm and wet **–see usage note at** TEMPERATURE

**hu·mid·i·fier** /hyuˈmɪdəˌfaɪɚ/ *n* a machine that makes the air in a room less dry **–humidify** *v* [T]

**hu·mid·i·ty** /hyuˈmɪdəti/ *n* [U] the amount of water that is contained in the air: *The humidity will be lower tomorrow.*

**hu·mil·i·ate** /hyuˈmɪliˌeɪt/ *v* [T] to make someone feel ashamed or embarrassed by making him/her seem stupid or weak: *Mrs. Banks humiliated me in front of the whole class.* **–humiliation** /ˌhyumɪliˈeɪʃən/ *n* [C,U] **–humiliated** /hyuˈmɪliˌeɪtɪd/ *adj*

**hu·mil·i·at·ing** /hyuˈmɪliˌeɪtɪŋ/ *adj* making you feel ashamed or embarrassed: *a humiliating experience*

**hu·mil·i·ty** /hyuˈmɪləti/ *n* [U] APPROVING the quality of not being too proud about yourself

**hu·mor**[1] /ˈhyumɚ/ *n* [U] **1** the ability to laugh at things and think that they are funny: *Dale has **no sense of humor** at all.* (=cannot understand when something is funny) **2** the quality in something that makes it funny and makes people laugh: *There's a lot of humor in his songs.* **3 good humor** a cheerful friendly attitude to people and events

**humor**[2] *v* [T] to do what someone wants so s/he will not become angry or upset: *Just humor me and listen, please.*

**hu·mor·ist** /ˈhyumərɪst/ *n* someone, especially a writer, who tells jokes and funny stories

**hu·mor·less** /ˈhyumɚlɪs/ *adj* too serious and not able to laugh at things that are funny

**hu·mor·ous** /ˈhyumərəs/ *adj* funny and enjoyable: *a humorous account of her trip to Egypt* **–humorously** *adv*

**hump** /hʌmp/ *n* **1 be over the hump** to have finished the most difficult part of something **2** a round shape that rises above a surface **3** a raised part on the back of a person or animal: *a camel's hump*

H

**hunch**[1] /hʌntʃ/ *n* a feeling that something is true or that something will happen, even if you do not have any facts or proof about it: *I had a **hunch** that you'd call today.*

**hunch**[2] *v* [I] to bend down and lean forward so that your back forms a curve —**hunched** *adj*

**hunch·back** /'hʌntʃbæk/ *n* OFFENSIVE someone who has a large raised part on his/her back

**hun·dred**[1] /'hʌndrɪd/ *number* **1** 100: *a hundred years | two hundred miles* **2** **hundreds of sth** a very large number of something: *Hundreds of people marched in protest.* **3** **a hundred times** SPOKEN a phrase meaning many times, used when you are annoyed: *I've told you a hundred times to turn off the lights!* **4** **a/one hundred percent** completely: *I agree one hundred percent.* **5** **give a hundred percent** to do everything you can in order to achieve something: *Everyone on the team gave a hundred percent.* —**hundredth** /'hʌndrɪdθ/ *number*

**hundred**[2] *n* a piece of paper money worth $100

**hun·dred·weight** /'hʌndrɪd,weɪt/ written abbreviation **cwt.** *n* a measure of weight equal to 100 pounds or 45.36 kilograms

**hung** /hʌŋ/ the past tense and PAST PARTICIPLE of HANG

**hun·ger**[1] /'hʌŋgɚ/ *n* [U] **1** the feeling that you want or need to eat: *babies crying from hunger* ✗ DON'T SAY "I have hunger." SAY "I am hungry." ✗ **2** a severe lack of food, especially for a long period of time: *people dying from hunger* —compare THIRST

**hunger**[2] *v* [I] **hunger for sth** to want something very much: *an actor hungering for success*

**hunger strike** /'.. ,./ *n* a situation in which someone refuses to eat, in order to protest about something

**hung ju·ry** /ˌ. '../ *n* [singular] a JURY that cannot agree about whether someone is guilty of a crime

**hung o·ver** /ˌ. '../ *adj* feeling sick because you drank too much alcohol the previous day

**hun·gry** /'hʌŋgri/ *adj* **1** wanting to eat something: *I'm hungry, let's eat! | If you **get hungry**, there's some turkey in the fridge.* **2** **go hungry** to not have enough food to eat: *Many people in our city go hungry day after day.* **3** **be hungry for sth** to want something very much: *Rick was hungry for a chance to work.* —**hungrily** *adv* —compare THIRSTY

**hung up** /ˌ. '.◂/ *adj* INFORMAL worrying too much about someone or something: *You shouldn't get all hung up over him, it's not worth it!*

**hunk** /hʌŋk/ *n* **1** a thick piece of something that has been taken from a bigger piece: *a hunk of bread* **2** INFORMAL an attractive man who has a strong body

**hun·ker** /'hʌŋkɚ/ *v* [I]

**hunker down** *phr v* [I] **1** INFORMAL to not do things that may be risky, so that you are safe and protected: *People are **hunkering down** and waiting for the economy to get better.* **2** to sit on your heels with your knees bent in front of you; SQUAT

**hunt**[1] /hʌnt/ *v* **1** [I,T] to chase animals in order to catch and kill them: *Tigers hunt at night.* **2** to look for someone or something very carefully: *Police are still **hunting for** the murderer.*

**hunt sb/sth ↔ down** *phr v* [T] to find an enemy or criminal after searching hard: *a plan to **hunt down** fathers who don't pay child support*

**hunt**[2] *n* **1** a careful search for someone or something: *The **hunt for** the missing child continues today.* **2** an occasion when people chase animals in order to catch and kill them

**hunt·er** /'hʌntɚ/ *n* a person or animal that hunts wild animals

**hunt·ing** /'hʌntɪŋ/ *n* [U] **1** the act of chasing animals in order to catch and kill them **2** **job-hunting/house-hunting etc.** the activity of looking for a job, a house to live in etc. —**hunting** *adj*

**hur·dle**[1] /'hɚdl/ *n* **1** a problem or difficulty that you must deal with before you can do something else: *the final hurdle in buying a house* **2** a type of small fence that a person or a horse jumps over during a race

**hurdle**[2] *v* [T] to jump over something while you are running —**hurdler** *n*

**hurl** /hɚl/ *v* [T] **1** to throw something using a lot of force: *He **hurled** a brick **through/out** the window.* **2** **hurl insults/abuse etc. at sb** to shout an insult in a loud and angry way **3** SPOKEN ⇨ VOMIT[1]

**hur·ray** /həˈreɪ, hʊˈreɪ/, **hur·rah** /hʊˈrɑ/ *interjection* OLD-FASHIONED ⇨ HOORAY

**hur·ri·cane** /'hɚɪ,keɪn, 'hʌr-/ *n* a storm that has very strong fast winds —compare TORNADO —see usage note at WEATHER

**hur·ried** /'hɚid, 'hʌrid/ *adj* done more quickly than usual: *We ate a hurried breakfast and left.* —**hurriedly** *adv*

**hur·ry**[1] /'hɚi, 'hʌri/ *v* [I,T] to do something or go somewhere more quickly than usual, or to make someone or something do this: *Their mother **hurried** the children **across** the road. | We will **have to hurry** if we don't want to miss the start of the movie.*

**hurry up** *phr v* **1** **hurry up!** SPOKEN said in order to tell someone to do something more quickly **2** [I,T **hurry sb/sth up**] to do something or go somewhere more quickly than usual, or to make someone or something do this: *I tried to **hurry** the kids **up** so they wouldn't be late for school. | I wish the bus would **hurry up** and get here.*

**hurry**[2] *n* **1** **be in a hurry** to need to do something, go somewhere etc. more quickly than usual: *I can't talk now, I'm in a hurry.*

**2 (there's) no hurry** SPOKEN said in order to tell someone that s/he does not have to do something quickly or soon: *You can pay me back next week, there's no hurry.* **3 not be in any hurry/be in no hurry** to be able to wait because you have a lot of time in which to do something: *Take your time, I'm not in any hurry.* **4 what's (all) the hurry?** SPOKEN said when you think someone is doing something too quickly

**hurt¹** /hɚt/ *v* **hurt, hurt, hurting** **1** [T] to injure yourself or someone else, especially not very seriously: *She hurt her knee playing volleyball.* | *Sammy! Don't throw sand, you might hurt somebody!* **2** [I,T] to feel pain or cause pain in a part of your body: *My feet really hurt after all that walking!* | *It hurts my knees to run.* **3** [I,T] to make someone feel very upset or unhappy: *I'm sorry, I didn't mean to hurt your feelings.* **4** [T] to have a bad effect on someone or something: *Will this hurt my chances of getting the job?* **5 it won't/doesn't hurt to do sth** SPOKEN said when you think someone should do something: *It won't hurt him to clean his room.* **6 be hurting** INFORMAL to feel upset or unhappy about something −**hurt** *n* [C,U] −see usage note at WOUND²

**hurt²** *adj* **1** suffering pain or injury: *It's okay, nobody got hurt.* | *Kerry was badly/seriously/ slightly hurt in a skiing accident.* **2** very upset or unhappy: *I was very hurt by what you said.* ✗ YOU SAY "seriously/badly/slightly hurt" about an injury, but "very hurt" when someone upsets you. ✗

**hurt·ful** /hɚtfəl/ *adj* making you feel upset or unhappy

**hur·tle** /hɚtl/ *v* [I] to move or fall very fast: *cars hurtling down the freeway at 90 miles per hour*

**hus·band** /hʌzbənd/ *n* the man that a woman is married to −see picture at FAMILY

**hush¹** /hʌʃ/ *v* SPOKEN said in order to tell someone to be quiet, or to comfort a child who is crying

**hush sth up** *phr v* [T] to prevent people from knowing about something dishonest: *The bank tried to hush the scandal up.*

**hush²** *n* [singular] a peaceful silence: *A hush fell over the room.* (=everyone suddenly became quiet)

**hushed** /hʌʃt/ *adj* quiet: *hushed voices*

**hush-hush** /ˌ. ˈ.◂/ *adj* INFORMAL secret

**husk** /hʌsk/ *n* [C,U] the dry outer part of some grains, nuts, corn etc. −see picture at PEEL²

**husk·y¹** /hʌski/ *adj* APPROVING **1** a husky voice is deep and sounds rough **2** a husky man is big and strong −**huskily** *adv* −**huskiness** *n* [U]

**husky²** *n* a dog with thick hair, often used for pulling SLEDs over the snow

**hus·tle¹** /hʌsəl/ *v* **1** [T] to make someone move quickly, often by pushing him/her: *Jackson was hustled into his car by bodyguards.* **2** [I] to hurry in doing something or going somewhere: *We've got to hustle, or we'll be late!* **3** [I,T] INFORMAL to cheat someone to get money etc.

**hustle²** *n* **1 hustle and bustle** busy and noisy activity **2** INFORMAL a way of getting money that is illegal and dishonest

**hus·tler** /hʌslɚ/ *n* someone who gets money in a way that is illegal and dishonest

**hut** /hʌt/ *n* a small house with only one or two rooms

**hutch** /hʌtʃ/ *n* a small wooden box in which you can keep rabbits

**hy·brid** /haɪbrɪd/ *n* **1** an animal or plant that is produced from parents of different breeds or types **2** something that is a mixture of two or more things: *The car is a hybrid that can run on gas or batteries.* −**hybrid** *adj*

**hy·drant** /haɪdrənt/ *n* ➪ FIRE HYDRANT

**hy·drau·lic** /haɪdrɔlɪk/ *adj* moved or operated by the pressure of water or other liquids: *hydraulic brakes* −**hydraulically** *adv*

**hy·drau·lics** /haɪdrɔlɪks/ *n* [plural] the study of how to use water pressure to produce power

**hy·dro·e·lec·tric** /ˌhaɪdroʊɪˈlɛktrɪk/ *adj* using water power to produce electricity: *a hydroelectric dam*

**hy·dro·gen** /haɪdrədʒən/ *n* [U] a gas that is an ELEMENT and is lighter than air, and that becomes water when it combines with OXYGEN

**hydrogen bomb** /ˈ... ˌ./ *n* an extremely powerful NUCLEAR bomb

**hy·dro·plane** /haɪdrəˌpleɪn/ *v* [I] if a car hydroplanes, it slides on a wet road

**hy·e·na** /haɪinə/ *n* a wild animal like a dog that makes a loud sound like a laugh

**hy·giene** /haɪdʒin/ *n* [U] the practice of keeping yourself and the things around you clean in order to prevent diseases: *Hygiene is very important when preparing a baby's food.*

**hy·gi·en·ic** /haɪdʒɛnɪk, -ˈdʒinɪk/ *adj* clean and likely to prevent diseases from spreading

**hymn** /hɪm/ *n* a song of praise to God

**hym·nal** /hɪmnəl/ *n* a book of HYMNs

**hype¹** /haɪp/ *n* [U] attempts to make people think something is good or important by talking about it a lot on television, the radio etc.: *the media hype surrounding Spielberg's new movie*

**hype²** *v* [T] also **hype sth ↔ up** to try to make people think something is good or important by advertising or talking about it a lot on television, the radio etc.: *The author has been hyped as the next Raymond Chandler.*

**hyped up** /ˌ. ˈ./ *adj* INFORMAL very excited or anxious about something: *They're all hyped up about getting into the playoffs.*

H

# hyper

**hy·per** /ˈhaɪpɚ/ *adj* INFORMAL extremely excited or nervous

**hy·per·ac·tive** /ˌhaɪpɚˈæktɪv/ *adj* someone, especially a child, who is hyperactive is too active, and not able to keep still or quiet for very long —**hyperactivity** /ˌhaɪpɚækˈtɪvəti/ *n* [U]

**hy·per·bo·le** /haɪˈpɚbəli/ *n* [U] a way of describing something by saying that it is much bigger, smaller, heavier etc. than it really is

**hy·per·link** /ˈhaɪpɚˌlɪŋk/, **hy·per·text link** /ˌhaɪpɚtɛkst ˈlɪŋk/ *n* a special picture or word on a computer screen that you CLICK on in order to move quickly to a place where you can find more information

**hy·per·sen·si·tive** /ˌhaɪpɚˈsɛnsəṭɪv/ *adj* very easily offended or made upset

**hy·per·ten·sion** /ˌhaɪpɚˈtɛnʃən, ˈhaɪpɚˌtɛnʃən/ *n* [U] TECHNICAL a medical condition in which someone's BLOOD PRESSURE is too high

**hy·per·ven·ti·late** /ˌhaɪpɚˈvɛnṭl̩ˌeɪt/ *v* [I] to breathe too quickly because you are very excited or upset

**hy·phen** /ˈhaɪfən/ *n* a mark (-) used in writing to join words or parts of words

**USAGE NOTE hyphens**

Use a hyphen (-) to join two or more words that are used as an adjective in front of a noun: *a two-car garage* | *a ten-year-old boy.* You can also say: *a garage for two cars* | *a boy who is ten years old.*

**hy·phen·ate** /ˈhaɪfəˌneɪt/ *v* [T] to join words or parts of words with a HYPHEN —**hyphenated** *adj*

**hyp·no·sis** /hɪpˈnoʊsɪs/ *n* [U] a state similar to sleep in which someone's thoughts and actions can be influenced by someone else, or the act of producing this state: *He remembered details of the crime under hypnosis.*

**hyp·not·ic** /hɪpˈnɑṭɪk/ *adj* **1** making someone feel tired, especially because sound or movement is repeated **2** relating to HYPNOSIS —**hypnotically** *adv*

**hyp·no·tize** /ˈhɪpnəˌtaɪz/ *v* [T] to produce a sleep-like state in someone, so that you can influence his/her thoughts or actions —**hypnotism** /ˈhɪpnəˌtɪzəm/ *n* [U] —**hypnotist** /ˈhɪpnətɪst/ *n*

**hy·po·chon·dri·ac** /ˌhaɪpəˈkɑndriˌæk/ *n* someone who worries all the time about his/her health, even when s/he is not sick —**hypochondriac** *adj* —**hypochondria** /ˌhaɪpoʊˈkɑndriə/ *n* [U]

**hy·poc·ri·sy** /hɪˈpɑkrəsi/ *n* [U] DISAPPROVING the act of saying you have particular beliefs, feelings etc., but behaving in a way that shows you do not really have these beliefs etc.: *the hypocrisy of divorced politicians talking about family values*

**hyp·o·crite** /ˈhɪpəˌkrɪt/ *n* someone who pretends to believe something or behave in a good way when really s/he does not —**hypocritical** /ˌhɪpəˈkrɪṭɪkəl/ *adj*

**hy·po·der·mic** /ˌhaɪpəˈdɚmɪk/ *n* an instrument with a hollow needle used for putting drugs into someone's body through the skin —**hypodermic** *adj* —compare SYRINGE

**hy·pot·e·nuse** /haɪˈpɑtˈn-us/ *n* TECHNICAL the longest side of a TRIANGLE that has a RIGHT ANGLE

**hy·po·ther·mi·a** /ˌhaɪpəˈθɚmiə/ *n* [U] TECHNICAL a serious medical condition in which someone's body temperature becomes very low, caused by extreme cold

**hy·poth·e·sis** /haɪˈpɑθəsɪs/ *n, plural* **hypotheses** an idea that is suggested as an explanation of something, but that has not yet been proved to be true —**hypothesize** /haɪˈpɑθəˌsaɪz/ *v* [T]

**hy·po·thet·i·cal** /ˌhaɪpəˈθɛṭɪkəl/ *adj* based on a situation that is not real but that might happen: *Students were given a hypothetical law case to discuss.* —**hypothetically** *adv*

**hys·ter·ec·to·my** /ˌhɪstəˈrɛktəmi/ *n* [C,U] a medical operation to remove a woman's UTERUS

**hys·ter·i·a** /hɪˈstɛriə, -ˈstɪriə/ *n* [U] extreme excitement, anger, fear etc. that you cannot control

**hys·ter·i·cal** /hɪˈstɛrɪkəl/ *adj* **1** INFORMAL extremely funny: *Robin Williams' act was hysterical!* **2** unable to control your behavior or emotions because you are very upset, afraid, excited etc. —**hysterically** *adv*

**hys·ter·ics** /hɪˈstɛrɪks/ *n* [plural] **1** a state of being unable to control your behavior or emotions because you are very upset, afraid, excited etc.: *She went into hysterics when she found out her husband had died.* **2 be in hysterics** INFORMAL to be laughing and not be able to stop

**I, i** /aɪ/ **1** the ninth letter of the English alphabet **2** the ROMAN NUMERAL for 1

**I** /aɪ/ *pron* used as the subject of a verb when you are the person speaking: *I saw Mike yesterday.* | *I've been playing softball.* | *I'm really hot.* | *My husband and I are going to Mexico.* ✗ DON'T SAY "I and my husband." ✗

**IA** the written abbreviation of Iowa

**ice¹** /aɪs/ *n* **1** [U] water that has frozen into a solid state: *Do you want some ice in your drink?* | *Drive carefully, there's ice on the roads.* **2 break the ice** to begin to be friendly to someone by talking to him/her: *Stan tried to break the ice by asking her where she was from.*

**ice**² v **1** [I,T] to put ice on a part of your body that is injured **2** [T] ⇨ FROST²
**ice over/up** phr v [I] to become covered with ice: *The lake **iced over** during the night.*

ice / ice cubes

**ice·berg** /ˈaɪsbɔɡ/ n an extremely large piece of ice floating in the sea

icicle

**ice·break·er** /ˈaɪsˌbreɪk-ɚ/ n **1** something you say or do to make someone less nervous **2** a ship that can sail through ice

**ice cap** /ˈ. ./ n an area of thick ice that always covers the North and South Poles

**ice-cold** /ˌ. ˈ◂/ adj extremely cold: *ice-cold drinks*

**ice cream** /ˈ. ./ n [U] a frozen sweet food made of milk or cream and sugar, usually with fruit, nuts, chocolate etc. added to it

**ice cream cone** /ˈ. . ˌ./ n a hard thin cookie shaped like a CONE, that you put ice cream in: *a vanilla ice cream cone* –see picture at CONE

**ice cube** /ˈ. ./ n a small block of ice that you put in cold drinks

**ice hock·ey** /ˈ. ˌ../ n [U] ⇨ HOCKEY

**ice pack** /ˈ. ./ n a bag of ice used for keeping something cold

**ice skate**¹ /ˈ. ./ v [I] to slide on ice wearing ICE SKATES –**ice skater** n –**ice skating** n [U]

**ice skate**² n [C usually plural] one of two special boots with metal blades on the bottom that let you slide quickly on ice

**i·ci·cle** /ˈaɪsɪkəl/ n a thin pointed stick of ice that hangs down from something such as a roof –see picture at ICE¹

**ic·ing** /ˈaɪsɪŋ/ n [U] **1** ⇨ FROSTING **2 icing on the cake** something that makes a good situation even better: *I love the new job - the extra money is just icing on the cake!*

**ick·y** /ˈɪki/ adj SPOKEN very unpleasant to look at, taste, or feel: *The soup tasted icky.*

**i·con** /ˈaɪkɑn/ n **1** a small picture on a computer screen that makes the computer do something when you use the MOUSE to choose it **2** someone or something famous, that people think represents an important idea: *The peace symbol is an icon of the sixties.* **3** also **ikon** a picture or figure of a holy person

**ic·y** /ˈaɪsi/ adj **1** extremely cold: *an icy wind* **2** covered in ice: *an icy road* **3** unfriendly and frightening: *an icy stare* –**icily** adv –**iciness** n [U]

**I'd** /aɪd/ **1** the short form of "I had": *I'd never met Kurt before today.* **2** the short form of "I would": *I'd love to come!*

**ID**¹ n [C,U] identification; something that shows your name, address, the date you were born etc.,

usually with a photograph: *May I see some ID, please?*

**ID**² the written abbreviation of Idaho

**i·de·a** /aɪˈdiə/ n **1** a plan or suggestion, especially one you think of suddenly: *Where did you get the **idea** for the book?* | *Going to the beach is a **good idea**!* | *I **have an idea** - let's get Dad a set of golf clubs.* **2** [C,U] understanding or knowledge of something: *The book gives you a pretty good **idea of** what it was like to grow up during the Depression.* | *Can you give me a **rough idea** (=a not very exact understanding) of how much it will cost?* | *Roman **had no idea** (=did not know) where Celia had gone.* | *I explained it twice, but she didn't seem to **get the idea.** (=did not understand).* **3** the aim or purpose of doing something: *The **idea of** the game is to hit the ball into the holes.* **4** an opinion or belief: *Bill has some strange **ideas about** religion.* | *Somewhere he's **gotten the idea** (=begun to believe) that I'm in love with him.*

**i·de·al**¹ /aɪˈdiəl/ adj **1** being the best that something could possibly be: *an ideal place for a picnic* **2** perfect, but not likely to exist: *In an ideal world no one would ever get sick.*

**ideal**² n **1** a principle or standard that you would like to achieve: *the ideal of perfect equality* **2** a perfect example of something

**i·de·al·ism** /aɪˈdiəˌlɪzəm/ n [U] the belief that you should live according to your high standards or principles, even if it is difficult

**i·de·al·is·tic** /ˌaɪdiəˈlɪstɪk/ adj APPROVING believing in principles and high standards, even if they cannot be achieved in real life: *In the movie, Stewart is an idealistic young senator.* –**idealist** /aɪˈdiəlɪst/ n

**i·de·al·ize** /aɪˈdiəˌlaɪz/ v [T] to imagine that something is perfect or better than it really is: *The show idealizes family life.* –**idealization** /aɪˌdiələˈzeɪʃən/ n [C,U] –**idealized** /aɪˈdiəˌlaɪzd/ adj

**i·de·al·ly** /aɪˈdiəli/ adv **1** in a way that you would like things to be, even if it is not possible: *Ideally I'd like to work at home.* **2** perfectly: *Don is ideally suited for the job.*

**i·den·ti·cal** /aɪˈdɛnɾɪkəl, ɪ-/ adj exactly the same: *Your shoes **are identical to** mine.* | *William and David are **identical twins**.* (=two babies that are born together and look the same) –**identically** adv

**i·den·ti·fi·a·ble** /aɪˌdɛnɾəˈfaɪəbəl, ɪ-/ adj able to be recognized

**i·den·ti·fi·ca·tion** /aɪˌdɛnɾəfəˈkeɪʃən, ɪ-/ n [U] **1** official documents that prove who you are: *You can use a passport as identification.* **2** the act of recognizing someone or something: *The bodies have been brought to the hospital for identification.*

**i·den·ti·fy** /aɪˈdɛnɾəˌfaɪ, ɪ-/ v [T] to recognize and name someone or something: *Can you identify the man who robbed you?*

**identify with** *phr v* [T] **1** [**identify with** sb] to be able to share or understand the feelings of someone else: *It was easy to **identify with** the novel's main character.* **2** **be identified with** to be closely connected with an idea or group of people: *The Peace Corps will always be **identified with** Kennedy.*

**i·den·ti·ty** /aɪˈdɛnɾəti, ɪ-/ *n* **1** [C,U] who someone is: *The identity of the killer is still unknown.* **2** [U] the qualities someone has that make him/her different from other people: *Many people's **sense of identity** comes from their job.*

**i·de·o·log·i·cal** /ˌaɪdiəˈlɑdʒɪkəl, ɪdiə-/ *adj* based on a particular set of beliefs or ideas –**ideologically** *adv*

**i·de·ol·o·gy** /ˌaɪdiˈɑlədʒi, ˌɪdi-/ *n* [C,U] a set of beliefs or ideas, especially political beliefs

**id·i·o·cy** /ˈɪdiəsi/ *n* [C,U] something that is extremely stupid

**id·i·om** /ˈɪdiəm/ *n* a group of words that have a special meaning that is very different from the ordinary meaning of the separate words: –**idiomatic** /ˌɪdiəˈmætɪk/ *adj*

**id·i·o·syn·cra·sy** /ˌɪdiəˈsɪŋkrəsi/ *n* an unusual habit or way of behaving that someone has –**idiosyncratic** /ˌɪdioʊsɪnˈkrætɪk/ *adj*

**id·i·ot** /ˈɪdiət/ *n* a stupid person or someone who has done something stupid –**idiotic** /ˌɪdiˈɑtɪk/ *adj*

**i·dle**[1] /ˈaɪdl/ *adj* **1** not working or being used: *a tractor **sitting idle** in the field* **2** OLD-FASHIONED lazy **3** having no useful purpose: *idle gossip* –**idleness** *n* [U] –**idly** *adv*

**idle**[2] *v* [I] if an engine idles, it runs slowly because it is not doing much work

**i·dol** /ˈaɪdl/ *n* **1** someone or something that you admire very much: *a teen idol* **2** an image or object that people pray to as a god

**i·dol·a·try** /aɪˈdɑlətri/ *n* [U] the practice of praying to IDOLs –**idolatrous** *adj* –**idolater** *n*

**i·dol·ize** /ˈaɪdlˌaɪz/ *v* [T] to admire someone so much that you think s/he is perfect: *She idolizes her mother.*

**i·dyl·lic** /aɪˈdɪlɪk/ *adj* very happy and peaceful

**i.e.** /ˈaɪ ˈi/ a written abbreviation used when you want to explain the exact meaning of something: *The movie is only for adults, i.e. those over 18.*

**if**[1] /ɪf; *weak* əf/ *conjunction* **1** used in order to talk about something that might happen: *If I call her now, she should still be at home.* | *We'll have to go on Monday instead, if it snows today.* ✗ DON'T SAY "if it will snow." ✗ **2** used in order to mean "whether," when you are asking or deciding something: *Would you mind if I used your phone?* **3** used when you are talking about something that always happens: *If I don't go to bed by 11:00, I feel terrible the next day.* **4** said when you are surprised, angry, or upset because something has happened or is true: *I'm sorry if I upset you.* | *I don't care if he is your brother - he's acting like an idiot.* **5** **if I were**

**you** used in order to give advice to someone: *If I were you, I'd call him instead of writing to him.* –see also **even if** (EVEN[1]) **as if/though** (AS[2]) **if only** (ONLY[1])

**if**[2] *n* **1** INFORMAL a condition or possibility: *There are still too many ifs to know if this will succeed.* **2** **no ifs, ands, or buts** if you want something done with no ifs, ands, or buts, you want it done quickly, without any arguing

**if·fy** /ˈɪfi/ *adj* INFORMAL an iffy situation is one in which you do not know what will happen: *The weather looks iffy today.*

**ig·loo** /ˈɪglu/ *n* a round house made from blocks of hard snow and ice

**ig·nite** /ɪgˈnaɪt/ *v* FORMAL **1** [T] to start a dangerous situation, angry argument etc.: *actions that could ignite a civil war* **2** [I,T] to start burning, or to make something do this

**ig·ni·tion** /ɪgˈnɪʃən/ *n* **1** [singular] the electrical part of an engine in a car that makes it start working: *Put the key in the ignition.* –see picture on page 469 **2** [U] FORMAL the act of making something start to burn

**ig·no·min·i·ous** /ˌɪgnəˈmɪniəs/ *adj* FORMAL making you feel ashamed or embarrassed: *an ignominious defeat*

**ig·no·rance** /ˈɪgnərəns/ *n* [U] DISAPPROVING lack of knowledge or information about something: *We talked about how racism comes from ignorance and fear.*

**ig·no·rant** /ˈɪgnərənt/ *adj* not knowing facts or information that you should know: *students who are **ignorant of** geography*

**ig·nore** /ɪgˈnɔr/ *v* [T] to not pay any attention to someone or something: *Jeannie ignored me all night!* | *The school board has ignored our complaints.*

**i·gua·na** /ɪˈgwɑnə/ *n* a large tropical American LIZARD

**i·kon** /ˈaɪkɑn/ *n* ⇨ ICON

**IL** the written abbreviation of Illinois

**I'll** /aɪl/ the short form of "I will": *I'll be there in a minute.*

**ill**[1] /ɪl/ *adj* **1** suffering from a disease or not feeling well; SICK: *The doctor said Patty was **seriously/critically ill**.* (=extremely ill) **2** bad or harmful: *Has he suffered any **ill effects** from the treatment?* **3** **ill at ease** nervous or embarrassed

**ill**[2] *adv* **1** badly or not pleasantly: *We were ill-prepared for the cold weather.* **2** **can ill afford (to do sth)** to not be able to do something because it would make your situation more difficult: *Congress can ill afford to raise taxes so close to an election.*

**ill**[3] *n* a bad thing, especially a problem or something that makes you worry: *the social ills caused by poverty*

**ill-ad·vised** /ˌ. .ˈ./ *adj* not sensible or not wise

**il·le·gal**[1] /ɪˈligəl/ *adj* not allowed by the law: *Did you know **it is illegal to** park your car* *here?* | *illegal drugs* **–illegally** *adv* –opposite LEGAL

**il·le·gal**[2] *n* also **illegal immigrant/alien** someone who comes into a country to live or work without official permission

**il·leg·i·ble** /ɪˈlɛdʒəbəl/ *adj* difficult or impossible to read: *illegible handwriting* **–illegibly** *adv*

**il·le·git·i·mate** /ˌɪləˈdʒɪtəmɪt/ *adj* **1** born to parents who are not married to each other. *an illegitimate child* **2** not allowed by the rules: *an illegitimate use of public money* **–illegitimacy** /ˌɪləˈdʒɪtəmɪsi/ *n* [U]

**ill-e·quipped** /ˌ. .ˈ.◂/ *adj* not having the necessary equipment or skills for something: *The hospitals there are dirty and ill-equipped.*

**ill-fat·ed** /ˌ. ˈ..◂/ *adj* not likely to have a good result

**il·lic·it** /ɪˈlɪsɪt/ *adj* not allowed by the law, or not approved of by society: *an illicit love affair* **–illicitly** *adv*

**il·lit·er·ate** /ɪˈlɪtərɪt/ *adj* not able to read or write **–illiteracy** /ɪˈlɪtərəsi/ *n* [U]

**ill-man·nered** /ˌ. ˈ..◂/ *adj* FORMAL not polite

**ill·ness** /ˈɪlnɪs/ *n* [C,U] a disease of the body or mind, or the state of having a disease or sickness: *mental illness* | *a serious illness* –see usage note at DISEASE

**il·log·i·cal** /ɪˈlɑdʒɪkəl/ *adj* not sensible or reasonable

**ill-treat** /ˌ. ˈ./ *v* [T] to be cruel to someone: *The prisoners were beaten and ill-treated.* **–ill-treatment** *n* [U]

**il·lu·mi·nate** /ɪˈluməˌneɪt/ *v* [T] to make a light shine on something: *The room was illuminated by candles.* **–illuminated** *adj*

**il·lu·mi·nat·ing** /ɪˈluməˌneɪtɪŋ/ *adj* FORMAL making something easier to understand: *an illuminating lecture on physics*

**il·lu·mi·na·tion** /ɪˌluməˈneɪʃən/ *n* [U] FORMAL the light provided by a lamp, fire etc.

**il·lu·sion** /ɪˈluʒən/ *n* **1** something that seems to be different from what it really is: *The design of the room gave an illusion of space.* **2** an idea or belief that is false: *Terry is under the illusion that* (=wrongly believes that) *he's going to pass the test.* | *We have no illusions about the hard work that lies ahead.*

**il·lu·so·ry** /ɪˈlusəri, -zəri/ *adj* FORMAL false, but seeming to be true or real

**il·lus·trate** /ˈɪləˌstreɪt/ *v* [T] **1** to explain or make something clear by giving examples: *The charts will help to illustrate this point.* **2** to draw, paint etc. pictures for a book: *a children's book illustrated by Dr. Seuss* **–illustrative** /ɪˈlʌstrətɪv, ˌɪləˈstreɪtɪv/ *adj*

**il·lus·tra·tion** /ˌɪləˈstreɪʃən/ *n* **1** a picture in a book: *watercolor illustrations* **2** an example that helps you understand something: *an illustration of how big the planets are, in comparison to Earth*

**il·lus·tra·tor** /ˈɪləˌstreɪtɚ/ *n* someone whose job is to draw pictures for a book, magazine etc.

**il·lus·tri·ous** /ɪˈlʌstriəs/ *adj* FORMAL very famous and admired by a lot of people

**ill will** /ˌ. ˈ./ *n* [U] unfriendly feelings for someone

**I'm** /aɪm/ the short form of "I am": *I'm not sure where he is.* | *Hello, I'm Donna.*

**im·age** /ˈɪmɪdʒ/ *n* **1** the opinion that people have about someone or something, especially because of the way he, she, or it is shown on television, in newspapers etc.: *The President will have to improve his image if he wants to be re-elected.* **2** a picture that you can see through a camera, on a television, in a mirror etc.: *a baby looking at his image in the mirror* **3** a picture that you have in your mind: *She had a clear image of how he would look in 20 years.* **4** a word, picture, or phrase that describes an idea in a poem, book, movie etc.

**im·age·ry** /ˈɪmɪdʒri/ *n* [U] the use of words, pictures, or phrases to describe ideas or actions in poems, books, movies etc.: *the disturbing imagery of Bosch's paintings*

**i·mag·i·na·ble** /ɪˈmædʒənəbəl/ *adj* able to be imagined: *I had the worst/best day imaginable.*

**i·mag·i·nar·y** /ɪˈmædʒəˌnɛri/ *adj* not real, but imagined: *Many children have imaginary friends.* –compare IMAGINATIVE

**i·mag·i·na·tion** /ɪˌmædʒəˈneɪʃən/ *n* [C,U] the ability to form pictures or ideas in your mind: *Teachers encouraged the students to use their imaginations in solving the problem.* | *Sheila realized that her fears had all been in her imagination.* (=were not true) –compare FANTASY

**i·mag·i·na·tive** /ɪˈmædʒənətɪv/ *adj* **1** able to think of new and interesting ideas: *an imaginative writer* **2** containing new and interesting ideas: *an imaginative story* **–imaginatively** *adv* –compare IMAGINARY

**i·mag·ine** /ɪˈmædʒɪn/ *v* [T] **1** to form pictures or ideas in your mind: *Imagine that you're lying on a beach somewhere.* | *Bobby couldn't imagine why she had lied to him.* **2** to have a false or wrong idea about something: *No one is out there, you're just imagining things.* **3** to think that something may happen or may be true: *I imagine Kathy will be there tomorrow.*

**im·bal·ance** /ɪmˈbæləns/ *n* [C,U] a lack of balance between two things, so they are not equal or correct: *a trade imbalance* **–imbalanced** *adj*

**im·be·cile** /ˈɪmbəsəl/ *n* someone who is extremely stupid

**im·bibe** /ɪmˈbaɪb/ *v* [I,T] FORMAL to drink something, especially alcohol

**im·bue** /ɪmˈbyu/ *v*
   **imbue sb/sth with** *phr v* [T] to make someone feel an emotion very strongly, or to make some-

thing contain a strong emotion: *songs imbued with a romantic tenderness*

**im·i·tate** /ˈɪməˌteɪt/ *v* [T] to do something in exactly the same way as someone or something else: *The tape was made with an actor imitating his voice.* —**imitative** *adj* —**imitator** *n* —compare COPY²

**im·i·ta·tion¹** /ˌɪməˈteɪʃən/ *n* **1** [C,U] a copy of someone's speech, behavior etc., or the act of copying: *Harry does an excellent imitation of Elvis.* | *Children learn by imitation.* **2** a copy of something: *It's not an antique; it's an imitation.*

**imitation²** *adj* **imitation leather/wood/ivory etc.** something that looks real, but that is a copy

**im·mac·u·late** /ɪˈmækyəlɪt/ *adj* **1** very clean and neat: *an immaculate house* **2** perfect and without any mistakes: *dancing with immaculate precision* —**immaculately** *adv*

**im·ma·te·ri·al** /ˌɪməˈtɪriəl/ *adj* not important in a particular situation

**im·ma·ture** /ˌɪməˈtʃʊr, -ˈtʊr/ *adj* **1** DISAPPROVING not behaving in a sensible way that is correct for your age: *Stop being so childish and immature!* **2** not fully formed or developed —**immaturity** *n* [U]

**im·me·di·a·cy** /ɪˈmidiəsi/ *n* [U] the quality of seeming to be important and urgent, and directly relating to what is happening now

**im·me·di·ate** /ɪˈmidiɪt/ *adj* **1** happening or done at once with no delay: *Police demanded the immediate release of the hostages.* **2** existing now, and needing to be dealt with quickly: *Our immediate concern was to stop the fire from spreading.* **3** near something or someone in time or place: *We have no plans to expand the business in the immediate future.* **4 immediate family** your parents, children, brothers, and sisters

**im·me·di·ate·ly** /ɪˈmidiɪtli/ *adv* **1** at once and with no delay: *Mandy answered the phone immediately.* **2** very near to something in time or place: *We left immediately afterwards.* | *They live immediately above us.*

**im·mense** /ɪˈmɛns/ *adj* extremely large: *an immense palace* —**immensity** *n* [U]

**im·mense·ly** /ɪˈmɛnsli/ *adv* very much: *I enjoyed your party immensely.*

**im·merse** /ɪˈmɔrs/ *v* [T] **1 be immersed in sth/immerse yourself in sth** to be completely involved in something: *Grant is completely immersed in his work.* **2** to put something completely in a liquid —**immersion** /ɪˈmɔrʒən/ *n* [U]

**im·mi·grant** /ˈɪməgrənt/ *n* someone who enters another country to live there: *an immigrant from Russia* —compare EMIGRANT

**im·mi·grate** /ˈɪməˌgreɪt/ *v* [I] to enter another country in order to live there —compare EMIGRATE —see usage note at EMIGRATE

**im·mi·gra·tion** /ˌɪməˈgreɪʃən/ *n* [U] **1** the process of entering another country in order to live there **2** the place in an airport, at a border etc. where officials check your documents, such as your PASSPORT

**im·mi·nent** /ˈɪmənənt/ *adj* happening or likely to happen very soon: *We believe that an attack is imminent.* | *The city is not in imminent danger.* —**imminently** *adv*

**im·mo·bile** /ɪˈmoʊbəl/ *adj* not moving, or not able to move

**im·mor·al** /ɪˈmɔrəl, ɪˈmɑr-/ *adj* morally wrong, and not accepted by society: *immoral sexual acts* —**immorality** /ˌɪməˈræləṭi, ˌɪmɔ-/ *n* [U]

**im·mor·tal** /ɪˈmɔrṭl/ *adj* **1** living or continuing always: *your immortal soul* **2** an immortal poem, song etc. is so famous that it will never be forgotten: *the immortal writings of Charles Dickens* —**immortality** /ˌɪmɔrˈtæləṭi/ *n* [U]

**im·mov·a·ble** /ɪˈmuvəbəl/ *adj* impossible to move, change, or persuade

**im·mune** /ɪˈmyun/ *adj* **1** not able to be affected by a disease or illness: *Pregnant women should make sure they are immune to German measles.* **2** not affected by unpleasant things that affect people, organizations etc. in similar situations: *The company seems to be immune to economic pressures.* | *The Governor is popular, but not immune from criticism.*

**immune sys·tem** /.ˈ. ˌ../ *n* the system by which your body protects itself against disease

**im·mu·ni·ty** /ɪˈmyunəṭi/ *n* [U] **1** the state or right of being IMMUNE to laws or punishment: *Congress granted immunity* (=gave immunity) *to both men.* **2** the state of being IMMUNE to diseases or illnesses: *The patient's immunity is low.*

**im·mu·ni·za·tion** /ˌɪmyənəˈzeɪʃən/ *n* [C,U] the act of immunizing (IMMUNIZE) someone: *the immunization of babies in the U.S. against hepatitis B*

**im·mu·nize** /ˈɪmyəˌnaɪz/ *v* [T] to protect someone from disease by giving him/her a VACCINE: *Have you been immunized against cholera?*

**im·mu·ta·ble** /ɪˈmyuṭəbəl/ *adj* FORMAL never changing, or impossible to change

**imp** /ɪmp/ *n* a child who behaves badly, but in a funny way

**im·pact¹** /ˈɪmpækt/ *n* **1** the effect that an event or situation has on someone or something: *Every decision at work has an impact on profit.* | *the environmental impact of the three new housing developments* **2** the force of one object hitting another: *The impact of the crash made the car flip over.* **3 on impact** at the moment when one thing hits another: *a missile that explodes on impact*

**im·pact²** /ɪmˈpækt/ *v* [I,T] to have an important or noticeable effect on someone or something: *The growth of the airport has impacted the city's economy.*

**im·pair** /ɪmˈpɛr/ *v* [T] to damage something or make it less good: *Her sight was impaired as a result of the disease.* —**impairment** *n* [U]

**im·paired** /ɪmˈpɛrd/ *adj* **1** damaged, less strong, or less good: *Radio reception was impaired after the storm.* | *impaired vision* **2** hearing/visually impaired etc. someone who is hearing impaired or visually impaired cannot hear, see etc. very well or at all

**im·pale** /ɪmˈpeɪl/ *v* [T] to push a sharp pointed object through something or someone

**im·part** /ɪmˈpɑrt/ *v* [T] FORMAL **1** to give information, knowledge etc. to someone: *He accused the universities of failing to impart moral values.* **2** to give a particular quality to something: *Burned butter imparts a bitter flavor to the sauce.*

**im·par·tial** /ɪmˈpɑrʃəl/ *adj* not giving special attention or support to any one person or group: *impartial advice* | *impartial observers of the election* —**impartially** *adv* —**impartiality** /ɪmˌpɑrʃiˈæləti/ *n* [U]

**im·pass·a·ble** /ɪmˈpæsəbəl/ *adj* impossible to travel along or through: *Some streets are impassable because of the snow.*

**im·passe** /ˈɪmpæs/ *n* [singular] a situation in which it is impossible to continue with a discussion or plan because the people involved cannot agree: *Discussions about pay have reached an impasse.*

**im·pas·sioned** /ɪmˈpæʃənd/ *adj* full of strong feelings and emotion: *an impassioned speech*

**im·pas·sive** /ɪmˈpæsɪv/ *adj* not showing any emotions: *His face was impassive as the judge spoke.* —**impassively** *adv*

**im·pa·tient** /ɪmˈpeɪʃənt/ *adj* **1** annoyed because of delays or mistakes that make you wait: *After an hour's delay, the airline passengers were becoming impatient.* | *Rob's teacher seems very impatient with some of the slower kids.* **2** very eager for something to happen, and not wanting to wait: *Gary was impatient to leave.* —**impatience** *n* [U] —**impatiently** *adv*

**im·peach** /ɪmˈpitʃ/ *v* [T] LAW to say that a public official is guilty of a serious crime —**impeachment** *n* [U]

**im·pec·ca·ble** /ɪmˈpɛkəbəl/ *adj* completely perfect and impossible to criticize: *She has impeccable taste in clothes.* —**impeccably** *adv*

**im·pede** /ɪmˈpid/ *v* [T] FORMAL to make it difficult for someone or something to make progress: *Rescue attempts were impeded by storms.*

**im·ped·i·ment** /ɪmˈpɛdəmənt/ *n* **1** a fact or event that makes action difficult or impossible: *The country's debt has been an impediment to development.* **2** a physical problem that makes

speaking, hearing, or moving difficult: *a speech impediment*

**im·pel** /ɪmˈpɛl/ **-elled, -elling** *v* [T] FORMAL to make you feel very strongly that you must do something: *He felt impelled to explain why he had acted the way he did.*

**im·pend·ing** /ɪmˈpɛndɪŋ/ *adj* likely to happen soon: *the impending legal battle*

**im·pen·e·tra·ble** /ɪmˈpɛnətrəbəl/ *adj* **1** impossible to get through, see through, or get into: *impenetrable fog* **2** very difficult or impossible to understand: *impenetrable scientific language*

**im·per·a·tive¹** /ɪmˈpɛrətɪv/ *adj* FORMAL **1** extremely important and urgent: *It's imperative that you leave immediately.* **2** TECHNICAL an imperative verb expresses a command

**imperative²** *n* **1** something that must be done urgently: *Reducing air pollution has become an imperative.* **2** TECHNICAL the form of a verb that expresses a command. In the sentence "Do it now!" the verb "do" is in the imperative

**im·per·cep·ti·ble** /ˌɪmpɚˈsɛptəbəl/ *adj* impossible to notice: *an almost imperceptible change* —**imperceptibly** *adv*

**im·per·fect¹** /ɪmˈpɚfɪkt/ *adj* not completely perfect: *an imperfect legal system* —**imperfectly** *adv*

**imperfect²** *n* [singular] TECHNICAL the form of a verb that shows an incomplete action in the past, that is formed with "be" and the PAST PARTICIPLE. In the sentence "We were walking down the road" the verb phrase "were walking" is in the imperfect

**im·per·fec·tion** /ˌɪmpɚˈfɛkʃən/ *n* [C,U] the state of being IMPERFECT, or something that is imperfect: *human imperfection* | *There may be slight imperfections in the cloth.*

**im·pe·ri·al** /ɪmˈpɪriəl/ *adj* relating to an EMPIRE or to the person who rules it

**im·pe·ri·al·ism** /ɪmˈpɪriəˌlɪzəm/ *n* [U] USUALLY DISAPPROVING a political system in which one country controls a lot of other countries —**imperialist** *n* —**imperialist, imperialistic** /ɪmˌpɪriəˈlɪstɪk/ *adj*

**im·per·il** /ɪmˈpɛrəl/ *v* [T] FORMAL to put something or someone in danger

**im·per·son·al** /ɪmˈpɚsənəl/ *adj* not showing any feelings of sympathy, friendliness etc.: *an impersonal letter* —**impersonally** *adv*

**im·per·so·nate** /ɪmˈpɚsəˌneɪt/ *v* [T] **1** to pretend to be someone else by copying his/her appearance, voice etc., in order to deceive people: *They were arrested for impersonating police officers.* **2** to copy someone's voice and behavior in order to make people laugh: *a comedian who impersonates politicians* —**impersonator** *n* —**impersonation** /ɪmˌpɚsəˈneɪʃən/ *n* [U]

**im·per·ti·nent** /ɪmˈpɚt̚n-ənt/ *adj* rude and not respectful, especially to an older person:

*asking impertinent questions* **–impertinence** *n* [U]

**im·per·vi·ous** /ɪmˈpɜːviəs/ *adj* **1** not affected or influenced by something: *He seemed* **impervious to** *the noise around him.* **2** not allowing anything to pass through: *Clothing must be impervious to cold and rain for the climbers to survive.*

**im·pet·u·ous** /ɪmˈpɛtʃuəs/ *adj* tending to do things quickly, without thinking: *an impetuous decision to get married | She is impetuous and stubborn.* **–impetuously** *adv*

**im·pe·tus** /ˈɪmpətəs/ *n* [U] **1** an influence that makes something happen, or happen more quickly: *The Surgeon General has provided the impetus for health prevention programs.* **2** TECHNICAL a force that makes an object start moving, or keeps it moving

**im·pinge** /ɪmˈpɪndʒ/ *v*
**impinge on/upon** sth *phr v* [T] FORMAL to have an effect, often an unwanted one, on someone or something: *International politics have* **impinged on** *decisions made in Congress.*

**imp·ish** /ˈɪmpɪʃ/ *adj* behaving like an IMP: *an impish laugh* **–impishly** *adv*

**im·plac·a·ble** /ɪmˈplækəbəl/ *adj* very determined to continue opposing someone or something: *an implacable enemy* **–implacably** *adv*

**im·plant**[1] /ɪmˈplænt/ *v* [T] **1** to put something into someone's body by a medical operation: *Doctors implanted a new lens in her eye.* **2** to influence someone so that s/he believes or feels something strongly: *the patriotism implanted in him by his father*

**im·plant**[2] /ˈɪmplænt/ *n* something that has been put into someone's body in a medical operation: *silicon breast implants*

**im·plau·si·ble** /ɪmˈplɔːzəbəl/ *adj* difficult to believe and not likely to be true: *an implausible excuse*

**im·ple·ment**[1] /ˈɪmpləˌmɛnt/ *v* [T] if you implement a plan, process etc., you begin to make it happen: *When will Congress implement its welfare reforms?* **–implementation** /ˌɪmpləmənˈteɪʃən/ *n* [U]

**im·ple·ment**[2] /ˈɪmpləmənt/ *n* a large tool or instrument with no motor: *farming implements*

**im·pli·cate** /ˈɪmplɪˌkeɪt/ *v* [T] to show that someone is involved in something wrong: *The witness* **implicated** *two other men* **in** *the robbery.*

**im·pli·ca·tion** /ˌɪmplɪˈkeɪʃən/ *n* **1** a possible effect or result of a plan, action etc.: *What are the implications of a disaster in the nuclear power industry?* **2** [C,U] something you do not say directly but that you want people to understand: *I don't like the* **implication that** *I was lying.* **3** [U] the act of making a statement that suggests someone has done something

wrong or illegal: *the implication of the bank president in the theft*

**im·plic·it** /ɪmˈplɪsɪt/ *adj* **1** suggested or understood but not stated directly: *There was implicit criticism in the principal's statement.* **2** complete and containing no doubts: *an implicit faith in her husband's faithfulness* **3 be implicit in** FORMAL to be a central part of something, without being stated: *Risk is implicit in owning a business.* **–implicitly** *adv* **–compare** EXPLICIT

**im·plode** /ɪmˈploʊd/ *v* [I] to explode inward

**im·plore** /ɪmˈplɔr/ *v* [T] FORMAL to ask for something in an emotional way; BEG: *Joan implored him not to leave.*

**im·ply** /ɪmˈplaɪ/ *v* [T] to suggest that something is true without saying or showing it directly: *He implied that the money hadn't been lost, but was stolen.* **–compare** INFER

**im·po·lite** /ˌɪmpəˈlaɪt/ *adj* not polite: *It would be impolite not to call her back and say "thank you."*

**im·port**[1] /ˈɪmpɔrt/ *n* **1** [C,U] the business of bringing products into one country from another in order to be sold, or the products that are sold: *Car imports have risen recently.* **–compare** EXPORT[1] **2** FORMAL importance or meaning: *a matter of import*

**im·port**[2] /ɪmˈpɔrt/ *v* [T] to bring something into a country from abroad in order to sell it: *oil imported from the Middle East* **–importer** *n* **–compare** EXPORT[2]

**im·por·tance** /ɪmˈpɔrtⁿns, -pɔrtⁿns/ *n* [U] **1** the quality of being important: *the importance of regular exercise | political issues* **of great importance** **2** the reason why something is important: *Explain the importance of the Monroe Doctrine in a 750 word essay.*

**im·por·tant** /ɪmˈpɔrtⁿnt, -ˈpɔrtⁿt/ *adj* **1** having a big effect or influence: *important questions | It's important to explain things carefully to the patient.* **2** having a lot of power or influence: *an important senator* **–importantly** *adv* **–opposite** UNIMPORTANT

**im·por·ta·tion** /ˌɪmpɔrˈteɪʃən/ *n* [U] the business of bringing goods from another country to sell in your country

**im·pose** /ɪmˈpoʊz/ *v* **1** [T] to introduce a rule, tax, punishment etc. and force people to accept it: *Many countries* **imposed** *economic sanctions* **on** *South Africa during apartheid.* **2** [T] to force someone to have the same ideas, beliefs etc. as you: *parents imposing their values on their children* **3** [I] to unreasonably ask or expect someone to do something: *I didn't ask you, because I didn't want to impose.*

**im·pos·ing** /ɪmˈpoʊzɪŋ/ *adj* large and impressive: *an imposing building*

**im·po·si·tion** /ˌɪmpəˈzɪʃən/ *n* **1** something that someone unreasonably expects or asks you to do for him/her: *They stayed for a month?*

*What an imposition!* **2** [U] the introduction of something such as a rule, tax, or punishment: *the imposition of taxes on cigarettes*

**im·pos·si·ble** /ɪmˈpɑsəbəl/ *adj* **1** not able to be done or to happen: *It's impossible to sleep with all this noise.* **2** extremely difficult to deal with: *an impossible situation* **3** behaving in an unreasonable and annoying way: *You're impossible; you change your mind every day.* **–impossibly** *adv* **–impossibility** /ɪmˌpɑsəˈbɪləti/ *n* [C,U]

**im·pos·ter** /ɪmˈpɑstɚ/ *n* someone who pretends to be someone else in order to trick people

**im·po·tent** /ˈɪmpət̮ənt/ *adj* **1** unable to take effective action because you do not have enough power, strength, or control: *an impotent city government* **2** a man who is impotent is unable to have sex because he cannot have an ERECTION **–impotence** *n* [U]

**im·pound** /ɪmˈpaʊnd/ *v* [T] LAW if the police or law courts impound your possessions, they take them and keep them until you claim them

**im·pov·er·ished** /ɪmˈpɑvərɪʃt/ *adj* very poor

**im·prac·ti·cal** /ɪmˈpræktɪkəl/ *adj* **1** an impractical plan, suggestion etc. is not sensible because it would be too expensive or difficult **2** not good at dealing with ordinary practical matters **–impractically** *adv* **–impracticality** /ɪmˌpræktɪˈkæləti/ *n* [U]

**im·pre·cise** /ˌɪmprɪˈsaɪs/ *adj* not exact: *John's directions were imprecise.* **–imprecisely** *adv* **–imprecision** /ˌɪmprɪˈsɪʒən/ *n* [U]

**im·preg·na·ble** /ɪmˈprɛgnəbəl/ *adj* very strong and unable to be entered: *an impregnable fort*

**im·preg·nate** /ɪmˈprɛgˌneɪt/ *v* [T] FORMAL **1** to make a substance spread completely through something, or to spread completely through something: *paper impregnated with perfume* **2** to make a woman or female animal PREGNANT

**im·press** /ɪmˈprɛs/ *v* [T] **1** to make someone feel admiration and respect: *She dresses like that to impress people.* | *We were impressed by the size of his art collection.* **2** to make the importance of something clear to someone: *My parents impressed on me the value of an education.*

**im·pres·sion** /ɪmˈprɛʃən/ *n* **1** the opinion or feeling you have about someone or something because of the way she, he, or it seems: *What were your first impressions of New York?* | *I get the impression that something's wrong here.* | *It's important to make a good impression at your interview.* **2** **be under the impression (that)** to think that something is true when it is not true: *I was under the impression that Marcie was coming to dinner too.* **3** the act of copying the speech or behavior of a famous person in order to make people laugh: *Rich Little did a great impression of Nixon.*

**4** the mark left by pressing something into a soft surface

**im·pres·sion·a·ble** /ɪmˈprɛʃənəbəl/ *adj* easy to influence: *The girls are at an impressionable age.*

**im·pres·sion·is·tic** /ɪmˌprɛʃəˈnɪstɪk/ *adj* based on a general feeling of what something is like rather than on details: *an impressionistic account of the events*

**im·pres·sive** /ɪmˈprɛsɪv/ *adj* causing admiration: *an impressive performance on the piano* **–impressively** *adv*

**im·print¹** /ˈɪmˌprɪnt/ *n* the mark left by an object that has been pressed into or onto something: *the imprint of her thumb on the clay*

**im·print²** /ɪmˈprɪnt/ *v* **be imprinted on your mind/memory** if something is imprinted on your mind or memory, you can never forget it

**im·pris·on** /ɪmˈprɪzən/ *v* [T] to put someone in prison or to keep him/her in a place s/he cannot escape from: *The government imprisoned the leader of the rebellion.* **–imprisonment** *n* [U]

**im·prob·a·ble** /ɪmˈprɑbəbəl/ *adj* **1** not likely to happen or to be true: *It is highly improbable that you will find sharks in these waters.* **2** surprising and slightly strange: *an improbable partnership* **–improbably** *adv* **–improbability** /ɪmˌprɑbəˈbɪləti/ *n* [C,U]

**im·promp·tu** /ɪmˈprɑmptu/ *adj* done or said without any preparation or planning: *an impromptu speech* **–impromptu** *adv*

**im·prop·er** /ɪmˈprɑpɚ/ *adj* **1** unacceptable according to professional, moral, or social rules of behavior: *Many cases of "stomach flu" result from improper cooking of food.* **2** illegal or dishonest: *The bank's director made an improper use of funds held by the bank.* **–improperly** *adv*: *improperly dressed*

**im·pro·pri·e·ty** /ˌɪmprəˈpraɪəti/ *n* [C,U] FORMAL behavior or an action that is unacceptable according to moral, social, or professional standards

**im·prove** /ɪmˈpruv/ *v* [I,T] to become better, or to make something better: *exercises to improve muscle strength* | *Your math skills have improved this year.* **–improved** *adj*

**improve on/upon** sth *phr v* [T] to do something better than before, or make it better: *No one's been able to improve on her Olympic record.*

**im·prove·ment** /ɪmˈpruvmənt/ *n* **1** [C,U] an act of improving, or the state of being improved: *There's certainly been an improvement in Danny's behavior.* | *Your German is getting better, but there's still room for improvement.* (=the possibility of more improvement) **2** a change or addition that makes something better: *home improvements*

**im·pro·vise** /ˈɪmprəˌvaɪz/ *v* **1** [I,T] to make or do something without any preparation, using what you have: *I left my lesson plans at home, so I'll have to improvise.* **2** [I] to perform music, sing, etc. from your imagination: *Jazz musicians are good at improvising.* –**improvisation** /ɪmˌprɑvəˈzeɪʃən/ *n* [C,U]

**im·pu·dent** /ˈɪmpyədənt/ *adj* rude and not showing respect –**impudence** *n* [U]

**im·pulse** /ˈɪmpʌls/ *n* **1** a sudden desire to do something without thinking about the results: *She resisted the impulse to hit him.|I bought this shirt* **on impulse**, *and now I don't like it.* **2** TECHNICAL a short electrical signal sent in one direction along a wire or nerve, or through the air

**im·pul·sive** /ɪmˈpʌlsɪv/ *adj* tending to do things without thinking about the results, or showing this quality: *an impulsive shopper|an impulsive decision* –**impulsively** *adv*

**im·pu·ni·ty** /ɪmˈpyunəṭi/ *n* [U] **with impunity** without risk of punishment: *We cannot let them break laws with impunity.*

**im·pure** /ɪmˈpyʊr/ *adj* mixed with other substances: *impure drugs*

**im·pu·ri·ty** /ɪmˈpyʊrəṭi/ *n* [C,U] a part of an almost pure substance that is of a lower quality, or the state of being IMPURE: *minerals containing impurities*

**IN** the written abbreviation of Indiana

**in¹** /ɪn; *weak* ən, n/ *prep* **1** used with the name of a container, place, or area to show where something is: *The paper is in the top drawer in the desk.|I was still in bed at 11:30.|cows standing in a field|He lived in Boston/Spain for 15 years.|Grandpa's in the hospital.* (=because he is sick or injured) **2** used with the names of months, years, seasons etc. to say when something happened: *We bought our car in April.|In 1969 the first astronauts landed on the moon.|In the winter, we use a wood stove.* **3** during a period of time: *We finished the whole project in a/one week.* **4** at the end of a period of time: *Gerry should be home in an hour.|I wonder if the business will still be going in a year.* **5** included as part of something: *One of the people in the story is a young doctor.|In the first part of the speech, he talked about the environment.* **6** **not done sth in years/months/weeks** if you have not done something in years etc., you have not done it for that amount of time: *I haven't been to the circus in years!* **7** using a particular kind of voice, or a particular way of speaking or writing: *"I'm afraid," Violet said in a quiet voice.|Their parents always talk to them in Italian.|Do not write in pen on this test.* **8** working on a particular kind of job: *She's in advertising.* **9** arranged in a particular way, often to form a group or shape: *Stand against the wall in a line.|He had made a bowl in the shape of a heart.|Put the words in alphabetical order.* **10** used in order to show the connection between two ideas or subjects: *I was never interested in sports as a kid.*

**11** used before the bigger number when you are talking about a relationship between two numbers: *1 in 10 women* (=of all women) *have the disease.* **12** **in shock/horror etc.** used in order to describe a strong feeling someone has when s/he does something: *She looked at me in shock as I told her how everything had gone wrong.* **13** **in all** used when giving a total amount: *Lots of my cousins came to the party. I think there were 25 of us in all.*

**in²** *adj, adv* **1** so as to be contained inside or surrounded by something: *She pushed the box towards me so that I could put my money in.* **2** inside a building, especially the one where you live or work: *Ms. Robinson isn't in yet this morning.|You're never in when I call.* **3** if a plane, bus, train, or boat is in, it has arrived at the airport, station etc.: *What time does his bus get in?* **4** given or sent to a particular place in order to be read or looked at: *Your final papers have to be in by Friday.* **5** if you write, paint, or draw something in, you write it etc. in the correct place: *Fill in the blanks, using a number 2 pencil.* **6** if clothes, colors, etc. are in, they are fashionable: *Long hair is in again.* **7** if a ball is in during a game, it is inside the area where the game is played **8** **be in for sth** if someone is in for something unpleasant, it is about to happen to him/her: *She's in for a shock if she thinks we're going to help her pay for it.* **9** **be in on sth** to be involved in doing, talking about, or planning something: *The movie asks questions about who was in on the plan to kill Kennedy.* **10** if the TIDE comes in or is in, the ocean water is at its highest level **11** **in joke** an in joke is one that is only understood by a small group of people

**in·a·bil·i·ty** /ˌɪnəˈbɪləṭi/ *n* [singular, U] a lack of the ability, skill etc. to do something: *an inability to work quickly*

**in·ac·ces·si·ble** /ˌɪnəkˈsɛsəbəl/ *adj* difficult or impossible to reach: *roads that are inaccessible in winter*

**in·ac·cu·ra·cy** /ɪnˈækyərəsi/ *n* [C,U] a mistake, or a lack of correctness: *There were several inaccuracies in the report.*

**in·ac·cu·rate** /ɪnˈækyərɪt/ *adj* not completely correct: *an inaccurate description* –**inaccurately** *adv*

**in·ac·tion** /ɪnˈækʃən/ *n* [U] lack of action: *The city council was criticized for its inaction on the parking problem.*

**in·ac·tive** /ɪnˈæktɪv/ *adj* not doing anything or not working: *inactive members of the club|The rate of heart disease among inactive men* (=men who do not exercise) *is much higher than in active men.* –**inactivity** /ˌɪnækˈtɪvəṭi/ *n* [U]

**in·ad·e·qua·cy** /ɪnˈædəkwəsi/ *n* **1** [U] a feeling that you are unable to deal with situations because you are not as good as other people: *Not having a job can cause strong feelings of inadequacy.* **2** [C,U] the fact of not being good enough for a particular purpose, or something that is not good enough: *the inadequacy of safety standards in the coal mines.* | *The airlines don't want the public to know about the system's inadequacies.*

**in·ad·e·quate** /ɪn'ædəkwɪt/ *adj* not good enough for a particular purpose: *inadequate health care services* –**inadequately** *adv*

**in·ad·mis·si·ble** /ˌɪnəd'mɪsəbəl/ *adj* FORMAL not allowed: *Some of the evidence was inadmissible in court.*

**in·ad·vert·ent·ly** /ˌɪnəd'vɚ̩tntli/ *adv* without intending to do something: *She inadvertently hit the brakes.* –**inadvertent** *adj*

**in·ad·vis·a·ble** /ˌɪnəd'vaɪzəbəl/ *adj* an inadvisable decision is not sensible; UNWISE: *It's inadvisable to take medicine without asking your doctor.*

**in·al·ien·a·ble** /ɪn'eɪlyənəbəl/ *adj* FORMAL an inalienable right cannot be taken away from you

**in·ane** /ɪ'neɪn/ *adj* extremely stupid or without much meaning: *inane jokes*

**in·an·i·mate** /ɪn'ænəmɪt/ *adj* not living: *Rocks are inanimate objects.*

**in·ap·pro·pri·ate** /ˌɪnə'proupriɪt/ *adj* not suitable or correct for a particular purpose or situation: *Martin's behavior at the funeral was inappropriate.* –**inappropriately** *adv*

**in·ar·tic·u·late** /ˌɪnɑr'tɪkyəlɪt/ *adj* not able to express yourself or speak clearly: *His grief made him inarticulate.*

**in·as·much as** /ˌɪnəz'mʌtʃ əz/ *conjunction* FORMAL used in order to begin a phrase that explains the rest of your sentence by showing the limited way that it is true: *She's guilty, inasmuch as she knew what the other girls were planning to do.*

**in·au·di·ble** /ɪn'ɔdəbəl/ *adj* too quiet to be heard: *Her reply was inaudible.* –**inaudible** *adv*

**in·au·gu·rate** /ɪ'nɔgyəˌreɪt/ *v* [T] **1** to have an official ceremony in order to show that someone is beginning an important job: *The President is inaugurated in January.* **2** to open a new building or start a new service with a ceremony –**inaugural** /ɪ'nɔgyərəl/ *adj* –**inauguration** /ɪˌnɔgyə'reɪʃən/ *n* [C,U]

**in·aus·pi·cious** /ˌɪnɔ'spɪʃəs/ *adj* FORMAL seeming to show that the future will be unlucky: *an inauspicious start to our trip*

**in·be·tween** /ˌ. .'./ *adj* INFORMAL in the middle of two points, sizes, etc.: *She's at that in-between age, neither a girl nor a woman.*

**in·born** /ˌɪn'bɔrn‹/ *adj* an inborn quality or ability is one that you have had naturally since birth: *an inborn sense of justice*

**in·bred** /ˌɪn'brɛd‹/ *adj* **1** having developed as a natural part of your character: *an inbred sense of respect* **2** produced by the breeding of closely related members of a family, which often causes problems: *an inbred genetic defect* –**inbreeding** /'ɪnˌbridɪŋ/ *n* [U]

**Inc.** /ɪŋk, ɪn'kɔrpəˌreɪṭɪd/ the written abbreviation of INCORPORATED: *General Motors Inc.*

**in·cal·cu·la·ble** /ɪn'kælkyələbəl/ *adj* too many or too great to be measured: *The scandal has done incalculable damage to the college's reputation.*

**in·can·des·cent** /ˌɪnkən'dɛsənt/ *adj* giving a bright light when heated –**incandescence** *n* [U]

**in·can·ta·tion** /ˌɪnkæn'teɪʃən/ *n* [C,U] a set of special words that someone uses in magic, or the act of saying these words

**in·ca·pa·ble** /ɪn'keɪpəbəl/ *adj* unable to do something or to feel a particular emotion: *Debbie is incapable of being sympathetic.* –**incapably** *adv*

**in·ca·pac·i·tate** /ˌɪnkə'pæsəˌteɪt/ *v* [T] to make someone too sick or weak to live or work normally: *He was incapacitated for a while after the operation.*

**in·ca·pac·i·ty** /ˌɪnkə'pæsəṭi/ *n* [U] lack of ability, strength, or power to do something, especially because you are sick

**in·car·cer·ate** /ɪn'kɑrsəˌreɪt/ *v* [T] FORMAL to put someone in a prison –**incarceration** /ɪnˌkɑrsə'reɪʃən/ *n* [U]

**in·car·nate** /ɪn'kɑrnɪt, -ˌneɪt/ *adj* **the devil/evil etc. incarnate** someone who is considered to be the human form of evil etc.

**in·car·na·tion** /ˌɪnkɑr'neɪʃən/ *n* **1** a time before or after the life you are living now, when, according to some religions, you were alive in the form of a different person or animal **2 be the incarnation of goodness/evil etc.** to represent perfect goodness etc. in the way you live

**in·cen·di·ar·y** /ɪn'sɛndiˌɛri/ *adj* **1 incendiary bomb/device etc.** a bomb etc. designed to cause a fire **2** an incendiary speech or piece of writing is intended to make people angry and is likely to cause trouble

**in·cense¹** /'ɪnsɛns/ *n* [U] a substance that has a pleasant smell when you burn it

**in·cense²** /ɪn'sɛns/ *v* [T] to make someone extremely angry: *I was incensed by his racist attitudes!*

**in·cen·tive** /ɪn'sɛnṭɪv/ *n* [C,U] something that encourages you to work harder, start new activities etc.: *The government provides incentives for new businesses.*

**in·cep·tion** /ɪn'sɛpʃən/ *n* [singular] FORMAL the start of an organization or institution: *He has worked for the company since its inception in 1970.*

**in·ces·sant** /ɪn'sɛsənt/ *adj* without stopping: *the incessant traffic noise* –**incessantly** *adv*

**in·cest** /'ɪnsɛst/ *n* [U] illegal sex between people who are closely part of the same family

**in·ces·tu·ous** /ɪn'sɛstʃuəs/ *adj* relating to INCEST –**incestuously** *adv*

**inch¹** /ɪntʃ/ written abbreviation **in.** *n*, *plural* **inches 1** a unit for measuring length, equal to

1/12 of a foot or 2.45 centimeters **2 every inch** all of someone or something: *Pictures cover every inch of wall space.* **3 inch by inch** very slowly or by a small amount at a time: *The area was searched inch by inch for landmines.* **4 not give/budge an inch** to refuse to change your opinions at all: *At first Will refused to give an inch in the argument.*

**inch²** *v* [I,T] to move very slowly and carefully, or to move something this way: *I got a glass of wine and **inched my way** across the crowded room.*

**in·ci·dence** /'ɪnsədəns/ *n* [singular] FORMAL the number of times something happens: *an increased incidence of heart attacks*

**in·ci·dent** /'ɪnsədənt/ *n* something unusual, serious, or violent that happens: *Any witnesses to the incident should speak to the police.*

**in·ci·den·tal** /ˌɪnsə'dɛntl/ *adj* happening or existing in connection with something else that is more important: *Keep a record of your **incidental expenses** on your trip.*

**in·ci·den·tal·ly** /ˌɪnsə'dɛntli/ *adv* used when giving additional information, or when changing the subject of a conversation: *Incidentally, Jenny's coming over tonight.*

**in·cin·er·ate** /ɪn'sɪnəˌreɪt/ *v* [T] to burn something in order to destroy it **–incineration** /ɪnˌsɪnə'reɪʃən/ *n* [U]

**in·cin·er·a·tor** /ɪn'sɪnəˌreɪtɚ/ *n* a machine that burns things at very high temperatures

**in·cip·i·ent** /ɪn'sɪpiənt/ *adj* FORMAL starting to happen or exist

**in·ci·sion** /ɪn'sɪʒən/ *n* TECHNICAL a cut that a doctor makes in someone's body during an operation

**in·ci·sive** /ɪn'saɪsɪv/ *adj* incisive words, remarks etc. are very direct and deal with the most important part of a subject

**in·ci·sor** /ɪn'saɪzɚ/ *n* one of your eight front teeth that have sharp edges

**in·cite** /ɪn'saɪt/ *v* [T] to deliberately make someone feel so angry or excited that s/he does something bad: *One man was jailed for inciting a riot.*

**in·cli·na·tion** /ˌɪnklə'neɪʃən/ *n* **1** [C,U] the desire to do something: *I didn't have the time or inclination to go with them.* **2** [C,U] a tendency to think or behave in a particular way: *his **inclination to** act violently*

**in·cline¹** /ɪn'klaɪn/ *v* [I,T] to slope at a particular angle, or make something do this

**in·cline²** /'ɪnklaɪn/ *n* a slope: *a steep incline*

**in·clined** /ɪn'klaɪnd/ *adj* **1 be inclined to agree/believe/think etc.** to have a particular opinion, but not have it very strongly: *I'm inclined to agree with you, but I don't really know.* **2** wanting to do something: *My client is not **inclined to** speak with reporters.* **3** likely or tending to do something: *He's **inclined to** get upset over small things.*

**in·clude** /ɪn'klud/ *v* [T] **1** if a group or set includes something or someone, it has that person or thing as one of its parts: *The price includes your flight, hotel, and car rental.* **2** to make someone or something part of a larger group or set: *Is my name **included on** the list?* | *Try to **include** Rosie more **in** your games, Sam.* **–**opposite EXCLUDE

**in·clud·ing** /ɪn'kludɪŋ/ *prep* used in order to show that someone or something is part of a larger group or set that you are talking about: *There were 20 people in the room, including the teacher.* | *We only paid $12 for dinner, including the tip.* **–**opposite EXCLUDING

**in·clu·sion** /ɪn'kluʒən/ *n* **1** [U] the action of including someone or something in a larger group or set, or the fact of being included in one: *Here's the list of books we're considering for inclusion on the reading list.* **2** someone or something that is included

**in·clu·sive** /ɪn'klusɪv/ *adj* including all the possible information, parts, numbers etc.: *an **all inclusive** guide to the restaurants in Manhattan*

**in·cog·ni·to** /ˌɪnkɑg'nitoʊ/ *adv* if a famous person does something incognito, s/he is hiding who s/he really is

**in·co·her·ent** /ˌɪnkoʊ'hɪrənt/ *adj* **1** badly explained and unable to be understood: *a dull incoherent speech* **2** not talking clearly: *The two women were incoherent after their ordeal.* **–incoherently** *adv*

**in·come** /'ɪnkʌm, 'ɪŋ-/ *n* [C,U] the money that you earn from working or making INVESTMENTs: *a good/high/low income* **–**see usage note at PAY²

**income tax** /'.. ˌ./ *n* [U] tax paid on the money you earn

**in·com·ing** /'ɪnˌkʌmɪŋ/ *adj* **1 incoming call/letter/fax** a telephone call, letter, or FAX that you receive **2** coming toward a place, or about to arrive: *the incoming tide*

**in·com·mu·ni·ca·do** /ˌɪnkəˌmyunɪ'kɑdoʊ/ *adj, adv* not allowed or not wanting to communicate with anyone

**in·com·pa·ra·ble** /ɪn'kɑmpərəbəl/ *adj* so impressive, beautiful etc. that nothing or no one is better: *her incomparable beauty/talents* **–incomparably** *adv*

**in·com·pat·i·ble** /ˌɪnkəm'pæt̮əbəl/ *adj* too different to be able to work together well or have a good relationship: *The software is **incompatible with** the operating system.* | *Tony and I have always been incompatible.* **–incompatibility** /ˌɪnkəmˌpætə'bɪlət̮i/ *n* [U]

**in·com·pe·tence** /ɪn'kɑmpət̮əns/ *n* [U] lack of ability or skill to do your job: *The doctor is being charged in court with incompetence.*

**in·com·pe·tent** /ɪn'kɑmpət̮ənt/ *adj* not having the ability or skill to do your job: *a totally incompetent waitress* **–incompetent** *n*

**in·com·plete** /ˌɪnkəmˈplit/ *adj* not having all its parts or not finished yet: *an incomplete sentence | The report is still incomplete.*

**in·com·pre·hen·si·ble** /ˌɪnkɑmprɪˈhɛnsə-bəl/ *adj* impossible to understand: *incomprehensible legal language*

**in·con·ceiv·a·ble** /ˌɪnkənˈsivəbəl/ *adj* too strange or unusual to seem real or possible: *It was inconceivable that such a quiet man could be violent.* —**inconceivably** *adj*

**in·con·clu·sive** /ˌɪnkənˈklusɪv/ *adj* not leading to any decision or result: *Our experiments are inconclusive. | inconclusive evidence* (=not proving anything) —**inconclusively** *adv*

**in·con·gru·ous** /ɪnˈkɑŋgruəs/ *adj* seeming to be wrong or unusual in a particular situation: *Her quiet voice seemed incongruous with her hard face.* —**incongruity** /ˌɪnkənˈgruəti/ *n* [C,U] —**incongruously** /ɪnˈkɑŋgruəsli/ *adv*

**in·con·se·quen·tial** /ˌɪnkɑnsəˈkwɛnʃəl/ *adj* FORMAL not important; INSIGNIFICANT: *an inconsequential role in a soap opera* —**inconsequentially** *adv*

**in·con·sid·er·ate** /ˌɪnkənˈsɪdərɪt/ *adj* not caring about other people's needs or feelings: *It was really inconsiderate of you not to call and say you'd be late.* —**inconsiderately** *adv* —opposite CONSIDERATE

**in·con·sist·en·cy** /ˌɪnkənˈsɪstənsi/ *n* **1** [C, U] information or a statement that cannot be true if the rest of the information or statement is true, or the state of being INCONSISTENT in this way: *The police became suspicious because of the inconsistencies in her statement.* **2** [U] the quality of changing your ideas too often or of doing something differently each time, so that people do not know what you think or want: *The team's inconsistency last season disappointed many fans.* —opposite CONSISTENCY

**in·con·sist·ent** /ˌɪnkənˈsɪstənt/ *adj* **1** two ideas or statements that are inconsistent are different and cannot both be true: *We're getting inconsistent results from the lab tests.* **2** not doing things in the same way each time, or not following an expected principle or standard: *I'm not being inconsistent! This is a different situation. | What they have done is inconsistent with the agreement that they made with us.* —**inconsistently** *adv* —opposite CONSISTENT

**in·con·sol·a·ble** /ˌɪnkənˈsoʊləbəl/ *adj* so sad that you cannot be comforted: *His widow was inconsolable.*

**in·con·spic·u·ous** /ˌɪnkənˈspɪkyuəs/ *adj* not easily seen or noticed: *I sat in the corner, trying to be as inconspicuous as possible.* —opposite CONSPICUOUS

**in·con·ti·nent** /ɪnˈkɑntˈn-ənt, -tənənt/ *adj* unable to control your BLADDER or BOWELS —**incontinence** *n* [U]

**in·con·tro·vert·i·ble** /ˌɪnkɑntrəˈvəṭəbəl/ *adj* an incontrovertible fact is definitely true:

*The police have incontrovertible evidence that he committed the crime.* —**incontrovertibly** *adv*

**in·con·ven·ience¹** /ˌɪnkənˈvinyəns/ *n* [C,U] something that causes you problems or difficulties, or the state of having problems or difficulties: *We apologize for any inconvenience caused by the delay to the bus service.*

**inconvenience²** *v* [T] to cause problems or difficulties for someone: *"I'll drive you home." "Are you sure? I don't want to inconvenience you."*

**in·con·ven·ient** /ˌɪnkənˈvinyənt/ *adj* causing problems or difficulties, especially in an annoying way: *I hope I haven't called at an inconvenient time.* —**inconveniently** *adv*

**in·cor·po·rate** /ɪnˈkɔrpəˌreɪt/ *v* [T] **1** to include something as part of a group, system etc.: *Several safety features have been incorporated into the car's design.* **2** to form a CORPORA-TION —**incorporation** /ɪnˌkɔrpəˈreɪʃən/ *n* [U]

**In·cor·po·rat·ed** /ɪnˈkɔrpəˌreɪṭɪd/ written abbreviation **Inc.** *adj* used after the name of a company in the US to show that it is a CORPORA-TION

**in·cor·rect** /ˌɪnkəˈrɛkt/ *adj* not correct; wrong: *incorrect spelling* —**incorrectly** *adv*

**in·cor·ri·gi·ble** /ɪnˈkɔrədʒəbəl, -ˈkɑr-/ *adj* someone who is incorrigible is bad in some way and cannot be changed: *an incorrigible liar*

**in·cor·rupt·i·ble** /ˌɪnkəˈrʌptəbəl/ *adj* too honest to be persuaded to do anything that is wrong: *an incorruptible judge*

**in·crease¹** /ɪnˈkris/ *v* [I,T] to become larger in number, amount, or degree or make something do this: *The price of gas has increased by 4%. | City populations are steadily increasing. | Smoking increases your chances of getting cancer.* —**increasing** *adj*: *increasing concern about job security* —opposite DECREASE¹

increase

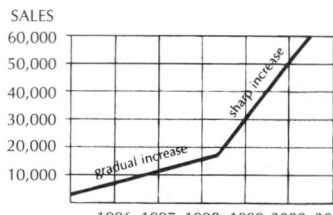

**in·crease²** /ˈɪŋkris/ *n* [C,U] a rise in number, amount, or degree: *There's been a huge increase in profits. | Crime in the city is on the increase.* (=increasing) —opposite DECREASE²

**in·creased** /ɪnˈkrist/ *adj* larger or more than before: *an increased awareness of environmental issues*

**in·creas·ing·ly** /ɪnˈkrisɪŋli/ *adv* more and more: *It's becoming increasingly difficult to find employment.*

**in·cred·i·ble** /ɪnˈkrɛdəbəl/ *adj* **1** extremely good, large, or impressive: *They serve the most incredible food there.* | *an incredible bargain* **2** very hard to believe: *It's incredible how much you remind me of your father.*

**in·cred·i·bly** /ɪnˈkrɛdəbli/ *adv* extremely: *It's incredibly beautiful here in the spring.*

**in·cred·u·lous** /ɪnˈkrɛdʒələs/ *adj* showing that you are unable or unwilling to believe something: *"They don't have a phone?" asked one incredulous woman.* —**incredulously** *adv* —**incredulity** /ˌɪnkrɪˈduləti/ *n* [U]

**in·cre·ment** /ˈɪnkrəmənt, ˈɪŋ-/ *n* an amount by which a value, number, or amount of money increases: *an annual salary increment of 2.9%* —**incremental** /ˌɪnkrəˈmɛnt̮l/ *adj*

**in·crim·i·nate** /ɪnˈkrɪməˌneɪt/ *v* [T] to make someone seem guilty of a crime: *He refused to incriminate himself by answering questions.* —**incriminating** *adj*: *incriminating evidence* —**incrimination** /ɪnˌkrɪməˈneɪʃən/ *n* [U]

**in·cu·bate** /ˈɪŋkyəˌbeɪt/ *v* [I,T] if a bird incubates its egg or if an egg incubates, it is kept warm under a bird's body until it HATCHes (=the baby bird comes out) —**incubation** /ˌɪŋkyəˈbeɪʃən/ *n* [U]

**in·cu·ba·tor** /ˈɪŋkyəˌbeɪt̮ɚ/ *n* **1** a machine for keeping eggs warm until the young birds HATCH (=come out) **2** a machine used by hospitals for keeping very small or weak babies alive

**in·cul·cate** /ˈɪnkʌlˌkeɪt, ɪnˈkʌlˌkeɪt/ *v* [T] FORMAL to make someone accept an idea by repeating it to him/her often

**in·cum·bent**[1] /ɪnˈkʌmbənt/ *n* a word meaning someone who has previously been elected to an official position, used during elections: *The election will be tough for the incumbents on the city council.*

**incumbent**[2] *adj* FORMAL **it is incumbent on/upon sb to do sth** if it is incumbent upon you to do something, it is your duty or responsibility to do it

**in·cur** /ɪnˈkɚ/ *v* **-rred, -rring** [T] to have something bad, such as a punishment or debt, happen because of something you have done: *The oil company incurred a debt of $5 million last year.*

**in·cur·a·ble** /ɪnˈkyʊrəbəl/ *adj* impossible to cure or stop: *an incurable disease* | *He's an incurable romantic.* (=he will never stop being romantic) —**incurably** *adv* —opposite CURABLE

**in·cur·sion** /ɪnˈkɚʒən/ *n* FORMAL a sudden attack or arrival into an area that belongs to other people

**in·debt·ed** /ɪnˈdɛt̮ɪd/ *adj* **be indebted to** to be very grateful to someone for the help s/he has given you: *I am indebted to my friend Catherine, who edited my manuscript.* —**indebtedness** *n* [U]

**in·de·cent** /ɪnˈdisənt/ *adj* **1** indecent behavior, clothes, or actions are likely to offend or shock people because they are against social or moral standards, or because they involve sex: *You can't wear a skirt that short - it's indecent!* | *indecent photographs* **2 indecent exposure** LAW the crime of deliberately showing your sex organs in a public place —**indecency** *n* [C,U] —compare DECENT

**in·de·ci·sion** /ˌɪndɪˈsɪʒən/ *n* [U] the state of not being able to make decisions: *After a week of indecision, we agreed to buy the house.*

**in·de·ci·sive** /ˌɪndɪˈsaɪsɪv/ *adj* **1** unable to make decisions: *He was criticized for being a weak indecisive leader.* **2** not having a clear result; INCONCLUSIVE: *an indecisive battle* —**indecisiveness** *n* [U]

**in·deed** /ɪnˈdid/ *adv* **1** used when adding more information to a statement: *Most people at that time were illiterate. Indeed, only 8% of the population could read.* **2** used when emphasizing a statement or a question: *"Vernon is one of the best pilots around." "Yes, indeed."*

**in·de·fen·si·ble** /ˌɪndɪˈfɛnsəbəl/ *adj* too bad to be excused or defended: *indefensible behavior*

**in·de·fin·a·ble** /ˌɪndɪˈfaɪnəbəl/ *adj* difficult to describe or explain: *For some indefinable reason she felt afraid.*

**in·def·i·nite** /ɪnˈdɛfənɪt/ *adj* **1** an indefinite action or period of time has no definite end arranged for it: *He was away in Alaska for an indefinite period.* **2** not clear or definite; VAGUE: *Our plans are still indefinite.*

**in·def·i·nite·ly** /ɪnˈdɛfənɪtli/ *adv* for a period of time without an arranged end: *I'll be staying here indefinitely.*

**in·del·i·ble** /ɪnˈdɛləbəl/ *adj* impossible to remove or forget; PERMANENT: *indelible ink* | *The movie left an indelible impression on her.* (=she could not forget it) —**indelibly** *adv*

**in·del·i·cate** /ɪnˈdɛlɪkɪt/ *adj* slightly impolite or offensive: *an indelicate question* —**indelicately** *adv*

**in·dem·ni·fy** /ɪnˈdɛmnəˌfaɪ/ *v* [T] LAW to promise to pay someone if something s/he owns becomes lost or damaged, or if s/he is injured

**in·dem·ni·ty** /ɪnˈdɛmnəti/ *n* LAW **1** [U] protection in the form of a promise to pay for any damage or loss **2** money that is paid to someone for any damages, losses, or injury

**in·dent** /ɪnˈdɛnt/ *v* [T] to start a line of writing closer to the middle of the page than the other lines

**in·den·ta·tion** /ˌɪndɛnˈteɪʃən/ *n* **1** a space at the beginning of a line of writing **2** a cut or space in the edge of something

**in·de·pend·ence** /ˌɪndɪˈpɛndəns/ *n* [U] **1** the freedom and ability to make your own decisions and take care of yourself without having to ask other people for help, money, or permission: *The apartments allow older people to keep their independence, while having medical care available.* **2** political freedom from control by another country: *The United States declared its independence in 1776.*

**Independence Day** /..'.. ,./ *n* [U] ⇨ FOURTH OF JULY

**in·de·pend·ent** /ˌɪndɪ'pɛndənt◂/ *adj* **1** confident, free, and not needing to ask other people for help, money, or permission to do something: *I feel so much more independent now that I'm working.* **2** not controlled by another government or organization: *India became an independent nation in 1947.* | *a European army independent of NATO* **3** not influenced by other people: *an independent report on the experiment* **–independently** *adv*

**in-depth** /ˌ. '.◂/ *adj* **in-depth study/report** a study or report that is very thorough and considers all the details

**in·de·scrib·a·ble** /ˌɪndɪ'skraɪbəbəl/ *adj* too good, strange, frightening etc. to be described: *My joy at seeing him was indescribable.*

**in·de·struct·i·ble** /ˌɪndɪ'strʌktəbəl/ *adj* impossible to destroy: *The tank was built to be indestructible.*

**in·de·ter·mi·nate** /ˌɪndɪ'tɚmənɪt/ *adj* impossible to find out or calculate exactly: *a dog of indeterminate breed* **–indeterminacy** /ˌɪndɪ'tɚmənɪsi/ *n* [U]

**in·dex¹** /'ɪndɛks/ *n, plural* **indexes** *or* **indices** /'ɪndə,siz/ **1** an alphabetical list at the end of a book, that lists all the names, subjects etc. in the book and the pages where you can find them **2** a set of cards with information, or a DATABASE in alphabetical order **3** a standard or level you can use for judging or measuring something by

**index²** *v* [T] to make an INDEX for something **–indexation** /ˌɪndɛk'seɪʃən/ *n*

**index card** /'.. ,./ *n* a small card for writing information on, used especially for INDEX*es*

**index fin·ger** /'.. ,../ *n* the finger next to the thumb; FOREFINGER **–see picture at** HAND¹

**In·di·an¹** /'ɪndiən/ *adj* **1** ⇨ NATIVE AMERICAN **2** relating to or coming from India

**Indian²** *n* **1** ⇨ NATIVE AMERICAN **2** someone from India

**Indian O·cean** /ˌ... '../ *n* **the Indian Ocean** the ocean between Africa in the west, India in the north, and Australia in the east

**Indian sum·mer** /ˌ... '../ *n* a period of warm weather in the fall

**in·di·cate** /'ɪndə,keɪt/ *v* [T] **1** to show that something exists or is likely to be true: *Research indicates that women live longer than men.* **2** to point at something: *Indicating a chair, he said, "Please, sit down."* **3** to say or do something that shows what you want or intend to do: *He indicated that he had no desire to come with us.*

**in·di·ca·tion** /ˌɪndə'keɪʃən/ *n* [C,U] a sign that something exists or is likely to be true: *Did Rick ever give any indication that he was unhappy?*

**in·dic·a·tive** /ɪn'dɪkət̮ɪv/ *adj* **be indicative of** to show that something exists or is likely to be true: *His reaction is indicative of how frightened he is.*

**in·di·ca·tor** /'ɪndə,keɪt̮ɚ/ *n* an event, fact etc. that shows that something exists, or shows you the way something is developing: *All the main economic indicators suggest that business is improving.*

**in·di·ces** /'ɪndə,siz/ *n* a plural of INDEX

**in·dict** /ɪn'daɪt/ *v* [I,T] LAW to officially charge someone with a crime **–indictable** /ɪn'daɪt̮əbəl/ *adj*

**in·dict·ment** /ɪn'daɪtmənt/ *n* **1 be an indictment of** to be a very clear sign that a system, method etc. is very bad or wrong: *It is an indictment of TV today that it doesn't make people think.* **2** LAW an official written statement saying that someone has done something illegal, or the act of making this statement

**in·dif·fer·ence** /ɪn'dɪfrəns/ *n* [U] lack of interest or concern: *I am amazed at the local government's indifference to the homeless people in our city.*

**in·dif·fer·ent** /ɪn'dɪfrənt/ *adj* not interested in someone or something, or not having any feelings or opinions about him, her, or it: *The industry seems indifferent to environmental concerns.*

**in·dig·e·nous** /ɪn'dɪdʒənəs/ *adj* indigenous plants, animals etc. have always lived or grown naturally in the place where they are: *plants indigenous to the Amazon region*

**in·di·gest·i·ble** /ˌɪndɪ'dʒɛstəbəl, -daɪ-/ *adj* food that is indigestible is difficult for the stomach to deal with **–see also** DIGEST¹

**in·di·ges·tion** /ˌɪndə'dʒɛstʃən, -daɪ-/ *n* [U] the pain caused by eating food that your stomach has difficulty DIGEST*ing*

**in·dig·nant** /ɪn'dɪgnənt/ *adj* angry because you feel you have been insulted or unfairly treated: *Indignant nurses said the hospital cared more about money than health care.* **–indignantly** *adv*

**in·dig·na·tion** /ˌɪndɪg'neɪʃən/ *n* [U] the feeling of being INDIGNANT: *Rich's indignation at not being chosen for the team was obvious.*

**in·dig·ni·ty** /ɪn'dɪgnət̮i/ *n* [C,U] a situation that makes you feel very ashamed and not respected: *They suffered the indignity of being tied up like animals.*

**in·di·rect** /ˌɪndə'rɛkt◂, -daɪ-/ *adj* **1** not directly caused by something or relating to it: *The accident was an indirect result of the heavy rain.* **2** not using the straightest or most direct way to get to a place: *an indirect route* **3** suggesting something without saying it directly or clearly: *He never mentioned my work,* *which I felt was an indirect criticism of its quality.* —**indirectly** *adv*

**indirect ar·ti·cle** /ˌ... '.../ *n* ⇨ ARTICLE

**indirect ob·ject** /ˌ... '../ *n* TECHNICAL in grammar, the person or thing that received something as the result of the action of the verb in a sentence. In the sentence "Pete gave me the money," "me" is the indirect object

**indirect speech** /ˌ... './ *n* TECHNICAL ⇨ RE-PORTED SPEECH

**in·dis·creet** /ˌɪndɪˈskrit/ *adj* careless about what you say or do, so that you let people know too much: *Try to stop him from saying anything indiscreet.*

**in·dis·cre·tion** /ˌɪndɪˈskrɛʃən/ *n* [C,U] an action, remark, or behavior that shows bad judgment and is usually considered socially or morally unacceptable: *his embarrassing sexual indiscretions | youthful indiscretion*

**in·dis·crim·i·nate** /ˌɪndɪˈskrɪmənɪt/ *adj* without considering whom or what you should choose, or without thinking about how he, she, or it will be affected: *indiscriminate acts of violence*

**in·dis·pen·sa·ble** /ˌɪndɪˈspɛnsəbəl/ *adj* someone or something that is indispensable is so important or useful that you cannot manage without him, her, or it: *The information he provided was **indispensable to** our research.*

**in·dis·pu·ta·ble** /ˌɪndɪˈspyut̮əbəl/ *adj* a fact that is indisputable must be accepted because it is definitely true —**indisputably** *adv*

**in·dis·tinct** /ˌɪndɪˈstɪŋkt/ *adj* not able to be seen, heard, or remembered very clearly: *indistinct voices in the next room* —**indistinctly** *adv*

**in·dis·tin·guish·a·ble** /ˌɪndɪˈstɪŋgwɪʃəbəl/ *adj* things that are indistinguishable are so similar that you cannot see any difference between them: *This material is **indistinguishable from** real silk.*

**in·di·vid·u·al**[1] /ˌɪndəˈvɪdʒuəl/ *adj* **1** considered separately from other people or things in the same group: *Each individual drawing is slightly different.* **2** belonging to or intended for one person rather than a group: *Individual attention must be given to each student.*

**individual**[2] *n* one person, considered separately from the rest of the group or society that s/he lives in: *the rights of the individual*

**in·di·vid·u·al·ism** /ˌɪndəˈvɪdʒuəlɪzəm/ *n* the belief or practice of allowing people to do things their own way without being influenced by other people —**individualist** *n* —**individualistic** /ˌɪndəˌvɪdʒuəˈlɪstɪk/ *adj*

**in·di·vid·u·al·i·ty** /ˌɪndəˌvɪdʒuˈæləti̮/ *n* [U] the quality that makes someone or something different from all others: *His individuality shows in his art work.*

**in·di·vid·u·al·ly** /ˌɪndəˈvɪdʒuəli, -dʒəli/ *adv*

separately, not together in a group: *Mr. Wong met with each employee individually.*

**in·di·vis·i·ble** /ˌɪndəˈvɪzəbəl/ *adj* not able to be separated or divided into parts —**indivisibly** *adv*

**in·doc·tri·nate** /ɪnˈdɑktrəˌneɪt/ *v* [T] to teach someone to accept a particular set of beliefs and not consider any others: *Schools may not indoctrinate children with religious beliefs.* —**indoctrination** /ɪnˌdɑktrəˈneɪʃən/ *n* [U]

**in·do·lent** /ˈɪndələnt/ *adj* FORMAL lazy —**indolently** *adv* —**indolence** *n* [U]

**in·dom·i·ta·ble** /ɪnˈdɑmət̮əbəl/ *adj* **indomitable spirit/courage etc.** FORMAL determination, courage etc. that can never be defeated

**in·door** /ˈɪndɔr/ *adj* used or happening inside a building: *an indoor swimming pool* —opposite OUTDOOR

**in·doors** /ˌɪnˈdɔrz/ *adv* into or inside a building: *It's raining - let's go indoors. | He stayed indoors all morning.* —opposite OUTDOORS

**in·duce** /ɪnˈdus/ *v* FORMAL **1** [T] to make someone decide to do something: *What **induced** you to spend so much money on a car?* **2** [T] to cause a particular physical condition: *This drug may induce drowsiness.* **3** [I,T] to make a woman give birth to her baby by giving her a special drug

**in·duce·ment** /ɪnˈdusmənt/ *n* [C,U] something that you are offered to persuade you to do something: *He was given $10,000 as an **inducement to** leave the company.*

**in·duct** /ɪnˈdʌkt/ *v* [T] to officially introduce someone into a group or organization, especially the army, navy etc. —**inductee** /ɪnˌdʌkˈti/ *n*

**in·duc·tion** /ɪnˈdʌkʃən/ *n* [C,U] the act or ceremony of officially introducing someone into a group or organization, especially the army, navy etc.

**in·dulge** /ɪnˈdʌldʒ/ *v* **1** [I,T] to let yourself do or have something that you enjoy, especially something that is considered bad for you: *I sometimes **indulge in** a cigarette at a party.* **2** [T] to let someone do or have whatever s/he wants, even if it is bad for him/her: *Ralph indulges his dogs terribly.*

**in·dul·gence** /ɪnˈdʌldʒəns/ *n* **1** [U] the habit of eating too much, drinking too much etc.: *a life of indulgence* **2** something that you do or have for pleasure, not because you need it: *Chocolate is my only indulgence.*

**in·dul·gent** /ɪnˈdʌldʒənt/ *adj* allowing someone to do or have whatever s/he wants, even if it is bad for him/her: *indulgent parents* —**indulgently** *adv*

**in·dus·tri·al** /ɪnˈdʌstriəl/ *adj* **1** relating to industry or the people working in industry: *industrial waste* **2** having many industries, or industries that are well developed: *an industrial region* —**industrially** *adv*

**in·dus·tri·al·ist** /ɪnˈdʌstriəlɪst/ *n* the owner of a factory, industrial company etc.

**in·dus·tri·al·ize** /ɪnˈdʌstriəˌlaɪz/ *v* [I,T] if a country or place is industrialized or if it industrializes, it develops a lot of industry —**industrialization** /ɪnˌdʌstriələˈzeɪʃən/ *n* [U]

**industrial park** /.ˌ.. ˈ./ *n* an area of land that has offices, businesses, small factories etc. on it

**in·dus·tri·ous** /ɪnˈdʌstriəs/ *adj* FORMAL tending to work hard: *an industrious young woman* —**industriously** *adv*

**in·dus·try** /ˈɪndəstri/ *n* **1** [U] the production of goods, especially in factories: *The country's economy is supported by industry.* **2** a particular type of trade or service that produces things: *the clothing industry*

**in·e·bri·at·ed** /ɪˈnibriˌeɪtɪd/ *adj* FORMAL drunk —**inebriation** /ɪˌnibriˈeɪʃən/ *n* [U]

**in·ed·i·ble** /ɪnˈɛdəbəl/ *adj* not suitable for eating: *inedible mushrooms*

**in·ef·fec·tive** /ˌɪnəˈfɛktɪv/ *adj* not achieving the correct effect or result: *an ineffective treatment for this disease* —**ineffectiveness** *n* [U]

**in·ef·fec·tu·al** /ˌɪnəˈfɛktʃuəl/ *adj* not achieving what someone or something is trying to do: *an ineffectual leader* —**ineffectually** *adv*

**in·ef·fi·cient** /ˌɪnəˈfɪʃənt/ *adj* not working well and wasting time, money, or energy: *an inefficient use of good farm land* —**inefficiently** *adv* —**inefficiency** *n* [C,U]

**in·el·e·gant** /ɪnˈɛləgənt/ *adj* not graceful or well done: *Her writing is sloppy and inelegant.*

**in·el·i·gi·ble** /ɪnˈɛlədʒəbəl/ *adj* not allowed to do or have something: *Non-citizens are* **ineligible to** *vote in the election.* —**ineligibility** /ɪnˌɛlədʒəˈbɪləti/ *n* [U]

**in·ept** /ɪˈnɛpt/ *adj* having no skill: *an inept driver* —**ineptitude** /ɪˈnɛptəˌtud/ *n* [U]

**in·e·qual·i·ty** /ˌɪnɪˈkwɑləti/ *n* [C,U] an unfair situation, in which some groups in society have less money or influence, or fewer opportunities than others: *There are many inequalities in our legal system.*

**in·eq·ui·ty** /ɪnˈɛkwəti/ *n* [C,U] FORMAL lack of fairness, or something that is unfair: *gross* **inequities** (=something very clearly unfair) *in the distribution of aid*

**in·ert** /ɪˈnɚt/ *adj* **1** TECHNICAL not producing a chemical reaction when combined with other substances: *inert gases* **2** not moving: *He checked her inert body for signs of life.*

**in·er·tia** /ɪˈnɚʃə/ *n* [U] **1** TECHNICAL the force that keeps an object in the same position or keeps it moving until it is moved or stopped by another force **2** a tendency for a situation to stay unchanged for a long time: *the problem of inertia in large bureaucracies* **3** a feeling that you do not want to do anything at all

**in·es·cap·a·ble** /ˌɪnəˈskeɪpəbəl/ *adj* FORMAL impossible to avoid: *The effects of the war are inescapable.* —**inescapably** *adv*

**in·es·sen·tial** /ˌɪnəˈsɛnʃəl/ *adj* FORMAL not necessary

**in·es·ti·ma·ble** /ɪnˈɛstəməbəl/ *adj* FORMAL too much or too great to be calculated —**inestimably** *adv*

**in·ev·i·ta·ble** /ɪˈnɛvətəbəl/ *adj* **1** certain to happen and impossible to avoid: *Death is inevitable.* **2 the inevitable** something that is certain to happen: *Finally, the inevitable happened and he lost his job* —**inevitability** /ɪˌnɛvətəˈbɪləti/ *n* [U]

**in·ev·i·ta·bly** *adv* /ɪnˈɛvətəbli/ as was certain to happen: *Inevitably, there were a few mistakes.* | *People inevitably gain some weight as they get older.*

**in·ex·act** /ˌɪnɪɡˈzækt/ *adj* not exact: *Psychology is an inexact science.* (=you cannot measure things exactly in it)

**in·ex·cus·a·ble** /ˌɪnɪkˈskyuzəbəl/ *adj* inexcusable behavior is too bad to be excused —**inexcusably** *adv*

**in·ex·haust·i·ble** /ˌɪnɪɡˈzɔstəbəl/ *adj* a supply that is inexhaustible exists in such large amounts that it can never be used up: *Warton seems to have an inexhaustible supply of energy.* —**inexhaustibly** *adv*

**in·ex·o·ra·ble** /ɪnˈɛksərəbəl/ *adj* FORMAL an inexorable process cannot be stopped: *the inexorable aging of the body* —**inexorably** *adv*

**in·ex·pen·sive** /ˌɪnɪkˈspɛnsɪv/ *adj* low in price: *an inexpensive vacation* —**inexpensively** *adv*

**in·ex·pe·ri·enced** /ˌɪnɪkˈspɪriənst/ *adj* not having much experience or knowledge: *an inexperienced driver* —**inexperience** *n* [U]

**in·ex·pli·ca·ble** /ˌɪnɪkˈsplɪkəbəl/ *adj* too unusual or strange to be explained or understood: *the inexplicable disappearance of the young man* —**inexplicably** *adv*

**in·ex·tri·ca·bly** /ˌɪnɪkˈstrɪkəbli/ *adv* FORMAL things that are inextricably connected or related cannot be separated from each other: *Smoking and lung cancer are* **inextricably linked.** —**inextricable** *adj*

**in·fal·li·ble** /ɪnˈfæləbəl/ *adj* **1** always right, and never making mistakes: *Many Catholics consider the Pope to be infallible.* **2** always having the intended effect: *an infallible cure for hiccups* —**infallibility** /ɪnˌfæləˈbɪləti/ *n* [U]

**in·fa·mous** /ˈɪnfəməs/ *adj* well known for being bad or evil: *an infamous criminal* —**infamously** *adv* —compare FAMOUS

**in·fa·my** /ˈɪnfəmi/ *n* [U] the state of being evil or of being well known for evil things

**in·fan·cy** /ˈɪnfənsi/ *n* [singular, U] **1** the period in a child's life before s/he can walk or talk: *Their son died in infancy.* **2 in its infancy** something that is in its infancy is just starting to be developed: *The project is still in its infancy.*

**in·fant** /'ɪnfənt/ *n* FORMAL a baby, especially one that cannot walk

**in·fan·tile** /'ɪnfən,taɪl, -təl/ *adj* **1** infantile behavior seems silly in an adult because it is typical of a child: *his infantile jokes* **2** affecting very small children: *infantile illnesses*

**in·fan·try** /'ɪnfəntri/ *n* [U] soldiers who fight on foot

**in·fat·u·at·ed** /ɪn'fætʃu,eɪtɪd/ *adj* having unreasonably strong feelings of love for someone: *He's infatuated with her.* —**infatuation** /ɪn,fætʃu'eɪʃən/ *n* [C,U]

**in·fect** /ɪn'fɛkt/ *v* [T] **1** to give someone a disease: *a young man infected with the AIDS virus* **2** to make food, water etc. dangerous and able to spread disease: *a bacteria that can infect fruit* **3** if a feeling that you have infects other people, it makes them begin to feel the same way: *Lucy's enthusiasm soon infected the rest of the class.*

**in·fect·ed** /ɪn'fɛktɪd/ *adj* **1** a wound that is infected has harmful BACTERIA in it that prevent it from getting better: *an infected finger* (=a finger with an infected wound) **2** food, water etc. that is infected contains BACTERIA that spread disease: *water infected with cholera*

**in·fec·tion** /ɪn'fɛkʃən/ *n* [C,U] a disease or sickness in a part of your body caused by BACTERIA or a VIRUS: *Wash the cut thoroughly to protect against infection.* | *an ear infection*

**in·fec·tious** /ɪn'fɛkʃəs/ *adj* **1** an infectious disease can be passed from one person to another **2** someone who is infectious has a disease that could be passed to other people **3** infectious feelings or laughter spread quickly from one person to another

**in·fer** /ɪn'fɚ/ *v* **-rred, -rring** [T] FORMAL to begin to have an opinion that something is probably true because of information that you have learned: *What can you infer from the available data?* —compare IMPLY

**in·fer·ence** /'ɪnfərəns/ *n* a belief or opinion you have, based on information that you already know: *You'll have to draw your own inferences from the evidence.* (=decide what you think is true)

**in·fe·ri·or**[1] /ɪn'fɪriɚ/ *adj* not good, or not as good in quality, value, or skill as someone or something else: *Larry always makes me feel inferior.* | *Her work is inferior to mine.* —**inferiority** /ɪn,fɪri'ɑrəti, -'ɔr-/ *n* [U] —opposite SUPERIOR[1]

**inferior**[2] *n* someone who has a lower position or rank than you in an organization —opposite SUPERIOR[2]

**in·fer·no** /ɪn'fɚnoʊ/ *n* LITERARY a very large and dangerous fire: *a raging inferno* (=an extremely violent fire)

**in·fer·tile** /ɪn'fɚtl/ *adj* **1** an infertile person or animal cannot have babies **2** infertile land

or soil is not good enough to grow plants in —**infertility** /,ɪnfɚ'tɪləti/ *n* [U]

**in·fest** /ɪn'fɛst/ *v* [T] if insects, rats etc. infest a place, they are there in large numbers and usually cause damage: *an old carpet infested with fleas* —**infestation** /,ɪnfɛ'steɪʃən/ *n* [C,U]

**in·fi·del** /'ɪnfədl, -,dɛl/ *n* OLD-FASHIONED a disapproving word for someone who does not believe in what you consider to be the true religion

**in·fi·del·i·ty** /,ɪnfə'dɛləti/ *n* [C,U] an act of being unfaithful to your wife or husband by having sex with someone else

**in·field** /'ɪnfild/ *n* [singular] the part of a baseball field inside the four bases —**infielder** *n* —see picture on page 472

**in·fight·ing** /'ɪn,faɪtɪŋ/ *n* [U] unfriendly competition and disagreement among members of the same group or organization: *political infighting*

**in·fil·trate** /ɪn'fɪl,treɪt, 'ɪnfɪl-/ *v* [I,T] to join an organization or enter a place, especially in order to find out secret information about it or to harm it: *The police have made several attempts to infiltrate the Mafia.* —**infiltrator** *n* —**infiltration** /,ɪnfɪl'treɪʃən/ *n* [U]

**in·fi·nite** /'ɪnfənɪt/ *adj* very great or without limits: *a teacher with infinite patience* | *an infinite universe*

**in·fi·nite·ly** /'ɪnfənɪtli/ *adv* very much: *This stove is infinitely better/worse than the other one.*

**in·fin·i·tes·i·mal** /,ɪnfɪnə'tɛsəməl/ *adj* extremely small: *infinitesimal changes in temperature* —**infinitesimally** *adv*

**in·fin·i·tive** /ɪn'fɪnətɪv/ *n* TECHNICAL in grammar, the basic form of a verb, used with "to." In the sentence "I forgot to buy milk," "to buy" is an infinitive

**in·fin·i·ty** /ɪn'fɪnəti/ *n* **1** [U] a space or distance without limits or an end **2** TECHNICAL a number that is larger than all others

**in·firm** /ɪn'fɚm/ *adj* FORMAL weak or ill, especially because of being old: *Aunt Louise has become old and infirm.*

**in·fir·ma·ry** /ɪn'fɚməri/ *n* FORMAL a place where sick people can receive medical treatment, especially in a place such as a school

**in·fir·mi·ty** /ɪn'fɚməti/ *n* [C,U] FORMAL bad health or a particular illness

**in·flame** /ɪn'fleɪm/ *v* [T] LITERARY to make someone have strong feelings of anger, excitement etc.

**in·flam·ma·ble** /ɪn'flæməbəl/ *adj* inflammable materials or substances will start to burn very easily: *Gasoline is highly inflammable* —opposite NONFLAMMABLE —compare FLAMMABLE —see usage note at FLAMMABLE

**in·flam·ma·tion** /,ɪnflə'meɪʃən/ *n* [C,U] swelling and soreness on or in a part of your

body, which is often red and hot to touch
–**inflamed** *adj*

**in·flam·ma·to·ry** /ɪnˈflæməˌtɔri/ *adj* FORMAL
an inflammatory speech, piece of writing etc. is
likely to make people angry

**in·flat·a·ble** /ɪnˈfleɪtəbəl/ *adj* an inflatable
object has to be filled with air before you can
use it: *an inflatable mattress*

Inflate

**in·flate** /ɪnˈfleɪt/ *v* **1** [I,T] to fill something
with air or gas, so that it becomes larger, or to
make something do this: *The machine quickly
inflates the tires.* **2** [T] to make something
larger in size, amount, or importance: *a policy
that inflates land prices* –opposite DEFLATE

**in·flat·ed** /ɪnˈfleɪtɪd/ *adj* **1** greater or larger
than is reasonable: *He has an inflated opinion of
his own importance.* **2** filled with air or gas:
*an inflated balloon*

**in·fla·tion** /ɪnˈfleɪʃən/ *n* [U] **1** a continuing
increase in prices or the rate at which prices increase: *the Mexican government's efforts to control inflation* **2** the process of filling something
with air or gas

**in·fla·tion·a·ry** /ɪnˈfleɪʃəˌnɛri/ *adj* relating to
or causing price increases: *inflationary wage increases*

**in·flex·i·ble** /ɪnˈflɛksəbəl/ *adj* **1** impossible
to influence or change: *a school with inflexible
rules* **2** inflexible material is stiff and will not
bend –**inflexibility** /ɪnˌflɛksəˈbɪləti/ *n* [U]

**in·flict** /ɪnˈflɪkt/ *v* [T] to make someone suffer
something unpleasant: *the damage inflicted on/
upon the enemy* –**infliction** /ɪnˈflɪkʃən/ *n* [U]

**in·flu·ence**[1] /ˈɪnfluəns/ *n* **1** [C,U] the
power to have an effect on the way someone or
something develops, behaves, or thinks: *Vince
used his influence with the union to get his
nephew a job.* **2** someone or something that
has an effect on other people or things: *Alex's
parents always thought that I was a good/bad
influence on him.* **3** under the influence
drunk or feeling the effects of a drug

**influence**[2] *v* [T] to have an effect on the way
someone or something develops, behaves, or
thinks: *I don't want to influence your deci-
sion.* | *He lets his brother influence him too
much.*

**in·flu·en·tial** /ˌɪnfluˈɛnʃəl/ *adj* having a lot of
influence: *an influential politician* –**influ-
entially** *adv*

**in·flu·en·za** /ˌɪnfluˈɛnzə/ *n* [U] FORMAL ⇨ FLU

**in·flux** /ˈɪnflʌks/ *n* [C usually singular] the
arrival of large numbers of people or things: *an
influx of cheap imported goods*

**in·fo** /ˈɪnfoʊ/ *n* [U] INFORMAL ⇨ INFORMATION

**in·fo·mer·cial** /ˈɪnfoʊˌmɚʃəl/ *n* a long television advertisement that is made to seem like a
regular program

**in·form** /ɪnˈfɔrm/ *v* [T] to formally tell someone about something: *Please inform us of any
progress.*

  **inform against/on** sb *phr v* [T] to tell the police, an enemy etc. about what someone has
done

**in·for·mal** /ɪnˈfɔrməl/ *adj* **1** relaxed and
friendly: *an informal meeting* **2** suitable for
ordinary situations or conversations: *an informal
letter to your family* –**informally** *adv*
–**informality** /ˌɪnfɔrˈmæləti/ *n* [U]

**in·form·ant** /ɪnˈfɔrmənt/ *n* someone who
gives secret information to the police, a government department etc.: *a CIA informant*

**in·for·ma·tion** /ˌɪnfɚˈmeɪʃən/ *n* [U] **1** facts
or details that tell you something about a situation, person, event etc.: *I need some more in-
formation about/on this machine.* | *Goodwin
was able to provide several new pieces of information.* **2** a telephone service that you can
call to get someone's telephone number

**Information su·per·high·way** /...,.. '.'../ *n*
[singular] the system of computer connections
that people anywhere in the world can use in
order to electronically send or obtain information, pictures, sounds etc.

**information tech·nol·o·gy** /...,.. .'.../, **IT** *n*
[U] the use of electronic processes, especially
computers, for gathering information, storing it,
and making it available

**in·form·a·tive** /ɪnˈfɔrmətɪv/ *adj* providing
many useful facts or ideas: *a very informative
book* –**informatively** *adv*

**in·formed** /ɪnˈfɔrmd/ *adj* having a lot of
knowledge or information about a particular
subject or situation: *Women should be able
to make an informed choice about con-
traception.* | *well-informed voters* –opposite
UNINFORMED

**in·form·er** /ɪnˈfɔrmɚ/ *n* ⇨ INFORMANT

**in·fo·tain·ment** /ˌɪnfoʊˈteɪnmənt/ *n* [U]
television programs that present news and other
types of information in an entertaining way

**in·frac·tion** /ɪnˈfrækʃən/ *n* [C,U] FORMAL an
act of breaking a rule or law

**in·fra·red** /ˌɪnfrəˈrɛd◂/ *adj* infrared light produces heat but cannot be seen –compare ULTRA-
VIOLET

**in·fra·struc·ture** /ˈɪnfrəˌstrʌktʃɚ/ *n* the basic systems that a country or organization needs
in order to work in the right way: *Japan's economic infrastructure*

**in·fre·quent** /ɪnˈfrikwənt/ *adj* not happening often: *one of our infrequent visits to Uncle Edwin's house* —**infrequently** *adv*

**in·fringe** /ɪnˈfrɪndʒ/ *v* [T] to do something that is against the law or that limits someone's legal rights: *The new law infringes on our basic right to freedom of speech.* —**infringement** *n* [C,U]

**in·fu·ri·ate** /ɪnˈfyʊri‚eɪt/ *v* [T] to make someone very angry: *He really infuriates me!*

**in·fu·ri·at·ing** /ɪnˈfyʊri‚eɪtɪŋ/ *adj* very annoying: *an infuriating delay of four hours* —**infuriatingly** *adv*

**in·fuse** /ɪnˈfyuz/ *v* **1** [T] to fill someone or something with a particular feeling or quality: *The coach has managed to infuse the team with new enthusiasm.* **2** [I,T] to put a substance such as tea in very hot water, so that its taste passes into the water —**infusion** /ɪnˈfyuʒən/ *n* [C,U]

**in·ge·nious** /ɪnˈdʒinyəs/ *adj* **1** an ingenious plan, idea, etc. works well and is the result of intelligent thinking and new ideas **2** an ingenious person is very good at inventing things, thinking of new ideas etc. —**ingeniously** *adv*

**in·ge·nu·i·ty** /‚ɪndʒəˈnuəti/ *n* [U] skill at inventing things, thinking of new ideas etc.

**in·gest** /ɪnˈdʒɛst/ *v* [T] TECHNICAL to eat something —**ingestion** *n* [U]

**in·grained** /ɪnˈgreɪnd, ˈɪngreɪnd/ *adj* **1** ingrained attitudes or behavior are firmly established and difficult to change **2** ingrained dirt is under the surface of something and difficult to remove

**in·gra·ti·ate** /ɪnˈgreɪʃi‚eɪt/ *v* **ingratiate yourself (with)** DISAPPROVING to try to get someone's approval by doing things to please him/her, expressing admiration etc.: *a politician trying to ingratiate himself with the voters* —**ingratiating** *adj* —**ingratiatingly** *adv*

**in·grat·i·tude** /ɪnˈgrætə‚tud/ *n* [U] the quality of not being grateful for something —**ingrate** /ˈɪngreɪt/ *n*

**in·gre·di·ent** /ɪnˈgridiənt/ *n* **1** one of the things that goes into a mixture from which a type of food is made: *Flour, water, and eggs are the main ingredients.* **2** a quality that helps to achieve something: *Imagination and hard work are the ingredients of success.*

**in·hab·it** /ɪnˈhæbɪt/ *v* [T] to live in a particular place: *a forest inhabited by bears and moose* —**inhabitable** *adj*

**in·hab·it·ant** /ɪnˈhæbətənt/ *n* one of the people who live in a particular place: *the inhabitants of large cities*

**in·hale** /ɪnˈheɪl/ *v* [I,T] to breathe in air, smoke, or gas: *Try not to inhale the fumes from the glue.* —**inhalation** /‚ɪnhəˈleɪʃən/ *n* [C,U]

**in·hal·er** /ɪnˈheɪlɚ/ *n* a plastic tube containing medicine that someone, especially someone with

ASTHMA, breathes in order to make his/her breathing easier

**in·her·ent** /ɪnˈhɪrənt, -ˈhɛr-/ *adj* a quality that is inherent in something is a natural part of it and cannot be separated from it: *a problem that is inherent in the system* —**inherently** *adv*

**in·her·it** /ɪnˈhɛrɪt/ *v* **1** [I,T] to receive something from someone after s/he has died: *I inherited the house from my uncle.* **2** [T] to get a quality, type of behavior, appearance etc. from one of your parents: *Tony inherited his father's nose.*

**in·her·i·tance** /ɪnˈhɛrɪţəns/ *n* [C,U] money, property etc. that you receive from someone after s/he has died

**in·hib·it** /ɪnˈhɪbɪt/ *v* [T] **1** to prevent something from growing or developing in the usual or expected way: *new treatments to inhibit the spread of the disease* **2** to make someone feel embarrassed or less confident, so s/he cannot do or say what s/he wants to: *Fear of criticism may inhibit a child's curiosity.*

**in·hib·it·ed** /ɪnˈhɪbɪţɪd/ *adj* not confident or relaxed enough to express how you really feel or do what you really want to do: *Julie's too inhibited to talk about sex.* —opposite UNINHIBITED

**in·hi·bi·tion** /‚ɪnhɪˈbɪʃən, ‚ɪnə-/ *n* [C,U] a feeling of worry or embarrassment that stops you from expressing how you really feel or doing what you really want to do: *She soon loses her inhibitions* (=stops feeling worried etc.) *when she's had a few glasses of wine.*

**in·hos·pi·ta·ble** /‚ɪnhɑˈspɪţəbəl/ *adj* **1** not friendly, welcoming, or generous to visitors **2** difficult to live or stay in because of severe weather conditions or lack of shelter: *an inhospitable climate* —**inhospitably** *adv*

**in-house** /‚ɪnˈhaʊs‹ / *adj, adv* within a company or organization rather than outside it: *an in-house training department*

**in·hu·man** /ɪnˈhyumən/ *adj* **1** very cruel and without any normal feelings of pity: *inhuman punishment* **2** lacking any human qualities in a way that seems strange or frightening: *an inhuman scream*

**in·hu·mane** /‚ɪnhyuˈmeɪn/ *adj* treating people or animals in a cruel and unacceptable way: *inhumane living conditions* —**inhumanely** *adv*

**in·hu·man·i·ty** /‚ɪnhyuˈmænəţi/ *n* [C,U] extreme cruelty or an act of cruelty: *the inhumanities of war*

**in·im·i·ta·ble** /ɪˈnɪməţəbəl/ *adj* too good for anyone else to copy: *Sinatra sings in his own inimitable style.*

**i·ni·tial¹** /ɪˈnɪʃəl/ *adj* happening at the beginning; first: *the initial stages of the disease* —**initially** *adv*

**initial²** *n* the first letter of a name: *a suitcase with the initials S.H. on it*

**initial³** *v* [T] to write your INITIALs on a document: *Could you initial this form for me, please?*

**i·ni·ti·ate** /ɪˈnɪʃiˌeɪt/ v [T] **1** FORMAL to arrange for something important to start: *The prison has recently initiated new security procedures.* **2** to introduce someone into an organization, club etc., usually with a special ceremony: *students initiated into the school's honor society* −**initiation** /ɪˌnɪʃiˈeɪʃən/ n [C,U]

**i·ni·tia·tive** /ɪˈnɪʃətɪv/ n **1** [U] the ability to make decisions and take action without waiting for someone to tell you what to do: *Try using your own initiative.* (=doing something without being told what to do) **2** a plan or process that has been started in order to achieve a particular aim or to solve a particular problem: *state initiatives to reduce spending* **3** **take the initiative** to be the first one to take action to achieve a particular aim or solve a particular problem

**in·ject** /ɪnˈdʒɛkt/ v [T] **1** to put a liquid, especially a drug, into your body by using a special needle: *The rat has been injected with a new drug.* **2** to improve something by adding an important thing or quality to it: *remarks that injected some humor into the situation*

**in·jec·tion** /ɪnˈdʒɛkʃən/ n **1** [C,U] an act of putting a liquid, especially a drug, into your body by using a special needle: *The nurse gave me an injection.* **2** an addition of an important thing or quality to something in order to improve it: *The business received a cash injection of $20,000.*

**in·junc·tion** /ɪnˈdʒʌŋkʃən/ n LAW an official order given by a court that stops someone from being allowed to do something

**in·jure** /ˈɪndʒɚ/ v [T] to hurt a person or animal: *She was badly injured in the accident.* −**injured** adj −**injurious** /ɪnˈdʒʊriəs/ adj −see usage note at WOUND²

**in·ju·ry** /ˈɪndʒəri/ n [C,U] physical harm or damage that is caused by an accident or attack, or a particular example of this: *serious injuries to the head and neck*

**in·jus·tice** /ɪnˈdʒʌstɪs/ n [C,U] a situation in which people are treated very unfairly: *a history of injustices against Black people*

**ink** /ɪŋk/ n [U] a colored liquid used for writing, printing etc.

**ink·ling** /ˈɪŋklɪŋ/ n **have an inkling** to have a slight idea about something: *We had no inkling that he was leaving.*

**in·laid** /ˈɪnleɪd, ɪnˈleɪd/ adj having a thin layer of a material set into the surface for decoration: *a wooden box inlaid with gold*

**in·land¹** /ˈɪnlənd/ adj an inland area, city etc. is not near the coast

**in·land²** /ɪnˈlænd, ˈɪnlænd, -lənd/ adv in a direction away from the coast and toward the center of a country: *driving inland*

**in-laws** /ˈ. ./ n [plural] INFORMAL your relatives by marriage, especially the mother and father of your husband or wife: *We're spending Christmas with my in-laws.*

**in·lay** /ˈɪnleɪ/ n [C,U] a material that has been set into the surface of another material as a decoration, or the pattern made by this

**in·let** /ˈɪnlɛt, ˈɪnlət/ n **1** a narrow area of water reaching from the sea or a lake into the land, or between islands **2** the part of a machine through which liquid or gas flows in

**in-line skate** /ˌ. . ˈ./ n a special boot with a single row of wheels fixed under it −compare ROLLER SKATE

**in·mate** /ˈɪnmeɪt/ n someone who is kept in a prison or in a hospital for people with mental illnesses

**inn** /ɪn/ n a small hotel, especially one that is not in a city

**in·nards** /ˈɪnɚdz/ n [plural] INFORMAL **1** the parts inside your body, especially your stomach **2** the parts inside a machine: *the innards of the computer*

**in·nate** /ˌɪˈneɪt◂/ adj an innate quality has been part of your character since you were born: *an innate sense of fun* −**innately** adv

**in·ner** /ˈɪnɚ/ adj **1** on the inside or close to the center of something: *the inner ear* −opposite OUTER **2** inner feelings, thoughts, meanings etc. are secret and not expressed **3** **inner circle** the few people in an organization, political party etc. who control it or share power with its leader

**inner cit·y** /ˌ.. ˈ../ n the part of a city that is near the middle, especially the part where the buildings are in a bad condition and the people are poor: *Crime in our inner cities seems to be getting worse.* −**inner city** adj: *an inner city school*

**in·ner·most** /ˈɪnɚˌmoʊst/ adj **1** your innermost feelings, desires etc. are the ones you feel most strongly and keep private **2** FORMAL farthest inside −opposite OUTERMOST

**inner tube** /ˈ.. ˌ./ n the rubber tube that is filled with air inside a tire

**in·ning** /ˈɪnɪŋ/ n one of the nine playing periods in a game of baseball

**inn·keep·er** /ˈɪnˌkipɚ/ n OLD-FASHIONED someone who owns or manages an INN

**in·no·cence** /ˈɪnəsəns/ n [U] **1** the fact of not being guilty of a crime: *How did they prove her innocence?* **2** the state of not having much experience of life, especially experience of bad or complicated things: *a child's innocence*

**in·no·cent** /ˈɪnəsənt/ adj **1** not guilty of a crime: *Nobody would believe that I was innocent.* | *He was found innocent of murder by the jury.* (=they decided he was innocent) **2** not having much experience of life, especially so that you are easily deceived: *I was 13 years old and very innocent.* **3** done or said without intending to harm or offend anyone: *an innocent remark* −**innocently** adv

**in·noc·u·ous** /ɪ'nɑkyuəs/ *adj* not offensive, dangerous, or harmful: *an innocuous but boring movie* **–innocuously** *adv*

**in·no·va·tion** /ˌɪnə'veɪʃən/ *n* [C,U] the introduction of new ideas, methods, or inventions, or the idea, method, or invention itself: *recent innovations in computing | The west coast has been the center of innovation in the computer industry.* **–innovate** /'ɪnə͵veɪt/ *v* [I] **–innovative** *adj* **–innovator** *n*

**in·nu·en·do** /ˌɪnyu'ɛndoʊ/ *n, plural* **innuendoes** *or* **innuendos** [C,U] an indirect remark about sex or about something bad that someone has done, or the act of making this type of remark: *nasty innuendos about Laurie and the boss*

**in·nu·mer·a·ble** /ɪ'numərəbəl/ *adj* too many to be counted: *innumerable stars*

**in·oc·u·late** /ɪ'nɑkyə͵leɪt/ *v* [T] to protect someone against a disease by introducing a weak form of it into his/her body: *Children should be inoculated against measles.* **–inoculation** /ɪ͵nɑkyə'leɪʃən/ *n* [C,U]

**in·of·fen·sive** /ˌɪnə'fɛnsɪv/ *adj* unlikely to offend anyone: *a quiet inoffensive man*

**in·op·por·tune** /ɪn͵ɑpɚ'tun, ͵ɪnɑ-/ *adj* FORMAL not suitable or not good for a particular situation: *They arrived at an inopportune moment.*

**in·or·di·nate** /ɪn'ɔrdn-ɪt/ *adj* FORMAL much greater than is reasonable: *an inordinate amount of work* **–inordinately** *adv*

**in·or·gan·ic** /ˌɪnɔr'gænɪk/ *adj* not consisting of anything that is living: *inorganic matter* **–inorganically** *adv*

**in·pa·tient** /'ɪnpeɪʃənt/ *n* someone who stays in a hospital at least one night for medical treatment **–compare** OUTPATIENT

**in·put** /'ɪnpʊt/ *n* [singular, U] **1** ideas, advice, money, or effort that you put into a job, meeting etc. in order to help it succeed: *Students are allowed input into what they learn in class.* **2** information that is put into a computer **3** electrical power that is put into a machine for it to use **–compare** OUTPUT

**in·quest** /'ɪnkwɛst/ *n* LAW an official process to find out the cause of a sudden or unexpected death, especially if there is a possibility that the death is the result of a crime

**in·quire** /ɪn'kwaɪɚ/ *v* [I,T] FORMAL to ask someone for information: *I am writing to inquire about your advertisement in the New York Post.* **–inquirer** *n* **–see usage note at** ASK

**inquire into** sth *phr v* [T] to ask questions in order to get more information about something or to find out why something happened: *The investigation will inquire into the reasons for the disaster.*

**in·quir·ing** /ɪn'kwaɪərɪŋ/ *adj* wanting to find out more about something: *Dad taught us to have inquiring minds.* (=taught us to ask questions about things) **–inquiringly** *adv*

**in·quir·y** /ɪn'kwaɪəri, 'ɪŋkwəri/ *n* **1** a question you ask in order to get information: *We're getting a lot of inquiries about our new train service.* **2** [C,U] the act of asking questions in order to get information about something or to find out why something happened, or the series of meetings in which this is done: *There will be an official inquiry into the incident.*

**in·qui·si·tion** /ˌɪnkwə'zɪʃən/ *n* [singular] FORMAL a series of questions that someone asks in a threatening or unpleasant way

**in·quis·i·tive** /ɪn'kwɪzətɪv/ *adj* interested in a lot of different things and wanting to find out more about them: *a cheerful inquisitive little boy*

**in·roads** /'ɪnroʊdz/ *n* **make inroads into/on** to become more and more successful, powerful, or popular and so take away power, trade, votes etc. from a competitor or enemy: *Their new soft drink is already making huge inroads into the market.*

**ins and outs** /ˌ. . '. / *n* [plural] all the exact details of a complicated situation, system, problem etc.: *I'm still learning the ins and outs of my new job.*

**in·sane** /ɪn'seɪn/ *adj* **1** INFORMAL completely stupid or crazy, often in a way that is dangerous: *You must've been totally insane to go with him! | an insane idea* **2** someone who is insane is permanently and seriously mentally ill **–insanely** *adv*

**in·san·i·ty** /ɪn'sænəti/ *n* [U] **1** very stupid actions that may cause you serious harm: *the insanity of war* **2** the state of being seriously mentally ill

**in·sa·tia·ble** /ɪn'seɪʃəbəl/ *adj* always wanting more and more of something: *an insatiable appetite*

**in·scribe** /ɪn'skraɪb/ *v* [T] to cut, print, or write words on something, especially on the surface of a stone or coin: *a tree inscribed with the initials J.S.* **–inscription** /ɪn'skrɪpʃən/ *n*

**in·scru·ta·ble** /ɪn'skrutəbəl/ *adj* not easily understood, because you cannot tell what someone is thinking or feeling: *an inscrutable smile* **–inscrutably** *adv*

**in·sect** /'ɪnsɛkt/ *n* a small creature such as an ANT or a fly, with six legs and a body divided into three parts

**in·sec·ti·cide** /ɪn'sɛktə͵saɪd/ *n* [U] a chemical substance used for killing insects

**in·se·cure** /ˌɪnsɪ'kyʊr/ *adj* **1** not feeling confident about yourself, your abilities, your relationships etc.: *She's very shy and insecure.* **2** not safe or not protected: *She feels that her position in the company is insecure.* (=she may lose her job) **–insecurity** *n* [U] **–insecurely** *adv*

**in·sem·i·na·tion** /ɪn͵sɛmə'neɪʃən/ *n* [U] the act of putting SPERM into a female's body in order to make her have a baby: *the artificial insemination of cattle* (=done by medical treatment, not sex)

**in·sen·si·tive** /ɪnˈsɛnsəṭɪv/ *adj* **1** not noticing other people's feelings, and not realizing that something that you do will upset them: *Sue asked several insensitive questions about Carla's recent divorce.* **2** not affected by physical effects or changes: *Some people are more insensitive to pain than others.* −**insensitively** *adv* −**insensitivity** /ɪnˌsɛnsəˈtɪvəṭi/ *n* [U]

**in·sep·a·ra·ble** /ɪnˈsɛpərəbəl/ *adj* **1** people who are inseparable are always together and are very friendly with each other: *When they were younger, the boys were inseparable.* **2** unable to be separated or not able to be considered separately: *The patient's mental and physical problems are inseparable.* −**inseparably** *adv*

**in·sert**[1] /ɪnˈsɚt/ *v* [T] to put something inside or into something else: *Insert the key in/into the lock.* −**insertion** /ɪnˈsɚʃən/ *n* [C,U]

**in·sert**[2] /ˈɪnsɚt/ *n* **1** something that is designed to be put inside something else: *Dan wears special inserts in his shoes to make him look taller.* **2** printed pages that are put inside a newspaper or magazine in order to advertise something

**in·side**[1] /ɪnˈsaɪd, ˈɪnsaɪd/ *prep adv* **1** in a container, room, building etc.: *He opened the box to find two kittens inside.* | *Go/come inside* (=into the house) *and get your jacket.* −opposite OUTSIDE[1] **2** if you have a feeling or thought inside you, you feel or think it but do not always express it: *You never know what's happening inside his head.* | *Don't keep the anger inside.* **3** used in order to emphasize that what is happening in a country or organization is only known by people who live there: *People inside the organization have told us that changes are happening.* **4** in less time than: *We'll be there inside of an hour.*

**inside**[2] *n* **1** **the inside** the inner part of something: *The inside of the house was nicer than the outside.* **2** **inside out** with the usual outside parts on the inside: *Your shirt is on inside out.* **3** **know/learn sth inside out** to know everything about a subject: *She knows the business inside out.* −opposite OUTSIDE

**inside**[3] *adj* **1** on or facing the inside of something: *the inside pages of a magazine* **2** **inside information/the inside story** information that is known only by people who are part of an organization, company etc.

**in·sid·er** /ɪnˈsaɪdɚ/ *n* someone who has a special knowledge of a particular organization because s/he is part of it

**in·sid·i·ous** /ɪnˈsɪdiəs/ *adj* happening gradually without being noticed, but causing great harm: *the insidious effects of breathing polluted air* −**insidiously** *adv*

**in·sight** /ˈɪnsaɪt/ *n* [C,U] the ability to understand something clearly, or an example of this: *The article gives us a real insight into Chinese culture.*

**in·sig·ni·a** /ɪnˈsɪɡniə/ *n, plural* **insignia** a BADGE or other object that shows what official or military rank someone has, or which group or organization s/he belongs to

**in·sig·nif·i·cant** /ˌɪnsɪɡˈnɪfəkənt/ *adj* too small or unimportant to consider or worry about: *an insignificant change in the unemployment rate* −**insignificantly** *adv* −**insignificance** *n* [U]

**in·sin·cere** /ˌɪnsɪnˈsɪr/ *adj* pretending to be pleased, sympathetic etc., but not really meaning what you say: *an insincere smile* −**insincerely** *adv* −**insincerity** /ˌɪnsɪnˈsɛrəṭi/ *n* [U]

**in·sin·u·ate** /ɪnˈsɪnyuˌeɪt/ *v* [T] to say something that seems to mean something unpleasant, without saying it directly: *Are you insinuating that she didn't deserve the promotion?* −**insinuation** /ɪnˌsɪnyuˈeɪʃən/ *n* [C,U]

**in·sip·id** /ɪnˈsɪpɪd/ *adj* not interesting, exciting, or attractive: *the movie's insipid story* | *his insipid voice* | *the insipid taste of weak tea* −**insipidly** *adv*

**in·sist** /ɪnˈsɪst/ *v* [I] **1** to say firmly and again and again that something is true, especially when other people think it may not be true: *Mike insisted that Joelle would never have gone by herself.* **2** to demand that something should happen: *I insisted that he leave.* | *They're insisting on your resignation.* −see usage note at RECOMMEND

**in·sist·ence** /ɪnˈsɪstəns/ *n* [U] the act of INSISTing that something should happen: *He came, but only at my insistence.*

**in·sist·ent** /ɪnˈsɪstənt/ *adj* INSISTing that something should happen: *She's very insistent that we should all be on time.* −**insistently** *adv*

**in so far as, insofar as** /ˌɪnsoʊˈfɑr əz/ *conjunction* FORMAL to the degree that something affects another thing: *Insofar as sales are concerned, the company is doing very well.*

**in·so·lent** /ˈɪnsələnt/ *adj* rude and not showing any respect: *He was suspended for being insolent to the principal.* −**insolence** *n* [U] −**insolently** *adv*

**in·sol·u·ble** /ɪnˈsɑlyəbəl/ *adj* **1** an insoluble substance does not DISSOLVE when you put it into a liquid **2** *also* **insolvable** impossible to explain or solve: *a number of seemingly insoluble conflicts in the region*

**in·sol·vent** /ɪnˈsɑlvənt/ *adj* FORMAL not having enough money to pay what you owe −**insolvency** *n* [U]

**in·som·ni·a** /ɪnˈsɑmniə/ *n* [U] the condition

of not being able to sleep –**insomniac** /ɪnˈsɑmniˌæk/ *n*

**in·spect** /ɪnˈspɛkt/ *v* [T] **1** to examine something carefully: *Inspect the car for dents before you buy it.* **2** to make an official visit to a building, organization etc. to check that everything is satisfactory and that rules are being obeyed: *The building is regularly inspected by the fire department.*

**in·spec·tion** /ɪnˈspɛkʃən/ *n* [C,U] the act of carefully checking an object's condition, or an organization, in order to be sure that it is obeying rules: *The restaurant is due for a health inspection this month.* | *a close inspection of the soldiers' living areas*

**in·spec·tor** /ɪnˈspɛktɚ/ *n* **1** an official whose job is to INSPECT something: *a health inspector* **2** a police officer of middle rank

**in·spi·ra·tion** /ˌɪnspəˈreɪʃən/ *n* [C,U] **1** something or someone that encourages you to do or produce something good: *Dante was the **inspiration for** my book on Italy.* | *Her hard work and imagination should be an **inspiration** to everyone.* **2** a good idea: *I've had an inspiration - let's go to the lake!* –**inspirational** *adj*

**in·spire** /ɪnˈspaɪɚ/ *v* [T] **1** to encourage someone to do or produce something good: *We were inspired by the coach's pre-game pep talk.* **2** to make someone have a particular feeling: *The captain **inspires** confidence **in** his men.* –**inspiring** *adj*

**in·spired** /ɪnˈspaɪɚd/ *adj* having very exciting special qualities: *Abraham Lincoln was an inspired leader.*

**in·sta·bil·i·ty** /ˌɪnstəˈbɪləti/ *n* [U] the state of being uncertain and likely to change suddenly: *the political instability in the region*

**in·stall** /ɪnˈstɔl/ *v* [T] **1** to put a piece of equipment somewhere and connect it so that it is ready to be used: *The school is installing a new furnace.* **2** to put someone in an important job or position, especially with a ceremony: *The college is installing a new chancellor.* –**installation** /ˌɪnstəˈleɪʃən/ *n* [C,U]

**in·stall·ment** /ɪnˈstɔlmənt/ *n* **1** one of a series of regular payments that you make until you have paid all the money you owe: *I'm paying for the car **in** monthly **installments**.* **2** one of the parts of a story that appears as a series in a magazine, newspaper etc.

**in·stance** /ˈɪnstəns/ *n* **1** **for instance** for example: *You can't depend on her. For instance, she arrived an hour late for an important meeting yesterday.* **2** an example of a particular fact, event etc.: *reports on **instances** of police brutality*

**in·stant¹** /ˈɪnstənt/ *adj* **1** happening or produced immediately: *The movie was an instant success.* **2** instant food, coffee etc. is in the

form of powder and is prepared by adding hot water

**instant²** *n* **1** [C usually singular] a moment in time: *I didn't believe her for an instant.* **2** **this instant** SPOKEN now, without delay: *Come here this instant!*

**in·stan·ta·ne·ous** /ˌɪnstənˈteɪniəs/ *adj* happening immediately: *an instantaneous reaction to the drug* –**instantaneously** *adv*

**in·stant·ly** /ˈɪnstəntli/ *adv* immediately: *He was killed instantly.*

**instant re·play** /ˌ.. ˈ../ *n* the immediate repeating of an important moment in a sports game on television by showing the film again

**in·stead** /ɪnˈstɛd/ *adv* **1** **instead of** in place of someone or something: *I'll have lamb instead of beef.* | *Why don't you do something, instead of just talking about it!* **2** in place of someone or something that has just been mentioned: *I can't go, but Lilly could go instead.*

**in·step** /ˈɪnstɛp/ *n* the raised part of your foot between your toes and your ANKLE, or the part of a shoe that this is under

**in·sti·gate** /ˈɪnstəˌɡeɪt/ *v* [T] to make something start to happen, especially to start something that will cause trouble: *Gang leaders were accused of instigating the riot.* –**instigator** *n* –**instigation** /ˌɪnstəˈɡeɪʃən/ *n* [U]

**in·still** /ɪnˈstɪl/ *v* [T] to teach someone a way of thinking or behaving over a long time: *We tried to **instill** good manners **into** all our children.*

**in·stinct** /ˈɪnstɪŋkt/ *n* [C,U] a natural tendency or ability to behave or react in a particular way, without having to learn it or think about it: *a lion's **instinct** to hunt*

**in·stinc·tive·ly** /ɪnˈstɪŋktɪvli/ *adv* reacting to something because of INSTINCT: *He heard a crash and instinctively turned his head.* –**instinctive** *adj*

**in·sti·tute¹** /ˈɪnstəˌtut/ *n* an organization that has a particular purpose, such as scientific or educational work: *research institutes*

**institute²** *v* [T] FORMAL to introduce or start a system, rule, legal process etc.: *The President agreed to institute welfare reforms.*

**in·sti·tu·tion** /ˌɪnstəˈtuʃən/ *n* **1** a large organization that has a particular purpose, such as scientific, educational, or medical work: *one of the most advanced medical institutions in the world* **2** an established system or custom in society: *the institution of marriage* **3** the act of introducing or starting a system, rule, legal process etc.: *the institution of a new law* –**institutional** *adj* –see also MENTAL INSTITUTION

**in·sti·tu·tion·al·ized** /ˌɪnstəˈtuʃənlˌaɪzd/ *adj* **1** **institutionalized violence/racism/corruption** violence etc. that has happened for so long in an organization or society that it has become accepted as normal **2** someone who has become institutionalized has lived for a long time in a prison, hospital for people who are mentally ill etc. and cannot now live normally in society

**in·struct** /ɪn'strʌkt/ v [T] **1** to officially tell someone what to do: *I've been instructed to wait here until Mr. Borman arrives.* **2** to teach someone or show him/her how to do something: *She's instructing the class in oil painting.*

**in·struc·tion** /ɪn'strʌkʃən/ n **1** [C usually plural] information or advice that tells you how to do something, especially printed material that explains how to use a piece of equipment, machine etc.: *Follow the instructions on the back of the box.|Don't forget to read the instructions.|He gave us instructions on/about how to fix the toilet.* **2** [U] teaching that you are given in a particular skill or subject: *He's under instruction to become a pilot.* –**instructional** adj

**in·struc·tive** /ɪn'strʌktɪv/ adj giving useful information: *a very instructive book on grammar*

**in·struc·tor** /ɪn'strʌktɚ/ n someone who teaches a particular subject, sport, skill etc.: *a ski instructor*

**in·stru·ment** /'ɪnstrəmənt/ n **1** a tool used in work such as science or medicine: *medical instruments* **2** an object such as a piano, horn, VIOLIN etc., used for producing musical sounds **3** a piece of equipment for measuring and showing distance, speed etc.: *a pilot examining her instruments*

**in·stru·men·tal** /ˌɪnstrə'mɛnt̮l/ adj **1 be instrumental in** to be important in making something happen: *a clue that was instrumental in solving the mystery* **2** instrumental music is for instruments, not voices

**in·sub·or·di·nate** /ˌɪnsə'bɔrdn-ɪt/ adj refusing to obey someone who has a higher rank than you in the army, navy etc. –**insubordination** /ˌɪnsəˌbɔrdn'eɪʃən/ n [U]

**in·sub·stan·tial** /ˌɪnsəb'stænʃəl/ adj not solid, large, strong, or satisfying: *The evidence against him was insubstantial.* (=not good enough)

**in·suf·fer·a·ble** /ɪn'sʌfərəbəl/ adj very annoying or unpleasant: *insufferable rudeness* –**insufferably** adv

**in·suf·fi·cient** /ˌɪnsə'fɪʃənt/ adj not enough: *insufficient supplies of food* –**insufficiently** adv –**insufficiency** n [singular, U]

**in·su·lar** /'ɪnsələ, 'ɪnsyə-/ adj FORMAL not interested in anything except your own group, country, way of life etc. –**insularity** /ˌɪnsʊ'lærət̮i/ n [U]

**in·su·late** /'ɪnsəˌleɪt/ v [T] **1** to cover or protect something so that electricity, sound, heat etc. cannot get in or out: *The pipes should be insulated so they don't freeze.* **2** to protect someone from unpleasant experiences or unwanted

influences: *college students insulated from the hardships of real life*

**in·su·la·tion** /ˌɪnsə'leɪʃən/ n [U] **1** the material used in order to INSULATE something, especially a building: *Insulation can save money on heating bills.* **2** the act of insulating something or the state of being insulated

**in·su·lin** /'ɪnsələn/ n [U] a substance produced naturally by your body that allows sugar to be used for energy

**in·sult¹** /ɪn'sʌlt/ v [T] to say or do something that offends someone, by showing that you do not respect him/her: *I was insulted when he refused to shake my hand.* –**insulting** adj

**in·sult²** /'ɪnsʌlt/ n a rude or offensive remark or action: *shouting insults at the police* –see also **add insult to injury** (ADD)

**in·sur·ance** /ɪn'ʃʊrəns/ n **1** [U] an arrangement with a company in which you pay it money each year and it pays the costs if anything bad happens to you or your property, such as having an illness or an accident: *Do you have insurance on/for your car?* **2** [U] the business of providing insurance: *My cousin works in insurance.* **3** [singular, U] protection against something bad happening: *We bought an alarm as insurance against burglary.*

**in·sure** /ɪn'ʃʊr/ v **1** [I,T] to buy or provide insurance: *My house is insured against fire.|This painting is insured for $5000.|Many companies won't insure young drivers.* **2** [T] to protect yourself against something bad happening: *We've done everything we can to insure that the project succeeds.*

**in·sur·gent** /ɪn'sɚdʒənt/ n one of a group of people fighting against the government of their own country –**insurgency** n [U] –**insurgent** adj

**in·sur·mount·a·ble** /ˌɪnsɚ'maʊnt̮əbəl/ adj a difficulty or problem that is insurmountable is too large or too difficult to deal with

**in·sur·rec·tion** /ˌɪnsə'rɛkʃən/ n [C,U] an attempt by a group of people within a country to take control using force and violence: *an armed insurrection led by the army* –**insurrectionist** n

**in·tact** /ɪn'tækt/ adj not broken, damaged, or spoiled: *The package arrived intact.*

**in·take** /'ɪnteɪk/ n [singular] **1** the amount of food, FUEL etc. that is taken in by someone or something: *I've been told to lower my intake of fat and alcohol.* **2** the number of people allowed to enter a school, profession etc.: *the yearly intake of students*

**in·tan·gi·ble** /ɪn'tændʒəbəl/ adj an intangible quality or feeling cannot be clearly felt or described, although you know it exists –**intangibly** adv

**in·te·ger** /'ɪnt̮ədʒɚ/ n TECHNICAL a whole number

**in·te·gral** /'ɪnt̮əgrəl, ɪn'tɛgrəl/ adj forming a

necessary part of something: *an integral part of the contract* —**integrally** *adv*

**in·te·grate** /ˈɪntəˌgreɪt/ *v* **1** [I,T] to end the practice of separating people of different races in a place or institution; DESEGEGRATE: *Many cities transported children long distances in order to integrate schools.* **2** [I,T] to join in the life and customs of a group or society, or to help someone do this: *It will take time for new members to integrate into the group.* **3** [T] to combine two or more things in order to make an effective system: *This software integrates moving pictures with sound.* —**integration** /ˌɪntəˈgreɪʃən/ *n* [U] —**integrated** /ˈɪntəˌgreɪtɪd/ *adj* —compare SEGREGATE

**in·teg·ri·ty** /ɪnˈtɛgrəti/ *n* [U] **1** the quality of being honest and having high moral principles: *a man of integrity* **2** FORMAL the state of being united as one complete thing: *the integrity of the economic system*

**in·tel·lect** /ˈɪntəlˌɛkt/ *n* [C,U] the ability to understand things and think intelligently: *a man of superior intellect*

**in·tel·lec·tu·al**[1] /ˌɪntəlˈɛktʃuəl/ *adj* concerning the ability to think and understand ideas and information: *the intellectual development of children* —**intellectually** *adv*

**intellectual**[2] *n* someone who is intelligent and who thinks about complicated ideas

**in·tel·li·gence** /ɪnˈtɛlədʒəns/ *n* [U] **1** the ability to learn, understand, and think about things: *a child of average intelligence* **2** information about the secret activities of other governments, or the group of people who gather this

**in·tel·li·gent** /ɪnˈtɛlədʒənt/ *adj* having a high level of ability to learn, understand, and think about things —**intelligently** *adv*

**in·tel·li·gi·ble** /ɪnˈtɛlədʒəbəl/ *adj* able to be understood —**intelligibly** *adv* —opposite UNINTELLIGIBLE

**in·tend** /ɪnˈtɛnd/ *v* **1** [T] to have something in your mind as a plan or purpose: *She never really intended to marry him.* **2 be intended for sb/sth** to be provided or designed for someone or something: *a program intended for the families of deaf children* —**intended** *adj*

**in·tense** /ɪnˈtɛns/ *adj* **1** having a very strong effect, or felt very strongly: *the intense heat of the desert* **2** making you do a lot of work, think hard etc.: *They finished in three days after an intense effort.* **3** serious and having very strong feelings or opinions: *an intense young woman* —**intensely** *adv*

**in·ten·si·fi·er** /ɪnˈtɛnsəˌfaɪɚ/ *n* TECHNICAL in grammar, a word that changes the meaning of another word, phrase, or sentence, in order to make its meaning stronger or weaker —see study note on page 463

**in·ten·si·fy** /ɪnˈtɛnsəˌfaɪ/ *v* [I,T] to increase in strength, size, or amount etc., or to make

something do this: *spices will intensify the flavor* | *The smell intensified as it grew hotter.* —**intensification** /ɪnˌtɛnsəfəˈkeɪʃən/ *n* [U]

**in·ten·si·ty** /ɪnˈtɛnsəti/ *n* [U] the quality of being felt very strongly or of having a strong effect: *the intensity of his anger*

**in·ten·sive** /ɪnˈtɛnsɪv/ *adj* involving a lot of activity, effort, or attention in order to achieve something: *The class is four weeks of intensive study.* —**intensively** *adv*

**intensive care** /.ˌ.. ˈ./ *n* [U] a department in a hospital that treats people who are very seriously ill or injured

**in·tent**[1] /ɪnˈtɛnt/ *n* **1** FORMAL what you intend to do: *The intent was to keep the area safe.* **2 to/for all intents and purposes** almost completely, or very nearly: *Their marriage was over for all intents and purposes.*

**intent**[2] *adj* **1 be intent on (doing) sth** to be determined to do something: *Alan is intent on going to Spain this summer.* **2** giving careful attention to something: *an intent look*

**in·ten·tion** /ɪnˈtɛnʃən/ *n* [C,U] something that you plan to do: *I have no intention of retiring anytime soon.*

**in·ten·tion·al** /ɪnˈtɛnʃənəl/ *adj* done deliberately: *an intentional attempt to mislead the public* —**intentionally** *adv* —opposite UNINTENTIONAL

**in·ter** /ɪnˈtɚ/ *v* **-rred, -rring** [T] FORMAL to bury a dead body

**in·ter·act** /ˌɪntəˈrækt/ *v* [I] **1** to talk to other people and work together with them: *Craig hasn't learned how to interact with the other kids.* **2** if two or more things interact, they have an effect on each other: *How will the drug interact with other medicines?*

**in·ter·ac·tion** /ˌɪntəˈrækʃən/ *n* [C,U] the activity of talking with other people and working together with them: *social interaction between teenagers*

**in·ter·ac·tive** /ˌɪntəˈræktɪv/ *adj* **1** involving communication between a computer, television etc. and the person using it: *an interactive software program for children* **2** involving people talking and working together

**in·ter·cede** /ˌɪntɚˈsid/ *v* [I] to talk to someone in authority or do something in order to prevent something from happening: *Hansen interceded on our behalf.* (=for us) —**intercession** /ˌɪntɚˈsɛʃən/ *n* [U]

**in·ter·cept** /ˌɪntɚˈsɛpt/ *v* [T] to stop someone or catch something that is going from one place to another: *O'Neill intercepted the ball.* —**interception** /ˌɪntɚˈsɛpʃən/ *n* [C,U]

**in·ter·change** /ˈɪntɚˌtʃeɪndʒ/ *n* a place where two HIGHWAYs or FREEWAYs meet

**in·ter·change·a·ble** /ˌɪntɚˈtʃeɪndʒəbəl/ *adj* things that are interchangeable can be used instead of each other: *a toy with interchangeable parts* —**interchangeably** *adv*

**in·ter·com** /'ɪntɚˌkɑm/ *n* a communication system by which people in different parts of a building, aircraft etc. can speak to one another: *An announcement came over the intercom telling everyone to get out of the building.*

**in·ter·con·ti·nen·tal** /ˌɪntɚˌkɑntəˈnɛntl, -ˌkɑntˈnˈɛntl/ *adj* happening between or going from one CONTINENT (=Africa, Asia, Europe etc.) to another: *an intercontinental flight*

**in·ter·course** /'ɪntɚˌkɔrs/ *n* [U] FORMAL the act of having sex

**in·ter·de·pend·ent** /ˌɪntɚdɪˈpɛndənt/ *adj* depending on or necessary to each other: *the interdependent group of countries called the European union* –**interdependence** *n* [U]

**in·ter·est¹** /'ɪntrɪst/ *n* **1** [singular, U] a feeling that makes you want to pay attention to something and find out more about it: *We share an* **interest in** *music.*|*Kelly* **lost interest** (=stopped showing an interest) *halfway through the movie.* **2** a subject or activity that you enjoy studying or doing: *What sort of interests do you have?* **3** [U] **a)** money that you must pay for borrowing money **b)** money that a bank pays you when you keep your money there **4** [U] a quality of something that attracts your attention and makes you want to know more about it: *a tourist guide to local places of* **interest 5 be in sb's interest** to be an advantage to someone

**interest²** *v* [T] to make someone want to pay attention to something and find out more about it: *I have some books that might interest you.*

**in·ter·est·ed** /'ɪntrɪstɪd, 'ɪntəˌrɛstɪd/ *adj* **1** giving a lot of attention to something because you want to find out more about it: *Peter is* **interested in** *Mexican politics.* **2** eager to do or have something: *Lisa is* **interested in** *studying law.*

**in·ter·est·ing** /'ɪntrɪstɪŋ, 'ɪntəˌrɛstɪŋ/ *adj* unusual or exciting in a way that keeps your attention: *a very interesting idea/book/person* –**interestingly** *adv*

**in·ter·face** /'ɪntɚˌfeɪs/ *n* TECHNICAL the HARDWARE and SOFTWARE needed for a computer to do things such as print documents, use a MOUSE etc.

**in·ter·fere** /ˌɪntɚˈfɪr/ *v* [I] to deliberately get involved in a situation when you are not wanted or needed: *It's better not to* **interfere in** *their arguments.*
**interfere with** sth *phr v* [T] **1** to prevent something from happening in the way it was planned: *Don't let sports* **interfere with** *your schoolwork.* **2** to spoil the sound or picture of a radio or television broadcast

**in·ter·fer·ence** /ˌɪntɚˈfɪrəns/ *n* [U] **1** an act of interfering (INTERFERE): *I resented his* **interference in** *my personal life.* **2** in sports, the act of illegally preventing another player from doing something **3** unwanted noise, a

spoiled picture etc. on the radio, telephone, or television

**in·ter·im¹** /'ɪntɚəm/ *adj* an interim report, payment, agreement etc. is used or accepted for a short time until a final one is made

**interim²** *n* **in the interim** in the period of time between two events: *There are two parts to the tour, so the visitors will need a place to rest in the interim.*

**in·te·ri·or¹** /ɪnˈtɪriɚ/ *n* the inner part or inside of something: *a car with brown leather interior* –opposite EXTERIOR¹

**interior²** *adj* inside or indoors: *an interior decorator* –opposite EXTERIOR²

**interior de·sign** /.,... .'./ *n* [U] the job or skill of choosing and arranging furniture, paints, art etc. for the inside of houses, buildings etc.

**in·ter·ject** /ˌɪntɚˈdʒɛkt/ *v* [I,T] FORMAL to interrupt what someone is saying with a sudden remark

**in·ter·jec·tion** /ˌɪntɚˈdʒɛkʃən/ *n* in grammar, a word or phrase that is used in order to express surprise, shock, pain etc. In the sentence "Ouch! That hurt!", "ouch" is an interjection

**in·ter·lock·ing** /ˌɪntɚˈlɑkɪŋ‹/ *adj* connected firmly together: *the Olympic symbol of interlocking circles* –**interlock** *v* [I,T]

**in·ter·lop·er** /'ɪntɚˌloʊpɚ/ *n* someone who enters a place where s/he should not be

**in·ter·lude** /'ɪntɚˌlud/ *n* a period of time between activities or events: *a brief interlude of peace before the fighting began again*

**in·ter·mar·ry** /ˌɪntɚˈmæri/ *v* [I] if people from different races, religions etc. intermarry, someone from one group marries someone from another group –**intermarriage** /ˌɪntɚˈmærɪdʒ/ *n* [U]

**in·ter·me·di·ar·y** /ˌɪntɚˈmidiˌɛri/ *n* someone who tries to help two other people or groups to agree with one another

**in·ter·me·di·ate** /ˌɪntɚˈmidiɪt/ *adj* done or happening between two other stages, levels etc.: *an intermediate Spanish class*

**in·ter·mi·na·ble** /ɪnˈtɚmənəbəl/ *adj* very boring and taking a lot of time: *interminable delays* –**interminably** *adv*

**in·ter·mis·sion** /ˌɪntɚˈmɪʃən/ *n* a short period of time between the parts of a play, concert etc.

**in·ter·mit·tent** /ˌɪntɚˈmɪtˈnt/ *adj* happening at some times but not regularly or continuously: *clouds and intermittent rain* –**intermittently** *adv*

**in·tern¹** /'ɪntɚn/ *n* **1** someone who has almost finished training as a doctor and is working in a hospital **2** someone, especially a student, who works for a short time in a particular job in order to gain experience

**in·tern²** /ɪnˈtɚn/ *v* [T] to put someone in prison, especially for political reasons –**internment** *n* [C,U]

**in·ter·nal** /ɪnˈtɚnl/ *adj* **1** inside something such as your body rather than outside: *a lot of internal bleeding* **2** within a particular country, company, organization etc.: *an internal flight from Denver to Chicago* —**internally** *adv* —opposite EXTERNAL

**Internal Rev·e·nue Serv·ice** /.,.. '... ,../ *n* [singular] ⇨ IRS

**in·ter·na·tion·al** /ˌɪntɚˈnæʃənəl/ *adj* concerning more than one nation: *an international agreement* —**internationally** *adv*

**In·ter·net** /ˈɪntɚˌnɛt/ *n* **the Internet** also **the Net** a system of connected computers that allows computer users around the world to exchange information: *Are you on the Internet yet?*

---

**CULTURE NOTE  The Internet**

**The Internet** is a system of many computers all around the world that allows people to communicate with each other and share information. Through **the Internet** you can find information about almost anything you can think of. You can read information from books and magazines that are **on line** (=available electronically instead of on paper). You can also use **the Internet** to send **e-mail** (=electronic mail), which is a way of sending letters and documents very quickly using a computer. The **World Wide Web** is what makes it possible for you to see and use the information on **the Internet** in an easy way.

---

**in·ter·nist** /ˈɪntɚnɪst/ *n* a doctor who treats people using medicines etc., rather than by using SURGERY —compare SURGEON

**in·tern·ship** /ˈɪntɚnˌʃɪp/ *n* the period of time when an INTERN works, or the particular job s/he does: *an internship in a law firm*

**in·ter·per·son·al** /ˌɪntɚˈpɚsənl/ *adj* involving relationships between people

**in·ter·plan·e·tar·y** /ˌɪntɚˈplænəˌtɛri/ *adj* happening or done between the PLANETs

**in·ter·play** /ˈɪntɚˌpleɪ/ *n* [U] the way that two people or things affect each other: *the interplay of light and color in her films*

**in·ter·pose** /ˌɪntɚˈpoʊz/ *v* [T] FORMAL to put something between two other things, people etc., usually to stop something: *a neutral group was interposed between the warring sides*

**in·ter·pret** /ɪnˈtɚprɪt/ *v* **1** [I,T] to change words spoken in one language into another: *Gina spoke enough Spanish to be able to interpret for me.* —compare TRANSLATE **2** [T] to explain or decide on the meaning of an event, statement etc.: *His silence was interpreted as guilt.*

**in·ter·pre·ta·tion** /ɪnˌtɚprəˈteɪʃən/ *n* [C,U] an explanation for an event, someone's actions etc.: *one scientist's interpretation of the data*

**in·ter·pret·er** /ɪnˈtɚprətɚ/ *n* someone who changes the spoken words of one language into another —compare TRANSLATOR

**in·ter·ra·cial** /ˌɪntɚˈreɪʃəl/ *adj* between different races of people: *an interracial marriage*

**in·ter·re·lat·ed** /ˌɪntɚrɪˈleɪtɪd/ *adj* many things that are interrelated all have an effect on each other

**in·ter·ro·gate** /ɪnˈtɛrəˌgeɪt/ *v* [T] to ask someone a lot of questions, sometimes in a threatening way: *Police are interrogating the suspect now.* —**interrogation** /ɪnˌtɛrəˈgeɪʃən/ *n* [C,U] —**interrogator** /ɪnˈtɛrəˌgeɪtɚ/ *n* —see usage note at ASK

**in·ter·rupt** /ˌɪntəˈrʌpt/ *v* **1** [I,T] to stop someone from speaking by suddenly saying or doing something: *I'm sorry, I didn't mean to interrupt you.|We'd only said a few words when Brian interrupted.* **2** [T] to stop a process or activity for a short time: *The war interrupted the supply of oil.* —**interruption** /ˌɪntəˈrʌpʃən/ *n* [C,U]

**in·ter·sect** /ˌɪntɚˈsɛkt/ *v* [I,T] if two lines, roads etc. intersect, they meet or go across each other

**in·ter·sec·tion** /ˈɪntɚˌsɛkʃən, ˌɪntɚˈsɛkʃən/ *n* the place where two roads, lines etc. meet and go across each other

**in·ter·sperse** /ˌɪntɚˈspɚs/ *v* [T] to mix something together with something else: *Music videos were interspersed with interviews.*

**in·ter·state¹** /ˈɪntɚˌsteɪt/ *n* a road that goes between states

**interstate²** *adj* between or involving different states in the US: *interstate trade*

**in·ter·twined** /ˌɪntɚˈtwaɪnd/ *adj* twisted together or closely related: *several intertwined stories*

**in·ter·val** /ˈɪntɚvəl/ *n* **1** a period of time between two events, activities etc.: *The Bijou Theater opened again after an interval of five years.* **2** **at daily/weekly/monthly etc. intervals** every day, week, month etc. **3** **at regular intervals** with the same amount of time or distance between each thing, activity etc: *Water your plants at regular intervals.* **4** **at intervals of** with a particular amount of time or distance between things, activities etc.: *at intervals of six feet*

**in·ter·vene** /ˌɪntɚˈvin/ *v* [I] **1** to do something to try to stop an argument, problem, war etc.: *The police had to intervene in the march to stop the fighting.* **2** to happen between two events, especially in a way that interrupts or prevents something: *They had planned to get married, but the war intervened.* —**intervening** *adj*

**in·ter·ven·tion** /ˌɪntɚˈvɛnʃən/ *n* [C,U] the act of intervening (INTERVENE)

**in·ter·view¹** /'ɪntɚˌvyu/ *n* **1** an occasion when someone famous is asked questions about his/her life, opinions etc.: *Michael Jackson gave an interview to Barbara Walters.* (=he answered her questions) **2** [C,U] a formal meeting in which someone is asked questions, usually to find out if s/he is good enough for a job

**interview²** *v* [T] to ask someone questions during an INTERVIEW —**interviewer** *n*

**In·ter·weave** /ˌɪntɚ'wɪv/ *v* **interwove** /-'wouv/, **interwoven** /-'wouvən/, **interweaving** [T] if two or more ideas or situations are interwoven, they are too closely related to be separated easily: *The histories of the two countries are closely interwoven.*

**in·tes·tate** /ɪn'tɛˌsteɪt/ *adj* LAW **die intestate** to die without a WILL

**in·tes·tine** /ɪn'tɛstɪn/ *n* the long tube that takes food from your stomach out of your body —**intestinal** *adj*

**in·ti·ma·cy** /'ɪntəməsi/ *n* a state of having a close personal relationship with someone: *the intimacy of good friends*

**in·ti·mate¹** /'ɪntəmɪt/ *adj* **1** having a very close relationship with someone: *She only told a few intimate friends that she was pregnant.* **2** relating to very private or personal matters: *the intimate nature of the doctor's relationship with a patient* **3** FORMAL relating to sex: *The virus can only be transmitted through intimate contact.* —**intimately** *adv*

**in·ti·mate²** /'ɪntəˌmeɪt/ *v* [T] FORMAL to make someone understand what you mean without saying it directly —**intimation** /ˌɪntə'meɪʃən/ *n* [C,U]

**in·tim·i·date** /ɪn'tɪməˌdeɪt/ *v* [T] to make someone afraid, often by using threats, so that s/he does what you want —**intimidation** /ɪnˌtɪmə'deɪʃən/ *n* [U]

**in·tim·i·dat·ed** /ɪn'tɪməˌdeɪṭɪd/ *adj* feeling worried or frightened because you are in a difficult situation: *Ben felt intimidated by the older boys.*

**in·tim·i·dat·ing** /ɪn'tɪməˌdeɪṭɪŋ/ *adj* making you feel worried and less confident: *Interviews can be an intimidating experience.*

**in·to** /'ɪntə; *before vowels* 'ɪntu; *strong* 'ɪntu/ *prep* **1** in order to be inside something or in a place: *Charlie went into the kitchen.* | *The child had fallen into the water.* **2** involved in a situation or activity: *He decided he would try to go into business for himself.* (=start his own business) | *Don't get into trouble, and be home by 10:00!* **3** in a different situation or physical form: *Make the bread dough into a ball.* (=the shape of a ball) | *I couldn't get into the Art History class, so I'm taking photography.* **4** to a point where you hit something, usually causing damage: *The car had run into a tree.* **5 be into sth** SPOKEN to like and be interested in something: *I was into ice skating when I was 10.*

**6** in a particular direction: *Look into my eyes.* **7** at or until a particular time: *We talked into the night.*

**in·tol·er·a·ble** /ɪn'tɑlərəbəl/ *adj* too difficult, unpleasant, or painful for you to bear: *an intolerable pain in my back* —**intolerably** *adv*

**in·tol·er·ant** /ɪn'tɑlərənt/ *adj* not willing to accept ways of thinking and behaving that are different from your own: *He's very intolerant of other people's political opinions.* —**intolerance** *n* [U]

**in·to·na·tion** /ˌɪntə'neɪʃən, -tou-/ *n* [C,U] the rise and fall in the level of your voice

**in·tox·i·cat·ed** /ɪn'tɑksəˌkeɪṭɪd/ *adj* **1** drunk: *He was intoxicated at the time of the accident.* **2** happy and excited because of success, love, power etc. —**intoxicating** *adj*

**in·tox·i·ca·tion** /ɪnˌtɑksə'keɪʃən/ *n* [U] the state of being drunk

**in·trac·ta·ble** /ɪn'træktəbəl/ *adj* FORMAL very difficult to control, manage, or solve: *intractable problems*

**in·tra·mu·ral** /ˌɪntrə'myurəl/ *adj* intended for the students of one school: *intramural sports*

**in·tran·si·gent** /ɪn'trænsədʒənt, -zə-/ *adj* FORMAL not willing to change your opinions or behavior —**intransigence** *n* [U]

**in·tran·si·tive verb** /.ˌ... '../ *n* TECHNICAL in grammar, an intransitive verb has a subject but no object. In the sentence, "They arrived early," "arrive" is an intransitive verb —compare TRANSITIVE VERB —see study note on page 468

**in·tra·ve·nous** /ˌɪntrə'vinəs/ *adj* within or connected to a VEIN (=a tube that takes blood to your heart): *an intravenous injection* —**intravenously** *adv*

**in·trep·id** /ɪn'trɛpɪd/ *adj* LITERARY willing to do dangerous things or go to dangerous places

**in·tri·ca·cy** /'ɪntrɪkəsi/ *n* **1** [U] the state of containing a lot of parts or details: *the intricacy of the plot* **2 the intricacies of sth** the complicated details of something: *the intricacies of Bach's music*

**in·tri·cate** /'ɪntrɪkɪt/ *adj* containing a lot of parts or details: *an intricate pattern in the rug*

**in·trigue¹** /ɪn'trig/ *v* [T] to interest someone a lot, especially by being strange or mysterious: *I was intrigued by her story.*

**in·trigue²** /'ɪntrig, ɪn'trig/ *n* [C,U] the practice of making secret plans to harm or deceive someone: *a book about political intrigue*

**in·tri·guing** /ɪn'trigɪŋ/ *adj* very interesting because it is strange or mysterious: *an intriguing idea* —**intriguingly** *adv*

**in·trin·sic** /ɪn'trɪnzɪk, -sɪk/ *adj* being part of the basic nature or character of someone or something: *The art has an intrinsic value that is not connected to how much it is worth.* —**intrinsically** *adv*

**in·tro** /'ɪntrou/ *n* INFORMAL the introduction to a song, television program etc.

**in·tro·duce** /ˌɪntrəˈdus/ v [T] **1** if you introduce someone to another person, you tell them each other's name for the first time: *Alice, may I introduce you to Megan?* **2** to make a change, plan, etc. happen or exist for the first time: *The company has introduced a new insurance plan.* **3** **introduce sb to sth** to show someone something or tell him/her about it for the first time: *He introduced us to Thai food.* **4** to speak at the beginning of a television program, public speech etc. to say what will happen next

**in·tro·duc·tion** /ˌɪntrəˈdʌkʃən/ n **1** [C,U] the act of making a change, plan etc. happen or exist for the first time: *the introduction of personal computers into the schools* **2** the act of telling two people each other's names when they first meet **3** a written or spoken explanation at the beginning of a book or speech

---

**USAGE NOTE** introductions

When you are introduced to someone, you usually shake hands with that person and say, "Hello, it's nice to meet you." In an informal situation, you can say, "Hi, nice to meet you." In a formal situation, you say, "How do you do?" When you introduce people to each other, you say, "This is..." You introduce each person: *"Ron, this is Jan Brown. Jan, this is Ron Jackson."* In an informal situation, you can say, "Do you know my daughter/friend/wife Kate?" In a formal situation, you say, "May I introduce you to my daughter/friend/wife Kate?"

---

**in·tro·duc·to·ry** /ˌɪntrəˈdʌktəri/ adj **1** concerning the beginning of a book, speech, course etc.: *the introductory chapter* **2** **introductory offer** a special low price to encourage you to buy something new

**in·tro·spec·tive** /ˌɪntrəˈspɛktɪv/ adj thinking deeply about your own thoughts and feelings –**introspection** /ˌɪntrəˈspɛkʃən/ n [U]

**in·tro·vert·ed** /ˈɪntrəˌvɚtɪd/ adj thinking a lot about your own problems, interests etc. and not wanting to be with other people –**introvert** n –compare EXTROVERTED

**in·trude** /ɪnˈtrud/ v [I] to go into a place or get involved in a situation where you are not wanted: *newspapers that intrude into/on people's private lives*

**in·trud·er** /ɪnˈtrudɚ/ n someone who enters a building or area where s/he is not supposed to be

**in·tru·sion** /ɪnˈtruʒən/ n [C,U] an unwanted person, event etc. that interrupts or annoys you: *He resented her intrusion into his work time.* –**intrusive** /ɪnˈtrusɪv/ adj

**in·tu·i·tion** /ˌɪntuˈɪʃən/ n [C,U] the ability to understand or know that something is true based on your feelings rather than facts, or an example

of this: *My intuition told me not to trust Reynolds.*

**in·tu·i·tive** /ɪnˈtuətɪv/ adj based on feelings rather than facts: *an intuitive understanding of the problem* –**intuitively** adv

**In·u·it** /ˈɪnuɪt/ n **the Inuit** [plural] a group of people who live in ARCTIC places such as northern Canada, Greenland, Alaska, and Eastern Siberia –**Inuit** adj

**in·un·date** /ˈɪnənˌdeɪt/ v [T] **1** **be inundated with/by sth** to receive so much of something that you cannot deal with all of it: *We were inundated with requests for tickets.* **2** FORMAL to flood a place –**inundation** /ˌɪnənˈdeɪʃən/ n [C,U]

**in·vade** /ɪnˈveɪd/ v **1** [I,T] to enter a place using military force: *Germany invaded Poland in 1939.* **2** [T] to go into a place in large numbers: *Every Christmas Jerusalem is invaded by tourists.* –**invader** n

**in·val·id**[1] /ɪnˈvælɪd/ adj not legally or officially acceptable: *an invalid bus pass*

**in·va·lid**[2] /ˈɪnvələd/ n someone who needs to be cared for because s/he is ill, injured, or very old –**invalid** adj

**in·val·i·date** /ɪnˈvæləˌdeɪt/ v [T] **1** to make a document, ticket etc. no longer legally acceptable **2** to show that something such as a belief, explanation etc. is wrong: *New research has invalidated the theory.* –**invalidity** /ˌɪnvəˈlɪdəti/ n [U]

**in·val·u·a·ble** /ɪnˈvælyəbəl, -yuəbəl/ adj extremely useful: *Your advice has been invaluable.*

**in·var·i·a·bly** /ɪnˈvɛriəbli, -ˈvær-/ adv always, without changing: *They invariably go to Florida on their vacation.* –**invariable** adj

**in·va·sion** /ɪnˈveɪʒən/ n [C,U] **1** an occasion when an army enters a country using military force **2** the arrival of people or things at a place where they are not wanted: *the yearly invasion of mosquitoes* **3** **invasion of privacy** a situation in which someone tries to find out about someone else's personal life, in a way that is upsetting and often illegal –**invasive** /ɪnˈveɪsɪv/ adj

**in·vent** /ɪnˈvɛnt/ v [T] **1** to make, design, or produce something for the first time: *Who invented the light bulb?* **2** to think of an idea, story etc. that is not true, usually to deceive people

**in·ven·tion** /ɪnˈvɛnʃən/ n [C,U] **1** the act of inventing something, or the thing that is invented: *The fax machine is an amazing invention.* **2** an idea, story etc. that is not true

**in·ven·tive** /ɪnˈvɛntɪv/ adj able to think of new and interesting ideas: *an inventive cook* –**inventiveness** n [U]

**in·ven·tor** /ɪnˈvɛntɚ/ n someone who has invented something

**in·ven·to·ry** /ˈɪnvənˌtɔri/ *n* **1** [U] all the goods in a store **2** a list of all the things in a place: *The store will be closed on Friday to take inventory.* (=make a list of its goods)

**in·verse** /ɪnˈvɚs, ˈɪnvɚs/ *adj* TECHNICAL **in inverse proportion/relation etc. to** getting larger as something else gets smaller, or getting smaller as something else gets larger –**inversely** *adv* –**inverse** *n*

**in·vert** /ɪnˈvɚt/ *v* [T] FORMAL to put something in the opposite position, especially by turning it upside down –**inversion** /ɪnˈvɚʒən/ *n* [C,U]

**in·vest** /ɪnˈvɛst/ *v* **1** [I,T] to give money to a company, bank etc., or to buy something, in order to get a profit later: *investing in stocks and bonds* **2** [T] to use a lot of time or effort to make something succeed –**investor** *n*

**in·ves·ti·gate** /ɪnˈvɛstəˌgeɪt/ *v* [I,T] to try to find out the truth about a crime, accident etc.: *The police are investigating the fraud charges.* –**investigator** *n*

**in·ves·ti·ga·tion** /ɪnˌvɛstəˈgeɪʃən/ *n* an official attempt to find out the reasons for something, such as a crime or scientific problem: *an investigation into the plane crash* –**investigative** /ɪnˈvɛstəˌgeɪtɪv/ *adj*

**in·vest·ment** /ɪnˈvɛstmənt/ *n* **1** [C,U] the money that you give to a company, bank etc. in order to get a profit later, or the act of doing this: *a $5000 investment in stocks* **2** something that you buy or do because it will be more valuable or useful later: *We bought the house as an investment.*

**in·vet·er·ate** /ɪnˈvɛtərɪt/ *adj* having done something over a long time, and not likely to stop: *an inveterate liar*

**in·vig·o·rat·ing** /ɪnˈvɪgəˌreɪtɪŋ/ *adj* making you feel more active and healthy: *an invigorating swim* –**invigorate** *v* [T] –**invigorated** *adj*

**in·vin·ci·ble** /ɪnˈvɪnsəbəl/ *adj* too strong to be defeated or destroyed: *Bubka is invincible in the pole vault.* –**invincibly** *adv*

**in·vis·i·ble** /ɪnˈvɪzəbəl/ *adj* not able to be seen: *organisms that are invisible without using a microscope* –**invisibly** *adv* –**invisibility** /ɪnˌvɪzəˈbɪləti/ *n* [U]

**in·vi·ta·tion** /ˌɪnvəˈteɪʃən/ *n* a request to someone that invites him/her to go somewhere or do something, or the card this is written on: *Did you get an invitation to the wedding?*

**in·vite¹** /ɪnˈvaɪt/ *v* [T] **1** to ask someone to come to a party, meal, wedding etc.: *I invited the Rosens to dinner next Friday.* **2 invite trouble/criticism etc.** to make trouble, criticism etc. more likely to happen to you

**invite** sb **along** *phr v* [T] to ask someone to come with you when you go somewhere: *You can invite one of your friends along.*

**invite** sb **in** *phr v* [T] to ask someone to come into your home, usually when they are standing at the door

**invite** sb **over** *phr v* [T] to ask someone to come to your home for a party, meal etc.: *I invited the Blackmers over for a meal.*

USAGE NOTE **invite**

**Invite** is usually used only to talk about the fact that you have been asked to go somewhere: *I've been invited to Barbara's party.* When you invite someone, say, "Would you like to come to my party?"

**in·vite²** /ˈɪnvaɪt/ *n* INFORMAL an invitation

**in·vit·ing** /ɪnˈvaɪtɪŋ/ *adj* an inviting sight, smell etc. is attractive and makes you want to do something: *The lake looked inviting.* (=made me want to swim in it) –**invitingly** *adv*

**in·voice** /ˈɪnvɔɪs/ *n* a list that shows how much you owe for goods, work etc. –**invoice** *v* [T]

**in·voke** /ɪnˈvoʊk/ *v* [T] FORMAL **1** to use a law, principle etc. to support your opinions or actions **2** LITERARY to ask for help from someone, especially a god

**in·vol·un·tar·y** /ɪnˈvɑlənˌtɛri/ *adj* an involuntary movement, reaction etc. is one that you make suddenly without intending to –**involuntarily** /ɪnˌvɑlənˈtɛrəli/ *adv*

**in·volve** /ɪnˈvɑlv/ *v* [T] **1** to include or affect someone or something: *a riot involving 45 prisoners* **2** to ask or allow someone to take part in something: *We're trying to involve as many of the parents as possible in the PTA.* **3** to include something as a necessary part or result of something else: *Taking the job involves moving to Texas.*

**in·volved** /ɪnˈvɑlvd/ *adj* **1** taking part in an activity or event. *More than 50 nations were involved in the war effort.* **2** difficult to understand because it is complicated or has a lot of parts: *a long involved answer* **3 be involved with sb** to be having a sexual relationship with someone

**in·volve·ment** /ɪnˈvɑlvmənt/ *n* [U] the act of taking part in an activity or event

**in·ward¹** /ˈɪnwɚd/ *adj* **1** felt in your own mind, but not expressed to other people: *Her calm face hid her inward fear.* ✗ DON'T SAY *"Her fear was inward."* ✗ **2** on or toward the inside of something –**inwardly** *adv*: *Ginny was inwardly disappointed that she hadn't seen him at the party.*

**inward²** inwards *adv* toward the inside –opposite OUTWARD²

**i·o·dine** /ˈaɪəˌdaɪn, -ˌdɪn/ *n* [U] a chemical that is often used on wounds to prevent infection

**i·on** /ˈaɪən, ˈaɪɑn/ *n* TECHNICAL an atom that has been given a positive or negative force

**i·o·ta** /aɪˈoʊtə/ *n* [singular] **not one/an iota of sth** not even a small amount of something: *There's not an iota of truth in what he says.*

**IOU** *n* INFORMAL an abbreviation for "I owe you"; a note that you sign to say that you owe someone some money

**IPA** *n* [singular] the International Phonetic Alphabet; a system of signs that represent the sounds made in speech

**IQ** *n* Intelligence Quotient; the level of someone's intelligence, with 100 being the average level

**IRA** *n* Individual Retirement Account; a special bank account in which you can save money for your RETIREMENT without paying tax on it until later

**i·ras·ci·ble** /ɪˈræsəbəl/ *adj* FORMAL becoming angry easily

**i·rate** /ˌaɪˈreɪt‹ / *adj* extremely angry **–irately** *adv*

**ir·i·des·cent** /ˌɪrəˈdɛsənt/ *adj* showing colors that seem to change in different lights **–iridescence** *n* [U]

**i·ris** /ˈaɪrɪs/ *n* **1** the round colored part of your eye **–**see picture at EYE¹ **2** a tall plant with purple, yellow, or white flowers and long thin leaves

**I·rish¹** /ˈaɪrɪʃ/ *adj* relating to or coming from Ireland

**Irish²** *n* **the Irish** [plural] the people of Ireland

**irk** /ɚk/ *v* [T] to trouble or annoy someone

**i·ron¹** /ˈaɪən/ *n* **1** an object that is heated and that you push across a piece of clothing to make it smooth **2** [U] a common heavy metal that is used in making steel

iron

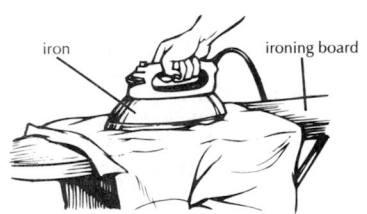

iron        ironing board

**iron²** *v* [T] to make your clothes smooth using an iron: *Can you iron my shirt for me?*

**iron sth ↔ out** *phr v* [T] to solve a small problem or difficulty: *Jim and Sharon are iron-ing out their differences.*

**iron³** *adj* **1** made of iron: *iron bars on the gate* **2** very firm or strict: *He ruled the country with an iron fist.* (=in a very strict and powerful way)

**Iron Cur·tain** /ˌ.. ˈ../ *n* **the Iron Curtain** a name used in past times for the border between the Communist countries of eastern Europe and the rest of Europe

**i·ron·ic** /aɪˈrɑnɪk/ *adj* **1** using words that are the opposite of what you really mean in order to be amusing, or show that you are annoyed **2** an ironic situation is unusual or amusing be-

cause something strange or unexpected happens **–ironically** *adv*

**i·ron·ing** /ˈaɪənɪŋ/ *n* [U] the activity of making clothes smooth with an iron

**ironing board** /ˈ... ˌ./ *n* a narrow board on which you make your clothes smooth with an iron **–**see picture at IRON²

**i·ro·ny** /ˈaɪrəni/ *n* [U] **1** the use of words that are the opposite of what you really mean in order to be amusing, or show that you are annoyed **2** the part of a situation that is unusual or amusing because something strange happens, or the opposite of what is expected happens: *The irony is that the drug was supposed to save lives.*

**ir·ra·tion·al** /ɪˈræʃənəl/ *adj* not reasonable or not based on good reasons: *an irrational fear of spiders* **–irrationally** *adv* **–irrationality** /ɪˌræʃəˈnæləti/ *n* [U]

**ir·rec·on·cil·a·ble** /ɪˌrɛkənˈsaɪləbəl/ *adj* so different that it is impossible to reach an agreement: *irreconcilable opinions* **–irreconcilably** *adv*

**ir·re·fut·a·ble** /ˌɪrɪˈfyuṭəbəl/ *adj* FORMAL an irrefutable statement, argument etc. cannot be proved wrong

**ir·reg·u·lar** /ɪˈrɛgyələ/ *adj* **1** having a shape, surface etc. that is not even or smooth: *a face with irregular features* **2** not happening at regular times or at the usual time: *an irregular heartbeat* **3** not following the usual pattern in grammar: *an irregular verb* **–irregularity** /ɪˌrɛgyəˈlærəṭi/ *n* [C,U] **–irregularly** /ɪˈrɛgyələli/ *adv*

**ir·rel·e·vance** /ɪˈrɛləvəns/, **ir·rel·e·van·cy** /ɪˈrɛləvənsi/ *n* [U] a lack of importance in a particular situation

**ir·rel·e·vant** /ɪˈrɛləvənt/ *adj* not useful in or relating to a particular situation, and therefore not important: *His age is irrelevant if he can do the job.* **–irrelevantly** *adv*

**ir·rep·a·ra·ble** /ɪˈrɛpərəbəl/ *adj* so bad that it cannot be repaired or made better **–irreparably** *adv*

**ir·re·place·a·ble** /ˌɪrɪˈpleɪsəbəl/ *adj* too special, valuable, or rare to be replaced by anything else: *an irreplaceable work of art*

**ir·re·press·i·ble** /ˌɪrɪˈprɛsəbəl/ *adj* full of energy and happiness that is too strong to be controlled: *Nathan's excitement was irrepress-ible.*

**ir·re·proach·a·ble** /ˌɪrɪˈproutʃəbəl/ *adj* FOR-MAL so good that you cannot criticize it: *Her behavior was irreproachable.*

**ir·re·sist·i·ble** /ˌɪrɪˈzɪstəbəl/ *adj* **1** so attractive or desirable that you cannot stop yourself from wanting it: *The dessert looks irre-sistible.* **2** too strong or powerful to be stopped: *an irresistible force* **–irresistibly** *adv*

**ir·re·spec·tive of** /ˌɪrɪˈspɛktɪv əv/ *prep* used in order to show that a particular fact does not affect a situation at all: *Anyone can play, irrespective of age.*

**ir·re·spon·si·ble** /ˌɪrɪˈspɑnsəbəl/ *adj* doing things that are careless without thinking about the possible results: *It was irresponsible of John to leave the kids alone.* –**irresponsibly** *adv* –**irresponsibility** /ˌɪrɪˌspɑnsəˈbɪləti/ *n* [U]

**ir·rev·er·ent** /ɪˈrɛvərənt/ *adj* not showing respect for religion, customs etc. –**irreverence** *n* [U] –**irreverently** *adv*

**ir·re·ver·si·ble** /ˌɪrɪˈvɚsəbəl/ *adj* impossible to change something back to the way it was before: *irreversible brain damage*

**ir·rev·o·ca·ble** /ɪˈrɛvəkəbəl/ *adj* not able to be changed or stopped: *an irrevocable decision* –**irrevocably** *adv*

**ir·ri·gate** /ˈɪrəˌgeɪt/ *v* [T] to supply water to land or crops

**ir·ri·ga·tion** /ˌɪrəˈgeɪʃən/ *n* [U] the act of supplying water to land or crops

**ir·ri·ta·ble** /ˈɪrətəbəl/ *adj* easily annoyed or made angry: *He's always irritable in the morning.* –**irritably** *adv* –**irritability** /ˌɪrətəˈbɪləti/ *n* [U]

**ir·ri·tant** /ˈɪrətənt/ *n* FORMAL **1** something that makes you feel angry or annoyed **2** a substance that makes part of your body painful and sore

**ir·ri·tate** /ˈɪrəˌteɪt/ *v* [T] **1** to make someone angry or annoyed: *The way she yells at her kids really irritates me.* **2** to make a part of your body painful and sore: *Wool irritates my skin.*

**ir·ri·tat·ing** /ˈɪrəˌteɪtɪŋ/ *adj* annoying: *an irritating habit of always being late* –**irritatingly** *adv*

**ir·ri·ta·tion** /ˌɪrəˈteɪʃən/ *n* **1** [C,U] the feeling of being annoyed, or something that makes you feel this way: *the irritation of constant traffic noise outside* **2** [U] a painful, sore feeling on a part of your body

**IRS** *n* **the IRS** the Internal Revenue Service; the government organization in the US that deals with taxes

**is** /z, s, əz; *strong* ɪz/ the third person singular of the present tense of BE

**Is·lam** /ˈɪzlɑm, ɪzˈlɑm, ˈɪslɑm/ *n* [U] the religion that was started by Muhammed and whose holy book is the Koran –**Islamic** /ɪzˈlɑmɪk, ɪs-/ *adj*

**is·land** /ˈaɪlənd/ *n* a piece of land completely surrounded by water: *a hotel development on the island*

**is·land·er** /ˈaɪləndɚ/ *n* someone who lives on an island

**isle** /aɪl/ *n* LITERARY an island

**is·n't** /ˈɪzənt/ *v* the short form of "is not": *That isn't the same car I saw yesterday.*

**i·so·late** /ˈaɪsəˌleɪt/ *v* [T] **1** to make or keep one person or thing separate from others: *The town was isolated by the floods.* **2** to prevent a country, political group etc. from getting support from other countries or groups

**i·so·lat·ed** /ˈaɪsəˌleɪtɪd/ *adj* **1** far away from other things: *an isolated farm* **2** feeling alone or separated from other people: *Newly retired people can often feel isolated and useless.* **3 an isolated case/example etc.** a case, example etc. that happens only once: *an isolated case of the disease*

**i·so·la·tion** /ˌaɪsəˈleɪʃən/ *n* [U] **1** the state of being separate from other places, things, or people: *the city's geographical isolation* (=its location far away from other cities) **2 in isolation** separately: *These events cannot be examined in isolation from one another.* **3** a feeling of being lonely

**is·sue¹** /ˈɪʃu/ *n* **1** a subject or problem that people discuss: *We should raise the issue* (=begin to discuss it) *at our next meeting.* **2** a magazine, newspaper etc. printed for a particular day, week, month, or year: *the new issue of Sports Illustrated* **3 at issue** FORMAL being discussed or considered: *Only the nurse's contract was at issue.* **4 make an issue (out) of sth** to argue about something: *There's no need to make an issue out of this!* **5 take issue with** to disagree or argue with someone about something: *He took issue with Mayor Farrell's statement.*

**issue²** *v* [T] **1** to officially make a statement or give a warning: *a statement issued by the White House* **2** to officially provide or produce something: *Every player was issued with a new uniform.*

**isth·mus** /ˈɪsməs/ *n* a narrow piece of land with water on both sides, that connects two larger areas of land

**IT** *n* [U] ⇨ INFORMATION TECHNOLOGY

**it** /ɪt/ *pron* [used as a subject or object] **1** a thing, situation, person, or idea that has been mentioned or is known about: *"Did you bring your umbrella?" "No, I left it at home."* | *"Where's the bread?" "It's* (=it is) *on the shelf."* | *You two are married? I can't believe it.* **2** the situation that someone is in now: *It's fun at school right now.* | *How's it going, Bob?* (=How are you?) **3** used as the subject or object of a sentence when the real subject or object is later in the sentence: *It costs less to drive than to take the bus.* **4** used with the verb "be" to talk about the weather, time, distance etc.: *It's raining again.* | *It's only a few miles from here to the beach.* | *I forgot that it was her birthday.* | *I was surprised that it was only 3:00.* **5** used in order to emphasize one piece of information in a sentence: *I don't know who took your book, but it wasn't me.* | *It must have been Ben* (=not any other person) *because nobody else was here.* | *It was yesterday* (=not any other day) *that we went to the Chinese restaurant.* **6** used as the subject of the words "seem," "appear," "look," and "happen": *It looks like Henry's not going to be able to come to lunch.*

**7 it's me/John/a pen etc.** used in order to give the name of a person or thing when it is not already known: *"What's that?" "It's a pen."* | *"Who's on the phone?" "It's Jill."*

**8** used in order to talk about a child or animal when you do not know what sex s/he is: *"Marilyn had a baby." "Is it a boy or girl?"* –see also **that's it** (THAT¹)

**I·tal·ian**¹ /ɪˈtælyən/ *adj* **1** relating to or coming from Italy **2** relating to the Italian language

**Italian**² *n* **1** [U] the language used in Italy **2** someone from Italy

**i·tal·i·cize** /ɪˈtæləˌsaɪz/ *v* [T] to put or print written words in ITALICS –**italicized** *adj*

**i·tal·ics** /ɪˈtælɪks, aɪ-/ *n* [plural] a type of printed letters that lean to the right: *This example is printed* **in italics**.

**itch**¹ /ɪtʃ/ *v* **1** [I,T] to have an unpleasant ITCH: *My back is itching.* **2 be itching to do sth** INFORMAL to want to do something very much: *Ian's been itching to try out his new bike.*

**itch**² *n* **1** an unpleasant feeling on your skin that makes you want to rub it with your nails **2** INFORMAL a strong desire to do or have something: *an itch for travel* –**itchy** *adj* –**itchiness** *n* [U]

**it'd** /ˈɪt̮əd/ **1** the short form of "it would": *It'd be easier if we both did it.* **2** the short form of "it had": *It'd been raining since Sunday.*

**i·tem** /ˈaɪt̮əm/ *n* **1** a single thing in a set, group, or list: *There are over 20 items on the menu.* **2** a piece of news in the newspaper or on television: *I saw an item about the kidnapping in the paper.* **3 be an item** INFORMAL to be having a sexual or romantic relationship with someone

**i·tem·ize** /ˈaɪt̮əˌmaɪz/ *v* [T] to write down all of the parts of something in a list –**itemized** *adj*

**i·tin·er·ant** /aɪˈtɪnərənt/ *adj* FORMAL traveling from place to place

**i·tin·er·ar·y** /aɪˈtɪnəˌrɛri/ *n* a plan of a trip, usually including the places you want to see

**it'll** /ˈɪt̮l/ the short form of "it will" : *It'll be nice to see Martha again.*

**it's** /ɪts/ **1** the short form of "it is": *It's snowing!* **2** the short form of "it has": *It's been snowing all day.*

**its** /ɪts/ *possessive adj* belonging or relating to a thing, situation, person, or idea that has been mentioned or is known about: *The tree has lost all of its leaves.*

**it·self** /ɪtˈsɛlf/ *pron* **1** the REFLEXIVE form of "it": *The cat was licking itself.* **2 in itself** only the thing mentioned, and not anything else: *We're proud you finished the race. That in itself is an accomplishment.*

**it·sy-bit·sy** /ˌɪtsi ˈbɪtsi‹ / also **it·ty-bit·ty** /ˌɪt̮i ˈbɪt̮i‹ / *adj* INFORMAL very small

**IUD** *n* intrauterine device; a small plastic or met-

al object placed in a woman's UTERUS to prevent her from having a baby

**IV** *n* the abbreviation of "intravenous"; medical equipment that is used for putting liquid directly into your body

**I've** /aɪv/ the short form of "I have": *I've seen you somewhere before.*

**i·vo·ry** /ˈaɪvəri/ *n* **1** [C,U] the hard smooth yellow-white substance from an ELEPHANT's tooth, or something made from this substance **2** [U] a pale yellow-white color –**ivory** *adj*

**i·vy** /ˈaɪvi/ *n* [U] a climbing plant with dark green shiny leaves –see also POISON IVY

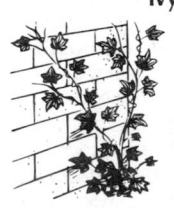

ivy

**Ivy League** /ˌ.. ˈ./ *adj* relating to a small group of old respected colleges in the north east of the US: *an Ivy League graduate* –**Ivy League** *n* [singular]

# J

**J, j** /dʒeɪ/ the tenth letter of the English alphabet

**jab** /dʒæb/ *v* [I,T] to quickly push something pointed into something else, or toward it: *The nurse jabbed a needle into his arm.* –**jab** *n*

**jab·ber** /ˈdʒæbɚ/ *v* [I] to talk quickly, in an excited way, and not very clearly

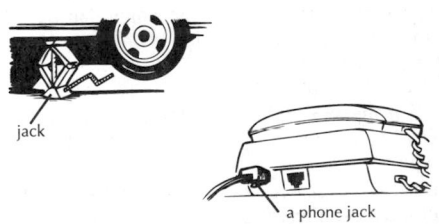

jack

jack

a phone jack

**jack**¹ /dʒæk/ *n* **1** a piece of equipment used for lifting something heavy, such as a car, and supporting it **2** an electronic connection for a telephone or other electronic machine

**jack**² *v*

**jack** sb/sth ↔ **up** *phr v* [T] **1** to lift something heavy using a JACK: *Dad jacked the car up so I could change the tire.* **2** to increase prices, sales etc. by a large amount: *Stores have jacked up their prices since July.*

**jack·al** /ˈdʒækəl/ *n* a wild animal like a dog that lives in Africa and Asia

**jack·ass** /ˈdʒækæs/ *n* **1** SPOKEN an impolite word meaning an annoying stupid person **2** a male DONKEY

**jack·et** /'dʒækɪt/ n **1** a short light coat −see picture at CLOTHES **2** the part of a SUIT that covers the top part of your body **3** ⇨ DUST JACKET

**jack·ham·mer** /'dʒæk,hæmɚ/ n a large powerful tool used for breaking hard materials such as the surface of a road

**jack-in-the-box** /'... ,./ n a toy shaped like a box from which a figure jumps out when the box's lid is lifted

**jack knife** /'. ./ n ⇨ POCKET KNIFE

**jack·knife** /'dʒæknaɪf/ v [I] if a truck or train with two or more parts jackknifes, the back part swings toward the front part

**jack-of-all-trades** /,. . ,. './ n [singular] someone who can do many different types of jobs

**jack-o-lan·tern** /'dʒæk ə ,læntɚn/ n a PUMPKIN with a face cut into it, usually with a light inside, made at HALLOWEEN

**jack·pot** /'dʒækpɑt/ n **1** a very large amount of money that you can win in a game **2 hit the jackpot a)** to win a lot of money **b)** to be very successful or lucky: *The movie "Total Recall" hit the jackpot.*

**Ja·cuz·zi** /dʒə'kuzi/ n TRADEMARK ⇨ HOT TUB

**jade** /dʒeɪd/ n [U] a usually green stone used for making jewelry and ORNAMENTS

**jad·ed** /'dʒeɪdɪd/ adj not interested in or excited by things because you have seen them or done them too much

**jag·ged** /'dʒægɪd/ adj having a rough uneven edge with a lot of sharp points: *jagged rocks*

**jag·uar** /'dʒægwɑr/ n a large wild cat with black spots from Central and South America

**jail**[1] /dʒeɪl/ n [C,U] a place where someone is sent to be punished for a crime; prison: *over-crowded jails | He was in jail for 15 years.*

**jail**[2] v [T] to put someone in JAIL

**jail·er, jailor** /'dʒeɪlɚ/ n someone whose job is to guard a prison or prisoners

**ja·lop·y** /dʒə'lɑpi/ n INFORMAL a very old car in bad condition

**jam**[1] /dʒæm/ v -mmed, -mming **1** [T] to push someone or something using a lot of force, especially into a small place: *Mr. Braithe jammed the letters into his pockets and left.* **2** [I,T] also **jam up** if a machine jams up or if you jam it, it stops working because something is stuck inside it: *Every time I try to use the Xerox machine it jams.* **3** [T] to fill a place with a lot of people or things, so that nothing can move: *The roads were jammed with cars.* **4** [I] to play music for fun with a group of people without practicing first

**jam**[2] n **1** [U] a thick sticky sweet substance made from fruit, usually eaten on bread: *strawberry jam* **2** also **traffic jam** a situation in which there are so many cars on the road that you cannot move: *Sorry I'm late −I got stuck in a jam.* **3 be in a jam/get into a jam** to be or

become involved in a difficult or bad situation: *Sarah, I'm in a jam −could you do me a favor?* **4** a situation in which something is stuck somewhere: *a jam in the fax machine*

**jamb** /dʒæm/ n the side post of a door or window

**jam·bo·ree** /,dʒæmbə'ri/ n a big noisy party or celebration

**jammed** /dʒæmd/ adj impossible to move because of being stuck: *The stupid door's jammed again.*

**jam-packed** /,. '.◂/ adj INFORMAL completely full of people or things: *a cereal jam-packed with vitamins*

**jam ses·sion** /'. ,../ n an occasion when people meet to play music together for fun

**Jane Doe** /,dʒeɪn 'dou/ n [singular] a name used in legal forms, documents etc. when a woman's name is not known

**jan·gle** /'dʒæŋgəl/ v [I,T] to make a noise that sounds like metal objects hitting against each other: *keys jangling in his pocket.*

**jan·i·tor** /'dʒænətɚ/ n someone whose job is to clean and take care of a large building: *the school janitor*

**Jan·u·ar·y** /'dʒænyu,ɛri/ written abbreviation **Jan.** n the first month of the year

> **USAGE NOTE January**
>
> When you use a month without a date, say "in January/February" etc. If you use it with a date, write "on January 9/10/11" etc. and say "on January ninth/tenth/eleventh" etc.

**Jap·a·nese**[1] /,dʒæpə'niz◂/ adj **1** relating to or coming from Japan **2** relating to the Japanese language

**Japanese**[2] n **1** [U] the language used in Japan **2 the Japanese** [plural] the people of Japan

**jar**[1] /dʒɑr/ n **1** a rounded glass container with a lid, used for storing food −see picture at CONTAINER **2** the amount of food contained in a jar: *half a jar of peanut butter*

**jar**[2] v -rred, -rring **1** [I,T] to shake or hit something with enough force to damage it or make it become loose: *Alice jarred her knee when she jumped off the wall.* **2** [I,T] to shock someone, especially by making an unpleasant noise: *The alarm jarred her awake.* **3** [I] to be very different in style and therefore look strange or unsuitable: *a modern building that jars with the historic surroundings*

**jar·gon** /'dʒɑrgən/ n [U] technical words and phrases that are difficult to understand unless you work in a particular profession: *medical jargon*

**jaun·dice** /'dʒɔndɪs, 'dʒɑn-/ n [U] a medical condition in which your skin and the white part of your eyes become yellow

**jaun·diced** /ˈdʒɔndɪst, ˈdʒɑn-/ *adj* **1** tending to judge people, things, or situations in a negative way: *a jaundiced view of the world* **2** suffering from JAUNDICE

**jaunt** /dʒɔnt, dʒɑnt/ *n* a short trip for pleasure

**jaun·ty** /ˈdʒɔnɾi, ˈdʒɑnɾi/ *adj* showing that you feel confident and cheerful –**jauntily** *adv*

**jav·e·lin** /ˈdʒævəlɪn, -vlɪn/ *n* **1** [U] a sport in which you throw a SPEAR (=a long pointed stick) as far as you can **2** the stick used in this sport

**jaw** /dʒɔ/ *n* **1** one of the two bones that form your mouth and that have all your teeth: *a broken jaw* **2** **sb's jaw dropped** used in order to say that someone looked very surprised or shocked: *Sam's jaw dropped when Katy walked into the room.*

**jaws** /dʒɔz/ *n* [plural] the mouth of an animal or person: *the powerful grip of the lion's jaws*

**jay·walk·ing** /ˈdʒeɪˌwɔkɪŋ/ *n* [U] the action of walking across a street in an area that is not marked for walking –**jaywalker** *n*

**jazz¹** /dʒæz/ *n* [U] **1** a type of popular music that usually has a strong beat and parts for performers to play alone **2** **and all that jazz** SPOKEN and things like that: *I'm sick of rules, responsibilities, and all that jazz.*

**jazz²** *v*

**jazz** sth ↔ **up** *phr v* [I,T] to make something more exciting and interesting: *We need a few pictures to jazz up the walls.*

**jazzed** /dʒæzd/ *adj* SPOKEN excited: *I'm really jazzed about going to New York.*

**jazz·y** /ˈdʒæzi/ *adj* **1** bright, colorful, and easily noticed: *a jazzy tie* **2** similar to the style of JAZZ music

**jeal·ous** /ˈdʒɛləs/ *adj* **1** feeling angry or unhappy because someone else has a quality, thing, or ability that you wish you had: *Diane was jealous of me because I got better grades.* **2** feeling angry or unhappy because someone you love is paying attention to another person, or because another person is showing too much interest in someone you love: *It used to make me jealous when he danced with other women.*

---

**USAGE NOTE jealous and envious**

If someone is **jealous**, s/he feels angry or unhappy because s/he cannot have something that someone else has: *Bill was jealous of his brother's success.* | *The older kids were jealous of the attention the new baby was getting.* If someone is **envious**, s/he wants to have the qualities or things that someone else has: *Linda was envious of Marcy's new car.*

---

**jeal·ous·y** /ˈdʒɛləsi/ *n* [C,U] the feeling of being JEALOUS

**jeans** /dʒinz/ *n* [plural] a popular type of pants made from DENIM

**Jeep** /dʒip/ *n* TRADEMARK a type of car made to travel over rough ground

**jeer** /dʒɪr/ *v* [I,T] to shout, speak, or laugh in order to annoy or frighten someone you dislike: *The crowd jeered at the speaker.* –**jeer** *n*

**jeez** /dʒiz/ *interjection* said in order to express sudden feelings such as surprise, anger, or shock

**Je·ho·vah's Wit·ness** /dʒɪˌhoʊvəz ˈwɪt⁻nɪs/ *n* a member of a religious organization that believes in every word of the Bible and will not fight in a war

**Jell-O, jello** /ˈdʒɛloʊ/ *n* [U] TRADEMARK a soft solid substance made from GELATIN and sweet fruit juice –see picture at DESSERT

**jel·ly** /ˈdʒɛli/ *n* [U] a thick sticky sweet substance made from fruit but having no pieces of fruit in it, usually eaten on bread: *a peanut butter and jelly sandwich*

**jel·ly·fish** /ˈdʒɛliˌfɪʃ/ *n* a round transparent sea animal with long things that hang down from its body

**jeop·ard·ize** /ˈdʒɛpəˌdaɪz/ *v* [T] to risk losing or destroying something that is valuable or important: *Junot was too worried about jeopardizing his career to say anything.*

**jeop·ard·y** /ˈdʒɛpədi/ *n* [U] **in jeopardy** in danger of being lost or destroyed

**jerk¹** /dʒɚk/ *v* **1** [I,T] to move with a quick movement, or to make something move this way: *Her head jerked up when Matt walked into the room.* **2** [I,T] to pull something suddenly and quickly: *Tom jerked open the door.*

**jerk** sb **around** *phr v* [T] INFORMAL to deliberately annoy someone by causing difficulties

**jerk²** *n* **1** INFORMAL someone who is stupid or very annoying: *What a jerk!* **2** a quick movement, especially a pulling movement: *He pulled the cord with a jerk.* –**jerky** *adj*

**jerk·y** /ˈdʒɚki/ *n* [U] pieces of dried meat, usually with a salty or SPICY taste

**jer·sey** /ˈdʒɚzi/ *n* [U] a shirt worn as part of a sports uniform

**jest** /dʒɛst/ *n* **1** **in jest** intending to be funny: *The criticisms were said in jest.* **2** a joke

**jest·er** /ˈdʒɛstər/ *n* a man employed in past times to entertain important people with jokes, stories etc.

**Je·sus¹** /ˈdʒizəs/, **Jesus Christ** /ˈ.. ˌ./ *n* the man on whose life and teachings Christianity is based

**Jesus²** *interjection* TABOO said when you are annoyed, angry, or surprised

**jet¹** /dʒɛt/ *n* **1** a fast plane with a jet engine **2** a narrow stream of gas, liquid etc. that is forced out of a small hole, or the small hole this comes from: *a strong jet of water*

**jet²** *v* **-tted, -tting** [I] INFORMAL to travel in a JET: *He jetted in from Paris yesterday.*

**jet en·gine** /ˌ. ˈ../ *n* an engine that forces out a

stream of hot air and gases, used in planes –see picture at AIRPLANE

**jet lag** /'. ./ *n* [U] the feeling of being very tired after traveling a long distance in a plane –**jet-lagged** *adj*

**jet-pro·pelled** /ˌ. .'.◂/ *adj* using a JET ENGINE for power –**jet propulsion** /ˌ. .'../ *n* [U]

**jet set** /'. ./ *n* [singular] rich and fashionable people who travel a lot –**jet setter** *n*

**jet·ti·son** /'dʒɛtəsən, -zən/ *v* [T] **1** to decide not to use an idea, plan, object etc.: *Jones & Co. had to jettison the project for lack of funds.* **2** to throw something from a plane or moving vehicle: *The pilot accidentally jettisoned some of their fuel.*

**jet·ty** /'dʒɛti/ *n* **1** a wide wall built out into the water, as protection against large waves **2** ⇨ WHARF

**jew·el** /'dʒuəl/ *n* a small valuable stone, such as a DIAMOND

**jew·eled** /'dʒuəld/ *adj* decorated with valuable stones

**jew·el·er** /'dʒuələ/ *n* someone who buys, sells, makes, or repairs jewelry

**jewelry**

ring

earrings

bracelet

necklace

brooch

**jew·el·ry** /'dʒuəlri/ *n* [U] small decorations you wear that are usually made from gold, silver, and jewels, such as rings and NECKLACEs

**jew·els** /'dʒuəlz/ *n* [plural] jewelry or decorations that are made with valuable stones

**Jew·ish** /'dʒuɪʃ/ *adj* belonging to a group of people whose religion is Judaism, or to a family that in ancient times lived in the land of Israel –**Jew** *n*

**jibe¹** /dʒaɪb/ *n* ⇨ GIBE

**jibe²** *v* [I] if two statements, actions etc. jibe with each other, they agree or make sense together: *Your statement to the police does not jibe with the facts.*

**jif·fy** /'dʒɪfi/ *n* SPOKEN **in a jiffy** very soon: *I'll be back in a jiffy.*

**jig** /dʒɪg/ *n* a type of quick dance, or the music for this dance

**jig·ger** /'dʒɪgə/ *n* a unit for measuring alcohol, equal to 1.5 OUNCEs

**jig·gle** /'dʒɪgəl/ *v* -**ggled**, -**ggling** [I,T] to move from side to side with short quick movements, or to make something do this: *Don't jiggle my arm while I'm pouring!*

**jig·saw puz·zle** /'dʒɪgsɔ ˌpʌzəl/ *n* a picture cut up into many small pieces that you try to fit together for fun

jigsaw puzzle

**jilt** /dʒɪlt/ *v* [T] to suddenly end a relationship with someone: *His girlfriend jilted him.* –**jilted** *adj*

**jin·gle¹** /'dʒɪŋgəl/ *v* [I,T] to shake small metal objects together so that they produce a noise, or to make this noise: *He jingled his keys in his pocket.*

**jingle²** *n* **1** a short song used in television and radio advertisements: *I can't get the jingle from that beer ad out of my head.* **2** the noise of something jingling (JINGLE)

**jinx** /dʒɪŋks/ *n* [singular] someone or something that brings bad luck, or a period of bad luck that results from this

**jinxed** /dʒɪŋkst/ *adj* often having bad luck, or making people have bad luck: *We must be jinxed, we've lost every game!*

**jit·ters** /'dʒɪtəz/ *n* **the jitters** the feeling of being nervous and anxious, especially before an important event: *I always get the jitters before I go on stage.*

**jit·ter·y** /'dʒɪtəri/ *adj* worried and nervous: *The recession has made consumers jittery.*

**jive¹** /dʒaɪv/ *v* [T] SLANG to try to make someone believe something that is not true: *You're jiving me!*

**jive²** *n* **1** a very fast type of dance, often performed to fast JAZZ music **2** [U] SLANG statements that you do not believe are true: *Don't you go giving me any of that jive!*

**job** /dʒɑb/ *n*
**1** ▶WORK◀ work that you do regularly in order to earn money: *I got a **part-time/full-time job** as a waitress.* | *She **applied for a job** at the bank.* | *He **quit/left his job** so he could go back to school.*
**2** **on the job** while doing work or at work: *Our reporters are on the job now.* | *All our employees get on-the-job training.*
**3** ▶DUTY◀ a particular duty or responsibility that you have: *It's my job to take care of my little brother.* | *It's Jim's job as secretary of the club to communicate with the members.*
**4** ▶IMPROVE STH◀ something you do to fix or improve something: *The car needs a paint job.* | *a nose job* (=an operation to change the shape of your nose)
**5** ▶STH YOU MUST DO◀ a piece of work

you must do, usually without being paid: *I have a lot of **odd jobs** (=different things) to do on Saturday.*

**6 ▶KIND OF THING◀** also **jobby** SPOKEN used in order to say that something is of a particular type: *His new computer's one of those little portable jobs.*

**7 do a nice/great etc. job** to do something very well: *Tina did a nice job on your makeup.*

**8 Good job!** SPOKEN said when you are proud that someone has done something well: *"Guess what? I passed the test!" "Good job!"*

**9 do the job** INFORMAL to make something have the result that you want or need: *A little more glue should do the job.*

**10 ▶CRIME◀** INFORMAL a crime such as robbing a bank

---

**USAGE NOTE    job, work, occupation, position, trade, career,** and **profession**

Use **work** as a general word to talk about what you do every day in order to earn money: *I have to go to work.* Your **job** is the particular type of work that you do: *Jeff just got a job as a waiter.* **Occupation** is a formal word for **job** that is used on official forms: *Please state your name, address, and occupation.* **Position** is a formal word that is used when a **job** is advertised in the newspaper. **Position** is also used by someone who is answering the advertisement: *I am writing to apply for the position of Teaching Assistant.* A **trade** is a job that you do with your hands and that needs skill: *She's an electrician by trade.* A **career** is a professional **job** that you do for most of your life, or for a long time: *Her political career began 20 years ago.* A **profession** is a **career** that you need a lot of formal training to do: *He decided to enter the medical profession.*

---

**jock** /dʒɑk/ *n* INFORMAL a student who plays a lot of sports

**jock·ey¹** /'dʒɑki/ *n* someone who rides horses in races

**jockey²** *v* [T] **jockey for position** to try to be in the best position or situation

**jock·strap** /'dʒɑkstræp/ *n* a piece of underwear that men wear when playing sports to support their sex organs

**joc·u·lar** /'dʒɑkyələ/ *adj* FORMAL joking or humorous —**jocularity** /ˌdʒɑkyə'lærəṭi/ *n* [U]

**jog¹** /dʒɑg/ *v* **-gged, -gging 1** [I] to run slowly and in a steady way, especially for exercise: *Julie jogs every morning.* —see picture on page 473 **2 jog sb's memory** to make someone remember something: *This picture might jog your memory.* **3** [T] to knock or push something lightly by mistake: *Someone jogged my elbow and I dropped the plate.*

**jog²** *n* [singular] a slow steady run, especially for exercise: *Let's go for a jog.*

**jog·ging** /'dʒɑgɪŋ/ *n* [U] the activity of running as a way of exercising: *Let's go jogging before breakfast.* —**jogger** *n*

**john** /dʒɑn/ *n* SPOKEN a toilet

**John Doe** /ˌdʒɑn 'doʊ/ *n* [singular] a name used in legal forms, documents etc. when a man's name is not known

**join** /dʒɔɪn/ *v* **1** [T] also **join in** to begin to take part in an activity that other people are involved in: *joining a political campaign* **2** [I,T] to become a member of an organization, society, or group: *He joined a health club to get in shape.* | *It doesn't cost anything to join.* **3** [T] to do something together with someone else: *Why don't you join us for dinner?* | *Please join with me in welcoming tonight's speaker.* **4** [I,T] to connect or fasten things together, or to be connected: *the place where the pipes join* **5 join the club!** SPOKEN said when you and other people are in the same situation: *You can't find a job? Join the club!* **6 join hands** if two or more people join hands, they hold each other's hands

**joint¹** /dʒɔɪnt/ *adj* **1** involving two or more people or groups, or owned or shared by them: *They have to reach a joint decision.* | *a joint bank account* | *"Who cooked dinner?" "It was a joint effort."* (=we did it together) **2 joint resolution** LAW a decision or law agreed by both houses of the US Congress and signed by the President —**jointly** *adv*: *The two of you will be jointly responsible for the project.*

**joint²** *n* **1** a part of the body where two bones meet, that can bend: *the knee joint* **2** SLANG a place, especially a BAR, club, or restaurant: *a fast-food joint* **3** SLANG a MARIJUANA cigarette **4** a place where two things or parts of an object are joined together: *One of the pipe joints was leaking.* **5 out of joint** a bone that is out of joint has been pushed out of its correct position —see also **put sb's nose out of joint** (NOSE¹)

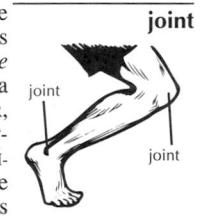
joint

**joint ven·ture** /ˌ. '../ *n* a business arrangement in which two or more companies work together to achieve something: *The two computer giants announced a joint venture in Malaysia.*

**joke¹** /dʒoʊk/ *n* **1** something funny that you say or do to make people laugh: *We stayed up telling jokes until two a.m.* **2** INFORMAL a situation that is so silly or unreasonable that it makes you angry: *What a joke that meeting was.* **3 take a joke** to be able to laugh at a joke about yourself: *Come on - can't you take a joke?*

**joke²** *v* [I] to say things that are intended to be

funny: *Owen's always **joking about** something.* —**jokingly** *adv*

**jok·er** /'dʒoʊkɚ/ *n* someone who makes a lot of jokes

**jol·ly** /'dʒɑli/ *adj* happy and cheerful

**jolt¹** /dʒoʊlt/ *n* **1** a sudden rough or violent movement: *We felt a big jolt, and then things started shaking* **2** a sudden shock: *a jolt of electricity | It was kind of an emotional jolt for me.*

**jolt²** *v* **1** [I,T] to move suddenly and roughly, or to make someone or something do this: *an earthquake that jolted southern California* **2** [T] to give someone a sudden shock: *companies jolted by the tax changes*

**jos·tle** /'dʒɑsəl/ *v* [I,T] to push or knock against someone in a crowd: *Spectators jostled for a better view.*

**jot** /dʒɑt/ *v* **-tted, -tting**
**jot sth ↔ down** *phr v* [T] to write something quickly: *Let me just **jot down** your phone number.*

**jour·nal** /'dʒɚnl/ *n* **1** a written record that you make of the things that happen to you each day **2** a magazine or newspaper for people who are interested in a particular subject: *The Wall Street Journal | a medical journal*

**jour·nal·is·m** /'dʒɚnl,ɪzəm/ *n* [U] the job or activity of writing reports for newspapers, magazines, television, or radio

**jour·nal·ist** /'dʒɚnl-ɪst/ *n* someone who writes reports for newspapers, magazines, television, or radio

**jour·ney** /'dʒɚni/ *n* a trip from one place to another, especially over a long distance —see usage note at TRAVEL²

**jo·vi·al** /'dʒoʊviəl/ *adj* friendly and cheerful: *a jovial face*

**jowls** /dʒaʊlz/ *n* [plural] loose skin on someone's lower jaw

**joy** /dʒɔɪ/ *n* [C,U] great happiness and pleasure, or something that gives you this feeling: *She laughed **with joy** at the news.*

**joy·ful** /'dʒɔɪfəl/ *adj* very happy, or likely to make people very happy: *joyful laughter* —**joyfully** *adv*

**joy·ous** /'dʒɔɪəs/ *adj* LITERARY full of happiness, or likely to make people happy: *a joyous song* —**joyously** *adv*

**joy·ride** /'dʒɔɪraɪd/ *n* a fast dangerous drive in a car, often after someone has stolen it for fun —**joyriding** *n* [U] —**joyrider** *n*

**joy·stick** /'dʒɔɪ,stɪk/ *n* a handle that you use in order to control something such as an aircraft or a computer game

**Jr.** *adj* the written abbreviation of JUNIOR

**ju·bi·lant** /'dʒubələnt/ *adj* extremely happy and pleased because you have been successful: *a jubilant smile* —**jubilation** /,dʒubə'leɪʃən/ *n* [U]

**Ju·da·ism** /'dʒudi,ɪzəm, -deɪ-, -də-/ *n* [U] the Jewish religion based on the Old Testament, the Talmud, and later teachings of the RABBIs

**judge¹** /dʒʌdʒ/ *n* **1** the official in control of a court who decides how criminals should be punished **2** someone who decides on the result of a competition: *a panel of judges at the Olympics* **3** someone who has a natural ability or the knowledge and experience to give an opinion about something: *a good judge of character*

**judge²** *v* **1** [I,T] to form or give an opinion about someone or something after thinking about all the information: *Employees should be **judged on** the quality of their work. | **Judging by** her clothes, I'd say she's rich.* **2** [T] to decide in court whether someone is guilty of a crime **3** [I,T] to decide the result in a competition: *Who's judging the pie-eating contest?* **4** [I,T] to form an opinion about someone in an unfair or criticizing way: *I just want Mom to stop judging me.*

**judg·ment** /'dʒʌdʒmənt/ *n* **1** [C,U] an opinion that you form after thinking about something: *It's time to **make** your own **judgments about** what to do. | People were right in their judgment of him.* **2** [U] the ability to make decisions about situations or people: *She seems to have pretty good judgment.* **3** [C,U] an official decision given by a judge or a court of law **4 judgment call** a decision you have to make yourself because there are no fixed rules in a situation

**judg·men·tal** /dʒʌdʒ'mɛntl/ *adj* too quick to form opinions and criticize other people

**Judgment Day** /'.. ,./ *n* a time after death when everyone is judged by God, according to some religions

**ju·di·cial** /dʒu'dɪʃəl/ *adj* relating to a court of law, judges etc.: *the judicial system*

**ju·di·ci·ar·y** /dʒu'dɪʃi,ɛri, -ʃəri/ *n* **the judiciary** FORMAL all the judges in a country who, as a group, form part of the system of government

**ju·di·cious** /dʒu'dɪʃəs/ *adj* FORMAL sensible and careful: *a judicious use of money*

**jug** /dʒʌg/ *n* a large deep container for liquids that has a narrow opening and a handle —see picture at CONTAINER

**jug·gle** /'dʒʌgəl/ *v*
**1** [I,T] to keep three or more objects moving through the air by throwing and catching them very quickly **2** [T] to try to fit two or more jobs, activities etc. into your life: *It's hard trying to juggle work and children.* —**juggler** *n*

juggle

**jug·u·lar** /'dʒʌgyələ/ *n* **1 go for the jugular** INFORMAL to criticize or attack someone very strongly **2** the large VEIN in your neck that takes blood from your head to your heart

**juice** /dʒus/ *n* **1** [C,U] the liquid that comes from fruit and vegetables, or a drink made from this: *a glass of orange juice* **2** [U] the liquid that comes out of meat when it is cooked **3** [U] INFORMAL electricity

**juic·y** /'dʒusi/ *adj* **1** containing a lot of juice: *a juicy peach* **2** **juicy gossip/details** INFORMAL interesting or shocking information **–juiciness** *n* [U]

**juke box** /'dʒuk bɑks/ *n* a machine in BARS and restaurants that plays music when you put money in it

**Ju·ly** /dʒʊ'laɪ, dʒə-/ written abbreviation **Jul.** *n* the seventh month of the year –see usage note at JANUARY

**jum·ble** /'dʒʌmbəl/ *n* [singular] a messy mixture of things: *a jumble of clothes on the floor* **–jumble** *v* [T]

**jum·bo** /'dʒʌmboʊ/ *adj* larger than other things of the same type: *a jumbo jet*

**jump¹** /dʒʌmp/ *v*
**1** ►UP◄ [I,T] to push yourself suddenly up in the air using your legs, or to go over something doing this: *Several fans tried to **jump onto** the stage.* | *kids **jumping up and down** on the bed* –see picture on page 473
**2** ►DOWN◄ [I] to let yourself drop from a place that is above the ground: *During the fire, two people jumped out of a window.*
**3** ►MOVE FAST◄ [I] to move quickly or suddenly in a particular direction: *Paul **jumped** up to answer the door.*
**4** ►IN SURPRISE/FEAR◄ [I] to make a sudden movement because you are surprised or frightened: *The sudden ring of the telephone **made us jump.***
**5** ►INCREASE◄ [I] to increase suddenly and by a large amount: *Profits **jumped** 20% last month.*
**6** **jump down sb's throat** INFORMAL to suddenly speak angrily to someone: *All I did was ask a question, and he **jumped down my throat!***
**7** **jump to conclusions** to form an opinion about something before you have all the facts: *Don't **jump to conclusions** when you don't know the facts!*
**8** **jump the gun** to start doing something too soon

**jump at** sth *phr v* [T] to eagerly accept the chance to do something: *Ruth **jumped at the chance** to study at Harvard.*

**jump on** sb *phr v* [T] INFORMAL to criticize or punish someone, especially unfairly: *Dad **jumps on Jeff** for every little mistake.*

**jump²** *n* **1** an act of pushing yourself suddenly up into the air using your legs **2** an act of letting yourself drop from a place that is above the ground: *a parachute jump* **3** a sudden large increase in an amount or value: *a jump in prices* **4** **get a jump on** to gain an advantage by doing something earlier than usual or earlier

than someone else: *I want to **get a jump on** my Christmas shopping.*

**jump·er** /'dʒʌmpɚ/ *n* a dress without SLEEVEs usually worn over a shirt

**jumper ca·ble** /'.. ˌ../ *n* [C usually plural] one of two thick wires used in order to send electricity from a car BATTERY that works to one that has stopped working

**jump rope** /'. ./ *n* a long piece of rope that children use for jumping over

**jump-start** /'. ./ *v* [T] **1** to do something to help a process or activity start working better or more quickly: *the government's efforts to jump-start the economy* **2** to start a car whose BATTERY has lost power by connecting it to the battery of a car that works

**jump·suit** /'dʒʌmpsut/ *n* a single piece of clothing like a shirt attached to a pair of pants, worn especially by women

**jump·y** /'dʒʌmpi/ *adj* worried or excited because you are expecting something bad to happen

**junc·tion** /'dʒʌŋkʃən/ *n* a place where one road, track etc. meets another one: *a railroad junction*

**junc·ture** /'dʒʌŋktʃɚ/ *n* **at this juncture** SPOKEN FORMAL at this point in an activity or time

**June** /dʒun/ written abbreviation **Jun.** *n* the sixth month of the year –see usage note at JANUARY

**jun·gle** /'dʒʌŋgəl/ *n* [C,U] a thick tropical forest with many large plants that grow very close together

**Jun·ior** /'dʒunyɚ/, written abbreviation **Jr.** *adj* used after the name of a man who has the same name as his father: *William Jones Jr.* –compare SENIOR

**junior¹** *n* **1** a student in the third year of HIGH SCHOOL or college **2** **be two/five/ten years sb's junior** to be two, five etc. years younger than someone else –compare SENIOR¹

**junior²** *adj* younger or of a lower rank: *a junior partner* –compare SENIOR²

**junior col·lege** /ˌ.. '../ *n* [C,U] a college where students take a course of study that continues for two years

**junior high school** /ˌ.. '. ˌ./ **junior high** /ˌ.. '. ./ *n* [C,U] a school in the US and Canada for students who are aged between 12 and 14 or 15

**junk** /dʒʌŋk/ *n* [U] old or unwanted things that have no use or value: *an attic filled with junk*

**jun·ket** /'dʒʌŋkɪt/ *n* a trip that is paid for by government money

**junk food** /'. ./ *n* [U] INFORMAL food that is not healthy because it has a lot of fat or sugar

**junk·ie** /'dʒʌŋki/ *n* **1** INFORMAL someone who takes dangerous drugs and is dependent on them **2** HUMOROUS someone who likes something so much that s/he seems to need it: *My dad's a TV junkie.*

**junk mail** /'. ./ *n* [U] letters that advertisers send to people

**junk·yard** /'dʒʌŋkˌyɑrd/ *n* **a)** a business that buys old cars, broken furniture etc. and sells the parts of them that can be used again **b)** the place where this business keeps the things it collects

**jun·ta** /'huntə, 'dʒʌntə/ *n* a military government that has gained power by using force

**Ju·pi·ter** /'dʒupətɚ/ *n* [singular] the largest PLANET that is the fifth farthest from the sun

**jur·is·dic·tion** /ˌdʒʊrɪs'dɪkʃən/ *n* [U] the right to use official authority to make legal decisions: *a matter outside the court's jurisdiction*

**ju·ror** /'dʒʊrɚ/ *n* a member of a JURY

**ju·ry** /'dʒʊri/ *n* **1** a group of 12 people who listen to details of a case in court and decide whether someone is guilty or not **2** a group of people chosen to judge a competition

**just¹** /dʒʌst/ *adv* **1** exactly: *My brother looks just like my dad.* **2** only: *I just play the piano for fun.* | *It happened just a few weeks ago.* | *Can you wait five minutes? I just have to iron this.* (=it's the last thing I have to do) **3** if something has just happened, it happened only a short time before: *I just got back from Marilyn's house.* **4 just about** almost: *She calls her grandfather just about every day.* | *I'm just about finished.* **5 be just about to do sth** to be going to do something soon: *We were just about to go riding when it started raining.* **6 be just doing sth** to be starting to do something: *I'm just making dinner now.* **7 just before/after etc.** only a short time before, after etc.: *Theresa got home just before us.* **8 (only) just** if something just happens, it does happen, but it almost did not: *Kurt only just made it home before the storm.* **9 just as** equally as: *The $250 TV is just as good as the $300 one.* **10 sth is just around the corner** used in order to say that something will happen or arrive soon: *Summer is just around the corner.*

SPOKEN PHRASES

**11** used for politely asking or telling someone something: *Could I just use your phone for a minute?* **12 just a minute/second** said in order to ask someone to wait for a short time: *Just a second - I can't find my keys.* **13** used in order to emphasize something that you are saying: *I just couldn't believe what she was saying.* | *Just shut up and listen!* **14 it's just that** used in order to explain the reason for something when someone thinks there is a different reason: *Boston is nice, it's just that I don't know anybody there.* **15 just now** a short time before now: *Your mother called just now.* **16 would just as soon** if you would just as soon do something, you would prefer to do it: *I'd just as soon go with you, if that's*

okay. **17 it's just as well** said when it is lucky that something has happened in the way it did, because if not, there may have been problems: *It's just as well Scott didn't go to the party, because Lisa was there.* **18 just because** used in order to say that although one thing is true, it does not mean that something else is true: *Just because you're older than me doesn't mean you can tell me what to do!*

---

USAGE NOTE just, already, and yet

In formal or written English, you must use these words with the present perfect tense: *I've already seen him.* | *The bell has just rung.* | *Have you eaten yet?* However, in informal speech, we often use these words with the simple past tense: *I already saw him.* | *The bell just rang.* | *Did you eat yet?*

---

**just²** *adj* morally right and fair: *a just punishment* —opposite UNJUST

**jus·tice** /'dʒʌstɪs/ *n* [U] **1** fairness in the way people are treated: *Children have a strong sense of justice.* **2** the system by which people are judged in courts of law and criminals are punished: *the criminal justice system* **3 do sb/sth justice** to treat or represent someone or something in a way that is fair and shows his, her, or its best qualities: *This picture doesn't do you justice.*

**Justice of the Peace** /ˌ... . . './ *n* FORMAL an official who judges offenses that are not serious, performs marriages, etc.

**jus·ti·fi·a·ble** /ˌdʒʌstə'faɪəbəl/ *adj* done for good reasons: *justifiable decisions* —**justifiably** *adv*

**jus·ti·fi·ca·tion** /ˌdʒʌstəfə'keɪʃən/ *n* [C,U] a good and acceptable reason for doing something: *There is no justification for terrorism.*

**jus·ti·fied** /'dʒʌstəˌfaɪd/ *adj* having an acceptable explanation or reason: *Your complaints are certainly justified.* —opposite UNJUSTIFIED

**jus·ti·fy** /'dʒʌstəˌfaɪ/ *v* [T] to give an acceptable explanation for something, especially when other people think it is unreasonable: *How can you justify spending so much money on a coat?*

**jut** /dʒʌt/ *v* **-tted, -tting** [I] also **jut out** to stick up or out farther than the other things in the same area: *a point of land that juts out into the ocean*

**ju·ve·nile** /'dʒuvənl, -ˌnaɪl/ *adj* **1** LAW relating to young people who are not yet adults: *juvenile crime* **2** typical of a child rather than an adult: *a juvenile sense of humor* —**juvenile** *n*

**juvenile de·lin·quent** /ˌ... .'../ *n* a child or young person who behaves in a criminal way

**jux·ta·pose** /'dʒʌkstəˌpoʊz, ˌdʒʌkstə'poʊz/ *v* [T] FORMAL to put things that are different to-

gether, especially in order to compare them
—**juxtaposition** /ˌdʒʌkstəpəˈzɪʃən/ *n* [C,U]

# K

**K, k** /keɪ/ the eleventh letter of the English
alphabet

**K** /keɪ/ *n* **1** the abbreviation of 1000: *He earns
$50K a year.* **2** the abbreviation of KILOBYTE

**ka·bob** /kəˈbɑb/ *n* small pieces of meat and
vegetables cooked on a stick

**ka·lei·do·scope** /kəˈlaɪdəˌskoʊp/ *n* a tube
with mirrors and pieces of colored glass at one
end, that shows colored patterns when you look
through and turn it

**kan·ga·roo** /ˌkæŋgəˈru/ *n* an Australian animal that has large strong back legs for jumping
and carries its babies in a pocket of skin on its
front

**ka·put** /kəˈpʊt/ *adj* SPOKEN broken: *The lawnmower's **gone kaput**.*

**kar·at** /ˈkærət/ *n* a unit for measuring how
pure a piece of gold is —see also CARAT

**ka·ra·te** /kəˈrɑṭi/ *n* [U] the Asian sport of
fighting in which you use your hands and feet to
hit and kick

**kar·ma** /ˈkɑrmə/ *n* [U] **1** INFORMAL the feeling
you get from a person, place, or action: *This
house has a lot of **good/bad karma**.* **2** the
force that is produced by the things you do in
your life and that will influence you in the future, according to some religions

**kay·ak** /ˈkaɪæk/ *n* a CANOE
(=type of boat) usually for
one person, that is enclosed
and has a hole for that
person to sit in

kayak

paddle

**keel¹** /kil/ *n* **on an even
keel** steady and without
any sudden changes

**keel²** *v*

  **keel over** *phr v* [I] to fall
over sideways

**keen** /kin/ *adj* **1** a keen sense of smell, sight,
or hearing is an extremely good ability to smell
etc. **2** someone with a keen mind can understand things quickly **3** very interested in something or eager to do it: *Most people are **keen to**
do a job well.* **—keenly** *adv*

**keep¹** /kip/ *v* **kept, kept, keeping**
**1** ▶NOT GIVE BACK◀ [T] to have something
and not give it back to the person who owned it
before: *You can keep the book. I don't need it
now.*
**2** ▶NOT LOSE◀ [T] to continue to have something and not lose it or get rid of it: *I kept the
letter for 35 years. | They're keeping the house
in Colorado and selling this one.*
**3** ▶CONTINUE IN STATE◀ [I,T] to make
someone or something continue to be in a
particular state or condition: *This blanket should
help you **keep warm**. | Her son **kept** her **waiting**
for an hour.*
**4 keep (on) doing sth** to continue doing something, or repeat an action many times: *If he
keeps on growing like this, he'll be taller than
Dad. | Rod kept calling them, but they weren't
home.*
**5** ▶STAY IN A PLACE◀ [T] to make someone
or something stay in a particular place: *They
kept him in jail for two weeks.*
**6** ▶DELAY◀ [T] to delay someone, or stop
someone from doing something: *I don't know
what's keeping her. It's 8:00 already. | Keep
those kids out of my yard!*
**7 keep a record/diary etc.** to regularly write
down information in a particular place: *Keep a
record of the food you eat for one week.*
**8 keep going** SPOKEN used in order to tell someone to continue doing something: *Keep going,
you're doing fine.*
**9 keep it down** SPOKEN said when you want
someone to be quiet: *Keep it down. I'm trying to
watch TV.*
**10 keep your promise** to do what you have
promised to do
**11 keep (sth) quiet** to not say anything in
order to avoid complaining, telling a secret, or
causing problems: *Let's keep quiet about this
until someone asks us.*
**12 keep a secret** to not tell anyone about a secret that you know
**13 keep sb posted** to continue to tell someone
the most recent news about someone or something: *Be sure to **keep us posted about** how
you're doing.*
**14** ▶FOOD◀ [I] if food keeps, it stays fresh
enough to still be eaten: *That yogurt won't keep
much longer.*

  **keep at** sth *phr v* [T] to continue working hard
at something: *Just keep at it until you get it
right.*

  **keep after** sb *phr v* [T] to tell someone to do
something again and again until s/he does it: *My
mother kept after me to practice.*

  **keep away** *phr v* [I,T **keep** sth/sb ↔ **away**] to
avoid going somewhere or seeing someone, or
to make someone do this: *Keep away from my
children! | Mom kept us away from school for a
week.*

  **keep** sth ↔ **down** *phr v* [T] **1** to control
something in order to prevent it from increasing:
*They promised to **keep** the rents **down**.* **2** to
stop yourself from VOMITing something: *I
couldn't keep any food down all week.*

  **keep from** *phr v* [T] **1** [**keep** sth **from** sb] to
not tell someone something that you know: *He
kept Angie's death from his family for 3 days.*
**2 keep (sb/sth) from doing sth** to prevent

someone or something from doing something: *It was hard to keep from telling him to shut up.* | *Put foil over the pie to keep it from burning.*

**keep** sth **off** *phr v* [T] to prevent something from affecting or damaging something else: *Wear a hat to keep the sun off your head.*

**keep** sb **on** *phr v* [T] to continue to employ someone: *We keep some of our Christmas workers on.*

**keep out** *phr v* **1 Keep Out!** used on signs to tell people that they are not allowed into a place **2** [T **keep** sb/sth **out**] to prevent someone or something from getting into a place: *a coat that keeps the rain out*

**keep out of** sth *phr v* [T] to not become involved with something: *My father's advice was to "keep out of trouble."*

**keep to** *phr v* **1** [T **keep to** sth] to continue to do, use, or talk about one thing and not change: *Keep to the main roads. They're better.* **2 keep** sth **to yourself** to not tell anyone else something that you know: *Kim kept Gina's secret to herself.* **3 keep to yourself** to not do things that involve other people, because you want to be alone: *Nina kept to herself at the party.*

**keep up** *phr v* **1** [T **keep** sth ↔ **up**] to prevent something from going to a lower level: *keeping up high standards of health care* **2** [I,T **keep** sth ↔ **up**] to continue doing something, or to make something continue: *Keep up the good work!* **3** [I] to move as fast as someone else: *Hey, slow down, I can't keep up!* **4** [I] to learn as fast or do as much as other people: *Davey isn't keeping up with the rest of the class in reading.* **5** [I] to continue to learn about a subject: *It's hard to keep up on/with changes in computer technology.* **6** [T **keep** sb **up**] to prevent someone from sleeping: *The racket next door kept us up all night.*

**keep²** *n* **1 earn your keep** to do a job in order to pay for the basic things you need such as food, clothing etc. **2 for keeps** a phrase meaning always, used especially by children

**keep·ing** /'kipɪŋ/ *n* [U] **1 for safe keeping** in order to avoid losing something: *I'll put the tickets here for safe keeping.* **2 in keeping/out of keeping** suitable or not suitable for a particular occasion or purpose: *a silly joke out of keeping with the solemn occasion*

**keep·sake** /'kipseɪk/ *n* a small object that reminds you of someone

**keg** /kɛg/ *n* a large container with curved sides and a flat top and bottom, used for storing beer

**ken·nel** /'kɛnl/ *n* a place where dogs are cared for while their owners are away, or the CAGE where they sleep

**kept** /kɛpt/ *v* the past tense and PAST PARTICIPLE of KEEP

**ker·nel** /'kɔnl/ *n* **1** the center part of a nut or seed, usually the part you can eat **2** something

that forms the most important part of a statement, idea, plan etc.: *There may be a kernel of truth in what he says.*

**ker·o·sene** /'kɛrə,sin, ,kɛrə'sin/ *n* [U] a type of oil that is burned for heat and light

**ketch·up** /'kɛtʃəp, 'kæ-/ *n* [U] a thick liquid made from TOMATOes

**ket·tle** /'kɛtl/ *n* a metal container used for boiling and pouring water

**key¹** /ki/ *n* **1** a specially shaped piece of metal that you put into a lock in order to lock or unlock a door, start a car etc. **2 the key** the part of a plan, action, etc. that everything else depends on: *Exercise is the key to a healthy body.* **3** the part of a musical instrument or a machine such as a computer that you press with your fingers to make it work **4** a set of seven musical notes that have a particular base note, or the quality of sound these notes have: *the key of G*

**key²** *adj* very important and necessary for success or to understand something: *a key witness*

**key³** *v*

**key** sth ↔ **in** *phr v* [T] to put information into a computer by using a KEYBOARD

**key·board** /'kibɔrd/ *n* a row or several rows of keys on a machine such as a computer, or a musical instrument such as a piano

**keyboard**

**keyed up** /,. './ *adj* worried or excited: *We were all very keyed up about the test.*

**key·hole** /'kihoʊl/ *n* the hole in a lock that you put a key in

**key·note** /'kinoʊt/ *adj* **keynote speaker/speech** the most important speaker at an official event, or the speech that s/he gives

**key ring** /'. ./ *n* a metal ring that you keep keys on

**kg.** *n* the written abbreviation of KILOGRAM

**kha·ki** /'kæki/ *n* [U] **1** a dull pale green-brown or yellow-brown color **2** cloth of this color, especially when worn by soldiers –**khaki** *adj*

**kha·kis** /'kækiz/ *n* [plural] pants that are made from KHAKI

K

**kick¹** /kɪk/ *v* **1** [T] to hit something with your foot: *She kicked the pile of books over.* | *Stop kicking me!* **2** [I,T] to move your legs as if you are kicking something: *a baby kicking its legs* **3 kick the habit** to stop doing something, such as smoking, that is a harmful habit **4 I could kick myself** SPOKEN

**kick**

said when you are annoyed because you have made a mistake or missed an opportunity: *I could have kicked myself for saying that.*

**5 kick the bucket** HUMOROUS to die

**kick around** *phr v* [T] **1** [kick sth ↔ **around**] to think about something a lot or get people's opinions about it before making a decision: *Doug's been kicking around an idea for the slogan.* **2** [kick sb ↔ **around**] to treat someone badly or unfairly: *He won't be kicking me around anymore!*

**kick back** *phr v* [I] INFORMAL to relax: *Here. Kick back and have a beer.*

**kick in** *phr v* **1** [I] INFORMAL to begin to have an effect: *Those pills should kick in any time now.* **2** [T kick sth ↔ **in**] to kick something so hard that it breaks: *The police had to kick the door in.*

**kick off** *phr v* [I,T kick sth ↔ **off**] INFORMAL to start, or to make an event start: *The festivities will kick off with a barbecue dinner.*

**kick** sb ↔ **out** *phr v* [T] INFORMAL to make someone leave a place

**kick²** *n* **1** an act of hitting something with your foot: *If the gate won't open, just give it a good kick.* (=kick it hard) **2** INFORMAL a strong feeling of excitement or pleasure: *Alan gets a real kick out of skiing.* | *She started stealing for kicks.* **3 be on a health/wine/swimming etc. kick** INFORMAL to have a new interest that you are very involved in

**kick·back** /ˈkɪkbæk/ *n* [C,U] INFORMAL money that you pay secretly or dishonestly for someone's help; BRIBE

**kick·off** /ˈkɪk-ɔf/ *n* [C,U] the time when a game of football starts, or the first kick that starts it: *Kickoff is at 3:00.*

**kick-start** /ˈ.. ./ *v* [T] to start a MOTORCYCLE using your foot

**kid¹** /kɪd/ *n* **1** INFORMAL a child: *How many kids do you have?* **2** INFORMAL a young person: *college kids* **3 kid stuff** INFORMAL something that is very easy or boring **4** [C,U] a young goat, or the leather made from its skin

**kid²** *v* **-dded, -dding** INFORMAL **1** [I,T] to say something that is not true, especially as a joke: *Don't get mad, I was just kidding.* **2** [T] to make yourself believe something that is untrue or unlikely: *Don't kid yourself; she'll never change.* **3 no kidding** SPOKEN used in order to ask someone if what s/he says is true, or to show that you already know it is true: *"You lived in Baltimore? I did, too." "No kidding."*

**kid³** *adj* **kid brother/sister** INFORMAL your brother or sister who is younger than you

**kid·do** /ˈkɪdoʊ/ *n* SPOKEN said when talking to a child or friend: *Okay, kiddo, it's time to go.*

**kid·nap** /ˈkɪdnæp/ *v* **-pped, -pping** [T] to take someone away illegally and demand money for returning him/her –**kidnapper** *n* –**kidnapping** *n* [C,U]

**kid·ney** /ˈkɪdni/ *n* one of the two organs in the body that separate waste liquid from blood and make URINE

**kidney bean** /ˈ.. ˌ./ *n* a dark red bean, shaped like a KIDNEY

**kill¹** /kɪl/ *v* **1** [I,T] to make a living thing die: *First she killed her husband, then she killed herself.* | *These chemicals can kill.* **2** [T] to make something stop, end, or finish: *Nothing that the doctor gives me kills the pain.* **3 sb will kill sb** SPOKEN used in order to say that someone will get very angry at someone else: *My wife will kill me if I don't get home soon.* **4 sth is killing me** SPOKEN used in order to say that a part of your body is hurting a lot: *My head is killing me.* **5 kill time** INFORMAL to do something that is not very interesting while you are waiting for something to happen **6 kill two birds with one stone** to achieve two things with one action

**kill** sb/sth ↔ **off** *phr v* [T] to cause the death of a lot of people, animals, or plants: *What killed off the dinosaurs?*

**kill²** *n* [singular] an animal killed by another animal, especially for food: *The lion dragged its kill into the bushes.*

**kill·er¹** /ˈkɪlɚ/ *n* a person, animal, or thing that kills or has killed: *The police are still looking for the girl's killer.* –**killer** *adj: a killer disease*

**killer²** *adj* SLANG extremely good, extremely difficult to deal with, extremely impressive etc.: *He's working a killer schedule.*

**kill·ing** /ˈkɪlɪŋ/ *n* **1** a murder: *a series of brutal killings* **2 make a killing** INFORMAL to make a lot of money very quickly

**kiln** /kɪln/ *n* a special OVEN for baking clay pots, bricks etc.

**ki·lo** /ˈkiloʊ, ˈkɪ-/ *n* ⇨ KILOGRAM

**ki·lo·byte** /ˈkɪləˌbaɪt/ *n* a unit for measuring computer information, equal to 1024 BYTES

**ki·lo·gram** /ˈkɪləˌgræm/ *n* a unit for measuring weight, equal to 1000 grams

**ki·lo·me·ter** /kɪˈlɑmətɚ, ˈkɪləˌmitɚ/ *n* a unit for measuring length, equal to 1000 meters

**ki·lo·watt** /ˈkɪləˌwɑt/ *n* a unit for measuring electrical power, equal to 1000 WATTS

**kilt** /kɪlt/ *n* a type of thick PLAID skirt, traditionally worn by Scottish men

**ki·mo·no** /kəˈmoʊnoʊ/ *n* a loose piece of clothing with wide SLEEVES, traditionally worn in Japan

**kin** /kɪn/ *n* [plural] **1 next of kin** FORMAL your most closely related family **2** OLD-FASHIONED your family

**kind¹** /kaɪnd/ *n* **1** a type or sort of person or thing: *What kind of pizza do you want?* | *We sell all kinds of hats.* **2 kind of** SPOKEN **a)** slightly, or in some ways: *You must be kind of disappointed.* **b)** used when you are explaining something and want to avoid giving the details: *I kind of made it look like the post office had lost*

**kitchen**

his letter. **3 a kind of (a)** SPOKEN used in order to say that your description of something is not exact: *a kind of a reddish-brown color* **4 of a kind** of the same type: *Each vase is handmade and is one of a kind.* (=the only one of its type) **5 in kind** by doing the same thing that has just been done to or for you: *The US should respond in kind if other countries do not trade fairly.*

**kind²** *adj* helpful, friendly, and caring toward other people: *Thank you for your kind invitation. | That was very kind of you.* ✗ DON'T SAY "That was very kindly" ✗

**kind·a** /ˈkaɪndə/ SPOKEN NONSTANDARD a short form of "kind of": *I'm kinda tired.*

**kin·der·gar·ten** /ˈkɪndəˌgɑrtˀn, -ˌgɑrdn/ *n* a class for young children, usually aged five, that prepares them for school

**kind-heart·ed** /ˌ. ˈ...◂/ *adj* kind and generous: *a kind-hearted woman*

**kin·dle** /ˈkɪndl/ *v* **1** [I,T] to start burning, or to make something start burning: *They taught us how to kindle a fire.* **2 kindle excitement/ interest etc.** to make someone excited, interested etc.

**kin·dling** /ˈkɪndlɪŋ/ *n* [U] small pieces of dry wood, leaves etc. that you use for starting a fire

**kind·ly¹** /ˈkaɪndli/ *adv* **1** in a kind way; generously: *Mr. Thomas has kindly offered to let us use his car.* **2** SPOKEN a word meaning "please," often used when you are annoyed: *Would you kindly go away?* **3 not take kindly to sth** to be annoyed or upset by something that someone says or does: *He didn't take kindly to my remark about his brother.*

**kindly²** *adj* kind and caring about other people; SYMPATHETIC: *a kindly woman*

**kind·ness** /ˈkaɪndnɪs/ *n* [C,U] kind behavior, or a kind action: *kindness to animals | It would be a kindness to tell him the truth.*

**kin·dred** /ˈkɪndrɪd/ *adj* **a kindred spirit** someone who thinks and feels the way you do

**kin·folk** /ˈkɪnfoʊk/, **kinfolks** *n* [plural] OLD-FASHIONED your family

**king** /kɪŋ/ *n* **1** a man from a royal family who rules a country: *the King of Spain | King Edward* **2** someone who is considered to be the most important or best member of a group: *the king of rock'n'roll*

**king·dom** /ˈkɪŋdəm/ *n* **1** a country ruled by a king or queen **2 the animal/plant/mineral kingdom** one of the three parts into which the natural world is divided

**king·fish·er** /ˈkɪŋˌfɪʃə/ *n* a small brightly colored wild bird that eats fish from rivers and lakes

**king·pin** /ˈkɪŋˌpɪn/ *n* the most important person in an organized group: *a drug kingpin*

**king-size** /ˈ. ./, **king-sized** *adj* very large, and usually the largest of its type: *a king-size bed*

**kink** /kɪŋk/ *n* **1** a twist in something that is normally straight: *The hose has a kink in it.* **2 work out the kinks** to solve all the problems in a plan, situation etc.

**kink·y** /ˈkɪŋki/ *adj* INFORMAL **1** someone who is kinky or who does kinky things has strange ways of getting sexual excitement **2** kinky hair has very tight curls

**ki·osk** /ˈkiɑsk/ *n* a small building where you can buy things such as newspapers or tickets

**kiss¹** /kɪs/ *v* **1** [I,T] to touch someone with your lips as a greeting, or to show love: *She kissed me on the cheek. | Matt kissed her goodnight and left the room.* **2 kiss sth goodbye** SPOKEN used in order to say that someone will lose his/her chance to get or do something: *If you don't work harder you can kiss medical school goodbye.*

kiss

**K**

**kiss**[2] *n* the action of touching someone with your lips as a greeting, or to show love: *Come here and give me a kiss.*

**kit** /kɪt/ *n* **1** a set of tools, equipment etc. that you use for a particular purpose or activity: *a first-aid kit* **2** something that you buy in parts and put together yourself: *He made the model from a kit.*

**kitch·en** /'kɪtʃən/ *n* the room where you prepare and cook food

**kite** /kaɪt/ *n* a toy that you fly in the air on the end of a long string, made from a light frame covered in paper or plastic

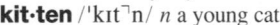

kite

**kitsch** /kɪtʃ/ *n* [U] kitsch decorations, movies etc. seem to be cheap and without style, and often amuse people because of this —**kitsch, kitschy** *adj*

**kit·ten** /'kɪt⌐n/ *n* a young cat

**kit·ty** /'kɪti/ *n* [C usually singular] **1** SPOKEN also **kittycat** a word meaning a cat, used by children or when calling to a cat: *Here, kitty kitty!* **2** INFORMAL the money that people have collected for a particular purpose

**kitty-cor·ner** /'.. ˌ../ *adv* INFORMAL on the opposite corner of a street from a particular place: *His store is kitty-corner from the bank.*

**ki·wi** /'kiwi/, **kiwi fruit** /'.. ./ *n* a soft green fruit with small black seeds and a thin brown skin

**Kleen·ex** /'klinɛks/ *n* [C,U] TRADEMARK a piece of soft thin paper, used especially for blowing your nose

**klep·to·ma·ni·ac** /ˌklɛptə'meɪniˌæk/ *n* someone who has a mental illness in which s/he has an uncontrollable desire to steal things

**klutz** /klʌts/ *n* INFORMAL someone who often drops things, falls easily etc. —**klutzy** *adj*

**km** *n* the written abbreviation of KILOMETER

**knack** /næk/ *n* [singular] INFORMAL a natural ability to do something well: *Harry **has the knack of** making friends wherever he goes.* —see usage note at ABILITY

**knap·sack** /'næpsæk/ *n* a bag that you carry on your back

**knead** /nid/ *v* [T] to press a mixture of flour and water many times with your hands: *Knead the bread dough for three minutes.*

**knee**[1] /ni/ *n* **1** the joint that bends in the middle of your leg —see picture at BODY **2** the part of your pants that covers your knee: *His jeans had holes in both knees.* **3 bring sb/sth to their knees a)** to defeat a country or group of people in a war **b)** to have such a bad effect on an organization, activity etc. that it cannot continue

**knee**[2] *v* [T] to hit someone with your knee: *Victor **kneed** him **in** the stomach.*

**knee·cap** /'nikæp/ *n* the bone at the front of your knee

**knee-deep** /ˌ. '.◂/ *adj* **1** deep enough to reach your knees: ***knee-deep in** mud* **2** INFORMAL greatly affected by something that you cannot avoid: *Ralph lost his job, and we ended up **knee-deep in** debt.*

**knee-high** /ˌ. '.◂/ *adj* tall enough to reach your knees: *knee-high grass*

**knee-jerk** /'. ./ *adj* DISAPPROVING relating to the reactions someone always has to particular questions or situations, without thinking about them first: *a **knee-jerk reaction** | a knee-jerk liberal*

**kneel** /nil/, **kneel down** *v* **knelt** /nɛlt/ *or* **kneeled, knelt** *or* **kneeled, kneeling** [I] to be in or move into a position where your body is resting on your knees: *She **knelt down on** the floor to pray.* —see picture on page 473

**knew** /nu/ *v* the past tense of KNOW

**knick·ers** /'nɪkɚz/ *n* [plural] old-fashioned loose pants that are short and fit tightly at the knees

**knick-knack** /'nɪk næk/ *n* INFORMAL a small object used as a decoration

**knife**[1] /naɪf/ *n, plural* **knives** a tool used for cutting or as a weapon, consisting of a metal blade attached to a handle: *a knife and fork*

**knife**[2] *v* [T] to STAB someone: *They got into a fight, and Raul was **knifed in** the stomach.*

**knight**[1] /naɪt/ *n* in the Middle Ages, a man with a high rank who fought while riding a horse

**knight**[2] *v* [T] to give someone a KNIGHTHOOD: *He was knighted in 1977.*

**knight·hood** /'naɪthʊd/ *n* [C,U] a special title or rank that is given to someone by the King or Queen in Britain

**knit** /nɪt/ *v* **knitted** *or* **knit, knitted** *or* **knit, knitting** [I,T] **1** to make clothes out of YARN (=thick thread) using special sticks to weave or tie the stitches together: *She's knitting me a sweater.* **2** to join people, things, or ideas more closely, or to be closely connected: *The broken bone should **knit together** smoothly. | a tightly knit family* **3 knit your brows** to show you are worried, thinking hard etc. by moving your EYEBROWs together

**knit·ting** /'nɪtɪŋ/ *n* [U] something that is being KNITted: *Margaret keeps her knitting in a canvas bag.*

**knitting nee·dle** /'.. ˌ../ *n* one of the two long sticks that you use to KNIT something —see picture at NEEDLE[1]

**knives** /naɪvz/ *n* the plural of KNIFE

**knob** /nɑb/ *n* a round handle that you turn or pull to open a door or drawer, turn on a radio etc.

**knob·by** /'nɑbi/ *adj* with hard parts that stick out from under the surface of something: *knobby knees*

K

knock     knock over

**knock**[1] /nak/ v **1** [I] to hit a door or window with your closed hand in order to attract someone's attention: *I've been knocking at/on the door for five minutes.* **2** [I,T] to hit someone or something with a quick hard hit, so that he, she, or it moves or falls down: *Don't knock my beer over.* | *Scott Payton got knocked down by a truck.* | *The ball was knocked loose, and Benjamin grabbed it.* | *A car knocked into a pole in the parking lot.* **3** **knock sb unconscious** to hit someone so hard that s/he becomes unconscious

---
SPOKEN PHRASES

**4** **Knock it off!** SPOKEN used in order to tell someone to stop doing something because it is annoying you **5** [T] to criticize someone or something: *"I hate this job." "Don't knock it - lots of people would like to have it."* **6** **knock some sense into sb** to make someone learn to behave in a more sensible way: *Maybe getting arrested will knock some sense into him.* **7** **knock on wood** an expression that is used after a statement about something good, in order to prevent your luck from becoming bad: *I haven't had a cold all winter, knock on wood.*

---

**knock** sth ↔ **back** phr v [T] to drink a large amount of alcohol very quickly: *We knocked back a bottle of tequila in an hour.*

**knock** sth ↔ **down** phr v [T] INFORMAL to reduce the price of something: *The new stove we bought was knocked down from $800 to $550.*

**knock off** phr v INFORMAL **1** [I] to stop working: *It's late; let's knock off for the day.* **2** [T **knock** sth ↔ **off**] to reduce the price of something by a particular amount: *I got him to knock $10 off the regular price.*

**knock out** phr v [T] **1** [**knock** sb ↔ **out**] to make someone become unconscious, especially by hitting him/her: *He knocked out his opponent in the fifth round.* **2** [**knock** sb/sth ↔ **out**] to defeat a person or team in a competition so that he, she, or it cannot continue to be in it: *Indiana knocked Kentucky out of the tournament.* **3** **knock yourself out** INFORMAL to work very hard: *I really knocked myself out to finish the essay on time.*

**knock** sb/sth ↔ **over** phr v [T] to hit someone or something so hard that he, she, or it falls down: *Scott knocked the lamp over.*

**knock** sb ↔ **up** phr v [T] SLANG to make a woman PREGNANT

**knock**[2] n **1** the sound of something hard hitting a hard surface: *a loud knock at the door* **2** the action of something hard hitting your body: *a knock on the head* **3** **take a knock** INFORMAL to have some bad luck or trouble: *Lee's taken quite a few hard knocks lately.*

**knock·down-drag-out** /,.. '. ./ adj using all kinds of methods to win, sometimes including violence: *a knockdown-drag-out election campaign*

**knock·er** /'nakɚ/ n a piece of metal on an outside door that you use to KNOCK loudly

**knock-on** /'. ./ adj **have a knock-on effect** to start a process in which each part is directly influenced by the one before it: *The price rises will have a knock-on effect throughout the economy.*

**knock·out** /'nak-aʊt/ n **1** an act of hitting your opponent so hard in BOXING that s/he cannot get up again **2** INFORMAL someone who is very attractive: *Barbara is a real knockout.*

**knoll** /noʊl/ n a small round hill

**knot**[1] /nat/ n **1** a place where two ends or pieces of rope, string etc. have been tied together: *Her Brownie troop is learning how to tie knots.* **2** many hairs, threads etc. that are twisted together: *My hair always ends up in knots.* **3** a unit for measuring the speed of a ship, equal to 6080 feet per hour or about 1853 meters per hour **4** a hard round place in a piece of wood where a branch once joined the tree **5** a small group of people standing close together **6** a tight painful place in a muscle, or a tight uncomfortable feeling in your stomach: *My stomach is in knots.* **7** **tie the knot** INFORMAL to get married

knot

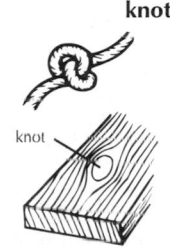

knot

**knot**[2] v -tted, -tting **1** [T] to tie together two ends or pieces of rope, string etc. **2** [I,T] if hairs, threads etc. knot or something knots them, they become twisted together

**knot·ty** /'nati/ adj knotty wood contains a lot of knots

**know**[1] /noʊ/ v knew, known, knowing **1** ▶HAVE INFORMATION◀ [I,T] to have information about something: *Do you know the answer?* | *She knows a lot about rare coins.* | *We don't know what we're supposed to be doing.* | *Martin didn't know that Ricky was coming.* | *He wants to know* (=wants to be told) *what happened.* **2** ▶BE SURE◀ [I,T] to be sure about something: *I knew she didn't like him.* | *Barry didn't know what to say.* **3** ▶BE FAMILIAR WITH◀ [T] to be familiar

K

with a person, place, system etc.: *I knew Hilary in high school. | She knows the city well because she grew up there. | He said he'd like to get to know us better.* (=would like to know more about us)

**4** ▶REALIZE◀ [T] to realize or understand something: *I don't think he knows how stupid he sounds. | I know exactly how you feel!*

**5** ▶RECOGNIZE◀ [T] to be able to recognize someone or something: *She knew it was Gail by her voice.* (=she recognized Gail because of her voice)

**6 know better** to be old or experienced enough to avoid making mistakes: *Ben should have known better than to tell his mother.*

**7 know your way around** to be familiar with a place, organization, system etc. so that you can use it effectively

**8 know full well/know perfectly well** used in order to emphasize that someone realizes or understands something: *You know perfectly well what I mean.*

---

SPOKEN PHRASES

**9 you know a)** said when you cannot quickly think of what to say next: *It has, you know, cherry pie filling.* **b)** said when you are trying to explain something by giving more information: *I have some clothes for Matthew, you know, for the baby, if Carrie wants them.* **c)** said when you begin talking about a subject: *You know, I worked in Arizona before I came here.* **d)** said in order to check if someone understands what you are saying: *I feel like New Mexico is really my home, you know?*

**10 I know a)** used in order to agree with someone: *"Trey's shoes are so ugly!" "I know, aren't they awful?"* **b)** said when you suddenly have an idea or think of the answer to a problem: *I know, let's ask Mr. McMillan for help.*

**11 as far as I know** said when you think something is true, but you are not sure: *As far as I know, Gail left at 6:00.*

**12 you never know** used in order to say that you are not sure about what will happen: *You never know. You might be lucky and win!*

---

—see also **how do you know** (HOW)

**know of** sb/sth *phr v* [T] **1** to have been told about or have read about someone or something, but not know much about it: *Do you know of any good restaurants around here?* **2 not that I know of** used in order to say that the answer to a question is "no," but that there may be other facts you do not know about: *"She was married before, wasn't she?" "Not that I know of."*

**know²** *n* **in the know** having a position in which you know more about something than most people: *Those in the know say that gas prices will go up next month.*

**know-how** /'. ./ *n* [U] INFORMAL practical ability or skill

**know·ing** /'nouɪŋ/ *adj* showing that you know all about something: *Glenn gave her a knowing look when she came in late.*

**know·ing·ly** /'nouɪŋli/ *adv* **1** in a way that shows you know all about something: *Brenda smiled knowingly at me.* **2** deliberately: *He'd never knowingly hurt you.*

**know-it-all** /'. . ,./ *n* INFORMAL someone who behaves as if s/he knows everything

**knowl·edge** /'nɑlɪdʒ/ *n* [U] **1** the information and understanding that you have gained through learning or experience: *His knowledge of American history is impressive.* **2** what someone knows or has information about: *To the best of my knowledge, none of the staff has complained.* (=I think this is true, although I may not have all the facts) | *The decision to attack was made without my knowledge.* (=without my knowing about it) | *"Is she really leaving?" "Not to my knowledge."* (=I do not think this is true, based on what I know)

**knowl·edge·a·ble** /'nɑlɪdʒəbəl/ *adj* knowing a lot: *Steve's very knowledgeable about politics.*

**known¹** /noun/ *v* the PAST PARTICIPLE of KNOW

**known²** *adj* known about, especially by many people: *a known criminal*

**knuck·le¹** /'nʌkəl/ *n* one of the joints in your fingers —see picture at HAND¹

**knuckle²** *v*

**knuckle down** *phr v* [I] INFORMAL to suddenly start working hard: *You just have to knuckle down and do it.*

**knuckle under** *phr v* [I] INFORMAL to accept someone's authority or orders without wanting to: *She refused to knuckle under to company regulations.*

**KO** *n* the abbreviation of KNOCKOUT

**ko·a·la** /kou'ɑlə/, **koala bear** /.'.. ,./ *n* an Australian animal like a small bear that climbs trees and eats leaves

**Ko·ran** /kə'ræn, -'rɑn/ *n* **1 the Koran** the holy book of the Muslim religion **2** a copy of this book

**Ko·re·an¹** /kə'riən/ *adj* **1** relating to or coming from Korea **2** relating to the Korean language

**Korean²** *n* **1** [U] the language used in Korea **2** someone from Korea

**ko·sher** /'kouʃɚ/ *adj* **1** kosher food is prepared according to Jewish law **2** kosher restaurants or stores sell food prepared in this way **3** INFORMAL honest and legal, or socially acceptable: *Are you sure their offer is kosher?*

**kow·tow** /'kautau/ *v* [I] INFORMAL to be too eager to please or obey someone who has more power than you: *Be polite, but don't kowtow to him.*

**Krem·lin** /'krɛmlɪn/ *n* **the Kremlin** the government of Russia and the former USSR, or the buildings that are this government's offices

**KS** the written abbreviation of Kansas

**ku·dos** /'kudoʊs, -doʊz/ *n* [U] admiration and respect that you get for being important or doing something important

**kung fu** /ˌkʌŋ 'fu/ *n* [U] a Chinese method of fighting in which you attack people with your feet and hands

**kW** *n* the written abbreviation of KILOWATT

**KY** the written abbreviation of Kentucky

**L, l** /ɛl/ **1** the twelfth letter of the English alphabet **2** the ROMAN NUMERAL (=number) for 50

**LA** the written abbreviation of Louisiana

**lab** /læb/ *n* INFORMAL ⇨ LABORATORY

**la·bel¹** /'leɪbəl/ *n* **1** a piece of paper or cloth that is attached to something and has information about that thing printed on it: *a label on a wine bottle | Always read the instructions on the label.* **2** a famous name that represents the company that is selling a product: *a clothing designer's label* **3** a word or phrase that is used in order to describe someone or something: *As a writer, he's proud of his "liberal" label.*

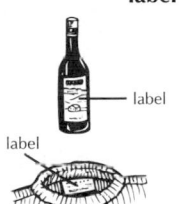

label

**label²** *v* [T] **1** to attach a LABEL to something, or to write information on something: *Make sure your charts are clearly labeled.* **2** to use a particular word or phrase in order to describe someone: *Teachers labeled the child a "slow learner."*

**la·bor¹** /'leɪbɚ/ *n* **1** [C,U] work, especially work using a lot of physical or mental effort: *farm labor | manual labor* (=physical work) **2** [U] all the people who work in an industry or country: *The auto industry needs skilled labor.* (=trained workers) **3** [U] the process of a baby being born, or the period when this happens: *Sandra was in labor for 17 hours.*

**labor²** *v* **1** [I] to work very hard: *farmers laboring in the fields* **2** [I,T] to try to do something that is difficult: *He labored over the report for hours.*

**lab·ora·to·ry** /'læbrəˌtɔri/ *n* a room or building in which a scientist does special tests and RESEARCH

**labor camp** /'.. ˌ./ *n* a place where prisoners are forced to do hard physical work

**Labor Day** /'.. ˌ./ *n* a national holiday in the US and Canada on the first Monday in September, to show support for workers

**la·bor·er** /'leɪbərɚ/ *n* someone whose job involves a lot of physical work

**la·bo·ri·ous** /lə'bɔriəs/ *adj* needing to be done slowly, and with a lot of effort: *the laborious process of examining all the data*

**labor u·nion** /'.. ˌ../ *n* an organization that represents workers in a particular industry, usually to discuss wages and working conditions with employers

**Lab·ra·dor** /'læbrəˌdɔr/ *n* a large dog with black or yellow fur, often used for guiding blind people

**lab·y·rinth** /'læbəˌrɪnθ/ *n* ⇨ MAZE

**lace¹** /leɪs/ *n* [U] a type of fine cloth with patterns of very small holes in it: *white lace on a wedding dress* –see also LACES

**lace²** *v* [T] also **lace up** to fasten clothes or shoes by tying their LACES: *Paul laced up his boots.*

**lac·er·ate** /'læsəˌreɪt/ *v* [T] to badly cut or tear the skin –**laceration** /ˌlæsə'reɪʃən/ *n*

**lac·es** /'leɪsɪz/ *n* [plural] strings that are pulled through special holes in clothing or shoes in order to fasten them –see picture at SHOE¹

**lack¹** /læk/ *n* [singular, U] the state of not having something or not having enough of something: *The project was canceled for lack of money.* (=because there was not enough) | *a total lack of interest*

**lack²** *v* [T] to not have something or enough of something: *Unfortunately, he lacks confidence.*

**lack·ing** /'lækɪŋ/ *adj* **1 be lacking in** to not have enough of a particular thing or quality: *No one said she was lacking in determination.* **2** not existing or available: *Information about the cause of the crash was lacking.*

**lack·lus·ter** /'lækˌlʌstɚ/ *adj* not very exciting or impressive: *a lackluster performance*

**la·con·ic** /lə'kɑnɪk/ *adj* tending to use only a few words when you talk

**lac·quer** /'lækɚ/ *n* a clear substance painted on wood or metal to give it a hard shiny surface –**lacquered** *adj: a lacquered box*

**lac·y** /'leɪsi/ *adj* decorated with LACE, or looking like lace: *black lacy underwear | lacy flowers*

**lad** /læd/ *n* OLD-FASHIONED a boy or young man

**lad·der** /'lædɚ/ *n* **1** a piece of equipment used for climbing up to high places, consisting of two long BARs connected with RUNGs (=steps) **2** the jobs you have to do in an organization in order to gradu-

**ladder**

L

ally become more powerful or important: *Stevens worked his way to the top of the corporate ladder*.

**lad·en** /'leɪdn/ *adj* carrying or loaded with a lot of something: *Grandma walked in, laden with presents*.

**la·dies' room** /'.. ,./ *n* a room in a public building with toilets for women – see usage note at TOILET

**la·dle** /'leɪdl/ *n* a deep spoon with a long handle – **ladle** *v* [T]: *ladling soup into bowls*

**la·dy** /'leɪdi/ *n* **1** a word meaning a woman, used in order to be polite: *Good afternoon, ladies.* | *a sweet old lady* **2** SPOKEN OFFENSIVE said when talking to a woman you do not know: *Hey, lady, get out of the way!*

**la·dy·bug** /'leɪdi,bʌg/ *n* a small round BEETLE (=insect) that is red with black spots

**lag**[1] /læg/ *v* **-gged, -gging** [I] **lag behind** to move or develop more slowly than other things or people: *Many small firms are lagging behind their larger rivals.*

**lag**[2] *n* a delay between two events – see also JET LAG

**la·goon** /lə'gun/ *n* an area of ocean that is not very deep, and is nearly separated from the ocean by rocks, sand, or CORAL

**laid** /leɪd/ *v* the past tense and PAST PARTICIPLE of LAY

**laid-back** /,. '.◂/ *adj* relaxed and not seeming to worry about anything: *He's easy to talk to, and very laid-back.*

**lain** /leɪn/ *v* the PAST PARTICIPLE of LIE

**lair** /lɛr/ *n* the place where a wild animal hides and sleeps: *a wolf's lair*

**lake** /leɪk/ *n* a large area of water surrounded by land: *We're going swimming in the lake.* | *Lake Michigan*

**lamb** /læm/ *n* [C,U] a young sheep, or the meat of a young sheep – see usage note at MEAT

**lam·bast** /læm'beɪst, 'læmbeɪst/ *v* [T] to severely criticize someone or something: *The governor lambasted state workers for wasting money.*

**lame**[1] /leɪm/ *adj* **1** unable to walk easily because your leg or foot is injured **2** INFORMAL too silly or stupid to believe: *a lame excuse*

**lame**[2] *v* [T] to make a person or animal LAME

**lame duck** /,. './ *n* someone in an official position, such as a president, who is powerless because his/her period in office will soon end

**la·ment**[1] /lə'mɛnt/ *v* [I,T] to express feelings of great sadness or disappointment about something

**lament**[2] *n* something such as a song that expresses great sadness

**lam·en·ta·ble** /lə'mɛntəbəl/ *adj* very disappointing: *her lamentable performance at the tennis match*

**lam·i·nate** /'læmə,neɪt/ *v* [T] to cover paper or wood with a thin layer of plastic in order to protect it – **laminated** *adj*

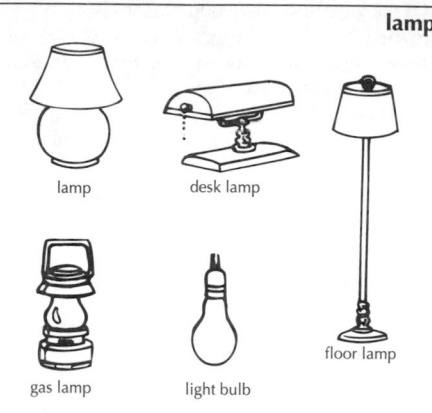

**lamp**

lamp          desk lamp

gas lamp          light bulb          floor lamp

**lamp** /læmp/ *n* an object that produces light by using electricity, oil, or gas: *a desk lamp*

**lam·poon** /læm'pun/ *v* [T] to write about someone such as a politician in a funny way that makes him/her seem stupid – **lampoon** *n*

**lamp·shade** /'læmpʃeɪd/ *n* a decorative cover put over the top of a lamp in order to make the light less bright

**lance** /læns/ *n* a long thin pointed weapon used in past times by soldiers on horses

**land**[1] /lænd/ *n* **1** [U] the ground, especially when owned by someone and used for buildings or farming: *A mall is being built on the land near the lake.* | *5000 acres of agricultural land* **2** [U] the solid dry part of the Earth's surface: *Frogs live on land and in the water.* **3** LITERARY a country or place, especially one with a particular quality: *a faraway land* – see usage note at EARTH

**land**[2] *v* **1** [I,T] if a plane lands, or if a pilot lands a plane, the plane moves down until it is safely on the ground: *My flight landed in Chicago an hour late.* **2** [I] to fall or come down onto something after moving through the air: *Chris slipped and landed on his back.* **3** [I] to arrive somewhere in a boat, plane etc.: *The Pilgrims landed on Cape Cod in 1620.* **4** [T] to put someone or something on land from a plane or boat: *They landed 1200 troops on the beach.* **5** [T] INFORMAL to finally succeed in getting a particular job, contract, or deal: *Kelly's landed a job with a big law firm.*

**land·fill** /'lændfɪl/ *n* a place where waste is buried in large amounts

**land·ing** /'lændɪŋ/ *n* **1** the floor at the top of a set of stairs **2** the action of arriving on land, or of making something such as a plane or boat come onto land – compare TAKEOFF

**landing gear** /'.. ,./ *n* [U] an aircraft's wheels and wheel supports – see picture at AIRPLANE

**landing pad** /'.. ,./ *n* the area where a HELICOPTER comes down to earth

**landing strip** /'.. ,./ *n* a special road on which a plane lands, especially not at an airport −compare RUNWAY

**land·la·dy** /'lænd,leɪdi/ *n* a woman who owns a building or other property and rents it to people

**land·locked** /'lændlɑkt/ *adj* surrounded by land: *a landlocked country*

**land·lord** /'lændlɔrd/ *n* someone who owns a building or other property and rents it to other people

**land·mark** /'lændmɑrk/ *n* **1** something that helps you recognize where you are, such as a famous building **2** one of the most important events, changes, or discoveries that influences someone or something: *a scientific landmark*

**land·own·er** /'lænd,oʊnɚ/ *n* someone who owns a large amount of land

**land·scape¹** /'lændskeɪp/ *n* **1** a view across an area of land, including hills, forests, fields etc.: *the sandy landscape of the desert* −compare SCENERY **2** a photograph or painting of a landscape

**landscape²** *v* [T] to arrange where the plants should grow in a park, yard, or garden

**land·slide** /'lændslaɪd/ *n* **1** the sudden falling of a lot of soil and rocks down the side of a hill, cliff, or mountain: *Part of Highway 101 is blocked by a landslide.* **2** a victory in which a person or political party wins a lot more votes than the others in an election: *Reagan won by a landslide in 1984.*

**lane** /leɪn/ *n* **1** one of the parts of a main road that is divided by painted lines: *driving in the fast/slow lane* (=in the lane that is farthest left or farthest right) **2** a narrow country road **3** one of the narrow areas that a pool or race track is divided into

**lan·guage** /'læŋgwɪdʒ/ *n* **1** a system of speaking, and usually writing, used by people in one country or area: *the English language | "Do you speak any foreign languages?" "Yes, I speak French."* ✗ DON'T SAY "I speak French language." ✗ **2** [U] the system of written and spoken words that people use to communicate: *language skills* **3** [C,U] TECHNICAL a system of commands and instructions used for operating a computer **4** [C,U] the way that something such as poetry or music expresses feelings **5** [U] INFORMAL words and phrases that most people consider to be offensive; swearing: *Watch your language!* (=stop swearing!)

**language lab·ora·to·ry** /'.. ,..../ *n* a room in a school or college where students can listen to TAPEs of a foreign language and practice speaking it

**lan·guid** /'læŋgwɪd/ *adj* moving slowly and weakly, but in an attractive way −**languorous** /'læŋgərəs/ *adj* −compare LISTLESS

**lan·guish** /'læŋgwɪʃ/ *v* [I] to be prevented from developing, improving, or being dealt with: *a case that has languished for years in the courts*

**lank·y** /'læŋki/ *adj* someone who is lanky is very tall and thin

**lan·tern** /'læntɚn/ *n* a type of lamp you can carry, that usually has a metal frame and glass sides

**lap¹** /læp/ *n* **1** the upper part of your legs when you are sitting down: *sitting on Grandma's comfortable lap* **2** a single trip around a race track or between the two ends of a pool: *Patty swims 30 laps a day.*

**lap²** *v* **-pped, -pping** **1** [I,T] if water laps something or laps against something, it touches something with small waves: *the sound of the lake lapping against the shore* **2** [T] also **lap up** to drink using quick movements of the tongue: *a cat lapping milk*

**lap sth ↔ up** *phr v* [T] DISAPPROVING to enjoy or believe something without criticizing or doubting it at all: *She's flattering him and he's just lapping it up!*

**la·pel** /lə'pɛl/ *n* the front part of a coat or JACKET that is attached to the collar and folds back on both sides

**lapse¹** /læps/ *n* **1** a short period of time when you forget something, do not pay attention, or fail to do something you should: *a memory lapse* **2** the period of time between two events: *a lapse of 5 years*

**lapse²** *v* [I] to end, especially because an agreed time limit is finished: *a book on which the copyright has lapsed*

**lapse into sth** *phr v* [T] **1** to start behaving or speaking in a very different way, especially one that is more normal or usual for you: *Without thinking, he lapsed into French.* **2** to become very quiet, less active, or unconscious: *She lapsed into silence. | a country lapsing back into recession*

**lap·top** /'læptɑp/ *n* a small computer that you can carry with you

**lar·ce·ny** /'lɑrsəni/ *n* [C,U] LAW the action or crime of stealing something

**larch** /lɑrtʃ/ *n* [C,U] a tree with bright green leaves shaped like needles that fall off in winter

**lard** /lɑrd/ *n* [U] the thick white fat from pigs, used in cooking

**large** /lɑrdʒ/ *adj* **1** big, or bigger than usual in size, number, or amount: *I'd like a large pepperoni pizza, please. | What's the largest city in Canada?* −opposite SMALL −see usage note at BIG **2** **at large** in general: *The risk is to American society at large.* **3** **be at large** to not yet be caught by the police: *Police say the murderer is still at large.* **4** **larger than life** more attractive, exciting, or interesting than other people or things **5** **by and large** used in order to say that something is generally true or

usually happens, but not always: *By and large, the decisions are all made by the students.*
—**largeness** *n* [U]

**large·ly** /ˈlɑrdʒli/ *adv* mostly or mainly: *The delay was largely due to bad weather.*

**large-scale** /ˌ. ˈ.◂/ *adj* involving a lot of people, effort, money, supplies etc.: *large-scale unemployment*

**lark** /lɑrk/ *n* a small wild brown bird that sings and has long pointed wings

**lar·va** /ˈlɑrvə/ *n, plural* **larvae** /ˈlɑrvi/ a young insect with a soft tube-shaped body, that will become an insect with wings

**lar·yn·gi·tis** /ˌlærənˈdʒaɪt̮ɪs/ *n* [U] an illness in which your throat and LARYNX are swollen, making it difficult for you to talk

**lar·ynx** /ˈlærɪŋks/ *n* TECHNICAL the part of your throat from which your voice is produced

**las·civ·i·ous** /ləˈsɪviəs/ *adj* DISAPPROVING showing a very strong sexual desire

**la·ser** /ˈleɪzɚ/ *n* a piece of equipment that produces a powerful narrow beam of light, or the beam of light itself: *laser surgery*

**lash**[1] /læʃ/ *v* **1** [T] to hit someone very hard with a whip, stick etc. **2** [T] to tie something tightly to something else using a rope **3** [I,T] to hit sharply against something: *waves lashing the rocks*

**lash out** *phr v* [I] **1** to suddenly speak loudly and angrily: *Georgie **lashed out at** him, screaming abuse.* **2** to suddenly try to hit someone with a lot of violent uncontrolled movements

**lash**[2] *n* **1** a hit with a whip, especially as a punishment **2** ⇨ EYELASH

**las·so** /ˈlæsoʊ/ *n* a rope with one end tied in a circle, used for catching cattle and horses —**lasso** *v* [T]

**last**[1] /læst/ *determiner, adj* **1** most recent: *Did you go to the last football game?* | *I saw Tim **last night/week/Sunday**.* | *The **last time** we went to that restaurant, I got sick afterward.* —compare NEXT[1] **2** at the end, after everyone or everything else: *The last part of the song is sad.* | *He's **the last person** I'd ask for help.* (=I do not want to ask him) **3** remaining after all others have gone: *Chris is always the last person to leave a party.* | *my last cigarette* **4 on its last legs** likely to fail or break: *The truck was on its last legs.* **5 have the last word** to make the last statement in an argument, which gives you an advantage

**last**[2] *adv* **1** most recently before now: *When I last saw her she was pregnant.* **2** after everything or everyone else: *Harris is going to speak last.* **3 last but not least** said when making a final statement, to show that it is just as important as your other statements: *...and last but not least, I'd like to thank my mother.*

**last**[3] *n, pron* **1 the last** the person or thing that comes after all the others: *Joe was the last of nine children.* (=he was born last) | *Les was*

the last to go to bed that night. **2 the day/week/year before last** the day, week etc. before the one that has just finished **3 the last I/we...** INFORMAL used when telling someone the most recent news that you know: *The last we heard, Paul was in Cuba.* | *The last I talked to her, she seemed fine.* **4 the last of** the remaining part of something: *We ate the last of that bread yesterday.*

**last**[4] *v* [I] **1** to continue for a particular length of time: *Jeff's operation lasted 3 hours.* **2** to continue to be effective, useful, or in good condition: *Most batteries will last for up to 8 hours.* **3** to be involved in a situation for a long time, especially when it is difficult: *I doubt their relationship will last.*

**last-ditch** /ˌ. ˈ.◂/ *adj* **last-ditch effort/attempt etc.** a final attempt to achieve something before it becomes impossible to do

**last·ing** /ˈlæstɪŋ/ *adj* continuing for a long time: *a lasting peace agreement*

**last·ly** /ˈlæstli/ *adv* FORMAL used when telling someone the last thing in a series of statements: *And lastly, we ask you all to be patient.*

**last name** /ˌ. ˈ./ *n* your family's name, which in English comes after your other names —compare FIRST NAME, MIDDLE NAME —see usage note at NAMES

**latch**[1] /lætʃ/ *n* a small metal BAR used for fastening a door, gate, window etc.

**latch**[2] *v*

**latch onto** sth *phr v* [T] INFORMAL if you latch onto an idea, style, phrase etc. you think it is so good, important etc. that you start using it too

**late**[1] /leɪt/ *adj* **1** arriving, happening, or done after the expected time: *Sorry I'm late. I got stuck in traffic.* | *Peggy was **late for** school.* | *a late breakfast* **2** near the end of a period of time: *a house built in the late 19th century* | *working until **late at night*** **3** happening at night, especially when most people are asleep: *I watched the late show on TV.* **4** paid or given back after the arranged time: *Oh no, my library books are late.* **5** FORMAL dead: *Mrs. Clausen's late husband*

**late**[2] *adv* **1** after the usual or expected time: *Most restaurants stay open late on Fridays.* | *I probably won't be home until late.* | *Our flight arrived 2 hours late.* **2** near the end of a period of time: *late in the afternoon* | *taking a walk **late at night***

**late·ly** /ˈleɪtli/ *adv* recently: *Lately I've been really busy.*

---

**USAGE NOTE** **lately** and **recently**

Use both of these words with the present perfect tenses to talk about something that began in the recent past and continues until now: *Lately I've been thinking about buying a new car.* | *Recently I've been thinking about buying a new car.* You can also use **recently** with the past tense to talk about a particular action in the recent past: *She recently got married.* ✘ DON'T SAY "She lately got married." ✘

**la·tent** /'leɪˀnt/ *adj* present but not yet noticeable, active, or completely developed: *a latent disease*

**lat·er**[1] /'leɪtɚ/ *adv* **1** after the present time or a time you are talking about: *I'll see you later.* | *They met in July, and two months later they were married.* **2 later on** at some time in the future, or after something else: *Later on in the movie the hero gets killed.*

**later**[2] *adj* **1** coming in the future, or after something else: *This will be decided at a later time/date.* | *information in a later chapter* **2** more recent: *Later models of the car are much improved.* ✘ DON'T SAY "models that are later." ✘

**lat·er·al** /'lætərəl/ *adj* TECHNICAL relating to the side of something, or movement to the side

**lat·est**[1] /'leɪtɪst/ *adj* the most recent or the newest: *What's the latest news?* | *the latest fashions* —see usage note at NEW

**latest**[2] *n* **at the latest** no later than the time mentioned: *I want you home by 11 at the latest.*

**la·tex** /'leɪtɛks/ *n* [U] a thick white liquid used for making products such as rubber, glue, and paint, and produced artificially or by some plants

**lath·er**[1] /'læðɚ/ *n* [singular, U] a lot of small white BUBBLES produced by rubbing soap with water

**lather**[2] *v* [I,T] to produce a LATHER, or cover something with lather

**Lat·in**[1] /'lætˀn/ *adj* **1** relating to or coming from Mexico, Central America, or South America **2** relating to the Latin language

**Latin**[2] *n* [U] an old language that is now used mostly for legal, scientific, or medical words

**La·ti·na** /lə'tinə/ *n* a woman in the US whose family comes from a country in LATIN AMERICA

**Lat·in A·mer·i·ca** /ˌlætˀn ə'mɛrɪkə/ *n* the land including Mexico, Central America, and South America —**Latin American** *adj*

**La·ti·no** /lə'tinoʊ/ *n* a man in the US whose family comes from a country in LATIN AMERICA. In the plural, Latinos can mean a group of men and women, or just men

**lat·i·tude** /'lætə,tud/ *n* **1** [C,U] TECHNICAL the distance north or south of the EQUATOR, measured in degrees —compare LONGITUDE —see picture at AXIS **2** [U] freedom to do or say what you like: *Students now have greater latitude in choosing their classes.*

**la·trine** /lə'trin/ *n* an outdoor toilet at a camp or military area

**lat·ter**[1] /'lætɚ/ *n* **the latter** FORMAL the second of two people or things that are mentioned: *Either glass or plastic would be effective, but the latter (=plastic) weighs less.* —compare FORMER[2]*

**latter**[2] *adj* **1** FORMAL being the last person or thing that has just been mentioned: *Of the phrases "go crazy" and "go nuts," the latter term is used less frequently.* **2** closer to the end of a period of time: *the latter part of the 19th century*

**laud·a·ble** /'lɔdəbəl/ *adj* FORMAL deserving praise or admiration

**laugh**[1] /læf/ *v* **1** [I] to make a sound with your voice, usually while smiling, because you think something is funny: *How come no one ever laughs at my jokes?* | *Then Tom's pants fell down and we all burst out laughing.* **2 laugh in sb's face** to show that you do not respect someone or will not obey him/her: *I told him he had to leave, but he just laughed in my face.*

**laugh at** sb/sth *phr v* [T] to make unkind or funny remarks about someone because s/he does or says something stupid: *Mommy, all the kids at school were laughing at me!*

**laugh** sth ↔ **off** *phr v* [T] to joke about something in order to pretend that it is not very serious or important: *She laughed off their insults.*

**laugh**[2] *n* **1** the sound you make when you laugh: *a big hearty laugh* **2 have the last laugh** to finally be successful after someone has criticized or defeated you

**laugh·a·ble** /'læfəbəl/ *adj* impossible to be treated seriously because of being so silly, bad, or difficult to believe

**laugh·ing·stock** /'læfɪŋ,stɑk/ *n* someone who has done something so silly or stupid that people laugh unkindly at him/her

**laugh·ter** /'læftɚ/ *n* [U] the action of laughing, or the sound of people laughing: *a roar of laughter from the audience*

**launch**[1] /lɔntʃ, lɑntʃ/ *v* [T] **1** to start something new, such as an activity, plan, or profession: *the movie that launched his acting career* **2** to send a weapon or a space vehicle into the sky or into space **3** to put a boat or ship into the water

**launch into** sth *phr v* [T] to suddenly start describing something or criticizing something: *He launched into the story of his life.*

**launch**[2] *n* an occasion at which a new product is shown or made available

**launch pad** *n* /'. ./ the area from which a space vehicle, ROCKET etc. is sent into space

**laun·der** /'lɔndɚ, 'lɑn-/ *v* [T] **1** to put stolen money into legal businesses or bank accounts in order to hide it or use it **2** FORMAL to wash clothes

**laun·dro·mat** /'lɔndrə,mæt, 'lɑn-/ *n* a place where you pay money to wash your clothes in machines

**laun·dry** /'lɔndri, 'lɑn-/ *n* [U] clothes, sheets etc. that need to be washed, or that have already

L

been washed: *I have to **do the laundry**.* (=wash clothes, sheets etc.)

**lau·re·ate** /'lɔriɪt, 'lɑr-/ *n* someone who has been given an important prize: *a Nobel laureate*

**lau·rel** /'lɔrəl, 'lɑr-/ *n* a small tree with smooth shiny dark green leaves that do not fall off in winter

**la·va** /'lɑvə, 'lævə/ *n* [U] **1** hot melted rock that flows from a VOLCANO **2** this rock when it becomes cold and solid

**lav·a·to·ry** /'lævə‚tɔri/ *n* FORMAL the room a toilet is in −see usage note at TOILET

**lav·en·der** /'lævəndɚ/ *n* a plant with purple flowers that have a strong pleasant smell

**lav·ish¹** /'lævɪʃ/ *adj* very generous and often expensive or complicated: *lavish gifts* | *He is **lavish with** his praise.*

**lavish²** *v*

**lavish sth on sb** *phr v* [T] to give someone a lot of something good: *They **lavish** a lot of attention **on** their children.*

**law** /lɔ/ *n* **1** [singular, U] the system of rules that people in a country, city, or state must obey: *Drunk driving is **against the law**.* (=illegal) | ***breaking the law*** (=doing something illegal) **2** a rule that people in a particular country, city, or local area must obey: *The city is trying to **pass a** new **law** allowing overnight parking.* **3 the law** the police: *Is he in trouble with the law?* **4 law and order** a situation in which people respect the law, and crime is controlled by the police, the prison system etc.: *The national guard was sent in to restore law and order.* **5** a statement that describes and explains how something works: *the law of gravity* | *the economic law of supply and demand*

**law-a·bid·ing** /'. .‚../ *adj* respectful of the law and obeying it

**law·ful** /'lɔfəl/ *adj* FORMAL considered by the government or law courts to be legal −opposite UNLAWFUL

**law·less** /'lɔlɪs/ *adj* FORMAL not obeying the law, or not controlled by law

**lawn** /lɔn/ *n* an area of ground around a house or in a park that is covered with grass −see picture on page 471

**lawn mow·er** /'lɔn ‚mouɚ/ *n* a machine that you use to cut the grass

**law·suit** /'lɔsut/ *n* a problem or complaint that someone brings to a court of law to be settled, especially for money

**law·yer** /'lɔyɚ/ *n* someone whose job is to advise people about laws, write formal agreements, or represent people in court

**lax** /læks/ *adj* not strict or careful about standards of behavior, work, safety etc.: *lax security for the building* −**laxity** *n* [U]

**lax·a·tive** /'læksəţɪv/ *n* a medicine or something that you eat that makes your BOWELs empty easily −**laxative** *adj*

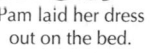

Pam laid her dress out on the bed.  Pam lay down on the bed.

**lay¹** /leɪ/ *v* **laid, laid, laying** **1** [T] to put someone or something carefully into a particular position: *Guests can **lay** their coats **on** the bed.* | *Martha **laid** the baby **down**.* **2 lay bricks/carpet/cable etc.** to put or attach something in the correct place, especially onto something or under the ground: *laying down a new bedroom carpet* **3** [I,T] if a bird, insect etc. lays eggs, it produces them from its body **4 lay a finger/hand on sb** to hurt someone, especially to hit him/her: *If you lay a hand on her, I'll call the police.* **5 lay blame/criticism/emphasis etc** FORMAL to blame, criticize, emphasize etc. **6 lay yourself open to blame/criticism etc.** to do something that makes you likely to be blamed, criticized etc. −compare LIE¹

**lay sth↔down** *phr v* [T] to officially state rules, methods etc. that someone must obey or use: *strict safety regulations **laid down** by the government*

**lay into sb** *phr v* [T] INFORMAL to attack someone physically or criticize him/her angrily: *You should have heard Dad **laying into** Tommy.*

**lay off** *phr v* **1** [T **lay sb ↔ off**] to stop employing someone, especially when there is not much work to do: *Jerry's just been **laid off** again.* **2** [I,T **lay off** sth/sb] SPOKEN to stop doing, having, or using something that is bad or annoying: *Don't you think you should **lay off** alcohol for a while?* | *Just **lay off*** (=stop criticizing) *- I don't care what you think!*

**lay sth ↔ on** *phr v* [T] to provide food, entertainment etc. in a very generous way: *Lola really **laid on** a great meal for us.*

**lay sb/sth ↔ out** *phr v* [T] **1** to spread something out: *Pam **laid** her dress **out** on the bed.* **2** INFORMAL to spend a lot of money: *We've just **laid out** $500 on a new fridge.*

**lay up** *phr v* [T] **be laid up (with)** to have to stay in bed because you are ill or injured: *He's **laid up** with a broken collarbone.*

**Lay** means "to put something somewhere": *Just lay the papers on the desk.* The other forms of this verb are **laid**, **laid**, and **laying**. **Lie** has two different meanings. Use one meaning of **lie** to talk about someone or something that is flat on a surface: *He likes to lie on his stomach and* read the paper. | *Don't leave your socks lying on the floor!* The other forms of this verb are **lain** and **lying**. The other meaning of **lie** is "to say something that is not true": *Are you lying to me?* The other forms of this verb are **lied** and **lying**.

**lay**² *v* the past tense of LIE

**lay**³ *adj* not trained in a particular profession or subject: *a lay preacher*

**lay·a·way** /'leɪəˌweɪ/ *n* [U] a method of buying goods in which the goods are kept by the seller for a small amount of money until the full price is paid

**lay·er**¹ /'leɪɚ/ *n* **1** an amount of a substance that covers all of a surface: *a layer of dust on the desk* **2** something that is placed on or between other things: *several layers of clothing*

**layer**² *v* [T] to put something down in layers: *macaroni layered with cheese*

**lay·man** /'leɪmən/ *n* someone who is not trained in a particular subject or type of work: *a book on astronomy written for **the layman*** (=people in general)

**lay·off** /'. ./ *n* the act of stopping a worker's employment because there is not enough work: *lay-offs in the steel industry*

**lay·out** /'leɪaʊt/ *n* **1** the way things are arranged in a particular area or place: *changes in the office layout* **2** the way in which writing and pictures are arranged on a page

**lay·o·ver** /'leɪˌoʊvɚ/ *n* a short stay somewhere between parts of a trip

**lay·per·son** /'leɪˌpɚsən/ *n* a word meaning a LAYMAN that is used when the person could be a man or a woman

**laze** /leɪz/ *v* [I] to relax and enjoy yourself without doing very much: *Jeff spent the morning just lazing in the yard.*

**la·zy** /'leɪzi/ *adj* **1** not liking and not doing work or physical activity: *the laziest boy in the class* **2** a lazy time is spent relaxing: *lazy summer afternoons* **3** moving slowly: *a lazy river*

**lb.** *n* the written abbreviation of POUND

**lead**¹ /lid/ *v* **led, led, leading**

**1** ▶GUIDE◀ [T] to guide a person or animal to a place, especially by going with or in front of the person or animal: *Aid workers led the refugees to safety.* | *Carl led his horse into the judging ring.*

**2** ▶GO IN FRONT◀ [I,T] to go in front of a group of people or vehicles: *The high school band is leading the parade.*

**3** ▶DOOR/ROAD/WIRE◀ [I] if a door, road etc. leads to somewhere, you can get there by

using it: *The second door **leads to** the principal's office.*

**lead**

leading a horse          The stairs lead to
                          the back door.

**4** ▶CONTROL◀ [T] to be in charge of something, especially an activity or a group of people: *Who is leading the investigation?*

**5** ▶WIN◀ [I,T] to be winning a game or competition: *At half-time, Green Bay was leading 12-0.*

**6** ▶CAUSE STH◀ [T] to be the thing that makes someone do something or think something: *What led you to study geology?* | *Rick **led me to believe** (=made me believe) he was going to return the money.*

**7 lead a normal/dull etc. life** to have a normal, boring etc. type of life

**8** ▶SUCCESS◀ [I,T] to be more successful than other people, companies, or countries in a particular activity or area of business: *The US leads the world in coal production.*

**9 lead the way a)** to guide someone in a particular direction **b)** to be the first to do something good or successful: *The Japanese led the way in using robots in industry.*

**10** ▶CONVERSATION◀ [I,T] to direct a conversation or discussion so that it develops in the way you want: *She finally led the topic around to pay raises.*

**lead off** sth *phr v* [T] to begin an event by doing something: *They **led off** the concert **with** a Beethoven Overture.*

**lead** sb **on** *phr v* [T] to make someone believe something that is not true: *He said it would only cost $15, but I think he was **leading** me **on**.*

**lead to** sth *phr v* [T] to make something happen or exist as a result of something else: *Opening the new lumber mill has **led to** the creation of 200 jobs.*

**lead up to** sth *phr v* [T] **1** to come before something and be a cause of it: *events **leading up to** the trial* **2** to gradually introduce a subject into a conversation: *remarks **leading up to** a request for money*

USAGE NOTE lead, guide, and direct                    L

**Lead** means "to show the way by going first": *He led us down the mountain.* **Guide** means "to show the way and explain things": *She guides tourists around the White House.* **Direct** means "to explain to someone how to get some-

*where"*: *Could you direct me to the station?*

as someone or something else: *He knows a lot more than I do - he's way out of my league.*

**lead**[2] *n* **1** [singular] the position or situation of being in front of or better than everyone else in a race or competition: *Lewis is still in the lead.* | *Joyner has taken the lead.* (=moved into the front position in a race) | *The US has taken the lead* (=is more advanced than others) *in space technology.* **2** the distance, number of points etc. by which one competitor is ahead of another: *The Bulls have a 5-point lead over the Celtics at halftime.* **3** a piece of information that may help you to make a discovery or find the answer to a problem: *Do the police have any leads in the robbery?* **4** the main acting part in a play, movie etc., or the main singer etc. in a musical group: *Who has the lead in the school play?* | *the lead guitarist*

**lead**[3] /lɛd/ *n* [U] **1** a soft gray-blue metal that melts easily **2** [C,U] the substance in a pencil that makes the marks when you write

**lead·er** /'lidɚ/ *n* **1** the person who directs or controls a team, organization, country etc.: *Most world leaders will attend the conference.* **2** the person, organization etc. that is better than all the others in a race or competition: *leaders in the field of medical science*

**lead·er·ship** /'lidɚˌʃɪp/ *n* **1** [U] the quality of being good at leading a team, organization, country etc.: *America needs strong leadership.* **2** [U] the position of being the leader of a team, organization etc.: *The bill was passed when the Senate was under Dole's leadership.* **3** [singular] the people who lead a country, organization etc.

**lead·ing** /'lidɪŋ/ *adj* **1** best, most important, or most successful: *a leading athlete* **2** **a leading question** a question asked in a way that makes you give a particular answer

**leaf**[1] /lif/ *n, plural* **leaves** **1** one of the flat green parts of a plant that are joined to its stem or branches **2** a part of the top of a table that can be added to make the table larger **3** [U] gold or silver in a very thin sheet −see also **turn over a new leaf** (TURN[1])

**leaf**[2] *v*

**leaf through** sth *phr v* [T] to turn the pages of a book quickly, without reading it carefully

**leaf·let** /'liflɪt/ *n* a small piece of printed paper that gives information or advertises something

**leaf·y** /'lifi/ *adj* having a lot of leaves: *green leafy vegetables*

**league** /lig/ *n* **1** a group of sports teams or players who play games against each other to see who is best: *Our team finished second in the league this year.* **2** a group of people or countries that have joined together because they have similar aims, political beliefs etc.: *the League of Nations* **3** **not in the same league/out of sb's league** not having the same abilities or qualities

**leak**[1] /lik/ *v* **1** [I,T] to let a liquid or gas in or out of a hole or crack: *Somebody's car must be leaking oil.* | *The roof's leaking!* **2** [I] to pass through a hole or crack: *Gas was leaking out of the pipes.* **3** [T] to deliberately give secret information to a newspaper, television company etc.: *Details of the President's speech were leaked to reporters.* −**leakage** *n* [U]

**leak out** *phr v* [I] if secret information leaks out, a lot of people find out about it

**leak**[2] *n* **1** a small hole that lets liquid or gas flow into or out of something: *a leak in the water pipe* **2** a situation in which someone has secret information: *leaks about a secret deal* **3** **take/have a leak** SLANG TO URINATE

**leak·y** /'liki/ *adj* having a hole or crack so that liquid or gas can pass through: *a leaky faucet*

**lean**[1] /lin/ *v* **1** [I] to move or bend your body in a particular position: *Celia leaned forward and whispered to Angie.* **2** [I] to support yourself or be supported in a position that is not straight or upright: *Brad was leaning on/against a wall.* **3** [T] to put something in a sloping position against something else: *Dad leaned the ladder against the wall.*

lean

**lean on** sb/sth *phr v* [T] to get support and encouragement from someone: *I know I can always lean on my friends.*

**lean toward** sth *phr v* [T] to tend to agree with or support a particular set of opinions, beliefs etc.: *Most of the church's members lean toward the political right.*

**lean**[2] *adj* **1** thin in a healthy and attractive way: *lean and athletic* **2** lean meat does not have much fat on it **3** difficult as a result of bad economic conditions or lack of money: *a lean year for the business* **4** a lean organization, company etc. uses only as much money and as many people as it needs

**lean·ing** /'linɪŋ/ *n* a tendency to prefer or agree with a particular set of beliefs, opinions etc.: *socialist leanings*

**leap**[1] /lip/ *v* **leaped** or **leapt** /lɛpt/, **leaped** or **leapt**, **leaping** [I] **1** to jump high into the air or over something: *a dog leaping over a puddle* −see picture on page 473 **2** to move very quickly and with a lot of energy: *Jon leaped up to answer the phone.*

**leap at** sth *phr v* [T] to accept an opportunity very eagerly: *I leapt at the chance to go to India.*

**leap**[2] *n* **1** a big jump **2** **by/in leaps and bounds** very quickly: *Your English is improving in leaps and bounds.*

**leap·frog** /'lipfrɑg/ *n* [U] a children's game in which someone bends over and someone else jumps over him/her –**leapfrog** *v* [I,T]

**leap year** /'. ./ *n* a year when February has 29 days instead of 28, which happens every four years

**learn** /lɜ·n/ *v* **1** [I,T] to gain knowledge of a subject or of how to do something, through experience or study: *Lisa's learning Spanish.* | *I'd like to learn (how) to sew.* | *We've been learning about electricity in school.* **2** [T] to get to know something so well that you can easily remember it: *Have you learned your lines for the play?* **3** [I,T] FORMAL to find out information, news etc. by hearing it from someone else: *We only learned about the accident later.* **4 learn sth the hard way** to understand something by learning from your mistakes and experiences: *I learned the hard way that bicycle helmets are necessary.* **5 learn your lesson** to suffer so much after doing something wrong that you will not do it again: *I didn't punish him because I thought he had learned his lesson.* –**learner** *n*: *a fast learner*

> **USAGE NOTE learn, teach, and show**
>
> Both **teach** and **learn** are used about things that take time to be able to do. **Learn** means to study or practice so that you can know facts or know how to do something: *Bev's learning how to drive.* **Teach** means to explain to someone what to do or how to do it, over a period of time: *Who taught you how to dance?* **Show** means to use actions to explain how to do something: *Let me show you how the stove works.*

**learn·ed** /'lɜ·nɪd/ *adj* FORMAL having a lot of knowledge because you have read and studied a lot

**learn·ing** /'lɜ·nɪŋ/ *n* [U] knowledge gained through reading and study

**learning dis·a·bil·i·ty** /'.. ..,.../ *n* a mental problem that affects a child's ability to learn

**lease¹** /lis/ *n* **1** a legal agreement that allows you to use a building, property etc. when you pay rent: *a two-year lease on the apartment* **2 a new/fresh lease on life** the feeling of being healthy, active, or happy again after being sick or unhappy

**lease²** *v* [T] to use or let someone use buildings, property etc. when s/he pays rent: *The offices have been leased to a new company.*

**leash** /liʃ/ *adj* a piece of rope, leather etc. fastened to a dog's collar in order to control the dog

**least¹** /list/ *determiner, pron* [the superlative of "little"] **1 at least a)** not less than a particular number or amount: *The thunderstorm lasted at least two hours.* **b)** used when mentioning an advantage to show that a situation is not as bad as it seems: *Well, at least you got your money back.* **c)** said when you want to correct or change something you have just said: *His name is Jerry. At least, I think it is.* **d)** even if nothing else is said or done: *Will you at least say you're sorry to her?* **2 the least sb could do** said when you think someone should do something to help someone else: *The least he could do is help you clean up.* **3 to say the least** used in order to show that something is more serious than you are actually saying: *Mrs. Caferelli was upset, to say the least.* **4** the smallest number or amount: *Even the least amount of the poison can kill you.* –see study note on page 457

**least²** *adv* **1** less than anything or anyone else: *It always happens when you least expect it.* | *I'm the least experienced person on the team.* **2 least of all** especially not: *I don't like any of them, least of all Debbie.*

**leath·er** /'lɛðɚ/ *n* [U] animal skin that has been treated to preserve it, and is used for making shoes etc.: *a leather belt*

**leath·er·y** /'lɛðəri/ *adj* hard and stiff like LEATHER: *leathery hands*

**leave¹** /liv/ *v* **left, left, leaving**
**1 ►GO AWAY◄** [I,T] to go away from a place or person: *Nick doesn't want to leave California.* | *When are you leaving for Calgary?* (=leaving the place you are in now to go to Calgary) | *I feel a little lonely now the kids have all left home* (=are no longer living at home)
**2 leave sb alone** SPOKEN used in order to tell someone to stop annoying or upsetting someone else: *Just stop asking questions and leave me alone.*
**3 leave sth alone** SPOKEN used in order to tell someone to stop touching something: *Timmy! Leave that alone, you'll break it!*
**4 ►STAY IN POSITION/STATE◄** [T] to make or let something stay in a particular state, place, or position when you are not there: *Why did you leave the windows open?*
**5 ►PUT STH IN A PLACE◄** [T] to put something in a place for someone: *Just leave the map on the table.* | *Please leave a message and I'll get back to you.*
**6 ►FORGET◄** [T] to forget to take something with you when you leave a place: *I think I left my keys in the car.*
**7 ►REMAIN◄** [T] to remain after everything else has been taken away: *Is there any coffee left?*
**8 ►NOT DO STH◄** [T] to not do something until later: *Can we leave the ironing for tomorrow?*
**9 ►HUSBAND/WIFE◄** [I,T] to stop living with your husband or wife: *Tammy's husband left her last year.*
**10 ►LET SB DECIDE◄** [T] to let someone decide something or be responsible for something:

*Leave the details **to** me; I'll arrange everything.*
**11** ▶GIVE AFTER DEATH◀ [T] to give something to someone after you die: *She **left** a lot of money to her son.*
**12 leave it at that** SPOKEN to not say or do anything more about a situation: *He's not going - let's just leave it at that.*
**13 leave a mark/stain etc.** to make a mark etc. that remains afterwards
**14 leave a lot to be desired** to be very unsatisfactory: *Your work in this class leaves a lot to be desired.*
**15 from where sb left off** from the place where you stopped: *Tomorrow we'll start the reading from where we left off.*
**16 leave sb in the lurch** INFORMAL to not help someone when you should stay and help him/her or when you promised to help
**leave** sb/sth **behind** *phr v* [T] to forget to take something with you when you leave a place, or to not take something on purpose: *Did you **leave** your umbrella **behind** in the restaurant?*
**leave** sb/sth **out** *phr v* [T] **1** to not include someone or something in a group, list, activity etc.: *The stew will still taste okay if we **leave out** the wine.* **2 be/feel left out** to feel as if you are not accepted or welcome in a social group: *I always felt **left out** when I played with my sister and her friends.*

---

**USAGE NOTE** leave and forget

Use **leave** to say that you have not brought something with you that you need: *I left my umbrella at home.* You can also use **forget** in this way: *I forgot my umbrella at home.* However, in written or formal English, it is better to say: *I forgot to bring my umbrella.*

---

**leave²** *n* [U] **1** time that you are allowed to spend away from your work because you are ill, have had a baby etc.: *How much **sick leave** have you taken?* **2 leave of absence** a period of time that you are allowed to spend away from work for a particular purpose – see usage note at VACATION
**leaves** /livz/ *n* the plural of LEAF
**lech·er·ous** /'lɛtʃərəs/ *adj* a lecherous man is always thinking about sex
**lec·tern** /'lɛktən/ *n* a high desk that you stand behind when you give a speech
**lec·ture¹** /'lɛktʃə/ *n* **1** a long talk to a group of people about a particular subject: *She's **giving** a **lecture on** modern art.* **2** a long serious talk that criticizes someone or warns him/her about something: *My parents **gave** me another **lecture about** my school work.*
**lecture²** *v* **1** [T] to talk angrily or seriously to someone in order to criticize or warn him/her: *I wish you'd stop **lecturing** me **about** smoking.* **2** [I] to teach a group of people about a particular subject, especially at a college

**led** /lɛd/ *v* the past tense and PAST PARTICIPLE of LEAD
**ledge** /lɛdʒ/ *n* **1** a narrow flat surface like a shelf that sticks out from the side of a building: *a window ledge* **2** a narrow flat surface of rock that is parallel to the ground
**ledg·er** /'lɛdʒə/ *n* a book in which a bank, business etc. records the money received and spent
**leech** /litʃ/ *n* a small soft creature that attaches itself to an animal in order to drink its blood
**leek** /lik/ *n* a vegetable with long straight green leaves, that tastes like onion
**leer** /lɪr/ *v* [I] to look at someone in an unpleasant way that shows that you think s/he is sexually attractive – **leer** *n*
**leer·y** /'lɪri/ *adj* worried and unable to trust someone or something: *The girl was **leery of** strangers.*
**lee·way** /'liweɪ/ *n* [U] freedom to do things in the way you want to: *Students have some leeway in what they can write about.*
**left¹** /lɛft/ *adj* **1** on the side of your body that contains your heart: *He broke his left leg.* **2** on, by, or in the direction of your left side: *the first house on the left side of the street* –opposite RIGHT¹
**left²** *adv* toward the left side: *Turn left at the next street.* –opposite RIGHT²
**left³** *n* **1** the left side or direction: *It's the second door on your left.* **2 the left** in politics, the left are people who believe that the government has a duty to pay for social services and to limit the power of businesses –opposite RIGHT³
**left⁴** *v* the past tense and PAST PARTICIPLE of LEAVE
**left field** /ˌ. './ *n* **1 in/from left field** INFORMAL unusual or strange compared to the way that people usually behave: *Some of his ideas are way **out in left field**.* (=very strange) **2** [singular] the area in baseball in the left side of the OUTFIELD
**left-hand** /'. ./ *adj* on the left side of something: *the top left-hand drawer*
**left-hand·ed** /ˌ. '..◀/ *adj* **1** someone who is left-handed uses his/her left hand to do most things **2** done with the left hand: *a left-handed punch* **3** made to be used with the left hand: *a left-handed iron* –**left-handed** *adv* –see picture at RIGHT-HANDED
**left·o·vers** /'lɛftˌoʊvəz/ *n* [plural] food that remains at the end of a meal and is kept to be eaten later
**left-wing** /'. ./ *adj* supporting the political aims of groups such as Socialists and Communists: *a left-wing newspaper* –**left-wing** /ˌ. './ *n* –**left-winger** /ˌ. '../ *n*
**leg** /lɛg/ *n*
**1** ▶BODY PART◀ either of the two long parts of your body that you use to stand or walk, or a similar part on an animal or insect: *How did you hurt your leg?* –see picture at BODY

**2** ▶FURNITURE◀ one of the upright parts that supports a piece of furniture: *a table leg*

**3** ▶PANTS◀ the part of your pants that covers your leg

**4** ▶FOOD◀ [C,U] the leg of an animal eaten as food: *roast leg of lamb*

**5** ▶TRIP/RACE ETC.◀ a part of a long trip, race, process etc. that is done one part at a time: *the last leg of our vacation*

**6** **-legged** having a particular number or type of legs: *a three-legged cat*

**7** **leg room** space in which to put your legs comfortably when you are sitting in a car, theater etc.

**8** **not have a leg to stand on** INFORMAL to be in a situation where you cannot prove or legally support what you say –see also **on its last legs** (LAST¹)

**leg·a·cy** /ˈlɛgəsi/ *n* **1** a situation that exists as a result of things that happened at an earlier time: *a legacy of good government* **2** money or property that you receive from someone after s/he dies

**le·gal** /ˈligəl/ *adj* **1** allowed, ordered, or approved by law: *a legal agreement* –opposite ILLEGAL¹ **2** relating to the law: *the legal system* | *If you don't pay soon, we'll be forced to take legal action.* (=go to court) –**legally** *adv*: *You can't legally buy alcohol until you're 21.* –**legality** /lɪˈgæləţi/ *n* [U]

**le·gal·ize** /ˈligəˌlaɪz/ *v* [T] to make something legal that was not legal before: *a campaign to legalize marijuana* –**legalization** /ˌligələˈzeɪʃən/ *n*

**leg·end** /ˈlɛdʒənd/ *n* **1** [C,U] an old well-known story, often about brave people or adventures, or all stories of this kind: *the legend of King Arthur* **2** someone who is famous and admired for being extremely good at doing something: *Elvis Presley, the rock and roll legend*

**leg·end·ar·y** /ˈlɛdʒənˌdɛri/ *adj* **1** famous and admired: *the legendary baseball player Ty Cobb* **2** talked or read about in LEGENDs

**leg·gings** /ˈlɛgɪnz/ *n* [plural] women's pants that stretch to fit the shape of the body

**leg·gy** /ˈlɛgi/ *adj* having long legs

**leg·i·ble** /ˈlɛdʒəbəl/ *adj* written or printed clearly enough for you to read: *His writing was barely legible.* –**legibly** *adv* –opposite ILLEGIBLE

**le·gion** /ˈlidʒən/ *n* a large group of soldiers or people

**leg·is·late** /ˈlɛdʒəˌsleɪt/ *v* [I] to make a law about something: *plans to legislate against abortion*

**leg·is·la·tion** /ˌlɛdʒəˈsleɪʃən/ *n* [U] **1** a law or set of laws: *human rights legislation* **2** the act of making laws

**leg·is·la·tive** /ˈlɛdʒəˌsleɪţɪv/ *adj* relating to laws or to making laws: *a legislative assembly* | *legislative measures to control illegal drugs*

**leg·is·la·tor** /ˈlɛdʒɪˌsleɪţɚ/ *n* an elected government official who is involved in making laws

**leg·is·la·ture** /ˈlɛdʒəˌsleɪtʃɚ/ *n* an institution that has the power to make or change laws: *the Ohio state legislature*

**leg·it** /lɪˈdʒɪt/ *adj* SPOKEN ⇨ LEGITIMATE

**le·git·i·mate** /ləˈdʒɪtəmɪt/ *adj* **1** correct, allowable, or operating according to the law: *legitimate business activities* **2** fair, correct, or reasonable according to accepted standards of behavior: *a legitimate question* **3** legitimate children are born to parents who are legally married to each other –**legitimacy** *n* [U] –opposite ILLEGITIMATE

**lei·sure** /ˈliʒɚ/ *n* [U] **1** time when you are not working or studying and can relax and do things you enjoy: *How do you spend your leisure time?* **2** **at sb's leisure** as slowly as you want and when you want: *Read it at your leisure.*

**lei·sure·ly** /ˈliʒɚli/ *adj* moving or done in a relaxed way: *a leisurely walk around the park*

**lem·on** /ˈlɛmən/ *n* [C,U] **1** a yellow fruit that has a sour-tasting juice –see picture on page 470 **2** INFORMAL something that does not work correctly: *This car's a real lemon.*

**lem·on·ade** /ˌlɛməˈneɪd/ *n* [U] a drink made with LEMON juice, sugar, and water

**lend** /lɛnd/ *v* **lent, lent, lending 1** [T] to let someone borrow something that you own, which s/he will give back to you later: *Could you lend me your bike?* –see picture at BORROW **2** [T] if a bank lends money, it lets someone borrow it if s/he pays it back with an additional amount of money: *Our bank lends money at low interest rates.* **3** **lend (sb) a hand** to help someone do something, especially something that needs physical effort: *Lend me a hand with this box.* **4** **lend itself to** to be suitable to be used in a particular way: *The story lends itself to a lot of pictures.* **5** [T] FORMAL to give something, especially an event, a particular quality: *The music lent a little elegance to the event.* –**lender** *n*

---

**USAGE NOTE lend, borrow, and loan**

Use **lend** when you let someone use something that s/he will give back to you: *I can lend you a pen if you don't have one.* Use **borrow** when you use something that belongs to someone else, that you will give back to him/her: *Could I borrow your pen for a minute?* Use **loan** to say that a bank or a person is lending money to someone: *I asked the bank manager if he could loan me $1000.* You also use **loan** when a museum, art gallery etc. borrows a work of art: *The paintings have been loaned to the Smithsonian for an exhibi-*

L

*tion.* In informal speech, we often use **loan** instead of **lend**: *Could you loan me your pen?* However, you should always use **lend** in written or formal English.

**length** /lɛŋkθ, lɛnθ/ *n* **1** [C,U] the measurement of something from one end to the other: *The length of the room is five feet.* | *a whale 3 meters in length* —see picture at HEIGHT **2** [C,U] the amount of time that you spend doing something or that something continues for: *the length of your stay in the hospital* **3** [C,U] the amount of writing in a book, or the amount of time that a movie, play etc. continues for: *We thought the length of the play was fine.* **4 go to great lengths to do sth** to be willing to use a lot of different methods to achieve something you want: *She went to great lengths to help us.* **5 at length** for a long time: *She spoke at length on the dangers of smoking.* **6** a piece of something that is long and thin: *two lengths of rope*

**length·en** /ˈlɛŋkθən/ *v* [I,T] to make something longer or to become longer: *I need this dress lengthened.*

**length·wise** /ˈlɛŋkθwaɪz/, **length·ways** /ˈlɛŋkθweɪz/ *adv* in the direction or position of the longest side: *Fold the cloth lengthwise.*

**length·y** /ˈlɛŋkθi/ *adj* continuing for a long time: *a lengthy speech/process/interview*

**le·ni·ent** /ˈliniənt, ˈlinyənt/ *adj* not strict in the way you punish someone or control his/her behavior: *Her parents are too lenient.* —**leniency** *n* [U]

**lens** /lɛnz/ *n* **1** a piece of curved glass or plastic that makes things look bigger or smaller: *He wore glasses with thick lenses.* | *a telescope lens* —see also picture at GLASSES **2** the clear part inside your eye that FOCUS*es* so you can see things clearly

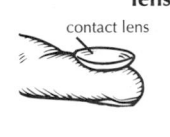
**lens**
contact lens

lens

**Lent** /lɛnt/ *n* the 40 days before Easter, when some Christians stop eating particular things or stop particular habits

**lent** *v* the past tense and PAST PARTICIPLE of LEND

**len·til** /ˈlɛnt̮əl/ *n* a small round seed like a bean, dried and used for food

**Le·o** /ˈlioʊ/ *n* **1** [singular] the fifth sign of the ZODIAC, represented by a lion **2** someone born between July 23 and August 22

**leop·ard** /ˈlɛpəd/ *n* a large and strong wild cat with yellow fur and black spots, from Africa and South Asia

**le·o·tard** /ˈliə,tɑrd/ *n* a tight-fitting piece of woman's clothing that covers the body from the neck to the top of the legs, worn especially while exercising

**lep·er** /ˈlɛpə/ *n* someone who has LEPROSY

**lep·ro·sy** /ˈlɛprəsi/ *n* [U] an infectious disease in which someone's skin becomes hard and is gradually destroyed —**leprous** /ˈlɛprəs/ *adj*

**les·bi·an** /ˈlɛzbiən/ *n* a woman who is sexually attracted to other women; HOMOSEXUAL —see also GAY

**less**[1] /lɛs/ *determiner, pron* [the comparative of "little"] **1** a smaller amount: *The job involves much less stress than my last one.* | *Skimmed milk has less fat than whole milk.* | *She spends less of her time playing tennis now.* **2 no less than** used in order to emphasize that an amount or number is large: *It took no less than nine policemen to hold him down.* **3 nothing less than** used in order to emphasize how serious or important something is: *He demands nothing less than perfection.*

**less**[2] *adv* [the comparative of "little"] **1** not so much, or to a smaller degree: *I'm trying to exercise more and eat less.* —compare MORE[1] **2 less and less** continuing to become smaller in amount or degree: *We seem to be spending less and less time together.* —see study note on page 457

---

**USAGE NOTE less and fewer**

Use **less** before an uncountable noun: *You get more food for less money at Shop 'n' Save.* Use **fewer** before a countable noun: *There are fewer trees in the neighborhood now.*

---

**less·en** /ˈlɛsən/ *v* [I,T] to become less, or to make something become less: *A low-fat diet can lessen the risk of heart disease.* —**lessening** *n* [U] —compare REDUCE

**less·er** /ˈlɛsə/ *adj* **1** FORMAL not as large or important as something else, or not as much as something else: *A lesser man* (=someone not as strong or brave) *would have quit before now.* **2 the lesser of two evils** the less harmful or unpleasant of two bad choices —**lesser** *adv*

**les·son** /ˈlɛsən/ *n* a period of time in which someone is taught a particular subject or how to do something: *Hannah is taking guitar lessons.* —see also **teach sb a lesson** (TEACH)

**let** /lɛt/ *v* **let, let, letting 1** [T] to allow someone to do something, or allow something to happen: *I wanted to go but my mother wouldn't let me.* | *Let the other car go past before you turn.* | *Let me finish this, then we can go.* | *He let Chris have one of his CDs.* **2 let go** to stop holding something: *Marlon let go of the horse, and it ran away.* **3 let sb go a)** to allow someone to be free after s/he has been kept somewhere: *The police let her go after two hours.* **b)** a phrase meaning to dismiss someone from his/her job, used in order to avoid saying this directly: *I'm afraid we have to let you go.* **4 let sb know** to tell someone something:

*Could you let me know when you're done?*
**5 let alone** used in order to say that one thing is not true or does not happen, so another thing cannot possibly be true or happen: *Davey can't even crawl yet, let alone walk!* **6 let sth go** to decide not to react to something bad or annoying that someone has said or done: *We'll let it go this time, but don't be late again.* **7 let me tell you** SPOKEN said in order to emphasize that something is true: *It was a really great party, let me tell you.* **8 let sb/sth be** to stop annoying someone, asking questions, or trying to change things: *Your mother's had a hard day, so just let her be.*

---

SPOKEN PHRASES

**9 let's** the short form of "let us," used when you want to suggest that someone do something with you: *Come on, let's dance! | I'm hungry, let's eat.* **10 let's see a)** said when you are going to try to do something: *Let's see if/whether Andy's home.* **b)** said when you pause because you cannot remember or find something: *Now let's see, where did I put it?* **c)** said when you want someone to show you something: *"I got a new dress." "Really? Let's see."* **11 let me do sth** said when you are offering to help someone: *Let me carry that for you.* **12 let's hope** said when you hope something is true or will happen: *Let's hope they get here before it snows.*

---

**let** sb ↔ **down** *phr v* [T] to make someone feel disappointed because you have not done what you promised: *You won't let me down, will you?* —see also LETDOWN

**let** sb ↔ **in** *phr v* [T] **1** to open the door of a house or building so that someone can come in: *She unlocked the door to let him in.* **2 let sb in on sth** to tell someone a secret: *I'll let you in on a little secret.*

**let** sb ↔ **into** sth *phr v* [T] to allow someone to come into a house or building: *Maria wouldn't let Billy into her house.*

**let** sb ↔ **off** *phr v* [T] to not punish someone, or to not make him/her do something s/he was supposed to do: *I'll let you off this time, but don't do it again.*

**let on** *phr v* [I] to behave in a way that shows you know a secret: *Don't let on (that) you know!*

**let out** *phr v* **1** [T **let** sb ↔ **out**] to allow someone to leave a building, room etc.: *Let the dog out, please.* **2** [I] if a school, college, movie etc. lets out, the people attending it can leave: *School lets out at 3:30.* **3** [T **let** sth ↔ **out**] to allow light, air etc. to escape from a place: *Close the door - you're letting all the heat out.* **4 let out a scream/cry etc.** to make a sound, especially a loud one: *Suddenly, Ben let out a yell and jumped up.*

**let up** *phr v* [I] if rain or snow lets up, it stops or there is less of it —see also LETUP

**let·down** /'letdaʊn/ *n* [singular] INFORMAL something that makes you feel disappointed because it is not as good as you expected: *The movie was a real letdown!*

**le·thal** /'liθəl/ *adj* able to kill someone: *a lethal dose of heroin*

**le·thar·gic** /lə'θɑrdʒɪk/ *adj* having no energy so that you feel lazy or tired —**lethargy** /'leθərdʒi/ *n* [U]

**let's** /lɛts/ ⇨ **let's** (LET)

**let·ter** /'letər/ *n* **1** a written message that you put into an envelope and send to someone by mail: *Mollie wrote a letter to her friend Gail.* **2** one of the signs in writing that represents a sound in speech: *There are 26 letters in the English alphabet.* **3 (do sth) to the letter** to do exactly what you are told to do: *He followed their instructions to the letter.*

**let·ter·head** /'letər,hɛd/ *n* the name and address of a person or business printed at the top of a piece of paper

**let·tuce** /'letɪs/ *n* [C,U] a round green vegetable with large thin leaves, eaten raw in SALADS —see picture on page 470

**let·up** /'letʌp/ *n* [singular, U] an end to an activity, or a decrease in activity: *There has been no letup in the requests for help.*

**leu·ke·mia** /lu'kimiə/ *n* [U] a serious disease that affects the blood and that can cause death

**lev·ee** /'levi/ *n* a special wall that is built to stop a river from flooding

**lev·el**[1] /'levəl/ *n* **1** the amount, degree, or number of something, as compared to another amount, degree, or number: *There were high levels of radiation after the explosion. | We can expect the temperature to stay at these levels until Friday.* **2** the height or position of something in relation to the ground or another thing: *Check the water level in the radiator. | All the pictures were hung at eye level.* (=at the same height as people's eyes) **3** a standard of skill or ability in a particular subject, sport etc.: *reading exercises designed for every level of student | Few athletes can compete at this level.* **4** a particular position in a system that has different ranks: *high-level talks* (=discussions between important people) **5** a floor in a building that has several floors: *Housewares is on Level 3.* **6** a tool used for checking if a surface is flat —see also SEA LEVEL

**level**[2] *adj* **1** flat, with no surface higher than the rest: *The floor was level but the walls sloped inward.* **2** at the same height or position as something else: *My head was level with his chin.*

**level**[3] *v* [T] **1** to knock something down to the ground and destroy it: *An earthquake leveled several buildings in the city.* **2 level a charge**

**against sb** to say that you think someone has done something wrong; ACCUSE

**level off/out** *phr v* [I] to stop going up or down, and continue at the same height or amount: *The plane climbed to 20,000 feet, then leveled off.* | *Oil prices have leveled off at $25 a barrel.*

**level with** sb *phr v* [T] INFORMAL to speak honestly with someone and tell him/her what you really think

**level-head·ed** /ˌ.. '..◂/ *adj* calm and sensible in making decisions

**lev·er** /ˈlɛvɚ, ˈliː-/ *n* **1** a long metal BAR that you use to lift something by putting one end under the object and pushing the other end down **2** a stick or handle on a machine that you move to make the machine work −**lever** *v* [T]

**lev·er·age**[1] /ˈlɛvərɪdʒ, ˈliː-/ *n* [U] **1** influence that you use to make people do what you want: *Small businesses have less leverage in dealing with banks.* **2** the action, use, or power of a LEVER

**leverage**[2] *v* [T] to buy INVESTMENTs using money you have borrowed

**lev·i·tate** /ˈlɛvəˌteɪt/ *v* [I] to rise and float in the air as if by magic −**levitation** /ˌlɛvə-ˈteɪʃən/ *n* [U]

**lev·i·ty** /ˈlɛvəti/ *n* [U] FORMAL the quality of telling jokes and having fun instead of being serious

**lev·y**[1] /ˈlɛvi/ *v* [T] **levy a tax/charge etc.** to officially make someone pay a tax etc.

**levy**[2] *n* an official demand for someone to pay a tax

**lewd** /lud/ *adj* using rude words or behaving in a way that makes someone think of sex: *lewd comments*

**lex·i·con** /ˈlɛksɪˌkɑn/ *n* all the words used in a language or a particular profession, or a book containing lists of these words: *a lexicon of cooking terms* −**lexical** /ˈlɛksɪkəl/ *adj*

**li·a·bil·i·ty** /ˌlaɪəˈbɪləti/ *n* **1** [U] the state of being responsible for something, especially for injury or damage: *The company has admitted liability for the accident.* **2** [singular] something that makes it difficult to do something, or that causes problems for you: *Johnson was a real liability to the team.* −compare ASSET

**li·a·ble** /ˈlaɪəbəl/ *adj* **1 be liable to do sth** to be likely to do something or likely to behave in a particular way: *She's liable to watch programs that aren't good for her.* | *The car's liable to overheat on long trips.* **2** legally responsible for the cost of something: *The university was not held liable for the damage done by its students.*

**li·aise** /liˈeɪz/ *v* [I] to exchange information with someone who works in a different office or job, so that everyone knows what is happening

**li·ai·son** /liˈeɪˌzɑn/ *n* **1** a sexual relationship between two people who are not married **2** [singular, U] a working relationship between two groups, companies etc.

**li·ar** /ˈlaɪɚ/ *n* someone who tells lies

**lib** /lɪb/ *n* INFORMAL ⇨ LIBERATION

**li·bel**[1] /ˈlaɪbəl/ *n* [C,U] the illegal act of writing or printing something about someone that is not true, and that would make people have a bad opinion of him/her: *He is suing the magazine for libel.* −compare SLANDER

**libel**[2] *v* [T] to write or print a LIBEL against someone −**libelous** *adj*

**lib·er·al**[1] /ˈlɪbrəl, -bərəl/ *adj* **1** willing to understand or respect the different behavior, ideas etc. of other people: *a liberal attitude toward sex* **2** supporting changes in political, social, or religious systems that allow people more freedom to do what they want: *a liberal democracy* **3** FORMAL generous: *a liberal donation to charity*

**liberal**[2] *n* someone with LIBERAL opinions or principles

**liberal arts** /ˌ.. './ *n* [plural] subjects that increase someone's general knowledge, rather than teach technical skills

**lib·er·al·is·m** /ˈlɪbrəˌlɪzəm/ *n* [U] opinions or principles that support changes in politics, religion etc.

**lib·er·al·ize** /ˈlɪbrəˌlaɪz/ *v* [T] to make a system, law, or moral attitude less strict

**lib·er·al·ly** /ˈlɪbrəli/ *adv* in large amounts; generously

**lib·er·ate** /ˈlɪbəˌreɪt/ *v* [T] **1** to make someone free from feelings or situations that make his/her life difficult: *In the 1930s, electricity liberated farmers from many hard chores.* **2** to free a place and the people in it from political or military control: *The city was liberated by the Allies in 1944.* −**liberator** *n*

**lib·er·at·ed** /ˈlɪbəˌreɪtɪd/ *adj* free to do the things you want, and not controlled by rules or other people

**lib·er·a·tion** /ˌlɪbəˈreɪʃən/ *n* [U] the state of being LIBERATED

**lib·er·ty** /ˈlɪbəti/ *n* **1** [C,U] the freedom to do what you want without having to ask permission from people in authority: *principles of liberty and democracy* | **civil liberties** (=the things you have a legal right to do) **2 be at liberty to do sth** to have permission to do something: *I'm not at liberty to say where he is at the moment.* **3 take the liberty of doing sth** to do something without asking permission, because you do not think it will upset or offend anyone: *I took the liberty of helping myself to a piece of cake.* **4 take liberties with sth** to make unreasonable changes in something such as a piece of writing

**li·bi·do** /lɪˈbidoʊ/ *n* [C,U] TECHNICAL someone's desire to have sex

**Li·bra** /'librə/ *n* **1** [singular] the seventh sign of the ZODIAC, represented by a SCALE **2** someone born between September 23 and October 23

**li·brar·i·an** /laɪˈbrɛriən/ *n* someone who works in a library

**li·brar·y** /'laɪˌbrɛri/ *n* a room or building containing books that you can read there or borrow

**lice** /laɪs/ *n* the plural of LOUSE

**li·cense**¹ /'laɪsəns/ *n* **1** an official document that gives you permission to own something or do something: *a driver's license* **2** [U] FORMAL freedom to do or say whatever you think is best

**license**² *v* [T] to give official permission for someone to own or do something: *He is licensed to carry a gun.*

**license plate** /'.. ˌ./ *n* a sign with numbers and letters on it at the front and back of your car –see picture on page 469

**li·chen** /'laɪkən/ *n* [C,U] a gray, green, or yellow plant that spreads over the surface of trees and stones –compare MOSS

**lick**¹ /lɪk/ *v* [T] **1** to move your tongue across the surface of something in order to eat it, taste it etc.: *Judy's dog jumped up to lick her face.* **2** INFORMAL to defeat an opponent or solve a problem: *"It looks like we have the fire licked," said Chief Grafton.* **3** lick your lips INFORMAL to feel eager or excited because you are expecting something

lick

**lick**² *n* **1** [C usually singular] an act of LICKing something with your tongue: *Can I have a lick of your ice cream cone?* **2 a lick of paint** INFORMAL a small amount of paint **3 not do a lick of work** INFORMAL to not do any work at all

**lick·e·ty-split** /ˌlɪkəti 'splɪt/ *adv* OLD-FASHIONED very fast

**lick·ing** /'lɪkɪŋ/ *n* [singular] INFORMAL the act of hitting someone as a punishment

**lic·o·rice** /'lɪkərɪʃ/ *n* [U] a strong-tasting sweet black substance used in candy and medicine

**lid** /lɪd/ *n* **1** a cover for a pot, box, or other container: *Where's the lid for this jar?* –see picture at PAN¹ **2 keep/put a lid on** INFORMAL to control a situation so that it does not become worse: *putting a lid on government spending* **3** ⇨ EYELID

**lie**¹ /laɪ/ *v* lay, lain, lying [I] **1 a)** to be in a position in which your body is flat on the floor, a bed etc.: *We lay on the beach for a couple of hours.* **b)** also **lie down** to put yourself in this position: *I'm going upstairs to lie down.* **2** to be in a particular place or position: *The town lies to the east of the lake.* | *Letters and bills were lying on the kitchen table.* **3** used in order to

say where something such as a reason or answer can be found: *The solution lies in alternative sources of power.* **4** to remain in a particular condition or place: *The letters lay hidden in her attic for forty years.* **5 lie low** to remain hidden because you do not want someone to find you **6 lie ahead** if something lies ahead, it is going to happen in the future: *There are difficulties that lie ahead.* **7 lie in wait (for sb/sth)** to remain hidden in order to attack someone or something –see also **not take sth lying down** (TAKE¹) –see picture at LAY¹ –see usage note at LAY¹

**lie around** *phr v* **1** [I,T] to be left out of the correct place, so that things look messy: *Books and papers were lying around everywhere.* **2** [I] to spend time relaxing, especially by lying down: *We just lay around on the beach the whole time.*

**lie behind** sth *phr v* [T] to be the true reason for an action, decision etc.: *I wonder what really lay behind her decision to quit her job.*

**lie**² *v* lied, lied, lying [I] to tell someone a lie: *I was pretty sure she was lying to me about where she'd been that night.*

**lie**³ *n* something that you say or write that you know is not true: *Mom spanked her for telling lies.*

**lie de·tect·or** /'. .ˌ../ *n* a machine used by the police to find out if someone is lying

**lien** /lin, 'liən/ *n* TECHNICAL a legal right to take someone's property if s/he does not pay a debt

**lieu** /lu/ *n* FORMAL **in lieu of** instead of: *property given in lieu of payment*

**lieu·ten·ant, Lieutenant** /luˈtɛnənt/ *n* an officer who has a middle rank in the Army, Navy, Air Force, or Marines

**life** /laɪf/ *n, plural* **lives**
**1** ▶PERIOD OF LIFE◀ [C,U] the period of time between someone's birth and death: *Charles lived in New York City all his life.* | *It was one of the happiest days of my life.* | *He became a father late in life.* (=when he was fairly old)
**2** ▶BEING ALIVE◀ [C,U] the state or quality of being alive: *a baby's first moments of life* | *Firemen risked their lives* (=did something during which they could have been killed) *to save the children.*
**3** ▶WAY OF LIVING◀ [C,U] all the experiences and activities that are typical of a particular way of living: *Life in L.A. is exciting.* | *country life* | *He's spent most of his working life* (=time spent working) *with one company.* | *the American way of life* | *This is the life, Joan!* (=what we are doing is the most enjoyable way to live)
**4** ▶EXPERIENCES◀ the type of experience that someone has during his/her life: *Tia had a full and happy life.* | *I'm hoping to win the lottery and live a life of luxury!* | *Then he started telling me his whole life story.* (=all the things that happened in his life)

**5** ▶LIVING THINGS◀ [U] living things such as people, animals, or plants: *Do you think there is life on other planets?* | *studying the island's plant life*

**6** private/sex/social etc. life activities in your life that are private, relate to sex, are done with friends etc.

**7** ▶MOVEMENT◀ [U] activity or movement: *There were no* **signs of life** *in the house.* | *Katie was young and* **full of life**. (=very cheerful and active)

**8** quality of life the level or quality of health, success, and comfort in someone's life

**9** ▶EXISTENCE◀ [U] human existence, and all the things that can happen during someone's life: *Life can be hard sometimes.*

**10** ▶PRISON◀ [U] also **life in prison** ⇨ LIFE SENTENCE

**11** ▶WORKING/EXISTING◀ [singular] the period of time that something continues to work or exist: *long-life batteries*

**12** (in) real life what really happens rather than what only happens in stories or someone's imagination

**13** bring sth to life/come to life to make something more exciting, or to start to become more exciting

SPOKEN PHRASES

**14** Not on your life! used in order to say that you will definitely not do something

**15** Get a life! said when you are annoyed with someone because you think s/he is boring

**16** for the life of me said when you cannot do something even when you try very hard: *I can't remember her name for the life of me!*

**17** that's life said when something bad has happened that you must accept

**18** life is too short said when telling someone that something is not important enough to worry about

**life·boat** /'laɪfbout/ *n* a small boat that is used for helping people who are in danger on the ocean

**life buoy** /'. ./ *n* a large ring that you can throw to someone in the water, so that s/he will float

**life ex·pect·an·cy** /'. .,.../ *n* the length of time that a person or animal is expected to live

**life·guard** /'laɪfgɑrd/ *n* someone whose job is to help swimmers who are in danger at the beach or a pool

**life in·sur·ance** /'. .,../ *n* [U] a type of insurance that someone buys so that when s/he dies, his/her family will receive money

**life jack·et** /'. ,../ *n* a piece of equipment that you wear around your chest so that you float in the water

**life·less** /'laɪflɪs/ *adj* **1** lacking interest, excitement, or activity: *a lifeless party* **2** dead or seeming to be dead

**life·like** /'laɪflaɪk/ *adj* very much like a real person or thing: *a very lifelike statue*

**life·line** /'laɪflaɪn/ *n* something that someone depends on completely: *She isn't able to leave the house, so the phone is her lifeline.*

**life·long** /'laɪflɔŋ/ *adj* continuing all through your life: *a lifelong friend*

**life·sav·er** /'laɪf,seɪvɚ/ *n* **1** someone or something that helps you in a very important way **2** Lifesaver TRADEMARK a small ring-shaped hard candy

**life sen·tence** /,. '../ *n* the punishment of sending someone to prison for the rest of his/her life

**life-size** /'. ./, **life-sized** *adj* a life-size model, picture etc. is the same size as the person or object it represents

**life·style** /'. ./ *n* the way that someone lives, including his/her work and activities, and what things s/he owns: *Getting married can mean a sudden change in your lifestyle.*

**life sup·port sys·tem** /'. ., ,../ *n* medical equipment that keeps someone alive who is extremely sick

**life-threat·en·ing** /'. ,.../ *adj* a life-threatening illness can kill you

**life·time** /'laɪftaɪm/ *n* the period of time during which someone is alive

**life vest** /'. ./ *n* ⇨ LIFE JACKET

**lift¹** /lɪft/ *v* **1** [T] to take something in your hands and raise it or move it higher: *Can you help me lift this box and put it in the car?* –see picture on page 473 **2** [I,T] also **lift up** to move something up into the air, or to move up into the air: *Lift up your feet so I can sweep the floor.* **3** [T] to remove a rule or law that prevents someone from doing something: *The US has lifted trade restrictions with the country.* **4** [I] if clouds or FOG lifts, it disappears **5** [T] INFORMAL to steal something

**lift²** *n* **1** give sb/sth a lift to make someone feel happier, or to make something more likely to be successful: *The end of the war is expected to give the economy a lift.* **2** give sb a lift to take someone somewhere in your vehicle **3** a movement in which something is lifted or raised

**lift-off** /'. ./ *n* [C,U] the moment when a space vehicle leaves the ground and rises up into the air

**lig·a·ment** /'lɪgəmənt/ *n* a band of strong material in your body that joins your bones together

**light¹** /laɪt/ *n*

**1** ▶LIGHT TO SEE◀ [U] the energy from the sun, a lamp etc. that allows you to see things: *Light was streaming in through the window.* | *The light in here isn't very good.*

**2** ▶ELECTRIC LIGHT◀ something such as a lamp that produces light using electricity: *Can you* **turn the lights on/off** *for me?*

**3** ▶TRAFFIC◀ one of a set of red, green, and

yellow lights that are used for controlling traffic: *Turn left at the lights.* | *Moore drove straight through a red light.*
**4 a light** something such as a match that starts a cigarette burning: *Excuse me, do you have a light?*
**5 bring sth to light/come to light** to make something known, or to become known: *New information about the case has come to light.*
**6 in light of sth** after considering something; because of: *In light of the low profits, we will have to make budget cuts.*
**7 see sth in a new/different light** to understand something in a new or different way
**8 shed/throw/cast light on sth** to provide new information about something so it is easier to understand
**9 a light at the end of the tunnel** something that gives you hope that a bad situation will end soon: *Kids often drop out of school because they can't see a light at the end of the tunnel.*
**10 see the light** to finally realize and understand something: *Maybe Gus will see the light and do what's good for the team.*

**light²** *adj*
**1** ▶COLOR◀ pale and not dark: *a light blue dress* —compare DARK¹
**2** ▶WEIGHT◀ not weighing very much: *Your backpack's lighter than mine.* —compare HEAVY
**3** ▶FORCE◀ not having much force or power: *a light wind*
**4** ▶CLOTHES◀ thin and not very warm: *a light sweater*
**5** ▶IN A ROOM/HOUSE◀ having plenty of light in it, especially from the sun: *The house was light and airy.*
**6** ▶FOOD◀ having less fat or fewer CALORIES that usual, or not having a strong taste: *light cream cheese* | *a light wine* —see also LITE
**7** ▶NOT SERIOUS◀ not serious in meaning or style: *a light comedy on TV*
**8 it is light** used in order to say that there is enough light outside to see by: *It was still light when we got home.*
**9** ▶SMALL AMOUNT◀ small in amount or degree: *Traffic was lighter than usual today.*
**10 make light of sth** to joke about something or to treat it as if it were not important

**light³** *v* lit *or* lighted, lit *or* lighted, lighting
**1** [I,T] to start burning, or to make something do this: *Dad is trying to light a fire in the fireplace.* —see picture at FIRE¹ **2** [T] to give light to something: *The room was lit by two lamps.*
**light up** *phr v* **1** [I,T] to become bright or to make something bright: *The fireworks lit up the night sky.* **2** [I] if your face or eyes light up, you show that you are pleased or excited **3** [I] INFORMAL to light a cigarette

**USAGE NOTE lit and lighted**

Use **lit** as the past participle of **light**: *Dean had already lit the candles.* Use **lighted** as

an adjective before a noun: *a lighted candle.*

**light⁴** *adv* **travel light** to travel without carrying too many of your possessions
**light bulb** /'. ./ *n* the glass object in a lamp that produces light —see picture at LAMP
**light·ed** /'laɪtɪd/ *adj* used before some nouns to mean "lit": *a lighted cigarette/match/lamp*
**light·en** /'laɪtⁿn/ *v* **1** [T] to reduce the amount of work, worry, debt etc. that someone has: *The new computers were supposed to lighten our work load.* **2** [I,T] to become brighter, or make something become brighter **3 lighten up!** SPOKEN used in order to tell someone not to be so serious about something: *Hey, lighten up, it was just a joke!* **4** [I,T] to reduce the weight of something
**light·er** /'laɪtɚ/ *n* a small object that produces a flame to light a cigarette
**light-head·ed** /'. ,../ *adj* not able to think clearly or move steadily because you are sick or have drunk too much alcohol
**light-heart·ed** /'. ,../ *adj* **1** cheerful and happy **2** not intended to be serious
**light·house** /'laɪthaʊs/ *n* a tower with a bright light that warns ships of danger
**light·ing** /'laɪtɪŋ/ *n* [U] the lights that light a room, building etc., or the quality of the light: *soft/bright/dim lighting*
**light·ly** /'laɪtli/ *adv* **1** with only a small amount of weight or force: *He kissed the child lightly on the head.* **2** using or having only a small amount of something: *Sprinkle sugar lightly over the cake* **3 not take sth lightly** to treat something in a serious way: *A bomb threat is not to be taken lightly.*
**light·ning¹** /'laɪtⁿnɪŋ/ *n* [U] a bright flash of light in the sky that happens during a storm: *a tall oak tree that was struck by lightning*

lightning

**lightning²** *adj* extremely fast or sudden: *a lightning attack by the army*
**light·weight¹** /'laɪt-weɪt/ *adj* **1** weighing less than average: *a lightweight jacket* **2** not needing much thinking or skill to understand or do: *a lightweight novel*
**lightweight²** *n* someone who is not important enough to have any influence, or who does not have enough intelligence: *a political/intellectual lightweight*
**light year** /'. ./ *n* the distance that light travels from the sun in one year
**lik·a·ble** /'laɪkəbəl/ *adj* likable people are nice, and are easy to like
**like¹** /laɪk/ *prep* **1** similar in some way to something else: *The lamp was round - like a ball.* | *You two are behaving like children.* | *I'd*

L

love to have a car like yours. | Ken **looks like** his brother. | Was the movie **anything like** the book? (=was it similar in any way?) | There's **nothing like** (=nothing better than) Mom's chicken soup! **2** typical of a particular person or thing: It's not like Dad to be late. (=it is unusual that Dad is late) **3** NONSTANDARD such as: Foods like spinach and broccoli are high in iron. **4 what is sb/sth like?** used when asking someone to describe something or to give his/her opinion: What's the new house like?

---

SPOKEN PHRASES

**5 like this** said when showing someone how something is or was done: She had her arms around his neck, like this. **6 more like** said when giving someone a number or amount that is more correct than the one s/he has mentioned: "He's been in there for 15 minutes!" "More like half an hour."

---

—see also **something like** (SOMETHING) —see usage note at AS

**like²** adv SPOKEN **1** I'm like/he's like/Bob's like etc. NONSTANDARD **a)** used in order to tell someone the exact words someone used: I asked him if he thought Liz was cute, and he's like, yeah, definitely. **b)** said when describing an event, feeling, or person, when it is difficult to do this exactly or when you use a noise instead of a word: I'm like, ooh! (=I was really surprised) | We were like, oh no! (=we realized something was wrong) | Their music has like, weird lyrics. (=weird is not the best word, but I cannot think of a better one) **2** said when you pause because you do not know what to say, you are embarrassed etc.: Do you think you could, like, just lend me $25? **3** said in order to give an example: The problem is that sushi is so expensive. Like last week I paid $40 for a meal. **4** said when what you are saying is not exact: It was like 9 o'clock and she still wasn't home. **5** said in order to emphasize something: That's like so stupid.

**like³** v [T] **1** to enjoy something, or think that someone or something is nice or pleasant: Do you like oranges? | I like Billy a lot. | I really like swimming in the ocean. | Pam doesn't **like to** walk home late at night. | Mom doesn't **like it** when we make a lot of noise. —opposite DISLIKE¹ **2** to think that it is good to do something in a particular way, so that you do it regularly: prefer: Jim likes to get to the airport early. | How do you like your hamburger cooked?

---

SPOKEN PHRASES

**3** used in order to ask politely for something, to ask someone to do something, or to offer someone something: **I'd like** a cheeseburger, please. | We **would like** you **to be** there if you can. | He'd **like to** know how much it will cost. | **Would you like** some more coffee? **4 How do you like...?** said when you want to know someone's opinion

---

about something: "How did you like the movie?" "It was okay." **5 not like the sound of sth** to be worried because of something you have heard or read: I don't like the sound of that weather report **6 (whether you) like it or not** used in order to tell someone that something unpleasant will happen and cannot be changed: You're going to the dentist, like it or not!

**like⁴** conjunction NONSTANDARD **1** as if: He acted like he owned the place. **2 like I said/told you/was saying** said when you are repeating something you have already said: Like I said, we'll probably be there around ten. **3** in the same way as: Do it like I told you to.

**like⁵** adj FORMAL **1** similar in some way: two people of **like mind** (=who think in a similar way) **2 -like** typical of or similar to something: moving with cat-like grace

**like⁶** n sb's likes and dislikes all the things someone likes and does not like

**like·li·hood** /ˈlaɪkliˌhʊd/ n [singular, U] **1** how likely something is to happen: Clean water decreases the **likelihood of** disease. **2 in all likelihood** almost definitely

**like·ly** /ˈlaɪkli/ adj, adv probably or almost definitely: It's **likely to** rain tomorrow. —**likely** adv: I'd very likely have done the same thing as you did.

**like-mind·ed** /ˌ. ˈ..◂/ adj two or more people who are like-minded have similar interests or opinions

**lik·en** /ˈlaɪkən/ v

**liken sb/sth to sb/sth** phr v [T] FORMAL to describe someone or something as similar to someone or something else: The writer **likens** marriage **to** slavery.

**like·ness** /ˈlaɪknɪs/ n **1** [U] the quality of being similar in appearance to something else **2** the image of someone in a painting or photograph: It's a good likeness of Eva.

**like·wise** /ˈlaɪk-waɪz/ adv **1** FORMAL in the same way: The dinner was amazing; likewise, the concert. **2** SPOKEN said in order to return someone's greeting or polite remark: "It's great to see you here." "Likewise."

**lik·ing** /ˈlaɪkɪŋ/ n **1 have a liking for sth** to like or enjoy something: She has a liking for chocolate cake. **2 take a liking to sb** INFORMAL to like someone you have just met

**li·lac** /ˈlaɪlɑk, -lək/ n **1** a small tree with pale purple and white flowers **2** [U] a pale purple color —**lilac** adj

**lilt** /lɪlt/ n [singular] the pleasant rise and fall in the sound of someone's voice or a piece of music

**lil·y** /ˈlɪli/ n a plant with large, usually bell-shaped white flowers

**li·ma bean** /ˈlaɪmə ˌbin/ n a pale green flat bean

**limb** /lɪm/ *n* **1** a large branch of a tree **2 go out on a limb** to do something alone and without help or support: *I'm glad it worked because I'd gone out on a limb to try it.* **3** FORMAL an arm or leg

**lim·bo** /'lɪmboʊ/ *n* **be in limbo** to be in an uncertain situation because you are waiting for something: *I'm kind of in limbo until I know which college I'm going to.*

**lime** /laɪm/ *n* **1** [C,U] a bright green fruit with a sour taste, or the tree this grows on **2** [U] a white powdery substance used in making CEMENT

**lime·light** /'laɪmlaɪt/ *n* **the limelight** attention from the public

**lim·er·ick** /'lɪmərɪk/ *n* a humorous short poem with five lines

**lim·it**[1] /'lɪmɪt/ *n* **1** the greatest amount, number etc. that is allowed or is possible: *There is a **limit on/to** the amount of time we have.* | *a 65 mph speed limit* | *Our finances are **stretched to the limit**.* (=we do not have any more money to spend) **2** the border or edge of something: *A fence marks the limit of the school fields.* **3 off limits** beyond the area where someone is allowed to go: *The beach is off limits after midnight.* **4 within limits** within the time, using the effort etc. that is reasonable and acceptable

**limit**[2] *v* [T] **1** to prevent an amount, number etc. from increasing beyond a particular point: *The economy will be limited to a 4% growth rate.* **2** to allow someone to use only a particular amount of something: *He's been **limited to** one hour of TV per night.* **3 be limited to** to exist or happen only in a particular place or group: *The damage was limited to the roof.* **–limiting** *adj*

**lim·i·ta·tion** /ˌlɪmə'teɪʃən/ *n* **1** [U] the act of limiting something: *the limitation of nuclear testing* **2** a limit on what you are able to do or how good something can be: *Computers **have their limitations**.*

**lim·it·ed** /'lɪmɪtɪd/ *adj* not very great in amount, number, degree etc.: *a family living on a **limited income*** –opposite UNLIMITED

**lim·o** /'lɪmoʊ/ *n* INFORMAL ⇨ LIMOUSINE

**lim·ou·sine** /'lɪməˌzin, ˌlɪmə'zin/ *n* a big expensive car

**limp**[1] /lɪmp/ *adj* without strength or firmness: *The dog's body **went limp** as the drug took effect.*

**limp**[2] *v* [I] to walk with difficulty because one leg is hurt: *He limped to the chair and sat down.*

**limp**[3] *n* the way someone walks when s/he is LIMPing: *The man we're looking for **walks with a limp**.*

**linch·pin** /'lɪntʃˌpɪn/ *n* **the linchpin of** someone or something that a system depends on, so that it will not work without him, her, or it: *My uncle was the linchpin of the family.*

line

They're standing in line to buy tickets.

**line**[1] /laɪn/ *n*
**1** ▶LONG THIN MARK◀ a long thin mark on a surface, especially one that has been drawn: *She **drew a line** on the map to show him how to get to the museum.* –see also DOTTED LINE
**2** ▶LIMIT/BORDER◀ a long thin mark used in order to show a limit or border: *Carol fell as she crossed the **finish line**.* (=the line that marks the end of a race) | *the dividing line between the lanes on the road*
**3 be/stand/wait in line** to stand in a row of people who are waiting for something: *We stood in line for two hours for tickets.*
**4** ▶ROW◀ a row of people or things: *toys arranged in a line on the floor*
**5** ▶DIRECTION◀ a direction something travels, or the imaginary path between two points in space: *Light travels **in a straight line**.*
**6** ▶SKIN◀ a very small fold in the skin; WRINKLE: *tiny lines around his eyes*
**7 county/state line** the border between two counties (COUNTY) or states in the US
**8** ▶WAY◀ a way of thinking about or doing something: *This meeting will be organized **along the same lines** (=in the same way) as the last one.*
**9 in line/out of line** happening or behaving in the correct or expected way, or not happening or behaving in this way: *The company's actions are **in line** with the state laws.* | *I thought what Kenny said was way out of line!*
**10** ▶TELEPHONE◀ a telephone wire, or the connection between two telephones: *The line was bad, so we hung up and tried again.* –see usage note at TELEPHONE
**11** ▶PRODUCTS◀ a particular type of goods: *The new line of shoes should sell really well.*
**12 be first/next in line for sth** to be very likely to be the next person to get something: *I'm sure Carl is next in line for a raise.*
**13** ▶SHAPE◀ the outer shape of something long or tall: *The building has beautiful lines.*
**14** ▶SPORTS◀ a row of players with a particular purpose in a sport: *the Bears' defensive line*
**15** ▶COMPANY◀ a company that provides a system for moving goods by road, water, or air: *a large shipping line*
**16 the line** ⇨ CLOTHESLINE
**17** ▶FAMILY◀ the people that existed before you in your family: *She comes from a long line of politicians.*

L

# STUDY NOTES

This special section contains helpful information about the most common usage problems for students of English, plus five picture pages that show vocabulary in context.

■ **Adjective word order** *page 456*  ■ **Numbers** *page 460*  ■ **Quantity** *page 466*
■ **Capitalization** *page 456*  ■ **Phrasal verbs** *page 462*  ■ **Verbs** *page 468*
■ **Comparatives** *page 457*  ■ **Intensifiers** *page 463*  ■ **Pictures** *beginning page 469*
■ **Modal verbs** *page 458*  ■ **Prepositions** *page 464*

## STUDY NOTES adjective word order

■ When you use more than one adjective to describe a noun, the adjectives are usually in the following order:

1. what something is like
2. what color it is
3. what type of thing it is:

|  | QUALITY/SIZE | TEMPERATURE | FEATURE/SHAPE | COLOR | TYPE | NOUN |
|---|---|---|---|---|---|---|
| *a* | beautiful |  | new | white | wool | *sweater* |
| *a* | long | hot | dry | . | summer | *day* |
| *a* | big |  | square | green | wooden | *box* |
| *a* | nice | cold |  |  |  | *glass of milk* |
|  | delicious | warm | fresh |  | homemade | *bread* |

■ Comparatives (like **better**) and superlatives (like **best**) are used before all the other adjectives in a group:
*It was the most beautiful white wool sweater I've ever seen.*
*Do you want the smaller yellow metal box or the bigger green wooden one?*

## STUDY NOTES capitalization

■ The first word of a sentence is capitalized in English: *How are you today?*

■ The names of people, places, and things that are trademarks are capitalized:
*Mary Johnson | Los Angeles, California | Pepsi-Cola*

■ In titles of books, movies, essays etc., capitalize the first word, the last word, and most of the other words. Do not capitalize prepositions (*of, by, at* etc.), the determiners *a, an,* and *the,* or the conjunctions *and, but, so, yet, or, for,* and *nor*:
*The Call of the Wild | Money, Banking, and the Economy*

■ Words like *college, high school,* and *place* are capitalized when they are part of a name:
*I'm in college.*
BUT
*I go to City College.*

*Do you know a good place to have lunch?*
BUT
*There's a good restaurant near Walton Place.*

■ In titles of professions, words are also capitalized when they are part of a name:
*I'm going to see the doctor.*
BUT
*I'm going to see Dr. Taylor/Doctor Taylor.*

■ In titles of family members, words are capitalized when you are using that word as a name:
*My grandma is 83 years old.*
BUT
*Can I have some milk, Grandma?*

# STUDY NOTES comparatives

The COMPARATIVE and SUPERLATIVE forms of adjectives and adverbs show an increase in quality, quantity, or degree. Comparatives are formed in three ways:

by adding **-er** and **-est** to the end of short words, like this:

*All of the girls' presents are big.*
*Anita's present is **bigger than** Jody's.*
*Melissa's present is **bigger than** both Anita's and Jody's.*
*Melissa's present is **the biggest** of the three.*

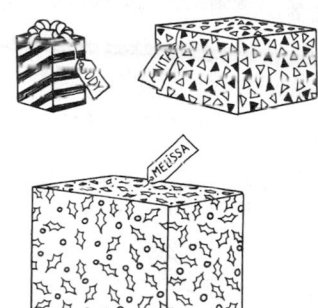

by adding **more** and **most** or **less** and **least** before longer words, like this:

*The watch with the leather band is **more expensive than** the child's watch.*
*The watch with the leather band is **less expensive than** the gold watch.*
*The gold watch is **the most expensive**.*
*The child's watch is **the least expensive**.*

by using a different word, like these comparatives of **good**:

*Brad's work is **the worst** of the three.*
*Jamie's work is **better than** Brad's, but **worse than** Jerome's.*
*Jerome's work is **the best**.*

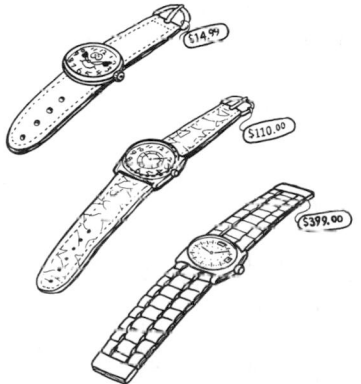

# STUDY NOTES modal verbs

■ The verbs in the charts below are modal verbs. They are used as auxiliary verbs with another verb to change its meaning in some way. This list tells you what the modal verbs mean and how to use them.

| | IN STATEMENTS | IN QUESTIONS | IN NEGATIVE STATEMENTS |
|---|---|---|---|
| **SHOWING ABILITY** **can** is used for talking about an ability or skill. **could** is the past tense form | *Deena* **can** *speak Russian.* *I* **could** *ride a bike when I was six.* | **Can** *Deena speak Russian?* **Could** *you ride a bike when you were little?* | *Deena* **can't/cannot** *speak Russian.* *I* **couldn't/could not** *ride a bike until I was seven.* |
| **be able to** is used for talking about actions or achievements. | *Pete* **was able to** *get there on time.* | **Was** *Pete* **able to** *get there on time?* | *Pete* **wasn't/was not** *able to get there on time.* |
| **ASKING AND GIVING PERMISSION** **could** and **may** are more polite than **can**. **may** is more formal than **could** or **can**. Use **could** in this way only in questions. | *You* **can** *have a cookie if you want.* *You* **may** *have a cookie if you like.* | **Can** *I have a cookie?* **May** *I have a cookie?* **Could** *you speak more clearly?* | *No, you* **can't/cannot** *have one.* *No, you* **may not** *have one.* |
| **MAKING REQUESTS AND SUGGESTIONS** **could** is more polite than **can**. Use **should** or **shall** with *I* and *we* to make suggestions. | *I* **can** *help if you want.* *We* **could** *barbecue some chicken.* *We* **should** *get that door fixed.* | **Can** *you hand me that pen?* **Could** *you do me a favor?* *What* **should/shall** *we do tonight?* **should** is now used much more than **shall** in questions. | |
| **SHOWING THAT SOMETHING IS NECESSARY** **need to** means that something is necessary. **have to** means that something is necessary, and that you have no choice about doing it. **must** is used by people in authority. **have got to** is a stronger way to say this. Never use **have got to** in questions or negative statements. | *Perry* **needs to** *talk to us.* *I* **have to** *ask my mom first.* *I've* **got to** *leave right now.* *We* **had to** *wait a long time.* *Paige, you* **must** *come wash your hands.* | **Does** *Perry* **need to** *talk to us?* **Do** *you* **have to** *ask your mom first?* **Do** *you* **have to** *leave right now?* **Did** *you* **have to** *wait a long time?* **Do** *I* **have to** *wash my hands, Dad?* **must** is not used in questions very often. | *Perry* **doesn't need** *to talk to us.* *I* **don't have to** *ask my mom first.* *I* **don't have to** *leave right now.* *We* **didn't have to** *wait a long time.* *You* **don't have to** *wash your hands.* **don't need to** and **don't have to** are the only modal verbs you can use to say that something is not necessary. |

# STUDY NOTES modal verbs

|  | IN STATEMENTS | IN QUESTIONS | IN NEGATIVE STATEMENTS |
|---|---|---|---|
| **GIVING COMMANDS**<br>**be to** is stronger than **must**. | *You **must** tell them everything you know.*<br><br>*You **are to** tell them everything you know.* |  | *You **mustn't/must not** tell them anything.*<br><br>*You **are not to** tell them anything.* |
| **GIVING ADVICE**<br>**should** is the most common modal verb for giving advice.<br>**ought to** is a little stronger than **should**.<br>**must** is used in order to emphasize that something is a good idea. | *You **should** hang the painting there.*<br><br>*Reggie **ought to** try to find a different job.*<br><br>*You **must** try some of this cake.*<br><br>*I really **must** go to the dentist's.* | ***Should** I hang the painting here?*<br><br>***Should** Reggie try to find a different job?*<br><br>**ought to** and **must** are almost never used in questions. | *You **shouldn't/should not** hang the painting there.*<br><br>*Reggie **shouldn't/should not** try to find a different job.*<br><br>*You **shouldn't/should not** leave without trying this cake.*<br><br>**ought not to** is fairly formal, and is not used very often.<br>**must not** and **mustn't** are not used very often for giving advice. |
| **SHOWING THAT SOMETHING IS ALMOST CERTAIN, OR IS IMPOSSIBLE** | *She **must be** sick, because she hasn't been to work.*<br><br>*Craig **must have** forgotten his keys.* |  | *She **can't be** sick, because I saw her at the mall.*<br><br>*Craig **can't have** forgotten his keys, because the house is locked.* |
| **SHOWING THAT SOMETHING IS POSSIBLE** | *I **might/may** take chemistry next semester.*<br><br>*They **could be** lost.* | ***Could** they be lost?* | *I **might not/may not** take chemistry next semester.* |
| **TALKING ABOUT THE FUTURE** | *Kathy **will** be there tomorrow.*<br><br>*The weatherman said it **would** rain tomorrow.* | ***Will** Kathy be there tomorrow?* | *Kathy **won't/will not** be there tomorrow.*<br><br>*The weatherman said it **wouldn't/would not** rain tomorrow.* |
| **TALKING ABOUT THE PAST**<br><br>Use **used to** to talk about states, situations, or actions in the past.<br>Use **would** only for talking about past actions. | *I **used to** have a car, but now I don't.*<br><br>*We **would** often go camping when we were younger.* | ***Did** you **use to** have a car?* | *I **didn't use to** have a car, but now I do.* |

# STUDY NOTES numbers

## USING AND SAYING NUMBERS

We say numbers differently, depending on the situation.

### "A" AND "ONE"

- In speech, we use "a" (a hundred), not "one" (one hundred): *My watch cost a hundred dollars.* | *There were about a hundred people at the wedding.* We use "one" (one hundred, one fourth) in math: *One fourth plus one fourth is* (OR *equals*) *one half.* | *One plus one is* (OR *equals*) *two.*

- We use "a" instead of "one" when we are talking in general about one of something: *I need a nail.* | *I have a sister.* We use "one" when we are emphasizing that we need only one thing, or when we are answering a question about numbers: *I only need one nail, not two.* | *"How many brothers and sisters do you have?" "I have one sister and two brothers."*

### DATES Examples of incorrect or nonstandard use have an ✗ beside them.

- In the US, we write the date in the order month, day, year: *July 1, 1999* (in personal or business letters) | *7/1/99* (on documents). We say, "July first, nineteen ninety-nine" OR "the first of July, nineteen ninety-nine." We can write *I'm leaving on July 1st* OR *I'm leaving on July 1.* We say both of these as *"I'm leaving on July first."* We do not write ✗*July 1st, 1999.* ✗

- If the third digit in a year is a zero, we say "oh," not "zero": *1904* (=nineteen oh four). Years that start with 10, 20 etc. are said this way: *2001* (=twenty oh one OR two thousand one) | *2010* (=twenty ten OR two thousand ten) | *2021* (=twenty twenty-one OR two thousand twenty-one).

### CLASSROOMS, CLASS NUMBERS, HOTEL ROOMS, APARTMENTS

- Numbers with two digits are said just like normal numbers: *room 21* (=room twenty-one) | *apartment 12* (=apartment twelve).

- For numbers with three digits, we say the first digit, then the other two digits are said as one number: *English 221* (=English two twenty-one) | *apartment 518* (=apartment five eighteen). EXCEPTIONS: If the second digit is a zero, we say each digit separately: *English 203* (=English two oh three) | *apartment 708* (=apartment seven oh eight). If the number is 100, 200, 300 etc., we say the whole number: *room 100* (=room one hundred)

- For numbers with four digits, we say the numbers in groups of two: *English 2220* (=English twenty-two twenty) | *apartment 1146* (=apartment eleven forty-six). EXCEPTIONS: if the third digit is a zero, we say the last two digits separately: *English 2102* (=English twenty-one oh two) | *apartment 1305* (=apartment thirteen oh five). If the number is 1000, 2000, 3000 etc., we say the whole number: *room 1000* (=room one thousand).

### ADDRESSES

We usually say addresses the same way we say numbers, but there are some exceptions.

- For house numbers with five digits, we say each digit separately: *20619 W. 182nd St.* (two oh six one nine west a hundred and eighty-second street)

- For post office boxes with three digits, we say each digit separately: *Box 150* (=box one five oh)

- For ZIP codes, we say each digit separately: *98119* (=nine eight one one nine) | *02134* (=oh two one three four) | *10011* (=one oh oh one one)

### TELEPHONE NUMBERS

- For telephone numbers, we say each digit separately: *The number for Information is 555-1212.* (=five five five one two one two) | *area code 206* (=two oh six)

### "OH" AND "ZERO"

- In math, we usually say "zero" instead of "oh," especially when 0 is a whole number: *0.05%* (=zero point zero five percent OR point zero five percent)

- In the scores of sports games, we say "zero" or "nothing": *The final score was 18-0.* (=eighteen (to) zero) | *They had a 2-0 lead at half time.* (=two (to) nothing OR two (to) zero) We also say "zip" and "zilch" in informal use: *We beat them 35-0!* (=thirty-five zip OR thirty-five zilch)

# STUDY NOTES numbers

| HOW MANY | | ORDER | FRACTIONS | | USING THESE NUMBERS IN SENTENCES |
|---|---|---|---|---|---|
| IN NUMERALS | IN WORDS | IN A LIST | IN NUMERALS | IN WORDS | |
| 1 | one | first | 1 | a whole | Two halves make **a whole.** |
| 2 | two | second | 1/2 | a/one half | Cut the pie **in half.** |
| 3 | three | third | 1/3 | a/one third | Cut the pie **in thirds.** |
| 4 | four | fourth | 1/4 | a/one fourth OR a/one quarter | Cut the pie **in fourths/ quarters.** |
| 5 | five | fifth | 1/5 | a/one fifth | Cut the pie **in fifths.** |
| 6 | six | sixth | 1/6 | a/one sixth | Cut the pie **in sixths.** |
| 7 | seven | seventh | 1/7 | a/one seventh | Cut the pie **in sevenths.** |
| 8 | eight | eighth | 1/8 | a/one eighth | Cut the pie **in eighths.** |
| 9 | nine | ninth | 1/9 | a/one ninth | |
| 10 | ten | tenth | 1/10 | a/one tenth | |
| 11 | eleven | eleventh | 1/11 | an/one eleventh | |
| 12 | twelve | twelfth | 1/12 | a/one twelfth | |
| 13 | thirteen | thirteenth | 1/13 | a/one thirteenth | My kids are **in their teens.** (between 13 and 19 years old) |
| 14 | fourteen | fourteenth | 1/14 | a/one fourteenth | |
| 15 | fifteen | fifteenth | 1/15 | a/one fifteenth | |
| 16 | sixteen | sixteenth | 1/16 | a/one sixteenth | |
| 17 | seventeen | seventeenth | 1/17 | a/one seventeenth | |
| 18 | eighteen | eighteenth | 1/18 | an/one eighteenth | |
| 19 | nineteen | nineteenth | 1/19 | a/one nineteenth | |
| 20 | twenty | twentieth | 1/20 | a/one twentieth | Jack is **in his twenties.** (between 20 and 29 years old) |
| 21 | twenty-one | twenty-first | 1/21 | a/one twenty-first | |
| 22 | twenty-two | twenty-second | 1/22 | a/one twenty-second | |
| 30 | thirty | thirtieth | 1/30 | a/one thirtieth | It's **in the thirties.** (between 30 and 39 degrees in temperature) |
| 40 | forty | fortieth | 1/40 | a/one fortieth | |
| 50 | fifty | fiftieth | 1/50 | a/one fiftieth | |
| 60 | sixty | sixtieth | 1/60 | a/one sixtieth | I was born **in the sixties.** (between 1960 and 1969) |
| 70 | seventy | seventieth | 1/70 | a/one seventieth | |
| 80 | eighty | eightieth | 1/80 | an/one eightieth | |
| 90 | ninety | ninetieth | 1/90 | a/one ninetieth | |
| 100 | a/one hundred | hundredth | 1/100 2/100 | a hundredth/ one one hundredth two hundredths/ two one hundredths | |
| 200 | two hundred | two hundredth | 1/200 | a/one two hundredth | |
| 1000 | a/one thousand | thousandth | 1/1000 | a/one thousandth | |
| 100,000 | a/one hundred thousand | | 1/100,000 | a/one hundred thousandth | |
| 1,000,000 | a/one million | millionth | 1/100,000,000 | a/one millionth | |
| | | | | | |

# STUDY NOTES phrasal verbs

## WHAT A PHRASAL VERB IS

Verbs like **get to, pull off,** and **come down on** are very common in English. These are called phrasal verbs, and they include a verb and one or more prepositions or adverbs.

- When these words are used together, they mean something different from what they mean when they are used separately. For example, **get** usually means to receive something, and **to** usually shows direction. However, to **get to** someone means "to upset or annoy someone."

- This dictionary makes it easy for you to understand and use phrasal verbs. They are listed under the main verb so that it is easy to find them. For example, **get to** is listed under **get**, after the meanings of the main verb. The phrasal verb in the example sentence is always in **_dark letters_** so you can see clearly how it is used in a sentence:

- The entry for **get to** shows that in informal speech and writing, you can say
  *Don't let him **get to** you, honey.*
  instead of
  *Don't let him **annoy** you, honey.*

> **get to** sb *phr v* [T] INFORMAL to upset or annoy someone: *Don't let him **get to** you, honey. He's just teasing you.*

## THE GRAMMAR OF PHRASAL VERBS

Phrasal verbs can be INTRANSITIVE or TRANSITIVE (see Study Note on p. 468). When they are intransitive, this dictionary shows them like this:

> **look out** *phr v* [I] to pay attention to what is happening around you: *Look out! You almost hit the cat.*

When phrasal verbs are transitive, they can be very difficult to use. To help you use them correctly, this dictionary shows whether the DIRECT OBJECT is a person or a thing, and where the object can be used in the sentence.

- The abbreviation **sb** means that the object is a person:

> **take after** sb *phr v* [T] to look or behave like another member of your family: *Jenny **takes after** her dad.*

- The abbreviation **sth** means that the object is a thing:

> **plow into** sth *phr v* [T] to hit something hard with a car, truck etc.: *A train derailed and **plowed into** two houses.*

- The abbreviation **sb/sth** means that the object can be a person or a thing:

> **think of** sb/sth *phr v* [T] **1** to produce a new idea, suggestion etc.: *Can you **think of** anything better to do?* **2** to remember a name or fact: *I can't **think of** his name now.* **3** to show that you want to treat other people well: *Bill's always **thinking of** others.*

- When the object can only follow the preposition or adverb, the entry looks like this:

> **run up** sth *phr v* [T] to make a debt, cost, price etc. greater: *We **ran up** a huge phone bill.*

- When the object can only follow the verb, the entry looks like this:

> **follow** sb **around** *phr v* [T] to keep following someone everywhere s/he goes: *My little brother is always **following** me **around**.*

## STUDY NOTES phrasal verbs

■ When the object can follow either the verb or the preposition or adverb, the entry uses the symbol ↔ and looks like this:

> **bring** sth ↔ **out** *phr v* [T] **1** to make something become easier to notice, see, taste etc.: *The red paint **brings out** the red in the curtains.*

■ Sometimes a phrasal verb can have two objects. These phrasal verbs are shown like this:

> **hit** sb **up for** sth *phr v* [T] SPOKEN to ask someone for something: *Mitch will probably try to **hit** you **up for** a loan.*

## STUDY NOTES intensifiers

■ Some adverbs like **very**, **fairly**, and **extremely** can be used in order to change the meaning of a word, phrase, or sentence.
They can make the meaning stronger:
   *They live **very** close to the beach.* (=more than just close)
Or, they can make the meaning less strong:
   *They live **fairly** close to the beach.* (=not really close, but definitely not far)

In the chart below, the meaning of the group of words gets stronger as you move from top to bottom:

| WORD GROUP | MEANING | EXAMPLES |
|---|---|---|
| **pretty** (INFORMAL) **kind of** (INFORMAL) **sort of** (INFORMAL) **fairly** **a little (bit)** | to some degree, but not too much | *I'm **pretty** tired.* *They're **kind of** busy.* *It made me **sort of** curious.* *It's a **fairly** expensive restaurant.* *The hamburgers are **a little** burned.* |
| **really** **very** **quite** **rather** (FORMAL) | more than just | *He's a **really** nice guy.* *I think it's **very** pretty.* *It's **quite** useful to know that.* *We have a **rather** long list.* |
| **quite** **amazingly** **surprisingly** **incredibly** **remarkably** | more than expected | *In fact, the wine was **quite** nice.* *Nina is **amazingly** smart.* *Bats can fly **surprisingly** fast.* *You've been **incredibly** kind.* *The sound is **remarkably** clear.* |
| **awfully** (INFORMAL) **extremely** | very much | *He's **awfully** cute.* *Erin's **extremely** shy.* |
| **completely** **totally** **absolutely** **entirely** **utterly** (FORMAL) | as much as possible | *The snake is **completely** harmless.* *Wait, I'm **totally** confused.* *I'm **absolutely** sure.* *This is an **entirely** different case.* *Dr. Lallas is **utterly** wrong.* |

**Answers to the questions on pages 464 and 465**

| 1 | in/on | 7 | in/near | 13 | behind |
| 2 | in/on | 8 | between | 14 | between |
| 3 | over | 9 | beside/between | 15 | in front of |
| 4 | above/over | 10 | in | 16 | toward |
| 5 | under/beside | 11 | on/on | 17 | out of |
| 6 | on/beside | 12 | on | | |

# STUDY NOTES prepositions

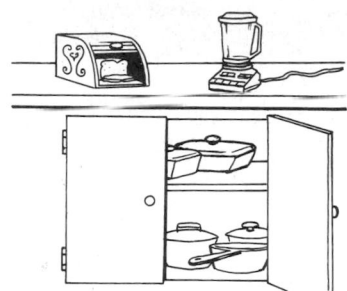

The casseroles are **in** the cupboard **on** the top shelf.
The blender is **on** the counter.

**Fill in the blanks with *in* or *on*.**

1. "Where are your pans?"

   "They're ____ the cupboard under the counter ____ the bottom shelf."

2. The bread is ____ the breadbox ____ the counter.

There are cobwebs **over** everything in the house.
There's an old chandelier **above/over** the big table.

**Fill in the blanks with *over* or *above*.**

3. There are old sheets ____ the furniture.

4. There's a spider hanging down ____ the chair.

There's a campground **below** the hill, **beside** the river **near** the bridge.
There's a bridge **over** the river.
Cars are **on** the bridge, driving **over** it.
The river flows **through** the valley **under** the bridge **past** the campground.
There's a rowboat **on** the river and someone is fishing **in** the river.

**Fill in the blanks with the correct preposition.**

5. There's a tent ____ the tree ____ the river.

6. A boy is walking ____ a log ____ the river.

7. A beaver is swimming ____ the river ____ the bank.

# STUDY NOTES prepositions

One candlestick is **beside** the vase.
The picture frames are **between** the other candlestick and the clock.

**Fill in the blanks with *beside* or *between*.**

8. The clock is right in the middle, ____ the vase and the picture frames.

9. The vase is ____ the clock, ____ it and a candlestick.

Shawn and Terry live **in** this house.
They live **on** East 135th Street.
They live **on** the corner of East 135th and Ferndale Avenue.
They live **in** a city.

**Fill in the blanks with *in, on,* or *at*.**

10. "Where do you live?"
    "I live ____ a small town in Iowa."

11. "Where is that Mexican restaurant you like?"
    "It's ____ Larch Way, ____ the corner of Larch Way and 130th."

12. We live ____ 20033 7th Avenue West.

The truck is in **front of** the station wagon.
The convertible is **between** the truck and the motorcycle.
All the other vehicles are **behind** the motorcycle.

**Fill in the blanks with *in front of, behind,* or *between*.**

13. The station wagon is ____ the truck.

14. The truck is ____ the station wagon and the convertible.

15. The motorcycle is ____ the convertible.

A woman is coming **out of** the bookstore. Two teenagers are going **into** the shoe store. A group of children are walking **toward** the toy store. A man is walking **away from** it.

**Fill in the blanks with *out of, into, toward,* or *away from*.**

16. A mother is walking ____ the shoe store with her kids.

17. An old man is coming ____ the toy store.

Answers are on page 463

# STUDY NOTES quantity

## NOUNS THAT SHOW QUANTITY

### COUNTABLE NOUNS
**(no grammar code)**

■ Words like **egg** and **cup** are COUNTABLE nouns because they are separate things that can be counted:

*an egg*        *a cup*

*two eggs*        *two cups*

■ These nouns have plural forms, and can be used with **a** or **an** when they are singular.

### UNCOUNTABLE NOUNS
**(grammar code [U])**

■ Words like **lemonade** and **aluminum** are UNCOUNTABLE nouns because they are substances that cannot be counted:

*There's some*        *a can made of*
*lemonade left.*        *aluminum*

■ These nouns do not have plural forms, and they cannot be used with **a** or **an.** Many other nouns that are not physical substances are also uncountable, such as **music, laughter, knowledge, swimming,** and **marriage.**

### NOUNS THAT ARE BOTH COUNTABLE AND UNCOUNTABLE
**(grammar code [C,U])**

■ Some nouns, such as **jam** and **lipstick**, can be countable in one meaning and uncountable in another. When they are countable, they can be used in their plural forms; when they are uncountable, they cannot. For example:

**jam** [C,U]

*a nice thick layer of **jam***        *lots of different **jams***

**lipstick** [C,U]

*Rosa is putting on her **lipstick**.*        *Rosa has several **lipsticks**.*

### PLURAL NOUNS
**(grammar code [plural])**

Some nouns, such as **pants** and **manners**, are used only in their plural form, with a plural verb:

*My **pants are** too small.*

*His **manners were** really bad.*

Sometimes these nouns do not look like plurals, such as the plural noun **media**:

*The **media are** now interested in her story.*

### SINGULAR NOUNS
**(grammar code [singular])**

Some nouns, such as **feel, collapse, electorate**, and **Neptune** are only used in their singular form, with a singular verb. They can be used with **a, an,** or **the,** or without any determiner at all:

*Silk has a wonderful **feel**.*

*Floods caused **the collapse** of the bridge.*

*The idea is not popular with **the electorate**.*

***Neptune** is far away from the Sun.*

# STUDY NOTES quantity

## TALKING ABOUT QUANTITIES

The sentences on the left show which words to use with COUNTABLE nouns in order to show quantity, and the sentences on the right show which words to use with UNCOUNTABLE nouns.

**all**

### HOW MANY? (for countable nouns)

### HOW MUCH? (for uncountable nouns)

- *Every* class was full.
  *All (of)* the classes were full.

- *All (of)* the money will go in Audrey's account.

- *Most of* the kids in my class take the bus.

- We worked in the lab *most of* the time.

- Use **a lot of** with the object of a sentence:
  I have **a lot of** relatives in Ohio.

- Use **a lot of** with the object of a sentence:
  They wanted **a lot of** money for the guitar.

- Use **many (of)** with the subject of a sentence.
  **Many of** my relatives live in Ohio.
  **Many** roads are full of litter.

- Use **much (of)** with the subject of a sentence:
  **Much of** our money is gone.
  **Much** work remains to be done. (FORMAL)

- Use **many** in questions:
  Do you have **many** relatives in Idaho?

- Use **much** in questions:
  Is there **much** money left?

- Use **many** or **a lot of** in negative statements:
  I don't have **many** relatives in Idaho.
  I don't have **a lot of** relatives In Idaho. (INFORMAL)

- Use **much** or **a lot of** in negative statements:
  There isn't **much** money left.
  There isn't **a lot of** money left. (INFORMAL)

- It will take **several** days to complete.

- I've read **some of** his short stories.
  We need to buy **some** new towels.

- **Some of** your stuff just fell off the table.
  There's **some** glue here if you need it.

- Use **some (of)** in questions when you expect the answer to be yes:
  Can I use **some of** your paper clips?

- Use **some (of)** in questions when you expect the answer to be yes:
  Do you want **some** carrot cake?

- Use **a few** in positive statements, and **few** or **not many** in negative statements:
  **A few** people did show up.
  **Not many** people showed up.
  **Few** visitors came that year.

- Use **a little** in positive statements, and **little** or **not much** in negative statements:
  There's **a little** work left to do.
  There's **not much** work left to do.
  The bill has **little** support in Congress.

- Use **any** in negative statements, and in questions when you do not know if the answer will be yes or no:
  They never had **any** children.
  Are there **any** gas stations near here?

- Use **any** in negative statements, and in questions when you do not know if the answer will be yes or no:
  No one paid **any** attention to them.
  Is there **any** coffee left?

- The camera broke, so we have **no** pictures of the picnic - **none** at all.
  **None of** the schools in the area has a pool.

- This fax makes **no** sense, **none** at all.
  **None of** their stock was on sale yet.

**none**

# STUDY NOTES verbs

## TRANSITIVE VERBS
### (grammar code [T])

■ **fix** and **thank** are both TRANSITIVE verbs. This means that they must be followed by a noun or noun phrase as a DIRECT OBJECT. If you take away the direct object, the sentence no longer makes sense. So we can say:

Alicia **thanked** Mr. Quintero.
Darren **was fixing** his bike.

Alicia     thanked     Mr. Quintero.
[subject]  [verb]      [object]

Darren     was fixing     his bike.
[subject]  [verb]         [object]

■ In this dictionary, transitive verbs are shown like this:

**fix¹** /fɪks/ *v* [T]
**1** ▶REPAIR◀ to repair something broken or not working: *Do you* |

## INTRANSITIVE VERBS
### (grammar code [I])

■ **bounce** and **argue** are both INTRANSITIVE verbs. This means that their meaning is complete without a DIRECT OBJECT. So we can say:

The ball **bounced**.
Kate and Rob **were arguing**.

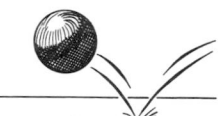

The ball     bounced.
[subject]    [verb]

Kate and Rob     were arguing.
[subject]        [verb]

■ In this dictionary, intransitive verbs are shown like this:

**ar·gue** /'ɑrgyu/ *v* **1** [I] to disagr someone, usually by talking or shou angry way, or getting upset: *Mo always seem to be arguin*

## VERBS THAT ARE BOTH INTRANSITIVE AND TRANSITIVE
### (grammar code [I, T])

■ Many verbs like **speak** and **see** can be both [T] (TRANSITIVE) and [I] (INTRANSITIVE). In this dictionary, these verbs are shown like this:

**speak** /spik/ *v* **spoke, spoken, speaking**
**1** ▶TALK TO SB◀ [I] to talk to someone about something or have a conversation: *Hello, can I*

**3** ▶LANGUAGE◀ [T] to be able to talk in a particular language: *My brother speaks English/ French.* ✗ DON'T SAY "My brother speaks in

**see** /si/ *v* **saw, seen, seeing**
**1** ▶USE EYES◀ [I,T] to use your eyes to notice people or things: *I can't see without my glas-*

## LINKING VERBS
### (grammar code [linking verb])

■ Some verbs like **become** do not have an [I] or a [T] after them in some or all of their meanings. These are called LINKING VERBS. These verbs must be followed by another word for their meaning to be complete, but the word can be a noun, an adjective, or an adverb. These nouns, adjectives, and adverbs always tell us something about the subject of a sentence. In this dictionary, linking verbs are shown like this:

**be·come** /bɪ'kʌm/ *v* **became, become, becoming 1** [linking verb] to begin to be something, or to develop in a particular way: *The weather had become warmer.* | *In 1960 Kennedy became the first Catholic president.* | *It is becoming harder to find good housing for low-income*

Other linking verbs are **appear, be, feel, look, remain,** and **seem.**

# cars

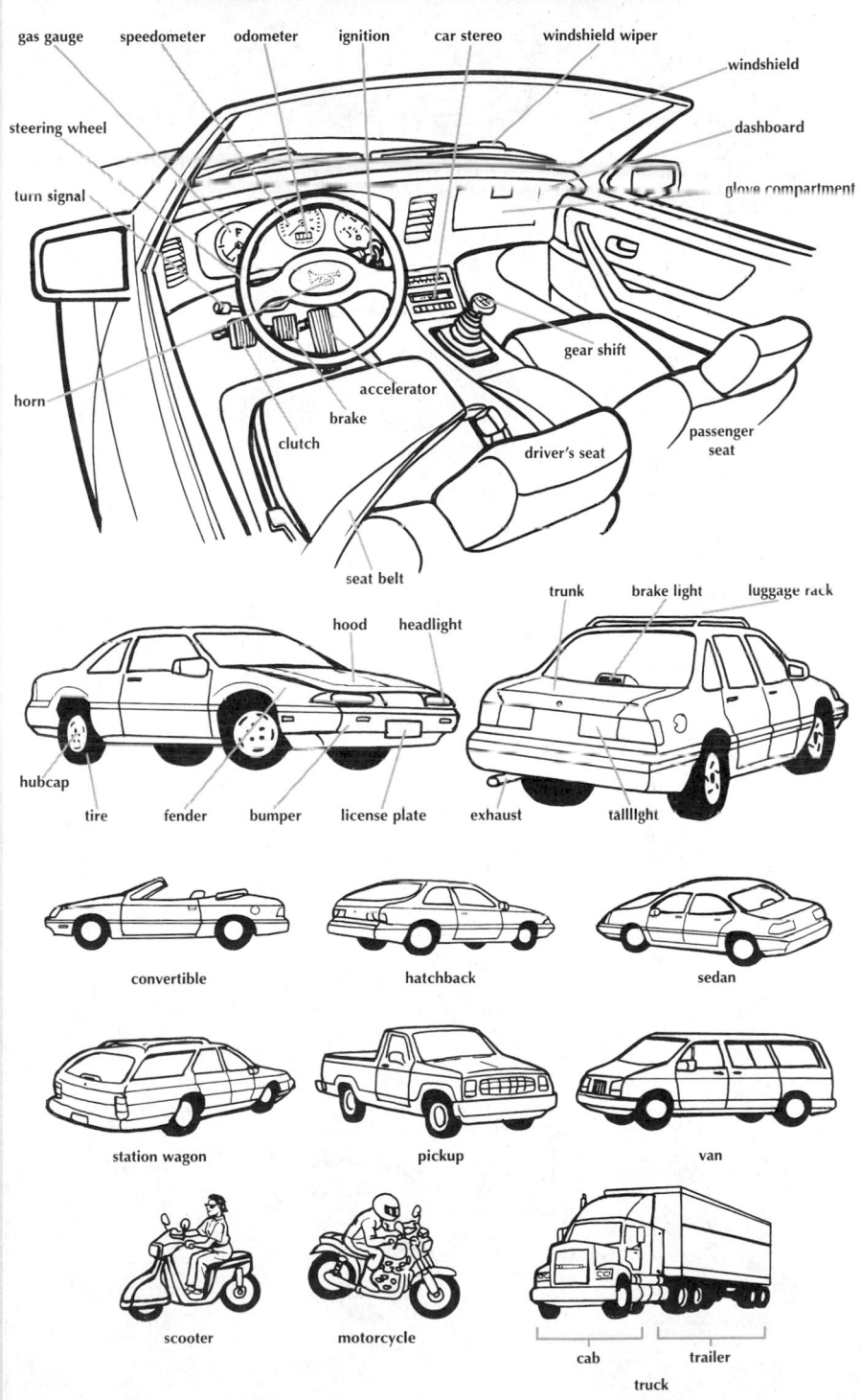

gas gauge speedometer odometer ignition car stereo windshield wiper

windshield

steering wheel

dashboard

turn signal

glove compartment

gear shift

horn

accelerator

brake

clutch

passenger seat

driver's seat

seat belt

trunk   brake light   luggage rack

hood   headlight

hubcap

tire   fender   bumper   license plate   exhaust   taillight

convertible

hatchback

sedan

station wagon

pickup

van

scooter

motorcycle

cab   trailer

truck

# fruit and vegetables

## fruit

apple

apricot

bananas

blueberries

cantaloupe

cherries

coconut

grapes

grapefruit

lemon

orange

peach

pear

pineapple

plum

raspberries

strawberries

watermelon

tangerine

## vegetables

artichoke

avocado

broccoli

asparagus

cabbage

carrots

cauliflower

celery

chili

corn

cucumber

eggplant

garlic

green beans

lettuce

mushrooms

onion

peas

pepper

potatoes

pumpkin

radishes

squash

tomato

zucchini

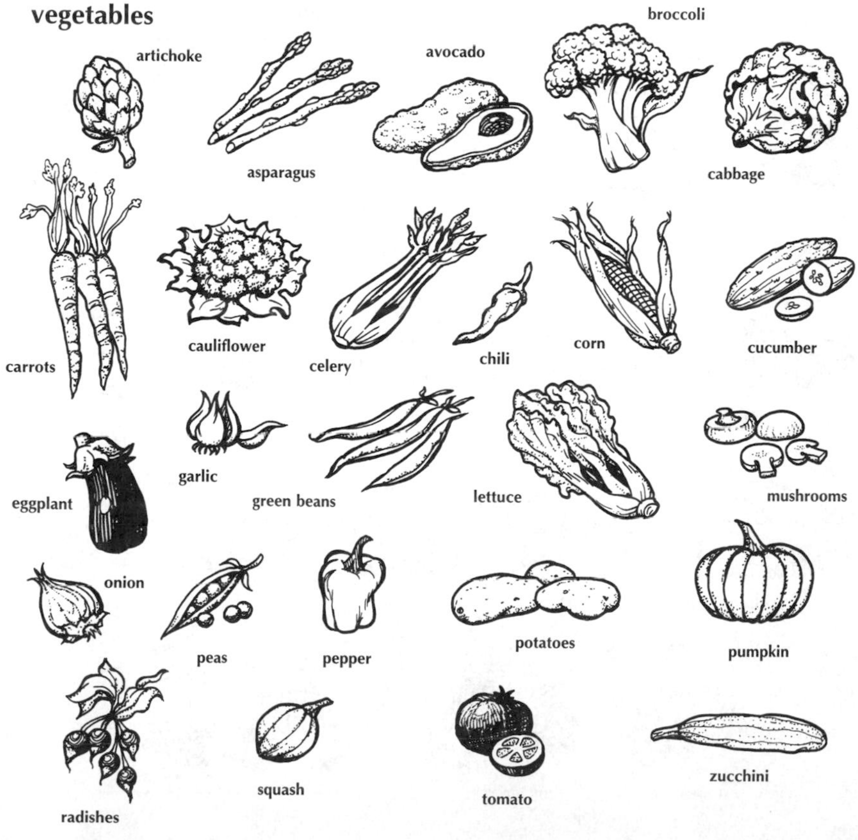

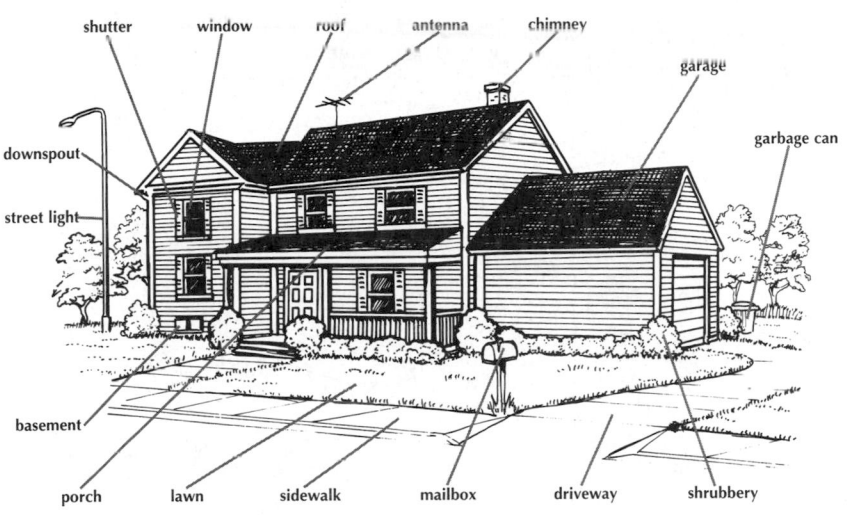

shutter   window   roof   antenna   chimney

garage

garbage can

downspout

street light

basement

porch   lawn   sidewalk   mailbox   driveway   shrubbery

balcony

**apartment building**

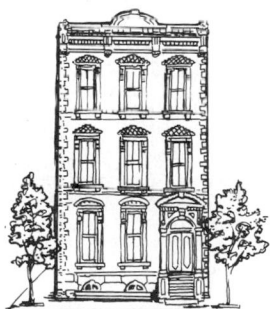

**townhouse/brownstone**

**ranch house**

## baseball

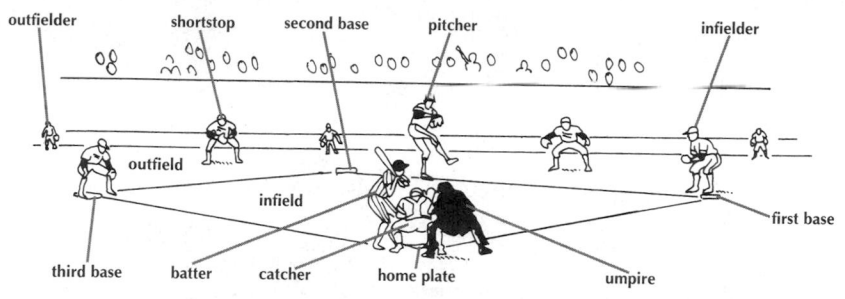

outfielder · shortstop · second base · pitcher · infielder · outfield · infield · first base · third base · batter · catcher · home plate · umpire

## football

yard line · end zone · goalpost · goal line · linebackers · defense · sideline · line men · offense · receiver · quarterback · running backs

## basketball

dunk · guard · free throw line · forward · center

# verbs of movement

push      pull

jump      leap      pick up

put down

walk      jog      run      crouch      kneel

lift      carry      hold

**18** ▶WORDS◀ a line of words in a poem, play, film, or song

**19** ▶FISHING◀ a strong thin piece of string you use to catch fish −see also ON LINE **somewhere along the line/way** (SOMEWHERE)

**line²** v [T] **1** to cover the inside of a piece of material, a container etc. with another material or substance: *We **lined** the box **with** newspapers.* | *a lined skirt* **2** to form rows along the edge of something: *a wide road **lined with** trees*

**line up** phr v **1** [I,T **line** sb/sth ↔ **up**] to make a row, or arrange people or things in a row: *OK class, **line up** by the door.* | *We **lined** the jars **up** on the shelf.* **2** [T **line** sb/sth ↔ **up**] to organize the activities that will happen at an event: *They've **lined up** some dancers for the show.*

**lin·e·age** /ˈlɪniɪdʒ/ n [C,U] the way in which members of a family are related to other members who lived in past times

**lin·e·ar** /ˈlɪniɚ/ adj **1** consisting of lines, or in the form of a straight line: *a linear drawing* **2** related to length: *linear measurements*

**line·back·er** /ˈlaɪnˌbækɚ/ n [C,U] in football, a player on the DEFENSE who stands behind the TACKLEs and ENDs −see picture on page 472

**lined** /laɪnd/ adj **1** a skirt, coat etc. that is lined has a piece of material covering the inside: *a fur-lined coat* **2** lined paper has straight lines printed on it

**line·man** /ˈlaɪnmən/ n in football, one of the players who face each other in a line and try to stop the other team or to help their own team to move forward −see picture on page 472

**lin·en** /ˈlɪnən/ n [U] **1** sheets, TABLECLOTHs etc.: *bed/table linen* **2** cloth used for making good quality summer clothes

**lin·er** /ˈlaɪnɚ/ n **1** a large ship for carrying people **2** a thick layer of material that can be attached to the inside of a piece of clothing to make it warmer

**lin·er notes** /ˈ.. ˌ./ n [plural] the writing on the case of a CD, record etc. that tells about the performers and music on it

**line·up** /ˈlaɪnʌp/ n **1** a group of people arranged in a row by the police so that a person who saw a crime can try to recognize the criminal **2** a set of events, programs, performers etc. that are arranged to follow each other: *The lineup of performers included Tony Curtis and Diana Ross.* −see also STARTING LINEUP

**lin·ger** /ˈlɪŋgɚ/ v [I] **1** to stay somewhere longer or to take longer to do something than usual: *We like to **linger over** breakfast on Saturday morning.* **2** also **linger on** to be slow to disappear: *The smell of smoke lingered for a week after the party.*

**lin·ge·rie** /ˌlɑnʒəˈreɪ, ˌlɑndʒə-/ n [U] women's underwear

**lin·ger·ing** /ˈlɪŋgərɪŋ/ adj continuing a long time: *a long lingering kiss*

**lin·go** /ˈlɪŋgoʊ/ n INFORMAL **1** words used only by a group of people who do a particular job or activity: *medical lingo* **2** a language

**lin·guist** /ˈlɪŋgwɪst/ n **1** someone who studies LINGUISTICS **2** someone who speaks several languages well

**lin·guis·tic** /lɪŋˈgwɪstɪk/ adj relating to language, words, or LINGUISTICS: *a child's linguistic development*

**lin·guis·tics** /lɪŋˈgwɪstɪks/ n [U] the study of languages, including their structures, grammar, and history

**lin·i·ment** /ˈlɪnəmənt/ n [C,U] an oily liquid you rub on your skin when your muscles are sore or stiff

**lin·ing** /ˈlaɪnɪŋ/ n [C,U] a piece of material covering the inside of something such as a box, a coat etc.: *a jacket with a silk lining*

**link¹** /lɪŋk/ v [T] **1** to make a connection between two or more situations, events, or people: *Lung cancer has been **linked to** smoking cigarettes.* **2** also **link up** to connect computers, communication systems, etc. so that sound, pictures, or information can be shared among them: *Our computers are **linked to** the central system.* **3** to join one place to another: *a highway linking two major cities* **4** **link arms** to bend your arm and put it through someone else's bent arm

**link²** n **1** a relationship or connection between two or more events, people, or ideas: *Latin is the **link between** all of the Romance languages.* | *He has **links with** the Socialist party.* **2** one of the rings that makes up a chain −see picture at CHAIN¹ **3** also **linkup** a connection between two places that allows people to travel or communicate between them: *a telephone/satellite link* −see also CUFF LINK

**link·age** /ˈlɪŋkɪdʒ/ n **1** [C,U] a LINK or connection between two things **2** [U] a situation in which one country agrees to do something only if another country does something as well

**link·ing verb** /ˈ.. ˌ./ n TECHNICAL in grammar, a verb that connects the subject of a sentence to its COMPLEMENT. In the sentence, "She seems friendly," "seems" is a linking verb −see study note on page 468

**li·no·le·um** /lɪˈnoʊliəm/ n [U] smooth shiny material that is used for covering floors

**lint** /lɪnt/ n [U] soft light pieces of thread or wool that come off cotton, wool, or other material

**li·on** /ˈlaɪən/ n a large African and Asian wild cat, the male of which has long thick hair around his neck

**li·on·ess** /ˈlaɪənɪs/ n a female lion

**lip** /lɪp/ n **1** one of the two edges of your mouth: *a kiss on the lips* −see picture at HEAD¹ **2** the edge of a container that will hold liquid: *the lip of the cup* **3** **my lips are sealed** SPOKEN said when promising someone that you will not tell a secret **4 -lipped** with lips of a particular type: *a thin-lipped woman* **5 pay/give lip service** to say that you support or agree with something, without doing anything to prove this: *They're only paying lip service to pollution prevention.*

**lip gloss** /'. ./ *n* [C,U] a substance that women use to make their lips very shiny

**lip-read** /'lɪp ˌrid/ *v* [I,T] to watch someone's lips move in order to understand what s/he is saying, especially because you cannot hear **–lip-reading** *n* [U]

**lip·stick** /'lɪpˌstɪk/ *n* [C,U] a colored substance that women put on their lips, or a small tube containing this

**lip synch** /'lɪpˌsɪŋk/ *v* [I] to pretend to sing by moving your lips at the same time as a recording is being played

**liq·ue·fy** /'lɪkwəˌfaɪ/ *v* [I,T] to become liquid, or to make something become liquid

**li·queur** /lɪ'kɚ, lɪ'kʊɚ/ *n* [C,U] a sweet alcoholic drink usually drunk after a meal

**liq·uid** /'lɪkwɪd/ *n* [C,U] a substance such as water, that is not solid or a gas, but that can flow and be poured **–liquid** *adj*: *liquid soap* –see also FLUID

**liq·ui·date** /'lɪkwəˌdeɪt/ *v* **1** [I,T] to close a business or company and sell its goods in order to pay a debt **2** [T] INFORMAL to kill someone **–liquidation** /ˌlɪkwɪ'deɪʃən/ *n* [C,U]

**liq·uor** /'lɪkɚ/ *n* [U] a strong alcoholic drink such as WHISKEY

**liquor store** /'.. ˌ./ *n* a store where alcohol is sold

**lisp** /lɪsp/ *v* [I,T] to pronounce the "s" sound like "th," so the word "sing" sounds like "thing" **–lisp** *n*

**list¹** /lɪst/ *n* a set of names, things, numbers etc. that are written one below the other so you can remember them: *Make a list of the equipment you'll need.* | *Butter wasn't on the shopping list.* ✗ DON'T SAY "in the list." ✗

**list²** *v* [T] to write a list, or to mention things one after the other: *All the players must be listed on the scoresheet.*

**lis·ten** /'lɪsən/ *v* [I] **1** to pay attention to what someone is saying or to something that you hear: *Have you listened to any of these tapes yet?* | *Are you listening to me?* –see picture at HEAR **2** SPOKEN used in order to tell someone to pay attention to what you are saying: *Listen, can I call you back later?* **3** to pay attention and accept what someone tells you: *I told him it was dangerous, but he wouldn't listen.*

**listen for** sth/sb *phr v* [T] to pay attention so that you are sure you will hear a sound: *I was listening for Bill's car in the street.*

**listen in** *phr v* [I] to listen to what someone is saying without him/her knowing it: *I think someone's listening in on the other phone.*

**listen up** *phr v* [I] SPOKEN used in order to get people's attention so they will hear what you are going to say: *OK people, listen up. I'm only going to say this once.*

---

**USAGE NOTE listen and hear**

Use both of these words to talk about sounds. **Listen** means "to pay attention to a sound or to what someone says": *She never listens to what I say.* **Hear** usually means "to know that a sound is being made": *Couldn't you hear the doorbell?* You can also use **hear** to talk about listening to music, or to ask if someone understands you: *Would you like to hear my new CD?* | *Make sure you come home at 6:00, do you hear me?*

---

**lis·ten·er** /'lɪsənɚ/ *n* **1** someone who listens, especially to the radio **2 good listener** someone who listens in a sympathetic way to other people

**list·ing** /'lɪstɪŋ/ *n* a printed or written list: *movie listings*

**list·less** /'lɪstlɪs/ *adj* feeling tired and uninterested in doing things

**list price** /ˌ. './ *n* a price for a product that is set by the company that makes it

**lit¹** /lɪt/ *v* the past tense and PAST PARTICIPLE of LIGHT

**lit²** *adj* having light or burning: *a well-lit room* | *a lit cigarette*

**lit·a·ny** /'lɪt̚n-i/ *n* **a litany of sth** a long list of problems, questions, complaints etc.: *a litany of economic problems*

**lite** /laɪt/ *adj* NONSTANDARD having fewer CALORIES than usual: *lite beer*

**li·ter** /'litɚ/ *written abbreviation* **l** *n* a unit for measuring liquid, equal to 2.12 PINTS or 0.26 gallons

**lit·er·a·cy** /'lɪtərəsi/ *n* [U] the ability to read and write

**lit·er·al** /'lɪtərəl/ *adj* relating to the most basic or original meaning of a word, statement, book etc.: *a literal interpretation of the Bible* –compare FIGURATIVE

**lit·er·al·ly** /'lɪtərəli/ *adv* **1** according to the most basic meaning of a word or expression: *There are literally millions of students in these programs.* **2** SPOKEN used in order to emphasize something you have just said: *The place was literally crawling with cops.* (=there were a lot of police officers there) **3 take sb/sth literally** to think that a word or statement is LITERAL when it is not: *Lou was joking, but Sara took it literally.*

**lit·er·ar·y** /'lɪtəˌrɛri/ *adj* **1** relating to literature **2** typical of writing used in literature rather than in ordinary writing and talking

**lit·er·ate** /'lɪtərɪt/ *adj* **1** able to read and write **2** well educated –opposite ILLITERATE

L

**lit·er·a·ture** /'lɪtərətʃə, 'lɪtrə-/ *n* [U]
**1** books, plays etc. that are considered very good and that people have liked for a long time: *the great classics of English literature*
**2** printed information designed by a company or organization to sell you something or give you advice

**lithe** /laɪð/ *adj* able to bend and move your body easily and gracefully

**lit·i·gate** /'lɪtə̩geɪt/ *v* [I,T] LAW to take a legal case to a court of law

**lit·i·ga·tion** /ˌlɪtə'geɪʃən/ *n* [U] the process of taking a legal case to a court of law

**lit·mus test** /'lɪt⁻məs ˌtɛst/ *n* a single action, situation, or quality that allows you to measure someone's attitude, beliefs etc.: *The elections will be a litmus test of the political mood in the US.*

**lit·ter¹** /'lɪtə/ *n* **1** [U] pieces of waste paper etc. that people leave on the ground in public places **2** a group of baby animals born at the same time to one mother

**litter²** *v* **1** [I,T] to leave pieces of waste paper etc. on the ground in a public place: *The sign says: Please Do Not Litter.* **2** [T] if a lot of things litter a place, they are spread all over it in a messy way: *The floor was littered with clothes.*

**lit·ter·bug** /'lɪtə̩bʌg/ *n* DISAPPROVING someone who LITTERS

**lit·tle¹** /'lɪtl/ *adj* **1** small in size: *a little house* **2** a little bit not very much: *It will only hurt a little bit.* | *Can I have a little bit of* (=a small amount of) *milk in my coffee, please?* **3** short in time or distance: *I'll wait a little while and then call again.* | *Anna walked a little way down the road with him.* **4** young and small: *a little boy* **5** not important: *He gets angry over little things.* **6** used in order to emphasize the adjective in a sentence: *She owns a nice little restaurant in the city.*

**little²** *quantifier* **less**, **least 1** only a small amount of something: *Little is known about the planet.* | *I have very little money right now, but he has even less.* **2** a little a small amount: *I only know a little Spanish.* | *She told him a little about it.* | *Would you like a little more cake?* | *I explained a little of the family's history.* **3** a short time or distance: *He must be a little over 60.* (=slightly older than 60) | *Phoenix is a little under 50 miles from here.* (=slightly fewer than 50 miles) —see usage note at FEW

**little³** *adv* **1** not much or only slightly: *He moved the table a little closer to the wall.* | *I was a little afraid of the dog.* | *She goes out very little.* —compare LESS², LEAST² **2** little by little gradually: *Little by little, she became more confident.*

**little fin·ger** /ˌ.. '../ *n* the smallest finger on your hand —see picture at HAND¹

**Little League Base·ball** /ˌ.. ˌ. '. ./ *n* TRADEMARK a group of baseball teams for children

**lit·ur·gy** /'lɪtədʒi/ *n* [C,U] prayers, songs etc. that are said in a particular order in a religious ceremony —**liturgical** /lɪ'tədʒɪkəl/ *adj*

**liv·a·ble**, **liveable** /'lɪvəbəl/ *adj* suitable to live in: *The apartment isn't fancy but it's livable.*

**live¹** /lɪv/ *v* **1** [I] to be alive or to continue to stay alive: *My grandmother lived to be 88.* | *Pythagoras lived a century before Socrates.* **2** [I] to have your home in a particular place: *"Where do you live?" "I live in Boston."* | *The Reyes family live on White Oak Avenue.* **3** [I,T] to have a particular type of life, or to live in a particular way: *We can live comfortably on the money that I earn.* | *children living in poverty* **4** live together to live with another person in a sexual relationship without being married: *Mark and I have been living together for two years.* **5** [I] to keep yourself alive by doing a particular thing or eating a particular food: *These animals live on insects.*

**live for** sb/sth *phr v* [T] to be the most important thing in your life: *She lives for ballet.*

**live off** sth/sb *phr v* [T] to get your food or money from someone or something: *He's living off money from his investments.*

**live** sth **down** *phr v* [T] **not live** sth **down** to not be able to make people forget about something bad or embarrassing you have done: *You'll never live this evening down!*

**live on** *phr v* [I] to continue to exist: *She will live on in our memories.*

**live through** sth *phr v* [T] to experience difficult or dangerous conditions and continue living: *Don didn't expect to live through the war.*

**live up to** sth *phr v* [T] to do something as well, or be as good as someone expects: *Charles could never live up to his father's expectations.*

**live with** *phr v* [T] **1** [live with sth] to accept a difficult situation even when it continues for a long time: *living with pain* **2** [live with sb] to live with another person, especially in a sexual relationship without being married: *Tim's living with a girl he met in college.*

**live²** /laɪv/ *adj* **1** not dead or artificial; LIVING: *He fed the snake live rats.* —compare DEAD¹ **2** broadcast as an event happens: *a live broadcast of the Rose Parade* **3** performed for people who are watching: *The Dew Drop Inn has live music every weekend.* **4** having electricity flowing through it: *a live wire* **5** ready to explode: *a live bomb* —see also **real live** (REAL¹)

**live³** /laɪv/ *adv* **1** to broadcast something at the same time that it happens: *Live, from New York, it's "Saturday Night!"* **2** performing in front of people: *I'd love to see the band play live!*

**live·li·hood** /'laɪvli̩hʊd/ *n* [C,U] the way you

earn money in order to live: *Farming is their livelihood.*

**live·ly** /'laɪvli/ *adj* **1** very active and cheerful: *a lively group of children* **2** very exciting and interesting: *a lively debate* —**liveliness** *n* [U]

**liv·en** /'laɪvən/ *v*

**liven up** *phr v* [I,T **liven** sth **up**] to become more exciting, or to make something more exciting: *Better music might liven the party up.*

**liv·er** /'lɪvɚ/ *n* **1** a large organ in your body that cleans your blood **2** [U] the liver of an animal used as food

**lives** /laɪvz/ *n* the plural of LIFE

**live·stock** /'laɪvstɑk/ *n* [U] animals that are kept on a farm

**liv·id** /'lɪvɪd/ *adj* **1** extremely angry; FURIOUS: *Dad will be livid when he finds out!* **2** a livid BRUISE is blue and black **3** pale because you are angry

**liv·ing**[1] /'lɪvɪŋ/ *adj* **1** alive now: *She is one of our greatest living writers.* —opposite DEAD[1] **2** existing or being used now: *a living language* **3** **living things** anything that lives, such as animals, plants, and people

**living**[2] *n* **1** the way that you earn money: *What does he do for a living?* | *It's hard to make a living* (=earn enough money) *as an actor.* **2** [U] the way that someone lives his/ her life: *Martha has always believed in healthy living.* **3** **the living** all the people who are alive —see also COST OF LIVING

**living room** /'.. ,./ *n* the main room in a house, where you relax, watch television etc.

**living will** /,.. './ *n* a document that explains what legal and medical decisions should be made for you if you are too sick to make them yourself

**liz·ard** /'lɪzɚd/ *n* a REPTILE that has rough skin, four short legs, and a long tail

**-'ll** /l, əl/ the short form of "will" or "shall": *He'll be here soon.*

**lla·ma** /'lɑmə/ *n* a large South American animal with thick hair like wool and a long neck

**Ln.** the written abbreviation of LANE

**load**[1] /loʊd/ *n* **1** a large quantity of something that is carried by a person, a vehicle etc.: *a ship carrying a full load of fuel and supplies* **2** **carload/truckload etc.** the largest amount or number that a car etc. can carry: *a busload of kids* **3** the amount of work that a machine or a person has to do: *a heavy work load* **4** a quantity of clothes that are washed at the same time: *Can you do a load of clothes later today?*

SPOKEN PHRASES

**5** **a load of sth/loads of sth** a lot of something: *Don't worry, there's loads of time.* **6** **a load of crap/shit etc.** used in order to say that something is wrong or very stupid **7** **get a load of sb/sth** said when you want someone to notice something funny or

surprising: *Get a load of that guy in the silver pants!*

**load**[2] *v* **1** [I,T] also **load up** to put a load of something on or into a vehicle: *He loaded up the car with camping gear.* **2** [T] to put bullets into a gun, film into a camera etc. **3** [T] to put a program into a computer

**load** sb/sth ↔ **down (with)** *phr v* [T] to make someone carry too many things or do too much work: *I was loaded down with luggage.*

**load up on** sth *phr v* [T] to get a lot of something: *People were loading up on bottled water.*

**load·ed** /'loʊdɪd/ *adj* **1** containing bullets, film etc.: *Is the camera loaded?* | *a loaded gun* **2** carrying a load of something: *a loaded truck* **3** INFORMAL very rich: *His grandmother is loaded.* **4** **loaded question** a question that is unfair because it makes you give a particular answer **5** **loaded with** full of a particular quality, or containing a lot of something: *a cake loaded with nuts* **6** INFORMAL very drunk

**loaf**[1] /loʊf/ *n, plural* **loaves** bread that is shaped and baked in one large piece —see picture at BREAD

**loaf**[2] *v* [I] INFORMAL to waste time in a lazy way when you should be working: *He spends his days loafing around the house.*

**Loaf·er** /'loʊfɚ/ *n* TRADEMARK a flat leather shoe without LACES —see picture at SHOE[1]

**loan**[1] /loʊn/ *n* **1** an amount of money that you borrow from a bank: *We'll take out a loan to buy the car.* **2** **on loan** being borrowed: *The book is on loan from the library.* **3** [singular] the act of lending something

**loan**[2] *v* [T] to lend someone something, especially money: *Can you loan me $20 until Friday?* —see usage note at LEND

**loan shark** /'. ./ *n* DISAPPROVING someone who lends money to people and charges a very high rate of INTEREST

**loath** /loʊθ, loʊð/ *adj* **be loath to do sth** FORMAL to be unwilling to do something: *I was loath to leave her alone.*

**loathe** /loʊð/ *v* [T] to hate someone or something —**loathing** *n* [C,U]

**loath·some** /'loʊðsəm, 'loʊθ-/ *adj* very unpleasant; DISGUSTING

**loaves** /loʊvz/ *n* the plural form of LOAF

**lob** /lɑb/ *v* **-bbed, -bbing** [T] to throw or hit a ball so that it moves slowly in a high curve

**lob·by**[1] /'lɑbi/ *n* **1** a large hall inside the entrance of a building: *waiting in the hotel lobby* **2** a group of people who try to persuade the government to change or approve a particular law: *the environmental lobby*

**lobby**[2] *v* [I,T] to try to persuade the government to change a particular law: *a group lobbying for/against the law* —**lobbyist** *n*

**lobe** /loʊb/ *n* ⇨ EARLOBE

**lob·ster** /ˈlɑbstɚ/ n [C,U] an ocean animal with eight legs, a shell, and two large CLAWS, or the meat of this animal

**lo·cal**[1] /ˈloʊkəl/ adj **1** relating to a particular place or area, especially the place you live in: *a good local hospital* | *reading the **local** paper* (=a newspaper for the place you live) | *It costs a quarter to make a **local call**.* (=a telephone call to someone in the same area as you) **2** TECHNICAL affecting a particular part of your body: *a local anesthetic*

**local**[2] n **the locals** the people who live in a particular place: *I asked one of the locals for directions.*

**lo·cale** /loʊˈkæl/ n FORMAL the place where something happens: *The novel is set in a tropical locale.*

**lo·cal·i·ty** /loʊˈkæləti/ n FORMAL a small area of a country, city etc.

**lo·cal·ized** /ˈloʊkəˌlaɪzd/ adj FORMAL only within a small area: *localized pain*

**lo·cal·ly** /ˈloʊkəli/ adv in or near the area where you are or the area you are talking about: *Do you live locally?*

**lo·cate** /ˈloʊkeɪt/ v **1** [T] to find the exact position of something: *Divers have located the shipwreck.* **2 be located** to be in a particular place or position: *The bakery is located in the middle of town.* **3** [I,T] to come to a place and start a business there: *The company located its offices in New Jersey when rents went up in New York.*

**lo·ca·tion** /loʊˈkeɪʃən/ n **1** a particular place or position: *a map showing the **location** of the school* **2** [C,U] a place where a movie is filmed, away from the STUDIO: *scenes shot on **location** in Montana*

**lock**[1] /lɑk/ v **1** [I,T] to be fastened with a lock, or to fasten something with a lock: *Lock the door when you leave.* –opposite UNLOCK **2 lock sth up/away/in etc.** to put something in a safe place and fasten it with a lock: *He locked the money in a safe.* **3** [I] to become set in one position and be unable to move: *The brakes locked and we skidded.*

**lock** sb **in** phr v [T] to prevent someone from leaving a place by locking the door

**lock into** sth phr v **be locked into** to be unable to change a situation: *The company is locked into a three-year contract with PARCO.*

**lock** sb **out** phr v [T] to prevent someone from entering a place by locking the door

**lock up** phr v **1** [T **lock** sb **up**] INFORMAL to put someone in prison **2** [T **lock** sth ↔ **up**] to make a building safe by locking all the doors

**lock**[2] n **1** a thing that keeps a door, drawer etc. fastened or shut and is usually opened with a key: *There's no lock on the door.* **2 lock, stock, and barrel** including every part of something: *They sold everything, lock, stock, and barrel.* **3 under lock and key** kept safely in

something that is locked **4** a small number of hairs on your head that hang together **5** a special area on a river where the water level can go up or down to raise or lower boats

**lock·er** /ˈlɑkɚ/ n a small cupboard with a lock where you leave books, clothes etc., especially at school or when you are playing sports

**locker room** /ˈ.. ˌ./ n a room where you change your clothes and leave them in a LOCKER

**lock·et** /ˈlɑkɪt/ n a piece of jewelry like a small round box in which you put a picture of someone, worn on a chain around your neck

**lock·smith** /ˈlɑkˌsmɪθ/ n someone who makes and repairs locks

**lo·co·mo·tive** /ˌloʊkəˈmoʊtɪv/ n a train engine

**lo·cust** /ˈloʊkəst/ n an insect similar to a GRASSHOPPER that flies in large groups and often destroys crops

**lodge**[1] /lɑdʒ/ v **1** [I] to become stuck somewhere: *He had a fish bone **lodged in** his throat.* –opposite DISLODGE **2 lodge a complaint/ protest etc.** to officially complain, protest etc. about something: *He has lodged a formal complaint with the club.* **3** [I] to pay someone rent in order to live in a room in his/her house

**lodge**[2] n **1** a building in the country where people can stay for a short time, especially in order to do a particular activity: *a ski/hunting lodge* **2** a local meeting place for some organizations: *the Masonic lodge*

**loft** /lɔft/ n **1** a raised level in a BARN where HAY is kept **2** a raised area above the main part of a room, usually used for sleeping, or an apartment with one of these

**loft·y** /ˈlɔfti/ adj **1** showing high standards or high moral qualities: *lofty ideals* **2** LITERARY high

**log**[1] /lɔg, lɑg/ n **1** a thick piece of wood cut from a tree **2** an official record of events on a ship or plane –see also **sleep like a log** (SLEEP[1])

**log**[2] v -gged, -gging **1** [T] to make an official record of events, facts etc., especially on a ship or plane **2** [I,T] to cut down trees –**logger** n

**log off/out** phr v [I] to stop using a computer or computer system by typing (TYPE) a special word

**log on/in** phr v [I] to start using a computer or computer system by typing (TYPE) a special word

**log cab·in** /ˌ. ˈ../ n a small house made of LOGS

**log·ger·heads** /ˈlɔgɚˌhɛdz, ˈlɑ-/ n **be at loggerheads** to disagree very strongly with someone: *The two Senators have been at loggerheads for years.*

**log·ging** /ˈlɔgɪŋ, ˈlɑ-/ n [U] the industry of cutting down trees for LUMBER, paper etc.

**log·ic** /ˈlɑdʒɪk/ n [U] **1** a set of sensible and correct reasons: *There is no **logic in** releasing criminals just because the prisons are crowded.*

**2** the science or study of thinking carefully about something, using formal methods

**log·i·cal** /'lɑdʒɪkəl/ *adj* **1** seeming reasonable and sensible: *It's the logical place to build a new supermarket.* –opposite ILLOGICAL **2** based on the rules of LOGIC: *a logical conclusion* –**logically** *adv*

**lo·gis·tics** /loʊ'dʒɪstɪks, lə-/ *n* **the logistics of sth** the practical organizing that is needed to make a complicated plan or activity successful –**logistical** *adj* –**logistically** *adv*

**log·jam** /'lɔgdʒæm, 'lɑg-/ *n* a lot of problems or other things that are preventing something from being done: *a logjam of work*

**lo·go** /'loʊgoʊ/ *n* a small design that is the official sign of a company or organization

**loin·cloth** /'lɔɪnklɔθ/ *n* a piece of cloth that men in some hot countries wear around their LOINS

**loins** /lɔɪnz/ *n* [plural] LITERARY the part of the body below your waist where the sexual organs are

**loi·ter** /'lɔɪtɚ/ *v* [I] to stand in a public place without having a reason to be there –**loitering** *n* [U]

**loll** /lɑl/ *v* [I] **1** to hang down in a loose or relaxed way: *The dog's tongue lolled out of its mouth.* **2** to sit or lie in a lazy or relaxed way

**lol·li·pop** /'lɑli,pɑp/ *n* a hard candy made of boiled sugar on the end of a stick

**lone** /loʊn/ *adj* LITERARY being the only person or thing in a place, or the only person or thing that does something: *a lone figure standing in the snow | Thea was the lone voice against the idea.*

**lone·ly** /'loʊnli/ *adj* **1** unhappy because you are alone: *She was very lonely after her husband died.* **2** LITERARY far from where people live: *a lonely country road* –**loneliness** *n* [U]

**lon·er** /'loʊnɚ/ *n* someone who wants to be alone or who has no friends

**lone·some** /'loʊnsəm/ *adj* ⇨ LONELY

**long¹** /lɔŋ/ *adj*

**1** ▶MEASUREMENT◀ measuring a great length, distance, or time: *There was a long line at the bank. | It's a long walk home from here. | The meeting was long and boring. | It takes a long time to drive to work.* –opposite SHORT¹

**2** ▶PARTICULAR LENGTH/TIME◀ having a particular length or continuing for a particular amount of time: *The snake was at least 3 feet long. | How long is the movie?*

**3** ▶SEEMING LONG◀ INFORMAL seeming too long in time or distance because you are tired, bored etc.: *It's been a long day.*

**4** **long hours** a large amount of time: *She spent long hours working at the computer.*

**5** ▶BOOK/LIST/NAME ETC.◀ a long book, list etc. has a lot of pages, details etc.

**6** **long weekend** three days, including Satur-

day and Sunday, when you do not have to go to work or school

**7** **in the long run** when something is finished, or at a later time: *All our hard work will be worth it in the long run.*

**8** ▶CLOTHES◀ long dresses, pants, SLEEVEs etc. cover all of your arms or legs

**long²** *adv* **1** for a long time: *Have you been waiting long?* **2** **long before/after** for a long time before or after a particular time or event: *The farm was sold long before you were born.* **3** **for long** for a long time: *Have you known the Garretts for very long?* **4** **as long as** if: *You can go as long as you're back by four o'clock.* **5** **no longer** used in order to show that something happened in the past, but does not happen now: *Mr. Allen no longer works for the company.* **6** **so long** SPOKEN goodbye **7** **before long** soon: *It will be Christmas before long.*

**long³** *v* [I] FORMAL to want something very much: *The children longed to get outside.*

**long-dis·tance** /ˌ. '.◀ / *adj* **1** a long-distance telephone call is to a place that is far away **2** traveling, running etc. between two places that are far away from each other: *long-distance flights* –**long-distance** *adv*

**long-drawn-out** /ˌ. ˌ. './ *adj* continuing for a longer time than is necessary: *a long-drawn-out discussion*

**lon·gev·i·ty** /lɑn'dʒɛvəti, lɔn-/ *n* [U] FORMAL long life

**long·hand** /'lɔŋhænd/ *n* [U] writing full words by hand rather than using a machine such as a computer –compare SHORTHAND

**long·ing** /'lɔŋɪŋ/ *n* [singular, U] a strong feeling of wanting someone or something very much: *a longing for peace* –**longing** *adj* –**longingly** *adv*

**lon·gi·tude** /'lɑndʒə,tud/ *n* [C,U] a position on the Earth measured in degrees east or west of an imaginary line running from the top of the Earth to the bottom –**longitudinal** /ˌlɑndʒə'tudn-əl/ *adj* –compare LATITUDE –see picture at AXIS

**long johns** /'. ./ *n* [plural] warm underwear that covers your legs

**long jump** /'. ./ *n* [U] a sport in which you jump as far as possible

**long-last·ing** /ˌ. '..◀ / *adj* continuing for a long time: *the long-lasting effects of child abuse*

**long-lived** /ˌlɔŋ 'laɪvd◀ / *adj* living or existing for a long time

**long-lost** /'. ./ *adj* lost or not seen for a long time: *a long-lost friend*

**long-range** /ˌ. '.◀ / *adj* **1** relating to a time that continues far into the future: *long-range development plans* **2** covering a long distance: *a long-range missile*

**long-run·ning** /ˌ. '..◀ / *adj* having existed or happened for a long time: *a long-running show on Broadway*

**long·shore·man** /ˌlɒŋˈʃɔːrmən, ˈlɒŋˌʃɔːr-mən/ *n* someone whose job is to load and unload ships

**long shot** /'. ./ *n* INFORMAL **1** someone or something with very little chance of success: *This plan is a real long shot.* **2 not by a long shot** not at all or not nearly: *This isn't over, not by a long shot.*

**long-stand·ing** /ˌ. '..◂/ *adj* having continued or existed for a long time: *a long-standing agreement between the two countries*

**long-suf·fer·ing** /ˌ. '...◂/ *adj* patient in spite of problems or unhappiness

**long-term** /ˌ. '.◂/ *adj* continuing for a long period of time into the future: *The long-term effects of the drug are not known.* —see also **in the long/short term** (TERM) —compare SHORT-TERM

**long·time** /ˈlɒŋtaɪm/ *adj* having existed for a long time, or having had a particular position for a long time: *her longtime boyfriend | a longtime goal*

**long-wind·ed** /ˌ. '..◂/ *adj* continuing to talk for too long in a way that is boring: *a long-winded speech*

**look¹** /lʊk/ *v* **1** [I] to turn your eyes toward something so that you can see it: *I didn't see it. I wasn't looking. | Patrick looked down at his shoes.* —see picture at WATCH¹ **2** [I] to try to find someone or something using your eyes: *I've looked everywhere for the money. | Have you looked in here? | Brad was looking for you last night.* **3** [linking verb] to seem to be something, especially by having a particular appearance: *You look nice/good in that dress. | He looks like he hasn't slept for days. | Gina and Ron looked very happy.* **4** **-looking** having a particular type of appearance: *That was a funny-looking dog! | healthy-looking children* **5 look sb in the eye** to look directly at someone in order to show that you are not afraid of him/her

SPOKEN PHRASES
**6 Look...** said when you are annoyed and you want to emphasize what you are saying: *Look, I'm very serious about this.* **7** [T] said in order to make someone notice something: *Look how tall he's gotten! | Mom, look what I made!* **8** (**I'm) just looking** used in a store in order to tell someone who works there that you do not need help: *"Can I help you?" "No thanks, I'm just looking."*

—see usage note at SEE

**look after** sb/sth *phr v* [T] to take care of someone or something: *We look after Rodney's kids after school.*

**look ahead** *phr v* [I] to think about what will happen in the future: *We need to look ahead and plan for next year.*

**look around** *phr v* [I,T **look around** sth] to see, study, read etc. many different things in order to find something or to learn about something: *We have 3 or 4 hours to look around the city.*

**look at** sth *phr v* [T] **1** to read something quickly: *Jane was looking at a magazine while she waited.* **2** to study and consider something in order to decide what to do: *The doctor looked at the cut on her head.* **3** SPOKEN said when you are using someone or something as an example of a situation: *We need insurance! Look at what happened to Tom when he didn't have any.*

**look back** *phr v* [I] to think about something that happened in the past: *Looking back (on it), I see my mistake.*

**look down on** sb/sth *phr v* [T] to think that you are better than someone or something else: *Ted seems to look down on poor people.*

**look for** sb/sth *phr v* [T] **1** to try to find a particular type of thing or person that you need or want: *How long have you been looking for a job?* **2 be looking for trouble** INFORMAL to be behaving in a way that makes it likely that problems will happen: *You're looking for trouble if you argue with her.*

**look forward to** sth *phr v* [T] to be excited and happy about something that is going to happen: *We're really looking forward to skiing in Tahoe.*

**look into** sth *phr v* [T] to try to find out the truth about something: *The FBI will look into the cause of the fire.*

**look on** *phr v* **1** [I] to watch something, without being involved in it: *The crowd looked on as the two men fought.* **2** [T **look on** sth] also **look upon** to think about something in a particular way: *My family looks on divorce as a sin.*

**look out** *phr v* [I] to pay attention to what is happening around you: *Look out! You almost hit the cat.*

**look** sth/sb ↔ **over** *phr v* [T] to examine something or someone quickly: *Can you look this letter over for me before I send it?*

**look through** *phr v* [T] **1** [**look through** sth] to look for something in a pile of papers, a drawer, someone's pockets etc.: *Her mother was looking through her stuff.* **2 look right through** sb to pretend that you have not seen someone

**look up** *phr v* **1** [I] if a situation is looking up, it is becoming better: *Things are looking up since I found a job.* **2** [T **look** sth ↔ **up**] to try to find information in a book, on a computer etc.: *If you don't know the word, look it up in the dictionary.* **3** [T **look** sb ↔ **up**] to visit someone you know, especially when you go to the place where s/he lives for another reason: *Don't forget to look up my parents when you're in Boston.*

**look up to** sb *phr v* [T] to admire and respect someone: *He looks up to his older brother.*

L

**look**² *n* **1** [C usually singular] an act of looking at something: *Let me take a look at that map again.* **2** an expression that you make with your eyes or face to show how you feel: *She gave me an angry look.* **3** the appearance of someone or something: *I don't like the look of that bruise - maybe you should see a doctor.* —see also LOOKS

**look·a·like** /'lʊkəˌlaɪk/ *n* INFORMAL someone who looks very similar to someone else, especially someone famous: *a Madonna lookalike*

**look·out** /'lʊk-aʊt/ *n* **1** be on the lookout to continually watch a place or pay attention to a situation because you are looking for someone or something: *Be on the lookout for snakes!* **2** someone whose duty is to watch carefully for danger, or the place where s/he does this

**looks** /lʊks/ *n* [plural] how beautiful or attractive someone is: *Stop worrying about your looks.*

**loom**¹ /lum/ *v* [I] **1** to appear as a large unclear threatening shape: *The mountain loomed in front of us.* **2** if a problem or difficult situation looms, it is likely to happen soon: *economic changes that loom ahead* **3 loom large** to seem important, worrying, and difficult to avoid: *Fear of failure loomed large in his mind.*

**loom**² *n* a frame or machine used for weaving cloth

**loon·y** /'luni/ *adj* INFORMAL extremely silly or crazy

**loop**¹ /lup/ *n* **1** a shape like a curve or a circle, or a line, piece of wire, string etc. that has this shape: *belt loops* (=cloth loops used for holding a belt on pants) **2 be out of the loop** to not be part of a group of people that make decisions: *Gaynor says he was out of the loop when the order was given.*

**loop**² *v* [I,T] to make a LOOP or to make something into a loop

**loop·hole** /'luphoʊl/ *n* a small mistake in a law or rule that makes it possible to legally avoid doing what the law says: *tax loopholes*

**loose**¹ /lus/ *adj*
**1** ▶NOT FIRMLY ATTACHED◀ not firmly attached to something: *The buttons on my shirt are coming loose.*
**2** ▶NOT TIED/FASTENED◀ not tied or fastened very tightly: *My shoe laces are loose.*
**3** ▶CLOTHES◀ loose clothes are big and do not fit tightly on your body
**4** ▶NOT CONTROLLED◀ free from being controlled in a CAGE, prison, or institution: *Two of the prisoners broke loose from the guards.* | *Don't let your dog loose on the beach.*
**5** a **loose translation/interpretation** something that has been translated etc. in a way that is not exact: *My French isn't very good, but I can give you a loose translation.*
**6 loose ends** parts of something such as work or an agreement that have not yet been completed: *I have to tie up a few loose ends before we go away.*
**7 loose cannon** someone who cannot be trusted because s/he says or does things you do not want him/her to
**8** ▶NOT MORAL◀ OLD-FASHIONED behaving in an immoral way: *a loose woman* —**loosely** *adv*

**loose**² *n* **on the loose** if a criminal is on the loose, s/he has escaped from prison

**loose-leaf** /'lus lif/ *adj* having pages that can be put in or taken out easily: *a loose-leaf notebook*

**loos·en** /'lusən/ *v* [I,T] to become less tight or less firmly attached to something, or to make something do this: *He loosened his tie.* | *The screws in the shelf had loosened.*

**loosen up** *phr v* **1** [I] to become more relaxed and feel less worried: *Claire loosened up after a few drinks.* **2** [I,T] if your muscles loosen up, or if you loosen them up, they stop feeling stiff

**loot**¹ /lut/ *v* [I,T] to steal things, especially from stores that have been damaged in a war or RIOT —**looting** *n* [U] —**looter** *n*

**loot**² *n* [U] goods that are stolen by thieves or taken by soldiers who have won a battle

**lop** /lɑp/ *v* **-pped, -pping** [T] also **lop off** to cut part of something off

**lope** /loʊp/ *v* [I] to run easily using long steps —**lope** *n*

**lop·sid·ed** /'lɑpˌsaɪdɪd/ *adj* having one side that is heavier, larger, or lower than the other side: *The cake was lopsided when it came out of the oven.*

**Lord** /lɔrd/ *n* **1** also **the Lord** a title used for God or Jesus Christ **2 good/oh/my Lord!** SPOKEN said when you are surprised, worried, or angry

**lord** *n* a man who has a particular position in the ARISTOCRACY

**lore** /lɔr/ *n* [U] knowledge and TRADITIONs that people learn from other people rather than from books

**lose** /luz/ *v* **lost, lost, losing**
**1** ▶NOT HAVE◀ [I] to stop having something important that you need: *Michelle lost her job.* | *We lost a lot of money on that deal.*
**2** ▶NOT FIND◀ [T] to be unable to find someone or something: *Danny's always losing his keys.*
**3** ▶NOT WIN◀ [I,T] to not win a game, argument, war etc.: *We lost to the Red Sox, 5-0.* | *Sanders lost the election by 371 votes.*
**4** ▶HAVE LESS◀ [T] to have less of something than before: *I need to lose weight.* | *She's lost a lot of blood.*
**5 lose your sight/memory/voice etc.** to stop being able to see, remember things, talk etc.
**6** ▶STOP HAVING A QUALITY◀ [T] to no longer have a particular quality, belief, attitude etc.: *The kids were losing interest in the*

L

game. | *Jake **lost** his **temper/cool*** (=became angry) *and started shouting.*

**7 lose an arm/eye etc.** to have a serious injury in which your arm etc. is cut off

**8 lose your balance** to become unsteady, especially so that you fall

**9 lose your husband/mother etc.** if you lose your husband etc., he dies: *Janet **lost the baby**.* (=the baby died before being born)

**10 lose your life** to die: *5000 soldiers lost their lives.*

**11 ▶WASTE◀** [T] to waste time or opportunities: *She **lost no time** in changing jobs.* | *You lost your chance!*

**12 lose sb** INFORMAL to confuse someone when explaining something to him/her: *You've lost me. Can you repeat that?*

**13 have nothing to lose** to be in a situation in which you can attempt to do something because you may be successful, and you will not be in a worse situation if you fail

**14 lose touch (with) a)** to not speak, see, or write to someone for so long that you do not know where s/he is: *I've lost touch with all my high school friends.* **b)** to not know the most recent information about a particular place, situation, event etc.

**15 lose it** SPOKEN **a)** to suddenly start shouting, laughing, or crying a lot because you think something is very bad, funny, or wrong: *I saw him hit the child and I lost it.* **b)** to become crazy: *You're losing it, Mabel.*

**16 lose your head** INFORMAL to stop being calm, so that you do the wrong thing: *I lost my head and started yelling.*

**17 lose heart** to become disappointed and unhappy: *The team lost heart after they lost their fifth game.*

**18 lose sight of** to forget about the most important part of something you are doing: *We can't lose sight of our goals.*

**19 lose your touch** to stop having a special ability or skill

**lose out** *phr v* [I] to not get something important such as a job because someone else gets it: *He **lost out on** a scholarship because his grades were low.*

---

**USAGE NOTE** lose, miss, lost, missing, and **disappear**

Use **lose** if you cannot find something: *I think I've lost my wallet.* Use **miss** if you do not attend a class, meeting etc. that you regularly go to: *Bill's been sick and has missed several days of work.* Use **lost** to describe someone who does not know where s/he is, or someone or something that you cannot find: *Will the parents of the lost girl please come to the information desk?* Use **missing** to describe someone or something that you have been looking for, especially when the situation is serious: *the*

---

missing jewels | *Detectives are searching for two missing boys, aged 10 and 12.* Use **disappear** when the way in which someone or something has been lost seems very strange: *My favorite pen seems to have disappeared.* | *Two soldiers disappeared over the weekend.* ✗ DON'T SAY "the disappeared pen/soldiers." ✗

**los·er** /'luzɚ/ *n* **1** someone who does not win: *a **bad/sore loser** (=someone who becomes too upset when s/he loses)* **2** someone who is never successful in life, work, or relationships: *Pam's boyfriend is such a loser!*

**loss** /lɔs/ *n* **1** [C,U] the fact of not having something any longer, or the action of losing something: *The loss of their home was a shock to the family.* | *weight loss* **2** [C,U] money that has been lost by a company, government, person, etc.: *The coal industry **made a loss of** $2 million last year.* **3** an occasion when you do not win a game: *3 wins and 4 losses so far this season* **4** [C,U] the death of someone: *Troops suffered **heavy losses** (=many deaths) in the first battle.* **5** [singular, U] the sadness you feel or disadvantage you have because someone or something leaves: *She felt a great sense of loss when her son left home.* **6 be at a loss** to not know what you should do or say: *I'm at a loss to know what to do.* **7 it's his/your loss** SPOKEN said when you think someone is stupid for not taking a good opportunity: *Well, if he doesn't take the job, it's his loss.*

**lost¹** /lɔst/ *adj* **1** not knowing where you are or how to find your way: *We **got lost** driving around the city.* **2** unable to be found: *a lost dog* **3** wasted: *lost opportunities* **4 be/feel lost** to not feel confident or able to take care of yourself: *I'd be lost without all your help.* **5** destroyed, ruined, or killed: *200 men were **lost in battle**.* **6 be lost on sb** if humor or intelligent thinking is lost on someone, s/he cannot understand it or does not want to accept it: *The joke was lost on him.* **7 Get lost!** SPOKEN used in order to tell someone rudely to go away **8 lost cause** something that has no chance of succeeding —see usage note at LOSE

**lost²** *v* the past tense and PAST PARTICIPLE of LOSE

**lost-and-found** /ˌ. . './ *n* an office used for keeping things that people have lost until their owners can get them

**lot** /lɑt/ *n* **1 a lot** also **lots** INFORMAL **a)** a large amount, quantity, or number of something: *A **lot** of people at work have the flu.* | *Mrs. Ruiz has **lots** of money.* | *A **lot of times** (=usually or often) we just sat and talked.* **b)** much: *You'll get there a lot quicker if you drive.* —see usage note at MUCH¹ —see study note on page 466 **2 have a lot on your mind** to have many problems you are thinking about **3** an area of land used especially for building on —see also PARKING LOT

**lo·tion** /ˈloʊʃən/ n [C,U] a liquid mixture that you put on your skin in order to make it soft or to protect it: *suntan lotion*

**lot·ter·y** /ˈlɑt̬əri/ n a game of chance in which people buy tickets in order to try to win a lot of money

**loud¹** /laʊd/ adj **1** making a lot of noise; not quiet: *The TV's too loud!* **2** loud clothes are too brightly colored —**loudly** adv

**loud²** adv loudly: *Can you talk a little louder please?* —see also **out loud** (OUT¹)

**loud-mouth** /ˈ. ./ n someone who talks too much, too loudly, and often in an offensive way —**loud-mouthed** adj

**loud·speak·er** /ˈlaʊdˌspikɚ/ n a piece of equipment that makes messages loud enough to be heard in a store, office, or station

**lounge¹** /laʊndʒ/ n a public room in a hotel or airport, where people can relax, sit down, or drink

**lounge²** v [I] to stand or sit in a lazy way: *We were lounging by the pool.*

**louse¹** /laʊs/ n, plural **lice** a very small insect that lives on the skin and hair of animals and people

**louse²** v

  **louse up** phr v [I,T **louse** sth ↔ **up**] to make a mistake or do something badly, especially so that it affects other people: *Why are you blaming me? You loused up!*

**lous·y** /ˈlaʊzi/ adj INFORMAL very bad or unimportant: *I've had a lousy day!*

**lov·a·ble** /ˈlʌvəbəl/ adj easy to love: *a lovable child*

**love¹** /lʌv/ v **1** [T] to like something very much, or enjoy doing something very much: *Tom loves to read.* | *Mom really loved her new dress.* **2** [T] to care very much about someone or something that is very special to you: *I love you very much.* | *He loves his country.* **3 I would love to/I'd love to** SPOKEN said when you really want to do something: *I'd love to come with you but I have work to do.*

**love²** n **1** [U] a strong romantic feeling for someone: *I fell in love with her the first time we met.* **2** [U] the strong feeling of caring very much about someone or something: *a mother's love for her child* **3** [C,U] something that you like very much, or that you enjoy doing very much: *his love of music/nature/singing etc.* **4** someone who you have romantic feelings about: *Mike was my first love.* **5 make love** to have sex with someone you love romantically **6 love/lots of love/all my love** INFORMAL written at the end of a letter to a friend, parent, husband etc.: *Take care. Lots of love, Dad.*

**love af·fair** /ˈ. .ˌ./ n a romantic sexual relationship: *a secret love affair*

**love·ly** /ˈlʌvli/ adj very nice, beautiful, or enjoyable: *Thank you for a lovely evening.*

**lov·er** /ˈlʌvɚ/ n **1** a sexual partner, usually someone who you are not married to: *I think my wife has a lover.* **2** someone who enjoys something very much: *a chocolate lover*

**love seat** /ˈ. ./ n a small SOFA for two people

**love·sick** /ˈlʌvˌsɪk/ adj sad because the person you love is not with you or does not love you

**love tri·an·gle** /ˈ. ˌ.../ n a situation in which one person is romantically involved with two other people

**lov·ing** /ˈlʌvɪŋ/ adj very caring: *a wonderful, loving husband*

**low¹** /loʊ/ adj **1** not high, or not far above the ground: *These shelves are a little too low for me.* | *a low ceiling* | *low clouds* **2** small in degree or amount: *a low temperature* | *new low prices* **3** bad, or below an acceptable standard: *a low grade in math* | *a low opinion of his work* **4** if a supply is low, you have used almost all of it: *We're **running/getting low on** gas.* **5** unhappy: *Kerry's been pretty low lately.* **6** a low voice, sound etc. is quiet or deep **7** lights that are low are not bright —opposite HIGH¹

**low²** adv in a low position or at a low level: *The sun sank low on the horizon.* | *He scored low on the SAT.* —opposite HIGH²

**low³** n a low price, level, degree etc.: *Prices dropped to an **all-time low**.* (=the lowest they have ever been) | *Tomorrow's low will be 25°F.*

**low·brow** /ˈloʊbraʊ/ adj a lowbrow book, movie etc. is not serious or not of very good quality

**low-cal** /ˌloʊˈkæl◂/ adj INFORMAL low-cal food or drinks do not have many CALORIES

**low·down** /ˈloʊdaʊn/ n **get the lowdown on sb/sth** INFORMAL to be given the important facts about someone or something

**low-end** /ˈ. ./ adj INFORMAL not the most expensive or not of the best quality: *low-end home computers*

**low·er¹** /ˈloʊɚ/ adj being the bottom part of something, or at the bottom of something: *I injured my lower back.* | *the lower floors of the building*

**lower²** v **1** [I,T] to become less, or to reduce something in amount, degree, strength etc.: *We're lowering prices on all our products!* | *Please **lower your voice**!* (=speak more quietly) **2** [T] to move something down: *The flag was lowered at sunset.*

**lower·case** /ˌ.. ˈ.◂/ n [U] letters written in their small form, such as a, b, c etc. —compare CAPITAL¹, UPPERCASE

**low-fat** /ˌ. ˈ.◂/ adj low-fat food, cooking etc. has or uses very little fat

**low-key** /ˌ. ˈ.◂/ adj not intended to attract a lot of attention: *The reception was very low-key.*

**low-life** /ˈ. ./ adj INFORMAL bad and usually involved in crimes: *a bunch of low-life criminals*

L

**low·ly** /ˈloʊli/ *adj* low in rank or importance

**low·ly·ing** /ˌ.ˈ..◂/ *adj* **1** low-lying land is not much higher than the level of the ocean **2** not very high: *low-lying fog*

**loy·al** /ˈlɔɪəl/ *adj* never changing your feelings for a particular person, set of beliefs, or country: *a loyal friend* —opposite DISLOYAL

**loy·al·ty** /ˈlɔɪəlti/ *n* **1** [U] the quality of being LOYAL to a particular person, set of beliefs, or country: *The company demands loyalty from its workers.* **2** [C usually plural] a feeling of wanting to help and encourage someone or something: *political loyalties*

**loz·enge** /ˈlɑzəndʒ/ *n* a small candy that has medicine in it

**LP** *n* long playing record; a record that plays for about 25 minutes on each side

**LSD** *n* [U] an illegal drug that makes people HALLUCINATE

**lube** /lub/ *v* [T] INFORMAL to LUBRICATE the parts of a car's engine

**lu·bri·cant** /ˈlubrəkənt/ *n* [C,U] a substance such as oil that is used on things that rub together, making them move more smoothly and easily

**lu·bri·cate** /ˈlubrəˌkeɪt/ *v* [T] to put a LUBRICANT on something —**lubrication** /ˌlubrəˈkeɪʃən/ *n* [U]

**lu·cid** /ˈlusɪd/ *adj* **1** clearly expressed and easy to understand: *a lucid and interesting article* **2** able to think clearly and understand what is happening around you: *He was rarely lucid during his long illness.*

**luck¹** /lʌk/ *n* [U] **1** success or something good that happens by chance: *Have you had any luck finding a new roommate?* | **Wish me luck!** | **Good luck** with your interview! **2** the way in which good or bad things happen to people by chance: *I've had bad luck all day. I missed the bus, was late for work, and I lost my keys.* **3 be in luck** to be able to do or get something that you want: *You're in luck —there's one ticket left!* **4 be out of luck** to not be able to do or get something you want: *We're out of luck —the park is closed.* **5 just my luck!** SPOKEN said when you are disappointed but not surprised that something bad has happened: *Just my luck! The guys just left.* **6 better luck next time** SPOKEN said when you hope that someone will be more successful the next time s/he tries to do something —see also **tough!/tough luck!** (TOUGH¹)

---

**USAGE NOTE** luck and lucky

Use the noun **luck** without an adjective to mean the good things that happen to you by chance: *Winning the game was just a matter of luck.* | *With luck, you'll find the right job.* You can use "have" with **luck**, but only if a word such as an adjective or determiner comes before **luck**: *He's had a*

---

*lot of bad luck lately.* | *We didn't have any luck getting tickets.* Use **lucky** to describe a situation that is good by chance, or someone who always has good luck: *We're lucky we haven't gone out of business like some other small companies.* ✗ DON'T SAY "we have luck." ✗

**luck²** *v*

**luck out** *phr v* [I] INFORMAL to be lucky: *We lucked out and found someone who spoke English.*

**luck·y** /ˈlʌki/ *adj* **1** having good luck; fortunate: *He's lucky to still be alive.* | *"I just got the last bus." "That was lucky!"* **2 I'll be lucky if** SPOKEN said when you think something is very unlikely: *I'll be lucky if I can pay my bills this month.* —**luckily** *adv*: *Luckily, no one was hurt.* —opposite UNLUCKY —see usage note at LUCK¹

**lu·cra·tive** /ˈlukrətɪv/ *adj* FORMAL making you earn a lot of money: *lucrative job opportunities*

**lu·di·crous** /ˈludɪkrəs/ *adj* silly, wrong, and unreasonable; RIDICULOUS: *The newspaper has printed some ludicrous stories.*

**lug** /lʌg/ *v* **-gged, -gging** [T] INFORMAL to pull or carry something that is very heavy: *We lugged our suitcases up to our room.*

**lug·gage** /ˈlʌgɪdʒ/ *n* [U] the bags etc. carried by people who are traveling; BAGGAGE

**lu·gu·bri·ous** /ləˈgubriəs/ *adj* LITERARY very sad and serious

**luke·warm** /ˌlukˈwɔrm◂/ *adj* **1** a liquid that is lukewarm is only slightly warm —see usage note at TEMPERATURE **2** not showing very much interest or excitement: *a lukewarm response*

**lull¹** /lʌl/ *v* [T] **1** to make someone feel calm or sleepy: *Singing softly, she lulled us to sleep.* **2** to make someone feel so safe and confident that you can easily deceive him/her: *She was lulled into believing that there was no danger.*

**lull²** *n* a short period when there is less activity or noise than usual: *a lull in the conversation*

**lul·la·by** /ˈlʌləˌbaɪ/ *n* a song that you sing to children in order to make them calm and sleepy

**lum·ber¹** /ˈlʌmbɚ/ *n* [U] trees that are cut down and used as wood for building

**lumber²** *v* [I] **1** to move in a slow, awkward way, usually because you are heavy: *The bear lumbered towards us.* **2 get/be lumbered with** to get a job or duty that you do not want: *I get lumbered with the work he doesn't want.*

**lum·ber·ing** /ˈlʌmbərɪŋ/ *n* [U] ⇨ LOGGING

**lum·ber·jack** /ˈlʌmbɚˌdʒæk/ *n* someone whose job is to cut down trees for wood

**lu·mi·nar·y** /ˈluməˌnɛri/ *n* someone who is famous and respected because of his/her knowledge or skills

**lu·mi·nous** /ˈlumənəs/ *adj* able to shine in the dark without being lit: *luminous paint*

**lump¹** /lʌmp/ *n* **1** a small piece of something solid that does not have a definite shape: *a lump of clay* −see picture at PIECE¹ **2** a hard swollen area on someone's skin or in his/her body **3 a lump in your throat** the tight feeling in your throat that happens when you want to cry

**lump²** *v* [T] to put two or more different people or things together and consider them as a single group: *Do you think I can lump these ideas into one paragraph?*

**lump sum** /ˌ. ˈ./ *n* an amount of money given in a single payment

**lump·y** /ˈlʌmpi/ *adj* having LUMPs and therefore not smooth: *a lumpy mattress*

**lu·na·cy** /ˈlunəsi/ *n* [U] actions or behavior that seem very stupid and unreasonable

**lu·nar** /ˈlunɚ/ *adj* relating to the moon: *a lunar eclipse*

**lu·na·tic** /ˈlunəˌtɪk/ *n* someone who behaves in a crazy, stupid, or very strange way −**lunatic** *adj*

**lunch** /lʌntʃ/ *n* [C,U] a meal eaten in the middle of the day, or that time of day: *What do you want for lunch? | When do you usually eat lunch? | We've already had lunch. | Dad usually goes jogging at lunch.* −see usage note at MEAL TIMES

**lunch·eon** /ˈlʌntʃən/ *n* [C,U] FORMAL ⇨ LUNCH

**lunch·time** /ˈlʌntʃtaɪm/ *n* [C,U] the time in the middle of the day when people usually eat LUNCH: *Is it lunchtime yet?*

**lung** /lʌŋ/ *n* one of two organs in the body used for breathing

**lunge** /lʌndʒ/ *v* [I] to make a sudden forceful movement toward someone or something: *Greg lunged forward to grab her arm.* −**lunge** *n*

**lurch** /lɚtʃ/ *v* [I] to walk or move in an unsteady, uncontrolled way: *He lurched drunkenly towards us.* −**lurch** *n* −see also **leave sb in the lurch** (LEAVE¹)

**lure¹** /lʊr/ *v* [T] to persuade someone to do something by making it seem attractive, exciting etc.; TEMPT: *Another company tried to lure him over by offering more money.*

**lure²** *n* **1** something that attracts people, or the quality of being able to do this: *the lure of power and money* **2** an object used in order to attract animals or fish so that they can be caught

**lu·rid** /ˈlʊrɪd/ *adj* DISAPPROVING deliberately shocking and involving sex or violence: *the lurid details of the murder*

**lurk** /lɚk/ *v* [I] to wait somewhere secretly, usually before doing something bad: *men lurking in the alley*

**lus·cious** /ˈlʌʃəs/ *adj* **1** extremely good to eat: *luscious ripe strawberries* **2** INFORMAL very sexually attractive

**lush¹** /lʌʃ/ *adj* having lots of very green and healthy plants or leaves

**lush²** *n* INFORMAL someone who drinks too much alcohol

**lust¹** /lʌst/ *n* [C,U] DISAPPROVING a very strong feeling of sexual desire, or a strong desire for something such as power or money

**lust²** *v*

**lust after/for** sb/sth *phr v* [T] DISAPPROVING **1** to have a strong feeling of sexual desire for someone **2** to want something very much because you do not have it yet: *politicians lusting for power*

**lus·ter** /ˈlʌstɚ/ *n* [singular, U] an attractive shiny appearance: *the luster of her long dark hair* −**lustrous** /ˈlʌstrəs/ *adj*

**lust·y** /ˈlʌsti/ *adj* strong and healthy; powerful: *The baby gave a lusty cry.* −**lustily** *adv*

**Lu·ther·an** /ˈluθərən/ *adj* relating to the Protestant church whose members follow the ideas of Martin Luther −**Lutheran** *n*

**lux·u·ri·ant** /lʌgˈʒʊriənt, lʌkˈʃʊ-/ *adj* healthy and growing thickly and strongly

**lux·u·ri·ate** /lʌgˈʒʊriˌeɪt, lʌkˈʃʊ-/ *v*

**luxuriate in** sth *phr v* [T] to relax and enjoy the pleasure you feel: *She luxuriated in the hot bath.*

**lux·u·ri·ous** /lʌgˈʒʊriəs, lʌkˈʃʊ-/ *adj* very comfortable, beautiful, and expensive: *a luxurious room in a hotel on the coast*

**lux·u·ry** /ˈlʌkʃəri, ˈlʌgʒəri/ *n* **1 luxury car/hotel/vacation etc.** a luxury car etc. is of the highest standard **2** something expensive that you want but do not need: *We can't afford the luxury of a new car.*

**Ly·cra** /ˈlaɪkrə/ *n* [U] TRADEMARK a cloth that stretches, used especially for making tight-fitting sports clothes

**ly·ing** /ˈlaɪ-ɪŋ/ *v* the PRESENT PARTICIPLE of LIE

**lynch** /lɪntʃ/ *v* [T] if a crowd of people lynches someone, they illegally hang him/her as a punishment −**lynching** *n*

**lynch·pin** /ˈlɪntʃˌpɪn/ *n* ⇨ LINCHPIN

**lyr·i·cal** /ˈlɪrɪkəl/ *adj* expressing strong emotions in a beautiful way: *lyrical music/poetry*

**lyr·i·cist** /ˈlɪrəsɪst/ *n* someone who writes LYRICS

**lyr·ics** /ˈlɪrɪks/ *n* [plural] the words of a song

# M

**M, m** /ɛm/ **1** the thirteenth letter of the English alphabet **2** the ROMAN NUMERAL (=number) for 1000

**m** *n* **1** the written abbreviation of "meter" **2** the written abbreviation of "million" **3** the written abbreviation of "male" **4** the written abbreviation of "mile" **5** the written abbreviation of "married" **6** the written abbreviation of "medium", used especially in clothes

**M.A.** *n* Master of Arts; a university degree in a subject such as history or literature that you can get after you have your first degree –compare M.S.

**MA** the written abbreviation of Massachusetts

**ma** /mɑ, mɔ/ *n* OLD-FASHIONED mother

**ma'am** /mæm/ *n* SPOKEN used in order to speak politely to a woman when you do not know her name: *Excuse me, ma'am.*

**mac** /mæk/ *n* SPOKEN used in order to speak to a man when you do not know his name: *Hey, mac! Is that your car?*

**ma·ca·bre** /məˈkɑbrə, məˈkɑb/ *adj* strange, frightening, and relating to death or injury: *a macabre tale*

**mac·a·ro·ni** /ˌmækəˈroʊni/ *n* [U] a type of PASTA in the shape of small curved tubes, that you cook in boiling water

**Mace** /meɪs/ *n* TRADEMARK a chemical that some people carry to defend themselves, which makes your eyes and skin sting painfully if it is SPRAYed in your face

**Mach** /mɑk/ *n* [U] a unit for measuring the speed of a plane in relation to the speed of sound

**ma·che·te** /məˈʃɛti, -ˈtʃɛ-/ *n* a large knife with a broad heavy blade, used as a tool for cutting or as a weapon

**ma·chine**[1] /məˈʃin/ *n* a piece of equipment that uses power such as electricity to do a particular job: *a sewing machine* | *The machines in the lab were running all night.*

---

**USAGE NOTE machine, appliance, device, gadget, and tool**

**Machine** is a general word for a piece of equipment that uses electricity or another form of power: *We've just bought a new sewing machine.* An **appliance** is a large **machine** that is used in the home: *Now, save 30% off all applicances, including refrigerators and dishwashers!* A **device** is a piece of equipment that is usually small and usually electronic, that does a special job: *A seismograph is a device that measures earthquake activity.* A **gadget** is a small piece of equipment that makes a particular job easier to do: *Have you seen this new gadget for opening wine bottles?* A **tool** is a small object that is used for making and repairing things, and that usually does not use electricity: *We keep most of the tools in the garage.*

---

**machine**[2] *v* [T] to make or shape something, especially metal parts for something, using a machine

**ma·chine gun** /.ˈ. ˌ./ *n* a gun that fires a lot of bullets very quickly

**machine-read·a·ble** /.ˌ. ˈ...◂/ *adj* able to be understood and used by a computer: *machine-readable text*

**ma·chin·er·y** /məˈʃinəri/ *n* [U] **1** machines, especially large ones: *agricultural machinery* | *The machinery in the factory is controlled by computers.* **2** the parts inside a machine that make it work **3** an official system or set of processes for organizing or achieving something: *The machinery of the law works slowly.*

**ma·chin·ist** /məˈʃinɪst/ *n* someone who operates or makes machines

**ma·cho** /ˈmɑtʃoʊ/ *adj* INFORMAL a man who is macho has qualities such as strength that are typical of men, but is not sensitive or sympathetic

**mack·er·el** /ˈmækərəl/ *n* [C,U] a common sea fish, that has a strong taste, or the meat from this fish

**mac·ro·cos·m** /ˈmækrəˌkɑzəm/ *n* a large complicated system such as the whole universe or a society, considered as a single unit –compare MICROCOSM

**mad** /mæd/ *adj* **-dder, -ddest 1** INFORMAL angry: *You make me so mad!* | *Lisa was really mad at me for telling.* **2 do sth like mad** INFORMAL to do something as quickly as you can: *Carlos was writing like mad at the end of the exam.* **3** behaving in a wild way, without thinking about what you are doing: *We made a mad dash for* (=ran wildly towards) *the door.* **4 power-mad/money-mad etc.** only interested in or only thinking about power, money etc.: *a power-mad dictator*

**mad·am** /ˈmædəm/ *n* **1** used in order to speak politely to a woman when you do not know her name: *May I help you, madam?* | *Dear Madam* (=used at the beginning of a business letter to a woman when you do not know her name) **2** a woman who is in charge of a group of PROSTITUTEs

**mad·den·ing** /ˈmædn-ɪŋ, ˈmædnɪŋ/ *adj* very annoying: *maddening behavior*

**made**[1] /meɪd/ *v* the past tense and PAST PARTICIPLE of MAKE

**made**[2] *adj* **1 be made of** to be built from or consist of something: *The frame is made of silver.* **2 be made for** to be perfectly suitable for a particular person, group, or situation: *I think Anna and Juan were made for each other.* **3 sb has (got) it made** used in order to say that someone is sure of success or happiness: *You have a wonderful family, plenty of money - you've got it made!*

**mad·house** /ˈmædhaʊs/ *n* a place that is very busy and noisy: *The airport is a madhouse at Christmas.*

**mad·ly** /ˈmædli/ *adv* **1 madly in love** very much in love **2** in a wild way: *Allen was beating madly on the door.*

**mad·man** /ˈmædmæn, -mən/ *n* like a mad-

**man** in a wild uncontrolled way: *He drives like a madman.*

**mad·ness** /'mædnɪs/ *n* [U] very stupid and often dangerous behavior: *It would be absolute madness to try to cross the desert on your own.*

**Ma·don·na** /mə'dɑnə/ *n* a picture or figure of Mary, the mother of Jesus Christ

**mael·strom** /'meɪlstrəm/ *n* a situation full of events that you cannot control or strong emotions that make people feel confused or frightened: *Forbes was pulled into the maelstrom of newspapers and TV attention.*

**mae·stro** /'maɪstroʊ/ *n* someone who can do something very well, especially a musician

**ma·fi·a** /'mɑfiə/ *n* **the Mafia** a large organization of criminals who control many illegal activities

**mag·a·zine** /,mægə'zin, 'mægə,zin/ *n* **1** a large thin book usually with a large picture on the cover, that is sold weekly or monthly and contains articles, photographs etc.: *a fashion magazine* **2** the part of a gun that holds the bullets

**ma·gen·ta** /mə'dʒɛntə/ *n* [U] a dark purplered color – **magenta** *adj*

**mag·got** /'mægət/ *n* the LARVA (=young insect) of a fly that lives in decaying food or flesh

**mag·ic** /'mædʒɪk/ *n* [U] **1** a secret power used for controlling events or doing impossible things, by saying special words or doing special actions: *a witch's magic* **2** the skill of doing tricks that look like magic, or the tricks themselves: *Dad always did a magic show at my birthday parties.* **3** an attractive quality that makes someone or something interesting or exciting: *These old stories still retain their magic.*

**mag·i·cal** /'mædʒɪkəl/ *adj* **1** very enjoyable and exciting, in a strange or special way: *a magical evening beneath the stars* **2** containing magic, or done using magic: *magical powers* – **magically** *adv*

**ma·gi·cian** /mə'dʒɪʃən/ *n* someone who performs magic tricks and makes things appear and disappear

**ma·gis·trate** /'mædʒɪ,streɪt, -strɪt/ *n* someone who judges less serious crimes in a court of law

**mag·nan·i·mous** /mæg'nænəməs/ *adj* kind and generous toward other people – **magnanimity** /,mægnə'nɪmət̮i/ *n* [U]

**mag·nate** /'mægneɪt, -nɪt/ *n* **steel/oil/shipping etc. magnate** a wealthy and powerful person in the steel etc. industry

**mag·ne·si·um** /mæg'niziəm, -ʒəm/ *n* [U] a light silver-white metal that is often used in medicine and to make other metals

**mag·net** /'mægnɪt/ *n* **1** a piece of iron or steel that can make other metal objects move toward it **2** a person or place that attracts many other people or things: *The city has become*

**a magnet for** many new industries. – **magnetize** /'mægnə,taɪz/ *v* [T]

magnet

**mag·net·ic** /mæg'nɛt̮ɪk/ *adj* **1** having the power of a MAGNET: *There's a magnetic strip on the back so that you can hang it up.* **2 magnetic personality** a quality that someone has that makes other people feel strongly attracted to him/her **3 magnetic tape/disk etc.** TAPE etc. that uses MAGNETs to record and store information, for example in a computer system

**mag·net·ism** /'mægnə,tɪzəm/ *n* [U] **1** a quality that makes other people feel attracted to you: *Her magnetism is a great asset in her career on television.* **2** the qualities of a MAGNET

**mag·nif·i·cent** /mæg'nɪfəsənt/ *adj* very impressive because of being big, beautiful etc.: *a magnificent painting/sunset* – **magnificence** *n* [U]

**mag·ni·fy** /'mægnə,faɪ/ *v* [T] **1** to make something appear larger than it is: *A microscope magnifies the image so you can see the cells.* **2** to make something seem more important or worse than it really is: *The reports tend to magnify the risks involved.* – **magnification** /,mægnəfə'keɪʃən/ *n* [C,U]

**magnifying glass** /'.... ,./ *n* a round piece of glass with a handle, that magnifies (MAGNIFY) things when you look through it

**mag·ni·tude** /'mægnə,tud/ *n* [U] **1** how large or important something is: *I hadn't realized the magnitude of the problem.* **2** TECHNICAL how strong an EARTHQUAKE is, or how bright a star is

**mag·no·lia** /mæg'noʊlyə/ *n* a tree or bush with large white, yellow, pink, or purple sweet-smelling flowers

**mag·pie** /'mægpaɪ/ *n* a wild bird with black and white feathers and a loud cry

**ma·hog·a·ny** /mə'hɑgəni/ *n* [C,U] a tropical American tree, or the hard dark wood of this tree

**maid** /meɪd/ *n* a female servant, especially in a large house

**maid·en**[1] /'meɪdn/ **maid** *n* LITERARY a young woman or girl who is not married

**maiden**[2] *adj* **maiden flight/voyage** the first trip that a plane or ship makes

**maiden name** /,.. './ *n* the family name that a woman had before she got married and began using her husband's name

**maid of hon·or** /,. . './ *n* the main BRIDESMAID in a wedding

**mail**[1] /meɪl/ *n* **1 the mail** the system of collecting and delivering letters, packages etc.: *I just put the letter in the mail.|What time does the mail come?* **2** [U] the letters, packages etc., that are delivered to a particular person or

M

at a particular time: *They sent his mail to the wrong address.* —see also AIRMAIL

**mail²** *v* [T] to send a letter, package etc. to someone: *I'll mail it to you tomorrow.*

**mail·box** /'meɪlbɑks/ *n* **1** a box outside your house or in a POST OFFICE where your letters are delivered or collected —see picture on page 471 **2** a special box in the street or at a POST OFFICE where you mail letters

**mail·ing** /'meɪlɪŋ/ *n* [C,U] the act of sending a large number of letters, advertisements etc. at the same time, or the total number of letters that you send

**mail·ing list** /'.. ˌ./ *n* a list of people's names and addresses that a company keeps in order to send information or advertisements to them

**mail·man** /'meɪlmæn, -mən/ *n* a man who delivers mail to people's houses

**mail or·der** /'. ˌ../ *n* [U] a method of selling in which you buy goods from a company that sends them by mail: *a mail order catalog*

**maim** /meɪm/ *v* [T] to wound or injure someone very seriously and often permanently: *The accident maimed her for life.*

**main¹** /meɪn/ *adj* **1** bigger or more important than all other things, ideas etc. of the same kind: *the main meal of the day | the main points of his speech* **2** **the main thing** SPOKEN used in order to say what the most important thing is in a situation: *As long as you're not hurt, that's the main thing.*

**main²** *n* a large pipe carrying water or gas that is connected to people's houses by smaller pipes: *a broken water/gas main*

**main·frame** /'meɪnfreɪm/ *n* a large computer that can work very fast and that a lot of people can use at the same time

**main·land** /'meɪnlænd, -lənd/ *n* **the mainland** the main area of land that forms a country, as compared to islands near it that are also part of that country

**main·ly** /'meɪnli/ *adv* **1** used in order to show that something is true of most members of a group: *The workforce mainly consists of men.* **2** used in order to show that something is generally true: *I bought the answering machine mainly for business reasons.* ✗ DON'T SAY "Mainly I bought the answering machine..." ✗

**main·stay** /'meɪnsteɪ/ *n* the most important part of something that makes it possible for it to work correctly or to continue to exist: *Farming is still the mainstay of our country's economy.*

**main·stream** /'meɪnstrim/ *n* **the mainstream** the beliefs and opinions that represent the most usual way of thinking about or doing something, or the people who have these beliefs and opinions: *His beliefs are very much those of the mainstream.* —**mainstream** *adj*

**main·tain** /meɪn'teɪn/ *v* [T] **1** to make something continue in the same way or at the same standard as before: *We have always main-*

tained good relations with our customers. **2** to keep something in good condition by taking care of it: *It costs a lot of money to maintain a big house.* **3** to strongly express an opinion or attitude: *I've always maintained that any changes in the law will hurt the poor more than the rich.* **4** to provide someone with the things he, she, or it needs, such as money or food: *He's too poor to maintain a wife and children.*

**main·te·nance** /'meɪntˈn-əns/ *n* [U] the work that is necessary to keep something in good condition: *car maintenance*

**ma·jes·tic** /mə'dʒɛstɪk/ *adj* looking very big and impressive: *a majestic view of the lake* —**majestically** *adv*

**maj·es·ty** /'mædʒəsti/ *n* **1** [U] the quality of being impressive and beautiful: *the majesty of the Great Pyramids* **2** **Your/Her/His Majesty** used when talking to or about a king or queen

**ma·jor¹** /'meɪdʒɚ/ *adj* very large or important, especially when compared to other things or people of a similar kind: *The car needs major repairs. | a major operation* ✗ DON'T SAY "major than." SAY "more important than" or "bigger than." ✗ —compare MINOR¹

**major²** *n* **1** the main subject that you study at a college or university: *His major is history.* —compare MINOR² **2** also **Major** an officer who has a middle rank in the Army, Air Force, or Marines

**major³** *v*

**major in** sth *phr v* [T] to study something as your main subject at a college or university: *I'm majoring in biology.*

**ma·jor·i·ty¹** /mə'dʒɔrəti, -'dʒɑr-/ *n* **1** [singular] most of the people or things in a particular group: *The majority of Americans do not want advertisements to be shown before a movie.* **2** [C usually singular] the difference between the number of votes gained by the winning party or person in an election and the number gained by other parties or people: *a majority of 500 votes* —compare MINORITY²

**majority²** *adj* happening as a result of the decision of most members of a group: *a majority decision/ruling*

**major-league** /'.. ˌ./ *adj* INFORMAL important or having a lot of power: *a major-league player in Michigan politics*

**Major Leagues** /ˌ.. './ **Majors** *n* [plural] the group of teams that make up the highest level of American professional baseball

**ma·jor·ly** /'meɪdʒɚli/ *adv* SPOKEN NONSTANDARD very or extremely: *My parents weren't majorly upset about the dent in the car.*

**make¹** /meɪk/ *v* made, made, making
**1** ▶PRODUCE STH◀ [T] to produce something by working or doing something: *I'll make the cake, and you make dinner. | Grandma made dolls for us. | The toy says "Made in Taiwan" on it. | The scissors slipped, and she made a hole in*

*the cloth.*

**2 ▶DO STH◀** [T] used before some nouns to show that someone does the action of the noun: *They made a mistake on the electricity bill.* | *Roger made a good suggestion.* | *Do you want to make an appointment with the doctor?*

**3 ▶CAUSE◀** [T] to cause a particular state or situation to happen: *Everything he says makes her mad.* | *That button makes the machine stop.* | *Look at the mess you made!* | *What made you decide to become a lawyer?* ✗ DON'T SAY "What made you to decide to become a lawyer?" ✗

**4 ▶FORCE◀** [T] to force someone to do something: *I wasn't hungry, but I made myself eat something.* | *The police made them stand up against the wall.*

**5 ▶EARN MONEY◀** [T] to earn or get money: *Irene makes about $60,000 a year.* | *You can make a lot of money working with computers.*

**6 ▶NUMBER◀** [linking verb] to be a particular number or amount when added together: *2 and 2 make 4.* | *If you include us, that makes eight people for dinner.*

**7 make a phone call** to talk to someone using the telephone

**8 make time** to leave enough time to do something: *Don't forget to make time to visit Grandpa this week.*

**9 ▶BE SUITABLE◀** [linking verb] to have the qualities that are necessary for a particular job, use, or purpose: *John will make a good father.* | *Her idea would make a good book.*

**10 make believe** to pretend that something is true, especially as a game: *The kids make believe they're cowboys.*

**11 make it a)** to arrive somewhere: *We made it to the station just as the bus was leaving.* **b)** to be able to go to an event, meeting etc.: *I'm sorry I can't make it to your play.* **c)** to be successful in a particular business or activity: *He's made it big* (=was very successful) *in Hollywood.* **d)** to live after a serious illness or injury, or to deal with a very difficult situation: *Mom made it through the operation all right.*

**12 make a difference** to cause a change, especially one that improves a situation: *The tax cuts will make a big difference in my salary.*

**13 make the bed** to pull the sheets and BLANKETs over a bed to make it look neat when you are not sleeping in it

**14 that makes two of us** SPOKEN used in order to say that you feel the same way that someone else does: *"I'm so tired!" "Yeah, that makes two of us."*

**15 make or break** to cause either great success or failure: *The first year can make or break a new business.*

**16 make do** to manage to do something using the things you already have, even though they are not exactly what you want: *We'll have to make do with these old clothes.* —see also **be made of** (MADE²) **make sure** (SURE¹) **make a**

(big) difference/make all the difference (DIFFERENCE) **make love** (LOVE²) **make sense** (SENSE¹) **make the best of sth** (BEST³) **make/ be friends (with)** (FRIEND) **make up your mind** (MIND¹)

**make for** sth *phr v* [T] to have a particular result or effect: *His laziness makes for a lot of work for the rest of us.* —see also **be made for** (MADE²)

**make** sth **of** sb/sth *phr v* [T] **1** to have a particular opinion about someone or something, or a particular way of understanding something: *What do you make of* (=what is your opinion of) *Robert's new idea?* **2 make the most of** to use an opportunity in a way that gives you as much advantage as possible: *I want to make the most of the time I have left in Europe.* **3 make much of** to treat a situation or person as if he, she, or it is extremely important: *He doesn't like us to make too much of his birthday.* —see also **make a fool of yourself** (FOOL¹)

**make off with** sth *phr v* [T] to steal something: *They made off with our TV.*

**make out** *phr v* **1** [T make sth ↔ out] to be able to hear, see, or understand something: *I can't make out what the sign says.* **2 make a check out to sb** to write a check so that the money is paid to a particular person, company, store etc.: *Make the check out to Ms. Linda Wright.* **3 make out (that)** INFORMAL to say that something is true when it is not: *Brian was making out he had won all the prizes.* **4 How did sb make out...?** SPOKEN used in order to ask if someone did something well: *"How did you make out in the interview?" "I think it went well."* **5** [I] SPOKEN to kiss and touch someone in a sexual way **6 make out like a bandit** SPOKEN to get a lot of money or gifts, win a lot etc.: *My nephew makes out like a bandit every Christmas.*

**make** sth ↔ **over** *phr v* [T] to change something: *The basement has been made over into a playroom.*

**make up** *phr v* **1** [T make sth ↔ up] to invent the words of a poem or story or the music for a song: *"What are you singing?" "I don't know, I just made it up."* **2** [T make sth ↔ up] to invent a story, explanation etc. in order to deceive someone: *Ron made up an excuse so his mother wouldn't be mad.* **3** [T make up sth] to combine together to form a substance, group, system etc.: *Chapter 5 is about the rocks and minerals that make up the earth's outer layer.* | *Women make up 60% of our employees.* **4** [T make sth ↔ up] to work at times when you do not usually work, because you have not done enough work at some other time: *I have to leave early, but I'll make up the time/work tomorrow.* **5 make it up to sb** to do something good for someone because you feel responsible for something bad that happened to him/her: *I'm sorry I forgot! I promise I'll make it up to you.*

**6** [I] to become friends with someone again, after you have had an argument: *Have you two made up?*

**make up for** sth *phr v* [T] **1** to make a bad situation or event seem better: *I bought her flowers to try to **make up for** the nasty things I said.* **2** to have so much of one quality that it does not matter that you do not have others: *Jay lacks experience, but he **makes up for it** with hard work.* **3 make up for lost time** to do something very quickly because you started late or something made you work too slowly: *I've been reading a lot at night to **make up for** lost time.*

---

**USAGE NOTE make and do**

Although there are no fixed rules about when to use **make** and when to use **do**, we tend to use **make** to talk about producing things, and **do** to talk about actions: *Who made your dress? | We need to make plans for our trip. | I'll make you a drink. | Could you do me a favor? | Thanks for all you've done to help. | It's my turn to do the dishes.*

---

**make²** *n* **1** a product made by a particular company: *"What make is your car?" "It's a Chevy."* **2 be on the make** DISAPPROVING to be trying hard to get something such as money or sex

**make-be·lieve** /ˌ. .'.ˌ / *n* [U] a state of imagining or pretending that something is real: *Don't be afraid, honey - the monster is only make-believe*

**mak·er** /'meɪkɚ/ *n* **1** a person or company that makes something or does something: *The maker of the drug is studying new ways to use it.* | *a dress maker* **2 decision maker/peace maker etc.** someone who is good at or responsible for making decisions, stopping arguments etc.

**make·shift** /'meɪkˌʃɪft/ *adj* made for temporary use when you need something and there is nothing better available: *a makeshift table made from boxes*

**make·up** /'meɪk-ʌp/ *n* **1** [U] substances such as powder, creams, and LIPSTICK that some people, usually women or actors, put on their faces: *I waited for Ginny to put on her makeup.* **2** all the parts, members, or qualities that make up something: *We haven't yet been told what the makeup of the new government will be.* (=who the members will be)

**mak·ing** /'meɪkɪŋ/ *n* **1** the process or business of making something: *The making of the movie took four years.* | *the art of rug making* **2 in the making** in the process of being made or produced: *The deal was 11 months in the making.*

**mak·ings** /'meɪkɪŋz/ *n* [plural] **have the makings of** to have the qualities or skills needed

to become a particular type of person or thing: *Sandy has the makings of a good doctor.*

**mal·a·dy** /'mælədi/ *n* FORMAL **1** an illness **2** something that is wrong with a system or organization

**mal·aise** /mæˈleɪz/ *n* [U] a feeling of anxiety, and a lack of confidence and satisfaction

**ma·lar·i·a** /məˈlɛriə/ *n* [U] a disease common in hot countries that is caused by the bite of an infected MOSQUITO —**malarial** *adj*

**male** /meɪl/ *adj* **1** belonging to the sex that cannot have babies: *a male lion* **2** typical of this sex: *a male voice* —**male** *n* —see usage note at MASCULINE

**male chau·vin·ist** /ˌmeɪl ˈʃoʊvənɪst/, **male chauvinist pig** /ˌ. ˌ... '. / *n* a man who believes that men are better than women —**male chauvinism** *n* [U]

**ma·lev·o·lent** /məˈlɛvələnt/ *adj* FORMAL showing a desire to harm other people —**malevolence** *n* [U]

**mal·func·tion** /mælˈfʌŋkʃən/ *n* a fault in the way a machine works: *a malfunction in the computer system* —**malfunction** *v* [I]

**mal·ice** /'mælɪs/ *n* [U] the desire to harm or upset someone: *Corran wasn't **acting out of malice**.* (=did not desire to harm someone)

**ma·li·cious** /məˈlɪʃəs/ *adj* showing a desire to harm or upset someone: *malicious gossip* —**maliciously** *adv*

**ma·lign** /məˈlaɪn/ *v* [T] FORMAL to say or write unpleasant and untrue things about someone: *He's been **much maligned** by the press.*

**ma·lig·nant** /məˈlɪgnənt/ *adj* **1** TECHNICAL a malignant TUMOR (=a group of growing cells) contains CANCER and may kill someone **2** FORMAL showing hatred and a strong desire to harm someone: *a malignant grin* —**malignancy** *n* [U] —compare BENIGN

**mall** /mɔl/ *n* a very large building with a lot of stores in it

**mal·lard** /'mælɚd/ *n* a type of common wild duck

**mal·le·a·ble** /'mæliəbəl/ *adj* **1** something that is malleable is easy to press, pull, or bend into a new shape: *a malleable metal* **2** someone who is malleable is easily influenced or changed by people

**mal·let** /'mælɪt/ *n* a wooden hammer

**mal·nour·ished** /ˌmælˈnɚɪʃt, -ˈnʌrɪʃt/ *adj* ill or weak because of not eating enough food, or because of not eating good food

**mal·nu·tri·tion** /ˌmælnuˈtrɪʃən/ *n* [U] illness or weakness as a result of being MALNOURISHED

**mal·prac·tice** /ˌmælˈpræktɪs/ *n* [C,U] the act of failing to do a professional duty, or of making a mistake while doing it

**malt** /mɔlt/ *n* **1** [U] grain, usually BARLEY, that is used for making beer, WHISKEY etc. **2** a

M

drink made from milk, malt, ICE CREAM, and something such as chocolate

**malt·ed** /'mɔlt̬ɪd/, **malted milk** /ˌ.. './ *n* ⇨ MALT

**mal·treat** /mæl'trit/ *v* [T] FORMAL to treat an animal or person cruelly −**maltreatment** *n* [U]

**ma·ma** /'mɑmə/ *n* INFORMAL ⇨ MOTHER¹

**ma·ma's boy** /'.. ˌ./ *n* INFORMAL a boy or man that people think is weak because his mother is too protective of him

**mam·mal** /'mæməl/ *n* the group of animals including humans that drink milk from their mother's breasts when they are young

**mam·moth** /'mæməθ/ *adj* very large: *a mammoth job*

**man¹** /mæn/ *n, plural* **men**
1 ▶MALE◀ an adult male human: *What did the man look like?* | *We met a Polish man and his wife.*
2 ▶ALL PEOPLE◀ [U] all people, both male and female, considered as a group: *one of the worst disasters in the history of man* | *All men must die.* ✗ DON'T SAY "all the men." ✗
3 ▶SOLDIER/EMPLOYER◀ [C usually plural] a man who works for an employer such as a builder, or who has a low rank in the Army, Navy etc.: *Call the men to meet here at 11:00 for an important announcement*
4 ▶GAMES◀ one of the pieces you use in a game such as CHESS
5 ▶WHAT SB LIKES◀ used in order to say that a man likes, or likes doing, a particular thing: *a gambling man* | *He's a meat and potatoes man.* (=likes eating food like meat and potatoes)
6 **the man in the street** the average person, who represents the general opinion of many people: *What the man in the street wants is a reduction in taxes.*
7 **be/become man and wife** FORMAL to be or become married
8 SPOKEN used in order to speak to someone, especially an adult male: *Hey, man! How're you doing?*
9 **my man** SPOKEN said by some men when talking to a male friend

---

**USAGE NOTE** man, mankind, people, humankind

**Man** can mean "people in general": *Man has always tried to understand the stars.* **Mankind** means "all people, considered as a group": *It was the richest country in the history of mankind.* However, many people think that using **man** and **mankind** in this way is wrong because it seems not to include women. Therefore, it is more usual to use **people** to mean "people in general" and **humankind** instead of **mankind**: *People have always tried to understand the stars.* | *It was the richest country in the history of humankind.*

---

**man²** *v* **-nned, -nning** [T] to use or operate a vehicle, piece of equipment etc.: *the astronauts who manned the first spacecraft* −see also MANNED

**man³** *interjection* used in order to emphasize what you are saying: *Oh man! I'm going to be really late.*

**man·a·cle** /'mænəkəl/ *n* an iron ring on a chain that is put around the hand or foot of a prisoner

**man·age** /'mænɪdʒ/ *v* [I,T] 1 to succeed in doing something difficult, such as dealing with a problem, living in a difficult situation: *It was heavy, but I managed to get it up the stairs.* | *I don't know how we'll manage* (=how we'll buy the things we need) *now that Keith's lost his job.* 2 to direct or control a business and the people who work in it: *I spent 16 years managing a hotel in Wilmington.* 3 SPOKEN HUMOROUS to do something that causes problems: *The kids managed to spill paint all over the carpet.*

**man·age·a·ble** /'mænɪdʒəbəl/ *adj* easy to control or deal with: *My hair's more manageable since I had it cut.*

**man·age·ment** /'mænɪdʒmənt/ *n* 1 [U] the act or process of controlling and organizing the work of a company or organization and the people who work for it: *He studied Business Management.* 2 [singular, U] the people who are in charge of controlling and organizing a company or organization: *The management has agreed to talk with our union.* | *There are several jobs open at management level.*

**man·ag·er** /'mænɪdʒə/ *n* someone who directs the work of something such as a business, a sports team, an actor etc.: *That meal was terrible - I want to speak to the manager!* | *the manager of the Boston Red Sox*

**man·a·ge·ri·al** /ˌmænə'dʒɪriəl/ *adj* relating to the job of being a manager: *good managerial skills*

**Man·da·rin** /'mændərɪn/ *n* [U] the official language of China

**man·date** /'mændeɪt/ *n* FORMAL 1 the right or power that a government has to do something, given by the people in an election: *The party has been given a mandate to raise taxes.* 2 an official command given to a person or organization to do something −**mandate** *v* [T]

**man·da·to·ry** /'mændəˌtɔri/ *adj* something that is mandatory must be done: *mandatory safety inspections*

**mane** /meɪn/ *n* the long hair on the back of a horse's neck, or around the face and neck of a male lion

**ma·neu·ver¹** /mə'nuvə/ *n* a skillful movement or carefully planned action, especially to avoid something or go around it: *basic skiing maneuvers* −see also MANEUVERS

M

**maneuver²** *v* [I,T] to move or turn skillfully, or to move or turn something skillfully: *It was hard to maneuver the piano through the door.| The car behind me was so close, I didn't have room to maneuver.*

**ma·neu·ver·a·ble** /mə'nuvərəbəl/ *adj* easy to move or turn: *a very maneuverable car* –**maneuverability** /mə,nuvrə'bɪləti/ *n* [U]

**ma·neu·vers** /mə'nuvərz/ *n* [plural] a military exercise like a battle used for training soldiers

**mange** /meɪndʒ/ *n* [U] a skin disease of animals that makes them lose small areas of fur –**mangy** *adj*

**man·ger** /'meɪndʒɚ/ *n* a long open container that horses, cows etc. eat from

**man·gle** /'mæŋgəl/ *v* [T] to damage something badly by crushing or twisting it: *The car was badly mangled in the accident.*

**man·go** /'mæŋgoʊ/ *n* a sweet juicy tropical fruit with a large seed

**man·grove** /'mæŋgroʊv/ *n* a tropical tree that grows in or near water and grows new roots from its branches

**man·han·dle** /'mæn,hændl/ *v* [T] to move someone or something roughly, using force: *She complained that she had been manhandled by the police.*

**man·hole** /'mænhoʊl/ *n* a hole on the surface of a road covered by a lid, that people go down to examine pipes, wires etc.

**man·hood** /'mænhʊd/ *n* [U] **1** the qualities that people think a man should have: *He feels the remark is an insult to his manhood* **2** the state of being a man rather than a boy: *The tribe performs special ceremonies when the boys reach manhood.*

**man·hunt** /'mænhʌnt/ *n* an organized search, usually for a criminal

**ma·ni·a** /'meɪniə/ *n* **1** a very strong desire for something or interest in something, that changes your behavior: *a **mania for** driving fast cars* **2** TECHNICAL a type of mental illness in which someone is extremely excited and active

**ma·ni·ac** /'meɪni,æk/ *n* INFORMAL **1** someone who is not responsible and behaves in a stupid or dangerous way: *He drives like a maniac.* **2** someone who has such a strong desire for something that it makes him/her very dangerous: *a dangerous sex maniac*

**ma·ni·a·cal** /mə'naɪəkəl/ *adj* behaving like you are crazy: *maniacal laughter*

**man·ic** /'mænɪk/ *adj* behaving in a very excited and often anxious way: *We were feeling really manic after the exam.*

**man·i·cure** /'mæni,kyʊr/ *n* [C,U] a treatment for the hands and FINGERNAILS that includes cleaning, cutting etc. –**manicure** *v* [T] –**manicurist** *n*

**man·i·fest¹** /'mænə,fɛst/ *v* FORMAL to become easy to see: *The disease can **manifest** itself in many ways.*

**manifest²** *adj* FORMAL plain and easy to see: *a manifest error in his judgment* –**manifestly** *adv*

**man·i·fes·ta·tion** /,mænəfə'steɪʃən/ *n* [C,U] a very clear sign that a particular situation or feeling exists: *These latest riots are a clear manifestation of growing unhappiness.*

**man·i·fes·to** /,mænə'fɛstoʊ/ *n* a written statement by a group, especially a political group, saying what it thinks and intends to do: *the Communist manifesto*

**man·i·fold** /'mænə,foʊld/ *adj* FORMAL many, and of different kinds: *The problems facing the government are manifold.*

**ma·nil·a en·ve·lope** /mə,nɪlə 'ɛnvəloʊp/ *n* an envelope made of strong brown paper

**ma·nip·u·late** /mə'nɪpyə,leɪt/ *v* [T] **1** to make someone do exactly what you want by deceiving or influencing him/her: *I don't like the way he manipulates people.* **2** to skillfully handle, control, or move something –**manipulation** /mə,nɪpyə'leɪʃən/ *n* [U]

**ma·nip·u·la·tive** /mə'nɪpyələtɪv/ *adj* good at controlling or deceiving people to get what you want: *a manipulative person* –**manipulator** /mə'nɪpyə,leɪtɚ/ *n*

**man·kind** /,mæn'kaɪnd/ *n* [U] all humans, considered as a group: *the worst war in the history of mankind* –see usage note at MAN¹

**man·ly** /'mænli/ *adj* having qualities such as strength or courage that are considered to be typical of a man –**manliness** *n* [U]

**man-made** /,. '. ◄/ *adj* made of substances such as plastic that are not natural: *man-made fibers*

**manned** /mænd/ *adj* controlled or operated by people: *a manned space flight* –opposite UN-MANNED

**man·ne·quin** /'mænəkən/ *n* a model of a human body used for showing clothes

**man·ner** /'mænɚ/ *n* **1** [singular] FORMAL the way in which something is done or happens: *The disease is usually treated **in this manner**.* **2** [singular] the way in which someone talks or behaves with other people: *Caleb has a pleasant manner.* **3** **all manner of** FORMAL many different kinds of things or people –see also MAN-NERS

**man·nered** /'mænɚd/ *adj* **1** **well-mannered/bad-mannered** polite or not polite to other people: *a bad-mannered old man* **2** DISAPPROVING relating to behavior that seems unnatural because it is only done to impress people: *a mannered way of talking*

**man·ner·ism** /'mænə,rɪzəm/ *n* [C,U] a way of speaking, behaving, moving etc. that is typical of a particular person or group of people: *Some of his mannerisms are exactly like his father's.*

**man·ners** /'mænɚz/ *n* [plural] polite ways of behaving in social situations: *Her children have such **good manners**.*

**man·nish** /'mænɪʃ/ *adj* a woman who is mannish looks or behaves like a man

**man·or** /'mænɚ/ *n* a large country house with a large area of land around it

**man·pow·er** /'mæn,paʊɚ/ *n* [U] all the workers available to do a particular type of work: *We don't have enough manpower right now to start the project.*

**man·sion** /'mænʃən/ *n* a very large house

**man·slaugh·ter** /'mæn,slɔtɚ/ *n* [U] LAW the crime of killing someone without intending to −compare MURDER¹

**man·tel** /'mæntl/, **man·tel·piece** /'mæntl,pis/ *n* the shelf above a FIREPLACE

**man·tle** /'mæntl/ *n* **1 take on/assume/wear the mantle of** to accept or have a particular duty or responsibility: *He assumed the mantle of leadership when the Prime Minister died.* **2 a mantle of snow/darkness etc.** LITERARY something that covers a surface or area **3** TECHNICAL the part of the inside of the earth that surrounds its center

**man·tra** /'mɑntrə/ *n* a repeated word or sound used as a prayer or to help people MEDITATE

**man·u·al¹** /'mænyuəl/ *adj* **1** involving the use of the hands: *manual skills* **2** using human power or skill, not electricity, machines etc.: *a manual pump* −**manually** *adv*

**manual²** *n* a book that gives instructions about how to do something such as use a machine: *a computer manual*

**manual la·bor** /,... '../ *n* [U] work done with your hands that does not need a lot of skill

**man·u·fac·ture¹** /,mænyə'fæktʃɚ/ *v* [T] to use machines to make goods, usually in large numbers: *I work for a company that manufactures aircraft engine parts.*

**manufacture²** *n* [U] FORMAL the process of making goods usually in large numbers

**man·u·fac·tur·er** /,mænyə'fæktʃərɚ/ *n* a company that makes goods usually in large numbers: *the world's largest shoe manufacturer*

**man·u·fac·tur·ing** /,mænyə'fæktʃərɪŋ/ *n* [U] the process of making goods in factories

**ma·nure** /mə'nʊɚ/ *n* [U] waste matter from animals that is put into the soil to produce better crops

**man·u·script** /'mænyə,skrɪpt/ *n* **1** a book or piece of writing before it is printed: *She sent a 350 page manuscript to the publisher.* **2** an old book written by hand before printing was invented: *an ancient Chinese manuscript*

**man·y** /'mɛni/ *quantifier, pron* **more, most** **1** used in formal English and in questions or negatives to mean a large number of people or things: *Many animals do not eat meat.* | *How many people are in your class?* | *There aren't many* (=are not many) *tickets left.* | *Many of our teachers are Japanese.* | *I've eaten too many doughnuts* (=more than you should) *already!* | *Why did you bring so many* (=such a large number of) *pencils?* **2 as many** the same number: *There weren't as many people at the meeting as we had hoped.* **3 a good/great many** FORMAL a large number: *A great many men died in that battle.* −see usage note at MUCH¹ −see study note on page 466

**map¹** /mæp/ *n* a drawing of an area or country showing rivers, roads, cities etc: *a map of Texas*

**map²** *v* **-pped, -pping** [T] to make a map of a particular area: *a device used to map the ocean floor*

**map sth ↔ out** *phr v* [T] to plan something carefully: *The UN mapped out a plan to rebuild the country.*

**ma·ple** /'meɪpəl/ *n* [C,U] a tree in northern countries that has leaves with many points, or the wood from this tree

**mar** /mɑr/ *v* **-rred, -rring** [T] to make something less attractive or enjoyable; SPOIL: *The table had been marred by cigarette burns.*

**mar·a·thon¹** /'mærə,θɑn/ *n* a race in which competitors run 26 miles and 385 yards

**marathon²** *adj* continuing for a very long time: *a marathon session of Congress*

**ma·raud·ing** /mə'rɔdɪŋ/ *adj* searching for something to kill, steal, or destroy: *marauding soldiers*

**mar·ble** /'mɑrbəl/ *n* **1** [U] a hard white rock that can be polished and used for building, STATUEs etc.: *a marble floor* **2** a small colored glass ball

**March** /mɑrtʃ/ *written abbreviation* **Mar.** *n* the third month of the year −see usage note at JANUARY

**march**

Their marching band marched in the parade.

**march¹** *v* [I] **1** to walk with firm regular steps like a soldier: *The Union army marched across the field.* **2** to walk quickly because you are angry or determined: *She marched out of the room without looking at us.* **3** to walk somewhere in a large group to protest about something: *The group plans to march on the White House next week.*

**march²** *n* **1** an organized event in which many people walk together to protest about something: *a civil rights march* **2** the act of walking with firm regular steps like a soldier **3** a piece of music with a regular beat for soldiers to MARCH to

**march·ing band** /'.. ,./ *n* a group of musicians who march while they play instruments

M

**Mar·di Gras** /'mɑrdi ˌgrɑ/ *n* [singular] the day before Lent, or the music, dancing etc. that celebrate this day

**mare** /mɛr/ *n* a female horse or DONKEY

**mar·ga·rine** /'mɑrdʒərɪn/ *n* [U] a yellow food often used instead of butter

**mar·gin** /'mɑrdʒɪn/ *n* **1** the empty space at the side of a printed page: *I wrote some notes in the margin.* **2** the difference in the number of votes, points etc. that exists between the winners and the losers of an election or competition: *The democrats won by a wide margin.* (=by a lot of votes) **3 margin of error** the degree to which a calculation can be wrong without affecting the final results **4** ⇨ PROFIT MARGIN

**mar·gin·al** /'mɑrdʒənl/ *adj* small in importance or amount: *Doctors only had marginal success in fighting the virus.* —**marginally** *adv*

**mar·i·jua·na** /ˌmærə'wɑnə/ *n* [U] a drug in the form of dried leaves that people smoke

**ma·ri·na** /mə'rinə/ *n* an area of water where people pay to keep their boats

**mar·i·nate** /'mærəˌneɪt/, **mar·i·nade** /ˌmærə'neɪd, 'mærəˌneɪd/ *v* [T] to put meat or fish in a mixture of oil, wine, SPICES etc. before you cook it —**marinade** *n*

**ma·rine**[1] /mə'rin/ *adj* relating to the sea: *marine life*

**marine**[2] *n* someone who is in the MARINES

**mar·i·ner** /'mærənɚ/ *n* LITERARY a sailor

**Ma·rines** /mə'rinz/, **Marine Corps** /ˌ.ˈ. ˌ./ *n* [U] the military organization of the US consisting of soldiers who work on ships

**mar·i·o·nette** /ˌmæriə'nɛt/ *n* a toy that looks like a person, animal etc. that is moved by pulling strings attached to its body —compare PUPPET

**mar·i·tal** /'mærətl/ *adj* relating to marriage: *marital problems*

**mar·i·time** /'mærəˌtaɪm/ *adj* **1** relating to the sea or ships: *maritime trade* **2** near the sea: *the maritime provinces*

**mark**[1] /mɑrk/ *v* [T] **1** to make a sign, shape, or word using a pen or pencil: *Check the envelopes that are marked "urgent" first.* **2** to show where something is: *The grave is marked by a stone cross.* **3** to represent the fact that something has happened or is true: *This year marks the company's 50th anniversary.* **4** if a teacher marks a test, paper etc., s/he corrects mistakes and gives it a grade **5** to make a mark on something in a way that spoils or damages it: *The heels of his boots had marked the floor.*

**mark** sth ↔ **down** *phr v* [T] to reduce the price of things that are being sold: *All items in the store have been marked down for one week only.* —see also MARKDOWN

**mark** sth ↔ **up** *phr v* [T] to increase the price of an item in order to sell it for more than you paid for it: *We could mark the prices up a little and still be competitive.* —see also MARKUP

**mark**[2] *n*

**1** ▶DIRTY SPOT◀ a spot or small dirty area on something that spoils its appearance: *What are these black marks on the couch?*

**2** ▶DAMAGE◀ a small area of something or on someone that has been damaged: *He had teeth marks* (=marks made by teeth) *on his arm.*

**3** ▶WRITING◀ a sign or shape that is written or printed: *She made a mark on the map to show where her house was.*

**4 make your mark** to become successful or famous: *Muis made his mark as a leader, journalist, and novelist.*

**5 a mark of** a sign that something is true or exists: *We'd like to give you this gift as a mark of our respect.*

**6 off the mark/wide of the mark** not correct: *My estimate was way off the mark.*

**7 on your mark, get set, go!** SPOKEN said in order to start a race

**8** a particular type of car, machine etc.: *a Lincoln Mark V*

**mark·down** /'mɑrkdaʊn/ *n* a reduction in the price of something: *Huge markdowns on all stock!*

**marked** /mɑrkt/ *adj* very easy to notice: *There has been a marked increase in crime in the last year.* —**markedly** /'mɑrkɪdli/ *adv*

**mark·er** /'mɑrkɚ/ *n* **1** an object, sign etc. that shows the position of something: *a marker at the edge of the football field* **2** a large pen with a thick point

**mar·ket**[1] /'mɑrkɪt/ *n*

**1** ▶PLACE TO SELL◀ an area outside where people buy and sell goods, food etc.: *We buy all our vegetables from the farmer's market.* —compare SUPERMARKET

**2 the market** ⇨ STOCK MARKET

**3 on the market** available for someone to buy: *That house has been on the market for a year now.*

**4** ▶COUNTRY/AREA◀ a particular country or area where a company sells its goods: *Is China the company's biggest overseas market?*

**5** ▶BUYERS◀ the number of people who want to buy something: *The market for used cars in the US seems to be getting smaller.*

**6 be in the market for** to be interested in buying something: *Are you in the market for a new boat?*

**7 a buyer's/seller's market** a time when it is better for buyers because prices are low, or better for sellers because prices are high

**market**[2] *v* [T] to try to persuade someone to buy something by advertising it in a particular way: *The game is being marketed as a learning toy.* —**marketer** *n*

**mar·ket·a·ble** /'mɑrkɪtəbəl/ *adj* marketable goods, skills etc. are easy to sell —**marketability** /ˌmɑrkɪtə'bɪləti/ *n* [U]

**mar·ket·ing** /ˈmɑrkɪtɪŋ/ *n* [U] the activity of deciding how to advertise a product, what price to charge for it etc., or the type of job in which you do this: *new marketing strategy* | *Reed works in marketing.*

**mar·ket·place** /ˈmɑrkɪtˌpleɪs/ *n* **1** **the marketplace** the business of buying and selling goods in competition with other companies **2** ⇨ MARKET[1]

**mark·ing** /ˈmɑrkɪŋ/ *n* [C usually plural] the colored shapes, patterns etc. on something such as an animal: *a cat with black and gray markings*

**marks·man** /ˈmɑrksmən/ *n* someone who can shoot a gun very well

**mark·up** /ˈmɑrk-ʌp/ *n* an increase in the price of something: *The usual markup is 20%.*

**mar·ma·lade** /ˈmɑrməˌleɪd/ *n* [U] a JAM made with fruit such as oranges

**ma·roon[1]** /məˈrun/ *n* [U] a very dark red-brown color –**maroon** *adj*

**maroon[2]** *v* **be marooned** to be left in a place where there are no people or from which you cannot escape: *The sailors were marooned on an island for 14 weeks.*

**mar·quee** /mɑrˈki/ *n* a large sign above a theater that gives the name of the movie or play

**mar·riage** /ˈmærɪdʒ/ *n* **1** the relationship between two people who are married: *a long and happy marriage* **2** [U] the state of being married: *He is not interested in marriage.*

**mar·riage·a·ble** /ˈmærɪdʒəbəl/ *adj* OLD-FASHIONED suitable for marriage

**mar·ried** /ˈmærid/ *adj* having a husband or a wife: *Are you married or single?* –see also MARRY

**mar·row** /ˈmæroʊ/ *n* the soft substance in the hollow center of bones

**mar·ry** /ˈmæri/ *v* **1** [I,T] to become someone's husband or wife: *When are you going to get married?* | *Tony is married to my sister.* ✗DON'T SAY "married with." ✗ **2** [T] to perform the ceremony at which two people get married: *Rabbi Feingold will marry us.*

 **marry into** sth *phr v* [T] to join a family by marrying someone who belongs to it

**Mars** /mɑrz/ *n* [singular] a small red PLANET, fourth from the sun

**marsh** /mɑrʃ/ *n* [C,U] an area of low ground that is soft and wet –**marshy** *adj*

**mar·shal[1]** /ˈmɑrʃəl/ *n* the officer in charge of a city's police or fire fighting department: *the fire marshal*

**marshal[2]** *v* [T] **marshal your arguments/ forces etc.** to organize your facts, people etc. so that they are most effective

**marsh·mal·low** /ˈmɑrʃˌmɛloʊ/ *n* [C,U] a soft white food made of sugar

**mar·su·pi·al** /mɑrˈsupiəl/ *n* an animal such as

a KANGAROO that carries its babies in a pocket of skin on its body

**mart** /mɑrt/ *n* an abbreviation of MARKET

**mar·tial** /ˈmɑrʃəl/ *adj* related to war or the army

**martial art** /ˌ.. ˈ./ *n* a sport such as KARATE in which you fight using your hands and feet

**martial law** /ˌ.. ˈ./ *n* [U] a situation in which the army controls a city, country etc.

**Mar·tian** /ˈmɑrʃən/ *n* an imaginary creature from Mars

**Mar·tin Lu·ther King Day** /ˌmɑrtˈn ˌluθəˈkɪŋ ˌdeɪ/ *n* an American holiday on the third Monday in January to remember the day that Martin Luther King Jr. was born

**mar·tyr[1]** /ˈmɑrtɚ/ *n* **1** someone who tries to make people feel sympathy by talking about how difficult his/her life is **2** someone who dies for his/her religious or political beliefs, and whose death makes people believe more strongly in those beliefs

**martyr[2]** *v* **be martyred** to become a MARTYR by dying for your religious or political beliefs

**mar·tyr·dom** /ˈmɑrtɚdəm/ *n* [U] the death or suffering of a MARTYR

**mar·vel[1]** /ˈmɑrvəl/ *v* [I,T] to feel surprise and admiration for the quality of something: *We marveled at the technology involved in creating such a tiny computer.*

**marvel[2]** *n* something or someone that makes you MARVEL: *Laser surgery is one of the marvels of modern medicine.*

**mar·vel·ous** /ˈmɑrvələs/ *adj* extremely good, enjoyable, and sometimes surprising: *a marvelous book by Sue Grafton*

**Marx·is·m** /ˈmɑrkˌsɪzəm/ *n* [U] a political system based on Karl Marx's ideas that explains the changes in history as the result of the struggle between social classes

**Marx·ist** /ˈmɑrksɪst/ *adj* relating to MARXISM –**Marxist** *n*

**masc** the written abbreviation of MASCULINE

**mas·car·a** /mæˈskærə/ *n* [U] a dark substance that you use to color your EYELASHes

**mas·cot** /ˈmæskɑt/ *n* an animal that represents a sports team or organization, and brings good luck

**mas·cu·line** /ˈmæskyəlɪn/ *adj* **1** having qualities that are considered to be typical of men: *a masculine voice* **2** TECHNICAL in grammar, a masculine noun or pronoun has a form that means it relates to a male, such as "widower" or "him" –compare FEMININE

---

**USAGE NOTE** masculine, feminine, male, female

Use **masculine** to talk about things that people think are typical of men: *a masculine voice.* Use **feminine** to talk about things that people think are typical of women: *a feminine voice.* Use **male** and

M

**female** to describe the sex of a person or animal: *Is your cat male or female?*

**mas·cu·lin·i·ty** /ˌmæskyəˈlɪnəti/ *n* [U] qualities that are considered to be typical of men −compare FEMININITY

**mash** /mæʃ/ *v* [T] to crush something, such as food that has been cooked, until it is soft: *Mash the potatoes in a bowl.*

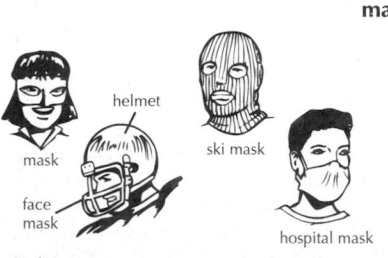

mask

helmet

mask

ski mask

face mask

hospital mask

**mask¹** /mæsk/ *n* **1** something that covers all or part of your face in order to protect or hide it: *a ski mask | The doctor wore a mask over his mouth and nose.* **2** something that covers your face and has another face painted on it: *a Halloween mask*

**mask²** *v* [T] keep something from being seen, heard, noticed etc: *The horrible smell was barely masked by the cheap perfume.*

**masked** /mæskt/ *adj* wearing a MASK

**mask·ing tape** /ˈmæskɪŋ ˌteɪp/ *n* [U] a special type of TAPE, made of paper

**mas·och·ism** /ˈmæsəˌkɪzəm/ *n* [U] sexual behavior in which you get pleasure from being hurt −**masochistic** /ˌmæsəˈkɪstɪk/ *adj*

**ma·son** /ˈmeɪsən/ *n* **1** someone whose job is cutting stone into pieces to be used in buildings **2 Mason** a man who belongs to a secret society, in which each member helps the other members to become successful

**ma·son·ry** /ˈmeɪsənri/ *n* [U] brick or stone from which a building or wall is made

**mas·quer·ade¹** /ˌmæskəˈreɪd/ *n* a dance or party where people wear MASKs and unusual clothes

**masquerade²** *v* [I] to pretend to be someone or something else

**Mass** /mæs/ *n* **1** [C,U] the main religious ceremony in the Roman Catholic Church **2** a piece of music written to be played at a Mass

**mass¹** *n* **1** a large amount or quantity of something: *The train wreck was a mass of twisted steel.* **2** [singular] a large crowd: *A mass of people were marching in the street.* **3** [U] TECHNICAL the amount of material in something: *the mass of a star* −see also MASSES

**mass²** *adj* involving or intended for a large number of people: *mass communication*

**mass³** *v* [I,T] to gather together in a large group, or to make people or things do this

**mas·sa·cre¹** /ˈmæsəkɚ/ *n* the act of massacring (MASSACRE) people: *a bloody massacre*

**massacre²** *v* [T] to kill a lot of people, especially people who cannot defend themselves: *In the middle ages whole villages were massacred by the king's soldiers.*

**mas·sage¹** /məˈsɑʒ, -ˈsɑdʒ/ *n* [C,U] the action of pressing and rubbing someone's body with your hands to reduce pain or make him/her relax: *Larry gave me a massage to help my back.*

**massage²** *v* [T] to give someone a MASSAGE

**massage par·lor** /ˈ. ˌ../ *n* **1** a place where people pay to have sex **2** a place where people pay to have a MASSAGE

**mass·es** /ˈmæsɪz/ *n* **the masses** [plural] all the ordinary people in a society: *music that appeals to the masses*

**mas·seur** /mæˈsɚ, mə-/ *n* someone who gives MASSAGEs

**mas·seuse** /mæˈsuz, mə-/ *n* a woman who gives MASSAGEs

**mas·sive** /ˈmæsɪv/ *adj* **1** very large, heavy, or powerful: *massive oil reserves beneath the ocean | a massive dog* **2** causing a lot of damage: *Carl had a massive heart attack at the age of 52.* −**massively** *adv*

**mass me·di·a** /ˌ. ˈ.../ *n* **the mass media** all the people and organizations that provide information and news for the public

**mass mur·der·er** /ˌ. ˈ.../ *n* someone who has murdered a lot of people

**mass-pro·duce** /ˌ. .ˈ./ *v* [T] to make a large number of goods using machinery so that each one can be sold cheaply: *The computers will be mass-produced in Korea.* −**mass production** /ˌ. .ˈ./ *n* [U]

**mass-pro·duced** /ˌ. .ˈ./ *adj* made in large numbers using machinery so that each object can be sold cheaply: *manufacturers of mass-produced cars*

**mast** /mæst/ *n* a tall pole on which the sails of a ship are hung

**mas·ter¹** /ˈmæstɚ/ *n* **1** OLD-FASHIONED a man who has authority over servants or animals: *the master of the house | the dog's master* **2** someone who is very skillful at doing a particular job, activity etc.: *a master of kung fu* **3** a document, record etc. from which other copies are made

**master²** *v* [T] to learn something so well that you understand it completely and have no difficulty with it: *It only took him a few months to master French.*

**master³** *adj* **1 master copy/list/tape etc.** the original copy, list etc. from which other copies are made **2 master plumber/chef etc.** someone who is very skillful at doing a particular job **3** most important or main: *the master bedroom*

**mas·ter·ful** /ˈmæstɚfəl/ *adj* skillfully done, made, or dealt with: *a masterful performance*

M

**master key** /ˌ.. ˈ./ *n* a key that will open all the doors in a building

**mas·ter·mind**[1] /ˈmæstəˌmaɪnd/ *n* [singular] someone who organizes a complicated plan, especially a criminal plan: *Corran was the mastermind behind the hijacking.*

**mastermind**[2] *v* [T] to think of and organize a complicated plan

**Master of Arts** /ˌ.. ˈ./ *n* ⇨ M.A.

**master of cer·e·mo·nies** /ˌ.. . ˈ..../ *n* ⇨ EMCEE

**Master of Sci·ence** /ˌ.. ˈ../ *n* ⇨ M.S.

**mas·ter·piece** /ˈmæstəˌpis/ *n* a work of art, piece of writing, music etc. that is of the highest quality compared to others of its kind

**master's de·gree** /ˈ.. ˌ../ **master's** *n* a university degree that you can get by studying for two years after your first degree

**mas·ter·y** /ˈmæstəri/ *n* [U] **1** complete control of a situation or complete understanding of a subject: *Early explorers could not match the Inuit mastery of the seas.* **2** thorough understanding or great skill

**mas·tur·bate** /ˈmæstəˌbeɪt/ *v* [I,T] to rub your sexual organs in order to get sexual pleasure −**masturbation** /ˌmæstəˈbeɪʃən/ *n* [U]

**mat** /mæt/ *n* **1** a small piece of thick material that covers part of a floor **2** a large piece of thick soft material used in some sports for people to fall on

**mat·a·dor** /ˈmætəˌdɔr/ *n* someone who fights and tries to kill a BULL during a BULLFIGHT

**match**[1] /mætʃ/ *n* **1** a short wooden stick that produces a flame when it is rubbed against a rough surface: *a box of matches* | *He lit a match so we could see.* **2** a game or sports event: *a tennis match* **3** [singular] something that is the same color or pattern as something else: *These shoes are a perfect match for the hat.* **4 be no match for** to be much less strong, fast etc. than an opponent: *Our defense was no match for theirs.*

**match**[2] *v* **1** [I,T] if one thing matches another, or if two things match, they look good together because they have a similar color, pattern etc.: *We found carpet to match the curtains in this room.* **2** [I,T] to be the same or look the same as something else: *The story she told about the accident doesn't match her husband's story.* | *Do these socks match?* **3** [T] to find something that is similar or related to something else: *Match the words on the left with the meanings on the right.* **4** [T] to be of the same quality or amount as someone or something else: *No one can match Rogers' speed on the football field.* **5** [T] to provide something that is suit-

able for a particular situation: *We'll try to help you find a job to match your skills.*

**match up** *phr v* [I] **1** to belong with or fit together with something: *The edges of the cloth don't match up.* **2** to be of a similar level or of similar quality as something: *If the product doesn't match up to our standards, we don't sell it.*

**match·book** /ˈmætʃbʊk/ *n* a small piece of thick folded paper containing paper matches

**match·box** /ˈmætʃbɑks/ *n* a small box containing matches

**match·ing** /ˈmætʃɪŋ/ *adj* having the same color, style, pattern etc. as something else: *a sapphire necklace with matching earrings*

**match·less** /ˈmætʃlɪs/ *adj* FORMAL better than all other things of the same kind

**match·mak·er** /ˈmætʃˌmeɪkə/ *n* someone who is always trying to find suitable people for his/her friends to have romantic relationships with −**matchmaking** *n* [U]

**mate**[1] /meɪt/ *n* **1** one of a pair of objects: *I can't find the mate to this glove.* **2** HUMOROUS someone's wife, husband, or sexual partner: *He's still searching for the perfect mate.* **3** the sexual partner of an animal −see also CLASSMATE, ROOMMATE

**mate**[2] *v* **1** [I] if animals mate they have sex to produce babies: *Most birds mate in the spring.* **2** [T] to put animals together so that they will have sex and produce babies

**ma·te·ri·al**[1] /məˈtɪriəl/ *n* **1** [C,U] cloth used for making things like clothes, curtains etc.: *Mom bought some velvet material for the dress.* −see usage note at CLOTH **2** [C,U] things such as wood, plastic, paper etc. from which things can be made: *building materials* **3** [U] information or ideas used in books, movies etc.: *The director added some new material to the play.*

**material**[2] *adj* **1** relating to someone's money, possessions, living conditions etc.: *the material comforts that money can buy* **2** relating to the real world or to physical objects, rather than religious or SPIRITUAL things: *the material world* **3** LAW very important and needing to be considered when making a decision: *a material witness for the defense*

**ma·te·ri·al·ism** /məˈtɪriəˌlɪzəm/ *n* [U] DISAPPROVING the belief that getting money and possessions is the most important thing in life −**materialist** *adj* −**materialistic** /məˌtɪriəˈlɪstɪk/ *adj*

**ma·te·ri·al·ize** /məˈtɪriəˌlaɪz/ *v* [I] **1** if a possible event or plan materializes, it happens: *His dream of building a hospital failed to materialize.* (=did not happen) **2** to appear suddenly in a way that is strange or unexpected: *A man materialized from the shadows.*

**ma·ter·nal** /məˈtɜnl/ *adj* **1** typical of the way a mother feels or acts: *maternal feelings*

match

These socks don't match.

M

**ma·ter·ni·ty** /mə'tɚnəti/ *adj* relating to a woman who is PREGNANT, or who has had a baby, or to the time when she is pregnant: *maternity clothes*

**maternity leave** /.'... ,./ *n* [U] time that a woman is allowed away from her job when she has a baby

**maternity ward** /.'... ,./ *n* a department in a hospital where a woman is cared for after having a baby

**math** /mæθ/ *n* [U] INFORMAL the study or science of numbers and of the structure and measurement of shapes

**math·e·mat·i·cal** /,mæθ'mætɪkəl/ *adj* related to or using mathematics: *a mathematical equation*

**math·e·ma·ti·cian** /,mæθmə'tɪʃən/ *n* someone who studies or teaches mathematics

**math·e·mat·ics** /,mæθ'mætɪks, ,mæθə-/ *n* [U] FORMAL ⇨ MATH

**mat·i·née** /,mæt⁻n'eɪ/ *n* a performance of a play or movie in the afternoon

**ma·tri·arch** /'meɪtri,ɑrk/ *n* a woman who leads or controls a family or social group –compare PATRIARCH –**matriarchal** /,meɪtri-'ɑrkəl/ *adj*

**ma·tri·ar·chy** /'meɪtri,ɑrki/ *n* [C,U] a social system that is led or controlled by women

**ma·tric·u·late** /mə'trɪkyə,leɪt/ *v* [I] FORMAL to officially start a course of study at a university –**matriculation** /mə,trɪkyə'leɪʃən/ *n* [U]

**mat·ri·mo·ny** /'mætrə,moʊni/ *n* [U] FORMAL the state of being married –**matrimonial** /,mætrə'moʊniəl/ *adj*

**ma·tron** /'meɪtrən/ *n* **1** a woman who is in charge of women and children in a school or prison **2** LITERARY an older married woman

**ma·tron·ly** /'meɪtrənli/ *adj* used when politely describing a woman who is slightly older and fatter than what is considered attractive

**matt, mat, matte** /mæt/ *adj* matt paint, color, or photographs are not shiny

**mat·ted** /'mætɪd/ *adj* matted hair or fur is twisted and stuck together

**mat·ter¹** /'mætɚ/ *n*
**1** ▶SUBJECT/SITUATION◀ a subject or situation that you have to think about or deal with, often one that causes problems: *Several important matters were discussed at the meeting.*|*Whether he is guilty is **a matter for** the jury to decide.*|*financial matters*|*It will only **make matters worse** if you complain.*
**2 sth is a matter of money/principle etc** a decision or situation that involves money etc.: *The planning is finished. Now it's just a matter of money and time.*
**3 sth is a matter of opinion** used to say that people have different opinions about

something
**4 a matter of seconds/days/inches etc.** only a few seconds, days, inches etc.: *The bullet missed him by a matter of inches.*
**5 no matter how/where/what etc.** said when a situation does not change even though things happen that could change it: *No matter how hard she tried, she couldn't get the door open.*
**6 for that matter** said when what you have said about one thing is also true about another: *I don't like him or, for that matter, his girlfriend either!*
**7** ▶SUBSTANCE/THINGS◀ [U]  **a)** TECHNICAL the material that everything in the universe is made of  **b)** things of a particular kind or for a particular use: *waste/vegetable matter*|*reading matter*
**8 it's only/just a matter of time** used in order to say that something will definitely happen even though you cannot say exactly when: *It's only a matter of time, until he is too old to live alone.*
**9 a matter of life and death** a very dangerous or serious situation

---
SPOKEN PHRASES
**10 what's the matter?** used in order to ask someone why s/he is upset, angry etc.: *What's the matter? Why are you crying?*
**11 as a matter of fact** said when giving a surprising or unexpected answer to a question or statement: *"Have you ever been to Paris?" "As a matter of fact I just came from there."*
**12 there's something/nothing the matter with** said when there is or is not a problem with something: *There's something the matter with the TV - the picture is bad.*
---

**matter²** *v* [I] **1** to be important, or to have an effect on what happens: *Money is the only thing that **matters to** him.*|*"Does it matter which road I take?" "No, it's the same distance."*
**2 it doesn't matter** SPOKEN  **a)** used in order to say that you do not care which one of two things you have: *"Do you want tea or coffee?" "Oh, it doesn't matter."*  **b)** used in order to tell someone you are not angry or upset: *"I'm sorry - I didn't realize you were eating dinner." "It doesn't matter!"*

**matter-of-fact** /,.. . '.◂/ *adj* showing no strong emotions when you are talking about something: *The doctor was very matter-of-fact when he explained the problem.* –**matter-of-factly** *adv*

**mat·ting** /'mætɪŋ/ *n* [U] strong rough material used for covering a floor

**mat·tress** /'mætrɪs/ *n* the soft part of a bed that you lie on: *a king-size mattress*

**ma·ture¹** /mə'tʃʊr, mə'tʊr/ *adj* **1** behaving in a reasonable way like an adult: *She's young, but she's very mature for her age.* **2** fully grown or developed: *Meat from mature animals*

**me**

*is often tough.* | *mature wine* −opposite IMMATURE

**mature**[2] *v* [I] **1** to become fully grown or developed: *The fly matures in only seven days.* **2** to begin to behave in a reasonable way like an adult: *Pat's matured a lot since going to college.* **3** if a BOND or POLICY matures, it becomes ready to be paid

**ma·tur·i·ty** /məˈtʃʊrəti, ˈtʊr-/ *n* [U] **1** the quality of behaving in a sensible way like an adult: *He has a lot of maturity for a fifteen year old.* **2** the time when a person, animal, or plant is fully grown or developed: *Rabbits reach maturity in only five weeks.* **3** TECHNICAL the time when a financial arrangement is ready to be paid

**maud·lin** /ˈmɔdlɪn/ *adj* talking or behaving in a sad and silly way; SENTIMENTAL

**maul** /mɔl/ *v* [T] to injure someone by tearing his/her flesh

**mau·so·le·um** /ˌmɔsəˈliəm, -zə-/ *n* a large stone building containing many graves or built over a grave

**mauve** /moʊv/ *n* [U] a pale purple color −**mauve** *adj*

**mav·er·ick** /ˈmævərɪk/ *n* someone who thinks or behaves in a way that is surprising and different from most people: *a political maverick* −**maverick** *adj*

**mawk·ish** /ˈmɔkɪʃ/ *adj* showing too much emotion in a way that is embarrassing −**mawkishly** *adv*

**max**[1] /mæks/ *n* [U] **1** SPOKEN at the most: *It'll cost $50 max.* **2** the written abbreviation for MAXIMUM **3** to the max SLANG to the greatest degree possible

**max**[2] *v*
**max out** *phr v* **max out (on sth)** SLANG to have or do too much of something so that you are tired or bored: *No more chocolate. I maxed out on it last night.*

**max·im** /ˈmæksɪm/ *n* a well-known phrase that shows how to behave in a reasonable way: *"A penny saved is a penny earned" is a maxim.*

**max·i·mize** /ˈmæksəˌmaɪz/ *v* [T] to increase something as much as possible: *We want to maximize the services available to our customers.* −opposite MINIMIZE

**max·i·mum**[1] /ˈmæksəməm/ *adj* being the largest that is possible, allowed, or needed: *The car has a maximum speed of 125 mph.* −opposite MINIMUM[1]

**maximum**[2] *n* the largest number, amount etc. that is possible, allowed, or needed: *"How much tax will I have to pay?" "20% is the maximum you could pay."* −opposite MINIMUM[2]

**May** /meɪ/ *n* the fifth month of the year −see usage note at JANUARY

**may** *modal verb* **1** used in order to talk about what was, is, or will be possible: *It may snow tonight.* | *This may not be enough money.* ✗ DON'T SAY "mayn't." ✗ **2 may I** SPOKEN used in order

to politely ask if you can do or have something: *May I borrow your pen?* | *May I have some more coffee?* **3** FORMAL used in order to allow someone to do something: *You may start writing on your test forms now.* **4 may as well** ⇨ **might as well** (MIGHT[1]) −compare MIGHT[1] −see usage note at PERHAPS −see study note on page 458

**may·be** /ˈmeɪbi/ *adv* **1** used in order to say that something may be true or may happen, but that you are not sure: *Maybe Anna's stuck in traffic.* | *There were 300 or maybe 400 people there.* | *Maybe I'll wear my blue suit.* **2** used in order to make a suggestion: *Maybe Jeff could help you.* −see usage note at PERHAPS

**May Day** /ˈ. ./ *n* [C,U] the first day of May, when LEFT-WING political parties have celebrations, and when people traditionally celebrate the arrival of spring

**may·day** /ˈmeɪdeɪ/ *n* a radio signal used in order to ask for help when a ship or plane is in danger

**may·hem** /ˈmeɪhɛm/ *n* [U] an extremely confused situation in which people are very frightened or excited: *There was complete mayhem after the explosion.*

**may·on·naise** /ˈmeɪəˌneɪz, ˈmæneɪz/ *n* [U] a thick white SAUCE made of egg and oil, often eaten on sandwiches (SANDWICH)

**may·or** /ˈmeɪɚ, mɛr/ *n* someone who is elected to lead the government of a town or city

**maze** /meɪz/ *n* **1** a specially designed system of paths that is difficult to find your way through, or something like this drawn on paper: *We got lost in the maze.* **2** a place that is difficult to find your way through: *a maze of dark hallways* **3** something that is complicated and difficult to understand: *a maze of government rules*

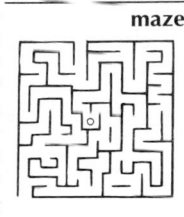
maze

**M.B.A.** *n* Master of Business Administration; a GRADUATE degree that teaches you the skills you need to be in charge of a business

**Mc·Coy** /məˈkɔɪ/ *n* **the real McCoy** INFORMAL something that is real and not a copy: *Paste jewels cost hundreds less than the real McCoy.*

**M.D.** *n* the abbreviation of Doctor of Medicine

**MD** the written abbreviation of Maryland

**ME** the written abbreviation of Maine

**me** /mi/ *pron* **1** the object form of "I": *Cathy called me last night.* | *My parents gave me a necklace for my birthday.* **2 me too** SPOKEN said when you agree with someone: *"I'm hungry!" "Me too."* **3 me neither** SPOKEN said when you agree with a negative statement someone has just made: *"I don't like fruitcake." "Me neither."*

**M**

**mead·ow** /'mɛdoʊ/ *n* a field with wild grass and flowers

**mea·ger** /'migɚ/ *adj* very small in amount: *a meager breakfast*

**meal** /mil/ *n* a particular time when you eat food, or the food that is eaten then: *Would you like wine with your meal?* | *It's important to eat regular meals.* —see also CORNMEAL, OATMEAL

**meal·time** /'miltaɪm/ *n* the usual time for eating a meal

**meal·y-mouthed** /ˌmili 'maʊðd/ *adj* not brave or honest enough to say clearly what you think

**mean¹** /min/ *v* **meant, meant, meaning** [T] **1** to express or have a particular meaning or message: *"What does the word 'Konbanwa' mean?" "It means 'Good Evening.'"* | *The red light means "stop."* ✗DON'T SAY "is meaning." ✗ **2** to intend a particular meaning when you say something: *I didn't mean to sound like I was mad.* | *I said Monday but I meant Tuesday.* ✗DON'T SAY "I am meaning." ✗ **3** to have a particular result: *It's snowing, which means that it will take longer to get there.* ✗DON'T SAY "which is meaning." ✗ **4 mean to do sth** to intend to do something: *I've been meaning to ask you something.* | *He says he didn't mean for her to get hurt.* **5 sb/sth means a lot (to sb)** used in order to say that someone or something is very important or special to someone: *It would mean a lot to your father if you offered to help.* **6 mean business** to be very serious about something such as a threat: *You have to be strict about the rules so they know you mean business.* **7 sth is meant to be** used in order to say that you think a situation was certain to happen: *I'm sure this marriage was meant to be.*

SPOKEN PHRASES

**8 I mean a)** said when you stop to think

about what to say next: *She's just so nice. I mean, she's a really gentle person.* **b)** said when you want to quickly change what you have just said: *She plays the violin, I mean the viola.* **9 I mean it!** said in order to emphasize what you are saying when you are very angry: *Don't ever say that word again, and I mean it!* **10 (Do) you mean ...?** said when you want to check that you understand something: *You mean you want me to call you, or will you call me?* **11 (Do) you know what I mean?** said in order to ask someone if s/he understands you: *I want to go somewhere different on vacation. You know what I mean?* **12 I know what you mean** said in order to show that you understand someone: *"I'm so tired of his complaining." "I know what you mean."* **13 what do you mean? a)** said when you do not understand someone **b)** said when you are very surprised and annoyed by something someone has done: *What do you mean, you sold the car?*

**mean²** *adj* **1** unkind or nasty: *Why do you say such mean things to me?* **2** cruel and having a bad temper: *a mean old man* **3** INFORMAL very good: *Ray plays a mean game of tennis.* **4 no mean** used in order to say that something is very good, or that someone does something very well: *It was no mean achievement for a woman to become a doctor in 1920.* **5** average: *The mean temperature in Akron was 18.2°F this month.*

**mean³** *n* TECHNICAL an average amount, figure, or value: *The mean of 7, 9, and 14 is 10.* —see also MEANS

**me·an·der** /mi'ændɚ/ *v* [I] to move slowly and turn many times: *a meandering stream* —**meanderings** *n* [plural]

**mean·ing** /'minɪŋ/ *n* **1** [C,U] the thing or idea that a word, phrase, or sign represents: *I don't understand the meaning of this word.* **2** [C,U] the idea that someone intends to express when s/he says something, writes a book, makes a film etc.: *There seemed to be very little meaning in the film's violence.* | *The poem could have two meanings.* **3** [U] the quality that makes something seem important and valuable: *Until today, I hadn't realized the full meaning of what had happened.* **4 not know the meaning of** used in order to say that someone has no understanding of a particular situation or feeling: *Those kids don't know the meaning of hard work.*

**mean·ing·ful** /'minɪŋfəl/ *adj* **1** serious, useful, or important: *a meaningful relationship* | *You need a meaningful sample for the experiment to work.* | *Congress hasn't made any meaningful changes to the bill.* **2** easy to understand: *The data isn't very meaningful to anyone but a scientist.* **3 a meaningful look/**

M

smile etc. a look that clearly expresses the way someone feels

**mean·ing·less** /ˈminɪŋlɪs/ adj without any purpose or meaning that you can understand or explain: *Her whole life felt meaningless.*

**means** /minz/ n [plural] **1** a method, system, object etc. that is used as a way of doing something: *We'll use any means we can to raise the money.* | *She took up photography as a means of earning a living.* | *The oil is transported by means of* (=using) *a pipeline.* **2 by all means** said in order to emphasize that someone should do or is allowed to do something: *By all means, drink while you are exercising.* **3 by no means** FORMAL not at all: *The results are by no means certain.* **4 a means to an end** something that you do or use only to achieve a result: *Bev always says her job is just a means to an end.* **5** the money or things that you have that make it possible for you to buy or do things: *They don't have the means to buy a car.* | *a man of means* (=who is rich)

**meant** /ment/ v the past tense and PAST PARTICIPLE of MEAN

**mean·time** /ˈmintaɪm/ n **in the meantime** until something happens, or in the time between two events: *We want to buy a house, but in the meantime we're renting the apartment.*

**mean·while** /ˈminwaɪl/ adv while something else is happening, or in the time between two events: *Chris was gone for hours; meanwhile, she got some work done.*

**mea·sles** /ˈmizəlz/ n **the measles** an infectious illness in which you have a fever and small red spots on your face and body

**mea·sly** /ˈmizli/ adj INFORMAL too small in amount or value: *I only won a measly $5.*

**meas·ur·a·ble** /ˈmɛʒərəbəl/ adj **1** able to be measured: *A manager should set measurable goals.* **2** important or large enough to have an effect: *The changes have not achieved any measurable results.* —**measurably** adv

**meas·ure¹** /ˈmɛʒɚ/ n **1** an official action that is intended to deal with a problem: *Congress passed a measure to control spending today.* **2 a measure of sth** enough to be noticed, but not a large amount: *He ought to be treated with a measure of respect.* **3 take measures** to use your authority in order to do whatever is necessary to achieve an aim: *We have taken measures to limit smoking to one area in the building.* **4 be a measure of sth** FORMAL to be a sign of the importance, strength etc. of something **5** [C,U] a system for measuring weight, length etc. of something, or the unit of weight, length etc. that is used: *The Richter scale is a measure of the strength of earthquakes.* | *The pint is a liquid measure.* **6 for good measure** in addition, so that what you do or give is enough: *Add a little more salt for good measure.*

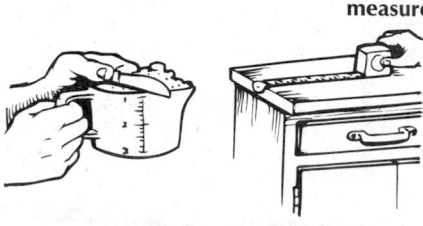

measuring cup                    measuring tape

**measure²** v **1** [T] to find the size, length, or amount of something: *Let's measure the wall to see if the bookshelves will fit.* | *Measure one cup of flour and add it to the mixture.* **2** [T] to judge the importance or value of something: *It's difficult to measure educational success.* **3** [linking verb] to be a particular size, length, or amount: *The table measures four feet by six feet.*

**measure sb/sth against** phr v [T] to judge someone or something by comparing him, her, or it to another person or thing: *All managers should be measured against the same standard.*

**measure up** phr v [I] to be good enough to do a particular job or to reach a particular standard: *The steak didn't measure up to his expectations.*

**meas·ure·ment** /ˈmɛʒəmənt/ n [C,U] the length, height, value etc. of something, or the act of measuring this: *We had to make/take a lot of measurements for the new carpet.*

**meat** /mit/ n [U] the flesh of animals and birds eaten as food: *I don't eat much meat.* —see also **dead meat** (DEAD¹)

---

**USAGE NOTE** meat

The meat from some animals has a different name from the animal itself. For example, the meat from a **cow** is **beef**. The meat from a **pig** is **pork** or **ham**. The meat from a **calf** (a young cow) is **veal**. But the meat from a **lamb** is **lamb**, and for birds and fish we use the same word for the meat and the animal: *They raise chickens and ducks on their farm.* | *Should we have chicken or duck for dinner?*

---

**meat·ball** /ˈmitbɔl/ n a type of food made of very small pieces of meat pressed together into a ball and cooked

**meat·loaf** /ˈmitloʊf/ n [C,U] a dish made from a meat mixture and baked in the shape of a LOAF

**meat·y** /ˈmiti/ adj containing a lot of meat or tasting strongly of meat: *a meaty stew*

**mec·ca** /ˈmɛkə/ n [singular] **1** a place that many people want to visit for a particular reason: *Florence is a mecca for art students.* **2 Mecca** a city in Saudi Arabia which many Muslims visit because it is holy to them

**me·chan·ic** /mɪˈkænɪk/ n someone whose job

M

is to repair vehicles and machinery: *an auto mechanic* – see also MECHANICS

**me·chan·i·cal** /mɪ'kænɪkəl/ *adj* **1** relating to machines, or using power from a machine: *mechanical engineering | a mechanical toy* **2** done or said without thinking, as if you were a machine: *a mechanical answer* –**mechanically** *adv*

**me·chan·ics** /mɪ'kænɪks/ *n* [U] **1** the science that deals with the effects of forces on objects **2** **the mechanics of (doing) sth** the way in which something works or is done: *the mechanics of the stock market*

**mech·a·nism** /'mɛkə,nɪzəm/ *n* **1** the part of a machine that does a particular job: *a car's steering mechanism* **2** a way in which something works or the process by which it is done: *the mechanisms of the brain | a mechanism for controlling the flow of traffic*

**mech·a·nize** /'mɛkə,naɪz/ *v* [I,T] to change a process so that machines do it instead of people

**mech·a·nized** /'mɛkə,naɪzd/ *adj* done by machines, or using machines: *a highly mechanized factory | farming techniques that are completely mechanized*

**med·al** /'mɛdl/ *n* a round flat piece of metal given as a prize to someone who has won a competition or who has done something brave: *an Olympic gold medal*

**med·al·ist** /'mɛdl-ɪst/ *n* someone who has won a MEDAL in a competition: *the 1996 silver medalist*

**me·dal·lion** /mə'dælyən/ *n* a piece of metal like a large coin, worn as jewelry on a chain around the neck

**med·dle** /'mɛdl/ *v* [I] DISAPPROVING to try to influence a situation that does not concern you: *meddling in other countries' affairs* –**meddler** *n*

**med·dle·some** /'mɛdlsəm/ *adj* tending to become involved in other people's private lives when they do not want you to

**me·di·a** /'midiə/ *n* **1** [plural] television, radio, and newspapers: *There's been a lot of media coverage* (=information on television, in newspapers etc.) *of the President's visit.* **2** the plural of MEDIUM – see also MASS MEDIA

**me·di·an** /'midiən/ *n* **1** something that divides a road or HIGHWAY, such as a thin piece of land **2** TECHNICAL the middle number in a set of numbers that are arranged in order

**me·di·ate** /'midi,eɪt/ *v* [I,T] to try to help two groups, countries etc. to stop arguing and make an agreement: *The court had to mediate between Hassel and his neighbors. | mediating a marriage dispute* –**mediator** *n* –**mediation** /,midi'eɪʃən/ *n* [U]

**Med·i·caid** /'mɛdɪ,keɪd/ *n* [U] a system by which the government helps to pay the cost of medical treatment for poor people

**med·i·cal** /'mɛdɪkəl/ *adj* relating to medicine and the treatment of disease or injury: *medical school | families who cannot afford medical care | The man was taken to St. Luke's hospital for medical treatment.* –**medically** *adv*

**Med·i·care** /'mɛdɪ,kɛr/ *n* [U] a system by which the government helps to pay the medical treatment of old people

**med·i·cat·ed** /'mɛdɪ,keɪtɪd/ *adj* containing medicine: *medicated soap/shampoo*

**med·i·ca·tion** /,mɛdɪ'keɪʃən/ *n* [C,U] medicine given to people who are ill: *Has the medication helped? | He's on medication for his heart.*

**me·dic·i·nal** /mə'dɪsənəl/ *adj* helping to cure illness or disease: *Cough drops should be used for medicinal purposes only.*

**med·i·cine** /'mɛdəsən/ *n*

**1** [C,U] a substance used for treating illness: *Remember to **take** your medicine. | Medicines should be kept away from children.* **2** [U] the treatment and study of illnesses and injuries: *She plans to study medicine at Harvard.*

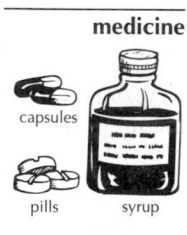

medicine

capsules

pills     syrup

**me·di·e·val** /,mɪd'ivəl, ,mɛ-, ,mi-/ *adj* relating to the MIDDLE AGES: *medieval poetry*

**me·di·o·cre** /,midi'oukə/ *adj* neither good nor bad: *a mediocre book | The food at the cafe was mediocre.* –**mediocrity** /,midi'ɑkrəti/ *n* [U]

**med·i·tate** /'mɛdə,teɪt/ *v* [I] to make yourself feel calm by being silent and still, and thinking only about one thing such as a sound or a simple religious idea –**meditation** /,mɛdə'teɪʃən/ *n* [U]

**med·i·ta·tive** /'mɛdə,teɪtɪv/ *adj* thinking deeply and seriously about something, or showing that you are doing this: *He was in a meditative mood.*

**Med·i·ter·ra·ne·an**[1] /,mɛdətə'reɪniən/ *adj* relating to or coming from the Mediterranean

**Mediterranean**[2] *n* **the Mediterranean** the areas of land surrounding the Mediterranean Sea (=sea between northern Africa and southern Europe), and the islands in it

**me·di·um**[1] /'midiəm/ *adj* of middle size or amount: *"What size do you wear?" "Medium." | Cook the soup over medium heat for 30 minutes. | a man of medium height*

**medium**[2] *n* **1** *plural* **media** a way of communicating or expressing something: *The Internet is a powerful advertising medium.* **2** *plural* **media** the material, paints etc. that an artist uses: *This sculptor's favorite medium is wood.* **3** *plural* **mediums** someone who claims to speak to dead people and receive messages from them

M

**medium-sized** /'... ,./, **medium-size** adj not small, but not large either: *medium-sized apples/cars | a medium-size business*

**med·ley** /'mɛdli/ n **1** tunes from different songs that are played one after the other as a single piece of music: *a medley of folk songs* **2** a mixture of things or people: *a vegetable medley*

**meek** /mik/ adj very quiet and gentle, and not willing to argue –**meekly** adv –**meekness** n [U]

**meet**[1] /mit/ v met, met, meeting
**1** ▸SEE SB FOR THE FIRST TIME◂ [I,T] to see and talk to someone for the first time, or to be introduced to someone: *Mike and Sara met in college. | "Do you know Rick Jones?" "I've never met him."*
**2** ▸BE IN THE SAME PLACE◂ [I,T] to come to the same place as someone else because you have arranged to find him/her there: *Let's meet for lunch tomorrow. | I'll meet you at the bank.*
**3** (it's) nice to meet you SPOKEN said when you meet someone for the first time: *"Paul, this is Jack." "Nice to meet you."*
**4** (it was) nice meeting you SPOKEN used when saying goodbye to someone you have just met for the first time
**5** ▸MEETING◂ [I] to be together in the same place in order to discuss something: *What time does the committee meet?*
**6** meet a need/demand etc. to have or do enough of what is needed, or be good enough to reach a particular standard: *She didn't meet all of the requirements for the job.*
**7** ▸SB ARRIVING◂ [T] to be at an airport, station etc. when someone arrives: *I'm going to meet John's plane.*
**8** ▸JOIN◂ [I,T] to join together at a particular place: *the place where two roads meet*
**9** meet sth head-on to deal with a problem without trying to avoid it
**10** meet (sb) halfway to do some of the things that someone wants, if s/he does some of the things you want: *Democrats plan to meet the governor halfway on welfare cuts.*

**meet up** phr v [I] to meet someone informally in order to do something together: *Let's meet up after the game.*

**meet with** sb/sth phr v [T] **1** to have a meeting with someone: *The President met with European leaders today in Paris.* **2** to get a particular reaction or result: *His proposal met with some criticism.*

**meet**[2] n a sports competition: *a swim meet*

**meet·ing** /'mitɪŋ/ n **1** an organized gathering of people for the purpose of discussing something: *There's a faculty meeting this afternoon.* **2** a meeting of the minds a situation in which people agree about something

**meeting house** /'.. ,./ n a building where Quakers go to WORSHIP

**meg·a** /'mɛgə/ adj SLANG very big, impressive, and enjoyable: *What a mega party!*

**meg·a·byte** /'mɛgə,baɪt/ n a unit for measuring computer information equal to a million BYTES

**meg·a·lo·ma·ni·a** /,mɛgəlou'meɪniə/ n [U] the belief that you are extremely important and powerful –**megalomaniac** /,mɛgəlou'meɪni,æk/ adj

**meg·a·phone** /'mɛgə,toun/ n a thing like a large horn, that you talk through when speaking to a crowd in order to make your voice sound louder

**meg·a·ton** /'mɛgə,tʌn/ n a measure of the power of an explosive that is equal to that of a million TONs of TNT (=a powerful explosive)

**mel·an·chol·y**[1] /'mɛlən,kɑli/ adj sad, or making you feel sad: *a melancholy look*

**melancholy**[2] n [U] LITERARY a feeling of sadness

**meld** /mɛld/ v to mix or combine two or more different things together: *a record that melds many different styles of music*

**me·lee** /'meɪleɪ, meɪ'leɪ/ n a confusing, noisy and sometimes violent situation: *Several people were hurt in the melee.*

**mel·low**[1] /'mɛlou/ adj **1** pleasant and smooth in sound or taste: *mellow jazz | a mellow wine* **2** gentle or calm because of age or experience: *Tim's more mellow now that he's older.*

**mellow**[2] mellow out v [I,T] to become more relaxed and calm, or to make someone do this: *She's mellowed over the years.*

**me·lod·ic** /mə'lɑdɪk/ adj **1** having a pleasant tune or a pleasant sound like music: *a sweet melodic voice* **2** relating to the main tune in a piece of music: *the melodic structure of Beethoven's symphonies*

**me·lo·di·ous** /mə'loudiəs/ adj having a pleasant tune or a pleasant sound like music: *a melodious voice*

**mel·o·dra·ma** /'mɛlə,drɑmə/ n [C,U] a story or play with many exciting events in which people's emotions are shown very strongly

**mel·o·dra·mat·ic** /,mɛlədrə'mætɪk/ adj having or showing emotions that are strong and unreasonable: *Stop being melodramatic!*

**mel·o·dy** /'mɛlədi/ n **1** [C,U] a song or tune **2** the main tune in a complicated piece of music

**mel·on** /'mɛlən/ n [C,U] one of several types of large sweet juicy fruits with hard skins and flat seeds

**melt** /mɛlt/ v **1** [I,T] to change something from solid to liquid by heating: *The snow's melting. | Melt the butter, and add the chopped onion.* **2** [I] to suddenly feel love or sympathy: *Whenever I hear his voice, I just melt.* **3** melt in your mouth if food melts in your mouth, it is smooth and tastes extremely good

M

**melt away** *phr v* [I] to disappear quickly and easily: *He began to exercise regularly, and the weight melted away.*

**melt·down** /'mɛltdaʊn/ *n* [C,U] a very dangerous situation in which the material in a NUCLEAR REACTOR melts and burns through its container

**melting pot** /'.. ,./ *n* a place where people from different races, countries, or social classes come and live together: *The US is often called a melting pot.*

**mem·ber** /'mɛmbɚ/ *n* **1** someone who has joined a particular club, group, or organization: *Are you a member of the French club? | Two of the band members quit yesterday.* **2** one of a group of similar people or things: *Cats and tigers are members of the same species.*

**mem·ber·ship** /'mɛmbɚˌʃɪp/ *n* **1** [C,U] the state of being a member of a club, group, organization, or system: *I forgot to renew my membership in the sailing club.* **2** [singular] all the members of a club, group, or organization: *The membership will vote for a chairman tonight.*

**mem·brane** /'mɛmbreɪn/ *n* [C,U] a very thin substance similar to skin that covers or connects parts of the body: *a membrane in the ear that helps us hear*

**me·men·to** /mə'mɛntoʊ/ *n* a small object that you keep to remind you of someone or something: *a memento of my college days*

**mem·o** /'mɛmoʊ/ *n* a short official note to another person in the same company

**mem·oirs** /'mɛmwɑrz/ *n* [plural] a book written by a famous person about his/her life and experiences

**mem·o·ra·bil·i·a** /ˌmɛmərə'bɪliə, -'bɪl-/ *n* [plural] things that you keep or collect because they relate to a famous person, event, or time: *Kennedy memorabilia*

**mem·o·ra·ble** /'mɛmrəbəl/ *adj* worth remembering: *Brando's memorable performance in "On the Waterfront" | a memorable weekend* –**memorably** *adv*

**mem·o·ran·dum** /ˌmɛmə'rændəm/ *n* FORMAL ⇨ MEMO

**me·mo·ri·al**[1] /mə'mɔriəl/ *n* made or done in order to remind people of someone who has died: *a memorial service for my grandfather*

**memorial**[2] *n* a public structure with writing on it that reminds people of someone who has died: *the Lincoln memorial | The wall was built as a memorial to soldiers who died in Vietnam.*

**Memorial Day** /.'... ,./ *n* [U] a US national holiday on the last Monday in May, to remember soldiers killed in wars

**mem·o·rize** /'mɛməˌraɪz/ *v* [T] to learn and remember words, music, or other information: *You all should have your lines memorized by Friday.*

**mem·o·ry** /'mɛmri, -məri/ *n* **1** [C,U] the ability to remember things, places, experiences etc.: *My memory isn't as good as it used to be. | Could you draw the map from memory?* (=by remembering it) **2** something that you remember from the past about a person, place, or experience: *I have a lot of happy memories of that summer. | That sound brings back memories of my childhood.* (=makes me remember it) –compare SOUVENIR **3** [U] the amount of space that can be used for storing information on a computer: *30 megabytes of memory* **4** the part of a computer in which information can be stored **5** in memory of for the purpose of remembering someone who has died: *She started a scholarship fund in memory of her husband.*

**men** /mɛn/ *n* the plural of MAN

**men·ace**[1] /'mɛnɪs/ *n* **1** something or someone that is dangerous or extremely annoying: *That man is a menace to society! | The mosquitoes are a menace at this time of year.* **2** [U] a threatening quality or manner: *There was menace in her voice*

**menace**[2] *v* [T] FORMAL to threaten someone or something with danger or harm

**men·ac·ing** /'mɛnɪsɪŋ/ *adj* making you expect something dangerous or bad; THREATENING: *a menacing laugh*

**me·nag·er·ie** /mə'nædʒəri, -ʒə-/ *n* a collection of animals kept privately or for people to see

**mend**[1] /mɛnd/ *v* **1** [T] to repair a tear or hole in a piece of clothing: *You'd better mend that shirt.* **2** mend your ways to improve the way you behave after behaving badly for a long time

**mend**[2] *n* be on the mend INFORMAL to be getting better after an illness

**me·ni·al** /'miniəl, -nyəl/ *adj* menial work is boring and needs no skill

**men·o·pause** /'mɛnəˌpɔz/ *n* [U] the time when a woman stops menstruating (MENSTRUATE)

**me·no·rah** /mə'nɔrə/ *n* a special CANDLESTICK, used in Jewish ceremonies

**men's room** /'. ./ *n* a room in a public place with toilets for men –see usage note at TOILET

**men·stru·ate** /'mɛnstruˌeɪt, -streɪt/ *v* [I] TECHNICAL when a woman menstruates every month, blood flows from her body –**menstruation** /ˌmɛnstru'eɪʃən, mɛn'streɪʃən/ *n* [U] –**menstrual** /'mɛnstruəl, -strəl/ *adj*

**men·tal** /'mɛnṭəl/ *adj* **1** relating to the mind, or happening in the mind: *your mental abilities | a mental illness | I made a mental note* (=made an effort to remember) *to call Julie.* **2** SLANG crazy: *That guy's mental!* –**mentally** *adv*: *mentally ill*

**mental health** /ˌ.. './ *adj* relating to the treatment of mental illnesses: *mental health workers/programs*

**mental in·sti·tu·tion** /'.. ..,../ *n* a hospital for people who are mentally ill

**men·tal·i·ty** /mɛn'tæləţi/ *n* [U] a particular type of attitude or way of thinking: *an aggressive mentality*

**men·thol** /'mɛnθɔl, -θɑl/ *n* [U] a substance that smells and tastes like MINT, used in medicine, candy, and cigarettes — **mentholated** /'mɛnθə,leɪţɪd/ *adj*

**men·tion**[1] /'mɛnʃən/ *v* [T] **1** to say or write about something in a few words: *Yes, Sheila did mention to me that her brother was ill. | Cooper wasn't mentioned in the article.* **2 don't mention it** SPOKEN used in order to politely say that there is no need for someone to thank you: *"Thanks for helping me out." "Don't mention it."* **3 not to mention** said when you are adding a piece of information that emphasizes what you have been saying: *He already has two houses and two cars, not to mention the boat.*

**mention**[2] *n* [C,U] the act of mentioning someone or something in a conversation or piece of writing: *Any mention of the accident upsets her. | He's had a couple of mentions in the newspaper. | The report made no mention of any profit figures.*

**men·tor** /'mɛntɔr, -tɚ/ *n* an experienced person who advises and helps a less experienced person

**men·u** /'mɛnyu/ *n* **1** a list of all the kinds of food that are available for a meal in a restaurant: *Let's see what's on the menu.* **2** a list of things that you can choose from or ask a computer to do, that is shown on the screen

**me·ow** /mi'aʊ/ *n* the crying sound that a cat makes — **meow** *v* [I]

**mer·ce·nar·y**[1] /'mɚsə,nɛri/ *n* someone who fights for any country who pays him/her

**mercenary**[2] *adj* only concerned with making money

**mer·chan·dise** /'mɚtʃən,daɪz, -,daɪs/ *n* [U] goods that are for sale in stores: *We've ordered the merchandise from a company in San Diego.*

**mer·chant**[1] /'mɚtʃənt/ *n* someone who buys and sells large quantities of goods

**merchant**[2] *adj* relating to trade in large quantities of goods: *a merchant vessel* (=ship)

**mer·ci·ful** /'mɚsɪfəl/ *adj* kind to people rather than being cruel

**mer·ci·ful·ly** /'mɚsɪfli/ *adv* fortunately, because a situation could have been much worse: *At least her death was mercifully quick.*

**Mer·cu·ry** /'mɚkyəri/ *n* [singular] the smallest PLANET, nearest the sun

**mer·cu·ry** *n* [U] a liquid silver-white metal that is used in THERMOMETERS

**mer·cy** /'mɚsi/ *n* **1** [U] kindness, pity, and a willingness to forgive: *Three of the attackers apologized and asked for mercy.* **2 at the mercy of** unable to do anything to protect yourself from someone or something: *The*

*houses near the forest fire are at the mercy of the winds.*

**mercy kill·ing** /'.. ,../ *n* ⇨ EUTHANASIA

**mere** /mɪr/ *adj* **1** used in order to emphasize how small or unimportant someone or something is: *She was a mere two years younger than the Princess.* **2** used in order to say that something small or unimportant has a big effect: *The mere thought that he might be hurt made her want to cry.*

**mere·ly** /'mɪrli/ *adv* **1** used in order to emphasize that something is exactly what you say it is, not better or worse, not more or less, etc; just: *I'm not making criticisms, merely suggestions.* **2** used in order to emphasize that something or someone is small or unimportant, compared to someone or something else; only: *We want more from work than merely a paycheck.*

**merge** /mɚdʒ/ *v* **1** [I,T] to combine or join together to form one thing: *The two unions merged to form a larger one.* **2 merge into sth** to seem to disappear into something and become part of it: *a point where the mountains merged into the sky* **3** if traffic merges, the cars from two roads come together onto the same road

**merg·er** /'mɚdʒɚ/ *n* the act of joining together two more companies or organizations to form one larger one

**me·rid·i·an** /mə'rɪdiən/ *n* the line drawn from the NORTH POLE to the SOUTH POLE to show the positions of places on a map

**me·ringue** /mə'ræŋ/ *n* [C,U] a light sweet food made by baking a mixture of sugar and the white parts of eggs

**mer·it**[1] /'mɛrɪt/ *n* **1** one of the good qualities or features of something or someone: *Living downtown has its merits.* **2** [U] FORMAL a good quality that makes something deserve praise or admiration: *a book of great merit*

**merit**[2] *v* [T] FORMAL to deserve something: *The play merits the awards it's won.*

**mer·maid** /'mɚmeɪd/ *n* a woman in stories who has a fish's tail instead of legs

**mer·ry** /'mɛri/ *adj* happy and having fun: *Merry Christmas!* (=used in order to tell someone you hope s/he has a good Christmas)

**merry-go-round** /'.. . ,./ *n* a machine at a FAIR that turns around and around, and has model animals and seats for children to sit on

**mesh**[1] /mɛʃ/ *n* [U] a piece of material made of threads or wires that have been woven together like a net: *a wire mesh screen*

**mesh**[2] *v* [I] **1** if two or more ideas, qualities, people etc. mesh, they go well together: *Their two management styles never meshed successfully.* **2** TECHNICAL if two parts of an engine or machine mesh, they fit closely together

**mes·mer·ize** /'mɛzmə,raɪz/ *v* [T] to make someone become completely interested in some-

**M**

thing: *The video game kept the kids mesmerized for hours.* – **mesmerizing** *adj*

**mess**[1] /mɛs/ *n* **1** [singular, U] a place or a group of things that is not organized or arranged neatly: *This house is a mess!* | *The kids made a mess in their room again.* **2** [singular] INFORMAL a situation in which there are a lot of problems and difficulties, especially as a result of mistakes or people not being careful: *His personal life was a mess.* | *I'm sorry, I've really made a mess of things.* **3** INFORMAL someone who behaves or thinks in a disorganized way: *I'd been crying for hours - I was a mess.* **4** a room in which members of the military eat and drink together

**mess**[2] *v*

**mess around** *phr v* INFORMAL **1** [I] to play or do silly things when you should be working or paying attention: *Stop messing around and do your homework!* **2** [T **mess** sb **around**] to make someone angry by lying, or by not giving him/her something s/he wants: *Don't mess me around. Tell me where she went!*

**mess around with** sb/sth *phr v* [T] INFORMAL **1** [mess around with sth] to play with something or make small changes to it: *I told you not to mess around with my camera!* **2** [mess around with sb] to have a sexual relationship with someone, especially someone who is married

**mess up** *phr v* INFORMAL **1** [T] to spoil something or make it dirty and disorganized: *I hope I haven't messed up your big plans.* | *Who messed up my clean kitchen?* **2** [I,T **mess** sth ↔ **up**] to make a mistake or do something badly: *"How did you do on the test?" "Oh, I really messed up."* – see also MESSED UP

**mess with** sb/sth *phr v* [T] **1** [mess with sth] to deal with something or use something that you do not understand: *You don't have to mess with any gears; the car's automatic.* **2** [mess with sb] to annoy or argue with someone: *I'm not in a bad mood, just don't mess with me.*

**mes·sage** /'mɛsɪdʒ/ *n* **1** a small amount of written or spoken information that you pass from one person to another: *"Janet just called." "Did she leave a message?"* | *Sorry, Tony's not home yet. Can I take a message?* (=used during phone calls) **2** [singular] the main idea or the most important idea in a movie, book, speech etc.: *The movie has a clear message: don't take drugs.* **3** **get the message** INFORMAL to understand what someone means or what s/he wants you to do: *Hopefully he got the message and will stop bothering me!*

**messed up** /ˌ. '.◄/ *adj* INFORMAL if someone is messed up, s/he has a lot of emotional problems: *Fred's all messed up from the divorce.*

**mes·sen·ger** /'mɛsəndʒɚ/ *n* someone who takes messages to other people

**mess hall** /'. ./ *n* a large room where soldiers eat

**mes·si·ah** /mə'saɪə/ *n* **the Messiah** Jesus Christ in the Christian religion, or the leader sent by God to save the world in the Jewish religion

**Messrs.** /'mɛsɚz/ *n* FORMAL the written plural of Mr.

**mess·y** /'mɛsi/ *adj* **1** dirty, or not arranged in an organized way: *a messy desk* **2** a messy situation is complicated and unpleasant to deal with: *a messy divorce*

**met** /mɛt/ *v* the past tense and PAST PARTICIPLE of MEET

**me·tab·o·lism** /mə'tæbə,lɪzəm/ *n* [C,U] the chemical processes in your body that change food into the energy you need for working and growing – **metabolic** /ˌmɛtə'balɪk/ *adj*

**met·al** /'mɛtl/ *n* [C,U] a hard, usually shiny substance such as iron, gold, or steel

**metal de·tec·tor** /'.. ..,../ *n* a machine used for finding metal, especially one used at airports for finding weapons

**me·tal·lic** /mə'tælɪk/ *adj* made of metal, or similar to metal in color, appearance, or taste: *a car painted metallic blue*

**met·al·lur·gy** /'mɛtl,ɚdʒi/ *n* [U] the scientific study of metals and their uses – **metallurgical** /ˌmɛtə'lɚdʒɪkəl/ *adj* – **metallurgist** /'mɛtl-,ɚdʒɪst/ *n*

**met·a·mor·pho·sis** /ˌmɛtə'mɔrfəsɪs/ *n*, *plural* **metamorphoses** /-fəsiz/ [C,U] the process in which something changes into a completely different form: *a caterpillar's metamorphosis into a butterfly*

**met·a·phor** /'mɛtə,fɔr/ *n* [C,U] a way of describing something by comparing it to something else that has similar qualities, without using the words "like" or "as." "A river of tears" is a metaphor – **metaphorical** /ˌmɛtə'fɔrɪkəl/ *adj* – **metaphorically** *adv*

**met·a·phys·i·cal** /ˌmɛtə'fɪzɪkəl/ *adj* relating to a study of PHILOSOPHY that is concerned with trying to understand and describe what REALITY is – **metaphysics** *n* [U] – **metaphysically** *adv*

**mete** /mit/ *v*

**mete** sth ↔ **out** *phr v* [T] FORMAL to give someone a punishment

**me·te·or** /'mitiɚ/ *n* a small piece of rock or metal that produces a bright burning line in the sky when it falls from space into the earth's ATMOSPHERE

**me·te·or·ic** /ˌmiti'ɔrɪk, -'ar-/ *adj* happening very suddenly and usually continuing for only a short time: *his meteoric rise to fame*

**me·te·or·ite** /'mitiə,raɪt/ *n* a small METEOR that has landed on the earth's surface

**me·te·or·ol·o·gy** /ˌmitiə'ralədʒi/ *n* [U] the scientific study of weather – **meteorologist** *n*

**meter** /'mitɚ/ *n* **1** written abbreviation **m.** a unit for measuring length, equal to 100 centimeters or 39.37 inches **2** a piece of equipment that measures the amount of gas, electricity, time etc. you have used: *The cab driver looked* *at the meter and said, "$5.70, please."* – see also PARKING METER **3** [C,U] the way that the words of a poem are arranged into a pattern of weak and strong beats

**meter maid** /'.. ./ *n* OLD-FASHIONED a woman whose job is to check that cars are not parked illegally

**meth·a·done** /'mɛθə,doʊn/ *n* [U] TECHNICAL a drug that is often given to people who are trying to stop taking HEROIN

**meth·ane** /'mɛθeɪn/ *n* [U] a gas with no color or smell, which can be burned to give heat

**meth·od** /'mɛθəd/ *n* a planned way of doing something: *This is the simplest method of payment.* | *Her teaching methods are unusual.*

**me·thod·i·cal** /mə'θɑdɪkəl/ *adj* done in a careful and well organized way, or always doing things this way: *They made a methodical search of the building.* | *a methodical woman* – **methodically** *adv*

**Meth·od·ist** /'mɛθədɪst/ *adj* relating to the Protestant church whose members follow the ideas of John Wesley – **Methodist** *n*

**meth·od·ol·o·gy** /,mɛθə'dɑlədʒi/ *n* [C,U] the set of methods and principles used when studying a particular subject or doing a particular type of work: *the methodology used in genetic research* – **methodological** /,mɛθədə-'lɑdʒɪkəl/ *adj*

**me·tic·u·lous** /mə'tɪkyələs/ *adj* very careful about details, and always trying to do things correctly: *The hospital keeps meticulous records.* – **meticulously** *adv*

**met·ric** /'mɛtrɪk/ *adj* using the metric system, or relating to it. *metric tons*

**metric sys·tem** /'.. ./ *n* [singular] the system of weights and measures based on the kilogram and the meter

**me·tro** /'mɛtroʊ/ *adj* relating to or belonging to a very large city: *the metro area*

**me·trop·o·lis** /mə'trɑpəlɪs/ *n* a very large city, or the most important city of a country or area: *Las Vegas is America's fastest growing metropolis.* – **metropolitan** /,mɛtrə'pɑlət⁻n/ *adj*

**met·tle** /'mɛtl/ *n* [U] LITERARY courage and determination

**Mex·i·can¹** /'mɛksɪkən/ *adj* relating to or coming from Mexico

**Mexican²** *n* someone from Mexico

**mez·za·nine** /'mɛzə,nin, ,mɛzə'nin/ *n* the floor or BALCONY just above the main floor in a theater, hotel, store etc.

**mg.** the written abbreviation of MILLIGRAM

**MI** the written abbreviation of Michigan

**mice** /maɪs/ *n* the plural of MOUSE

**mi·crobe** /'maɪkroʊb/ *n* an extremely small living creature that cannot be seen without a MICROSCOPE

**mi·cro·bi·ol·o·gy** /,maɪkroʊbaɪ'ɑlədʒi/ *n* [U] the scientific study of very small living things – **microbiologist** *n*

**mi·cro·chip** /'maɪkroʊ,tʃɪp/ *n* ⇨ CHIP¹

**mi·cro·cosm** /'maɪkrə,kɑzəm/ *n* a small group, society etc. that has the same qualities as a much larger one: *San Jose's mix of people is a microcosm of America.* – compare MACROCOSM

**mi·cro·fiche** /'maɪkroʊ,fiʃ/ *n* [C,U] a sheet of MICROFILM that can be read using a special machine, especially at a library

**mi·cro·film** /'maɪkrə,fɪlm/ *n* [C,U] film used for making very small photographs of important documents, newspapers, maps etc.

**mi·cro·or·ga·nism** /,maɪkroʊ'ɔrgə,nɪzəm/ *n* an extremely small living creature that cannot be seen without a MICROSCOPE

**mi·cro·phone** /'maɪkrə,foʊn/ *n* a piece of electrical equipment for making your voice sound louder, that you hold in front of your mouth when you are singing, giving a speech etc.

**mi·cro·proc·es·sor** /,maɪkroʊ'prɑsɛsɚ/ *n* the main CHIP in a computer that controls most of its operations

**mi·cro·scope** /'maɪkrə,skoʊp/ *n* a scientific instrument that makes extremely small things appear large enough to be seen

**mi·cro·scop·ic** /,maɪkrə'skɑpɪk/ *adj* **1** extremely small: *microscopic animals/organisms* **2** using a MICROSCOPE: *a microscopic examination*

**mi·cro·wave** /'maɪkrə,weɪv/ *n* **1** also **microwave oven** a type of OVEN that cooks food very quickly by using MICROWAVEs instead of heat – see picture at KITCHEN **2** a very short electric wave used especially for cooking food, sending radio messages, and in RADAR

**mid·air** /,mɪd'ɛr/ *n* **in midair** in the air or sky: *The plane exploded in midair.*

**mid·day** /'mɪd-deɪ/ *n* [U] the middle of the day, around 12:00 p.m.; NOON – compare MIDNIGHT

---

**middle**

Billy  Tom  Chris

Tom is in the middle.

**mid·dle¹** /'mɪdl/ *n* **1 the middle a)** the center part of a thing, place, or position: *Why's your car parked **in the middle of** the road?* | *Tom's the guy in the middle.* **b)** the part that is between the beginning and the end of a story, event, period etc.: *I fell asleep **in the middle of** class.* | *Who'd call us in the middle of the*

M

*night?* **2 be in the middle of doing something** to be busy doing something: *Can I call you back later? I'm right in the middle of cooking dinner.*

---

**USAGE NOTE middle and center**

Use both of these words to talk about where something is. The **middle** of something is the area or part that is farthest away from the sides or edges: *Someone left a toy in the middle of the floor.* The **center** of something is exactly in the middle: *Put the vase in the center of the table.*

---

**middle²** *adj* **1** nearest to the center of something: *Do you mind if we sit in the middle row? | The middle lane was blocked off because of an accident.* **2** half way through an event, action, or period of time, or between the beginning and the end: *I missed the middle act of the play.*

**middle-aged** /ˌ.. './ *n* belonging or relating to the period of your life when you are about 40 to 60 years old: *a middle-aged woman* **–middle age** *n* [U]

**Middle Ag·es** /ˌ.. '../ *n* **the Middle Ages** the period in European history between the 5th and 15th centuries A.D.

**Middle A·mer·i·ca** /ˌmɪdl əˈmɛrɪkə/ *n* [U] **1** ⇨ MIDWEST **2** Americans who are neither rich nor poor, who usually have traditional values: *Cars that attract Middle America - people who are looking for comfort and value.*

**middle class** /ˌ.. '.◂/ *n* **the middle class** the social class that includes people who are neither rich nor poor: *a tax reduction for the middle class* **–middle-class** *adj* –see usage note at CLASS¹

**Middle East** /ˌ.. '.◂/ *n* **the Middle East** the part of Asia that is between the Mediterranean Sea and the Arabian Sea, including countries such as Turkey and Iran **–Middle Eastern** *adj*

**middle fin·ger** /ˌ.. '../ *n* the longest finger in the middle of the five fingers on your hand –see picture at HAND¹

**mid·dle·man** /ˈmɪdlˌmæn/ *n* someone who buys things in order to get a profit by selling them to someone else

**middle name** /ˌ.. './ *n* the name that, in English, comes between your first name and your family name –see usage note at NAMES

**middle-of-the-road** /ˌ.. . . '.◂/ *adj* middle-of-the-road ideas, opinions etc. are not extreme, so many people agree with them: *a politician that appeals to middle-of-the-road voters*

**middle school** /'.. ˌ./ *n* a school in the US for students between the ages of 11 and 14

**midg·et** /ˈmɪdʒɪt/ *n* a very small person

**mid·life crisis** /ˌmɪdlaɪf ˈkraɪsɪs/ *n* the worry and lack of confidence that some people feel when they are about 40 or 50 years old

**mid·night** /ˈmɪdnaɪt/ *n* [U] 12 o'clock at night, or 0:00 a.m.: *I fell asleep a little after midnight.* –compare MIDDAY

**mid·riff** /ˈmɪdrɪf/ *n* the part of the body between your chest and your waist

**midst** /mɪdst/ *n* **in the midst of** in the middle of something such as an event, situation, place, or group: *a reason for hope in the midst of a war*

**mid·term** /ˈmɪdtɚm/ *n* **1** an examination that students take in the middle of a SEMESTER: *When are your midterms?* **2** [U] the middle of the period when an elected government has power **–midterm** *adj*

**mid·way** /ˌmɪdˈweɪ◂/ *adj, adv* at the middle point between two places, or in the middle of a period of time or an event: *There's a gas station* **midway between** *here and Fresno. | He went silent* **midway through** *his speech.*

**mid·week** /ˌmɪdˈwik◂/ *adj, adv* on one of the middle days of the week, such as Tuesday, Wednesday, or Thursday: *midweek classes | I can see you midweek.*

**Mid·west** /ˌmɪdˈwɛst/ *n* **the Midwest** the central area of the US **–Midwestern** /mɪdˈwɛstɚn/ *adj*

**mid·wife** /ˈmɪdwaɪf/ *n* a specially trained nurse, usually a woman, whose job is to help women when they are having a baby

**miffed** /mɪft/ *adj* INFORMAL annoyed

**might¹** /maɪt/ *modal verb* **1** used in order to talk about what was, is, or might be possible: *I might be wrong, but I'm almost positive she said that. | I might not be able to go - my son is sick. | She might have tried calling, but I've been out.* **2** used in CONDITIONAL sentences to show possibility: *If Hawaii is too expensive, we might go to Florida.* **3** used instead of "may" when reporting what someone said or thought: *This morning I thought it might rain, so I brought an umbrella.* **4 might as well** SPOKEN used in order to say that you will do something even though you are not very interested in it or excited about it: *I might as well go with you. I don't have anything else to do.* **5** FORMAL used in order to give advice: *You might try calling the manager of the store. | You* **might want to** *get your blood pressure checked.*

**might²** *n* [U] LITERARY strength and power: *She tried* **with all her might** *to push him away.*

**might·y¹** /ˈmaɪṭi/ *adj* strong and powerful: *mighty warriors*

**mighty²** *adv* INFORMAL very: *That chicken smells mighty good, Jenny.*

**mi·graine** /ˈmaɪgreɪn/ *n* an extremely bad HEADACHE

**mi·grant** /ˈmaɪgrənt/ *n* a person, bird, or animal that regularly moves from one area or country to another: *migrant workers hired during the war* –compare EMIGRANT, IMMIGRANT

M

**mi·grate** /'maɪgreɪt/ v [I] **1** if birds or animals migrate, they travel to a different part of the world, especially in the fall and spring **2** to go to another area or country for a short time, usually in order to find a place to live or work: *farmworkers who migrate from state to state, harvesting crops* –compare EMIGRATE, IMMIGRATE –see usage note at EMIGRATE

**mi·gra·tion** /maɪ'greɪʃən/ n the action of a large group of birds, animals, or people moving from one area or country to another: *the yearly migration of geese* –**migratory** /'maɪgrə,tɔri/ adj

**mike** /maɪk/ n INFORMAL ⇨ MICROPHONE

**mild** /maɪld/ adj **1** not too severe or serious: *a mild case of flu* | *mild criticism* **2** not strong-tasting or hot-tasting: *mild cheddar cheese* | *a mild green chili* **3** if the weather is mild, it is not too cold or wet and not too hot **4** if a soap or beauty product is mild, it is gentle to your skin, hair etc.

**mil·dew** /'mɪldu/ n [U] a very small white or gray FUNGUS (=plant without leaves) that grows on walls, leather, and other surfaces in warm, slightly wet places –**mildew** v [I]

**mild·ly** /'maɪldli/ adv **1** slightly: *McKee was only mildly interested.* **2 to put it mildly** SPOKEN said when you are saying something unpleasant in the most polite way that you can: *Well, to put it mildly, I don't think Greg likes you very much.* **3** in a gentle way: *"Perhaps," he answered mildly.*

**mile** /maɪl/ n **1** a unit for measuring distance, equal to 1760 yards or 1609 meters: *The city is about 15 miles north of here.* | *Mark jogs at least 5 miles a day.* **2 miles** INFORMAL a very long distance: *We walked for miles without seeing anyone.* **3 talk a mile a minute** SPOKEN to talk very quickly without stopping **4 be miles away** SPOKEN to not be paying attention to what is happening around you: *Sorry, I was miles away. What did you say?*

**mile·age** /'maɪlɪdʒ/ n **1** [singular, U] the number of miles that a car has traveled since it was new: *a used car with low mileage* **2** [U] the number of miles a car travels using each gallon of gasoline: *Our car gets really good mileage.* (=a lot of miles per gallon) **3 get a lot of mileage out of sth** to make something as useful for you as it can be: *I've gotten a lot of mileage out of that old joke.*

**mile·stone** /'maɪlstoʊn/ n a very important event in the development of something: *Winning the election was a milestone in his political career.*

**mi·lieu** /mil'yu, mil'yʊ/ n, plural **milieus** [C,U] FORMAL all the things and people that surround you and influence you: *Always consider the writer's social and political milieu.*

**mil·i·tant¹** /'mɪlətənt/ adj willing to use force

or violence: *Militant groups were still protesting against the new law.* –**militancy** n [U]

**militant²** n someone who uses violence to achieve social or political change

**mil·i·ta·ris·m** /'mɪlɪtə,rɪzəm/ n [U] the belief that a country should increase its army, navy etc. and use them to get what it wants –**militaristic** /,mɪlətə'rɪstɪk/ adj

**mil·i·tar·y¹** /'mɪlə,tɛri/ adj used by the Army, Navy, or Air Force, or relating to war: *military aircraft* | *a military base in Greece* | *My brother was sent to military academy.* (=military school) –**militarily** /,mɪlə'tɛrəli/ adv

**military²** n [C usually singular] the military organizations of a country, such as the army and navy: *My father is in the military.*

**mil·i·tate** /'mɪlə,teɪt/ v

**militate against** sth phr v [T] FORMAL to prevent something from happening or from being likely to happen: *factors that militated against her becoming a political leader*

**mi·li·tia** /mə'lɪʃə/ n a group of people trained as soldiers who are not members of the permanent army: *a militia of 300,000*

**milk¹** /mɪlk/ n [U] **1** a white liquid that people drink, which is usually produced by cows or goats: *a glass of milk* | *Would you like milk in your coffee?* **2** a white liquid produced by female animals and women for feeding their babies

**milk²** v [T] **1** to take milk from a cow or goat **2 milk sb/sth for sth** INFORMAL to get all the money, advantages etc. that you can from a person, thing, or situation: *I'm going to milk her for every penny she has.*

**milk·man** /'mɪlkmæn/ n someone who delivers milk to houses each morning

**milk·shake** /'mɪlkʃeɪk/ n a drink made from milk and ICE CREAM: *a chocolate milkshake*

**milk·y** /'mɪlki/ adj **1** if water or a liquid is milky, it is not clear and looks slightly white, like milk **2** milky skin is white and smooth

**Milky Way** /,.. './ n **the Milky Way** the pale white band made up of large numbers of stars that you can see across the sky at night

**mill¹** /mɪl/ n **1** a large machine used for crushing food such as corn, grain, or coffee into a powder **2** a building where materials such as paper, steel, or cotton cloth are made **3** a small tool or machine used especially for crushing pepper or coffee

**mill²** v [T] to crush grains in a MILL –see picture at GRIND¹

**mill around** phr v [I] INFORMAL if a lot of people are milling around, they are moving around a place and do not seem to have a particular purpose: *Tourists were milling around the streets.*

**mil·len·ni·um** /mə'lɛniəm/ n, plural **millennia 1** a period of time equal to 1000 years **2** the time when a new 1000 year period be-

M

gins: *projects planned for the start of the new millennium* –**millennial** *adj*

**mil·li·gram** /'mɪlə,græm/ written abbreviation **mg.** *n* a unit for measuring weight, equal to 1/1000th of a gram

**mil·li·li·ter** /'mɪlə,litɚ/ *n* a unit for measuring liquids, equal to 1/1000th of a liter or .00212 of a PINT

**mil·li·me·ter** /'mɪlə,mitɚ/ written abbreviation **mm.** *n* a unit for measuring length, equal to 1/1000th of a meter or 0.03937 inches

**mil·li·ner·y** /'mɪlə,nɛri/ *n* [U] OLD-FASHIONED women's hats, or the activity of making these hats –**milliner** /'mɪlənɚ/ *n*

**mil·lion** /'mɪlyən/ *number* **1** 1,000,000: *$350 million* | *4 million people* ✗ DON'T SAY "4 million of people." ✗ **2** also **millions** an extremely large number of people or things: *I've heard that excuse a million times.* **3 not/never in a million years** SPOKEN said in order to emphasize how impossible or unlikely something is: *I never would have guessed in a million years!* **4 look/feel like a million dollars** INFORMAL to look very attractive or feel very happy and healthy **5 one in a million** the best of all possible people or things: *My wife is one in a million!* –**millionth** /'mɪlyənθ/ *number*

**mil·lion·aire** /,mɪlyə'nɛr/ *n* someone who is very rich and has at least one million dollars

**mime¹** /maɪm/ *n* an actor who performs without using words, or a performance in which no words are used

**mime²** *v* [I,T] to perform using actions and movements instead of using words: *She stretched out her arms, miming a swimmer.*

**mim·ic¹** /'mɪmɪk/ *v* **mimicked, mimicked, mimicking** [T] **1** to copy the way someone speaks, moves, or behaves, usually to make people laugh: *Lily mimicked Sue's Southern accent.* **2** to have the same behavior, appearance, or qualities as someone or something else: *a computer that mimics human abilities, such as walking and speaking* –**mimicry** *n* [U]

**mimic²** *n* a person or animal that is good at MIMIC*king* someone or something else

**mince** /mɪns/ *v* **1** [T] to cut food into extremely small pieces: *Mince the onion and garlic.* **2 not mince words** to say exactly what you think, even if this may offend people: *He's a brash New Yorker who doesn't mince words.* **3** [I] to walk, using very small steps and moving your hips a lot: *models mincing down/along the runway*

**mince·meat** /'mɪnsmit/ *n* [U] a sweet mixture of apples, dried fruit, and SPICE*s*, but no meat, used in PIE*s*

**mind¹** /maɪnd/ *n*
**1** ▶BRAIN◀ your thoughts, or the part of your brain used for thinking and imagining things: *What kind of plans did you have in mind?*

(=what plans were you thinking about) | *What's on your mind?* (=what are you thinking about)
**2 change your mind** to change your opinions or decision about something: *If you change your mind and want to come, give us a call.*
**3 make up your mind** to decide something, or become very determined to do something: *Have you made up your mind which college you want to go to?*
**4 come/spring to mind** if something comes to mind, you suddenly think of it
**5 state of mind** the way you are feeling, such as how happy or sad you are
**6 cross/enter your mind** if something crosses your mind, you think about it for a short period: *It never crossed my mind that she might be unhappy.*
**7 -minded** having a particular attitude or believing that a particular thing is important: *He was a mean, narrow/closed-minded old man.* (=he did not accept other ideas and opinions) | *politically-minded students*
**8 keep/bear sth in mind** to remember something: *Keep in mind that the bank will be closed tomorrow.*
**9 have a lot on your mind** to be unable to think clearly because you are very busy or have a lot of problems
**10 out of your mind** INFORMAL crazy: *Are you out of your mind!*
**11 go out of your mind/lose your mind** INFORMAL to start to become mentally ill or to behave in a strange way: *I have so much to do, I feel like I'm going out of my mind.*
**12 no one in his/her right mind** INFORMAL no one who is sensible: *No woman in her right mind would walk alone at night around here.*
**13 your mind goes blank** INFORMAL if your mind goes blank, you suddenly cannot remember something: *As soon as Mr. Daniels asked me for the answer, my mind went blank.*
**14 put your mind to** to decide to do something and use a lot of effort in order to succeed: *You can win if you just put your mind to it.*
**15 have/keep an open mind** to be willing to accept other ideas and opinions
**16 take your mind off sth** to make you stop thinking about something: *Dad needs a vacation to take his mind off work.* –see also ONE-TRACK MIND **blow sb's mind** (BLOW¹) **slip your mind** (SLIP¹)

**mind²** *v* **1** [I,T] to feel annoyed, worried, or angry about something: *It's not my job, but I don't mind doing it.* | *Do you think she'd mind if we didn't come?* **2 mind your manners/language** OLD-FASHIONED to behave or speak in a polite way

SPOKEN PHRASES
**3 do you mind/would you mind** used in order to politely ask if you can do something, or if someone will do something for you: *Do you mind if I use your*

*phone?* | *Would you mind waiting here a minute?* **4 I wouldn't mind doing sth** said when you would like to do something: *I wouldn't mind living in Minneapolis.* **5 mind your own business** to not try to find out what other people are doing: *"So, did he kiss you?" "Mind your own business!"*

**mind-bog·gling** /'maɪnd,bɑgəlɪŋ/ *adj* INFORMAL strange or complicated, and difficult to imagine or believe: *a mind-boggling amount of money*

**mind·ful** /'maɪndfəl/ *adj* behaving in a way that shows you remember a rule or fact: *Mindful of the guide's warning, they returned before dark.*

**mind·less** /'maɪndlɪs/ *adj* so simple that you do not have to think carefully about what you are doing: *Stuffing envelopes is mindless work.* −**mindlessness** *n* [U]

**mine¹** /maɪn/ *possessive pron* the thing or things belonging or relating to the person who is speaking: *That's her car. This is mine.* | *He didn't have a pencil so I let him borrow mine.* | *Theresa's coat is black. Mine is blue.*

**mine²** *n* **1** a type of bomb that is hidden below the surface of the ground or in the water, which explodes when someone or something touches it **2** a deep hole or series of holes in the ground from which gold, coal etc. is dug: *He's worked in the coal mines all his life.*

**mine³** *v* **1** [I,T] to dig into the ground in order to get gold, coal etc.: *men mining for gold* **2** [T] to hide bombs under the ground or in the water: *The entire field was mined by the enemy.*

**mine·field** /'maɪnfild/ *n* an area of land that has mines hidden in it

**min·er** /'maɪnɚ/ *n* someone who works in a mine: *a coal miner*

**min·er·al** /'mɪnərəl/ *n* a natural substance such as CALCIUM, iron, coal, or salt, that is present in some foods and in the earth: *Milk is full of valuable vitamins and minerals.*

**mineral wa·ter** /'... ,../ *n* water that comes from under the ground and contains MINERALS

**min·gle** /'mɪŋgəl/ *v* **1** [I] to meet and talk with a lot of different people at a social event: *Reporters mingled with movie stars at the awards ceremony.* **2** [I,T] if two or more smells, sounds, feelings etc. mingle or are mingled, they combine with each other: *anger mingled with disappointment and fear*

**min·i** /'mɪni/ *adj* INFORMAL very small; MINIATURE: *mini bottles of shampoo*

**min·i·a·ture¹** /'mɪniətʃɚ, 'mɪnɪtʃɚ/ *adj* very small: *a miniature doll house*

**miniature²** *n* **1** something that has the same appearance as someone or something, but is much smaller: *This painting is a miniature of the one in the museum.* **2 in miniature** exactly

the same as someone or something else, except much smaller: *She has her mother's face in miniature.*

**miniature golf** /,... './ *n* [U] a GOLF game, played for fun, in which you hit a small ball through passages, over small bridges and hills etc.

**min·i·mal** /'mɪnəməl/ *adj* extremely small in amount or degree and therefore not worth worrying about: *The new operation causes a minimal amount of pain to the patient.* −**minimally** *adv*

**min·i·mize** /'mɪnə,maɪz/ *v* [T] to make the degree or amount of something as small as possible: *To minimize the risk of getting heart disease, eat well and exercise daily.* −opposite MAXIMIZE

**min·i·mum¹** /'mɪnəməm/ *adj* the minimum number, amount, or degree is the smallest that it is possible to have: *$30,000 is the minimum price that we would accept.* | *You will need to make a minimum payment of $50 a month.* −opposite MAXIMUM¹

**minimum²** *n* the smallest number, amount, or degree that it is possible to have: *Jim works a minimum of* (=at least) *50 hours a week.* | *Costs were kept to a minimum.* (=as small as possible) −opposite MAXIMUM²

**minimum wage** /,... './ *n* [U] the lowest amount of money that can legally be paid per hour to a worker: *I'm only earning minimum wage, but it's a fun job.*

**min·ing** /'maɪnɪŋ/ *n* [U] the industry of digging gold, coal etc. out of the ground, or the action of digging for gold etc.: *coal mining in Oklahoma* | *mining companies*

**min·i·se·ries** /'mɪni,sɪriz/ *n* [plural] a television DRAMA that is divided into several parts and shown on different nights

**min·i·skirt** /'mɪni,skɚt/ *n* a very short skirt

**min·is·ter¹** /'mɪnəstɚ/ *n* **1** a religious leader in some Christian churches −compare PRIEST **2** a politician who is in charge of a government department: *a meeting of European ministers*

**minister²** *v*

**minister to** sb/sth *phr v* [T] FORMAL to give help to someone or something: *doctors who minister to the needs of their patients*

**min·is·te·ri·al** /,mɪnə'stɪriəl/ *adj* relating to a minister, or done by a minister: *ministerial decisions*

**min·is·try** /'mɪnəstri/ *n* **1** [U] the profession of being a church leader, or the work done by a religious leader: *Our son entered/joined the ministry two years ago.* (=became a minister) **2** a government department: *the Defense Ministry*

**min·i·van** /'mɪni,væn/ *n* a large vehicle with seats for six or more people

**mink** /mɪŋk/ *n* [C,U] a small animal with soft brown fur, or the valuable fur from this animal

M

**min·now** /ˈmɪnoʊ/ *n* a very small fish that lives in rivers, lakes etc.

**mi·nor¹** /ˈmaɪnɚ/ *adj* small and not very important or serious: *We made a few minor changes to the plan.* | *It's only a minor injury.* ✗ DON'T SAY "minor than." ✗ —opposite MAJOR¹

**minor²** *n* **1** LAW someone who is not old enough to be considered legally responsible for his/her actions, usually someone under the age of 18 **2** the second main subject that you study at college for your degree: *"What's your minor?" "Math."* —compare MAJOR²

**minor³** *v*

**minor in** sth *phr v* [T] to study a second main subject as part of your college degree: *I'm minoring in African Studies.*

**mi·nor·i·ty¹** /məˈnɔrəṭi, maɪ-, -ˈnɑr-/ *adj* relating to a group of people who do not have the same opinion, religion, race etc. as most of the larger group that they are in: *help for minority groups* | *minority students*

**minority²** *n* **1** a group of people of a different race or religion than most people in a country, or someone in one of these groups: *job opportunities for minorities and women* **2** [singular] a small part of a larger group of people or things: *Only a minority of the committee voted against the new rule.* **3** **be in the minority** to be less in number than any other group: *Male teachers are very much in the minority at public schools.* —compare MAJORITY¹

**Minor Leagues** /ˌ.. ˈ./ *n* [plural] the groups of teams that form the lower levels of American professional baseball

**min·strel** /ˈmɪnstrəl/ *n* **1** a singer or dancer who pretended to be a black person and who performed in shows in the early part of the 20th century **2** a singer or musician in the Middle Ages

**mint¹** /mɪnt/ *n* **1** a candy with a sweet hot taste: *an after dinner mint* **2** [U] a plant with sweet hot-tasting leaves used in cooking and making medicine —see also PEPPERMINT, SPEARMINT **3** **a mint** INFORMAL a large amount of money: *Bill made a mint when he sold his company.* **4** a place where coins are officially made

**mint²** *adj* **in mint condition** looking new and in perfect condition: *a 1957 Chevy in mint condition*

**mint³** *v* [T] to make a coin

**mint·y** /ˈmɪnti/ *adj* tasting or smelling of MINT: *minty mouthwash*

**mi·nus¹** /ˈmaɪnəs/ *prep* **1** used in mathematics when you SUBTRACT one number from another: *17 minus 5 is 12 (17-5=12)* **2** INFORMAL without something that would normally be there: *He came back from the fight minus a couple of front teeth.*

**minus²** *n* **1** ⇨ MINUS SIGN **2** something bad about a situation: *There are pluses and minuses to living in a big city.* —compare PLUS⁴

**minus³** *adj* **1** **A minus/B minus** etc. a mark used in a system of marking a student's work. "A minus" is lower than "A," but higher than "B plus" —compare PLUS³ **2** **minus 5/20/30** etc. less than zero, especially less than zero degrees in temperature: *At night the temperature can go as low as minus 30.*

**min·us·cule** /ˈmɪnəˌskyul/ *adj* extremely small: *a minuscule amount of food*

**minus sign** /ˈ.. ˌ./ *n* a sign (-) showing that a number is less than zero, or that the second of two numbers is to be SUBTRACTed from the first

**min·ute¹** /ˈmɪnɪt/ *n* **1** a period of time equal to 60 seconds: *Ethel's train arrives in fifteen minutes.* | *It's three minutes to 4:00.* (=three minutes before 4:00) **2** a very short period of time: *For a minute I thought he was serious.* | *I'll be ready in a minute.* **3** **wait/just a minute** SPOKEN **a)** used in order to ask someone to wait a short period of time for something: *"Are you coming with us?" "Yes, just a minute."* **b)** used when you do not agree with someone or do not think that s/he is doing or saying something that is right: *Wait a minute here! I can't believe you think that $20 is a fair price!* **4** **the minute (that)** as soon as: *I knew it was Jill the minute I heard her voice.* **5** **last minute** at the last possible time, just before something must be done or completed: *Frank changed his mind at the last minute and decided to come with us after all.* | *a few last minute arrangements* **6** **any minute (now)** very soon: *She should get here any minute now.*

**mi·nute²** /maɪˈnut/ *adj* **1** extremely small: *Her handwriting is minute - I can't read what the note says.* **2** paying attention to the smallest things or parts: *Johnson explained the plan in minute detail.*

**min·utes** /ˈmɪnɪts/ *n* [plural] an official written record of what is said at a meeting and what decisions are made there

**mir·a·cle** /ˈmɪrəkəl/ *n* **1** something lucky that happens, that you did not think was possible: *It's a miracle (that) you weren't killed!* **2** an action or event that is impossible according to the ordinary laws of nature, believed to be done or caused by God: *the miracles of Jesus*

**mi·rac·u·lous** /mɪˈrækyələs/ *adj* completely unexpected and very lucky: *The doctors thought she might die, but she made a miraculous recovery.* —**miraculously** *adv*

**mi·rage** /mɪˈrɑʒ/ *n* a strange effect caused by hot air in a desert, in which you can see things when they are not actually there

**mire¹** /maɪɚ/ *v* **be mired (down) in a)** to be in a very difficult situation: *an economy mired* *in recession* **b)** to be stuck in deep mud: *The car's wheels became mired in mud and snow.*

**mire²** *n* **1** [singular, U] a very difficult situation: *The company sank deeper into the mire of debt.* **2** [U] LITERARY deep mud

**mir·ror¹** /ˈmɪrɚ/ *n* **1** a piece of special flat glass that you can look at and see yourself in: *the bathroom mirror* | *a rearview mirror* (=a mirror in a car, for looking at the area behind you) **2 mirror image** a system or pattern that is almost exactly the same as another one: *Some experts believe that this economic recession is a mirror image of the events leading up to the Great Depression in the 1930s.*

**mirror²** *v* [T] to represent or be very similar to something else: *The election results mirrored public opinion.*

**mirth** /mɝθ/ *n* [U] LITERARY happiness and laughter

**mis·ad·ven·ture** /ˌmɪsədˈvɛntʃɚ/ *n* [C,U] bad luck or an accident

**mis·ap·pre·hen·sion** /ˌmɪsˌæprɪˈhɛnʃən/ *n* FORMAL a mistaken belief or a wrong understanding of something: *I was under the misapprehension that the work would be completed by Friday.*

**mis·ap·pro·pri·ate** /ˌmɪsəˈproupriˌeɪt/ *v* [T] FORMAL to dishonestly take something, especially money, that a company, organization etc. has trusted you to keep safe: *One of the partners in the firm misappropriated company funds.* —**misappropriation** /ˌmɪsəˌproupriˈeɪʃən/ *n* [U]

**mis·be·have** /ˌmɪsbɪˈheɪv/ *v* [I] to behave badly: *Anne's being punished for misbehaving in class.* —**misbehavior** /ˌmɪsbɪˈheɪvyɚ/ *n* [U]

**misc.** the written abbreviation of MISCELLANEOUS

**mis·cal·cu·late** /ˌmɪsˈkælkyəˌleɪt/ *v* [I,T] **1** to make a mistake in calculating the number, length, cost etc. of something: *We miscalculated the time it would take to drive to Long Island.* **2** to make a mistake when you are judging a situation: *I think politicians have miscalculated the strength of public feeling about the tax issue.*

**mis·cal·cu·la·tion** /ˌmɪsˌkælkyəˈleɪʃən/ *n* **1** a mistake made in calculating the number, length, cost etc. of something: *The builders made a huge miscalculation in the cost of repairs to the building.* **2** a wrong judgment about a situation: *A slight miscalculation by either country could lead to war.*

**mis·car·riage** /ˈmɪsˌkærɪdʒ, ˌmɪsˈkærɪdʒ/ *n* [C,U] **1** the act of accidentally giving birth to a baby too early for him/her to live: *Did you hear that Sharon had a miscarriage?* —compare ABORTION **2 miscarriage of justice** a situation in which someone is wrongly punished by a court of law for something s/he did not do

**mis·car·ry** /ˌmɪsˈkæri/ *v* [I] to accidentally give birth to a baby too early for him/her to live

**mis·cel·la·ne·ous** /ˌmɪsəˈleɪniəs/ *adj* made up of many different things or people that do not seem to be related to each other: *a miscellaneous assortment of books*

**mis·chief** /ˈmɪstʃɪf/ *n* [U] bad behavior, especially by children, that causes trouble or damage but no serious harm: *He's always getting into mischief.* (=behaving in a way that causes trouble) | *I knew those kids were up to some mischief* (=doing or planning to do something that will cause trouble)

**mis·chie·vous** /ˈmɪstʃəvəs/ *adj* liking to have fun by playing tricks on people or doing things to annoy or embarrass them: *a mischievous child*

**mis·con·cep·tion** /ˌmɪskənˈsɛpʃən/ *n* [C,U] an idea that is wrong or untrue, but that people still believe: *At first, there was a misconception that only gay people could get AIDS.*

**mis·con·duct** /ˌmɪsˈkɑndʌkt/ *n* [U] FORMAL bad or dishonest behavior by someone in a position of authority or trust: *an investigation into police misconduct*

**mis·con·strue** /ˌmɪskənˈstru/ *v* [T] FORMAL to not understand correctly what someone has said or done: *The research results have been misconstrued.*

**mis·deed** /ˌmɪsˈdid/ *n* FORMAL a wrong or illegal action

**mis·de·mean·or** /ˌmɪsdɪˈminɚ/ *n* LAW a crime that is not very serious

**mis·di·rect** /ˌmɪsdəˈrɛkt/ *v* [T] FORMAL to use your efforts, emotion, or abilities in a way that is wrong or unsuitable: *misdirected anger* —**misdirection** /ˌmɪsdəˈrɛkʃən/ *n* [U]

**mi·ser** /ˈmaɪzɚ/ *n* DISAPPROVING someone who hates spending money and likes saving it —**miserly** *adj*

**mis·er·a·ble** /ˈmɪzərəbəl/ *adj* **1** very unhappy, especially because you are lonely or sick: *She's at home feeling miserable with the flu.* **2** very bad in quality: *miserable weather* —**miserably** *adv*

**mis·er·y** /ˈmɪzəri/ *n* [U] great suffering or unhappiness: *the misery of life in the refugee camps*

**mis·fit** /ˈmɪsˌfɪt/ *n* someone who does not seem to belong in the place where s/he lives or works, because s/he is very different from the other people there

**mis·for·tune** /mɪsˈfɔrtʃən/ *n* [C,U] bad luck, or something that happens to you as a result of bad luck: *We had the misfortune of being in a hotel in Boston when the snow storm hit.*

**mis·giv·ing** /mɪsˈgɪvɪŋ/ *n* [C,U] a feeling of doubt or fear about what might happen or about whether something is right: *I knew he had some misgivings about letting me use his car.*

**mis·guid·ed** /mɪsˈgaɪdɪd/ *adj* **1** intended to be helpful but actually making a situation worse: *The song is a misguided attempt to turn popular*

M

*music into poetry.* **2** wrong because of being based on a wrong understanding of a situation: *The belief that communism must be opposed was misguided.*

**mis·han·dle** /ˌmɪsˈhændl/ *v* [T] to deal with a situation badly, or not skillfully: *University officials are being criticized for mishandling the student protest.*

**mis·hap** /ˈmɪshæp/ *n* [C,U] a small accident or mistake that does not have a very serious effect

**mis·in·form** /ˌmɪsɪnˈfɔrm/ *v* [T] to give someone information that is incorrect or untrue, either deliberately or accidentally: *The public has been misinformed about the nature of our work.*

**mis·in·ter·pret** /ˌmɪsɪnˈtɜprɪt/ *v* [T] to not understand the correct meaning of something that someone says or does: *I think she misinterpreted my joke - I didn't mean to upset her.* −**misinterpretation** /ˌmɪsɪnˌtɜprəˈteɪʃən/ *n* [C,U]

**mis·judge** /ˌmɪsˈdʒʌdʒ/ *v* [T] **1** to form a wrong or unfair opinion about a person or situation: *The White House has badly misjudged Congress's support for his bill.* **2** to guess an amount, distance etc. wrongly: *Don misjudged the turn and wrecked his car.* −**misjudgment** *n* [C,U]

**mis·lay** /mɪsˈleɪ/ *v* mislaid /-ˈleɪd/, mislaid, mislaying [T] ⇨ MISPLACE

**mis·lead** /mɪsˈlid/ *v* misled /-ˈlɛd/, misled, misleading [T] to make someone believe something that is not true by giving him/her false or incomplete information: *I wasn't trying to mislead anyone, I just didn't know all the facts.*

**mis·lead·ing** /mɪsˈlidɪŋ/ *adj* likely to make someone believe something that is not true: *It is illegal to put misleading information into an advertisement.* −**misleadingly** *adv*

**mis·man·age** /ˌmɪsˈmænɪdʒ/ *v* [T] to deal with something you are in charge of in a way that is not effective or organized: *This project's been completely mismanaged from the beginning.* −**mismanagement** *n* [U]

**mis·match** /ˈmɪsmætʃ/ *n* a combination of things or people that are not equal in quality, strength, ability, or looks: *Saturday's game was a complete mismatch.* (=one team was much better than the other) −**mismatched** *adj*

**mis·no·mer** /ˌmɪsˈnoʊmɚ/ *n* a wrong or unsuitable name: *The police chief said it would be a misnomer to call their actions "big drug raids."*

**mi·sog·y·nist** /mɪˈsɑdʒənɪst/ *n* FORMAL a man who hates women −**misogyny** *n* [U] −**misogynistic** /mɪˌsɑdʒəˈnɪstɪk/ *adj*

**mis·place** /ˌmɪsˈpleɪs/ *v* [T] to put something somewhere and then forget where you put it: *I've misplaced my glasses again.*

**mis·placed** /ˌmɪsˈpleɪst/ *adj* misplaced feelings of trust, love etc. are unsuitable because the person that you have these feelings for does not deserve them: *a misplaced sense of loyalty*

**mis·print** /ˈmɪsˌprɪnt/ *n* a mistake in a book, magazine etc.

**mis·quote** /ˌmɪsˈkwoʊt/ *v* [T] to make a mistake in reporting what someone else has said or written: *The governor's speech was misquoted in the newspapers.*

**mis·read** /ˌmɪsˈrid/ *v* misread /-ˈrɛd/, misread, misreading [T] **1** to make a judgment about a situation or person that is wrong: *Fischer misread her silence as anger.* **2** to read something in the wrong way: *Did you misread the date on the letter?* −**misreading** *n* [C,U]

**mis·rep·re·sent** /ˌmɪsrɛprɪˈzɛnt/ *v* [T] to deliberately give a wrong description of someone's opinions or of a situation, especially in order to get an advantage for yourself: *Some of these ideas about welfare reform have been misrepresented in the press.* −**misrepresentation** /mɪsˌrɛprɪzənˈteɪʃən/ *n* [C,U]

**miss¹** /mɪs/ *v* **1** [T] to not go somewhere or do something, especially when you want to but cannot: *Sorry I have to miss your barbecue.* | *He'd never miss the chance/opportunity to go to Acapulco!* **2** [T] to not arrive in time for something: *By the time we got there, we'd missed the beginning of the movie.* **3** [T] to feel sad because you are not with a particular person, or because you no longer have something or are no longer doing something: *I've missed you so much!* | *Do you miss living in the city?* **4** [I,T] to not hit or catch something: *She fired at the target but missed.* | *Jackson missed an easy catch and the A's scored.* **5** [T] to not see, hear, or notice something: *Jody found an error that everyone else had missed.* **6** [T] to notice that something or someone is not in the place you expect him, her, or it to be: *I didn't miss my key until I got home.* **7 miss the boat** INFORMAL to fail to take an opportunity that will give you an advantage: *You'll be missing the boat if you don't buy these shares now.* −see usage note at LOSE

**miss out** *phr v* [I] to not have the chance to do something that you enjoy: *You're the one who'll miss out if you don't come.* | *She got married very young, and now she feels she's missing out on life.*

**miss²** *n* **1 Miss Smith/Jones** etc. used in front of the family name of a woman who is not married in order to speak to her politely, to write to her, or talk about her **2** a failed attempt to hit, catch, or hold something **3** used in order to speak politely to a young woman when you

miss

Lucia just missed the bus.

M

do not know her name: *Excuse me, miss, you've dropped your umbrella.* **4 Miss Italy/Ohio/World etc.** used before the name of a country, city etc. that a woman represents in a beauty competition

**mis·shap·en** /ˌmɪsˈʃeɪpən, ˌmɪʃˈeɪ-/ *adj* not the normal or natural shape: *He was born with a misshapen spine.*

**mis·sile** /ˈmɪsəl/ *n* **1** a weapon that can fly over long distances and that explodes when it hits something **2** FORMAL an object that is thrown at someone in order to hurt him/her

**miss·ing** /ˈmɪsɪŋ/ *adj* **1** someone or something that is missing is not in the place where you would normally expect him, her, or it to be: *Police are still searching for the missing child.│a kid with his two front teeth missing* **2** not included, although it ought to have been: *Why is my name **missing from** the list?* –see usage note at LOSE

**mis·sion** /ˈmɪʃən/ *n* **1** an important job that someone has been given to do: *Our mission was to blow up the airport.* **2** a group of people who go to another country for a particular purpose: *a Canadian trade mission to Japan* **3** a special trip made by a space vehicle or military plane: *a mission to Mars* **4** the work of a MISSIONARY, or a building where s/he does this work **5** something that you feel you must do because it is your duty: *She feels her **mission in life** is to help poor people.*

**mis·sion·ar·y** /ˈmɪʃəˌnɛri/ *n* someone who has gone to a foreign country in order to teach people about Christianity

**mis·spell** /ˌmɪsˈspɛl/ *v* [T] to spell a word incorrectly –**misspelling** *n* [C,U]

**mis·step** /ˈmɪs-stɛp/ *n* a mistake, especially one that offends or upsets people: *political missteps*

**mist¹** /mɪst/ *n* [C,U] a light cloud low over the ground that makes it difficult for you to see very far: *Heavy mists followed the rain.*

**mist²** *v* [I,T] to become covered with very small drops of water, or to make something do this: *The windows are all misted up/over.*

**mis·take¹** /mɪˈsteɪk/ *n* **1** something that has been done in the wrong way, or an opinion or statement that is incorrect: *Ivan's work is full of spelling mistakes.│I think you've **made a mistake** - I ordered fish, not beef.* **2** something you do that you later realize was not the right thing to do: *Marrying him was a big mistake.│I **made the mistake** of giving him my phone number.* **3 by mistake** without intending to do something: *Someone must have left the door open by mistake.* –see usage note at ERROR

**mistake²** *v* mistook, mistaken, mistaking [T] to understand something wrongly: *He'd mistaken the address and gone to the wrong house.*

**mistake sb/sth for** sb/sth *phr v* [T] to think that

one person or thing is someone or something else: *I mistook him for his brother.*

**mis·tak·en** /mɪˈsteɪkən/ *adj* wrong about something: *I had the mistaken idea that it would be quicker to take the bus.* –**mistakenly** *adv*

**mis·ter** /ˈmɪstɚ/ *n* **1** ⇨ MR. **2** SPOKEN said in order to speak to a man when you do not know his name: *Hey mister, is this your wallet?*

**mis·tle·toe** /ˈmɪsəlˌtoʊ/ *n* [U] a plant with small round white fruit that is often used as a decoration at Christmas

**mis·took** /ˌmɪˈstʊk/ *v* the past tense of MISTAKE

**mis·treat** /ˌmɪsˈtrit/ *v* [T] to treat a person or animal cruelly: *The hostages said they had not been mistreated.* –**mistreatment** *n* [U]

**mis·tress** /ˈmɪstrɪs/ *n* a woman that a man has a sexual relationship with even though he is married to someone else

**mis·tri·al** /ˈmɪstraɪl/ *n* a TRIAL during which a mistake in the law is made, so that a new trial has to be held

**mis·trust** /mɪsˈtrʌst/ *n* [U] the feeling that you cannot trust someone or his/her reasons for behaving in a particular way: *We both have a deep **mistrust of** politicians.* –**mistrust** *v* [T]

**mist·y** /ˈmɪsti/ *adj* **1** misty weather is weather with a lot of mist **2** LITERARY full of tears: *her eyes became misty*

**mis·un·der·stand** /ˌmɪsʌndɚˈstænd/ *v* **1** [I,T] to think that something means one thing when in fact it means something different: *I think you misunderstood what I was trying to say.* **2** [T] to fail to recognize someone's true character or qualities: *Why am I always misunderstood by people who work with me?*

**mis·un·der·stand·ing** /ˌmɪsʌndɚˈstændɪŋ/ *n* **1** [C,U] a failure to understand a question, situation, or instruction: *I think there's been a misunderstanding about what time we were supposed to meet.* **2** an argument or disagreement that is not very serious: *We've had our misunderstandings in the past, but we're good friends now.*

**mis·use¹** /ˌmɪsˈyuz/ *v* [T] to use something in the wrong way or for the wrong purpose: *an attempt to prevent the telephones at work from being misused for personal calls*

**mis·use²** /ˌmɪsˈyus/ *n* [C,U] the use of something in the wrong way or for the wrong purpose: *a misuse of power*

**mite¹** /maɪt/ *n* **1** a very small insect that lives in plants, CARPETs etc.: *dust mites* **2** a small child, especially one you feel pity for

**mite²** *adv* INFORMAL a small amount: *She's a mite shy.*

**mit·i·gate** /ˈmɪtəˌgeɪt/ *v* [T] FORMAL to make a situation or the effects of something less unpleasant, harmful, or serious: *Only foreign aid can*

M

*mitigate the terrible effects of the war.* —**mitigation** /ˌmɪtəˈgeɪʃən/ *n* [U]

**mitt** /mɪt/ *n* **1** a type of leather GLOVE used for catching a ball in baseball **2** a GLOVE made of thick material, worn to protect your hand: *an oven mitt*

**mit·ten** /ˈmɪt̚n/ *n* a type of GLOVE that has one part that covers your fingers and a separate part for your thumb

**mix**[1] /mɪks/ *v* **1** [I,T] if you mix two or more substances or if they mix, they combine to become a single substance: *You can't mix oil and water.* | *Mix the butter and sugar **together**, then add the milk.* **2** [I,T] to combine two or more different activities, ideas, groups of things etc.: *This record **mixes** jazz **with** rock.* **3** [I] to enjoy meeting, talking, and spending time with other people, especially people you do not know very well: *Charlie doesn't **mix** well with the other children.*

**mix up** *phr v* [T] **1** [mix sb/sth ↔ up] to make the mistake of thinking that someone or something is another person or thing: *It's easy to **mix** him **up** with his brother; they look so much alike.* **2** [mix sth ↔ up] to change the way things have been arranged so that they are no longer in the same order: *Don't **mix up** those papers, or we'll never find the ones we need.* **3** [mix sb up] INFORMAL to make someone feel confused: *They kept asking me questions and trying to **mix** me **up**.* – see also MIXED UP, MIX-UP

**mix**[2] *n* **1** [C,U] a combination of substances that you mix together to make something: *cake mix* **2** [singular] the particular combination of things or people that form a group: *There was a strange **mix** of people at Larry's party.*

**mixed** /mɪkst/ *adj* **1** consisting of many different types of things, people, ideas etc.: *a mixed diet of fruit and vegetables* | *We had **mixed feelings** (=felt both happy and sad) about moving so far away.* **2** a **mixed blessing** something that is good in some ways but bad in others: *Having the kids at home for the summer is always a mixed blessing - I miss the time alone.* **3** a **mixed bag** a group of things or people that are all very different from each other

**mixed mar·riage** /ˌ. ˈ../ *n* [C,U] a marriage between two people from different races or religions

**mixed up** /ˌ. ˈ◂/ *adj* **1** **be mixed up in something/be mixed up with someone** to be involved with a bad or dishonest situation or person: *kids getting mixed up with gang members* **2** confused: *I got mixed up and went to the wrong restaurant.* – see also **mix up** (MIX[1]), MIX-UP

**mix·er** /ˈmɪksɚ/ *n* **1** a piece of equipment used for mixing different substances together: *a food mixer* **2** a drink that can be mixed with alcohol: *Use the orange juice as a mixer.*

**mix·ture** /ˈmɪkstʃɚ/ *n* **1** [C,U] a single substance made by mixing two or more different substances together: *Pour the cake mixture into a pan and bake it for 45 minutes.* **2** [singular] a combination of two or more people, things, feelings, or ideas that are different: *I listened to his excuse with a mixture of amusement and disbelief.*

**mix-up** /ˈ. ./ *n* INFORMAL a mistake that causes confusion about details or arrangements: *There was a mix-up at the station and Eddie got on the wrong bus.* – see also **mix up** (MIX[1]), MIXED UP

**ml.** the written abbreviation of MILLILITER

**mm.** the written abbreviation of MILLIMETER

**MN** the written abbreviation of Minnesota

**MO** the written abbreviation of Missouri

**moan**[1] /moʊn/ *v* **1** [I] to make the sound of a MOAN: *An injured soldier moaned in the bed next to mine.* **2** [I,T] to complain in an annoying way, especially in an unhappy voice: *Stop moaning about your problems and get to work!* —**moaner** *n*

**moan**[2] *n* a long low sound expressing pain or sadness

**moat** /moʊt/ *n* a deep wide hole, usually filled with water, that is dug around a building such as a castle as a defense

**mob**[1] /mɑb/ *n* **1** a large noisy crowd, especially one that is angry and violent **2** **the Mob** INFORMAL ⇨ MAFIA

**mob**[2] *v* **-bbed, -bbing** [T] to move forward and form a crowd around someone in order to express admiration or to attack him/her: *She's mobbed by her fans wherever she goes.*

**mo·bile**[1] /ˈmoʊbəl/ *adj* able to move or be moved quickly and easily: *a mobile phone* | *I'm much more mobile now that I have a car.* —**mobility** /moʊˈbɪləti/ *n* [U] —opposite IMMOBILE

**mo·bile**[2] /ˈmoʊbil/ *n* a decoration made of small objects tied to string and hung up so that they move when air blows around them

**mobile home** /ˌ. ˈ./ *n* a type of house made of metal that can be pulled by a large vehicle and moved to another place

**mo·bi·lize** /ˈmoʊbəˌlaɪz/ *v* [I,T] to gather together or be brought together in order to work to achieve something difficult: *Forces have been mobilized to defend the capital.* —**mobilization** /ˌmoʊbələˈzeɪʃən/ *n* [C,U]

**mob·ster** /ˈmɑbstɚ/ *n* INFORMAL a member of the Mafia

**moc·ca·sin** /ˈmɑkəsən/ *n* a flat comfortable shoe made of soft leather –see picture at SHOE[1]

**mock**[1] /mɑk/ *v* [I,T] to laugh in an unkind way at someone or something and try to make him, her, or it seem stupid or silly, especially by copying his or her actions or speech: *Wilson mocked Joe's southern accent.* —**mockingly** *adv* —compare **make fun of sb/sth** (FUN[1])

M

**mock**[2] *adj* not real, but intended to be very similar to a real situation, substance etc.: *law students arguing cases in mock trials*

**mock·er·y** /ˈmɑkəri/ *n* **1** [U] the act of laughing at someone or something and trying to make him, her, or it seem stupid or silly **2** [singular] something that you expect to be a good example of what it is, but instead is completely useless or ineffective. *The trial made a mockery of justice.* (=the trial was expected to produce justice, but it did not)

**mock·ing·bird** /ˈmɑkɪŋˌbɚd/ *n* an American bird that copies the songs of other birds

**mo·dal verb** /ˌmoʊdl ˈvɚb/ **modal** *n* TECHNICAL in grammar, a verb that is used with other verbs to change their meaning by expressing ideas such as possibility, permission, or intention. In English, the modals are "can," "could," "may," "might," "shall," "should," "will," "would," "must," "ought to," "have to," and "had better" — see study note on page 458

**mode** /moʊd/ *n* FORMAL a particular way or style of behaving, living, or doing something: *a very efficient mode of transportation*

**mod·el**[1] /ˈmɑdl/ *n* **1** someone whose job is to show clothes, hair styles etc. by wearing them and being photographed: *a top fashion model* **2** a small copy of something such as a vehicle, building, or machine, especially one that can be put together from separate parts: *a toy store with a large selection of models* **3** someone who is employed by an artist or photographer in order to be painted or photographed **4** a particular type or design of a vehicle, machine, weapon etc.: *Ford has two new models coming out in October.* **5** a person or thing that is a perfect example of something good and is therefore worth copying: *Shelly's essay is a model of care and neatness.*

**model**[2] *adj* **1** model airplane/train/car etc. a small copy of a plane etc., especially one that can be put together from separate parts **2** model wife/employee/prison/school etc. a person or thing that is a perfect example of its type

**model**[3] *v* **1** [I,T] to have a job in which you show clothes, hair styles etc. by wearing them and being photographed **2** [I,T] to have a job in which you are employed by an artist or photographer in order to be painted or photographed **3** [T] to copy a system or way of doing something: *Their education system is modeled on the French one.* **4** model yourself on to try to be like someone else because you admire him/her: *James had always modeled himself on his hero, Martin Luther King.* **5** [T] to make small objects from materials such as wood or clay

**mod·el·ing** /ˈmɑdl-ɪŋ/ *n* [U] **1** the work of a model: *a career in modeling* **2** the activity of making model ships, planes, cars etc.

**mo·dem** /ˈmoʊdəm/ *n* a piece of electronic equipment that allows information from one computer to be sent along telephone wires to another computer

**mod·er·ate**[1] /ˈmɑdərɪt/ *adj* **1** neither very big nor very small, neither very hot nor very cold, neither very fast nor very slow etc.: *students of moderate ability | a moderate temperature* **2** having opinions or beliefs, especially about politics, that are not extreme and that most people consider reasonable or sensible: *a senator with moderate views*

**mod·e·rate**[2] /ˈmɑdəˌreɪt/ *v* [I,T] to make something less extreme or violent, or to become this: *To lose weight, moderate the amount of food you eat.*

**mod·e·rate**[3] /ˈmɑdərɪt/ *n* someone whose opinions or beliefs, especially about politics, are not extreme and are considered reasonable or sensible by most people

**mod·er·ate·ly** /ˈmɑdərɪtli/ *adv* fairly but not very: *a moderately successful company*

**mod·er·a·tion** /ˌmɑdəˈreɪʃən/ *n* [U] **1 in moderation** if you do something in moderation, you do not do it too much: *You've got to learn to drink in moderation.* **2** FORMAL control of your behavior, so that you keep your actions, feelings, habits etc. within reasonable or sensible limits

**mod·er·at·or** /ˈmɑdəˌreɪtɚ/ *n* someone whose job is to control a discussion or argument and to help people reach an agreement

**mod·ern** /ˈmɑdɚn/ *adj* **1** belonging to the present time or the most recent time: *modern American history | modern medical techniques* **2** using or willing to use very recent ideas, fashions, or ways of thinking: *The school is very modern in its approach to sex education.* —**modernity** /mɑˈdɚnəti, -ˈdɛr-/ *n* [U] —see usage note at NEW

**mod·ern·ize** /ˈmɑdɚˌnaɪz/ *v* [T] to change something, using new things or methods so that it is more suitable to be used in the present time: *We're modernizing the whole house, starting with a new bathroom.* —**modernization** /ˌmɑdɚnəˈzeɪʃən/ *n* [C,U]

**mod·est** /ˈmɑdɪst/ *adj* **1** APPROVING unwilling to talk proudly about your abilities and achievements: *He's very modest about his success.* **2** not very big in size, quantity, value etc.: *a modest salary* **3** APPROVING shy about showing your body or attracting sexual interest —**modestly** *adv* —opposite IMMODEST

**mod·es·ty** /ˈmɑdəsti/ *n* [U] APPROVING **1** the quality of being MODEST about your abilities or achievements **2** the quality of being MODEST about your body

**mod·i·cum** /ˈmɑdɪkəm/ *n* FORMAL **a modicum of** a small amount of something, especially a good quality: *Even children need a modicum of privacy.*

M

**mod·i·fi·ca·tion** /ˌmɑdəfəˈkeɪʃən/ n **1** a small change made in something, in order to improve it: *We've made a few **modifications** to the original design.* **2** [U] the act of modifying (MODIFY) something, or the process of being modified

**mod·i·fi·er** /ˈmɑdəˌfaɪɚ/ n TECHNICAL in grammar, an adjective, adverb, or phrase that gives additional information about another word. In the sentence "The dog is barking loudly," "loudly" is a modifier

**mod·i·fy** /ˈmɑdəˌfaɪ/ v [T] **1** to make small changes to something in order to improve it: *The car's been modified to use less fuel.* **2** TECHNICAL to act as a MODIFIER

**mod·u·lar** /ˈmɑdʒələ/ adj based on MODULEs or made using modules: *modular furniture*

**mod·u·late** /ˈmɑdʒəˌleɪt/ v [T] TECHNICAL to change the sound of your voice or another sound –**modulation** /ˌmɑdʒəˈleɪʃən/ n [U]

**mod·ule** /ˈmɑdʒul/ n **1** one of several separate parts that can be combined to form a larger object, such as a machine or building **2** a part of a SPACECRAFT that can be separated from the main part and used for a particular purpose

**mo·hair** /ˈmoʊhɛr/ n [U] expensive wool made from ANGORA

**Mo·ham·med** /moʊˈhæməd/ ⇨ MUHAMMAD

**moist** /mɔɪst/ adj slightly wet, in a pleasant way: *Make sure the soil is moist before planting the seeds.*｜*a moist chocolate cake* –compare DAMP

**moist·en** /ˈmɔɪsən/ v [I,T] to become MOIST, or to make something do this: *Moisten the clay with a little water.*

**mois·ture** /ˈmɔɪstʃɚ/ n [U] small amounts of water that are present in the air, in a substance, or on a surface: *The desert air contains hardly any moisture.*

**mois·tur·iz·er** /ˈmɔɪstʃəˌraɪzɚ/ n a creamy liquid you put on your skin to keep it soft

**mo·lar** /ˈmoʊlɚ/ n one of the large teeth at the back of the mouth, used for crushing food

**mo·las·ses** /məˈlæsɪz/ n [U] a thick dark sweet liquid that is obtained from raw sugar plants when they are being made into sugar

**mold**[1] /moʊld/ n **1** [U] a green or black FUNGUS (=plant without leaves) that grows on old food and on walls or objects that are in warm, slightly wet places **2** a hollow container that you pour liquid into, so that when the liquid becomes solid, it takes the shape of the container: *a candle mold shaped like a star*

mold

**mold**[2] v [T] **1** to shape a solid substance by pressing or rolling it or by putting it into a MOLD: *a figure of a man molded out of clay*

**2** to influence the way someone's character or attitudes develop: *His character has been molded more by his experiences than by his education.*

**mold·ing** /ˈmoʊldɪŋ/ n [C,U] a thin decorative line of stone, wood, plastic etc. around the edge of something such as a wall, car, or piece of furniture

**mold·y** /ˈmoʊldi/ adj covered with MOLD: *moldy bread*

**mole** /moʊl/ n **1** a small dark brown mark on the skin that is often slightly higher than the skin around it **2** a small animal with brown fur that cannot see very well and lives in holes in the ground **3** someone who works for an organization, especially a government, while secretly giving information to its enemy

**mol·e·cule** /ˈmɑləˌkyul/ n the smallest unit into which any substance can be divided without losing its own chemical nature, usually consisting of two or more atoms –**molecular** /məˈlɛkyələ/ adj

**mo·lest** /məˈlɛst/ v [T] to attack or harm someone by touching him/her in a sexual way or trying to have sex with him/her: *Tina was molested by her uncle when she was 13.* –**molester** n –**molestation** /ˌmoʊləˈsteɪʃən, ˌmɑ-/ n [U]

**mol·li·fy** /ˈmɑləˌfaɪ/ v [T] FORMAL to make someone feel less angry and upset about something

**mol·lusk** /ˈmɑləsk/ n a type of sea or land animal, for example a SNAIL or CLAM, with a soft body covered by a hard shell

**molt** /moʊlt/ v [I] when a bird or animal molts, it loses hair, feathers, or skin so that new hair, feathers, or skin can grow

**mol·ten** /ˈmoʊltn/ adj molten metal or rock has been made into a liquid by being heated to a very high temperature

**mom** /mɑm/ n INFORMAL mother: *Can I go to David's house, Mom?*

**mo·ment** /ˈmoʊmənt/ n **1** a very short period of time: *I'll be back in a moment.*｜*Your food will be ready in a moment.* **2** a particular point in time: *At that moment, the door opened and Danny walked in.*｜*I knew it was you the moment (that) I heard your voice.* **3** at the moment now: *We're living in an apartment at the moment, but we'll be moving into our house in six weeks.* **4** for the moment used in order to say that something is happening now but will probably change in the future: *The rain has stopped for the moment.* **5** [C usually singular] a particular period of time when you have a chance to do something: *It was her big moment* (=her chance to show other people how skilled she is)*; she took a deep breath and began to play.* –compare MINUTE[1]

**mo·men·tar·i·ly** /ˌmoʊmənˈtɛrəli/ adv **1** for a very short time: *Jason was mo-*

*mentarily stunned by the explosion.* **2** very soon: *I'll be with you momentarily.*

**mo·men·tar·y** /'moumən,tɛri/ *adj* continuing for a very short time: *a momentary silence*

**mo·men·tous** /mou'mɛntəs, mə-/ *adj* a momentous event, occasion, decision etc. is very important, especially because of the effects it will have in the future: *the momentous changes in Central Europe*

**mo·men·tum** /mou'mɛntəm, mə-/ *n* [U] **1** the force that makes a moving object keep moving: *The rock* **gained/gathered momentum** (=moved faster and faster) *as it rolled down the hill.* **2** the ability to keep increasing, developing, or being more successful: *The business did very well at first but now it seems to be* **losing momentum**.

**mom·ma** /'mamə/ *n* SPOKEN mother

**mom·my** /'mami/ *n* SPOKEN a word meaning mother, used especially by a child or when speaking to a child

**mon·arch** /'manək, 'manark/ *n* a king or queen

**mon·ar·chy** /'manəki/ *n* **1** [U] the system in which a country is ruled by a king or queen **2** a country that is ruled by a king or queen

**mon·as·ter·y** /'manə,stɛri/ *n* a building or group of buildings in which MONKs live

**mo·nas·tic** /mə'næstɪk/ *adj* relating to MONKs or a MONASTERY

**Mon·day** /'mʌndi, -deɪ/ written abbreviation **Mon.** *n* the second day of the week –see usage note at SUNDAY

**mon·e·tar·y** /'manə,tɛri/ *adj* relating to money, especially all the money in a particular country: *a monetary system based on the value of gold*

**mon·ey** /'mʌni/ *n* [U] **1** what you earn by working and use in order to buy things, usually in the form of coins or pieces of paper with their value printed on them: *How much money do you have?* | *That car must have cost a lot of money.* | *We're trying to* **save** *enough* **money** *for a trip to Europe.* | *Zach's* **making** *a lot of* **money** (=earning money or making a profit) *selling his paintings.* | *I left my wallet at home - do you* **have** *enough* **money on you** (=carry money with you) *to pay for the meal?* | *She's making about $40,000 a year, which is pretty* **good money**. (=good wages for your work) **2** wealth: *Money isn't everything.* | *Fred lost all his money when he was forced to close his business.* | *I think he made his money on the stock market.* **3** **get your money's worth** to think that something you have paid to do or see was worth the price that you paid: *The tickets were expensive, but we felt that we got our money's worth.*

SPOKEN PHRASES

**4 kind of money** a phrase meaning a lot of money, used when you think something

costs too much, when someone earns a lot more than other people etc.: *They wanted $5000, and I just* **don't have that kind of money**. | *People with that kind of money* (=rich people) *don't need to work.* **5 pay good money for** to spend a lot of money on something: *I paid good money for that sofa, so it should last.* **6 there's money (to be made) in** used in order to say that you can get a lot of money from a particular activity or from buying and selling something: *There's a lot of money in selling antiques.* **7 for my money** used when giving your opinion about something, to emphasize that you believe it strongly: *For my money, the Chicago Bears are one of the best teams in the league.* **8 money talks** used in order to say that people who have money can usually get whatever they want **9 be (right) on the money** used when something is perfect or exactly right for the situation: *Her solution was right on the money - the clients loved it.* **10 money is no object** used in order to say that you can spend as much money as you want to on something: *Choose whatever you like, money is no object.*

**money mar·ket** /'.. ,../ *n* the banks and other financial institutions that buy and sell BONDs, CURRENCY (=paper money) etc.

**money or·der** /'.. ,../ *n* a special type of check that you buy and send to someone so that s/he can exchange it for money

**mon·grel** /'maŋgrəl, 'mʌŋ-/ *n* a dog that is a mix of several breeds of dog

**mon·i·ker** /'manikə/ *n* INFORMAL someone's name or NICKNAME

**mon·i·tor¹** /'manətə/ *n* **1** a piece of equipment that looks like a television and that shows information or pictures, especially on a computer **2** a child who is chosen to help a teacher in some way: *The blackboard monitor cleans the boards.*

**monitor²** *v* [T] to carefully watch, listen to, or examine something over a period of time, to check for any changes or developments: *Army intelligence has been monitoring the enemy's radio broadcasts.* | *Doctors are monitoring the patient's condition.*

**monk** /mʌŋk/ *n* a man who is a member of a group of religious men who live together in a MONASTERY (=special building)

**mon·key¹** /'mʌŋki/ *n* **1** a type of active animal that lives in hot countries and has a long tail, that it uses with its hands to climb trees **2 monkey business** behavior that may cause trouble or be dishonest: *The boys are awfully quiet - I think they're up to some monkey business.* **3 make a monkey out of sb** to make someone seem stupid

M

**monkey² v**

**monkey around** *phr v* [I] INFORMAL to behave in a stupid or careless way: *They were monkeying around in the playground and one of them got hurt.*

**monkey (around) with** sth *phr v* [T] to touch or use something, usually when you do not know how to do it correctly: *You'll break the TV if you don't stop monkeying with it.*

**monkey wrench** /'.. ,./ *n* a tool that is used for holding or turning things of different widths, especially NUTs

**mon·o** /'mɑnoʊ/ *n* [U] INFORMAL an infectious illness that makes you feel weak and tired for a long time

**mon·o·chrome** /'mɑnə,kroʊm/ *adj* having, using, or appearing in only black, white, and gray: *a monochrome computer monitor*

**mo·nog·a·my** /mə'nɑgəmi/ *n* [U] the custom or practice of being married to only one person at one time – **monogamous** /mə'nɑgəməs/ *adj*

**mon·o·gram** /'mɑnə,græm/ *n* a design made from the first letters of someone's names, that is put on things such as shirts or writing paper – **monogrammed** *adj*

**mon·o·lith·ic** /,mɑnl'ɪθɪk/ *adj* 1 a monolithic organization, political system etc. is very large and difficult to change 2 very large, solid, and impressive: *a monolithic building* – **monolith** /'mɑnəlɪθ/ *n*

**mon·o·logue, monolog** /'mɑnl,ɔg, -,ɑg/ *n* a long speech by one character in a play, movie, or television show

**mon·o·nu·cle·o·sis** /,mɑnoʊ,nukli'oʊsɪs/ *n* [U] ⇨ MONO

**mo·nop·o·lize** /mə'nɑpə,laɪz/ *v* [T] to have complete control over something, especially a type of business, so that other people cannot get involved: *The tobacco industry is monopolized by a few large companies.* – **monopolization** /mə,nɑpələ'zeɪʃən/ *n* [U]

**Mo·nop·o·ly** /mə'nɑpəli/ *n* [U] TRADEMARK a game using artificial money in which you try to get more money and property than your opponents

**mo·nop·o·ly** *n* the control of all or most of a business activity: *The government broke up Bell Telephone's monopoly on telephone services.* – **monopolistic** /mə,nɑpə'lɪstɪk/ *adj*

**mon·o·rail** /'mɑnə,reɪl/ *n* [C,U] a type of railroad that uses a single RAIL, or the train that travels on this type of railroad

**mon·o·tone** /'mɑnə,toʊn/ *n* [singular] a sound that continues on the same note without getting any louder or softer: *He spoke in a monotone.*

**mo·not·o·nous** /mə'nɑt⌐n-əs/ *adj* boring because there is no variety: *a monotonous job* – **monotony** *n* [U] – **monotonously** *adv*

**mon·soon** /mɑn'sun/ *n* the season when it rains a lot in India and other southern Asian countries, or the rain or wind that happens during this season

**mon·ster** /'mɑnstɚ/ *n* 1 an imaginary large ugly frightening creature: *a sea monster* 2 someone who is cruel and evil: *Only a monster could kill an innocent child.* 3 an object, animal etc. that is unusually large: *That dog's a real monster!* – **monster** *adj*

**mon·stros·i·ty** /mɑn'strɑsəti/ *n* something large that is very ugly, especially a building

**mon·strous** /'mɑnstrəs/ *adj* 1 very wrong, immoral, or unfair: *a monstrous crime* 2 unusually large: *a monstrous piece of pie | a monstrous truck* – **monstrously** *adv*

**mon·tage** /mɑn'tɑʒ, moʊn-/ *n* 1 [U] an art form in which a picture, movie etc. is made from parts of different pictures etc. that are combined to form a whole 2 a picture, movie etc. made using this process

**month** /mʌnθ/ *n* 1 one of the 12 periods of time that a year is divided into: *the month of May | He's starting college at the end of this month. | last/next month* (=the month before or after this one) 2 any period of time equal to about four weeks: *Jeff is away for two months. | We'll be back a month from today/tomorrow/Friday.* (=a month after today, etc.)

**month·ly** /'mʌnθli/ *adj* 1 happening or done every month: *a monthly meeting* 2 relating to a single month: *his monthly rate of pay* – **monthly** *adv*

**mon·u·ment** /'mɑnyəmənt/ *n* 1 a building or other large structure that is built to remind people of an important event or famous person: *a monument to soldiers killed in the war* 2 **be a monument to** to be a very clear example of what can happen as a result of a particular quality: *The huge empty office buildings are a monument to bad planning.*

**mon·u·men·tal** /,mɑnyə'mɛnṭl◂/ *adj* 1 a monumental achievement, piece of work etc. is very important and has a lot of influence: *Darwin's monumental work on evolution* 2 extremely large, bad, good, impressive etc.: *monumental stupidity*

**moo** /mu/ *n* the sound that a cow makes – **moo** *v* [I]

**mooch** /mutʃ/ *v* [T] INFORMAL to get something by asking someone to give it to you instead of paying for it yourself: *Tim's always mooching my cigarettes.*

**mood** /mud/ *n* 1 the way you feel at a particular time, or the way a group of people feel: *You're certainly in a good/bad mood today. | The mood after the game was one of extreme gloom.* 2 **be in the mood** to want to do something or feel that you would enjoy doing something: *Are you in the mood for a walk?*

**mood·y** /'mudi/ *adj* 1 having MOODs that change often and quickly, especially angry or bad moods: *a moody teenager* **2** making people feel particular MOODs: *moody music*

**moon**[1] /mun/ *n* **1 the moon** the round object that can be seen shining in the sky at night **2** [singular] the shape of this object as it appears at a particular time: *There's no moon tonight.* (=it cannot be seen) | *a full moon* (=the moon appearing as a full circle) **3** a large round object that moves around PLANETs other than the earth: *Saturn has several moons,* –see also **once in a blue moon** (ONCE[1]) –see picture at ORBIT[1]

**moon**[2] *v* [I,T] INFORMAL to bend over and show your uncovered BUTTOCKs to someone as a rude joke

**moon over** sb/sth *phr v* [T] INFORMAL to spend your time thinking about someone or something that you love: *She's been mooning over his photograph for hours.*

**moon·beam** /'munbim/ *n* a beam of light from the moon

**moon·less** /'munlıs/ *adj* without the moon showing in the sky: *a cloudy moonless night*

**moon·light**[1] /'munlaɪt/ *n* [U] the light of the moon

**moonlight**[2] *v* [I] INFORMAL to have a second job in addition to your main job: *Clayton's been moonlighting as a security guard.* –**moonlighting** *n* [U] –**moonlighter** *n*

**moon·lit** /'mun,lɪt/ *adj* made brighter by the light of the moon: *a beautiful moonlit night*

**moor** /mur/ *v* [I,T] to fasten a ship or boat to the land or the bottom of the sea, lake etc. with a rope or chain

**moor·ing** /'murɪŋ/ *n* the place where a ship or boat MOORs

**moose** /mus/ *n* a large wild North American, European, or Asian animal with large ANTLERs (=flat horns that look like branches) and a head like a horse

**moot** /mut/ *adj* **1 a)** a question or point that is moot is one that has not yet been decided, and about which people have different opinions: *Whether these laws will really reduce violent crime is a moot point.* **2** a situation or possible action that is moot is no longer likely to happen or exist, or is no longer important: *Questions about planning the project are moot, because there is no money to finance it.*

**mop**[1] /map/ *n* **1** a thing for washing floors, made of a long stick with threads of thick string or a piece of SPONGE fastened to one end **2** INFORMAL a large amount of thick messy hair: *a mop of curly hair*

**mop**[2] *v* **-pped, -pping** [T] **1** to wash a floor with a wet MOP **2** to remove liquid from a surface by rubbing it with a cloth or something soft: *Earl mopped the sweat from his face.*

**mop** sth ↔ **up** *phr v* [T] to clean liquid off a surface using a mop, cloth, or something soft: *Can you mop up the milk you've spilled?*

**mope** /moup/ *v* [I] to pity yourself and feel sad, without making any effort to be more cheerful: *Don't just sit there moping - go out and play!*

**mope around** *phr v* [I,T] to do nothing because you are sad and you pity yourself: *Since Jerry left, she's just been moping around the house.*

**mo·ped** /'moupɛd/ *n* a vehicle like a bicycle with a small engine

**mor·al**[1] /'morəl, 'marəl/ *adj* **1** relating to the principles of what is right and wrong, and the difference between good and evil: *Terry refused to join the army for moral reasons.* | *a woman of high moral standards* | *a moral responsibility/duty* to help the poor –opposite IMMORAL **2 moral support** encouragement that you give by expressing approval or interest, rather than by giving practical help **3 moral victory** a situation in which you show that your beliefs are right and fair, or that you are the most skillful, even if you do not win the argument, game etc. **4** always behaving in a way that is based on strong principles about what is right and wrong: *a moral man*

**moral**[2] *n* a practical lesson about how to behave, that you learn from a story or from something that happens to you: *The moral of the story is that crime doesn't pay.* –see also MORALS

**mo·rale** /mə'ræl/ *n* [U] the level of confidence and positive feelings a person or group has, especially a group that works together, belongs to the same team etc.: *Rumors of job losses are bad for morale.*

**mor·al·ist·ic** /ˌmorə'lıstık, ˌmar-/ *adj* having very strong and fixed beliefs about what is right and wrong and about how people should behave –**moralist** /'morəlıst, 'ma-/ *n*

**mo·ral·i·ty** /mə'ræləti/ *n* [U] **1** beliefs or ideas about what is right and wrong and about how people should behave: *declining standards of morality* **2** the degree to which something is right or acceptable: *a discussion on the morality of the death penalty*

**mor·al·ize** /'morə,laɪz, 'mar-/ *v* [I] DISAPPROVING to tell other people your ideas about right and wrong behavior and about how people should behave

**mor·al·ly** /'morəli, 'mar-/ *adv* **1** according to moral principles about what is right and wrong: *It wasn't actually against the law, but it was morally wrong.* **2** in a way that is good and right: *the difficulty of behaving morally in a corrupt society*

**mor·als** /'morəlz, 'mar-/ *n* [plural] principles or standards of good behavior, especially in matters of sex: *His book reflects the morals and customs of the time.*

**mo·rass** /mə'ræs/ *n* [singular] **1** a complicated and confusing situation that is very

M

difficult to get out of: *California's economic morass* **2** a complicated amount of information: *a morass of details*

**mor·a·to·ri·um** /ˌmɔrəˈtɔriəm, ˌmɑr-/ *n* [C usually singular] an official announcement stopping an activity for a period of time: *a moratorium on nuclear weapons testing*

**mor·bid** /ˈmɔrbɪd/ *adj* having a strong and unhealthy interest in unpleasant subjects, especially death: *a morbid interest in fatal diseases* −**morbidly** *adv*

**more**¹ /mɔr/ *adv* **1** used before many adjectives and adverbs that have two or more SYLLABLEs in order to make the COMPARATIVE form: *My meal was more expensive than Dan's.* | *You'll have to be more careful next time.* | *The students will feel much more confident if they work in groups.* | *The troops were becoming more and more tired as the weeks went on.* −opposite LESS¹ **2** happening a greater number of times or for longer: *I promised Mom I'd help her more with the housework.* | *We see our grandchildren more than we used to.* | *He goes out a lot more now that he has a car.* −opposite LESS¹ **3** **not...any more** used in order to show that something that used to happen or be true does not happen or is not true now: *Sarah doesn't live here any more.* −see also ANY² ANYMORE **once more** (ONCE¹) −see study note on page 457

---

**USAGE NOTE more**

Use **more** as the opposite of both "less" and "fewer": *I think I'll need more money.* | *There were more people there than yesterday.* If an adjective has more than one syllable, you should usually use **more** instead of a COMPARATIVE form of the adjective: *He's more intelligent than the others.* ✗ DON'T SAY "intelligenter." ✗

---

**more**² *quantifier* [the comparative of "many" and "much"] **1** a greater amount or number: *There were more accidents on the highways this year than last year.* | *They haven't been gone more than 2 or 3 days.* | *These days, more and more people travel long distances in their jobs.* **2** an additional number or amount: *Would you like some more coffee?* | *I have to make a few more phone calls.* | *We had 5/12/20 more people at the meeting than we expected.* **3** **more or less** almost: *This report says more or less the same thing as the other one.*

**more·o·ver** /mɔrˈoʊvɚ/ *adv* FORMAL a word meaning "in addition to this," that is used in order to add information to something that has just been said: *A new design would not be acceptable, and, moreover, would delay the project even further.*

**mo·res** /ˈmɔreɪz/ *n* [plural] FORMAL the customs, social behavior, and moral values of a particular group: *American social mores*

**morgue** /mɔrg/ *n* a building or room where dead bodies are kept before they are buried or burned

**Mor·mon** /ˈmɔrmən/ *adj* relating to a religious organization called The Church of Jesus Christ of Latter-Day Saints, that has strict moral rules such as not allowing its members to drink alcohol and coffee −**Mormon** *n* −**Mormonism** *n* [U]

**morn·ing** /ˈmɔrnɪŋ/ *n* **1** [C,U] the early part of the day, especially from when the sun rises until the middle of the day: *I got a letter from Wayne this morning.* | *The freeway is usually jammed in the morning.* **2** **(Good) Morning** SPOKEN said in order to greet someone when you meet him/her in the morning: *Morning, Rick.*

**morning sick·ness** /ˈ.. ˌ../ *n* [U] a feeling of sickness that some women have when they are going to have a baby

**mo·ron** /ˈmɔrɑn/ *n* someone who is very stupid −**moronic** /məˈrɑnɪk/ *adj*

**mo·rose** /məˈroʊs/ *adj* unhappy, silent, and having a bad temper −**morosely** *adv*

**mor·phine** /ˈmɔrfin/ *n* [U] a powerful drug used for stopping pain

**morph·ing** /ˈmɔrfɪŋ/ *n* [U] a computer method that is used in order to make one image gradually change into a different one −**morph** *v* [I,T]

**Morse code** /ˌmɔrs ˈkoʊd/ *n* [U] a system of sending messages in which the alphabet is represented by short and long signals of sound or light

**mor·sel** /ˈmɔrsəl/ *n* a small piece of food: *a morsel of bread*

**mor·tal**¹ /ˈmɔrtl/ *adj* **1** not living for ever: *mortal creatures* −opposite IMMORTAL **2** **mortal injuries/blow/danger etc.** injuries etc. that will cause death or are likely to cause death **3** **mortal fear/terror/dread** extreme fear −**mortally** *adv*

**mor·tal**² *n* **1** **lesser/ordinary/mere mortals** HUMOROUS an expression meaning ordinary people, as compared with people who are more important or more powerful **2** LITERARY a human

**mor·tal·i·ty** /mɔrˈtæləti/ *n* [U] **1** also **mortality rate** the number of deaths during a particular period of time among a particular group of people or from a particular cause: *a decrease in the infant mortality rate* (=the rate at which babies die) **2** the condition of being human and having to die

**mor·tar** /ˈmɔrtɚ/ *n* **1** a heavy gun that fires explosives in a high curve **2** [U] a mixture of LIME, sand, and water, used in building for joining bricks or stones together

**mor·tar·board** /ˈ.. ˌ./ *n* a cap with a flat square top that you wear when you GRADUATE from a HIGH SCHOOL or university

M

**mort·gage**[1] /ˈmɔrgɪdʒ/ *n* **1** an agreement in which you borrow money from a bank in order to buy a house, and pay back the money over a period of years: *We've taken out a mortgage* (=borrowed money for a mortgage) *on a new house*. **2** the amount of money lent on a mortgage: *a mortgage of $100,000*

**mortgage**[2] *v* [T] to borrow money by giving someone, usually a bank, the right to own your house, land, or property if you do not pay back the money he, she, or it lent you within a certain period of time: *We mortgaged the house to pay for Sarah's college education.*

**mor·ti·cian** /mɔrˈtɪʃən/ *n* someone whose job is to arrange funerals and prepare bodies before they are buried

**mor·ti·fy** /ˈmɔrtəˌfaɪ/ *v* **be mortified** to feel extremely embarrassed or ashamed: *I was mortified by my father's behavior.* –**mortifying** *adj* –**mortification** /ˌmɔrtəfəˈkeɪʃən/ *n* [U]

**mor·tu·ar·y** /ˈmɔrtʃuˌɛri/ *n* the place where a body is kept before a funeral and where the funeral is sometimes held

**mo·sa·ic** /mouˈzeɪ-ɪk/ *n* [C,U] a pattern or picture made by fitting together small pieces of colored stone, glass etc.

mosaic

**mo·sey** /ˈmouzi/ *v* [I] INFORMAL to walk somewhere in a slow relaxed way: *I guess I'll mosey on down to the store now.*

**mosey along** *phr v* [I] to leave: *It's getting late; we'd better mosey along.*

**Mos·lem** /ˈmɑzləm, ˈmɑs-/ ⇨ MUSLIM

**mosque** /mɑsk/ *n* a building where Muslims go to have religious services

**mos·qui·to** /məˈskitou/ *n* a small flying insect that bites and sucks the blood of people and animals, making you ITCH and sometimes spreading diseases

**moss** /mɔs/ *n* [U] a small flat green or yellow plant that looks like fur and often grows on trees and rocks –**mossy** *adj*

**most**[1] /moust/ *adv* **1** used before many adjectives and adverbs that have two or more SYLLABLES in order to make the SUPERLATIVE form: *I think Anna is one of the most beautiful women I know.* | *I forgot to tell you the most important thing!* | *This style of management is most frequently used in Japan.* **2** more than anything else: *She liked the dark beer most.* | *I was angry at her, but, most of all I felt sad that the marriage was over.* **3** SPOKEN NONSTANDARD almost: *We eat at Joe's most every weekend.* –see study note on page 457

**most**[2] *quantifier* [the superlative of "many" and "much"] **1** almost all of a particular group of people or things: *Most of the kids I know have parents who are divorced.* | *Most computers*

have two disk drives. **2** more than anyone or anything else: *Ricardo's restaurant gives you the most food for your money.* | *Diane had the most to say of all of us.* (=she said more than everyone else) **3** the largest number or amount of something: *He spent most of his time in Milwaukee.* | *How can we get the most power from the engine?* **4 at (the) most** used in order to say that a number or amount will not be larger than you say. *The book should cost $10 or $12 at the most.* **5 for the most part** used in order to say that something is generally true or usually happens, but not always: *Everyone was talking except for Grandpa who, for the most part, was silent.* **6 make the most of sth** to get the most advantage that is possible from a situation: *You'll have to make the most of the small amount of information you have.*

**most·ly** /ˈmoustli/ *adv* in most cases, or most of the time: *Mostly, he travels by car or in his own plane.* | *The room was full of athletes, mostly football players.* ✗ DON'T SAY "mostly all," "mostly everybody," etc. SAY "almost all," "almost everybody," etc. ✗

**mo·tel** /mouˈtɛl/ *n* a hotel for people traveling by car, with a place for the car near each room

**moth** /mɔθ/ *n* an insect similar to a BUTTERFLY that usually flies at night, especially toward lights

**moth·ball**[1] /ˈmɔθbɔl/ *n* a small ball made of a strong-smelling chemical, used for keeping MOTHs away from clothes

**mothball**[2] *v* [T] INFORMAL to close a factory or operation, and keep all its equipment or plans for a long time without using them: *Our Denver factory is now mothballed.*

**moth-eat·en** /ˈ. ˌ../ *adj* **1** clothing that is moth-eaten has holes eaten in it by moths **2** old and in bad condition: *a moth-eaten old chair*

**moth·er**[1] /ˈmʌðɚ/ *n* **1** a female parent: *My mother said I have to be home by 9:00.* | *Mother, can I have some ice cream?* | *a mother hen and her chicks* –see picture at FAMILY **2** SPOKEN something that is very large: *a real mother of a car* **3** SPOKEN something that is a very good or very bad example of its type: *I woke up with the mother of all hangovers.*

**mother**[2] *v* [T] to take care of and protect someone in the way that a mother does: *Tom resented being constantly mothered by his wife.*

**moth·er·board** /ˈmʌðɚˌbɔrd/ *n* TECHNICAL the main CIRCUIT BOARD inside a computer

**moth·er·fuck·er** /ˈmʌðɚˌfʌkɚ/ *n* SPOKEN TABOO someone who you dislike very much or with whom you are very angry –**motherfucking** *adj*

**moth·er·hood** /ˈmʌðɚˌhʊd/ *n* [U] the state of being a mother

**mother-in-law** /ˈ.. . ˌ./ *n* the mother of your husband or wife –see picture at FAMILY

M

**moth·er·ly** /ˈmʌðəli/ *adj* typical of a kind or concerned mother: *I remember Mrs. Sederman as a motherly woman who always had a cookie for us.*

**Mother Na·ture** /ˌ.. ˈ../ *n* [U] an expression used in order to talk about the force that controls and organizes the Earth, its weather, and the living creatures and plants on it

**mother-of-pearl** /ˌ.. . ˈ./ *n* [U] a pale-colored smooth shiny substance on the inside of some shells, used for making buttons, jewelry etc.

**Mother's Day** /ˈ.. ˌ./ *n* a holiday in honor of mothers, celebrated in the US and Canada on the second Sunday in May

**mo·tif** /mouˈtif/ *n* an idea, subject, or pattern that is regularly repeated and developed in a book, movie, work of art etc.

**mo·tion**[1] /ˈmouʃən/ *n* **1** [U] the process of moving, or the way that someone or something moves: *the gentle rolling motion of the ship* **2** a single movement of your head, hand etc.: *He made a motion with his hand, as if to tell me to keep back.* **3** a proposal that is made formally at a meeting and then decided on by voting: *The motion to increase the club's membership charges was passed/carried by 15 votes to 10.* **4 in slow motion** if something on television or in the movies is shown in slow motion, it is shown more slowly than usual so that all the actions can be clearly seen: *Let's look at that touchdown in slow motion.* **5 go through the motions** to do something because you have to do it, without being very interested in it: *I thought they had a great marriage, but he says they've just been going through the motions for years.*

**motion**[2] *v* [I,T] to give someone directions or instructions by moving your head, hand etc.: *The police officer motioned for me to stop the car.*

**mo·tion·less** /ˈmouʃənlɪs/ *adj* not moving at all

**motion pic·ture** /ˌ.. ˈ../ *n* ⇨ MOVIE

**mo·ti·vate** /ˈmouṭəˌveɪt/ *v* [T] to be the reason that someone is willing or eager to do something: *Every one of his actions is motivated by a desire for more power.*

**mo·ti·vat·ed** /ˈmouṭəˌveɪṭɪd/ *adj* **1** very eager to do or achieve something: *an intelligent and highly motivated student* **2** done for a particular reason: *The police believe the attack was racially motivated.* (=done because someone hates other races) | *a politically motivated decision* (=done to gain an advantage in politics)

**mo·ti·va·tion** /ˌmouṭəˈveɪʃən/ *n* **1** [U] eagerness and willingness to do something: *Jack is smart, but he lacks motivation.* **2** the reason why you want to do something: *the motivation for the lawsuit*

**mo·tive** /ˈmouṭɪv/ *n* the reason that makes someone do something, especially when this reason is kept hidden: *We believe that the motive for the murder was jealousy.*

**mot·ley** /ˈmɑtli/ *adj* **a motley crew/bunch/ assortment etc.** a group of people or other things that do not seem to belong together, especially people or things that you do not approve of

**mo·tor**[1] /ˈmouṭɚ/ *n* the part of a machine that makes it work or move by changing power into movement: *The drill is powered by a small electric motor.* –compare ENGINE

**motor**[2] *adj* using power provided by an engine: *a motor vehicle*

**mo·tor·bike** /ˈmouṭɚˌbaɪk/ *n* a MOTORCYCLE, often a small one

**mo·tor·cade** /ˈmouṭɚˌkeɪd/ *n* a group of cars and other vehicles that travel together and surround a very important person's car

**mo·tor·cy·cle** /ˈmouṭɚˌsaɪkəl/ *n* a fast, usually large, two-wheeled vehicle with an engine –see picture on page 469

**motor home** /ˌ.. ˈ./ *n* a large vehicle with beds, a kitchen etc. in it, used for traveling; RV –compare MOBILE HOME

motor home

**mo·tor·ist** /ˈmouṭərɪst/ *n* FORMAL someone who drives a car

**mo·tor·ized** /ˈmouṭəˌraɪzd/ *adj* having an engine, especially when something does not usually have an engine: *a motorized wheelchair*

**mo·tor·mouth** /ˈmouṭɚˌmauθ/ *n* INFORMAL someone who talks too much

**motor scoot·er** /ˈ.. ˌ../ *n* ⇨ SCOOTER

**motor ve·hi·cle** /ˌ.. ˈ.../ *n* FORMAL a car, bus, truck etc.

**mot·tled** /ˈmɑtld/ *adj* covered with patterns of light and dark colors of different shapes: *a mottled brown snake*

**mot·to** /ˈmɑtou/ *n* a short statement that expresses the aims or beliefs of a person, school, or institution: *The school motto is "Never lose hope."*

**mound** /maund/ *n* **1** a pile of dirt, stones, sand etc. that looks like a small hill **2** a large pile of something: *a mound of papers*

**mount**[1] /maunt/ *v* **1** [I] also **mount up** to gradually increase in size or amount: *His debts continued to mount up.* **2** [T] to plan, organize, and begin an event or a course of action: *mounting an attack on the enemy camp* **3** [I,T] FORMAL to get on a horse, bicycle etc.: *She mounted the horse and rode off.* **4** [T] FORMAL to go up something such as a set of stairs: *Reporters shouted as Mayor Bradley mounted the steps of City Hall.* **5** [T] to be attached to something and supported by it: *I mounted his picture on a piece of stiff paper.*

M

**mount²** *n* **1** **Mount** part of the name of a mountain: *Mount Everest* **2** LITERARY an animal, especially a horse, that you ride on

**moun·tain** /'maʊntˀn/ *n* **1** a very high hill: *climbing a mountain* **2** a very large pile or amount of something: *a mountain of work to do.* **3** **make a mountain out of a molehill** to treat a problem as if it were very serious when in fact it is not

**mountain bike** /'.. ,./ *n* a strong bicycle with wide thick tires

**moun·tain·eer·ing** /,maʊntˀn'ɪrɪŋ/ *n* [U] an outdoor activity in which you climb mountains —**mountaineer** *n*

**mountain goat** /'.. ,./ *n* an animal that looks like a goat and lives in the western mountains of North America

**mountain li·on** /'.. ,../ *n* ⇨ COUGAR

**moun·tain·ous** /'maʊntˀn-əs/ *adj* having a lot of mountains: *a mountainous region of Europe*

**moun·tain·side** /'maʊntˀn,saɪd/ *n* the side of a mountain

**moun·tain·top** /'maʊntˀn,tɑp/ *n* the top part of a mountain

**Mount·ie** /'maʊnɾi/ *n* INFORMAL a member of the national police force of Canada

**mount·ing** /'maʊnɾɪŋ/ *adj* gradually increasing or becoming worse: *The Senator can hardly ignore the mounting criticism.*

**mourn** /mɔrn/ *v* [I,T] to feel very sad because someone has died, and show this in the way you behave: *The whole country mourned Kennedy's death.* | *The old woman still **mourns for** her son, 30 years after his death*

**mourn·er** /'mɔrnɚ/ *n* someone who attends a funeral, especially a relative of the dead person

**mourn·ful** /'mɔrnfəl/ *adj* very sad: *slow mournful music*

**mourn·ing** /'mɔrnɪŋ/ *n* [U] **1** great sadness because someone has died: *People wore black as a sign of mourning.* **2** **be in mourning** to be very sad because someone has died: *She's still **in mourning for** her son.*

**mouse** /maʊs/ *n* **1** a small object connected to a computer, that you move with your hand and press to give commands to the computer **2** *plural* **mice** a small animal like a rat with smooth fur, a long tail, and a pointed nose, that lives in buildings or in fields

**mousse** /mus/ *n* [C,U] **1** a cold sweet food made from a mixture of cream, eggs, and fruit or chocolate: *chocolate mousse* **2** a slightly sticky substance that you put in your hair to make it look thicker or to hold it in place

**mous·tache** /'mʌstæʃ, mə'stæʃ/ *n* ⇨ MUSTACHE

**mous·y** /'maʊsi, -zi/ *adj* **1** mousy hair is a dull brownish-gray color **2** a mousy girl or woman is small, quiet, uninteresting, and unattractive

**mouth¹** /maʊθ/ *n* **1** the part of your face that you put food into, or that you use for speaking —see picture at HEAD¹ **2** **keep your mouth shut** INFORMAL to not say anything: *I was getting really mad, but I kept my mouth shut.* **3** **open/shut your mouth** to start to speak, or to stop speaking: *Everything was fine until you opened your mouth!* **4** an opening, entrance, or way out: *the mouth of a river* (=where it joins the sea) | *the mouth of a jar* **5** **big mouth** INFORMAL someone who is a big mouth or has a big mouth often says things that s/he should not say **6** **make your mouth water** if food makes your mouth water, it looks so good you want to eat it immediately —see also MOUTH-WATERING **7** **open-mouthed/wide-mouthed** etc. with an open, wide etc. mouth —see also **shoot your mouth off** (SHOOT¹)

**mouth²** /maʊð/ *v* [T] **1** to move your lips as if you are saying words, but without making any sound: *When the teacher wasn't looking, Carter looked at me and mouthed "Don't laugh."* **2** to say things that you do not really believe or that you do not understand: *people mouthing "politically correct" attitudes*

**mouth off** *phr v* [I] INFORMAL to talk angrily or rudely to someone: *He was suspended for mouthing off to the principal.*

**mouth·ful** /'maʊθfʊl/ *n* **1** an amount of food or drink that you put into your mouth at one time: *I'm too full to eat another mouthful.* **2** **a mouthful** INFORMAL a long word or phrase that is difficult to say: *Her real name is quite a mouthful, so we just call her Dee.*

**mouth·piece** /'maʊθpis/ *n* **1** the part of a musical instrument, telephone etc. that you put in your mouth or next to your mouth **2** a person, newspaper etc. that expresses the opinions of a government or a political organization, especially without ever criticizing these opinions: *Pravda used to be the mouthpiece of the Communist Party.*

**mouth·wash** /'maʊθwɑʃ, -wɔʃ/ *n* [C,U] a liquid used in order to make your mouth smell fresh or to get rid of an infection in your mouth

**mouth-wa·ter·ing** /'. ,.../ *adj* food that is mouth-watering looks or smells extremely good

**mov·a·ble** /'muvəbəl/ *adj* able to be moved: *toy soldiers with movable arms and legs* —opposite IMMOVABLE

**move¹** /muv/ *v*

**1** ▶**CHANGE POSITION**◀ [I,T] to change from one place or position to another, or to make something do this: *I saw the dog's leg move, so I knew he was alive.* | *He moved the chair into the corner of the room.* | *She could hear someone **moving around** in Gail's room.*

**2** ▶**NEW PLACE**◀ [I,T] to go to a new place to live, work, or study, or to make someone do this: *They **moved to** Atlanta in May.* | *The company is **moving into** larger offices next*

M

*year.* | *They're **moving** Carrie **into** a different class next year.*

**3** ►FEEL EMOTION◄ [T] to make someone feel a strong emotion, especially sadness or sympathy: *The story moved me to tears.* (=made me cry)

**4** ►PROGRESS◄ [I] to progress or change in a particular way: *He moved easily from teaching into administration.*

**5** **get moving** SPOKEN used in order to say that someone needs to hurry: *If you don't get moving, you'll miss the bus.*

**6** ►START DOING STH◄ [I] to start doing something in order to achieve something: *We'll have to move quickly if we want to give the report at the conference.* | *The Senate has not yet moved on* (=not done anything as a result of) *the suggestions from the committee.*

**7** ►MEETING◄ [I] FORMAL to make an official suggestion at a meeting: *Dr. Reder moved that the proposal be accepted.*

**8** ►CHANGE ARRANGEMENTS◄ [T] to change the time or order of something: *We'll have to move the party to another day.*

**9** ►GO FAST◄ [I] INFORMAL to travel very fast: *That truck was really moving.*

**move away** *phr v* [I] to go to a new home in a different area: *They sold the house and moved away to a town in Ohio.*

**move in** *phr v* [I] **1** to start living in a new house: *We just moved in to the apartment yesterday.* **2** to start living with someone in the same house: *Jack asked Caroline to move in with him.* **3** to begin to control a situation using your power or high rank: *huge companies moving in on small businesses*

**move off** *phr v* [I] to leave a place: *As we moved off in the car, Mom stood waving goodbye.*

**move on** *phr v* [I] **1** [I] to leave a place where you have been staying in order to continue on a trip: *After three days we decided it was time to move on.* **2** to start talking or writing about a new subject in a speech, book, discussion etc.: *I'd like to move on now to the subject of education.* **3** to progress, improve, or become more modern as time passes: *The music business has certainly moved on since the days of vinyl records.*

**move out** *phr v* [I] to leave the house where you are living in order to go to live somewhere else: *We have to move out by next Friday.*

**move over** *phr v* [I] to change position in order to make room for someone or something else: *Move over a little so I can sit down.*

**move up** *phr v* [I] to get a better job than the one you had before: *She's been moved up to the managerial level.*

**move²** *n* **1** something that you decide to do in order to achieve something or make progress: *"I called Tom to say I don't want to see him again." "Good move!"* | *The White House says the Premier's statement is a move towards peace.* | *Brian won't make the first move* (=be the first one to do something to change a situation) *because he says he didn't start the argument.* **2** an action in which someone moves in a particular direction, especially in order to attack someone or to escape: *Grodin made a move toward the door.* | *They watched us but made no move to stop us.* **3** **be on the move** to be going or traveling to different places all the time: *He was constantly on the move, visiting customers all over the state.* **4** **get a move on** SPOKEN said when you want someone to hurry: *Get a move on, or we'll be late!* **5** the process of leaving the place where you live or work and going to live or work somewhere else: *The move to the new house took three days.* **6** the act of changing the position of one of the objects in a game, or the time when a particular player does this: *It's your move.*

**move·ment** /'muvmənt/ *n* **1** [C,U] a change in the place or position of something or someone: *I noticed a sudden movement behind the curtain.* **2** a group of people who share the same ideas or beliefs and work together to achieve a particular aim: *the anti-war movement* **3** a change or development in people's attitudes or behavior: *a movement away from traditional values* **4** one of the main parts into which a piece of music such as a SYMPHONY is divided **5** the moving parts of a piece of machinery, especially a clock

**mov·er** /'muvɚ/ *n* **1** someone whose job is to help people move from one house to another **2** **mover and shaker** an important person who has power and influence over what happens in a situation

**mov·ie** /'muvi/ *n* a story that is told using sound and moving pictures; FILM

**mov·ies** /'muviz/ *n* **the movies** the theater where you go to watch a movie: *Do you want to go to the movies with us?*

**movie star** /'.. ,./ *n* a famous movie actor or actress

**mov·ing** /'muvɪŋ/ *adj* **1** making you feel strong emotions, especially sadness or sympathy: *a moving story* **2** changing from one position to another: *Oil the moving parts of this machine regularly.* –**movingly** *adv*

**moving van** /'.. ,./ *n* a large vehicle used for moving furniture from one house to another

**mow** /mou/ *v* **mowed, mowed** *or* **mown** /moun/, **mowing** [I,T] to cut grass or crops with a machine: *When are you going to mow the lawn?*

**mow** sb ↔ **down** *phr v* [T] to kill people or knock them down, especially in large numbers: *soldiers mowed down by enemy guns*

**mow·er** /'mouɚ/ *n* a machine that you use to cut grass

M

**mpg** the written abbreviation of "miles per gallon"; used when describing the amount of GASOLINE used by a car: *a car that gets 35 mpg*

**mph** the written abbreviation of "miles per hour"; used when describing the speed of a vehicle: *driving along at 60 mph*

**Mr.** /'mɪstə/ *n* **1** Mr. Smith/Jones etc. used in front of the family name of a man to speak to him politely, to write to him, or to talk about him **2** a title used when speaking to a man in an official position: *Mr. Chairman | Mr. President*

**Mrs.** /'mɪsɪz/ *n* Mrs. Smith/Jones etc. used in front of the family name of a woman who is married to speak to her politely, to write to her, or to talk about her

**M.S., M.Sc.** *n* Master of Science; a university degree in science that you can earn after your first degree —compare M.A.

**MS** the written abbreviation of Mississippi

**Ms.** /mɪz/ *n* Ms. Smith/Jones etc. used in front of the family name of a woman who does not want to call herself "Mrs." or "Miss"

**MT** the written abbreviation of Montana

**Mt.** the written abbreviation for MOUNT: *Mt. Everest*

**much**[1] /mʌtʃ/ *adv* **more, most 1** used before COMPARATIVES and SUPERLATIVES to mean a lot: *Wayne looked much older than the last time I saw him. | Dad's feeling much better now. | The fair this year was much more fun than last year.* **2 too much/so much/very much/how much** etc. used in order to show the degree to which someone does something or something happens: *Thank you very much! | I know how much he likes Ann. | He's feeling so much better today that he went out for a walk.* **3 not much a)** only a little, only to a small degree etc.: *She isn't much younger than me. | Rob didn't like the movie very much.* **b)** used in order to say that something does not happen very often: *We don't go out much since the baby was born.* **4 much less** used in order to say that one thing is even less true or less possible than another: *He doesn't have enough money to buy new shoes, much less a new car.*

---

**USAGE NOTE   much, very, a lot, and many**

Use **much** with adjectives that come from the PASSIVE form of verbs: *The painting is much admired.* **Very** is used in the same way with ordinary adjectives: *The painting is very beautiful.* Use **much** with uncountable nouns in negative sentences and in questions: *These plants aren't getting much sunlight. | How much money do we have?* Use **a lot** or **many** with countable nouns: *She knows a lot of people. | There weren't many cars on the road.*

---

**much**[2] *quantifier* **1** used in spoken questions and negatives and in formal or written English to mean a lot of something: *Was there much traffic? | We don't have much time. | The storm is bringing rain to **much** of the state.* **2 how much** used in order to ask about the amount or cost of something: *How much is that green shirt?* (=what does it cost) *| She didn't know how much milk was left.* **3 so much/too much** used in order to talk about an amount that is very large, especially one that is too large: *I have so much reading to do for tomorrow. I'll never get it done. | He says the government has spent too much money on weapons.* **4 not much** used in order to say that something is not important, interesting etc.: *"What's been happening with you this week?" "Not much."* (=nothing that is interesting or important) **5 so much for** SPOKEN said when something that seemed useful or important before, does not seem that way now: *He didn't listen to me, but he won anyway. So much for my good advice!* **6 be too much for** to be too hard for someone: *Climbing stairs is too much for me since the operation.*

**muck** /mʌk/ *n* [U] something such as dirt, mud, or another sticky substance: *shoes covered in thick black muck*

**mu·cus** /'myukəs/ *n* [U] a liquid produced by parts of your body such as your nose —**mucous** *adj*

**mud** /mʌd/ *n* [U] **1** wet earth that is soft and sticky: *The kids tracked mud all over the carpet.* **2 sb's name is mud** SPOKEN said when people are annoyed at someone because s/he has caused trouble

**mud·dle**[1] /'mʌdl/ *v*
**muddle through/on** *phr v* [I] to continue doing something even though it is confusing or difficult

**muddle**[2] *n* a state of confusion or a lack of order: *papers in a muddle on the floor*

**mud·dy**[1] /'mʌdi/ *adj* covered with mud or containing mud: *muddy boots | muddy water*

**muddy**[2] *v* [T] **1 muddy the issue/waters** to make a situation more complicated or more confusing than it was before **2** to make something dirty with mud

**mud·guard** /'mʌdgard/ *n* a piece of rubber that hangs behind the wheel of a vehicle to prevent mud from getting on the vehicle

**mud·slide** /'mʌdslaɪd/ *n* a lot of very wet mud that has slid down the side of a hill

**mud·sling·ing** /'mʌd,slɪŋɪŋ/ *n* [U] the practice of saying bad things about someone so that other people will have a bad opinion of him/her —**mudslinger** *n*

**muff** /mʌf/ *v* [T] INFORMAL to do something badly or make a mistake so that something is not successful: *Fonseca muffed the catch.*

M

**muf·fin** /'mʌfən/ *n* a small, slightly sweet type of bread that often has fruit in it: *a blueberry muffin*

**muf·fle** /'mʌfəl/ *v* [T] to make a sound less loud or clear: *Thick curtains muffled the traffic noise.*

**muf·fled** /'mʌfəld/ *adj* muffled voices or sounds cannot be heard clearly: *He could barely hear Lisa's muffled voice.*

**muf·fler** /'mʌfləʳ/ *n* **1** a piece of equipment on a vehicle that makes the noise from the engine quieter **2** OLD-FASHIONED ⇨ SCARF¹

**mug¹** /mʌg/ *n* a large cup with straight sides and a handle used for drinking coffee, tea etc., or a large glass with a handle used for drinking beer

**mug²** *v* **-gged, -gging** [T] to attack someone and take his/her money: *She was mugged and her purse stolen.* **–mugging** *n* [U]

**mug·ger** /'mʌgəʳ/ *n* someone who attacks someone else to take his/her money –see usage note at THIEF

**mug·gy** /'mʌgi/ *adj* INFORMAL muggy weather is unpleasant because it is too warm and HUMID **–mugginess** *n* [U] –see usage note at TEMPERATURE

**mug·shot** /'mʌgʃɑt/ *n* INFORMAL a photograph of a criminal's face taken by the police

**Mu·ham·mad** /mou'hæməd/ *a* PROPHET who taught ideas on which Islam is based

**mu·lat·to** /mə'lɑtou/ *n* OLD-FASHIONED a word for someone with one white parent and one black parent, that is now considered offensive

**mulch** /mʌltʃ/ *n* [singular, U] decaying leaves that you put on the soil to improve its quality and to protect the roots of plants

**mule** /myul/ *n* an animal that has a DONKEY and a horse as parents

**mull** /mʌl/ *v* [T] to heat wine or beer with sugar and SPICEs

  **mull sth ↔ over** *phr v* [T] to think about something carefully: *I mulled over his offer for a day or two and then accepted it.*

**mul·lah** /'mʌlə/ *n* a religious leader or teacher in Islam

**mul·ti·col·ored** /'mʌltɪˌkʌləd/ *adj* having many different colors: *a multicolored shirt*

**mul·ti·cul·tur·al** /ˌmʌlti'kʌltʃərəl, -tɪ-/ *adj* involving people or ideas from many different countries, races, religions etc.: *The US is a multicultural society.* **–multiculturalism** *n* [U]

**mul·ti·lat·er·al** /ˌmʌltɪ'læṭərəl/ *adj* involving several different countries, companies etc.: *a multilateral agreement to stop the fighting* –compare BILATERAL, UNILATERAL

**mul·ti·me·di·a** /ˌmʌltɪ'midiə, -ti-/ *adj* using a mixture of sounds, words, pictures etc. to give information, especially on a computer program **–multimedia** *n* [U]

**mul·ti·na·tion·al** /ˌmʌlti'næʃənl/ *adj* **1** a multinational company has offices, businesses etc. in several different countries **2** involving people from several different countries: *a multinational peace-keeping force*

**mul·ti·ple¹** /'mʌltəpəl/ *adj* including or involving many parts, people, events etc.: *He suffered multiple injuries to his legs.*

**multiple²** *n* a number that can be divided by a smaller number an exact number of times: *20 is a multiple of 4 and 5.*

**multiple choice** /ˌ... '.../ *adj* a multiple choice test or question shows several possible answers and you must choose the correct one

**mul·ti·plex** /'mʌltɪˌplɛks/ *n* a movie theater that has several rooms in which different movies are shown

**mul·ti·pli·ca·tion** /ˌmʌltəplə'keɪʃən/ *n* [U] **1** a method of calculating in which you MULTIPLY numbers **2** FORMAL a large increase in the size, amount, or number of something: *the multiplication of the white blood cells* –compare DIVISION

**mul·ti·plic·i·ty** /ˌmʌltə'plɪsəṭi/ *n* [C,U] FORMAL a large number or great variety of things: *a multiplicity of views on the issue*

**mul·ti·ply** /'mʌltəˌplaɪ/ *v* [I,T] **1** to increase greatly, or to make something do this: *The company's problems have multiplied over the past year.* **2** to do a calculation in which you add one number to itself a particular number of times: *4 multiplied by 5 is 20. (=4 × 5 = 20)* –compare DIVIDE

**mul·ti·pur·pose** /ˌmʌltɪ'pəpəs◂, -ti-/ *adj* having many different uses or purposes: *a multipurpose room*

**mul·ti·ra·cial** /ˌmʌltɪ'reɪʃəl◂, -ti-/ *adj* including or involving many different races of people

**mul·ti·tude** /'mʌltəˌtud/ *n* FORMAL a multitude of a very large number of things or people: *Poems often have a multitude of interpretations.*

**mum·ble** /'mʌmbəl/ *v* [I,T] to say something too quietly or not clearly enough for someone to understand you: *He mumbled his name and I had to ask him to repeat it.*

**mum·bo-jum·bo** /ˌmʌmbou 'dʒʌmbou/ *n* [U] INFORMAL something that is difficult to understand or that makes no sense: *She was telling me some New Age mumbo-jumbo about crystals.*

**mum·mi·fy** /'mʌməˌfaɪ/ *v* [T] to preserve a dead body as a MUMMY

**mum·my** /'mʌmi/ *n* a dead body that has been preserved and often wrapped in cloth, especially in ancient Egypt

**mumps** /mʌmps/ *n* [U] an infectious illness in which your throat swells and becomes painful

**munch** /mʌntʃ/ *v* [I,T] to eat something in a noisy way: *The rabbit munched happily on its lettuce.*

M

**munch·ies** /'mʌntʃiz/ *n* [plural] INFORMAL
**1 have the munchies** to feel hungry, especially for food such as cookies or POTATO CHIPs
**2** foods such as cookies or POTATO CHIPs that are served at a party

**mun·dane** /mʌn'deɪn/ *adj* DISAPPROVING ordinary and not interesting or exciting; dull: *a mundane life in the suburbs* –**mundanely** *adv*

**mu·nic·i·pal** /myu'nɪsəpəl/ *adj* relating to the government of a town or city

**mu·nic·i·pal·i·ty** /myu,nɪsə'pæləti/ *n* a town or city that has its own government

**mu·ni·tions** /myu'nɪʃənz/ *n* [plural] military supplies such as bombs and large guns –**munition** *adj*

**mu·ral** /'myʊrəl/ *n* a painting that is painted on a wall

**mur·der¹** /'mɚdɚ/ *n* **1** [C,U] the crime of deliberately killing someone: *a man charged with the murder of two young girls | 4600 murders were committed in the US in 1975.*
**2 get away with murder** INFORMAL to not be punished for doing something wrong, or to be allowed to do anything you want: *Those kids of theirs get away with murder!* **3** SPOKEN used in order to say that something is very difficult or unpleasant: *Traffic was murder this morning!*

**murder²** *v* [T] to kill someone deliberately and illegally: *He murdered his wife in a jealous rage.* –**murderer** *n*

**mur·der·ous** /'mɚdərəs/ *adj* very dangerous or violent and likely to kill someone: *murderous gangs*

**murk·y** /'mɚki/ *adj* dark and difficult to see through: *murky water*

**mur·mur¹** /'mɚmɚ/ *v* [I,T] to say something in a soft quiet voice: *He softly murmured her name.* –**murmuring** *n* [C,U]

**murmur²** *n* a soft quiet sound made by someone's voice: *She answered in a low murmur.*

**mus·cle** /'mʌsəl/ *n* **1** [C,U] one of the pieces of flesh inside your body that join bones together and make your body move: *Weight lifting will strengthen your arm muscles.*
**2 military/political etc. muscle** military etc. power or influence **3** [U] physical strength and power: *It takes muscle to move a piano.* **4 not move a muscle** to not move at all

**mus·cu·lar** /'mʌskyələ/ *adj* **1** having a lot of big muscles: *strong muscular arms*
**2** related to or affecting the muscles: *a muscular disease*

**muse** /myuz/ *v* [I] FORMAL to imagine or think a lot about something: *new college graduates musing on/over what the future might hold* –**musing** *n*

**mu·se·um** /myu'ziəm/ *n* a building where important objects are kept and shown to the public: *an art museum*

**mush** /mʌʃ/ *n* [singular, U] DISAPPROVING a soft food that is part solid and part liquid: *I can't eat this mush!*

**mush·room¹** /'mʌʃrum/ *n* a FUNGUS (=plant without leaves) that has a stem and a round top, of which some types can be eaten and some are poisonous –see picture on page 470

**mushroom²** *v* [I] to grow in size or numbers very quickly: *The city's population has mushroomed to over one million.*

**mushroom cloud** /'.. ,./ *n* a large cloud shaped like a MUSHROOM that is caused by a NUCLEAR explosion

**mush·y** /'mʌʃi/ *adj* **1** DISAPPROVING very emotional: *mushy love stories* **2** soft and wet: *mushy old potatoes*

**mu·sic** /'myuzɪk/ *n* [U] **1** the arrangement of sounds made by musical instruments or voices: *What kind of music do you like? | My favorite piece of music is Bach's "Magnificat."*
**2** the art of writing or playing music: *music lessons* **3** a set of written marks representing music, or the paper that this is written on: *Jim plays the piano well, but he can't read music.*
**4 put on some music** to turn on a radio etc. to listen to music **5 face the music** to admit that you have done something wrong and accept punishment: *If he took the money, he'll have to face the music.*

**mu·si·cal¹** /'myuzɪkəl/ *adj* **1** relating to music or consisting of music: *musical instruments*
**2** good at playing or singing music: *I wasn't very musical as a child.* –**musically** *adv*

**musical²** *n* a play or movie that uses songs and music to tell a story

**mu·si·cian** /myu'zɪʃən/ *n* someone who plays a musical instrument very well or as a job

**musk** /mʌsk/ *n* [U] a strong smelling substance used for making PERFUME –**musky** *adj*

**mus·ket** /'mʌskɪt/ *n* a type of gun used in past times

**Mus·lim** /'mʌzləm, 'muz-, 'mus-/ *n* someone whose religion is Islam –**Muslim** *adj*

**muss** /mʌs/ **muss up** *v* [T] INFORMAL to make someone's hair, clothes etc. messy

**mus·sel** /'mʌsəl/ *n* [C,U] a small sea animal with a black shell and a soft body that can be eaten

**must¹** /məst; *strong* mʌst/ *modal verb* **1** *past form* **had to** used in order to say that something is necessary because of a rule, or because it is the best thing to do: *All passengers must wear seatbelts. | You must not allow your dog out without a leash. | It's getting late, I really must go.* **2** *past form* **must have** used in order to say that something is very likely to be true: *George must be almost eighty years old now. | That car must have been doing (=traveling) 90 miles an hour!* **3** used in order to suggest that someone do something: *You must see Robin Williams' new movie. It's really* *funny.* −see usage note at HAVE TO −see study note on page 458

**must**[2] /mʌst/ *n* **a must** INFORMAL something that you must do or must have: *If you visit Florida, going to Disney World is a must.*

**mus·tache** /ˈmʌstæʃ, məˈstæʃ/ *n* hair that grows on a man's upper lip −see picture at HAIRSTYLE

**mus·tang** /ˈmʌstæŋ/ *n* a small wild horse

**mus·tard** /ˈmʌstɚd/ *n* [U] **1** a yellow SAUCE usually eaten with meat **2** a hot-tasting seed or the yellow powder made from it, used in making mustard

**mus·ter**[1] /ˈmʌstɚ/ *v* **1 muster (up) courage/support etc.** to find or gather as much courage etc. as you can in order to do something difficult: *I'm still trying to muster up the courage to speak to her.* **2** [T] to gather a group of people such as soldiers into one place: *mustering an army*

**muster**[2] *n* **pass muster** to be accepted as good enough for a particular job

**must·n't** /ˈmʌsnt/ *modal verb* OLD-FASHIONED the short form of "must not": *You mustn't forget to tell her what I said.*

**must·y** /ˈmʌsti/ *adj* having a wet unpleasant smell: *musty old books*

**mu·ta·ble** /ˈmyuṭəbəl/ *adj* FORMAL able or likely to change −**mutability** /ˌmyuṭəˈbɪləṭi/ *n* [U] −opposite IMMUTABLE

**mu·tant** /ˈmyutⁿnt/ *n* an animal or plant that is different from others of the same kind because of a change in its GENES −**mutant** *adj*

**mu·tate** /ˈmyuteɪt/ *v* [I] if an animal or plant mutates, it becomes different from others of the same kind because of a change in its GENES −**mutation** /myuˈteɪʃən/ *n* [C,U]

**mute**[1] /myut/ *v* [T] to make a sound quieter: *The thick walls muted the sounds of the city.*

**mute**[2] *n* someone who cannot or will not speak −**mute** *adj* −**mutely** *adv*

**mut·ed** /ˈmyuṭɪd/ *adj* **1 muted criticism/response etc.** criticism etc. that is not strong or forceful **2** quieter than usual: *the muted sound of snoring from the next room* **3** a muted color is less bright than usual

**mu·ti·late** /ˈmyuṭlˌeɪt/ *v* [T] to damage someone or something severely, especially by removing part of it: *bodies mutilated in the explosion* −**mutilation** /ˌmyuṭlˈeɪʃən/ *n* [C,U]

**mu·ti·nous** /ˈmyutⁿn-əs/ *adj* not satisfied with the behavior of someone in authority, and refusing to obey his/her orders: *mutinous soldiers*

**mu·ti·ny** /ˈmyutⁿn-i/ *n* [C,U] a situation in which people, especially soldiers or SAILORS, refuse to obey someone in authority and try to take control for themselves: *a mutiny on the ship* −**mutiny** *v* [I]

**mutt** /mʌt/ *n* INFORMAL a dog that does not belong to a particular breed

**mut·ter** /ˈmʌtɚ/ *v* [I,T] to speak in a quiet voice, especially when you are complaining about something but do not want other people to hear you: *He walked away muttering about how the world was going crazy.*

**mut·ton** /ˈmʌtⁿn/ *n* [U] the meat from a sheep

**mu·tu·al** /ˈmyutʃuəl/ *adj* **1** a feeling or action that is mutual is felt or done by two or more people toward one another: *A good marriage is marked by mutual respect.* **2** shared by two or more people: *We were introduced by a mutual friend.* (=someone we both know) **3 the feeling is mutual** SPOKEN said when you have the same feeling about someone as s/he has toward you: *"You really drive me crazy sometimes!" "The feeling is mutual!"* −**mutuality** /ˌmyutʃuˈæləṭi/ *n* [U]

**mutual fund** /'... ˌ./ *n* a company through which you can buy SHAREs of other companies

**mu·tu·al·ly** /ˈmyutʃuəli, -tʃəli/ *adv* **1** done, felt, or experienced by two or more people: *a mutually rewarding business arrangement* **2 mutually exclusive** if two ideas, beliefs etc. are mutually exclusive, they cannot both exist or be true at the same time

**Mu·zak** /ˈmyuzæk/ *n* [U] TRADEMARK recorded music that is played continuously in airports, offices etc.

**muz·zle**[1] /ˈmʌzəl/ *n* **1** the nose and mouth of an animal such as a dog or horse **2** the end of the BARREL of a gun **3** something that you put over a dog's mouth so it cannot bite someone

**muzzle**[2] *v* [T] **1** to prevent someone from speaking freely or from expressing his/her opinions: *an attempt to muzzle the press* **2** to put a MUZZLE over a dog's mouth so that it cannot bite someone

**my** /maɪ/ *possessive adj* belonging or relating to the person who is speaking: *I'd like you to meet my mother.|That's my car over there.|I tried not to let my feelings show.*

**my·op·ic** /maɪˈɑpɪk, -ˈoʊ-/ *adj* **1** TECHNICAL ⇨ NEARSIGHTED **2** unwilling or unable to think about the future results of an action: *a myopic view of crime prevention* −**myopia** /maɪˈoʊpiə/ *n* [U]

**myr·i·ad** /ˈmɪriəd/ *n* LITERARY a very large number of something: *a myriad of stars in the sky* −**myriad** *adj*

**my·self** /maɪˈsɛlf/ *pron* **1** the REFLEXIVE form of "me": *I burned myself on the stove.|I made myself a cup of coffee.* **2** the strong form of "me," used in order to emphasize the subject or object of a sentence: *I went to the grocery store myself to buy it.* **3 (all) by myself a)** without help: *Look, Mommy - I tied my shoes all by myself!* **b)** alone: *I went to the movie by myself.* **4 (all) to myself** for my own use: *I had the whole swimming pool to myself today.* **5 not be myself** SPOKEN said when you are not behaving or feeling as you usually do, because you are sick or upset: *I'm sorry for what I said - I'm not myself these days.*

**mys·te·ri·ous** /mɪˈstɪriəs/ *adj* **1** strange and difficult to explain or understand: *a mysterious illness for which the doctors could not find a cause* **2** not saying much about something, because you want it to be a secret: *John and Randi are being very **mysterious about** something - do you think they might be engaged?* —**mysteriously** *adv*

**mys·ter·y** /ˈmɪstəri/ *n* **1** something that is difficult to explain or understand: *The location of the stolen money **remains a mystery**.* **2** a story, especially about a murder, in which events are not explained until the end: *the Sherlock Holmes mystery stories* **3** [U] a quality that makes someone or something seem strange, interesting, and difficult to explain or understand: *old legends full of mystery*

**mys·ti·cal** /ˈmɪstɪkəl/, **mys·tic** /ˈmɪstɪk/ *adj* relating to religious or magical powers that people cannot understand: *the mystical experiences of the Navajo religion* —**mystically** *adv*

**mys·ti·cism** /ˈmɪstəˌsɪzəm/ *n* [U] a religious practice in which someone tries to gain knowledge about God and truth by praying and thinking very seriously –**mystic** /ˈmɪstɪk/ *n*

**mys·ti·fy** /ˈmɪstəˌfaɪ/ *v* [T] to make someone feel confused and unable to explain or understand something: *a case that mystified the police* –**mystifying** *adj*

**mys·tique** /mɪˈstik/ *n* [U] FORMAL the quality that makes something seem mysterious, special, or interesting: *the mystique of Hollywood in the 1940s*

**myth** /mɪθ/ *n* **1** [C,U] an ancient story, especially one that explains a natural or historical event, or this type of story in general: *the Greek myths that deal with the creation of the world* **2** an idea or story that many people believe, but that is not true: *the myth that older workers are not productive*

**myth·i·cal** /ˈmɪθɪkəl/ *adj* **1** relating to MYTH: *mythical creatures such as the Minotaur* **2** not real or true, but only imagined: *the mythical Wild West of popular fiction*

**my·thol·o·gy** /mɪˈθɑlədʒi/ *n* [C,U] ancient MYTHs in general, or the beliefs that they represent: *stories from Greek mythology* –**mythological** /ˌmɪθəˈlɑdʒɪkəl/ *adj*

# N

**N, n** /ɛn/ the fourteenth letter of the English alphabet

**N** the written abbreviation of NORTH or NORTHERN

**n** the written abbreviation of NOUN

**'n'** /n, ən/ *conjunction* a short form of AND: *rock 'n' roll music*

**N/A** the written abbreviation of "not applicable"; used on a form to show that you do not need to answer a particular question

**nab** /næb/ *v* **-bbed, -bbing** [T] INFORMAL to catch someone doing something illegal: *You'd be surprised who gets **nabbed for** riding without a ticket.*

**nag**[1] /næg/ *v* **-gged, -gging** [I,T] **1** to complain continuously to someone in order to get him/her to do something: *Shawna has been **nagging** me **to** fix the kitchen sink.* **2** to be annoyed, worried, or upset about something again and again over a period of time: *White has been nagged by various injuries throughout the season.*

**nag**[2] *n* INFORMAL someone who NAGs continuously

**nag·ging** /ˈnægɪŋ/ *adj* making you worry or feel pain all the time: *a nagging headache*

**nail**[1] /neɪl/ *n* **1** a thin pointed piece of metal with a flat end, that you push into a piece of wood etc. using a hammer **2** the hard flat part that covers the top end of your fingers and toes: *Taryn's trying hard to stop biting her nails.* –see picture at HAND[1] –see also **fight (sb/sth) tooth and nail** (TOOTH)

nail

**nail**[2] *v* [T] **1** to fasten something to something else with a nail: *The windows were **nailed shut**.* **2** INFORMAL to catch someone who has done something wrong and prove that s/he is guilty: *They finally managed to nail the guy who killed those girls.* **3** INFORMAL to do something exactly right, or to be exactly correct: *Taylor nailed a jump shot with 1.1 seconds left in the game.* **4** INFORMAL to hit something or someone: *Somebody drove through a stop light and nailed her.*

**nail** sb/sth ↔ **down** *phr v* [T] **1** to fasten something with nails **2** to reach a final and definite decision about something: *It will take some more work befor the agreement is **nailed down**.*

**nail·brush** /ˈneɪlbrʌʃ/ *n* a small stiff brush used for cleaning your nails

**nail file** /ˈ. ./ *n* a thin piece of metal with a rough surface, used for shaping your nails

**nail pol·ish** /ˈ. ˌ../ *n* [U] colored or clear liquid that women paint on their nails to make them look attractive

**na·ive** /nɑˈiv/ *adj* lacking experience, so that you believe most people are honest and kind and that good things will happen to you: *Perhaps it*

N

was naive, but I never regretted giving him my phone number. **–naively** adv **–naivety, naiveté** /naˈivəˌteɪ, nɑˌivˈteɪ/ n [U]

**na·ked** /ˈneɪkɪd/ adj **1** not wearing any clothes; NUDE **2 with the naked eye** without an instrument such as a MICROSCOPE to help you see **–nakedness** n [U] **–nakedly** adv

**name¹** /neɪm/ n **1** the word that someone or something is called or known by: *Hi, what's your name? | Peter is his **first name**, and Nolan is his **last name**. | What's the name of the street the school is on?* **2 a big/famous/household name** INFORMAL someone who is famous **3** [singular] the opinion that people have about a person, company etc.; REPUTATION: *He has given baseball a **bad name**.* (=made people have a bad opinion about it) | *Carl returned to Bay City to clear his **good name**.* (=make people have a good opinion of him again) **4 be in sb's name** to officially belong to someone: *The house is in my wife's name.* **5 the name of the game** the most important thing or quality in a particular activity: *Beating the competition is the whole name of the game.* **6 (do sth) in the name of science/religion etc.** to use science, religion etc. as the reason for doing something, even if it is wrong

---

**USAGE NOTE names**

Use someone's first name when you know him/her, unless s/he is quite a lot older than you are: *What do you think, Pat?* Use someone's title and last name in formal situations, or in order to show respect for someone who is quite a lot older than you are: *Professor Taylor, could I make an appointment to see you? | How are your grandchildren, Mr. Fox?* You can use titles such as Doctor and Professor alone, without a name: *What's wrong with me, Doctor?* However, the titles "Mr.," "Ms.," "Mrs.," and "Miss" can only be used if you are also saying someone's last name: *Hello, Mrs. Radnor! | Will Mrs. Fran Radnor please come to the information desk?* ✗ DON'T SAY "Hello, Mrs.!" or "Hello, Mrs. Fran!" ✗ Last names are not used alone, except by people who know each other very well. ✗ DON'T SAY "Hello, Radnor!" ✗

---

**name²** v [T] **1** to give someone or something a particular name: *Sarah **named** the baby Henry, **after** his grandfather.* (=gave him the same name as his grandfather) | *The stadium was **named for** Brady, who provided the money.* (=it was given the name of someone who was related in some way to the thing being named) **2** to say what the name of someone or something is: *Can you name this song? | The police have not yet named the murder victim.* **3** to officially choose someone for a particular job:

*Roy Johnson was **named as** the new manager.* **4 you name it** SPOKEN said after a list of things to mean that there are many more that you could mention: *Beer, whiskey, wine - you name it and I've got it!* **5 name names** to give the names of people who have done something wrong or illegal to someone in authority

**name-cal·ling** /ˈ. ˌ../ n [U] the act of saying or shouting rude words at someone

**name·drop** /ˈneɪmdrɑp/ v **-pped, -pping** [I] DISAPPROVING to mention famous people's names and pretend that you know them so people will admire you **–namedropping** n [U]

**name·less** /ˈneɪmlɪs/ adj **1** not known by a name; ANONYMOUS: *a gift from a nameless businessman* **2** having no name: *millions of nameless stars*

**name·ly** /ˈneɪmli/ adv used in order to make it clear exactly who or what you are talking about: *The movie won two Oscars, namely "Best Actor" and "Best Director."*

**name·sake** /ˈneɪmseɪk/ n sb's namesake someone or something that has the same name as someone or something else

**name tag** /ˈ. ./ n a small sign with your name on it that you attach to your clothes so that people at a party, meeting etc. know who you are

**nan·ny** /ˈnæni/ n a woman whose job is to take care of a family's children, usually in the children's own home

**nap¹** /næp/ n a short sleep during the day: *Dad usually **takes a nap** in the afternoon.*

**nap²** v **-pped, -pping** **1** [I] to sleep for a short time during the day **2 be caught napping** INFORMAL to not be ready when something happens, although you should have been ready

**na·palm** /ˈneɪpɑm/ n [U] a thick liquid made from GASOLINE that is used in bombs

**nape** /neɪp/ n [singular] the back of your neck

**nap·kin** /ˈnæpkɪn/ n a small piece of cloth or paper used for cleaning your mouth or hands when you are eating

**narc¹** /nɑrk/ n INFORMAL a police officer who deals with catching people who use and sell illegal drugs

**narc²** v [I] SLANG to tell the police about something illegal that someone is doing, especially when it involves drugs

**nar·cis·sis·m** /ˈnɑrsəˌsɪzəm/ n [U] FORMAL too much admiration for your own appearance or abilities **–narcissistic** /ˌnɑrsəˈsɪstɪk/ adj **–narcissist** /ˈnɑrsəsɪst/ n

**nar·cot·ic** /nɑrˈkɑtɪk/ n [C usually plural] a type of drug that takes away pain and makes you feel sleepy, which may be used in hospitals but is usually illegal: *The pair were arrested for possession of narcotics.* **–narcotic** adj

**nar·rate** /ˈnæreɪt, næˈreɪt/ v [T] if someone narrates a movie or television program, s/he describes or explains what is happening in the pictures: *a documentary narrated by Robert Redford*

**nar·ra·tion** /næˈreɪʃən/ *n* [C,U] FORMAL
**1** the act of telling what happens in a story: *The narration switches from the past to the present and back again.* **2** a spoken description or explanation during a play, movie etc.

**nar·ra·tive** /ˈnærət̬ɪv/ *n* [C,U] FORMAL a description of events that is told as a story: *a narrative that is set during the Civil War* **–narrative** *adj*

**nar·ra·tor** /ˈnæˌreɪt̬ɚ/ *n* someone who tells the story in a movie, book etc.

**narrow**

a narrow street

a wide street

**nar·row**[1] /ˈnæroʊ/ *adj* **1** only measuring a small distance from side to side: *a long narrow street* –opposite WIDE[1] **2** DISAPPROVING too limited, and not allowing other possibilities: *I am disappointed by the narrow viewpoint given by the author.* **3** **win/lose etc. by a narrow margin** to win, lose etc. by a small amount **4** **narrow defeat/victory etc.** a defeat, victory etc. that you only just lose or win **5** **narrow escape** a situation in which you only just avoid danger or trouble **–narrowly** *adv* **–narrowness** *n* [U]

**narrow**[2] *v* [I,T] **1** to become more narrow, or to make something do this: *The road narrows here.* | *She narrowed her eyes and frowned.* **2** also **narrow down** to become less in number, range etc., or to make something do this: *There were over 800 entries, and it was hard to narrow down the list of finalists.*

**narrow**[3] *n* ⇨ **the straight and narrow** (STRAIGHT)

**narrow-mind·ed** /ˈ.. ˌ../ *adj* not willing to accept ideas or beliefs that are new and different

**na·sal** /ˈneɪzəl/ *adj* **1** a nasal sound or voice comes mostly through your nose: *a high nasal voice* **2** relating to the nose: *the nasal cavity* **–nasally** *adv*

**nas·ty** /ˈnæsti/ *adj* **1** having a bad appearance, smell, or taste: *a nasty looking apartment* **2** unkind and unpleasant: *a nasty thing to say* | *a nasty old man* **3** very severe, painful, or unpleasant: *a nasty cut on his hand* | *nasty weather* **4** morally bad or offensive; OBSCENE: *a nasty mind* **–nastiness** *n* [U] **–nastily** *adv*

**na·tion** /ˈneɪʃən/ *n* **1** a word meaning a country and its people, used especially when considering its political and economic structures:

*The President is addressing the nation tomorrow.* | *the richest nation in the world* **2** a large group of people of the same race and speaking the same language: *the Cherokee nation* –see usage note at RACE[1]

**na·tion·al**[1] /ˈnæʃənl/ *adj* **1** relating to a whole nation rather than to part of it or to other nations: *the national news* | *an issue of national importance* –compare INTERNATIONAL **2** typical of a particular nation: *national dress*

**national**[2] *n* someone who is a citizen of one country but is living in another country: *a Korean national living in the US* –compare ALIEN[2], CITIZEN

**national an·them** /ˌ... ˈ../ *n* the official song of a nation that is sung or played at public occasions

**na·tion·al·ism** /ˈnæʃənlˌɪzəm/ *n* [U] **1** the belief that your country is better than any other country **2** the desire of people who have the same race or who speak the same language etc. to have their own country: *the rise of nationalism in Eastern Europe*

**na·tion·al·ist** /ˈnæʃənl-ɪst/ *adj* wanting to become politically independent, or wanting to remain this way: *African nationalist movements* **–nationalist** *n*

**na·tion·al·is·tic** /ˌnæʃnəˈlɪstɪk/ *adj* believing that your country is better than other countries: *a nationalistic speech*

**na·tion·al·i·ty** /ˌnæʃəˈnæləti/ *n* [C,U] the legal right of belonging to a particular country; CITIZENSHIP: *a man who has British nationality* ✗ DON'T SAY "My nationality is Mexican/Swedish etc." SAY "I come from Mexico/Sweden etc." ✗

**na·tion·al·ize** /ˈnæʃənəˌlaɪz/ *v* [T] if a government nationalizes an organization, industry etc., it buys it in order to take control of it –compare PRIVATIZE, SOCIALIZE

**na·tion·al·ly** /ˈnæʃənl-i/ *adv* by or to everyone in a nation: *a series of nationally televised debates*

**national mon·u·ment** /ˌ... ˈ.../ *n* a building or a special place that is protected by the government for people to visit

**national park** /ˌ... ˈ./ *n* a large area of beautiful land that is protected by the government for people to visit: *Yellowstone National Park*

**national se·cu·ri·ty** /ˌ... .ˈ.../ *n* [U] the idea that a country must protect its citizens, especially by having a strong army, or the state of having this protection: *The US Army says that releasing the document would damage national security.*

**na·tion·wide** /ˌneɪʃənˈwaɪd◂ / *adj* happening or existing in every part of a nation: *nationwide price increases* | *The brewery employs about 3000 people nationwide.* **–nationwide** *adv*

**na·tive**[1] /ˈneɪt̬ɪv/ *adj* **1** **native country/land etc.** the place where you were born: *The Pope is* visiting his *native Poland.* (=Poland is where he was born) **2 native Californian/New Yorker** etc. someone who was born in California etc. **3 native language/tongue** the language you spoke when you first learned to speak **4** growing, living, or produced in a particular area: *a plant native to Ecuador* **5 native speaker** someone who speaks the language s/he learned as a baby: *Practice your German with native speakers.* —opposite NON-NATIVE

**native²** *n* **1** a native of someone who was born in a particular place: *She's a native of southern Brazil.* **2** [C usually plural] OFFENSIVE a member of a race who lived in Africa, South America etc. before the Europeans arrived

**Native A·mer·i·can** /ˌ... .'.../ *n* someone who belongs to one of the tribes who were living in North America before the Europeans arrived –**Native American** *adj*

**NATO** /'neɪtoʊ/ *n* [singular] the North Atlantic Treaty Organization; a group of countries in North America and Europe that give military help to each other

**nat·u·ral¹** /'nætʃərəl/ *adj* **1** normal or usual, and what you would expect in a particular situation: *It's only natural to have doubts before your wedding.* (=it is completely normal) | *It's not natural for a four-year-old to be so quiet.* —opposite UNNATURAL **2** not caused, made, or controlled by people: *earthquakes and other natural disasters* | *natural fibers like cotton* **3** having a particular skill or ability without being taught: *a natural athlete* **4** not looking or sounding unusual: *Was he really that nervous? He acted natural enough.* —**naturalness** *n* [U]

**natural²** *n* **be a natural** to be very good at doing something without being taught: *Look how he swings that bat - he's a complete natural!*

**natural gas** /ˌ... './ *n* [U] gas used for cooking or heating that is taken from under the earth or ocean

**natural his·to·ry** /ˌ... '.../ *n* [U] the study of plants, animals, and minerals

**nat·u·ral·ist** /'nætʃrəlɪst/ *n* someone who studies plants, animals, and other living things

**nat·u·ral·ize** /'nætʃrə,laɪz/ *v* [T] to make someone a citizen of a country that s/he was not born in –**naturalization** /ˌnætʃrələ'zeɪʃən/ *n* [U]

**nat·u·ral·ly** /'nætʃrəli/ *adv* **1** in a way that you would expect: *Students naturally make mistakes when translating another language.* **2** SPOKEN used in order to agree with what someone has said, or to answer "of course" to a question: *"Are you excited to be home?" "Naturally."* **3** as a natural feature or quality: *naturally curly hair* | *Golf seemed to come naturally to him.* (=he was good at it without being taught) **4** in a manner that is no different from

usual: *Speak naturally into the microphone, please.*

**natural re·sourc·es** /ˌ... '.../ *n* [plural] all the land, minerals, energy etc. that exist in a country

**natural se·lec·tion** /ˌ... .'.'./ *n* [U] TECHNICAL the process by which only the plants and animals that are suitable to their environment will continue to live

**na·ture** /'neɪtʃɚ/ *n* **1** [U] everything that exists in the world that is not made or controlled by humans, such as animals, plants, weather etc.: *We like camping; it makes us feel closer to nature.* **2** [C,U] the character or particular qualities of someone or something: *She is a trusting person by nature.* | *The nature of my work requires a lot of traveling.* **3** a particular type of thing: *He provided support of a political/ financial nature.* **4 let nature take its course** to allow events to happen without doing anything to change the results: *The medicine didn't work, so we let nature take its course.* –see also SECOND NATURE

**nature re·serve** /'.. .,./ *n* an area of land in which animals and plants are protected

**naught** /nɔt/ *n* [U] OLD-FASHIONED nothing: *All their plans came to naught.* (=failed)

**naugh·ty** /'nɔti/ *adj* a naughty child behaves badly and is rude or does not obey adults –**naughtiness** *n* [U] –**naughtily** *adv*

**nau·se·a** /'nɔziə, 'nɔʒə, 'nɔʃə/ *n* [U] FORMAL the feeling you have when you think you are going to VOMIT

**nau·se·at·ed** /'nɔzi,eɪtɪd/ *adj* feeling NAUSEA: *When I was pregnant I felt nauseated all the time.* –**nauseate** *v* [T]

**nau·se·at·ing** /'nɔzi,eɪtɪŋ/ *adj* making you feel NAUSEA: *the nauseating smell of cigar smoke*

**nau·seous** /'nɔʃəs, -ʒəs/ *adj* **1** NONSTANDARD ⇨ NAUSEATED **2** making you feel NAUSEA: *nauseous odors* –**nauseously** *adv*

**nau·ti·cal** /'nɔt̪ɪkəl/ *adj* relating to ships or sailing –**nautically** *adv*

**na·val** /'neɪvəl/ *adj* relating to the navy: *a naval battle*

**na·vel** /'neɪvəl/ *n* FORMAL ⇨ BELLY BUTTON

**nav·i·ga·ble** /'nævɪgəbəl/ *adj* deep and wide enough for ships to travel on: *Part of the St. Lawrence River is navigable.*

**nav·i·gate** /'nævə,geɪt/ *v* **1** [I,T] to find the way to a place, especially by using maps: *Rick usually drives and I navigate.* **2** [T] to sail all the way across or along an area of water

**nav·i·ga·tion** /ˌnævə'geɪʃən/ *n* [U] **1** the science of planning the way along which you travel from one place to another: *a compass and other navigation instruments* **2** the act of sailing a ship or flying a plane along a particular line of travel: *Navigation along this canal should be easy.* –**navigational** *adj*

**nav·i·ga·tor** /ˈnævəˌgeɪtɚ/ *n* the officer on a ship or aircraft who plans the way along which it travels

**na·vy** /ˈneɪvi/ *n* **1** the part of a country's military forces that is organized for fighting a war at sea: *My dad was 20 when he joined the navy.* **2** the war ships belonging to a country: *the need for a larger navy* **3** ⇨ NAVY BLUE

**navy blue** /ˌ.. ˈ.◂/ *adj* very dark blue – **navy blue** *n* [U]

**NBC** *n* National Broadcasting Company; one of the national television and radio companies in the US

**NC** the written abbreviation of North Carolina

**NCAA** *n* National Collegiate Athletic Association; the organization that is in charge of sports at American colleges and universities

**NCO** *n* Noncommissioned Officer; a soldier such as a CORPORAL or SERGEANT

**ND** the written abbreviation of North Dakota

**NE 1** the written abbreviation of NORTHEAST **2** the written abbreviation of Nebraska

**near**[1] /nɪr/ *adv, prep* **1** only a short distance from someone or something: *Don't go too near the road.* | *I'd like to live nearer the ocean.* **2** close in time to a particular event: *She got more and more nervous as the wedding **drew near**.* (=became closer in time) | *The construction work is now near completion.* **3** **nowhere near** not at all close to a particular quality or state: *The new jazz station is nowhere near as good as the old one.* | *We're nowhere near finished.* **4** **near perfect/impossible etc.** INFORMAL almost perfect, impossible etc.; nearly: *a near perfect test score*

---

**USAGE NOTE near and close**

Use **near** and **close** to talk about short distances. **Close** is usually followed by the word "to," but **near** is not: *There's a new supermarket near our house.* | *We live close to the bus stop.* We also use **close** to talk about something that is not far away in time: *It's close to your bedtime, kids.*

---

**near**[2] *adj* **1** only a short distance from someone or something: *The nearest town (=the town that is the closest) is 20 miles away.* **2** very close to having a particular quality or being a particular thing: *His explanation is as **near to** the truth as we'll get.* | *Honestly, it was a **near miracle**.* **3** **in the near future** at a time that is not very far in the future: *We will have a new teacher joining us in the near future.* **4** **near miss** a situation in which something almost hits something else: *Two planes had a near miss above the airport today.*

**near·by** /ˌnɪrˈbaɪ◂/ *adj* not far away: *We used to go swimming in a nearby lake.* – **nearby** *adv*

**near·ly** /ˈnɪrli/ *adv* almost, but not completely or exactly: *This isn't nearly as hard as the last*

test. | *Frozen vegetables are nearly always cheaper than fresh ones.*

**near·sight·ed** /ˈnɪrˌsaɪtɪd/ *adj* unable to see things clearly unless they are close to you – **nearsightedness** *n* [U]

**neat** /nit/ *adj* **1** SPOKEN very good or pleasant: *The fireworks were really neat - I've never seen so many different kinds!* **2** carefully arranged and not messy: *She wears her hair in a neat braid.* | *They keep their house **neat and clean**.* **3** a neat person does not like his/her things or house to be messy **4** simple and effective: *a neat solution to the problem* – **neatly** *adv* – **neatness** *n* [U]

**nec·es·sar·i·ly** /ˌnɛsəˈsɛrəli/ *adv* **1** **not necessarily** used in order to say that something is not certain, even if it might be reasonable to expect it to be: *Expensive restaurants do not necessarily have the best food.* **2** in a way that has to happen and cannot be avoided: *Income tax laws are necessarily complicated.*

**nec·es·sar·y** /ˈnɛsəˌsɛri/ *adj* **1** needed in order to do something or have something; ESSENTIAL: *Don't call me unless it's absolutely necessary.* | *Will you make all the necessary arrangements?* | *It may be **necessary to** operate on your knee.* **2 a necessary evil** something bad or unpleasant that you have to accept in order to achieve what you want: *Parking fees are a necessary evil in the region's fight against air pollution.*

**ne·ces·si·tate** /nəˈsɛsəˌteɪt/ *v* [T] FORMAL to make it necessary for you to do something: *The new law necessitated a change in the health and safety guidelines.*

**ne·ces·si·ty** /nəˈsɛsəti/ *n* **1** something that you need to have or that must happen: *A car is a necessity for this job.* | *Election reforms are an absolute necessity.* **2** [U] the fact of something being necessary: *the necessity of eating well* **3** **of necessity** in a way that you cannot avoid: *A doctor must, of necessity, make decisions that no one else can.*

**neck**[1] /nɛk/ *n* **1** the part of your body that joins your head to your shoulders: *Swans have long slender necks.* – see picture at HEAD[1] **2** the part of a piece of clothing that goes around your neck **3** the narrow part of a bottle **4 be up to your neck in sth** INFORMAL to be in a very difficult situation, or to be very busy doing something: *Mason is up to his neck in debt.* **5 -neck, -necked** having a particular type of neck: *a V-neck sweater* | *a long-necked bottle* **6 neck and neck** INFORMAL if two people, teams etc. are neck and neck in a competition, they both have an equal chance of winning **7 in this neck of the woods** INFORMAL in this area or part of the country: *What are you doing in this neck of the woods?*

**neck**[2] *v* [I] OLD-FASHIONED SLANG if two people neck, they kiss for a long time in a sexual way – **necking** *n* [U]

N

**neck·lace** /'nɛk-lɪs/ *n* a piece of jewelry that hangs around your neck: *a pearl necklace* –see picture at JEWELRY

**neck·line** /'nɛk-laɪn/ *n* the shape made by the edge of a woman's dress, shirt etc. around or below the neck: *a low neckline*

**neck·tie** /'nɛktaɪ/ *n* FORMAL ⇨ TIE²

**nec·tar** /'nɛktɚ/ *n* [U] **1** thick juice made from some fruits: *peach nectar* **2** the sweet liquid that BEES collect from flowers

**nec·ta·rine** /ˌnɛktəˈrin/ *n* a round juicy yellow-red fruit that has a large rough seed and smooth skin

**née** /neɪ/ *adj* used in order to show the family name that a woman had before she was married: *Lorna Brown, née Wilson*

**need¹** /nid/ *v* [T] **1** to feel that you must have or do something, or that something is necessary: *I need a vacation.* | *The roast needs to cook a little longer.* | *You need a background in computer programming for this job.* | *David, I need you to go to the store for some milk.* **2** to have to do something: *You need to make reservations for Yosemite campgrounds.* | *Do we need to dress up for the party?* | *You don't need to fill in any forms.* **3** sb does not need sth SPOKEN used in order to say that something will make someone's life more difficult: *"He's always questioning everything I do." "Yeah, you don't need that."* –see study note on page 458

**need²** *n* **1** [singular] a situation in which something must be done, especially to improve the situation: *There is an urgent need to improve teaching standards.* | *the need for stricter safety regulations* | *We will work all night if need be.* (=if it is necessary) **2** be in need of to need attention, help, money etc.: *a large population in need of doctors* **3** [C usually plural] what someone needs to have in order to live a normal healthy life: *a school that meets the educational needs of the deaf* **4** [U] the state of not having enough food or money: *We're collecting donations for families in need.*

**needle**

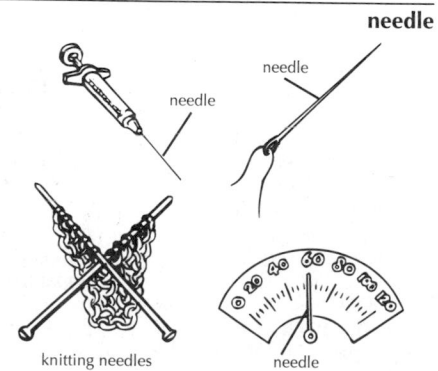

knitting needles

needle

**nee·dle¹** /'nidl/ *n* **1** a small thin piece of

steel used for sewing, that has a point at one end and a hole at the other end –see also picture at SEW **2** the sharp hollow metal part on the end of a SYRINGE **3** a small thin pointed leaf, especially from a PINE tree **4** a long thin stick used in knitting (KNIT) **5** the very small pointed part in a RECORD PLAYER that picks up sound from the records **6 it's like looking for a needle in a haystack** used in order to say that something is almost impossible to find

**needle²** *v* [T] INFORMAL to deliberately annoy someone by making a lot of unkind remarks or stupid jokes: *She's always needling Jim about his weight.*

**need·less** /'nid-lɪs/ *adj* **1 needless to say** used when you are telling someone something that s/he probably already knows or expects: *Needless to say, with four children we're always busy.* **2** not necessary, and often easily avoided: *Why take needless risks?* –**needlessly** *adv*

**nee·dle·work** /'nidl,wɚk/ *n* [U] the activity or art of sewing, or things made by sewing

**need·y** /'nidi/ *adj* **1** having very little food or money: *a needy family* **2 the needy** people who do not have enough food or money

**ne·gate** /nɪˈgeɪt/ *v* [T] FORMAL **1** to prevent something from having any effect: *The decision would effectively negate last year's Supreme Court ruling.* **2** to state that something does not exist or is not true; DENY –**negation** /nɪˈgeɪʃən/ *n* [U]

**neg·a·tive¹** /'nɛgətɪv/ *adj* **1** having a bad or harmful effect: *Raising taxes could have a negative effect on the economy.* **2** considering only the bad aspects of a situation, person etc.: *She's being very negative about school lately.* **3** saying or meaning no: *a negative answer* –compare AFFIRMATIVE **4** a medical or scientific test that is negative does not show any sign of what was being looked for: *Their test for phosphates came out/up negative.* **5** TECHNICAL having the type of electrical charge that is carried by ELECTRONS, shown by a (-) sign on a BATTERY **6** TECHNICAL a negative number or quantity is lower than zero. (-) is the negative sign –**negatively** *adv* –opposite POSITIVE

**negative²** *n* **1** a statement or expression that means no **2** a piece of film that shows dark areas as light and light areas as dark, from which a photograph is printed

**negative**

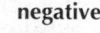

**ne·glect¹** /nɪˈglɛkt/ *v* [T] **1** to not pay enough attention to someone or something, or to not take care of him, her, or it very well: *Each year, 700,000 children are abused or neglected.* **2** to not do something or forget to do it, often because you are lazy or careless: *The manufacturer had neglected to* warn users about the possible health risks. | Four security guards were accused of neglecting their duties. —**neglected** adj

**neglect**[2] n [U] **1** failure to take care of something or someone well: I'm afraid my house plants are suffering from neglect! **2** the condition something or someone is in when he, she, or it has not been taken care of: inner cities in a state of neglect

**ne·glect·ful** /nɪ'glɛkfəl/ adj FORMAL not taking care of something very well, or not giving it enough attention: He had been neglectful of his work. | We have been too **neglectful** of educating the new generation.

**neg·li·gee** /ˌnɛglɪ'ʒeɪ, 'nɛglɪˌʒeɪ/ n a very thin pretty piece of clothing that a woman wears over a NIGHTGOWN

**neg·li·gence** /'nɛglɪdʒəns/ n [U] the failure to do something that you are responsible for in a careful enough way, so that something bad happens or may happen: They're suing the doctor for negligence.

**neg·li·gent** /'nɛglɪdʒənt/ adj not being careful enough about something that you are doing, so that serious mistakes are made: The company had been **negligent in** its safety procedures. —**negligently** adv

**neg·li·gi·ble** /'nɛglɪdʒəbəl/ adj too slight or unimportant to have any effect: There is negligible damage to the car. —**negligibly** adv

**ne·go·tia·ble** /nɪ'goʊʃəbəl/ adj **1** prices, agreements etc. that are negotiable can be discussed and changed: Is the salary negotiable? **2** a road that is negotiable can be traveled along **3** TECHNICAL a check that is negotiable can be exchanged for money

**ne·go·ti·ate** /nɪ'goʊʃiˌeɪt/ v **1** [I,T] to discuss something in order to reach an agreement: UN representatives are trying to negotiate a ceasefire. **2** [T] to succeed in getting past or over a difficult place on a road, path etc.: an old man carefully negotiating the steps

**ne·go·ti·a·tion** /nɪˌgoʊʃi'eɪʃən/ n [C usually plural, U] official discussions between two groups who are trying to agree on something: Johnson and Co. has **entered into negotiations** with City Hall over its bid to build the new freeway. | He was offered the job after some negotiation over the salary.

**Ne·gro** /'nigroʊ/ n OLD-FASHIONED OFFENSIVE a Black person

**neigh** /neɪ/ v [I] to make a loud sound like a horse —**neigh** n

**neigh·bor** /'neɪbɚ/ n **1** someone who lives in a house or apartment very near you: The Nelsons are our **next-door neighbors**. (=they live in the house next to ours) **2** someone who is sitting or standing next to you: Write down your name and then pass the paper to your neighbor. **3** a country that has a border with

another country —**neighbor** adj: the neighbor kids | my neighbor lady

**neigh·bor·hood** /'neɪbɚˌhʊd/ n **1** a small area of a town, or the people who live there: a nice neighborhood in Boston | a neighborhood school | Are there any good restaurants **in the neighborhood**? (=in this area of town) **2 in the neighborhood of** either a little more or a little less than a particular number or amount: Do you have any stereos costing in the neighborhood of $300?

**neigh·bor·ing** /'neɪbɚɪŋ/ adj near the place where you are or the place you are talking about: There's a good bus service to neighboring towns.

**neigh·bor·ly** /'neɪbɚli/ adj friendly and helpful toward your NEIGHBORs —**neighborliness** n [U]

**nei·ther**[1] /'niðɚ, 'naɪ-/ determiner, pron not one or the other of two people or things: Neither of them was hungry, but they had a cup of coffee. | Neither leader would admit to being wrong. —compare EITHER[2], NONE[1] —see usage note at EITHER[2]

**neither**[2] adv used in order to agree with a negative statement that someone has made, or to add a negative statement to one that has just been made: "I don't like herb tea." "Neither do I." | Bill can't sing at all, and neither can his brother. (=both Bill and his brother can't sing) | "I haven't seen Greg in a long time." "Me neither." —compare **me either** EITHER[3]

**neither**[3] conjunction **neither...nor...** used when mentioning two statements, facts, actions etc. that are not true or possible: Neither his mother nor his father spoke English. —see usage note at EITHER[1]

**ne·on** /'niɑn/ n [U] a gas that is an ELEMENT and that produces a bright light when electricity is passed through it

**neon light** /ˌ.. './ n a glass tube filled with NEON that produces a bright, usually colored light when electricity is passed through it

**neph·ew** /'nɛfyu/ n the son of your brother or sister, or the son of your husband's or wife's brother or sister —compare NIECE —see picture at FAMILY

**nep·o·tism** /'nɛpəˌtɪzəm/ n [U] the practice of giving the best jobs to members of your family when you are in a position of power

**Nep·tune** /'nɛptun/ n [singular] the eighth PLANET from the sun

**nerd** /nɚd/ n INFORMAL someone who is not fashionable and does not know how to behave in social situations: a computer nerd (=someone who is only interested in computers and does not know how to behave with people) —**nerdy** adj

**nerve** /nɚv/ n **1** [U] the ability to stay calm in a dangerous, difficult, or frightening situation: It **takes a lot of nerve** to give a speech in front

N

*of so many people.* **2 have the nerve to do sth** INFORMAL to be rude without being ashamed or embarrassed about it: *He had the nerve to criticize my cooking.* **3** one of the thin parts like threads inside your body that help control your movements, and along which your brain sends and receives feelings of heat, cold, pain etc. **4 hit/touch/strike a nerve** to do or say something that makes someone angry or upset because it relates to a subject that is important to him/her: *I accidentally hit a raw nerve by asking him about his wife.*

**nerve-rack·ing** /'nɚv ˌrækɪŋ/ *adj* very worrying or frightening: *a nerve-racking drive through a snowstorm*

**nerves** /nɚvz/ *n* [plural] INFORMAL **1** the feeling of being nervous because you are worried or a little frightened: *What's wrong? You're a **bundle of nerves**.* (=extremely worried or frightened) **2 get on sb's nerves** INFORMAL to annoy someone, especially by doing something again and again: *Joyce's complaining is getting on my nerves.*

**nerve-wrack·ing** /'nɚv ˌrækɪŋ/ *n* ⇨ NERVE-RACKING

**nerv·ous** /'nɚvəs/ *adj* **1** worried or frightened about something, and unable to relax: *Sam's **nervous about** taking his driving test again.* | *The way she was watching him **made** him **nervous**.* **2** often becoming worried or frightened and easily upset: *a thin nervous man* | *All the pressure to do well in college has made her a **nervous wreck**.* (=someone who is too anxious all the time) **3** relating to the nerves in your body: *a nervous disorder* **–nervously** *adv* **–nervousness** *n* [U]

---

**USAGE NOTE** nervous, concerned, and anxious

Use **nervous** when you feel worried and frightened about something that is going to happen soon: *Jack was nervous about speaking in front of everyone.* **Concerned** also means "worried," but is used especially when someone is worried about a particular problem: *We are concerned about the number of homeless people in our city.* Use **anxious** when you are worried that something bad has happened or will happen, especially to someone you know: *Her parents became anxious when she didn't come home that night.*

---

**nervous break·down** /ˌ.. '../ *n* a mental illness in which someone becomes extremely anxious and tired and cannot live and work normally

**nervous sys·tem** /'.. ˌ../ *n* the system of nerves in your body, through which you feel pain, heat etc. and control your movements

**nest¹** /nɛst/ *n* **1** a hollow place made or chosen by a bird to lay its eggs in and to live in

**2** a place where insects or small animals live: *a hornets' nest* **3** INFORMAL your parents' house: *children leaving the nest to go off to college*

**nest²** *v* [I] to build or use a NEST: *owls nesting in a tree hole*

**nest egg** /'. ./ *n* an amount of money that you save to use later

**nes·tle** /'nɛsəl/ *v* **1** [I,T] to move into a comfortable position by pressing against someone or something: *The girl was still in her arms, her head nestled on Heather's chest.* **2** [I] to be in a position that is protected from wind, rain etc.: *a village **nestled among** the hills*

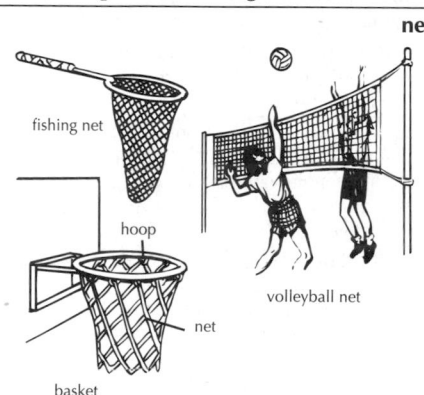

net

fishing net

hoop

volleyball net

net

basket

**net¹** /nɛt/ *n* **1** [C,U] a material made of strings, wires, or threads woven across each other with regular spaces between them: *a fishing net* **2** [C usually singular] a net used in particular games: *I can't play tennis; I'm always hitting the ball into the net.* **3 the Net** ⇨ INTERNET

**net²** *v* **-tted, -tting** [T] **1** to earn a particular amount of money as a profit after paying taxes: *Last year, they netted $52,000.* –compare GROSS² **2** to catch a fish in a net

**net³** *adj* **1** a net amount of money is the amount that remains after things such as taxes etc. have been taken away: *a net profit of $500,000* –compare GROSS¹ **2 net weight** the weight of something without its container **3 net result** the final result, after all the effects are known: *The net result of the policy was higher prices in the stores.*

**net·tle¹** /'nɛtl/ *n* [C,U] a wild plant with rough leaves that sting you

**nettle²** *v* [T] to annoy someone: *Al realized he had nettled Eileen, and went silent.*

**net·work¹** /'nɛt⌐wɚk/ *n* **1** a group of radio or television stations that broadcasts many of the same programs in different parts of the country: *the four*

network

a computer network

*biggest TV networks* **2** a system of lines, tubes, wires, roads etc. that cross each other and are connected to each other: *the freeway network* **3** a set of computers that are connected to each other so that they can share information **4** a group of people, organizations etc. that are connected or that work together: *Trina had developed a good network of business contacts.*

**network²** *v* **1** [T] to connect several computers together so that they can share information **2** [I] to meet other people who do the same type of work in order to share information, help each other etc.

**net·work·ing** /'net¬ˌwɚkɪŋ/ *n* [U] the practice of meeting other people who do the same type of work, in order to share information, help each other etc.

**neu·rol·o·gy** /nʊ'ralədʒi/ *n* [U] the scientific study of the NERVOUS SYSTEM and the diseases that are related to it −**neurological** /ˌnʊrə-'ladʒɪkəl/ *adj* −**neurologist** /nʊ'ralədʒɪst/ *n*

**neu·ro·sis** /nʊ'roʊsɪs/ *n* a mental illness that makes someone worried or frightened in an unreasonable way

**neu·rot·ic** /nʊ'raṭɪk/ *adj* **1** unreasonably anxious or afraid: *My aunt is neurotic about cleanliness.* **2** relating to a NEUROSIS: *neurotic disorders* −**neurotically** *adv* −**neurotic** *n*

**neu·ter¹** /'nuṭɚ/ *adj* TECHNICAL in English grammar, a neuter pronoun such as "it" relates to something that has no sex, or does not show the sex of the person or animal that it relates to

**neuter²** *v* [T] to remove part of the sex organs of a male animal so that it cannot produce babies −compare SPAY

**neu·tral¹** /'nutrəl/ *adj* **1** not supporting either side in an argument, competition, or war: *The paper was praised for its neutral reporting of the elections.* | *Switzerland was neutral during World War II.* **2** a neutral color such as gray or brown is not strong or bright **3** TECHNICAL a neutral wire has no electrical CHARGE **4** TECHNICAL a neutral substance is neither acid nor alkaline (ALKALI)

**neutral²** *n* **1** [U] the position of the GEARs of a car or machine when it will not move forward or backward: *Start the car in neutral.* **2** a country or person that is not fighting for or helping a country that is in a war

**neu·tral·i·ty** /nu'træləṭi/ *n* [U] the state of not supporting either side in an argument, competition, or war

**neu·tral·ize** /'nutrəˌlaɪz/ *v* [T] **1** to prevent something from having any effect: *Higher taxes will neutralize increased wages.* **2** TECHNICAL to make a substance chemically NEUTRAL −**neutralization** /ˌnutrələ'zeɪʃən/ *n* [U]

**neu·tron** /'nutran/ *n* a part of an atom that has no electrical CHARGE

**nev·er** /'nevɚ/ *adv* **1** not at any time, or not once: *I've never been to Hawaii.* | *We waited*

until 11:00, but they never came. | *I never thought I'd pass the class.* | *I never knew* (=I did not know until now) *that you played the guitar!* **2 never mind** SPOKEN used in order to tell someone that something was not important or that you do not want to say something again: *"What did you say?" "Never mind, it doesn't matter."* **3 you never know** SPOKEN used in order to say that something that seems unlikely could happen: *You never know, maybe you'll be lucky and win the lottery.*

**nev·er·the·less** /ˌnevɚðə'les◂/ *adv* in spite of what has just been mentioned: *I know he's telling the truth. Nevertheless, I don't trust him.*

**new**

old

new

**new** /nu/ *adj* **1** recently made, built, invented, or developed: *I went to see Mel Gibson's new movie.* | *Can the new drugs help her?* | *the new nations of Eastern Europe* **2** recently bought: *Do you like my new dress?* **3** not used or owned by anyone before: *A used car costs a lot less than a new one.* | *a brand new CD player* (=completely new) **4** not experienced by someone before: *Do you like your new teacher?* | *Eve decided to move to a new town and start over.* | *We had fruit there that was completely new to me.* (=I had never seen it before) **5** having recently arrived in a place, or started a different job or activity: *Are you a new student here?* | *It's hard being the new kid on the block.* (=the newest person in a job, school etc.) **6** recently discovered: *Scientists have identified a new herpes-type virus.* **7 what's new?** SPOKEN used as a friendly greeting to ask what is happening in someone's life −**newness** *n* [U]

**USAGE NOTE** new, recent, modern, current, up-to-date, and latest

Use **new** to talk about something that has existed for only a short time: *Have you read Alice Walker's new book?* Use **recent** to talk about something, especially an event, that happened a short time ago: *He won a medal in the recent Olympics.* Use **modern** to describe things that exist now, especially in order to emphasize that they are different from earlier things of the same kind: *modern machinery* | *modern teaching methods.* Use **current** to describe something that exists now but that may change: *the current economic crisis.* Use

N

up-to-date to describe the newest knowledge, information, way of doing things etc.: *an up-to-date computer system.* Use latest to talk about the newest thing in a series of similar things: *the latest issue of Time magazine.*

**New Age** /ˌ. ˈ.ᵈ / *adj* relating to a set of beliefs about religion, medicine, and ways of life that are not part of traditional Western religions

**new·born** /ˈnubɔrn/ *n* a baby that has only recently been born –**newborn** /ˌnuˈbɔrnᵈ/ *adj*

**new·com·er** /ˈnuˌkʌmɚ/ *n* someone who has recently arrived somewhere or recently started a particular activity: *a **newcomer to** the real estate business*

**new·fan·gled** /ˈnuˌfæŋgəld/ *adj* DISAPPROVING newfangled ideas, machines etc. have been recently invented but seem complicated or unnecessary: *newfangled ideas about raising children*

**new·ly** /ˈnuli/ *adv* very recently: *a newly married couple*

**new·ly·weds** /ˈnuliˌwɛdz/ *n* [plural] a man and a woman who have recently gotten married

**news** /nuz/ *n* **1** [U] information about something that has happened recently: *Have you heard (=received) any **news about** your job application?* | *I have some **good/bad news** for you.* | *an interesting **piece of news*** **2** [U] reports of recent events in the newspapers or on the radio or television: *There is more **news of** fighting in the area.* | *a **news story/report/item** on the plane crash* | *I usually watch CNN for national and international news.* | *Reports about the disabled rarely **make the news**. (=are rarely reported in newspapers etc.)* **3 the news** a regular television or radio program that gives you reports of recent events: *Did you see/hear that story **on the news**?* **4 that's news to me** SPOKEN said when you are surprised or annoyed because you have not been told something earlier: *The meeting's been canceled? That's news to me.* **5 news blackout** a period of time when particular pieces of news are not allowed to be reported

**news a·gen·cy** /ˈ. ˌ.../ *n* a company that supplies reports on recent events to newspapers, radio, and television

**news bul·le·tin** /ˈ. ˌ.../ *n* a very short news program about something important that has just happened, that is broadcast suddenly in the middle of a television or radio program

**news·cast** /ˈnuzkæst/ *n* a news program on the radio or television

**news·cast·er** /ˈnuzˌkæstɚ/ *n* someone who reads the news on the radio or television

**news·let·ter** /ˈnuzˌlɛtɚ/ *n* a short written report of news about a club, organization, or particular subject that is sent regularly to people: *our church newsletter*

**news·pa·per** /ˈnuzˌpeɪpɚ/ *n* **1** a set of large folded sheets of paper containing news, pictures, advertisements etc., that is printed and sold daily or weekly: *the local newspaper* | *an interesting article **in the newspaper*** **2** [U] sheets of paper from old newspapers: *We just use newspaper for packing dishes.*

**news·print** /ˈnuzˌprɪnt/ *n* cheap paper used mostly for printing newspapers on

**news·stand** /ˈnuzstænd/ *n* a place on a street where newspapers are sold

**news·wor·thy** /ˈnuzˌwɚði/ *adj* important or interesting enough to be reported as news: *newsworthy events*

**new·sy** /ˈnuzi/ *adj* a newsy letter is from a friend or relative and contains a lot of news about him/her

**newt** /nut/ *n* a small animal with a long body, four legs, and a tail, that lives in water

**New Tes·ta·ment** /ˌ. ˈ...ᵈ / *n* **the New Testament** the part of the Bible that is about Jesus Christ's life and what he taught –compare OLD TESTAMENT

**new wave** /ˌ. ˈ./ *n* people who are trying to introduce new ideas in music, movies, art, politics etc. –**new wave** *adj*

**New World** /ˌ. ˈ./ *n* **the New World** a word meaning North, Central, and South America, used when talking about the time that Europeans first discovered these areas: *Columbus' arrival in the New World*

**New Year** /ˈ. ./, **New Year's** *n* the time when you celebrate the beginning of the year: *Happy New Year!* | *Have you made any **New Year's resolutions**? (=promises to improve yourself)*

**new year** /ˌ. ˈ.ᵈ / *n* **the new year** the year after the present year, especially the months at the beginning of it: *We're opening three new stores **in the new year**.*

**New Year's Day** /ˌ. . ˈ./ *n* [singular, U] a holiday on January 1, the first day of the year in Western countries

**New Year's Eve** /ˌ. . ˈ./ *n* [singular, U] a holiday on December 31, the last day of the year in Western countries

**next¹** /nɛkst/ *determiner, adj* **1** the next day, time, event etc. is the one that happens after the present one: ***The next** flight leaves in 45 minutes.* | *They returned to New York **the next day**.* | ***Next time** (=when this happens again) be more careful.* | *Why don't we have lunch **next week**?* | *I'll see you **next Monday**.* ✗ DON'T SAY "the next Monday/month/year etc." ✗ **2** the next place is the one closest to where you are now: *Turn left at the **next corner**.* | *the people at the **next table*** **3** the next person or thing in a list, series etc. is the one you deal with after the present one: *Can I help the **next person**, please?* | *Read the **next** two chapters by Friday.* **4** slightly bigger, heavier etc. than the one you have: *Can I try the **the next size up**? (=a slightly bigger size) | *I'd like to exchange this shirt for the next biggest/smallest size.* **5 the next best thing** the thing or situation that is almost as good as the one you really want: *Visiting Victoria, in Canada, is the next best thing to being in England.*

**next**[2] *adv* **1** immediately afterward: *What should we do next?* | *First, write your name at the top of the page. Next, read the instructions.* **2 next to** very close to someone or something, with nothing in between: *I sat next to a really nice lady on the plane.* | *Your glasses are there, next to the phone.* **3 next to nothing** very little: *I actually bought the car for next to nothing.* (=very little money) **4 next to impossible** very difficult: *It's next to impossible to get tickets for the game.*

**next**[3] *pron* the person or thing in a list, series etc. that comes after the person or thing you are dealing with now: *Carrots. Milk. What's next on the shopping list?* | *Pauline was next in line.*

**next door** /ˌ. ˈ./ *adv* **1** in the room, building etc. that is next to yours: *The Simpsons live next door.* **2 next door to** next to a building: *Our apartment is right next door to the post office.*

**next-door** /ˌ. ˈ.◂/ *adj* relating to the room, building etc. that is next to yours: *I'd like you to meet my next-door neighbor, Lara Hughes.*

**next of kin** /ˌ. . ˈ./ *n, plural* **next of kin** LAW the person or people who are most closely related to you, and who are still alive: *The victim will not be named until her next of kin are informed.*

**NFC** *n* National Football Conference; a group of teams that is part of the NFL −see also AFC

**NFL** *n* National Football League; the organization that is in charge of professional football in the US

**NH** the written abbreviation of New Hampshire

**NHL** *n* National Hockey League; the organization that is in charge of professional HOCKEY in the US and Canada

**nib·ble** /ˈnɪbəl/ *v* [I,T] to eat a small amount of food with a lot of very small bites: *a rabbit nibbling on a carrot* −**nibble** *n*

**nice** /naɪs/ *adj* **1** good, pleasant, attractive, or enjoyable: *Did you have a nice time at the beach?* | *That's a nice sweater.* | *I'm going to take a nice hot shower.* | *Come on inside where it's nice and warm.* | *You look nice today.* **2** friendly or kind: *They're all very nice people.* | *It was nice of you to visit me in the hospital.* | *Be nice to your little sister!* **3** nice weather is warm and sunny: *It's really nice out today.*

SPOKEN PHRASES
**4 it is nice/it would be nice** said when you think something is good or when you wish you could do something: *It's nice (that) your family visits you so often.* | *It'd be nice to go to Spain some day.* **5 (it's) nice to meet you** a polite phrase used when you

meet someone for the first time **6 (it was) nice meeting you** a polite phrase used when you say goodbye after meeting someone for the first time **7 Nice going/move/one!** said as a joke when someone makes a mistake or does something wrong: *"I just spilled my coffee!" "Nice going!"*

−**niceness** *n* [U]

**USAGE NOTE** nice

Use **nice** when you are speaking in order to show that you like someone or something: *We had a nice time at the party.* However, many teachers think it is better to use a more specific adjective in formal and written English: *They have a beautiful house.* | *He tells interesting stories.*

**nice-look·ing** /ˌ. ˈ.◂/ *adj* fairly attractive: *He's a really nice-looking guy.*

**nice·ly** /ˈnaɪsli/ *adv* **1** in a satisfactory, pleasing, or skillful way; WELL: *Belinda is always so nicely dressed.* (=wearing attractive clothes) | *His arm is healing nicely.* **2** in a polite or friendly way: *I hope you thanked Mrs. Chang nicely.*

**ni·ce·ty** /ˈnaɪsəţi/ *n* a small and exact detail or difference: *legal niceties*

**niche** /nɪtʃ/ *n* **1** a job or activity that is perfect for the skills, abilities, and character that you have: *After many years, she found her niche as a fashion designer.* **2** a small hollow place in a wall, often used for holding STATUEs

**nick**[1] /nɪk/ *n* **1 in the nick of time** just before it is too late or before something bad happens: *The doctor arrived just in the nick of time.* **2** a very small cut on the surface or edge of something

**nick**[2] *v* [T] to accidentally make a small cut on the surface or edge of something: *I nicked my chin when I was shaving.*

**nick·el** /ˈnɪkəl/ *n* **1** a coin used in the US and Canada worth 5 cents (=$\frac{1}{20}$ of a dollar) **2** [U] a hard silver-white metal that is an ELEMENT and is used for making other metals

**nickel-and-dime** /ˌ... . ˈ./ *adj* INFORMAL not large, important, or effective enough: *We face problems that can't be solved with nickel-and-dime solutions.*

**nick·name**[1] /ˈnɪkneɪm/ *n* a silly name or a shorter form of someone's real name, usually given by friends or family: *His nickname was "Elephant" because of his ears.*

**nickname**[2] *v* [T] to give someone a NICKNAME

**nic·o·tine** /ˈnɪkəˌtin/ *n* [U] a dangerous substance in tobacco

**niece** /nis/ *n* the daughter of your brother or sister, or the daughter of your husband's or wife's brother or sister −compare NEPHEW −see picture at FAMILY

**nif·ty** /'nɪfti/ *adj* INFORMAL very good, fast, or effective: *John taught me a nifty little card trick.*

**nig·ger** /'nɪgɚ/ *n* TABOO an extremely offensive word for a Black person

**nig·gling** /'nɪglɪŋ/ *adj* not very important, but continuing to annoy someone: *a niggling doubt*

**nigh** /naɪ/ *adv, prep* LITERARY **1** near **2 well nigh/nigh on** almost: *Edna was well nigh fifty when at last she married.*

**night** /naɪt/ *n* **1** [C,U] the dark part of each 24-hour period, when the sun cannot be seen: *a store that is open all night* | *You can see the stars really clearly here at night.* **2** [C,U] the evening: *Some friends are coming over to-morrow night.* | *Mom had to go to the hospital last night.* | *I fly back to New Orleans on Thursday night.* | *We had a good night out.* (=when you go to a restaurant, party etc.) ✗ DON'T SAY "this night." SAY "tonight." ✗ **3** [C,U] the time when most people are sleeping: *The baby cried all night long.* | *I woke up in the middle of the night.* | *What you need is a good night's sleep.* (=to sleep well all night) **4 night after night** every night for a long period: *He goes out drinking night after night.* **5 night and day/ day and night** all the time: *The store is guarded day and night.* – see also DAY, NIGHTS, TONIGHT²

**night·club** /'naɪt¬klʌb/ *n* a place where people can drink and dance that is open late at night

**night·fall** /'naɪtfɔl/ *n* [U] LITERARY the time in the evening when the sky becomes darker; DUSK

**night·gown** /'naɪt¬gaʊn/, **night·ie** /'naɪti/ *n* a piece of loose clothing, like a dress, that women wear in bed

**night·in·gale** /'naɪt¬n,geɪl, 'naɪtɪŋ-/ *n* a small European wild bird that sings very beautifully, especially at night

**night·life** /'naɪt¬laɪf/ *n* [U] entertainment in places where you can dance, drink etc. in the evening: *Las Vegas is famous for its nightlife.*

**night light** /'. ./ *n* a small, not very bright light, often put in a child's BEDROOM to stop him/her from being afraid

**night·ly** /'naɪtli/ *adj, adv* happening every night: *the nightly news* | *The restaurant is open nightly.*

**night·mare** /'naɪt¬mɛr/ *n* **1** a very frightening dream **2** a person, thing, situation etc. that is very bad or very difficult to deal with: *It was a nightmare driving home in the snow.* –**nightmarish** *adj*

**night owl** /'. ./ *n* INFORMAL someone who enjoys being awake or working late at night

**nights** /naɪts/ *adv* regularly or often at night: *Juan works nights.*

**night school** /'. ./ *n* [U] classes taught at night, for people who work during the day: *I'm studying Spanish at night school.*

**night·stand** /'naɪtstænd/, **night ta·ble** /'. ,../ *n* a small table beside a bed

**night·time** /'naɪt-taɪm/ *n* [U] the time during the night when the sky is dark –opposite DAY-TIME

**nil** /nɪl/ *n* [U] nothing or zero: *His chances of winning the election are almost nil.* (=not likely)

**nim·ble** /'nɪmbəl/ *adj* **1** able to move quickly, easily, and skillfully; AGILE: *nimble fingers* | *a nimble climber* **2 a nimble mind/ wit etc.** an ability to think quickly or understand things easily

**nin·com·poop** /'nɪŋkəm,pup/ *n* OLD-FASHIONED someone who has done something stupid; IDIOT

**nine** /naɪn/ *number* **1** 9 **2** 9 o'clock: *I have to be in the office by nine.*

**nine·teen** /,naɪn'tin‹/ *number* 19 –**nineteenth** *number*

**nine-to-five** /,. . '.‹/ *adj, adv* from 9:00 a.m. until 5:00 p.m.; the hours that most people work in an office: *You work nine-to-five, right?* | *a nine-to-five job*

**nine·ty** /'naɪnti/ *number* **1** 90 **2 the nineties a)** the years between 1990 and 1999 **b)** the numbers between 90 and 99, especially when used for measuring temperature **3 be in my/his/their etc. nineties** to be aged between 90 and 99 –**ninetieth** /'naɪntiiθ/ *number*

**ninth** /naɪnθ/ *number* **1** 9th **2** 1/9

**nip¹** /nɪp/ **-pped, -pping** *v* **1** [I,T] to bite someone or something with small sharp bites, or to try to do this: *This stupid dog keeps nipping at my ankles.* **2 nip sth in the bud** to prevent something from becoming a problem by stopping it as soon as it starts

**nip²** *n* **1** a small sharp bite, or the action of biting someone or something **2 nip and tuck** equally likely to happen or not happen: *I made it to the airport, but it was nip and tuck.*

**nip·ple** /'nɪpəl/ *n* **1** the dark raised circle in the middle of a woman's breast, that a baby sucks in order to get milk –compare TEAT **2** one of the two dark raised circles on a man's chest **3** the small piece of rubber on the end of a baby's bottle **4** something shaped like a nipple, for example on a machine

**nip·py** /'nɪpi/ *adj* weather that is nippy is cold enough that you need a coat

**nit** /nɪt/ *n* the egg of a LOUSE (=small insect)

**nit·pick·ing** /'nɪt,pɪkɪŋ/ *n* [U] the act of criticizing people about unimportant details –**nitpicking** *adj*

**ni·trate** /'naɪtreɪt/ *n* [C,U] a chemical compound that is mainly used for improving the soil that crops are grown in

**ni·tro·gen** /'naɪtrədʒən/ *n* [U] a gas that is an ELEMENT and is the main part of the earth's air

**nit·ty-grit·ty** /'nɪti ,grɪti, ,nɪti 'grɪti/ *n* **the nitty-gritty** INFORMAL the basic and practical facts and details of an agreement or activity: *Let's get down to the nitty-gritty and work out the cost.*

**nit·wit** /'nɪt¬,wɪt/ *n* INFORMAL a silly stupid person

**NJ** the written abbreviation of New Jersey

**NM** the written abbreviation of New Mexico

**no.** *plural* **nos.** the written abbreviation of NUMBER

**no**[1] /nou/ *adv* **1** SPOKEN said in order to give a negative reply to a question, offer, or request: *"Is she married?" "No, she's not." | "Do you want some more coffee?" "No, thanks." | I asked Dad if I could have a dog, but he said no.* **2** SPOKEN said when you disagree with a statement: *"Gary's weird." "No, he's just shy."* **3** SPOKEN said when you do not want someone to do something: *No, Jimmy, don't touch that.* —opposite YES

**no**[2] *determiner* **1** not any, or not at all: *I'm sorry, there are no more tickets available. | He has no control over his children. | There's no reason to be afraid. | I'm no fool.* (=I am not stupid) **2** used on a sign in order to show that something is not allowed: *No smoking | No parking* —see also **in no time** (TIME[1])

---

**USAGE NOTE no and not**

Use **no** before nouns to mean "not any," or to say that something is not allowed: *He has no job and no money. | a "no smoking" sign.* You can also use **no** in order to agree with negative questions: *"It's not raining, is it?" "No, it isn't."* Use **not** in order to make a verb negative: *I'm not going camping.* When the word "all" and words that begin with "every-" are the subject of a sentence, use **not** to make the subject negative: *Not all of the students finished the test. | Not everyone likes horror movies.* You can also use **not** before names, pronouns, adverbs of frequency, and prepositions: *"George and Diane are getting a divorce." "Not them!" | "Do you watch sports on TV?" "Not very often." | It's open on Saturday, but not on Sunday.*

---

**no**[3] *n* a negative answer or decision: *Her answer was a definite no.*

**no·bil·i·ty** /nou'bıləti/ *n* **1 the nobility** the group of people in particular countries who have the highest social class **2** [U] the quality of being NOBLE

**no·ble**[1] /'noubəl/ *adj* **1** morally good or generous in a way that should be admired: *a noble young man | a noble achievement* **2** belonging to the NOBILITY: *noble families* —**nobly** *adv*

**no·ble**[2], **no·ble·man** /'noubəlmən/, **no·ble·wom·an** /'noubəl,wumən/ *n* someone who belongs to the NOBILITY

**no·bod·y**[1] /'nou,bʌdi, -,badi/ *pron* ⇨ NO ONE —see usage note at ANYONE

**nobody**[2] *n* someone who is not important, successful, or famous: *I feel like a nobody!*

**no-brain·er** /'. ,../ *n* [C usually singular] SLANG something that you do not have to think about,

because it is easy to understand: *an action movie that's a real no-brainer*

**noc·tur·nal** /nak'tɜnl/ *adj* **1** TECHNICAL nocturnal animals are active at night **2** FORMAL happening at night

**nod** /nad/ *v* **-dded, -dding 1** [I,T] to move your head up and down, especially to show that you agree with or understand something: *The committee nodded their heads in agreement. | "Are you having fun?" he asked. Jill smiled and nodded.* **2** to move your head up and down once toward someone or something, in order to greet someone or to give him/her a sign to do something: *I nodded to the waiter and asked for the bill. | "Sally's in there," Jim said, nodding toward the door.*

**nod off** *phr v* [I] to begin to sleep, often without intending to: *His speech was so boring I kept nodding off.* —**nod** *n*

**node** /noud/ *n* **1** a place where lines in a network, GRAPH etc. meet or join **2** ⇨ LYMPH NODE

**no-fault** /. '.◂/ *adj* **1** no-fault car insurance will pay for the damage done in an accident, even if you caused the accident **2** a no-fault DIVORCE does not blame either the husband or the wife

**no-frills** /. '.◂/ *adj* without any features that are not completely necessary; basic: *a no-frills airline*

**noise** /nɔız/ *n* [C,U] a sound or sounds that is too loud, annoying, or not intended: *the noise of the traffic | What was that cracking noise? | The washing machine is making a weird noise. | There was a lot of noise outside.*

---

**USAGE NOTE noise and sound**

Use **sound** to talk about something that you hear: *I love the sound of birds singing.* **Noise** means "loud unpleasant sounds": *Could you kids stop making so much noise?*

---

**noise·less·ly** /'nɔızlısli/ *adv* not making any sound: *walking noiselessly* —**noiseless** *adj*

**noise pol·lu·tion** /'. .,../ *n* [U] very loud continuous noise in the environment that is harmful to people

**nois·y** /'nɔızi/ *adj* making a lot of noise, or full of noise: *a group of noisy kids | a noisy restaurant* —**noisily** *adv* —**noisiness** *n* [U]

**no·mad** /'noumæd/ *n* a member of a tribe that travels from place to place, usually to find fields for his/her animals —**nomadic** /nou'mædık/ *adj*

**no-man's land** /'. . ,./ *n* [singular, U] land that no one owns or controls, especially between two opposing armies

**no·men·cla·ture** /'noumən,kleıtʃɚ/ *n* [C,U] FORMAL a system of naming things

**nom·i·nal** /ˈnɑmənl/ *adj* **1 nominal leader/head etc.** someone who has the title of leader etc. but does not actually do that job **2 nominal price/fee/sum etc.** a small amount of money

**nom·i·nal·ly** /ˈnɑmənl-i/ *adv* officially described as something or as doing something, although the truth may be different: *The President nominally commands the armed forces.*

**nom·i·nate** /ˈnɑməˌneɪt/ *v* [T] **1** to officially choose someone so that s/he can be one of the competitors in an election, competition etc.: *Ferraro was the first woman to be nominated for the job of vice president.* **2** to choose someone for a particular job or position: *Margaret was nominated (as) club representative.*

**nom·i·na·tion** /ˌnɑməˈneɪʃən/ *n* [C,U] **1** the act of officially choosing someone to be a competitor in an election, competition etc., or the official choice: *Clinton got the Democratic nomination for President.* **2** the act of choosing someone for a particular job, or the person chosen: *the nomination of O'Connor to the United States Supreme Court*

**nom·i·nee** /ˌnɑməˈni/ *n* someone who has been NOMINATEd for a prize, duty etc.: *Oscar nominee Winona Ryder*

**non·ag·gres·sion** /ˌnɑnəˈgrɛʃən/ *n* [U] the state of not fighting or attacking: *a nonaggression pact/treaty* (=a country's promise not to attack)

**non·al·co·hol·ic** /ˌnɑnælkəˈhɔlɪk/ *adj* a nonalcoholic drink does not have any alcohol in it

**non·cha·lant** /ˌnɑnʃəˈlɑnt/ *adj* calm and not seeming interested in or worried about anything: *young men trying to appear nonchalant* –**nonchalance** *n* [U] –**nonchalantly** *adv*

**non·com·bat·ant** /ˌnɑnkəmˈbætⁿnt/ *n* someone in the army, navy etc. who does not do any fighting during a war, such as an army doctor

**non·com·mit·al** /ˌnɑnkəˈmɪtəl/ *adj* not giving a definite answer, or not willing to express your opinions: *The lawyer was noncommittal about Jones' chances of going to prison.* –**noncommittally** *adv*

**non·con·form·ist** /ˌnɑnkənˈfɔrmɪst/ *n* someone who deliberately does not accept the beliefs and customs that most people in a society accept: *a political nonconformist*

**non·dair·y** /ˌ. ˈ..◂/ *adj* containing no milk, and used instead of a product that contains milk: *non-dairy whipped topping*

**non·de·nom·i·na·tion·al** /ˌ. ...ˈ.../ *adj* not related to a particular religion or religious group: *a non-denominational chapel*

**non·de·script** /ˌnɑndɪˈskrɪpt◂/ *adj* not having any noticeable or interesting qualities: *a nondescript man in a plain gray suit*

**none¹** /nʌn/ *quantifier, pron* **1** not any of something: *"Can I have some more pie?" "Sorry, there's none left."* **2** not one person or thing: *None of my friends has a car.* | *Any decision is better than none at all.* **3 none other than** used in order to emphasize a fact when you are surprised that it is true: *Her uncle is none other than the President.* –see usage note at EITHER² –see study note on page 466

### USAGE NOTE none of

**None of** is a singular subject, and is used with a singular verb in formal and written English: *None of the three countries wants to be a nuclear state.* However, in informal speech, we usually use a plural verb: *None of my friends have a car.*

**none²** *adv* **1 none the worse/wiser etc.** not any worse than before, not knowing any more than before etc.: *The cat's none the worse for having stayed out all night.* **2 none too soon/likely etc.** not at all soon, not at all likely etc.: *The ambulance arrived none too soon.*

**non·en·ti·ty** /nɑnˈɛnɾəti/ *n* someone who has no importance, power, or ability

**none·the·less** /ˌnʌnðəˈlɛs◂/ *adv* FORMAL in spite of what has just been mentioned; NEVERTHELESS: *It won't be as fast as a supercomputer, but it will do the job nonetheless.*

**non·e·vent** /ˈnɑnɪˌvɛnt, ˌnɑnɪˈvɛnt/ *n* INFORMAL an event that is disappointing and much less exciting or interesting than you expected: *The concert was a total nonevent.*

**non·ex·ist·ent** /ˌnɑnɪgˈzɪstənt◂/ *adj* not existing at all in a particular place or situation: *Airplanes were practically nonexistent in those days.*

**non·fat** /ˌnɑnˈfæt◂/ *adj* nonfat milk, YOGURT etc. has no fat in it

**non·fic·tion** /ˌnɑnˈfɪkʃən/ *n* [U] articles, books etc. about real facts or events, not imagined ones –**nonfiction** *adj* –compare FICTION

**non·flam·ma·ble** /ˌnɑnˈflæməbəl/ *adj* difficult or impossible to burn –opposite INFLAMMABLE, FLAMMABLE

**non·in·ter·ven·tion** /ˌnɑnɪntɚˈvɛnʃən/ *n* [U] the refusal of a government to become involved in the affairs of other countries

**no-no** /ˈnoʊnoʊ/ *n* INFORMAL something that is not allowed, or not socially acceptable: *My parents think sex before marriage is a definite no-no.*

**no-non·sense** /ˌnoʊˈnɑnsɛns◂/ *adj* very practical, direct, and unwilling to waste time: *a no-nonsense attitude toward work*

**non·pay·ment** /ˌnɑnˈpeɪmənt/ *n* [U] failure to pay bills, taxes, or debts

**non·plussed** /ˌnɑnˈplʌst/ *adj* so surprised that you do not know what to say or do: *I was momentarily nonplussed by his news.*

**non·prof·it** /ˌnɑnˈprɑfɪt/ *adj* a nonprofit organization, school, hospital etc. uses the money it earns to help people instead of making a profit, and therefore does not have to pay taxes

**non·pro·lif·er·a·tion** /ˌnɑnprəˌlɪfəˈreɪʃən/ *n* [U] the act of limiting the number of NUCLEAR or chemical weapons that are being made across the world

**non·re·fund·a·ble** /ˌ.ˈ...◂/ *adj* if something you buy is non-refundable, you cannot get your money back after you have paid for it: *non-refundable airline tickets*

**non·re·new·a·ble** /ˌ. .ˈ...◂/ *adj* non-renewable types of energy such as coal or gas cannot be replaced after they have been used

**non·sense** /ˈnɑnsɛns, -səns/ *n* [U] **1** ideas, statements, or opinions that are not true or that seem very stupid: *"This dress makes me look fat." "Nonsense, you look great!"* **2** behavior that is stupid and annoying: *I'm not putting up with any more of your nonsense!* **3** speech or writing that has no meaning or cannot be understood: *Children often make up nonsense songs.* –**nonsensical** /nɑnˈsɛnsɪkəl/ *adj*

**non se·qui·tur** /ˌnɑn ˈsɛkwɪt̮ɚ/ *n* FORMAL a statement that does not seem related to the statements that were made before it

**non·smok·er** /ˌnɑnˈsmoʊkɚ/ *n* someone who does not smoke –opposite SMOKER

**non·smok·ing** /ˌnɑnˈsmoʊkɪŋ◂/ *adj* a non-smoking area, building etc. is one where people are not allowed to smoke

**non·stand·ard** /ˌnɑnˈstændɚd◂/ *adj* TECHNICAL nonstandard words, expressions, or pronunciations are usually considered to be incorrect by educated speakers of a language –compare STANDARD²

**non·stick** /ˌnɑnˈstɪk◂/ *adj* nonstick pans have a special surface inside that food will not stick to

**non·stop** /ˌnɑnˈstɑp◂/ *adj, adv* without stopping or without a stop: *Dan worked nonstop for 12 hours.* | *a nonstop flight to New York*

**non·ver·bal** /ˌ. ˈ..◂/ *adj* not using words: *non-verbal communication* –**non-verbally** *adv*

**non·vi·o·lence** /ˌnɑnˈvaɪələns/ *n* [U] the practice of opposing a government without fighting, for example by not obeying laws: *an environmental group with a policy of nonviolence*

**non·vi·o·lent** /ˌnɑnˈvaɪələnt/ *adj* not using or not involving violence: *nonviolent protests against the government* | *nonviolent mental patients*

**noo·dle** /ˈnudl/ *n* [C usually plural] a long thin piece of soft food made from flour, water, and usually eggs, that is cooked by being boiled: *chicken noodle soup*

**nook** /nʊk/ *n* **1** a small, quiet, safe place: *a shady nook* **2 every nook and cranny** every part of a place: *We've searched every nook and cranny for that key.*

**noon** /nun/ *n* 12 o'clock in the middle of the day; MIDDAY: *Lunch will be right at noon.* | *the noon meal*

**no one** /ˈ. ./ *pron* not anyone: *I tried calling last night but no one was home.* | *No one could remember her name.* –see usage note at ANYONE

**noose** /nus/ *n* a circle of a rope that becomes tighter as it is pulled, used for hanging people as a punishment –compare LASSO

**nope** /noʊp/ *adv* SPOKEN no: *"Aren't you hungry?" "Nope."*

**no·place, no place** /ˈnoʊpleɪs/ *adv* INFORMAL ⇨ NOWHERE –see usage note at ANYONE

**nor** /nɚ; *strong* nɔr/ *conjunction* **1 neither ... nor** used in order to show that not one of a set of facts, people, qualities, actions etc is true: *My mother's family were neither rich nor poor.* | *Neither Matt nor Julie nor Mark said anything.* **2** used after a negative statement, meaning "and not," "or not," "neither," or "not either": *He wasn't at the meeting, nor was he at work yesterday.*

**norm** /nɔrm/ *n* the usual way of doing something, or the acceptable way of behaving: *the values, norms, and traditions of North American families* | *Working at home is becoming the norm for many employees.*

**nor·mal** /ˈnɔrməl/ *adj* usual, typical, or expected: *Greg just isn't acting like his normal self.* | *normal everyday life* –opposite ABNORMAL

**nor·mal·i·ty** /nɔrˈmæləti/, **nor·mal·cy** /ˈnɔrməlsi/ *n* [U] a situation in which everything happens in the usual way

**nor·mal·ize** /ˈnɔrməˌlaɪz/ *v* [I,T] to become normal again, or to make a situation become normal again: *In March 1944 Russia normalized relations with Italy.* (=became friendly again after a period of disagreement) –**normalization** /ˌnɔrmələˈzeɪʃən/ *n* [U]

**nor·mal·ly** /ˈnɔrməli/ *adv* **1** usually: *I normally go to bed around eleven.* **2** in the usual expected way: *Try to relax and breathe normally.*

**north¹, North** /nɔrθ/ *n* [singular, U] **1** the direction toward the top of the world, or to the left of someone facing the rising sun: *Which way is north?* **2 the north** the northern part of a country, state etc.: *Rain will spread to the north later today.* **3 the North** the part of the US east of the Mississippi River and north of Washington, D.C. **4 up North** in or to the North of the US: *Douglas comes from somewhere up North.*

**north²** *adj* **1** in, to, or facing north: *a town 20 miles north of Salem* | *the north end of the field* **2 north wind** a wind that comes from the north

**north**³ *adv* **1** toward the north: *Go north on I-5 to Portland.* | *The window faces north.* **2 up north** in the north or to the north: *The Simpsons are moving up north in May.*

---

**USAGE NOTE** north/south/east/west of and in the north/south/east/west of

Use **north/south/east/west of** as an adjective phrase to describe where a place is in relation to another place: *Chicago is south of Milwaukee.* Use **in the north/south/east/west/ of** as a noun phrase to say which part of a place you are talking about: *The mountains are in the north of the province.* However, you must use **northern, southern, eastern,** or **western** with the name of a place: *They have a cabin in northern Ontario.* ✗ DON'T SAY "in the north of Ontario." ✗

---

**North A·mer·i·can** /ˌ. .'.../ *n* one of the seven CONTINENTS, that includes land between the Arctic Ocean and the Caribbean Sea **–North American** *adj*

**north·bound** /'nɔrθbaʊnd/ *adj* traveling or leading toward the north: *northbound traffic* | *the northbound lanes of the freeway*

**north·east**¹ /ˌnɔrθ'ist◄/ *n* [U] **1** the direction that is exactly between the north and the east **2 the Northeast** the northeast part of a country, state etc. **–northeastern** *adj*

**northeast**² *adj, adv* in, from, or toward the northeast: *traveling northeast* | *a northeast wind*

**north·er·ly** /'nɔrðəli/ *adj* **1** in or toward the north: *sailing in a northerly direction* **2** a northerly wind comes from the north

**north·ern** /'nɔrðən/ *adj* in or from the north part of an area, country, state etc.: *northern California* **–see usage note at** NORTH³

**north·ern·er, Northerner** /'nɔrðənə/ *n* someone who comes from the NORTHERN part of a country or the northern HEMISPHERE

**Northern Lights** /ˌ.. './ *n* [plural] bands of colored lights that are seen in the night sky in the most northern parts of the world

**north·ern·most** /'nɔrðən,moust/ *adj* farthest north: *the northernmost tip of Maine*

**North Pole** /ˌ. './ *n* **the North Pole** the most northern point on the surface of the earth, or the area around it

**north·ward** /'nɔrθwəd/ *adj, adv* toward the north

**north·west**¹ /ˌnɔrθ'wɛst◄/ *n* **1** the direction that is exactly between north and west **2 the Northwest** the northwest part of a country, state etc. **–northwestern** *adj*

**northwest**² *adj, adv* in, from, or toward the northwest: *driving northwest* | *a northwest wind*

**nose**¹ /noʊz/ *n*
**1** ▶FACE◄ the part of a person's or animal's face used for smelling and breathing through:

Someone punched him and broke his nose. | *the dog's cold wet nose* | *Don't* **pick your nose.** (=clean it with your finger) **–see picture at** HEAD¹

**2 sb's nose is running** if someone's nose is running, liquid is slowly coming out of it because s/he has a cold

**3 (right) under sb's nose** so close to someone that s/he should notice, but does not: *The man escaped right under the noses of the guards.*

**4 stick/poke your nose into sth** INFORMAL to show too much interest in private matters that do not concern you: *Jana's always sticking her nose into other people's business.*

**5 put sb's nose out of joint** INFORMAL to annoy someone by attracting everyone's attention away from him/her

**6** ▶PLANE◄ the pointed front end of a plane, ROCKET etc. **–see picture at** AIRPLANE

**7 red-nosed/long-nosed etc.** having a nose that is red, long etc.

**8 on the nose** INFORMAL exactly: *Tanya guessed the price right on the nose.*

**9 turn your nose up (at sth)** to refuse to accept something because you do not think it is good enough for you: *Five years ago, lawyers were turning their noses up at bankruptcy work.*

**10 keep your nose to the grindstone** to continue working very hard, without stopping to rest **–see also blow your nose** (BLOW¹) **pay through the nose** (PAY¹)

**nose**² *v* [I,T] move forward slowly and carefully: *The boat* **nosed out** *into the lake.*

**nose around/about** *phr v* [I] to try to find out private information about someone or something: *Why were you* **nosing around** *my office?*

**nose·bleed** /'noʊzblid/ *n* have a nosebleed to have blood coming out of your nose

**nose·dive** /'noʊzdaɪv/ *n* **1 take a nosedive** to suddenly become less in amount, price, rate etc.: *The company's profits took a nosedive last year.* **2** a sudden steep drop by a plane, with its front end pointing toward the ground **–nosedive** *v* [I]

**nose job** /'. ./ *n* INFORMAL a medical operation on someone's nose in order to improve its appearance

**no-show** /'. ./ *n* INFORMAL someone who does not go to an event that s/he has promised to go to **–no-show** *v* [I,T]

**nos·tal·gia** /nɑ'stældʒə, nə-/ *n* [U] the slightly sad feeling you have when you remember happy events from the past: *nostalgia for his life on the farm* **–nostalgic** *adj* **–nostalgically** *adv*

**nos·tril** /'nɑstrəl/ *n* one of the two holes at the end of your nose, through which you breathe **–see picture at** HEAD¹

**nos·y** /'noʊzi/ *adj* always trying to find out private information about someone or something: *Our neighbors are really nosy.* **–nosiness** *n* [U]

**not** /nɑt/ *adv* **1** used in order to make a word, statement, or question negative: *Most stores are not open until 9:30 a.m.* | *Is anyone not coming to the party?* | *I don't* (=do not) *smoke.* —compare NO¹ **2** used instead of a whole phrase, to mean the opposite of what has been mentioned before it: *No one knows if the story is true or not.* (=or if it is not true) | *"Is Mark still sick?" "I hope not."* (=I hope he is not still sick) —compare SO¹ **3** used in order to make a word or phrase have the opposite meaning: *Not a lot/not much* (=little) *is known about the disease.* | *Most of the hotels were not very expensive/not that great/not too bad.* (=slightly cheap, slightly bad, or acceptable) **4 not only ... (but) also** in addition to being or doing something: *She's not only funny, she's also smart.* **5 not a/not one** not any person or thing; none: *Not one of the students knew the answer.* | *Look! Not a cloud in the sky!* **6 not bad!** SPOKEN said when you are proud of a small achievement: *"See, I got a B+ on my test!!" "Not bad!"* **7 not that ...** used before a negative sentence: *Sarah has a new boyfriend - not that I care.* **8 ...not!** SLANG said when you mean the opposite of what you have just been saying: *Yeah, she's pretty - not!* —see usage note at NO²

**no·ta·ble** /'noʊt̬əbəl/ *adj* important, interesting, or unusual enough to be noticed: *It's their worst team ever, with the notable exception of Rawlings* (=he is the only good player)

**no·ta·bly** /'noʊt̬əbli/ *adv* **1** especially; particularly: *Some politicians, most notably the President, refused to comment.* **2** in a way that is noticeable: *a notably successful project*

**no·ta·rize** /'noʊt̬ə,raɪz/ *v* [T] to have a NOTARY PUBLIC make a document official

**no·ta·ry pub·lic** /,noʊt̬əri 'pʌblɪk/, **notary** *n* someone who has the legal power to make a signed document official

**no·ta·tion** /noʊ'teɪʃən/ *n* [C,U] a system of written marks or signs used for representing musical sounds, mathematical problems, or scientific ideas

**notch¹** /nɑtʃ/ *n* **1** a V-shaped cut in a surface or edge: *Cut a notch near one end of the stick.* **2** a level of achievement or a social position: *Losing the game brought the team down a few notches.*

**notch²** *v* [T] to cut a V-shaped mark into something

**note¹** /noʊt/ *n* **1** a short informal letter: *I wrote Tina a note to thank her for helping.* **2** something that you write down in order to remind you of something: *She made a note of my new address.* **3** a particular musical sound or PITCH, or the sign in written music that represents this **4 take note (of sth)** to pay careful attention to something: *Take note of the instructions at the top of the page.* **5 a note of anger/sadness etc.** a particular quality or feel-

ing that you notice in a particular person or situation: *The movie ended on a note of hope.* **6 of note** important or famous: *a writer of note* —see also NOTES

**note²** *v* [T] **1** to notice or pay careful attention to something: *Please note that the museum is closed on Monday.* **2** also **note down** to write something down so you will remember it: *He noted my telephone number.*

**note·book** /'noʊtbʊk/ *n* **1** a book of plain paper in which you can write notes **2** a small computer that is about the size of a book

**not·ed** /'noʊt̬ɪd/ *adj* well-known; famous: *a noted author*

**note·pa·per** /'noʊt̬,peɪpɚ/ *n* [U] paper used for writing letters or notes on

**notes** /noʊts/ *n* [plural] information that a student writes down during a class, from a book etc. so s/he will remember it: *Did you take any notes* (=write them) *in history class?* —see also **compare notes (with sb)** (COMPARE¹)

**note·wor·thy** /'noʊt̬,wɚði/ *adj* FORMAL important or interesting enough to deserve your attention: *a noteworthy event*

**noth·ing¹** /'nʌθɪŋ/ *pron* **1** not anything; no thing: *There's nothing in the bag.* | *I had nothing else* (=nothing more) *to do, so I went to bed.* | *Nothing you say will change what he thinks.* | *There's nothing left to eat.* (=there was something but it is gone) | *I have nothing against New York,* (=I have no reason for not liking it) *I just don't want to live there.* **2** something that you do not consider to be important or interesting: *I have nothing to wear tonight!* | *"What did you say?" "Oh, nothing."* **3** zero: *The Red Sox won the game three nothing.* (=the Red Sox had 3, the other team had no points) **4 for nothing a)** without having a purpose or a good reason: *I did all that work for nothing. The teacher didn't even look at it.* **b)** without paying or being paid: *My dad said he'd fix it for nothing.* **5 have nothing to do with a)** if something has nothing to do with a fact or situation, it is not related to that fact or situation: *"He's mad because of what I said, isn't he?" "No, that has nothing to do with it."* **b)** if someone has nothing to do with a situation or person, he or she is not involved in it or with him/her: *"What happened?" "I don't know. I had nothing to do with it."* **6 nothing special** having no very good or very bad qualities: *The story was nothing special, but the pictures were beautiful.* **7 nothing but** only: *We've had nothing but rain for two weeks now.*

SPOKEN PHRASES

**8 nothing much** SPOKEN very little: *"Hi Judy! What's new?" "Oh, nothing much."* **9 it was nothing** used when someone thanks you, in order to say that you did not mind helping: *"Thanks a lot!" "It was nothing."* **10** NONSTANDARD anything: *I never said nothing about taking you swimming.*

N

**11 nothing doing** SPOKEN OLD-FASHIONED used in order to say that you refuse to do something

**nothing**[2] *adv* **1 be nothing like** to have no qualities that are similar to someone or something else: *We have hills at home, but they're nothing like the mountains here!* **2 be nothing less than/nothing short of** if something is nothing less than or nothing short of a particular quality, then it has that quality: *She thought his ideas were nothing less than ridiculous.*

**noth·ing·ness** /'nʌθɪŋnɪs/ *n* [U] the state of complete emptiness where nothing exists

**no·tice**[1] /'noʊt̬ɪs/ *v* [I,T] to see, feel, or hear someone or something: *She noticed that I was getting nervous.* | *I said "hello," but she didn't notice.*

**notice**[2] *n* **1** a written or printed statement that gives information or a warning to people: *Put the notice up here so everyone can see it.* **2** [U] information or a warning about something that will happen: *You must give the bank three days'/two weeks'/a month's notice before closing the account.* **3 not take any notice/take no notice** to pay no attention to someone or something: *Don't take any notice of her, she's just angry.* **4 at short notice/at a moment's notice** without much warning, so that you have only a short time to do something: *You can't expect us to leave at a moment's notice!* **5 until further notice** from now until another change is announced: *The store will be closed until further notice.*

**no·tice·a·ble** /'noʊt̬ɪsəbəl/ *adj* easy to notice: *There's been a noticeable improvement in your work.* **–noticeably** *adv*

**no·ti·fi·ca·tion** /ˌnoʊt̬əfə'keɪʃən/ *n* [C,U] FORMAL an act of officially informing someone about something

**no·ti·fy** /'noʊt̬ə,faɪ/ *v* [T] FORMAL to tell someone something formally or officially; INFORM: *Have you notified the police?*

**no·tion** /'noʊʃən/ *n* an idea, belief, or opinion about something, especially one that you think is wrong

**no·to·ri·e·ty** /ˌnoʊt̬ə'raɪət̬i/ *n* [U] the state of being famous for doing something bad

**no·to·ri·ous** /noʊ'tɔriəs/ *adj* famous for something bad: *The city is notorious for rainy weather.* | *a notorious criminal* **–notoriously** *adv*

**not·with·stand·ing** /ˌnɑt̬wɪθ'stændɪŋ/ *prep* FORMAL if something is true notwithstanding something else, it is true even though the other thing has happened: *Their friendship notwithstanding, the two Senators have very different ideas.*

**noun** /naʊn/ *n* in grammar, a word or group of words that represents a person, place, thing, quality, action, or idea. In the sentence "Pollu-

tion is a problem in some cities," "pollution," "problem," and "cities" are nouns

**nour·ish** /'nɔɪʃ, 'nʌrɪʃ/ *v* [T] **1 well-nourished/under-nourished** having had enough food or not enough food to eat to keep you healthy: *a well-nourished baby* **2** to give a person or plant the food that is needed in order to live, grow, and be healthy

**nour·ish·ing** /'nɔɪʃɪŋ, 'nʌr-/ *adj* food that is nourishing makes you strong and healthy: *a nourishing meal*

**nour·ish·ment** /'nɔɪʃmənt, 'nʌr-/ *n* [U] FORMAL food that is needed so you can live, grow, and be healthy

**nov·el**[1] /'nɑvəl/ *n* a long written story in which the characters and events are usually imaginary: *a novel by Hemingway*

**novel**[2] *adj* new, different, and unusual: *a novel idea*

**nov·el·ist** /'nɑvəlɪst/ *n* someone who writes NOVELS

**nov·el·ty** /'nɑvəlti/ *n* **1** something new and unusual that attracts people's attention and interest: *Cars are still a novelty on the island.* **2** [U] the quality of being new, different, and unusual: *the novelty of using E-mail* **3** a small cheap object often bought as a present

**No·vem·ber** /noʊ'vɛmbɚ, nə-/ *written abbreviation* **Nov.** *n* the eleventh month of the year —see usage note at JANUARY

**nov·ice** /'nɑvɪs/ *n* someone who has only begun learning a skill or activity

**now**[1] /naʊ/ *adv* **1** at the present time: *Seattle is now one of the computer industry's major centers.* | *Judy should have been home by now.* (=before now) | *Mom says we have to be home by 9:00 from now on.* (=starting now and continuing into the future) | *For now* (=for a short time), *Jim will be in charge of marketing.* **2** immediately: *You'd better go now - you're late.* | *Call her right now, before she leaves.* **3** used when you know or understand something because of something you have just seen, just been told etc.: *"I've just been talking to the landlord." "So, now do you see why I'm worried?"* **4 (every) now and then** used in order to say that something happens sometimes but not always: *He sees her every now and then at church.*

---
SPOKEN PHRASES

**5** said when you pause because you cannot think what to say or when you want to get someone's attention: *Now, what did you say your name was?* | *OK now. Watch me.*
**6 now you tell me!** said when you are annoyed because someone has just told you something s/he should have told you before
**7 now now** said in order to try to make someone feel better when s/he is sad: *Now now, don't cry.*

**now**[2], **now that** *conjunction* because or after something has happened: *Now that I've bought the skirt, I don't like it.*

**now·a·days** /'nauə,deɪz/ *adv* in the present, compared to what happened in past times: *People tend to live longer nowadays.*

**no·where** /'nouwɛr/ *adv* **1** not any place: *There's nowhere to put anything in our new apartment.* | *There are plants on the island that grow nowhere else.* (−in no other place) see usage note at ANYONE **2 get nowhere** to have no success, or make no progress: *The committee is getting nowhere with the report.* **3 be nowhere to be seen/found** to be impossible to find: *The book I needed to finish my paper was nowhere to be found.* **4 nowhere near a)** far from a particular place: *Buffalo is in New York State, but it's nowhere near New York City.* **b)** not at all: *They've sold a lot of bikes, but nowhere near as many as they needed to.* **5 out of nowhere** happening or appearing suddenly and unexpectedly: *The car came out of nowhere and just missed hitting her.*

**nox·ious** /'nakʃəs/ *adj* FORMAL harmful or poisonous: *a noxious gas*

**noz·zle** /'nazəl/ *n* a short tube attached to the end of a pipe or HOSE that controls the flow of liquid coming out

**NPR** National Public Radio; a company in the US that broadcasts radio programs without advertisements

**-n't** /ənt/ *adv* the short form of NOT: *He isn't* (=is not) *here.* | *She can't* (=cannot) *see him.* | *I didn't* (=did not) *do it.* −see usage note at NOT

**nu·ance** /'nuɑns/ *n* [C,U] a very slight difference in meaning, color, or feeling −**nuanced** *adj*

**nu·cle·ar** /'nukliɚ/ *adj* **1** relating to or involving the use of nuclear weapons: *nuclear war* **2** using nuclear power, or relating to nuclear energy: *a nuclear submarine* **3** relating to the NUCLEUS (=central part) of an atom: *nuclear physics*

**nuclear arm** /,... './ *n* [C usually plural] ⇨ NU-CLEAR WEAPON

**nuclear dis·ar·ma·ment** /,... .'.../ *n* [U] the activity of getting rid of NUCLEAR WEAPONS

**nuclear en·er·gy** /,... './ *n* [U] the power that comes from splitting atoms, used for making electricity and the explosive part of some bombs

**nuclear fam·i·ly** /,... './ *n* a family that has a father, mother, and children −compare EX-TENDED FAMILY

**nuclear pow·er** /,... '../ *n* [U] power, usually in the form of electricity, produced from NU-CLEAR ENERGY

**nuclear re·ac·tion** /,... .'.../ *n* a process in which the central part of an atom splits and forms new substances and produces a lot of energy

**nuclear re·ac·tor** /,... .'../ *n* a large machine that produces NUCLEAR ENERGY

**nuclear weap·on** /,... '../ *n* a very powerful weapon that uses NUCLEAR ENERGY to destroy large areas

**nu·cle·us** /'nukliəs/ *n, plural* **nuclei** /-kliaɪ/ **1** the central part of an atom, made up of PRO-TONs and NEUTRONs **2 the nucleus of sth** the central or most important part of something: *Photographs by Adams, Weston, and Lange form the nucleus of the collection.* **3** the central part of a cell

**nude**[1] /nud/ *adj* not wearing any clothes; NAKED

**nude**[2] *n* **1 in the nude** without wearing any clothes: *sleeping in the nude* **2** a painting or STATUE of someone who is not wearing clothes

**nudge** /nʌdʒ/ *v* [T] to push someone or something gently, especially with your elbow: *Ken nudged me and said, "Look, there's Cindy."* −**nudge** *n*

**nu·dist** /'nudɪst/ *n* someone who believes it is natural and healthy not to wear clothes −**nudist** *adj*

**nu·di·ty** /'nudəti/ *n* [U] the state of not wearing any clothes

**nug·get** /'nʌgɪt/ *n* a small rough piece of a valuable metal found in the earth: *a gold nugget*

**nui·sance** /'nusəns/ *n* [C usually singular] someone or something that annoys you or causes problems: *Jon is making a nuisance of himself, always phoning Rachel late at night.*

**nuke**[1] /nuk/ *v* [T] INFORMAL **1** to attack a place using NUCLEAR WEAPONS **2** SPOKEN to cook food in a MICROWAVE

**nuke**[2] *n* INFORMAL ⇨ NUCLEAR WEAPON

**null and void** /,nʌl ən 'vɔɪd/ *adj* LAW having no effect : *The court declared the contract to be null and void.* (=not legal, and therefore completely without an effect)

**nul·li·fy** /'nʌlə,faɪ/ *v* [T] LAW to state officially that something will have no legal effect: *The new government nullified the 1964 treaty.*

**numb**[1] /nʌm/ *adj* **1** unable to feel anything: *My feet are getting numb from the cold.* **2** unable to think, feel, or react in a normal way: *She was numb with grief after her mother's death.* −**numbness** *n* [U] −**numbly** *adv*

**numb**[2] *v* [T] to make someone unable to feel anything: *The cold wind numbed my face.*

**num·ber**[1] /'nʌmbɚ/ *n*

**1** ▶SIGN◄ a word or sign that represents an amount or quantity: *Choose a number between one and ten.* | *Add the numbers 7, 4, and 3.* | *a round number* (=a number ending in 0, such as 10, 20 etc.) | *an even number* (=2,4,6,8 etc.) | *an odd number* (=1,3,5,7 etc.)

**2** ▶ON A PHONE◄ a set of numbers that you press on a telephone when you are calling someone: *I think I dialed the wrong number.* | *He* *gave me his* **work**/**home** **number**. −see usage note at TELEPHONE

**3** ▶IN A SERIES◀ a sign used in order to show the position of something in an ordered set, list, series etc.: *Look at question number five.* | *What's his room number?*

**4** ▶FOR RECOGNIZING PEOPLE/THINGS◀ a set of numbers used in order to name or recognize someone or something: *a social security number* | *the serial number on the car's engine*

**5** ▶AMOUNT◀ [C,U] an amount of something that can be counted: *There are* **a large/great/small number** *of cars on the road today.* | **The number** *of smokers is decreasing.* | **A number of** (=several) *people have complained to the company.*

**6 number one** INFORMAL the best or most important person or thing in a group: *The fans shouted, "We're number one!"* | *California continues to be the number one travel destination in the US.*

**7** ▶MUSIC◀ a piece of popular music, a song, a dance etc. that forms part of a larger performance −see study note on page 460

> ### USAGE NOTE number
>
> When we use **numbers** in a sentence, we usually use a plural verb: *Twenty bottles of wine were drunk at the party.* However, when we give an opinion about the amount itself, we use a singular verb: *Twenty bottles of wine is too much for the party.*

**number**[2] *v* [T] **1** to give a number to something that is part of a set or list: *Number the items from one to ten.* **2** if people or things number a particular amount, that is how many there are: *The crowd numbered around 20,000.* **3 sb's/sth's days are numbered** used in order to say that someone or something cannot live or continue much longer: *These injuries mean his days as a player are numbered.*

**number crunch·er** /'.. ,../ *n* INFORMAL **1** a computer designed to work with numbers and calculate results **2** someone who works using numbers, such as an ACCOUNTANT −**number-crunching** *n* [U]

**nu·mer·al** /'numərəl, 'numrəl/ *n* a written sign that represents a number, such as 5, 22 etc. −**numeral** *adj*

**nu·mer·i·cal** /nu'merɪkəl/ *adj* expressed in numbers, or relating to numbers: *Are the pages in numerical order?* (=numbered 1, 2, 3 etc.) −**numerically** *adv*

**num·er·ous** /'numərəs/ *adj* FORMAL many: *We discussed the plans on numerous occasions.*

**nun** /nʌn/ *n* a woman who is a member of a group of Christian women who live together in a CONVENT (=special building) −compare MONK

**nup·tial** /'nʌpʃəl/ *adj* FORMAL relating to marriage

**nup·tials** /'nʌpʃəlz/ *n* [plural] FORMAL a wedding

**nurse**[1] /nɚs/ *n* someone whose job is to take care of people who are ill or injured, usually in a hospital

**nurse**[2] *v* **1** [T] to take care of people who are ill or injured **2** [T] to rest when you have an illness or injury so you will get better: *He's nursing a sprained ankle.* **3** [I,T] ⇨ BREAST-FEED

**nurs·er·y** /'nɚsəri/ *n* **1** a place where plants and trees are grown and sold **2** OLD-FASHIONED a young child's room **3** a place where young children are taken care of for a short time while their parents are shopping, in church etc.

**nursery rhyme** /'... ,./ *n* a short well-known song or poem for children

**nursery school** /'... ,./ *n* a school for children from three to five years old −compare KINDERGARTEN

**nurs·ing** /'nɚsɪŋ/ *n* [U] the job of taking care of people who are ill, injured, or very old

**nursing home** /'.. ,./ *n* a small private hospital for people who are too old or injured to take care of themselves

**nur·ture**[1] /'nɚtʃɚ/ *v* [T] FORMAL **1** to feed and take care of a child, plant etc. while it is growing: *children nurtured by loving parents* **2** to help a plan, idea, feeling etc. develop: *nurturing new democracies in the Third World*

**nurture**[2] *n* [U] FORMAL the help, education, care etc. that is given to a child who is growing and developing

**nut** /nʌt/ *n* **1** a large seed that you can eat that usually grows in a hard brown shell: *a cashew nut* **2** INFORMAL someone who is crazy or behaves strangely **3** a small piece of metal with a hole in the middle that is screwed onto a BOLT to fasten things together **4** INFORMAL someone who is extremely interested in a particular activity: *a golf nut* **5** [C usually plural] SLANG ⇨ TESTICLE **6 the nuts and bolts of sth** the practical details of a subject, plan, job etc. −see also NUTS

**nut**

nut

nut

**nut·crack·er** /'nʌt‚krækɚ/ *n* a tool for cracking the shells of nuts

**nu·tri·ent** /'nutriənt/ *n* a chemical or food that helps plants, animals, or people to live and grow: *Plants take nutrients from the soil.* −**nutrient** *adj*

**nu·tri·tion** /nu'trɪʃən/ *n* [U] the process of getting the right type of food for good health and growth −**nutritional** *adj*: *nutritional information on food packages* −**nutritionally** *adv*: *a nutritionally balanced diet*

**nu·tri·tious** /nu'trɪʃəs/ *adj* food that is nutritious has a lot of substances that your body needs to stay healthy and grow

**nuts** /nʌts/ *adj* INFORMAL crazy, silly, or angry: *My sister will go nuts* (=become very angry) *when she finds out I wrecked her car.*

**nut·shell** /'nʌt⌐ʃɛl/ *n* **1** (to put it) in a nutshell INFORMAL used in order to show that you are going to give the main facts about something in a way that is short and clear **2** the hard outer part of a nut

**nut·ty** /'nʌti/ *adj* **1** tasting like nuts: *a nutty flavor* **2** INFORMAL crazy: *a nutty idea*

**nuz·zle** /'nʌzəl/ *v* [I,T] **1** to gently rub your face or head against someone in a loving way: *a new mother gently nuzzling her baby's head* **2** if an animal nuzzles someone or nuzzles up against someone, it gently rubs its nose against him/her

**NV** the written abbreviation of Nevada

**NW** the written abbreviation of NORTHWEST

**NY** the written abbreviation of New York

**ny·lon** /'naɪlɑn/ *n* [U] a strong artificial material that is used for making plastic, cloth, rope etc.: *a nylon parka*

**ny·lons** /'naɪlɑnz/ *n* [plural] a piece of clothing that women wear on their legs, that is very thin and made of NYLON

**nymph** /nɪmf/ *n* one of the spirits of nature who appears in the form of a young girl, in ancient Greek and Roman stories

**nym·pho·ma·ni·ac** /ˌnɪmfə'meɪniˌæk/ *n* a woman who wants to have sex often, usually with a lot of different men —**nymphomania** /ˌnɪmfə'meɪnlə/ *n* [U]

# O

**O, o** /oʊ/ **1** the fifteenth letter of the English alphabet **2** SPOKEN zero: *room 203* (=two o three)

**o'** /ə/ *prep* NONSTANDARD a way of writing "of" as it is often said in speech: *a cup o' coffee*

**oaf** /oʊf/ *n* a stupid or awkward person, especially a man or boy

**oak** /oʊk/ *n* [C,U] a large tree that is common in northern countries, or the hard wood of this tree

**oar** /ɔr/ *n* a long pole with a wide blade at one end, used for rowing a boat

**o·a·sis** /oʊ'eɪsɪs/ *n, plural oases* /oʊ'eɪsiz/ a place with trees and water in a desert

oasis

**oath** /oʊθ/ *n* **1** a formal and serious promise: *He swore an oath* (=gave a promise) *to support the Constitution.* **2** be under oath to have made an official promise to tell the truth in a court of law

**oat·meal** /'oʊt⌐mil/ *n* [U] crushed OATS that are boiled and eaten for breakfast, or used in cooking

**oats** /oʊts/ *n* [plural] a grain that is eaten by people and animals

**o·be·di·ence** /ə'bidiəns, oʊ-/ *n* [U] doing what you are supposed to do, according to a law or to someone in authority: *He acted in obedience to the law.*

**o·be·di·ent** /ə'bidiənt, oʊ-/ *adj* always obeying laws, rules, or people in authority: *an obedient dog* —**obediently** *adv* —opposite DISOBEDIENT

**o·bese** /oʊ'bis/ *adj* extremely fat —**obesity** *n* [U] —see usage note at FAT

**o·bey** /ə'beɪ, oʊ-/ *v* [I,T] to do what you are supposed to do, according to the law or to what someone in authority says: *Children should be taught to obey the law.* | *The sergeant yells an order and the men obey immediately.* —opposite DISOBEY

**o·bit·u·ar·y** /ə'bɪtʃuˌɛri, oʊ-/ *n* a report of someone's death in a newspaper

**ob·ject¹** /'ɑbdʒɪkt, 'ɑbdʒɛkt/ *n* **1** a thing that you can see, hold, or touch: *Cubes, balls, and other objects were set out for the students to draw.* **2** [singular] the purpose of a plan, action, or activity: *The object of this game is to score points by kicking the ball into the goal.* **3** an object of desire/pity etc. someone or something that you desire, pity etc. **4** TECHNICAL in grammar, the person or thing that is affected by the action of the verb in a sentence. In the sentence "Sheila closed the door," "door" is the object

**ob·ject²** /əb'dʒɛkt/ *v* [I] to say that you do not like or approve of something: *He objected to Bianchi's suggestion, saying it would cost too much.*

**ob·jec·tion** /əb'dʒɛkʃən/ *n* a reason you give for not approving of an idea or plan: *Does anyone have any objections to Mr. Ducin's proposal?* | *Several Senators made/raised/voiced objections to the bill.* (=they objected)

**ob·jec·tion·a·ble** /əb'dʒɛkʃənəbəl/ *adj* unpleasant and likely to offend people; OFFENSIVE

**ob·jec·tive¹** /əb'dʒɛktɪv/ *n* something that you are working hard to achieve: *The company's main objective is to increase sales overseas.*

**objective²** *adj* **1** not influenced by your own feelings, beliefs, or ideas: *an objective opinion from the judge* **2** FORMAL not imagined; real —**objectively** *adv* —**objectivity** /ˌɑbdʒɛk'tɪvəti/ *n* [U] —compare SUBJECTIVE

**ob·li·gate** /'ɑbləˌgeɪt/ *v* [T] **1** to make someone feel that s/he has to do something, because it is right, a duty etc.: *The city was obli-*

*gated to* make drastic spending cuts. **2 be/feel obligated** to do something only because someone has done something nice for you: *I hope he doesn't feel obligated to wear the shirt just because I gave it to him.*

**ob·li·ga·tion** /ˌɑblə'geɪʃən/ *n* [C,U] a moral or legal duty to do something: *Every father has an obligation to take care of his child.*

**o·blig·a·to·ry** /ə'blɪgə,tɔri/ *adj* FORMAL having to be done because of a law, rule etc.; COMPULSORY

**o·blige** /ə'blaɪdʒ/ *v* **1** [T] FORMAL to make someone feel that it is necessary to do something, especially because it is a right, duty etc.: *Doctors are obliged to keep their patients' records secret.* **2 I/we would be obliged if** used in formal letters to ask someone to do something for you: *I would be obliged if you could send me a copy of the contract as soon as possible.* **3** [I,T] to do something that someone has asked you to do: *He asked to borrow my car, and I was happy/glad to oblige.*

**o·blig·ing** /ə'blaɪdʒɪŋ/ *adj* willing and eager to help: *a cheerful and obliging woman* **–obligingly** *adv*

**o·blique** /ə'blik, oʊ-/ *adj* not expressed in a direct way: *oblique references to his drinking problem*

**ob·lit·er·ate** /ə'blɪtə,reɪt/ *v* [T] to destroy something completely: *Large areas of the city were obliterated during World War II.* **–obliteration** /ə,blɪtə'reɪʃən/ *n* [U]

**ob·liv·i·on** /ə'blɪviən/ *n* [U] FORMAL **1** the state of being completely forgotten: *Old movie stars who have faded into oblivion.* **2** the state of being unconscious or of not knowing what is happening: *He spent the night drinking himself into oblivion.*

**ob·liv·i·ous** /ə'blɪviəs/ *adj* not knowing about or not noticing something happening around you; UNAWARE: *Maxwell walked on, completely oblivious to/of the danger.*

**ob·long** /'ɑblɔŋ/ *adj* having a shape that is longer than it is wide: *an oblong mirror* **–oblong** *n*

**ob·nox·ious** /əb'nɑkʃəs/ *adj* extremely unpleasant or rude: *obnoxious behavior|Robin gets so obnoxious when she's drunk.* **–obnoxiously** *adv*

**o·boe** /'oʊboʊ/ *n* a wooden musical instrument shaped like a narrow tube, that you play by blowing into it

**ob·scene** /əb'sin, ɑb-/ *adj* **1** dealing with sex or violence in a way that is offensive and shocking: *obscene photographs/language* **2** extremely immoral or unfair: *obscene wealth*

**ob·scen·i·ty** /əb'sɛnəṭi/ *n* **1** [C usually plural] a sexually offensive word or action: *kids shouting obscenities* **2** [U] offensive language or behavior involving sex, especially in a book, play etc.: *laws against obscenity*

**ob·scure¹** /əb'skyʊr/ *adj* **1** unclear or difficult to understand: *Jarrett didn't like the plan for some obscure reason.* **2** known about only by a few people: *an obscure poet*

**obscure²** *v* [T] **1** to prevent something from being seen: *Clouds obscured the hills in the distance.* **2** to make something difficult to know or understand: *legal language that seems to obscure meaning*

**ob·scur·i·ty** /əb'skyʊrəṭi/ *n* **1** [U] the state of not being known or remembered: *O'Brien retired from politics and died in obscurity.* **2** [C,U] something that is difficult to understand, or the quality of being difficult to understand

**ob·serv·a·ble** /əb'zɚvəbəl/ *adj* able to be seen or noticed

**ob·serv·ance** /əb'zɚvəns/ *n* [U] **1** the celebration of a religious or national event: *the observance of Yom Kippur* **2** the practice of obeying a law or rule

**ob·serv·ant** /əb'zɚvənt/ *adj* good or quick at noticing things: *An observant guard reported that there were three boxes missing.*

**ob·ser·va·tion** /ˌɑbzɚ'veɪʃən, -sɚ-/ *n* **1** [C,U] the act or process of carefully watching someone or something, or one of the facts you learn from doing this: *Scientists are making careful observations of the meteor's path through space.|The patient is under close observation.* (=being continuously watched) **2** a remark about something that you have noticed: *He made several humorous observations about the state of our local theaters.*

**ob·serv·a·to·ry** /əb'zɚvə,tɔri/ *n* a special building from which scientists watch the moon, stars, weather etc.

**ob·serve** /əb'zɚv/ *v* [T] **1** to watch someone or something carefully: *Advertisers observed consumers' buying habits.* **2** to obey a law, agreement, or religious rule: *Both sides are observing the ceasefire.* **3** FORMAL to see or notice something in particular: *Doctors observed that the disease only occurs in women over 50.* **4** FORMAL to say what you have noticed about something

**ob·serv·er** /əb'zɚvɚ/ *n* **1** someone whose job is to watch a situation, system, business etc. carefully in order to report any changes or illegal actions or to say what will happen in the future: *International observers criticized the use of military force in the region.* **2** someone who sees or notices something

**ob·sessed** /əb'sɛst/ *adj* thinking about someone or something all the time, so that you cannot think of anything else: *William is obsessed with making money.* **–obsess** *v* [I,T]

**ob·ses·sion** /əb'sɛʃən/ *n* something that you cannot stop thinking or worrying about: *an unhealthy obsession with sex*

**ob·ses·sive** /əbˈsɛsɪv/ *adj* thinking or worrying too much about someone or something so that you do not think about other things enough: *She has an obsessive need to control everything.* —**obsessively** *adv*

**ob·so·lete** /ˌɑbsəˈlit‹/ *adj* no longer useful or needed because something newer and better has been made: *Our computer system will soon be obsolete.* —**obsolescence** /ˌɑbsəˈlɛsəns/ *n* [U]

### obstacle

an obstacle in the road    causing an obstruction

**ob·sta·cle** /ˈɑbstɪkəl/ *n* **1** something that makes it difficult for you to succeed: *Sylvia has had to overcome the obstacles of racism and sexism at work.* **2** something that blocks your way, so that you must go around it: *an obstacle in the road*

**obstacle course** /ˈ... ˌ./ *n* a line of objects that a runner must jump over, go under etc.

**ob·stet·rics** /əbˈstɛtrɪks, ɑb-/ *n* [U] the part of medical science that deals with the birth of children —**obstetrician** /ˌɑbstəˈtrɪʃən/ *n*

**ob·sti·nate** /ˈɑbstənɪt/ *adj* DISAPPROVING determined not to change your opinions, ideas, behavior etc.; STUBBORN —**obstinacy** *n* [U]

**ob·struct** /əbˈstrʌkt/ *v* [T] **1** to block a road, path, passage, or someone's view of something: *The new airport terminal partially obstructs the view from the tower.| The truck was on its side, obstructing two lanes of traffic.* **2** to try to prevent someone from doing something by making it difficult: *Federal officers accused Robbins of obstructing their investigation.* —**obstructive** *adj*

**ob·struc·tion** /əbˈstrʌkʃən/ *n* **1** [C,U] something that blocks a road, passage, tube etc., or the fact of blocking a road etc.: *The accident caused an obstruction on the freeway.* **2** [U] the act of preventing something from happening: *The judge is charged with the obstruction of justice in the Martel case.* —see picture at OBSTACLE

**ob·tain** /əbˈteɪn/ *v* [T] FORMAL to get something that you want: *Information about passports can be obtained from the embassy.*

**ob·tain·a·ble** /əbˈteɪnəbəl/ *adj* able to be obtained

**ob·tru·sive** /əbˈtrusɪv/ *adj* noticeable in an unpleasant way: *The signs are obtrusive, blocking one of the city's most beautiful views.| The waitresses were friendly but never obtrusive.* —opposite UNOBTRUSIVE

**ob·tuse** /əbˈtus, ɑb-/ *adj* **1** FORMAL stupid or slow to understand something **2 obtuse angle** TECHNICAL an angle between 90 and 180 degrees

**ob·vi·ous** /ˈɑbviəs/ *adj* easy to notice or understand: *an obvious mistake| Kyman is the obvious choice for team captain.|* ***It was obvious that** he was lying.*

**ob·vi·ous·ly** /ˈɑbviəsli/ *adv* used when something is easily noticed or understood, or when you expect that other people already know the thing you have just said: *Obviously, we won't have time to finish.| She was obviously feeling terrible.*

**oc·ca·sion** /əˈkeɪʒən/ *n* **1** a time when something happens: *I met with him **on several occasions**.* **2** an important event or ceremony: *We're saving the champagne for **a special occasion**.| Larsky **rose to the occasion** (=achieved something difficult) and scored the winning goal.* **3** [singular] a suitable time, or reason to do something: *Veteran's day is the occasion when we remember people who died in war.* **4 on occasion** sometimes but not often: *He has a drink on occasion.*

**oc·ca·sion·al** /əˈkeɪʒənl/ *adj* happening sometimes but not often: *strong winds and occasional rain*

**oc·ca·sion·al·ly** /əˈkeɪʒənl-i/ *adv* sometimes, but not regularly or often: *Stir the soup occasionally and add the milk before serving.*

**oc·cult** /əˈkʌlt/ *n* **the occult** the knowledge and study of magic and spirits —**occult** *adj*

**oc·cu·pan·cy** /ˈɑkyəpənsi/ *n* [U] FORMAL someone's use of a building or other space for living or working in

**oc·cu·pant** /ˈɑkyəpənt/ *n* FORMAL someone who lives in a building, room etc., or who is in it at a particular time: *a letter addressed to the occupant*

**oc·cu·pa·tion** /ˌɑkyəˈpeɪʃən/ *n* **1** FORMAL a job or profession; EMPLOYMENT: *Please state your name and occupation.* —see usage note at JOB **2** [U] the act of entering a place and getting control of it, especially by military force **3** FORMAL something that you spend time doing, especially for pleasure: *One of my childhood occupations was collecting baseball cards.*

**oc·cu·pa·tion·al** /ˌɑkyəˈpeɪʃənəl/ *adj* relating to your job

**oc·cu·pied** /ˈɑkyəˌpaɪd/ *adj* **1** being used: *All the beds in the youth hostel were already occupied.* **2** busy doing or thinking about something: *I brought along some toys to **keep** the kids **occupied**.*

**oc·cu·py** /ˈɑkyəˌpaɪ/ *v* [T] **1** to live, work etc. in a particular place: *Salem Press occupies the seventh floor of the building.* **2** if something occupies you or your time, you are busy doing it: *Fishing occupies most of my spare time.* **3** to fill a particular amount of space: *Family photos occupied almost the entire wall.*

**4** to enter a place and get control of it, especially by military force

**oc·cur** /əˈkɚ/ *v* **-rred, -rring** [I] FORMAL **1** to happen, especially without being planned first: *Earthquakes occur without any warning signs.* **2** to exist or be present in a particular place: *The disease mainly **occurs in** young children.* −see usage note at HAPPEN

**occur to** sb *phr v* [T] to suddenly come into your mind: *I washed it in hot water - it never occurred to me to check the label.*

**o·cean** /ˈouʃən/ *n* **1 the ocean** the great quantity of salt water that covers most of the Earth's surface **2** a particular area of salt water somewhere on Earth: *the Indian Ocean* −**oceanic** /ˌouʃiˈænɪk/ *adj*

**o·cean·og·ra·phy** /ˌouʃəˈnɑgrəfi/ *n* [U] the scientific study of the ocean −**oceanographer** *n*

**o'clock** /əˈklɑk/ *adv* **one/two/three etc. o'clock** one of the times when the clock shows the exact hour as a number from 1 to 12

**oc·ta·gon** /ˈɑktəˌgɑn/ *n* a flat shape with eight sides and eight angles −**octagonal** /ɑkˈtægənəl/ *adj* −see picture at SHAPE

**Oc·to·ber** /ɑkˈtoubɚ/ written abbreviation **Oct.** *n* the tenth month of the year −see usage note at JANUARY

**oc·to·pus** /ˈɑktəpəs/ *n,* *plural* **octopuses** *or* **octopi** /ˈɑktəpaɪ/ a sea creature with a soft body and eight TENTACLES (=arms)

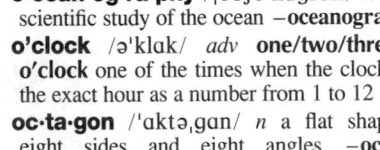
octopus
tentacle

**OD** *v* [I] SLANG to take too much of a dangerous drug; OVERDOSE

**odd** /ɑd/ *adj* **1** different from what is expected; strange: *It's odd that she hasn't phoned by now. | an odd guy* **2 odd jobs** small jobs of different kinds that someone does, especially fixing or cleaning things: *The boys are earning money doing odd jobs for the neighbors.* **3** an odd number cannot be divided by 2: *1, 3, 5, 7, etc. are odd numbers* −compare EVEN² **4** separated from its pair or set: *an odd sock* **5 20-odd/30-odd etc.** INFORMAL a little more than 20, 30 etc. −see also ODDS

**odd·i·ty** /ˈɑdəti/ *n* a strange or unusual person or thing

**odd·ly** /ˈɑdli/ *adv* in a strange or unusual way −see also **strangely/oddly/funnily enough** ENOUGH

**odds** /ɑdz/ *n* [plural] **1** how likely it is that something will or will not happen, often expressed as a number: *The odds are about 1 in 12 that a boy will be colorblind.* **2 at odds (with sb)** disagreeing with someone: *Briggs found himself at odds with his colleagues at NASA.* **3** difficulties that make a good result seem very unlikely: *Our team won the title against all the odds.* (=in spite of difficulties)

**odds and ends** /ˌ. . ˈ./ *n* [plural] INFORMAL various small things, usually ones that have little value

**ode** /oud/ *n* a long poem that is written in order to praise a person or thing

**o·di·ous** /ˈoudiəs/ *adj* FORMAL very bad or unpleasant: *an odious greedy little man*

**o·dom·e·ter** /ouˈdɑmətɚ/ *n* an instrument in a vehicle that records the distance it travels −see picture on page 469

**o·dor** /ˈoudɚ/ *n* a smell, especially an unpleasant one −see usage note at SMELL²

**o·dor·less** /ˈoudɚlɪs/ *adj* not having a smell: *an odorless gas*

**od·ys·sey** /ˈɑdəsi/ *n* LITERARY a long trip

**of** /əv, ə; *strong* ʌv/ *prep* **1** used in order to show a quality or feature that someone or something has: *I love the color of his shirt. | the size of the building | It was stupid of me to say that.* **2** used in order to show that something is a part of something else: *The first part of the story is funny. | the tips of your fingers* **3** used in order to show that something belongs to or relates to someone or something: *He gave her an old shirt of his. | a friend of Bobby's* **4** used with words that show a particular type of group: *a pack of cigarettes | a bunch of grapes | a herd of elephants* **5** used in order to show an amount or measurement: *a cup of coffee | lots of room | a drop of water* **6** used in order to show that someone or something is from a larger group of similar people or things: *That's one of her best poems. | members of a rock group | a familiar brand of coffee* **7** used in dates: *the 23rd of January, 2003* **8** SPOKEN used when you are giving the time to mean before: *It's ten of five.* (=ten minutes before 5:00) **9** used when giving the name of something: *the city of New Orleans | the game of chess* **10** used when giving the reason for or the cause of something: *She died of cancer.* **11** used in order to say what something shows: *a picture of his family | a map of the world* **12** used in order to say what something is about or what type of thing it is: *Do you know the story of Tom Thumb? | the problem of crime in schools* **13** used in order to show direction or distance: *I live just north of here. | The school is within a mile of the park.* (=it is less than a mile from the park) **14** used after nouns describing actions to show to whom the action is done or who did the action: *the testing of river water for chemicals | the crying of a child* **15** LITERARY made from: *a dress of pure silk* **16** written, made, produced etc. by: *the early plays of Shakespeare* **17** used in order to say where someone lives: *the people of Malaysia* −see also **of course** (COURSE¹)

**off¹** /ɔf/ *adv* **1** away from or out of a place or position: *She waved goodbye as she drove off. | My button fell off! | The bus stopped, and she got off.* **2 turn/shut sth ↔ off** to make a machine or light stop working by pushing a button: *Turn the lights off when you leave.* | *Does the machine shut itself off?* **3** lower in price: *You get 10%/15% off if you buy $100 worth of groceries.* **4** far in distance or long in time: *Spring is still* **a long way off.** | *mountains* **way off** *in the distance* **5** not at work or school because you are sick or on vacation: *I'm taking the day/week off.* **6 off and on/on and off** for short periods of time, but not regularly: *I worked as a secretary off and on for three years.* –see also WELL-OFF

**off**[2] *adj* **1** removed or no longer connected: *old paint cans with their lids off* **2** a machine, light, or other piece of equipment that is off is not operating or not working: *Why are all the lights off?* –opposite ON[3] **3** not at work or school because you are sick or on vacation: *I'm off tomorrow, but I'll see you the next day.* **4** not correct or not of good quality: *His calculations are off by 20%.* **5** an event that is off will not happen even though it has already been planned: *The wedding is off. Scott and Liz had another fight.* –compare ON[3] **6 have an off day/week etc.** SPOKEN to have a day, week etc. when you are not doing something as well as you usually do **7 off season** the time in the year when a place or a business is not as busy as it usually is

**off**[3] *prep* **1** not on something, or not touching something: *Get your feet off the couch!* | *I'm taking the picture off the wall.* **2** away from a particular place: *The boat was seen* **just off** (=a short distance from) *the coast of Florida.* **3** if a room, road, building etc. is off a particular place, it is very near that place: *Oak Hills - isn't that off Route 290?*

**off**[4] *v* [T] SLANG to kill someone

**off·beat** /ˌɔfˈbit◂/ *adj* INFORMAL unusual and not what people expect: *an offbeat style of comedy*

**off·col·or** /ˌ. '..◂/ *adj* offensive, especially in a sexual way: *an off-color joke*

**of·fend** /əˈfɛnd/ *v* **1** [T] to make someone angry or upset: *Several people were offended by Blaine's joke.* **2** [I] FORMAL to do something that is a crime

**of·fend·er** /əˈfɛndɚ/ *n* someone who is guilty of a crime

**of·fense**[1] /əˈfɛns/ *n* **1** a crime: *Drinking and driving is a serious offense.* | *He was charged with* **committing** *several burglary* **offenses.** **2 no offense** SPOKEN said in order to show that you hope what you are saying will not offend someone: *No offense, but your sister isn't very smart.* **3 take offense/cause offense** to feel OFFENDed or to OFFEND someone: *Many women took offense at the tone of his speech.*

**of·fense**[2] /ˈɔfɛns/ *n* [U] the players in a game such as football, whose main job is to try to get points –**offensive** *adj* –see picture on page 472

**of·fen·sive**[1] /əˈfɛnsɪv/ *adj* **1** used or intended for attacking: *offensive weapons* –opposite DEFENSIVE[1] **2** very rude and likely to upset people: *offensive jokes* –**offensively** *adv* –**offensiveness** *n* [U]

**offensive**[2] *n* **1** an attack made on a place by an army **2 be on the offensive** to attack or criticize people

**of·fer**[1] /ˈɔfɚ, ˈɑfɚ/ *v* **1** [T] to say that you are willing to give something to someone, or to hold something out to someone so that s/he can take it: *They've* **offered** *us $175,000* **for** *the house.* | *I was about to offer them some cookies.* **2** [I,T] to say that you are willing to do something: *She didn't even* **offer to** *help.*

**offer**[2] *n* **1** a statement that you are willing to give something to someone or to do something for someone: *Thanks for your* **offer of** *help.* **2** something that is offered, especially an amount of money: *He made me* **an offer of** *$50* **for** *the bike.*

**of·fer·ing** /ˈɔfrɪŋ, ˈɑ-/ *n* something you give someone, especially God

**off·hand**[1] /ˌɔfˈhænd◂/ *adj* not giving people much time or attention when you are talking to them: *an offhand manner*

**offhand**[2] *adv* immediately, without time to think: *I can't give you an answer offhand - I'll have to check my notes.*

**of·fice** /ˈɔfɪs, ˈɑ-/ *n* **1** a room with a desk, telephone etc. in it where you do your work: *the manager's office* **2** the building of a company or organization where people work: *Are you going to the office today?* **3** [C,U] an important job or position, especially in government: *She's been* **in office** *for too long.* | *He holds the office of secretary.*

**of·fi·cer** /ˈɔfəsɚ, ˈɑ-/ *n* **1** someone who has a position of authority in the army, navy etc. **2** a policeman: *What's the problem, officer?* | *Officer O'Leary* **3** someone who has an important position in an organization –see also CEO

---

**USAGE NOTE** officer, official, and the authorities

An **officer** is someone in the police force or the military: *This club is for army officers and their wives.* An **official** is someone in a business or government organization who has a position of authority: *A factory official announced that 100 workers would be laid off.* **Authorities** are the people in an organization, especially in the government, who have the power to make decisions: *Authorities said the cause of the crash was unknown.*

---

**of·fi·cial**[1] /əˈfɪʃəl/ *adj* approved of or done by someone in authority, especially the government: *an official investigation*

**official²** *n* someone who has a responsible position in an organization: *a union official* –see usage note at OFFICER

**of·fi·cial·ly** /əˈfɪʃəli/ *adv* **1** publicly and formally: *The new bridge was officially opened this morning.* **2** according to what you say publicly, even though this may not be true: *Officially, he's on vacation, but actually he's in the hospital.*

**of·fi·ci·ate** /əˈfɪʃiˌeɪt/ *v* [I] FORMAL to perform special duties, especially at a religious ceremony

**of·fi·cious** /əˈfɪʃəs/ *adj* DISAPPROVING someone who is officious is always telling other people what to do

**off·ing** /ˈɔfɪŋ/ *n* **be in the offing** to be about to happen: *I heard that there might be a promotion in the offing for you.*

**off-ramp** /ˈ. ./ *n* a road for driving off a HIGHWAY or FREEWAY –opposite ON-RAMP

**off·set** /ˌɔfˈsɛt, ˈɔfsɛt/ *v* **offset, offset, offsetting** [T] if something offsets another thing, it has an opposite effect so that the situation remains the same: *The cost of the flight was offset by the cheapness of the hotel.*

**off·shoot** /ˈɔfʃut/ *n* an organization, system of beliefs etc. that has developed from a larger or earlier one: *The business was an offshoot of IBM.*

**off·shore** /ˌɔfˈʃɔr/ *adj, adv* in the water, at a distance from the shore: *America's offshore oil reserves | The ship is anchored offshore.*

**off·spring** /ˈɔfˌsprɪŋ/ *n, plural* **offspring** **1** someone's child or children **2** an animal's baby or babies

**off·stage** /ˌɔfˈsteɪdʒ/ *adv* **1** just behind or to the side of a stage in a theater: *There was a loud crash offstage.* **2** when an actor is not acting: *What does the book tell us about Olivier's life offstage?*

**off-the-rec·ord** /ˌ. . ˈ..ˌ/ *adj* an off-the-record remark is not supposed to be made public –**off-the-record** *adv*

**off-the-wall** /ˌ. . ˈ.ˌ/ *adj* INFORMAL a little strange or unusual: *an off-the-wall TV show*

**of·ten** /ˈɔfən, ˈɔftən/ *adv* many times; frequently: *That was fun! We should do it more often! | How often do you come to New Orleans?*

**o·gle** /ˈoʊgəl/ *v* [I,T] to look at someone in an offensive way that shows you think s/he is sexually attractive

**o·gre** /ˈoʊgɚ/ *n* **1** someone who seems cruel and frightening **2** a large ugly person in children's stories who eats people

**OH** the written abbreviation of Ohio

**oh** /oʊ/ *interjection* **1** used in phrases in order to express strong emotions or to emphasize what you think about something: *"I didn't get the job." "Oh, that's too bad." | Oh no! I've lost my wallet!* **2** said in order to make a slight pause, especially before replying to a question

or giving your opinion on something: *"What time are you going to lunch?" "Oh, I haven't decided yet."*

**ohm** /oʊm/ *n* a unit for measuring electrical RESISTANCE

**oil¹** /ɔɪl/ *n* **1** [U] a smooth thick dark liquid that is burned to produce heat or used for making machines run easily: *motor oil* **2** [U] a thick dark liquid from under the ground, from which oil and GASOLINE are made; PETROLEUM **3** [C,U] a smooth thick liquid made from plants or animals, used in cooking or for making beauty products: *olive oil* –see also OILS

**oil²** *v* [T] to put oil into or onto something

**oiled** /ɔɪld/ *adj* covered with oil

**oil paint·ing** /ˈ. ˌ../ *n* [C,U] a picture painted with paint that contains oil, or all of these kinds of paintings considered as art

**oils** /ɔɪlz/ *n* [plural] paints that contain oil

**oil slick** /ˈ. ./ *n* a layer of oil floating on water

**oil·y** /ˈɔɪli/ *adj* **1** covered with oil, or containing a lot of oil: *an oily fish* **2** looking or feeling like oil: *an oily liquid*

**oink** /ɔɪŋk/ *n* the sound that a pig makes –**oink** *v* [I]

**oint·ment** /ˈɔɪntˈmənt/ *n* [C,U] a soft oily substance that you rub into your skin, especially as a medical treatment

**OJ** *n* [U] SPOKEN orange juice

**OK¹, okay** /oʊˈkeɪ/ *adj* SPOKEN **1** not ill, injured, unhappy etc.: *Do you feel OK now?* **2** satisfactory or acceptable: *Does my hair look OK?* **3** used in order to ask if you can do something, or to tell someone that s/he can do something: *"Is it OK if I leave early?" "Yes, that's OK." | I'll go first, okay?* –**OK** /ˌoʊˈkeɪ/ **okay** *adv*: *Is your computer working OK?* –see usage note at YES

**OK², okay** *interjection* **1** said when you start talking, or continue to talk after a pause: *OK, can we go now?* **2** said when you agree with someone: *"We'd better be there by four." "Okay."*

**OK³, okay** *v* [T] INFORMAL to say officially that you will agree to something or allow it to happen: *Are you sure the bank will OK the loan?*

**OK⁴, okay** *n* INFORMAL **give the OK/get the OK** to give or get permission to do something: *I got the OK to leave early.*

**OK⁵** the written abbreviation of Oklahoma

**old** /oʊld/ *adj* **1** having lived or existed for a long time: *an old man | We sell old and new books.* –see picture at NEW **2** having been used a lot: *an old pair of shoes* –see picture at NEW **3** having a particular age: *Our dog is three years old. | my ten-year-old daughter | How old is Kenny?* **4** **old house/job/teacher** etc. INFORMAL a house etc. that you had before but do not have now: *I saw your old girlfriend last night.* **5** **good old/poor old** etc. sb SPOKEN used in order to talk to or about someone you know and like: *"Keith drove me home."* *"Good old Keith!"* **6** experienced, heard, or seen many times before; familiar: *I'm tired of listening to the same old music all the time.* **7** **an old friend/enemy etc.** a friend etc. that you have known for a long time **8** **the old** old people —compare ANCIENT, ELDERLY —see usage note at ELDER

---

**USAGE NOTE** old and elderly

Use **old** to talk about the age of things or people: *How old are your children?* | *How old is your car?* Use **elderly** to be more polite when talking about people who are very old: *an elderly gentlemen in his 80s.*

---

**old·en** /'oʊldən/ *adj* LITERARY **in olden days/ times** a long time ago

**old-fash·ioned** /ˌ. '..◂/ *adj* not modern and considered no longer fashionable: *old-fashioned ideas*

**old·ie** /'oʊldi/ *n* INFORMAL someone or something that is old, especially a song or movie

**Old Tes·ta·ment** /ˌ. '...◂/ *n* **the Old Testament** the part of the Bible that is about the time before the birth of Christ

**old-tim·er** /ˌ. '../ *n* INFORMAL **1** an old man **2** someone who has been in a particular job, place etc. for a long time

**Old World** /ˌ. './ *n* **the Old World** Europe, and parts of Asia and Africa —**Old World** *adj* —compare NEW WORLD

**ol·ive** /'ɑlɪv/ *n* **1** a small black or green fruit, eaten as a vegetable or used for making oil **2** [U] also **olive green** a dull pale green color —**olive** *adj*

**O·lym·pic Games** /əˌlɪmpɪk 'geɪmz, oʊ-/ **Olympics** *n* [plural] an international sports event held every four years —**Olympic** *adj*

**ome·let, omelette** /'ɑmlɪt/ *n* eggs beaten together and cooked, often with other foods added: *a cheese omelet*

**o·men** /'oʊmən/ *n* a sign of what will happen in the future: *a good/bad omen*

**om·i·nous** /'ɑmənəs/ *adj* making you feel that something bad is going to happen: *ominous black clouds* —**ominously** *adv*

**o·mis·sion** /oʊ'mɪʃən, ə-/ *n* **1** [U] the act of not including or doing something: *He's angry about the omission of his name from the list.* **2** something that has been OMITted: *The report is full of mistakes and omissions.*

**o·mit** /oʊ'mɪt, ə-/ *v* **-tted, -tting** [T] to not include something, either deliberately or because you forgot to do it: *We decided to omit the third paragraph.*

**om·nip·o·tent** /ɑm'nɪpətənt/ *adj* FORMAL able to do everything —**omnipotence** *n* [U]

**om·ni·scient** /ɑm'nɪʃənt/ *adj* FORMAL knowing everything —**omniscience** *n* [U]

**on¹** /ɔn, ɑn/ *prep* **1** touching, being supported by, or hanging from: *I got mud on my pants.* | *pictures hanging on the wall* | *She was sitting on the bed.* **2** in a particular place or area of land: *The answer is on page 44.* | *Henry grew up on a farm.* | *My brother lives on Brady Road.* **3** at the side of something such as a road or river: *a restaurant on the river* | *cars parked on the road* **4** at some time during a particular day: *The ad was in the newspaper on Monday.* | *It happened on my birthday.* | *On May 10th Jo had a baby girl.* **5** being broadcast by a television or radio station: *I heard it on the radio.* | *The movie's on HBO tonight.* **6** about a particular subject: *a book on China* **7** used in order to show who or what is affected by an action: *a new tax on imported wine* | *The divorce was hard on Jill.* | *medical testing done on rats* **8** used in order to say what has been used for doing something or to say what has made something happen: *Did you do these graphs on a computer?* | *I cut myself on a piece of glass.* **9** in a particular direction: *The Mayor was sitting on my right.* (=on the right side of me) **10** in a vehicle such as a bus, plane, train etc.: *I got a ticket on the last bus.* **11** **on a trip/ vacation etc.** during a trip etc.: *They met on a trip to Spain.* **12** part of a team or group that works together: *Are you on the soccer team?* **13** **have/carry sth on you** to have something with you now: *Do you have a pen on you?* **14** SPOKEN used in order to say that someone is paying for something: *Dinner's on me, tonight.* **15** INFORMAL if something bad happens on someone, it happens when s/he is not expecting it: *You can't just quit on me!* **16** INFORMAL taking a medicine or drugs: *She's on antibiotics.*

**on²** *adv* **1** continuing without stopping: *"I'm not sure if...." "Go on, what were you going to say?"* | *The peace talks dragged on* (=continued slowly) *for months.* **2** forward or ahead, toward a particular place: *We were tired from the climb, but Steve wanted to go on.* **3** continuing into the future: *From that day on he hasn't drunk any alcohol.* **4** if you have a piece of clothing on, you are wearing it: *Put your coat on, it's cold out.* **5** operating or working: *Could you* **turn/switch on** *the lights, please?* (=push the button that makes them work) —opposite OFF¹ **6** into a vehicle such as a bus, plane, or train: *I got on at Vine Street.* **7** ⇨ **off and on/on and off** (OFF¹) —see also HEAD-ON **later on** (LATER¹)

**on³** *adj* **1** if a film or television show is on, it is being broadcast or shown: *The local news will be on in a minute.* | *What's on at the Rialto Theater tonight?* **2** operating or working: *The fax machine isn't on.* —opposite OFF² **3** if an event is on, it will happen: *There's a Jazz Festival on at the lake this weekend.*

**once¹** /wʌns/ *adv* **1** on one occasion, or at one time: *"Have you been to Texas?" "Yes, but* *only once."* | *He told me once he didn't like Thai food.* | *He tried skiing* **once before** *but he didn't like it.* **2 once a week/year etc.** one time every week, year etc. as a regular activity: *She goes to the gym once a week.* **3 (every) once in a while** sometimes, but not often: *My uncle sends us money every once in a while.* **4 once more** one more time; again: *I'll call him once more, but then we have to leave.* **5 at once a)** at the same time: *I can't do two things at once!* **b)** FORMAL immediately or without waiting: *Everybody knew at once how serious the situation was.* **6 all at once** suddenly: *All at once, the room went quiet.* **7** in the past, but not now: *He must have been good-looking once.* **8 for once** SPOKEN used in order to say that something should happen more often: *"Where's Mark?" "He's washing the dishes, for once."* **9 once and for all** definitely and finally: *Let's settle this once and for all.* **10 once upon a time** a phrase meaning a long time ago, used in children's stories **11 once in a blue moon** very rarely: *He comes to see us once in a blue moon.*

**once²** *conjunction* from the time something happens: *Once you try this, you'll never want to stop.*

**once-o·ver** /'. ˌ../ *n* INFORMAL **give sb/sth the once-over** to look at or examine someone or something quickly: *Ollie gave the car the once-over and decided not to buy it.*

**on·com·ing** /'ɔnˌkʌmɪŋ, 'ɑn-/ *adj* **oncoming car/traffic etc.** a car etc. that is coming toward you

**one¹** /wʌn/ *number* **1** 1 **2** one o'clock: *I have a meeting at one.*

**one²** *pron* **1** someone or something that has been mentioned or is known about: *"Do you have a bike?" "No, but I'm getting one for my birthday."* | *"Do you know where those books are?" "Which ones?"* | *"Which candy bar do you want?" "This/that one."* | *Jane's* **the one** *with the red hair.* **2 one by one** if people do something one by one, first one person does it, then the next etc.: *One by one, the passengers got off the bus.* **3 one after the other/one after another** if events or actions happen one after the other, they happen without much time between them: *He's had one problem after another this year.* **4 (all) in one** used in order to say that something has many functions or works in many ways: *This is a TV, radio, and VCR all in one.* **5** FORMAL **a)** people in general: *One must be careful to keep exact records.* **b)** used in order to mean "I": *One is tempted to ignore the whole problem.* **6 have had one too many** INFORMAL to have drunk too much alcohol

**one³** *determiner* **1** a word meaning a particular thing or person, used especially when there are others of the same kind: *One reason I like the house is because of the big kitchen.* |

**One of** *the children is sick.* ✗ DON'T SAY "One of the children are sick." ✗ **2 one day/afternoon etc. a)** a particular day etc. in the past: *There was one week in April last year when we had two feet of snow.* **b)** any day etc. in the future: *Let's go shopping one Saturday when we're less busy.* **3** only: *My one worry is that she will decide to leave college.* **4** SPOKEN used in order to emphasize your description of someone or something: *That is one cute kid!*

**one⁴** *n* a piece of paper money worth $1

**one an·oth·er** /ˌ. .'../ *pron* FORMAL ⇨ EACH OTHER: *The two men shook hands and thanked one another.* —see usage note at EACH OTHER

**one-lin·er** /ˌ. '../ *n* a very short joke

**one-night stand** /ˌ. . './ *n* INFORMAL an occasion when two people have sex, but do not intend to meet each other again

**one-of-a-kind** /ˌ. . . '.◄/ *adj* special because no one else or nothing else is like him, her, or it: *one-of-a-kind handmade carpets*

**one-on-one** /ˌ. . './ *adv* between only you and one other person: *We're working one-on-one with the students to help them.*

**on·er·ous** /'ɑnərəs, 'oʊ-/ *adj* FORMAL difficult and tiring: *onerous duties*

**one-sid·ed** /ˌ. '..◄/ *adj* **1** considering or showing only one side of a question, subject etc. in a way that is unfair: *a one-sided view of the problem* **2** an activity or competition that is one-sided is one in which one person or team is much stronger than the other: *a one-sided football game*

**one-time** /'wʌntaɪm/ *adj* former: *Mitchell, a onetime carpenter, is now a successful writer.*

**one-to-one** /ˌ. . '.◄/ *adj* **1** between only two people: *tuition on a one-to-one basis* **2** matching one other person, thing etc. exactly: *a one-to-one correspondence between sound and symbol*

**one-track mind** /ˌ. . './ *n* **have a one-track mind** to think about only one thing all the time: *All you ever talk about is baseball! You have a one-track mind.*

**one-up·man·ship** /ˌwʌn'ʌpmənˌʃɪp/ *n* [U] attempts to make yourself seem better than other people

**one-way** /ˌ. '.◄/ *adj* **1** moving or allowing movement in only one direction: *one-way traffic* | *a one-way street* **2** a one-way ticket is for taking a trip from one place to another but not back again —see also ROUND-TRIP

**on·go·ing** /'ɔnˌgoʊɪŋ, 'ɑn-/ *adj* continuing: *ongoing discussions*

**on·ion** /'ʌnyən/ *n* [C,U] a round white yellow or red vegetable with many layers, that has a strong taste and smell —see picture on page 470

**on-line, online** /ˌ. '.◄/ *adj, adv* **1** directly connected to or controlled by a computer: *an on-line printer* **2** connected to many other computers, especially computers that are on the

**INTERNET:** *All of our local schools will be/go on line by the end of the year.* –see culture note at INTERNET

**on·look·er** /'ɔn,luka, 'ɑn-/ *n* someone who watches something happening without being involved in it

**on·ly¹** /'ounli/ *adv* **1** not more than a particular amount, number, age etc., especially when this is unusual: *Tammy was only 9 months old when she learned to walk.* | *That TV only costs $55!* **2** nothing or no one except the person or thing mentioned: *You're only wearing a T-shirt. No wonder you're cold.* | *This parking lot is for restaurant customers only.* **3** in one place, situation, or way and no other, or for one reason and no other: *You can only get to the lake with a four-wheel-drive vehicle.* | *You're only doing this because you think he'll pay you for it!* **4** not better, worse, or more important than someone or something: *Steph's only the assistant manager.* | *I was only kidding.* **5 not only...(but)** used in order to say that something is even better, worse, or more surprising than what you have just said: *Math is not only easy for her, it's fun.* **6** FORMAL no earlier than a particular time: *Congress passed the law only last year.* **7 only just a)** a very short time ago: *We're only just beginning the treatment.* **b)** almost not; hardly: *There's only just room here for two people.* **8 if only a)** used in order to give a reason for something, and say that it is not a good one: *Just call her, if only to say you're sorry.* **b)** used in order to express a strong wish: *If only I could have gone to the funeral.* **9 only too** very or completely: *He was only too ready to earn some more money.*

---

**USAGE NOTE only**

The meaning of a sentence can change depending on where you use **only**. Always put **only** just before the word that it describes: *Only John saw the lion.* (=no one except John saw the lion) | *John only saw the lion.* (=he saw it, but he did not do anything else to it, such as take a photograph of it) | *John saw only the lion.* (=the lion was the only animal he saw)

---

**only²** *adj* **1** with no others of the same kind: *She's the only person I know who doesn't like chocolate.* | *Walking is the only exercise I get.* **2** an only child does not have any brothers or sisters **3 the only thing is...** SPOKEN used before you begin to talk about something that might be a problem: *I'd like to come see you, the only thing is my car's being fixed.*

**only³** *conjunction* except that; but: *We were going to go fishing, only it started raining.*

**on-ramp** /'. ./ *n* a road for driving onto a HIGHWAY or FREEWAY –opposite OFF-RAMP

**on·rush** /'ɔnrʌʃ, 'ɑn-/ *n* [singular] a strong movement forward: *a sudden onrush of water*

**on·set** /'ɔnsɛt, 'ɑn-/ *n* **the onset of** the beginning of something: *the onset of a bad cold*

**on·slaught** /'ɑnslɔt, 'ɔn-/ *n* a very strong attack

**on·to** /*before consonants* 'ɔntə, 'ɑn-; *before vowels and strong* 'ɔntu, 'ɑn-/ *prep* **1** used with verbs showing movement, to mean in or on a particular place: *The cat jumped onto the kitchen table.* | *How did he get onto the roof?* | *When you turn onto River Road, you'll see the church.* **2 be onto sb** INFORMAL to know who did something wrong or illegal: *He was scared. He knows we're onto him.*

**o·nus** /'ounəs/ *n* **the onus** the responsibility for something: *The onus is on the company to provide safety equipment.*

**on·ward¹** /'ɔnwəd, 'ɑn-/, **onwards** *adv* **1 from...onward** beginning at a particular time and continuing into the future: *European History from 1900 onward* **2** forward: *The ship moved onward through the fog.*

**on·ward²** *adj* **1** moving forward or continuing: *the onward journey* **2** developing over a period of time: *the onward march of scientific progress*

**oo·dles** /'udlz/ *n* [plural] INFORMAL a large amount of something: *oodles of fun*

**oops** /ups, ʊps/ *interjection* said when someone has fallen, dropped something, or made a small mistake: *Oops! I spilled the milk!*

**ooze¹** /uz/ *v* [I,T] **1** if a liquid oozes from something or if something oozes a liquid, liquid flows from it very slowly: *blood was oozing from the cut* **2** INFORMAL to show a lot of a particular quality: *Leo's voice oozed sarcasm.*

**ooze²** *n* [U] very soft mud, especially at the bottom of a lake or river

**o·pal** /'oupəl/ *n* [C,U] a white stone used in jewelry that has other colors in it that show when light shines on it

**o·paque** /ou'peɪk/ *adj* **1** not transparent **2** hard to understand –compare TRANSPARENT

**open**

**o·pen¹** /'oupən/ *adj*
**1** ▶OPEN◀ not closed: *Who left the window open?* | *I can barely keep my eyes open, I'm so tired.* | *A book lay open on the table.*
**2** ▶STORES/BANKS ETC.◀ ready for business, and letting customers come in: *We're open until six o'clock.* | *Are the bars still open?*
**3** ▶PUBLIC USE◀ ready or available to be

used by the public: *When is the new library going to be open?* | *The pool is only open to the public* in the summer.

**4 ▶NOT RESTRICTED◀** available to anyone, so that anyone can take part: *Few jobs were open to women before World War I.* | *an open meeting*

**5 ▶NOT ENCLOSED◀** not enclosed or covered by buildings, walls etc.: *driving in the open country* | *an open fire*

**6 ▶NOT SECRET◀** not hiding anything: *Ralph looked at her with open admiration.*

**7 ▶WILLING TO LISTEN◀** willing to listen to other people: *Keep an open mind* (=listen without judging) *until you've heard everyone's ideas.* | *We're open to suggestions on how to improve our service.*

**8 ▶HONEST◀** honest and not wanting to hide anything: *My husband and I try to be open with each other.*

**9 be open to criticism/discussion etc.** able to be criticized, discussed etc.: *Her comments were open to misunderstanding.*

**10 ▶NOT DECIDED◀** not finally decided: *The location of the peace talks is still an open question.* | *We'll leave the discussion open until more information is available.*

**11 keep your eyes/ears open** SPOKEN to keep looking or listening so that you will notice anything that is important

**12 welcome/greet sb with open arms** to greet someone with happiness and excitement: *The European visitors were welcomed by local people with open arms.*

**open²** *v* also **open up 1** [I,T] to become open, or to make something open: *Dan's opening his birthday presents.* | *Open up the window.* | *a door that opens automatically* **2** [I] if a store, bank, or public building opens at a particular time, it begins to allow people inside at that time: *What time does the bookstore open on Sundays?* **3** [I,T] to start, or to make something do this: *The restaurant opens next month.* | *a new play opening on Broadway* | *He opened up a checking account at First National Bank.* **4** [I,T] to spread something out, or become spread out: *I can't open my umbrella.* | *The roses are starting to open up.* | *Open your books to page 153.* **5** [T] to make something available to be used or visited: *They're plowing the snow to open up the roads.* | *Parts of the White House will be opened to the public.*

**6 open fire (on)** to start shooting at someone or something

**open into/onto** sth *phr v* [T] to lead directly into a place: *The kitchen opens onto the back yard.*

**open up** *phr v* **1** [I] to stop being shy and say what you really think: *Once Ann gets to know you, she'll open up.* **2** [I,T **open** sth ↔ **up**] to become available or possible, or to make some-

thing available or possible: *Education opens up all kinds of opportunities.*

**USAGE NOTE open, close, turn on,** and **turn off**

Use **open** and **close** to talk about objects such as doors, windows, or boxes: *Let's open a window; it's warm in here.* Use **turn on** and **turn off** to talk about water or gas, or about things that use electricity: *Turn on the TV; there's a good show on now.*

**open³** *n* **(out) in the open a)** outdoors: *It's fun to eat out in the open.* **b)** not hidden or secret: *The truth is finally out in the open.*

**open-air** /ˌ.. ˈ.◂/ *adj* outdoor: *open-air concerts*

**open-and-shut case** /ˌ.. . ˌ. ˈ./ *n* something such as a law case that is very easy to prove

**open-end·ed** /ˌ.. ˈ..◂/ *adj* without a fixed ending time: *an open-ended job contract*

**o·pen·er** /ˈoʊpənɚ/ *n* **1** a tool or machine used in order to open letters, bottles, or cans: *an electric can opener* **2** the first of a series of things such as sports competitions: *the opener against the Celtics*

**open-heart sur·gery** /ˌ.. ˌ. ˈ.../ *n* [U] a medical operation in which doctors operate on someone's heart

**open house** /ˌ.. ˈ./ *n* **1** an occasion when a school or business allows the public to come in and see the work that is done there **2** a party that you can come to or leave at any time during a particular period: *an open house from 2-6 p.m.*

**o·pen·ing¹** /ˈoʊpənɪŋ/ *n* **1** an occasion when a new business, building etc. is ready for use: *the opening of the new art gallery* **2** the beginning of something: *The chairman made a speech at the opening of the conference.* **3** a job or position that is available: *Are there any openings for gardeners?* **4** a hole or space in something: *an opening in the fence* **5** an opportunity to do or say something: *He waited for an opening to ask his question.*

**opening²** *adj* first or beginning: *the President's opening remarks* | *Are you going to opening night?* (=the first night of a new play, movie etc.)

**o·pen·ly** /ˈoʊpənli/ *adv* honestly and not secretly: *They talk openly about their problems.*

**open-mind·ed** /ˌ.. ˈ..◂/ *adj* willing to consider and accept new ideas, opinions etc.: *My doctor isn't very open-minded about new treatments.* **−open-mindedness** /ˌ.. ˈ.../ *n* [U]

**o·pen·ness** /ˈoʊpənɪs/ *n* [U] **1** the quality of being honest and not keeping things secret: *the openness of a small child* **2** the quality of being willing to accept new ideas or people: *Her openness to suggestions makes her easy to work with.*

**open-plan** /ˌ.. '.'/ adj an open-plan office, school etc. does not have walls dividing it into separate rooms

**open sea·son** /ˌ.. '..'/ n [singular] **1** the time each year when it is legal to kill particular animals or fish as a sport: *open season for deer* **2** HUMOROUS a time during which someone or something is criticized a lot: *It's been open season on the President since he made his budget speech.*

**op·er·a** /'ɑprə, 'ɑpərə/ n [C,U] a musical play in which all of the words are sung, or these plays considered as a form of art –**operatic** /ˌɑpəˈrætɪk/ adj

**op·er·a·ble** /'ɑprəbəl/ adj **1** able to be treated by a medical operation: *The cancer is operable.* **2** working and ready to use: *an operable machine* –opposite INOPERABLE

**op·er·ate** /'ɑpəˌreɪt/ v **1** [I,T] if a machine operates or you operate it, it works or you make it work: *He doesn't know how to operate the equipment.* | *The machine seems to be operating smoothly.* **2** [I] to cut open someone's body in order to remove or fix a part that is damaged: *Doctors operated on him for appendicitis.* **3** [I,T] to organize and manage a business or activity: *large banks that operate nationwide* | *an agreement to build and operate a cellular phone network* **4** [I,T] to have a particular effect, or to do something in a particular way: *How does the new security system operate?* | *The computer network will operate as an information resource for all universities in the state.*

**operating sys·tem** /'... ,../ n a system in a computer that helps all the programs to work

**op·er·a·tion** /ˌɑpəˈreɪʃən/ n **1** the process of cutting into someone's body to fix or remove a part that is damaged: *a knee operation* | *Mom had to have an operation on her back.* **2** a set of planned actions or activities for a particular purpose: *a rescue operation* **3** [U] the way the parts of a machine or system work together: *Wear protective glasses when the machine is in operation.* **4** [C,U] a business or company, or the work of a business: *The company's overseas operations are expanding.* | *Their delivery service has been in operation* (=been working) *for ten years.* **5** TECHNICAL an action done by a computer: *a machine performing millions of operations per second* **6** [U] the way something such as a law has an effect or achieves a result: *a close look at the operation of the tax laws*

**op·er·a·tion·al** /ˌɑpəˈreɪʃənl/ adj **1** working and ready to be used: *The new airport will soon be operational.* **2** relating to the operation of a business, government etc.: *operational costs* –**operationally** adv

**op·er·a·tive** /'ɑpərətɪv/ adj working or having an effect: *The law will become operative in a month.*

**op·er·a·tor** /'ɑpəˌreɪtɚ/ n **1** someone who works on a telephone SWITCHBOARD: *Ask the operator to help you with the call.* –see usage note at TELEPHONE **2** someone who operates a machine or piece of equipment: *a computer operator*

**oph·thal·mol·o·gy** /ˌɑfθəlˈmɑlədʒi, -θəˈmɑ-, ˌɑp-/ n [U] TECHNICAL the medical study of the eyes and diseases that affect them –**ophthalmologist** n

**o·pin·ion** /əˈpɪnyən/ n **1** [C,U] your ideas or beliefs about a particular subject: *What's your opinion on nuclear testing?* | *In my opinion, getting a divorce is too easy.* | *people who aren't afraid to express/give their opinions* **2** judgment or advice from a professional person about something: *We got a second opinion* (=we asked two people) *before replacing the furnace.* **3** **have a high/low/good etc. opinion of** to think that someone or something is very good or very bad: *The management seems to have a high opinion of her work.* **4** [U] what people in general think about something: *Public opinion is strongly in favor of changing the election system.* –see usage note at VIEW[1]

**o·pin·ion·at·ed** /əˈpɪnyəˌneɪtɪd/ adj DISAPPROVING expressing very strong opinions about things: *an opinionated letter*

**opinion poll** /.'., ,./ n ⇒ POLL[1]

**o·pi·um** /'oupiəm/ n [U] an illegal drug made from POPPY seeds

**o·pos·sum** /əˈpɑsəm, 'pɑsəm/ n an American animal that looks like a large rat and can hang from trees by its tail

**op·po·nent** /əˈpounənt/ n **1** someone who tries to defeat another person in a competition, game etc.: *His opponent is twice as big as he is.* **2** someone who disagrees with a plan, idea etc.: *opponents of federal aid to education*

**op·por·tune** /ˌɑpɚˈtun/ adj FORMAL **an opportune moment/time/place etc.** a time etc. that is suitable for doing something

**op·por·tun·ist** /ˌɑpɚˈtunɪst/ n DISAPPROVING someone who uses every chance to gain power or advantages over others –**opportunistic** /ˌɑpɚtuˈnɪstɪk/ adj –**opportunism** /ˌɑpɚˈtuˌnɪzəm/ n [U]

**op·por·tu·ni·ty** /ˌɑpɚˈtunəti/ n **1** an occasion when it is possible for you to do something: *I haven't had an opportunity to think about this yet.* | *The meeting will give you the/an opportunity to introduce yourself to the team.* | *I'd like to take this opportunity to thank everyone who helped me.* **2** a chance to get a job: *There are good opportunities for graduates in your field.* –compare CHANCE[1] –see usage note at CHANCE[1]

**op·pose** /əˈpouz/ v [T] to disagree strongly with an idea or action: *A local group opposes the plan for environmental reasons.*

**op·posed** /ə'pouzd/ *adj* **1** disagreeing strongly with someone or something, or feeling strongly that someone or something is wrong: *I'm* **opposed to** *the death penalty.* **2 as opposed to** used in order to show that two things are different from each other: *The group gave out 300 food boxes this year, as opposed to 200 last year.*

**op·pos·ing** /ə'pouzɪŋ/ *adj* **1** opposing teams, groups etc. are competing, arguing etc. with each other **2** opposing ideas, opinions etc. are completely different from each other

**op·po·site¹** /'ɑpəzɪt, -sɪt/ *adj* **1** completely different: *I thought the music would relax me, but it had the opposite effect.* | *Ray started walking in the opposite direction.* **2** facing something or directly across from something: *a building on the opposite side of the river* | *Louise and I work* **at opposite ends of** (=on different sides of) *the city, so it's hard to meet.*

**opposite²** *prep, adv* if one thing or person is opposite another, they are facing each other: *Put the piano opposite the sofa.* | *He's moved into the house opposite.*

**opposite³** *n* a person or thing that is completely different from someone or something else: *Hot and cold are opposites.* | *David loves to read, but Mike's* **the opposite**.

**op·po·si·tion** /ˌɑpə'zɪʃən/ *n* [U] strong disagreement with, or protest against something: *the residents'* **opposition to** *plans for a new highway*

**op·press** /ə'prɛs/ *v* [T] to treat people in an unfair and cruel way

**op·pressed** /ə'prɛst/ *adj* treated unfairly or cruelly: *oppressed minority groups* | *the poor and* **the oppressed** (=people who are oppressed)

**op·pres·sion** /ə'prɛʃən/ *n* [U] the act of OP-PRESSing people, or the state of being oppressed: *People are demanding an end to the oppression.*

**op·pres·sive** /ə'prɛsɪv/ *adj* **1** cruel and unfair: *an oppressive military government* **2** making you feel uncomfortable: *oppressive heat*

**op·pres·sor** /ə'prɛsɚ/ *n* a person or group that OPPRESSes people

**opt** /ɑpt/ *v* [I,T] to choose one thing instead of another: *We've* **opted for** *a smaller car.* | *More high school students are* **opting to** *go to college.*

**opt out** *phr v* [I] to choose not to join in a group or system: *Several countries may* **opt out** *of NATO.*

**op·tic** /'ɑptɪk/ *adj* relating to the eyes: *the optic nerve*

**op·ti·cal** /'ɑptɪkəl/ *adj* relating to the way light is seen, or relating to the eyes: *an optical instrument* **–optically** *adv*

**optical il·lu·sion** /ˌ... .'../ *n* a picture or image that tricks your eyes and makes you see something that is not actually there

**op·ti·cian** /ɑp'tɪʃən/ *n* someone who makes GLASSES

**op·ti·mism** /'ɑptə,mɪzəm/ *n* [U] a tendency to believe that good things will happen: *At the moment, there is optimism about the country's economic future* –opposite PESSIMISM

**op·ti·mist** /'ɑptə,mɪst/ *n* someone who believes that good things will happen –opposite PESSIMIST

**op·ti·mis·tic** /ˌɑptə'mɪstɪk/ *adj* believing that good things will happen in the future: *Tom's* **optimistic about** *finding a job.* **–optimistically** *adv* –opposite PESSIMISTIC

**op·ti·mum** /'ɑptəməm/ *adj* best or most suitable for a particular purpose: *the optimum diet for good health*

**op·tion** /'ɑpʃən/ *n* **1** a choice you can make in a particular situation: *Consider all your options carefully.* | *If these talks fail, war may be the only option we have left.* | *Dropping out of school* **is not an option.** (=you cannot do it) **2 keep/leave your options open** to wait before making a decision: *Leave your options open until you have the results of the test.* **3** the right to buy or sell something in the future: *You can rent the piano, with an option to buy.*

**op·tion·al** /'ɑpʃənl/ *adj* something that is optional is something you do not need to do or have, but can choose if you want it: *A sun roof is optional in this car.*

**op·tom·e·trist** /ɑp'tɑmətrɪst/ *n* someone who examines people's eyes and orders GLASSES for them **–optometry** /ɑp'tɑmətri/ *n* [U]

**op·u·lent** /'ɑpyələnt/ *adj* decorated in an expensive way: *an opulent hotel* **–opulence** *n* [U]

**OR** the written abbreviation of Oregon

**or** /ɚ; *strong* ɔr/ *conjunction* **1** used between two possibilities or before the last in a series of possibilities: *Would you like pie, cake, or some ice cream?* | *Is she coming back with Nancy or with her aunt?* | *Tickets cost $4 or $5.* (=they cost around $5, but you are not sure exactly how much) | *You can use* **either** *milk* **or** *cream in the sauce.* | *I'll see him this afternoon,* **or else** *I'll call him tomorrow.* –compare EITHER¹ **2 or anything/something** SPOKEN or something that is similar to what you have just mentioned: *Do you want to go out for a drink or anything?* **3** used after a negative verb when you mean not one thing and not another thing: *They don't go to movies or plays.* **4** used in order to warn or advise someone: *Hurry* **or** *you'll miss your plane.* | *We can't go over 65,* **or else** *we'll get a speeding ticket.* | *Don't be late,* **or else...** (=used as a threat) **5 or so** used with a number, time, distance etc. to show that it is not exact: *There's a gas station a mile* **or so** *down the road.* **6** used before a word or phrase that explains what has been said before: *biology, or the study of living things* **7** used in order to explain why something happened or why something must be true: *She must be tired, or she wouldn't have yelled at us.*

**o·ral¹** /ˈɔrəl/ *adj* **1** spoken, not written: *an oral report* **2** relating to the mouth: *oral hygiene*

**oral²** *n* a test in a university in which questions and answers are spoken rather than written

**or·ange** /ˈɔrɪndʒ, ˈɑr-/ *n* [U] **1** a round fruit that has a sweet-tasting juice and a thick skin that you do not eat −see picture on page 470 **2** the color of an orange −**orange** *adj*

**o·rang·u·tang** /əˈræŋəˌtæŋ/, also **o·rang·u·tan** /əˈræŋəˌtæn/ *n* a large APE (=animal like a monkey) that has long arms and long orange hair

**or·a·tor** /ˈɔrət̬ə, ˈɑr-/ *n* someone who makes speeches and is good at persuading people −**oration** /əˈreɪʃən, ə-/ *n*

**or·at·o·ry** /ˈɔrətɔri, ˈɑr-/ *n* [U] the skill or art of making public speeches

**or·bit¹** /ˈɔrbɪt/ *n* the path traveled by an object that is moving around a larger object: *the Moon's orbit around the Earth* −**orbital** *adj*

**orbit**

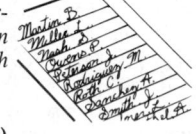

**orbit²** *v* [I,T] to travel in a circle around a larger object: *a satellite that orbits the Earth*

**or·chard** /ˈɔrtʃəd/ *n* a place where fruit trees are grown

**or·ches·tra** /ˈɔrkɪstrə/ *n* a large group of musicians who play CLASSICAL MUSIC on different instruments −**orchestral** /ɔrˈkɛstrəl/ *adj*

**orchestra pit** /ˈ... ˌ./ *n* the place at the front of a theater next to the stage and below the main floor, where the ORCHESTRA sits to play during a musical theater performance

**or·ches·trate** /ˈɔrkɪˌstreɪt/ *v* [T] to organize an important event or a complicated plan, especially secretly: *a rebellion orchestrated by the army*

**or·ches·tra·tion** /ˌɔrkɪˈstreɪʃən/ *n* [C,U] the way a piece of music is arranged for an ORCHESTRA, or the act of arranging it

**or·chid** /ˈɔrkɪd/ *n* a tropical, often brightly colored, flower with three PETALS

**or·dain** /ɔrˈdeɪn/ *v* [T] to officially make someone a religious leader −see also ORDINATION

**or·deal** /ɔrˈdil/ *n* a terrible or painful experience: *School can be an ordeal for children with learning problems.*

**or·der¹** /ˈɔrdə/ *n*

**1** **in order (for sb/sth) to do sth** so that something can happen or so that

**order**

These names are in alphabetical order.

someone can do something: *In order for you to graduate next year, you'll have to go to summer school.* | *Sunlight is needed in order for this chemical process to take place.*

**2** ▸**ARRANGEMENT**◂ [C,U] the way that several things are arranged, organized, or put on a list: *names written in alphabetical order* | *Are these pictures in order?* (=arranged in a particular order) | *Some of the book's pages were out of order.* (=not correctly arranged) | *I need to put the files in order.* (=organize them)

**3** ▸**GOODS/MEAL**◂ a request for goods from a company or for food in a restaurant, or the goods or food that you ask for: *The school's just placed an order for more books.* | *Has anyone taken your order?* (=written down what you want in a restaurant) | *I'll have an order of fries and a coke.*

**4** ▸**NO CRIME/TROUBLE**◂ [U] a situation in which people obey rules and respect authority: *Police are working hard to maintain law and order in the area.*

**5** ▸**COMMAND**◂ a command given by someone in authority: *Captain Marshall gave the order to advance.* | *He refused to obey the judge's order.*

**6** **out of order** a phrase meaning not working, used especially on signs: *The photocopier is out of order again.*

**7** **in order** legal and correct: *Your passport seems to be in order*

**8** ▸**POLITICS ETC.**◂ the political, social, or economic situation at a particular time: *the present economic order*

**9** **on the order of sb/sth** similar in some way to someone or something: *a car that averages on the order of 35 miles per gallon* −see also **in short order** (SHORT¹)

**order²** *v* **1** [I,T] to ask for goods or services: *"What did you order?" "Spaghetti."* | *I've ordered a new table for the kitchen.* **2** [T] to command someone to do something: *The judge ordered the jury not to discuss the trial.* **3** [T] to arrange something in a particular way: *a list of names ordered alphabetically*

---

**USAGE NOTE order and command**

Use **order** for most situations when someone who is in a position of authority tells other people to do something: *The governor ordered an investigation into the shootings.* Use **command** when it is someone in the military who is telling other people to do something: *The general commanded his troops to fire.*

---

**or·der·ly¹** /ˈɔrdəli/ *adj* **1** arranged or organized in a neat way: *an orderly desk* **2** peaceful or behaving well: *an orderly crowd* −opposite DISORDERLY

**orderly²** *n* someone who does unskilled jobs in a hospital

**or·di·nal num·ber** /ˌɔrdn-əl 'nʌmbɚ/ *n* one of the numbers such as first, second, third etc. that show the order of things –compare CAR-DINAL NUMBER

**or·di·nance** /'ɔrdn-əns/ *n* a law of a city or town that does not allow an activity or that re-stricts an activity: *parking ordinances*

**or·di·nar·i·ly** /ˌɔrdn'ɛrəli/ *adv* usually: *I don't ordinarily go to movies in the after-noon. | Ordinarily, he doesn't repair trucks, just cars.*

**or·di·nar·y** /'ɔrdn̩ɛri/ *adj* **1** average, usual, or not different: *laws written in language that ordinary people can understand | A videophone costs much more than an ordinary tele-phone. | ordinary items like toothpaste and soap* **2** not special in any way: *It was just an ordi-nary working day.* **3** **out of the ordinary** very different from what is usual: *I didn't notice any-thing out of the ordinary when I came home.*

**or·di·na·tion** /ˌɔrdn'eɪʃən/ *n* [C,U] the act or ceremony making someone a religious leader –see also ORDAIN

**ore** /ɔr/ *n* [C,U] rock or earth from which metal can be obtained

**or·gan** /'ɔrgən/ *n* **1** part of the body of an animal or plant that has a particular purpose: *the heart, liver, and other internal organs* **2** a large musical instrument like a piano, with large pipes to make the sound, or an electric instru-ment that makes similar sounds

**or·gan·ic** /ɔr'gænɪk/ *adj* **1** living, or related to living things: *organic matter | organic chem-istry* –opposite INORGANIC **2** using farming methods that do not use chemicals, or produced by these methods: *organic vegetables* –**or-ganically** *adv*

**or·gan·ism** /'ɔrgəˌnɪzəm/ *n* a living thing: *a microscopic organism*

**or·gan·ist** /'ɔrgənɪst/ *n* someone who plays the ORGAN

**or·ga·ni·za·tion** /ˌɔrgənə'zeɪʃən/ *n* **1** a group such as a club or business that has been formed for a particular purpose: *a charity organization | an organization of Christian stu-dents* **2** [U] the act of planning and arranging things effectively: *She was responsible for the organization of the fund-raising campaign.* **3** [U] the way in which the different parts of a system are arranged and work together: *the so-cial organization of twelfth century Europe* –**organizational** *adj*

**or·ga·nize** /'ɔrgəˌnaɪz/ *v* **1** [T] to plan or arrange something: *Who's organizing the New Year's party? | Organize your ideas on paper before you write your essay.* **2** [I,T] to form a UNION (=an organization that protects workers' rights) or persuade people to join one

**or·ga·nized** /'ɔrgəˌnaɪzd/ *adj* **1** planned or arranged in an effective way: *The meeting's always well organized when Donita's in*

charge. **2** an organized activity is arranged for and done by many people: *organized sports | organized religion*

**organized crime** /ˌ... './ *n* [U] a large and powerful organization of criminals

**or·ga·niz·er** /'ɔrgəˌnaɪzɚ/ *n* someone who organizes an event or group of people: *Last year the organizers of the event sent out 3000 invita-tions.*

**or·gasm** /'ɔrˌgæzəm/ *n* [C,U] the moment when you have the greatest sexual pleasure dur-ing sex

**or·gy** /'ɔrdʒi/ *n* a wild party with a lot of eat-ing, drinking, and sexual activity

**O·ri·ent** /'ɔriənt/ *n* **the Orient** OLD-FASHIONED the eastern part of the world, especially China and Japan

**o·ri·ent** /'ɔriˌɛnt/ *v* [T] **1** to make someone familiar with a place or situation: *It takes a while to orient yourself in a new city.* **2** to find someone's position using a map etc.

**O·ri·en·tal** /ˌɔri'ɛntl/ *adj* **1** relating to Asia: *Oriental culture* **2** a word used for describing someone from Asia, that is sometimes con-sidered offensive –compare ASIAN

**o·ri·en·ta·tion** /ˌɔriən'teɪʃən/ *n* **1** [C,U] the beliefs, aims, or interests that a person or group chooses to have: *the group's right-wing political orientation* **2** [U] training and preparation for a new job or activity: *orientation week for new students* **3** **sexual orientation** the fact of being HETEROSEXUAL or HOMOSEXUAL **4** the direction in which something faces

**o·ri·ent·ed** /'ɔriˌɛntɪd/ *adj* giving attention to a particular type of person or thing: *male-oriented movies like "Die Hard" | a service ori-ented towards the needs of business people*

**or·i·gin** /'ɔrədʒɪn, 'ɑr-/ *n* the situation or place from which something comes, or where it began to exist: *a word of Latin origin | Scientists be-lieve the origin of the disease is an illness common in monkeys.* –see also ORIGINS

**o·rig·i·nal** [1] /ə'rɪdʒənl/ *adj* **1** first or earliest: *The house still has its original stone floor. | Our original plan was too expensive.* **2** completely new and different: *Students had to invent an original design for a chair.* **3** not copied, or not based on something else: *an original screen-play*

**original** [2] *n* a painting, document etc. that is not a copy

**o·rig·i·nal·i·ty** /əˌrɪdʒə'næləti/ *n* [U] the quality of being completely new and different: *the originality of her performance*

**o·rig·i·nal·ly** /ə'rɪdʒənl-i/ *adv* in the begin-ning: *Her family originally came from Thai-land. | Originally, we hoped to be finished by June.*

**o·rig·i·nate** /ə'rɪdʒəˌneɪt/ *v* [I] FORMAL to start to develop in a particular place or from a particular situation: *The custom of having a Christmas tree* **originated in** *Germany.*

**or·i·gins** /'ɔrədʒɪnz, 'ɑr-/ *n* [plural] the country, race, or class from which someone comes: *He's proud of his Italian origins.*

**o·ri·ole** /'ɔri,oʊl, 'ɔriəl/ *n* a wild bird that is black with a red and a yellow stripe on its wing

**or·na·ment** /'ɔrnəmənt/ *n* an object that you keep in your house because it is beautiful rather than useful: *Christmas ornaments*

**or·na·men·tal** /,ɔrnə'mɛntl/ *adj* designed to decorate something: *ornamental vases*

**or·nate** /ɔr'neɪt/ *adj* having a lot of decoration: *ornate furniture* –**ornately** *adv*

**or·ne·ry** /'ɔrnəri/ *adj* HUMOROUS behaving in an unreasonable and angry way

**or·ni·thol·o·gy** /,ɔrnə'θɑlədʒi/ *n* [U] the scientific study of birds –**ornithologist** *n*

**or·phan**¹ /'ɔrfən/ *n* a child whose parents are dead

**orphan**² *v* [T] **be orphaned** to become an ORPHAN

**or·phan·age** /'ɔrfənɪdʒ/ *n* a place where ORPHANed children live

**or·tho·don·tist** /,ɔrθə'dɑntɪst/ *n* a DENTIST who makes teeth straight when they have not been growing correctly –**orthodontics** *n* –**orthodontic** *adj*

**or·tho·dox** /'ɔrθə,dɑks/ *adj* **1** officially accepted, or considered to be normal by most people: *orthodox methods of treating disease* **2** following the traditional beliefs of a religion: *an orthodox Jew* –**orthodoxy** *n* [C,U]

**Orthodox Church** /,... './ *n* **the Orthodox Church** one of the Christian churches in eastern Europe and parts of Asia

**or·tho·pe·dics** /,ɔrθə'pidɪks/ *n* [U] the area of medicine that deals with bones –**orthopedic** *adj*

**Os·car** /'ɑskə/ *n* one of the prizes given each year to the best movies, actors etc. in the movie industry: *an Oscar for best director*

**os·ten·ta·tious** /,ɑstən'teɪʃəs/ *adj* DISAPPROVING designed or done in order to be impressive to other people: *ostentatious furniture | an ostentatious lifestyle* –**ostentation** *n* [U]

**ostracize** /'ɑstrə,saɪz/ *v* [T] to behave in a very unfriendly way toward someone and not allow him/her to be part of a group –**ostracism** /'ɑstrə,sɪzəm/ *n* [U]

**os·trich** /'ɑstrɪtʃ, 'ɔ-/ *n* a very large African bird with long legs, that runs very quickly but cannot fly

**oth·er**¹ /'ʌðə/ *determiner, adj* **1** used in order to mean one or more of the rest of a group of people or things, when you have already mentioned one person or thing: *Nora's home, but the other girls are at school. | Here's one sock, where's* **the other one***?* **2** used in order

to mean someone or something that is different from, or exists in addition to, the person or thing you have already mentioned: *He shares an apartment with three other guys. | I'm busy now; could we talk some other time? | a cottage on* **the other side** *of the lake* (=on the side opposite you) | *Everyone else seemed to be going* **the other way***.* (=in a different direction, especially an opposite direction) **3 the other day/ morning etc.** SPOKEN recently: *I talked to Ted the other day.* **4 other than** except: *I know she has brown hair, but other than that I don't remember much about her.* **5 every other day/ week etc.** on one of every two days, weeks etc.: *Her husband cooks dinner every other day.* **6 in other words** used in order to express an idea or opinion in a way that is easier to understand: *There are TV sets in 68.5 million homes; in other words, 97 percent of the population watch TV.* –compare ANOTHER –see also EACH OTHER **on the one hand...on the other hand** (HAND¹)

---

**USAGE NOTE other, others, and another**

Use all of these words to mean "more people or things of the same type." **Other** is a determiner that is used with plural nouns: *Do you have any other shoes to wear?* **Others** is a plural pronoun: *Besides these shoes, do you have any others?* **Another** is a singular pronoun, or a determiner that is used with a singular noun: *Besides these shoes, I have another pair. | Finish that hot dog first, then maybe you can have another.*

---

**other**² *pron* **1** one or more people or things that form the rest that you are talking about: *We ate one pizza and froze the other. | John's here; where are the others?* (=the other people) | *Some stereos are better than others.* **2 someone/ something etc. or other** used when you cannot be certain or definite about what you are saying: *We'll get the money somehow or other.*

**oth·er·wise** /'ʌðə,waɪz/ *adv* **1** a word meaning "if not," used when there will be a bad result if something does not happen: *You'd better get the tickets now; otherwise, there may not be any left.* **2** except for what has just been mentioned: *The sleeves are long, but otherwise the dress fits.* **3** in a different way: *Adam was ready to buy the house, but his wife decided otherwise.*

**ot·ter** /'ɑtə/ *n* a small animal that can swim, has brown fur, and eats fish

**ouch** /aʊtʃ/ *interjection* said when you feel sudden pain: *Ouch! That hurt!*

**ought to** /'ɔt̬ə; *strong* 'ɔt̬u/ *modal verb* **1** used in order to make a suggestion: *You ought to take a day off.* **2** used in order to say that someone should do something because it is right: *He ought to apologize to her. | We ought* *not to be eating such high fat food.* **3** used in order to say that you expect something to happen or be true: *The weather ought to be nice there in October.* —see study note on page 458

**ounce** /aʊns/ *written abbreviation* **oz.** *n* **1** a unit for measuring weight equal to ⅟₁₆ of a pound or 28.35 grams **2** a unit for measuring the weight of a liquid, equal to ⅟₁₆ of a PINT or 29.574 MILLILITERS **3 an ounce of truth/sense etc.** a small amount or a particular quality: *Don't you have even an ounce of sense?*

**our** /ɑr; *strong* aʊɚ/ *possessive adj* belonging or relating to the person who is speaking and one or more other people: *We don't have curtains on our windows.* | *Our daughter is at college.*

**ours** /aʊɚz, ɑrz/ *possessive pron* the thing or things belonging or relating to the person who is speaking and one or more other people: *"Whose car is that?" "It's ours."* | *They have their tickets, but ours haven't come yet.*

**our·selves** /aʊɚˈsɛlvz, ɑr-/ *pron* **1** the REFLEXIVE form of "we": *We cook for ourselves.* **2** the strong form of "we," used in order to emphasize the subject or object of a sentence: *We started this business ourselves.* **3 (all) by ourselves a)** without help: *Amy and I made supper all by ourselves.* **b)** alone: *Dad left us by ourselves for an hour.* **4 to ourselves** not having to share with other people: *After Mom leaves, we'll have the house to ourselves.*

**oust** /aʊst/ *v* [T] to force someone out of a position of power

**oust·er** /ˈaʊstɚ/ *n* [C usually singular] the act of removing someone from a position of power

**out¹** /aʊt/ *adj, adv* **1** away from the inside of a place or container: *Close the door on your way out.* | *All his tools were out of their box on the floor.* **2** away from the place where you usually are, such as home or work: *Ms. Jackson is out right now. She'll be back at 1:00.* | *He asked me out for dinner tonight.* (=invited me to dinner) **3** away from a place: *The sign said "Keep Out."* **4** outside: *Why don't you go out and play?* **5** in or to a place that is far away or difficult to get to: *Do you want me to come out and get you?* | *He's moved out to Arizona.* **6** completely or carefully: *Clean out the cupboard before you put the dishes in.* | *I'm worn out.* (=very tired) **7** if power, electricity etc. is out, it is not working correctly, or not on: *The electricity was out for an hour last night.* | *OK, kids. Put the lights out.* **8** not having power any more: *The only way to lower taxes is to vote the Democrats out!* **9** used in order to say that something has appeared: *The sun wasn't out at all today.* | *leaves coming out on the trees* **10 out loud** done in a way so that people can hear your voice: *parents reading out loud to their kids* **11** if a number or amount is out, it is not correct: *My calculations are way out!* **12** available to be bought: *Morrison has a*

*new book out this month.* **13** SPOKEN not possible: *"Where should we go?" "Well, skiing's out because it costs too much."* **14 be out for sth/be out to do sth** INFORMAL to intend to do or get something: *Don't listen to Danny - he's just out to get attention.* **15** INFORMAL **a)** asleep: *Billy was out like a light by 6:00.* **b)** not conscious: *You must have hit him pretty hard. He's out cold.* **16** a player in a game who is out is no longer allowed to play, or has lost one of his/her chances to get a point **17** clothes or styles that are out are no longer fashionable **18** someone who is out has told people that s/he is a HOMOSEXUAL **19** if the tide is out, the ocean is at its lowest level

**out²** *prep* **1** from inside something, or through something: *She pulled out a $20 bill.* | *He was looking out the window at the beach.* **2 out of a)** from a particular place or time: *I took the books out of the box.* | *a nail sticking out of the wall* | *It was one of the best movies to come out of the 1980s.* **b)** from a larger group of the same kind: *Three out of four dentists recommend the toothpaste.* | *Kathy was chosen out of all the kids in her class.* **c)** having none of something that you had before: *We're almost out of gas.* | *The car was completely out of control.* **d)** used in order to show what something is made from: *a box made out of wood* **3 out of it** INFORMAL not able to think clearly because you are very tired, drunk etc.: *I'm really out of it today.* **4 out of the way a)** a place that is out of the way is far from any towns: *an out of the way motel* **b)** finished: *Good. Now that's out of the way, we can start working.*

**out³** *n* **an out** INFORMAL an excuse for not doing something: *I'm busy Sunday, so that gives me an out.*

**out⁴** *v* [T] to publicly say that someone is HOMOSEXUAL when that person wants it to be a secret

**out·age** /ˈaʊtɪdʒ/ *n* a period of time when a service, especially the electricity supply, is not provided: *a power outage*

**out-and-out** /ˌ. . ˈ./ *adj* having all the qualities of a particular type of person or thing; complete: *an out-and-out lie*

**out·bid** /aʊtˈbɪd/ *v* **outbid, outbid, outbidding** [T] to offer more money than someone else for something that you want to buy

**out·break** /ˈaʊtbreɪk/ *n* the start or sudden appearance of something bad such as a war or disease: *an outbreak of malaria*

**out·burst** /ˈaʊtbɚst/ *n* a sudden powerful expression of strong emotion: *an angry outburst*

**out·cast** /ˈaʊtkæst/ *n* someone who is not accepted by other people and is forced to live away from them: *a social outcast*

**out·class** /aʊtˈklæs/ *v* [T] to be much better than someone else at doing something: *Baltimore outclassed the Mets in the first game of the World Series.*

**out·come** /ˈaʊtˌkʌm/ *n* [singular] the final result of a meeting, process etc.: *We were eager to know what the **outcome of** the experiment would be.*

**out·crop·ping** /ˈaʊtˌkrɑpɪŋ/ *n* a rock or group of rocks that sticks out from the surface of the ground

**out·cry** /ˈaʊtˌkraɪ/ *n* [singular] an angry protest by a lot of people: *The killings led to a **public outcry for** new gun restrictions.*

**out·dat·ed** /ˌaʊtˈdeɪtɪd⁴/ *adj* **1** no longer useful or modern: *outdated computers* **2** no longer effective: *an outdated map*

**out·dis·tance** /aʊtˈdɪstəns/ *v* [T] to go faster or farther than someone else in a race

**out·do** /aʊtˈdu/ *v* [T] to be better or more successful than someone else: *My brothers are always trying to outdo each other.*

**out·door** /ˈaʊtdɔr/ *adj* happening, existing, or used outside and not in a building: *outdoor activities | an outdoor swimming pool* –compare INDOOR

**out·doors** /aʊtˈdɔrz/ *adv* outside, not inside a building: *I prefer working outdoors.* –compare INDOORS

**out·er** /ˈaʊtɚ/ *adj* **1** on the outside of something: *Peel off the outer leaves of lettuce.* **2** far from the middle of something: *an outer office* –opposite INNER

**out·er·most** /ˈaʊtɚˌmoʊst/ *adj* farthest from the middle: *the outermost planets* –opposite INNERMOST

**outer space** /ˌ.. ˈ./ *n* [U] the space outside the Earth's air where the stars and PLANETs are

**out·field** /ˈaʊtfild/ *n* [singular] the part of a baseball field that is farthest from the player who is BATting –**outfielder** *n* –see picture on page 472

**out·fit¹** /ˈaʊtˌfɪt/ *n* **1** a set of clothes worn together: *I love your outfit!* **2** INFORMAL a group of people who work together as an organization: *When did you join this outfit?*

**outfit²** *v* **-tted, -tting** [T] to provide someone with a set of clothes or equipment for a special purpose, such as camping

**out·fit·ter** /ˈaʊtˌfɪtɚ/ *n* a person or business that OUTFITs people for a particular activity

**out·go·ing** /ˈaʊtˌgoʊɪŋ/ *adj* **1** wanting to meet and talk to new people, or showing this quality; friendly: *Sally is really outgoing and easy to talk to. | an outgoing personality* **2** **the outgoing president/CEO etc.** someone who is finishing a job as president etc. **3** going out from or leaving a place: *outgoing phone calls*

**out·grow** /aʊtˈgroʊ/ *v* [T] **1** to grow too big for something: *Kara's already outgrown her shoes.* **2** to no longer enjoy something you used to enjoy

**out·growth** /ˈaʊtˌgroʊθ/ *n* a natural result of something: *Pollution is an outgrowth of industry.*

**out·house** /ˈaʊthaʊs/ *n* a small building outside the house, in which there is a toilet

**out·ing** /ˈaʊtɪŋ/ *n* a short enjoyable trip for a group of people: *a Sunday outing to the park*

**out·land·ish** /aʊtˈlændɪʃ/ *adj* strange and unusual: *outlandish clothes*

**out·last** /aʊtˈlæst/ *v* [T] to continue to exist or do something longer than someone else: *The whole point of the game is to outlast your opponent*

**out·law¹** /ˈaʊtˌlɔ/ *v* [T] to say officially that something is illegal: *Gambling was outlawed here in 1980.*

**outlaw²** *n* OLD-FASHIONED a criminal who is hiding from the police

**out·lay** /ˈaʊtˌleɪ/ *n* [C,U] an amount of money that is spent for a particular purpose: *Even after a huge outlay on the new building, the progress was slow.*

**out·let** /ˈaʊtˌlɛt, -lɪt/ *n* **1** a place on a wall where you can connect electrical equipment to the electricity supply **2** a store that sells things for less than the usual price: *a clothes outlet* **3** a way of expressing or getting rid of strong feelings: *I use judo as **an outlet for** stress.* **4** a way out through which something such as a liquid or gas can flow

**out·line¹** /ˈaʊtˌlaɪn/ *n* **1** the main ideas or facts about something without all the details: *Here is an outline of the company's plan.* **2** a line around the edge of something that shows its shape

**outline²** *v* [T] **1** to describe the main ideas or facts about something, but not all the details: *He gave us a five page memo outlining his theory.* **2** to draw or put a line around the edge of something to show its shape: *I've **outlined** the names on the cards **in** silver.*

**out·live** /aʊtˈlɪv/ *v* [T] to live longer than someone else

**out·look** /ˈaʊtˌlʊk/ *n* **1** your general attitude to life and the world: *Nels has a very **positive outlook on** life.* **2** what is expected to happen in the future: *The **outlook for** travelers is for higher prices on overseas flights.*

**out·ly·ing** /ˈaʊtˌlaɪ-ɪŋ/ *adj* far from cities, people etc.: *There may be some frost in **outlying** areas.*

**out·ma·neu·ver** /ˌaʊtməˈnuvɚ/ *v* [T] to gain an advantage over someone by using skillful movements or plans

**out·mod·ed** /aʊtˈmoʊdɪd/ *adj* ⇨ OUTDATED

**out·num·ber** /aʊtˈnʌmbɚ/ *v* [T] to be more in number than another group: *Men outnumber women in Congress.*

**out of bounds** /ˌ.. ˈ.⁴/ *adj* **1** not inside the official playing area in a sports game: *The referee said the ball was out of bounds.* **2** not allowed or acceptable: *Some topics, such as sex, are out of bounds for discussion.* –**out of**

**bounds** *adv*: *The ball was knocked out of bounds.*

**out-of-date** /ˌ. . '.ˌ/ *adj* ⇨ OUTDATED

**out-of-state** /ˌ. . '.ˌ/ *adj, adv* from, to, or in another state: *out-of-state license plates* | *I could have gone out-of-state for college.*

**out-of-the-way** /ˌ. . . '.ˌ/ *adj* far from cities and people and often difficult to find: *They met in an out-of-the-way hotel.*

**out·pa·tient** /'aʊtˌpeɪʃənt/ *n* someone who goes to the hospital for treatment but does not stay there —compare INPATIENT

**out·per·form** /ˌaʊtpɚ'fɔrm/ *v* [T] to do something better than other things or people: *Mart Stores continued to outperform other large retailers.*

**out·place·ment** /'aʊtˌpleɪsmənt/ *n* [U] a service that a company provides to help its workers find other jobs when it cannot continue to employ them

**out·post** /'aʊtˌpoʊst/ *n* a small town or group of buildings in a place that is far away from big cities

**out·pour·ing** /'aʊtˌpɔrɪŋ/ *n* a large amount of something that is produced suddenly, such as strong emotions, ideas, or help: *an outpouring of help from the public*

**out·put** /'aʊtˌpʊt/ *n* [C,U] the amount of work, goods etc. produced by someone or something: *Economic output is down 10% this year.* —compare INPUT

**out·rage¹** /'aʊtˌreɪdʒ/ *n* [C,U] a feeling of great anger or shock, or something that causes this: *a deep sense of moral outrage* | *"This is an outrage - they owe me at least another $350!"*

**outrage²** *v* [T] to make someone feel very angry or shocked: *Shorman's comments outraged leaders of the African-American community.* —**outraged** *adj*

**out·ra·geous** /aʊt'reɪdʒəs/ *adj* very shocking and offensive: *an outrageous comedy show* —**outrageously** *adv*

**out·reach** /'aʊtˌritʃ/ *n* [U] the practice of trying to help people with particular problems, especially through an organization: *the church's community outreach program*

**out·right¹** /'aʊtˌraɪt/ *adj* **1** complete and total: *an outright refusal to sell the house* **2** clear and direct: *an outright lie*

**out·right²** /aʊt'raɪt, 'aʊtˌraɪt/ *adv* **1** not trying to hide your feelings; OPENLY: *Nadine laughed outright at the suggestion.* **2** completely: *My parents own their home outright, after having worked hard to pay it off.*

**out·run** /aʊt'rʌn/ *v* [T] **1** to run faster or further than someone **2** to develop more quickly than something else: *Social needs have outrun the state's ability to provide help.*

**out·set** /'aʊtˌsɛt/ *n* **at/from the outset** at or from the beginning of an event or process: *The rules were agreed at the outset of the game.*

**out·shine** /aʊt'ʃaɪn/ *v* [T] to be much better at something than someone else

**out·side¹** /ˌaʊt'saɪd, 'aʊtsaɪd/ **outside of** *prep* **1** out of a particular building or room, but still near it: *He left an envelope outside my door.* —opposite INSIDE¹ **2** beyond the limits of a city, country etc.: *Perry lives just outside of Billings, Montana.* **3** beyond the limits of a situation, activity etc.: *She's crying, but outside of that, I don't know anything.* | *Teachers can't control what students do outside school.*

**outside²** *adv* **1** not inside any building: *Mom, can I go outside and play?* | *No, it's dark outside.* **2** not in a room or building, but close to it: *Wait outside; I want to talk to him alone.*

**outside³** *n* **1** the outer part or surface of something: *They painted the outside of the building pink.* —opposite INSIDE² **2** the area of land around something such as a building: *From the outside the house looked very nice.* **3 on the outside** used in order to describe the way someone or something appears to be: *Their marriage seemed so perfect on the outside.*

**out·sid·er** /aʊt'saɪdɚ/ *n* someone who does not belong to a particular group, organization etc.: *Corran is a Washington outsider who has never been in office before.*

**out·skirts** /'aʊtskɚts/ *n* [plural] the parts of a city or town that are farthest from the center: *He lived on the outskirts of town.*

**out·smart** /aʊt'smɑrt/ *v* [T] to gain an advantage over someone using tricks or your intelligence: *He was mad because he had been outsmarted by his brother.*

**out·sourc·ing** /'aʊtsɔrsɪŋ/ *n* [U] the practice of using workers from outside a company, or of buying supplies, parts etc. from another company instead of producing them yourself

**out·spo·ken** /aʊt'spoʊkən/ *adj* expressing your opinions honestly even if they shock or offend other people: *an outspoken critic of the program* —**outspokenness** *n* [U]

**out·stand·ing** /aʊt'stændɪŋ/ *adj* **1** better than anyone or anything else; excellent: *an outstanding performance* **2** not yet done, paid, or solved: *an outstanding debt*

**out·stretched** /ˌaʊt'strɛtʃt/ *adj* reaching out to full length: *I took hold of his outstretched arm.*

**out·strip** /aʊt'strɪp/ *v* [T] to be larger, greater, or better than someone or something else: *The gains will outstrip the losses.*

**out·ward¹** /'aʊtwɚd/ *adj* **1** relating to how people, things etc. seem to be rather than how they are: *Amy answered with a look of outward calm.* **2** going away from a place or toward the outside: *The outward flight was bumpy.* —compare INWARD¹

**outward²**, **outwards** *adv* toward the outside: *The door opens outward.* —compare INWARD²

**out·ward·ly** /ˈaʊtˈwɚdli/ *adv* according to how people, things etc. seem to be rather than how they are inside: *Outwardly he seems to be very happy.*

**out·weigh** /aʊtˈweɪ/ *v* [T] to be more important or valuable than something else: *The advantages far outweigh the disadvantages.*

**out·wit** /aʊtˈwɪt/ *v* -witted, -witting [T] ⇨ OUTSMART

**o·val** /ˈoʊvəl/ *n* a shape like a circle, but longer than it is wide —**oval** *adj* —see picture at SHAPE

**o·va·ry** /ˈoʊvəri/ *n* the part of a female that produces eggs —**ovarian** /oʊˈvɛriən/ *adj*

**o·va·tion** /oʊˈveɪʃən/ *n* FORMAL if people give someone an ovation, they CLAP their hands to show approval: *The performance received a standing ovation.* —compare ENCORE

**ov·en** /ˈʌvən/ *n* a piece of equipment that food is cooked inside, shaped like a metal box with a door on it —see picture at KITCHEN

**over**

The truck is driving over the bridge.
The ferry is going across the river.

**o·ver¹** /ˈoʊvɚ/ *prep* **1** above or higher than something, without touching it: *I leaned over the desk.* | *The sign over the door said "No Exit."* | *The ball went way over* (=a long way above) *my head.* —opposite UNDER¹ —compare ABOVE¹, ACROSS¹ —see also picture at ABOVE¹ **2** moving across the top of something, or from one side of it to the other: *We walked over the hill.* | *The boy leaped over the stream.* —compare ACROSS¹ **3** on something or someone so that he, she, or it is covered: *Put this blanket over him.* —opposite UNDER¹ **4** more than a particular amount, number, or age: *He told me he spent over $1000 last week.* | *a game for children over seven* **5 over on** on the opposite side of something from where you are: *Jamie lives over on Wicker Ave.* **6** during: *I saw Julie over the summer.* **7** down from the edge of something: *Hang the towel over the back of the chair.* **8 be/get over sth** to feel better after being sick or upset: *He's mad, but he'll get over it.* **9** about or concerning something: *They had an argument over who would take the car.* **10** using the telephone or a radio: *The sales-*

man explained it to me over the phone. —see also **all over** (ALL²)

**over²** *adv* **1** down from an upright position: *Kate fell over and hurt her ankle.* | *I saw him push the bike over.* **2** used in order to show where someone or something is: *I'm over here!* | *There's a mailbox over on the corner.* **3** to or in a particular place: *We drove over to Macon County to the fair.* | *The weather's awful. Why don't you stay over?* (=in my house) **4** above: *You can't hear anything when the planes fly over.* **5** again: *I got mixed up and had to start over.* | *She sings the same song over and over (again).* (=repeatedly) **6 think/talk sth over** to think or talk about something carefully or thoroughly before deciding what to do: *Think it over, and give us your answer tomorrow.* **7** so that another side is showing: *He rolled over and went to sleep.* **8** from one person or group to another: *The land was handed over* (=given) *to the government.* **9** more or higher than a particular amount, number, or age: *"Did you guess the right number?" "No, I was over by two."* (=the number I guessed was two higher) | *a game for children aged six and over*

**over³** *adj* **1** finished: *The game's over - Dallas won.* **2 get sth over with** to do something unpleasant so that you do not have to worry about it any more: *Well, call her and get it over with.*

**o·ver·all¹** /ˈoʊvɚˌɔl/ *adj* including everything: *The overall cost of the trip is $500.*

**o·ver·all²** /ˌoʊvɚˈɔl/ *adv* **1** generally: *Overall, the situation looks good.* **2** including everything: *Inflation is growing at 3% a year overall.*

**overalls**

overalls          coveralls

**o·ver·alls** /ˈoʊvɚˌɔlz/ *n* [plural] heavy cotton pants with a piece that covers your chest, held up by two bands that go over your shoulders

**o·ver·awed** /ˌoʊvɚˈɔd/ *adj* feeling great respect or fear: *Laura was overawed by the size of the house.*

**o·ver·bear·ing** /ˌoʊvɚˈbɛrɪŋ/ *adj* always trying to control other people without considering their feelings or needs; DOMINEERING

**o·ver·board** /ˈoʊvɚˌbɔrd/ *adv* **1** over the side of a ship into the water: *He fell overboard by accident.* **2 go overboard** INFORMAL to do or say something that is too extreme for a particular situation, for example by being too emotional or expensive: *She managed to find a nice present, without going overboard.*

**o·ver·bur·dened** /ˌoʊvəˈbɚdnd/ *adj* carrying or doing too much: *overburdened freeways | the overburdened court system*

**o·ver·cast** /ˈoʊvəˌkæst/ *adj* dark because of clouds: *a gray overcast sky*

**o·ver·charge** /ˌoʊvəˈtʃɑrdʒ/ *v* [I,T] to charge someone too much money for something

**o·ver·coat** /ˈoʊvəˌkoʊt/ *n* a long thick warm coat

**o·ver·come** /ˌoʊvəˈkʌm/ *v* **1** [T] to succeed in controlling a feeling or problem: *I'm trying to overcome my fear of flying.* **2 be overcome (by sth)** to be made weak, unconscious, or unable to control your feelings: *She was overcome by smoke.* **3** [I,T] to fight and win against someone or something: *Antiaircraft guns were used to overcome the enemy.*

**o·ver·com·pen·sate** /ˌoʊvəˈkɑmpənˌseɪt/ *v* [I] to try to correct a weakness or mistake by doing too much of the opposite thing –**overcompensation** /ˌoʊvəˌkɑmpənˈseɪʃən/ *n* [U]

**o·ver·crowd·ed** /ˌoʊvəˈkraʊdɪd◂/ *adj* filled with too many people or things: *an overcrowded classroom*

**o·ver·do** /ˌoʊvəˈdu/ *v* [T] to do or use too much of something: *When exercising you have to be careful not to **overdo it**.*

**o·ver·done** /ˌoʊvəˈdʌn/ *adj* cooked too much: *an overdone steak*

**o·ver·dose** /ˈoʊvəˌdoʊs/ *n* too much of a drug taken at one time: *He died from a heroin overdose.* –**overdose** *v* [I]

**o·ver·draw** /ˌoʊvəˈdrɔ/ *v* [T] to have spent more money than the amount you have in the bank

**o·ver·due** /ˌoʊvəˈdu◂/ *adj* **1** not done or happening when expected; late: *an overdue library book* **2 be overdue (for sth)** to have needed something done for a long time: *Salary increases are **long overdue**.*

**o·ver·eat** /ˌoʊvəˈit/ *v* [I] to eat too much, or more than is healthy

**o·ver·es·ti·mate** /ˌoʊvəˈɛstəˌmeɪt/ *v* **1** [I,T] to think that something is larger, more expensive, or more important than it really is **2** [T] to think that someone is more skillful, intelligent etc. than s/he really is –opposite UNDERESTIMATE

**o·ver·ex·tend** /ˌoʊvəɪkˈstɛnd/ *v* [T] to try to do too much or use too much of something, causing problems: *Even with extra people working, they're **overextending themselves**.* –**overextended** *adj*

**o·ver·flow**[1] /ˌoʊvəˈfloʊ/ *v* [I,T] **1** if a liquid or river overflows, it goes over the edges of the container or place where it is: *a sink **overflowing with** water* **2** if people overflow a place, there are too many of them to fit into it

**o·ver·flow**[2] /ˈoʊvəˌfloʊ/ *n* [C,U] the people, water etc. that cannot be contained in a place because it is already full: *the **overflow** of people from the concert*

overflow

**o·ver·grown** /ˌoʊvəˈgroʊn◂/ *adj* covered with plants that have grown without being controlled: *a yard **overgrown with** weeds*

**o·ver·hand** /ˈoʊvəˌhænd/ *adj, adv* thrown with your arm above the level of your shoulder: *an overhand pitch*

**o·ver·hang** /ˌoʊvəˈhæŋ/ *v* [I,T] to hang over something or stick out above it: *tree branches overhanging the path* –**overhang** /ˈoʊvəˌhæŋ/ *n*

**o·ver·haul** /ˌoʊvəˈhɔl, ˈoʊvəˌhɔl/ *v* [T] to repair or change all the parts of a machine, system etc. that need it –**overhaul** /ˈoʊvəˌhɔl/ *n*

**o·ver·head**[1] /ˌoʊvəˈhɛd◂/ *adj, adv* above your head: *A plane flew overhead. | an overhead light*

**o·ver·head**[2] /ˈoʊvəˌhɛd/ *n* money that you spend for rent, electricity etc. to keep a business operating

**o·ver·hear** /ˌoʊvəˈhɪr/ *v* [T] to hear by accident what other people are saying when they do not know that you are listening: *I overheard some people saying that the food was bad.* –compare EAVESDROP

**o·ver·joyed** /ˌoʊvəˈdʒɔɪd/ *adj* extremely happy because something good has happened: *We were **overjoyed to hear** that they are getting married.*

**o·ver·kill** /ˈoʊvəˌkɪl/ *n* [U] INFORMAL more of something than is necessary or desirable: *Starting Christmas advertising in August seems like overkill.*

**o·ver·land** /ˈoʊvəˌlænd/ *adj, adv* across land, not by sea or air: *traveling overland to Ayers Rock*

**o·ver·lap** /ˌoʊvəˈlæp/ *v* **-pped, -pping** [I,T] **1** if two or more things overlap, part of one thing covers part of another thing: *a pattern of overlapping circles* **2** if two subjects, activities, ideas etc. overlap, they share some but not all of the same parts or qualities –**overlap** /ˈoʊvəˌlæp/ *n* [C,U]

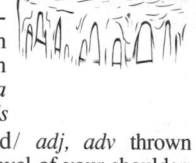
overlap

overlapping roof tiles

**o·ver·load** /ˌoʊvəˈloʊd/ *v* [T] **1** to load something with too many things or people: *Don't **overload** the washing machine **with** clothes.* **2** to give someone too much work to do **3** to damage an electrical system by causing too much electricity to flow through it –**overload** /ˈoʊvəˌloʊd/ *n* [C,U]

**o·ver·look** /ˌoʊvɚ'lʊk/ *v* [T] **1** to not notice something or to not realize how important it is: *It's easy to overlook mistakes when reading your own writing.* **2** to forgive someone's mistake, bad behavior etc.: *I'm willing to overlook what you said this time.* **3** to have a view of something from above: *a room overlooking the beach*

**o·ver·ly** /'oʊvɚli/ *adv* too much, or very: *We weren't overly impressed with the movie.*

**o·ver·night**[1] /ˌoʊvɚ'naɪt/ *adv* **1** for or during the night: *She's staying overnight at a friend's house.* **2** INFORMAL suddenly: *You can't expect to lose the weight overnight.*

**o·ver·night**[2] /'oʊvɚnaɪt/ *adj* continuing all night: *an overnight flight to Japan*

**o·ver·pass** /'oʊvɚpæs/ *n* a structure like a bridge that allows one road to go over another road

**o·ver·pop·u·lat·ed** /ˌoʊvɚ'pɑpyəˌleɪtɪd/ *adj* having too many people: *an overpopulated city* –**overpopulation** /ˌoʊvɚˌpɑpyə'leɪʃən/ *n* [U]

**o·ver·pow·er** /ˌoʊvɚ'paʊɚ/ *v* [T] to defeat someone because you are stronger

**o·ver·pow·er·ing** /ˌoʊvɚ'paʊərɪŋ/ *adj* very strong; INTENSE: *an overpowering smell*

**o·ver·priced** /ˌoʊvɚ'praɪst/ *adj* too expensive

**o·ver·rat·ed** /ˌoʊvɚ'reɪtɪd/ *adj* something or someone that is overrated is not as good or important as some people think: *I think rave music is overrated.* –**overrate** *v* [T] –compare UNDERRATED

**o·ver·re·act** /ˌoʊvɚri'ækt/ *v* [I] to react to something with too much anger or surprise, or by doing more than is necessary: *The fight started when Mark made a joke about Wayne, and Wayne overreacted.* –**overreaction** /ˌoʊvɚri'ækʃən/ *n* [C,U]

**o·ver·ride** /ˌoʊvɚ'raɪd/ *v* [T] **1** to change someone's decision because you have the authority to do so: *Congress has overridden the President's veto.* **2** to be more important than something else: *The state of the economy seems to override other political and social questions.*

**o·ver·rid·ing** /ˌoʊvɚ'raɪdɪŋ/ *adj* more important than anything else: *Security is of overriding importance.*

**o·ver·rule** /ˌoʊvɚ'rul/ *v* [T] to officially change someone's order or decision because you think that it is wrong: *"Objection overruled," said Judge Klein.*

**o·ver·run** /ˌoʊvɚ'rʌn/ *v* **1** [T] to spread over a place quickly and in great numbers, harming that place: *a town overrun with tourists* **2** to continue beyond a limit: *The meeting overran by half an hour.* –**overrun** /'oʊvɚˌrʌn/ *n*

**o·ver·seas** /ˌoʊvɚ'siz/ *adj, adv* to or in a foreign country that is across the ocean: *I'm going to study overseas.* | *an overseas tour*

**o·ver·see** /ˌoʊvɚ'si/ *v* [T] to watch a group of workers to be sure that a piece of work is done correctly; SUPERVISE: *Bentley is overseeing the project.* –**overseer** /'oʊvɚˌsiɚ/ *n*

**o·ver·shad·ow** /ˌoʊvɚ'ʃædoʊ/ *v* [T] to make someone seem less important by being more successful than s/he is: *He felt constantly overshadowed by his older brother.*

**o·ver·shoot** /ˌoʊvɚ'ʃut/ *v* [I,T] to miss a TARGET or a place where you wanted to stop or turn, by going too far past it: *I overshot the turn, and had to go back.*

**o·ver·sight** /'oʊvɚsaɪt/ *n* [C,U] a mistake that you make by not noticing something or by forgetting to do something: *We apologize for the oversight; your refund will be mailed to you immediately.*

**o·ver·sim·pli·fy** /ˌoʊvɚ'sɪmpləˌfaɪ/ *v* [I,T] to make a problem or situation seem more simple than it really is, by ignoring important facts –**oversimplification** /ˌoʊvɚˌsɪmpləfə'keɪʃən/ *n* [C,U]

**o·ver·sleep** /ˌoʊvɚ'slip/ *v* [I] to sleep for longer than you intended

**o·ver·state** /ˌoʊvɚ'steɪt/ *v* [T] to talk about something in a way that makes it seem more important, serious etc. than it really is; EXAGGERATE: *I don't believe I'm overstating the danger of hiking alone.* –opposite UNDERSTATE

**o·ver·step** /ˌoʊvɚ'stɛp/ *v* [T] to go beyond an acceptable limit: *Wilson has clearly overstepped his authority.*

**o·vert** /oʊ'vɚt, 'oʊvɚt/ *adj* FORMAL done or shown in public or in an open way: *overt discrimination* –**overtly** *adv*

**o·ver·take** /ˌoʊvɚ'teɪk/ *v* [T] **1** to have a sudden and unexpected effect on someone: *He was overtaken by exhaustion.* **2** to develop or increase more quickly than someone else

**over-the-count·er** /ˌ.. . '..ɪ/ *adj* over-the-counter drugs can be bought without a PRESCRIPTION (=written order) from a doctor

**o·ver·throw** /ˌoʊvɚ'θroʊ/ *v* [T] to remove a leader or government from power by force: *Rebel forces have made an attempt to overthrow the government.* –**overthrow** /'oʊvɚˌθroʊ/ *n* [U]

**o·ver·time** /'oʊvɚˌtaɪm/ *n* [U] time that you work on your job in addition to your usual working hours: *Are you going to work any overtime this weekend?*

**o·ver·ture** /'oʊvɚtʃɚ, -ˌtʃʊr/ *n* **1** a piece of music written as an introduction to a longer musical piece, especially an OPERA **2** also **overtures** an attempt to be friendly with a person, group, or country: *Neither country is willing to make peace overtures to the other.*

**o·ver·turn** /ˌoʊvɚ'tɚn/ *v* **1** [I,T] if something overturns or you overturn it, it turns upside down or falls over on its side: *The truck had overturned.* | *The kids overturned the table while* they were playing. **2 overturn a ruling/ verdict/law** to change a decision made by a court so that it becomes the opposite of what it was before

**o·ver·view** /ˈoʊvɚˌvyu/ *n* a short description of a subject or situation that gives the main ideas without explaining all the details: *an overview of the history of the region*

**o·ver·weight** /ˌoʊvɚˈweɪt◂/ *adj* too heavy or too fat: *I'm ten pounds overweight.* —see usage note at FAT

**o·ver·whelm** /ˌoʊvɚˈwɛlm/ *v* [T] if a feeling overwhelms someone, s/he feels it very strongly: *Gary was overwhelmed with sadness.* —**overwhelmed** *adj*

**o·ver·whelm·ing** /ˌoʊvɚˈwɛlmɪŋ/ *adj* **1** affecting someone very strongly: *Shari felt an overwhelming urge/need to cry.* **2** extremely large or great: *an overwhelming number/ majority* —**overwhelmingly** *adv*

**o·ver·worked** /ˌoʊvɚˈwɚkt◂/ *adj* working too much and for too long: *an overworked teacher* —**overwork** *n* [U]

**o·ver·wrought** /ˌoʊvɚˈrɔt◂/ *adj* very upset, nervous, and worried

**ow** /aʊ/ *interjection* said in order to show that something hurts you: *Ow! That hurt!*

**owe** /oʊ/ *v* [T] **1** to have to pay someone because s/he has allowed you to borrow money: *Bob owes me $20.* **2** to feel grateful to someone, or to feel that you should do something for someone because s/he has done something for you: *Jane will watch the kids - she owes me a favor anyway.*

**owing to** /ˈ.. ./ *prep* because of: *Work on the building has stopped, owing to lack of money.*

**owl** /aʊl/ *n* a bird that hunts at night and has large eyes and a loud call —see also NIGHT OWL

**own**[1] /oʊn/ *determiner, pron* **1** belonging to or done by a particular person and no one else: *She wants her own room.* | *You have to learn to make your own decisions.* | *He decided to start a business of his own.* **2 (all) on your own a)** alone: *Rick is home on his own.* **b)** without help: *Did you make that all on your own?*

**own**[2] *v* [T] to legally have something because you bought it or have been given it: *He owns two houses in Utah.*

**own up** *phr v* [I] to admit that you have done something wrong: *He'll never own up to his mistakes.*

**own·er** /ˈoʊnɚ/ *n* someone who owns something: *the owner of the dog* | *a home owner* —**ownership** *n* [U]

**ox** /aks/ *n, plural* **oxen** /ˈaksən/ a male cow that has had part of its sex organs removed

**ox·ide** /ˈaksaɪd/ *n* [C,U] TECHNICAL a chemical compound of an ELEMENT and oxygen

**ox·i·dize** /ˈaksəˌdaɪz/ *v* [I,T] TECHNICAL to combine with oxygen, especially when this causes RUST, or to make something do this

**ox·y·gen** /ˈaksɪdʒən/ *n* [U] a gas in the air that has no color, smell, or taste, and that all plants and animals need in order to live

**oys·ter** /ˈɔɪstɚ/ *n* [C,U] a small sea animal that has a shell and can produce a jewel called a PEARL, or the meat of this animal

**oz.** the written abbreviation of OUNCE or ounces

**o·zone lay·er** /ˈoʊzoʊn ˌleɪɚ/ *n* [singular] a layer of gases that prevents harmful RADIATION from the sun from reaching the Earth

# P

**P, p** /pi/ the sixteenth letter of the English alphabet

**p.** *plural* **pp.** the written abbreviation of PAGE and PAGEs

**PA**[1] the written abbreviation of Pennsylvania

**PA**[2] *n* [C usually singular] public address system; electronic equipment that makes someone's voice loud enough to be heard by a large group of people

**pa** /pɑ/ *n* OLD-FASHIONED father

**PAC** /pæk/ *n* [singular] political action committee; an organization that tries to influence politicians so that they support the group's aims, for example by voting in a particular way

**pace**[1] /peɪs/ *n* **1** [singular] the speed or rate at which something happens or at which you do something such as move, work etc.: *We were walking at a steady/slow pace.* | *He likes to work at his own pace.* **2 keep pace (with)** to move or change as fast as something or someone else: *Supply has to keep pace with increasing demand.*

**pace**[2] *v* [I,T] **1** to walk backward and forward when you are waiting or worried about something: *Darren paced back and forth in the waiting room.* **2 pace yourself** to do something at a steady speed so you do not get tired too quickly

**pace·mak·er** /ˈpeɪsˌmeɪkɚ/ *n* a very small machine that is attached to someone's heart to help it beat regularly

**pace·set·ter** /ˈpeɪsˌsɛt̬ɚ/ *n* someone or something that sets an example for others: *The pacesetter for high-speed trains is the French TGV.*

**Pacific O·cean** /pəˌsɪfɪk ˈoʊʃən/ *n* **the Pacific** the large ocean between Asia and Australia in the west, and North and South America in the east

**Pacific Rim** /.,.. ˈ./ *n* **the Pacific Rim** the land and islands that are around the edges of the Pacific Ocean, especially in Asia

**pac·i·fi·er** /ˈpæsəˌfaɪɚ/ *n* a rubber object that a baby sucks on so that s/he does not cry

**pac·i·fism** /ˈpæsəˌfɪzəm/ *n* [U] the belief that all wars and forms of violence are wrong – **pacifist** *n*

**pac·i·fy** /ˈpæsəˌfaɪ/ *v* [T] to make someone calm and quiet after s/he has been angry or upset: *a father pacifying a crying child*

**pack**[1] /pæk/ *v* **1** [I,T] also **pack up** to put things into boxes, SUITCASEs, bags etc. in order to take or store them somewhere: *I never pack until the night before a trip. | Juanita packed up the glassware. | Can you pack the kids' lunches?* **2** [I,T] if a crowd of people packs a place, there are so many of them that the place is too full: *Thousands of people packed the stadium.* **3** [T] to cover, fill, or surround something closely with material to protect it: *Pack some newspaper around the bottles.* **4** [T] to press soil, snow etc. down firmly: *The packed snow crunched under our feet.*

**pack** sb/sth ↔ **in** *phr v* [T] INFORMAL to attract a lot of people, or to try to put a lot of people or things somewhere: *Bryan Adams' concerts always **pack** them **in**.*

**pack** sth **into** sth *phr v* [T] to fit a lot of something into a space, place, or period of time: *We packed a lot of travel into our vacation.*

**pack** sb/sth **off** *phr v* [T] INFORMAL to send someone away quickly in order to get rid of him/her: *Our folks **packed** us **off** to camp every summer.*

**pack up** *phr v* [I] INFORMAL to finish work: *I think I'll **pack up** and go home early.*

**pack**[2] *n* **1** a small container that holds a set of things: *a pack of cigarettes/cards/gum* – see picture at CONTAINER **2** a group of wild animals that live and hunt together: *a wolf pack* **3** a group of people: *a pack of reporters yelling questions* **4** several things wrapped or tied together to make them easy to sell, carry, or send: *a gift pack of beauty products | a six-pack of beer* **5** ⇨ BACKPACK[1]

**pack·age**[1] /ˈpækɪdʒ/ *n* **1** the box, bag etc. that food is put in for selling: *a package of peanut butter cookies* **2** something packed into a box, wrapped in paper, especially for mailing **3** a set of related things or services that are sold or offered together: *a new software package | a package tour to the Southwest* (=including room, meals etc.)

**package**[2] *v* [T] **1** to put something in a special package, especially to be sold: *candy packaged in cellophane bags* **2** to try to make an idea, person etc. seem interesting or attractive so that people will like it or buy it: *a new band packaged to appeal to teenage girls*

**pack·ag·ing** /ˈpækɪdʒɪŋ/ *n* [U] **1** bags, boxes etc. that contain a product that is sold in a store: *Putting apples in packaging seems completely unnecessary.* **2** a way of making something seem attractive or interesting to people so that they will buy it: *the packaging of a best-selling novel*

**packed** /pækt/ *adj* **1** extremely full of people or things: *The theater was packed. | a box packed full of books* **2** if you are packed, you have put everything you need into boxes or cases before going on a trip: *OK, I'm all packed.*

**pack·er** /ˈpækɚ/ *n* someone whose job is to pack goods that are to be moved or sold

**pack·et** /ˈpækɪt/ *n* a small envelope containing a group of things: *a packet of carrot seeds* – see picture at CONTAINER

**pack·ing** /ˈpækɪŋ/ *n* [U] **1** the act of putting things into cases or boxes so that you can send or take them somewhere: *I usually do my packing the night before I leave.* **2** paper, plastic, cloth etc. used for packing things

**packing case** /ˈ.. ˌ./ *n* a large strong wooden box in which things are packed in order to be sent somewhere or stored

**pack rat** /ˈ. ./ *n* INFORMAL someone who collects and stores things that s/he does not really need

**pact** /pækt/ *n* a formal agreement between two groups, nations, or people: *The two countries will sign a non-aggression pact.*

**pad**[1] /pæd/ *n* **1** a thick piece of soft material used for protecting something or making it more comfortable: *the knee and shoulder pads that football players wear | Ken slept on a foam pad on the floor.* **2** many sheets of paper fastened together, used for writing letters, drawing pictures etc.: *a memo pad*

**pad**[2] *v* **-dded, -dding 1** [T] to protect something, shape it, or make it more comfortable by covering or filling it with soft material: *Doug padded a box for the kitten to sleep in.* **2** [I] to walk softly and quietly: *a cat padding across the floor* **3** [T] INFORMAL to add something unnecessary to a document or speech to make it longer, or to a price to make it higher: *They realized that their lawyer was padding the court fees.*

**pad·ding** /ˈpædɪŋ/ *n* [U] material that fills or covers something to make it softer or more comfortable: *The padding is coming out of the car seat.*

**pad·dle**[1] /ˈpædl/ *n* **1** a short pole with a wide flat end, used for moving a small boat along – compare OAR – see picture at KAYAK **2** an object used for hitting the ball in PING-PONG, consisting of a round flat top on a short handle

**paddle**[2] *v* [I,T] to move a small boat through water, using a PADDLE: *We paddled across the lake to the beach.* – see also DOG PADDLE

**pad·dock** /'pædək/ *n* a small enclosed field in which horses are kept

**pad·dy** /'pædi/, **rice paddy** *n* a field in which rice is grown in water

**pad·lock** /'pædlɑk/ *n* a small metal lock that hangs, that you can put on a door, bicycle etc. —**padlock** *v* [T]

**padlock**

**pa·dre** /'pɑdrɪ, -dɪi/ *n* INFORMAL a priest, especially one in the army

**pa·gan** /'peɪgən/ *n* someone who does not believe in any of the main religions of the world, but believes instead in many gods —**pagan** *adj*

**page¹** /peɪdʒ/ *n* **1** one side of a sheet of paper in a book, newspaper, etc., or the sheet itself: *Do the exercises on page 10 for homework.* | *The story was on the **front page** of every newspaper.* | *There's a page missing from this comic book.* **2** a young person who works in a government office for a short time in order to gain experience

**page²** *v* [T] **1** to call someone's name in a public place, especially using a LOUDSPEAKER: *We couldn't find Jan at the airport, so we **had her paged.*** **2** to call someone using a BEEPER (=small machine that receives messages)

**pag·eant** /'pædʒənt/ *n* **1** a public show or ceremony that usually shows an event in history **2** a competition for young women in which their beauty and other qualities are judged

**pag·eant·ry** /'pædʒəntri/ *n* [U] impressive ceremonies or events, involving many people wearing special clothes: *the pageantry of a royal wedding*

**pag·er** /'peɪdʒɚ/ *n* ⇨ BEEPER

**pa·go·da** /pə'goudə/ *n* an Asian TEMPLE that has several levels, with a decorated roof at each level

**paid** /peɪd/ *v* the past tense and PAST PARTICIPLE of PAY

**pail** /peɪl/ *n* a container with a handle, used for carrying liquids or by children when playing on the beach; BUCKET: *We picked two pails of blackberries.* (=enough to fill two pails)

**pain¹** /peɪn/ *n* **1** [C,U] the feeling you have when part of your body hurts: *Soldiers lay groaning **in pain** (=feeling pain) on the ground.* | *The drugs don't do much to **relieve** her pain.* (=make it hurt less) | *Wes **has a pain in** his lower back.* **2 be a pain in the ass/butt** SPOKEN an impolite expression meaning to be extremely annoying **3 be a pain (in the neck)** SPOKEN to be very annoying: *This pan is great to cook with, but it's a pain to wash.* **4** [C,U] emotional or mental suffering: *the pain children feel when their parents divorce* —see also PAINS

**pain²** *v* [T] FORMAL to make someone feel unhappy: *It pains me to see my mother growing old.*

**pained** /peɪnd/ *adj* worried and upset: *a pained look on his face*

**pain·ful** /'peɪnfəl/ *adj* **1** making you feel physical pain: *a painful injury* **2** making you feel very unhappy: *painful memories of the war* **3** very bad and embarrassing for other people to watch, hear etc.: *The acting in the movie was so bad, it was painful to watch.*

**pain·ful·ly** /'peɪnfəli/ *adv* **1** with pain, or causing pain: *Mike walked slowly and painfully to the door.* | *People can be painfully cruel to each other.* **2 painfully obvious/clear etc.** a fact or situation that is painfully obvious etc., is so easy to notice that it is embarrassing: *It was painfully clear that Lynn would never be a ballet dancer.* **3** needing a lot of effort, or causing a lot of trouble: *Rebuilding the bridge was a painfully slow process.* **4** in a way that makes you sad or upset: *I was painfully aware that she didn't like me.*

**pain·kill·er** /'peɪn,kɪlɚ/ *n* a medicine that reduces or removes pain

**pain·less** /'peɪnlɪs/ *adj* **1** without pain, or causing no pain: *Giving blood is a nearly painless process.* **2** INFORMAL needing no effort or hard work: *a painless way to learn Spanish*

**pains** /peɪnz/ *n* [plural] **1 take pains** to make a special effort to do something well: *Bonnie always **takes pains to** have a nice Thanksgiving dinner.* **2 be at pains to do sth** to be very careful to do something: *The two leaders were at pains to avoid an argument.*

**pains·tak·ing** /'peɪnz,teɪkɪŋ, 'peɪn,steɪ-/ *adj* very careful and thorough: *painstaking research* —**painstakingly** *adv*

**paint¹** /peɪnt/ *n* [U] a liquid that you put on a surface to make it a particular color: *a can of yellow paint* | *The kitchen needs a fresh **coat of paint.*** (=layer of paint) —see also PAINTS

**paint**

**paint²** *v* [I,T] **1** to put paint on a surface: *What color are you painting the house?* **2** to make a picture of someone or something using paint: *Who painted your wife's portrait?* | *She likes to paint in watercolors.* **3 paint a picture of sth** to describe something in a particular way: *The letters paint an interesting picture of her life.*

**paint·box** /ˈpeɪntˌbɑks/ *n* a special box with dry blocks of colored paint in it

**paint·brush** /ˈpeɪntˌbrʌʃ/ *n* a special brush used for painting pictures or to paint rooms etc.

**paint·er** /ˈpeɪntɚ/ *n* **1** someone who paints pictures; ARTIST: *a landscape painter* **2** someone whose job is painting houses, rooms etc.: *a house painter*

**paint·ing** /ˈpeɪntɪŋ/ *n* **1** a painted picture; *a painting of a mountain landscape* **2** [U] the act of making a picture using paint: *Monet's style of painting* **3** [U] the act of covering a wall, house etc. with paint: *We spent Saturday painting the bedrooms.*

**paints** /peɪnts/ *n* [plural] a set of small tubes or blocks of paint of different colors, used for painting pictures: *a set of oil paints*

**paint thin·ner** /ˈ. ˌ../ *n* [U] a liquid that you add to paint to make it less thick

**pair**[1] /pɛr/ *n, plural* **pairs** *or* **pair** **1** something made of two parts that are joined and used together: *a pair of scissors | two pairs of jeans* **2** two things of the same kind that are used together: *a pair of socks/earrings | She has 12 pairs of shoes!* **3** two people who are standing or doing something together: *a pair of dancers | Work in pairs* (=in groups of two) *on the next exercise.* –see usage note at COUPLE[1]

---

### USAGE NOTE pair

**Pair** is a singular noun, and should be used with a singular verb: *This pair of pants doesn't fit.* | *You gave me a pair of scissors that isn't sharp.*

---

**pair**[2] **pair up** *v* [I,T] to form or be put into groups of two: *We were paired with partners in French class.*

**pair off** *phr v* [I,T] to come together or bring two people together: *The guests paired off for the first dance.*

**pa·ja·mas** /pəˈdʒɑməz, -ˈdʒæ-/ *n* [plural] a pair of loose pants and a loose shirt that you wear in bed

**pal**[1] /pæl/ *n* OLD-FASHIONED a close friend: *a college pal*

**pal**[2] *v* **-lled, -lling** OLD-FASHIONED

**pal around** *phr v* [I] to go places and do things with a friend: *Rob and Dave have been palling around with each other for years.*

**pal·ace** /ˈpælɪs/ *n* a large house where a king or queen officially lives: *Buckingham Palace*

**pal·at·a·ble** /ˈpælətəbəl/ *adj* **1** an idea, suggestion etc. that is palatable is acceptable: *It's the only health care proposal that is palatable to the voters.* **2** having an acceptable taste: *a palatable wine*

**pal·ate** /ˈpælɪt/ *n* **1** the top inside part of the mouth **2** FORMAL someone's ability to taste things: *Each course was a delight to the palate.*

**pa·la·tial** /pəˈleɪʃəl/ *adj* very large and beautifully decorated: *a palatial hotel*

**pale**[1] /peɪl/ *adj* **1** having a much lighter skin color than usual, because you are sick, frightened etc.: *Jan looked tired and pale.* **2** lighter than the usual color: *pale green walls*

**pale**[2] *v* [I] **1 pale into insignificance** to seem much less important when compared to something else: *All our troubles paled into insignificance when we heard about the war.* **2 pale in/by comparison** to seem less important, good etc. when compared to something else: *This year's profits pale in comparison to last year's.* **3** if you pale, your face becomes much whiter than usual, because you are sick, frightened etc.: *Myra paled at the sight of the blood on the floor.*

**pa·le·on·tol·o·gy** /ˌpeɪliɑnˈtɑlədʒi, -liɑn-/ *n* [U] the study of FOSSILS (=ancient animals and plants that have been preserved in rock) **–paleontologist** *n*

**pal·ette** /ˈpælɪt/ *n* a board with a curved edge and a hole for the thumb, on which a painter mixes colors

**pal·i·mo·ny** /ˈpæləˌmoʊni/ *n* [U] money that someone must pay regularly to a former partner, when they have lived together for a long time without being married

**pall**[1] /pɔl/ *n* **1** a low dark cloud of smoke, dust etc. **2** [singular] something that spoils an event or occasion that should have been happy: *The drug scandal cast a pall over* (=spoiled the happy feelings at) *the Olympics.*

**pall**[2] *v* [I] to become uninteresting or unpleasant: *The excitement of the new job began to pall after a while.*

**pall·bear·er** /ˈpɔlˌbɛrɚ/ *n* someone who helps to carry a COFFIN (=a box with a dead body inside) at a funeral

**pal·lid** /ˈpælɪd/ *adj* looking pale and unhealthy: *pallid skin*

**pal·lor** /ˈpælɚ/ *n* [singular] a pale unhealthy color of your skin or face

**palm**[1] /pɑm/ *n* **1** the inside surface of your hand between the base of your fingers and your wrist: *She held out the sea shell in the palm of her hand.* –see picture at HAND[1] **2** ⇨ PALM TREE

**palm**[2] *v* [T]

**palm sth ↔ off** *phr v* [T] to persuade someone to accept or buy something, especially by deceiving him/her: *He tried to palm off the jewelry as antiques.*

**palm read·er** /ˈ. ˌ../ *n* someone who tells you about your character or about what will happen to you by looking at your hand

**Palm Sun·day** /ˌ. ˈ../ *n* the Sunday before Easter in Christian religions

**palm tree** /ˈ. ./ *n* a tall tropical tree with large pointed leaves at its top, that grows near beaches or in deserts

**pal·pa·ble** /ˈpælpəbəl/ *adj* FORMAL easily and clearly noticed: *a palpable lie* **–palpably** *adv*

**pal·pi·ta·tions** /ˌpælpəˈteɪʃənz/ *n* [plural] irregular or extremely fast beating of your heart

**pal·try** /ˈpɔltri/ *adj* too small to be useful or important: *a paltry pay raise*

**pam·per** /ˈpæmpər/ *v* [T] to give someone too much care and attention: *She pampers her son too much.*

**pam·phlet** /ˈpæmflɪt/ *n* a very thin book with paper covers, giving information about something: *a pamphlet about evening classes at the college*

pan

lid
frying pan
saucepan
wok

**pan¹** /pæn/ *n* **1** a round metal container used for cooking, usually with a handle: *Melt the butter in a heavy pan, and stir in the flour.* **2** a metal container for baking things, or the food that this contains: *a pan of sweet rolls baking in the oven* **3** a container with low sides, used for holding liquids: *an oil pan*

**pan²** *v* **-nned, -nning** **1** [T] INFORMAL to strongly criticize a movie, play etc. in a newspaper or on television or radio: *The critics panned his first play.* **2** [I,T] to move a camera while taking a picture or follow a moving object with a camera: *The camera panned across the crowd.*

**pan for** sth *phr v* to wash soil in a pan in order to separate gold from it

**pan out** *phr v* [I] to happen or develop in the expected way: *If this trip doesn't pan out, I might go to Indonesia instead.*

**pan·a·ce·a** /ˌpænəˈsiə/ *n* something that people think will make everything better or cure any illness: *Money is not a panacea for the problems in our schools, but it can help.*

**pa·nache** /pəˈnæʃ, -ˈnɑʃ/ *n* [U] a way of doing things that is exciting and makes them seem easy: *Mr. Seaton danced with panache.*

**pan·cake** /ˈpænkeɪk/ *n* a flat round type of bread made from flour, milk, and eggs, that is cooked in a pan and eaten for breakfast

**pan·cre·as** /ˈpæŋkriəs/ *n* a GLAND in your body that helps your body to use the food you eat **–pancreatic** /ˌpæŋkriˈætɪk/ *adj*

**pan·da** /ˈpændə/ *n* a large black and white animal similar to a bear, that lives in China

**pan·de·mo·ni·um** /ˌpændəˈmoʊniəm/ *n* [U] a situation in which there is a lot of noise and confusion because people are angry, frightened, excited etc.: *There was pandemonium after UCLA won the football game.*

**pan·der** /ˈpændər/ *v*

**pander to** sth/sb *phr v* [T] to give someone what s/he wants, even though you know it is not good for him/her: *I won't read newspapers that pander to people's interest in sex and scandal.*

**pane** /peɪn/ *n* a piece of glass in a window or door

**pan·el¹** /ˈpænl/ *n* **1** a group of people who are chosen to discuss something, decide something, or answer questions: *A panel of experts was there to give advice on gardening.* **2** a sheet of wood, glass, etc. that fits into a frame to form part of a door, wall, or ceiling: *an oak door with three panels* **3** **instrument/control panel** the place in a plane, boat etc. on which the instruments or controls are fixed

**pan·el²** *v* [T] to cover or decorate something such as a wall with flat pieces of wood, glass etc.: *an oak-paneled room*

**pan·el·ing** /ˈpænl-ɪŋ/ *n* [U] wood in long pieces that is used for covering walls etc.: *pine paneling*

**pan·el·ist** /ˈpænl-ɪst/ *n* a member of a PANEL, especially on a radio or television program

**pang** /pæŋ/ *n* a sudden strong and unpleasant feeling: *hunger pangs* | *She had pangs of guilt over the way she had treated Pete.*

**pan·han·dle** /ˈpænˌhændl/ *v* [I] to ask for money in the streets; BEG **–panhandler** *n*

**pan·ic¹** /ˈpænɪk/ *n* [C,U] a sudden feeling of fear or anxiety that makes you do things without thinking carefully about them: *People ran into the streets **in a panic** when the earthquake hit.* | *There was panic on Wall Street as prices fell.*

**pan·ic²** *v* **panicked, panicked, panicking** [I,T] to suddenly feel so frightened that you do things without thinking clearly, or to make someone feel this way: *Office workers panicked when fire broke out in the building.* | *Don't shout - you'll panic the horses.* **–panicky** *adj*

**panic-strick·en** /ˈ.. ˌ../ *adj* so frightened that you cannot think clearly: *I remember the panic-stricken look on her face.*

**pan·o·ram·a** /ˌpænəˈræmə, -ˈrɑ-/ *n* a view over a wide area of land: *a **panorama of** the Rocky Mountains* **–panoramic** *adj*

**pan·sy** /ˈpænzi/ *n* **1** a small flat brightly colored garden flower **2** SPOKEN an insulting word for a man who seems weak

**pant** /pænt/ *v* [I] to breathe quickly with short noisy breaths, especially after exercising or because it is hot: *a dog panting in the heat*

**pan·the·ism** /ˈpænθiˌɪzəm/ *n* [U] the religious idea that God is present in all natural things in the universe

**pan·ther** /ˈpænθər/ *n* a large wild black cat that is good at hunting

**pant·ies** /'pænɾiz/ n [plural] a piece of women's underwear that covers the area between the waist and the top of the legs

**pan·to·mime** /'pænɾə,maɪm/ n [C,U] a method of performing using only actions and not words, or a play performed using this method

**pan·try** /'pæntri/ n a small room near the kitchen where food, dishes etc. are kept

**pants** /pænts/ n [plural] a piece of clothing that covers you from your waist to your feet and has separate parts for each leg: *Jason needs a new **pair of pants** for school.*

**pants leg** /'. ./, **pant leg** n the part of a pair of pants that covers one leg

**pant·suit** /'pæntsut/ n a women's suit consisting of a JACKET and matching pants

**pan·ty·hose** /'pænɾi,hoʊz/ n [plural] a very thin piece of women's clothing that covers the legs from the feet to the waist, usually worn with dresses or skirts

**pan·ty·lin·er** /'pænɾi,laɪnɚ/ n a very thin SANITARY NAPKIN

**pa·pa** /'pɑpə/ n OLD-FASHIONED ⇨ FATHER¹

**pa·pa·cy** /'peɪpəsi/ n **the papacy** the position and authority of the POPE

**pa·pal** /'peɪpəl/ adj relating to the POPE

**pa·pa·ya** /pə'paɪə/ n [C,U] a sweet juicy tropical fruit with many small seeds inside it

**pa·per¹** /'peɪpɚ/ n **1** [U] thin sheets used for writing or drawing on, wrapping things in etc.: *a piece of writing paper | a paper plate* **2** a newspaper: *Have you seen today's paper? | an ad in the **local paper*** (=the newspaper for the area you live in) **3** a piece of writing that is done as part of a class: *My history paper is due tomorrow.* **4 on paper** if an idea seems good on paper, it seems good or true but has not been tested in a real situation yet: *It looks good on paper, but I still don't think it will work.* **5** a piece of writing or a speech by someone who has studied a particular subject: *She's **giving a paper on** global warming at the conference.* **6** [C,U] ⇨ WALLPAPER¹ −see also PAPERS

**paper²** v [T] to decorate the walls of a room by covering them with WALLPAPER

**pa·per·back** /'peɪpɚ,bæk/ n a book with a stiff paper cover: *Her novel's just come out **in paperback**.* −compare HARDBACK

**paper boy** /'.. ,./ n a boy who delivers newspapers to people's houses

**paper clip** /'.. ,./ n a small piece of curved wire used for holding sheets of paper together

**paper girl** /'.. ,./ n a girl who delivers newspapers to people's houses

**pa·pers** /'peɪpɚz/ n [plural] important or official documents or letters, such as your WILL or your PASSPORT

**pa·per·weight** /'peɪpɚ,weɪt/ n a small heavy object that you put on top of papers so that they stay on a desk

**pa·per·work** /'peɪpɚ,wɚk/ n [U] work such as writing letters or reports, or putting information on forms, especially when done as part of a job: *I have a lot of paperwork to do tonight.*

**pa·pier-mâ·ché** /,peɪpɚ mə'ʃeɪ/ n [U] a soft substance made from a mixture of paper, water, and glue, which becomes hard when it dries

**Pap smear** /'pæp əmɪr/ n a medical test that takes cells from a woman's CERVIX and examines them for signs of CANCER

**par** /pɑr/ n [U] **1 be on a par (with)** to be of the same standard as something else: *Bruce thinks shopping is on a par with going to the dentist.* (=is as bad as going to the dentist) **2 not be up to par/be below par** to be less good than usual: *Beth is still not up to par after her operation.* **3 par for the course** to be what you would normally expect to happen: *"Lisa was late again." "That's par for the course."*

**par·a·ble** /'pærəbəl/ n a short simple story that teaches a moral or religious lesson

**par·a·chute¹** /'pærə-,ʃut/ n a large piece of cloth that is attached to your back to make you fall through the air slowly when you jump out of a plane

parachute

**parachute²** v **1** [I] to jump from a plane using a PARACHUTE: *Soldiers **parachuted into** the field during the night.* **2** [T] to drop something from a plane with a parachute: *We can **parachute** supplies **to** the troops.*

**pa·rade¹** /pə'reɪd/ n **1** a public celebration when musical bands, decorated vehicles etc. move down the street: *The city has a parade every Fourth of July.* **2** a military ceremony in which soldiers stand or march together so that they can be examined

**parade²** v **1** [I] to march together to celebrate or protest something: *Peace demonstrators **paraded** toward the Capitol Building.* **2** [I] to walk around an area in order to attract attention: *A couple of teenage girls were **parading** around the pool in their bikinis.* **3** [T] to show a particular quality or possession in order to make people notice you: *Sara tends to **parade** her money in front of her friends.* **4** [T] to show someone to the public, especially in order to prove that you have control or power over him/her: *The prisoners were **paraded** in front of the TV cameras.*

**par·a·digm** /'pærə,daɪm/ n FORMAL a model or typical example of something that explains an idea or process very clearly: *The Holocaust is a*

P

**par·a·digm** of *evil.* –**paradigmatic** /ˌpærədɪg-ˈmætɪk/ *adj*

**par·a·dise** /ˈpærəˌdaɪs, -ˌdaɪz/ *n* **1** [U] a place or situation that is as pleasant or beautiful as possible: *Hawaii is often referred to as a natural paradise.* **2** a place that has everything you need to do a particular activity: *This mall is a shopper's paradise.* **3** ⇨ HEAVEN

**par·a·dox** /ˈpærəˌdɑks/ *n* a statement or situation that seems strange or impossible because it contains two opposing ideas: *It's a paradox that a rich country has so many poor people.* –**paradoxical** /ˌpærəˈdɑksɪkəl/ *adj* –**paradoxically** *adv*

**par·af·fin** /ˈpærəfɪn/ *n* [U] a soft white substance used as a FUEL or for making CANDLES

**par·a·gon** /ˈpærəˌgɑn/ *n* someone who is a perfect example of something: *Mrs. Ives considered herself to be a paragon of virtue.*

**par·a·graph** /ˈpærəˌgræf/ *n* a group of several sentences that deal with one idea in a piece of writing

**par·a·keet** /ˈpærəˌkit/ *n* a small brightly colored bird with a long tail, that is often kept as a pet

**par·a·le·gal** /ˌpærəˈligəl/ *n* someone whose job is to help a lawyer do his/her work

**par·al·lel**[1] /ˈpærəˌlɛl/ *n* a connection or SIMILARITY between two things that happen or exist in different places or at different times: *The article draws a **parallel between** the political situation now and the situation in the 1930s.* (=it shows how they are similar)

**parallel**[2] *adj* two lines that are parallel to each other are the same distance apart along their whole length: *a street **running parallel to** (=that is parallel to) the railroad*

**parallel**[3] *v* [T] FORMAL to be very similar to something else: *The Greek stories about Dionysus parallel the Roman ones about Bacchus.*

**pa·ral·y·sis** /pəˈræləsɪs/ *n* [U] **1** the loss of the ability to move or feel part of your body: *Such injuries can cause permanent paralysis.* **2** a lack of ability to operate correctly or to do anything: *So what's causing the tax bill paralysis in Congress?*

**par·a·lyt·ic** /ˌpærəˈlɪtɪk/ *n* someone who is completely PARALYZEd –**paralytic** *adj*

**par·a·lyze** /ˈpærəˌlaɪz/ *v* [T] **1** to make someone lose the ability to move part of his/her body, or to feel anything in it **2** to make something stop being able to operate, or to make someone unable to do anything: *Heavy snow has paralyzed several cities in the eastern States.* –**paralyzed** *adj*: *The stroke left him paralyzed and unable to feed himself.*

**par·a·med·ic** /ˌpærəˈmɛdɪk/ *n* someone who usually works in an AMBULANCE and is trained to help sick or injured people, but is not a doctor or nurse

**pa·ram·et·er** /pəˈræmətɚ/ *n* a limit that controls the way that something should be done: *Congress will decide on **parameters for** the investigation.*

**par·a·mil·i·tar·y** /ˌpærəˈmɪləˌtɛri/ *adj* organized like an army, but not part of the legal military forces of a country: *a paramilitary force* –**paramilitary** *n*

**par·a·mount** /ˈpærəˌmaʊnt/ *adj* more important than anything else: *The needs of the customer should be paramount.*

**par·a·noid** /ˈpærəˌnɔɪd/ *adj* **1** DISAPPROVING extremely worried because you believe that you cannot trust other people: *Ever since her keys were stolen she's been paranoid about going into the house alone.* **2** suffering from a mental illness that makes you believe that other people are trying to harm you –**paranoia** /ˌpærəˈnɔɪə/ *n* [U]

**par·a·pher·na·lia** /ˌpærəfəˈneɪlyə, -fə-ˈneɪl-/ *n* [U] a lot of small things that belong to someone or that are used for a particular activity: *photographic paraphernalia*

**par·a·phrase** /ˈpærəˌfreɪz/ *v* [T] to express what someone has written or said in a way that is shorter or easier to understand: *Write a paragraph that paraphrases the story.* –**paraphrase** *n*

**par·a·ple·gic** /ˌpærəˈplidʒɪk/ *n* someone who is unable to move the lower part of his/her body

**par·a·site** /ˈpærəˌsaɪt/ *n* **1** a plant or animal that lives on or in another plant or animal and gets food from it **2** a lazy person who does not work but depends on other people –**parasitic** /ˌpærəˈsɪtɪk/ *adj*

**par·a·sol** /ˈpærəˌsɔl, -ˌsɑl/ *n* a type of UMBRELLA used for protection from the sun

**par·a·troop·er** /ˈpærəˌtrupɚ/ *n* a soldier who is trained to jump out of a plane using a PARACHUTE

**par·cel**[1] /ˈpɑrsəl/ *n* **1** ⇨ PACKAGE[1] **2** an area of land that is part of a larger area that has been divided

**parcel**[2] *v*

**parcel** sth ↔ **out** *phr v* [T] to divide or share something among several people or groups: *The foundation receives the money, then **parcels** it **out** to various projects.*

**parcel post** /ˌ.. ˈ./ *n* [U] the cheapest way of sending packages by mail, because it uses trains and trucks rather than planes

**parched** /pɑrtʃt/ *adj* **1** be **parched** INFORMAL to be very THIRSTY: *I'm parched!* **2** LITERARY extremely dry: *parched land*

**parch·ment** /ˈpɑrtʃmənt/ *n* [U] thick yellow-white writing paper that in past times was made of sheep or goat skin

**par·don**[1] /ˈpɑrdn/ *v* [T] **1 pardon (me)** SPOKEN **a)** used in order to politely say you are sorry when you have done something that is embarrassing or rude: *Pardon me - I hope I* *didn't hurt you.* **b)** used in order to ask someone politely to move so you can go past him/her: *Pardon me, can I just get to my seat?* **c)** said when you want to politely get someone's attention in order to ask a question: *Pardon me, is this the way to City Hall?* **d)** used in order to politely ask someone to repeat what s/he has just said: *Pardon me, could you repeat that last number again?* **e)** used before politely disagreeing with something that someone has said: *Pardon me, but I don't think that's true.* **2** to officially allow someone not to be punished, although a court has proved that s/he is guilty of a crime: *His only chance now is for the governor to pardon him.*

**pardon**[2] *n* an official order allowing someone to be free and stopping his/her punishment: *Tyler was later* **granted a pardon.** (=given one) −see also **I beg your pardon** (BEG)

**par·don·a·ble** /ˈpɑrdn-əbəl/ *adj* FORMAL possible to forgive or excuse: *a pardonable error*

**pare** /pɛr/ *v* [T] to cut off the thin outer part of something, especially a fruit or vegetable: *Pare the apples and slice them into chunks.*

**pare** sth **down** *phr v* [T] to gradually reduce an amount or number: *Production costs have to be* **pared down.**

**par·ent** /ˈpɛrənt, ˈpær-/ *n* the father or mother of a person or animal: *My parents are coming to visit next week.* −**parental** /pəˈrɛntl/ *adj*: *parental love* see picture at FAMILY

**par·ent·age** /ˈpɛrəntɪdʒ, ˈpær-/ *n* [U] someone's parents and the country they are from: *children of French-Canadian parentage*

**pa·ren·the·sis** /pəˈrɛnθəsɪs/ *n, plural* **parentheses** /-siz/ one of the marks ( ), used in writing to separate additional information from the main information: *The numbers* **in parentheses** *refer to page numbers.*

**par·ent·hood** /ˈpɛrəntˌhʊd, ˈpær-/ *n* [U] the state of being a parent

**par·ish** /ˈpærɪʃ/ *n* **1** the area served by a particular church **2** the members of a particular church −**parishoner** /pəˈrɪʃənɚ/ *n*

**par·i·ty** /ˈpærəti/ *n* [U] the state of being equal, especially having equal pay, rights, or power: *Our employees are demanding* **parity with** *other workers in the industry.*

**park**[1] /pɑrk/ *n* a large open area with grass and trees in a town, where people can walk, play games etc. −see also BALL PARK

**park**[2] *v* [I,T] to put a car in a particular place for a period of time: *Is it okay if I park here?* | *Park your car in the back lot.*

**par·ka** /ˈpɑrkə/ *n* a thick warm coat with a HOOD

**park and ride** /ˌ. . ˈ./ *n* [U] a system in which you leave your car in a special place in one part of a city and then take a bus or train from there to the center of town

**park·ing** /ˈpɑrkɪŋ/ *n* [U] **1** the act of parking a car: *Seth parked right under a "No Parking" sign.* **2** spaces in which you can leave a car: *Parking is available on Lemay Street.* | *We got a* **parking space** *near the door.*

**parking ga·rage** /ˈ.. .ˌ./ *n* an enclosed building for cars to be parked in

**parking lot** /ˈ.. ˌ./ *n* an open area for cars to be parked in

**parking me·ter** /ˈ.. ˌ./ *n* a machine that you must put money into so that you can park your car in the space next to it

**park·way** /ˈpɑrkweɪ/ *n* a wide road in or around a city, usually with grass and trees in the middle or along the sides

**par·lia·ment** /ˈpɑrləmənt/ *n* the group of people who are elected in some countries to make laws and discuss important national affairs −**parliamentary** /ˌpɑrləˈmɛntri, -ˈmɛntəri/ *adj*

**par·lor** /ˈpɑrlɚ/ *n* **1** a store or type of business that provides a particular service: *a beauty parlor* | *a funeral parlor* **2** OLD-FASHIONED a formal room in a house used especially for entertaining visitors in

**pa·ro·chi·al** /pəˈroʊkiəl/ *adj* **1** only interested in the things that affect you and your local area: *My cousin's views are fairly parochial.* **2** relating to a particular church: *a parochial school*

**par·o·dy**[1] /ˈpærədi/ *n* [C,U] a performance or a piece of writing or music that copies a particular style in a funny way: *a parody of Walt Whitman's poetry*

**parody**[2] *v* [T] to copy someone's style or attitude in a funny way: *a comedian who parodies politicians*

**pa·role** /pəˈroʊl/ *n* [U] permission for someone to leave prison, on the condition that s/he continues to behave well: *He was released* **on parole** *after serving 5 years.* −**parole** *v* [T]

**par·quet** /pɑrˈkeɪ, ˈpɑrkeɪ/ *n* [U] small flat blocks of wood laid in a pattern that covers the floor of a room

**par·rot** /ˈpærət/ *n* a brightly colored tropical bird with a curved beak that can be taught to copy human speech

**pars·ley** /ˈpɑrsli/ *n* [U] a plant with groups of curled leaves, used in cooking or as a decoration on food

**pars·nip** /ˈpɑrsnɪp/ *n* [C,U] a large thick white or pale yellow root that is eaten as a vegetable

**part**[1] /pɑrt/ *n*

**1** ▶**OF A WHOLE**◀ [C,U] a piece of something or some of something, such as an object, area, event, or period of time: *Which* **part of** *town do you live in?* | *The* **best part** *of the movie was when she hit him.* | *The* **front part** *of the car was badly damaged.* | *A* **large part of** (=a lot of) *my time is spent reading.* | *We waited for the* *better part of* (=most of) *an hour.*

**2** ▶SEPARATE PIECE◀ one of the separate pieces that something is made of: *Do you sell parts for Ford cars?*

**3 play/have a part in** to be one of several things that make something happen or be successful: *Our planes played a big part in the attack.*

**4 take part** to be involved in an activity, event etc. together with other people: *Ten runners took part in the race.*

**5** ▶WHAT SB DID◀ what someone did in an activity, especially one that was shared by several people: *We'd like to thank Walter for his part in organizing the concert.| It was a huge mistake on her part.* (=that she made)

**6** ▶IN A PLAY/MOVIE◀ the words and actions of a particular character in a play, movie etc., performed by an actor: *Kessler played/had the part of Hamlet.*

**7** ▶QUANTITY◀ a particular quantity used when measuring different substances together into a mixture: *Mix two parts sand to one part cement.*

**8** ▶HAIR◀ the line on your head made by dividing your hair with a comb

**9 for the most part** mostly, in most places, or most of the time: *She is, for the most part, a fair person.*

**10 in part** to some degree, but not completely: *The accident was due in part to the bad weather.*

**part**² *v* **1** [T] to pull the two sides of something apart, making a space in the middle: *He parted the curtains and looked out into the street.* **2** [I] FORMAL to separate from someone, or end a relationship with him/her: *The time came for them to part.* **3** [T] to divide the hair on your head into two parts with a comb so that it makes a line **4 part company a)** to separate from someone, or end a friendship or business relationship with someone **b)** to no longer agree with someone

**part with** sth *phr v* [T] to get rid of something although you do not want to: *I hated to part with those boots, but they were too old.*

**part**³ *adv* if something is part one thing, part another, it consists of both those things: *The English test is part written, part spoken.*

**par·tial** /ˈpɑrʃəl/ *adj* **1** not complete: *The party was only a partial success.* **2 be partial to sth** FORMAL to like something very much: *I'm very partial to chocolate.* **3** ⇨ BIASED

**par·ti·al·i·ty** /ˌpɑrʃiˈæləti/ *n* [U] the fact of unfairly supporting one person or group more than another: *The city council was accused of partiality in awarding contracts.*

**par·tial·ly** /ˈpɑrʃəli/ *adv* not completely: *He's only partially to blame.*

**par·tic·i·pant** /pɑrˈtɪsəpənt, pɚ-/ *n* someone who is taking part in an activity or event

**par·tic·i·pate** /pɑrˈtɪsəˌpeɪt, pɚ-/ *v* [I] to take part in an activity or event: *I'd like to thank everyone who participated in tonight's show.*

**par·ti·ci·pa·tion** /pɑrˌtɪsəˈpeɪʃən, pɚ-/ *n* [U] the act of taking part in something: *The participation of the public in the recycling program has been really great.*

**par·ti·ci·ple** /ˈpɑrtəˌsɪpəl/ *n* TECHNICAL in grammar, the form of a verb, usually ending in "-ing" or "-ed," that is used in compounds to make verb tenses, or as an adjective or GERUND —see also PAST PARTICIPLE, PRESENT PARTICIPLE

**par·ti·cle** /ˈpɑrtɪkəl/ *n* a very small piece of something: *dust particles*

**par·tic·u·lar**¹ /pɚˈtɪkyələ/ *adj* **1** a particular thing or person is the one that you are talking about, and not any other: *I'm looking for a particular book; can you help me?* ✗ DON'T SAY "a book that is particular." ✗ **2** special or important enough to mention separately: *There was nothing in the letter of particular importance.* **3** very careful about choosing exactly what you like, and not easily satisfied; FUSSY: *He's very particular about what he eats.*

**particular**² *n* **in particular** special or specific: *Is there anything in particular I can help you with?*

**par·tic·u·lar·ly** /pɚˈtɪkyələli, -ˈtɪkyəli/ *adv* especially: *She isn't particularly attractive.*

**part·ing**¹ /ˈpɑrtɪŋ/ *n* [C,U] FORMAL an occasion when two people leave each other

**parting**² *adj* **a parting kiss/gift/glance etc.** something that you give someone as you leave

**par·ti·san** /ˈpɑrtəzən, -sən/ *adj* **1** showing support for a particular political party, plan, or leader, and criticizing all others: *a partisan speech* **2 a partisan struggle/conflict** the continuing fight of a group of people against an enemy that has defeated its country —**partisan** *n*

**par·ti·tion**¹ /pɑrˈtɪʃən, pɚ-/ *n* **1** a thin wall that separates one part of a room from another **2** [U] the separation of a country into two or more independent countries

**partition**² *v* [T] to divide a country, room, building etc. into two or more parts

**partition** sth ↔ **off** *phr v* [T] to divide a room into two parts using a PARTITION

**part·ly** /ˈpɑrtli/ *adv* to some degree, but not completely: *The accident was partly my fault.*

**part·ner** /ˈpɑrtnɚ/ *n* **1** someone with whom you do a particular activity, for example dancing, or playing a game against two other people: *my tennis partner* **2** one of the owners of a business **3** one of two people who are married, or who live together and have a sexual relationship

**part·ner·ship** /ˈpɑrtnɚˌʃɪp/ *n* **1** a relationship in which two or more people, organizations etc. work together to achieve something: *We're trying to build a partnership between the business community and colleges.* **2** [U] the state of being a partner, especially in business: *We've been in partnership for five years.* **3** a business owned by two or more partners

**part of speech** /ˌ. . ˈ./ *n* TECHNICAL in grammar, any of the types into which words are divided according to their use, such as noun, verb, or adjective

**par·tridge** /ˈpɑrtrɪdʒ/ *n* [C,U] a fat bird with a short tail that is hunted for food and sport, or the meat from this bird

**part-time** /ˌ. ˈ.ˑ/ *adj, adv* working or studying for fewer than the number of hours that work is usually done: *Brenda works part-time in our office.* | *a part-time job* –compare FULL-TIME

**part·way** /ˌpɑrtˈweɪˑ/ *adv* some of the distance into or along a place, or after some of a period of time has passed: *The house sat partway up a canyon.* | *Dave arrived partway through the lecture.*

**par·ty**[1] /ˈpɑrt̮i/ *n* **1** an occasion when people meet together to enjoy themselves by eating, drinking, dancing etc.: *We're having/giving/throwing a party on Saturday.* | *a birthday party* **2** an organization of people with the same political aims, that you can vote for in elections: *the Democratic Party* **3** a group of people that has been organized in order to do something: *A search party was formed to find the missing girl* | *Foster, party of six, your table is ready.* **4** one of the people or groups involved in an argument, agreement etc., especially a legal one **5 party animal** INFORMAL someone who enjoys parties a lot

---

**CULTURE NOTE** political parties

The two main political parties in the US are the **Democratic Party** and the **Republican Party**. When the **Democrats** are the party that is in power, they tend to use taxes to pay for social programs. When the **Republicans** are the party that is in power, they tend to encourage business to help the economy.

---

**party**[2] *v* [I] INFORMAL to enjoy yourself, especially by drinking alcohol, eating, dancing etc.: *We were out partying until 4 a.m.*

**pass**[1] /pæs/ *v*
**1** ▸**GO PAST**◂ [I,T] also **pass by** to move to a particular point, object, person etc. and go past him, her, or it: *Angie waved at me as she passed.* | *A car passed us doing at least 90 miles an hour.*
**2** ▸**MOVE IN A DIRECTION**◂ [I] to move from one place to another, following a particular direction: *We passed through Texas on our way to Mexico.* | *Pass over the bridge and turn left.*
**3** ▸**GO THROUGH/ACROSS ETC.**◂ [I,T] to go across, through, around etc. something else, or to make something do this: *The new road passes behind our house.* | *Pass the rope around the tree.*

**4** ▸**GIVE**◂ [T] to take something and put it in someone's hand: *Please pass the salt.*
**5** ▸**SPORTS**◂ [I,T] to kick, throw, or hit a ball or other object to another member of your team: *Dad taught me to pass a football when I was seven.*
**6** ▸**TIME**◂ **a)** [I] if time passes, it goes by: *A year passed before I learned the truth.* **b)** [T] to spend time in a particular way: *She passed the time by reading.* | *birds that pass the winter in Canada* –see usage note at TIME[1]
**7** ▸**TEST/CLASS**◂ **a)** [I,T] to succeed in a test or class: *Do you think you'll pass?* | *He's worried he won't pass history.* **b)** [T] to officially decide that someone has passed a test: *The driving tester passed me even though I failed parallel parking.*
**8** ▸**LAW/DECISION**◂ [T] to officially accept a law or proposal, especially by voting: *The motion was passed, 15 votes to 3.*
**9** ▸**END**◂ [I] to stop existing or happening; end: *The storm soon passed.* | *Deirdre will be upset for a while, but it'll pass.*
**10** ▸**CHANGE**◂ [I] FORMAL to change: *When ice melts, it passes from a solid to a liquid state.*
**11 pass judgment** to say whether you think someone or something is right or wrong: *I'm only here to listen, not to pass judgment.*
**12** ▸**DON'T KNOW ANSWER**◂ [I] SPOKEN said when you cannot answer a question because you do not know the answer: *"What year was Einstein born?" "Pass."* –see also **pass the buck** (BUCK[1])

**pass away** *phr v* [I] a phrase meaning to die, used in order to avoid saying this directly

**pass** sb ↔ **by** *phr v* [T] if something passes you by, it exists or happens but you do not have the chance to be involved in it or get any advantage from it: *Robin felt that life was passing her by.*

**pass** sth ↔ **down** *phr v* [T] to give or teach something to people who are younger than you or who live after you: *These traditions have been passed down from one generation to the next.*

**pass for** sb/sth *phr v* [T] to be very similar to someone or something, so that people think you are that person, or that something is that thing: *With her hair cut like that, she could pass for a boy.*

**pass** sb/sth **off as** sth *phr v* [T] to try to make people think that someone or something is something that he, she, or it is not: *He managed to pass himself off as a doctor for three years!*

**pass on** *phr v* **1** [T **pass** sth ↔ **on**] to tell someone a piece of information that someone else has told you: *She said she'd pass the message on to Ms. Chen.* **2** [T **pass** sth ↔ **on**] to give something to someone else: *Take one and pass the rest on to the next person.*

**pass out** *phr v* **1** [I] to suddenly become unconscious **2** [T **pass** sth ↔ **out**] to give some-

thing to each one of a group of people: *Please
**pass out** the dictionaries.*

**pass over** *phr v* [I,T **pass** sb ↔ **over**] to ignore
someone's ability and not give him/her a job
s/he wants or deserves

**pass up** *phr v* [T] **pass up a chance/
opportunity/offer** to not use a chance to do
something

---

**USAGE NOTE** pass, passed, and past

**Passed** is the PAST PARTICIPLE of the verb
**pass**: *I think we've just passed the store.*
**Past** is an adjective: *I've been busy the past
week.*

---

**pass²** *n* **1** the act of kicking, throwing, or
hitting a ball or other object to another member
of your team: *a 30-yard pass* **2** an official
document that proves you are allowed to enter a
building or that you have already paid to do
something: *a bus pass | a zoo pass* **3** a way
through a place that is difficult to cross: *a
narrow mountain pass* **4 make a pass at sb**
INFORMAL to try to kiss or touch another person
with the intention of having sex with him/her
**5** the act of moving past something: *Can you
make a pass through the room and see if there
are any dirty glasses left?*

**pass·a·ble** /ˈpæsəbəl/ *adj* **1** a road or river
that is passable is not blocked, so you can travel
along or across it −opposite IMPASSABLE **2** just
good enough to be acceptable, but not very
good: *a passable piece of work*

**pas·sage** /ˈpæsɪdʒ/ *n* **1** also **pas·sage·way**
/ˈpæsɪdʒ,weɪ/ a narrow area with walls on
each side, that connects one room or place to
another: *a dark passage at the back of the building* **2** a short part of a book, poem, speech,
piece of music etc.: *an interesting passage on
page 32* **3** [U] the action of going across, over,
or along something: *The bridge isn't strong enough to allow the passage of heavy vehicles.*
**4** a tube in your body that air or liquid can
pass through: *nasal passages* **5 the passage
of time** LITERARY the passing of time: *Her condition improved with the passage of time.*
**6** [singular] a trip on a ship, or the cost of this:
*She paid for his passage to Bermuda.*

**pass·book** /ˈpæsbʊk/ *n* a book for keeping a
record of the money you put into and take out of
your bank account

**pas·sé** /pæˈseɪ/ *adj* no longer modern or fashionable: *a writing style that has become passé*

**pas·sen·ger** /ˈpæsəndʒɚ/ *n* someone who is
traveling in a car, plane, boat etc., but is not
driving it

**pass·er·by** /ˌpæsɚˈbaɪ/ *n, plural* **passersby**
someone who is walking past a place by chance:
*Several passersby saw the accident.*

**pass·ing¹** /ˈpæsɪŋ/ *adj* **1** going past: *Our cat
likes to watch the passing traffic.* **2** done

quickly while you are doing something else: *He
gave the report only a passing glance.*
**3** continuing for only a short time: *Eating
organic food is more than just a passing fad.*

**passing²** *n* **1 in passing** if you say something
in passing, you mention it while you are mainly
talking about something else: *The actress mentioned in passing that she had once worked in a
factory.* **2** a word meaning someone's death,
used in order to avoid saying this directly

**pas·sion** /ˈpæʃən/ *n* **1** [C,U] a very strongly
felt emotion, especially of love, hatred, or anger:
*He spoke **with passion** about the situation in his
country. | the passions that influence polit-
ics | sexual passion* **2** a strong liking for some-
thing: *a **passion for** fast cars*

**pas·sion·ate** /ˈpæʃənɪt/ *adj* showing PAS-
SION, or full of passion: *a passionate kiss | a
passionate speech* −**passionately** *adv*

**pas·sive¹** /ˈpæsɪv/ *adj* **1** tending to accept
situations or things that other people do, without
attempting to change or fight against them; SUB-
MISSIVE: *"I'm a very passive person," she
admitted.* **2** not having a lot of involvement in
something that is happening: *Traditional classroom learning is usually very passive.* −**pas-
sively** *adv* −**passivity** /pæˈsɪvəti/ *n* [U]

**passive²** *n* **the passive (voice)** TECHNICAL in
grammar, in the passive voice, the action of the
verb has an effect on the subject of the sentence.
It is shown in English by the verb "be" followed
by a PAST PARTICIPLE. In the sentence, "Oranges
are grown in California," the verb is in the
passive voice −compare ACTIVE²

**passive smo·king** /ˌ.. ˈ../ *n* [U] the act of
breathing in smoke from someone else's cigarette, pipe etc., although you do not want to

**Pass·o·ver** /ˈpæs,oʊvɚ/ *n* [singular] a Jewish
holiday in the spring to remember when the
Jews in ancient Egypt became free

**pass·port** /ˈpæspɔrt/ *n* a small official book
that proves who you are and what country you
are a citizen of, which you must have in order to
leave your country and enter other ones

**pass·word** /ˈpæswɚd/ *n* a secret word or
phrase that you must use before being allowed
to enter a place that is guarded, or use a computer system

**past¹** /pæst/ *adj* **1** having happened, existed,
or been experienced before now: *He knew from
past experience not to argue. | She was
obviously trying to make up for past mistakes.*
**2** a little earlier than the present, or up until
now: *Tim's been out of town for the past week.*
**3** finished or having come to an end: *The time
for discussion is past.* **4** achieving something
in the past, or holding an important position in
the past: *She's a past president of the club.* −see
usage note at PASS¹

**past²** *prep* **1** farther than: *My house is a mile
past the bridge.* **2** up to and beyond: *Tanya*

*walked right past me!* **3** after a particular time, or older than a particular age: *It's ten past nine.* (=ten minutes after nine o'clock) | *She must be past eighty.* **4 I wouldn't put it past sb (to do sth)** SPOKEN used in order to say that you would not be surprised if someone did something because it is typical of him/her: *I don't know if he stole the car, but I wouldn't put it past him!*

**past³** *n* [singular] **1** the time that existed before now: *People travel more now than they did in the past.* **2** all the things that have happened to someone or that s/he has done before now: *She'd like to forget her past and start all over.*

**past⁴** *adv* **1** up to and beyond a particular place: *Hal and his friends drove past at top speed.* **2 go past** if a period of time goes past, it passes: *Several weeks went past without any news from home.*

**pas·ta** /'pɑstə/ *n* [U] an Italian food made from flour, eggs, and water and cut into various shapes, usually eaten with a SAUCE

**paste¹** /peɪst/ *n* [C,U] **1** a type of thick glue that is used for sticking paper together or onto another surface **2** a soft thick mixture that can be easily shaped or spread: *Mix the water and the powder into a smooth paste.* **3** a food made by crushing solid foods into a smooth soft mixture: *tomato paste*

**paste²** *v* [T] to stick paper together or onto another surface with PASTE

**pas·tel** /pæ'stɛl/ *n* **1** a soft pale color, such as pale blue or pink **2** [C,U] a small colored stick for drawing pictures with, made of a substance like oily CHALK —**pastel** *adj*

**pas·teur·ize** /'pæstʃə,raɪz, -stə,raɪz/ *v* [T] to heat a liquid, especially milk, in a special way that kills any BACTERIA in it —**pasteurization** /,pæstʃərə'zeɪʃən/ *n* [U]

**pas·time** /'pæs-taɪm/ *n* something enjoyable that you do when you are not working: *His pastimes include watching TV and reading.*

**pas·tor** /'pæstə/ *n* a minister in some PROTESTANT churches

**pas·tor·al** /'pæstərəl/ *adj* **1** relating to the duties of a priest, minister etc. toward the members of his/her religious group: *Pastoral visits are made on Fridays.* **2** LITERARY typical of the simple peaceful life in the country: *a pastoral scene*

**past par·ti·ci·ple** /,. '..../ *n* TECHNICAL in grammar, a PARTICIPLE that is usually formed by adding "-ed" to a verb, but that can be IRREGULAR. It can be used in compounds to make PERFECT tenses, or as an adjective. In the sentence "Look what you have done," "done" is a past participle

**past per·fect** /,. '../ *n* **the past perfect** TECHNICAL in grammar, the tense of a verb that shows that an action was completed before another event or time in the past. In the sentence

"I had finished my breakfast before Rick called," "had finished" is in the past perfect

**pas·try** /'peɪstri/ *n* **1** [U] a mixture of flour, fat, and milk or water, used for making the outer part of baked foods such as PIEs **2** a small sweet cake

**past tense** /,. './ *n* **the past tense** TECHNICAL in grammar, the tense of a verb that shows that an action or state began and ended in the past. In the sentence, "We walked to school yesterday," "walked" is in the past tense

**pas·ture** /'pæstʃə/ *n* [C,U] land that is covered with grass and is used for cattle, sheep etc. to feed on —**pasture** *v* [I,T]

**past·y** /'peɪsti/ *adj* looking very pale and unhealthy: *a pasty face*

**pat¹** /pæt/ *v* **-tted, -tting 1** [T] to touch someone or something lightly again and again, with your hand flat: *Giles patted her hand sympathetically.* **2 pat sb/yourself on the back** INFORMAL to praise someone or yourself for doing something well

**pat²** *n* **1** an act of touching someone or something with your hand flat, especially in a friendly way: *He gave the dog a pat on the head.* **2 a pat of butter** a small amount of butter, often in a flat square shape **3 a pat on the back** INFORMAL praise for something that has been done well: *Alex deserves a pat on the back for all his hard work.*

**pat³** *adv* **have sth down pat** to know something thoroughly so that you can say it, perform it etc. without thinking about it

**patch¹** /pætʃ/ *n* **1** a small piece of material used for covering a hole in something, especially clothes **2** a part of an area that is different or looks different from the parts that surround it: *There may be a few patches of rain near the coast.* **3** a small area of ground for growing fruit or vegetables: *a cabbage patch*

**patch², patch up** *v* [T] to put a small piece of material over a hole, especially in a piece of clothing: *patched pants*

**patch sth ↔ up** *phr v* [T] to end an argument and become friendly with someone: *I've patched it up with my girlfriend.*

**patch·work** /'pætʃwək/ *n* [U] a type of sewing in which many different colored pieces of cloth are sewn together to make one large piece: *a patchwork quilt*

**patch·y** /'pætʃi/ *adj* **1** happening or existing in a number of small separate areas: *patchy fog* **2** not complete enough to be useful: *My knowledge of biology is pretty patchy.*

**pâ·té** /pɑ'teɪ, pæ-/ *n* [U] a thick smooth food made from meat or fish, that you spread on bread

**pa·tent¹** /'pæt⁻nt/ *n* a special document that says that you have the right to make or sell a new invention or product and that no one else is allowed to do so

**patent**[2] *v* [T] to obtain a PATENT

**patent**[3] *adj* FORMAL clear and easy to notice; OBVIOUS: *a patent lie*

**pat·ent leath·er** /ˌ.. '../ *n* [U] thin shiny leather, usually black: *patent leather shoes*

**pa·tent·ly** /'pæt⁻ntli/ *adv* **patently obvious/false/unfair etc.** completely clear, untrue, unfair etc., in a way that anyone can notice: *patently offensive language*

**pa·ter·nal** /pə'tɚnl/ *adj* **1** typical of the way a father feels or acts **2 paternal grandmother/uncle etc.** your father's mother, brother etc. –**paternally** *adv* –compare MATERNAL

**pa·ter·nal·ism** /pə'tɚnl,ɪzəm/ *n* [U] practice of making decisions for people or organizations, so that they are never able to be responsible themselves –**paternalistic** /pə,tɚnə'lɪstɪk/ *adj*

**pa·ter·ni·ty** /pə'tɚnəti/ *n* [U] LAW the state of being a father

**path** /pæθ/ *n* **1** a track that people walk along over an area of ground: *a path through the woods* **2** a way that allows you to move forward through something: *The police cleared a path through the crowd.* **3** the direction or line along which someone or something moves: *The storm destroyed everything in its path.*

**pa·thet·ic** /pə'θɛtɪk/ *adj* **1** making you feel pity or sympathy: *the pathetic sight of starving children* **2** very bad, useless, or weak: *Vicky made a pathetic attempt to apologize.* –**pathetically** *adv*

**path·o·log·i·cal** /ˌpæθə'lɑdʒɪkəl/ *adj* **1** pathological behavior or feelings are unreasonable, impossible to control, and caused by a mental illness: *a pathological liar* **2** TECHNICAL relating to the causes and effects of disease: *a pathological condition*

**pa·thol·o·gy** /pə'θɑlədʒi, pæ-/ *n* [U] the study of the causes and effects of diseases –**pathologist** *n*

**pa·thos** /'peɪθous, -θɑs, 'pæ-/ *n* [U] LITERARY the quality that a person or a situation has that makes you feel pity and sadness

**path·way** /'pæθweɪ/ *n* [U] ⇨ PATH

**pa·tience** /'peɪʃəns/ *n* [U] the ability to wait calmly for a long time or deal with difficulties without becoming angry, anxious, or annoyed: *Finally I **lost my patience with** him and started shouting.* | *The kids are beginning to **try my patience**.* (=make me stop being patient) | *I don't **have the patience** to sew my own clothes.*

**pa·tient**[1] /'peɪʃənt/ *n* someone who is getting medical treatment

**patient**[2] *adj* able to wait calmly for a long time or to deal with difficulties without becoming angry, anxious, or annoyed: *Try to be **patient with** your students.* –**patiently** *adv* –opposite IMPATIENT

**pat·i·o** /'pæti,ou/ *n* an outside area near a

house with a stone floor and no roof, where people can sit, eat etc.

**pa·tri·arch** /'peɪtri,ɑrk/ *n* an old man who is respected and who is the most important person in a family or tribe –compare MATRIARCH

**pa·tri·arch·al** /ˌpeɪtri'ɑrkəl/ *adj* **1** ruled or controlled only by men: *a patriarchal society* **2** relating to being a PATRIARCH, or typical of a patriarch

**pa·tri·arch·y** /'peɪtri,ɑrki/ *n* [C,U] a social system in which men hold all the power

**pat·ri·cide** /'pætrə,saɪd/ *n* [U] the crime of killing your father

**pat·ri·mo·ny** /'pætrə,mouni/ *n* [C,U] FORMAL property that is passed on to you after your father dies

**pa·tri·ot** /'peɪtriət/ *n* someone who loves and respects his/her country and is willing to defend it

**pa·tri·ot·ic** /ˌpeɪtri'ɑtɪk/ *adj* willing to defend your country because you love and respect it, or showing pride for your country: *a patriotic citizen* | *patriotic songs* –**patriotism** /'peɪtriə,tɪzəm/ *n* [U]

**pa·trol**[1] /pə'troul/ *n* **1** the action of regularly checking different parts of an area to prevent problems or crime: *Guards were **on patrol** throughout the night.* **2** a group of police, soldiers, planes etc. that PATROL a particular area: *the California Highway Patrol*

**patrol**[2] *v* **-lled, -lling** [I,T] to regularly check an area in order to prevent problems or crime: *soldiers patrolling a prisoner-of-war camp*

**pa·trol·man** /pə'troulmən/ *n* a police officer who PATROLs a particular area

**pa·tron** /'peɪtrən/ *n* **1** someone who supports an organization, artist, musical performer etc., especially by giving money: *a patron of the arts* **2** someone who often uses a particular store, restaurant, company etc.: *We offer a 20% discount for all our regular patrons.*

**pa·tron·age** /'peɪtrənɪdʒ, 'pæ-/ *n* [U] **1** the action of using a particular store, restaurant, company etc.: *Thank you for your patronage.* **2** the support that a PATRON gives to an organization etc.: *her patronage of the Boston Symphony* **3** a system in which a powerful person gives money or important jobs to people who support him/her: *political patronage*

**pa·tron·ize** /'peɪtrə,naɪz, 'pæ-/ *v* [T] **1** to behave or talk in a way that shows you think someone is less important or intelligent than you: *Don't patronize me.* | *a manager who patronizes his employees* **2** to regularly use a particular store, restaurant, company etc.

**pa·tron·iz·ing** /'peɪtrə,naɪzɪŋ, 'pæ-/ *adj* showing that you think someone is less important or intelligent than you: *a patronizing attitude*

**pat·ter** /'pæṭɚ/ *n* [singular] **1** the sound of something lightly hitting a hard surface: *the* *patter of raindrops on the ground* **2** very fast and continuous talk: *a car salesman's patter* −**patter** *v* [I]

**patterns**

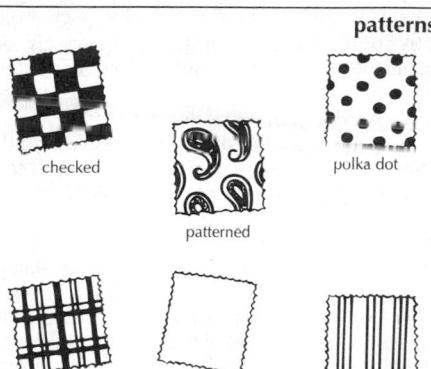

checked

polka dot

patterned

plaid

plain

striped

**pat·tern** /ˈpætɚn/ *n* **1** the regular way in which something happens, develops, or is done: *Romantic novels tend to **follow** a similar **pattern**.| the behavior patterns of young children* **2** a design made from shapes, colors, lines etc. that are arranged in a regular way: *a pattern of small red and white squares| a dress with a rose pattern* −see picture at ELABORATE¹ **3** a shape that you copy onto cloth, paper etc. when making something, especially clothing: *a skirt pattern*

**pat·terned** /ˈpætɚnd/ *adj* decorated with a pattern: *patterned sheets* −see picture at PATTERN

**pat·ty** /ˈpæti/ *n* a round flat piece of cooked meat or other food: *beef patties*

**pau·ci·ty** /ˈpɔsəti/ *n* [U] **a paucity of** FORMAL less than is needed of something: *a paucity of information*

**paunch** /pɔntʃ, pɑntʃ/ *n* a man's fat stomach −**paunchy** *adj*

**pau·per** /ˈpɔpɚ/ *n* OLD-FASHIONED someone who is very poor

**pause¹** /pɔz/ *v* [I] to stop speaking or doing something for a short time before starting again: *Tom paused for a moment, and then asked, "So what should I do?"*

**pause²** *n* a short time when you stop speaking or doing something: *After a pause Rick said, "You're right." | a long **pause in** the conversation*

**pave** /peɪv/ *v* [T] **1** to cover a path, road etc. with a hard level surface such as CONCRETE **2 pave the way** to do something that will make an event, development etc. possible in the future: *Galileo's achievements paved the way for Newton's scientific laws.*

**pave·ment** /ˈpeɪvmənt/ *n* [U] the hard surface of a road

**pa·vil·ion** /pəˈvɪlyən/ *n* **1** a structure built in a park or at a FAIR, and used as a place for public entertainment, EXHIBITIONs etc. **2** a very large tent

**paw¹** /pɔ/ *n* the foot of an animal, such as a lion or dog, that has CLAWs (=sharp strong nails)

**paw²** *v* [I,T] **1** if an animal paws something, it touches something with its PAW: *Tyler's cat pawed at the buttons on Hank's coat.* **2** INFORMAL to touch someone in a way that is too rough or too sexual: *He kept trying to paw me in the car.*

**pawn¹** /pɔn/ *n* someone who is used by a more powerful person or group: *"We're pawns in a big political game," said the miners' spokesman.*

**pawn²** *v* [T] to leave a valuable object with a PAWNBROKER in order to borrow money

**pawn·bro·ker** /ˈpɔnˌbroʊkɚ/ *n* someone whose business is to lend people money in exchange for valuable objects

**pay¹** /peɪ/ *v* **paid, paid, paying** **1** ▶GIVE MONEY◀ [I,T] to give someone money for something in order to buy it, or for something s/he has done for you: *We get paid monthly. | Have you paid the babysitter yet? | I can't afford to **pay** that much **for** a pair of shoes. | Plumbers are paid $40 an hour. | The company's **paying for** my plane tickets.* ✗ DON'T SAY "The company's paying my plane tickets." ✗ **2** ▶BILL/DEBT◀ [T] to give a person, company etc. the money that you owe him, her, or it: *We need to pay the electricity bill soon.* **3 pay attention** to carefully listen to or watch someone or something, or to be careful about what you are doing: *Sorry, I wasn't paying attention. What did you say?* **4 pay a visit** to go to see a particular place or person: *It's about time you paid a visit to the dentist.* **5 pay sb a compliment** to tell someone that you think s/he is nice, attractive, intelligent etc. **6 pay your way** to pay for your bills, food etc. without needing to use anyone else's money: *She paid her own way through law school.* **7** ▶GOOD RESULT◀ [I] to be worth doing, and result in an advantage for you: *Crime doesn't pay. | **It pays to** be on time.* **8** ▶PROFIT◀ [I] to be profitable: *We worked hard but couldn't make the business pay.* **9 pay tribute to sb/sth** to show how much you admire or respect someone or something: *an evening of jazz to pay tribute to Ella Fitzgerald* **10 pay your respects (to sb)** FORMAL to greet someone politely or visit a place, especially in order to say or show that you are sorry that someone has died: *Sam came over to pay his respects to the family.* **11 pay your dues** to work hard for a long time before you get much money or thanks, or

P

before you become famous: *He deserves a break; he's paid his dues as an actor.*

**12 pay through the nose** INFORMAL to pay far too much money for something −see also **pay/give lip service** (LIP)

**pay** sb/sth ↔ **back** *phr v* [T] to give someone the money that you owe him/her; REPAY: *Can I borrow $10? I'll **pay** you **back** tomorrow.*

**pay for** sth *phr v* [T] to suffer or be punished for doing something. *If you drink any more you'll be **paying for** it in the morning.*

**pay** sth ↔ **in/into** *phr v* [T] to put money into a bank account: *The check was **paid into** your account on Friday.*

**pay off** *phr v* **1** [T **pay** sth ↔ **off**] to pay all the money that you owe for something: *We've finally **paid off** the mortgage.* **2** [I] if something that you try to do pays off, it is successful: *Their crazy idea actually **paid off.*** **3** [T **pay** sb ↔ **off**] to give someone money so that s/he will not tell people about something illegal or dishonest

**pay out** *phr v* [I,T **pay** sth ↔ **out**] to pay a lot of money for something: *How much do we **pay out** in salaries? | Last year, $123 million was **paid out** in health benefits.*

**pay up** *phr v* [I] INFORMAL to pay all the money that you owe

**pay²** *n* [U] money that you are given for working; SALARY: *The **pay** will be better at my new job.*

---

**USAGE NOTE** pay, income, salary, and wage

**Pay** is a general word for money that someone gets for doing work: *The pay in her new job isn't very good.* **Income** is the money that you or your family receive from any place: *an investment income | Their income is fairly high, with both of them working.* A **salary** is the pay that professional people earn every year: *What's the yearly salary for a teacher?* A **wage** is the pay that someone earns every hour or every week: *The minimum wage is $5.25 an hour. | Our wages have been increased to $500 a week.*

---

**pay·a·ble** /ˈpeɪəbəl/ *adj* **1** a bill, debt etc. that is payable must be paid: *A standard fee of $35 is payable every three months.* **2** **payable to** able to be paid to a particular person or organization: *Please **make the check payable to** "Al's Service Station."* (=write this name on the check)

**pay·check** /ˈpeɪtʃɛk/ *n* a check used for paying a worker his/her wages: *a monthly paycheck*

**pay·day** /ˈpeɪdeɪ/ *n* [C usually singular] the day when you get your PAYCHECK

**pay dirt** /ˈ. ./ *n* [U] **hit/strike pay dirt** INFORMAL to make a valuable or useful discovery: *In finding the 10,000-year-old elephant, scientists had hit pay dirt.*

**pay·ee** /peɪˈi/ *n* TECHNICAL the person who should be paid money, especially by check

**pay·load** /ˈpeɪloʊd/ *n* [C,U] the goods or equipment carried by a truck, plane, or SPACECRAFT

**pay·ment** /ˈpeɪmənt/ *n* **1** an amount of money that should be paid or that has been paid: *How much are your car payments?* **2** [U] the act of paying: *Late payment will result in a $10 fine.*

**pay·off** /ˈpeɪɔf/ *n* INFORMAL **1** the good result or the advantage that you get because of doing something: *There's a big payoff for companies that keep their employees happy.* **2** money that is paid to someone so that s/he will not cause problems, for example by telling people about something illegal or dishonest

**pay phone** /ˈ. ./ *n* a public telephone that you can use when you put a coin or your CREDIT CARD in it

**pay·roll** /ˈpeɪroʊl/ *n* **1** the list of people who are employed by a company and the amount of money they are paid: *We have 127 staff **on the payroll**.* **2** the total amount of wages that a particular company pays

**pay-TV** /ˌ. .ˈ./ *n* [U] television CHANNELs or programs that you must pay to watch

**PBS** *n* [U] Public Broadcasting System; a company in the US that broadcasts television programs without advertisements

**PC¹** *n* personal computer; a small computer that is used by one person at a time, at work or at home

**PC²** *adj* ⇨ POLITICALLY CORRECT

**PE** *n* [U] physical education; sports and exercises that are taught as a school subject

**pea** /pi/ *n* [C usually plural] a small round green seed that is cooked and eaten as a vegetable −see picture on page 470

**peace** /pis/ *n* **1** [U] a situation or period of time in which there is no war or fighting: *working for **world peace** | Germany has **been at peace with** France since 1945.* **2** [U] a situation that is very calm, quiet, and pleasant: *All I want is some **peace and quiet**. | Mary, let your sister read **in peace**.* (=without being interrupted) **3** [U] a feeling of being calm, happy, and not worried: *Will you please call if you're going to be late, just for my **peace of mind**?* **4 disturbing the peace** LAW the crime of being too noisy or too violent in a public place **5 make (your) peace** to agree to stop fighting with a person or group: *He was anxious to **make peace with** Jill before she left.*

**peace·a·ble** /ˈpisəbəl/ *adj* not liking to argue, or not causing any arguments or fights: *peaceable citizens* −**peaceably** *adv*

**peace·ful** /ˈpisfəl/ *adj* **1** calm, quiet, and without problems or excitement: *a peaceful va-*

*cation in the country | a peaceful night's sleep* **2** not fighting a war, or deliberately not being violent: *a peaceful relationship between countries | a peaceful protest against nuclear weapons* —**peacefully** *adv*

**peace·keep·ing** /'pis,kipɪŋ/ *adj* trying to prevent fighting or violence: *the UN's peacekeeping role*

**peace·mak·er** /'pis,meɪkɚ/ *n* someone who tries to persuade people or countries to stop fighting

**peace·time** /'pis-taɪm/ *n* [U] a period when a country is not fighting a war —opposite WAR-TIME

**peach** /pitʃ/ *n* **1** a round juicy yellow-red fruit that has a large rough seed and skin that feels FUZZY, or the tree on which it grows —see picture on page 470 **2** [U] a pale pink-orange color

**pea·cock** /'pikɑk/ *n* a large bird, the male of which has long blue and green tail feathers that it can spread out

**peak¹** /pik/ *n* **1** the time when someone or something is biggest, most successful, or best: *Trenton is now at the peak of his career. | The company's profits reached a peak in 1992.* **2** the pointed top of a mountain, or a mountain with a pointed top: *the Alps' snow-covered peaks*

**peak²** *v* [I] to become the biggest, most successful, or best that someone or something can be: *In the 1950s, Chicago's population peaked at around 3.6 million.*

**peaked** /pikt/ *adj* pale, and looking sick

**peal** /pil/ *n* a sudden loud repeated sound, such as laughter, THUNDER, or bells RINGing: *Peals of laughter came from the audience.* —**peal** *v* [I]

**pea·nut** /'pinʌt/ *n* a small nut you can eat that has a soft light brown shell

**peanut but·ter** /'.. ,../ *n* [U] a soft food made from crushed PEANUTs, usually eaten on bread: *a peanut butter and jelly sandwich*

**pea·nuts** /'pinʌts/ *n* [U] INFORMAL a very small amount of money: *I'm tired of working for peanuts.*

**pear** /pɛr/ *n* a sweet juicy fruit with a round wide bottom that becomes thinner on top near the stem, or the tree on which it grows —see picture on page 470

**pearl** /pɚl/ *n* **1** a valuable small white round object, that forms inside an OYSTER and is used in jewelry: *a pearl necklace* **2** [U] a pale silver-white color

**peas·ant** /'pɛzənt/ *n* a word meaning someone who does farm work on the piece of land where s/he lives, used especially to describe people who did this in past times

**peat** /pit/ *n* [U] a substance formed under the surface of the ground from decaying plants, used as soil or as FUEL

**peb·ble** /'pɛbəl/ *n* a small smooth stone that is usually in a river or on a beach

**pe·can** /pə'kɑn, -'kæn/ *n* a long thin sweet nut with a dark smooth shell, or the tree on which these nuts grow

**peck¹** /pɛk/, **peck at** *v* [I,T] if a bird pecks something, it quickly moves its beak to hit or pick up something, especially food

**peck²** *n* **1 give sb a peck on the cheek** to kiss someone quickly and lightly **2** the action of a bird hitting something with its beak

**pe·cu·liar** /pɪ'kyulyɚ/ *adj* **1** strange and a little surprising: *She has the peculiar habit of blinking a lot when she talks.* **2 be peculiar to** to be a quality that only one particular person, place, or thing has: *the strong flavor that is peculiar to garlic* —**peculiarly** *adv*

**pe·cu·li·ar·i·ty** /pɪ,kyuli'ærəti/ *n* [C,U] an unusual or slightly strange habit or quality, especially one that only a particular person, place etc. has: *At least she knew about his peculiarities before she married him!*

**ped·a·go·gi·cal** /,pɛdə'gɑdʒɪkəl/ *adj* FORMAL relating to methods of teaching —**pedagogy** /'pɛdə,gɑdʒi/ *n* [U]

**ped·al¹** /'pɛdl/ *n* the part of a bicycle, car, or MOTORCYCLE that you push with your foot in order to make it move: *the gas pedal*

**pedal²** *v* [I,T] to ride a bicycle by pushing the PEDALs with your feet

**pe·dan·tic** /pə'dæntɪk/ *adj* paying too much attention to small details and rules, especially because you are trying to prove how much you know: *a pedantic professor*

**ped·dle** /'pɛdl/ *v* [T] to go from place to place trying to sell something, especially something illegal or cheap: *Eric was caught peddling drugs.* —**peddler** *n*: *a drug peddler*

**ped·es·tal** /'pɛdəstl/ *n* **1** the base that you put a STATUE or a PILLAR on **2 put sb on a pedestal** to admire someone too much because you think s/he is perfect

**pe·des·tri·an¹** /pə'dɛstriən/ *n* someone who is walking instead of driving a car or riding a bicycle

**pedestrian²** *adj* **1** relating to PEDESTRIANs, or used by pedestrians: *a pedestrian crossing* (=where cars must stop to allow people to walk across the street) **2** ordinary, and not very interesting or exciting: *It is a piece of real journalism, rather than the usual pedestrian stuff.*

**pe·di·a·tri·cian** /,pidiə'trɪʃən/ *n* a doctor who treats children

**pe·di·at·rics** /,pidi'ætrɪks/ *n* [U] the area of medicine that deals with children and their illnesses

**ped·i·cure** /'pɛdɪ,kyʊr/ *n* [C,U] a treatment for the feet that includes cleaning them and cutting the TOENAILs

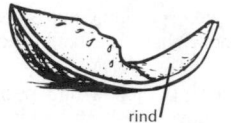
rind

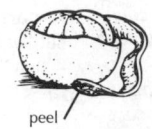
peel

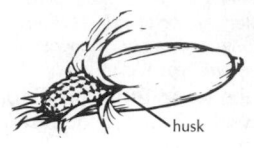
husk

skin

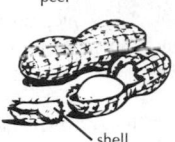
shell

pod

**ped·i·gree** /'pɛdə,gri/ *n* [C,U] the parents and other past family members of an animal or person, or the written record of them –**pedigree** *adj*: *a pedigree Great Dane*

**pee** /pi/ *n* [singular, U] INFORMAL URINE, or the act of urinating (URINATE): *Andy, do you need to go pee before we leave?* –**pee** *v* [I]

**peek**[1] /pik/ *v* [I] to quickly look at something, especially something you are not supposed to see: *The door was open, so I peeked into his office.*

**peek**[2] *n* a quick look at something: *Take a peek in the oven and see if the cake's done.*

**peek·a·boo** /'pikə,bu/ *interjection, n* [U] a game played with babies and young children, in which you hide your face and then show it again and again, saying "peekaboo!"

**peel**[1] /pil/ *v* **1** [T] to remove the skin of a fruit or vegetable: *Peel the potatoes and cut them in half.* **2** [I,T] to remove a thin outside layer from the surface of an object: *Peel the labels off/from the jars before recycling.* **3** [I] if skin, paper, or paint peels, it is loose and coming off in small thin pieces: *I got sunburned and now my face is peeling.*

**peel** sth ↔ **off** *phr v* [I,T] to take off your clothes, especially if they are wet or tight: *He peeled off his T-shirt and put it in the wash.*

**peel**[2] *n* [U] the thick skin of a fruit or vegetable such as an orange, a potato, or a BANANA

**peel·ings** /'pilɪŋz/ *n* [plural] pieces of skin that are removed from a fruit or vegetable before cooking it: *carrot peelings*

**peep**[1] /pip/ *v* [I] **1** to look at something quickly and secretly: *I saw Joe peeping through the curtains.* **2** to appear: *The sun finally peeped out from behind the clouds.*

**peep**[2] *n* **1** a quick or secret look at something: *Did you get a peep at the audience?* **2** **not (hear) a peep** used to say that a child is not making any sounds: *I didn't hear a peep out of the kids all afternoon.*

**peep·hole** /'piphoul/ *n* a small hole in a door that you can look through

**peep·ing Tom** /,pipɪŋ 'tam/ *n* someone who secretly watches people, especially people who are undressing

**peer**[1] /pɪr/ *n* someone who is the same age as you, or who has the same type of job, rank etc.: *Barton has gained the respect of his peers.*

**peer**[2] *v* [I] to look very carefully, especially because you cannot see something well: *Harris peered into the dark closet.*

**peer·less** /'pɪrlɪs/ *adj* better than any other: *his peerless achievements in science*

**peer pres·sure** /'. ,../ *n* the strong feeling that young people have that they should do the same things that their PEERs are doing

**peeve** /piv/ *n* ⇨ **pet peeve** (PET[3])

**peg**[1] /pɛg/ *n* **1** a short piece of wood or metal that fits into a hole or is fastened to a wall, used for fastening furniture together, for hanging things on etc.: *a coat peg* **2** also **tent peg** a pointed piece of wood or metal used for keeping a tent attached to the ground

**peg**[2] **-gged, -gging** *v* **1** **have sb pegged (as)** to say that someone has a particular type of character: *I never had him pegged as a winner.* **2** [T] to set prices, wages etc. in relation to a particular value: *loan payment rates that are pegged to the national rates*

**pe·jor·a·tive** /pɪ'dʒɔrətɪv, -'dʒɑr-/ *adj* FORMAL a pejorative word or phrase is used in order to insult someone or to show disapproval

**pe·king·ese, pek·in·ese** /,pikə'niz/ *n* a very small dog with a short flat nose and long silky hair

**pel·i·can** /'pɛlɪkən/ *n* a large bird that catches fish for food and holds them in the part of its large beak that is shaped like a bag

**pel·let** /'pɛlɪt/ *n* a small hard ball made from metal, ice, paper, food etc.

**pelt**[1] /pɛlt/ *v* [T] to attack someone by throwing a lot of things at him/her: *Two kids were pelting each other with snowballs.*

**pelt**[2] *n* the skin of a dead animal with the fur or hair still on it

**pel·vis** /'pɛlvɪs/ *n* the set of large wide curved bones at the base of your SPINE, to which your legs are joined –**pelvic** *adj*

**pen**[1] /pɛn/ *n* **1** [C,U] an instrument used for writing and drawing in ink: *a ballpoint pen | Write your essays in pen* (=using a pen), *not pencil.* **2** a small area surrounded by a fence, that farm animals are kept in – see also PIGPEN

**pen²** v **-nned, -nning** [T] LITERARY **1** to write a letter or note with a pen **2** [I,T] to prevent a person or animal from leaving an enclosed area: *The flu kept him* **penned in** *the house for a week.*

**pe·nal** /'pinl/ adj **1** relating to the legal punishment of criminals: *a penal institution* (=type of prison) **2 penal offense** a crime

**penal code** /'.. ,./ n a set of laws and the punishments for not obeying these laws: *the Oregon Penal Code*

**pe·nal·ize** /'pinl,aɪz, 'pɛn-/ v [T] **1** to punish someone or treat him/her unfairly: *If Glenda's been trying her best, she shouldn't be* **penalized for** *her low grades.* **2** to punish a player or sports team by giving an advantage to the other team: *The Bears were* **penalized for** *taking too much time.*

**pen·al·ty** /'pɛnlti/ n **1** a punishment for not obeying a law, rule, or legal agreement: *a* **penalty** *of $120* **for** *speeding* | *He was given* **the death penalty**. (=the punishment of being killed) **2** a disadvantage given to a player or sports team for not obeying the rules

**pen·ance** /'pɛnəns/ n [C,U] a punishment that you accept, especially for religious reasons, to show that you are sorry for doing a bad thing

**pen·chant** /'pɛntʃənt/ n a liking for something that you do as a habit: *Philip has a* **penchant for** *smoking French cigarettes.*

**pen·cil** /'pɛnsəl/ n [C,U] an instrument used for writing and drawing, made of wood with a gray or colored center: *Do the math problems* **in pencil** (=using a pencil), *not pen.* | *an editor's blue pencil*

**pencil sharp·en·er** /'.. ,..../ n an object with a small blade inside it, used for making the pointed end of a pencil sharp

**pend·ant** /'pɛndənt/ n a jewel or small decoration that hangs from a chain you wear around your neck: *a diamond pendant*

**pend·ing¹** /'pɛndɪŋ/ prep FORMAL until something happens, or while something happens: *The decision has been delayed pending further research.*

**pending²** adj FORMAL not yet decided, agreed on, or finished: *Their divorce is still pending.*

**pen·du·lum** /'pɛndʒələm/ n a long stick with a weight on the end of it, that hangs down and swings from side to side, especially in a large clock

**pen·e·trate** /'pɛnə,treɪt/ v **1** [I,T] to enter something or pass through it, especially when this is difficult: *bullets that can penetrate metal* | *Dampness had* **penetrated into** *the walls.* **2** [T] to join and be accepted by an organization, business etc. in order to find out secret information: *CIA agents had penetrated several left-wing groups.* **3** [T] to understand something difficult: *scientists trying to penetrate the mysteries of nature*

**pen·e·trat·ing** /'pɛnə,treɪtɪŋ/ adj **1 penetrating eyes/look/gaze** someone who has penetrating eyes etc. seems able to see what another person is thinking **2** a penetrating noise or voice is so loud that you hear it very clearly **3** showing an ability to understand things quickly and completely: *a penetrating mind* – **penetration** /,pɛnə'treɪʃən/ n [U]

**pen·guin** /'pɛŋgwɪn/ n a large black and white Antarctic sea bird, that cannot fly but uses its wings for swimming

**pen·i·cil·lin** /,pɛnə'sɪlən/ n [U] a substance used as a medicine to destroy BACTERIA

**pe·nin·su·la** /pə'nɪnsələ/ n a piece of land that is almost completely surrounded by water: *the Italian peninsula* – **peninsular** adj

**pe·nis** /'pinɪs/ n the outer sex organ of males

**pen·i·tent** /'pɛnətənt/ adj FORMAL feeling sorry about doing something bad, and showing you do not intend to do it again – **penitence** n [U]

**pen·i·ten·tia·ry** /,pɛnə'tɛnʃəri/ n a prison: *the state penitentiary*

**pen·knife** /'pɛn-naɪf/ n ⇨ POCKET KNIFE

**pen name** /'. ./ n a name used by a writer instead of his/her real name; PSEUDONYM

**pen·nant** /'pɛnənt/ n a long pointed flag used by schools, sports teams etc., or on ships as a sign

**pen·ni·less** /'pɛnɪlɪs/ adj having no money

**pen·ny** /'pɛni/ n, plural **pennies 1** a coin used in the US and Canada worth 1 cent (=¹⁄₁₀₀ of a dollar) **2 a penny/every penny** any of your money or all of your money: *I don't owe her a penny!* | *He spent every penny on his car.*

**pen pal** /'. ./ n someone in another country to whom you write letters in order to become his/her friend

**pen·sion** /'pɛnʃən/ n the money that a company pays regularly to someone after s/he RETIRES (=stops working)

**pension fund** /'.. ,./ n the large amount of money that a company, organization etc. INVESTs and uses for paying PENSIONs

**pension plan** /'.. ,./ n a system for organizing the type of PENSION that a company will give you

**pen·sive** /'pɛnsɪv/ adj thinking about something a lot and seeming slightly sad: *He sat by the river, looking pensive.*

**Pen·ta·gon** /'pɛntə,gɑn/ n **the Pentagon** the US government building from which the army, navy etc. are controlled, or the military officers who work in this building

**pentagon** n a flat shape with five sides and five angles – **pentagonal** /pɛn'tægənl/ adj – see picture at SHAPE

P

**Pen·te·cos·tal** /ˌpɛntɪˈkɑstl/ *adj* relating to the Christian church whose members believe that the spirit of God can help them to heal diseases and pray in special languages –Pentecostal *n*

**pent·house** /ˈpɛnthaʊs/ *n* a very expensive and comfortable apartment on the top floor of a tall building

**pent-up** /ˌ. ˈ.‹ / *adj* pent-up emotions are not expressed for a long time: *All the pent-up anger she was feeling came out as she cried.*

**pe·on** /ˈpiɑn/ *n* OFTEN HUMOROUS someone who works at a boring or physically hard job for low pay: *I don't know anything - I'm just one of the peons.*

**peo·ple**[1] /ˈpipəl/ *n* **1** [plural] men, women, and children: *I like the people I work with. | How many people were at the wedding?* **2 the people** [plural] all the ordinary people in a country or a state: *The US is meant to have "a government of the people, by the people, and for the people."* **3** FORMAL a race or nation: *the peoples of Asia* **4 of all people** SPOKEN used in order to say that someone is the only person who you would not have expected to do something: *It was Michael Jordan, of all people, who missed the shot that made the Bulls lose.* –see usage notes at MAN[1], PERSON

**people**[2] *v* **be peopled with** LITERARY to be filled with people or things of a particular type: *Her books are peopled with imaginary creatures.*

**pep**[1] /pɛp/ *v* **-pped, -pping**
**pep sb/sth ↔ up** *phr v* [T] INFORMAL to make something or someone more active, interesting, or full of energy: *I've added some chilies to pep up the chicken a little.*

**pep**[2] *n* [U] OLD-FASHIONED physical energy: *Ed's always full of pep.* –**peppy** *adj*

**pep·per**[1] /ˈpɛpɚ/ *n* **1** [U] a black, pale yellow, or red hot-tasting powder, used in cooking **2** a hollow red, green, or yellow fruit with a sweet or hot taste that is eaten as a vegetable, or added to other foods –see picture on page 470

**pepper**[2] *v* [T] **1** to scatter things all over or all through something: *The article is peppered with quotations.* **2** to put pepper in food

**pep·per·mint** /ˈpɛpɚˌmɪnt/ *n* [U] **1** a MINT plant with sweet-smelling hot-tasting leaves used in making candy, tea, and medicine **2** a candy with this taste

**pep·pe·ro·ni** /ˌpɛpəˈroʊni/ *n* [C,U] a hot-tasting dry Italian SAUSAGE

**pep ral·ly** /ˈ. ˌ../ *n* a meeting when people give speeches or shout to encourage and support a team: *The pep rally will be in the gym a half hour before the game starts.*

**pep talk** /ˈ. ./ *n* INFORMAL a speech that is intended to encourage people to work harder, win a game etc.: *a pre-game pep talk from the football coach*

**per** /pɚ/ *prep* for each: *Bananas are 60¢ per pound. | You need at least half a bottle of wine per person for the party.*

**per ca·pi·ta** /pɚ ˈkæpətə/ *adj, adv* FORMAL calculated by dividing the total amount of something by the number of people in a particular place: *The average per capita income in the area is $40,000 a year.*

**per·ceive** /pɚˈsiv/ *v* [T] FORMAL **1** to understand or think about something in a particular way: *It is a difficult situation, but we don't perceive it as anything we can't deal with. | I think the public perceives that our industry has a problem.* **2** to notice something that is difficult to notice: *The sound is too high to be perceived by humans.*

**percent**[1] /pɚˈsɛnt/ *adj, adv* **1** equal to a particular amount in every hundred: *Leave the waitress a 15% tip.* (=a tip of 15 cents for every dollar you have spent on the meal) **2 a/one hundred percent** completely: *I agree with you a hundred percent.*

**percent**[2] *n* **five/ten etc. percent** five, ten etc. in every hundred: *The interest rate at the bank is six percent.* (=6%, or six cents on every dollar)

**per·cent·age** /pɚˈsɛntɪdʒ/ *n* **1** [C,U] a particular amount out of every hundred: *A high percentage of Internet users are men. | The percentage of deaths caused by highway accidents has decreased recently.* **2** a share of profits equal to a particular amount in every dollar: *He gets a percentage for every book that is sold.*

**per·cep·ti·ble** /pɚˈsɛptəbəl/ *adj* FORMAL noticeable: *The accounts show a barely perceptible increase in profits.* –opposite IMPERCEPTIBLE

**per·cep·tion** /pɚˈsɛpʃən/ *n* **1** the way you understand something and your beliefs about what it is like: *The local library is trying to change the perception that the library is not a fun place to be.* **2** [U] the way you use your senses to notice things: *Drugs can change your perception of sounds and sights.* **3** [U] the natural ability to understand or notice something quickly: *I was amazed at the perception of Rachel's five-year-old girl.*

**per·cep·tive** /pɚˈsɛptɪv/ *adj* good at noticing and understanding what is happening or what someone is thinking or feeling: *A perceptive teacher can really help a shy child.*

**perch**[1] /pɚʃ/ *n* **1** a branch, stick etc. where a bird sits **2** INFORMAL a high place where someone can sit or where a building is placed: *He watches from his perch halfway up the mountain.* **3** [C,U] a fish with sharp pointed FINs that lives in rivers, lakes etc., or the meat from this fish

**perch**[2] *v* **1 be perched on/over etc.** to be in a position on top of or on the edge of something: *a house perched on a hill* **2 perch (yourself) on** to sit on top of or on the edge of something: *Wally perched on the gate and stared at us.* **3** [I] if a bird perches on something, it sits on it

**per·co·late** /ˈpɚkəˌleɪt/ v [I] if a liquid percolates through something, it passes slowly through a material that has small holes in it

**per·co·la·tor** /ˈpɚkəˌleɪtɚ/ n a pot in which coffee is made by passing hot water again and again through crushed coffee beans

**per·cus·sion** /pɚˈkʌʃən/ n [U] the part of an ORCHESTRA that consists of drums and other related instruments

**pe·remp·to·ry** /pəˈrɛmptəri/ adj FORMAL DISAPPROVING showing an expectation of being obeyed immediately: *a peremptory order*

**pe·ren·ni·al**[1] /pəˈrɛniəl/ adj **1** happening again and again, or existing for a long time: *the perennial problem of poverty* **2** a plant that is perennial lives for more than two years

**perennial**[2] n a plant that lives for more than two years

**per·fect**[1] /ˈpɚfɪkt/ adj **1** of the best possible type or standard: *They seemed to have a perfect marriage.* **2** exactly right for a particular purpose: *This rug's* **perfect for** *the living room.* | *We've found the perfect place for a vacation.* **3** complete and without any mistakes or problems: *a perfect diamond* | *a car in perfect condition* | *Your English is perfect.* —opposite IMPERFECT[1] **4** complete or total: *She has a date with a perfect stranger.* **5 nobody's perfect** SPOKEN used when you are answering someone who has criticized you: *Yes, I made a mistake - nobody's perfect.*

**per·fect**[2] /pɚˈfɛkt/ v [T] to make something perfect or as good as you are able to: *She's spending a year in France to perfect her French.*

**per·fect**[3] /ˈpɚfɪkt/ n TECHNICAL ⇨ FUTURE PERFECT, PAST PERFECT, PRESENT PERFECT

**per·fec·tion** /pɚˈfɛkʃən/ n [U] **1** the state of being perfect: *Claire's parents demanded perfection from her.* | *The steak was cooked* **to perfection.** **2** the process of making something perfect: *The perfection of the technology will take years.* **3** a perfect example of something: *His acting is perfection.*

**per·fec·tion·ist** /pɚˈfɛkʃənɪst/ n someone who is not satisfied with anything unless it is completely perfect: *You look fine. Don't be such a perfectionist.*

**per·fect·ly** /ˈpɚfɪktli/ adv **1** in a perfect way: *She's always perfectly dressed.* **2** a word meaning very or completely, used when you are annoyed about something: *You know perfectly well what I'm talking about!*

**per·fo·rat·ed** /ˈpɚfəˌreɪtɪd/ adj **1** a piece of paper that is perforated has a line of small holes in it so that part of it can be torn off easily **2** a part of your body that is perforated has had a

hole torn in it: *a perforated eardrum* —**perforate** v [T]

**per·form** /pɚˈfɔrm/ v **1** [I,T] to do something to entertain people: *We saw "Hamlet" performed last week.* | *Karen will be performing with her band on Friday.* **2** [T] to do something such as a job or piece of work, especially something difficult or complicated: *Surgeons can perform this operation in less than three hours.* | *a minister performing a wedding ceremony* **3 perform well/badly** if a machine performs well or badly, it works in that way: *The bike performs well on mountain trails.*

**per·form·ance** /pɚˈfɔrməns/ n **1** an act of performing a play, piece of music etc., or the occasion when this is performed: *a beautiful performance of Swan Lake* | *The next performance is at 8 o'clock.* **2** [U] how successful someone or something is, and how well he, she, or it works: *The country's economic performance has been poor recently.* | *The car's performance on wet roads was good.* **3** [U] the act of doing something, especially your work: *The accident occurred during the performance of his duties.*

**per·form·er** /pɚˈfɔrmɚ/ n an actor, musician etc. who performs to entertain people: *a circus performer*

**per·form·ing arts** /.ˌ.. ˈ./ n [plural] arts such as dance, music, or DRAMA, that are performed to entertain people

**per·fume** /ˈpɚfyum, pɚˈfyum/ n [C,U] **1** a liquid with a strong pleasant smell, that you put on your skin: *What kind of perfume are you wearing?* **2** a pleasant smell: *the rose's sweet perfume* —**perfumed** adj: *perfumed soap*

**per·func·to·ry** /pɚˈfʌŋktəri/ adj done quickly, carelessly, and without interest: *The guard made a perfunctory check of the room and then left.* —**perfunctorily** adv

**per·haps** /pɚˈhæps/ adv **1** possibly; MAYBE: *"Where's Nancy?" "Perhaps she's caught in traffic."* | *This is perhaps Irving's finest novel.* **2** SPOKEN used in order to politely ask or suggest something: *Perhaps you'd like to join us?*

---

**USAGE NOTE perhaps, maybe, and may be**

Use **perhaps** or **maybe** to talk about something that is possible. **Maybe** is usually used at the beginning of a sentence or CLAUSE: *Maybe we can get together this weekend.* **Perhaps** is a little more formal, and can be used in other places in a clause: *We can perhaps meet this weekend.* **May** is a modal verb that is sometimes used with the verb "be": *She may be here later.*

**per·il** /ˈpɛrəl/ *n* LITERARY **1** [U] danger of being harmed or killed: *Everyone feared that the sailors were in great peril.* **2 the perils of** the dangers involved in a particular activity: *They weren't aware of the perils of climbing a mountain alone.*

**per·il·ous** /ˈpɛrələs/ *adj* LITERARY very dangerous: *a perilous journey*

**pe·rim·e·ter** /pəˈrɪmətɚ/ *n* **1** the border around an area of land: *the perimeter of the airfield* **2** the whole length of the border around an area or shape: *the perimeter of a triangle*

**pe·ri·od** /ˈpɪriəd/ *n* **1** a length of time: *the period from Christmas Day until New Year's Day | a 3-day waiting period for the purchase of a gun* **2** a particular length of time in history or in a person's life: *a short period of calm during the Civil War | the blue period in Picasso's painting* **3** the monthly flow of blood from a woman's body **4** the mark (.) used in writing that shows the end of a sentence or an abbreviation **5** one of the equal parts that the school day is divided into: *I have a history test during first/second/third period on Tuesday.* **6** one of the equal parts that a game is divided into in a sport such as HOCKEY **7 period!** SPOKEN said when you have made a decision and you do not want to discuss the subject any more: *I just won't do it, period!*

**pe·ri·od·ic** /ˌpɪriˈɑdɪk/, **periodical** *adj* happening again and again, usually at regular times: *Dale gets periodic headaches.*

**pe·ri·od·i·cal** /ˌpɪriˈɑdɪkəl/ *n* a magazine, especially one about a serious or technical subject

**pe·ri·od·i·cal·ly** /ˌpɪriˈɑdɪkli/ *adv* happening again and again, usually at regular times: *The river periodically floods the valley. | Athletes are periodically tested for drugs.*

**periodic ta·ble** /ˌ..ˌ.. ˈ../ *n* [singular] a specially arranged list of the ELEMENTs (=simple chemical substances)

**pe·riph·e·ral**[1] /pəˈrɪfərəl/ *adj* **1** relating to the main idea, question, activity etc., but less important than it: *The building of jet engines is a peripheral business for BMW.* **2** in the outer area of something, or relating to an outer area: *the peripheral suburbs of a big city | peripheral vision* (=what you can see to the side of you when you look straight ahead) **3** peripheral equipment can be connected to a computer and used with it

**peripheral**[2] *n* a piece of equipment that is connected to a computer and used with it

**pe·riph·er·y** /pəˈrɪfəri/ *n* the outside area or edge of something: *a new neighborhood on the periphery of the city* —compare OUTSKIRTS

**per·i·scope** /ˈpɛrəˌskoʊp/ *n* a long tube with mirrors fitted in it that is used for looking over the top of something, especially in a SUBMARINE

**per·ish** /ˈpɛrɪʃ/ *v* [I] LITERARY to die: *Hundreds perished when the Titanic sank.*

**periscope**

periscope

**per·ish·a·ble** /ˈpɛrɪʃəbəl/ *adj* food that is perishable can become bad quickly: *milk and other perishable items* —**perishables** *n* [plural]

**per·jure** /ˈpɚdʒɚ/ *v* [I] **perjure yourself** to tell a lie in a court of law

**per·ju·ry** /ˈpɚdʒəri/ *n* [U] the crime of telling a lie in a court of law

**perk**[1] /pɚk/ *n* money, goods, or other advantages that you get from your work in addition to your pay: *A car and travel expenses are perks of the job.*

**perk**[2] *v* [I,T] INFORMAL to make coffee using a PERCOLATOR

**perk up** *phr v* **1** [I,T **perk sb ↔ up**] to become more cheerful and interested in what is happening around you, or to make someone feel this way: *Meg perked up when the music started. | A cup of tea will perk you up.* **2** [I,T **perk sth ↔ up**] to become better, more interesting etc., or to make something do this: *Lower interest rates may be needed to perk up the economy.*

**perk·y** /ˈpɚki/ *adj* cheerful and full of interest: *a perky little girl*

**perm**[1] /pɚm/ *n* a way of putting curls into straight hair by treating it with chemicals: *Debbie's getting a perm today.*

**perm**[2] *v* [T] to put curls into straight hair using chemicals: *Did you have your hair permed?*

**per·ma·nent**[1] /ˈpɚmənənt/ *adj* continuing to exist for a long time or for all time: *a permanent job | The UN Security Council has five permanent members.* —**permanence** *n* [U] —compare TEMPORARY

**permanent**[2] *n* ⇨ PERM[1]

**per·ma·nent·ly** /ˈpɚmənəntli/ *adv* always, or for a very long time: *Do you plan to live here permanently? | The school has been permanently closed.*

**per·me·ate** /ˈpɚmiˌeɪt/ *v* [I,T] to spread through every part of something: *The smell of smoke permeated the house.*

**per·mis·si·ble** /pɚˈmɪsəbəl/ *adj* FORMAL allowed by law or by the rules: *In some religions, divorce is not permissible.*

**per·mis·sion** /pɚˈmɪʃən/ *n* [U] the act of allowing someone to do something: *You have to ask permission if you want to leave class early. | Did your dad give you permission to use the car?* ✗ DON'T SAY "the permission." ✗

**per·mis·sive** /pɚˈmɪsɪv/ *adj* allowing actions or behavior that many people disapprove of: *the permissive society of the 1970s*

**per·mit**[1] /pɚˈmɪt/ v **-tted, -tting** FORMAL **1** [T] to allow something to happen, especially by a rule or law: *Smoking is not permitted inside the building.* **2** [I] to make it possible for something to happen: *We'll probably go to the beach, weather permitting.* (=if the weather is good enough)

**per·mit**[2] /ˈpɚmɪt/ n an official written statement giving you the right to do something: *You can't park here without a permit.* | *a travel/work permit*

**per·mu·ta·tion** /ˌpɚmyʊˈteɪʃən/ n one of the different ways in which a set of things can be arranged, or put together to make something else: *Over the years, I've found several permutations of this recipe.*

**per·ni·cious** /pɚˈnɪʃəs/ adj FORMAL very harmful, especially in a way that is not easily noticeable: *the pernicious effect of racial segregation in schools*

**per·ox·ide** /pəˈrɑkˌsaɪd/ n [U] a chemical liquid used in order to make dark hair lighter, or to kill BACTERIA

**per·pen·dic·u·lar** /ˌpɚpənˈdɪkyəlɚ/ adj **1** be **perpendicular to** if one line is perpendicular to another line, they form an angle of 90° **2** exactly upright and not leaning to one side or the other: *a perpendicular pole* —compare HORIZONTAL, VERTICAL

**per·pe·trate** /ˈpɚpəˌtreɪt/ v [T] FORMAL to do something that is morally or legally wrong: *Goodwin denied he had perpetrated the fraud.*

**per·pe·tra·tor** /ˈpɚpəˌtreɪtɚ/ n FORMAL someone who does something that is a crime

**per·pet·u·al** /pɚˈpɛtʃuəl/ adj **1** continuing all the time without changing: *the perpetual noise of the machinery* **2** repeated many times in a way that annoys you: *I'm tired of her perpetual complaining.* —**perpetually** adv

**per·pet·u·ate** /pɚˈpɛtʃuˌeɪt/ v [T] to make something continue: *We are trying to get rid of books that perpetuate stereotypes.*

**per·plex** /pɚˈplɛks/ v [T] a problem that perplexes you, confuses you and worries you because it is difficult to understand: *Shea's symptoms perplexed the doctors.* —**perplexed** adj —**perplexity** n [U]

**per·qui·site** /ˈpɚkwəzɪt/ n FORMAL ⇨ PERK[1]

**per se** /ˌpɚ ˈseɪ/ adv LATIN used in order to show that something is being considered alone, apart from anything else: *Money, per se, is not usually why people change jobs.*

**per·se·cute** /ˈpɚsɪˌkyut/ v [T] **1** to treat someone cruelly and unfairly, especially because of his/her religious or political beliefs: *a writer persecuted for criticizing the government* **2** to deliberately cause trouble for someone: *Duke said he was being persecuted by a hostile media.* —**persecutor** n

**per·se·cu·tion** /ˌpɚsɪˈkyuʃən/ n [U] the act of persecuting (PERSECUTE) someone: *Several re-ligious groups suffered persecution under the old Communist regime.*

**per·se·ver·ance** /ˌpɚsəˈvɪrəns/ n [U] determination to keep trying to do something difficult: *You have to admire the perseverance and skill required to build a road through the pass.*

**per·se·vere** /ˌpɚsəˈvɪr/ v [I] to continue trying to do something difficult in a determined way: *Jeff persevered in his efforts to learn how to ski.*

**per·sist** /pɚˈsɪst/ v [I] **1** to continue to do something, even though it is difficult or other people do not like it: *Her boss persisted in his efforts to ask her for a date.* **2** to continue to exist or happen: *The pain persisted for months, even though the injury had healed.*

**per·sist·ence** /pɚˈsɪstəns/ n [U] the act or state of being PERSISTENT: *Brancusi's persistence was finally rewarded with a small part in a TV show.*

**per·sist·ent** /pɚˈsɪstənt/ adj **1** continuing to exist or happen, especially for longer than is usual: *Congress needs to address the problem of persistent unemployment.* **2** continuing to do something even though it is difficult or other people oppose it: *You may not be able to find them easily, but be persistent.* —**persistently** adv: *He persistently denies doing anything wrong.*

**per·son** /ˈpɚsən/ n, plural **people 1** a man, woman, or child: *Bert's kind of a hard person to talk to.* | *Abby's a computer/cat etc. person.* (=someone who likes computers, cats etc.) **2 in person** if you do something in person, you do it when you are in a place, not by using a letter or the telephone: *You'll have to apply for your passport in person.* —see also FIRST PERSON, SECOND PERSON, THIRD PERSON

---

**USAGE NOTE** person, persons, people, and peoples

**Person** means one man, woman, or child: *She's a really generous person.* The plural of **person** is **persons**, but this is only used in very official language. When talking about more than one **person**, use **people** as the plural: *There were about 100 people at the wedding.* **People** is also a countable noun that means a particular race or group that lives in a particular country. The plural is **peoples**: *the peoples of the Caribbean.*

---

**per·so·na** /pɚˈsoʊnə/ n, plural **personas** or **personae** /-ni/ the way you behave when you are with other people: *You always wonder how different movie stars are from their **public personas**.*

**per·son·a·ble** /ˈpɚsənəbəl/ adj having a pleasant way of talking and behaving: *Beth is a charming personable young woman.*

**per·son·al** /'pɚsənəl/ *adj*
**1** ▶RELATING TO YOU◀ belonging to you, or relating to what you know, have done, have experienced etc.: *Please keep all bags and other personal belongings with you.* | *These women know from personal experience about the problems facing single mothers.*
**2** ▶PRIVATE◀ private and concerning only you: *That's a personal question.* (=a question about things that are private) | *Owen has a lot of personal problems.*
**3** ▶ONLY YOU◀ used in order to emphasize that no one else did or will do something: *Whoopi Goldberg made a personal appearance at the charity event.* | *I will give this my personal attention.*
**4** ▶CRITICISM◀ involving rude or upsetting criticism of someone: *Making personal remarks like that isn't professional.* | *It's nothing personal* (=I am not criticizing you) - *I just don't agree with you.*
**5 personal friend** someone you know well, especially someone famous or important: *The editor is a personal friend of his.*
**6** ▶NOT WORK◀ not relating to your work or business: *We're not allowed to make personal phone calls at work.*
**7** ▶YOUR BODY◀ relating to your body or the way you look: *personal hygiene*

**personal com·put·er** /ˌ... .'../ *n* ⇨ PC¹

**per·son·al·i·ty** /ˌpɚsə'næləti/ *n* **1** [C,U] someone's character, especially the way s/he behaves toward other people: *Alice has an outgoing personality.* **2** someone who is well known to the public: *a TV personality* **3** [U] INFORMAL the qualities that make someone or something interesting: *We liked the name because we thought it had personality.*

**per·son·al·ize** /'pɚsənəˌlaɪz/ *v* **1** to put your name or INITIALs on something: *I hate cars with personalized license plates.* **2** to decorate something in a way you like: *Becky has personalized her office with photos and drawings.* **3** to make something suitable for what a particular person needs: *a school that personalizes language courses* **4** to talk about and criticize people rather than dealing with facts: *Both candidates began personalizing the campaign.*

**per·son·al·ly** /'pɚsənəli/ *adv* **1** SPOKEN used in order to emphasize that you are only giving your own opinion: *Personally, I don't like horror movies.* **2** doing or having done something yourself: *She's personally responsible for all the arrangements.* **3** said as a criticism of someone's character or appearance: *Dora's in a bad mood - don't take anything she says personally.* (=don't think that she is criticizing you) **4** as a friend, or as someone you have met: *I don't know her personally, but I like her books.*

**personal pro·noun** /ˌ... '../ *n* TECHNICAL in grammar, a PRONOUN used for the person who is speaking, being spoken to, or being spoken about, such as "I," "you," and "they"

**per·so·nals** /'pɚsənəlz/ *n* **the personals** a part of a newspaper in which people can have private messages printed

**per·son·i·fi·ca·tion** /pɚˌsɑnəfə'keɪʃən/ *n* **1 the personification of** someone who has a lot of a particular quality, so that s/he is used as an example of that quality: *Mrs. Grant is the personification of kindness.* **2** [C,U] the representation of a thing or a quality as a person: *the personification of Justice as a woman holding scales*

**per·son·i·fy** /pɚ'sɑnəˌfaɪ/ *v* [T] **1** to think of or represent a quality or thing as a person: *Time is usually personified as an old man with a beard.* **2** to represent a particular quality or thing by being a typical example of it: *Nathan personifies truthfulness.*

**per·son·nel** /ˌpɚsə'nɛl/ *n* **1** [plural] the people who work in a company or for a particular kind of employer: *All personnel need to have identification cards.* | *military personnel* **2** [U] ⇨ HUMAN RESOURCES

**per·spec·tive** /pɚ'spɛktɪv/ *n* **1** a way of thinking about something that is influenced by the type of person you are or the work you do: *We'll need to ask Dr. Havani for a scientific perspective on the problem.* **2** [U] the ability to think about something sensibly, so that it does not seem worse than it is: *She's having trouble keeping her problems in perspective.* **3** [U] a method of drawing a picture that makes objects look solid and shows distance and depth: *Children's drawings often have no perspective.*

**per·spi·ra·tion** /ˌpɚspə'reɪʃən/ *n* [U] FORMAL ⇨ SWEAT²

**per·spire** /pɚ'spaɪɚ/ *v* [I] FORMAL ⇨ SWEAT¹

**per·suade** /pɚ'sweɪd/ *v* [T] **1** to make someone decide to do something by giving good reasons: *Ken finally persuaded Jo to apply for the job.* **2** to make someone believe something or feel sure about something; CONVINCE: *She persuaded the jury (that) her client was not guilty.* | *Valdez believed he could persuade any reporter of anything.*

**per·sua·sion** /pɚ'sweɪʒən/ *n* **1** [U] the act or skill of persuading someone to do something: *With a little persuasion, Debbie agreed to come with us.* **2** a particular belief, especially a political or religious one: *Jake and his brother are of different political persuasions.*

**per·sua·sive** /pɚ'sweɪsɪv/ *adj* able to influence other people to believe or do something: *a number of persuasive arguments* | *Erin can be very persuasive.*

**pert** /pɚt/ *adj* **1** amusing in a way that shows a slight lack of respect: *a pert answer* **2** neat and attractive in a cheerful way: *a pert red ribbon in her hair*

**per·tain** /pɚˈteɪn/ v
  **pertain to** sth phr v [T] FORMAL to relate directly to something: *laws **pertaining to** welfare benefits*

**per·ti·nent** /ˈpɚt̚n-ənt/ adj FORMAL directly relating to something that is being considered; RELEVANT: *Reporters asked a few pertinent questions.*

**per·turbed** /pɚˈtɚbd/ adj FORMAL worried and annoyed: *Kerry was **perturbed that** the doctors only allowed her to talk to her father for ten minutes.* –**perturb** v [T]

**pe·ruse** /pəˈruz/ v [T] FORMAL to read something in a careful way: *an evening spent perusing the job advertisements* –**perusal** n [U]

**per·vade** /pɚˈveɪd/ v [T] to be in all parts of something: *The smoke from the factory pervaded the city.*

**per·va·sive** /pɚˈveɪsɪv/ adj existing or spreading everywhere: *a pervasive fear of crime*

**per·verse** /pɚˈvɚs/ adj behaving in an unreasonable way by doing the opposite of what people want you to do: *He takes perverse pleasure in arguing with everyone.*

**per·ver·sion** /pɚˈvɚʒən/ n [C,U] **1** a type of sexual behavior that is considered unnatural and unacceptable **2** the act of changing something so that it is no longer right, reasonable, or true: *a perversion of the truth*

**per·vert**[1] /pɚˈvɚt/ v [T] to change someone or something in a harmful way: *These genetic experiments pervert nature.*

**per·vert**[2] /ˈpɚvɚt/ n someone whose sexual behavior is considered unnatural and unacceptable

**per·vert·ed** /pɚˈvɚtɪd/ adj **1** relating to unacceptable and unnatural sexual thoughts or behavior: *They were the most perverted pictures I had ever seen!* **2** morally wrong or unnatural: *perverted logic*

**pes·ky** /ˈpɛski/ adj INFORMAL annoying and causing trouble: *a pesky fly*

**pes·si·mis·m** /ˈpɛsəˌmɪzəm/ n [U] the feeling of being PESSIMISTIC: *There is a lot of pessimism in the country about the economy.*

**pes·si·mist** /ˈpɛsəmɪst/ n someone who always expects that the worst thing will happen: *Don't be such a pessimist - things will work out.* –opposite OPTIMIST

**pes·si·mis·tic** /ˌpɛsəˈmɪstɪk/ adj expecting that bad things will happen or that a situation will have a bad result: *Jonathan is **pessimistic about** his chances.* –opposite OPTIMISTIC

**pest** /pɛst/ n **1** a small animal or insect that destroys crops or food **2** INFORMAL an annoying person: *The kids next door can be real pests.*

**pes·ter** /ˈpɛstɚ/ v [T] to annoy someone by asking for something again and again: *Lisa **pestered** her mother **to** let her go swimming.*

**pes·ti·cide** /ˈpɛstəˌsaɪd/ n a chemical substance that kills insects that destroy crops

**pet**[1] /pɛt/ n an animal that you keep at home: *Do you have any pets?* –see also TEACHER'S PET

**pet**[2] v [T] **1** to move your hand over an animal's fur, in order to show it affection **2** to kiss and touch someone in a sexual way

**pet**[3] adj **1 pet project/subject etc.** a plan, subject etc. that you particularly like or are interested in: *Congressmen are always looking for funding for their pet projects.* **2** a pet animal is one that someone keeps at home: *a pet hamster* **3 pet peeve** something that always annoys you, that may not annoy other people. *One of my pet peeves is people being late for meetings.*

**pet·al** /ˈpɛtl/ n the colored part of a flower that is shaped like a leaf: *Sunflowers have large petals.*

**pe·ter** /ˈpitɚ/ v [I]
  **peter out** phr v [I] to gradually become smaller, fewer, quieter etc. and then no longer exist or happen: *The trail became narrower and eventually **petered out** altogether.*

**pe·tite** /pəˈtit/ adj a woman who is petite is short and thin in an attractive way

**pe·ti·tion**[1] /pəˈtɪʃən/ v [I,T] to formally ask someone in authority to do something, especially by sending him/her a PETITION: *Residents are petitioning against a new prison in the area.*

**petition**[2] n a piece of paper that asks someone in authority to do or change something, and is signed by a lot of people: *Will you sign a **petition against** nuclear testing?* | *Locals **drew up a petition** to protest the building of a new highway.*

**pet·ri·fied** /ˈpɛtrəˌfaɪd/ adj **1** extremely frightened: *We were so petrified by the noise in the attic that we couldn't move.* **2 petrified wood** wood that has changed into stone over millions of years –**petrify** v [T]

**pet·ro·chem·i·cal** /ˌpɛtroʊˈkɛmɪkəl/ n a chemical substance obtained from PETROLEUM or natural gas: *the petrochemical industry*

**pe·tro·le·um** /pəˈtroʊliəm/ n [U] oil that is obtained from below the surface of the Earth and is used in order to make GASOLINE and other chemical substances: *petroleum-based products*

**pet·ty** /ˈpɛti/ adj **1** something that is petty is not serious or important: *Don't bother me with petty details.* **2** someone who is petty cares too much about things that are not very important or serious: *Sometimes he's so petty about money.* (=he thinks too much about exactly how much people owe him) **3 petty crime** a crime that is not serious, for example, stealing things that are not expensive –**pettiness** n [U]

**petty cash** /ˌ.. './ n [U] money that is kept in an office for making small payments

**petty of·fi·cer**, **Petty Officer** /ˌ.. '...◂/ n an officer who has the lowest rank in the Navy

**pet·u·lant** /ˈpɛtʃələnt/ adj behaving in an impatient and angry way, like a child: *You're acting like a petulant four-year-old.*

**pew**¹ /pyu/ *n* a long wooden seat in a church

**pew**² *interjection* said when something smells very bad: *Pew! There must be a farm near here.*

**pew·ter** /'pyuṯɚ/ *n* [U] a gray metal made by mixing LEAD and TIN

**PG** *adj* the abbreviation of "parental guidance," used in order to show that a movie may include parts that are not suitable for young children to see

**phal·lic** /'fælɪk/ *adj* like a PENIS, or relating to the penis. *a phallic symbol* (=something that represents a penis)

**phal·lus** /'fæləs/ *n* the male sex organ, or a model of it

**phan·tom** /'fænṯəm/ *n* LITERARY **1** ⇨ GHOST **2** something that exists only in your imagination

**Phar·aoh** /'fɛrou, 'fær-/ *n* a ruler of ancient Egypt

**phar·ma·ceu·ti·cal** /ˌfɑrməˈsuṯɪkəl/ *adj* relating to the production of drugs and medicine: *large pharmaceutical companies*

**phar·ma·cist** /'fɑrməsɪst/ *n* someone whose job is to prepare drugs and medicine

**phar·ma·col·o·gy** /ˌfɑrməˈkɑlədʒi/ *n* [U] the scientific study of drugs and medicines −**pharmacologist** *n*

**phar·ma·cy** /'fɑrməsi/ *n* a store or a part of a store where medicines are prepared and sold

**phase**¹ /feɪz/ *n* **1** one part of a process in which something develops or grows: *the last phase of the project | It's normal for a 2-year-old to have tantrums; your child is just **going through a phase**.* **2** one of the changes in the appearance of the moon or a PLANET when it is seen from the Earth

**phase**² *v* [T]

**phase** sth ↔ **in** *phr v* [T] to introduce something gradually: *New rules about claiming overtime will be **phased in** over the next two months.*

**phase** sth ↔ **out** *phr v* [T] to gradually stop using or providing something: *Leaded gas was **phased out** in the 1970s.*

**Ph.D.** /ˌpi eɪt ʃ 'di/ *n* Doctor of Philosophy; the highest university degree that can be earned, or someone who has this degree

**pheas·ant** /'fɛzənt/ *n* a large colorful bird with a long tail, that is hunted for food and sport, or the meat from this bird

**phe·nom·e·nal** /fɪˈnɑmənl/ *adj* very unusual and impressive: *We have a phenomenal view of the harbor at night from here.* −**phenomenally** *adv*

**phe·nom·e·non** /fɪˈnɑmənɑn, -ˌnɑn/ *n* **1** *plural* **phenomena** something that happens or exists in society, science, or nature that is unusual or difficult to understand: *Homelessness is not a **new phenomenon**.* **2** *plural* **phenomenons** a person or thing that has a rare ability or quality: *Gillespie called him one of the phenomenons of our century.*

**phew** /fyu, hwyu/ *interjection* said when you feel tired, hot, or RELIEVED: *Phew! I'm glad that's over.*

**phial** /'faɪl/ *n* a small bottle for liquid medicine

**phi·lan·der·er** /fɪˈlændərɚ/ *n* OLD-FASHIONED a man who has sex with many women and does not want a serious relationship −**philandering** *n* [U]

**phi·lan·thro·pist** /fɪˈlænθrəpɪst/ *n* someone who gives a lot of money and help to people who need it

**phi·lan·thro·py** /fɪˈlænθrəpi/ *n* [U] the practice of giving money and help to people who need it −**philanthropic** /ˌfɪlənˈθrɑpɪk/ *adj*

**phil·is·tine** /'fɪləˌstin/ *n* DISAPPROVING someone who does not like or understand art, music, literature etc.

**phi·los·o·pher** /fɪˈlɑsəfɚ/ *n* **1** someone who studies or teaches PHILOSOPHY: *ancient Greek philosophers* **2** someone who thinks a lot and asks questions about the world, life, death etc.

**phil·o·soph·i·cal** /ˌfɪləˈsɑfɪkəl/ *adj* **1** relating to PHILOSOPHY: *a philosophical discussion* **2** accepting difficult or unpleasant things calmly: *Anderson remains **philosophical about** his defeat.* −**philosophically** *adv*

**phi·los·o·phize** /fɪˈlɑsəˌfaɪz/ *v* [I] to talk or think about important subjects and ideas in a serious way

**phi·los·o·phy** /fɪˈlɑsəfi/ *n* **1** [U] the study of what it means to exist, what good and evil are, what knowledge is, or how people should live **2** a set of ideas about these subjects: *the philosophy of Plato* **3** a set of beliefs about how you should live your life, do your job etc.: *a new business philosophy*

**phlegm** /flɛm/ *n* [U] a thick sticky substance produced in your nose and throat, especially when you have a cold; MUCUS

**phleg·mat·ic** /flɛgˈmæṯɪk/ *adj* FORMAL calm and not easily excited or worried

**pho·bi·a** /'foubiə/ *n* a strong, usually unreasonable, fear of something: *Holly **has a phobia about** snakes.* −**phobic** *adj*

**phoe·nix** /'finɪks/ *n* a bird in ancient stories that burns itself at the end of its life and is born again from the ASH*es*

**phone**¹ /foun/ *n* **1** a piece of equipment that you use in order to talk with someone in another place; telephone: *What's your phone number? | a car phone* **2** **be on the phone** to be talking to someone else using a telephone: *I was on the phone for an hour, talking to Lynn.* −see usage note at TELEPHONE

**phone**² *v* [I,T] to talk to someone using a telephone; call: *Several people phoned the radio station to complain.*

**phone book** /'. ./ *n* a book containing an

alphabetical list of the names, addresses, and telephone numbers of all the people in the area

**phone booth** /'. ./ *n* a partly enclosed structure containing a telephone that the public can use

**pho·net·ic** /fə'nɛtɪk/ *adj* relating to the sounds of human speech: *a phonetic alphabet* (=that uses signs to represent the sounds) −**phonetically** *adv*

**pho·net·ics** /fə'nɛtɪks/ *n* [U] TECHNICAL the science and study of speech sounds

**pho·no·graph** /'founə,græf/ *n* OLD-FASHIONED ⇨ RECORD PLAYER

**pho·ny** /'founi/ *adj* INFORMAL false or not real, and intended to deceive someone; FAKE: *Dirk gave the cops a phony address.* −**phony** *n*: *She's such a phony!*

**phoo·ey** /'fui/ *interjection* used in order to express strong disbelief or disappointment

**phos·phate** /'fasfeɪt/ *n* [C,U] one of the various forms of a salt of PHOSPHORUS, used in industry

**phos·pho·res·cent** /,fasfə'rɛsənt/ *adj* a substance that is phosphorescent shines slightly because it contains PHOSPHORUS, but produces little or no heat −**phosphorescence** *n* [U]

**phos·pho·rus** /'fasfərəs/ *n* [U] a poisonous chemical that starts to burn when it is brought out into the air −**phosphoric** /fas'fɔrɪk, -'fur-/ *adj*

**pho·to** /'foutou/ *n* INFORMAL ⇨ PHOTOGRAPH: *Who's the girl in this photo?*

**pho·to·cop·i·er** /'foutə,kapiə/ *n* a machine that quickly copies documents onto paper by photographing them

**pho·to·cop·y** /'foutə,kapi/ *n* a copy of a document made by a PHOTOCOPIER: *Make a photocopy of this article for me.* −**photocopy** *v* [T]

**photo fin·ish** /,.. '../ *n* the end of a race in which the leaders finish so close together that a photograph has to be taken to show who won

**pho·to·gen·ic** /,foutə'dʒɛnɪk/ *adj* always looking attractive in photographs: *Julie is very photogenic.*

**pho·to·graph** /'foutə,græf/ *n* a picture that is made using a camera: *an old photograph of my grandfather* | *Visitors are not allowed to take photographs.* −see also PICTURE¹ −**photograph** *v* [T]

**pho·tog·ra·pher** /fə'tagrəfə/ *n* someone who takes photographs, especially as a job: *a news photographer*

**pho·to·graph·ic** /,foutə'græfɪk/ *adj* **1** relating to photographs: *a photographic image* **2 photographic memory** the ability to remember exactly every detail of something you have seen

**pho·tog·ra·phy** /fə'tagrəfi/ *n* [U] the art, profession, or process of taking photographs: *I'm taking a photography class in the evenings.*

**pho·to·syn·the·sis** /,foutou'sɪnθəsɪs/ *n* [U] TECHNICAL the way that green plants make their food using the light from the sun

**phras·al verb** /,freizəl 'vɚb/ *n* TECHNICAL in grammar, a verb that changes its meaning when it is used with an adverb or preposition. In the sentence "The rocket blew up," "blew up" is a phrasal verb −see study note on page 462

**phrase¹** /freiz/ *n* **1** a group of words that has a special meaning: *Darwin's famous phrase, "the survival of the fittest"* **2** TECHNICAL in grammar, a group of words without a main verb that together make a subject, an object, or a verb tense. In the sentence, "We have a brand new car," "a brand new car" is a noun phrase −compare CLAUSE, SENTENCE¹

**phrase²** *v* [T] to express something in a particular way: *He phrased his question politely.* −**phrasing** *n* [U]

**phys·i·cal¹** /'fɪzɪkəl/ *adj* **1** relating to someone's body rather than his/her mind or soul: *physical exercise/contact* | *a woman of great physical strength* **2** relating to real things that can be seen, tasted, felt etc.: *our physical environment* **3** someone who is physical touches people a lot **4** involving very forceful body movements: *a very physical dancing style* **5** relating to or following the laws of nature: *the physical force of gravity* **6** a physical science such as PHYSICS studies things that are not living: *physical chemistry* −compare ORGANIC

**physical²**, **physical ex·am·i·na·tion** /,... ...'../ *n* a medical examination by a doctor, for example, before someone is allowed to start a job

**physical ed·u·ca·tion** /,... ..'../ *n* ⇨ PE

**phys·i·cally** /'fɪzɪkli/ *adv* **1** in relation to the body rather than the mind or soul: *I try to keep myself physically fit.* (=having strong muscles and not much fat) **2 physically impossible** not possible according to the laws of nature or what is known to be true: *It's physically impossible for penguins to fly.*

**physical ther·a·py** /,... '.../ *n* [U] a treatment for injuries and muscle problems that uses special exercises, rubbing, heat etc. −**physical therapist** *n*

**phy·si·cian** /fɪ'zɪʃən/ *n* FORMAL ⇨ DOCTOR¹ −see usage note at DOCTOR¹

**phys·ics** /'fɪzɪks/ *n* [U] the science that deals with the study of physical objects and substances, and natural forces such as light, heat, movement etc. −**physicist** /'fɪzəsɪst/ *n*

**phys·i·ol·o·gy** /,fɪzi'alədʒi/ *n* [U] a science that deals with the study of how the bodies of living things work −**physiological** /,fɪziə'ladʒɪkəl/ *adj* −compare ANATOMY

**phys·i·o·ther·a·py** /,fɪziou'θɛrəpi/ *n* [U] ⇨ PHYSICAL THERAPY

**phy·sique** /fɪ'zik/ *n* the shape, size, and

appearance of someone's body: *a man with a powerful physique*

**pi·an·ist** /ˈpiːænɪst, ˈpiənɪst/ *n* someone who plays the piano

**pi·an·o** /piˈænoʊ/ *n* a large musical instrument that you play by pressing a row of narrow black and white BARs with your fingers

**pic·co·lo** /ˈpɪkəˌloʊ/ *n* a musical instrument like a small FLUTE

**pick¹** /pɪk/ *v* [T]

**1** ▶CHOOSE◀ to choose something or someone from a group of people or things: *Katie picked the blue one.* | *Have you **picked** a date for the wedding yet?* | *He **picked** the Giants to win the division.* | *Phillips is now so successful that he can **pick and choose** the projects he wants.* (=he can choose only the ones he likes)

**2** ▶FLOWER/FRUIT◀ to pull or break off a flower or fruit from a plant or tree: *We're going out to the farm on Saturday to pick apples.*

**3** ▶REMOVE/PULL OFF◀ to remove small things from something, or to pull off small pieces from something: ***picking** meat off the bone* | *Michael, stop **picking** your nose.* (=cleaning the inside of it with your finger)

**4** **pick your way** to move carefully through an area, choosing exactly where to walk or drive: *Rescue workers picked their way through the rubble.*

**5** **pick a fight (with sb)** to deliberately begin an argument or fight with someone: *Adam's always picking fights with the younger kids.*

**6** **pick sb's brain(s)** to ask someone who knows a lot about a subject for information or advice about it: *If you have time later, could I pick your brains about some legal issues?*

**7** **pick a lock** to use something that is not a key to unlock a door, window etc. −see also PICKPOCKET

**pick at** sth *phr v* [T] to eat only a small amount of your food, as if you are not really hungry: *I was so nervous I could only **pick at** my lunch.*

**pick** sb/sth ↔ **off** *phr v* [T] to shoot people or animals one at a time from a long distance away: *Snipers were **picking off** anyone who came outdoors.*

**pick on** sb *phr v* [T] to unfairly criticize someone again and again, treat someone in an unkind way, or hurt someone: *Greg, stop **picking on** your sister!*

**pick** sb/sth ↔ **out** *phr v* [T] **1** to choose something carefully from a group of things: *We had a lot of fun **picking out** a present for Leslie's baby.* **2** to recognize or notice someone or something in a group of people or things: *The victim was able to **pick out** her attacker from a police lineup.*

**pick** sth ↔ **over** *phr v* [T] to carefully examine a group of things in order to choose only the ones you want: *Wash and **pick over** the beans.*

**pick up** *phr v*

**1** ▶LIFT UP◀ [T **pick** sb/sth ↔ **up**] to hold

someone or something and lift him, her, or it from a surface: ***Pick** me **up**, Daddy!* | *kids **picking up** shells at the beach* | *I **picked up** the phone* (=answered the phone) *just as it stopped ringing.* −see picture on page 473

**2** ▶GO GET SB/STH◀ [T **pick** sb/sth ↔ **up**] to go somewhere, usually in a vehicle, in order to get someone or something. *I'll **pick up** my stuff around six, okay?* | *What time should we **pick** you **up** at the airport?*

**3** ▶BUY◀ [T **pick** sth ↔ **up**] INFORMAL to buy something: *Will you **pick up** something for dinner on your way home?* | *The company is **picking up** the bill for my computer.* (=it is paying for it)

**4** ▶CLEAN A PLACE◀ [I,T **pick** sth ↔ **up**] to put things away neatly, or to clean a place by doing this: *Straighten your room and **pick up** all those papers.* | ***Pick up** the living room, please.* | *He never **picks up** after himself.* (=he does not put away the things he has used)

**5** ▶GET BETTER◀ [I] to improve: *Sales should **pick up** before Christmas.*

**6** ▶INCREASE◀ [I,T **pick up** sth] to increase or get faster: *The car was gradually **picking up** speed.* (=going faster) | *The wind had **picked up** considerably.*

**7** ▶LEARN◀ [T **pick** sth ↔ **up**] to learn something without deliberately trying to: *Craig **picked up** the guitar from his dad.*

**8** ▶ILLNESS◀ [T **pick** sth ↔ **up**] to get an illness from someone: *She's **picked up** a cold from a child at school.*

**9** ▶NOTICE◀ [T **pick** sth ↔ **up**] to notice, see, or hear something, or to receive signals from something, especially when this is difficult; DETECT: *We didn't **pick** anything **up** on radar.* | *The dogs were able to **pick up** the scent.*

**10** ▶START AGAIN◀ [T **pick** sth ↔ **up**] to begin a conversation, meeting etc. again, starting from the point where it stopped earlier; RESUME: *We'll **pick up where we left off** after lunch.*

**11** ▶POLICE◀ [T **pick** sb ↔ **up**] if the police pick someone up, they find him/her and take him/her to the police station; ARREST: *Carr was **picked up** and taken in for questioning.*

**12** ▶SEX◀ [T **pick** sb ↔ **up**] to talk to someone you do not know and try to start a sexual relationship with him/her: *a guy trying to **pick up** girls at the bar*

**13** **pick up the pieces (of sth)** to get a situation back to normal after something bad has happened: *Ralph's trying to **pick up** the pieces of his business.*

**pick up on** sth *phr v* [T] to notice or understand something that is not easy to notice, and react to it: *Children quickly **pick up on** tensions between their parents.*

**pick²** *n* **1** [U] choice: *There are four kinds of cake, so you can **take your pick**.* (=choose one) | *She'll be able to **have her pick of** colleges.* (=choose any one she wants) **2** the

**pick of sth** INFORMAL the best thing or things in a group: *The Doles will get the pick of the puppies.* **3** a sharp pointed tool, such as a PICK-AX **4** a small flat object that you use for playing an instrument such as a GUITAR

**pick·ax** /'pɪk-æks/ *n* a large tool that has a long handle and a curved iron end with two sharp points, used for breaking up a road, rocks etc.

**pick·er** /'pɪkɚ/ *n* a person or machine that picks things such as fruit, cotton etc.

**pick·et¹** /'pɪkɪt/, **picket line** /'.. ./ *n* a group or line of people who PICKET a factory, store etc.: *Two workers were hurt today trying to cross the picket line.* (=trying to work during a STRIKE)

**picket²** *v* [I,T] to stand or march in front of a factory, store etc. to protest something, or to stop people from going in to work during a STRIKE (=time when everyone refuses to work)

**picket fence** /ˌ.. '. / *n* a fence made of a line of strong pointed sticks fixed in the ground

**pick·le¹** /'pɪkəl/ *n*
**1** [C,U] a CUCUMBER (=vegetable) preserved in VINEGAR and salt or sugar, or a thin piece of this: *a dill pickle* **2 be in a pickle** OLD-FASHIONED to be in a difficult situation

**picket fence**

**pickle²** *v* [T] to preserve food in VINEGAR with salt or sugar and various SPICES –**pickled** *adj*: *pickled onions/herring*

**pick-me-up** /'. . ,./ *n* INFORMAL something that makes you feel cheerful or gives you more energy, especially a drink or medicine

**pick·pock·et** /'pɪkˌpɑkɪt/ *n* someone who steals things from people's pockets, especially in public –see usage note at THIEF

**pick·up** /'pɪkʌp/ *n* **1** also **pickup truck** /'.. ˌ./ a vehicle with a large open part at the back that is used for carrying goods –see picture on page 469 **2** the act of taking something from a place using a vehicle: *There is a regular garbage pickup on Tuesdays.* **3** [U] INFORMAL the ability of a car to reach a high speed in a short time: *The new models have a lot of pickup.* **4** INFORMAL the act or process of improving: *a pickup in sales*

**pick·y** /'pɪki/ *adj* INFORMAL, DISAPPROVING someone who is picky is difficult to make happy, because s/he only likes a small range of things: *a picky eater | Kelly's so picky about her clothes!*

**pic·nic¹** /'pɪknɪk/ *n* **1** an occasion when people take food and eat it outdoors, for example in a park: *We used to have picnics down by the creek. | Do you want to go for a picnic this Saturday?* **2 be no picnic** INFORMAL

to be difficult or unpleasant: *Riding the bus to work every day is no picnic!*

**picnic²** *v* **picnicked, picnicking** [I] to have a PICNIC

**pic·to·ri·al** /pɪk'tɔriəl/ *adj* relating to or using pictures: *a pictorial history of Montana*

**pic·ture¹** /'pɪktʃɚ/ *n*
**1** ▶IMAGE◀ a painting, drawing, or photograph. *I have a picture of my family on the wall. | Draw/paint a picture of your house. | a group of tourists taking pictures (=taking photographs) | Leo's picture (=photograph of him) is in the newspaper.*
**2** ▶SITUATION◀ [singular] the general situation in a place, organization etc.: *The political picture has greatly changed since March.*
**3** ▶DESCRIPTION◀ [C usually singular] a description that gives you an idea of what something is like: *The report paints a clear picture of life in the army.*
**4 be in/out of the picture** INFORMAL to be involved or not be involved in a situation: *With his main rival out of the picture, the mayor has a chance of winning the election.*
**5** ▶ON A SCREEN◀ the image that you see on a television or in a movie: *Something's wrong with the picture.*
**6 get the picture** SPOKEN to understand something: *I don't want you around here any more, get the picture?*
**7** ▶MOVIE◀ OLD-FASHIONED ⟶ MOVIE: *Grandma loved going to the pictures.*

**picture²** *v* [T] **1** to imagine something, especially by making an image of it in your mind: *I can still picture him standing there with his uniform on. | I can't picture myself as a mother.* **2** to show something or someone in a photograph, painting, or drawing: *The girl is pictured sitting on a horse.*

**picture book** /'.. ,./ *n* a children's story book that has a lot of pictures in it

**pic·tur·esque** /ˌpɪktʃə'rɛsk/ *adj* attractive and interesting: *a picturesque sunset/village*

**pid·dling** /'pɪdlɪŋ/ *adj* INFORMAL small and unimportant: *a piddling amount of money*

**pidg·in** /'pɪdʒən/ *n* [C,U] a language that is a mixture of two other languages and is used by people who do not speak each other's language very well

**pie** /paɪ/ *n* [C,U] **1** a food usually made with fruit baked inside a covering of PASTRY: *an apple pie* –see picture at DESSERT **2 as easy as pie** INFORMAL very easy **3 a piece/share/slice of the pie** INFORMAL a share of something such as money or profit: *Landers wants a bigger slice of the pie.* **4 pie in the sky** INFORMAL a good plan or promise that you do not think will ever happen: *The whole idea is pie in the sky, but it's nice to dream about it.*

**piece¹** /pis/ *n*
**1** ▶PART OF A WHOLE◀ a part of something

that has been separated, broken, or cut off from the rest of it: *Do you want a **piece of** pizza?* | *The vase lay **in pieces** (=broken into many pieces) on the floor.*
**2** ▶PART OF A SET◀ a single thing of a particular type, often part of a set of things or part of a larger thing: *a **piece of** paper* | *a chess piece* | *a **five-piece** band (=one with five members)* | *a beautiful **piece of** land on the river*
**3** ▶CONNECTED PART◀ one of several different parts that can be connected together to make something: *the **pieces of** a jigsaw puzzle*
**4 a piece of advice/information/gossip etc.** some advice, information etc.: *Let me give you a piece of advice: don't ask her about her mother.*
**5 go to pieces** to become so upset or nervous that you cannot think or behave normally: *When she found out what Joe had done, Liz just went to pieces.*
**6 smash/tear/rip etc. sth to pieces** to damage something severely: *She tore the letter to pieces and burned it.*
**7 (all) in one piece** not damaged or injured: *I'm glad the china arrived all in one piece.*
**8 give sb a piece of your mind** INFORMAL to tell someone that you are very angry with him/her: *If I see her, I'll give her a piece of my mind!*
**9 be a piece of cake** INFORMAL to be very easy to do: *Raising four children hasn't been a piece of cake.*
**10** ▶ART/MUSIC ETC.◀ something that has been written or made by an artist, musician, or writer: *a beautiful **piece of work***
**11 be a piece of shit/crap/junk etc.** SPOKEN an impolite way of saying that something is of very low quality: *I had one of those bikes once - it was a piece of junk!*

**pieces**

a piece of cake

a slice of bread

a lump of sugar

**piece²** *v*

**piece** sth ↔ **together** *phr v* [T] **1** to use all the facts or information that you have in order to understand a situation: *Police are still trying to **piece together** a motive for the shooting.* **2** to put all the parts of something back into their correct position or order

**piece·meal** /'pismil/ *adj, adv* happening or done slowly in separate stages that are not planned or related: *The house was filled with old furniture they'd bought piecemeal.*

**piece·work** /'piswɚk/ *n* [U] work that is paid by the amount that you do rather than by the number of hours you work

**pie chart** /'. ./ *n* a circle divided into several parts that shows how something such as business income is divided

**pier** /pɪr/ *n* **1** a structure that is built out into the water so that boats can stop next to it **2** a thick post of stone or metal used for supporting something such as a bridge

**pierce** /pɪrs/ *v* [T] **1** to make a hole in or through something using an object with a sharp point: *Tiffany's **getting** her **ears pierced**. (=having a hole put in her ears for wearing jewelry)* | *A bullet pierced his body.* **2** LITERARY if a bright light or a loud sound pierces something, it is suddenly seen or heard very clearly: *The lights from the boat pierced the fog.*

**pierc·ing** /'pɪrsɪŋ/ *adj* **1** sounding or feeling very sharp and unpleasant: *a piercing cry/scream* | *an icy piercing wind* **2** piercing eyes or looks show that someone notices or understands something more than other people would: *He looked away from Mr. Darden's piercing eyes.*

**pi·e·ty** /'paɪəṭi/ *n* [U] respect for God and religion, shown in the way you behave

**pig¹** /pɪg/ *n* **1** a farm animal with short legs, a fat, usually pink body, and a curled tail **2** SPOKEN an impolite word meaning someone who eats too much, is very dirty, or is unpleasant in some way: *You ate all the pizza, you pig.* **3** SPOKEN OFFENSIVE a police officer

**pig**

**pig²** *v* **-gged, -gging**
**pig out** *phr v* [I] INFORMAL to eat too much of something you like: *We **pigged out on** ice cream last night.*

**pi·geon** /'pɪdʒən/ *n* a gray bird with short legs that is common in cities

**pi·geon·hole¹** /'pɪdʒən,hoʊl/ *n* one of the small open boxes in a frame inside a desk, in which letters or papers can be put

**pigeonhole²** *v* [T] to decide unfairly that someone or something belongs to a particular group or type: *People find out you've been a bartender and pigeonhole you, so you can never do anything else.*

**pigeon-toed** /'.. ,./ *adj* having feet that point in rather than straight forward

**pig·gy** /'pɪgi/ *n* SPOKEN a word meaning a pig, used when speaking to children

**pig·gy·back ride** /'pɪgi,bæk ,raɪd/ *n* a way of carrying a child by putting him/her on your back —**piggyback** *adv*

**pig·gy bank** /'.. ,./ *n* a small container, sometimes in the shape of a pig, used by children for saving coins

**pig·head·ed** /'pɪg,hɛdɪd/ *adj* DISAPPROVING determined to do things the way you want even if there are good reasons not to; STUBBORN

**pig·let** /'pɪglɪt/ *n* a young pig

**pig·ment** /'pɪgmənt/ *n* [C,U] **1** a colored substance that is mixed with oil, water etc. to make paint **2** the natural substance in plants and animals that gives color to hair, skin, leaves etc.

**pig·men·ta·tion** /,pɪgmən'teɪʃən/ *n* [U] the color that a living thing has, or the general color of someone's hair and skin

**pig·pen** /'pɪgpɛn/, **pig·sty** /'pɪgstaɪ/ *n* **1** a place on a farm where pigs are kept **2** INFORMAL a place that is very dirty or messy: *Your bedroom is a pigpen!*

**pig·tail** /'pɪgteɪl/ *n* one of two long lengths of hair that has been pulled together and tied at either side of the head, worn especially by young girls: *a girl with her hair in pigtails* —compare BRAID[1], PONYTAIL —see picture at HAIRSTYLE

**pike** /paɪk/ *n* [C,U] **1** a large fish that eats other fish and lives in rivers and lakes **2** INFORMAL ⇨ TURNPIKE

**pile**[1] /paɪl/ *n* **1** a large group of similar things collected or thrown together: *Stuart sighed and looked at the pile of bills and letters on his desk.* **2** a neat collection of similar things put one on top of the other; STACK: *a pile of folded clothes* **3** **piles of/a pile of** INFORMAL a lot of something: *I have piles of work to do tonight.* **4** [C,U] the soft short threads on a CARPET: *a deep pile carpet* **5** ⇨ PILING

**pile**[2] *v* **1** [I,T] also **pile up** to make a pile by collecting things together; STACK: *A lot of dishes had piled up in the sink.* **2** [T] to fill something or cover a surface with a lot of something: *a plate piled high with spaghetti*

**pile in/into** sth *phr v* [T] INFORMAL if a group of people pile into a place or vehicle, they all try to get into it quickly and at the same time: *We all piled into the car and left.*

**pile out** *phr v* [I] INFORMAL if a group of people pile out of a place or vehicle, they all try to get out of it quickly and at the same time: *As soon as we stopped, the kids piled out and ran to the beach.*

**pile up** *phr v* [I,T] to become larger in quantity or amount, or to make something do this; ACCUMULATE: *Debts from the business were piling up quickly.*

**pile·up** /'paɪlʌp/ *n* INFORMAL a traffic accident in which several vehicles have crashed into each other: *a 16-car pileup*

**pil·fer** /'pɪlfɚ/ *v* [I,T] to steal small amounts of things, or things that are not worth much: *He's been pilfering envelopes from work.*

**pil·grim** /'pɪlgrəm/ *n* someone who travels a long way to a holy place for a religious reason

**pil·grim·age** /'pɪlgrəmɪdʒ/ *n* [C,U] a trip to a holy place for a religious reason: *a pilgrimage to Mecca*

**pil·ing** /'paɪlɪŋ/ *n* a heavy post made of wood, cement, or metal, used for supporting a building or bridge

**pill** /pɪl/ *n* **1** a small solid piece of medicine that you swallow: *She's taking pills to control her blood pressure.* —see picture at MEDICINE **2 the Pill** a pill that women can take in order to avoid having babies: *Mary has been on the pill for years now.* **3** INFORMAL someone who annoys you, often a child: *Stop being such a pill, Darren.*

**pil·lage** /'pɪlɪdʒ/ *v* [I,T] to steal things from a place using violence, especially during a war

**pil·lar** /'pɪlɚ/ *n* **1** a tall solid post used as a support for part of a building; COLUMN **2 a pillar of the community/church etc.** an active and important member of a group, organization etc.

**pil·low** /'pɪloʊ/ *n* a cloth bag filled with soft material, that you put your head on when you sleep

**pil·low·case** /'pɪloʊ,keɪs/ *n* a cloth bag for a PILLOW

**pi·lot** /'paɪlət/ *n* **1** someone who flies an aircraft or STEERS a ship: *an airline pilot* **2** a single television program that is made in order to test whether people like it and want to watch more programs **3 pilot program/study** a test that is done to see if an idea or product will be successful: *We'll start a pilot program to find the best way of collecting bottles for recycling.* —**pilot** *v* [T]

**pilot light** /'.. ,./ *n* a small gas flame that burns all the time in a piece of equipment such as a STOVE, that is used for lighting the whole piece of equipment

**pimp** /pɪmp/ *n* a man who controls PROSTITUTEs and makes money from them

**pim·ple** /'pɪmpəl/ *n* a small raised red spot on your skin, especially on your face —**pimply** *adj*

**PIN** /pɪn/ *n* Personal Identification Number; a number that only you know, that you must use in order to use a service such as getting money from a bank machine

**pin**[1] /pɪn/ *n* **1** a short thin piece of metal with a sharp point at one end, used especially for fastening pieces of cloth together **2** a piece of jewelry fastened to your clothes by a pin: *What a pretty pin!* **3** a thin piece of metal used as a support for something: *He has to have pins put in his ankle.* —see also CLOTHESPIN, PINS AND NEEDLES, ROLLING PIN, SAFETY PIN

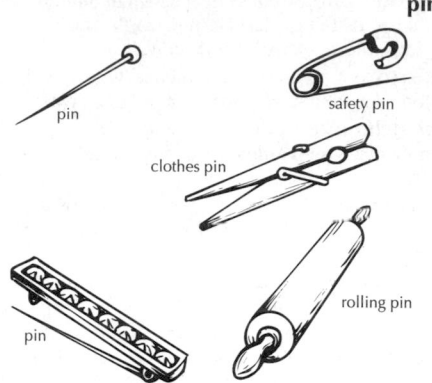

pin

safety pin

clothes pin

rolling pin

pin

P

**pin²** *v* **-nned, -nning** **1** [T] to fasten something or join things together with a pin or pins: *Can you **pin** this announcement **on** the bulletin board for me? | He wore campaign buttons **pinned to** his lapels.* **2 pin your hopes on** to hope that something will happen, because all your plans depend on it: *I hope she's not pinning all her hopes on winning.* **3 pin the blame on sb** to blame someone for something, often unfairly: *Don't try to pin the blame on me!* **4** [T] to trap someone so that s/he is unable to move: *He was pinned under the car.*

**pin** sb/sth **down** *phr v* [T] **1** to make someone decide something, or tell you what the decision is: *I couldn't **pin** him **down** to a definite date for the meeting.* **2** to understand something clearly or be able to describe exactly what it is: *I can't **pin down** his accent.*

**pin·ball** /ˈpɪnbɔl/ *n* [U] a game played on a machine with lights and bells and a sloping board in which you push buttons to try to keep a ball from rolling off the board: *a pinball machine*

**pin·cer** /ˈpɪnsɚ, ˈpɪntʃɚ/ *n* one of the pair of CLAWs (=sharp curved nails) that some insects and SHELLFISH have

**pinch¹** /pɪntʃ/ *v* **1** [T] to press a part of someone's flesh very tightly, either between two hard surfaces or between your finger and thumb: *Ow! Dad, Carlo pinched me!* **2** [I,T] if your clothes, shoes etc. pinch you, they are too tight and hurt you **3 pinch pennies** to be careful to spend as little money as possible **4** INFORMAL to steal something that is small or not worth much: *I pinched a newspaper from the doctor's office.*

**pinch²** *n* **1 pinch of salt/pepper etc.** a small amount of salt, pepper etc. that you can hold between your finger and thumb: *Sprinkle each bun with a pinch of sugar.* **2** an act of PINCHing someone: *She gave him a pinch on the cheek.* **3 in a pinch** if necessary in a difficult or urgent situation: *I could get $300, maybe $400 dollars in a pinch.*

**pinched** /pɪntʃt/ *adj* **1** not having enough money to do what you want: *financially pinched schools* **2** a pinched face looks thin and unhealthy because someone may be ill, too cold, very old, or tired

**pinch-hit** /ˌ. ˈ./ *v* [I] **1** to BAT for someone else in a game of baseball **2** to do something for someone else because s/he is suddenly not able to do it: *Could you pinch-hit for Larry in the meeting today?* **—pinch-hitter** *n*

**pin·cush·ion** /ˈpɪnˌkʊʃən/ *n* a small PILLOW into which you stick pins until you need to use them

**pine¹** /paɪn/, **pine tree** /ˈ. ./ *n* [C,U] a tree with long leaves shaped like needles, or the wood of this tree

**pine²**, **pine away** *v* [I] to gradually become weaker and less healthy because you are very sad and lonely

**pine for** sb/sth *phr v* [T] to become unhappy or ill because you cannot be with someone you love or in a place you love

**pine·ap·ple** /ˈpaɪnˌæpəl/ *n* [C,U] a large brown tropical fruit with pointed leaves that stick out of the top, or its sweet yellow flesh —see picture on page 470

**pine cone** /ˈ. ./ *n* the brown seed container of the PINE —see picture at CONE

**ping** /pɪŋ/ *n* a short high RINGing sound —**ping** *v* [I]

**ping-pong** /ˈpɪŋpɑŋ, -pɔŋ/ *n* [U] an indoor game played on a large table, in which two people use PADDLEs to hit a small ball to each other across a low net

**pin·ion** /ˈpɪnyən/ *v* [T] FORMAL to hold or tie up someone's arms or legs very tightly so s/he cannot move

**pink** /pɪŋk/ *adj* **1** pale red: *a pink dress* **2** used when talking about things relating to HOMOSEXUAL people: *the pink vote in the local election* —**pink** *n* [C,U]

**pink·ie**, **pinky** /ˈpɪŋki/ *n* the smallest finger on your hand

**pink slip** /ˈ. ./ *n* a written warning you get when your job is going to end because there is not enough work

**pin·na·cle** /ˈpɪnəkəl/ *n* **1** [singular] the most successful, powerful, or exciting part of something: *She reached the pinnacle of success as a writer at the age of 45.* **2** a high mountain top **3** a pointed stone decoration like a small tower on top of a church or castle

**pin·point¹** /ˈpɪnpɔɪnt/ *v* [T] **1** to say exactly what the facts about something really are: *It was impossible to pinpoint the cause of the crash.* **2** to find or show the exact position of something: *First, we have to pinpoint the location of the leak.*

**pinpoint²** *adj* **with pinpoint accuracy** without even the smallest mistake: *the plane's ability to drop bombs with pinpoint accuracy*

**pinpoint**³ *n* a very small area or amount of something: *a tiny pinpoint of light*

**pin·prick** /'pɪnˌprɪk/ *n* a very small hole or mark in something, like one made by a pin

**pins and nee·dles** /ˌ. . '../ *n* **1** the uncomfortable feeling of being PRICKed that you get when your blood returns to a part of your body after it was blocked **2** be on pins and needles to be very nervous: *Mom's been on pins and needles waiting to hear from you.*

**pin·stripe** /'pɪnstraɪp/ *n* dark-colored cloth with a pattern of thin light-colored lines on it: *a blue pinstripe suit* –**pinstriped** *adj*

**pint** /paɪnt/ *n* a unit for measuring liquid, equal to 16 FLUID OUNCES or 0.4732 liters

**pin·up** /'pɪnʌp/ *n* a picture of an attractive person, especially someone famous or someone with few clothes on, that is put up on a wall

**pi·o·neer**¹ /ˌpaɪə'nɪr/ *n* **1** one of the first people to travel to a new or unknown place and begin living there, farming etc.: *Grandpa's family were pioneers in the Oregon Territory.* **2** one of the first people to do something that other people will later develop or continue to do: *the pioneers of modern space travel*

**pioneer**² *v* [T] to be the first one to do, invent, or use something new: *a hospital pioneering a new type of surgery*

**pi·ous** /'paɪəs/ *adj* having strong religious beliefs, and showing this in the way you behave –opposite IMPIOUS

**pipe**¹ /paɪp/ *n* **1** a tube through which a liquid or gas flows: *a sewer pipe* **2** a thing used for smoking tobacco, consisting of a small tube with a container shaped like a bowl at one end: *Harry smiled and lit his pipe.* **3** one of the metal tubes that air is forced through in an ORGAN **4** a simple musical instrument like a tube that you blow through

**pipe**² *v* [T] to send a liquid or gas through a pipe to another place: *oil piped from Alaska*

**pipe down** *phr v* [I] SPOKEN used in order to tell someone rudely to stop talking or making a noise: *Pipe down! I'm trying to listen to this!*

**pipe up** *phr v* [I] INFORMAL to start speaking, or speak more loudly: *Dennis piped up, saying he didn't agree.*

**pipe dream** /'. ./ *n* a hope, idea, plan etc. that will probably never work or happen: *Money and fame - isn't that all a pipe dream?*

**pipe·line** /'paɪp-laɪn/ *n* **1** a long line of connecting pipes, used for carrying gas, oil etc. over long distances **2** be in the pipeline if a plan, idea or event is in the pipeline, it is still being prepared, but it will happen or be completed soon

**pip·ing**¹ /'paɪpɪŋ/ *n* [U] **1** several pipes, or a system of pipes, used for carrying a liquid or gas: *Something's wrong with the piping in the building.* **2** thin cloth CORDS used as decorations on clothes and furniture

**piping**² *adj* **piping hot** very hot: *piping hot soup*

**pip·squeak** /'pɪpskwik/ *n* SPOKEN someone whom you think is not worth attention or respect, especially because s/he is small or young: *Shut up, you little pipsqueak!*

**pi·quant** /pi'kɑnt, 'pikənt/ *adj* FORMAL **1** having a pleasantly hot taste: *a piquant chili sauce* **2** interesting and exciting: *piquant photos of life in Paris* –**piquancy** /'pikənsi/ *n* [U]

**pique**¹ /pik/ *v* [T] **1** pique sb's interest/curiosity to make someone very interested in something: *Go on, you've piqued my interest.* **2** FORMAL to make someone feel annoyed or upset

**pique**² *n* [U] FORMAL a feeling of being annoyed or upset: *Greta left in a fit of pique.*

**pi·ra·cy** /'paɪrəsi/ *n* [U] **1** the act of illegally copying and selling other people's work: *software piracy* **2** the crime of attacking and stealing from ships

**pi·ra·nha** /pə'rɑnə, -'ræn-/ *n* a South American fish with sharp teeth that lives in rivers and eats flesh

**pi·rate**¹ /'paɪrɪt/ *n* **1** someone who illegally copies and sells another person's work: *We're losing thousands of dollars to video pirates.* **2** someone who sails on the oceans, attacking other boats and stealing things from them

**pirate**² *v* [T] to illegally copy and sell other people's work: *pirated CDs*

**pir·ou·ette** /ˌpɪru'ɛt/ *n* a very fast turn made on one toe or the front part of one foot, especially by a BALLET dancer –**pirouette** *v* [I]

**Pis·ces** /'paɪsiz/ *n* **1** [singular] the twelfth sign of the ZODIAC, represented by two fish **2** someone born between February 19 and March 20

**piss**¹ /pɪs/ *v* SPOKEN an impolite word meaning to URINATE

**piss sb ↔ off** *phr v* [T] SPOKEN an impolite expression meaning to annoy someone very much: *It really pisses me off when you treat me like a child.*

**piss**² *n* SPOKEN **1** [singular] an impolite word meaning an act of urinating (URINATE): *I need to take a piss.* **2** [U] an impolite word meaning URINE

**pissed** /pɪst/, **pissed off** /ˌ. './ *adj* SPOKEN an impolite expression meaning very annoyed: *Frank's really pissed off.*

**pis·ta·chi·o** /pɪ'stæʃiˌoʊ/ *n* a small green nut that you can eat

**pis·tol** /'pɪstl/ *n* a small gun that you can use with one hand

**pis·ton** /'pɪstən/ *n* a part of an engine consisting of a short solid piece of metal inside a tube, that moves up and down to make the other parts of the engine move

**pit¹** /pɪt/ *n*

**1** ▶HOLE◀ a hole or a low area in the ground, especially one made by digging: *a barbecue pit | an open pit mine* (=where minerals are dug out from the surface of the earth)

**2** ▶MARK◀ a small hollow mark in the surface of something: *There are tiny scratches and pits on the windshield.*

**3** ▶MESSY PLACE◀ SPOKEN a house or room that is messy or in bad condition: *Erica's house is a total pit!*

**4** **be the pits** SPOKEN used in order to say that a thing or situation is very bad: *That would be the pits if you got sick.*

**5** **in the pit of your stomach** if you feel bad emotions in the pit of your stomach, they are so strong that you almost feel sick: *The strange noises gave her a funny feeling in the pit of her stomach.*

**6** ▶IN FRUIT◀ the single large hard seed in some fruits: *a peach pit*

**7** ▶FOR CARS◀ a place beside a race track where a race car can quickly get more gas or be repaired

**8** ⇨ ORCHESTRA PIT

**9** ⇨ MINE²

**pit²** *v* **-tted, -tting** [T] **1** to take out the single large hard seed inside some fruits **2** to put small marks or holes in the surface of something: *The disease had pitted and scarred his skin.*

**pit** sb/sth **against** sb/sth *phr v* [T] to test your strength, ability, power etc. against someone else: *This week's big game pits Houston against Miami.*

**pit bull ter·ri·er** /ˌ. . '.../ *n* a short, extremely strong, and often violent dog

**pitch¹** /pɪtʃ/ *v*

**1** ▶THROW◀ [T] to throw something, especially with a lot of force: *Carl tore up Amy's letter and pitched it into the fire. | a group of men pitching horseshoes in the park*

**2** ▶BASEBALL◀ [I,T] to throw the ball in a game of baseball: *Who's pitching for the Red Sox today?*

**3** ▶FALL◀ [I,T] to fall suddenly and heavily in a particular direction, or to make someone or something fall in this way: *A sudden stop pitched her into the windshield. | He tripped and pitched forward into the bushes.*

**4** ▶VOICE/MUSIC◀ [T] to make a sound produced at a particular level: *The song is pitched too high for me.*

**5** **pitch a tent** to set up a tent

**6** ▶SELL/PERSUADE◀ [I,T] INFORMAL to try to persuade someone to buy or do something: *The meeting is your chance to pitch your ideas to the boss.*

**7** ▶SAY/WRITE◀ [T] to say or write something in a way that you know will be understood by particular people; aim: *a TV show pitched at children*

**8** ▶SHIP/PLANE◀ [I] to move roughly with the back and front going up and down

**pitch in** *phr v* [I] INFORMAL to start to work eagerly as a member of a group: *If we all pitch in, it won't take very long to finish.*

**pitch²** *n* **1** how high or low a musical note or someone's voice is **2** a throw of the ball in a game of baseball, or a way in which it can be thrown **3** [singular, U] the strength of your feelings or opinions about something: *Their excitement rose to fever pitch.* (=a very excited level) **4** INFORMAL the things someone says in order to persuade people to buy or do something: *a sales pitch* **5** [U] a dark sticky substance that is used on roofs, the bottoms of ships etc. to stop water coming through

**pitch black** /ˌ. '.◀/ *adj* completely black or dark: *It was pitch black in the basement and really scary.*

**pitch·er** /'pɪtʃɚ/ *n* **1** a container used for holding and pouring liquids: *a pitcher of beer* –see picture at CONTAINER **2** the baseball player who throws the balls for the BATTER to hit –see picture on page 472

**pitch·fork** /'pɪtʃfɔrk/ *n* a tool with a long handle and two or three long curved metal points at one end, used especially for lifting HAY (=dried cut grass)

**pit·e·ous** /'pɪtiəs/ *adj* LITERARY making you feel pity: *a piteous cry*

**pit·fall** /'pɪtfɔl/ *n* a problem or difficulty that is likely to happen, or a mistake that is likely to be made: *Following the instructions now can help you avoid a number of pitfalls later on.*

**pith·y** /'pɪθi/ *adj* spoken or written in strong clear language without wasting any words: *pithy comments*

**pit·i·ful** /'pɪtɪfəl/ *adj* **1** making you feel pity or sympathy: *a pitiful sight* **2** not good enough to deserve respect: *His performance last night was pitiful.* **–pitifully** *adv*

**pit·i·less** /'pɪtɪlɪs/ *adj* showing no pity: *a pitiless dictator*

**pit stop** /'. ./ *n* **1** a time when a race car stops beside the track in order to get more gas or be quickly repaired **2** **make a pit stop** SPOKEN **a)** to stop when driving on a long trip in order to get food, gas etc. **b)** to go to the toilet

**pit·tance** /'pɪt⌐ns/ *n* [singular] a very small amount of money

**pit·y¹** /'pɪti/ *n* **1** [U] sympathy for someone who is suffering or unhappy: *I don't need your pity!* **2** [singular] a sad or unfortunate situation: *It's a pity (that) so much time was wasted.* **3** **take/have pity on sb** to feel sympathy for someone and do something to help him/her

**pit·y²** *v* [T] to feel sympathy for someone because s/he is in a bad situation: *I pity anyone who has to live with Sherry.*

P

**piv·ot**[1] /'pɪvət/ *n* a fixed central point or pin on which something balances or turns

**pivot**[2] *v* [I,T] to turn or balance on a central point, or to make something do this: *McGee pivots, and throws the ball to second base.*

**piv·ot·al** /'pɪvətəl/ *adj* a pivotal event/moment/role etc. an event, moment etc. that has a very important effect on the way something develops: *Parker played a pivotal role in getting the deal.*

**pix·el** /'pɪksəl/ *n* TECHNICAL the smallest unit of an image on a computer screen

**pix·ie** /'pɪksi/ *n* a very small imaginary creature with magic powers, that looks like a person

**piz·za** /'pitsə/ *n* [C,U] a thin flat round bread, baked with TOMATO, cheese, and usually vegetables or meat on top

**piz·zazz** /pə'zæz/ *n* [U] an exciting quality or style: *a theater show that needs more pizzazz*

**pj's, P.J's** /'pidʒeɪz/ *n* [plural] SPOKEN ⇨ PAJAMAS

**plac·ard** /'plækəd, -kɑrd/ *n* a large sign or advertisement that you carry or put on a wall

**pla·cate** /'pleɪkeɪt, 'plæ-/ *v* [T] FORMAL to make someone stop feeling angry by doing special things for him/her —**placatory** /'pleɪkə-,tɔri/ *adj*

**place**[1] /pleɪs/ *n*

**1** ▶POINT/POSITION◀ **a)** any area, point, or position in space; LOCATION: *Make sure you keep your passport in a safe place.* | *a beautiful place surrounded by mountains* **b)** a particular point on a larger area or thing: *a sore place on my knee* | *Paint is coming off the wall in places.* (=in some areas, but not others)

**2** ▶WHERE YOU DO STH◀ a building or area that is used for, or is suitable for, a particular purpose or activity: *What this town needs is a really good place to eat/drink/dance.* | *Mexico's a great place for a vacation.* | *A library is no place for a party.*

**3** ▶BUILDING/TOWN ETC.◀ a particular building, town, country etc.: *She was born in a place called Black River Falls.* | *I'm going over to Jeff's place* (=his house) *for dinner.*

**4** ▶RIGHT POSITION/ORDER◀ the right or usual position or order: *Put the CDs back in their place.* | *By six o'clock, everything was in place for the party.*

**5** take place to happen: *When did the robbery take place?* –see usage note at HAPPEN

**6** ▶IMPORTANCE◀ the importance or position that someone or something has, compared to other people or things: *No one could ever take her place.* (=be as important or loved as she is) | *Carla has friends in high places.* (=with important ranks in society) | *By the 1950s, cars had taken the place of trains.* (=were used instead of them) | *There will always be a place for you here.* (=a position for you to have)

**7** in place of instead of: *Try using mixed herbs in place of salt on vegetables.*

**8** ▶RIGHT OCCASION◀ the right occasion or situation: *This isn't the place to discuss that, Alanna.*

**9** sb's place someone's duty or right because of the position s/he has: *It's not your place to tell me what to do.*

**10** first/second/third etc. place first, second etc. position in a race or competition: *Jerry finished in third place.*

**11** in the first/second/third place SPOKEN used in order to introduce a series of points in an argument or discussion: *Well, in the first place, I can't afford it, and in the second place I'm not really interested.*

**12** ▶SEAT/SPACE◀ a seat on a bus, train etc., or a position in a line: *Is this place taken?* (=being used) | *Can you save my place?* (=not let anyone else use it)

**13** all over the place INFORMAL everywhere: *There were policemen all over the place!*

**14** put sb in his/her place to show someone that s/he is not as important, intelligent etc. as s/he thinks s/he is: *I'd like to put her in her place - the little snob!*

**15** out of place not suitable for or comfortable in a particular situation: *I felt really out of place at Cindy's wedding.*

**16** go places INFORMAL to become successful: *Nick's the kind of guy who could really go places.*

**17** also **Place** used in the names of short streets: *I live at 114 Seaview Place.*

---

**USAGE NOTE place, space, and room**

Use **place** to talk about an area or a particular part of an area: *The best place to sit is right in front of the stage.* Use both **space** and **room** to talk about empty areas. **Space** can mean the size of an area, or it can mean the area itself: *There's a lot of space in the back of these cars.* | *I had trouble finding a parking space.* **Room** means that there is enough space for a particular purpose: *There's room in the back seat for all three of you.* ✗ DON'T SAY "There's enough place." ✗

---

**place**[2] *v* **1** [T] to put something carefully in an exact place: *Seth placed his trophy on the top shelf.* **2** [T] to put someone or something in a particular situation: *You'll be placed with the advanced students.* **3** [T] to decide that someone or something is important or valuable: *Your father has placed great trust in you.* | *a teacher who places an emphasis on good grammar* **4** can't place sb/sth to be unable to remember exactly why you recognize someone or something: *I recognize her name, but I can't place her.* **5** [T] to find a job for someone: *The agency had placed her in/with a local firm.*

**6 place an order** to ask a store or business to get something for you so you can buy it

**pla·ce·bo** /pləˈsiboʊ/ n a substance given to someone instead of medicine, without telling him/her it is not real, either because the person is not really sick or because this is part of a test

**place·ment** /ˈpleɪsmənt/ n [C,U] **1** the act of finding a place for someone to live or work, or the place itself: *a job placement | the college placement office* (=where they help you find work) **2** the act of putting something or someone in a position, or the position itself: *He wasn't satisfied with the furniture placement. | You'll need to take a placement test.* (=test that decides which level of class you can take)

**pla·cen·ta** /pləˈsɛntə/ n a body organ like thick flesh inside the UTERUS that feeds an unborn baby

**plac·id** /ˈplæsɪd/ adj calm and peaceful: *a placid expression | the placid surface of the lake* −**placidly** adv

**pla·gia·rism** /ˈpleɪdʒəˌrɪzəm/ n [C,U] the act of plagiarizing (PLAGIARIZE), or the idea, phrase, story etc. that has been plagiarized: *an article full of plagiarisms | She was accused of plagiarism in writing her thesis.* −**plagiarist** n

**pla·gia·rize** /ˈpleɪdʒəˌraɪz/ v [I,T] to take someone else's words, ideas, etc. and copy them, pretending that they are your own

**plague¹** /pleɪg/ n **1** [C,U] an attack of a disease that spreads easily, and kills a large number of people **2 a plague of rats/locusts etc.** a very large and dangerous number of rats etc.

**plague²** v [T] to make someone suffer over a long period of time, or to cause trouble again and again: *Gloria had always been plagued by ill health.*

**plaid** /plæd/ n [C,U] a pattern of squares and lines, originally from Scotland and used especially on material for clothing −**plaid** adj: *a plaid work shirt* −see picture at PATTERN

**plain¹** /pleɪn/ adj **1** very clear, and easy to understand or recognize: *It's quite plain that you don't agree. | Why don't you tell me in plain English?* (=clearly, without technical language) **2** without anything added or without decoration; simple: *plain food | a plain blue suit* −see picture at PATTERN **3** a word meaning ugly or unattractive, used in order to be polite: *She's kind of plain, but she has a great personality.*

**plain²** n a large area of flat land: *a grassy plain | countless miles of plains*

**plain³** adv **plain stupid/wrong/rude etc.** SPOKEN clearly and simply stupid, wrong etc.: *They're just plain lazy.*

**plain·clothes** /ˈ. ./ adj plainclothes police wear ordinary clothes so that they can work without being recognized

**plain·ly** /ˈpleɪnli/ adv **1** in a way that is easy to see, hear, or understand: *The price is plainly marked on the tag. | Let me speak plainly.* **2** simply or without decoration: *a plainly dressed young girl*

**plain·tiff** /ˈpleɪntɪf/ n LAW the person in a court of law who ACCUSEs someone else of doing something illegal −compare DEFENDANT

**plain·tive** /ˈpleɪntɪv/ adj a plaintive sound is high, like someone crying, and sounds sad: *the plaintive cry of the wolf*

**plan¹** /plæn/ n **1** something that you have decided to do or achieve: *Her plan is to finish school and then travel for a year. | We haven't made any fixed plans yet. | Sorry, I have plans for tonight. | There's been a change of plan.* (=we have decided to do something else) **2** a set of actions for achieving something in the future: *NASA has announced plans for a new space station. | We'll finish in April if everything goes according to plan.* (=if things happen in the way that we arranged or expected) **3** a drawing of something such as a building, room, or machine, as it would be seen from above, showing the shape, measurements, parts etc.: *Have you seen the plans for the new library?*

**plan²** v **-nned, -nning 1** [I,T] also **plan out** to think about something you want to do, and how you will do it: *We've been planning our vacation for months.* **2** [T] to intend to do something: *How long do you plan on staying? | Where do you plan to go next year?* **3** [T] to think about something you are going to make or build, and decide what it will look like

**plane** /pleɪn/ n **1** a vehicle that flies by using wings and one or more engines; AIRPLANE −see picture at AIRPLANE **2** a particular level: *Let's try to keep the conversation on a friendly plane.* **3** a tool that has a flat bottom with a sharp blade in it, used for making wooden surfaces smooth **4** TECHNICAL a completely flat surface in GEOMETRY

**plan·et** /ˈplænɪt/ n **1** a very large round object in space that moves around a star, such as the sun: *Mercury is the smallest planet. | Planet Earth* **2 what planet is sb on?** SPOKEN HUMOROUS used in order to say that someone's ideas are not sensible −**planetary** /ˈplænəˌtɛri/ adj

**plan·e·tar·i·um** /ˌplænəˈtɛriəm/ n a building where lights on a curved ceiling show the movements of PLANETs and stars

**plank** /plæŋk/ n **1** a long flat piece of wood used for building: *a bridge/floor/dock made out of planks* **2** one of the main principles of a political party's statement of its aims: *Low taxation is the main plank in the party platform.*

**plank·ton** /ˈplæŋktən/ n [U] very small plants and animals that live in the ocean and are eaten by fish

**plan·ner** /ˈplænɚ/ n someone who plans

something, especially someone who plans the way towns grow and develop

**plant**[1] /plænt/ n **1** a living thing that has leaves and roots and usually grows in the ground, especially one that is smaller than a tree: *Don't forget to water the plants. | a tomato plant* **2** a factory and all its equipment: *They've just built a new chemical plant.* **3** INFORMAL someone who has been sent to work for a company or organization in order to find out secret information for the police or another company

**plant**[2] v [T] **1** to put plants or seeds in the ground to grow: *planting carrots | a hillside planted with pine trees* **2** INFORMAL to hide stolen or illegal goods in someone's clothes, bags, room etc. in order to make him/her seem guilty: *Someone must have planted the drugs on her.* **3** to put something firmly somewhere, or to move somewhere and stay there: *Tony planted himself in a chair by the fire.* **4 plant an idea/doubt/suspicion** to mention something that makes someone begin to have an idea, doubt etc.: *Their conversation had planted doubts in Yuri's mind.* –**planting** n [C,U]: *seasonal planting*

**plan·ta·tion** /plæn'teɪʃən/ n a large farm, especially in a hot country, where a single crop such as tea, cotton, or sugar is grown: *a rubber plantation*

**plant·er** /'plæntɚ/ n **1** a container for growing plants in **2** someone who owns or is in charge of a PLANTATION

**plaque** /plæk/ n **1** a piece of flat metal or stone with writing on it that reminds people of a particular event or person: *A bronze plaque tells of the building's historic past.* **2** [U] a harmful substance that forms on your teeth, that BACTERIA can live and breed in

**plas·ma** /'plæzmə/ n [U] the yellowish liquid part of the blood that carries the blood cells

**plas·ter**[1] /'plæstɚ/ n [U] a substance used for covering walls and ceilings to give them a smooth surface

**plaster**[2] v [T] **1** to spread or stick something all over a surface so that it is thickly covered: *a wall plastered with signs* **2** to cover a surface with PLASTER

**plas·tered** /'plæstɚd/ adj INFORMAL very drunk: *I got plastered with Sharon last night.*

**plaster of Par·is** /ˌplæstɚ əv 'pærɪs/ n [U] a mixture of a white powder and water that dries quickly, used especially for making STATUEs

**plas·tic**[1] /'plæstɪk/ adj **1** made of plastic: *a plastic bag | plastic spoons/cups/bowls* **2** seeming artificial or unnatural: *a plastic smile | plastic-tasting food* **3** TECHNICAL a plastic substance such as clay can be formed into many different shapes and then keep the shape

**plastic**[2] n [C,U] a light strong material that is chemically produced, that can be made into

different shapes when soft and keeps its shape when hard: *toys made of plastic*

**plas·tic·i·ty** /plæ'stɪsəti/ n [U] TECHNICAL the quality of being easily made into any shape

**plastic sur·ger·y** /ˌ.. '.../ n [U] the medical practice of changing the appearance of people's faces or bodies, either to improve their appearance or to repair injuries

**plate** /pleɪt/ n **1** a flat, usually round, dish that you eat from or serve food from: *a china plate* **2** also **plateful** /'pleɪtfʊl/ the amount that a plate will hold: *a plate of chicken* **3** a flat piece of metal, glass, bone etc.: *An iron plate covered the hole in the sidewalk.* **4 gold/silver etc. plate** ordinary metal with a thin covering of gold, silver etc. **5** ⇨ LICENSE PLATE: *New Jersey plates* **6** a thin piece of plastic with false teeth set into it

**pla·teau** /plæ'toʊ/ n **1** a large area of flat land that is higher than the land around it **2** a period during which the level or amount of something does not change: *Inflation rates have reached a plateau.* –**plateau** v [I]

**plat·ed** /'pleɪtɪd/ adj covered with a thin layer of metal, especially gold or silver: *a silver-plated spoon*

**plate glass** /ˌ. './ n [U] clear glass made in large thick sheets for use especially in store windows –**plate-glass** /ˌ. '.ı / adj

**plat·form** /'plætfɔrm/ n **1** a raised structure for people to stand or work on: *He climbed on to the platform and began to address the crowd. | an oil platform off the California coast* **2** the main ideas and aims of a political party, especially the ones that they state just before an election: *Republicans continued to argue about the party platform.* **3** the type of computer OPERATING SYSTEM or HARDWARE you are using: *an IBM platform* **4** a chance for someone to express his/her opinions: *He used the TV interview as a platform for his views on education.* **5** the raised place in a railroad station where you get on and off a train

**plat·ing** /'pleɪtɪŋ/ n [U] a thin layer of metal that covers another metal surface: *silver plating*

**plat·i·num** /'plætˀnəm, 'plætˀn-əm/ n [U] an expensive heavy silver-white metal that is an ELEMENT and is used in making jewelry

**plat·i·tude** /'plætəˌtud/ n a boring statement that has been made many times before: *a speech full of platitudes*

**pla·ton·ic** /plə'tɑnɪk/ adj a relationship that is platonic is friendly but not sexual

**pla·toon** /plə'tun/ n a small group of soldiers that is part of a COMPANY

**plat·ter** /'plætɚ/ n **1** a large plate, used for serving food **2 chicken/seafood etc. platter** chicken etc. arranged on a plate with other foods and served in a restaurant

**plat·y·pus** /'plætəpəs/ n a small Australian

animal that lays eggs and has a beak, but also has fur and feeds milk to its babies

**plau·dit** /ˈplɔdɪt/ *n* [C usually plural] FORMAL things you say in order to show praise and admiration: *The magazine has* ***won plaudits*** *from media critics.*

**plau·si·ble** /ˈplɔzəbəl/ *adj* easy to believe and likely to be true: *a plausible story* –opposite IMPLAUSIBLE

**play¹** /pleɪ/ *v*

**1** ▶SPORT/GAME◀ **a)** [I,T] to take part or compete in a sport: *The guys are out playing basketball.* | *Garcia* ***plays for*** *the Hornets.* | *The 49ers are playing the Vikings on Saturday.* (=they are competing against the Vikings) **b)** [T] to use a particular piece, card, person etc. in a game or sport: *Play the ace of clubs.* | *Coach plans to play Williams at quarterback.*

**2** ▶CHILDREN/TOYS◀ [I,T] to do things that you enjoy, especially to pretend things or to use toys: *He has a lot of toys to* ***play with.*** | *Andy spends too much time playing computer games.* | *Mom, can I go over and* ***play with*** *Zachary?*

**3** ▶MUSIC◀ **a)** [I,T] to perform a piece of music on an instrument: *There's a good band playing on Saturday night.* | *Matt plays drums.* **b)** [I,T] to make a radio, STEREO etc. produce sounds, especially music: *I brought a few CDs to play tonight.*

**4** **play a part/role** to have an effect or influence on something: *Political concerns played no part in my decision.*

**5** ▶THEATER/MOVIE◀ **a)** [T] to act one of the characters in a movie, TV, or theater performance: *Polly is playing Celia in "As You Like It."* **b)** [I] to be performed or shown at a theater etc.: *Have you checked to see where the movie's playing?*

**6** ▶BEHAVE◀ [I,T] INFORMAL to behave in a particular way, or pretend to have a particular quality, in order to achieve something: *If he asks, just* ***play dumb.*** (=pretend you do not know the answer) | *Doctors warned parents to* ***play it safe*** (=do the safest thing) *by immunizing their children.* | *Tracy forced herself to* ***play it cool*** (=stay calm and not be too eager) *with Brad.*

**7** **play ball** **a)** to play by throwing, kicking, hitting, or catching a ball: *Just don't play ball in the house.* **b)** INFORMAL to agree to do something that someone wants you to do: *If you guys play ball with us, we'll all avoid problems.*

**8** **play a trick/joke on sb** to do something to surprise or deceive someone, and make other people laugh: *It was only some boys playing jokes on each other.*

**9** **play it by ear** INFORMAL to decide what to do as things happen, instead of planning anything: *"Are you having a barbecue Saturday?" "We'll*

*have to play it by ear; it depends on the weather."*

**10** **play with fire** to do something that could have a very bad result: *If you invest in high-risk stocks, you're playing with fire.*

**11** **play games** DISAPPROVING to use a person or situation in order to get what you want, without caring about what is best for other people: *We're sick of politicians* ***playing games with*** *the budget.*

**12** **play sth by ear** to be able to play music after you have heard it instead of by reading the notes

**13** **play your cards right** to behave in an effective way in a situation, in order to get what you want: *If you play your cards right, he'll probably pay for your dinner.*

**14** **play second fiddle to sb/sth** to be involved in an activity, but not be as important as the main person or group that is involved in it

**15** **play possum** to pretend to be asleep or dead

**play around** *phr v* [I] **1** to spend time having fun, but without having a particular purpose: *The kids are* ***playing around*** *outside.* **2** INFORMAL to have a sexual relationship with someone who is not your husband or wife

**play** sth ↔ **back** *phr v* [T] to let someone hear or see again something that has been recorded on a TAPE, VIDEO etc.: *Can you* ***play back*** *the trumpet solo to me?*

**play** sth ↔ **down** *phr v* [T] to make something seem less important or bad than it really is: *The White House tried to* ***play down*** *the latest economic figures.*

**play on** sth *phr v* [T] to use a feeling or idea in order to gain an advantage: *His campaign* ***plays on*** *people's fear of losing their jobs.*

**play** sth ↔ **up** *phr v* [T] to make something seem better or more important than it really is: *The town has* ***played up*** *its location to attract tourists.*

**play with** sth *phr v* [T] **1** to keep touching or moving something: *Stop* ***playing with*** *the remote control!* **2** to organize or think about something in different ways, to see what works: *I've been* ***playing with*** *the design of the newsletter.*

**play²** *n* **1** a story that is written to be performed by actors, especially in a theater: *a* ***play about*** *two men on trial for murder* | *The theater arts class is* ***putting on a play*** (=performing one) *in the spring.* **2** [C,U] the actions of the people who are playing a game or sport: *Rain stopped play at 5:30 p.m.* | *Jackson scores with a three-point play!* (=he makes three points by doing one action) **3** [U] the things that people, especially children, do for fun, such as using toys: *children* ***at play*** *in the sandbox* | *a play area with slides and swings* **4** **come into play** to be used or have an effect: *Laws on immigration come into play in this case.*

**5 bring/put sth into play** to use something or make it have an effect: *This is where you should bring your experience into play.* **6 play on words** a use of a word or phrase that is interesting or funny because it has more than one meaning – see also PUN

**play·act·ing** /'. ,../ behavior in which someone pretends to be serious or sincere, but is not

**play·boy** /'pleɪbɔɪ/ *n* a rich man who does not work and who spends time enjoying himself with beautiful women, fast cars etc.

**play-by-play** /,. . '. ◂/ *adj* **play-by-play commentary/description** a description of the action in a sports game as it happens, given on television or the radio

**Play-Doh** /'pleɪdoʊ/ *n* [U] TRADEMARK a soft substance like colored clay, used by children for making shapes

**play·er** /'pleɪɚ/ *n* **1** someone who plays a game, sport, or musical instrument: *a piano player | a basketball player* **2** one of the people, companies, or organizations that is involved in a situation: *a major player in the UN peace talks*

**play·ful** /'pleɪfəl/ *adj* **1** intended to be fun rather than serious, or showing that you are having fun: *a playful discussion | Michael Gibb's playful music and performances | a playful grin* **2** very active and happy: *a playful little kitten* – **playfully** *adv* – **playfulness** *n* [U]

**play·ground** /'pleɪɡraʊnd/ *n* a small area of land, usually next to a school or in a park, where children can play

**play·house** /'pleɪhaʊs/ *n* **1** a word meaning "theater," often used as part of a theater's name: *the Pasadena Playhouse* **2** a small structure like a house that children can play in

**play·ing card** /'.. ,./ *n* ⇨ CARD¹

**play·ing field** /'.. ,./ *n* **1** a large piece of ground with particular areas marked off for playing football, baseball etc. **2 level playing field** a situation in which different people, companies, countries etc. can all compete fairly with each other because no one has special advantages: *"We would like to do business on a more level playing field," said Kokado.*

**play·mate** /'pleɪmeɪt/ *n* OLD-FASHIONED a friend you play with when you are a child

**play·off** /'pleɪɔf/ *n* a game or series of games played by the best teams or players in a sports competition, in order to decide the final winner

**play·pen** /'pleɪpɛn/ *n* a piece of equipment with a net or wooden BARs around it, which young children can play in safely

**play·room** /'pleɪrum/ *n* a room for children to play in

**play·thing** /'pleɪ,θɪŋ/ *n* **1** someone whom you use only for your own amusement, without considering his/her feelings or needs: *I'm not just your plaything, you know.* **2** ⇨ TOY¹

**play·wright** /'pleɪraɪt/ *n* someone who writes plays

**pla·za** /'plɑzə, 'plæzə/ *n* an outdoor public place, usually with a lot of stores and small businesses: *South Shore Plaza*

**plea** /pli/ *n* **1** a request that is urgent and full of emotion: *a mother's plea for help* **2** LAW a statement by someone in a court of law saying whether s/he is guilty or not: *The defendant entered a plea of "not guilty."*

**plea bar·gain** /'. ,../ *v* [I] to avoid punishment for a serious crime by agreeing to say you are guilty of a less serious one

**plead** /plid/ *v* **pleaded** *or* **pled, pleaded** *or* **pled, pleading** **1** [I] to ask for something you want very much, in an urgent and anxious way; BEG: *Amy pleaded with the stranger to help her.* **2** [I,T] LAW to officially say in a court of law whether or not you are guilty of a crime: *"How do you plead?" "Not guilty." | Parker pled guilty to four charges of theft.*

**pleas·ant** /'plɛzənt/ *adj* **1** enjoyable, nice, or good: *He had a pleasant laugh. | a pleasant surprise* **2** polite, friendly, or kind: *a really nice, pleasant man* – **pleasantly** *adv* – opposite UNPLEASANT

**pleas·ant·ry** /'plɛzəntri/ *n* FORMAL a slightly funny or not very serious remark that you say in order to be polite

**please¹** /pliz/ *interjection* **1** used in order to be polite when asking for something: *May I please have a glass of water? | Could you answer the door for me, please?* **2** used in order to be polite when asking someone to do something: *Please put the dirty plates here. | Patty, sit down, please.* **3** SPOKEN said in order to politely accept something that someone offers you: *"Want some cake, Heather?" "Please."*

---

### USAGE NOTE **please** and **thank you**

Use **please** when asking for something or asking someone to do something: *Could I please borrow your pen? | Will you put the milk in the fridge, please? | Hello. May I speak with Alice, please?* Use **please** when saying "yes" in order to be polite: *"Would you like more coffee?" "Yes, please."* Use **thank you** when someone gives you something, does what you have asked, or does or says something that is polite or kind: *"Here's your coat." "Thank you." | Thank you for watering my plants. | "You look nice today." "Thank you!"* Use **thank you** with "no" in order to be polite: *"Would you like more coffee?" "No, thank you."* If someone gives you a present or does something special for you, it is polite to thank him/her in a stronger way: *Thank you very much. That's very kind of you.* In informal situations you can say: *Thanks a lot. That's really nice of you.* When someone thanks you, the most common answer is **you're welcome**: *"Thank you for the card, Uncle Chet." "You're welcome."* In informal speech, we can also say "that's okay," "no problem," or "sure": *"Thanks for the lift." "No problem."*

**please²** *v* **1** [I,T] to make someone feel happy or satisfied: *Mark has always been **hard to please**. | We always **aim to please**.* (=try to make people satisfied) **2 whatever/however etc. sb pleases** whatever, however etc. someone wants: *You can do whatever you please, but I'm going out.* **3 if you please** SPOKEN FORMAL used in order to politely emphasize a demand: *Close the door, if you please.* –**pleasing** *adj: a pleasing flavor*

**pleased** /plizd/ *adj* **1** happy or satisfied: *Our lawyers are **pleased with** the judge's decision.* **2 (I'm) pleased to meet you** SPOKEN said in order to be polite when you meet someone for the first time

**pleas·ur·a·ble** /'plɛʒərəbəl/ *adj* FORMAL enjoyable: *We want to make this a pleasurable experience for everyone.*

**pleas·ure** /'plɛʒɚ/ *n* **1** [U] a feeling of happiness, satisfaction, or enjoyment: *I often read **for pleasure**. | Marie takes great **pleasure in** working at the school.* (=she enjoys it a lot) **2** an activity or experience that you enjoy very much: *It's a pleasure to finally meet you.* **3 (it is) my pleasure** SPOKEN a polite phrase used in order to say that you are glad you can do something nice for someone: *"Thanks for walking me home." "It was my pleasure."*

**pleat** /plit/ *n* a flat fold in a skirt, pair of pants, dress etc. –**pleat** *v*

**pleat·ed** /'plitɪd/ *adj* a pleated skirt, pair of pants, dress etc. has a lot of flat narrow folds

**pleb·i·scite** /'plɛbə,saɪt/ *n* [C,U] a system by which everyone in a country votes on an important national decision

**pled** /plɛd/ *v* a past tense and PAST PARTICIPLE of PLEAD

**pledge¹** /plɛdʒ/ *n* **1** a serious promise or agreement to do something or to give money to help a CHARITY: *Several countries **made pledges** totalling $6 million in aid. | a pledge of $15,000* **2** someone who promises to become a member of a college FRATERNITY or SORORITY

**pledge²** *v* [T] **1** to make a formal, usually public, promise: *Several companies have **pledged to** cut pollution by 50% or more.* **2** to make someone formally promise something: *We were all **pledged to** secrecy.* **3** to promise to become a member of a college FRATERNITY or SORORITY

**Pledge of Al·le·giance** /ˌ. . .'../ *n* the **Pledge of Allegiance** an official statement said by Americans in which they promise to be loyal to the United States. It is usually said by children every morning at school

**ple·na·ry** /'plinəri, 'plɛ-/ *adj* FORMAL involving all of the members of a committee, organization etc.: *a plenary meeting | a plenary speech* (=to all the members)

**plen·ti·ful** /'plɛnt̬ɪfəl/ *adj* more than enough in amount or number: *a plentiful supply of fish in the bay* –**plentifully** *adv*

**plen·ty¹** /'plɛnt̬i/ *quantifier, n* [U] a large amount that is enough or more than enough: *We have **plenty of** time to get to the airport. | There should be plenty to eat at the picnic.*

**plenty²** *adv* SPOKEN more than enough; a lot: *There's plenty more room in the car.*

**pleth·o·ra** /'plɛθərə/ *n* **a plethora of** FORMAL a very large number: *a plethora of complaints*

**Plex·i·glass** /'plɛksi,glæs/ *n* [U] TRADEMARK a strong clear type of plastic that can be used instead of glass

**pli·a·ble** /'plaɪəbəl/, **pli·ant** /'plaɪənt/ *adj* **1** able to bend without breaking or cracking: *Roll the clay until it is soft and pliable.* **2** easily influenced by others, or willing to accept new ideas: *Craig had always been too pliant.*

**pli·ers** /'plaɪɚz/ *n* [plural] a small metal tool used for bending wire or cutting it: *a pair of pliers*

**plight** /plaɪt/ *n* a bad, serious, or sad situation that someone is in: *The Governor has done nothing to help the **plight of** the homeless. | the university's financial plight*

**plod** /plɑd/ *v* **-dded, -dding** [I] to move or do something too slowly, because you are tired or bored: *The movie just **plods along** without enough action. | cattle **plodding through** mud*

**plod·ding** /'plɑdɪŋ/ *adj* without any variety or excitement; boring: *a plodding writing style*

**plop¹** /plɑp/ *v* **-pped, -pping** [T] to sit down, fall down, or drop somewhere in a careless way: *Jaime **plopped down** on a sofa. | His golf ball drifted and **plopped into** a pond. | She plopped the book on the table and stood up.*

**plop²** *n* the sound made by something when it falls or is dropped into liquid

**plot¹** /plɑt/ *n* **1** the events that form the main story of a book, movie, or play: *The plot was boring, but the special effects were good.* **2** a secret plan you make with other people to do something illegal or harmful: *a plot to kill the President* **3** a small piece of land for building or growing things on

**plot²** **-tted, -tting** *v* **1** [I,T] to make a secret plan to harm a particular person or organization: *Brown had **plotted to** kill his first wife.* **2** [T] also **plot out** to make lines and marks on a CHART or map that represent facts, numbers etc.: *plotting earthquakes on a map | graphs that plot the company's progress*

**plow¹, plough** /plaʊ/ *n* a large piece of equipment used on farms, that cuts up the surface of the ground so that seeds can be planted – see also SNOWPLOW

**plow², plough** *v* **1** [I,T] to use a PLOW in order to cut earth, push snow off streets etc.: *We drove through miles of newly plowed fields.* **2** [I] to move with a lot of effort or force through something: *a ship plowing through large waves*

**plow** sth ↔ **back** *phr v* to use profits to reinvest in the same company that made them: *Much of their funds are plowed back into equipment and training.*

**plow into** sth *phr v* [T] to hit something hard with a car, truck etc.: *A train derailed and plowed into two houses.*

**plow through** sth *phr v* [T] to read all of something even though it is difficult, long, or boring

**ploy** /plɔɪ/ *n* a way of tricking someone in order to gain an advantage: *He thought the boy's screams were just a ploy to get attention.*

**pluck¹** /plʌk/ *v* **1** [T] to pull something quickly in order to remove it: *She plucks her eyebrows.* (=pulls out hairs from the edges of them) **2 pluck up the courage** to make yourself be brave or confident enough to do something: *I finally plucked up the courage to ask for a raise.* **3** to pull the feathers off a chicken or other bird before cooking it **4** to quickly pull the strings of a musical instrument

**pluck²** *n* [U] courage and determination to do something that is difficult – **plucky** *adj*

**plug¹** /plʌg/ *n* **1** the small object at the end of a wire that is used for connecting a piece of electrical equipment to a SOCKET (=supply of electricity) **2** a round flat piece of rubber used for blocking the hole in a bathtub or SINK **3** INFORMAL a way of advertising a book, movie etc. by talking about it on a radio or television program

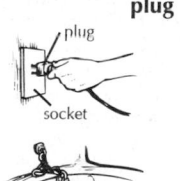

**plug** ... plug ... socket ... plug

**plug²** *v* **-gged, -gging** [T] **1** also **plug up** to fill a hole or block it: *Firefighters plugged a leak from an explosion at a chemical plant.* **2** to advertise a book, movie etc. by talking about it on a radio or television program

**plug away** *phr v* [I] to continue working hard at something: *He's been plugging away at his essay all week.*

**plug** sth ↔ **in** *phr v* [T] to connect a piece of electrical equipment to a SOCKET (=supply of electricity): *Is the TV plugged in?* – opposite UNPLUG

**plug** sth **into** *phr v* [T] to connect one piece of electrical equipment to another: *Can you plug the speakers into the stereo for me?*

**plum** /plʌm/ *n* a soft round, usually purple fruit with a single large seed, or the tree on which it grows – see picture on page 470

**plum·age** /ˈpluːmɪdʒ/ *n* [U] the feathers covering a bird's body

**plumb·er** /ˈplʌmɚ/ *n* someone whose job is to repair water pipes, SINKs, toilets etc.

**plumb·ing** /ˈplʌmɪŋ/ *n* [U] the system of water pipes in a house or building: *Isaac's apartment has a lot of plumbing problems.*

**plume** /pluːm/ *n* **1** a small cloud of smoke, dust, gas etc.: *Neighbors noticed plumes of smoke coming from the garage.* **2** a large feather

**plum·met** /ˈplʌmɪt/ *v* [I] **1** to suddenly and quickly decrease in value: *House prices have plummeted over the past year.* **2** to fall suddenly and very quickly from a very high place: *Two small planes collided and plummeted to the ground.*

**plump¹** /plʌmp/ *adj* **1** attractively round and slightly fat: *plump juicy strawberries | plump cushions* **2** a word meaning fat, used in order to be polite: *He was 67, short, and a little plump.* – see usage note at FAT¹

**plump²** *v*

**plump for** sth *phr v* [T] INFORMAL to choose something after thinking about all your choices: *I think I'll plump for the Spanish class.*

**plump** sth ↔ **up** *phr v* [T] to make a PILLOW bigger and softer by shaking and hitting it

**plun·der¹** /ˈplʌndɚ/ *v* [I,T] to steal money or property from a place while fighting in a war: *Every building was plundered, even the church.*

**plunder²** *n* [U] things that are stolen by the fighters during an attack or war

**plunge¹** /plʌndʒ/ *v* **1** [I,T] to fall down, especially into water, or to push something down with a lot of force: *A van ran off a curve and plunged into the river early today. | Barton plunged his hands into his pockets and strode away.* **2** [I] to suddenly decrease in amount or value: *The price of gas plunged to 99 cents a gallon.*

**plunge into** *phr v* [T] **plunge sb/sth into sth** to put someone or something into a bad or difficult situation: *The US was suddenly plunged into war.*

**plunge²** *n* **1 take the plunge** to decide to do something risky, usually after delaying or worrying about it: *I finally took the plunge and moved to Washington.* **2** a sudden decrease in amount, or a sudden fall

**plung·er** /ˈplʌndʒɚ/ *n* a tool used for unblocking a pipe in a toilet or SINK, consisting of a straight handle with a large rubber cup on its end

**plunk¹** /plʌŋk/ *v* [T] INFORMAL

**plunk down** sth *phr v* [T] to spend a lot of money for something, or to put something down quickly and loudly: *Plunk down $300,000 and you could have a new house in Sun City.*

**plunk²** *n* the sound made by something when it is dropped

**plu·per·fect** /ˌpluˈpɔfɪkt/ *n* **the pluperfect** TECHNICAL ⇨ PAST PERFECT

**plu·ral** /ˈplʊrəl/ *n* **the plural** TECHNICAL in grammar, the form of a word that represents more than one person or thing. For example, "dogs" is the plural of "dog" **–plural** *adj*: *a plural noun/verb* –compare SINGULAR¹ –see study note on page 466

**plu·ral·i·ty** /plʊˈræləti/ *n* [C,U] the largest number of votes in an election, especially when this is less than the total number of votes that all the other people or parties have received

**plus¹** /plʌs/ *prep* used when one number or amount is added to another: *Three plus six equals nine. (3+6=9)|The jacket costs $49.95 plus tax.*

**plus²** *conjunction* and also: *He's going to college, plus he's working 20 hours a week.*

**plus³** *adj* **1 A plus/B plus/C plus etc.** a grade used in a system of marking students' work; a C plus is higher than a C, but lower than a B MINUS **2** greater than zero or than a particular amount: *a temperature of plus 12°|She makes $50,000 a year plus.* **3 plus or minus** used in order to give the amount by which another amount can vary: *The results are accurate within plus or minus 3 percentage points.* –compare MINUS³

**plus⁴** *n* **1** ⇨ PLUS SIGN **2** something that is an advantage or a quality that you think is good: *The restaurant's convenient location is a plus.*

**plush** /plʌʃ/ *adj* comfortable, expensive, and of good quality: *a large plush office*

**plus sign** /ˈ. ./ *n* the sign (+)

**Plu·to** /ˈplutoʊ/ *n* [singular] a small PLANET, ninth from the sun

**plu·toc·ra·cy** /pluˈtɑkrəsi/ *n* a country that is ruled by rich people, or a government that is controlled by them

**plu·to·ni·um** /pluˈtoʊniəm/ *n* [U] a metal that is an ELEMENT and is used for producing NUCLEAR power

**ply¹** /plaɪ/ *n* [U] a unit for measuring the thickness of thread, rope, PLYWOOD etc. based on the number of threads or layers that it has

**ply²** *v* **plied, plied, plying 1 ply your trade** to work at your business or special skill: *Blues bands were plying their trade in bars around town.* **2** [I,T] LITERARY a boat or vehicle that plies between two places travels to those two places regularly

**ply** sb sth **with** *phr v* [T] to continue giving someone large amounts of something, especially food and drinks

**ply·wood** /ˈplaɪwʊd/ *n* [U] a material made of thin sheets of wood stuck together to form a hard board

**p.m.** the abbreviation of "post meridiem"; used after numbers to show times from NOON until just before MIDNIGHT: *I get off work at 5:30 p.m.*

**PMS** *n* [U] Premenstrual Syndrome; the anger or sadness and physical pain that many women experience before each PERIOD

**pneu·mat·ic** /nʊˈmætɪk/ *adj* **1** TECHNICAL filled with air: *a pneumatic tire* **2** able to work using air pressure: *a pneumatic drill* **–pneumatically** *adv*

**pneu·mo·nia** /nʊˈmoʊnyə/ *n* [U] a serious disease of the lungs, which makes people have difficulty breathing

**P.O.** *n* the written abbreviation of POST OFFICE

**poach** /poʊtʃ/ *v* **1** [T] to cook food such as eggs or fish in slightly boiling liquid **2** [I,T] to illegally catch or shoot animals, birds, or fish, especially from private land

**poach·er** /ˈpoʊtʃɚ/ *n* someone who illegally catches or shoots animals, birds, or fish, especially on private land

**P.O. Box** /ˌpi ˈoʊ ˌbɑks/ *n* Post Office Box; a box in a POST OFFICE that has a special number, to which you can have mail sent instead of to your home

**pock·et¹** /ˈpɑkɪt/ *n* **1** a small bag sewn onto shirts, coats, pants, or skirts, often used for putting keys or money in: *Julie stuck her hands in her pockets.|Dad always keeps pens in his shirt pocket.* **2** the amount of money you have that you can spend: *Over $20 million was taken out of the pockets of American taxpayers.* **3** a small bag, net, or piece of material that is attached to something such as a car seat, used for holding maps, magazines etc. **4** a small area or amount that is different from what surrounds it: *Pockets of the Midwest will have thunderstorms tonight.*

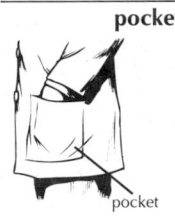
pocket

**pocket²** *v* [T] to get money in a slightly dishonest way, or by stealing it: *He admitted pocketing $5300 of his own campaign money.*

**pocket³, pocket-sized** /ˈ.. ˌ./ *adj* small enough to fit into a pocket: *a pocket calendar|a pocket-sized notebook*

**pock·et·book** /ˈpɑkɪtˌbʊk/ *n* **1** ⇨ WALLET **2** OLD-FASHIONED ⇨ PURSE¹

**pock·et·ful** /ˈpɑkɪtˌfʊl/ *n* the amount that will fill a pocket, or a large amount: *a pocketful of small change*

**pock·et knife** /ˈpɑkɪtˌnaɪf/ *n, plural* **pocket knives** a small knife with a blade that you can fold into its handle

**pock·mark** /ˈpɑkmɑrk/ *n* a small hollow mark on someone's skin, made by a skin disease **–pockmarked** *adj*

**pod** /pɑd/ *n* the long green part of plants such

as beans and PEAs, that the seeds grow in: *a pea pod* −see picture at PEEL²

**po·di·a·trist** /pə'daɪətrɪst/ *n* a doctor who takes care of people's feet and treats foot diseases −**podiatry** *n* [U]

**po·di·um** /'poʊdiəm/ *n* **1** a tall thin desk you stand behind when giving a speech to a lot of people **2** a small raised area for a performer, speaker, or musical conductor to stand on

**po·em** /'poʊəm/ *n* a piece of writing that expresses emotions, experiences, and ideas, especially in short lines using words that RHYME (=have a particular pattern of sounds)

**po·et** /'poʊɪt/ *n* someone who writes poems

**po·et·ic** /poʊ'ɛtɪk/ *adj* **1** relating to poetry or typical of poetry: *poetic language* **2** graceful and expressing deep emotions: *a poetic and powerful ballet* −**poetically** *adv*

**poetic jus·tice** /.,.. '../ *n* [U] a situation in which someone who has done something bad suffers in a way that you think s/he deserves

**poetic li·cense** /.,.. '../ *n* [U] the freedom to change facts, not obey grammar rules etc. because you are writing poetry

**po·et·ry** /'poʊətri/ *n* [U] **1** poems: *a book of Emily Dickenson's poetry* −compare PROSE **2** the art of writing poems: *a poetry class*

**pog·rom** /'poʊgrəm/ *n* a planned killing of large numbers of people, especially Jews, done for reasons of race or religion

**poign·ant** /'pɔɪnyənt/ *adj* making you have strong feelings of sadness or pity: *poignant childhood memories* −**poignancy** *n* [U] −**poignantly** *adv*

**poin·set·ti·a** /pɔɪn'sɛtiə/ *n* a plant with groups of large bright red or white leaves that look like flowers

**point¹** /pɔɪnt/ *n*
**1** ▶ONE IDEA◀ a single fact, idea, or opinion in an argument or discussion: *That's a very interesting point.* | *Jackie pounded the table to* ***make her point.***
**2** ▶MAIN IDEA◀ the main meaning or idea in something that is said or done: *Get to the point!* (=say your idea directly) | ***The point is that I*** *don't trust him anymore.* | *What's your point?* | *That's* ***beside the point.*** (=it does not relate to the subject)
**3** ▶IN TIME/DEVELOPMENT◀ a specific moment or time, or a stage in something's development: ***At some point*** *we'll need to get some more gas.* | *They* ***reached the point*** *where they thought they should get married.*
**4** ▶PLACE◀ an exact position or place: *the point where two lines cross each other*
**5** ▶PURPOSE◀ [U] the purpose or aim of doing something: ***The whole point of*** *traveling is to experience new things.* | ***There's no point in*** *going now - we're already too late.* ✗ DON'T SAY "There's no point to go now." ✗

**6** ▶QUALITY◀ a particular quality that someone or something has: *Public speaking is one of the Mayor's* ***strong points.*** (=best qualities)
**7** ▶GAME/SPORT◀ a unit used for showing the SCORE in a game or sport: *The Rams beat the Giants by six points.*
**8** ▶IN NUMBERS◀ the sign (.) used for separating a whole number from the DECIMALs that follow it: *four point seven five percent* (=4.75%)
**9** ▶MEASURE◀ a measure on a scale: *Stocks were down 12 points today at 5098.*
**10 the high/low point of** the best or worst part of something, or the best or worst moment: *The high point in my life was having my son.*
**11** ▶SHARP END◀ the sharp end of something: *the point of a needle*
**12 up to a point** partly, but not completely: *He believed her story, up to a point.*
**13 make a point of doing something** to deliberately do something: *Make a point of going to the French Quarter when you visit New Orleans.*
**14** ▶SMALL SPOT◀ a very small spot: *a tiny point of light*
**15** ▶LAND◀ a long thin piece of land that stretches out into the ocean
**16 to the point** only talking about the most important facts or ideas: *Your business letters should be short and to the point.*
**17 on the point of doing sth** going to do something very soon: *I was just on the point of leaving for work when the phone rang.*
**18 the point of no return** the moment when you become so involved in an activity, situation etc. that it is impossible for you to stop doing it

---

SPOKEN PHRASES
**19 you/they have a point** said when you think someone's idea or opinion is right: *"The tickets might be too expensive." "You have a point."*
**20 that's not the point** said when facts or explanations do not relate to the main facts or ideas: *"But I gave you the money back." "That's not the point; you shouldn't have stolen it."*
**21 I see your point** used in order to say that you accept what someone has said: *Grandma refuses to go to a nursing home, and I see her point.*

---

−see also GUNPOINT −see usage note at VIEW¹

**point²** *v* **1** [I] to show someone something by holding your finger out toward it: *John* ***pointed to*** *a chair. "Please, sit down."* | *"That's my car," she said,* ***pointing at*** *a white Ford.* **2** [I,T] to aim something or to be aimed in a particular direction: *He* ***pointed*** *a gun* ***at*** *the old man's head.* | *Hold the bat so that your fingers* ***point toward*** *its end.* **3** [T] to show someone which direction to go: *There should be signs* ***pointing the way*** *to her house.* **4 point the finger at sb** INFORMAL to blame someone; ACCUSE

**point out** *phr v* **1** [T **point** sth ↔ **out**] to tell someone something that s/he does not already know or has not yet noticed: *Hobart pointed out that Washington hadn't won a game in L.A. since 1980.* **2** [T **point** sb/sth ↔ **out**] to show a person or thing to someone by pointing at him, her, or it: *Mrs. Lucas pointed out her new students to us.*

**point to/toward** sb/sth *phr v* [T] to show that something is probably true: *The report points to stress as a cause of heart disease.*

**point-blank** /ˌ. ˈ./ *adv* **1** if you say something point-blank, you say it in a very direct way: *They refused my offer point-blank.* **2** if you shoot a gun point-blank, the person or thing you are shooting is directly in front of you: *Ralston was shot at point-blank range.*

**point·ed** /ˈpɔɪntɪd/ *adj* **1** having a point at the end: *cowboy boots with pointed toes* **2 a pointed question/look/remark etc.** a direct question, look etc. that deliberately shows that you are bored, annoyed, or do not approve of something

**point·ed·ly** /ˈpɔɪntɪdli/ *adv* deliberately, so that people notice: *Wilton pointedly avoided asking Reiter for advice.*

**point·er** /ˈpɔɪntɚ/ *n* **1** a helpful piece of advice; TIP: *I can give you some pointers on how to cook a turkey.* **2** the thin ARROW that points to a particular place, number, or direction on a piece of equipment such as a computer, watch, or scale **3** a long stick used for pointing at things on a map, board etc. **4** a hunting dog that points its nose at animals and birds that are hiding

**point·less** /ˈpɔɪntlɪs/ *adj* **1** without any purpose or meaning: *pointless violence on TV* **2** not likely to have any effect: *It's pointless trying to talk to him - he won't listen.*

**point man** /ˈ. ./ *n* someone, especially a soldier, who goes ahead of a group to see what a situation is like or if there is any danger

**point of view** /ˌ. . ˈ./ *n* **1** a particular way of thinking about or judging a situation: *From a purely practical point of view, this is not a good decision.* **2** someone's own personal opinion or attitude about something: *My parents never seem to be able to see my point of view.*

**poin·ty** /ˈpɔɪnti/ *adj* INFORMAL ⇨ POINTED

**poise¹** /pɔɪz/ *n* [U] **1** behavior that shows you are calm, confident, and able to control how you feel: *Throughout the discussion he never lost his poise.* **2** a graceful way of moving or standing: *Miss Gaines was tall, thin, and lacking in poise.*

**poise²** *v* [T] to put something in a carefully balanced position, or to hold it there: *The reporter sat with his pen poised over a notebook.*

**poised** /pɔɪzd/ *adj* **1** completely prepared for something to happen, because it is likely to happen very soon: *The army was poised to attack.* | *property that is poised for development* **2** not moving, but completely ready to move: *runners poised at the start of a race* **3** behaving in a calm confident way that shows you are able to control how you feel: *an attractive poised college graduate*

**poi·son¹** /ˈpɔɪzən/ *n* [C,U] **1** a substance that can kill you or make you sick if you eat it, breathe it etc.: *A child was rushed to the hospital after eating rat poison.* **2** INFORMAL a person, feeling, idea etc. that persuades you to do bad things or makes you feel very unhappy: *She's poison, Dale! Don't listen to her!*

**poison²** *v* [T] **1** to kill or harm someone by giving him/her poison: *Two of the victims had been poisoned with arsenic.* **2** to make the land, lakes, rivers, air etc. dangerous by adding harmful chemicals to it: *Chemical waste has poisoned the city's water supply.* **3** to influence someone in a bad way or make him/her feel very unhappy: *Sex on TV is poisoning our children's minds!*

**poi·son·ing** /ˈpɔɪzənɪŋ/ *n* [C,U] an illness that is caused by swallowing, touching, or breathing a poisonous substance: *lead poisoning*

**poison i·vy** /ˌ.. ˈ../ *n* [U] a bush or VINE with an oily substance on its leaves that makes your skin hurt if you touch it

**poi·son·ous** /ˈpɔɪzənəs/ *adj* containing poison or producing poison: *a poisonous chemical* | *poisonous snakes* —**poisonously** *adv*

**poke** /poʊk/ *v* **1** [I,T] to press something quickly and with a lot of force using a pointed object, such as your finger or a stick: *Stop poking me!* | *He poked at the campfire with a stick.* **2** [I,T] to push something through a space or out of an opening, so that you can see part of it: *David poked his head around the door and smiled at us.* | *The roots of the trees are poking up through the sidewalk.* **3 poke a hole** to make a hole in something by pushing a pointed object through it **4 poke fun at** to joke about someone in an unkind way: *Stop poking fun at your sister!* —**poke** *n*

**pok·er** /ˈpoʊkɚ/ *n* **1** [U] a card game that people usually play for money **2** a metal stick used for moving coal or wood in a fire to make it burn better

**poker-faced** /ˈ.. ˌ./ *adj* showing no expression on your face: *His poker-faced secretary led us into the office.* —**poker face** *n* [singular]

**pok·ey, poky** /ˈpoʊki/ *adj* **1** doing things very slowly, especially in a way that you find annoying: *a pokey driver* **2** too small and not very pleasant or comfortable: *a pokey apartment*

**po·lar** /ˈpoʊlɚ/ *adj* **1** relating to the North Pole and the South Pole: *polar ice caps* **2 polar opposite** someone or something that is completely opposite to another person or thing in character or style: *Louise and her sister are polar opposites.*

**polar bear** /ˈ.. ˌ./ n a large white bear that lives near the North Pole

**po·lar·i·ty** /pouˈlærəti, pə-/ n [C,U] FORMAL a state in which two ideas or sides in an argument are completely opposite: *the growing polarity between workers and management*

**po·lar·ize** /ˈpouləˌraɪz/ v [I,T] FORMAL to divide into two opposing groups, or to make people do this: *The election polarized the city.* –**polarization** /ˌpoulərəˈzeɪʃən/ n [U]

**Po·lar·oid** /ˈpouləˌrɔɪd/ n TRADEMARK a camera that uses a special film to produce a photograph very quickly, or a picture taken with this kind of camera

**Pole** /poul/ n someone from Poland

**pole** n **1** a long stick or post: *a telephone pole* (=holding up telephone wires outside) | *a fishing pole* **2** the most northern and southern point on a PLANET: *an expedition to the North Pole* **3 be poles apart** to be very different from someone else: *Dad's and Mark's political views are poles apart.* **4** one of two points at the end of a MAGNET where its power is strongest **5** one of the two points at which wires can be fixed onto a BATTERY in order to use its electricity

**po·lem·ic** /pəˈlemɪk/ n strong arguments that criticize or defend a particular idea, opinion, or person –**polemical** adj

**pole vault** /ˈ. ./ n [U] a sport in which you jump over a high BAR using a special long pole

**po·lice¹** /pəˈlis/ n **1 the police** an official organization that protects people and property and makes sure that everyone obeys the law: *We'll have to tell the police.* **2** [plural] the people who work for this organization: *Police arrived soon after the alarm went off.*

**police²** v [T] **1** to keep order in a place using police: *new ways of policing the neighborhood* **2** to control a particular activity or industry by making sure people obey the rules: *an agency that polices the nuclear power industry*

**police de·part·ment** /ˈ. ˌ./ n the official police organization in a particular area or city

**police force** /ˈ. ˌ./ n all the police officers that work for a particular police organization

**po·lice·man** /pəˈlismən/ n a male police officer

**police of·fi·cer** /ˈ. ˌ./ n a member of the police

**police state** /ˈ. ˌ./ n a country where the government strictly controls most of the activities of its citizens

**police sta·tion** /ˈ. ˌ./ n the local office of the police in a town or city

**po·lice·wom·an** /pəˈlisˌwumən/ n a female police officer

**pol·i·cy** /ˈpɑləsi/ n **1** [C,U] a way of doing things that has been officially agreed and chosen by a political party or organization: *the government's foreign policy* | *the company's policy on*

maternity leave **2** a written agreement with an insurance company: *a homeowner's policy* **3** [C,U] a particular principle that you believe in: *I make it my policy not to gossip.*

**po·li·o** /ˈpouliˌou/ n [U] a serious infectious disease of the nerves in your BACKBONE, often resulting in PARALYSIS (=the inability to move your muscles)

**Po·lish¹** /ˈpoulɪʃ/ adj relating to or coming from Poland

**Polish²** n **1** [U] the language used in Poland **2 the Polish** [plural] the people of Poland

**pol·ish¹** /ˈpɑlɪʃ/ v [T] to make something smooth, bright, and shiny by rubbing it: *Davy spent all morning polishing his car.* –**polisher** n

polish

**polish** sth ↔ **off** phr v [T] INFORMAL to finish food, work etc. quickly or easily: *The kids polished off the rest of the cake.*

**polish** sth ↔ **up** phr v [T] to improve a skill or an ability: *Barney's taking a class to polish up his writing skills.*

**polish²** n **1** a liquid, powder, or other substance used for rubbing into a surface to make it shiny: *furniture polish* | *shoe polish* **2** [U] great skill and style in the way someone performs, writes, or behaves: *Your paper is okay, but it needs a little polish.* **3** an act of polishing a surface to make it smooth and shiny: *An occasional polish will keep the table looking new.* –see also NAIL POLISH

**pol·ished** /ˈpɑlɪʃt/ adj **1** shiny because of being rubbed with polish: *polished furniture* **2** done with great skill and style: *a polished performance* **3** polite and confident: *polished manners*

**po·lite** /pəˈlaɪt/ adj **1** behaving or speaking in a way that is correct for the social situation you are in: *It's not polite to talk with food in your mouth.* | *a polite smile* **2 just being polite** SPOKEN saying something you may not really believe, in order to avoid offending someone: *Did she really like the gift, or was she just being polite?* –**politely** adv –**politeness** n [U]

**po·lit·i·cal** /pəˈlɪtɪkəl/ adj **1** relating to the government, politics, and the public affairs of a country: *The US has two main political parties.* | *political campaigns* | *political activists* **2** relating to the way that people, groups, companies etc. try to get advantages for themselves: *Each side had a political reason for being there.* | *It gets too political in the office sometimes.* (=too many people try to get advantages for themselves) **3** interested in or active in politics: *Mike's never been political.* –**politically** adv

**po·lit·i·cally cor·rect** /.,... .'./, **PC** adj politically correct language, behavior, and attitudes are considered acceptable because they do not offend women, people of a particular race, DISABLED people etc.: *It's not politically correct to say "handicapped" anymore.* –**political correctness** n [U]

**political pris·on·er** /.,... '.../ n someone who is put in prison because s/he criticizes the government

**political sci·ence** /.,... '../ n [U] the study of politics and government

**pol·i·ti·cian** /,palə'tɪʃən/ n someone who works in politics: *Unfortunately politicians are not highly trusted these days.*

**po·lit·i·cize** /pə'lɪtəsaɪz/ v [T] to make a situation, position, or organization more political or more involved in politics: *The issue has recently been politicized.* –**politicized** adj

**pol·i·tics** /'palə,tɪks/ n 1 [U] ideas and activities that are concerned with gaining and using power in a country, city etc.: *She's involved in city politics.* | *Politics doesn't interest me.* 2 [U] the profession of being a politician: *He'll retire from politics before the next election.* 3 [plural] the activities of people who are concerned with gaining personal advantage within a group: *Colin tries not to get involved in office politics.* 4 [plural] someone's political beliefs and opinions: *I'm not sure what Ellen's politics are.*

**pol·ka** /'poulkə, 'poukə/ n a very quick simple dance for people dancing in pairs, or the music for this dance –**polka** v [I]

**polka dot** /'.. ,./ n one of a number of spots that form a pattern, especially on material for clothing: *a white dress with red polka dots* –**polka-dot** adj: *a polka-dot scarf* –see picture at PATTERN

**poll**[1] /poul/ n the process of finding out what people think about something by asking many people the same question, or the record of the result: *Recent polls show that support for the President is strong.* –see also POLLS

**poll**[2] v [T] to try to find out what people think about a subject by asking many people the same question: *We polled 600 teachers, asking their opinion on the new education policy.*

**pol·len** /'palən/ n [U] a powder produced by flowers that is carried by the wind or insects to make other flowers produce seeds

**pollen count** /'.. ,./ n a measurement of the amount of POLLEN in the air

**pol·li·nate** /'palə,neɪt/ v [T] to make a flower or plant produce seeds by giving it POLLEN –**pollination** /,palə'neɪʃən/ n [U]

**polling place** /'.. ,./, **polling sta·tion** /'.. ,../ n the place where you can go to vote in an election

**polls** /poulz/ n [plural] **the polls** the voting in

an election: *Voters go to the polls* (=vote) *on Tuesday.*

**poll·ster** /'poulstɚ/ n someone who prepares and asks questions to find out what people think about a particular subject

**pol·lut·ant** /pə'lutˀnt/ n a substance that makes air, water, soil etc. dangerously dirty

**pol·lute** /pə'lut/ v [I,T] to make air, water, soil etc. dangerously dirty: *Gold miners entered the territory, polluting rivers with mercury.* –**polluter** n

**pol·lut·ed** /pə'lutɪd/ adj full of POLLUTION: *heavily polluted air/rivers*

**pol·lu·tion** /pə'luʃən/ n [U] 1 the process of polluting (POLLUTE) a place: *Toxic waste is a major cause of pollution.* 2 substances that POLLUTE a place: *Pollution levels are dangerously high in some cities.* –see also NOISE POLLUTION

**po·lo** /'poulou/ n [U] an outdoor game played between two teams riding horses, who use long wooden hammers to hit a small ball

**polo shirt** /'.. ,./ n a shirt with short SLEEVEs and a collar, usually made of cotton

**pol·y·es·ter** /'pali,ɛstɚ, ,pali'ɛstɚ/ n [U] an artificial material used especially to make cloth

**po·lyg·a·my** /pə'lɪgəmi/ n [U] TECHNICAL the practice of having more than one wife at the same time –**polygamous** adj –**polygamist** n

**pol·y·gon** /'pali,gan/ n TECHNICAL a flat shape with three or more sides

**pol·y·graph** /'pali,græf/ n TECHNICAL ⇨ LIE DETECTOR

**pol·y·mer** /'paləmɚ/ n a chemical compound that has a simple structure of large MOLECULEs

**pol·yp** /'paləp/ n a small LUMP that grows inside a passage in the body, that is usually not harmful but that can block the passage

**pol·y·tech·nic** /,pali'tɛknɪk/ n a college where you can study technical or scientific subjects

**pol·y·un·sat·u·rat·ed fat** /,paliʌn,sætʃə'reɪt̬ɪd 'fæt/ adj a kind of fat that comes from vegetables and plants and is healthier than SATURATED FAT from animals

**pom·e·gran·ate** /'pamə,grænɪt/ n a round fruit with thick red skin and many juicy red seeds that you can eat

**pomp** /pamp/ n [U] FORMAL all the impressive clothes, decorations, music etc. that are traditional for an important public ceremony

**pom·pom** /'pampam/, **pom·pon** /'pampan/ n 1 a ball of wool, feathers etc. used as a decoration on clothing 2 a large round ball of loose paper or plastic strings connected to a handle, used by CHEERLEADERs

**pomp·ous** /'pampəs/ adj trying to make people think you are important, especially by using a lot of formal words: *a pompous speech* –**pomposity** /pam'pasət̬i/ n [U]

**pon·cho** /'pɑntʃoʊ/ n **1** a kind of coat that is made from a single piece of thick cloth, with a hole in the middle for your head to go through **2** a coat like this that keeps out the rain and has a HOOD (=cover for your head)

**pond** /pɑnd/ n a small area of fresh water that is smaller than a lake

**pon·der** /'pɑndɚ/ v [I,T] LITERARY to spend time thinking carefully and seriously about something: *She pondered her answer for a long time.*

**pon·der·ous** /'pɑndərəs/ adj **1** moving slowly or awkwardly because of being very big: *an elephant's ponderous walk* **2** boring and too serious: *a ponderous voice*

**pon·tiff** /'pɑntɪf/ n FORMAL the POPE

**pon·tif·i·cate** /pɑn'tɪfə,keɪt/ v [I] to give your opinion about something in a way that shows you think you are always right: *Anthony likes to pontificate about how wonderful capitalism is.*

**pon·toon** /pɑn'tun/ n one of the floating metal containers that are attached to bridges, SEA PLANEs etc. in order to make them float

**po·ny¹** /'poʊni/ n a small horse

**pony²** v

**pony up** phr v [I,T] INFORMAL to pay for something: *Opera fans who pony up $34.95 will see a four-hour opera special.*

**Pony Ex·press** /ˌ.. .ˈ./ n [singular] a mail service in the 1860s that used horses and riders to carry the mail

**po·ny·tail** /'poʊni,teɪl/ n hair tied together at the back of your head – see picture at HAIRSTYLE

**pooch** /putʃ/ n INFORMAL HUMOROUS a dog

**poo·dle** /'pudl/ n a dog with thick curly hair that is often cut in a special shape

**pooh-pooh** /'pupu, pu'pu/ v [T] INFORMAL to say that you think that an idea, suggestion etc. is not very good: *At first they pooh-poohed the idea.*

**pool¹** /pul/ n **1** a structure that has been specially built and filled with water so that people can swim or WADE in it **2** [U] an indoor game played on a cloth-covered table, in which you hit balls with a long stick into pockets at the corners and sides of the table **3 a pool of oil/light etc.** a small area of liquid or light on a surface: *Creighton lay there in a pool of blood.* **4** a small area of still water in the ground: *A shallow pool had formed among the rocks.* **5** a group of people who are available to work or to do an activity when they are needed: *a secretarial pool* | *a talent pool of great student athletes* **6** a number of things or an amount of money that is shared by a group of people: *Each ticket won $63 from a prize pool of $376,141.*

**pool²** v [T] to combine your money, ideas, skills etc. with those of other people so that you can

all use them: *If we pool our resources, we can start our own business.*

**pool hall** /'. ./ n a building where people go to play POOL

**pool ta·ble** /'. ˌ../ n a cloth-covered table with pockets at the corners and sides, used for playing POOL

**poop¹** /pup/ n **1** [U] SPOKEN a word meaning solid waste from your BOWELs, or the act of passing waste, used especially by children **2 the poop** SPOKEN the latest news about someone or something: *So what's the poop on the new guy?*

**poop²** v [I,T] INFORMAL a word meaning to pass solid waste from your BOWELs, used especially by children

**poop out** phr v [I] SPOKEN to stop trying to do something because you are tired: *She pooped out halfway through the race.*

**pooped** /pupt/, **pooped out** adj SPOKEN very tired: *I'm pooped!*

**poop·er scoop·er** /'.. ˌ../ n INFORMAL a small SHOVEL and a container, used by dog owners for removing their dogs' solid waste from the streets

**poor** /pʊr, pɔr/ adj **1** having very little money and not many possessions: *She comes from a poor family.* | *a poor country* **2 the poor** people who are poor: *a charity that distributes food to the poor* **3** not as good as it could be or should be: *The soil in this part of the country is poor.* | *poor health* **4 poor girl/ Mom/man etc.** SPOKEN said in order to show pity for someone because s/he is unlucky, unhappy etc.: *Poor Dad - everything's going wrong today.* **5** not good at doing something: *a poor reader*

**poor·ly** /'pʊrli/ adv badly: *a poorly lit room*

**pop¹** /pɑp/ v **-pped, -pping 1** [I,T] to do something that suddenly lets the air out of a container or BALLOON so that a sound like a small explosion is made, or to make a sound like this: *Oh, Jodie, did your balloon pop?* | *popping a champagne cork* **2** [I] if your ears pop, you feel the pressure in them suddenly change, for example, when you go up in a plane **3** [I,T] to cook POPCORN until it bursts open: *Why don't we pop some popcorn?* **4 pop the question** INFORMAL to ask someone to marry you: *Has Dan popped the question yet?* **5** [I] SPOKEN to go somewhere or do something quickly, suddenly, or without planning: *Maybe I'll just pop in on Terry.* (=visit him for a short time) | *I didn't mean to say that - it just popped out!* **6** SPOKEN to hit someone: *If you say that again, I'll pop you.* **7 pop a pill** INFORMAL to take a PILL

**pop up** phr v [I] INFORMAL to happen or appear suddenly or without warning: *Every once in a while a good new band pops up.*

**pop²** n **1** [U] modern music that is popular with young people: *a pop record* **2** OLD-

FASHIONED ⇨ FATHER¹ **3** [U] INFORMAL ⇨ SOFT DRINK −see culture note at SODA **4** a sudden short sound like a small explosion: *the pop of an air rifle*

**pop·corn** /'pɑpkɔrn/ *n* [U] a type of corn that swells and bursts open when heated, usually eaten warm with butter and salt

**Pope** /poʊp/ *n* **the Pope** the leader of the Roman Catholic Church

**pop·lar** /'pɑplɚ/ *n* [C] a tall thin tree with light green BARK

**pop psy·chol·o·gy** /ˌ. .'.../ *n* [U] ways of dealing with problems in life that are made popular on television or in books, but that are not considered scientific

**pop·py** /'pɑpi/ *n* a brightly colored flower, usually red, with small black seeds

**pop quiz** /ˌ. './ *n* a short test that is given without any warning in order to check that students have been studying

**pops** /pɑps/ *adj* **pops concert/orchestra** a concert or ORCHESTRA that performs popular CLASSICAL MUSIC

**Pop·si·cle** /'pɑpsɪkəl/ *n* TRADEMARK a food made of ice that tastes like fruit, that is frozen onto sticks

**pop·u·lace** /'pɑpyələs/ *n* [singular] FORMAL the ordinary people who live in a country

**pop·u·lar** /'pɑpyələ/ *adj* **1** liked by a lot of people, or by most of the people in a group: *a song that's really popular right now* | *the most popular kid in school* **2** shared, accepted, or done by a lot of people: *The party had managed to gain massive popular support.* | *Popular opinion* (=what most people think) *in Peru seems to support the new president.*

**pop·u·lar·i·ty** /ˌpɑpyə'lærəṭi/ *n* [U] the quality of being liked or supported by a large number of people: *The band's popularity has grown steadily in the last five years.*

**pop·u·lar·ize** /'pɑpyələˌraɪz/ *v* [T] to make an unknown or difficult subject or idea become well known, accepted, or understood: *Jane Fonda popularized aerobic exercise.* | *popularizing science*

**pop·u·lar·ly** /'pɑpyələli/ *adv* by most people: *It's popularly believed that people need eight hours of sleep every night.*

**pop·u·late** /'pɑpyəˌleɪt/ *v* [T] to fill an area with people or animals who move or live there: *a suburb that is densely/heavily populated by students* (=has a lot of students living there) | *a sparsely populated area* (=with few people)

**pop·u·la·tion** /ˌpɑpyə'leɪʃən/ *n* [C,U] **1** the number of people or animals living in a particular area, country etc.: *What's the population of New York?* | *There was a population explosion* (=a sudden large increase in population) *between 1944 and 1964 in the US.* **2** all of the people who live in a particular area or share a particular condition: *Most of the popula-tion of Canada lives near the US border.* | *an increasingly elderly population*

**pop·u·lous** /'pɑpyələs/ *adj* FORMAL having a large population: *the most populous country in Africa*

**por·ce·lain** /'pɔrsəlɪn/ *n* [U] a hard shiny white substance that is used for making expensive plates, cups etc., or objects made of this

**porch** /pɔrtʃ/ *n* a structure built onto a house at its front or back entrance, with a floor and roof but no walls −see picture on page 471

**por·cu·pine** /'pɔrkyəˌpaɪn/ *n* a small animal with thick QUILLs (=needle-shaped parts) on its back and sides

**pore¹** /pɔr/ *n* one of the small holes in the skin or in a leaf that liquid can pass through

**pore²** *v*

**pore over** sth *phr v* [T] to read or look at something very carefully for a long time: *We spent all day poring over wedding magazines.*

**pork** /pɔrk/ *n* **1** the meat from pigs: *pork chops* −see usage note at MEAT **2** SLANG government money spent in a particular area in order to get political advantages

**por·nog·ra·phy** /pɔr'nɑgrəfi/, **porn** /pɔrn/ *n* [U] magazines, movies etc. that show sexual acts and images in a way that is intended to make people feel sexually excited −**pornographic** /ˌpɔrnə'græfɪk/ *adj* −**pornographer** /pɔr'nɑgrəfə/ *n*

**po·rous** /'pɔrəs/ *adj* allowing liquid, air etc. to pass through slowly: *porous rock*

**por·poise** /'pɔrpəs/ *n* a large sea animal similar to a DOLPHIN, that breathes air

**por·ridge** /'pɔrɪdʒ, 'pɑr-/ *n* [U] cooked OATMEAL

**port** /pɔrt/ *n* **1** [C,U] a place where ships can load and unload people or things; HARBOR: *The ship was back in port after a week at sea.* **2** a town or city with a HARBOR: *the port of Wilmington, North Carolina* **3** a place on the outside of a computer where you can connect another piece of equipment such as a PRINTER **4** [C,U] a strong sweet Portuguese wine **5** [U] the left side of a ship or aircraft when you are looking toward the front

**port·a·ble** /'pɔrtəbəl/ *adj* light and easily carried or moved: *a portable phone/computer* −**portable** *n*

**por·tal** /'pɔrtl/ *n* LITERARY a large gate or entrance to a building

**por·tend** /pɔr'tɛnd/ *v* [T] LITERARY to be a sign that something is going to happen, especially something bad: *strange events that portend some great disaster* −**portent** /'pɔrtɛnt/ *n*

**por·ter** /'pɔrtɚ/ *n* **1** someone whose job is to carry travelers' bags at airports, hotels etc. **2** someone whose job is to take care of the part of a train where people sleep

**port·fo·li·o** /pɔrt'fouli,ou/ n **1** a large flat case used for carrying drawings, documents etc. **2** a collection of drawings or other pieces of work by an artist, photographer etc. **3** a collection of SHAREs owned by a particular person or company: *an investment portfolio*

**port·hole** /'pɔrthoul/ n a small window on the side of a ship or plane

**por·ti·co** /'pɔrtɪ,kou/ n a covered entrance to a building, consisting of a roof supported by PILLARs

**por·tion**[1] /'pɔrʃən/ n **1** a part of something larger: *The news showed only a portion of the interview.* | *We put a portion of our pay into a savings account.* **2** an amount of food for one person, especially when served in a restaurant: *Do you have children's portions?* **3** a share of something such as blame or a duty: *Both drivers must bear a portion of the blame.*

**portion**[2] v
  **portion** sth ↔ **out** phr v [T] to divide something into parts and give them to several people

**port·ly** /'pɔrtli/ adj used in order to describe an older man who is fat in a fairly attractive way: *a portly gentleman*

**por·trait** /'pɔrtrɪt/ n **1** a painting, drawing, or photograph of a person: *a family portrait* **2** the story or a description of someone or something, often in the form of a movie: *The movie is a portrait of life in Harlem in the 1940s.*

**por·trai·ture** /'pɔrtrɪtʃɚ/ n [U] the art of painting or drawing pictures of people

**por·tray** /pɔr'treɪ, pɚ-/ v [T] **1** to describe something or someone in the form of a story or film: *a movie that portrays the life of Charlie Chaplin* **2** **portray sb/sth as sth** to describe or show someone or something in a particular way, according to your opinion of him/her: *In the novel, Elaine's father is portrayed as a cruel tyrant.* **3** to act the part of a character in a play: *Robin Williams portrayed Peter Pan in the movie.*

**por·tray·al** /pɔr'treɪəl, pɚ-/ n [C,U] the action of PORTRAYing someone or something, or the book, film, play etc. that results from this: *an accurate portrayal of pioneer life*

**Por·tu·guese**[1] /,pɔrtʃə'giz/ adj relating to or coming from Portugal

**Portuguese**[2] n **1** [U] the language used in Portugal **2** **the Portuguese** [plural] the people of Portugal

**pose**[1] /pouz/ v **1** **pose a problem/threat/danger** to cause a problem or danger: *Nuclear waste poses a threat to the environment.* **2** [I,T] to sit or stand in a particular position in order to be photographed or painted, or to make someone do this: *The astronauts posed for pictures near the shuttle.* **3** **pose a question** to ask a question that needs to be carefully thought about: *His speech poses an interesting question.*

**4** **pose as sb** to pretend to be someone else in order to deceive people: *The thief got in by posing as a repairman.*

**pose**[2] n a position in which someone deliberately stands or sits: *She **struck a pose** (=stood or sat in a particular position) with her head to one side.*

**pos·er** /'pouzɚ/ n INFORMAL someone who pretends to have a quality or social position s/he does not have, in order to seem impressive to other people

**posh** /paʃ/ adj expensive and used by rich people: *a posh restaurant*

**po·si·tion**[1] /pə'zɪʃən/ n
**1** ▶STANDING/SITTING◀ the way someone stands or sits, or the direction in which an object is pointing: *Keep your arms in this position as you dance.* | *This exercise is done in a sitting position.*
**2** ▶SITUATION◀ [C usually singular] the situation that someone is in, or the situation concerning a particular subject: *The company is in a dangerous financial position right now.* | *I'm afraid I'm **not in a position to** help you.* (=do not have the power or money to help you)
**3** ▶RANK◀ the level or rank someone has in a society or organization: *Ask someone in a **position of authority**.* | *a study on the **position of** minorities **in** our society*
**4** ▶OPINION◀ an opinion about a particular subject: *What's the party's **position on** foreign aid?*
**5** ▶PLACE◀ [U] the place where someone or something is, in relation to other things: *Help me put the furniture back in position.*
**6** ▶JOB◀ a job: *He's applied for a position at the bank.* —see usage note at JOB
**7** ▶SPORTS◀ the area where someone plays in a sport, or the type of actions s/he is responsible for doing in a game: *"What position do you play?" "Second base."*
**8** ▶RACE/COMPETITION◀ the place that someone has during a race or competition: *Paldi has moved into second position.*

**position**[2] v [T] to put something or someone in a particular place: *Police positioned themselves around the bank.*

**pos·i·tive**[1] /'pazətɪv/ adj **1** very sure that something is right: *"Are you sure you don't want a drink?" "Positive."* **2** considering the good qualities of a situation, person etc., and expecting success: *Sharon has a positive attitude to work.* | *So far, we've had mostly positive reactions to the new show.* **3** a medical or scientific test that is positive shows signs of what is being looked for: *Her pregnancy test came out/up positive.* **4** having a good or useful effect, especially on someone's character: *Living abroad has been a positive experience for Jim.* **5** TECHNICAL a positive number or quantity is higher than zero. (+) is the positive sign **6** TECHNICAL having the type of electrical

**p**

charge that is carried by PROTONs, shown by a (+) sign on a BATTERY —opposite NEGATIVE[1]

**positive**[2] *n* a number that is higher than zero

**pos·i·tive·ly** /'pɑzətɪvli, ˌpɑzə'tɪvli‹/ *adv*
**1** SPOKEN used in order to emphasize that you mean what you are saying: *This is positively the last time I'm going to say this.* **2** INFORMAL used in order to emphasize a strong opinion or a surprising statement: *Some patients positively enjoy being in the hospital.* **3** in a way that shows you agree with something and want it to succeed: *News of the changes was received positively.* —see also **think positively** (THINK)

**pos·se** /'pɑsi/ *n* a group of men gathered together in past times by a SHERIFF (=local law officer) to help catch criminals

**pos·sess** /pə'zɛs/ *v* [T] **1** FORMAL to own or have something: *The country possesses nuclear arms.* | *She possesses a great talent for poetry.* **2 what possessed sb to...?** SPOKEN said when you cannot understand why someone did something: *What possessed you to buy such an expensive gift?* —**possessor** *n*

**pos·sessed** /pə'zɛst/ *adj* controlled by an evil spirit

**pos·ses·sion** /pə'zɛʃən/ *n* **1** [C usually plural] something that you own: *When they left, they had to sell most of their possessions.* **2** [U] FORMAL the state of having or owning something: *He was found in possession of illegal drugs.* | *When can we take possession of the house?* (=begin to use the house after buying it)

**pos·ses·sive**[1] /pə'zɛsɪv/ *adj* **1** wanting someone to have feelings of love or friendship only for you: *I love Dave, but he's very possessive.* **2** unwilling to let other people use something you own: *As a child, she was very possessive of her toys.*

**possessive**[2] *n* **the possessive** TECHNICAL in grammar, a word such as "my," "its," "their" etc., used in order to show that one thing or person belongs to another thing or person, or is related to that thing or person —**possessive** *adj*: *a possessive adjective/pronoun*

**pos·si·bil·i·ty** /ˌpɑsə'bɪləti/ *n* **1** something that may happen or may be true: *There's a possibility (that) they'll come this weekend.* | *a possibility of getting a scholarship* **2** something that gives you an opportunity to do what you want: *Fuel cells are another possibility for powering electric cars.*

**pos·si·ble** /'pɑsəbəl/ *adj* **1 as long/much/soon as possible** as long, soon etc. as you can: *They need the tapes as quickly as possible.* | *We kept going for as long as possible.* **2** able to be done, to happen, or to exist: *Is it possible to give the report to you tomorrow?* | *Computer technology makes it possible for people to work at home now.* | *This is the best/worst possible result.* (=it can be no better or worse) **3 would it**

**be possible to...?** SPOKEN said when asking politely if you can do or have something: *Would it be possible to exchange these gloves?* **4** likely to be done, to happen, or to exist: *Icy conditions are possible along the coast.* | *I'm looking for possible research topics.* **5 whenever/wherever possible** every time or place that you have an opportunity to do something: *She visits her grandmother whenever possible.* —compare IMPOSSIBLE

**pos·si·bly** /'pɑsəbli/ *adv* **1** used when saying that something may be true or likely: *The trial will take place soon, possibly next week.* | *Picasso is quite possibly* (=very likely) *the best painter of this century.* **2** used with MODAL VERBs, especially "can" and "could," to emphasize that something is or is not possible: *I couldn't possibly eat all that!* | *We did everything we possibly could to help them.* | *Tracey might possibly have forgotten.* **3 could/can you possibly...?** SPOKEN said when politely asking someone to do something: *Could you possibly turn the radio down?*

**pos·sum** /'pɑsəm/ *n* INFORMAL ⇨ OPOSSUM —see also **play possum** (PLAY[1])

**post**[1] /poʊst/ *n* **1** a strong upright piece of wood, metal etc. that is fixed into the ground: *a fence post* **2** an important job, especially in the government or military: *Biddle was given a new post in the Middle East.* **3** the place where someone has to be in order to do his/her job: *The guards cannot leave their posts.* **4** a military BASE

**post**[2] *v* [T] **1** to put a public notice about something on a wall or BULLETIN BOARD: *They've posted warning signs on the gate.* **2** to give someone a government job in a foreign country: *Officials posted in the area were told to leave.* **3** if a company posts its profits, sales, losses etc., it records the money gained or lost in its accounts: *In the final quarter, the company posted $12.4 million in earnings.*

**post·age** /'poʊstɪdʒ/ *n* [U] the money charged for sending a letter, package etc. by mail

**post·al** /'poʊstl/ *adj* relating to the official mail system that takes letters from one place to another: *postal workers*

**postal serv·ice** /'.. ˌ../ *n* the public service for carrying letters, packages etc. from one part of the country to another

**post·card** /'poʊstkɑrd/ *n* a card, often with a picture on the front, that can be sent in the mail without an envelope: *a postcard of Niagara Falls* —see picture at CARD[1]

**post·date** /ˌpoʊst'deɪt/ *v* [T] to write a check with a date that is later than the actual date, so that it cannot be used until that time

**post·doc·tor·al** /ˌpoʊst'dɑktərəl/ *adj* relating to study done after a PH.D.

**post·er** /'pousta/ n a large printed notice, picture etc. used in order to advertise something or as a decoration: *We designed the posters for the concert.*

**pos·te·ri·or** /pa'stiria, pou-/ n HUMOROUS the part of the body you sit on

**pos·ter·i·ty** /pa'stɛrəti/ n [U] the people who will live after you are dead: *I'm saving these pictures for posterity.*

**post·grad·u·ate**[1] /,poust'grædʒuɪt/ n someone who is studying to obtain a higher degree after high school or college

**postgraduate**[2] adj relating to studies done by a POSTGRADUATE: *a postgraduate scholarship*

**post·hu·mous** /'pastʃəməs/ adj happening after someone's death: *a posthumous award* −**posthumously** adv

**Post-it** /'poust,ɪt/ n TRADEMARK a small piece of paper that sticks to things, used for leaving notes for people

**post·man** /'poustmən/ n ⇨ MAILMAN

**post·mark** /'poustmark/ n an official mark made on a letter, package etc. that shows the place and time it was sent −**postmark** v [T]: *The card is postmarked Dec. 2.*

**post·mas·ter** /'poust,mæstə/ n the person in charge of a POST OFFICE

**post·mor·tem** /,poust'mɔrtəm/ n **1** an examination of a dead body to discover why the person died **2** an examination of why something has failed

**post·na·tal** /,poust'neɪtl/ adj TECHNICAL relating to the time after a baby is born: *postnatal care* compare PRENATAL

**post of·fice** /'. ,../ n a place where you can buy stamps, and send letters, packages etc.

**post of·fice box** /'. .. ,./ ⇨ P.O. BOX

**post·pone** /poust'poun/ v [T] to change an event to a later time or date: *The game was postponed because of rain.* −**postponement** n [C,U]

**post·script** /'poust,skrɪpt/ n ⇨ P.S.

**pos·tu·late** /'pastʃə,leɪt/ v [T] FORMAL to suggest that something might have happened or might be true −**postulate** /'pastʃəlɪt, -,leɪt/ n

**pos·ture** /'pastʃə/ n [C,U] the position you hold your body in when you sit or stand: *Poor posture can lead to back trouble.*

**po·sy** /'pouzi/ n LITERARY a small BUNCH of flowers

**pot**[1] /pat/ n **1** a container used for cooking, that is round, deep, and usually made of metal: *pots and pans* **2** a container with a handle and a small tube for pouring, used for making coffee or tea: *a coffee pot* −see picture at CONTAINER **3** a container for a plant: *The plant needs a new pot.* −see picture at CONTAINER **4 go to pot** INFORMAL if an organization or a place goes to pot, its condition becomes worse because no one takes care of it: *The university has gone to pot since we were there.* **5 the pot** INFORMAL all

the money that people have risked in a game of cards **6** ⇨ MARIJUANA

**pot**[2] v [T] to put a plant in a pot filled with soil

**po·tas·si·um** /pə'tæsiəm/ n [U] a silver-white soft metal that is used in making soaps and FERTILIZERs

**po·ta·to** /pə'teɪtou, -tə/ n, plural **potatoes** [C,U] a hard round white root with a brown or pale yellow skin, cooked and eaten as a vegetable −see also HOT POTATO −see picture on page 470

**potato chip** /.'.. ,./ n one of many thin hard pieces of potato that have been cooked in oil, and that are sold in packages −see picture at CHIP[1]

**pot·bel·ly** /'pat,bɛli/ n a large round stomach that sticks out −**potbellied** adj

**po·ten·cy** /'poutnsi/ n [U] **1** the strength of the effect of a drug, medicine, alcohol etc. on your mind or body: *high-potency vitamins* **2** a man's ability to have sex

**po·tent** /'poutnt/ adj powerful and effective: *a potent weapons system | potent drugs*

**po·ten·tial**[1] /pə'tɛnʃəl/ adj possible: *It's a new system with many potential problems. | He's having lunch with some potential clients.* (=people who may use his services)

**potential**[2] n [U] **1** [singular] the possibility that something will develop or happen in a particular way: *There's a potential for conflict in the area.* **2** [U] a natural ability that could develop to make you very good at something: *She was told she had great potential as a singer.*

**po·ten·tial·ly** /pə'tɛnʃəli/ adv if something is potentially dangerous, useful, embarrassing etc., it does not have that quality now, but it may develop it later: *potentially dangerous fireworks | a potentially fatal disease* (=one that could kill you)

**pot·hold·er** /'pat,houldə/ n a piece of thick material used for holding hot cooking pans

**pot·hole** /'pathoul/ n a hole in the surface of a road that makes driving difficult

**po·tion** /'pouʃən/ n LITERARY a drink intended to have a special or magic effect on the person who drinks it: *a love potion*

**pot luck** /,. './ n **take pot luck** INFORMAL to choose something without knowing very much about it: *Nobody knew about any good restaurants, so we took pot luck.*

**pot·luck** /,pat'lʌk/ adj **a potluck dinner/lunch etc.** a meal in which everyone who is invited brings something to eat

**pot pie** /,. './ n meat and vegetables covered with PASTRY and baked in a deep dish

**pot·pour·ri** /,poupu'ri/ n [U] a mixture of dried flowers and leaves kept in a bowl to make a room smell nice

**pot shot** /,. './ n **take a pot shot at** INFORMAL to shoot at someone or something without aiming carefully

**pot·ter·y** /'patəri/ *n* [U] **1** objects made out of baked clay: *a pottery bowl* **2** the activity of making objects out of baked clay: *a pottery class* –**potter** *n*

**pot·ty** /'pati/ *n* SPOKEN a word meaning a toilet, used when speaking to children

**pouch** /paʊtʃ/ *n* **1** a small leather or cloth bag used for keeping and carrying things in, especially in past times **2** a pocket of skin that MARSUPIALs keep their babies in

**poul·try** /'poʊltri/ *n* [U] birds that are kept on farms for supplying eggs and meat, or the meat from these birds

**pounce** /paʊns/ *v* [I] to suddenly jump on a person or animal after waiting to catch him, her, or it: *The cat likes to pounce on people when they come through the door.*

**pound¹** /paʊnd/ *n* **1** written abbreviation **lb.** a unit for measuring weight, equal to 16 OUNCEs or 453.6 grams: *a pound of apples | She's lost/ gained 10 pounds this year.* (=her weight has gone down or up by 10 pounds) **2 the pound** a place where lost dogs and cats are kept until the owner claims them **3 5-pounder/2-pounder etc.** INFORMAL an animal or fish that weighs a particular number of pounds: *Ben caught a 5-pounder in the Kootenai River.*

**pound²** *v* **1** [I,T] to hit something hard many times, in order to make a loud sound or to damage something: *Someone was pounding on their door late last night. | The boys pounded the bottles with their sticks until they had all broken.* **2** [I] if your heart pounds, it beats very quickly **3** [I] to walk or run quickly with heavy steps: *I heard the sound of heavy boots pounding on the floor.* **4** [T] to attack a person or place for a long time: *Enemy guns pounded the city until morning.*

**pound cake** /'. ./ *n* a heavy cake made from flour, sugar, eggs, and butter

**pour** /pɔr/ *v* **1** [T] to make a liquid or a substance such as salt or sand flow out of or into something: *Shall I pour more champagne? | Pour yourself more coffee if you'd like some.* **2 it pours (down)** if it pours, a lot of rain comes out of the sky: *It's been pouring all afternoon.* –see usage note at WEATHER **3** [I] to flow quickly and in large amounts: *Fuel poured out of the plane.* **4** [I] if people or things pour into or out of a place, a lot of them arrive or leave at the same time: *Letters are pouring in from people all over the state. | People poured out of their houses into the streets.* **5 pour money/aid etc. into** to provide a lot of money over time to pay for something: *Thomas has poured thousands of dollars into his shop.*

pour

**pour** sth ↔ **out** *phr v* [T] to tell someone everything about your thoughts, feelings etc.: *Sonia poured out all her frustrations to Val.*

**pout** /paʊt/ *v* [I,T] to push out your lips because you are annoyed, or in order to look sexually attractive: *Stop pouting and eat your dinner.* –**pout** *n*

**pov·er·ty** /'pavəti/ *n* **1** the situation or experience of being poor: *He worked all his life to avoid the poverty he knew as a child. | families living in extreme poverty* **2 the poverty line** the income below which a person or a family is officially considered to be very poor and in need of help: *Her salary keeps the family just above the poverty line.*

**poverty-strick·en** /'... ,../ *adj* extremely poor: *a poverty-stricken neighborhood*

**P.O.W.** *n* the abbreviation of PRISONER OF WAR: *a P.O.W. camp*

**pow·der¹** /'paʊdɚ/ *n* **1** [C,U] a dry substance in the form of very small grains: *talcum powder | baking powder* **2 powder keg** a dangerous situation or place where violence or trouble could suddenly start: *The city has become a powder keg since the demonstration.*

**powder²** *v* [T] **1** to put powder on your skin **2 powder your nose** a phrase meaning to go to the toilet, used by women in order to be polite

**pow·dered** /'paʊdɚd/ *adj* produced or sold in the form of powder: *powdered milk*

**powder room** /'.. ,./ *n* a polite phrase meaning a women's public toilet

**pow·der·y** /'paʊdəri/ *adj* like powder or easily broken into powder: *powdery snow*

**pow·er¹** /'paʊɚ/ *n*
**1** ▶CONTROL SB/STH◀ [U] the ability or right to control people or events: *The factory has too much power over its employees. | People go into politics because of power, not money.*
**2** ▶POLITICAL◀ [U] political control of a country or government: *The current leader has been in power for ten years. | He came to power* (=began to control the country) *after the revolution.*
**3** ▶ENERGY◀ [U] energy such as electricity that can be used to make a machine, car etc. work: *The storm caused a power failure/cut* (=a time when there is no electricity) *in our area. | electricity produced by nuclear/solar power*
**4** ▶AUTHORITY◀ [C,U] the legal right or authority to do something: *Congress has the power to declare war. | Only the police have the power of arrest.*
**5** ▶COUNTRY◀ a country that is very strong and important: *Germany is a major industrial power in Europe. | a meeting of world powers* (=the strongest countries in the world)
**6** ▶PHYSICAL◀ [U] the physical strength of something such as an explosion, natural force, or animal: *The power of the eruption blew away*

*the whole mountainside.*

**7 ▶NATURAL ABILITY◀** [C,U] a natural or special ability to do something: *the **power** of sight/speech | She has the **power** to make an audience laugh or cry.*

**8 be in sb's power** to be in a situation in which someone has control over you

**9 do everything in your power** to do everything that you are able or allowed to do: *I did everything in my power to save her.*

**10 earning/purchasing etc. power** the ability to earn money, buy things etc.: *the purchasing power of middle-class teenagers*

**11 the powers that be** INFORMAL the people who have positions of authority, and whose decisions affect your life: *The hardest part will be persuading the powers that be at City Hall to agree.*

**12 to the power of 3/4/5 etc.** TECHNICAL if a number is increased to the power of 3, 4, 5 etc., it is multiplied by itself 3, 4, 5 etc. times —see usage note at FORCE[1]

**power**[2] *v* **1 solar-powered/nuclear-powered etc.** working or moving by means of a BATTERY etc.: *a battery-powered flashlight* **2** [T] to supply power to a vehicle or machine: *a car **powered by** solar energy* **3** [I,T] to do something quickly and with a lot of strength: *Ms. Graf has **powered** her way **through** the first three rounds at Wimbledon.*

**power** sth ↔ **up** *phr v* [T] to make a machine, especially a computer, start working: *Never move a computer while it is **powered up**.*

**power base** /'.. ,./ *n* the group of people in a particular area that supports a politician or leader

**pow·er·boat** /'.. ,./ *n* a boat with a powerful engine that is used for racing

**pow·er·ful** /'pauɚfəl/ *adj* **1** able to control and influence events and other people's actions: *a meeting of the world's most powerful leaders* **2** having a lot of power, strength, or force: *a powerful engine | a powerful man | a powerful explosion* **3** having a strong effect on someone's feelings or ideas: *Hate is a dangerously powerful emotion, Krista. | a powerful argument against eating meat* **4** having a strong effect on your body: *a powerful drug/medicine* **–powerfully** *adv*

**pow·er·house** /'pauɚ,haus/ *n* INFORMAL **1** a country, company, organization etc. that has a lot of power or influence **2** someone who has a lot of energy

**pow·er·less** /'pauɚlıs/ *adj* unable to stop or control something because you do not have the power, strength, or right to do so: *The small group of soldiers was **powerless** to stop the attack.* **–powerlessness** *n* [U]

**power line** /'.. ,./ *n* a large wire above or under the ground that takes electricity from one place to another

**power of at·tor·ney** /,.. ..'../ *n* [C,U] LAW the legal right to do things for someone else in his/her business or personal life, or the document that gives this right

**power plant** /'.. ,./, **power sta·tion** /'.. ,../ *n* a building where electricity is made

**power steer·ing** /,.. '../ *n* [U] a special system that makes it easier for the driver of a vehicle to STEER (=change the direction of the vehicle)

**power tool** /'.. ,./ *n* a tool that works by using electricity

**pow·wow** /'pau wau/ *n* a meeting or discussion, especially a meeting of a Native American tribe

**pp.** the written abbreviation of "pages": *Read pp. 20-35.*

**PR** *n* **1** [U] ⇨ PUBLIC RELATIONS **2** the written abbreviation for Puerto Rico

**prac·ti·ca·ble** /'præktıkəbəl/ *adj* FORMAL able to be used successfully in a particular situation: *a practicable idea*

**prac·ti·cal** /'præktıkəl/ *adj* **1** relating to real situations and events rather than ideas: *Do you have a lot of **practical experience** as a mechanic? | I deal with practical matters, like finding people places to stay.* **2** sensible and likely to succeed or be effective: *We have to be **practical** and not spend so much money. | Is that a practical solution to the problem?* **3** designed to be useful, or to be suitable for a particular purpose: *She gives practical gifts, such as clothes. | a practical car for a family* **4 for all practical purposes** used in order to describe what the real situation is, although it might seem to be different: *For all practical purposes, the election is over. (=we already know who the winner is)*

**prac·ti·cal·i·ty** /,præktı'kæləti/ *n* **1 practicalities** [plural] the real facts of a situation, rather than ideas about how it might be: *We have to think about practicalities, like how long it will take, and how much it will cost.* **2** [U] how sensible and suitable an idea is: *It's a nice idea, but I'm not sure about the practicality of it.*

**practical joke** /,... './ *n* a trick that is intended to surprise someone and make other people laugh

**prac·ti·cally** /'præktıkli/ *adv* **1** SPOKEN almost: *Practically everyone was there. | She practically jumped out of her chair.* **2** in a sensible way: *Vasko just doesn't think practically.*

**prac·tice**[1] /'præktıs/ *n*
**1 ▶SKILL◀** [U] **a)** regular activity that you do in order to improve a skill or ability: *It **takes** a lot of **practice** to be a good piano player.* **b)** the period of time in which you do this: *We have football practice tonight.*
**2 ▶STH THAT IS USUALLY DONE◀** [C,U]

**a)** something that people do often and in a particular way: *unsafe sexual practices* **b)** something that people do in a particular way because it is usually done that way in their religion, society, organization etc.; CUSTOM: *the practice of kissing someone as a greeting | It's standard/normal practice to do the payroll in this way.*
**3 in practice** used in order to describe what the real situation is rather than what seems to be true: *Annette is the head of the company, but in practice Sue runs everything.*
**4 ▶DOCTOR/LAWYER◀** the work of a doctor or lawyer, or the place where s/he works: *She has a successful medical/legal practice.*
**5 be out of practice** to be unable to do something well because you have not done it for a long time: *I'd like to sing with you, but I'm really out of practice.*
**6 put sth into practice** to start using an idea, plan, method etc. instead of just thinking about it or studying it: *Now's your chance to put the skills you've learned into practice.*

**practice**[2] *v* **1** [I,T] to do an activity regularly to improve your skill or ability: *Gail practices the piano more than an hour every day.* **2** [I,T] to work as a doctor or lawyer: *Bill is practicing law/medicine in Ohio now.* **3** [T] to do an activity as a habit, or to live according to the rules of a religion: *The posters encourage young people to practice safe sex.*

**prac·ticed** /ˈpræktɪst/ *adj* good at doing something because you have done it many times before: *a practiced pilot*

**prac·tic·ing** /ˈpræktɪsɪŋ/ *adj* **1 a practicing doctor/lawyer/architect etc.** someone who has trained as a doctor, lawyer etc., and who still works as one **2 a practicing Catholic/Jew/Muslim etc.** someone who obeys the rules of a particular religion

**prac·ti·tion·er** /prækˈtɪʃənɚ/ *n* FORMAL someone who is trained to do a particular type of work that involves a lot of skill: *a tax practitioner | Dr. Reynolds is a family/general practitioner.* (=a doctor who treats general medical problems)

**prag·mat·ic** /prægˈmætɪk/ *adj* dealing with problems in a sensible and practical way rather than following a set of ideas that are considered correct: *The diet gives you pragmatic suggestions for eating healthily.*

**prag·ma·tism** /ˈprægmə,tɪzəm/ *n* [U] a tendency to deal with problems in a PRAGMATIC way *–pragmatist n*

**prai·rie** /ˈprɛri/ *n* a large area of flat land in North America that is covered in grass

**prairie dog** /ˈ.. ,./ *n* a North American animal with a short tail that is related to a SQUIRREL, that lives in holes on a PRAIRIE

**praise**[1] /preɪz/ *v* [T] **1** to say publicly that someone has done something well or that you admire him/her: *Mr. Bonner praised Jill for the*

*quality of her work.* **2** to give thanks or honor to God

**praise**[2] *n* [U] **1** words that you say or write to praise someone or something: *The papers were full of praise for the quick actions of the fire department.* **2** an expression of respect or thanks to God

**praise·wor·thy** /ˈpreɪz,wɚði/ *adj* FORMAL deserving praise

**prance** /præns/ *v* [I] to walk, moving your body in a confident way so people will notice you: *He started prancing around in front of the video camera.*

**prank** /præŋk/ *n* a trick that is intended to make someone look silly: *Ms. Jong pulled the prank* (=tricked someone) *with the help of her college roommate.*

**prank·ster** /ˈpræŋkstɚ/ *n* someone who plays PRANKs on people

**prat·tle** /ˈprætl/ *n* silly or unimportant things that someone talks about continuously *–prattle v* [I]

**prawn** /prɔn/ *n* a sea animal like a large SHRIMP, that is often eaten in restaurants

**pray** /preɪ/ *v* [I,T] **1** to speak to a god or gods in order to ask for help or give thanks: *You don't have to go to church to pray. | people praying for peace at the Wailing Wall* **2** to wish or hope for something very strongly: *We're praying for good weather tomorrow.*

**prayer** /prɛr/ *n* **1** words that you say when praying to a god or gods: *Have you said your prayers yet?* **2** [U] the act or regular habit of praying: *a time of prayer* **3 not have a prayer** INFORMAL to have no chance of succeeding: *The Seahawks don't have a prayer of winning.*

**preach** /pritʃ/ *v* **1** [I,T] to give a speech, usually in a church, about a religious subject: *Pastor Young preached a sermon on forgiveness.* **2** [T] to talk about how good or important something is and to try to persuade other people to do or accept it: *You're the one who's always preaching honesty, and then you lie to me!* **3** [I] to give advice in a way that annoys people: *My dad's been preaching at me about not studying enough.*

**preach·er** /ˈpritʃɚ/ *n* someone who talks about religious subjects, usually in a church

**preach·y** /ˈpritʃi/ *adj* INFORMAL trying very hard to persuade people to accept a particular opinion, in a way that annoys them

**pre·am·ble** /ˈpri,æmbəl/ *n* FORMAL a statement at the beginning of a book, speech etc.: *the preamble to the Constitution*

**pre·ar·ranged** /,priəˈreɪndʒd/ *adj* planned before: *We can have a driver pick you up at a prearranged time.*

**pre·car·i·ous** /prɪˈkɛriəs, -ˈkær-/ *adj* **1** likely to become dangerous: *The newspaper is in a precarious financial position/situation.* **2** likely to fall, or likely to cause something to fall: *The cup was in a precarious position at the edge of the table.* –**precariously** *adv*

**pre·cau·tion** /prɪˈkɔʃən/ *n* something that you do to prevent something bad or dangerous from happening: *Always take precautions when riding your bicycle at night.* | *The nuclear power station was shut down as a precaution against any other accidents.*

**pre·cau·tion·a·ry** /prɪˈkɔʃəˌnɔri/ *adj* done as a PRECAUTION: *The doctors have put him in the hospital as a precautionary measure.*

**pre·cede** /prɪˈsid/ *v* [T] FORMAL to happen or exist before something else: *The fire was preceded by a loud explosion.*

**prec·e·dence** /ˈprɛsədəns/ *n* [U] **take/have precedence** to be more important or urgent than someone or something else: *This project takes precedence over everything else, until it is finished.*

**prec·e·dent** /ˈprɛsədənt/ *n* FORMAL an action or official decision that is used as an example for a similar action or decision at a later time: *The trial set a precedent for civil rights legislation.*

**pre·ced·ing** /prɪˈsidɪŋ, ˈprisidɪŋ/ *adj* FORMAL happening or coming before something else: *The events of the preceding week worried him.*

**pre·cept** /ˈprisɛpt/ *n* FORMAL a rule that helps you decide how to think or behave in a situation: *the moral precepts of Judaism*

**pre·cinct** /ˈprisɪŋkt/ *n* **1** a part of a city that has its own police force, government officials etc.: *the 12th precinct* **2 precincts** FORMAL the area around an important building

**pre·cious**[1] /ˈprɛʃəs/ *adj* **1** extremely important to you: *Those memories of my wife are the most precious to me.* **2** valuable because of being rare or expensive: *a precious jewel/stone/metal* **3** SPOKEN used in order to describe someone or something that is small and pretty: *What a precious little girl!*

**precious**[2] *adv* **precious little/few** INFORMAL very little or very few: *We had precious little time to prepare for the trip.*

**prec·i·pice** /ˈprɛsəpɪs/ *n* a very steep side of a mountain or cliff

**pre·cip·i·tate**[1] /prɪˈsɪpəˌteɪt/ *v* FORMAL to make something happen suddenly: *Massive selling precipitated the stock market crash of 1929.*

**pre·cip·i·tate**[2] /prɪˈsɪpətɪt/ *adj* FORMAL done too quickly, especially without thinking carefully enough: *Be careful of taking precipitate action.*

**pre·cip·i·ta·tion** /prɪˌsɪpəˈteɪʃən/ *n* [C,U] TECHNICAL rain or snow that falls on the ground, or the amount that falls

**pre·cip·i·tous** /prɪˈsɪpətəs/ *adj* FORMAL **1** a precipitous change is sudden and unpleasant: *a precipitous drop in property values* **2** a precipitous action or event happens too quickly and

is not well planned **3** dangerously high or steep: *precipitous cliffs*

**pré·cis** /ˈpreɪsi/ *n, plural* **pré·cis** /-siz/ FORMAL a statement that gives the main ideas of a piece of writing, speech etc.

**pre·cise** /prɪˈsaɪs/ *adj* **1** exact and correct in every detail: *I can't tell you the precise amount I paid.* | *We need a more precise method of measurement.* **2 to be precise** used when you add exact details about something: *He was born in April, on the 4th to be precise.*

**pre·cise·ly** /prɪˈsaɪsli/ *adv* **1** exactly: *I do not remember precisely what happened.* | *The numbers were not precisely accurate.* **2** SPOKEN used in order to agree with what someone has just said: *"So Clark is responsible for the mistake." "Precisely."*

**pre·ci·sion** /prɪˈsɪʒən/ *n* [U] the quality of being very exact: *The weight of an atom can be measured with great precision.* –**precision** *adj*: *precision bombing*

**pre·clude** /prɪˈklud/ *v* [T] FORMAL to prevent something or make it impossible to happen: *Poor eyesight may preclude you from driving at night.*

**pre·co·cious** /prɪˈkouʃəs/ *adj* a precocious child behaves like an adult in some ways, especially by asking intelligent questions

**pre·con·ceived** /ˌprikənˈsivd/ *adj* preconceived ideas are formed about something before you know what it is really like: *He has a lot of preconceived ideas/notions about what living in America is like.*

**pre·con·cep·tion** /ˌprikənˈsɛpʃən/ *n* an idea that is formed about something before you know what it is really like

**pre·con·di·tion** /ˌprikənˈdɪʃən/ *n* something that must happen before something else can happen: *An end to the fighting is a precondition for peace negotiations.*

**pre·cur·sor** /ˈpriˌkɚsɚ, prɪˈkɚsɚ/ *n* FORMAL something that happened or existed before something else and influenced its development: *This machine is a precursor of the computer.*

**pre·date** /priˈdeɪt/ *v* [T] to happen or exist earlier than something else: *These animals predate humans.*

**pred·a·tor** /ˈprɛdətɚ/ *n* an animal that kills and eats other animals

**pred·a·to·ry** /ˈprɛdəˌtɔri/ *adj* **1** predatory animals kill and eat other animals **2** eager to use someone's weakness to get an advantage: *The danger is from predatory foreign companies who buy other businesses and shut them down.*

**pred·e·ces·sor** /ˈprɛdəˌsɛsɚ/ *n* **1** someone who had a job before someone else began to do it: *My predecessor worked here for ten years.* **2** something such as a machine or system that existed before another one: *a computer that is much faster than its predecessors*

**pre·des·ti·na·tion** /ˌpridɛstəˈneɪʃən/ *n* [U] the belief that God or FATE has decided everything that will happen and that no one can change this

**pre·des·tined** /priˈdɛstɪnd/ *adj* something that is predestined is certain to happen and cannot be changed

**pre·de·ter·mined** /ˌpridɪˈtəmɪnd/ *adj* FORMAL decided or arranged before: *The doors unlock at a predetermined time.*

**pre·dic·a·ment** /prɪˈdɪkəmənt/ *n* a difficult or unpleasant situation in which you must decide what to do: *It was Raoul who got us **in this predicament** in the first place.*

**pred·i·cate** /ˈprɛdɪkɪt/ *n* TECHNICAL in grammar, the part of a sentence that has the main verb, and that tells what the subject is doing or describes the subject. In the sentence, "He ran out of the house," "ran out of the house" is the predicate —compare SUBJECT¹

**pred·i·ca·tive** /ˈprɛdɪˌkətɪv, -ˌkeɪtɪv/ *adj* TECHNICAL in grammar, a predicative adjective or phrase comes after a verb and describes the subject, such as "sad" in "She is sad"

**pre·dict** /prɪˈdɪkt/ *v* [T] to say that something will happen before it happens: *The newspapers are predicting a close election.* | *My grandmother predicted (that) Sal and I would be married within a year.*

**pre·dict·a·ble** /prɪˈdɪktəbəl/ *adj* behaving or happening in a way that you expect: *You're so predictable!* | *The snow had a predictable effect on traffic.* —**predictably** *adv*: *Predictably, the new TV series was as bad as the old one.* —**predictability** /prɪˌdɪktəˈbɪləti/ *n* [U]

**pre·dic·tion** /prɪˈdɪkʃən/ *n* [C,U] a statement saying that something is going to happen, or the act of making statements of this kind: *I don't want to **make a prediction** about how popular the book will be.* —**predictive** *adj*

**pred·i·lec·tion** /ˌprɛdlˈɛkʃən, ˌprid-/ *n* FORMAL the tendency to like a particular kind of person or thing: *a predilection for chocolate*

**pre·dis·posed** /ˌpridɪˈspoʊzd/ *adj* **predisposed to/toward** likely to behave or think in a particular way, or to have a particular health problem: *The judge said that Stein was "predisposed to violence."*

**pre·dis·po·si·tion** /ˌpridɪspəˈzɪʃən/ *n* a tendency to behave in a particular way or suffer from a particular health problem: *a predisposition to/toward skin cancer*

**pre·dom·i·nance** /prɪˈdɑmənəns/ *n* FORMAL **1** [singular] a larger number or amount of one type of thing or person in a group than of any other type: *the **predominance of** auto workers in our city* **2** [U] the most power or importance in a particular group or area: *American **predominance in** world economics*

**pre·dom·i·nant** /prɪˈdɑmənənt/ *adj* more powerful, common, or noticeable than others:

*The environment is the predominant social issue in the nineties.*

**pre·dom·i·nant·ly** /prɪˈdɑmənəntli/ *adv* mostly or mainly: *a college in a predominantly middle class neighborhood*

**pre·dom·i·nate** /prɪˈdɑməˌneɪt/ *v* [I] to have the most importance, or to be the most in number: *a district where Democrats predominate*

**pre·em·i·nent** /priˈɛmənənt/ *adj* much more important or powerful than all others in a particular group: *a preeminent political figure* —**preeminence** *n* [U]

**pre·empt** /priˈɛmpt/ *v* [T] to make what someone is about to do unnecessary or not effective, by doing something else first: *Approval of the plan would preempt a strike by 110,000 city employees.* —**preemptive** *adj*: *a preemptive attack on an enemy naval base*

**preen** /prin/ *v* **1** **preen yourself** DISAPPROVING to spend a lot of time making yourself look good: *He's always preening himself in the mirror.* **2** [I,T] if a bird preens or preens itself, it cleans itself and makes its feathers smooth

**pre·ex·ist·ing** /ˌpriɪgˈzɪstɪŋ◂/ *adj* existing already, or before something else: *Most insurance policies exclude all pre-existing medical conditions.*

**pre·fab·ri·cat·ed** /priˈfæbrəˌkeɪtɪd/, **pre·fab** /priˈfæb, ˈprifæb/ *adj* built from parts made in a factory and put together somewhere else: *prefabricated homes*

**pref·ace¹** /ˈprɛfɪs/ *n* an introduction at the beginning of a book or speech

**preface²** *v* [T] FORMAL to say or do something first before saying or doing something else: *He prefaced his remarks **with** an expression of thanks to the audience.*

**pre·fer** /prɪˈfə/ *v* **-rred, -rring** [T] **1** to like someone or something more than someone or something else: *She prefers walking **to** driving.* | *Which color do you prefer?* | *I would prefer not to come on Tuesday.* | *I prefer to watch movies with other people.* ✗ DON'T SAY "I prefer watching." ✗ **2** **I would prefer it if** used in order to tell someone politely not to do something: *I'd prefer it if you didn't smoke in the house.*

**pref·er·a·ble** /ˈprɛfərəbəl/ *adj* better or more suitable: *Anything is **preferable to** war.*

**pref·er·a·bly** /ˈprɛfərəbli/ *adv* used in order to show which person, thing, place, or idea you think would be the best choice: *You should see a doctor, preferably a specialist.*

**pref·er·ence** /ˈprɛfrəns, -fərəns/ *n* **1** if someone has a preference for something, s/he likes it more than another thing: *We have always had a **preference for** small cars.* | *Many travelers carry US dollars **in preference to** their own currency.* **2** **give/show preference to** to treat someone better than you treat other people:

*Teachers sometimes show preference to smarter students.*

**pref·er·en·tial** /ˌprɛfəˈrɛnʃəl/ *adj* treating one person or group better than others: *Bank officials denied that the senator was getting **preferential treatment**.*

**pre·fix** /ˈpriˌfɪks/ *n* TECHNICAL in grammar, a group of letters that is added to the beginning of a word in order to make a new word, such as "mis-" in "misunderstand" −compare SUFFIX

**preg·nan·cy** /ˈprɛgnənsi/ *n* [C,U] the condition of being PREGNANT, or the period of time when a woman is pregnant: *You should not drink alcohol during your pregnancy.*

**preg·nant** /ˈprɛgnənt/ *adj* **1** having an unborn baby growing in your body: *She's three months pregnant.* | *I didn't intend to get pregnant.* **2** LITERARY full of meaning or importance that is not expressed: *a pregnant silence*

**pre·heat** /priˈhit/ *v* [T] to heat an OVEN to a particular temperature before cooking food in it

**pre·his·tor·ic** /ˌprihɪˈstɔrɪk/ *adj* relating to the time in history before anything was written down: *prehistoric cave drawings* −**prehistorically** *adv* −**prehistory** /priˈhɪstəri/ *n* [U]

**pre·judge** /ˌpriˈdʒʌdʒ/ *v* [T] to form an opinion about someone or something before knowing all the facts

**prej·u·dice**[1] /ˈprɛdʒədɪs/ *n* [C,U] an unfair feeling of dislike against someone who is of a different race, sex, religion etc.: *There are laws that discourage **racial/sexual prejudice** in society.* | *public **prejudice against** single mothers*

**prejudice**[2] *v* [T] to influence someone so that s/he has an unfair opinion about someone or something before s/he knows all the facts: *Watson's wild appearance may **prejudice** the jury **against** him.*

**prej·u·diced** /ˈprɛdʒədɪst/ *adj* having an unfair feeling of dislike for someone who is of a different race, sex, religion etc.: *Kurt is so **prejudiced against** gay people!*

**prej·u·di·cial** /ˌprɛdʒəˈdɪʃəl/ *adj* FORMAL influencing people to think in a particular way about someone or something, especially so that they have a bad opinion of him, her, or it: *prejudicial remarks*

**pre·lim·i·nar·y**[1] /prɪˈlɪməˌnɛri/ *adj* happening before something that is more important, often in order to prepare for it: *a preliminary investigation*

**preliminary**[2] *n* [C usually plural] something that is done at the beginning of an activity, event etc., often in order to prepare for it: *the preliminaries of the competition*

**prel·ude** /ˈprɛlud, ˈprɛlyud/ *n* **1** be a **prelude to** to happen just before something else, often as an introduction to it: *The attack may be*

a prelude to full-scale war. **2** a short piece of music that comes before a large musical piece

**pre·mar·i·tal** /ˌpriˈmærətl/ *adj* happening or existing before marriage: *premarital sex*

**pre·ma·ture** /ˌpriməˈtʃʊr, -ˈtʊr/ *adj* **1** happening too early or before the right time: *He suffered a premature death at the age of 35.* **2** a premature baby is born before the usual time

**pre·ma·ture·ly** /ˌpriməˈtʃʊrli/ *adv* before the time that something usually happens or is supposed to happen: *The sun causes your skin to age prematurely.* | *a baby born prematurely*

**pre·med·i·tat·ed** /priˈmɛdəˌteɪtɪd/ *adj* a premeditated action has been planned and done deliberately: *a premeditated murder* −**premeditation** /priˌmɛdəˈteɪʃən/ *n* [U]

**pre·men·stru·al** /priˈmɛnstrəl/ *adj* TECHNICAL happening just before a woman's PERIOD (=monthly flow of blood)

**premenstrual syn·drome** /ˌ.ˌ.. '../ *n* [U] ⇨ PMS

**pre·mier**[1], **Premier** /prɪˈmɪr, -ˈmyɪr, ˈprimɪr/ *n* the head of a government

**premier**[2] *adj* FORMAL best or most important: *a premier wine from Bordeaux*

**pre·miere** /prɪˈmɪr, -ˈmyɪr, -ˈmyɛr/, **pre·mière** *n* the first public performance of a movie or play: *the 1955 premiere of "Cat on a Hot Tin Roof"* −**premiere** *v* [I,T]

**prem·ise** /ˈprɛmɪs/ *n* FORMAL a statement or idea that you think is true and use as a base for developing other ideas: *The proposal is based on the **premise that** the budget will be balanced in three years.*

**prem·is·es** /ˈprɛmɪsɪz/ *n* [plural] the buildings and land that a store, company etc. uses: *He was ordered **off the premises**.* (=out of the building) | *Do not smoke **on the premises**.* (=in the building)

**pre·mi·um** /ˈprimiəm/ *n* **1** an amount of money that you pay for something such as insurance: *annual premiums* **2** **be at a premium** difficult to get because a lot of people want it: *Hotel rooms are at a premium around major holidays.* **3** **put/place a premium on sth** to think that one quality or activity is much more important than others: *The club puts a premium on loyalty.*

**pre·mo·ni·tion** /ˌpriməˈnɪʃən, ˌprɛ-/ *n* a feeling that something bad is about to happen: *She **had a** horrible **premonition that** something would happen to the children.*

**pre·mon·i·to·ry** /prɪˈmɑnəˌtɔri/ *adj* FORMAL giving a warning that something bad is going to happen

**pre·na·tal** /ˌpriˈneɪtl/ *adj* TECHNICAL relating to unborn babies and the care of women who are PREGNANT −compare POSTNATAL

**pre·oc·cu·pa·tion** /priˌɑkyəˈpeɪʃən/ *n* **1** [singular, U] the state of being PREOCCUPIED: *His growing **preoccupation with** his health be-*

P

gan *to affect his work.* **2** something that you think about a lot: *I have the usual preoccupations of job, money, and family.*

**pre·oc·cu·pied** /pri'ɑkyə,paɪd/ *adj* thinking or worrying about something a lot, so that you do not pay attention to other things: *What's wrong? You seem* **preoccupied with** *something.*

**pre·oc·cu·py** /pri'ɑkyə,paɪ/ *v* [T] if something preoccupies you, you think or worry about it a lot: *Rowan had let the deal preoccupy him completely.*

**pre·or·dained** /,priɔr'deɪnd/ *adj* FORMAL certain to happen because God or FATE has already decided it

**prep** /prɛp/ *v* **-pped, -pping** [T] INFORMAL to prepare someone for an operation in a hospital

**pre·paid** /,pri'peɪd / *adj* a prepaid envelope does not need a stamp because the person receiving it has already paid the cost

**prep·a·ra·tion** /,prɛpə'reɪʃən/ *n* **1** [U] the act or process of preparing something: *The church was cleaned* **in preparation for** *the wedding.* | *Fresh fish needs very little preparation.* **2** **preparations** [plural] arrangements for something that is going to happen: *They are* **making preparations for** *the President's visit.*

**pre·par·a·to·ry** /prɪ'pærə,tɔri, -'pɛr-, 'prɛprə-/ *adj* done in order to get ready for something: *preparatory work*

**pre·pare** /prɪ'pɛr/ *v* **1** [T] to make something ready to be used: *The rooms still need to* **be prepared for** *the guests.* | *I haven't* **prepared** *my report* **for** *the meeting yet.* **2** [I,T] to make plans or arrangements for something that will happen soon: *I hope you've begun to* **prepare for** *the test.* | *The Bears are* **preparing to** *play the Redskins next week.* **3** [T] to make yourself or someone else ready to deal with something that will happen soon: *You should probably* **prepare yourself for** *some bad news.* **4** [T] to give someone the training, skill etc. that s/he needs to do something: *My job is to* **prepare** *these soldiers* **for** *war.* **5** [T] to make food or a meal ready to eat: *This dish can be prepared the day before.*

---

**USAGE NOTE prepare and get ready**

Use **prepare** to talk about making or producing something that is ready to be used: *Edwards only had two days to prepare the report.* | *This dish can be prepared ahead of time.* Use **get ready** to talk about doing the things that you need to do so you are ready for an activity: *You guys still have to get your stuff ready for school.* | *Natalie's upstairs getting ready for her date.* ✗Don't say "preparing for her date." ✗ In informal speech, you can usually use **get ready** instead of **prepare**: *I have to get supper ready now.*

---

**pre·pared** /prɪ'pɛrd/ *adj* **1** ready to do something or to deal with a particular situation: *She was not mentally* **prepared for** *the shock of losing her job.* **2** **be prepared to do sth** to be willing to do something if it is necessary: *Is he prepared to accept the offer?* | *I am not prepared to discuss this any further with you now.* **3** arranged and ready to be used, before it is needed: *The police read out a prepared statement to the press, and refused to make any other comment.*

**pre·par·ed·ness** /prɪ'pɛrɪdnɪs/ *n* [U] the state of being ready for something: *military preparedness*

**pre·pon·der·ance** /prɪ'pɑndərəns/ *n* FORMAL a larger number or amount of one type of thing or person in a group than of any other type: *There's* **a preponderance of** *women in the orchestra.*

**prep·o·si·tion** /,prɛpə'zɪʃən/ *n* TECHNICAL in grammar, a word or phrase that is used before a noun, pronoun, or GERUND to show place, time, direction etc. In the phrase "at the bank," "at" is a preposition −**prepositional** *adj* −see study note on page 464

**pre·pos·ter·ous** /prɪ'pɑstərəs/ *adj* completely unreasonable or silly; ABSURD: *That's a preposterous story!*

**prep·py** /'prɛpi/ *adj* INFORMAL preppy styles or clothes are very neat and CONSERVATIVE in a way that is typical of people who go to expensive private schools

**prep school** /'. ./ *n* INFORMAL a private school that prepares students for college

**pre·reg·is·ter** /pri'rɛdʒɪstɚ/ *v* [I] to put your name on a list for a particular course of study, school etc. before the official time to do so −**preregistration** /,prirɛdʒɪ'streɪʃən/ *n* [U]

**pre·req·ui·site** /pri'rɛkwəzɪt/ *n* FORMAL something that is necessary before something else can happen or be done: *A degree in French is a* **prerequisite for** *the job.*

**pre·rog·a·tive** /prɪ'rɑgətɪv/ *n* a special right that someone has because of his/her importance or position: *It's my prerogative as his mother to take him out of school.*

**pres·age** /'prɛsɪdʒ, prɪ'seɪdʒ/ *v* [T] LITERARY to be a warning or sign that something is going to happen, especially something bad

**Pres·by·te·ri·an** /,prɛzbə'tɪriən, prɛs-/ *adj* relating to the Protestant church that follows the teachings of John Knox, which includes strict rules for behavior −**Presbyterian** *n*

**pre·school** /'priskul/ *n* a school for young children between two and five years of age −**preschool** *adj* −**preschooler** *n*

**pre·scribe** /prɪ'skraɪb/ *v* [T] **1** to say what medicine or treatment a sick person should have: *Dr. Dawson* **prescribed** *some sleeping pills* **for** *me.* **2** FORMAL to state officially what should be done in a particular situation: *a punishment prescribed by the law*

**pre·scrip·tion** /prɪˈskrɪpʃən/ *n* **1** a piece of paper on which a doctor writes what medicine a sick person should have, or the medicine itself: *a prescription for his chest pains* **2** an idea or suggestion about how to solve a problem or improve a situation: *What's your prescription for a happy marriage?*

**pre·scrip·tive** /prɪˈskrɪptɪv/ *adj* FORMAL saying how something should be done or what someone should do

**pres·ence** /ˈprɛzəns/ *n* **1** [U] the state of being present in a particular place: *The UN is concerned about the presence of nuclear weapons in Asia.|The jury's presence is not needed for this part of the trial.* **2 in sb's presence** with someone or in the same place as him/her: *Everyone was afraid to voice an opinion in his presence.* **3** [U] the ability to impress people with your appearance or manner: *The best actors always have great presence on stage.* **4** [singular] a group of people from another country who are in a place to watch or influence what is happening: *the end of the American military presence in Vietnam* **5 have the presence of mind to do sth** to have the ability to deal with a dangerous situation calmly and quickly: *Bill had the presence of mind to call 911 after the fire started.* **6 make your presence felt** to have a strong effect on other people or situations: *Hanley has made his presence felt since joining the company.*

**pres·ent**[1] /ˈprɛzənt/ *adj* **1 be present** FORMAL to be in a particular place: *How many people were present at the board meeting?* **2** happening or existing now: *We are unable to answer your questions at the present time.*

**pre·sent**[2] /prɪˈzɛnt/ *v* [T] **1** to give something to someone, especially at an official or public occasion: *Mr. Davis presented the winning team with a gold cup.* **2** to give or show information about something or someone in a particular way: *Her book is presented as an answer to the problems of modern marriage.|The way you present yourself is very important.* **3** to cause something such as a problem or difficulty to happen or exist: *The heavy rains presented a new difficulty for the rescue workers.* **4** to give a performance in a theater etc., or broadcast it on television or radio: *The Roxy is presenting a production of "Waiting for Godot" this week.* **5** to introduce someone formally to someone else: *May I present my parents, Mr. and Mrs. Benning.*

**pres·ent**[3] /ˈprɛzənt/ *n* **1** something that you give to someone on a special occasion; GIFT: *a birthday/Christmas/anniversary present* **2 the present** a) the time that is happening now: *The ensemble will play works from the Renaissance up to the present.* b) TECHNICAL in grammar, the

form of a verb that shows what exists or is happening now **3 at present** at this time; now: *We have no plans at present for closing the factory.*

**pre·sent·a·ble** /prɪˈzɛntəbəl/ *adj* attractive and neat enough to be seen or shown in public: *Do I look presentable?*

**pres·en·ta·tion** /ˌprɪzənˈteɪʃən, ˌprɛ-/ *n* **1** the act of giving someone a prize or present at a formal ceremony: *the presentation of the Oscars* **2** a formal talk about a particular subject: *She gave a short presentation on/about the new product.* **3** the way in which something is shown, said etc. to others: *As a chef I care about the presentation of food as well as its taste.* **4** FORMAL the act of giving something to someone: *Most airlines will refund your money on presentation of* (=when you give them) *a letter from a doctor.*

**pres·ent-day** /ˌ.. ˈ.◂/ *adj* modern or existing now: *The colonists settled near present-day Charleston.*

**pres·ent·ly** /ˈprɛzəntli/ *adv* FORMAL **1** at this time; now: *Presently I am unemployed.* **2** OLD-FASHIONED in a short time; soon

**present par·ti·ci·ple** /ˌ.. ˈ..../ *n* TECHNICAL in grammar, a PARTICIPLE that is formed by adding "-ing" to a verb. It can be used in compounds to make CONTINUOUS tenses, as in "she's sleeping," as an adjective, as in "the sleeping child," or as a GERUND, as in "I like cooking"

**present per·fect** /ˌ.. ˈ../ *n* **the present perfect** TECHNICAL in grammar, the tense of a verb that shows a time up to and including the present, and is formed with "have" and the PAST PARTICIPLE. In the sentence "Ken has traveled all over the world," "has traveled" is in the present perfect

**pres·ent tense** /ˌ.. ˈ./ *n* **the present tense** TECHNICAL in grammar, the form of a verb that shows what is true, what exists, or what is happening now. In the sentence "I always leave for work at 8:00," "leave" is in the present tense

**pres·er·va·tion** /ˌprɛzɚˈveɪʃən/ *n* [U] the act of keeping something unharmed or unchanged, or the degree to which it is unharmed or unchanged: *the preservation of the rainforest|The painting was in a good/bad state of preservation.*

**pres·erv·a·tive** /prɪˈzɚvətɪv/ *n* [C,U] a chemical substance that prevents food or wood from decaying

**pre·serve**[1] /prɪˈzɚv/ *v* [T] **1** to keep something or someone from being harmed, destroyed, or changed too much: *The house is part of local history, and should be preserved.|It is important to preserve the achievements of the last few years.* **2** to keep food for a long time by treating it so that it will not decay: *cucumbers preserved in vinegar*

**preserve**[2] *n* **1 be the preserve of** if an activity or place is the preserve of a particular group of people, only that group is able or allowed to do it or use it: *Politics is no longer the preserve of wealthy white males.* **2** an area of land or water that is kept for private hunting and fishing: *the Denali National Park and Preserve* **3** a sweet food such as JAM made from large pieces of fruit boiled with sugar

**pre·shrunk** /ˌpriˈʃrʌŋk◂/ *adj* preshrunk clothes are sold after they have been made smaller by being washed: *preshrunk jeans*

**pre·side** /prɪˈzaɪd/ *v* [I] to be in charge of a formal meeting, ceremony, important situation etc.: *Judge Baxter presided over the trial.*

**pres·i·den·cy** /ˈprɛzədənsi/ *n* **1** the job or office of president: *Robinson has again been elected to the presidency.* **2** the period of time that someone is president: *the early days of her presidency*

**pres·i·dent, President** /ˈprɛzədənt/ *n* **1** the official leader of a country that does not have a king or queen: *the President of Mexico* | *President Lincoln* **2** someone who is in charge of a business, bank, club, college etc.: *the President of Brown University*

**pres·i·den·tial** /ˌprɛzəˈdɛnʃəl/ *adj* relating to the job or office of president: *the presidential candidate/election*

**President's Day** /ˈ... ˌ./ *n* a US holiday on the third Monday in February to remember the BIRTHDAYs of George Washington and Abraham Lincoln

**press**[1] /prɛs/ *v*

**1 ▶WITH FINGER◀** [T] to push something with your finger to make a machine do something, make a bell ring etc.: *Mrs. Mott pressed the doorbell again.* | *Press F8 to copy a file.*

press

**2 ▶PUSH AGAINST◀** [T] to push something firmly against something else and keep it there for a period of time: *He pressed his hand down over the wound.* | *Their faces were pressed against the window.*

**3 ▶IRON◀** [T] to make clothes smooth using heat; IRON: *I need to have this suit cleaned and pressed.*

**4 ▶PERSUADE◀** [T] to try very hard to persuade someone to do something or tell you something: *Detectives had been pressing him for details.*

**5 ▶MOVE◀** [I] to move in a particular direction by pushing: *The crowd pressed forward to see what was happening.*

**6 ▶HEAVY WEIGHT◀** [T] to put pressure or weight on something to make it flat, crush it etc.: *a machine for pressing olives/grapes*

**7 press charges** to say officially that someone

has done something illegal so that a court must decide if s/he is guilty

**press on/ahead** *phr v* [I] to continue doing something without stopping: *The army crossed the river and pressed on/ahead to the border.*

**press**[2] *n* **1 the press** the people who write news reports for newspapers, radio, or television, or the reports that are written: *Members of the press were waiting outside.* | *Of course, the incident was in the national press the next day.* **2** a business that prints and sometimes sells books: *the University Press* **3** ⇨ PRINTING PRESS **4 good/bad press** the good or bad opinion of something given by newspapers, radio, or television **5** a piece of equipment that makes something flat or forces liquid out of something: *a flower press* | *a wine press* **6 go to press** if a newspaper, magazine, or book goes to press, it begins to be printed

**press a·gent** /ˈ. ˌ../ *n* someone whose job is to give photographs or information about a famous person to newspapers, radio, or television

**press con·fer·ence** /ˈ. ˌ../ *n* a meeting at which someone makes official statements to people who write news reports: *The Governor held a press conference last night.*

**press corps** /ˈ. ./ *n* a group of people who usually write the news reports that come from a particular place: *the White House press corps*

**pressed** /prɛst/ *adj* **be pressed for time/ money etc.** to not have enough time, money etc.: *I can't stop now - I'm pressed for time.*

**press·ing** /ˈprɛsɪŋ/ *adj* needing to be dealt with very soon; URGENT: *Environmental pollution is our most pressing concern.* (=what we are most worried about)

**press re·lease** /ˈ. .ˌ./ *n* an official statement that gives information to the newspapers, radio, or television: *The movie studio issued a press release announcing that the contract had been signed.*

**pres·sure**[1] /ˈprɛʃɚ/ *n* **1** [U] an attempt to make someone do something by using influence, arguments, threats etc.: *The group is putting pressure on the state to change the smoking laws.* | *NASA was under political pressure to start a new space program.* **2** [C,U] the conditions of your work, family, or way of living that make you anxious and cause problems: *Their team always plays best under pressure.* | *the pressures of modern life* **3** [C,U] the force or weight that is being put on something, or the strength of this force or weight: *The pressure of the water turns the wheel.* | *The gas is stored at high/low pressure.*

**pres·sure**[2] *v* [T] to try to make someone do something by using influence, arguments, threats etc.: *Some parents pressure their kids too much.*

**pressure cook·er** /ˈ.. ˌ../ *n* a tightly covered cooking pot that cooks food very quickly using hot steam

**pres·sured** /'prɛʃəd/ *adj* feeling a lot of worry because of the number of things that you have to do: *Her job makes her feel pressured all the time.*

**pressure group** /'.. ,./ *n* a group of people or an organization that tries to influence what the public thinks about things, and what the government does about things

**pres·sur·ized** /'prɛʃə,raızd/ *adj* in an aircraft that is pressurized, the air pressure inside it is similar to the pressure on the ground

**pres·tige** /prɛ'stiʒ, -'stidʒ/ *n* [U] the respect or admiration that someone or something receives, usually as a result of success, high quality etc.: *Being a doctor has a certain amount of prestige.* –**prestige** *adj*: *a prestige automobile* (=one that a rich person drives)

**pres·tig·ious** /prɛ'stıdʒəs, -'sti-/ *adj* admired or respected as one of the best and most important: *a prestigious award for writers*

**pre·sum·a·bly** /prı'zuməbli/ *adv* used in order to say that something is likely to be true, although you are not certain: *Presumably, your suitcase was put on the wrong flight.*

**pre·sume** /prı'zum/ *v* **1** [T] to think that something is likely to be true, although you are not certain: *I presume (that) this price includes all transportation and hotels.* **2** [T] to accept that something is true until it is proved untrue, especially in law: *She is missing and is presumed dead.* **3** [I] FORMAL to behave rudely by doing something that you do not have the right to do: *Don't presume to tell me how to raise my children!*

  **presume on/upon** sb/sth *phr v* [T] FORMAL to use someone's kindness, trust etc. in a way that is wrong, usually by asking him/her for more than you should: *She has no right to presume on us by asking us to invite her friends.*

**pre·sump·tion** /prı'zʌmpʃən/ *n* **1** an act of thinking that something must be true: *There should always be a presumption of innocence until someone is proven guilty.* **2** [U] FORMAL behavior that is not respectful or polite, and that shows you are too confident

**pre·sump·tu·ous** /prı'zʌmptʃuəs/ *adj* showing disrespect as a result of being too confident: *It was a little presumptuous of him to assume he spoke for me as well.*

**pre·sup·pose** /,prisə'pouz/ *v* [T] FORMAL to depend on something that is thought to be true; ASSUME: *All your plans presuppose that the bank will be willing to lend us the money.* –**presupposition** /,prisʌpə'zıʃən/ *n* [C,U]

**pre·tend¹** /prı'tɛnd/ *v* [I,T] **1** to behave as if something is true when you know it is not: *Terry pretended to be asleep.* | *She pretended (that) she didn't remember me.* **2** to imagine that something is true or real, as a game: *Let's pretend we're on the moon!*

**pretend²** *adj* a word meaning IMAGINARY, used especially by or when talking to children: *We sang songs around a pretend campfire.*

**pre·tense** /'pritɛns, prı'tɛns/ *n* **1** [singular, U] an attempt to pretend that something is true: *Kevin made a pretense of enjoying his dinner, but I know he didn't like it.* **2** **under false pretenses** if you do something under false pretenses, you do it by pretending that something is true when it is not: *He would get women to come into his home under false pretenses, and then attack them.*

**pre·ten·sion** /prı'tɛnʃən/ *n* [C usually plural] an attempt to seem more important, wealthy etc. than you really are: *a nice young man without pretensions*

**pre·ten·tious** /prı'tɛnʃəs/ *adj* trying to seem more important, wealthy etc. than you really are: *There were a bunch of pretentious people at the gallery opening.* –opposite UNPRETENTIOUS

**pre·text** /'pritɛkst/ *n* a reason that is given for doing something, in order to hide the real reason: *He got into the building on the pretext of checking the heating.*

**pret·ty¹** /'prıti/ *adv* INFORMAL **1** fairly, but not completely: *My parents were pretty strict.* | *"How are you feeling?" "Oh, pretty good."* **2** very: *Dad was pretty angry about it.* **3** **pretty much** almost completely: *I'm pretty much done with my homework.*

**pretty²** *adj* **1** a woman or child who is pretty is attractive: *a very pretty little girl* **2** attractive or pleasant to look at or listen to: *a pretty pink dress* | *a song with a pretty tune* **3** **not a pretty picture/sight** very ugly, upsetting, or worrying: *With the fire still burning at 2 a.m., the area wasn't a pretty sight.* –see usage note at BEAUTIFUL

**pret·zel** /'prɛtsəl/ *n* a salty type of bread, baked in the shape of a loose knot –see picture at BREAD

**pre·vail** /prı'veıl/ *v* [I] FORMAL **1** to manage to win or to remain in control after a struggle or argument: *The Celtics have prevailed all season.* **2** if a belief, attitude etc. prevails, it exists among a group of people: *A belief in magic still prevails in some societies.*

  **prevail on/upon** sb *phr v* [T] FORMAL to persuade someone: *I might be willing to prevail upon the committee to reconsider its decision.*

**pre·vail·ing** /prı'veılıŋ/ *adj* **1** very common in a particular place at a particular time; CURRENT: *Williams' books challenged prevailing views of US history.* **2** **prevailing wind** a wind that blows over a particular area for most of a period of time

**prev·a·lent** /'prɛvələnt/ *adj* common at a particular time or in a particular place: *The disease is more prevalent among young people.* –**prevalence** *n* [U]

P

**pre·vent** /prɪ'vɛnt/ v [T] to stop something from happening, or stop someone from doing something: *I'm trying to prevent a fight.* | *A knee injury has prevented Larry from playing tennis.* –**preventable** adj

**pre·ven·ta·tive** /prɪ'vɛnʈɪv/ adj ⇨ PREVENTIVE

**pre·ven·tion** /prɪ'vɛnʃən/ n [U] the act of preventing something, or the actions that you take in order to prevent something: *crime prevention* | *the prevention of war*

**pre·ven·tive** /prɪ'vɛnʈɪv/ adj intended to prevent something you do not want to happen: *preventive medicine* (=that prevents people from becoming sick)

**pre·view** /'privyu/ n 1 an occasion when you see a movie, play etc. before it is shown to the public 2 an advertisement for a movie or television program that often consists of short parts of it –**preview** v [T]

**pre·vi·ous** /'priviəs/ adj 1 happening or existing before a particular event, time, or thing: *She has two children from a previous marriage.* 2 **previous to sth** FORMAL before a particular time or event: *Previous to becoming a writer, Cathy taught history.*

**pre·vi·ous·ly** /'priviəsli/ adv before now, or before a particular time: *They offered Bill a position that had not existed previously.*

**pre·war** /ˌpri'wɔr◂/ adj, adv happening or existing before a war, especially World War I or World War II: *the country's prewar population*

**prey¹** /preɪ/ n 1 [U] an animal that is hunted and eaten by another animal: *a tiger stalking its prey* 2 **bird/beast of prey** a bird or animal that lives by killing and eating other animals 3 **fall prey to sth** to be affected by something unpleasant: *More teenagers are falling prey to gang violence.*

**prey²** v

**prey on** sb/sth phr v [T] 1 if an animal or bird preys on another animal or bird, it hunts and eats it 2 to try to influence or deceive weaker people: *dishonest salesmen who prey on old people*

**price¹** /praɪs/ n 1 [C,U] the amount of money that must be paid in order to buy something: *House prices have gone up again.* | *The price is $49.95.* | *I can't believe how high/low their prices are.* | *Fish is lower in price in the coastal towns.* –compare COST¹ 2 [C,U] something bad that you must deal with in order to have or do something else: *Bad health is the price you pay for smoking.* 3 **at a price a)** used in order to say that you can buy something, but only if you pay a lot of money: *You can buy excellent wine here - at a price.* **b)** used in order to say that something can be achieved, but that it involves something unpleasant: *She was finally made department manager, but at what price!* 4 **at any price** even if

something is extremely difficult: *They were determined to have a child at any price.* 5 **asking price** the price that someone who is selling something says s/he wants for it: *The asking price was $500, but we paid $350 for it.*

**price²** v [T] 1 to give a price to something that is for sale: *a reasonably priced pair of shoes* 2 to put a sign on goods that shows how much they cost

**price·less** /'praɪslɪs/ adj 1 so valuable that you cannot calculate a financial value: *priceless antiques* 2 extremely important or useful: *priceless skills/information* 3 INFORMAL very funny or silly: *The look on his face when I walked in the room was priceless.*

**pric·ey, pricy** /'praɪsi/ adj INFORMAL expensive: *a pricey restaurant*

**prick¹** /prɪk/ v 1 [T] to make a small hole in the surface of something, using a sharp point: *Prick the pie dough all over with a fork.* 2 **prick up its ears** if an animal pricks up its ears, it raises them and points them toward a sound

**prick²** n 1 a slight pain you get when something sharp goes into your skin: *She felt a sharp prick when the needle went into her finger.* 2 SPOKEN OFFENSIVE a stupid unpleasant man 3 a small hole in the surface of something, made by a sharp point 4 SPOKEN TABOO ⇨ PENIS

**prick·le¹** /'prɪkəl/ n 1 a long thin sharp point on the skin of some plants and animals 2 a stinging feeling on your skin

**prickle²** v [I,T] to have an unpleasant stinging feeling on your skin, or to make someone feel this: *That sweater always prickles me.*

**prick·ly** /'prɪkli/ adj 1 covered with PRICKLEs: *prickly bushes* 2 making you have a stinging feeling on your skin: *a prickly wool jacket*

**pride¹** /praɪd/ n [U] 1 a feeling of satisfaction and pleasure in what you have done, or in what someone connected with you has done: *Everyone on our team takes great pride in the quality of their work.* | *They always talk about their son with pride.* 2 a feeling that you like and respect yourself and that you deserve to be respected by other people: *I think you hurt his pride by laughing at the way he speaks English.* 3 a feeling that you are better than other people: *Beattie's pride kept him from asking for a loan.* 4 **sb's pride and joy** someone or something that is very important to someone: *Ken's new car is his pride and joy.* 5 **swallow your pride** to ignore your feelings of pride and do something that seems necessary, even though you do not want to do it: *You're just going to have to swallow your pride and apologize.*

**pride²** v **pride yourself on sth** to be very proud of something that you do well, or of a quality that you have: *Sandy prides herself on her ability to speak four languages.*

**priest** /prist/ *n* someone who is specially trained to perform religious duties and ceremonies, for example, in the Roman Catholic Church

**priest·ess** /'pristis/ *n* a woman with religious authority and duties in some non-Christian religions

**priest·hood** /'pristhʊd/ *n* **the priesthood** the position of being a priest: *Angelo has decided to enter the priesthood.* (=become a priest)

**prim** /prɪm/ *adj* very formal in the way you behave, and easily shocked by anything rude: *Janet's much too **prim and proper** to laugh at a joke like that.* **–primly** *adv*

**pri·ma·cy** /'praɪməsi/ *n* [U] the state of being the thing or person with the most importance or authority: *No one ever questioned the primacy of the church in their lives.*

**pri·ma don·na** /ˌprimə 'dɑnə, ˌprɪmə-/ *n* someone who thinks that s/he is very good at what s/he does, and demands a lot of attention and admiration from other people

**pri·mal** /'praɪməl/ *adj* primal emotions or attitudes are very strong, and seem to come from a part of someone's character that is ancient or like an animal

**pri·mar·i·ly** /praɪ'mɛrəli/ *adv* mainly: *We do sell paintings, but this is primarily a furniture store.*

**pri·mar·y**[1] /'praɪˌmɛri, -məri/ *adj* most important; main: *I used his book as my primary source of information.*

**primary**[2] *n* an election in the US in which people vote to decide who will be their political party's CANDIDATE for a political position

**primary care** /ˌ... './ *n* [U] the main medical help that you get, unless your doctor decides that you need to see a SPECIALIST (=doctor with special skills)

**primary col·or** /ˌ... '../ *n* one of the three colors - red, yellow, and blue - that you can mix together to make any other color

**primary school** /'... ˌ./ *n* ⇨ ELEMENTARY SCHOOL

**pri·mate** /'praɪmeɪt/ *n* a member of the group of MAMMALs that includes humans and monkeys

**prime**[1] /praɪm/ *adj* **1** most important: *Smoking is the prime cause of heart disease.* **2** of the very best quality or kind: *The house is in a prime location.* **3 prime example** a very good example of something: *There are excellent children's facilities - a prime example is the Children's Science Museum.*

**prime**[2] *n* **be in your prime/be in the prime of life** to be at the time in your life when you are strongest and most active

**prime**[3] *v* [T] **1** to prepare someone for a situation so that s/he knows what to do: *The senators were primed to ask some tough questions.* **2** to put a special layer of paint on a surface, to prepare it for the main layer **3** to prepare a PUMP to work by filling it with a liquid

**prime min·is·ter** /ˌ. '.../ *n* the leader of the government in countries that have a PARLIAMENT

**prime num·ber** /ˌ. '../ *n* a number that can only be divided by itself and the number one

**prim·er** /'praɪmɚ/ *n* [C,U] a special paint that is spread over the bare surface of wood, metal etc. before the main layer of paint is put on

**prime time** /ˌ. '.ᴖ/ *n* [U] the time in the evening when the largest number of people are watching television

**pri·me·val** /praɪ'mivəl/ *adj* belonging to the earliest period of the Earth's existence: *primeval forests*

**prim·i·tive** /'prɪmətɪv/ *adj* **1** belonging to an early stage of the development of humans or animals: *primitive societies* **2** very simple, uncomfortable, or without modern features: *primitive living conditions*

**pri·mor·di·al** /praɪ'mɔrdiəl/ *adj* existing at the beginning of time or the beginning of the Earth: *the primordial seas*

**primp** /prɪmp/ *v* [I,T] DISAPPROVING to try to make yourself look attractive by arranging your hair, putting on MAKEUP etc.

**prim·rose** /'prɪmroʊz/ *n* a very brightly colored spring flower

**prince** /prɪns/ *n* **1** the son of a king or queen, or one of his or her close male relatives **2** a male ruler of some small countries: *Prince Rainier of Monaco*

**prince·ly** /'prɪnsli/ *adj* good enough for a prince, or typical of a prince: *a princely gift*

**prin·cess** /'prɪnsɪs, -sɛs/ *n* **1** the daughter of a king or queen, or one of his or her close female relatives **2** the wife of a prince

**prin·ci·pal**[1] /'prɪnsəpəl/ *adj* most important; main: *Her principal reason for taking the job is to travel.*

**principal**[2] *n* **1** someone who is in charge of a school **2** [singular] **a)** an amount of money lent to someone, on which INTEREST is paid **b)** an amount of money that you have saved or INVESTed, and that earns interest **3** the main person in a business or organization, who can make business decisions

**prin·ci·pal·i·ty** /ˌprɪnsə'pæləti/ *n* a country ruled by a prince

**prin·ci·pal·ly** /'prɪnsəpli/ *adv* mainly: *Bus drivers are on strike, principally over wages.*

**prin·ci·ple** /'prɪnsəpəl/ *n* **1** [C,U] a moral rule or set of ideas that makes you behave in a particular way: *Our beliefs are based **on the principle that** everyone is equal.* | *She doesn't eat meat **on principle**.* (=because of a moral idea) **2** a rule that explains the way something works: *the principle of the steam engine* **3 in principle a)** if something is possible in principle, there is no good reason why it should not happen: *In principle, you can leave work early on Friday, but it's not always possible.* **b)** if you agree in principle, you agree about a

**P**

general plan or idea without the details: *We're hoping the contract will be approved in principle.*

**prin·ci·pled** /ˈprɪnsəpəld/ *adj* having strong beliefs about what is morally right and wrong: *Most of them were **highly principled** and able people.*

**prin·ci·ples** /ˈprɪnsəpəlz/ *n* [plural] **1** strong ideas about what is morally right or wrong, that you try to follow in everything you do: *That guy has no principles - he'd cheat his own mother.* **2** the general rules on which a skill, science etc. is based: *the principles of geometry*

**print¹** /prɪnt/ *v* **1** [I,T] to produce words, numbers, or pictures on paper, using a machine that puts ink onto the surface: *The books are printed in Canada. | a machine that can print 60 pages a minute* **2** [T] to produce many copies of a book, newspaper etc.: *We're printing 10,000 copies to start with.* **3** [T] to print a letter, speech etc. in a newspaper, book, or magazine: *Newspapers no longer print the kind of news most people want to read.* **4** [I,T] to write words by hand without joining the letters: *Please print your name in capital letters.* **5** [T] to produce a photograph on special paper

**print** sth ↔ **off/out** *phr v* [T] to produce a printed copy of a computer document

**print²** *n* **1** [U] writing that has been printed in books, newspapers etc.: *I can't read small print without my glasses. | Just because you see something **in print**, it doesn't mean it's true.* **2** **be in print/be out of print** if a book is in print or out of print, it is or is not available to buy **3** **the fine/small print** the details of a legal document, often in very small writing: *The small print said we couldn't sublet the apartment.* **4** a picture that has been printed from a small sheet of metal or block of wood, or a copy of a painting **5** a photograph printed on paper: *You can pick up your prints on Friday.* **6** a mark made on a surface or in a soft substance by something that has been pressed onto it: *a cat's paw print in the yard* −see also FOOTPRINT **7** [C,U] cloth that has a colored pattern on it: *She was wearing a print dress and white shoes.*

**print·er** /ˈprɪntɚ/ *n* **1** a machine connected to a computer that can copy documents from a computer onto paper **2** someone who owns or works in a printing business

**print·ing** /ˈprɪntɪŋ/ *n* [U] **1** the act or process of making a book, magazine etc. using a machine: *a printing error* **2** all the copies of a book that are printed at one time: *a novel in its third printing*

**printing press** /ˈ.. ˌ./ *n* a machine that prints newspapers, books etc.

**print·out** /ˈprɪntaʊt/ *n* [C,U] paper with printed information on it, produced by a PRINTER

**pri·or** /ˈpraɪɚ/ *adj* FORMAL **1** **prior to** before: *We didn't know what had been discussed prior*

to the meeting. **2** done, planned, or existing earlier than something else; PREVIOUS: *I couldn't attend because of a **prior commitment**.*

**pri·or·i·tize** /praɪˈɔrəˌtaɪz/ *v* [T] to put the things you must deal with in order of importance, so that you can deal with the most important ones first: *The mayor promises to prioritize neighborhood improvement projects.* −**prioritization** /praɪˌɔrətəˈzeɪʃən/ *n* [U]

**pri·or·i·ty** /praɪˈɔrəti/ *n* **1** the thing that you think is most important and that needs attention before anything else: *Let's decide what our priorities are.* **2** **have priority (over)** to be considered most important and dealt with before anything or anyone else: *Help the children first - they have priority over everyone else.*

**prism** /ˈprɪzəm/ *n* a transparent block of glass that breaks up white light into different colors

**pris·on** /ˈprɪzən/ *n* [C,U] a large building where people are kept as a punishment for a crime, or while waiting to go to court for their TRIAL: *Williams was **sent to prison** for six years for rape.*

**pris·on·er** /ˈprɪzənɚ/ *n* **1** someone who is kept in a prison as a punishment for a crime **2** someone who is taken by force and kept somewhere, for example during a war: *The captain was **taken prisoner** by enemy soldiers. | They **kept/held** her **prisoner** for three months.*

**prisoner of war** /ˌ.... ˈ./, **P.O.W.** *n* a member of the military who is caught by the enemy during a war and kept as a prisoner

**pris·sy** /ˈprɪsi/ *adj* INFORMAL too worried about behaving correctly, and easily shocked by anything rude

**pris·tine** /ˈprɪˌstin, prɪˈstin/ *adj* extremely clean, and not spoiled at all by use: *a 1973 Volkswagen Beetle **in pristine condition** | pristine wilderness areas*

**pri·va·cy** /ˈpraɪvəsi/ *n* [U] **1** the state of being able to be alone, and not seen or heard by other people: *Joan read the letter **in the privacy** of her own room.* **2** the state of being able to keep your own affairs secret: *our legal right to privacy*

---

**CULTURE NOTE privacy**

In the US and Canada, privacy is important. This does not just mean having time or a place to be alone. It also means that there are particular subjects that are considered private, that you should not usually talk about with other people. For example, you should not ask how old someone is, how much money s/he makes, or how much s/he paid for something. You should only talk about religion or politics with friends, and it is not polite to ask someone whom s/he voted for.

**pri·vate**[1] /ˈpraɪvɪt/ *adj* **1** only for use by one particular person or group, not for everyone: *The family has a private plane.* | *Rooms are available for private parties.* **2** secret or personal and not for sharing with others: *her private thoughts* | *You had no right to look at my private papers.* **3** not relating to, owned by, or paid for by the government: *a private school* **4** separate from your work or your official position, and not related to it: *The president will be making a private visit to Mexico.* **5** quiet and without lots of people: *Is there a private corner where we can talk?* **–privately** *adv*: *Is there someplace we can talk privately?*

**private**[2] *n* **1** **in private** without other people listening or watching: *Miss Schultz, I need to speak to you in private.* **2** also **Private** someone who has the lowest rank in the Army or Marines

**private en·ter·prise** /ˌ.. ˈ.../ *n* [U] the economic system in which private businesses can compete, and the government does not control industry

**private in·ves·ti·gat·or** /ˌ.. .ˈ..../, **private detec·tive** /ˌ.. .ˈ../ *n* someone whom you pay to do things such as look for information or missing people, or follow someone and report on what s/he does

**private parts** /ˌ.. ˈ./, **pri·vates** /ˈpraɪvɪts/ *n* [plural] INFORMAL an expression meaning "sex organs," used in order to avoid naming them directly

**pri·va·tion** /praɪˈveɪʃən/ *n* [C,U] FORMAL a lack of the things that everyone needs, such as food, warmth, and shelter

**pri·vat·ize** /ˈpraɪvəˌtaɪz/ *v* [T] if a government privatizes an industry, service etc. that it controls or owns, it sells it to private owners –compare NATIONALIZE, SOCIALIZE

**priv·i·lege** /ˈprɪvlɪdʒ, -vəlɪdʒ/ *n* **1** a special advantage that is given only to one person or group of people: *In some poorer countries, education is a privilege, not a right.* **2** [U] the state of having more advantages or rights than other people, for example because you are rich or powerful: *a position of privilege* **3** [singular] something that you are lucky to have the chance to do, and that you enjoy very much: *It's been a privilege to meet you, sir.* **–privileged** *adj*

**priv·y**[1] /ˈprɪvi/ *adj* FORMAL **privy to sth** sharing secret knowledge of something: *Only three people were privy to our plans.*

**privy**[2] *n* ⇨ OUTHOUSE

**prize**[1] /praɪz/ *n* something that is given to someone who is successful in a competition, race, game of chance etc.: *Her roses won first/second/third prize at the flower show.*

**prize**[2] *adj* **1** good enough to win a prize or to have won a prize: *prize cattle* **2** **prize money** money that is given to the person who wins a competition, race etc.

**prize**[3] *v* [T] to think that someone or something is very important or valuable: *a necklace that his mother had prized*

**prized** /praɪzd/ *adj* very important or valuable to someone: *Nick's motorbike is his most prized possession.*

**prize·fight** /ˈpraɪzfaɪt/ *n* a BOXING match in which the competitors are paid

**pro** /proʊ/ *n* **1** INFORMAL ⇨ PROFESSIONAL[2]: *It's a pleasure to watch a real pro like Browning skate.* **2** something that is an advantage: *We discussed the pros and cons* (=the advantages and disadvantages) *of starting our own business.*

**prob·a·bil·i·ty** /ˌprɑbəˈbɪləti/ *n* **1** [singular, U] how likely it is that something will happen, exist, or be true: *There is little probability of the hostages being released soon.* **2** **in all probability** very probably: *There will, in all probability, be parts that you do not understand.* **3** something that is likely to happen or exist: *War is a real probability unless the talks succeed.*

**prob·a·ble** /ˈprɑbəbəl/ *adj* likely to happen, exist, or be true: *It is highly probable that the mayor will be reelected.* | *The probable cause of the plane crash was ice on the wings.*

**prob·a·bly** /ˈprɑbəbli/ *adv* likely to happen, exist, or be true: *We'll probably go to Florida next year.*

**pro·ba·tion** /proʊˈbeɪʃən/ *n* [U] **1** a system that allows some criminals to leave prison early or not to go to prison at all, if they promise to behave well for a specific period of time: *Preston's been on probation for three years.* **2** a period of time during which someone who has just started a job is tested to see whether s/he is suitable for what s/he is doing –**probationary** /proʊˈbeɪʃəˌnɛri/ *adj*

**probation of·fi·cer** /.ˈ.. ,.../ *n* someone whose job is to watch, advise, and help people who have broken the law and are on PROBATION

**probe**[1] /proʊb/ *v* [I,T] **1** to ask questions in order to find things out: *Reporters are already probing into the affair.* **2** to look for something or examine something, using a long thin instrument –**probing** *adj*

**probe**[2] *n* **1** a long thin instrument that doctors and scientists use to examine parts of the body **2** a SPACECRAFT without people in it, that is sent into space to collect information **3** a word meaning a very thorough process of asking questions in order to find things out, used especially by newspapers; INQUIRY

**prob·lem** /ˈprɑbləm/ *n* **1** a difficult situation or person that has to be dealt with or thought about: *I've been having a few problems with my car.* | *Wilson insists there isn't a drug problem in the school.* | *When did the problem first arise/*

*occur?* ✗ DON'T SAY "When did the problem happen?" ✗ | *Unemployment remains a* **serious problem** *here.* ✗ DON'T SAY "an important problem." ✗ **2** a question that must be answered, especially one relating to numbers or facts: *The test will have 20 algebra problems.*

---

SPOKEN PHRASES

**3 no problem a)** used in order to say that you are very willing to do something: *"Could you go to the store for me?" "Sure, no problem."* **b)** used after someone has thanked you or said s/he is sorry: *"Thanks so much for all your help." "Oh, no problem."*
**4 that's your/his/their etc. problem** used in order to say that someone else is responsible for dealing with a situation, not you: *If you can't get yourself there on time, that's your problem.* **5 What's your problem?** used in order to ask someone what is wrong, in a way that shows you think s/he is not being reasonable: *Look, what's your problem? It's my decision!*

---

**prob·lem·at·ic** /ˌprɑbləˈmætɪk/ *adj* full of problems and difficult to deal with: *The situation has become somewhat problematic.* −**problematically** *adv*

**pro·ce·dure** /prəˈsidʒɚ/ *n* [C,U] the correct or normal way of doing something: *the procedure for shutting down a computer* | *a common medical procedure* (=treatment that follows a set of rules) −**procedural** *adj*

**pro·ceed** /prəˈsid, proʊ-/ *v* [I] **1** to continue to do something that has already been started, especially after a short pause: *Talks are proceeding smoothly.* **2 proceed to do sth** to do something next: *Larry joined us, and proceeded to take over the whole conversation.* **3** FORMAL to move in a particular direction: *Please* **proceed to** *the nearest exit.*

**pro·ceed·ings** /prəˈsidɪŋz, proʊ-/ *n* [plural] **1** an event or series of actions: *We watched the proceedings from a third floor window.* **2** actions taken in a law court or in a legal case: *legal proceedings*

**pro·ceeds** /ˈproʊsidz/ *n* [plural] the money that has been gained from doing something or selling something: *All the* **proceeds from** *the bake sale will go toward buying new uniforms.*

**pro·cess¹** /ˈprɑsɛs, ˈproʊ-/ *n* **1** a series of actions, developments, or changes that happen naturally: *the aging process* | *the digestive process* **2** a series of actions that someone does in order to achieve a particular result: *She's learning to read, but it's a slow process.* **3 be in the process of doing sth** to have started doing something and not yet be finished: *We're in the process of moving to a new office building.* **4** a system or a treatment of materials that is used for producing goods: *an industrial process*

**process²** *v* [T] **1** to treat food or some other substance by adding other substances to it, for

example to give it color or keep it fresh: *processed cheese* **2** to deal with information in an official way: *Your membership application is still being processed.* **3** to put information into a computer to be examined −**processing** *n* [U]

**pro·ces·sion** /prəˈsɛʃən/ *n* **1** a line of people or vehicles moving slowly as part of a ceremony: *a funeral procession* −compare PARADE¹ **2** several people or things of the same kind, appearing or happening one after the other: *an endless* **procession of** *people giving speeches*

**pro·ces·sion·al** /prəˈsɛʃənl/ *adj* relating to or used during a PROCESSION: *processional music*

**pro·ces·sor** /ˈprɑsɛsɚ/ *n* ⇨ CPU −see also FOOD PROCESSOR

**pro·claim** /proʊˈkleɪm, prə-/ *v* [T] FORMAL to say officially and publicly that something is true or exists: *A national holiday was proclaimed.*

**proc·la·ma·tion** /ˌprɑkləˈmeɪʃən/ *n* an official public statement that tells citizens what will be done about something important: *the Emancipation Proclamation* (=that freed the US SLAVES)

**pro·cras·ti·nate** /prəˈkræstəˌneɪt/ *v* [I] to delay doing something that you ought to do: *If you keep on procrastinating, you won't have time to do it right.* −**procrastination** /prəˌkræstəˈneɪʃən/ *n* [U] −**procrastinator** /prəˈkræstəˌneɪtɚ/ *n*

**pro·cre·ate** /ˈproʊkriˌeɪt/ *v* [I,T] FORMAL to produce children or baby animals −**procreation** /ˌproʊkriˈeɪʃən/ *n* [U]

**pro·cure** /proʊˈkyʊr, prə-/ *v* [T] FORMAL to obtain something, especially something that is difficult to get: *Clark was accused of procuring guns for the rebels.* −**procurement** *n* [U]

**prod¹** /prɑd/ *v* -dded, -dding [I,T] **1** to strongly encourage someone to do something: *We had to* **prod** *Randall* **into** *applying for the job.* **2** ⇨ POKE

**prod²** *n* something you POKE animals with in order to make them move in a particular direction

**prod·i·gal** /ˈprɑdɪgəl/ *adj* FORMAL tending to waste what you have, especially money

**pro·di·gious** /prəˈdɪdʒəs/ *adj* FORMAL impressively large or skillful in a way that surprises people; AMAZING: *He eats a* **prodigious amount** *of food.* | *a* **prodigious feat** (=impressive achievement) −**prodigiously** *adv*

**prod·i·gy** /ˈprɑdədʒi/ *n* a young person who is extremely good at doing something: *Mozart was a* **child prodigy**. −compare GENIUS

**pro·duce¹** /prəˈdus/ *v* **1** [T] to grow something or make it naturally: *This region produces most of the state's corn.* | *Trees produce carbon dioxide.* **2** [T] to make something happen or develop, or have a particular result or effect: *The announcement produced shouts of anger.* | *The drug can produce side effects in some people.*

**3** [T] to show something so it can be seen or considered: *Officer Ryan asked the suspect to produce his driver's license.* **4** [I,T] to make something using an industrial process: *The challenge is to produce cheap electricity.* **5** [T] to control the preparation of a play, movie etc. and then show it to the public **6** [T] to make something using skill and imagination: *Diane produced a fantastic meal.*

**prod·uce**[2] /'pradus, 'prou-/ *n* [U] food that has been grown or farmed, especially fresh fruits and vegetables: *the produce section of the supermarket*

**pro·duc·er** /prə'dusɚ/ *n* **1** a person, company, or country that makes or grows goods, foods, or materials: *Scotland is a producer of high quality wool.* **2** someone who controls the preparation of a play, movie etc., but who does not direct the actors

**prod·uct** /'pradʌkt/ *n* **1** [C,U] something useful that is grown, made in a factory, or taken from nature: *None of our products are tested on animals.* | *dairy products* **2** **be the product of sth** to be the result of experiences or of good or bad conditions: *Criminals are often the product of bad homes.* **3** the number you get by multiplying two or more numbers

**pro·duc·tion** /prə'dʌkʃən/ *n* **1** [U] the process of making or growing things, or the amount that is produced: *Steel production has decreased by 35%.* **2** something produced by skill or imagination, such as a play or movie: *a new Broadway production of "Follies"*

**pro·duc·tive** /prə'dʌktɪv/ *adj* producing or achieving a lot: *productive land* | *a very productive conference* —**productively** *adv* —opposite UNPRODUCTIVE

**pro·duc·tiv·i·ty** /,proudək'tɪvəti, ,pra-/ *n* [U] the rate at which goods are produced, and the amount produced: *Factory managers want to increase the workers' productivity.*

**prof** /praf/ *n* **1** SPOKEN ⇨ PROFESSOR **2** **Prof.** the written abbreviation of PROFESSOR

**pro·fane** /prou'feɪn, prə-/ *adj* showing disrespect for God or for holy things, by using rude words or religious words wrongly: *profane language*

**pro·fan·i·ty** /prou'fænəti, prə-/ *n* [C,U] a rude word, or a religious word used wrongly, that shows disrespect for God or for holy things

**pro·fess** /prə'fɛs, prou-/ *v* [T] FORMAL **1** to make a claim about something, especially a false one: *Although he professes to be a vegetarian, he eats fish.* **2** to express a personal feeling or belief freely, and not try to hide it: *Fabian longed to profess his love for her.* —**professed** *adj*

**pro·fes·sion** /prə'fɛʃən/ *n* **1** a job that needs special education and training: *He's a lawyer by profession.* (=as his job) —see usage note at JOB **2** [singular] all the people in a particular profession: *the teaching profession* **3** FORMAL a statement of your belief, opinion, or feeling

**pro·fes·sion·al**[1] /prə'fɛʃənl/ *adj* **1** doing a job, sport, or activity for money: *a professional baseball player* **2** professional sports are played by people who are paid **3** relating to a job that needs special education and training: *You should speak to a lawyer for professional advice.* **4** showing that someone has been well trained and is good at his/her work. *This report looks very professional.* —**professionally** *adv*

**professional**[2] *n* **1** someone who earns money by doing a job, sport, or activity that other people do just for enjoyment —compare AMATEUR[2] **2** someone who works in a job that needs special education and training: *a health care professional* **3** someone who has a lot of experience and does something very well: *Holt thinks his co-workers don't see him as a true professional.*

**pro·fes·sion·al·ism** /prə'fɛʃnəl,ɪzəm, -ʃnl-/ *n* [U] the skill and high standards of behavior expected of a PROFESSIONAL person

**pro·fes·sor** /prə'fɛsɚ/ *n* a teacher at a university or college, especially one who has a high rank: *Thank you, Professor Drexler.* | *my history professor*

**prof·fer** /'prafɚ/ *v* [T] FORMAL to offer something to someone —**proffer** *n*

**pro·fi·cien·cy** /prə'fɪʃənsi/ *n* [U] the ability to do something with a high level of skill: *a math proficiency test*

**pro·fi·cient** /prə'fɪʃənt/ *adj* able to do something with a high level of skill: *Gwen's proficient in three languages.* —**proficiently** *adv*

**pro·file**[1] /'proufaɪl/ *n* **1** a side view of someone's head: *a drawing of her in profile* **2** a short description that gives important details about someone or something: *a profile of her career* **3** **keep a low profile** to behave quietly and avoid doing things that will make people notice you

**profile**[2] *v* [T] to write or give a short description of someone or something: *His new play was profiled in last Sunday's newspaper.*

**prof·it**[1] /'prafɪt/ *n* **1** [C,U] money that you gain by selling things or doing business: *Eric made a profit of $23,000 when he sold his house.* | *They sold the company at a huge profit.* **2** [U] an advantage that you gain from doing something: *reading for profit and pleasure*

**profit**[2] *v* [T] FORMAL to be useful or helpful to someone: *It might profit you to meet her in person.*

**profit by/from** sth *phr v* [T] to learn from something that happens, or get something good from a situation: *The rebels will profit from the army's mistakes.*

**prof·it·a·bil·i·ty** /,prafɪtə'bɪləti/ *n* [U] the

state of producing a profit, or the degree to which a business or activity is PROFITABLE

**prof·it·a·ble** /ˈprɑfɪṭəbəl/ *adj* producing a profit or a useful result: *The company has had a profitable year.* –**profitably** *adv*

**prof·it·eer** /ˌprɑfəˈtɪr/ *n* a person or company that makes unfairly large profits, especially by selling things at very high prices when they are difficult to get –**profiteering** *n* [U]

**profit mar·gin** /ˈ.. ˌ../ *n* the difference between the cost of producing something and the price you sell it at

**profit shar·ing** /ˈ.. ˌ../ *n* [U] a system in which workers are allowed to share some of their company's profits

**prof·li·gate** /ˈprɑfləgɪt/ *adj* FORMAL **1** wasting money in a careless way **2** behaving in an immoral way

**pro·found** /prəˈfaʊnd/ *adj* **1** having a strong influence or effect: *Her death was a profound shock to all of us.* **2** showing strong serious feelings: *a profound apology* **3** showing great knowledge and understanding: *a profound book* –**profoundly** *adv* –**profundity** /prəˈfʌndəṭi/ *n* [C,U]

**pro·fuse·ly** /prəˈfyusli/ *adv* many times, or in large numbers or amounts: *Keiko thanked them profusely.* –**profuse** *adj*

**pro·fu·sion** /prəˈfyuʒən/ *n* [singular, U] a very large amount: *Poppies grew in profusion over the hillsides.*

**prog·e·ny** /ˈprɑdʒəni/ *n* [U] LITERARY the babies of a person or animal

**prog·no·sis** /prɑgˈnoʊsɪs/ *n, plural* **prognoses** /-siz/ TECHNICAL **1** a doctor's opinion of how an illness or disease will develop **2** a judgment about what will happen in the future, based on information or experience

**pro·gram¹** /ˈproʊgræm, -grəm/ *n* **1** a show on television or radio: *There's a program about whales on channel 9.* **2** a set of instructions given to a computer to make it do a particular job: *a software program that helps you with household finances* **3** a set of planned activities with a specific purpose: *Stanford's MBA program | a government program to house the homeless | Lucy's exercise program includes weight lifting and swimming.* **4** a printed description of what will happen at a play, concert etc. and of the people who will be performing **5 get with the program** SPOKEN used in order to tell someone to pay attention to what needs to be done, and do it

**program²** *v* **-mmed, -mming** [T] **1** to set a machine to operate in a particular way: *I've programmed the VCR to record that movie you wanted.* **2** to give a set of instructions to a computer to make it do a particular job

**pro·gram·mer** /ˈproʊˌgræmɚ, -grəmɚ/ *n* someone whose job is to write programs for computers –**programming** *n* [U]

**prog·ress¹** /ˈprɑgrəs, -grɛs/ *n* [U] **1** the process of getting better at doing something, or getting closer to finishing or achieving something: *Nick has made a lot of progress since coming to our school. | We've been watching the progress of the trial with interest.* **2** all of the improvements, developments, and achievements that happen in science, society, work etc.: *technological progress* **3 in progress** happening now, and not yet finished: *Please do not enter while there is a class in progress.* **4** movement toward a place: *The ship made slow progress through the rough sea.*

**pro·gress²** /prəˈgrɛs/ *v* [I] **1** to develop, improve, or become more complete over a period of time: *Work on the new building progressed quickly.* **2** to move forward: *We progressed slowly toward the front of the arena.*

**pro·gres·sion** /prəˈgrɛʃən/ *n* [singular, U] **1** a process of change or development: *Doctors are worried by the rapid progression of her illness.* **2** movement toward a particular place

**pro·gres·sive¹** /prəˈgrɛsɪv/ *adj* **1** supporting new or modern ideas and methods: *a progressive attitude* **2** becoming better, worse, or more complete over a period of time: *a progressive disease* –**progressively** *adv*

**progressive²** *n* TECHNICAL the progressive ⇨ CONTINUOUS²

**pro·hib·it** /proʊˈhɪbɪt, prə-/ *v* [T] **1** to officially make an activity illegal, or to officially not allow it: *Smoking in this building is prohibited. | Stores are prohibited from selling alcohol to people under 21.* **2** to make something impossible or prevent it from happening: *His bad eyesight prohibited him from becoming a pilot.*

**pro·hi·bi·tion** /ˌproʊəˈbɪʃən/ *n* **1** [C,U] FORMAL the act of officially making something illegal or officially not allowing it, or an order that does this: *a prohibition on cigarette advertising* **2 Prohibition** the period from 1919 to 1933 in the US when the production and sale of alcoholic drinks was illegal

**pro·hib·i·tive** /proʊˈhɪbəṭɪv, prə-/ *adj* preventing people from doing or buying something: *The cost of property in some large cities is prohibitive.* –**prohibitively** *adv*

**proj·ect¹** /ˈprɑdʒɛkt, -dʒɪkt/ *n* **1** a carefully planned piece of work: *the new highway project | My school project is on Virginia State history.* **2 the projects** ⇨ HOUSING PROJECT

**pro·ject²** /prəˈdʒɛkt/ *v* **1** [T] to use the information you have now to calculate or plan what will happen in the future: *projected sales for next year | A visit by the president is projected for March.* **2** [T] to make other people have a particular idea about you: *Jim always projects an image of self-confidence.* **3** [I,T] to speak or sing loudly enough to be heard by everyone in a big room or theater **4** [T] to use light to make an image appear on a screen or surface **5** [I,T] to stick out beyond an edge or surface: *The garage roof projects over the driveway.* **6** [T] FORMAL to throw something through the air with great force

**pro·jec·tile** /prə'dʒɛktl, -,taɪl/ *n* FORMAL an object that is thrown or fired from a weapon

**pro·jec·tion** /prə'dʒɛkʃən/ *n* **1** a statement about something you think will happen: *this year's sales projections* **2** something that sticks out beyond an edge or surface **3** [C,U] the act of using light to make an image appear on a screen or surface, or the image itself: *film projection*

**pro·jec·tion·ist** /prə'dʒɛkʃənɪst/ *n* someone whose job is to operate a PROJECTOR

**pro·jec·tor** /prə'dʒɛktɚ/ *n* a piece of equipment that uses light to make a movie or pictures appear on a screen

**pro·le·tar·i·at** /ˌproʊlə'tɛriət/ *n* the **proletariat** the people in a society who are poor, own no property etc. –**proletarian** *adj*

**pro·lif·er·ate** /prə'lɪfə,reɪt/ *v* [I] FORMAL to rapidly increase in number and spread to many different places: *Projects to clean up the environment are proliferating.* –**proliferation** /prəˌlɪfə'reɪʃən/ *n* [singular, U]

**pro·lif·ic** /prə'lɪfɪk/ *adj* producing a lot of something: *Agatha Christie was a prolific writer.* –**prolifically** *adv*

**pro·logue** /'proʊlɑg, -lɔg/ *n* the introduction to a book, movie, or play

**pro·long** /prə'lɔŋ/ *v* [T] to make something such as a feeling, activity, or state continue longer: *high-tech machinery that prolongs people's lives*

**pro·longed** /prə'lɔŋgd/ *adj* continuing for a long time: *a prolonged illness*

**prom** /prɑm/ *n* a formal dance party for HIGH SCHOOL students, that usually happens at the end of a school year: *the senior prom* (=dance for students in their last year of school)

**prom·e·nade** /ˌprɑmə'neɪd, -'nɑd/ *n* OLD-FASHIONED a walk for pleasure in a public place, or a wide path where you can do this –**promenade** *v* [I]

**prom·i·nence** /'prɑmənəns/ *n* [U] the fact of being important and famous: *Stallone rose to prominence* (=became famous) *with the movie "Rocky."*

**prom·i·nent** /'prɑmənənt/ *adj* **1** famous or important: *prominent politicians* **2** large and sticking out: *a prominent nose* **3** **a prominent place/position** somewhere that is easily seen: *The family portrait was hung in a prominent place on the wall.* –**prominently** *adv*

**pro·mis·cu·ous** /prə'mɪskyuəs/ *adj* having sex with a lot of people: *In the study, single men under 30 were the most promiscuous group.* –**promiscuity** /ˌprɑmɪ'skyuəti/ *n* [U]

**prom·ise¹** /'prɑmɪs/ *v* **1** [I,T] to make a statement that you will definitely do something

or that something will definitely happen: *You promised me (that) you wouldn't be late!* | *She's promised to clean her room.* | *I've already promised them a ride to the dance.* **2** [T] to make people expect that something will happen: *The game promises to be exciting.* **3** **I can't promise anything** SPOKEN used in order to tell someone that you will try to do what s/he wants, but you may not be able to

**promise²** *n* **1** a statement that you will definitely do something or that something will definitely happen: *You made me a promise, and I expect you to keep it.* (=do what you said you would do) | *Christy broke her promise to practice the flute every day.* (=she failed to practice) | *a promise of help* **2** [U] signs that something or someone will be good or successful: *He shows a lot of promise as a writer.*

**prom·is·ing** /'prɑmɪsɪŋ/ *adj* showing that someone or something is likely to be successful in the future: *a promising young singer* –**promisingly** *adv*

**pro·mo** /'proʊmoʊ/ *n adj* INFORMAL ⇨ PROMOTIONAL

**prom·on·to·ry** /'prɑmən,tɔri/ *n* a high piece of land that goes out into the ocean

**pro·mote** /prə'moʊt/ *v* [T] **1** to help something develop and be successful: *Davis works to promote understanding between cultures.* **2** to advertise a product or event: *The company is spending millions promoting its new software.* **3** to give someone a better, more responsible position at work: *Ted was promoted to senior sales manager.* **4** to be responsible for arranging a large public event such as a concert or a sports game

**pro·mot·er** /prə'moʊtɚ/ *n* someone whose job is to arrange large public events such as concerts or sports games

**pro·mo·tion** /prə'moʊʃən/ *n* **1** [C,U] a move to a better, more responsible position at work: *She received a promotion to Lieutenant.* **2** [C,U] an activity intended to advertise a product or event, or the thing that is being advertised: *a sales promotion*

**pro·mo·tion·al** /prə'moʊʃənl/ *adj* promotional products and activities are made or organized in order to advertise something

**prompt¹** /prɑmpt/ *v* **1** [T] to make someone do something, or to help him/her remember to do it: *News of the scandal prompted a Senate investigation.* | *Alex does practice his drums, but he needs prompting.* **2** [I,T] to remind someone, especially an actor, of the next words in a speech

**prompt²** *adj* **1** done quickly, immediately after something else, or at the right time: *We request prompt payment of bills.* **2** someone who is prompt arrives at the right time or does something on time –**promptly** *adv*: *The disease is* *not fatal if treated promptly.* | *He gave the roses to Joanna, who promptly burst into tears.*

**prompt**[3] *n* a sign on a computer screen that shows that the computer has finished one operation and is ready to begin the next

**prone** /proun/ *adj* **1** likely to do something or suffer from something: *a narrow river that is prone to flooding* | *As a child she was accident prone.* (=often had accidents) **2** FORMAL lying down flat, especially with the front of your body facing down

**prong** /prɔŋ, praŋ/ *n* **1** one of the thick sharp pointed parts on the end of some tools, such as a PITCHFORK —compare TINE **2** **two-pronged, three-pronged etc.** a two-pronged or three-pronged attack, approach, plan etc. comes from two or three directions or uses two or three methods at the same time

**pro·noun** /'prounaun/ *n* TECHNICAL in grammar, a word that is used instead of a noun or noun phrase. In the sentence "He brought me a chair and I sat on it," the words "he," "me," "I," and "it" are pronouns

---

**USAGE NOTE** pronoun agreement

Pronouns such as **everyone**, **anyone**, and **someone** are singular, and should be used with singular verbs and pronouns: *Has everyone finished his or her drink?* However, in speech and informal writing, we usually use plural pronouns instead: *Anyone can use the library, can't they?* | *Someone has left their backpack behind.*

---

**pro·nounce** /prə'nauns/ *v* [T] **1** to make the sound of a letter, word etc. in the correct way: *How do you pronounce your name?* **2** to state something officially and formally: *He was pronounced dead at 11:00 p.m.*

**pro·nounced** /prə'naunst/ *adj* very strong or noticeable: *Harold walks with a pronounced limp.*

**pro·nounce·ment** /prə'naunsmənt/ *n* FORMAL an official public statement

**pron·to** /'prantou/ *adv* SPOKEN a word meaning quickly or immediately, used especially when you are annoyed: *Get in the house, pronto!*

**pro·nun·ci·a·tion** /prə,nʌnsi'eɪʃən/ *n* **1** [C,U] the way in which a language or a particular word is pronounced: *There are two different pronunciations of "read."* **2** [singular, U] a particular person's way of pronouncing a word or words

**proof** /pruf/ *n* **1** [U] facts, information, documents etc. that prove something is true: *Do you have any proof that this is your bag?* | *Returns will be accepted with proof of purchase.* (=something that proves that you bought the thing) **2** TECHNICAL a printed copy of a piece of writing, used in order to find and remove mistakes before the final printing is done **3** [U] a

measurement of how much alcohol is in a drink. For example, 40 proof is 20% alcohol

**proof·read** /'pruf-rid/ *v* [I,T] to read something in order to correct any mistakes in it —**proofreader** *n*

**prop**[1] /prap/ *v* **-pped, -pping** [T] to support something or keep it in a particular position: *He propped his bike against the fence.* | *The gate had been propped open with a brick.*

**prop** sth ↔ **up** *phr v* [T] **1** to prevent something from falling by putting something against it or under it: *Steel poles prop up the crumbling walls.* **2** to help something to continue to exist: *Willis sold stocks to prop up his failing company.*

**prop**[2] *n* **1** an object placed under or against something to hold it in a position **2** an object such as a book, weapon etc. used by actors in a play or movie

**prop·a·gan·da** /,prapə'gændə/ *n* [U] false or partly false information that is given to the public by a government or political party in order to make people agree with them —**propagandist** *n* —**propagandize** *v* [I,T]

**prop·a·gate** /'prapə,geɪt/ *v* FORMAL **1** [T] to share ideas, information, or beliefs with many people: *a journal that propagates scientific developments* **2** [I,T] to grow or produce new plants, or to make a plant do this —**propagation** /,prapə'geɪʃən/ *n* [U]

**pro·pel** /prə'pɛl/ *v* **-lled, -lling** [T] **1** to make someone achieve something, or to make something happen or develop: *The actress's striking good looks helped propel her to stardom.* **2** to move, drive, or push something forward: *old ships propelled by steam*

**pro·pel·ler** /prə'pɛlɚ/ *n* a piece of equipment that consists of two or more blades that spin around to make a ship or aircraft move

**pro·pen·si·ty** /prə'pɛnsəti/ *n* FORMAL a natural tendency to behave or develop in a particular way: *Bubba had a propensity to gain weight.*

**prop·er** /'prapɚ/ *adj* **1** correct, or right for a particular situation: *Put that back in its proper place.* | *You have to go through the proper procedures.* **2** socially correct and acceptable: *I didn't think it was proper to ask for her phone number so soon.* **3** inside the limits of an area or subject: *We no longer live in Dallas proper; we moved to Mesquite.*

**prop·er·ly** /'prapɚli/ *adv* correctly, in a way that is right or suitable: *She can read German but has trouble speaking it properly.*

**proper noun** /,.. './, **proper name** *n* TECHNICAL in grammar, a noun such as "Mike," "Paris," or "Easter" that is the name of a particular person, place, or thing and is spelled with a capital letter

**prop·er·ty** /'prapɚti/ *n* **1** [U] something that someone owns: *Police recovered some of the stolen property.* **2** [C,U] land, buildings, or both together: *We have several lovely properties* *for sale in that area.*| *Get off! This is **private property!*** **3** a natural quality of something: *an herb with healing properties*

**proph·e·cy** /ˈprɑfəsi/ *n* a statement that tells what will happen in the future, often made by someone with religious or magical power

**proph·e·sy** /ˈprɑfəˌsaɪ/ *v* [I,T] to use religious or magical knowledge to say what will happen in the future

**proph·et** /ˈprɑfɪt/ *n* someone who says what will happen in the future and teaches people more about a religion

**pro·phet·ic** /prəˈfɛtɪk/ *adj* relating to correctly saying what will happen in the future: *The Ambassador's warnings **proved prophetic.*** (=what he warned about actually happened) –**prophetically** *adv*

**pro·pi·tious** /prəˈpɪʃəs/ *adj* FORMAL likely to bring good results; FAVORABLE: *Circumstances were propitious for investment.*

**pro·po·nent** /prəˈpoʊnənt/ *n* someone who supports something or persuades people to do something: *a **proponent of** gay rights* –compare OPPONENT

**pro·por·tion** /prəˈpɔrʃən/ *n* **1** a part or share of a larger amount or number of something: *The **proportion of** adults who smoke is lower than before.* **2** [C,U] the relationship between the amounts, numbers, or sizes of related things: *Girls outnumber boys at the school by a **proportion of** three to one.*| *Taxes rise **in proportion to** the amount you earn.* **3** [U] the correct relationship between the size or shape of the different parts of something: *The porch is **out of proportion with** the rest of the house.* **4 sense of proportion** the ability to judge what is most important and what is not important in a situation **5 get/blow things out of proportion** to react to a situation as if it is worse or more serious than it really is

**pro·por·tion·al** /prəˈpɔrʃnəl, -ˈpɔrʃənl/, **pro·por·tion·ate** /-ʃənɪt/ *adj* staying in a particular relationship with another thing in size, amount, or importance: *The number of Representatives each state has **is proportional to** its population.* –**proportionally** *adv*

**pro·pos·al** /prəˈpoʊzəl/ *n* **1** [C,U] a plan or idea that is officially suggested for someone to consider, or the act of suggesting this: *a **proposal to** build a new hospital* **2** the act of asking someone to marry you: *Did you accept his proposal?*

**pro·pose** /prəˈpoʊz/ *v* **1** [T] to officially suggest that something be done: *I **propose that** we close the meeting.* **2** [I] to ask someone to marry you: *Has he proposed yet?* **3** [T] FORMAL to intend to do something: *What do you **propose to do** about it?*

**prop·o·si·tion**¹ /ˌprɑpəˈzɪʃən/ *n* **1** a statement in which you express a judgment or opinion: *a nation dedicated to the **proposition that**

*all people are created equal under the law* **2** an offer, plan, or idea, especially in business or politics: *Her latest proposition seemed to be a good investment.*| *Proposition 13 on the ballot*

**prop·o·si·tion**² *v* [T] to suggest to someone that s/he have sex with you, especially in exchange for money

**pro·pri·e·tar·y** /prəˈpraɪəˌtɛri/ *adj* information or products that are proprietary can only be known about or sold by a particular company

**pro·pri·e·tor** /prəˈpraɪətrɪs/ *n* FORMAL an owner of a business

**pro·pri·e·ty** /prəˈpraɪəti/ *n* [singular, U] FORMAL correct social or moral behavior: *We doubt the propriety of her going there alone.*

**pro·pul·sion** /prəˈpʌlʃən/ *n* [U] TECHNICAL the force that moves a vehicle forward, or the system used in order to make this happen: *jet propulsion*

**pro ra·ta** /ˌproʊ ˈreɪtə, -ˈrɑtə/ *adj* TECHNICAL calculated or paid according to exactly how much of something is used or how much work is done

**pro·sa·ic** /proʊˈzeɪ·ɪk/ *adj* FORMAL boring, ordinary, or lacking in imagination: *a prosaic style of writing* –**prosaically** *adv*

**pro·scribe** /proʊˈskraɪb/ *v* [T] FORMAL to officially stop the existence or use of something: *laws to proscribe child labor* –**proscription** /proʊˈskrɪpʃən/ *n* [C,U]

**prose** /proʊz/ *n* [U] written language in its usual form, not as poetry

**pros·e·cute** /ˈprɑsəˌkyut/ *v* [I,T] to say officially that you think someone is guilty of a crime and must be judged by a court of law: *He was prosecuted for theft.*

**pros·e·cu·tion** /ˌprɑsəˈkyuʃən/ *n* **1 the prosecution** the people in a court of law who are trying to prove that someone is guilty of a crime: *a witness for the prosecution* –compare DEFENSE¹ **2** [C,U] the process or act of prosecuting (PROSECUTE) someone

**pros·e·cu·tor** /ˈprɑsəˌkyutɚ/ *n* a lawyer who is trying to prove in a court of law that someone is guilty of a crime

**pros·e·lyt·ize** /ˈprɑsələˌtaɪz/ *v* [I,T] FORMAL to try to persuade someone to join a religious group, political party etc.

**pros·pect**¹ /ˈprɑspɛkt/ *n* **1** [C,U] something that is possible or likely to happen in the future, or the possibility itself: *There's every **prospect of** ending the war soon.*| *a company with good **prospects for** growth*| *Valerie couldn't bear the **prospect of** returning to Miami.* **2 (sb's) prospects** someone's chances of success in the future: *His job prospects are not very good.*

**pros·pect**² *v* [I,T] to look for things such as gold, silver, and oil in the ground or under the ocean: *men **prospecting for** gold* –**prospector** *n*

**pro·spec·tive** /prə'spɛktɪv/ *adj* **1** likely to do a particular thing: *a prospective buyer for the house* **2** likely to happen: *the prospective costs of the deal*

**pro·spec·tus** /prə'spɛktəs/ *n* **1** a small book that gives details about a university, or that advertises a new business **2** an official statement that describes a business opportunity

**pros·per** /'prɑspɚ/ *v* [I] to be successful and become rich: *an environment in which small businesses can prosper*

**pros·per·i·ty** /prɑ'spɛrəti/ *n* [U] the condition of having money and being successful: *a time of economic prosperity*

**pros·per·ous** /'prɑspərəs/ *adj* successful and rich: *a prosperous community*

**pros·the·sis** /prɑs'θisɪs/ *n, plural* **prostheses** /prɑs'θisiz/ TECHNICAL an artificial leg, tooth, arm or other part of the body – **prosthetic** /prɑs'θɛtɪk/ *adj*

**pros·ti·tute**[1] /'prɑstə,tut/ *n* someone who has sex with people to earn money

**prostitute**[2] *v* **1 prostitute yourself** to have sex with someone for money **2** [T] to use your skills and abilities to do something people do not think is valuable, usually in order to earn money: *He's prostituting his acting talent doing TV commercials.*

**pros·ti·tu·tion** /,prɑstə'tuʃən/ *n* [U] the work of PROSTITUTEs

**pros·trate**[1] /'prɑstreɪt/ *adj* **1** FORMAL so shocked or upset that you can no longer do anything: *Mrs. Klinkman was prostrate with grief.* **2** lying flat on the ground with your face down: *His body was found prostrate on the floor.*

**prostrate**[2] *v* [T] **prostrate yourself** to lie flat on the ground with your face down, in order to show praise or respect

**pro·tag·o·nist** /prou'tægənɪst/ *n* FORMAL the main character in a play, movie, or story

**pro·tect** /prə'tɛkt/ *v* [T] to prevent someone or something from being harmed or damaged: *a lotion to protect you from sunburn | a plan to protect the town against another attack* – **protected** *adj*: *a protected species* – **protector** *n*: *a chest protector*

**pro·tec·tion** /prə'tɛkʃən/ *n* **1** [U] the act of protecting, or the state of being protected: *Heidi's thin coat gave little protection against the cold.* **2** [singular] something that protects someone or something: *A car alarm provides/ gives some protection against theft.*

**pro·tec·tive** /prə'tɛktɪv/ *adj* **1** used or intended for protection: *a protective covering for the computer* **2** wanting to protect someone from danger or harm: *She's overly protective of her children.*

**pro·té·gé** /'proutə,ʒeɪ, ,proutə'ʒeɪ/ *n* a young person who is guided and helped by

someone who has power, wealth, or more experience

**pro·tein** /'proutin/ *n* [C,U] one of the many substances in foods such as meat and eggs that helps your body to grow and be healthy

**pro·test**[1] /'proutɛst/ *n* **1** a strong public complaint about something that you disagree with or think is unfair: *Almirez led a protest against the construction of a new shopping mall.* **2 do sth under protest** to do something in a way that shows you do not want to do it, because you think it is wrong or unfair

**pro·test**[2] /'proutɛst, prə'tɛst/ *v* **1** [I,T] to say or do something publicly to show that you disagree with something or think that it is unfair: *a group protesting against human rights abuses | Students carried signs protesting the war.* – compare COMPLAIN **2** [T] to state very strongly that something is true, especially when other people do not believe you: *Throughout the trial, he kept protesting his innocence.* – **protestation** /,prɑtə'steɪʃən, ,prou-/ *n*

**Prot·es·tant** /'prɑtəstənt/ *adj* relating to a part of the Christian church that separated from the Roman Catholic Church in the 16th century – **Protestant** *n* – **Protestantism** *n* [U]

**pro·to·col** /'proutə,kɔl, -,kɑl/ *n* **1** [singular, U] the system of rules for the correct way to behave on official occasions: *Even touching the Queen is a breach of protocol.* (=it is not allowed) **2** an official statement of the rules that a group of countries have agreed to follow in dealing with a particular problem: *the Montreal Protocol on greenhouse gases*

**pro·ton** /'proutɑn/ *n* TECHNICAL a part of an atom that has a positive electrical CHARGE

**pro·to·type** /'proutə,taɪp/ *n* a model of a new car, machine etc., used in order to test the design before it is produced

**pro·tract·ed** /prou'træktɪd, prə-/ *adj* continuing for a long time, usually longer than necessary: *a messy protracted divorce* – **protraction** /prou'trækʃən, prə-/ *n* [U]

**pro·trac·tor** /prou'træktɚ, prə-/ *n* a flat tool shaped like a half circle, used for measuring and drawing angles

**pro·trude** /prou'trud/ *v* [I] FORMAL to stick out from somewhere: *a rock protruding from the water* – **protruding** *adj* – **protrusion** /prou'truʒən/ *n* [C,U]

**proud** /praud/ *adj* **1** feeling pleased with your achievements, family, country etc. because you think they are very good: *We're really proud of you for getting straight A's. | We're proud to announce the birth of our son. | I'm proud (that) the team's done so well.* **2** thinking that you are more important, skillful etc. than you really are: *Raffery had always been a proud man.* **3 do sb proud** to make someone feel proud of you by doing something well: *Congratulations, Natalie - you've sure done us* *proud.* **4** too embarrassed or ashamed to allow other people to help you when you need it: *Terry was too proud to ask his family for money.* –**proudly** *adv* –see also PRIDE¹

**prove** /pruv/ *v* **proved, proved** *or* **proven, proving** [T] **1** to show that something is definitely true: *They have enough evidence to prove that she is guilty.* **2** to show over time that someone or something has a particular quality: *The answering machine has proven to be very useful.* **3 prove yourself** to show how good you are at doing something: *At seventeen years old, she had yet to prove herself on the pro golf tour.* –**provable** *adj*

**prov·en**¹ /'pruvən/ *adj* shown to be real or true: *a proven method of learning*

**proven**² *v* a PAST PARTICIPLE of PROVE

**prov·erb** /'pravɚb/ *n* a short statement that most people know, that contains advice about life

**pro·ver·bi·al** /prə'vɚbiəl/ *adj* known by most people, and usually relating to a PROVERB: *I was running around like the proverbial headless chicken!* –**proverbially** *adv*

**pro·vide** /prə'vaɪd/ *v* [T] **1** to give or supply something to someone: *I work with a service that provides shelter for the homeless.* | *This should provide you with all the details you need.* **2 provide that** FORMAL if a law or rule provides that something must happen, it states that something must happen

**provide for** sb/sth *phr v* [T] **1** to give someone the things s/he needs, such as money, food, or clothing: *Dad always thought a man should provide for his family.* **2** to make plans in order to deal with something that might happen in the future: *The hotel is examining ways to provide for the disabled.*

**pro·vid·ed** /prə'vaɪdɪd/, **provided that** *conjunction* used in order to say that something will only happen if another thing happens first: *Talks will take place in July, provided that enough progress has been made.*

**prov·i·dence** /'pravədəns/ *n* [singular, U] a force that some people believe controls our lives in the way God wants: *an act of divine providence*

**prov·i·den·tial** /ˌpravə'dɛnʃəl/ *adj* FORMAL happening just when you need it; LUCKY: *a providential opportunity*

**pro·vid·er** /prə'vaɪdɚ/ *n* **1** a person or company that provides something such as a service: *a health-care provider* **2** someone who gives his/her family the money, food, clothes etc. that they need

**pro·vid·ing** /prə'vaɪdɪŋ/, **providing that** *conjunction* ⇨ PROVIDED

**prov·ince** /'pravɪns/ *n* **1** one of the large areas into which some countries are divided: *the provinces of Canada* **2 sb's province** FORMAL a subject that someone is responsible for or knows

a lot about: *Sales forecasts are not within my province.*

**pro·vin·cial** /prə'vɪnʃəl/ *adj* **1** unwilling to accept new ideas or to think about things in a new way: *They were narrowly provincial in their outlook.* **2** relating to a PROVINCE: *the provincial government of Quebec*

**pro·vi·sion** /prə'vɪʒən/ *n* **1** [C,U] the act of providing something that someone needs now or will need in the future: *the provision of services for the elderly* | *He has made provisions for his wife in his will.* **2** a condition in an agreement or law: *the provisions of the treaty* –see also PROVISIONS

**pro·vi·sion·al** /prə'vɪʒənl/ *adj* existing for only a short time and likely to be changed in the future: *A provisional government was set up after the revolution.*

**pro·vi·sions** /prə'vɪʒənz/ *n* [plural] food supplies, especially for a trip: *We had enough provisions for two weeks.*

**pro·vi·so** /prə'vaɪzou/ *n* FORMAL a condition that you ask for before you will agree to something: *Tom's grandson inherited his money with the proviso that he go to college.*

**prov·o·ca·tion** /ˌpravə'keɪʃən/ *n* [C,U] an action or event that makes someone angry, or that is intended to do this: *My client was attacked without provocation!*

**pro·voc·a·tive** /prə'vakətɪv/ *adj* **1** intending to make someone angry or cause a lot of discussion: *a provocative new book on the meanings of dreams* **2** intending to make someone sexually excited: *a provocative dress*

**pro·voke** /prə'vouk/ *v* [T] **1** to make someone very angry, especially by annoying him/her: *She did hit him, but he provoked her into doing it.* **2** to cause a sudden reaction or feeling: *Miller scored a touchdown, provoking cheers from the crowd.*

**pro·vost** /'prouvoust/ *n* an important official at a university, one rank below its president

**prow** /prau/ *n* the front part of a ship or boat

**prow·ess** /'prauɪs/ *n* [U] FORMAL strength and skill at doing something: *a man of great athletic prowess*

**prowl**¹ /praul/ *v* [I,T] to move around an area quietly, trying not to be seen or heard: *a tiger prowling through the jungle*

**prowl**² *n* **be on the prowl** to be moving quietly, hunting for an animal or person to attack

**prowl·er** /'praulɚ/ *n* someone who moves around quietly at night, especially near your house, in order to steal something or harm you

**prox·im·i·ty** /prak'sɪməti/ *n* [U] FORMAL nearness in distance or time: *We chose this house because of its proximity to the school.*

**prox·y** /'praksi/ *n* **1** someone whom you choose to represent you, especially to vote instead of you at an election **2 (do sth) by**

**proxy** to do something by arranging for someone else to do it for you

**prude** /prud/ *n* DISAPPROVING someone who is very easily shocked by anything relating to sex −**prudish** *adj*

**pru·dent** /'prudnt/ *adj* sensible and careful, especially by avoiding risks that are not necessary: *It would not be prudent to spend so much money now.* −**prudence** *n* [U]

**prune**¹ /prun/, **prune back** *v* [T] to cut off some of the branches of a tree or bush to make it grow better

**prune**² *n* a dried PLUM

**pru·ri·ent** /'pruriənt/ *adj* showing too much interest in sex −**prurience** *n* [U]

**pry** /praɪ/ *v* **pried, pried, prying** **1** [T] to force something open, or to force it away from something else: *They finally pried the window open.\ I had to use a screwdriver to pry the lid off the paint can.* **2** [I] to try to find out details about someone's private life in an impolite way: *I didn't mean to pry into your personal life.*

**P.S.** *n* the abbreviation of POSTSCRIPT; a note that you add to the end of a letter, that gives more information

**psalm** /sɑm/ *n* a song or poem praising God

**pseu·do·nym** /'sudn,ɪm, 'sudə,nɪm/ *n* a false name used by someone, especially a writer, instead of his/her real name

**psych** /saɪk/ *v*
  **psych sb** ↔ **out** *phr v* [T] INFORMAL to do or say things that will make your opponent feel nervous or confused: *Ignore him - he's just trying to psych you out.*
  **psych sb/yourself up** *phr v* [T] INFORMAL to prepare someone mentally before doing something so s/he feels confident: *soldiers trying to psych themselves up for combat*

**psy·che** /'saɪki/ *n* TECHNICAL someone's mind or basic nature that controls how s/he thinks or behaves

**psyched** /saɪkt/, **psyched up** *adj* SPOKEN be **psyched (up)** to be mentally prepared for and excited about an event, activity etc.: *Bryony's totally psyched about/for her date.*

**psy·che·del·ic** /,saɪkə'dɛlɪk/ *adj* **1** psychedelic drugs such as LSD make you see things that do not really exist **2** psychedelic art, clothing etc. has a lot of bright colors and patterns

**psy·chi·a·trist** /saɪ'kaɪətrɪst, sə-/ *n* a doctor who studies and treats mental illness −compare PSYCHOLOGIST

**psy·chi·a·try** /saɪ'kaɪətri, sə-/ *n* [U] the study and treatment of mental illness −**psychiatric** /,saɪki'ætrɪk/ *adj*: *a psychiatric hospital*

**psy·chic**¹ /'saɪkɪk/ *adj* **1** relating to strange events involving the power of the human mind: *a mysterious psychic phenomenon* **2** affecting the mind rather than the body: *a psychic disorder*

**psychic**² *n* someone who has strange powers such as the ability to know what will happen in the future

**psy·cho** /'saɪkoʊ/ *n* SLANG someone who is likely to behave in a violent or crazy way

**psy·cho·anal·y·sis** /,saɪkoʊə'næləsɪs/ *n* [U] a way of treating someone who is mentally ill by talking to him/her about his/her past life, feelings etc. to find out the cause of the illness −**psychoanalyze** /,saɪkoʊ'ænl,aɪz/ *v* [T]

**psy·cho·an·a·lyst** /,saɪkoʊ'ænl-ɪst/ *n* someone who treats people using PSYCHOANALYSIS

**psy·cho·log·i·cal** /,saɪkə'lɑdʒɪkəl/ *adj* **1** relating to the way people's minds work and the way this affects their behavior: *Loss of memory is often a psychological problem that can be treated.* **2** relating to PSYCHOLOGY: *a psychological test* −**psychologically** *adv*

**psy·chol·o·gist** /saɪ'kɑlədʒɪst/ *n* someone who is trained in PSYCHOLOGY −compare PSYCHIATRIST

**psy·chol·o·gy** /saɪ'kɑlədʒi/ *n* **1** [U] the scientific study of the mind and how it works, and how mental problems can be treated: *a professor of psychology* **2** [C,U] the usual way that a particular person or group thinks and reacts: *a study into the psychology of soldiers in the field*

**psy·cho·path** /'saɪkə,pæθ/ *n* someone who has a mental illness that makes him/her behave in a violent or criminal way −**psychopathic** /,saɪkə'pæθɪk/ *adj*

**psy·cho·sis** /saɪ'koʊsɪs/ *n*, *plural* **psychoses** /saɪ'koʊsiz/ [C,U] TECHNICAL a serious mental illness that may cause changes in someone's behavior

**psy·cho·so·mat·ic** /,saɪkoʊsə'mætɪk/ *adj* TECHNICAL a psychosomatic illness is caused by fear or anxiety rather than by any physical problem

**psy·cho·ther·a·py** /,saɪkoʊ'θɛrəpi/ *n* [U] the treatment of mental illness by using PSYCHOLOGY rather than drugs or medicine −**psychotherapist** *n*

**psy·chot·ic** /saɪ'kɑtɪk/ *adj* TECHNICAL relating to mental illness, or resulting from it: *psychotic behavior* −**psychotic** *n*

**pt.** the written abbreviation of PART and PINT

**PTA** *n* Parent-Teacher Association; an organization of teachers and parents that works to improve a particular school

**pub** /pʌb/ *n* a comfortable BAR that often serves food

**pu·ber·ty** /'pyubɚti/ *n* [U] the stage of physical development when you change from a child to an adult who is able to have children: *Our daughter is just reaching puberty.* (=starting to develop physically)

**pu·bes·cent** /pyu'bɛsənt/ *adj* a pubescent boy or girl is going through PUBERTY

**pu·bic** /'pyubɪk/ *adj* relating to or near the sex organs: *pubic hair*

**pub·lic**[1] /'pʌblɪk/ *adj* **1** relating to all the ordinary people in a country or city: *We acted out of concern for public welfare.* **2** available for anyone to use: *a public swimming pool* | *public transportation* **3** relating to the government and the services that it provides: *It has been eight years since she was elected to* **public office.** (=a job in the government) | *the public library system* **4** known about by most people: *Last night the name of the killer was* **made public.** | *a* **public figure** (=well-known person) **5** intended for anyone to know, see, or hear: *I think* **public displays** *of emotion are embarrassing!* **6 go public a)** to tell everyone about something that was secret: *They finally went public with news of their engagement.* **b)** to begin to sell SHAREs in your company –opposite PRIVATE[1] –see also PUB-LICLY

**public**[2] *n* **1 the public** all the ordinary people in a country or city: *The museum is* **open to the public** *five days a week.* | *This product is not for sale to the* **general public.** **2 in public** in a place where anyone can know, see, or hear: *He was always very nice to her in public.* **3** [singular, U] the people who like to listen to a particular singer, read a particular writer etc.: *A star has to try to please her public.*

**public ac·cess** /,.. '../ *n* [U] a situation in which anyone can enter a place or use a service: *a public access TV channel* (=one that will allow anyone to make a program)

**public ad·dress sys·tem** /,.. .'. ,../ *n* ⇒ PA[2]

**public as·sist·ance** /,.. .'../ *n* [U] the government programs that help poor people get food, homes, and medical care –compare WELFARE

**pub·li·ca·tion** /,pʌblə'keɪʃən/ *n* **1** [U] the process of printing a book, magazine etc. and offering it for sale to the public: *There may be a delay of up to eight weeks before publication.* **2** a book, magazine etc.: *a monthly publication for stamp collectors* **3** [U] the act of making something known to the public: *The authorities tried to stop the publication of the test results.*

**public de·fen·der** /,.. .'../ *n* a lawyer who is paid by the government to defend people who cannot pay for a lawyer themselves

**public hous·ing** /,.. '../ *n* [U] houses or apartments built by the government for poor people

**pub·li·cist** /'pʌbləsɪst/ *n* someone whose job is to make sure that famous people or new products, movies, books etc. get a lot of PUBLICITY

**pub·lic·i·ty** /pə'blɪsəti/ *n* [U] **1** attention that someone or something gets from newspapers, television etc.: *a murder trial that received a lot of* **publicity** **2** the business of making sure that people know about what a famous person is doing, or about a new product, movie, book etc. –**publicize** /'pʌblə,saɪz/ *v* [T]

**pub·lic·ly** /'pʌblɪkli/ *adv* **1** in way that is intended for anyone to know, see, or hear: *I don't like to talk publicly about what I say to players privately.* | *Lozansky was jailed for publicly criticizing the government.* **2** by the government, as part of its services: *The hospitals are publicly operated in cities, suburbs, and rural areas.* **3** a company that is publicly owned has sold SHAREs in it to the public **4** among the ordinary people in a country or city: *the publicly unpopular Vietnam war*

**public re·la·tions** /,.. .'../, PR *n* **1** [plural] the relationship between an organization and the public: *Organizing events for charity is always good for public relations.* **2** [U] the work of explaining what a company does so the public will approve of it: *the public relations department*

**public school** /'.. ,./ *n* a free local school that is controlled and paid for by the government

**public tel·e·vi·sion** /,.. '..../ *n* [U] a television program or service that is paid for by the government, large companies, and the public

**pub·lish** /'pʌblɪʃ/ *v* **1** [I,T] to arrange for a book, magazine etc. to be written, printed, and sold: *a book that was first published in 1851* **2** [T] if a newspaper, magazine etc. publishes something such as a letter, it prints it for people to read: *The article was published in the Los Angeles Times.* **3** [T] to make official information available for everyone to use: *New guidelines for social studies education were published this year.* –**publishing** *n* [U]

**pub·lish·er** /'pʌblɪʃɚ/ *n* a person or company that arranges the writing, printing, and sale of books, newspapers etc. –**publishing** *n* [U]: *I work in publishing.*

**puck** /pʌk/ *n* a hard flat circular piece of rubber that you hit with a stick in the game of HOCKEY

**puck·er** /'pʌkɚ/ **pucker up** *v* **1** [I,T] INFORMAL if your mouth puckers or you pucker it, your lips are pulled together tightly: *She puckered up, ready for his kiss.* **2** [I] if cloth puckers, it gets folds in it so that it is no longer flat –**puckered** *adj* –**pucker** *n*

**pud·ding** /'pʊdɪŋ/ *n* [C,U] a thick sweet creamy food made with milk, eggs, sugar, and flour, that is eaten cold: *chocolate pudding*

**pud·dle** /'pʌdl/ *n* a small pool of water on a road, path etc., often caused by rain: *children splashing in the puddles*

**pudg·y** /'pʌdʒi/ *adj* fatter than usual: *short pudgy fingers* –**pudginess** *n* [U]

**pu·er·ile** /'pyʊrəl, -raɪl/ *adj* FORMAL silly and stupid; CHILDISH: *puerile humor*

**puff**[1] /pʌf/ *v* **1** [I] to breathe quickly and with difficulty as the result of a physical effort: *Max was puffing heavily after climbing the stairs.* **2** [I,T] to breathe smoke from a cigarette, pipe etc. in and out: *William sat there* **puffing on** *his*

P

*pipe.* **3** [I,T] to blow steam or smoke out of something: *an old car puffing fumes*

**puff** sth ↔ **out** *phr v* [T] to make something bigger by filling it with air: *a frog with its throat puffed out*

**puff up** *phr v* **1** [I,T also **puff** sth ↔ **up**] to become bigger by filling with air, or to make something do this: *Birds puff up their feathers to stay warm.* **2** [I] if your eye, face etc. puffs up, it swells: *My eye puffed up where he hit me.*

**puff²** *n* **1** the action of breathing smoke into your mouth and blowing it out again: *He took a puff on his cigar.* **2** a sudden short movement of air, smoke, or wind: *puffs of smoke coming from the chimney* **3** a word used for various things that are light or seem full of air: *a cream puff* (=light PASTRY)|*a powder puff* (=for putting powder on your body)

**puf·fin** /'pʌfɪn/ *n* a North Atlantic bird with a black and white body and a large, brightly colored beak

**puff·y** /'pʌfi/ *adj* puffy eyes, cheeks, faces etc. are swollen: *Her eyes were red and puffy from crying.* –**puffiness** *n* [U]

**pug·na·cious** /pʌg'neɪʃəs/ *adj* FORMAL very eager to quarrel or fight with people

**puke** /pyuk/ *v* [I,T] SLANG ⇨ VOMIT¹ –**puke** *n* [U]

**pull¹** /pʊl/ *v*

**1** ▶MOVE TOWARD YOU◀ [I,T] to use your hands to move something toward you: *Mom, Sara's pulling my hair!*|*Wilson quickly pulled the door open.*|*Help me pull the trunk into the corner.* –opposite PUSH¹ –see picture on page 473

**2** ▶REMOVE◀ [T] to remove something from its place, especially by using force: *She has to have her wisdom teeth pulled.*|*The baby's pulled everything out of the cupboards.*|*Some guy pulled a gun on one of the bank tellers.* (=he took out a gun and pointed it at someone)

**3** ▶MAKE STH FOLLOW YOU◀ [I,T] to use a rope, chain etc. to make something move behind you in the direction you are moving: *a car pulling a camper behind it* –opposite PUSH¹

**4** ▶MUSCLE◀ [T] to injure a muscle by stretching it too much while exercising: *I pulled a muscle in my thigh playing volleyball.*

**5 pull sb's leg** INFORMAL to tell someone something that is not true, as a joke: *He never said that! You're pulling my leg!*

**6 pull strings** to use a special position or relationship that you have in order to get something: *Samuels pulled strings to get her daughter a job in Mitchell's office.*

**7** ▶MOVE YOUR BODY◀ [I,T] to use force to move your body somewhere: *She pulled away from him in horror.*|*The kids pulled themselves up onto the platform.*

**8 pull the strings** to control something, especially when you are not the person who is supposed to be controlling it: *Who is really pull-ing the strings in the White House?*

**9 pull your weight** to do your share of the work: *If you don't start pulling your weight around here, you'll be fired!*

**10 pull a stunt/trick/joke/prank** INFORMAL to do something that annoys or harms other people: *kids pulling practical jokes*

**11** ▶CLOTHING◀ [I,T] if you pull a piece of clothing on or off, you put it on or take it off quickly

**12 pull the rug out from under sb** to suddenly take away something that someone was depending on to achieve what s/he wanted

**13 pull a fast one** SPOKEN to deceive someone: *Are you trying to pull a fast one on me?*

**pull** sth ↔ **apart** *phr v* [T] to separate something into two or more pieces or groups: *Loosen the roots and gently pull the plants apart.*|*the ethnic problems that pulled Yugoslavia apart*

**pull away** *phr v* [I] **1** to move ahead of a competitor by going faster or being more successful: *Chicago pulled away in the third quarter to win, 107-76.* **2** to start to drive away from the place your car was stopped: *Grant pulled away from the curb.*

**pull** sth ↔ **down** *phr v* [T] to destroy something or make it no longer exist: *Citizens of Berlin pulled down the wall dividing their city.*

**pull for** sb *phr v* [T] INFORMAL to encourage a person or team to succeed: *Good luck, Joey, we're pulling for you.*

**pull in** *phr v* **1** [I,T **pull** sth ↔ **in**] to move a car into a particular space and stop it: *Kevin pulled in behind me and parked.* **2** [T **pull in** sth] INFORMAL to get money, business etc., by doing something to attract people's attention: *Hall pulled in 58% of the vote.*

**pull off** *phr v* **1** [T **pull** sth ↔ **off**] INFORMAL to succeed in doing something difficult: *The Huskies pulled off a win in Saturday's game against WSU.* **2** [T **pull off** sth] to leave a road in order to stop or to turn into another road: *I had to pull off the road, I was laughing so hard.*

**pull out** *phr v* **1** [I] to drive a car onto a road from where you have stopped **2** [I,T **pull** sb/ sth ↔ **out**] to get yourself or someone else out of a bad or dangerous situation: *Investors can pull out at any time by selling their shares.* **3 pull out all the stops** to do everything you can in order to make something succeed: *Fred's pulling out all the stops for his daughter's wedding.*

**pull over** *phr v* [I,T **pull** sb/sth ↔ **over**] to drive to the side of a road and stop your car, or to make someone do this: *We didn't realize we were speeding until the highway patrol pulled us over.*

**pull through** *phr v* [I,T **pull** sb **through**] INFORMAL **1** to stay alive after a serious injury or illness, or to help someone do this: *We all prayed that he would pull through.* **2** to continue to live or exist after being in a difficult or upsetting situation: *The city managed to* **pull through** *its financial crisis.*

**pull together** *phr v* **1** [I] to work hard with other people to achieve something: *After the hurricane, neighbors* **pulled together** *to help each other.* **2 pull yourself together** INFORMAL to force yourself to stop being nervous, afraid, or disorganized: *It's time you* **pulled yourself together** *and got a job.*

**pull up** *phr v* **1** [I] to stop the car you are driving: *A red Buick* **pulled up** *at the stop lights.* **2 pull up a chair** to get a chair and sit down near someone **3** [T **pull** sth ↔ **up**] to use force to take plants out of the ground

**pull**[2] *n* **1** an act of using force to move something toward you or in the same direction as you are going: *Give the rope a strong pull.* **2** [C usually singular] a strong force such as GRAVITY that makes things move in a particular direction: *the gravitational pull of the moon* **3** [singular, U] INFORMAL power that gives you an unfair advantage: *a family with a lot of political pull*

**pul·ley** /'pʊli/ *n* a piece of equipment consisting of a wheel over which you pull a chain or rope to lift heavy things

**pull·out** /'pʊlaʊt/ *n* **1** the act of an army, business etc. leaving a particular place: *the pullout of NATO troops from the region* **2** part of a book or magazine that can be removed

**pull·o·ver** /'pʊl,oʊvɚ/ *n* a SWEATER without buttons

**pull-up** /'. ./ *n* an exercise in which you use your arms to pull yourself up to a metal BAR that is above your head

**pul·mo·nar·y** /'pʊlmə,nɛri, 'pʌl-/ *adj* TECHNICAL relating to or affecting the lungs: *pulmonary disease*

**pulp**[1] /pʌlp/ *n* [U] **1** the soft inside part of a fruit or vegetable **2** a very soft substance that is almost liquid: *wood pulp* **3 beat sb to a pulp** INFORMAL to hit someone again and again until s/he is seriously injured

**pulp**[2] *adj* pulp books, magazines etc. are usually of poor quality and tell stories about sex and violence: *pulp novels*

**pulp**[3] *v* [T] to beat or crush something until it becomes soft and like a liquid

**pul·pit** /'pʊlpɪt, 'pʌl-/ *n* a structure like a tall box at the front of a church, from which someone speaks

**pul·sate** /'pʌlseɪt/ *v* [I] to make sounds or movements that are strong and regular like a heart beating: *loud pulsating music* **–pulsation** /pʌl'seɪʃən/ *n* [C,U]

**pulse**[1] /pʌls/ *n* **1** [C usually singular] the regular beat that can be felt as your heart pumps blood around your body: *When I found him he didn't have a pulse.* **2** [C usually singular] also **pulse rate** the number of regular beats per minute as your heart pumps blood around your

body: *A nurse came in and* **took my pulse**. (=counted the number of beats) **3** [C usually plural] a seed such as beans and PEAs that can be eaten **4** an amount of light, sound, or energy that continues for a very short time: *an electric pulse*

**pulse**[2] *v* [I] to move or flow with a steady rapid beat or sound: *blood* **pulsing through** *the veins*

**pul·ver·ize** /'pʌlvə,raɪz/ *v* [T] **1** to crush something into powder: *a machine that pulverizes rocks* **2** INFORMAL to defeat someone completely, especially in a sport or game **–pulverization** /,pʌlvərə'zeɪʃən/ *n* [U]

**pu·ma** /'pumə, 'pyumə/ *n* ⇨ COUGAR

**pum·ice** /'pʌmɪs/ *n* [C,U] very light rock from a VOLCANO, or a piece of this that you rub on your skin to make it soft

**pum·mel** /'pʌməl/ *v* [T] to hit someone or something many times with your FISTs

**pump**[1] /pʌmp/ *n* **1** a machine that forces liquid or gas into or out of something: *a water/air/gas pump* **2** a woman's shoe that is plain and does not fasten: *a pair of black pumps* –see picture at SHOE[1]

**pump**[2] *v* **1** [T] to make liquid or gas move in a particular direction using a pump: *a machine that* **pumps** *water* **into** *the fields* **2** [I] to move liquid very quickly in and out or up and down: *His heart was pumping fast.* **3 pump sb (about sth)** INFORMAL to ask someone a lot of questions about something in order to find out information **4 pump money into sth** INFORMAL to spend a lot of money on something such as a project **5 pump iron** INFORMAL to lift heavy weights regularly in order to get bigger and stronger muscles

**pump out** *phr v* **1** [I,T **pump** sth ↔ **out**] to produce or supply something in large amounts: *Loud music was* **pumping out** *of the speakers.* **2** [T **pump** sth ↔ **out**] to remove liquid from something using a pump: *We had to* **pump** *the basement out after the pipes burst.*

**pump up** *phr v* [T] **1** [**pump** sb ↔ **up**] to increase someone's interest or excitement about something: *cheerleaders* **pumping up** *a crowd* **2** [**pump** sth ↔ **up**] to fill something such as a tire with air; INFLATE

**pum·per·nick·el** /'pʌmpɚ,nɪkəl/ *n* [U] a heavy dark brown bread

**pump·kin** /'pʌmpkɪn, 'pʌŋkɪn/ *n* [C,U] a very large orange fruit that grows on the ground, or the inside of this eaten as food: *pumpkin pie* –see picture on page 470

**pun** /pʌn/ *n* an amusing use of a word or phrase that has two meanings, or of words with the same sound but different meanings. For example: *Seven days without water makes one weak.* (=week) **–pun** *v* [I]

**punch**[1] /pʌntʃ/ *v* [T] **1** to hit someone or something hard with your FIST (=closed hand): *Zach punched his brother right in the face.*

**2** to make a hole in something using a metal tool or other sharp object: *The conductor came along and punched our tickets.* **3 punch a clock** to record the time that you start or finish work by putting a card into a special machine

**punch in** *phr v* [I] to record the time that you arrive at work by putting a card into a special machine

**punch out** *phr v* [I] to record the time that you leave work by putting a card into a special machine

**punch²** *n* **1** a quick strong hit made with your FIST (=closed hand): *a punch in the stomach* **2** [U] a drink made from fruit juice, sugar, water, and sometimes alcohol **3** a metal tool for cutting holes or for pushing something into a small hole: *a three-hole punch* **4** [U] a strong effective quality that makes people interested: *We need something to give the ad campaign some punch.*

**punch·ing bag** /'.. ,./ *n* **1** a heavy leather bag that hangs from a rope, that is hit for exercise **2 use sb as a punching bag** INFORMAL to hit someone hard, or to criticize someone a lot

**punch line** /'. ./ *n* the last few words of a joke or story, that make it funny or surprising

**punc·tu·al** /'pʌŋktʃuəl/ *adj* arriving, happening etc. at exactly the time that has been arranged: *They're always punctual for appointments.* —**punctuality** /ˌpʌŋktʃu'æləti/ *n* [U]

**punc·tu·ate** /'pʌŋktʃu,eɪt/ *v* [T] **1** to divide written work into sentences, phrases etc. using COMMAS, PERIODS etc. **2 be punctuated by/with sth** to be interrupted many times by a noise: *A conversation with the Morgans is punctuated with brotherly insults and jokes.*

**punc·tu·a·tion** /ˌpʌŋktʃu'eɪʃən/ *n* [U] the way that PUNCTUATION MARKS are used in a piece of writing

**punctuation mark** /..'.. ,./ *n* a sign, such as a COMMA or QUESTION MARK, that is used in dividing a piece of writing into sentences, phrases etc.

**punc·ture¹** /'pʌŋktʃɚ/ *n* a small hole made when something is PUNCTUREd

**puncture²** *v* [I,T] to make or get a small hole in something, so that air or liquid can get out: *Jay's in the hospital with a punctured lung.*

**pun·dit** /'pʌndɪt/ *n* someone who knows a lot about a particular subject, and is often asked for his/her opinion: *political pundits*

**pun·gent** /'pʌndʒənt/ *adj* having a strong smell or taste: *the pungent smell of onions*

**pun·ish** /'pʌnɪʃ/ *v* [T] to make someone suffer because s/he has done something wrong or broken the law: *Danny was punished for breaking a window.*

**pun·ish·a·ble** /'pʌnɪʃəbəl/ *adj* deserving legal punishment: *Murder is punishable by life imprisonment.*

**pun·ish·ing** /'pʌnɪʃɪŋ/ *adj* making you feel very tired and weak: *a punishing walk*

**pun·ish·ment** /'pʌnɪʃmənt/ *n* **1** a way in which a person or an action is punished: *There are harsh/severe punishments for drug dealing.* ✗ DON'T SAY "strict/strong punishments." ✗ **2** [U] the act of punishing someone, or the process of being punished: *We are determined that the terrorists will not escape punishment.* | *As punishment, Marshall had to stay after school.* —see also CAPITAL PUNISHMENT

**pu·ni·tive** /'pyunəṭɪv/ *adj* intended as punishment: *The government's first punitive action/measure was to take away the organization's federal funding.* | *punitive damages* (=money that is paid as a punishment)

**punk** /pʌŋk/ *n* [U] **1** also **punk rock** /ˌ. './ a type of loud violent music popular in the late 1970s and 1980s, played by people with brightly colored hair, who wore chains, pins, and torn clothing **2** INFORMAL a boy or young man who likes to start fights, do things that are illegal, etc.

**punt** /pʌnt/ *n* in football, a long kick that you make after dropping the ball from your hands —**punt** *v* [I,T]

**pu·ny** /'pyuni/ *adj* small, thin, and weak: *a puny little kid*

**pup** /pʌp/ *n* **1** ⇨ PUPPY **2** a young SEAL or OTTER

**pu·pil** /'pyupəl/ *n* **1** a child or young person in school **2** the small black round area in the middle of your eye —see picture at EYE¹

**pup·pet** /'pʌpɪt/ *n* **1** a model of a person or animal that you can move by pulling strings that are attached to parts of its body, or by putting your hand inside it: *a puppet show* **2** a person or organization that is no longer independent, and is controlled by someone else: *a puppet government*

**pup·pet·eer** /ˌpʌpɪ'tɪr/ *n* someone who performs with PUPPETS

**pup·py** /'pʌpi/ *n* a young dog

**puppy love** /'.. ,./ *n* [U] a young boy's or girl's love for someone, that people do not think of as serious

**pur·chase¹** /'pɚtʃəs/ *v* [T] to buy something: *The insurance company will try to convince customers to purchase the full range of insurance.* | *Maybe the best gift is one that has not been purchased.*

**purchase²** *n* **1** [C,U] the act of buying something: *The two women had just made several large purchases.* **2** something that has been bought: *The store will deliver your purchases.*

**pure** /pyʊr/ *adj* **1** not mixed with anything else: *pure gold* **2** complete: *It was pure chance that we were there at the same time.* ✗ DON'T SAY "the chance was pure." ✗ **3** clean, without anything harmful or unhealthy: *pure drinking water* **4 pure science/math etc.** work done in order to increase our knowledge of something rather than to make practical use of it: *pure research* –compare APPLIED **5** LITERARY having the quality of being completely good or moral

**pu·ree** /pyʊˈreɪ/ *n* [C,U] food that is boiled or crushed until it is almost a liquid: *tomato puree* –**puree** *v* [T]

**pure·ly** /ˈpyʊrli/ *adv* completely and only: *He did it for purely selfish reasons.* | *We met purely by chance.*

**pur·ga·to·ry** /ˈpɚɡəˌtɔri/ *n* [U] a place where, according to Roman Catholic beliefs, the souls of dead people must suffer for the bad things they have done, until they are good enough to enter heaven

**purge** /pɚdʒ/ *v* [T] **1** to force your opponents to leave an organization or place, often by using violence: *The army was purged of anyone the government considered dangerous.* **2** TECHNICAL to get rid of something bad that is in your body, or of bad feelings –**purge** *n*

**pu·ri·fy** /ˈpyʊrəˌfaɪ/ *v* [T] to remove the dirty or unwanted parts from something: *The water should be purified before drinking.* –**purification** /ˌpyʊrəfəˈkeɪʃən/ *n* [U]

**pur·ist** /ˈpyʊrɪst/ *n* someone who has very strict ideas about what is right or correct in a particular subject

**Pur·i·tan** /ˈpyʊrətən, -rətⁿn/ *n* a member of a Protestant religious group in the 16th and 17th centuries, who wanted to make religion simpler

**pu·ri·tan·i·cal** /ˌpyʊrəˈtænɪkəl/ *adj* having strict attitudes about religion and moral behavior: *puritanical parents who won't let their children go to dances*

**pu·ri·ty** /ˈpyʊrəti/ *n* [U] the quality or state of being pure: *The purity of the sound/colors was incredible.* | *religious purity*

**pur·ple** /ˈpɚpəl/ *n* [U] a dark color made from red mixed with blue –**purple** *adj*

**pur·port** /pɚˈpɔrt/ *v* **1 purport to be** FORMAL to claim to be someone or to do something, especially when it is possible that the claim is not true: *He purports to be the son of the wealthy Italian banker.* **2 be purported to be** to claim that something is true, especially when it is possible that it is not true: *The painting is purported to be the work of Monet.* –**purport** /ˈpɚpɔrt/ *n*

**pur·pose** /ˈpɚpəs/ *n* **1** the aim that an event, process, or activity is supposed to achieve: *The purpose of this exercise is to increase your strength.* | *The Red Cross sent supplies for medical purposes.* | *For the purposes of the report, low income was defined as $30,000 a year for a family of four.* **2 on purpose** deliberately: *Firefighters believe the fire was started on purpose.* **3** [U] determination to succeed in what you want to do: *She came back from vacation with a new sense of purpose.*

**pur·pose·ful** /ˈpɚpəsfəl/ *adj* having a clear aim or purpose; determined: *a purposeful ambitious young woman*

**pur·pose·ly** /ˈpɚpəsli/ *adv* deliberately: *They purposely left him out of the discussion.*

**purr** /pɚ/ *v* [I] **1** if a cat purrs, it makes a soft low sound in its throat **2** if an engine purrs, it works perfectly and makes a quiet smooth sound –**purr** *n*

**purse¹** /pɚs/ *n* **1** a bag used by women to carry money and personal things. *I think my glasses are still in my purse.* **2 control/hold the purse strings** to control the money in a family, company etc.

**purse²** *v* [T] **purse your lips** to bring your lips together tightly in a circle, especially to show disapproval

**purs·er** /ˈpɚsɚ/ *n* an officer who is responsible for the money on a ship and is in charge of the passengers' rooms, comfort etc.

**pur·sue** /pɚˈsu/ *v* [T] FORMAL **1** to continue doing an activity or trying to achieve something over a long time: *Thomas is pursuing a doctorate in biology.* **2** to chase or follow someone or something in order to catch him, her, or it: *The police are pursuing the suspect along Nordhoff Blvd.* **3 pursue the matter/question** to continue trying to persuade someone, ask, or find out about a particular subject: *The company plans to pursue the matter in court.*

**pur·suit** /pɚˈsut/ *n* **1** [U] the act of chasing or following someone: *police cars in hot pursuit of the robbers* (=following close behind them) **2** FORMAL the act of trying to achieve something in a determined way: *the right to life, liberty, and the pursuit of happiness* **3** FORMAL an activity that you spend a lot of time doing: *Nancy enjoys outdoor pursuits.*

**pur·vey·or** /pɚˈveɪɚ/ *n* FORMAL someone who supplies information, goods, or services to people as a business: *purveyors of fine cheeses* –**purvey** *v* [T]

**pus** /pʌs/ *n* [U] a thick yellowish liquid produced in an infected part of your body

**push¹** /pʊʃ/ *v*
**1** ▶MOVE◀ [I,T] to move a person or thing away from you by pressing with your hands: *A couple of guys were pushing an old Volkswagen down the street.* | *Lisa pushed Amy into the pool.* | *Can you push harder? It's not moving.* –opposite PULL¹ –see picture on page 473
**2** ▶MAKE STH START/STOP◀ [I,T] to press a button, SWITCH etc. to make a machine start or stop working: *Just push the off button.*
**3** ▶TRY TO GET PAST SB◀ [I,T] to move somewhere by pushing people away from you: *Heather pushed past us without speaking.* | *people trying to push their way to the front*
**4** ▶PERSUADE◀ [I,T] to try to persuade someone to accept or do something: *The agency is*

*pushing to increase US exports.* | *citizens* **push- ing for** *stricter gun controls* | *My parents* **pushed** *me* **into** *going to college.*

**5 ►WORK HARD◄** [T] to make someone work very hard: *Royce has been* **pushing** *himself too much lately.*

**6 ►INCREASE/DECREASE◄** [I,T] to increase or decrease an amount, number, or value: *New medical technology has* **pushed** *the cost of health care* **up/higher.** | *The recession has* **pushed** *stock market prices* **down/lower.**

**7 ►DRUGS◄** [T] INFORMAL to sell illegal drugs

**8 push your luck/push it** INFORMAL to do some- thing or ask for something again, when this is likely to annoy someone or be risky: *Don't push it! I'll tell you when I'm ready.*

**push ahead** *phr v* [I] to continue with a plan or activity in a determined way: *The airport is* **pushing ahead** *with its program to expand.*

**push around** *phr v* [T **push** sb ↔ **around**] INFORMAL to tell someone who is less important or weaker than you what to do in a rude or threatening way: *Don't let your boss* **push** *you* **around.** | *A bunch of boys were* **pushing** *one of the younger kids* **around.**

**push on** *phr v* [I] to continue traveling some- where or trying to achieve something: *The others stopped for a rest, but I* **pushed on** *to the top.*

**push** sth ↔ **through** *phr v* [T] to persuade someone to accept a law, policy, plan etc., even though there is opposition to it: *Wilson* **pushed through** *a measure to increase the state sales tax.*

**push²** *n* [C usually singular] **1** the act of push- ing someone or something: *Just* **give** *the door a* **push** *if it's stuck.* **2** an attempt to get or achieve something: *Eastern Europe's* **push** *to modernize their economies* **3 if/when push comes to shove** when or if a situation becomes extremely difficult: *If push comes to shove, I can always rent out the house.* **4** an attack in which an army goes into a particular area: *the army's push into enemy territory*

**push·er** /ˈpʊʃɚ/ *n* INFORMAL someone who sells illegal drugs

**push·o·ver** /ˈpʌʃˌoʊvɚ/ *n* INFORMAL **be a pushover** to be easy to persuade, influence, or defeat

**push-up** /ˈ. ./ *n* an exercise in which you lie on the floor on your front and push yourself up with your arms

**push·y** /ˈpʊʃi/ *adj* so determined to succeed and get what you want that you behave in a rude way: *pushy salespeople*

**puss·y·cat** /ˈpʊsiˌkæt/ *n* INFORMAL **1** also **puss** a word meaning a cat, used when talking to children **2** INFORMAL someone who is kind and gentle

**puss·y·foot** /ˈpʊsiˌfʊt/ *v* [I] INFORMAL to be too careful and afraid to do something: *Stop pussy- footing around and decide!*

**puss·y wil·low** /ˌpʊsi ˈwɪloʊ/ *n* a tree with long thin branches and soft round flowers that look like fur

**put** /pʊt/ *v* **put, put, putting** [T]

Bill put on his jacket.

**1 ►MOVE TO PLACE/ POSITION◄** to move some- one or something into a particular place or position: *Where did you put the newspaper?* | *Put every- thing in the dishwasher and start it, okay?* | *I put some money into our account.* | *It's time to* **put** *the kids* **to bed.** (=make them go into their beds) –see also picture on page 473

**2 ►CHANGE◄** to change someone's situation or the way s/he feels: *The recent layoffs put 250 people out of work.* | *Ohio State's win put them in the playoffs.* | *music to put you in a relaxed mood*

**3 ►WRITE◄** to write or print something in a particular place: *Put your name at the top of your answer sheet.* | *We put an ad in the paper.*

**4 put emphasis/pressure/blame etc. on** to emphasize something, make someone feel pressure, blame someone etc.: *People are start- ing to put pressure on Congress to pass gun control laws.*

**5 put an end/stop to sth** to stop something such as an activity that is harmful or not accept- able: *The pollution is caused by too many people driving to work; the city wants to put a stop to this practice.*

**6 ►EXPRESS◄** to say or express something in a particular way: *To put it bluntly, a lot of people just don't like her.* | *Well, let me put it this way: he's lied to us before.*

**7 ►HAVE IMPORTANCE/QUALITY◄** to con- sider something to have a particular level of importance or quality: *Almeida says he "puts his family first." | The new study puts UCLA among the top five research universities in the US.*

**8 put sth behind you** to try to forget about a bad experience or a mistake so that it does not affect you now: *Vietnam veterans talked of the need to put the war behind them.*

**9 put faith/confidence/trust etc. in** to trust or believe in someone or something: *These people put little trust in doctors.* –see also **put your mind to** (MIND¹)

**put** sth ↔ **aside** *phr v* [T] **1** to ignore a problem or disagreement in order to achieve something: *Try to* **put** *your feelings* **aside** *and look at the facts.* **2** to save something to be used or dealt with later: *I have money* **put aside** *for emergencies.*

**put** sth ↔ **away** *phr v* [T] to put something in the place where it is usually kept: *Those kids never* **put** *anything* **away!**

**put** sth ↔ **back** *phr v* [T] to put things or people in the place or situation they were before: *Put the milk back in the fridge, please.* | *a program to put people back to work*

**put down** *phr v* [T] **1** [**put** sb **down**] INFORMAL to criticize someone and make him/her feel silly or stupid. *The teachers here never put you down.* **2** [**put** sth ↔ **down**] INFORMAL to write something on a piece of paper: *I put down that I'd be available to work on Saturdays.* **3** [**put** sth/sth ↔ **down**] to use force to stop people who are fighting against a government: *Soldiers were sent to put down the rebellion.*

**put** sth ↔ **forward** *phr v* [T] to suggest a plan, idea etc.: *a treaty put forward by the Dutch*

**put** sth ↔ **in** *phr v* [T] **1** to add or replace equipment: *We had to have a new furnace put in.* **2** to ask for something in an official way: *Sawyer put in his expenses claim last week.* **3** to spend time doing something: *Doug is putting in a lot of hours at work.* (=he is working a lot)

**put** sth **into** sth *phr v* [T] **1 put energy/ effort/enthusiasm etc. into** sth to use energy etc. when you are doing something: *Koskoff put a lot of time and effort into this project.* **2 put sth into action/effect/practice** to start using something such as an idea or plan: *The college hopes to put the changes into effect by August 1.*

**put off** *phr v* [T] **1** [**put** sth ↔ **off**] to delay something, or to delay doing something: *Many Americans put off filling out their tax forms as long as possible.* **2** [**put** sb ↔ **off**] to make someone dislike something or someone, or to make him/her not want to do something: *Don't be put off by the restaurant's decor; the food is excellent.*

**put on** *phr v* [T]
**1** ▶CLOTHES◀ [**put** sth ↔ **on**] to dress yourself in a piece of clothing: *Put your coat on - it's cold.* −see usage note at DRESS[1]
**2** ▶AFFECT/INFLUENCE◀ [**put** sth ↔ **on** sth] to do something that affects or influences something else: *The government put a freeze on the construction of new nuclear power plants.* (=they stopped it)
**3 put on weight/5 pounds etc.** to become fatter
**4** ▶ON SKIN◀ [**put** sth ↔ **on**] to use MAKEUP etc. on your skin: *I hardly ever put on lipstick.*
**5** ▶MUSIC◀ [**put** sth ↔ **on**] to begin to play a record, TAPE, VIDEO etc.: *Let's put on some music.*
**6** ▶EVENT/PLAY◀ [**put** sth ↔ **on**] to arrange an event, concert, play etc., or to perform in one: *The West Valley Symphony is putting on a concert for charity.*
**7** ▶START EQUIPMENT◀ [**put** sth ↔ **on**] to make something such as a piece of equipment begin working: *It's cold in here. Why don't you put on the heat?*
**8** ▶FOOD◀ [**put** sth ↔ **on**] to begin to cook

something on a STOVE: *Let me just put the potatoes on.*

**put out** *phr v* [T] **1** [**put** sth ↔ **out**] to stop a fire, cigarette etc. from burning: *The fire caused $500,000 in damage before they put it out.* **2** [**put** sth ↔ **out**] to produce something, especially something such as a book, record, movie etc.: *They've put out three books now on vegetarian cooking.* **3** [**put** sth ↔ **out**] to place things where people can find and use them: *I'm just going to put out cold cuts, bread, and stuff for lunch.* **4** [**put** sth ↔ **out**] to put something outside the house: *Has anybody put the cat out yet?* **5** [**put** sb ↔ **out**] to make more work or cause problems for someone: *Will it put you out if I bring another guest?* **6 put out your hand/foot etc.** to move your hand etc. away from your body: *Jack put out his foot and tripped her.*

**put through** *phr v* [T] **1** [**put** sb **through** sth] to make someone do something that is very unpleasant or difficult: *My father's drinking problem put my mother through hell.* **2 put sb through school/university etc.** to pay for someone to go to school etc. **3** [**put** sb **through**] to connect someone to someone else on the telephone

**put** sth **to** sb *phr v* [T] to suggest something such as a plan to a person or group: *The proposal was put to the committee on January 9.*

**put** sth ↔ **together** *phr v* [T] **1** to build or fix something by joining its different parts together: *The store will put together bicycles and other large toys for you.* **2** to organize, collect, or prepare the different parts of something such as a plan: *Franklin has put together a program to help families in need.* **3 put together** combined: *He earns more than the rest of us put together.*

**put up** *phr v* [T] **1** [**put** sth ↔ **up**] to build something such as a wall or building, or to raise something so that it is upright: *The developers plan to put up a 15-storey office building.* **2** [**put** sth ↔ **up**] to attach a picture etc. to a wall or decorate things, so people can see them: *putting up Christmas decorations* **3 put sth up for sale/discussion/review etc.** to make something available to be sold, discussed etc. **4** [**put** sb **up**] INFORMAL to let someone stay in your house: *I can put Jared up for the night.* **5 put up money/$500/$3 million etc.** to give money to be used for a particular purpose: *Furth put up $42,000 in prize money for the contest.* **6 put up resistance/a fight/a struggle** to argue against or oppose something in a determined way, or to fight against someone who is attacking you: *Opponents of the bill are putting up a good fight in the Assembly.*

**put** sb **up to** sth *phr v* [T] to suggest or encourage someone to do something wrong, silly, or dangerous: *Jim wouldn't usually play such a* *stupid trick; someone must have **put** him **up to** it.*

  **put up with** sth *phr v* [T] to accept a bad situation without complaining: *I'm not going to **put up with** being treated like that.* —see usage note at BEAR¹

**put-down** /'. ./ *n* INFORMAL something you say that is intended to make someone feel stupid and unimportant

**put out** /,. './ *adj* **be/feel put out** to feel upset or offended: *I was put out because it was obvious that she didn't like my cooking.*

**pu·tre·fy** /'pyutrə,faɪ/ *v* [I,T] FORMAL to decay and smell very bad

**pu·trid** /'pyutrɪd/ *adj* very decayed and bad-smelling

**putt** /pʌt/ *v* [I,T] to hit a GOLF ball gently along the ground toward the hole —**putt** *n*

**put·ter** /'pʌt̬ɚ/ *v* [I] to spend time doing things that are not very important, in a relaxed way: *He's been **puttering around** the yard all morning.*

**put·ty** /'pʌti/ *n* [U] a soft substance that becomes hard when it dries, used for example for fixing glass into window frames

**put up·on** /'. .,./ *adj* **be/feel put upon** to think that other people are treating you unfairly by expecting too much of you: *She makes me feel that she is being put upon if I ask her to help.*

**puz·zle¹** /'pʌzəl/ *n* **1** a game or toy that has a lot of pieces that you have to fit together: *a 500-piece **jigsaw puzzle*** **2** a game in which you have to think hard to solve a difficult question or problem: *a book of crossword puzzles* **3** something that is difficult to understand or explain: *The way the stock market works has always been a puzzle to me.*

**puzzle²** *v* **1** [T] to make someone confused or unable to understand something: *At first, doctors were puzzled by the infection.* **2** [I,T] to think for a long time about something because you cannot understand it: *Jill **puzzled over** the first question on the exam for ten minutes.*

**puz·zled** /'pʌzəld/ *adj* confused and unable to understand something, or showing this: *a puzzled expression*

**pyg·my** /'pɪgmi/ *n* **1** also **Pygmy** someone who belongs to a race of very small people from parts of Asia and Africa **2** a very small type of animal: *a pygmy rabbit*

**py·lon** /'paɪlɑn/ *n* one of the tall metal structures that supports wires carrying electricity across the country

**pyr·a·mid** /'pɪrəmɪd/ *n* **1** a large stone building with a flat base and sides shaped like TRIANGLEs that form a point at the top **2** something that has this shape

**pyre** /paɪɚ/ *n* a high pile of wood on which a dead body is placed to be burned in a funeral ceremony

**Py·rex** /'paɪrɛks/ *n* [U] TRADEMARK a special type of strong glass that does not break at high temperatures and is used for making cooking dishes

**py·thon** /'paɪθɑn, -θən/ *n* a large tropical snake that kills animals for food by crushing them

**Q, q** /kyu/ *n* the seventeenth letter of the English alphabet

**Q-tip** /'kyu tɪp/ *n* TRADEMARK a small thin stick with cotton at each end, used for cleaning places that are difficult to reach, such as your ears

**quack¹** /kwæk/ *v* [I] to make the sound that ducks make

**quack²** *n* **1** INFORMAL someone who pretends to be a doctor **2** the sound a duck makes

**quad** /kwɑd/ *n* INFORMAL a square open area with buildings all around it, especially in a school or college

**quad·ran·gle** /'kwɑdræŋgəl/ *n* **1** ⇨ QUAD **2** TECHNICAL a flat shape that has four straight sides

**quad·rant** /'kwɑdrənt/ *n* **1** a quarter of a circle **2** a quarter of an area, especially of land: *the town's southwest quadrant* **3** a tool for measuring angles

**quad·ra·phon·ic** /,kwɑdrə'fɑnɪk◂/ *adj* using a system of sound recording, broadcasting etc. in which sound comes from four different SPEAKERs at the same time

**quad·ri·lat·er·al** /,kwɑdrə'læt̬ərəl/ *n* a flat shape with four straight sides —**quadrilateral** *adj*

**quad·ri·ple·gic** /,kwɑdrə'plidʒɪk/ *n* someone who has PARALYSIS of both arms and both legs —**quadriplegic** *adj*

**quad·ru·ped** /'kwɑdrə,pɛd/ *n* TECHNICAL an animal that has four feet

**quad·ru·ple¹** /kwɑ'drupəl/ *v* [I,T] to increase and become four times as big or as high, or to make something do this: *The number of car owners quadrupled in just five years.*

**quadruple²** *adj, quantifier* four times as big, as many, or as much: *Patients were given quadruple the normal dose of the drug.*

**quad·ru·plet** /kwɑ'druplɪt/ *n* one of four babies born at the same time to the same mother

**quag·mire** /'kwægmaɪɚ, 'kwɑg-/ *n* **1** a difficult or complicated situation: *Income tax regulations are sometimes a quagmire.* **2** an area of soft wet muddy ground

**quail** /kweɪl/ *n* [C,U] a small fat bird with a short tail, that is hunted and shot for food and sport, or the meat from this bird

**quaint** /kweɪnt/ *adj* unusual and attractive, especially in an old-fashioned way: *a quaint restaurant*

**quake**[1] /kweɪk/ *v* [I] **1** to shake in an uncontrolled way, usually because you are afraid **2** if the earth, a building etc. quakes, it shakes violently

**quake**[2] *n* INFORMAL ⇨ EARTHQUAKE

**Quak·er** /'kweɪkɚ/ *adj* relating to the Society of Friends, a Christian religious group that opposes violence, has no religious leaders or ceremonies, and holds its religious meetings in silence **–Quaker** *n*

**qual·i·fi·ca·tion** /ˌkwɑləfə'keɪʃən/ *n* **1** [C usually plural] a skill, personal quality, or type of experience that makes you suitable for a particular job or position: *Her qualifications include teaching math and science.* **2** [C,U] the achievement of an official standard in order to do a job, enter a sports competition etc.: *her qualification for the Olympic swimming team* **3** [C,U] something that you add to a statement to limit its effect or meaning: *You have the right to refuse without qualification.*

**qual·i·fied** /'kwɑləˌfaɪd/ *adj* **1** having the right knowledge, experience, skills etc. for a particular job: *a qualified teacher* **2** qualified agreement, approval etc. is limited in some way because you do not completely agree

**qual·i·fi·er** /'kwɑləˌfaɪɚ/ *n* **1** someone who has reached the necessary standard for entering a competition **2** TECHNICAL in grammar, a word or phrase that acts as an adjective or adverb, that limits or adds to the meaning of another word or phrase. In the sentence "She rode off happily on her new red bike," "happily," "new," and "red" are qualifiers

**qual·i·fy** /'kwɑləˌfaɪ/ *v* **1** [I] to pass an examination or reach the standard of knowledge or skill that you need in order to do something: *Those who* **qualify as** *stock brokers must work for the company for five years.* | *He's hoping to* **qualify for** *the US Open.* **2** [I] to have the right to claim something: *Only members of the credit union can qualify for loans.* **3** [T] to mean that someone is suitable to do or be something: *The fact that you've been to France doesn't* **qualify** *you* **as** *an expert on the French.* **4** [T] to add something to what has already been said in order to limit its effect or meaning: *Let me qualify that statement.*

**qual·i·ta·tive** /'kwɑləˌteɪtɪv/ *adj* relating to the quality or standard of something, rather than amount or number: *a qualitative study of the health care program* **–compare** QUANTITATIVE

**qual·i·ty**[1] /'kwɑləti/ *n* **1** the good parts of someone's character: *The boys follow Lucas because he has qualities they admire.* | *the qualities of honesty and independence* **2** [C,U] the degree to which something is good or bad: *high/low quality recording equipment* | *a sewing machine* **of poor/good quality** | *We're trying to*

*improve* **the quality of life** *for the people in this area.* **3** [U] a high standard: *a company that guarantees quality in its service* **4** something that is typical of something and makes it different from other things: *There is a wild quality in his books that keeps you reading.*

**quality**[2] *adj* of a high standard: *quality products*

**quality con·trol** /'... .ˌ./ *n* [U] the practice of checking goods as they are produced, to make sure their quality is good enough

**quality time** /'... ˌ./ *n* [U] the time that you spend giving someone, especially a family member, your full attention

**qualm** /kwɑm, kwɔm/ *n* [C usually plural] a feeling of slight worry because you are not sure that what you are doing is right: *He has no* **qualms about** *saying "no" to his children.*

**quan·da·ry** /'kwɑndri, -dəri/ *n* **be in a quandary about/over sth** to be unable to decide what to do about a difficult problem or situation: *The college is* **in a quandary** *as to whether it should build more student housing or give more financial aid.*

**quan·ti·fi·er** /'kwɑntəˌfaɪɚ/ *n* TECHNICAL in grammar, a word or phrase that is used with a noun to show quantity. In the sentence "There were only a few people at the party," "few" is a quantifier

**quan·ti·fy** /'kwɑntəˌfaɪ/ *v* [T] to measure something and express it as a number: *People's attitudes have changed, but it is difficult to quantify this change.* **–quantifiable** /ˌkwɑntə'faɪəbəl/ *adj*

**quan·ti·ta·tive** /'kwɑntəˌteɪtɪv/ *adj* relating to amounts rather than to the quality or standard of something: *a quantitative difference* | *quantitative studies/data* **–compare** QUALITATIVE

**quan·ti·ty** /'kwɑntəti/ *n* [C,U] an amount of something that can be counted or measured: *a small* **quantity of** *ice cream* | *large* **quantities of** *water* | *an increase in the quantity of new business*

**quan·tum leap** /ˌkwɑntəm 'lip/ *n* a very large and important improvement: *a quantum leap in medical science*

**quar·an·tine** /'kwɔrənˌtin, 'kwɑr-/ *n* [U] a time when a person or animal is kept apart from others in case she, he, or it has a disease: *The dogs were kept* **in quarantine** *for three months.* **–quarantine** *v* [T]

**quark** /kwɑrk/ *n* TECHNICAL a very small piece of matter that forms part of an atom

**quar·rel**[1] /'kwɔrəl, 'kwɑrəl/ *n* **1** an angry argument: *The shooting was a result of a quarrel between neighbors.* **2 have no quarrel with** FORMAL to have no reason to dislike someone or disagree with an idea, decision etc.: *We have no quarrel with the court's decision.*

**quarrel**[2] *v* [I] to have an angry argument: *We*

can hear the people who live next door *quarreling* with each other.

**quar·rel·some** /'kwɔrəlsəm, 'kwɑr-/ *adj* too ready to argue about things

**quar·ry**[1] /'kwɔri, 'kwɑri/ *n* **1** a place where large amounts of stone, sand etc. are dug out of the ground **2** an animal or person that you are hunting or chasing

**quarry**[2] *v* [T] to dig out stone, sand etc. from a QUARRY

**quart** /kwɔrt/ written abbreviation **qt.** *n* a unit for measuring liquid, equal to 2 PINTs or 0.9463 liters

**quar·ter** /'kwɔrtɚ/ *n*
**1** one of four equal parts into which something can be divided: *Cut the sandwiches into quarters.* | *A quarter of Canada's population is French speaking.*
**2** one of the four periods of 15 minutes into which each hour can be divided: *Can you be ready in **a quarter (of an) hour**? | It's **a quarter to/after five**.* (=15 minutes before or after 5 o'clock) **3** a coin used in the US and Canada worth 25 cents (= ¼ of a dollar) **4** a word meaning a period of three months, used when discussing bills, wages, and income: *Profits were down in the fourth quarter.* **5** one of the four periods into which a year at school or college is divided −compare SEMESTER **6** one of the four equal times into which games of some sports are divided −see also QUARTERS

quarter

quarter

**quar·ter·back** /'kwɔrtɚ,bæk/ *n* the player in football who directs the OFFENSE and throws the ball −see picture on page 472

**quar·ter·fi·nal** /ˌkwɔrtɚ'faɪnl/ *n* one of the set of four games near the end of a competition, whose winners play in the two SEMIFINALs

**quar·ter·ly**[1] /'kwɔrtɚli/ *adj, adv* produced or happening four times a year: *a quarterly report*

**quarterly**[2] *n* a magazine that is produced four times a year

**quar·ters** /'kwɔrtɚz/ *n* [plural] the house or rooms where you live, especially if you are in the army

**quar·tet** /kwɔr'tɛt/ *n* **1** a piece of music written for four performers **2** a group of four things or people

**quartz** /kwɔrts/ *n* [U] a hard mineral substance that is used in making electronic watches and clocks

**qua·sar** /'kweɪzɑr/ *n* TECHNICAL a very bright, very distant object similar to a star

**quash** /kwɑʃ/ *v* [T] FORMAL **1** to officially state that a judgment or decision is no longer legal or correct: *The judge quashed the decision of a lower court.* **2** to use force to end protests or to stop people who are not obeying the law

**qua·ver** /'kweɪvɚ/ *v* [I,T] if your voice quavers, it shakes as you speak, especially because you are nervous

**quay** /keɪ, ki/ *n* a place where boats can be tied up or loaded

**quea·sy** /'kwizi/ *adj* feeling sick; NAUSEOUS −**queasiness** *n* [U]

**queen** /kwin/ *n* **1** also **Queen** the female ruler of a country who is from a royal family, or the wife of a king **2** SLANG OFFENSIVE a male HOMOSEXUAL, especially one who behaves like a woman **3** a large female BEE, ANT etc. that lays the eggs for a whole group **4** the woman who wins a beauty competition

**queen-size** /'. ./ *adj* larger than the standard size: *a queen-size bed*

**queer**[1] /kwɪr/ *adj* **1** OLD-FASHIONED strange: *a queer expression* **2** OFFENSIVE ⇨ HOMOSEXUAL

**queer**[2] *n* OFFENSIVE ⇨ HOMOSEXUAL

**quell** /kwɛl/ *v* [T] **1** to make a violent situation end: *The military were sent out to **quell the rioting**.* **2** to stop feelings of doubt, worry, and anxiety from getting stronger: *City officials were trying to quell public fears about the spread of the disease.*

**quench** /kwɛntʃ/ *v* [T] **quench your thirst** if a drink quenches your thirst, it makes you stop feeling thirsty

**que·ry** /'kwɪri/ *n* FORMAL a question −**query** *v* [T]

**quest** /kwɛst/ *n* LITERARY a long search for something −**quest** *v* [I]

**ques·tion**[1] /'kwɛstʃən, 'kwɛʃtʃən/ *n* **1** a type of phrase used in order to ask for information: *I have a **question about** the math homework. | Do you mind if I ask you a personal question?* **2** a subject that needs to be discussed or a problem that needs to be solved; ISSUE: *The question is whether more troops should be sent. | a debate on **the question of** tax cuts* **3** a feeling of doubt about something: *The recent fighting has **called into question** (=made people have doubts about) the government's power to keep the peace.* **4 without question a)** definitely: *Their weapons technology is without question a threat to us.* **b)** without complaining or asking why: *They accepted our demands without question.* **5 in question** the person or thing that is in question is the one that is being discussed: *The document in question is a report dated June 18, 1948.* **6 be out of the question** used in order to emphasize that what someone wants to do is not possible or not allowed: *A career in basketball is out of the question, unless he works harder at it.* **7 (that's a) good question!** SPOKEN said when you are admitting you do not know the answer to a question: *"If we don't have enough people to help, how can we finish the job?" "Good question!"*

**question**² *v* [T] **1** to ask someone questions, especially about a crime: *Police are questioning three men about the murder.* **2** to stop trusting someone or start to have doubts about something: *Are you questioning my honesty?* –see usage note at ASK

**ques·tion·a·ble** /'kwɛstʃənəbəl/ *adj* **1** questionable actions or behavior are likely to be dishonest or morally wrong **2** uncertain or possibly not correct: *It is questionable what the law would accomplish.* **3** used in order to describe someone or something that you think is not legal or not morally correct: *Barton has been involved in some questionable financial deals.*

**ques·tion·ing** /'kwɛstʃənɪŋ/ *adj* a questioning look or expression shows that you need more information or that you doubt something

**question mark** /'.. ,./ *n* the mark (?), used in writing at the end of a question

**ques·tion·naire** /ˌkwɛstʃə'nɛr/ *n* a written set of questions about a particular subject given to a large number of people, in order to collect information

**quib·ble** /'kwɪbəl/ *v* [I] to argue about something that is not very important: *They're just quibbling over the details now.*

**quiche** /kiʃ/ *n* a type of food that consists of PASTRY filled with a mixture of eggs, cheese, vegetables etc.

**quick**¹ /kwɪk/ *adj* **1** quick actions or events are done or happen in a very short time: *I'll just take a quick shower first.* | *Snyder is quick to reward her employees for good work.* | *Don't make any quick movements, or you'll scare the rabbit.* | *I promise I'll be quick - just give me a minute to talk to her.* **2** able to learn and understand things in a short time; intelligent: *Carolyn's a quick learner.*

**quick**² *adv* SPOKEN NONSTANDARD ⇨ QUICKLY: *Come quick! Larry's on TV!* | *It was all over pretty quick.*

**quick·en** /'kwɪkən/ *v* [I,T] to become quicker, or to make something do this: *Realizing they were late, they quickened their pace.* (=walked faster)

**quick·ie** /'kwɪki/ *adj* happening or done quickly: *a quickie divorce* (=one that is done cheaply and quickly) –**quickie** *n*

**quick·ly** /'kwɪkli/ *adv* **1** fast, or done in a short amount of time: *Don't eat too quickly.* | *It's amazing how quickly she's grown.* **2** for a short amount of time: *I'll just run to the store quickly, and then we can eat.*

**quick·sand** /'kwɪksænd/ *n* [C,U] wet sand that is dangerous because it pulls you down into it if you walk on it

**quid pro quo** /ˌkwɪd prou 'kwou/ *n* FORMAL something that you give or do in exchange for something else, especially when this arrangement is not official

**qui·et**¹ /'kwaɪət/ *adj* **1** not making a lot of noise: *Be quiet! Daddy has a headache.* **2** not busy, or not full of people or activity: *We live in a quiet neighborhood.* | *Business has been really quiet recently.* **3** not speaking or not likely to say much: *She was described as quiet and hardworking.* –see also **keep (sth) quiet** (KEEP)

**qui·et**², **quiet down** *v* [I,T] to become calmer and less active or noisy, or to make someone do this; *Quiet down and get ready for bed!*

**quiet**³ *n* the state of being quiet and not active: *Can't we have some peace and quiet around here!*

**qui·et·ly** /'kwaɪətli/ *adv* **1** without making much or any noise: *Ron shut the door quietly.* | *"I'm sorry," he said quietly.* **2** in a way that does not attract attention: *The meeting was quietly arranged to keep the reporters away.*

**quill** /kwɪl/ *n* **1** a large feather, or a pen made from a large feather, used in past times **2** one of the sharp needles on the backs of some animals, such as the PORCUPINE

**quilt** /kwɪlt/ *n* a warm thick cover for a bed, made by sewing two layers of cloth together with a filling of cloth or feathers: *a patchwork quilt*

quilt

**quilt·ed** /'kwɪltɪd/ *adj* quilted cloth has a thick layer of material sewn to it in a pattern of stitches

**quint·es·sen·tial** /ˌkwɪntə'sɛnʃəl/ *adj* being a perfect example of a particular type of person or thing: *New York is the quintessential big city.* –**quintessentially** *adv* –**quintessence** /kwɪn'tɛsəns/ *n* [U]

**quin·tet** /kwɪn'tɛt/ *n* five singers or musicians who perform together

**quin·tu·plet** /kwɪn'tʌplɪt, -'tu-/ *n* one of five babies who are born at the same time to the same mother

**quip** /kwɪp/ *v* **-pped, -pping** [I] to make an amusing remark –**quip** *n*

**quirk** /kwɚk/ *n* **1** a strange habit or feature that someone or something has: *The fact that we don't say the "g" in the word "gnat" is just a quirk of language.* **2** something strange that happens by chance: *By a quirk of timing, her granddaughter was born on her birthday.*

**quirk·y** /'kwɚki/ *adj* slightly strange or unusual: *a quirky sense of humor*

**quit** /kwɪt/ *v* **quit, quit, quitting 1** [I,T] INFORMAL to leave a job, school etc., especially because it makes you annoyed or unhappy: *They gave the position to someone else, so I quit.* | *When did you quit your job?* **2** [T] INFORMAL to stop doing something that is bad: *I quit smoking three years ago.*

**quite** /kwaɪt/ *adv, quantifier* **1** very, but not extremely: *His hair is quite thin on top now.* | *I thought the instructions were quite clear.* **2 not quite** not completely or not exactly: *I'm not quite sure how the system works.* | *It happened not quite thirty years ago.* | *Lewis **isn't** quite as fast as he used to be.* **3** used when an amount or number is large, but not extremely large: *They've had **quite a bit** of snow this year.* (=a lot of snow) | *There were **quite a few** people at the party.* (=a lot of people) | *We haven't seen each other in **quite a while**.* (=a long time) **4** used in order to emphasize the fact that something is unusually good, bad etc.: *That's **quite a** coat, where did you buy it?* | *Roby made **quite an** impression on the kids.*

**quits** /kwɪts/ *adj* INFORMAL **call it quits a)** to agree that an argument or debt is settled: *If you give me $20, we'll call it quits.* **b)** to stop doing something: *Baird will call it quits after two terms as mayor.*

**quit·ter** /'kwɪtɚ/ *n* INFORMAL DISAPPROVING someone who stops doing a job, activity, or duty because it becomes difficult

**quiv·er**[1] /'kwɪvɚ/ *v* [I] to shake slightly because you are angry, upset, or anxious: *The girl **quivered** with fear.*

**quiver**[2] *n* **1** a slight shaking movement **2** a long case used for carrying ARROWs

**quix·ot·ic** /kwɪk'sɑtɪk/ *adj* having ideas and plans that are based on hopes and are not practical

**quiz**[1] /kwɪz/ *n* **1** a small test: *We have a math quiz on Friday.* **2** a competition in which you have to answer questions: *a quiz show on TV*

**quiz**[2] *v* **-zzed, -zzing** [T] to ask someone a lot of questions: *His parents quizzed him about who he was out with the night before.*

**quiz·zi·cal** /'kwɪzɪkəl/ *adj* **a quizzical look/smile/expression** a look etc. that shows you have a question

**quo·rum** /'kwɔrəm/ *n* the smallest number of people that must be at a meeting in order for official decisions to be made

**quo·ta** /'kwoʊtə/ *n* a particular amount that you are expected to have, or the limit on the amount of something you are allowed to have: *a salesman trying to **fill** his **quota** (=sell the amount he is expected to sell)*

**quot·a·ble** /'kwoʊtəbəl/ *adj* a quotable remark is interesting and worth repeating

**quo·ta·tion** /kwoʊ'teɪʃən/ *n* **1** words from a book, poem etc. that you repeat in your own speech or piece of writing: *a quotation from Shakespeare* **2** a written statement of the exact amount of money that a service will cost: *The insurance company sent us a quotation.* **3** [U] the act of quoting (QUOTE) something

**quotation mark** /. . . . / *n* [C usually plural] a

mark ("or") used in writing before and after any words that are being QUOTEd

**quote**[1] /kwoʊt/ *v* **1** [I,T] to repeat exactly what someone else has said or written: *The papers **quoted** Hanson **as** saying, "I'm guilty, but I'm not going to jail!"* | *a line **quoted from** her famous poem* **2** [T] to give proof for what you are saying by mentioning a particular example of something: *Dr. Morse quoted three successful cases in which patients used the new drug.* **3** [T] to tell a customer the price you will charge him/her for a particular service: *The first insurance company quoted me the lowest price.* **4 quote ... unquote** SPOKEN used when you are repeating the exact words someone else used: *... and Mr. Wigan said, quote, "Go to hell," unquote.*

**quote**[2] *n* INFORMAL ⇨ QUOTATION

**quo·tient** /'kwoʊʃənt/ *n* TECHNICAL a number that is the result of one number being divided by another

# R

**R**[1]**, r** /ɑr/ the eighteenth letter of the English alphabet

**R**[2] *adj* the abbreviation of "restricted," used in order to show that no one under the age of 17 can go to a particular movie unless a parent comes with him/her

**R & B** *n* [U] rhythm and blues; a type of popular music that is a mixture of BLUES and JAZZ, usually played on electric instruments

**R & D** *n* [U] research and development; the part of a business concerned with studying new ideas and planning new products

**R & R** *n* [U] rest and relaxation; a vacation given to people in the army, navy etc. after a long time of hard work or during a war

**rab·bi** /'ræbaɪ/ *n, plural* **rabbis** a Jewish religious leader

**rab·bit** /'ræbɪt/ *n* a common small animal with long ears and soft fur, that lives in the ground

**rab·ble** /'ræbəl/ *n* a noisy crowd of people who are likely to cause trouble

**rab·id** /'ræbɪd/ *adj* suffering from RABIES: *a rabid dog*

**ra·bies** /'reɪbiz/ *n* [U] a disease that kills animals and people that are bitten by an infected animal

**rac·coon** /ræ'kun/ *n* an animal with black fur around its eyes and black and white bands on its tail

**race**[1] /reɪs/ *n* **1** a competition to find out who can run, drive, swim etc. the fastest: *Greg finished third in the race.* **2** [C,U] one of the groups that humans are divided into, based on their skin color, the shape of their face or body, their type of hair etc.: *Our company employs people from all races and religions* **3** a group of people with the same customs, language, history etc. **4** a competition for power or a political position: *Chirac lost the 1988 presidential race.* **5 a race against time** a situation in which something difficult must be done before a particular time –see also ARMS RACE, HUMAN RACE

---

**USAGE NOTE race, nation, state,** and **tribe**

Use these words to talk about groups of people. The largest group is a **race**, which means people who have the same skin color, type of hair, and physical features: *The survey was given to people of different races and ages.* A **nation** is a country and its social and political structure, or a group of people with the same history and language: *Leaders of several Western nations are meeting in Paris this week.* Use **state** when talking about politics or the government of a country: *The state still owns much of the country's media.* A **tribe** is a group of families within a country who are the same **race**, and have the same traditions and the same leader: *The Navajo tribe is the second largest in the US.*

---

**race**[2] *v* **1** [I,T] to compete in a race, or to ride a horse, car etc. in a race: *Schumacher will be racing in the Monaco Grand Prix.* | *Which boat will you be racing?* **2** [I,T] to go very quickly, or to make someone or something do this: *I raced down the stairs to answer the phone.* | *The crash victims were raced to Pacific Hospital.* **3** if your heart or mind races, it is working harder and faster than usual **4** if an engine races, its parts are moving too fast

**race·course** /ˈreɪs-kɔrs/ *n* a track that runners, cars, horses etc. use in a race

**race re·la·tions** /ˈ. .,../ *n* [plural] the relationship between two groups of people who are from different RACEs but who live in the same city, country, or area

**rac·es** /ˈreɪsɪz/ *n* **the races** an event at which horses are raced against each other, especially for money

**race·track** /ˈreɪs-træk/ *n* a track around which runners, cars, horses etc. race

**ra·cial** /ˈreɪʃəl/ *adj* **1** relating to the relationships between different races of people: *a fight against racial discrimination* (=unfair treatment of people because of their race) **2** relat-

ing to people's race: *racial groups* –**racially** *adv*

**rac·ing** /ˈreɪsɪŋ/ *n* [U] **horse/car/bicycle/dog etc. racing** the sport of racing horses, cars etc.

**rac·ism** /ˈreɪsɪzəm/ *n* [U] **1** unfair treatment of people, or violence against them, because they belong to a different race from yours: *claims of police brutality and racism* **2** the belief that some races of people are better than others –**racist** *adj n*

**rack**[1] /ræk/ *n* a frame or shelf for holding things, usually with BARs or hooks: *a spice rack* | *towel racks*

**rack**[2] *v* [T] **1 rack your brain(s)** to think very hard or for a long time: *I had to rack my brains to remember his name.* **2 be racked with pain/guilt** feeling great physical pain, or feeling very guilty

**rack** sth ↔ **up** *phr v* [T] INFORMAL to make the value, amount, or level of something increase; ACCUMULATE: *The Seahawks have racked up enough wins to get into the playoffs.*

**rack·et** /ˈrækɪt/ *n* **1** INFORMAL a loud noise: *What's all the racket?* **2** INFORMAL a dishonest way of obtaining illegal goods: *He runs a drugs racket.* **3** a thing used for hitting the ball in games such as tennis, consisting of a light stick with a round firm net at the top

**rack·et·ball** /ˈrækɪtˌbɔl/ *n* [U] an indoor game in which two players use RACKETs to hit a small rubber ball against the four walls of a square court

**rack·et·eer·ing** /ˌrækəˈtɪrɪŋ/ *n* [U] a crime that consists of getting money dishonestly, using a carefully planned system –**racketeer** *n*

**rac·quet** /ˈrækɪt/ *n* ⇨ RACKET

**rac·y** /ˈreɪsi/ *adj* exciting in a sexual way

**ra·dar** /ˈreɪdɑr/ *n* [C,U] a method of finding the position of things such as planes by sending out radio waves, or the piece of equipment that does this: *The aircraft is designed to be difficult to spot on radar.*

**ra·di·al tire** /ˌreɪdiəl ˈtaɪɚ/, **radial** *n* a car tire with wires inside the rubber to make it stronger and safer

**ra·di·ance** /ˈreɪdiəns/ *n* [U] **1** great happiness or love that shows in the way someone looks: *the radiance of youth* **2** soft light that shines from or onto something

**ra·di·ant** /ˈreɪdiənt/ *adj* **1** full of happiness and love, in a way that shows in your face: *a radiant smile* **2** TECHNICAL sending out light or heat –**radiantly** *adv*

**ra·di·ate** /ˈreɪdiˌeɪt/ *v* **1** [I,T] if someone radiates a feeling or quality, or if it radiates from him/her, s/he shows it in a way that is easy to see: *Janine radiates confidence.* **2** [I,T] if something radiates light or heat, or if light or heat radiates, it is sent out in all directions: *warmth radiating from the heater* **3** [I] to

**R**

spread out from a central point: *pain radiating down his leg*

**ra·di·a·tion** /ˌreɪdiˈeɪʃən/ *n* [U] **1** a form of energy that comes from NUCLEAR reactions, that is harmful to living things in large amounts: *radiation exposure* **2** energy in the form of heat or light sent out as beams that you cannot see: *ultraviolet radiation from the sun*

**ra·di·a·tor** /ˈreɪdiˌeɪtɚ/ *n* **1** a piece of equipment used for heating a room, consisting of a hollow metal container fixed to a wall and connected to hot water pipes **2** the part of a car or plane that stops the engine from getting too hot

**rad·i·cal**[1] /ˈrædɪkəl/ *adj* **1** thorough and complete, so that something is very different: *radical changes to the tax system | a radical new idea for treating the disease* **2** supporting complete political or social change: *radical demands for reform* **–radically** *adv*

**radical**[2] *n* someone who wants thorough and complete social and political change **–radicalism** *n* [U]

**ra·di·o**[1] /ˈreɪdiˌoʊ/ *n* **1** a piece of electronic equipment that you use to listen to music or programs that are broadcast, or the programs themselves: *Have you heard Sting's new song on the radio? | I listen to the radio in the car on the way home from work.* **2** [U] the activity of making and broadcasting programs that can be heard on a radio: *He'd like a job in radio.* **3** [C,U] a piece of electronic equipment that can send and receive spoken messages, or the sending or receiving of these messages: *the ship's radio | We've lost radio contact.*

**radio**[2] *v* [I,T] to send a message using a radio: *We'll have to radio Chicago for permission to land.*

**ra·di·o·ac·tive** /ˌreɪdioʊˈæktɪv/ *adj* containing RADIATION: *radioactive waste*

**ra·di·o·ac·tiv·i·ty** /ˌreɪdioʊækˈtɪvəti/ *n* [U] **1** a quality that some substances have that makes them send out RADIATION **2** the energy produced in this way: *High levels of radioactivity remained in the area after the explosion.*

**ra·di·ol·o·gist** /ˌreɪdiˈɑlədʒɪst/ *n* a hospital doctor who is trained in the use of RADIATION to treat people

**ra·di·ol·o·gy** /ˌreɪdiˈɑlədʒi/ *n* [U] the study of the use of RADIATION and X-RAYS in medical treatment

**ra·di·o·ther·a·py** /ˌreɪdioʊˈθɛrəpi/ *n* [U] the treatment of illnesses using RADIATION

**rad·ish** /ˈrædɪʃ/ *n* a small red or white root that has a slightly hot taste and is eaten raw as a vegetable

**ra·di·um** /ˈreɪdiəm/ *n* [U] a very RADIOACTIVE metal that is an ELEMENT

**ra·di·us** /ˈreɪdiəs/ *n, plural* **radii** /ˈreɪdiaɪ/ **1** the distance from the center to the edge of a circle –see picture at DIAMETER **2 within a 10 mile/100 meter** etc. **radius** within a distance

of 10 miles etc. in all directions from a particular place

**ra·don** /ˈreɪdɑn/ *n* [U] a RADIOACTIVE gas that is an ELEMENT

**raf·fle**[1] /ˈræfəl/ *n* a type of competition or game in which people buy tickets with numbers on them in order to try to win prizes

**raffle**[2], **raffle off** *v* [T] to offer something as a prize in a RAFFLE

**raft** /ræft/ *n* **1** a flat floating structure used as a boat or to sit on, jump from etc. when you are swimming **2** a small flat rubber boat filled with air **3 a raft of** a large number of things or a large amount of something: *There are plenty of restaurants and a raft of motels.*

**raf·ter** /ˈræftɚ/ *n* one of the large sloping pieces of wood that form the structure of a roof

**raft·ing** /ˈræftɪŋ/ *n* [U] the sport of traveling down a fast-flowing river in a rubber RAFT

**rag**[1] /ræg/ *n* **1** a small piece of old cloth: *a rag for washing the car* **2 in rags** wearing old torn clothes: *beggars dressed in rags* **3 go from rags to riches** to become very rich after starting your life very poor

**rag**[2] *v* **-gged, -gging**

**rag on** sb *phr v* [T] SPOKEN **1** to make jokes and laugh at someone in order to embarrass him/her: *Everybody's ragging on Steve about his new haircut.* **2** to criticize someone in an angry way: *Stop ragging on me - I'll apologize to her later.*

**rag·a·muf·fin** /ˈrægəˌmʌfɪn/ *n* LITERARY a dirty young child wearing torn clothes

**rag·bag** /ˈrægbæg/ *n* **a ragbag of** a confused mixture of things that do not seem to go together or make sense: *a ragbag of ideas*

**rag doll** /ˈ. ./ *n* a soft DOLL made of cloth

**rage**[1] /reɪdʒ/ *n* [C,U] a strong feeling of anger that you cannot control: *When he refused to help, she flew into a rage.* (=suddenly became very angry)

**rage**[2] *v* [I] **1** to continue happening with great force or violence: *The battle raged for several days. | Outside a storm was raging.* **2** to feel extremely angry about something and to show this: *Tom raged at himself for having been so stupid.*

**rag·ged** /ˈrægɪd/, **raggedy** /ˈrægɪdi/ *adj* **1** torn and in bad condition: *raggedy blankets* **2** not straight or neat, but with rough uneven edges: *a ragged beard* **3** wearing clothes that are old, torn, and dirty: *ragged children*

**rag·tag** /ˈrægtæg/ *adj* looking messy and wearing dirty torn clothes: *a ragtag army*

**rag·time** /ˈrægtaɪm/ *n* [U] a type of JAZZ music with a quick strong beat, popular in the US in the early 1900s

**rah-rah** /ˈrɑrɑ/ *interjection, adj* an expression meaning HOORAY, often used in order to describe someone who supports something without thinking about it enough: *I'm just not a rah-rah American.*

**raid**[1] /reɪd/ *n* **1** a short attack on a place by soldiers, planes, or ships, intended to cause damage but not to take control: *an air raid* **2** a sudden visit by the police when they are searching for something: *Drug dealers were arrested after a police raid.*

**raid**[2] *v* [T] **1** if the police raid a place, they enter it suddenly to search for something illegal **2** to make a sudden attack on a place: *A group of soldiers raided enemy headquarters.* **3** INFORMAL to take or steal a lot of things from a place: *The kids raided the refrigerator after school.* (=ate a lot of food) –**raider** *n*

**rail**[1] /reɪl/ *n* **1** a long piece of wood or metal that is fixed along or around something, especially to keep you from falling: *Tourists stood at the rail taking pictures of the falls.* | *a bath rail* **2** one of the two long metal tracks fixed to the ground that trains move along

**rail**[2] *v* [I] LITERARY to complain angrily about something that you think is unfair

**rail·ing** /'reɪlɪŋ/ *n* a fence consisting of a piece of wood or metal supported by upright posts, which keeps people from falling over an edge or helps support them going up stairs: *kids climbing over the railings*

**rail·road**[1] /'reɪlroʊd/ *n* **1** a method of traveling or moving things around by train **2 the railroad** all the work, equipment etc. relating to a train system: *My grandfather works on/for the railroad.*

**railroad**[2] *v* [T] to force or persuade someone to do something without giving him/her enough time to think about it: *This complex bill should not be railroaded through the House.*

**rain**[1] /reɪn/ *n* [U] water that falls in small drops from clouds in the sky: *We'd better hurry; it looks like rain.* (=it is probably going to rain) –see usage note at WEATHER

**rain**[2] *v* **it rains** if it rains, drops of water fall from clouds in the sky: *Is it still raining?*

**rain down** *phr v* [I,T **rain down** sth] if something rains down or is rained down, it falls in large quantities: *Falling rocks rained down on cars and houses.*

**rain** sth ↔ **out** *phr v* [T] if an event is rained out, it has to stop because there is too much rain: *We had tickets to the Blue Jays game, but it was rained out.*

**rain·bow** /'reɪnboʊ/ *n* a large curve of different colors that can appear in the sky when there is both sun and rain

**rain check** /'. ./ *n* **1 take a rain check** SPOKEN used in order to say that you would like to accept an invitation or offer later, but you cannot right now: *I'm sorry, but I'm busy on Saturday - can I take a rain check?* **2** a ticket for an outdoor event, game etc. that you can use

another day, given to people if the event has to stop because of rain

**rain·coat** /'reɪnkoʊt/ *n* a coat that you wear to protect yourself from the rain

**rain·drop** /'reɪndrɑp/ *n* a single drop of rain

**rain·fall** /'reɪnfɔl/ *n* [C,U] the amount of rain that falls on an area in a particular time: *The rainfall this winter has been unusually low.*

**rain forest** /'. ,. / *n* an area of thick forest with tall trees that are very close together, growing in a place where it rains a lot

**rains** /reɪnz/ *n* **the rains** a time in the year when there is a lot of rain in tropical countries; MONSOON

**rain·storm** /'reɪnstɔrm/ *n* a storm with a lot of rain and strong winds

**rain·water** /'reɪn,wɔtɚ, -,wɑ-/ *n* [U] water that has fallen as rain

**rain·y** /'reɪni/ *adj* **1** having a lot of rain: *a rainy weekend* **2 rainy day** a difficult time when you will need money that you do not need now: *"You'd better save that money for a rainy day."* (=for a time when you need it)

**raise**[1] /reɪz/ *v* [T]
**1** ▶MOVE◀ to move or lift something to a higher position or to an upright position: *The flag is raised at school every morning.* | *Raise your hand if you know the answer*
**2** ▶INCREASE◀ to increase an amount, number, or level: *a plan to raise taxes* | *Don't raise your voice at me, young man.* (=speak loudly and angrily)
**3** ▶IMPROVE◀ to improve the quality or standard of something: *This bill is all about raising standards in our schools.*
**4** ▶CHILDREN/ANIMALS/CROPS◀ to take care of children, animals, or crops until they are fully grown: *They've raised seven children.* | *He wants to try raising corn.*
**5** ▶GET MONEY/SUPPORT◀ to collect money, support etc. so that you can use it to help people: *We've raised $10,000 for cancer research.*
**6** ▶FARMING◀ to grow plants or keep animals to sell: *Most of their income is from raising pigs.*
**7 raise a question/objection etc.** to begin to talk or write about a something that you want someone to consider: *Maryann raised the issue of marriage again.*
**8 raise hell/Cain etc.** INFORMAL **a)** to behave in a wild noisy way that upsets other people: *The guys were out raising hell in the bars last night.* **b)** to protest something in an angry and threatening way: *Jenny raised a fuss when the nurse tried to give her a shot.* –see usage note at RISE[1]

R

**raise**

**raise**[2] *n* an increase in the money you earn: *a raise of $100 a month*

**rai·sin** /'reɪzən/ *n* a dried GRAPE

**rake**[1] /reɪk/ *n* a gardening tool used for gathering dead leaves etc.

**rake**[2] *v* **1** [I,T] also **rake up** to move a RAKE across a surface in order to make the soil level, gather dead leaves etc.: *raking up the leaves in the fall* **2** [T] to separate or tear apart things that are part of a group by moving something through it with force: *She raked her fingers through her hair and screamed.* **3 rake sb over the coals** to speak angrily to someone who has done something wrong

**rake** sth ↔ **in** *phr v* [T] INFORMAL to earn a lot of money without trying very hard: *The toy stores rake it in during Christmas*

**rake** sth ↔ **up** *phr v* [T] to talk about something from the past that people would rather not mention: *Why do you have to rake up that old argument again?*

**ral·ly**[1] /'ræli/ *n* **1** a large public meeting to support a political idea, sports event etc.: *a campaign rally* **2** a car race on public roads: *the Monte Carlo Rally*

**rally**[2] *v* **1** [I,T] to come together or bring people together to support an idea, a political party etc.: *The President's speech rallied more supporters.* **2** [I] to become stronger again after a time of weakness or defeat: *The price of gold rallied after a slight drop.*

**rally around** *phr v* [I,T **rally around** sb/sth] if a group of people rally around, they all try to help you in a difficult situation: *Her friends all rallied around when her father died.*

**RAM** /ræm/ *n* [U] TECHNICAL random access memory; the part of a computer that keeps information for a short time so that it can be used immediately –compare ROM

**ram**[1] /ræm/ **-mmed, -mming** *v* [T] **1** to run or drive into something, or to push something using a lot of force: *The bus had rammed into the truck.* | *He rammed the key into the lock.* **2 ram sth down sb's throat** to try to force someone to accept an idea or opinion by repeating it again and again: *I don't like people who try to ram their religious beliefs down my throat.*

**ram**[2] *n* a fully grown male sheep

**Ram·a·dan** /'rɑmə,dɑn/ *n* [singular] the ninth month of the Muslim year, during which no food may be eaten during the hours of the day when it is light

**ram·ble**[1] /'ræmbəl/ *v* [I] **1** to talk in a very confused way, not staying with one subject: *His speeches tend to ramble.* **2** to go on a walk for pleasure: *We rambled through the woods all afternoon.*

**ramble on** *phr v* [I] to talk or write for a long time in a way that other people think is boring: *Sara rambled on about her trip to New York.*

**ramble**[2] *n* a long walk for pleasure

**ram·bling** /'ræmblɪŋ/ *adj* **1** speech or writing that is rambling is very long and does not seem to have any clear organization or purpose: *a long rambling letter* **2** a building that is rambling has an irregular shape and covers a large area: *a rambling old house*

**ram·bunc·tious** /ræm'bʌŋkʃəs/ *adj* noisy, full of energy, and behaving in a way that cannot be controlled: *rambunctious children*

**ram·i·fi·ca·tion** /,ræməfə'keɪʃən/ *n* FORMAL a result of something that happens or that you do, that has an effect on other things: *the economic ramifications of rising oil prices*

**ramp** /ræmp/ *n* **1** a road for driving onto or off a large main road **2** a slope that has been built to connect two places that are at different levels: *ramps for wheelchair users*

**ram·page**[1] /'ræmpeɪdʒ, ræm'peɪdʒ/ *v* [I] to rush around in groups and behave wildly or violently: *drunken college students rampaging through the streets*

**ram·page**[2] /'ræmpeɪdʒ/ *n* **on the rampage** rushing around in a wild and violent way: *gangs on the rampage*

**ramp·ant** /'ræmpənt/ *adj* spread across or affecting a large area and difficult to control: *rampant inflation* –**rampantly** *adv*

**ram·rod** /'ræmrɑd/ *n* **ramrod stiff/straight** sitting or standing with your back straight and your body stiff

**ram·shack·le** /'ræm,ʃækəl/ *adj* badly built and needing to be repaired: *a ramshackle farm house*

**ran** /ræn/ *v* the past tense of RUN

**ranch** /ræntʃ/ *n* a very large farm where cattle, horses, or sheep are raised

**ranch·er** /'ræntʃɚ/ *n* someone who owns or works on a RANCH: *a cattle rancher* –**ranch** *v* [I] –**ranching** *n* [U]

**ranch house** /'. ./ *n* a house built on one level, with a roof that does not slope much –see picture on page 471

**ran·cid** /'rænsɪd/ *adj* food such as milk or butter that is rancid smells or tastes unpleasant because it is no longer fresh: *rancid butter*

**ran·cor** /'ræŋkɚ/ *n* [U] FORMAL a feeling of hatred, especially when you cannot forgive someone: *The discussion proceeded honestly and without rancor.* –**rancorous** /'ræŋkərəs/ *adj*

**ran·dom** /'rændəm/ *adj* **1** happening or chosen without any definite plan, aim, or pattern: *a random survey* **2 at random** in a completely unplanned way: *The winning numbers will be chosen at random.* –**randomly** *adv*

**random ac·cess mem·o·ry** /,.. ,.. '.../ *n* [C,U] ⇨ RAM

**rang** /ræŋ/ *v* the past tense of RING

**range**[1] /reɪndʒ/ *n*
**1** ▶GROUP◀ a group of things that are different, but belong to the same general type: *books on a **wide range of** subjects*
**2** ▶NUMBER LIMITS◀ the limits within which amounts, levels, ages etc. can vary: *The house is **beyond/out of** our **price range**.* (=more than our limit) | *games for the 8-12 age range*
**3** ▶LIMITS TO POWER/ACTIVITY◀ the limits to the amount of power or responsibility that a person or organization has, or the types of activity they are allowed to do: *The issue falls outside the range of the investigation.*
**4** ▶PRODUCTS◀ a set of similar products made by a particular company or available in a particular store: *a new range of mountain bikes*
**5** ▶DISTANCE◀ **a)** [U] the distance within which something can be seen or heard or at which a particular weapon can hit things: *He was shot at **point-blank range**.* (=from very close) | *I was out of her range of vision.* **b)** the distance at which a vehicle such as an aircraft can travel before it needs more FUEL: *missiles with a **range of** more than 300 miles*
**6** ▶MOUNTAINS◀ a line of mountains or hills: *the Cascade Range*
**7** ▶FOR PRACTICE◀ an area of land where you can practice using weapons: *a rifle range*
**8** ▶LAND◀ [C,U] a large area of grassy land used by cattle
**9** ▶COOKING◀ ⇨ STOVE

**range**[2] *v* [I] **1** to vary between particular limits: *toys **ranging in price** from $5 to $25* **2** to deal with a large number of subjects: *Her speech **ranged over** several topics.* **3** if animals range somewhere, they move over a wide area of land

**rang·er** /'reɪndʒɚ/ *n* someone whose job is to watch and take care of a forest or area of public land and the people and animals that use it: *a forest ranger*

**rank**[1] /ræŋk/ *n* [C,U] the position or level that someone has in an organization: *He's just been promoted to the rank of Sergeant.*

**rank**[2] *v* **1** [I] to have a particular position in a list of people or things that are put in order of quality or importance: *Gail ranks third in her class at school.* **2** [T] to decide the position someone or something should have on a list, based on quality or importance: *a list of wines ranked by quality and price*

**rank**[3] *adj* having a very strong and unpleasant smell or taste: *rank meat*

**rank and file** /ˌ. . './ *n* **the rank and file** the ordinary members of an organization rather than the leaders

**rank·ing**[1] /'ræŋkɪŋ/ *n* the position or level that someone has on a list of people who have a particular skill: *the skater's national ranking*

**ranking**[2] *adj* a ranking person has a high position in an organization or is one of the best at an activity: *the ranking officer*

**ran·kle** /'ræŋkəl/ *v* [I,T] if something rankles or rankles you, it still annoys you a long time after it happened

**ran·sack** /'rænsæk/ *v* [T] **1** to go through a place stealing things and causing damage: *The victim's house had been ransacked.* **2** to search a place very thoroughly: *He ransacked his drawers but couldn't find his birth certificate.*

**ran·som** /'rænsəm/ *n* [C,U] an amount of money paid to free someone who is held as a prisoner: *The kidnappers demanded $50,000 in ransom.* **–ransom** *v* [T]

**rant** /rænt/ *v* [I] to talk or complain in a loud, excited, and confused way: *She ranted about how unfairly her boss treated her.* | *You can **rant and rave** (=rant continuously), but I won't change my mind.*

**rap**[1] /ræp/ *n* **1** [C,U] a type of popular music in which the words are not sung, but spoken in time to music with a steady beat **2** a quick light hit or knock: *a rap at the door* **3** [singular] blame or punishment for a mistake or crime: *a murder rap* | *He got himself a good lawyer to **beat the rap**.* (=avoid punishment) | *I'd rather drive, so I don't have to **take the rap** (=be blamed) for getting lost.* **4 get a bad/ bum rap** to be unfairly criticized, or to be treated badly: *The city got a bum rap in the 1980s as being a center of crime and drug trafficking.*

**rap**[2] *v* **-pped, -pping** **1** [I,T] to hit or knock something quickly and lightly: *It sounded like someone was rapping on the window.* **2** [T] to criticize or blame someone: *a movie rapped by critics for its violence* **3** [I] to say the words of a RAP song

**rape**[1] /reɪp/ *v* [T] to force someone to have sex by using violence

**rape**[2] *n* **1** [C,U] the crime of forcing someone to have sex by using violence: *a rape victim* **2** sudden unnecessary destruction, especially of the environment: *the rape of our rain forests*

**rap·id** /'ræpɪd/ *adj* done very quickly, or happening in a short time: *the tree's rapid growth* | *rapid political changes* **–rapidly** *adv* **–rapidity** /rə'pɪdəti/ *n* [U]

**rap·ids** /'ræpɪdz/ *n* [plural] part of a river where the water looks white because it is moving very fast over rocks

**rap·ist** /'reɪpɪst/ *n* someone who has forced someone else to have sex by using violence

**rap·port** /ræ'pɔr, rə-/ *n* [C,U] friendly agreement and understanding between people: *She can create an immediate **rapport with** her audience.*

**rap·proche·ment** /ˌræprouʃ'mɑn/ *n* [singular, U] FORMAL increasing good relations between two countries or groups of people, after a time of unfriendly relations: *Both sides are hoping for a swift rapprochement.*

R

**rapt** /ræpt/ *adj* so interested in something that you do not notice anything else: *The children were listening, rapt, to the story teller.*

**rap·ture** /'ræptʃɚ/ *n* [U] great excitement, pleasure, and happiness: *a look of rapture on her face* –**rapturous** *adj*

**rare** /rɛr/ *adj* **1** not seen or found very often, or not happening very often: *Thunderstorms are rare here.* | *a rare form of cancer* **2** meat that is rare has only been cooked for a short time and is still red: *Antonio likes his steaks rare.*

---

### USAGE NOTE rare and scarce

Use **rare** to talk about something that is valuable and that there is not much of: *Rare coins are usually worth a lot of money.* Use **scarce** to talk about something that is difficult to get at a particular time: *During the war, food and clothing were scarce.*

---

**rare·ly** /'rɛrli/ *adv* not often: *She's rarely home these days.* | *Secretaries are rarely given the thanks they deserve.*

**rar·ing** /'rɛrɪŋ/ *adj* **raring to go** INFORMAL very eager to start an activity: *We got up early, raring to go.*

**rar·i·ty** /'rɛrəti/ *n* **be a rarity** to not happen or exist very often: *Old cars in good condition are a rarity.*

**ras·cal** /'ræskəl/ *n* HUMOROUS a child who behaves badly but whom you still like

**rash**¹ /ræʃ/ *adj* done too quickly without thinking carefully first, or behaving in this way: *rash decisions* | *a rash and reckless young man*

**rash**² *n* **1** a lot of red spots on someone's skin, caused by an illness or a reaction to a substance such as food, plants, or medicine **2** **a rash of** INFORMAL a large number of unpleasant events, changes etc. within a short time: *a rash of drive-by shootings*

**rasp·ber·ry** /'ræz,bɛri/ *n* a soft sweet red BERRY –see picture on page 470

**rasp·y** /'ræspi/ *adj* making a rough unpleasant sound: *Marlon Brando's raspy voice in "The Godfather"* –**rasp** *v* [I] –**rasp** *n*

**rat**¹ /ræt/ *n* **1** an animal that looks like a large mouse with a long tail **2** INFORMAL someone who has been disloyal to you or has deceived you: *That rat Bruce just did it for the money.*

**rat**² *v* **-tted, -tting** [I] OLD-FASHIONED to be disloyal to someone by telling someone in authority about something wrong that s/he has done: *You'd better not rat on me!*

**rate**¹ /reɪt/ *n* **1** the number of times something happens over a period of time: *a country with a low birth rate* | *a high crime rate* **2** a charge or payment set according to a standard scale: *What's the going rate* (=the usual amount paid for work) *for a piano teacher?* | *The Federal Reserve lowered interest rates today.*

**3** the speed at which something happens over a period of time: *Our money was running out at an alarming rate.* **4** **at this rate** SPOKEN used in order to say what will happen if things continue to happen in the same way: *At this rate, we'll never finish on time.* **5** **at any rate** SPOKEN used when you are giving one definite fact in a situation that is not sure or not satisfactory: *He's planning to come. At any rate, I think that's what he said.* **6** **first-rate/second-rate/third-rate** of good, bad, or very bad quality: *a third-rate movie* **7** the speed a vehicle is traveling: *Jet fighters sped past at an amazing rate.*

**rate**² *v* **1** [T] to have a particular opinion about the value or worth of something: *Johnson is rated one of the best basketball players.* **2** **X-rated/R-rated etc.** used in order to show that a movie has been officially approved for people of a particular age to see **3** [T] INFORMAL to deserve something: *You all rate a big thank-you for your work.*

**rath·er** /'ræðɚ/ *adv, quantifier* **1** **rather than** a phrase meaning instead of, used when you are comparing two things or situations: *We decided to have the wedding in the summer rather than in the spring.* | *Religious instruction belongs in church rather than in the public schools.* **2** **would rather** used when you would prefer to do or have one thing more than another: *I hate sitting doing nothing; I'd rather be busy.* | *Dave would rather have a dog than a cat, but I like cats.* | *He said he would rather not risk it.* **3** FORMAL used in order to give more correct or specific information about what you have said: *Lucy, or Susie rather, asked me to come tonight.* **4** fairly or to some degree: *Some of the photographs are rather grainy and blurred.*

**rat·i·fy** /'ræṭə,faɪ/ *v* [T] to make a written agreement official by signing it: *Both nations ratified the treaty.* –**ratification** /,ræṭəfə-'keɪʃən/ *n* [U]

**rat·ing** /'reɪtɪŋ/ *n* a level on a scale that shows how popular, good, important etc. someone or something is: *The governor's approval rating is high.*

**ra·tings** /'reɪtɪŋz/ *n* **the ratings** [plural] a list that shows which movies, television programs etc. are the most popular: *Her show is at the top of the ratings.*

**ra·ti·o** /'reɪʃi,oʊ, 'reɪʃoʊ/ *n* a relationship between two amounts, represented by two numbers that show how much bigger one amount is than the other: *The ratio of boys to girls in the class is 2:1.* (=two boys for each girl)

**ra·tion**¹ /'ræʃən, 'reɪ-/ *n* a limited amount of something such as food or gas that you are allowed to have when there is not much available: *a ration of sugar*

**ration**² *v* [T] to control the supply of something by allowing people to have only a limited amount of it: *Coffee was rationed during the war.* −**rationing** *n* [U]

**ra·tion·al** /ˈræʃənəl/ *adj* **1** based on reason rather than on emotion: *a rational decision* | *There must be a rational explanation for their disappearance.* **2** able to think clearly and make good decisions; SENSIBLE: *a rational person* −**rationally** *adv* −**rationality** /ˌræʃəˈnælət̬i/ *n* [U]    opposite IRRATIONAL

**ra·tion·ale** /ˌræʃəˈnæl/ *n* [C,U] FORMAL the reasons and principles on which a decision, plan etc. is based: *I can't see the rationale behind his plan.*

**ra·tion·al·ize** /ˈræʃnəˌlaɪz, -nlˌaɪz/ *v* [I,T] to think of reasons, especially reasons that are not good or sensible, to explain your behavior or attitudes: *He rationalized that his parents would have given him the money anyway, so why not just take it?* −**rationalization** /ˌræʃnələˈzeɪʃən/ *n* [C,U]

**ra·tions** /ˈræʃənz, ˈreɪ-/ *n* [plural] the food that is given to a soldier each day during a war

**rat race** /ˈ. ./ *n* [U] **the rat race** INFORMAL the unpleasant situation in business, politics etc. in which people are always competing against each other

**rat·tle**[1] /ˈræt̬l/ *v* **1** [I,T] to shake with quick repeated knocking sounds, or to make something do this: *There was something rattling around in the trunk.* **2** [T] INFORMAL to make someone lose his/her confidence and become nervous: *Don't get rattled - just stay calm.*

**rattle** sth ↔ **off** *phr v* [T] to say something very quickly and easily without effort: *She rattled off the names of all the states.*

**rattle**[2] *n* **1** a baby's toy that makes a noise when it is shaken **2** [singular] the noise that you hear when the parts of something knock against each other

**rat·tler** /ˈræt̬lɚ, ˈræt̬l-ɚ/ *n* INFORMAL ⇨ RATTLESNAKE

**rat·tle·snake** /ˈræt̬lˌsneɪk/ *n* a poisonous American snake that makes a noise with its tail

**rau·cous** /ˈrɔkəs/ *adj* a raucous voice or noise is very loud and unpleasant: *a raucous laugh* −**raucously** *adv*

**raun·chy** /ˈrɔntʃi, ˈrɑn-/ *adj* INFORMAL intended to make you think about sex: *a raunchy movie*

**rav·age** /ˈrævɪdʒ/ *v* [T] to destroy, ruin, or damage something badly; DEVASTATE: *a forest ravaged by fire*

**rav·ag·es** /ˈrævɪdʒɪz/ *n* **the ravages of sth** LITERARY damage or destruction caused by something such as war, disease, time etc.

**rave**[1] /reɪv/ *v* [I] **1** to talk in an excited way about something because you think it is very good: *Everybody raved about the movie, but I hated it.* **2** to talk in a wild angry way

**rave**[2] *adj* **rave reviews** strong praise for a new movie, book, restaurant, or product: *The book had/got rave reviews.*

**rave**[3] *n* an event at which young people dance all night to loud music with a strong beat

**ra·ven** /ˈreɪvən/ *n* a large black bird

**rav·en·ous** /ˈrævənəs/ *adj* extremely hungry

**ra·vine** /rəˈvin/ *n* a deep narrow valley with steep sides

**rav·ing** /ˈreɪvɪŋ/ *adj* INFORMAL talking or behaving in a crazy way: *a raving lunatic* −**raving** *adv* : *raving mad/drunk*

**rav·ings** /ˈreɪvɪŋz/ *n* [plural] things that someone says that are crazy

**rav·ish·ing** /ˈrævɪʃɪŋ/ *adj* a word meaning "very beautiful," used especially to describe people

**raw** /rɔ/ *adj* **1** not cooked: *raw onions* **2** raw cotton, sugar, and other materials are still in their natural state, and have not been prepared for people to use: *natural gas and other raw materials* **3** skin that is raw is red and sore **4** not experienced, fully trained, or completely developed: *raw recruits in the army* (=people who have just joined the army) | *This idea was the raw material* (=an idea that is not developed) *for his new play.* **5** a raw emotion or quality is strong, natural, and easy to notice: *raw courage* **6 a raw deal** unfair treatment: *She deserved a raise; I think she's getting a raw deal.*

**ray** /reɪ/ *n* **1** a narrow beam of light from the sun, a lamp etc.: *the sun's rays* −see picture at GREENHOUSE EFFECT **2 ray of hope/comfort** etc. something that provides a small amount of hope, comfort etc.

**ray·on** /ˈreɪɑn/ *n* [U] a smooth material like silk used for making clothes

**raze** /reɪz/ *v* [T] to destroy a city, building etc. completely: *Three buildings had been razed to make way for a new mall.*

**ra·zor** /ˈreɪzɚ/ *n* a sharp instrument for removing hair from the body: *an electric razor*

**razor blade** /ˈ.. ˌ./ *n* a small flat blade with a very sharp cutting edge, used in some RAZORs

**razz** /ræz/ *v* [T] INFORMAL to try to embarrass or annoy someone by making jokes about him/her; TEASE: *The kids were razzing Tom about Jenny.*

**Rd.** *n* the written abbreviation of ROAD

**-'re** /ɚ/ *v* the short form of "are": *We're* (=we are) *ready to go.*

**re** /ri/ *prep* a word meaning "about" or "regarding," used in business letters to introduce the main subject: *Re your letter of June 10...*

**reach**[1] /ritʃ/ *v* **1** [T] to arrive at a particular place: *It took four days for the letter to reach me.* **2** [I,T] to move your hand or arm in order to touch, hold, or pick up something: *He threatened me and reached for his knife.* | *Mike*

**reach**

She can't reach the top of the tree.

reached out and took her hand. | Jean can't reach the cans on the top shelf. **3** [I,T] to be big enough, long enough etc. to get to a particular level or point: Will the ladder reach the roof? | The rope won't reach. **4** [T] to increase, decrease, or develop to a particular level or standard over time: The temperature will reach 95° today. | The land has **reached the point** (=reached a situation) at which no crops can be grown on it. **5 reach a decision/agreement etc.** to succeed in deciding something, agreeing on something etc. **6** [T] to speak to someone, especially by telephone: I wasn't able to reach him yesterday. **7** [T] if something such as a message reaches a lot of people, it is seen or heard by them: a TV program that reaches millions of homes

**reach²** n **1** [singular, U] the distance that you can stretch out your arm to touch something: The box on top of the table was just **out of her reach**. **2 within reach (of sth) a)** within a distance that you can easily travel: We live **within easy reach of** the city. **b)** also **in reach** easy to achieve or get with the skills, power, money etc. that you have: This house is **within reach of** the first-time home buyer. **3 beyond the reach/out of reach** difficult to achieve or get because you do not have enough skill, power, or money: Computer crime is **beyond the reach of** the regular police force.

**re·act** /ri'ækt/ v [I] **1** to behave in a particular way because of what someone has done or said to you: How did she **react to** the news? | The audience **reacted by** shouting and booing. **2 react against sth** to show that you do not like or agree with something by deliberately doing the opposite: He reacted against his parents' strictness by running away. **3** TECHNICAL to change when mixed with another substance −compare OVERREACT

**re·ac·tion** /ri'ækʃən/ n **1** [C,U] something that you feel or do because of what has happened to you or been said to you: What was his **reaction to** the question? −see also **gut reaction/feeling etc.** (GUT¹) **2** a bad effect, such as an illness from food that you have eaten or from a drug that you have taken: Grant **had a reaction to** the medicine. **3** [singular] a change in someone's attitudes, behavior etc. because s/he does not agree with something that was done in the past: strong public **reaction against** nuclear tests **4** [C,U] a change that happens when two or more chemical substances are mixed together −see also REACTIONS

**re·ac·tion·ar·y** /ri'ækʃə,nɛri/ adj DISAPPROVING strongly opposed to social or political change −**reactionary** n

**reactions** /ri'ækʃənz/ n [plural] your ability to move quickly when something dangerous happens: an athlete with quick reactions

**re·ac·tor** /ri'æktɚ/ n ⇨ NUCLEAR REACTOR

**read** /rid/ v **read** /rɛd/, **read** /rɛd/, **reading 1** [I,T] to look at written words, numbers, or signs and understand what they mean: Can Billy read yet? | She sat reading a magazine. | I can't actually read music, but I can play the guitar. **2** [I,T] to find out information from books, newspapers etc.: I **read about** the accident in the paper. | I **read that** you can buy that new pain killer now. **3** [I,T] to say written or printed words to other people: Each student had to read his or her report. | Read to me, Mommy. **4 read between the lines** to guess what someone really feels or means, even when his/her words do not show it: You have to read between the lines to understand what the writer is saying. **5 read sb's mind/thoughts** to guess what someone is thinking: "Hey," said Sarah, reading Kate's thoughts, "I'm scared too." **6** [T] if a measuring instrument reads a particular number, it shows that number: What does your gas meter read? **7** [T] to understand a remark, situation etc. in a particular way: The movie could be read as a protest against the Church. **8 well-read** having read a lot of books

**read sth into** sth phr v [T] to think that a situation, action etc. means more than it really does: You shouldn't **read** so much **into** what she says.

**read up on** sth phr v [T] to read a lot about something so that you know a lot about it: We need to **read up on** the new tax laws.

**read·a·ble** /'ridəbəl/ adj **1** interesting, enjoyable, or easy to read: The magazine is now more readable and stylish. **2** clear and able to be read; LEGIBLE −see also MACHINE-READABLE

**read·er** /'ridɚ/ n **1** someone who reads a lot, or reads in a particular way: an **avid reader** (=someone who likes to read a lot) | a fast/slow reader **2** someone who reads a particular book, newspaper etc.: Many of our readers wrote in to complain.

**read·er·ship** /'ridɚ,ʃɪp/ n [C,U] the people who read a particular newspaper, magazine etc.

**read·i·ly** /'rɛdl·i/ adv **1** quickly and easily: The information is readily available on computer. **2** quickly, willingly, and without complaining: Chip readily agreed to help.

**read·i·ness** /'rɛdɪnɪs/ n **1** [singular, U] willingness to do something: I admire his **readiness to** help people. **2** [U] the state of being prepared and ready for something that might happen: The army was standing by **in readiness for** an attack.

**read·ing** /'ridɪŋ/ n **1** [C,U] the activity of looking at and understanding written words: I enjoy reading and swimming. | a careful reading of the contract **2** the way that you understand something, or your opinion about what a statement, event, article, piece of music etc. means; INTERPRETATION: What's your **reading of the situation**, Herb? (=what do you think has caused the situation, or what might happen?) **3** the books, articles etc. that you read: *I have a lot of reading to do for class.* **4** a number or amount shown on a measuring instrument: *The man came to take a reading from the electric meter.*

**re·ad·just** /ˌriːəˈdʒʌst/ v **1** [I] to change the way you do things because of a new job, situation, or way of life: *After the war, I needed time to readjust to life at home.* **2** [T] to make a small change to something, or move something to a new position: *Remember to readjust the mirrors in the car.* —**readjustment** n [C,U]

**read-on·ly mem·o·ry** /ˌ. ˌ. ˈ.../ n [C,U] ⇨ ROM

**read·out** /ˈriːd-aʊt/ n a record of information produced by a computer that is shown on a screen or in print

**read·y** /ˈrɛdi/ adj **1** someone that is ready is prepared or able to do something: *Aren't you ready yet?* | *We're just about ready to eat.* | *Go get ready* (=do the things you need to do) *for bed.* | *I don't think Joey is ready for school yet.* **2** something that is ready has been prepared and can be used, eaten etc. immediately: *Is supper ready?* | *The dry cleaning will be ready to be picked up on Monday.* | *Are you getting ready for* (=preparing things for) *the camping trip?* | *The bus only takes exact change, so have your money ready.* **3** willing or likely to do something: *She looked really upset and ready to cry.* **4** **ready cash/money** money that is available to be used immediately **5** **(get) ready, (get) set, go!** used in order to tell people to start a race –see usage note at PREPARE

**ready-made** /ˌ.. ˈ.ˌ / adj ready to be used immediately: *ready-made clothing*

**real¹** /riːl/ adj **1** not imaginary but actually existing: *The new system has real advantages.* | *There is a very real danger/possibility/ risk of an explosion.* **2** true and not pretended: *What's the real reason you were late?* **3** not false; GENUINE: *real gold* | *"Jack" isn't his real name.* **4** used in order to emphasize what you are saying: *Matt's a real jerk.* | *It's a real pleasure to meet you.* **5** **the real world** also **real life** the world that people actually live in, as opposed to an imaginary one: *Things don't happen like that in the real world.* **6** **the real thing/McCoy** INFORMAL a thing or person that is the actual one and not a copy: *This isn't Mexican food from a box. This is the real thing!*

SPOKEN PHRASES

**7** said when something is the way you think it should be: *Now that's real coffee!* **8** **real live** used in order to emphasize how rare or unusual something is: *Wow! A real live movie star!* **9** **be for real** used in order to say that someone or something is actually what s/he seems to be, or actually means what s/he says: *Are you for real?* (=do you really mean what you are saying?) **10** **get real** used in order to tell someone that what s/he is suggesting is not sensible or possible:

*You may just have to get real and get a job like everybody else!*

**real²** adv SPOKEN NONSTANDARD very: *I'm real sorry!*

**real es·tate** /ˈ. .ˌ./ n [U] **1** property such as houses or land: *Real estate prices fell again last year.* | *Japanese investment in US real estate* **2** the business of selling houses or land

**real estate a·gent** /ˈ. .. ..ˌ./ n someone whose job is to sell houses or land

**re·al·ism** /ˈriːəˌlɪzəm/ n [U] the ability to deal with situations in a practical or sensible way

**re·al·ist** /ˈriːəˌlɪst/ n someone who thinks in a REALISTIC way

**re·al·is·tic** /ˌriːəˈlɪstɪk/ adj practical and sensible, or dealing with situations in this way: *You have to be realistic about your chances of winning.* (=realize that you may not win) | *realistic sales targets* (=sensible ones, that can be achieved) –opposite UNREALISTIC

**re·al·is·tic·al·ly** /ˌriːəˈlɪstɪkli/ adv **1** in a REALISTIC way: *We can't realistically hire new people without any money.* **2** described or shown in a way that is very similar to real life: *a realistically drawn picture*

**re·al·i·ty** /riˈæləti/ n **1** [C,U] what is true or what actually happens, not what is imagined or not real: *Being aware of dangers on the street at night is one of the realities of living in the city.* | *It's best to accept the reality of the situation.* **2** **in reality** used in order to say that something is different from what seems to be true: *He said he'd retired, but in reality, he was fired.* **3** **become a reality/make sth a reality** to begin to exist or happen, or to make something do this: *Money from two major companies helped to make the Children's Center a reality.* **4** **reality check** INFORMAL an occasion when you consider the facts of a situation, as opposed to what you would like or what you have imagined: *It's time for a reality check: the team isn't as good as people think.*

**re·al·i·za·tion** /ˌriːələˈzeɪʃən/ n [singular, U] **1** the act of understanding or realizing something that you did not know before: *We finally came to the realization that the business wasn't going to work.* **2** the act of achieving what you had planned or hoped to do: *Harry sacrificed everything for the realization of his dream.*

**re·al·ize** /ˈriːəˌlaɪz/ v [T] **1** to know or understand the importance of something that you did not know before: *I'm sorry, I didn't realize (that) it was so late.* | *He obviously didn't realize the dangers involved.* **2** **realize a hope/goal/ dream** etc. to achieve something you have been hoping for, working for etc. **3** **sb's (worst) fears were realized** used in order to say that the thing that someone was afraid of actually happened: *Morris's worst fears were realized when the police came to his door.*

**real·ly** /'rili/ *adv* **1** a word meaning "very" or "very much," used in order to emphasize something: *Yeah, he's a really nice guy.* | *I don't really trust him.* **2** used in order to emphasize that something is true, especially when people might think something else is true: *This doll might really be valuable.* | *No, really, I'm fine.*

---
SPOKEN PHRASES

**3 really?** used when you are surprised about or interested in what someone has said: *"Jay got promoted." "Really? When?"* **4 not really** used in order to say "no," especially when something is not completely true: *"Is that salsa hot?" "Not really."* (=not too hot) **5 (yeah) really** used in order to agree with someone: *"I just want to meet a nice guy." "Yeah, really."*

---

**realm** /rɛlm/ *n* **1** an area of knowledge, interest, or thought: *new discoveries in the realm of science* **2** LITERARY a country ruled over by a king or queen

**real-time** /'. ./ *adj* TECHNICAL a real-time computer system deals with information as fast as it receives it —**real time** *n* [U]

**real·tor** /'riltɚ/ *n* ⇨ REAL ESTATE AGENT

**real·ty** /'rilti/ *n* [U] ⇨ REAL ESTATE

**ream** /rim/ *n* **1 reams of sth** INFORMAL a lot of something: *He took reams of notes in the class.* **2** TECHNICAL 500 sheets of paper

**reap** /rip/ *v* [I,T] to get something good because of the hard work that you have done: *The company has reaped the benefits of their advertising campaign.*

**rear**[1] /rɪr/ *n* **1 the rear** the back part of an object, vehicle, building etc.: *There are more seats at the rear of the theater.* **2** ⇨ REAR END **3 bring up the rear** to be at the back of a line or group of people that is moving forward: *The kids came around the corner with Donny bringing up the rear.*

**rear**[2] *v* **1** [T] to care for a person, animal, or plant until s/he or it is fully grown: *She reared seven children by herself.* **2** [I] also **rear up** if an animal rears, it rises up on its back legs **3 rear its ugly head** if a problem rears its ugly head, it appears or happens: *We must attack racism whenever it rears its ugly head.*

**rear**[3] *adj* relating to the back of something: *the rear wheels of the car* | *the rear entrance of the hospital*

**rear end** /,. './ *n* SPOKEN the part of your body that you sit on: *He fell right on his rear end!*

**rear-end** /,. './ *v* [T] INFORMAL to hit the back of someone's car with another car: *Someone rear-ended us on the freeway.*

**re·ar·range** /,riə'reɪndʒ/ *v* [T] to change the position or order of things: *We rearranged the furniture in the living room.* —**rearrangement** *n* [C,U]

**rear·view mir·ror** /,.. '../ *n* the mirror in a car that you use to see what is behind you when you are driving

**rear·ward** /'rɪrwɚd/ *adv* in, toward, or at the back of something: *a rearward facing seat*

**rea·son**[1] /'rizən/ *n* **1** [C,U] the cause or fact that explains why something happens or exists: *Did he give any reason for quitting?* | *There is no reason to believe that he is guilty.* —see usage note at EXCUSE[2] **2** [U] sensible judgment and understanding: *Randy is not the kind of man who listens to reason.* (=is persuaded by reason) | *You can choose the car you want, within reason.* (=within sensible limits) **3** [U] the ability to think, understand, and form judgments that are based on facts: *a conflict between reason and emotion* **4 all the more reason to do sth** used in order to say that what has just been mentioned is another reason for doing what you have suggested: *"I have no money." "All the more reason to stay home with me tonight."*

**rea·son**[2] *v* **1** [T] to form a particular judgment about something after thinking about the facts: *The jury reasoned that he could not have committed the crimes.* **2** [I] to think about facts clearly and make judgments: *Small children do not have the ability to reason.*

**reason with** sb *phr v* [T] to talk to someone in order to persuade him/her to be more sensible: *I tried to reason with her, but she wouldn't listen.*

**rea·son·a·ble** /'riznəbəl, -zən-/ *adj* **1** fair and sensible: *a reasonable suggestion* | *He seemed like a reasonable guy.* **2** a reasonable amount, number, or price is not too much or too big: *The store sells good furniture at reasonable prices* —**reasonableness** *n* [U] —opposite UN-REASONABLE

**rea·son·a·bly** /'riznəbli/ *adv* **1** fairly but not completely: *I did reasonably well on the test.* **2** in a way that is fair or sensible: *"I'm sure we can find an answer," Steve said reasonably.*

**rea·soned** /'rizənd/ *adj* based on careful thought; SENSIBLE: *a reasoned argument*

**rea·son·ing** /'rizənɪŋ/ *n* [U] the process of thinking carefully about something in order to make a judgment: *a decision based on sound reasoning* (=good reasoning) | *I don't understand your line of reasoning.* (=the way you are thinking)

**re·as·sur·ance** /,riə'ʃʊrəns/ *n* [C,U] something that you say or do to make someone feel less worried about a problem: *I need some reassurance that I won't be fired.* | *He didn't give me any reassurances.*

**re·as·sure** /,riə'ʃʊr/ *v* [T] to make someone feel calm and less worried about a problem: *Kids need to be reassured that their parents love them no matter what.*

**re·as·sur·ing** /,riə'ʃʊrɪŋ/ *adj* making someone feel calm and less worried: *a quiet reassuring voice* −**reassuringly** *adv*

**re·bate** /'ribeɪt/ *n* an amount of money that is paid back to you when you have paid too much rent, taxes etc.: *a tax rebate*

**reb·el**[1] /'rɛbəl/ *n* **1** someone who REBELS against people in authority: *Rebels have overthrown the government.* **2** someone who does not do things in the way that other people want him/her to do them: *She was a rebel at school.*

**rebel**[2] *v* **-lled, -lling** [I] to oppose or fight against someone who is in authority: *Brando played a character who rebels against small-town attitudes.*

**re·bel·lion** /rɪ'bɛlyən/ *n* [C,U] **1** an organized attempt to change the government using violence: *He led an armed rebellion against the government.* **2** opposition to someone in authority: *teenage rebellion* −compare REVOLUTION

**re·bel·lious** /rɪ'bɛlyəs/ *adj* **1** deliberately disobeying someone in authority: *I was a rebellious child.* **2** fighting against the government by using violence: *rebellious troops*

**re·birth** /ri'bɚθ, 'ribɚθ/ *n* [singular] a change that results in an old idea, method etc. becoming popular again

**re·bound**[1] /'ribaʊnd, rɪ'baʊnd/ *v* **1** [I] if a ball rebounds, it moves quickly back after hitting something solid: *The ball rebounded off the hoop.* **2** to increase again after decreasing; IMPROVE: *Oil prices rebounded this week.*

**re·bound**[2] /'ribaʊnd/ *n* **on the rebound** someone who is on the rebound is upset or confused because a romantic relationship has ended

**re·buff** /rɪ'bʌf/ *v* [T] FORMAL to be unkind to someone who is trying to be friendly or helpful: *His offer of help was rebuffed.* −**rebuff** *n*

**re·build** /ri'bɪld/ *v* [T] **1** to build something again, after it has been damaged or destroyed: *The freeway system was quickly rebuilt after the earthquake.* **2** to make something strong and successful again: *attempts to rebuild the area's economy*

**re·buke** /rɪ'byuk/ *v* [T] FORMAL to criticize someone because s/he has done something wrong: *The band has been rebuked by the critics for writing racist songs.* −**rebuke** *n* [C,U]

**re·but** /rɪ'bʌt/ *v* **-tted, -tting** [T] FORMAL to give reasons to show that a statement or a legal charge that has been made against you is false −**rebuttal** /rɪ'bʌtl/ *n*

**re·cal·ci·trant** /rɪ'kælsətrənt/ *adj* FORMAL refusing to obey or be controlled, even after being punished −**recalcitrance** *n* [U]

**re·call**[1] /rɪ'kɔl/ *v* [T] **1** to remember something: *I don't recall meeting him.* | *He couldn't recall who he had spoken to.* **2** to ask people to return a product they bought from your

company because something may be wrong with it

**re·call**[2] /rɪ'kɔl, 'rikɔl/ *n* **1** [U] the ability to remember something you have learned or experienced: *She has total recall* (=ability to remember everything) *of what she has read.* **2** a situation in which a company RECALLs a product

**re·cant** /rɪ'kænt/ *v* [I,T] FORMAL to say publicly that you no longer have a particular religious or political belief

**re·cap** /'rikæp, ri'kæp/ *n* [C usually singular] INFORMAL the act of repeating the main points of something that has just been said: *And now for a recap of tonight's news.* −**recap** *v* [I,T]

**re·cap·ture** /ri'kæptʃɚ/ *v* [T] **1** to make someone experience or feel something again: *a movie that recaptures the innocence of childhood* **2** to win a piece of land back that you have lost in a war, or to win a political position again after losing it: *Christians recaptured Budapest from the Ottoman Empire in 1686.* **3** to catch a prisoner or animal that has escaped: *Both men were recaptured by the police.*

**re·cede** /rɪ'sid/ *v* [I] **1** if something you see, feel, or hear recedes, it gets further and further away until it disappears: *The sound receded into the distance.* | *Tensions between the two countries have receded for the moment.* **2** if your hair recedes, you gradually lose the hair at the front of your head **3** if water recedes it moves back from an area that it was covering

**re·ceipt** /rɪ'sit/ *n* **1** a piece of paper that shows that you have received money or goods: *Be sure and keep your receipts for tax purposes.* **2** [U] FORMAL the act of receiving something: *The contract becomes valid on/upon receipt of* (=when we receive) *your letter.*

**re·ceive** /rɪ'siv/ *v* [T] **1** to be given something officially: *He received an award from the college.* **2** FORMAL to get a letter, telephone call etc.: *Have you received my letter?* **3** FORMAL if you receive medical treatment, an injury etc., it happens or is done to you: *My father is receiving chemotherapy.* **4** FORMAL to accept or welcome someone officially as a guest or member of a group: *Perez was received at the White House and given the award.*

**re·ceiv·er** /rɪ'sivɚ/ *n* **1** the part of a telephone that you hold next to your mouth and ear −see usage note at TELEPHONE **2** a piece of electronic equipment in a STEREO that changes electrical signals into sound, then makes them loud enough to hear **3** someone who is officially in control of a company or business that is BANKRUPT (=has no money) **4** in football, the player who is allowed to catch the ball −see picture on page 472

**re·ceiv·er·ship** /rɪ'sivɚˌʃɪp/ *n* [U] **go into receivership** if a company or business goes into receivership, it starts to be controlled by an official RECEIVER

R

**re·cent** /'risənt/ adj having happened or begun to exist only a short time ago: *In a recent interview, she said she wanted to try a singing career.* | *The **most recent** edition of the magazine has Roseanne's picture on it.* | *Their businesses have had troubles **in recent years/months**.* —see usage note at NEW

**re·cent·ly** /'risəntli/ adv **1** not long ago: *We recently moved from Ohio.* **2** during the recent period of days or weeks; lately: *I haven't seen him recently.* —see usage note at LATELY

**re·cep·ta·cle** /rɪ'sɛptəkəl/ n FORMAL a container

**re·cep·tion** /rɪ'sɛpʃən/ n **1** a large formal party to celebrate something or to welcome someone: *a wedding reception* | *a reception for the visiting professors* **2** a way of reacting to a person or idea that shows what you think of him, her, or it: *He got a **warm reception** (=a friendly greeting) from the crowd.* **3** [U] the quality of the sound of your radio or the picture of your television: *My TV **gets good reception**.*

**re·cep·tion·ist** /rɪ'sɛpʃənɪst/ n someone whose job is to welcome and help people at a hotel, business office etc.

**re·cep·tive** /rɪ'sɛptɪv/ adj willing to listen to new ideas or new opinions: *Ron isn't very **receptive to** other people's suggestions.*

**re·cess** /'risɛs, rɪ'sɛs/ n **1** [U] a time when children are allowed to go outside to play during the school day: *Charlie got into a fight **during/at recess**.* **2** [C,U] a time of rest during the working day or year at a law court, government etc.: *Congress is **in recess** until January.* **3** a space in the wall of a room for shelves, cupboards etc.

**re·ces·sion** /rɪ'sɛʃən/ n a period of time when there is less business activity, trade etc. than usual

**re·charge** /ri'tʃɑrdʒ/ v [T] to put a new supply of electricity into a BATTERY —**rechargeable** adj

**rec·i·pe** /'rɛsəpi/ n **1** a set of instructions that tells you how to cook something: *a recipe for chocolate cake* **2** INFORMAL **be a recipe for sth** to be likely to cause a particular result: *Inviting Paul and his ex-wife to the party was a recipe for disaster.*

**re·cip·i·ent** /rɪ'sɪpiənt/ n FORMAL someone who receives something: *Bauer has been the recipient of many honors.*

**re·cip·ro·cal** /rɪ'sɪprəkəl/ adj FORMAL a reciprocal agreement, relationship etc. is one where two groups of people do or give the same things to each other

**re·cip·ro·cate** /rɪ'sɪprə,keɪt/ v [I,T] FORMAL to do or give something because something similar has been done or given to you

**re·cit·al** /rɪ'saɪtl/ n a public performance of a piece of music or poetry, usually by one person: *a piano recital*

**re·cite** /rɪ'saɪt/ v [I,T] to say something such as a poem, story etc. that you know by memory: *Everyone had to recite a poem today at school.* —**recitation** /,rɛsə'teɪʃən/ n [C,U]

**reck·less** /'rɛklɪs/ adj not caring about danger or the bad results of your behavior, or showing this quality: *As a boy he was wild and reckless.* | *reckless driving* | *reckless decisions* —**recklessly** adv —**recklessness** n [U]

**reck·on** /'rɛkən/ v [T] **1** to guess a number, amount etc. without calculating it exactly: *The software company reckons it will sell 2.5 million units this year.* **2** SPOKEN to think or suppose: *I reckon they'll be late.*

**reckon with** sb/sth phr v [T] to consider a possible problem when you think about the future: *The new team is a **force to be reckoned with**.* (=something to consider seriously)

**reck·on·ing** /'rɛkənɪŋ/ n [U] calculation that is not exact: *By my reckoning, we should be there by now.*

**re·claim** /rɪ'kleɪm/ v [T] **1** to ask for something to be given back to you: *reclaiming lost luggage* **2** to make something able to be used, when it has never been used or has not been used for a while: *The organization is trying to reclaim desert land for farming.* —**reclamation** /,rɛklə'meɪʃən/ n [U]

**re·cline** /rɪ'klaɪn/ v **1** [I,T] to push the back of a seat or chair so that it slopes backward, so that you can lean back in it: *The front seats of the car recline.* **2** [I] to lie or sit back in a relaxed way: *people reclining on the grass in the sunshine*

**rec·luse** /'rɛklus/ n someone who likes to live alone and avoids other people —**reclusive** /rɪ'klusɪv/ adj

**rec·og·ni·tion** /,rɛkəg'nɪʃən/ n **1** [singular, U] public admiration and thanks for someone's work or achievements: *She was given an award **in recognition of** 25 years of service.* | *His music didn't **receive recognition** in his lifetime.* **2** [U] the act of recognizing someone or something

**rec·og·niz·a·ble** /,rɛkəg'naɪzəbəl/ adj able to be easily recognized: *The car was barely recognizable when they pulled it out of the river.*

**rec·og·nize** /'rɛkəg,naɪz/ v [T] **1** to know someone or something that you have seen before: *I recognized him from an old photograph.* **2** to accept officially that an organization, government etc. is legal: *The UN has refused to recognize the new government.* **3** to accept and admit that something is true or real: *Dr. Campbell **recognizes that** the treatment may cause problems for some patients.* **4** to thank someone officially for something that s/he has done: *Tonight we'd like to recognize some people who have worked very hard for us.*

**re·coil** /'rikɔɪl, rɪ'kɔɪl/ v [I] to move back suddenly from something that you do not like or are afraid of: *Emily recoiled at the sight of the snake.*

**rec·ol·lect** /ˌrɛkəˈlɛkt/ v [T] OLD-FASHIONED to remember something: *I don't recollect her name.*

**rec·ol·lec·tion** /ˌrɛkəˈlɛkʃən/ n [C,U] FORMAL something from the past that you remember, or the act of remembering it: *He has no recollection of the crash.*

**rec·om·mend** /ˌrɛkəˈmɛnd/ v [T] **1** to advise someone to do something: *She recommended that I try the soup.* | *We recommend hiring a professional designer.* **2** to praise someone or something as being good for a particular purpose: *Can you recommend a local restaurant?* **3 sth has little/nothing etc. to recommend it** used in order to say that something has few or no good qualities: *The hotel has little to recommend it, except that it's cheap.*

> **USAGE NOTE recommend, suggest, ask, insist, request, demand**
>
> When you use these verbs with "that," use only the INFINITIVE form of the verb without "to," even if the subject is singular: *I recommend that this plan be accepted.* | *May I suggest that he meet us later?* | *We ask that the committee review the facts.*

**rec·om·men·da·tion** /ˌrɛkəmənˈdeɪʃən/ n **1** advice given to someone, especially about what to do: *The committee was able to make detailed recommendations to the school.* | *the department's recommendation that he be fired* **2** [U] the action of saying that someone or something is good for a particular purpose: *We took the tour on a friend's recommendation.* **3** a letter or statement that someone is suitable for a particular job, course of study etc.: *Can you write a recommendation for me?*

**rec·om·pense** /ˈrɛkəmˌpɛns/ v [T] FORMAL to give someone a payment for trouble or losses that you have caused –**recompense** n [singular, U]

**rec·on·cile** /ˈrɛkənˌsaɪl/ v **1 be reconciled (with)** to have a good relationship with someone again after arguing with him/her: *His parents are now reconciled with each other.* **2** [T] to show that two different ideas, situations etc. can exist together and are not opposed to each other: *How can he reconcile his religious beliefs with all this gambling?*
**reconcile** sb/yourself **to** sth phr v [T] to make someone able to accept an unpleasant situation: *She never reconciled herself to her son's drug problem.*

**rec·on·cil·i·a·tion** /ˌrɛkənˌsɪliˈeɪʃən/ n [C,U] a situation in which two people, countries etc. become friendly again after arguing or fighting with each other: *There is still hope of a reconciliation between the two groups.*

**re·con·di·tion** /ˌrikənˈdɪʃən/ v [T] to repair something so that it works well or looks good again: *a reconditioned vacuum cleaner*

**re·con·nais·sance** /rɪˈkɑnəsəns, -zəns/ n [C,U] the activity of sending out aircraft or soldiers in order to get information about the enemy –**reconnoiter** /ˌrikəˈnɔɪtə/ v [I,T]

**re·con·sid·er** /ˌrikənˈsɪdə/ v [I,T] to think again about something in order to decide if you should change your opinion: *Won't you reconsider our offer?* –**reconsideration** /ˌrikənˌsɪdəˈreɪʃən/ n [U]

**re·con·sti·tute** /riˈkɑnstəˌtut/ v [T] **1** to make a group, organization etc. exist in a different form: *The four political groups will be reconstituted as a new party.* **2** to change dried food into its original form by adding water to it

**re·con·struct** /ˌrikənˈstrʌkt/ v [T] **1** to produce a complete description of something that happened by collecting pieces of information: *Police have reconstructed the events leading up to the crime.* **2** to build something again after it has been destroyed or damaged

**re·con·struc·tion** /ˌrikənˈstrʌkʃən/ n **1** [U] work that is done to repair damage to a city, industry etc. especially after a war: *the reconstruction of the former East Germany* **2** a medical operation to replace a bone or part of the body that has been damaged: *hip reconstruction*

**re·cord¹** /ˈrɛkəd/ n **1** [C,U] information about something that is written down so that it can be looked at in the future: *Keep a record of how much you spend on this trip.* | *the highest water levels on record* (=that have been written in records ) **2** the fastest speed, longest distance, highest or lowest level etc. ever: *She broke the record for the 1500 meter run.* | *a record high/low temperature* **3** the known facts about someone's past behavior and how good or bad it has been: *Our company has a good/bad record for giving money to charity.* **4** a round flat piece of plastic on which music is stored: *a record collection* **5 off/on the record** not official and not meant to be repeated, or official and able to be repeated: *Canelli told us off the record that he had new evidence.* **6 for the record** used in order to tell someone that what you are saying should be remembered: *For the record, my salary has never been close to $1 million!*

**re·cord²** /rɪˈkɔrd/ v **1** [T] to write information down so that it can be looked at in the future: *All the data is recorded on computer.* **2** [I,T] to store pictures, a television show etc. on VIDEO: *Will you record "The X-Files" for me?* | *A friend who owns a camcorder recorded their wedding for them.* –compare FILM² **3** [I,T] to store music, sound etc. on something so that it can be listened to again: *Recently the group finished recording their third album.*

R

**4** [T] to measure the size, speed, temperature etc. of something so that it can be seen

**re·cord-break·ing** /'.. ,../ adj better, higher, faster etc. than anything done before: *a record-breaking speed/flight etc.*

**re·cord·er** /rɪ'kɔrdɚ/ n **1** ⇨ TAPE RECORDER **2** a small wooden musical instrument shaped like a tube, that you play by blowing into it

**re·cord·ing** /rɪ'kɔrdɪŋ/ n a piece of music, speech etc. that has been recorded: *a recording of Vivaldi's "Gloria"*

**record play·er** /'.. ,../ n a piece of equipment for playing records

**re·count¹** /rɪ'kaʊnt/ v [T] **1** FORMAL to tell a story or describe a series of events: *a TV movie recounting the war years* **2** to count something again

**re·count²** /'rikaʊnt/ n a process of counting votes again

**re·coup** /rɪ'kup/ v [T] to get back money you have lost or spent: *The agency should recoup its investment in a year.*

**re·course** /'rikɔrs, rɪ'kɔrs/ n [U] FORMAL something you can do to help yourself in a difficult situation, or the act of doing this: *The police **had no recourse but to** shoot.* (=shooting was their only choice)

**re·cov·er** /rɪ'kʌvɚ/ v **1** [I] to get better after an illness, injury, shock etc.: *My uncle is **recovering from** a heart attack.* **2** [I] to return to a normal condition after a period of trouble or difficulty: *The economy will take at least three years to recover.* **3** [T] to get back something that was taken from you, lost, or almost destroyed: *The police managed to recover the stolen goods.* **4** [T] to get back your ability to control your feelings or your body: *He never recovered the use of his arm.*

**re·cov·er·y** /rɪ'kʌvəri/ n **1** [C,U] the process of getting better after an illness, injury etc.: *a quick **recovery from** the flu* **2** [C,U] the process of returning to a normal condition after a period of trouble or difficulty: *Oklahoma's economic recovery* **3** [U] the act of getting something back: *the **recovery** of the stolen jewels*

**re·cre·ate** /,rikri'eɪt/ v [T] to make something exist again or be experienced again: *a museum that recreates a Native American settlement*

**rec·re·a·tion** /,rɛkri'eɪʃən/ n [C,U] an activity that you do for pleasure or fun: *The new park is being built to provide recreation especially for kids. | the city's Parks and Recreation department* —**recreational** adj —see usage note at SPORT

**re·crim·i·na·tion** /rɪ,krɪmə'neɪʃən/ n [C usually plural, U] a situation in which people blame each other, or the things they say when they are blaming each other

**re·cruit¹** /rɪ'krut/ v [I,T] to find new people to work in a company, join an organization, do a

job etc.: *The coaches are visiting colleges in order to recruit new players.* —**recruitment** n [U] —**recruiter** n

**recruit²** n someone who has recently joined a company or an organization

**rec·tan·gle** /'rɛk,tæŋgəl/ n a shape with four straight sides, two of which are usually longer than the other two, and four RIGHT ANGLES —**rectangular** /rɛk'tæŋgyəlɚ/ adj —see picture at SHAPE

**rec·ti·fy** /'rɛktə,faɪ/ v [T] FORMAL to correct something that is wrong: *All efforts to rectify the problem have failed.*

**rec·tor** /'rɛktɚ/ n **1** a priest who is in charge of a local Episcopal church **2** the person in charge of some colleges or schools

**rec·tum** /'rɛktəm/ n TECHNICAL the lowest part of your BOWELs —**rectal** /'rɛktl/ adj

**re·cu·per·ate** /rɪ'kupə,reɪt/ v [I] to get better after an illness, injury etc.: *Jan is still **recuperating from** her operation.* —**recuperation** /rɪ,kupə'reɪʃən/ n [U]

**re·cur** /rɪ'kɚ/ v **-rred, -rring** [I] to happen again, or to happen several times: *a recurring dream* —**recurrence** n [C,U] —**recurrent** adj

**re·cy·cla·ble** /ri'saɪkləbəl/ adj able to be RECYCLEd: *recyclable bottles* —**recyclable** n [C usually plural]

**re·cy·cle** /ri'saɪkəl/ v [I,T] to put used objects or materials through a special process, so that they can be used again: *bottles that can be recycled* —**recycled** /,ri'saɪkəld/ adj: *recycled paper* —**recycling** n [U]

**red¹** /rɛd/ **-dder, -ddest** adj **1** having the color of blood: *a red dress* **2** hair that is red is an orange-brown color **3** skin that is red is a bright pink color **4** a wording meaning COMMUNIST that is considered to be offensive —**redness** n [U]

**red²** n **1** [C,U] a red color **2** **be in the red** to owe more money than you have —opposite **be in the black** (BLACK²) **3** **see red** to become very angry: *The way he treated his dog just made me see red.*

**red-blood·ed** /,. '..◂/ adj **red-blooded male/American/capitalist etc.** HUMOROUS used in order to emphasize that someone has all of the qualities that a typical man, American etc. is supposed to have: *As any red-blooded male will tell you, football is one of America's major religions.*

**red car·pet** /,. '../ n [singular] special treatment that you give someone important who is visiting you: *Hollywood stars who visit the restaurant are given the **red carpet treatment**.*

**Red Cres·cent** /,. '../ n [singular] a part of the Red Cross that works in Muslim countries

**Red Cross** /,. './ n [singular] an international organization that helps people who are suffering as a result of war, floods, disease etc.

**red·den** /'rɛdn/ v [I,T] to become red, or to make something do this: *Tina's face reddened with embarrassment.*

**re·deem** /rɪ'dim/ v [T] FORMAL **1** **redeeming quality/value etc.** a good quality etc. that keeps something from being completely bad or wrong: *The TV programs he watches have no redeeming social value.* **2** to exchange a piece of paper representing an amount of money for the money that it is worth: *Redeem this coupon for 20¢ off a jar of coffee.* **3** **redeem yourself** to do something to improve other people's opinion of you, after you have behaved badly or failed **4** a word meaning to free someone from the power of evil, used especially in the Christian religion –**redeemable** *adj*

**re·demp·tion** /rɪ'dɛmpʃən/ n [U] **1** **past/beyond redemption** too bad to be saved, improved, or fixed **2** the state of being freed from the power of evil, believed by Christians to be made possible by Jesus Christ

**re·de·vel·op** /,ridə'vɛləp/ v [T] to make an area more modern by putting in new buildings or changing old ones –**redevelopment** n [C,U]

**red-eye** /'. ./ n [U] INFORMAL a plane with PASSENGERS on it that makes a trip that starts late at night and arrives early in the morning: *the red-eye from Chicago to Seattle*

**red-hand·ed** /,. '..⸴/ adj **catch sb red-handed** INFORMAL to catch someone at the moment when s/he is doing something wrong: *She was caught red-handed taking money from the register.*

**red·head** /'rɛdhɛd/ n someone who has red hair

**red her·ring** /,. '../ n a fact or idea that is not important but is introduced in order to take your attention away from something that is important

**red-hot** /,. '.⸴/ adj extremely hot: *red-hot metal*

**re·di·rect** /,ridɪ'rɛkt, -daɪ-/ v [T] to send something in a different direction, or use something for a different purpose: *Our mail has been redirected to the new house. | She needs to redirect her energy into something more useful.*

**red-light dis·trict** /,. '. ,../ n the area of a city where there are many PROSTITUTES

**red meat** /,. './ n [U] dark colored meat such as BEEF

**red·neck** /'rɛdnɛk/ n INFORMAL DISAPPROVING someone who lives in a country area, is not educated, and has strong unreasonable opinions

**re·do** /ri'du/ v [T] to do something again: *You'll have to redo this essay.*

**re·dou·ble** /ri'dʌbəl/ v [T] **redouble your efforts** to greatly increase your efforts to do something

**re·dress** /rɪ'drɛs/ v [T] FORMAL to correct something that is wrong, not equal, or unfair: *Tax laws help the rich, not the poor; Congress*

should *redress the balance.* –**redress** /'ridrɛs, rɪ'drɛs/ n [U]

**red tape** /,. './ n [U] official rules that seem unnecessary and that delay action

**re·duce** /rɪ'dus/ v [I,T] to become smaller or less in size, amount, price etc., or to make something do this: *a jacket reduced from $75 to $35 | Reduce the heat and simmer the rice for another 10 minutes.*

**reduce** sb/sth **to** sth phr v [T] **1** **reduce sb to tears/silence/poverty etc.** to make someone cry, be silent, become poor etc.: *They were reduced to begging on the streets.* **2** **reduce sth to rubble/ashes/ruins** to destroy something completely, especially a building or city

**re·duc·tion** /rɪ'dʌkʃən/ n [C,U] a decrease in size, amount, price etc.: *a reduction in the price of gasoline*

**re·dun·dant** /rɪ'dʌndənt/ adj not necessary because something else means or does the same thing. For example, "female sister" is a redundant phrase –**redundancy** n [U]

**red·wood** /'rɛdwʊd/ n [C,U] a very tall tree that grows near the coast in Oregon and California

**reed** /rid/ n **1** a tall plant like grass that grows near water **2** a thin piece of wood in some musical instruments that produces a sound when you blow over it

**re·ed·u·ca·tion** /,. ..'../ n [U] the process of teaching someone to think or behave differently, especially about politics –**re-educate** /. '.../ v [T]

**reef** /rif/ n a line of sharp rocks or a raised area of sand near the surface of the sea

**reek** /rik/ v [I] to smell strongly of something unpleasant: *His breath reeked of garlic.* –**reek** n [singular]

**reel**[1] /ril/ n **1** a round object onto which things such as special string for FISHING or film can be wound **2** the amount that one of these objects will hold: *a reel of film*

**reel**[2] v **1** [I] to walk in an unsteady way and almost fall over, as if you are drunk: *A guy came reeling down the hallway.* **2** **be reeling** to be so badly affected or shocked by a situation that you do not know what to do next : *The hotel chain is still reeling from the effects of their financial and legal problems.* **3** [T] to wind or unwind string for FISHING on a REEL

**reel** sth ↔ **off** phr v [T] INFORMAL to repeat a lot of information quickly and easily: *Andy can reel off the names of all the state capitals.*

**re·e·lect** /,riə'lɛkt/ v [T] to elect someone again –**reelection** /riə'lɛkʃən/ n [C,U]

**re·en·act** /,. .'./ v [T] to perform the actions of a story, crime etc. that happened in the past: *children re-enacting the Christmas story* –**reenactment** n

**re·en·try** /ri'ɛntri/ n [C,U] an act of entering a

place or situation again: *a spacecraft's **reentry** into the Earth's atmosphere.*

**ref** /rɛf/ *n* SPOKEN ⇨ REFEREE[1]

**re·fer** /rɪˈfɚ/ *v* **-rred, -rring**
  **refer to** *phr v* [T] **1** [**refer to** sb/sth] to mention or speak about someone or something: *He referred to her simply as "my friend."*
  **2** [**refer to** sth] to look at a book, map, piece of paper etc. for information: ***Refer to** page 14 for instructions.* **3** [**refer to** sb/sth] if a statement, number, report etc. refers to someone or something, it is about that person or thing: *The blue line on the graph **refers to** sales.* **4** [**refer** sb/sth **to** sb/sth] to send someone or something to another place or person for information, advice, or a decision: *Professor Harris **referred** me **to** an article she had written.*

**ref·er·ee[1]** /ˌrɛfəˈri/ *n* someone who makes sure that the rules are followed during a game in sports such as football, basketball, or BOXING

**R**

---
**USAGE NOTE referee and umpire**

Both of these words mean the person who makes sure that the rules are followed in a sports game. Use **referee** with basketball, boxing, football, hockey, soccer, and wrestling. Use **umpire** with baseball, tennis, and volleyball.

---

**referee[2]** *v* [I,T] to be the REFEREE for a game

**ref·er·ence** /ˈrɛfrəns/ *n* **1** [C,U] something you say or write that mentions another person or thing: *In his letter, Sam **made** no **reference to** his illness.* **2** [C,U] the act of looking at something for information, or the book, magazine etc. you get the information from: *Keep a dictionary on your desk for easy reference.* | *the reference section of the library* **3** **a)** a letter containing information about you that is written by someone who knows you well, usually to a new employer **b)** the person who writes this letter **4** a note that tells you where the information that is used in a book, article etc. comes from

**reference book** /ˈ.. ˌ./ *n* a book, such as a dictionary, that you look at to find information

**reference li·brar·y** /ˈ.. ˌ..../, **reference room** /ˈ.. ˌ./ *n* a public library or a room in a library, that contains REFERENCE BOOKs that you can use but not take away

**ref·er·en·dum** /ˌrɛfəˈrɛndəm/ *n, plural* **referenda** /-də/ *or* **referendums** [C,U] an occasion when you vote in order to make a decision about a particular subject, rather than voting for a person

**re·fill[1]** /riˈfɪl/ *v* [T] to fill something again: *Could you refill the glasses, please?* **–refillable** *adj*

**re·fill[2]** /ˈrifɪl/ *n* **1** a container filled with a particular substance that you use to REFILL something: *refills for an ink pen* **2** SPOKEN

another drink to REFILL your glass: *Would you like a refill?*

**re·fi·nance** /riˈfaɪnæns, ˌrifəˈnæns/ *v* [T] to borrow or lend money in order to change the way someone pays back a debt: *We'd like to refinance the house to make the payments smaller.*

**re·fine** /rɪˈfaɪn/ *v* [T] **1** to make a substance more pure using an industrial process: *Gasoline is refined from crude oil.* **2** to improve a method, plan, system etc. by making some changes to it: *Ideas from Lopez's short stories are further refined in his novels.*

**re·fined** /rɪˈfaɪnd/ *adj* **1** made more pure using an industrial process: *refined flour* **2** improved and made more effective: *a refined method of measurement* **3** polite, educated, and interested in art, music, and literature

**re·fine·ment** /rɪˈfaɪnmənt/ *n* **1** [U] the process of improving something or making a substance more pure: *the **refinement of** sugar* | *the **refinement** of their economic theories* **2** a change to an existing product, plan, system etc. that improves it: *We've added a number of refinements to the design.* **3** [U] the quality of being REFINED

**re·fin·er·y** /rɪˈfaɪnəri/ *n* a factory where something such as oil, sugar, or metal is REFINED

**re·fin·ish** /riˈfɪnɪʃ/ *v* [T] to give the surface of something, especially wood, a new appearance by painting or polishing it: *Dad refinished Grandma's old desk.*

**re·flect** /rɪˈflɛkt/ *v*

reflect

**1** [T] to show or be a sign of a particular situation, idea, or feeling: *Children's behavior reflects their environment.* | *People's opinions about Congress have been reflected in the election results.* **2** [I] to think carefully: *Please take some time to **reflect on** our offer.*

**3** [I,T] if a surface reflects light, heat, or an image, it throws back the light etc. that hits it: *mountains **reflected in** the lake* | *sunlight **reflecting off** the whitewashed houses*

  **reflect on** sb/sth *phr v* [T] to influence people's opinion of someone or something, especially in a bad way: *behavior that **reflects** badly **on** the school*

**re·flec·tion** /rɪˈflɛkʃən/ *n* **1** [C,U] careful thought, or an idea or opinion based on this: *a writer's **reflections on** America in the 1920s* | *taking time for reflection* **2** something that shows, or is a sign of, a particular situation, fact, or feeling: *The rise in crime is a **reflection** of a violent society.* | *If your kids are bad, it's a **reflection on** you.* (=a sign that you are a bad parent) **3** an image REFLECTed in a mirror or a similar surface: *We looked at our reflections in the pool.* –see picture at REFLECT **4** [U] the light or heat that is REFLECTed from something

**re·flec·tive** /rɪˈflɛktɪv/ *adj* **1** a reflective surface REFLECTs light **2** thinking quietly, or showing that you are doing this: *He was in a reflective mood.*

**re·flec·tor** /rɪˈflɛktɚ/ *n* a small piece of plastic that REFLECTs light

**re·flex** /ˈriflɛks/ *n* [C usually plural] a sudden physical reaction that you have without thinking about it: *basketball players with good reflexes* (=the ability to react quickly)

**re·flex·ive** /rɪˈflɛksɪv/ *n* TECHNICAL in grammar, a verb or a pronoun that shows that an action affects the person or thing that does the action. In the sentence "I enjoyed myself," "myself" is reflexive —**reflexive** *adj*

**re·form¹** /rɪˈfɔrm/ *v* **1** [T] to improve an organization or system by making a lot of changes to it: *plans to reform the tax laws* **2** [I,T] to improve your behavior by making a lot of changes to it, or to make someone do this: *a reformed criminal/alcoholic etc.* (=someone who is no longer a criminal etc.) | *No one believes that Uncle Max has reformed.*

**reform²** *n* [C,U] a change made to an organization or system in order to improve it: *educational reforms*

**ref·or·ma·tion** /ˌrɛfɚˈmeɪʃən/ *n* [C,U] an improvement made by changing something a lot: *the reformation of the welfare system*

**re·form·er** /rɪˈfɔrmɚ/ *n* someone who works hard to make a lot of changes in order to improve a government or society

**reform school** /.'. ,./ *n* a special school where young people who have broken the law are sent

**re·frain¹** /rɪˈfreɪn/ *v* [I] FORMAL to stop yourself from doing something: *Please refrain from smoking.*

**refrain²** *n* part of a song that is repeated, especially at the end of each VERSE

**re·fresh** /rɪˈfrɛʃ/ *v* [T] to make someone feel less tired or less hot: *A shower will refresh you.* **2 refresh sb's memory** to say something that makes someone remember something: *Please refresh my memory - what was your last job?* —**refreshed** *adj*

**re·fresh·er course** /.'.. ,./ *n* a training class that teaches you about new developments in a subject or skill you have already studied or learned

**re·fresh·ing** /rɪˈfrɛʃɪŋ/ *adj* **1** making you feel less tired or less hot: *a refreshing drink* **2** pleasantly different from what is familiar and boring: *Their music makes a refreshing change from typical radio songs.* —**refreshingly** *adv*

**re·fresh·ment** /rɪˈfrɛʃmənt/ *n* **1** [C usually plural] food and drinks that are provided at a meeting, party, sports event etc.: *Refreshments will be served after the concert.* **2** [U] food and drinks in general

**re·frig·er·ate** /rɪˈfrɪdʒəˌreɪt/ *v* [T] to make something such as food and drinks cold in order to preserve them: *Refrigerate the sauce overnight.* —**refrigeration** /rɪˌfrɪdʒəˈreɪʃən/ *n* [U]

**re·frig·er·a·tor** /rɪˈfrɪdʒəˌreɪtɚ/ *n* a large piece of kitchen equipment used for keeping food and drinks cold, shaped like a metal cupboard and kept cold by electricity –see picture at KITCHEN

**re·fuel** /rɪˈfyul/ *v* [I,T] to fill a vehicle or plane with FUEL again before continuing on a trip

**ref·uge** /ˈrɛfyudʒ/ *n* a place that provides protection or shelter from bad weather or danger: *About 50 families have taken refuge* (=found protection) *in a Red Cross shelter.*

**ref·u·gee** /ˌrɛfyʊˈdʒi / *n* someone who has been forced to leave his/her country, especially during a war

**re·fund¹** /ˈrifʌnd/ *n* an amount of money that is given back to you if you are not satisfied with the goods or services you have paid for: *Two cups were broken, so they gave me a refund.*

**re·fund²** /rɪˈfʌnd/ *v* [T] to give someone his/her money back because something is wrong with the goods or services s/he paid for

**re·fur·bish** /rɪˈfɚbɪʃ/ *v* [T] to thoroughly repair and improve a building by painting it, cleaning it etc. —**refurbishment** *n* [C,U]

**re·fus·al** /rɪˈfyuzəl/ *n* [C,U] an act of saying or showing that you will not do, accept, or allow something: *His refusal to take the drug test caused him to lose his job.*

**re·fuse¹** /rɪˈfyuz/ *v* **1** [I,T] to say or show that you will not do or accept something: *I asked her to marry me, but she refused.* | *Cindy refuses to go to school.* | *an offer that's too good to refuse* (=so good that you cannot say no) **2** [T] to not give or allow someone to have something that s/he wants: *We were refused permission to enter the country.*

---

**USAGE NOTE** reject, turn down, refuse, and decline

Use all of these words in order to show that you do not accept something. If you **reject** something or someone, you say firmly that you will not accept an offer, a suggestion, someone's friendship etc.: *They have until December 19 to accept or reject the proposal.* | *Kieran's book got rejected by every publisher.* **Turn down** is an informal way to say **reject**: *You'd be stupid to turn down such a good job offer.* If you **refuse** something, you say no, although someone very much wants you to accept it: *Peggy refused all offers of help.* If you **decline** an offer, you say politely that you cannot or will not accept it: *I'm sorry, but I'll have to decline the invitation.*

R

**ref·use**² /'rɛfjus/ *n* [U] FORMAL waste material; TRASH

**re·fute** /rɪ'fyut/ *v* [T] FORMAL to prove that a statement or idea is not correct or fair: *Jamieson refuted the charges in court.*

**re·gain** /rɪ'geɪn/ *v* [T] to get something back: *Valerie's slowly regaining her health after her operation.*

**re·gal** /'rigəl/ *adj* typical of a king or queen or suitable for a king or queen

**re·ga·lia** /rɪ'geɪlyə/ *n* [U] traditional clothes and decorations, used at official ceremonies: *academic regalia*

**re·gard**¹ /rɪ'gɑrd/ *n* FORMAL **1** [U] respect for someone or something, or careful attention that shows this: *He's always been **held in high regard** (=respected very much) by the entire department.* | *You have no **regard for** my feelings!* **2 with/in regard to** FORMAL used in order to say what you are talking or writing about: *Several changes have been made with regard to security.*

**regard**² *v* [T] **1** to think about someone or something in a particular way: *I've always **regarded** you **as** my friend.* **2** FORMAL to look at someone or something, especially in a particular way: *She regarded him thoughtfully.*

**re·gard·ing** /rɪ'gɑrdɪŋ/ *prep* FORMAL a word used especially in business letters to introduce the particular subject you are writing about: *Regarding your recent inquiry, I've enclosed a copy of our new brochure.*

**re·gard·less** /rɪ'gɑrdlɪs/ *adv* **1 regardless of** in spite of difficulties or opposition: *He'll sign that contract regardless of what anyone says!* **2** without being affected by different situations, problems etc.: *You get a lot of criticism but you just have to continue, regardless.*

**re·gards** /rɪ'gɑrdz/ *n* [plural] good wishes: *My cousin **sends his regards**.*

**re·gat·ta** /rɪ'gɑt̬ə, -'gæ-/ *n* a race for rowing or sailing boats

**re·gen·er·ate** /ri'dʒɛnə,reɪt/ *v* [I,T] FORMAL to develop and grow strong again, or to make something do this: *Given time, the forest will regenerate.* –**regeneration** /rɪ,dʒɛnə'reɪʃən/ *n* [U]

**re·gent** /'ridʒənt/ *n* a member of a small group of people that makes decisions about education in a US state, or that governs a university: *the Iowa Board of Regents*

**reg·gae** /'rɛgeɪ/ *n* [U] a type of popular music from Jamaica

**re·gime** /reɪ'ʒim, rɪ-/ *n* **1** a government that has not been elected in fair elections **2** a particular system of government or management, especially one you disapprove of: *the Communist regime* **3** ⇨ REGIMEN

**re·gi·men** /'rɛdʒəmən/, **regime** *n* a special plan for eating, exercising etc. that is intended to improve your health

**reg·i·ment** /'rɛdʒəmənt/ *n* a large group of soldiers consisting of several BATTALIONs –**regimental** /,rɛdʒə'mɛnt̬l/ *adj*

**reg·i·ment·ed** /'rɛdʒə,mɛntɪd/ *adj* controlled very strictly: *Prisoners follow a highly regimented schedule.* –**regimentation** /,rɛdʒə-mən'teɪʃən/ *n* [U]

**re·gion** /'ridʒən/ *n* **1** a fairly large area of a state, country etc., usually without exact limits: *Snow is expected in mountain regions.* **2** the area around a particular part of your body: *pain in the lower back region* **3 (somewhere) in the region of** about; APPROXIMATELY: *It will cost in the region of $750.*

**re·gion·al** /'ridʒənl/ *adj* relating to a particular REGION: *regional customs* –**regionally** *adv*

**reg·is·ter**¹ /'rɛdʒəstɚ/ *n* **1** a book containing an official list or record of something: *the National Register of Historic Places* **2** the place where the warm or cool air of a heating system comes into a room, with a metal cover you can open or close **3** ⇨ CASH REGISTER

**register**² *v* **1** [I,T] to record a name, details about something etc. on an official list: *The car is registered in my sister's name.* **2** [I,T] to officially arrange to attend a particular school, university, or course; ENROLL: *How many students have **registered for** the European History class?* **3** [T] to express a feeling or opinion about something: *Her face registered surprise and shock.* **4** [I,T] if an instrument registers an amount or if an amount registers on it, the instrument shows or records that amount: *The thermometer registered 74°F.* **5** to send a package or letter by REGISTERED MAIL

**registered mail** /,... './ *n* [U] a service in which the post office records the time when your mail is sent and delivered

**registered nurse** /,... './, **RN** *n* someone who has been trained and is officially allowed to work as a nurse

**reg·is·trar** /'rɛdʒə,strɑr/ *n* someone who is in charge of official records, especially in a college

**reg·is·tra·tion** /,rɛdʒə'streɪʃən/ *n* **1** [U] the process of officially arranging to attend a particular school, university, or class; ENROLLMENT: *fall quarter registration* **2** [U] the act of recording names and details on an official list **3** an official piece of paper containing details about a vehicle and the name of its owner

**reg·is·try** /'rɛdʒəstri/ *n* a place where official records are kept

**re·gress** /rɪ'grɛs/ *v* [I] FORMAL to go back to an earlier, less developed state –**regression** /rɪ'grɛʃən/ *n* [U] –compare PROGRESS²

**re·gret**¹ /rɪ'grɛt/ *v* **-tted, -tting** [T] **1** to feel sorry about something you have done and wish you had not done it: *I've always regretted selling my dad's old fishing rod.* | *He **regrets that** he never went to college.* **2** FORMAL to be sorry and

R

sad about a situation: *I regret that I will be unable to attend.*

**regret**² *n* [C,U] sadness that you feel about something because you wish it had not happened or that you had not done it: *The company expressed deep regret at the accident.* | *Carl said he had no regrets about his decision.* –**regretfully** *adv* –**regretful** *adj*

**re·gret·ta·ble** /rɪ'grɛtəbəl/ *adj* something that is regrettable makes you feel sorry or sad because it has unpleasant results: *a regrettable mistake* –**regrettably** *adv*

**re·group** /ˌri'grup/ *v* [I,T] to form a group again in order to be more effective, or to make people do this: *The party needs time to regroup politically.*

**reg·u·lar**¹ /'rɛgyələ/ *adj*
**1** ▶REPEATED◀ repeated, with the same amount of time or space between each thing and the next: *His heartbeat is strong and regular.* | *Planes were taking off at regular intervals.*
**2** ▶NORMAL SIZE◀ of standard size: *fries and a regular coke*
**3** ▶SAME TIME◀ happening or planned for the same time every day, month, year etc.: *regular meetings* | *Once I start working regular hours, things should get better.*
**4** ▶HAPPENING OFTEN◀ happening or doing something very often: *He's one of our regular customers.*
**5** ▶USUAL◀ normal or usual: *She's not our regular babysitter.*
**6** ▶ORDINARY◀ ordinary: *I'm just a regular doctor, not a specialist.*
**7** ▶EVENLY SHAPED◀ evenly shaped with parts or sides of equal size: *regular features* (=an evenly shaped face)
**8** ▶GRAMMAR◀ TECHNICAL a regular verb or noun changes its forms in the same way as most verbs or nouns. The verb "walk" is regular, but "be" is not –**regularity** /ˌrɛgyə'lærəti/ *n* [U]

**regular**² *n* **1** INFORMAL a customer who goes to the same store, restaurant etc. very often **2** [U] gas that contains LEAD –compare UNLEADED

**reg·u·lar·ly** /'rɛgyələli, 'rɛgyəli/ *adj* **1** at regular times, for example every day, week, or month: *Brush your teeth and see your dentist regularly.* **2** often: *Janet comes to visit regularly.*

**reg·u·late** /'rɛgyəˌleɪt/ *v* [T] **1** to control an activity or process, usually by having rules: *The use of these drugs is strictly regulated.* **2** FORMAL to make a machine work at a particular speed, temperature etc.: *Use this dial to regulate the sound.*

**reg·u·la·tion** /ˌrɛgyə'leɪʃən/ *n* **1** an official rule or order: *safety regulations* **2** [U] control over something, especially by rules: *the regulation of public spending*

**reg·u·la·to·ry** /'rɛgyələˌtɔri/ *adj* FORMAL having the purpose of controlling an activity or

process, especially by rules: *the Nuclear Regulatory Commission*

**re·gur·gi·tate** /rɪ'gədʒəˌteɪt/ *v* FORMAL **1** [I,T] VOMIT **2** [T] to repeat facts, ideas etc. without understanding them clearly: *I want my students to think for themselves - not to regurgitate what they've read.* –**regurgitation** /rɪˌgədʒə'teɪʃən/ *n* [U]

**re·hab** /'rihæb/ *n* [U] INFORMAL ⇨ REHABILITATION: *Frank's been in rehab for six weeks.*

**re·ha·bil·i·tate** /ˌriə'bɪləˌteɪt, ˌrihə-/ *v* [T]
**1** to help someone to live a healthy or useful life again after s/he has been sick or in prison: *rehabilitating young criminals* **2** to improve a building or area so that it is in a good condition again

**re·ha·bil·i·ta·tion** /ˌriəˌbɪlə'teɪʃən, ˌrihə-/ *n* [U] the process of curing someone who has an alcohol or drug problem

**re·hash** /ri'hæʃ/ *v* [T] INFORMAL to use the same ideas again in a new form that is not really different or better: *He keeps rehashing the same old speech.* –**rehash** /'rihæʃ/ *n*

**re·hears·al** /rɪ'həsəl/ *n* [C,U] a period of time or a particular occasion when all the people in a play, concert etc. practice it before giving a public performance: *We only have one more rehearsal before the concert.*

**re·hearse** /rɪ'həs/ *v* [I,T] to practice something such as a play or concert before giving a public performance

**re·house** /ˌri'haʊz/ *v* [T] to put someone in a new or better home: *Many people had to be rehoused after the war.*

**reign**¹ /reɪn/ *n* **1** the period of time during which someone rules a country: *the reign of Queen Anne* **2** the period of time during which a particular situation or state exists: *a reign of terror* (=when a government kills many of its opponents)

**reign**² *v* [I] **1** the reigning champion the most recent winner of a competition **2** LITERARY to exist for a period of time as a very important or noticeable feature: *Confusion reigned this week over the budget proposals.* **3** to be the ruler of a country

**re·im·burse** /ˌriɪm'bəs/ *v* [T] FORMAL to pay money back to someone: *The company will reimburse you for your travel expenses.* –**reimbursement** *n* [U]

**rein** /reɪn/ *n* **1** [C usually plural] a long narrow band of leather that is fastened around a horse's head in order to control it **2** (a) free rein complete freedom to say or do things the way you want to: *The magazine gives free rein to its writers in matters of style.* **3** keep a tight rein on to control someone or something strictly: *The government is trying to keep a tight rein on public spending.*

**re·in·car·nate** /ˌriɪn'karˌneɪt/ *v* be re-

R

**incarnated** to be born again in another body after you have died

**re·in·car·na·tion** /ˌriːɪnkɑrˈneɪʃən/ *n* **1** [U] the act of being born again in another body after you have died **2** the person or animal that a REINCARNATED person has become: *Many Hindus view him as the reincarnation of the god Vishnu.*

**rein·deer** /ˈreɪndɪr/ *n* a type of DEER with long horns that lives in very cold places

**re·in·force** /ˌriːɪnˈfɔrs/ *v* [T] **1** to do something to make an opinion, statement, feeling etc. stronger or to support it: *The fire safety rules will be reinforced by regular drills.* **2** to make something such as a part of a building, a piece of clothing etc. stronger: *a wall reinforced with concrete*

**re·in·force·ment** /ˌriːɪnˈfɔrsmənt/ *n* [U] **1** the act of doing something to make an opinion, statement, feeling etc. stronger: *Positive reinforcement helps kids behave better.* **2** the act of reinforcing (REINFORCE) a wall, building etc.

**re·in·force·ments** /ˌriːɪnˈfɔrsmənts/ *n* [plural] more soldiers who are sent to an army to make it stronger

**re·in·state** /ˌriːɪnˈsteɪt/ *v* [T] **1** to put someone back into a job that s/he had before: *Two employees who were wrongfully fired will be reinstated.* **2** if a law, system, or practice is reinstated, it begins to be used after not being used −**reinstatement** *n* [C,U]

**re·in·vent** /ˌriːɪnˈvɛnt/ *v* [T] **1** to produce an idea, method etc. that is based on something that existed in the past, but is slightly different: *plans to reinvent the American educational system* **2** **reinvent the wheel** INFORMAL to waste time trying to find a way of doing something, when someone else has already discovered the best way to do it

**re·is·sue** /riˈɪʃu/ *v* [T] to produce a record, book etc. again, after it has not been available for some time −**reissue** *n*

**re·it·e·rate** /riˈɪtəˌreɪt/ *v* [T] FORMAL to say something more than once −**reiteration** /riˌɪtəˈreɪʃən/ *n* [C,U]

**re·ject¹** /rɪˈdʒɛkt/ *v* [T] **1** to refuse to accept, believe in, or agree with something: *I rejected the company's offer.* **2** to refuse to accept someone for a job, school etc.: *Yale rejected his application.* **3** to stop giving someone love or attention: *She feels rejected by her parents.* −see usage note at REFUSE¹

**re·ject²** /ˈridʒɛkt/ *n* a product that is thrown away because it is damaged or imperfect

**re·jec·tion** /rɪˈdʒɛkʃən/ *n* **1** [C,U] the act of not accepting, believing in, or agreeing with something: *The council's rejection of the proposal was unexpected.* **2** the act of not accepting someone for a job, school etc.: *She got a lot of rejections before the book was finally published.* **3** [U] a situation in which someone

stops giving you love or attention: *I couldn't deal with any more rejection.*

**re·joice** /rɪˈdʒɔɪs/ *v* [I] LITERARY to feel or show that you are very happy

**re·joic·ing** /rɪˈdʒɔɪsɪŋ/ *n* [U] FORMAL extreme happiness that is shown by a lot of people

**re·join** /riˈdʒɔɪn/ *v* [T] to go back to a group of people, organization etc. that you were with before: *Hiroko rejoined her family in Japan.*

**re·join·der** /rɪˈdʒɔɪndɚ/ *n* FORMAL a reply, especially a rude one

**re·ju·ve·nate** /rɪˈdʒuvəˌneɪt/ *v* [T] **1** to make someone feel or look young and strong again: *Exercise rejuvenates the body.* **2** to make a system or place better again: *the rejuvenated downtown area* −**rejuvenation** /rɪˌdʒuvəˈneɪʃən/ *n* [singular, U]

**re·kin·dle** /riˈkɪndl/ *v* [T] **1** to make someone have a particular feeling, thought etc. again: *a chance to rekindle an old romance* **2** to start a fire again

**re·lapse** /rɪˈlæps/ *n* [C,U] **1** a situation in which someone feels sick again after feeling better: *He's had/suffered a relapse.* **2** a situation in which someone or something gets worse after being good for a while: *a relapse into drug abuse* −**relapse** *v* [I]

**re·late** /rɪˈleɪt/ *v* **1** [I,T] to make or show a connection between two or more ideas or subjects: *I don't understand how the two ideas relate.* **2** **war-related/drug-related etc.** caused by or relating to war, drugs etc.: *There were very few alcohol-related deaths on the roads this month.* **3** [T] FORMAL to tell a story to someone

**relate to** sb/sth *phr v* [T] **1** to be concerned with or connected to a particular subject: *Mr. Harrison's point relates to the first question he was asked.* **2** to be able to understand someone's problems, feelings etc.: *I find it hard to relate to kids.*

**re·lat·ed** /rɪˈleɪtɪd/ *adj* **1** connected by similar ideas or dealing with similar subjects: *lung cancer and related medical problems* | *The study compares Czech, Polish, and other related Slavic languages.* −opposite UNRELATED **2** connected by a family relationship: *Are you related to Paula?*

**re·la·tion** /rɪˈleɪʃən/ *n* **1** **in relation to** used when comparing two things or showing the relationship between them: *The area of land is tiny in relation to the population.* **2** [C,U] a connection between two things: *Doctors say there was no relation between the drugs he was taking and his death* | *This case bears no relation to* (=is not connected with or similar to) *the Goldman trial.* **3** a member of your family; RELATIVE: *Joan Bartell, the author, is no relation to Governor Bartell.*

**re·la·tions** /rɪˈleɪʃənz/ *n* [plural] **1** official connections between companies, countries etc.:

Nixon's visit to China strengthened East-West relations. | The US has maintained **diplomatic relations** with Laos. **2** the way people or groups of people behave toward each other: *Relations between the two families were never good.* –see also PUBLIC RELATIONS

**re·la·tion·ship** /rɪ'leɪʃən,ʃɪp/ *n* **1** the way in which two people or groups behave toward each other: *The police have a good relationship with the community.* **2** a situation in which two people have sexual or romantic feelings for each other: *My parents had a strong relationship.* | *He's much happier now that he's in a relationship.* **3** [C,U] the way in which two or more things are related to each other: *the relationship between pay and performance at work*

**rel·a·tive**[1] /'rɛlətɪv/ *n* a member of your family: *I have relatives in Minnesota.*

**relative**[2] *adj* **1** having a particular quality when compared with something else: *The 1950s were a time of relative peace/calm/prosperity for the country.* **2 relative to sth** relating to or compared with a particular subject: *Demand for corn is low relative to the supply.*

**relative clause** /ˌ... './ *n* TECHNICAL in grammar, a part of a sentence that has a verb in it and is joined to the rest of the sentence by a RELATIVE PRONOUN. In the sentence "The dress that I bought is too small," "that I bought" is the relative clause

**rel·a·tive·ly** /'rɛlətɪvli/ *adv* to a particular degree, especially when compared to something similar: *I woke up relatively early this morning.*

**relative pro·noun** /ˌ... '../ *n* TECHNICAL in grammar, a PRONOUN such as "who," "which," or "that," which connects a RELATIVE CLAUSE to the rest of the sentence. In the sentence "The dress that I bought is too small," "that" is the relative pronoun

**rel·a·tiv·i·ty** /ˌrɛlə'tɪvəti/ *n* [U] **1** TECHNICAL the relationship between time, space, and movement, which changes with increased speed: *Einstein's theory of relativity* **2** the state of being RELATIVE

**re·lax** /rɪ'læks/ *v* **1** [I,T] to become more calm and less worried, or to make someone do this: *It's hard to relax after work.* | *The whiskey relaxed me.* **2** [I,T] if a part of your body relaxes or you relax it, it becomes less stiff and tight: *Try to relax your neck.* | *Let your muscles relax.* **3** [T] to make rules, controls etc. less strict: *relaxing the immigration laws*

**re·lax·a·tion** /ˌrilæk'seɪʃən/ *n* **1** [C,U] the state of being relaxed in your mind and body, or the process of becoming this way: *Make time for exercise and relaxation.* | *relaxation of the back muscles* **2** [U] the process of making rules, controls etc. less strict: *the relaxation of travel restrictions*

**re·lay**[1] /'rileɪ, rɪ'leɪ/ *v* [T] **1** to pass a message from one person or place to another:

Could you **relay** the message **to** Mary for me? **2** to send out a radio or television signal

**re·lay**[2] /'rileɪ/ also **relay race** /'.. ,./ *n* a race in which each member of a team runs or swims part of the distance

**re·lease**[1] /rɪ'lis/ *v* [T] **1** to let someone be free after keeping him/her as a prisoner: *Three hostages were released this morning.* **2** to stop holding something; *He released her arm when she screamed.* **3** to let news or information be known publicly: *Details of the crime have not been released.* **4** to make a movie or record available for people to buy or see: *Simon has released a new album.* **5** to allow a patient to leave a hospital

**release**[2] *n* **1** [singular] the act of releasing (RELEASE) someone: *After his release from prison, he worked as a carpenter.* **2** a new movie or record that is available for people to see or buy: *the singer's latest release* **3** [U] a feeling that you are free from worry or pain: *a sense of emotional release* –see also PRESS RELEASE

**rel·e·gate** /'rɛlə,geɪt/ *v* [T] FORMAL to make someone or something less important than before: *He's been relegated to the role of assistant.*

**re·lent** /rɪ'lɛnt/ *v* [I] to let someone do something that you refused to let him/her do before: *Park officials relented, and allowed campers to stay.*

**re·lent·less** /rɪ'lɛntlɪs/ *adj* **1** continuous and strong: *the relentless heat of the desert* **2** continuing to do something in a determined way: *the lawyer's relentless questioning* –**relentlessly** *adv*

**rel·e·vance** /'rɛləvəns/ also **rel·e·van·cy** /'rɛləvənsi/ *n* [U] the degree to which something relates to a particular subject or problem: *a statement with no relevance to the issue* –opposite IRRELEVANCE

**rel·e·vant** /'rɛləvənt/ *adj* directly relating to the subject or problem being discussed: *The question is not relevant to my point.* –opposite IRRELEVANT

**re·li·a·ble** /rɪ'laɪəbəl/ *adj* able to be trusted; DEPENDABLE: *a reliable car* | *reliable financial information* –**reliably** *adv* –**reliability** /rɪ,laɪə'bɪləti/ *n* [U] –opposite UNRELIABLE

**re·li·ance** /rɪ'laɪəns/ *n* [singular, U] the state of being dependent on something: *the country's reliance on imported oil*

**re·li·ant** /rɪ'laɪənt/ *adj* **be reliant on/upon** to depend on something or someone: *The country is reliant on foreign aid.*

**rel·ic** /'rɛlɪk/ *n* an old object or habit that reminds people of the past: *ancient Roman relics*

**re·lief** /rɪ'lif/ *n* **1** [singular, U] a feeling of comfort and happiness because something bad did not happen or is finished: *It was a relief to know that the children were safe.* | *Exams are* *finally over.* **What a relief!** **2** [U] the reduction of pain: *a medicine for* **pain relief** **3** [U] money, food, clothing etc. given to people who need them: *federal relief* (=money from the government) *for farmers* **4** TECHNICAL a raised shape or decoration on a surface: *a marble relief*

**relief map** /.'. ,./ *n* a map on which mountains, hills etc. are raised

**re·lieve** /rɪ'liv/ *v* [T] **1** to make a pain, problem, bad feeling etc. less severe: *The county is building a new school to relieve overcrowding.* | *We tried to* **relieve the boredom/tension** *by singing.* **2** to replace someone else at a job or duty when s/he is finished for the day: *The guards are relieved at six o'clock.* **3** **relieve yourself** a polite expression meaning to URINATE

**relieve** sb **of** sth *phr v* [T] FORMAL to help someone by carrying something heavy or by doing something difficult for him/her

**re·lieved** /rɪ'livd/ *adj* feeling happy because something bad did not happen or is finished: *I was* **relieved to be** *out of the hospital.* | *We were* **relieved that** *Brian was home safe.*

**re·li·gion** /rɪ'lɪdʒən/ *n* [C,U] a belief in one or more gods and the activities relating to this belief, or a particular system of belief: *the study of religion* | *the Muslim religion*

**re·li·gious** /rɪ'lɪdʒəs/ *adj* **1** relating to religion: *religious beliefs* **2** believing strongly in your religion and obeying its rules: *a very religious woman*

**re·li·gious·ly** /rɪ'lɪdʒəsli/ *adv* **1** regularly and thoroughly or completely: *He exercises religiously.* **2** in a way that is related to religion

**re·lin·quish** /rɪ'lɪŋkwɪʃ/ *v* [T] FORMAL to give up your position, power, rights etc.: *The party refused to relinquish power.*

**rel·ish**[1] /'rɛlɪʃ/ *v* [T] to enjoy something or like it: *Jamie* **didn't relish the idea** *of getting up early.*

**relish**[2] *n* **1** [C,U] a cold SAUCE eaten especially with meat to add taste: *pickle relish* **2** [U] great enjoyment of something: *Barry ate with* **great relish.**

**re·live** /,ri'lɪv/ *v* [T] to experience something again that happened in past times, or to remember it clearly: *Tarrant was forced to relive the experience by watching it on film.*

**re·lo·cate** /ri'loʊ,keɪt/ *v* [I,T] to move to a new place: *Our company* **relocated to** *the West Coast.* –**relocation** /,riloʊ'keɪʃən/ *n* [U]

**re·luc·tant** /rɪ'lʌktənt/ *adj* unwilling and slow to do something: *She* **was** *very* **reluctant to** *ask for help.* –**reluctance** *n* [singular, U] –**reluctantly** *adv*

**re·ly** /rɪ'laɪ/ *v*

**rely on/upon** sb/sth *phr v* [T] to trust or depend on someone or something: *We're* **relying on** *him to help.*

**re·main** /rɪ'meɪn/ *v* [I] **1** to continue to be in the same state or condition: *The communist party remains in power.* | *Veltman remained silent.* **2** to continue to exist after others have gone or been destroyed: *Only half the statue remains.* **3** **it remains to be seen** used when it is still uncertain whether something will happen: *It remains to be seen whether the operation was successful.* **4** FORMAL to stay in the same place or position without moving or leaving: *He remained in his office, unwilling to speak to anyone.* –see also REMAINS

**re·main·der** /rɪ'meɪndɚ/ *n* **the remainder (of sth)** the rest of something after everything else has gone or been dealt with: *the remainder of the semester*

**re·main·ing** /rɪ'meɪnɪŋ/ *adj* having been left when other similar things or people have gone or been dealt with: *The remaining puppies were given away.*

**re·mains** /rɪ'meɪnz/ *n* [plural] **1** the parts of something that are left after the rest has been destroyed: *We visited* **the remains of** *the temple.* **2** FORMAL a person's body after s/he has died

**re·make** /'rimeɪk/ *n* a movie or song that has the same story as one that was made before: *a remake of "The Wizard of Oz"* –**remake** /ri'meɪk/ *v* [T]

**re·mark**[1] /rɪ'mɑrk/ *n* something that you say: *Carl* **made** *a sarcastic* **remark.**

**remark**[2] *v* [T] to say something: *One woman* **remarked that** *Galen was handsome.*

**remark on/upon** sth *phr v* [T] to notice that something has happened and to say something about it: *Everyone* **remarked on** *the new carpet.*

**re·mar·ka·ble** /rɪ'mɑrkəbəl/ *adj* very unusual or noticeable in a way that deserves attention or praise: *He called Gorbachev "one of the most remarkable men in history."*

**re·mar·ka·bly** /rɪ'mɑrkəbli/ *adv* in an amount or to a degree that is surprising: *Charlotte and her cousin look remarkably similar.*

**re·marry** /ri'mæri/ *v* [I,T] to marry again: *He's been divorced and remarried several times.* –**remarriage** *n* [C,U]

**re·me·di·al** /rɪ'midiəl/ *adj* **1** **remedial class/education etc.** a special class etc. for students who are having difficulty learning something **2** FORMAL intended to provide a cure or improvement in something: *remedial exercises for a weak back*

**rem·e·dy**[1] /'rɛmədi/ *n* **1** a successful way of dealing with a problem: *an economic* **remedy** *for unemployment* **2** a medicine that cures pain or illness: *an excellent* **remedy** *for teething pain*

**remedy**[2] *v* [T] to deal successfully with a problem or improve a bad situation: *The hospital is trying to remedy the problem.*

**re·mem·ber** /rɪˈmɛmbɚ/ v **1** [I,T] to have a picture or idea in your mind of people, events etc. from the past: *Do you remember the first job you ever had?* | *Mr. Daniels has lived there for as long as I can remember.* **2** [I,T] to bring information or facts that you know back into your mind: *She suddenly remembered (that) she had to go to the dentist.* | *Can you remember her name?* **3** [I,T] to not forget to do something: *Remember to get some milk at the store today!* —compare REMIND **4** [T] to think about someone who has died, with special respect and honor: *remembering those who fought in Korea* **5 be remembered for/as sth** to be famous for something important that you did: *She'll be remembered as one of the best female athletes of the decade.* | *He is remembered for his achievements in the world of quantum physics.*

---

**USAGE NOTE** remember and remind

Use **remember** to say that you are the one who is remembering something: *Do you remember that guy we met at the party?* | *I can't remember how much I paid for it.* | *He suddenly remembered he had to go to the bank.* Use **remind** to say that it is someone or something else that is making you remember something: *Doesn't she remind you of Nicole?* | *Please remind me to call him later today.* ✗ DON'T SAY "remember me to call him." ✗

---

**re·mem·brance** /rɪˈmɛmbrəns/ n the act of remembering and giving honor to someone who has died: *She planted a tree in remembrance of her husband.*

**re·mind** /rɪˈmaɪnd/ v [T] **1** to make someone remember something that s/he must do: *Remind me to stop by the post office.* **2 remind sb of** to make someone remember someone or something from past times: *Wendy reminds me of* (=looks or acts like) *her mother.* —see usage note at REMEMBER

**re·mind·er** /rɪˈmaɪndɚ/ n something that makes you notice or remember something else: *The photos were a painful reminder of his first wife.*

**rem·i·nisce** /ˌrɛməˈnɪs/ v [I] to talk or think about pleasant events in your past: *Petty sat reminiscing about the old days of rock 'n' roll.* —reminiscence n [C,U]

**rem·i·nis·cent** /ˌrɛməˈnɪsənt/ adj **reminiscent of sth** reminding you of something: *His voice is reminiscent of Frank Sinatra's.*

**re·miss** /rɪˈmɪs/ adj FORMAL careless about doing something that you ought to do: *The nurses were accused of being remiss in their duties.*

**re·mis·sion** /rɪˈmɪʃən/ n [C,U] a period of time when an illness improves: *Her cancer is in remission.*

**re·mit** /rɪˈmɪt/ v **-tted, -tting** [I,T] FORMAL to send a payment by mail

**re·mit·tance** /rɪˈmɪtˈns/ n [C,U] FORMAL the act of sending money by mail, or the amount of money that is sent

**rem·nant** /ˈrɛmnənt/ n a small part of something that remains after the rest has been used or destroyed: *the remnants of a 14th century castle*

**ro·mod·el** /ˌriˈmɑdl/ v [T] to change the shape or appearance of something: *We've had the kitchen remodeled.*

**rem·on·strate** /ˈrɛmənˌstreɪt, rɪˈmɑnˌstreɪt/ v [I] FORMAL to tell someone that you strongly disapprove of what s/he has done

**re·morse** /rɪˈmɔrs/ n [U] a strong feeling of being sorry for doing something very bad: *Keating showed no remorse for his crime.* —remorseful adj —remorseless adj

**re·mote** /rɪˈmoʊt/ adj **1** far away in distance or time: *a remote planet* | *the remote past* **2** very slight or small: *There's a remote possibility/chance that the operation will not work.* **3** very different from something else, or not closely related to it: *subjects that are remote from everyday life* —remoteness n

**remote con·trol** /ˌ·ˌ · ˈ·/ also **remote** n a piece of equipment that you use to control a radio, television, toy etc. from a distance —remote-controlled adj: *a remote-controlled airplane*

**re·mote·ly** /rɪˈmoʊtli/ adv used in order to emphasize a negative statement: *The two situations are not even remotely similar.*

**re·mov·a·ble** /rɪˈmuvəbəl/ adj able to be removed: *a table with a removable middle*

**re·mov·al** /rɪˈmuvəl/ n [C,U] the act of removing something: *the removal of foreign troops from the country*

**re·move** /rɪˈmuv/ v [T] **1** to take something away from, out of, or off the place where it is: *Remove the pan from the oven to cool.* | *The old paint will have to be removed first.* **2** to end something such as a problem, law, system etc.: *The threat of a world war had been removed.* **3 be (far) removed from sth** to be very different from something else: *This job is far removed from anything that I've done before.* **4** to make someone leave a job: *The Mayor has been removed from office.*

**re·mov·er** /rɪˈmuvɚ/ n [C,U] **paint/stain etc. remover** a substance that removes paint etc. from something else

**re·mu·ner·ate** /rɪˈmyunəˌreɪt/ v [T] FORMAL to pay someone for something s/he has done —remuneration /rɪˌmyunəˈreɪʃən/ n [C,U]

**Ren·ais·sance** /ˈrɛnəˌzɑns, -ˌsɑns, ˌrɛnəˈsɑns/ n **1 the Renaissance** the time in Europe between the 14th and 17th centuries when a lot of new art and literature was produced **2** [singular] a new interest or development in something that has not been popular: *a jazz renaissance*

**re·name** /riˈneɪm/ v [T] to change the name of something: *They renamed the airport in honor of President Kennedy.*

**rend** /rɛnd/ v **rent, rent, rending** [T] LITERARY to tear or break something into pieces

**ren·der** /ˈrɛndər/ v [T] FORMAL **1** to give someone something: *The management discussed the issue before rendering a decision.* | *payment for services rendered* (=for work someone has done) **2** to cause someone or something to be in a particular state: *The accident rendered her left leg useless.* **3** to express or present something in a particular way: *In her paintings she renders feelings by using specific colors.*

**ren·der·ing** /ˈrɛndərɪŋ/ n the particular way a painting, story etc. is expressed: *Coppola's rendering of the Dracula story*

**ren·dez·vous¹** /ˈrɑndeɪˌvu, -dɪ-/ n, plural **rendezvous** an arrangement to meet someone at a particular time and place, or the place where you meet: *The rendezvous is set for Central Park.*

**rendezvous²** v [I] to meet someone at a particular place and time: *The boat rendezvoused with two others near Cuba.*

**ren·di·tion** /rɛnˈdɪʃən/ n [U] the way that a play, piece of music, art etc. is performed or made: *a wonderful rendition of "Turandot"*

**ren·e·gade** /ˈrɛnəˌgeɪd/ n someone who joins an opposing side in a war, political or religious organization etc. **–renegade** adj: *renegade soldiers*

**re·nege** /rɪˈnɛg, -ˈnɪg/ v [I] to not do something that you promised to do: *The company claims that the city reneged on the deal/promise.*

**re·new** /rɪˈnu/ v [T] **1** to arrange for a contract, official document etc. to continue: *It's time to renew our insurance.* **2** to begin to do something again: *Congress renewed its demand for tax cuts.* **3** to give someone new strength **–renewal** n [C,U]

**re·new·a·ble** /rɪˈnuəbəl/ adj **1** able to be replaced by natural processes so that it is never used up: *a renewable energy source* **2** a renewable contract, ticket etc. can be made to continue after the date that it is supposed to end **–opposite** NONRENEWABLE

**re·newed** /rɪˈnud/ adj increasing again after not being very strong: *Kathleen began her paper again with renewed energy/interest.*

**re·nounce** /rɪˈnaʊns/ v [T] **1** to say publicly that you will no longer try to keep something, or will not stay in an important position: *Grayson renounced his claim to the family fortune.* **2** to say publicly that you no longer believe in or support an idea, religion etc.: *He renounced his faith in Judaism.*

**ren·o·vate** /ˈrɛnəˌveɪt/ v [T] to repair something such as building so that it is in good condition again **–renovation** /ˌrɛnəˈveɪʃən/ n [C,U]

**re·nowned** /rɪˈnaʊnd/ adj famous for a special skill or for something that you have done: *a renowned singer of the late 19th century* **–renown** n [U]

**rent¹** /rɛnt/ v **1** [I,T] to pay money regularly to live in a place that belongs to someone else: *They're renting an apartment near the beach.* | *We'll rent for six months.* **2** [T] to pay money for the use of something for a short period of time: *rent a movie/car* **3** [T] also **rent** sth ↔ **out** to let someone live in a place that you own in return for money: *They've rented out their house for the summer.* **–renter** n

**rent²** n [C,U] **1** the amount of money you pay for the use of a house, room, car etc. that belongs to someone else: *Office rents are very high here.* **2 for rent** available to be rented

**rent·al¹** /ˈrɛntl/ n **1** [C,U] an arrangement by which you rent something: *a video rental store* **2** [U] the money that you pay to rent something: *Ski rental is $14.*

**rental²** adj available to be rented or being rented: *a rental car* | *rental properties*

**rent con·trol** /ˈ. .ˌ./ n [U] a situation in which a city or state uses laws to limit the price of renting apartments

**re·nun·ci·a·tion** /rɪˌnʌnsiˈeɪʃən/ n [C,U] FORMAL the act of renouncing (RENOUNCE) something

**re·or·ga·nize** /riˈɔrgəˌnaɪz/ v [I,T] to arrange or organize something in a new and better way: *The filing system needs to be reorganized.* **–reorganization** /riˌɔrgənəˈzeɪʃən/ n [U]

**rep** /rɛp/ n **1** INFORMAL someone who represents an organization or a company and its products; representative: *a sales rep* **2** SLANG ⇨ REPUTATION

**re·pair¹** /rɪˈpɛr/ n **1** [C usually plural, U] something that you do to fix something that is broken or damaged: *They're doing repairs on the bridge.* | *The car's in the shop for repair.* **2 in good/bad repair** in good or bad condition: *The roads are in good repair.*

**repair²** v [T] to fix something that is broken or damaged: *I have to get the TV repaired.*

**re·pair·man** /rɪˈpɛrmən/ n someone whose job it is to fix a particular type of thing: *a TV repairman*

**rep·a·ra·tion** /ˌrɛpəˈreɪʃən/ n [C,U] FORMAL payment made to someone for damage, injury etc. that you have caused

**re·pa·tri·ate** /riˈpeɪtriˌeɪt/ v [T] to send someone or something back to the country he, she, or it comes from **–repatriation** /riˌpeɪtriˈeɪʃən/ n [U]

**re·pay** /rɪˈpeɪ/ v [T] **1** to pay back money that you have borrowed: *How long will it take to repay the loan?* **2** to show someone that you are grateful for his/her help: *How can I ever repay you?* **–repayment** n [C,U]

**re·peal** /rɪˈpil/ v [T] to officially end a law: *In 1933, Prohibition was finally repealed.* **–repeal** n [U]

**re·peat¹** /rɪˈpit/ v [T] **1** to say or do something again: *Sally kept repeating, "It wasn't me, it wasn't me." | You'll have to repeat the class.* **2** to say something that you have heard someone else say: *Please don't repeat any of this to Bill.*

**repeat²** n **1** an event that is just like something that happened before: *I don't want to see a repeat performance of last year.* (=I do not want something bad to happen again) **2** ⇨ RERUN

**re·peat·ed** /rɪˈpitɪd/ adj done or happening again and again: *Repeated attempts to fix the satellite have failed.* **–repeatedly** adv

**re·pel** /rɪˈpɛl/ v **-lled, -lling 1** [T] if something repels you, it forces you to go away in order to avoid it: *Tear gas was used to repel the rioters.* **2** [I,T] TECHNICAL if two things repel each other, they push each other away with a MAGNETIC force

**re·pel·lent¹** /rɪˈpɛlənt/ n [C,U] a substance that keeps insects away from you: *mosquito repellent*

**repellent²** adj extremely unpleasant or nasty: *repellent behavior*

**re·pent** /rɪˈpɛnt/ v [I,T] FORMAL a word meaning to be sorry for something that you have done, used especially by religious people **–repentance** n [U] **–repentant** adj

**re·per·cus·sion** /ˌripɚˈkʌʃən/ n [C usually plural] the effect that an action or event has, even a long time after it has happened: *Their civil war had international repercussions.*

**rep·er·toire** /ˈrɛpɚˌtwɑr/ n [C usually singular] all the plays, pieces of music etc. that a performer or group can perform

**rep·e·ti·tion** /ˌrɛpəˈtɪʃən/ n [C,U] the act of saying or doing the same thing again, or many times: *the repetition of old stories | kids learning the times tables by repetition*

**rep·e·ti·tious** /ˌrɛpəˈtɪʃəs/ adj saying or doing the same thing many times, so that people become bored: *a repetitious speech*

**re·pet·i·tive** /rɪˈpɛtətɪv/ adj done many times in the same way: *repetitive exercises*

**re·phrase** /riˈfreɪz/ v [T] to express something in different words so that its meaning is clearer or more acceptable: *OK, let me rephrase the question.*

**re·place** /rɪˈpleɪs/ v [T] **1** to start doing something or being used instead of another person or thing: *Val will be replacing Brian as editor.* **2** to buy something that is newer or better in order to use it instead of something that is old or broken: *Our VCR isn't working, but we can't afford to replace it.* **3** to put something back in its correct place: *Please replace the books when you are finished.*

**re·place·ment** /rɪˈpleɪsmənt/ n **1** someone or something that replaces another person or thing: *We're waiting for Mr. Dunley's replacement.* **2** [U] the act of replacing something

**re·play** /ˈriˌpleɪ/ n [C,U] an action in a sport that you see on television, that is immediately shown again: *On the replay you can see the foul.*

**re·plen·ish** /rɪˈplɛnɪʃ/ v [T] FORMAL to fill something again or make something complete again: *The charity urgently needs to replenish food supplies.* **–replenishment** n [U]

**re·plete** /rɪˈplit/ adj FORMAL full: *He said the report was "replete with errors."*

**rep·li·ca** /ˈrɛplɪkə/ n a very good copy of a piece of art, a building etc.: *an exact replica of the White House*

**rep·li·cate** /ˈrɛpləˌkeɪt/ v [T] FORMAL to do or make something again, so that you get the same result or make an exact copy: *Scientists are trying to replicate Hudson's experiment.* **–replication** /ˌrɛpləˈkeɪʃən/ n [C,U]

**re·ply¹** /rɪˈplaɪ/ v [I,T] to answer someone by saying or writing something: *"Of course," she replied. | I haven't replied to his letter yet.* –see usage note at ANSWER¹

**reply²** n [C,U] something that is said, written, or done in order to reply to someone: *There have been no replies to our ad. | Marcy said nothing in reply.* (=as a reply)

**re·port¹** /rɪˈpɔrt/ n **1** a written or spoken description of a situation or event that gives people information: *a police report on the accident | a weather report* **2** a piece of writing in which someone carefully examines a particular subject: *the company's annual report | a book report* **3** FORMAL the noise of an explosion or shot

**report²** v **1** [I,T] to tell someone about something, especially in newspapers and on television: *The Daily Gazette reported the story. | Here's Kathy Levy, reporting on the latest developments.* **2** [T] to tell someone in authority that a crime or accident has happened: *Who reported the fire?* **3** [T] to complain officially about someone to people in authority: *Somebody reported Kyle for smoking in school.* **4** [I] to state officially to someone in authority that you have arrived in a place: *Visitors must report to the main reception desk. | One of the soldiers had not reported for duty.*

**report back** phr v [I] to bring someone information that s/he asked you to find: *The committee reported back to Congress.*

**report card** /.ˈ. ˌ./ n a written statement giving a student's grades

**re·port·ed·ly** /rɪˈpɔrtɪdli/ adv according to what people say: *She's reportedly one of the richest women in Europe.*

**re·port·ed speech** /.ˌ.. ˈ./ n [U] TECHNICAL in grammar, the style of speech or writing that is used for reporting what someone says, without repeating the actual words. The sentence "She

R

said she didn't feel well" is an example of reported speech

**re·port·er** /rɪ'pɔrtɚ/ *n* someone whose job is to write or tell about events in a newspaper or on radio or television

**re·pos·i·to·ry** /rɪ'pɑzə,tɔri/ *n* a place where things are kept safely: *a repository for nuclear waste*

**re·pos·sess** /,ripə'zɛs/ *v* [T] to take back something that someone has paid part of the money for, because s/he cannot pay the rest of the money: *I have to pay them $450 or they'll repossess the car.*

**rep·re·hen·si·ble** /,rɛprɪ'hɛnsəbəl/ *adj* FORMAL reprehensible behavior is very bad and deserves criticism

**rep·re·sent** /,rɛprɪ'zɛnt/ *v* [T] **1** to do things or speak officially for someone else: *Craig hired a lawyer to represent him.* | *She represents the 5th congressional district of Texas.* **2** to be a sign or mark for something else: *The green triangles on the map represent campgrounds.* **3** if art represents something, it shows or means a thing or idea: *a painting representing heaven and hell* **4 represent yourself as sth** to say that you are something that you are not: *He represents himself as an expert in prison law.*

**rep·re·sen·ta·tion** /,rɛprɪzɛn'teɪʃən, -zən-/ *n* **1** [U] the state of having someone to speak, vote, or make good decisions for you: *There is no representation on the council for the Hispanic community.* **2** something, for example, a painting or sign, that shows or describes something else: *The model is a representation of how the atom is split.*

**rep·re·sen·ta·tive¹** /,rɛprɪ'zɛntət̬ɪv/ *n* **1** someone who is chosen to act, speak, vote etc. for someone else **2 Representative** a member of the House of Representatives in US Congress

**representative²** *adj* **1** like other members of the same group; typical: *The sample is representative of the total population.* **2** relating to a system of government in which people elect other people to represent them: *representative democracy*

**re·press** /rɪ'prɛs/ *v* [T] **1** to stop yourself from expressing a feeling: *It's not healthy to repress your emotions.* **2** to control people by using force

**re·pressed** /rɪ'prɛst/ *adj* DISAPPROVING having feelings or desires that you do not express: *a sexually repressed man*

**re·pres·sion** /rɪ'prɛʃən/ *n* [U] **1** the use of force to control people: *Stalin's repression of religious groups* **2** the action of stopping yourself from feeling an emotion, or the state of having done this

**re·pres·sive** /rɪ'prɛsɪv/ *adj* cruel and severe: *a repressive political system*

**re·prieve** /rɪ'priv/ *n* **1** a delay before something unpleasant continues: *a reprieve from the pain* **2** an official order that prevents a prisoner from being killed as a punishment —compare PARDON² **–reprieve** *v* [T]

**rep·ri·mand** /'rɛprə,mænd/ *v* [T] to tell someone officially that s/he has done something wrong: *Several managers were reprimanded for their treatment of women.* **–reprimand** *n* [C,U]

**re·pris·al** /rɪ'praɪzəl/ *n* [C,U] a violent action that punishes your enemy for something bad that s/he has done: *He's afraid to help the police for fear of reprisals against his family.*

**re·prise** /rɪ'priz/ *v* [I,T] to perform a particular character from a play, movie etc. again, or to sing a particular song again: *Hamilton refused to reprise her role as the Wicked Witch.*

**re·proach¹** /rɪ'proutʃ/ *n* **1** [C,U] criticism or disapproval, or a remark that expresses this: *His mother gave him a look full of reproach.* **2 above/beyond reproach** impossible to criticize; perfect: *The actions of the police should be above reproach.*

**reproach²** *v* [T] to criticize someone and try to make him/her sorry for doing something: *Mrs. Winters reproached her son for his rude behavior.*

**re·pro·duce** /,riprə'dus/ *v* **1** [I,T] to produce young plants or animals: *Most birds and fish reproduce by laying eggs.* **2** [T] to make a copy of something: *The colors were difficult to reproduce.*

**re·pro·duc·tion** /,riprə'dʌkʃən/ *n* **1** [U] the act or process of producing young plants or animals: *Cold weather affects the insect's reproduction.* **2** [C,U] the act of copying something such as a book or painting, or the copy itself: *a reproduction of Homer's painting*

**re·pro·duc·tive** /,riprə'dʌktɪv/ *adj* relating to the process of producing young plants and animals: *the reproductive system of mammals*

**re·prove** /rɪ'pruv/ *v* [T] FORMAL to criticize someone for doing something bad

**rep·tile** /'rɛptaɪl, 'rɛptl/ *n* an animal such as a snake or LIZARD that lays eggs, and whose blood changes temperature with the environment around it **–reptilian** /rɛp'tɪliən/ *adj*

**re·pub·lic** /rɪ'pʌblɪk/ *n* a country governed by elected representatives and led by a president —compare MONARCHY

**re·pub·li·can¹** /rɪ'pʌblɪkən/ *adj* **1 Republican** relating to or supporting the Republican Party: *a Republican candidate for the Senate* **2** relating to a REPUBLIC: *a republican system of government* **–Republicanism** *n* [U]

**republican²** *n* **1 Republican** someone who supports the Republican Party or is a member of it —see culture note at PARTY¹ **2** someone who believes in REPUBLICs, or works to make his/her country become one —compare DEMOCRAT

**Republican Par·ty** /.,... '../ *n* [singular] one of the two main political parties of the US

**re·pu·di·ate** /rɪ'pyudi,eɪt/ *v* [T] FORMAL to disagree strongly with someone or something and refuse to have any association with him, her, or it; REJECT: *Angelides publicly repudiated his friend's statements.* —**repudiation** /rɪ,pyudi-'eɪʃən/ *n* [U]

**re·pug·nance** /rɪ'pʌgnəns/ *n* [U] FORMAL a feeling of strong dislike; DISGUST

**re·pug·nant** /rɪ'pʌgnənt/ *adj* FORMAL very unpleasant and offensive: *behavior that is morally repugnant*

**re·pulse** /rɪ'pʌls/ *v* [T] **1** if something repulses you, it makes you feel sick even to think about it: *The nation was repulsed by the crime.* **2** to defeat a military attack: *The enemy forces were repulsed with the help of French troops.*

**re·pul·sion** /rɪ'pʌlʃən/ *n* **1** [singular, U] a sick feeling that you get from seeing or thinking about something unpleasant **2** [U] TECHNICAL the electric or MAGNETIC force by which one object pushes another one away from it

**re·pul·sive** /rɪ'pʌlsɪv/ *adj* so unpleasant that you almost feel sick: *morally repulsive behavior*

**rep·u·ta·ble** /'rɛpyətəbəl/ *adj* respected for being honest and doing good work: *a reputable construction company*

**rep·u·ta·tion** /,rɛpyə'teɪʃən/ *n* the opinion that people have of someone or something because of what has happened in the past: *a man with a reputation for honesty*

**re·pute** /rɪ'pyut/ *n* [U] FORMAL ⇨ REPUTATION: *a pianist of great repute*

**re·put·ed** /rɪ'pyutɪd/ *adj* FORMAL according to what most people think or say: *He is reputed to be a millionaire.* —**reputedly** *adv*

**re·quest**[1] /rɪ'kwɛst/ *n* the act of asking for something politely or formally: *We've made a request for new equipment.* | *Drinks are available on request.* (=if you ask for them) | *I called the police at her request.* (=because she asked me to)

**request**[2] *v* [T] to ask for something politely or formally: *We request that everyone be quiet.* —see usage notes at ASK, RECOMMEND

**req·ui·em** /'rɛkwiəm/ *n* [C,U] a Christian ceremony of prayers for someone who has died, or a piece of music written for this ceremony

**re·quire** /rɪ'kwaɪɚ/ *v* [T] **1** to need something: *Roses require a lot of sunshine.* **2** FORMAL to demand officially that someone do something because of a law or rule: *Everyone is required by law to wear seat belts.*

**re·quire·ment** /rɪ'kwaɪɚmənt/ *n* **1** a quality or skill that is needed or asked for in a particular situation: *Each state has different requirements for its government workers.* **2 meet sb's requirements** to provide or do everything that someone needs: *The contract meets all our requirements.*

**req·ui·site** /'rɛkwəzɪt/ *adj* FORMAL needed for a particular purpose

**req·ui·si·tion** /,rɛkwə'zɪʃən/ *n* [C,U] FORMAL an official demand to have something, usually made by the army —**requisition** *v* [T]

**re·route** /ri'raʊt, ri'rut/ *v* [T] to make vehicles, aircraft etc. go a different way from the way they usually go: *Traffic has been rerouted across the bridge.*

**re·run** /'rirʌn/ *n* a television program or a movie that is being shown again: *a rerun of "Cheers"* —**rerun** /ri'rʌn/ *v* [T]

**re·sale** /'riseɪl/ *n* the state of being sold again: *the resale value of the house*

**re·scind** /rɪ'sɪnd/ *v* [T] to officially end a law, agreement, or decision

**res·cue**[1] /'rɛskyu/ *v* [T] to save someone or something from harm or danger: *He rescued two people from the fire.* —**rescuer** *n*

**rescue**[2] *n* an act of saving someone or something from harm or danger: *They are trained for air rescues.* | *A nearby boat came to the rescue.* (=saved or helped someone)

**re·search**[1] /'risɚtʃ, rɪ'sɚtʃ/ *n* [U] serious study of a subject that is intended to discover new facts about it: *scientific research on/into heart disease* | *Holmes is doing research* (=finding information) *for a book on the Middle Ages.*

**research**[2] *v* [I,T] to study a subject in detail so you can discover new facts about it: *Conner spent eight years researching the history of the region.* —**researcher** *n*

**re·sem·blance** /rɪ'zɛmbləns/ *n* [C,U] if there is a resemblance between two things or people, they are similar to each other: *There's a slight resemblance between Mike and his cousin.* (=they look like each other)

**re·sem·ble** /rɪ'zɛmbəl/ *v* [T] to look like, or be similar to, someone or something: *She resembles her mother in many ways.*

**re·sent** /rɪ'zɛnt/ *v* [T] to feel angry and upset about something that someone has done to you: *I've always resented my father for leaving the family.*

**re·sent·ful** /rɪ'zɛntfəl/ *adj* feeling angry and upset about something that someone has done, or showing this: *a resentful look*

**re·sent·ment** /rɪ'zɛntmənt/ *n* [U] a feeling of anger about something that someone has done to you

**res·er·va·tion** /,rɛzɚ'veɪʃən/ *n* **1** an arrangement that you make so that a place in a hotel, on a plane etc. is kept for you to use: *Have you made reservations at the restaurant yet?* **2** [C,U] a feeling of doubt because you do not agree completely with a plan, idea etc.: *I still have reservations about promoting O'Neil.* **3** an area of land in the US on which some Native Americans live

R

**re·serve**[1] /rɪˈzɚv/ v [T] **1** to arrange for a place in a hotel, on a plane etc. to be kept for you to use: *I'd like to reserve a table for 8:00.* **2** to keep something separate so that it can be used for a particular purpose: *a parking space reserved for the disabled*

**reserve**[2] n **1** an amount of something that is kept to be used in the future when it may be needed: *Water reserves are dangerously low.* | *We **keep** some money **in reserve** for emergencies.* **2** [U] the quality of being unwilling to express your emotions or talk about your problems: *His natural reserve stopped him from saying anything.* **3** an area of land where wild animals, plants etc. are protected: *a nature reserve* **4** [U] also **reserves** a military force that a country has in addition to its usual army

**re·served** /rɪˈzɚvd/ adj unwilling to express your emotions or talk about your problems: *a cool reserved young man*

**res·er·voir** /ˈrɛzəˌvwɑr, -zɚ-, -ˌvwɔr/ n **1** a special lake where water is stored to be used by people in a city **2** a large amount of something that has not been used yet: *a reservoir of oil beneath the desert*

**re·shuf·fle** /riˈʃʌfəl/ v [T] to change the jobs of people who work in an organization: *The company is expected to reshuffle its top managers.* —reshuffle n

**re·side** /rɪˈzaɪd/ v [I] FORMAL to live in a particular place: *Mexican citizens who legally reside in the US*

**res·i·dence** /ˈrɛzədəns/ n FORMAL **1** the place where you live: *a private residence* **2** [U] the state of living in a place **3** in residence living or working in a place: *Mr. Moreau is our artist in residence.*

**res·i·den·cy** /ˈrɛzədənsi/ n a period of time during which a doctor receives special training in a particular type of medicine

**res·i·dent** /ˈrɛzədənt/ n **1** someone who lives in a place such as a house or apartment: *a park for local residents* **2** a doctor working at a hospital where s/he is being trained —resident adj

**res·i·den·tial** /ˌrɛzəˈdɛnʃəl/ adj a residential area consists of private houses, with no offices or businesses

**re·sid·u·al** /rɪˈzɪdʒuəl/ adj FORMAL remaining after a process, event etc. is finished: *the residual effects of radiation exposure*

**res·i·due** /ˈrɛzəˌdu/ n a substance that remains after something else has disappeared or been removed: *an oily residue*

**re·sign** /rɪˈzaɪn/ v [I,T] **1** to leave your job or position officially because you want to: *Burton resigned from the company yesterday.* **2** resign yourself to sth/to doing sth to accept something that is unpleasant but cannot be changed: *I've resigned myself to living in the city for a while.*

**res·ig·na·tion** /ˌrɛzɪgˈneɪʃən/ n **1** [C,U] the act of RESIGNing, or a written statement to say you are doing this: *Did Johnson **hand in his resignation**?* (=give his resignation to the manager) **2** [U] the feeling of accepting an unpleasant situation that you cannot change: *I could hear the resignation in his voice.*

**re·signed** /rɪˈzaɪnd/ adj accepting an unpleasant situation that you cannot change, or showing that you feel this: *He's **resigned to** the fact that she's leaving.* | *a resigned voice/look*

**re·sil·ience** /rɪˈzɪlyəns/ n [U] **1** the ability to quickly become strong, healthy, or happy, after a difficult situation, illness etc.: *Experts say this is a sign of the economy's resilience.* **2** the ability of a substance such as rubber to return to its usual shape when pressure is removed —resilient adj

**res·in** /ˈrɛzən/ n **1** [U] a thick sticky liquid that comes from some trees **2** a chemical substance used for making plastics

**re·sist** /rɪˈzɪst/ v **1** [I,T] to not accept changes, or to try to prevent changes from happening: *People generally resist change.* | *Residents were ordered to evacuate, but they resisted.* **2** [I,T] to oppose or fight against someone or something: *resisting enemy attacks against the city* | *When the girls resisted, the man let go of them.* **3** [I,T] to try hard not to do something that you want to do: *I couldn't resist laughing at him.* | *Carter found their offer **hard to resist**.* **4** [T] to not be changed or harmed by something: *They say vitamin C helps you resist colds.*

**re·sist·ance** /rɪˈzɪstəns/ n **1** [singular, U] a refusal to accept new ideas or changes: *There is strong public **resistance to** the new taxes.* **2** [singular, U] fighting against someone or something: *The rebels **put up** fierce **resistance** against the army.* **3** [singular, U] the ability to avoid the effects of a disease or drug: *Your body has built up a **resistance to** the penicillin.* **4** [U] TECHNICAL the degree to which a substance can stop electricity from going through it

**re·sis·tant** /rɪˈzɪstənt/ adj **1** not easily harmed or damaged by something: *a heat-resistant/fire-resistant cover* **2** unwilling to accept something: *people who are **resistant to** change*

**res·o·lute** /ˈrɛzəˌlut/ adj doing something because you feel very strongly that you are right —resolutely adv

**res·o·lu·tion** /ˌrɛzəˈluʃən/ n **1** a formal or official decision agreed on by a group, especially after a vote: *a budget resolution in Congress* **2** [singular, U] the final solution to a problem or difficulty: *a peaceful **resolution to** the crisis* **3** a promise that you make to yourself to do something: *Have you made any **New Year's resolutions**?* **4** [U] the quality of having strong beliefs and determination

**re·solve**[1] /rɪˈzalv/ v **1** [T] to find an answer to a problem or a way of dealing with it: *The president is trying to resolve the situation quickly.* **2** [I] to make a definite decision to do something: *Joan resolved to continue working after she had children.* **3** [I,T] to make a formal decision to do something, especially by voting

**resolve**[2] n [U] FORMAL strong determination to succeed in doing something

**res·o·nant** /ˈrezənənt/ adj having a deep clear loud sound that continues for a long time: *a resonant voice* —**resonance** n [U]

**res·o·nate** /ˈrezəˌneɪt/ v [I] to make a deep clear loud sound that continues for a long time

**re·sort**[1] /rɪˈzɔrt/ n **1** a place where many people can go for a vacation, with hotels, swimming pools etc.: *a beach resort* **2** **as a last resort** if everything else that you have tried fails: *You could, as a last resort, sleep in the car.*

**resort**[2] v

**resort to** sth phr v [T] to do something or use something in order to succeed, even if it is bad: *She finally resorted to threats to get him to stop smoking.*

**re·sound** /rɪˈzaʊnd/ v [I] **1** to be full of sound; ECHO: *a room resounding with laughter* **2** if a sound resounds, it continues loudly and clearly for a long time

**re·sound·ing** /rɪˈzaʊndɪŋ/ adj **1** a resounding noise is loud and clear: *a resounding crash* **2** **a resounding success/victory etc.** a very great and complete success, victory etc. —**resoundingly** adv

**re·source** /ˈrisɔrs, rɪˈsɔrs/ n **1** [C usually plural] something such as land, minerals, or natural energy that exists in a country and can be used in order to increase its wealth: *a country rich in natural resources* **2** something that can be used in order to make a job or activity easier: *resource materials for teachers* —see also RESOURCES

**re·source·ful** /rɪˈsɔrsfəl/ adj good at finding ways to deal with problems effectively —**resourcefulness** n [U]

**re·sour·ces** /ˈriˌsɔrsɪz/ n [plural] all the money, property, skills etc. that you have available to use: *Our financial resources are limited.* —see also HUMAN RESOURCES

**re·spect**[1] /rɪˈspɛkt/ n **1** [U] admiration for someone because of his/her knowledge, skill etc.: *I have great respect for her work as a writer.* **2** [U] the attitude of not being rude to someone or not damaging something because you think he, she, or it is important or impressive: *You ought to show more respect to your grandfather.* | *These kids have no respect for other people's property.* —opposite DISRESPECT **3** **in one respect/in some respects/in every respect** used in order to say that something is true in one way, some ways, or in every

way: *In some respects, Leon is right.* **4** **with (all due) respect** FORMAL used before disagreeing with someone, in order to be polite: *With all due respect to you sir, that is not the point.* **5** **with respect to** FORMAL concerning a particular thing, or concerning something that has just been mentioned; REGARDING: *With respect to your question about jobs, all our positions are filled.* —see also RESPECTS

**respect**[2] v [T] **1** to admire someone because of his/her knowledge, skill etc.: *The students like and respect him.* **2** **respect sb's wishes/rights etc.** to be careful not to do anything against someone's wishes, rights etc. **3** **respect the law/Constitution etc.** to be careful not to disobey the law, Constitution etc.

**re·spect·a·ble** /rɪˈspɛktəbəl/ adj **1** having standards of behavior or appearance that people approve of and admire: *a respectable family* | *Go wash up and make yourself look respectable.* **2** showing skills, knowledge etc. that people admire: *Kemp has done a respectable job.* —**respectably** adv —**respectability** /rɪˌspɛktəˈbɪləti/ n [U]

**re·spect·ed** /rɪˈspɛktɪd/ adj admired by many people because of your work, skills etc.: *a respected leader*

**re·spect·ful** /rɪˈspɛktfəl/ adj feeling or showing respect —**respectfully** adv —opposite DISRESPECTFUL

**re·spec·tive** /rɪˈspɛktɪv/ adj people's respective jobs, houses etc. are the separate ones that each of them has: *the two sisters and their respective husbands*

**re·spec·tive·ly** /rɪˈspɛktɪvli/ adv each separately in the order mentioned: *The dollar and yen rose 2% and 3% respectively.*

**re·spects** /rɪˈspɛkts/ n [plural] **1** polite greetings: *Give my respects to your parents.* **2** **pay your (last/final) respects** to go to a funeral to show that you liked and respected someone

**res·pi·ra·tion** /ˌrɛspəˈreɪʃən/ n [U] TECHNICAL the process of breathing —see also ARTIFICIAL RESPIRATION

**res·pi·ra·tor** /ˈrɛspəˌreɪtɚ/ n a piece of equipment that covers the nose and mouth and helps someone to breathe

**res·pi·ra·to·ry** /ˈrɛsprəˌtɔri/ adj TECHNICAL relating to breathing: *the respiratory system*

**res·pite** /ˈrɛspɪt/ n [singular, U] a short time of rest from something unpleasant such as pain, effort, or trouble: *The Northwest should have a brief respite from the rain today.*

**re·splend·ent** /rɪˈsplɛndənt/ adj FORMAL very beautiful in appearance, in a way that looks expensive

**re·spond** /rɪˈspand/ v **1** [I] to react to something that has been said or done: *Voters responded to the tax increases by voting against the Democrats.* **2** [I] to say or write something

R

as a reply: *How did he respond to your question?* **3** [I] to improve as a result of a particular medical treatment: *Her cancer is responding well to the drugs.* −see usage note at ANSWER[1]

**re·sponse** /rɪ'spɑns/ *n* [C,U] something that is said, written, or done as a reaction or reply to something else: *I am writing in response to your advertisement.* | *We've had a good response to our appeal for help.*

**re·spon·si·bil·i·ty** /rɪ,spɑnsə'bɪləti/ *n* **1** [U] a duty to be in charge of or take care of something: *Do you think he's ready for more responsibility?* | *Terry said he'd take responsibility for* (=agree to be in charge of) *organizing the trip.* **2** something that you have a duty to do, be in charge of, or take care of: *The president has many responsibilities.* **3** [U] blame for something bad: *No one has accepted/taken responsibility for the bombing.*

**re·spon·si·ble** /rɪ'spɑnsəbəl/ *adj* **1** if you are responsible for something bad, it is your fault: *a gang responsible for several robberies* **2** in charge of or taking care of something: *She's responsible for our foreign sales.* **3** responsible job/position/post a job in which the ability to make good judgments and decisions is needed **4** sensible and able to be trusted: *a responsible young man* **5** be responsible to if you are responsible to someone, that person is in charge of your work and you must explain your actions to him/her

**re·spon·si·bly** /rɪ'spɑnsəbli/ *adv* in a sensible way that makes people trust you: *Can I trust you to behave responsibly while I'm gone?*

**re·spon·sive** /rɪ'spɑnsɪv/ *adj* **1** ready to react in a useful or helpful way: *a company that is responsive to your business needs* **2** able or willing to give answers or show your feelings about something: *Utley was awake and responsive after the surgery.* −**responsiveness** *n* [U] −opposite UNRESPONSIVE

**rest**[1] /rɛst/ *n* **1** the rest a) what is left after everything else has been used, dealt with etc.: *What should I do with the rest of the pizza?* b) the others in a group, or the other part of something: *Sam's here today, but he'll be away for the rest of the week.* | *I'll read you the rest tomorrow night.* **2** [C,U] a period of time when you can relax or sleep: *I need to get some rest.* **3** put/set sb's mind at rest to make someone feel less anxious or worried **4** come to rest to stop moving: *The truck went off the road and came to rest at the bottom of the hill.* **5** lay/put sth to rest to get rid of a false idea or belief by showing that it is not true: *I'm glad those rumors have been put to rest.* **6** at rest TECHNICAL not moving

**rest**[2] *v* **1** [I] to stop doing something and relax or sleep for a period of time: *Do you want to rest before we go on?* **2** rest your feet/legs/ eyes etc. to stop using a part of your body for a

period of time because it is feeling sore or tired: *We stopped at a cafe for a while to rest our legs.* **3** [T] to support an object or part of your body by putting it on or against something: *The baby rested his head on my shoulder.* | *Rest your bike against the wall.* **4** rest assured (that) FORMAL used in order to tell someone that what you say is true: *You can rest assured that we'll do all we can.* **5** sb will not rest until LITERARY if someone will not rest until something happens, s/he will not be satisfied until it happens **6** rest in peace a phrase written on a grave stone **7** rest on your laurels to be satisfied with what you have done, and not do anything more: *We can't rest on our laurels; the market is too competitive.*

**rest on/upon** sth *phr v* [T] FORMAL to depend on or be based on something: *His future in sports rests on this meeting with the coaches.*

**rest with** sb *phr v* [T] if a decision rests with someone, s/he is responsible for it: *The final decision rests with you.*

**re·state** /ri'steɪt/ *v* [T] to say something again in a different way, so that it is clearer or more strongly expressed: *Hersh restated his confidence in Glidden's abilities.* −**restatement** *n* [C,U]

**res·tau·rant** /'rɛs,trɑnt, 'rɛstə,rɑnt, 'rɛstə-rənt/ *n* a place where you can buy and eat a meal

---

**CULTURE NOTE** getting attention in a restaurant

In the US and Canada, when you are in a restaurant and want to get the attention of a waiter or waitress, you can look at him or her and raise your hand slightly. This shows that you are ready to order, would like the check etc.

---

**rest·ful** /'rɛstfəl/ *adj* peaceful and quiet: *a restful weekend*

**rest home** /'. ./ *n* ⇨ NURSING HOME

**res·ti·tu·tion** /,rɛstə'tuʃən/ *n* [U] FORMAL the act of giving back to the owner something that was lost or stolen, or of paying for damage

**res·tive** /'rɛstɪv/ *adj* FORMAL ⇨ RESTLESS

**rest·less** /'rɛstlɪs/ *adj* **1** unable to keep still, especially because you are impatient, anxious, or bored: *The children are getting restless.* **2** not satisfied and wanting new experiences: *I could see she was restless and thinking about a new job.* −**restlessness** *n* [U] −**restlessly** *adv*

**re·store** /rɪ'stɔr/ *v* [T] **1** to make something as good as it was before: *restoring antique furniture* **2** to make something exist again: *The army was called in to restore order.* **3** FORMAL to give back to someone something that was lost or stolen: *The stolen horses were restored to their rightful owner.* −**restoration** /,rɛstə'reɪʃən/ *n* [C,U]

**re·strain** /rɪ'streɪn/ v [T] **1** to physically prevent someone from doing something: *He had to be restrained by his teammates from attacking the referee.* **2** to control something: *new taxes to restrain the demand for foreign goods*

**re·strained** /rɪ'streɪnd/ adj behavior that is restrained is calm and controlled

**re·straint** /rɪ'streɪnt/ n **1** [U] calm and controlled behavior: *I think you showed great restraint, considering what she said.* **2** [C,U] something that controls what you can say or do: *Budget cuts have put restraints on public spending.*

**re·strict** /rɪ'strɪkt/ v [T] to control something or keep it within limits: *new laws to restrict the sale of guns*

**re·strict·ed** /rɪ'strɪktɪd/ adj **1** controlled or limited: *The sale of alcohol is restricted to people over the age of 21.* **2** only allowed to be seen or used by a particular group of people: *a restricted area used by the army*

**re·stric·tion** /rɪ'strɪkʃən/ n [C,U] a rule or set of laws that limits what you can do or what is allowed to happen: *There's a restriction on how many tickets you can buy.| freedom to travel without restriction*

**re·stric·tive** /rɪ'strɪktɪv/ adj tending to restrict you too much: *complaints about restrictive trade policies*

**rest·room** /'rɛstrum/ n a room with a toilet, in a public place such as a restaurant or theater —see usage note at TOILET

**re·struc·ture** /ˌri'strʌktʃɚ/ v [T] to change the way in which something such as a business or system is organized —restructuring n [U]

**re·sult**[1] /rɪ'zʌlt/ n **1** [C,U] something that happens or exists because of something else: *As a result of (=because of) the snow storm, there is no school today in most of the tri-city area.| Ann missed several tests, with the result that she failed the class.* **2** the answers that are produced by a scientific or medical study or test: *When will you have the results of my blood test?*

**result**[2] v [I] to happen or exist because of something: *an illness resulting from eating bad food*
**result in** sth phr v [T] to make something happen: *The fire resulted in the death of two children.*

**re·sult·ant** /rɪ'zʌltənt, -t⁻nt/ adj FORMAL happening or existing because of something else

**re·sume** /rɪ'zum/ v [I,T] FORMAL to start doing something again after a pause: *Thielen hopes to resume his duties soon.* —resumption /rɪ'zʌmpʃən/ n [singular, U]

**ré·su·mé** /'rɛzəˌmeɪ, ˌrɛzə'meɪ/ n a written list and description of your education and your previous jobs, that you use when you are looking for a job

**re·sur·face** /ˌri'sɚfɪs/ v **1** [I] to appear again: *Old arguments began to resurface at last week's meeting.* **2** [I] to come back up to the

surface of the water **3** [T] to put a new surface on a road

**re·sur·gence** /rɪ'sɚdʒəns/ n [singular, U] if there is a resurgence of a harmful belief or activity, it reappears and becomes stronger: *a resurgence of racial violence* —resurgent adj

**res·ur·rect** /ˌrɛzə'rɛkt/ v [T] to bring an old practice, belief etc. back into use or fashion: *Designers in the 1990s resurrected the styles of the 1960s.*

**res·ur·rec·tion** /ˌrɛzə'rɛkʃən/ n [U] the act of bringing an old practice, belief etc. back into use or fashion

**re·sus·ci·tate** /rɪ'sʌsəˌteɪt/ v [T] to make someone breathe again after s/he has almost died —resuscitation /rɪˌsʌsə'teɪʃən/ n [U]

**re·tail**[1] /'riteɪl/ n [U] the sale of goods in stores to people for their own use —compare WHOLESALE[2]

**retail**[2] v retail for/at to be sold at a particular price in stores: *This item retails for $469.*

**retail**[3] adv from a RETAILER: *We bought it retail.*

**re·tail·er** /'riˌteɪlɚ/ n someone who sells goods to the public, using a store —compare WHOLESALER

**re·tain** /rɪ'teɪn/ v [T] **1** to keep something or to continue to have something: *Steamed vegetables retain more of their flavor and color.| a town that has retained its colonial charm* **2** to keep facts in your memory: *She retains most of what she reads.* —retention /rɪ'tɛnʃən/ n [U]

**re·tain·er** /rɪ'teɪnɚ/ n **1** an amount of money that you pay regularly to someone such as a lawyer, so that s/he will continue to work for you **2** a small plastic and wire object that you wear in your mouth to make your teeth stay straight

**re·take** /ˌri'teɪk/ v [T] to get control of something again: *Rebels have retaken the city.*

**re·tal·i·ate** /rɪ'tælieɪt/ v [I] to do something bad to someone because s/he has done something bad to you: *When the police moved in, the angry crowd retaliated by throwing rocks.*

**re·tal·i·a·tion** /rɪˌtæli'eɪʃən/ n [U] the act of retaliating (RETALIATE): *The teenager was killed in retaliation for a similar killing in a nearby neighborhood.*

**re·tard**[1] /rɪ'tɑrd/ v [T] FORMAL to delay the development of something, or to make something happen more slowly —retardation /ˌritɑr'deɪʃən/ n [U]

**retard**[2] /'ritɑrd/ n SLANG OFFENSIVE a stupid person

**re·tard·ed** /rɪ'tɑrdɪd/ adj less mentally developed than other people: *training programs for retarded adults*

---

**USAGE NOTE retarded**

Using the word **retarded** to talk about someone who has difficulty learning things is offensive. It is more polite to say that a

R

person is "mentally challenged" or has "special needs."

**retch** /rɛtʃ/ v [I] if you retch, you feel like you are VOMITing but nothing comes out of your stomach

**re·think** /ˌriˈθɪŋk/ v [I,T] to think about a plan or idea again in order to decide if any changes should be made

**ret·i·cent** /ˈrɛtəsənt/ adj unwilling to talk about what you know or how you feel: *She was very reticent about her reasons for leaving.* −**reticence** n [U]

**ret·i·na** /ˈrɛt⁻nə/ n the area at the back of your eye that sends an image of what you see to your brain

**ret·i·nue** /ˈrɛt⁻nˌu/ n a group of helpers or supporters who are traveling with an important person: *the president's retinue*

**re·tire** /rɪˈtaɪɚ/ v **1** [I,T] to stop working, usually because of old age, or to make someone do this: *Barney wants to retire next year.* **2** [I] FORMAL to go away to a quiet place: *He retired to his room.* **3** [I] FORMAL to go to bed

**re·tired** /rɪˈtaɪɚd/ adj retired people have stopped working, usually because they are old: *a retired teacher*

**re·tire·ment** /rɪˈtaɪɚmənt/ n **1** [C,U] the act of retiring (RETIRE)) from your job: *a party for Bill's retirement* **2** [singular, U] the period of time after you have retired: *a long and happy retirement*

**re·tir·ing** /rɪˈtaɪərɪŋ/ adj **1** not wanting to be with other people: *a shy and retiring woman* **2 the retiring president/manager etc.** a president etc. who is soon going to RETIRE

**re·tort** /rɪˈtɔrt/ v [T] to reply quickly, in an angry or humorous way: *"It's all your fault!" he retorted.* −**retort** n

**re·trace** /rɪˈtreɪs/ v [T] **1** to go back the way you have come: *She retraced her steps to try to find her ring.* **2** to repeat exactly the same trip that someone else has made: *The ships are retracing Columbus's route across the Atlantic to North America.*

**re·tract** /rɪˈtrækt/ v **1** [T] to make an official statement saying that something you said earlier is not true: *He confessed to the crime but later retracted his statement.* **2** [I,T] if a part of something retracts or is retracted, it moves back into the main part −**retraction** /rɪˈtrækʃən/ n [C,U]

**re·tract·a·ble** /rɪˈtræktəbəl/ adj a retractable part of something can be pulled back into the main part: *a knife with a retractable blade*

**re·tread** /ˈritrɛd/ n an old tire with a new rubber surface put onto it

**re·treat¹** /rɪˈtrit/ v [I] **1** to decide not to do what you have promised or planned because it seems too difficult or extreme: *The president seems to be retreating from his pledge to cut*

taxes. **2** to move away from a place or person: *"We need another lamp," she called after the retreating servant.* **3** to stop being involved with society or other people at all: *After her death, he retreated into himself and stopped working altogether.* **4** if an army retreats it stops fighting and moves away from the enemy

**retreat²** n **1** the act of deciding to do or believe something that is less extreme or difficult than what you had planned, promised, or believed before: *a retreat from his original position on welfare spending* **2** a place you can go to that is quiet or safe: *a mountain retreat* **3** [C,U] a decision to no longer be involved with society or other people at all: *The philosopher's retreat from society produced some of his greatest works.* **4** [C,U] an army's movement away from the enemy: *Napoleon's retreat from Moscow* **5** [C,U] a movement away from a place or person

**re·tri·al** /ˌriˈtraɪl, ˈritraɪl/ n the process of judging a law case in court again: *My lawyer demanded a retrial.*

**ret·ri·bu·tion** /ˌrɛtrəˈbyuʃən/ n [singular, U] punishment that is deserved: *Employees need to feel they can express their views without fear of retribution.*

**re·trieve** /rɪˈtriv/ v [T] to find something and bring it back: *You can retrieve the document by clicking on the icon.* | *He retrieved the book from the shelf and handed it to me.* −**retrieval** n [U]

**re·triev·er** /rɪˈtrivɚ/ n a type of dog that can be trained to find and bring back birds that its owner has shot

**ret·ro·ac·tive** /ˌrɛtrouˈæktɪv/ adj a law or decision that is retroactive is effective from a particular date in the past: *a retroactive pay increase* −**retroactively** adv

**ret·ro·spect** /ˈrɛtrəˌspɛkt/ n **in retrospect** when you think about the past, and know more now than you did then: *In retrospect, it was the wrong time to leave my job.*

**ret·ro·spec·tive** /ˌrɛtrəˈspɛktɪv/ adj concerned with the past: *a retrospective look at Capra's movies*

**re·try** /riˈtraɪ/ v [I] to judge a law case in court again

**re·turn¹** /rɪˈtɚn/ v

**1 ▶GO BACK◀** [I] to go back to a place where you were before, or to come back from a place: *Kevin has just returned from Texas.* | *She didn't return until after 8 o'clock.* ✗ DON'T SAY "return back." ✗

**2 ▶PREVIOUS STATE◀** [I] to be in a previous state or condition again: *Things will soon return to normal.*

**3 ▶GIVE BACK◀** [T] to give something back, or put something back in its place: *Will you return these books to the library for me?* | *It didn't fit, so I returned it.* (=took it back to the store)

**4 ▶HAPPEN AGAIN◀** [I] to start to happen or

exist again: *Take two of these pills if the pain returns.*

**5** ▶START AGAIN◀ [I] to go back to an activity, discussion etc. that was stopped or interrupted: *Let's return to the subject of your previous employment.* | *Does she plan to return to work after the baby is born?*

**6** ▶DO STH SIMILAR◀ [T] to react to something someone has done, by doing something similar: *Why didn't you return my call?* | *She's really helped me recently, and I wanted to return the favor.*

**7 return a verdict** if a JURY returns their VERDICT, they say whether someone is guilty or not

**8** ▶MONEY◀ [T] if an INVESTMENT returns a particular amount of money, that is how much profit it produces

**return**[2] *n*

**1** ▶GOING BACK◀ [singular, U] the act of going back to a place where you were before, or of coming back from a place: *We're all looking forward to your return!* | *I expect to meet her on/upon her return.* (=when she returns)

**2** ▶GIVING STH BACK◀ [U] the act of giving something back, or of putting something back in its place: *a reward for the return of the stolen necklace*

**3** ▶STH HAPPENING AGAIN◀ the fact of something starting to happen or to exist again: *the return of spring*

**4** ▶STH STARTING AGAIN◀ [singular] the act of going back to an activity, discussion, way of doing something etc. that was stopped or interrupted: *her return to full-time work* | *There cannot be a return to the old way of life.*

**5** ▶MONEY◀ [C,U] the amount of profit an INVESTMENT produces: *He expects a big return on his shares.*

**6 in return (for)** in exchange for, or as payment for something: *I'd like to buy you a drink in return for all you've done.*

**7** ▶STATEMENT◀ a statement or set of figures given as a reply to an official demand: *a tax return*

**re·turn·a·ble** /rɪ'tɜnəbəl/ *adj* returnable bottles, containers etc. can be given back to the store

**re·un·ion** /ri'yunyən/ *n* **1** a meeting of people who have not met for a long time: *a college reunion* **2** [U] the state of being brought together again after a period of being separated: *an emotional reunion after a long separation*

**re·u·nite** /,riyu'naɪt/ *v* [I,T] to come together again, or to be brought together again after a period of being separated: *That spring, he was at last reunited with his children.*

**Rev.** the written abbreviation of REVEREND

**rev**[1] /rɛv/ *n* [C usually plural] INFORMAL one REVOLUTION of an engine

**rev**[2] **rev up** *v* **-vved, -vving** [I,T] if you rev an engine, or if it revs, it works faster

**re·val·ue** /ri'vælyu/ *v* [T] to examine something again in order to calculate its present value −**revaluation** /ri,vælyu'eɪʃən/ *n* [C,U] −compare DEVALUE

**re·vamp** /ri'væmp/ *v* [T] INFORMAL to change something in order to improve it: *a bill that would revamp federal banking laws*

**re·veal** /rɪ'vil/ *v* [T] **1** to show something that was previously hidden: *The curtains opened to reveal a darkened stage.* **2** to make something known that was previously secret: *The newspaper story revealed a huge cover-up.* | *She suddenly revealed that she had once been married.*

**re·veal·ing** /rɪ'vilɪŋ/ *adj* **1** showing someone's character or feelings: *Some of her comments were very revealing.* **2** revealing clothes show parts of your body that are usually kept covered

**rev·el** /'rɛvəl/ *v*
**revel in** sth *phr v* [T] to enjoy something very much: *Bobby seemed to revel in my undivided attention.*

**rev·e·la·tion** /,rɛvə'leɪʃən/ *n* [C,U] a surprising and previously secret fact that suddenly becomes known, or the act of making this fact known: *strange revelations about her past*

**rev·el·er** /'rɛvələ/ *n* someone who is enjoying drinking, dancing, and eating, especially at a party

**rev·el·ry** /'rɛvəlri/ *n* [C,U] wild noisy dancing, eating, drinking etc.

**re·venge**[1] /rɪ'vɛndʒ/ *n* [U] something you do in order to punish someone who has harmed or offended you: *I think that Brennan lied in order to get/take revenge on the company for firing him.* | *a bomb attack in revenge for the killing of ten prisoners*

**revenge**[2] *v* [T] to punish someone who has harmed or offended you −see also AVENGE

**rev·e·nue** /'rɛvə,nu/ *n* [U] **1** money that is earned by a company **2** money that the government receives from tax

**re·ver·ber·ate** /rɪ'vɜbə,reɪt/ *v* [I] **1** if a loud sound reverberates, it is heard many times as it is sent back from different surfaces: *Their voices reverberated around the empty church.* **2** to have a strong effect that continues for a long time: *The fall of stock prices continues to reverberate in the market.* −**reverberation** /rɪ,vɜbə'reɪʃən/ *n* [C,U]

**re·vere** /rɪ'vɪr/ *v* [T] FORMAL to greatly respect and admire someone: *He was revered as a leader.*

**rev·er·ence** /'rɛvrəns/ *adj* FORMAL respect and admiration: *a reverence for tradition* −**reverent** *adj* −**reverently** *adv* −opposite IRREVERENT

**Rev·er·end** /'rɛvrənd, -ərənd/ *n* a minister in the Christian church: *Reverend Larson*

R

**rev·er·ie** /'rɛvəri/ *n* [C,U] a state of imagining or thinking about pleasant things

**re·ver·sal** /rɪ'vɜ·səl/ *n* [C,U] the act of changing an arrangement, process, or action in order to do the opposite: *a reversal of their usual policy* | *a reversal of the court's decision*

**re·verse**[1] /rɪ'vɜ·s/ *v* **1** [T] to change something, such as a decision, judgment, or process, so that it is the opposite of what it was before: *The judge reversed his original decision and set her free.* **2** [I,T] to move backward, especially in a vehicle: *Reverse the car through the gate.* | *reversing out of a driveway* **3** [T] to change around the usual order of the parts of something: *Let's reverse the order of the songs and sing "Freedom" first.* –**reversible** *adj: a reversible coat*

**reverse**[2] *n* **1** [U] the control in a vehicle that makes it go backward: *Put the car in reverse.* **2 the reverse** the opposite: *He did the reverse of what we expected and bought us all a drink.* **3 in reverse** done in the opposite way or with the opposite effect: *Welfare is taxation in reverse.*

**reverse**[3] *adj* opposite of what is usual or to what has just been stated: *Put the letters of the words in reverse order and see what it spells.*

**reverse dis·crim·i·na·tion** /.,. ...'..'../ *n* [U] a phrase meaning a situation in which a woman or a MINORITY such as an African-American is chosen for a job even though s/he is not the best person for the job, used by people who do not approve of this –compare AFFIRMATIVE ACTION

**re·vert** /rɪ'vɜ·t/ *v* **revert to sth** to go back to a previous situation, condition, use, or habit: *Leningrad reverted to its former name of St. Petersburg.* –**reversion** /rɪ'vɜ·ʒən/ *n* [singular, U]

**re·view**[1] /rɪ'vyu/ *n* **1** [C,U] an act of carefully examining, considering, and judging a situation or process: *an urgent review of safety procedures* | *Our salaries are currently under review.* (=being examined and considered) **2** an article that gives an opinion about a new book, play, movie etc.: *His book got very good reviews.*

**review**[2] *v* **1** [T] to examine, consider, and judge a situation or process carefully: *The state is reviewing its education policy.* **2** [I,T] to write an article that gives your opinion about a new book, play, movie etc.: *He reviews movies for our local newspaper.* **3** [I,T] to prepare for a test by studying books, notes, reports etc.

**re·view·er** /rɪ'vyuɚ/ *n* someone who writes articles that give his/her opinion about new books, plays, movies etc.

**re·vile** /rɪ'vaɪl/ *v* [T] FORMAL to express hatred of someone or something

**re·vise** /rɪ'vaɪz/ *v* [T] **1** to change your opinions, plans etc. because of new information or ideas: *The hotel operator said it will revise*

*plans for the new building.* **2** to improve a piece of writing

**re·vi·sion** /rɪ'vɪʒən/ *n* **1** [C,U] the process of improving something, especially a piece of writing **2** a piece of writing that has been improved

**re·vi·tal·ize** /ri'vaɪṭl,aɪz/ *v* [T] to make something become strong, active, or powerful again: *The city has begun to revitalize the downtown area.* (=make businesses stronger, rebuild buildings etc.) –**revitalization** /ri,vaɪṭl-ə'zeɪʃən/ *n* [U]

**re·viv·al** /rɪ'vaɪvəl/ *n* **1** [C,U] a process in which something becomes active, strong, or popular again: *the revival of the fishing industry* **2** a new performance of a play that has not been performed for a long time: *a revival of "Oklahoma!"* **3** a public religious meeting that is intended to make people interested in Christianity

**re·vive** /rɪ'vaɪv/ *v* [I,T] **1** to become conscious or healthy, or make someone do this: *We revived her with cold water.* **2** to come back into use or existence, or bring something back into use or existence: *The television station decided to revive some old TV shows from the 1950s and 60s.*

**re·voke** /rɪ'voʊk/ *v* [T] to officially state that a law, decision etc. is no longer effective: *Her driver's license has been revoked.*

**re·volt**[1] /rɪ'voʊlt/ *v* **1** [I] to refuse to obey a government, law etc., often using violence against it: *The people revolted against the military government.* **2** [T] to make you feel sick and shocked: *I was revolted by what I saw.*

**revolt**[2] *n* [C,U] strong and often violent action against a government, law etc.: *The entire nation is in revolt.* | *The revolt is over.*

**re·volt·ing** /rɪ'voʊltɪŋ/ *adj* extremely unpleasant: *What a revolting meal!*

**rev·o·lu·tion** /,rɛvə'luʃən/ *n* **1** [C,U] a time of great, usually sudden, social and political change, especially when force is used in order to change a ruler or political system: *the Russian Revolution* **2** a complete change in ways of thinking, methods of working etc.: *Computer technology has caused a revolution in business practices.* **3** [C,U] one complete circular movement or spin around a central point: *The earth makes one revolution around the sun each year.* | *a wheel turning at a speed of 100 revolutions per minute*

**rev·o·lu·tion·ar·y**[1] /,rɛvə'luʃə,nɛri/ *adj* **1** completely new and different: *a revolutionary new treatment for cancer* **2** relating to a political or social REVOLUTION: *a revolutionary army*

**revolutionary**[2] *n* someone who joins in or supports a political or social REVOLUTION

**rev·o·lu·tion·ize** /,rɛvə'luʃə,naɪz/ *v* [T] to completely change the way people think or do things: *new machines that revolutionized the entire industry*

**re·volve** /rɪ'vɑlv/ *v* [I,T] to spin around a central point, or to make something do this: *The wheels began to revolve slowly.* –**revolving** *adj*: *a revolving door*

  **revolve around** sb/sth *phr v* [T] **1** to have something as a main subject or purpose: *Her life seems to revolve around her job.* **2** to move in circles around something: *The moon revolves around the earth.*

**re·volv·er** /rɪ'vɑlvɚ/ *n* a type of small gun that you hold in one hand

**re·vue** /rɪ'vyu/ *n* a show in a theater that includes singing, dancing, and telling jokes

**re·vul·sion** /rɪ'vʌlʃən/ *n* [U] a strong feeling of being sick and shocked

**re·ward¹** /rɪ'wɔrd/ *n* [C,U] something, especially an amount of money, that is given to someone for doing something good, providing information etc.: *The police are offering a reward for information.* –compare AWARD²

**reward²** *v* [T] to give something to someone, especially an amount of money, for doing something good, providing information etc.: *To train a dog, reward him with food and praise.* | *She was generously rewarded for her work.*

**re·ward·ing** /rɪ'wɔrdɪŋ/ *adj* making you feel happy and satisfied: *a rewarding job*

**re·wind** /ri'waɪnd/ *v* [I,T] to make a TAPE go back to the beginning

**re·work** /ri'wɚk/ *v* [T] to change or improve a plan, piece of music, story etc. so that you can use it

**re·write** /ri'raɪt/ *v* [T] to write something again using different words in order to make it clearer or more effective – **rewrite** /'riraɪt/ *n*

**rhap·so·dy** /'ræpsədi/ *n* a piece of music that is written to express emotion, and does not have a regular form

**rhet·o·ric** /'rɛt̮ərɪk/ *n* [U] **1** speech or writing that sounds impressive, but is not actually sincere or very useful: *There's a lot of rhetoric about supporting education, but very little is actually done.* **2** the art of speaking or writing in order to persuade or influence people –**rhetorical** /rɪ'tɔrɪkəl/ *adj* –**rhetorically** *adv*

**rhe·tor·i·cal ques·tion** /.,... '../ *n* a question that you ask as a way of making a statement, without expecting an answer

**rheu·ma·tism** /'rumə,tɪzəm/ *n* [U] a disease that makes your joints or muscles painful and stiff

**rhine·stone** /'raɪnstoun/ *n* [C,U] a jewel made from glass or a rock that is intended to look like a DIAMOND

**rhi·noc·er·os** /raɪ'nɑsərəs/, **rhi·no** /'raɪnou/ *n* a large heavy animal with thick rough skin and one or two horns on its nose

**rho·do·den·dron** /,roudə'dɛndrən/ *n* a large bush with groups of red, purple, pink, or white flowers

**rhu·barb** /'rubɑrb/ *n* [U] a plant with long thick red stems that are cooked and eaten as a fruit

**rhyme¹** /raɪm/ *n* **1** a word that ends with the same sound as another word: *I can't find a rhyme for "donkey."* **2** a short poem or song, especially for children, using words that rhyme –see also NURSERY RHYME **3** [U] the use of words that rhyme in poetry, especially at the ends of lines: *Parts of Shakespeare's plays are written in rhyme.* **4 without rhyme or reason** in a way that cannot be reasonably explained: *Joe's moods change without rhyme or reason.*

**rhyme²** *v* **1** [I] if two words or lines of poetry rhyme, they end with the same sound: *"House" rhymes with "mouse."* **2** [T] to put two or more words together to make them rhyme: *You can't rhyme "box" with "backs."*

**rhythm** /'rɪðəm/ *n* [C,U] a regular repeated pattern of sounds in music, speech etc.

**rhythm and blues** /,... './ *n* [U] ⇨ R & B

**rhyth·mic** /'rɪðmɪk/ *adj* having RHYTHM: *fast rhythmic music*

**RI** the written abbreviation of Rhode Island

**rib¹** /rɪb/ *n* **1** one of the 12 pairs of curved bones that surround your lungs, or one of the similar bones in an animal **2** a piece of meat that includes an animal's rib: *beef ribs*

**rib²** *v* **-bbed, -bbing** [T] INFORMAL to make jokes about someone and laugh at him/her, but in a friendly way: *John always gets ribbed about being bald.*

**rib·ald** /'raɪbɔld, 'rɪbəld/ *adj* ribald jokes, remarks, songs etc. are humorous, rude and usually about sex

**ribbed** /rɪbd/ *adj* having a pattern of raised lines: *a ribbed sweater*

**rib·bon** /'rɪbən/ *n* **1** [C,U] a long narrow piece of cloth, used for tying things or as a decoration: *a red ribbon in her hair* **2** a colored ribbon that is given as a prize in a competition –see also BLUE RIBBON **3** a long narrow piece of cloth with ink on it that is used in a TYPEWRITER

**rib cage** /'. ./ *n* the structure of RIBs around your lungs and heart

**rice** /raɪs/ *n* [U] a white or brown grain grown in wet fields, that is eaten after it has been boiled

**rice pad·dy** /'. ,../ *n* ⇨ PADDY

**rich** /rɪtʃ/ *adj* **1** having a lot of money or valuable possessions: *a very rich man* | *a rich and powerful nation* **2** rich foods contain a lot of butter, cream, sugar, or eggs, and make you feel full very quickly: *a rich chocolate cake* **3** containing a lot of something good: *foods that are rich in vitamins* | *a rich cultural heritage* **4 the rich** people who have a lot of money or valuable possessions **5** very deep and strong: *a rich dark blue* | *the rich tone of a*

R

cello **6** good for growing plants in: *rich soil*
**7** expensive and beautiful: *rich silk* **–richness**
*n* [U]

**rich·es** /'rɪtʃɪz/ *n* [plural] LITERARY a lot of
money or valuable possessions

**rich·ly** /'rɪtʃli/ *adv* **1** in a beautiful or
expensive way: *a richly decorated fabric*
**2 richly deserve** to completely deserve something: *They got the punishment they so richly
deserved.* **3** in large amounts: *He was richly
rewarded for his work.*

**rick·et·y** /'rɪkəti/ *adj* a rickety piece of
furniture, stair etc. is in bad condition and is
likely to break if you use it

**rick·shaw** /'rɪkʃɔ/ *n* a small vehicle used in
Asia for carrying one or two passengers, that is
pulled by someone walking or riding a bicycle

**ric·o·chet** /'rɪkə,ʃeɪ/ *v* [I] if something such
as a bullet or a thrown rock ricochets, it changes
direction when it hits a surface **–ricochet** *n*

**rid¹** /rɪd/ *adj* **1 get rid of a)** to throw away
something you do not want or use: *Do you want
to get rid of these old shirts?* **b)** to make something that is unpleasant go away, stop happening, or stop existing: *I can't get rid of this cold.*
**c)** to make someone who annoys you leave: *I
couldn't get rid of her - she just sat there talking
about herself all night.* **2 be rid of** to have
gotten rid of someone who annoys you or something that is unpleasant: *He's gone, and I'm glad
to be rid of him.*

**rid²** *v* **rid, rid, ridding**
**rid** sb/sth **of** sth *phr v* [T] **1** to remove something or someone that is bad or harmful from a
place, organization etc.: *efforts to **rid** the
government **of** corrupt officials* **2 rid yourself
of** sth to stop having a feeling, thought, or
problem that was causing you trouble

**rid·dance** /'rɪdns/ *n* **good riddance** SPOKEN
said when you are glad that someone or something has gone away

**rid·dle** /'rɪdl/ *n* **1** a difficult and amusing
question that you must guess the answer to **2** a
mysterious action, event, or situation that you do
not understand and cannot explain: *His disappearance is a riddle.*

**rid·dled** /'rɪdld/ *adj* **riddled with** very full of
something, especially something bad or unpleasant: *Your paper is good, but it is riddled with
spelling mistakes.*

**ride¹** /raɪd/ *v* **rode, ridden** /'rɪdn/, **riding**
**1** [I,T] to sit on an animal, especially a horse,
or on a bicycle, and make it move along: *We
went riding* (=horses) *in the mountains.* | *Can
you ride a bike?* **2** [I,T] to travel in a car, train,
or other vehicle: *She feels sick when she rides in
the car for too long.* | *Fred rides the subway to
work everyday.* **3 let** sth **ride** SPOKEN to take no
action about something that is wrong or unpleasant: *I didn't like what he was saying, but I let it
ride.* **4** [T] SPOKEN to annoy someone by repeat-

edly criticizing him/her again and again, or asking him/her to do things again and again: *Stop
riding her - she's doing her best!*

**ride on** sth *phr v* [T] if something is riding on
something else, it depends on it: *He knew he
had to win - his reputation was **riding on** it.*

**ride** sth ↔ **out** *phr v* [T] to come out of a
difficult situation, bad experience etc. without
being harmed by it: *The company managed to
ride out the scandal.*

**ride²** *n* **1** a trip in a car, train, or other vehicle:
*Have you **gone for a ride in** Peggy's new car
yet?* | *Mick **gave** me **a ride** to work.* **2** a large
machine that people ride on for pleasure at a
FAIR or AMUSEMENT PARK: *Have you been on the
new ride at Disneyland?* **3** a trip on an animal,
especially a horse, or on a bicycle: *It's a beautiful day - do you want to **go for a ride**.*

**rid·er** /'raɪdɚ/ *n* someone who rides a horse,
bicycle etc.

**ridge** /rɪdʒ/ *n* **1** a long area of high land,
especially at the top of a mountain: *the ridge
along the Virginia-Kentucky border* **2** a long
narrow raised part of a surface: *ridges on the
soles of her shoes*

**rid·i·cule¹** /'rɪdə,kyul/ *n* [U] unkind laughter,
or remarks intended to make someone or something seem stupid: *Tracy has become an **object
of ridicule**.* (=a person that everyone laughs at)

**ridicule²** *v* [T] to laugh at a person, idea etc., or
to make unkind remarks about him, her, or it:
*They all ridiculed my plan.*

**ri·dic·u·lous** /rɪ'dɪkyələs/ *adj* silly or unreasonable: *What a ridiculous idea!* **–ridiculously**
*adv*

**rid·ing** /'raɪdɪŋ/ *n* [U] the sport of riding
horses

**rife** /raɪf/ *adj* **1** if something bad is rife, it is
very common: *Disease is rife in the region.*
**2 rife with** full of something bad: *The office is
rife with rumors about his resignation.*

**riff** /rɪf/ *n* a repeated series of notes in popular
music

**ri·fle¹** /'raɪfəl/ *n* a gun with a long BARREL
(=tube-shaped part) that you hold up to your
shoulder to shoot

**rifle²** *v* [T] to search through a place and steal
things from it: *It looked like someone had been
rifling through my desk.*

**rift** /rɪft/ *n* **1** a serious disagreement: *a growing rift between the two countries* **2** a crack or
narrow opening in a large piece of rock, group
of clouds etc.

**rig¹** /rɪg/ *v* **-gged, -gging** [T] **1** to arrange or
influence an election, competition etc. in a dishonest way so that you get the result that you
want: *The newspapers claimed that the election
had been rigged.* **2** to provide a ship with
ropes, sails etc.

**rig** sth ↔ **up** *phr v* [T] INFORMAL to make simple
equipment, furniture etc. out of materials that

R

you can find quickly and easily: *We rigged up a shelter using a big piece of plastic we found.*

**rig**² *n* **1** a large structure used for digging to find oil **2** INFORMAL a large TRUCK

**rig·a·ma·role** /'rɪgəmə,roʊl/ *n* [singular, U] ⇨ RIGMAROLE

**rig·ging** /'rɪgɪŋ/ *n* [U] all the ropes, sails etc. on a ship

**right**¹ /raɪt/ *adj* **1** correct or true: *Did you get the right answer? | Their predictions were right.* **2** on the right, which is the side of the body that has the hand most people write with: *Make a right turn after the gas station. | Raise your right hand.* **3** best or most suitable for a particular situation or purpose: *You need to have the right people running it to make it work.* **4** morally correct, or done according to the law: *What he did wasn't right, but he was angry.* **5 be in the right place at the right time** to be in a place or position that allows you to gain an advantage for yourself

SPOKEN PHRASES
**6 that's right** said when something that is said or done is correct, or when you remember something or are reminded of it: *"Dave just turned 60?" "That's right." | "No, you taped over Star Trek." "Oh, that's right."* **7** said in order to ask if what you have said was correct: *You wanted to go to the mall, right?* **8 yeah, right** said when you do not believe what has just been said: *He says, "I'll call you," and I'm like, "yeah, right."* **9** said in order to agree with what someone has said, to show that you are listening, or to show that what s/he has said is correct: *"I got so bored..." "Right." "...and I quit."* **10** used in order to check that someone understands and agrees with what you have said: *If people are comfortable, they're more likely to talk, right?*

–**rightness** *n* [U] –see also ALL RIGHT

**right**² *adv* **1** exactly in a particular position or place: *Shut up, he's right behind you! | His phone number's right there on the desk.* **2** immediately: *Send back your copy of the contract right away. | I need it right now! | I'll be right there.* (=I am coming now) *| She went to the grocery store, but she'll be right back.* (=come back soon) **3** correctly: *They didn't spell my name right.* **4** toward the direction or side that is on the right: *Turn right at the lights.* **5** all the way to something, through something etc.: *Go right to the end of the road. | You can see right through her bathing suit!* **6 sb will be right with you** used in order to say that someone will come soon to help or talk to you: *Your waitress will be right with you.*

**right**³ *n* **1** something that you are allowed to do or have according to the law or according to moral ideas: *Women didn't have the right to vote until 1920. | the right to free speech | a*

country in which every citizen enjoys **equal rights** (=rights that are the same for everyone) –see also CIVIL RIGHTS, HUMAN RIGHTS **2** [singular] the side of your body that has the hand that most people write with, or the direction toward this side: *Our house is on the right. | The matches are in the top drawer to your right.* **3** [U] behavior that is morally correct: *The lawyers said that Snyder did not know right from wrong* (=know what is morally correct and what is not) *at the time of the crime* **4 in his/her/its own right** considered alone, without depending on anyone or anything else: *San Jose is a city in its own right, not just a suburb of San Francisco.* **5 have a right to be/do sth** to have a good reason to do something, feel something, expect something etc.: *Weil has every right to be suspicious of him. | We didn't promise them anything; they have no right to be angry.* **6 the right** in politics, the right are people who believe that the government should not try to change or control social problems or businesses by making too many rules or limits; CONSERVATIVE –see also RIGHTS

**right**⁴ *v* [T] **1** to put something back in an upright position: *We finally managed to right the canoe.* **2** to correct something: *an attempt to right the wrong* (=correct something bad that was done) *of discrimination*

**right an·gle** /ˌ. '../ *n* an angle of 90°, like the angles at the corners of a square –**right-angled** /ˌ. '..⊣/ *adj*

**right·eous** /'raɪtʃəs/ *adj* **1 righteous indignation/anger etc.** strong feelings of anger when you think a situation is not morally right or fair **2** LITERARY morally good and fair: *a righteous man* **3** SLANG extremely good: *a righteous dude* –**righteousness** *n* [U] –**righteously** *adv*

**right field** /ˌ. './ *n* [singular] the area in baseball in the right side of the OUTFIELD

**right·ful** /'raɪtfəl/ *adj* according to what is legally and morally correct: *the property's rightful owner* –**rightfully** *adv*

**right-hand** /'. ./ *adj* **1** on your right side: *Make a right-hand turn.* **2 sb's right-hand man** the person who supports and helps someone the most, especially in his/her job

**right-hand·ed** /ˌ. '..⊣/ *adj* **1** someone who is right-handed uses his/her right hand for most things **2** done with the right hand: *a right-handed punch* –**right-handed** /ˌ. '../ *adv*

**right-handed**

Chrissie is right-handed.

**right·ly** /'raɪtli/ *adv* **1** correctly, or for a good reason: *She rightly pointed out that this won't solve the problem. | The book has rightly been called "an American Classic."* **2 I can't rightly say/I don't rightly know** SPOKEN said when you are not sure whether something is correct

**right of way** /ˌ. . '. / n [U] the right to drive into or across a road before other vehicles

**rights** /raɪts/ n [plural] legal permission to print or use a story, movie etc. in another form: *Several movie studios are bidding for the rights to Crichton's last book.*

**right-wing** /ˌ. '.◂ / adj supporting the political aims of the RIGHT: *a right-wing newspaper* **–right-winger** n **–right wing** n [singular]

**rig·id** /'rɪdʒɪd/ adj **1** rigid methods, systems etc. are very strict and difficult to change: *a rigid belief in the Bible* **2** someone who is rigid is very unwilling to change his/her ideas **3** stiff and not moving or bending: *a tent supported on a rigid frame* **–rigidly** adv **–rigidity** /rɪ'dʒɪdəti/ n [U]

**rig·ma·role** /'rɪgmə,roul/ n [singular, U] a set of actions that seems silly: *the rigmarole of filling out all these forms*

**rig·or** /'rɪgɚ/ n **1** [U] great care and thoroughness in making sure that something is correct: *the rigor of scientific proof* **2** **the rigors of** the unpleasant conditions of a difficult situation: *the rigors of a Canadian winter* **3** [U] FORMAL the state of being strict or severe: *the full rigor of the law*

**rig·or mor·tis** /ˌrɪgɚ 'mɔrṭɪs/ n [U] the condition in which someone's body becomes stiff after s/he dies

**rig·or·ous** /'rɪgərəs/ adj **1** careful and thorough: *rigorous safety checks* **2** very strict or severe: *a school with a rigorous curriculum* **–rigorously** adv

**rile** /raɪl/, **rile sb up** v [T] INFORMAL to make someone very angry

**rim** /rɪm/ n **1** the outside edge of something circular, such as a glass or a wheel **2** **-rimmed** with a particular type of rim: *gold-rimmed glasses*

**rind** /raɪnd/ n [C,U] the thick outer skin of some foods or fruits, such as BACON, cheese, and LEMONs **–see picture at** PEEL²

**ring¹** /rɪŋ/ n **1** a piece of jewelry that you wear on your finger **–see picture at** JEWELRY **2** a circular line or mark: *counting the rings in a tree trunk* **3** an object in the shape of a circle: *a key ring* **4** a group of people or things arranged in a circle: *surrounded by a ring of enemy tanks* **5** a group of people who illegally control a business or criminal activity: *a drug ring* **6** the sound made by a bell or the act of making this sound: *a ring at the door* **7** a small square area where people BOX or WRESTLE, or the large circular area surrounded by seats at a CIRCUS

**ring²** v **rang, rung, ringing 1** [I,T] to make a bell make a sound, especially to call someone's attention to you: *I rang the bell but there was no answer.* | *Please ring for assistance.* **2** [I] if a

bell rings, it makes a noise: *The telephone's ringing.* **–see usage note at** TELEPHONE **3** [I] if your ears ring, they are filled with a continuous sound **4** **ring a bell** INFORMAL if something rings a bell, you think you have heard it before: *Her name rings a bell, but I can't remember her face.* **5** **not ring true** if something does not ring true, you do not believe it: *His excuse didn't really ring true.*

**ring out** phr v [I] if a voice, bell etc. rings out, it makes a loud and clear sound: *The sound of a shot rang out.*

**ring sth ↔ up** phr v [T] to press buttons on a CASH REGISTER to record how much money needs to be put inside it: *She rang up our purchases.*

**ring³** v **ringed, ringed, ringing** [T] **1** to surround something: *The police ringed the building.* **2** to draw a circular mark around something

**ring·lead·er** /'rɪŋ,lidɚ/ n someone who leads a group that is doing something illegal or wrong: *Police arrested the two ringleaders last night.*

**ring·let** /'rɪŋlɪt/ n a long curl of hair that hangs down

**ring·side** /'rɪŋsaɪd/ n [singular] the area nearest to the performance in a CIRCUS, BOXING match etc.: *a ringside seat*

**ring·worm** /'rɪŋwɚm/ [U] a common disease that gives you red rough circles on your skin

**rink** /rɪŋk/ n a building with a specially prepared area with a smooth surface where you can SKATE

**rink·y-dink** /'rɪŋki ˌdɪŋk/ adj INFORMAL cheap and of bad quality

**rinse¹** /rɪns/ v [T] to use clean water in order to remove dirt, soap, etc. from something: *Rinse the lettuce in cold water.* | *Let me just rinse the sand off my feet.*

**rinse sth ↔ out** phr v [T] to wash something with clean water but not soap: *Please rinse out your bottles before recycling them.*

**rinse²** n **1** an act of rinsing (RINSE) something: *a dishwasher's rinse cycle* **2** [C,U] a product used for slightly changing the color of hair: *a brown rinse*

**ri·ot¹** /'raɪət/ n **1** a situation in which a crowd of people behaves in a violent and uncontrolled way: *Rises in food prices caused riots and strikes.* **2** [singular] someone or something that is very funny or enjoyable: *Jack's a real riot at a party.* **3** **read sb the riot act** INFORMAL to warn someone angrily that s/he must stop doing something wrong

**riot²** v [I] if a crowd of people riots, they all behave violently in a public place **–rioter** n

**ri·ot·ing** /'raɪəṭɪŋ/ n [U] violent and uncontrolled behavior from a crowd that is out of control: *Rioting broke out in the city late last night.*

**ri·ot·ous** /ˈraɪətəs/ *adj* **1** wild, exciting, and not controlled: *riotous celebrations* **2** noisy, possibly dangerous, and not controlled: *riotous crowds*

**RIP** the abbreviation of "Rest in Peace," written on the stone over a grave

rip

rip　　　　　　　　rip up

**rip**[1] /rɪp/ *v* **-pped, -pping** **1** [I,T] to tear something or be torn quickly and violently: *Oh, no! I've just ripped my sleeve.* | *Don't pull the curtain; it'll rip.* | *Impatiently, Sue ripped the letter open.* **2** [I] to move quickly and violently: *a tornado ripping through an area* **3 Let 'er rip!** SPOKEN used in order to tell someone to make a car, boat etc. go as fast as it can

**rip off** *phr v* [T] SPOKEN **1** [rip sb ↔ off] to charge someone too much money for something: *The taxi driver tried to rip me off!* **2** [rip sth] to steal something: *Someone ripped off Dan's car stereo.*

**rip** sth ↔ **up** *phr v* [T] to tear something into several pieces: *Fran ripped up her contract.*

**rip**[2] *n* a long tear or cut

**rip·cord** /ˈrɪpkɔrd/ *n* the string that you pull to open a PARACHUTE

**ripe** /raɪp/ *adj* **1** ripe food or crops are ready to eat: *Those peaches don't look ripe yet.* **2 be ripe for** to be in the right condition for something: *The area is ripe for a major earthquake.* **3 the time is ripe (for)** used in order to say it is the right time for something to happen: *The time is ripe for trade talks.* **4 ripe old age** if you live to a ripe old age, you are very old when you die –**ripeness** *n* [U]

**rip·en** /ˈraɪpən/ *v* [I,T] to become RIPE, or to make something do this: *Corn ripens quickly in hot weather.*

**rip·off** /ˈrɪpɔf/ *n* SPOKEN something that is unreasonably expensive, and makes you feel cheated: *The drinks in the hotel bar are a ripoff!*

**rip·ple**[1] /ˈrɪpəl/ *v*
**1** [I,T] to move in small waves, or to make something do this: *a flag rippling in the wind* **2** [I] to make a noise like water that is flowing gently: *water rippling over rocks* **3** [I] to pass from one person to the next like a wave: *Laughter rippled through/around the crowd.*

ripple

ripple

**ripple**[2] *n* **1** a small low wave on the surface of a liquid: *a breeze making ripples on the lake* **2** a feeling or sound that spreads through a person or group because of something that happens: *A ripple of laughter/nervousness ran through the audience.*

**rip-roar·ing** /ˌ. ˈ.. / *adj, adv* INFORMAL noisy, exciting, and not controlled: *We were having a rip-roaring time!* | *rip-roaring drunk*

**rise**[1] /raɪz/ *v* rose, risen /ˈrɪzən/, rising [I]
**1** ▶INCREASE◀ to increase in number, amount, quality, or value: *World oil prices are rising.* | *Tourism rose by 4% last year.* | *The population has risen steadily/sharply since the 1950s.*
**2** ▶GO UP◀ to go up: *Smoke rose from the chimney.* | *Flood waters are still rising in parts of Missouri.* –opposite FALL[1]
**3** ▶STAND◀ to stand up: *Thornton rose to his feet and turned to speak to them.*
**4** to become important, powerful, successful, or rich: *the story of how Marilyn Monroe rose to stardom*
**5** ▶VOICE/SOUND◀ to be heard, especially by getting louder or stronger: *Traffic noise rose from the street below.*
**6** ▶SUN/MOON/STAR◀ to appear in the sky: *We'd been traveling for over an hour before the sun rose.* –opposite SET[1]
**7** ▶EMOTION◀ to get stronger: *You could feel the excitement rising as we waited.*
**8** ▶MOUNTAIN/BUILDING◀ to be or seem taller than anything else around: *Then they could see Mount Shasta rising in the distance.*
**9** ▶BREAD/CAKES◀ if bread, cakes etc. rise, they become bigger as they bake, or because they contain YEAST
**10 rise to the occasion/challenge** to deal with a difficult situation or problem successfully by doing things better than you have done them before
**11 all rise** SPOKEN FORMAL used in order to tell people to stand up when a judge enters a court of law
**12** ▶BED◀ LITERARY to get out of bed in the morning
**13** ▶AGAINST A GOVERNMENT◀ LITERARY also **rise up** to try to defeat the government or army that is in control of your country; REBEL

**rise above** sth *phr v* [T] to be good or wise enough to deal with an insult or unpleasant situation without becoming upset by it: *You ought to be able to rise above all that silly fighting.*

R

---

**USAGE NOTE** rise and raise

**Rise** means "to move to a higher position" and does not have an object: *The curtain rose and the play began.* **Raise** means "to move someone or something to a higher position" and always has an object: *They raised the curtain and the play began.*

**rise**[2] *n* **1** an increase in number, amount, or value: *a 10% rise in car sales | a tax rise* **2** [singular] the achievement of importance, success, or power: *a book about his rise to fame/power* **3 give rise to sth** to be the reason something happens or begins to exist: *a new industry that gave rise to scores of new companies* **4** an upward slope: *a slight rise in the road* **5 get a rise out of sb** to make someone annoyed or embarrassed by making a joke about him/her: *Ask about his car - that always gets a rise out of him.*

**ris·er** /ˈraɪzɚ/ *n* **early/late riser** someone who usually wakes up very early or very late

**ris·ers** /ˈraɪzɚz/ *n* [plural] a set of wooden or metal steps for a group of people to stand on

**risk**[1] /rɪsk/ *n* **1** [C,U] the chance that something bad may happen: *Think about the risks in starting a new business. | the risk of cancer from smoking | There was a risk (that) he would say no.* **2 take a risk/run the risk** to do something even though there is a chance that something bad will happen: *You'll be running the risk of getting caught.* **3 at risk** likely to be harmed or put in a bad situation: *I'm not going to put my officers at risk.* (=make them do something dangerous) *| people at risk from radiation poisoning | He's at risk of losing his job.* **4 at your own risk** if you do something at your own risk, no one else is responsible if something bad happens: *Customers may park here at their own risk.* **5** something that is likely to hurt you or be dangerous: *health risks from air pollution | the risk factors for heart disease* (=things that make you likely to get sick) **6 insurance/credit risk** a person or business to whom it is a good or bad idea to give insurance or lend money: *Drivers under 21 are considered poor insurance risks.*

**risk**[2] *v* [T] **1** to put something in a situation in which it could be lost, destroyed, or harmed: *I'm not going to risk my life/neck to save a cat! | She risked her career by running for governor.* **2** to do something that you know may have bad results: *Some people have risked returning home, although the war is not over.*

**risk·y** /ˈrɪski/ *adj* involving a risk that something bad will happen: *a risky financial investment | Buying a used car is a risky business.* (=a situation or action that may be bad) **–riskiness** *n* [U]

**ris·qué** /rɪsˈkeɪ/ *adj* a joke, remark etc. that is risqué is slightly shocking because it is about sex

**rite** /raɪt/ *n* **1** a ceremony that is always performed in the same way, often for a religious purpose: *funeral rites* **2 rite of passage** a special ceremony or action that is a sign of a new time in someone's life

**rit·u·al**[1] /ˈrɪtʃuəl/ *n* [C,U] a ceremony or set of actions that is always done in the same way: *I*

*love all the rituals of making food at Thanksgiving.*

**ritual**[2] *adj* **1** done as part of a RITE or RITUAL: *ritual prayers* **2** done in a fixed and expected way, but without really meaning anything: *ritual campaign promises*

**ritz·y** /ˈrɪtsi/ *adj* INFORMAL fashionable and expensive: *a ritzy neighborhood*

**ri·val**[1] /ˈraɪvəl/ *n* a person, group, or organization that you compete with: *a business/football rival*

**rival**[2] *adj* **rival company/team/player etc.** a person, group, or organization that competes against you: *rival airlines*

**rival**[3] *v* [T] to be as good or important as someone or something else: *As a writer, Laurier could not rival Blake.*

**ri·val·ry** /ˈraɪvəlri/ *n* [C,U] continuous competition: *rivalry in the auto industry*

**riv·er** /ˈrɪvɚ/ *n* **1** a natural and continuous flow of water in a long line that goes into an ocean, lake etc.: *the Colorado River | up river* (=in the opposite direction that a river is flowing) *| down river* (=in the same direction that a river is flowing) **2** a large amount of moving liquid: *a river of lava from the volcano*

**riv·er·bed** /ˈrɪvɚˌbɛd/ *n* the ground over which a river flows

**riv·er·side** /ˈrɪvɚˌsaɪd/ *n* [singular] the land on the sides of a river: *a cottage on the riverside*

**riv·et**[1] /ˈrɪvɪt/ *n* a metal pin for fastening flat pieces of metal together

**rivet**[2] *v* [T] **1** to attract and hold someone's attention: *People sat riveted to their TVs during the trial.* **2** to fasten something with RIVETs

**riv·et·ing** /ˈrɪvətɪŋ/ *adj* extremely interesting: *a riveting movie*

**R.N.** *n* the abbreviation of REGISTERED NURSE

**roach** /routʃ/ *n* ⇨ COCKROACH

**road** /roud/ *n* **1** [C,U] also **Road** a specially prepared hard surface for vehicles to travel on: *The gas station's just up/down the road.* (=farther along the road) *| the main road out of town | a side/back road* (=a small one that is not used very much) *| She lives out on Park Road. | Watch out for ice on the roads.* (=all the streets and roads in an area) –see usage note at STREET **2 on the road (to)** traveling for a long distance, especially in a car: *We've been on the road since 7:00 a.m.* **3 on the road to success/recovery etc.** developing in a way that will result in success, health etc.

**road·block** /ˈroudblak/ *n* **1** something that stops the progress of something you want to achieve: *The greatest roadblock to success is the men's lack of skill.* **2** something that is put across a road to stop traffic: *Police put up roadblocks to catch drunk drivers.*

**road·house** /ˈroudhaus/ *n* a restaurant or BAR on a road outside a city

**road·kill** /'roʊdkɪl/ *n* [U] INFORMAL animals that are killed by cars on a road or HIGHWAY

**road·run·ner** /'roʊd,rʌnɚ/ *n* a small bird that runs very fast and lives in the southwest US

**road·side** /'roʊdsaɪd/ *n* [singular] the edge of a road: *a roadside restaurant*

**road test** /'. ./ *n* an occasion when a company tests the quality of a car it has made by driving it in bad conditions −compare TEST DRIVE

**road trip** /'. ./ *n* SLANG a long trip in a car, taken for pleasure

**road·way** /'roʊdweɪ/ *n* [singular] the part of the road that is used by vehicles

**road·wor·thy** /'roʊd,wɚði/ *adj* if a vehicle is roadworthy it is in good enough condition to be driven

**roam** /roʊm/ *v* [I,T] to walk or travel for a long time with no clear purpose: *gangs roaming the city* | *bears roaming through the forest*

**roar**[1] /rɔr/ *v* **1** [I] to make a deep, very loud noise: *lions roaring* **2** [I] to travel very fast, making a loud noise: *planes roaring overhead* **3** [I,T] to say something with a deep loud voice: *"Get out of here now!" he roared.*

**roar**[2] *n* a deep loud continuous sound: *a roar of laughter* | *the roar of the engine*

**roar·ing** /'rɔrɪŋ/ *adj* **1** making a deep, very loud continuous noise: *roaring floodwaters* **2 roaring fire** a fire that burns with a lot of flames and heat

**roast**[1] /roʊst/ *v* [I,T] to cook something in an OVEN or over a fire

**roast**[2] *n* **1** a large piece of ROASTed meat **2** an outdoor party at which food is cooked on an open fire: *a hot dog roast*

**roast**[3] *adj* ROASTed: *roast beef*

**rob** /rɑb/ *v* **-bbed, -bbing** [T] to steal money or things from a person, bank etc.: *Two men were arrested for robbing a supermarket.*

---

### USAGE NOTE rob and steal

Use these words to talk about taking something that belongs to someone else. **Rob** is used to describe the act of taking money or property from a person or place: *Someone robbed the bank last night.* | *We don't carry cash because we're afraid we'll get robbed.* ✗ DON'T SAY "someone stole a bank" or "we're afraid we'll get stolen." ✗ **Steal** is used to talk about the actual things that are taken: *Matt's bike was stolen while he was on vacation.* | *They caught him trying to steal some cigarettes.* ✗ DON'T SAY "Matt's bike was robbed" or "rob some cigarettes." ✗

---

**rob·ber** /'rɑbɚ/ *n* someone who steals things, especially from stores or banks: *an armed robber* (=one that carries a gun) −see usage note at THIEF

**rob·ber·y** /'rɑbəri/ *n* [C,U] the crime of stealing money or things from a person or place: *Several robberies took place over the weekend.* | *They're in prison for armed robbery.* (=robbery using a gun)

**robe** /roʊb/ *n* a long loose piece of clothing: *pajamas and a matching robe* | *a judge's robe*

**rob·in** /'rɑbɪn/ *n* a common wild bird with a red chest and brown back

**ro·bot** /'roʊbɑt, -bʌt/ *n* a machine that can move and do some of the work of a person, and is controlled by a computer: *industrial robots* −**robotic** /roʊ'bɑtɪk, rə-/ *adj*

**ro·bot·ics** /roʊ'bɑtɪks/ *n* [U] the study of how ROBOTs are made and used

**ro·bust** /roʊ'bʌst, 'roʊbʌst/ *adj* strong and healthy or not likely to have problems: *a surprisingly robust 70-year-old* | *a more robust economy*

**rock**[1] /rɑk/ *n* **1** [U] a type of stone that forms part of the Earth's surface: *a tunnel cut through solid rock* **2** a large piece of stone: *Let's sit down on that rock and rest.* **3** a type of popular modern music with a strong loud beat, played on GUITARs and drums **4** INFORMAL a DIAMOND or other jewel **5 be between a rock and a hard place** to have a choice between two things, both of which are unpleasant −see also ROCKS

**rock**[2] *v* **1** [I,T] to move gently, leaning from one side to the other, or to make something do this: *Jane sat rocking the baby.* | *Waves were making the boat rock.* **2** [T] to make the people in a place feel very shocked or surprised: *a city rocked by violence* **3** to play or dance to ROCK'N'ROLL music **4 rock the boat** INFORMAL to cause problems for other members of a group by criticizing something or trying to change the way something is done

**rock and roll** /ˌ. . './ *n* [U] ⇨ ROCK'N'ROLL

**rock bot·tom** /ˌ. '../ *n* [U] **hit/reach rock bottom** INFORMAL to become as bad as something can possibly be: *By June, their marriage had hit rock bottom.*

**rock-bottom** /ˌ. '..◂/ *adj* rock-bottom prices are as low as they can possibly be

**rock·er** /'rɑkɚ/ *n* **1** ⇨ ROCKING CHAIR **2 be off your rocker** SPOKEN to be crazy

**rock·et**[1] /'rɑkɪt/ *n* **1** a machine that is shaped like a tube, used for traveling or carrying things into space, or to carry bombs **2** an explosive that goes high in the air and explodes with many bright colors

**rock·et**[2] *v* [I] **1** to move somewhere very fast: *a train rocketing through a tunnel* **2** to achieve a successful position very quickly: *a song that has rocketed to number one in the charts*

**rock·ing chair** /'.. ,./ *n* a chair that has two curved pieces of wood fixed under it, so that it ROCKs −see picture on page 698

R

**rocking horse** /ˈ.. ˌ./ *n* a wooden horse for children that ROCKs when you sit on it

rocking chair

**rock'n'roll** /ˌrakənˈroʊl/ *n* [U] a type of music with a strong loud beat and played on GUITARs and drums, that became popular in the 1950s

**rocks** /raks/ *n* [plural] INFORMAL **on the rocks a)** alcoholic drinks that are served on the rocks have ice in them **b)** a relationship or marriage that is on the rocks is failing

**rock·y** /ˈraki/ *adj* **1** covered with rocks or made of rock: *the rocky coast of Maine* **2** INFORMAL a relationship or situation that is rocky is difficult and may not continue: *He had a rocky start as chairman.*

**rod** /rad/ *n* a long thin pole or stick, made of wood, metal, or plastic: *a fishing rod*

**rode** /roʊd/ *v* the past tense of RIDE

**ro·dent** /ˈroʊdnt/ *n* one of a group of small animals with long sharp front teeth, such as rats or rabbits

**ro·de·o** /ˈroʊdiˌoʊ, roʊˈdeɪoʊ/ *n* a competition in which COWBOYs ride wild horses, and catch cattle with ropes

**roe** /roʊ/ *n* [C,U] fish eggs

**rogue**[1] /roʊg/ *adj* **1** a rogue person or organization does not follow the usual rules or methods and often causes trouble **2** a rogue animal leaves its group and starts causing damage

**rogue**[2] *n* a man who often behaves in a slightly bad or dishonest way, but whom people still like

**rogu·ish** /ˈroʊgɪʃ/ *adj* typical of a ROGUE, or behaving like a rogue: *a roguish smile*

**role** /roʊl/ *n* **1** the position, job, or function someone or something has in a particular situation or activity: *We're looking seriously at the **role** of education in our society.* | *companies that **play a major/key role** in the world's economy* **2** the character played by an actor: *Brendan will **play the role of** Romeo.* **3** the position someone has or the way s/he is expected to behave in an organization, relationship etc.: *women's **role in** society*

**role mod·el** /ˈ. ˌ../ *n* someone whom people try to copy because they admire him/her

**role-play** /ˈ. ./ *n* [C,U] an exercise in which you behave in the way that someone else would behave in a particular situation: *ideas for classroom role-plays* **–role-play** *v* [I,T]

**roll**[1] /roʊl/ *v*

**1** ▶BALL/BODY◀ [I,T] to move by turning over and over, or from side to side, or to make something do this: *Don't let the ball roll into the street.* | *Roll the wine barrels into the corner.* | *a ship rolling on the waves* | *The dog's been **rolling in** something stinky.*

**2** ▶LIQUID/VEHICLE◀ [I] to move steadily and smoothly: *Tears rolled down his cheeks.* | *The van was starting to roll backward .*

**3** ▶PAPER/STRING◀ [T] to curl or wind something into the shape of a tube or ball: *Roll the string **into** a ball.* | *Bob rolled another cigarette.* –see picture at FOLD[2]

**4** ▶SUBSTANCE◀ [T] also **roll out** to make something flat by moving something round and heavy over it: *Roll the pie crust thin.*

**5** ▶SOUND◀ [I] if a drum or THUNDER rolls, it makes a long deep sound

**6 roll your eyes** to move your eyes around and up to show that you think someone or something is stupid

**7** ▶MACHINE◀ [I] if a machine rolls, it operates: *Keep the camera rolling!*

**8 be rolling in the aisles** INFORMAL if people in a theater are rolling in the aisles, they are laughing a lot

**9 (all) rolled into one** including several things in one thing: *The class was a history, art, and language course all rolled into one.*

---

SPOKEN PHRASES

**10** ▶ACTION◀ [I] to begin doing something: *Are we ready to roll here?*

**11** ▶LEAVE◀ [I] to leave a place: *Okay, let's roll.*

**12 be rolling in it** to be extremely rich

---

**roll around** *phr v* [I] INFORMAL if a regular time or event rolls around, it arrives or happens again: *By the time Friday night **rolled around**, we were too tired to go out.*

**roll** sth ↔ **back** *phr v* [T] to reduce the price of something: *a promise to **roll back** taxes*

**roll** sth ↔ **down** *phr v* [T] **roll a window down** to open a car window

**roll in** *phr v* [I] **1** INFORMAL to arrive in large numbers or quantities: *Money started **rolling in** after the first calls for help.* **2** INFORMAL to arrive later than expected: *They finally **rolled in** at 4:00.* **3** if mist, clouds etc. roll in, they begin to cover an area of the sky or land

**roll** sth ↔ **out** *phr v* [T] to make something flat and straight after it has been curled into a tube shape: ***Roll out** your sleeping bag.*

**roll over** *phr v* [I] to turn your body around once so that you are lying in a different position: *Ralph **rolled over** onto his stomach.*

**roll up** *phr v* **1** [T **roll** sth ↔ **up**] to curl something such as cloth or paper into a tube shape **2 roll a window up** to close a car window

**roll**[2] *n* **1** a piece of paper, film, money etc. that has been curled into the shape of a tube: *a roll of dollar bills* –see picture at FOLD[2] **2** a small round LOAF of bread for one person –see picture at BREAD **3** an official list of the names of people at a meeting, in a class etc.: *the union membership roll* –see also ROLL CALL **4 be on a roll** INFORMAL to be having a lot of success with what you are trying to do: *I don't want to stop playing - I'm on a roll!* **5** [singular] the movement of a ship or plane when it leans from side to side **6** a long deep sound: *the roll of drums/thunder*

**roll call** /'. ./ *n* [C,U] the act of reading out an official list of names to check who is present at a meeting or in a class

**roll·er** /'roulə/ *n* **1** a tube-shaped piece of wood, metal etc. that can be rolled over and over: *paint rollers* **2** one of several tubes that women wind their hair around to make it curl

**Roll·er·blade** /'roulə,bleɪd/ *n* TRADEMARK a special boot with a single row of wheels fixed under it −compare ROLLER SKATE

**roller coast·er** /'.. ,../ *n* **1** a track with sudden steep slopes and curves, that people ride on in special cars at FAIRs and AMUSEMENT PARKs **2** a situation that is impossible to control because it keeps changing very quickly: *I feel like I'm on an emotional roller coaster.*

**roller skate** /'.. ,./ *n* a special boot with four wheels fixed under it −**rollerskate** *v* [I] −**rollerskating** *n* [U]

**rol·lick·ing** /'ralɪkɪŋ/ *adj* noisy and cheerful: *a rollicking good time*

**roll·ing** /'roulɪŋ/ *adj* rolling hills have many long gentle slopes

**rolling pin** /'.. ,./ *n* a long tube-shaped piece of wood used for making PASTRY flat and thin before you cook it −see picture at PIN¹

**ro·ly-po·ly** /,.. '..◂/ *adj* a roly-poly person or animal is short and fat

**ROM** /ram/ *n* [U] TECHNICAL Read-Only Memory; the part of a computer where permanent instructions or information are stored −compare RAM

**Ro·man Cath·o·lic** /,roumən 'kæθlɪk/ *adj* relating to the part of the Christian religion whose leader is the Pope: *the Roman Catholic Church* −**Roman Catholic** *n*

**ro·mance** /'roumæns, rou'mæns/ *n* **1** a relationship between two people who love each other: *a summer romance* **2** a story about love between two people **3** [U] the feeling of excitement and adventure that is connected with a particular place, activity etc.: *the romance of the theater*

**Roman nu·mer·al** /,.. '.../ *n* a number in a system that was used in ancient Rome, that uses letters instead of numbers: *XXVII is the Roman numeral for 27.*

**ro·man·tic¹** /rou'mænɪk/ *adj* **1** showing strong feelings of love: *"Paul gave me roses for our anniversary." "How romantic!"* **2** involving feelings of love: *a romantic relationship* **3** a romantic story or movie is about love: *a new romantic comedy* **4** not practical, and basing your actions too much on an imagined idea of the world: *romantic ideas about becoming famous* −**romantically** *adv*

**romantic²** *n* **1** someone who shows strong feelings of love and likes doing things relating to love: *Oh Jim, you're so romantic!* **2** someone who is not practical and bases his/her actions too much on an imagined idea of the world: *You're a* **hopeless romantic**.

**ro·man·ti·cize** /rou'mæntə,saɪz/ *v* [T] to talk or think about things in a way that makes them seem more attractive: *a romanticized idea of country life*

**romp** /ramp/ *v* [I] to play in a noisy way by running, jumping etc.: *puppies romping in the yard* −**romp** *n*

**roof¹** /ruf, ruf/ *n* **1** the outside surface on top of a building or vehicle: *The storm ripped the roof off our house.* | *a ski rack for the car roof* −see picture on page 471 **2** the top of a passage under the ground: *The roof of the tunnel suddenly collapsed.* **3** **a roof over your head** a place to live: *They're worried about keeping a roof over their heads.* **4** the hard upper part of the inside of your mouth **5** **the roof caves/falls in** INFORMAL if the roof caves or falls in, something bad suddenly happens to you **6** **under one roof** in one building: *It's a restaurant and three bars all under one roof.*

**roof²** *v* [T] to put a roof on a building: *a house roofed with tiles*

**roof·ing** /'rufɪŋ/ *n* [U] material for making or covering roofs

**roof·top** /'ruftap/ *n* the top surface of a building: *Beyond the rooftops she could see the bay.*

**rook·ie** /'ruki/ *n* someone who has just started doing a job or playing a professional sport, and has little experience: *a rookie policeman*

**room¹** /rum, rum/ *n* **1** a part of the inside of a building that has its own walls, floor, and ceiling: *the living room* | *Is Sally still in the computer room?* **2** [U] enough space for a particular purpose: *Save room for dessert!* | *There isn't enough* **room** *in my closet* **for** *my coats.* −see usage note at PLACE¹ **3** **there's room for improvement** used in order to say that someone's work needs to be improved

**room²** *v* [I] **room with sb** to share the room that you live in with someone, for example at college

**room and board** /,. . './ *n* [U] a room to sleep in, and meals: *How much do you pay for room and board?*

**room·mate** /'rum-meɪt/ *n* someone with whom you share a room, apartment, or house

**room serv·ice** /'. ,../ *n* [U] a service provided by a hotel, by which food, drinks etc. can be brought to a guest's room

**room·y** /'rumi, 'rumi/ *adj* with plenty of space inside: *a roomy car*

**roost** /rust/ *n* a place where birds rest and sleep −**roost** *v* [I]

**roost·er** /'rustɚ/ *n* a male chicken

R

**root**

**root**¹ /rut, rʊt/ *n* **1** the part of a plant or tree that grows under the ground: *Be careful of the roots when you plant the roses.* **2** the basic or main part of a problem or idea: *Allergies are often the root of* (=are the cause of) *health problems.| We need to try to deal with the root causes of drug abuse.| the roots of Marxism* **3** the part of a tooth, hair etc. that is fixed to the rest of the body **4 take root a)** if an idea takes root, people begin to accept or believe it: *helping democracy take root* **b)** if a plant takes root, it grows into the ground **5** TECHNICAL in grammar, the basic part of a word that shows its main meaning. For example, the root of "disagree" is "agree" –see also ROOTS, SQUARE ROOT

**root**² *v* **1 be rooted in** to have developed from something and be strongly influenced by it: *a holiday that is rooted in old customs* **2** [I] to search for something by moving things around: *"Now where are my gloves?" she said, rooting around in the closet.* **3** [I,T] to grow roots or to fix a plant firmly by its roots: *The bulbs will root in spring.*

**root for** sb *phr v* [T] INFORMAL **1** to support a sports team or player by shouting and cheering: *We always root for the Yankees.* **2** to support and encourage someone in a competition, test, or difficult situation: *Good luck - I'll be rooting for you!*

**root** sth ↔ **out** *phr v* [T] to find out where a particular problem exists and get rid of it: *We are doing all we can to root out violence in the schools.*

**root beer** /ˈ. ./ *n* [C,U] a sweet non-alcoholic drink made from the roots of some plants

**root·less** /ˈrutlɪs/ *adj* having nowhere that you feel is really your home

**roots** /ruts, rʊts/ *n* [plural] **1** the origins of a custom or TRADITION that has continued for a long time: *Jazz has its roots in African music.* **2** sb's **roots** someone's connection with a place because s/he was born there or his/her family lived there: *her rural roots in southern Illinois* **3 put down roots** to start to feel that a place is your home

**rope**¹ /roʊp/ *n* [C,U] very strong thick string, made by twisting together many threads: *The rope was there to keep the climbers from falling.* –see also ROPES

**rope**² *v* **1** [T] to tie things together using rope: *Harvey roped his horse to a nearby tree.* **2** [T] to catch an animal using a circle of rope

**rope** sb ↔ **in/into** *phr v* [T] INFORMAL to persuade someone to help you in a job or activity: *Who roped you into doing the dishes?*

**rope** sth ↔ **off** *phr v* [T] to surround an area with ropes in order to separate it from another area: *Police roped off the area of the robbery.*

**ropes** /roʊps/ *n* [plural] **1 know the ropes** to know how to do all the parts of a job because you have a lot of experience of it **2 show sb**

**the ropes** to show someone the things s/he needs to know in order to do a job

**ro·sa·ry** /ˈroʊzəri/ *n* a string of BEADs used by Roman Catholics for counting prayers

**ro·sé** /roʊˈzeɪ/ *n* [U] pink wine

**rose**¹ /roʊz/ *n* **1** a common sweet-smelling flower that grows on a bush that has THORNs (=sharp points on a stem) **2** [U] a pink color

**rose**² *v* the past tense of RISE

**Rosh Ha·sha·nah** /ˌraʃ həˈʃanə/ *n* Jewish New Year, in late September or early October

**ros·ter** /ˈrastɚ/ *n* a list of people's names showing the jobs they must do and when they must do them

**ros·trum** /ˈrastrəm/ *n* a small PLATFORM (=raised area) that you stand on in front of an AUDIENCE

**ros·y** /ˈroʊzi/ *adj* **1** pink: *rosy cheeks* **2** seeming to offer hope of success or happiness: *a rosier future*

**rot**¹ /rat/ *v* **-tted, -tting** [I,T] to decay by a gradual natural process, or to make something do this: *Sugar rots your teeth.| old buildings that were left to rot*

**rot**² *n* [U] the natural process of decaying, or the part of something that has decayed: *a tree full of rot*

**ro·ta·ry** /ˈroʊtəri/ *adj* **1** turning in a circle around a fixed point, like a wheel: *the rotary movement of helicopter blades* **2** having a main part that does this: *a rotary engine*

**ro·tate** /ˈroʊteɪt/ *v* **1** [I,T] to turn around a fixed point, or to make something do this: *The Earth rotates every 24 hours.| Rotate the handle to the right.* **2** [I,T] if a job rotates or people rotate jobs, they each do the job for a fixed period of time: *We try to rotate the boring jobs.* **3** [T] to regularly change the crops grown on a piece of land

**ro·ta·tion** /roʊˈteɪʃən/ *n* **1** [C,U] the action of turning around a fixed point, or one complete turn: *the rotation of the Earth on its axis| The wheel makes 10 rotations a minute.* **2** [U] the practice of changing regularly from one thing to another or changing the person who does a particular job: *We work in rotation.| crop rotation* **3** a complete turn around a fixed point

**ROTC** /ˈratsi, ˌar oʊ ti ˈsi/ *n* Reserve Officer's Training Corp; an organization that trains students to be US army officers

**rote** /roʊt/ *n* [U] **learn sth by rote** to learn something by repeating it until you remember it, without understanding the meaning

**ro·tis·ser·ie** /roʊˈtɪsəri/ *n* a piece of equipment for cooking meat by turning it around and around on a metal ROD

**ro·tor** /ˈroʊtɚ/ *n* the part of a machine that turns around on a fixed point

**rot·ten** /ˈratᵊn/ *adj* **1** badly decayed: *rotten apples* **2** INFORMAL very nasty or unpleasant: *What a rotten thing to do!* **3** INFORMAL very bad at doing something, or badly done: *I'm a rotten cook.* **4 feel rotten** to feel ill or unhappy about something: *She felt rotten about having to fire him.*

**ro·tund** /roʊˈtʌnd/ *adj* having a fat round body

**ro·tun·da** /roʊˈtʌndə/ *n* a round building or hall, especially one with a DOME

**rouge** /ruːʒ/ *n* [U] ⇨ BLUSH[2]

**rough[1]** /rʌf/ *adj* **1** having an uneven surface: *Our jeep's good for traveling over rough ground.* **2** not exact or not containing many details: *Can you give us a rough idea of the cost?* | *a rough draft of the speech* **3** using force or violence; not gentle: *Ice hockey is a rough sport.* **4** a rough area has a lot of violence and crime: *a rough part of the city* **5** a rough period of time is one when you have a lot of problems and difficulties: *She's had a rough couple of weeks.* | *I had a rough night.* (=I did not sleep well) **6** with strong winds or storms: *A sailboat sank in rough seas.* **7** not fair or kind: *Don't be so rough on her.* (=be kinder) —**roughness** *n* [U]

**rough[2]** *v* **rough it** INFORMAL to live in conditions that are not very comfortable: *We're going to rough it in the mountains for a few days.*

**rough** sb ↔ **up** *phr v* [T] INFORMAL to attack someone by hitting him/her

**rough[3]** *adv* **play rough** to play in a fairly violent way

**rough·age** /ˈrʌfɪdʒ/ *n* [U] a substance in some foods that helps your BOWELs to work

**rough-and-tum·ble** /ˌ. . ˈ..◂/ *adj* full of people competing, often in a nasty way: *the rough-and-tumble world of politics*

**rough·house** /ˈrʌfhaʊs/ *v* [I] to play in a noisy physical way

**rough·ly** /ˈrʌfli/ *adv* **1** not exactly; about: *Roughly 100 people came.* **2** not gently or carefully: *Don't pet the cat so roughly!*

**rough·neck** /ˈrʌfnɛk/ *n* INFORMAL a large strong rude man who enjoys fighting

**rough·shod** /ˈrʌfʃɑd/ *adv* **ride roughshod over sb/sth** to behave in a way that ignores other people's feelings or opinions

**rou·lette** /ruˈlɛt/ *n* [U] a game played for money in which you try to guess which hole a small ball on a spinning wheel will fall into

**round[1]** /raʊnd/ *adj* **1** shaped like a circle, a ball, or the letter "o": *a round table* | *a tree with round berries* | *the baby's round cheeks* **2 in round figures/numbers** not expressed as an exact number but as the nearest 10, 100, 1000 etc.: *What's the annual profit, in round figures?* —**roundness** *n* [U]

**round[2]** *n*
**1** ▶CONNECTED EVENTS◀ a number of events that are related: *the latest round of peace talks*
**2 round of applause** a time when people are

clapping (CLAP) to show that they enjoyed a performance
**3** ▶DRINKS◀ alcoholic drinks bought for all the people in a group, usually by one person
**4** ▶SPORTS◀ **a)** a complete game of GOLF **b)** one of the periods of fighting in BOXING or WRESTLING **c)** one of the parts of a competition that you have to finish before you can go to the next part: *Graf has made it to the third round.*
**5** ▶SHOT◀ a single shot from a gun: *The soldier fired several rounds before escaping.*
**6** ▶SONG◀ a song for three or four singers who each start the same tune at different times, until all of them are singing —see also ROUNDS

**round[3]** *v* [T] **1** to go around something such as a bend or the corner of a building: *The Porsche rounded the bend at 120 mph.* **2** also **round off** to make something round: *Round the corners of the table with a jigsaw.*

**round** sth ↔ **off** *phr v* [I,T] to change an exact figure to the nearest whole number

**round** sth ↔ **out/off** *phr v* to make something complete by adding something to it, or by doing one final thing: *Jeff rounded out his degree by studying in Spain for a year.*

**round** sth ↔ **up** *phr v* [T] to find and gather together a group of people or things: *Police rounded up 20 people for questioning.*

**round[4]** *adv* ⇨ **all year round** (YEAR) —see also AROUND

**round·a·bout** /ˈraʊndəˌbaʊt/ *adj* not done in the shortest most direct way: *a roundabout route to avoid heavy traffic*

**rounds** /raʊndz/ *n* [plural] the usual visits or checks that someone makes as a part of his/her job, especially a doctor

**round-the-clock** /ˌ. . ˈ.◂/ *adj* all the time, both day and night: *round-the-clock hospital care*

**round-trip** /ˌ. ˈ.◂/ *adj* a round-trip ticket is for taking a trip from one place to another and back again —see also ONE-WAY

**round·up** /ˈraʊndʌp/ *n* an occasion when a lot of people or animals are brought together, often by force: *a roundup of criminal suspects*

**rouse** /raʊz/ *v* [T] **1** to wake up, or wake someone up: *We were roused from a deep sleep.* **2** to make someone become excited enough to start doing something: *King's speech roused his supporters toward greater efforts.*

**rous·ing** /ˈraʊzɪŋ/ *adj* making people feel excited and eager to do something: *a rousing speech/song*

**rout** /raʊt/ *v* [T] to defeat someone completely in a battle, competition, election etc. —**rout** *n* [singular]

**route[1]** /rut, raʊt/ *n* the way from one place to another, especially one that is shown on a map: *What is the shortest route from Memphis to Atlanta?* | *We had to take a longer route because of the snow.*

**route**² *v* [T] to send something or someone by a particular ROUTE: *All the military supplies were routed through* Turkey.

**rou·tine**¹ /ru'tin/ *n* [C,U] the usual or normal way in which you do things: *Harry doesn't like any change in his daily routine.* | *We shouldn't accept TV violence as routine.*

**routine**² *adj* **1** regular and usual: *a routine medical test* | *a few routine questions* **2** ordinary and boring: *a routine job* —**routinely** *adv*

**rov·ing** /'roʊvɪŋ/ *adj* traveling or moving from one place to another: *a roving reporter*

**row**

There are two seats in the front row.

**row**¹ /roʊ/ *n* **1** a line of things or people next to each other: *a row of houses* **2** **three/four etc. in a row** three times, four times etc. together and in the same way: *We've lost four games in a row.* **3** a line of seats in a theater, large room etc.: *I sat in the front row.*

**row**² *v* [I,T] to make a boat move by using OARs: *Slowly, she rowed across the lake.*

**row·boat** /'roʊboʊt/ *n* a small boat that you move by using OARs

**row·dy** /'raʊdi/ *adj* behaving in a noisy way that is not controlled: *a group of rowdy children* —**rowdiness** *n* [U]

**row·ing** /'roʊɪŋ/ *n* [U] the sport or activity of making a boat move by using OARs

**roy·al** /'rɔɪəl/ *adj* relating to or belonging to a king or queen: *the royal family* | *the royal palace*

**roy·al·ties** /'rɔɪəltiz/ [plural] payments made to the writer of a book or piece of music

**roy·al·ty** /'rɔɪəlti/ *n* [U] members of a royal family

**rpm** *n* revolutions per minute; a unit for measuring the speed of an engine

**RSVP** an abbreviation that is written on invitations in order to ask someone to reply

**rub**¹ /rʌb/ *v* **-bbed, -bbing 1** [I,T] to move your hand, a cloth etc. over a surface while pressing against it: *The stain should come out if you rub harder.* | *Can you rub some lotion on my back please?* **2** [I] to move around while pressing against another surface: *My shoes are rubbing against my heels.* **3 rub it in** INFORMAL to remind someone of something that s/he wants to forget, especially because s/he is embarrassed about it or ashamed of it: *"You went out with Wanda in sixth grade, didn't you?" "Yeah, don't rub it in!"* **4 rub sb the wrong way**

INFORMAL to annoy someone by the way you talk or behave toward him/her: *I think Marilyn rubs him the wrong way.* **5 rub shoulders with sb** INFORMAL to spend time with rich famous people **6 rub off on sb** if a feeling, habit etc. rubs off on someone, s/he starts to have it because someone else has it: *Her positive attitude seemed to rub off on everyone.*

**rub down** *phr v* [T] **1** [rub sth ↔ down] to make a surface dry or smooth by pressing against it with a cloth **2** [rub sb down] to press someone's muscles to make him/her relax, especially after exercise

**rub**² *n* an act of rubbing something or someone: *Could you give me a back rub?*

**rub·ber** /'rʌbɚ/ *n* **1** [U] a substance used for making tires, boots etc., that is made from chemicals or the liquid that comes out of tropical trees: *rubber gloves* **2** INFORMAL ⇨ CONDOM

**rubber band** /ˌ.. '.', '.. ,./ *n* a thin circular piece of rubber used for keeping things together

**rub·ber·neck** /'rʌbɚˌnɛk/ *v* [I] INFORMAL to look around at something such as an accident while you are driving or walking past

**rubber-stamp** /ˌ.. '.'./ *v* [T] to give official approval to something without really thinking about it

**rub·ber·y** /'rʌbəri/ *adj* **1** looking or feeling like rubber: *a rubbery steak* **2** if your legs or knees are rubbery, they are weak and unsteady

**rub·bish** /'rʌbɪʃ/ *n* [U] ⇨ GARBAGE

**rub·ble** /'rʌbəl/ *n* [U] broken stones or bricks from a building, wall etc. that has been destroyed: *a pile of rubble*

**rub·down** /'rʌbdaʊn/ *n* **give sb a rubdown** to rub someone's body in order to make him/her relax, especially after exercise

**ru·bel·la** /ru'bɛlə/ *n* [U] TECHNICAL ⇨ MEASLES

**ru·by** /'rubi/ *n* [C,U] a dark red jewel, or the color of this jewel —**ruby** *adj*

**ruck·us** /'rʌkəs/ *n* [singular] INFORMAL a noisy argument or confused situation: *What's all the ruckus about?*

**rud·der** /'rʌdɚ/ *n* a flat part at the back of a boat or aircraft that is turned in order to change the direction in which the vehicle moves —see picture at AIRPLANE

**rud·dy** /'rʌdi/ *adj* a ruddy face looks pink and healthy

**rude** /rud/ *adj* **1** speaking or behaving in a way that is not polite: *a rude remark* | *Don't be rude to your grandmother!* ✗ DON'T SAY "rude with." ✗ **2** relating to sex in an offensive way: *a rude gesture* **3 a rude awakening** a situation in which someone suddenly realizes something unpleasant —**rudely** *adv* —**rudeness** *n* [U]

**ru·di·men·ta·ry** /ˌrudə'mɛntri, -'mɛnˌtəri/ *adj* FORMAL **1** rudimentary knowledge or understanding is very simple and basic: *a rudi-*

**mentary knowledge of** geometry **2** not very advanced or developed: *rudimentary equipment*

**ru·di·ments** /'rudəmənts/ *n* [plural] FORMAL the most basic parts of a subject: *They know* **the rudiments of** *grammar.*

**rue** /ru/ *v* [T] LITERARY to wish that you had not done something; REGRET: *She'll* **rue the day that** *she met him.*

**rue·ful** /'rufəl/ *adj* showing that you wish you had not done something: *a rueful smile* **–ruefully** *adv*

**ruf·fle**[1] /'rʌfəl/ *v* [T] **1** to make a smooth surface uneven or messy: *Brian's dad reached over and ruffled his hair.* **2** also **ruffle sb's feathers** to offend, annoy, or upset someone: *Don't let yourself* **get ruffled** *over what he said.*

**ruffle**[2] *n* a band of cloth sewn in folds as a decoration around the edges of a shirt, skirt, etc. **–ruffled** *adj*

**rug** /rʌg/ *n* **1** a piece of thick cloth, wool etc. that is put on the floor as a decoration **–compare** CARPET[1] **2** HUMOROUS ⇨ TOUPEE **–see** also **pull the rug out from under sb** (PULL[1])

**rug·by** /'rʌgbi/ *n* [U] an outdoor game played by two teams with an OVAL ball that you kick or carry

**rug·ged** /'rʌgɪd/ *adj* **1** land that is rugged is rough, rocky, and uneven **2** attractively strong: *a rugged face* | *She's really a rugged character in this play.*

**ru·in**[1] /'ruɪn/ *v* [T] **1** to spoil or destroy something completely: *He ruined our evening by getting drunk.* | *Our credit will be ruined if we don't pay the bills right now.* **2** to make someone lose all his/her money

**ruin**[2] *n* **1** [U] a situation in which something is damaged, spoiled, or destroyed: *The old barn has* **fallen into ruin.** | *financial ruin* **2** **be in ruins** to be badly damaged or destroyed: *The country's economy is in ruins.* **3** [U] a situation in which someone has lost his/her social position, or all his/her money: *Jack's gambling eventually* **led to his ruin.** **4** also **ruins** [plural] the part of a building that is left after the rest has been destroyed: *the* **ruins of** *the Artemis temple*

**ru·in·ous** /'ruɪnəs/ *adj* causing great destruction or loss of money: *a ruinous decision*

**rule**[1] /rul/ *n* **1** an instruction that says how something is to be done or what is allowed: *Erin knows the rules of the game.* | *Well, that's what happens if you* **break the rules.** (=disobey them) | *It's* **against the rules** *to have alcohol in your room.* **2** [U] the government of a country by a particular group of people or by using a particular system: *a country* **under** *foreign* **rule** | **majority rule** (=government by the political party that most people voted for) **3** **as a (general) rule** usually: *As a rule, I try to drink a pint of water a day.* **4** **bend/stretch the rules** to allow something to happen even if it is against

the rules: *Can't we bend the rules just this once?* **5** **rule of thumb** a principle that is based on practical experience, and that works most of the time: *As a rule of thumb, chicken should be cooked 15 minutes for each pound.* **6** **rule the roost** INFORMAL to be the most powerful person in a group: *She likes to think she rules the roost around here.* **7** **sb/sth rules** INFORMAL used in order to say that the team, school etc. mentioned is better than anyone else: *Midland High rules!*

**rule**[2] *v* **1** [I,T] to have the official power to control a country and its people, especially as a MONARCH: *The story is set during the time when the Pharaohs* **ruled (over)** *Egypt.* **2** [I,T] to make an official decision about something such as a legal problem: *The judge* **ruled that** *the baby belonged with his real father.* | *The board* **rules on** *matters between unions and city government.* **3** [T] if a feeling or desire rules someone, it controls his/her life, so that s/he does not have time for other things: *Don't let your job* **rule your life.** (=control you)

**rule sth/sb out** *phr v* [T] to decide that something is not possible or suitable: *We can't* **rule out the possibility that** *he has left the country.*

**ruled** /ruld/ *adj* ruled paper has parallel lines printed across it

**rul·er** /'rulɚ/ *n* **1** someone such as a king who has official power over a country and its people **2** a flat narrow piece of plastic, metal etc. with straight edges that you use for measuring things and drawing straight lines: *a 12-inch ruler*

**rul·ing**[1] /'rulɪŋ/ *n* an official decision, especially one made by a law court: *the Supreme Court's* **ruling on** *the case*

**ruling**[2] *adj* **the ruling class/party** the group that controls a country or organization

**rum** /rʌm/ *n* [C,U] a strong alcoholic drink made from sugar

**rum·ble** /'rʌmbəl/ *v* **1** [I] to make a lot of long low sounds: *Thunder rumbled in the distance.* **2** [I,T] OLD-FASHIONED to fight with someone **–rumble** *n* [singular]

**ru·mi·nate** /'rumə,neɪt/ *v* [I] FORMAL to think about something for a long time: *He sat* **ruminating on** *the meaning of life.*

**rum·mage** /'rʌmɪdʒ/ *v* [I] to search for something by moving things around: *Kerry was* **rummaging through** *a drawer looking for a pen.*

**rummage sale** /'.. ,./ *n* an event at which old clothes, furniture, toys etc. are sold

**rum·my** /'rʌmi/ *n* [U] any of several simple card games for two or more players

**ru·mor** /'rumɚ/ *n* [C,U] information that is passed from one person to another and which may not be true: *Have you heard the* **rumor about** *Sam and Kelly?* | **Rumor has it (that)**

R

(=there is a rumor that) *Jean's getting married again.*

**ru·mored** /'rumərd/ *adj* if something is rumored to be true, people are saying that it may be true but no one knows for certain: *It was rumored that a magazine had offered a lot of money for her story.*

**rump** /rʌmp/ *n* **1** [C,U] the part of an animal's back that is just above its legs, or the meat from this part **2** INFORMAL the part of your body on which you sit; BOTTOM

**rum·ple** /'rʌmpəl/ *v* [T] to make hair, clothes etc. messy or WRINKLed –**rumpled** *adj*: *a rumpled shirt*

**run¹** /rʌn/ *v* **ran, run, running**

**1** ▶MOVE◀ **a)** [I] to move very quickly, moving your legs faster than when you walk: *Some kids were running down the street. | If we run, we can still catch the bus.* –see picture on page 473 **b)** [I,T] to move quickly or make something do this: *A car ran off the road right here. | Let me just run the vacuum cleaner over the carpet.*

**2** ▶BE IN CHARGE OF◀ [T] to control, organize, or operate a business, organization etc.: *The company runs cross-country skiing tours in Vermont. | He simply ran that business into the ground.* (=made it fail)

**3** ▶MACHINES◀ [I,T] to operate or be operated: *The radio runs on/off batteries.* (=uses batteries to work) | *I forgot to run the dishwasher. | Nate left the engine running. | The ad says the computer can be up and running* (=working) *in less than an hour.*

**4** ▶MONEY/NUMBERS◀ [I,T] to be at a particular level, length, amount, price etc.: *Unemployment is running at 5%. | The report runs to 700 pages. | debts running into millions of dollars*

**5** ▶GO SOMEWHERE◀ [I,T] SPOKEN to go somewhere quickly, either walking or in a car: *I need to run out to my car; I left my books in it. | Jean's downtown, running a few errands.* (=going places to buy or do things)

**6** ▶NEWS/STORIES/ADVERTISEMENTS◀ [I,T] to print or broadcast a story etc.: *What does it cost to run an ad in the local paper? | They ran the item on the 6 o'clock news.*

**7 run smoothly/run according to plan** to happen in the way that you want or expect: *The tour guide helps to keep things running smoothly.*

**8** ▶ELECTION◀ [I] to try to be elected: *Barbara Boxer ran for the Senate in 1992. | Dole ran against Clinton.*

**9** ▶TEST/PROCESS◀ [T] to do something such as a medical test or an EXPERIMENT, in which you do things in a particular order: *The doctors say they need to run a few tests first.*

**10 run late/run on time/run early** to arrive, go somewhere, or do something late, at the right

time, or early: *Sorry you had to wait; I've been running late all day.*

**11** ▶WATER/LIQUIDS◀ [I] to flow: *The sweat was just running down my face. | Who left the water running?* (=still flowing from a pipe) | *I need a Kleenex; my nose is running.* (=producing liquid)

**12** ▶CONTINUE◀ [I] to continue to be used, performed etc. for a particular length of time: *The contract runs through to 2002. | "WKRP" ran for five seasons, from 1978-1982.*

**13** ▶ROADS/PIPES/FENCES◀ [I,T] to exist in a particular place or continue in a particular direction, or to make something do this: *They want to run a pipeline through protected parts of Alaska. | A small path runs between the two beaches.*

**14** ▶BUSES/TRAINS◀ [I] to take people from one place to another: *Subway trains run every 7 minutes.*

**15 be running short/low** to have very little of something left: *Hospitals in the war-torn nation are running low on medical supplies. | Lend me $20, will you? I'm running short of cash.*

**16** ▶TOUCH◀ [T] to touch something by moving your hand along its surface: *Doug ran his fingers through her silky black hair.*

**17 run deep** if a feeling runs deep, people feel it very strongly: *Resentment against the military runs deep around here.*

**18 run in the family** if something such as a quality, disease, or skill runs in the family, many people in that family have it

**19 run drugs/guns etc.** to bring drugs etc. into a country illegally

**20** ▶COLOR◀ [I] if color or MAKEUP runs, it spreads from one area of cloth or skin to another when it gets wet

**21** ▶CLOTHING◀ [I] if a woman's PANTY HOSE run, they get a long thin hole in them

**22 run a temperature/fever** to have a body temperature that is higher than normal, because you are sick

**23** ▶FEELING◀ [I] to move from one part of your body to another: *a pain running down her leg*

**24 run the show** to be in charge of an event or situation: *Who's running this show anyway?*

**25 run aground/ashore** if a ship runs aground or ashore, it cannot move because the water is not deep enough

**run across** sb/sth *phr v* [T] to meet or find someone or something by chance: *I ran across some old love letters the other day.*

**run after** sb/sth *phr v* [T] to chase someone or something: *She started to leave, but Smith ran after her.*

**run around** *phr v* [I,T] to go to different places and do different things, especially in a disorganized way: *Everyone was running around trying to help us get ready for the party, and causing more problems in the process.*

**run away** *phr v* [I] **1** to leave a place in order to escape from someone or something: *Kathy ran away from home at the age of 16.* **2** to try to avoid an unpleasant situation: *He used drugs as a way of running away from his problems.*

**run sth by** sb *phr v* [T] to ask someone about something in order to get his/her opinion or permission: *You'd better run that contract by a lawyer.*

**run down** *phr v* **1** [T run sb ↔ down] to hit a person or animal with a car while you are driving, and kill or injure him, her, or it: *A drunk driver ran down a 14-year-old girl in Landsdowne Road yesterday.* **2** [I,T run sth ↔ down] to gradually lose power, or to make something do this: *Don't leave it switched on - you'll run down the batteries.*

**run into** *phr v* [T] **1** [run into sb] INFORMAL to meet someone by chance: *I run into her sometimes on campus.* **2** run into trouble/debt/ problems etc. to begin to have difficulties: *Bond's company ran into trouble when it couldn't repay its debts.* **3** [run into sb/sth] to hit someone or something with a car or other vehicle: *He lost control of the car and ran into a guardrail.*

**run off** *phr v* **1** [I] to leave a place or person when you are not supposed to: *Our dog keeps running off.* **2** [T run sth ↔ off] to quickly print copies of something: *Please run off 100 photocopies.*

**run off with** *phr v* [T] **1** [run off with sb] to go away with someone because you are having a sexual relationship with him/her and other people do not approve: *Her husband ran off with an old girlfriend.* **2** [run off with sth] to steal something and leave on foot: *Looters smashed windows and ran off with TVs and VCRs.*

**run out** *phr v* [I] **1** to use all of something, so that there is none left: *My pen's running out of ink.* | *I'm running out of ideas.* (=I do not have any more) **2** to be used or finished: *They need to make a deal, but time is running out.* **3** to come to the end of a period of time when something is allowed to be done or used: *My contract runs out in September.*

**run** sb/sth ↔ **over** *phr v* [T] to hit someone or something with a car or other vehicle, and drive over him, her, or it: *I think you just ran over some broken glass.*

**run through** sth *phr v* [T] **1** to read, check, or explain something quickly, especially a list: *I'd like to run through the agenda with you before the meeting.* **2** to repeat something, so that you will remember it: *Let's run through that scene again.* **3** to be present in many parts of something: *Unfortunately, there's a racist streak that runs through this community.*

**run up** sth *phr v* [T] to make a debt, cost, price etc. greater: *We ran up a huge phone bill.*

**run up against** sth *phr v* [T]

to suddenly have to deal a problem when you are trying to do something: *The campaign ran up against stiff opposition.*

**run²** *n*

**1** ▶RUNNING◀ an act of running: *He usually goes for a run before breakfast.* | *a 10K fun run*

**2 in the short/long run** from now until a period of time that will come soon, or from now until far in the future: *In the long run, the rain forest itself is worth more than the timber in it.*

**3** ▶BASEBALL◀ a point in a baseball game: *The Cubs had 3 runs in the sixth inning.*

**4** ▶PLAY/MOVIE ETC.◀ a period of time during which a play, movie, or television show is shown or performed regularly: *The play starts an 8-week run on Friday.*

**5 be on the run** to be trying to escape from someone, especially the police: *In his book, he describes what it's like to live on the run.*

**6** ▶CLOTHES◀ a long hole in a pair of NYLONS

**7** ▶REGULAR TRIP◀ a regular trip made by a person or a vehicle that carries a lot of people: *I'm doing the school run this week.* (=taking my children to school) | *the daily ferry run*

**8** ▶MONEY◀ [singular] an occasion when a lot of people take their money out of a bank or buy a lot of one particular thing at the same time: *Managers were trying to prevent a run on the bank.*

**9** ▶ELECTION◀ [singular] an attempt to be elected: *Turner is making his first run for public office.*

**10 make a run for it** to try to get away from a place quickly: *The soldiers made a run for it, trying to get across the border without getting caught.*

**11 a run of** a series of events that happen one right after another: *Sondheim's run of successful musicals*

**12 have the run of** sth to be allowed to go anywhere or do anything in a place: *Their dog has free run of the house.*

**13 give** sb **a run for his/her money** to make an opponent or competitor work very hard to beat you: *The White Sox gave the A's a run for their money, but lost in the ninth inning.*

**14** ▶SPORTS◀ a special area for people to SKI down, or a track for people to slide down in a BOBSLED etc.

**run·a·round** /ˈrʌnəˌraʊnd/ *n* **give/get the runaround** INFORMAL to not give someone the information or help s/he has asked for, and send him/her to another place to get it: *I keep calling to find out about my car, but I just get the runaround - nobody will tell me what's wrong with it.*

**run·a·way¹** /ˈrʌnəˌweɪ/ *n* someone, especially a child, who has left home or the place where s/he is supposed to be

**runaway**[2] *adj* moving fast and out of control: *a runaway train*

**run·down** /ˈrʌndaʊn/ *n* a quick report or explanation of a situation, event etc.: *Can you give me* **a rundown on** *what happened while I was gone?*

**run-down** /ˌ. ˈ.◂/ *adj* **1** a building or area that is run-down is in very bad condition: *a run-down motel* **2** someone who is run-down is very tired and not very healthy: *He's been feeling run-down lately.*

**rung**[1] /rʌŋ/ *v* the PAST PARTICIPLE OF RING

**rung**[2] *n* **1** one of the steps of a LADDER —see picture at LADDER **2** INFORMAL a particular level or position in an organization: *The changes didn't affect people on the lower rungs of the company.*

**run-in** /ˈ. ./ *n* an argument or disagreement with someone in authority: *Barry* **had a run-in with** *the police.*

**run·ner** /ˈrʌnɚ/ *n* **1** someone who runs as a sport: *a long-distance runner* **2** one of the long thin blades of metal on the bottom of a SLED

**runner-up** /ˌ.. ˈ./ *n, plural* **runners-up** the person or team that finishes second in a race or competition

**run·ning**[1] /ˈrʌnɪŋ/ *n* [U] **1** the activity of running: *Do you want to* **go running**? **2** **be in the running/be out of the running** to have some chance of winning or being successful, or to have no chance: *Is MERC still in the running for the contract?* **3** **the running of sth** the way that a business, organization etc. is managed or organized: *He is not involved in the day-to-day running of the business.*

**running**[2] *adj* **1** **running water** water that comes from a FAUCET: *a house with no running water* **2** **running battle/argument** an argument that continues over a long period of time: *They're in a running battle with the neighbors about the fence between their yards.* **3** **running commentary** a spoken description of an event while it is happening, especially a sports event **4** done while you are running: *a running jump* **5** **running total** a total that is always being increased as new costs, amounts etc. are added to it

**running**[3] *adv* **three years/five times etc. running** for three years, five times etc. without change or interruption: *This is the fourth day running that it has rained.*

**running back** /ˈ.. ˌ./ *n* [C,U] in football, a player whose main job is to run with the ball —see picture on page 472

**running mate** /ˈ.. ˌ./ *n* the person who is chosen by someone who wants to become the US President to be the Vice President if they win the election

**run·ny** /ˈrʌni/ *adj* INFORMAL **1** a runny nose has liquid coming out of it because you are sick **2** not solid or thick enough: *runny eggs*

**run-of-the-mill** /ˌ. . . ˈ.◂/ *adj* not special or interesting; ORDINARY: *It's not the usual run-of-the-mill job.*

**runs** /rʌnz/ *n* INFORMAL **the runs** ⇨ DIARRHEA

**run-up** /ˈ. ./ *n* **the run-up to sth** the period of time just before an important event: *Most stores are hiring more staff in the run-up to Christmas.*

**run·way** /ˈrʌnweɪ/ *n* a very long surface like a wide road that aircraft leave from and come down on

**rup·ture**[1] /ˈrʌptʃɚ/ *n* **1** [C,U] an occasion when something suddenly breaks apart or bursts: *the rupture of a blood vessel* **2** a situation in which two people, groups, countries etc. disagree and end their relationship

**rupture**[2] *v* [I,T] to break or burst, or to make something do this: *An oil pipeline ruptured early this morning.*

**ru·ral** /ˈrʊrəl/ *adj* relating to country areas rather than the city: *a peaceful rural setting* —compare URBAN

**ruse** /ruz/ *n* FORMAL something you do in order to deceive someone; trick

**rush**[1] /rʌʃ/ *v* **1** [I,T] to move or do something very quickly: *It's an important decision; don't rush it.* | *There's no need to rush - we have plenty of time.* | *Everyone was* **rushing to** *catch the last bus.* **2** [T] to take or send something somewhere very quickly: *We had to* **rush** *Helen* **to** *the hospital.* **3** [T] to try to make someone do something quickly: *Don't rush me - let me think.*

**rush around** *phr v* [I] to try to do a lot of things quickly in a short period of time

**rush into** sth *phr v* [T] to get involved in something quickly without thinking carefully about it: *My mother's worried that I'm* **rushing into** *getting married.*

**rush** sth ↔ **through** *phr v* [T] to get something such as a new law approved more quickly than usual

**rush**[2] *n* **1** [singular] a sudden fast movement of things or people: *They all made a rush for the door.* **2** [singular, U] a situation in which you need to hurry, especially because a lot of people want to do or get something: *There's a big rush to get tickets.* **3** **the rush** the time when a place or group of people are very busy: *the Christmas rush for shoppers* **4** INFORMAL a strong, usually pleasant feeling that you get from taking a drug or from doing something exciting

**rush hour** /ˈ. ./ *n* [C,U] the time of day when there are a lot of vehicles on the road because people are going to and from work

**Rus·sian**[1] /ˈrʌʃən/ *adj* **1** relating to or coming from Russia **2** relating to the Russian language

**Russian**[2] *n* **1** [U] the language used in Russia **2** someone from Russia

**rust**[1] /rʌst/ *n* [U] the reddish-brown substance that forms on iron, steel etc. when it gets wet: *spots of rust on the fender*

**rust**[2] *v* [I,T] to become covered with RUST, or to make something do this: *a lock that has rusted shut*

**rus·tic** /ˈrʌstɪk/ *adj* APPROVING simple and old-fashioned in a way that is typical of the country: *a rustic mountain cabin*

**rus·tle**[1] /ˈrʌsəl/ *v* **1** [I,T] if leaves, papers etc. rustle, or you rustle them, they make a soft noise as they rub against each other **2** [T] to steal farm animals such as cattle or horses

**rustle** sth ↔ **up** *phr v* [T] INFORMAL to find or make something quickly, especially food for a meal

**rustle**[2] *n* [singular] the noise made when something RUSTLEs: *the rustle of dry leaves*

**rus·tler** /ˈrʌslɚ/ *n* someone who steals farm animals such as cattle or horses

**rust·proof** /ˈrʌstpruf/ *adj* metal that is rust-proof will not RUST

**rust·y** /ˈrʌsti/ *adj* **1** covered with RUST: *rusty nails* **2** if someone's skill is rusty, it is not as good as it once was because s/he has not practiced: *My tennis is a little rusty.*

**rut** /rʌt/ *n* **1** **in a rut** INFORMAL living or working in a situation that does not change, and so is boring: *Meredith felt she was **stuck in a rut** in her job at the library.* **2** a deep narrow track left in the ground by a wheel

**ru·ta·ba·ga** /ˈrutəˌbeɪgə/ *n* a large round yellow vegetable

**ruth·less** /ˈruθlɪs/ *adj* **1** cruel and without pity: *a ruthless killer* **2** very determined to do whatever is necessary to succeed, or showing this quality: *a ruthless businessman* | *ruthless determination* –**ruthlessly** *adv* –**ruthlessness** *n* [U]

**RV** *n* recreational vehicle; a large vehicle with cooking equipment, beds etc. that a family uses for traveling or camping

**rye** /raɪ/ *n* [U] a type of grain that is used for making bread and WHISKEY (=alcohol) –see picture at BREAD

# S

**S, s** /ɛs/ *n* the nineteenth letter of the English alphabet

**S** the written abbreviation of SOUTH or SOUTHERN

**-'s** /z, s, ɪz/ **1** the short form of "is": *What's that?* **2** the short form of "has": *He's gone out.* **3** used in order to show the POSSESSIVE form of nouns: *Bill is one of Jason's*

*friends.* | *the company's plans* **4** the short form of "us," used only with "let" to form "let's": *Let's go, or we'll be late.*

**Sab·bath** /ˈsæbəθ/ *n* [singular] **the Sabbath** the day of the week that Jews or Christians consider to be a day for resting and praying, either Saturday or Sunday

**sab·bat·i·cal** /səˈbætɪkəl/ *n* [C,U] a period when someone who teaches stops doing his/her usual work to travel and study: *Prof. Morris is away* **on sabbatical** *this semester.*

**sa·ber** /ˈseɪbɚ/ *n* a military sword

**sa·ble** /ˈseɪbəl/ *n* [C,U] an expensive fur used for making coats, or the small animal this fur comes from

**sab·o·tage**[1] /ˈsæbəˌtɑʒ/ *v* [T] to secretly damage or destroy something so that an enemy cannot use it, or so that a situation has the result you want: *Four sailors threatened to sabotage the boat's nuclear reactor.* | *Rebels tried to sabotage the elections by killing candidates.* –**saboteur** /ˌsæbəˈtɚ/ *n*

**sabotage**[2] *n* [U] damage that has been done deliberately to something in order to harm an enemy: *The company claimed the crash was caused by sabotage.*

**sac** /sæk/ *n* TECHNICAL a part shaped like a small bag inside a plant or animal, that contains air or liquid

**sac·cha·rin** /ˈsækərɪn/ *n* [U] a chemical substance that tastes very sweet and is used instead of sugar

**sac·cha·rine** /ˈsækərɪn/ *adj* too romantic in a way that seems silly and not sincere: *a saccharine love story*

**sa·chet** /sæˈʃeɪ/ *n* a very small plastic, paper, or cloth bag containing a liquid or powder: *a sachet of dried lavender*

**sack**[1] /sæk/ *n* **1** a large bag made of strong cloth, plastic, or paper in which you carry or keep things: *a sack of potatoes* **2** also **sackful** the amount that a sack can contain –see also **hit the sack** (HIT)

**sack**[2] *v* [T] to steal and destroy things in a city that has been defeated by an army: *The Vandals sacked Rome in 455 A.D.*

**sack out** *phr v* [I] INFORMAL to go to sleep: *The*

*party went on so late that everyone just* **sacked out on** *the floor.*

**sac·ra·ment** /'sækrəmənt/ *n* an important Christian ceremony such as marriage or COMMUNION

**sa·cred** /'seɪkrɪd/ *adj* **1** relating to a god or religion, and believed to be holy: *sacred writings/music/rituals* **2** extremely important to someone: *The Big Sur coastline is seen as a sacred resource.*

**sacred cow** /ˌ.. './ *n* DISAPPROVING a belief, object etc. that is so important to someone that s/he will not let anyone criticize or change it

**sac·ri·fice¹** /'sækrəˌfaɪs/ *n* [C,U] **1** something that you decide not to have or not to do in order to get something that is more important: *Her parents* **made** *a lot of* **sacrifices** *to put her through college.* **2** an object or animal that is SACRIFICEd —**sacrificial** /ˌsækrə'fɪʃəl/ *adj*

**sacrifice²** *v* **1** [T] to not have or do something that is valuable or important in order to get something that is more important: *It's not worth* **sacrificing** *your health* **for** *your job.* **2** [I,T] to offer something to a god as part of a ceremony, often by killing it: *Priests sacrificed two bulls on the altar.*

**sac·ri·leg·ious** /ˌsækrə'lɪdʒəs/ *adj* treating something holy or important in a bad way that does not show respect for it: *It would be sacrilegious to tear down the old city library.* —**sacrilege** /'sækrəlɪdʒ/ *n* [C,U]

**sac·ro·sanct** /'sækroʊˌsæŋkt/ *adj* too important to be changed or criticized in any way: *Our time spent together as a family is sacrosanct.*

**sad** /sæd/ *adj* **-dder, -ddest** **1** unhappy, especially because something unpleasant has happened to you: *Linda* **looks** *very* **sad** *today.* | *I liked living in Vancouver, and I was sad to leave it.* —opposite HAPPY **2** a sad event, story etc. makes you feel unhappy: *Have you heard the* **sad news** *about Mrs. Winters?* | *It's sad that two city parks had to close down.* **3** very bad or unacceptable: *It's* **a sad state of affairs** (=bad situation) *when a person isn't safe at home anymore.* —**sadness** *n* [singular, U]

**sad·den** /'sædn/ *v* [T] FORMAL to make someone feel sad or disappointed: *It saddened me to hear of your father's death.*

**sad·dle¹** /'sædl/ *n* **1** a seat made of leather that is put on a horse's back so that you can ride it **2** a seat on a bicycle or a MOTORCYCLE

**saddle²** *v* [T] to put a SADDLE on a horse

**saddle up** *phr v* [I,T] to put a SADDLE on a horse, or to sit on the saddle that is on a horse

**saddle** sb **with** sth *phr v* [T] to give someone a job, problem etc. that is difficult or boring: *Wesley managed to saddle Harris with all the photocopying.*

**sad·dle·bag** /'sædlˌbæg/ *n* a bag that you carry things in that is attached to a SADDLE on a horse or a bicycle

**sa·dism** /'seɪdɪzəm/ *n* [U] the practice of getting pleasure, especially sexual pleasure, from being cruel to someone —**sadistic** /sə'dɪstɪk/ *adj*: *a sadistic ruler* —**sadist** /'seɪdɪst/ *n* —compare MASOCHISM

**sad·ly** /'sædli/ *adv* **1** in a sad way: *Jimmy nodded sadly.* **2 sadly (enough)** unfortunately: *Sadly, most small businesses fail in the first year.*

**sa·fa·ri** /sə'fari/ *n* a trip through the country areas of Africa in order to watch wild animals: *The Bakers are* **on safari** *in Zaire.*

**safe¹** /seɪf/ *adj* **1** not in danger of being harmed or stolen: *I'd feel safer driving with someone else.* | *Nothing can* **keep** *a city* **safe from** *terrorist attacks.* | *Both children were found,* **safe and sound.** (=unharmed) **2** not likely to cause or allow any physical injury or harm: *a safe water supply* | *Is it safe to swim here?* | *Have a* **safe trip/drive.** | *The kids watched* **from a safe distance.** **3** a safe place is one where something is not likely to be stolen or lost: *Keep your passport in a safe place.* **4** not involving any risk and very likely to succeed: *Gold is a safe investment.* | *I think it's a safe bet that he'll remember your birthday.* **5 to be on the safe side** used when you are being very careful in order to avoid an unpleasant situation: *We'll each keep a copy of the lease to be on the safe side.* **6** not likely to cause disagreement: *It is safe to say that most Internet users are men.* —**safely** *adv*: *Drive safely!*

**safe²** *n* a strong metal box or cupboard with a lock on it, where you keep money and valuable things

**safe-de·pos·it box** /ˈ. .ˌ.. ˌ./ *n* a small box used for keeping valuable objects, usually in a special room in a bank

**safe·guard** /'seɪfɡɑrd/ *n* a law, agreement etc. that is intended to protect someone or something from possible dangers or problems: *safeguards against misuse of medications* —**safeguard** *v* [T]: *laws to safeguard wildlife in the area*

**safe ha·ven** /ˌ. '../ *n* a place where someone can go in order to escape from possible danger or attack

**safe·keep·ing** /ˌseɪf'kipɪŋ/ *n* [U] **for safekeeping** if you put something somewhere for safekeeping, you put it in a place where it will not get damaged, lost, or stolen

**safe sex** /ˌ. './ *n* [U] ways of having sex that reduce the risk of getting a sexual disease, especially by the use of a CONDOM

**safe·ty** /'seɪfti/ *n* [U] **1** the state of being safe from danger or harm: *Some students are concerned about safety on campus.* **2** how safe someone or something is: *There are fears for* *the safety of the hostages.* | *Parents are worried about the safety of the toy.*

**safety belt** /'.. ,./ *n* ⇨ SEAT BELT

**safety net** /'.. ,./ *n* **1** a system or arrangement that helps people who have serious problems: *Too many people do not have the safety net of insurance.* **2** a large net used for catching someone who is performing high above the ground if s/he falls

**safety pin** /'.. ,./ *n* a wire pin with a cover that its point fits into so that it cannot hurt you – see picture at PIN¹

**safety ra·zor** /'.. ,../ *n* a RAZOR that has a cover over part of the blade to protect your skin

**safety valve** /'.. ,./ *n* **1** something you do that allows you to express strong feelings such as anger, without doing any harm: *Exercise is a good safety valve for stress.* **2** a part of a machine that allows gas, steam etc. to be let out when the pressure is too high

**sag** /sæg/ *v* **-gged, -gging** [I] **1** to sink or bend down and away from the usual position: *The branches sagged under the weight of the snow.* **2** to become weaker or less valuable: *efforts to boost the sagging economy*

**sa·ga** /'sagə/ *n* a long story or description of events

**sage** /seɪdʒ/ *adj* LITERARY very wise, especially as a result of being old

**sage·brush** /'seɪdʒbrʌʃ/ *n* [U] a small bush with a strong smell, that grows on dry land in western North America

**Sag·it·tar·i·us** /ˌsædʒəˈtɛriəs/ *n* **1** [singular] the ninth sign of the ZODIAC, represented by a man with a BOW and ARROWS **2** [C] someone born between November 22 and December 21

**said¹** /sɛd/ *v* the past tense and PAST PARTICIPLE of SAY

**said²** *adj* LAW used when giving more information about someone or something that has just been mentioned: *The said robbery happened about 5:00.*

**sail¹** /seɪl/ *v* **1** [I] to travel across an area of water in a boat or ship: *We sailed along the coast of Alaska.* **2** [I,T] to direct or control the movement of a boat or ship: *The captain sailed the ship safely past the toy.* | *I'd like to learn how to sail.* **3** [I] to start a trip by boat or ship: *What time do we sail?*

**sail²** *n* **1** a large piece of strong cloth fixed onto a boat, so that the wind will push the boat along: *a yacht with white sails* **2** **set sail** to begin a trip by boat or ship: *The ship will set sail at dawn.*

**sail·boat** /'seɪlboʊt/ *n* a small boat with one or more sails

**sail·ing** /'seɪlɪŋ/ *n* [U] the sport of traveling through water in a SAILBOAT

**sail·or** /'seɪlɚ/ *n* **1** someone who works on a ship **2** someone who is in the Navy

**saint** /seɪnt/ *n* **1** also **Saint** someone who is honored by the Catholic Church after death because s/he has suffered for his/her religious beliefs **2** SPOKEN someone who is very good, kind, or patient: *You're a real saint to help us like this.* –**sainthood** /'seɪnthʊd/ *n* [U]

**Saint Ber·nard** /ˌseɪnt bɚˈnɑrd/ *n* a very large strong dog with long hair

**sake** /seɪk/ *n* [U] **1** **for the sake of/for sb's sake** in order to help, improve, or please someone or something: *Both sides are willing to take risks for the sake of peace.* | *I have to be nice to her, for Kathy's sake.* **2** **for goodness'/Pete's/heaven's etc. sake** SPOKEN said when you are annoyed, surprised, impatient etc.: *Why didn't you tell me, for heaven's sake?*

**sal·a·ble, saleable** /'seɪləbəl/ *adj* something that is salable can be sold, or is easy to sell: *salable merchandise*

**sal·ad** /'sæləd/ *n* [C,U] **1** a mixture of raw vegetables, for example LETTUCE, CUCUMBER, and TOMATO **2** raw or cooked food cut into small pieces and served cold: *potato salad*

**salad bar** /'.. ,./ *n* a place in a restaurant where you can make your own SALAD

**salad dress·ing** /'.. ,../ *n* [C,U] a liquid mixture for putting on SALADs to give them a special taste

**sal·a·man·der** /'sælə,mændɚ/ *n* a small animal similar to a LIZARD, that can live in water and on land

**sa·la·mi** /səˈlɑmi/ *n* [C,U] a large SAUSAGE with a strong taste, that is eaten cold

**sal·a·ried** /'sælərid/ *adj* receiving a SALARY: *salaried workers*

**sal·a·ry** /'sæləri/ *n* [C,U] money that you receive every month as payment from the organization you work for: *She earns a good salary.* –compare WAGES –see usage note at PAY²

**sale** /seɪl/ *n* **1** [C,U] the act of giving property, food, or other goods to someone in exchange for money: *The sale of alcohol is strictly controlled by state laws.* | *Business is slow; I haven't made a sale (=sold something) all day.* **2** **for sale** available to be bought: *They had to put their home up for sale.* | *Is this table for sale?* **3** a time when stores sell their goods at lower prices than usual: *There's a great sale on at Macy's now.* **4** **on sale** available to be bought in a store, or available for a lower price than usual: *Don found a really good CD player on sale.*

**sales** /seɪlz/ *n* [plural] **1** the total number of products that a company sells during a particular time, measured in the amount of money they bring to the company: *a company with sales of $60 million per year* **2** [U] the part of a company that deals with selling products: *Sally got a job as sales manager.*

**sales clerk** /'. ./ *n* someone who sells things in a store

**sales·man** /'seɪlzmən/ n a man whose job is to sell things: *a used car salesman | a traveling salesman*

**sales·person** /'seɪlz,pɚsən/ n someone whose job is to sell things

**sales rep·re·sent·a·tive** /'. ..,.../ also **sales rep** /'. ./ someone who travels around selling his/her company's products

**sales slip** /'. ./ n a small piece of paper that you are given in a store when you buy something; RECEIPT

**sales tax** /'. ./ n [C,U] a tax that you pay in addition to the cost of something you are buying

**sales·wom·an** /'seɪlz,wʊmən/ n a woman whose job is selling things

**sa·li·ent** /'seɪliənt/ adj FORMAL most noticeable or important: *the salient points of the plan* –**salience** n [U]

**sa·line** /'seɪlin, -laɪn/ adj containing or consisting of salt: *a saline solution* (=liquid with salt in it) –**saline** n [U]

**sa·li·va** /sə'laɪvə/ n [U] the liquid that is produced naturally in your mouth

**sal·i·vate** /'sælə,veɪt/ v [I] TECHNICAL to produce more SALIVA in your mouth than usual because you see or smell food

**sal·low** /'sæloʊ/ adj sallow skin looks slightly yellow and unhealthy

**salm·on** /'sæmən/ n [C,U] a large ocean fish with silver skin and pink flesh, or the meat from this fish

**sa·lon** /sə'lɑn/ n a place where you can get your hair cut, have a MANICURE etc.: *a beauty salon*

**sa·loon** /sə'lun/ n a place where alcoholic drinks were sold and drunk in the western US in the 19th century

**sal·sa** /'sælsə, 'sɔl-/ n [U] **1** a SAUCE made from onions, TOMATOes, and hot-tasting PEPPERs that you put on Mexican food **2** a type of Latin American dance music

**salt¹** /sɔlt/ n **1** [U] a natural white mineral that is added to food to make it taste better **2** TECHNICAL a type of chemical, formed by combining an acid with another substance

**salt²** v [T] to add salt to food to make it taste better
**salt sth** ↔ **away** phr v [T] to save money for future use, especially dishonestly

**salt³** adj **1** preserved by salt: *salt pork* **2** containing salt or salt water: *a salt lake*

**salts** /sɔlts/ n [plural] a mineral substance like salt that is used as a medicine or to make your bath smell good

**salt shak·er** /'. ,../ n a small container for salt

**salt·wa·ter** /'sɔlt,wɔtɚ, -,wɑ-/ adj living in SALTY water: *saltwater fish*

**salt·y** /'sɔlti/ adj tasting of or containing salt –**saltiness** n [U]

**sal·u·ta·tion** /,sælyə'teɪʃən/ n [C,U] FORMAL a greeting, especially one at the beginning of a letter, such as "Dear Mr. Roberts"

**sa·lute¹** /sə'lut/ v [I,T] to move your right hand to your head in order to show respect to an officer in the Army, Navy etc.

**salute²** n **1** an act of saluting (SALUTE) **2** an occasion when guns are fired into the air in order to show respect for someone: *a 21-gun salute*

**sal·vage¹** /'sælvɪdʒ/ v [T] to save something from a situation in which other things have already been damaged, destroyed, or lost: *Farmers are trying to salvage their wheat from the heavy rains.*

**salvage²** n [U] the act of salvaging (SALVAGE) something, or the things that are salvaged: *salvage crews* (=people who are salvaging things)

**sal·va·tion** /sæl'veɪʃən/ n [U] **1** the state of being saved from evil by God, according to the Christian religion **2** something that prevents danger, loss, or failure: *Donations of food and clothing have been the salvation of the refugees.*

**Salvation Ar·my** /.,.. '../ n **the Salvation Army** a Christian organization that tries to help poor people

**salve** /sæv/ n [C,U] **1** a substance that you put on sore skin to make it less painful **2** something you do to make a situation better –**salve** v [T]

**sal·vo** /'sælvoʊ/ n FORMAL **1** the first of a series of actions or statements, especially in a situation in which people are arguing: *His opening salvo was an angry criticism of his former employer.* **2** the firing of several guns in a battle or as part of a ceremony

**Sa·mar·i·tan** /sə'mærət̚n/ also **good Samaritan** n someone who helps you when you have problems

**same¹** /seɪm/ adj **1 the same person/place etc. a)** one particular person, place etc. and not a different one: *They go to the same place for their vacation every summer. | Kim's birthday and Roger's are on the same day.* **b)** used in order to say that two or more people, things etc. are exactly like each other; IDENTICAL: *She does the same job as I do, but in a bigger company.* ✗ DON'T SAY "She does the same job like I do." ✗ **2** used in order to say that a particular person or thing does not change: *She keeps playing the same songs.* **3 at the same time** if two things happen at the same time they happen together: *How can you type and talk at the same time?* **4 the same old story/excuse etc.** INFORMAL something that you have heard many times before: *It's the same old story - his wife doesn't understand him.* **5 same difference** SPOKEN used in order to say that different actions, behavior etc. have the same result: *"Should I e-mail them or fax a letter?" "Same difference."* **6 by the same token** in the same way or for the same reasons: *You need to try to understand Dave's work, but by the same token, Dave should try to come home earlier.* **7 be in the same boat** to be in the same difficult situation that someone else is in: *Everyone has to work overtime - we're all in the same boat.*

**same**² *pron* **1 the same a)** used in order to say that two or more people, actions, or things are exactly like each other: *Thanks - I'll do the same for you one day. | The houses may look the same, but one's slightly larger.* **b)** used in order to say that a particular person or thing does not change: *She keeps playing the same songs. | "How's Danny?" "Oh, he's the same as ever." ✗ DON'T SAY "He's same as ever." ✗* **2 (and the) same to you!** SPOKEN used as a reply to a greeting or as an angry reply to a rude remark: *"Have a good weekend!" "Thanks, same to you!"* **3 same here** SPOKEN said in order to tell someone that you feel the same way as him/her: *"I hate shopping malls." "Same here."*

**same·ness** /ˈseɪmnɪs/ *n* [U] a boring lack of variety, or the quality of being very similar to something else: *There's a sameness to all these highrise buildings.*

**sam·ple**¹ /ˈsæmpəl/ *n* **1** a small part or amount of something that is examined or used in order to find out what the rest is like: *Do you have a sample of your work? | free samples of a new shampoo* **2** a group of people who have been chosen to give information by answering questions: *a random sample of 500 college students* (=one in which you choose people without knowing anything about them)

**sample**² *v* [T] **1** to taste a food or drink in order to see what it is like: *We sampled several kinds of cheese.* **2** to choose some people from a larger group in order to ask them questions: *Over 25% of the people sampled said TV is their favorite form of entertainment.*

**san·a·to·ri·um** /ˌsænəˈtɔriəm/ *n* a hospital for sick people who are getting better but still need rest and care

**sanc·ti·fy** /ˈsæŋktəˌfaɪ/ *v* [T] to make something holy

**sanc·ti·mo·ni·ous** /ˌsæŋktəˈmoʊniəs/ *adj* behaving as if you are morally better than other people: *Don't talk to me in that sanctimonious way!*

**sanc·tion**¹ /ˈsæŋkʃən/ *n* **1** [U] official permission, approval, or acceptance: *The protest march was held without government sanction.* **2** something, such as a punishment, that makes people obey a rule or law: *Cranley's behavior deserves the severest sanction the committee can give.* –see also SANCTIONS

**sanction**² *v* [T] FORMAL to officially accept or allow something: *The UN refused to sanction the use of force.*

**sanc·tions** /ˈsæŋkʃənz/ *n* [plural] official orders or laws stopping trade, communication etc. with another country, as a way of forcing its leaders to make political changes: *Several governments* **imposed** *trade* **sanctions on** (=started using sanctions against) *countries that use chemical weapons.*

**sanc·ti·ty** /ˈsæŋktəti/ *n* [U] **the sanctity of sth** the quality that makes something so important that it must be respected and preserved: *the sanctity of marriage*

**sanc·tu·ar·y** /ˈsæŋktʃuˌeri/ *n* **1** [C,U] a peaceful place that is safe and provides protection, especially for people who are in danger: *The rebel leader* **took sanctuary** *in an embassy.* **2** an area for birds or animals where they are protected and cannot be hunted **3** the room where Christian religious services take place

**sanc·tum** /ˈsæŋktəm/ *n* **1 the inner sanctum** HUMOROUS a place that only a few important people are allowed to enter: *We were only allowed into the director's inner sanctum for a few minutes.* **2** a holy place inside a TEMPLE

**sand**¹ /sænd/ *n* [U] the substance that forms deserts and BEACHes, and consists of many small grains

**sand**² *v* [T] **1** to make a surface smooth by rubbing it with SANDPAPER or a special piece of equipment **2** to put sand on a frozen road to make it safer

**san·dal** /ˈsændl/ *n* a light open shoe that you wear in warm weather –see picture at SHOE¹

**sand·bag**¹ /ˈsændbæg/ *n* a bag filled with sand, used for protection from floods, explosions etc.

**sandbag**² *v* **-gged, -gging** [I,T] **1** to build small walls with SANDBAGs in order to protect a place from a flood, explosion etc. **2** to deliberately do something to prevent a process from happening or being successful: *Senator Murphy has been accused of sandbagging the investigation.*

**sand·bank** /ˈsændbæŋk/ *n* a raised area of sand in a river, ocean etc.

**sand·blast** /ˈsændblæst/ *v* [T] to clean or polish metal, stone, glass etc. with a machine that sends out a powerful stream of sand

**sand·box** /ˈsændbɑks/ *n* a special area of sand for children to play in

**sand·cas·tle** /ˈsændˌkæsəl/ *n* a small model of a castle made out of sand, usually by children on a BEACH

**sand dune** /ˈ. ./ *n* ⇨ DUNE

**sand·man** /ˈsændmæn/ *n* [singular] a man in children's stories who makes children sleep by putting sand in their eyes

**sand·pa·per** /ˈsændˌpeɪpɚ/ *n* [U] strong paper covered with a rough substance, used for rubbing wood in order to make it smooth –**sandpaper** *v* [T]

S

**sand·pip·er** /'sænd,paɪpɚ/ *n* a small bird with long legs and a long beak, that lives by the ocean

**sand·stone** /'sændstoʊn/ *n* [U] a type of soft yellow or red rock

**sand·storm** /'sændstɔrm/ *n* a storm in the desert in which sand is blown around by strong winds

**sand·wich**[1] /'sændwɪtʃ/ *n* two pieces of bread with cheese, meat, egg etc. between them, usually eaten for LUNCH: *tuna fish sandwiches*

**sandwich**[2] *v* [T] **be sandwiched between** to be in a very small space between two other things: *a motorcycle sandwiched between two vans*

**sand·y** /'sændi/ *adj* **1** covered with sand: *My towel's so sandy!* **2** sandy hair is dark BLOND

**sane** /seɪn/ *adj* **1** able to think in a normal and reasonable way –opposite INSANE **2** reasonable and based on sensible thinking: *a sane solution to a difficult problem*

**sang** /sæŋ/ *v* the past tense of SING

**san·guine** /'sæŋgwɪn/ *adj* FORMAL cheerful and hopeful about the future: *Smith's lawyers aren't very sanguine about the outcome of the trial.*

**san·i·tar·i·um** /,sænə'tɛriəm/ *n* ⇨ SANA-TORIUM

**san·i·tar·y** /'sænə,tɛri/ *adj* **1** relating to health, especially to the removal of dirt, infection, or human waste: *Workers complained about sanitary arrangements at the factory.* **2** clean and not involving any danger to your health: *All food is stored under sanitary conditions.*

**sanitary nap·kin** /,.... '../ *n* a piece of soft material that a woman wears in her underwear when she has her PERIOD

**san·i·ta·tion** /,sænə'teɪʃən/ *n* [U] the protection of public health by removing and treating waste, dirty water etc.

**san·i·tize** /'sænə,taɪz/ *v* [T] **1** to make news, literature etc. less offensive by taking out anything unpleasant: *The coach's actual remarks have been sanitized so they can be printed.* **2** to clean something thoroughly, removing dirt and BACTERIA

**san·i·ty** /'sænəti/ *n* [U] **1** the ability to think in a normal and reasonable way: *I went away for the weekend to try and keep my sanity.* **2** the condition of being mentally healthy: *He lost his sanity after his children were killed.*

**sank** /sæŋk/ *v* the past tense of SINK

**San·ta Claus** /'sænɾə ,klɔz/, **Santa** *n* an old man with red clothes and a long white BEARD, who children believe brings them presents at Christmas

**sap**[1] /sæp/ *n* **1** [U] the watery substance that carries food through a plant **2** INFORMAL a stupid person who is easy to deceive or treat badly

**sap**[2] *v* **-pped, -pping** [T] to gradually make something weak or destroy it: *The illness sapped her strength.*

**sap·phire** /'sæfaɪɚ/ *n* [C,U] a transparent bright blue jewel

**sap·ling** /'sæplɪŋ/ *n* a young tree

**sap·py** /'sæpi/ *adj* expressing love and emotions in a way that seems silly: *a sappy love song*

**Sa·ran Wrap** /sə'ræn ,ræp/ *n* [U] TRADEMARK thin transparent plastic used for wrapping food

**sar·casm** /'sɑr,kæzəm/ *n* [U] a way of speaking or writing in which you say the opposite of what you mean in order to make an unkind joke or to show that you are annoyed: *"I'm glad you came early," said Jim, with heavy sarcasm.*

**sar·cas·tic** /sɑr'kæstɪk/ *adj* using SARCASM: *Do you have to be so sarcastic?* **–sarcastically** *adv*

**sar·dine** /sɑr'din/ *n* [C,U] **1** a young HERRING (=a type of fish), or the meat from this fish, usually sold in cans **2** **be packed like sardines** to be crowded tightly together in a small space

**sar·don·ic** /sɑr'dɑnɪk/ *adj* speaking or smiling in an unpleasant way that shows you do not have a good opinion of someone or something

**sa·ri** /'sɑri/ *n* a type of loose clothing worn by many Indian and Bangladeshi women, and some Pakistani women

**SASE** *n* self addressed stamped envelope; an envelope that you put your name, address, and a stamp on, so that someone else can send you something

**sash** /sæʃ/ *n* **1** a long piece of cloth that you wear around your waist like a belt: *a white dress with a blue sash* **2** a long piece of cloth that you wear over one shoulder and across your chest as a sign of a special honor **3** a frame that has a sheet of glass fixed into it to form part of a window

**sass** /sæs/ *v* [T] SPOKEN to talk in a rude way to someone you should respect: *Don't sass me, young lady!*

**sass·y** /'sæsi/ *adj* INFORMAL rude to someone you should respect: *a sassy child*

**sat** /sæt/ *v* the past tense and PAST PARTICIPLE of SIT

**Sa·tan** /'seɪt̚n/ *n* [singular] the Devil, considered to be the main evil power and God's opponent

**sa·tan·ic** /sə'tænɪk, seɪ-/ *adj* **1** relating to practices that treat the Devil like a god: *satanic rites* **2** extremely cruel or evil: *satanic laughter*

**sa·tan·is·m** /'seɪt̚n,ɪzəm/ *n* [U] the practice of treating the Devil like a god **–satanist** *n*

**sat·el·lite** /'sæt̚l,aɪt/ *n* **1** a machine that has been sent into space and goes around the Earth, moon etc., used for electronic communication: *a broadcast coming in by satellite* **2** a moon that moves around a PLANET **3** a country, town, or organization that is controlled by or is dependent on another larger one

**satellite dish** /'... ,./ *n* a large circular piece of metal that receives the signals for SATELLITE TELEVISION

**satellite tel·e·vi·sion** /,... '..../, **satellite TV** *n* [U] television programs that are broadcast using SATELLITEs in space

**sat·in** /'sæt⁻n/ *n* [U] a type of cloth that is very smooth and shiny

**sat·in·y** /'sæt⁻n-i/ *adj* smooth, shiny, and soft like SATIN: *satiny material*

**sat·ire** /'sætaɪɚ/ *n* **1** [U] a way of talking or writing about something that is funny and also makes people see its faults **2** a play, story etc. written in this way: *a social satire* –**satirical** /sə'tɪrɪkəl/ *adj* –**satirically** *adv*

**sat·i·rist** /'sætərɪst/ *n* someone who writes SATIRE

**sat·i·rize** /'sætə,raɪz/ *v* [T] to use SATIRE to make people see someone or something's faults: *a movie satirizing the fashion industry*

**sat·is·fac·tion** /,sætɪs'fækʃən/ *n* **1** [C,U] a feeling of happiness or pleasure because you have achieved something or got what you wanted: *He looked around the room with satisfaction.* | *Both leaders expressed satisfaction with the talks.* **2** [U] the act of filling a need, demand, claim etc.: *the satisfaction of our spiritual needs* **3** **to sb's satisfaction** as well or completely as someone wants: *I'm not sure I can answer that question to your satisfaction.*

**sat·is·fac·to·ry** /,sætɪs'fæktəri, tri/ *adj* **1** good enough for a particular situation or purpose: *The students are not making satisfactory progress.* **2** making you feel pleased and happy: *a satisfactory result* –**satisfactorily** *adv* –opposite UNSATISFACTORY –compare SATISFYING

**sat·is·fied** /'sætɪs,faɪd/ *adj* **1** pleased because something has happened in the way that you want, or because you have achieved something: *Most of our customers are satisfied with the food we provide.* **2** feeling sure that something is right or true: *I'm satisfied (that) he's telling the truth.* **3 satisfied?** SPOKEN said in order to ask if someone is pleased with what has happened, especially when you are not: *Okay, okay, I was wrong - satisfied?* –opposite DISSATISFIED

**sat·is·fy** /'sætɪs,faɪ/ *v* [T] **1** to make someone happy by providing what s/he wants or needs: *She doesn't feel she works hard enough to satisfy her boss.* **2** to provide someone with enough information to show that something is true or has been done correctly: *The evidence isn't enough to satisfy us that he's innocent.* **3** FORMAL to be good enough for a particular purpose, standard etc.: *I'm afraid you haven't satisfied the college entrance requirements.*

**sat·is·fy·ing** /'sætɪs,faɪ-ɪŋ/ *adj* **1** making you feel pleased and happy, especially because you have got what you wanted: *a satisfying career* **2** food that is satisfying makes you feel that you have eaten enough: *a satisfying meal* –opposite UNSATISFYING –compare SATISFACTORY

**sat·u·rate** /'sætʃə,reɪt/ *v* [T] **1** to make something completely wet: *The rain saturated the soil.* **2** to make something very full of a particular type of thing: *The market was saturated with too many exercise videos.* –**saturation** /,sætʃə'reɪʃən/ *n* [U]

**sat·u·rat·ed fat** /,.... './ *n* [C,U] a type of fat from meat and milk products

**Sat·ur·day** /'sætɚdi, -,deɪ/ written abbreviation **Sat.** *n* the seventh day of the week –see usage note at SUNDAY

**Sat·urn** /'sætɚn/ *n* [singular] the second largest PLANET, sixth from the sun

**sauce** /sɔs/ *n* [C,U] a thick cooked liquid that is served with food to give it a particular taste: *spaghetti with tomato sauce*

**sauce·pan** /'sɔs-pæn/ *n* a deep round metal container with a handle, used for cooking –see picture at PAN¹

**sau·cer** /'sɔsɚ/ *n* a small round plate that you put a cup on

**sau·cy** /'sɔsi/ *adj* slightly rude, in a way that is amusing: *a saucy look*

**sau·er·kraut** /'sauɚ,kraut/ *n* [U] a salty German food made of CABBAGE

**sau·na** /'sɔnə/ *n* **1** a room that is filled with steam to make it very hot, in which people sit because it is considered healthy **2** a time when you sit or lie in a room like this: *It's nice to have a sauna after swimming.*

**saun·ter** /'sɔntɚ, 'sɑn-/ *v* [I] to walk in a slow and confident way: *He sauntered up to her and grinned.*

**sau·sage** /'sɔsɪdʒ/ *n* [C,U] a mixture of meat and SPICEs eaten hot or cold, often for breakfast

**sau·té** /sɔ'teɪ/ *v* [T] to cook something quickly in a little hot oil or fat

**sav·age¹** /'sævɪdʒ/ *adj* **1** very cruel and violent: *savage fighting* **2** criticizing someone or something very severely: *a savage attack on the newspaper industry* **3** very severe and harmful: *savage measures to control the budget* **4** OLD-FASHIONED ⇨ PRIMITIVE –**savagely** *adv*

**savage²** *n* OLD-FASHIONED an insulting word for someone from a country where the way of living seems simple and undeveloped

**savage³** *v* [T] **1** to attack someone violently, causing serious injuries: *The boy was savaged by dogs.* **2** to criticize someone or something very severely: *a movie savaged by the critics*

**sav·age·ry** /'sævɪdʒri/ *n* [C,U] extremely cruel and violent behavior

**save¹** /seɪv/ *v*

**1** ▸FROM HARM/DANGER◂ [T] to make

someone or something safe from danger, harm, or destruction: *We are working to **save** the rain forest **from** destruction.* | *The new speed limit should save more lives.*
**2** ▶MONEY◀ [I,T] also **save up** to keep money so that you can use it later: *I'm saving up to buy a car.* | *Brian's saved $6000 to put toward a new house.*
**3** ▶NOT WASTE◀ [T] to use less time, money, energy etc. so that you do not waste any: *We'll save time if we take a cab.*
**4** ▶TO USE LATER◀ [T] to keep something so that you can use or enjoy it in the future: *Let's save the rest of the pie for later.*
**5** ▶HELP TO AVOID◀ [T] to help someone by making it unnecessary for him/her to do something unpleasant or difficult: *If you could pick up the medicine, it would save me a trip to the pharmacy.*
**6** ▶COLLECT◀ [T] also **save** sth ↔ **up** to keep all the objects of a particular kind that you can find, so that they can be used for a special purpose: *She's saving foreign coins for her son's collection.*
**7** ▶KEEP FOR SB◀ [T] to stop people from using something so that it is available for someone else: *We'll save you a seat in the theater.*
**8** ▶COMPUTER◀ [I,T] to make a computer keep the work that you have done on it —see also **save your breath/don't waste your breath** (BREATH) **lose/save face** (FACE[1])
**save on** sth *phr v* [T] to avoid wasting something by using as little as possible of it: *We turn the heat off at night to **save on** electricity.*
**save[2]** *n* an action by the GOALKEEPER in SOCCER, HOCKEY etc. that prevents the other team from getting a point
**sav·er** /'seɪvɚ/ *n* **1** **-saver** something that prevents loss or waste: *time-savers like instant food and microwave cooking* **2** someone who saves money in a bank
**sav·ing grace** /ˌ.. './ *n* a good or acceptable quality that makes something not completely bad: *The movie's only saving grace is its beautiful scenery.*
**sav·ings** /'seɪvɪŋz/ *n* **1** [plural] all the money that you have saved, especially in a bank **2** [singular] an amount of something that you have not used or do not have to spend: *Enjoy 25% **savings on** our regular prices.*
**savings ac·count** /'.. .ˌ./ *n* a bank account that pays INTEREST on the money you have in it
**savings and loan** /ˌ.. . './ *n* a business similar to a bank where you can save money, and that also lends money for things such as houses
**savings bank** /'.. ˌ./ *n* a bank whose business is mostly from SAVINGS ACCOUNTS and from LOANS for houses
**sav·ior** /'seɪvyɚ/ *n* **1** someone or something that saves you from a difficult or dangerous situation **2** **the/our Savior** another name for Jesus Christ, used in the Christian religion

**sa·vor** /'seɪvɚ/ *v* [T] to make an activity or experience last as long as you can, because you are enjoying every moment of it: *Drink it slowly and savor every drop.*
**sa·vor·y** /'seɪvəri/ *adj* having a pleasant smell or taste, especially one that is related to salty foods: *a savory aroma* —see also UNSAVORY
**sav·vy** /'sævi/ *n* [U] INFORMAL practical knowledge and ability: *marketing savvy* —**savvy** *adj*: *a savvy businesswoman*
**saw[1]** /sɔ/ *v* the past tense of SEE
**saw[2]** *n* a tool that has a flat blade with a row of sharp points, used for cutting wood
**saw[3]** *v* **sawed, sawn** *or* **sawed, sawing** [I,T] to cut something using a SAW: *We decided to **saw off** the lower branches of the apple tree.*
**saw·dust** /'sɔdʌst/ *n* [U] very small pieces of wood that are left when you cut wood with a SAW
**saw·mill** /'sɔmɪl/ *n* [U] a factory where trees are cut into boards
**sawn** /sɔn/ *v* the PAST PARTICIPLE of SAW
**sax** /sæks/ *n* INFORMAL ⇨ SAXOPHONE
**sax·o·phone** /'sæksəˌfoʊn/ *n* a metal musical instrument that you play by blowing into it and pressing special buttons, used especially in JAZZ and dance music
**say[1]** /seɪ/ *v* **said, said, saying,** *third person singular, present tense* **says**
**1** ▶SPEAK◀ [T] to speak words: *He said he'd call back.* | *Tell her I said hi.* | *Say bye-bye, Melissa.*
**2** ▶EXPRESS STH◀ [I,T] to express a thought, feeling, opinion etc. in words: *He didn't seem to understand what I said.* | *Did she say what time to come?* | *The doctor **says (that)** I can't go home yet.* | *That's a pretty mean **thing to say.*** | *Every time I want to cook, Mom **says no**.* (=refuses to let me)
**3** ▶WITHOUT WORDS◀ [I,T] to express something without using words: *Her smile **says it all**.* (=her smile expresses her happiness) | *What is Hopper trying to say in this painting?*
**4** ▶GIVE INFORMATION◀ [T] to give information in writing, pictures, or numbers: *The clock said quarter after six.* | *What do the instructions say?*
**5** **to say the least** used when what you have said could have been stated much more strongly: *The house needs work, to say the least.*
**6** **go without saying** used when what you have said or written is so clear that it really did not need to be stated: *It goes without saying that the taxpayers will be outraged.*
**7** **that is to say** used before describing what you mean in more detail or more clearly: *Things still aren't equal. That is to say, women still are not paid as much as men.*
**8** **having said that** used before saying something that makes the opinion you have given

seem less strong: *The movie is sloppily made, but having said that, it's still a cute picture to take the kids to.*

---
SPOKEN PHRASES
---

**9 be saying** used in phrases to emphasize that you are trying to explain what you mean in a way that someone will understand better: *All I'm saying is that he should have been more careful.* (=used when you do not want someone to be angry about what you have said) | *I'm not saying this is more important, I'm just saying that I'm more interested in it.* | *Well, you're not really being fair, (do you) see what I'm saying?* (=do you understand me?)
**10 say to yourself** to think something: *I was worried about it, but I said to myself, "You can do this."*
**11** [T] to suggest or suppose something: *Meet me at, let's say, 7 o'clock.* | *Say you were going to an interview. What would you wear?*
**12 say when** used when you want someone to tell you when you have given him/her the correct amount of something, especially a drink
**13 Say what?** said when you have not heard something that someone said, or when you cannot believe that something is true

---
USAGE NOTE **say, tell, speak, and talk**
---

**Say** and **tell** are always followed by objects. **Tell** can be followed by a direct object or an indirect object: *Keith is good at telling stories.* | *Could you tell me how to get to the library?* **Say** is never used with an indirect object: *She won't say anything.* | *Dad said "no."* ✗ DON'T SAY "Dad said me 'no.'" ✗ **Say** can be followed by CLAUSES beginning with "that": *He said that he saw Marcia yesterday.* **Tell** can also be used in this way, but only with an indirect object: *He told me that he saw Marcia yesterday.* You can also use **tell** to give orders or to talk about giving orders: *Tell Jan to come home right now!* | *She told us to sit down.* Both **speak** and **talk** are used in situations in which one person is talking, but **speak** is more formal: *He spoke for an hour about the economy.* | *He talked for hours about his girlfriend.* You can also use **talk** to show that two people are having a conversation: *Ron was talking to Helen in the corner.* Use **speak** to ask politely for someone on the telephone: *Hello, may I speak to Sandra Wright, please?*

**say²** *n* [singular, U] **1** the right to help decide something: *Members felt that they had **had no say in** the proposed changes.* | *Who has the final say?* **2 have your/their say** to give your opin-

ion on something: *You'll all have the chance to have your say.*

**say·ing** /ˈseɪ-ɪŋ/ *n* a well-known statement that expresses an idea most people believe is true and wise; PROVERB

**SC** the written abbreviation of South Carolina

**scab** /skæb/ *n* **1** a hard layer of dried blood that forms over a cut or wound **2** INFORMAL an insulting word for someone who works in a place where other people refuse to work because they are on STRIKE

**scads** /skædz/ *n* [plural] INFORMAL large numbers or quantities of something: *scads of money*

**scaf·fold** /ˈskæfəld, -foʊld/ *n* **1** a structure built next to a building or high wall, for people to stand on while they work on the building or wall **2** a structure used in past times for killing criminals by hanging them from it

**scaf·fold·ing** /ˈskæfəldɪŋ/ *n* [U] poles and boards that are built into a structure for people to stand on when they are working on a high wall or the outside of a building

**scald** /skɔld/ *v* [T] to burn yourself with hot liquid or steam: *Ow! That coffee scalded my tongue.* −**scald** *n*

**scald·ing** /ˈskɔldɪŋ/ *adj, adv* extremely hot: *scalding hot water*

**scale¹** /skeɪl/ *n*
**1** ▶SIZE◀ [singular, U] the size or level of something, when compared to what is normal: *a large/small scale project* | *They built their new house on a grand scale.* (=it is very big)
**2** ▶MEASURING SYSTEM◀ [C usually singular] a system for measuring the force, speed, amount etc. of something, or for comparing it with something else: *a company's pay scale* | *On a scale from 1 to 10, I'd give it an 8.*
**3** ▶FOR WEIGHING◀ [C usually plural] a machine or piece of equipment for weighing people or objects: *Here, put the bag of apples on the scales.*
**4** ▶MEASURING MARKS◀ a set of marks with regular spaces between them on an instrument that is used for measuring: *a ruler with a metric scale*
**5** ▶MAP/DRAWING◀ [C,U] the relationship between the size of a map, drawing, or model and the actual size of the place or thing that it represents: *a scale of 1 inch to the mile*
**6** ▶MUSIC◀ a series of musical notes that have a fixed order and become gradually higher or lower in PITCH
**7** ▶ON FISH◀ [C usually plural] one of the small flat pieces of hard skin that cover the bodies of fish, snakes etc.

**scale²** *v* [T] **1** to climb to the top of something that is high: *scaling a 40-foot wall* **2** to remove the SCALEs from a fish

**scale** sth ↔ **back/down** *phr v* [T] to reduce the size of something such as an organization or plan: *The factory managers have made a decision to scale back production.*

**scal·lop** /'skæləp, 'skɑləp/ *n* [C,U] a small sea animal that has a hard flat shell, or the meat from this animal

**scal·loped** /'skæləpt, 'skɑ-/ *adj* cloth or objects that have scalloped edges are cut in a series of small curves as a decoration

**scalp**[1] /skælp/ *n* the skin on the top of your head, where your hair grows

**scalp**[2] *v* [T] **1** INFORMAL to buy tickets for an event and sell them again at a much higher price **2** to cut off a dead enemy's SCALP as a sign of victory

**scal·pel** /'skælpəl/ *n* a small and very sharp knife used by doctors during operations

**scal·y** /'skeɪli/ *adj* **1** an animal that is scaly is covered with small flat pieces of hard skin **2** scaly skin is dry and rough

**scam** /skæm/ *n* SLANG a dishonest plan, usually to get money

**scam·per** /'skæmpɚ/ *v* [I] to run with short quick steps, like a child or small animal: *A mouse scampered into its hole.*

**scan** /skæn/ *v* **-nned, -nning** **1** [I,T] also **scan through** to read something quickly in order to understand its main meaning or to find a particular piece of information: *I had a chance to scan through the report on the plane.* **2** [T] to examine an area carefully, because you are looking for a particular person or thing: *Lookouts were scanning the sky for enemy planes.* **3** [T] if a machine scans an object or a part of your body, it produces a picture of what is inside: *All luggage has to be scanned at the airport.* **4** if a piece of computer equipment scans an image, it copies it from paper onto the computer −**scan** *n* −see also SCANNER

**scan·dal** /'skændl/ *n* [C,U] something that has happened that people think is immoral or shocking: *a scandal involving several important politicians* | *Reporters are always looking for scandal and gossip.*

**scan·dal·ize** /'skændl,aɪz/ *v* [T] to do something that shocks people very much: *a crime that has scandalized the entire city*

**scan·dal·ous** /'skændl-əs/ *adj* completely immoral and shocking: *scandalous behavior*

**scan·ner** /'skænɚ/ *n* TECHNICAL **1** a machine that passes a BEAM of ELECTRONs over an object or a part of your body in order to produce a picture of what is inside **2** a piece of computer equipment that copies an image from paper onto the computer

**scant** /skænt/ *adj* not enough: *After two weeks, they had made scant progress.*

**scant·y** /'skænti/ *adj* not big enough for a particular purpose: *a scanty bikini* −**scantily** *adv*: *scantily dressed*

**scape·goat** /'skeɪpgoʊt/ *n* someone who is

blamed for something bad that happens, even if it is not his/her fault −**scapegoat** *v* [T]

**scar**[1] /skɑr/ *n* **1** a permanent mark on your skin from a cut or wound **2** a permanent emotional or mental problem caused by a bad experience

**scar**[2] *v* **-rred, -rring** [T] **1** to have or be given a permanent mark on your skin from a cut or wound: *The fire had left him scarred for life.* **2** to have or be given permanent emotional or mental problems because of a bad experience: *Rob's parents' divorce left him emotionally scarred.*

**scarce** /skɛrs/ *adj* if food, clothing, water etc. is scarce, there is not enough of it available −see usage note at RARE

**scarce·ly** /'skɛrsli/ *adv* **1** almost not at all, or almost none at all: *Their teaching methods have scarcely changed in the last 10 years.* **2** definitely not, or almost certainly not: *Owen is really angry, and you can scarcely blame him.*

**scar·ci·ty** /'skɛrsəti/ *n* [C,U] a situation in which there is not enough of something: *a scarcity of quality child care*

**scare**[1] /skɛr/ *v* INFORMAL **1** [I,T] to become frightened, or to make someone feel frightened: *Walter scares easily.* | *Don't do that! You scared me to death/scared the hell out of me!* (=scared me very much) **2** scare sb into doing sth to make someone do something by frightening or threatening him/her: *Maybe we can scare the kids into behaving till their mom comes back.*

**scare sb/sth ↔ off/away** *phr v* [T] **1** to make someone or something go away by frightening him, her, or it: *We lit fires to scare away the wild animals.* **2** to make someone uncertain or nervous so that s/he does not do something s/he was going to do: *I'd like to call him, but I don't want to scare him off.*

**scare sth ↔ up** *phr v* [T] SPOKEN to make something although you have very few things to make it from: *I'll try to scare up some breakfast.*

**scare**[2] *n* **1** [singular] a sudden feeling of fear: *What a scare you gave me!* **2** a situation in which a group of people become frightened about something: *a bomb scare*

**scare·crow** /'skɛrkroʊ/ *n* an object made to look like a person, that a farmer puts in a field to frighten birds

**scared** /skɛrd/ *adj* INFORMAL frightened by something or nervous about something; afraid: *We were scared (that) something terrible might happen.* | *I'm scared of flying.* | *Steve heard some noise, and he was scared stiff/scared to death.* (=extremely frightened)

**scarf**[1] /skɑrf/ *n, plural* **scarves** *or* **scarfs** a piece of material that you wear around your neck, head, or shoulders to keep warm or to look attractive

**scarf**² *v* [I,T] SLANG
  **scarf** sth ↔ **down/up** *phr v* [T] to eat something very quickly

**scar·let** /'skɑrlɪt/ *n* [U] a very bright red color —**scarlet** *adj*

**scarves** /skɑrvz/ *n* the plural of SCARF

**scar·y** /'skɛri/ *adj* INFORMAL frightening: *a scary movie*

**scat** /skæt/ *interjection* said in order to tell a small animal to go away: *Go on, cat! Scat!*

**scath·ing** /'skeɪðɪŋ/ *adj* scathing remarks, COMMENTS etc. criticize someone or something very severely

**scat·ter** /'skætɚ/ *v* **1** [I,T] to move or be made to move in many different directions: *He pulled out a gun and the crowd scattered.* **2** [T] to throw or drop a lot of things over a wide area: *Clothes had been scattered across the floor.*

**scat·ter·brained** /'skætɚˌbreɪnd/ *adj* INFORMAL tending to forget or lose things because you do not think in a practical way

**scav·enge** /'skævɪndʒ/ *v* [I,T] to search for things to eat or use among unwanted food or objects: *wild dogs scavenging for food* —**scavenger** *n*

**sce·nar·i·o** /sɪ'nɛriˌoʊ, -'nær-/ *n* **1** a situation that could possibly happen but has not happened yet: *Even in the worst-case scenario* (=if the worst possible thing happens), *we'll still get the money back.* **2** a description of the story in a movie, play etc.

**scene** /sin/ *n*
  **1** ▶PLAY/MOVIE◀ a part of a play or movie during which the action all happens in one place over a short period of time: *She comes on in Act 2, Scene 3.* | *a love scene*
  **2** ▶VIEW/PICTURE◀ a view of a place as you see it, or as it appears in a picture: *a peaceful country scene* ✗ DON'T SAY "There's a nice scene from my window." SAY "There's a nice view." ✗
  **3** ▶ACCIDENT/CRIME◀ [singular] the place where something bad happened: *Firefighters arrived on/at the scene within minutes.* | *the scene of the crime*
  **4** **the music/fashion/political etc. scene** a particular set of activities and the people who are involved in them: *Lisa always knows what's happening on the fashion scene.*
  **5** ▶ARGUMENT◀ a loud angry argument, especially in a public place: *Sit down and stop making a scene!*
  **6** **not sb's scene** INFORMAL not the type of thing someone likes: *Loud parties aren't really my scene.*
  **7** **behind the scenes** secretly: *You have no idea what goes on behind the scenes.*
  **8** **set the scene a)** to provide the conditions in which an event can happen: *Interest in fitness set the scene for the success of sport shoes.*

**b)** to describe the situation before you begin to tell a story —see usage note at VIEW²

**sce·ner·y** /'sinəri/ *n* [U] **1** the natural features of a place, such as mountains, forests etc.: *What beautiful scenery!* **2** the painted background, furniture etc. used on a theater stage

**sce·nic** /'sinɪk/ *adj* with beautiful views of nature: *Let's take the scenic route home.*

**scent** /sɛnt/ *n* **1** a particular smell, especially a pleasant one: *the scent of roses* **2** the smell left behind by an animal or person: *The dog ran for the door when he picked up his owner's scent.* **3** [C,U] ⇨ PERFUME —see usage note at SMELL²

**scent·ed** /'sɛntɪd/ *adj* having a particular smell, especially a pleasant one: *a room scented with spring flowers*

**scep·ter** /'sɛptɚ/ *n* a short decorated stick carried by kings and queens at special ceremonies

**sched·ule**¹ /'skɛdʒəl, -dʒul/ *n* **1** [C,U] a plan of what someone is going to do and when s/he is going to do it: *I have a very full schedule this week.* (=I am very busy) | *We're on schedule to finish in May.* (=we will finish by the planned date) **2** a list that shows the times that buses, trains etc. leave or arrive at a particular place

**schedule**² *v* [T] to plan that something will happen at a particular time: *The meeting has been scheduled for Friday.* | *Another new store is scheduled to open in three weeks.*

**scheme**¹ /skim/ *n* **1** a plan, especially to do something bad or illegal: *a scheme to avoid paying taxes* **2** a system that you use to organize something: *a bright color scheme for decorating the kitchen*

**scheme**² *v* [I] to secretly make dishonest plans to get or achieve something; PLOT: *politicians scheming to win votes* —**schemer** *n*

**schism** /'sɪzəm, 'skɪzəm/ *n* [C,U] FORMAL the separation of a group of people into two groups as the result of a disagreement

**schiz·o·phre·ni·a** /ˌskɪtsə'friniə/ *n* [U] a mental illness in which someone's thoughts and feelings become separated from what is really happening around him/her —**schizophrenic** /ˌskɪtsə'frɛnɪk/ *adj, n*

**schlep**¹, **schlepp** /ʃlɛp/ *v* -pped, -pping [T] INFORMAL to carry something heavy, or to go somewhere in a tired way: *I don't want to schlep this all the way across town.*

**schlep**², **schlepp** *n* INFORMAL **1** a lazy stupid person **2** a long trip that makes you tired

**schlock** /ʃlɑk/ *n* [U] INFORMAL things that are cheap, bad, or useless

**schmaltz·y** /'ʃmɔltsi, 'ʃmɑl-/ *adj* INFORMAL dealing with strong emotions such as love and sadness in a way that seems silly and insincere:

*schmaltzy music* **–schmaltz** *n* [U] –compare SENTIMENTAL

**schmooze** /ʃmuz/ *v* [I] INFORMAL to talk about things that are not important: *drinking and schmoozing at a party*

**schmuck** /ʃmʌk/ *n* INFORMAL an insulting word meaning someone who is stupid or does things you do not like

**schnapps** /ʃnæps/ *n* [U] a strong alcoholic drink

**schol·ar** /'skɑlɚ/ *n* **1** someone who knows a lot about a particular subject **2** someone who has been given a SCHOLARSHIP to study at a college or university

**schol·ar·ly** /'skɑlɚli/ *adj* **1** concerned with serious study of a particular subject: *a scholarly journal* **2** someone who is scholarly spends a lot of time studying, and knows a lot about a particular subject

**schol·ar·ship** /'skɑlɚˌʃɪp/ *n* **1** an amount of money that is given to someone by an organization to help pay for his/her education **2** [U] the methods that are used in serious studying, or the knowledge that comes from this

**scho·las·tic** /skə'læstɪk/ *adj* relating to schools or teaching: *an excellent scholastic record*

**school**[1] /skul/ *n*
**1** ▶BUILDING◀ [C,U] a place where children are taught: *Which school did you go to? | I can get some work done while the kids are at school.* (=studying in the school building)
**2** ▶TIME AT SCHOOL◀ [U] the time spent at school: *What are you doing after school?*
**3** ▶TEACHERS/STUDENTS◀ the students and teachers at a school: *The whole school was sorry when she left.*
**4** in school attending a school: *Are your boys still in school?*
**5** ▶FOR ONE SUBJECT◀ [C,U] a place where a particular subject or skill is taught: *an art school*
**6** ▶UNIVERSITY◀ a) a department that teaches a particular subject at a university: *the Harvard School of Law* b) INFORMAL a college or university: *"Where did you go to school?" "UC San Diego."*
**7** ▶ART/IDEAS◀ a number of people who are considered as a group because of their style of work, or their ideas: *the Dutch school of painting*
**8** school of thought an opinion or way of thinking about something that is shared by a group of people: *One school of thought says that red wine is good for you.*
**9** ▶FISH◀ a large group of fish or other sea creatures that are swimming together: *a school of dolphins*

**school**[2] *v* [T] FORMAL to train or teach someone: *The children are schooled in music and art from a very early age.*

**school·ing** /'skulɪŋ/ *n* [U] education at school

**schoo·ner** /'skunɚ/ *n* a fast sailing ship with two sails

**sci·ence** /'saɪəns/ *n* **1** [U] knowledge that is based on testing and proving facts, or the study that produces this knowledge: *the application of science and technology to everyday life* **2** [C,U] a particular area of science, such as BIOLOGY or chemistry, or a subject that is studied like a science: *the social sciences*

**science fic·tion** /ˌ.. '../ *n* [U] books and stories about imaginary worlds or imaginary developments in science, such as travel in space

**sci·en·tif·ic** /ˌsaɪən'tɪfɪk/ *adj* **1** relating to science, or using its methods: *scientific discoveries | a scientific experiment* **2** done very carefully, using an organized system: *We do keep records, but we're not very scientific about it.* –opposite UNSCIENTIFIC

**sci·en·tist** /'saɪəntɪst/ *n* someone who works in science

**sci-fi** /ˌsaɪ'faɪ/ *n* [U] INFORMAL ⇨ SCIENCE FICTION

**scin·til·lat·ing** /'sɪntl̩ˌeɪtɪŋ/ *adj* interesting, amusing, and intelligent: *a scintillating speech*

**scis·sors** /'sɪzɚz/ *n* [plural] a tool for cutting paper, made of two sharp blades that are joined in the middle and that have handles on one end: *Hand me that pair of scissors, please.*

**scoff** /skɔf, skɑf/ *v* [I] to laugh at a person or idea, or to make unkind remarks, in a way that shows you think he, she, or it is stupid: *Other lawyers scoffed at his methods.*

**scold** /skoʊld/ *v* [T] to tell someone in an angry way that s/he has done something wrong: *Mom scolded me for wasting electricity.* –scolding *n* [C,U]

**scoop**[1] /skup/ *n* **1** a deep spoon for picking up or serving food such as flour or ICE CREAM **2** also **scoopful** the amount that a scoop will hold: *two scoops of sugar* **3** an important or exciting news story that is printed in one newspaper before any of the others know about it

**scoop**[2] *v* [T] to pick something up with a SCOOP, a spoon, or with your curved hand: *She scooped up a handful of sand.*

**scoot** /skut/ *v* [I] INFORMAL to leave a place quickly: *Go to bed, Andrew - scoot!*

**scoot·er** /'skutɚ/ *n* **1** a small two-wheeled vehicle like a bicycle with an engine –see picture on page 469 **2** a child's vehicle with two small wheels, an upright handle, and a narrow board that you stand on with one foot, while the other foot pushes the vehicle along the ground

**scope**[1] /skoʊp/ *n* [U] **1** the range of things that a subject, activity, book etc. deals with: *A thorough discussion of this subject is beyond the scope of this paper.* **2** the opportunity to do or develop something: *I want a job with scope for promotion.*

**scope²** *v*

**scope** sb/sth ↔ **out** *phr v* [T] SPOKEN to look at someone or something to see what he, she, or it is like: *Let's scope out that new bar tonight.*

**scorch¹** /skɔrtʃ/ *v* [I,T] if you scorch something, or if it scorches, its surface burns slightly and changes color: *Turn down the iron or you'll scorch your shirt.*

**scorch** *scorch*

**scorch²** *n* a mark made on something where its surface has been burned

**scorch·er** /ˈskɔrtʃɚ/ *n* INFORMAL an extremely hot day: *It's going to be a real scorcher.*

**scorch·ing** /ˈskɔrtʃɪŋ/ *adj* INFORMAL extremely hot: *It's scorching outside!*

**score¹** /skɔr/ *n* **1** the number of points that a person or team wins or earns in a game, competition, or test: *The final score was 35 to 17.* | *I got a higher/lower score than Tracy on the geometry test.* | *Who's going to keep score?* (=record the scores as a game is played) **2** a paper copy of a piece of music for a group of performers, or the music itself: *a movie score* **3 know the score** INFORMAL to know the real facts of a situation, including any unpleasant ones: *He knew the score when he decided to get involved.* **4 on that score** SPOKEN concerning the subject you have just mentioned: *We've got plenty of money, so don't worry on that score.* **5** OLD-FASHIONED twenty: *four-score years ago* (=80 years ago) −see also **settle the score** (SETTLE)

**score²** *v* **1** [I,T] to win or earn points in a game, competition, or test: *Dallas scored right before the end of the game.* | *Mr. Burke's class scored about six points higher than the others.* **2** [T] to give a particular number of points in a game, competition, or test: *The exams will be scored by computer.* **3 score points** INFORMAL to do or say something to please someone or to make him/her feel respect for you: *Does she think she can score points with me by making me cookies?* **4** [I,T] INFORMAL to be very successful in something you do: *Barnes has scored again with another popular book.* **5** [I,T] SLANG to manage to get something you want, especially sex or illegal drugs −see also SCORES

**score·board** /ˈskɔrbɔrd/ *n* a sign on which the SCORE of a game is shown as it is played

**score·card** /ˈskɔrkɑrd/ *n* a printed card used for writing the SCORE of a game as it is played

**scor·er** /ˈskɔrɚ/ *n* **1** someone who earns a point in a game **2** also **scorekeeper** someone who records the number of points won in a game or competition as it is played

**scores** /skɔrz/ *n* [plural] a large number, but usually less than a hundred: *On the playground, scores of children ran and screamed.*

**scorn¹** /skɔrn/ *n* [U] strong criticisms of someone or something that you think is not worth any respect at all: *The media has heaped/ poured scorn on the President's speech.* −**scornful** *adj*

**scorn²** *v* [T] FORMAL to show in an unkind way that you think that a person, idea, or suggestion is stupid or not worth accepting: *He scorned the opinions of anyone who disagreed with him*

**Scor·pi·o** /ˈskɔrpiˌoʊ/ *n* **1** [singular] the eighth sign of the ZODIAC, represented by a SCORPION **2** someone born between October 24 and November 21

**scor·pi·on** /ˈskɔrpiən/ *n* a creature like a large insect, that has a poisonous tail

**Scotch** /skɑtʃ/ *n* [C,U] a type of WHISKEY (=a strong alcoholic drink) made in Scotland, or a glass of this drink

**scotch** *v* **scotch a rumor** stop a RUMOR (=story about someone) from spreading

**Scotch tape** /ˌ. ˈ./ *n* [U] TRADEMARK sticky thin clear plastic in a long narrow band, used for sticking paper and other light things together

**scot-free** /ˌskɑt ˈfri/ *adv* **get off scot-free** INFORMAL to avoid being punished although you deserve to be

**Scot·tish** /ˈskɑtɪʃ/ *adj* relating to or coming from Scotland

**scoun·drel** /ˈskaʊndrəl/ *n* OLD-FASHIONED a bad or dishonest man

**scour** /skaʊɚ/ *v* [T] **1** to search very carefully and thoroughly through an area or a document: *Detectives scoured her letters for clues.* **2** also **scour out** to clean something very thoroughly by rubbing it with a rough material

**scourge** /skɜrdʒ/ *n* FORMAL something that causes a lot of harm or suffering: *the scourge of war* −**scourge** *v* [T]

**scout¹** /skaʊt/ *n* **1** a soldier who is sent to search an area in front of an army and get information **2** someone whose job is to look for good sports players, musicians etc. in order to employ them: *a talent scout*

**scout²** *v* **1** [I] also **scout around** to look for something in a particular area: *I'm going to scout around for a place to buy some beer.* **2** [T] also **scout out** to examine a place or area in order to get information about it, especially for military reasons: *Two men went off to scout out the woods ahead.* **3** [T] also **scout for** to look for good sports players, musicians etc. in order to employ them

**scowl** /skaʊl/ *v* [I] to look at someone or something in an angry or disapproving way: *Tom just scowls at me when we meet.* −**scowl** *n*

**Scrab·ble** /ˈskræbəl/ *n* [U] TRADEMARK a game using a special board and small objects with letters on them, in which you try to make words out of the letters

**scrab·ble** v [I] to quickly feel around with your fingers, especially in order to look for something: *Police scrabbled through garbage cans looking for the wallet.*

**scrag·gly** /'skrægli/ adj growing in a way that looks uneven and messy: *a scraggly beard*

**scram** /skræm/ v -mmed, -mming [I] INFORMAL to leave a place very quickly, especially because you are not wanted: *Get out of here! Scram!*

**scram·ble**[1] /'skræmbəl/ v **1** [I] to climb up or over something quickly, using your hands to help you: *Andy scrambled easily over the wall.* **2** [I] to rush and struggle with other people in order to get or do something: *people scrambling for safety* **3** [T] to mix electronic signals so that they cannot be understood without a special piece of equipment: *All messages are scrambled for security reasons.* —opposite UNSCRAMBLE **4** [T] to mix up the order of letters, words etc., so that the meaning is not clear **5 scramble an egg** to cook an egg by mixing the white and yellow parts together and heating it

**scramble**[2] n [singular] **1** a quick and difficult climb in which you have to use your hands to help you: *a rough scramble over loose rocks* **2** a situation in which people rush and struggle with each other in order to get or do something: *a scramble for the best seats | a scramble for federal funding*

**scrap**[1] /skræp/ n **1** a small piece of paper, cloth etc.: *a scrap of paper* **2** [U] materials or objects that are no longer suitable for the purpose they were made for, but can be used again in another way: *scrap metal* **3** a small piece of information: *There isn't a scrap of evidence to support her story.* **4** INFORMAL a short fight or argument that is not very serious: *Katie got into a little scrap at school.*

**scrap**[2] v -pped, -pping **1** [T] INFORMAL to decide not to do or use something because it is not practical: *We've decided to scrap the whole idea of renting a car.* **2** [T] to take apart an old machine, vehicle etc., and use its parts in some other way: *equipment to be sold or scrapped*

**scrap·book** /'skræpbʊk/ n a book with empty pages in which you can stick pictures, newspaper articles, or other things you want to keep

**scrape**[1] /skreɪp/ v **1** [T] to remove something from a surface, using the edge of a knife, stick etc.: *Jerry bent to scrape the mud off his boots.* **2** [I,T] to rub against a rough surface in a way that causes slight damage or injury, or to make something do this: *I scraped my knee on the sidewalk.* **3** [I,T] to make a noise by rubbing roughly against a surface: *Metal scraped when he turned the key.*

**scrape by** phr v [I] to have just enough money to live: *They just manage to scrape by on her salary.*

**scrape** sth ↔ **together/up** phr v [T] to get enough money for a particular purpose, when this is difficult: *We're trying to scrape together enough money for a vacation.*

**scrape**[2] n **1** a mark or slight injury caused by rubbing against a rough surface: *Steve only got a few cuts and scrapes.* **2** INFORMAL a situation in which you get into trouble or have difficulties: *Harper has had previous scrapes with the law.*

**scrap·py** /'skræpi/ adj INFORMAL always wanting to argue or fight

**scraps** /skræps/ n [plural] pieces of food that are left after you have finished eating: *Save the scraps for the dog.*

**scratch**[1] /skrætʃ/ v **1** [I,T] to rub a part of your body with your FINGERNAILs: *Will you scratch my back? | a dog scratching itself* **2** [T] to make a small cut in a surface, or to remove something from a surface, using something sharp: *Did the cat scratch you? | The paint's been scratched off the wall here.* **3** [I] to make a noise by rubbing something sharp or rough on a hard surface: *Didn't you hear the dog scratching at the door?* **4 scratch the surface** to deal with only a very small part of a subject: *We've been studying the stars for years, but we've only scratched the surface.* **5** [T] INFORMAL to stop planning to do something because it is no longer possible or practical: *I guess we can scratch that idea.* **6** [T] to remove a person or thing from a list: *Her name had been scratched from/off the list of competitors.*

**scratch**[2] n **1** a small cut or mark on the surface of something or on someone's skin: *Where did this scratch on the car come from?* **2 from scratch** without using anything that was prepared before: *I made the cake from scratch.* **3 not come/be up to scratch** INFORMAL to not be good enough for a particular standard: *Your work hasn't really been up to scratch lately.* **4** a sound made by something sharp or rough being rubbed on a hard surface: *You could hear the dry scratch of his pen as he wrote.* **5** [singular] the act of rubbing a part of your body with your FINGERNAILs: *My back needs a good scratch.* **6 without a scratch** INFORMAL without being injured at all: *Stuart was hurt in the accident, but Max escaped without a scratch.*

**scratch pa·per** /'. ,../ n [U] cheap paper, or paper that has already been used on one side, that you can write notes or lists on

**scratch·y** /'skrætʃi/ adj **1** scratchy clothes or materials have a rough surface and are uncomfortable to wear or touch: *a scratchy pair of wool socks* **2** a voice that is scratchy sounds deep and rough **3** a scratchy throat is sore

**scrawl** /skrɔl/ v to write something in a fast, careless, or messy way: *a telephone number scrawled on a piece of paper* —**scrawl** n

**scraw·ny** /ˈskrɔni/ *adj* looking thin and weak in an unattractive way: *a scrawny little kid*

**scream¹** /skrim/ *v* [I,T] to make a loud high noise with your voice, or shout something loudly because you are hurt, frightened, excited etc.: *Suddenly she screamed, "Look out!"* | *The baby was* ***screaming for*** *her bottle.*

**scream²** *n* **1** a loud high noise that you make when you are hurt, frightened, excited etc.: *I thought I heard a child's scream* **2** a very loud high sound: *the scream of the jet engines* **3 be a scream** INFORMAL to be very funny: *"How was the show?" "It was a scream."*

**screech** /skritʃ/ *v* **1** [I,T] to make a very high loud unpleasant sound: *The motor screeched when we turned it on.* | *"Get out of my way!" she screeched.* **2 screech to a halt/stop/standstill** if a vehicle screeches to a halt, it stops very suddenly, so that its BRAKE*s* make an unpleasant high sound –**screech** *n*

**screen¹** /skrin/ *n* **1** the flat glass part of a television or a computer: *It's easier to correct your work* ***on screen*** *than on paper.* **2** a large flat white surface that movies are shown on in a movie theater **3** a wire net that covers an open door or window so that air can get inside a house but insects cannot: *screens on the windows* | *a screen door* **4** a piece of material on a frame that can be moved, used for dividing one part of a room from another **5** [singular, U] movies, or the business of making movies: *a chance to appear* ***on the big screen*** (=in a movie) *with Robert DeNiro*

**screen**

**screen²** *v* [T] **1** to do medical tests on people in order to discover whether they have a particular illness: *Women over the age of 50 are screened for breast cancer.* **2** to test people in order to find out whether they are suitable for a particular job or organization: *Every job applicant is screened before the interview.* **3** also **screen off** to hide or protect something by putting something in front of it: *Part of the murder victim's house was screened off by the police.* **4 screen calls** to find out who is calling you on the telephone, especially by using an ANSWERING MACHINE, so that you do not have to speak to someone you do not want to

**screen·play** /ˈskrinpleɪ/ *n* a story written for a movie or a television show

**screen·writ·er** /ˈskrin,raɪt̬ɚ/ *n* someone who writes SCREENPLAY*s*

**screw¹** /skru/ *n* **1** a thin pointed piece of metal that you push and turn in order to fasten pieces of wood or metal together **2 have a screw loose** INFORMAL OFTEN HUMOROUS to be slightly crazy

**screw²** *v* **1** [T] to fasten two objects together using a screw: *Screw the boards together using the half-inch screws.* **2** [T] to fasten or close something by turning it until it cannot be turned any more: *Don't forget to screw the top back on.* **3** [I,T] SLANG an impolite word meaning to have sex with someone **4** [T] SPOKEN an impolite word meaning to treat someone dishonestly or unfairly: *We really* ***got screwed*** *on that deal.* **5 screw you/him/that etc.** SPOKEN OFFENSIVE said when you are very angry with someone or something

**screw around** *phr v* [I] SPOKEN to waste time or behave in a silly way: *Stop* ***screwing around*** *and get back to work!*

**screw up** *phr v* **1** [I,T **screw** sth ↔ **up**] INFORMAL to make a bad mistake that ruins what you intended to do: *I can't believe they* ***screwed up*** *our plane tickets.* **2** [T **screw** sb ↔ **up**] INFORMAL to make someone feel extremely unhappy, confused, or anxious, especially for a long time: *Carole's family really* ***screwed*** *her* ***up***. **3 screw up your face/lips/eyes etc.** to tighten the muscles in your face etc.

**screw·ball** /ˈskrubɔl/ *n* INFORMAL someone who seems very strange, silly, or crazy –**screwball** *adj*

**screw·driv·er** /ˈskru,draɪvɚ/ *n* a tool with a long thin metal end, used for turning screws

**screwed up** /,. ˈ.◂ / *adj* INFORMAL **1** very unhappy, confused, or anxious because you have had bad experiences in the past: *These poor kids, they're so screwed up from their parents' divorce.* **2** not working, or in a bad condition: *My left leg* ***got screwed up*** *playing football.*

**screw·y** /ˈskrui/ *adj* INFORMAL slightly strange or crazy: *a screwy plan*

**scrib·ble** /ˈskrɪbəl/ *v* **1** also **scribble down** [T] to write something quickly in a messy way: *He scribbled down his phone number on a business card.* **2** [I] to draw marks that do not mean anything: *Stop scribbling on the desk!* –**scribble** *n* –**scribbles** *n* [plural]

**scribe** /skraɪb/ *n* someone in past times whose job was to copy or record things by writing them

**scrimp** /skrɪmp/ *v* **scrimp and save** to try to save as much money as you can, even though you have very little: *We had to scrimp and save the first few years we were married.*

**script** /skrɪpt/ *n* **1** the written form of a speech, play, television or radio show, or movie: *Bring your script to rehearsal.* **2** [C,U] the set of letters used in writing a language; ALPHABET: *Arabic script* **3** [singular, U] writing done by hand, especially so that the letters of the words are joined: *cursive script*

**script·ed** /ˈskrɪptɪd/ *adj* a scripted speech or broadcast has been planned and written down so that it can be read

**scrip·ture** /ˈskrɪptʃɚ/ *n* **1** [U] also **the (Holy) Scripture** the Bible **2** [C,U] the holy books of a particular religion –**scriptural** *adj*

**script·writ·er** /'skrɪpt,raɪtɚ/ n someone who writes SCRIPTs for movies, television programs etc.

**scroll**[1] /skroʊl/ n a long piece of paper that is rolled up and has official writing on it

**scroll**[2] v [I,T] to move information up or down a computer screen so that you can read it

**scrooge** /skrudʒ/ n INFORMAL someone who hates to spend money

**scro·tum** /'skroʊtəm/ n the bag of flesh on a man or male animal that contains the TESTICLEs

**scrounge** /skraʊndʒ/ v INFORMAL **1** [T] to get money or something you want by asking other people to give it to you instead of earning it or paying for it yourself: *Sarah was scrounging cigarettes off the guys all night.* **2** [I] to search for something such as food or supplies: *a sculpture built from materials scrounged from junkyards*

**scrub**[1] /skrʌb/ v **-bbed, -bbing** [I,T] to clean something by rubbing it very hard with a stiff brush or rough cloth: *Don't forget to scrub behind your ears.* | *scrub the floor*

**scrub**[2] n [U] low bushes and trees that grow in very dry soil

**scruff** /skrʌf/ n **by the scruff of the neck** if you hold an animal or person by the scruff of the neck, you hold the fur, flesh, or clothes at the back of his, her, or its neck: *The cat had a kitten by the scruff of its neck.*

**scruff·y** /'skrʌfi/ adj dirty and messy: *a scruffy kid*

**scrump·tious** /'skrʌmpʃəs/ adj INFORMAL food that is scrumptious tastes very good

**scrunch** /skrʌntʃ/ v
**scrunch** sth ↔ **up** phr v [T] to twist or crush something into a small shape: *He scrunched up his napkin.*

**scru·ple** /'skrupəl/ n [C usually plural] an idea of what is right and wrong, that prevents you from doing something that is considered bad: *He wondered if Gwen had any religious scruples about sex.*

**scru·pu·lous** /'skrupyələs/ adj **1** done very carefully so that every detail is correct: *his scrupulous attention to detail* **2** careful to be honest, fair, and morally correct: *He carried out his task with great care and scrupulous fairness.* **–scrupulously** adv **–opposite** UNSCRUPULOUS

**scru·ti·nize** /'skrutˈn,aɪz/ v [T] to examine someone or something very carefully and completely: *Sherman got out and scrutinized the fender.*

**scru·ti·ny** /'skrutˈn-i/ n [U] the process of examining something carefully and completely: *Closer scrutiny shows that the numbers don't add up.*

**scu·ba div·ing** /'skubə ,daɪvɪŋ/ n [U] the sport of swimming under water while breathing from a container of air on your back

**scuff** /skʌf/ v [T] to make a mark on a smooth surface by rubbing something rough against it: *I've already scuffed my new shoes.*

**scuf·fle** /'skʌfəl/ n a short fight that involves only a few people and is not very serious: *A policeman was injured in a scuffle with demonstrators yesterday.* **–scuffle** v [I,T]

**sculp·tor** /'skʌlptɚ/ n an artists who makes SCULPTUREs

**sculp·ture** /'skʌlptʃɚ/ n **1** [C,U] objects made from clay, wood, metal etc. as a form of art and often shaped like people or animals: *a bronze sculpture by Peter Helzer* **2** [U] the art of making these objects: *a sculpture class*

**sculp·tured** /'skʌlptʃɚd/ adj **1** decorated with SCULPTUREs: *the sculptured entrance of the church* **2 sculptured muscles/features etc.** muscles etc. that look like an artist shaped them because they are so smooth and perfect

**scum** /skʌm/ n **1** [singular, U] the thick messy substance that forms on the surface or at the bottom of a liquid: *Green scum covered the old pond.* **2** SPOKEN ⇨ SCUMBAG

**scum·bag** /'skʌmbæg/ n SPOKEN an unpleasant person that you do not like, trust, or respect: *What a scumbag!*

**scur·ri·lous** /'skɚ-ələs, 'skʌr-/ adj a scurrilous remark, article etc. contains untrue statements that are intended to make someone or something seem bad

**scur·ry** /'skɚi, 'skʌri/ v [I] to move very quickly with small steps: *squirrels scurrying around*

**scut·tle** /'skʌtl/ v **1** [T] INFORMAL to ruin someone's plans or chance of being successful: *Plans for the freeway have been scuttled due to lack of money.* **2** [I] to run quickly with small steps: *crabs scuttling along the beach* **3** [T] to sink a ship, especially in order to prevent it from being used by an enemy

**scythe** /saɪð/ n a farming tool with a long curved blade, used for cutting grain or long grass

**SD** the written abbreviation of South Dakota

**SE** the written abbreviation of SOUTHEAST

**sea** /si/ n **1** a large area of salty water that is smaller than an ocean, or that is enclosed by land: *the North Sea* | *the Mediterranean Sea* **2** a word meaning the ocean that is used when talking about traveling in a ship or boat: *The boat was heading out to sea.* (=traveling away from land) **3 a sea of** a large number or amount of something: *a sea of people* **4 the seas** LITERARY the ocean

**sea·bed** /'sibɛd/ n the land at the bottom of the sea

**sea·far·ing** /'si,fɛrɪŋ/ adj LITERARY relating to ships that travel in the ocean, and the people who work on them

**sea·food** /'sifud/ n [U] ocean animals such as fish and SHELLFISH that can be eaten

S

**sea·gull** /'sigʌl/ *n* a common gray and white bird that lives near the sea and has a loud cry

**sea·horse** /'sihɔrs/ *n* a small sea fish that has a head and neck that look like those of a horse

**seal**¹ /sil/ *n* **1** a large sea animal that has smooth fur, eats fish, and lives by the ocean in cold areas **2** an official mark that is put on documents, objects etc. in order to prove that they are legal or real: *The letter had the seal of the Department of Justice at the top.* **3** a piece of rubber or plastic used on a pipe, machine, container etc. in order to prevent something such as water or air from going into or out of it **4** a piece of WAX, plastic etc. that you break in order to open a new container: *Do not use this product if the seal on the bottle is broken.* **5 seal of approval** if you give something your seal of approval, you say that you accept or approve of it, especially officially: *The board denied the film its seal of approval.*

**seal**² *v* [T] **1** also **seal up** to close an entrance, container, or hole so tightly that no air, water etc. can go into or out of it: *Many of the tombs have remained sealed since the 16th century.* **2** to close an envelope, package etc. using something sticky, such as TAPE or glue **3 seal a deal/agreement etc.** to do something that makes a promise, agreement etc. seem more definite or official: *Everything is finished - we just have to seal the deal with our signatures.*

**seal sth ↔ in** *phr v* [T] to stop something from going out of the thing it is contained in: *Our hamburgers are flame-grilled to **seal in** freshness and flavor.*

**seal sth ↔ off** *phr v* [T] to stop people entering a particular area or building, especially because it is dangerous. *Soldiers **sealed off** the area after the recent bombing.*

**sealed** /sild/ *adj* something that is sealed is completely closed and cannot be opened unless it is broken, cut, or torn: *a sealed envelope | a sealed window*

**sea lev·el** /'. ,../ *n* [U] the average level of the sea, used as a standard for measuring the height of an area of land, such as a mountain: *200 feet above sea level*

**sea li·on** /'. ,../ *n* a large type of SEAL that lives on the coasts of the Pacific Ocean

**seam** /sim/ *n* **1** the line where two pieces of cloth have been sewn together: *His jacket was ripped at the shoulder seams.* **2** a layer of a mineral, such as coal, that is under the ground **3** the line where two pieces of metal, wood etc. have been joined together

**sea·man, Seaman** /'simən/ *n* someone who has the lowest rank in the Navy

**seam·less** /'simlɪs/ *adj* **1** done or made so well, that you do not notice where one part ends and another part begins: *The show is a seamless blend of song, dance, and storytelling.* **2** not having any SEAMs: *seamless stockings*

**seam·stress** /'simstrɪs/ *n* a woman whose job is to make and sew clothes

**seam·y** /'simi/ *adj* unpleasant and involving crime, violence, POVERTY, or immoral behavior: *the seamy streets of the city*

**sé·ance** /'seɪɑns/ *n* a meeting where people try to talk to the spirits of dead people, or to receive messages from them

**sea plane** /'. ./ *n* a plane that can land on water

**sear** /sɪr/ *v* [T] **1** to burn something with a sudden very strong heat: *The heat from the fire seared her skin.* **2** to cook the outside of a piece of meat quickly at a very high temperature **–searing** *adj*

**search**¹ /sɚtʃ/ *n* **1** [C] an attempt to find someone or something that is difficult to find: *Police **called off** the **search for** (=officially stopped looking for) the missing girl. | Denise went off **in search of** a hammer.* **2** [singular] an attempt to find the answer to or explanation of a difficult problem: *He traveled around the world **in search of** the truth.*

**search**² *v* [I,T] to look carefully for someone or something that is difficult to find: *I searched all over the house, but I couldn't find them anywhere. | animals searching for food* **2** [T] if the police etc. search someone, they look in his/her pockets, clothes, or bags for guns, drugs etc.: *We were all **searched** at the airport.* **3** [I] to try to find an answer or explanation for a difficult problem: *Scientists have spent years **searching for** a solution.*

**search·ing** /'sɚtʃɪŋ/ *adj* trying hard to find out details, facts, or someone's feelings and thoughts: *He gave me a searching look. | searching questions*

**search·light** /'sɚtʃlaɪt/ *n* a large bright light used for finding people, vehicles etc. at night

**search par·ty** /'. ,../ *n* a group of people organized to look for someone who is lost

**search war·rant** /'. ,../ *n* a legal document that officially allows the police to search a building

**sea·shell** /'siʃɛl/ *n* the shell that covers some types of ocean animals

**sea·shore** /'siʃɔr/ *n* [U] **the seashore** the land along the edge of the ocean –compare BEACH –see usage note at SHORE

**sea·sick** /'si,sɪk/ *adj* feeling sick because of the movement of a boat or ship **–seasickness** *n* [U]

**sea·side** /'sisaɪd/ *adj* relating to the land next to the sea or the ocean: *a seaside inn*

**sea·son**¹ /'sizən/ *n* **1** one of the four main periods in the year; winter, spring, summer, or fall **2** a period of time in a year when something happens most often or when something is usually done: *The **rainy/wet season** usually starts in May. | It's **football/baseball/basketball season**. (=the period when football etc. is played regularly) | *Everything gets so busy during the* *holiday season.* (=the period from Thanksgiving to New Year's) **3 be in season** if particular vegetables or fruit are in season, it is the time of year when they are ready to be eaten **4 out of season** if someone hunts or catches fish out of season, s/he is doing it when it is not legal

**season²** *v* [T] to add salt, pepper etc. to food in order to make it taste better: *The salad was seasoned with fresh herbs.*

**sea·son·a·ble** /ˈsiznəbəl/ *adj* **seasonable weather/temperatures** weather that seems typical for a particular season −opposite UNSEASONABLE

**sea·son·al** /ˈsizənəl/ *adj* only happening, available, or needed during a particular season: *Jim hires high school kids for seasonal help at the farm.*

**sea·soned** /ˈsizənd/ *adj* **seasoned soldier/ lawyer/dancer etc.** someone who has had a lot of experience as a soldier etc.: *Even the seasoned professionals were impressed by her speech.*

**sea·son·ing** /ˈsizənɪŋ/ *n* [C,U] salt, pepper, SPICEs etc. that you add to food to make it taste better

**S**

**season tick·et** /ˌ.. ˈ../ *n* a ticket that allows you to go on a trip, go to a theater, watch a sports team etc. as often as you want during a period of time

**seat¹** /sit/ *n* **1** something such as a BENCH or chair that you can sit on, especially one in a restaurant, plane, or theater: *I think I left my sweater **in the front/back seat** of Mom's car.* | *We had great seats at the Giants game.* −see picture at ROW¹ **2 take/have a seat** to sit down: *Please take a seat, Ms. Carson.* **3** the part of a chair, bicycle etc. that you sit on **4** a position as a member of the government or a group that makes official decisions: *The Republican Party won two more seats in the Senate.* **5 seat of learning/government etc.** FORMAL a place, usually a city, where a university or government is based −see also **take a back seat** (BACK SEAT)

**seat²** *v* [T] **1 be seated a)** to be sitting down: *Schultz was seated next to the President throughout the speech.* **b)** SPOKEN FORMAL used in order to politely ask someone to sit down: *Would everyone please be seated.* **2 seat yourself** to sit down somewhere: *Seating himself on a nearby chair, he asked, "So how can I help?"* **3** to make someone sit in a particular place: *The hostess will seat you soon.* **4** if a room, vehicle, theater etc. seats a particular number of people, it has enough seats for that number: *The new Olympic stadium seats over 70,000.*

**seat belt** /ˈ. ./ *n* a strong belt attached to the seat of a car or plane, that you fasten around yourself for protection in an accident: *Please fasten your seat belts.* −see picture on page 469

**seat·ing** /ˈsitɪŋ/ *n* [U] seats that are available or arranged in a particular way: *Have you made the **seating arrangements/plans** for your wedding reception yet?* (=planned where people will sit)

**sea ur·chin** /ˈ. ˌ../ *n* a small round sea animal that is covered with sharp points

**sea·weed** /ˈsiwid/ *n* [U] a common plant that grows in the ocean

**sec** /sɛk/ *n* SPOKEN a short form of "second": *Wait a sec - I'm coming too!*

**se·cede** /sɪˈsid/ *v* [I] FORMAL to formally stop being part of a country, especially because of a disagreement: *The southern states wanted to **secede from** from the US in the 1850s.* −**secession** /sɪˈsɛʃən/ *n* [singular, U]

**se·clud·ed** /sɪˈkludɪd/ *adj* very private and quiet: *a relaxing vacation on a secluded island*

**se·clu·sion** /sɪˈkluʒən/ *n* [U] the state of being private and away from other people: *He lives **in seclusion** inside the old castle.*

**sec·ond¹** /ˈsɛkənd/ *number, pron* **1** 2nd; someone or something that is after the first one: *Debbie **came in second** in the women's marathon.* (=was the one after the winner in a race) | *September 2nd* (=second day of September) **2 be second to none** to be better than anyone or anything else: *The service in that hotel is second to none.*

**second²** *n* **1** a period of time equal to $\frac{1}{60}$ of a minute: *It takes about 30 seconds for the computer to start up.* **2** SPOKEN a very short period of time: *I'll be off the phone **in a second!*** | *Wait **just a second**.*

**sec·ond·ar·y** /ˈsɛkənˌdɛri/ *adj* **1** not as important or valuable as something else: *For many students, academic life is secondary.* **2** developing from something of the same type, or coming from it: *a secondary infection*

**secondary school** /ˈ.... ˌ./ *n* a school in the US or Canada that children go to after ELEMENTARY SCHOOL and before college

**second base** /ˌ.. ˈ./ *n* [singular] in baseball, the second place that a player must touch before s/he can gain a point −see picture on page 472

**second class** /ˌ.. ˈ./ *n* [U] a way of traveling, especially on trains, that is cheaper but not as comfortable as FIRST CLASS

**second-class** /ˌ.. ˈ.◂/ *adj* **1** considered to be less important than other people or things: *They treated us like **second-class citizens**.* (=people who are not as important as other people in society) **2** relating to cheaper and less comfortable seats on a train, bus etc.: *second-class tickets*

**second-guess** /ˌ.. ˈ./ *v* [T] **1** to criticize something after it has already happened: *There's no point in second-guessing what should have been done.* **2** to try to guess what will happen, or to say what someone will do before s/he does it: *You have to try to second-guess the other team's moves.*

**second·hand** /ˌ.. '.◂/ *adj* **1** secondhand clothes, furniture, books etc. have already been owned or used by someone else: *We bought a cheap secondhand car.* **2** a secondhand report, information etc. is something that you are told by someone different than the person who originally said it –**secondhand** /ˌ.. '../ *adv*

**sec·ond·ly** /'sɛkəndli/ *adv* used in order to introduce the second fact, reason etc. that you want to talk about: *And secondly, a large number of her poems deal with love.*

**second na·ture** /ˌ.. '../ *n* [U] something you have done so often that you now do it without thinking a lot about it: *After you get used to driving a car, it becomes second nature.*

**second per·son** /ˌ.. '../ *n* [singular] TECHNICAL in grammar, a form of a verb or PRONOUN that you use to show the person you are speaking to. "You" is a second person pronoun, "you are" is the second person singular of the verb "to be"

**second-rate** /ˌ.. '.◂/ *adj* not very good: *second-rate hospitals*

**sec·onds** /'sɛkəndz/ *n* [plural] **1** another serving of the same food after you have eaten your first serving: *Would anyone like seconds?* **2** goods sold cheaply because they are not perfect: *factory seconds*

**second wind** /ˌsɛkənd 'wɪnd/ *n* [singular] a feeling of energy that you get after you have been working or exercising very hard, so that you thought you were too tired to continue: *Susan got her second wind in the last lap of the race.*

**se·cre·cy** /'sikrəsi/ *n* [U] the act of keeping something such as information secret, or the state of being secret: *They had to meet in secrecy because of the war.*

**se·cret**[1] /'sikrɪt/ *adj* known about by only a few people: *I can't believe you've kept your wedding secret from your parents.* (=did not tell them about it) | *secret government files* –**secretly** *adv*

**secret**[2] *n* an idea, plan, fact etc. that you try to hide because you do not want everyone to know about it: *Can you keep a secret?* (=not tell a secret)

**secret a·gent** /ˌ.. '../ *n* someone who secretly collects information or watches people for a government

**sec·re·tar·y** /'sɛkrəˌtɛri/ *n* **1** someone whose job is to TYPE letters, keep records, arrange meetings, answer telephones etc. in an office **2** an official who is in charge of a large government department in the US: *the Secretary of Defense* **3** an official in an organization whose job is to write down notes from meetings, write letters etc.: *Julie was elected secretary of the poetry club.* –**secretarial** /ˌsɛkrə'tɛriəl/ *adj*

**se·crete** /sɪ'krit/ *v* [T] **1** if part of a plant or animal secretes a substance, it produces that substance: *The animal secretes a scent to keep attackers away.* **2** FORMAL to hide something –**secretion** /sɪ'kriʃən/ *n* [C,U]

**se·cre·tive** /'sikrətɪv/ *adj* behaving in a way that shows you do not want to tell people your thoughts, plans etc.

**secret serv·ice** /ˌ.. '../ *n* **the Secret Service** a US government department whose main purpose is to protect the President

**sect** /sɛkt/ *n* a group of people with its own set of beliefs or religious habits, especially one that has separated from a larger group

**sec·tar·i·an** /sɛk'tɛriən/ *adj* supporting a particular religious group and its beliefs, or relating to the differences between religious groups: *sectarian violence* –opposite NON-SECTARIAN

**sec·tion**[1] /'sɛkʃən/ *n* **1** one of the parts that an object, group, place etc. is divided into: *the poorer sections of Brooklyn* | *Does this restaurant have a smoking section?* | *The rocket is built in sections.* (=in parts that are then fitted together) **2** one of the parts of a book or newspaper: *Are you still reading the sports section?* –**sectional** *adj*

**section**[2] *v* [T] TECHNICAL to cut or draw a SECTION of something such as a part of the body or a building

**section sth off** *phr v* [T] to divide an area into SECTIONs: *The old part of the graveyard had been sectioned off by trees.*

**sec·tor** /'sɛktɚ/ *n* **1** a part of a particular economic system, such as a business, industry, or trade: *the public/private sector of the health industry* (=the part controlled by the government or by private companies) **2** one of the parts that an area is divided into for military purposes: *the former eastern sector of Berlin*

**sec·u·lar** /'sɛkyələ/ *adj* not religious or not controlled by a religious authority: *secular universities*

**se·cure**[1] /sɪ'kyʊr/ *adj* **1** not likely to change or be at risk: *a secure job* **2** safe and protected from danger: *The garage isn't a very secure place.* **3** fastened, locked, or guarded: *He made sure the knife was secure on his belt.* **4** confident and having no doubts or worries: *financially secure* (=not needing to worry about having enough money)

**secure**[2] *v* [T] **1** to get or achieve something important, especially after a lot of effort: *a treaty designed to secure peace* **2** to make something safe from being attacked or harmed: *Armed forces were called out to secure the border.* **3** to fasten or tie something tightly in a particular position: *We secured the boat and jumped onto the rocks.*

**se·cu·ri·ty** /sɪ'kyʊrəti/ *n* [U] **1** the state of being safe, or the things you do to keep someone or something safe: *national security* | *Allow plenty of time for airport security checks.* **2** protection from change, risks, or bad situations: *the security of working for a large, powerful corporation* | *economic security* **3** the guards who protect a business's buildings, equipment, and workers: *Security is coming over to check the area.* **4** a feeling of being safe and protected: *Rules and order can give a child a sense of security.*

**se·cu·ri·ty de·pos·it** /.'... .,../ *n* an amount of money you give to a LANDLORD before you move into a place, that will be returned to you later if you do not damage his/her property

**se·dan** /sɪˈdæn/ *n* a large car that has seats for at least four people and has a TRUNK — see picture on page 469

**se·date** /sɪˈdeɪt/ *adj* slow, formal, or not very exciting: *his calm sedate manner*

**se·dat·ed** /sɪˈdeɪt̬ɪd/ *adj* made sleepy or calm by being given a special drug

**sed·a·tive** /ˈsɛdət̬ɪv/ *n* a drug used in order to make someone sleepy or calm

**sed·en·tar·y** /ˈsɛdn̩ˌtɛri/ *adj* a sedentary job involves sitting down or not moving very much

**sed·i·ment** /ˈsɛdəmənt/ *n* [singular, U] the solid material, such as dirt, that settles at the bottom of a liquid

**sed·i·men·ta·ry** /ˌsɛdəˈmɛntri, -ˈmɛnt̬əri/ *adj* made of the SEDIMENT at the bottom of lakes, oceans etc.: *sedimentary rock*

**se·di·tion** /sɪˈdɪʃən/ *n* [U] FORMAL speech, writing, or actions that try to encourage people to disobey a government — **seditious** *adj*

**se·duce** /sɪˈdus/ *v* [T] to persuade someone to do something, especially to have sex, by making it seem extremely attractive: *It's the story of a teenage girl who seduces an older man.* — **seduction** /sɪˈdʌkʃən/ *n* [C,U]

**se·duc·tive** /sɪˈdʌktɪv/ *adj* **1** sexually attractive: *a woman with a seductive voice* **2** very attractive to you: *a seductive job offer*

**see** /si/ *v* **saw, seen, seeing**
**1** ▶USE EYES◀ [I,T] to use your eyes to notice people or things: *I can't see without my glasses.* | *I saw a necklace I really liked at the mall.* | *He's seen "Star Wars" about eight times.*
**2** ▶UNDERSTAND◀ [I,T] to understand or realize something: *Do you see how it works?* | *I can see (that) Yolanda might not like it.* | *(You) see, she's not really old enough for this book yet.* (=used when you are explaining something to someone) | *"It goes in the red box." "Oh, I see."* (=I understand) | *At 14, he couldn't see the* **point of** (=understand the reason) *staying in school.* | *Do you see what I mean about the camera being broken?*
**3** ▶VISIT/MEET◀ [T] to visit, meet, or have a meeting with someone: *I saw BJ the other day.* | *You ought to see a doctor.*
**4** ▶FIND OUT◀ [T] to find out information or

a fact: *Plug it in and see if it's working.* | *I'll see what's playing at the movie theater.* | *I guess we'll have to wait and see what happens.*
**5** ▶CONSIDER◀ [T] to consider someone or something in a particular way: *Fights on TV can make children see violence as normal.* | *He sees himself as the next John Wayne.* | *Well, the way I see it, that school is no worse than any other.*
**6** ▶EXPERIENCE◀ [T] to have experience of something: *The attorney said he had never seen a case like this before.*
**7** ▶HAPPEN◀ [T] to be the time when or place where something happens: *This year has seen a 5% increase in burglaries.*
**8** ▶THINK◀ [I,T] to think something, especially about what is going to happen in the future: *We were supposed to have a vacation in May, but I don't see that happening.*
**9** ▶MAKE SURE◀ [T] to make sure or check that something is done correctly: *Please see that everything is put back where it belongs.*
**10 be seeing sb** to be having a romantic relationship with someone
**11 see eye to eye** to agree with someone: *My mother and I have never seen eye to eye about things.*

---

SPOKEN PHRASES
**12 see you** used in order to say goodbye to someone you will meet again: *Okay, I'll see you.* (=later) | *See you, Ben.*
**13 let's see/let me see** said when you are trying to remember something or think about something: *Let's see. Was it a week ago I talked to you?*
**14 I don't see why not** said when you mean yes: *"Would that be legal?" "I don't see why not."*
**15 I'll/we'll see** said when you do not want to make a decision immediately, especially when you are talking to a child: *"Can we go to Disney World this year?" "We'll see."*
**16 you should have seen sb/sth** said when you think someone or something you have seen was very funny, surprising etc.: *You should've seen the look on her face!*

---

— see also **see clear to sth** (CLEAR³)

**see about** sth *phr v* [T] **1** to make arrangements or deal with something: *Tran went to see about a job.* **2 we'll see about that** SPOKEN said when you intend to stop someone doing something s/he has planned: *"I'm going to Tim's." "We'll see about that. I need help with dinner."*

**see** sb ↔ **off** *phr v* [T] to go to an airport, station etc. to say goodbye to someone who is leaving: *The soldiers were seen off by friends and relatives.*

**see** sb **out** *phr v* [T] to go with someone to the door when s/he leaves: *No, that's okay, I'll see myself out.* (=go by myself to the door)

**see through** phr v [T] **1** [see through sb/sth] to be able to recognize the truth when someone is trying to persuade or deceive you: *I can see right through his lies.* **2** [see sb/sth through] to continue doing something difficult until it is finished, or to continue helping someone during a difficult time: *Miller is determined to see the project through.* | *Mom was always there to help see me through.*

**see to** sth phr v [T] to deal with something or make sure that it happens: *"We'll see to it that he does well," said Coach Green.*

> **USAGE NOTE see, look, and watch**
>
> **See** is a general word that means "to notice something with your eyes": *I can't see any signs for the highway.* Use **look** when someone deliberately turns his/her eyes toward someone or something and pays attention to him, her, or it: *Look at all the balloons!* Use **watch** for activities or programs that you pay attention to for a period of time: *Jeff's watching the game on TV.*

**seed**[1] /sid/ n, plural **seed** or **seeds 1** [C,U] a small hard object produced by plants, from which a new plant will grow: *an apple seed* **2 (the) seeds of sth** the beginning of something that will grow and develop: *He was able to sow the seeds of doubt in the minds of the jury.*

**seed**[2] v [T] to plant seeds in the ground

**seed·ling** /'sidlɪŋ/ n a young plant grown from seed

**seed·y** /'sidi/ adj INFORMAL looking dirty or poor, and often being related to illegal or immoral activity: *the seedy side of town*

**see·ing** /'siɪŋ/ conjunction because a particular fact or situation is true: *You can stay out later tonight, seeing that/as it's the weekend.*

**seeing eye dog** /ˌ.. '. ˌ./ n a dog that is trained to guide blind people

**seek** /sik/ v **sought, sought, seeking 1** [I,T] to try to find or get something: *The UN is seeking a political solution to the crisis.* **2** [T] FORMAL to try to achieve or do something: *The Governor will not say whether he will seek re-election next year.* **3 seek advice/help etc.** FORMAL to ask someone for advice, help etc.

**seem** /sim/ v [linking verb] **1** to appear to be a particular thing or to have a particular quality or feeling: *Henry seems very confused.* | *There seems to be a problem with the brakes.* | *The dream seemed very real to me.* **2** to appear to exist or be true: *We seem to have turned onto the wrong road.*

**seem·ing** /'simɪŋ/ adj FORMAL appearing to be true even though it may not be: *her seeming calm* −compare APPARENT

**seem·ing·ly** /'simɪŋli/ adv in a way that

appears to be true but may not be: *a seemingly endless stretch of land* −compare APPARENTLY

**seen** /sin/ v the PAST PARTICIPLE of SEE

**seep** /sip/ v [I] to flow slowly through small holes or cracks: *Water was seeping through the ceiling.* −**seepage** n [singular, U]

**see·saw**[1] /'sisɔ/ n a long board on which children play, that is balanced in the middle so that when one end goes up the other end goes down

**seesaw**[2] v [I] to move suddenly up and down or from one condition to another and back again: *Stock prices seesawed throughout the morning.*

**seethe** /sið/ v [I] to be so angry that you are almost shaking: *Holly was seething with rage.* −**seething** adj

**seg·ment** /'sɛgmənt/ n a part of something that is divided from the whole: *a large segment of the population* | *an orange segment*

**seg·ment·ed** /'sɛgmɛntɪd/ adj divided into separate parts: *the segmented body of an insect*

**seg·re·gate** /'sɛgrəˌgeɪt/ v [T] to separate one group of people from others because of race, sex, religion etc.: *The Group Areas Act segregated housing along racial lines.* −**segregation** /ˌsɛgrəˈgeɪʃən/ n [U] −compare INTEGRATE

**seg·re·gat·ed** /'sɛgrəˌgeɪtɪd/ adj segregated buildings or areas can only be used by members of a particular race, sex, religion etc.: *racially segregated schools*

**seis·mic** /'saɪzmɪk/ adj TECHNICAL relating to or caused by EARTHQUAKEs: *a period of seismic activity*

**seis·mol·o·gy** /ˌsaɪzˈmɑlədʒi/ n [U] the scientific study of EARTHQUAKEs −**seismologist** n

**seize** /siz/ v **1** [T] to take hold of something quickly and forcefully; GRAB: *Ron seized the child's arm and lifted her into the boat.* **2 seize control/power** to take control of a place suddenly using military force: *Rebels seized control of the embassy.* **3** [T] to take away something such as illegal guns, drugs etc.: *Police seized 10 kilos of cocaine.*

**sei·zure** /'siʒɚ/ n **1** [U] the act of taking control or possession of something suddenly: *the seizure of illegal firearms* **2** a short time when someone is unconscious and cannot control the movements of his/her body: *an epileptic seizure*

**sel·dom** /'sɛldəm/ adv very rarely: *Glenn seldom eats breakfast.*

**se·lect**[1] /sɪˈlɛkt/ v [T] to choose something or someone: *Regina was selected to read her story first.*

**select**[2] adj FORMAL consisting of or used by a small group of specially chosen people: *a select club*

**se·lec·tion** /sɪˈlɛkʃən/ n **1** [C,U] the act of choosing something or someone, or the thing or person that is chosen: *Would you care to* **make** *a* **selection** *from our dessert tray?* **2** a collection of things, especially things for sale: *a store with a wide selection of jewelry*

**se·lec·tive** /sɪˈlɛktɪv/ *adj* careful about what you choose to do, buy etc.: *She's very selective about what kind of clothes she wears.*

**self** /sɛlf/ *n, plural* **selves** [C,U] the type of person you are, including your character, abilities etc.: *He's starting to feel* **like his old self** *again.* (=feel normal again, after feeling bad or sick) | *trying to develop a child's sense of self*

**self-ab·sorbed** /ˌ. .ˈ.◂/ *adj* so concerned about yourself or your own problems that you forget about other people

**self-ap·point·ed** /ˌ. .ˈ..◂/ *adj* thinking that you are the best person to do something when you are not: *a self-appointed guardian of morality*

**self-as·sured** /ˌ. .ˈ.◂/ *adj* confident about what you are doing −**self-assurance** *n* [U]

**self-cen·tered** /ˌ. ˈ..◂/ *adj* interested only in yourself and never caring about other people; SELFISH: *You're acting like a self-centered child.*

**self-con·fi·dent** /ˌ. ˈ...◂/ *adj* being confident in your abilities, appearance etc., and not shy or nervous with people −**self-confidence** *n* [U]

**self-con·scious** /ˌ. ˈ..◂/ *adj* worried and embarrassed about what you look like or what other people think of you: *She feels self-conscious about wearing glasses.*

**self-con·tained** /ˌ. .ˈ.◂/ *adj* complete in itself and not needing other things to make it work: *a self-contained economy*

**self-con·trol** /ˌ. .ˈ./ *n* [U] the ability to control your feelings and behavior even when you are angry, excited, or upset: *His lack of self-control caused problems in the classroom.*

**self-de·feat·ing** /ˌ. .ˈ..◂/ *adj* making a situation have a bad result for you: *He made several self-defeating statements during the interview.*

**self-de·fense** /ˌ. .ˈ./ *n* [U] the use of force to protect yourself from attack: *She shot the man* **in self-defense**.

**self-de·ni·al** /ˌ. .ˈ../ *n* [U] the practice of not having or doing the things that you enjoy, either because you cannot afford it or for moral or religious reasons

**self-de·struc·tive** /ˌ. .ˈ..◂/ *adj* self-destructive actions are likely to harm or kill the person who is doing them

**self-dis·ci·pline** /ˌ. ˈ.../ *n* [U] the ability to make yourself do the things that you ought to do without someone else making you do them −**self-disciplined** *adj*

**self-em·ployed** /ˌ. .ˈ.◂/ *adj* working for yourself rather than for a company

**self-es·teem** /ˌ. .ˈ./ *n* [U] the feeling that you are someone who deserves to be liked, respected, and admired

**self-ev·i·dent** /ˌ. ˈ...◂/ *adj* clearly true and needing no proof; OBVIOUS

**self-ex·plan·a·to·ry** /ˌ. .ˈ..../ *adj* clear and easy to understand, with no need for explanation: *The instructions are self-explanatory.*

**self-ful·fil·ling proph·e·cy** /ˌ. .ˌ.. ˈ../ *n* a statement about what will happen in the future, that becomes true because you changed your behavior to make it happen

**self-help** /ˌ. ˈ./ *n* the use of your own efforts to deal with your problems instead of depending on other people

**self-i·mage** /ˌ. ˈ../ *n* the idea that you have of your own abilities, appearance, and character: *a man with a* **poor self-image**

**self-im·por·tant** /ˌ. .ˈ..◂/ *adj* thinking you are more important than other people

**self-im·prove·ment** /ˌ. .ˈ../ *n* [U] the activity of trying to learn more skills or to deal with your problems better

**self-in·dul·gent** /ˌ. .ˈ..◂/ *adj* allowing yourself to have or enjoy something that you do not need: *spoiled self-indulgent teenagers* −**self-indulgence** *n* [singular, U]

**self-in·flict·ed** /ˌ. .ˈ..◂/ *adj* a self-inflicted injury, problem etc. is one that you have caused yourself: *a self-inflicted gunshot wound*

**self-in·terest** /ˌ. ˈ../ *n* [U] concern for what is best for you rather than for other people: *It's* **in** *the employer's* **self-interest** *to help employees with health care.*

**self·ish** /ˈsɛlfɪʃ/ *adj* caring only about yourself rather than about other people: *a selfish and ambitious man* −**selfishness** *n* [U] −**selfishly** *adv* −opposite UNSELFISH

**self·less** /ˈsɛlflɪs/ *adj* caring about other people more than about yourself

**self-made** /ˌ. ˈ.◂/ *adj* successful and wealthy because of your own efforts: *a self-made millionaire*

**self-pit·y** /ˌ. ˈ../ *n* [U] the feeling of being too sorry for yourself: *Ryan was always patient and never gave in to self-pity.*

**self-por·trait** /ˌ. ˈ../ *n* a picture that you make of yourself

**self-pos·sessed** /ˌ. .ˈ.◂/ *adj* calm and confident because you are in control of your feelings

**self-pres·er·va·tion** /ˌ. ..ˈ../ *n* [U] keeping yourself from being harmed or killed: *White had a strong* **instinct for self-preservation**.

**self-re·li·ance** /ˌ. .ˈ../ *n* [U] the ability to act and make decisions by yourself without depending on other people −**self-reliant** *adj*

**self-re·spect** /ˌ. .ˈ./ *n* [U] a feeling of confidence and pride in your abilities, ideas, and character −**self-respecting** *adj*: *No self-respecting union would give up its right to strike.*

**self·re·straint** /ˌ. .ˈ./ *n* [U] the ability to control what you do or say in situations that upset you

**self·right·eous** /ˌ. ˈ../ *adj* too proud and sure that your beliefs, attitudes etc. are right, in a way that annoys other people

**self·sac·ri·fice** /ˌ. ˈ.../ *n* [U] the act of giving up what you need or want in order to help someone else –**self-sacrificing** *adj*

**self·sat·is·fied** /ˌ. ˈ.../ *adj* → SMUG

**self·seek·ing** /ˌ. ˈ.. / *adj* doing things only to get an advantage for yourself: *a dishonest and self-seeking politician*

**self·serv·ice** /ˌ. ˈ..◂ /, **self serve** /ˌ. ˈ./ *adj* used in order to describe places where you get things for yourself, rather than being served: *a self-service gas station*

**self·start·er** /ˌ. ˈ../ *n* someone who is able to work without needing other people's help or a lot of instructions

**self·styled** /ˌ. ˈ.◂ / *adj* having given yourself a title, position etc. without having a right to it: *a self-styled computer expert*

**self·suf·fi·cient** /ˌ. .ˈ..◂ / *adj* able to provide for all your needs without help from other people: *a country that is self-sufficient in food production* –**self-sufficiency** *n* [U]

**self·sup·port·ing** /ˌ. .ˈ..◂ / *adj* able to earn enough money to support yourself: *a self-supporting museum*

**sell** /sɛl/ *v* **sold, sold, selling** **1** [I,T] to give something in exchange for money: *We sold the car for $5000. | Scott wants to sell his stereo to me.* –compare BUY¹ **2** [T] to offer something for people to buy: *Do you sell oriental rugs?* **3** [T] to make someone want to buy something: *Sensational headlines are what sell newspapers.* **4** [I] to be bought by people in large numbers or amounts: *Toys based on the movie are really selling.* **5** [I,T] to try to make someone accept a new plan, idea etc., or to become accepted: *Now we have to try to sell Monica on the idea.* **6** **sell yourself short** INFORMAL to not have the confidence in your abilities that you should have, so that you do not take advantage of opportunities

**sell** sth ↔ **off** *phr v* [T] to sell a large number of things because you need the money: *They're selling off her paintings in an auction today.*

**sell out** *phr v* [I] **1** to sell all of what was for sale so that there is none left: *I'm sorry, but the tickets are all sold out.* **2** INFORMAL to do something that is against your beliefs or principles, in order to get power or money: *Neil accused him of selling out to big business.*

**sell up** *phr v* [I] to sell everything you have because you want the money: *The Martins eventually sold up and moved to Florida.*

**sell·er** /ˈsɛlɚ/ *n* **1** a person or company that sells something: *the largest seller of microwave ovens* –compare BUYER **2** **good/best/biggest**

etc. **seller** a product that a company sells a lot of: *The multi-CD player is our biggest seller.*

**sell·ing point** /ˈ.. ˌ./ *n* a special feature of a product that will make people want to buy it

**sell·out** /ˈsɛlaʊt/ *n* [singular] **1** a performance, sports event etc. for which all the tickets have been sold: *a sellout crowd of 45,769* **2** INFORMAL a situation in which someone does something that is against his/her beliefs or principles, especially in order to get power or money: *Some people may call the deal a sellout.*

**selves** /sɛlvz/ *n* the plural of SELF

**se·man·tics** /səˈmæntɪks/ *n* [U] the study of the meaning of words –**semantic** *adj*

**sem·blance** /ˈsɛmbləns/ *n* a condition or quality that is at least slightly like another one: *I'm just trying to create some semblance of order here.*

**se·men** /ˈsimən/ *n* [U] the liquid that is produced by the male sex organs and contains SPERM

**se·mes·ter** /səˈmɛstɚ/ *n* one of two periods into which a year at school or college is divided –compare QUARTER

**sem·i·cir·cle** /ˈsɛmiˌsɚkəl/ *n* **1** half a circle **2** a group arranged in a curved line: *Could everyone please sit in a semicircle?* (=sit in a curved line)

**sem·i·co·lon** /ˈsɛmiˌkoʊlən/ *n* the mark (;) used in writing to separate independent parts of a sentence or list

**sem·i·con·duct·or** /ˈ.. .ˌ../ *n* a substance such as SILICON that is used in electronic equipment to allow electricity to pass through it

**sem·i·fi·nal** /ˈsɛmiˌfaɪnl, ˈsɛmaɪ-, ˌsɛmiˈfaɪnl/ *n* one of two sports games whose winners then compete against each other to decide who wins the whole competition –compare QUARTERFINAL

**sem·i·nal** /ˈsɛmənəl/ *adj* new and important, and influencing the way something develops in the future: *a seminal book | seminal research*

**sem·i·nar** /ˈsɛməˌnɑr/ *n* a short course or a special meeting that people attend in order to study a particular subject: *a seminar on teaching English in China | a series of management seminars*

**sem·i·nary** /ˈsɛməˌnɛri/ *n* a college at which people study religion and can train to be priests or ministers

**sem·i·pre·cious** /ˌsɛmiˈprɛʃəs◂ / *adj* a semiprecious jewel or stone is valuable, but not as valuable as a DIAMOND or RUBY

**Se·mit·ic** /səˈmɪtɪk/ *adj* relating to the race of people that includes Jews, Arabs, and other ancient peoples from the Middle East

**sen·ate** /ˈsɛnɪt/ *n* **the Senate** the smaller of the two groups of people who make the laws in countries such as the US and Australia –compare HOUSE OF REPRESENTATIVES

**sen·a·tor, Senator** /'sɛnətɚ/ *n* a member of the Senate: *Senator Feinstein* —**senatorial** /ˌsɛnə'tɔriəl/ *adj*

**send** /sɛnd/ *v* **sent, sent, sending** [T] **1** to arrange for something to go or be taken to another place, especially by mail: *Have you **sent** the bank **a letter** yet?* | *Valerie's asking us to send her more money.* **2** to make someone go somewhere: *The UN is **sending** troops **to** the region.* | *We all got **sent** home from school at noon.* | *If anyone knocks, please **send** them **away**.* **3** to arrange for someone to go somewhere and stay there: *Morrison was **sent to** jail for five years.* **4 send your love/best wishes etc.** to ask someone to give your greetings, good wishes etc. to someone else: *Mark sends his love.* **5** to make someone or something do something: *A shortage of oil **sent** prices **up** this week.* (=made them increase) | *The blast **sent** people running for safety.* **6** INFORMAL to make someone feel happy: *Oh, doesn't his music just **send you**?*

**send away for** sth *phr v* [T] to order something through the mail: *I **sent away for** a pair of sandals.*

**send** sth ↔ **down** *phr v* [T] to make something lose value: *The news **sent** the price of gold **down**.*

**send for** sb/sth *phr v* [T] to ask or order someone to come to you, or that something be brought or mailed to you: *An ambulance was **sent for**, but it was too late.* | *Send now **for** your free catalog.*

**send in** *phr v* [T] **1** [**send** sth ↔ **in**] to send something, usually by mail, to a place where it can be dealt with: *Did you **send in** your application?* **2** [**send** sb ↔ **in**] to send soldiers, police etc. somewhere to deal with a dangerous situation: *Finally, the mayor had to **send in** the police.*

**send off** *phr v* [T] **1** [**send** sth ↔ **off**] to mail something somewhere: *Riley **sent off** copies to everyone in the family.* **2** [**send** sb ↔ **off**] to make someone go somewhere: *We got **sent off** to camp every summer.*

**send** sb/sth ↔ **out** *phr v* [T] to make something or someone go from one place to various other places: *The wedding invitations were **sent out** weeks ago.*

**send-off** /'. ./ *n* INFORMAL an occasion when people gather together to say goodbye to someone who is leaving: *We wanted to **give** you a big send-off.*

**se·nile** /'sinaɪl/ *adj* mentally confused or behaving strangely, because of old age —**senility** /sɪ'nɪləti/ *n* [U]

**Se·nior** /'sinyɚ/ written abbreviation **Sr.** *adj* used after the name of a man who has the same name as his son: *Robert Burrelli, Sr.* —compare JUNIOR

**senior**[1] *n* **1** a student in the last year of HIGH SCHOOL or college **2** be two/five/ten etc.

**years** sb's **senior** to be two, five, ten etc. years older than someone —compare JUNIOR[1]

**senior**[2] *adj* older, or of higher rank: *a senior officer in the Navy* —compare JUNIOR[2]

**senior cit·i·zen** /ˌ.. '.../ *n* an old person, especially someone over the age of 65

**senior high school** /ˌ.. '. ˌ./ *n* ⇨ HIGH SCHOOL

**se·nior·i·ty** /ˌsin'yɔrəti, -'yɑr-/ *n* [U] the state of being older or higher in rank than someone else, which often gives you an advantage: *a worker with ten years' seniority at the plant*

**sen·sa·tion** /sɛn'seɪʃən/ *n* **1** [C,U] the ability to feel, or a feeling that you get from your senses or an experience: *Matt had a burning sensation in his arm.* | *I had the strangest sensation that I was being watched.* **2** extreme excitement or interest, or someone or something that causes this: *News of the discovery **caused a** great sensation in the art world.*

**sen·sa·tion·al** /sɛn'seɪʃənl/ *adj* **1** DISAPPROVING intended to shock or excite people: *a sensational news report of the murder* **2** very interesting or exciting: *a sensational finish to the race*

**sen·sa·tion·al·ism** /sɛn'seɪʃənlˌɪzəm/ *n* [U] DISAPPROVING a way of reporting events or stories that is intended to shock or excite people

**sense**[1] /sɛns/ *n*

**1** ▸**JUDGMENT**◂ [U] good understanding and judgment, especially about practical things: *Earl **had the sense** not to move the injured man much.* —compare COMMON SENSE

**2** ▸**FEELING**◂ [singular] a feeling about something: *She felt a strong **sense of** accomplishment.* | *At the end you have that sense of a shared experience.* | *a child's **sense of** self-esteem* (=his/her feelings about himself/herself)

**3 make sense a)** to have a clear meaning that is easy to understand: *Do these instructions **make** any **sense** to you?* | *I can't **make sense of** the report.* **b)** to have a good reason or explanation: *Why would she wander off alone? It doesn't make sense.* **c)** to be a sensible thing to do: *It **makes sense to** take care of your health while you're young.*

**4 in a sense/in some senses** in only one way or only some ways, when there are more things to be considered: *In one sense he's right, but things are more complicated than that.*

**5** ▸**SEE/SMELL ETC.**◂ one of the five natural powers of sight, hearing, touch, taste, and smell: *a dog with a strong **sense of smell***

**6 in the sense that** used in order to say that something you have just said is true in a particular way: *The experiment was a success in the sense that we got the results we were looking for.*

**7** sb's **senses** someone's ability to know and do what is sensible in a situation: *I'm glad that Lisa finally **came to her senses** (=realized what was sensible) and sold that car.* | *Have you **lost***

*your senses?* (=are you crazy?)

**8** ▶ABILITY◀ [singular] a natural ability to judge something: *When we were in the woods, I lost all **sense of direction**.* (=ability to know where I was)

**9 sense of humor** the ability to understand and enjoy things that are funny, or to make people laugh: *Larry **has a great sense of humor**.*

**10** ▶MEANING◀ the meaning of a word, phrase, sentence etc.: *Many words have more than one sense.* | *In what sense is the term used?*

**11 there's no sense in (doing) sth** SPOKEN used in order to say that it is not sensible to do something: *There's no sense in getting upset about it now.*

**sense**[2] *v* [T] to feel that something exists or is true without being told or having proof: *Sonya **sensed that** David wanted to be alone.*

**sense·less** /'sɛnslɪs/ *adj* **1** happening or done for no good reason or with no purpose: *the senseless killing of innocent people* **2** INFORMAL not conscious: *The pitcher missed, hit him in the head, and knocked him senseless.*

**sen·si·bil·i·ty** /ˌsɛnsə'bɪləṭi/ *n* [C,U] the way that someone reacts to particular subjects or types of behavior: *We apologize if we have **offended the sensibilities** of our viewers.* | *our moral sensibility*

**sen·si·ble** /'sɛnsəbəl/ *adj* **1** showing good judgment; reasonable: *Come on, be sensible.* | *The question is how to manage profits in a sensible way.* **2** suitable for a particular purpose; practical: *sensible clothes for camping in* — **sensibly** *adv*

---

**USAGE NOTE** sensible and sensitive

Use **sensible** to talk about someone who makes good, reasonable decisions and who does not behave in a stupid or dangerous way: *She's sensible enough not to drive when she's drunk.* Use **sensitive** to talk about someone who is easily upset or offended: *He's sensitive about his height, so don't mention it.*

---

**sen·si·tive** /'sɛnsəṭɪv/ *adj* **1** able to understand the feelings, problems etc. of other people: *a husband who is **sensitive to** his wife's needs* — opposite INSENSITIVE **2** easily offended or hurt by the things that other people do or say: *Chrissy is very **sensitive about** her weight.* **3** having a greater ability than usual to feel or measure a physical effect: *My teeth are really **sensitive to** cold.* | *a **highly sensitive** thermometer* **4** a sensitive situation or subject needs to be dealt with very carefully because it may offend people: *The interviewer avoided asking questions on **sensitive issues**.* — **sensitivity** /ˌsɛnsə'tɪvəṭi/ *n* [U] — **sensitively** *adv* /'sɛnsəṭɪvli/ — see usage note at SENSIBLE

**sen·sor** /'sɛnsɚ, -sɔr/ *n* TECHNICAL a piece of

equipment that finds heat, light, sound etc., even in very small amounts

**sen·so·ry** /'sɛnsəri/ *adj* relating to your senses of sight, hearing, smell, taste, or touch: *sensory perception*

**sen·su·al** /'sɛnʃuəl/ *adj* relating to or enjoying physical pleasure, especially sexual pleasure: *a sensual massage* | *Tina's very sensual.* — **sensuality** /ˌsɛnʃu'æləṭi/ *n* [U]

**sen·su·ous** /'sɛnʃuəs/ *adj* pleasing to your senses: *the sensuous feel of a silk scarf*

**sent** /sɛnt/ *v* the past tense and PAST PARTICIPLE of SEND

**sen·tence**[1] /'sɛntⁿns, -təns/ *n* **1** TECHNICAL in grammar, a group of written or spoken words that has a subject and a verb, and expresses a complete thought or asks a question **2** a punishment that a judge gives to someone who is guilty of a crime: *a 10-year sentence for arson*

**sentence**[2] *v* [T] to give a legal punishment to someone who is guilty of a crime: *He was **sentenced to** life in prison for the murder.*

**sen·ti·ment** /'sɛntəmənt/ *n* **1** [C,U] FORMAL an opinion or feeling that you have about something: *Pacifist sentiment was strong among the demonstrators.* | *"Anderson ought to be fired." "My sentiments exactly."* (=I completely agree) **2** [U] feelings such as pity, love, or sadness that are considered to be too strong: *There's no room for sentiment in business!*

**sen·ti·men·tal** /ˌsɛntə'mɛntl◀/ *adj* **1** showing emotions such as love, pity, and sadness too strongly: *a sentimental movie* | *Laurie still gets **sentimental about** our old house.* **2** based on or relating to feelings rather than being practical: *a sentimental view of the past* | *The watch wasn't worth much, but it had great **sentimental value**.* — **sentimentality** /ˌsɛntəmən'tæləṭi/ *n* [U]

**sen·try** /'sɛntri/ *n* OLD-FASHIONED a soldier standing outside a building as a guard

**sep·a·ra·ble** /'sɛpərəbəl/ *adj* able to be separated from something else — opposite INSEPARABLE

**sep·a·rate**[1] /'sɛprɪt/ *adj* **1** not relating to each other or affecting each other in any way: *He keeps his professional life **separate from** his private life.* | *It's a completely separate issue.* **2** not joined to each other or touching each other: *There is a small smoking area **separate from** the main dining room.* **3** different: *a word with four separate meanings* — **separately** *adv*

**sep·a·rate**[2] /'sɛpəˌreɪt/ *v* **1** [I,T] to divide or split something into two or more parts, or to make something do this: *Ms. Barker **separated** the class **into** four groups.* | *At this point the satellite **separates from** the launcher.* **2** [T] to be between two things so that they cannot touch each other or connect to each other: *A curtain **separated** one patient's area **from** another.* **3** [I,T] to move apart, or to make people do

this: *Police moved in to separate the crowd.*
**4** [I] to start to live apart from your husband,
wife, or sexual partner: *When did Lyle and Jan
separate?*

**sep·a·rat·ed** /ˈsɛpəˌreɪtɪd/ *adj* no longer living with your husband, wife, or sexual partner:
*Her parents are separated.*

**sep·a·ra·tion** /ˌsɛpəˈreɪʃən/ *n* **1** [U] FORMAL
the act of separating or the state of being separate: *the separation of powers between Congress
and the President* **2** [C,U] a period of time
when two or more people live apart from each
other: *Kim asked Bob for a legal separa-
tion.* | *Separation from the family is hard on
children.*

**Sep·tem·ber** /sɛpˈtɛmbɚ/ written abbreviation **Sept.** *n* the ninth month of the year – see
usage note at JANUARY

**sep·ul·cher** /ˈsɛpəlkɚ/ *n* LITERARY a large
TOMB

**se·quel** /ˈsikwəl/ *n* **1** a movie, book etc. that
continues the story of an earlier one **2** an
event that is related to an earlier event

**se·quence** /ˈsikwəns/ *n* [C,U] **1** a series of
related events or actions that have a particular
result: *This quarter we'll study the **sequence of
events** that led to World War I.* **2** the order
that things are supposed to have, or in which
actions are supposed to be done: *Two of the
pages were **out of sequence**.* (=not in
order) | *Try to place the following pictures **in se-
quence**.* —**sequential** /sɪˈkwɛnʃəl/ *adj*

**se·quin** /ˈsikwɪn/ *n* a small round piece of flat
metal that is shiny and is sewn on clothes for
decoration

**se·quoi·a** /sɪˈkwɔɪə/ *n* ⇨ REDWOOD

**ser·e·nade**[1] /ˌsɛrəˈneɪd/ *n* a song or piece of
music that someone performs outside at night
for the person s/he loves —**serenade** *v* [T]

**se·rene** /səˈrin/ *adj* **1** someone who is serene is very calm and not at all worried **2** a
place that is serene is peaceful and quiet —**se-
renity** /sɪˈrɛnəti/ *n* [U]

**ser·geant, Sergeant** /ˈsɑrdʒənt/ *n* a low rank
in the army, police etc., or someone who has
this rank

**se·ri·al**[1] /ˈsɪriəl/ *adj* arranged or happening
one after the other in the correct order: *serial
processing on a computer*

**serial**[2] *n* a story that is broadcast or printed in
several separate parts

**serial kill·er** /ˈ... ˈ../ *n* someone who has killed
several people in the same way, one after the
other

**serial num·ber** /ˈ... ˌ../ *n* one of a series of
numbers printed on a large number of similar
things such as televisions, so that you can tell
them apart

**se·ries** /ˈsɪriz/ *n, plural* **series** **1** a group of
events or actions of the same kind that happen
one after the other: *There has been a series of*

accidents along this road. **2** a set of television
or radio programs with the same characters or
on the same subject: *a new comedy series*

**se·ri·ous** /ˈsɪriəs/ *adj* **1** a serious problem,
situation etc. is bad or dangerous and makes
people worry: *Her mother's been in a serious
accident.* **2 be serious** to be sincere about
what you say or do: *John **is serious about**
finding a new career.* | *You can't be serious!* (=I
do not believe you) **3** important and deserving
a lot of attention: *Raising children is a **serious
business**.* **4** a serious romantic relationship is
intended to continue for a long time: *So, are you
two serious?* —**seriousness** *n* [U]

**se·ri·ous·ly** /ˈsɪriəsli/ *adv* **1** in a serious
way: *I'm seriously worried about Ben.* **2 take
sb/sth seriously** to believe that someone or
something is important and worth paying attention to: *You can't take everything he says so
seriously.*

**ser·mon** /ˈsɚmən/ *n* **1** a talk about a religious subject, usually given at a church and
based on the Bible **2** INFORMAL a talk in which
someone gives you unwanted moral advice
—see also PREACH

**ser·pent** /ˈsɚpənt/ *n* LITERARY a snake

**ser·rat·ed** /səˈreɪtɪd, ˈsɛˌreɪtɪd/ *adj* **serrated
knife/edge** with a sharp edge made of a row of
connected V shapes like teeth

**se·rum** /ˈsɪrəm/ *n* [C,U] TECHNICAL a liquid tak-
en from animal's blood that is put into someone's blood in order to fight an infection
—compare VACCINE

**serv·ant** /ˈsɚvənt/ *n* someone who is paid to
clean someone's house, cook food for him/her
etc.

**serve**[1] /sɚv/ *v*

**1** ▶FOOD/DRINKS◀ [I,T] to give someone
food or drinks as part of a meal: *Dinner will be
served at 8:00.* | *pie served with ice cream* | *Why
aren't you out there serving the guests?*

**2** ▶BE USED◀ [I,T] to be for a particular
purpose: *The couch can also serve as a bed.*

**3** ▶DO A JOB◀ [I,T] to spend time doing a
particular job, especially one that is helpful:
*Kelly served a three-year term in the Army.*

**4** ▶PROVIDE STH◀ [T] to provide someone
with something that is useful or necessary:
*We're your local Ford dealers, serving Sioux
Falls for over 25 years.*

**5** ▶IN PRISON◀ [T] to spend a particular
amount of time in prison: *Baxter **served a** five-
year **sentence for** theft.*

**6** ▶LEGALLY◀ [T] to officially give or send
someone a legal document: *Jones was served a
summons to appear in court.*

**7** ▶SPORTS◀ [I,T] to start playing a game
such as tennis by throwing the ball into the air
and hitting it to your opponent

**8 it serves sb right** SPOKEN used in order to say
that someone deserves something unpleasant,
because s/he has done something stupid or un-

kind: *I'm sorry Eddie had an accident, but it serves him right for driving so fast!*

**serve²** *n* the action in a game such as tennis in which you throw the ball into the air and hit it to your opponent

**serv·er** /'sɚvɚ/ *n* **1** a special spoon, fork etc. used for putting a particular type of food on a plate: *a pair of wooden salad servers* **2** the main computer on a NETWORK that controls all the others **3** someone who brings you food in a restaurant **4** a player who hits the ball to begin a game such as tennis

**serv·ice¹** /'sɚvɪs/ *n*

**1** ▶IN A STORE ETC.◀ [U] the help that people who work in a restaurant, hotel, store etc. give you: *The food is terrific but the service is lousy.* | *the customer service department*

**2** **public services** things such as hospitals, schools etc. that are provided for the public to use

**3** ▶WORK DONE◀ [C,U] the work that you do for someone or an organization: *He retired after 20 years of service.* | *You may need the services of a lawyer.*

**4** ▶CEREMONY◀ a formal religious ceremony, especially in a church: *Father Palmer will be conducting the funeral service.* (=be in charge of the ceremony)

**5** ▶BUSINESS◀ a business that provides help or does jobs for people rather than producing things: *She operates a cleaning service.*

**6** ▶HELP◀ [singular, U] help that you give to someone: *"Thank you so much." "I'm glad to be of service."* (=to help)

**7** **the service** a country's military forces, especially considered as a job: *Stan joined the service after high school.*

**8** ▶GOVERNMENT◀ an organization that works for government: *the diplomatic service*

**9** **be at your service** FORMAL to be available to help you if you need something: *We're at your service, Ma'am.*

**10** ▶SPORTS◀ an act of hitting the ball to your opponent to start a game such as tennis

**11** **in service/out of service** to be available or not available for people to use: *an elevator/bus/telephone that is out of service*

**service²** *v* [T] **1** to examine a machine or vehicle and fix it if necessary: *When's the last time you had the car serviced?* **2** to provide people with something that they need: *buses that service the local community*

**serv·ice·a·ble** /'sɚvɪsəbəl/ *adj* ready or suitable to be used for a particular purpose

**service charge** /'.. ,./ *n* an amount of money that is added to the price of something in order to pay for extra services that you use when buying it: *For phone orders, there's a $1 service charge.*

**serv·ice·man** /'sɚvɪs,mæn, -mən/ *n* a man who is a member of the military

**service sta·tion** /'.. ,../ *n* ⇨ GAS STATION

**serv·ice·wom·an** /'sɚvɪs,wʊmən/ *n* a woman who is a member of the military

**ser·vile** /'sɚvəl, -vaɪl/ *adj* willing to obey someone completely

**serv·ing** /'sɚvɪŋ/ *n* an amount of food that is enough for one person; HELPING

**ser·vi·tude** /'sɚvə,tud/ *n* [U] the condition of being a SLAVE or being forced to obey someone

**ses·sion** /'sɛʃən/ *n* **1** a period of time used for a particular purpose, especially by a group of people: *a question-and-answer session after the meeting* **2** a formal meeting, especially of a law court or government organization: *The State Court is now in session.* **3** a part of the year when classes are given at a university

**set¹** /sɛt/ *v* set, set, setting

**1** ▶RECORD/STANDARD ETC.◀ [T] to do or decide something that other things are compared to or measured against: *Carl Lewis set a world record.* | *The agency has set standards for water cleanliness.* | *Parents should set an example for their children.* (=behave in the way they want their children to behave)

**2** ▶PRICE/TIME ETC.◀ [T] to decide that something will happen at a particular time, cost a particular amount etc.: *The price was set too high.* | *The satellite launch date was set for May.*

**3** ▶PUT STH SOMEWHERE◀ [T] to put something somewhere carefully: *Just set that bag down on the floor.*

**4** ▶MAKE STH READY◀ [T] to arrange something or put it in a particular position, so that it is ready to be used or done: *I set my alarm for 6:30.* | *How many people should I set the table for?* (=put knives, plates etc. on it)

**5** ▶FIRE◀ to make something start burning: *Angry mobs set the building on fire.* | *Careless campers set fire to the dry brush.*

**6** ▶MOVIE/STORY ETC.◀ [T] if a play, movie, story etc. is set in a place or at a particular time, the events in it happen there or at that time: *Clavell's epic novel is set in 17th century Japan.*

**7** **set sb/sth straight** to correct something or someone: *The company wants to set the record straight* (=explain the true situation) *about its safety procedures.*

**8** **set the stage/scene** to make it possible for something to happen: *Recent pay cuts set the stage for a strike.*

**9** **set sth in motion** to make something start happening: *Once the process is set in motion, we cannot stop it.*

**10** ▶SUN/MOON◀ [I] when the sun or moon sets, it moves lower in the sky until it can no longer be seen

**11** **set your sights on sth** to decide that something is your aim: *Annie set her sights on the most popular boy in school.*

**12** **set your mind to sth** to decide that you are willing to work hard for something: *You can do anything that you set your mind to.*

**13** **set foot in/on** to go into or onto a place:

*The event is attracting people who have never before set foot in a museum.*

**14 set sb free/loose** to allow a person or animal to leave a prison or CAGE, or to untie him, her, or it: *Do you mean he set all the lab animals loose?*

**15 set sail** to start sailing somewhere

**16 set to work** to start doing something, or to make someone start doing something: *Volunteers set to work clearing trash from the field.*

**17 ▶BECOME SOLID◀** [I] if a liquid mixture sets, it becomes hard and solid: *The concrete will set within two hours.*

**18 set sth to music a)** to write music for a story or poem: *poems set to music by Lloyd Webber* **b)** to arrange something so that it can be done while music plays: *exercise routines set to music*

**19 set a trap a)** to invent a plan that will catch someone doing something wrong: *Police set a trap for the thieves.* **b)** to make a trap ready to catch an animal

**20 ▶BONE◀** [T] to put the ends of a broken bone back together so that it will heal

**21 ▶ATTACH◀** [T] to attach or glue something into a surface: *a diamond set in a gold ring*

**22 ▶HAIR◀** [T] to arrange someone's hair while it is wet, so that it will have a particular style when it is dry

**23 set great store by** to consider something to be very important: *Greg sets great store by his friends' trust.* – see also **(get) ready, (get) set, go!** (READY)

**set about** sth *phr v* [T] **set about doing sth** to begin doing something: *Johnny set about improving his Spanish before his trip.*

**set** sb **against** sb *phr v* [T] to make someone start to argue or fight with someone else: *The issue sets Republicans against one another.*

**set** sth ↔ **apart** *phr v* [T] to make someone or something different from other similar people or things: *The movie's realistic characters set it apart from other gangster pictures.*

**set** sth ↔ **aside** *phr v* [T] **1** to save something for a special purpose: *Hotels must set aside 50% of their rooms for non-smokers.* **2** to decide not to be affected or influenced by a particular belief, idea etc.: *They should set politics aside and do what is best for the country.*

**set back** *phr v* [T] **1** [set sb/sth ↔ **back**] to delay the progress or development of someone or something: *Officials fear that the incident will set back race relations.* **2** [set sb **back**] to cost someone a lot of money: *Dinner set us back $300.*

**set** sth ↔ **down** *phr v* [T] to make a rule or write something in an official document: *The rules of the game were clearly set down.*

**set forth** sth *phr v* [T] FORMAL **1** to establish rules, principles etc.: *a document setting forth guidelines for behavior* **2** to write or talk

about an idea, rule etc., in order to explain it: *Rousseau set forth his educational theories in the book "Emile."*

**set in** *phr v* [I] if something sets in, especially something unpleasant, it begins and is likely to continue: *As warm weather set in, the ice began to melt.*

**set off** *phr v* **1** [T set sth ↔ **off**] to make something start happening or make people suddenly start doing something: *The attack set off another round of fighting.* | *The rains set off a mudslide that killed 15 people.* **2** [T set sth ↔ **off**] to make something explode: *The bomb was set off by a remote control device.* **3** [T set sth ↔ **off**] to make machinery or electronic equipment, especially an ALARM, start working: *A fire in the kitchen set off the smoke alarms.* **4** [I] to leave a place in order to go somewhere, especially somewhere far away: *Thousands of people set off for the West during the 1800s.*

**set out** *phr v* **1** **set out to do sth** to deliberately start doing something: *He set out to make a movie about his experiences in Vietnam.* **2** [I] to leave a place, especially to begin a trip: *The couple set out for Fresno at about 9:30.* **3** [T set out sth] to write or talk about ideas, rules etc. in a clear and organized way: *He is the first candidate to set out his foreign policy proposals.*

**set up** *phr v* **1** [I,T set sth ↔ **up**] to start a company, organization, business etc.: *The county has set up a special education program for teenage mothers.* **2** [T set sth ↔ **up**] to prepare something or make arrangements for something: *Chris, could you help me set up the computer?* | *I called the doctor's to set up an appointment.* **3** [T set sth ↔ **up**] to build something or put it somewhere: *The police set up a roadblock to try to catch the criminals.* **4** [T set sb ↔ **up**] to deliberately make people think that someone has done something wrong: *Hudson accused his partners of setting him up.* **5 set up shop** to start a business: *They set up shop in 1993 in Mason's basement.*

**set²** *n* **1** a group of things that belong together: *a set of dishes* | *a chess set* **2** a television or radio: *a color TV set* **3** a place where a movie or television program is acted and filmed: *OK, everybody, quiet on the set!* **4** one part of a game such as tennis or VOLLEYBALL: *Sampras leads two sets to one.* **5** the things that are put on a stage to make the background for a play

**set³** *adj* **1** a set time, amount, price etc. is fixed and cannot be changed: *We meet at a set time each week.* **2** INFORMAL ready to do something: *If everyone is all set, we'll start the meeting.* **3 be set on/upon/against sth** INFORMAL to be very determined about something: *Jerry's dead set against paying the extra money for the trip.* **4** being in a particular place or position: *a castle set on a hill*

**set·back** /'sɛt‾bæk/ *n* something that delays your progress or makes things worse than they were: *The peace talks suffered a setback when fighting resumed this week.*

**set·ter** /'sɛtə-/ *n* a dog with long hair, often used in hunting to find birds and animals

**set·ting** /'sɛtɪŋ/ *n* [C usually singular] **1** all the things that surround someone or something: *a cabin in a mountain setting* **2** a position of the controls on a machine, piece of electronic equipment etc.: *Turn the microwave to its highest setting.* **3** the place or time in which the events in a book or movie happen: *London is the setting for his most recent novel.*

**set·tle** /'sɛtl/ *v*

**1** ▶END ARGUMENT◀ [I,T] to end an argument or a bad situation by agreeing to do something: *They can't seem to settle their arguments without fighting.* | *The company agreed to settle with them out of court.* (=without arguing in a court of law)

**2** ▶COMFORTABLE POSITION◀ [I,T] to put yourself or someone else in a comfortable position: *Dave settled back and turned on the TV.* | *Grandpa settled himself in the car.*

**3** ▶DECIDE STH◀ [T] to decide on something, or organize the details of something that will happen in the future: *We have to get the details of the trip settled soon.*

**4** ▶IN A NEW PLACE◀ **a)** [I,T] to start a new town or city in a place where no one has lived before: *They came from England to settle in America.* | *the men and women who settled Alaska* **b)** [I] to begin to live in a place where you intend to live for a long time: *My family moved around a lot before settling in Los Angeles.*

**5** ▶SNOW/DUST◀ [I] if snow, dust etc. settles, it falls to the ground and stays there: *When the dust settled, we could see the damage done by the tornado.*

**6** ▶BILL/DEBT◀ [T] if you settle a bill, account, debt etc. you pay the money that you owe

**7 settle a score** to do something bad to someone because s/he has done something bad to you

**8 settle your stomach/nerves** to do something that makes you stop feeling sick or nervous: *Drink some mint tea. It'll settle your stomach.*

**settle down** *phr v* [I] **1** to become calmer and less active or noisy: *Kids, settle down and eat your dinner.* **2** to start living in one place, working, and behaving in a responsible way: *My parents want me to marry Jim and settle down.* **3** to begin to do something and to give it all your attention: *When he finally settled down to work, it was 10:30.*

**settle for** *phr v* [T] to accept something that is less than you wanted: *We looked at some nice apartments, but we had to settle for the cheapest one.*

**settle in, settle into** *phr v* [I] to become happier and more comfortable in a new situation or place: *Adam seems to have settled in at his new school.*

**settle on/upon** *phr v* [T] to decide to do or have something after thinking about many possibilities: *They haven't settled on a name for the baby yet.*

**settle up** *phr v* [I] INFORMAL to pay money that you owe for something

**set·tled** /'sɛtld/ *adj* **1** unlikely to change: *the settled life of a farmer* **2 feel/be settled** to feel comfortable about living or working in a particular place: *We don't feel settled in our new house yet.* –compare UNSETTLED

**set·tle·ment** /'sɛtlmənt/ *n* **1** an official agreement or decision that ends an argument: *The two sides have reached a settlement* (=made an agreement) *in the land dispute.* **2** [C,U] a payment of money that you owe someone or that someone owes to you: *He accepted a financial settlement of $500.* **3** [U] the movement of a large number of people into a new place in order to live there: *the settlement of the Oklahoma territory* **4** a place where people live, especially where no one lived before: *a Stone Age settlement*

**set·tler** /'sɛtlə-, 'sɛtl-ə-/ *n* someone who goes to live in a new place, usually where there were few people before: *early settlers of the American West*

**set·up** /'. ./ *n* [C usually singular] **1** a way of organizing or arranging something: *Do you like the new setup at work?* **2** INFORMAL a dishonest plan that is intended to trick someone: *I knew immediately that the whole thing was a setup.*

**sev·en** /'sɛvən/ *number* **1** 7 **2** seven o'clock: *The movie starts at seven.*

**sev·en·teen** /,sɛvən'tin‹/ *number* 17 –seventeenth *number*

**sev·enth** /'sɛvənθ/ *number* **1** 7th **2** 1/7 **3 be in seventh heaven** INFORMAL to be extremely happy: *The kids were in seventh heaven when we were staying on the farm.*

**Seventh Day Ad·vent·ist** /,.. ,. .'../ *adj* relating to a Christian group that believes that Christ will soon come again to Earth –**Seventh Day Adventist** *n*

**sev·en·ty** /'sɛvənti/ *number* **1** 70 **2 the seventies a)** the years between 1970 and 1979 **b)** the numbers between 70 and 79, especially when used for measuring temperature –**seventieth** /'sɛvəntiɪθ/ *number*: *her seventieth birthday*

**sev·er** /'sɛvə-/ *v* [T] FORMAL **1** to cut through something completely: *His finger was severed in the accident.* **2** to end a relationship or agreement with someone: *The deal severs all ties between the two organizations.* –**severance** *n* [U]

**sev·er·al** /'sɛvrəl/ *quantifier* a number of people or things that is more than a few, but not a lot: *I called her several times on the phone.* | *I've talked to **several of** my students about this.* −compare FEW −see study note on page 466

**sev·e·rance pay** /'sɛvrəns ˌpeɪ/ *n* [U] money you get from a company that you worked for because you no longer have a job

**se·vere** /sə'vɪr/ *adj* **1** very bad or serious: *severe head injuries* | *severe problems* **2** not kind or friendly: *severe criticism* | *a severe look on her face* −compare STRICT −**severity** /sɪ'vɛrəti/ *n* [C,U]

**se·vere·ly** /sə'vɪrli/ *adv* very badly or to a great degree: *a country severely affected by drought* | *She was punished severely for her actions.*

**sew** /soʊ/ *v* sewed, sewn or sewed, sewing [I,T] to join pieces of cloth together or attach something to a piece of cloth using a needle and thread: *Can you sew a button on this shirt for me?* −**sewing** *n* [U]

sew — needle

**sew** sth ↔ **up** *phr v* [T] **1** to close or repair something by sewing it: *I need to sew up this hole in my jeans.* **2** INFORMAL to gain control over a situation so that you are sure to win or get an advantage: *The Republicans think they have the election sewn up.*

**sew·age** /'suɪdʒ/ *n* [U] the waste material and used water that is carried away from houses by SEWERs

**sew·er** /'suɚ/ *n* a pipe or passage under the ground that carries away waste material and used water from houses, factories etc.

**sewn** /soʊn/ *v* a PAST PARTICIPLE of SEW

**sex** /sɛks/ *n* **1** [U] the activity that a male and a female do together in order to produce children or for pleasure; SEXUAL INTERCOURSE: *She said she wouldn't **have sex** with him until she knew him better.* | *There are some sex scenes in the movie.* **2** [U] the condition of being male or female: *I don't care what sex the baby is, as long as it's healthy.* **3** one of the two groups of people or animals, male and female: *He isn't comfortable with members of **the opposite sex**.* (=people that are not his own sex)

**sex ed·u·ca·tion** /'. ..ˌ.../ *n* [U] education in schools about sexual activity and sexual relationships

**sex·ism** /'sɛkˌsɪzəm/ *n* [U] the belief that one sex, especially the female sex, is weaker, less intelligent, or less important than the other

**sex·ist** /'sɛksɪst/ *adj* relating to or showing SEXISM: *a book about sexist attitudes in the military* −**sexist** *n*

**sex sym·bol** /'. ,../ *n* someone famous who many people think is very sexually attractive

**sex·u·al** /'sɛkʃuəl/ *adj* **1** relating to sex: *sexual contact* | *sexual passion* **2** involving a male and a female: *children learning their sexual roles* −**sexually** *adv*

**sexual ha·rass·ment** /ˌ... .'.., ˌ... '.../ *n* [U] sexual remarks, looks, or touching that you do not want, especially from someone that you work with

**sexual in·ter·course** /ˌ... '.../ *n* [U] FORMAL the physical act of sex between two people

**sex·u·al·i·ty** /ˌsɛkʃu'æləti/ *n* [U] all the things that someone does or feels that are related to sexual activity

**sex·y** /'sɛksi/ *adj* sexually exciting or attractive: *a sexy woman*

**Sgt.** *n* the written abbreviation of SERGEANT

**sh** /ʃʃ/ *interjection* ⇨ SHH

**shab·by** /'ʃæbi/ *adj* **1** old and in bad condition because of being used a lot: *shabby hotel rooms* **2** unfair or wrong: *I don't deserve this kind of **shabby treatment**.* −**shabbily** *adv*

**shack**[1] /ʃæk/ *n* a small building that has not been built very well

**shack**[2] *v*

**shack up** *phr v* [I] INFORMAL to start living with someone and having sex with him/her: *I found out that she was **shacked up with** some guy from Florida.*

**shack·le**[1] /'ʃækəl/ *n* one of a pair of metal rings joined by a chain, that is used for keeping a prisoner's hands or feet together

**shackle**[2] *v* [T] **1** be shackled by sth to be prevented from doing what you want to do by something: *a company shackled by debts* **2** to put SHACKLEs on someone

shade

shadow

shade

**shade**[1] /ʃeɪd/ *n* **1** [singular, U] an area that is cooler and darker because the light of the sun cannot reach it: *boys sitting **in the shade** of a tree* −compare SHADOW[1] **2** something that reduces or blocks light, especially a cover that you pull across a window: *Can you **close/open the shades** in the living room?* **3** a particular degree of a color: *a darker **shade of** red/green/ blue* **4 shade of meaning/opinion etc.** a slight difference in things such as a meaning etc.: *a word with many shades of meaning* **5 a shade** very slightly, a little bit: *The room is a shade too hot for me.*

**Shade** is an area where there is no sunlight: *It's too hot here - let's find some shade.* A **shadow** is a dark shape you see on a surface that is caused by something blocking the light: *Mommy, my shadow is longer than yours!*

**shade²** *v* [T] to protect something from direct light or heat: *She used her hand to shade her eyes from the sun.*

**shades** /'ʃeɪdz/ *n* [plural] INFORMAL ⇨ SUN-GLASSES

**shad·ow¹** /'ʃædoʊ/ *n* **1** a dark shape that an object or a person makes on a surface when it is between that surface and the light: *The bright lights behind us cast strange shadows on the wall.* −compare SHADE¹ −see picture at SHADE¹ **2** [C,U] darkness caused when light is prevented from coming into a place: *Most of the room was in shadow. | He waited in the shadows.* **3 without/beyond a shadow of a doubt** without any doubt at all: *I think he's guilty beyond any shadow of a doubt.* −see usage note at SHADE¹

**shadow²** *v* [T] to follow someone closely in order to watch what s/he is doing

**shad·ow·y** /'ʃædoʊi/ *adj* **1** mysterious and difficult to know anything about: *a shadowy figure from his past* **2** full of shadows and difficult to see: *a shadowy corner*

**shad·y** /'ʃeɪdi/ *adj* **1** protected from the sun or producing shade: *a shady spot for a picnic | a shady tree* **2** INFORMAL not honest or legal: *a shady business deal*

**shaft** /ʃæft/ *n* **1** a passage that goes up through a building or down into the ground: *an elevator shaft* **2** a long handle on a tool, SPEAR etc. **3 shaft of light/sunlight** a narrow beam of light

**shag·gy** /'ʃægi/ *adj* **1** shaggy hair or fur is long and messy: *a shaggy red beard* **2** having shaggy hair

**shake¹** /ʃeɪk/ *v* shook, shaken, shaking **1** [I,T] to move up and down or from side to side with quick movements, or to make something do this: *His hands were shaking. | Shake the bottle to mix the oil and vinegar.* **2 shake your head** to move your head from side to side as a way of saying no −compare NOD **3 shake hands (with sb)** to hold someone's hand in your hand and move it up and down, as a greeting or a sign that you have agreed on something **4** [T] to hold someone by his/her shoulders and quickly push and pull him/her backward and forward:

**shake hands**

*He shook Gus and threw him to the floor.* **5** [I] if your voice shakes, it sounds nervous and unsteady **6 be/look/feel shaken** to be frightened, shocked, or upset: *Mark looked shaken as he put down the phone.*

**shake sb down** *phr v* [T] INFORMAL to get money from someone by using threats

**shake off** *phr v* [T] **1** [shake sth ↔ off] to get rid of an illness, problem etc.: *I can't seem to shake off this cold.* **2** [shake sb ↔ off] to escape from someone who is chasing you

**shake sth ↔ out** *phr v* [T] to shake something such as a cloth so that small pieces of dirt, dust etc. come off

**shake sb/sth ↔ up** *phr v* [T] **1** if an unpleasant experience shakes someone up, s/he is shocked or upset by it: *The accident really shook her up.* **2** to make changes to an organization, country etc. to make it more effective −see also SHAKEUP

**shake²** *n* **1** an act of shaking: *Give the ketchup bottle a good shake.* **2** ⇨ MILKSHAKE

**shake·down** /'ʃeɪkdaʊn/ *n* **1** INFORMAL the act of getting money from someone by using threats **2** a final test of a vehicle or system for problems before it is put into general use: *a shakedown process*

**shak·en** /'ʃeɪkən/ *v* the PAST PARTICIPLE of shake

**shake·up** /'ʃeɪk-ʌp/ *n* a process in which an organization, company etc. makes a lot of changes in order to be more effective

**shak·y** /'ʃeɪki/ *adj* **1** weak and unsteady because of illness, old age, or shock: *a shaky voice* **2** not likely to last a long time or be successful: *a shaky marriage* **3** not solid or firm: *a shaky ladder*

**shall** /ʃəl; *strong* ʃæl/ *modal verb* **1** FORMAL used in order to say what will happen or what must happen: *The right to a trial by jury shall be preserved.* **2** used in order to ask a question, especially as a way of suggesting something: *Shall I turn on the air conditioner?* **3** FORMAL used in order to say what you are going to do in the future: *I shall keep her picture always.* −see study note on page 458

Use both **shall** and **will** to talk about future time. Use **will** to talk about what you are planning to do: *I'll* (=I will) *call the travel agency tomorrow.* Use **shall** to mean "do you want me to?": *Shall I call the travel agency for you?* In informal speech, we often use **should** instead of **shall**: *Should I call the travel agency for you?*

**shal·lot** /'ʃælət, ʃə'lɑt/ *n* a vegetable like a small onion

**shal·low** /'ʃæloʊ/ *adj* **1** not deep, measuring only a short distance from the top to the bottom:

*a shallow baking dish\a shallow pool* **2** not showing any serious or careful thought: *a shallow argument* –see picture at DEEP¹

**sham¹** /ʃæm/ *n* [singular] something that deceives people by seeming good or true when it is not: *We found out later that the insurance company was a sham.*

**sham²** *adj* not real; FAKE: *sham jewelry*

**sham·bles** /'ʃæmbəlz/ *n* [singular] INFORMAL **be (in) a shambles a)** to be very badly organized, and fail completely: *The whole evening was a shambles - the food never even arrived.* **b)** to be very messy or damaged: *The apartment was a shambles.*

**shame¹** /ʃeɪm/ *n* **1** the feeling of being guilty or embarrassed that you have after doing something that is wrong: *a deep sense of shame* –compare EMBARRASSED, ASHAMED **2 it's/ what a shame** SPOKEN used in order to say that a situation is disappointing, and you wish things had happened differently: *It's such a shame (that) Margaret couldn't come.* **3 Shame on you!** SPOKEN used in order to tell someone that s/he should feel ashamed of something that s/he has done: *Shame on you for not telling me about that sooner.* **4 put sth/sb to shame** to be much better than something or someone else and make the other seem bad when you compare the two: *This party puts my little dinner to shame.* **5** [U] loss of honor; DISGRACE: *His behavior brought shame on the whole family.*

**shame²** *v* [T] to make someone feel ashamed: *He was shamed into admitting he'd stolen the money.*

**shame·faced** /'ʃeɪmfeɪst/ *adj* looking ashamed or embarrassed

**shame·ful** /'ʃeɪmfəl/ *adj* so bad that someone should be ashamed: *a shameful and cowardly action* –**shamefully** *adv*

**shame·less** /'ʃeɪmlɪs/ *adj* feeling no shame: *a shameless liar* –**shamelessly** *adv*

**sham·poo¹** /ʃæm'pu/ *n* [C,U] a liquid soap used for washing your hair, a CARPET etc.

**shampoo²** *v* [T] to wash something with SHAMPOO

**sham·rock** /'ʃæmrɑk/ *n* a small green plant with three leaves on each stem, that is the national sign of Ireland

**shan·ty** /'ʃænti/ *n* a small building that has not been built very well; SHACK

**shape¹** /ʃeɪp/ *n* **1** [C,U] the outer form of something that you can see or feel: *a cake in the shape of a heart* **2 in good/bad/poor shape** in good, bad etc. condition or health: *The old car's still in good shape.* **3 in shape/out of shape** in a good or bad state of health or physical FITNESS: *What do you do to keep in shape?* **4** [singular] a particular combination of qualities and features that something has: *These trade laws are responsible for the shape of Ja-*

panese industry today. **5** a particular form such as a circle, square, TRIANGLE etc. **6 take shape** to develop into a clear and definite form: *His plan was beginning to take shape.* **7** something or someone that you cannot see clearly enough to recognize: *He was just a shape in the mist.*

**shape²** *v* [T] **1** to influence something such as a belief or opinion and make it develop in a particular way: *an event that shaped public opinion* **2** to make something have a particular shape: *Shape the clay into small balls.*

**shape up** *phr v* [I] INFORMAL to develop and improve: *Our plans to visit Germany are shaping up.* | *You better shape up John, or you're off the team.*

shape

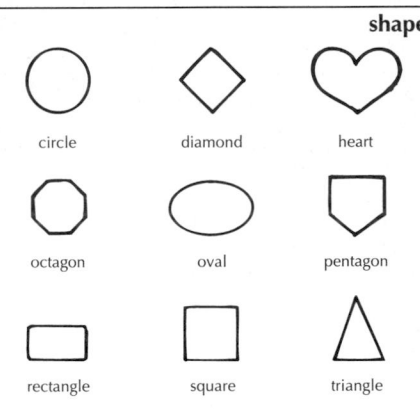

circle    diamond    heart

octagon    oval    pentagon

rectangle    square    triangle

**shaped** /ʃeɪpt/ *adj* having a particular shape: *The box is egg-shaped.*

**shape·ly** /'ʃeɪpli/ *adj* having an attractive shape: *her long shapely legs*

**share¹** /ʃɛr/ *v* **1** [I,T] to have or use something that other people have or use at the same time: *All the kids had to share the same bathroom.* | *There's only one book - we'll have to share.* **2** [T] to let someone have or use something that belongs to you: *Will you share your toys with Ronnie?* **3** [I,T] to divide something between two or more people: *I took the cookies to work to share with everybody.* | *We share the expenses for the house.* **4** [T] to have the same interest, opinion etc. as someone else: *Does Molly share your interest in stamp collecting?* **5** [I,T] to tell someone else about an idea, secret, problem etc.: *Thank you for sharing your feelings with me.*

**share²** *n* **1** [singular] the part of something that is owned, done, or used by you: *I paid my share of the bill and left.* **2 have/get your share** as much of something as you could reasonably expect to have: *Rob's certainly getting his share of attention from the women.* **3** one of the equal parts into which the ownership of a company is divided: *He wants to buy/ sell 500 shares in CNN.* –compare STOCK¹

**shark** /ʃɑrk/ *n* a large sea fish with very sharp teeth

**sharp¹** /ʃɑrp/ *adj*

sharp

a sharp pencil

a blunt pencil

**1** ▶ABLE TO CUT◀ having a very thin edge or point that can cut things easily: *a sharp knife* −compare DULL¹, BLUNT¹

**2** ▶DIRECTION◀ making a sudden change in direction: *a sharp turn in the road*

**3** ▶INTELLIGENT◀ able to think and understand things very quickly: *She's a very sharp lawyer.*

**4** ▶REMARK◀ criticizing in a severe and angry way

**5** ▶PAIN◀ sudden and very bad: *a sharp pain in my chest*

**6** ▶CHANGE◀ a sharp increase or decrease is big and very sudden: *a sharp increase in prices* −see picture at INCREASE²

**7** ▶EYES◀ able to see or notice things very easily: *Lenny has a sharp eye for detail.*

**8** ▶CLOTHES◀ attractive and stylish: *My grandfather was a sharp dresser.* (=wore stylish clothes)

**9** ▶SOUNDS◀ loud, short, and sudden: *a sharp cry*

**10** ▶PICTURE◀ having a shape that is clear and detailed: *a sharp picture on the TV* −see picture at GRAINY

**11 a sharp tongue** the ability to express anger or unkind thoughts well

**12** ▶MUSIC◀ a musical note that is sharp is played or sung slightly higher than it should be −compare FLAT¹

**13** ▶TASTE◀ having a strong taste: *sharp Cheddar cheese* −**sharply** *adv* −**sharpness** *n* [U]

**sharp²** *adv* **at 8 o'clock/two-thirty etc. sharp** at exactly 8:00, 2:30 etc.: *I expect you to be here at 10:30 sharp.*

**sharp·en** /ʃɑrpən/ *v* [I,T] to make something sharper, or become sharper: *sharpening a pencil*

**sharp·en·er** /ʃɑrpənɚ/ *n* a tool or machine that SHARPENS pencils, knives etc.

**shat·ter** /ʃætɚ/ *v* **1** [I,T] to break suddenly into very small pieces, or to make something do this: *My cup fell to the floor and shattered.* **2 shatter sb's hopes/dreams etc.** to completely destroy someone's hopes or beliefs: *A knee injury shattered his hopes of becoming a baseball player.*

**shave¹** /ʃeɪv/ *v* **1** [I,T] to cut off hair very close to the skin, especially from your face, legs etc. **2** to remove very thin pieces from the surface of something using a sharp tool

**shave²** *n* **1** [C usually singular] an act of shaving (SHAVE): *I need a shave.* **2 a close shave** a situation in which you only just avoid an accident or something bad: *We had a close shave on the highway yesterday - a huge truck almost pushed us off the road.*

**shav·er** /ʃeɪvɚ/ *n* a tool used for shaving (SHAVE)

**shav·ings** /ʃeɪvɪŋz/ *n* [plural] very thin pieces of something such as wood that are cut from a surface

**shawl** /ʃɔl/ *n* a piece of cloth that is worn around the shoulders or head for warmth

**s/he** /ʃi ɚ hi/ *pron* used in writing when the subject of the sentence can be either male or female

**she¹** /ʃi/ *pron* **1** a female person or animal who has been mentioned or is known about: *"Where's Kate?" "She went out to the car." | "I saw Suzy today." "Oh really, how is she?" | She's* (=she is) *my sister.* **2** used when talking about a car or ship that has been mentioned

**she²** *n* [singular] a female: *What a cute dog! Is it a she or a he?*

**sheaf** /ʃif/ *n, plural* **sheaves 1** wheat, corn etc. that is tied together after it has been cut **2** several pieces of paper held or tied together

**shear** /ʃɪr/ *v* **sheared, sheared** *or* **shorn, shearing** [T] to cut the wool off a sheep

**shears** /ʃɪrz/ *n* [plural] a tool like a large pair of scissors

**sheath** /ʃiθ/ *n* a cover for the blade of a knife or sword

**sheathe** /ʃið/ *v* [T] to put a knife or sword into a SHEATH

**sheaves** /ʃivz/ *n* the plural of SHEAF

**she'd** /ʃid/ **1** the short form of "she had": *She'd forgotten to close the door.* **2** the short form of "she would": *She said she'd love to come.*

**shed¹** /ʃɛd/ *n* a small building used especially for storing things: *a tool shed in the back yard*

**shed²** *v* **shed, shed, shedding** [T] **1** to drop something or allow it to fall off, especially as part of a natural process: *Snakes regularly shed their skin.* **2** to get rid of something that you do not want: *I'd like to shed a few pounds before summer.* (=lose some weight)

**sheen** /ʃin/ *n* [singular, U] a smooth shiny appearance: *the beautiful sheen of her hair*

**sheep** /ʃip/ *n, plural* **sheep** a farm animal that eats grass and is kept for its wool and its meat

**sheep·ish** /ʃipɪʃ/ *adj* uncomfortable or embarrassed because you have done something silly or wrong: *Renny apologized, looking sheepish.* −**sheepishly** *adv*

**sheer** /ʃɪr/ *adj* **1 sheer joy/luck/bliss etc.** joy, luck etc. with no other feeling or quality mixed with it: *people dancing and singing with sheer joy* **2 the sheer size/weight/numbers etc.** used in order to emphasize how big, heavy etc. something is: *The most impressive thing*

S

*about Alaska is its sheer size.* **3** a sheer drop, cliff etc. is extremely steep

**sheet** /ʃit/ *n* **1** a large piece of thin cloth that you put on a bed to lie on or under: *Have you changed the sheets?* (=put clean sheets on the bed) **2** a thin flat piece of something such as paper, metal, or glass: *a sheet of paper* **3** a large flat area of something such as ice or water that is spread over a surface: *The road was covered with a sheet of ice.*

**sheik, sheikh** /ʃik, ʃeɪk/ *n* **1** an Arab chief or prince **2** a Muslim religious teacher or leader

**shelf** /ʃɛlf/ *n, plural* **shelves** a long flat board fixed on a wall, in a frame etc. on which you put or store things: *two shelves for books* | *a jar on the top shelf*

**she'll** /ʃil, ʃil/ the short form of "she will": *She'll be here around 8:00.*

**shell**[1] /ʃɛl/ *n* **1** the hard outer covering of a nut, egg, seed, and some types of animal: *looking for sea shells on the beach* | *The turtle pulled its head into its shell.* –see picture at PEEL[2] **2** an explosive that is fired from a large gun, or the metal container that this is in

**shell**[2] *v* [T] to fire SHELLs at something

**shell out** *phr v* [T] INFORMAL to pay money for something, often when you do not want to: *We had to shell out over $400 to get the car fixed.*

**shell·fish** /ˈʃɛlˌfɪʃ/ *n, plural* **shellfish** [C,U] a small sea or water animal that has a shell, or this animal eaten as a food

**shel·ter**[1] /ˈʃɛltɚ/ *n* **1** [C,U] a place with a roof over it that protects you from danger or the weather, or the protection that it gives: *a shelter for battered women* | *The family took shelter in the cellar when the tornado hit.* **2** [U] a place to live, considered as one of the basic needs of life: *providing food and shelter for the homeless*

**shelter**[2] *v* [I,T] to provide a place where someone or something is protected, especially from danger or from the weather, or to stay in such a place: *People were sheltering in doorways, under bridges, anywhere.* | *familes who sheltered Jews from the Nazis*

**shel·tered** /ˈʃɛltɚd/ *adj* **1** protected from anything that might hurt, upset, or shock you: *Gina had a sheltered childhood.* **2** protected from the weather: *a sunny sheltered beach*

**shelve** /ʃɛlv/ *v* [T] **1** to decide not to continue with a plan, although you might continue with it later: *The project has been shelved due to lack of funding.* **2** to put something, usually a book, on a shelf

**shelves** /ʃɛlvz/ *n* the plural of SHELF

**shelv·ing** /ˈʃɛlvɪŋ/ *n* [U] a set of shelves, or the material used for them

**she·nan·i·gans** /ʃəˈnænɪgənz/ *n* [plural] INFORMAL tricks or slightly dishonest behavior; MISCHIEF

**shep·herd** /ˈʃɛpɚd/ *n* someone whose job is to take care of sheep

**sher·bet** /ˈʃɚbɪt/ *n* [U] a frozen sweet food made from water, fruit, sugar, and sometimes milk and eggs

**sher·iff** /ˈʃɛrɪf/ *n* a chief police officer in a COUNTY who is elected

**sher·ry** /ˈʃɛri/ *n* [C,U] a pale or dark brown strong wine, or a glass of this drink

**she's** /ʃiz/ **1** the short form of "she is": *She's my little sister.* **2** the short form of "she has": *She's invited us to a party.*

**shh** /ʃʃ/ *interjection* used in order to tell someone to be quiet: *Shh! I can't hear what he's saying.*

**shield**[1] /ʃild/ *n* **1** something that protects someone or something from being hurt or damaged: *police carrying riot shields* | *the heat shield on a rocket* **2** a broad piece of metal used in past times by soldiers to protect themselves in battle, or something that has this shape

shield

shield

riot shield

**shield**[2] *v* [T] to protect someone or something from being hurt, damaged, or upset: *Of course, you try to shield your children from bad influences.* | *a hat to shield your face from the sun*

**shift**[1] /ʃɪft/ *n* **1** a change in the way most people think about something, or in the way something is done: *Polls show a shift in public opinion.* **2** one of the three 8-hour periods in a day during which a particular group of workers are at work: *Lou's on the night/day shift this week.* –see also GEAR SHIFT

**shift**[2] *v* **1** [I] to change your opinion or attitude: *Washington's policy toward Taiwan appears to have shifted.* **2** [I,T] to move something from one place to another, or to change your body's position: *We have to shift the couch that way.* | *Jan shifted uncomfortably in her seat.* **3** [I,T] to change the GEARs when you are driving: *Shift into second gear.*

**shift·less** /ˈʃɪftlɪs/ *adj* not at all interested in working; lazy

**shift·y** /ˈʃɪfti/ *adj* someone who is shifty or has shifty eyes looks like s/he cannot be trusted

**shim·mer** /ˈʃɪmɚ/ *v* [I] to shine with a soft light that seems to shake slightly: *a lake shimmering in the moonlight* –**shimmer** *n* [singular]

**shin** /ʃɪn/ *n* the front part of your leg between your knee and your foot –see picture at BODY

**shine**[1] /ʃaɪn/ *v* **shone, shone, shining** **1** [I] to produce light: *The sun was shining brightly all day.* **2** [I] to look bright and smooth: *Dan polished the car until it shone.* **3** [T] to point a light toward a particular place or in a particular direction: *Shine the flashlight over here.* **4** [I] if your eyes or face shine, they show you are happy: *Jenny's eyes* **shone with** *excitement.* **5** [I] to be extremely good at doing something so that other people notice you: *How can you expect to shine in a job that doesn't interest you?*

**shine²** *v* **shined, shined, shining** [T] to make the surface of something such as a shoe smooth and bright by rubbing it

**shine³** *n* [singular, U] the brightness that something has: *hair with lots of shine*

**shin·gle** /ˈʃɪŋgəl/ *n* [C,U] one of many thin pieces of wood or other material used for covering a roof or a wall

**shin·ny** /ˈʃɪni/ *v* [I] **shinny up/down** INFORMAL to climb quickly up or down a tree or a pole

**shin·y** /ˈʃaɪni/ *adj* bright and smooth looking: *shiny hair | shiny leather boots*

**ship¹** /ʃɪp/ *n* **1** a large boat used for carrying people and things on the ocean: *a cruise ship* **2** a space vehicle: *a rocket ship*

**ship²** *v* **-pped, -pping** [T] **1** to deliver goods: *They ship food all over the country.* **2** to send or carry something by sea

**ship·load** /ˈʃɪploʊd/ *n* the number of people or things a ship can carry

**ship·ment** /ˈʃɪpmənt/ *n* [C,U] a load of goods being delivered, or the act of sending them: *a shipment of TVs | the shipment of goods by rail*

**ship·ping** /ˈʃɪpɪŋ/ *n* [U] **1 shipping and handling** the price charged for delivering goods: *Please add $2.95 to cover* **shipping and handling.** **2** ships considered as a group, or anything that is related to business done by ships: *The canal has been closed to shipping.*

**ship·wreck¹** /ˈʃɪp-rɛk/ *n* [C,U] the destruction of a ship by a storm or an accident, or the damaged ship itself: *survivors of a shipwreck*

**shipwreck²** *v* **be shipwrecked** to have been in a ship that has been destroyed by a storm or an accident

**ship·yard** /ˈʃɪp-yɑrd/ *n* a place where ships are built or repaired

**shirk** /ʃɚk/ *v* [I,T] to avoid doing something you should do: *We cannot simply* **shirk** *our* **duty/responsibility** *to the UN.*

**shirt** /ʃɚt/ *n* **1** a piece of clothing that covers the upper part of your body and your arms, and has a collar and usually buttons down the front −compare BLOUSE −see picture at CLOTHES −see also T-SHIRT **2 keep your shirt on** SPOKEN used in order to tell someone who is angry or upset to stay calm

**shirt·sleeves** /ˈʃɚtslivz/ *n* **in your shirt-sleeves** wearing a shirt but no JACKET

**shit** /ʃɪt/ *n* SPOKEN TABOO **1 shit!/oh shit!** said when you are angry or annoyed about something: *Shit! I haven't finished yet.* **2** something that is bad, badly made, untrue etc.: *This radio is a* **piece of shit.** *| You're* **full of shit,** *Wayne.* (=what you are saying is stupid) *| Maria put up with a lot of shit from Howard.* **3** solid waste that comes out of your body from your BOWELS **4** SLANG ⇨ STUFF¹: *What's this shit?* −**shitty** *adj* −**shit** *v* [I,T]

**shiv·er¹** /ˈʃɪvɚ/ *v* [I] to shake slightly because you are cold or frightened: *a dog shivering with cold/fear*

**shiver²** *n* a shaking movement of your body that happens when you are cold or afraid: *a shiver of cold | A* **shiver ran down my spine.** (=I felt afraid) −**shivery** *adj*

**shoal** /ʃoʊl/ *n* **1** a small hill of sand just below the surface of water, that is dangerous for boats **2** a large group of fish that swim together

**shock¹** /ʃak/ *n* **1** [C usually singular] an unexpected and unpleasant event or piece of news that makes you extremely upset: *Rob's death* **came as a complete shock** *to us.* **2** [singular, U] the feeling of surprise and DISBELIEF you have when something unexpected and unpleasant happens: *He'll* **get a shock** *when he sees the phone bill. | Everyone was* **in shock** *at the news of the bombing.* **3** a sudden painful feeling caused by a flow of electricity passing through your body: *Ow! The toaster* **gave me a shock.** **4** [U] TECHNICAL a medical condition in which someone is very weak, often after an unpleasant experience: *The crash victims are being treated*

**S**

---

**shoes**

flats

high heels

Loafers         sandals

moccasins

pumps

laces

tennis shoes

*for shock.* **5** ⇨ SHOCK WAVE **6** ⇨ SHOCK ABSORBER

**shock²** *v* [I,T] **1** to make someone feel very surprised, and usually upset or offended: *The shooting has shocked the entire community.* | *It shocked us to learn what the real price was.* **2** [T] to give someone an electric shock —**shocked** *adj*

**shock ab·sorb·er** /'. .,../ *n* a piece of equipment connected to each wheel of a vehicle to make traveling more comfortable and less BUMPY

**shock·ing** /'ʃɑkɪŋ/ *adj* very offensive or upsetting: *a shocking crime*

**shock wave** /'. ./ *n* **1** [C usually plural] a strong feeling of shock that people have when something bad happens unexpectedly: *The stock market crash sent shock waves through Wall Street.* **2** [C,U] a strong movement of air, heat, or the earth from an explosion, EARTHQUAKE etc.

**shod¹** /ʃɑd/ *adj* LITERARY wearing shoes

**shod²** *v* the past tense and PAST PARTICIPLE of SHOE

**shod·dy** /'ʃɑdi/ *adj* **1** done or made cheaply or carelessly: *Whoever fixed the roof did a shoddy job.* **2** unfair and dishonest: *a shoddy trick*

**shoe¹** /ʃu/ *n* **1** something that you wear to cover your feet, that is made of leather or some other strong material: *a pair of high-heeled shoes* | *tennis shoes* **2 be in sb's shoes** to be in the situation that someone else is in: *I'm glad I'm not in his shoes, with all those debts to pay.* **3 if the shoe fits, (wear it)** SPOKEN used in order to say that if a remark that has been made about you is true, then you should accept it: *"Are you saying I'm a liar?" "If the shoe fits, ..."*

**shoe²** *v* **shod, shod, shoeing** [T] to put a strong metal cover on the bottom of a horse's foot

**shoe·horn** /'ʃuhɔrn/ *n* a curved piece of plastic or metal that you use to help you put a shoe on easily

**shoe·lace** /'ʃuleɪs/ *n* a thin piece of string or leather that you use to tie your shoes

**shoe·string** /'ʃu,strɪŋ/ *n* **on a shoestring** done or made without spending very much money: *a movie made on a shoestring*

**shone** /ʃoʊn/ *v* the past tense and PAST PARTICIPLE of SHINE

**shoo** /ʃu/ *interjection* said in order to tell an annoying child or animal to go away —**shoo** *v* [T]: *Aunt Betty shooed us out of the kitchen.*

**shoo-in** /'. ./ *n* INFORMAL someone who is expected to win easily in an election or race: *Senator Perry is a shoo-in for reelection.*

**shook** /ʃʊk/ *v* the past tense of SHAKE

**shook-up** /, '.◂/ *adj* SPOKEN NONSTANDARD ⇨ **be/look/feel shaken** (SHAKE¹)

**shoot¹** /ʃut/ *v* **shot, shot, shooting**
**1** ▶KILL/INJURE◀ [T] to kill or injure some-

one with a gun: *One police officer was shot dead in the incident.* | *Did you hear that Dean shot a moose?*
**2** ▶FIRE A GUN◀ [I,T] to fire a weapon at someone or something, or to make a weapon fire: *They drove up and just started shooting at people.* | *learning to shoot a gun*
**3** ▶MOVE◀ [I,T] to move quickly in a particular direction, or to make something move in this way: *The fountain shot a stream of water 10 feet high.* | *A severe pain shot through his chest.*
**4** ▶PHOTO/MOVIE◀ [I,T] to take photographs or make a movie: *Spielberg is shooting on location.*
**5** ▶SPORTS◀ [I,T] to throw, kick, or hit a ball toward the place where you can make points: *Let's go shoot some hoops/baskets.*
**6** ▶GO AHEAD◀ SPOKEN said in order to tell someone you are ready to listen: *"I've got a question." "Okay, shoot."*
**7 shoot the breeze** INFORMAL to have a friendly conversation about unimportant things
**8 shoot your mouth off** INFORMAL to talk too much, especially about your opinions or a secret: *Don't go shooting your mouth off about this.*

**shoot** ↔ **sb/sth down** *phr v* [T] **1** to destroy an enemy plane while it is flying: *The plane was shot down over the ocean.* **2** to say that what someone suggests is wrong or stupid: *Terry's boss shot down all her ideas.*

**shoot for** sth *phr v* [T] INFORMAL to try to achieve something: *Okay, we'll shoot for 1:30.* (=try to do something by then)

**shoot up** *phr v* **1** [I] to quickly increase in number, size, or amount: *Oil prices have shot up again.* | *Your son's really shot up* (=grown very tall) *lately.* **2** [I,T] INFORMAL to put illegal drugs into your body using a needle

**shoot²** *n* **1** an occasion when someone takes photographs or makes a movie: *a photo/fashion shoot* **2** a new part of a plant

**shoot³** *interjection* said when you are annoyed, disappointed, or surprised: *Oh shoot, I forgot to get Dan's stuff from the dry cleaners.*

**shoot·ing** /'ʃutɪŋ/ *n* **1** a situation in which someone is killed or injured by a gun: *Two teenagers were killed in a drive-by shooting.* **2** [U] the sport of killing animals and birds with guns; HUNTING

**shooting star** /,.. './ *n* a piece of rock or metal from space that burns brightly as it falls toward the earth; METEOR

**shop¹** /ʃɑp/ *n* **1** a small store that sells only a particular type of goods: *a card shop* **2** a place where things are made or repaired: *a bicycle repair shop* **3** [U] a subject taught in school, in which students use tools and machinery to make things out of wood and metal, or learn to fix things such as cars and electrical objects —see also **set up shop** (SET¹)

S

**shop**² v **-pped, -pping** [I] to go to one or more stores to buy things: *I've been out* **shopping for** *some things I need for the house.* **–shopper** n –see also SHOPPING

**shop around** phr v [I] to compare the price and quality of different things before you decide which to buy: *It's a good idea to* **shop around** *before buying a laptop.*

**shop·lift** /'ʃɑpˌlɪft/ v [I,T] to take something from a store without paying for it **–shoplifter** n –see usage note at THIEF

**shop·lift·ing** /'ʃɑpˌlɪftɪŋ/ n [U] the crime of taking things from stores without paying for them

**shop·ping** /'ʃɑpɪŋ/ n [U] **1** the activity of going to stores to buy things: *We'd better start our Christmas shopping early.* **2 go shopping** to go to stores to buy things, especially clothes **3** [singular] the things you have bought, usually food: *The boys helped me bring the shopping in from the car.*

**shopping cen·ter** /'.. ˌ../ n a group of stores built together in one area

**shopping mall** /'.. ˌ./ n ⇨ MALL

**shore**¹ /ʃɔr/ n [C,U] the land along the edge of a large area of water: *a house on the eastern shore of the bay*

---

**USAGE NOTE** shore, bank, coast, and seashore

Use **shore** to talk about the land along the edge of the ocean or a lake: *We watched as the boat came closer to shore.* Use **bank** to talk about the land along the edge of a river: *The river overflowed its banks during the storm.* Use **coast** to talk about the total area of land near the ocean: *They live in a little town on the southeast coast.* **Seashore** is similar in meaning to **coast**, and is used especially in the names of places: *The state has set up a research center at the Cape Hatteras National Seashore.* A **beach** is a part of the **shore**, usually covered by sand or smooth stones, where you go for pleasure: *Let's take a walk on the beach.*

---

**shore**² v

**shore** sth **up** phr v [T] **1** to support a wall with large pieces of wood, metal etc. to stop it from falling down **2** to help or support something that is likely to fail or is not working well: *The money is needed to* **shore up** *the failing bank.*

**shorn** /ʃɔrn/ v a PAST PARTICIPLE of SHEAR

**short**¹ /ʃɔrt/ adj

**1** ▶LENGTH/DISTANCE◀ not long: *Sophie has got short blond hair.* | *It's only a short distance from here to the river.*

**2** ▶TIME◀ happening for only a little time or for less time than usual: *Last week's meeting was really short.*

**3** ▶PERSON◀ not as tall as average height: *I'm too short to reach the shelf.*

**4** ▶NOT ENOUGH◀ not having enough of something you need: *I'm* **short of cash** *right now.* | *I'm five dollars short.* | *We're two players short of a team.* (=we need two more players)

**5 be in short supply** to not be available in large quantities: *Fruit and sugar were in short supply then.*

**6 on short notice** with very little warning that something is going to happen: *Sorry, we can't come on such short notice.*

**7 in short order** very quickly: *His demands were met in short order.*

**8 be short for** to be a shorter way of saying a name: *Her name is Becky, short for Rebecca.*

**9 for short** as a shorter way of saying a name: *It's called the Message Handling System - MHS for short.*

**10 in the short run/term** during a short period of time after the present: *These policies will only help us in the short term - in 10 years things will change.*

**11 get the short end of the stick** INFORMAL to be the one in a group who has to do a job that no one wants to do

**12 be short with** to speak to someone in a rude or unfriendly way: *Sorry I was so short with you on the phone.* **–shortness** n [U]

**short**² adv **short of (doing) sth** without actually doing something: *They've cut the budget and the workforce - everything short of canceling the project altogether.* –see also **cut sth short** (CUT¹) **fall short (of)** (FALL¹) **be running short/low** (RUN¹) **stop short of sth** (STOP¹)

**short**³ n **1 in short** used when you want to say the most important point in a few words: *In short, I don't think we can do it.* **2** INFORMAL a short movie that is shown before the main movie in a theater **3** INFORMAL ⇨ SHORT CIRCUIT

**short**⁴ v [I,T] INFORMAL to have a bad electrical connection that makes a machine stop working correctly, or to make something do this

**short·age** /'ʃɔrtɪdʒ/ n [C,U] a situation in which there is not enough of something that people need: *food shortages* | *a shortage of medicine*

**short·bread** /'ʃɔrt⌐brɛd/ n [U] a hard sweet cookie made with a lot of butter

**short-change** /ˌ. './ v [T] **1** to treat someone unfairly by not giving him/her what s/he deserves: *The miners felt short-changed by the new contract.* **2** to give back too little money to someone who has paid you for something

**short circuit** /ˌ. '../ n a bad electrical connection that makes a machine stop working correctly **–short circuit** v [I,T]

**short·com·ing** /'ʃɔrt⌐ˌkʌmɪŋ/ n [C usually plural] a fault in someone's character, or in a product, system etc.: *shortcomings in the public health system*

**short cut** /ˈ. ./ *n* **1** a quicker more direct way of going somewhere: *Let's take a short cut across the park.* **2** a quicker way of doing something: *There are no short cuts to finding a job.*

**short·en** /ˈʃɔrtⁿn/ *v* [I,T] to become shorter, or to make something shorter: *Can you help me shorten this skirt?*

**short·en·ing** /ˈʃɔrtⁿn-ɪŋ, -nɪŋ/ *n* [U] fat made from vegetable oil that you mix with flour when making PASTRY

**short·fall** /ˈʃɔrtfɔl/ *n* the difference between the amount you have and the amount you need or expect: *shortfalls in the city's budget*

**short·hand** /ˈʃɔrthænd/ *n* [U] a fast method of writing using special signs or shorter forms to represent letters, words, and phrases: *taking notes in shorthand*

**short-lived** /ˌʃɔrtˈlɪvd◂/ *adj* existing only a short time: *a short-lived fashion*

**short·ly** /ˈʃɔrtli/ *adv* **1** very soon: *I expect him home shortly.* | *The President left for Washington shortly before noon.* **2** speaking in a way that is not patient: *"Yes, yes, I understand," he said shortly.*

**short-or·der cook** /ˌ. ˌ. ˈ./ *n* someone in a restaurant kitchen who makes the food that can be prepared easily or quickly

**short-range** /ˌ. ˈ.◂/ *adj* designed to travel or operate only within a short distance: *short-range nuclear weapons*

**shorts** /ʃɔrts/ *n* [plural] **1** pants that end at or above the knees: *a pair of tennis shorts* **2** men's UNDERPANTS

**short·sight·ed, short-sighted** /ˌʃɔrtˈsaɪtɪd◂/ *adj* **1** not considering the future effects of something: *short-sighted planning* **2** unable to see very far without GLASSES

**short·stop** /ˈʃɔrtstɑp/ *n* [C,U] the position in baseball between SECOND BASE and THIRD BASE, or the person who plays this position −see picture on page 472

**short sto·ry** /ˌ. ˈ../ *n* a short written story, usually about imaginary events

**short-term** /ˌ. ˈ.◂/ *adj* continuing for only a short time into the future: *short-term loans* −compare LONG-TERM −see also **in the short/long term** (TERM)

**short wave** /ˌ. ˈ.◂/ *n* [U] radio broadcasting that can be sent around the world

**shot¹** /ʃɑt/ *n*
**1** ▶GUNS◀ an act of firing a gun: *Troops fired a warning shot.*
**2** ▶DRUG◀ the act of putting medicine or legal drugs into your body using a needle: *Have you had your flu shot?*
**3** ▶MOVIES/PHOTOGRAPHS◀ **a)** a photograph: *a beautiful shot of the countryside around Prague* **b)** the view of something in a movie, television program, or photograph: *close-up shots of the actress*

**4** ▶ATTEMPT◀ INFORMAL an attempt to do something or achieve something: *Marty always wanted to take a shot at acting.*
**5** ▶DRINK◀ a small amount of a strong alcoholic drink
**6** ▶SPORT◀ an attempt to throw, kick, or hit the ball toward the place where you can get a point: *Nice shot!*
**7 a shot in the arm** something that makes you more confident or successful: *Winning the scholarship was a real shot in the arm for Mike.*
**8 like a shot** very quickly: *He jumped up like a shot and ran to the door.* −see also BIG SHOT, LONG SHOT

**shot²** *adj* **be shot** INFORMAL to be in bad condition or useless: *This battery is shot - do we have another one?*

**shot³** *v* the past tense and PAST PARTICIPLE of SHOOT

**shot·gun** /ˈʃɑtˌɡʌn/ *n* a long gun, used for shooting animals and birds

**shotgun wed·ding** /ˌ.. ˈ../ *n* a wedding that has to take place immediately because the woman is going to have a baby

**shot put** /ˈ. ./ *n* [singular] a sport in which you throw a heavy metal ball as far as you can −**shot putter** *n*

**should** /ʃəd; *strong* ʃʊd/ *modal verb* **1** used when giving or asking for advice or an opinion: *You shouldn't (=should not) get mad so easily.* | *The county should purchase the land to make a park.* | *They should have called the police.* | *Should I wear my gray dress?* **2** used in order to say that you expect something to happen or be true: *Yvonne should be back by 8:00.* | *He's a good cook, so there should be good food.* **3** FORMAL used like "if" in formal CONDITIONAL sentences that use the present tense: *Should you decide to accept the offer, please return the enclosed form.* −see usage note at SHALL −see study note on page 458

**shoul·der¹** /ˈʃoʊldɚ/ *n* **1** one of the two parts of the body at each side of the neck where the arm is connected: *Andy put his arm around his wife's shoulder.* | *When we asked him what was wrong, he just shrugged his shoulders.* (=raised them to show that he did not know or care) −see picture at BODY **2** the part of a shirt, coat etc. that covers your shoulders **3 a shoulder to cry on** someone who gives you sympathy: *Diane's always there when I need a shoulder to cry on.* **4** an area of ground beside a road where drivers can stop their cars if they are having trouble

**shoul·der²** *v* **1** [T] **shoulder the responsibility/burden/costs etc.** to accept a difficult or unpleasant responsibility, duty etc.: *Carrie shouldered the burden of taking care of three young kids alone.* **2** to push through a crowd of people using your shoulders: *He shouldered his way to the front of the room.*

**shoulder bag** /'.. ,./ n a woman's PURSE that hangs from the shoulder by a long piece of material

**shoulder blade** /'.. ,./ n one of the two flat bones on each side of your back

**should·n't** /'ʃʊdnt/ modal verb the short form of "should not": *You shouldn't work so hard.*

**shout¹** /ʃaʊt/ v [I,T] to say something very loudly: *Someone shouted, "She's over here!" | "Welcome everyone!" he shouted to the crowd.*

**shout at** sb phr v [T] to say something loudly to someone because you are angry: *The two women were shouting at each other outside the supermarket.*

**shout** sb ↔ **down** phr v [T] to shout in order to prevent someone from being heard: *The mayor was shouted down at the meeting.*

**shout²** n **1** a loud call that expresses anger, excitement etc.: *suddenly there was a shout from upstairs* **2 give sb a shout** SPOKEN to go and find someone and tell him/her something: *If you can find out any more information, give me a shout.*

**shove** /ʃʌv/ v **1** [I,T] to push someone or something in a rough or careless way, using your hands or shoulders: *Some reporters were pushed and shoved* (=pushed in a crowd) *as they tried to get near the President.* **2** INFORMAL to put something somewhere carelessly or without thinking much: *Just shove those papers into the drawer for now.* **3 shove it** SPOKEN an impolite phrase said when you are very annoyed or angry and you do not want to talk to someone any longer: *"Just shove it, Tony," she said as she walked out.* —**shove** n

**shove off** phr v [I] to push a boat away from the land, usually with a pole

**shov·el¹** /'ʃʌvəl/ n **1** a tool with a long handle, used for digging or moving earth, stones etc. —see picture at DIG¹ **2** a part of a large vehicle or machine used for digging or moving earth

**shovel²** v **1** [I,T] to dig or move earth, stones etc. with a SHOVEL: *When are you going to shovel the driveway?* (=shovel snow from the driveway) **2 shovel sth into/onto sth** to put large amounts of something into a place quickly: *He sat at the table shoveling his dinner into his mouth.*

**show¹** /ʃoʊ/ v showed, shown, showing
**1** ▶MAKE SOMETHING CLEAR◀ [T] to make it clear that something is true or exists by providing facts or information: *The report shows a rise in employment. | a receipt showing that they had already paid | The article shows how attitudes have changed in the South.*
**2** ▶HOW YOU FEEL◀ [T] to show how you feel by the way that you behave: *Even after a long hike, he showed no signs of being tired. | Her face showed her disappointment.*
**3** ▶INFORMATION◀ [T] if a picture, map etc.

shows something, you can see it on the picture, map etc.: *a figure showing the digestive system*
**4** ▶LET SB SEE◀ [T] to let someone see something: *Karen showed us her wedding pictures. | He's showing his paintings at the art gallery.*
**5** ▶EXPLAIN STH◀ [T] to tell someone how to do something or where something is: *Show Beth where to put the cake for the party. | Can you show me how to play the game?*
**6** ▶GUIDE SB◀ [T] to go with someone and guide him/her to a place: *Thanks for showing us around the new building.*
**7** ▶CAN BE SEEN◀ [I,T] if something shows, it can be seen: *His muscles showed beneath his shirt.*
**8 have something/nothing to show for** to have achieved something or nothing after working towards an aim: *I've been practicing so hard, and I still have nothing to show for it.*
**9** ▶MOVIE◀ [I,T] if a movie is showing at a theater, or if a theater is showing a movie, you can see it there: *What's showing at the Carlton?*
**10 show a profit/loss** if a business shows a profit or loss, its accounts show that it made a profit or a loss —see usage note at LEARN

**show** sb ↔ **around** (sth) phr v [T] to go with someone around a place when s/he first arrives in order to show what is important, interesting etc.: *Mrs. Doney will show you around the museum.*

**show off** phr v **1** [I] to try to do things that will make people admire you or what you have: *Jason's showing off in front of the girls.* **2** [T **show** sth ↔ **off**] to show something to many people because you are very proud of it: *The Wilsons are having a party to show off their new house.* **3** [T **show** sth ↔ **off**] if one thing shows off another thing, it makes the other thing look especially attractive: *Your blue tablecloth really shows off the white dishes.*

**show up** phr v **1** [I] INFORMAL to arrive at the place where someone is waiting for you: *The coach was mad because Bill showed up late for the game.* **2** [I] to be easy to see or notice: *The doctor said that the bacteria didn't show up at first under the microscope.* **3** [T **show** sb ↔ **up**] to do something in order to embarrass someone or make him/her seem stupid when other people are there: *I don't like the way you try to show me up.*

**show²** n **1** a performance in a theater or on radio or television: *a new show opening on Broadway | a popular TV show* **2** a collection of things for the public to look at: *the spring flower show* **3 be on show** to be shown to the public: *The photographs will be on show until the end of the month.* **4 a show of** a) something that shows what something is like, how someone feels etc.: *The army marched through the town in a show of force.* b) something that you do to make people think that something is true: *She made a show of interest.* **5 let's get this show on the road** SPOKEN said when you want to tell people it is time to start working or start a trip

**show and tell** /ˌ. . '. / *n* [U] a time during the school day when young children tell the other children in their class about a favorite object they have brought with them

**show biz** /ˈʃoʊ bɪz/ *n* [U] INFORMAL ⇨ SHOW BUSINESS

**show busi·ness** /ˈ. ˌ../ *n* [U] the entertainment industry: *She started in show business as a child.*

**show·case** /ˈʃoʊkeɪs/ *n* **1** an event or situation that is designed to show the good qualities of a person, organization etc.: *Bryan Adams's new album is a showcase for his talents.* **2** a glass box showing objects for people to look at in a store, an art show etc.

**show·down** /ˈʃoʊdaʊn/ *n* a meeting, argument, fight etc. that will settle a disagreement or competition that has continued for a long time: *a showdown between the top two teams in the league*

**show·er¹** /ˈʃaʊɚ/ *n* **1** a thing that you stand under to wash your whole body: *The phone always rings when I'm in the shower.* **2** an act of washing your body while standing under the shower: *Hurry up! I want to take a shower too.* **3** a short period of rain: *Showers are expected later today.* —see usage note at WEATHER **4** a party at which presents are given to a woman who is going to get married or have a baby: *We're having a baby shower for Paula on Friday.*

**shower²** *v* **1** [I] to wash your whole body while standing under a SHOWER: *Is there time to shower before we leave?* **2** [T] to generously give someone a lot of things: *The children are showering the new puppy with attention.*

**show·er·y** /ˈʃaʊəri/ *adj* raining frequently for short periods: *a showery day*

**show·ing** /ˈʃoʊɪŋ/ *n* **1** an occasion when a movie, art show etc. can be seen or looked at: *a special showing of Georgia O'Keeffe's paintings* **2** something that shows how well or badly you are doing: *The senator made a strong showing at the polls.*

**show·man** /ˈʃoʊmən/ *n* someone who is good at entertaining people and getting a lot of public attention —**showmanship** *n* [U]

**shown** /ʃoʊn/ *v* the PAST PARTICIPLE of SHOW

**show-off** /ˈ. ./ *n* INFORMAL someone who always tries to show how smart or how much skill s/he has so that other people will admire him/her: *Don't be such a show-off!*

**show·piece** /ˈʃoʊpis/ *n* something that an organization, government etc. wants people to see because it is a successful example of what they are doing

**show·room** /ˈʃoʊrum/ *n* a large room where you can look at things that are for sale: *a car showroom*

**show·y** /ˈʃoʊi/ *adj* very colorful, big, expensive etc. in a way that attracts people's attention: *showy clothes*

**shrank** /ʃræŋk/ *v* the past tense of SHRINK

**shrap·nel** /ˈʃræpnəl/ *n* [U] small pieces of metal from a bomb, bullet etc. that are scattered when it explodes

**shred¹** /ʃrɛd/ *n* **1** a small thin piece that is torn or cut roughly from something: *The kitten had torn/ripped the toy to shreds.* **2** a very small amount: *There's not a shred of evidence to prove he's guilty.* (=none at all)

**shred²** *v* **-dded, -dding** [T] **1** to cut or tear something into SHREDs **2** to put a document into a SHREDDER

**shred·der** /ˈʃrɛdɚ/ *n* a machine that cuts documents into small pieces so that no one can read them

**shrewd** /ʃrud/ *adj* good at judging what people or situations are really like, especially in a way that makes you successful: *a shrewd businesswoman*

**shriek** /ʃrik/ *n* **1** a very high loud sound: *the shriek of an owl* **2** a high loud sound that you make with your voice because you are frightened, excited, angry etc.: *She gave a shriek of delight and hugged him.* —**shriek** *v* [I]

**shrill** /ʃrɪl/ *adj* very high and unpleasant: *shrill voices*

**shrimp** /ʃrɪmp/ *n* [C,U] **1** a small curved sea animal that has ten legs and a soft shell, or the meat from this animal **2** INFORMAL an unkind word for someone who is very small

**shrine** /ʃraɪn/ *n* **1** a place that is related to a holy event or holy person, and that people visit to pray **2** a place that people visit and respect because it is related to a famous person: *Elvis Presley's home has become a shrine.*

**shrink¹** /ʃrɪŋk/ *v* **shrank, shrunk, shrinking 1** [I,T] to become smaller or to make something smaller: *My sweater shrank in the wash.* **2** [I] to become smaller in amount, size, or value: *The economy has shrunk by 20% in the last two years.*

**shrink from** sth *phr v* [T] to avoid doing something difficult or unpleasant: *She shrank from telling us the news.*

**shrink²** *n* INFORMAL HUMOROUS a PSYCHIATRIST

**shrink·age** /ˈʃrɪŋkɪdʒ/ *n* [U] the act of shrinking, or the amount that something shrinks: *Make the pants longer to allow for shrinkage.*

**shrink-wrapped** /ˈ. ˌ./ *adj* goods that are shrink-wrapped are wrapped tightly in plastic —**shrink-wrap** *n* [U]

**shriv·el** /ˈʃrɪvəl/ **shrivel up** *v* [I,T] if something shrivels or is shriveled, it becomes smaller and its surface is covered in lines because it is dry or old —**shriveled** *adj*: *a shriveled old man*

S

**shroud**[1] /ʃraʊd/ *n* **1** a cloth that is wrapped around a dead person's body before it is buried **2** something that hides or covers something

**shroud**[2] *v* **be shrouded in mist/smoke etc.** to be covered and hidden by mist, smoke etc.: *mountains shrouded in clouds*

**shrub** /ʃrʌb/ *n* a small bush

**shrub·ber·y** /'ʃrʌbəri/ *n* [U] SHRUBs planted close together in a group —see picture on page 471

**shrug** /ʃrʌg/ *v* **-gged, -gging** [I,T] to raise and then lower your shoulders in order to show that you do not know something or do not care about something: *Dan shrugged and went back to what he was doing.* —**shrug** *n*

**shrug** sth ↔ **off** *phr v* [T] to treat something as unimportant and not worry about it: *Marge tried to **shrug** off the boss's criticism.*

**shrunk** /ʃrʌŋk/ *v* the PAST PARTICIPLE of SHRINK

**shrunk·en** /'ʃrʌŋkən/ *adj* having become smaller or been made smaller: *a shrunken old woman*

**shuck** /ʃʌk/ *v* [T] to remove the outer cover of a vegetable such as corn or PEAs, or the shell of OYSTERs or CLAMs

**shucks** /ʃʌks/ *interjection* OLD-FASHIONED said in order to show you are a little disappointed about something

**shud·der** /'ʃʌdə/ *v* [I] to shake because you are frightened or cold, or because you think something is very unpleasant: *Gwen shuddered as she described the man who had attacked her.* —**shudder** *n*

**shuf·fle**[1] /'ʃʌfəl/ *v* **1** [I] to walk slowly and noisily, without lifting your feet off the ground: *an old man shuffling across the room* **2** [T] to move something such as papers or cards into a different position: *Ginny shuffled the papers on her desk.* **3 shuffle your feet** to move your feet slightly because you are bored or embarrassed: *Ernie looked nervous and shuffled his feet.*

**shuf·fle**[2] *n* **1** the act of shuffling (SHUFFLE) your feet **2** the act of shuffling (SHUFFLE) papers or cards **3** the act of officially changing the members of an organization: *a management shuffle*

**shuf·fle·board** /'ʃʌfəlˌbɔrd/ *n* [U] a game in which you use a long stick to push a flat round object along a smooth surface toward an area with numbers on it

**shun** /ʃʌn/ *v* **-nned, -nning** [T] to avoid someone or something deliberately

**shunt** /ʃʌnt/ *v* [T] to give someone or something a less important position than he, she, or it deserves: *Too often the needs and problems of education are **shunted aside**.*

**shush** /ʃʌʃ, ʃʊʃ/ *v* **1 shush!** SPOKEN said in order to tell someone, especially a child, to be quiet: *"Shush!" said Tim. "Don't talk so loud."*

**2** [T] to tell someone to be quiet: *She started to complain, but Betty shushed her.*

**shut**[1] /ʃʌt/ *v* **shut, shut, shutting 1** [I,T] to close something, or to become closed: *Do you want me to shut the window?* | *I heard the back door shut.* | *She leaned back and shut her eyes.*

**2 shut your mouth/trap/face!** SPOKEN used in order to rudely and angrily tell someone to stop talking

**shut down** *phr v* [I,T **shut** sth ↔ **down**] if a company, factory, large machine etc. shuts down or is shut down, it stops operating: *Three nuclear generators were **shut down** for safety reasons.* | *The factory will **shut down** for two weeks this month.*

**shut off** *phr v* **1** [I,T **shut** sth ↔ **off**] if a machine, tool etc. shuts off or if you shut it off, it stops operating: *We **shut** the engine **off** when it overheated.* | *The heat **shuts off** automatically.* **2** [T **shut** sth ↔ **off**] to prevent goods or supplies from being available or being delivered: *Food, oil, and gas supplies were **shut off** during the fighting.*

**shut** sb/sth **out** *phr v* [T] **1** [**shut** sb ↔ **out**] to deliberately not let someone join in an activity, process etc.: *Some people are being **shut out** of the health care system.* **2** [**shut** sth ↔ **out**] to stop yourself from seeing, hearing, or thinking about something: *He can **shut out** the rest of the world when he's working.* **3** [**shut out** sb] to defeat an opposing team and prevent them from getting any points: *The Blue Jays **shut out** the Phillies 3-0.*

**shut** sb/sth **up** *phr v* **1 shut up!** SPOKEN said in order to tell someone rudely to stop talking: *Just **shut up**; I'm trying to think.* **2** [T **shut** sb **up**] to make someone stop talking or be quiet: *The only way to **shut** her **up** is to feed her.*

**shut**[2] *adj* not open; closed: *Is the door shut tight?*

**shut·down** /'ʃʌtdaʊn/ *n* the closing of a factory, business, or piece of machinery: *the shutdown of a paper mill*

**shut-eye** /'. ./ *n* [U] INFORMAL sleep: *I really need some shut-eye.*

**shut-in** /'. ./ *n* someone who is sick or DISABLED and cannot leave the house easily

**shut·ter** /'ʃʌtə/ *n* **1** one of a pair of wooden or metal covers on the outside of a window, that can be closed —see picture on page 471 **2** a part of a camera that opens to let light onto the film

**shut·tle**[1] /'ʃʌtl/ *n* **1** a plane, bus, or train that makes regular short trips between two places: *the Washington-New York shuttle* **2** a space vehicle that can fly into space and return to Earth and be used more than once: *the launch of the Atlantis space shuttle*

**shuttle**[2] *v* **1** [T] to move people from one place to another place that is close: *Passengers are shuttled to the hotel by bus.* **2** [I] to travel frequently between two places: *The visitors* *were **shuttled between** the hotel and the conference center twice a day.*

**shut·tle·cock** /'ʃʌtl̩ˌkɑk/ *n* a small light object that you hit over the net in the game of BADMINTON

**shy¹** /ʃaɪ/ *adj* **1** too nervous and embarrassed to talk to people in a confident way: *Cal's **painfully** shy.* (=extremely shy) **2** unwilling to do something or get involved in something: *He's not **shy about** showing off his wealth.* —**shyly** *adv* —**shyness** *n* [U]

**shy²** *v* [I] if a horse shies, it makes a sudden movement away from something because it is frightened

**shy away from** sth *phr v* [T] to avoid doing something because you are not confident enough about it: *Erik had always **shied away from** speaking in public.*

**shy·ster** /'ʃaɪstɚ/ *n* INFORMAL a dishonest person, especially a lawyer or politician

**sib·ling** /'sɪblɪŋ/ *n* **1** FORMAL your brother or sister **2 sibling rivalry** competition between brothers and sisters for the attention of their parents

**sic¹** /sɪk/ *adv* LATIN used after a word that you have copied into a piece of writing in order to show that you know it was not spelled or used correctly

**sic²** *v* **-cced, -ccing** [T] INFORMAL to tell a dog to attack someone

**sick¹** /sɪk/ *adj* **1** suffering from a disease or illness: *Nina's not coming in today; she's sick.* | *Everyone ate the same thing, but I was the only one who **got sick**.* **2 be sick** to bring food up from your stomach through your mouth; VOMIT: *Uh oh, the dog's going to be sick!* **3 feel sick (to your stomach)** to feel as if you are going to VOMIT: *I felt so sick after eating all that popcorn.* **4 be sick (and tired) of/be sick to death of** to be angry and bored with something that has been happening for a long time: *I'm sick to death of all this arguing.* **5 make me sick** SPOKEN to make you feel strong anger and disapproval: *People who treat animals like that make me sick.* **6** someone who is sick does things that are strange and cruel: *The murders are obviously the work of a sick mind.* **7** sick stories, jokes etc. deal with death and suffering in a cruel or unpleasant way

**sick²** *n* [plural] **the sick** people who are sick: *nurses taking care of the sick and wounded*

**sick·en** /'sɪkən/ *v* **1** [T] to make you feel strong anger and disapproval: *We were sickened by newspaper reports of child abuse.* **2** [I] to become sick

**sick·en·ing** /'sɪkənɪŋ/ *adj* **1** making you feel sick: *The plane dropped with sickening speed.* **2** making you feel strong anger and disapproval: *It's sickening to see so many poor people in such a wealthy country.*

**sick·le** /'sɪkəl/ *n* a tool with a blade in the shape of a hook, used for cutting wheat

**sick leave** /'. ./ *n* [U] the time you are allowed to be away from work because of sickness

**sick·ly** /'sɪkli/ *adj* **1** weak, unhealthy, and often sick: *a sickly child* **2** unpleasant and making you feel sick: *the sickly smell of rotten eggs*

**sick·ness** /'sɪknɪs/ *n* **1** [U] the state or feeling of being sick; ILLNESS: *soldiers suffering from hunger and sickness* **2** an illness: *common sicknesses such as colds and ear infections* **3 air/travel/car etc. sickness** a feeling that you are going to VOMIT, that you get when you travel in a plane, car etc. —see also MORNING SICKNESS —see usage note at DISEASE

**sick pay** /'. ./ *n* [U] wages paid by an employer to a worker who cannot work because of illness

**side¹** /saɪd/ *n*
**1** ▶PART OF AN AREA◀ one of the two areas that something is divided into: *Jim grew up on Detroit's east side.* | *They own a house **on the other side** of the lake.* | *A computer sits **to one side** of the desk.*
**2** ▶NEXT TO◀ the place or area directly next to someone or something: *They walked **side by side**.* (=next to each other) | *Her mother was always **at her side** in the hospital.*
**3** ▶EDGE◀ the part of an object or area that is farthest from the middle: *He was standing at the side of the field.*
**4** ▶OF A BUILDING/VEHICLE ETC.◀ a surface of something that is not its front, back, top, or bottom: *A truck ran into the left side of the bus.*
**5** ▶FLAT SURFACE◀ one of the flat surfaces of something: *A cube has six sides.*
**6** ▶OF A THIN OBJECT◀ one of the two surfaces of a thin flat object: *You can write on both sides of the paper.*
**7 -sided** having a particular number of sides: *a set of eight-sided dishes*
**8 from side to side** moving continuously from right to left: *They sang and danced, swaying from side to side.*
**9 from all sides** from every direction: *enemy gunfire coming from all sides*
**10** ▶SUBJECT/SITUATION◀ one part of a subject, problem, or situation: *I'd like to hear her side of the story.* | *We need to look at the issue from all sides.*
**11** ▶IN AN ARGUMENT/WAR/COMPETITION◀ one of the people, groups, teams, or countries opposing each other in a quarrel, war, competition etc.: *Nancy's **on our side**.* (=agrees with us) | *The two team captains **chose sides**.* (=chose who would be on his/her team)
**12** ▶FOOD◀ a dish that you eat in addition to the main dish of a meal in a restaurant: *I'll have the roast beef sandwich with **a side of** fries.*
**13 on the side a)** in addition to your regular job, sometimes illegally: *He runs a little business **on the side**.* **b)** in addition to the main dish

that you order in a restaurant: *Could I have a salad on the side?*

**14 ▶PART OF YOUR BODY◀** the part of your body from your shoulder to the top of your leg: *She was wounded in her right side.*

**15 ▶OF A FAMILY◀** the parents, grandparents etc. of your mother or father: *Her father's side of the family is German.*

**16 ▶MOUNTAIN/VALLEY◀** one of the sloping areas of a hill, valley etc.

**side²** *adj* **1** in or on the side of something: *You can leave by the side door.* **2 side street/road etc.** a street, road etc. that is smaller than a main street: *They live on a side street off Reseda Blvd.* **3** from the side of something: *a side view of the statue*

**side³** *v* [I] **side with/against** to support or argue against a person or group in a quarrel, fight etc.: *Democrats **sided with** the President on the issue of gun control.*

**side·board** /'saɪdbɔrd/ *n* a long low piece of furniture in a DINING ROOM that you store dishes and glasses in

**side·burns** /'saɪdbɚnz/ *n* [plural] hair that grows down the sides of a man's face in front of his ears

**side·car** /'saɪdkɑr/ *n* an enclosed seat that is joined to the side of a MOTORCYCLE and has a separate wheel

**side dish** /'. ./ *n* a dish that is served along with the main food at a meal: *grilled chicken with a side dish of roasted peppers*

**side ef·fect** /'. .,./ *n* **1** an effect that a drug has on your body in addition to the intended effect: *The most common side effect is a slight fever.* **2** an unexpected result of an activity, situation, or event: *A side effect of tuna fishing was the death of thousands of dolphins.*

**side·kick** /'saɪd,kɪk/ *n* INFORMAL a friend or helper of someone who is more important: *Batman's sidekick, Robin*

**side·line¹** /'saɪdlaɪn/ *n* **1** one of the two lines that form the edges of a field where sports are played, and the area just outside these lines −see picture on page 472 **2** something that you do to earn money in addition to your regular job: *Mark does translation work **as a sideline**.* **3 on the sidelines** not taking part in an activity even though you want to: *There are still buyers on the sidelines waiting to get stocks.*

**sideline²** *v* [I,T] **be sidelined** to not be included in a game or event because you are injured or because you are not as good as someone else: *Their quarterback was sidelined with a knee injury.*

**side·long** /'saɪdlɔŋ/ *adj* **sidelong look/glance** a way of looking at someone by moving your eyes to the side, done secretly or when you are nervous

**side or·der** /'. ,../ *n* ⇒ SIDE¹

**side·show** /'saɪdʃou/ *n* a separate small part of a CIRCUS or a FAIR, that often has very unusual performers

**side·step** /'saɪdstɛp/ *v* **1** [T] to avoid talking about or dealing with something that is unpleasant or difficult: *Congressman Howell sidestepped the reporters' questions.* **2** [I,T] to step quickly to one side to avoid an accident

**side·swipe** /'saɪdswaɪp/ *v* [T] to hit the side of a car or other vehicle with the side of your car

**side·track** /'saɪdtræk/ *v* [T] to make someone stop doing or saying something by making him/her interested in something else: *I think we're **getting sidetracked** from the main issue here.*

**side·walk** /'saɪdwɔk/ *n* a hard surface or path for people to walk on along the side of a street −see picture on page 471

**side·ways** /'saɪdweɪz/ *adj* toward one side, or with the side facing forward: *Mel's car slid sideways as it hit the ice.|They had to turn the couch sideways to get it through the door.*

**sid·ing** /'saɪdɪŋ/ *n* [U] wood, metal, or plastic in long narrow pieces, used for covering the sides of houses

**si·dle** /'saɪdl/ *v* [I] to walk toward someone or something slowly, as if you do not want to be noticed: *Theo **sidled up** to me with an embarrassed look.*

**siege** /sidʒ/ *n* a situation in which an army surrounds a place and stops supplies of food, weapons etc. from getting to it: *a city **under siege** (=surrounded by an army)*

**si·es·ta** /si'ɛstə/ *n* a NAP (=short period of sleep) taken in the afternoon by people who live in hot countries

**sieve** /sɪv/ *n* a kitchen tool that looks like a wire net, used for separating solids from liquids or small pieces from large pieces −**sieve** *v* [T]

**sift** /sɪft/ *v* [T] **1** to put flour, sugar etc. through a SIEVE in order to remove large pieces **2** also **sift through** to examine something very carefully in order to find something: *It will take a while to sift through all these files.*

**sigh¹** /saɪ/ *v* [I] to breathe out loudly and slowly, especially when you are tired or in order to express a strong emotion: *She **sighed with** satisfaction.*

**sigh²** *n* an act of SIGHing, or the sound of sighing: *Judy sat down with a **sigh of relief**.*

**sight¹** /saɪt/ *n*

**1 ▶ABILITY TO SEE◀** [U] the physical ability to see: *My grandmother is **losing her sight**.*

**2 ▶ACT OF SEEING◀** [singular, U] the act of seeing something: *I always faint **at the sight of** blood.|We **caught sight of** (=suddenly saw) Henry as we turned the corner.*

**3 ▶STH YOU SEE◀** something you can see, especially if it is something beautiful, unusual etc.: *The Wrigley Building is one of the most famous sights in Chicago.*

**4 in/within sight a)** inside the area that you can see: *There was nobody in sight.* | *We camped within sight of the beach.* **b)** likely to happen soon: *Peace is in sight.*

**5 out of sight** outside the area that you can see: *The police parked down the road, out of sight of the house.*

**6 lose sight of** to be so concerned with unimportant details that you forget to think about the thing you are supposed to be doing or aiming for: *I think the party has lost sight of its ideals.*

**7 out of sight, out of mind** used in order to say that you will soon forget someone or something if you do not see him, her, or it for a period of time

**8 ▶ON A WEAPON◀** [C usually plural] the part of a gun or weapon that helps you aim at something —see usage note at VIEW²

**sight²** *v* [T] to see something from a long distance away, especially something you have been looking for: *Two bears have been sighted in the area.*

**sight·ed** /'saɪtɪd/ *adj* able to see; not blind

**sight·ing** /'saɪtɪŋ/ *n* an occasion when something is seen, especially when it is something unusual or rare: *Many UFO sightings have been reported in the area.*

**sight·less** /'saɪtlɪs/ *adj* LITERARY blind

**sight·read** /'saɪt ͡rid/ *v* [I,T] to play or sing written music that you have never looked at or practiced before

**sight·see·ing** /'saɪtˌsiɪŋ/ *n* [U] the activity of visiting famous or interesting places, especially as a tourist: *After the conference was over, we went sightseeing.* —sightseer *n*

**sign¹** /saɪn/ *n* **1** a piece of paper, metal etc. in a public place that gives information such as directions or prices, or tells people what to do: *Just follow the signs that say "Montlake Bridge."* | *a no smoking sign* **2** an event, fact etc. that shows that something exists or is happening, or that it will happen in the future: *The train showed no signs of slowing down.* | *Extreme tiredness is an early sign of the disease.* **3** a picture or shape that has a particular meaning; SYMBOL: *A dollar sign looks like "$."* **4** a movement or sound that you make without speaking, in order to tell someone something: *a sign of greeting* **5** one of the SYMBOLs of the ZODIAC: *I'm a Cancer. What's your sign?*

**sign²** *v* **1** [I,T] to write your name on a letter or document to show that you wrote it or agree with it: *Please sign on the dotted line.* | *Sign your name here.* | *Did you sign the check?* **2** [T] to officially agree to employ someone: *Columbia Records signed*

sign

signature

her *to a three-year contract.* **3** [I] to tell someone something by using movements: *She signed to us to get out of the way.*

**sign** sth ↔ **away** *phr v* [T] to sign a document that gives something you own to someone else: *The Puyallup Tribe signed away much of their land rights.*

**sign for** sth *phr v* [T] to sign a document to prove that you have received something: *Can you please sign for the package?*

**sign in** *phr v* [I] to write your name in a book when you enter a hotel, an office building etc.

**sign off** *phr v* **1** [I] to say goodbye at the end of a radio or television broadcast, or at the end of a letter **2** [I,T **sign** sth ↔ **off**] to officially say or show that you approve of a document, plan, or idea: *Garcia claimed he had never signed off on the deal.*

**sign out** *phr v* **1** [I] to write your name in a book when you leave a hotel, an office building etc. **2** [T **sign** sth **out**] to write your name on a form or in a book to show that you have taken or borrowed something: *Who do I see about signing out a company car?*

**sign** sth ↔ **over** *phr v* [T] to sign an official document that gives something you own to someone else: *Dad signed his truck over to me when he got his new car.*

**sign up** *phr v* **1** [T **sign** sb ↔ **up**] to officially allow someone to work for a company or organization: *The Yankees signed him up when he finished college.* **2** [I] to put your name on a list because you want to take a class, belong to a group etc: *About 20 people signed up for the workshop.*

**sig·nal¹** /'sɪgnəl/ *n* **1** a sound, action, or event that gives information or tells someone to do something: *The runners waited for the signal to go.* | *a traffic signal* (=a light telling drivers when to stop or go) **2** a series of light waves, sound waves etc. that carry an image, sound, or message to something such as a radio or television: *broadcasting signals*

**signal²** *v* **1** [I,T] to make a movement or sound, without speaking, that gives information or tells someone to do something: *Marshall pushed his plate away and signaled for coffee.* **2** [T] to be a sign or proof of something: *The March elections signaled the end of a nine-year civil war.* **3** [T] to make something clear by what you say or do: *Carter has signaled his intention to run for mayor.*

**signal³** *adj* FORMAL important: *a signal achievement/failure*

**sig·na·to·ry** /'sɪgnəˌtɔri/ *n* FORMAL one of the people or countries that sign an agreement

**sig·na·ture** /'sɪgnətʃɚ/ *n* your name written the way you usually write it, for example at the end of a letter, on a check etc. —see picture at SIGN²

**sig·nif·i·cance** /sɪg'nɪfəkəns/ *n* [U] the importance or meaning of something, especially something that might affect you in the future: *I hope you all understand the significance of this contract.*

**sig·nif·i·cant** /sɪgˈnɪfəkənt/ *adj* **1** noticeable or important: *Picasso is one of the most significant artists of the 20th century.* **2** having a special meaning that is not known to everyone: *Ginger and Tom exchanged significant looks.* **significantly** *adv* –opposite INSIGNIFICANT

**significant oth·er** /.,... '../ *n* HUMOROUS someone you have a serious sexual relationship with

**sig·ni·fy** /ˈsɪgnəˌfaɪ/ *v* [T] **1** to represent, mean, or be a sign of something: *Changes in the weather may signify that pollution is affecting our climate.* **2** to express a wish, feeling, or opinion by doing something: *Everyone nodded to signify their agreement.*

**sign·ing** /ˈsaɪnɪŋ/ *n* [U] the act of signing something such as an agreement or a contract: *Twelve representatives were present for the **signing of** the agreement.*

**sign lan·guage** /'. ,../ *n* [C,U] a language that uses hand movements instead of spoken words, used by people who cannot hear

**sign·post** /ˈsaɪnpoʊst/ *n* **1** something that is used for holding a street sign up **2** something that shows you what is happening or what you should do: *The employment figures are a key signpost of the economy's performance.*

**si·lence**[1] /ˈsaɪləns/ *n* **1** [U] complete absence of sound or noise: *Nothing disturbed the silence of the night.* **2** [C,U] complete quiet because no one is talking, or a period of complete quiet: *There was a long silence before he spoke again. | The Judge called for silence in the courtroom.*

**silence**[2] *v* [T] **1** to make someone stop criticizing or giving his/her opinions: *Independent media reports have been silenced by the state.* **2** to stop someone from talking, or to stop something from making noise: *Kim tried to silence the shrieking baby by giving her a bottle.*

**si·lenc·er** /ˈsaɪlənsɚ/ *n* a thing that is put on the end of a gun so that it makes less noise when it is fired

**si·lent** /ˈsaɪlənt/ *adj* **1** not saying anything or making any noise; quiet: *The crowd **fell silent** (=became quiet) when the President appeared.* **2** failing or refusing to talk about something: *John **remained silent** when asked about the money.* **3 give sb the silent treatment** to not talk to someone to show that you are angry or upset about something s/he did –**silently** *adv*

**silent part·ner** /,.. '../ *n* someone who owns part of a business but does not make decisions about how it operates

**sil·hou·ette**[1] /ˌsɪluˈɛt, ˈsɪluˌɛt/ *n* a dark shape or shadow, seen against a light background

**silhouette**[2] *v* [T] to appear as a SILHOUETTE: *skyscrapers silhouetted against the sky*

**sil·i·con** /ˈsɪlɪˌkɑn, -kən/ *n* [U] an ELEMENT that is often used for making glass, bricks, parts for computers etc.

**silk** /sɪlk/ *n* [C;U] a thin thread produced by a SILKWORM, or the soft, usually shiny cloth made from this thread: *a silk shirt*

**silk·en** /ˈsɪlkən/ *adj* LITERARY soft and smooth like silk, or made of silk: *her silken hair*

**silk·worm** /ˈsɪlkˌwɚm/ *n* a type of CATERPILLAR (=insect) that produces silk

**silk·y** /ˈsɪlki/ *adj* soft and smooth like silk: *silky fur*

**sill** /sɪl/ *n* the narrow flat piece of wood at the base of a window frame

**sil·ly** /ˈsɪli/ *adj* not sensible or serious; stupid: *I felt very silly wearing that huge hat. | a silly joke* –**silliness** *n* [U]

**si·lo** /ˈsaɪloʊ/ *n* **1** a tall round building used for storing grain, animal food etc. **2** a large structure under the ground from which a MISSILE can be fired

**silt** /sɪlt/ *n* [U] sand or mud that is carried by the water in a river, and settles in a bend of the river or in the entrance to a port

**sil·ver**[1] /ˈsɪlvɚ/ *n* [U] **1** a valuable shiny white metal that is an ELEMENT and is used for making jewelry, spoons etc. **2** the color of this metal

**silver**[2] *adj* **1** made of silver: *a silver spoon* **2** colored silver: *a silver dress* **3 be born with a silver spoon in your mouth** to be born into a rich family

**silver an·ni·ver·sa·ry** /,.. ..'.../ *n* the date that is exactly 25 years after an important event, especially a wedding

**silver med·al** /,.. '../ *n* a prize that is given to someone who finishes second in a race, competition etc., and that is usually made of silver

**silver plate** /,.. './ *n* [U] metal with a thin covering of silver –**silver-plated** /,.. '..◂/ *adj*: *silver-plated bowl*

**sil·ver·smith** /ˈsɪlvɚˌsmɪθ/ *n* someone who makes things out of silver

**sil·ver·ware** /ˈsɪlvɚˌwɛr/ *n* [U] objects such as knives, spoons, and forks that are made of silver or any other metal

**sim·i·lar** /ˈsɪmələ/ *adj* almost the same but not exactly the same: *His interests are **similar to** mine. | The two paintings are very **similar in** style. | kids with similar backgrounds* –opposite DISSIMILAR

**sim·i·lar·i·ty** /ˌsɪməˈlærəti/ *n* **1** [U] the quality of being similar to something else; RESEMBLANCE: *There's **a similarity between** the two men.* **2** a particular way in which things or people are similar: *Discuss the **similarities and differences between** the two writers.*

**sim·i·lar·ly** /ˈsɪmələ·li/ *adv* in a similar way: *two men who were dressed similarly | Men must wear suits; similarly, women must wear a skirt or dress and not pants.*

**sim·i·le** /ˈsɪməli/ *n* an expression in which you compare two things using the words "like" or "as," for example "as red as blood" –compare METAPHOR

**sim·mer** /ˈsɪmə·/ *v* **1** [I,T] to cook food slowly and not allow it to boil: *Let the soup simmer for 5 minutes.* **2 simmer down!** SPOKEN said in order to tell someone to be less excited or angry and more calm –**simmer** *n* [singular]

**sim·per** /ˈsɪmpə·/ *v* [I] to smile in a way that is silly and annoying

**sim·ple** /ˈsɪmpəl/ *adj* **1** not difficult or complicated; easy: *a simple math problem* **2** without a lot of decoration or things that are not necessary; plain: *a simple white dress | a simple meal* –see picture at ELABORATE¹ **3** not involving anything else: *The simple fact/truth is she was hired because she can do the job.* ✗ DON'T SAY "The fact is simple." ✗ **4** consisting of only one or a few necessary parts: *simple tools like a hammer and saw* **5** ordinary and not special in any way: *the simple life of a farmer* **6** OLD-FASHIONED not very intelligent **7 simple past/present/future** TECHNICAL a tense of a verb that is formed without using a PARTICIPLE

**simple in·ter·est** /ˌ.. ˈ.../ *n* [U] INTEREST that you pay on an amount of money that you INVEST, which does not include the interest that it has earned –compare COMPOUND INTEREST

**simple-mind·ed** /ˌ.. ˈ.., ˌ.. ˈ../ *adj* not able to understand complicated things; FOOLISH

**sim·plic·i·ty** /sɪmˈplɪsəti/ *n* [U] **1** the quality of being easy to do or understand, and not complicated: *For the sake of simplicity* (=to make things easier) *the questions can only be answered "True" or "False."* **2** the quality of being plain rather than having a lot of decoration

**sim·pli·fy** /ˈsɪmpləˌfaɪ/ *v* [T] to make something clearer and easier to do or understand: *How can we simplify these instructions?* –**simplification** /ˌsɪmpləfəˈkeɪʃən/ *n* [U] –see also OVERSIMPLIFY –compare COMPLICATE

**sim·plis·tic** /sɪmˈplɪstɪk/ *adj* DISAPPROVING treating difficult subjects in a way that is too SIMPLE

**sim·ply** /ˈsɪmpli/ *adv* **1** only; just: *You can't hit someone simply because you want to.* **2** used in order to emphasize what you are saying; really: *What he said simply isn't true!* **3** in a way that is easy to understand: *To put it simply* (=explain it in a simple way), *the bank decided not to lend us the money.* **4** in a plain and ordinary way: *Alanna was dressed quite simply.*

**sim·u·late** /ˈsɪmyəˌleɪt/ *v* [T] to make or do something that is not real but looks, sounds, or feels as though it is real: *an experiment to simulate the effects of being weightless* –**simulator** *n: a flight simulator* –**simulated** *adj*

**sim·u·la·tion** /ˌsɪmyəˈleɪʃən/ *n* [C,U] something you do or make in order to practice what you would do in a real situation: *Students have had to learn about the planes by computer simulation and from textbooks.*

**si·mul·ta·ne·ous** /ˌsaɪməlˈteɪniəs/ *adj* happening or done at exactly the same time: *a simultaneous broadcast on TV and radio* –**simultaneously** *adv*

**sin¹** /sɪn/ *n* **1** something you do that is against religious laws: *the sin of greed* **2** [singular] INFORMAL something that you do not approve of: *It's a sin to waste food - eat what's on your plate!*

**sin²** *v* **-nned, -nning** [I] to do something wrong that is against religious laws

**since¹** /sɪns/ *conjunction* **1** at or from a particular time in the past: *I haven't seen him since we graduated from high school.* **2** during the period of time after another time or event in the past: *Jim's been working at Citibank ever since he finished college.* **3** because: *You'll have to get up early, since the bus leaves at 7 a.m.* –see usage note at AGO

**since²** *prep* **1** at or from a time or event in the past: *I've been here since 8 o'clock. | Trade has improved since the end of the war.* **2 since when?** SPOKEN used in questions to show anger or surprise: *Since when does having a fast car mean you're a success?*

> **USAGE NOTE since and for**
>
> When you use **since** and **for** with the PRESENT PERFECT tense, they both mean "from a time in the past until now." Use **since** with specific dates: *I've lived here since 1996.* Use **for** with periods of time: *I've lived here for two years.* ✗ DON'T SAY "I've lived here since two years." ✗

**since³** *adv* **1** at a time in the past after another time or event in the past: *His ex-wife has since remarried, but he's still single.* **2** for the whole of a period of time after an event or time in the past: *He graduated in 1983 and has lived in San Diego ever since.*

**sin·cere** /sɪnˈsɪr/ *adj* honest and true, or based on what you really feel or believe: *As a friend, he is both sincere and loyal. | a sincere apology* –opposite INSINCERE

**sin·cere·ly** /sɪnˈsɪrli/ *adv* **1** in a sincere way: *I sincerely hope we meet again.* **2 Sincerely/Sincerely yours** an expression you write at the end of a formal letter before you sign your name

**sin·cer·i·ty** /sɪn'sɛrəti/ *n* [U] the quality of being honest, and really meaning or believing what you say

**sin·ew** /'sɪnju/ *n* [C,U] TECHNICAL a strong CORD in the body that connects a muscle to a bone

**sin·ew·y** /'sɪnyui/ *adj* having strong muscles: *sinewy arms*

**sin·ful** /'sɪnfəl/ *adj* **1** morally wrong; WICKED: *a sinful man* **2** INFORMAL very bad or wrong: *a sinful waste of money/time*

**sing** /sɪŋ/ *v* **sang, sung, singing** **1** [I,T] to make musical sounds, songs etc. with your voice: *Do you like singing folk songs? | Jana sings in the church choir.* **2** [I] if birds sing, they produce high musical sounds **3** **sing sb to sleep** to sing to a child until s/he goes to sleep —**singing** *n* [U]: *a career in singing*
**sing along** *phr v* [I] to sing with someone else who is already singing or playing music
**sing out** *phr v* [I,T] to sing or shout loudly and clearly

**sing.** the written abbreviation of SINGULAR

**singe** /sɪndʒ/ *v* [I,T] to burn something slightly on the surface or edge, or to be burned in this way: *Fortunately, the fire only singed his hair.* —**singe** *n*

**sing·er** /'sɪŋɚ/ *n* someone who sings, especially as a job: *an opera singer*

**sin·gle¹** /'sɪŋgəl/ *adj* **1** only one: *We lost the game by a single point. | a single sheet of paper* **2** not married: *Terry is 34 years old and he's still single. | a club for single men/women* **3** intended to be used by only one person: *a single room/bed* —compare DOUBLE¹ **4** used in order to emphasize a separate thing: *The single biggest/greatest problem we have is money. | She visits her mother every single day.*

**single²** *n* **1** a musical recording of only one song: *Have you heard his new single?* **2** a one-dollar bill — see also SINGLES

**single³** *v*
**single sb/sth ↔ out** *phr v* [T] to choose someone or something from among a group, especially in order to praise or criticize him, her, or it: *The medical center has been singled out for criticism because of its high death rates.*

**sin·gle-breast·ed** /ˌ.. '..◂/ *adj* a single-breasted jacket (=coat) has one row of buttons on the front

**single file** /ˌ.. './ *n* [U] **in single file** in a line with one person behind the other: *Soldiers marched in single file along the quay.*

**single-hand·ed·ly** /ˌ.. '..../, **single-handed** /ˌ.. '../ *adv* done by one person with no help from anyone else

**single-mind·ed** /ˌ.. '..◂/ *adj* having one clear purpose and working hard to achieve it: *a single-minded determination to succeed*

**sin·gles** /'sɪŋgəlz/ *n* [plural] people who are

not married: *a singles bar* (=where single people can go to drink and meet people)

**sin·gly** /'sɪŋgli/ *adv* one at a time: *We sell doughnuts singly or by the dozen.*

**sing·song** /'sɪŋsɔŋ/ *n* [singular] a way of speaking in which your voice rises and falls repeatedly in a boring way —**singsong** *adj*: *a singsong voice*

**sin·gu·lar** /'sɪŋgyəlɚ/ *n* **the singular** TECHNICAL in grammar, the form of a word that represents only one person or thing. For example, "child" is in the singular —**singular** *adj*: *a singular noun/verb* —compare PLURAL —see study note on page 466

**sin·gu·lar·ly** /'sɪŋgyələli/ *adv* FORMAL very noticeably; PARTICULARLY: *She wore a singularly inappropriate dress to the ceremony.*

**sin·is·ter** /'sɪnɪstɚ/ *adj* seeming to be bad or evil: *There was something sinister about the way he looked.*

**sink¹** /sɪŋk/ *v* **sank** or **sunk, sunk, sinking**
**1** ▶IN WATER◀ [I,T] to go down or make something go down below the surface of water: *Bill dove for his wallet, but it sank to the bottom of the lake. | The submarine sank four ships before it was destroyed.* —compare DROWN
**2** ▶MOVE DOWNWARD◀ **a)** [I] to fall down heavily, especially because you are weak or tired: *Lee sank into a chair and went to sleep.* **b)** [I] to move down slowly to a lower level: *The sun sank behind the horizon.*
**3** ▶GET WORSE◀ [I] to gradually get into a worse state: *Krista could see Ari sinking into depression.*
**4** ▶DECREASE◀ [I] to decrease in amount, number, value etc.: *House prices in the area are sinking fast.*
**5** **be sunk** INFORMAL to be in a situation in which you are certain to fail or have a lot of problems: *If he doesn't lend us the money, we're sunk!*
**6** **your heart sinks/your spirits sink** if your heart or spirits sink, you lose your hope or confidence
**7** ▶MONEY◀ [T] to spend a lot of money on something; INVEST: *They had sunk thousands into that house.*
**8** ▶SPORTS◀ [T] to get a basketball or GOLF ball into a basket or hole
**sink in** *phr v* [I] if information, facts etc. sink in, you begin to understand them or realize their full meaning: *At first, what she said didn't really sink in.*

**sink²** *n* an open container in a kitchen or BATHROOM that you fill with water to wash dishes, your hands etc. —see picture at KITCHEN

**sink·hole** /'sɪŋkhoʊl/ *n* a hole in the ground that is made when the roof of a CAVE falls in

**sink·ing** /'sɪŋkɪŋ/ *adj* **a sinking feeling** a feeling that you get when you realize that something very bad is beginning to happen

**sin·ner** /ˈsɪnɚ/ *n* someone who does something wrong that is against religious laws

**si·nus** /ˈsaɪnəs/ *n* TECHNICAL one of the pair of hollow spaces in the bones of your face behind your nose

**sip¹** /sɪp/ *v* [I,T] to drink something slowly, swallowing only small amounts: *Mrs. Hong sat sipping her tea.*

**sip²** *n* a very small amount of a drink: *He took a **sip of** coffee.*

**si·phon¹** /ˈsaɪfən/ *n* a bent tube that you use to get liquid out of a container by holding one end of the tube at a lower level than the container

**siphon²** *v* [T] **1** to remove liquid from a container using a SIPHON **2** to take money from an organization's account over a period of time, especially secretly: *The cash was stolen, **siphoned off** to the black market.*

**sir** /sɚ/ *n* **1** SPOKEN used in order to speak politely to a man when you do not know his name: *Can I help you, sir?* | *Dear Sir* (=used at the beginning of a business letter to a man when you do not know his name) **2 Sir** a title used before the name of a KNIGHT: *Sir Lancelot*

**sire** /saɪɚ/ *v* [T] to be the father of an animal, especially a horse −**sire** *n*

**si·ren** /ˈsaɪrən/ *n* a piece of equipment that makes very loud warning sounds, used on police cars, fire engines etc.

**sir·loin** /ˈsɚlɔɪn/, **sirloin steak** /ˌ.. ˈ./ *n* [C,U] a good piece of meat cut from the back of a cow

**sis·sy** /ˈsɪsi/ *n* INFORMAL a boy that other boys do not approve of because he likes doing things that girls do −**sissy** *adj*

**sis·ter** /ˈsɪstɚ/ *n* **1** a girl or woman who has the same parents as you: *Isn't that your **big/little** (=older or younger) sister?* −see picture at FAMILY **2** a woman who belongs to the same race, religion, organization etc. as you **3** also **Sister** ⇨ NUN: *Sister Frances* −**sisterly** *adv* −compare BROTHER¹

**sis·ter·hood** /ˈsɪstɚˌhʊd/ *n* [U] a strong loyalty among women who share the same ideas and aims −compare BROTHERHOOD

**sister-in-law** /ˈ.. . ˌ./ *n, plural* **sisters-in-law 1** the sister of your husband or wife **2** the wife of your brother, or the wife of your husband or wife's brother −see picture at FAMILY

sitting on a chair · sitting at a desk

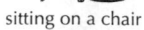

**sit** /sɪt/ *v* **sat, sat, sitting**
**1** ▶ON A SEAT◀ [I] **a)** to be in a chair, on a

seat etc. with the top half of your body upright and your weight resting on your BUTTOCKS: *The children **sat** around her **on** the floor.* | *I was **sitting at my desk** writing a letter.* **b)** to move to a sitting position after you have been standing: *He came and **sat beside/next to** her.*

**2** ▶IN A POSITION◀ [I] to lie or be in a particular position: *A number of old books **sat** on the shelf.*

**3** ▶NOT DO ANYTHING◀ [I] to stay in one place for a long time, especially doing nothing useful: *I can't **sit here** all day, I have work to do.* | *Don't just **sit there** - help me!*

**4** ▶MAKE SB SIT◀ [T] to make someone sit somewhere: *She **sat** the boy **in** a corner.*

**5 sit tight** to stay where you are and not move, or to stay in the same situation and not do anything, while you are waiting for something: *Investors should **sit tight** and see what happens in a few days.*

**6 sit still** to sit somewhere without moving around in your seat: *Sit still and let me fix your hair.*

**7 not sit well with sb** if a situation, plan etc. does not sit well with someone, it makes him/her feel anxious and unhappy

**8** ▶MEET◀ [I] to have an official meeting: *The court sits once a month.*

**sit around** *phr v* [I] to spend time resting or not doing anything useful: *Dan just **sits around** and watches TV all the time.*

**sit back** *phr v* [I] to get into a comfortable position, or not get involved in something: *Just **sit back** and relax - I'll make dinner.*

**sit down** *phr v* [I] to move into a sitting position after you have been standing: *Bobby, get over here and **sit down**.*

**sit in** *phr v* [I] **1 sit in for sb** to do a job, go to a meeting etc. instead of the person who usually does it: *He's only **sitting in for** Sally while she's gone.* **2 sit in on sth** to be present somewhere but not get involved in the activity: *Do you mind if I **sit in on** your class?*

**sit on** sth *phr v* [T] [I] to be a member of an organization or other official group: *Hawkins **sits on** several government committees.*

**sit** sth ↔ **out** *phr v* [T] to stay where you are until something finishes and not get involved in it: *I think I'll **sit** this dance **out**.*

**sit through** sth *phr v* [T] to go to a meeting, performance etc. and stay until it finishes, even if it is very long or boring: *We had to **sit through** a three-hour meeting this morning.*

**sit up** *phr v* **1** [I] to move to a sitting position after you have been lying down: *He finally was able to **sit up** in bed and eat something.* **2** [I] to stay awake and not got to bed: *We **sat up** all night waiting for her to come home.* **3 sit up and take notice** to suddenly start paying attention to someone or something: *The success of writers like Paretsky has **made** publishers **sit up and take notice**.*

**sit·com** /'sɪt˺kɑm/ *n* [C,U] a funny television program in which the same characters appear in different situations each week

**sit-down** /ˌ. '.◂/ *adj* **1** a sit-down meal or restaurant is one in which you sit at a table and eat a formal meal **2 sit-down protest/strike etc.** an occasion when a large group of people protest something by not moving from a particular area until the problem is solved

**site¹** /saɪt/ *n* **1** a place where something important or interesting happened: *the site where the Pilgrims landed* **2** an area where something is being built or will be built: *a construction site*

**site²** *v* **be sited** to be put or built in a particular place

**sit-in** /'. ./ *n* a protest in which people sit down and refuse to leave a place until their demands are dealt with

**sit·ter** /'sɪtɚ/ *n* SPOKEN a word meaning BABY-SITTER, used especially when the person is taking care of older children

**sit·ting** /'sɪt̪ɪŋ/ *n* **at/in one sitting** during one continuous period of time when you are sitting in a chair: *Morris read the whole book in one sitting.*

**sit·u·at·ed** /'sɪtʃu,eɪt̪ɪd/ *adj* **be situated** to be in a particular place or position: *The hotel is situated in the old market district.*

**sit·u·a·tion** /ˌsɪtʃu'eɪʃən/ *n* a combination of all that is happening and all the conditions that exist at a particular time and place: *The present economic/political situation in the country is very unstable.* | *What would you do if you were in my situation?*

**situation comedy** /ˌ.... '.../ *n* ⇨ SITCOM

**sit-up** /'. ./ *n* [C usually plural] exercises for your stomach, in which you sit up from a lying position while keeping your feet on the floor

**six** /sɪks/ *number* **1** 6 **2** six o'clock: *I get out of class at six.*

**six-pack** /'. ./ *n* six bottles or CANs of a drink sold together as a set: *a six-pack of beer*

**six·teen** /ˌsɪk'stin◂/ *number* 16 **–sixteenth** *number*

**sixth** /sɪksθ/ *number* **1** 6th **2** 1/6

**sixth sense** /ˌ. './ *n* [singular] a special ability to feel or know something without using any of your five usual senses such as hearing or sight; INTUITION

**six·ty** /'sɪksti/ *number* **1** 60 **2 the sixties a)** the years between 1960 and 1969 **b)** the numbers between 60 and 69, especially when used for measuring temperature **–sixtieth** /'sɪkstiɪθ/ *number*

**siz·a·ble, sizeable** /'saɪzəbəl/ *adj* fairly large: *a sizable crowd of people*

**size¹** /saɪz/ *n* **1** [C,U] how big or small something is: *A diamond's value depends on its size and color.* | *They wanted so much money for houses half the size of ours!* **2** [U] the fact of being very big: *I couldn't believe the sheer size of the ship.* **3** one of the standard measures in which clothes, goods etc. are made and sold: *This shirt is the wrong size.* ✗ DON'T SAY "have a size." ✗ | *They didn't have anything in my size.: a size 10 shoe* **4 large-sized/medium-sized etc.** large, average etc. in size: *a pocket-sized calculator*

**size²** *v*

**size** *sb/sth* ↔ **up** *phr v* [T] INFORMAL to think carefully about a situation or person so that you can decide how to react: *Julie is able to size up people quickly.*

**siz·zle** /'sɪzəl/ *v* [I] to make a sound like water falling on hot metal: *bacon sizzling in the pan*

**skate¹** /skeɪt/ *n* **1** ⇨ ICE SKATE² **2** ⇨ ROLLER SKATE **3** [C,U] a large flat sea fish

**skate²** *v* [I] to move on SKATEs: *I never learned how to skate.* **–skating** *n* [U]: *Let's go skating.* **–skater** *n*

**skate·board** /'skeɪt˺bɔrd/ *n* a short board with two wheels at each end, on which you stand and ride, pushing your foot along the ground in order to move **–skateboarding** *n* [U]

**skel·e·ton** /'skɛlət˺n/ *n* **1** the structure consisting of all the bones in a human or animal body: *the human skeleton* **2 have a skeleton in the closet** to have a secret about something embarrassing or unpleasant that happened to you in the past **3 skeleton staff/crew/service** only enough people to keep an operation or organization working **–skeletal** *adj*

**skep·tic** /'skɛptɪk/ *n* someone who does not believe something unless s/he has definite proof

**skep·ti·cal** /'skɛptɪkəl/ *adj* doubting or not believing something: *He's very skeptical about astrology.* **–skepticism** /'skɛptə,sɪzəm/ *n* [U]

**sketch¹** /skɛtʃ/ *n* **1** a drawing that you do quickly and without a lot of details: *a pencil sketch of a bird* **2** a short written or spoken description without a lot of details: *The New Yorker had an interesting sketch of E.B. White's life.* **3** a short humorous scene that is part of a longer performance: *a comic sketch*

**sketch²** *v* [I,T] to draw a SKETCH of something

**sketch in** *sth phr v* [T] to add more information without giving too many details: *I'll try to sketch in the historical background.*

**sketch** *sth* ↔ **out** *phr v* [T] to describe something in a few words, giving only the basic details: *Rob sketched out a plan for next year's advertising campaign.*

**sketch·y** /'skɛtʃi/ *adj* not thorough or complete, and not having enough details to be useful: *We only have sketchy information as to the cause of the fire.*

**skew** /skyu/ *v* [T] to affect a test, election, RESEARCH etc. so that the results are not balanced, and therefore not correct **–skewed** *adj*: *Sometimes the data can be badly skewed.*

**skew·er** /'skyuɚ/ *n* a long metal or wooden stick that you put through a piece of raw food that you want to cook −**skewer** *v* [T]

**ski¹** /ski/ *n, plural* **skis** one of a pair of long narrow pieces of wood or plastic that you fasten to boots so you can move easily on snow

**ski²** *v* **skied, skied, skiing** [I] to move over snow on SKIs: *Do you know how to ski?* −**skiing** /'skiɪŋ/ *n* [U]: *We're going skiing this weekend.* −**skier** *n*

**skid¹** /skɪd/ *v* **-dded, -dding** [I] if a vehicle skids, it slides sideways suddenly and you cannot control it: *A car skidded on the ice and went in a ditch.*

**skid²** *n* a sudden sliding movement of a vehicle that you cannot control

**skids** /skɪdz/ *n* [plural] **be on the skids/hit the skids** INFORMAL to begin to fail: *That was when his career hit the skids.*

**skies** /skaɪz/ *n* **the skies** a word meaning the sky, used especially when describing the weather

**skill** /skɪl/ *n* [C,U] an ability to do something very well, especially because you have learned and practiced it: *All you need are some basic computer skills.* | *a painter of great skill* −see usage note at ABILITY

**skilled** /skɪld/ *adj* having the training and experience needed to do something well: *a highly skilled mechanic* −opposite UNSKILLED

**skil·let** /'skɪlɪt/ *n* a heavy FRYING PAN, usually made of iron

**skill·ful** /'skɪlfəl/ *adj* good at doing something that you have learned and practiced: *a skillful doctor* −**skillfully** *adv*

**skim** /skɪm/ *v* **-mmed, -mming** **1** [T] to remove something that is floating on the surface of a liquid: *Skim the fat off the soup.* **2** [I,T] also **skim through** to read something quickly to find the main facts or ideas in it: *Jim skimmed the contract until he found the section on money.* **3** [T] to move along quickly, nearly touching the surface of something: *birds skimming the tops of the trees*

**skim milk** /ˌ. './ *n* [U] milk that has had most of its fat removed from it

**skimp** /skɪmp/ *v* [I,T] to not use enough money, time, effort etc. on something, so it is unsuccessful or of bad quality: *You shouldn't skimp on buying good shoes for the children.*

**skimp·y** /'skɪmpi/ *adj* too small in size or quantity: *a skimpy little dress* | *a skimpy meal*

**skin¹** /skɪn/ *n*
**1** ▶ON A BODY◀ [C,U] the natural outer covering of a human's or animal's body: *I can't wear wool; it makes my skin itch.* | *a skin disease*
**2** ▶ANIMAL SKIN◀ [C,U] the skin of an animal used as leather, clothes etc.: *a tiger skin rug*
**3** ▶FOOD◀ [C,U] the natural outer layer of some fruits and vegetables: *banana skins* | *the skin of an onion* −see picture at PEEL²

**4** **-skinned** having a particular type or color of skin: *a dark-skinned woman*
**5** ▶LAYER◀ [C,U] a thin solid layer that forms on the top of a liquid such as paint or milk when it gets cool or is left uncovered
**6** **make sb's skin crawl** to make someone feel uncomfortable, nervous, or slightly afraid: *He also had a way of making your skin crawl.*
**7** **(do sth) by the skin of your teeth** INFORMAL to only just succeed in doing something: *We made it there by the skin of our teeth.*
**8** **get under sb's skin** INFORMAL to annoy someone, especially by the way you behave: *Her silly voice really gets under my skin.*
**9** **have thin/thick skin** to be easily upset or not easily upset by criticism

**skin²** *v* **-nned, -nning** [T] to remove the skin from an animal, fruit, or vegetable

**skin-deep** /ˌ. '.◂/ *adj* **beauty is only skin deep** a phrase meaning that being a good person is better than being beautiful

**skin·flint** /'skɪnˌflɪnt/ *n* INFORMAL someone who does not want to spend or give away money; MISER

**skin·head** /'skɪnhɛd/ *n* a young person who SHAVEs off his/her hair and often behaves violently against people who are not white

**skin·ny** /'skɪni/ *adj* extremely thin, or too thin: *I was a really skinny kid.* −see usage note at THIN¹

**skinny dip·ping** /'.. ˌ../ *n* [U] INFORMAL swimming without any clothes on

**skin-tight** /ˌ. '.◂/ *adj* clothes that are skin-tight fit tightly against your body: *skin-tight jeans*

**skip** /skɪp/ *v* **-pped, -pping** **1** [T] to not do something that you would usually do or that you should do: *I tend to skip breakfast.* | *Butch got in trouble for skipping school.* **2** [I] to move forward with quick jumps from one foot to the other: *children skipping down the street* **3** [I] to go from one subject, place etc. to another in no particular order: *The speaker skipped around from one topic to another.* **4** [I,T] to not notice or do something, either deliberately or by accident, even though it is the next thing you would usually do: *Oh, I skipped over that question.* **5** [I] also **skip rope** to play with a JUMP ROPE

**skip·per** /'skɪpɚ/ *n* INFORMAL someone who is in charge of a ship; CAPTAIN

**skir·mish** /'skɚmɪʃ/ *n* a military fight between small groups of people or soldiers: *a border skirmish*

**skirt¹** /skɚt/ *n* a piece of women's clothing that fits around the waist and hangs down like a dress −see picture at CLOTHES

**skirt²**, **skirt around** *v* [T] **1** to go around the outside edge of a place: *The soldiers skirted around the town and crossed the river.* **2** to avoid an important problem, subject etc.: *Would you just stop skirting the issue?*

**skit** /skɪt/ n a short funny performance: *a skit about buying a car*

**skit·tish** /'skɪtɪʃ/ adj nervous, frightened, or not sure about something: *He was skittish about lending her money.*

**skulk** /skʌlk/ v [I] to hide or move around quietly because you do not want to be seen: *Two men were skulking in the shadows.*

**skull** /skʌl/ n the bones of a person's or animal's head

**skull·cap** /'skʌlkæp/ n a small cap worn sometimes by priests or Jewish men

**skunk** /skʌŋk/ n a small black and white animal that produces an unpleasant smell if it is attacked

**sky** /skaɪ/ n [singular, U] **1** the space above the earth where the sun, clouds, and stars are: *a clear blue sky|a patch of sky between the clouds* **2 the sky's the limit** SPOKEN used in order to say that there is no limit to what someone can achieve, spend, win etc. −see also SKIES

**sky·div·ing** /'skaɪ,daɪvɪŋ/ n [U] the sport of jumping from an aircraft and falling through the sky before opening a PARACHUTE −**skydiver** n [U]

**sky-high** /ˌ. '.◂/ adj INFORMAL extremely high or expensive: *Prices at the auction were sky-high.* −**sky-high** adj

**sky·light** /'skaɪlaɪt/ n a window in the roof of a building

---

**skyline**

skyscraper

**sky·line** /'skaɪlaɪn/ n the shape made by tall buildings or hills against the sky

**sky·rock·et** /'skaɪ,rɑkɪt/ v [I] to increase suddenly and by large amounts: *Property values have skyrocketed in the past year.*

**sky·scrap·er** /'skaɪ,skreɪpɚ/ n a very tall building in a city

**slab** /slæb/ n a thick flat piece of a hard material such as stone: *a concrete slab*

**slack¹** /slæk/ adj **1** hanging loosely, or not pulled tight: *a slack rope* **2** with less business activity than usual: *a slack period in the travel business* **3** not taking enough care to do things correctly: *Rich is starting to get slack in his work.*

**slack²** n **1 take/pick up the slack a)** to do additional work that needs to be done because the person who usually does it is not there: *With McGill gone, I expect the rest of you to take up the slack.* **b)** to make a rope tighter **2 cut/**

**give sb some slack** INFORMAL to allow someone to make mistakes without getting angry at him/her: *Cut her some slack - she's only been working here two weeks!* **3** [U] looseness in the way something such as a rope hangs or is fastened

**slack³, slack off** v [I] **1** to not work as quickly as you should on your job: *She's always slacking off near the end of the day.* **2** ⇨ SLACKEN −**slacker** n

**slack·en** /'slækən/, **slacken off** v [I,T] to gradually become slower, weaker, or less active, or to make something do this: *We left the cabin once the rain slackened off.*

**slacks** /slæks/ n [plural] ⇨ PANTS

**slag** /slæg/ n [U] waste material that is left when metal is obtained from rock

**slain** /sleɪn/ v the PAST PARTICIPLE OF SLAY

**slake** /sleɪk/ v [T] LITERARY **slake your thirst** to drink so that you are not THIRSTY

**slam¹** /slæm/ v **-mmed, -mming 1** [I,T] if a door, gate etc. slams, or someone slams it, it shuts loudly with a lot of force: *Baxter left the room, slamming the door.* **2** [T] to hit something or someone against a surface, quickly and violently: *Manya slammed the phone down.|Muggers had slammed him up against a wall.* **3** INFORMAL to criticize someone strongly, especially in a newspaper report: *Mayor Watson was slammed in the press for not acting sooner.*

**slam²** n [C usually singular] the noise or action of hitting or closing something hard

**slan·der** /'slændɚ/ n [C,U] a spoken statement about someone that is not true and is intended to damage the good opinion that people have of him/her −**slander** v [T] −**slanderous** adj −compare LIBEL¹

**slang** /slæŋ/ n [U] very informal language that uses new or rude words instead of the usual word for something, often used only by people who belong to a particular group −**slangy** adj

**slant¹** /slænt/ v [I] to slope or move in a sloping line: *a two-door car with a slanted rear window*

**slant²** n **1** a sloping position or angle: *The house sits on a slant.* **2** a way of writing or thinking about a subject that shows support for a particular set of ideas or beliefs: *a feminist slant on Dickens's novels*

**slap¹** /slæp/ v **-pped, -pping** [T] to hit someone quickly with the flat part of your hand: *She spun around and slapped his face.*

**slap sth ↔ on** phr v [T] to put or spread something quickly on a surface in a careless way: *Just slap a coat of paint on, and it'll be as good as new.*

**slap²** n **1** a quick hit with the flat part of your hand **2 a slap in the face** something that someone does that shocks and upsets you, because it makes you realize s/he does not support you: *This decision is a slap in the face to the*

S

*Florida Legislature.* **3 a slap on the wrist** INFORMAL a punishment that is not very severe

**slap·dash** /'slæpdæʃ/ *adj* careless and done too quickly: *a slapdash job of painting the house*

**slap·stick** /'slæp,stɪk/ *n* [U] humorous acting in which the actors fall over, throw things at each other etc.

**slash**[1] /slæʃ/ *v* **1** [I,T] to cut or try to cut something in a violent way with a sharp weapon, making a long deep cut: *Police said the victim had her throat slashed with a razor.* **2** [T] INFORMAL to greatly reduce an amount or price: *Many companies are slashing jobs to reduce spending.*

**slash**[2] *n* **1** a quick movement that you make with a sharp weapon in order to cut someone or something **2** also **slash mark** a line (/) used in writing to separate words, numbers etc. **3** a long narrow wound on your body, or a long narrow cut in a piece of material

**slat** /slæt/ *n* a thin flat piece of wood, plastic, or metal

**slate**[1] /sleɪt/ *n* **1** [U] a dark gray rock that can be easily split into thin flat pieces **2** a list of people that voters can choose in an election

**slate**[2] *v* **1** **be slated to be/do sth** to be expected to get a particular position or job: *Manley is slated to become the next principal.* **2** **be slated for** to be expected to happen at a time in the future: *The corner office buildings are slated for demolition.*

**slath·er** /'slæðɚ/ *v* [T] to put a thick layer of a soft substance onto something: *fresh bread slathered with butter*

**slaugh·ter** /'slɔtɚ/ *v* [T] **1** to kill a lot of people in a cruel or violent way **2** to kill an animal for food **3** INFORMAL to defeat an opponent by a large number of points –**slaughter** *n* [U]

**slaugh·ter·house** /'slɔtɚ,haʊs/ *n* a building where animals are killed

**slave**[1] /sleɪv/ *n* **1** someone who is owned by another person and works without pay for him/her **2** **be a slave to/of** to be completely influenced by something so that you cannot make decisions based on your own opinions: *a slave to fashion*

**slave**[2] *v* [I] to work very hard: *Michael's been slaving in the kitchen all day.*

**slave driv·er** /'. ,../ *n* INFORMAL someone who makes people work extremely hard

**slave la·bor** /,. '../ *n* [U] **1** INFORMAL work for which you are paid a very small amount of money: *$2.00 an hour? That's slave labor!* **2** work done by SLAVEs, or the slaves that do this work

**slav·er·y** /'sleɪvəri/ *n* [U] the system of having SLAVEs, or the condition of being a slave: *Slavery was abolished after the Civil War.*

**slav·ish** /'sleɪvɪʃ/ *adj* DISAPPROVING showing that someone is too willing to behave like or obey someone else: *a slavish imitation of Scorsese's style* | *slavish devotion to duty*

**slay** /sleɪ/ *v* **slew, slain, slaying** [T] LITERARY to kill someone violently: *Kennedy was slain in Dallas.* –**slaying** *n*

**slea·zy** /'slizi/ *adj* low in quality, immoral, and unpleasant: *sleazy bars* | *a sleazy lawyer*

**sled** /slɛd/ *n* a vehicle that slides over snow, often used by children –**sled** *v* [I]

**sledge ham·mer** /'slɛdʒ ,hæmɚ/ *n* a large heavy hammer

**sleek** /slik/ *adj* **1** smooth and shiny: *a cat's sleek fur* **2** attractive and expensive: *a sleek car*

**sleep**[1] /slip/ *v* **slept, slept, sleeping** **1** [I] to be asleep: *I slept well last night.* | *If you're tired, why don't you sleep late tomorrow?* (=sleep until late in the morning) ✗ DON'T SAY "I slept early." SAY "I went to sleep/bed early." ✗ **2** **sleep on it** SPOKEN to think about something carefully before you make a decision: *Sleep on it, and we'll discuss it tomorrow.* **3** **sleep tight** said in order to tell someone, especially a child, that you hope s/he sleeps well **4** [T] to have enough beds for a particular number of people: *The tent sleeps six.* **5** **sleep like a log** SPOKEN to sleep very well without waking up

**sleep around** *phr v* [I] DISAPPROVING to have sex with many people

**sleep in** *phr v* [I] to sleep later than usual in the morning: *I slept in till 10:00 on Saturday.*

**sleep sth ↔ off** *phr v* [T] to sleep until you no longer feel sick, especially after being drunk: *drunks sleeping it off in the jail cells*

**sleep over** *phr v* [I] to sleep at someone's house for a night: *Mom, can I sleep over at Ann's tonight?*

**sleep through** sth *phr v* [T] to sleep while something noisy is happening: *How could you have slept through the earthquake?*

**sleep together** *phr v* [I] INFORMAL to have sex with someone you are not married to: *Are you sure they're sleeping together?*

**sleep with** *phr v* [I] INFORMAL to have sex with someone you are not married to: *Everyone knows he's sleeping with Diana.*

**sleep**[2] *n* **1** [U] the natural state of being asleep: *I had trouble getting to sleep last night.* (=succeeding in sleeping) | *Ed sometimes talks in his sleep.* (=while he is sleeping) **2** [singular] a period of sleeping: *You'll feel better after a good night's sleep.* (=a night when you sleep well) **3** **go to sleep** to start sleeping: *Katherine went to sleep about 7:00 last night.* –compare **fall asleep** (ASLEEP) **4** **don't lose sleep over it** SPOKEN said in order to tell someone not to worry about something **5** **put sth to sleep** to give an animal drugs so that it dies without pain

**sleep·er** /'slipɚ/ *n* **1** someone who is asleep: *Sam's a **heavy/light sleeper**.* (=he sleeps well or wakes up easily) **2** a movie, book etc. that is suddenly and unexpectedly successful

**sleeping bag** /'.. ,./ *n* a large warm bag for sleeping in

**sleeping pill** /'.. ,./ *n* a PILL that helps you to sleep

**sleep·less** /'sliplɪs/ *adj* unable to sleep: *We spent a sleepless night waiting for her to call.* −**sleeplessness** *n* [U]

**sleep·walk·er** /'slip,wɔkɚ/ *n* someone who walks while s/he is sleeping −**sleepwalk** *v* [I] −**sleepwalking** *n* [U]

**sleep·y** /'slipi/ *adj* **1** tired and ready for sleep: *I don't know why I'm so sleepy.* **2** quiet and without much activity: *a sleepy little town* −**sleepily** *adv* −**sleepiness** *n* [U]

**sleep·y·head** /'slipi,hɛd/ *n* SPOKEN someone, especially a child, who looks as if s/he wants to go to sleep: *It's time for bed, sleepyhead.*

**sleet** /slit/ *n* [U] freezing rain −**sleet** *v* [I] −see usage note at WEATHER

**sleeve** /sliv/ *n* **1** the part of a piece of clothing that covers your arm or part of your arm: *a blouse with short sleeves* **2** **-sleeved** having a particular type of sleeve: *long-sleeved shirts* **3** **have sth up your sleeve** INFORMAL to have a secret plan that you are going to use later: *Janssen usually has a few surprises up his sleeve.*

**sleeve·less** /'slivlɪs/ *adj* without SLEEVES: *a sleeveless dress*

**sleigh** /sleɪ/ *n* a large vehicle pulled by animals, used for traveling on snow

**sleight of hand** /,slaɪt əv 'hænd/ *n* [U] quick skillful movements with your hands when performing magic tricks

**slen·der** /'slɛndɚ/ *adj* thin and graceful: *long slender fingers* −see usage note at THIN[1]

**slept** /slɛpt/ *v* the past tense and PAST PARTICIPLE of SLEEP

**sleuth** /sluθ/ *n* OLD-FASHIONED someone who tries to find out information about a crime

**slew[1]** /slu/ *n* **a slew of** INFORMAL a large number: *a slew of new TV programs*

**slew[2]** *v* the past tense of SLAY

**slice[1]** /slaɪs/ *n* **1** a flat piece of bread, meat etc. cut from a larger piece: *Cut the tomato into thin slices.* −see picture at PIECE[1] **2** a part or a piece of something: *The German company wants a slice of the US market.* **3** **a slice of life/history etc.** something that seems typical of life, the history of a place etc.: *The old theater is a real slice of history.*

**slice[2]** *v* [T] **1** also **slice up** to cut meat, bread etc. into thin flat pieces: *Could you slice the bread?* **2** to reduce the size or amount of something: *The budget for schools was sliced by $100 million.* **3** **no matter how you slice it** INFORMAL used in order to say that even if you

consider a situation in many different ways, it is always the same: *No matter how you slice it, we have a big problem.*

**slick[1]** /slɪk/ *adj* **1** good at persuading people, often in a way that is slightly dishonest: *a slick salesman | slick commercials* **2** smooth and slippery: *The roads are **slick with** ice.*

**slick[2]** *n* ⇨ OIL SLICK

**slick[3]** *v*
**slick sth ↔ down/back** *phr v* [T] to make hair smooth and shiny by using oil, water etc.

**slide[1]** /slaɪd/ *v* **slid** /slɪd/, **slid, sliding** **1** [I,T] to move smoothly on or along a surface, or to make something move in this way: *children sliding on the ice | She slid the box across the floor.* **2** [I] to become lower in value, number, or amount etc.: *Car sales slid 0.5% in July.* **3** [T] to gradually start to have a particular problem, attitude etc.: *Morrison gradually slid into alcohol and drug abuse.* **4** **let sth slide** INFORMAL to ignore something: *I didn't agree, but I let it slide.*

**slide[2]** *n* **1** a large structure for children to slide down while playing **2** a small piece of film in a frame that shows a picture on a screen, when you shine light through it: *slides of our vacation* **3** a decrease in the price, value, etc. of something: *a slide in the President's popularity* **4** a situation in which someone gradually begins to have a particular problem, attitude etc.: *School officials are worried about the slide in student performance.* **5** a sudden fall of earth, stones, snow etc. down a slope: *a rock slide* **6** a small piece of thin glass used for holding something when you look at it under a MICROSCOPE

**slide pro·jec·tor** /'. .,../ *n* a piece of equipment that makes SLIDES appear on a screen

**sliding scale** /,.. './ *n* a system for paying taxes, wages etc. in which the amount that you pay changes when there are different conditions

**sli·er** /'slaɪɚ/ *adj* the COMPARATIVE OF SLY

**sli·est** /'slaɪ-ɪst/ *adj* the SUPERLATIVE OF SLY

**slight[1]** /slaɪt/ *adj* **1** not serious or important: *I'm afraid there will be a slight delay.* (=short delay) **2** thin and delicate: *a slight old lady*

**slight[2]** *v* [T] to offend someone by treating him/her rudely: *Meg **felt slighted** at not being invited to the party.* −**slighting** *adj*

**slight[3]** *n* FORMAL a remark or action that offends someone: *I consider the comment a **slight on** the quality of our work!*

**slight·ly** /'slaɪtli/ *adv* **1** a little: *She raised her eyebrow slightly.* **2** **slightly built** having a thin and delicate body

**slim[1]** /slɪm/ *adj* **1** attractively thin: *tall and slim* −see usage note at THIN[1] **2** very small in amount: *a slim lead in the polls* **3** **slim chance/hopes etc.** very little chance etc. of getting what you want: *We have a slim chance of winning.*

**slim²** *v* **-mmed, -mming**

**slim down** *phr v* [I,T] **1** to become thinner by eating less, exercising etc.: *I've been trying to **slim down** since Christmas.* **2** to reduce the size or number of something: *Apex Co. is slimming down its workforce to cut costs.* **−slimming** *n* [U]

**slime** /slaɪm/ *n* [U] a thick slippery substance that looks or smells unpleasant

**slim·y** /ˈslaɪmi/ *adj* **1** covered with SLIME: *slimy rocks* **2** INFORMAL friendly in a way that is not pleasant or sincere, because you want to get something for yourself: *He's so slimy!*

**sling¹** /slɪŋ/ *v* **slung, slung, slinging** [T] to throw something somewhere with a wide uncontrolled movement: *She slung her purse over her shoulder.*

**sling²** *n* **1** a piece of cloth tied around your neck to support your injured arm or hand: *Emily's arm has **been in a sling** for six weeks.* **2** ropes or strong pieces of cloth for holding heavy objects that need to be lifted or carried

**sling·shot** /ˈslɪŋʃɑt/ *n* a stick in the shape of a Y with a thin band of rubber attached, used by children to throw stones

**slink** /slɪŋk/ *v* **slunk, slunk, slinking** [I] to move somewhere quietly and secretly: *The cat slunk behind the chair.*

**slip¹** /slɪp/ *v* **-pped, -pping** **1** [I] to accidentally slide a short distance quickly, or to fall by sliding in this way: *Joan slipped and fell.* | *The knife slipped and cut her finger.* **2** [I] to move quietly or secretly: *After dinner, Al slipped outside.* **3** [T] to put something somewhere or give someone something quietly or secretly: *She slipped his wallet out of his pocket.* | *Dad slipped me $50 when Mom wasn't looking.* **4** [I] to become worse or lower than before: *Standards have slipped in the restaurant since the head chef left.* **5** **slip your mind** if something slips your mind, you forget to do it: *I'm so sorry - it completely slipped my mind.*

**slip into** *phr v* [T] to put clothes on quickly: *I'll just **slip into** something more comfortable.*

**slip** sth ↔ **off** *phr v* [T] to take clothes off quickly: *He **slipped off** his coat and went upstairs.*

**slip** sth ↔ **on** *phr v* [T] to put clothes on quickly: *She **slipped** the dress **on** over her head.*

**slip out** *phr v* [I] if something slips out, you say it without intending to: *I'm sorry I spoiled the surprise; it just **slipped out**.*

**slip out of** sth *phr v* [T] to take clothes off quickly: *Ken **slipped out of** his shoes.*

**slip up** *phr v* [I] to make a mistake: *They **slipped up** and sent me the wrong form.*

**slip²** *n* **1** a small or narrow piece of paper: *a slip of paper with her phone number on it* **2** a piece of clothing worn under a dress or skirt, that hangs from the shoulders or waist **3** **a slip of the tongue** something that you say when you meant to say something else **4** **give sb the slip**

INFORMAL to succeed in escaping from someone who is chasing you: *He gave the police the slip.*

**slip·knot** /ˈslɪpnɑt/ *n* a knot that you can make tighter or looser by pulling one of its ends

**slipped disc, slipped disk** /ˌ. ˈ./ *n* a painful injury caused when a part between the bones in your back moves out of place

**slip·per** /ˈslɪpɚ/ *n* a light soft shoe that you wear in your house

**slip·per·y** /ˈslɪpəri/ *adj* **1** smooth and difficult to hold, walk on etc., especially because of being wet: *Careful, the sidewalk's slippery.* **2** INFORMAL not to be trusted: *a slippery character*

**slip·shod** /ˈslɪpʃɑd/ *adj* done too quickly and carelessly: *slipshod work*

**slip-up** /ˈ. ./ *n* a careless mistake that spoils a process or plan: *One slip-up cost us $100,000.*

**slit** /slɪt/ *v* **slit, slit, slitting** [T] to make a straight narrow cut in cloth, paper etc.: *Slit the pie crust before baking.* **−slit** *n*

**slith·er** /ˈslɪðɚ/ *v* [I] to slide across a surface, twisting and moving like a snake

**sliv·er** /ˈslɪvɚ/ *n* a very small thin pointed piece of something that has been cut or broken off something else: *a small sliver in his finger* (=a sliver of wood) | *a sliver of pie* **−sliver** *v* [T] **−compare** SPLINTER¹

**slob** /slɑb/ *n* INFORMAL someone who is lazy, dirty, messy, or rude: *The guy is a total slob.*

**slob·ber** /ˈslɑbɚ/ *v* [I] to let SALIVA (=liquid produced in your mouth) come out of your mouth and run down: *The dog's slobbered all over the rug!*

**slog** /slɑg/ *v* **-gged, -gging** [I] **1** to walk somewhere with difficulty: *soldiers **slogging through** the mud* **2** to work very hard at something without stopping: *I've been **slogging through** a boring 400 page novel.*

**slo·gan** /ˈsloʊgən/ *n* a short phrase that is easy to remember, used by politicians, companies that are advertising etc.: *The crowd shouted anti-racist slogans.*

**slop¹** /slɑp/ *v* **-pped, -pping** **1** [I,T] to make liquid move around or over the edge of something, or to move in this way: *The coffee slopped out of the cup and all over me.* **2** [T] to feed SLOP to pigs

**slop²** *n* [U] **1** food waste that is used for feeding animals **2** food that is too soft and tastes bad: *I'm not eating that slop!*

**slope¹** /sloʊp/ *n* **1** a piece of ground or a surface that is higher at one end than the other: *a ski slope* **2** the angle at which something slopes: *a slope of 30°*

**slope²** *v* [I] if the ground or a surface slopes, it is higher at one end than the other: *fields sloping to the road*

**slop·py** /ˈslɑpi/ *adj* **1** not neat, careful, or thorough: *sloppy work* **2** loose-fitting and not looking neat: *big sloppy sweatshirts* **3** wet and dirty: *a sloppy lick from the dog* −**sloppily** *adv* −**sloppiness** *n* [U] −compare MESSY

**slosh** /slɑʃ/ *v* [I] **1** to walk through water or mud noisily: *kids sloshing through puddles* **2** if a liquid in a container sloshes, it moves against the sides of the container: *water sloshing around in the bottom of the boat*

**sloshed** /slɑʃt/ *adj* INFORMAL drunk: *Gus was sloshed even before the party started.*

**slot**[1] /slɑt/ *n* **1** a long narrow hole made in a surface: *Which slot do the coins go in?* **2** a time, position, or opportunity for something: *the top-rated TV show in its time slot*

**slot**[2] *v* **-tted, -tting** [I,T] to put something into a SLOT, or to go in a slot: *The cassette slots in here.* | *The instructions tell you how to slot the shelf together.*

  **slot in** *phr v* [I,T **slot** sb/sth **in**] INFORMAL to find a time or a place for someone or something in a plan, organization etc.: *Can you slot me in today?*

**sloth** /slɔθ, sloυθ/ *n* **1** a slow-moving animal from Central and South America **2** [U] LITERARY laziness −**slothful** *adj*

**slot ma·chine** /'. .,./ *n* a machine in which you put a coin, and which gives you more money back if three of the same pictures appear

**slouch**[1] /slaυtʃ/ *v* [I] to stand, sit, or walk with your shoulders bent forward: *Don't slouch like that; you'll hurt your back.*

**slouch**[2] *n* **1** the position of your body when you SLOUCH **2** **be no slouch (at)** INFORMAL to be very good or skillful at something: *He's no slouch at football.*

**slough**[1] /slaυ, slu/ *n* a wet area that is full of mud and dirty water that does not flow

**slough**[2] /slʌf/ *v*

  **slough** sth ↔ **off** *phr v* [T] **1** TECHNICAL to get rid of a dead outer layer of skin **2** LITERARY to get rid of a feeling, belief etc.

**slov·en·ly** /'slʌvənli, 'slɑ-/ *adj* dirty, messy, and careless: *slovenly housekeeping*

**slow**[1] /sloυ/ *adj* **1** not moving, being done, or happening quickly: *They've been slow in answering our letters.* | *The slowest runners started at the back.* | *businesses that are slow to react to market trends* **2** a clock that is slow shows a time earlier than the true time: *My watch is a few minutes slow.* **3** if business is slow, there are not many customers: *It's been a slow day.* **4** not quick at understanding things: *The school gives extra help for slower students.*

**slow**[2] *v* [I,T] also **slow up** to become slower or make something slower: *Road work slowed up traffic this morning.*

  **slow down** *phr v* [I,T **slow** sth ↔ **down**] to become slower or make something slower: *Dave's back trouble is slowing him down.* | *Slow down - no running by the pool.*

**slow**[3] *adv* NONSTANDARD ⇨ SLOWLY

**slow·down** /'sloυdaυn/ *n* a time when an activity takes place slowly, especially when workers are protesting about something: *Sales have fallen since workers began their slowdown.* | *a slowdown in the tourist trade*

**slow·ly** /'sloυli/ *adv* at a slow speed or rate: *The car was moving slowly down the street.* | *The medicine is slowly decreased until the patient is better.*

**slow mo·tion** /ˌ. '../ *n* [U] movement in a movie or television program that is shown at a much slower speed than the speed at which it happened: *a replay of the goal shown in slow motion*

**slow·poke** /'sloυpoυk/ *n* SPOKEN someone who moves or does things too slowly: *Hurry up, slowpoke, or we'll be late.*

**slow-wit·ted** /ˌ. '..◂/ *adj* not quick to understand things

**sludge** /slʌdʒ/ *n* [U] a soft thick substance made of mud, waste, oil etc.

**slug**[1] /slʌg/ *n* **1** INFORMAL a bullet **2** a small creature with a soft body and no legs, like a SNAIL without a shell **3** INFORMAL a small amount of a drink, especially alcohol: *a slug of whiskey* **4** INFORMAL a piece of metal used illegally instead of a coin in machines that sell things **5** a hard hit: *a slug on the jaw*

**slug**[2] *v* **-gged, -gging** [T] **1** INFORMAL to hit someone hard with your closed hand: *I stood up and he slugged me again.* **2** to hit a ball hard **3** **slug it out** to argue or fight until someone wins or something has been decided: *The two sides are slugging it out in court.*

**slug·gish** /'slʌgɪʃ/ *adj* moving, working, or reacting more slowly than normal: *The traffic was sluggish downtown.*

**sluice**[1] /slus/ *n* a passage for water to flow through, with a gate that can stop the water if necessary

**sluice**[2] *v* [T] to wash something with a lot of water

**slum**[1] /slʌm/ *n* an area of a city with old buildings in very bad condition, where many poor people live: *She grew up in the slums of L.A.*

**slum**[2] *v* **-mmed, -mming** [I,T] to spend time in conditions that are much worse than those you are used to: *We traveled around the country, slumming it.*

**slum·ber** /'slʌmbɚ/ *n* [singular] LITERARY sleep −**slumber** *v* [I]

**slumber par·ty** /'.. ,../ *n* a party in which a group of children, especially girls, sleep at one child's house

**slump**[1] /slʌmp/ *v* [I] **1** to suddenly go down in price, value, or number: *Car sales have slumped recently.* **2** **be slumped** to be sitting with your body leaning forward: *He was found slumped over the steering wheel of his car.*

**slump**[2] *n* **1** a sudden fall in prices, sales, profits etc.: *a slump in the housing market*

**2** a time when companies or sports teams are not successful: *The Yankees needed this win to pull them out of a slump.*

**slung** /slʌŋ/ *v* the past tense and PAST PARTICIPLE of SLING

**slunk** /slʌŋk/ *v* the past tense and PAST PARTICIPLE of SLINK

**slur¹** /slɚ/ *v* **-rred, -rring 1** [I,T] to speak unclearly without separating words or sounds: *After a few drinks, he started to slur his words.* **2** [T] to criticize someone or something unfairly

**slur²** *n* **1** an unfair criticism: *racial slurs* **2** an unclear way of speaking in which the words are not separated: *an injury that caused a slur in her speech*

**slurp** /slɚp/ *v* [I,T] to drink a liquid while making a noisy sucking sound: *Stop slurping your soup!* **–slurp** *n*

**slush** /slʌʃ/ *n* **1** [U] partly melted snow **2** a drink made by partly freezing a sweet liquid: *orange slush* **–slushy** *adj*

**slush fund** /'. ./ *n* money that is available to be used but is not kept for one particular purpose

**slut** /slʌt/ *n* OFFENSIVE a woman who has sex with many different people

**sly** /slaɪ/ *adj* **slyer** or **slier, slyest** or **sliest 1** using tricks and dishonesty to get what you want: *He's sly and greedy.* **2** showing that you know something that others do not know: *a sly smile* **3 on the sly** INFORMAL secretly doing something you are not supposed to be doing: *He's been smoking on the sly.* **–slyly** *adv*

**smack¹** /smæk/ *v* [T] **1** to hit someone or something, especially with your open hand: *She smacked him hard across the face.* **2 smack your lips** to make a short loud noise with your lips, especially because something looks good to eat

**smack of** sth *phr v* [T] to seem to have a particular quality: *a policy that smacks of age discrimination*

**smack²** *n* **1** a hit with your open hand, or a noise like the sound of this: *a smack on the head* **2** [U] SLANG ⇨ HEROIN

**smack³** *adv* INFORMAL **1** exactly or directly in, on, or through something: *an old building smack (dab) in the middle of campus* **2** to hit something directly with a lot of force: *The van ran smack into the wall.*

**small** /smɔl/ *adj* **1** not large in size or amount: *Rhode Island is the smallest state.* | *a store selling small appliances* **2** unimportant or easy to deal with: *a small problem* **3** a small child is young: *She has two small children.* **4 small business/farm** a business etc. that does not produce or use large amounts of money: *Magill started a small business publishing reference works.* **5 small fortune** a lot of money: *That house must have cost him a small fortune.* **6 the small of your back** the part of

your back just above your BUTTOCKS **–small** *adv*: *He writes so small I can't read it.*

**small change** /,. './ *n* [U] money in coins of low value

**small claims court** /,. '. ,./ *n* a court that deals with cases that involve small amounts of money

**small fry** /'. ./ *n* [U] INFORMAL **1** children **2** unimportant people or things

**small-mind·ed** /,. '..◂/ *adj* DISAPPROVING only interested in things that affect you, and too willing to judge people according to your own opinions: *greedy small-minded people*

**small po·ta·toes** /,. .'../ *adj* INFORMAL not very big or important: *Compared to his salary, mine is small potatoes.*

**small·pox** /'smɔlpɑks/ *n* [U] a serious disease that causes spots that leave marks on your skin

**small-scale** /,. '.◂/ *adj* not very big, or not involving a lot of people: *small-scale map* | *small-scale development*

**small talk** /'. ./ *n* [U] polite friendly conversation about unimportant subjects: *He's not very good at making small talk.*

**small-time** /,. '.◂/ *adj* unimportant or not successful: *a small-time gangster*

**smart¹** /smɑrt/ *adj* **1** intelligent: *Jill's a smart kid.* **2** making good judgments or decisions: *I don't think that would be a very smart move.* (=good decision or plan) **3** smart machines, weapons etc. use computers or advanced TECHNOLOGY to work **4** saying funny or intelligent things in a way that is rude and not respectful: *Don't get smart with me, young lady!* **5** OLD-FASHIONED neat and fashionable **–smartly** *adv*: *smartly dressed men*

**smart²** *v* [I] **1** to be upset because someone has offended you: *He's still smarting from the insult.* **2** if a part of your body smarts, it hurts with a stinging pain

**smart al·eck** /'smɑrt ˌælɪk/, **smart ass** *n* INFORMAL someone who says funny or intelligent things in a rude way

**smart card** /'. ./ *n* a small plastic card that can be used in many ways, for example as a key, a bank card, as IDENTIFICATION etc.

**smart·y pants** /'smɑrti ˌpænts/ *n* HUMOROUS ⇨ SMART ALECK

**smash¹** /smæʃ/ *v* **1** [I,T] to break into many small pieces violently, or to make something do this: *The plates smashed on the floor.* | *Rioters smashed store windows and set fire to cars.* **2** [I,T] to hit an object or surface violently, or to make something do this: *Murray smashed his fist against the wall.* **3** [T] to destroy something such as a political system or criminal organization: *Police have smashed a drug smuggling ring.*

**smash** sth ↔ **in** *phr v* [T] to hit something so violently that you damage it: *Pete's window was smashed in by the driver of the other car.*

**smash** sth ↔ **up** *phr v* [T] to damage or destroy something: *She smashed up the truck in an accident.*

**smash²** *n* also **smash hit** a very successful new play, movie, song etc.: *the band's latest smash-hit single*

**smashed** /smæʃt/ *adj* INFORMAL drunk

**smat·ter·ing** /'smætərɪŋ/ *n* a small number or amount of something: *a smattering of applause* | *He has a smattering of French.* (=he knows a little French)

**smear¹** /smɪr/ *v* **1** [I,T] to spread a liquid or soft substance on a surface, or to become spread on a surface: *Jill smeared lotion on Rick's back.* | *The note was damp and the ink had smeared.* **2** [T] to spread an untrue story about someone in order to harm him/her

**smear²** *n* **1** a mark that is left when a substance is spread on a surface: *a dirty smear* **2** an untrue story about someone that is meant to harm him/her

**smell¹** /smɛl/ *v* **1** [I] to have a particular smell: *The room smelled of fresh flowers.* | *This wine smells like berries.* **2** [I] to have an unpleasant smell; STINK: *Something in the refrigerator smells.* **3** [I,T] to notice or recognize a particular smell, or to be able to do this: *I smell something burning!* | *I've got a cold and I can't smell at all.* **4** [T] to put your nose near something and breathe in, to discover what type of smell it has: *Come and smell these roses.*

**smell²** *n* **1** the quality that you recognize by using your nose: *the smell of fresh bread* **2** an unpleasant smell; STINK: *What's that smell in the basement?* **3** [U] the ability to notice or recognize smells: *an excellent sense of smell*

---

**USAGE NOTE smell, odor, scent, fragrance, and aroma**

Use **smell** in a general way to talk about something that you notice or recognize using your nose: *the smell of rotten eggs* | *There are some wonderful smells coming from the kitchen.* An **odor** is an unpleasant smell: *The odor of stale smoke was in the air.* A **scent** is what something smells like, especially something that smells pleasant: *a cleaning liquid with a pine scent.* A **fragrance** is an extremely pleasant scent: *the deliciously sweet fragrance of the flowers.* An **aroma** is a pleasant smell from food or drinks: *The aroma of fresh coffee filled the house.*

---

**smell·y** /'smɛli/ *adj* having an unpleasant smell: *smelly socks*

**smelt** /smɛlt/ *v* [T] to melt a rock that contains metal in order to remove the metal

**smidg·en** /'smɪdʒən/, **smidge** /smɪdʒ/ *n* [singular] INFORMAL a small amount of some-

thing: *"Want some more wine?" "Just a smidgen."*

**smile** /smaɪl/ *v* **1** [I] to have a happy expression on your face in which your mouth curves up: *Keith smiled at me.* | *a smiling baby* **2** [T] to say or express something with a smile: *She smiled her thanks.* **–smile** *n*: *a wide smile*

**smirk** /smɚk/ *v* [I] to smile in an unpleasant or unkind way: *Both officers smirked and laughed at him* **–smirk** *n*

**smith** /smɪθ/ *n* **1** goldsmith/silversmith etc. someone who makes things from gold, silver etc. **2** ⇨ BLACKSMITH

**smith·er·eens** /ˌsmɪðə'rinz/ *n* **blown/smashed etc. to smithereens** INFORMAL broken into very small pieces

**smit·ten** /'smɪtˀn/ *adj* **be smitten** to suddenly feel that you love someone or like something very much: *He's absolutely smitten with that new girl.*

**smock** /smɑk/ *n* a loose piece of clothing like a long shirt, worn to protect your clothes

**smog** /smɑg, smɔg/ *n* [U] unhealthy air in cities that is a mixture of smoke, gases, chemicals etc. **–smoggy** *adj*

**smoke¹** /smoʊk/ *n* **1** [U] the white, gray, or black gas that is produced by something burning **2** INFORMAL a cigarette or drugs that are smoked: *Do you have a smoke?* **3 go up in smoke** INFORMAL if your plans go up in smoke, you cannot do what you intended to do

**smoke²** *v* **1** [I,T] to suck or breathe in smoke from your cigarette, PIPE etc.: *Do you mind if I smoke?* | *Ed smokes Cuban cigars.* **2** [I] to send out smoke: *a smoking chimney* **3** [T] to give fish or meat a special taste by hanging it in smoke **–smoking** *n* [U]

**smok·er** /'smoʊkɚ/ *n* someone who smokes **–opposite** NONSMOKER

**smoke screen** /'. ./ *n* something that you say or do to hide your real plans or actions

**smoke·stack** /'smoʊkstæk/ *n* a tall CHIMNEY at a factory or on a ship

**smok·ing gun** /ˌ.. './ *n* INFORMAL definite proof of who is responsible for something or how something really happened: *It was strong evidence, but certainly no smoking gun.*

**smok·y** /'smoʊki/ *adj* **1** filled with smoke: *a smoky room* **2** producing a lot of smoke: *a smoky fire* **3** having the taste, smell, or appearance of smoke: *smoky cheese*

**smol·der** /'smoʊldɚ/ *v* [I] **1** to burn slowly without a flame: *The factory is still smoldering after last night's blaze.* **2** to have strong feelings that are not expressed: *Nick left Judy smoldering with anger.*

**smooch** /smutʃ/ *v* [I] INFORMAL to kiss someone in a romantic way **–smooch** *n*

**smooth¹** /smuð/ *adj* **1** having an even surface: *a smooth road* | *smooth skin* **2** a substance that is smooth is thick but has no big pieces in it: *smooth peanut butter* **3** a way of doing something that is smooth is graceful and has no sudden changes: *Swing the tennis racket in one smooth motion.* **4** operating or happening without problems: *No one said marriage would always be smooth.* **5** polite and confident in a way that people do not trust: *a smooth talker* −**smoothly** *adv* −**smoothness** *n* [U]

**smooth**[2] *v* [T] **1** also **smooth out/down** to make something flat by moving your hands across it: *Tanya sat down, smoothing her skirt.* **2** also **smooth away** to take away the roughness from a surface: *a face cream that smoothes away lines*

**smooth** sth ↔ **over** *phr v* [T] to make problems or difficulties seem less important: *He depended on Nancy to **smooth over** any troubles.*

**smor·gas·bord** /'smɔrgəs,bɔrd/ *n* [C,U] a meal in which people serve themselves from a large number of different foods

**smoth·er** /'smʌðɚ/ *v* [T] **1** to kill someone by putting something over his/her face so that s/he cannot breathe **2** to put a large amount of a substance on or into something: *a cake smothered with/in chocolate* **3** to express your feelings for someone so strongly that your relationship cannot develop normally **4** to make a fire stop burning by preventing air from reaching it

**smudge**[1] /smʌdʒ/ *n* a dirty mark −**smudgy** *adj*

**smudge**[2] *v* [I,T] if a substance such as ink or paint smudges or is smudged, it becomes messy or unclear because someone has touched or rubbed it: *Now look, you've smudged my drawing! | Your lipstick is smudged.*

**smug** /smʌg/ *adj* **-gger, -ggest** DISAPPROVING showing that you are very satisfied with how smart, lucky, or good you are: *a smug smile* −**smugly** *adv*

**smug·gle** /'smʌgəl/ *v* [T] to take something illegally from one place to another: *cocaine smuggled from South America into the United States* −**smuggler** *n* −**smuggling** *n* [U]

**smut** /smʌt/ *n* [U] DISAPPROVING books, stories, pictures etc. that are about sex −**smutty** *adj*

**snack** /snæk/ *n* a small amount of food that you eat between meals or instead of a meal

**snack bar** /'. ./ *n* a place where you can buy SNACKs

**sna·fu** /'snæfu, snæ'fu/ *n* [singular] INFORMAL a situation in which something does not happen the way it should

**snag**[1] /snæg/ *n* **1** INFORMAL a sudden difficulty or problem: *The project **hit a snag** when costs got out of hand.* **2** a thread that has been accidentally pulled out of a piece of cloth because it has gotten stuck on something sharp or pointed

**snag**[2] *v* **-gged, -gging** **1** [I,T] to become stuck on something sharp or pointed, or to make

something do this: *Marty's fishing line **snagged on** a tree branch.* **2** [T] INFORMAL to get someone to notice you, or to manage to get something: *Can you snag that waiter for me? | "That's mine!" she yelled, snagging the necklace.*

**snail** /sneɪl/ *n* **1** a small creature with a soft body and no legs that has a round shell on its back **2 at a snail's pace** extremely slowly

**snake**[1] /sneɪk/ *n* a REPTILE (=type of animal) with a long thin body and no legs

**snake**[2] *v* [I] LITERARY to move in long twisting curves: *The train **snaked its way through** the hills.*

**snap**[1] /snæp/ *v* **-pped, -pping** **1** [I,T] if something long and thin snaps, or if you snap it, it breaks with a short loud noise: *He **snapped** the chalk **in two**.* (=into two pieces) | *Dry branches snapped under their feet.* **2** [I,T] to move into a particular position with a short loud noise, or to make something move like this: *The pieces just **snap together** like this. | She **snapped** her briefcase **open/shut**.* **3** [I] to speak quickly in an angry way: *I'm sorry I **snapped at** you.* **4** [I] if an animal such as a dog snaps, it tries to bite you **5 snap your fingers** to make a short loud noise by moving a finger quickly across the thumb on the same hand **6** [T] to stop a series of events: *Tampa snapped an eight-game losing streak on Saturday.* **7** [I] to suddenly become unable to control a strong feeling such as anger or worry: *I don't know what happened - I guess I just snapped.*

**snap out of** sth *phr v* [T] INFORMAL to suddenly stop being sad, tired, upset, etc.: *Come on, Gary, snap out of it.*

**snap up** *phr v* [T] **1** [**snap** sth ↔ **up**] to buy something immediately, especially because it is very cheap: *snapping up bargains at a sale* **2** [**snap** sb ↔ **up**] to eagerly take an opportunity to have someone as part of your company, team etc.

**snap**[2] *n* **1** [singular] a sudden short loud noise, especially of something breaking or closing: *I heard a snap, and then the tree just fell over.* **2** a small metal object that fastens clothes by pressing two parts together **3 be a snap** INFORMAL to be very easy to do: *Making pie crust is a snap.* **4** ⇨ SNAPSHOT −see also **cold snap** (COLD[1])

**snap**[3] *adj* **snap judgment/decision** a judgment or decision made too quickly

**snap·drag·on** /'. ,../ *n* a white, yellow, or red garden flower

**snap·per** /'snæpɚ/ *n* [C,U] a common fish that lives in warm seas, or the meat from this fish

**snap·py** /'snæpi/ *adj* **1 make it snappy** SPOKEN said in order to tell someone to hurry **2** spoken or written in a short, clear, and often funny way: *a snappy answer* **3** quick to react in an angry or annoyed way: *You don't have to be so snappy!* **4** INFORMAL snappy clothes are attractive and fashionable: *a snappy blue blazer*

**snap·shot** /'snæpʃɑt/ *n* an informal photograph

**snare**[1] /snɛr/ *n* a trap for catching an animal

**snare**[2] *v* [T] **1** to catch an animal using a SNARE **2** to catch someone, especially by tricking him/her: *Ships patrol the coast to snare drug dealers*

**snarl** /snɑrl/ *v* **1** [I,T] to speak or say something in an angry way: *"Shut up!" he snarled.* **2** [I] if an animal snarls it makes a low angry sound and shows its teeth **3** [I,T] also **snarl up** if traffic snarls or is snarled, it cannot move **4** [I] if hair, thread, wires etc. snarl, they become twisted and messy −**snarl** *n*

**snarl-up** /'. ./ *n* INFORMAL a situation that prevents work from continuing or traffic from moving

**snatch**[1] /snætʃ/ *v* [T] **1** to take away from someone, especially by force: *Huong saw two youths snatch a woman's purse.* **2** to quickly take the opportunity to do something: *I managed to snatch an hour's sleep on the bus.*

**snatch**[2] *n* **a snatch of conversation/song etc.** a short and incomplete part of something that you hear

**snaz·zy** /'snæzi/ *adj* INFORMAL very bright, attractive, and fashionable: *a snazzy new car*

**sneak**[1] /snik/ *v* sneaked *or* snuck, sneaked *or* snuck, sneaking **1** [I] to go somewhere quietly and secretly: *Three boys tried to sneak past the guard.* **2** [T] to take something somewhere secretly: *students sneaking beer up to their dorm rooms* **3** **sneak a look/glance at** to look at something quickly and secretly: *I sneaked a look at her diary.*

**sneak up** *phr v* [I] to come near someone very quietly, so s/he does not see or hear you: *Don't sneak up on me like that!* | *Erickson snuck up behind him and grabbed the gun.*

**sneak**[2] *n* INFORMAL someone who does things secretly and cannot be trusted

**sneak·er** /'snikɚ/ *n* ⇨ TENNIS SHOE

**sneak·ing** /'snikɪŋ/ *adj* **have a sneaking suspicion/feeling** to think you know something without being sure: *I have a sneaking suspicion that he's dating someone else.*

**sneak·y** /'sniki/ *adj* doing things in a secret and often dishonest way

**sneer** /snɪr/ *v* [I] to show you have no respect for a person or idea by the expression on your face, or by the way you talk about him, her, or it: *Ned always sneered at the type of people who went to the opera.* −**sneer** *n*

**sneeze** /sniz/ *v* [I] **1** to suddenly have air burst out of your nose in an uncontrolled way, for example when you are sick: *I've been sneezing all night!* **2** **sth is nothing to sneeze at** INFORMAL used in order to say that something is

impressive enough to be considered important: *With 35 nations involved, the competition is nothing to be sneezed at.* −**sneeze** *n*

**snick·er** /'snɪkɚ/ *v* [I] to laugh quietly at something that is not supposed to be funny −**snicker** *n*

**snide** /snaɪd/ *adj* funny but unkind: *a snide remark about her clothes*

**sniff** /snɪf/ *v* **1** [I] to breathe air into your nose with a loud sound, especially in short breaths: *Stop sniffing and blow your nose!* **2** [I,T] to breathe in through your nose in order to smell something: *cats sniffing at their food* −**sniff** *n*

**sniff at** sth *phr v* [T] to refuse something in a proud way: *A job with them is nothing to sniff at.* (=something you should not refuse)

**sniff** sth ↔ **out** *phr v* [T] to discover or find something by its smell: *dogs that sniff out drugs*

**snif·fle** /'snɪfəl/ *v* [I] to SNIFF again and again, especially when you are crying or are sick

**snif·fles** /'snɪfəlz/ *n* **the sniffles** a slight cold: *Max has had the sniffles all week.*

**snig·ger** /'snɪgɚ/ *v* [I] ⇨ SNICKER

**snip** /snɪp/ *v* **-pped, -pping** [I,T] to cut something with scissors using quick small cuts −**snip** *n*

**snipe** /snaɪp/ *v* [I] **1** to criticize someone in an unkind way: *I wish you two would stop sniping at each other.* **2** to shoot at unprotected people from a hidden position

**snip·er** /'snaɪpɚ/ *n* someone who shoots at unprotected people from a hidden position

**snip·pet** /'snɪpɪt/ *n* **snippet of information/ news etc.** a small piece of information etc.

**snit** /snɪt/ *n* **be in a snit** INFORMAL to be unreasonably annoyed about something: *Dan's in a snit because I used his flashlight.*

**snitch** /snɪtʃ/ *v* INFORMAL **1** [I] DISAPPROVING to tell someone that someone else has done something wrong because you want him/her to be punished **2** [T] to steal something, especially something that is small and not valuable: *I snitched a couple of cookies.* −**snitch** *n*

**sniv·el·ing** /'snɪvəlɪŋ/ *adj* behaving or speaking in a weak complaining way, especially while crying: *a sniveling little brat*

**snob** /snɑb/ *n* **1** someone who thinks s/he is better than people from a lower social class **2** **music/wine etc. snob** someone who knows a lot about music etc. and thinks his/her opinions are better than other people's

**snob·ber·y** /'snɑbəri/ *n* [U] the attitudes and behavior of SNOBs

**snob·bish** /'snɑbɪʃ/, **snob·by** /'snɑbi/ *adj* having attitudes and behavior that are typical of a SNOB

**snoop** /snup/ *v* [I] to try to find out about someone's private affairs by secretly looking at his/her things: *I caught her snooping in/around my office.* −**snoop** *n*

**snoot·y** /'snuti/ *adj* typical of people who think they are better than other people, or full of people like this: *snooty restaurant service | a snooty East Coast private college*

**snooze** /snuz/ *v* [I] INFORMAL to sleep for a short time: *Dad was snoozing on the sofa.* —**snooze** *n*

**snore** /snɔr/ *v* [I] to make a loud noise each time you breathe while you are asleep —**snore** *n*

**snor·kel¹** /'snɔrkəl/ *n* a tube that allows a swimmer to breathe air when s/he is under water

**snorkel²** *v* [I] to swim using a SNORKEL —**snorkeling** *n* [U]

**snort** /snɔrt/ *v* **1** [I,T] to make a noise by forcing air out through your nose, in order to express anger or annoyance, or while laughing: *Olsen **snorted at** the suggestion.* **2** [T] SLANG to take illegal drugs by breathing them in through your nose —**snort** *n*

**snot** /snɑt/ *n* INFORMAL **1** [U] an impolite word meaning the thick liquid that is produced in your nose **2** someone who is SNOTTY

**snot·ty** /'snɑti/ *adj* INFORMAL **1** showing that you think you are better than other people; SNOBBISH: *a snotty rich woman* **2** an impolite word meaning wet and dirty with the thick liquid that is produced in your nose: *a snotty handkerchief*

**snout** /snaʊt/ *n* the long nose of some kinds of animals, such as pigs

**snow¹** /snoʊ/ *n* **1** [U] water frozen into soft white pieces that fall like rain in cold weather **2** a period of time during which snow falls: *the first snow of the winter* —see usage note at WEATHER

**snow²** *v* **1 it snows** if it snows, snow falls from the sky: *Look, it's snowing!* **2 be snowed in** to be unable to leave a place because so much snow has fallen there: *We were snowed in for a week.* **3 be snowed under (with sth)** to have more work than you can deal with: *I'd love to go, but I'm totally snowed under right now.* **4** [T] INFORMAL to make someone believe or support something that is not true: *Even the banks were snowed by this charming conman.*

**snow·ball¹** /'snoʊbɔl/ *n* **1** a ball made out of snow: *kids throwing snowballs* **2 not have a snowball's chance (in hell)** INFORMAL to have no possibility of success

**snowball²** *v* [I] if a problem or situation snowballs, it gets bigger or harder to control at a faster and faster rate

**snow·bound** /'snoʊbaʊnd/ *adj* unable to leave a place because there is too much snow

**snow·drift** /'snoʊˌdrɪft/ *n* a large amount of snow piled up by the wind

**snow·fall** /'snoʊfɔl/ *n* [C,U] an occasion when snow falls from the sky, or the amount that falls in a particular period of time: *Their average annual snowfall is 24 inches. | a light snowfall*

**snow·flake** /'snoʊfleɪk/ *n* a small soft white piece of frozen water that falls as snow

**snow job** /'. ./ *n* INFORMAL an act of making someone believe something that is not true

**snow·man** /'snoʊmæn/ *n* a figure of a person made out of snow

**snow·plow** /'snoʊplaʊ/ *n* a vehicle or piece of equipment for pushing snow off roads

**snow·shoe** /'snoʊʃu/ *n* one of a pair of wide flat frames used for walking on snow without sinking

**snow·storm** /'snoʊstɔrm/ *n* a storm with strong winds and a lot of snow

**snow-white** /ˌ. '.◂/ *adj* pure white

**snow·y** /'snoʊi/ *adj* **1** snowing, or full of snow: *snowy weather* **2** LITERARY pure white: *snowy white hair*

**snub** /snʌb/ *v* **-bbed, -bbing** [T] to be rude to someone, especially by ignoring him/her: *Despite her success, the critics snubbed her.* —**snub** *n*

**snuck** /snʌk/ *v* a past tense and PAST PARTICIPLE of SNEAK

**snuff¹** /snʌf/, **snuff out** *v* **1** [T] to put out a CANDLE flame by covering it or pressing the burning part with your fingers **2** INFORMAL to stop something completely: *laws intended to snuff out smoking in public places* **3** SLANG to kill someone

**snuff²** *n* [U] tobacco made into a powder, which people SNIFF through their noses

**snug** /snʌg/ *adj* **-gger, -ggest** **1** warm and comfortable: *a snug little room* **2** clothes that are snug fit fairly tightly —**snugly** *adv*

**snug·gle** /'snʌgəl/, **snuggle up** *v* [I] INFORMAL to get into a warm comfortable position: *couples snuggling up on cold winter nights*

**so¹** /soʊ/ *adv* **1 so...that** used in order to describe or emphasize a quality: *Jack is so fat that he can't get through the door.* **2** SPOKEN NONSTANDARD said in order to emphasize an adjective: *That party was so boring!* **3** used in order to talk about an idea, situation etc. that has already been mentioned: *"Will I need my coat?" "I don't think so."* **4** a word meaning "also," used at the beginning or in the middle of sentences: *Vince is an idiot and so is his wife.* **5** a word meaning "very," used in order to emphasize feelings: *I'm so glad you could come.* **6 or so** used when you cannot be exact about a number, amount, or period of time: *He left a week or so ago. | Dena had five drinks or so.* **7 and so on/forth** used after a list to show that there are other similar things that could also be mentioned: *a room full of old furniture, paintings, rugs, and so forth* **8 so as (not) to do sth** in order to do or not do something: *Try to remain calm so as not to alarm anyone.*

SPOKEN PHRASES

**9** said in order to get someone's attention, especially in order to ask him/her a question:

*So, what do you think of the school?*
**10** said when you are making sure that you have understood something: *So you aren't actually leaving until Friday?*
**11** used with a movement of your hand when you are describing how big, tall etc. something or someone is, or how to do something: *It was about so big.│Then you fold the paper like so.* **12** also **so what?** used in order to say impolitely that you do not think that something is important· *"I'm going to tell Mom what you said." "So?"│Yes, I'm late. So what?* **13 so long!** used in order to say goodbye **14 so help me** said in order to threaten someone, although you will probably not do what you say: *Shut up or so help me I'll kill you!*
**15 so much for** used in order to say that something you tried to do did not work, or something that was promised did not happen: *Well, so much for getting out of here at five o'clock.*

—see usage notes at AS¹, SUCH

**so²** *conjunction* **1** used in order to show why something happens; therefore: *I got hungry, so I made a sandwich.* ✗ DON'T SAY "Since I got hungry, so I made a sandwich." ✗ **2 so (that)** in order to make something happen, or make something possible: *I put your keys in the drawer so they wouldn't get lost.*

**so³** *adj* **sth is so** used in order to say that something is true: *Please, say it isn't so!│Is that so?*

**soak** /souk/ *v* [I,T] **1** if you soak something or let it soak, you cover it with liquid for a period of time: *Just put that dish in the sink to soak.│Soak the beans overnight.* **2** if water soaks somewhere or soaks something, it makes something completely wet: *The rain had soaked through her jacket.* **3** [T] INFORMAL to make someone pay a very large amount of money for something: *a tax designed to soak the rich*
**soak** sth ↔ **up** *phr v* [T] **1** if something soaks up a liquid, it takes the liquid into itself; ABSORB: *Serve grilled bread for soaking up the broth.* **2** to enjoy everything about an experience: *I'm going to spend a week just soaking up the sunshine.* **3** INFORMAL to learn a lot quickly

**soaked** /soukt/ *adj* very wet: *I'm absolutely soaked.*

**soak·ing** /'soukɪŋ/, **soaking wet** /ˌ.. './ *adj* completely wet: *Your shoes are soaking wet!*

**so-and-so** /'. . ./ *n* SPOKEN used in order to talk about someone, without saying his/her name

**soap¹** /soup/ *n* **1** [U] the substance that you use with water to wash things, especially your body: *a bar of soap* **2** INFORMAL ⇨ SOAP OPERA

**soap²** *v* [T] to rub soap on someone or something

**soap·box** /'soupbaks/ *n* **get on your soap-**

**box** INFORMAL to tell people your opinions about something in a loud and forceful way

**soap ope·ra** /'. ,../ *n* a television or radio story about the daily lives of the same group of people, which is broadcast regularly

**soap·y** /'soupi/ *adj* containing soap: *soapy water*

**soar** /sɔr/ *v* [I] **1** to increase quickly to a high level: *The temperature soared to 97°.* **2** to fly, especially very fast or very high up in the air: *birds soaring overhead* **3** to look very tall and impressive: *The cliffs soar 500 feet above the sea.* —**soaring** *adj*

**S.O.B.** *n* SLANG ⇨ **son of a bitch** (SON)

**sob** /sab/ *v* **-bbed, -bbing** [I] to cry while breathing in short sudden bursts —**sob** *n*

**so·ber¹** /'soubɚ/ *adj* **1** not drunk **2** extremely serious: *Much sober thought is required to make the right choice.* **3** plain and not at all brightly colored: *a sober gray suit* —**soberly** *adv* —**sobriety** /sou'braɪəti, sə-/ *n* [U]

**sober²** *v* [I,T] to become more serious, or to make someone do this —**sobering** *adj*: *a sobering thought*
**sober** (sb) ↔ **up** *phr v* [I,T] to gradually become less drunk, or to make someone do this: *Some black coffee might sober you up.*

**sob sto·ry** /'. ,../ *n* INFORMAL a story that someone tells you in order to make you feel sorry for him/her

**so-called** /ˌ. '.◄/ *adj* **1** used in order to show that you think the name that someone or something is called is wrong: *the so-called freedom fighters* **2** used in order to show that something or someone is usually called a particular name: *Only so-called "safe and sane" fireworks are allowed.*

**soc·cer** /'sakɚ/ *n* [U] an outdoor game in which two teams of 11 players try to kick a ball into their opponents' GOAL

**so·cia·ble** /'souʃəbəl/ *adj* friendly and liking to be with other people —opposite UNSOCIABLE

**so·cial** /'souʃəl/ *adj* **1** relating to human society and its organization, or the quality of people's lives: *We ought to be dealing with the real social issues such as unemployment.* **2** relating to the position in society that you have: *friends from different social backgrounds* **3** relating to the things that you do with other people, especially for enjoyment: *Ellis always had an active social life.* **4** social animals live together in groups, rather than alone —**socially** *adv*

**social climb·er** /'.. ,../ *n* DISAPPROVING someone who does anything s/he can to move into a higher social class

**so·cial·is·m** /'souʃə,lɪzəm/ *n* [U] an economic and political system that tries to give equal opportunities to all people, and in which most businesses belong to the government —**socialist** n, adj

**so·cia·lite** /ˈsouʃəˌlaɪt/ n someone who is well known for going to many fashionable parties

**so·cial·ize** /ˈsouʃəˌlaɪz/ v **1** [I] to spend time with other people in a friendly way: *I hate having to socialize with strangers.* **2** [T] if a government socializes an industry, service etc., it takes it away from private owners in order to control it: *socialized medicine* —opposite PRI-VATIZE

**social sci·ence** /ˌ.. ˈ../ n **a)** [U] the study of people in society, that includes history, politics, ECONOMICS, SOCIOLOGY, and ANTHROPOLOGY **b)** any one of these subjects

**Social Se·cu·ri·ty** /ˌ.. .ˈ.../ n [U] a US government program into which workers must pay money, that gives money to old people and others who cannot work

**social stud·ies** /ˈ.. ˌ../ n [plural] ⇨ SOCIAL SCIENCE

**social work·er** /ˈ.. ˌ../ n someone who is trained to help people with particular social problems, such as being unable to work —**social work** n [U]

**so·ci·e·ty** /səˈsaɪəṭi/ n **1** [C,U] a large group of people who share the same laws, ways of doing things, religions, etc.: *a study of 19th century Western society | a democratic society* **2** [U] people in general: *Society's attitude to-ward smoking has changed a lot in recent years.* **3** an organization with members who share similar interests, aims etc.: *the American Cancer Society* **4** [U] the fashionable group of people who are rich: *a society wedding*

**so·ci·o·ec·o·nom·ic** /ˌsousiouˌɛkəˈnɑmɪk, -ˌikə-/ adj relating to both social and economic conditions: *people with a low socioeconomic status*

**so·ci·ol·o·gy** /ˌsousiˈɑlədʒi/ n [U] the scientific study of societies and the behavior of people in groups —**sociologist** n

**so·cio·path** /ˈsousiəˌpæθ, -ʃiə-/ n TECHNICAL someone whose behavior toward other people is strange and possibly dangerous

**sock**¹ /sɑk/ n a piece of clothing that you wear on your foot inside your shoe: *a pair of socks*

**sock**² v INFORMAL **1** [I,T] to affect something or someone very badly: *They were socked with a $5000 tax bill.* **2** [T] to hit someone very hard: *Somebody socked him in the mouth.* **3 be socked in** to be completely covered by FOG: *The airport was socked in for six hours.*

**sock·et** /ˈsɑkɪt/ n **1** the place in a wall where you can connect electrical equipment to the supply of electricity —see picture at PLUG¹ **2** the hollow part of something such as a joint, into which another round part fits: *the shoulder/elbow socket*

**sod** /sɑd/ n [U] a piece of dirt with grass grow-ing on top of it

**so·da** /ˈsoudə/ n [C,U] **1** also **soda pop** ⇨ SOFT DRINK **2** also **soda water** water that con-tains BUBBLEs, often added to alcoholic drinks

---

**CULTURE NOTE** soda, soda pop, pop, and soft drink

All of these words mean the same thing, but **pop** and **soda** are used in different parts of the US. In the Midwest and West, people usually say **pop**. In the Northeast, people usually say **soda**. The general word used by everyone is **soft drink**.

---

**sod·den** /ˈsɑdn/ adj very wet and heavy: *sodden clothing*

**so·di·um** /ˈsoudiəm/ n [U] a silver-white met-al that is an ELEMENT, that produces salt when mixed with CHLORINE

**so·fa** /ˈsoufə/ n a comfortable seat that is wide enough for two or three people to sit on

**soft** /sɔft/ adj **1** not hard, firm, or stiff, but easy to press: *a soft pillow* **2** smooth and pleasant to touch: *soft skin* **3** soft sounds are quiet **4** soft colors or lights are not too bright **5** not of the strongest or most harmful kind: *soft drugs* **6** INFORMAL a soft job, life etc. does not involve hard work or difficulties **7** INFORMAL not strict enough: *The Governor does not want to seem soft on crime.* **8** soft water does not contain a lot of minerals **9 have a soft spot for sb** to like someone: *She's always had a soft spot for Grant.* —**softly** adv —**softness** n [U]

**soft·ball** /ˈsɔftbɔl/ n **a)** [U] an outdoor game similar to baseball but played with a slightly larger and softer ball **b)** [C] the ball used in this game

**soft-boiled** /ˌ. ˈ.ᐊ / adj an egg that is soft-boiled has been boiled until the white part is sol-id, but the yellow part is still liquid

**soft drink** /ˈ. ./ n a sweet drink that contains BUBBLEs and has no alcohol in it: *cola and other soft drinks* —see culture note at SODA

**soft·en** /ˈsɔfən/ v [I,T] **1** to become softer, or to make something do this: *a lotion that helps to soften your skin* **2** to become less strict or severe, or to make something do this: *Goldberg tried to soften the blow* (=make bad news less upsetting) *with a joke. | Pale flowered wallpaper softens the look of the room.* —opposite HARDEN

**soften** sb ↔ **up** phr v [T] INFORMAL to be nice to someone so that s/he will do something for you

**soft-heart·ed** /ˌsɔftˈhɑrṭɪdᐊ / adj kind and sympathetic

**soft-ped·al** /ˈsɔftˌpɛdl/ v [T] INFORMAL to make something seem less extreme than it really is: *While meeting the voters, he soft-pedaled his racist views.*

**soft sell** /ˌ. './ n [singular] a way of selling something in which you are gently persuaded to buy it

**soft-spok·en** /ˌ. '..‹ / adj having a quiet gentle voice

**soft touch** /ˌ. './ n INFORMAL someone who is easy to deceive or persuade to do something

**soft·ware** /'sɔft-wɛr/ n [U] a set of PROGRAMS (=instructions) that you put into a computer when you want it to do a particular job: *word processing software* —compare HARDWARE

**soft·y** /'sɔftli/ n INFORMAL someone who is very kind and sympathetic, or is easily persuaded: *He seems aggressive, but really he's just a big softy.*

**sog·gy** /'sɑgi/ adj very wet and soft: *She thought the pie crust was kind of soggy.*

**soil**[1] /sɔɪl/ n [C,U] the top layer of the earth in which plants grow: *sandy soil*

**soil**[2] v [T] FORMAL to make something dirty —soiled adj

**so·journ** /'soʊdʒɚn/ n FORMAL a period of time that you stay in a place that is not your home —sojourn v [I]

**sol·ace** /'sɑlɪs/ n [U] a feeling of happiness after having been very sad or upset: *Since Mom's death we've found solace in our family.*

**so·lar** /'soʊlɚ/ adj relating to the sun or the sun's power: *a solar eclipse | solar energy*

**solar pan·el** /ˌ.. './ n a piece of equipment that changes the sun's light into electricity

**solar sys·tem** /'.. ˌ../ n 1 **the solar system** the earth and all the PLANETs, moons etc. that move around the sun 2 a similar type of system that moves around another star

**sold** /soʊld/ v the past tense and PAST PARTICIPLE of SELL

**sol·der**[1] /'sɑdɚ, 'sɔ-/ v [T] to join metal surfaces together or to repair them using melted metal

**solder**[2] n [U] the metal that is used in order to SOLDER something

**sol·dier** /'soʊldʒɚ/ n a member of the army, especially someone who is not an officer

**sold-out** /ˌ. './ adj if a concert, movie etc. is sold out, all the tickets for it have been sold

**sole**[1] /soʊl/ adj 1 the sole person, thing etc. is the only one of its type: *the sole survivor of the plane crash* 2 only concerning or belonging to one group or person: *sole ownership of the company*

**sole**[2] n 1 the bottom of your foot 2 the bottom part of a shoe, not including the heel 3 [C,U] a common flat sea fish, or the meat from this fish

**sole·ly** /'soʊli/ adv only, or not involving anyone or anything else: *We were solely responsible for the mistakes.*

**sol·emn** /'sɑləm/ adj very serious: *a solemn humorless man | a solemn ceremony | a solemn*

promise (=one that you will definitely keep) —solemnly adv —solemnity /səˈlɛmnəti/ n [U]

**so·lic·it** /səˈlɪsɪt/ v 1 [T] to ask someone for something such as money, help, or information: *We were unable to solicit any support from the government.* 2 [I] to offer to have sex with someone for money: *Twelve women were arrested for soliciting.* —solicitation /səˌlɪsəˈteɪʃən/ n [C,U]

**so·lic·i·tor** /səˈlɪsətɚ/ n 1 someone who goes from place to place trying to sell goods: *The sign said "No Solicitors."* 2 the main law officer of a city, town, or government department

**so·lic·it·ous** /səˈlɪsətəs/ adj very eager to make someone feel safe or comfortable: *Our tour guide was extremely solicitous.*

**sol·id**[1] /'sɑlɪd/ adj 1 firm and usually hard, without spaces or holes: *solid rock | The lake in the park is frozen solid.* 2 **solid gold/silver/ oak etc.** completely made of gold etc.: *a solid gold necklace* 3 strong and well made: *a good solid chair* 4 continuously, without any pauses: *She didn't talk to me for three solid weeks.* 5 based on definite facts or a definite principle: *solid information* 6 loyal and able to be trusted or depended on: *a solid citizen* —solidly adv —solidity /səˈlɪdəti/ n [U]

**solid**[2] n TECHNICAL an object or substance that has a firm shape and is not a gas or liquid —see also SOLIDS

**sol·i·dar·i·ty** /ˌsɑləˈdærəti/ n [U] the loyalty and support of a group of people that share the same aim or opinions: *Hundreds of workers went to the meeting to show their solidarity.*

**so·lid·i·fy** /səˈlɪdəˌfaɪ/ v 1 [I,T] to become solid, or to make something solid. *Crystals form when the liquid solidifies.* 2 [T] to make a plan, agreement, or feeling more definite: *Working together has solidified our friendship.*

**solids** /'sɑlɪdz/ n [plural] food that is not liquid: *The doctor says I can't eat solids for another week.*

**solid-state** /ˌ.. '.‹ / adj a solid-state electrical system uses TRANSISTORs

**so·lil·o·quy** /səˈlɪləkwi/ n a speech in a play that a character says to himself/herself so that the people watching know his/her thoughts

**sol·i·taire** /'sɑləˌtɛr/ n [U] 1 a card game for one player 2 a piece of jewelry that has only one jewel in it: *a diamond solitaire ring*

**sol·i·tar·y** /'sɑləˌtɛri/ adj 1 a solitary person or thing is the only one in a place: *A solitary figure waited by the door.* 2 done alone or spending time alone: *a solitary game | a solitary life*

**solitary con·fine·ment** /ˌ..... '.../ n [U] a punishment in which a prisoner is kept alone and is not allowed to talk to or see anyone else

**sol·i·tude** /'sɑləˌtud/ n [U] the state of being

alone and away from other people: *She spent the last years of her life living in solitude.*

**so·lo**[1] /'soʊloʊ/ *adj* done alone, without anyone else helping you: *his first solo flight* —**solo** *adv*

**solo**[2] *n* **1** a piece of music written for one performer **2** a job or performance that is done alone, such as flying a plane, dancing, singing etc.

**so·lo·ist** /'soʊloʊɪst/ *n* a musician who performs a SOLO

**sol·stice** /'sɑlstɪs, 'sɔl-/ *n* the day on which there is either the most or the least hours of light from the sun: *the summer/winter solstice*

**sol·u·ble** /'sɑlyəbəl/ *adj* a soluble substance can be DISSOLVEd in a liquid —opposite INSOLUBLE

**so·lu·tion** /sə'luʃən/ *n* **1** a way of solving a problem or dealing with a difficult situation: *Has anyone found a solution to question 7? | The only solution was to move into a quieter apartment.* **2** a liquid mixed with a solid or a gas, usually without a chemical change

**solve** /sɑlv/ *v* [T] to find an answer to a problem or a way of dealing with a difficult situation: *The tax may be the only way to solve the city's budget crisis.* —**solvable** *adj*

**sol·vent**[1] /'sɑlvənt/ *adj* having enough money to pay your debts —**solvency** *n* [U]

**solvent**[2] *n* a substance, usually a liquid, that can change a solid substance into a liquid

**som·ber** /'sɑmbɚ/ *adj* **1** sad and serious; GRAVE: *a somber mood | a somber funeral service for 10 Marines* **2** dark, or not having any bright colors: *a somber room*

**some**[1] /səm; *strong* sʌm/ *quantifier* **1** an amount or number of something that is not specific: *Do you want some coffee? | I need to buy some new socks.* **2** a few of the people or things in a group, or part of an amount of something: *Some guys at work have extra tickets to the Superbowl. | I've lost some weight.* **3** a fairly large amount of something: *It was some time before the police finally arrived.* —see study note on page 466

> ### USAGE NOTE some, somebody, any, and anybody
>
> Use **some** and **somebody** in questions when you think that the answer will be "yes": *Is there still some pizza in the fridge? | Can somebody help me with this box?* Use **any** and **anybody** in questions when you do not know what the answer will be: *Is there any mail for me? | Did anybody call while I was out?*

**some**[2] *pron* **1** an amount or number of something that is not specific: *Can I use some of your lotion? | She likes flowers, so I bought her some for her birthday.* **2** a few of the people or

things in a group, or part of an amount of something: *Some of the roads were closed because of the snow.* **3 and then some** INFORMAL and more: *He has enough money to buy the house and then some!*

**some**[3] *determiner* **1** INFORMAL used when you are talking about a person or thing that you do not know, remember, or understand: *I read about it in some magazine. | For some reason or other they decided to move to Detroit.* **2 some friend/help! etc.** SPOKEN said when you are annoyed because someone or something has disappointed you: *I can't believe you told Mom. Some brother you are!*

**some**[4] *adv* **1** a little more or a little less than a particular number or amount: *Some 700 homes were damaged by the storm.* **2 some more** an additional number or amount of something: *Would you like some more cake?*

**some·bod·y** /'sʌm,bɑdi, -,bʌdi/ *pron* ⇨ SOMEONE —see usage notes at ANYONE, SOME[1]

**some·day** /'sʌmdeɪ/ *adv* at an unknown time in the future: *Someday I'm going to go to Spain.*

**some·how** /'sʌmhaʊ/ *adv* **1** in some way, although you do not know how: *We'll find your bag somehow.* **2** for some reason that you cannot understand: *Somehow I don't trust him.*

**some·one** /'sʌmwʌn/ *pron* a word meaning a particular person, used when you do not know or do not say who that person is: *Be careful! Someone could get hurt. | "Does Mike still live here?" "No, someone else (=a different person) is renting it now."* —see usage notes at ANYONE, PRONOUN

**some·place** /'sʌmpleɪs/ *adv* SPOKEN ⇨ SOMEWHERE —see usage note at ANYONE

**som·er·sault** /'sʌmɚ,sɔlt/ *n* the action of rolling forward until your feet go over your head and touch the ground again —**somersault** *v* [I]

**some·thing** /'sʌmθɪŋ/ *pron* **1** a word meaning a particular thing, used when you do not know its name, exactly what it is etc.: *He said something about a Halloween party. | There's something in my eye. | I don't eat eggs. Could I have something else? (=something different)* **2 something like** used when you cannot be exact about a number or amount: *There are something like 3000 homeless people in this city.* **3 have something to do with** to be connected or related to a person, thing, or activity in a way that you are not sure about: *High-fat diets may have something to do with the disease.* **4 something to eat/drink** some food or a drink: *We went out for something to eat after the movie.* **5 something to do** an activity or job: *I'll go to the store; it'll give me something to do.* **6 twenty-something/thirty-something** INFORMAL used when someone is between the ages of 20 to 29, 30 to 39 etc.

SPOKEN PHRASES

**7 or something...** said when you cannot

remember or cannot be exact: *Maybe I cooked it too long or something.* | *I saw him on "The Tonight Show" or something like that.* **8 be (really) something** used when something is impressive or unusual: *It's really something to see all the hot air balloons taking off together.*

**some·time** /'sʌmtaɪm/ *adv* at an unknown time in the past or future: *I'll call you sometime next week.*

**some·times** /'sʌmtaɪmz/ *adv* on some occasions, but not always: *Sometimes I don't get home until 9:00 at night.*

**some·way** /'sʌmweɪ/ *adv* INFORMAL ⇨ SOMEHOW

**some·what** /'sʌmwʌt/ *adv* a little; slightly: *I feel somewhat responsible for the accident.*

**some·where** /'sʌmwɛr/ *adv* **1** in a place or to a place that is not specific: *I think he wants you to drive him somewhere.* | *Do you want to eat lunch here or somewhere else?* (=somewhere different) −see usage note at ANYONE **2 somewhere around/between etc.** a little more or a little less than a particular number or amount: *A good CD player costs somewhere around $500.* **3 somewhere along the line/way** used in order to say that you are not sure when something happened: *Somewhere along the line I made a mistake.*

**son** /sʌn/ *n* **1** your male child: *My son is 12.* −see picture at FAMILY

SPOKEN PHRASES

**2** [singular] used by an older person as a friendly way to talk to a boy or young man: *What's your name, son?* **3** **son of a bitch** a rude expression that shows you are angry or surprised **4** **son of a gun** used in order to talk to a man you know and like: *John, you old son of a gun, how are you?*

**so·na·ta** /sə'natə/ *n* a piece of CLASSICAL MUSIC usually for two instruments, one of which is a piano

**song** /sɔŋ/ *n* **1** a short piece of music with words: *Turn up the radio; this is my favorite song.* **2** [C,U] the musical sounds made by birds **3** [U] the act of singing, or the art of singing **4** **for a song** very cheaply: *We bought it for a song at the flea market.*

**son·ic** /'sanɪk/ *adj* TECHNICAL relating to sound

**sonic boom** /ˌ.. './ *n* the loud sound that an aircraft makes when it reaches the SOUND BARRIER

**son-in-law** /'. . ˌ./ *n* the husband of your daughter −see picture at FAMILY

**son·net** /'sanɪt/ *n* a poem that has 14 lines that RHYME with each other in a particular pattern

**so·no·rous** /'sanərəs/ *adj* having a deep pleasantly loud sound: *a sonorous voice*

**soon** /sun/ *adv* **1** in a short time from now, or a short time after something has happened: *"How soon* (=how quickly) *can you leave for New York?"* | *Soon another fire truck arrived.* **2** **as soon as** immediately after something has happened: *I tried to call you as soon as I heard the news.* **3** **sooner or later** used when you think something will definitely happen: *Sooner or later Joe's going to get hurt.* **4** **the sooner...the better** used in order to say that it is important that something happen soon: *The sooner you finish this report, the better.* **5** **no sooner had...than** used when something has happened almost immediately after something else: *No sooner had I stepped in the shower than the phone rang.* −see also **would (just) as soon** (WOULD)

**soot** /sʊt/ *n* [U] black powder that is produced when something burns

**soothe** /suð/ *v* [T] **1** to make someone feel less worried, angry, or upset: *School officials were trying to soothe anxious parents.* **2** to make a pain stop hurting as much: *a gel that soothes aching muscles*

**sooth·ing** /'suðɪŋ/ *adj* making someone feel less worry, anger, sadness, or pain: *She spoke in a soothing voice.* | *a soothing oil*

**sop** /sap/ *v* **-pped, -pping**
**sop sth ↔ up** *phr v* [T] INFORMAL to remove a liquid from a surface using something that will ABSORB the liquid: *I took a piece of bread to sop up the gravy.*

**so·phis·ti·cat·ed** /sə'fɪstəˌkeɪtɪd/ *adj* **1** confident and having knowledge about subjects that are considered socially important such as art, literature, music etc.: *a sophisticated young man* **2** made or designed well, and often complicated: *highly sophisticated nuclear missiles* | *a sophisticated technique* −opposite UNSOPHISTICATED

**so·phis·ti·ca·tion** /səˌfɪstə'keɪʃən/ *n* [U] the quality of being SOPHISTICATED: *He has a reputation for wealth and sophistication.* | *the sophistication of new technology*

**soph·o·more** /'safmɔr/ *n* a student in the second year of HIGH SCHOOL or college

**soph·o·mor·ic** /ˌsaf'mɔrɪk/ *adj* very silly and unreasonable: *sophomoric humor*

**sop·o·rif·ic** /ˌsapə'rɪfɪk/ *adj* FORMAL making you feel ready to sleep

**sop·ping** /'sapɪŋ/, **sopping wet** /ˌ.. './ *adj* very wet: *By the time I got home, I was sopping wet.*

**so·pra·no** /sə'prænoʊ/ *n* [C,U] a woman, girl, or young boy singer with a very high voice

**sor·bet** /'sɔrbeɪ, 'sɔrbət/ *n* [C,U] a sweet frozen food made from fruit juice, sugar, and water

**sor·cer·er** /'sɔrsərɚ/, **sor·ce·ress** /'sɔrsərəs/ *n* a man or woman who uses magic and gets help from evil spirits

S

**sor·cer·y** /ˈsɔrsəri/ n [U] magic that uses the power of evil spirits

**sor·did** /ˈsɔrdɪd/ adj involving immoral or dishonest behavior: *all the sordid details of the Watergate scandal*

**sore**[1] /sɔr/ adj **1** painful as a result of a wound, infection, or too much exercise: *My knee's a little sore from running yesterday.* | *a sore throat* **2 sore point/spot** something that is likely to make someone upset or angry if you talk about it: *Don't mention marriage - it's a sore point with him.* **3** OLD-FASHIONED upset, angry, or annoyed —**soreness** n [U]

**sore**[2] n an infected place on the body

**sore·ly** /ˈsɔrli/ adv very much: *He will be sorely missed by everyone.*

**so·ror·i·ty** /səˈrɔrəṭi, -ˈrɑr-/ n a club for women at a college or university —compare FRATERNITY

**sor·row** /ˈsɑrou, ˈsɔ-/ n [C,U] a feeling of great sadness, or an event that makes you feel great sadness: *Our prayers are with you in your time of sorrow.* | *the joys and sorrows of family life* —**sorrowful** adj

**sor·ry** /ˈsɑri, ˈsɔri/ adj **1 sorry/I'm sorry** SPOKEN **a)** said when you feel ashamed or unhappy about something bad that you have done: *I'm sorry, I didn't mean to scare you.* **b)** said as a polite way to excuse or correct yourself: *Sorry for calling so late.* | *I'm sorry about that!* (=used as an apology) ✗ DON'T SAY "I'm sorry for that." ✗ **2** feeling ashamed, embarrassed, or unhappy about something you have done: *Keith looked really sorry after he yelled at you.* **3** to feel pity or sympathy for someone because s/he is in a bad situation: *Stop feeling sorry for yourself!* | *I'm sorry to hear that* your mother died. —see usage note at SYMPATHY **4** feeling disappointed about a situation: *Dad's still sorry that he never joined the army.* **5** INFORMAL very bad: *That's the sorriest excuse I've ever heard.* —see usage note at APOLOGIZING

**sort**[1] /sɔrt/ n **1 sort of** SPOKEN **a)** slightly; a little: *I still feel sort of tired.* **b)** used when you cannot be exact or do not want to give details: *He got a sort of special degree from the university.* **2** a type of person, thing, action etc.: *What sort of damage do these insects do?* **3** an action done by a computer in order to organize information in a particular way —compare **kind of** (KIND[1])

**sort**[2] v [T] to put things in a particular order, or to arrange them in groups according to size, type etc.: *All the letters have to be sorted and delivered by Friday.*

**sort** sth ↔ **out** phr v [T] **a)** to organize something that is messy, complicated, or in the wrong order: *It took us three hours to sort out our tax receipts.* **b)** to separate something from a group: *I need to sort out which clothes I should pack.*

**sort through** sth phr v [T] to look at many similar things in order to find the one you want: *Greg sorted through the mail, looking for the letter.*

**sort·a** /ˈsɔrṭə/ SPOKEN NONSTANDARD a short form of "sort of": *Don't you think he's sorta cute?*

**SOS** n [singular] used as a signal by a ship or plane that needs help

**so-so** /ˈ. ./ adj, adv SPOKEN neither very good nor very bad: *"How was the movie?" "So so."*

**souf·flé** /suˈfleɪ/ n [C,U] a baked dish that is light and made from eggs, flour, milk, and sometimes cheese

**sought** /sɔt/ v the past tense and PAST PARTICIPLE of SEEK

**sought-af·ter** /ˈ. ,../ adj wanted by a lot of people, but difficult to get: *one of the world's most sought-after chefs*

**soul** /soul/ n **1** the part of a person that is not physical and contains his/her thoughts, feelings, character etc., which many people believe exists after death **2** a person: *Don't you dare tell a soul!* **3** [U] a type of popular modern music that often expresses deep emotions, usually performed by Black singers and musicians **4** [U] a special quality that makes you feel strong emotions: *His poetry lacks soul.*

**soul·ful** /ˈsoulfəl/ adj expressing deep sad emotions: *a soulful cry*

**soul·less** /ˈsoul-lɪs/ adj lacking the qualities that make people feel interest, emotions, or excitement: *a soulless town*

**soul-search·ing** /ˈ. ,../ n [U] the act of carefully examining your thoughts and feelings in order to make a decision: *After much soul-searching, she decided that she could never marry him.*

**sound**[1] /saund/ n **1** [C,U] something that you hear, or something that can be heard: *the sound of breaking glass* | *There's no sound coming from the TV.* —see usage note at NOISE **2 by the sound of it/things** SPOKEN according to what you have heard or read about something: *By the sound of it, he's being forced out of his job.* **3** a long wide area of water that connects two larger areas of water

**sound**[2] v **1** [linking verb] someone or something that sounds good, strange etc. seems that way when you hear or read about him, her, or it: *Your friend sounds like a nice guy.* **2** [linking verb] to seem to show a particular quality or emotion with your voice: *You sound upset. Are you OK?* **3 sounds good** SPOKEN said in order to accept something that someone has suggested: *"Do you want Thai food tonight?" "Sounds good."* **4** [I,T] to produce a noise, or to make something do this: *The church bells sounded.*

**sound off** phr v [I] to express a strong opinion or complaint, often in a loud or annoying way:

*We were told not to **sound off about** our problems to the press.*

**sound out** *phr v* [T] [**sound sb/sth ↔ out**] to talk to someone in order to find out what s/he thinks about a plan or idea: *We've found a way of **sounding out** public opinion on the issue.*

**sound**[3] *adj* **1** practical, based on good judgment, and likely to produce good results: *Our helpline offers **sound advice** to new parents.* | *a sound investment* **2** in good condition and not damaged in any way: *The roof leaks, but the floors are sound.* **3 of sound mind** LAW not mentally ill −opposite UNSOUND

**sound**[4] *adv* **sound asleep** completely asleep: *Bonita was sound asleep.*

**sound bar·ri·er** /ˈ. ˌ.../ *n* **the sound barrier** the point when an aircraft reaches the speed of sound

**sound bite** /ˈ. ./ *n* a short phrase used by politicians or companies that are advertising, that is supposed to represent the most important part of what they are saying

**sound ef·fects** /ˈ. ˌ./ *n* [plural] special sounds used in order to make a movie, television show etc. seem more real

**sound·ing board** /ˈ.. ˌ./ *n* someone you discuss your ideas with before using them

**sound·ly** /ˈsaʊndli/ *adv* **1 sleep soundly** to sleep well, without waking up or dreaming: *I always sleep soundly at my parents' house.* **2** completely or severely: *Washington was soundly defeated in the final match.* **3** in a way that is strong and unlikely to break: *The building is soundly designed.*

**sound·proof**[1] /ˈsaʊndpruf/ *adj* a soundproof wall, room etc. is one that sound cannot go through or go out of

**soundproof**[2] *v* [T] to make something SOUND-PROOF

**sound·track** /ˈsaʊndtræk/ *n* the recorded music from a movie

**soup**[1] /sup/ *n* [C,U] a hot liquid food that usually has pieces of meat or vegetables in it: *chicken noodle soup*

**soup**[2] *v*

**soup sth ↔ up** *phr v* [T] to improve something such as a car by making it more powerful or more exciting −**souped-up** /ˌ. ˈ.◂/ *adj*

**soup kitch·en** /ˈ. ˌ.../ *n* a place where free food is given to people who have no home

**sour**[1] /saʊɚ/ *adj* **1** having an acid taste, like the taste of a LEMON: *sour green apples* **2** milk or other food that is sour is not fresh and has an unpleasant taste and smell: *The milk has **gone sour**.* **3** unfriendly or unhappy: *a sour expression* **4 go/turn sour** INFORMAL to stop being enjoyable or satisfactory: *By that time, their relationship had turned sour.*

**sour**[2] *v* **1** [I] to stop being enjoyable or satisfactory: *Relations between the two countries*

had soured. **2** [I,T] to become sour, or make a food do this

**source** /sɔrs/ *n* **1** the thing, place, person etc. that you obtain something from: *Tourism is the city's greatest source of income.* | *gasoline and other sources of energy* **2** the cause of a problem, or the place where it starts: *Grant has always been a source of trouble in the classroom.* **3** a person, book, or document that you get information from: *Reliable sources say the company is going bankrupt.* **4** the place where a stream or river starts

**sour cream** /ˌ. ˈ./ *n* [U] a thick white cream with a sour taste, used in cooking

**sour·dough** /ˈsaʊɚdoʊ/, **sourdough bread** /ˈ.. ˌ./ *n* [U] a type of bread with a slightly sour taste −see picture at BREAD

**south**[1], **South** /saʊθ/ *n* [singular, U] **1** the direction toward the bottom of the world, or to the right of someone facing the rising sun: *Which way is south?* **2 the south** the southern part of a country, state etc.: *Rain will spread **to the south** later today.* **3 the South** the southeastern states of the US **4 down South** in or to the South of the US: *We moved down South in 1996.* −see usage note at NORTH[3]

**south**[2] *adj* **1** in, to, or facing south: *The hotel's about two miles **south of** Monterey.* | *the south wall of the building* **2 south wind** a wind coming from the south

**south**[3] *adv* toward the south: *Go south on I-35 to Des Moines.* | *The window faces south.*

**South A·mer·i·ca** /ˌsaʊθ əˈmɛrəkə/ *n* one of the seven CONTINENTs, that includes land south of the Caribbean Sea and north of Antarctica −**South American** *adj*

**south·bound** /ˈsaʊθbaʊnd/ *adj* traveling or leading toward the south: *southbound traffic* | *the southbound lanes of the freeway*

**south·east**[1] /ˌsaʊθˈist◂/ *n* [U] **1** the direction that is exactly between south and east: *southeast Utah* **2 the Southeast** the southeast part of a country, state etc. −**southeastern** *adj*

**southeast**[2] *adj, adv* in or toward the southeast: *flying southeast* | *a southeast wind*

**south·er·ly** /ˈsʌðɚli/ *adj* **1** in or toward the south: *sailing in a southerly direction* **2** a southerly wind comes from the south

**south·ern** /ˈsʌðɚn/ *adj* in or from the south part of an area, state, country etc.: *southern New Mexico* −see usage note at NORTH[3]

**south·ern·er** /ˈsʌðɚnɚ/ *n* someone who comes from the SOUTHERN part of a country or the southern HEMISPHERE

**south·ern·most** /ˈsʌðɚnˌmoʊst/ *adj* farthest south: *the southernmost tip of the island*

**South Pa·cif·ic** /ˌ. ˈ.../ *n* **the South Pacific** the southern part of the Pacific Ocean where there are groups of islands, such as New Zealand and Polynesia

**S**

**South Pole** /ˌ. './ *n* **the South Pole** the most southern point on the surface of the earth, or the area around it

**south·ward** /'saʊθwəd/ *adj adv* toward the south

**south·west¹** /ˌsaʊθ'wɛst◂/ *n* **1** the direction that is exactly between south and west **2 the Southwest** the southwest part of a country, state etc. —**southwestern** *adj*

**southwest²** *adj, adv* in, from, or toward the southwest: *driving southwest* | *a southwest wind*

**sou·ve·nir** /ˌsuvə'nɪr, 'suvə,nɪr/ *n* an object that you keep to remind yourself of a special occasion or a place that you have visited

**sov·er·eign¹** /'savərɪn/ *adj* **1** having the highest power or authority in a country **2** a sovereign country is independent and governs itself —**sovereignty** *n* [U]

**sovereign²** *n* FORMAL a king or queen

**So·vi·et** /'souviɪt, -vi,ɛt/ *adj* relating to or coming from the former Soviet Union

**sow¹** /soʊ/ *v* **sowed, sown** or **sowed, sowing** [I,T] to plant or scatter seeds on a piece of ground: *We sow the corn in the early spring.*

**sow²** /saʊ/ *n* a female pig

**soy·bean** /'sɔɪbin/ *n* a bean used especially for making foods that can be eaten instead of meat

**spa** /spɑ/ *n* a place that people go to in order to improve their health, especially a place where the water has special minerals in it

**space¹** /speɪs/ *n* **1** [U] the amount of an area, room, container etc. that is empty or available to be used: *Is there any more space in the basement?* | *There's not enough space in the computer's memory.* **2** [C,U] an empty area that is used for a particular purpose: *There were no parking spaces.* | *6900 square feet of office space for sale* **3** the empty area between two things; GAP: *There's a space for it there - between the books.* **4** [U] the area outside the Earth's air where the stars and PLANETs are: *a satellite traveling through space* **5 in/during the space of** within a particular period of time: *In the space of a few seconds it was done.* **6** [C,U] empty land that does not have anything built on it: *a fight to save the city's open spaces* **7** [U] opportunities to do what you want or to be alone: *I need more space, Joe.* —see usage note at PLACE¹

**space²** *v* [T] **1** to arrange objects, events etc. so that they have an equal amount of space or time between them: *Space the plants four inches apart.* **2** also **space out** [I] SLANG to stop paying attention and begin to look in front of you without thinking —**spacing** *n* [U]

**space-age** /'. ./ *adj* INFORMAL very modern: *space-age design*

**space ca·det** /'. .,./, **space case** /'. ,./ *n* SLANG someone who is SPACEY

**space·craft** /'speɪs-kræft/ *n* a vehicle that can travel in space

**spaced** /speɪst/, **spaced out** /ˌ. '.◂/ *adj* SLANG ⇨ SPACEY

**space·ship** /'speɪs,ʃɪp/ *n* a word meaning SPACECRAFT, used especially in stories

**space shut·tle** /'. ,../ *n* a SPACECRAFT for carrying people into space, that can be used more than once

**space·y** /'speɪsi/ *adj* SPOKEN behaving as if you do not know what is happening: *Is she on drugs or just really spacey?*

**spa·cious** /'speɪʃəs/ *adj* having a lot of space in which you can move around: *a spacious car/room/house*

**spade** /speɪd/ *n* **1** ⇨ SHOVEL¹ **2** a playing card with one or more black shapes like pointed leaves on it

**spa·ghet·ti** /spə'gɛti/ *n* [U] long thin pieces of PASTA that look like strings

**span¹** /spæn/ *n* **1** the amount of time during which something continues to exist or happen: *Most children have a short attention span.* | *The mayfly has a two-day life span.* (=lives for two days) **2** a period of time between two dates or events: *Over a span of five years, they planted 10,000 new trees.* **3** the distance from one side of something to the other: *a wing span of three feet*

**span²** *v* **-nned, -nning** [T] **1** to include all of a period of time: *Mariani's career spanned 45 years of change in Hollywood.* **2** to go from one side of something to the other: *a bridge spanning the river*

**span·gle** /'spæŋgəl/ *n* ⇨ SEQUIN —**spangled** *adj*

**span·iel** /'spænyəl/ *n* a dog with long hair and long ears

**Span·ish¹** /'spænɪʃ/ *adj* **1** relating to or coming from Spain **2** relating to the Spanish language

**Spanish²** *n* **1** [U] the language used in places such as Mexico, Spain, and South America **2 the Spanish** [plural] the people of Spain, considered as a single group

**spank** /spæŋk/ *v* [T] to hit a child on the BUTTOCKS with your open hand —**spanking** *n* [C,U]

**spar** /spɑr/ *v* **-rred, -rring** [I] to practice BOXING or MARTIAL ARTS with someone

**spare¹** /spɛr/ *adj* **1 spare key/battery etc.** a key etc. that you have in addition to the one you usually use, so that it is available if it is needed **2** not being used by anyone and therefore available for use: *a spare bedroom* **3 spare time** time when you are not working: *I play tennis in my spare time.* **4 spare change** coins that you can afford to give to someone

**spare²** *v* [T] **1** to prevent someone from having to do something difficult or unpleasant: *I was trying to spare you unnecessary work.*

**2** **$20/an hour etc. to spare** $20, one hour etc. that is left in addition to what you use or need to do something: *We made it to the airport with 10 minutes to spare.* **3** **Could you spare (me)...?** SPOKEN used in order to ask someone if s/he could lend or give you something, or if s/he has time to talk to you: *Could you spare me 20 minutes of your time?* **4** **spare no expense/effort etc.** to use as much money, effort etc. as necessary to do something: *We will spare no expense in buying new equipment.* **5** to not damage or harm someone or something, when other people or things are being killed or damaged: *Only the children's lives were spared.*

**spare**[3] *n* an additional key, BATTERY etc. that you keep so that it is available if it is needed: *The back left tire is flat - is there a spare in the trunk?*

**spar·ing·ly** /'spɛrɪŋli/ *adv* using or giving only a little of something: *People are being asked to use water sparingly this summer.* –**sparing** *adj*

**spark**[1] /spɑrk/ *n* **1** a very small flash of fire coming from a larger fire or from hitting two hard objects together **2** a flash of light caused by electricity passing across a small space **3** **spark of interest/intelligence etc.** a small amount of interest, etc. that you see in someone's expression or behavior: *As she spoke, she saw a spark of hope in Tony's eyes.*

**spark**[2] *v* **1** [T] also **spark off** to make something start happening: *The speech sparked off riots in the city.* **2** [I] to produce SPARKs

**spar·kle** /'spɑrkəl/ *v* [I] **1** to shine in small bright flashes: *diamonds sparkling in the light* **2** if someone's eyes sparkle, they shine because s/he is happy or excited –**sparkle** *n* [C,U]

**spark·ler** /'spɑrklɚ/ *n* a thin stick that you hold, which makes SPARKs when you burn it

**spark plug** /'. ./ *n* a part in a car engine that produces the SPARK to make the gas burn

**spar·row** /'spæroʊ/ *n* a common small brown or gray bird

**sparse** /spɑrs/ *adj* small in number or amount, and usually scattered over a large area: *sparse vegetation* –**sparsely** *adv*: *sparsely populated*

**spar·tan** /'spɑrᵗn/ *adj* very simple and without comfort: *spartan living conditions*

**spasm** /'spæzəm/ *n* **1** a sudden movement in which your muscles become tight in an uncontrolled way: *back spasms* **2** a short period during which a strong feeling or reaction to something happens: *spasms of laughter*

**spas·mod·ic** /spæz'mɑdɪk/ *adj* **1** happening for short periods of time but not regularly or continuously: *my spasmodic efforts to stop smoking* **2** relating to a muscle SPASM –**spasmodically** *adv*

**spas·tic** /'spæstɪk/ *adj* OLD-FASHIONED having uncontrolled SPASMs as a result of a disease

**spat**[1] /spæt/ *n* INFORMAL an argument or disagreement that is not important; quarrel

**spat**[2] *v* a past tense and the PAST PARTICIPLE of SPIT

**spate** /speɪt/ *n* **a spate of sth** a large number of similar events that happen in a short period of time: *a spate of burglaries in the area*

**spa·tial** /'speɪʃəl/ *adj* TECHNICAL relating to the position, size, or shape of things

**spat·ter** /'spætɚ/ *v* [I,T] if a liquid spatters or you spatter it, drops of it fall onto a surface: *Rain began to spatter on the steps.*

**spat·u·la** /'spætʃələ/ *n* a kitchen tool with a wide flat part, used for lifting and spreading food

**spawn**[1] /spɔn/ *v* **1** [T] to make something happen or start to exist: *The book "Dracula" has spawned a number of movies.* **2** [I,T] if a fish or FROG spawns, it lays a lot of eggs together

**spawn**[2] *n* [U] the eggs of a fish or FROG laid together in a soft group

**spay** /speɪ/ *v* [T] to remove part of a female animal's sex organs so that she cannot produce babies

**speak** /spik/ *v* **spoke, spoken, speaking** **1** ▶TALK TO SB◀ [I] to talk to someone about something or have a conversation: *Hello, can I speak to Mr. Sherwood please?* | *We need to speak with/to you before you leave.* **2** ▶SAY WORDS◀ [I] to use your voice to say words: *Most children don't begin to speak until they are over a year old.* **3** ▶LANGUAGE◀ [T] to be able to talk in a particular language: *My brother speaks English/French.* ✗ DON'T SAY "My brother speaks in English/French." ✗ **4** **generally/technically etc. speaking** used in order to say that you are expressing a general, technical etc. opinion: *Generally speaking, I agree with you, but this case is different.* **5** **so to speak** SPOKEN used in order to say that the expression you have used does not have its usual meaning: *He found the problem in his own back yard, so to speak.* (=affecting him or his family, or the area he lives in) **6** **speaking of...** SPOKEN used when you want to say more about someone or something that has just been mentioned: *Speaking of Jody, how is she?* **7** ▶ABOUT SB/STH◀ [I] to tell someone about a particular subject or person: *He spoke of/about his love of the theater.* **8** **speak your mind** to say exactly what you think: *Dana always speaks her mind.* **9** **none/nothing to speak of** nothing large or important enough to mention: *"Did you get any snow last week?" "None to speak of."* **10** ▶GIVE A SPEECH◀ [I] to make a formal speech: *I get so nervous if I have to speak in public.* –see usage note at SAY

*S*

**speak for** sb/sth *phr v* [T]  **1** to express the feelings, thoughts etc. of another person or group of people: *I'm **speaking for** the whole family when I say "thank you" to all of you.*  **2 sth speaks for itself** to show something so clearly that no explanation is necessary: *Our profits **speak for themselves**.* (=our profits show how good or bad our business is)  **3 be spoken for** to be promised to someone else: *This puppy is already **spoken for**.*

**speak out** *phr v* [I] to say publicly what you think about something, especially as a protest: *people **speaking out against** human rights abuses*

**speak up** *phr v* [I]  **1** SPOKEN used in order to ask someone to speak more loudly: *Could you **speak up** please, I can't hear you.*  **2** to say publicly what you think about something: *If we don't **speak up** nobody will help us.*

**speak·er** /'spikɚ/ *n*  **1** someone who makes a speech: *Our speaker this evening is Professor Gill.*  **2 English/French etc. speaker** someone who speaks English, French etc.  **3** the part of a radio, CD PLAYER etc. where the sound comes out

**spear**[1] /spɪr/ *n* a pole with a sharp pointed blade at one end, used as a weapon

**spear**[2] *v* [T]  **1** INFORMAL to push a pointed object such as a fork into something so you can pick it up  **2** to push or throw a SPEAR into something to kill it

**spear·head** /'spɪrhɛd/ *v* [T] to lead an attack or an organized action: *a labor strike spearheaded by the workers*

**spe·cial**[1] /'spɛʃəl/ *adj*  **1** better, more important, or deserving more love and attention than ordinary things, events, or people: *I want to go somewhere special for our anniversary. | This is a **special occasion**. | Gordon's a special friend of ours.*  **2** different from what is usual: *special facilities for language learners*  **3 special care/attention etc.** more care, attention etc. than is usual: *We try to **give special care** to the youngest patients.*

**special**[2] *n*  **1** something that is not ordinary or usual, but is made or done for a particular purpose: *a two-hour TV special on the election*  **2** a meal, dish, or cheaper price that a restaurant, supermarket etc. offers for a short time only: *What are today's lunch specials? | Chickens are on special this week.*

**special ed·u·ca·tion** /ˌ.. ..ˈ../ *n* [U] education for children who have physical or mental problems

**special ef·fects** /ˌ.. .ˈ./ *n* [plural] images or sounds of something that does not really exist or did not really happen, made especially for a movie or television program

**spe·cial·ist** /'spɛʃəlɪst/ *n* someone who knows a lot about a particular subject or has a lot of skill in it: *a heart specialist*

**spe·cial·ize** /'spɛʃəˌlaɪz/ *v* [I] to limit most of your study, business etc. to a particular subject or activity: *a lawyer who **specializes in** divorce cases* —**specialization** /ˌspɛʃələ'zeɪʃən/ *n* [C,U]

**spe·cial·ized** /'spɛʃəˌlaɪzd/ *adj* developed for a particular purpose: *a job that requires specialized knowledge*

**spe·cial·ly** /'spɛʃəli/ *adv*  **1** for one particular purpose: *The plane is specially designed for spying.*  **2** SPOKEN especially: *I had it made specially for you.*

**spe·cial·ty** /'spɛʃəlti/ *n*  **1** a subject that you know a lot about, or a skill that you have: *His specialty is mid-19th century literature.*  **2** a food or product that is very good, produced in a particular restaurant, area etc.: *The grilled fish is their specialty.*

**spe·cies** /'spiʃiz, -siz/ *n, plural* **species** a group of animals or plants of the same kind that can breed with each other

**spe·cif·ic** /spɪ'sɪfɪk/ *adj*  **1** used when talking about a particular thing, person, time etc.: *There are three specific types of treatment for this disease. | specific issues to discuss*  **2** detailed and exact: *Can you **be more specific**?*

**spe·cif·i·cal·ly** /spɪ'sɪfɪkli/ *adv*  **1** for a particular type of person or thing: *a book written specifically for young teenagers*  **2** in a detailed or exact way: *I was told specifically to arrive 10 minutes early.*

**spec·i·fi·ca·tion** /ˌspɛsəfə'keɪʃən/ *n* [C usually plural] a detailed instruction about how something should be done, made etc.: *a rocket built to exact specifications*

**spe·cif·ics** /spɪ'sɪfɪks/ *n* [plural] particular and exact details: *We can discuss **the specifics** of the deal later.*

**spe·ci·fy** /'spɛsəˌfaɪ/ *v* [T] to state something in an exact and detailed way: *The original plan didn't **specify how** the money should be spent.*

**spec·i·men** /'spɛsəmən/ *n*  **1** blood, skin, etc. that is taken from your body to be tested or examined: *We need a urine specimen for drug testing.*  **2** a single example of something from a larger group of similar things: *This specimen was found in northwestern China.*

**spe·cious** /'spiʃəs/ *adj* FORMAL seeming to be true or correct, but really false: *a specious argument*

**speck** /spɛk/ *n* a very small mark, spot, or piece of something: *a speck of dirt/dust/blood*

**speck·led** /'spɛkəld/ *adj* covered with a lot of small spots or marks: *speckled eggs*

**spec·ta·cle** /'spɛktəkəl/ *n*  **1** an unusual or strange thing or situation that you see: *Watching my parents dance was quite a spectacle.*  **2** a public scene or show that is very impressive: *the spectacle of the Thanksgiving parade*

**spec·ta·cles** /'spɛktəkəlz/ *n* [plural] FORMAL ⇨ GLASSES

**spec·tac·u·lar**[1] /spɛk'tækyələ/ *adj* very impressive or exciting: *a spectacular view of the Grand Canyon* −**spectacularly** *adv*

**spectacular**[2] *n* an event or performance that is very big and impressive

**spec·ta·tor** /'spɛkteɪtə/ *n* someone who watches an event, game etc.: *Over 50,000 spectators saw the final game.*

**spec·ter** /'spɛktə/ *n* **1 the specter of sth** something that frightens you because it will cause problems for you if it happens: *The specter of war lingered over the talks.* **2** LITERARY ⇨ GHOST

**spec·trum** /'spɛktrəm/ *n* **1** a complete or very wide range of opinions, ideas, situations etc.: *The officials represent a **wide spectrum of** political opinion.* **2** the set of different colors that is produced when light passes through a PRISM

**spec·u·late** /'spɛkyə,leɪt/ *v* **1** [I,T] to guess why something happened or what will happen next without knowing all the facts: *Police refuse to speculate on the murderer's motives at this time.* **2** [I] to buy goods, property etc., hoping to make a large profit when you sell them −**speculator** *n*

**spec·u·la·tion** /,spɛkyə'leɪʃən/ *n* [C,U] the act of speculating (SPECULATE): *There is continued **speculation about** the future of the company.*

**spec·u·la·tive** /'spɛkyələtɪv, -,leɪtɪv/ *adj* **1** based on SPECULATION: *a speculative story in the newspapers* **2** bought or done in order to make a profit later: *a speculative investment in real estate*

**sped** /spɛd/ *v* the past tense and PAST PARTICIPLE of SPEED

**speech** /spitʃ/ *n* **1** a talk, especially a formal one about a particular subject, given to a group of people: *The President **gave a speech** in Congress on the state of the nation.* | *My dad will **make a short speech** at the wedding.* **2** [U] the ability to speak, or the way someone speaks: *Her speech was slow and distinct.* **3** [U] spoken language rather than written language

**speech·less** /'spitʃlɪs/ *adj* unable to speak because you are angry, shocked, upset etc.: *Boyd's answer **left her speechless**.*

**speed**[1] /spid/ *n* **1** [C,U] how fast something moves or travels: *The cyclists were riding **at a speed of** 35 mph.* | *a car traveling **at high speed*** ✗ DON'T SAY "in high speed" ✗ **2** [U] the rate at which something happens or is done: *I'm amazed by the **speed at** which computers have changed modern life.* **3** −**speed** having a particular number of GEARS: *a 10-speed bicycle* **4** [U] SLANG an illegal drug that makes you very active

**speed**[2] *v* **sped** *or* **speeded, sped** *or* **speeded, speeding** **1** [I] to move or happen quickly: *The train **sped along** at over 80 miles an hour.*

**2 be speeding** to be driving faster than the legal limit

**speed up** *phr v* [I,T] to move or happen faster, or to make something do this: *an attempt to **speed up** production at the factory* | *We **sped up** to pass the car in front of us.*

**speed·boat** /'spidbout/ *n* a small boat with a powerful engine that can go very fast

**speed·ing** /'spidɪŋ/ *n* [U] the action of traveling too fast in a vehicle: *I got a ticket for speeding.*

**speed lim·it** /'. ,../ *n* the fastest speed that you are allowed to drive on a particular road: *a 40 mph speed limit*

**speed·om·e·ter** /spɪ'dɑmətə/ *n* an instrument in a vehicle that shows how fast it is going −see picture on page 469

**speed·y** /'spidi/ *adj* happening or done quickly, or working quickly: *We're hoping for a speedy end to the troubles.* | *a speedy computer chip* −**speedily** *adv*

**spell**[1] /spɛl/ *v* **1** [I,T] to form a word by writing or saying the letters in the correct order: *My last name is Haines, spelled H-A-I-N-E-S.* | *Our three-year-old is already learning to spell.* **2 spell trouble/defeat/danger etc.** if a situation spells trouble etc., it makes you expect trouble: *The latest setback may spell defeat for the Democrats in the election.* **3** [T] if letters spell a word, they form it

**spell** sth ↔ **out** *phr v* [T] to explain something clearly and in detail: *Do I have to **spell** it **out** for you? John's seeing another woman.*

**spell**[2] *n* **1** magic, or the special words or ceremonies used in making it happen: *The witches **cast a spell on** the young prince.* **2** a period of a particular type of weather, activity etc.: *We've had a **cold/warm/wet/dry spell** for most of January.*

**spell·bound** /'spɛlbaʊnd/ *adj* extremely interested in something you are listening to: *We were spellbound by his stories.*

**spell·ing** /'spɛlɪŋ/ *n* **1** [U] the ability to spell words in the correct way: *His spelling has improved.* **2** the way that a word is spelled: *There are two different spellings for this word.*

**spelling bee** /'.. ,./ *n* a spelling competition done by students

**spend** /spɛnd/ *v* **spent, spent, spending** **1** [I,T] to use your money to buy or pay for something: *I spent $40 **on** these shoes.* | *How much do you want to spend?* **2** [T] to use time doing a particular activity: *I need to **spend** more **time with** my family.* | *We spent the whole morning by the pool.* −see usage note at TIME[1]

**spend·ing** /'spɛndɪŋ/ *n* [U] the amount of money spent on something, especially by the government: *a cut in **defense/public spending***

**spend·thrift** /'spɛnd,θrɪft/ *n* someone who spends a lot of money in a careless way

**spent¹** /spɛnt/ *v* the past tense and PAST PARTI-CIPLE of SPEND

**spent²** *adj* **1** already used and now empty or useless: *spent cartridges* **2** LITERARY extremely tired

**sperm** /spɚm/ *n* **1** *n, plural* **sperm** a cell produced by the male sex organ that joins with an egg to produce new life **2** [U] ⇨ SEMEN

**spew** /spyu/, **spew out** *v* [I,T] to flow out of something in large quantities, or to make something do this: *Smoke and gas were **spewing out** of the volcano.*

**sphere** /sfɪr/ *n* **1** something in the shape of a ball: *The earth is a sphere.* **2** a particular area of work, interest, knowledge etc.: *He works mainly in the sphere of international banking.*

**spher·i·cal** /ˈsfɪrɪkəl, ˈsfɛr-/ *adj* having a round shape like a ball

**sphinx** /sfɪŋks/ *n* an ancient Egyptian image of a lion with a human head

**spice¹** /spaɪs/ *n* **1** [C,U] a powder or seed taken from plants that is put into food to give it a special taste: *herbs and spices* **2** [singular, U] interest or excitement that is added to something: *Variety is the spice of life!* —**spiced** *adj*

**spice²** also **spice up** *v* [T] **1** to add interest or excitement to something: *I need a few jokes to spice up my speech.* **2** to add SPICE to food

**spick-and-span** /ˌspɪk ən ˈspæn/ *adj* very clean and neat

**spic·y** /ˈspaɪsi/ *adj* food that is spicy contains a lot of SPICEs: *spicy meatballs*

**spi·der** /ˈspaɪdɚ/ *n* a small creature with eight legs that makes WEBs (=sticky nets) to catch insects

**spi·der·y** /ˈspaɪdəri/ *adj* writing that is spidery has long thin lines and is normally not very neat

**spiel** /ʃpil, spil/ *n* INFORMAL a long explanation of something, often used in order to try to persuade someone that something is good or true: *I **gave** her **the spiel** about how good the product was, but she didn't buy any.*

**spif·fy** /ˈspɪfi/ *adj* INFORMAL fashionable or attractive: *a spiffy little car*

**spike¹** /spaɪk/ *n* something that is long and thin with a sharp point, especially a piece of metal —**spiky** *adj*

**spike²** *v* [T] **spike sb's drink** to add alcohol or a drug to what someone is drinking

**spill¹** /spɪl/ *v* **1** [I,T] if a liquid spills or you spill it, it flows over the edge of a container by accident: *I spilled coffee on my shirt.* **2** [I] if people spill out of a place, they move out in large groups **3** **spill your guts** INFORMAL to tell someone a lot of personal things, especially because you are upset: *The*

spill

guy next to me at the bar tried to spill his guts to me.

**spill over** *phr v* [I] if a problem or bad situation spills over, it begins to affect other places, people etc.: *There's a danger that the war will **spill over into** other countries.*

**spill²** *n* an act of SPILLing something or the amount that is spilled: *a huge oil spill in the Atlantic*

**spin¹** /spɪn/ *v* **spun, spun, spinning** **1** [I,T] to turn around and around very quickly, or to make something do this: *skaters spinning on the ice* | *He grabbed Lisa by the arm and **spun her around**.* (=turned her around) **2** [I,T] to make cotton, wool etc. into thread by twisting it together **3** [T] if an insect spins a WEB or a CO-COON, it produces thread and makes it **4** **spin a tale/yarn/story** to tell a story that you have invented

**spin²** *n* **1** an act of turning around quickly: *The truck **went into a spin**.* **2** a way of saying or showing something that makes it seem to have particular qualities, used especially in politics and advertising: *a news report with a pro-abortion spin* —see also SPIN DOCTOR **3** **spin control** the act or skill of describing a bad situation in a way that makes it seem better than it is, used especially in politics and advertising **4** INFORMAL a short trip in a car for pleasure: *Would you like to **go for a spin**?*

**spin·ach** /ˈspɪnɪtʃ/ *n* [U] a vegetable with large dark green leaves

**spi·nal** /ˈspaɪnl/ *adj* relating to or affecting the SPINE: *a spinal injury*

**spinal cord** /ˈ.. ˌ./ *n* the long string of nerves that go from your brain down your back, through your SPINE

**spin·dly** /ˈspɪndli/ *adj* long and thin and not strong: *spindly legs*

**spin doc·tor** /ˈ. ˌ../ *n* INFORMAL someone who describes a situation in a way that makes it seem better than it is: *a White House spin doctor*

**spine** /spaɪn/ *n* **1** also **spinal column** the long row of bones down the center of your back **2** a stiff sharp point on an animal or plant: *cactus spines* **3** the part of a book that the pages are attached to

**spine·less** /ˈspaɪnlɪs/ *adj* lacking courage and determination: *He's too spineless to speak for himself.*

**spinning wheel** /ˈ.. ˌ./ *n* a small machine used in past times to make thread

**spin-off** /ˈ. ./ *n* **1** a useful product that developed unexpectedly from something else **2** a television program using characters that were originally on a different program

**spin·ster** /ˈspɪnstɚ/ *n* OLD-FASHIONED an older unmarried woman who is not likely to marry

**spi·ral¹** /ˈspaɪrəl/ *n* a curve in the form of a continuous line that winds around a central point —**spiral** *adj*: *a spiral staircase*

**spiral**[2] *v* [I] to move up or down in the shape of a spiral: *a leaf spiraling to the ground*

**spire** /spaɪɚ/ *n* a tower that rises steeply to a point, especially on a church

**spir·it**[1] /'spɪrɪt/ *n* **1** [C,U] the qualities that make someone live the way s/he does, and make him/her different from other people, and that are often believed to continue to exist after death: *I'm 85, but I still feel young in spirit.* | *I can still feel her spirit in this house.* **2** a living thing without a physical body such as an ANGEL or GHOST **3** [U] courage and determination: *I admired the spirit with which she fought for her rights.* **4** [singular] the attitude that you have toward something: *There's a real spirit of co-operation between the two clubs.* **5** team/community/public etc. spirit the strong feeling that you belong to a particular group and you want to help it **6** [C usually plural] a strong alcoholic drink such as WHISKEY – see also SPIRITS

**spirit**[2] *v* [T] **spirit sb/sth away** to remove someone or something from a place in a secret or mysterious way: *After the concert the band was spirited away in a cab.*

**spir·it·ed** /'spɪrɪtɪd/ *adj* having a lot of courage and determination: *She made a spirited defense of the plan.* –opposite DISPIRITED

**spir·its** /'spɪrɪts/ *n* [plural] how happy or sad someone feels at a particular time: *The children were in high spirits* (=happy and excited) | *Her spirits rose* (=she became happy) *when she heard the news.*

**spir·i·tu·al**[1] /'spɪrɪtʃuəl, -tʃəl/ *adj* **1** relating to the spirit rather than the body or mind: *spiritual health and well-being* **2** relating to religion: *spiritual songs* | *a very spiritual woman* –**spiritually** *adv*

**spiritual**[2] *n* a religious song first sung by the black people of the US when they were SLAVEs

**spit**[1] /spɪt/ *v* **spit** *or* **spat, spat, spitting** **1** [I,T] to force a small amount of liquid, blood, food etc. from your mouth: *He spat on the ground.* **2** **spit it out** SPOKEN used in order to tell someone to say something s/he does not want to say, or is having trouble saying: *Tell me what you did - come on, spit it out.*

**spit**[2] *n* **1** [U] INFORMAL ⇨ SALIVA **2** a long thin stick that you put through meat to cook it over a fire

**spite**[1] /spaɪt/ *n* **1** **in spite of** although; DE-SPITE: *She loved him in spite of the fact that he drank too much.* **2** a feeling of wanting to hurt, annoy, or upset someone: *Lola refused to let her ex-husband see the children out of spite.* (=because of spite)

**spite**[2] *v* [T] to annoy or upset someone deliberately: *He's doing this just to spite me!*

**spite·ful** /'spaɪtfəl/ *adj* intending to annoy or upset someone

**splash**[1] /splæʃ/ *v* **1** [I,T] if a liquid splashes or you make it splash, it falls on something or hits against it: *He splashed some cold water on his face.* | *water splashed down onto the rocks* **2** [I,T] to make water go up into the air by hitting it or moving around in it: *We were splashing each other in the pool.* | *children splashing around in puddles*

**splash**[2] *n* **1** the sound of SPLASHing: *Jerry jumped into the water with a loud splash.* **2** a small amount of a liquid that has SPLASHed onto something, or a mark made by this: *splashes of paint on my pants* **3** **a splash of color** color that you add to something to make it brighter

**splash·y** /'splæʃi/ *adj* big, bright, and very easy to notice: *a splashy tie*

**splat** /splæt/ *n* [singular] the sound made when something wet hits a hard surface

**splat·ter** /'splætɚ/ *v* [I,T] if a liquid splatters, it hits against a surface: *rain splattering against the window*

**splay** /spleɪ/ **splay out** *v* [I,T] to spread something apart such as your fingers or legs

**splen·did** /'splɛndɪd/ *adj* **1** excellent: *a splendid vacation* **2** beautiful or impressive: *a splendid view from the balcony* –**splendidly** *adv*

**splen·dor** /'splɛndɚ/ *n* [U] impressive beauty: *the splendor of Yosemite Valley*

**splice** /splaɪs/ *v* [T] to join the ends of two pieces of film, wire etc. so they form one piece

**splint** /splɪnt/ *n* a flat piece of wood, metal etc. that is attached to someone's arm or leg to prevent a broken bone from moving

**splin·ter** /'splɪntɚ/ *n* **1** a small sharp piece of wood, glass, or metal that has broken off of a larger piece: *I have a splinter in my finger.* –compare SLIVER **2** **splinter group/organization** a group of people that separate from a larger organization because they have different ideas

**splinter**[2] *v* [I,T] to break into thin sharp pieces, or to cause something to do this

**split**[1] /splɪt/ *v* **split, split, splitting** **1** [I,T] also **split up** to divide or make something divide into two or more groups, parts etc.: *We'll split up into three work groups.* | *Try splitting this section into two.* **2** [I,T] to tear or break something along a straight line, or to be torn or broken in this way: *He split his pants when he bent over.* | *The board had split in two.* **3** [T] to divide something among two or more people in equal parts: *We decided to split the money between us.* **4** [I] SLANG to leave quickly

**split up** *phr v* [I] to end a marriage or a relationship: *Eve's parents split up when she was three.*

**split**[2] *n* **1** a long straight hole caused when something breaks or tears: *a split in the seam of my skirt* **2** a serious disagreement that divides an organization or group of people: *a split in the Republican Party*

S

**split·lev·el** /ˌ. '..◂/ *adj* a split-level house has a ground floor that is on two different levels

**split sec·ond** /ˌ. '../ *n* **a split second** an extremely short period of time: *I only had a split second to decide.* **–split-second** /ˌ. '..◂/ *adj*

**split·ting** /ˈsplɪtɪŋ/ *adj* **splitting headache** a very painful HEADACHE

**splurge** /splɜ˞dʒ/ *v* [I] INFORMAL to spend more money than you can usually afford: *We went shopping and splurged on clothes.*

**spoil** /spɔɪl/ *v* **spoiled** *or* **spoilt** /spɔɪlt/, **spoiled** *or* **spoilt, spoiling** **1** [T] to ruin something by making it less attractive, enjoyable, useful etc.: *Don't let his bad mood spoil your evening.* **2** [I] to start to decay: *The meat has spoiled.* **3** [T] to treat someone in a way that is very kind or too generous: *a hotel that spoils its guests*

**spoiled** /spɔɪld/ *adj* a child who is spoiled is rude and behaves badly because s/he is always given what s/he wants: *a spoiled brat*

**spoils** /spɔɪlz/ *n* [plural] things taken by an army from a defeated enemy, or things taken by thieves

**spoil·sport** /ˈspɔɪlspɔrt/ *n* INFORMAL someone who spoils other people's fun: *Come on and play, don't be a spoilsport.*

**spoke¹** /spouk/ *v* the past tense of SPEAK

**spoke²** *n* one of the thin metal BARs that connect the outer ring of a wheel to the center, especially on a bicycle

**spok·en¹** /ˈspoukən/ *v* the PAST PARTICIPLE of SPEAK

**spoken²** *adj* **1 spoken English/language** the form of language that you speak rather than write **2 -spoken** speaking in a particular way: *a soft-spoken man* (=he speaks quietly)

**spokes·man** /ˈspouksmən/ *n* a male SPOKESPERSON

**spokes·per·son** /ˈspouksˌpɚsən/ *n* someone who has been chosen to speak officially for a group, organization, government etc.

**spokes·wom·an** /ˈspouksˌwumən/ *n* a female SPOKESPERSON

**sponge¹** /spʌndʒ/ *n* **1** [C,U] a piece of a very light substance that is full of small holes and is used for washing or cleaning something **2** a sea animal with a soft body, from which sponges are made

**sponge²** *v* **1** [T] also **sponge down** to wash something with a wet SPONGE **2** [T] to remove liquid from a surface using a sponge **3** [I] to get money, food etc. from someone without working for it: *He's been sponging off his friends for years.*

**sponge cake** /ˈ. ./ *n* [C,U] a light cake made with eggs, sugar, and flour but usually no fat

**spong·y** /ˈspʌndʒi/ *adj* soft and full of holes like a SPONGE: *spongy wet earth*

**spon·sor¹** /ˈspɑnsɚ/ *n* **1** a person or company that SPONSORs a television show, sports event etc.: *the sponsor of the French Open* **2** someone who SPONSORs a person for CHARITY

**sponsor²** *v* [T] **1** to give money to a television show, sports event etc. in exchange for the right to advertise your products at the event **2** to officially support a proposal for a new law **3** to give someone money for a CHARITY if s/he walks, runs, swims etc. a particular distance

**spon·ta·ne·i·ty** /ˌspɑntəˈneɪəti, ˌspɑntʰ-ˈneɪ-/ *n* [U] the quality or state of being SPONTANEOUS

**spon·ta·ne·ous** /spɑnˈteɪniəs/ *adj* happening or done without being planned or organized, because you suddenly want to do it: *a spontaneous decision* **–spontaneously** *adv*

**spoof** /spuf/ *n* a funny performance that copies a serious book, play, movie etc. and makes it seem silly: *a spoof on/of one of Shakespeare's tragedy plays* **–spoof** *v* [T]

**spook¹** /spuk/ *n* INFORMAL ⇨ GHOST

**spook²** *v* [T] INFORMAL to frighten someone: *Being alone all night really spooked me.*

**spook·y** /ˈspuki/ *adj* INFORMAL strange or frightening; EERIE: *a spooky old house*

**spool** /spul/ *n* an object shaped like a small wheel that you wind wire, thread, camera film etc. around

**spoon¹** /spun/ *n* a tool used for eating, cooking, and serving food, shaped like a small bowl with a long handle

**spoon²** *v* [T] to pick up or move food with a spoon: *Spoon the sauce over the fish.*

**spoon-feed** /ˈ. ./ *v* [T] **1** to give too much help to someone: *Spoon-feeding students does not help them remember things.* **2** to feed a baby with a spoon

**spoon·ful** /ˈspunfʊl/ *n* the amount that a spoon can hold: *a spoonful of sugar*

**spo·rad·ic** /spəˈrædɪk/ *adj* not happening regularly, or happening only in a few places: *sporadic bombing* **–sporadically** *adv*

**sport¹** /spɔrt/ *n* **1** a physical activity in which people compete against each other, and that has rules: *Baseball's my favorite sport.* | *Do you play any sports?* **2 good/bad sport** someone who can or cannot deal with defeat or being joked about without becoming angry or upset

---

**USAGE NOTE**    sport, recreation, game, and **hobby**

Use **sport** to talk about an activity that uses physical effort and skill, has rules, and is done in competition: *Her favorite sport is basketball.* | *I'm no good at sports.* Use **recreation** to talk about all the activities that people do in order to relax: *the city's Parks and Recreation Department.* Use **game** to talk about a particular competition in a

**sport**: *We went to my brother's football game last night.* You can also use **game** to talk about a competition that involves using mental skill, knowledge, or luck: *How about a game of cards?* Use **hobby** to talk about an activity that you do in your free time, usually alone: *Her hobbies are reading and music.*

**sport²** *v* **be sporting sth** to be wearing or showing something in a proud way: *He walked in today sporting a new suit.*

**sport·ing** /'spɔrṭɪŋ/ *adj* **1** relating to sports: *a new sporting goods* (=sports equipment) *store* **2 a sporting chance** a good chance of succeeding or winning

**sports** /spɔrts/ *adj* **1** relating to sports or used for sports: *a sports club* **2** on the subject of sports: *I like reading the sports pages.* (=in a newspaper)

**sports car** /'. ./ *n* a low fast car, often with a roof that can be folded back

**sports·cast** /'spɔrts-kæst/ *n* a television program of a sports game

**sports jack·et** /'. ,../, **sports coat** /'. ./ *n* a man's comfortable JACKET worn on informal occasions

**sports·man·ship** /'spɔrtsmən‚ʃɪp/ *n* [U] behavior that is fair, honest, and polite in a game or sports competition. *I was very impressed with the team's spirit and sportsmanship.*

**sports·wear** /'spɔrtswɛr/ *n* [U] clothes that are suitable for informal occasions

**sport·y** /'spɔrṭi/ *adj* designed to look attractive in a bright informal way: *a sporty red car*

**spot¹** /spɑt/ *n*
**1** ▶PLACE◀ a particular place: *Oh, sorry, I'm sitting in your spot.* | *a popular vacation spot*
**2** ▶COLORED AREA◀ a small round area on a surface, that is a different color from the rest: *a white dog with black spots*
**3** ▶MARK◀ a dirty mark on something: *paint spots on the floor*
**4 on the spot** INFORMAL **a)** immediately: *Cathy was offered the job on the spot.* **b)** at the place where something is happening: *He had a heart attack and died on the spot.*
**5** ▶APPEARANCE◀ a short appearance on TV, radio etc.: *an advertising spot*
**6** ▶POSITION◀ a position in a competition: *a movie in the number one spot*
**7 put sb on the spot** to make someone do something or answer a question that s/he does not want to, by making him/her feel embarrassed not to do it: *Don't put me on the spot like that in front of your parents.*
**8 bright spot** something that is good in a bad situation: *Foreign trade is the one bright spot in the economy.* −see also **hit the spot** (HIT¹)

**spot²** *v* **-tted, -tting** [T] **1** to notice or recognize something that is difficult to see, or that

you are looking for: *A helicopter pilot spotted the wreckage of the plane.* | *She has a good eye for spotting talent.* **2** to give the other player in a game an advantage: *Come on, I'll spot you 10 points if you play.*

**spot check** /'. ./ *n* a quick examination of a few things or people in a group, to see whether everything is correct or satisfactory: *Health inspectors will make spot checks throughout the state.*

**spot·less** /'spɑtlɪs/ *adj* **1** completely clean: *Donna keeps her car spotless.* **2** completely honest and good: *a spotless reputation*

**spot·light¹** /'spɑtlaɪt/ *n* **1** a very powerful light that can be directed at someone or something, or the light made by this: *theater spotlights* **2 the spotlight** something that makes people pay attention to someone or something: *Russia is back in the media spotlight again.*

**spotlight²** *v* [T] to make people pay attention to someone or something: *a music festival that spotlights modern composers*

**spot·ty** /'spɑṭi/ *adj* **1** good in some parts but not in others: *The stock market showed spotty gains.* **2** covered with spots: *a spotty camera lens*

**spouse** /spaʊs/ *n* FORMAL a husband or wife

**spout¹** /spaʊt/ *n* an opening through which liquid comes out: *a teapot with a wide spout* −see picture at TEAPOT

**spout²** *v* **1** [I,T] if a liquid spouts or is spouted, it comes out of a narrow place with a lot of force: *A leak spouted from the garden hose.* | *a whale spouting water* **2** [I] INFORMAL also **spout off** to talk a lot in a boring way: *He's always spouting off about politics.*

**sprain** /spreɪn/ *v* [T] to injure a joint in your body by suddenly twisting it: *Amy sprained her ankle when she fell.* −**sprain** *n*

**sprang** /spræŋ/ *v* the past tense of SPRING

**sprawl** /sprɔl/ *v* [I] **1** also **sprawl out** to lie or sit with your arms or legs stretched out: *When we got home, Carey was sprawled on the sofa.* **2** if a building or town sprawls, it spreads out over a wide area −**sprawl** *n* [singular, U]: *urban sprawl*

**spray¹** /spreɪ/ *v* [T] **1** to make a liquid come out of a container, HOSE etc. in a stream of very small drops: *Spray a little perfume on the backs of your knees too.* **2** [I] to be scattered in small drops or pieces through the air: *He started to fire, bullets spraying everywhere.*

spray

**spray²** *n* **1** [C,U] liquid that is forced out of a container to spread out in very small drops: *hair spray* **2** a special container that makes liquid SPRAY: *a non-aerosol spray* **3** [U] water that is

thrown up in very small drops from the ocean
**4** leaves and flowers arranged as a decoration:
*a spray of violets*

**spread**¹ /sprɛd/ *v* **spread, spread, spreading**
**1** ▶OPEN/ARRANGE◀ [T] also **spread out** to
open something so that it covers a big area, or to
arrange a number of things over a big area:
*Tracy had a map spread out over the floor.* | *The
population is evenly **spread across** the state.* | *He
sat with books and papers **spread over** the table.*
**2** ▶GET BIGGER/WORSE◀ [I,T] to get bigger
or worse by having an effect on more people or
places, or on a larger area: *Rain will **spread
throughout** the area by tonight.* | *Cancer has
**spread to** her lungs.*
**3** ▶INFORMATION/IDEAS◀ [I,T] to make
something widely known, or to become widely
known: *News of her arrest quickly
spread.* | *Don't listen to him; he's always
**spreading rumors**.*
**4** ▶SOFT SUBSTANCE◀ [T] to put a soft substance onto a surface in order to cover it: *toast
**spread with** butter and jam*
**5** ▶PUSH APART◀ [I,T] also **spread apart** to
push your arms, legs, or fingers wide apart:
*"Spread your legs!" one cop shouted.*
**6** ▶DO STH GRADUALLY◀ [T] also **spread
out** to do something gradually over time: *You
can **spread** the payments **over** a year.*
**7** **spread yourself thin** to accept too many
duties so you are always too busy: *You've been
spreading yourself too thin lately.*
**8** ▶WINGS◀ [T] also **spread open** if a bird or
insect spreads it wings, it stretches them wide
**spread out** *phr v* [I] if a group of people spread
out, they move apart from each other in order to
cover a wide area: *If we **spread out**, it should be
easier to find her.*

**spread**² *n* **1** [singular] the increase in the area
or number of people that something has an
effect on: *More education is needed to control
the spread of TB.* **2** [C,U] a soft food that you
put on bread: *cheese spread* | *a low-fat spread*
**3** INFORMAL a large meal for several people on a
special occasion: *Kay always **puts on a** great
**spread**.* **4** a special article or advertisement in
a newspaper or magazine: *a two-page spread*
**5** a large farm or RANCH **6** TECHNICAL the
difference between two amounts, such as the
buying and selling price of a SHARE on the
STOCK MARKET

**spread·sheet** /'sprɛdʃit/ *n* TECHNICAL a type
of computer program that can show and calculate information about sales, taxes, payments
etc.

**spree** /spri/ *n* a short period in which you do
something that you enjoy, especially spending
money or drinking: *I see you **went on a** shopping **spree**!*

**sprig** /sprɪg/ *n* a small stem or part of a branch
with leaves or flowers on it: *a sprig of parsley*

**spring**¹ /sprɪŋ/ *v* **sprang, sprung, springing**
**1** [I] to jump suddenly and quickly in a
particular direction: *He turned off the alarm and
sprang out of bed.* | *a cat **springing at** a mouse*
**2** [I] to appear suddenly on someone's face or
in his/her eyes: *Tears **sprang to** her eyes as she
spoke.* **3** **spring to mind** to immediately be
thought of: *Pam's name springs to mind as
someone who could do the job.* **4** **spring into
action/spring to life** to suddenly become active
or start doing things: *The whole school springs
into action at Homecoming.* **5** **spring open/
shut** to open or close suddenly and quickly: *The
lid of the box sprang open.* **6** **spring to sb's
defense** to immediately help someone who is
being attacked or criticized: *Molly sprang to her
daughter's defense.* **7** **spring a leak** if a boat
or a container springs a leak, it begins to let
liquid in or out through a crack or hole
**spring for** sth *phr v* [T] INFORMAL to pay for
something: *I might **spring for** a pizza.*
**spring** sth **on** sb *phr v* [T] INFORMAL to tell
someone news that surprises or shocks him/her:
*I'm sorry to have to **spring** this **on** you.*
**spring up** *phr v* [I] to suddenly appear or start
to exist: *All along the railroad, new towns
sprang up.*

**spring**² *n* **1** the season between winter and
summer, when leaves and flowers appear: *The
park opens **in (the) spring**.* | *I'm going to
Cancun **this spring**.* | *last/next spring* (=the
spring before or after this one) **2** a place where
water comes up naturally from the ground **3** a
twisted piece of metal that will return to its original shape after it has been pressed or pulled
**4** [U] the ability of a chair, bed etc. to return to
its normal shape after being pressed down **5** a
sudden quick movement or jump in a particular
direction

**spring·board** /'sprɪŋbɔrd/ *n* **1** something
that helps you to become involved in an activity:
*His computer knowledge provided a **spring-
board for** his career.* **2** a strong board that
bends, used in order to jump high

**spring break** /ˌ. './ *n* a vacation from school
in the spring, that is usually two weeks long

**spring chick·en** /ˌ. '../ *n* **be no spring chick-
en** HUMOROUS to no longer be young

**spring fe·ver** /ˌ. '../ *n* [U] a sudden feeling of
energy and wanting to do something new and
exciting, that you get in the spring

**spring·time** /'sprɪŋtaɪm/ *n* [U] the time of
year when it is spring

**spring·y** /'sprɪŋi/ *adj* returning quickly to its
original shape after being pressed: *springy grass*

**sprin·kle**¹ /'sprɪŋkəl/ *v* **1** [T] to scatter
small drops of liquid or small pieces of something onto something else: *spaghetti sprinkled
with parmesan* **2** [I] to rain lightly: *It was
sprinkling when we left.*

**sprinkle**[2] *n* **1** small pieces of food, or a light layer of these: *chocolate sprinkles | a sprinkle of grated cheese* **2** a light rain: *There will be sprinkles of rain over Oregon.*

**sprin·kler** /'sprɪŋklɚ/ *n* a piece of equipment used for scattering drops of water on grass to make it grow

**sprint** /sprɪnt/ *v* [I] to run very fast for a short distance, usually in a race –**sprinter** *n* –**sprint** *n*

**sprout**[1] /spraʊt/ *v* **1** [I,I] to start to grow or send up new growth: *a plant sprouting new flowers | seeds beginning to sprout* **2** also **sprout up** to appear suddenly in large numbers: *new homes sprouting up in the suburbs*

**sprout**[2] *n* **1** a new growth on a plant **2** a BEAN or other plant that is not fully grown and is eaten in SALADs: *alfalfa sprouts* **3** ⇨ BRUSSELS SPROUT

**spruce**[1] /sprus/ *n* [C,U] a tree with short leaves shaped like needles, or the wood of this tree

**spruce**[2] *v*

**spruce up** *phr v* [I,T] INFORMAL to make yourself or a place look better or neater: *I want to spruce up a little before dinner.*

**sprung** /sprʌŋ/ *v* the past tense and PAST PARTICIPLE of SPRING

**spry** /spraɪ/ *adj* a spry old person is active and cheerful

**spud** /spʌd/ *n* INFORMAL ⇨ POTATO

**spun** /spʌn/ *v* the past tense and PAST PARTICIPLE of SPIN

**spunk·y** /'spʌŋki/ *adj* INFORMAL brave and full of energy: *The movie is about a spunky girl who wants to play basketball.* –**spunk** *n* [U]

**spur**[1] /spɚ/ *n* **1** a sharp pointed object on the heel of a rider's boot **2** on the spur of the moment without planning ahead of time: *You can't just get married like that, on the spur of the moment.*

**spur**[2] *v* **-rred, -rring** [T] **1** to make an improvement or change happen faster: *Growth in the city was spurred by cheap housing.* **2** also **spur on** to encourage someone to do or continue doing something: *Her sister's success spurred her on to practice harder.*

**spu·ri·ous** /'spyʊriəs/ *adj* FORMAL **1** based on incorrect reasoning: *spurious arguments* **2** not sincere: *spurious sympathy*

**spurn** /spɚn/ *v* [T] LITERARY to refuse to accept something or to have a relationship with someone, in an unkind way: *a spurned lover*

**spurt**[1] /spɚt/ *v* [I] **1** to flow out suddenly with a lot of force: *Blood spurted from his arm.* **2** to suddenly move forward very quickly: *Liz spurted past the other runners.*

**spurt**[2] *n* **1** a stream of liquid that comes out suddenly: *Water was coming out of the faucet in spurts.* (=quickly for short periods) **2** a short

sudden increase in activity, effort, or speed: *a growth spurt*

**sput·ter** /'spʌtɚ/ *v* **1** [I] to make several quick soft sounds: *The engine sputtered and died.* **2** [I,T] to talk quickly in short confused phrases, especially because you are angry

**spy** /spaɪ/ *v* [I] to secretly collect information or watch people, usually for a government or company: *He's in prison for spying. | Stop spying on the neighbors! –spy n; a government spy*

**squab·ble** /'skwɑbəl/ *v* [I] to argue continuously about something unimportant: *What are those kids squabbling about now? –squabble n*

**squad** /skwɑd/ *n* an organized group of people who do a job that needs special skills: *a cheerleading squad | soldiers in the bomb squad*

**squad car** /'. ./ *n* a car used by police on duty

**squad·ron** /'skwɑdrən/ *n* a military force consisting of a group of aircraft or ships: *a bomber squadron*

**squal·id** /'skwɑlɪd/ *adj* **1** extremely dirty, unhealthy, and unsafe: *squalid living conditions* **2** ⇨ IMMORAL

**squall** /skwɔl/ *n* a sudden strong wind that brings rain or snow

**squal·or** /'skwɑlɚ/ *n* [U] extremely dirty, unhealthy, and unsafe conditions: *people living in squalor*

**squan·der** /'skwɑndɚ/ *v* [T] to waste your time, or spend money carelessly on useless things: *They've squandered thousands on that old house.*

**square**[1] /skwɛr/ *adj* **1** having four equal sides and four right angles: *a square window* **2** square inch/meter etc. a measurement of an area whose length is equal to its width: *two square acres of land* **3** like a square in shape: *a square jaw* **4** a square deal honest and fair treatment from someone: *a car dealer that gives customers a square deal* **5** a square meal a complete satisfying meal **6** be square if two people are square, they do not owe each other any money: *Here's your $20, so now we're square.* **7** INFORMAL someone who is square is boring and unfashionable **8** OLD-FASHIONED honest: *I'm being square with you.*

**square**[2] *n* **1** a shape with four straight equal sides forming four right angles –see picture at SHAPE **2** a broad open area with buildings around it in the middle of a town: *Times Square* **3** be back to square one to be back in exactly the same situation that you started from: *If things go wrong, we're back to square one.* **4** TECHNICAL the result of multiplying a number by itself. For example, the square of 5 is 25 **5** OLD-FASHIONED DISAPPROVING someone who always obeys the rules and never seems to have fun

**square**[3] *v* [T] TECHNICAL to multiply a number by itself

S

**square** sth ↔ **away** *phr v* [T] to finish dealing with something: *Peter needs another day to get things squared away at home.*

**square off** *phr v* [I] to get ready to fight someone by facing him/her

**square up** *phr v* [I] to pay money that you owe: *I'll get the drinks, and we can square up later.*

**square**[4] *adv* SPOKEN NONSTANDARD ⇨ SQUARELY

**square dance** /'. ./ *n* a type of dance in which four pairs of dancers face each other in a square

**square·ly** /'skwɛrli/ *adv* **1** exactly or completely: *The report puts the blame squarely on the senior managers. | Clark was hit squarely on the right elbow by a fast ball.* **2** directly and with confidence: *I promise I will squarely face the challenges of leadership.*

**square root** /ˌ. './ *n* TECHNICAL the number that, when multiplied by itself, equals a particular number. For example, the square root of 9 is 3

**squash**[1] /skwɑʃ, skwɔʃ/ *v* INFORMAL **1** [T] to press something into a flat shape, often damaging it; CRUSH: *My hat got squashed on the flight.* **2** [I,T] to push yourself or someone else into a space that is too small: *Seven of us squashed into the car.*

**squash**[2] *n* **1** [C,U] one of several types of heavy hard fruits, such as a PUMPKIN, that is cooked and eaten as a vegetable – see picture on page 470 **2** [U] an indoor game similar to RACKETBALL

**squat**[1] /skwɑt/ *v* [I] **1** also **squat down** to sit with your knees bent under you and balancing on your feet **2** to live in a building or on a piece of land without permission and without paying rent

**squat**[2] *adj* short and thick, or low and wide: *small squat houses | a squat cartoon figure*

**squawk** /skwɔk/ *v* [I] if a bird squawks, it makes a loud angry cry –**squawk** *n*

**squeak**[1] /skwik/ *v* [I] **1** to make a very short high noise or cry: *Is that your chair squeaking?* **2 squeak by/through** INFORMAL to manage to succeed, but not by very much: *The Bulls have squeaked through into the playoffs.*

**squeak**[2] *n* a very short high noise or cry: *the squeak of a mouse*

**squeak·y** /'skwiki/ *adj* **1** making very high noises that are not loud: *a squeaky voice | squeaky bed springs* **2 squeaky clean** INFORMAL **a)** never having done anything morally wrong **b)** completely clean: *squeaky clean hair*

**squeal**[1] /skwil/ *v* [I] **1** to make a long loud high sound or cry: *squealing tires | children squealing with excitement* **2 squeal (on sb)** INFORMAL to tell the police about someone you know who has done something wrong

**squeal**[2] *n* a long loud high sound or cry: *squeals of delight*

**squeam·ish** /'skwimɪʃ/ *adj* easily upset by the sight of unpleasant things: *I couldn't be a doctor - I'm too squeamish.*

**squeeze**[1] /skwiz/ *v* **1** [T] to press something firmly inwards, especially with your hand: *She squeezed Jim's shoulder gently.* **2** [T] to twist or press something in order to get liquid out of it: *Squeeze some lemon juice onto the salad.* **3** [I,T] to try to make a person or thing fit into a small space: *Can you squeeze in next to Rick?* **4 squeeze sb out (of sth)** to not let someone take part in something: *Some small businesses are being squeezed out of the market.* **5 squeeze sb/sth in** INFORMAL to manage to do something although you are very busy: *Professor Lang can squeeze you in* (=have time to see you) *at 2:00.* **6** [T] to strictly limit the amount of money that is available to an organization: *a school squeezed by budget cuts*

**squeeze**[2] *n* **1 a (tight) squeeze** a situation in which there is only just enough room for things or people to fit somewhere: *It'll be a tight squeeze with six of us in the car.* **2** an act of pressing something firmly inwards with your hand: *Laurie gave his hand a little squeeze.* **3** a small amount of something you get by squeezing: *a squeeze of lime juice* **4 a/the squeeze** a situation in which wages, prices, borrowing money etc. are strictly controlled: *Congress is likely to put the squeeze on farm programs.*

**squelch** /skwɛltʃ/ *v* **1** [T] INFORMAL to stop something such as an idea or action from spreading or continuing: *Store owners said the law would squelch competition.* **2** [I] ⇨ SQUISH

**squid** /skwɪd/ *n* a sea creature with a long soft body and 10 TENTACLEs (=arms)

**squig·gle** /'skwɪgəl/ *n* a short line in writing or drawing that curls and twists –**squiggly** *adj*

**squint** /skwɪnt/ *v* [I] to look at something with your eyes partly closed in order to see better or because of bright light: *He looked at me, squinting in the sun.* –**squint** *n*

**squire** /skwaɪɚ/ *n* a man who owned most of the land around a country village in past times

**squirm** /skwɚm/ *v* [I] to twist your body from side to side because you are uncomfortable or nervous: *Stop squirming so I can comb your hair!*

**squir·rel** /'skwɚəl/ *n* a small animal with a long FURRY tail that lives in trees and eats nuts

**squirt**[1] /skwɚt/ *v* **1** [I,T] if you squirt liquid or it squirts, it is forced out of a narrow hole in a thin fast stream: *Orange juice squirted onto her dress. | You need to squirt some oil onto the lock.* **2** [T] to hit or cover someone or something with a stream of liquid: *Mom! Tom's squirting me with the hose!*

**squirt**[2] *n* **1** a fast thin stream of liquid: *a squirt of ketchup* **2** SPOKEN an insulting word for someone who is young, short, or not important: *Get out of my way, squirt.*

**squish** /skwɪʃ/ *v* **1** [I,T] INFORMAL ⇨ SQUASH[1] **2** [I] to make a sucking sound by moving through something soft and wet, such as mud

**squish·y** /'skwɪʃi/ *adj* soft and wet, or easy to SQUEEZE: *squishy mud*

**Sr.** *n* the written abbreviation of SENIOR

**St.** *n* **1** the written abbreviation of STREET **2** the written abbreviation of SAINT

**stab**[1] /stæb/ *v* **-bbed, -bbing** **1** [T] to push a sharp object into someone or something, using a lot of force: *She says he **stabbed** her **with** the bread knife.* **2 stab sb in the back** INFORMAL to do something bad to someone who likes and trusts you; BETRAY

**stab**[2] *n* **1** an act of STABbing or trying to stab someone: *The victim had four stab wounds.* **2 take a stab at (doing) sth** INFORMAL to try to do something that is difficult or that you have never done: *Carla decided to take a stab at learning to sail.*

**stab·bing** /'stæbɪŋ/ *n* a crime in which someone is STABbed

**sta·bil·i·ty** /stə'bɪləti/ *n* [U] the condition of being strong, steady, and not changing: *a long period of political stability* —opposite INSTABILITY

**sta·bi·lize** /'steɪbə,laɪz/ *v* [I,T] to become firm and steady or not change any more, or to make something do this: *The financial markets are finally stabilizing.* | *A rod is put in to stabilize the broken bone.* —**stabilization** /,steɪbələ-'zeɪʃən/ *n* [U] —opposite DESTABILIZE

**sta·ble**[1] /'steɪbəl/ *adj* **1** steady and not likely to move or change: *Be careful - the ladder doesn't look stable.* | *a stable marriage* **2** calm, reasonable, and not easy to upset: *mentally stable* —opposite UNSTABLE

**stable**[2] *n* a building where horses are kept

**stack**[1] /stæk/ *n* a neat pile of things: *a stack of magazines on the table*

**stack**[2] *v* **1** [I,T] also **stack up** to form a neat pile, or put things into a neat pile: *Just stack the dishes in the sink for now.* | *chairs that are designed to stack easily* **2** [T] to put piles of things on or in a place: *Al has a job stacking shelves in the supermarket.*

**stack up** *phr v* [I] INFORMAL to compare with something else of the same kind: *a new PC that **stacks up** well **against** the others on the market*

**stacks** /stæks/ *n* [plural] **the stacks** the part of a library where most of the books are kept

**sta·di·um** /'steɪdiəm/ *n, plural* **stadiums** *or* **stadia** /'steɪdiə/ a large field for playing sports, surrounded by a building that has many rows of seats: *a football stadium*

**staff**[1] /stæf/ *n* the group of people who work

for an organization: *Lisa's **on** the city planning staff.* | *a meeting of library **staff members***

**staff**[2] *v* [T] to provide the workers for an organization: *a hospital staffed by experienced nurses* —**staffing** *n* [U]: *staffing costs*

**staff·er** /'stæfɚ/ *n* one of the people who works for an organization: *a Mercury News staffer since 1967*

**stag** /stæg/ *n* a fully grown male DEER —see also STAG NIGHT

**stage**[1] /steɪdʒ/ *n* **1** a particular state or level that someone or something reaches in a process: *The disease is still **in its early stages**.* | *At this stage no one is sure what to do next.* | *Children go through various **stages** of development.* | *the planning **stage** of the project* **2** the raised floor in a theater where plays are performed **3** [singular, U] the profession of acting: *Lina's always wanted to be **on stage**.* **4** a place where something important happens: *the world political stage* **5 s/he's going through a stage** INFORMAL used in order to say that someone young will soon stop behaving in a particular way —see also **set the stage/scene (for sth)** (SET[1])

**stage**[2] *v* [T] **1** to organize an event that people will notice or come to see: *They're staging five plays this summer.* | *factory workers **staging** a strike* **2** to start doing something again after you have stopped for a while: *After five years, Johnson **is staging a comeback** in basketball.*

**stage·coach** /'steɪdʒkoʊtʃ/ *n* a closed vehicle pulled by horses, that carried passengers in past times

**stage fright** /'. ./ *n* [U] nervousness that some people feel before they perform in front of a lot of people

**stage man·ag·er** /'. ,.../ *n* someone who is responsible for a theater stage during a performance

**stag·ger**[1] /'stægɚ/ *v* **1** [I] to walk or move in an unsteady way: *A man came **staggering** down the stairs.* **2** [T] to arrange for things to be done at different times, so that they do not all happen at the same time: *Student registration will be staggered to avoid delays.*

**stagger**[2] *n* an unsteady movement of someone who has difficulty walking

**stag·ger·ing** /'stægərɪŋ/ *adj* very surprising or shocking, and almost unbelievable: *She spends a staggering amount of money on clothes.*

**stag·ing** /'steɪdʒɪŋ/ *n* [C,U] the art of performing a play, or the way this is done: *a modern staging of "Romeo and Juliet"*

**stag·nant** /'stægnənt/ *adj* **1** stagnant water or air does not move or flow and often smells bad **2** not changing or improving: *Steel production has stayed stagnant.*

**stag·nate** /'stægneɪt/ v [I] to stop developing or improving: *a stagnating economy* —**stagnation** /stæg'neɪʃən/ n [U]: *political stagnation*

**stag night** /'. ./ n a night before a man's wedding that he spends with his male friends, drinking and having noisy fun

**staid** /steɪd/ adj serious, old-fashioned, and boring in the way you live, work, or dress: *a staid old bachelor*

**stain**¹ /steɪn/ v **1** [I,T] to accidentally make a colored mark on something, especially one that is difficult to remove, or to be marked in this way: *This carpet stains easily.| a tablecloth stained with wine* **2** [T] to paint wood with a STAIN

**stain**² n **1** a mark that is difficult to remove: *I got coffee stains on my shirt.* **2** [C,U] thin paint used for protecting wood and making it darker

**stain·less steel** /ˌ.. './ n [U] a type of steel that does not RUST

**stair** /stɛr/ n one of the steps in a set of stairs: *Jane sat on the bottom stair.*

**stair·case** /'stɛrkeɪs/ n a set of stairs inside a building, and the structure that supports it

**stairs** /stɛrz/ n [plural] a set of steps built for going from one level of a building to another: *Bev ran up/down the stairs. | The office is up one flight of stairs.* (=the stairs between two floors of a building) —see also DOWNSTAIRS, UPSTAIRS¹ —compare STEP¹

**stair·way** /'stɛrweɪ/ n a set of stairs and the structure that supports it, either inside or outside a building

**stake**¹ /steɪk/ n **1** a pointed piece of wood, metal etc. that is pushed into the ground to hold a rope, mark a particular place etc. **2 be at stake** if something is at stake, you will lose it if a plan or action is not successful **3 have a stake in** to have an important part or share in a business, plan etc.: *a 5% stake in the company* **4** [C usually plural] money risked on the result of a game, race etc.; BET

**stake**² v [T] **1** to risk something on the result of a game, race etc., or on the result of a plan or action: *The President is staking his reputation on the peace plan.* **2 stake (out) a claim** to say publicly that you think you have a right to have or own something: *The two tribes have both staked a claim to the territory.*

**stake** sth ↔ **out** phr v [T] INFORMAL to watch a place secretly and continuously: *The police have been staking out the club for weeks.*

**stake·out** /'steɪkaʊt/ n the act of watching a place secretly and continuously

**stale** /steɪl/ adj **1** no longer fresh: *stale bread* **2** no longer interesting: *a stale old joke*

**stale·mate** /'steɪlmeɪt/ n [C,U] a situation in which neither side in an argument, battle etc. can gain an advantage

**stalk**¹ /stɔk/ n the main stem of a plant

**stalk**² v **1** [T] to follow a person or animal quietly in order to catch or kill him, her, or it **2** [I] to walk in a proud or angry way: *Sheryl turned and stalked out of the room.*

**stalk·er** /'stɔkɚ/ n someone who often follows someone else, often in order to annoy or harm him/her —**stalking** n [U]

**stall**¹ /stɔl/ n **1** a small enclosed area for washing or using the toilet: *a shower stall* **2** an enclosed area in a building for an animal, especially a horse **3** an occasion when an engine suddenly stops working: *Then the plane went into a stall.*

**stall**² v [I,T] **1** if an engine stalls or you stall it, it suddenly stops working: *My car always stalls when it's cold.* **2** INFORMAL to deliberately delay doing something, or to make someone else do this: *Quit stalling and answer my question! | I'll try to stall him for a few minutes.*

**stal·lion** /'stælyən/ n a fully grown male horse

**stal·wart** /'stɔlwɚt/ n someone who strongly supports a particular organization or set of ideas —**stalwart** adj: *a stalwart supporter*

**stam·i·na** /'stæmənə/ n [U] physical or mental strength that lets you continue doing something for a long time

**stam·mer** /'stæmɚ/ v [I,T] to repeat the first sound of a word because you have a speech problem, or because you are nervous —**stammer** n [singular] —see also STUTTER

**stamp**¹ /stæmp/ n **1** a small piece of paper that you stick onto an envelope or package that shows you have paid to mail it **2** a tool for printing a mark onto a surface, or the mark made by this tool: *a passport stamp* **3 have/ bear the stamp of sth** to clearly have a particular quality: *a speech that bears the stamp of authority*

**stamp**² v **1** [I] to lift up your foot and put it down hard, or to walk in this way: *Tony stamped upstairs.* **2** [T] to put a pattern, sign, or letters on something using a special tool: *Please stamp the date on all incoming mail.* **3** [T] to stick a stamp onto an envelope or package

**stamp** sth ↔ **out** phr v [T] to get rid of something: *efforts to stamp out drug abuse*

**stam·pede** /stæm'pid/ n **1** an occasion when a large number of animals suddenly start running together **2** a sudden rush by a lot of people who all want to do the same thing or go to the same place: *a stampede to buy gold before the price goes up* —**stampede** v [I,T]

**stance** /stæns/ n **1** an opinion that is stated publicly: *Senator, what is your stance on nuclear tests?* **2** the way in which you stand during a particular activity

**stanch** /stæntʃ/ v [T] ⇨ STAUNCH²

**stand¹** /stænd/ v stood, stood, standing

**1** ▶STAND◀ [I] to be on your feet in an upright position: *Jeff and I were standing there and saw it all.* | *Hundreds of people stood watching.* | *Stand still* (=stand without moving) *and let me comb your hair.* | *A policeman told everyone to stand back/aside.* (=stand farther away from something)

**2** ▶START STANDING◀ [I] also **stand up** to move so that you are standing· *Please stand for the singing of the National Anthem* | *Everybody stood up to applaud.*

**3** ▶UPRIGHT POSITION◀ [I,T] to be in an upright position somewhere, or to put something in an upright position: *We'll stand the Christmas tree in the corner.* | *There's now a parking lot where the theater once stood.* | *The house has stood empty* (=not been lived in) *for 20 years.*

**4** ▶LEVEL/AMOUNT◀ [I] to be at a particular level or amount: *The unemployment rate stood at 8% in January.*

**5 can't stand** SPOKEN to dislike something or someone very much: *Dave can't stand dogs.* | *I can't stand to waste anything.* —see usage note at BEAR¹

**6 stand to do sth** to be likely to do or have something: *The company stands to make more than $12 million on the deal.*

**7** ▶NOT CHANGE◀ [I] to continue to exist or be correct, and not change: *The Supreme Court let stand the ruling of the lower court.* | *Horowitz has stood firm on his refusal.* (=refused to change it)

**8** ▶HEIGHT◀ [I] to have a particular height: *The Eiffel Tower stands 300 meters high.*

**9 stand a chance (of doing sth)** to be likely to succeed in doing something: *You don't stand a chance of going out with her.*

**10** ▶BE GOOD ENOUGH◀ [T] to be good enough or strong enough to remain unharmed or unchanged by something: *jeans that can stand the rough wear kids give them* | *Their marriage has certainly stood the test of time.*

**11** ▶IN STATE/SITUATION◀ [I, linking verb] to be in or remain in a particular state or situation: *US warships stood ready to block all trade in the area.* | *The offer, as it stands, is not acceptable.*

**12 stand in the way/in sb's way** to prevent someone from doing something, or prevent something from happening or developing: *Some important objections still stand in the way of an agreement.*

**13** ▶BEAR/ACCEPT◀ [T] to be able to accept or deal with something unpleasant or difficult: *He could hardly stand the pain any longer.*

**14 where/how you stand** what your opinion about something is: *Voters are not sure where she stands on the issue of immigration.*

**15 know where you stand** to know what someone's opinion of you is, or to know what s/he wants you to do: *You just never know where you stand with Walter.*

**16 stand on your own two feet** to be independent and not need help from other people

**17 it stands to reason** used in order to say that something is clearly true: *It stands to reason that children will imitate their parents.*

**18 could stand** used in order to say that someone should do something or that something should be different: *I could stand to lose a little weight.* | *That skirt could stand to be longer.*

**19 stand pat** to refuse to change a decision, plan etc.: *Lurie has been standing pat, waiting for the best offer.*

**20 stand on your head/hands** to support yourself on your head or hands in an upright position, with your feet in the air —see also **be on guard/stand guard** (GUARD¹)

**stand around** phr v [I] to stand somewhere and not do anything: *Everybody was just standing around talking.*

**stand by** phr v **1** [T **stand by** sth] to decide what to do, say, or believe, and not change this: *The doctors are standing by their original statements.* | *If you don't stand by your principles, they won't respect you.* **2** [T **stand by** sb] to stay loyal to someone and support him/her in a difficult situation: *Matt's parents have stood by him through his drug problem.* **3** [I] to be ready to do something: *Fire crews are now standing by.* **4** [I] to not do anything to help someone, or to not prevent something from happening: *Muldrow said that while one officer stood by, another hit the boy.*

**stand for** sth phr v [T] **1** to represent a word, phrase, or idea: *VA stands for Veterans Administration.* **2** to support an idea, principle etc.: *Martin Luther King stood for fairness and racial equality.*

**stand out** phr v [I] **1** to be clearly better than other things or people: *Morrison stands out as the most experienced candidate.* **2** to be very easy to see or notice: *In her red dress, she really stood out in the crowd.*

**stand up** phr v **1** [I] to be proven to be true or correct: *The accusations will never stand up in court.* | *Lo's studies stood up to close scrutiny from experts.* **2** [T **stand** sb **up**] to not meet someone when you have promised to meet him/her: *My date stood me up last night.* **3** [I] to remain in good condition after being used a lot or in a bad situation: *The equipment did not stand up under battlefield conditions.*

**stand up for** sb/sth phr v [T] to support or defend someone or something when s/he or it is being attacked or criticized: *Don't be afraid to fight by standing up for your rights.*

**stand up to** sb phr v [T] to be brave and refuse to do or say what someone is trying to make you do or say: *He became a kind of hero for standing up to the local gangs.*

**stand²** n **1** a piece of furniture or equipment for supporting something: *a music stand* **2** a table or small structure, usually outside or in a large building, where you can buy something: *a hotdog stand* **3** an opinion that you state publicly: *Bradley was unwilling to* **take a stand** (=say what his opinion was) *on the issue*. **4** the place in a court of law where someone sits when the lawyers ask him/her questions: *Shaw had lied* **on the stand**. (=when he was answering questions) | *Epstein will* **take the stand** (=begin answering questions) *Friday*. **5** an effort to defend yourself or to oppose something: *Lassiter feels he has to* **make a stand** *to protect the Alaska wilderness*. —see also STANDS

**stand-a·lone** /ˌ. .ˈ.ˌ/ *adj* working on its own without being controlled by anything else: *a stand-alone computer*

**stan·dard¹** /ˈstændɚd/ *n* **1** a level of quality, skill, or ability that is considered to be acceptable: *They have to* **meet/reach a** *certain* **standard** *or they won't pass.* | *Mr. Williams* **sets** *very* **high standards** *for all his students.* **2** the ideas of what is good or normal that someone uses to compare one thing with another: *By American* **standards**, *Rafael's salary is pretty low*.

**standard²** *adj* normal or usual: *Security checks are now* **standard practice/procedure**. —compare NONSTANDARD, SUBSTANDARD

**stan·dard·ize** /ˈstændɚˌdaɪz/ *v* [T] to make all the things of one particular type the same as each other: *national standardized tests* —**standardization** /ˌstændɚdəˈzeɪʃən/ *n* [U]

**standard of liv·ing** /ˌ.. . ˈ../ *n* the amount of wealth and comfort that a person, group, or country has

**stand·by** /ˈstændbaɪ/ *n* **1** someone or something that is ready to be used when needed: *a standby power generator* **2 on standby a)** ready to be used when needed: *The police have been kept* **on standby** *in case of trouble.* **b)** ready to travel on a plane if there are any seats left when it is ready to leave: *The flight is full, but we can put you* **on standby**.

**stand-in** /ˈ. ./ *n* someone who does the job or takes the place of someone else for a short time

**stand·ing¹** /ˈstændɪŋ/ *adj* **1** continuing to exist; permanent: *We have a standing offer to use their beach cabin.* **2** done from a standing position: *a* **standing ovation** (=when people stand to CLAP after a performance)

**standing²** *n* [U] someone's rank or position in a system, organization, etc., based on what other people think of him/her: *the President's standing in the opinion polls*

**stand·off** /ˈstændɔf/ *n* a situation in which neither side in a fight or battle can gain an advantage

**stand·out** /ˈstændaʊt/ *n* someone who is better at doing something than other people in a group —**standout** *adj*

**stand·point** /ˈstændpɔɪnt/ *n* a particular person's or group's way of thinking about a problem or subject; POINT OF VIEW

**stands** /stændz/ *n* [plural] the place where people sit to watch a sports game

**stand·still** /ˈstændˌstɪl/ *n* [singular] a situation in which there is no movement or activity at all: *Strikes* **brought** *production* **to a standstill**.

**stand·up** /ˈstændʌp/ *adj* INFORMAL standup COMEDY involves one person telling jokes as a performance —**standup** *n* [C,U]

**stank** /stæŋk/ *v* the past tense of STINK

**stan·za** /ˈstænzə/ *n* a group of lines that forms part of a poem

**sta·ple¹** /ˈsteɪpəl/ *n* **1** a small thin piece of metal with ends that bend, used in order to hold pieces of paper together or to hold something in place **2** a food that is needed and used all the time: *staples like flour and rice* —**staple** *adj*

**staple²** *v* [T] to fasten things together with a STAPLE

**sta·pler** /ˈsteɪplɚ/ *n* a tool used for putting STAPLEs through paper, wood etc.

**star¹** /star/ *n* **1** a very large amount of burning gases in space, that looks like a point of light in the sky at night **2** a shape with five or six points sticking out of it, that is sometimes used as a sign of quality or rank **3** a famous performer in entertainment or sports: *a movie star* **4** INFORMAL someone who is particularly good at something: *Jim is definitely our* **star** *player*. **5 the stars/sb's stars** the power of the stars to affect what happens, that some people believe in

**star²** *v* **-rred, -rring 1** [T] if a movie, play etc. stars someone, that person acts the part of the main character: *a movie starring Bruce Willis* **2** [I] to act the part of the main character in a movie, play etc.: *This is her first time* **starring in** *a TV comedy*.

**star·board** /ˈstarbɚd/ *n* [U] the right side of a ship or aircraft when you are looking toward the front

**starch¹** /startʃ/ *n* **1** [C,U] a substance in such foods as bread, rice, and potatoes **2** [U] a substance used for making cloth stiff

**starch²** *v* [T] to make cloth stiff using STARCH

**starch·y** /ˈstartʃi/ *adj* containing a lot of STARCH: *starchy foods*

**star·dom** /ˈstardəm/ *n* [U] the situation of being a famous performer

**stare¹** /stɛr/ *v* [I] **1** to look at someone or something for a long time without moving your eyes: *Stop staring at me!* **2 be staring sb in the face** INFORMAL to be very clear and easy to see or understand; OBVIOUS

**stare²** *n* the expression on your face when you STARE

**star·fish** /ˈstarˌfɪʃ/ *n* a flat sea animal that is shaped like a star

**stark**[1] /stɑrk/ *adj* **1** very simple and severe in appearance: *the stark beauty of the desert* **2** unpleasantly clear and impossible to avoid: *the stark realities of drug addiction* **–starkly** *adv*

**stark**[2] *adv* **stark naked** INFORMAL not wearing any clothes

**star·let** /'stɑrlɪt/ *n* a young actress who plays small parts in movies and is hoping to become famous

**star·light** /'stɑrlaɪt/ *n* [U] the light that comes from the stars

**star·ling** /'stɑrlɪŋ/ *n* a common European bird that is black and slightly green

**star·lit** /'stɑr,lɪt/ *adj* made brighter by the light of the stars: *a starlit night*

**star·ry** /'stɑri/ *adj* having many stars: *a starry sky*

**starry-eyed** /'.. ,./ *adj* INFORMAL hopeful about things in a way that is silly or unreasonable: *a starry-eyed teenager*

**Stars and Stripes** /,. . './ *n* [singular] the flag of the US

**Star-Span·gled Ban·ner** /,. .. '../ *n* [singular] the national ANTHEM (=song) of the US

**star-stud·ded** /'. ,./ *adj* including many famous performers: *a star-studded cast*

**start**[1] /stɑrt/ *v*
**1** ▶BEGIN DOING STH◀ [I,T] to begin doing something: *Have you started making dinner? | I didn't start work until 9:30. | It's starting to rain.*
**2** ▶BEGIN HAPPENING◀ [I,T] to begin happening, or to make something do this: *The race starts in 10 minutes. | The fire was started by a loose wire.*
**3 to start with** SPOKEN **a)** said in order to emphasize the first of a list of facts or opinions: *There's a lot wrong with those kids; to start with, they're rude.* **b)** said when talking about the beginning of a situation that later changes: *I was nervous to start with, but then I was fine.*
**4** ▶JOB/SCHOOL◀ [I,T] to begin a new job, or to begin going to school, college etc.: *How soon can you start? | Mark's starting school/ college in the fall.*
**5** ▶TRIP◀ [I] also **start off/out** to begin a trip: *You'll have to start early if you want to get there by noon. | We didn't get started until after dark.*
**6** ▶CAR◀ [I,T] also **start up** if you start a car or engine, or if it starts, it begins to work: *Can't you get that engine started?*
**7** ▶ROAD/RIVER◀ [I] if a road, river etc. starts somewhere, it begins in that place: *The Red River starts in New Mexico.*
**8** ▶PRICES◀ [I] if prices start at or from a particular figure, that is the lowest figure at which you can buy something
**9** ▶BUSINESS/CLUB◀ [T] also **start up** to make something begin to exist: *Sally decided to*

*start up a club for single mothers.*
**10** ▶MOVE SUDDENLY◀ [I] to move suddenly because you are surprised or afraid

**start sb/sth ↔ off** *phr v* [I,T] to begin an activity, or to help someone do this: *Let's start off by reviewing what we did last week.*

**start on** *phr v* [T] **1** [start on sth] to begin working on something: *You'd better get started on your homework.* **2** [start sb on sth] to make someone start doing or using something: *How old was she when you started her on solid food?*

**start over** *phr v* [I] to start doing something again from the beginning so that you can correct what was wrong the first time: *Coming back home was like a chance to start over.*

---

**USAGE NOTE start and begin**

Usually, these words mean the same thing. However **start** has some special meanings for which **begin** cannot be used. Use **start** to talk about making a machine work: *Bob couldn't start the car.* You should also use **start** to talk about making something begin to exist: *Starting a new business is hard work.*

---

**start**[2] *n* **1** the beginning of an activity, event, or situation: *Hurry, or we'll miss the start of the show. | They've had problems (right) from the start. | It was a close race from start to finish.* **2 it's a start** used in order to say that something you have achieved may not be impressive, but it will help with a bigger achievement: *We only have $92 million of the $600 million needed, but it's a start.* **3 for a start** INFORMAL said in order to emphasize the first of a list of facts or opinions: *I don't think she'll get the job. She's too young, for a start.* **4** [singular] a sudden movement caused by fear or surprise: *Ed woke up with a start.*

**start·er** /'stɑrtɚ/ *n* **1** a person, horse etc. that is in a race when it starts: *Of the eight starters, only three finished the race.* **2** someone who gives the signal for a race to begin **3** also **starter motor** a piece of equipment for starting an engine

**start·ing line·up** /,.. '../ *n* the best players on a sports team, who play when the game begins

**star·tle** /'stɑrtl/ *v* [T] to make someone suddenly surprised or slightly shocked: *The sudden noise behind her startled her.* **–startling** *adj*: *startling news*

**start-up** /'. ./ *adj* start-up costs are related to beginning and developing a new business

**star·va·tion** /stɑr'veɪʃən/ *n* [U] suffering or death caused by not having enough to eat

**starve** /stɑrv/ *v* **1** [I,T] to suffer or die because you do not have enough to eat, or to make someone do this: *animals that have been starved to death | starving refugees* **2 be starving/ starved** SPOKEN to be very hungry: *When do we*

S

eat? I'm starving! **3 be starved for/of sth** to not be given something very important: *That poor kid's just **starved for** attention.*

**stash**[1] /stæʃ/ v [T] INFORMAL to keep something in a safe, often secret, place: *He has money **stashed away** in a Swiss bank.*

**stash**[2] n INFORMAL an amount of something, especially an illegal drug, that is kept in a secret place

**state**[1] /steɪt/ n **1** the condition that someone or something is in at a particular time: *Your car's in a bad state.* | *The driver was in a **state of shock.** | You can't take a test in this **state of mind.*** **2** also **State** one of the areas with limited law-making powers that some countries, such as the US, are divided into: *the state of Oklahoma* **3** [C,U] also **State** a country or its government: *a meeting between heads of state* **4** [U] the official ceremonies and events relating to governments and rulers: *the President's **state visit** to Moscow* **5 be in a state/get into a state** SPOKEN to be or become very nervous or anxious —see usage note at RACE[1]

**state**[2] v [T] FORMAL **1** to give a piece of information or your opinion about something by saying or writing it clearly: *The witness **stated** that he had never seen the woman before.* **2** if a document, ticket etc. states information, it contains the information written clearly

**state·ly** /'steɪtli/ adj impressive in style or size: *a stately mansion*

**state·ment** /'steɪtˈmənt/ n **1** an opinion or a piece of information that is spoken or written officially and publicly: *The company will **make a statement about** the accident later today.* **2** a list showing amounts of money paid, received etc. and their total: *a bank statement* **3 make a statement** to do something that shows your beliefs or political opinions: *Why get your nose pierced? Are you trying to make a statement?*

**state-of-the-art** /ˌ. . . '.◂/ adj using the newest methods, materials, or knowledge: *state-of-the-art technology*

**States** /steɪts/ n INFORMAL **the States** the US

**states·man** /'steɪtsmən/, **states·wom·an** /'steɪts₁wʊmən/ n a political or government leader, especially one who is known as being wise and fair —**statesmanlike** adj —**statesmanship** n [U]

**stat·ic**[1] /'stætɪk/ adj **1** not moving, changing, or developing: *static prices* **2** static electricity collects on the surface of objects and can give you a small electric shock

**static**[2] n [U] noise caused by electricity in the air that spoils the sound on a radio or TV

**sta·tion**[1] /'steɪʃən/ n **1** a place where public vehicles stop so that passengers can get on and off, goods can be loaded etc.: *a bus/train station* **2** a building or place that is a center for a particular type of service or activity: *a police station* | *a gas station* **3** a company that broad-

casts on radio or television, or its programs that you receive: *a country music station*

**station**[2] v [T] to put someone in a particular place in order to do a particular job or military duty: *My uncle's stationed in Germany right now.*

**sta·tion·a·ry** /'steɪʃə₁nɛri/ adj not moving: *a stationary vehicle*

**sta·tion·er·y** /'steɪʃə₁nɛri/ n [U] materials that you use for writing, such as paper, pens, pencils etc.

**station wag·on** /'.. ₁../ n a car with a door at the back, and a lot of space for boxes, cases etc. —see picture on page 469

**sta·tis·tic** /stə'tɪstɪk/ n [singular] a single number that represents a fact or measurement: *Is he aware of the statistic that two out of three marriages fail?* —**statistical** adj: *statistical analysis* —**statistically** adv

**stat·is·ti·cian** /ˌstætəs'tɪʃən/ n someone who works with STATISTICS

**sta·tis·tics** /stə'tɪstɪks/ n **1** [plural] a collection of numbers that represent facts or measurements: *Statistics show that 35% of new businesses fail in their first year.* **2** [U] the science of dealing with and explaining such numbers

**stat·ue** /'stætʃu/ n something that looks like a person or animal, and is made of stone, metal etc.

**stat·u·ette** /ˌstætʃu'ɛt/ n a very small STATUE

**stat·ure** /'stætʃɚ/ n [U] FORMAL **1** the degree to which someone is admired or regarded as important: *a musician of great stature* **2** someone's height

**sta·tus** /'steɪtəs, 'stæ-/ n **1** [C,U] the legal or official position or condition of a person, group, country etc.: *Please state your name, age and **marital status.** (=whether you are married or not)* **2** [U] a high social position that makes people recognize and respect you: *a **status symbol** (=something that shows your high social position)* **3 the status of sth** what is happening at a particular time in a situation: *No one would comment on the status of her application.*

**status quo** /ˌsteɪtəs 'kwoʊ, ˌstæ-/ n the state of a situation at a particular time

**stat·ute** /'stætʃut/ n FORMAL a law or rule that has been formally written down

**stat·u·to·ry** /'stætʃə₁tɔri/ adj FORMAL fixed or controlled by law: *statutory rights*

**statutory rape** /ˌ.... './ n the crime of having sex with someone who is below a particular age

**staunch**[1] /stɔntʃ, stɑntʃ/ adj very loyal: *a staunch supporter* —**staunchly** adv

**staunch**[2] v [T] to stop the flow of a liquid, especially of blood from a wound

**stave** /steɪv/ v

**stave** sth ↔ **off** phr v [T] to stop someone or something from reaching you or affecting you for a period of time: *White blood cells* **stave off** *infection and disease.*

**stay**[1] /steɪ/ v **1** [I] to continue to be in a particular position, place, or state: *How long is it going to stay this cold?* | *Stay right there! I'll be back in a minute.* | **Stay away** *from my wife!* | *I had to* **stay late** *at work.* | *I stayed up* (=stayed awake) *all night.* | *Are you going to* **stay in** (=not leave your home) *tonight?* | *Someone has to* **stay behind** (=stay after others have left) *and clean up this mess.* **2** [I] to live in a place for a short time as a visitor or guest: *She's* **staying with** *us for a week.* | *Where are you staying while you're here?* ✗ DON'T SAY "Where do you stay?" ✗ **3 stay put** INFORMAL to remain in one place and not move

**stay on** *phr v* [I] to continue to do a job or to study after the usual or expected time for leaving: *Rachelle is staying on for a fifth year in college.*

**stay**[2] n **1** a limited time of living in a place: *a stay in the hospital* **2** [C,U] LAW the stopping or delay of an action because a judge has ordered it

**stead·fast** /'stɛdfæst/ *adj* LITERARY faithful and very loyal: *Carlos remained* **steadfast in** *his beliefs.*

**stead·y**[1] /'stɛdi/ *adj* **1** firmly in one place without moving, shaking, or falling: *Keep the ladder steady.* **2** moving, happening, or developing in a continuous gradual way: *steady progress* **3** a steady level, speed etc. stays about the same **4 steady job/work/income** a job etc. that will continue over a long period of time – **steadily** *adv* – **steadiness** *n* [U] – opposite UNSTEADY

**steady**[2] v [I,T] to become more calm or controlled, or to make someone or something do this: *"Watch the steps," he said, steadying her with his hand.*

**steady**[3] *adv* **go steady (with sb)** to have a long romantic relationship with someone – **steady** *n*

**steak** /steɪk/ n [C,U] a thick flat piece of meat or fish

**steal**[1] /stil/ v **stole, stolen, stealing 1** [I,T] to take something that belongs to someone else without his/her permission, and not give it back: *Two local men were arrested for stealing a car.* | *When did you find out your partner was* **stealing from** *you?* – see usage note at ROB **2** [I] LITERARY to move quietly without anyone noticing you

**steal**[2] n INFORMAL something that costs much less than it is worth: *At $15 a bottle, their Merlot is a real steal.*

**stealth** /stɛlθ/ n [U] the action of doing something quietly and secretly – **stealthily** *adv*: *moving stealthily* – **stealthy** *adj*

**steam**[1] /stim/ n **1** [U] the gas that water produces when it is boiled: *a steam engine* (=that uses steam to operate) **2 let/work/blow off**

**steam** to get rid of your anger, excitement, or energy by shouting or doing something active **3 run out of steam** to no longer have the energy or the support you need to continue doing something

**steam**[2] v [U] **1** [I] to send out steam: *steaming coffee* **2** [T] to cook something using steam: *Steam the vegetables for five minutes.*

**steam** sth ↔ **up** *phr v* [I,T] to cover or be covered with steam: *My glasses are* **steamed up**.

**steam·roll** /'stimroʊl/ v [T] INFORMAL to defeat an opponent or force someone to do something by using all your power or influence

**steam·roll·er** /'stim,roʊlɚ/ n a heavy vehicle with very wide wheels for making road surfaces flat

**steam·y** /'stimi/ *adj* **1** full of steam, or covered with steam: *steamy windows* **2** sexually exciting: *a steamy love scene*

**steel**[1] /stil/ n [U] **1** a strong hard metal that can be shaped easily, made of iron and CARBON **2 nerves of steel** the ability to be brave and calm in a dangerous or difficult situation

**steel**[2] v [T] **steel yourself** to prepare yourself to do something that you know will be unpleasant

**steel wool** /ˌ. './ n [U] a rough material made of steel wires, used in order to make surfaces smooth, remove paint etc.

**steel·y** /'stili/ *adj* extremely strong and determined: *a steely expression*

**steep**[1] /stip/ *adj* **1** a road, hill etc. that is steep slopes at a high angle **2** a steep increase or rise in something is large and happens quickly **3** INFORMAL steep prices, charges etc. are very expensive – **steeply** *adv* – **steepen** *v* [I,T]

**steep**[2] v [I,T] to put something in a liquid and leave it there, or to be left in a liquid

**stee·ple** /'stipəl/ n a tall pointed tower on a church

**steer**[1] /stɪr/ v **1** [I,T] to control the direction that a vehicle goes in: *The bumps in the road were making it hard to steer.* **2** [T] to influence someone's behavior or the way a situation develops: *Helen tried to* **steer the conversation** *away from school.* **3** [T] to guide someone to a place: *Bobby took my arm and steered me into the next room.* **4 steer clear (of)** INFORMAL to try to avoid someone or something that is unpleasant

**steer**[2] n a young male cow that has had part of its sex organs removed

**steer·ing** /'stɪrɪŋ/ n [U] the parts of a vehicle that allow you to control the direction it goes in

**steering wheel** /'.. ˌ./ n a wheel that you turn to control the direction a vehicle goes in – see picture on page 469

**stel·lar** /'stɛlɚ/ *adj* **1** done extremely well: *a stellar performance* **2** TECHNICAL relating to the stars

**stem**[1] /stɛm/ *n* **1** a long thin part of a plant, from which leaves or flowers grow **2** the thin part of a wine glass, between the base and the wide top —see picture at GLASS

**stem**[2] *v* **-mmed, -mming** [T] **stem the tide/ flow of** to stop something from spreading or growing: *Even the Great Fire could not stem the tide of immigrants to Chicago.*

**stem from** sth *phr v* [T] to develop as a result of something else: *Her back problems stem from holding her baby on one hip.*

**stench** /stɛntʃ/ *n* a strong unpleasant smell

**sten·cil**[1] /'stɛnsəl/ *n* a piece of plastic, paper etc. in which patterns or letters have been cut

**stencil**[2] *v* [T] to put a pattern or letter on a surface by painting or drawing through the holes in a STENCIL

**ste·nog·ra·pher** /stə'nɑɡrəfər/ *n* someone whose job is to write down what someone else is saying by using SHORTHAND —**stenography** *n* [U]

**step**[1] /stɛp/ *n*
**1** ▶MOVEMENT◀ the act of putting one foot down in front of the other one in order to move along: *Take two steps forward and one step back.*
**2** ▶ACTION◀ one of a series of things that you do in order to deal with a problem or to produce a particular result: *We must take steps* (=take action) *to make sure it never happens again.* | *an important first step toward peace*
**3** ▶STAIR◀ a flat narrow surface, especially one in a series, that you put your foot on when you are going up or down, especially outside a building: *Jenny waited on the church steps.* —compare STAIRS
**4** ▶IN A PROCESS◀ a stage in a process or a position on a scale: *That promotion was quite a step up for her.* —see also STEP-BY-STEP
**5** ▶DANCING◀ a movement of your feet in dancing: *I'm always getting the steps wrong.*
**6 watch your step** SPOKEN **a)** to be careful about what you say or how you behave **b)** to be careful when you are walking
**7 in step/out of step a)** having ideas that are the same as, or different from, other people's: *"Perhaps I haven't kept in step with the voters,"* Hannigan admitted. **b)** moving your feet in the same way as, or a different way from, people you are walking or marching with
**8** ▶SOUND◀ the sound you make when you take a step —see also FOOTSTEP

**step**[2] *v* **-pped, -pping** [I] **1** to put one foot down in front of the other one in order to move along: *Step aside/back and let the doctor through.* **2** to bring your foot down on something: *Yuck! What did you step in?* **3 step out of line** to behave badly by doing something that you are not expected to do or told not to do
**4 step on it** SPOKEN said when you want someone to go somewhere faster, especially in a car: *If you don't step on it we'll miss the plane.*

**5 step on sb's toes** to offend or upset someone, especially by trying to do his/her work

**step down/aside** *phr v* [I] to leave your job or official position because you want to or think you should: *He's decided to step down at the end of the year.*

**step forward** *phr v* [I] to come and offer help: *Several volunteers have kindly stepped forward.*

**step in** *phr v* [I] to become involved in a discussion or disagreement, especially in order to stop the trouble: *The referee stepped in to separate the players.*

**step out** *phr v* [I] to go out for a short time: *Molly just stepped out but she'll be back soon.*

**step** sth ↔ **up** *phr v* [T] to increase the amount of an activity or the speed of a process: *The industry has stepped up efforts to clean up its pollution.*

**step·broth·er** /'stɛpˌbrʌðər/ *n* a boy or man whose father or mother has married your mother or father

**step-by-step** /ˌ. . '.◂/ *adj* a step-by-step plan, method etc. deals with things carefully and in a particular order

**step·child** /'stɛp-tʃaɪld/ *n* a child that your husband or wife has from a relationship before your marriage

**step·daugh·ter** /'stɛpˌdɔtər/ *n* a daughter that your husband or wife has from a relationship before your marriage

**step·fa·ther** /'stɛpˌfɑðər/ *n* a man who is married to your mother but who is not your father

**step·lad·der** /'stɛpˌlædər/ *n* a LADDER with two sloping parts that are attached at the top so that it can stand without support

**step·moth·er** /'stɛpˌmʌðər/ *n* a woman who is married to your father but who is not your mother

**stepped-up** /ˌ. '.◂/ *adj* done more quickly or with more effort than before: *stepped-up factory production*

**stepping-stone** /'.. ˌ./ *n* **1** something that helps you to improve or become more successful: *a stepping-stone to a better job* **2** one of a row of stones that you walk on to get across a stream

**step·sis·ter** /'stɛpˌsɪstər/ *n* a girl or woman whose father or mother has married your mother or father

**step·son** /'stɛpsʌn/ *n* a son that your husband or wife has from a relationship before your marriage

**ster·e·o** /'stɛriˌoʊ, 'stɪr-/ *n* **1** a machine for playing records, CDs etc. that produces sound from two SPEAKERs **2 in stereo** if music or a broadcast is in stereo, the sound it makes is directed through two SPEAKERs

**ster·e·o·type**[1] /'stɛriəˌtaɪp, 'stɪr-/ *n* an idea of what a particular type of person is like that

many people have, and that is wrong or unfair
−**stereotypical** /ˌstɛriouˈtɪpɪkəl/ *adj*

**stereotype²** *v* [T] DISAPPROVING to decide that
some people have particular qualities or abilities
because they belong to a particular race, sex
etc.: *Homeless people are often stereotyped as a
bunch of alcoholics.*

**ster·ile** /ˈstɛrəl/ *adj* **1** sterile people or animals are not able to produce babies
**2** completely clean and not containing any
BACTERIA: *a sterile bandage* **3** lacking new
ideas or imagination: *sterile concepts* −**sterility**
/stəˈrɪləti/ *n* [U]

**ster·il·ize** /ˈstɛrəˌlaɪz/ *v* [T] **1** to make
something completely clean and kill any
BACTERIA in it: *sterilized surgery equipment*
**2** to make a person or animal unable to have
children −**sterilization** /ˌstɛrələˈzeɪʃən/ *n*
[C,U]

**ster·ling** /ˈstɚlɪŋ/ *adj* **sterling quality/effort/
character etc.** the best quality, effort etc.

**sterling sil·ver** /ˌ.. ˈ../, **sterling** *n* [U] a metal
that is over 92% pure silver

**stern¹** /stɚn/ *adj* very strict and severe: *stern
discipline* | *a stern expression* −**sternly** *adv*

**stern²** *n* the back part of a ship

**ste·roid** /ˈstɛrɔɪd, ˈstɪrɔɪd/ *n* a drug used
especially for treating injuries, that people sometimes use illegally to improve their sports
performance

**steth·o·scope** /ˈstɛθəˌskoʊp/ *n* an instrument used by doctors to listen to someone's
heart or breathing

**stew¹** /stu/ *n* a food made of meat and vegetables, cooked in liquid

**stew²** *v* **1** [T] to cook something slowly in liquid: *stewed tomatoes* **2** INFORMAL to worry because of something that has happened or that
you have done

**stew·ard** /ˈstuɚd/ *n* **1** OLD-FASHIONED a man
who is a FLIGHT ATTENDANT **2** also **shop stew-
ard** a worker who represents the members of a
UNION **3** a man who is responsible for the
comfort of the passengers on a ship

**stew·ard·ess** /ˈstuɚdɪs/ *n* OLD-FASHIONED a
woman who is a FLIGHT ATTENDANT

**stick¹** /stɪk/ *v* **stuck, stuck, sticking** **1** [I,T]
to attach something to something else using a
sticky substance, or to become attached to a surface: *Did you remember to stick a stamp on the
envelope?* | *leaves sticking to the windshield*
**2** [T] INFORMAL to put something somewhere:
*Just stick your coat on that chair.* **3** [I,T] to
push a pointed object into something, or to be
pushing into something in this way: *Ow! That
pin stuck me!* | *There's a nail sticking through
the board here.* **4** [I,T] if something sticks or
is stuck, it is fixed and difficult to move: *Hey,
this door is stuck.*

**stick around** *phr v* [I] INFORMAL to stay or wait
in a particular place

**stick by** sb/sth *phr v* [T] INFORMAL **1** to continue to give your support to someone: *Laura
has always stuck by me.* **2** to decide what to
do, say, or believe, and not change this: *Barnes
is sticking by his decision to testify.*

**stick out** *phr v* **1** [I] if a part of something
sticks out, it comes out further than the rest of a
surface or comes out through a hole **2** [T **stick
sth ↔ out**] to deliberately make something come
forward or out: *Jamie stuck out his foot to trip
his brother.* **3** **stick out (like a sore thumb)**
INFORMAL to look very unsuitable and different
from everyone or everything else **4** **stick your
neck out** INFORMAL to take the risk of saying or
doing something that may be wrong, or that
other people may disagree with **5** **stick your
tongue out (at sb)** to quickly put your tongue
outside your mouth and back in again, in order
to be rude **6** **stick it out** INFORMAL to continue
doing something that is difficult, boring etc.

**stick to** *phr v* [T] **1** to decide what to do,
say, or believe, and not change this: *That's my
story and I'm sticking to it.* | *If you're driving,
stick to soft drinks.* **2** **stick to your guns** to
continue to say or do something, although
people disagree with you

**stick together** *phr v* [I] INFORMAL if people stick
together, they continue to support each other

**stick up** *phr v* [I] if a part of something sticks
up, it is raised up or points upward above a surface

**stick up for** sb *phr v* [T] INFORMAL to defend
someone who is being criticized

**stick with** *phr v* [T] INFORMAL **1** [**stick with**
sb] to stay close to someone when there is a risk
you could be separated **2** [**stick with** sb/sth] to
continue doing something or supporting someone: *Let's just stick with the original plan.*
**3** [**stick** sb **with** sth] to give someone a
difficult or unpleasant responsibility: *I'll go as
long as I don't get stuck with paying the bill
again!* **4** **stick with it** to continue doing something that is difficult, boring etc. **5** [**stick with**
sb] to remain in your memory: *One thing he
said has stuck with me ever since.*

**stick²** *n* **1** a long thin piece of wood that has
fallen or been cut from a tree **2** **stick of
celery/gum etc.** a long thin piece of something
**3** a long thin piece of wood or metal that you
use for a particular purpose: *a walking stick* | *a
hockey stick* −see also **get the short end of the
stick** (SHORT¹), STICKS

**stick·er** /ˈstɪkɚ/ *n* a small piece of paper or
plastic with a picture or writing on it, that you
can stick onto something

**stick-in-the-mud** /ˈ. . . ˌ./ *n* someone who is
not willing to try anything new, or does not
want to go out and have fun

**stick·ler** /ˈstɪklɚ/ *n* **be a stickler for rules/
punctuality etc.** to think that rules etc. are
extremely important, and expect people to
follow them

**sticks** /stɪks/ *n* SPOKEN **the sticks** an area that is very far from a town or city

**stick shift** /'. ./ *n* **1** a piece of equipment in a car that you move with your hand to control its GEARS **2** a car that uses this system −compare AUTOMATIC²

**stick·y** /'stɪki/ *adj* **1** made of or covered with a substance that sticks to surfaces: *sticky candy* | *Your hands are sticky.* **2** weather that is sticky is very hot and the air feels wet **3** INFORMAL a sticky situation, question, or problem is difficult or dangerous to deal with −**stickiness** *n* [U]

**stiff¹** /stɪf/ *adj* **1** difficult to bend or move: *stiff cardboard* **2** if a part of your body is stiff, your muscles hurt and it is difficult to move **3** more difficult, strict, or severe than usual: *a stiff fine* **4** thick and almost solid: *Beat the egg whites until stiff.* **5** unfriendly or very formal: *a stiff smile* **6 a stiff wind/breeze** a fairly strong wind or BREEZE **7 a stiff drink** a very strong alcoholic drink −**stiffly** *adv* −**stiffness** *n* [U]

**stiff²** *adv* INFORMAL **bored/scared/worried stiff** extremely bored etc.

**stiff³** *n* **1** SLANG the body of a dead person **2 working stiff** INFORMAL an ordinary person who works

**stiff⁴** *v* [T] INFORMAL to not pay someone money that you owe him/her or that s/he expects to be given

**stiff·en** /'stɪfən/ *v* **1** [I] to suddenly become unfriendly or anxious: *Harold stiffened, sensing danger.* **2** [I,T] also **stiffen up** to become difficult to bend or move, or to make something do this: *My knee has stiffened up.*

**sti·fle** /'staɪfəl/ *v* **1** [T] to stop something from happening, developing, or being expressed: *Annette felt college was stifling her creativity.* **2** [I,T] to make someone feel unable to breathe comfortably, or to feel this way −**stifling** *adj*: *stifling heat*

**stig·ma** /'stɪgmə/ *n* [singular, U] shame or difficulty caused by a strong feeling in society that a type of behavior is wrong or bad: *the stigma attached to AIDS* −**stigmatize** /'stɪgmə,taɪz/ *v* [T]

**still¹** /stɪl/ *adv* **1** up to a particular point in time and continuing at that moment: *Do you still play tennis?* **2** even later or for even longer than expected: *Why are you still here?* **3** in spite of what has just been said or done: *Well, I still think Eric's weird.* **4 still colder/harder/better etc.** also **colder/harder/better etc. still** even colder, harder etc. than something else: *Could we do still better? Of course.* **5 be still going strong** to continue to be active or successful, even after a long time: *We've been partners for 25 years, and we're still going strong.*

Use **still** to talk about a situation that continues to exist at the present time. **Still** is usually used before the verb: *I still see Jeannie from time to time.* | *The club still sends him the newsletter.* However, if the verb is "be", **still** is used after it: *I hope these potatoes are still good.* | *She's still on the phone.* If the sentence has a group of verbs in it, **still** is used after the first verb: *You can still catch up with them if you hurry.* | *We're still waiting to hear from Tim.* If a sentence has a negative word in it, **still** is used before it: *I still don't understand today's assignment.* | *We bought more food, but there's still not enough for everyone.* Use **yet** in negative sentences and questions to talk about something that you expect to happen, but which has not happened. Usually, **yet** is used at the end of a sentence: *I haven't finished the book yet.* | *Is Mark back from lunch yet?*

**still²** *adj* **1** not moving: *Just keep/stand/stay still while I tie your shoes.* **2** quiet and without any activity: *At that time of day, the forest was still.* −**stillness** *n* [U]

**still³** *n* **1** a piece of equipment for making alcoholic drinks out of grain or potatoes **2** a photograph of a scene from a movie **3 the still of the night/evening etc.** LITERARY the calm and quiet time of the night etc.

**still·born** /ˌstɪl'bɔrn◂/ *adj* born dead −**stillbirth** /'stɪlbɚθ/ *n* [C,U]

**still life** /'. ./ *n, plural* **still lifes** [C,U] a picture of an arrangement of objects, especially flowers and fruit

**stilt·ed** /'stɪltɪd/ *adj* stilted writing or speaking is formal and unnatural

**stilts** /stɪlts/ *n* [plural] a pair of poles you can stand on, used for walking high above the ground

**stim·u·lant** /'stɪmyələnt/ *n* **1** a drug or substance that makes you feel more active **2** something that encourages more of an activity or helps a process to develop faster

**stim·u·late** /'stɪmyə,leɪt/ *v* [T] **1** to encourage more of an activity, or to help a process develop faster: *efforts to stimulate the economy* | *Light stimulates plant growth.* **2** to make someone excited about and interested in something: *projects designed to stimulate children's curiosity* **3** to increase the energy of someone or something −**stimulating** *adj*: *a stimulating conversation* −**stimulation** /ˌstɪmyə'leɪʃən/ *n* [U]

**stim·u·lus** /'stɪmyələs/ *n, plural* **stimuli** /-laɪ/ **1** [singular, U] something that encourages more of an activity or helps a process to

develop faster  **2** something that makes someone or something move or react

**sting**[1] /stɪŋ/ *v* **stung, stung, stinging  1** [T] if
an insect or plant stings you, it hurts you with its
sharp point or points: *Jamie was stung by a bee.*
**2** [I,T] to feel a sharp pain in your eyes, throat,
or skin, or to make someone feel this: *My eyes
sting.* | *The smoke stung my throat.*  **3 be stung
by sth** to be upset or badly affected by something: *Paul was stung by her criticisms.*

**sting**[2] *n*  **1** a wound made when an insect or
plant stings you: *a bee sting*  **2** [singular] a
sharp pain that you feel in your eyes, throat, or
skin  **3** a trick used for catching someone while
s/he is doing something illegal

**sting·er** /'stɪŋɚ/ *n* the point on a creature's
body that contains poison, for example on a BEE

**sting·ray** /'stɪŋreɪ/ *n* a large flat fish that has a
long tail like a whip with stingers on it

**stin·gy** /'stɪndʒi/ *adj* not willing to spend
money or share something even though you
have enough: *She's so stingy.* —**stinginess** *n* [U]

**stink**[1] /stɪŋk/ *v* **stank, stunk, stinking  1** [I]
to have a very strong and unpleasant smell: *The
dog's breath stinks!*  **2 sth stinks!** SPOKEN said
when you think something is bad or unfair:
*Don't eat there - the food stinks.* —**stinky** *adj*

**stink** sth ↔ **up** *phr v* [T] INFORMAL to fill a place
with a very strong and unpleasant smell: *He's
stinking up the house with cigar smoke!*

**stink**[2] *n*  **1 make/cause/raise a stink** to complain about something so that people pay attention to you: *I'm going to raise a stink if they
don't change our tickets.*  **2** a strong unpleasant
smell

**stink·er** /'stɪŋkɚ/ *n* INFORMAL someone who behaves badly, or something that is of bad quality

**stink·ing** /'stɪŋkɪŋ/ *adj*  **1** having a strong
unpleasant smell: *stinking socks*  **2** SPOKEN said
when you think something is bad, unfair, or untrue: *I won't work for a stinking $2.50 an hour!*

**stint**[1] /stɪnt/ *n* a job or position that you have
for a limited period: *a five-year stint teaching
English in Korea*

**stint**[2] *v* [I] ⇨ SKIMP

**sti·pend** /'staɪpɛnd, -pənd/ *n* an amount of
money paid regularly to someone such as a
priest or student so that s/he can live: *a monthly
stipend*

**stip·u·late** /'stɪpyəˌleɪt/ *v* [T] to say that
something must be done because of an agreement: *The contract stipulates that we receive
25% of the profits.*

**stip·u·la·tion** /ˌstɪpyə'leɪʃən/ *n* something
specific that must be done as part of an agreement: *Mr. Gleason agreed, with the stipulation
that his name was not used.*

**stir**[1] /stɚ/ *v* **-rred, -rring  1** [T] to mix a liquid or food by moving a spoon around in it:
*Stir the mixture until smooth.*  **2** [I,T] to move

slightly, **or to make
someone or something
do this**: *Rachel stirred in
her sleep.*  **3** [T] to make
someone feel a strong emotion: *The killings stirred citizens to protest.*

stir

**stir** sth ↔ **up** *phr* [T] to
deliberately try to cause
problems or make people
argue: *If you let him stay, he'll just stir up more
trouble.*

**stir**[2] *n*  **1** a strong feeling such as excitement or
anger, felt by many people: *The movie caused
such a stir that it was finally banned.*
**2** [singular] an act of STIRring something

**stir-fry** /'. ./ *v* [T] to quickly cook meat,
vegetables etc. in a little oil over very high heat
—**stir-fry** *n*

**stir·rup** /'stɚəp, 'stɪrəp/ *n* one of the two
metal parts on a horse's SADDLE that you put
your foot in

**stitch**[1] /stɪtʃ/ *n*  **1** one of the small lines of
thread where a piece of cloth has been sewn:
*tiny stitches in the sleeves*  **2** [C usually plural]
a piece of thread, plastic etc. used for fastening
together the edges of a wound: *Nancy had 14
stitches in her leg.*  **3** one of the small circles
that you KNIT when you are making a SWEATER
**4** [singular] a sharp pain in a muscle near your
waist, that you get from exercising too much
**5 not a stitch (of clothing)** INFORMAL no
clothes at all: *He stood there without a stitch on.*
—see also STITCHES

**stitch**[2] *v* [T] to sew two pieces of cloth together, or to sew something onto a piece of
cloth: *a shirt stitched with gold thread*
—**stitching** *n* [U]

**stitch** sth ↔ **up** *phr v* [T] to sew together the
edges of a wound or two pieces of cloth

**stitch·es** /'stɪtʃɪz/ *n* [plural] **in stitches**
INFORMAL unable to stop laughing: *Tony kept us
in stitches all night.*

**stock**[1] /stɑk/ *n*  **1** [C,U] a supply of something that is kept to be sold or used later: *"Do
you sell batteries?" "Sorry, they're out of
stock."* (=we do not have any more) | *stocks of
canned food in the cupboard*  **2** [C] a SHARE in
a company  **3** [U] the number of SHAREs that a
person owns, or the total value of a company's
shares  **4** [U] a liquid made from boiling meat,
bones, or vegetables, used especially for making
soups: *chicken stock*  **5 take stock (of sth)** to
think carefully about everything that has happened so that you can decide what to do next:
*We need to take stock of the situation.*
**6** someone's family, especially those that lived
in a particular place in past times: *She comes
from old New England stock.*  **7** ⇨ LIVESTOCK

**stock**[2] *v* [T] to have a supply of something
available to be sold or used: *Do you stock camping equipment?*

**stock up** *phr v* [I] to buy a lot of something that you intend to use later: *stocking up on groceries*

**stock·ade** /stɑˈkeɪd/ *n* a wall built to defend a place, made from large upright pieces of wood, or the area inside this

**stock·brok·er** /ˈstɑkˌbroʊkɚ/ *n* someone whose job is to buy and sell STOCKs, BONDs, and SHAREs for other people —**stockbroking** *n* [U]

**stock cer·tif·i·cate** /ˈ. .ˌ,.../ *n* an official document that proves you own SHAREs of a company

**stock ex·change** /ˈ. .ˌ,./ *n* the business of buying and selling STOCKs and SHAREs, or the place where this happens

**stock·hold·er** /ˈstɑkˌhoʊldɚ/ *n* someone who owns STOCK

**stock·ing** /ˈstɑkɪŋ/ *n* **1** a very thin piece of clothing that fits closely over a woman's foot and most of her leg: *silk stockings* **2** a thing like a large sock that is hung by the FIREPLACE before Christmas to be filled with presents

**stock mar·ket** /ˈ. .ˌ,./ *n* **1** ⇨ STOCK EXCHANGE **2** the average value of STOCKs sold in the STOCK EXCHANGE

**stock·pile** /ˈstɑkpaɪl/ *n* a large supply of something that you collect in order to use it in the future: *a stockpile of weapons* —**stockpile** *v* [T]

**stock-still** /ˌ. ˈ./ *adv* not moving at all: *The deer stood stock-still, listening.*

**stock·y** /ˈstɑki/ *adj* having a short, heavy, strong-looking body: *a stocky man*

**stock·yard** /ˈstɑkyard/ *n* a place where cattle are kept before being sold or killed for their meat

**stodg·y** /ˈstɑdʒi/ *adj* a stodgy person is boring and formal: *a stodgy old professor*

**sto·ic** /ˈstoʊɪk/, **sto·i·cal** /ˈstoʊɪkəl/ *adj* not showing your emotions or not complaining when something bad happens to you —**stoicism** /ˈstoʊɪˌsɪzəm/ *n* [U]

**stoke** /stoʊk/ *v* [I,T] to add more wood or FUEL to a fire

**stoked** /stoʊkt/ *adj* SLANG very happy and excited about something

**stole**[1] /stoʊl/ *v* the past tense of STEAL

**stole**[2] *n* a long straight piece of cloth or fur that a woman wears over her shoulders

**sto·len** /ˈstoʊlən/ *v* the PAST PARTICIPLE of STEAL

**stol·id** /ˈstɑlɪd/ *adj* not showing a lot of emotion —**stolidly** *adv*

**stom·ach**[1] /ˈstʌmək/ *n* **1** the organ in your body that DIGESTs the food you eat: *My stomach hurts.* **2** the front part of your body, below your chest: *I always sleep on my stomach.* —see picture at BODY **3** the ability and willingness to do something unpleasant: *I didn't* **have the stomach** *to watch him fight.*

**stomach**[2] *v* [T] to be able to deal with something that is unpleasant: *I just* **can't stomach** *moving to another place.*

**stom·ach·ache** /ˈstʌmək,eɪk/ *n* a pain in your stomach

**stomp** /stamp, stɔmp/ *v* [I] to step very hard on the ground or to walk this way, usually because you are angry: *"Shut up!" Peter yelled, and* **stomped off.**

**stone**[1] /stoʊn/ *n* **1** a small rock or a piece of rock **2** [U] rock, or a hard mineral substance: *stone benches | a wall made of stone* **3** a jewel: *a gold-plated necklace with fake stones* **4** a ball of hard material that can form in an organ such as the KIDNEY or BLADDER

**stone**[2] *adv* **stone cold/deaf/dead** completely cold, DEAF, or dead: *The pasta was stone cold when it was served.*

**stone**[3] *v* [T] to kill or hurt someone by throwing stones at him/her

**stoned** /stoʊnd/ *adj* SLANG feeling very calm, or unable to control your behavior, because you have taken an illegal drug

**stone·wall** /ˈstoʊnwɔl/ *v* [I,T] to deliberately delay doing something or refuse to give information about it: *The union is stonewalling on the contract.*

**stone·work** /ˈstoʊnwɚk/ *n* [U] the parts of a building made of or decorated with stone

**ston·y** /ˈstoʊni/ *adj* **1** covered with stones or containing stones: *a stony path* **2** showing no emotion or pity: *a stony silence*

**stony-faced** /ˌ.. ˌ./ *adj* showing no emotion, pity, or friendliness

**stood** /stʊd/ *v* the past tense and PAST PARTICIPLE of STAND

**stool** /stul/ *n* **1** a chair without a support for your back: *a bar stool | a piano stool* **2** TECHNICAL a piece of solid waste from the body

**stoop**[1] /stup/ *v* [I] **1** to bend your body forward and down, especially your head and shoulders: *Troy stooped to pick up his pencil.* **2** to do something that other people consider to be bad or morally wrong: *No one believed he would* **stoop to** *lying.*

**stoop**[2] *n* **1** the position you hold your body in when you STOOP **2** a set of stairs leading up to a city house, or the flat area at the top of them

**stop**[1] /stɑp/ *v* **-pped, -pping** **1** [I,T] to end an action, activity, movement, or event, or to make something end: *Stop! I can't run that fast. | We couldn't stop laughing. | I hope the rain stops soon. | How did they stop the fight?* **2** [T] to prevent someone from doing something: *She can't* **stop** *me* **from** *leaving!* **3** [I] to pause during an activity, trip etc. in order to do something: *Let's* **stop at** *a cafe and get some lunch. | We* **stopped for** *gas in Louisville.* **4 stop it/that!** SPOKEN said when you want someone to stop annoying or upsetting you: *Stop* *it! That hurts!* **5** [T] to make someone stop walking or traveling, especially to talk to him/her: *He's been stopped twice by the police for speeding.* **6 stop short of sth** to stop before you do one more thing that would be too dangerous, risky etc.: *Tom stopped short of calling her a liar.* **7 stop (dead) in your tracks** to stop suddenly, especially because something has surprised or frightened you

**stop by** *phr v* [I] to quickly visit a person or place, especially before going somewhere else: *It was nice of Judy to stop by.*

**stop in** *phr v* [I] INFORMAL to make a short visit to a place or person, especially when you are going somewhere else: *Let's stop in at Gary's on the way.*

**stop off** *phr v* [I] to quickly visit a place that is near to where you are going: *I need to stop off at the post office.*

**stop** sth ↔ **up** *phr v* [T] **1** to block a hole in something, especially a pipe: *The sink's stopped up again.* **2 be stopped up** if your nose or head is stopped up, it is blocked with thick liquid because you have a cold −see also PLUG²

**stop²** *n* **1** the action of stopping or of being stopped: *The taxi came to a stop outside his hotel. | Mrs. Drayton put a stop to the gossip.* (=stopped it from continuing) **2** a place where you stop during a trip, or the short period you spend at that place: *Our first stop is Brussels, and then we're going to Paris.* **3** a place where a bus or train regularly stops for its passengers: *I get off at the next stop.* −see also **pull out all the stops** (PULL¹)

**stop·gap** /'stɑpgæp/ *n* a solution, plan, person etc. that you use until you have a better one: *a stopgap measure to deal with the parking problem*

**stop·light** /'stɑplaɪt/ *n* a set of red, yellow, and green lights used for controlling traffic

**stop·o·ver** /'stɑp,oʊvɚ/ *n* a short time between parts of a trip, especially a long plane trip: *a three-hour stopover in Atlanta*

**stop·page** /'stɑpɪdʒ/ *n* **1** an occasion when workers stop working as a protest: *a two-month work stoppage* **2** something that blocks a tube, pipe, or container

**stop·per** /'stɑpɚ/ *n* a piece of plastic, CORK etc. that you put in the top of a bottle to close it

**stop·watch** /'stɑpwɑtʃ/ *n* a watch used for measuring the exact time it takes to do something, such as run a race

**stor·age** /'stɔrɪdʒ/ *n* [U] the act or state of keeping something in a special place when it is not being used: *the safe storage of chemical weapons | There's storage space in the garage. | The furniture is in storage until we find a new house.*

**store¹** /stɔr/ *n* **1** a large room or building where goods are sold to the public: *a book/shoe/liquor store | I'm going to the store to get*

some milk. −see also DEPARTMENT STORE **2** a supply of something, especially something that you can use later: *a store of information | secret stores of weapons* **3 be in store** to be about to happen to someone: *There's a surprise in store for you tomorrow!*

**store²** *v* [T] **1** also **store away** to put things away and keep them there until you need them: *All my old clothes are stored in the basement.* **2** to keep facts or information in a computer: *You can store your files on this disk.*

**store·house** /'stɔrhaʊs/ *n* **1** a storehouse of information/methods etc. something that can give you a lot of information, methods etc.: *The craft shop is a storehouse of ideas for gifts and decorations.* **2** OLD-FASHIONED ⇨ WAREHOUSE

**store·keep·er** /'stɔr,kipɚ/ *n* someone who owns or is in charge of a store

**store·room** /'stɔr-rum/ *n* a room where goods are stored

**sto·rey** /'stɔri/ *n* ⇨ STORY

**stork** /stɔrk/ *n* a tall white water bird with long legs and a long beak

**storm¹** /stɔrm/ *n* **1** a period of bad weather when there is a lot of wind, rain, snow etc.: *a snow storm* −see usage note at WEATHER **2** a situation in which people suddenly become angry and excited: *The mayor's policies caused a storm of opposition.* **3 dance/talk/work etc. up a storm** INFORMAL to do something with a lot of excitement and effort: *Jenny and I cooked up a storm.* **4 take sb/sth by storm** to suddenly become very successful and admired in a particular place: *a new show that's taking Broadway by storm*

**storm²** *v* **1** [T] to attack a place and enter it with a lot of force: *Enemy troops stormed the city.* **2** [I] to go somewhere fast because you are very angry: *Jack stormed in, demanding an explanation.*

**storm·y** /'stɔrmi/ *adj* **1** full of rain, strong winds, snow etc.: *stormy weather | a stormy day* **2** a stormy relationship or situation is one in which people are very angry, excited, and unreasonable

**sto·ry** /'stɔri/ *n* **1** a description of an event that is intended to entertain people: *The movie is based on a true story. | a ghost/bedtime/love story | Grandma used to read/tell us stories every night.* **2** a report in a newspaper or news broadcast about a recent event: *a front-page story in "The Chronicle"* **3** a floor or level of a building: *There's a balcony on the third story. | a three-story building* (=with three levels) **4 it's a long story** SPOKEN said when you think something will take too long to explain: *It's a long story - I'll tell you later.* **5 to make a long story short** SPOKEN said when you want to finish explaining something quickly: *To make a long story short, she got mad and left.* **6** an excuse, explanation, or lie: *Do you believe his story?*

**sto·ry·tell·er** /'stɔri,tɛlɚ/ *n* someone who tells stories

**stout**[1] /staʊt/ *adj* **1** fairly fat and heavy: *a stout middle-aged man* **2** brave and determined: *a stout defender of human rights*

**stout**[2] *n* [U] a strong dark beer

**stove** /stoʊv/ *n* a piece of kitchen equipment on which you cook food in pots and pans, and that contains an OVEN

**stow** /stoʊ/, **stow away** *v* [T] to put something away neatly in a place until you need it again: *Please stow all carry-on baggage under your seat.*

**stow·a·way** /'stoʊə,weɪ/ *n* someone who hides on an aircraft, ship etc. in order to travel without paying

**strad·dle** /'strædl/ *v* [T] **1** to sit or stand with your legs on either side of something: *boys straddling the railings* **2** to seem to agree about two different opinions about something: *The government is straddling the issue of lowering taxes.*

**strag·gle** /'strægəl/ *v* [I] if people in a large group straggle, they move away from the group one at a time: *Travelers were beginning to straggle out of Customs.*

**strag·gly** /'strægli/ *adj* INFORMAL growing or spreading out in a messy, uneven way: *straggly hair*

**straight**[1] /streɪt/ *adv* **1** in a straight line: *Stand up straight!* | *The bathroom's straight down the hall.* | *She kept staring straight ahead.* **2** immediately, directly, or without any delay: *Why didn't you go straight to the police?* | *Come home straight after school.* **3** happening one after the other in a series: *He worked 18 hours straight without a break.* **4** not see/think straight to be unable to see or think clearly: *It was so noisy, I could hardly think straight.* **5** get/keep sth straight SPOKEN to correctly understand the facts about a situation without being confused: *Let me get this straight: Don's not coming, but Peggy is?* | *I can't keep all their names straight.*

**straight**[2] *adj* **1** not bent or curved: *a straight line* | *My sister has straight hair.* (=without curls) **2** level or upright, and not bent or leaning: *Is this sign straight?* | *straight teeth* **3** honest and direct: *I wish you'd give me a straight answer.* **4** one after the other: *The Australian team won three straight victories.* **5** get straight A's to earn the grade "A" in all of your school subjects **6** a straight face a serious expression on your face even though you want to laugh or smile: *How did you manage to keep a straight face?* **7** INFORMAL ⇨ HETEROSEXUAL **8** alcoholic drinks that are straight do not have any ice, water etc. added to them **9** INFORMAL unwilling to take risks or do exciting things: *"What's his girlfriend like?" "She's pretty straight."*

**straight**[3] *n* the straight and narrow a sensible and moral way of living: *Without his father to keep him on the straight and narrow, Abe went into debt*

**straight·en** /'streɪtn/ *v* **1** [I,T] to become straight or make something straight: *Try straightening out your legs.* **2** [T] also **straighten up** to clean a room that is messy

**straighten** sb/sth ↔ **out** *phr v* [T] to deal with a difficult situation or solve a problem: *I'll talk to him and see if I can straighten things out.*

**straighten up** *phr v* [I] to start behaving well: *You straighten up right now, young man!*

**straight·for·ward** /,streɪt'fɔrwɚd◂/ *adj* **1** simple or easy to understand: *The exam questions are fairly straightforward.* **2** honest and not hiding what you think: *a straightforward response*

**straight·jack·et** /'streɪt,dʒækɪt/ *n* ⇨ STRAITJACKET

**strain**[1] /streɪn/ *n* **1** [C,U] worry that you feel because you are always busy or always dealing with problems: *He couldn't cope with the strain of being a lawyer.* **2** a problem or difficulty caused by using too much of something: *Paying for our kids' educations put a huge strain on our savings.* **3** [U] a force that pulls, stretches, or pushes something: *The rope snapped under the strain.* (=because of the force) **4** [C,U] an injury caused by stretching a muscle or using part of your body too much: *eye strain* —compare SPRAIN **5** [C,U] a difficult situation, that causes problems in a relationship, so that two people or groups are no longer friendly or no longer trust each other: *The strain was beginning to show in their marriage.* **6** one of the particular varieties of a plant, animal, or living thing: *a new strain of the virus*

**strain**[2] *v* **1** [T] to injure part of your body by stretching it too much: *Kevin strained a muscle in his neck.* **2** [I,T] to use a lot of effort, supplies, or money to try to do something: *She moved closer, straining to hear what they said.* | *The lack of federal money is straining the University's finances.* **3** [T] to cause problems in a relationship: *It's one of the issues that is straining relations between the countries.* **4** [T] to separate solid things from a liquid by pouring the mixture through a STRAINER or cloth **5** [I] to pull hard at something or push hard against something: *a boat straining against the wind*

**strained** /streɪnd/ *adj* **1** unfriendly, uncomfortable, and showing a lack of trust: *a strained conversation* **2** worried and tired: *Alex looks strained.*

**strain·er** /'streɪnɚ/ *n* a kitchen tool used for separating solid food from a liquid

**strait** /streɪt/ *n* a narrow passage of water that joins two larger areas of water: *the Strait of Gibraltar*

**strait·jack·et** /'streɪt,dʒækɪt/ *n* a special coat for violent or mentally ill people that prevents them from moving their arms

**strand** /strænd/ *n* a single thin piece of thread, hair, wire etc.

**strand·ed** /'strændɪd/ *adj* needing help because you are unable to move from a particular place: *I was stranded at the airport without any money.*

**strange**[1] /streɪndʒ/ *adj* **1** unusual, surprising, or difficult to understand: *I had a strange dream last night.* | *It's strange that Brad isn't here yet.* | *That's strange - I thought I left my keys on the table.* | *At first the city seemed* **strange to me.** ✗ DON'T SAY "the city seemed strange for me." ✗ **2** not familiar: *I was all alone in a strange country.* –**strangeness** *n* [U]

**strange**[2] *adv* SPOKEN NONSTANDARD strangely: *Reed has been acting strange.*

**strange·ly** /'streɪndʒli/ *adv* in an unusual or surprising way: *Cathy was strangely silent at dinner.*

**strang·er** /'streɪndʒɚ/ *n* **1** someone you do not know: *Mom told us never to talk to strangers.* **2** someone in a new and unfamiliar place or situation: *a stranger to New York*

**stran·gle** /'stræŋgəl/ *v* [T] to kill someone by tightly pressing his/her throat with your hands, a rope etc. –**strangulation** /,stræŋgyə'leɪʃən/ *n* [U]

**stran·gle·hold** /'stræŋgəl,hoʊld/ *n* the power to completely control something: *The government had a **stranglehold on** the media.*

**strap**[1] /stræp/ *n* a strong band of cloth or leather that is attached to a shoe, bag etc. so that it does not fall down or off: *a watch strap* | *bra straps*

**strap**[2] *v* -pped, -pping [T] to fasten someone or something to a place using one or more STRAPs: *Make sure your backpack is **strapped on** tightly.*

**strap·less** /'stræplɪs/ *adj* a strapless dress, BRA, etc. does not have any STRAPs over the shoulders

**strapped** /stræpt/ *adj* INFORMAL having little or no money to spend: *I'd offer to pay, but I'm **strapped for cash.***

**stra·ta** /'st;ætə, 'streɪtə/ *n* the plural of STRATUM

**strat·a·gem** /'st;ætədʒəm/ *n* a trick or plan used for deceiving an enemy or gaining an advantage

**stra·te·gic** /strə'tidʒɪk/ *adj* **1** done as part of a military, business, or political plan: *the strategic position of US armed forces in Europe* **2** useful for a particular purpose, especially fighting a war: *strategic missiles*

**strat·e·gy** /'st;ætədʒi/ *n* **1** [C,U] the set of plans and skills used in order to gain success or achieve an aim: *a strategy for improving adult education programs* **2** [U] a country's plans for how to use its armies, equipment etc. effectively during a war

**strat·i·fied** /'st;ætə,faɪd/ *adj* **1** [U] separated into different social classes: *a stratified society* **2** [C,U] rocks or soil that are stratified have separated into different layers –**stratify** *v* [T]

**strat·o·sphere** /'st;ætə,sfɪr/ *n* **the stratosphere** the outer layer of air surrounding the earth, starting about six miles above the earth

**stra·tum** /'st;ætəm, 'streɪ-/ *n, plural* **strata** /-tə/ **1** a layer of a particular type of rock or dirt **2** a social class in society

**straw** /strɔ/ *n* **1** [C,U] dried stems of wheat or similar plants, used for making things such as baskets, or a single stem of this: *a straw hat* **2** a thin tube of plastic used for sucking a drink from a bottle or cup –see picture at GLASS **3** **the last/final straw** the last problem in a series of problems that makes you finally get angry

**straw·ber·ry** /'strɔ,bɛri/ *n* a sweet red BERRY with small pale seeds on its surface –see picture on page 470

**stray**[1] /streɪ/ *v* [I] to move away from a safe or familiar area without intending to: *The kitten had **strayed from** its mother.*

**stray**[2] *adj* **1** a stray animal is lost or has no home **2** accidentally separated from a larger group: *a few stray hairs*

**stray**[3] *n* an animal that is lost or has no home

**streak**[1] /strik/ *n* **1** a colored line or thin mark: *a few gray streaks in her hair* **2** a quality you have that seems different from the rest of your character: *Richard has a wild streak in him.* **3** a period when you are always successful or always failing: *Our team was **on a winning streak.*** –**streaky** *adj*

**streak**[2] *v* **1** [T] to cover something with STREAKs: *Marcia's face was streaked with sweat.* **2** [I] to move or run very quickly: *A fighter jet streaked across the sky.*

**stream**[1] /strim/ *n* **1** a natural flow of water that is smaller than a river: *We used to go fishing in this stream.* **2** a long continuous series of people, vehicles, events etc.: *a stream of cars* | *a stream of ideas* **3** a flow of water, gas, smoke etc.: *a stream of warm air*

**stream**[2] *v* [I] to move quickly and continuously in one direction, especially in large amounts: *Tears were streaming down his cheeks.* | *People streamed out of the movie theater.*

**stream·er** /'strimɚ/ *n* a long narrow flag or piece of colored paper used as a decoration for special events

**stream·line** /'strimlaɪn/ *v* [T] **1** to make something such as a business or process become simpler and more effective: *The hospital has streamlined the paperwork for nurses.* **2** to make something have a smooth shape so that it moves easily through the air or water −**streamlined** *adj*: *streamlined cars*

**street** /strit/ *n* **1** a road in a town or city with houses, stores etc. on one or both sides: *What street do you live on?* | *the corner of Main Street and 4th Avenue* **2 the streets** used when talking about the busy part of a city, where there is a lot of activity, excitement, and crime: *homeless people living on the streets*

> **USAGE NOTE** street and road
>
> A **street** is in a town or city. A **road** is usually in the country. Sometimes however, the word **road** is used in the names of **streets**, especially wide ones.

**street·car** /'strit˺kɑr/ *n* an electric bus that moves along metal tracks in the road

**street light, street·light** /'strit-laɪt/ *n* a light on a long pole that stands next to a street −see picture on page 471

**strength** /streŋkθ, streŋθ/ *n*
**1** ▸**PHYSICAL**◂ [U] the physical power and energy that you have: *I didn't have the strength to get up.* | *Bruce is lifting weights to build up his strength.*
**2** ▸**DETERMINATION**◂ [U] the quality of being brave or determined in dealing with difficult situations: *It took great strength to raise three children by herself.*
**3** ▸**COUNTRY/SYSTEM ETC.**◂ [U] the power of an organization, country, or system: *The US increased its military strength in the region.*
**4** ▸**FEELING/BELIEF ETC.**◂ [U] how strong a feeling, belief, or relationship is: *The strength of their marriage was being tested.*
**5** ▸**QUALITY/ABILITY**◂ a particular quality or ability that makes someone or something successful and effective: *His ambition is both a strength and a weakness.* | *the strengths of the argument*
**6** ▸**ALCOHOL/MEDICINE**◂ [C,U] how strong a liquid such as an alcoholic drink, medicine, or cleaning liquid is: *a full-strength fabric cleaner*
**7** ▸**MONEY**◂ the value of a particular type of money when compared to other types: *The yen gained in strength against the dollar today.*
**8 on the strength of sth** because of something that persuaded or influenced you: *We chose this car on the strength of his advice.* −compare WEAKNESS −see usage note at FORCE[1]

**strength·en** /'streŋkθən, 'strenθən/ *v*
**1** [I,T] to become stronger, or to make something such as a feeling, belief, or relationship stronger: *The problems had strengthened their relationship.* **2** [T] to make something such as your body or a building stronger: *an exercise to strengthen your arms* | *extra supports to strengthen the bridge* **3** [I,T] to increase in value or improve, or to make something do this:

*new trade agreements to strengthen the economy* −opposite WEAKEN

**stren·u·ous** /'strɛnyuəs/ *adj* using a lot of effort or strength: *strenuous exercise* | *strenuous objections to the plan* −**strenuously** *adv*

**strep throat** /ˌstrep 'θrout/ *n* [U] INFORMAL a fairly common medical condition in which your throat is very sore

**stress[1]** /strɛs/ *n* **1** [C,U] continuous feelings of worry caused by difficulties in your life that prevent you from relaxing: *Baxter's under a lot of stress at work.* | *the stresses and strains of modern life* **2** [U] special attention or importance given to an idea or activity; EMPHASIS: *In his report, he laid stress on the need for more teachers.* **3** [C,U] the physical force or pressure on an object: *rocks subjected to stress and high temperatures* **4** [C,U] the degree to which you emphasize a word or part of a word when you say it

**stress[2]** *v* [T] **1** to emphasize a statement, fact, or idea: *She stressed the need for more health education for teens.* **2** also **stress out** SPOKEN to become STRESSED: *Terry's stressing about his midterms.* **3** to say a word or part of a word loudly or with more force

**stressed** /strɛst/ also **stressed out** *adj* SPOKEN so worried and tired that you cannot relax: *She was really stressed out about all the problems at home.*

**stress·ful** /'strɛsfəl/ *adj* making you worry a lot: *They're living under very stressful conditions.*

**stretch[1]** /strɛtʃ/ *v* **1** [I,T] also **stretch out** to become bigger or looser as a result of being pulled, or to make something do this by pulling it: *Dad stretched my T-shirt!* | *My new sweater has stretched.* **2** [I,T] to reach out your arms, legs, or body to full length: *He stretched his arms out to try to reach the branch.* | *Be sure to stretch before you exercise.* **3** [I] to spread out over a large area, or continue for a long period: *The desert stretched to the horizon.* | *The project will probably stretch into next year.* **4** [I] if cloth stretches, it changes shape when you pull or wear it, and becomes its original shape when you stop: *The shorts stretch to fit your shape.* **5** [T] to pull something so it is tight: *We can stretch a rope between two trees.* **6 stretch sth to the limit** to use as much of a supply of something as is available, without having enough for anything else: *Our resources are already stretched to the limit.* **7 stretch your legs** INFORMAL to go for a walk

**stretch out** *phr v* [I] INFORMAL to lie down so you can rest or sleep: *I'll just stretch out on the couch for a while.*

**stretch[2]** *n* **1** an area of water or land: *a dangerous stretch of road* **2** a continuous period of time: *During the summer we worked 12 hours at a stretch.* (=without stopping) **3** the action of stretching part of your body

**4** [U] the ability of a material to become bigger or longer without tearing **5 not by any stretch (of the imagination)** SPOKEN used in order to say that something is definitely not true: *She's not fat, by any stretch of the imagination.*

**stretch·er** /'stretʃɚ/ *n* a covered frame on which you carry someone who is injured or too sick to walk

**strew** /stru/ *v* **strewed, strewn** /strun/ *or* **strewed, strewing** [T] to throw or drop a number of things over an area in a messy way: *Papers were **strewn all over** the floor.*

**strick·en** /'strɪkən/ *adj* FORMAL experiencing the bad effects of trouble, illness, sadness etc.: *a woman **stricken by** grief* —see also POVERTY-STRICKEN

**strict** /strɪkt/ *adj* **1** demanding that rules should be obeyed: *Her parents are very strict.* | *Strictly speaking* (=to be exact about what I am saying) *the drug has not yet been approved for use.* **2** a strict rule, order etc. must be obeyed: *I have strict instructions not to let you stay up late.* **3** very exact and correct: *It's not a restaurant **in the strictest sense** of the word - it's more like a cafe.*

**strict·ly** /'strɪktli/ *adv* **1** exactly and correctly: *That is not strictly true.* **2** used in order to emphasize what you are saying: *Our drug treatment program is strictly voluntary.* **3** only used for a particular purpose or by a particular person: *These bowls are **strictly for** decoration; they're too delicate to be used.* **4** in a way that must be obeyed: *Smoking is strictly forbidden in the hospital.*

**stride**[1] /straɪd/ *v* **strode, stridden** /'strɪdn/, **striding** [I] to walk with quick long steps: *He strode across the room.*

**stride**[2] *n* **1** a long step that you take when you walk **2 make (great) strides** to develop or make progress quickly: *The city has made great strides in cleaning up its streets.* **3 take sth in stride** to deal with a problem calmly without becoming annoyed or upset: *He took it in his stride when I said "no."*

**stri·dent** /'straɪdnt/ *adj* **1** showing determination and a strong opinion that may be unpleasant to other people: *a strident denial of the charges* **2** a sound that is strident is loud and unpleasant: *her strident voice*

**strife** /straɪf/ *n* [U] FORMAL trouble or disagreement between two people or groups; CONFLICT

**strike**[1] /straɪk/ *v* **struck, struck** *or* **stricken, striking**
**1** ▶HIT◀ [T] FORMAL to hit someone or something: *He was **struck** on the head **by** a falling rock.* | *The car stopped when it struck a tree.*
**2** ▶THOUGHT/IDEA◀ [T] if a thought or idea strikes you, you suddenly realize it or think of it: *It suddenly **struck** me **that** Nora had told the truth.*
**3 strike sb as sth** to seem to someone to have

a particular quality: *She strikes me as being a very intelligent woman.*
**4** ▶WORK◀ [I] to deliberately stop working for a time because of a disagreement about pay, working conditions etc.: *The dock workers are preparing to strike for shorter work days.*
**5** ▶ATTACK◀ [I] to attack quickly and suddenly: *The police are waiting for the killer to strike again.*
**6 strike a balance** to give the correct amount of attention or importance to two opposing ideas or situations. *It's never easy to **strike a balance between** work and family.*
**7** ▶STH UNPLEASANT◀ [I] if something unpleasant strikes, it happens suddenly: *The tornado struck in the middle of the night.*
**8 strike a deal** to agree to do something if someone else does something for you: *The dispute ended when the company struck a deal with the union.*
**9 strike a chord** to make someone feel that s/he agrees with, likes, or is similar to someone or something: *The way he writes strikes a chord with me.*
**10 strike a match** to make a match burn
**11 strike oil/gold etc.** to discover oil, gold etc. in the ground
**12** ▶CLOCK◀ [I,T] if a clock strikes or strikes one, three, six etc., its bell sounds one, three, six etc. times to show the time: *The clock **struck** four.* (=4 o'clock) —see usage note at HIT[1]

**strike down** *phr v* to make a law or formal decision stop being legal or officially accepted: *An appeals court **struck down** the decision to set him free.*

**strike out** *phr v* **1** [I] INFORMAL to be unsuccessful at something: *"Did she say she'd go out with you?" "No, I **struck out**."* **2** [I,T **strike sb ↔ out**] to get three STRIKEs in baseball so that you are not allowed to continue to try to hit, or to make someone do this **3** [I] to start a difficult trip or experience: *We **struck out** for home in the blinding snow.*

**strike up** *phr v* [T] **1 strike up a conversation/friendship etc.** to start a conversation, friendship etc. with someone **2** [I,T] to begin to play or sing something: *The band **struck up** an Irish tune.*

**strike**[2] *n* **1** a time when a group of workers STRIKE: *The union decided to **go on strike**.* **2** a military attack: *threats of an **air strike*** **3 two/three etc. strikes against** two, etc. qualities that are considered to be wrong, bad, or a disadvantage: *It's expensive and too big - that's two strikes against it.* **4** in baseball, an attempt to hit the ball that fails, or a ball that is thrown toward the hitter within the correct area, but is not hit

**strik·er** /'straɪkɚ/ *n* someone who does not work because s/he is on STRIKE

**strik·ing** /'straɪkɪŋ/ *adj* **1** unusual or interesting enough to be noticed: *There's a striking* *similarity between the two girls.* **2** very attractive, often in an unusual way: *a man with a striking face*

**string**[1] /strɪŋ/ *n* **1** [C,U] a strong thread made of several threads twisted together, used for tying things: *We tied a string around the box.* **2** a number of similar things or events that happen one after the other: *The police asked me a string of questions.* **3** no strings attached having no special conditions or limits on an agreement, relationship etc.: *a guaranteed interest-free loan - no strings attached* **4** first/second/third string in sports, a player who is judged to have the highest, second highest etc. level of skill in playing a particular position: *the second string quarterback.* **5** a string of pearls/beads etc. a lot of PEARLS, BEADS etc. on a string **6** one of the long thin pieces of wire that is stretched across a musical instrument to produce sound −see also STRINGS

**string**[2] *v* strung, strung, stringing [T] to join things together using string, or hang up decorations in this way: *Dad was busy stringing up Christmas lights.* −see also STRUNG-OUT

**string** sb **along** *phr v* [T] INFORMAL to continue to promise to do something that you do not intend to do, especially in relationships: *Jerry's been stringing her along for years - he'll never marry her.*

**string bean** /'. ./ *n* ⇨ GREEN BEAN

**strin·gent** /'strɪndʒənt/ *adj* stringent rules, laws etc. strictly control something: *stringent laboratory conditions*

**strings** /strɪŋz/ *n* [plural] **the strings** the people in an ORCHESTRA who play instruments such as the VIOLIN, CELLO etc.

**string·y** /'strɪŋi/ *adj* food that is stringy has thin hard pieces in it that are difficult to CHEW

**strip**[1] /strɪp/ *v* -pped, -pping **1** [I,T] also **strip off** to take off your clothes, or take someone else's clothes off of him/her: *He stripped and got into the shower.* **2** [T] to remove something that is covering the surface of something else: *It took all day to strip the paint off the walls.* **3** strip sb of sth to take away something important from someone such as his/her possessions, rank, or property

**strip**[2] *n* **1** a long narrow piece of cloth, paper etc.: *Tear the paper into one-inch strips.* **2** a long narrow area of land: *a strip of sand*

**stripe** /straɪp/ *n* a long narrow line of color: *a shirt with blue and red stripes*

**striped** /straɪpt, 'straɪpɪd/ *adj* having a pattern of STRIPEs: *a blue and white striped shirt* −see picture at PATTERN

**strip·per** /'strɪpɚ/ *n* someone whose job is to perform by taking off his/her clothes in a sexually exciting way

**strip·tease** /'strɪptiz/ *n* [C,U] the dance that a STRIPPER does

**strive** /straɪv/ *v* strove or strived, striven /'strɪvən/or strived, striving [I] FORMAL to try very hard to get or do something: *Ross is constantly striving for perfection.*

**strode** /stroʊd/ *v* the past tense of STRIDE

**stroke**[1] /stroʊk/ *n* **1** a sudden illness in which an ARTERY (=tube) in your brain bursts or becomes blocked: *Since Tom had a stroke he's had trouble talking.* **2** a repeated movement of your arms in a sport such as swimming: *back stroke.* **3** stroke of luck something lucky that happens to you: *By some stroke of luck, we got the last hotel room.* **4** a single movement of a pen or brush, or a line made by doing this

**stroke**[2] *v* [T] to move your hand gently over something: *She stroked the baby's face.*

**stroll** /stroʊl/ *v* [I] to walk in a slow relaxed way: *We strolled along the beach.* −stroll *n*

**stroke**

**stroll·er** /'stroʊlɚ/ *n* a chair on wheels in which a small child sits and is pushed along

**strong** /strɔŋ/ *adj* **1** ▸PHYSICAL◂ having a lot of physical power: *We need a few strong people to help move these boxes.* | *the strongest muscles in your body* **2** ▸NOT EASILY BROKEN◂ not easily broken or damaged: *a strong rope* | *a strong adhesive* **3** ▸POWER◂ having a lot of power or influence: *a strong leader* | *a strong army* **4** ▸FEELINGS◂ strong feelings, ideas etc. are ones that are very important to you: *a strong belief in God* | *As a child she showed a strong interest in art.* **5** ▸ARGUMENT◂ a strong reason, opinion, etc. is one that is likely to persuade other people: *There's strong evidence to suggest that he's innocent.* **6** ▸NOT TOO UPSET◂ able to deal with problems without becoming too upset or worried by them: *Do you think she's strong enough to handle this?* **7** ▸TASTE/SMELL◂ having a taste, smell, color etc. that is easy to notice: *strong coffee* **8** ▸RELATIONSHIP◂ a strong relationship or friendship is likely to last a long time: *a strong bond between the two brothers* **9** 50/1000/75,000 etc. strong used in order to give the number of people in a group: *Our staff is over a thousand strong.* −compare WEAK

**strong·hold** /'strɔŋhoʊld/ *n* **1** an area where there is a lot of support for a particular attitude, way of life, political party etc.: *a Republican stronghold* **2** an area that is strongly defended: *a rebel stronghold*

**strong·ly** /'strɔŋli/ *adv* **1** if you feel or believe something strongly, you are very sure and serious about it: *I feel strongly that medical rec-*

*ords should be private.* **2** in a way that persuades someone to do something: *I strongly urge/advise/encourage you to get more facts before deciding.* | *The company strongly believes that it's time for a change.* **3** in a way that is easy to notice: *The house smelled strongly of gas.*

**strong-willed** /ˌ. ˈ.◂ / *adj* having a lot of determination to do what you want; STUBBORN: *a strong-willed child*

**strove** /stroʊv/ *v* the past tense of STRIVE

**struck** /strʌk/ *v* the past tense and PAST PARTICIPLE of STRIKE

**struc·tur·al** /ˈstrʌktʃərəl/ *adj* relating to the structure of something: *structural damage to the aircraft*

**struc·ture**[1] /ˈstrʌktʃɚ/ *n* **1** [C,U] the way in which the parts of something connect with each other to form a whole: *Children need a stable family structure to feel secure.* | *chemical structure* | *sentence structure* **2** something that has been built: *The bridge was an impressive structure.* | *a huge steel structure*

**structure**[2] *v* [T] to arrange something carefully in an organized way: *The business should be structured to meet demand.*

**strug·gle**[1] /ˈstrʌgəl/ *v* [I] **1** to try very hard to achieve something, even though it is difficult: *After Hal lost his job we had to struggle to pay the bills.* **2** to fight someone who is attacking you or holding you: *She struggled with the man and screamed for help.* **3** to move somewhere with a lot of difficulty: *He struggled up the stairs with the luggage.*

**struggle**[2] *n* **1** a long hard fight for freedom, political rights etc.: *His death led to a struggle for power within the country.* **2** a fight between two people for something

**strum** /strʌm/ *v* **-mmed, -mming** [I,T] to play an instrument such as a GUITAR by moving your fingers across the strings

**strung** /strʌŋ/ *v* the past tense and PAST PARTICIPLE of STRING

**strung-out** /ˌ. ˈ.◂ / *adj* INFORMAL badly affected by a drug so that you cannot react normally, or so tired or worried that you cannot react normally

**strut**[1] /strʌt/ *v* **-tted, -tting** [I] **1** to walk in a proud way with your head up and your chest pushed forward: *Ray was strutting around telling everyone how he'd won.* **2** **strut your stuff** HUMOROUS to show proudly what you can do or what you have

**strut**[2] *n* a long thin piece of metal or wood used for supporting a part of a bridge, the wing of an aircraft etc.

**stub**[1] /stʌb/ *n* **1** the short part of something that is left after the rest has been used: *a pencil stub* **2** the part of a ticket that is returned to you as proof that you have paid

**stub**[2] *v* **-bbed, -bbing** [T] **stub your toe** to hurt your toe by hitting it against something

**stub** sth ↔ **out** *phr v* [T] to stop a cigarette from burning by pressing the end of it against something

**stub·ble** /ˈstʌbəl/ *n* [U] the very short stiff hairs on a man's face when he has not SHAVEd —**stubbly** *adj*

**stub·born** /ˈstʌbɚn/ *adj* refusing to change your opinions, beliefs etc. because you believe you are right: *Pat's a stubborn woman.*

**stub·by** /ˈstʌbi/ *adj* short and thick or fat: *his stubby fingers*

**stuc·co** /ˈstʌkoʊ/ *n* [U] a CEMENT mixture used especially for covering the outside walls of houses

**stuck**[1] /stʌk/ *v* the past tense and PAST PARTICIPLE of STICK

**stuck**[2] *adj* **1** not able to move: *Our car got stuck in the mud.* **2** not able to continue working on something because it is too difficult: *Can you help me with this? I'm stuck.* **3** not able to get away from a boring or unpleasant situation: *I'm tired of being stuck at home all day with the kids.*

**stuck-up** /ˌ. ˈ.◂ / *adj* INFORMAL proud and unfriendly because you think you are better than other people

**stud** /stʌd/ *n* **1** [C,U] an animal such as a horse that is kept for breeding: *a stud farm* **2** SLANG a man who is very active sexually **3** a small round piece of metal that is put on a surface for decoration: *a leather jacket with silver studs* **4** a small round EARRING

**stud·ded** /ˈstʌdɪd/ *adj* decorated with a lot of STUDs or jewels: *a bracelet studded with diamonds* —see also STAR-STUDDED

**stu·dent** /ˈstudnt/ *n* **1** someone who is studying at a school, university etc.: *a first-year medical student* | *She has 30 students in her class.* **2** **a student of sth** someone who is very interested in a particular subject

**student bod·y** /ˌ.. ˈ../ *n* all the students in a school, university etc.: *Molly is president of the student body.*

**stud·ied** /ˈstʌdid/ *adj* studied behavior is deliberate and intended to have a particular effect on other people: *a studied manner of speaking*

**stud·ies** /ˈstʌdiz/ *n* [plural] subjects that people study: *Are you doing well in your studies?*

**stu·di·o** /ˈstudiˌoʊ/ *n* **1** a room where television and radio programs are made and broadcast **2** a movie company or the place where movies are made: *the big Hollywood studios* **3** a room where a painter or photographer works: *an art studio* **4** also **studio apartment** a small apartment with one main room

**stu·di·ous** /ˈstudiəs/ *adj* spending a lot of time reading and studying

**stud·y**[1] /'stʌdi/ *n* **1** a piece of work that is done to find out more about a particular subject or problem, and that is usually written in a report: *My nephew is doing a study of teenagers' language for his thesis.* **2** [U] the activity of studying a particular subject: *the study of ancient history* **3** a room in a house that is used for work or study –see also STUDIES

**study**[2] *v* **1** [I,T] to spend time going to classes, reading etc. to find out more about a particular subject: *I'm studying medicine at NYU.* | *Are you* ***studying to be*** *a lawyer?* **2** [T] to examine something carefully to find out more about it: *Dr. Brock is* ***studying how*** *the disease affects children.*

**stuff**[1] /stʌf/ *n* [U] INFORMAL **1** a substance or material of any sort: *What's this stuff on the floor?* | *Don't drink that stuff!* **2** a number of different things: *I need a place to store my stuff for a while.* **3** all the activities that someone does: *We have a load of stuff to do before we leave.*

**stuff**[2] *v* [T] **1** to push things into a small space quickly: *He* ***stuffed*** *some clothes* ***into*** *a bag and left.* **2** to fill something with a soft material until it is full: *a pillow stuffed with feathers* **3** **be stuffed** INFORMAL to be so full of food that you cannot eat any more: *The cake looks great, but I'm stuffed!* **4** to fill a chicken, vegetable etc. with a mixture of food before cooking it **5** to fill the skin of a dead animal in order to make the animal look alive

**stuffed-up** /ˌ. '.◂/ *adj* INFORMAL having a STUFFY nose or head

**stuff·ing** /'stʌfɪŋ/ *n* [U] **1** a mixture of food that you put inside a chicken, vegetable etc. before cooking it **2** material that is used for filling something such as a PILLOW

**stuff·y** /'stʌfi/ *adj* **1** not having enough fresh air: *a stuffy room* **2** boring and old-fashioned: *Rob's family is really stuffy.* **3** a stuffy nose is filled with thick liquid because you are sick

**stum·ble** /'stʌmbəl/ *v* [I] **1** to almost fall down while you are walking: *She stumbled coming out of the house.* **2** to stop or make a mistake when you are reading or speaking to people: *He was* ***stumbling over*** *the words of his speech.*

**stumble on/across** sth *phr v* [T] to discover something or meet someone by chance: *We thought that we'd* ***stumbled on*** *a cure for the disease.*

**stumbling block** /'.. ˌ./ *n* a problem that prevents you from achieving something: *The question of funding is still our major stumbling block.*

**stump**[1] /stʌmp/ *n* **1** the part of a tree that remains in the ground after the rest has been cut down **2** the part of an arm, leg etc. that remains when the rest has been cut off

**stump**[2] *v* **1** **be stumped (by sth)** to be unable to think of an answer to a difficult question: *We were completely stumped by her question.* **2** [T] to ask someone a difficult question so that s/he is unable to think of an answer: *The question stumped everyone in the room.*

**stump for** sb *v* [T] to try to influence people to vote for a particular person

**stun** /stʌn/ *v* **-nned, -nning** [T] **1** to surprise or shock someone so much that s/he does not react: *Everyone was stunned by Betty's answer.* **2** to make someone unconscious for a short time by hitting him/her on the head

**stung** /stʌŋ/ *v* the past tense and PAST PARTICIPLE of STING

**stunk** /stʌŋk/ *v* the past tense and PAST PARTICIPLE of STINK

**stun·ning** /'stʌnɪŋ/ *adj* **1** extremely attractive or beautiful: *You look stunning in that dress.* **2** very surprising or shocking: *a stunning answer*

**stunt**[1] /stʌnt/ *n* **1** a dangerous action that is done to entertain people, usually in a movie **2** something silly or dangerous that you do, especially to make someone pay attention to you: *Don't ever* ***pull a stunt like that*** *(=do something like that) again!*

**stunt**[2] *v* [T] to stop someone or something from growing or developing correctly: *Lack of food has* ***stunted*** *their* ***growth***.

**stunt man** /'. ./, **stunt wom·an** /'. ˌ../ *n* a man or woman whose job is to take the place of an actor when something dangerous has to be done in a movie

**stu·pe·fied** /'stupəˌfaɪd/ *adj* so surprised or bored that you cannot think clearly –**stupefy** *v* [T]

**stu·pe·fy·ing** /'stupəˌfaɪ·ɪŋ/ *adj* making you feel so surprised or bored that you cannot think clearly –**stupefied** *adj*

**stu·pen·dous** /stu'pɛndəs/ *adj* extremely large or impressive: *a stupendous achievement*

**stu·pid** /'stupɪd/ *adj* **1** showing a lack of good sense or judgment; silly: *How could you be so stupid?* | *He's always saying stupid things and getting into fights.* **2** an insulting word used in order to describe someone who is not intelligent: *I know that - I'm not stupid!* **3** SPOKEN used when talking about something that annoys you: *I can't get this stupid door open!* –**stupidity** /stu'pɪdəti/ *n* [C,U]

**stu·por** /'stupɚ/ *n* [C,U] a state in which you cannot think, see etc. clearly: *We found him in a* ***drunken stupor***.

**stur·dy** /'stɚdi/ *adj* strong and not likely to break or be hurt: *a sturdy table*

**stut·ter** /'stʌtɚ/ *v* [I,T] to speak with difficulty because you repeat the first sound of a word: *"I w-w-want to g-g-go too," he stuttered.* –**stutter** *n* [singular] –see also STAMMER

**style**[1] /staɪl/ *n* **1** [C,U] a way of doing, making, painting etc. something that is typical of a particular period of time or group of people: *He's trying to copy Van Gogh's style of painting.* | *architecture in the Gothic style* **2** the particular way that someone behaves, works, or deals with other people: *Carolyn has an informal style of teaching.* **3** [C,U] a fashion or design, especially in clothes or hair: *His clothes are always in style.* **4** [U] the particular way you do things that makes people admire you: *You may not like him, but you have to admit that he has style.*

**style**[2] *v* [T] to cut someone's hair in a particular way

**styl·ish** /ˈstaɪlɪʃ/ *adj* attractive in a fashionable way: *a very stylish woman* | *stylish clothes*

**sty·lis·tic** /staɪˈlɪstɪk/ *adj* relating to the style of a piece of writing or art: *I've made a few stylistic changes to your report.*

**styl·ized** /ˈstaɪəˌlaɪzd/ *adj* done in an artificial style that is not natural or like real life

**sty·mie** /ˈstaɪmi/ *v* [T] INFORMAL to prevent someone from doing what s/he has planned or wants to do: *All of our efforts to talk with him have been stymied.*

**suave** /swɑv/ *adj* attractive, confident, and relaxed, but often in a way that is not sincere

**sub** /sʌb/ *n* **1** INFORMAL ⇨ SUBMARINE **2** INFORMAL ⇨ SUBSTITUTE[1] **3** a very large long SANDWICH

**sub·com·mit·tee** /ˈsʌbkəˌmɪti/ *n* a small group formed from a committee to deal with a particular problem in more detail

**sub·con·scious** /ˌsʌbˈkɑnʃəs/ *adj* ⇨ UNCONSCIOUS **—subconscious** *adj* **—subconsciously** *adv*

**sub·con·ti·nent** /ˌsʌbˈkɑntɪn-ənt, -tənənt/ *n* a large area of land that forms part of a CONTINENT: *the Indian subcontinent*

**sub·cul·ture** /ˈsʌbˌkʌltʃɚ/ *n* the behavior, beliefs, activities etc. of a particular group of people in a society that are different from the rest of the society: *the drug subculture*

**sub·di·vide** /ˌsʌbdəˈvaɪd, ˈsʌbdəˌvaɪd/ *v* [T] to divide something into smaller parts

**sub·di·vi·sion** /ˈsʌbdəˌvɪʒən/ *n* an area of land for building a number of houses on, or these houses once they are built

**sub·due** /səbˈdu/ *v* [T] to control someone, especially by using force: *The nurses were trying to subdue a violent patient.*

**sub·dued** /səbˈdud/ *adj* **1** a person or sound that is subdued is unusually quiet: *Jason looked subdued after talking to the principal.* **2** subdued colors, lights etc. are less bright than usual

**sub·ject**[1] /ˈsʌbdʒɪkt/ *n* **1** something that you are talking or writing about: *Stop trying to change the subject!* (=talk about something else) | *She's written several books on the subject*

*of ancient Ireland.* **2** an area of knowledge that you study at a school or university: *"What's your favorite subject?" "Science."* **3** TECHNICAL in grammar, a noun, noun phrase, or pronoun that usually comes before the verb in a sentence, and represents the person or thing that does the action of the verb or about which something is stated. In the sentence "Jean loves her cats," "Jean" is the subject **4** subject matter the subject that is being discussed in a book, shown in a movie or play etc.: *The subject matter of this film may not be suitable for young children.* **5** a person or animal that is used in a test or EXPERIMENT: *All the subjects were men between the ages of 18 and 25.* **6** the particular person, object etc. that you paint or photograph **7** someone who is from a country that has a king or queen

**subject**[2] *adj* **be subject to sth** to be likely to be affected by something, or to be dependent on something: *All prices are subject to change.* | *The pay raise is subject to the management's approval.*

**sub·ject**[3] /səbˈdʒɛkt/ *v*
**subject sb/sth to sth** *phr v* [T] to force someone or something to experience something unpleasant: *He subjected his victims to extreme torture.*

**sub·jec·tive** /səbˈdʒɛktɪv/ *adj* a statement, attitude etc. that is subjective is influenced by personal opinion or feelings rather than facts **—compare** OBJECTIVE[2]

**sub·ju·gate** /ˈsʌbdʒəˌgeɪt/ *v* [T] FORMAL to force a person or group to obey you **—subjugation** /ˌsʌbdʒəˈgeɪʃən/ *n* [U]

**sub·junc·tive** /səbˈdʒʌŋktɪv/ *n* TECHNICAL in grammar, a verb form used in order to express doubt, wishes, or possibility. In the sentence "He suggested we leave early," "leave" is in the subjunctive

**sub·let** /sʌbˈlɛt, ˈsʌblɛt/ *v* **-tted, -tting** [I,T] to take rent from someone for a room, house etc. that you rent from someone else: *I'm subletting the room for the summer.* **—sublet** /ˈsʌblɛt/ *n*

**sub·lime** /səˈblaɪm/ *adj* excellent in a way that makes you feel very happy

**sub·lim·i·nal** /ˌsʌbˈlɪmənl/ *adj* subliminal messages, suggestions etc. affect the way you think without you noticing it

**sub·ma·rine** /ˈsʌbməˌrin, ˌsʌbməˈrin/ *n* a ship that can travel under water

**sub·merged** /səbˈmɚdʒd/ *adj* completely under the surface of the water: *cars submerged by the flood* **—submersion** /səbˈmɚʒən/ *n* [U]

**sub·mis·sion** /səbˈmɪʃən/ *n* **1** [U] the state of accepting that someone else has power over you: *The prisoners were starved into submission.* **2** [C,U] the act of giving a piece of writing to someone so s/he can consider or approve it, or the piece of writing itself: *All submissions must be received by the 15th of March.*

**sub·mis·sive** /səbˈmɪsɪv/ *adj* always willing to obey someone: *a submissive wife*

**sub·mit** /səbˈmɪt/ *v* **-tted, -tting** **1** [T] to give a piece of writing to someone so s/he can consider or approve it: *I submitted my plan to the committee yesterday.* **2** [I,T] to obey someone who has power over you, especially because you have no choice: *We refused to submit to the kidnapper's demands.*

**sub·or·di·nate¹** /səˈbɔrdənɪt/ *n* FORMAL someone who has a lower position or less authority than someone else: *He ignored the suggestions from his subordinates.*

**subordinate²** *adj* FORMAL less important than something else, or lower in rank or authority: *a subordinate position*

**sub·or·di·nate³** /səˈbɔrdnˌeɪt/ *v* [T] to put someone or something in a SUBORDINATE position **–subordination** /səˌbɔrdnˈeɪʃən/ *n* [U]

**sub·poe·na** /səˈpinə/ *n* LAW an official document that orders someone to go to and talk in a TRIAL in a court of law **–subpoena** *v* [T]

**sub·scribe** /səbˈskraɪb/ *v* [I] to pay money regularly to have a newspaper or magazine sent to you: *What magazines do you subscribe to?* **–subscriber** *n*

**subscribe to** sth *phr v* [T] to agree with or support an idea, opinion etc.: *They obviously don't subscribe to his theory.*

**sub·scrip·tion** /səbˈskrɪpʃən/ *n* an amount of money that you pay regularly to receive copies of a newspaper or magazine

**sub·se·quent** /ˈsʌbsəkwənt/ *adj* FORMAL coming after or following something else: *Her physical condition improved in subsequent years.* **–subsequently** *adv*: *The charges against him were subsequently dropped.*

**sub·ser·vi·ent** /səbˈsɜrviənt/ *adj* too willing to do what other people want you to do **–subservience** *n* [U]

**sub·side** /səbˈsaɪd/ *v* [I] to become less strong or loud: *The storm subsided around dawn.*

**sub·sid·i·ar·y¹** /səbˈsɪdiˌɛri/ *n* a company that is owned or controlled by another company

**subsidiary²** *adj* relating to the main situation or business, but less important or smaller than it: *He played a subsidiary role in the negotiations.*

**sub·si·dize** /ˈsʌbsəˌdaɪz/ *v* [T] to pay a SUBSIDY: *housing that is subsidized by the government*

**sub·si·dized** /ˈsʌbsəˌdaɪzd/ *adj* to be paid for by a SUBSIDY: *subsidized meals/education*

**sub·si·dy** /ˈsʌbsədi/ *n* money that is paid by the government in order to help with the cost of something

**sub·sist** /səbˈsɪst/ *v* [I] to stay alive using only small amounts of food or money: *The prisoners subsisted on rice and water.* **–subsistence** *n* [U]: *subsistence farming*

**sub·stance** /ˈsʌbstəns/ *n* **1** a type of solid or liquid that has particular qualities: *The bag was covered with a sticky substance.* | *a poisonous/hazardous/toxic substance* | *illegal substances* (=drugs) **2** [singular, U] the most important ideas in a document, speech, report etc.: *The news report said little about the substance of the peace talks.* **3** FORMAL facts that are true and important: *There's no substance to his arguments.*

**substance a·buse** /ˈ.. .ˌ./ *n* [U] TECHNICAL the habit of taking too many illegal drugs so that you are harmed by them

**sub·stand·ard** /ˌsʌbˈstændərd◄/ *adj* not as good as the average, or not as good as usual: *substandard health care*

**sub·stan·tial** /səbˈstænʃəl/ *adj* **1** large enough in amount or numbers to be noticed: *She earns a substantial income.* **2** large and strongly made

**sub·stan·tial·ly** /səbˈstænʃəli/ *adv* very much: *Prices have increased substantially.*

**sub·stan·ti·ate** /səbˈstænʃiˌeɪt/ *v* [T] FORMAL to prove the truth of something that someone has said

**sub·sti·tute¹** /ˈsʌbstəˌtut/ *n* **1** someone who does someone else's job while s/he is away, sick etc.: *Rona is working as a substitute teacher.* **2** something new or different that you use or do instead of what you used or did before: *a sugar substitute* | *There is no substitute for* (=nothing better than) *a good diet.*

**substitute²** *v* **1** [T] to use something new or different instead of something else: *You can substitute margarine for butter in this recipe.* **2** [I,T] to do someone's job for a short time until s/he is able to do it again **–substitution** /ˌsʌbstəˈtuʃən/ *n* [C,U]

**sub·ter·fuge** /ˈsʌbtərˌfyudʒ/ *n* [C,U] FORMAL a trick or dishonest way of doing something, or the use of this

**sub·ter·ra·ne·an** /ˌsʌbtəˈreɪniən/ *adj* TECHNICAL beneath the surface of the earth; UNDERGROUND: *a subterranean lake*

**sub·ti·tles** /ˈsʌbˌtaɪtlz/ *n* [plural] words on a movie screen that translate what the actors are saying when the movie is in a foreign language **–subtitled** *adj*

**sub·tle** /ˈsʌtl/ *adj* **1** not easily noticed unless you pay careful attention: *She noticed some subtle changes in his personality.* **2** a subtle taste or smell is pleasant and delicate: *the subtle scent of mint in the air* **3** a subtle person, plan etc. skillfully hides what he, she, or it intends to do or achieve **–subtly** /ˈsʌtl-i, ˈsʌtli/ *adv*

**sub·tle·ty** /ˈsʌtlti/ *n* [C,U] the quality of being SUBTLE, or something that is subtle: *the subtlety of the wine's flavor* | *The subtleties of the story do not translate well into other languages.*

**sub·tract** /səbˈtrækt/ *v* [T] to take a number or amount from something larger: *If you subtract 15 from 25 you get 10.* **–subtraction** /səbˈtrækʃən/ *n* **–compare** ADD

**sub·urb** /'sʌbɚb/ *n* an area away from the center of a city, but still part of it, where a lot of people live: *We moved to* **the suburbs** *last year.* | *a suburb of Chicago*

**sub·ur·ban** /sə'bɚbən/ *adj* relating to a SUB-URB: *suburban life* | *suburban Cleveland* (=the suburban areas around Cleveland)

**sub·ur·bi·a** /sə'bɚbiə/ *n* [U] all SUBURBS in general: *life in suburbia*

**sub·ver·sive** /səb'vɚsɪv/ *adj* intending to destroy or damage a government, society, religion etc.: *a subversive speech*

**sub·vert** /səb'vɚt/ *v* [T] FORMAL to act in a SUBVERSIVE way

**sub·way** /'sʌbweɪ/ *n* a railroad that runs under the ground in cities

**suc·ceed** /sək'sid/ *v* **1** [I] to do what you have tried to do, or to reach a high position in something such as your job: *Finally, I* **succeeded in** *convincing Anna that I was right.* | *She gave herself five years to* **succeed as** *a writer.* **2** [I] to have the result or effect that something is intended to have: *Our advertising campaign* **succeeded in** *attracting more customers.* **3** [I,T] to be the next person to take a position or do a job after someone else: *Mr. Harvey will* **succeed** *Mrs. Lincoln* **as** *chairman.* −compare FAIL¹

**suc·ceed·ing** /sək'sidɪŋ/ *adj* coming after something else: *Sales improved in succeeding years.*

**suc·cess** /sək'sɛs/ *n* **1** [U] the achievement of doing what you have tried to do or want to do: *We had no/some success in developing a better engine.* **2** something that has the result or effect that you intended: *Jackie's wedding* **was a big/huge/great success.** **3** someone who does very well or reaches a high position in something such as his/her job: *He wants to* **be a success.** **4 success story** someone or something that succeeds when other people or things do not −opposite FAILURE

**suc·cess·ful** /sək'sɛsfəl/ *adj* **1** having the result or effect that you intended: *The surgery was completely successful.* **2** respected and successful as a result of earning a lot of money: *a successful businessman* −**successfully** *adv* −opposite UNSUCCESSFUL

**suc·ces·sion** /sək'sɛʃən/ *n* **1 in succession** happening one after the other: *The team has won four championships in succession.* **2 a succession of sth** a number of people or things that happen or follow one after another: *A succession of bad investments led to the failure of the business.* **3** [U] the act of taking over an important job, position etc., or the right to be next to take it

**suc·ces·sive** /sək'sɛsɪv/ *adj* happening, existing, or following one after the other: *Babe Ruth hit three successive home runs in one game.* −**successively** *adv*

**suc·ces·sor** /sək'sɛsɚ/ *n* someone who takes a job or position that was held before by someone else: *No one was certain who Mao's successor would be.*

**suc·cinct** /sək'sɪŋkt, sə'sɪŋkt/ *adj* clearly expressed in a few words −**succinctly** *adv*

**suc·cor** /'sʌkɚ/ *n* LITERARY help

**suc·cu·lent** /'sʌkyələnt/ *adj* juicy and tasting very good: *a succulent steak* −**succulence** *n* [U]

**suc·cumb** /sə'kʌm/ *v* [I] FORMAL **1** to stop trying to oppose a person or a strong desire, and allow him, her, or it to persuade or influence you; YIELD: *Eventually, she* **succumbed to** *his charms.* **2** to become very sick or die from an illness

**such** /sʌtʃ/ *determiner, pron* **1** used in order to talk about a person or thing that is like the one that you have just mentioned: *Such behavior is not acceptable here.* | *What would you do in* **such a** *situation?* | *"Did you get the job?"* **"No such luck."** (=I wasn't lucky) **2 such as** used when giving an example of something: *He likes dangerous sports such as mountain climbing.* | *big cities such as New York, Tokyo, and London* **3** used in order to emphasize an amount or degree: *We had* **such** *fun at your party!* | *I was in* **such a** *hurry* **that** *I left my lunch at home.* | *Mandy's* **such a** *nice person.* **4 there's no such person/thing as** used in order to say that a particular type of person or thing does not exist: *There's no such thing as a perfect job.* **5 as such** exactly what the word used is understood to mean: *He doesn't have a degree as such, just a lot of business courses.*

> **USAGE NOTE** such and so
>
> Use **such** and **so** to emphasize a particular quality that a person or thing has. Use **so** just before an adjective: *Your dress is so pretty.* | *Some people are so rude.* However, if the adjective is used before a noun, use **such**: *She has such pretty eyes.* | *Mark is such a good swimmer.* You can also use **so** to emphasize an adverb: *He always sings so loudly.*

**such-and-such** /'. . ,./ *determiner* SPOKEN used instead of the name of something: *You can say that when you press such-and-such a key, such-and-such happens.*

**suck** /sʌk/ *v* **1** [I,T] to hold something in your mouth and pull on it with your tongue and lips: *Don't suck your thumb, Katie.* | *Ben was* **sucking on** *a piece of candy.* **2** [T] to pull someone or something with a lot of force: *A man almost got* **sucked under** *by the current.* **3 get sucked into (doing) sth** to make someone become involved in something unpleasant: *I'm not going to get* **sucked into** *an argument with you guys.* **4** [I] SPOKEN to be bad or unpleasant: *It* **sucks** *having to stay inside all* _day._ | _The band was great, but his singing sucked._

**suck up to** sb _phr v_ [I] SPOKEN to say or do things someone wants in order to make him/her like you or to get what you want: _She's always **sucking up to** the director._

**suck·er** /'sʌkɚ/ _n_ **1** INFORMAL someone who is easily tricked: _Ellen always was a sucker._ **2** SPOKEN a thing: _Do you know how much this sucker cost me?_ **3 be a sucker for sth** to like something so much that you cannot refuse it: _I'm a sucker for old movies._ **4** ⇨ LOLLIPOP

**suc·tion** /'sʌkʃən/ _n_ [U] the process of removing air or liquid from a container or space so that another substance can be pulled in, or so that two surfaces stick together

**sud·den** /'sʌdn/ _adj_ **1** done or happening unexpectedly: _We've had a sudden change of plans._ **2 all of a sudden** without any warning: _All of a sudden, the lights went out._

**sud·den·ly** /'sʌdnli/ _adv_ quickly and unexpectedly: _She suddenly realized what she'd done._ | _"Now I remember!" Bill said suddenly._

**suds** /sʌdz/ _n_ [plural] the BUBBLEs that form on top of water with soap in it —**sudsy** _adj_

**sue** /su/ _v_ [I,T] to make a legal claim against someone, especially for money, because s/he has harmed you in some way: _She plans to **sue** the company **for** $1 million._

**suede** /sweɪd/ _n_ [U] soft leather with a slightly rough surface

**suf·fer** /'sʌfɚ/ _v_ **1** [I,T] to experience something bad, such as pain, sickness, or the effects of a bad situation: _Neil suffered a heart attack last year._ | _Marnie **suffers from** headaches._ | _Small businesses are suffering financially right now._ **2** [T] if someone suffers a bad experience, it happens to him/her: _The mayor has **suffered a defeat** in the election._ **3** [I] to become worse in quality: _Andy's work began to suffer after his divorce._ —**sufferer** _n_ —**suffering** _n_ [C,U]

**suf·fice** /sə'faɪs/ _v_ [I] FORMAL to be enough: _A few examples will **suffice to** show this is true._

**suf·fi·cient** /sə'fɪʃənt/ _adj_ FORMAL as much as you need for a particular purpose; enough: _They had **sufficient** evidence **to** send him to prison._ —**sufficiency** _n_ [singular, U] —opposite INSUFFICIENT

**suf·fix** /'sʌfɪks/ _n_ TECHNICAL in grammar, a letter or letters added to the end of a word in order to make a new word, such as "ness" at the end of "kindness" —compare PREFIX, AFFIX

**suf·fo·cate** /'sʌfə,keɪt/ _v_ **1** [I,T] to die or kill someone by preventing him/her from breathing: _One firefighter was suffocated by the smoke._ **2 be suffocating** INFORMAL to feel uncomfortable because there is not enough fresh air —**suffocation** /,sʌfə'keɪʃən/ _n_ [U]

**suf·frage** /'sʌfrɪdʒ/ _n_ [U] FORMAL the right to vote

**sug·ar** /'ʃʊgɚ/ _n_ [U] a sweet white or brown substance that is obtained from plants and used for making food and drinks sweet: _Do you **take** sugar in your coffee?_ —**sugary** _adj: sugary snacks_

**sug·ared** /'ʃʊgɚd/ _adj_ covered in sugar: _sugared almonds_

**sug·gest** /səg'dʒɛst, sə'dʒɛst/ _v_ [T] **1** to tell someone your ideas about what should be done: _They suggested meeting for drinks first._ | _Don **suggested that** we go swimming._ **2** to say that someone or something is good for a particular purpose; RECOMMEND: _Gina Reed's name has been **suggested for** the job._ **3** to make someone think that a particular thing is true; INDICATE: _The article **suggested that** Nachez might run for mayor._ —see usage note at RECOMMEND

**sug·gest·i·ble** /səg'dʒɛstəbəl, sə'dʒɛs-/ _adj_ easily influenced by other people or by things you see and hear

**sug·ges·tion** /səg'dʒɛstʃən, sə'dʒɛs-/ _n_ **1** an idea or plan that someone mentions: _We've **had** some **suggestions** on good plays to see in New York._ | _Can I **make a suggestion**?_ | _They accepted the **suggestion that** Todd go first._ **2** [U] the act of telling someone your idea about what should be done: _I took the class **at** my adviser's **suggestion**._ **3 suggestion that/of** a slight possibility: _The police said that there was no suggestion of murder._

**sug·ges·tive** /səg'dʒɛstɪv, sə'dʒɛs-/ _adj_ **1** making you think of sex: _a suggestive remark_ **2** reminding you of something: _a spotted rug, **suggestive of** leopard skin_

**su·i·ci·dal** /,suə'saɪdl/ _adj_ **1** wanting to kill yourself: _Fay's very unhappy - suicidal, in fact._ **2** behavior that is suicidal is dangerous and likely to result in death

**su·i·cide** /'suə,saɪd/ _n_ **1** [C,U] the act of killing yourself: _Her brother **committed suicide** last year._ **2 political/social etc. suicide** something you do that ruins your job or position in society

**suit¹** /sut/ _n_ **1** a set of clothes made of the same material, including a short coat with pants or a skirt: _a dark gray suit_ **2** a piece of clothing used for a special purpose: _a swimming suit_ **3** [C,U] ⇨ LAWSUIT: _A homeowner **filed suit against** the county and lost._ **4** one of the four types of cards in a set of playing cards

**suit²** _v_ [T] **1** to be acceptable or right for you: _"Is tomorrow at 10:00 okay?" "**That suits me fine**." (=is acceptable to me)_ **2** to make someone look attractive: _Short hair suits you._ **3 suit yourself** SPOKEN said in order to tell someone that s/he can do whatever s/he wants to do, usually in a way that shows you are annoyed or upset: _"I'm not sure I want to go tonight." "Suit yourself."_ **4** to have the right qualities to do something: _Lucy's **ideally suited for** the job._ —see usage note at APPROPRIATE¹

**suit·able** /'sutəbəl/ *adj* right or acceptable for a particular purpose or situation: *This book isn't suitable for young children.* −**suitably** *adv* −**suitability** /ˌsutəˈbɪləti/ *n* [U] −opposite UNSUITABLE −see usage note at APPROPRIATE[1]

**suit·case** /'sut͡keɪs/ *n* a bag or box with a handle, for carrying your clothes when you travel

**suite** /swit/ *n* **1** a set of expensive rooms in a hotel: *the honeymoon suite* **2** a set of matching furniture for a room: *a living room suite* **3** a piece of music made up of several short parts: *the Nutcracker Suite*

**suit·or** /'sutɚ/ *n* OLD-FASHIONED a man who wants to marry a particular woman

**sul·fur** /'sʌlfɚ/ *n* [U] a yellow strong-smelling chemical that is an ELEMENT

**sulk** /sʌlk/ *v* [I] to show that you are annoyed about something by being silent and looking unhappy: *Stop sulking; you can go out and play later.* −**sulky** *adj*

**sul·len** /'sʌlən/ *adj* silently showing anger or bad temper

**sul·phur** /'sʌlfɚ/ *n* [U] ⇨ SULFUR

**sul·tan** /'sʌlt͡n/ *n* a ruler in some Muslim countries

**sul·try** /'sʌltri/ *adj* **1** weather that is sultry is hot with no wind **2** a woman who is sultry is very sexually attractive

**sum**[1] /sʌm/ *n* **1** an amount of money: *The city has spent a large sum of money on parks.* **2 the sum of** the total when you add two or more numbers together: *The sum of 4 and 5 is 9.*

**sum**[2] *v* -mmed, -mming
**sum up** *phr v* [I,T] to end a discussion or speech by giving the main information about it in a short statement: *So, to sum up, we need to organize our time better.*

**sum·ma·rize** /'sʌməˌraɪz/ *v* [I,T] to make a short statement that gives only the main information about an event, plan, report etc.

**sum·ma·ry** /'sʌməri/ *n* a short statement that gives the main information about an event, plan, report etc.: *Read the article and write a summary of it.* | *In summary, more research is needed.* −**summary** *adj: summary information*

**sum·mer** /'sʌmɚ/ *n* the season between spring and fall, when the weather is hottest: *The pool is open in (the) summer.* | *We're going to Mt. Whitney this summer.* | *last/next summer* (=the summer before or after this one )

**summer school** /'.. ./ *n* [C,U] classes that you can take in the summer at a school or college

**sum·mer·time** /'sʌmɚˌtaɪm/ *n* [U] the time of year when it is summer

**summer va·ca·tion** /ˌ.. .ˈ../ *n* [C,U] the time during the summer when schools are closed, or a trip you take during this time

**sum·mit** /'sʌmɪt/ *n* **1** a set of meetings among the leaders of several governments: *an economic summit* **2** the top of a mountain

**sum·mon** /'sʌmən/ *v* [T] FORMAL **1** to officially order someone to come to a particular place: *I was summoned to the principal's office.* **2** also **summon up** to make a great effort to use your strength, courage, etc.: *Tim summoned up his courage to ask Kay for a date.*

**sum·mons** /'sʌmənz/ *n, plural* **summonses** an official order to appear in a court of law

**sump·tu·ous** /'sʌmpt͡ʃuəs/ *adj* very impressive and expensive: *a sumptuous meal*

**sun**[1] /sʌn/ *n* **1** the large bright star in the sky that gives us light and heat, and around which the Earth moves −see picture at GREENHOUSE EFFECT **2** [U] the heat and light that come from the sun: *Val lay in the sun, listening to the radio.* **3** any star around which PLANETs move

**sun**[2] *v* -nned, -nning [T] **sun yourself** to sit or lie outside when the sun is shining

**sun·bathe** /'sʌnbeɪð/ *v* [I] to sit or lie outside in the sun in order to become tan (=brown) −**sunbathing** *n* [U]

**sun·block** /'sʌnblɑk/ *n* [U] a cream that you put on your skin that completely prevents the sun from burning you

**sun·burn** /'sʌnbɚn/ *n* [U] the condition of having skin that is red and painful as a result of spending too much time in the sun −**sunburned** *adj*

**sun·dae** /'sʌndi, -deɪ/ *n* a dish of ICE CREAM, fruit, nuts, and sweet SAUCE: *a hot fudge sundae* −see picture at DESSERT

**Sun·day** /'sʌndi, -deɪ/ written abbreviation **Sun.** *n* the first day of the week

---

**USAGE NOTE Sunday**

Use the preposition "on" to talk about a particular day in the week that has just passed or the week that is coming: *Let's go to the mall on Friday.* | *Susan arrived on Saturday.* Use "last" before the name of a day to talk about something that happened the week before this one: *I had lunch with Lucy last Tuesday.* ✗ DON'T SAY "on last Tuesday." ✗ Use "next" before the name of a day to talk about something that will happen during the week after this one: *We'll see you next Thursday.* ✗ DON'T SAY "on next Thursday." ✗ Use the name of the day to say that something happens every week on that particular day: *Monday is my day off.* | *We always go bowling on Wednesdays.* Only use "the" in front of the name of a day if you are talking about a particular day of a particular week: *Can we meet on the Monday before Thanksgiving?*

---

**Sunday School** /'.. ./ *n* [C,U] a class in a

church where children go to be taught about their religion

**sun·dial** /'sʌndaɪl/ *n* an object that shows the time by the shadow of a POINTER on a flat surface that is marked with the hours

**sun·down** /'sʌndaʊn/ *n* [U] ⇨ SUNSET

**sun·dry** /'sʌndri/ *adj* FORMAL ⇨ MISCELLANEOUS

**sun·flow·er** /'sʌn,flaʊɚ/ *n* a tall plant with large yellow flowers whose seeds can be eaten or used for making oil

**sung** /sʌŋ/ *v* the PAST PARTICIPLE of SING

**sun·glass·es** /'sʌn,glæsɪz/ *n* [plural] dark glasses that you wear in order to protect your eyes when the sun is bright

**sunk**[1] /sʌŋk/ *v* the past tense and PAST PARTICIPLE of SINK

**sunk**[2] *adj* INFORMAL in a lot of trouble, or having failed: *If we can't finish by 5:00, we're sunk.*

**sunk·en** /'sʌŋkən/ *adj* **1** having fallen to the bottom of the sea: *a sunken ship* **2** built or placed at a lower level than the surrounding area: *a sunken garden*

**sun·light** /'sʌnlaɪt/ *n* [U] natural light that comes from the sun: *These plants don't need much sunlight.*

**sun·lit** /'sʌn,lɪt/ *adj* made brighter by light from the sun: *a sunlit kitchen*

**sun·ny** /'sʌni/ *adj* **1** full of light from the sun: *a sunny day* **2** cheerful and happy: *a sunny personality*

**sun·rise** /'sʌnraɪz/ *n* [U] the time when the sun first appears in the morning

**sun·roof** /'sʌnruf/ *n* a part of the roof of a car that you can open

**sun·screen** /'sʌnskrin/ *n* [C,U] a cream that you put on your skin that will stop the sun from burning you for a period of time

**sun·set** /'sʌnsɛt/ *n* [U] the time of day when the sun disappears and night begins

**sun·shine** /'sʌnʃaɪn/ *n* [U] the light and heat that comes from the sun: *Let's go out and enjoy the sunshine.*

**sun·tan** /'sʌntæn/ *n* ⇨ TAN[2]

**sun·up** /'sʌnʌp/ *n* [U] ⇨ SUNRISE

**su·per**[1] /'supɚ/ *adj* INFORMAL extremely good: *He's a super soccer player.*

**super**[2] *n* SPOKEN a building SUPERINTENDENT

**super**[3] *adv* SPOKEN extremely: *a super expensive restaurant*

**su·perb** /su'pɚb/ *adj* extremely good; excellent: *a superb dinner* –**superbly** *adv*

**Super Bowl** /'.. ,./ *n* a football game played once a year in order to decide which professional team is the best in the US

**su·per·fi·cial** /,supɚ'fɪʃəl/ *adj* **1** based only on the first things you notice, not on complete knowledge: *There are superficial similarities between the two novels, but that's all.* | *He's made only a superficial study of law.*

**2** affecting only the surface of your skin or the outside part of something: *She had some superficial cuts on her arm.* **3** someone who is superficial does not think about things that are serious or important; SHALLOW –**superficially** *adv*

**su·per·flu·ous** /su'pɚfluəs/ *adj* FORMAL more than is needed or wanted; unnecessary: *superfluous details*

**su·per·high·way** /,supɚ'haɪweɪ/ *n* a very large road on which you can drive fast for long distances between cities –see also INFORMATION SUPERHIGHWAY

**su·per·hu·man** /,supɚ'hyumən◂/ *adj* using powers that are much greater than ordinary ones: *a superhuman effort to finish the job*

**su·per·in·tend·ent** /,supɚɪn'tɛndənt/ *n* **1** someone who is responsible for a place, job, activity etc.: *Mel's just been hired as superintendent of sales.* **2** someone who takes care of an apartment building **3** someone who is responsible for of all the schools in a particular area of the US

**su·pe·ri·or**[1] /sə'pɪriɚ, su-/ *adj* **1** better than other similar people or things: *I believe Matisse's work is superior to Picasso's.* ✗ DON'T SAY "superior than." ✗ **2** extremely good in quality: *superior wines* **3** showing that you think you are better than other people: *a superior attitude* –opposite INFERIOR[1]

**superior**[2] *n* someone who has a higher rank or position than you in a job: *I'll have to discuss it with my superiors.* –opposite INFERIOR[2]

**su·pe·ri·or·i·ty** /sə,pɪri'ɔrəti, -'ɑr-/ *n* [U] **1** the quality of being better than other things: *the country's military superiority over its neighbors* **2** an attitude that shows you think you are better than other people: *Janet always spoke with an air of superiority.*

**su·per·la·tive**[1] /sə'pɚlətɪv, su-/ *adj* excellent: *a superlative actor*

**superlative**[2] *n* **1** **the superlative** TECHNICAL in grammar, the form of an adjective or adverb that shows the highest degree of a particular quality. For example, "fastest" is the superlative of "fast" **2** a word in this form, used when expressing praise or admiration –see study note on page 457

**su·per·mar·ket** /'supɚ,mɑrkɪt/ *n* a very large store that sells many different kinds of food and things people need for the house

**su·per·nat·u·ral** /,supɚ'nætʃərəl◂, -tʃrəl◂/ *n* **the supernatural** events, powers, abilities, or creatures that are impossible to explain by science or natural causes –**supernatural** *adj*: *supernatural powers*

**sup·er·pow·er** /'supɚ,paʊɚ/ *n* a country that has very great military and political power

**su·per·sede** /,supɚ'sid/ *v* [T] to replace something that is older or less effective with something new or better: *TV had superseded radio by the 1960s.*

**su·per·son·ic** /ˌsupɚ'sɑnɪk◂/ *adj* faster than the speed of sound: *supersonic jets*

**su·per·star** /'supɚˌstɑr/ *n* an extremely famous performer, especially a musician or movie actor

**su·per·sti·tion** /ˌsupɚ'stɪʃən/ *n* [C,U] DISAPPROVING a belief that some objects or actions are lucky and some are unlucky

**su·per·sti·tious** /ˌsupɚ'stɪʃəs/ *adj* DISAPPROVING believing that some objects or actions are lucky or unlucky

**su·per·struc·ture** /'supɚˌstrʌktʃɚ/ *n* [singular, U] a structure that is built on top of the main part of something such as a ship or building

**su·per·vise** /'supɚˌvaɪz/ *v* [I,T] to be responsible for a group of workers or students and make sure that they do their work correctly −**supervision** /ˌsupɚ'vɪʒən/ *n* [U]: *working under supervision*

**su·per·vis·or** /'supɚˌvaɪzɚ/ *n* someone who SUPERVISEs workers or students −**supervisory** *adj*: *a supervisory role*

**sup·per** /'sʌpɚ/ *n* an informal meal that is eaten in the evening; dinner: *What's for supper?* (=what will we eat?) −see usage note at MEAL TIMES

**sup·plant** /sə'plænt/ *v* [T] FORMAL to take the place of another person or thing: *The old factories have all been supplanted by new high-tech industries.*

**sup·ple** /'sʌpəl/ *adj* able to bend and move easily: *a supple dancer* | *supple leather*

**sup·ple·ment¹** /'sʌpləmənt/ *n* **1** something that is added to something else to improve it. *dietary supplements* **2** an additional part of something such as a newspaper, magazine etc.: *the Sunday supplement*

**sup·ple·ment²** /'sʌpləˌmɛnt/ *v* **supplement a salary/income/diet** to add something to what you earn or eat in order to improve it: *He took a night job to supplement their income.*

**sup·ple·men·tal** /ˌsʌplə'mɛnṭl/, **supplemen·tary** /-'mɛntri, -'mɛntəri/ *adj* additional: *The doctor recommended taking supplementary vitamins.*

**sup·pli·er** /sə'plaɪɚ/ *n* a company that provides a particular product: *medical suppliers*

**sup·plies** /sə'plaɪz/ *n* [plural] food, clothes, and things that are necessary for daily life, especially for a particular period: *supplies for a camping trip*

**sup·ply¹** /sə'plaɪ/ *n* **1** [C,U] an amount of something that is available to be used, or the process of providing this: *Supplies of fresh fruit arrive daily.* | *Oklahoma's large supply of oil* | *the supply of oxygen to the brain* **2** a system that is used in order to provide gas,

water etc.: *We've had problems with the water supply lately.*

**supply²** *v* [T] to provide people with something that they need or want, especially regularly over a long time: *Workers are supplied with masks and special clothing.* | *He was arrested for supplying drugs to dealers.*

**supply and de·mand** /.ˌ. . .'./ *n* [U] the relationship between the amount of goods for sale and the amount that people want to buy, especially the way this relationship influences prices

**sup·port¹** /sə'pɔrt/ *v* [T] **1** to say that you agree with an idea, group, person etc. and want him, her, or it to succeed: *The union will support workers' demands for a pay raise.* **2** to hold the weight of something in order to prevent it from falling: *an arch supported by two columns* **3** to help and encourage someone: *I appreciate your supporting me during my divorce.* **4** to provide enough money for someone to live: *How can Brad support a family on his salary?* **5** to get money in order to pay for a bad habit: *He's started stealing to support his drug habit.* **6** to prove that something is true: *There is now enough data to support the theory.*

**support²** *n* **1** [U] the things people do to help an idea, plan, group etc. succeed, or the act of encouraging it: *The proposal has won the support of local businesses.* **2** [U] help and encouragement that you give someone: *My parents have given me a lot of support.* **3** [C,U] an object that holds up something else: *supports for the roof*

**sup·port·er** /sə'pɔrtɚ/ *n* someone who supports a particular person, group, or plan: *Supervisor Carter's supporters say he has been treated unfairly.*

**sup·port·ive** /sə'pɔrtɪv/ *adj* giving help or encouragement to someone in a particular situation: *Larry's always been supportive of my working.*

**sup·pose¹** /sə'pouz/ *v* [T] **1 be supposed to do sth a)** used in order to say what someone should or should not do, especially because of official rules: *You're supposed to wear a seat belt in the car.* **b)** used in order to say or ask what should happen: *The checks were supposed to arrive two weeks ago.* | *What time is the movie supposed to start?* **2 be supposed to be sth** to be believed to be true or real by many people: *This is supposed to be the oldest theater in New York.* **3** to think that something is probably true: *I suppose it's not very important.*

SPOKEN PHRASES

**4 I suppose (that)** used when saying in an angry way that you think something is true: *I suppose you thought that was funny!* **5 suppose/supposing** used in order to ask someone to imagine what might happen: *Suppose you do get the job. Who'd take care of the kids?* **6 What's that supposed to mean?** said when you are annoyed by what someone has just said: *"I'll keep your idea in mind." "Keep it in mind! What's that supposed to mean?"*

**suppose**[2] *conjunction* SPOKEN **1** used in order to ask what might happen: *Don't do it. Suppose Mom found out?* **2** used in order to suggest something: *Suppose we try to finish this part first.*

**sup·posed** /sə'pouzd/ *adj* used in order to show that you do not think something is true or real, although other people claim it is: *the supposed link between violent movies and crime*

**sup·pos·ed·ly** /sə'pouzɪdli/ *adv* used when saying what other people claim is true or real, especially when you do not think they are right: *He had to deliver supposedly important papers.* | *Supposedly, he's rich and handsome.*

**sup·pos·ing** /sə'pouzɪŋ/ *conjunction* ⇨ SUPPOSE[2]

**sup·po·si·tion** /ˌsʌpə'zɪʃən/ *n* [C,U] something that you think is true even though you are not certain and cannot prove it

**sup·press** /sə'prɛs/ *v* [T] **1** to stop people from opposing the government, especially by using force: *The army was called in to suppress the revolt.* **2** to stop yourself from showing your feelings: *Andy could barely suppress his anger.* **3** to prevent important information or opinions from becoming known: *His lawyer suppressed some of the evidence.* —**suppression** /sə'prɛʃən/ *n* [U]

**su·prem·a·cy** /sə'prɛməsi, su-/ *n* [U] a position in which a group or idea is more powerful or advanced than anything else: *the supremacy of their army*

**su·preme** /sə'prim, su-/ *adj* **1** having the highest position of power, importance, or influence: *the Supreme Commander of the UN forces* **2** the greatest possible: *a supreme honor* —**supremely** *adv*

**Supreme Court** /ˌ. '. / *n* [singular] the court of law with the most authority in the US

**sur·charge** /'sɚtʃɑrdʒ/ *n* money that you have to pay in addition to the basic price of something

**sure**[1] /ʃʊr, ʃɚ/ *adj* **1** certain about something: *Are you sure (that) you've met him before?* | *I knew I'd like it, but I wasn't sure about/of the kids.* | *Garvey isn't sure who he can trust.* **2 make sure a)** to check that something is true or that something has been done: *He called to make sure (that) we got home okay.* **b)** to do something so that you are certain that something will happen: *I wanted to make sure (that) I got an appointment.* **3** certain to happen or succeed: *The county fair is sure to appeal to everyone.* | *Investing in the stock market is not a sure thing.* (=it is risky) **4 be sure of sth** to be certain to get something or certain that something will happen: *The*

*Giants are now sure of a place in the playoffs.* **5 sure of yourself** confident about your own abilities and opinions: *Hirsch appeared very calm and sure of himself.* **6 sure thing** SPOKEN said in order to agree to something: *"See you Friday." "Yeah, sure thing."*

**sure**[2] *adv* **1 for sure** INFORMAL **a)** certainly: *I think he's married, but I don't know for sure.* **b)** used in order to emphasize that something is true: *It's a lot better than it was, that's for sure.* **2 sure enough** INFORMAL used in order to say that something happened in the way someone thought it would: *Sure enough, by the age of 30, I was bald too.* **3** INFORMAL used in order to admit that something is true, before you say something very different: *Sure, he's cute, but I'm still not interested.*

SPOKEN PHRASES

**4** said in order to say yes to someone: *"Can I read your paper?" "Sure."* **5** said in order to emphasize a statement: *It's sure nice outside tonight.* | *Well, it sure doesn't make my job any easier.* **6** used as a way of replying when someone thanks you: *"Hey, thanks for your help." "Sure."*

—see usage note at YES

**sure-fire** /ˌ. '. ◂/ *adj* INFORMAL certain to succeed: *a sure-fire way to make a million bucks*

**sure·ly** /'ʃʊrli, 'ʃɚli/ *adv* used in order to show that you think something must be true: *Surely you won't go there alone!*

**surf**

**surf**[1] /sɚf/ *v* [I] **1** to ride on ocean waves standing on a special board **2 surf the net** to look quickly through the information on the INTERNET for information that interests you

−**surfer** *n* −**surfing** *n* [U]: *Didn't you go surfing at Ventura?* −see also **channel hop/ surf** (CHANNEL)

**surf**[2] *n* [U] waves that come onto the beach and have white BUBBLEs on top of them

**sur·face**[1] /'sɚfəs/ *n* **1** the outside or top layer of something: *a cleaner for all your kitchen surfaces | the Earth's surface | leaves floating **on the surface** of the lake* **2 the surface** the qualities that someone or something seems to have until you learn more about him, her, or it: *He seems quiet **on the surface**, but he really likes to talk. | **Under the surface**, there were problems at the bank.*

**surface**[2] *v* **1** [I] to rise to the surface of water: *Whales were surfacing near our boat.* **2** [I] to become known about or easy to notice: *Old arguments are starting to surface.* **3** [T] to put a surface on a road

**surf·board** /'sɚfbɔrd/ *n* a long special board that you stand on to ride on ocean waves

**surge**[1] /sɚdʒ/ *v* [I] **1** if a crowd of people surges, it suddenly moves forward together very quickly **2** also **surge up** to begin to feel an emotion very strongly: *Rage surged up inside her.*

**surge**[2] *n* **1** a sudden large increase in something: *a **surge of** excitement | a **surge in** oil prices* **2** a sudden movement of a lot of people: *a **surge of** refugees into the country*

**sur·geon** /'sɚdʒən/ *n* a doctor who does operations in a hospital −see usage note at DOCTOR[1]

**sur·ger·y** /'sɚdʒəri/ *n* [U] medical treatment in which a doctor cuts open your body to fix, change or remove something inside: *heart surgery | plastic surgery*

**sur·gi·cal** /'sɚdʒɪkəl/ *adj* relating to or used for medical operations: *surgical gloves*

**sur·ly** /'sɚli/ *adj* bad-tempered, unfriendly, and often rude: *surly behavior*

**sur·mise** /sɚ'maɪz/ *v* [T] FORMAL to guess that something is true using information you have

**sur·mount** /sɚ'maunt/ *v* [T] FORMAL to succeed in dealing with a problem or difficulty

**sur·pass** /sɚ'pæs/ *v* [T] to be better or greater than someone or something else: *Japan has surpassed other countries in technology. | His success had surpassed their hopes/expectations.*

**sur·plus**[1] /'sɚplʌs/ *n* [C,U] **1** more of something than is needed or used: *a surplus of goods* **2** money that a country or company has after it has paid for the things it needs: *a budget surplus* −opposite DEFICIT **3** the state of having sold more goods to another country than you have bought from it: *a trade surplus with China*

**surplus**[2] *adj* more than what is needed or used: *surplus corn*

**sur·prise**[1] /sɚ'praɪz, sə'praɪz/ *n* **1** [C,U] something that is unexpected or unusual: *What a surprise to see you here! | It **came as no sur-**

*prise** when Jeff moved to Chicago.* (=we expected it would happen) | *Dad, I have a sur-prise for you!* **2** [U] the feeling you have when something unexpected or unusual happens: *Imagine our surprise when we heard the news!* **3 catch/take sb by surprise** to happen in an unexpected way: *The heavy snowfall had caught everyone by surprise.* **4 Surprise!** SPOKEN said at the same time as you show someone something that s/he did not expect, such as a gift. *Close your eyes, Joanne - Surprise!*

**sur·prise**[2] *v* [T] **1** to make someone feel surprised: *"Pam got fired." "It doesn't surprise me."* **2** to find, catch, or attack someone when s/he does not expect it: *A security guard surprised the robber.*

**sur·prised** /sɚ'praɪzd, sə-/ *adj* having a feeling of surprise: *We were surprised (that) David got the job. | I'm surprised at how much it costs. | Judy seemed surprised by his answer.* ✗ DON'T SAY "surprised for." ✗

**sur·pris·ing** /sɚ'praɪzɪŋ, sə-/ *adj* unusual or unexpected: *surprising news | It's hardly/ scarcely surprising that they lost the game.* −**surprisingly** *adv*: *The test was surprisingly easy.*

**sur·real** /sə'ril/ *adj* very strange, like something from a dream: *a surreal movie*

**sur·re·al·is·tic** /sə,riə'lɪstɪk/ *adj* using qualities, images etc. that are SURREAL: *a surrealistic painter*

**sur·ren·der** /sə'rɛndɚ/ *v* **1** [I] to say officially that you want to stop fighting because you know that you cannot win: *The hijackers were given one hour to surrender.* **2** [T] FORMAL to give up something such as a ticket or PASSPORT to an official **3** [T] FORMAL to give up something that is important or necessary, often because you feel forced to: *She agreed to surrender her baby for adoption.* −**surrender** *n* [U]

**sur·rep·ti·tious·ly** /,sɚəp'tɪʃəsli, ,sʌrəp-/ *adv* done secretly or quietly so that other people do not notice −**surreptitious** *adj*

**sur·ro·gate** /'sɚəgɪt, 'sʌrə-/ *adj* taking the place of someone or something else: *The organization acts as a surrogate family for runaways.* −**surrogate** *n*

**surrogate moth·er** /,... '../ *n* a woman who has a baby for another woman who cannot have children

**sur·round** /sə'raund/ *v* [T] **1** to be all around someone or something: *a lake surrounded by trees* **2** to be closely related to a situation or event: *Secrecy surrounded the President's visit to Geneva.* −**surrounding** *adj*: *the surrounding countryside*

**sur·round·ings** /sə'raundɪŋz/ *n* [plural] all the things that are around you, and where they are: *It took me a few weeks to get used to my new surroundings.*

**sur·veil·lance** /sɚˈveɪləns/ n [U] the act of carefully watching a particular person or place that might be related to a crime: *Police have the suspect **under surveillance**.*

**sur·vey**[1] /ˈsɚveɪ/ n **1** a set of questions that you ask a large number of people, in order to find out about their opinions and behavior: *We're **taking a survey** of people's eating habits.* **2** a careful examination of an area, used for making a map of that area

**sur·vey**[2] /sɚˈveɪ/ v [T] **1** to ask a large number of people a set of questions in order to find out about their opinions or behavior: *More than 50% of the students surveyed said they exercise regularly.* **2** to look at someone or something carefully so that you can make a decision, or find out more information: *Kramer surveyed the damage to his car.* **3** to examine and measure an area of land in order to make a map

**sur·vey·or** /sɚˈveɪɚ/ n someone whose job is to measure and record the details of an area of land

**sur·viv·al** /sɚˈvaɪvəl/ n [U] the state of continuing to live or exist, especially after a difficult or dangerous situation: *Doctors say the operation will increase his **chances of survival**.*

**sur·vive** /sɚˈvaɪv/ v [I,T] **1** to continue to live after an accident, illness, etc.: *Only one person survived the crash.* **2** to continue to exist or be involved in an activity in spite of difficulties: *Few small businesses survived the recession.* | *The surviving teams will play each other on Sunday.*

**sur·vi·vor** /sɚˈvaɪvɚ/ n **1** someone who continues to live after an accident, illness etc: *Two of the survivors were hospitalized.* **2** someone who continues trying and is unwilling to lose hope in spite of difficulties

**sus·cep·ti·ble** /səˈsɛptəbəl/ adj **1** likely to be affected by a particular illness or problem: *I've always been very **susceptible to** colds.* **2** easily influenced or affected by something: *Children are particularly **susceptible to** horror movies.*

**sus·pect**[1] /ˈsʌspɛkt/ n someone who may be guilty of a crime: *the police's main suspect*

**sus·pect**[2] /səˈspɛkt/ v [T] **1** to think that someone may be guilty of a crime: *a woman who is **suspected of** murder* **2** to think that something is likely, especially something bad: *She **suspected (that)** Sandra had been lying.* **3** to doubt that someone or something is completely honest, sincere, or real: *Do you have reason to suspect his motives?*

**sus·pect**[3] /ˈsʌspɛkt/ adj difficult to believe or trust: *Her explanation seems suspect.*

**sus·pend** /səˈspɛnd/ v [T] **1** to officially stop something from continuing, usually for a short time: *The bus service has been suspended until further notice.* **2** to officially stop some-

one from working, driving, or going to school for a fixed period, because s/he has broken the rules: *Joey was **suspended from** school.* | *Drunk drivers will **have their licenses suspended**.* **3** to hang something from something else: *a chandelier suspended from the ceiling*

**sus·pend·ers** /səˈspɛndɚz/ n [plural] two bands of cloth that go over your shoulders and are attached to your pants to hold them up

**sus·pense** /səˈspɛns/ n [U] a feeling of not knowing what is going to happen next: *Don't **keep** us **in suspense**. What happened?*

**sus·pen·sion** /səˈspɛnʃən/ n **1** [U] the act of officially stopping something from continuing for a period of time: *Bad weather led to the suspension of the game.* **2** an act of removing someone from a school or job for a short time, in order to punish him/her: *a three-day suspension for cheating* **3** [U] equipment attached to the wheels of a vehicle to make it BOUNCE less

**sus·pi·cion** /səˈspɪʃən/ n **1** [C,U] a feeling or belief that something is probably true: *Potter was arrested **on suspicion of** robbery.* | *I'm not sure who erased the file, but **I have my suspicions**.* **2** [U] lack of trust: *She always treated us **with suspicion**.*

**sus·pi·cious** /səˈspɪʃəs/ adj **1** not willing to trust someone or something: *I'm **suspicious of** her intentions.* **2** making you think that something bad or illegal is happening: *Passengers should report any bags that look suspicious.* —**suspiciously** adj: *It looks suspiciously like someone has tampered with the lock.*

**sus·tain** /səˈsteɪn/ v [T] **1** to make it possible for someone or something to continue to exist over a period of time: *The nation's economy was largely sustained by foreign aid.* **2 sustain injuries/damages/losses** FORMAL to be injured or damaged, or to lose a lot of money or soldiers: *Three firefighters sustained minor injuries from the blaze.*

**sus·tained** /səˈsteɪnd/ adj continuing for a long time: *A sustained effort is needed to fight drug abuse.*

**svelte** /svɛlt/ adj thin and graceful: *a svelte young woman*

**SW** the written abbreviation of southwest

**swab** /swɑb/ n a small stick with a piece of material on the end, used for cleaning wounds or putting on medicine: *a cotton swab* —**swab** v [T]

**swag·ger** /ˈswægɚ/ v [I] to walk proudly, swinging your shoulders in a way that seems too confident —**swagger** n [singular, U]: *an arrogant swagger*

**swal·low**[1] /ˈswɑloʊ/ v **1** [T] to make food or drink go down your throat **2** [I] to make this type of a movement, especially because you are nervous: *He swallowed anxiously before answering.* **3** [T] INFORMAL to believe a story or explanation that is not actually true: *You didn't*

*swallow that story about Harry, did you?*
**4 swallow your pride** to do something that seems necessary even though you feel embarrassed or ashamed

**swallow** sb/sth ↔ **up** *phr v* [T] to make someone or something disappear by surrounding or taking control of him, her, or it: *Most of the forest was swallowed up by the growing city.*

**swallow**² *n* **1** an act of making food or drink go down your throat: *Mike drank his beer in one swallow.* **2** a common small bird with pointed wings and a tail with two points

**swam** /swæm/ *v* the past tense of SWIM

**swamp**¹ /swamp, swɔmp/ *n* [C,U] land that is always very wet and sometimes covered with water

**swamp**² *v* [T] **1** INFORMAL to suddenly give someone more work, problems etc. than s/he can deal with: *We've been swamped with job applications.* **2** to suddenly cover something with a lot of water so that it causes damage

**swan** /swɑn/ *n* a large white bird with a long neck, that lives near lakes and rivers

**swank** /swæŋk/, **swank·y** /'swæŋki/ *adj* INFORMAL very fashionable or expensive: *a swank New York hotel*

**swap** /swɑp/ *v* **-pped, -pping** [I,T] to exchange something you have for something that someone else has: *Can I swap seats with you?* **–swap** *n*

**swarm**¹ /swɔrm/ *v* [I] to move in a large uncontrolled crowd: *Tourists swarmed around the museum.*
**swarm with** sth *phr v* [T] to be full of a moving crowd of people, birds, or insects: *The beaches were swarming with people all summer long.*

**swarm**² *n* a large group of insects that move together: *a swarm of bees*

**swarth·y** /'swɔrði, -θi/ *adj* DISAPPROVING having dark skin

**swat** /swɑt/ *v* **-tted, -tting** [T] to hit something with a swinging movement of your hand: *trying to swat a fly* **–swat** *n*

**swatch** /swɑtʃ/ *n* a small piece of cloth that is used as a SAMPLE to show what a material is like

**swath** /swɑθ, swɔθ/ *n* a long area that is different from the areas on either side of it: *The hurricane cut a wide swath through South Carolina.*

**sway**¹ /sweɪ/ *v* **1** [I,T] to move slowly from one side to another: *palm trees swaying in the breeze* **2** [T] to try to influence someone to make a particular decision: *Nothing you say will sway her.*

**sway**² *n* [singular, U] **1** a swinging movement from one side to another: *the sway of her hips* **2** LITERARY the power to rule or influence people

**swear** /swɛr/ *v* **swore, sworn, swearing 1** [I] to use offensive language: *Don't swear in front of the children.* **2** [I,T] to make a very serious promise or threat: *Do you swear to tell the truth?* | *I swear I'll kill him!* **3** [T] SPOKEN used in order to emphasize that something is true: *I swear (to God) that's the ugliest dog I've ever seen!* | *I could've sworn* (=I was certain) *I put the receipt in my pocket.* –see also **swear/dirty/cuss word** (WORD¹)

**swear by** sth *phr v* [T] to strongly believe that something is effective: *Heidi swears by vitamin C for preventing colds.*

**swear** sb ↔ **in** *phr v* [T] **1** to make someone publicly promise to be loyal to a country or an important job: *The new governor was sworn in today.* **2** to make someone give an official promise in a court of law: *The bailiff was swearing in the jury.*

**swear off** sth *phr v* [T] to decide to stop doing something that is bad for you: *I'm swearing off alcohol after last night!*

**sweat**¹ /swɛt/ *v* **1** [I] to have liquid coming out through your skin, especially when you are hot or nervous: *Lynn was sweating after the long climb.* **2** [I] INFORMAL to work hard: *I spent all night sweating over my term paper.* **3 don't sweat it** SPOKEN used in order to tell someone not to worry about something: *Mom, don't sweat it. I'll eat later.*

**sweat** sth ↔ **out** *phr v* [T] to continue doing something until it is finished, even though it is difficult: *Just sweat it out until the end of the month.*

**sweat**² *n* **1** [U] liquid that comes out through your skin, especially when you are hot or nervous; PERSPIRATION: *By noon, Ian was dripping with sweat.* **2** [singular] a condition in which you are SWEATing: *Steve broke into a sweat* (=started to sweat) *as soon as he went on stage.* **3 no sweat** SPOKEN used in order to say that you can do something easily: *"Can you give Kara a ride home?" "Yeah, no sweat!"*

**sweat·er** /'swɛtɚ/ *n* a piece of warm KNITted clothing for the top half of your body –see picture at CLOTHES

**sweats** /swɛts/ *n* [plural] INFORMAL **1** a set of clothes made of thick soft cotton, usually worn for playing sports **2** pants of this type –see picture at CLOTHES

**sweat·shirt** /'swɛt-ʃɚt/ *n* a thick soft cotton shirt, usually worn for playing sports –see picture at CLOTHES

**sweat·shop** /'swɛt-ʃɑp/ *n* a factory where people work hard in bad conditions for very little money

**sweat·y** /'swɛti/ *adj* covered with SWEAT, or smelling of sweat: *I've just been working out, so I'm all sweaty.*

**sweep**¹ /swip/ *v* **swept, swept, sweeping 1** [T] also **sweep up** to clean the dirt from the floor or ground using a BROOM **2** [I] to move quickly or with a lot of force: *Ms. Ellis swept into the meeting demanding an explanation.* **3 sweep the country/nation** to quickly affect or become popular with most of the people in a country: *a fashion trend that is sweeping the nation*

**sweep** sth ↔ **away** *phr v* [T] to completely destroy something or make something disappear: *Entire houses were swept away by the floods.*

**sweep²** *n* **1** a long swinging movement of your arm, a weapon etc. **2** a long curved line or area of land: *the sweep of the bay* **3** [C usually singular] a search or attack that moves through a particular area: *Soldiers made a sweep of the village.*

**sweep·ing** /'swipɪŋ/ *adj* **1** affecting many things, or affecting one thing very much: *sweeping changes* **2 sweeping statement/generalization** a statement that is unfair because it is too general and includes people or things that should not be included

**sweep·stakes** /'swipsteɪks/ *n* a type of BETting in which the winner gets all the money risked by everyone else

**sweet** /swit/ *adj* **1** having a taste like sugar: *Is your lemonade too sweet?* | *a sweet apple* **2** having a pleasant smell or sound: *a sweet-smelling rose* | *the sweet sounds of the cello* **3** kind, gentle, and friendly: *a sweet smile* | *a sweet little boy* **4 have a sweet tooth** to like to eat sweet foods **5** making you feel pleased and satisfied: *Revenge is sweet!* —**sweetly** *adv* —**sweetness** *n* [U]

**sweet·en** /'switʌn/ *v* **1** [I,T] to become or make something sweeter: *Sweeten the mixture with honey.* **2 sweeten the deal/pot/offer etc.** to make a deal seem more acceptable, usually by offering more money: *They sweetened the deal with a 10% discount.*

**sweet·en·er** /'switʌn-ɚ, -nɚ/ *n* **1** [C,U] a substance used instead of sugar to make food or drinks taste sweeter **2** INFORMAL something that you give to someone to persuade him/her to do something: *Car dealers are offering sweeteners like 15% financing.*

**sweet·heart** /'swithɑrt/ *n* **1** someone that you love, or a way of talking to him/her: *Good night, sweetheart.* **2** ⇨ SWEETIE

**sweet·ie** /'switi/ *n* SPOKEN **1** used in order to speak to someone that you love, especially a child: *Do you want some ice cream, sweetie?* **2** someone who is kind and generous: *Pat's such a sweetie!*

**sweet po·ta·to** /'. .,../ *n* a root that looks like an orange potato, cooked and eaten as a vegetable

**sweets** /swits/ *n* [plural] INFORMAL sweet food or candy

**swell¹** /swɛl/ *v* **swelled, swollen, swelling** **1** [I] also **swell up** to gradually increase in size, especially because of an injury: *My ankle swelled up like a balloon.* **2** [I,T] to gradually increase in amount or number: *The city's popu-*

*lation has swollen to 2 million.* **3 swell with pride/anger etc.** to feel very proud, angry etc.

**swell²** *n* a long smooth wave in the ocean

**swell³** *adj* OLD-FASHIONED very good: *I had a really swell time.*

**swell·ing** /'swɛlɪŋ/ *n* [C,U] an area on your body that becomes larger than usual because of injury or sickness: *the pain and swelling in her knee*

**swel·ter·ing** /'swɛltərɪŋ/ *adj* unpleasantly hot: *a sweltering summer day* —see usage note at TEMPERATURE

**swept** /swɛpt/ *v* the past tense and PAST PARTICIPLE of SWEEP

**swerve** /swɚv/ *v* [I] to turn suddenly and dangerously while driving or flying: *Mark swerved to avoid hitting a deer.*

**swift** /swɪft/ *adj* happening or moving very quickly: *a swift response* | *a swift river* —**swiftly** *adv*

**swig** /swɪg/ *v* **-gged, -gging** [T] INFORMAL to drink something quickly and in large amounts —**swig** *n*: *Zach took a swig of Coke.*

**swill¹** /swɪl/ *n* [U] food for pigs; SLOP

**swill²** *v* [T] to drink something in large amounts: *swilling beer all day*

**swim¹** /swɪm/ *v* **swam, swum, swimming** **1** [I] to move through the water by using your arms, legs etc.: *Can Lucy swim?* | *fish swimming up the stream* **2** [T] to cross a pool, lake etc. or go a particular distance by swimming: *He swims 20 laps a day.* **3** [I] if your head swims, you feel confused or DIZZY **4** [I] if something you are looking at swims, it seems to move around, usually because you are sick **5 be swimming in/with sth** to be covered or surrounded by liquid: *meatballs swimming in sauce* —**swimming** *n* [U]: *Do you want to go swimming?*

**swim²** *n* a period when you swim: *Would you like to go for a swim after work?*

**swimming pool** /'.. ,./ *n* ⇨ POOL¹

**swim·suit** /'swɪmsut/ *n* ⇨ BATHING SUIT

**swin·dle¹** /'swɪndl/ *v* [T] to get money from someone by tricking him/her —**swindler** *n*

**swindle²** *n* a situation in which someone gets money from someone else by tricking him/her

**swine** /swaɪn/ *n, plural* **swine** OLD-FASHIONED **1** a pig **2** INFORMAL someone who is rude or morally bad

**swing¹** /swɪŋ/ *v* **swung, swung, swinging** [I,T] **1** to move backward and forward while hanging from a particular point, or to make something move in this way: *They walked hand in hand, swinging their arms.* | *a sign swinging in the wind* **2** to move smoothly in a curved direction, or to make something move this way: *The screen door kept swinging open/shut.*

**swing around** *phr v* [I,T] to turn around

quickly, or to make something do this: *Mitch swung around to face her.*

**swing at** sb/sth *phr v* [T] to try to hit someone or something with your hand or with an object that you are holding: *He swung at the ball and missed.*

**swing by** *phr v* [I,T] INFORMAL to quickly visit a person or place before going somewhere else: *Can we swing by the store on the way home?*

**swing**² *n* **1** a seat hanging from ropes or chains, on which children swing: *a bunch of kids playing on the swings* **2** an attempt to hit someone or something by swinging your arm, an object etc.: *Then he tried to take a swing at me.* **3** a change from one feeling, opinion etc. to another: *a big swing in public opinion* **4 be in full swing** if a party, event etc. is in full swing, it is at its highest level of activity

**swing·ing** /ˈswɪŋɪŋ/ *adj* HUMOROUS exciting, fun, and enjoyable: *a swinging party*

**swipe**¹ /swaɪp/ *v* **1** [I,T] also **swipe at** to hit or try to hit someone or something by swinging your arm very quickly **2** [T] INFORMAL to steal something: *Somebody swiped my wallet.*

**swipe**² *n* the act of hitting someone or something by swinging your arm very quickly: *Shelly took a swipe at her brother.*

**swirl**¹ /swɚl/ *v* [I,T] to turn around and around, or to make something do this: *Swirl the wine around in the glass like this.*

**swirl**² *n* a SWIRLing movement or pattern: *decorative swirls in the cake frosting*

**swish** /swɪʃ/ *v* [I,T] to move quickly through the air with a soft sound like a whistle, or to make something do this: *a cow swishing its tail* –**swish** *n* [singular]

**Swiss**¹ /swɪs/ *adj* relating to or coming from Switzerland

**Swiss**² *n* **the Swiss** [plural] the people of Switzerland, considered as a single group

---

**switch**

switch on                                switch off

**switch**¹ /swɪtʃ/ *v* **1** [I,T] to change from doing or using one thing to doing or using something else: *He studied biology before switching (over) to law.* | *Here, switch hands and see if that works better.* **2** [T] to replace someone or something with a different person or object: *We must have accidentally switched umbrellas.*

**switch off** *phr v* **1** [I,T **switch** sth ↔ **off**] to turn off a machine, radio, light etc. by using a SWITCH: *Be sure to switch off the lights when you leave.* **2** [I] INFORMAL to stop listening or paying attention to someone: *He just switches off when he's tired.*

**switch on** *phr v* [I,T **switch** sth ↔ **on**] to turn on a machine, radio, light etc. by using a SWITCH

**switch**² *n* **1** the part that you move up or down on a machine, radio, light etc. so that it starts or stops operating: *Where's the on/off switch?* | *a light switch* **2** a change: *Tom's glad he made the switch from his old job.* **3** a thin stick that bends easily

**switch·board** /ˈswɪtʃbɔrd/ *n* a piece of equipment that directs all the telephone calls made to or from a particular business, hotel etc.

**swiv·el** /ˈswɪvəl/, **swivel around** *v* [I,T] to turn around while remaining in the same place, or to make something do this: *She wants a chair that swivels.*

**swol·len**¹ /ˈswoʊlən/ *v* the PAST PARTICIPLE of SWELL

**swollen**² *adj* **1** a part of your body that is swollen is bigger than usual because of injury or sickness **2** a swollen river has more water in it than usual

**swoon** /swun/ *v* [I] OLD-FASHIONED to feel so much emotion that you almost FAINT (=lose consciousness)

**swoop** /swup/ *v* [I] to suddenly and quickly move downwards through the air, especially to attack something: *An owl swooped down and grabbed a mouse.* –**swoop** *n*

**sword** /sɔrd/ *n* a weapon with a long sharp blade and a handle

**sword·fish** /ˈsɔrdˌfɪʃ/ *n* a large fish with a long pointed upper jaw shaped like a sword

**swore** /swɔr/ *v* the past tense of SWEAR

**sworn**¹ /swɔrn/ *v* the PAST PARTICIPLE of SWEAR

**sworn**² *adj* **1 sworn statement/testimony** something you say or write that you have officially promised is the truth **2 sworn enemies** two people or groups who will always hate each other

**swum** /swʌm/ *v* the PAST PARTICIPLE of SWIM

**swung** /swʌŋ/ *v* the past tense and PAST PARTICIPLE of SWING

**syc·a·more** /ˈsɪkəˌmɔr/ *n* [C,U] an eastern North American tree with broad leaves, or the wood from this tree

**syc·o·phant** /ˈsɪkəfənt/ *n* FORMAL someone who always praises someone else in order to gain an advantage

**syl·la·ble** /ˈsɪləbəl/ *n* TECHNICAL each part of a word that contains a single vowel sound

**syl·la·bus** /ˈsɪləbəs/ *n, plural* **syllabuses** *or* **syllabi** /-baɪ/ a plan that shows a student what s/he will be studying in a particular subject

**sym·bol** /ˈsɪmbəl/ *n* **1** a picture, person, object etc. that represents a particular quality, idea, organization etc.: *the five-ring* **symbol** *of the Olympic Games* | *De Gaulle became a* **symbol of** *French pride and patriotism.* —see also SEX SYMBOL **2** a letter, number, or sign that represents a sound, amount, chemical substance etc.: *What's the chemical* **symbol** *for iron?*

**sym·bol·ic** /sɪm'bɑlɪk/ *adj* representing a particular event, process, situation etc.: *a red rose,* **symbolic** *of love* —**symbolically** *adv*

**sym·bol·ism** /'sɪmbə,lɪzəm/ *n* [U] the use of SYMBOLS to represent things: *There's a lot of religious symbolism in his paintings.*

**sym·bol·ize** /'sɪmbə,laɪz/ *v* [T] **1** to be a SYMBOL of something: *A wedding ring symbolizes a couple's vows to each other.* **2** to represent something by using a SYMBOL: *Death is often* **symbolized by** *the color black.*

**sym·met·ri·cal** /sə'mɛtrɪkəl/, **sym·met·ric** /sə'mɛtrɪk/ *adj* having two halves that are exactly the same size and shape —opposite ASYMMETRICAL

**sym·me·try** /'sɪmətri/ *n* [U] exact likeness in size and shape between two halves or sides of something

**sym·pa·thet·ic** /,sɪmpə'θɛtɪk/ *adj* **1** showing that you understand how sad, hurt, lonely etc. someone feels: *a sympathetic nurse* **2** willing to support someone's plans, actions, ideas etc.: *He's fairly* **sympathetic to** *the staff's concerns.* —**sympathetically** *adv* —opposite UNSYMPATHETIC

**sym·pa·thize** /'sɪmpə,θaɪz/ *v* [I] **1** to understand how sad, hurt, lonely etc. someone feels: *I* **sympathize with** *those people who lost their jobs.* **2** to support a country, plan, action etc.: *Very few people* **sympathize with** *his views on racial separation.*

**sym·pa·thy** /'sɪmpəθi/ *n* [C,U] **1** a feeling of support for someone who is sad, hurt, lonely etc.: *I* **have no sympathy for** *people like her.* | *I'm sorry to hear Bill died; you* **have my sympathies.** **2** support for someone's plan, actions, ideas etc.: *Students marched* **in sympathy with** *the strikers.* (=to show support for them)

---

---

**sym·pho·ny** /'sɪmfəni/ *n* a long piece of music written for an ORCHESTRA

**symp·tom** /'sɪmptəm/ *n* **1** a physical condition that shows you may have a particular disease: *medicine that helps relieve your cold symptoms* **2** a sign that a serious problem exists: *Rising crime rates are another* **symptom** *of a society in trouble.* —**symptomatic** /,sɪmptə'mætɪk/ *adj*

**syn·a·gogue** /'sɪnə,gɑg/ *n* a building where Jewish people go to have religious services

**sync** /sɪŋk/ *n* INFORMAL **in sync/out of sync a)** happening or moving at the same time or rate, or not doing this: *Unfortunately, the band wasn't* **in sync with** *the drummer.* **b)** doing or saying things that are suitable or not suitable for a situation: *His message was* **out of sync with** *the mood of the country.*

**syn·chro·nize** /'sɪŋkrə,naɪz/ *v* **1** [T] to make two or more things happen or move at the same time or rate: *The attack was synchronized with a bombing in Washington.* **2** to make two or more watches or clocks show exactly the same time —**synchronization** /,sɪŋkrənə'zeɪʃən/ *n* [U]

**syn·di·cate** /'sɪndəkɪt/ *n* [C,U] **1** a group of people, companies etc. that join together to achieve a particular aim: *the city's largest crime syndicate* **2** an organization that sells someone's articles, photographs, television shows etc. to several different newspapers or broadcasting companies

**syn·di·cat·ed** /'sɪndə,keɪtɪd/ *adj* a syndicated newspaper COLUMN, television program etc. is bought and used by several different newspapers or broadcasting companies —**syndication** *n* /,sɪndə'keɪʃən/ [U]

**syn·drome** /'sɪndroʊm/ *n* TECHNICAL a set of physical or mental conditions that show you have a particular disease

**syn·od** /'sɪnəd/ *n* an important meeting of church members to make decisions concerning the church

**syn·o·nym** /'sɪnə,nɪm/ *n* TECHNICAL a word with the same meaning or almost the same meaning as another word. For example, "mad" and "angry" are synonyms —opposite ANTONYM

**syn·on·y·mous** /sɪ'nɑnəməs/ *adj* **1** having a strong association with another quality, idea, situation etc.: *He thinks that being poor is* **synonymous with** *being a criminal.* **2** having the same or nearly the same meaning

**syn·op·sis** /sɪ'nɑpsɪs/ *n, plural* **synopses** /-siz/ a short description of the main parts of a story

**syn·tax** /'sɪntæks/ *n* [U] TECHNICAL the way words are arranged in order to form sentences or phrases

**syn·the·sis** /'sɪnθəsɪs/ *n* [C,U] the act of combining several things into a single complete unit, or the combination that is produced: *the study of protein synthesis* | *a* **synthesis of** *reports from Canada and Sweden*

**syn·the·size** /'sɪnθə,saɪz/ *v* [T] to combine several ideas, styles, methods, substances etc. in order to produce something: *Scientists can now synthesize the drug.*

**syn·the·siz·er** /'sɪnθəˌsaɪzɚ/ *n* an electronic musical instrument that can sound like various different musical instruments

**syn·thet·ic** /sɪn'θɛtɪk/ *adj* **1** made by combining several different substances: *synthetic fabrics like acrylic and polyester* **2** not natural; artificial —**synthetically** *adv*

**syph·i·lis** /'sɪfəlɪs/ *n* [U] a very serious disease that is passed from one person to another during sex

**sy·ringe** /sə'rɪndʒ/ *n* a hollow tube and needle used for removing blood or other liquids from your body, or putting drugs etc. into it

**syr·up** /'sɚəp, 'sɪrəp/ *n* [U] thick sticky liquid made from sugar —**syrupy** *adj* —see picture at MEDICINE

**sys·tem** /'sɪstəm/ *n* **1** a set of related or connected things that work together as a single unit: *Oregon's school system | the public transportation system | a car alarm system | the company's computer system* **2** an organized set of rules, methods, or plans used by a particular group or for a particular purpose: *a system for electing city officials | the nation's legal system* **3** a set of parts in your body, such as bones or particular organs, considered as a single unit: *the digestive system* **4 the system** INFORMAL the rules, TRADITIONs, government, institutions etc. in a society that seem to control how you live: *Believe me, you can't beat the system!* (=do things in a different way than the system says) **5 get sth out of your system** INFORMAL to do something that helps you stop feeling angry, annoyed, or upset

**sys·tem·at·ic** /ˌsɪstə'mætɪk/ *adj* as part of an organized plan or process; THOROUGH: *a systematic search* —**systematically** *adv*

# T

**T, t** /ti/ **1** the twentieth letter of the English alphabet **2 to a T/to a tee** INFORMAL exactly or perfectly: *a dress that fit her to a T*

**tab** /tæb/ *n* **1** the amount you owe for a restaurant meal or a service that many people use: *Our lunch tab came to $53. | The city is picking up the tab for street repairs.* (=is paying for them) **2 keep tabs on sb/sth** INFORMAL to carefully watch what someone or something is doing: *The police are keeping close tabs on her.* **3** a small piece of metal, plastic, or paper that you pull to open a container **4** a small piece of paper on plastic you attach to a page, FILE etc. in order to find it easily

**tab·by** /'tæbi/ *n* a cat with orange, gray, or brown marks on its fur

**tab·er·na·cle** /'tæbɚˌnækəl/ *n* a church or other building used by some religious groups

**ta·ble**[1] /'teɪbəl/ *n* **1** a piece of furniture with a flat top supported by legs: *the kitchen table* **2** a list of numbers, facts, or information arranged in rows across and down a page: *Check the book's table of contents. | learning your multiplication tables* **3 set the table** to put knives, forks, dishes etc. on a table before a meal **4 clear the table** to take all the empty dishes off a table after a meal **5 turn the tables on sb** to change a situation completely so that someone loses an advantage and you gain one **6 at the table** when sitting at a table having a meal: *It's not polite to blow your nose at the table.* **7 under the table** INFORMAL done secretly and usually illegally: *Payments were made under the table to avoid taxes.* **8** the group of people sitting around a table: *The whole table got up and left.*

**table**[2] *v* [T] **table a bill/proposal/offer etc.** to decide to deal with an offer, idea etc. later

**ta·ble·cloth** /'teɪbəlˌklɔθ/ *n* a cloth used for covering a table

**ta·ble·spoon** /'teɪbəlˌspun/ *n* **1** a special large spoon used for measuring food **2** a large spoon used for eating food **3** also **tablespoonful** the amount this spoon holds

**tab·let** /'tæblɪt/ *n* **1** a small round piece of medicine; PILL: *vitamin C tablets* **2** a set of pieces of paper for writing on that are glued together at the top **3** a flat piece of hard clay or stone that has words cut into it

**table ten·nis** /'.. ˌ../ *n* [U] ⇨ PING-PONG

**tab·loid** /'tæblɔɪd/ *n* a newspaper that has small pages, a lot of photographs, short stories, and not much serious news

**ta·boo** /tə'bu, tæ-/ *n* [C,U] something you must avoid doing or saying because society thinks it is offensive, embarrassing, or wrong —**taboo** *adj*: *a taboo subject*

**tab·u·late** /'tæbyəˌleɪt/ *v* [T] to arrange facts, numbers, or information together in lists, rows etc. —**tabulation** /ˌtæbyə'leɪʃən/ *n* [U]

**tac·it** /'tæsɪt/ *adj* tacit agreement, approval, or support is given without being spoken or officially agreed —**tacitly** *adv*

**tac·i·turn** /'tæsəˌtɚn/ *adj* not usually talking a lot, so that you seem unfriendly

**tack**[1] /tæk/, **tack up** *v* [T] to attach a notice on a wall, board etc. using a THUMBTACK

**tack sth** ↔ **on** *phr v* [T] INFORMAL to add something to something that already exists or is complete: *Joan tacked a few words on the end of my letter.*

**tack**[2] *n* **1 a different/new/similar etc. tack** to do something that is different, new, or similar to what someone else does: *If polite requests don't work, you'll have to try a different tack.*

**2** ⇨ THUMBTACK **3** a small nail with a sharp point and a flat top: *carpet tacks*

**tack·le¹** /'tækəl/ *v* [T] **1** to make a determined effort to deal with a difficult problem: *a new attempt to tackle homelessness* **2** to force someone to the ground to stop him/her from running, especially in football: *Edwards was tackled on the play.*

**tackle²** *n* **1** the act of tackling (TACKLE) someone **2** [C,U] in football, one of the players who play on the outside of the GUARDs **3** [U] the equipment used in some sports such as FISHING **4** ropes and PULLEYs (=wheels) used for moving a ship's sails, heavy weights etc.

**tack·y** /'tæki/ *adj* **1** INFORMAL not fashionable and of bad quality: *tacky furniture* **2** slightly sticky —**tackiness** *n* [U]

**ta·co** /'takoʊ/ *n* a Mexican-American food made from a fried corn TORTILLA, that is folded and filled with meat, beans etc.

**tact** /tækt/ *n* [U] the ability to say or do things carefully and politely so that you do not embarrass or upset someone

**tact·ful** /'tæktfəl/ *adj* careful not to say or do something that will upset or embarrass someone else: *a tactful response* —**tactfully** *adv*

**tac·tic** /'tæktɪk/ *n* [C usually plural] **1** a skillfully planned action used for achieving something: *the aggressive tactics of the salesman* **2** the way the military uses its armies, weapons etc. in order to win a battle

**tac·ti·cal** /'tæktɪkəl/ *adj* **1** tactical weapon/missile/aircraft etc. a weapon etc. that is used over a short distance **2** done in order to help you achieve what you want: *a tactical move to avoid criticism* —**tactically** *adv*

**tad** /tæd/ *n* SPOKEN a tad a small amount: *Could you turn up the sound just a tad?*

**tad·pole** /'tædpoʊl/ *n* a small creature with a long tail that lives in water and becomes a FROG or TOAD

**taf·fy** /'tæfi/ *n* [U] a soft CHEWY candy, usually made from brown sugar or MOLASSES

**tag¹** /tæg/ *n* **1** a small piece of paper, metal, or plastic that is put on something or on someone's clothes and shows information about him, her, or it: *I can't find the price tag on these jeans.* | *Where's your name tag?* **2** [U] a children's game in which one player chases and tries to touch the others

**tag²** *v* -**gged, -gging** [T] to fasten a TAG onto something: *Scientists have now tagged most of the bay's seals.*

**tag along** *phr v* [I] INFORMAL to go somewhere with someone, especially when s/he does not want you to: *My little brother always tagged along with us.*

**tail¹** /teɪl/ *n* **1** the movable part at the back of an animal's body: *a dog wagging its tail* **2** the back part of an aircraft —see picture at AIRPLANE **3** the end or back part of something,

especially something long and thin: *the tail of a comet* **4** the tail end of sth the last part of an event, situation, or period of time: *the tail end of the century* **5** INFORMAL someone whose job is to secretly watch and follow someone such as a criminal —see also TAILS

**tail²** *v* [T] INFORMAL to secretly watch and follow someone such as a criminal

**tail off** *phr v* [I] to gradually become quieter, smaller, weaker etc.: *His voice tailed off as he saw his father approaching.*

**tail·coat** /'teɪlkoʊt/ *n* ⇨ TAILS

**tail·gate¹** /'teɪlgeɪt/ *v* [I,T] to drive too closely behind another vehicle

**tailgate²** *n* a door at the back of a vehicle, especially a PICKUP, that opens down

**tail·light** /'teɪl-laɪt/ *n* one of the two red lights at the back of a vehicle —see picture on page 469

**tai·lor¹** /'teɪlɚ/ *n* someone whose job is to make clothes, especially men's clothes, that are measured to fit each customer perfectly

**tailor²** *v* [T] **tailor sth to/for sb** to make something be exactly what someone wants or needs: *a special music class tailored to young children*

**tai·lor·ing** /'teɪlərɪŋ/ *n* [U] the way that clothes are made, or the job of making them

**tailor-made** /ˌ.. '.ɪ / *adj* **1** exactly right for only one particular person, place, situation, purpose etc.: *The job seems tailor-made for him.* **2** made by a TAILOR: *a tailor-made suit*

**tail·pipe** /'teɪlpaɪp/ *n* ⇨ EXHAUST²

**tails** /teɪlz/ *n* **1** [plural] a man's suit coat with two long parts that hang down the back, worn to formal events **2** the side of a coin that does not have a picture of someone's head on it —opposite HEADS

**tail·spin** /'teɪlspɪn/ *n* **1** go into a tailspin to begin to have great problems you cannot control: *government programs that sent the economy into a tailspin* **2** an uncontrolled fall of a plane through the air, in which the back spins in a wider circle than the front

**taint** /teɪnt/ *v* [T] **1** to make someone or something seem less honest, respectable, or good: *Her reputation was tainted by the murder trial.* **2** to ruin something by adding an unwanted substance to it: *All the blood supplies were tainted with bacteria.* —**taint** *n*

**taint·ed** /'teɪntɪd/ *adj* **1** food or drink that is tainted is not safe to eat because it is spoiled or contains poison **2** affected or influenced by something illegal, dishonest, or morally wrong: *tainted witnesses*

**Tai·wan·ese** /ˌtaɪwɑˈnizɪ / *adj* relating to or coming from Taiwan

**take¹** /teɪk/ *v* **took, taken, taking** [T]

**1** ▶MOVE◄ to move someone or something from one place to another: *I was going to take some work home.* | *Take a piece of cake for your* *husband.* | *Merritt was taken by ambulance to the nearest hospital.*

---

**take after**

He takes after his father.

**2** ▶DO STH◀ used with a noun to show that something is being done: *Here, take a look.* | *Let me just take a quick shower first.* | *The new rules* **take effect** *October 1.*

**3** **take a picture/photograph/video etc.** to photograph, VIDEOTAPE etc. something: *Here's a picture of me that was taken at camp.* | *They took an X-ray of her leg.*

**4** ▶NEED STH◀ to need something in order to do something or for something to happen: *It takes about three days to drive up there.* | *It'll take a lot of planning, but I think it can be done.* | *What kind of gas does your car take?*

**5** ▶ACCEPT◀ to accept or receive something: *Are you going to take the job?* | *Do you take Visa?* | *Take my advice and go see a doctor.* | *Why should I take the blame?*

**6** ▶STUDY◀ to study a particular subject: *We had to take three years of English.* | *She wants to take ballet.*

**7** **take a test/exam** to write or do a test: *I'm taking my driving test next week.*

**8** ▶GET/STEAL◀ to steal something or borrow it without someone's permission: *They took all her jewelry.*

**9** ▶REMOVE◀ to remove something from a particular place: *Can you* **take** *the turkey* **out** *of the oven for me?*

**10** ▶HOLD/PUT◀ to reach for something and then hold it or put it somewhere: *Let me take your coat.*

**11** ▶GET CONTROL◀ to get possession or control of something: *Rebel forces have taken control of the airport.*

**12** ▶BEAR◀ to bear or accept something unpleasant: *Jeff can't take the stress.* | *She's taken a lot of abuse from him.* | *Losing the game by only one point was* **hard to take.** (=difficult to accept)

**13** **not take sth lying down** to refuse to accept being treated badly: *I'm not going to take this lying down! You'll be hearing from my lawyer!*

**14** ▶MEDICINE/DRUG◀ to swallow or INJECT a medicine or drug: *He doesn't smoke, drink, or take drugs.* (=illegal drugs) | *Why don't you take an aspirin or something?*

**15** ▶TRAVEL◀ to use a car, bus, train etc. to go somewhere, or to travel using a particular

road: *I'll take the subway home.* | *Take the next turn on the right.* –see usage note at TRANSPORTATION

**16** ▶UNDERSTAND/CONSIDER◀ to understand or consider something in a particular way: *He takes his job very seriously.* | *I didn't mean for you to take what I said literally.*

**17** ▶WRITE◀ also **take down** to write down information: *He's not here; can I take a message?* | *Let me take down your phone number.*

**18** ▶MEASURE/TEST◀ to test or measure something: *Sit here and we'll take your blood pressure.*

**19** ▶USE◀ a word meaning to use something, used when giving instructions: *Take some flour and add enough water to make a paste.*

**20** ▶HAVE SPACE FOR◀ to have enough space to contain a particular number of people or things: *The station wagon takes six people.*

**21** ▶FEELINGS/REACTIONS◀ to have a particular feeling or reaction when something happens: *His family* **took** *the news pretty* **hard.** (=were very upset) | *She doesn't seem to take a lot of interest in her kids.*

**22** ▶BUY◀ to decide to buy something: *He gave me a discount so I said I'd take it.*

**23** ▶SIZE◀ to wear a particular size of clothing or shoes: *Jim takes an extra large shirt.*

**24** **take it upon yourself** to decide to do something even though no one has asked you to do it: *Parents have taken it upon themselves to raise extra cash for the school.*

**25** ▶FOOD/DRINKS◀ [T] to use something such as salt, sugar, milk etc. in your food or drinks: *Do you take cream in your coffee?* –see also **take care** (CARE²) **take care of** (CARE²) **take part** (PART¹) **take place** (PLACE¹)

**take after** sb *phr v* [T] to look or behave like another member of your family: *Jenny* **takes after** *her dad.*

**take** sth ↔ **apart** *phr v* [T] to separate something into pieces: *Vic* **took apart** *the faucet and put in a new washer.*

**take away** *phr v* [T] **1** [take sth ↔ away] to remove something from someone or somewhere: *One more ticket and your license will be* **taken away.** **2** [take sb ↔ away] to bring someone to a prison or hospital from his/her home: *Hyde was* **taken away** *in handcuffs.*

**take** sth ↔ **back** *phr v* [T] **1** to return something to the store where you bought it: *You should* **take it back** *if it doesn't fit.* **2** to admit that something you said was wrong: *All right, I'm sorry, I* **take it back.**

**take** sth ↔ **down** *phr v* [T] to remove something from its place, especially by separating it into pieces: *We* **take down** *the Christmas tree on January 6.* –opposite **put up** (PUT)

**take in** *phr v* [T] **1** [take sth ↔ in] to collect or earn an amount of money: *We've* **taken in** *$100,000 so far for charity.* **2** [take sth ↔ in] to notice, understand, and remember things: *Babies **take in** an amazing amount of information.* **3** [take sth ↔ in] to bring something to a place in order to be repaired: *I need to **take** the car **in** for a tune-up.* **4** [take sb/sth ↔ in] to let someone or something stay in your house or a shelter, because she, he, or it has nowhere else to stay: *The Humane Society **took in** almost 38,000 cats and dogs last year.* **5** [take in sth] to go to see something, such as a movie, play etc.: *tourists **taking in** the sights* **6 be taken in** to be deceived by someone or something: *The bank had **been taken in** by the forged receipts.* **7** [take sth ↔ in] to make part of a piece of clothing smaller: *If we **take in** the waist, Doris's wedding dress will fit you.*

**take off** *phr v* **1** [T take sth ↔ off] to remove something: *Your name has been **taken off** the list.* | **Take** your shoes **off** in the house. **2** [I] if an aircraft or space vehicle takes off, it rises into the air **3** [I] INFORMAL to leave a place: *We packed everything in the car and **took off**.* **4** [T take sth off] also **take off work** to not go to work for a period of time: *I'm **taking** some time **off** work to go to the wedding.* **5** [I] to suddenly become successful: *Her career **took off** after she won a prize on TV's "Star Search."*

**take on** *phr v* [T] **1** [take sb ↔ on] to compete or fight against someone: *The winner of this game will **take on** Houston in the championships.* **2** [take on sth] to begin to have a different quality or appearance: *Once we had children, Christmas **took on** a different sort of importance.* **3** [take sth ↔ on] to start doing some work or to start being responsible for something: *Ethel agreed to **take on** the treasurer's position.* **4** [take sb on] to start to employ someone: *The team has **taken on** a new coach.*

**take out** *phr v* [T] **1** [take sb out] to go with someone to a restaurant, movie, party etc., and pay for his/her meal and entertainment: *We're **taking** Sabina **out** for dinner.* **2** [take sth ↔ out] to arrange to get something from a bank, court, insurance company etc.: *The couple **took out** a $220,000 mortgage.*

**take** sth ↔ **out on** sb *phr v* [T] to behave angrily toward someone because you are upset or angry about something else: *Why are you **taking** it **out on** me? It's not my fault!*

**take over** *phr v* [I,T take sth ↔ over] to get control of or become responsible for something: *Jack is supposed to **take over** for Carmen while she's on maternity leave.* | *His son will **take over** the business.*

**take to** *phr v* [T] **1** [take to sb/sth] to quickly start to like someone or something: *The two women **took to** each other right away.* **2** [take to sth] to go out and walk somewhere, for a particular reason: *Thousands of protesters **took to** the streets.* **3 take to doing sth** to begin

doing something regularly: *Sandra has taken to getting up early to go jogging.*

**take up** *phr v* [T] **1** [take up sth] to begin doing a job or activity: *I've just **taken up** tennis.* **2** [take up sth] if something takes up time or space, it fills or uses it: *The program **takes up** a lot of memory on the hard drive.* **3** [take sth ↔ up] to begin discussing or considering something: *The Senate will **take up** the bill in the next few weeks.*

**take** sb **up on** sth *phr v* [T] to accept an offer, invitation etc.: *A number of students have **taken** him **up on** his offer of extra help.*

**take up with** *phr v* [T] **1** [take sth ↔ up with sb] to discuss something with someone, especially a complaint or problem: *You should **take** it **up** with the union.* **2** [take up with sb] to begin a friendship or a romantic relationship, especially with someone you should not have a relationship with: *Nina has **taken up with** her boss.*

**take²** *n* **1** the act of filming a scene for a movie or television program: *We had to shoot five takes for the explosion scene.* **2** [singular] INFORMAL ⇨ TAKINGS

**tak·en** /'teɪkən/ *v* the PAST PARTICIPLE OF TAKE

**take-off** /'teɪk-ɔf/ *n* [C,U] **1** the time when an aircraft rises into the air **2** a funny performance that copies the style of a particular show, movie, or performer

**take-out** /'teɪk-aʊt/ *n* **1** a meal you buy from a restaurant that you eat somewhere else **2** a restaurant that sells this food —**take-out** *adj*

**take·o·ver** /'teɪkˌoʊvɚ/ *n* the act of getting control of something such as a company, country, or political group: *a military takeover*

**tak·ings** /'teɪkɪŋz/ *n* [plural] the amount of money earned by a small business or from an activity: *the day's takings*

**tal·cum pow·der** /'tælkəm ˌpaʊdɚ/ *n* [U] a fine powder that you put on your skin to keep it dry

**tale** /teɪl/ *n* a story about imaginary events: *a book of fairy tales*

**tal·ent** /'tælənt/ *n* **1** [C,U] a natural ability to do something well: *great musical talent* | *a talent for painting* —see usage note at ABILITY **2** [singular] a person or people who have talent: *She's the best legal talent in the city.* | *scouts checking out the talent* (=people who have talent)

**tal·ent·ed** /'tæləntɪd/ *adj* very good at something that not everyone can do: *a talented actor*

**tal·is·man** /'tælɪsmən, -lɪz-/ *n* an object that some people think can protect them

**talk¹** /tɔk/ *v* **1** [I] to say things to someone; speak: *Who's he **talking to** on the phone?* | *How old was your baby when she started to talk?* ✗ DON'T SAY "talk English/Chinese etc." SAY "speak English/Chinese etc." ✗ **2** [I,T] to discuss something with someone: *I'd like to **talk with** you in private.* | *Grandpa never **talks about** the war.* | *Those guys are always **talking sports**.* (=discussing them) **3 talk your way out of sth** INFORMAL to use excuses or explanations to avoid an unpleasant situation: *He always manages to talk his way out of trouble.* **4** [I] to tell someone secret information because you are forced to: *Prisoners who refused to talk were shot.*

> SPOKEN PHRASES
>
> **5 talk dirty** to swear or make sexual suggestions to someone **6 talk tough** to tell people very strongly what you want, or to threaten them **7 what are you talking about?** said when someone has just said something stupid or annoying: *Aliens? UFOs? What are you talking about?* **8 we're/you're talking** used in order to tell someone an amount: *We're talking at least ten days to fix the car.* **9 talk about funny/stupid/rich etc.** said in order to emphasize a quality that someone or something has: *Talk about smart! Kim got straight A's at Harvard.*

−see usage note at SAY
  **talk back** *phr v* [I] to rudely answer someone who is older or has more authority than you: *Don't **talk back to** your father!*
  **talk down to** sb *phr v* [T] to speak to someone as if you think you are smarter or more important than s/he is: *He always explained things but never **talked down to** me.*
  **talk** sb **into** sth *phr v* [T] to persuade someone to do something: *Maybe I can **talk** Vicky **into** driving us to the mall.*
  **talk** sb **out of** sth *phr v* [T] to persuade someone not to do something: *Brenda **talked** me **out of** quitting my job.*
  **talk** sth ↔ **over** *phr v* [T] to discuss all the details of something, usually before making a decision about it
**talk²** *n* **1** a conversation: *Steve and I **had a long talk** last night.* **2** a speech or LECTURE: *Ms. Mason will be **giving a talk** on the Civil War.* **3** [U] news that is not official or not completely true: *There was talk of the factory closing down.* **4** [U] a particular type of speech: *Carrie still uses baby talk.* **5 it's just/only talk** used in order to say that something is likely to be untrue: *Don't worry about it; it's just talk.* −see also SMALL TALK, TALKS
**talk·a·tive** /'tɔkətɪv/ *adj* liking to talk a lot
**talk·er** /'tɔkɚ/ *n* INFORMAL someone who talks a lot
**talks** /tɔks/ *n* [plural] a series of formal discussions between two governments, organizations etc.: *the latest trade talks*
**talk show** /'. ./ *n* a television or radio show in which people answer questions about themselves or discuss important subjects

**tall** /tɔl/ *adj* **1** having a greater than average height: *the tallest boy in the class* | *tall buildings* −see picture at HEIGHT **2** having a particular height: *My brother's almost 6 feet tall.* −see picture at HEIGHT **3 a tall order** INFORMAL a piece of work or a request that will be extremely difficult to do **4 a tall tale** a story you tell to make something sound more exciting, dangerous etc. than it really was
**tal·low** /'tælou/ *n* [U] hard animal fat used for making CANDLEs and soap
**tal·ly¹** /'tæli/ *n* a record of how much you have won, spent, used etc. so far: *Somebody should be **keeping a tally** of how much we owe.*
**tally²** *v* **1** [T] also **tally up** to calculate the total number of points won, things done etc.: *Can you tally up the scores?* **2** [I] if two numbers, statements, dates etc. tally, they match each other exactly: *The signatures should **tally with** the names on the list.*
**Tal·mud** /'tɑlmud, 'tælməd/ *n* **the Talmud** the collection of writings that Jewish laws are based on
**tal·on** /'tælən/ *n* one of the sharp curved nails on the feet of some birds that hunt
**tam·bou·rine** /ˌtæmbə'rin/ *n* a circular musical instrument with small pieces of metal around the edge, played by hitting or shaking it
**tame¹** /teɪm/ *adj* **1** a tame animal has been trained to live with people or work for them **2** INFORMAL not as exciting, violent, or offensive as you had expected: *"How was the movie?" "Pretty tame."*
**tame²** *v* [T] to train a wild animal so that it will not hurt people
**tam·per** /'tæmpɚ/ *v*
  **tamper with** sth *phr v* [T] to change something without permission, usually in order to damage it: *Several bottles of aspirin had been **tampered with**.*
**tam·pon** /'tæmpɑn/ *n* a tube-shaped piece of cotton that a woman puts in her VAGINA during her PERIOD
**tan¹** /tæn/ *adj* **1** having a pale yellow-brown color: *tan leather shoes* **2** having darker skin after spending a lot of time in the sun: *Your face is really tan.*
**tan²** *n* **1** the darker skin some people get when they spend a lot of time in the sun; SUNTAN: *I want to **get a tan**.* **2** [U] a pale yellow-brown color
**tan³** *v* **-nned, -nning** **1** [I] to get darker skin by spending time in the sun: *I don't tan easily.* **2** [T] to change animal skin into leather by putting a special acid on it
**tan·dem** /'tændəm/ *n* **1 in tandem** FORMAL together or at the same time: *Police are working **in tandem with** local schools to reduce car thefts.* **2** a bicycle built for two riders sitting one behind the other

**tan·gent** /ˈtændʒənt/ *n* **go off on a tangent** to suddenly start talking or thinking about a completely different subject: *It was hard to keep Maria from going off on a tangent.* —**tangential** /tænˈdʒɛnʃəl/ *adj: tangential comments*

**tan·ger·ine** /ˌtændʒəˈrin/ *n* a sweet fruit that looks like a small orange –see picture on page 470

**tan·gi·ble** /ˈtændʒəbəl/ *adj* real, definite, and able to be shown or touched: *tangible proof* –opposite INTANGIBLE

**tan·gle**¹ /ˈtæŋgəl/ *n* hair, threads, knots etc. that have become twisted together: *tangles in her hair | a tangle of branches*

**tangle**² *v* [I,T] to become twisted together, or to make the parts of something do this: *My hair tangles easily.*

**tangle with** sb *phr v* [T] INFORMAL to argue or fight with someone

**tan·gled** /ˈtæŋgəld/, **tangled up** *adj* **1** twisted together: *tangled string/hair/branches* **2** complicated and confusing: *tangled emotions*

**tan·go** /ˈtæŋgoʊ/ *n* **the tango** a slow dance from South America, or the music for this dance

**tang·y** /ˈtæŋi/ *adj* tasting or smelling both sweet and sour –**tang** *n* [singular]

**tank**¹ /tæŋk/ *n* **1** a large container for holding liquid or gas: *a fish tank | a car's* **gas tank** **2** a heavy military vehicle with a large gun and metal belts over its wheels

**tank**² *v*

**tank** sth ↔ **up** *phr v* [T] to fill a car's TANK with gas

**tan·kard** /ˈtæŋkəd/ *n* a large metal cup used for drinking beer

**tank·er** /ˈtæŋkə/ *n* a vehicle or ship used for carrying a large amount of liquid or gas: *an oil tanker*

**tan·ta·lize** /ˈtænṭlˌaɪz/ *v* [T] to make someone feel a very strong desire for something that is difficult to get

**tan·ta·liz·ing** /ˈtænṭlˌaɪzɪŋ/ *adj* making you want something very much: *tantalizing smells coming from the kitchen*

**tan·ta·mount** /ˈtænṭəˌmaʊnt/ *adj* **be tantamount to sth** to be almost the same thing as something else: *His refusal to speak was tantamount to admitting he was guilty.*

**tan·trum** /ˈtæntrəm/ *n* **have/throw a tantrum** to suddenly become very angry, noisy, and unreasonable

**tap**¹ /tæp/ *v* **-pped, -pping** **1** [I,T] to gently hit your finger or foot against something: *Someone was* **tapping on** *the window outside. | Caroline tapped her feet in time to the music.* **2** [I,T] to use something or become able to use something: *With the Internet you can* **tap into** *information from around the world. | tapping the country's natural resources* **3** [T] to put a TAP on someone's telephone

**tap**² *n* **1** an act of hitting something gently, especially to get someone's attention: *Suddenly I felt a tap on my shoulder.* **2** an object used for letting liquid out of a BARREL **3** a small electronic object that allows you to secretly listen to someone's telephone conversations **4** **on tap** **a)** beer that is on tap comes from a BARREL **b)** INFORMAL available to be used: *unlimited data on tap* **5** [U] ⇨ FAUCET –see also TAPS

**tap danc·ing** /ˈ. ˌ../ *n* [U] a type of dancing in which you make a noise with special shoes that have metal pieces on the bottom –**tap dance** *v* [I]

**tape**¹ /teɪp/ *n* **1 a)** [U] a thin narrow band of plastic material used for recording sounds, VIDEO pictures, or computer information: *Did you get the interview* **on tape**? (=recorded on tape) –see also VIDEOTAPE¹ **b)** a flat plastic case that contains this type of tape: *Can I borrow your old Beatles tape? | a* **blank tape** (=with nothing recorded on it) **2** [C,U] a narrow band of sticky material used for sticking things together, such as paper or packages

**tape**² *v* **1** [I,T] to record sounds or pictures onto a TAPE –see also VIDEOTAPE² **2** to stick something onto something else using TAPE: *He has lots of postcards taped to his wall.* **3** [T] also **tape up** to firmly tie a BANDAGE around an injury

**tape deck** /ˈ. ./ *n* the part of a STEREO used for recording and playing sounds on a TAPE

**tape meas·ure** /ˈ. ˌ../ *n* a long band of cloth or metal with inches, CENTIMETERs etc. marked on it, used for measuring things

**ta·per**¹ /ˈteɪpə/ *v* [I,T] to become gradually narrower towards one end –**tapered** *adj: pants with tapered legs*

**taper off** *phr v* [I] to decrease gradually: *The rain finally* **tapered off** *in the afternoon.*

**taper**² *n* a long thin CANDLE

**tape re·cord·er** /ˈ. .ˌ../ *n* a piece of electronic equipment used for recording and playing sounds on a TAPE –**tape record** *v* [T]

**tap·es·try** /ˈtæpɪstri/ *n* [C,U] heavy cloth with colored threads woven into it to make a picture, or a large piece of this cloth

**tape·worm** /ˈteɪpwəm/ *n* a long flat PARASITE that can live inside the INTESTINEs of people and animals

**taps** /tæps/ *n* [singular] a tune played on the BUGLE at night in an army camp or at a military funeral

**tap wa·ter** /ˈ. ˌ../ *n* [U] water that comes out of a FAUCET

**tar**¹ /tɑr/ *n* [U] a black substance that is thick and sticky, and is used on road surfaces, roofs etc. to protect them from water

**tar**² *v* **-rred, -rring** [T] to cover something with TAR

**ta·ran·tu·la** /təˈræntʃələ/ *n* a large hairy poisonous SPIDER

**tavern**

**tar·dy** /'tɑrdi/ *adj* late, or done too slowly: *If you are tardy once more you'll have to stay after school.* –**tardiness** *n* [U]

**tar·get** /'tɑrgɪt/ *n* **1** an object, person, or place that is deliberately chosen to be attacked: *a military target* **2** an aim or result that you try to achieve: *We're trying to reach a target of $2 million in sales.* **3** something that you practice shooting at: *Pete missed the target by two inches.*

**target² v [T] 1** to aim something at someone or something: *missiles targeted on/at European cities* **2** to try to make something have an effect on a limited group or area: *welfare programs targeted at the unemployed* **3** to deliberately attack someone or something: *Smaller banks with less security have been targeted.*

**tar·iff** /'tærɪf/ *n* a tax on goods that are brought into a country or taken out of it

**tar·mac** /'tɑrmæk/ *n* ⇨ ASPHALT

**tar·nish** /'tɑrnɪʃ/ *v* **1** [T] to make someone or something less impressive or respectable: *More violence will tarnish the school's reputation.* **2** [I] if a metal tarnishes, it becomes darker and less shiny

**tar·ot** /'tæroʊ/ *n* [singular, U] a set of cards used for telling what might happen to someone in the future

**tarp** /tɑrp/, **tar·pau·lin** /tɑr'pɔlən/ *n* [C,U] a cloth that water cannot go through, used for protecting things from the rain

**tar·ry** /'tæri/ *v* [I] LITERARY to stay in a place too long, or delay going somewhere

**tart¹** /tɑrt/ *adj* pleasantly sour: *tart green apples*

**tart²** *n* a small PIE without a top, usually containing fruit

**tar·tan** /'tɑrt⁻n/ *n* [C,U] a traditional Scottish PLAID pattern, or cloth with this pattern

**tar·tar** /'tɑrtɚ/ *n* [U] a hard substance that forms on teeth and can damage them

**tartar sauce** /'.. ,./ *n* [U] a cold white thick SAUCE often eaten with fish

**task** /tæsk/ *n* **1** a job or particular thing that you have to do, especially a difficult or annoying one: *the dangerous task of rescuing crash victims* **2** **take sb to task** to angrily criticize someone for doing something wrong

**task force** /'. ./ *n* a group that is formed in order to do a particular job, especially a military or political one

**tas·sel** /'tæsəl/ *n* a group of threads tied together at one end and hung as a decoration on curtains, clothes etc. –**tasseled** *adj*

**taste¹** /teɪst/ *n* **1** the feeling that is produced when your tongue touches a particular food or drink: *I don't like the taste of garlic.* | *a bitter taste* **2** [C,U] the particular type of music, clothes, art etc. that someone prefers: *Sheila has strange taste in clothes.* **3** [U] the enjoyment of something: *She never lost her taste for*

*travel.* **4** a small amount of a food or drink, eaten to find out what it is like: *Here, have a taste and tell me what you think.* **5** **be in good/bad/poor taste** to be suitable or unsuitable for a particular occasion: *a joke in very bad taste*

**taste²** *v* **1** [I] to have a particular type of taste: *What does the soup taste like?* | *This milk tastes a little sour.* ✗ DON'T SAY "is tasting." ✗ **2** [T] to put a small amount of food or drink in your mouth in order to find out what it is like. *Taste this and see if it needs more salt.* **3** [T] to experience the particular taste of a food or drink: *My cold's so bad I can't taste a thing.* ✗ DON'T SAY "I am not tasting." ✗

**taste·ful** /'teɪstfəl/ *adj* chosen, decorated, or made in a way that is attractive and of good quality: *Frank was dressed in casual but tasteful clothes.* –**tastefully** *adv*: *a tastefully furnished apartment*

**taste·less** /'teɪstlɪs/ *adj* **1** offensive, unsuitable, or of bad quality: *tasteless jokes* **2** not having any taste: *tasteless food*

**tast·er** /'teɪstɚ/ *n* someone whose job is to test the quality of a food or drink by tasting it: *wine tasters*

**tast·ing** /'teɪstɪŋ/ *n* an event where you can try different kinds of food and drinks: *a cheese tasting*

**tast·y** /'teɪsti/ *adj* having a very good taste: *tasty fish*

**tat·tered** /'tætɚd/ *adj* old and torn: *tattered curtains*

**tat·ters** /'tætɚz/ *n* [plural] **in tatters a)** clothes that are in tatters are old and torn **b)** completely ruined: *All his great plans lay in tatters.*

**tat·tle** /'tætl/ *v* [I] if a child tattles, s/he tells a parent or teacher that another child has done something bad

**tat·tle·tale** /'tætl,teɪl/ *n* SPOKEN a word meaning someone who TATTLEs, used especially by children

**tat·too** /tæ'tu/ *n* a picture, word etc. that is put permanently onto your skin using a needle and ink –**tattooed** *adj* –**tattoo** *v* [T]

**taught** /tɔt/ *v* the past tense and PAST PARTICIPLE of TEACH

**taunt** /tɔnt, tɑnt/ *v* [T] to try to make someone upset or angry by saying something unkind: *The other kids taunted him about his weight.* –**taunt** *n*

**Tau·rus** /'tɔrəs/ *n* **1** [singular] the second sign of the ZODIAC, represented by a BULL **2** someone born between April 20 and May 20

**taut** /tɔt/ *adj* **1** stretched tight: *a taut rope* **2** seeming worried: *a taut look on his face* –**tautly** *adv*

**tav·ern** /'tævɚn/ *n* a BAR that usually only serves beer and wine

**taw·dry** /ˈtɔdri/ *adj* cheap and of bad quality: *tawdry jewelry* —**tawdriness** *n* [U]

**taw·ny** /ˈtɔni/ *adj* having a light gold-brown color: *tawny fur*

**tax**[1] /tæks/ *n* [C,U] the money you must pay the government, based on how much you earn, what you buy, where you live etc.: *a 13% tax on cigarettes* | *I only earn $25,000 a year after taxes*. (=after paying tax)

**tax**[2] *v* [T] **1** to charge a tax on something: *Incomes of under $30,000 are taxed at 15%.* **2 tax sb's patience/strength etc.** to use almost all of someone's PATIENCE, strength etc.: *His constant questions had begun to tax her patience.*

**tax·a·tion** /tækˈseɪʃən/ *n* [U] the system of charging taxes, or the money collected from taxes

**tax ex·empt** /ˈ. .ˌ./ *adj* not TAXed, or not having to pay tax: *tax-exempt savings* | *a tax-exempt charity*

**tax·i**[1] /ˈtæksi/, **tax·i·cab** /ˈtæksiˌkæb/ *n* a car with a driver whom you pay to drive you somewhere: *We'll just take a taxi home.*

**taxi**[2] *v* [I] if a plane taxis, it moves slowly on the ground

**tax·i·der·my** /ˈtæksəˌdɝmi/ *n* [U] the process of specially treating and filling the body of a dead animal, bird, or fish so that it still looks alive

**tax·ing** /ˈtæksɪŋ/ *adj* making you feel very tired, weak, or annoyed: *a taxing job*

**taxi stand** /ˈ.. .ˌ./ *n* a place where TAXIs wait in order to get passengers

**tax·pay·er** /ˈtæksˌpeɪɚ/ *n* someone who pays taxes

**tax shel·ter** /ˈ. .ˌ./ *n* a plan or method that allows you to legally avoid paying tax

**TB** *n* the abbreviation of TUBERCULOSIS

**tbsp.** *n* the written abbreviation of TABLESPOON

**tea** /ti/ *n* **1** [U] a drink made by pouring boiling water onto dried leaves: *a cup of tea* **2** [C,U] dried leaves, flowers etc., used for making a hot drink: *mint tea* | *herbal teas*

**tea bag** /ˈ. ./ *n* a small paper bag with dried leaves in it, used for making tea

**teach** /titʃ/ *v* **taught, taught, teaching** **1** [I,T] to give lessons in a school or college: *Mr. Rochet has been teaching for 17 years.* | *She teaches math at Jackson High School.* **2** [T] to show someone how to do something: *My dad taught me how to swim.* **3 teach sb a lesson** INFORMAL to make someone avoid doing something bad or unwise again: *Well, I hope that being locked out teaches him a lesson.* —see usage note at LEARN

**teach·er** /ˈtitʃɚ/ *n* someone whose job is to teach: *Mr. Paulin is my history teacher.*

**teacher's pet** /ˌ.. ˈ./ *n* a teacher's favorite student, especially one that the other students dislike

**teach·ing** /ˈtitʃɪŋ/ *n* [U] the work that a teacher does, or the profession of being a teacher: *I'd like to go into teaching when I finish college.*

**tea co·sy** /ˈ. .ˌ./ *n* a thick cover that you put over a TEAPOT to keep the tea hot

**tea·cup** /ˈtikʌp/ *n* a cup that you serve tea in

**teak** /tik/ *n* [C,U] a tall South Asian tree, or the very hard wood of this tree used for making ships and furniture

**team**[1] /tim/ *n* **1** a group of people who compete against another group in a sport, game etc.: *Which team is winning?* | *Manuel is on the swimming team.* **2** a group of people who are chosen to work together to do a particular job: *a team of doctors* **3** two or more animals that are used for pulling a vehicle

**team**[2] *v*

**team up** *phr v* [I] to form a team with another person, company etc. in order to work together: *We're teaming up with another publisher to do the book.*

**team·mate** /ˈtim-meɪt/ *n* someone who plays or works on the same team as you

**team play·er** /ˌ. ˈ../ *n* INFORMAL someone who works well with other people so that the whole group is successful

**team·ster** /ˈtimstɚ/ *n* someone whose job is to drive a TRUCK

**team·work** /ˈtimwɝk/ *n* [U] the ability of a group to work well together, or the effort the group makes

**tea·pot** /ˈtipɑt/ *n* a container used for serving tea, that has a handle and a SPOUT

teapot
spout

**tear**[1] /tɛr/ **tore, torn, tearing** *v* **1 a)** [T] to put a hole in a piece of paper, cloth etc. by pulling it very hard or by accidentally letting it touch something sharp: *You've torn your sleeve.* | *He tore the envelope open.* | *Oh no, I tore a hole in my jeans!* **b)** [I] to become damaged in this way: *Be careful, you don't want your dress to tear!* **2** [I] INFORMAL to move very quickly, often in a careless or violent way: *Two kids came tearing around the corner.* **3** [T] to remove something by tearing it: *The storm actually tore the door off its hinges.*

**tear apart** *phr v* [T] **1** [**tear** sb **apart**] to make someone feel extremely unhappy or upset: *It tears me apart to see Lisa cry.* **2** [**tear** sth ↔ **apart**] to make a group, organization etc. start having problems: *Your drinking is tearing this family apart!*

**tear** sth ↔ **down** *phr v* [T] to deliberately destroy a building: *My old school was **torn down** last year*.

 **tear into** sb/sth *phr v* [T] INFORMAL to strongly criticize someone or something: *Then he started **tearing into** her for spending money*.

 **tear** sth ↔ **up** *phr v* [T] to destroy something, especially paper, by tearing it into a lot of little pieces: *He **tore up** all of Linda's old letters*.

**tear**[2] /tɪr/ *n* a drop of liquid that flows from your eyes when you cry: *She ran away with tears in her eyes* | *Suddenly Brian **burst into** tears*. (=started crying)

**tear**[3] /tɛr/ *n* a hole in a piece of paper, cloth etc. where it has been torn

**tear·drop** /'tɪrdrɑp/ *n* a single tear

**tease**[1] /tiz/ *v* **1** [I,T] to try to embarrass or annoy someone by making jokes about him/her: *Don't cry. I was just teasing.* | *Johnny, stop teasing your sister!* **2** [T] to comb your hair in the wrong direction so that it looks thicker

**tease**[2] *n* someone who enjoys teasing (TEASE) people

**tea·spoon** /'tispun/ *n* **1** a small spoon used for STIRring a cup of tea or coffee **2** a special spoon used for measuring food **3** also **tea·spoonful** the amount this spoon can hold

**teat** /tit/ *n* a NIPPLE on a female animal

**tech·ni·cal** /'tɛknɪkəl/ *adj* **1** relating to the practical skills, knowledge, and methods used in science or industry: *technical experts* | *technical training* **2** relating to a particular subject or profession: *a legal document full of technical terms*

**tech·ni·cal·i·ties** /ˌtɛknɪ'kælətiz/ *n* [plural] the details of a system or process that you need special knowledge to understand

**tech·ni·cal·i·ty** /ˌtɛknɪ'kæləti/ *n* a small detail in a law or rule

**tech·ni·cally** /'tɛknɪkli/ *adv* according to the exact details of a rule or law: *Technically, he's responsible for fixing all the damage*.

**tech·ni·cian** /tɛk'nɪʃən/ *n* a trained worker who does a job relating to science or industry: *a lab technician*

**tech·nique** /tɛk'nik/ *n* [C,U] a special method of doing something: *new techniques for teaching English* | *the artist's talent and technique*

**tech·nol·o·gy** /tɛk'nɑlədʒi/ *n* [C,U] a combination of all the knowledge, equipment, methods etc. that is used in scientific or industrial work: *medical technology* | *developing new technologies* –**technological** /ˌtɛknə'lɑdʒɪkəl/ *adj*

**ted·dy bear** /'tɛdi ˌbɛr/ *n* a soft toy shaped like a bear

**te·di·ous** /'tidiəs/ *adj* boring, and continuing for a long time: *a tedious discussion*

**te·di·um** /'tidiəm/ *n* [U] the quality of being TEDIOUS

**tee** /ti/ *n* a small object used for holding a GOLF ball, or the raised area from which you hit the ball

**teem** /tim/ *v*

 **teem with** sth *phr v* [T] to be full of people or animals that are all moving around: *lakes **teeming with** fish* –**teeming** *adj*: *the teeming streets of Cairo*

**teen** /tin/ *n* INFORMAL ⇨ TEENAGER –**teen** *adj*

**teen·age** /'tineɪdʒ/ *adj* aged between 13 and 19, or relating to someone who is: *our teenage son* ✗ DON'T SAY "our son is teenage." ✗

**teen·ag·er** /'tiˌneɪdʒɚ/ *n* someone who is between 13 and 19 years old

**teens** /tinz/ *n* [plural] the period in your life when you are aged between 13 and 19: *She got married when she was still **in her teens***.

**tee·ny** /'tini/, **tee·ny-wee·ny** /ˌtini 'wini◂/ *adj* SPOKEN very small; TINY

**tee shirt** /'. ./ *n* ⇨ T-SHIRT

**tee·ter** /'titɚ/ *v* [I] **1** to move or stand in an unsteady way: *teetering in high-heeled shoes* **2** **be teetering on the brink/edge of** to be very likely to become involved in a dangerous situation: *a country teetering on the brink of revolution*

**teeth** /tiθ/ *n* the plural of TOOTH

**teethe** /tið/ *v* [I] if a baby is teething, his/her first teeth are growing

**tee·to·tal·er** /ˌti'toutlɚ◂/ *n* someone who never drinks alcohol

**Tef·lon** /'tɛflɑn/ *n* [U] TRADEMARK a special material that stops things from sticking to it, often used in making pans

**tel·e·com·mu·ni·ca·tions** /ˌtɛləkəˌmyunə'keɪʃənz/ *n* [U] the process or business of sending and receiving messages by telephone, radio, SATELLITE etc.

**tel·e·com·mut·er** /'tɛləkəˌmyutɚ/ *n* someone who works at home instead of in an office, but uses the telephone and a computer to communicate with the people s/he works with

**tel·e·gram** /'tɛləˌgræm/ *n* a message sent by TELEGRAPH

**tel·e·graph** /'tɛləˌgræf/ *n* [C,U] a method of sending messages using electrical signals, or the equipment used for sending these messages

**te·lep·a·thy** /tə'lɛpəθi/ *n* [U] the ability to communicate thoughts directly to someone else's mind without speaking, writing, or using signs

**tel·e·phone**[1] /'tɛləˌfoun/ *n* ⇨ PHONE[1]

**telephone**[2] *v* [I,T] ⇨ PHONE[2]

---

**USAGE NOTE** telephone, phone, call, and other words used for telephoning

Use each of these words as a verb. **Call** is the most common, and **telephone** is not very common: *I think I'll call Pedro.* | *Chris phoned to say he'd be late.* A **call, phone**

**call**, or **telephone call** is the action of tele-phoning: *Give me a call later in the week.* | *Kerry, there's a phone call for you.* To make a telephone call, you find the **phone number** in the **telephone/phone book.** Then you **dial** the number. If you need help with a call, you dial the **operator**. The phone will **ring**, and if the person is there, s/he will **answer** by **picking up the receiver**. If s/he is not there, you can leave a message on the **answering machine** If s/he is already talking on the phone, the **line** will be **busy**. When you finish talking, you **hang up**. To make a telephone call in a public place, you can go to a **telephone/phone booth**.

**tel·e·pho·to lens** /ˌtɛləˌfoʊtoʊ ˈlɛnz/ *n* a camera LENS that makes things that are far away seem closer and larger

**tel·e·scope**[1] /ˈtɛləˌskoʊp/ *n* a piece of equip-ment shaped like a tube, used for making things that are far away seem closer and larger so you can look at them

**telescope**[2] *v* to make a series of events seem to happen in a shorter amount of time

**tel·e·scop·ic** /ˌtɛləˈskɑpɪk/ *adj* relating to a TELESCOPE, or using a telescope: *a telescopic lens* | *telescopic observation*

**tel·e·thon** /ˈtɛləˌθɑn/ *n* a special television program that continues for several hours and is intended to persuade people to give money to a CHARITY

**tel·e·vise** /ˈtɛləˌvaɪz/ *v* [T] to broadcast some-thing on television: *Is the game going to be televised?*

**tel·e·vi·sion** /ˈtɛləˌvɪʒən/ *n* **1** also **televi-sion set** /ˈ.... ˌ./ a thing shaped like a box with a screen, on which you can see programs that are broadcast: *a big-screen television* **2** [U] the programs that you can watch and listen to on a television: *He's been watching television all day.* | *Guess who's being interviewed on televi-sion tonight?* **3** [U] the activity of making and broadcasting programs that can be seen and heard on a television: *a job in television*

**tell** /tɛl/ *v* told, told, tell-ing

**1** ▶INFORMATION◀ [T] to give someone facts or information in speech or writing: *Tell Mark I said hi.* | *Did you tell Jennifer about the party?* | *Could you tell me how to make that cheesecake?* | *Dad used to tell us bedtime stories.*

**2** ▶RECOGNIZE◀ [I,T] to be able to recognize or judge something correctly: *I could tell it was a serious discussion.* | *Carol puts the twins in different color booties so you can tell them apart.* | *Use plain yogurt instead of sour cream -*

*you can't tell the difference.* | *"How long will it take?" "It's hard to tell."*

**3** ▶WHAT SB SHOULD DO◀ [T] to say that someone should or must do something: *Tell her to put on her coat - it's cold.* | *Stop telling me what to do all the time!*

**4** **tell yourself** to encourage yourself to do something, or remind yourself of the facts of a situation that upsets or worries you: *I kept tell-ing myself to relax.*

**5** ▶SIGN◀ [T] to give information in a way other than using speech or writing: *This red light tells you it's recording.*

**6** **there's no telling what/how/whether etc.** used in order to say that it is impossible to know what will happen next: *There's just no telling what kids will say next.*

**7** **all told** in total: *All told, 40,000 airline workers have lost their jobs this year.*

**8** ▶STH WRONG◀ [I,T] SPOKEN to tell some-one in authority about something wrong that someone else has done: *Don't, Connie! I'm going to tell on you!*

---

SPOKEN PHRASES

**9** **(I'll) tell you what** said in order to suggest something: *Tell you what, call me on Friday, and we'll make plans then.*

**10** **I tell you/I'm telling you/let me tell you** said in order to emphasize something: *I'm telling you, the gossip in this place is un-believable!*

**11** **tell me about it** said in order to say that you already know how bad something is: *"She's so arrogant!" "Yeah, tell me about it."*

**12** **(I) told you (so)** said when someone does something you have warned him/her about, and it has a bad result: *Told you. I knew that car was a bad buy.*

**13** **to tell (you) the truth** said in order to emphasize or admit that what you are saying is true: *I don't know how you cope, to tell you the truth.*

**14** **you never can tell/you can never tell** used in order to say that you can never be certain about what will happen in the future: *They're not likely to win, but you never can tell.*

**15** **to hear sb tell it** used in order to say that someone is giving his/her opinion of an event, and it may not be the exact truth: *Well, to hear her tell it, it was all Monica's fault.*

---

—see usage note at SAY

**tell** sb ↔ **off** *phr v* [T] to talk angrily to some-one when s/he has done something wrong: *I'm going to get told off for being late.*

**tell·er** /ˈtɛlɚ/ *n* someone whose job is to receive money from, and pay out money to, the customers in a bank

T

**tell off**

**tell·ing** /ˈtɛlɪŋ/ *adj* **1** a remark that is telling shows what you really think, although you may not intend it to **2** having a great or important effect; SIGNIFICANT: *a telling argument*

**tell·tale** /ˈtɛlteɪl/ *adj* clearly showing something that is unpleasant or supposed to be secret: *the telltale signs of drug addiction*

**temp**[1] /tɛmp/ *n* an office worker who is only employed for a limited period of time

**temp**[2] *v* [I] to work as a TEMP: *Anne's temping until she can find another job.*

**tem·per**[1] /ˈtɛmpɚ/ *n* **1** [C,U] a tendency to become suddenly angry: *John needs to learn to control his temper.* **2** [singular, U] an uncontrolled feeling of anger that continues for a short time: *You're certainly in a foul temper this morning.* **3 lose/keep your temper** to suddenly become very angry, or to stay calm **4 have a quick/hot/slow temper** to get angry very easily, or not very easily **5 -tempered** having a particular type of temper: *a bad-tempered old man* | *a good-tempered child* (=a happy one)

**temper**[2] *v* [T] **1** to make metal harder by heating it and then making it cold: *tempered steel* **2** FORMAL to make something less difficult or severe: *criticism tempered with humor*

**tem·per·a·ment** /ˈtɛmprəmənt/ *n* [C,U] the part of your character that makes you likely to be happy, angry, sad etc.: *a baby with a calm temperament*

**tem·per·a·men·tal** /ˌtɛmprəˈmɛnt̮l/ *adj* **1** tending to get upset, excited, or angry very easily **2** a temperamental machine does not always work correctly

**tem·per·ance** /ˈtɛmprəns/ *n* [U] the practice of never drinking alcohol

**tem·per·ate** /ˈtɛmprɪt/ *adj* weather or a part of the world that is temperate is never very hot or very cold: *a temperate climate*

**tem·per·a·ture** /ˈtɛmprətʃɚ/ *n* **1** [C,U] how hot or cold something is: *Water freezes at a temperature of 32°F.* | *a gradual rise/fall in temperature* | *Store this product at room temperature.* (=the normal temperature in a room) **2 sb's temperature** the temperature of your body, used as a measure of whether you are sick or not: *It's time to take your temperature.* (=measure it) | *I think I have a temperature.* (=have one that is higher than normal)

---

**USAGE NOTE temperature**

Many words are used in order to describe the temperature of the air or of a substance. Air or a substance that is **cold** has a low temperature: *a nice cold drink* | *It's too cold to go swimming.* Air or a substance that is **cool** has a low temperature but is not **cold**: *cool breezes* | *Serve the Beaujolais cool.* Air or a substance that is **warm** is

pleasant: *It's warm enough outside to go to the beach.* | *The water in the pool is nice and warm.* Air or a substance that is **hot** has a high temperature: *The coffee's still too hot to drink.* | *It's too hot to sit in the sun.* Some words are used only to describe the temperature of air. **Bitter** and **freezing** mean "extremely cold and unpleasant": *a bitter wind* | *It's freezing in here!* Air that is **chilly** is cold enough to make you feel uncomfortable. A day that is **humid** or **muggy** makes you feel uncomfortable because the air feels wet, heavy, and warm. Weather that is **sweltering** is very hot and makes you feel wet and uncomfortable. A room that is **stifling** is very hot and is difficult to breathe in. Some words are used only to describe substances. Water or a drink that is **tepid** is only slightly warm in a way that is unpleasant. Water or food that is **luke-warm** is slightly warm and not as warm or cold as it should be. Water or a subtance that is **boiling** is so hot that it BUBBLES.

---

**tem·pest** /ˈtɛmpɪst/ *n* LITERARY a violent storm

**tem·pes·tu·ous** /tɛmˈpɛstʃuəs/ *adj* always full of strong emotions: *a tempestuous relationship*

**tem·plate** /ˈtɛmpleɪt/ *n* **1** a sheet of paper, plastic, or metal in a special shape, used in order to help you cut other materials in the same shape **2** a system for arranging information on a computer screen

**tem·ple** /ˈtɛmpəl/ *n* **1** a building where people go to WORSHIP in some religions **2** the fairly flat area on the side of your head, between your eye and your ear

**tem·po** /ˈtɛmpoʊ/ *n* **1** the speed at which music is played **2** the speed at which something happens; PACE: *the tempo of city life*

**tem·po·rar·y** /ˈtɛmpəˌrɛri/ *adj* existing or happening for only a limited period of time: *Linda is here on a temporary basis while Jane is away.* —**temporarily** /ˌtɛmpəˈrɛrəli/ *adv*: *The library is temporarily closed.* —compare PERMANENT[1]

**tempt** /tɛmpt/ *v* **1** [T] to make someone want to have or do something although it is wrong, bad, silly etc., by making it seem attractive: *They're offering free gifts to tempt people to join.* | *Can I tempt you with another piece of cake?* **2 be tempted to do sth** to consider doing something that may not be a good idea: *I'm tempted to just go out and buy a new car.* **3 tempt fate** to do or say something that might end the good luck you have had —**tempting** *adj*

**temp·ta·tion** /tɛmpˈteɪʃən/ *n* [C,U] **1** a strong desire to have or do something although it is wrong, bad, silly etc., because it seems attractive: *I really had to resist the temptation to slap her.* **2** something that makes you have this desire: *Having candy in the house is a great temptation!*

**ten**[1] /tɛn/ *number* **1** 10 **2** ten o'clock: *I have a meeting at ten.*

**ten**[2] *n* a piece of paper money worth $10

**te·na·cious** /tə'neɪʃəs/ *adj* very determined to do something, and unwilling to stop trying −**tenacity** /tə'næsəṭi/ *n* [U]

**ten·an·cy** /'tɛnənsi/ *n* [C,U] the right to use a house, room etc. that is rented, or the period of time during which you have this right

**ten·ant** /'tɛnənt/ *n* someone who lives in a house, room etc. and pays rent to the person who owns it

**tend** /tɛnd/ *v* **1 tend to do sth** to be likely to do a particular thing: *It tends to be very wet at this time of year.* **2 tend bar** to work as a BARTENDER **3** [T] also **tend to** to take care of someone or something: *Rescue teams were tending to the survivors.*

**tend·en·cy** /'tɛndənsi/ *n* **1** a part of your character that makes you likely to develop, think, or behave in a particular way: *He has a **tendency to** talk too much.* **2** a change or development that is happening, or an action that usually happens: *There's a **tendency for** men to marry younger women.*

**ten·der**[1] /'tɛndɚ/ *adj* **1** tender food is easy to cut and eat −opposite TOUGH[1] **2** a tender part of your body is painful if someone touches it **3** gentle in a way that shows love: *a tender look* **4** LITERARY young and inexperienced: *He lost his father **at the tender age of** seven.* −**tenderly** *adv* −**tenderness** *n* [U]

**tender**[2] *v* **1** [I] to make a formal offer to buy all or part of a company **2** [T] to make a formal offer to do something: *The senator has offered to **tender his resignation.** (=officially say that he is going to leave his job)*

**tender**[3] *n* a formal offer to buy all or part of a company

**ten·der·heart·ed** /,tɛndɚ'hɑrṭɪd◂/ *adj* very kind and gentle

**ten·der·ize** /'tɛndɚ,raɪz/ *v* [T] to make meat softer by preparing it in a special way

**ten·don** /'tɛndən/ *n* a thick strong string-like part of your body that connects a muscle to a bone

**ten·dril** /'tɛndrəl/ *n* a thin curling piece of something such as hair or the stem of a plant

**ten·e·ment** /'tɛnəmənt/ *n* a large building divided into apartments, especially in a poor area of a city

**ten·et** /'tɛnɪt/ *n* a principle or belief: *the tenets of Buddhism*

**ten·nis** /'tɛnɪs/ *n* [U] a game in which two or four people use RACKETs to hit a ball to each other across a net

**tennis shoe** /'.. ,./ *n* a light shoe used for sports −see picture at SHOE[1]

**ten·or** /'tɛnɚ/ *n* [C,U] **1** a male singer with a high voice **2 the tenor of** FORMAL the general meaning or quality of something: *the tenor of the president's speech*

**tense**[1] /tɛns/ *adj* **1** nervous and anxious: *You seem really tense - what's wrong? | a tense situation* **2** unable to relax because your muscles feel tight and stiff

**tense**[2] **tense up** *v* [I,T] to become tight and stiff, or to make your muscles do this

**tense**[3] *n* [C,U] TECHNICAL in grammar, one of the forms of a verb that shows actions or states in the past, now, or in the future. For example, "he studied" is in the past tense, "he studies" is in the present tense, and "he will study" is in the future tense

**ten·sion** /'tɛnʃən/ *n* **1** [C,U] the feeling that exists when people do not trust each other and may suddenly attack each other: *efforts to calm racial tensions* **2** [U] a nervous and anxious feeling: *The tension became unbearable and I wanted to scream.* **3** [U] tightness or stiffness in a wire, rope, muscle etc.: *You can increase the tension by turning this screw.*

**tent** /tɛnt/ *n* a shelter that you can easily move, made of cloth or plastic and supported by poles and ropes: *Where should we **pitch the tent**? (=put up the tent)*

**ten·ta·cle** /'tɛntəkəl/ *n* one of the long thin parts like arms of a creature such as an OCTOPUS −see picture at OCTOPUS

**ten·ta·tive** /'tɛntəṭɪv/ *adj* **1** not definite or certain: *tentative plans* **2** done without confidence: *a tentative smile* −**tentatively** *adv*

**tenth** /tɛnθ/ *number* 10th

**ten·u·ous** /'tɛnyuəs/ *adj* **tenuous link/ relationship etc.** a connection, relationship etc. that seems weak or not real −**tenuously** *adv*

**ten·ure** /'tɛnyɚ/ *n* [U] **1** the right to stay permanently in a teaching job at a university **2** FORMAL the period of time when someone has an important job: *the Mayor's tenure in office*

**te·pee, teepee** /'tipi/ *n* a round tent used by some Native Americans

**tep·id** /'tɛpɪd/ *adj* tepid liquid is slightly warm

**te·qui·la** /tə'kilə/ *n* [U] a strong alcoholic drink made in Mexico

**term**[1] /tɚm/ *n* **1** a word or expression that has a particular meaning, especially in a technical or scientific subject: *I don't understand these legal terms.* **2** a fixed or limited period of time, especially in politics or education: *a four-year **term of office*** **3 in the long/short term** during a long or short period from now: *The company's prospects look better in the long term.* −see also TERMS

**term**[2] *v* [T] FORMAL to name or describe something in a particular way: *The meeting could hardly be termed a success.*

**ter·mi·nal**[1] /'tɚmənəl/ *adj* **1** a terminal disease cannot be cured, and causes death: *terminal*

**cancer 2 terminal decline/decay** the state of becoming worse and worse and never getting better **–terminally** adv: *terminally ill*

**terminal**² n **1** a big building where you go to get onto planes, buses, or ships, or where goods are loaded on them **2** a computer KEYBOARD and screen connected to a computer that is somewhere else **3** one of the points at which you can connect wires to an electrical CIRCUIT

**ter·mi·nate** /'tɚmə,neɪt/ v [I,T] FORMAL **1** ⇨ END² **2** FORMAL to FIRE someone from his/her job **– termination** /,tɚmə'neɪʃən/ n [C,U]

**ter·mi·nol·o·gy** /,tɚmə'nɑlədʒi/ n [C,U] the technical words or expressions that are used in a particular subject: *scientific terminology*

**ter·mi·nus** /'tɚmənəs/ n the place at the end of a railroad or bus line

**ter·mite** /'tɚmaɪt/ n an insect that eats wood from trees and buildings

**terms** /tɚmz/ n [plural] **1** the parts of an agreement, contract etc.: *Sign here to say you agree to the terms and conditions.* **2 in terms of** used when explaining or discussing how a particular fact or event is related to something: *In terms of sales, the book hasn't been very successful.* **3 in financial/artistic etc. terms** if you describe or consider something in financial etc. terms, you are thinking of it in a financial etc. way: *A million years isn't a very long time in geological terms.* **4 in no uncertain terms** in a clear and usually angry way: *He told me in no uncertain terms not to come back.* **5 be on good/bad/friendly etc. terms** to have a particular type of relationship with someone: *He hasn't been on good terms with his father for years.* **6 be on speaking terms** to be friendly with someone and able to talk to him/her: *We're barely on speaking terms now.* **7 come to terms with** to understand and deal with a difficult problem or situation: *It was hard to come to terms with Marie's death.*

**ter·race** /'tɛrɪs/ n **1** a flat outdoor area next to a building or on a roof, where you can eat, relax etc. **2** a flat area cut out of the side of a hill, often used for growing crops on

**ter·ra·cot·ta** /,tɛrə'kɑtə/ n [U] hard red-brown baked clay: *a terracotta pot*

**ter·rain** /tə'reɪn/ n [C,U] land of a particular type: *rocky/hilly/rough terrain*

**ter·res·tri·al** /tə'rɛstriəl/ adj TECHNICAL **1** relating to the earth rather than to the moon, stars, or other PLANETs **2** living on or relating to land rather than water

**ter·ri·ble** /'tɛrəbəl/ adj **1** extremely severe and causing harm or damage: *a terrible accident* **2** INFORMAL very bad or unpleasant: *a terrible movie* **3** making you feel afraid or shocked: *a terrible noise*

**ter·ri·bly** /'tɛrəbli/ adv **1** very badly: *We played terribly, and that's why we lost.*

**2** extremely: *I'm terribly sorry, but the answer is no.*

**ter·ri·er** /'tɛriɚ/ n a small active type of dog

**ter·rif·ic** /tə'rɪfɪk/ adj INFORMAL **1** very good or enjoyable: *a terrific party* **2** very large in size or degree: *It's a terrific honor to win this award.* **–terrifically** adv

**ter·ri·fy** /'tɛrə,faɪ/ v [T] to make someone extremely afraid: *The thought of giving a speech terrified her.* **–terrifying** adj

**ter·ri·to·ri·al** /,tɛrə'tɔriəl/ adj **1** relating to land that is owned or controlled by a particular country, ruler etc.: *US territorial waters* **2** territorial animals or people closely guard the place they consider to be their own

**ter·ri·to·ry** /'tɛrə,tɔri/ n **1** [C,U] land that is owned or controlled by a particular country, ruler etc.: *Canadian territory* **2** [U] land of a particular type: *unexplored territory* **3** [C,U] the area that an animal, person, or group considers to be its own **4** [C,U] an area of business for which someone is responsible: *the Chicago sales territory* **5 come/go with the territory** to be a natural and accepted part of a particular job, situation, place etc.: *You'd better get used to criticism from the press - it comes with the territory.*

**ter·ror** /'tɛrɚ/ n **1** [C,U] a feeling of extreme fear, or something that causes this: *She ran away in terror.* | *the terrors of war* **2** INFORMAL a very annoying person, especially a child

**ter·ror·ism** /'tɛrə,rɪzəm/ n [U] the use of violence to obtain political demands **–terrorist** n **–terrorist** adj: *terrorist bombings*

**ter·ror·ize** /'tɛrə,raɪz/ v [T] to deliberately frighten people by threatening to harm them, especially so they will do what you want

**ter·ry·cloth** /'tɛri,klɔθ/ n [U] thick cotton cloth used for making TOWELs

**terse** /tɚs/ adj a terse reply, message etc. uses very few words and often shows that you are annoyed **–tersely** adv

**test**¹ /tɛst/ n **1** a set of questions or exercises to measure someone's skill, ability, or knowledge: *I have a history test tomorrow.* | *Paul passed/failed his driver's test the first time.* | *All students must take a placement test.* ✗ DON'T SAY "make a test." SAY "take a test." ✗ **2** the process of examining something carefully in order to see what it is like or to find out something: *They're going to run/do some tests on my blood.* **3** a situation in which the qualities of something are clearly shown: *Living together will really put their relationship to the test.* (=find out how good it is) | *Today's race is a real test of skill.*

**test**² v [T] **1** to measure someone's skill, ability, or knowledge, using a test: *We're being tested on grammar tomorrow.* **2** to examine or use something in order to see what it is like or to find out something: *testing nuclear weapons*

T

**3** to show how good or strong something is: *The next six months will test your powers of leadership.*

**tes·ta·ment** /ˈtɛstəmənt/ *n* FORMAL **1 a testament to sth** something that shows or proves something else very clearly: *His latest record is a testament to his growing musical abilities.* **2** ⇨ WILL² –see also NEW TESTAMENT, OLD TESTAMENT

**test ban** /ˈ. ./ *n* an agreement between countries to stop testing NUCLEAR WEAPONS

**test case** /ˈ. ./ *n* a legal case that makes a particular principle clear and is used as a standard for similar cases

**test drive** /ˈ. ./ *n* an occasion when you drive a car and decide if you want to buy it –**test-drive** *v* [T]

**tes·ti·cle** /ˈtɛstɪkəl/ *n, plural* **testicles** or **testes** /ˈtɛstiz/ one of the two round organs below a man's PENIS that produce SPERM

**tes·ti·fy** /ˈtɛstəˌfaɪ/ *v* [I,T] to make a formal statement of what is true, especially in a court of law: *Two men testified that they saw you there.* | *You can't make me testify against my husband.*

**tes·ti·mo·ni·al** /ˌtɛstəˈmoʊniəl/ *n* something that is given or said to someone to show thanks or admiration

**tes·ti·mo·ny** /ˈtɛstəˌmoʊni/ *n* [C,U] **1** a formal statement of what is true, especially one made in a court of law **2** something that shows or proves something else very clearly: *an achievement that's a testimony to his hard work*

**test pi·lot** /ˈ. ˌ../ *n* a pilot who flies new aircraft in order to test them

**test tube** /ˈ. ./ *n* a small glass container shaped like a tube that is used in scientific tests

**tes·ty** /ˈtɛsti/ *adj* impatient and easily annoyed: *a testy old man* –**testily** *adv*

**tet·a·nus** /ˈtɛtˈn-əs, -nəs/ *n* [U] a serious disease caused by infection in a cut or wound, that makes your muscles become stiff

**teth·er** /ˈtɛðɚ/ *n* a rope or chain to which something is tied

**text** /tɛkst/ *n* **1** [U] the writing in a book, magazine etc. rather than the pictures, or any written material **2 the text of sth** the exact words of something: *The entire text of the speech was printed in the newspaper.*

**text·book¹** /ˈtɛksrbʊk/, **text** *n* a book that contains information about a subject: *a history textbook*

**textbook²** *adj* **a textbook example/case** a very clear and typical example of how something should happen or be done

**tex·tile** /ˈtɛkstaɪl/ *n* any material that is made by weaving

**tex·tiles** /ˈtɛkstaɪlz/ *n* [plural] the industry that makes cloth

**tex·ture** /ˈtɛkstʃɚ/ *n* [C,U] the way that a surface, material etc. feels when you touch it, and how smooth or rough it looks: *fabric with a coarse texture*

**tex·tured** /ˈtɛkstʃɚd/ *adj* having a surface that is not smooth: *a wall with a textured surface*

**than** /ðən, ðɛn; *strong* ðæn/ *conjunction, prep* used when comparing two things, amounts etc. that are different: *He's been unemployed for more than a year.* | *Jean's taller than Stella.* | *I can swim better than you.*

**thank** /θæŋk/ *v* [T] **1** to tell someone that you are pleased and grateful for a gift or something that s/he has done: *We would like to thank everyone for helping.* **2 thank God/ goodness/heavens** SPOKEN said when you are very glad about something: *Thank God no one was hurt!* **3 have sb to thank (for sth)** SPOKEN used in order to say who is responsible for something happening: *The team has Jones to thank for keeping them in the game.*

**thank·ful** /ˈθæŋkfəl/ *adj* glad and grateful that something good has happened: *Our family does have a lot to be thankful for.* | *I'm thankful (that) I didn't have to go to the dentist.* –**thankfully** *adv*: *Thankfully, everything turned out all right.*

**thank·less** /ˈθæŋklɪs/ *adj* a thankless job is difficult and you do not get much praise for doing it

**thanks¹** /θæŋks/ *interjection* INFORMAL **1** ⇨ THANK YOU¹: *Can I borrow your pen? Thanks a lot.* | *Thanks for giving me a ride to school.* **2 thanks/no thanks** said in order to accept or refuse something that someone is offering you: *"Can I give you a hand?"* (=help you) *"Oh, thanks."*

**thanks²** *n* [plural] **1** the things that you say or do to show that you are grateful to someone: *He left without saying a word of thanks.* **2 thanks to** because of: *We're late, thanks to you.*

**Thanks·giv·ing** /ˌθæŋksˈgɪvɪŋ/ *n* [C,U] **1** a holiday in the US and Canada in the fall when families have a large meal together to celebrate and be thankful for food, health, families etc. **2** the period of time just before and after this day: *Where are you going for Thanksgiving?*

**thank you¹** /ˈ. ./ *interjection* **1** said in order to tell someone that you are grateful for something that s/he has done: *"Here's the book you wanted, Katy." "Oh, thank you."* | *Thank you for coming to my birthday party.* ✗ DON'T SAY *"I thank you for coming."* ✗ **2 thank you/no thank you** said in order to accept or refuse something that someone is offering you: *"Would you like another cookie?" "No thank you."* –see usage note at PLEASE¹

**thank you²** *adj* **thank you letter/gift/note etc.** a letter, gift etc. that is given to someone to thank him/her for something

**thank you**[3] *n* something that you say or do to thank someone for something: *Please accept this gift as a thank you for your support.*

**that**[1] /ðæt/ *determiner, pron, plural* **those** **1** used when talking about someone or something that is farther away in time, distance, etc. than someone or something else: *Her mother gave her that necklace.* (=the one she is wearing) | *What should I do with that?* (=something you are pointing to) —compare THIS[1] **2** used when talking about someone or something that has already been mentioned or is already known about: *"Here's a picture of Kelly and me." "Oh, that's cute."* | *I had to park in that lot by the library.* | *We met for coffee later that day.* **3 that's it a)** used when what you have mentioned is all of something or the end of something: *It rains in February and that's it for the year.* **b)** SPOKEN used in order to tell someone that s/he has done something correctly: *Wave bye-bye, Ian. That's it!* **4 that is** used in order to correct a statement or give more exact information about something: *It's a seven day trip. That is, it's five days there plus two days driving.*

SPOKEN PHRASES

**5 at that** said in order to give more information: *She's pregnant, and having twins at that!* **6 that's that** said when something is completely finished or when a decision will not be changed: *You're not going and that's that!* **7 that's all there is to it** said in order to emphasize that something is simple to do, explain etc.: *We lost because we didn't play well. That's all there is to it.*

USAGE NOTE **that, who, whom, and which**

Use **that** to talk about people and things, but **whom** only for people: *There's the car that I saw yesterday.* | *There's the girl that I saw yesterday.* | *There's the girl whom I saw yesterday.* If you add more information to a sentence that is about an idea or thing, use **which**: *He broke his leg, which meant he couldn't come with us.* If you add information about a person, use **who**: *I'm going to visit my parents, who live in San Diego.* In informal speech and writing, if a noun phrase is used after **that** or **whom**, we often leave out these words: *The question (that) she asked was impolite.* | *The man (whom) the police arrested is my neighbor.*

**that**[2] /ðət; *strong* ðæt/ *conjunction* used in order to introduce a CLAUSE that is the object of a sentence, shows a result, or gives information about a person, thing, time etc. that has already been mentioned: *The rules state that if the ball hits the line, it's in.* | *Is it true that the Nelsons*

are moving? | *I was so hungry that I ate the whole pizza.* | *They're showing the movie that you wanted to see.* | *Have you gotten the letter that I sent you?* —see also **so...that** (SO[1])

**that**[3] /ðæt/ *adv* **1 that long/much/big etc.** SPOKEN used when talking about the size, number, or amount of something: *I hadn't been waiting that long.* **2 not that much/long/big etc.** SPOKEN not very much, long etc.: *His parents are big people, but he's not that tall.*

**thatch** /θætʃ/ *n* dried STRAW used for making roofs —**thatched** *adj*

**thaw**[1] /θɔ/ *v* **1** [I,T] also **thaw out** if ice or snow thaws or is thawed, it becomes warmer and turns into water **2** [I,T] also **thaw out** if frozen food thaws or is thawed, it becomes soft so it is ready to be cooked **3** [I] to become more friendly and less formal: *Relations between the two countries are beginning to thaw.* —compare MELT

**thaw**[2] *n* **1** [singular] a period of warm weather during which snow and ice melt: *the spring thaw* **2** a time when a relationship becomes more friendly

**the**[1] /ðə, *before a vowel* ði; *strong* ði/ *definite article, determiner* **1** used before nouns to show that you are talking about a particular person or thing, especially when it has already been mentioned or when there is only one: *I need to go to the grocery store.* | *That's the dress I want.* | *Hand me the red book.* —compare A **2** used as part of some names: *the United States* | *The Morrisons are planning to buy a new house.* (=used when you are talking about the whole family) **3** used before an adjective to make it into a noun: *They provide services for the blind.* **4** used before a singular noun to show that you are talking about that thing in general: *The computer has changed the way people work.* **5** used instead of "each" or "every": *Our car gets about 35 miles to the gallon.* **6** used before the names of musical instruments: *Kira's learning to play the piano.* **7** used in order to mention a part of the body or something that belongs to someone: *The ball hit him right in the eye!* | *The car* (=our car) *broke down again.* **8** used when talking about a particular period of time, especially a DECADE or date, or the time when a particular event happened: *music of the fifties* (=the 1950s) | *Immigrants poured into America in the late 1800s.* | *the Depression years* **9** used in order to emphasize that someone or something is important or famous: *It's definitely the movie to see.*

USAGE NOTE **using the**

Do not use **the** with uncountable nouns when you are using the general sense of the noun: *My favorite food is ice cream.* ✗ DON'T SAY *"My favorite food is the ice cream."* ✗ Use **the** with uncountable nouns when you mean a particular thing: *The ice cream we bought yesterday is already gone!* Do not use **the** with plural uncountable nouns when you are using the general sense of the noun: *Beth likes cats.* ✗ DON'T SAY "Beth likes the cats." ✗ Use **the** with plural uncountable nouns when you mean a particular group of things: *The cats we saw in the pet store were cute.* Use **the** to talk about something that is the only one of its type: *The sun is really hot today.*

**the²** *adv* used in comparisons: *She's the smartest kid in her class.* | *The more you practice, the better you'll play.*

**the·a·ter** /'θiəṭɚ/ *n* **1** a building with a stage where plays are performed: *the Apollo Theater* **2** [U] the work of acting in, writing, or organizing plays: *She's been working* **in theater** *for many years.* **3** a building where movies are shown

**the·at·ri·cal** /θi'ætrɪkəl/ *adj* **1** relating to the theater: *an expensive theatrical production* **2** behaving in a way that is intended to make people notice you: *a theatrical gesture* **–theatrics** *n* [plural]

**theft** /θɛft/ *n* [C,U] the act or crime of stealing something: *car theft* | *the theft of their luggage*

**their** /ðɚ; *strong* ðɛr/ *possessive adj* **1** belonging or relating to the people, animals, or things that have been mentioned, or are known about: *The guests left their coats on the bed.* | *Their little boy plays with Morgan sometimes.* **2** NONSTANDARD used instead of "his" or "her" after words such as someone, anyone etc.: *Everybody has their own ideas about it.*

**theirs** /ðɛrz/ *possessive pron* **1** the thing or things belonging to or relating to the people or things that have been mentioned, or are known about: *Some friends of theirs are staying with them.* | *When our washing machine broke the neighbors let us use theirs.* **2** NONSTANDARD used instead of "his" or "hers" after words such as someone, anyone, everyone etc.: *Okay, get your coats. Does everyone have theirs?*

**them** /ðəm, əm; *strong* ðɛm/ *pron* **1** the object form of "they": *Has anybody seen my keys? I can't find them.* | *My folks wanted me to tell them all about my trip.* **2** NONSTANDARD used instead of "him" or "her" after words such as someone, anyone, everyone etc.: *Somebody phoned for you, so I told them to call back later.* –see usage note at ME

**theme** /θim/ *n* **1** the main subject or idea in a book, movie, speech etc.: *The theme of the movie is how people react to death.* **2 theme music/song/tune** music or a song that is always played with a particular television or radio program **–thematic** /θi'mæṭɪk/ *adj*

**theme park** /'. ./ *n* an AMUSEMENT PARK that

is based on one subject such as water or space travel

**them·selves** /ðəm'sɛlvz, ðɛm-/ *pron* **1** the REFLEXIVE form of "they": *People usually like to talk about themselves.* **2** the strong form of "they," used in order to emphasize the subject or object of a sentence: *Doctors themselves admit that the treatment does not always work.* **3** (all) by themselves **a)** without help: *The kids made cookies all by themselves.* **b)** alone: *Many old people live by themselves* **4** (all) to themselves for their own use: *The kids had the pool to themselves today.*

**then¹** /ðɛn/ *adv* **1** after something has happened; next: *We could have lunch and then go shopping.* **2** at a particular time in the past or future: *I'll have to leave by then.* | *My family lived in New York back then.* **3** SPOKEN said in order to show that what you are saying is related in some way to what has been said before: *"He can't come on Friday." "Then how about Saturday?"* | *So you're going into nursing then?* **4** used in order to say that if one thing is true, the other thing is also true or should be the correct result: *"I have to pick Bobby up at school." "Then you should leave by 2:30."* **5** used in order to add something to what you have just said: *He's really busy at work, and then there's the new baby, too!* **6 then and there** immediately: *I would have given up then and there if my parents hadn't encouraged me.* –see also **but then (again)...** (BUT¹) **(every) now and then** (NOW¹)

**then²** *adj* at that time in the past: *the then President of the US*

**the·o·lo·gian** /ˌθiə'loudʒən/ *n* someone who studies or writes about THEOLOGY

**the·ol·o·gy** /θi'ɑlədʒi/ *n* [U] the study of religion, religious beliefs, and God **–theological** /ˌθiə'lɑdʒɪkəl/ *adj*

**the·o·rem** /'θiərəm, 'θɪrəm/ *n* TECHNICAL a statement that can be shown to be true, especially in mathematics

**the·o·ret·i·cal** /ˌθiə'rɛṭɪkəl/ *adj* **1** relating to THEORY: *theoretical physics* **2** a theoretical situation or condition could exist but does not yet exist **–theoretically** *adv*

**the·o·rist** /'θiərɪst/, **the·o·re·ti·cian** /ˌθiərə'tɪʃən/ *n* someone who develops ideas that explain why particular things happen or are true

**the·o·rize** /'θiəˌraɪz/ *v* [I,T] to think of a possible explanation or reason for a particular event, fact etc.: *Doctors theorize that the infection is passed from animals to humans.*

**the·o·ry** /'θiəri, 'θɪri/ *n* **1** an explanation for something that may be reasonable, but it has not yet been proven to be true: *Darwin's theory of evolution* | *a theory that light is made up of waves* **2 in theory** something that is true in theory is supposed to be true but may not be true: *In theory, the crime rate should decrease* *as employment increases.* **3** [U] the general principles or ideas of a subject such as science or music: *studying music theory*

**ther·a·peu·tic** /ˌθɛrə'pyuţɪk/ *adj* **1** relating to the treatment or cure of a disease: *therapeutic drugs* **2** making you feel calm and relaxed: *Long walks can be therapeutic.*

**ther·a·py** /'θɛrəpi/ *n* [C,U] the treatment of an illness or injury, or of a mental or emotional problem, especially without using drugs or SURGERY: *Ted's having physical therapy for his back.* | *He's been **in therapy** for years.* —**therapist** *n*

**there¹** /ðɛr/ *pron* used as the subject of a sentence in order to say that something exists or happens: *There were several people hurt in the accident.* | *Suddenly, there was a loud crash.* | *Are there any questions?*

**there²** *adv* **1** in or to a particular place that is not where you are or near you: *Would you hand me that glass over there?* | *He was just sitting there.* | *The party was almost over by the time I got there.* (=arrived) —compare HERE¹ **2** at a particular point in time, in a story etc.: *I'll read this chapter and stop there.* **3** **be there (for sb)** if someone is there for you, s/he will always help and support you when you have problems: *My folks are great - they're always there for me.*

---
SPOKEN PHRASES

**4** **there (you go)** INFORMAL **a)** used when giving something to someone or when you have done something for someone: *Come on Aaron, let's get you your bottle - there you go.* **b)** used in order to encourage someone: *Just one more situp, there.* **5** **there** used when you have finished something: *There, that's the last piece of the puzzle.* **6** **there's...** said in order to make someone look at or pay attention to someone or something: *There's that restaurant I was telling you about.* **7** **hello/hi there** used when greeting someone, especially when you have just noticed him/her: *Hi there. You must be Liane.* **8** **there, there** used in order to comfort a child: *There, there, it's all right.*

---

—see also **then and there** (THEN¹)

**there·a·bouts** /ˌðɛrə'baʊts, 'ðɛrəˌbaʊts/ *adv* near a particular number, amount, time etc.: *The chair costs $50 **or thereabouts**.*

**there·af·ter** /ðɛr'æftɚ/ *adv* FORMAL after a particular event or time; AFTERWARDS: *The store caught fire and closed **shortly thereafter**.*

**there·by** /ðɛr'baɪ, 'ðɛrbaɪ/ *adv* FORMAL with the result that: *Expenses were cut 12%, thereby increasing efficiency.*

**there·fore** /'ðɛrfɔr/ *adv* FORMAL for the reason that has just been mentioned: *His health continued to decline, and therefore he retired from his job.*

**there·in** /ðɛr'ɪn/ *adv* FORMAL **1** in that place, or in that piece of writing: *the contract and all the rules therein* **2** **therein lies** used in order to state the cause of something: *He speaks the truth, and therein lies his power.*

**there·of** /ðɛr'ʌv/ *adv* FORMAL relating to something that has just been mentioned: *insurance for the home and the contents thereof*

**there·up·on** /'ðɛrəˌpɑn, ˌðɛrə'pɑn/ *adv* FORMAL ⇨ THEREFORE

**ther·mal** /'θɚməl/ *adj* relating to or caused by heat: *thermal underwear* | *thermal energy*

**ther·mom·e·ter** /θɚ'mɑməţɚ/ *n* a piece of equipment that measures the temperature of the air, your body etc.

**ther·mo·nu·cle·ar** /ˌθɚmoʊ'nukliɚ/ *adj* relating to a NUCLEAR reaction caused by very high heat

**Ther·mos** /'θɚməs/, **Thermos bot·tle** /'.. ˌ../ *n* TRADEMARK a special container like a bottle that keeps hot drinks hot or cold drinks cold

**ther·mo·stat** /'θɚməˌstæt/ *n* an instrument that controls the temperature of a room, machine etc.

**the·sau·rus** /θɪ'sɔrəs/ *n, plural* **thesauruses** *or* **thesauri** /-'sɔraɪ/ a book in which words are put into groups with other words that have a similar meaning

**these** /ðiz/ *determiner, pronoun* the plural form of THIS

**the·sis** /'θisɪs/ *n, plural* **theses** /'θisiz/ **1** a long piece of writing about a particular subject that you do for a university degree: *She's writing her thesis on Victorian women criminals.* **2** FORMAL an idea or statement that tries to explain why something happens

**they** /ðeɪ/ *pron* **1** the people, animals, or things that have been mentioned or are known about: *Ken gave me flowers, aren't they beautiful?* | *I stopped at Doris and Ed's place, but they weren't home.* | *They're* (=they are) *not coming until 9:00.* **2** a particular group or organization, or the people involved in it: *They sell all different kinds of candles.* | *They took my appendix out last year.* | *They're going to build a new road.* **3** used in order to say what people in general believe, think, are saying etc.: *They say it's bad luck to spill salt.* **4** NONSTANDARD used instead of "he" or "she" after words such as someone, anyone, everyone etc.: *Somebody at work said that they had known you in college.*

**they'd** /ðeɪd/ **1** the short form of "they had": *They'd had a lot to drink.* **2** the short form of "they would": *They'd like to visit us soon.*

**they'll** /ðeɪl, ðɛl/ the short form of "they will": *They'll have to wait.*

**they're** /ðɚ; *strong* ðɛr/ the short form of "they are": *They're very nice people.*

**they've** /ðeɪv/ the short form of "they have": *They've been here before.*

thick

a thick book          a thin book

**thick¹** /θɪk/ *adj* **1** measuring a large distance, or a larger distance than usual, between two opposite sides or surfaces: *a nice thick piece of bread* | *The clouds were getting thicker.* −opposite THIN¹ **2** used in order to describe the distance between two opposite sides or surfaces: *The ice is two feet/five inches thick on the lake.* **3** a substance that is thick has very little water in it: *thick soup* **4** filling the air so it is difficult to see through or breathe in: *The air was thick with smoke from the fire.* **5** growing very close together with not much space in between: *He has thick black hair.* −**thickly** *adv*

**thick²** *n* **1 be in the thick of sth** to be involved in the most active, dangerous etc. part of a situation: *US troops are right in the thick of the action.* **2 through thick and thin** in spite of any difficulties or problems: *They stayed married through thick and thin.*

**thick·en** /'θɪkən/ *v* [I,T] to become thick, or make something thick: *Thicken the soup with flour.*

**thick·et** /'θɪkɪt/ *n* a group of bushes and small trees

**thick·ness** /'θɪknɪs/ *n* [C,U] how thick something is: *Roll out the dough to a thickness of 1 inch.*

**thick·set** /ˌθɪk'sɛt◂/ *adj* having a body that is wide and strong

**thick-skinned** /ˌ. '.◂/ *adj* not being offended if people criticize you or do not like you

**thief** /θif/ *n, plural* **thieves** /θivz/ someone who steals things: *a car thief*

**thigh** /θaɪ/ *n* the top part of your leg between your knee and your HIP −see picture at BODY

**thim·ble** /'θɪmbəl/ *n* a small hard cap that you put over the end of your finger to protect it when you are sewing

**thin¹** /θɪn/ *adj* **thinner, thinnest 1** measuring a small distance, or a smaller distance than usual, between two opposite sides or surfaces: *a thin slice of cheese* | *a wire as thin as a human hair* | *The walls here are paper-thin.* (=very thin) −opposite THICK¹ −see picture at THICK¹ **2** having little fat on your body: *He's tall, very thin, and has dark hair.* **3** air that is thin is difficult to breathe because there is not much OXYGEN in it **4** not close together, and with spaces in between: *His hair is very thin on top.* **5** a substance that is thin has a lot of water in it: *thin broth* −**thinness** *n* [U] −**thin** *adv* NONSTANDARD −see also THINLY

**thin²** *v* **-nned, -nning** [T] to make something thinner or to become thinner: *his thinning hair* | *paint thinned with water*

**thin out** *phr v* [I] if a crowd thins out, people gradually leave so there are fewer of them

**thing** /θɪŋ/ *n* **1** a fact, idea, statement, action, or event: *A funny thing happened last week.* | *I said the first thing that came into my mind.* | *I have better things to do with my time.* | **One thing** is certain: we'll never go there again! **2** an object: *Do you know how to turn this thing off?* | *The box had all sorts of things in it.* | *I don't have a thing to wear!* **3 not know/feel/see etc. a thing** to know, feel, see etc. nothing: *He doesn't know a thing about fixing a car.* | *Sarah's leaving you, and you can't do a thing about it.* **4 there's no such thing (as sth)** used in order to emphasize that someone or something does not exist or does not happen: *There's no such thing as Santa Claus!* **5 be seeing/hearing things** to believe that you are seeing or hearing something that is not really there **6 the last thing sb wants/expects etc.** something that someone does not want, expect etc. at all: *The last thing we wanted was to start a fight.* **7 do your own thing**

INFORMAL to do what you want, and not what someone else wants you to do

---

SPOKEN PHRASES

**8 the thing is** said when explaining a problem or the reason for something: *We want to come, but the thing is we can't find a babysitter.* **9 for one thing** said when giving a reason for something: *I don't think she'll get the part - for one thing she can't sing!* **10 it's a good thing (that)** used in order to say that it is lucky or good that something happened: *It's a good thing the drug store's open late.* **11 first thing** at the beginning of the day or morning: *I'll call you first thing tomorrow, OK?* **12 (it's) just one of those things** used in order to say that something that has happened is not someone's fault or could not have been avoided **13 it's (just) one thing after another** said when a lot of unpleasant things happen to you

---

−see also THINGS

**thing·a·ma·jig** /'θɪŋəməˌdʒɪg/ n SPOKEN said when you cannot remember the real name of the thing you want to mention: *Where's the thingamajig for the garlic?*

**things** /θɪŋz/ n [plural] **1** life in general and the way it affects someone: *How are things with you?|Things couldn't be better.|I know things can be very hard at times.* **2** the things you own or the things you are carrying: *Just put your things there.*

**think** /θɪŋk/ thought, thought, thinking v **1** [T] to have an opinion or belief about something: *Fred thought (that) it was a good idea.|So, what do you think about/of my new car?|I didn't think you liked mayonnaise.* (=I believed you did not like it) **2** [I] to use your mind to decide something, solve problems, have ideas etc.: *She lay awake thinking about the money.|Just a second, I'm thinking.* **3 think about/of doing sth** to consider the possibility of doing something: *I'm thinking about moving to Albuquerque.* **4 think better of sth** to decide not to do something that you had intended to do, especially something bad or that could cause problems: *He reached for a cigar, but then thought better of it.* **5 think nothing of (doing sth)** to do something easily that other people consider to be difficult or unusual: *Purdey thinks nothing of driving two hours to work every day.* **6 think twice** to consider a decision very carefully before you decide if you will do it or not: *You should think twice about/before getting involved with a married man.* **7 who would have thought?** used in order to say that something is very surprising: *Who'd have thought being a mother would make you so happy?* **8 think well/highly of** to admire or approve of someone or his/her work: *People had always thought highly of her grandmother.*

**9 think positively** to believe that you are going to be successful or that a situation is going to have a good result

---

SPOKEN PHRASES

**10 I think** said when you believe something is true but you are not sure: *Quiet! I think I heard a burglar.* **11 I think so/I don't think so** used when answering a question to say that you do or do not believe something is true: *"Will she be back on Friday?" "I think so."* **12 I think I'll/I thought I'd** said when telling someone what you will probably do: *I think I'll stay with my parents through Christmas.|I thought I'd go jogging today.* **13 I thought...** **a)** used in order to say what you believed was true, when you discover it is not true: *Oh, I thought you were Catholic.* **b)** used in order to report exactly what was in your mind: *And I thought, wow, I can't believe she's 15 already.* **14 when you think about it** used in order to say that you realize something about the subject or fact that you are considering: *It's a crazy price for a car when you think about it.* **15 I'm thinking** NONSTANDARD used in order to tell someone your opinion or what you are considering: *I'm thinking it's a bad time to go on vacation.* **16 just think!** said when asking someone to imagine or consider something: *Just think - tomorrow we'll be in Hawaii!* **17 come to think of it** said when you have just remembered something that is related to your conversation: *Come to think of it, I did see Rita yesterday.*

---

−see also UNTHINKABLE

**think back** phr v [I] to think about something that you remember from the past: *Think back to what we learned last week about the Constitution.*

**think of** sb/sth phr v [T] **1** to produce a new idea, suggestion etc.: *Can you think of anything better to do?* **2** to remember a name or fact: *I can't think of his name now.* **3** to show that you want to treat other people well: *Bill's always thinking of others.*

**think** sth ↔ **out** phr v [T] to plan all the details of something very carefully: *Everything has been really well thought out.*

**think** sth ↔ **over** phr v [T] to consider something carefully before making a decision: *Take a few days to think over our offer.*

**think** sth ↔ **through** phr v [T] to think carefully about the possible results of doing something: *Give us time to think it through.*

**think** sth ↔ **up** phr v [T] to produce an idea, plan etc. that is completely new: *thinking up ways to get more customers*

**think·ing** /'θɪŋkɪŋ/ n [U] **1** an opinion about something, or an attitude toward something: *It is difficult to know what the Democratic party's* *thinking is on the issue.* **2** the activity of using your mind to solve a problem, produce thoughts etc.: *a situation that requires careful thinking*

**think tank** /'. ./ *n* a committee of people with experience in a particular subject that an organization or government establishes to produce ideas and give advice: *a right-wing think tank*

**thin·ly** /'θɪnli/ *adv* **1** in a way that leaves a very small distance between two opposite sides or surfaces: *a **thinly sliced** onion* **2** in a way that covers a large area but leaves a lot of space in between: *a **thinly populated** area*

**third** /θɚd/ *number* **1** 3rd **2** 1/3

**third base** /ˌ. './ *n* [singular] in baseball, the third place that a player must touch before s/he can gain a point −see picture on page 472

**third de·gree** /ˌ. .'.◂/ *n* **give sb the third degree** INFORMAL to ask someone a lot of questions in order to get information from him/her

**third-de·gree burn** /ˌ. .ˌ './ *n* a very severe burn that goes through someone's skin

**third per·son** /ˌ. '../ *n* [singular] TECHNICAL in grammar, a form of a verb or pronoun that you use to show the person or thing that is being mentioned. "He," "she," "it," and "they" are all third person pronouns −compare FIRST PERSON, SECOND PERSON

**third-rate** /ˌ. '.◂/ *adj* of very bad quality

**Third World** /ˌ. '.◂/ *n* **the Third World** a phrase meaning the poorer countries of the world that do not have developed industries, which some people consider to be offensive −**Third World** /ˌ. '.◂/ *adj*

**thirst** /θɚst/ *n* **1** [singular] the feeling of wanting a drink to **quench your thirst** (=get rid of it) ✗ DON'T SAY "I have thirst." ✗ **2** [U] the state of not having enough to drink: *The cattle died **of thirst**.* **3** **a thirst for sth** a strong desire for something such as knowledge, power, excitement etc.

**thirst·y** /'θɚsti/ *adj* **1** feeling that you want to drink something: *I'm thirsty - let's get some beer.* **2** **thirsty for sth** LITERARY having a strong desire for something −**thirstily** *adv*

**thir·teen** /ˌθɚ'tin◂/ *number* 13 −**thirteenth** /ˌθɚ'tinθ◂/ *number*

**thir·ty** /'θɚti/ *number* **1** 30 **2** **the thirties** **a)** the years between 1930 and 1939 **b)** the numbers between 30 and 39, especially when used for measuring temperature −**thirtieth** /'θɚtiɪθ/ *number*

**this¹** /ðɪs/ *determiner, pron, plural* **these** **1** used when talking about someone or something that is closer in time, distance etc. than someone or something else: *My mother gave me this necklace.* (=the one I am wearing) | *What should I do with this?* (=something I am holding and showing you) | *We're driving up to the lake this Sunday.* (=the Sunday that is coming) −compare THAT¹ **2** used when talking about a person, thing etc. that has already been men-

tioned or that is already known about: *We took these photos on our vacation last summer.* | *This is the third time he's been late this week.* **3** SPOKEN used in conversation to mention a particular person or thing: *This friend of mine said he could get us tickets.* | *We saw this really cool movie last night.* **4** **this is** SPOKEN used in order to introduce someone to someone else: *Nancy, this is my wife, Elaine.* **5** **this and that** various different things, subjects etc.: *We just talked about guys and this and that.*

**this²** *adv* used when talking about the size, number, degree, or amount of something: *I've never stayed up this late before.* | *Katie's about this tall now.* (=said when using your hands to show a size)

**this·tle** /'θɪsəl/ *n* a wild plant with purple flowers and leaves that have sharp points

**thong** /θɔŋ, θɑŋ/ *n* **1** a single string that forms part of a piece of clothing **2** a long thin piece of leather used for fastening things or as part of a whip **3** [C usually plural] a pair of summer shoes, usually made of rubber, with only a v-shaped band across the front that fits between your toes to hold the shoes on

**thorn** /θɔrn/ *n* **1** a sharp point that grows on a plant such as a rose **2** **a thorn in your side** someone or something that annoys you or causes you problems over a long time

**thorn·y** /'θɔrni/ *adj* **1** **thorny question/ problem/issue etc.** a question, problem etc. that is very difficult to deal with **2** having a lot of THORNS

**thor·ough** /'θɚou, 'θʌrou/ *adj* **1** including every possible detail: *The police conducted a thorough search of the property.* **2** careful to do everything that you should and avoid mistakes: *As a scientist, Madison is methodical and thorough.*

**thor·ough·bred** /'θɚəˌbrɛd, 'θɚou-, 'θʌr-/ *n* a horse that has parents of the same very good breed

**thor·ough·fare** /'θɚəˌfɛr, 'θɚou-, 'θʌr-/ *n* the main road through a city

**thor·ough·ly** /'θɚouli, 'θʌr-/ *adv* **1** completely or very much: *Thanks for dinner; I thoroughly enjoyed it.* **2** carefully and completely: *Rinse the vegetables thoroughly.*

**those** /ðouz/ *determiner, pron* the plural of THAT

**though¹** /ðou/ *conjunction* **1** used in order to introduce a statement that is surprising, unexpected, or different from your other statements: *Though Beattie is almost 40, she still plans to compete.* | *I seem to keep gaining weight, **even though** I'm exercising regularly.* −compare ALTHOUGH **2** used like "but" in order to add a fact or opinion to what you have said: *I bought it at one of the department stores, though it's probably cheaper at K-Mart.* **3** **as though** used like "as if" in order to say how something seems or appears: *She was staring at me as though she knew me.*

**though**[2] *adv* SPOKEN in spite of that: *Raleigh's a nice city. Mark doesn't want to leave Georgia, though.*

**thought**[1] /θɔt/ *v* the past tense and PAST PARTICIPLE of THINK

**thought**[2] *n* **1** something that you think of, think about, or remember: *Do you have any thoughts on the subject? | Even the thought of flying scares me.* **2** [U] the act of thinking: *She sat at her desk, deep in thought.* (=thinking so much she did not notice anything else) **3** [U] the act of considering something carefully and seriously: *You need to give the decision plenty of thought.* **4** (it's) just a thought SPOKEN said when you have made a suggestion and you have not thought about it very much **5** [C,U] a feeling of caring about someone: *He had given no thought to the other passengers.* **6** [C,U] an intention to do something: *We worked with no thought of making money.*

**thought·ful** /'θɔtfəl/ *adj* **1** serious and quiet because you are thinking about something: *a thoughtful expression on his face* **2** careful to do things to make other people happy or comfortable: *You have a very thoughtful husband.* –**thoughtfully** *adv* –**thoughtfulness** *n* [U]

**thought·less** /'θɔtlɪs/ *adj* not thinking about the needs and feelings of other people: *a thoughtless remark/comment*

**thou·sand** /'θaʊzənd/ *number* **1** 1000 **2** **thousands of** INFORMAL a lot of: *a cottage thousands of miles from anywhere* –**thousandth** *adj*

**thrash** /θræʃ/ *v* **1** [T] to hit someone violently, often as a punishment **2** [I] to move from side to side in an uncontrolled way: *a fish thrashing around on dry land* –**thrashing** *n* [C,U]

**thrash** sth ↔ **out** *phr v* [T] to discuss a problem thoroughly until you find an answer: *Officials are still trying to thrash out an agreement.*

**thread**[1] /θrɛd/ *n* **1** [C,U] a long thin line of cotton, silk etc. that you use to sew cloth: *a spool of thread* **2** [singular] the relation between different parts of a story, explanation etc.: *He lost the thread* (=forgot the main part) *of his argument.* **3** a raised line of metal that winds around the bottom part of a screw

**thread**[2] *v* [T] **1** to put thread, string, rope etc. through a hole: *Will you thread the needle for me?* **2** **thread your way through/down etc.** to move through a place by carefully going around things that are in the way: *a biker threading his way through traffic*

**thread·bare** /'θrɛdbɛr/ *adj* clothes, CARPETs etc. that are threadbare are very thin because they have been used a lot

**threat** /θrɛt/ *n* **1** [C,U] a statement or warning that you will cause someone trouble, pain, or sadness: *He made a threat against my family. | a death threat from the kidnappers* **2** [C usually singular] the possibility that something bad will happen: *a threat of rain* **3** [C usually singular] someone or something that is a danger to something else: *a threat to national security*

**threat·en** /'θrɛtṇ/ *v* **1** [T] to say that you will cause someone trouble, pain etc. if s/he does not do what you want: *Samba threatened to run away from home. | Don't you threaten me!* **2** [T] to be likely to harm or destroy something: *Pollution is threatening the historical buildings of Athens.* **3** [I,T] if something unpleasant threatens to happen, it seems likely to happen: *The fighting threatens to become a major war.*

**threat·en·ing** /'θrɛtṇ-ɪŋ/ *adj* making threats or intended to threaten someone: *a threatening letter*

**three** /θri/ *number* **1** 3 **2** three o'clock: *I'll meet you at three.*

**three-di·men·sion·al** /ˌ. .'...◂/, **3-D** /ˌθri 'di◂/ *adj* having or seeming to have length, depth, and height: *a 3-D movie*

**thresh** /θrɛʃ/ *v* [I,T] to separate the grain from corn, wheat etc. by beating it –**thresher** *n*

**thresh·old** /'θrɛʃhoʊld, -ʃoʊld/ *n* **1** **on the threshold of sth** at the beginning of a new and important event or development: *We're on the threshold of a new period in telecommunications.* **2** the level at which something begins to happen or have an effect on something: *a plan to raise/lower the threshold for business tax | She has a high/low pain threshold.* **3** the entrance to a room, or the area of floor at the entrance

**threw** /θru/ *v* the past tense of THROW

**thrift** /θrɪft/ *n* [U] OLD-FASHIONED wise and careful use of money **thrifty** *adj*

**thrift store** /'. ./, **thrift shop** *n* a store that sells used goods, especially clothes, often in order to get money for a CHARITY

**thrill**[1] /θrɪl/ *n* a strong feeling of excitement and pleasure, or the thing that makes you feel this: *I'll never forget the thrill of my first parachute jump.*

**thrill**[2] *v* [I,T] to feel strong excitement and pleasure, or make someone else feel this: *Manley thrilled us with stories from his travels.*

**thrilled** /θrɪld/ *adj* very excited, pleased, or happy: *I'm thrilled to finally have my own car.*

**thrill·er** /'θrɪlɚ/ *n* a movie or book that tells an exciting story about murder, crime etc.

**thrill·ing** /'θrɪlɪŋ/ *adj* exciting and interesting: *a football game with a thrilling finish*

**thrive** /θraɪv/ *v* **thrived** *or* **throve, thrived, thriving** [I] FORMAL to become very successful or very strong and healthy: *a plant that is able to thrive in dry conditions*

**thriv·ing** /ˈθraɪvɪŋ/ *adj* very successful: *a thriving business*

**throat** /θroʊt/ *n* **1** the passage from the back of your mouth down the inside of your neck: *I have a sore throat.* **2** the front of your neck: *The attacker cut his throat with a razor.* **3 force/ram sth down sb's throat** to force someone to accept your ideas or listen to your opinions when s/he does not want to **4 be at each other's throats** if two people are at each other's throats, they are fighting or arguing with each other −see also **clear your throat** (CLEAR²) **jump down sb's throat** (JUMP¹)

**throat·y** /ˈθroʊti/ *adj* making a low rough sound when you speak, sing, cough etc.

**throb¹** /θrɑb/ *v* **-bbed, -bbing** [I] **1** if a part of your body throbs, you get a regular feeling of pain in it: *My head was throbbing with pain.* **2** to beat strongly and regularly

**throb²** *n* a strong regular beat: *the low throb of the music* −see also HEARTTHROB

**throes** /θroʊz/ *n* [plural] **in the throes of sth** in the middle of trying to deal with a very difficult situation: *a woman in the throes of childbirth*

**throne** /θroʊn/ *n* **1** the chair on which a king or queen sits **2 the throne** the position and power of being king or queen

**throng¹** /θrɔŋ, θrɑŋ/ *n* LITERARY ⇨ CROWD¹

**throng²** *v* [I,T] LITERARY if people throng a place, they go there in large numbers: *crowds thronging St. Peter's Square*

**throt·tle¹** /ˈθrɑtl/ *v* [T] ⇨ STRANGLE

**throttle²** *n* TECHNICAL a piece of equipment that controls the amount of gas going into an engine

**through¹** /θru/ *prep* **1** into one end of a passage, door etc. and out the other end or side: *He climbed in through the window.* | *a train going through a tunnel* | *water flowing through a pipe* **2** going into an area, group etc. and moving across it or within it: *He tried to push his way through the crowd.* | *a plane flying through the air* | *a trip through Europe* **3** by means of, or because of someone or something: *They reached a settlement through negotiations.* **4** if you see or hear something through a window, wall etc., the window, wall etc. is between you and it: *I could see him through the window.* | *music coming through the walls* **5** during and to the end of a period of time: *She slept calmly through the night.* **6** from one side of a thing or place to the other: *We drove through a red light by accident.* | *A dog chewed through the rope.* **7 Friday through Sunday/ through May 15th etc.** from Friday until the end of Sunday, from Friday until the end of May 15th etc.: *The exhibit will be here through July 31st.* **8 look/search/go etc. through sth** to look, search etc. among all the parts of something: *I've searched through my files but I can't find the receipt.* **9 get through sth** to deal with a difficult situation successfully: *Janet needed a lot of support to get through the divorce.*

**through²** *adv* **1** from one end or side of something to the other: *I held the door to let them through.* | *He walked through to the library.* **2 read/think/study etc. sth through** to read, think etc. about something very carefully from beginning to end: *Read it through before signing it.* **3 through and through** completely: *He came in from the rain soaked through and through.* −see also **come through** (COME) **get through** (GET) **go through** (GO¹) **pull through** (PULL¹)

**through³** *adj* **be through (with sb/sth)** INFORMAL **a)** to have finished using something, doing something etc.: *I'm through with the phone now if you still need it.* **b)** to no longer have a romantic relationship with someone: *Steve and I are through!*

**through·out** /θruˈaʊt/ *adv, prep* **1** in every part of a place: *Thanksgiving is celebrated throughout the US.* **2** during all of a particular time: *She was calm throughout the interview.*

**throve** /θroʊv/ *v* a past tense of THRIVE

**throw¹** /θroʊ/ *v* **threw, thrown, throwing**

throw away

**1** ▶THROW A BALL/ STONE ETC.◀ [I,T] to make an object move quickly through the air by moving your arm: *It's Ted's turn to throw.* | *Some kids are throwing bottles at the wall.* (=in order to hit it) | *Throw the ball to Daddy.*
**2** ▶PUT STH CARELESSLY◀ [T] to put something somewhere quickly and carelessly: *Just throw your coat on the bed.*
**3** ▶PUSH ROUGHLY◀ [T] to push someone roughly toward a particular direction or position: *Police threw the man to the ground and tied his hands.*
**4 throw yourself on/down etc.** to move somewhere suddenly and with force: *Elise threw herself on the bed and started to cry.*
**5** ▶MAKE SB FALL◀ [T] if a horse throws its rider, it makes him/her fall off
**6** ▶MOVE HANDS/HEAD ETC.◀ [T] to suddenly move your hands, arms, head etc. in a particular direction: *Vic threw his head back and laughed.*
**7 throw sb in jail** INFORMAL to put someone in prison
**8 throw sb** SPOKEN to confuse or shock someone, especially by suddenly saying something: *His reaction threw me for a loop.* (=completely confused me)
**9 throw a party** to organize a party and invite people
**10 throw your weight around** to use your

authority in an unreasonable way

**11 throw the book at sb** INFORMAL to punish someone as severely as possible

**throw** sth ↔ **away** *phr v* [T] **1** to get rid of something that you do not want or need: *Do you still want the newspaper, or can I **throw** it **away**?* **2** to lose or waste a chance, advantage etc.: *This is a good chance to study abroad; don't **throw** it **away**.*

**throw in** *phr v* [T] **1** [throw sth ↔ in] to add something, especially to what you are selling: *If you're really interested in the desk, we'll **throw in** the chair.* **2 throw in the towel** INFORMAL to admit that you have been defeated

**throw** sb/sth ↔ **off** *phr v* [T] **1** to take off a piece of clothing quickly and carelessly **2** to escape from someone: *Somehow he managed to **throw** them **off** his trail.*

**throw** sth ↔ **on** *phr v* [T] to put on a piece of clothing quickly and carelessly

**throw out** *phr v* [T] **1** [throw sth ↔ out] to get rid of something that you do not want or need: *The meat smells funny - you'd better **throw** it **out**.* **2** [throw sb ↔ out] to make someone leave a place quickly because s/he has behaved badly: *Jim got **thrown out of** the Navy for taking drugs.*

**throw** sth ↔ **together** *phr v* [T] to make something quickly and not very carefully: *How about **throwing** some sandwiches **together** for lunch?*

**throw up** *phr v* [I,T] INFORMAL ⇨ VOMIT¹

**throw²** *n* **1** an act of throwing something such as a ball: *The throw went right to first base.* **2** the distance that something is thrown: *a throw of 30 feet*

**throw·a·way** /'θroʊəˌweɪ/ *adj* **1 throwaway remark/line etc.** a short remark that is said quickly and without thinking carefully **2 throwaway society** a society that wastes things instead of caring about the environment

**throw·back** /'θroʊbæk/ *n* something that is like something that existed in the past: *His music is a **throwback to** the 1970s.*

**thrown** /θroʊn/ *v* the PAST PARTICIPLE of THROW

**thru** /θru/ *prep, adj, adv* NONSTANDARD ⇨ THROUGH¹

**thrust¹** /θrʌst/ *v* **thrust, thrust, thrusting** [T] to push something somewhere with a sudden or violent movement: *Dean **thrust** his hands **in** his pockets.*

**thrust²** *n* **1** [C,U] a sudden strong movement that pushes something forward: *the thrust of an airplane* **2 the thrust** the main meaning or most important part of what someone says or does: *The thrust of his argument is that all of life is political.*

**thru·way** /'θruweɪ/ *n* a wide road for fast traffic

**thud** /θʌd/ *n* the low sound that is made by a heavy object hitting something else: *The box fell with a thud.* –**thud** *v* [I]

**thug** /θʌg/ *n* a violent person

**thumb¹** /θʌm/ *n* **1** the thickest finger on your hand, that helps you hold things –see picture at HAND¹ **2 be under sb's thumb** to do everything that someone wants **3 give sth the thumbs up/down** to show that you approve or disapprove of something: *We give the movie a thumbs up!*

**thumb²** *v* **1 thumb a ride** INFORMAL ⇨ HITCHHIKE **2 thumb your nose at** to show that you do not respect rules, laws, someone's opinion etc.: *The Senator is basically thumbing his nose at the state's voters.*

**thumb through** *phr v* [T] to look through a book, magazine etc. quickly

**thumb·nail¹** /'θʌmneɪl/ *adj* **thumbnail sketch/description** a short description that gives only the main facts

**thumbnail²** *n* the nail on your thumb

**thumb·tack** /'θʌmtæk/ *n* a short pin with a wide flat top, used for attaching papers to walls

**thump** /θʌmp/ *v* **1** [I,T] to make a dull sound by beating or falling against a surface: *a dog thumping his tail on the floor* **2** [I] if your heart thumps, it beats very quickly because you are frightened or excited **3** [T] INFORMAL to hit someone very hard with your hand closed: *I'm going to thump you on the head if you don't stop talking!* –**thump** *n*

**thun·der¹** /'θʌndɚ/ *n* [U] the loud noise that you hear during a storm, usually after a flash of LIGHTNING

**thunder²** *v* **1 it thunders** if it thunders, a loud noise comes from the sky, usually after LIGHTNING **2** [I] to make a very loud noise: *The kids came thundering downstairs.*

**thun·der·bolt** /'θʌndɚˌboʊlt/ *n* a flash of LIGHTNING that hits something

**thun·der·clap** /'θʌndɚˌklæp/ *n* a loud noise of THUNDER

**thun·der·cloud** /'θʌndɚˌklaʊd/ *n* a large dark cloud in a storm

**thun·der·ous** /'θʌndərəs/ *adj* extremely loud: *thunderous applause*

**thun·der·storm** /'θʌndɚˌstɔrm/ *n* a storm with THUNDER and LIGHTNING

**thun·der·struck** /'θʌndɚˌstrʌk/ *adj* extremely surprised or shocked

**Thurs·day** /'θɚzdi, -deɪ/ *written abbreviation* **Thurs.** *n* the fifth day of the week –see usage note at SUNDAY

**thus** /ðʌs/ *adv* FORMAL **1** as a result of something that you have just mentioned; so: *Traffic will become heavier, thus increasing pollution.* **2** in this way: *The oil spill could thus contaminate the water supply.* **3 thus far** until now: *We've received only one offer thus far.*

**thwart** /θwɔrt/ *v* [T] to prevent someone from doing what s/he is trying to do

**thy·roid** /ˈθaɪrɔɪd/, **thyroid gland** /ˈ.. ˌ./ *n* an organ in your neck that produces HORMONEs (=substances that affect the way you develop and behave)

**ti·a·ra** /tiˈɑrə, tiˈɛrə/ *n* a piece of jewelry like a small CROWN

**tic** /tɪk/ *n* a sudden uncontrolled movement of a muscle in your face, usually because of being nervous

**tick¹** /tɪk/ *n* **1** the short repeated sound that a clock or watch makes every second **2** a small creature with eight legs that attaches itself to animals and sucks their blood

**tick²** *v* **1** [I] if a clock or watch ticks, it makes a short sound every second **2 what makes sb tick** INFORMAL the reasons that someone behaves in a particular way: *I can't figure out what makes him tick.*

**tick** sb ↔ **off** *phr v* [T] INFORMAL to annoy someone: *She got ticked off because she had to wait in line again.*

**tick·et¹** /ˈtɪkɪt/ *n* **1** a printed piece of paper that shows that you have paid for a movie or to travel on a bus, plane etc.: *cheap **tickets to** the theater | a plane ticket to Tampa* **2** a printed note saying that you must pay money because you have done something illegal, especially while driving or parking your car: *a speeding/ parking ticket* **3** a list of the people supported by a particular political party in an election: *the Democratic ticket*

**ticket²** *v* [T] to give someone a ticket for parking his/her car in the wrong place or for driving too fast

**tick·le¹** /ˈtɪkəl/ *v* **1** [T] to move your fingers lightly over someone's body in order to make him/her laugh **2** [I,T] if something touching your body tickles you, it makes you want to rub your body because it is uncomfortable: *Mommy, this blanket tickles.* **3** [T] if a situation, remark etc. tickles you, it amuses or pleases you: *Mom will be **tickled pink/tickled to death** (=very pleased) to know you're visiting.*

**tickle²** *n* a feeling in your throat that makes you want to cough

**tick·lish** /ˈtɪklɪʃ/ *adj* **1** someone who is ticklish is sensitive to tickling (TICKLE) **2** INFORMAL a ticklish situation or problem must be dealt with very carefully

**tic-tac-toe** /ˌtɪk tæk ˈtoʊ/ *n* [U] a children's game in which two players draw the marks X and O in a pattern of nine squares

**tid·al** /ˈtaɪdl/ *adj* relating to the regular rising and falling of the sea: *tidal pools*

**tidal wave** /ˈ.. ˌ./ *n* a very large ocean wave that flows over the land and destroys things

**tid·bit** /ˈtɪdˌbɪt/ *n* **1** a small piece of food that tastes good **2** a small piece of interesting information, news etc.

**tide¹** /taɪd/ *n* the regular rising and falling of the level of the ocean: *It's **high/low tide**. (=the ocean is at a high or low level)

**tide²** *v*

**tide** sb **over** *phr v* [T] to help someone deal with a difficult time: *Could you lend me $50 to **tide** me **over** until payday?*

**ti·dy** /ˈtaɪdi/ *adj* ⇨ NEAT

**tie¹** /taɪ/ *v* **tied, tied, tying** **1** [I,T] to fasten something or be fastened with a rope, string etc.: *The dress ties in the back. | She **tied** the scarf loosely **around** her neck.* **2** [T] to make a knot in a rope, string etc.: *Can you **tie** your shoelaces yet?* **3** [I] also **be tied** to have the same number of points in a competition: *two teams that are **tied for** first place | The score is tied.*

tie

**tie** sb **down** *phr v* [T] to stop someone from being free to do what s/he wants to do: *Neil doesn't like feeling **tied down**.*

**tie in** *phr v* [I] if one idea or statement ties in with another one, it helps to prove the same thing: *This data **ties** right **in with** ours.*

**tie up** *phr v* [T] **1** [**tie** sb ↔ **up**] to tie someone's arms, legs etc. so that s/he cannot move: *They **tied** Davis **up** and took his money.* **2** [**tie** sth ↔ **up**] to fasten something together by using string or rope: *a package **tied up with** heavy string* **3** [**tie** sth ↔ **up**] to prevent something from moving: *Sorry I'm late - I got **tied up** in traffic.* **4 be tied up a)** to be very busy: *I'm kind of **tied up** these days.* **b)** if your money is tied up in something, it is all being used for that thing: *Our money's **tied up** in a long-term savings plan.*

**tie²** *n* **1** a long narrow piece of cloth that men wear around their neck, tied in a knot outside their shirts **2** a relationship between two people, groups, or countries: *close family ties* **3** a piece of string, wire etc. used in order to fasten or close something such as a bag **4** the result of a game, competition, or election in which two or more people get the same number of points, votes etc.: *The game **ended in a tie**.*

**tie·break·er** /ˈtaɪˌbreɪkɚ/ *n* an additional question or point that decides the winner when two people or teams have the same number of points in a competition

**tier** /tɪr/ *n* **1** a row of seats that has other rows above or below it **2** one of several levels in an organization or system: *a company with four tiers of management*

**tiff** /tɪf/ *n* a slight argument between friends

**ti·ger** /ˈtaɪgɚ/ *n* a large strong wild cat with yellow and black lines on its fur

**tight¹** /taɪt/ *adj*
**1** ▶CLOTHES◀ fitting part of your body very

closely: *These shoes feel too tight.* | *tight jeans*

**2** ▶FIRMLY PULLED◀ pulled or stretched firmly so that it is straight: *Pull the thread tight.*

**3** ▶FIRMLY FIXED◀ firmly fixed and difficult to move: *Make sure the screws are tight.*

**4** ▶FIRMLY CONTROLLED◀ controlled very strictly and firmly: *Security is tight for the President's visit.*

**5** ▶MONEY◀ **a)** INFORMAL if money is tight, you do not have enough of it **b)** someone who is tight tries hard to avoid spending money

**6** ▶TIME◀ if time is tight, it is difficult for you to do the things you need to do in the time you have: *It's a **tight schedule**, but we can manage.*

**7** ▶PEOPLE◀ INFORMAL **a)** two people who are tight have a close friendship: *We're getting pretty tight.* **b)** INFORMAL drunk

**8 in a tight spot** INFORMAL in a difficult situation: *I'm in kind of a tight spot - could you lend me $20?* –**tightly** *adv*

**tight²** *adv* very firmly or closely; tightly: *Hold tight and don't let go of my hand.* | *Put the lid on tight.*

**tight·en** /'taɪtn/ *v* **1** [T] to close or fasten something firmly by turning it: *You'd better tighten the cap on the bottle.* **2** [T] to stretch something as far as possible: *The rope tightened and Arnie gave the climber some slack.* | *Tighten your seat belt before we start.* **3** [T] to make something fit as closely as possible **4** [I] to close firmly around something: *Richard's grip tightened on her arm.* **5** [T] to make a rule, law, or system more strict: *City Hall has decided to **tighten up on** security.* **6 tighten your belt** INFORMAL to try to spend less money than you usually spend

**tight-fist·ed** /ˌ. '..◀ / *adj* INFORMAL not generous with money; STINGY

**tight·rope** /'taɪtroʊp/ *n* a rope or wire high above the ground that someone walks along in a CIRCUS

**tights** /taɪts/ *n* [plural] girls' or women's clothing that fits closely around the feet and legs and up to the waist, that is thick and colored

**tight·wad** /'taɪtwɑd/ *n* INFORMAL DISAPPROVING someone who hates to spend or give money

**tile** /taɪl/ *n* a thin square piece of baked clay or other material that is used for covering roofs, walls, or floors –**tile** *v* [T]

**till¹** /tɪl, tl/ *prep, conjunction* SPOKEN until: *I was up till 1:00 a.m. studying for my test.*

**till²** *n* ⇨ CASH REGISTER

**tilt** /tɪlt/ *v* [I,T] to move into a position where one side is higher than the other, or to make something do this: *Don't tilt so far back in your chair.* | *She tilted her head and looked at him.* –**tilt** *n* [C,U]

**tim·ber** /'tɪmbɚ/ *n* trees that are cut down and used for building or making things

**time¹** /taɪm/ *n*

**1** ▶MINUTES/HOURS ETC.◀ [U] something that is measured in minutes, hours, years etc. using clocks: *Time goes by* (=passes) *so quickly these days.*

**2** ▶ON THE CLOCK◀ [singular] a particular point in time that is shown on a clock in hours and minutes: *What time is it?* | *Do you have the time?* (=used in order to ask someone what time it is)

**3** ▶OCCASION◀ an occasion when something happens or someone does something: *We visit him two or three times a month.* | *When was the last time you saw Kelly?* | *Every/each time I offer to cook, she says no.* | *The next time you come, we'll go to a show.* | *One time* (=once) *we went to Florida for spring break.* | *Smoking is not allowed at any time.*

**4** ▶HOW OFTEN/HOW LONG◀ [singular, U] used when talking about how often something happens or how long it continues: *I used to play tennis all the time.* (=often) | *Randy drives most of the time.* (=usually) | *Where's Mandy? She's been gone for a long time.* | *Patty whined the whole time.* (=during all of a period of time) | *These pictures were taken some time ago.* (=a fairly long time ago)

**5** ▶WHEN STH HAPPENS◀ [C,U] the particular minute, hour, day etc. when something happens or someone does something: *an arrival/departure time* (=time when a plane, train etc. arrives or leaves) | *The program's on at breakfast/supper time.* | *I was really hungry by the time I got home.* | *We left the building at the same time.* –see usage note at WHEN: ✗ DON'T SAY "in the same time." ✗

**6 it's time...** used in order to say when something should be done, should happen, or is expected to happen: *It's time for dinner.* | *It's time to go.*

**7** ▶TIME NEEDED◀ the amount of time that it takes to do something, or that is needed to do something: *Learning a language takes time.* (=takes a long time) | *I won't have time to shop for a gift before Friday.* | *I've spent a lot of time writing this paper.* | *Come on - stop wasting time.*

**8 be on time** to arrive or happen at the correct time or the time that was arranged: *The buses are never on time.* ✗ DON'T SAY "be in time." ✗

**9 in time** early or soon enough to do something: *We got there just in time to see the clowns.* | *They arrived in time for dinner.* ✗ DON'T SAY "on time to" or "on time for." ✗

**10 ahead of time** before an event or before you need to do something, in order to be prepared: *We need to get there ahead of time to get a good seat.*

**11** ▶GOOD/RIGHT TIME◀ [C,U] a suitable time for something to happen or be done: *You've caught me at a bad time - can I call you back later?* | *This isn't the right time to ask for a raise.*

**12 in no time** soon or quickly: *We'll be there*

*in no time.*

**13 it's about time** SPOKEN said when you feel strongly that something should happen soon or should already have happened: *It's about time you got a job!*

**14 when the time comes** when something that you expect to happen actually happens, or when something becomes necessary: *She'll make the right choice when the time comes.*

**15 at this/that/the time** now, or at a particular moment in the past: *We can't give you an answer at this time.* | *At that/the time* (=then) *I was still living in Phoenix.* –see usage note at WHEN

**16 one/two etc. at a time** allowing only a specific number of things to happen or exist at the same time: *You can borrow three books at a time from the library.*

**17 take your time** to do something slowly or carefully without hurrying: *Take your time - you don't have to rush.*

**18 for the time being** for a short time but not permanently: *They'll let us live here for the time being.*

**19 good/bad/difficult etc. time** a part of your life when you have experiences that are good, bad etc.: *That was the happiest time of my life.*

**20 ▶IN HISTORY◀** a particular period in history: *It happened in the time of the Romans.* –see also TIMES²

**21 time's up** SPOKEN said in order to tell people to stop doing something because there is no more time left: *Okay, time's up. You'll have to get out of the pool.*

**22 in time to sth** if you do something in time to a piece of music, you do it using the same RHYTHM and speed as the music

**23 do time** INFORMAL to spend time in prison –see also TIMES²

---

**USAGE NOTE time**

When talking about what people do with their time, use the verbs **spend**, **pass**, and **waste**. To **spend** time is to do something useful with your time: *We spent the day cleaning the house.* If you **pass** the time, you have a lot of time and not a lot of useful things to do with it: *How do you pass the time now that you're retired?* To **waste** time is to not use your time well: *I wasted an hour trying to find a parking space!*

---

**time²** *v* [T] **1** to do something or arrange for something to happen at a particular time: *The bomb was **timed to** go off at 5:00.* | *an ill-timed announcement* (=one that happens at a bad time) **2** to measure how fast someone or something is going, how long it takes to do something etc.: *Christie was **timed at** 10.02 seconds.* | *Okay, time how long it takes me to finish.*

**time and a half** /ˌ. . . './ *n* [U] one and a half times the normal rate of pay

**time bomb** /'. ./ *n* **1** a situation that is likely to become a very serious problem: *Unemployment has become a time bomb.* **2** a bomb that is set to explode at a particular time

**time card** /'. ./ *n* a card on which the hours you have worked are recorded by a machine

**time-con·sum·ing** /'. .ˌ../ *adj* needing a long time to do: *time-consuming work*

**time-hon·ored** /'. ˌ../ *adj* a time-honored method, custom etc. is one that has existed or worked well for a long time

**time·keep·er** /'taɪmˌkipɚ/ *n* someone who officially records how long it takes to do something, especially at a sports event

**time·less** /'taɪmlɪs/ *adj* always remaining beautiful, attractive etc.: *the timeless beauty of the ocean*

**time lim·it** /'. ˌ../ *n* the longest time that you are allowed to do something in: *There's a three-year time limit for writing a thesis.*

**time·ly** /'taɪmli/ *adj* done or happening at exactly the right time: *a timely decision* –opposite UNTIMELY

**time off** /ˌ. './ *n* [U] time when you are officially allowed not to be at work or studying

**time out** /ˌ. './ *n* **1 take time out** to rest or do something different from your usual job or activities **2** a short time during a sports game when the teams can rest and get instructions from the COACH

**tim·er** /'taɪmɚ/ *n* an instrument for measuring time, when you are doing something such as cooking

**times¹** /taɪmz/ *prep* multiplied by: *two times two equals four*

**times²** *n* [plural] the present time or a particular period in history, and the ways that people do or did things during that period: *modern times* | *Their technology is 30 years **behind the times**.*

**time·ta·ble** /'taɪmˌteɪbəl/ *n* **1** a plan of events and activities, with their dates and times **2** ⇨ SCHEDULE¹

**time warp** /'. ./ *n* [singular] INFORMAL the feeling that you are in a different time in history or in the future, instead of in the present

**time zone** /'. ./ *n* one of the 24 areas the world is divided into, each of which has its own time

**tim·id** /'tɪmɪd/ *adj* not brave or confident: *a timid child* –**timidly** *adv* –**timidity** /təˈmɪdəti/ *n* [U]

**tim·ing** /'taɪmɪŋ/ *n* [U] the ability to decide the right time to do something, or the act of deciding this: *It's bad timing, starting a diet before Christmas.*

**tin** /tɪn/ *n* [U] a soft white metal used for making cans, building materials etc: *a tin can*

**tin·der** /'tɪndɚ/ n [U] material that burns easily, used for lighting fires

**tin·der·box** /'tɪndɚ,bɑks/ n a place or situation that is dangerous because it is likely that there will be fighting

**tine** /taɪn/ n a pointed part of something that has several points, for example on a fork —compare PRONG

**tin·foil** /'tɪnfɔɪl/ n [U] OLD-FASHIONED ⇨ FOIL

**tinge** /tɪndʒ/ n a very small amount of color or emotion: *a **tinge** of sadness in her voice | white paint with a yellow tinge* —**tinged** adj: *black hair **tinged** with gray*

**tin·gle** /'tɪŋgəl/ v [I] to feel a slight sting on your skin: *My fingers **tingled** with the cold.* —**tingle** n

**tin·ker** /'tɪŋkɚ/ v [I] INFORMAL to try to improve something by making small changes to it, but without having a careful plan: *He's outside **tinkering** with his car again.*

**tin·kle** /'tɪŋkəl/ v **1** [I] to make high soft RINGing sounds: *a tinkling bell* **2** [I] a word meaning to URINATE, used when speaking to young children —**tinkle** n

**tin·ny** /'tɪni/ adj a tinny sound is unpleasant to listen to, like small pieces of metal hitting each other: *tinny music*

**tin·sel** /'tɪnsəl/ n [U] thin pieces of shiny silver paper, used especially as Christmas decorations

**tint**[1] /tɪnt/ n a pale or light shade of a particular color: *The sky had a pink tint.*

**tint**[2] v [T] to give something, especially your hair, a TINT

**ti·ny** /'taɪni/ adj extremely small: *a tiny room | thousands of tiny fish*

**tip**[1] /tɪp/ n **1** the end of something, especially something pointed: *the tip of your nose | Provincetown, on the northern tip of Cape Cod* **2** an additional amount of money that you give to someone such as a WAITER or taxi driver for his/her service: *Did you **leave a tip**?* **3** a helpful piece of advice: *He **gave** me some useful **tips on** how to take good pictures.* **4 on the tip of your tongue** if a word, name etc. is on the tip of your tongue, you know it but cannot remember it immediately **5 the tip of the iceberg** a small sign of a problem that is much larger: *What we have seen so far is just the tip of the iceberg.*

**tip**[2] v **-pped, -pping 1** [I,T] also **tip over** to fall or turn over, or to make something do this: *The baby tipped the plant over. | The ladder must have tipped over during the night.* **2** [I,T] to lean at an angle, or to make something do this: *I tipped the bucket to pour out the water. | a man with his hat tipped forward* **3** [I,T] to give a TIP to a WAITER, taxi driver etc. for his/her service: *Did you remember to tip the waitress?* —see culture note at TIP[1]

**tip** sb ↔ **off** phr v [T] INFORMAL to give someone such as the police secret information about something illegal: *The police must have been **tipped off** about the robbery.*

**ti·pi** /'tipi/ n ⇨ TEPEE

**tip-off** /'. ./ n INFORMAL **1** a warning or message about something illegal that is given secretly to the police, a government etc. **2** the beginning of a basketball game: *Tip-off is at 7:30 tonight in the Coliseum.*

**tip·per** /'tɪpɚ/ n INFORMAL someone who TIPs a WAITER, taxi driver, etc. for his/her service: *He's a **good tipper**.* (=someone who gives large tips)

**tip·ster** /'tɪpstɚ/ n someone who gives the police, a REPORTER etc. secret information about something that is going to happen

**tip·sy** /'tɪpsi/ adj INFORMAL slightly drunk

**tip·toe**[1] /'tɪptoʊ/ n **on tiptoe** standing on your toes, with the rest of your feet off the ground: *Matt stood on tiptoe to look over the wall.*

**tiptoe**[2] v [I] to walk on TIPTOE: *They tiptoed past the door.*

**ti·rade** /'taɪreɪd/ n a long angry speech criticizing someone or something: *The senator launched into a **tirade against** his critics.*

**tire**[1] /taɪɚ/ n a thick round piece of rubber that fits around the wheel of a car, bicycle etc.: *I had a **flat tire** (=one that has lost all its air) on the way home.* —see picture on page 469

**tire**[2] v **1** [I,T] to become tired, or to make someone feel tired: *Aunt Mary was beginning to tire. | Even short walks tire her.* **2 tire of sth** to become bored with something: *Sooner or later he'll tire of politics.*

**tire** sb ↔ **out** phr v [T] to make someone very tired: *Those kids have **tired** me **out**.*

**tired** /taɪɚd/ adj **1** feeling that you want to sleep or rest: *I'm really tired. | Ben looks tired too. | We're all pretty **tired out** (=completely tired) after the long flight.* **2** bored or annoyed with something: *I'm **tired of** your stupid comments.*

**tire·less** /'taɪɚlɪs/ adj very determined and never getting tired: *a tireless worker* —**tirelessly** adv

**tire·some** /ˈtaɪəʳsəm/ *adj* annoying and boring: *The winter had been long and tiresome.* —compare TIRING

**tir·ing** /ˈtaɪərɪŋ/ *adj* making you feel tired: *a tiring trip across the country by train*

**tis·sue** /ˈtɪʃu/ *n* **1** ⇨ KLEENEX **2** [U] the parts of a plant, animal, or human such as muscles, skin, leaves etc. that are made up of groups of similar cells: *damaged lung tissue*

**tit** /tɪt/ *n* SLANG OFFENSIVE a woman's breast

**tit-for-tat** /ˌtɪt fəʳ ˈtæt/ *adj* INFORMAL a tit-for-tat crime or action is something bad that has been done to someone because s/he has done something similar to you: *a series of tit-for-tat murders*

**tit·il·late** /ˈtɪtḷˌeɪt/ *v* [T] to make someone feel excited or interested, especially sexually: *a story to titillate the readers*

**ti·tle¹** /ˈtaɪtḷ/ *n* **1** the name given to a book, painting, play etc.: *"What's the title of this play?" "Heroes."* **2** a word such as "Mrs.," "Dr.," "Senator" etc. that is used before someone's name to show whether s/he is married or what his/her rank or position is **3** a word or name that describes someone's rank or position: *Her official title is editorial manager.* **4** [singular, U] TECHNICAL the legal right to own something: *Who has the **title to** this land?* **5** the most important game in a sport, that shows who the best team or player is: *Foreman first won his heavyweight title in 1974.*

**title²** *v* [T] to give a name to a book, play etc.: *a concert titled "Home for the Holidays"*

**title role** /ˌ.. ˈ./ *n* the main character in a play, after whom the play is named: *Elizabeth Taylor plays the title role in "Cleopatra."*

**tit·ter** /ˈtɪtəʳ/ *v* [I] to laugh quietly, especially in a nervous way —**titter** *n*

**tiz·zy** /ˈtɪzi/ *n* [singular] INFORMAL **in a tizzy** feeling nervous, upset, and sometimes confused: *Mom's in a tizzy because everyone's late.*

**TLC** *n* [U] INFORMAL tender loving care; kindness and love that you give to someone when s/he is sick or upset

**TN** the written abbreviation of Tennessee

**TNT** *n* [U] a powerful explosive

**to¹** /tə, *before vowels* tʊ; *strong* tu/ [used with the basic form of a verb to make the infinitive.] ✗ DO NOT USE "to" with modal verbs. ✗ **1** used after verbs: *I'd love to go! | She didn't want to bother you. | The men were told to leave the bar.* **2** used after "how," "where," "who," "whom," "whose," "which," "when," "what," or "whether": *Can you show me how to do this? | Maria didn't know whether to call Tim or not.* **3** used after some nouns: *If you get a chance to see the play, you should. | He has no reason to believe that.* **4** used after adjectives: *Dad says he's not ready to retire yet. | It's great to see you!* **5** used in order to show the purpose of an action: *He covered the child to keep her from getting cold.* **6** used after "too" and an adjective: *It's too cold to go outside.* **7** used after an adjective and "enough": *Are you feeling well enough to go back to work?* **8** used after "there is" and a noun: *There's nothing to do here.*

### USAGE NOTE to

In written English, you should try not to put a word between **to** and the verb that comes after it: *He tried quietly to play his guitar.* Sometimes, however, we separate **to** from the verb that comes after it in order to emphasize something or because the sentence is clearer: *Your job is to really help these children.*

**to²** *prep* **1** in order to be in a particular place, event, state etc.: *The drive to the city takes five hours. | I couldn't go to sleep last night. | Are you going to the wedding?* **2** toward or in the direction of a place: *She went to the door. | Throw the ball to me.* **3** used in order to show the position of something, especially in relation to something else: *The water came up to our knees. | a town 50 miles to the south of Indianapolis | My back was to the door.* (=facing the door) **4** used in order to show who receives or owns something, or to whom speech is directed: *Angie said "hi" to me this morning. | The ring belongs to her mother.* **5** starting with one thing or in one place and ending with or in another: *A to Z | Mom, I can count to 100. | It's 30 miles **from** here **to** Toronto.* **6** used when showing who or what is affected by an action or situation: *Mr. Reger is nice to everyone. | The chemicals are a danger to ocean life.* **7** fitting or being part of a machine or piece of equipment: *I have a key to the office.* **8** used when comparing two numbers, things etc.: *The Bears won, 27 to 10.* **9** used in order to mean "before" when you are giving the time: *It's ten to four.*

**to³** /tu/ *adv* ⇨ TO AND FRO **come to** (COME)

**toad** /toʊd/ *n* an animal like a large FROG but brown in color

**toad·stool** /ˈtoʊdstul/ *n* a plant that looks like a MUSHROOM, but is usually poisonous

**to and fro** /ˌtu ən ˈfroʊ/ *adv* moving in one direction and then back again: *walking to and fro*

**toast¹** /toʊst/ *n* **1** [U] bread that has been heated until it is brown and CRISP: *Could I have some toast with my eggs, please?* **2** an occasion when you TOAST someone: *I'd like to **propose a toast** to the happy couple.* **3** **be the toast of Broadway/Hollywood etc.** to be very popular and praised by many people in a particular place

**toast²** *v* [T] **1** to ask people to drink something with you in order to thank someone, wish someone luck etc.: *We toasted our victory with* *champagne.* **2** to make bread turn brown by heating it

**toast·er** /'toʊstəʳ/ *n* a machine used for making TOAST

**toast·y** /'toʊsti/ *adj* SPOKEN warm in a way that makes you feel comfortable

**to·bac·co** /tə'bækoʊ/ *n* [U] dried brown leaves that are smoked in cigarettes, CIGARs etc., or the plant that these come from

**to·bac·co·nist** /tə'hækənɪst/ *n* OLD-FASHIONED someone who owns a store that sells tobacco, cigarettes, etc.

**to·bog·gan·ing** /tə'bɑgənɪŋ/ *n* [U] the sport of sliding down snow covered hills on a special wooden board that curves up at the front —**toboggan** *n* —**toboggan** *v* [I]

**to·day**[1] /tə'deɪ/ *n* **1** the day that is happening now: *Today is Wednesday.* **2** the present time: *Video games are the obsession of today's youth.*

**today**[2] *adv* **1** during the day that is happening now: *Mom can we go to the park today?* **2** in the present time: *Today, cancer is the leading cause of death in women.*

**tod·dle** /'tɑdl/ *v* [I] to walk with short unsteady steps, like a very young child does

**tod·dler** /'tɑdləʳ/ *n* a child between the ages of about 1 and 3

**to·do** /tə 'du/ *n* [singular] INFORMAL unnecessary excitement or angry feelings about something; FUSS: *She's always **making** a big **to-do** over something.*

**toe**[1] /toʊ/ *n* **1** one of the five separate parts at the end of your foot: *I hurt my **big toe**.* (=largest toe) —see picture at BODY **2 on your toes** ready for anything that might happen: *Practicing every day really **keeps you on your toes***

**toe**[2] *v* **toe the line** to do what you are told to do by people in authority: *I refuse to toe the line anymore!*

**TOEFL** /'toʊfəl/ *n* Test of English as a Foreign Language; a test that students can take if their first language is not English, that proves that they can understand English

**toe·hold** /'toʊhoʊld/ *n* [singular] a position you have just gained, from which you can increase your power or success: *It took us five years to **gain a toehold** in the market.*

**toe·nail** /'toʊneɪl/ *n* the hard flat part that covers the top end of your toe

**toe-to-toe** /ˌ. . '. ◂/ *adj* ⇨ HEAD-TO-HEAD

**tof·fee** /'tɔfi, 'tɑfi/ *n* [C,U] a sticky brown candy made from sugar and butter, or a piece of this

**to·fu** /'toʊfu/ *n* [U] a soft white food that is made from SOYBEANs

**to·ga** /'toʊgə/ *n* a long loose piece of clothing worn by people in ancient Greece and Rome

**to·geth·er**[1] /tə'gɛðəʳ/ *adv* **1** if two or more things are put together, they form a single subject, group, mixture, or object: *Add the numbers*

*together.* | *We put the puzzle together last night.* **2** with or next to each other: *Kevin and I went to school together.* | *Together we can win.* | *We were **crowded/packed etc. together** in one little room.* **3** at the same time: *Why do all the bills seem to come together?* —see also **get your act together** (ACT[2])

**together**[2] *adj* SPOKEN thinking clearly, being very organized etc.: *Carla seems really together.*

**to·geth·er·ness** /tə'gɛðəʳnɪs/ *n* [U] a feeling of having a close relationship with other people

**tog·gle** /'tɑgəl/ *n* a piece of wood or plastic like a short stick that is used as a button on coats, bags etc.

**togs** /tɑgz, tɔgz/ *n* [plural] INFORMAL clothes

**toil** /tɔɪl/ *v* [I] LITERARY to work very hard for a long period of time —**toil** *n* [U]

**toi·let** /'tɔɪlɪt/ *n* a large bowl that you sit on to get rid of waste matter from your body

---

**USAGE NOTE** toilet

Do not use this word to talk about a room that has a **toilet** in it. Use **bathroom** for the room in a house that has a toilet in it. Use **restroom**, **ladies' room**, **women's room**, and **men's room** to talk about a room in a public place with one or more toilets. On a plane, this room is called a **lavatory**.

---

**toi·let·ries** /'tɔɪlətriz/ *n* [plural] things such as soap and TOOTHPASTE that are used for washing yourself

**to·ken**[1] /'toʊkən/ *n* **1** a piece of metal, shaped like a coin, that you use instead of money in some machines **2** something that represents a feeling, fact, event etc.: *He had given her the ring as **a token of** his love.*

**token**[2] *adj* a token action, change etc. is small and not very important, but shows that you are dealing with a problem or will keep a promise: *He receives a token salary for his help.*

**to·ken·ism** /'toʊkə,nɪzəm/ *n* [U] actions that are intended to make people think that an organization deals fairly with people or problems when in fact it does not

**told** /toʊld/ *v* the past tense and PAST PARTICIPLE of TELL

**tol·er·a·ble** /'tɑlərəbəl/ *adj* something that is tolerable is not very good but is acceptable: *The temperature was a tolerable 90 degrees.*

**tol·er·ance** /'tɑlərəns/ *n* **1** [U] willingness to allow people to do, say, or believe what they want: *He had little tolerance for laziness in his sons.* **2** [C,U] the degree to which someone or something can suffer pain, difficulty etc. without being harmed: *These plants have a very limited **tolerance for** cold weather.*

**tol·er·ate** /'tɑlə,reɪt/ *v* [T] to accept something even though you do not like it: *I couldn't tolerate the working conditions.* | *learning to tol-*

erate other people's views **–tolerant** /'talə-
rənt/ adj –see usage note at BEAR¹

**toll¹** /toʊl/ n **1** the number of people killed or
injured at a particular time: *The death toll has
risen to 83.* **2 take its toll (on)** to have a bad
effect on someone or something over a long
period of time: *Years of smoking have taken
their toll on his health.* **3** the money you have
to pay to use a particular road, bridge etc.

**toll²** v [I,T] if a bell tolls, or you toll it, it keeps
ringing slowly

**toll booth** /'. ./ n a place where you pay to use
a particular road, bridge etc.

**toll-free** /ˌ. '.◂/ adj a toll-free telephone call
does not cost any money: *Call our toll-free
number now.*

**toll·gate** /'toʊlgeɪt/ n a TOLL BOOTH with a
gate that opens when you pay money

**tom·a·hawk** /'tɑmə,hɔk/ n a HATCHET (=type
of weapon) used by some Native Americans in
past times

**to·ma·to** /tə'meɪtoʊ/ n, plural **tomatoes** a
soft round red fruit, eaten as a vegetable raw or
cooked: *a tomato sauce* –see picture on page
470

**tomb** /tum/ n a grave, especially a large one
above the ground

**tom·boy** /'tɑmbɔɪ/ n a girl who likes to play
the same games as boys

**tomb·stone** /'tumstoʊn/ n ⇨ GRAVESTONE

**tom·cat** /'tɑmkæt/ n a male cat

**tome** /toʊm/ n a large heavy book

**tom·fool·er·y** /ˌtɑm'fuləri/ n [U] OLD-
FASHIONED silly behavior

**to·mor·row¹** /tə'mɑroʊ, -'mɔr-/ n **1** the
day after today: *Tomorrow is Thursday.* **2** the
future, especially the near future: *the world of
tomorrow* **3 do sth like there's no tomorrow**
to do something without worrying about the future: *We're spending money like there's no tomorrow.*

**tomorrow²** adv on or during the day after today: *Are we playing football tomorrow?*

**ton** /tʌn/ n **1** a unit for measuring weight,
equal to 2000 pounds **2** INFORMAL a very large
quantity or weight: *Your suitcase weighs a ton!*
(=is very heavy)| *We ate tons of* (=a lot of)
*food.* **3 like a ton of bricks** INFORMAL happening unexpectedly in a way that shocks you: *I
hadn't missed my family much until that day, but
then it hit me like a ton of bricks.*

**tone¹** /toʊn/ n **1** [C,U] the way your voice
sounds that shows how you are feeling, or what
you mean: *I don't like your tone of voice.*
(=rude or angry way of speaking)| *He spoke in
a threatening tone.* **2** [singular, U] the general
feeling or attitude expressed in a piece of writing, activity etc.: *The argument set the tone
(=began a feeling that continued) for the evening.* **3** a sound made by a piece of electronic
equipment: *Please leave a message after the*

tone. **4** [U] the quality of a sound, especially
the sound of a musical instrument or someone's
voice **5** [U] how strong and firm your
muscles, skin etc. are: *muscle tone* **6** a SHADE
of a particular color

**tone²** **tone up** v [T] to make your muscles, skin
etc. feel healthier, stronger, firmer etc.: *I'm trying to tone up my stomach.*

**tone** sth ↔ **down** phr v [T] to make something
such as a speech or piece or writing less
offensive, exciting etc.: *They toned down the
words to the song so it could be played on the
radio.*

**tone-deaf** /'. ./ adj unable to hear the difference between different musical notes

**tongs** /tɑŋz, tɔŋz/ n [plural] a tool for picking
up objects, made of two movable BARs that are
attached at one end

**tongue** /tʌŋ/ n **1** the soft movable part in
your mouth that you use for tasting and speaking **2 bite/hold your tongue** to stop yourself
from saying something: *I wanted to argue but I
had to bite my tongue.* **3 mother/native
tongue** the language you spoke when you first
learned to speak **4** the part of a shoe under the
LACES (=strings that you tie them with) –see
also **on the tip of your tongue** (TIP¹) **slip of the
tongue** (SLIP²) **a sharp tongue** (SHARP¹)

**tongue-in-cheek** /ˌ. . '.◂/ adv said or done
seriously, but meant as a joke: *The show was
done in a tongue-in-cheek style.*

**tongue-tied** /'. ./ adj unable to speak easily
because you are nervous

**tongue twist·er** /'. ˌ../ n a word or phrase
with many similar sounds that is difficult to say
quickly: *"She sells sea shells by the seashore"
is a tongue twister.*

**ton·ic** /'tɑnɪk/ n **1** [C,U] also **tonic water** /'..
ˌ../ a bitter-tasting drink with BUBBLEs, that is
added to some alcoholic drinks **2** something,
especially a medicine, that gives you more energy or strength

**to·night¹** /tə'naɪt/ adv on or during the night
of today: *Do you want to go out tonight?*

**tonight²** n the night of today: *Tonight is a very
special occasion.*| *tonight's news*

**ton·nage** /'tʌnɪdʒ/ n [U] **1** the number of
TONs that something weighs, or the amount of
something that there is, measured in tons **2** the
size of a ship or the amount of goods it can
carry, shown in tons

**ton·sil** /'tɑnsəl/ n one of two small organs at
the sides of your throat near the back of your
tongue

**ton·sil·li·tis** /ˌtɑnsə'laɪtɪs/ n [U] an infection
of the TONSILs

**To·ny** /'toʊni/ n a prize given each year to the
best plays, actors etc. in New York's theaters

**too** /tu/ adv **1** more than is needed, wanted,
or possible: *You're going too fast!*| *This is too
busy a road to let the kids play near it.* ✗ DON'T

SAY "This is a too busy road." ✗ **2** also: *Sheila wants to come too.* | *"I'm really hungry." "I am too!"* **3** very: *It shouldn't be too long until dinner's ready.*

---

**USAGE NOTE too, very, and enough**

Use **too** before an adjective or adverb in order to say that something is more than you need or more than is acceptable: *This shirt is too big for me.* Use **very** before an adjective or adverb in order to emphasize it: *This shirt is very big.* Use **enough** after an adjective or adverb in order to say that something has as much of a quality as it needs: *The shirt is big enough for me.*

---

**took** /tʊk/ *v* the past tense of TAKE

**tool**[1] /tul/ *n* **1** something such as a hammer, SCREWDRIVER etc. that you use to make or repair things **2** something such as a piece of equipment or a treatment that is useful for a particular purpose: *Can television be used as a tool for learning?* —see usage note at MACHINE[1]

**tool**[2] *v* to decorate leather with a special tool

**tool along/down** *phr v* [I] INFORMAL to drive fast, especially for fun: *tooling along* at 90 miles an hour

**toot** /tut/ *v* [I,T] if a horn toots, or if you toot it, it makes a short sound —**toot** *n*

**tooth** /tuθ/ *n*, plural **teeth** **1** one of the hard objects in your mouth that you use to bite and CHEW your food: *Did you brush your teeth?* (=clean them) **2** one of the pointed parts that sticks out from a comb, SAW etc. **3 fight (sb/sth) tooth and nail** to work or fight as hard as you can to prevent something from happening or to achieve something: *The residents intend to fight the proposed shopping mall tooth and nail.* —see also **have a sweet tooth** (SWEET)

**tooth·ache** /'tuθeɪk/ *n* [C] a pain in a tooth

**tooth·brush** /'tuθbrʌʃ/ *n* a small brush for cleaning your teeth

**tooth·paste** /'tuθpeɪst/ *n* [U] a substance used for cleaning your teeth

**tooth·pick** /'tuθpɪk/ *n* a small pointed piece of wood for removing pieces of food from between your teeth

**top**[1] /tɑp/ *n*

**1** ▶HIGHEST PART◀ the highest part of something: *Write your name at the top of the page.* | *There was a flag on top of the tower.* —opposite BOTTOM[1]

**2** ▶UPPER SURFACE◀ the flat upper surface of an object: *The table has a glass top.* | *the top of my desk*

**3 on top of a)** in addition to: *On top of everything else, I need $700 to fix my car!* **b)** in control of a situation: *I'm on top of the problem.*

**4 the top** the highest position in a company, competition etc.: *The Rockets are at the top of the league.*

**5** ▶COVER◀ a cover for a pen, container etc., especially something that you push or turn: *I can't unscrew the top of this jar.*

**6** ▶CLOTHING◀ clothing that you wear on the upper part of your body: *Is that a new top?*

**7 off the top of your head** INFORMAL said without checking the facts: *Off the top of my head I'd say there were about 50.*

**8 at the top of your voice/lungs** shouted or sung as loudly as you can: *I yelled at the top of my lungs, but he didn't hear.*

**9** ▶TOY◀ a toy that spins and balances on its point when you twist it

**10 top-of-the-line** the best or most expensive: *a top-of-the-line video system*

**11 on top of the world** INFORMAL extremely happy —see also **blow your top/stack** (BLOW[1])

**top**[2] *adj* **1** at the top; highest: *the top button of my shirt* —opposite BOTTOM[2] **2** best or most successful: *Carl is one of our top salesmen* **3 top dog** INFORMAL the person in the highest or most important position: *Tony's top dog around here.*

**top**[3] *v* **-pped, -pping** [T] **1** to be higher, better, or more than something: *Their profits have topped $5,000,000 this year.* **2** to form or be the top for something: *ice cream topped with maple syrup*

**top sth ↔ off** *phr v* [T] **1 to top it (all) off** INFORMAL in addition to other bad things that have happened: *Then I lost my job, and to top it all off, my dog died.* **2** INFORMAL to do one final thing before finishing something: *We topped off the evening with a visit to a local bar.* **3** to add the last part of something that is needed to complete or fill it: *Can you top off the tank with unleaded gas, please?*

**top out** *phr v* [I] if something that is increasing tops out, it reaches its highest point and stops rising: *The Dow Jones average topped out at 5999.75 today.*

**top 40** /ˌtɑp 'fɔrti/ *n* **1** [U] music that is popular with young people, consisting of simple tunes with a strong beat: *I like top 40 better than hard rock.* **2 the top 40** the list of the 40 most popular records in a particular week

**top hat** /ˈ. ˌ./ *n* a man's tall hat with a flat top, worn in past times

**top-heav·y** /ˈ. ˌ../ *adj* **1** too heavy at the top and therefore likely to fall over **2** a top-heavy organization has too many managers

**top·ic** /'tɑpɪk/ *n* a subject that people talk or write about: *a discussion on the topic of human rights* | *Jackie's engagement was the main topic of conversation.* (=what was talked about)

**top·i·cal** /'tɑpɪkəl/ *adj* relating to something that is important at the present time: *a new TV show dealing with topical issues*

**top·less** /'tɑplɪs/ *adj* not wearing any clothes on the upper part of the body

**top·most** /'tɑpmoʊst/ *adj* highest: *the top-most branches of the tree*

**top-notch** /ˌ. '.◂/ *adj* INFORMAL having the highest quality or standard: *top-notch schools*

**to·pog·ra·phy** /tə'pɑgrəfi/ *n* [U] **1** the science of describing or making a map of an area of land **2** the shape of an area of land, including its hills, valleys etc. —**topographer** *n* —**topographical** /ˌtɑpə'græfɪkəl/ *adj*

**top·ping** /'tɑpɪŋ/ *n* [C,U] food that you put on top of other food to make it taste or look better: *a pizza with five toppings*

**top·ple** /'tɑpəl/ *v* **1** [I,T] to fall over, or to make something do this: *Several trees **toppled** over in the storm.* **2** [T] to take power away from a leader or government: *The scandal could topple the government.*

**top-se·cret** /ˌ. '..◂/ *adj* top-secret documents or information must be kept completely secret

**top·sy-tur·vy** /ˌtɑpsi 'tɚviˌ/ *adj* INFORMAL completely disorganized and in a state of confusion

**torch**[1] /tɔrtʃ/ *n* a long stick that you burn at one end for light or as a symbol: *the Olympic torch*

**torch**[2] *v* [T] INFORMAL to start a fire deliberately in order to destroy something: *Someone torched the old warehouse.*

**tore** /tɔr/ *v* the past tense of TEAR

**tor·ment**[1] /'tɔrmɛnt/ *n* [C,U] severe pain and suffering, or something that causes this: *The war left thousands of families **in torment**.*

**tor·ment**[2] /tɔr'mɛnt/ *v* [T] to make someone suffer a lot of mental or physical pain: *The cat's tormenting the birds again.* —**tormentor** *n*

**torn** /tɔrn/ *v* the PAST PARTICIPLE of TEAR

**tor·na·do** /tɔr'neɪdoʊ/ *n* an extremely violent storm with air that spins very quickly in the shape of a FUNNEL —see usage note at WEATHER

**tor·pe·do** /tɔr'pidoʊ/ *n* a weapon that is fired under the surface of the ocean from one ship at another —**torpedo** *v* [T]

**tor·rent** /'tɔrənt, 'tɑr-/ *n* **1** **a torrent of sth** a lot of something: *a torrent of criticism* **2** a large amount of water moving very quickly in a particular direction —**torrential** /tə'rɛnʃəl, tɔ-/ *adj*: *torrential rain*

**tor·rid** /'tɔrɪd, 'tɑr-/ *adj* **1** involving strong emotions, especially sexual excitement: *a torrid love affair* **2** extremely hot

**tor·so** /'tɔrsoʊ/ *n* the main part of your body, not including your arms, legs, or head

**tort** /tɔrt/ *n* LAW an action that is wrong but not criminal and can be dealt with in a CIVIL court of law

**tor·ti·lla** /tɔr'tiyə/ *n* a thin flat Mexican bread made from CORNMEAL or flour

**tor·toise** /'tɔrtəs/ *n* a kind of TURTLE with a sharp nose, that lives on land

**tor·tu·ous** /'tɔrtʃuəs/ *adj* **1** very complicated, long, and therefore confusing: *a tortuous process* **2** a tortuous road has a lot of turns and is difficult to travel on

**tor·ture**[1] /'tɔrtʃɚ/ *n* [C,U] **1** the act of torturing (TORTURE) someone **2** mental or physical suffering: *It was torture, watching her cry and not being able to help.*

**torture**[2] *v* [T] to make someone suffer severe physical punishment in order to make him/her give information: *He was tortured to death in prison.*

**toss** /tɔs/ *v* **1** [T] to throw something without much force: *Could you toss me my keys?* **2** **toss and turn** to change your position a lot in bed because you cannot sleep **3** also **toss sth ↔ out** INFORMAL to get rid of something: *"Where's the newspaper?" "I tossed it."* **4** [T] to cover one food with another food by gently moving them with a spoon: *Rinse the blueberries and **toss** them **with** sugar.* —**toss** *n* —see also **toss/flip a coin** (COIN[1])

**toss-up** /'. ./ *n* **it's a toss-up** SPOKEN said when you do not know which of two things will happen, or which of two things to choose: *So far the election is still a toss-up.*

**tot** /tɑt/ *n* INFORMAL a small child

**to·tal**[1] /'toʊtl/ *adj* **1** affecting or including everything; complete: *His farm has a total area of 100 acres.* | *the total absence of any sound* **2** **total number/amount/cost etc.** the number, amount etc. that you get when you add all the parts of something together: *The total cost of the building will be $6 million.* **3** SPOKEN used in order to emphasize the degree of something: *He's a total idiot!*

**total**[2] *n* the final number, amount etc. of something after all the parts have been added together; SUM: *The city spent **a total of** two million dollars on the library.* | *I was out of work for 34 days **in total**.*

**total**[3] *v* [T] **1** to add up to a particular amount: *Prize money totaling $5000 will be awarded.* **2** INFORMAL to damage a car so badly that it cannot be repaired

**to·tal·i·tar·i·an** /toʊˌtælə'tɛriən/ *adj* based on a political system in which people are completely controlled by the government —**totalitarianism** *n* [U]

**to·tal·i·ty** /toʊ'tæləti/ *n* [U] FORMAL the whole of something

**to·tal·ly** /'toʊtl-i/ *adv* completely: *I totally agree with you.* | *The whole game was totally unfair.*

**tote** /toʊt/ *v* [T] INFORMAL to carry something

**tote bag** /'. ./ *n* a large bag in which you carry things

**to·tem pole** /'toʊtəm ˌpoʊl/ *n* a tall wooden pole with images of animals or faces cut into it, made by some Native American tribes

**tot·ter** /'tɑtɚ/ v [I] to walk or move in an unsteady way as if you are about to fall down: *a woman **tottering around** in high heels*

**tou·can** /'tukæn, -kɑn/ n a tropical bird with bright feathers and a very large beak

**touch¹** /tʌtʃ/ v **1** [T] to put your finger, hand etc. on something or someone so you feel him, her, or it: *Don't touch the paint - it's still wet!* | *Can you touch your toes?* (=while standing up and without bending your knees) **2** [I,I] if two things are touching, there is no space in between them: *Make sure the wires aren't touching.* **3 not touch sth a)** to not use or handle something: *My brother won't let me touch his bike.* **b)** to not eat or drink something: *She didn't touch her breakfast.* **4 not touch sb** to not hurt someone physically: *I swear Mom, I didn't touch him!* **5** [T] to deal with or become involved in a particular situation or problem: *Clancy said he wouldn't touch the case.* **6 touch base** to talk for a short time with someone about something you are both working on in order to share information: *I wanted to **touch base with** you before the meeting.* **7** [T] to affect someone's emotions, especially by making him/her feel pity or sympathy: *His speech touched everyone present.* –see also TOUCHED

**touch down** *phr v* [I] if an aircraft touches down, it lands on the ground

**touch** sth ↔ **off** *phr v* [T] to cause a bad situation or violent event to begin: *The report **touched off** a fierce debate.*

**touch on/upon** sth *phr v* [T] to mention something when you are talking or writing: *Her songs **touch on** social issues.*

**touch** sth ↔ **up** *phr v* [T] to improve something by making small changes to it: *Norma **touched up** her makeup for the picture.*

**touch²** n **1** the action of putting your finger, hand etc. on someone or something: *Rita felt the touch of his hand on her arm.* **2 get in touch (with sb)** to communicate with someone by letter or telephone: *I've been trying to get in touch with you all morning.* **3 a)** the state of speaking or writing to someone regularly: *We try to **stay in touch** through e-mail.* | *I've **lost touch with** my high school friends.* **b)** the state of having the best information or knowledge about a situation or subject: *I think he's **out of touch with** the American people.* **4** [U] the sense that you use in order to feel things, especially by putting your finger, hand etc. on something: *Her skin was cool **to the touch**.* **5 a touch of sth** a very small amount of something: *a touch of sadness in her voice* | *salad dressing with a touch of lemon juice* **6** a small detail or change that improves something: *Becky put the **finishing touches** on the cake.* **7** [U] a particular way of doing something skillful: *I must be **losing my touch** - I can't hit anything today.*

**touch-and-go** /ˌ. . '.ˌ/ adj INFORMAL if a situation is touch-and-go, there is a risk that something bad could happen: *After Dad's operation, it was touch-and-go for a while.*

**touch·down** /'tʌtʃdaʊn/ n **1** the action in American football of moving the ball into the opponents' END ZONE in order to gain points **2** the moment that a space vehicle lands on the ground

**touched** /tʌtʃt/ adj feeling happy and grateful because of what someone has done for you: *We were touched by their concern.*

**touch·ing** /'tʌtʃɪŋ/ adj affecting your emotions, especially making you feel pity, sympathy, sadness etc.: *a touching movie about a boy and his dog*

**touch·stone** /'tʌtʃstoʊn/ n a standard used for measuring the quality of something

**touch·y** /'tʌtʃi/ adj **1** easily offended or annoyed: *You've been very touchy lately - what's wrong?* **2 touchy subject/question etc.** something that you have to be careful about saying, in order not to offend someone

**tough¹** /tʌf/ adj **1** INFORMAL difficult and needing a lot of effort: *Working as a fireman is tough.* | *a tough question on the test* | *a tough choice/decision* **2** very determined, and able to deal with difficult conditions: *She's a tough businesswoman.* **3** very strict: *tough anti-smoking laws* **4** difficult to cut or eat: *a tough steak* —opposite TENDER¹ **5 tough!/tough luck!** SPOKEN said when you do not have any sympathy for someone else's problems: *"I'm freezing!" "Tough! You should have worn your coat."* **6** a tough place, area etc. is likely to have a lot of violence and crime: *He grew up in a tough neighborhood.* –**toughness** n [U]

**tough²** v

**tough** sth ↔ **out** *phr v* [T] to deal with a very difficult situation by being determined to continue: *He could've gone home, but he stayed and **toughed it out**.*

**tough·en** /'tʌfən/ **toughen up** v [I,T] to become TOUGHer, or to make someone or something do this: *Hard work has toughened her up.*

**tou·pee** /tu'peɪ/ n a piece of artificial hair that a man can wear when he has no hair on part of his head

**tour¹** /tʊr/ n **1** a trip taken for pleasure, in which you visit several different places in a country, area etc.: *a 14-day tour of Egypt.* **2** a short trip through a place in order to see the things in it: *We **went on a tour through/of** the Smithsonian.* **3** a planned trip by a group of musicians, a sports team etc. in order to play in several places: *The band goes **on tour** later this year.*

**tour²** v [I,T] to visit a place on a tour: *We're going to tour New England this summer.*

**tour·ism** /'tʊrɪzəm/ n [U] the business of providing things for people to do and places for them to stay while they are on vacation: *The island depends on tourism for most of its income.*

**tour·ist** /'tʊrɪst/ *n* someone who is traveling or visiting a place for pleasure

**tour·na·ment** /'tʊrnəmənt, 'tɚ-/ *n* a competition in which many players compete against each other until there is one winner

**tour·ni·quet** /'tʊrnɪkɪt, 'tɚ-/ *n* a band of cloth that is twisted tightly around an injured arm or leg to make blood stop coming out

**tou·sle** /'taʊzəl, -səl/ *v* [T] to make someone's hair look messy —**tousled** *adj*

**tout** /taʊt/ *v* [T] to praise someone or something in order to persuade people that he, she, or it is important or worth a lot: *Paul's band is being touted as the next big thing.*

**tow**[1] /toʊ/ *v* [T] to pull a vehicle or ship using a rope, chain etc.: *Our car had to be towed away.*

**tow**[2] *n* **1** an act of TOWing a vehicle or ship **2** **in tow** following closely behind someone or something: *Mattie arrived with all her children in tow.*

**to·ward** /tɔrd, tə'wɔrd/, **towards** *prep* **1** in a particular direction: *traffic moving toward the coast* | *I saw a man coming toward me.* ✗ DON'T SAY "I saw a man coming to me." ✗ **2** concerning someone or something: *How do you feel toward her?* | *different attitudes towards divorce* **3** in order to achieve something: *working towards world peace* **4** just before a particular time: *I felt tired toward the end of the day.* **5** near a particular place: *We're building a pipeline down toward Abilene.*

**tow·el** /'taʊəl/ *n* a piece of cloth used for drying something: *a bath towel* (=for drying yourself) | *a dish towel*

**towel**[2], **towel off/down** *v* [I,T] to dry your body using a TOWEL

**tow·er**[1] /'taʊɚ/ *n* **1** a tall narrow part of a castle, church etc. **2** a tall structure used for signaling or broadcasting: *a radio/television tower*

**tower**[2] *v* to be much taller than the people or things around you: *O'Neal towered over the other players on the court.* —**towering** *adj*

**town** /taʊn/ *n* **1** a place with houses, stores, offices etc. where people live and work, that is smaller than a city: *a little town on the coast* | *She's from out of town.* (=lives in a different town) | *I'm coming into town* on the 5:30 flight from Dallas. **2** [U] the business or shopping center of a town: *"Where's Dad?" "He's gone into town."* **3** [singular] all the people who live in a particular town: *The whole town got involved in the celebrations.* **4** **go to town (on sth)** SPOKEN to do something eagerly and with a lot of energy: *Larry really went to town on those pancakes.* (=ate them quickly) **5** **on the town** INFORMAL going to restaurants,

theaters etc. for entertainment: *Everyone went out for a night on the town.*

**town hall** /ˌ. './ *n* a public building used for a town's local government

**town·house** /'taʊnhaʊs/ *n* a house in a group of houses that share one or more walls —see picture on page 471

**town·ship** /'taʊnʃɪp/ *n* an area where people live and work that is organized under a local government

**towns·peo·ple** /'taʊnzˌpipəl/, **towns·folk** /'taʊnzfoʊk/ *n* [plural] all the people who live in a particular town

**tow truck** /'. ./ *n* a strong truck that is used for pulling vehicles that cannot move on their own

**tox·ic** /'taksɪk/ *adj* poisonous, or containing poison: *toxic exhaust fumes* —**toxicity** /tak-'sɪsəṭi/ *n* [U]

**tox·i·col·o·gy** /ˌtaksɪ'kalədʒi/ *n* [U] the study of poisons and their effects

**toxic waste** /ˌ.. './ *n* [C,U] waste products from industry that are harmful to people, animals, or the environment

**tox·in** /'taksɪn/ *n* a poisonous substance, especially one made by BACTERIA

**toy**[1] /tɔɪ/ *n* an object for children to play with: *What kind of toys did you get for Christmas?*

**toy**[2] *v*

**toy with** sb/sth *phr v* [T] **1** [**toy with** sth] to think about an idea, plan etc. for a short time and not very seriously: *She had toyed with the idea of becoming an actress.* **2** [**toy with** sb/sth] INFORMAL to make someone think that you like or love him/her when you do not

**trace**[1] /treɪs/ *v* [T] **1** to study or describe the history, development, or origin of something: *He traced his family history back to the 17th century.* **2** to copy a drawing, map etc. by putting a piece of paper over it and drawing the lines that you can see through it **3** to find someone or something that has disappeared by searching carefully for him, her, or it: *Police are still trying to trace the missing child.* **4** to find out where a telephone call is coming from using electronic equipment —**traceable** *adj*

**trace**[2] *n* **1** [C,U] a small sign that someone or something was present or existed: *We found no trace of them on the island.* | *He simply disappeared without a trace.* (=completely) **2** a very small amount of a substance, quality, emotion etc. that is difficult to notice: *There was a trace of poison in the glass.* | *a trace of sorrow in his voice*

**trac·er** /'treɪsɚ/ *n* a search to find a package or letter that has been lost in the mail

**track**[1] /træk/ *n*

**1** ▶ROAD/PATH◀ a narrow road or path with a rough uneven surface: *a dirt track through the woods*

**2** **keep/lose track of sth** to pay attention to someone or something so that you know what is happening, or to fail to do this: *It's hard to keep track of everyone's birthdays.*

**3 be on the right/wrong track** to be doing or thinking things that are likely to make you succeed or fail: *Keep going, you're on the right track*

**4 be on/off track** to be in a state or situation that will lead to success or failure: *I feel that my career is back on track now.*

**5 ▶SONG◀** one of the songs or pieces of music on a record: *the best track on the album*

**6 ▶RAILROAD◀** the two metal lines along which a train travels: *railroad tracks*

**7 ▶FOR RACING◀** a course with a special surface on which people, cars, horses etc. race

**8 ▶SPORT◀** [U] the sport of running on a track: *He ran track in high school.*

**9 tracks** a series of marks on the ground made by a moving animal, person, or vehicle: *We saw bear tracks in the mud.*

**10 make tracks** INFORMAL to hurry when going somewhere: *Come on, we'd better make tracks.* –see also **off the beaten track/path** (BEATEN), ONE-TRACK MIND

**track²** *v* [T] **1** to search for a person or animal by following a smell or TRACKs on the ground: *We tracked the moose for hours.* **2** to follow the movements of an aircraft, ship etc. using RADAR **3** to leave mud or dirt behind you when you walk: *Who tracked mud all over the floor?*

**track** sb/sth ↔ **down** *phr v* [T] to find someone or something by searching for a long time in different places: *We finally were able to **track down** her parents.*

**track and field** /ˌ. . './ *n* [U] all the sports that involve running races, jumping, and throwing things

**track meet** /'. ./ *n* a sports competition with a variety of running, jumping, and throwing events

**track rec·ord** /'. ˌ../ *n* [singular] all the things that a person or organization has done in the past that show how good she, he, or it will be at doing similar things in the future: *Liz has a lousy track record in her relationships with men.*

**tract** /trækt/ *n* **1 digestive/respiratory/ urinary etc. tract** a system of connected organs in your body that have one purpose **2** a large area of land: *a tract of forest* **3** FORMAL a short piece of writing, especially on a religious or political subject

**trac·tion** /'trækʃən/ *n* [U] **1** the force that prevents a wheel from sliding on a road: *The car lost traction and ran off the road.* **2** a medical treatment in which an injured body part is gently pulled using weights

**trac·tor** /'træktɚ/ *n* a strong vehicle with large wheels, used for pulling farm equipment

**trade¹** /treɪd/ *n* **1** [U] the activity of buying, selling, or exchanging goods, especially between countries: *foreign trade banking/retail/tourist etc. trade* (=the business that comes from or is

done by banks etc.) **2** an exchange: *Let's make a trade - my frisbee for your baseball.* **3** a particular job, especially one in which you work with your hands: *Jerry's a plumber by trade.* –see usage note at JOB

**trade²** *v* **1** [I,T] to buy, sell, or exchange goods, especially between countries: *Our company has a lot of experience trading in Asia.* **2** to exchange one thing for another: *I'll trade my apple for your candy bar.* **3 trade insults (with sb)** if two people trade insults, they insult each other

**trade** sth ↔ **in** *phr v* [T] to give something old that you own as part of the payment for something new: *I traded my Chevy in for a Honda.*

**trade on** sth *phr v* to use a situation or someone's kindness in order to gain an advantage for yourself: *She's **trading on** her father's fame to try to make it in the music business.*

**trade up** *phr v* [I,T] to sell something such as a car or house so you can buy a better car or house

**trade-in** /'. ./ *n* a car, piece of equipment etc. that you give as part of the payment for the newer one that you are buying

**trade·mark** /'treɪdmɑrk/ *n* a special name, mark, or word on a product that shows it is made by a particular company

**trade-off** /'. ./ *n* an acceptable balance between two opposing things: *The boats are difficult to build, but the trade-off is that I get a good price for them.*

**trad·er** /'treɪdɚ/ *n* someone who buys and sells goods or STOCKs

**trade school** /'. ./ *n* a VOCATIONAL school

**trade se·cret** /'. ˌ../ *n* a piece of secret information about a particular business, that is only known by the people who work there

**tra·di·tion** /trə'dɪʃən/ *n* [C,U] **1** a belief, custom, or way of doing something that has existed for a long time: *a country **steeped in** (=full of) **tradition** | an old family/Jewish tradition* –see usage note at HABIT **2 (be) in the tradition of** to have many of the same features as something made or done in the past: *He was an entertainer in the great tradition of vaudeville.*

**tra·di·tion·al** /trə'dɪʃənəl/ *adj* **1** relating to the TRADITIONs of a country, group of people etc.: *a traditional greeting | traditional music* **2** following ideas, methods etc. that have existed for a long time rather than doing something new or different: *My father has very traditional ideas about marriage.* –**traditionally** *adv*

**tra·di·tion·al·ist** /trə'dɪʃənl-ɪst/ *n* someone who likes traditional ideas but does not like new ones

**traf·fic¹** /'træfɪk/ *n* [U] **1** the vehicles moving along a particular road: *There was **heavy traffic** (=a lot of traffic) on the roads this morning.* **2** the movement of aircraft, ships, trains etc. from one place to another: *air/shipping traffic*

**traffic²** *v* **trafficked, trafficked, trafficking**
 **traffic in** sth *phr v* [T] to buy and sell illegal goods: *He's accused of **trafficking in** cocaine.* —**trafficker** *n*

**traffic jam** /'.. ,./ *n* a long line of vehicles on the road that cannot move, or that move very slowly: *We were **stuck in a traffic jam** for two hours!*

**traf·fick·ing** /'træfɪkɪŋ/ *n* **drug/arms trafficking** the activity of buying and selling illegal drugs or weapons

**traffic light** /'.. ,./, **traffic sig·nal** /'.. ,../ *n* ⇨ LIGHT¹

**trag·e·dy** /'trædʒədi/ *n* [C,U] **1** an event that is extremely sad, especially one that involves death: *They never recovered from the tragedy of their son's death.* **2** a serious play that ends sadly, usually with the death of the main character, or this style of writing: *Shakespeare's tragedies*

**tra·gic** /'trædʒɪk/ *adj* a tragic event or situation is very sad, often because it involves death: *a tragic car accident* —**tragically** *adv*

**trail¹** /treɪl/ *v* **1** [I,T] also **trail behind** to be losing a game, competition, election etc.: *The Cowboys are trailing 21-14 in the third quarter.* **2** [I,T] if you trail something or it trails behind you, it gets pulled behind you as you move along: *She walked outside, her skirt trailing on the ground.* **3** [I] to follow a short distance behind someone: *The two mothers walked along with their kids **trailing behind** them.* **4** [T] to follow someone such as a criminal in order to try to catch him/her
 **trail off** *phr v* [I] if your voice or something you say trails off, it becomes quieter and quieter until it cannot be heard: *Her words **trailed off** as Mrs. Hellman walked into the room.*

**trail²** *n* **1** a path across open country or through the forest: *a hiking trail in the mountains* **2** **trail of blood/clues/destruction** etc. a series of marks or signs left behind by someone or something that is moving: *The wounded animal left a trail of blood behind it.* **3** **be on the trail of** looking for a person or information that is difficult to find: *a reporter on the trail of a big story*

**trail·blaz·er** /'treɪl,bleɪzɚ/ *n* INFORMAL someone who is the first to discover or develop new methods of doing something: *a trailblazer in the field of medical research*

**trail·er** /'treɪlɚ/ *n* **1** a vehicle that can be pulled behind a car, used for living in during a vacation **2** a frame that is pulled behind a vehicle, on which you carry something large such as a boat —see picture on page 469 **3** a short advertisement for a movie or television program

**trailer park** /'.. ,./ *n* an area where TRAILERs are parked and used as people's homes

**train¹** /treɪn/ *n* **1** a set of connected railroad cars pulled by an ENGINE **2** **train of thought** a related series of thoughts in an argument or discussion: *Sorry, I've **lost** my **train of thought**.* **3** a long line of moving people or animals: *a camel train* **4** a part of a dress that spreads out over the ground behind the person wearing it

**train²** *v* **1** [I,T] to teach someone or be taught the skills of a particular job or activity: *Sally spent two years **training as** a nurse.* **2** [T] to teach an animal to do something or to behave correctly: *I've trained the dog to sit.* **3** [I,T] to prepare for a sports event by exercising and practicing, or to make someone do this: *He is training for the Olympics.* —**trained** *adj* —**trainer** *n*

**train·ee** /treɪˈni/ *n* someone who is being trained for a job: *a trainee pilot/salesperson*

**train·ing** /'treɪnɪŋ/ *n* [U] **1** the process of teaching or being taught skills for a particular job: *Did you have any training on the computer?* **2** special physical exercises that you do to stay healthy or prepare for a sporting event: *He injured his knee **in training**.*

**trait** /treɪt/ *n* a particular quality in someone's character; CHARACTERISTIC: *His jealousy is one of his worst traits.*

**trai·tor** /'treɪtɚ/ *n* someone who is not loyal to his/her country, friends etc.

**tra·jec·to·ry** /trəˈdʒɛktəri/ *n* TECHNICAL the curved path of an object that is fired or thrown through the air

**tram** /træm/ *n* ⇨ STREETCAR

**tramp¹** /træmp/ *n* **1** ⇨ TRANSIENT² **2** OLD-FASHIONED a woman who has too many sexual partners

**tramp²** *v* [I,T] to walk somewhere with heavy steps: *kids tramping through the snow*

**tram·ple** /'træmpəl/ *v* [I,T] **1** to step on something heavily so that you crush it with your feet: *One woman was **trampled to death** by the crowd.* **2** to ignore or not care about someone's rights, ideas, hopes etc.: *a rule that **tramples on** people's right to free speech*

**tram·po·line** /ˌtræmpəˈlin, 'træmpə,lin/ *n* a piece of sports equipment that you jump up and down on, made of a sheet of material tightly stretched across a large frame

**trance** /træns/ *n* a state in which you seem to be asleep but you are still able to hear and understand what is said to you

**tran·quil** /'træŋkwəl/ *adj* pleasantly calm, quiet, and peaceful: *a tranquil spot for a picnic* —**tranquility** /træŋˈkwɪləti/ *n* [U]

**tran·qui·liz·er** /'træŋkwə,laɪzɚ/ *n* a drug used in order to make a person or animal calm or unconscious —**tranquilize** *v* [T]

**trans·act** /trænˈzækt/ *v* [I,T] FORMAL to do business

**trans·ac·tion** /træn'zækʃən/ *n* FORMAL a business deal: *The company keeps a report of all stock transactions.*

**trans·at·lan·tic** /ˌtrænzət'læntɪk/ *adj* crossing the Atlantic Ocean, or involving people on both sides of the Atlantic: *a transatlantic flight | a transatlantic business deal*

**tran·scend** /træn'sɛnd/ *v* [T] FORMAL to go above or beyond the limits of something: *The appeal of baseball transcends age and gender* **transcendence** *n* [U]

**tran·scen·den·tal** /ˌtrænsɛn'dɛntl/ *adj* existing above or beyond human knowledge or understanding

**trans·con·ti·nen·tal** /ˌtrænskɑntən'ɛntl, ˌtrænz-/ *adj* crossing a CONTINENT: *the first transcontinental railroad*

**tran·scribe** /træn'skraɪb/ *v* [T] to change information from one form to another: *recordings being transcribed onto disk* **–transcription** /træn'skrɪpʃən/ *n* [C,U]

**tran·script** /'træn,skrɪpt/ *n* **1** an exact written or printed copy of something that was said: *a transcript of the witness's testimony* **2** an official document that has a list of the classes you took as a student and the grades you received

**trans·fer**[1] /'trænsfɚ, træns'fɚ/ *v* **-rred, -rring 1** [I,T] to move from one place, job, etc. to another, or to make someone or something do this: *After his first year he transferred to UCLA. | They're transferring him from accounts to the shipping department.* **2** [T] LAW to officially give property or money to someone else **–transferable** /træns'fɚəbəl/ *adj*

**trans·fer**[2] /'trænsfɚ/ *n* [C,U] the process of TRANSFERring someone or something: *the transfer of funds between banks | a job transfer*

**trans·fixed** /træns'fɪkst/ *adj* **be transfixed** to be unable to move because you are shocked, frightened etc.: *We were transfixed by the pictures of the storm on TV.*

**trans·form** /træns'fɔrm/ *v* [T] to change the appearance, character etc. of someone or something completely: *the Soviet Union's attempts to transform the country into a democracy*

**trans·for·ma·tion** /ˌtrænsfɚ'meɪʃən/ *n* [U] a complete change in the appearance, character etc. of someone or something: *the transformation of the old house into a restaurant*

**trans·form·er** /træns'fɔrmɚ/ *n* a piece of electrical equipment that changes the electricity from one VOLTAGE to another

**trans·fu·sion** /træns'fyuʒən/ *n* [C,U] FORMAL the process of putting new blood into someone's body

**trans·gress** /trænz'grɛs/ *v* [I,T] FORMAL to do something that is against the rules of a religion or society **–transgression** /trænz'grɛʃən/ *n* [C,U]

**tran·sient**[1] /'trænʒənt/ *adj* FORMAL **1** continuing or existing for only a short time **2** passing quickly through a place, or staying there only a short time: *transient workers*

**transient**[2] *n* someone who has no home or job and moves from place to place, often asking people for money

**tran·sis·tor** /træn'zɪstɚ/ *n* a piece of electronic equipment that controls the flow of electricity in radios, televisions etc.

**tran·sit** /'trænzɪt/ *n* [U] the process of moving people, products etc. from one place to another: *The shipment must have been lost in transit.*

**tran·si·tion** /træn'zɪʃən/ *n* [C,U] FORMAL the process of changing from one form or condition to another: *The transition from a dictatorship to a democracy is difficult.*

**tran·si·tion·al** /træn'zɪʃənl/ *adj* relating to a period of change from one form or condition to another: *transitional government/housing | a transitional period between the two projects*

**tran·si·tive verb** /ˌtrænzətɪv 'vɚb/ *n* TECHNICAL in grammar, a transitive verb has an object. In the sentence "She makes her own clothes," "makes" is a transitive verb **–compare** INTRANSITIVE VERB **–see study note on page 468**

**tran·si·to·ry** /'trænzəˌtɔri/ *adj* ⇨ TRANSIENT[1]

**trans·late** /'trænzleɪt, ˌtrænz'leɪt/ *v* **1** [I,T] to change speech or writing from one language to another: *I have to translate from German into English* **–compare** INTERPRET **2 translate into sth** if one thing translates into another, the second thing happens as a result of the first: *Will more investment translate into more jobs?* **–translation** /trænz'leɪʃən/ *n* [C,U]

**trans·la·tor** /'trænzˌleɪtɚ/ *n* someone who changes writing or speech into a different language **–compare** INTERPRETER

**trans·lu·cent** /trænz'lusənt/ *adj* not transparent, but clear enough for some light to pass through **–translucence** *n* [U]

**trans·mis·sion** /trænz'mɪʃən/ *n* **1** [C,U] the process of sending out radio or television signals, or the program itself **2** the part of a vehicle that uses the power from the engine to turn the wheels **3** [U] FORMAL the process of sending or passing something from one place, person etc. to another: *the transmission of disease*

**trans·mit** /trænz'mɪt/ *v* **-tted, -tting 1** to send out electric signals for radio or television; broadcast **2** [T] to send or pass something from one place, person etc. to another: *The virus is transmitted through the blood.*

**trans·mit·ter** /trænz'mɪtɚ, 'trænz,mɪtɚ/ *n* equipment that sends out radio or television signals

**trans·par·ent** /træns'pærənt, -'pɛr-/ *adj* **1** clear and able to be seen through: *transparent glass* **2** easy to notice and not deceiving anyone; OBVIOUS: *a transparent attempt to fool the voters* –**transparency** *n* [U] –**transparently** *adv*

**tran·spire** /træn'spaɪɚ/ *v* [T] FORMAL to happen: *Nobody knows what transpired that day.*

**trans·plant**[1] /træns'plænt/ *v* [T] **1** to move a plant from one place and put it in another **2** to move an organ such as a heart from one person's body to another

**trans·plant**[2] /'trænsplænt/ *n* [C,U] the medical operation of TRANSPLANTing an organ, or the organ itself: *a heart transplant* –compare IMPLANT[2]

**trans·port** /træns'pɔrt/ *v* [T] to move or carry goods, people etc. from one place to another in a vehicle: *using helicopters to transport equipment*

**trans·por·ta·tion** /ˌtrænspɚ'teɪʃən/ *n* [U] the process or business of moving goods, people etc. from one place to another: *Buses are the main form of public transportation.* | *Sunny Tours provides free transportation from/to the airport.*

> **USAGE NOTE** transportation
>
> Use **by** with types of transportation to say how you traveled somewhere: *We came by car/by bus/by bicycle/by boat/by plane.* For walking, use **on foot**: *Pioneers crossed the Rockies on foot.* Use the verb **get** with a preposition to say how you enter or leave a vehicle. You **get on** or **get off** a subway, train, bicycle, motorcycle, plane, or boat. You **get in** or **get into** and **get out of** a car or taxi. Use **take** to talk about traveling by public transportation: *I usually take the bus/train/subway to work.* Use **go** to talk about traveling in a private car or on a bicycle: *I go to work by car.*

**trans·pose** /træns'poʊz/ *v* [T] FORMAL to change the order or position of two or more words, letters etc.

**trans·sex·u·al** /trænz'sɛkʃuəl/ *n* someone who has had a medical operation to become a person of the opposite sex

**trans·ves·tite** /trænz'vɛstaɪt/ *n* someone who enjoys dressing like a person of the opposite sex

**trap**[1] /træp/ *n* **1** a piece of equipment for catching animals: *a mouse trap* **2** an unpleasant situation from which it is difficult to escape: *the deadly trap of drug and alcohol addiction* **3** a trick that is intended to catch someone or make him/her say or do something that s/he did not intend to

**trap**[2] *v* **-pped, -pping** [T] **1** to force someone into a place from which s/he cannot escape: *Up to 25 people may be trapped in the burning building.* **2** to prevent something such as water, dirt, heat etc. from escaping or spreading:

*a filter that traps dust* **3** to trick someone so that s/he says or does something that s/he did not intend to: *He says that the police trapped him into confessing.* **4 be trapped** to be in an unpleasant situation from which it is difficult to escape: *She was trapped in a bad marriage.* **5** to catch an animal in a trap

**trap door** /ˌ. './ *n* a small door that covers an opening in a floor or roof

**tra·peze** /træ'piz/ *n* a short BAR hanging from two ropes high above the ground, used by ACROBATS

**trap·per** /'træpɚ/ *n* someone who traps wild animals for their fur

**trap·pings** /'træpɪŋz/ *n* [plural] clothes, possessions etc. that show someone's success, or his/her position in a particular job: *He has all the trappings of stardom.*

**trash**[1] /træʃ/ *n* [U] **1** waste material such as old food, dirty paper etc., or the container this is put in; GARBAGE: *Just put it in the trash.* **2** INFORMAL something that is of very poor quality: *There's so much trash on TV these days.*

**trash**[2] *v* [T] INFORMAL **1** to destroy something completely: *You can't have parties if your friends are going to trash the place.* **2** to criticize someone or something severely: *Critics have trashed the movie.*

**trash can** /'. ./ *n* ⇨ GARBAGE CAN

**trash com·pact·or** /'. .ˌ../ *n* a machine used in the home for pressing TRASH into a small block so that it takes less space

**trash·y** /'træʃi/ *adj* of extremely bad quality, and often about sex: *trashy novels*

**trau·ma** /'trɔmə, 'traʊmə/ *n* [U] a state of extreme shock that is caused by a very frightening or unpleasant experience, or the experience itself: *Children have trouble coping with the trauma of divorce.* | *soldiers suffering from trauma*

**trau·mat·ic** /trə'mæṭɪk, trɔ-/ *adj* shocking and upsetting: *a traumatic experience*

**trau·ma·tize** /'trɔməˌtaɪz, 'traʊ-/ *v* [T] to shock someone so badly that s/he is unable to do things normally

**trav·el**[1] /'trævəl/ *v* **1** [I] to make a trip from one place to another, especially to distant places: *Rick's traveling across/through the US with a backpack.* | *We always travel light.* (=without taking many bags) **2** [I] to move from one place or person to another: *News travels fast in a small town like this.* **3** [I,T] to go a particular distance or at a particular speed: *We traveled over 400 miles the first day of our trip.* | *The bus was traveling at a high speed.*

**travel**[2] *n* [U] the act or activity of traveling: *Heavy rain is making road travel difficult.*

> **USAGE NOTE** travel
>
> Although the verb "to travel" generally means "to go from one place to another,"

the nouns **travel** and **travels** are usually used about traveling for long distances and long periods of time: *Wade came home after years of foreign travel.* | *She wrote a book about her travels in South America.* A **trip** is the time spent and the distance traveled in going from one place to another: *The trip to work takes me about 25 minutes.* Use **journey** instead of **trip** for a trip that is a long distance or is very difficult: *It was an uncomfortable journey on a crowded train.* Use **voyage** to talk about traveling by sea or in a SPACECRAFT.

**travel a·gen·cy** /'.. ,.../ *n* a business that arranges travel and vacations

**travel a·gent** /'.. ,../ *n* someone who works in a TRAVEL AGENCY

**trav·el·er** /'trævələ/ *n* someone who is on a trip or who travels often

**traveler's check** /'... ,./ *n* a special check that can be exchanged for the money of a foreign country

**trav·els** /'trævəlz/ *n* [plural] trips, especially to places that are far away: *Kim has lots of photos of her travels.* –see usage note at TRAVEL[2]

**tra·verse** /trə'vɚs/ *v* [T] FORMAL to move across, over, or through something

**trav·es·ty** /'trævɪsti/ *n* a very bad example of something, that gives a completely false idea of it: *The trial was described as a travesty of justice.*

**trawl** /trɔl/ *n* a wide net that is pulled along the bottom of the ocean to catch fish –**trawl** *v* [I,T]

**trawl·er** /'trɔlɚ/ *n* a fishing boat that uses a TRAWL

**tray** /treɪ/ *n* a flat piece of plastic, metal, or wood with raised edges, that is used for carrying things such as plates, food etc.

**treach·er·ous** /'trɛtʃərəs/ *adj* **1** someone who is treacherous cannot be trusted because s/he secretly intends to harm you **2** extremely dangerous because you cannot see the dangers: *Black ice on the roads is making driving treacherous.*

**treach·er·y** /'trɛtʃəri/ *n* [U] actions that are not loyal to someone who trusts you

**tread[1]** /trɛd/ *v* **trod, trodden, treading** **1** **tread carefully/lightly etc.** to be very careful about what you say or do in a difficult situation: *It's best to tread lightly when the boss is in a bad mood.* **2** **tread water** to stay floating upright in deep water by moving your legs as if you were riding a bicycle **3** OLD-FASHIONED to walk or step on something

**tread[2]** *n* **1** [C,U] the pattern of thick deep lines on the part of a tire that touches the road **2** the part of a stair or step that you put your foot on **3** [singular] the sound that someone makes when s/he walks: *a heavy tread*

**tread·mill** /'trɛdmɪl/ *n* [singular] **1** work or a way of life that seems very boring because you always have to do the same things: *It's time for me to step off the treadmill and get a new job.* **2** a piece of exercise equipment that has a large belt around a set of wheels, that moves when you walk on it

**trea·son** /'trizən/ *n* [U] the crime of being disloyal to your country or government, especially by helping its enemies

**treas·ure[1]** /'trɛʒɚ/ *n* **1** [U] gold, silver, jewels etc.: *a story about buried treasure* **2** a very valuable and important object such as a painting or ancient document: *the treasures of the Art Institute of Chicago*

**treasure[2]** *v* [T] to treat something or someone as very special, important, or valuable: *I'll always treasure the memories of this day.*

**treas·ur·er** /'trɛʒərɚ/ *n* someone who takes care of the money for an organization

**treas·ur·y** /'trɛʒəri/ *n* **1** the money in an organization's accounts **2** a government office that controls a country's money

**treat[1]** /trit/ *v* [T] **1** to behave toward someone in a particular way: *Why do you* **treat** *me* **like** *an idiot?* | *She* **treats** *children* **the same as** *adults.* | *Mr. Parker* **treats** *everyone* **equally/ fairly.* **2** to consider something in a particular way: *You can* **treat** *these costs* **as** *business expenses.* **3** to give someone medical attention for a sickness or injury: *Eleven people were* **treated for** *minor injuries.* **4** to buy or arrange something special for someone: *We're* **treating** *Mom* **to** *dinner for her birthday.* **5** to put a special substance on something or use a chemical process in order to protect or clean it: *The wood has been treated to make it waterproof.*

**treat[2]** *n* **1** something special that you give someone or do for him/her: *If you're good, I'll buy you a treat.* **2** [singular] an unexpected event that gives you a lot of pleasure: *Getting your letter was a real treat.* **3** **my treat** SPOKEN used in order to tell someone that you will pay for something: *Put away your money - dinner's my treat.*

**treat·a·ble** /'tritəbəl/ *adj* able to be medically treated: *The disease is treatable with antibiotics.*

**trea·tise** /'tritəs/ *n* a serious book or article about a particular subject: *a treatise on political philosophy*

**treat·ment** /'tritmənt/ *n* **1** [C,U] a method that is intended to cure an injury or sickness: *He's trying a new* **treatment for** *cancer.* **2** [U] a particular way of behaving toward someone or of dealing with him/her: *He's not getting any special treatment even if he is the coach's son.* **3** [C,U] a particular way of dealing with or talking about a subject: *He gives a thoughtful treatment of the subject.* **4** [U] a process by which something is cleaned, protected etc.: *a waste treatment plant*

**trea·ty** /ˈtriti/ *n* a formal written agreement between two or more countries: *a peace treaty*

**tre·ble**[1] /ˈtrɛbəl/ *n* the upper half of the whole range of musical notes

**treble**[2] *v* [I,T] ⇨ TRIPLE[2]

**tree** /tri/ *n* a very tall plant that has a TRUNK, branches, and leaves, and lives for many years: *an apple tree*

**tree·top** /ˈtritɑp/ *n* [C usually plural] the top branches of a tree

**trek**[1] /trɛk/ *v* **-kked, -kking** to make a long and difficult trip on foot: *trekking across the Rockies* –**trek** *n*: *a trek across the country* –**trekking** *n* [U]

**trel·lis** /ˈtrɛlɪs/ *n* a wooden frame for supporting climbing plants

**trem·ble** /ˈtrɛmbəl/ *v* [I] to shake because you are upset, afraid, or excited: *Her lip trembled as she spoke.|Ray's voice was **trembling with fear/anger**.*

**tre·men·dous** /trɪˈmɛndəs/ *adj* **1** very great in amount, size, power etc.: *I have tremendous respect for her.|a runner with tremendous speed* **2** very good or impressive: *a tremendous success*

**trem·or** /ˈtrɛmɚ/ *n* **1** a small EARTHQUAKE **2** a slight shaking movement that you cannot control

**trench** /trɛntʃ/ *n* a long narrow hole that is dug along the ground

**tren·chant** /ˈtrɛntʃənt/ *adj* expressed very strongly, effectively, and directly: *a trenchant critic of big business*

**trench coat** /ˈ. ./ *n* a type of RAINCOAT that is similar to a military coat, with pockets and a belt

**trend** /trɛnd/ *n* **1** the way a situation is generally developing or changing: *There's a **trend** toward more part-time employment.|a **fashion trend** (=what is fashionable right now)* **2 set the trend** to start doing something that other people copy

**trend·y** /ˈtrɛndi/ *adj* INFORMAL modern and fashionable: *a trendy bar*

**trep·i·da·tion** /ˌtrɛpəˈdeɪʃən/ *n* [U] FORMAL a feeling of anxiety or fear about something that is going to happen

**tres·pass** /ˈtrɛspæs/ *v* [I] to go onto someone's land without permission –**trespasser** *n*

**tres·tle** /ˈtrɛsəl/ *n* a wooden support made of beams in an "A" shape under a table or bridge

**tri·al** /ˈtraɪəl/ *n* **1** [C,U] a legal process in which a court of law examines a case to decide whether someone is guilty of a crime: *a murder trial|Holt is **on trial for** bank robbery. (=being judged in a court of law)* **2** [C,U] a test to know if something works well and is safe: *clinical trials of a new drug* **3** [C,U] a time during which you employ someone in order to know if s/he is satisfactory for a particular job: *Bonnie's been hired **on a trial basis**.* **4 trial and error**

testing different ways of doing something in order to find the best one: *I learned to cook by trial and error.* –see also TRIALS

**trial run** /ˌ. ˈ./ *n* an occasion when you test something new in order to see if it works

**tri·als** /ˈtraɪəlz/ *n* [plural] **1** a sports competition that tests a player's ability: *the Olympic swimming trials* **2 trials and tribulations** difficult experiences and troubles: *all the trials and tribulations of being a teenager*

**tri·an·gle** /ˈtraɪˌæŋgəl/ *n* **1** a flat shape with three straight sides and three angles –see picture at SHAPE **2** a small musical instrument shaped like a triangle, that you play by hitting it with a small metal BAR

**tri·ath·lon** /traɪˈæθlɑn, -lən/ *n* a sports competition in which you run, swim, and bicycle

**tribe** /traɪb/ *n* a social group that consists of people of the same race who have the same beliefs, customs, language etc. and live in one area ruled by a chief: *the tribes of the Amazon jungle* –**tribal** *adj*: *tribal art|tribal leaders* –see usage note at RACE[1]

**trib·u·la·tion** /ˌtrɪbyəˈleɪʃən/ *n* [C,U] difficult experiences that you have to deal with –see also **trials and tribulations** (TRIALS)

**tri·bu·nal** /traɪˈbyunl, trɪ-/ *n* a type of court that has official authority to deal with a particular situation or problem: *a war crimes tribunal*

**tri·bu·tar·y** /ˈtrɪbyəˌtɛri/ *n* a river or stream that flows into a larger river

**trib·ute** /ˈtrɪbyut/ *n* [C,U] something that you say, do, or give in order to express your respect or admiration for someone: *The concert will be a **tribute to** Bob Dylan.* –see also **pay tribute to sb/sth** (PAY[1])

**tri·ceps** /ˈtraɪsɛps/ *n* the large muscle at the back of your upper arm

**trick**[1] /trɪk/ *n* **1** something you do in order to deceive someone: *It was just a trick to get me to agree.* **2** something you do to surprise someone and make other people laugh: *The kids like **playing tricks on** the grownups.* **3 do the trick** SPOKEN if something does the trick, it solves a problem or achieves what you want: *A little salt should do the trick.* **4** an effective way of doing something: *There's **a trick to** getting the audience's attention.* **5** a skillful set of actions that seem like magic, done in order to entertain people: *Mike's learning some new card tricks.* **6 How's tricks?** SPOKEN used in order to greet someone in a friendly way: *Hi, Bill. How's tricks?*

**trick**[2] *v* [T] to deceive someone in order to get something from him/her or make him/her do something: *Believe me, we're not trying to trick you.|Clients were **tricked into** believing he'd invest the money.*

**trick·er·y** /'trɪkəri/ n [U] the use of tricks to deceive or cheat people

**trick·le¹** /'trɪkəl/ v [I] **1** if liquid trickles somewhere, it flows slowly in drops or in a thin stream: Sweat **trickled down** his face. **2** if people, vehicles, goods etc. trickle somewhere, they move there slowly in small groups or amounts: cars **trickling into** the parking lot

**trickle²** n **1** a thin slow flow of liquid **2** a movement of people, vehicles, goods etc. into a place in very small numbers or amounts: Higher prices have **reduced** the number of visitors **to a trickle**.

**trick or treat** /ˌ. . './ v **1 go trick or treat-ing** if children go trick or treating, they put on COSTUMEs and go from house to house on HALLOWEEN in order to get candy **2** SPOKEN said to someone in order to get candy on Halloween

**trick·ster** /'trɪkstɚ/ n someone who deceives or cheats people

**trick·y** /'trɪki/ adj **1** a tricky job or situation is difficult to deal with: Finding out how the trouble started will be tricky. **2** a tricky person is likely to deceive you

**tri·cy·cle** /'traɪsɪkəl/ n a small vehicle with one wheel at the front and two wheels at the back, that you ride by pushing the PEDALs with your feet

**tri·dent** /'traɪdnt/ n a weapon with three points that looks like a large fork

**tried¹** /traɪd/ v the past tense and PAST PARTI-CIPLE of TRY

---
**USAGE NOTE try to do and try doing**

Saying Nick tried to climb the mountain means that he tried but he could not climb it. Saying Nick tried climbing the mountain means that he climbed it in order to have the experience of climbing.

---

**tried²** adj **tried and tested/true** used success-fully many times: tried and tested methods

**tri·fle¹** /'traɪfəl/ adj, adv **a trifle ...** slightly: It's a trifle salty, but otherwise delicious.

**trifle²** n something that has little value or importance

**trig·ger¹** /'trɪgɚ/ n **1** the part of a gun that you press with your finger to fire it: Carter aimed and **pulled/squeezed the trigger**. **2 be the trigger (for)** to be the thing that causes a serious problem: The doctor thinks stress was the trigger for Ben's heart attack.

**trigger²**, **trigger off** v [T] to make something happen: Heavy rain may trigger mudslides.

**trigger hap·py** /'.. ,../ adj too willing to use weapons to solve disagreements

**trig·o·nom·e·try** /ˌtrɪgə'nɑmətri/ n [U] the part of mathematics that is concerned with the relationship between the angles and sides of TRIANGLEs

**trike** /traɪk/ n INFORMAL ⇨ TRICYCLE

**tri·lat·er·al** /ˌtraɪ'lætərəl / adj including three groups or countries: a trilateral agreement

**trill** /trɪl/ n a musical sound made by quickly repeating two notes that are very similar: a bird's trill –**trill** v [I,T]

**tril·lion** /'trɪlyən/ number 1,000,000,000,000

**tril·o·gy** /'trɪlədʒi/ n a group of three books, plays, movies etc. that have the same subject or characters

**trim¹** /trɪm/ v **mmed, mming** [T] **1** to make something look neater by cutting a small amount off it: My hair needs to be trimmed. **2** to reduce the size or amount of something in order to save money: plans to trim the city's budget | The industry intends to trim more work-ers. **3** to decorate something around its edges: a beautifully trimmed Christmas tree | a coat **trimmed with** velvet

**trim sth ↔ off** phr v [T] to cut small pieces from the end of something so that it looks nea-ter: **Trim off** the stems before putting the roses in water.

**trim²** adj thin and healthy looking: a trim figure

**trim³** n **1** [singular] an act of cutting some-thing in order to make it look neater: Your beard needs a trim. **2** [singular, U] a decoration around the edges of a car, piece of clothing etc.: a blue car with white trim

**tri·mes·ter** /'traɪmɛstɚ, traɪ'mɛstɚ/ n **1** one of three periods into which a year at school or college is divided **2** one of the three-month periods of a woman's PREGNANCY

**trim·mings** /'trɪmɪŋz/ n [plural] **1** material or objects used for decorating things such as clothes **2 all the trimmings** all the other types of food that are traditionally served with the main dish of a meal: a turkey dinner with all the trimmings

**trin·ket** /'trɪŋkɪt/ n a piece of jewelry or a small pretty object that is not worth much money

**tri·o** /'trioʊ/ n a piece of music written for three performers

**trip¹** /trɪp/ n **1** an occasion when you go from one place to another: We're **taking a trip** to Florida. | You'll have to **make** two **trips** - there's too much to carry. | When are you **going on** your business **trip**? –see usage note at TRAVEL² **2** SLANG the experiences someone has while s/he is taking illegal drugs **3** SLANG a person or experience that is amusing and differ-ent from normal: Yeah, she's a real trip.

**trip² v -pped, -pping 1** [I] to hit something with your foot while you are walking or running so that you fall or almost fall: "How did you hurt your foot?" "I **tripped on/over** a cord." **2** [T] also **trip up**

trip

to make someone fall by putting your foot in front of him/her when s/he is moving **3 trip a switch/wire** to accidentally make an electrical system operate by moving part of it: *I tripped the switch accidentally and set off the alarm.* **4** [I] also **trip out** SLANG to experience the effects of illegal drugs

**trip up** *phr v* [I] to make a mistake: *It's easy to trip up on some of the details.*

**tripe** /traɪp/ *n* [U] the stomach of a cow or pig, used as food

**tri·ple**[1] /'trɪpəl/ *adj* having three parts, or involving three people or groups: *The skater fell while attempting a triple jump.*

**triple**[2] *v* [I,T] to become three times as much or as many, or to make something do this: *The population may triple in 20 years.*

**tri·plet** /'trɪplɪt/ *n* one of three children born at the same time to the same mother

**trip·li·cate** /'trɪpləkɪt/ *n* **in triplicate** if a document is written in triplicate, there are three copies of it

**tri·pod** /'traɪpɑd/ *n* a support with three legs, used for a camera, TELESCOPE etc.

**trite** /traɪt/ *adj* a trite remark, idea etc. has been used so often that it seems boring and not sincere

**tri·umph**[1] /'traɪəmf/ *n* **1** an important success or victory, especially after a difficult struggle: *Winning a gold medal was a personal triumph for Sylvie.* | *San Francisco's triumph over Cincinnati in the Super Bowl* **2** a feeling of pleasure and satisfaction that you get from victory or success: *shouts of triumph* **–triumphant** /traɪ'ʌmfənt/ *adj*: *a triumphant army*

**triumph**[2] *v* [I] to gain a victory or success, especially after a difficult struggle: *Once again, good triumphs over evil.*

**tri·um·phal** /traɪ'ʌmfəl/ *adj* done or made in order to celebrate a victory or success: *a triumphal march*

**triv·i·a** /'trɪviə/ *n* [plural] **1** unimportant or useless details: *Don't waste my time with trivia.* **2** detailed facts about past events, famous people, sports etc., used in QUIZ games

**triv·i·al** /'trɪviəl/ *adj* unimportant or of little value: *We do not view the issue as a trivial matter.*

**triv·i·al·ize** /'trɪviə,laɪz/ *v* [T] to make something important seem less important than it really is: *The media tried to trivialize the court's decision.*

**trod** /trɑd/ *v* the past tense of TREAD

**trod·den** /'trɑdn/ *v* the PAST PARTICIPLE of TREAD

**troll** /troʊl/ *n* an imaginary creature in ancient Scandinavian stories, like a very large or very small ugly person

**trol·ley** /'trɑli/ *n* an electric vehicle for carry-

ing passengers, that moves along the street on metal tracks

**trom·bone** /trɑm'boʊn/ *n* a metal musical instrument, that you play by blowing into it and moving a long sliding tube

**tromp** /trɑmp, trɔmp/ *v* [I,T] INFORMAL ⇨ TRAMP[2]

**troop**[1] /trup/ *n* **1** an organized group of people or animals: *a Girl Scout troop* **2** a group of soldiers, especially on horses or in TANKs – see also TROOPS

**troop**[2] *v* [I] INFORMAL to move together in a group: *We parked our cars and trooped over the grass to the picnic area.*

**troop·er** /'trupɚ/ *n* a member of a state police force in the US

**troops** /trups/ *n* [plural] organized groups of soldiers: *Troops were sent in to stop the riots.*

**tro·phy** /'troʊfi/ *n* a prize for winning a competition, especially a silver cup or a PLAQUE: *the first-place trophy*

**trop·i·cal** /'trɑpɪkəl/ *adj* **1** coming from or existing in the hottest and wettest parts of the world: *tropical flowers* **2** weather that is tropical is hot and the air seems wet

**trop·ics** /'trɑpɪks/ *n* **the tropics** the hottest and wettest parts of the world, between the Tropic of Cancer and the Tropic of Capricorn

**trot** /trɑt/ *v* **-tted, -tting** [I] **1** if a horse trots, it moves with quick small steps **2** to run fairly slowly with short steps: *Jimmy trotted along behind his parents.* **–trot** *n*

**trot** *sb/sth* ↔ **out** *phr v* [T] INFORMAL to bring something or someone out to show other people: *The Reids like to trot out photos of their grandchildren.*

**trou·ba·dour** /'trubə,dɔr/ *n* a singer and poet who traveled around in past times

**trou·ble**[1] /'trʌbəl/ *n*

**1** ▶PROBLEMS◀ [C,U] problems that make something difficult, make you worry, spoil your plans etc.: *They're having some trouble with their new car.* | *a plane with engine trouble* | *People often come to me with their troubles.*

**2** **the trouble with** SPOKEN used when explaining what is not satisfactory about something or someone: *The trouble with you is you don't listen.*

**3** ▶BAD SITUATION◀ [U] a difficult or dangerous situation: *We're in big/real/deep trouble now!* | *a call from a ship in trouble*

**4** ▶HEALTH◀ [U] INFORMAL a problem that you have with your health: *heart/back trouble*

**5** ▶EFFORT◀ [U] an amount of effort and time that is needed to do something: *She took the trouble to explain it to us again.* | *I'm sorry to put you to so much trouble.* | *"Could you help me carry this?" "Sure, it's no trouble."* (=I am happy to help)

**6** ▶BLAME◀ [U] a situation in which someone

in authority is angry with you or is likely to punish you: *My daughter's gotten into trouble at school.* | *Joe's in trouble with the police again.*
**7 be asking for trouble** INFORMAL to take risks or do something stupid that is likely to cause problems: *You're asking for trouble if you don't get those brakes fixed.*
**8 ▶ARGUMENT/VIOLENCE◀** a situation in which people quarrel or fight with each other: *recent troubles on college campuses*

**trouble²** *v* [T] FORMAL **1** to ask someone to do something for you when it is difficult for him/her: *I won't trouble you again.* **2 May I trouble you for...?** used in order to ask for something extremely politely: *May I trouble you for more wine?*

**trou·bled** /'trʌbəld/ *adj* having many emotional problems: *a deeply troubled man*

**trou·ble·mak·er** /'trʌbəl,meɪkɚ/ *n* someone who deliberately causes problems

**trou·ble·shoot·er** /'trʌbəl,ʃutɚ/ *n* someone who is employed by a company to deal with its most serious problems –**troubleshooting** *n* [U]

**trou·ble·some** /'trʌbəlsəm/ *adj* causing you trouble for a long time: *troublesome back pain*

**trou·ble·spot** /'trʌbəlspat/ *n* a place where there is trouble such as fighting, or where trouble may happen: *Tourists have been warned to stay away from troublespots.*

**trough** /trɔf/ *n* a long narrow open container that holds water or food for animals

**trounce** /traʊns/ *v* [T] to defeat someone completely: *Colorado trounced Minnesota 58-7 on Saturday.*

**troupe** /trup/ *n* a group of singers, actors, dancers etc. who work together

**trou·sers** /'traʊzɚz/ *n* [plural] ⇨ PANTS

**trout** /traʊt/ *n* [C,U] a common river fish, or the meat from this fish

**trove** /troʊv/ *n* a place where a large number of special or valuable things can be found: *The house contains a treasure trove of antique furniture.*

**tru·ant** /'truənt/ *n* a student who stays away from school without permission –**truancy** *n* [U]

**truce** /trus/ *n* an agreement between two enemies to stop fighting or arguing for a short time: *The warring sides have declared a truce.*

**truck¹** /trʌk/ *n* a large road vehicle that is used for carrying heavy loads –see picture on page 469

**truck²** *v* [T] to take something somewhere by truck: *Food and medicine were trucked in to flood victims.*

**truck farm** /'. ./ *n* a farm that grows vegetables and fruit for sale

**truck·ing** /'trʌkɪŋ/ *n* [U] the business of taking goods from place to place by truck

**truck·load** /'trʌkloʊd/ *n* the amount of something that a truck can carry

**truck stop** /'. ./ *n* a cheap place to eat and buy gas on a HIGHWAY, used especially by truck drivers

**truc·u·lent** /'trʌkyələnt/ *adj* FORMAL bad-tempered and always willing to argue with people

**trudge** /trʌdʒ/ *v* [I] to walk with slow heavy steps because you are tired or sad: *trudging home from shopping*

**true** /tru/ *adj* **1** based on facts and not imagined or invented: *Believe me, it's a true story.* | *Is it true that you're moving to Denver?* | *Answer the questions True or False.* –opposite FALSE **2** SPOKEN used when admitting that something is a fact: *True, he has a college degree, but he doesn't have enough job experience.* **3 true love/courage/friendship etc.** love, courage, etc. that is strong and has all the qualities that it should have **4 come true** if dreams, wishes etc. come true, they happen: *Their dream of owning a house in the mountains had finally come true.* **5** faithful and loyal to someone: *She stayed true to her husband during the trial.* **6 true friend/believer etc.** someone who behaves in the way that a good friend, believer etc. should behave: *You know who your true friends are at a time like this.*

**true-life** /,. '.◂/ *adj* based on what really happened, and not invented: *a true-life adventure*

**truf·fle** /'trʌfəl/ *n* **1** a soft chocolate candy **2** a FUNGUS you can eat that grows under the ground

**tru·ism** /'truɪzəm/ *n* a statement that is clearly true, so that there is no need to say it –compare CLICHÉ

**tru·ly** /'truli/ *adv* **1** used in order to emphasize that the way you are describing something is true; really: *They're truly the best athletes I've seen.* | *a truly amazing story* **2** in an exact or correct way: *A spider can't truly be called an insect.* –see also **yours (truly)** (YOURS)

**trump¹** /trʌmp/ *n* **1** a SUIT or a playing card that is chosen to be of a higher value than the others in a particular card game **2 play your trump card** to use an advantage that you have kept hidden until now, in order to make sure that you get what you want

**trump²** *v* [T] to play a TRUMP that beats someone else's card in a game

**trumped-up** /,. '.◂/ *adj* **trumped-up charges/evidence etc.** false information that has been used in order to make someone seem guilty of a crime

**trum·pet¹** /'trʌmpɪt/ *n* **1** a musical instrument that you blow into, that consists of a long bent metal tube that is wide at one end **2** the loud noise made by some animals, such as ELEPHANTS

**trumpet²** *v* [T] to tell as many people as you can about something you think is important or are proud of: *another new wine being trumpeted by its makers*

**trun·cat·ed** /'trʌŋ,keɪtɪd/ *adj* made short, or shorter than before: *a truncated speech*

**trun·dle** /'trʌndl/ *v* [I,T] to move slowly on wheels, or to make something do this by pushing it or pulling it

**trunk** /trʌŋk/ *n* **1** the thick central wooden stem of a tree that branches grow on **2** an enclosed space in the back of a car where you can put large bags, tools etc. —see picture on page 469 **3** the very long nose of an ELEPHANT **4** a large box that you store clothes, books etc. in, often used when traveling **5** TECHNICAL the main part of your body, not including your head, arms, or legs —compare TORSO

**trunks** /trʌŋks/ *n* [plural] very short pants that men wear when swimming

**trust¹** /trʌst/ *v* **1** [T] to believe that someone is honest and will not hurt you, cheat you, disobey you etc.: *I've never trusted her.* | *Can you* **trust him with** *your car?* (=believe he will not damage it) **2** [T] to depend on something: *Trust your instincts.* **3 I trust** SPOKEN FORMAL used in order to say that you hope something is true: *I* **trust that** *you had a successful business trip.*

**trust in** sb/sth *phr v* [T] FORMAL to believe that you can depend on someone or something

**trust²** *n* **1** [U] the belief that you can trust someone: *It took three years to earn his trust.* —opposite DISTRUST¹ **2** [U] an arrangement in which someone legally controls your money or property, usually until you are old enough to use it: *$100,000 is being* **held in trust** *for his daughter.* **3** a group of companies that work together to reduce competition

**trust·ee** /trʌ'sti/ *n* a person or company that legally controls someone else's property

**trust·ing** /'trʌstɪŋ/, **trust·ful** /'trʌstfəl/ *adj* willing or too willing to trust someone: *a trusting little child*

**trust·wor·thy** /'trʌst,wɚði/ *adj* able to be trusted or depended on

**trust·y** /'trʌsti/ *adj* HUMOROUS a trusty weapon, horse, friend etc. is one you can depend on

**truth** /truθ/ *n* **1** the truth the true facts about something: *Do you think he's* **telling the truth**? **2** [U] the state or quality of being true: *There was no truth in what she said.* | *a poem about truth and beauty* **3** FORMAL an important fact or idea that is accepted as being true: *scientific truths* **4 to tell (you) the truth** SPOKEN used when you admit something or tell someone your true opinion: *To tell you the truth, I don't care where she went.*

**truth·ful** /'truθfəl/ *adj* giving the true facts about something: *He swore his statement was truthful and accurate.* **—truthfully** *adv*

**try¹** /traɪ/ *v* **tried, tried, trying** **1** [I,T] to attempt to do something: *Please* **try to** *come*

early. | *Greg* **tried hard** *not to laugh.* | *Just* **try your best** *- it doesn't matter if you win or lose.* **2** [T] to do something, test something, or go somewhere, in order to find out if it is useful or will be successful: *Try the other light switch.* | *"Where's Bob?" "Try the next room."* **3** [T] to do, use, or taste something in order to find out if it is suitable or good: *Do they fit or do you want to try a bigger size?* | *Try some of this cake!* **4** [T] to examine and judge a person or a legal case in a court of law: *Three men were* **tried** *for murder.* **5 try sb's patience/ nerves/temper etc.** to make someone start to feel impatient, nervous, angry etc.

**try** sth **↔ on** *phr v* [T] to put on a piece of clothing to find out if it fits or makes you look attractive: *Would you like to* **try** *those jeans* **on**?

**try** sth **↔ out** *phr v* [T] to attempt to use something in order to find out if it works or is good: *When are you going to* **try out** *your new software?*

**try out for** sth *phr v* [T] to be tested in order to become a member of a team, an actor in a play etc.: *Sandra's* **trying out for** *the girls' basketball team.*

**try²** *n* [C usually singular] an attempt to do something: *I've never skated before, but I'll* **give it a try**.

**try·ing** /'traɪ-ɪŋ/ *adj* difficult and unpleasant to deal with: *It's been a very trying time for us all.*

**try·out** /'traɪ-aʊt/ *n* an occasion when someone is tested to decide whether s/he is good enough to be on a sports team

**tsar** /zɑr, tsɑr/ *n* ⇨ CZAR

**T-shirt** /'ti ʃɚt/ *n* a soft cotton shirt, with short SLEEVEs and no collar

**tsp.** *n* the written abbreviation of TEASPOON

**tub** /tʌb/ *n* **1** ⇨ BATHTUB **2** a plastic or paper container with a lid, that food is sold in: *a tub of ice cream* **3** a large round container used for washing things, storing things etc.

**tu·ba** /'tubə/ *n* a large metal musical instrument with a wide opening that points straight up, that you play by blowing

**tub·by** /'tʌbi/ *adj* INFORMAL short and fat

**tube** /tub/ *n* **1** a pipe made of metal, plastic, glass etc., especially one that liquids or gases go through: *tubes coming out of the patient's nose and mouth* **2** a container for a soft substance, that you SQUEEZE to push the substance out: *a tube of toothpaste* —see picture at CONTAINER **3** one of the parts inside the body shaped like a tube: *a fallopian tube* (=part of a woman's organs for having babies) **4 go down the tubes** if a situation goes down the tubes, it suddenly becomes bad: *My career's going down the tubes.* **5 the tube** SPOKEN the television: *What's on the tube?*

**tu·ber·cu·lo·sis** /tʊ,bɚkyə'loʊsɪs/ *n* [U] a serious infectious disease that affects the lungs and other parts of the body

**tub·ing** /'tubɪŋ/ *n* [U] tubes, usually connected together in a system: *copper tubing*

**tu·bu·lar** /'tubyələ/ *adj* made of tubes or shaped like a tube

**tuck¹** /tʌk/ *v* **1** [T] to push the edge of a cloth or piece of clothing into something so that it stays in place: *He **tucked in** his shirt and combed his hair.* **2** to put something in a small space, or a safe place: *She **tucked** the money **into** her pocket.* **3** to move the arms, legs, or head close to the body and keep it there: *The duck had its head tucked under its wing.* **4 tucked away** in a safe or hidden place: *a little cabin tucked away in the mountains*

**tuck** sb ↔ **in** *phr v* [T] to make a child feel comfortable in bed by tightly covering him/her with a BLANKET

**tuck²** *n* **1** a fold of cloth sewn flat in a piece of clothing **2** a medical operation to make someone look thinner or younger: *a tummy tuck*

**Tues·day** /'tuzdi, -deɪ/ written abbreviation **Tues.** *n* the third day of the week —see usage note at SUNDAY

**tuft** /tʌft/ *n* a short thick group of hairs, feathers, grass etc.: *a tuft of hair* —**tufted** *adj*

**tug¹** /tʌg/ *v* **-gged, -gging** [I,T] to pull something suddenly and hard: *Alice **tugged at** my hand, saying "Let's go!"*

**tug²** *n* **1** also **tug boat** a small strong boat used for pulling ships **2** a sudden strong pull

**tug-of-war** /ˌ. . './ *n* a competition in which two teams pull on the opposite ends of a rope

**tu·i·tion** /tu'ɪʃən/ *n* [U] **1** the money you pay for being taught: *Tuition went up to $3000 last semester.* **2** the act of teaching: *Ben improved his grades **under the tuition of** Mr. Neals.*

**tu·lip** /'tulɪp/ *n* a tall brightly colored garden flower, shaped like a cup

**tum·ble** /'tʌmbəl/ *v* [I] to fall or roll in a sudden uncontrolled way: *Losing her balance, she **tumbled down** the stairs.* | *They think California will tumble into the ocean one day.* —**tumble** *n*

**tum·bler** /'tʌmblə/ *n* a glass with a flat bottom and no handle

**tum·my** /'tʌmi/ *n* INFORMAL stomach: *Mommy, I have a tummy ache.*

**tu·mor** /'tumə/ *n* a group of cells in the body that grow too quickly and cause sickness or health problems: *a brain tumor*

**tu·mult** /'tumʌlt/ *n* [C,U] FORMAL a state of confusion, excitement, or other strong emotions: *the tumult of civil war* | *the tumult of angry thoughts in her head* —**tumultuous** /tu'mʌltʃuəs/ *adj*

**tu·na** /'tunə/ *n* [C,U] a large common ocean fish, or the meat from this fish, usually sold in cans

**tun·dra** /'tʌndrə/ *n* [U] the large flat areas of land in northern areas where it is very cold and there are no trees

**tune¹** /tun/ *n* **1** a series of musical notes that are nice to listen to: *Jill was humming a little tune to herself.* **2 in tune/out of tune** playing or singing the correct musical notes, or playing or singing notes that are slightly too high or low: *My guitar's completely out of tune.* **3 be in tune with/be out of tune with** to understand what someone needs, thinks, and wants, or to not understand this: *We try to stay in tune with students' needs.* **4 change your tune** to suddenly have a different opinion about something

**tune²** *v* [T] **1** to make a small change to a musical instrument so that it plays the correct PITCH: *We need to have the piano tuned.* **2** to make a television or radio receive broadcasts from a particular CHANNEL or STATION: ***Stay tuned** for more great music on KHPI, the city's best rock station.* **3** to make small changes to an engine so that it works better

**tune in** *phr v* **1** [I,T **tune** sth ↔ **in**] to watch or listen to a particular television or radio program, or to make your television or radio receive that program: *Over 3 million viewers **tune in to** our show daily.* **2 tuned in** INFORMAL knowing what is happening around you or what other people are thinking: *Jean's really **tuned in to** the local music scene.*

**tune out** *phr v* [I,T **tune** sb ↔ **out**] INFORMAL to ignore someone or something, or to stop listening to him, her, or it: *It's hard to **tune out** the noise in the office sometimes.*

**tune up** *phr v* **1** [T **tune** sth ↔ **up**] to fix and clean a car's engine **2** [I,T **tune** sth ↔ **up**] to prepare a musical instrument so that it plays at the same PITCH as other instruments

**tun·er** /'tunə/ *n* a piece of electronic equipment that lets you choose which electrical signal your radio, television etc. receives

**tune-up** /'. ./ *n* an occasion when someone fixes and cleans your car's engine, or the process of doing this

**tu·nic** /'tunɪk/ *n* a long loose piece of clothing, usually without SLEEVEs, often worn with a belt

**tun·nel¹** /'tʌnl/ *n* a passage that has been dug under the ground or through a mountain, usually for cars or trains

**tunnel²** *v* [I] to dig a TUNNEL

**tunnel vi·sion** /'.. ˌ../ *n* **1** the tendency to think about only one subject, so that you forget other things that may be important too **2** a condition in which someone's eyes are damaged so that they can only see straight ahead

**Tup·per·ware** /'tʌpəˌwɛr/ *n* [U] TRADEMARK a type of plastic container with a tight lid, used for storing food

**tur·ban** /'təbən/ *n* a long piece of cloth that is worn twisted around the top of your head

**tur·bine** /'tɔˈbaɪn, -bɪn/ *n* an engine that works when the pressure from liquid or steam moves a special wheel inside it

**tur·bu·lence** /'tɔˈbyələns/ *n* [U] **1** strong changing movements of air or water: *There was a lot of turbulence during the flight.* **2** a situation in which people's thoughts, actions, and emotions are always changing: *political turbulence*

**tur·bu·lent** /'tɔˈbyələnt/ *adj* **1** experiencing a lot of sudden changes and often wars or violence: *the turbulent years before the Revolution* **2** turbulent winds, oceans etc. are full of strong changing movements

**turd** /tɔˈd/ *n* **1** INFORMAL an impolite word for a piece of solid waste passed from the body **2** SPOKEN a very impolite word for an unpleasant person

**tu·reen** /tʊˈrin/ *n* a large dish with a lid, used especially for serving soup

**turf** /tɔˈf/ *n* **1** [U] grass and soil on the ground's surface, or an artificial substance made to look like this: *thick moist turf* | *The game was played on artificial turf.* **2** INFORMAL an area that someone knows well and feels that s/he controls or owns: *The gangs will not allow any non-members onto their turf.*

**tur·gid** /'tɔˈdʒɪd/ *adj* **1** boring and difficult to understand: *turgid poetry* **2** swollen, especially with liquid

**tur·key** /'tɔˈki/ *n* [C,U] a bird similar to a chicken but larger, or the meat from this bird — see also COLD TURKEY

**tur·moil** /'tɔˈmɔɪl/ *n* [singular, U] a state of confusion, excitement, and trouble: *In 1967 the country was in racial turmoil.*

**turn**

turn on          turn off

**turn¹** /tɔˈn/ *v*

**1** ▶YOUR BODY◀ [I] to move your body so that you are looking in a different direction: *Alison turned towards us.* | *Turn around so I can see the back of the dress.* | *He turned to look behind him.*

**2** ▶OBJECT◀ [T] to move an object so that it is facing in a different direction: *She turned the box around/over to look at the label.*

**3** ▶DIRECTION◀ [I] to go in a new direction when you are walking, driving etc.: *Turn right at the next stop light.*

**4** ▶MOVE AROUND A CENTRAL POINT◀ [I,T] to move around a central point that does not move: *The wheels turned slowly.*

**5** ▶AGE◀ [linking verb] to become a particular age: *Megan's just turned four.*

**6** ▶COLOR◀ [linking verb] **a)** to become a different color: *His hair is turning gray.* | *Helen turned bright red.* (=because she was embarrassed)

**7** ▶CHANGE◀ [linking verb] to become different from before: *The weather will turn colder.* | *The crowd turned violent when the soccer team lost.*

**8** ▶PAGE◀ [T] to move a page in a book or magazine so that you can see the next one

**9 turn your back (on)** to refuse to help or be involved with someone or something: *She wouldn't turn her back on her friends.*

**10 turn your nose up at** to refuse to accept something because you do not think it is good enough for you: *He won't turn his nose up at a $3000 pay raise.*

**11 turn over a new leaf** to decide that you will change your behavior to make it better: *I'm going to turn over a new leaf and start exercising.*

**12 turn a deaf ear/turn a blind eye** to ignore what someone is saying or doing: *The State has turned a deaf ear to the public's health needs.*

**13 turn the tables (on sb)** to become stronger or better than an opponent who has been stronger or better than you: *The team managed to turn the tables in the second half of the game.*

**14 turn sb/sth loose** to allow a person or animal to be free to do what she, he, or it wants

**15 turn a profit** to make a profit

**turn sb against** sb/sth *phr v* [T] to make someone stop liking or agreeing with someone or something: *His experiences in Vietnam turned him against the war.*

**turn sth ↔ around** *phr v* [T] **1** to complete the process of making a product or providing a service: *We can turn around 500 units by next week.* **2** to make a plan, business etc. that was not working well begin to work: *It's taken four years, but we've turned the business around.*

**turn away** *phr v* **1** [T turn sb ↔ away] to refuse to let people into a theater, restaurant etc. because it is too full: *By 6:00, we were turning people away.* **2** [I,T turn sb ↔ away] to refuse to give sympathy, help, or support: *We never turn patients away, even if they don't have money.* | *The US cannot just turn away from the world's problems.*

**turn back** *phr v* [I,T turn sb ↔ back] **1** to go in the opposite direction, or to tell someone to do this: *Travelers had to turn back because of the snow.* | *The journalists were turned back at the border.* **2 turn back the clock** to try do things the way they were done in the past

**turn down** *phr v* [T] **1** [turn sth ↔ down] to make a machine such as a television, OVEN etc. produce less sound, heat etc.: *Can you turn your radio down a little bit?* **2** [turn sb/sth ↔ down] to refuse an offer, request, or invitation:

*If he asks me, I'll* **turn** *him* **down.** | *Diane* **turned down** *the job offer.* —see usage note at REFUSE[1]

**turn in** *phr v* **1** [T **turn** sth ↔ **in**] to give something you find to someone in authority so that it can be returned to the owner: *Luckily someone had* **turned** *my purse* **in.** **2** [T **turn** sth ↔ **in**] to give work that you have done to the teacher to be given a grade: *Has everyone* **turned in** *last night's homework?* **3** [T **turn** sb ↔ **in**] to tell the police where a criminal is **4** [I] INFORMAL to go to bed. *I think I'll* **turn in.**

**turn into** sth *phr v* [T] | also **turn** sth **into** sth] to become something different, or to make someone or something do this: *The argument* **turned into** *a fight.* | *The witch* **turned** *the frog* **into** *a prince.*

**turn off** *phr v* **1** [T **turn** sth ↔ **off**] to stop a supply of water, electricity etc., especially so that a machine stops working: *Turn off the television - it's dinner time.* | *Who* **turned** *the water* **off?** —see usage note at OPEN[2] **2** [I,T **turn off** sth] to drive off one road and onto another, often a smaller one: *Make sure you* **turn off** *at the next exit.* | *We* **turned off** *the highway looking for a place to eat.* **3** [T **turn** sb **off**] to make someone decide that s/he does not like someone or something, often in a sexual way: *I was* **turned off** *by the doctor's attitude - he just didn't care.* | *She says skinny men* **turn** *her* **off.** —see also TURN-OFF

**turn on** *phr v* [T] **1** [**turn** sth ↔ **on**] to make the supply of water, electricity etc. begin to flow through a pipe, machine etc., so that it starts working: *Could you* **turn on** *the dishwasher/ TV?* | *Has the gas company* **turned on** *the gas yet?* —see usage note at OPEN[2] **2** [**turn on** sb] to suddenly attack someone physically or using unpleasant words, after being nice to him/her: *The dog* **turned on** *him and bit him.* **3** [**turn** sb **on**] to make someone sexually excited

**turn out** *phr v* **1** [linking verb] to happen in a particular way, or to have a particular result: *Are you happy with the way your essay* **turned out?** | *It* **turned out that** *he was married to someone else!* **2** [T **turn** sth ↔ **out**] if you turn out a light, you push a button to stop the flow of electricity: *Don't forget to* **turn out** *the lights when you leave.* **3** [I] if people turn out for an event, they come to it: *Only about 30 people* **turned out for** *the show.* —see also TURN-OUT **4** [T **turn** sth ↔ **out**] to produce or make something: *Why do our high schools* **turn out** *students who can't read?* **5** [T **turn** sb **out**] to make someone leave his/her home

**turn over** *phr v* [T] **1** [**turn** sth ↔ **over to** sb] to give someone the right to own something such as a plan, business, piece of property, or to make him/her responsible for it: *The industry is being* **turned over** *to private ownership.* **2** [**turn** sth ↔ **over**] to bring a criminal to the police or another official organization: *Benson was* **turned over** *to the FBI yesterday.* **3** [**turn over** sth] if a business turns over a particular amount of money, it makes that amount during a period of time: *We* **turned over** *$5000 in our third month.* ⇨ TURNOVER

**turn to** *phr v* [T] **1** [**turn to** sb/sth] to try to get help from someone or by doing something: *He still* **turns to** *us for advice.* | *Some kids* **turn to** *selling drugs to get money.* **2** [**turn to** sth] to go to a particular page in a book, magazine etc.: *Turn to page 45 in your math book.* **3** [**turn to** sth] to begin thinking about or doing something new: *Bateman* **turned to** *politics after law school.*

**turn up** *phr v* **1** [T **turn** sth ↔ **up**] to make a machine such as a radio, OVEN etc. produce more sound, heat etc.: *Turn up the radio - I love this song.* **2** [I] to be found after being searched for: *We looked for the ring for weeks, and then it* **turned up** *in my pocket.* **3** to arrive: *Danny* **turned up** *late as usual.* **4** [I] to happen, especially when you are not expecting it: *Don't worry, a job will* **turn up** *soon.* **5** [T **turn** sth ↔ **up**] to find something by searching for it thoroughly: *The police searched the house, but they didn't* **turn up** *anything.*

**turn[2]** *n*

**1** ▸**CHANCE TO DO STH**◂ the time when it is your chance, duty, or right to do something that a group of people are doing, one after another: *It's your* **turn** *to do the dishes tonight.* | *When do I get a turn?*

**2 take turns** if a group of people take turns doing something, each of them has a chance or a duty to do it: *Why don't you take turns using the computer?* | *We agreed to take turns driving*

**3 in turn** one after another: *He spoke to each of the students* **in turn.**

**4** ▸**CHANGE DIRECTION**◂ a change in the direction you are moving in: *Make a left/right* **turn** *at the stop sign.*

**5** ▸**MOVE STH**◂ the act of turning something: *Give the wheel another turn.*

**6** ▸**TWO ROADS JOIN**◂ a place where a road joins another road: *I think we missed our turn; we were supposed to go left on Holly St.*

**7 the turn of the century** the beginning of a century

**8 take a turn for the better/worse** to suddenly become better or worse: *Her health took a turn for the worse.*

**9 turn of events** an unexpected change in a situation: *By some unfortunate* **turn of events,** *the documents were lost.*

**10 do sb a good turn** to help someone

**turn·a·round** /'tənəˌraʊnd/ *n* an important and completely different change: *The win was a turnaround for the team.*

**turn·coat** /'tənkoʊt/ *n* someone who stops supporting a political party or group and joins the opposite group

**turning point** /'.. ˌ./ *n* the time when an

important change starts to happen: *Winning the race was a turning point in his athletic career.*

**tur·nip** /ˈtənɪp/ *n* [C,U] a large round pale yellow or white root, cooked and eaten as a vegetable

**turn-off** /ˈ. ./ *n* **1** a place where you can leave a main road to get onto another one.: *I think the turn-off was back there a few blocks.* **2** something that someone does that makes you dislike him/her, usually in a sexual way

**turn·out** /ˈtənaʊt/ *n* [singular] the number of people who go to an event such as a party, meeting, or election: *The voter turnout was 93%.*

**turn·o·ver** /ˈtənˌoʊvə/ *n* **1** [singular] the amount of money a business earns in a particular period: *an annual turnover of $35 million* **2** [U] the rate at which people leave an organization and are replaced by others: *The company has a high rate of turnover.* **3** a small fruit PIE: *apple turnovers*

**turn·pike** /ˈtənpaɪk/ *n* a main road that you have to pay a TOLL to use

**turn sig·nal** /ˈ. ˌ../ *n* one of the lights on a vehicle that is lit in order to show which direction the driver is turning, or the stick that you push up or down to turn on this light —see picture on page 469

**turn·stile** /ˈtənstaɪl/ *n* a gate that only lets one person through at a time

**turn·ta·ble** /ˈtənˌteɪbəl/ *n* a piece of equipment used for playing RECORDs

**tur·pen·tine** /ˈtəpənˌtaɪn/ *n* [U] a strong-smelling oil used for removing paint

**tur·quoise** /ˈtəkwɔɪz, -kɔɪz/ *n* [U] a bright blue-green color —**turquoise** *adj*

**tur·ret** /ˈtəɪt, ˈtʌrɪt/ *n* a small tower on a large building, especially a CASTLE

**tur·tle** /ˈtətl/ *n* a REPTILE (=type of animal) that has four legs and a hard shell and lives mainly in water

**tur·tle·neck** /ˈtətlˌnɛk/ *n* a type of shirt or SWEATER with a close-fitting collar that covers most of your neck

**tush** /tʊʃ/ *n* INFORMAL the part of your body that you sit on

**tusk** /tʌsk/ *n* one of the two very long teeth that stick out of an animal's mouth, for example an ELEPHANT's

**tus·sle** /ˈtʌsəl/ *n* a struggle or fight —**tussle** *v* [I]

**tu·tor** /ˈtutə/ *n* someone who is paid to teach only one or a few students, especially students who are having difficulty with a subject: *my French tutor* —**tutor** *v* [T]

**tu·to·ri·al** /tuˈtɔriəl/ *adj* relating to a TUTOR or the teaching that s/he does

**tux·e·do** /tʌkˈsidoʊ/, **tux** /tʌks/ *n* a man's suit, usually black, that is worn at formal occasions

**TV** *n* [C,U] ⇨ TELEVISION: *What's on TV?* | *Sue just bought a new TV.*

**TV din·ner** /ˌ. . ˈ../ *n* a frozen prepared meal you can buy from the store, that you heat up and eat at home

**twang** /twæŋ/ *n* **1** the quality of your voice when your speaking sounds come from your nose as well as your mouth **2** a short RINGing sound like the one made by quickly pulling a tight string —**twang** *v* [I,T]

**twas** /twʌz/ LITERARY a word meaning "it was," used in past times

**tweak** /twik/ *v* [T] **1** to quickly pull or twist something: *Grandpa tweaked my nose and laughed.* **2** to make small changes to something in order to improve it

**tweed** /twid/ *n* [U] a rough wool cloth used especially for making JACKETs

**tweet** /twit/ *v* [I] to make a quick high sound like a small bird —**tweet** *n*

**tweez·ers** /ˈtwizəz/ *n* [plural] a small tool made from two thin pieces of metal joined at one end, used for example for pulling out single hairs: *a pair of tweezers*

**twelfth** /twɛlfθ/ *number* **1** 12th **2** $\frac{1}{12}$

**twelve** /twɛlv/ *number* **1** 12 **2** twelve o'clock: *I'm going to lunch at twelve.*

**twen·ty¹** /ˈtwɛnti/ *number* **1** 20 **2 the twenties** a) the years between 1920 and 1929 b) the numbers between 20 and 29, especially when used for measuring temperature —**twentieth** /ˈtwɛntiθ/ *number*

**twenty²** *n* a piece of paper money worth $20

**twenty-one** /ˌ.. ˈ.ˌ/ *n* ⇨ BLACKJACK

**twerp** /twəp/ *n* SPOKEN a stupid or annoying person

**twice** /twaɪs/ *adv* two times: *I've seen that movie twice already.*

**twid·dle** /ˈtwɪdl/ *v* [T] to move your fingers around, or to turn something with them many times, usually because you are bored

**twig** /twɪg/ *n* a very thin branch that grows on a larger branch of a tree

**twi·light** /ˈtwaɪlaɪt/ *n* [U] the time between day and night when the sky starts to become dark, or the pale light at this time

**twin¹** /twɪn/ *n* one of two children who are born at the same time to the same mother: *Jenny and Julie are **identical twins**.* (=twins who look exactly the same) | *I have a twin brother.*

**twin²** *adj* like something else and considered with it as a pair: *twin towers* | *twin cities*

**twin bed** /ˌ. ˈ./ *n* a bed for one person

**twine¹** /twaɪn/ *n* [U] thick strong string

**twine²** *v* [I,T] to twist something, or to twist around something: *The plant had **twined around** the fence.*

**twinge** /twɪndʒ/ *n* a sudden pain, or a sudden feeling of a bad emotion: *a twinge of guilt*

**twin·kle** /'twɪŋkəl/ v **1** if a star or light twinkles, it continues to change from being bright to dark **2** if someone's eyes twinkle, s/he has a happy expression **–twinkle** n

**twin-size** /ˌ. '.◄/ adj relating to a TWIN BED: twin-size sheets

**twirl** /twɚl/ v [I,T] to continue turning around quickly, or to make something do this: dancers leaping and twirling on stage **–twirl** n

**twist**[1] /twɪst/ v **1** [I,T] to continue to turn something, such as hair, wire, or cloth, several times with your hands: Her hair was twisted into a bun. | Wash the green beans and **twist off** the stems. (=remove them by twisting) **2** [I,T] to turn around or bend part of your body into another position: She screamed, twisting in agony. | I **twisted my ankle** playing soccer. (=hurt it by turning in the wrong direction) **3** [T] to change the true or intended meaning of someone's statement: They twisted the story around and said we tried to cheat them. **4** [I] if a road, river etc. twists, it has a lot of curves in it **5 twist sb's arm** INFORMAL to persuade someone to do something that s/he does not want to do: I think she'll do it if we twist her arm a little.

**twist**[2] n **1** a shape made by twisting something, such as paper, rope, or hair: pasta twists **2** an unexpected change in a story or situation: Her disappearance added a new twist to the story. **3** a bend in a road, river etc.

**twist·ed** /'twɪstɪd/ adj strange and slightly cruel: a twisted joke

**twist·er** /'twɪstɚ/ n INFORMAL ⇨ TORNADO

**twit** /twɪt/ n SPOKEN a stupid or silly person

**twitch** /twɪtʃ/ v [I] if a part of your body twitches, it makes a sudden small uncontrolled movement: The cat's tail twitched irritably. **–twitch** n

**twit·ter** /'twɪtɚ/ v [I] if a bird twitters, it makes a lot of short high sounds **–twitter** n [singular]

**two** /tu/ number **1** 2 **2** two o'clock: The game begins **at two**. **–compare** SECOND[2]

**two-bit** /'. ./ adj SLANG not very good or important: a two-bit actor

**two-by-four** /'. . ./ n a long piece of wood that is two inches thick and four inches wide

**two-di·men·sion·al** /ˌ. .'...◄/ adj flat: a two-dimensional drawing

**two-faced** /ˌ. '.◄/ adj INFORMAL saying different things about something to different people, in a way that is not honest or sincere

**two-piece** /ˌ. '.◄/ adj a two-piece suit has a coat and pants that match

**two·some** /'tusəm/ n a group of two people

**two-time** /'. ./ v [T] INFORMAL to deceive your usual partner by having a secret sexual relationship with someone else

**two-tone** /ˌ. '.◄/ adj having two different colors: two-tone shoes

**two-way** /ˌ. '.◄/ adj **1** moving or allowing movement in both directions: two-way traffic **2** a two-way radio sends and receives messages

**TX** the written abbreviation of Texas

**ty·coon** /taɪ'kun/ n someone who is very successful in business and has a lot of money: an oil tycoon

**ty·ing** /'taɪ-ɪŋ/ v the PRESENT PARTICIPLE of TIE

**tyke** /taɪk/ n INFORMAL a small child

**type**[1] /taɪp/ n **1** a particular kind of person or thing, or a group of people or things that have similar features or qualities: What type of desserts do you have? | The least expensive model **of this type** sells for $400. **2** someone with particular qualities, interests, appearance etc.: the athletic type **3 not be sb's type** INFORMAL to not be the kind of person that someone is attracted to: Alex is OK - but he's not really my type. **4** [U] printed letters: italic type

**type**[2] v [I,T] to write something using a computer or TYPEWRITER

**type·cast** /'taɪpkæst/ v typecast, typecast, typecasting [T] to always give an actor the same type of character to play: He does not want to **be typecast as** a bad guy.

**type·face** /'taɪpfeɪs/ n a group of letters, numbers etc. of the same style and size, used in printing

**type·writ·er** /'taɪpˌraɪtɚ/ n a machine that prints letters, numbers etc. onto paper **–compare** PRINTER

**type·writ·ten** /'taɪpˌrɪtˀn/ adj written using a TYPEWRITER: a typewritten manuscript

**ty·phoid** /'taɪfɔɪd/, **typhoid fe·ver** /ˌ.. '../ n [U] a serious infectious disease that is caused by BACTERIA in food or water

**ty·phoon** /taɪ'fun/ n a very strong tropical storm

**ty·phus** /'taɪfəs/ n [U] a serious infectious disease that is caused by the bite of an insect

**typ·i·cal** /'tɪpɪkəl/ adj **1** having the usual features or qualities of a particular thing, person, or group: He looked like the typical tourist. | Cool weather is **typical of** early April. **2 typical!** SPOKEN said when you are annoyed that something bad has happened again: The car won't start - typical!

**typ·i·cal·ly** /'tɪpɪkli/ adv **1** in the way that something usually happens: Gasoline prices typically rise in the summer. **2** in the way that a person or group usually behaves: Nothing is more typically American than hamburgers.

**typ·i·fy** /'tɪpəˌfaɪ/ v [T] to be a typical example or feature of something: a dark painting that typifies her work

**typ·ing** /'taɪpɪŋ/ n [U] the activity of writing using a TYPEWRITER

**typ·ist** /'taɪpɪst/ n someone who uses a TYPEWRITER

**ty·po** /'taɪpoʊ/ n INFORMAL a mistake that you make when you write using a computer or TYPE-WRITER

**ty·ran·ni·cal** /tɪ'rænɪkəl/ adj behaving in an unfair or cruel way toward someone you have power over: *a brutal and tyrannical government* –**tyrannize** /'tɪrə‚naɪz/ v [T]

**tyr·an·ny** /'tɪrəni/ n **1** [U] strict, unfair, and often cruel control over someone: *the tyranny of poverty* **2** [C,U] government by a cruel ruler who has complete power

**ty·rant** /'taɪrənt/ n someone, especially a ruler, who uses his/her power in an unfair or cruel way: *Ginny sees her father as a harsh and selfish tyrant.*

**tzar** /zɑr, tsɑr/ n ⇨ CZAR

# U

**U, u** /yu/ the twenty-first letter of the English alphabet

**u·biq·ui·tous** /yu'bɪkwətəs/ adj FORMAL seeming to be everywhere: *New York's ubiquitous yellow cabs* –**ubiquity** n [U]

**ud·der** /'ʌdɚ/ n the part of a cow, goat etc. that produces milk

**UFO** n Unidentified Flying Object; a mysterious object in the sky, sometimes thought to be a space vehicle from another world

**ugh** /ʌg, ʌk, ʌh/ interjection used in order to show strong dislike: *Ugh! That tastes terrible!*

**ug·ly** /'ʌgli/ adj **1** very unattractive or unpleasant to look at: *an ugly face* **2** very unpleasant or violent in a way that makes you feel frightened: *an ugly scene at the bus stop* –**ugliness** n [U]

**uh** /ʌ/ interjection said when you are deciding what to say next: *I, uh, I'm sorry I'm late.*

**UHF** n [U] ultra-high frequency; a range of radio WAVES that produces very good sound quality

**uh huh** /n'hn, m'hm, ə'hʌ/ interjection INFORMAL used in order to say yes or to show that you understand something: *"Is this the one you want?" "Uh huh."*

**uh oh** /'ˉʌ ˉoʊ/ interjection INFORMAL said when you have made a mistake or have realized that something bad has happened: *Uh oh, I think I forgot my keys.*

**uh uh** /'ˉʌn ˉʌn, 'ˉm ˉm/ interjection INFORMAL used in order to say no: *"Did you go to Billy's game?" "Uh uh, I forgot."*

**ul·cer** /'ʌlsɚ/ n a sore area on your skin or inside your body, that may bleed: *a stomach ulcer*

**ul·te·ri·or** /ʌl'tɪriɚ/ adj **ulterior motive/reason** a reason for doing something that you hide in order to get an advantage for yourself: *Do you think she has an ulterior motive for helping us?*

**ul·ti·mate**[1] /'ʌltəmɪt/ adj **1** better, bigger, worse etc. than others of the same kind: *A Rolls Royce is the ultimate symbol of wealth.* | *the ultimate disgrace* **2** the ultimate purpose, aim, reason etc. is the final and most important one

**ultimate**[2] n **the ultimate in sth** the best example or highest level of something: *The Orient Express is the ultimate in rail travel.*

**ul·ti·mate·ly** /'ʌltəmɪtli/ adv in the end; FINALLY: *Ultimately it's your decision.*

**ul·ti·ma·tum** /‚ʌltə'meɪtəm/ n a statement saying that if someone does not do what you want, s/he will be punished: *The government issued an ultimatum* (=gave an ultimatum) *to the rebels to surrender.*

**ul·tra·son·ic** /‚ʌltrə'sɑnɪk◂/ adj TECHNICAL ultrasonic sounds are too high for humans to hear

**ul·tra·sound** /'ʌltrə‚saʊnd/ n [C,U] a medical process that uses sound waves to produce images of the inside of your body

**ul·tra·vi·o·let** /‚ʌltrə'vaɪəlɪt◂/ adj ultraviolet light is beyond the purple range of colors that humans can see –compare INFRARED

**um** /m/ interjection said when you are deciding what to say next: *I can't - um, maybe I won't be able to come.*

**um·bil·i·cal cord** /ʌm'bɪlɪkəl ‚kɔrd/ n a tube of flesh that joins an unborn baby to its mother

**um·brage** /'ʌmbrɪdʒ/ n **take umbrage (at sth)** FORMAL to be offended by something that someone has done or said: *Leiden took umbrage at O'Brian's comments.*

**um·brel·la** /ʌm'brɛlə/ n
**1** a thing that you hold above your head to protect you from the rain
**2 umbrella organization/group/agency** an organization that includes several smaller groups

umbrella

**ump** /ʌmp/ n INFORMAL ⇨ UMPIRE[1]

**um·pire**[1] /'ʌmpaɪɚ/ n someone who makes sure that the rules are followed during a game in sports such as baseball and tennis –see usage note at REFEREE –see picture on page 472

**umpire**[2] v [I,T] to be the UMPIRE for a game

**ump·teenth** /'ʌmptinθ, ‚ʌm'tinθ/ quantifier INFORMAL a word used when you do not know a specific number, but want to say that the number is unreasonably large: *They're showing "The Wizard of Oz" for the umpteenth time.* –**umpteen** quantifier

**UN** n [U] the United Nations; an international organization that tries to find peaceful solutions to world problems

**un·a·bashed** /‚ʌnə'bæʃt◂/ adj not shy or

embarrassed about something: *unabashed curiosity*

**un·a·bat·ed** /ˌʌnə'beɪtɪd/ *adj* continuing without becoming weaker or less forceful: *The storm continued unabated.*

**un·a·ble** /ʌn'eɪbəl/ *adj* not able to do something: *He delivers food to people who are unable to leave their homes.* −compare INABILITY

**un·a·bridged** /ˌʌnə'brɪdʒd◂/ *adj* a book that is unabridged is complete

**un·ac·cept·a·ble** /ˌʌnək'sɛptəbəl/ *adj* something that is unacceptable is so wrong or bad that it should not be allowed to continue: *Nancy's behavior is unacceptable.* −**unacceptably** *adv*

**un·ac·count·a·ble** /ˌʌnə'kaʊntəbəl/ *adj* **1** not having to explain your actions or decisions to anyone else **2** very surprising and difficult to explain: *a product that flopped for unaccountable reasons* −**unaccountably** *adv*

**un·a·dul·ter·at·ed** /ˌʌnə'dʌltə,reɪtɪd/ *adj* complete or pure, without having any other feelings, substances etc. mixed in: *unadulterated fun/evil*

**un·af·fect·ed** /ˌʌnə'fɛktɪd/ *adj* not changed or influenced by something: *Parts of the city remained unaffected by the fire.*

**un·aid·ed** /ʌn'eɪdɪd/ *adj* without help

**un·A·mer·i·can** /ˌʌn ə'mɛrɪkən◂/ *adj* not supporting or loyal to American customs, ideas etc.

**u·nan·i·mous** /yu'nænəməs/ *adj* a unanimous decision, vote etc. is one on which everyone agrees −**unanimously** *adv* −**unanimity** /ˌyunæ'nɪməti/ *n* [U]

**un·an·nounced** /ˌʌnə'naʊnst◂/ *adj* happening without anyone knowing about or expecting it: *Several people arrived unannounced.*

**un·an·swered** /ʌn'ænsəd◂/ *adj* an unanswered telephone, letter, question etc. has not been answered

**un·armed** /ˌʌn'ɑrmd◂/ *adj* not carrying any weapons: *An officer shot an unarmed man.*

**un·as·sum·ing** /ˌʌnə'sumɪŋ◂/ *adj* quiet and showing no desire for attention, or not attracting attention; MODEST: *an unassuming friendly Italian restaurant*

**un·at·tached** /ˌʌnə'tætʃt◂/ *adj* **1** not involved in a romantic relationship **2** not connected to anything

**un·at·tend·ed** /ˌʌnə'tɛndɪd◂/ *adj* left alone without being watched: *Small children should never be left unattended.*

**un·at·trac·tive** /ˌʌnə'træktɪv◂/ *adj* **1** not physically attractive or beautiful **2** not good or desirable: *High taxes make it an unattractive state in which to start a business.*

**un·au·thor·ized** /ʌn'ɔθə,raɪzd/ *adj* without official approval or permission: *an unauthorized biography of Marlon Brando*

**un·a·vail·a·ble** /ˌʌnə'veɪləbəl/ *adj* **1** not able or willing to meet with someone: *Mr. Foster is unavailable for comment.* **2** not able to be obtained: *an album previously unavailable on CD*

**un·a·void·a·ble** /ˌʌnə'vɔɪdəbəl/ *adj* if something is unavoidable, nothing can be done to prevent it: *an unavoidable delay*

**un·a·ware** /ˌʌnə'wɛr/ *adj* not noticing or knowing about something: *He was unaware of his legal rights.*

**un·a·wares** /ˌʌnə'wɛrz/ *adv* **catch/take sb unawares** to happen or do something to someone when s/he is not expecting it: *The events in the Middle East caught the CIA unawares.*

**un·bal·anced** /ˌʌn'bælənst◂/ *adj* **1** slightly crazy: *mentally unbalanced* **2** not balanced

**un·bear·a·ble** /ʌn'bɛrəbəl/ *adj* too painful, unpleasant etc. for you to be able to deal with; INTOLERABLE: *Her pain had become unbearable.* −**unbearably** *adv*

**un·beat·a·ble** /ʌn'biʈəbəl/ *adj* someone or something that is unbeatable will always be better than any other person or thing: *We guarantee our prices are unbeatable!*

**un·be·liev·a·ble** /ˌʌnbɪ'livəbəl/ *adj* extremely surprising: *The tapes are tiny, but the sound quality is unbelievable.* −**unbelievably** *adv*

**un·born** /ˌʌn'bɔrn◂/ *adj* not yet born: *an unborn child*

**un·bound·ed** /ˌʌn'baʊndɪd◂/ *adj* FORMAL very great and seeming to have no limit: *unbounded optimism*

**un·bri·dled** /ˌʌn'braɪdld◂/ *adj* not controlled: *unbridled anger*

**un·called-for** /ʌn'kɔld ˌfɔr/ *adj* behavior or remarks that are uncalled-for are unsuitable or rude

**un·can·ny** /ʌn'kæni/ *adj* very strange and difficult to explain: *He bears an uncanny resemblance to John Lennon.* −**uncannily** *adv*

**un·cer·tain** /ʌn'sət̩n/ *adj* **1** not sure or having doubts about something: *I'm uncertain about what to say to her.* **2** not known or not definite: *His future with the company is uncertain.* −**uncertainty** *n* [C,U] −**uncertainly** *adv*

**un·chart·ed** /ˌʌn'tʃɑrtɪd◂/ *adj* **uncharted territory/waters** a situation or activity that you have never experienced or tried before

**un·checked** /ˌʌn'tʃɛkt◂/ *adj* allowed to get worse because it is not controlled or stopped: *Left unchecked, the disease will spread.*

**un·cle** /'ʌŋkəl/ *n* the brother of your mother or father, or the husband of your AUNT −see picture at FAMILY

**un·clean** /ˌʌn'klin◂/ *adj* **1** dirty **2** not pure in a moral or religious way

**un·clear** /ˌʌn'klɪr◂/ *adj* difficult to understand

or be sure about: *It is unclear whether the law covers this case.*

**Uncle Sam** /ˌʌŋkəl ˈsæm/ *n* [singular] INFORMAL the US, or US government, represented by the figure of a tall man with a white BEARD and tall hat

**Uncle Tom** /ˌʌŋkəl ˈtɑm/ *n* DISAPPROVING a name for a Black person who is too friendly or respectful to white people

**un·com·fort·a·ble** /ʌnˈkʌmftəbəl, ʌnˈkʌm-fətəbəl/ *adj* **1** not feeling physically relaxed and satisfied, or not making someone feel this way: *The heat was making Irene uncomfortable.* | *an uncomfortable chair* **2** unable to relax because you are embarrassed or worried: *I feel uncomfortable talking about sex education.* —**uncomfortably** *adv*

**un·com·mon** /ʌnˈkɑmən/ *adj* rare or unusual: *It is not uncommon for children as young as ten to work in many countries.* (=it is fairly common) —**uncommonly** *adv*

**un·com·pro·mis·ing** /ʌnˈkɑmprəˌmaɪzɪŋ/ *adj* determined not to change your opinions or intentions: *Grigson took an uncompromising position on gun control.*

**un·con·cerned** /ˌʌnkənˈsɚnd/ *adj* not anxious or worried about something: *Americans cannot be unconcerned about the problem of the world's poor.*

**un·con·di·tion·al** /ˌʌnkənˈdɪʃənəl/ *adj* not limited by or depending on any agreements or conditions: *We are demanding the unconditional release of the hostages.* —**unconditionally** *adv*

**un·con·firmed** /ˌʌnkənˈfɚmd/ *adj* not proved or supported by official information: *an unconfirmed report/rumor of a nuclear accident*

**un·con·scion·a·ble** /ʌnˈkɑnʃənəbəl/ *adj* FORMAL morally wrong or unacceptable

**un·con·scious¹** /ˌʌnˈkɑnʃəs/ *adj* unable to see, move, feel etc. because you are not conscious: *The passenger was all right, but the driver was knocked unconscious.* —**unconsciously** *adv* —**unconsciousness** *n* [U]

**unconscious²** *n* **the/sb's unconscious** the part of your mind in which there are thoughts and feelings that you do not realize that you have

**un·con·sti·tu·tion·al** /ˌʌnkɑnstəˈtuʃənəl/ *adj* not allowed by the rules that govern a country or organization

**un·con·trol·la·ble** /ˌʌnkənˈtroʊləbəl/ *adj* something that is uncontrollable cannot be controlled or stopped: *uncontrollable rage/laughter*

**un·con·trolled** /ˌʌnkənˈtroʊld/ *adj* **1** not controlled or stopped: *the damage done by uncontrolled logging* **2** without rules or laws: *a uncontrolled free market*

**un·con·ven·tion·al** /ˌʌnkənˈvɛnʃənəl/ *adj* very different from the way people usually behave, think, dress, or do things

**un·count·a·ble** /ˌʌnˈkaʊntəbəl/ *adj* **uncountable noun** TECHNICAL in grammar, a noun that has no plural form, such as "water," "gold," or "furniture" —opposite COUNTABLE —see study note on page 466

**un·couth** /ʌnˈkuθ/ *adj* behaving or speaking in a way that is rude and unacceptable

**un·cov·er** /ʌnˈkʌvɚ/ *v* [T] **1** to discover something that had been kept secret or hidden: *A search of their baggage uncovered two pistols.* **2** to remove the cover from something

**un·cut** /ˌʌnˈkʌt/ *adj* **1** a movie, book etc. that is uncut has not had violent or sexual scenes removed from it **2** an uncut jewel has not yet been cut into a particular shape

**un·daunt·ed** /ˌʌnˈdɔntɪd, -ˈdɑn-/ *adj* not afraid to continue doing something in spite of difficulties or danger; DETERMINED: *Nelson was undaunted by the opposition to his plan.*

**un·de·cid·ed** /ˌʌndɪˈsaɪdɪd/ *adj* not having made a decision about something: *A majority of voters were undecided about which candidate to choose.*

**un·de·ni·a·ble** /ˌʌndɪˈnaɪəbəl/ *adj* definitely true or certain: *an undeniable fact* —**undeniably** *adv*

**un·der¹** /ˈʌndɚ/ *prep* **1** below something or covered by it: *He's hiding under the blanket.* | *a dog sleeping under the bed* **2** less than a particular age, number, amount, or price: *I can't buy beer - I'm under age.* (=not old enough) | *a ticket for under $10* **3** controlled or governed by a particular leader, government, system etc.: *a country under Marxist rule* **4** **be under discussion/construction/attack etc.** to be in the process of being discussed, built etc.: *The new city library is still under construction.* **5** **under way** happening or in the process of being done: *Construction is already under way on the new library.* **6** affected by a particular influence, condition, or situation: *She performs well under pressure.* **7** if you are under someone at your job, you have a lower position of authority than s/he does **8** **be under the impression** to believe that something is true, especially something that is later proved to be untrue: *I was under the impression that she really liked me.* **9** according to a particular law, agreement etc.: *Under section seven of the tax code, we are entitled to inspect your accounts.* **10** in a particular part of a list, book, system etc. where you can find information: *You'll find that topic under "Heart Disease" in the index.* —see also UNDERCOVER —compare BENEATH¹, OVER¹

**under²** *adv* **1** in or to a place that is below or covered by something: *He pushed Lonnie's head under the water.* **2** less than the age, number, or amount that is mentioned: *Children aged nine and under must be with a parent.*

**un·der·age** /ˌʌndɚˈeɪdʒ/ *adj* too young to

U

legally buy alcohol, drive a car etc.: *a campaign to stop underage drinking*

**un·der·class** /'ʌndɚ,klæs/ n [singular] the lowest social class, consisting of people who are very poor

**un·der·cov·er** /,ʌndɚ'kʌvɚ / adj acting or done secretly in order to catch criminals or find out information: *an undercover agent/cop*

**un·der·cur·rent** /'ʌndɚ,kɚənt, -,kʌr-/ n a feeling that someone does not express openly: *There was an undercurrent of suspicion about the newcomers.*

**un·der·cut** /,ʌndɚ'kʌt, 'ʌndɚ,kʌt/ v [T] **1** to make someone's work, plans etc. not be successful or effective: *Such activity could undercut public confidence in Congress.* **2** to sell something more cheaply than someone else: *Street vendors can undercut stores by up to 50%.*

**un·der·dog** /'ʌndɚ,dɔg/ n **the underdog** person or team in a competition that is not expected to win

**un·der·es·ti·mate** /,ʌndɚ'ɛstə,meɪt/ v **1** [I,T] to think that something is smaller, less expensive, or less important than it really is: *They underestimated the cost of the construction.* **2** [T] to think that someone is less skillful, intelligent etc. than s/he really is: *Don't underestimate Ronnie - he's very good at his job.* –opposite OVERESTIMATE

**un·der·go** /,ʌndɚ'goʊ/ v [T] if you undergo something unpleasant or hard to deal with, it happens to you or is done to you: *He'll have to undergo major heart surgery.*

**un·der·grad·u·ate** /,ʌndɚ'grædʒuɪt/ n a student in the first four years of college –**undergraduate** adj –compare GRADUATE[1], POST-GRADUATE[1]

**un·der·ground** /'ʌndɚ,graʊnd/ adj, adv **1** under the earth's surface: *an underground tunnel* | *creatures that live underground* **2** secret, becoming secret, or done secretly: *an underground rebellion* | *The Ukrainian church went underground during the Communist era.*

**un·der·growth** /'ʌndɚ,groʊθ/ n [U] bushes, small trees etc. that grow around and under bigger trees

**un·der·hand·ed** /,ʌndɚ'hændɪd/ adj dishonest and done secretly: *an underhanded deal*

**un·der·line** /'ʌndɚ,laɪn, ,ʌndɚ'laɪn/ v [T] **1** to draw a line under a word **2** to show that something is important: *The rise in crime underlines the need for more jobs.*

**un·der·ly·ing** /,ʌndɚ'laɪ-ɪŋ/ adj **underlying reason/cause/problem etc.** the reason, cause etc. that is most important but that is not easy to discover

**un·der·mine** /,ʌndɚ,maɪn, ,ʌndɚ'maɪn/ v [T] to gradually make someone or something less strong or effective: *He's trying to undermine Clinton's support in the South.*

**un·der·neath** /,ʌndɚ'niθ/ prep, adv directly below or under something: *We turned some rocks over to see what was underneath.* | *There's nice wood underneath all that paint.* –compare BENEATH[1]

**un·der·nour·ished** /,ʌndɚ'nɔɪʃt, -'nʌrɪʃt/ adj not healthy because you have not eaten enough food

**un·der·paid** /,ʌndɚ'peɪd / adj earning less money than you deserve –**underpay** /,ʌndɚ'peɪ/ v [I,T]

**un·der·pants** /'ʌndɚ,pænts/ n [plural] a short piece of underwear worn on the lower part of the body

**un·der·pass** /'ʌndɚ,pæs/ n a road or path that goes under another road or path

**un·der·priv·i·leged** /,ʌndɚ'prɪvlɪdʒd / adj very poor and not having the advantages of most other people in society: *clothing for underprivileged children*

**un·der·rat·ed** /,ʌndɚ'reɪtɪd / adj if someone or something is underrated, people do not think he, she, or it is as good, effective etc. as he, she or it really is: *He is underrated as an actor.* –**underrate** v [T] –opposite OVERRATED

**un·der·score** /'ʌndɚ,skɔr/ v [T] to emphasize something so people pay attention to it: *The survey underscores the division between rich and poor in America.*

**un·der·shirt** /'ʌndɚ,ʃɚt/ n a piece of underwear worn under a shirt

**un·der·side** /'ʌndɚ,saɪd/ n **the underside of sth** the bottom side or surface of something: *white spots on the underside of the leaves*

**un·der·sized** /,ʌndɚ'saɪzd / adj too small, or smaller than usual

**un·der·staffed** /,ʌndɚ'stæft / adj not having enough workers, or having fewer workers than usual

**un·der·stand** /,ʌndɚ'stænd/ v **understood**, **understood**, **understanding** **1** [I,T] to know the meaning of what someone is saying to you, or the language that s/he speaks: *Do you understand Spanish?* | *I could barely understand what he was saying.* ✗ DON'T SAY "I am understanding." ✗ **2** [I,T] to know how someone feels and why s/he behaves the way s/he does: *Believe me, John - I understand how you feel.* **3** [I,T] to know how or why a situation, event etc. happens, especially through learning or experience: *Do you understand how this works?* | *I don't understand why the experiment failed.* **4** **make yourself understood** to make what you say clear to other people **5** **I understand (that)** SPOKEN used in order to say politely or formally that someone has already told you something: *I understand that you want to buy a painting.* –compare MISUNDERSTAND

**un·der·stand·a·ble** /,ʌndɚ'stændəbəl/ adj **1** understandable behavior, reactions etc. seem reasonable because of the situation you are in:

U

*It's **understandable that** he's a little afraid - anyone would be.* **2** able to be understood: *legal documents written in understandable terms*

**un·der·stand·ing**[1] /ˌʌndɚˈstændɪŋ/ *n* **1** [singular, U] knowledge about something, based on learning and experience: *She **has a basic understanding** of computers.* **2** [singular, U] sympathy toward someone's character and behavior: *Harry thanked us for our understanding.* **3** an informal private agreement about something: *I thought we had **come to an understanding** about the price.* **4** [U] the ability to know or learn; INTELLIGENCE

**understanding**[2] *adj* showing sympathy and pity for other people's problems: *an understanding boss*

**un·der·state** /ˌʌndɚˈsteɪt/ *v* [T] to say that something is not as large or as important as it really is: *The report understates the severity of the problem.*

**un·der·stat·ed** /ˌʌndɚˈsteɪtɪd◂/ *adj* done in a way that is not very noticeable or seems unimportant: *the understated decoration of his office*

**un·der·state·ment** /ˈʌndɚˌsteɪt⁀mənt/ *n* a statement that is not strong enough to express how good, impressive, bad etc. something really is: *To say that the effects of the earthquake were severe **is an understatement**.*

**un·der·stood** /ˌʌndɚˈstʊd/ *v* the past tense and PAST PARTICIPLE of UNDERSTAND

**un·der·stud·y** /ˈʌndɚˌstʌdi/ *n* an actor who learns a part in a play so that s/he can act if the usual actor cannot perform

**un·der·take** /ˌʌndɚˈteɪk/ *v* [T] FORMAL **1** to start to do a piece of work for which you are responsible: *Baker undertook the task of writing the annual report.* **2 undertake to do sth** to promise to do something: *We undertook to publish within six months.*

**un·der·tak·er** /ˈʌndɚˌteɪkɚ/ *n* someone whose job is to arrange funerals

**un·der·tak·ing** /ˈʌndɚˌteɪkɪŋ/ *n* [C usually singular] an important job, piece of work etc. for which you are responsible: *Setting up the Summer Olympics was a **massive undertaking**.*

**un·der·tone** /ˈʌndɚˌtoʊn/ *n* a feeling or quality that you notice even though it is difficult to see, hear, taste etc.: *an **undertone** of sadness in her voice*

**un·der·tow** /ˈʌndɚˌtoʊ/ *n* a strong current under the ocean's surface, that pulls water away from the shore

**un·der·wa·ter** /ˌʌndɚˈwɔtɚ◂, -ˈwɑ-/ *adj* below the surface of the water: *underwater photography* –**underwater** *adv*

**un·der·wear** /ˈʌndɚˌwɛr/ *n* [U] clothes that you wear next to your body under your other clothes

**un·der·weight** /ˌʌndɚˈweɪt◂/ *adj* weighing less than is expected or usual: *an underweight baby* –opposite OVERWEIGHT –see usage note at THIN[1]

**un·der·world** /ˈʌndɚˌwɚld/ *n* **1** [singular] the criminals in a particular place and the activities they are involved in **2** the place where the spirits of the dead live, especially in ancient Greek stories

**un·der·write** /ˈʌndɚˌraɪt, ˌʌndɚˈraɪt/ *v* [T] FORMAL to support an activity, business etc. with money: *The project is underwritten by a National Science Foundation grant.*

**un·de·sir·a·ble** /ˌʌndɪˈzaɪrəbəl◂/ *adj* FORMAL bad and unpleasant, or not wanted because it may have a bad effect: *The treatment has no undesirable side effects.*

**un·de·ter·mined** /ˌʌndɪˈtɚmɪnd◂/ *adj* ⇨ INDETERMINATE

**un·de·vel·oped** /ˌʌndɪˈvɛləpt◂/ *adj* undeveloped land has not been built on or used for a particular purpose

**un·dis·closed** /ˌʌndɪsˈkloʊzd◂/ *adj* not known publicly: *Henderson was hired for an **undisclosed amount/sum**.*

**un·dis·guised** /ˌʌndɪsˈgaɪzd◂/ *adj* clearly shown and not hidden: *She looked at me with undisguised hatred.*

**un·dis·put·ed** /ˌʌndɪˈspyutɪd◂/ *adj* **undisputed leader/master/champion etc.** someone whom everyone agrees is the leader etc.

**un·dis·turbed** /ˌʌndɪsˈtɚbd◂/ *adj, adv* not interrupted, moved, or changed: *They let her rest undisturbed.*

**un·di·vid·ed** /ˌʌndɪˈvaɪdɪd◂/ *adj* complete: *Please give me your **undivided attention**.* (=full attention)

**un·do** /ʌnˈdu/ *v* [T] **1** to untie or open something that is tied or closed: *I can't get the clasp on my necklace undone.* **2** to try to remove the bad effects of something: *The courts have tried to undo the legal abuses of the past.*

**un·do·ing** /ʌnˈduɪŋ/ *n* **be sb's undoing** to cause someone's failure, defeat, shame etc.: *Borrowing too much money proved to be his undoing.*

**un·done** /ˌʌnˈdʌn◂/ *adj* **1** not tied or closed: *Your shirt button has **come undone**.* **2** not finished or completed: *Much of the work on the bridge has been **left undone**.*

undone

**un·doubt·ed·ly** /ʌnˈdaʊtɪdli/ *adv* used in order to emphasize that something is definitely true: *He's undoubtedly one of the best guitar players of all time.*

**un·dress** /ʌnˈdrɛs/ v [I,T] to take your clothes off, or take someone else's clothes off

**un·dressed** /ʌnˈdrɛst/ adj not wearing any clothes, or wearing only PAJAMAS: *Jessie got undressed quickly and snuggled into bed.*

**un·due** /ˌʌnˈduˈ/ adj FORMAL more than is reasonable, suitable, or necessary: *The tax creates an undue burden on farmers.*

**un·du·ly** /ʌnˈduli/ adv FORMAL much more than necessary, or much too extreme: *unduly harsh punishment*

**un·dy·ing** /ˌʌnˈdaɪ-ɪŋˈ/ adj LITERARY continuing for ever: *undying love*

**un·earth** /ʌnˈɚθ/ v [T] **1** to find something that was buried in the ground: *Scientists have unearthed eight more skeletons at Pompeii.* **2** to find out the truth: *New evidence has been unearthed that connects them to the crime.*

**un·earth·ly** /ʌnˈɚθli/ adj very strange and not seeming natural: *an unearthly greenish light*

**un·eas·y** /ˌʌnˈizi·/ adj not at all comfortable with what is happening in a situation: *We felt uneasy about his decision.* –**uneasiness** n [U] –**uneasily** adv

**un·ed·u·cat·ed** /ʌnˈɛdʒəˌkeɪtˌɪd/ adj not having much education, or showing that someone is not well educated

**un·em·ployed** /ˌʌnɪmˈplɔɪdˈ/ adj **1** without a job: *an unemployed teacher* **2 the unemployed** people who do not have jobs

**un·em·ploy·ment** /ˌʌnɪmˈplɔɪmənt/ n [U] **1** the condition of not having a job, or the number of people who do not have a job: *There is high unemployment in the cities.* **2** money that is paid regularly by the government to people who have no job: *Bill's drawing unemployment.* (=receiving money)

**un·e·qual** /ʌnˈikwəl/ adj **1** not having the same rights, chances etc. as other people: *the unequal treatment of minorities* **2** not the same in size, amount, value, rank etc.

**un·e·quiv·o·cal** /ˌʌnɪˈkwɪvəkəl/ adj FORMAL completely clear and definite with no doubts

**un·er·ring** /ʌnˈɛrɪŋ, ʌnˈɚɪŋ/ adj always exactly correct: *Madsen's unerring judgment*

**un·eth·i·cal** /ʌnˈɛθɪkəl/ adj considered to be morally wrong: *unethical behavior in business*

**un·e·ven** /ʌnˈivən/ adj **1** not flat, smooth, or level: *uneven ground* **2** not equal or balanced: *The racial mix of the school is uneven.* **3** good in some parts and bad in others: *a music album of uneven quality* –**unevenly** adv

**un·ex·cused** /ˌʌnɪkˈskuzdˈ/ adj **unexcused absence** an occasion when you are away from school or work without permission

**un·ex·pect·ed** /ˌʌnɪkˈspɛktɪdˈ/ adj surprising because of not being expected: *the unexpected death of his father* –**unexpectedly** adv

**un·fail·ing** /ʌnˈfeɪlɪŋ/ adj always happening or being shown, in spite of difficulties: *his unfailing kindness*

**un·fair** /ˌʌnˈfɛr·/ adj not right or fair: *an unfair decision* | *It's unfair to make her do most of the packing.* –**unfairly** adv –**unfairness** n [U]

**un·faith·ful** /ʌnˈfeɪθfəl/ adj someone who is unfaithful has sex with someone who is not his/her wife, husband, or usual partner

**un·fa·mil·iar** /ˌʌnfəˈmɪlyɚ/ adj **1** not known to you: *an unfamiliar face* **2** not knowing about something: *I am unfamiliar with his books.* –**unfamiliarity** /ˌʌnfəˌmɪlˈyærəti/ n [U] –compare UNKNOWN¹

**un·fas·ten** /ʌnˈfæsən/ v [T] ⇨ UNDO: *Lewis unfastened his seat belt and got out.*

**un·fa·vor·a·ble** /ʌnˈfeɪvərəbəl/ adj **1** unfavorable conditions or events are not as good as you want them to be: *an unfavorable weather report* **2** showing disapproval: *an unfavorable review of the movie*

**un·feel·ing** /ʌnˈfilɪŋ/ adj not showing sympathy or pity for others

**un·fet·tered** /ʌnˈfɛtɚdˈ/ adj not restricted in any way: *the unfettered free-market system*

**un·fit** /ʌnˈfɪt/ adj not suitable or good enough to do something or to be used for something: *That woman is unfit to raise a child!* | *land unfit for cultivation*

**un·fold** /ʌnˈfoʊld/ v [I,T] **1** if a story, plan etc. unfolds, it becomes clearer and you understand it: *The case began to slowly unfold in court.* **2** to open something that was folded: *She unfolded the map.*

**un·fore·seen** /ˌʌnfɔrˈsin·, -fɚ-/ adj an unforeseen situation is one that you were not able to plan for because you did not expect it: *an unforeseen delay*

**un·for·get·ta·ble** /ˌʌnfɚˈgɛtəbəl/ adj so beautiful, good, exciting etc. that you remember it for a long time: *The ships, with their billowing sails, were an unforgettable sight.*

**un·for·tu·nate** /ʌnˈfɔrtʃənɪt/ adj **1** happening because of bad luck: *an unfortunate accident* **2** unsuitable and causing embarrassment: *an unfortunate choice of words*

**un·for·tu·nate·ly** /ʌnˈfɔrtʃənɪtli/ adv used when you are mentioning a fact that you wish were not true: *Unfortunately, your computer needs more memory to run this program.*

**un·found·ed** /ˌʌnˈfaʊndɪdˈ/ adj not based on facts; wrong: *The company insisted that our complaints were unfounded.*

**un·furl** /ʌnˈfɚl/ v [T] to unroll and open a flag, sail etc.

**un·gain·ly** /ʌnˈgeɪnli/ adj awkward and not graceful: *an ungainly teenager*

**un·gra·cious** /ʌnˈgreɪʃəs/ adj not polite or friendly: *She gave us an ungracious welcome.* –**ungraciously** adv

**un·grate·ful** /ʌnˈgreɪtfəl/ adj not thanking someone for something s/he has given to you or done for you

U

**un·hap·py** /ʌnˈhæpi/ *adj* **1** not happy: *He had a very unhappy childhood.* **2** feeling worried or annoyed because you do not like what is happening: *Americans are deeply **unhappy with** the state of the nation.* —unhappiness *n* [U] —unhappily *adv*

**un·health·y** /ʌnˈhɛlθi/ *adj* **1** likely to make you ill: *unhealthy city air* **2** not physically healthy: *an unhealthy baby that was born too early* **3** not normal or natural and likely to cause harm: *an unhealthy relationship*

**unheard-of** /ʌnˈhɚd ʌv/ *adj* so unusual that it has never happened or been known before: *The opera raised the price of its seats to an unheard-of $100 each!*

**un·ho·ly** /ʌnˈhouli/ *adj* **1** INFORMAL unusual and offensive or upsetting: *an **unholy alliance** between greed and politics* **2** not holy or not respecting what is holy

**un·hook** /ʌnˈhʊk/ *v* [T] to unfasten or remove something from a hook: *Can you help me unhook my necklace?*

**UNICEF** /ˈyunəˌsɛf/ *n* [U] the United Nations Children's Fund; an organization that helps children who suffer from disease, HUNGER etc.

**u·ni·corn** /ˈyunəˌkɔrn/ *n* an imaginary animal like a white horse with a long straight horn on its head

**un·i·den·ti·fied** /ˌʌnaɪˈdɛntɪˌfaɪd, ˌʌnə-/ *adj* an unidentified person or thing is one that you do not recognize or know the name of: *An unidentified man was hit by a car.*

**u·ni·fi·ca·tion** /ˌyunəfəˈkeɪʃən/ *n* [U] the act of combining two more groups, countries etc. to make a single group or country: *the economic unification of Europe*

**u·ni·form¹** /ˈyunəˌfɔrm/ *n* **1** a particular type of clothing that the members of an organization wear to work: *a blue police uniform* **2** **be in uniform a)** to be wearing a uniform **b)** to be in the army, navy etc. —uniformed *adj*

**uniform²** *adj* a number of things that are a uniform size, weight etc. are all nearly the same size, weight etc. —uniformly *adv* —uniformity /ˌyunəˈfɔrməti/ *n* [U]

**u·ni·fy** /ˈyunəˌfaɪ/ *v* [T] **1** to combine the parts of a country, organization etc. to make a single unit: *Spain was unified in the 16th century.* **2** to change a group of things so that they are all the same: *a record that unifies different musical styles* —unified *adj*

**u·ni·lat·er·al** /ˌyunəˈlætərəl/ *adj* a unilateral action or decision is made by only one of the groups, organizations etc. that are involved in a situation: *a unilateral ceasefire* —compare BILATERAL MULTILATERAL

**un·im·por·tant** /ˌʌnɪmˈpɔrtˀnt/ *adj* not important

**un·in·sured** /ˌʌnɪnˈʃʊrd/ *adj* having no insurance: *uninsured drivers*

**un·in·tel·li·gi·ble** /ˌʌnɪnˈtɛlədʒəbəl/ *adj* impossible to understand: *Their radio transmissions were unintelligible.*

**un·in·ter·est·ed** /ʌnˈɪntrɪstɪd, -ˈɪntərəs-/ *adj* not interested —compare DISINTERESTED

**un·in·ter·rupt·ed** /ˌʌnɪntrəˈrʌptɪd/ *adj* continuous, without being stopped: *All I want is two hours of uninterrupted work.*

**un·ion** /ˈyunyən/ *n* **1** ⇨ LABOR UNION: *the auto workers' union* **2** a group of countries or states with the same central government **3** [singular, U] FORMAL the act of joining two or more things together, or the state of being joined together: *the **union** of East Germany **with** West Germany* **4** [singular, U] FORMAL the act of marriage, or the state of being married

**un·ion·ized** /ˈyunyəˌnaɪzd/ *adj* having formed a UNION, or belonging to one —unionize *v* [I,T]

**u·nique** /yuˈnik/ *adj* **1** INFORMAL unusually good and special: *a unique opportunity to study with an artist* | *unique Christmas presents* **2** being the only one of its kind: *a unique sculpture* —uniquely *adv*

---

**USAGE NOTE unique**

Use this word in order to talk about something that is the only one of its kind: *Glenn Gould had a unique way of playing the piano.* You may sometimes hear people say "very unique," "more unique," "the most unique," etc. However, using **unique** in this way is nonstandard.

---

**u·ni·sex** /ˈyunəˌsɛks/ *adj* suitable for both men and women: *a unisex jacket*

**u·ni·son** /ˈyunəsən/ *n* **in unison a)** if people speak in unison, they say the same words at the same time: *"Okay, Mom!" the twins said in unison.* **b)** if people do something in unison, they do it together because they agree with each other: *Congress needs to act in unison on this issue.*

**u·nit** /ˈyunɪt/ *n* **1** a person or thing that is one whole part of something larger: *The family is the smallest social unit.* | *an eight-unit apartment building* (=it has 8 apartments) **2** a group of people who work together as part of a larger group: *the emergency unit of the hospital* **3** an amount or quantity of something that is used as a standard of measurement: *The dollar is the basic **unit of** money in the US.* **4** a piece of furniture that can be fitted to others of the same type: *a kitchen unit* **5** a piece of machinery that is part of a larger machine: *The cooling unit is broken.*

**U·ni·tar·i·an** /ˌyunəˈtɛriən/ *adj* relating to a Protestant church whose members believe in religious freedom —Unitarian *n*

**u·nite** /yuˈnaɪt/ *v* [I,T] to join together with other people or organizations and act as one group, or to make people join together in this way: *Congress* **united behind** *the President.* | *The deal would unite two of the country's oldest electronics firms.*

**u·nit·ed** /yu'naɪṭɪd/ *adj* **1** involving or done by everyone: *a united effort to clean up the environment* **2** closely related by sharing feelings, aims etc.: *a united community*

**United Na·tions** /.ₐ.. '../ *n* [singular] ⇨ UN

**u·ni·ty** /'yunəṭi/ *n* [singular, U] the state of being UNITED: *a new political unity among countries*

**u·ni·ver·sal** /ˌyunə'vɚsəl‹ / *adj* **1** concerning all the members of a group or of the world: *universal voting rights* | *a universal health care program* **2** relating to everywhere in the world: *universal environmental problems* **3** true or suitable in every situation: *a universal truth* –**universally** *adv*

**u·ni·verse** /'yunə,vɚs/ *n* **the universe** all of space, including all the stars and PLANETs

**u·ni·ver·si·ty** /ˌyunə'vɚsəṭi/ *n* [C,U] a school at the highest level, where you study for a DE-GREE

**un·just** /ˌʌn'dʒʌst‹ / *adj* not fair or reasonable: *unjust laws*

**un·jus·ti·fied** /ˌʌn'dʒʌstə,faɪd/ *adj* done without a good reason: *Experts think the fears about the economy are unjustified.* –**unjustifiable** *adj*

**un·kempt** /ˌʌn'kɛmpt‹ / *adj* not neat; messy: *Her hair was dirty and unkempt.*

**un·kind** /ˌʌn'kaɪnd‹ / *adj* nasty, unpleasant, or cruel: *an unkind remark*

**un·know·ing·ly** /ʌn'noʊɪŋli/ *adv* without realizing what you are doing or what is happening: *Millions of people may have been unknowingly infected.*

**un·known¹** /ˌʌn'noʊn‹ / *adj* **1** not known about by most people: *An unknown number of rebels are in hiding.* **2** not famous: *an unknown musician* **3** **the unknown** things that you do not know about or understand: *a fear of the unknown* –compare UNFAMILIAR

**unknown²** *n* someone who is not famous: *Early in her career, she was still an unknown.*

**un·law·ful** /ʌn'lɔfəl/ *adj* not legal

**un·lead·ed** /ˌʌn'lɛdɪd‹ / *n* [U] gas that does not contain any LEAD –compare REGULAR²

**un·leash** /ʌn'liʃ/ *v* [T] to suddenly let a strong force or feeling have its full effect: *The ceremony unleashed memories of the war.*

**un·less** /ən'lɛs, ʌn-/ *conjunction* used in order to say what will happen or be true if another thing does not happen or is not true: *We can go in my car unless you want to walk.* | *He won't go to sleep unless you tell him a story.* ✗ DON'T SAY "unless if." ✗

**un·like¹** /ˌʌn'laɪk‹ / *prep* **1** completely different from another person or thing: *Unlike most commercials, this one is educational.*

**2** not typical of someone: *It's unlike Judy to leave without telling us.*

**unlike²** *adj* different: *I've never known two sisters so unlike.*

**un·like·ly** /ˌʌn'laɪkli‹ / *adj* not likely to happen: *I'll try to get an earlier flight, but it's **unlikely (that)** I'll be able to.* –**unlikelihood** *n* [U]

**un·lim·it·ed** /ˌʌn'lɪmɪṭɪd‹ / *adj* without a fixed limit: *unlimited mileage on the rental car*

**un·list·ed** /ˌʌn'lɪstɪd‹ / *adj* an unlisted phone number is not in the list of numbers in the telephone book because someone does not want his/her number to be known

**un·load** /ʌn'loʊd/ *v* **1** [I,T] to remove goods from a vehicle or large container, or to have them removed: *unloading the dishwasher* | *The ship took a long time to unload.* **2** [T] INFORMAL to get rid of something by selling it quickly: *The warehouse is trying to unload a huge quantity of goods at discount prices.* **3** [T] to get rid of work or a duty by giving it to someone else: *Don't let Donna unload those reports onto you.* **4** [I,T] to take film out of a camera or bullets out of a gun

**un·lock** /ʌn'lɑk/ *v* [T] to undo the lock on a door, box etc.: *I tried to unlock the door, but the key didn't fit.*

**un·luck·y** /ˌʌn'lʌki‹ / *adj* **1** having bad luck: *We were **unlucky with** the weather this weekend.* **2** happening as a result of bad luck: *It was **unlucky for** us **that** the bank closed just as we got there.* **3** causing bad luck: *Some people think black cats are unlucky.*

**un·marked** /ˌʌn'mɑrkt‹ / *adj* something that is unmarked has no words or signs on it: *an unmarked police car*

**un·mar·ried** /ˌʌn'mæɪid‹ / *adj* not married; SINGLE

**un·mask** /ʌn'mæsk/ *v* [T] to make a truth that has been hidden become known: *He was unmasked as an enemy spy.*

**un·mis·tak·a·ble** /ˌʌnmɪ'steɪkəbəl‹ / *adj* familiar and easy to recognize: *the unmistakable taste of garlic*

**un·mit·i·gat·ed** /ˌʌn'mɪṭəgeɪṭɪd‹ / *adj* **unmitigated disaster/failure etc.** something that is completely bad

**un·moved** /ˌʌn'muvd‹ / *adj* not worried, or not feeling pity: *The judge was unmoved by his excuses.*

**un·named** /ˌʌn'neɪmd‹ / *adj* an unnamed person, place, or thing is one whose name is not known publicly: *a reporter's unnamed source*

**un·nat·u·ral** /ˌʌn'nætʃərəl‹ / *adj* **1** different from what you would normally expect: *It's unnatural for a child to spend so much time alone.* **2** different from what is produced in nature: *unnatural colors* **3** different from normal human behavior in a way that seems morally wrong: *unnatural sexual practices*

U

**un·nec·es·sar·y** /ˌʌn'nɛsəˌsɛri/ *adj* **1** not needed, or more than is needed: *The rule prevents unnecessary delays.* **2** a remark or action that is unnecessary is unkind or unreasonable –**unecessarily** *adv*

**un·nerve** /ʌn'nɝv/ *v* [T] to upset or frighten someone so that s/he loses his/her confidence or ability to think clearly: *Dave was completely unnerved by the argument with Terry.* –**unnerving** *adj*: *She drove with unnerving speed up the dirt road.*

**un·no·ticed** /ˌʌn'noʊţɪst/ *adj* without anyone noticing someone or something: *She sat unnoticed at the back.*

**un·ob·served** /ˌʌnəb'zɝvd/ *adj, adv* not seen, or without being seen: *Bret left the meeting unobserved.*

**un·ob·tru·sive** /ˌʌnəb'trusɪv/ *adj* APPROVING not attracting attention and not likely to be noticed: *an efficient unobtrusive waiter*

**un·oc·cu·pied** /ʌn'ɑkyəˌpaɪd/ *adj* a seat, house, room etc. that is unoccupied has no one in it

**un·of·fi·cial** /ˌʌnə'fɪʃəl/ *adj* **1** without approval or permission from someone in authority: *Unofficial reports say about 25 people are dead.* **2** not made publicly known, or not done as part of official duties: *The President made an unofficial visit to a children's hospital.* –**unofficially** *adv*

**un·or·tho·dox** /ʌn'ɔrθəˌdɑks/ *adj* different from what is usual or accepted by most people: *unorthodox behavior*

**un·pack** /ʌn'pæk/ *v* [I,T] to take everything out of a box or SUITCASE and put it where it belongs

**un·paid** /ˌʌn'peɪd/ *adj* **1** an unpaid bill or debt has not been paid **2** done without getting any money: *unpaid work*

**un·par·al·leled** /ʌn'pærəˌlɛld/ *adj* FORMAL greater or better than all the others: *Those years were a time of unparalleled happiness in our lives.*

**un·pleas·ant** /ʌn'plɛzənt/ *adj* **1** not pleasant or enjoyable: *an unpleasant surprise* **2** not kind or friendly: *unpleasant neighbors*

**un·plug** /ʌn'plʌg/ *v* **-gged, -gging** [T] to disconnect a piece of electrical equipment by taking its PLUG out of a SOCKET

**un·plugged** /ʌn'plʌgd/ *adj* if a group of musicians performs unplugged, they perform without electric instruments

**un·pop·u·lar** /ʌn'pɑpyələ/ *adj* not liked by most people: *an unpopular decision*

**un·prec·e·dent·ed** /ʌn'prɛsəˌdɛnţɪd/ *adj* never having happened before, or never having happened so much: *The Steelers won an unprecedented four Super Bowls in six years.*

**un·pre·dict·a·ble** /ˌʌnprɪ'dɪktəbəl/ *adj* changing so much that you do not know what to expect: *unpredictable weather*

**un·pre·pared** /ˌʌnprɪ'pɛrd/ *adj* not ready to deal with something: *Their son seems unprepared for school.*

**un·pre·pos·sess·ing** /ˌʌnpripə'zɛsɪŋ/ *adj* not unusual, attractive, or interesting: *an unprepossessing girl of 14*

**un·prin·ci·pled** /ʌn'prɪnsəpəld/ *adj* FORMAL not caring about whether what you do is morally right or not

**un·print·a·ble** /ʌn'prɪnţəbəl/ *adj* words that are unprintable are rude or shocking

**un·pro·duc·tive** /ˌʌnprə'dʌktɪv/ *adj* not achieving any useful result: *a totally unproductive meeting*

**un·pro·fes·sion·al** /ˌʌnprə'fɛʃənəl/ *adj* not behaving according to the way that people in a particular profession or activity should behave: *Osborn was fired for unprofessional conduct.*

**un·prof·it·a·ble** /ʌn'prɑfɪţəbəl/ *adj* **1** making no profit: *an unprofitable business* **2** FORMAL bringing no advantage or gain

**un·pro·tect·ed** /ˌʌnprə'tɛktɪd/ *adj* **1** something that is unprotected could hurt someone or be damaged: *unprotected machinery* **2** **unprotected sex** sex without a CONDOM

**un·pro·voked** /ˌʌnprə'voʊkt/ *adj* unprovoked anger, attacks, etc. are directed at someone who has not done anything to deserve them

**un·qual·i·fied** /ʌn'kwɑləˌfaɪd/ *adj* **1** not having the right knowledge, experience, or education to do something: *The hospital was accused of hiring unqualified health workers.* **2** complete: *The movie is an unqualified success.*

**un·ques·tion·a·bly** /ʌn'kwɛstʃənəbli/ *adv* in a way that leaves no doubt: *This is unquestionably the coldest winter in years.*

**un·ques·tioned** /ʌn'kwɛstʃənd/ *adj* accepted by everyone: *his unquestioned right to rule*

**un·quote** /'ʌnkwoʊt/ *v* SPOKEN ⇨ **quote ... unquote** (QUOTE¹)

**un·rav·el** /ʌn'rævəl/ *v* **1** [I,T] if you unravel threads or if they unravel, they become separated **2** [T] to understand or explain something that is very complicated

**un·real** /ˌʌn'ril/ *adj* **1** an experience, situation etc. that is unreal seems so strange that you think you must be imagining it: *The trip took so long that it began to seem unreal.* **2** SPOKEN very exciting; excellent: *Some of the shots Magic Johnson made were unreal.* **3** not relating to real things that happen: *Test questions often deal with unreal situations.*

**un·re·al·is·tic** /ˌʌnriə'lɪstɪk/ *adj* unrealistic ideas are not based on fact: *unrealistic job expectations* | *You're being unrealistic - one new player is not going to change the way the whole team plays.* | *It's unrealistic to expect her to be happy all the time.*

**un·rea·son·a·ble** /ʌn'rizənəbəl/ *adj* **1** wrong or unfair: *It's unreasonable to give a*

*10-year-old so much responsibility.* **2** behaving in a way that is not pleasant, not sensible, and often silly: *He has a talent for dealing with the kids when they're being unreasonable.* **3** unreasonable prices, costs etc. are too high

**un·rec·og·niz·a·ble** /ˌʌnrɛkəgˈnaɪzəbəl/ *adj* changed or damaged so much that you cannot recognize someone or something: *The downtown area is almost unrecognizable.*

**un·rec·og·nized** /ʌnˈrɛkəgˌnaɪzd/ *adj* **1** not receiving the respect someone deserves: *an unrecognized jazz musician of the 1930s* **2** not noticed or not thought to be important: *Violence in the home had gone unrecognized in the courts for years.*

**un·re·cord·ed** /ˌʌnrɪˈkɔrdɪd/ *adj* not written down or recorded: *an event unrecorded in history books*

**un·re·fined** /ˌʌnrɪˈfaɪnd/ *adj* **1** an unrefined substance has not gone through the process of being separated from other substances that naturally combine with it: *unrefined sugar* **2** FORMAL not polite or educated

**un·re·lat·ed** /ˌʌnrɪˈleɪtɪd/ *adj* with no connection with something else: *unrelated events*

**un·re·lent·ing** /ˌʌnrɪˈlɛntɪŋ/ *adj* FORMAL an unpleasant situation that is unrelenting continues for a long time: *two days of unrelenting rain*

**un·re·li·a·ble** /ˌʌnrɪˈlaɪəbəl/ *adj* unable to be trusted or depended on: *unreliable information* | *He was found to be an unreliable witness.* (–he did not tell the truth in a court)

**un·re·lieved** /ˌʌnrɪˈlivd/ *adj* an unpleasant situation that is unrelieved continues for a long time because nothing happens to change it: *unrelieved pain*

**un·re·mit·ting** /ˌʌnrɪˈmɪtɪŋ/ *adj* FORMAL something that is unremitting continues for a long time and probably will not stop: *unremitting pressure at work*

**un·re·quit·ed** /ˌʌnrɪˈkwaɪtɪd/ *adj* **unrequited love** romantic love that you feel for someone who does not feel the same love for you

**un·re·served** /ˌʌnrɪˈzɚvd/ *adj* complete and without any doubts: *You have my unreserved support.*

**un·re·solved** /ˌʌnrɪˈzɑlvd/ *adj* an unresolved problem or question has not been answered or solved

**un·re·spon·sive** /ˌʌnrɪˈspɑnsɪv/ *adj* **1** not reacting to what people say to you: *The politicians seem to be unresponsive to the city's needs.* | *an unresponsive teenager* **2** not affected by something: *a disease that is unresponsive to drugs*

**un·rest** /ʌnˈrɛst/ *n* [U] a social or political situation in which people express their anger or dissatisfaction about something: *civil/political unrest in the former Soviet Union*

**un·re·strained** /ˌʌnrɪˈstreɪnd/ *adj* not controlled or limited: *unrestrained laughter*

**un·ri·valed** /ʌnˈraɪvəld/ *adj* FORMAL better than any other: *an unrivaled collection of 19th century art*

**un·roll** /ʌnˈroʊl/ *v* [T] to open something that was curled into the shape of a ball or tube, and make it flat: *unrolling a sleeping bag*

**un·ru·ly** /ʌnˈruli/ *adj* **1** behaving in an uncontrolled or violent way: *unruly children* **2** unruly hair is messy

**un·safe** /ʌnˈseɪf/ *adj* **1** a building, machine etc. that is unsafe is dangerous **2** if you are unsafe, you are in danger of being hurt

**un·said** /ʌnˈsɛd/ *adj* **be left unsaid** if something is left unsaid, you do not say it although you think it: *Some things are better left unsaid.*

**un·san·i·tar·y** /ʌnˈsænəˌtɛri/ *adj* very dirty and likely to cause disease: *unsanitary conditions*

**un·sat·is·fac·to·ry** /ˌʌnsætɪsˈfæktəri/ *adj* not good enough: *Your work is unsatisfactory.*

**un·sa·vor·y** /ʌnˈseɪvəri/ *adj* unpleasant or morally unacceptable: *unsavory business deals*

**un·scathed** /ʌnˈskeɪðd/ *adj* not hurt by a bad or dangerous situation: *The driver came out of the crash unscathed.*

**un·screw** /ʌnˈskru/ *v* [T] **1** to undo something by twisting it: *Turn off the light before unscrewing the bulb.* **2** to take the screws out of something

**un·scru·pu·lous** /ʌnˈskrupyələs/ *adj* behaving in an unfair or dishonest way: *an unscrupulous lawyer*

**un·sea·son·a·ble** /ʌnˈsizənəbəl/ *adj* unseasonable weather is unusual for the time of year

**un·seat** /ʌnˈsit/ *v* [T] to remove someone from a position of power: *Two candidates are trying to unseat the mayor.*

**un·seem·ly** /ʌnˈsimli/ *adj* FORMAL unseemly behavior is not polite or suitable: *an unseemly argument over money*

**un·seen** /ˌʌnˈsin/ *adj, adv* FORMAL not noticed or seen: *She left the office unseen.*

**un·set·tled** /ʌnˈsɛtld/ *adj* **1** an unsettled situation makes you feel unsure about what will happen: *Recent events have left the capital unsettled.* **2** worried or excited about something so that you feel upset or nervous: *The children are feeling unsettled by the divorce.* **3** an unsettled argument continues without reaching any agreement: *The issue remains unsettled.* **4** weather that is unsettled changes a lot in a short time **5** if your stomach is unsettled, you feel uncomfortable and a little sick

**un·set·tling** /ʌnˈsɛtl-ɪŋ/ *adj* causing worry: *unsettling changes in the software industry*

**un·sight·ly** /ʌnˈsaɪtli/ *adj* unpleasant to look at: *unsightly office buildings*

**un·skilled** /ˌʌnˈskɪld◂/ *adj* **1** not trained for a particular type of job: *unskilled workers* **2** unskilled work does not need people with special skills

**un·so·phis·ti·cat·ed** /ˌʌnsəˈfɪstəˌkeɪt̮ɪd◂/ *adj* **1** having little knowledge or experience of new ideas and fashions, and showing this in your behavior: *unsophisticated audiences* **2** unsophisticated tools, methods, or processes are simple or not very modern

**un·sound** /ˌʌnˈsaʊnd◂/ *adj* **1** unsound arguments, methods etc. are not based on fact or reason **2** an unsound building or structure is in bad condition

**un·speak·a·ble** /ʌnˈspikəbəl/ *adj* extremely bad: *unspeakable crimes*

**un·spe·ci·fied** /ʌnˈspɛsəˌfaɪd/ *adj* not clearly or definitely stated: *The ticket is valid for an unspecified period of time.*

**un·spo·ken** /ʌnˈspoʊkən/ *adj* understood but not talked about: *There was an unspoken agreement between us, that we would tell Dee.*

**un·sports·man·like** /ʌnˈspɔrtsmənˌlaɪk/ *adj* not behaving in a fair honest way in playing sports

**un·sta·ble** /ʌnˈsteɪbəl/ *adj* **1** likely to change suddenly, especially so that something difficult or dangerous happens: *an unstable economy | unstable behavior* **2** dangerous and likely to fall over: *an unstable wall*

**un·stead·y** /ʌnˈstɛdi/ *adj* **1** shaking when you try to walk, hold something etc: *I felt unsteady on my feet.* **2** not firm or likely to fall: *The old bridge had become unsteady.* **3** an unsteady situation is likely to become worse

**un·stop·pa·ble** /ʌnˈstɑpəbəl/ *adj* unable to be stopped: *The team seems unstoppable this year.*

**un·suc·cess·ful** /ˌʌnsəkˈsɛsfəl◂/ *adj* not achieving what you wanted to achieve: *an unsuccessful experiment/actor* **–unsuccessfully** *adv*: *We tried, unsuccessfully, to convince Herrera of the truth.*

**un·suit·a·ble** /ʌnˈsut̮əbəl/ *adj* not having the right qualities for a particular person, purpose, or situation: *This movie is **unsuitable for** young children.*

**un·sung** /ˌʌnˈsʌŋ◂/ *adj* not praised or famous for something you have done, although you deserve to be: *the **unsung heroes** of the war against crime*

**un·sure** /ˌʌnˈʃʊr◂/ *adj* **1** not certain about something or about what you have to do: *If you're **unsure of** the rules, ask the teacher.* **2** unsure of yourself lacking confidence: *Clara seemed shy and unsure of herself.*

**un·sus·pect·ing** /ˌʌnsəˈspɛktɪŋ◂/ *adj* not knowing that something bad is about to happen: *Criminals can make easy money from mugging unsuspecting tourists.*

**un·swerv·ing** /ʌnˈswɚvɪŋ/ *adj* never changing in spite of difficulties: *unswerving loyalty*

**un·tan·gle** /ʌnˈtæŋgəl/ *v* [T] to make things straight that are twisted together: *conditioner that helps untangle your hair*

**un·tapped** /ˌʌnˈtæpt◂/ *adj* an untapped RE-SOURCE, market etc. has not yet been used

**un·ten·a·ble** /ʌnˈtɛnəbəl/ *adj* an untenable argument, THEORY etc. is impossible to defend against criticism

**un·think·a·ble** /ʌnˈθɪŋkəbəl/ *adj* impossible to accept or imagine: *It was unthinkable a few years ago for a woman to run for President.*

**un·tie** /ʌnˈtaɪ/ *v* [T] to undo the knots in something or undo something that has been tied: *Mommy, can you untie my shoelaces?*

**un·til** /ən·tɪl, ʌn-/ *prep conjunction* **1** used in order to say that something stops happening or being done at a particular time or when something else happens: *I have classes until 7 p.m. today. | Debbie's on vacation until Monday.* **2** not until used in order to say that something will not happen before a particular time: *The movie doesn't start until 8 p.m. | The doctor's not available until tomorrow.*

**un·time·ly** /ʌnˈtaɪmli/ *adj* **1** happening earlier than it should or than you expected: *an untimely death* **2** not right for the occasion: *an untimely show of anger*

**un·tir·ing** /ʌnˈtaɪərɪŋ/ *adj* never stopping while working or trying to do something: *untiring efforts to help the homeless*

**un·told** /ˌʌnˈtoʊld◂/ *adj* too much or too many to be counted: *Floods did untold damage to farmland.*

**un·touch·a·ble** /ʌnˈtʌtʃəbəl/ *adj* someone who is untouchable is in such a strong position that s/he cannot be affected by, or punished for, anything: *These drug dealers think they're untouchable.*

**un·to·ward** /ˌʌnˈtɔrd/ *adj* FORMAL unexpected, unusual, or not wanted: *Neighbors say that **nothing untoward** had happened on the night of the shooting.*

**un·tried** /ˌʌnˈtraɪd◂/ *adj* new and not tested by being used: *an untried theory*

**un·true** /ʌnˈtru/ *adj* a statement that is untrue does not give the right facts; false

**un·truth·ful** /ʌnˈtruθfəl/ *adj* dishonest or not true

**un·used¹** /ˌʌnˈyuzd◂/ *adj* not being used, or never used: *unused apartments*

**un·used²** /ʌnˈjust/ *adj* unused to not experienced in dealing with something: *She's unused to driving at night.*

**un·u·su·al** /ʌnˈyuʒuəl, -ʒəl/ *adj* **1** different from what is usual or ordinary: *Our team has an unusual number of talented players.* **2** interesting or attractive because of being different: *unusual clothes*

**un·u·su·al·ly** /ʌnˈyuʒuəli, -ʒəli/ *adv* **1** unusually hot/difficult etc. more hot, difficult etc. than is usual: *an unusually rainy spring* **2** in a way that is different from what is usual or ordinary: *houses painted unusually bright colors*

**un·veil** /ʌnˈveɪl/ *v* [T] **1** to show or tell people something that was a secret: *The mayor will unveil plans for a new park.* **2** to remove the cover from something as part of a formal ceremony

**un·want·ed** /ˌʌnˈwɑnɪd◂, -ˈwɔn-, -ˈwɒn-/ *adj* not wanted or needed. *unwanted visitors*

**un·war·rant·ed** /ʌnˈwɔrənɪd, -ˈwɑr-/ *adj* not done for any good reason: *The judge decided a delay in the case was unwarranted.*

**un·wel·come** /ʌnˈwɛlkəm/ *adj* **1** not wanted, especially because it might cause embarrassment or problems: *unwelcome sexual advances* **2** unwelcome guests, visitors etc. are people that you do not want in your home

**un·wield·y** /ʌnˈwildi/ *adj* an unwieldy object is heavy and difficult to carry

**un·will·ing** /ʌnˈwɪlɪŋ/ *adj* **1** not wanting to do something and refusing to do it: *He's unwilling to take responsibility.* **2** not wanting to do something, but doing it: *an unwilling helper*

**un·wind** /ʌnˈwaɪnd/ *v* **1** [I] to relax and stop feeling anxious: *Swimming helps me unwind.* **2** [I,T] to undo something that is wrapped or twisted around something else:

**un·wise** /ˌʌnˈwaɪz◂/ *adj* likely to lead to a bad result: *an unwise decision*

**un·wit·ting·ly** /ʌnˈwɪtɪŋli/ *adv* without knowing or realizing something: *Several employees unwittingly became involved in illegal activities.* –unwitting *adj*

**un·writ·ten** /ˌʌnˈrɪtⁿ◂/ *adj* known about and understood by everyone but not written down. *There was an unwritten rule in our family that nobody questioned my father.*

**un·yield·ing** /ʌnˈyildɪŋ/ *adj* not changed by other people's wishes: *The terrorists are unyielding in their demands.*

**un·zip** /ʌnˈzɪp/ *v* -pped, -pping [T] to unfasten the ZIPPER on a piece of clothing, bag etc.

**up¹** /ʌp/ *adv* **1** toward a higher position: *Duncan climbed up into the tree.* | *Put the picture up higher.* | *Could you come up here and help us?* **2** at or in a high position: *"Where's Dave?" "He's up in his room."* | *a balloon floating up above us* **3** into an upright or raised position: *The choir stood up to sing.* | *The hair on the dog's back was sticking up.* **4** in or toward the North: *I'm driving up to see my parents.* | *His relatives all live up North.* **5** toward someone so that you are near him/her or in the place where s/he is: *The cop came up to the car and asked Chad for his license.* **6** increasing in loudness, strength, heat, activity etc.: *Turn up the TV.* | *The level of violent crime was up by 3% this month.* **7** completely: *All the space in*

the basement is filled up. | *Eat up your dinner!* **8** broken or divided completely: *She tore the letter up into tiny pieces.* | *We'll split the money up evenly.* **9** firmly fastened, covered, or joined: *a box tied up with string* | *Her dad covered her up and said goodnight.* **10** brought or gathered together in a group: *Add up the following numbers...* | *He gathered up all the pens he could find.* **11** so as to receive attention: *Payton brought that point up at the meeting.* **12** above and including a particular number or amount: *This movie is suitable for children aged 12 and up.* **13 up and down a)** higher and lower: *kids jumping up and down* **b)** to one end of something and then back again: *We walked up and down the street trying to find the house.* **14 it's up to you** SPOKEN said to tell someone that you want him/her to make a decision: *"Do you think I should get the dress?" "It's up to you."* **15 up close** very near someone or something: *If you look up close you can see the cracks.* **16 meet/see/know etc. up close** to experience something that you had previously only read or heard about, or to meet someone that you had only seen in newspapers, movies etc.: *I was surprised by how short he was when I met him up close.* **17 up to a)** used in order to show the highest amount or level of something, or the latest time something can happen: *Up to 10 people are allowed in the elevator at one time.* | *This offer is valid up to December 15.* **b)** good enough or well enough to do something: *Do you feel up to a walk today?* | *The new machines aren't up to our usual standard.* **c)** used in order to say or ask what someone is doing: *What have you been up to this week?* | *I'm sure Bob's up to something.* (=doing something secret)

**up²** *adj* **1** awake: *"Sorry, were you in bed?" "No, I'm still up."* **2** a computer system that is up is working –opposite DOWN **3** a level, number, or amount that is up is higher than before: *Profits were up by 4% this year.* –opposite DOWN **4 be up against** to have to deal with a difficult situation or fight an opponent: *We're up against some of the biggest companies in the world.* **5 be up for a)** to be intended for a particular purpose: *The house is up for sale.* | *the topic up for discussion at the meeting* **b)** SPOKEN to be interested in something, or feeling well enough to do something: *Is anybody up for a game of tennis?* **6 be up and running** if a machine or process is up and running, it is working correctly: *The equipment should be up and running in about three weeks.* **7 be up before** to be judged in a court of law: *He was up before the grand jury on charges of fraud.*

---

SPOKEN PHRASES
**8 What's up?** used in order to greet someone, or to ask if there is a problem: *Hey Mark! What's up?* | *What's up? Are you OK?* **9 be up** if someone is up, s/he is

happy: *Dario seemed really up for the first time today.* **10 be up on (sth)** to know a lot about something: *I'm not really up on the way things work here.*

**up³** *prep* **1** toward or in a higher place: *Walk up the hill and turn right.* **2** toward or at the top or far end of something: *The cat's up a tree.* | *I'm going up the road to see Jill.* **3** toward the place where a river starts: *sailing up the river*

**up⁴** *n* **ups and downs** the good things and bad things that happen in a particular situation: *the ups and downs of marriage*

**up⁵** *v* INFORMAL **1** **-pped, -pping** [T] to increase the amount or level of something: *They've upped Don's salary by $2500!* **2** **up and...** to suddenly start to do something different or surprising: *...and then Mike up and left, without telling anybody.*

**up-and-com·ing** /ˌ. . '..◄/ *adj* likely to be successful and popular: *an up-and-coming actor*

**up·beat** /ˌʌp'bit◄/ *adj* cheerful and making you feel that good things will happen: *a movie with an upbeat ending*

**up·bring·ing** /'ʌpˌbrɪŋɪŋ/ *n* [singular] the care and training that parents give their children when they are growing up: *a strict upbringing*

**up·chuck** /'ʌp-tʃʌk/ *v* [I] INFORMAL ⇨ VOMIT¹

**up·com·ing** /'ʌpˌkʌmɪŋ/ *adj* happening soon: *the upcoming elections*

**up·date¹** /'ʌpdeɪt, ˌʌp'deɪt/ *v* [T] **1** to add the most recent information to something: *The files need to be updated.* **2** to make something more modern in the way it looks or operates

**update²** *n* the most recent news about something: *an update on the earthquake*

**up·end** /ʌp'ɛnd/ *v* [T] to turn something over so that it is standing upside down

**up·front** /ʌp'frʌnt/ *adj* **1** **be upfront** to talk or behave in a direct and honest way: *Jill's always been upfront with him.* **2** an upfront payment, agreement etc. is done before anything else −**upfront** *adv*: *We'll need $300 upfront.*

**up·grade** /'ʌpgreɪd, ʌp'greɪd/ *v* [T] to improve something, or to exchange something for something better: *I was upgraded to first class on the flight back.* | *We need to upgrade our computer.* −**upgrade** *n*

**up·heav·al** /ʌp'hivəl, 'ʌpˌhivəl/ *n* [C,U] a very big change that often causes problems: *political upheaval in the former Soviet Union*

**up·hill** /ˌʌp'hɪl◄/ *adj, adv* **1** toward the top of a hill: *an uphill climb* −opposite DOWNHILL¹ **2** an uphill battle, job etc. is very difficult and needs a lot of effort

**up·hold** /ʌp'hoʊld/ *v* [T] **1** to defend or support a law, system, or principle so that it is not made weaker: *They want to uphold family values.* **2** if a court upholds a decision that is

made by another court, it states that the decision was correct

**up·hol·ster** /ə'poʊlstɚ, ʌp'hoʊl-/ *v* [T] to cover a chair or SOFA with material −**upholstered** *adj*

**up·hol·ster·y** /ə'poʊlstəri/ *n* [U] material that is used for covering chairs and SOFAs, or the process of doing this

**up·keep** /'ʌpkip/ *n* [U] the care that is needed to keep something in good condition: *the upkeep of a big house*

**up·lift·ing** /ˌʌp'lɪftɪŋ◄/ *adj* making you feel more cheerful: *uplifting music*

**up·on** /ə'pɑn, ə'pɔn/ *prep* FORMAL on: *We are completely dependent upon your help.* | *sitting upon the throne*

**up·per¹** /'ʌpɚ/ *adj* **1** in a higher position than something else: *the upper jaw* −opposite LOWER¹ **2** near or at the top of something: *the upper floors of the building* −opposite LOWER¹ **3** more important or higher in rank than other parts in an organization: *upper management* **4** **have/gain the upper hand** to have more power than someone else, so that you are able to control a situation: *Rebels have gained the upper hand in some areas.* **5** **the upper limit** the highest limit: *sounds that are at the upper limit of our hearing ability*

**upper²** *n* the top part of a shoe

**up·per·case** /ˌ.. '.◄/ *n* [U] letters written in their large form, such as A, B, C etc. −compare CAPITAL¹, LOWERCASE

**upper class** /ˌ.. '.◄/ *n* **the upper class** the group of people who belong to the highest social class −see usage note at CLASS¹

**up·per·most** /'ʌpɚˌmoʊst/ *adj* **1** most important: *Environmental concerns should be uppermost.* | *It's your safety that's uppermost in my mind.* (=I think is most important) **2** highest: *the uppermost branches of the tree*

**up·pi·ty** /'ʌpəti/ *adj* SPOKEN thinking that you are better or more important than other people in your social class

**up·right¹** /'ʌp-raɪt/ *adj* **1** standing straight up **2** always behaving in an honest way: *upright citizens*

**upright²** *adv* **1** standing or sitting with your back straight: *He sat bolt upright* (=completely upright), *terrified by the noise.* **2** made to stand straight up

**up·ris·ing** /'ʌpˌraɪzɪŋ/ *n* an occasion when a group of people use violence to try to change the rules, laws etc. in an institution or country

**up·riv·er** /ʌp'rɪvɚ/ *adv* in the opposite direction from the way the water is flowing in a river

**up·roar** /'ʌp-rɔr/ *n* [singular, U] a lot of noise or angry protest about something: *His accusations against the country's Prime Minister caused an uproar in the foreign press.*

**up·root** /ˌʌp'rut/ *v* [T] **1** to pull a plant and its roots out of the ground **2** to make someone leave his/her home for a new place, especially when this is difficult: *Steven's new job will mean uprooting the family.*

**up·scale** /ˌʌp'skeɪl◂/ *adj* relating to people from a high social class who have a lot of money: *upscale neighborhoods*

**up·set¹** /ˌʌp'sɛt◂/ *adj* **1** unhappy and worried because something unpleasant has happened: *They're still upset about/over losing the money.* | *Steve's upset that they forgot to make reservations.* **2** an upset stomach/tummy an illness that has an effect on the stomach and makes you sick

**up·set²** /ʌp'sɛt/ *v* upset, upset, upsetting **1** [T] to make someone feel unhappy or worried: *Kopp's comments upset many of his listeners.* **2** upset sb's stomach to make someone feel sick **3** [T] to change a plan or situation in a way that causes problems: *The ecological balance of the area has been upset.*

**up·set³** /'ʌpsɛt/ *n* **1** an occasion when a person or team surprisingly beats a stronger opponent in a competition **2** an unexpected problem or difficulty: *upsets in sales and marketing*

**up·set·ting** /ʌp'sɛtɪŋ/ *adj* making you feel upset: *I've just heard some very upsetting news.*

**up·shot** /'ʌpʃɑt/ *n* the upshot (of) the final result of a situation: *The upshot is that she's moving to another department.*

**up·side** /'ʌpsaɪd/ *n* the upside the positive part of a situation: *The upside is that the problem is simple to prevent.* –opposite DOWN-SIDE

**up·side down** /ˌʌpsaɪd 'daʊn/ *adj, adv* **1** with the top at the bottom and the bottom at the top: *Isn't that picture upside down?* **2** disorganized and messy: *We turned the house upside down looking for my keys.*

**up·stage** /ˌʌp'steɪdʒ/ *v* [T] to do something that takes people's attention away from someone else who is more important

**up·stairs¹** /ˌʌp'stɛrz◂/ *adv* on or going toward a higher floor of a building, especially a house: *Her office is upstairs on your right.* –opposite DOWN-STAIRS

upstairs

**upstairs²** *adj* **1** on the upper floor of a building: *the upstairs bathroom* **2** the upstairs the rooms in the upper floors of a house: *The upstairs has one very large bathroom.*

**up·start** /'ʌpstɑrt/ *n* someone who is new in his/her job and behaves as if s/he is more important than s/he is

**up·state** /ˌʌp'steɪt◂/ *adj, adv* in or toward the northern part of a state: *She lives upstate, near the lake.* –compare DOWNSTATE

**up·stream** /ˌʌp'strim/ *adv* along a river, in the opposite direction from the way the water is flowing –**upstream** /'. ./ *adj* –compare DOWN-STREAM

**up·surge** /'ʌpsɚdʒ/ *n* a sudden increase: *a recent upsurge in car sales*

**up·swing** /'ʌpswɪŋ/ *n* an improvement or increase in the level of something: *an upswing in the economy*

**up·take** /'ʌpteɪk/ *n* be slow/quick on the uptake INFORMAL to be slow or fast at learning or understanding things

**up·tight** /ˌʌp'taɪt◂/ *adj* INFORMAL behaving in an annoyed way because you are feeling nervous and worried

**up-to-date** /ˌ. . '.◂/ *adj* relating to or having the most recent knowledge, information etc.: *Our computer system is not up-to-date.* | *Doctors must keep up-to-date with medical research.* –see usage note at NEW

**up·town** /ˌʌp'taʊn/ *adv* to or in the northern area of a city or town, or the area where the richer people live: *The Parkers live uptown.* –**uptown** /'. ./ *adj* –compare DOWNTOWN²

**up·turn** /'ʌptɚn/ *n* a time when business activity is increased and conditions improve: *an upturn in oil production* –compare DOWNTURN

**up·turned** /'ʌptɚnd, ˌʌp'tɚnd/ *adj* **1** turning upward at the end: *an upturned nose* **2** turned upside down: *upturned boxes*

**up·ward¹** /'ʌpwɚd/ *adj* **1** moving or pointing toward a higher position: *an upward movement of the hand* **2** increasing to a higher level: *the upward trend in house prices*

**upward²**, **upwards** *adv* **1** from a lower place or position to a higher one: *Billy pointed upward at the clouds.* **2** increasing to a higher level: *Salaries have been moving upwards.* –opposite DOWNWARD¹

**u·ra·ni·um** /yʊ'reɪniəm/ *n* [U] a heavy RADIO-ACTIVE white metal that is used in producing nuclear energy and weapons

**U·ra·nus** /yʊ'reɪnəs, 'yʊrənəs/ *n* [singular] the seventh PLANET from the sun

**ur·ban** /'ɚbən/ *adj* relating to a town or city: *the urban population* –compare RURAL

**ur·bane** /ɚ'beɪn/ *adj* behaving in a relaxed and confident way in social situations: *Jerome's urbane charm*

**urban re·new·al** /ˌ.. .'../ *n* [U] the process of improving poor city areas by building new houses, stores etc.

**urban sprawl** /ˌ.. './ *n* [U] DISAPPROVING the spread of city buildings and houses into areas that were outside the city

**ur·chin** /'ɚtʃɪn/ *n* OLD-FASHIONED a small dirty child

**urge¹** /ɚdʒ/ *v* [T] **1** to strongly advise someone to do something: *Cal's family urged him to find another job.* | *I urge that you consider the problem carefully.* **2** FORMAL to strongly

U

suggest that something should be done: *Banks urged caution in raising interest rates.*

**urge** sb ↔ **on** *phr v* [T] to encourage a person or animal to work harder, go faster etc.: *Lewis was urged on by the crowd.*

**urge**² *n* a strong wish or need: *sexual urges* | *I felt a sudden urge to hit him.*

**ur·gent** /'ɔˈdʒənt/ *adj* very important and needing to be dealt with immediately: *an urgent message* | *She's in urgent need of medical attention.* −**urgency** /'ɔˈdʒənsi/ *n* [U]

**u·ri·nate** /'yʊrəˌneɪt/ *v* [I] TECHNICAL to make URINE flow out of your body

**u·rine** /'yʊrɪn/ *n* [U] the liquid waste that comes out of your body when you go to the toilet

**urn** /ɔˈn/ *n* **1** a container that holds and pours a large amount of coffee or tea **2** a decorated container, especially one that is used for holding the ASHes of a dead body

**US** *n* the abbreviation of the United States

**us** /əs; *strong* ʌs/ *pron* the object form of "we": *He walked by, but he didn't see us.* −see usage note at ME

**us·age** /'yusɪdʒ/ *n* **1** [C,U] the way that words are used in a language: *a book on modern English usage* **2** [U] the way in which something is used, or the amount of it that is used: *plans to cut water usage*

**use**¹ /yuz/ *v* [T] **1** if you use a tool, method, service etc., you do something with it: *Use a food processor to grate the vegetables.* | *Can I use your phone?* | *Most people use credit cards for shopping.* **2** to take something from a supply so that there is less left: *These light bulbs use less electricity.* | *Our car's using too much oil.* **3** to make someone do something for you in a way that is not fair or honest: *They used her to smuggle drugs into the country.* **4** to say or write a particular word or phrase: *I try not to use bad language around the kids.* **5** to regularly take illegal drugs

**use** sth ↔ **up** *phr v* [T] to use all of something: *Who used up the toothpaste?*

**use**² /yus/ *n*
**1** ▶ACT OF USING STH◄ [singular, U] the act of using something or the amount that is used: *We've saved a lot of money through the use of energy-saving technology.*
**2** ▶WAY STH IS USED◄ a way in which something can be used, or the purpose for which it can be used: *educational uses for computers*
**3** ▶RIGHT/ABILITY TO USE STH◄ the right or ability to use something: *Joe's given me the use of his office.* | *Mr. Wayne doesn't have the use of his legs.*
**4** **be any use/be no use** to be useful, or to not be useful: *Was that map any use?* | *The information is of no use to us.*
**5** **make use of** to get an advantage from something: *We need to make use of the people we*

have available before we hire new ones. | *I have to make better use of my time.* (=get more advantage from it)
**6** **it's no use doing sth** SPOKEN used in order to tell someone not to do something because it will have no effect: *It's no use arguing with Kathy; she won't listen.*
**7** **put sth to (good) use** to use knowledge, skills etc. for a particular purpose: *a chance to put your medical training to good use*
**8** **it's no use!** SPOKEN used in order to say that you are going to stop doing something because you do not think it will be successful: *It's no use! I can't fix this.*
**9** **have no/little use for sb/sth** to not like or respect someone or something: *Meisner has little use for rules about acting.*
**10** **in use** being used: *The computer room's in use all morning.*
**11** **for the use of** for a particular person or group to use: *The gym is for the use of employees only.*
**12** ▶WORDS◄ one of the meanings of a word, or the way that a particular word is used

**used**¹ /yust/ *adj* **be used to sth/be used to doing sth** be familiar with something so that it no longer seems surprising, difficult etc.: *Kathy is used to getting up early?* | *He hasn't gotten used to the weather here yet.* −opposite **unused to** (UNUSED²)

**used**² /yuzd/ *adj* **used cars/clothes etc.** cars, clothes etc. that have already had an owner; SECONDHAND

**used to** /'yustə; *final or before a vowel* 'yustu/ *modal verb* if something used to happen, it happened often or regularly in the past but does not happen now: *We used to go to the movies every week.* | *"Didn't you use to smoke?" "Yes, but I quit."* −see study note on page 458

**USAGE NOTE** **used to, be used to,** and **get used to**

Use **used to** to talk about something that someone did regularly in the past: *I used to play tennis twice a week, but I don't have time now.* Use **be used to** and **get used to** to talk about being or becoming more comfortable with a situation or activity, so that it does not seem strange or difficult: *Are you used to the cold winters yet?* | *I can't get used to living in a big city.*

**use·ful** /'yusfəl/ *adj* helping you to do or to get what you want: *useful information* | *a useful book for travelers* −**usefully** *adv* −**usefulness** *n* [U]

**use·less** /'yuslɪs/ *adj* not useful: *These scissors are completely/totally useless.* | *It's useless to complain.*

**us·er** /'yuzɔˈ/ *n* someone who uses a product, service etc.: *computer users*

**us·er-friend·ly** /ˌ.. ˈ..◂/ *adj* well designed and easy to use

**ush·er**[1] /ˈʌʃɚ/ *n* someone who shows people to their seats in a theater, wedding etc.

**usher**[2] *v* [T] to help someone to get from one place to another by showing him/her the way: *The secretary* **ushered** *us* **into** *the office.*

**u·su·al** /ˈyuʒuəl, -ʒəl/ *adj* **1** the same as what happens most of the time or in most situations: *Let's meet at the usual place.* | *It's* **colder/warmer than usual** *for March.* **?** **as usual** in the way that happens or exists most of the time: *They were late, as usual.*

**u·su·al·ly** /ˈyuʒuəli, -ʒəli/ *adv* used when describing what happens on most occasions or in most situations: *We usually go out for dinner on Saturday.*

**u·surp** /yuˈsɚp/ *v* [T] FORMAL to take someone else's power, position, job etc.

**UT** the written abbreviation of Utah

**u·ten·sil** /yuˈtɛnsəl/ *n* a tool or object with a particular use: *kitchen utensils*

**u·ter·us** /ˈyutərəs/ *n* TECHNICAL the organ in a woman or female MAMMAL where babies develop

**u·til·i·ty** /yuˈtɪləti/ *n* a service such as gas or electricity that is provided for people to use: *Does the rent include utilities?*

**u·til·ize** /ˈyutlˌaɪz/ *v* [T] FORMAL to use something effectively: *You're not utilizing your skills in your job.* **–utilization** /ˌyutl-əˈzeɪʃən/ *n* [U]

**ut·most**[1] /ˈʌtˌmoʊst/ *adj* used in order to emphasize how important, strong, or serious something is: *This is a matter of the utmost importance.* | *He was treated with the utmost care and respect.*

**utmost**[2] *n* [singular] **1 to the utmost** to the highest limit, extent, degree etc. possible: *The piece challenges singers to the utmost.* **2 do your utmost** to try as hard as you can in order to achieve something: *We've done our utmost to make them feel welcome.*

**u·to·pi·a** /yuˈtoupiə/ *n* [C,U] an imaginary perfect world where everyone is happy

**ut·ter**[1] /ˈʌtɚ/ *adj* complete or extreme: *We watched in utter amazement.* **–utterly** *adv*

**utter**[2] *v* [T] FORMAL to say something **–utterance** *n*

**U-turn** /ˈyu tɚn/ *n* a turn that you make in a vehicle, so that you go back in the direction you came from: *Shea* **made a U-turn** *on Oakland Road.*

# V

**V, v** /vi/ **1** the twenty-second letter of the English alphabet **2** the number 5 in the system of ROMAN NUMERALS

**V** *n* something that has a shape like the letter V; *a dress with a V neck*

**VA** the written abbreviation of Virginia

**va·can·cy** /ˈveɪkənsi/ *n* **1** a room or building that is not being used and is available for someone to stay in: *a motel sign saying "no vacancies"* **2** a job that is available for someone to start doing: *Are there any* **vacancies for** *cooks?*

**va·cant** /ˈveɪkənt/ *adj* **1** empty and available for someone to use: *vacant apartments* **2** a vacant job is available for someone to start doing

**va·cate** /ˈveɪkeɪt/ *v* [T] FORMAL to leave a seat, room etc. so that someone else can use it: *Guests must vacate their rooms by noon.*

**va·ca·tion** /veɪˈkeɪʃən, və-/ *n* a time that is spent not working or not at school: *They're* **on vacation** *for the next two weeks.* | *the kids'* **summer vacation** | *We'd like to* **take a vacation** *in the Virgin Islands.* **–vacation** *v* [I]

### USAGE NOTE vacation

We use **vacation** to talk about time you spend away from school or work: *Where are you* **going on vacation** *this summer?* Use **break** to talk about a time that you stop working in order to rest, or about a short vacation from school: *You've been studying for hours; why don't you take a break?* | *We're going skiing during spring break.* Use **holiday** to talk about a day when no one officially has to go to work or school: *Christmas is my favorite holiday.* Use **leave** to talking about time for when you are allowed not to work for a special reason: *Kate's on maternity leave for three months.*

**vac·ci·nate** /ˈvæksəˌneɪt/ *v* [T] to protect someone from a disease by giving him/her a VACCINE: *Have you been* **vaccinated against** *measles?* **–vaccination** /ˌvæksəˈneɪʃən/ *n* [U]

**vac·cine** /vækˈsin/ *n* [C,U] a substance that contains a weak form of the VIRUS that causes a disease and is used for protecting people from that disease: *polio vaccine*

**vac·il·late** /ˈvæsəˌleɪt/ *v* [I] FORMAL to continue to change your opinions, ideas etc. because you cannot decide between two choices

**vac·uum**[1] /'vækyum/ n **1** ⇨ VACUUM CLEANER **2** a space that is completely empty of all gas **3** [singular] a situation in which someone or something is missing or lacking: *Her husband's death left a vacuum in her life.* **4** in a vacuum if something happens in a vacuum, it happens without being influenced by anything: *You can't make decisions in a vacuum.*

**vacuum**[2] v [I,T] to clean a place using a VACUUM CLEANER

**vacuum clean·er** /'.. ,../ n a machine that cleans floors by sucking up the dirt from them

**vacuum-packed** /'.. ,./ adj vacuum-packed food is packed in a container from which the air is removed, in order to keep the food fresh

**va·gi·na** /və'dʒaɪnə/ n the passage from a woman's outer sexual organs to her UTERUS –**vaginal** /'vædʒənl/ adj

**va·grant** /'veɪgrənt/ n FORMAL someone who has no home or work

**vague** /veɪg/ adj **1** unclear because someone does not give enough details: *She's been vague about her plans for the summer.* **2** have a vague idea/feeling etc. to think that something might be true or that you remember something, although you cannot be sure

**vague·ly** /'veɪgli/ adv **1** slightly: *She looked vaguely familiar.* **2** in a way that shows you are not thinking about what you are doing: *He smiled vaguely.*

**vain** /veɪn/ adj **1** full of pride in yourself, your appearance, and your abilities **2** in vain without success: *I tried in vain to convince Paul to come.* **3** vain attempt/hope etc. an attempt, hope etc. that is not successful –**vainly** adv

**val·en·tine** /'vælən,taɪn/ n **1** a card given on Valentine's Day **2** a name for someone you love on VALENTINE'S DAY: *Will you be my valentine?*

**Valentine's Day** /'... ,./ n a holiday in some countries when people give special cards, candy, or flowers to people they love

**val·et** /væ'leɪ, 'væleɪ/ n **1** someone who parks your car for you at a hotel or restaurant **2** a male servant who takes care of a man's clothes, serves his meals etc.

**val·iant** /'vælyənt/ adj FORMAL very brave, especially in a difficult situation: *a valiant rescue attempt*

**val·id** /'vælɪd/ adj **1** a valid ticket, document, or agreement can be used legally or is officially acceptable: *a valid passport* **2** based on strong reasons or facts: *There is no valid data on the drug's safety.* –opposite INVALID[1]

**val·i·date** /'vælə,deɪt/ v [T] FORMAL to prove that something is true or correct, or to make a document or agreement officially and legally acceptable –opposite INVALIDATE

**va·lid·i·ty** /və'lɪdəti/ n [U] the state of being real, true, or based on facts: *Scientists are questioning the validity of the experiment.*

**val·ley** /'væli/ n an area of lower land between two lines of hills or mountains

**val·or** /'vælɚ/ n [U] LITERARY great courage, especially in war

**val·u·a·ble** /'vælyəbəl, -yuəbəl/ adj **1** worth a lot of money: *a valuable ring* **2** valuable help, advice etc. is very useful –compare INVALUABLE

**val·u·a·bles** /'vælyəbəlz/ n [plural] things that you own that are worth a lot of money, such as jewelry, cameras etc.

**val·ue**[1] /'vælyu/ n [U] **1** [C,U] the amount of money that something is worth: *Did the thieves take anything of value?* (=worth a lot of money) | *drugs with a street value of $50,000* (=the value of drugs when they are sold illegally) **2** [U] the importance or usefulness of something: *His research was of great value to doctors working with this disease.* | *These earrings have sentimental value.* (=are important to you because they were a gift, remind you of someone etc.)

**value**[2] v [T] **1** to think that something is important to you: *I value your friendship.* **2** to say how much something is worth: *a painting valued at $5 million*

**val·ues** /'vælyuz/ n [plural] your principles about what is right and wrong, or your ideas about what is important: *traditional family values*

**valve** /vælv/ n a part of a tube or pipe that opens and closes like a door in order to control the flow of liquid, gas, air etc. passing through

**vam·pire** /'væmpaɪɚ/ n an imaginary creature that looks like a person and sucks people's blood by biting their necks

**van** /væn/ n **1** a TRUCK with an enclosed back, used for carrying goods: *a moving van* **2** a large box-like car –see picture on page 469

**van·dal** /'vændl/ n someone who VANDALIZES public property

**van·dal·ism** /'vændl,ɪzəm/ n [U] the crime of deliberately damaging things, especially public property

**van·dal·ize** /'vændl,aɪz/ v [T] to damage or destroy things deliberately, especially public property

**van·guard** /'vængɑrd/ n in the vanguard in the most advanced position of development: *a group in the vanguard of political reform*

**va·nil·la** /və'nɪlə/ n [U] a sweet-smelling liquid from the bean of a plant, that is added to particular foods: *vanilla ice cream*

**van·ish** /'vænɪʃ/ v [I] to disappear suddenly, especially in a way that cannot be easily explained: *When I looked again, he'd vanished.* | *Police say the suspect seems to have*

V

*vanished without a trace*. (=disappeared so that no sign remains) −**vanishing** *adj*

**van·i·ty** /'vænəti/ *n* [U] the quality of being too proud of yourself

**van·quish** /'væŋkwɪʃ/ *v* [T] LITERARY to defeat someone or something completely

**van·tage point** /'væntɪdʒ ˌpɔɪnt/ *n* **1** a good position from which you can see something **2** a way of thinking about things that comes from your own situation: *Kopcek's ideas come from his vantage point as an immigrant*.

**va·por** /'veɪpɚ/ *n* [C,U] many small drops of liquid that float in the air: *water vapor*

**va·por·ize** /'veɪpəˌraɪz/ *v* [I,T] to be changed into a VAPOR, or change a liquid into a vapor

**var·i·a·ble¹** /'vɛriəbəl, 'vær-/ *adj* **1** likely to change often: *the variable nature of the weather* **2** sometimes good and sometimes bad: *The group's performance has been variable lately*.

**variable²** *n* something that may be different in different situations: *cultural variables*

**var·i·ance** /'vɛriəns, 'vær-/ *n* [U] FORMAL **be at variance with** if two people or things are at variance with each other, they do not agree or are very different

**var·i·ant** /'vɛriənt, 'vær-/ *n* something that is slightly different from the usual form of something: *a spelling variant* −**variant** *adj*

**var·i·a·tion** /ˌvɛri'eɪʃən, ˌvær-/ *n* [C,U] a difference or change from the usual amount or form of something: *variations in prices from store to store*

**var·i·cose veins** /ˌværəkoʊs 'veɪnz/ *n* [plural] a medical condition in which the VEINS in your leg become swollen and painful

**var·ied** /'vɛrid, 'vær-/ *adj* consisting of or including many different types of things or people: *They make products as varied as ash trays and toys*.

**va·ri·e·ty** /və'raɪəti/ *n* **1** [U] a lot of things of the same type that are different from each other in some way: *The data comes from a variety of sources.* | *The variety that cable TV provides makes it very popular.* **2** [U] the differences within a group, set of actions etc. that make it interesting: *There isn't much she could do to add variety to her work.* **3** a type of something that is different from others in the same group: *a new variety of rose* | *To preserve the flavor of the cookies, store each variety in a separate container*.

**variety show** /.'... ˌ./ *n* a television or radio program or a play that consists of many different performances, especially funny ones

**var·i·ous** /'vɛriəs, 'vær-/ *adj* several different: *This coat comes in various colors*.

**var·i·ous·ly** /'vɛriəsli, 'vær-/ *adv* in many different ways: *He's been variously called a genius and a madman*.

**var·nish¹** /'vɑrnɪʃ/ *n* [C,U] a clear liquid that is painted onto things that are made of wood, to protect them and give them a shiny surface

**varnish²** *v* [T] to paint something with VARNISH

**var·si·ty** /'vɑrsəti/ *n* [C,U] the main team that represents a university, college, or school in sports: *the varsity basketball team*

**var·y** /'vɛri, 'væri/ *v* **1** [I] if several things of the same type vary, they are all different from each other: *Teaching methods vary greatly/enormously from school to school.* | *Wines that vary in price/quality* **2** [I] to change often: *His moods seem to vary a lot.* **3** [T] to regularly change what you do or the way that you do it: *You need to vary your diet and get more exercise*.

**var·y·ing** /'vɛriɪŋ, 'væriɪŋ/ *adj* changing or different: *Races are over varying distances*.

**vase** /veɪs, veɪz, vɑz/ *n* a container used for decoration or to put flowers in

**va·sec·to·my** /və'sɛktəmi/ *n* [C,U] a medical operation to cut the small tube through which a man's SPERM passes, so that he is unable to produce children −compare HYSTERECTOMY

**vast** /væst/ *adj* **1** extremely large: *vast deserts* **2** **the vast majority of** almost all of a group of people or things

**vast·ly** /'væstli/ *adv* very greatly: *vastly improved educational programs*

**vat** /væt/ *n* a very large container for keeping liquids in

**vault¹** /vɔlt/ *n* **1** a room with thick walls and a strong door, where money, jewels etc. are kept safely **2** a room where people from the same family are buried **3** a jump over something

**vault², vault over** *v* [T] to jump over something in one movement, using your hands or a pole to help you: *He vaulted over the fence and ran off*.

**V chip** /'vi tʃɪp/ *n* a CHIP in a television that allows parents to prevent their children from watching programs that are violent or have sex in them

**VCR** *n* video cassette recorder; a machine that is used for recording television shows or watching VIDEOTAPES

**VD** *n* [U] OLD-FASHIONED venereal disease; a disease that is passed from one person to another during sex −see also STD

**VDU** *n* visual display unit; a machine like a television that shows the information from a computer

**-'ve** /v, əv/ the short form of "have": *I've/ We've finished*.

**veal** /vil/ *n* [U] the meat from a CALF (=young cow) −see usage note at MEAT

**veer** /vɪr/ *v* [I] to change direction suddenly: *The car veered sharply to the left*.

**veg** /vɛdʒ/, **veg out** *v* [I] INFORMAL to relax and not do anything important: *I just want to veg out in front of the TV*.

**veg·e·ta·ble** /'vɛdʒtəbəl/ *n* **1** a plant such as corn or potatoes, that is grown in order to be eaten **2** INFORMAL someone who cannot think or move because his/her brain has been damaged

**veg·e·tar·i·an** /ˌvɛdʒə'tɛriən/ *n* someone who does not eat meat or fish –**vegetarian** *adj*

**veg·e·ta·tion** /ˌvɛdʒə'teɪʃən/ *n* [U] plants in general, especially all the plants in one particular area: *a meadow with thick vegetation*

**veg·gies** /'vɛdʒiz/ *n* [plural] INFORMAL vegetables –**veggie** *adj*

**ve·he·ment** /'viəmənt/ *adj* showing very strong feelings or opinions: *vehement complaints* –**vehemently** *adv*

**ve·hi·cle** /'viːkəl/ *n* FORMAL **1** a thing such as a car, bus etc. that is used for carrying people or things from one place to another **2 a vehicle for (doing) sth** something that you use as a way of spreading your ideas, opinions, etc. –**vehicular** /vi'hɪkyələ/ *adj*

**veil**[1] /veɪl/ *n* **1** a thin piece of material that women wear to cover their faces: *a bridal veil* **2 a veil of secrecy/silence etc.** something that stops you knowing the full truth about a situation: *A veil of mystery surrounded Gomez's death.*

**veil**[2] *v* [T] **1 be veiled in mystery/secrecy** if something is veiled in mystery, secrecy etc., very little is known about it **2** to cover something with a VEIL

**veiled** /veɪld/ *adj* **veiled criticism/threats etc.** criticisms, threats etc. that are not said directly

**vein** /veɪn/ *n* **1** one of the tubes through which blood flows to your heart from other parts of your body –compare ARTERY **2** one of the thin lines on a leaf or on the wing of an insect **3** a thin layer of a valuable metal or mineral in rock: *a rich vein of gold* **4** a particular style of speaking or writing about something: *Her speech continued in a similar/humorous vein.*

**Vel·cro** /'vɛlkroʊ/ *n* [U] TRADEMARK a material used for fastening shoes, clothes etc., made from two special pieces of cloth that stick to each other

**ve·loc·i·ty** /və'lɑsəti/ *n* [C,U] TECHNICAL the speed at which something moves in a particular direction: *the velocity of light*

**ve·lour** /və'lʊr/ *n* [U] heavy cloth that has a soft surface

**vel·vet** /'vɛlvɪt/ *n* [U] cloth with a soft surface on one side

**vel·vet·y** /'vɛlvɪti/ *adj* looking, feeling, tasting, or sounding smooth and soft: *a velvety voice*

**ven·det·ta** /vɛn'dɛtə/ *n* a quarrel in which two families or groups try to harm each other over a long period of time

**vend·ing ma·chine** /'vɛndɪŋ məˌʃin/ *n* a machine that you can get cigarettes, candy, drinks etc. from by putting in money

**ven·dor** /'vɛndə/ *n* **1** someone who sells things, especially in the street: *That street vendor sells great hot dogs.* **2** LAW someone who is selling something such as a house or land

**ve·neer** /və'nɪr/ *n* [C,U] **1** a thin layer of good quality wood that covers the outside of a piece of furniture that is made of a cheaper material: *oak veneer* **2 a veneer of** FORMAL behavior that hides someone's real character or feelings: *a veneer of politeness*

**ven·er·a·ble** /'vɛnərəbəl/ *adj* FORMAL very old and respected because of age, experience, historical importance etc.: *a venerable gentleman*

**ven·er·ate** /'vɛnəˌreɪt/ *v* [T] FORMAL to treat someone or something with great respect, especially because she, he, or it is old: *The Chinese venerate their ancestors.*

**ve·ne·re·al dis·ease** /vəˌnɪriəl dɪ'ziz/ *n* [C,U] ⇨ VD

**Ve·ne·tian blind** /vəˌniʃən 'blaɪnd/ *n* a set of long flat BARs used for covering a window, that can be raised or lowered to let in light

**venge·ance** /'vɛndʒəns/ *n* **1** something violent or harmful that you do to someone in order to punish him/her for hurting you: *a desire for vengeance* **2 with a vengeance** much more than is expected or normal: *The music started up again with a vengeance.* –see also REVENGE, AVENGE

**venge·ful** /'vɛndʒfəl/ *adj* LITERARY very eager to punish someone who has hurt you

**ven·i·son** /'vɛnəsən/ *n* [U] the meat of a DEER

**ven·om** /'vɛnəm/ *n* [U] **1** a liquid poison that some snakes, insects etc. produce **2** extreme anger or hatred: *a speech full of venom*

**vent**[1] /vɛnt/ *n* **1** a hole or pipe through which gases, smoke, or liquid can enter or go out: *an air vent* **2 give vent to** FORMAL to do something to express a strong feeling

**vent**[2] *v* [T] to do something to express your feelings, often in a way that is unfair: *Jay vented his anger on his family.*

**ven·ti·late** /'vɛntlˌeɪt/ *v* [T] to let fresh air into a room, building etc. –**ventilated** *adj* –**ventilation** /ˌvɛntl'eɪʃən/ *n* [U]

**ven·ti·la·tor** /'vɛntlˌeɪtə/ *n* ⇨ RESPIRATOR

**ven·tril·o·quism** /vɛn'trɪləˌkwɪzəm/ *n* [U] the art of speaking without moving your lips, so that the sound seems to come from somewhere else –**ventriloquist** *n*

**ven·ture**[1] /'vɛntʃə/ *n* **1** a new business activity that involves taking risks: *a new joint venture* (=an agreement between two companies to do something together) **2** a trip or attempt to do something that involves taking risks

**venture**[2] *v* FORMAL **1** [I] to risk going somewhere when it could be dangerous: *Several boats ventured out to sea, despite the weather.* **2** [T] to say something although you are afraid of how someone may react to it: *Sandy shyly* *ventured a question.* **3** [T] to take the risk of losing something: *He **ventured** his savings on a new business.*

**ven·ue** /ˈvɛnyu/ *n* a place such as a theater, CLUB, or STADIUM where people go for an arranged activity: *a popular jazz venue*

**Ve·nus** /ˈvinəs/ *n* [singular] a small PLANET, second from the sun

**ve·ran·da** /vəˈrændə/ *n* ⇨ PORCH

**verb** /vɚb/ *n* TECHNICAL in grammar, a word or group of words that is used in order to describe an action, experience, or state. In the sentence, "They arrived late," "arrived" is a verb –see study note on page 468

**ver·bal** /ˈvɚbəl/ *adj* **1** spoken: *a verbal agreement* **2** relating to words or using words: *verbal skill* –**verbally** *adv*

**ver·ba·tim** /vɚˈbeɪtɪm/ *adj, adv* repeating the actual words that were spoken or written: *a verbatim report of our conversation*

**ver·bose** /vɚˈboʊs/ *adj* FORMAL using or containing too many words

**ver·dict** /ˈvɚdɪkt/ *n* **1** an official decision that is made by a JURY in a court of law about whether someone is guilty: *Has the jury **reached a verdict**?* (=made a decision) **2** an official decision or opinion made by a person or group that has authority: *The panel will **give** their **verdict** tomorrow.*

**verge**[1] /vɚdʒ/ *n* **be on the verge of** to be about to do something: *Andy was on the verge of tears.*

**verge**[2] *v*

 **verge on/upon** sth *phr v* [T] to be very close to a harmful or extreme state: *Their behavior sometimes **verges on** insanity.*

**ver·i·fi·ca·tion** /ˌvɛrəfəˈkeɪʃən/ *n* [U] proof that something is real, true, legal, or allowed: *Please send us written verification that you are a student.*

**ver·i·fy** /ˈvɛrəˌfaɪ/ *v* [T] **1** to find out if a fact, statement etc. is correct or true; CHECK: *This will have to be **verified with** the head office.* | *The bank will have to **verify that** you have an account.* **2** to state that something is true: *The suspect's statement was verified by a witness.*

**ver·i·ta·ble** /ˈvɛrət̬əbəl/ *adj* FORMAL used in order to emphasize a comparison that you think is correct: *His paintings are a veritable feast of color.*

**ver·min** /ˈvɚmɪn/ *n* [plural] small animals, birds, or insects that destroy crops, spoil food, or cause other problems and that are difficult to control

**ver·nac·u·lar** /vɚˈnækyələ/ *n* the language or DIALECT that people in a country or area speak, especially when this is not the official language

**ver·sa·tile** /ˈvɚsət̬l/ *adj* **1** good at doing a lot of different things and able to learn new skills quickly and easily: *a versatile singer* **2** having many different uses: *Cotton is a versatile material.* –**versatility** /ˌvɚsəˈtɪlət̬i/ *n* [U]

**verse** /vɚs/ *n* **1** a set of lines that forms one part of a poem or song, and that usually has a pattern that is repeated in other parts **2** [U] words arranged in the form of poetry: *a book of verse* **3** a sentence or group of sentences in the Bible that have a number

**versed** /vɚst/ *adj* **be (well) versed in** to know a lot about a subject or to have a lot of skill in doing something: *Tso is well versed in Navajo laws.*

**ver·sion** /ˈvɚʒən/ *n* **1** a copy of something that has been changed slightly: *This is a **simpler/later version of** the camera.* **2** a description of an event that is given by one person: *The two newspapers gave different **versions of** the accident.* **3** a play, movie etc. that is slightly different from the book, piece of music etc. on which it is based: *a shorter **version of** the book* **4** a TRANSLATION of a piece of writing: *an English **version of** an Italian poem*

**ver·sus** /ˈvɚsəs/ *written abbreviation* **vs.** *prep* used in order to show that two people or teams are against each other in a game or a court case: *the Knicks versus the Lakers*

**ver·te·bra** /ˈvɚt̬əbrə/ *n, plural* **vertebrae** /-breɪ, -bri/ one of the small hollow bones down the center of your back

**ver·ti·cal** /ˈvɚt̬ɪkəl/ *adj* pointing straight up and down in a line and forming an angle of 90 degrees with the ground or with another line: *a vertical rock face* –**vertically** *adv* –compare HORIZONTAL

vertical
a vertical line
a diagonal line
a horizontal line

**ver·ti·go** /ˈvɚt̬ɪˌgoʊ/ *n* [U] a sick DIZZY feeling that is caused by looking down from a very high place

**verve** /vɚv/ *n* [U] the quality of being cheerful and exciting: *He plays the piano with great verve.*

**ve·ry**[1] /ˈvɛri/ *adv* **1** used in order to emphasize an adjective, adverb, or expression: *We saw a very good movie the other night.* | *They only stay at the very best hotels.* | *Sid gets embarrassed very easily.* | *We must understand the very real problems these people have.* **2 your very own** used in order to emphasize that something belongs to one particular person: *She's glad to have her very own room at last.* **3 not very a)** used before a quality to mean exactly the opposite of that quality: *She wasn't very happy about working overtime.* (=she was angry) **b)** only slightly: *"Was the game very exciting?" "Not very."* **4 very much** a lot: *It didn't cost very much.* ✗ DON'T SAY "It cost very much." SAY "It cost a lot." ✗ | *I enjoyed* *my visit very much.* ✗ DON'T SAY "I very much enjoyed my visit." ✗   —see usage notes at MUCH¹, TOO

---

**USAGE NOTE very**

Use **very** in order to emphasize an adjective or adverb: *It's very cold outside.* | *She drives very fast.* Do not use **very** with adjectives that already have a strong meaning, such as "starving," "huge," "terrible" etc.: *By the time I got home, I was exhausted.* ✗ DON'T SAY "very exhausted." ✗   Do not use **very** in phrases that begin with "in," "on," "at" etc: *He was in love with Alice.* ✗ DON'T SAY "very in love with." ✗

---

**very²** *adj* used in order to emphasize a noun: *Start again from the very beginning.* | *You come here* **this very minute!** (=now) | *The* **very thought** *of food makes me feel sick.* (=just thinking about it)

**very high fre·quen·cy** /ˌ.. '.../ *n* [U] ⇨ VHF

**ves·sel** /'vɛsəl/ *n* FORMAL a ship or large boat —see also BLOOD VESSEL

**vest** /vɛst/ *n* **1** a piece of clothing without SLEEVEs that has buttons down the front, worn over a shirt **2** a piece of special clothing without SLEEVEs that is worn to protect your body: *a bullet-proof vest*

**vest·ed in·terest** /ˌ.. '../ *n* a strong reason, especially a reason relating to money, for wanting something to happen: *The company* **has a vested interest** *in attracting foreign trade.*

**ves·ti·bule** /'vɛstəˌbyul/ *n* FORMAL a wide passage or small room inside the front door of a public building

**ves·tige** /'vɛstɪdʒ/ *n* FORMAL a small part or amount of something that remains when most of it no longer exists: *a policy that is one of* **the last vestiges** *of the Cold War*

**vet** /vɛt/ *n* **1** the short form of VETERINARIAN; someone who is trained to give medical care and treatment to sick animals **2** INFORMAL the short form of VETERAN

**vet·er·an** /'vɛtərən/ *n* **1** someone who has been a soldier, sailor etc. in a war **2** someone who has had a lot of experience in a particular activity: *a veteran traveler*

**vet·er·i·nar·i·an** /ˌvɛtərə'nɛriən, ˌvɛtrə-, ˌvɛtʰn-/ *n* ⇨ VET

**vet·er·i·nar·y** /'vɛtərəˌnɛri, 'vɛtrə-/ *adj* TECHNICAL relating to the medical care and treatment of sick animals

**ve·to¹** /'vitou/ *v* [T] **1** to officially refuse to allow something to happen, especially something that other people or organizations have agreed: *The UN Security Council vetoed the proposal.* **2** to refuse to accept a particular plan or suggestion: *Sally wanted to invite 20*

*friends to her birthday party, but I vetoed that idea.*

**veto²** *n* [C,U] a refusal to give official permission for something, or the right to refuse to give such permission: *the governor's* **veto of** *a bill*

**vex** /vɛks/ *v* [T] OLD-FASHIONED to make someone feel annoyed or worried: *vexing computer problems*

**VHF** *n* [U] TECHNICAL very high frequency; radio waves that move very quickly and produce good sound quality

**VHS** *n* [U] the type of VIDEOTAPE used by most people in the US

**vi·a** /'vaɪə, 'viə/ *prep* **1** traveling through a place on the way to another place: *We're flying to Denver via Chicago.* —see picture at DIRECT³ **2** using a particular person, machine etc. to send something: *I sent a message to Jan via Ryan.*

**vi·a·ble** /'vaɪəbəl/ *adj* able to succeed without any problems: *a viable plan/solution* | *Solar energy is a* **viable alternative** *to coal or gas.* | *The plan isn't* **economically/commercially viable**.

**vi·a·duct** /'vaɪəˌdʌkt/ *n* a long high bridge across a valley

**vi·al** /'vaɪəl/ *n* a small bottle, especially for liquid medicines

**vibe** /vaɪb/ *n* [C usually plural] INFORMAL the feelings that a particular person, group, or situation seems to produce and that you react to: *I'm getting* **good/bad vibes** *from this guy.*

**vi·brant** /'vaɪbrənt/ *adj* **1** exciting, full of energy, and interesting: *a vibrant personality* **2** a vibrant color is bright and strong

**vi·brate** /'vaɪbreɪt/ *v* [I,T] to shake continuously with small fast movements, or to make something do this: *The vocal chords vibrate as air passes over them.*

**vi·bra·tion** /vaɪ'breɪʃən/ *n* [C,U] a continuous slight shaking movement: *the vibrations of the plane's engine*

**vic·ar** /'vɪkɚ/ *n* a religious leader in the Church of England

**vi·car·i·ous** /vaɪ'kɛriəs/ *adj* experienced by watching or reading about someone else doing something: *Parents get* **vicarious pleasure/satisfaction** *from their children's success.*

**vice** /vaɪs/ *n* **1** [U] criminal activities that involve sex or drugs: *Police have smashed a* **vice ring** *in the city.* (=a group of criminals involved in vice) **2** a bad habit: *Smoking is my only vice.* **3** a bad or immoral quality in someone's character: *the vice of greed*

**vice pres·i·dent** /ˌ. '...◂/ *n* **1** the person who is next in rank to the president of a country **2** someone who is responsible for a particular part of a company: *the vice president of marketing*

**vice squad** /'. ./ *n* the part of the police force that deals with VICE

**vi·ce ver·sa** /ˌvaɪs ˈvɚsə, ˌvaɪsə-/ *adv* used when the opposite of a situation you have just described is also true: *Whatever Susie wants, James doesn't, and vice versa.*

**vi·cin·i·ty** /vəˈsɪnəti/ *n* **in the vicinity (of)** in the area around a particular place: *The car was found in the vicinity of the bus station.*

**vi·cious** /ˈvɪʃəs/ *adj* **1** violent and dangerous, and likely to hurt someone: *a vicious dog* **2** cruel and deliberately trying to upset someone: *Someone's spreading a vicious rumor about Stan.* **–viciously** *adv*

**vicious cir·cle** /ˌ.. ˈ../ *n* [singular] a situation in which one problem causes another problem that then causes the first problem again

**vic·tim** /ˈvɪktɪm/ *n* **1** someone who has been hurt or killed by someone or something or who has been affected by a bad situation: *Eleven of the fire's 25 victims have died.* | *an aid program for flood/earthquake victims* | *An 18-year-old boy is the latest **AIDS/polio victim**.* **2** something that is badly affected or destroyed by a situation or action: *Some small businesses have **fallen victim to** budget cuts.*

**vic·tim·ize** /ˈvɪktəˌmaɪz/ *v* [T] to deliberately treat someone unfairly: *Some workers said they'd been victimized because of their political activity.*

**vic·tor** /ˈvɪktɚ/ *n* FORMAL the winner of a battle or competition

**vic·to·ri·ous** /vɪkˈtɔriəs/ *adj* successful in a battle or competition

**vic·to·ry** /ˈvɪktəri/ *n* [C,U] the success you achieve by winning a battle or competition: *the Lakers' **victory over** the Celtics* | *The Democrats easily **won a victory** at the polls.* –opposite DEFEAT²

**vid·e·o¹** /ˈvɪdioʊ/ *n* **1** a copy of a movie or television program that is recorded on VIDEOTAPE: *Let's rent a video tonight.* **2** [C,U] a VIDEOTAPE: *Do we have a blank video?* | *The movie "Toy Story" is now **on video**.* **3** [U] the process of recording and showing television programs, movies, real events etc. using video equipment: *Many teachers now use video in the classroom.*

**video²** *adj* relating to recording and broadcasting sound and pictures on a VIDEOTAPE: *video equipment* –compare AUDIO

**video cas·sette re·cord·er** /ˌ... .ˈ. .ˌ../ *n* ⇨ VCR

**vid·e·o·disk** /ˈvɪdioʊˌdɪsk/ *n* a round flat piece of plastic from which movies can be played in the same way as from a VIDEOTAPE

**video game** /ˈ... ˌ./ *n* a game in which you move images on a screen by pressing electronic controls

**vid·e·o·tape¹** /ˈvɪdioʊˌteɪp/ *n* a long narrow band of MAGNETIC material in a plastic container, on which movies, television programs etc. can be recorded

**videotape²** *v* [T] to record something on a VIDEOTAPE: *Detectives videotaped the interview with the suspect.*

**vie** /vaɪ/ *v* **vied, vied, vying** [I] to compete very hard with someone in order to get something: *The two brothers **vied for** her attention.*

view

From the window there was a beautiful view.

**view¹** /vyu/ *n* **1** your belief or opinion about something: *I'd like to have your **views on/about** this issue.* | *In my/her/our view, the movie is too violent.* | *What's your **point of view**, Kate?* **2** a way of considering or understanding something: *The President's **view of** the situation wasn't discussed.* | *This book gives the **artist's view of** nature.* | *We have to consider **religious/public/ world views on** the question.* **3** [C,U] what you are able to see or the possibility of seeing it: *From our window we **have a beautiful/great view of** the ocean.* | *The end of the tunnel finally **came into view**.* (=began to be seen) | *I sat behind a tall guy who **blocked my view**.* (–stopped me from seeing something) **4** the whole area that you can see from somewhere: *a spectacular view of the mountains* | *A new factory now **spoils the view** of the park.* (=makes it look less beautiful) **5** a photograph or picture that shows a beautiful or interesting place: *The postcards show **scenic views** of New York.* **6 in view of** used in order to introduce the reason for your decision or action: *In view of his unsportsmanlike behavior, Max has been suspended from the team.*

---

**USAGE NOTE** view, opinion, and **point of view**

Use **view** and **opinion** to talk about what someone thinks or believes about something: *There are different views on capital punishment.* | *I've always respected your opinion.* Use **point of view** to talk about one part of a problem or situation: *Try to see it from the landlord's point of view.*

---

**USAGE NOTE** view, sight, scene, and vision

Use all of these words as countable nouns in order to talk about things that you see. Use **view** to talk about what you can see from a window or a high place: *From my office window I have a good view of the park.* Use **sight** to talk about something that is unusual, beautiful, interesting etc.: *The Grand Canyon at dawn is a spectacular sight.* Use **scene** to talk about the place where something happened: *Police arrived within minutes at the scene of the accident.* Use **vision** to talk about an idea of what the future will be like: *He has a romantic vision of a world without war.* When **sight** and **vision** are used as uncountable nouns, they mean "the ability to see": *Dean lost his sight in a factory accident.* | *I've always had perfect vision.*

**view**² *v* **1** [T] FORMAL to look at something because you are interested: *Many people came to view the fireworks.* **2** [T] to think of something in a particular way: *Conflict is viewed as part of the child-parent relationship.* | *I view the change as an adventure.* **3** [I,T] FORMAL to watch a television program, movie etc.: *a chance to view the movie before it opens in theaters*

**view·er** /ˈvyuɚ/ *n* someone who watches television: *The series is watched by millions of viewers.*

**vig·il** /ˈvɪdʒəl/ *n* [C,U] **1** a silent political protest in which people wait outside a building: *500 people held a vigil outside the embassy.* **2** a time, especially during the night, when you stay awake in order to pray or stay with someone who is ill: *John's been keeping a vigil beside his son in the hospital.*

**vig·i·lance** /ˈvɪdʒələns/ *n* [U] careful attention that you give to what is happening

**vig·i·lant** /ˈvɪdʒələnt/ *adj* FORMAL giving careful attention to what is happening: *Health inspectors must be vigilant when examining restaurants.*

**vig·i·lan·te** /ˌvɪdʒəˈlænti/ *n* a member of an unofficial group of people who join together to catch or punish criminals

**vig·or** /ˈvɪgɚ/ *n* [U] physical and mental energy and determination

**vig·or·ous** /ˈvɪgərəs/ *adj* **1** using a lot of energy and strength or determination: *vigorous exercise* | *a vigorous debate on gun control* **2** **vigorous opponent/defender etc.** someone who opposes or defends something strongly: *a vigorous campaigner for human rights* **3** strong and very healthy: *a vigorous young man*

**vile** /vaɪl/ *adj* **1** INFORMAL very unpleasant: *a vile temper* **2** evil: *a vile book*

**vil·i·fy** /ˈvɪləˌfaɪ/ *v* [T] FORMAL to say bad things about someone in order to make other people have a bad opinion of him/her

**vil·la** /ˈvɪlə/ *n* a big country house

**vil·lage** /ˈvɪlɪdʒ/ *n* **1** a very small town **2** **the village** the people who live in the village: *The whole village came to the wedding.*

**vil·lag·er** /ˈvɪlɪdʒɚ/ *n* someone who lives in a village

**vil·lain** /ˈvɪlən/ *n* the main bad character in a movie, play, or story

**vil·lain·y** /ˈvɪləni/ *n* [U] evil or criminal behavior

**vin·di·cate** /ˈvɪndəˌkeɪt/ *v* [T] FORMAL **1** to prove that someone or something is right or true **2** to prove that someone who has been blamed for something is not guilty –**vindication** /ˌvɪndəˈkeɪʃən/ *n* [U]

**vin·dic·tive** /vɪnˈdɪktɪv/ *adj* deliberately cruel and unfair: *He became bitter and vindictive after the divorce.*

**vine** /vaɪn/ *n* a plant that grows long stems that attach themselves to other plants, trees, buildings etc.: *grape vines*

**vin·e·gar** /ˈvɪnɪgɚ/ *n* [U] an acid-tasting liquid that is made from wine, used for improving the taste of food or preserving it

**vine·yard** /ˈvɪnyɚd/ *n* a piece of land where GRAPES are grown in order to make wine

**vin·tage**¹ /ˈvɪntɪdʒ/ *adj* **1** vintage wine is good quality wine that is made in a particular year **2** old and showing high quality: *a vintage car*

**vintage**² *n* a particular year in which a wine is made

**vi·nyl** /ˈvaɪnl/ *n* [U] a type of strong plastic

**vi·o·la** /viˈoʊlə/ *n* a wooden musical instrument shaped like a VIOLIN but larger and with a lower sound

**vi·o·late** /ˈvaɪəˌleɪt/ *v* [T] **1** to disobey or do something against a law, agreement etc.: *Killing the elephants violated international agreements.* **2** FORMAL to enter and spoil a place that should be respected: *Vandals had violated the graveyard.*

**vi·o·la·tion** /ˌvaɪəˈleɪʃən/ *n* an action that breaks a law, agreement etc.: *human rights violations* | *traffic violations*

**vi·o·lat·or** /ˈvaɪəˌleɪtɚ/ *n* someone who has broken the law

**vi·o·lence** /ˈvaɪələns/ *n* [U] **1** behavior that is intended to hurt other people physically: *Kids see too much violence on TV.* | *acts of violence against the refugees* **2** an angry way of speaking or reacting: *"What?" she said, with sudden violence.*

**vi·o·lent** /ˈvaɪələnt/ *adj* **1** violent actions are intended to hurt people: *violent crimes such as murder and rape* | *violent attacks* **2** likely to hurt other people: *a violent and dangerous criminal* | *The demonstrators suddenly turned violent.* (=became violent) **3** showing very strong angry emotions or opinions: *a violent argument* **4** **violent movie/play etc.** a movie, play etc. that shows a lot of violent actions **5** **violent storm/earthquake etc.** a storm, EARTHQUAKE etc. that happens with a lot of force

**vi·o·let** /ˈvaɪəlɪt/ *n* a small sweet-smelling dark purple flower

**vi·o·lin** /ˌvaɪə'lɪn/ *n* a small wooden musical instrument, that you play by pulling a special stick across wire strings

**VIP** *n* a very important person; someone who is famous or powerful and is treated with respect

**vi·per** /'vaɪpɚ/ *n* a small poisonous snake

**vi·ral** /'vaɪrəl/ *adj* relating to or caused by a VIRUS: *viral pneumonia*

**vir·gin**[1] /'vɚdʒɪn/ *n* someone who has never had sex

**virgin**[2] *adj* **1** virgin land/forest etc. land, forest etc. that is still in its natural state and has not been used or changed by people **2** without sexual experience

**vir·gin·i·ty** /vɚ'dʒɪnəti/ *n* [U] the condition of never having had sex: *He was 20 when he lost his virginity.* (=had sex for the first time)

**Virgin Mar·y** /ˌvɚdʒɪn 'mɛri/ *n* in the Christian religion, the mother of Jesus

**Vir·go** /'vɚgoʊ/ *n* [U] **1** the sixth sign of the ZODIAC, represented by a VIRGIN **2** someone born between August 23 and September 22

**vir·ile** /'vɪrəl/ *adj* having or showing traditionally male qualities such as strength and sexual attractiveness: *a young virile man* **–virility** /və'rɪləti/ *n* [U]

**vir·tu·al** /'vɚtʃuəl/ *adj* almost or nearly something: *He was a virtual prisoner in his own home.*|*Most of the country lives in virtual poverty.*

**vir·tu·al·ly** /'vɚtʃuəli, -tʃəli/ *adv* almost completely: *He was virtually unknown until the elections.*

**virtual re·al·i·ty** /ˌ... .'.../ *n* [U] an environment produced by a computer that surrounds the person looking at it and seems almost real

**vir·tue** /'vɚtʃu/ *n* **1** [U] FORMAL moral goodness of character and behavior: *a woman of the highest virtue* **2** a particular good quality in someone's character: *Among his virtues are honesty and kindness.* **3** [C,U] an advantage that makes something better or more useful than something else: *Free trade has its virtues.* **4 by virtue of** FORMAL by means of or as a result of something: *He became chairman by virtue of hard work.*

**vir·tu·o·so** /ˌvɚtʃu'oʊsoʊ/ *n* someone who is a very skillful performer, especially in music: *a piano virtuoso* **–virtuoso** *adj*

**vir·tu·ous** /'vɚtʃuəs/ *adj* FORMAL behaving in a very honest and moral way

**vir·u·lent** /'vɪrələnt, 'vɪryə-/ *adj* **1** FORMAL full of hatred: *virulent racism* **2** a poison, disease etc. that is virulent is very dangerous and affects people very quickly

**vi·rus** /'vaɪrəs/ *n* **1** a very small living thing that causes infectious illnesses, or the illness caused by this: *the common cold virus* **2** a set of instructions secretly put into a computer, that can destroy information stored in the computer

**vi·sa** /'vizə/ *n* an official mark that is put on your PASSPORT, that allows you to enter or leave another country: *She's here on a **student visa**.*

**vis·age** /'vɪzɪdʒ/ *n* LITERARY a face

**vis-à-vis** /ˌvizə'vi/ *prep* FORMAL in relation to or in comparison with something or someone

**vis·cous** /'vɪskəs/ *adj* TECHNICAL a viscous liquid is thick and does not flow easily **–viscosity** /vɪs'kɑsəti/ *n* [U]

**vise** /vaɪs/ *n* a tool that holds an object firmly so that you can work on it using both of your hands

**vis·i·bil·i·ty** /ˌvɪzə'bɪləti/ *n* [U] the distance that it is possible to see at a particular time: *There is **poor visibility** on the roads due to heavy fog.*

**vis·i·ble** /'vɪzəbəl/ *adj* **1** something that is visible can be seen: *The mountains weren't visible because of the clouds.* –opposite INVISIBLE **2** an effect that is visible can be noticed: *a visible change in her attitude* **–visibly** *adv*

**vi·sion** /'vɪʒən/ *n* **1** [U] the ability to see: *Will the operation improve my vision?* **2** a picture or idea in your mind of the way a situation could happen: *I have a **vision of** a better future for this city.* **3** something you see in a dream as part of a religious experience: *The prophet Mohammed visited her in a vision.* **4** [U] the ability to make plans for the future with a clear purpose: *We need a leader with vision.* –see usage note at VIEW[2]

**vi·sion·ar·y** /'vɪʒəˌnɛri/ *adj* having clear ideas of how the world can be better in the future **–visionary** *n*

**vis·it**[1] /'vɪzɪt/ *v* **1** to go and spend time with someone: *My aunt is **coming to visit** next week.* **2** [I,T] to go and spend time in a place, especially as a tourist: *We want to visit the Grand Canyon on our trip.* **3** [I] INFORMAL to talk socially with someone: *We watched TV while Mom visited with Mrs. Levinson.*

**visit**[2] *n* **1** an occasion when someone visits a place or person: *When are you going to **pay us a visit**?*|*The Senator spoke to the girl during a **visit to** the hospital.*|*We've just **had a visit from** the police.* **2** INFORMAL an occasion when you talk socially with someone, or the time you spend doing this: *Barbara and I had a nice long visit.*

**vis·it·a·tion** /ˌvɪzə'teɪʃən/, **visitation rights** *n* [U] LAW the right that a parent who is DIVORCEd has to see his/her children

**vis·i·tor** /'vɪzətɚ/ *n* someone who comes to visit a place or a person: *a guide book for **visitors to** Mexico City*|*Let's not bother them now - they **have visitors**.* (=people are visiting them)

**vi·sor** /'vaɪzɚ/ *n* **1** the curved part of a hat or HELMET that sticks out above your eyes, or a special hat that consists only of this **2** the part of a HELMET that can be lowered to protect your face **3** a flat piece of material in the front window of a car that you pull down to keep the sun out of your eyes

**vis·ta** /'vɪstə/ *n* LITERARY a view, especially over a large area of land

**vis·u·al** /'vɪʒuəl/ *adj* relating to seeing or to your sight: *visual arts such as painting and sculpture* | *The movie has a strong visual impact.* –**visually** *adv*

**visual aid** /ˌ.. '. / *n* something such as a map, picture, or movie that is used for helping people to learn

**vis·u·al·ize** /'vɪʒuə,laɪz/ *v* [T] to form a picture of someone or something in your mind; imagine: *I tried to visualize the house as he described it.*

**vi·tal** /'vaɪtl/ *adj* **1** extremely important or necessary: *These computer systems are vital to our business.* | *Are nuclear weapons vital for national security?* **2** full of life and energy: *a vital person*

**vi·tal·i·ty** /vaɪ'tæləti/ *n* [U] life and energy: *He has the vitality of a man half his age.*

**vi·tal·ly** /'vaɪtl-i/ *adv* in an extremely important or necessary way: *It's vitally important that you attend the meeting.*

**vital sta·tis·tics** /ˌ.. '../ *n* [plural] facts about people such as their age, race, and whether they are married, especially in official records

**vi·ta·min** /'vaɪtəmɪn/ *n* a chemical substance found in food that is necessary for good health: *The doctor told me to get more vitamin A and vitamin C.*

**vit·ri·ol·ic** /ˌvɪtri'ɑlɪk/ *adj* something you say that is vitriolic is very cruel: *a vitriolic attack on homosexuals*

**vi·va·cious** /vɪ'veɪʃəs, vaɪ-/ *adj* someone, especially a woman, who is vivacious has a lot of energy and is fun to be with –**vivaciously** *adv* –**vivacity** /vɪ'væsəti/ *n* [U]

**viv·id** /'vɪvɪd/ *adj* **1** producing sharp clear pictures in your mind that makes something seem real: *a vivid description of the mountains* **2 vivid imagination** the ability to imagine things so clearly that even unreal things may seem real: *Your daughter has a vivid imagination.* **3** vivid colors or patterns are very bright –**vividly** *adv*

**viv·i·sec·tion** /ˌvɪvə'sɛkʃən/ *n* [U] the practice of operating on animals in order to do scientific tests on them

**VJ, video jock·ey** /'... ˌ../ *n* someone who introduces and plays VIDEOs of popular music on television

**V-neck** /'vi nɛk/ *n* a type of shirt or SWEATER with a collar that is shaped like the letter V

**VOA** *n* [U] Voice of America; a radio company that broadcasts American news and programs all over the world

**vo·cab·u·lar·y** /voʊ'kæbyə,lɛri, və-/ *n* **1** [C,U] all the words that someone knows, learns, or uses: *He has a huge vocabulary for a*

*five-year-old.* **2** [C,U] the words that are used when talking about a particular subject: *the vocabulary of doctors and scientists* **3** all the words in a particular language

**vo·cal**[1] /'voʊkəl/ *adj* **1** relating to the voice: *vocal music* **2** INFORMAL expressing your opinion strongly or loudly: *a vocal critic of the president* –**vocally** *adv*

**vocal**[2] *n* [C usually plural] the part of a piece of music that is sung rather than played on an instrument: *The song has Maria McKee on vocals.*

**vocal cords** /'.. ˌ./ *n* [plural] thin pieces of muscle in your throat that produce sound when you speak or sing

**vo·cal·ist** /'voʊkəlɪst/ *n* someone who sings, especially with a band

**vo·ca·tion** /voʊ'keɪʃən/ *n* [C,U] the feeling that the purpose of your life is to do a particular job because it allows you to help other people, or the ability to do this job: *Teaching isn't just a job to her - it's her vocation.*

**vo·ca·tion·al** /voʊ'keɪʃənəl/ *adj* **vocational school/training/education etc.** a school or method of training that teaches you the skills you need to do a particular job

**vo·cif·er·ous** /voʊ'sɪfərəs/ *adj* FORMAL loud and determined in expressing your opinions: *vociferous complaints* –**vociferously** *adv*

**vod·ka** /'vɑdkə/ *n* [U] a strong clear alcoholic drink, first made in Eastern Europe

**vogue** /voʊg/ *n* **be in vogue/be the vogue** to be fashionable and popular: *The preppy look was in vogue in the early 80s.*

**voice**[1] /vɔɪs/ *n* **1** [C,U] the sound you make when you speak or sing, or the ability to make this sound: *I thought I heard voices downstairs.* | *Andrea has a really beautiful voice.* (=singing voice) | *He's caught a bad cold and lost his voice.* (=cannot speak) | *I can hear you - you don't have to raise your voice.* (=speak in a loud angry way) | *Keep your voice down,* (=speak more quietly) *it's supposed to be a surprise.* | *"It won't work," he said in a loud/soft/ worried/booming voice.* ✗ DON'T SAY "...with a loud/soft/worried/booming voice." ✗ **2 deep-voiced/husky-voiced etc.** having a voice that is deep and low etc. **3** [C,U] an opinion or wish that is expressed: *Shouldn't parents have a voice in deciding how their children are educated?* **4** [singular] a person, organization, newspaper etc. that expresses the wishes or opinions of a group of people: *By the early 1960s, King had become the voice of the civil rights movement.* **5 the voice of reason/experience etc.** someone who is sensible, has experience etc. especially in a situation where other people do not

**voice**[2] *v* [T] to tell people your opinions or feelings about a particular subject: *We all voiced our concerns about the plan.*

**voice mail** /'. ./ *n* [U] a system, especially in a company, in which telephone calls are recorded so that someone can listen to them later

**void**[1] /vɔɪd/ *adj* **1** a contract or agreement that is void is officially no longer legal; INVA-LID[1]: *They were demanding that the elections be declared void.* **2 be void of** to completely lack something: *Her eyes were void of all expression.*

**void**[2] *n* **1** a feeling of great sadness that you have when someone you love dies or when something important is missing from your life: *Their son's death left a painful void in their lives.* **2** an empty space where nothing exists

**void**[3] *v* [T] to make a contract or agreement VOID so that it has no legal effect: *The cashier will void the sale.*

**vol·a·tile** /'vɑlət̬l/ *adj* **1** likely to change suddenly and become violent: *He's a pretty volatile character.* | *a volatile situation* **2** a volatile liquid or substance changes easily into a gas — **volatility** /ˌvɑlə'tɪlət̬i/ *n* [U]

**vol·ca·no** /vɑl'keɪnoʊ/ *n, plural* **volcanoes** *or* **volcanos** a mountain with a large hole at the top out of which rocks, LAVA, and ASH sometimes explode: *This island has several active volcanoes.* (–volcanoes that may explode at any time) — **volcanic** /vɑl'kænɪk/ *adj*: *volcanic rocks*

**vo·li·tion** /voʊ'lɪʃən, vou-/ *n* [U] FORMAL **of your own volition** because you want to do something and not because you are forced to do it: *Robin left the company of her own volition.*

**vol·ley** /'vɑli/ *n* **1** a large number of bullets, ARROWS, rocks etc. fired or thrown at the same time: *a volley of shots* **2** a lot of questions, insults, attacks etc. that are all said or made at the same time: *a volley of abuse*

**volleyball**

**vol·ley·ball** /'vɑli,bɔl/ *n* **1** [U] a game in which two teams hit a ball to each other across a net with their hands and try not to let it touch the ground **2** the ball used in this game

**volt** /voʊlt/ *n* a unit for measuring the force of an electric current

**volt·age** /'voʊltɪdʒ/ *n* [C,U] the force of an electric current measured in VOLTs

**vol·ume** /'vɑlyəm, -yum/ *n* **1** [U] the amount of sound produced by a television, radio etc.: *I can't hear the TV; can you turn up the volume?* **2** [U] the amount of space that a substance fills or an object contains: *Let the dough double in volume before you bake it.* **3** [C,U] the total amount of something: *an increase in the volume of traffic* **4** a book, especially one of the books into which a very long book is divided: *a 12-volume set of poetry*

**vo·lu·mi·nous** /və'lumənəs/ *adj* FORMAL **1** very large: *a voluminous skirt* **2** voluminous books, documents etc. are very long and contain a lot of information

**vol·un·tar·y** /'vɑlən,tɛri/ *adj* done willingly and without being forced or paid: *voluntary work* | *We're asking for people to help on a voluntary basis.* (=without being paid) — **voluntarily** /ˌvɑlən'tɛrəli/ *adv*

**vol·un·teer**[1] /ˌvɑlən'tɪr/ *v* **1** [I,T] to offer to do something without expecting any reward: *Ernie volunteered to wash the dishes.* | *I volunteered for the job.* **2** [T] to tell someone something without being asked: *Michael volunteered the information before I had a chance to say anything.* **3** [I] to offer to join the army, navy etc.: *When the war began, my brother immediately volunteered.*

**volunteer**[2] *n* **1** someone who offers to do something without expecting any reward or pay **2** someone who offers to join the army, navy etc.

**vo·lup·tu·ous** /və'lʌptʃuəs/ *adj* **1** a woman who is voluptuous has large breasts and a soft curved body **2** expressing or suggesting sexual pleasure: *a voluptuous mouth*

**vom·it**[1] /'vɑmɪt/ *v* [I,T] FORMAL to bring food or drink up from the stomach and out through the mouth

**vomit**[2] *n* [U] the food or drink that comes out when someone VOMITs

**voo·doo** /'vudu/ *n* [U] magical beliefs and practices used as a form of religion, especially in parts of Africa, Latin America, and the Caribbean

**vo·ra·cious** /və'reɪʃəs, vɔ-/ *adj* FORMAL **1** eating or wanting large quantities of food: *The dog has a voracious appetite.* **2** extremely eager to do something: *a voracious reader* — **voracity** /və'ræsət̬i/ *n* [U]

**vor·tex** /'vɔrtɛks/ *n, plural* **vortices** /'vɔrtəsiz/ LITERARY a large area of wind or water that spins rapidly and pulls things into its center

**vote**[1] /voʊt/ *v* **1** [I,T] to mark a paper or raise your hand in order to show which person you want to elect, which plan you support, who you want to win a particular prize etc.: *He's too young to vote.* (=in an election) | *Who did you vote for?* | *If we can't agree, we'll have to vote on it.* | *Congress voted to reduce taxes by 2%.* | *85% of union members voted against going on strike.* **2** [T] to agree to provide something as the result of voting: *Congress has voted an extra $20 million for road improvements.*

V

**vote**² *n* **1** a choice or decision that you make by voting: *He's certainly not going to get my vote!* | *There were 1079* **votes for** *Mr. Swanson, and 766 for Mr. Reynolds.* | *You have until 8:00 to* ***cast your vote***. (=vote) **2** an act of making a choice or decision by voting: *We couldn't decide so we* ***took a vote on*** *it.* | *Congress will* ***put*** *the bill* ***to a vote*** *tomorrow.* **3 the vote a)** the total number of votes made in an election or the total number of people who vote: *increasing our share of the vote* | *efforts to win* ***the African American/Irish/Jewish vote*** (=all the votes of African Americans etc.) **b)** the right to vote: *In France, women didn't get the vote until 1945.* **4 vote of confidence** the action of showing publicly that you support someone: *Darman got a vote of confidence from the committee and remained president.*

**vot·er** /'voʊṭɚ/ *n* someone who votes or has the right to vote: *The state decided to let the voters decide the issue.*

**voting booth** /'.. ˌ./ *n* an enclosed place where you can vote without being seen

**vouch** /vaʊtʃ/ *v*

**vouch for** sb/sth *phr v* [T] **1** to say that you have a firm belief that something is true or good because of your experience or knowledge of it: *I'll* ***vouch for*** *the accuracy of that report.* **2** to say that you will be responsible for someone's behavior, actions etc.: *I can* ***vouch for*** *my son, officer.*

**vouch·er** /'vaʊtʃɚ/ *n* a kind of ticket that can be used for a particular purpose instead of money

**vow**¹ /vaʊ/ *n* a serious promise: *She* ***made a vow*** *to herself* ***that*** *she would never tell anyone.* | *marriage vows*

**vow**² *v* [T] to make a serious promise to yourself or someone else: *He* ***vowed to*** *kill the man that destroyed his family.* | *I* ***vowed that*** *I would never drink again.*

**vow·el** /'vaʊəl/ *n* TECHNICAL the letter a, e, i, o, or u, and sometimes y

**voy·age** /'vɔɪ-ɪdʒ/ *n* a long trip, especially in a ship or a space vehicle: *the voyage from England to America* **–voyage** *v* [I] LITERARY **–see** usage note at TRAVEL²

**voy·eur** /vɔɪ'ɚ/ *n* [U] someone who gets sexual pleasure from secretly watching other people's sexual activities **–voyeurism** /'vɔɪə,rɪzəm/ *n* [U] **–voyeuristic** /ˌvɔɪə'rɪstɪk/ *adj*

**vs.** /'vɚsəs/ the written abbreviation of VERSUS

**VT** the written abbreviation of Vermont

**vul·gar** /'vʌlgɚ/ *adj* very rude, offensive, and often relating to sex: *vulgar language* **–vulgarity** /vʌl'gærəṭi/ *n* [U]

**vul·ner·a·ble** /'vʌlnərəbəl/ *adj* easily harmed, hurt, or attacked: *The army was in a vulnerable position.* | *She looked so young and vulnerable.* **–vulnerability** /ˌvʌlnərə'bɪləṭi/ *n* [U] **–opposite** INVULNERABLE

**vul·ture** /'vʌltʃɚ/ *n* **1** a large wild bird that eats dead animals **2** someone who uses other people's troubles for his/her own advantage

**vy·ing** /'vaɪ-ɪŋ/ *v* the PRESENT PARTICIPLE of VIE

# W

**W, w** /'dʌbəl,yu, 'dʌbəyu/ the twenty-third letter of the English alphabet

**W 1** the written abbreviation of WEST or WESTERN **2** the written abbreviation of WATT

**WA** the written abbreviation of Washington

**wack·y** /'wæki/ *adj* INFORMAL silly in an amusing way

**wad**¹ /wɑd/ *n* **1** a thick pile of thin sheets of something, especially money: *a wad of dollar bills* **2** a thick soft mass of material that has been pressed together: *a wad of cotton*

**wad**² *v* **-dded, -dding**

**wad** sth ↔ **up** *phr v* [T] INFORMAL to press something such as a piece of paper or cloth into a small tight ball: *Aaron* ***wadded up*** *the letter and threw it away.*

**wad·dle** /'wɑdl/ *v* [I] to walk with short steps, swinging from one side to another like a duck: *a fat man* ***waddling along/up etc.*** *the street* **–waddle** *n*

**wade** /weɪd/ *v* [I,T] to walk through water that is not deep: *We* ***waded across*** *the stream.*

**wade through** sth *phr v* [T] to read or deal with a lot of long and boring written work: *Preston was* ***wading through*** *a 500-page report.*

**wa·fer** /'weɪfɚ/ *n* a very thin cookie

**waf·fle**¹ /'wɑfəl/ *n* a flat bread with a pattern of holes in it, often eaten for breakfast

**waffle**² *v* [I] INFORMAL to be unable to decide what action to take: *He made his decision without waffling.*

**waft** /wɑft, wæft/ *v* [I,T] to move gently through the air: *The smell of bacon* ***wafted up*** *from the kitchen.*

**wag** /wæg/ *v* **-gged, -gging** [I,T] **1** if a dog wags its tail, or the tail wags, it shakes from one side to another **2** to shake your finger from one side to the other in order to tell someone not to do something: *"Don't go back there again," she said, wagging her finger.* **–wag** *n*

**wage**¹ /weɪdʒ/ *n* [singular] the amount of money you earn, usually for each hour that you work: *The job's not very exciting, but he earns a good wage.* | *an hourly wage* ✗ DON'T SAY "an annual wage." SAY "an annual salary". ✗ **–see** also WAGES **–see** usage note at PAY²

**wage**² *v* [T] to be involved in a war, struggle, or fight against someone or something: *The police*

W

*are* ***waging a campaign/war against*** *drug pushers.*

**wa·ger**[1] /ˈweɪdʒɚ/ *n* **1** an agreement to risk money on the result of a race, game etc.: *Higgins* ***had a wager on*** *the World Series.* **2** the money that you risk: *a $10 wager*

**wager**[2] *v* [T] to risk money on the result of a race, game etc.: *Brad* ***wagered*** *$20* ***on*** *the game.*

**wag·es** /ˈweɪdʒɪz/ *n* [plural] the money you get each day, week, or month, that is usually paid according to the number of hours that you work —compare SALARY

**wag·on** /ˈwægən/ *n* **1** a strong vehicle with four wheels, pulled by horses **2** a small CART with four wheels and a long handle in the front, used as a toy for children **3** INFORMAL ⇨ STATION WAGON **4** **be on the wagon** INFORMAL to no longer drink alcohol: *Harry's been on the wagon since he got married.*

**wagon train** /ˈ.. ˌ./ *n* a large group of WAGONs traveling together in past times

**waif** /weɪf/ *n* LITERARY a child or animal that is thin and unhealthy, and looks as if he, she, or it does not have a home

**wail** /weɪl/ *v* **1** [I] to make a long high sound with your voice because you are in pain or very sad, or to make a sound like this: *women wailing with grief* | *sirens wailing in the distance* **2** [T] to say something in a loud, sad, and complaining way: *"My money's gone!" she wailed.* **–wail** *n*

**waist** /weɪst/ *n* **1** the part in the middle of your body just above your HIPs: *She has a slim waist.* —see picture at BODY **2** the part of a piece of clothing that goes around your waist: *These pants are too big in the waist.*

**waist·band** /ˈweɪstbænd/ *n* the part of a skirt, pants etc. that fastens around your waist

**waist·line** /ˈweɪstlaɪn/ *n* **1** [singular] the measurement around your waist **2** the position of the waist of a piece of clothing

**wait**[1] /weɪt/ *v* **1** [I] to not do something until something else happens, someone arrives etc.: *Hurry up! Everyone's waiting.* | *Wait right here until I come back.* | *We had to* ***wait*** *45 minutes* ***for*** *a bus.* | *Are you* ***waiting to*** *use the phone?* **2** **wait tables** to serve food to people at their table in a restaurant: *I waited tables to earn money in college.*

SPOKEN PHRASES
**3** **wait a minute/second** said in order to ask someone to wait for a short time: *Wait a second, I'll get my coat and come with you.* **4** **I can't wait/I can hardly wait** said when you want to do something, go somewhere etc. very much: *I can't wait to see the look on his face.* **5** **(just) you wait** said in order to warn or threaten someone: *I'll get you back for what you've done, just you wait.*

**wait around** *phr v* [I] to do nothing while you are waiting for something to happen, someone to arrive etc.: *We were* ***waiting around for*** *Dad's plane to come in.*

**wait on** sb *phr v* [T] **1** to serve food to someone at his/her table, especially in a restaurant: *A very nice young woman* ***waited on*** *us at The Riverboat today.* **2** **wait on sb hand and foot** OFTEN HUMOROUS to do everything for someone

**wait** sth ↔ **out** *phr v* [T] to wait for something to finish: *They found a place to* ***wait out*** *the storm.*

**wait up** *phr v* [I] **1** to wait for someone to return before you go to bed: *Please don't* ***wait up*** *for me.* **2** **Wait up!** SPOKEN used to tell someone to stop and wait for you: *Wait up you guys - I've dropped my wallet.*

---

**USAGE NOTE** wait and expect

Use **wait** to talk about staying somewhere until someone comes or something happens: *Please wait until Mr. Fletcher arrives.* | *She's been waiting all day for that phone to ring.* Use **expect** to say that you think something will probably happen, arrive etc., whether you want it to or not: *I didn't expect her to be so angry.* | *Were you expecting a phone call?*

---

**wait**[2] *n* [singular] a period of time in which you wait for something to happen, someone to arrive etc.: *We had a three-hour* ***wait for*** *our flight.* —see also **lie in wait (for sb/sth)** (LIE[1])

**wait·er** /ˈweɪtɚ/ *n* a man who serves food in a restaurant

**waiting list** /ˈ.. ˌ./, **wait list** /ˈ. ./ *n* a list of people who want to do or buy something but who must wait for other people who are on the list before them: *Over 500 students are* ***on the waiting/wait list.***

**waiting room** /ˈ.. ˌ./ *n* a room for people to wait in, for example to see a doctor

**wait·ress** /ˈweɪtrɪs/ *n* a woman who serves food at the tables in a restaurant

**waive** /weɪv/ *v* [T] to state officially that a right, rule etc. can be ignored: *She* ***waived her right*** *to a lawyer.*

**waiv·er** /ˈweɪvɚ/ *n* an official statement saying that a right, rule etc. can be ignored

**wake**[1] /weɪk/ *v* **woke, woken, waking** [I,T] also **wake up** to stop sleeping, or to make someone stop sleeping: *Try not to wake the baby.* | *I woke up at 5:00 this morning.*

**wake up** *phr v* [I,T] to start to pay attention to something: *Hey! Wake up when I'm talking to you!*

**wake up to** *phr v* [T] to start to realize and understand a danger, an idea etc.: *You have to* ***wake up to*** *the fact that alcohol is killing you.*

**wake**[2] *n* **1** **in the wake of/in sth's wake** as a result of: *Five members of the city council re-*

*signed in the wake of the scandal.* **2** the track
or path made behind a car, boat etc. as it moves
along: *The car left clouds of dust in its wake.*
**3** the time before a funeral when people meet
to remember the dead person

**wak·en** /'weɪkən/ *v* [I,T] FORMAL to wake, or to
wake someone: *He was wakened by the sound
of a car horn outside.*

**wak·ing** /'weɪkɪŋ/ *adj* **waking hours/
moments etc.** all the time when you are awake:
*He spends every waking moment with that girl!*

**walk¹** /wɔk/ *v* **1** [I,T] to move along by
putting one foot in front of the other: *We must
have walked ten miles today.* | *Do you* **walk to**
*work?* | *She* **walked up to** *him and kissed
him.* | *tourists* **walking around** *the downtown
area* —see picture on page 473 **2** [T] to walk
through or across a particular area: *walking the
streets of Boston* **3** **walk the dog** to take a dog
outside to walk **4** **walk sb somewhere** to
walk somewhere with someone: *It's late - I'll
walk you home.* **5** **walk all over sb** INFORMAL to
treat someone very badly: *She lets those kids
walk all over her.* **6** [I] INFORMAL to leave a
court of law without being punished or sent to
prison: *I knew he'd walk - they didn't have enough evidence.*

  **walk away** *phr v* [I] to leave a situation without
caring what happens, even though you are responsible for it: *You can't just* **walk away from**
*eight years of marriage!*

  **walk away with** sth *phr v* [T] to win something easily: *Carrie* **walked away with** *the prize.*

  **walk in on** sb *phr v* [T] to go into a place and
interrupt someone whom you did not expect to
be there: *I* **walked in on** *Terry and Lisa in bed.*

  **walk into** sth *phr v* [T] to become involved in a
situation that is unpleasant or makes you look
stupid without intending to: *You* **walked straight
into** *that one!*

  **walk** sth **off** *phr v* [T] if you walk off an unpleasant feeling, you go for a walk to make it go
away: *If you get a cramp, just try to* **walk it off.**

  **walk off with** sth *phr v* to steal something, or
to take something by mistake: *Someone* **walked
off with** *my new jacket!*

  **walk out** *phr v* [I] **1** to stop working as a
protest: *The electricians at the factory have*
**walked out.** **2** to leave your husband, wife etc.
suddenly: *Mary just* **walked out on** *him one day.*

**walk²** *n* **1** the time you spend or the distance
you travel when you are walking: *Would you
like to* **go for a walk**? (=for pleasure) | *Let's* **take
a walk** *after lunch.* | *It's only a* **ten minute/two
mile walk** *from here.* **2** a particular path or
ROUTE for walking: *popular walks in Yellowstone National Park* **3** [U] the way someone
walks —see also WALK OF LIFE

**walk·er** /'wɔkɚ/ *n* **1** a metal frame that old
or sick people use to help them walk
**2** someone who walks at a particular speed, in

a particular place etc.: *A brisk walker can get
there in 25 minutes.*

**walk·ie-talk·ie** /ˌwɔki 'tɔki/ *n* a small radio
that you can carry and use to speak to other
people who have the same type of radio

**walk-in** /'. ./ *adj* big enough for a person to
walk inside: *a walk-in closet*

**walking stick** /'. ˌ./ *n* a long thin stick, used
to help support you when you walk

**Walk·man** /'wɔkmən/ *n* TRADEMARK a small
machine that plays TAPEs and has HEADPHONES,
that you carry with you to listen to music

**walk of life** /ˌ. . '. / *n* the position in society
that someone has: *The club has members from*
**all walks of life.**

**walk-on** /'. ./ *n* a small acting part in a play or
movie in which the actor has no words, or an
actor who has this part —**walk-on** *adj*

**walk·out** /'wɔk-aʊt/ *n* an occasion when
people stop working or leave somewhere as a
protest: *City employees* **staged a walkout** *in
protest of the budget cuts.*

**walk-up** /'. ./ *n* INFORMAL an apartment that you
have to walk up the stairs to, because there is no
ELEVATOR in the building

**walk·way** /'wɔk-weɪ/ *n* a path, often above
the ground, built to connect two parts of a building or two buildings

**wall** /wɔl/ *n* **1** one of the sides of a room or
building: *Hang that picture on the wall by the
door.* **2** an upright structure made of stone or
brick, that divides one area from another: *A
brick wall surrounds the building.* **3** the side
of something hollow, such as a pipe or tube: *The
walls of the blood vessels had been damaged.*
**4** something that prevents you from doing
something or going somewhere: *A wall of
people was blocking my view of the stage.*
—**walled** *adj* —see also **have your back to the
wall** (BACK¹)

**wal·let** /'wɑlɪt, 'wɔ-/ *n* a small flat folding
case for putting paper money in, usually made
of leather

**wal·lop** /'wɑləp/ *v* [T] INFORMAL to hit someone
or something very hard

**wal·low** /'wɑloʊ/ *v* **1** DISAPPROVING to allow
yourself to feel sad, upset, or full of pity, especially for too long a time: *wallowing in self-pity/
despair* **2** [I] to roll around in mud, water etc.
for pleasure: *pigs wallowing in the mud*

**wall·pa·per** /'wɔlˌpeɪpɚ/ *n* [U] paper that you
stick onto the walls of a room in order to decorate it —**wallpaper** *v* [T]

**Wall Street** /'. ./ *n* **1** a street in New York
City where the American STOCK EXCHANGE is
**2** the American STOCK EXCHANGE

**wall-to-wall** /ˌ. . '. ◂/ *adj* covering the whole
floor: *wall-to-wall carpeting*

**wal·nut** /'wɔlnʌt/ *n* **1** a slightly bitter nut
with a large light brown shell, or the tree on

W

which this grows **2** [U] the dark brown wood of this tree

**wal·rus** /'wɔlrəs, 'wɒl-/ *n* a large sea animal similar to a SEAL with two long thick teeth

**waltz**[1] /wɔlts/ *n* a fairly slow dance with a RHYTHM consisting of patterns of three beats, or the music for this dance

**waltz**[2] *v* [I] **1** to dance a WALTZ **2** INFORMAL to walk somewhere calmly and confidently: *Jeff waltzed up to the bar and poured himself a drink.*

**wan** /wɑn/ *adj* looking pale, weak, or tired: *a wan smile*

**wand** /wɑnd/ *n* a thin stick you hold in your hand to do magic tricks

**wan·der** /'wɑndər/ *v* **1** [I,T] to move or travel around an area without a clear direction or purpose: *I'll just wander around the mall for awhile.* | *wandering the streets* **2** [I] also **wander off** to move away from where you are supposed to stay: *Don't let her wander off.* **3** [I] to start to talk or write about something not related to the main subject that you were talking or writing about before: *The book's plot wanders a little.* **4** [I] if your mind, thoughts etc. wander, you no longer pay attention to something: *She's getting old, and sometimes her mind wanders.* −**wanderer** *n*

**wane**[1] /weɪn/ *v* [I] **1** if something such as power, influence, or a feeling wanes, it becomes gradually less strong or less important: *My enthusiasm for the project was waning.* **2** when the moon wanes, you gradually see less of it

**wane**[2] *n* **on the wane** becoming smaller, weaker, or less important: *The President's popularity seems to be on the wane.*

**wan·gle** /'wæŋgəl/ *v* [T] INFORMAL to get something by persuading or tricking someone: *I managed to wangle an invitation out of George.*

**wan·na** /'wɑnə, 'wɒnə/ SPOKEN NONSTANDARD **1** a short form of "want to": *I don't wanna go.* **2** a short form of "want a": *Do you wanna sandwich?*

**wan·na·be** /'wɑnəˌbi/ *n* INFORMAL someone who tries to look or behave like a famous or popular person, or wants to become involved in a famous or popular group: *young wanna-be gang members*

**want**[1] /wɑnt, wɒnt, wɔnt/ *v* [T] to have a desire or need for something: *What do you want for your birthday?* | *I don't want any more milk, thanks.* | *They talked about moving, but Mark doesn't want to leave Iowa.* | *Carlson wants him to take the work on vacation.* | *I can pick it up on my way to work if you want.* (=if you would like that) −see usage note at DESIRE[2]

**want for** sth *phr v* [T] to not have something that you need: *Those kids have never wanted for anything.*

**want**[2] *n* [C,U] something that you desire or

need but do not have: *We watched television for want of anything better to do.*

**want ad** /'. ./ *n* a small advertisement that you put in a newspaper if you want to employ someone to do a job

**want·ed** /'wɑntɪd/ *adj* someone who is wanted is being looked for by the police: *The man is wanted for murder.*

**want·ing** /'wɑntɪŋ/ *adj* proven to be not good enough. *Traditional solutions had been tried and found wanting.*

**wan·ton** /'wɑnˀn, 'wɔn-/ *adj* **1** deliberately causing damage or harm for no reason: *wanton destruction* **2** OLD FASHIONED a wanton woman is considered sexually immoral

**war** /wɔr/ *n* [C,U] **1** a time when two or more countries or opposing groups within a country fight each other with soldiers and weapons: *In 1793 England was at war with/against France.* | *Was your dad in the war?* | *What would happen if we lost this war?* | *the war between the states* **2** a struggle to control or stop a bad or illegal activity: *the war on/against drugs* **3** a situation in which a person or group is fighting for power, influence, or control: *a trade war* −**war** *v* [I]

**war·ble** /'wɔrbəl/ *v* [I,T] to sing with a high, continuous, but rapidly varying sound, the way a bird does

**war crime** /'. ./ *n* an illegal and cruel act done during a war −**war criminal** /'. ,.../ *n*

**ward**[1] /wɔrd/ *n* **1** a part of a hospital where people who need medical treatment stay: *the maternity ward* (=for women who are having babies) | *the children's ward* **2** LAW someone, especially a child, who is under the legal protection of another person or of a law court

**ward**[2] *v*

**ward** sth ↔ **off** *phr v* [T] to do something to protect yourself from an illness, danger, attack etc.: *a spray to ward off insects*

**war·den** /'wɔrdn/ *n* the person in charge of a prison

**war·drobe** /'wɔrdroub/ *n* the clothes that someone has: *This skirt is the newest addition to my wardrobe.*

**ware·house** /'wɛrhaus/ *n* a large building for storing large quantities of goods

**wares** /wɛrz/ *n* [plural] LITERARY things that are for sale, usually not in a store

**war·fare** /'wɔrfɛr/ *n* [U] a word meaning the activity of fighting in a war, used especially when talking about particular methods of fighting: *chemical warfare*

**war game** /'. ./ *n* an activity in which soldiers fight an imaginary battle in order to test military plans

**war·head** /'wɔrhɛd/ *n* the explosive part at the front of a MISSILE

**war·like** /'wɔrlaɪk/ *adj* **1** threatening war or

W

attack: *a warlike gesture* **2** liking war and being good at it: *a warlike reputation*

**war·lock** /ˈwɔrlɑk/ *n* a man who is supposed to have magic powers, especially to do bad things

**war·lord** /ˈwɔrlɔrd/ *n* a leader of a military or fighting group, usually an unofficial one

**warm**[1] /wɔrm/ *adj* **1** slightly hot, especially pleasantly: *Are you warm enough?* | *I hope we get some warmer weather soon.* | *a warm bath* −see usage note at TEMPERATURE **2** able to keep in heat or keep out cold: *warm clothes* **3** friendly: *a warm smile* −**warmly** *adv*

**warm**[2] *v* [I,T] also **warm up** to become warm or warmer, or to make someone or something do this: *Here, warm yourself by the fire.* | *There's some soup warming up in the pot.*

**warm to** sb/sth *phr v* [T] also **warm up to** to begin to like someone or something: *Bruce didn't warm to him as he had to Casey.*

**warm up** *phr v* [I,T **warm** sb **up**] to do gentle physical exercises to prepare your body for exercise, singing, etc.: *warming up before the race*

**warm-blood·ed** /ˌ. ˈ..◂ / *adj* having a body temperature that remains fairly high whether the temperature around it is hot or cold: *Mammals are warm-blooded animals.* −compare COLD-BLOODED

**warmed o·ver** /ˌ. ˈ..◂ / *adj* **1** food that is warmed over has been cooked before and then heated again for eating **2** an idea or argument that is warmed over has been used before and is no longer interesting or useful

**warm-heart·ed** /ˌ. ˈ..◂ / *adj* friendly and kind: *a warm-hearted old lady*

**war·mon·ger** /ˈwɔrˌmʌŋgɚ, -ˌmɑŋ-/ *n* someone who is eager to start a war −**warmongering** *n* [U]

**warmth** /wɔrmθ/ *n* [U] **1** a feeling of being warm: *the warmth of the sun* **2** friendliness: *the warmth of her smile*

**warm-up** /ˈ. ./ *n* a set of gentle exercises that you do to prepare your body for exercise, dancing, singing etc.

**warn** /wɔrn/ *v* [I,T] to tell someone that something bad or dangerous may happen, so that s/he can avoid it or prevent it: *Customers were* **warned of/about** *the risks involved.* | *I* **warned** *you* **not to** *walk home alone.* | *We* **warned** *her* **that** *something like that might happen.*

**warn·ing** /ˈwɔrnɪŋ/ *n* [C,U] something that prepares you for something bad or dangerous that might happen: *The planes attacked without warning.* | *a* **warning to** *women over 50* | *You've been* **given** *several* **warnings about** *this already.* | *Be aware of* **warning signs** (=pain etc. that shows that an illness is coming) *such as tiredness and headaches.*

**warp** /wɔrp/ *v* [I,T] **1** to become bent or twisted, or to make something do this: *The wet*

wood had warped in the heat. **2** to begin to have WARPED ideas, or to make someone do this

**war·path** /ˈwɔrpæθ/ *n* **be on the warpath** HUMOROUS to be angry about something and want to punish someone for it

**warped** /wɔrpt/ *adj* **1** having ideas or thoughts that most people think are not normal, or showing this quality: *a warped sense of humor* **2** bent or twisted into the wrong shape: *a warped cassette tape*

**war·rant**[1] /ˈwɔrənt, ˈwɑ-/ *v* [T] to be a good enough reason for something to happen or be done: *The story doesn't really warrant the attention it's been given in the press.* −compare UNWARRANTED

**warrant**[2] *n* an official paper that allows the police to do something: *The police have* **a warrant** *for Bryson's arrest.*

**war·ran·ty** /ˈwɔrənti, ˈwɑ-/ *n* [C,U] a written promise that a company will fix or replace something if it breaks after you have bought it: *The TV comes with a 3-year warranty.*

**war·ren** /ˈwɔrən, ˈwɑ-/ *n* **1** a set of holes and passages under the ground that rabbits live in **2** a lot of narrow passages in a building or between buildings: *a warren of alleyways and old tenement houses*

**war·ring** /ˈwɔrɪŋ/ *adj* fighting in a war: *warring factions*

**war·ri·or** /ˈwɔriɚ, ˈwɑ-/ *n* LITERARY a soldier, especially an experienced and skillful one

**war·ship** /ˈwɔrʃɪp/ *n* a navy ship with guns

**wart** /wɔrt/ *n* a small hard raised spot on your skin caused by a VIRUS

**war·time** /ˈwɔrtaɪm/ *n* [U] the time during which a war is happening: *a book about his wartime experiences*

**war·y** /ˈwɛri/ *adj* careful and worried about danger or problems: *Teach children to be* **wary** *of strangers.* −**warily** *adv*

**was** /wəz; *strong* wʌz, wɑz/ *v* the past tense of BE in the first and third person singular

**wash**[1] /wɑʃ, wɔʃ/ *v*

**wash**

**1** [T] to clean something with water: *These jeans need to be washed.* | *Go wash your hands!* | **Wash** *the mud* **off** *the truck.* **2** [I] to clean your body with water: *"I'm going upstairs to wash,"* *he called to Marge.* **3** [I,T] if water washes, it flows somewhere or makes something move somewhere: *waves* **washing** *softly* **against** *the shore* | *Floods* **washed** *much of the topsoil* **away**. | *Their boat* **washed up/ashore** *about five miles south.* **4 sth doesn't/won't wash** SPOKEN said when you do not believe someone or you think that other people will not believe him/her: *His explanation just didn't wash.* **5 wash your hands of sth** to refuse to be responsible for something: *They want to wash their hands of the whole thing.*

**wash** sth ↔ **down** *phr v* [T] **1** to drink something in order to help you swallow food or medicine: *He washed down a mouthful of toast with coffee.* **2** to clean something using a lot of water: *washing down the driveway*

**wash off** *phr v* [I] if a substance washes off, you can remove it from the surface of something by washing: *Will this paint wash off?*

**wash out** *phr v* [I,T **wash** sth ↔ **out**] to remove dirt, a spot etc. by washing something, or to be removed in this way: *Will you wash out the cups? | I don't know if that ink will wash out.*

**wash up** *phr v* [I] to wash your hands: *Go wash up for supper.*

**wash**² *n* **1** [C,U] clothing, sheets etc. that have been washed or that need washing: *I did three loads of wash this morning. | Your socks are in the wash.* (=being washed or waiting to be washed) **2** **it will all come out in the wash** SPOKEN said when you think that a problem will be solved without you having to do anything about it

**wash·a·ble** /ˈwɑʃəbəl/ *adj* able to be washed without being damaged: *a machine washable sweater*

**wash·bowl** /ˈwɑʃboʊl/, **wash·ba·sin** /ˈwɑʃ-ˌbeɪsən/ *n* ⇨ SINK

**wash·cloth** /ˈwɑʃklɔθ/ *n* a small square piece of cloth that you use to wash yourself

**washed-out** /ˌ. ˈ.◂ / *adj* very tired and pale: *My parents looked washed-out after the long trip.*

**washed-up** /ˌ. ˈ.◂ / *adj* INFORMAL someone who is washed-up is no longer successful: *a washed-up rock star*

**wash·er** /ˈwɑʃɚ/ *n* **1** a washing machine **2** a small ring of plastic or metal that you put between a NUT and a BOLT, or between two pipes, to make them fit together tightly

**wash·ing** /ˈwɑʃɪŋ/ *n* [U] clothes etc. that need to be washed or have just been washed: *Hang the washing on the line.*

**washing ma·chine** /ˈ.. .ˌ./ *n* a machine that washes clothes

**wash·out** /ˈwɑʃaʊt/ *n* [singular] INFORMAL a failure: *Rosie's date was a complete washout.*

**wash·room** /ˈwɑʃrum/ *n* OLD-FASHIONED ⇨ RESTROOM

**was·n't** /ˈwʌzənt, ˈwɑzənt/ *v* the short form of "was not": *He wasn't there.*

**WASP, Wasp** /wɑsp/ *n* White Anglo-Saxon Protestant; a white American whose religion is Protestant, and who is often fairly rich

**wasp** /wɑsp, wɔsp/ *n* a black and yellow flying insect similar to a BEE, that can sting you —see picture at BEE

**waste**¹ /weɪst/ *n* **1** [singular, U] the use of something in a way that is not useful or sensible, or the act of using more than you should of

something: *My father thought college would be a complete waste of time/money. | A lot of the food ended up going to waste.* **2** [C,U] things that are left after you have used something, or things you no longer want: *recycling household waste | laws on the safe disposal of nuclear/ toxic/hazardous wastes*

**waste**² *v* [T] **1** to use something in a way that is not effective, or to use more of it than you should: *Turn off those lights, you're wasting electricity. | They wasted a lot of time trying to fix the computer themselves.* —see usage note at TIME¹ **2** **be wasted on sb** if something is wasted on someone, s/he does not understand it or does not think it is worth anything: *All the romance in the movie was wasted on him.* **3** SLANG to kill someone —see also **save your breath/don't waste your breath** (BREATH)

**waste away** *phr v* [I] to gradually become thinner and weaker because you are sick: *He's wasting away to nothing.*

**waste**³ *adj* not being used effectively or no longer useful: *waste paper*

**waste·bas·ket** /ˈweɪstˌbæskɪt/ *n* a container into which you put paper etc. that you want to get rid of

**wast·ed** /ˈweɪstɪd/ *adj* **1** SPOKEN having drunk too much or taken drugs: *Chuck got wasted at Bryan's party.* **2** useless: *It had been a wasted trip.*

**waste·ful** /ˈweɪstfəl/ *adj* using more than is needed of something or using it badly, so that it is wasted: *wasteful packaging on groceries*

**waste·land** /ˈweɪstlænd/ *n* [C,U] a place that is too dry to be used for anything: *a wasteland unable to support human life*

**waste·pa·per bas·ket** /ˈweɪstˌpeɪpɚ ˌbæs-kɪt/ *n* ⇨ WASTEBASKET

**watch**¹ /wɑtʃ, wɔtʃ/ *v* **1** [I,T] to look at and pay attention to something or someone: *Harry was watching the game on TV. | I watched carefully for signs of emotion on her face.* **2** [T] to be careful about something, or about how you use something: *I should be watching my weight* (=being careful not to become fat). *| Billy, watch your language!* (=do not use rude words) *| Hey, watch it* - you stepped on my toes. **3** [T] to take care of someone or guard something: *Could you watch the kids for me Saturday night?* —see usage note at SEE

**watch for** sth *phr v* [T] to look for something, so that you are ready to deal with it: *Doctors are watching for any change in his condition.*

**watch out** *phr v* [I] to pay attention to what you are doing and be careful about it: *You can ride your bike here, but watch out for cars. | Watch out! You might cut yourself.*

**watch over** sth *phr v* [T] to take care of something or guard it: *The eldest child watches over the younger ones.*

W

**watch**

Lois is watching TV.

They are looking at the picture.

**watch**² *n* **1** [C] a small clock that you wear on your wrist or carry in your pocket: *My watch has stopped.* **2 keep a (close) watch on** to check a situation or a place carefully so that you always know what is happening and are ready to deal with it: *Police kept a 24-hour watch on the house.* | *Wall Street traders are keeping a close watch on gold prices.* **3 keep watch** to continue looking around an area in order to warn people of any danger: *Douglas kept watch while the others slept.* **4 keep a watch out for** to look carefully in order to try to find someone or something, while you are doing other things: *When you vacuum, could you keep a watch out for my ring?* **5 be on the watch for** to be looking and waiting for something that might happen or someone you might see: *Be on the watch for pickpockets around here.* **6** [C,U] people employed to guard or protect someone or something, or the fixed period of the day or night when they do this

**watch·dog** /'wɑtʃdɔg/ *n* **1** a person or group that makes sure other people follow rules: *a US Department of Energy watchdog committee* **2** a dog that protects someone's property

**watch·ful** /'wɑtʃfəl/ *adj* careful to notice what is happening, in order to prevent something bad happening: *keeping a watchful eye on the kids*

**watch·mak·er** /'wɑtʃ,meɪkɚ/ *n* someone who makes and repairs watches and clocks

**watch·man** /'wɑtʃmən/ *n* someone whose job is to guard a building or area: *the night watchman*

**watch·word** /'wɑtʃwɚd/ *n* [singular] the main principle or rule that you think about in a particular situation: *In the business of real estate, the watchword has been "buy" not "build."*

**wa·ter**¹ /'wɑtɚ, 'wɑ-/ *n* [U] **1** the clear colorless liquid that falls from the sky as rain, forms lakes, rivers, and oceans, and is necessary for life to exist: *Would you like a drink of water?* | *Ward waded out into the deepest water.* | *floods left the entire area* **under water** | *We sell only the finest* **fresh water** (=from a lake, river etc. not an ocean) *fish.* **2 in/into hot water** in a situation in which you have a lot of trouble: *My brother got into hot water borrowing all that money.*

**water**² *v* **1** [T] to pour water on a plant or seeds in the ground to help them grow: *I've had to water the lawn every day this week.* **2** [I] if your eyes water, they fill with water because they hurt: *The onions are making my eyes water.* **3** [I] if your mouth waters, it fills with water because you see something that looks good to eat

**water** sth ↔ **down** *phr v* [T] **1** to make something weaker by adding water: *The whiskey had been* **watered down**. **2** to make an idea, statement etc. less strong so that it does not offend or upset anyone: *We* **watered down** *the report a little for the broadcast.*

**wa·ter·bed** /'wɑtɚ,bɛd/ *n* a bed made of rubber or soft plastic and filled with water

**wa·ter·borne** /'wɑtɚ,bɔrn/ *adj* carried by water: *waterborne bacteria*

**wa·ter·col·or** /'wɑtɚ,kʌlɚ/ *n* [C,U] a special paint mixed with water, or a painting made with these: *Most of her works are watercolors.*

**wa·tered-down** /ˌ.. '.◂/ *adj* **1** a watered-down statement, plan etc. is not as strong or offensive as a previous one: *watered-down versions of horror movies* **2** a watered-down drink has been made weaker by having water added to it

**wa·ter·fall** /'wɑtɚ,fɔl/ *n* water that falls straight down over a rock or from the top of a mountain

**water foun·tain** /'.. ˌ../ *n* a piece of equipment in a public place that produces a stream of water that you can drink from; DRINKING FOUNTAIN

**wa·ter·front** /'wɑtɚ,frʌnt/ *n* [C] land at the edge of a lake, river etc.: *a new shopping center* **on the waterfront**

**wa·ter·hole** /'wɑtɚ,houl/ *n* a small area of water in a dry place where wild animals go to drink

**watering can** /'... ˌ./ *n* a container with a long hollow part on the front for pouring water on plants

**wa·ter·ing hole** /'... ˌ./ *n* INFORMAL a place such as a club or BAR where people can buy drinks: *the college students' favorite watering hole*

**wa·ter·logged** /'wɑtɚ,lɔgd, -ˌlɑgd/ *adj* land or an object that is waterlogged is so wet it cannot hold any more water

**wa·ter·mark** /'wɑtɚ,mɑrk/ *n* **1** a special design on a piece of paper that you can only see when it is held up to the light **2** the mark showing the highest level of a lake, river etc.

W

**wa·ter·mel·on** /ˈwɔtəˌmɛlən/ n [C,U] a large round green fruit with juicy dark pink flesh and black seeds —see picture on page 470

**water po·lo** /ˈ.. ˌ../ n [U] a game played in a swimming pool, in which two teams of players try to throw a ball into their opponents' GOAL

**wa·ter·proof** /ˈwɔtəˌpruf/ adj not allowing water to go through: *waterproof boots*

**water re·sis·tant** /ˈ.. .ˌ../ adj not letting water in easily, but not keeping all water out: *a water resistant watch*

**wa·ters** /ˈwɔtəz/ n [plural] **1** the part of the ocean near or belonging to a particular country: *fishing in Icelandic waters* **2** the water in a particular lake, river etc.: *the point where the waters of the Amazon flow into the sea*

**wa·ter·shed** /ˈwɔtəˌʃɛd/ n **1** [singular] the point at which an important change happens: *The beginning of television was **a watershed in** 20th century culture.* **2** the high land separating two river systems

**wa·ter·side** /ˈwɔtəˌsaɪd/ adj at the edge of a lake, river etc.: *a waterside restaurant* —**waterside** n [singular]

**water ski·ing** /ˈ.. ˌ../ n [U] a sport in which someone is pulled along on SKIs over water by a boat: *Do you want to **go water skiing**?* —**water ski** v [I] —**water skier** n

**wa·ter·tight** /ˈwɔtəˌtaɪt/ adj **1** not allowing water to get in: *a watertight container* **2** having no mistakes or weaknesses: *a watertight excuse/argument*

**wa·ter·way** /ˈwɔtəˌweɪ/ n an area of water, often part of a river, that ships can go through

**wa·ter·works** /ˈwɔtəˌwɜks/ n [plural] buildings, pipes, and supplies of water forming a public water system

**wa·ter·y** /ˈwɔtəri/ adj containing too much water: *watery soup | watery eyes*

**watt** /wɑt/ n a unit for measuring electrical power: *a 100 watt light bulb*

**wave¹** /weɪv/ v **waved, waving** **1** [I,T] to move your hand, or something you hold in your hand, as a signal or greeting, or to express something: *demonstrators waving their signs | Look! They're waving at us. | I **waved goodbye** as they pulled out of the driveway.* **2** [I] if a flag waves, it moves with the wind

**wave** sth ↔ **aside** phr v [T] to refuse to pay attention to a person or the things s/he suggests, offers etc.: *"Not true!" she said, **waving aside** any further comments.*

**wave²** n **1** a area of raised water that moves across the surface of a large area of water, especially the ocean: *Huge waves slammed onto the beach.* **2** a sudden increase in a particular

emotion, activity, number etc: *Police are trying to fight the recent **crime wave** in the suburbs. | a **wave of** nostalgia for his childhood | a huge **wave of** immigrants from Eastern Europe* **3** the movement you make when you wave your hand: *The Governor gave a wave to the crowd.* **4** a part of your hair that curls slightly: *tight waves of hair* **5** the form in which some types of energy move: *light/sound/radio waves* **6 make waves** INFORMAL to cause problems: *We have a job to finish, so don't make waves, OK?* —see also HEAT WAVE

**wave·length** /ˈweɪvlɛŋθ/ n **1** the size of a radio wave or the distance between two waves of energy such as sound or light **2 be on the same wavelength** INFORMAL to think in the same way about something as someone else does

**wa·ver** /ˈweɪvə/ v [I] to be uncertain or unsteady: *Mrs. Shreve wavered as she took a step towards us. | The president is **wavering between** two options.*

**wav·y** /ˈweɪvi/ adj having waves (=even curved shapes): *wavy hair*

**wax¹** /wæks/ n [U] a thick substance made of fats or oils, used for making things such as CANDLES

**wax²** v **1** [T] to put WAX on something, especially in order to polish it: *The floors had been waxed recently.* **2 wax romantic/eloquent etc.** OFTEN HUMOROUS to talk eagerly about someone or something you admire, especially for a long time: *Jamie sat at the bar, waxing poetical about Marcie.* **3** [I] when the moon waxes, you gradually see more of it

**waxed pa·per** /ˌ. ˈ../ , **wax paper** n [U] paper with a thin layer of WAX on it, used for wrapping food

**wax·y** /ˈwæksi/ adj **1** made of WAX or covered in wax: *apples with a waxy skin* **2** looking or feeling like WAX: *vines with waxy leaves* —**waxiness** n [U]

**way¹** /weɪ/ n

**1** ▶ROAD/PATH◀ the road, path etc. that you have to follow in order to get to a particular place: *Which way should we go? | Can you mail this on your **way downtown/home**? | Could you tell me the **way to** the police station **from** here? | I can give you a ride; it's **on my/the way**.* **2** ▶DIRECTION◀ a particular direction: *Which way is north from here? | Face this way, please. | Move three steps this way.* **3** ▶METHOD◀ [C] a manner or method of doing something or thinking about something: *Nobody could figure out a **way to** solve the problem. | I'd like to tell her **in my own way**. | Look at the way that guy's dressed! | Ryan has a funny **way of** talking.* **4 in a way/in some ways** used in order to say that something is partly true: *In a way, I like working alone better.* **5** ▶DISTANCE/TIME◀ [singular] also **ways** the distance or time between two places or events,

wave

especially if it is long: *a long way from home* | *We have a ways to go yet before we're done.* | *Did he actually come **all the way** (=the whole distance) from Bali?*

**6 have/get your way** to do what you want even if someone else wants something different: *They always let that kid **get his own way**.*

**7 the way/sb's way** where someone wants to go: *There was a big truck **in the way**.* (=preventing people from going past) | *Get **out of my way**!* (=move aside)

**8 get in the way of sth** to prevent something from happening: *Don't let your social life get in the way of your studying.*

**9 come a long way** to have developed a lot: *Psychiatry has come a long way since the 1920s.*

**10 a long way to go** to need a lot of time to develop or reach a particular standard: *There is a long way to go before democracy is accepted there.*

**11 under way** happening or moving: *Building work is scheduled to **get under way** (=start happening) today.*

**12 be on the way/its way/sb's way** to be arriving soon: *The check is on its way.* | *Carla's already on her way here.*

**13 way around** a particular order or position that something should be in: *Which way around does this skirt go?* | *Make sure all the pictures are the right way around.*

**14 give way to** if one thing gives way to another thing, this other thing replaces it or controls it: *fear gave way to anger*

**15 go out of your way to do sth** to do something that involves making a special effort, especially for someone else: *Ben went out of his way to help us.*

**16 you can't have it both ways** used in order to say that you cannot have the advantages of two different possible decisions

**17 make way a)** to move to one side so that someone or something can pass **b)** if one thing makes way for something else, this other thing replaces it: *Several houses were torn down to **make way for** a new fire station.*

---

SPOKEN PHRASES

**18 by the way** said when you want to begin talking about a new subject that you have just remembered: *Oh, by the way, I saw Marie yesterday.*

**19 no way! a)** used in order to say that you will definitely not do or allow something: *"Dad, can I have the car tonight?" "No way!"* **b)** used in order to say that you do not believe something or are surprised by it: *She's 45? No way!*

**20 way to go!** used in order to tell someone that s/he has done something good, or done something very well – see also **out of the way** (OUT²)

---

**way²** *adv* **1** long in distance or time: *We took the boat way out into the ocean.* | *a movie made way back before they used sound* **2 way more/bigger/longer etc.** SPOKEN NONSTANDARD a lot more, bigger, longer etc.: *This test was way harder than the last one.*

**way·lay** /ˈweɪleɪ/ *v* [T] LITERARY to stop someone so that you can talk to him/her, or in order to harm or rob him/her

**way of life** /ˌ . . ˈ./ *n, plural* **ways of life** the way someone lives, or the way people in a society usually live: *the **American way of life***

**way-out** /ˌ. ˈ.◄/ *adj* SPOKEN very modern and strange: *I like jazz, but not the way-out stuff.*

**way·side** /ˈweɪsaɪd/ *n* **fall/go by the wayside** to stop being successful, important, popular etc.: *With so many domestic problems, foreign policy issues fell by the wayside.*

**way·ward** /ˈweɪwɚd/ *adj* not following rules, and causing problems: *a wayward teenager*

**we** /wi/ *pron* **1** the person who is speaking and one or more other people: *We went to a bar that night.* | *We live in Dallas.* **2** people in general: *We know almost nothing about what causes the disease.* | *We all dream of being rich one day.*

**weak** /wik/ *adj* **1** not physically strong: *Kate's still weak from her illness.* | *a weak heart* **2** not strong in character, and easily influenced: *He's weak and afraid to make decisions.* **3** not having much ability or skill in a particular activity or subject: *I'm good at math, but weak at/in science.* **4** not having much power or influence: *a very weak leader* **5** not being good enough to persuade or influence people: *a weak excuse* **6** containing a lot of water or having little taste: *weak tea* **–weakly** *adv*

**weak·en** /ˈwikən/ *v* [I,T] **1** to become less powerful or physically strong, or to make someone or something do this: *The disease has weakened her heart.* | *a country weakened by war* **2** to become less determined, or to make someone do this: *Nothing could weaken her resolve.*

**weak·ling** /ˈwik-lɪŋ/ *n* DISAPPROVING someone who is not physically strong

**weak·ness** /ˈwiknɪs/ *n* **1** [U] the state of lacking strength in your body or character:

*weakness in the muscles* **2** a fault in someone's character or in a system, organization, design etc.: *What do you think are your strengths and weaknesses?* | *The cost of the plan is its main weakness.* **3 a weakness for sth** if you have a weakness for something, you like it very much even though it may not be good for you: *She's always had a weakness for chocolate.*

**wealth** /wɛlθ/ *n* **1** [U] a large amount of money and possessions: *a family of great wealth* **2 a wealth of experience/choices etc.** a large amount of experience, a large number of choices etc. that can help you do something: *the wealth of information that is available on the Internet*

**wealth·y** /'wɛlθi/ *adj* **1** having a lot of money or valuable possessions: *a very wealthy man* **2 the wealthy** people who have a lot of money or valuable possessions

**wean** /win/ *v* [I,T] to gradually stop feeding a baby on his/her mother's milk and start giving him/her ordinary food: *She was weaned at eight months.*

**wean** sb **off** sth *phr v* [T] to make someone gradually stop doing something you disapprove of: *I'm still trying to wean my daughter off sugary snacks.*

**wean** sb **on** sth *phr v* [T] **be weaned on** INFORMAL to be influenced by something from a very early age: *young movie directors who were weaned on MTV videos*

**weap·on** /'wɛpən/ *n* something that you use to fight with, especially a knife or gun –**weaponry** *n* [U]

**wear**[1] /wɛr/ *v* **wore, worn, wearing** **1** [T] to have something on your body, especially clothes or jewelry: *Why aren't you wearing your glasses?* | *I think I'll wear my black jeans to Pat's party.* **2** [T] to have your hair in a particular style: *Fay wore her hair in braids.* **3** [I,T] to become thinner, weaker etc. by continued use, or to make something do this: *The rug had worn in several places.* | *He's worn a hole in his pants already.* **4** [T] to have a particular expression on your face: *wearing a smile* **5 wear well** to remain in good condition after a period of time: *Expensive fabrics don't always wear well.* **6 sth is wearing thin** INFORMAL if an excuse, explanation, opinion etc. is wearing thin, it has been used so often that you no longer believe or accept it **7 wear the pants** INFORMAL to be the person in a family who makes the decisions –see usage note at DRESS[1]

**wear** sth ↔ **away** *phr v* [I,T] to gradually become thinner, weaker etc., or to make something do this by using it, rubbing it etc.: *Look at where the rocks have been worn away by the sea.*

**wear down** *phr v* **1** [I,T wear sth ↔ down] to gradually become smaller, or to make something do this by using it, rubbing it etc.: *My shoes have worn down at the heel.* **2** [T wear sb ↔ down] to make someone physically weaker or less determined: *He won simply by wearing down his opponent.*

**wear off** *phr v* [I] if pain or the effect of something wears off, it gradually stops: *The drug was starting to wear off.*

**wear on** *phr v* [I] if time wears on, it passes very slowly: *It became hotter as the day wore on.*

**wear out** *phr v* [I,T] **1** [wear sth ↔ out] to become weak, broken, or useless, or to make something do this by using it a lot or for a long time. *I think these batteries have worn out.* **2** [wear sb ↔ out] to feel extremely tired, or to make someone feel this way: *You look really worn out.* **3 wear out your welcome** to stay at someone's house longer than s/he wants you to

**wear**[2] *n* **1** [U] normal damage caused by continuous use over a long period: *The tires are showing signs of wear and tear.* **2** [U] the amount of use you can expect to get from something: *You'll get a lot of wear out of a sweater like that.* **3** clothes of a particular type, or worn for a particular activity: *evening wear*

**wea·ri·some** /'wɪrisəm/ *adj* FORMAL making you feel bored, tired, or annoyed: *a wearisome task*

**wea·ry**[1] /'wɪri/ *adj* very tired: *weary of arguing* | *The nation is weary of war and poverty.* –**wearily** *adv* –**weariness** *n* [U]

**weary**[2] *v* [I,T] FORMAL to become very tired especially because you have been doing something for a long time, or to make someone feel this way: *Jacobs soon wearied of his job at the bank.*

**wea·sel**[1] /'wizəl/ *n* **1** an animal like a long thin rat that kills other small animals **2** INFORMAL someone who has been disloyal to you or has deceived you

**weasel**[2] *v*

**weasel out of** sth *phr v* [I] INFORMAL to avoid doing something you should do by using dishonest excuses or lies: *We made a deal, and you can't weasel out of it.*

**weath·er**[1] /'wɛðɚ/ *n* **1** [singular, U] the temperature and other conditions such as sun, rain, and wind: *What was the weather like on your vacation?* | *very dry/wet/hot/cold weather* **2 under the weather** INFORMAL slightly sick: *I'm feeling a little under the weather.*

W

---

**USAGE NOTE weather**

There are many words for talking about the weather. **Wind** is a general word for the air when it moves. A **breeze** is a pleasant, gentle wind. A **gust** is a sudden strong wind, and a **gale** is an extremely strong wind. **Rain** is water that falls from clouds. If it is raining hard, it is **pouring**. If it is raining a little, it is a **drizzle**. When rain lasts only a short time, it is a **shower**. When rain begins to freeze, it is **sleet**. Hard, frozen drops of rain are **hail**. Frozen **rain** that falls in soft white pieces is **snow**. A **storm** is a general word for bad, wet weather. A **hurricane** is a storm with an extremely strong wind, that usually moves over water. A **tornado** is a cloud that spins and can destroy things, that moves as part of a storm over land. Both hurricanes and tornados are types of **cyclone**, which is a strong wind that moves in a circle. A **blizzard** is a bad winter storm with a lot of wind and snow. A **drought** is a long period with no water. When a lot of water suddenly covers an area that is usually dry, it is a **flood**.

**weather²** v **1** [T] to come through a very difficult situation without failing: *Business was bad, but we knew we would* **weather the storm**. **2** [I,T] to change or be changed in color or shape over a period of time because of sun, rain, wind etc.: *a weathered statue*

**weather fore·cast** /'.. ,../ n a report saying what the weather is expected to be like in the near future

**weather fore·cast·er** /'.. ,..../ n someone on television or radio who tells you what the weather will be like

**weath·er·man** /'wɛðɚ,mæn/ n a male WEATHER FORECASTER

**weather vane** /'wɛðɚ ,veɪn/ n a metal object attached to the top of a building, that moves to show the direction the wind is blowing

**weave¹** /wiv/ v **wove** *or* **weaved**, **woven** *or* **weaved**, **weaving** **1** [I] to make threads into cloth by crossing them under and over each other on a special machine: *They weave beautiful cloths in Ireland.* **2** [T] to make something by weaving or by twisting pieces of things together: *weaving a basket* **3** [I,T] to move somewhere by turning and changing direction a lot: *The snake was* **weaving through** *the grass towards us.* **−weave** n

**weave²** n the way in which a material is woven, and the pattern formed by this: *a fine weave*

**web** /wɛb/ n **1** a net of sticky thin threads made by a SPIDER to catch insects **2 a web of sth** a closely related set of things that can be very complicated: *a web of lies* **3 the Web** ⇨ WORLD WIDE WEB

**webbed** /wɛbd/ adj webbed feet or toes have skin between the toes: *a duck's webbed feet*

**web-foot·ed** /ˌ. '..‹ /, **web-toed** /ˌ. '.‹ / adj having toes that are joined by pieces of skin

**web·site** /'wɛbsaɪt/ n a program on a computer that is connected to the INTERNET and gives information about a particular subject or product

**we'd** /wid/ **1** the short form of "we had": *We'd better go now.* **2** the short form of "we would": *We'd rather stay.*

**wed** /wɛd/ v **wed** *or* **wedded**, **wed** *or* **wedded**, **wedding** **1** [I,T] LITERARY to marry someone **2 be wedded to sth** to be unable or unwilling to change a particular idea or way of doing things: *Most California commuters are wedded to their cars*

**wed·ding** /'wɛdɪŋ/ n a marriage ceremony, especially one with a religious service: *Have you been invited to their wedding?*

**wedding ring** /'.. ,./ n a ring worn to show that you are married, given to you on your wedding day

**wedge¹** /wɛdʒ/ n **1** a piece of wood, metal etc. that has one thick edge and one pointed edge, used for keeping a door open, splitting wood etc. **2** something shaped like a wedge: *a wedge of chocolate cake | shoes with wedge heels*

**wedge²** v [T] **1** to force something firmly into a narrow space: *We* **wedged** *a towel* **under** *the door to keep the cold air out.* **2 wedge sth open/shut** to put something under a door, window etc. to make it stay open or shut

**wed·lock** /'wɛdlɑk/ n [U] OLD-FASHIONED **1 born out of wedlock** if a child is born out of wedlock, his/her parents are not married when s/he is born **2** the state of being married

**Wednes·day** /'wɛnzdi, -deɪ/ written abbreviation **Wed.** n the fourth day of the week −see usage note at SUNDAY

**wee** /wi/ adj **1** LITERARY very small: *a wee child* **2 the wee hours** the early hours of the morning, just after MIDNIGHT

**weed¹** /wid/ n a wild plant that grows where you do not want it to grow

**weed²** v [I,T] to remove WEEDs from a place **weed** sb/sth ↔ **out** phr v [T] to get rid of people or things that are not very good: *These tests are supposed to* **weed out** *unsuitable recruits.*

**week** /wik/ n **1** a period of time equal to seven days, beginning on Sunday and ending on Saturday: *The movie starts* **this week**. *|* **last/next week** (=the week before or after this one) **2** any period of time equal to seven days and nights: *They spent three weeks in the tropics. |* **In a week**, (=a week after today) *the guests will begin to arrive. | I'll be back* **a week from today/tomorrow/Friday**. (=a week after today etc.) *| Are you busy* **the week after next**? (=the week that follows next week) **3** also **work week** the part of the week when you go to work, usually from Monday to Friday: *I don't see the kids much during the week.*

**week·day** /'wikdeɪ/ n any day of the week except Saturday and Sunday

**week·end** /'wikɛnd/ n Saturday and Sunday: *What are you doing* **this weekend**? (=the weekend that is coming) **last/next weekend** (=the weekend before or after this one) **over the week-**

**W**

*end* (=during the weekend that is past or that is coming) –see usage note at WEEKNIGHT

**week·ly** /'wikli/ *adj* **1** happening or done every week: *a weekly newspaper* **2** relating to a single week: *his weekly rate of pay* –**weekly** *adv*

**week·night** /'wiknaɪt/ *n* any night except Saturday or Sunday

---

**USAGE NOTE  weeknight**

Friday night is really a **weeknight**, but most people think of it as the beginning of the weekend because they do not have to go to school or work on Saturday. Sunday is part of the weekend, but people call it a **school night** because there is school on Monday.

---

**wee·nie** /'wini/ *n* SPOKEN **1** ⇨ HOT DOG **2** a word meaning someone who is weak, afraid, or stupid, used especially by children

**weep** /wip/ *v* **wept, wept, weeping** [I,T] to cry: *She wept as she described the man who had raped her.*

**weigh** /weɪ/ *v* **1** [linking verb] to have a particular weight: *The baby weighs 12 pounds.* **2** [T] to use a machine to find out what something or someone weighs: *Have you weighed yourself lately?* **3** [T] to consider something carefully: *I had to weigh the options pretty carefully.*

  **weigh down** *phr v* [T] **1** [weigh sb/sth ↔ down] to make someone or something bend or feel heavy under a load: *Sally was weighed down with shopping bags.* **2** [weigh sb ↔ down] to make someone feel worried: *a young man weighed down with responsibilities*

  **weigh in** *phr v* [I] **1** to have your weight tested before taking part in a BOXING fight or a horse race **2** weigh in (with) INFORMAL to add a remark to a discussion or an argument: *Everyone at the meeting weighed in with his own opinion.*

  **weigh on** sb *phr v* [T] to make someone feel worried: *The problem's been weighing on my mind for a long time.*

  **weigh** sth ↔ **out** *phr v* [T] to measure an amount of something by weighing it: *Could you weigh out half a pound of flour for me?*

**weight¹** /weɪt/ *n*

**1** ▶WHAT SB/STH WEIGHS◀ [U] how heavy someone or something is, which can be shown when measured by a particular system: *She's been putting on weight/losing weight lately.* (=becoming heavier/lighter)

**2** ▶HEAVINESS◀ [U] the fact of being heavy: *The weight of her boots made it hard for her to run.*

**3** ▶HEAVY THING◀ something that is heavy: *Omar can't lift heavy weights because he's hurt his back.* | *The gym has a rowing machine, step machine, and weights.*

**4** ▶FOR MEASURING QUANTITIES◀ a piece of metal weighing a particular amount that is balanced against something else to measure what it weighs

**5** ▶RESPONSIBILITY/WORRY◀ something that makes you worry: *Selling the house was a great weight off my mind.*

**6** ▶IMPORTANCE◀ [U] value, influence, or importance: *Tina's opinion doesn't carry much weight around here.*

**7** **throw your weight around** INFORMAL to use your position of authority to tell people what to do in an unpleasant and unreasonable way: *Paul is the only manager here who doesn't throw his weight around and give orders to people.*

**8** **pull your weight** INFORMAL to do all of the work that you are supposed to do: *If he's not pulling his weight, then talk to him about it!*

**weight²**, **weight down** *v* [T] to add something heavy to something or put a weight on it, especially in order to keep it in place: *fishing nets weighted with lead*

**weight·ed** /'weɪtɪd/ *adj* **weighted in favor/ weighted against** producing conditions that are favorable or unfavorable to one particular group: *The system is weighted against middle-class taxpayers.*

**weight·less** /'weɪtlɪs/ *adj* having no weight, especially when you are floating in space –**weightlessness** *n* [U]

**weight·lift·ing** /'. ,../ *n* [U] the sport of lifting specially shaped weights attached to the ends of a bar –**weight-lifter** *n*

**weight·y** /'weɪti/ *adj* important and serious: *a weighty problem*

**weird** /wɪrd/ *adj* INFORMAL unusual and strange: *It's weird, but I don't like ice cream very much.*

**weird·o** /'wɪrdoʊ/ *n* SPOKEN someone who behaves strangely, wears unusual clothes etc.

**welch** /wɛltʃ/ *v* [I] INFORMAL ⇨ WELSH

**wel·come¹** /'wɛlkəm/ *interjection* said in order to greet someone who has just arrived: *Welcome to Chicago!* | *Welcome back - it's good to see you again.*

**welcome²** *adj* **1** someone who is welcome is accepted by people as being part of a group: *I had the feeling I wasn't really welcome.* **2** something that is welcome is something people are happy to receive or be given because it helps them: *a welcome suggestion* | *a welcome breeze on a hot day*

---

SPOKEN PHRASES

**3** **you're welcome!** said in order to reply politely to someone who has just thanked you for something: *"Thanks for the coffee." "You're welcome."* **4** **be welcome to sb/ sth** used in order to say that someone can be with someone or have something if s/he wants to, because you do not want to: *If Rob wants that job he's welcome to it!* **5** **be welcome to do sth** used in order say that someone can do something if s/he wants to: *You're welcome to stay for lunch.*

**welcome**³ *v* [T] **1** to say hello in a friendly way to someone who has just arrived: *Jill was welcoming guests at the door.* **2** to gladly accept an idea, suggestion etc.: *We would welcome a change in the law.*

**welcome**⁴ *n* the greetings and acceptance you give to someone who has arrived as a guest: *Thank you for your warm welcome.* –see also **wear out your welcome** (WEAR¹)

**weld**¹ /wɛld/ *v* [I,T] to attach metal objects to each other by melting their edges and pressing them together when they are hot, or to be attached in this way –**weld** *n* –**welder** *n*

**wel·fare** /'wɛlfɛr/ *n* [U] **1** also **Welfare** money paid by the government to people who are very poor, not working, sick etc.: *Most of my neighbors are on welfare.* **2** health, comfort, and happiness: *We're only concerned with your welfare.*

**we'll** /wɪl; *strong* wil/ the short form of "we will": *We'll have to leave soon.*

**well**¹ /wɛl/ *adv* **better, best 1** in a good or satisfactory way: *Did you sleep well?* | *She doesn't hear very well.* | *Is the business doing well?* (=successful) | *a well-dressed young man* **2** in a thorough way: *I don't know her very well.* | *Mix the flour and eggs well.* **3** as well as in addition to something else: *I'm learning French as well as Italian.* **4** as well also: *I'd like a cup of coffee please, and a piece of apple pie as well.* **5** may/might/could well used in order to say that something is likely to happen or is likely to be true: *What you say may well be true.* **6** may/might as well do sth INFORMAL **a)** used when you do not particularly want to do something but you still do it: *We may as well get started.* **b)** used in order to say that doing something else would have an equally good result: *That train was so slow, we might just as well have taken the bus.* **7** very much, or very long in time: *It was well after 2:00 by the time we finished.* | *I'm well aware of the problem.* –see usage note at GOOD¹

**well**² *adj* **better, best 1** healthy: *My mother's not very well.* | *I'm feeling a lot better, thanks.* **2** it's just as well (that) SPOKEN used in order to say that things have happened in a way that is lucky or good, especially when they may have happened differently: *It's just as well I couldn't go to the game, we lost anyhow.* **3** it's/that's all very well SPOKEN used in order to say that you think something is not really good or satisfactory, even if someone else thinks it is: *It's all very well for you to say you're sorry, but I've been waiting here for two hours!*

**well**³ *interjection* **1** used in order to pause before saying something, to emphasize what you are saying, or to express surprise: *Mary's been acting strangely and, well, I was worried she*

might do something stupid. | *Well, all I can say is it's a total waste of time!* | *Well, so Steve's a senior manager now is he?* **2** also **oh well** said in order to show that you accept a situation even though it is not a good one: *Oh well, at least you did your best.* **3** said in order to connect two parts of a story that you are telling: *You know that guy I was telling you about? Well, he's been arrested!*

**well**⁴ *n* **1** a deep hole in the ground from which water is taken **2** a very deep hole in the ground from which oil is taken

**well**⁵ **well up** *v* [I] LITERARY **1** if liquids or well up, they rise and may start to flow: *Tears began to well up in her eyes.* **2** if feelings well or well up, they start to get stronger: *Anger welled up within him.*

**well-ad·just·ed** /ˌ. .'..◂/ *adj* able to deal well with your emotions and with the problems of life: *She seems pretty well-adjusted to me.*

**well-ad·vised** /ˌ. .'.◂/ *adj* FORMAL **you would be well-advised to do sth** used when you are strongly advising someone to do something: *You would be well-advised to see a doctor about that mole.*

**well-be·ing** /ˌ. '../ *n* [U] a feeling of being comfortable, healthy, and happy: *Regular exercise can improve your sense of well-being.*

**well-bred** /ˌ. '.◂/ *adj* OLD-FASHIONED very polite and knowing what to do in social situations

**well-de·fined** /ˌ. .'.◂/ *adj* something that is well-defined is very clear and easy to see, recognize, or understand: *well-defined muscles* | *well-defined rules*

**well-done** /ˌ. '.◂/ *adj* meat that is well-done has been cooked thoroughly: *He likes his steak well-done.*

**well-groomed** /ˌ. '.◂/ *adj* someone who is well-groomed has a very neat and clean appearance: *a well-groomed young man*

**well-heeled** /ˌ. '.◂/ *adj* rich: *a well-heeled family*

**well-in·ten·tioned** /ˌ. .'..◂/ *adj* ⇨ WELL-MEANING

**well-known** /ˌ. '.◂/ *adj* known by a lot of people: *a well-known artist and writer*

**well-mean·ing** /ˌ. '..◂/ *adj* intending or intended to be helpful, but often failing or making things worse: *well-meaning advice*

**well-off** /ˌ. '.◂/ *adj* having enough money to have a very good standard of living: *They're not extremely rich, but they're very well-off.*

**well-read** /ˌwɛl 'rɛd◂/ *adj* someone who is well-read has read many books and knows a lot about different subjects

**well-round·ed** /ˌ. '..◂/ *adj* **1** someone who is well-rounded has had a wide variety of experiences in life **2** a well-rounded education or background is complete and gives you knowledge of a wide variety of subjects

W

**well-spo·ken** /ˌ. ˈ..◂/ *adj* able to speak in a clear and polite way

**well-thought-of** /ˌ. ˈ. ˌ.◂/ *adj* liked and admired by other people

**well-timed** /ˌ. ˈ.◂/ *adj* said or done at the most suitable moment: *My arrival wasn't very well-timed.*

**well-to-do** /ˌ. . ˈ.◂/ *adj* rich: *a well-to-do family*

**well-wish·er** /ˈ. ˌ../ *n* someone who does something to show that s/he admires someone and wants him/her to succeed, be healthy etc.: *Hundreds of well-wishers waved as he climbed off the plane.*

**Welsh** /wɛlʃ/ *adj* relating to or coming from Wales

**welsh** *v* [I] INFORMAL to not do something you have agreed to do: *He welshed on the deal.*

**welt** /wɛlt/ *n* a raised mark on someone's skin where s/he has been hit

**wel·ter** /ˈwɛltɚ/ *n* FORMAL **a welter of** a large and confusing number of different details, emotions etc.: *a welter of information*

**went** /wɛnt/ *v* the past tense of GO

**wept** /wɛpt/ *v* the past tense and PAST PARTICIPLE of WEEP

**we're** /wɪr/ the short form of "we are": *We're going to the library.*

**were** /wɚ/ *v* the past tense of BE

**weren't** /wɚnt, ˈwɚənt/ *v* the short form of "were not": *Why didn't you tell me that you weren't happy?*

**were·wolf** /ˈwɛrwʊlf/ *n* a person in stories who changes into a WOLF

**west¹, West** /wɛst/ *n* **1** [singular, U] the direction toward which the sun goes down: *Which way is west?* **2 the west** the western part of a country, state etc.: *Rain will spread to the west later today.* **3 the West a)** the countries in North America and the western part of Europe **b)** the part of the US west of the Mississippi River **4 out West** in or to the west of the US: *I've always wanted to travel out west.* —see usage note at NORTH³

**west²** *adj* **1** in, to, or facing the west: *four miles west of Toronto | the west coast of the island* **2 west wind** a wind coming from the west

**west³** *adv* toward the west: *Go west on I-90 to Spokane. | The window faces west.*

**west·bound** /ˈwɛstbaʊnd/ *adj* traveling or leading toward the west: *westbound traffic | the westbound lanes of the freeway*

**west·er·ly** /ˈwɛstɚli/ *adj* **1** in or toward the west: *sailing in a westerly direction* **2** westerly winds come from the west

**west·ern¹** /ˈwɛstɚn/ *adj* **1** in or from the west part of an area, country, state etc.: *western Iowa* **2 Western** in or from the countries in North America and the western part of Europe: *Western technology* —see usage note at NORTH³

**western²** *n* a movie about life in the 19th century in the American West

**west·ern·er, Westerner** /ˈwɛstɚnɚ/ *n* someone who comes from the WESTERN part of a country or the western HEMISPHERE

**Western Eu·rope** /ˌ.. ˈ../ *n* the western part of Europe, including places such as Great Britain and Italy —**Western European** /ˌ.. ˌ..◂/ *adj*

**west·ern·ize** /ˈwɛstɚˌnaɪz/ *v* [T] to bring ideas, types of behavior, business methods etc. that are typical of North America and western Europe to other countries

**west·ern·most** /ˈwɛstɚnˌmoʊst/ *adj* farthest west: *the westernmost part of the island*

**west·ward** /ˈwɛstwɚd/ *adj, adv* toward the west

**wet¹** /wɛt/ *adj* **1** covered in or full of liquid: *Try not to get your feet wet. | a wet sponge* **2** rainy: *wet weather* **3** not yet dry: *wet paint* **4 wet behind the ears** INFORMAL very young and without much experience —**wetness** *n* [U]

**wet²** *v* **wet** *or* **wetted, wet, wetting** [T] **1** to make something wet: *Wet this cloth and put it on her forehead.* **2 wet the bed/wet your pants** to make your bed or pants wet because you URINATE by accident

**wet·back** /ˈwɛtˌbæk/ *n* TABOO an extremely offensive word for someone from Mexico who has come to the US, especially illegally

**wet suit** /ˈwɛtsut/ *n* a thick piece of clothing, usually made of rubber, that swimmers wear to keep warm when they are in the water

**we've** /wiv/ the short form of "we have": *We've got to leave by 6:00.*

**whack¹** /wæk/ *v* [T] INFORMAL to hit someone or something hard: *I got whacked in the mouth by a baseball.*

**whack²** *n* **1** the act of hitting something hard, or the noise this makes **2 out of whack** INFORMAL if a machine or system is out of whack, it is not working correctly **3 take a whack at** INFORMAL to try to do something: *I can't open this jar; do you want to take a whack at it?*

**whacked** /wækt/, **whacked out** *adj* SPOKEN **1** very tired **2** behaving in a very strange way

**whale¹** /weɪl/ *n* **1** a very large animal that swims in the ocean and breathes through a hole on the top of its head **2 have a whale of a time** INFORMAL to enjoy yourself very much

**whale²** *v*

**whale on** sb/sth *phr v* [T] SPOKEN to hit someone or something very hard: *Three guys were just whaling on him.*

**whal·er** /ˈweɪlɚ/ *n* **1** someone who hunts whales **2** a boat used for hunting whales

**whal·ing** /ˈweɪlɪŋ/ *n* [U] the activity of hunting whales

W

**wham**[1] /wæm/ *interjection* **1** said when describing the sound of one thing hitting another thing very hard: *The car went wham into the wall.* **2** said in order to show that something very unexpected suddenly happens: *Everything is going OK and then, wham, you lose your job.*

**wham**[2] *n* the sound made when something is hit very hard: *a loud wham*

**wharf** /wɔrf/ *n*, plural **wharves** /wɔrvz/ a structure that is built out into the water so that boats can stop next to it; PIER

**what** /wʌt, wɑt; *weak* wət/ *determiner pron*
**1** used when asking about something that you do not know anything about: *What are you doing?* | *What did Ellen say?* | *What kind of dog is that?* | *"I didn't think it would be like this." "What do you mean?"* **2** used in order to talk about things or information, especially in questions that are not direct: *I'm not sure what you can do.* | *I couldn't believe what he was saying.* | *He showed us what he'd made.* **3 have what it takes** to have the ability or courage to do something: *Whitman didn't have what it takes to do the job.*

---
SPOKEN PHRASES
---

**4 a)** said when you have not heard something that someone said: *"Do you want a fried egg?" "What?"* **b)** used in order to answer when someone calls your name: *"Anita?" "What?" "Can you come here for a minute?"* **5** used at the beginning of a sentence to emphasize what you are saying: *What an idiot!* | *What a nice day.* **6 what about...? a)** used in order to make a suggestion: *What about sending him an e-mail?* **b)** used in order to introduce a new person or thing into the conversation: *What about the salad - should I throw it away?* | *So, I've been enjoying work - what about you?* **7 What's up? a)** used when saying hello to someone you know well: *"Hey Chris! What's up, buddy?" "Not a lot!"* **b)** used in order to ask what is wrong or what is happening: *What's up with this printer - does it work?* **8 what's happening? a)** used in order to ask what people are doing or what a situation is: *What's happening? What's everyone staring at?* | *What's happening with your dad's business? (=how is it?)* **b)** used when saying hello to someone you know well: *Hi, Brad. What's happening, man?* **9 what (...) for?** used in order to ask the reason for something or purpose of something: *"Can I borrow your bike?" "What for?"* | *What's this thing for?* **10 what if...? a)** used in order to ask what will happen, especially when it could be something bad or frightening: *What if we get stuck out there in the snow?* **b)** used when making a suggestion: *What if you just take that part out of the speech?* **11** said when you are very surprised:

*"They won't let Martin back into the country." "What?"* **12 ...or what? a)** used in order to ask if there is another possibility: *Are they doing that to save money, or what?* **b)** used in order to show you are impatient when asking a question: *Are you coming now, or what?* **13 what's with...?** used in order to ask why someone is behaving strangely or why something strange is happening: *What's with Nicky? He seems really mad.*

−see also **guess what/you'll never guess** (GUESS[1]) **so what?** (SO[1]) −see also usage note at WHICH

---
**USAGE NOTE** what

When you are talking to someone and you do not understand what s/he says or you do not hear him/her clearly, it is polite to say, "I'm sorry, I didn't hear you" or "I'm sorry, I don't understand you." It is not polite to just say, "What?"

---

**what·cha·ma·call·it** /'wʌtʃəmə,kɔlɪt/ *n* SPOKEN a word you use when you cannot remember the name of something: *I've broken the whatchamacallit on my bag.*

**what·ev·er**[1] /wət'ɛvɚ/ *pron* **1** any or all of the things that are wanted, needed, or possible: *Just take whatever you need.* **2** used as a reply to mean that it does not matter what happens: *"Do you want to go to the movies?" "Whatever."* **3** SPOKEN said when you do not know the exact name of someone or something: *Why don't you invite Steve, or whatever he's called, to supper?*

**whatever**[2] *determiner* **1** used in order to talk about anything or everything of a particular type: *Whatever faults he may have, I still like him.* | *Whatever I suggest, she always disagrees.* **2 whatever you say/want** used in order to agree with someone, when you do not want to argue: *"I want to go to Canada this year." "OK, whatever you want."*

**whatever**[3], **what·so·ev·er** /,wʌtsoʊ'ɛvɚ/ *adv* used in order to emphasize a negative statement: *She had no money whatsoever.*

**wheat** /wit/ *n* [U] a plant that produces a grain, used for making flour and food such as bread

**whee·dle** /'widl/ *v* [I,T] to persuade someone to do something by saying pleasant things that you do not really mean: *He wheedled me into paying.* | *She managed to wheedle $15 out of him.*

**wheel**[1] /wil/ *n* **1** one of the round things under a car, bicycle etc. that turns and allows it to move **2** a flat round part in a machine that turns when the machine operates **3** ⇨ STEERING WHEEL **4 big wheel** INFORMAL an important person −see also WHEELS

**wheel**² *v* **1** [T] to move something that has wheels: *She **wheeled** her bike **into** the garage.* **2** [I] to turn around suddenly: *Anita **wheeled around** and started yelling at us.* –see also **wheeling and dealing**

**wheel·bar·row** /'wil,bærou/ *n* a small CART with one wheel in the front and two long handles for pushing it, that you use outdoors to carry things

**wheel·chair** /'wil-tʃɛr/ *n* a chair with wheels, used by people who cannot walk

**wheel·ie** /'wili/ *n* **do a wheelie** INFORMAL to balance on the back wheel of a bicycle or MOTORCYCLE that you are riding

**wheel·ing and deal·ing** /,.. . '../ *n* [U] activities that involve a lot of complicated and sometimes dishonest deals, especially in politics or business –**wheeler-dealer** /,.. '../ *n*

**wheels** /wilz/ *n* SPOKEN (**set of**) **wheels** a car: *Wow! Nice wheels!*

**wheeze** /wiz/ *v* [I] to breathe with difficulty, making a whistling sound in your chest –**wheezy** *adj*

**when**¹ /wɛn/ *adv* used when asking what time something will happen: *When are we leaving?* | *When did you notice he was gone?*

**when**² *conjunction* **1** used in order to give a specific time: *When I was little, I hated green beans.* | *They look like gold when the sun shines on them.* **2** used in order to show what happens in a particular situation: *When you think about it, you'll see I'm right.* **3** even though or in spite of the fact that something is true: *Why do you want a new bike when this one is perfectly good?* –see also **since when** (SINCE²)

---

**USAGE NOTE** when, at the time, by the time, and by that time

Use these phrases to talk about the relationship between two events. Use **when** at the beginning of a CLAUSE in order to say what was happening at the same time that another event happened: *When the doorbell rang, I was in the shower.* | *I was in the shower when the doorbell rang.* Use **at the time** to talk about a specific time in the past when two things happened at the same time: *I'm sorry I couldn't see you this morning.* | *I had an appointment at the time.* | *At the time, I had no idea what he was talking about.* Use **by the time** to say that one thing had already happened when something else happened, or that one thing will have already happened when something else happens. This phrase is used with dependent clauses (=clauses that cannot be used alone as sentences): *By the time he decided to go to the concert, there were no more tickets.* | *By the time she graduates, she will have lived in Boston for five years.* **By that time** means the same thing, but the phrase is used with inde-

---

pendent clauses (=clauses that could be used alone as sentences): *She said she'd phone us at 6:00, but by that time we'd already left.* | *"I can help you with the dishes in a few minutes." "By that time, I'll have finished washing them."*

---

**when·ev·er** /wɛ'nɛvɚ, wə-/ *adv, conjunction* **1** every time: *Whenever we come here we see someone we know.* **2** at any time: *Come over whenever you want.* **3** SPOKEN used in order to say that it does not matter when something happens: *"Should I come over around six?" "Whenever."*

**where** /wɛr/ *adv, conjunction* **1** used in order to ask or tell someone the place or position of something: *Where do you live?* | *Where did you park the car?* | *I know where Ramon is.* **2** used in order to ask or talk about the situation or state of something: *Where do we go from here?* (=what do we do now?) | *I wish I knew where it will all end.* (=I wish I knew what will happen)

**where·a·bouts**¹ /'wɛrə,bauts, ,wɛrə'bauts/ *adv* SPOKEN used in questions when you are asking where a place is: *Whereabouts do you live?*

**where·a·bouts**² /'wɛrə,bauts/ *n* [U] the place or area where someone or something is: *His whereabouts are still a mystery.*

**where·as** /wɛr'æz; weak wɛrəz/ *conjunction* used in order to say that although something is true of one thing, it is not true of another: *They want a house, whereas we would rather live in an apartment.*

**where·by** /wɛr'baɪ/ *adv* FORMAL by means of which, or according to which: *a law whereby all children receive free education*

**where·in** /wɛr'ɪn/ *adv, conjunction* FORMAL in what or in which: *a procedure wherein patients are given high doses of vitamin B*

**where·u·pon** /,wɛrə'pɑn, 'wɛrə,pɑn/ *conjunction* FORMAL after which: *One of them said he was a liar, whereupon a fight broke out.*

**wher·ev·er** /wɛr'ɛvɚ/ *adv* **1** to or at any place: *If you could go wherever you wanted to in the world, where would you go?* | *Sit wherever you like.* **2** used at the beginning of a question to show surprise: *Wherever did you find that old thing?*

**where·with·al** /'wɛrwɪ,ðɔl, -,θɔl/ *n* **the wherewithal to do sth** the money or ability you need in order to do something: *He just didn't have the wherewithal to do more with his life.*

**whet** /wɛt/ *v* **-tted, -tting** [T] **whet sb's appetite (for sth)** to make someone want more of something: *The trip to Paris has whetted my appetite for travel.*

**wheth·er** /'wɛðɚ/ *conjunction* **1** used when talking about a choice between different possibilities: *He asked me whether she was coming.* | *I couldn't decide **whether or not** I wanted to go.*

W

**2** used in order to say that something definitely will or will not happen in spite of what the situation is: *Whether you like it **or not**, you're going to have to take that test.*

**whew** /hwyu, hwu/ *interjection* ⇨ PHEW

**which** /wɪtʃ/ *determiner, pron* **1** used in order to ask or state what things you mean when a choice is to be made: *Which of these books is yours? | Ask him which one he wants.* **2** used in order to show what specific thing or things you mean: *The letters from fans, which have been coming every day, are mostly from teenagers.* **3** used in order to add more information about something, especially in written language after a COMMA: *The train only takes two hours, which is quicker than the bus.* –see also usage note at THAT¹

---

**USAGE NOTE which and what**

Use these words when asking a question about a choice you need to make. Use **what** when you make a choice from an unknown number of things or people: *What color would you like your room to be painted?* Use **which** when you make a choice from a limited number of things or people: *Which color would you like - blue or yellow?*

---

**which·ev·er** /wɪ'tʃɛvɚ/ *determiner, pron* used in order to say that it does not matter what thing you choose, what you do etc.: *You can have whichever you like best. | You get the same result whichever way you do it.*

**whiff** /wɪf/ *n* a smell of something that is not strong: *As she walked past, I **caught a whiff of** (=smelled) her perfume.*

**while¹** /waɪl/ *n* **a while** a period of time, especially a short one: *Can you wait a while or do you have to leave right now? | I've been alone **for a while**. | I'll be back in **a little while**.* –see also AWHILE, **worth your while** (WORTH¹)

**while²** *conjunction* **1** during the time that something is happening: *They arrived while we were having dinner. | I like to listen to music while I'm taking a bath.* **2** in spite of the fact that; though: *While she is a likable woman she can be extremely difficult to work with.* **3** used in order to say that although something is true of one thing, it is not true of another: *That region has plenty of water, while this one has little.*

**while³** *v* **while away the hours/evening/days etc.** to spend time in a pleasant and lazy way: *We whiled away the summer evenings talking and drinking wine.*

**whim** /wɪm/ *n* a sudden desire to do or have something, especially when there is no good reason for it: *I went to visit her **on a whim**.* (=because of a whim)

**whim·per** /'wɪmpɚ/ *v* [I] to make low crying sounds, or to speak in this way: *A dog*

*whimpered in the corner. | "Don't hurt me," he whimpered.* –**whimper** *n*

**whim·si·cal** /'wɪmzɪkəl/ *adj* unusual, but fun or showing that someone is having fun: *a whimsical smile*

**whine** /waɪn/ *v* [I] **1** to complain about something in a sad annoying voice: *Stop **whining about** everything!* **2** to make a long high sound because you are in pain or unhappy: *The dog was whining at the door.* **3** if a machine whines, it makes a continuous high sound –**whine** *n* –**whiner** *n*

**whin·ny** /'wɪni/ *v* [I] if a horse whinnies, it makes a quiet high sound –**whinny** *n*

**whip¹** /wɪp/ *n* a long thin piece of rope or leather with a handle, used for making animals move or for hitting people

**whip²** **-pped, -pping** *v* **1** [T] to hit someone with a whip **2** [T] INFORMAL to defeat someone easily: *Smith ran for three touchdowns as the Hawks whipped the Huskies 42-3.* **3** [T] INFORMAL to move something with a quick sudden movement: *He **whipped out** a gun.* **4** [I] to move suddenly or violently: *The wind **whipped across** the plain. | Bill **whipped around** to see what was happening.* **5 whip sb/sth into shape** INFORMAL to make a system, group of people etc. start to work in an organized way **6** [T] also **whip up** to continue to quickly mix something such as cream or the clear part of an egg very hard until it becomes stiff

**whip up** *phr v* [T] **1 whip up support/enthusiasm etc.** to deliberately try to make people feel or react strongly **2** [**whip** sth ↔ **up**] to quickly make something to eat: *I could whip up a salad or something.*

**whip·lash** /'wɪplæʃ/ *n* [U] a neck injury caused when your head moves forward and back again suddenly and violently, especially in a car accident

**whip·ping** /'wɪpɪŋ/ *n* a punishment given to someone by hitting him/her, especially with a whip

**whir** /wɚ/ *v* **-rred, -rring** [I] to make a fairly quiet regular sound, like the sound of something spinning or moving up and down in the air very quickly: *Somewhere, an electric motor whirred.* –**whir** *n*

**whirl¹** /wɚl/ *v* [I,T] to spin around very quickly, or to make something do this: *The falling leaves **whirled around** her feet.*

**whirl²** *n* **1 give sth a whirl** INFORMAL to try something that you are not sure you are going to like or be able to do **2** [singular] a lot of activity of a particular kind: *a whirl of social activity* **3 be in a whirl** to feel very excited or confused about something: *Debbie's head was all in a whirl.* **4** a spinning movement, or the shape of a substance that is spinning: *a whirl of dust*

**whirl·pool** /'wɚlpul/ *n* a powerful current of

**W**

water that spins rapidly and pulls things down into it

**whirl·wind** /'wɚˌwɪnd/ *n* **1 a whirlwind romance/tour etc.** something that happens much more quickly than usual **2** an extremely strong wind that moves quickly with a circular movement, causing a lot of damage **3 a whirlwind of activity/emotions etc.** a situation in which you quickly experience a lot of different activities or emotions one after another

**whisk**[1] /wɪsk/ *v* [T] **1** to stir liquids or soft food very quickly together: *Whisk the yolks and sugar in a bowl.* **2** to quickly take something or someone somewhere: *After the show, the band was* **whisked away/off** *to a secret location.*

**whisk**[2] *n* a small kitchen tool made of curved pieces of wire, used for WHISKing eggs, cream etc.

**whisk·er** /'wɪskɚ/ *n* one of the long stiff hairs that grow near the mouth of a cat, mouse etc.

**whisk·ers** /'wɪskɚz/ *n* [plural] the hair that grows on a man's face

**whis·key** /'wɪski/ *n, plural* **whiskeys** *or* **whiskies** [C,U] a strong alcoholic drink made from grain, or a glass of this drink

**whis·per**[1] /'wɪspɚ/ *v* **1** [I,T] to speak or say something very quietly, using your breath rather than your voice: *What are you two whispering about over there?* **2** [I] LITERARY to make a soft sound: *The wind whispered in the trees.*

**whisper**[2] *n* **1** a very quiet voice: *"Quiet - they're coming!"* *he said* **in a whisper.** **2** LITERARY a soft sound: *the whisper of the meadow grasses*

**whis·tle**[1] /'wɪsəl/ *v* **1** [I,T] to make a high or musical sound by blowing air out through your lips: *Adam* **whistled** *to/at me from across the street.* **2** [I] to make a high sound by blowing into a whistle: *The referee whistled and the game began.* **3** [I] to move quickly with a high sound: *Bullets were whistling through the air.* **4** [I] to make a high sound when air or steam is forced through a small hole: *a whistling kettle*

**whistle**[2] *n* **1** a small object that produces a high sound when you blow into it **2** a high sound made by blowing air through a whistle, your lips etc. **3** a high sound made by something moving quickly: *the whistle of the wind* −see also **blow the whistle (on sb)** (BLOW[1])

**white**[1] /waɪt/ *adj* **1** having a color that is lighter than every other color, like the color of snow or clouds: *white paint* **2** someone who is white has pale skin −**whiteness** *n* [U]

**white**[2] *n* **1** [U] a white color **2** also **White** someone who has pale skin **3** the white part of your eye **4** [C,U] the transparent part of the inside of an egg, that surrounds the yellow part and becomes white when cooked

**white-bread** /ˌ. '.◂/ *adj* relating to people who are white and who have traditional Ameri-

can values, and who are often considered boring: *a white-bread suburban family*

**white col·lar** /ˌ. '.◂/ *adj* white collar workers do jobs in offices, banks etc., and often manage other workers −compare BLUE COLLAR −see usage note at CLASS[1]

**White House** /'. ./ *n* **1** [singular] the President of the US and the people who advise him/her: *an election that resulted in a Democratic White House* **2 the White House** the official home in Washington, D.C. of the President of the US −**White House** *adj*: *a White House spokesperson*

**white lie** /ˌ. './ *n* INFORMAL a lie that is not very important, especially one that you tell in order to avoid hurting someone's feelings

**whit·en** /'waɪt̬n/ *v* [I,T] to become white, or to make something do this: *It whitens your teeth and freshens your breath!*

**white trash** /ˌ. './ *n* [U] INFORMAL an insulting expression meaning white people who are poor and uneducated

**white·wash** /'waɪt̬wɑʃ, -wɔʃ/ *n* **1** [C usually singular] an attempt to hide the true facts about a serious accident or illegal action: *One magazine called the report a whitewash.* **2** [U] a white liquid mixture used for painting walls, fences etc. −**whitewash** *v* [T]

**white·wa·ter** /'waɪt̬ˌwɔt̬ɚ, -ˌwɑ-/ *n* [U] a part of a river that looks white because the water is flowing very quickly over rocks

**whit·tle** /'wɪt̬l/ *v* [I,T] to cut a piece of wood into a particular shape by cutting off small pieces

**whittle** sth ↔ **away** *phr v* [T] to gradually reduce the size, amount, or value of something: *The country is slowly* **whittling away at** *its huge trade imbalance.*

**whittle** sth ↔ **down** *phr v* [T] to gradually make something smaller by taking parts away: *I've* **whittled down** *the list of guests from 30 to 16.*

**whiz**[1] /wɪz/ *v* **-zzed, -zzing** [I] **1** INFORMAL to move very quickly, often making a sound like something rushing through the air: *Marty* **whizzed by** *us on his motorbike.* **2** SLANG to URINATE

**whiz**[2] *n* **1** INFORMAL someone who is very fast, intelligent, or skilled in a particular activity, especially a young person: *a computer* **whiz kid** **2** [singular] SLANG an act of urinating (URINATE)

**who** /hu/ *pron* **1** used in order to ask about a person or group of people, or to make a statement about them: *"Who is that?"* *"That's Amy's brother."* | *"Who told you about the fire?"* *"Mr. Garcia."* | *I know who sent you that card.* | *The Wright brothers were the men who invented the airplane.* **2** used in order to add more information about someone: *She asked her English teacher, who had also studied Latin.* −see also usage note at THAT[1]

W

**whoa** /wou, hwou, hou/ *interjection* a command given to a horse to make it stop

**who'd** /hud/ **1** the short form of "who had": *a young girl who'd been attacked* **2** the short form of "who would": *Who'd know where I can get tickets?*

**who·dun·it** /hu'dʌnɪt/ *n* INFORMAL a book, movie etc. about a murder, in which you do not find out who the murderer is until the end

**who·ev·er** /hu'ɛvɚ/ *pron* **1** used in order to talk about someone when you do not know who s/he is: *Whoever did this is in big trouble.* **2** used in order to show that it does not matter which person does something: *Whoever gets there first can find a table.*

**whole¹** /houl/ *n* **1 the whole of** all of something: *The whole of the morning was wasted.* **2 on the whole** used in order to say that something is generally true: *On the whole, life was much quieter after John left.* **3 as a whole** used in order to say that all the parts of something are being considered: *We must look at our educational system as a whole.* **4** [C usually singular] something that consists of a number of parts, but is considered as a single unit: *Two halves make a whole.*

**whole²** *adj* all of something; ENTIRE: *She drank a whole bottle of wine.* | **The whole thing** (=everything about a situation) *just makes me sick.* | *Barney spent the whole day in bed.*

**whole·heart·ed** /ˌhoul'hartɪd◂/ *adj* involving all your feelings, interest etc.: *You have our wholehearted support.* **–wholeheartedly** *adv*

**whole·sale¹** /'houlseɪl/ *adj* **1** relating to the sale of goods in large quantities, usually at low prices to people or stores that then sell to other people: *a wholesale price* **2** affecting almost everything or everyone, and often done without any concern for the results: *wholesale destruction* **–wholesale** *adv*: *I can get it for you wholesale.* **–compare** RETAIL

**whole·sale²** *n* [U] the selling of goods in large quantities to RETAIL stores: *goods bought at wholesale prices* **–compare** RETAIL

**whole·sal·er** /'houlˌseɪlɚ/ *n* a person or business that sells goods WHOLESALE

**whole·some** /'houlsəm/ *adj* **1** likely to make you healthy: *a good wholesome breakfast* **2** considered to be morally good or acceptable: *a nice clean wholesome kid*

**whole wheat** /ˌ. '.◂/ *adj* whole wheat flour or bread is made using every part of the WHEAT grain, including the outer layer

**who'll** /hul/ the short form of "who will": *This is Denise, who'll be your guide today.*

**whol·ly** /'houli/ *adv* FORMAL completely: *The club is wholly responsible for the damage.*

**whom** /hum/ *pron* the object form of "who," used especially in formal speech or writing: *To whom am I speaking?* | *He spoke to a man with whom he used to work.* **–see** usage notes at THAT¹, WHO

**whoop** /hup, wup/ *v* [I] to shout loudly and happily **–whoop** *n*

**whoops** /wups/ *interjection* said when you make a small mistake, drop something, or fall

**whoosh** /wuʃ, wuʃ/ *v* [I] INFORMAL to move very fast with a soft rushing sound: *cars whooshing past* **–whoosh** *n*

**whop·per** /'wapɚ/ *n* INFORMAL **1** something that is unusually large **2** a lie

**who're** /'huɚ, hur/ the short form of "who are": *Who're those two guys?*

**whore** /hɔr/ *n* OFFENSIVE ⇨ PROSTITUTE¹

**who's** /huz/ **1** the short form of "who is": *Who's sitting next to Reggie?* **2** the short form of "who has": *That's Karl, the guy who's studied in Brazil.*

**whose** /huz/ *determiner, possessive pron* **1** used in order to ask which person or people a particular thing belongs to: *Whose jacket is this?* **2** used in order to show the relationship between a person and something that belongs to that person: *That's the man whose house burned down.*

**who've** /huv/ the short form of "who have": *There are a lot of people who've complained.*

**why** /waɪ/ *adv, conjunction* **1** for what reason: *Why are these books so cheap?* | *Why haven't you finished it yet?* **2 why don't you/why doesn't he...etc.** SPOKEN used in order to make a suggestion: *Why don't you try this one?* **3 why not?** SPOKEN **a)** used in order to ask someone why s/he has not done something: *"I haven't done my homework." "Why not?"* **b)** used in order to agree to do something: *"Do you want to come along?" "Yeah, why not?"*

**WI** the written abbreviation of Wisconsin

**wick** /wɪk/ *n* the string on a CANDLE or in an oil lamp that is burned

**wick·ed** /'wɪkɪd/ *adj* **1** morally bad; evil: *the wicked stepmother in "Cinderella"* **2** bad in a way that seems harmless and amusing; MISCHIEVOUS: *a wicked grin* **3** SLANG very good: *a wicked concert*

**wick·er** /'wɪkɚ/ *adj* made from thin dry branches woven together: *a white wicker chair*

**wick·et** /'wɪkɪt/ *n* one of the curved wires used in CROQUET

**wide¹** /waɪd/ *adj* **1** measuring a large distance from one side to the other: *a wide street* | *Jill has a wide mouth.* | *The quake was felt over a wide area.* **–see** picture at NARROW¹ **2** measuring a particular distance from one side to the other: *The bathtub's three feet wide and five feet long.* **3** including a large variety of different people, things, or situations: *We offer a wider range of vegetarian dishes.* **4** from many people: *The case has received wide attention.* **5 statewide/citywide/company-wide etc.** affecting all of a place or all of the people in it **6 wide difference/gap etc.** a large and noticeable difference, GAP etc.: *wide differences of opinion*

**wide²** *adv* **1** used instead of "completely" with the prepositions "open" and "apart": *Somebody left the door wide open.│wide open spaces│The guards stood with their legs wide apart.* **2 wide open for/to sth** making it easy for people to do something: *She left herself wide open to criticism.│Siberia is wide open for investment.* **3 wide awake** completely awake **4** away from the point that you were aiming at: *His shot went wide.*

**wide-eyed** /'. ./ *adj, adv* **1** with your eyes wide open, especially because you are surprised or frightened: *a wide-eyed stare* **2** too willing to believe, accept, or admire things because you do not have much experience of life

**wide·ly** /'waɪdli/ *adv* **1** in a lot of different places or by a lot of people: *products that are widely available│a widely read newspaper* **2** to a large degree; a lot: *Taxes vary widely from state to state.*

**wid·en** /'waɪdn/ *v* [I,T] **1** to become wider or to make something wider: *His eyes widened in fear.│The old trail was widened into a road.* **2** to become greater or larger: *The gap between low and high incomes began to widen after 1974.*

**wide·spread** /ˌwaɪd'sprɛd◂/ *adj* happening in many places, among many people, or in many situations: *the widespread use of illegal drugs*

**wid·ow** /'wɪdoʊ/ *n* a woman whose husband has died and who has not married again

**wid·owed** /'wɪdoʊd/ *adj* having become a WIDOW or WIDOWER: *He was widowed three years ago.*

**wid·ow·er** /'wɪdoʊɚ/ *n* a man whose wife has died and who has not married again

**width** /wɪdθ, wɪtθ/ *n* [C,U] the distance from one side of something to the other: *the width of the window│a width of 10 inches* –see picture at HEIGHT

**wield** /wild/ *v* [T] **1 wield power/control/authority etc.** to have a lot of power, control etc. and be ready to use it: *the influence wielded by the church* **2** to hold a weapon or tool and use it

**wife** /waɪf/ *n, plural* **wives** the woman that a man is married to: *This is my wife, Elaine.*

**wig** /wɪg/ *n* artificial hair that you wear to cover your head: *a blond wig*

**wig·gle** /'wɪgəl/ *v* [I,T] to make small movements from side to side or up and down, or to make something move this way: *wiggling your toes* –**wiggle** *n*

**wig·wam** /'wɪgwɑm/ *n* a type of tent that was used in past times by some Native Americans

**wild¹** /waɪld/ *adj* **1** living or growing in a natural state, and not controlled by people: *wild horses│wild flowers* **2** showing strong uncontrolled emotions such as excitement, anger, or happiness: *a wild look in her eyes│wild applause from the audience* **3** SPOKEN exciting, interesting, unusual, or strange: *Sarah's party was really wild.│a wild haircut│"He's a year old and already saying words." "That's wild."* **4** done or said without knowing all the facts or thinking carefully about them: *Take a wild guess.* (=guess without thinking carefully) **5 be wild about sth** SPOKEN to be very interested in or excited about something: *I'm not too wild about his movies.* **6** a wild card in a game can represent any card that you want it to be

**wild²** *adv* **1 run wild** to behave in an uncontrolled way because you have no rules or people to control you **2 go wild** to suddenly become very noisy and active because you are excited or angry: *The crowd went wild when the Giants won.*

**wild³** *n* **in the wild** in an area that is natural and not controlled or changed by people: *animals that live in the wild* –compare CAPTIVITY

**wil·der·ness** /'wɪldɚnɪs/ *n* [singular, U] a large natural area of land that has never been farmed or built on: *the Alaskan wilderness*

**wild goose chase** /ˌ. '. ˌ./ *n* [singular] a situation in which you waste a lot of time looking for something that cannot be found

**wild·life** /'waɪldlaɪf/ *n* [U] animals and plants that live in natural conditions: *the wildlife of the Rockies*

**wiles** /waɪlz/ *n* [plural] things you say or tricks you use in order to persuade someone to do what you want

**will¹** /wəl, əl, l; *strong* wɪl/ *modal verb* **1** used in order to make the simple future tense: *Kathy will be there tomorrow.│What time will she get here?│I'll* (=I will) *go shopping later.* **2** used in order to say that you are ready or willing to do something: *I'll do whatever you say.│Vern said he won't* (=will not) *work for Joe.* **3** used in order to ask someone to do something: *Will you do me a favor?* **4** used in CONDITIONAL sentences that use the present tense: *If it rains, we'll have the barbecue in the clubhouse.* **5** used like "can" to show what is possible: *This car will seat 5 people.* **6** used in order to say what always happens or what is generally true: *Prices will always go up.* **7 Will you...** SPOKEN said when you are angrily

wig

telling someone to do something: *Will you shut up!* –see usage note at SHALL –see study note on page 458

**will²** *n* **1** [C,U] the determination to do what you have decided to do: *He's lost the will to live*. **2** a legal document that shows whom you want to give your money and property to after you die: *Grandma Stacy left me $7000 in her will*. **3** [singular] what you decide should happen: *No one can force him to stay here against his will*. (=if he does not want to) **4** al will when or where you want, without any difficulty or opposition: *They can just change their policies at will*. **5** where there's a will there's a way SPOKEN used in order to say that if you are determined enough you will succeed

**will³** *v* [T] **1** to try to make something happen by thinking about it very hard: *He shut his eyes, willing her to win*. **2** to give something to someone after you die: *She willed the house to her son*.

**will·ful, wilful** /'wɪlfəl/ *adj* deliberately doing what you want even though people tell you not to: *a willful child* –**willfully** *adv*

**will·ing** /'wɪlɪŋ/ *adj* **1** be willing to do sth able to be persuaded to do something: *How much are they willing to pay?* **2** eager or wanting to do something: *willing helpers* –**willingness** *n* [U] –**willingly** *adv* –opposite UNWILLING

**wil·low** /'wɪloʊ/ *n* a tree with very long thin branches, that grows near water

**wil·low·y** /'wɪloʊi/ *adj* tall, thin, and graceful

**will·pow·er** /'wɪl,paʊɚ/ *n* [U] the ability to control your thoughts and actions in order to achieve something: *I don't have the willpower to diet*.

**wil·ly-nil·ly** /,wɪli 'nɪli/ *adv* something that happens to you willy-nilly happens whether or not you want it to

**wilt** /wɪlt/ *v* [I] if a plant or flower wilts, it bends because it needs water or is old

**wil·y** /'waɪli/ *adj* good at using tricks in order to get something that you want: *a wily politician*

**wimp** /wɪmp/ *n* INFORMAL **1** someone who is afraid to do something difficult or unpleasant: *Don't be such a wimp!* **2** a man who is small, weak, and not impressive –**wimpy** *adj*

**win¹** /wɪn/ *v* won, won, winning **1** [I,T] to be the best or first in a competition, game, election etc.: *Who do you think will win the Super Bowl?* | *Dad won at chess again.* | *Marcy's team is winning by 3 points*. **2** [T] to earn a prize at a competition or game: *winning a gold medal* | *I won $200 playing poker*. **3** [T] to gain something good because of all your efforts and skill: *Dr. Lee's work won her the admiration of scientists worldwide*. –opposite LOSE –see usage note at GAIN¹

**win out** *phr v* [I] to succeed after being un-

successful for a long time: *Sooner or later good sense will win out*.

**win sb ↔ over** *phr v* [T] to gain someone's support, friendship, trust etc.: *She completely won him over that evening*.

**win²** *n* a victory or success, especially in a sport: *a record of 7 wins and 6 losses*

**wince** /wɪns/ *v* [I] to react to something by looking upset or moving slightly, especially because you are in pain or embarrassed: *I still wince at the memory of how badly I sang*.

**winch** /wɪntʃ/ *n* a machine with a rope or chain used for lifting heavy objects –**winch** *v* [T]

**wind¹** /wɪnd/ *n* **1** [C,U] the air outside when it moves with a lot of force: *Expect strong winds and rain tomorrow.* | *The wind blew sand in my face.* | *A cold east wind* (=from the east) *was blowing*. –see usage note at WEATHER **2** get wind of sth to accidentally learn information that is private or secret **3** your ability to breathe easily: *Rae got the wind knocked out of her.* (=was hit in the stomach and could not breathe for a short time) **4** the winds of change/freedom etc. changes in people's ideas that will have important results **5** be in the wind to be likely to happen: *Something was in the wind, something important*. **6** take the wind out of sb's sails INFORMAL to make someone less excited, or to make someone or something seem less important or impressive **7** the winds the people in an ORCHESTRA or band who play musical instruments that you blow into, such as the FLUTE

**wind²** /waɪnd/ *v* wound, wound, winding **1** [I,T] to turn or twist something around and around, especially around something else: *Don't wind the cord around the iron.* | *yarn wound into a ball* –opposite UNWIND **2** [T] also **wind up** to make a machine, toy, clock etc. work by turning a small handle around and around: *I forgot to wind my watch*. **3** [I] if a road, river etc. winds, it curves or bends many times

**wind down** *phr v* [I,T] to gradually become slower, less active etc., or to make an activity do this: *The party started winding down after midnight*.

**wind up** *phr v* **1** [I] to do something, go somewhere, or become involved in something, without intending to: *We always wind up doing what she wants to do.* | *Most of them wound up in prison*. **2** [I,T **wind** sth ↔ **up**] to end an activity, meeting etc.: *It's almost 5:00 –we'd better wind things up*.

**wind·break·er** /'wɪnd,breɪkɚ/ *n* a type of coat made especially to protect you from the wind

**wind·chill fac·tor** /'wɪndtʃɪl ,fæktɚ/ *n* [U] the combination of cold weather and strong winds, that makes the temperature seem colder

**wind·ed** /'wɪndɪd/ *adj* having difficulty

breathing because you have exercised too much or have been hit in the stomach

**wind·fall** /'wɪndfɔl/ *n* an amount of money that you get unexpectedly: *a **windfall** profit*

**wind·ing** /'waɪndɪŋ/ *adj* curving or bending many times: *a long winding river*

**wind in·stru·ment** /'wɪnd ˌɪnstrəmənt/ *n* a musical instrument such as the FLUTE that you play by blowing into it

**wind·mill** /'wɪnd.mɪl/ *n* a building or structure with BLADES that the wind turns, used for producing electrical power or crushing grain

**win·dow** /'wɪndoʊ/ *n* **1** an opening with glass across it in the wall of a building, car etc., used for letting in air and light: *Can I open the window?* −see picture on page 471 **2** one of the areas on a computer screen where you can do different types of work

**window dress·ing** /'.. ˌ../ *n* [U] **1** an attempt to make something seem attractive when it is not **2** the art of arranging things in a store window

**win·dow·pane** /'wɪndoʊˌpeɪn/ *n* a whole piece of glass used in a window

**window shop·ping** /'.. ˌ../ *n* [U] the activity of looking at goods in store windows without intending to buy them

**win·dow·sill** /'wɪndoʊˌsɪl/ *n* a shelf that is attached to the bottom of a window

**wind·pipe** /'wɪndpaɪp/ *n* the tube through which air passes from your throat to your lungs

**wind·shield** /'wɪndʃild/ *n* the large window at the front of a car, bus, plane etc. −see picture on page 469

**windshield wip·er** /'.. ˌ../ *n* [C usually plural] a long thin piece of metal with a rubber edge, that moves across a WINDSHIELD to remove rain −see picture on page 469

**wind·surf·ing** /'wɪndˌsɚfɪŋ/ *n* [U] the sport of sailing across water by standing on a special board and holding onto a large sail

**wind·swept** /'wɪndswɛpt/ *adj* **1** a place that is windswept is usually windy and has few trees, buildings etc. **2** made messy by the wind: *windswept hair*

**wind·y** /'wɪndi/ *adj* with a lot of wind blowing, or getting a lot of wind: *It's been windy all day.* | *a windy beach*

**wine** /waɪn/ *n* [C,U] an alcoholic drink made from GRAPEs or other fruit, or a particular type of this drink: *a glass of wine* | *a fine selection of wines*

**wine·glass** /'waɪnglæs/ *n* a glass for wine, with a base, a thin upright part, and a bowl-shaped top

**wing¹** /wɪŋ/ *n* **1** the part of a bird's or insect's body used for flying: *ducks flapping their wings* **2** one of the two flat parts that stick out of a plane's sides and help it stay in the air −see picture at AIRPLANE **3** one of the parts that a large building is divided into: *the east wing of*

the library **4** one of the groups that a political party is divided into, based on the members' opinions and aims: *the conservative wing of the Democrats* −see also LEFT-WING, RIGHT-WING **5 take sb under your wing** to give advice, help, PROTECTION etc. to someone younger or less experienced than you

**wing²** *v* **1 wing it** INFORMAL to do or say something without any planning or preparation; IMPROVISE: *"I can't give a speech!" "Just wing it, you'll be fine."* **2** [I] LITERARY to fly

**winged** /wɪŋd/ *adj* having wings: *winged insects*

**wings** /wɪŋz/ *n* [plural] **1 the wings** the side parts of a stage where actors are hidden from people watching the play **2 waiting in the wings** ready to be used or ready to do something

**wing·span** /'wɪŋspæn/ *n* the distance from the end of one wing to the end of the other

**wing·tip** /'wɪŋtɪp/ *n* **1** the end of a wing **2** a type of shoe for men with a pattern of small holes on the toe

**wink¹** /wɪŋk/ *v* [I] to open and close one eye quickly, usually to show that you are joking, being friendly, or telling a secret: *"And don't tell Mom," he said, winking at her.*

**wink²** *n* the action of winking, usually as a signal: *He looked at Greta and gave her a wink.*

**win·ner** /'wɪnɚ/ *n* **1** someone who wins a competition, game, election etc.: *the winner of the poetry contest* **2** INFORMAL someone or something that is successful

**win·ning** /'wɪnɪŋ/ *adj* **winning smile/charm/personality etc.** a feature you have that is so attractive that many people like you

**win·nings** /'wɪnɪŋz/ *n* [plural] money that you win in a game or by GAMBLING

**win·o** /'waɪnoʊ/ *n* INFORMAL someone who drinks a lot of cheap wine and lives on the streets

**win·some** /'wɪnsəm/ *adj* LITERARY pleasant and attractive: *a winsome smile*

**win·ter** /'wɪntɚ/ *n* the season between fall and spring, when the weather is coldest: *The park closes in (the) winter.* | *I hope it snows this winter.* | *last/next winter* (=the winter before or after this one)

**win·ter·time** /'wɪntɚˌtaɪm/ *n* [U] the time of year when it is winter

**win·try** /'wɪntri/ *adj* like winter, or typical of winter, especially because it is cold or snowing

**win-win sit·u·a·tion** /ˌ. ˌ. ..'../ *n* a situation that will end well for everyone involved in it

**wipe** /waɪp/ *v* [T] **1** to clean something by rubbing it with a cloth or against a soft surface: *Could you **wipe off** the table for me?* | *Wipe your feet before you come in.* **2** to remove dirt, water etc. from something with a cloth or your hand: *He **wiped** the sweat **from** his face.* | *wiping away her tears* **3** to remove all the in-

W

formation that is stored on a TAPE, VIDEO, or computer DISK

**wipe out** *phr v* **1** [T **wipe** sb/sth ↔ **out**] to completely remove, destroy, or defeat someone or something: *Fires wiped out half of the city.* **2** [T **wipe** sb **out**] SPOKEN to make someone feel extremely tired: *All that running has wiped me out.* **3** [I] SPOKEN to fall down or hit something when driving a car, riding a bicycle etc.

**wipe** sth ↔ **up** *phr v* [T] to remove liquid from a surface using a cloth: *Quick! Get something to wipe up the mess!*

**wip·er** /'waɪpɚ/ *n* [C usually plural] ⇨ WINDSHIELD WIPER

**wire**[1] /waɪɚ/ *n* **1** [U] metal that is shaped like thick thread: *a wire fence* **2** a piece of metal like this used for carrying electrical currents or sound waves: *a telephone wire* **3** ⇨ TELEGRAM

**wire**[2] *v* [T] **1** also **wire up** to connect wires to something, usually in an electrical system: *I'm almost finished wiring up the alarm.* **2** to fasten two or more things or parts together using wire: *Lila had to have her jaw wired.* **3** to send money electronically **4** to send a TELEGRAM

**wired** /waɪɚd/ *adj* **1** a person, room etc. that is wired has a hidden piece of recording equipment attached to him, her, or it **2** SPOKEN feeling very active, excited, and awake

**wire·tap** /'waɪɚˌtæp/ *v* **-pped, -pping** [I,T] to listen to or record someone's telephone conversations using electronic equipment –**wiretap** *n*

**wir·ing** /'waɪərɪŋ/ *n* [U] the network of wires that form the electrical system in a building: *You'll have to replace the wiring.*

**wir·y** /'waɪəri/ *adj* **1** someone who is wiry is thin but has strong muscles **2** wiry hair is stiff and curly

**wis·dom** /'wɪzdəm/ *n* [U] **1** good judgment and the ability to make wise decisions **2** knowledge gained through a lot of learning and experience over a long period of time

**wisdom tooth** /'.. ,./ *n* one of the four large teeth at the back of your mouth that do not grow until you are an adult

**wise**[1] /waɪz/ *adj* **1** based on good judgment and experience: *It'd be wise to leave early.* | *a wise decision* –opposite UNWISE **2** able to make good decisions and give good advice: *a wise leader* **3 be none the wiser** to not understand something even though it has been explained to you or to not know about something that someone has done: *They sent me on a training course, but I'm still none the wiser.* **4 price-wise/time-wise etc.** SPOKEN when considering prices, time etc.: *It would have been a problem transportation-wise.* –**wisely** *adv*

**wise**[2] *v*

**wise up** *phr v* [I] INFORMAL to begin to understand the situation that you are in and deal with

it better: *Corporations should wise up and realize that employees aren't machines.*

**wise·crack** /'waɪzkræk/ *n* INFORMAL a quick funny, slightly unkind remark

**wise guy** /'. ./ *n* INFORMAL an annoying person who thinks that s/he knows more than someone else

**wish**[1] /wɪʃ/ *v* **1** [T] to hope that something will happen or that you can do something, even though it is very unlikely: *I wish they'd hurry up!* | *I wish (that) I could remember his name.* **2** [I,T] FORMAL to want to do something: *I wish to make a complaint.* **3** [T] to say that you hope someone will be happy, successful, lucky etc.: *Wish me luck!* **4 I/you wish!** SPOKEN said when you do not think something is true or possible, but you want it to be: *"I'm sure he likes you." "Yeah, I wish!"* –see usage note at DESIRE[2]

**wish for** sth *phr v* [T] to express what you hope for or want, often silently: *If you could have anything, what would you wish for?*

**wish**[2] *n* **1** the act of wishing for something that you want, or the thing that you wish for: *Close your eyes and make a wish!* | *Did you get your wish?* **2** FORMAL a desire to do something, or a hope that something will happen: *I had no wish to see him.* | *It was her wish that she be buried in Montana.* **3 best wishes** a phrase written in cards to say that you hope someone will be happy and successful

**wish·bone** /'wɪʃboʊn/ *n* a Y-shaped chicken bone that two people pull apart in order to find out who will get his/her wish

**wish·ful think·ing** /,.. '../ *n* [U] the false belief that something will happen just because you want it to

**wish·y-wash·y** /'wɪʃi ˌwɑʃi, -,wɔʃi/ *adj* INFORMAL a wishy-washy person, question, idea etc. does not seem to have a definite aim or purpose

**wisp** /wɪsp/ *n* **1** a small thin amount of hair, grass etc. **2** a small thin line of smoke, cloud etc. –**wispy** *adj*

**wist·ful** /'wɪstfəl/ *adj* showing slight sadness because you know you cannot have something you want: *a wistful expression* –**wistfully** *adv*

**wit** /wɪt/ *n* **1** the ability to say things that are funny, intelligent, and interesting: *a writer famous for his wit* **2** someone who has this ability –see also WITS

**witch** /wɪtʃ/ *n* a woman who is believed to have magic powers, especially ones that she uses for doing bad things –compare WARLOCK

**witch·craft** /'wɪtʃkræft/ *n* [U] the use of magic in order to make strange things happen

**witch doc·tor** /'. ,../ *n* a man who is believed to be able to cure people using magic, especially in some parts of Africa

W

**witch hunt** /'. ./ *n* DISAPPROVING an attempt to find and punish people whose opinions, political beliefs etc. are considered to be wrong or dangerous

**with** /wɪθ, wɪð/ *prep* **1** used in order to show that two or more people or things are together or near each other: *She went to the beach with her friends.* | *Put this bag with the other ones.* | *eggs mixed with milk.* **2** having a particular condition, thing, quality, or feeling: *a boy with a broken arm* | *Connie smiled with pride.* | *Where's the dish with the blue pattern?* **3** including: *Your dinner comes with fries.* **4** using something: *Don't eat with your fingers!* **5** because of something: *The room was bright with sunlight.* **6** used in order to say what covers or fills something: *a pillow filled with feathers* | *His hands were covered with blood.* **7** relating to something or someone: *What's wrong with the radio?* | *She's in love with you.* **8** supporting or liking someone: *I agree with you.* **9** against or opposing someone: *He's always arguing with his son.* **10** at the same time or rate as something else: *The wine will get better with age.* **11 with it** SPOKEN thinking clearly and not tired: *Sorry, I'm not very with it today.* **12 be with me/you** SPOKEN to understand what someone is saying: *Are you with me?* **13** in the same direction as something: *sailing with the wind*

**with·draw** /wɪθ'drɔ, wɪð-/ *v* **1** [T] to take money out of a bank account: *He withdrew $200 from his savings account.* **2** [T] to stop giving something or stop making something available, especially because of an official decision: *Congress threatened to withdraw support for the space project.* **3** [I,T] to stop being involved in something, or to make someone stop being involved: *She was withdrawn from Winston Academy.* | *The third candidate has withdrawn.* **4** [I,T] to move out of a place, or to make a person or group do this: *American troops were gradually withdrawn.*

**with·draw·al** /wɪθ'drɔəl/ *n* **1** [C,U] the action of taking money out of a bank account, or the amount you take out: *I'd like to make a withdrawal, please.* **2** [C,U] the action of moving an army, its weapons etc. away from the area where it was fighting: *the withdrawal of 1000 Russian tanks* **3** [C,U] the action of not continuing to give something or be involved in something: *the withdrawal of government aid* | *Hanson's withdrawal from the competition surprised everyone.* **4** [U] the pain, bad feelings etc. that someone suffers when s/he stops regularly taking a drug

**with·drawn** /wɪθ'drɔn/ *adj* quiet, thoughtful, and not willing to be around other people

**with·er** /'wɪðɚ/ *v* [I] **1** also **wither away** if a plant withers, it starts to become drier and smaller because it is dying **2** to gradually become less in size, importance etc.: *Small towns are withering away as the young people leave for the cities.*

**with·hold** /wɪθ'hoʊld, wɪð-/ *v* [T] to refuse to give something to someone: *They said McShane had withheld information from Congress.*

**with·in** /wɪ'ðɪn, wɪ'θɪn/ *adv, prep* **1** during a particular period of time: *The movie should start within the next 5 minutes.* | *Within a month of meeting him I knew I was in love.* **2** inside a particular area or distance, and not beyond it: *We need a hotel within a mile of the airport.* **3** inside an organization, society, or group of people: *They want to promote from within the department.* **4** obeying a particular set of rules, TRADITIONS, limits etc.: *driving within the speed limit*

**with·out** /wɪ'ðaʊt, wɪ'θaʊt/ *adv, prep* **1** not having, not using, or not doing something: *I can't see anything without my glasses.* | *He left without saying goodbye.* **2** not being with someone or not having someone to help you: *Why did you leave without me?* | *We can't finish this job without Jake.* **3 do/go without** to not have something that you really want or need, or to stop having it: *They went without food and water for 2 days.*

**with·stand** /wɪθ'stænd, wɪð-/ *v* [T] to be strong enough not to be harmed or changed by something: *The buildings have withstood earthquakes since 1916.*

**wit·ness**[1] /'wɪt⁻nɪs/ *n* **1** someone who sees an accident or a crime and can describe what happened: *Unfortunately there were no witnesses to the robbery.* **2** someone who describes in a court of law what s/he has seen or what s/he knows about a crime: *He asked the witness how well she knew the defendant.* **3** someone who watches another person sign an official document, and then signs it also to prove this

**witness**[2] *v* [T] **1** to see something happen, especially an accident or a crime: *Few people actually witnessed the event.* **2** to watch someone sign an official document, and then sign it also to prove this

**witness stand** /'.. ,./ *n* the raised area where WITNESSes sit when they are being questioned in a court of law

**wits** /wɪts/ *n* [plural] **1 lose your wits** to lose your ability to think quickly and make good decisions **2 be at your wits' end** to feel very annoyed, impatient, and upset because you do not know how to solve a problem **3 keep/ have your wits about you** to be ready to think quickly in order to deal with a problem **4 scare sb out of his/her wits** to frighten someone so much that s/he cannot think clearly

**wit·ti·cism** /'wɪtə,sɪzəm/ *n* a quick, funny, and interesting remark

**wit·ty** /'wɪti/ *adj* using words in a funny, intelligent, and interesting way: *a witty young man | a witty response*

**wives** /waɪvz/ *n* the plural of WIFE

**wiz·ard** /'wɪzə·d/ *n* **1** a man who is believed to have special magic powers **2** also **wiz** INFORMAL someone who is very good at doing something or using something: *a computer wizard*

**wiz·ened** /'wɪzənd/ *adj* old and having dry skin with a lot of WRINKLEs (=lines)

**wk.** *n* the written abbreviation of WEEK

**wob·ble** /'wɑbəl/ *v* [I] to move from side to side in an unsteady way —**wobbly** *adj*: *a wobbly chair* —**wobble** *n*

**woe** /woʊ/ *n* [U] LITERARY great sadness —see also WOES

**woe·be·gone** /'woʊbɪˌgɔn, -ˌgɑn/ *adj* looking very sad

**woe·ful·ly** /'woʊfəli/ *adv* **1** deserving to be criticized and pitied for being so bad: *a woefully disappointing performance* **2** in a very sad way: *He sighed and looked woefully around the room.*

**woes** /woʊz/ *n* [plural] FORMAL problems that are affecting someone greatly

**wok** /wɑk/ *n* a large wide pot, used especially to STIR-FRY meat and vegetables —see picture at PAN[1]

**woke** /woʊk/ *v* the past tense of WAKE

**wo·ken** /'woʊkən/ *v* the PAST PARTICIPLE of WAKE

**wolf**[1] /wʊlf/ **wolf down** *v* [T] INFORMAL to eat something very quickly: *She wolfed down a couple of hamburgers.*

**wolf**[2] *n*, *plural* **wolves** /wʊlvz/ a wild animal similar to a dog

**wom·an** /'wʊmən/ *n*, *plural* **women 1** an adult female human: *the women I work with | a woman doctor/lawyer/politician* **2** women in general: *It's not safe there for a woman traveling alone.*

**wom·an·hood** /'wʊmənˌhʊd/ *n* [U] the state of being a woman, or the time when a female person is an adult

**wom·an·iz·er** /'wʊməˌnaɪzə·/ *n* a man who tries to have sexual relationships with many different women

**wom·an·kind** /'wʊmənˌkaɪnd/ *n* [U] women considered together as a group

**womb** /wum/ *n* ⇨ UTERUS

**wom·en** /'wɪmɪn/ *n* the plural of WOMAN

**won** /wʌn/ *v* the past tense and PAST PARTICIPLE of WIN

**won·der**[1] /'wʌndə·/ *v* [I,T] **1** to think about something and want to know what is true about it or what is happening or will happen: *I wonder if she knows we're here. | I wonder how Wendy's feeling today. | We wondered where you'd gone.* **2 I was wondering if/whether** SPOKEN **a)** used in order to offer a polite invita-

tion: *We were wondering whether you'd like to come with us.* **b)** used in order to politely ask for something: *I was wondering if I could use your phone.* **3** to have doubts about whether someone or something is true, good, normal etc.: *I began to wonder about this business of his.* **4** to be surprised by something: *I wonder why she didn't call the police.*

**won·der**[2] *n* **1** [U] a feeling of admiration and surprise: *They listened to Lisa's story in/with wonder.* **2 no wonder** SPOKEN said when you are not surprised about something: *No wonder you feel sick if you ate the whole pizza!* **3** someone or something that makes you feel admiration and surprise: *the wonders of modern technology*

**won·der**[3] *adj* extremely good or effective: *a new wonder drug*

**won·der·ful** /'wʌndə·fəl/ *adj* extremely good: *Congratulations! That's wonderful news!* —**wonderfully** *adv*

**won't** /woʊnt/ *v* the short form of "will not": *Dad won't like it.*

**wont**[1] /wɔnt, woʊnt/ *adv* FORMAL **be wont to do sth** to have the habit of doing something

**wont**[2] *n* FORMAL **as is sb's wont** used in order to say that it is someone's habit to do something

**woo** /wu/ *v* [T] **1** to try to persuade someone to do something such as support you, vote for you, or buy something from you: *Politicians were busy wooing voters.* **2** OLD-FASHIONED to be romantic in order to gain someone's love

**wood** /wʊd/ *n* [C,U] the material that tree branches and TRUNKs are made of: *polished wood floors | a table made from three different types of wood* —see also WOODS

**wood·chuck** /'wʊdtʃʌk/ *n* ⇨ GROUNDHOG

**wood·ed** /'wʊdɪd/ *adj* having WOODS or covered with trees

**wood·en** /'wʊdn/ *adj* **1** made from wood: *a wooden box* **2** not showing enough expression, movement, or emotion: *a wooden performance*

**wood·land** /'wʊdlənd, -lænd/ *n* [C,U] an area of land that is covered with trees

**wood·peck·er** /'wʊdˌpɛkə·/ *n* a bird with a long beak that it uses to make holes in trees

**woods** /wʊdz/ *n* [plural] a small forest where a lot of trees grow: *We live next to the woods.*

**wood·wind** /'wʊdˌwɪnd/ *n* **the woodwinds** the people in an ORCHESTRA or band who play musical instruments that you blow into, such as the CLARINET or FLUTE

**wood·work** /'wʊdwə·k/ *n* [U] **1** the parts of a building that are made of wood, usually for decoration **2** the skill of making wooden objects

**wood·y** /'wʊdi/ *adj* looking, smelling, tasting, or feeling like wood: *woody plants*

**woof** /wʊf/ *n* a word that represents the sound a dog makes

**wool**[1] /wʊl/ *n* [U] the soft thick hair of a sheep, used for making cloth and YARN

**wool**[2], **wool·en** /'wʊlən/ *adj* made from wool: *a wool skirt | wool blankets*

**wool·ens** /'wʊlənz/ *n* [plural] clothes that are made from wool

**wool·y** /'wʊli/ *adj* looking or feeling like wool: *a wooly beard*

**woo·zy** /'wuzi/ *adj* INFORMAL feeling weak and unsteady; DIZZY

**word**[1] /wɚd/ *n*

**1** ▶LANGUAGE PART◀ the smallest unit of language used for making phrases and sentences, that usually represents an object, idea, action etc.: *"Casa" is the Spanish word for "house." | Write a 500-word essay about your family.*

**2** ▶STH SAID/WRITTEN◀ something that you say or write: *I didn't hear/understand a word you said. | Tell us what happened in your own words.* (=without being influenced by what others say) | *Promise you won't say a word about the accident to John.*

**3** ▶STATEMENT◀ a short important statement or discussion: *Mr. Gleeson would like a word with you in his office. | a word of advice/warning/encouragement*

**4 in other words** used when you are repeating a statement in simpler, clearer, or more direct words: *Some people aren't demonstrative. In other words, they don't express their feelings.*

**5** ▶NEWS◀ [singular, U] information, news, or a message: *The word is the company's closing its offices in Boston. | Have you had any word from your lawyers yet?*

**6** ▶PROMISE◀ a promise: *I give you my word: we'll take good care of him. | He's a man of his word.* (=does not break his promises)

**7 swear/dirty/cuss word** a word that is considered to be offensive or shocking by most people

**8 word for word** said, written, copied etc. with exactly the same words in exactly the same order: *That's not what he said word for word, but it's close.*

**9 take sb's word for it** to believe what someone says even though s/he has no proof: *Don't just take my word for it - ask them yourself!*

**10 by word of mouth** if information or news comes to you by word of mouth, someone tells you about it instead of you reading about it, seeing it on television etc.

**11 put in a good word for sb** to talk about someone's valuable qualities with an important person: *Could you put in a good word for me with your boss?*

**12 the last word** the last statement in a discussion or argument: *She's not content unless she has the last word.*

**13 my word!** SPOKEN OLD-FASHIONED said when you are very surprised: *My word! Isn't he tall!*

**14 not in so many words** not in a direct way: *"So Dad said he'd pay for it?" "Not in so many words."*

**15 give/say the word** to tell someone to start doing something: *Don't move until I give the word.*

**16 the final word** the power to decide whether or how to do something: *My boss has the final word on hiring staff.*

**word**[2] *v* [T] to use particular words when saying or writing something: *a carefully worded letter to the manager*

**word·ing** /'wɚdɪŋ/ *n* [U] the words and phrases used in order to express something

**word pro·ces·sor** /'. ,.../ *n* a small computer or a special computer program that you use for writing letters, reports etc. **– word processing** *n* [U]

**word·y** /'wɚdi/ *adj* using too many words: *a long wordy explanation*

**wore** /wɔr/ *v* the past tense of WEAR

**work**[1] /wɚk/ *v*

**1** ▶DO A JOB◀ [I] to do a job in order to earn money, or to do the activities and duties that are part of your job: *Heidi works for a law firm in Montreal. | I used to work at Burger King. | He's working with children who have learning difficulties.*

**2** ▶OPERATE◀ [I] if a machine or piece of equipment works, it does what it has been designed to do: *The CD player isn't working.*

**3** ▶USE A MACHINE◀ [T] to use a complicated machine or piece of equipment: *Does any of you know how to work the printer?*

**4** ▶BE EFFECTIVE◀ [I] if something works, it is effective, successful, or gives you the results that you want: *The glue didn't work, so I stapled it. | Did Gene's plan work? | I hope this cough medicine works.*

**5** ▶DO AN ACTIVITY◀ [I] to do an activity or a duty that involves a lot of time and effort: *I'd like you to work in small groups and discuss Chapter 7.*

**6 work your way** to move somewhere or achieve something gradually and with effort: *Dave worked his way to the top of the firm.*

**7** ▶MOVE SLOWLY◀ [I,T] to move into a position slowly with many small movements, or to move something in this way: *The screw must have worked loose.*

**8 work against sb** to prevent someone from being successful or getting the result s/he wants: *Unfortunately her bad grades worked against her.*

**9 work up an appetite/sweat** to do so much exercise that you become very hungry or SWEATY

**10** ▶SHAPE STH◀ [T] if you work a material such as clay, leather, or metal, you bend it, shape it etc. in order to make something

**11** ▶LAND◀ [T] if you work the land or the soil, you try to grow crops on it

**W**

**12 ►EXERCISE◄** [T] if you work a muscle or part of your body, you are exercising it

**work on** *phr v* [T] **1** [**work on** sth] to try to repair something, complete something, or improve something: *Dad's still working on the car.* | *Isn't Claire working on her Ph.D.?* | *I need to work on my essay.* **2** [**work on** sb] to try again and again to influence someone, so that s/he does what you want

**work out** *phr v* **1** [T **work** sth ↔ **out**] to calculate an amount, price, or value: *Have you worked out how much we owe them?* **2** [I] to cost a particular amount: *The hotel works out to/at about $50 a night.* **3** [T **work** sth ↔ **out**] to think carefully in order to solve a problem or plan something: *He still hasn't worked out which college he's going to.* **4** [I] if a problem or difficult situation works out, it gradually stops being a problem etc.: *Don't worry. I'm sure everything will work out fine.* **5** [I] to do a set of exercises regularly: *Sue works out in the gym twice a week.*

**work up to** sth *phr v* [T] to gradually prepare yourself to do something difficult: *I'm working up to being able to do 20 laps.*

**work**² *n* **1** [U] a job you are paid to do, or the duties and activities that are a part of your job: *Her father's been out of work for a year.* (=without a job) | *Much of our work involves meeting clients.* ✗ DON'T SAY "I have a work." SAY "I have a job." ✗ **2** [U] the place where you do your job, or the period during the day when you work: *I'll see you at work on Monday.* | *Do you want to go out to dinner after work?* **3** [U] the act of doing something useful that involves a lot of effort and time, or the useful activities you do: *Hey! Stop talking and get to work!* (=start working) | *Brenda and Lou have done a lot of work on their house.* **4** [U] the things that you produce as a result of working, studying, or RESEARCH: *We're pleased with your work.* | *Einstein's work on nuclear physics* **5** [C,U] something that an artist makes, or the type of things s/he makes: *great works of art* | *I admire Degas' work.* – see also WORKS **6 at work** doing a job or an activity: *Crews were at work repairing the roads.* **7 work clothes** clothes you wear to work in – see usage note at JOB

**work·a·ble** /'wɚkəbəl/ *adj* a workable plan, system, idea etc. can be used or done effectively: *a workable solution*

**work·a·hol·ic** /ˌwɚkə'hɔlɪk/ *n* INFORMAL someone who works much more than other people, and who does not have time and does not want to do anything else

**work·bench** /'wɚkbɛntʃ/ *n* a strong table with a hard surface, used when working with tools

**worked up** /ˌ. './ *adj* INFORMAL very upset or excited about something: *Don't get so worked up about your daughter.*

**work·er** /'wɚkɚ/ *n* **1** someone who works for a company, organization etc., but is not a manager: *Fifty workers lost their jobs.* | *a farm worker* **2** someone who works well or quickly: *Lisa's a good/hard/quick worker.*

**workers' com·pen·sa·tion** /ˌ.. ..'.. ../ *n* [U] money that a company must pay to a worker who is injured or becomes ill as a result of his/her job

**work·fare** /'wɚkfɛr/ *n* [U] a system under which poor people must do some work, in exchange for the money that they are given by the government

**work·force** /'wɚkfɔrs/ *n* [singular] all the people who work in a particular country, industry, or company

**work·ing** /'wɚkɪŋ/ *adj* **1** having a job: *working parents* **2** relating to work, or used for work: *bad working conditions* | *working clothes* **3 be in working order** to be working well and not be broken or have problems: *My father's watch is still in good working order.* **4 a working knowledge of sth** enough practical knowledge about something to use it effectively: *a working knowledge of Spanish*

**working class** /ˌ.. ˌ./ *n* **the working class** the social class that includes people who do not have much money or power and who usually do physical work –**working-class** *adj*

**work·ings** /'wɚkɪŋz/ *n* [plural] the ways in which something works: *the workings of government departments*

**work·load** /'wɚkloud/ *n* the amount of work that a person or machine is expected to do: *a heavy workload* (=a lot of work)

**work·man** /'wɚkmən/ *n* someone who does physical work such as building or repairing things

**work·man·like** /'wɚkmən,laɪk/ *adj* skillfully and carefully done

**work·man·ship** /'wɚkmən,ʃɪp/ *n* [U] skill in making things, or the quality of something that has been made: *the fine workmanship of this table*

**work·out** /'wɚk-aut/ *n* a period when you do a lot of exercise, especially as training for a sport

**works** /wɚks/ *n* **1** [plural] all the writing, paintings etc. that a writer or artist has done: *the complete works of Shakespeare* **2 the works** SPOKEN everything: *a hamburger with the works* (=with onions, cheese etc.) **3** OLD-FASHIONED a factory or industrial building: *a gas works*

**work·sheet** /'wɚkʃit/ *n* a piece of paper with questions, exercises etc. for students

**work·shop** /'wɚkʃap/ *n* **1** a room or building where tools and machines are used in order to make or repair things **2** a meeting at which people try to improve their skills by discussing their experiences and doing practical exercises

W

**work·sta·tion** /'wɚk,steɪʃən/ *n* the part of an office where you work, including your desk, computer etc.

**world** /wɚld/ *n* **the world** the PLANET we live on including all of the people, countries etc. on it; the Earth: *Athletes from **all over the world** compete in the Olympics.* | *the world's longest river*
**1** ►SOCIETY◄ the society we live in, or a society that is based on a particular type of activity: *Modern technology is changing the world.* | *the world of baseball* | *the music world*
**2 in the world** SPOKEN used in order to emphasize something you are saying: *You're the **best** dad **in the world**.* | *Why **in the world** should I listen to you?*
**3** ►COUNTRIES◄ [singular] a group of countries or a part of the world: *the Western World* | *the industrialized world*
**4** ►SB'S FEELINGS◄ the set of feelings, experiences, thoughts etc. that someone has: *Ever since the accident she's been living **in her own little world**.* (=not noticing anything except her own thoughts etc.)
**5 the animal/plant/insect world** animals etc. considered as a group
**6** ►ANOTHER WORLD◄ a PLANET in another part of the universe where other creatures might live: *a strange world light years away from earth*
**7 a world of** INFORMAL a lot of: *A vacation would **do you a world of good**.* (=make you feel a lot better)
**8 be out of this world** to be extremely good: *Have you tried their ice cream? It's out of this world!*
**9 be/feel on top of the world** to feel extremely happy
**10 mean the world to sb** to be the most important person or thing that someone cares about
**11 move/go up in the world** to become richer, more important, more responsible etc. in society
**12 have the best of both worlds** to have the advantages of two completely different things −see usage note at EARTH

**world-class** /ˌ. '.◄ / *adj* among the best in the world: *a world-class tennis player*

**world·ly** /'wɚldli/ *adj* **1 sb's worldly goods/possessions** everything someone owns
**2** knowing a lot about people and society, based on experience: *worldly young men*

**world pow·er** /ˌ. '../ *n* a powerful country whose trade, politics etc. affect other countries

**World Se·ries** /ˌ. '../ *n* **the World Series** the last series of baseball games that is played each year in order to decide the best professional team in the US and Canada

**world·wide** /ˌwɚld'waɪd◄ / *adj* everywhere in the world, or within the whole world: *worldwide*

*fame* | *The company employs 2000 people worldwide.*

**World Wide Web** /ˌ. ,. '. / written abbreviation **WWW** *n* [singular] **the World Wide Web** a popular system that makes it easier for people to see and use information on the INTERNET −see culture note at INTERNET

**worm¹** /wɚm/ *n* a small tube-shaped creature with a soft body and no legs that lives in the ground −see also **a (whole) can of worms** (CAN¹)

**worm²** *v* **1 worm your way into sth** to move slowly through a small or crowded place: *Reporters wormed their way into the court room.*
**2 worm sth out of sb** to get information from someone who does not want to give it

**worn** /wɔrn/ *v* the PAST PARTICIPLE of WEAR

**worn out, worn-out** /ˌ. '.◄ / *adj* **1** very tired because you have been working too much: *I'm all worn out.* **2** too old or damaged to be used: *a pair of worn-out sneakers*

**wor·ried** /'wɚid, 'wʌrid/ *adj* unhappy or nervous because you are worrying about someone or something: *We were really **worried about** you!* | *I **got worried** when you didn't call.*

**wor·ry¹** /'wɚi, 'wʌri/ *v* **1** [I] to think about someone or something all the time, because you feel nervous or anxious about him, her, or it: *I **worry about** Dave - he doesn't eat right* | *She's always **worrying about** her grades.* **2 don't worry** SPOKEN **a)** said when you are trying to make someone feel less anxious: *Don't worry, I'm sure they're both fine.* **b)** used in order to tell someone that s/he does not have to do something: *Don't **worry about** the kids - I can drive them to school.* **3** [T] to make someone feel nervous, unhappy, or upset: *It worries me that she hasn't called yet.*

**worry²** *n* **1** a problem or bad situation that makes you unhappy because you do not know how to solve it: *My only worry is that the report won't be ready on time.* **2** [U] the feeling of being anxious about something

**worse¹** /wɚs/ *adj* [the comparative of "bad"]
**1** not as good, more unpleasant, or having a lower quality: *The play was **worse than** I expected.* | *Traffic always **gets worse** after 4:30.*
**2** sicker or in a condition that is not as good: *If I feel any worse tomorrow I'll go see a doctor.* | *His hearing has gotten worse.* −see study note on page 457

**worse²** *n* [U] **1** something worse: *Moving from Georgia was **a change for the worse**.* (=a bad change) | *"How was the opera?" "I've seen/heard worse."* (=not bad but not excellent)
**2 go from bad to worse** to become even worse: *Things went from bad to worse and finally we got divorced.*

**worse³** *adv* **1** in a more severe or serious way than before: *The pain hurts worse than yester-*

W

*day.* **2** not as well, or less successfully: *Margo sings even worse than I do!*

**wors·en** /'wɚsən/ *v* [I,T] to become worse, or to make something become worse: *If the weather worsens, the flight will be canceled.*

**worse off** /ˌ. '.'/ *adj* poorer, less successful, or having fewer advantages than you did before: *We're actually worse off than I thought.*

**wor·ship** /'wɚʃɪp/ *v* **-ped, -ping** also **-pped, -pping** **1** [I,T] to show respect and love for a god, especially by praying in a church, TEMPLE etc. **2** [T] to love and admire someone very much: *She absolutely worships her Grandpa Jim!* **–worship** *n* [U]: *a house of worship* (=church or building where people can pray) **–worshiper** *n*

**worst**[1] /wɚst/ *adj* [the superlative of "bad"] worse than anything else of the same type: *It was the worst movie I've ever seen.* | *the worst snowstorm in years* –see study note on page 457

**worst**[2] *n* **1** also **the worst** someone or something that is worse than every other person, plan, quality, thing etc.: *She was rude, but worst of all she wouldn't leave me alone.* | *This is the worst I've ever done on a test.* **2** **the worst** the worst possible result, experience, or situation: *The worst of it is, he even took the car!* | *What's the worst that can happen if we lose?* **3** **at worst** if a thing or situation is as bad as it can be: *At worst the repairs will cost you around $700.* **4** **if (the) worst comes to (the) worst** if the worst possible thing happens: *If worst comes to worst, we'll have to sell the house.*

**worst**[3] *adv* in the worst way or most severely: *Their village was worst affected by the war.*

**worth**[1] /wɚθ/ *adj* **1** **be worth sth** to have a particular value, especially in money: *Our house is worth about $350,000.* | *Each question is worth 4 points.* **2** **be worth it/be worth doing** to be helpful, valuable, or good for you: *It might be worth it to call them first.* | *It's worth a try.* (=you might get what you want if you try doing something) | *Stop crying over him. He's not worth it.* | *It's not worth going if you get there late.* **3** **worth your while** valuable to you because you could gain something you want or need: *We can make it worth your while to fly to Miami.*

**worth**[2] *n* **1** **... worth of sth** an amount of something based on how much money you spend, how much time you use etc.: *twenty dollars' worth of gas* | *a year's worth of training* | *three trucks' worth of supplies* **2** **sb's worth** how important someone is, and how useful what s/he does is: *You need to let people know your real worth.*

**worth·less** /'wɚθlɪs/ *adj* **1** not valuable, not important, or not useful: *Are you saying the stocks are worthless?* | *I used to think studying was worthless.* **2** a worthless person has no good qualities or useful skills

**worth·while** /ˌwɚθ'waɪl◂/ *adj* worth all of the time, effort, or money you have used: *All that work finally seemed worthwhile.*

**wor·thy** /'wɚði/ *adj* **1** good enough to deserve respect, admiration, or attention: *a worthy opponent* | *worthy achievements* **2** **be worthy of sth** FORMAL to deserve something: *a leader who is worthy of our trust*

**would** /wəd, əd, d; *strong* wʊd/ *modal verb* **1** used instead of "will" when reporting what someone has said: *Mr. Thomas said it would be OK to go.* | *She told me she wouldn't* (=would not) *come.* **2** used in CONDITIONAL sentences that use the past tenses: *Dad would be really mad if he knew.* | *You know I would help you if I had time.* | *If you had listened to me, you wouldn't have gotten in trouble.* **3** used in order to show that you expected something to happen or be true, but it did not or was not: *I thought Caroline would be happy, but she got really mad at me.* **4** used in order to say that something happened regularly in the past: *Sometimes, Eva would come over and make dinner for the kids.* **5** **would not/wouldn't** used in order to say that someone refused to do something: *Blair wouldn't answer the question.* –see study note on page 458

---

SPOKEN PHRASES

**6** **would like/would love** used in order to say that you want something: *I would love to see your new house!* **7** **Would you...?** said in order to ask for or offer something politely: *Would you bring me that broom?* | *Would you like some coffee or something?* | *Would you mind waiting until tomorrow?* **8** **I would/I wouldn't** used in order to give advice: *"What should I do?" "I would tell him you're sorry."* | *I'd* (=I would) *go if I were you.* | *I wouldn't leave the car unlocked, if I were you.* **9** used before verbs that express what you think, when you want to make an opinion less definite: *I would guess the stores are closed by now.* | *I would have thought you'd be tired.* **10** **would (just) as soon** used in order to say that you would prefer something to happen or be done: *I'd just as soon you didn't tell her.* **11** **would rather** said when you prefer doing or having one thing instead of another: *I would rather stay home alone than go out with those idiots.* **12** used in order to show you are annoyed about something that someone has done: *You would go and tell the teacher!*

---

**would-be** /'. ./ *adj* **would-be actor/robber** etc. someone who hopes to have a particular job or intends to do a particular thing

**would·n't** /'wʊdnt/ *v* the short form of "would not": *She wouldn't answer.*

**would've** /'wʊdəv/ *v* the short form of "would have": *You would've hated my old boyfriend.*

**wound**[1] /wund/ *n* an injury, especially a deep cut made in your skin by a knife or bullet: *gunshot wounds*

**wound**[2] *v* [T]  **1** to injure someone, especially with a knife or gun: *Two officers were badly wounded.*  **2 wound sb's pride** to upset someone by criticizing him/her  −**wounded** *adj*

---

**USAGE NOTE   wounded, injured**, and **hurt**

Use **wounded** when a part of the body is damaged by a weapon: *a wounded soldier.* Use **injured** when someone has been hurt in an accident or in an event such as an earthquake: *One passenger was killed and four were injured.* Use **hurt** to say that a part of your body feels pain: *My neck hurts.*

---

**wound**[3] /waʊnd/ *v* the past tense and PAST PARTICIPLE of WIND

**wound up** /ˌwaʊnd ˈʌp/ *adj* very angry, nervous, or excited: *He got so wound up he couldn't sleep.*

**wove** /woʊv/ *v* the past tense of WEAVE

**wo·ven** /ˈwoʊvən/ *v* the PAST PARTICIPLE of WEAVE

**wow** /waʊ/ *interjection* said when you think something is impressive or surprising: *Wow! You look great!*

**wran·gle** /ˈræŋɡəl/ *v* [I] to argue with someone angrily for a long time

**wran·gler** /ˈræŋɡlɚ/ *n* INFORMAL ⇨ COWBOY

**wrap**

**wrap**[1] /ræp/ *v* [T] **-pped, -pping**  **1** to fold cloth, paper etc. around something, especially in order to cover it: *I haven't wrapped her present yet.* | *Wrap this blanket around you.*  **2 wrap your arms around** to hold someone or something by putting your arms around him, her, or it  **3 have sb wrapped around your finger** to be able to persuade someone to do whatever you want

**wrap** sth ↔ **up** *phr v* [T]  **1** to completely cover something by folding paper, cloth etc. around it: *sandwiches wrapped up in foil*  **2** to finish or complete a job, meeting etc.: *We should have the project wrapped up in a month.* | *That just about wraps up our show for tonight.*  **3 be wrapped up in your children/**

**work** etc. to give too much attention to your children, work, etc.

**wrap**[2] *n* OLD-FASHIONED ⇨ SHAWL

**wrap·per** /ˈræpɚ/ *n* the paper or plastic that covers a piece of food, especially candy: *gum wrappers*

**wrapping pa·per** /ˈ.. ˌ../ *n* [C,U] colored paper used for wrapping presents

**wrath** /ræθ/ *n* [U] FORMAL very great anger

**wreak** /rik/ *v* LITERARY **wreak havoc** to cause a lot of damage, problems, or suffering

**wreath** /riθ/ *n* a decoration made from flowers and leaves arranged in a circle

**wreck**[1] /rɛk/ *v* [T] INFORMAL to completely ruin, spoil, or destroy something or someone: *I hope he doesn't wreck the car.* | *Her drinking problem wrecked her marriage/health.*

**wreck**[2] *n*  **1** a car, plane, or ship that is so damaged it cannot be repaired  **2** INFORMAL someone who is very nervous, tired, or unhealthy: *I feel like a wreck!*  **3** a bad accident involving cars or planes: *Only one person survived the wreck.*  **4** INFORMAL something that is very messy and needs a lot of repairs: *The house was a wreck when we bought it.*

**wreck·age** /ˈrɛkɪdʒ/ *n* [U] the broken parts of a car, plane, or building that has been destroyed in an accident: *Ambulance crews removed a man from the wreckage.*

**wren** /rɛn/ *n* a very small brown bird that sings

**wrench**[1] /rɛntʃ/ *v* [T]  **1** to injure part of your body by twisting it suddenly: *Sam wrenched his back lifting furniture.*  **2** to twist and pull something from its position using force: *Prisoners had even wrenched doors off their hinges.*

**wrench**[2] *n*  **1** a metal tool with a round end, used for turning NUTs  **2 be a wrench** an experience that is a wrench is difficult and involves strong emotions: *It was a wrench to leave San Diego.*

**wrench·ing** /ˈrɛntʃɪŋ/ *adj* extremely difficult to deal with, and involving strong emotions: *a wrenching choice* | *a* **gut-wrenching/heart-wrenching** *story* (=one that makes you feel strong emotions)

**wrest** /rɛst/ *v* [T] FORMAL **wrest sth from sb** **a)** to take away someone's power or influence **b)** to violently pull something away from someone

**wres·tle** /ˈrɛsəl/ *v*  **1** [I,T] to fight by holding onto someone and trying to push or pull him/her down  **2** [I] to try to deal with a difficult problem or emotion: *For weeks he wrestled with his guilt.*

**wres·tling** /ˈrɛslɪŋ/ *n* [U] a sport in which you try to throw your opponent to the ground and hold him/her there  −**wrestler** /ˈrɛslɚ/ *n*

**wretch** /rɛtʃ/ *n* LITERARY someone whom you pity

W

**wretch·ed** /'rɛtʃɪd/ *adj* extremely unhappy, especially because you are lonely, sick, poor etc.

**wrig·gle** /'rɪgəl/ *v* [I,T] to twist from side to side with small quick movements, or to move part of your body this way: *a worm wriggling through the mud* —**wriggle** *n*

**wring** /rɪŋ/ *v* **wrung, wrung, wringing** [T] **1** also **wring out** to tightly twist wet clothes, sheets etc. in order to remove water from them **2 wring your hands** to rub and press your hands together because you are nervous or upset **3 wring sth's neck** to kill an animal or bird, such as a chicken, by twisting its neck

**wring·er** /'rɪŋɚ/ *n* **1 go through the wringer** INFORMAL to have an unpleasant or difficult experience **2** a machine used especially in past times for pressing water out of washed clothes

**wrin·kle¹** /'rɪŋkəl/ *n* **1** a line on your face or skin that you get when you are old **2** a line in cloth, paper etc. caused by crushing it or accidentally folding it: *wrinkles in his shirt* **3 iron out the wrinkles** to solve the last small problems that are preventing a plan, system, etc. from working

wrinkle

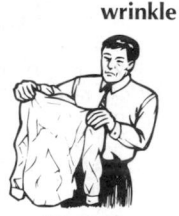

His shirt is wrinkled.

**wrin·kle²** *v* [I,T] to form small folds in something such as clothes or skin, or to be shaped in these folds: *Oh no, you wrinkled my dress.* | *Her nose wrinkles when she smiles.* —**wrinkled** *adj*

**wrist** /rɪst/ *n* the joint between your hand and your arm —see pictures at HAND¹, BODY

**wrist·watch** /'rɪst-wɑtʃ/ *n* a watch that you wear on your wrist

**writ** /rɪt/ *n* a legal document that orders someone to do something or not to do something

**write** /raɪt/ *v* **wrote, written, writing 1** [I,T] to produce a new book, story, song etc.: *I'm writing about the Civil War for my history essay.* | *a poem written by Walt Whitman* | *a sign written in Spanish* **2** [I,T] to write a letter to someone: *Have you written to Mom yet?* | *He finally wrote me a letter.* **3** [I,T] to form words, letters, or numbers with a pen or pencil: *We learned how to write in kindergarten.* | *Please write your name and address on the form.* **4** [I,T] to write stories, plays, articles etc. to earn money: *He writes for The Chronicle.*

**write back** *phr v* [I] to answer someone's letter by writing a letter and sending it to him/her: *Write back soon!*

**write** sth ↔ **down** *phr v* [T] to write information, ideas etc. on a piece of paper so that you do not forget them: *Why didn't you write her address down?*

**write in** *phr v* **1** [I] to write a letter to an organization in order to complain, ask for information, or give an opinion **2** [T **write** sb ↔ **in**] to add someone's name to your BALLOT in order to vote for him/her

**write off** *phr v* **1** [T **write** sb/sth ↔ **off**] to decide not to deal with someone or something any longer, because what you had hoped for did not succeed: *I didn't get the grades for the study abroad program, so I had to write it off.* **2** [T **write** sth ↔ **off**] to decide that a debt will never be paid to you, and officially accept it as a loss: *The credit company must have written off ten percent as bad charges*

**write** sth ↔ **out** *phr v* [T] to write all the information that is needed for a list, report, check etc.: *Gina wrote out a check for $820.*

**write** sth ↔ **up** *phr v* [T] to write something such as a report, article etc. based on notes you made earlier: *Doug's writing up his review for the school paper.*

**write-in** /'. ./ *n* a vote for someone who is not on the BALLOT, that you can give by writing his/her name on it

**write-off** /'. ./ *n* an amount of money that you lose from your income, for example because someone has not paid a debt: *a $149 million write-off to pay for legal fees*

**writ·er** /'raɪtɚ/ *n* someone who writes books, stories etc. in order to earn money

**write-up** /'. ./ *n* an opinion that is written in a magazine or newspaper about a new book, play, product etc.

**writhe** /raɪð/ *v* [I] to twist your body because you are suffering pain: *writhing in agony*

**writ·ing** /'raɪtɪŋ/ *n* [U] **1** words that are written or printed: *I can't read her writing.* **2 in writing** a promise, agreement etc. that is in writing has been written down, which proves that it is official **3** books, stories, and poems in general: *We're studying European writing from the 1930s.* **4** the activity or job of writing books, stories etc.: *creative writing*

**writ·ings** /'raɪtɪŋz/ *n* [plural] the books, stories, poems etc. that a particular person writes: *Mark Twain's writings*

**writ·ten** /'rɪt˺n/ *v* the PAST PARTICIPLE of WRITE

**wrong¹** /rɔŋ/ *adj* **1** not correct, not the one you intended, or not the one you should use: *Paul's wrong: Hilary's 17, not 18.* | *I bought the wrong size.* | *You must have dialed the wrong number.* (=not the telephone number you wanted) —opposite RIGHT¹ **2** not morally right or acceptable; bad: *He didn't do anything wrong!* | *What's wrong with making a profit?* **3** not suitable: *It's the wrong time of year to go skiing.* | *I think they're wrong for each other.* **4 what's wrong?** SPOKEN **a)** used in order to ask someone what problems s/he has, why s/he is unhappy etc.: *"What's wrong, Jenny?" "I miss Daddy."* | *What's wrong with your shoulder?* **b)** used in order to ask why something is not working: *What's wrong with the* *phone?* **5 be in the wrong place at the wrong time** to become involved in a bad situation without intending to **6 get the wrong end of the stick** INFORMAL to fail to understand the real meaning of something that someone says or does

**wrong**[2] *adv* **1** not done in the correct way: *You spelled my name wrong.* −opposite RIGHT[2] **2 go wrong** to develop problems and stop being good, successful, useful etc.: *Everything went wrong yesterday.* | *If anything goes wrong with your car, we'll fix it for free.* **3 get sth wrong** to remember or understand something incorrectly: *I got the answer wrong.* | *Don't get me wrong* −*I think it looks nice.*

**wrong**[3] *n* **1** [U] behavior that is not morally correct: *He doesn't know the difference between right and wrong.* **2** an action, decision, situation etc. that is not fair: *a chance to right the wrongs they suffered during the war* (=have a fair solution to an unfair situation) **3 be in the wrong** to make a mistake or deserve the blame for something **4 sb can do no wrong** used in order to say that someone seems to be perfect

**wrong**[4] *v* [T] FORMAL to treat someone unfairly or judge him/her unfairly

**wrong·do·ing** /'rɔŋ,duɪŋ/ *n* [C,U] FORMAL illegal actions or immoral behavior −**wrongdoer** *n*

**wrong·ful·ly** /'rɔŋfəli/ *adv* unfairly or illegally: *Tyrone was wrongfully accused of stealing.*

**wrote** /roʊt/ *v* the past tense of WRITE

**wrought** /rɔt/ *adj* LITERARY made or done

**wrought i·ron** /,. '..◂/ *n* [U] long thin pieces of iron formed into shapes: *a wrought iron gate*

**wrung** /rʌŋ/ *v* the past tense and PAST PARTICIPLE of WRING

**wry** /raɪ/ *adj* showing in a humorous way that you are not pleased by something: *a wry smile*

**wuss** /wʊs/ *n* SLANG someone who seems weak because s/he is afraid to do anything difficult or unpleasant: *You're such a wuss!*

**WV** the written abbreviation of West Virginia

**WWW** *n* the written abbreviation of WORLD WIDE WEB

**WY** the written abbreviation of Wyoming

**X, x** /ɛks/ the twenty-fourth letter of the English alphabet

**X** *adj* used in order to show that a movie has not been officially approved for anyone under the age of 18

**x** *n* a sign used in mathematics, representing a number or quantity that is not known but can be calculated: *If $3x = 6$, then $x = 2$.*

**xen·o·pho·bi·a** /,zɛnə'foʊbiə/ *n* [U] an extreme fear or dislike of people from other countries

**xe·rox, Xerox** /'zɪrɑks, 'zirɑks/ *n* TRADEMARK ⇨ PHOTOCOPY −**xerox** *v* [T]

**X·mas** /'krɪsməs, 'ɛksməs/ *n* INFORMAL a written form of the word Christmas

**x-ray**[1] /'ɛks reɪ/ *n* **1** a beam of RADIATION that can go through solid objects and is used for photographing the inside of the body **2** an x-ray photograph taken by doctors in order to search for broken bones, injuries etc. inside someone's body

**x-ray**[2] *v* [T] to photograph part of someone's body using X-RAYS

**xy·lo·phone** /'zaɪlə,foʊn/ *n* a musical instrument with flat metal BARS, that you play by hitting them with a stick

**Y, y** /waɪ/ the twenty-fifth letter of the English alphabet

**ya** /yʌ/ *pron* SPOKEN NONSTANDARD you: *See ya later!*

**yacht** /yɑt/ *n* a large expensive boat used for sailing, racing, and traveling for pleasure

yacht

**yak**[1] /yæk/ *n* a long-haired cow from central Asia

**yak**[2] *v* [I] **-kked, -kking** INFORMAL to talk continually about things that are not serious

**y'all** /yɔl/ *pron* SPOKEN a word meaning "you" or "all of you," used mainly in the southern US: *Will y'all be quiet for a minute?*

**yam** /yæm/ *n* [C,U] ⇨ SWEET POTATO

**yank** /yæŋk/ *v* [I,T] to pull something quickly and with force: *Stop yanking on my hair!*

**Yan·kee** /'yæŋki/ *n* **1** someone who fought against the southern states in the American Civil War **2** also **Yank** a word meaning a US citizen, often considered an insult when used by someone who is not American

**yap** /yæp/ *v* **-pped, -pping** [I] if a small dog yaps, it BARKS in an excited way −**yap** *n*

**yard** /yɑrd/ *n* **1** the land around a house, usually covered with grass: *Somebody kicked a ball into our front yard.* | *a swimming pool in the back yard* **2** written abbreviation **yd.** a unit for measuring length, equal to 3 feet or 0.9144 meters

**yard sale** /'. ./ *n* a sale of used clothes, furniture, toys etc., in someone's yard −compare GARAGE SALE

**yard·stick** /'yɑrd,stɪk/ *n* something that you compare another thing with, in order to judge how good or successful it is: *He used Deborah's career as a* **yardstick for** *his own achievements.*

**yar·mul·ke** /'yɑməkə, 'yɑrməlkə/ *n* a small round cap worn by some Jewish men

**yarn** /yɑrn/ *n* **1** a thick wooly type of thread used for knitting (KNIT) **2** INFORMAL a long story that is not completely true

**yawn¹** /yɔn/ *v* [I] **1** to open your mouth wide and breathe deeply, usually because you are tired or bored: *He looked at his watch and yawned.* **2** to be or become wide open: *The ground shook and yawned under their feet.*

yawn

**yawn²** *n* **1** an act of YAWNing **2** SPOKEN said in order to show that you think something is not interesting or exciting: *"We could go to Sherri's house." "Yawn!"*

**yd.** *n* the written abbreviation of YARD

**yeah** /yɛə/ *adv* SPOKEN yes – see usage note at YES

**year** /yɪr/ written abbreviation **yr.** *n* **1** also **calendar year** a period of time equal to about 365 days or 12 months, beginning on January 1 and ending on December 31: *Where are you spending Christmas* **this year**? | **last/next year** (=the year before or after this one) **2** any period of time equal to about 365 days or 12 months: *Jenny is five* **years old**. | *My passport expires* **in a year**. | *None of this will matter* **a year from now**. | *The* **tax year** *begins in April.* **3 years** INFORMAL many years: *It's been years since I played tag.* | *I haven't seen her* **in/for years**. **4 school/academic year** the period of time during a year when students are in school, college etc.: *Final exams are near the end of the school year.* **5 all year round** during the whole year: *It's sunny there all year round.*

**year·book** /'yɪrbʊk/ *n* a book printed once a year by a high school or college, about its students, sports events, clubs etc. during that year

**year·ling** /'yɪrlɪŋ/ *n* a young animal, especially a horse, between the ages of one and two

**year·ly** /'yɪrli/ *adj, adv* happening or done every year or once a year: *our yearly trip to Florida* | *Investments are reviewed yearly.*

**yearn** /yɚn/ *v* [I] LITERARY to want something very much, especially something extremely difficult to get: *They* **yearned to** *go home.* | *Trish* **yearns for** *affection.* **–yearning** *n* [U]

**yeast** /yist/ *n* [U] a substance used for making bread rise and for producing alcohol in beer or wine

**yell** /yɛl/ *v* [I,T] also **yell out** to shout or say something very loudly because you are angry, excited, or frightened: *You didn't have to* **yell at** *me!* **–yell** *n*

**yel·low¹** /'yɛloʊ/ *adj* having the same color as LEMONs or butter

**yellow²** *n* [U] a yellow color **–yellow** *v* [I,T]: *the yellowing pages of an old book*

**Yellow Pag·es** /ˌ.. '../ *n* TRADEMARK **the Yellow Pages** a book that lists the telephone numbers and addresses of stores, restaurants, and businesses in a particular area

**yelp** /yɛlp/ *v* [I] to make a short high cry like a dog makes, because of pain, excitement etc. **–yelp** *n*

**yen** /yɛn/ *n* **1** a standard unit of money used in Japan **2** SINGULAR a strong desire: *a yen to travel*

**yep** /yɛp/ *adv* SPOKEN yes –see usage note at YES

**yes** /yɛs/ *adv* SPOKEN **1** said in order to give a positive reply to a question, offer, or request: *"Is she back at college?" "Yes, she left two days ago."* | *"Nancy, did you want some pie?" "Yes, please."* | *"Antonio, will you come tomorrow?" "Yes, Becky, I will."* | *Why don't you ask Dad? I'm sure he'll* **say yes**. **2** said in order to agree with a statement: *"It's such a nice day." "Yes, it is."* | *"You're late again." "Yes. I'm sorry."* **3** said in order to show that you do not completely agree with a statement: *"John doesn't like me anymore." "Yes he does!"* | *"We need a vacation." "Yes, but we can't afford it."* **4** said when you have noticed that someone wants your attention: *"Linda!" "Yes?"* | *Yes, sir, how may I help you?* **5** said when you are very happy or excited: *Yes! I got the job!*

**USAGE NOTE** yes

In informal speech, we use many different answers instead of **yes**. Some of these are **yeah, uh huh, yep, okay**, and **sure**.

**yes·ter·day** /'yɛstɚdi, -ˌdeɪ/ *adv, n* **1** the day before today: *Yesterday was their tenth anniversary.* | *Did you go to the game yesterday?* **2** the past, especially the recent past: *yesterday's fashions*

**yet¹** /yɛt/ *adv* **1** a word meaning "at the present time" or "already," used in negative statements and questions: *I don't think she's awake yet.* | *Have you heard their new song yet?* **2** at some time in the future; still: *She may change her mind yet.* | *We* **have yet to** *hear from them.* (=we still have not heard) | *"Has Lori arrived?" "Not yet."* **3** in addition to what you have already gotten, done etc.: **yet another** *mistake* | *I'm sorry to ask for help* **yet again**. (=one more time after many others) **4** in spite of something; but: *a quiet* **yet** *powerful leader* –see usage notes at JUST¹, STILL¹

**yet²** *conjunction* in spite of something: *The story's unbelievable, yet supposedly it's all true.*

**yew** /yu/ *n* a tree or bush with leaves that look like flat needles, or the heavy wood of this tree

**Yid·dish** /'yɪdɪʃ/ *n* [U] a language similar to German, used in many places by Jewish people – **Yiddish** *adj*

**yield** /yild/ *v* **1** [T] to produce something: *Company investments yielded a profit of over $45,000.* **2** [I,T] to allow yourself to be forced or persuaded to do something: *The city council yielded to the public's demands for better bus services.* | *a leader who will yield power to someone younger* **3** [I] to allow the traffic from a bigger road to go first **4** [I] to move, bend, or break because of physical pressure

**yikes** /yaɪks/ *interjection* INFORMAL said when you suddenly notice or realize something that is shocking or that means you must do something quickly: *Yikes! I'm late!*

**yip·pee** /'yɪpi/ *interjection* said when you are very happy or excited about something

**YMCA** *n* Young Men's Christian Association; an organization that provides places to stay, sports centers, and training for young people, especially in large cities – see also YWCA

**yo** /you/ *interjection* SLANG said in order to greet someone or get his/her attention, or as a reply when someone says your name

**yo·del** /'youdl/ *v* [I] to sing while changing your natural voice to a very high voice and back again many times

**yo·ga** /'yougə/ *n* [U] a system of exercises in which you control your body and mind

**yo·gurt** /'yougɚt/ *n* [C,U] a smooth, slightly sour, thick liquid food made from milk

**yoke** /youk/ *n* a wooden BAR used for joining together two animals, especially cattle, in order to pull heavy loads – **yoke** *v* [T]

**yo·kel** /'youkəl/ *n* HUMOROUS someone from the country who has not experienced living in modern society

**yolk** /youk/ *n* [C,U] the yellow part in the center of an egg

**yon·der** /'yundɚ/ *adv, determiner* LITERARY over there

**you** /yə, yu; *strong* yu/ *pron* [used as a subject or object] **1** the person or people you are speaking or writing to: *You must be hungry.* | *Do you want a cigarette?* | *I can't hear you.* | *I hope you like the dress.* | *Who made that for you?* **2** people in general: *You can't trust anybody these days.* | *You never know what Jim will say.* – compare ONE² **3** used with nouns or phrases when you are talking to or calling someone: *You jerk!* | *You kids be quiet!* **4 you all** SPOKEN used instead of "you" when speaking to two or more people: *What do you all want to do tonight?*

**you'd** /yəd, yud; *strong* yud/ **1** the short form of "you would": *I didn't think you'd mind.* **2** the short form of "you had": *You'd better do what he says.*

**you'll** /yəl, yul; *strong* yul/ the short form of "you will": *You'll have to speak louder.*

**young¹** /yʌŋ/ *adj* **1** at an early stage of life or development; not old: *young children* | *I used to ski when I was young.* | *a young country* **2** seeming younger than you are, or looking younger than something is: *a lotion for healthier younger skin* **3** designed or intended for young people: *Is this dress too young for me?*

**young²** *n* **1 the young** young people considered as a group **2** [plural] young animals: *a turtle and her young*

**young·ster** /'yʌŋstɚ/ *n* a young person

**your** /yɚ; *strong* yur, yɔr/ *possessive adj* **1** belonging or relating to the person or people someone is speaking to: *Is that your mother?* | *Your hair looks really nice.* | *Don't worry, it's not your fault.* **2** belonging to any person: *When times are bad you can rely on your friends.*

**you're** /yɚ; *strong* yur, yɔr/ the short form of "you are": *You're bothering me.*

**yours** /yurz, yɔrz/ *possessive pron* **1** the thing or things belonging or relating to the person someone is speaking to: *Yours is the nicest car.* | *That bag is yours, isn't it?* | *Is he a friend of yours?* **2 yours (truly) a)** a phrase you write before you sign your name at the end of a letter **3 yours truly a)** HUMOROUS used instead of "I": *Yes, yours truly finally quit smoking.*

**your·self** /yɚ'sɛlf/ *pron, plural* **yourselves** /yɚ'sɛlvz/ **1** the REFLEXIVE form of "you": *Don't hurt yourself!* | *Make yourself a cup of coffee, if you want.* **2** the strong form of "you," used in order to emphasize the subject or object of a sentence: *Why don't you do it yourself?* **3 (all) by yourself a)** without help: *Did you move the sofa by yourself?* **b)** alone: *You're going to Ecuador by yourself?* **4 (all) to yourself** for your own use: *You'll have the house all to yourself this weekend.*

**youth** /yuθ/ *n* **1** [U] the period of time when someone is young, or the quality of being young: *During his youth he lived in France.* **2** [U] young people in general: *the youth of the 1960s* | *a youth hostel* (=a cheap hotel for young people) **3** a boy or young man, especially a TEENAGER: *A youth was arrested for stealing.*

**youth·ful** /'yuθfəl/ *adj* typical of young people, or seeming young: *his youthful strength* | *a youthful mother*

**you've** /yəv, yuv; *strong* yuv/ the short form of "you have": *You've got to take care of yourself.*

**yo-yo** /'youyou/ *n* **1** a toy you hold in your hand that is made of two circular parts joined together that go up and down a string as you lift your hand up and down **2** SLANG someone who does stupid things

**yr.** *n* the written abbreviation of YEAR

**yuck** /yʌk/ *interjection* said when you think something is unpleasant: *Yuck! This stuff tastes gross!* – **yucky** *adj*

**Yule** /yul/ *n* LITERARY Christmas

**Yule·tide** /'yultaɪd/ *n* [U] LITERARY the period from just before Christmas until just after it

**yum** /yʌm/ *interjection* said in order to emphasize that you think something tastes good: *Yum! Apple pie!*

**yum·my** /'yʌmi/ *adj* INFORMAL food that is yummy tastes very good

**yup·pie** /'yʌpi/ *n* INFORMAL a young person who only seems interested in having a professional job, earning a lot of money, and buying expensive things

**YWCA** *n* Young Women's Christian Association; an organization that provides places to stay, special help, and training for young women, especially in large cities —see also YMCA

# Z

**Z, z** /zi/ the last letter of the English alphabet

**za·ny** /'zeɪni/ *adj* unusual in a way that is amusing and exciting: *a zany new TV comedy*

**zap** /zæp/ *v* -pped, -pping [T] INFORMAL to kill, destroy, or attack something extremely quickly, especially by using electricity or a LASER beam

**zeal** /zil/ *n* [U] great interest in something and eagerness to be involved in it: *political zeal* —**zealous** *adj*

**ze·bra** /'zibrə/ *n* a wild African animal like a horse, that has black and white bands on its body

**ze·nith** /'zinɪθ/ *n* [C usually singular] **1** the most successful point in the development of something: *This album shows Simon at the zenith of his powers.* **2** the highest point that the sun or a star reaches in the sky

**ze·ro¹** /'zɪroʊ, 'zɪroʊ/ *number* **1** 0 **2** the point between - and + on a scale for measuring something, especially temperature: *zero degrees Fahrenheit* **3** the temperature at which water freezes in the Celsius system of measuring temperature: *20°C below zero*

**zero²** *v*

**zero in on** sb/sth *phr v* [T] to aim at one thing or give special attention to one person or thing: *war planes zeroing in on a target*

**zest** /zɛst/ *n* [U] a feeling of eagerness, excitement, and enjoyment: *a zest for life*

**zig·zag¹** /'zɪgzæg/ *n* a line that looks like a row of z's joined together

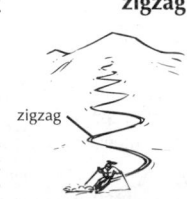
zigzag

**zigzag²** *v* -gged, -gging [I] to move forward by going to the left at an angle, and then to the right at an angle, and then to the left etc.: *a path that zigzags across the mountain*

**zil·lion** /'zɪlyən/ *number* INFORMAL an extremely large number or amount: *She asked a zillion questions.*

**zinc** /zɪŋk/ *n* [U] a white metal that is an ELEMENT that is often used in order to produce other metals

**zip¹** /zɪp/ *v* -pped, -pping **1** [T] also **zip up** to close or fasten something using a ZIPPER: *Zip up your coat.* —opposite UNZIP **2** [I] to go somewhere or do something very quickly: *A few cars zipped past us.*

**zip²** *n* [U] SPOKEN **1** a short form of ZIP CODE **2** none; zero

**zip code** /'. ./ *n* the number you write below an address in the US on an envelope, that helps the post office deliver the mail more quickly

**zip·per** /'zɪpɚ/ *n* an object for fastening clothes, bags etc., with two lines of small pieces of metal or plastic that slide together

**zipper**

**zit** /zɪt/ *n* SLANG ⇨ PIMPLE

**zo·di·ac** /'zoʊdi,æk/ *n* **the zodiac** an imaginary circle in space that the sun, moon, and PLANETs follow as a path, which some people believe influences people's lives

zipper

**zom·bie** /'zɑmbi/ *n* **1** INFORMAL someone who moves very slowly and cannot think clearly because s/he is very tired **2** a dead body that is made to move, walk etc. by magic

**zone** /zoʊn/ *n* part of an area that has a specific purpose or has a special quality: *a no-parking zone | the war/battle/combat zone* —see also TIME ZONE

**zon·ing** /'zoʊnɪŋ/ *n* [U] a system of choosing areas to be used for particular purposes, such as building houses —**zone** *v* [T]

**zoo** /zu/ *n* a place where many different types of animals are kept so that people can see them

**zo·ol·o·gy** /zoʊ'ɑlədʒi/ *n* [U] the scientific study of animals and their behavior —**zoologist** *n* —**zoological** /,zoʊə'lɑdʒɪkəl/ *adj*

**zoom¹** /zum/ *v* [I] INFORMAL to travel very quickly: *We zoomed down the highway.*

**zoom in/out** *phr v* [I] if a camera zooms in or out, it makes the object it is photographing seem closer or farther away

**zoom²** *n* the sound an engine makes or the sound of something moving very quickly

**zoom lens** /'. ./ *n* a camera LENS that moves in order to make the objects you are photographing seem closer and larger

**Zs, Z's** /ziz/ *n* [plural] SPOKEN **catch/get some Zs** to sleep

**zuc·chi·ni** /zu'kini/ *n* [C,U] a long smooth dark green fruit, cooked and eaten as a vegetable —see picture on page 470

**Zzz** used in writing to represent sleep

# Word Building

| prefix | meaning | example |
|---|---|---|
| a-, an- | opposite; without; not | amoral, atypical, antonym |
| anti- | opposed to; against | antifreeze, antidote |
| audi-, audio- | relating to sound; relating to hearing | audiovisual, auditorium |
| auto- | of or by yourself | autobiography, automobile |
| bi- | two; twice | bilingual, biannual |
| bio- | relating to living things | biology, biochemistry |
| cent-, centi- | 100, 100th part of something | centipede, centimeter |
| circum- | all the way around something | circumstance, circumference |
| co-, col-, com-, con-, cor- | with; together | coexist, collect, compassion, confederation, correlation |
| contra- | against | contraceptive |
| counter- | opposite; against | counterproductive |
| cyber- | relating to computers | cyberspace, cyberpunk |
| de- | to do or make the opposite of; remove from; reduce | decriminalize, decaffeinated, devalue |
| dis- | opposite | disapprove, dishonesty |
| down- | to a lower position; to or toward the bottom | downturn, downriver, downstairs |
| eco- | relating to the environment | ecological |
| electri-, electro- | relating to electricity | electrify, electrocute |
| em-, en- | to make something have a quality | empower, enlarge |
| ex- | no longer being or doing | ex-wife, ex-football player |
| ex- | out; from | exit, export |
| extra- | outside; beyond | extraterrestrial, extracurricular |
| geo- | relating to the earth | geology, geography |
| hydr-, hydro- | relating to or using water | hydroelectric, hydrant |
| il-, im-, in-, ir- | not | illogical, impossible, inconvenient, irrational |
| in-, im- | in; into | incoming, immerse |
| inter-, intro-, intra- | between; together; within | international, introduce, intravenous |
| mis- | bad; badly | misfortune, misbehave |
| mono- | one | monogram, monologue |
| multi- | many | multicolored, multicultural |
| non- | not | nonsmoking, nonstandard |
| over- | too much; beyond; outer; additional | overpopulate, overhang, overcoat, overtime |
| poly- | many | polygon |
| post- | later than; after | postgraduate, postpone |
| pre- | before | prewar, preview |
| pro- | in favor of | pro-American |
| re- | again | rewrite, redo, rewind |
| semi- | half; partly | semicircle, semiprecious |
| sub- | under; below; less important or powerful | subway, substandard, subcommittee |
| super- | larger; greater; more powerful | supermarket, superhuman, supervisor |
| sym-, syn- | with; together | sympathy, synthesis |
| tele- | at or over a long distance | telescope, television |
| theo- | relating to God or gods | theology |
| therm-, thermo- | relating to heat | thermostat, thermometer |
| trans- | on or to the far side of something; between two things | transatlantic, transportation |
| tri- | three | tricycle, triangle |
| ultra- | beyond; extremely | ultrasonic, ultramodern |
| un- | not; opposite | unhappy, unfair, undress |
| under- | too little | underdeveloped, underage |
| uni- | one | unilateral |
| vice- | next in rank below the most important person | Vice-President, vice-captain |

# Word Building

| suffix | meaning | example |
|---|---|---|
| -ability, -ibility | used in order to make nouns from adjectives that end in -able and -ible | accountability, flexibility |
| -able, -ible | capable of; having a particular quality | manageable, comfortable, reversible, responsible |
| -al, -ial | relating to something; the act of doing something | coastal, electrical, financial, refusal, denial |
| -an, -ian, -ean | from or relating to a place; someone who has a particular job or knows about a particular subject; relating to or similar to a time, thing, or person; someone who has a particular belief | American, suburban, librarian, historian, subterranean, Victorian, Christian |
| -ant, -ent | someone or something that does something | servant, disinfectant, resident, repellent |
| -ar | relating to something | muscular, stellar |
| -ary | relating to something | customary, planetary |
| -ation, -tion, -ion | the act of doing something; the state or result of doing something | examination, combination, completion, election |
| -cy | used in order to make nouns from adjectives | accuracy |
| -en | made of something; to make something have a particular quality | wooden, golden, darken, strengthen |
| -ence, -ance, -ency, -ancy | a state or quality; the act of doing something | intelligence, obedience, performance, tendency, presidency, pregnancy |
| -er, -or, -ar, -r | someone or something that does something | teacher, actor, beggar, writer, photocopier, accelerator |
| -ery, -ry | an act; a quality; a place where something is done or made | bribery, bravery, snobbery, distillery, bakery |
| -ful | full of | beautiful, harmful |
| -goer | someone who goes somewhere regularly | moviegoer, churchgoer |
| -graph, -graphy | something that is written or drawn | autograph, biography |
| -hood | the state or time of being something | childhood, manhood, womanhood |
| -ic, -ical | of; like; relating to a particular thing | photographic, historical |
| -ify | to affect in a particular way | purify, clarify, terrify |
| -ish | people or language; having a quality | Spanish, English, childish, selfish |
| -ism | a belief or set of ideas; the act of doing something | Buddhism, capitalism, criticism |
| -ist | relating to a political or religious belief | socialist, Methodist |
| -ity | having a particular quality | stupidity, regularity |
| -ive | having a particular quality | creative, descriptive |
| -ize | to make something have a quality; to change something into a different state | modernize, crystallize |
| -less | without something | childless, careless, endless |
| -logue, -log | relating to words | monologue, catalog |
| -ly | in a particular way; at regular times | slowly, quickly, hourly |
| -ment | the act or result of doing something | government, development |
| -ness | used in order to make nouns | happiness, softness |
| -ology | the study or science of something | geology, technology |
| -or | someone or something that does something | doctor, actor, inventor, radiator, incinerator, incubator |
| -ory | a place or thing used for doing something; having a particular quality | laboratory, satisfactory, obligatory |
| -ous, -ious | used in order to make adjectives from nouns | dangerous, furious |
| -proof | not allowing something to come in, come through, or destroy something | soundproof, waterproof, fireproof |
| -ship | having a particular position; an art or skill | membership, friendship, scholarship |
| -wear | clothes of a particular type | menswear, womenswear, sportswear |
| -y | full of or covered with something; tending to do something | hairy, fuzzy, sleepy, curly |

# Irregular Verbs

The list below shows the verbs that have irregular past tense, PAST PARTICIPLE, or PRESENT PARTICIPLE forms. When a verb has more than one form that is used, the most common form is given first.

| verb | past tense | past participle | present participle |
|---|---|---|---|
| **arise** | arose | arisen | arising |
| **awake** | awoke | awoken | awaking |
| **be** | —see BE | | |
| **bear** | bore | borne | bearing |
| **beat** | beat | beaten | beating |
| **become** | became | become | becoming |
| **begin** | began | begun | beginning |
| **behold** | beheld | beheld | beholding |
| **bend** | bent | bent | bending |
| **bet** | bet | bet | betting |
| **bid**[2] | bid | bid | bidding |
| **bid**[3] | bade or bid | bid or bidden | bidding |
| **bind** | bound | bound | binding |
| **bite** | bit | bitten | biting |
| **bleed** | bled | bled | bleeding |
| **blow** | blew | blown | blowing |
| **break** | broke | broken | breaking |
| **breed** | bred | bred | breeding |
| **bring** | brought | brought | bringing |
| **broadcast** | broadcast or broadcasted | broadcast or broadcasted | broadcasting |
| **build** | built | built | building |
| **burn** | burned | burned or burnt | burning |
| **burst** | burst | burst | bursting |
| **buy** | bought | bought | buying |
| **cast** | cast | cast | casting |
| **catch** | caught | caught | catching |
| **choose** | chose | chosen | choosing |
| **cling** | clung | clung | clinging |
| **come** | came | come | coming |
| **cost**[2] | cost | cost | costing |
| **creep** | crept | crept | creeping |
| **cut** | cut | cut | cutting |
| **deal** | dealt | dealt | dealing |
| **dig** | dug | dug | digging |
| **dive** | dived or dove | dived | diving |
| **do** | —see DO | | |
| **draw** | drew | drawn | drawing |
| **dream** | dreamed or dreamt | dreamed or dreamt | dreaming |
| **drink** | drank | drunk | drinking |
| **drive** | drove | driven | driving |
| **dwell** | dwelled or dwelt | dwelled or dwelt | dwelling |
| **eat** | ate | eaten | eating |
| **fall** | fell | fallen | falling |
| **feed** | fed | fed | feeding |
| **feel** | felt | felt | feeling |
| **fight** | fought | fought | fighting |
| **find** | found | found | finding |
| **fit** | fit or fitted | fitted | fitting |
| **flee** | fled | fled | fleeing |
| **fling** | flung | flung | flinging |
| **fly** | flew | flown | flying |
| **forbid** | forbade or forbid | forbid or forbidden | forbidding |
| **forecast** | forecast or forecasted | forecast or forecasted | forecasting |
| **foresee** | foresaw | foreseen | foreseeing |
| **forget** | forgot | forgotten | forgetting |
| **forgive** | forgave | forgiven | forgiving |
| **freeze** | froze | frozen | freezing |
| **get** | got | gotten | getting |
| **give** | gave | given | giving |

# Irregular Verbs

| verb | past tense | past participle | present participle |
|---|---|---|---|
| **go** | went | gone | going |
| **grind** | ground | ground | grinding |
| **grow** | grew | grown | growing |
| **hang**[1] | hung | hung | hanging |
| **have** | —see HAVE | | |
| **hear** | heard | heard | hearing |
| **hide** | hid | hidden | hiding |
| **hit** | hit | hit | hitting |
| **hold** | held | held | holding |
| **hurt** | hurt | hurt | hurting |
| **keep** | kept | kept | keeping |
| **kneel** | knelt *or* kneeled | knelt *or* kneeled | kneeling |
| **knit** | knitted *or* knit | knitted *or* knit | knitting |
| **know** | knew | known | knowing |
| **lay** | laid | laid | laying |
| **lead** | led | led | leading |
| **leap** | leaped *or* leapt | leaped *or* leapt | leaping |
| **leave** | left | left | leaving |
| **lend** | lent | lent | lending |
| **let** | let | let | letting |
| **lie**[1] | lay | lain | lying |
| **lie**[2] | lied | lied | lying |
| **light** | lit *or* lighted | lit *or* lighted | lighting |
| **lose** | lost | lost | losing |
| **make** | made | made | making |
| **mean** | meant | meant | meaning |
| **meet** | met | met | meeting |
| **mislead** | misled | misled | misleading |
| **mistake** | mistook | mistaken | mistaking |
| **misunderstand** | misunderstood | misunderstood | misunderstanding |
| **outbid** | outbid | outbid | outbidding |
| **outdo** | outdid | outdone | outdoing |
| **overcome** | overcame | overcome | overcoming |
| **overdo** | overdid | overdone | overdoing |
| **overhang** | overhung | overhung | overhanging |
| **overhear** | overheard | overheard | overhearing |
| **override** | overrode | overridden | overriding |
| **overrun** | overran | overrun | overrunning |
| **oversee** | oversaw | overseen | overseeing |
| **overtake** | overtook | overtaken | overtaking |
| **overthrow** | overthrew | overthrown | overthrowing |
| **pay** | paid | paid | paying |
| **prove** | proved | proved *or* proven | proving |
| **put** | put | put | putting |
| **read** | read | read | reading |
| **rebuild** | rebuilt | rebuilt | rebuilding |
| **redo** | redid | redone | redoing |
| **relay** | relayed | relayed | relaying |
| **repay** | repaid | repaid | repaying |
| **rewrite** | rewrote | rewritten | rewriting |
| **rid** | rid | rid | ridding |
| **ride** | rode | ridden | riding |
| **ring**[2] | rang | rung | ringing |
| **rise** | rose | risen | rising |
| **run** | ran | run | running |
| **saw** | sawed | sawn *or* sawed | sawing |
| **say** | said | said | saying |
| **see** | saw | seen | seeing |
| **seek** | sought | sought | seeking |
| **sell** | sold | sold | selling |
| **send** | sent | sent | sending |
| **set** | set | set | setting |
| **sew** | sewed | sewn *or* sewed | sewing |
| **shake** | shook | shaken | shaking |

| verb | past tense | past participle | present participle |
|------|-----------|----------------|--------------------|
| shed | shed | shed | shedding |
| shine | shone | shone | shining |
| shrink | shrank | shrunk | shrinking |
| shut | shut | shut | shutting |
| sing | sang | sung | singing |
| sink | sank or sunk | sunk | sinking |
| sit | sat | sat | sitting |
| slay | slew | slain | slaying |
| sleep | slept | slept | sleeping |
| slide | slid | slid | sliding |
| sling | slung | slung | slinging |
| slit | slit | slit | slitting |
| sow | sowed | sown or sowed | sowing |
| speak | spoke | spoken | speaking |
| speed | sped or speeded | sped or speeded | speeding |
| spend | spent | spent | spending |
| spin | spun | spun | spinning |
| spit | spit or spat | spat | spitting |
| split | split | split | splitting |
| spread | spread | spread | spreading |
| spring | sprang | sprung | springing |
| stand | stood | stood | standing |
| steal | stole | stolen | stealing |
| stick | stuck | stuck | sticking |
| sting | stung | sting | stinging |
| stink | stank or stunk | stunk | stinking |
| strew | strewed | strewn or strewed | strewing |
| stride | strode | stridden | striding |
| strike | struck | struck or stricken | striking |
| string | strung | strung | stringing |
| strive | strove or strived | striven or strived | striving |
| swear | swore | sworn | swearing |
| sweep | swept | swept | sweeping |
| swell | swelled | swollen | swelling |
| swim | swam | swum | swimming |
| swing | swung | swung | swinging |
| take | took | taken | taking |
| teach | taught | taught | teaching |
| tear | tore | torn | tearing |
| tell | told | told | telling |
| think | thought | thought | thinking |
| throw | threw | thrown | throwing |
| thrust | thrust | thrust | thrusting |
| tread | trod | trodden | treading |
| undergo | underwent | undergone | undergoing |
| understand | understood | understood | understanding |
| undertake | undertook | undertaken | undertaking |
| undo | undid | undone | undoing |
| unwind | unwound | unwound | unwinding |
| uphold | upheld | upheld | upholding |
| upset | upset | upset | upsetting |
| wake | woke | woken | waking |
| wear | wore | worn | wearing |
| weave | wove or weaved | woven or weaved | weaving |
| wed | wed or wedded | wed or wedded | wedding |
| weep | wept | wept | weeping |
| wet | wet or wetted | wet | wetting |
| win | won | won | winning |
| wind | wound | wound | winding |
| withdraw | withdrew | withdrawn | withdrawing |
| withhold | withheld | withheld | withholding |
| withstand | withstood | withstood | withstanding |
| wring | wrung | wrung | wringing |
| write | wrote | written | writing |

# PRONUNCIATION

## American English
This dictionary shows pronunciations used by speakers of the most common American English dialects. Sometimes more than one pronunciation is shown. For example, many Americans say the first vowel in *data* as /eɪ/, while others say this vowel as /æ/. We show *data* as /ˈdeɪtə, ˈdætə/. This means that both pronunciations are possible and are commonly used by educated speakers. We have not, however, shown all American dialects and all possible pronunciations. For example, *news* is shown only as /nuz/ even though a few Americans might pronounce this word as /nyuz/. The vowels /ɔ/ and /ɑ/ are both shown, but many speakers do not use the sound /ɔ/. These speakers say /ɑ/ in place of /ɔ/, so that *caught* and *cot* are both said as /kɑt/.

## Use of hyphen
When more than one pronunciation is given for a word, we usually show only the part of the pronunciation that is different from the first pronunciation, replacing the parts that are the same with a hyphen: **economics** /ˌɛkəˈnɑmɪks, ˌi-/. The hyphen is also used for showing the division between syllables when this might not be clear: **boyish** /ˈbɔɪ-ɪʃ/, **drawing** /ˈdrɔ-ɪŋ/, **clockwise** /ˈklɑk-waɪz/.

## Symbols
The symbols used in this dictionary are based on the symbols of the International Phonetic Alphabet (IPA) with a few changes. The symbol /y/, which is closer to English spelling than the /j/ used in the IPA, is used for the first sound in *you* /yu/. Other changes are described in the paragraph **American English Sounds**.

## Foreign words
English pronunciations have been shown for foreign words, even though some speakers may use a pronunciation closer to that of the original language.

## Abbreviations
No pronunciations are shown for most abbreviations. This is either because they are not spoken (and are defined as "written abbreviations"), or because they are pronounced by saying the names of the letters, with main stress on the last letter and secondary stress on the first: **VCR** /ˌvi si ˈɑr/. Pronunciations have been shown where an abbreviation is spoken like an ordinary word: **RAM** /ræm/.

## Words that are forms of main words
A form of a main word that is a different part of speech may come at the end of the entry for that word. If the related word is pronounced by saying the main word and adding an ending (see list on page 930), no separate pronunciation is given. If the addition of the ending causes a change in the pronunciation of the main word, the pronunciation for the related word is given. For example: **impossible** /ɪmˈpɑsəbəl/, **impossibility** /ɪmˌpɑsəˈbɪləti/. There are some pronunciation changes that we do not show at these entries, because they follow regular patterns: (1) When an *-ly* or *-er* ending is added to a main word ending in /-bəl/, /-kəl/, /-pəl/, /-gəl/, or /-dəl/, the /ə/ is usually omitted. For example, **practical** is shown as /ˈpræktɪkəl/. When *-ly* is added to it, it becomes **practically** /ˈpræktɪkli/. This difference is not shown. (2) When *-ly* or *-ity* is added to words ending in *-y* /i/, the /i/ becomes /ə/: **angry** /ˈæŋgri/ becomes **angrily** /ˈæŋgrəli/. This is not shown.

## Stress
In English words of two or more syllables, at least one syllable is said with more force than the others. The sign /ˈ/ is put before the syllable with the most force. We say it has *main stress*: **person** /ˈpɜsən/, **percent** /pɜˈsɛnt/. Some words also have a stress on another syllable that is less strong than the main

stress. We call this *secondary stress*, and the sign /ˌ/ is placed before such a syllable: **personality** /ˌpɜsəˈnæləti/, **personify** /pɜˈsɑnəˌfaɪ/. Secondary stress is not usually shown in the second syllable of a two-syllable word, unless it is necessary to show that the second syllable must not be shortened, as in **starlit** /ˈstɑrˌlɪt/ compared to **starlet** /ˈstɑrlɪt/.

## Unstressed Vowels
/ə/ and /ɪ/ Many unstressed syllables in American English are pronounced with a very short unclear vowel. This vowel is shown as /ə/ or /ɪ/; however, there is very little difference between them in normal connected speech. For example, the word *affect* /əˈfɛkt/ and *effect* /ɪˈfɛkt/ usually sound the same. The word *rabbit* is shown as /ˈræbɪt/, but it may also be pronounced /ˈræbət/.

/ə/ and /ʌ/ These sounds are very similar. The symbol /ə/ is used in unstressed syllables, and /ʌ/, which is longer, is used in stressed and secondary stressed syllables. When people speak more quickly, secondary stressed syllables become unstressed so that /ʌ/ may be pronounced as /ə/. For example, *difficult* /ˈdɪfɪˌkʌlt/ and *coconut* /ˈkoʊkəˌnʌt/ may be pronounced as /ˈdɪfɪkəlt/ and /ˈkoʊkənət/. Only the pronunciation with /ʌ/ is shown.

## Compound Words with a Space or Hyphen
Many compounds are written with either a space or a hyphen between the parts. When all parts of the compound appear in the dictionary as separate main words, the full pronunciation of the compound is not shown. Only its stress pattern is given. Each syllable is represented by a dot /./, and the stress marks are put before the dots that represent the syllables with stress. For example: **bus stop** /ˈ. ./, **town hall** /ˌ. ˈ./. Sometimes a compound contains a main word with an ending. If the main word is in the dictionary and the ending is a common one, only a stress pattern is shown. For example: **washing machine** /ˈ.. ˌ./. *Washing* is not a main word in the Dictionary, but *wash* is; so only a stress pattern is shown because *-ing* is a common ending. But if any part is not a main word, the full pronunciation is given: **helter-skelter** /ˌhɛltɚ ˈskɛltɚ/.

## Stress Shift
A number of compounds may have a shift in stress when they are used before nouns. For example, the compound *plate glass* would have the pattern /ˌ. ˈ./ when spoken by itself or in a sentence like *The window was made of plate glass*. But the phrase *plate glass window* would usually have the pattern /ˌ. . ˈ./. The mark /ˌ·/ shows this. For example: **plate glass** /ˌ. ˈ·/. Stress shift can also happen with some single words: **artificial** /ˌɑrtəˈfɪʃəl ·/, **independent** /ˌɪndɪˈpɛndənt ·/.

## Syllabic Consonants
The sounds /n/ and /l/ can be *syllabic*. That is, they can themselves form a syllable, especially when they are at the end of a word (and follow particular consonants, especially /t/ and /d/). For example, in **sudden** /ˈsʌdn/ the /n/ is syllabic; there is no vowel between the /d/ and the /n/, so no vowel is shown. In the middle of a word, a hyphen or stress mark after /n/ or /l/ shows that it is syllabic: **botanist** /ˈbɑtn̩-ɪst/ and **catalog** /ˈkætl̩ˌɔg/ are three-syllable words.

The sound *r* can be either a consonant, /r/, or a vowel, /ɚ/. When /ɚ/ is followed by an unstressed vowel, it may be pronounced as a sequence of two vowels, /ɚ/ plus the following vowel, or as /ə/ followed by a syllable beginning with /r/. For example, the word *coloring* may be pronounced as /ˈkʌlɚɪŋ/ instead of /ˈkʌlərɪŋ/. Only the pronunciation, /ˈkʌlərɪŋ/, is shown.